The
Harper
American
Literature

Compact
Edition

The Harper American Literature

Compact Edition

Donald McQuade
University of California, Berkeley
General Editor

Robert Atwan
Seton Hall University

Martha Banta
University of California at Los Angeles

Justin Kaplan

David Minter
Emory University

Cecelia Tichi
Boston University

Helen Vendler
Harvard University

Harper & Row, Publishers, New York
Cambridge, Philadelphia, San Francisco, Washington,
London, Mexico City, São Paulo, Singapore, Sydney

Cover Photo
Mary Cassatt, *The Banjo Lesson,*
c. 1894. Pastel on paper, 28 in. × 22 1/2 in.
The Williams Fund, 1958; Virginia
Museum, Richmond, Virginia.

Sponsoring Editor
Phillip Leininger

Coordinating Editor
Jonathan Haber

Development Editor
Nat LaMar

Project Editor
Lenore Bonnie Biller

Text and Cover Design
Karen Salsgiver

Text Art
Vantage Art, Inc.

Production Manager
Jeanie Berke

Production Assistant
Brenda DeMartini

Compositor
*ComCom Division of Haddon Crafts-
men, Inc.*

Printer and Binder
R. R. Donnelley & Sons, Company

For permission to use copyrighted
material, grateful acknowledgment
is made to the copyright holders
listed on pp. 2529–2538, which
are hereby made part of this copyright page.

The Harper American Literature,
Compact Edition

Copyright © 1987 by Harper &
Row, Publishers, Inc.

Library of Congress Cataloging in
Publication Data

The Harper American literature.

    Includes bibliographies and
indexes.
    I. American literature.
I. McQuade, Donald.
II. Harper & Row, Publishers.
PS507.H227 1987 810'.8 86-19412
ISBN 0-06-044372-3 (v. 1)
ISBN 0-06-044367-7 (pbk.: v. 1)
ISBN 0-06-044373-1 (v. 2)
ISBN 0-06-044368-5 (pbk.: v. 2)
ISBN 0-06-044374-x (Compact
Edition)
ISBN 0-06-044371-5 (pbk.: Com-
pact Edition)

94 95 RRD 10 9 8 7 6

Contents

The Literature of the New World: 1492–1620

41   The Literature of Colonial America: 1620–1776

205 The Literature of the New Republic: 1776–1836

419   The Literature of the American Renaissance: 1836–1865

The Literature of an Expanding Nation: 1865–1912

1501   # The Literature of Modernism: Prose / 1912–1940

1763   # The Literature of Modernism: Poetry / 1912–1940

The Literature of Postwar America: Prose / 1940–1973

       1; 2

The Literature of Postwar America: Poetry / 1940–1973

The Literature of Contemporary America: Prose

The Literature of Contemporary America: Poetry

Preface

The Harper American Literature reaffirms and invigorates what is now a nearly 150-year-old tradition of multivolume collections of American literature. From the publication in 1855 of Evert A. and George L. Duyckinck's two-volume *Cyclopaedia of American Literature,* readers wanting to explore what the Duyckincks called "the literary biography of America" have had ready access to what each succeeding generation judged the literature most worthy of its collective attention. But *The Harper American Literature* realizes for the first time a goal announced in the Duyckinck's preface and subsequently endorsed by the editors of virtually every collection of American literature—"to bring together in one book convenient for perusal and reference . . . memorials and records of the writers of the country and their works, from the earliest period to the present day." What distinguishes *The Harper American Literature* from its predecessors is its commitment to presenting fully the richness of American literature, its thematic and stylistic range as well as its geographical and ethnic diversity. To this end, we have worked to extend the conventional boundaries of the American literary tradition.

Virtually all collections of American literature now in print begin either with a generous selection of Puritan writings or, in fewer instances, with Captain John Smith and his engaging account of the early years of the Virginia colony. Yet such beginnings ignore a great deal of compelling literature written in and about America long before the first settlements at either Roanoke Island or Plymouth Plantation—from Cabeza de Vaca's harrowing sixteenth century narrative of his struggles to survive along the southeast coast of what is now Texas to the compelling creation myths of Native Americans. To supplant the narrow, northeastern, Puritan bias of currently available texts, we begin with a wealth of presettlement writing. "The Literature of the New World, 1492–1620," maps out new approaches to the important cultural forces that have helped shape American life.

The Harper American Literature extends America's literary tradition in another significant direction. Its final section, "The Literature of Contemporary America," gives unprecedented attention to our most recent—and eloquent—writers of fiction, poetry, and drama, far beyond the mid-1960s boundaries set by editors of nearly all other collections. Sampling the work of such important contemporary writers of fiction as Raymond Carver and Bobbie Ann Mason, poets Robert Pinsky and Jorie Graham, and playwright David Mamet—to name but a few of these many fresh and already celebrated voices—will enable readers to explore unexpected dimensions of American literature.

These unique sections, "The Literature of the New World" and "The Literature of Contemporary America," enlarge our presentation of the American literary scene. The earliest of our texts dates from 1492, the latest from 1986. We also reprint important but neglected works by classic writers, as well as important works by such neglected writers as Abigail Adams and Harriet Beecher Stowe. Throughout *The Harper American Literature,* the seven contributing editors aim to present the most comprehensive regathering and reassessment ever of America's literary tradition, including but extending beyond classic works. This Compact Edition steadfastly maintains the spirit and substance of the two-volume edition. For example, along with the most familiar sections of Washington Irving's *Sketch Book,* we include a representative chapter from his *History of the Life and Voyages of Christopher Columbus,* a rarely reprinted work that underscores both the continuity of American literature and the fascination of early nineteenth-century American writers with their distant past. Later, we give unprecedented attention to Gertrude Stein's role in the emergence of American modernism. By offering fresh perspectives on the work of America's literary masters, we provide evidence of the ways in which American literature helped shape, and in turn was influenced by, American culture during each period in its history. Throughout, we have taken special care to provide readers with ready access to unexpected and inviting selections without overburdening overcrowded reading schedules. We hope that inquisitive readers will be prompted to explore further the works, careers, and interconnections that give American literature its inexhaustible richness.

Committed to offering a broader range in the characteristic modes of America's most prominent literary figures, we established the following criteria to guide us in presenting the work of each writer: the literary merits of a particular selection, its significance in American literary history, its reflection of the range and depth of the writer's accomplishments, its connections to other themes and styles, and its power to document the literary values of the cultural context within which the writer works. Most often, we represent American writers by their most important work and by a sampling of other literary performances that show them engaging significant cultural issues.

A perennial problem of any collection of American literature is a structure that appears to isolate careers and periods without adequate attention to the interactions of these lives, works, and times. *The Harper American Literature* represents a concerted effort to weave selections, footnotes, author headnotes, and period introductions into a unified approach to American literature and the culture that informs it. In these two volumes, we seek not only to celebrate the classics of American literature and to locate neglected works of special literary merit, but also to suggest the many ways in which these works are enmeshed in a particular social and cultural context. We have designed the eleven period introductions to *The Harper American Literature* to show how major American writers were shaped by, how they were influential in, how they were responsive to their times—to offer a memorable view of the cultural immediacy of a period, what Gertrude Stein calls "the continuous present."

Each introduction focuses on the prevailing circumstances and competitions American writers faced in each period. What was it like for writers to work at different moments in American cultural history? Were writers peripheral or central figures in examining the major issues and crises of their eras? What major developments occurred in the related arts? What was the taste of the reading public in each period? What, more generally, was the state of language, literacy, and public discourse? The answers to these and similar questions create vivid images of what it was like for writers to live and work in their times.

Each period introduction highlights relevant American literary issues, cultural materials, and personalities. Brief "boxed inserts" include (but are not restricted to) selections from writers who otherwise may not warrant full representation, as well as literary and cultural documents. These literary and folk pieces, philosophical and historical statements, and illustrations add texture to the introductions. A short list of suggested further reading, arranged chronologically, follows each introduction.

A brief informative essay introduces each writer represented in *The Harper American Literature*. These headnote essays provide biographical details and the specific literary context for each writer's work. One major purpose of these headnotes is to show writers writing. In them, we trace the shape of an author's career and address the question of that writer's place in American literary history. We also consider how each writer feeds on, recoils from, or is in conflict with a particular literary, social, political, or cultural environment. At once biographical, contextual, and analytical, these essays counter the tendency to view writers in isolation from one another—by placing their contributions in the context of the main thematic and stylistic traditions of American literature. We designed the headnote essays to be informative enough to free our readers from the need to surround themselves with additional secondary sources before they read, but suggestions for further reading assist those who want to explore further the life and work of a particular author.

The Harper American Literature reprints virtually every recognized American literary classic. Yet we want these classics to reflect more than an attenuated literary tradition, one too often dismissed as elitist. We believe that America's literary classics can—and should—exemplify what the scholar Nathan Huggins calls a "pluralistic realism." No collection of American literature can be complete unless it includes a wide range of distinctive voices, including those of women, blacks, Asian-Americans, Mexican-Americans, and Native Americans. In our selections, headnote essays, and section introductions, we blend these works of literary and cultural merit with other, more traditional, selections so that these new voices can be heard as more than simply statistical responses or intellectual concessions to contemporary propriety.

The Harper American Literature broadens the restrictive notion of what constitutes an American classic. We include, for example, a representative selection of Native American oral and written literatures, stretching from the oral poetry of the sixteenth century to the fiction of such contemporary writers as N. Scott Momaday and Leslie Silko. In doing so, we seek to show how celebrated and less-heralded works of literature illumine each other and enable us to appreciate the diverse achievements that have shaped a distinctively American culture. For "major" and "minor" figures alike, our consistent editorial aim has been to preserve the writer's living complexity, his or her verbal struggles with the challenges of shaping a self, modifying a genre, extending a literary tradition, or enriching a cultural context—as these are reflected in individual acts of composition.

The Harper American Literature follows a simple chronological organization, established by the author's date of birth yet remaining responsive to such instructional clusters as the sequence of authors in the American Renaissance. We set no guidelines for the length of our selections, which vary from short poems to full-length novellas—including Melville's Billy Budd, Henry James's Daisy Miller, and Gertrude Stein's The Gentle Lena. We avoid excerpting whenever possible, but when a writer's most important work is principally in extended prose forms, we reprint self-contained chapters or passages. James Fenimore Cooper, for example, is represented by a chapter from each of The Leather-Stocking Tales, featuring the life and death of Natty Bumppo. Other selections, as in the case of Nabokov's Lolita, are justified by its author's having previously supervised publication of the material in an abbreviated format. Several authors, including Saul Bellow and David Mamet, offered recommendations on which of their works to include.

We have taken great care to provide reliable and readable texts, editing or modernizing only as needed (principally in spelling and punctuation). We have aimed to maintain the flavor of the original while making it accessible to contemporary readers. We note special textual problems and give the date of first publication at the end of each selection, preceded by the date of composition, if known. Footnotes, which are kept to a judicious minimum, explain obscure references, biblical and classical allusions, foreign words, and phrases having special or archaic meanings. We avoid interpretive footnotes. We have tried in every way possible to create conditions for reading that will enable students to discover and develop the integrity of their own responses with the support of their instructors.

We present The Harper American Literature as the most comprehensive collection ever assembled for the purpose of understanding—and reconstructing— American literary history. But we also intend it to be a flexible instructional resource. Because it contains virtually all the primary and supporting material required for instructional use and leisurely reading, The Harper American Literature enables instructors and students to concentrate on the literary merits of major American writing. Readers will find in these pages new forms, subjects, themes, and styles—each the product of a distinctive American literary imagination.

Projects with the scope and complexity of The Harper American Literature are by interest and necessity collaborative intellectual enterprises. The seven contributing editors of this project met for extended periods to plan the project—to articulate the principles and procedures that would guide its development, decide on the features that would distinguish it from its predecessors, and agree on the authors and selections to be included. Within this collaborative context, several of the editors made selections and wrote headnote essays for writers in periods outside their areas of primary responsibility. And while the eleven period introductions are unified by common principles and purposes, each essay in *The Harper American Literature* remains an extended individual critical statement summarizing the literary and cultural distinctiveness of each period in American literary history. Robert Atwan is the author of the introduction to "The Literature of the New World, 1492–1620"; Cecelia Tichi of "The Literature of Colonial America, 1620–1776"; Donald McQuade of "The Literature of the New Republic, 1776–1836"; and Justin Kaplan of "The Literature of the American Renaissance, 1836–1865." For "The Literature of an Expanding Nation, 1865–1912," Justin Kaplan treated the decade following the Civil War, Martha Banta the next thirty years. David Minter wrote the introductions to "The Literature of Modernism: Prose, 1912–1940"; "The Literature of Postwar America: Prose, 1940–1973"; and "The Literature of Contemporary America: Prose." Helen Vendler is the author of the introductions to "The Literature of Modernism: Poetry, 1912–1940"; "The Literature of Postwar America: Poetry, 1940–1973"; and "The Literature of Contemporary America: Poetry."

Donald McQuade,
General Editor

Acknowledgments

The publication of *The Harper American Literature* represents the collaborative efforts of numerous professionals. In many ways its final shape challenges the accuracy of a century-old American adage, first recorded in Henry Ward Beecher's *Proverbs from Plymouth Pulpit* (1887): "It is not the going out of port, but the coming in, that determines the success of a voyage." As *The Harper American Literature* comes to completion, its seven contributing editors would like to acknowledge those who contributed to this ambitious undertaking at both ends.

The Harper American Literature could not have been launched without the intelligence and vision of John J. McDermott, Distinguished Professor of Philosophy at Texas A & M University, who helped articulate the need for a substantially different collection of American writing. His generous advice and rich understanding of American culture have proven invaluable throughout the project's development. Helene Brewer, Queens College, CUNY, served as a limitless resource during the early phases of shaping this collection. John Frederick Nims, University of Illinois at Chicago Circle, and Joseph F. Trimmer, Ball State University, made significant contributions to the project's development, especially during the first several rounds of extended conversations about its distinctive features. We are grateful for their continued support.

During the several years that the contributing editors developed *The Harper American Literature,* many of our colleagues across the country offered incisive readings of various drafts of the manuscript. For their thoughtful critiques and helpful suggestions, we would like to thank the following reviewers: Daniel Aaron, Harvard University; Maurice Bassan, San Francisco State University; Calvin Bedient, University of California at Los Angeles; Frank Bergon, Vassar College; Dennis Berthold, Texas A & M University; Lynn Z. Bloom, Virginia Commonwealth University; Virginia W. Brumbach, Eastfield College; Louis J. Budd, Duke University; Lawrence Buell, Oberlin College; Robert P. Burke, Joliet Junior College; Edwin H. Cady, Duke University; Bonnie Costello, Radcliffe College; Michael Dunne, Middle Tennessee State University; Kathy Early, Middlesex County College; Emory Elliott, Princeton University; Suzanne Ferguson, Ohio State University; Steven Fink, Ohio State University; Benjamin Franklin Fisher IV, University of Mississippi; Michael T. Gilmore, Brandeis University; James Goodwin, University of California at Los Angeles; Robert C. Grayson, Southeast Missouri State University; Malcolm Griffith, University of Washington; Phillip F. Gura, University of Colorado, Boulder; William Howarth, Princeton University; J. G. Jannsen, Arizona State University; Donald Kartiganer, University of Washington; Merrill Lewis, Western Washington University; John S. Mann, Western Illinois University; Terence Martin, Indiana University; Lee Mitchell, Princeton University; James Moore, Mount San Antonio College; Elsa Nettels, College of William and Mary; Sarah Emily Newton, California State University, Chico; John Frederick Nims, University of Illinois at Chicago Circle; Thornton H. Parsons, Syracuse University; David Perkins, Harvard University; Marjorie Perloff, University of Southern California; Robert L. Phillips, Mississippi State University; Donald Pizer, Tulane University; Joel Porte, Harvard University; Carolyn Porter, University of California, Berkeley; John Reardon, Miami University, Ohio; Louis D. Rubin, University of North Carolina at Chapel Hill; Henry M. Sayre, Oregon State University; Richard Schramm, University of Utah; Dorothy U. Seyler, Northern Virginia Community College; Frank Shuffelton, University of Rochester; Ellen Hurt Smith, Stetson University; Haskell Springer, University of Kansas; William T. Stafford, Purdue University; Eric J. Sundquist, University of California, Berkeley; David O. Tomlinson, U. S. Naval Academy; Darwin T. Turner, University of Iowa; Emily S. Watts, University of Illinois at Urbana–Champaign; Robert P. Weeks, University of Michigan; Michael West, University of Pittsburgh; Ann Woodlief, Virginia Commonwealth University; Larzer Ziff, John Hopkins University.

We are especially grateful to the following colleagues and friends for their many helpful suggestions and generous encouragement: Daniel Aaron, Harvard University; Max Apple, Rice University; Helene Atwan; Anne Bernays; Joe Cuomo, Queens College, CUNY; Joan Feinberg; Joseph A. Finder; Steven Fink, Ohio State University; Sally Fitzgerald; Bruce Forer, Queens College; William Howarth, Princeton University; Dennis Huston, Rice University; Walter Isle, Rice University; Betsy B. Kaufman, Queens College; Bridget Gellert Lyons, Rutgers University; Robert B. Lyons, Queens College; Rosemary Magee, Emory University; Wendy Martin, Queens College; Larry McMurtry; Susanne B.

McQuade; Caroline Minter; Marie Ponsot, Queens College; Carolyn Porter, University of California, Berkeley; Edward Quinn, City College, CUNY; Harold Schechter, Queens College; Nancy Sommers, Rutgers University; Donald Stone, Queens College; Robert Towers, Columbia University; William Vesterman, Rutgers University; William P. Wilson, Queens College; and Thomas Wortham, University of California at Los Angeles. We are also indebted to Frederick Buell, Queens College, CUNY; his imaginative intelligence, critical acumen, and patient understanding made this a far more solid book than it otherwise would have been. William P. Kelly, Queens College, generously and repeatedly made his knowledge of American literature and culture available. Elissa Weaver, University of Chicago, provided what are at once highly reliable and readable new translations of materials relating to Columbus's voyages. Wallace Chafe, University of California at Santa Barbara; Russ Hall, Harper & Row; and William C. Sturtevant, Smithsonian Institution, helped strengthen our representation of Native American literature, as did the work of Paula Gunn Allen, University of California, Berkeley, and her colleagues on the Modern Language Association's Commission on the Languages and Literature of America. Sally McLendon, Hunter College, CUNY, contributed immeasurably to our efforts to call greater attention to the eloquence and significance of Native American oral and written literatures. H. Barbara Weinberg, Queens College, CUNY, served as an extraordinary resource for exploring the interrelations of American literature and art. Her command of American art history has made each volume of *The Harper American Literature* more attractive as well as more responsive to the interplay of artistic forces in our culture. We are grateful for her assistance.

We would like to acknowledge the first-rate research and editorial assistance of Dianne Armstrong, University of California at Los Angeles; Stephanie Bobo, Boston University; Ruth Burke, University of California at Los Angeles; Carolyn Denard, Kennesaw College; JoEllen Fisherkeller, University of California, Berkeley; Ken Houghton, University of California at San Diego; Karen Johnson, Indiana University–Purdue University, Indianapolis; Laura Parkington, Seton Hall University; John Pearson, Boston University; and David Wheeler. Virginia, Marise, and Tara McDermott ingeniously prepared a chart of American literature that helped clarify our work. We would also like to acknowledge the special contributions of Trudy Baltz, who devoted great intelligence and energy to the project long before it took final shape, as well as of Michael Arnold and James Barcscz, both of Rutgers University, who offered incisive readings and excellent advice as the project neared completion. The preparation of this manuscript benefited greatly from the skillful and genial assistance of Nora Elias and Jeannette Gilkison at the University of California at Los Angeles, as well as Sandy Quals and Jo Taylor at Emory University.

We would also like to express our appreciation to the staffs at the libraries of Boston, Columbia, Emory, Harvard, Indiana, Princeton, and Seton Hall Universities; the University of California, Berkeley; the University of California at San Diego; Queens College; and the Maplewood and South Orange public libraries. In addition, we often relied on the expertise of Anthony Shipps, Indiana University; Elizabeth Smith, slide collection manager of the art history program, CUNY Graduate Center; and Errol Somay, New York Public Library.

Our continuing thanks go to the skillful and gracious professionals at Harper & Row. This project could not have been published without the support of Neale Sweet, vice-president and publisher. His commitment to *The Harper American Literature* and the principles underlying it has been exemplary. Lauren Bahr, director of development, kept the project on course with a masterful blend of energy, intelligence, and good will. Nat LaMar, development editor, quickly became an indispensable intellectual presence. His editorial insights and his knowledge of American literature are everywhere apparent to the contributing editors. We are also indebted to Jonathan Haber, who deftly coordinated the in-house editorial process with rare intelligence and excellent literary taste. Bonnie Biller, project editor, managed the flow of several thousand pages of manuscript and page proof with intelligent exactness and irrepressible good cheer. For the elegant look of these volumes, we would like to thank Karen Salsgiver. Claudia Kohner successfully guided the manuscript through its early development. Cara Tate proved to be an inexhaustible resource for solving every conceivable editorial and administrative problem; she helped make *The Harper American Literature* a better book to work on and read. George Blaine and Kathy Vuignier quietly contributed to the project with daily examples of efficiency. We would also like to thank Barbara Cinquegrani, Peter Coveney, Carole Knoeller, and Mira Schachne for their fine work.

Our greatest debt is to Phil Leininger, sponsoring editor. His expansive and detailed knowledge of American literature as well as his understanding and appreciation of this project's purpose made him a constant source of imaginative recommendations and useful advice. He helped us in every way to refine and realize our vision. Quite simply, *The Harper American Literature* would not exist without his having cultivated the commitment he shared with us to reexamine— and reconstruct—America's distinctive literary heritage.

We trust that all those who contributed to putting *The Harper American Literature* in print will endorse Ralph Waldo Emerson's notion that "the reward of a thing well done is to have it done."

The Harper American Literature

Compact Edition

John White,
Indians Fishing,
watercolor, ca. 1585.
British Museum, London.
Photograph: Bettmann Archive.

The Literature of the New World 1492–1620

The Discoveries of America

 America has had many discoverers. The first arrived
some 22,000 years ago, when emigrants from Asia
crossed the land bridge that is now the Bering Strait
to become the earliest inhabitants of the New World.
From these prehistoric migrations eventually grew
the great Aztec, Inca, and Mayan civilizations.
Recent archaeological evidence suggests that early in
the eleventh century A.D. the Vikings set up
campsites in Newfoundland and even made a few
unsuccessful attempts at colonization. It is also highly
probable that English fishing vessels routinely coasted
Canadian shores a decade or so before Christopher
Columbus set out on his momentous journey.

At 2:00 A.M., Friday, October 12, 1492, Columbus
undeniably made the first recorded discovery of
America. Yet his reputation as the discoverer of the
New World is somewhat tainted by the fact that he
never understood *what* it was he had actually found.
Like all early navigators, Columbus wanted to
discover a route, not a region. He ventured out with
the hope of finding a convenient sea passage to the
Orient, a trade route that would give Spain
commercial access to the opulent world Marco Polo
described so vividly in his famous thirteenth-century
account of an overland journey to the court of
Kublai Khan. From the moment Columbus first
spotted the island of Guanahaní—which he promptly
renamed San Salvador—he was certain that his grand
calculation had been correct: He had reached the east
by sailing west. He was so convinced of this that

throughout the four voyages he made to the New World between 1492 and 1502 he saw and interpreted everything—every plant, animal, mineral, place, and person he encountered—within the context of his having successfully reached Asia. To Washington Irving, Columbus was a man "predisposed to be deceived." The world he found was truly new, yet he persisted in seeing it as old.

Columbus's grand illusion derived ultimately from a mental picture of the earth that he pieced together from his reading of the prophetic books of the Bible, Marco Polo, and the famous ancient geographer Ptolemy. In brief, Columbus's dream of sailing directly west to Asia depended on what could be called the "small-earth theory." In his mathematically oriented *Geography* (ca. 150 A.D.), Ptolemy had grossly underestimated the size of the earth and had greatly extended Asia's eastern coast. This world image fitted in nicely with Marco Polo's speculations concerning the position of Japan, which Columbus—accepting Polo's location—estimated lay only 2,760 miles from Portugal. (The actual distance is well over 12,000 miles.) Columbus reinforced his calculations with quotations from the Old Testament prophets. In the apocryphal Book of Esdras (2:6) he read that the earth consists of six parts land and only one part water, a ratio that he believed would result in a short sea voyage. And in the Book of Ezekiel (5:5) he read that Jerusalem had been placed at the center of the world, a location that led him during his third voyage to conclude that he had approached the "Terrestrial Paradise," the original Garden of Eden.

Not only did Columbus derive an image of the world from the prophetic books, but he also wrote his own *Book of Prophecies*. In it he saw his career as the fulfillment of Isaiah 11:10–12: "And he shall set up an ensign for the nations." In 1502 Columbus wrote: "In carrying out this Enterprise of the Indies, neither reason, nor mathematics nor maps were any use to me: fully accomplished were the words of Isaiah." By his fourth voyage Columbus had sailed beyond geography into a vast, visionary world, wandering, as Irving put it, "in lands of his imagination." It was a geography in which every new observation, every new discovery, was made to fit into a single overarching theory—the belief that he had discovered a passage to India.

Credit for the discovery of America as a distinctly new region of the earth is often, though not without controversy, awarded to the Florentine navigator Amerigo Vespucci. In 1501, sailing to Brazil under the Portuguese flag, Vespucci noted that "we arrived at a new land which . . . we observed to be a continent." When his *Mundus Novus* (*The New World*) appeared in 1503, it received far wider circulation than anything Columbus had written. Vespucci was imbued with a deeper spirit of the Renaissance than Columbus, whose views in many respects resembled the views of such medieval travelers as Marco Polo. Vespucci doubted Ptolemy's accuracy. Like his family's friend Leonardo da Vinci, Vespucci maintained that observation was a more trustworthy guide than authority.

Vespucci secured his reputation as the discoverer of the New World by claiming in his next published work that he had found the South American continent during a 1497 voyage. Clearly he fabricated this early voyage to get around the fact that Columbus had set foot on—though not convincingly identified—the Paria peninsula of Venezuela on his third voyage in 1498. Thus Vespucci promoted himself not only as the first explorer to recognize the existence of a new world, but also as the first to discover its mainland.

"We Arrived at a New Land"

Now we come to the reasoning animals. We found all the earth inhabited by people completely nude, men as well as women, without covering their shame. They have bodies well proportioned, white in color with black hair, and little or no beard. I tried very hard to understand their life and customs because for 27 days I ate and slept with them, and that which I learned of them follows:

They have no laws or faith, and live according to nature. They do not recognize the immortality of the soul, they have among them no private property, because everything is common; they have no boundaries of kingdoms and provinces, and no king! They obey nobody, each is lord unto himself; no justice, no gratitude, which to them is unnecessary because it is not part of their code. They live in common in houses made like very large cabins; and for people who have no iron or other metal, it is possible to say that their cabins are truly wonderful, for I have seen houses which are 200 *passi* long and 30 wide and artfully made by craftsmen, and in one of these houses were 500 or perhaps 600 souls. They slept in nets [hammocks] woven of cotton, exposed to the air without any other covering; they eat seated on the ground; their food is roots of herbs and many good fruits, an infinity of fish and great quantities of shellfish; crabs, oysters, lobsters, crayfish, and many other things which the sea produces. The meat which they eat commonly is human flesh, as shall be told. When they can have other flesh of animals and birds they eat that too but they do not hunt for it much because they have no dogs and their land is very full of woods which are filled with fierce wild beasts, so they do not ordinarily enter the woods unless with a crowd of people.

Amerigo Vespucci (1502), on his first Brazilian voyage
(translated by S. E. Morison)

When an obscure German geographer, Martin Waldseemüller, came across Vespucci's work while preparing an edition of Ptolemy, he decided that this new land ought to bear the name of its founder: "[Europe, Africa, and Asia] have been more widely explored, and another, fourth part has been discovered by Americus Vesputius . . . , and I do not see why anyone should rightly forbid naming it Amerigo, land of Americus as it were, after its discoverer Americus, a man of acute genius, or America, inasmuch as both Europe and Asia have received their names from women." The geographer then took the liberty of writing the word *America* across the new territory on his 1507 world map. Despite numerous objections (the Spanish and Portuguese continued to refer to the New World as "the Indies" until the eighteenth century), and despite Waldseemüller's own change of mind, the name stuck. Ralph Waldo Emerson thought it "strange" that Vespucci had "managed in this lying world to supplant Columbus and baptize half the earth with his own dishonest name."

Vespucci's writings and Waldseemüller's geography convinced Europeans that something was drastically amiss with Columbus's version of the world. Here was no string of Asian islands but a newly discovered continent, a fourth part of the world. Ptolemy's influential map required serious revision; the world was not what everyone supposed. As Vespucci cautiously admitted: "Let it be said in a whisper, experience is certainly worth more than theory."

A Literature of Experience

As a central issue of Renaissance thought, the conflict between experience and theory, between modern observation and ancient authority, understandably left its mark on the literature of exploration. The discovery of the New World was itself a product of the Renaissance: Leonardo da Vinci drew his designs for a flying machine in the same year Columbus claimed San Salvador for Spain. *Experience* became a key word of intellectual discourse: "To me it seems," da Vinci wrote, "that all sciences are vain and full of errors that are not born of Experience, mother of all certainty, and that are not tested by Experience." The tension between experience and authority informed all of the arts and sciences of the time. In geography the conflict was dramatized by two sorts of maps—the theoretical maps of the entire world *(mappi mundi)* elaborately devised by learned academicians and the practical cruising charts *(portolanos)* made from the direct experience of working navigators. The early mariners and explorers constantly found themselves confronted by a discrepancy between what the big maps led them to expect and what was actually there.

By means of the *portolanos,* generations of mariners gradually pieced together a precise outline of the known world, especially the heavily traveled Mediterranean. Closely related to the practical coastal chart was the written record of assorted observations and experiences navigators kept during a voyage. Known in Greek as a *periplus* ("sailing around"), such navigational records go back to the fifth century B.C. A *periplus* eventually came to signify the narrative of a voyage round a coastline. Henry David Thoreau, a voluminous reader, alludes in *Walden* to one of the most famous of these, *The Periplus of Hanno.* The classical *periplus* clearly served as an important model of composition for the early explorers of the New World and subsequently left its mark on the great nineteenth-century voyage literature of Cooper, Poe, Thoreau, Twain, and Melville. Ezra Pound in the *Cantos* also saw the form as a literary plunge into direct experience: "periplum, not as land looks on a map / but as sea bord seen by men sailing."

The attitude behind the *periplus*—that one's experiences be grounded in personal observation and oriented to a specific location—would become a conspicuous feature of American writing. "Nothing is so easy as to travel on a map," wrote Crèvecoeur. "Our fingers smoothly glide over brooks and torrents and mountains." Or as Melville put it in *Moby-Dick,* "It is not down in any map; true places never are." As a method of *knowing,* the supremacy of experience to doctrine in American literature would be vividly dramatized in *Old Times on the Mississippi,* where a young Mark Twain learns to "read" the river, and in Faulkner's "The Bear," where the young Ike McCaslin learns how to "read" the woods.

Ernest Hemingway's version of the ancient *periplus* involved a dialectical movement between detail and design in composition. In a 1924 letter he describes the literary method of his first collection of stories, *In Our Time,* by using the language of exploration:

> Finished the book of 14 stories with a chapter on *In Our Time* between each story—that is the way they were meant to go—to give the picture of the whole between examining it in detail. Like looking with your eye at something, say a passing coast line, and then looking at it with 15 × binoculars. Or rather, maybe, looking at it and then going in and living in it—and then coming out and looking at it again.

Hemingway's method, as he reports it here, especially resembles James Fenimore Cooper's rhetorical procedure in *The Leatherstocking Tales,* where topographical description alternates continually between a "bird's-eye view" of a vast landscape and an extreme close-up of a particular spot.

America and the Pastoral Ideal

For Renaissance writers Arcadia represented a lovely natural landscape comfortably inhabited by shepherds who live—mainly for love and song—in hardy simplicity. This highly conventionalized ideal, known as the pastoral, evolved into a cultural attitude that not only shaped the American writer's response to the natural world but also led to a persistent devaluation of civilized society in favor of a return to simpler ways of life. As the critic Leo Marx noted in *The Machine in the Garden,* his study of the pastoral ideal in America, the central theme of a remarkably large number of books is the "withdrawal from society into an idealized landscape."

Literary pastoral had long symbolized the European dream of a Golden Age, and with the discovery of the New World that dream seemed for a brief moment in history to have come true. It seemed, at last, that an actual physical world did indeed exist uncorrupted by man and resembling the original state of nature. Columbus on his third voyage thought that he had literally come near to the Terrestrial Paradise. Later explorers, possessing a less biblical sense of geography, would still see the primeval American landscape as offering the possibility for another earthly paradise. This view dominated most descriptions of the new land. Thus the great French essayist Montaigne would write of the inhabitants of America, "I think that what we have seen of these people with our own eyes surpasses not only the pictures with which poets have illustrated the golden age, and all their attempts to draw mankind in the state of happiness, but the ideas and the very aspirations of philosophers as well."

For nearly all the early explorers, the vision of the Golden Age was also a vision of actual gold. All other motives for exploration—the investigation of new regions, the religious conversion of native populations, the discovery of previously unknown natural phenomena—were secondary compared to the acquisition of gold and silver. "We came here to serve God," said the conquistador Bernal Díaz, "and also to get rich." Columbus never ceased quizzing native chieftains about gold, and the repeated failure of all the first explorers to find precious metals severely dampened the initial European enthusiasm for the new land. After all, what good was this new world if it were poorer than the old one? What was the point in financing expedition after expedition if all that could be brought back were colorful birds, strange plants, and poor naked people? If no wealth could be found, then this entire New World amounted to no more than the "obstacle" Verrazzano found it to be—a vast and useless mass of land inconveniently blocking the way to the fabulous Indies. The search for gold, not geographical curiosity, stimulated the earliest penetrations into the North American wilderness.

During the period of inland exploration, the pastoral ideal had little to do with what we now think of as the wilderness. The conventional landscape of pastoral poetry and romance took the form of a gentle, bountiful, and orderly garden, the type of landscape the early explorers would have recognized as a standard feature of Renaissance painting. An appreciation of such landscapes was more the result of an acquired taste for certain picturesque configurations of natural scenery than of a direct encounter with vast and impenetrable forests.

For the first explorers and settlers, *wilderness* had highly pejorative connotations. The word conjured up medieval images of bestiality, malevolence, and the horrors of hell. From the deck of the *Mayflower* in 1620, William Bradford looked out on a "hideous and desolate wilderness, full of wild beasts and wild men." His was a landscape far removed from any comfortable pastoral ideal:

> For summer being done, all things stand upon them with a weatherbeaten face; and the whole country, full of woods and thickets, represented a wild and savage hue. If they looked behind them, there was the mighty ocean which they had passed, and was now as a main bar and gulf to separate them from all the civil parts of the world.

Nonetheless, by the end of the eighteenth century, the wilderness came to possess a decidedly positive value. By the era of Cooper and Thoreau, it would replace the cultivated garden as the ideal American landscape.

The New American Hero

Survival in the wilderness—the central action of so many exploration narratives— would become a recurring theme of both popular and classic American literature. Out of the confrontation with the wilderness emerged a new type of hero: tough, self-reliant, experienced, in contact with life at its most elemental levels. We can trace the origins of this new heroic personality in such early exploration texts as *The Narrative of Alvar Núñez Cabeza de Vaca* (1542), one of the great documents in the literature of human endurance. Cabeza de Vaca's story is the harrowing account of how four shipwrecked men managed to keep themselves alive while wandering for eight years through the hard country of the Texas Gulf. Like many American survival and captivity tales, Cabeza de Vaca's narrative culminates in a spiritual rebirth—the survivors in this case literally saving themselves by becoming faith healers among the various Indian communities that held them prisoner.

The Sea Mark

Aloof, aloof; and come no near,
        the dangers do appear;
Which if my ruin had not been
        you had not seen:
I only lie upon this shelf
        to be a mark to all
        which on the same might fall,
That none may perish but myself.

If in or outward you be bound,
        do not forget to sound.
Neglect of that was cause of this
        to steer amiss.
The seas were calm, the wind was fair
        that made me so secure,
        that now I must endure
All weathers be they foul or fair.

The winter's cold, the summer's heat
        alternatively beat
Upon my bruised sides, that rue
        because too true
That no relief can ever come.
        But why should I despair
        being promised so fair
That there shall be a day of Doom.

Captain John Smith (ca. 1631)

The connection between physical survival and spiritual rebirth is best expressed by the explorer who more than any other typified the new American hero— Captain John Smith. "It is a happy thing to be born to strength, wealth and honor," Smith wrote, "but that which is got by prowess and magnanimity is the truest luster; and those can the best distinguish content, that have escaped most honorable dangers; as if, out of every extremity, he found himself now born to a new life."

In Smith's vigorous writing, the idea of experience takes on new significance. Experience is important not only as a method of testing a theory but also as a supreme value in and for itself. Experiences become cumulative and hierarchical. The hero has many experiences—the more extreme the better.

Though Smith's numerous accounts of the New World contain a few Edenic overtones ("And then the Country of Massachusetts, which is the Paradise of all those parts"), his Arcadia is mainly a utilitarian utopia. His descriptions seem pastoral insofar as they are textured with an imagery of natural abundance. But even though the new land abounded with resources, it required, Smith continually emphasized, discipline and hard work to forge out of the raw resources an independent subsistence. The bitter experiences Smith eventually suffered in Virginia left him skeptical of the "golden promises" that made colonists "slaves in hopes of recompenses." Instead of the lure of gold, Smith held out to future settlers the lure of fish. Men, women, and children, he promised more extravagantly than usual, "with a small hook and line, by angling may take divers sorts of excellent fish at their pleasures; and is it not pretty sport to pull up two pense, six pense, and twelve pense, as fast as you can haul and vere [pay out] a line." Throughout his writing, Smith scornfully dismissed the possibility of gold and silver mines and underscored—in terms Benjamin Franklin a century later could hardly disagree with—the inevitable convertibility of labor into wealth.

Smith wrote his books and pamphlets primarily to attract potential colonists to America. While Smith's writing stressed the "incredible abundance" of the New World, he went a step further by promoting the land as a means to individual well-being, liberty, and improved social status. In his books we find the earliest formulations of what would become a prevailing image of America: an open society where someone without benefit of family connections, inheritance, or formal education can by virtue of hard work alone enjoy a happy, independent, and prosperous life. The role Smith played in the "invention" of America may be far more important than the part he played in its discovery.

Toward a Pluralistic Culture

With Captain John Smith, the English language and the American experience became inseparably united. For that reason Smith has often been called the first writer in American literature. Yet it is important to remember that initially the English participated only minimally in the colonization of the New World. While Smith struggled with a disorganized band of lazy colonists in Jamestown to erect a dingy fort, Spain and France had already created a New World literature. French influence extended throughout Canada, the Northeast, and the Midwest. By the mid-eighteenth century, Spain controlled everything west of the Mississippi and south of the Oregon country as well as Florida and territories south of Tennessee. The Dutch, too, made a considerable effort at colonizing the New World, controlling Manhattan Island along with the rich and beautiful Hudson valley.

A cultural pluralism characterized the New World from the start. Long before Smith reached Virginia, an African black named Estevan had journeyed far into the wilderness of New Mexico. And about the time Smith finally gave up on Jamestown, Santa Fe had become a successfully settled community. "We Americans," wrote Walt Whitman in a letter commemorating the anniversary of Santa Fe,

> have yet to really learn our own antecedents, and sort them, to unify them. They
> will be found ampler as has been supposed, and in widely different sources. Thus
> far, impress'd by New England writers and schoolmasters, we tacitly abandon

ourselves to the notion that our United States have been fashioned from the British Islands only—which is a very great mistake."

Exploration writing did not end with Captain John Smith and Samuel de Champlain but evolved into an American literary tradition as men and women like William Bradford, Mary Rowlandson, William Byrd, Daniel Boone, Thomas Jefferson, and William Bartram conducted their various errands into the wilderness. America, as Thoreau reminds us in *The Maine Woods,* always seems in the process of being discovered. The sheer wonder of discovery, in fact, may be the Age of Exploration's most durable legacy to American literature. Steeped in the writings of the great discoverers and explorers, the major American authors, from Washington Irving and James Fenimore Cooper to Hart Crane and William Carlos Williams, repeatedly beheld a world that was excitingly and inexhaustibly new. The inescapable fact of that newness may be what is most essentially American about American literature.

Further Reading:
J. Fiske, *Discovery of America,* 2 vols., 1893.
F. J. Turner, *The Frontier in American History,* 1920.
H. N. Smith, *The Virgin Land,* 1950.
R. W. B. Lewis, *The American Adam,* 1955.
E. O'Gorman, *The Invention of America,* 1961.
C. L. Sanford, *The Quest for Paradise: Europe and the American Moral Imagination,* 1961.
L. Marx, *The Machine in the Garden: Technology and the Pastoral Ideal in America,* 1964.
H. M. Jones, *O Strange New World,* 1964.
J. J. McDermott, *The American Angle of Vision,* 1966.
R. Nash, *Wilderness and the American Mind,* 1967, 1973.

S. E. Morison, *The European Discovery of America: The Northern Voyages,* 1971, and *The Southern Voyages,* 1974.
E. Page, *American Genesis,* 1973.
R. Slotkin, *Regeneration Through Violence: The Mythology of the American Frontier, 1600–1860,* 1973.
J. Seelye, *Prophetic Waters: The River in Early American Life and Literature,* 1977.
W. Franklin, *Discoverers, Explorers, Settlers: The Diligent Writers of Early America,* 1979.
F. Turner, *Beyond Geography: The Western Spirit Against the Wilderness,* 1980.
T. Todorov, *The Conquest of America,* 1984.

Christopher Columbus
1451–1506

Between 1492 and 1502, Christopher Columbus, convinced that the world was much smaller than it is and that the Orient could be easily reached by sailing west, made four voyages to the New World. On the first journey, on October 12, 1492, he discovered the island of San Salvador, and from there he went on to find the Bahamas, Cuba, and Haiti (he named the island Hispaniola). Though he discovered none of the riches that Marco Polo had spoken about so glowingly, he nevertheless returned to Spain confident that he had indeed reached the East. He was so certain that he had found the Indies that he named the people of the islands "Indians."

During the voyage, Columbus kept a daily journal that, like so many other original documents of these expeditions, is now lost. Our information concerning the first voyage comes from an abstract made of Columbus's journal by the Spanish historian Bartolome de Las Casas. The abstract puts Columbus's observations into the third person, except when Las Casas thought the admiral's words should be left intact (these are noted by quotation marks). Otherwise, the abstract appears to retain all the essential facts of the journey.

Columbus set out on his second voyage in September 1493. Though he discovered Puerto Rico, Jamaica, parts of Cuba, the Virgin Islands, and the Lesser Antilles, the expedition proved to be a financial disaster: still no gold or silver, still no fabulous cities. Of this voyage there is neither a journal nor an abstract. An aristocratic friend of Columbus's, however, accompanied him on the expedition and left an informal account. Michele de Cuneo's record of the journey shows how quickly relations between the Europeans and the natives deteriorated. His cold-blooded narrative of the skirmish in which Columbus's crew surprised a band of Carib men and women near St. Croix represents the first recorded battle between the Old World and the New. It prefigures the many disastrous encounters that would occur between the two worlds for centuries.

On the third voyage, which departed in May 1498, Columbus discovered Trinidad and the Spanish Main and came very close to finding the Amazon. He set foot on the South American continent, but, believing it an island, sailed up to Cuba, which he ironically thought must be the mainland, the gateway to the land of the Great Khan. While sailing in the Gulf of Paria, off the coast of Venezuela, Columbus formed a fantastic theory, which he set out in his journals and in a formal letter to the queen and king of Spain. He imagined that the earth was not perfectly round but rather pear-shaped and that he had approached its highest point. Here was to be found the original Garden of Eden, the "Terrestrial Paradise."

A great navigator but a poor administrator, Columbus was eventually relieved of his governorship in the New World. He had not found riches, nor had he been able to establish a peaceful, successful colony. Arrested by a special delegation, Columbus was returned to Spain in chains. Frustrated, his mind turning more and more to visionary goals, he immersed himself in the prophetic books of the Bible and attempted to prove to the Crown that Spain was destined to liberate Jerusalem from Islam. To provide the finances for this religious goal, Columbus made yet another voyage to the New World, this time searching for a passage through the newly discovered islands. On this journey, though he discovered Honduras, Nicaragua, Costa Rica, Panama, and Colombia, he never found the illusory passage (none would exist until the opening of the Panama Canal in 1914). Throughout the trip, Columbus encountered fierce storms, smashed vessels, mutiny, and madness. He spent an entire year marooned in a small cove off Jamaica; physically ill and profoundly disillusioned, he dreamed of Cathay and recorded the voices he heard from heaven. He miraculously made it back to Spain in November 1504, and for the remaining year and a half of his life wrote report after report insisting on his great accomplishment—his discovery that the Malay peninsula could be reached by sailing west. He died never realizing the magnificence of what he actually did discover.

Further Reading:
W. Irving, *A History of the Life and Voyages of Christopher Columbus*, 1828.
S. E. Morison, *Admiral of the Ocean Sea: A Life of Christopher Columbus*, 1942.
B. Landstrom, *Columbus*, 1966.
E. Bradford, *Christopher Columbus*, 1973.

Text:
Journals and Other Documents on the Life and Voyages of Christopher Columbus, ed. S. E. Morison, 1963.

from The Journal of the First Voyage[*]

[The Discovery of the West Indies]

[October 12, 1492]

Friday, 12 October

At two hours after midnight appeared the land,[1] at a distance of 2 leagues. They handed all sails and set the *treo,* which is the mainsail without bonnets, and lay-to waiting for daylight Friday, when they arrived at an island of the Bahamas that was called in the Indians' tongue *Guanahaní.* Presently they saw naked people, and the Admiral went ashore in his barge, and Martín Alonso Pinzón and Vicente Yáñez, his brother, who was captain of the *Niña,* followed. The Admiral broke out the royal standard, and the captains [displayed] two banners of the Green Cross, which the Admiral flew on all the vessels as a signal, with an F and a Y,[2] one at one arm of the cross and the other on the other, and over each letter his or her crown.

Once ashore they saw very green trees, many streams, and fruits of different kinds. The Admiral called to the two captains and to the others who jumped ashore and to Rodrigo de Escobedo, secretary of the whole fleet, and to Rodrigo Sánchez of Segovia, and said that they should bear faith and witness how he before them all was taking, as in fact he took, possession of the said island for the King and Queen, their Lord and Lady, making the declarations that are required, as is set forth at length in the testimonies which were there taken down in writing. Presently there gathered many people of the island. What follows are the formal words of the Admiral, in his Book of the First Navigation and Discovery of these Indies:[3]

"I," says he, "in order that they might develop a very friendly disposition towards us, because I knew that they were a people who could better be freed and converted to our Holy Faith by love than by force, gave to some of them red caps and to others glass beads, which they hung on their necks, and many other things of slight value, in which they took much pleasure. They remained so much our [friends] that it was a marvel, later they came swimming to the ships' boats in which we were, and brought

---

[*] The first printed version of the *Journal* appeared in 1825. It was first translated into English in 1827. The present translation is by Samuel Eliot Morison.
[1] San Salvador.

[2] For Ferdinand and Isabella, the king and queen of Spain. (Isabella is spelled in Spanish with a Y.)
[3] Title of Columbus's original journal.

us parrots and cotton thread in skeins and darts and many other things, and we swopped them for other things that we gave them, such as little glass beads and hawks' bells.[4] Finally they traded and gave everything they had, with good will; but it appeared to me that these people were very poor in everything. They all go quite naked as their mothers bore them; and also the women, although I didn't see more than one really young girl. All that I saw were young men, none of them more than 30 years old, very well built, of very handsome bodies and very fine faces; the hair coarse, almost like the hair of a horse's tail, and short, the hair they wear over their eyebrows, except for a hank behind that they wear long and never cut. Some of them paint themselves black (and they are of the color of the Canary Islanders, neither black nor white), and others paint themselves white, and some red, and others with what they find. And some paint their faces, others the body, some the eyes only, others only the nose. They bear no arms, nor know thereof; for I showed them swords and they grasped them by the blade and cut themselves through ignorance. They have no iron. Their darts are a kind of rod without iron, and some have at the end a fish's tooth and others, other things. They are generally fairly tall and good looking, well built. I saw some who had marks of wounds on their bodies, and made signs to them to ask what it was, and they showed me that people of other islands which are near came there and wished to capture them, and they defended themselves. And I believed and now believe that people do come here from the mainland to take them as slaves. They ought to be good servants and of good skill, for I see that they repeat very quickly whatever was said to them. I believe that they would easily be made Christians, because it seemed to me that they belonged to no religion. I, please Our Lord, will carry off six of them at my departure to Your Highnesses, that they may learn to speak. I saw no animal of any kind in this island, except parrots." All these are the words of the Admiral.

[October 13, 1492]

Saturday, 13 October

At the time of daybreak there came to the beach many of these men, all young men, as I have said, and all of good stature, very handsome people. Their hair is not kinky but straight and coarse like horsehair; the whole forehead and head is very broad, more so than [in] any other race that I have yet seen, and the eyes very handsome and not small. They themselves are not at all black, but of the color of the Canary Islanders; nor should anything else be expected, because this is on the same latitude as the island of Ferro in the Canaries.[5] The legs of all, without exception, are very straight and [they have] no paunch, but are very well proportioned. They came to the ship in dug-outs which are fashioned like a long boat from the trunk of a tree, and all in one piece, and wonderfully made (considering the country), and so big that in some came 40 or 50 men, and others smaller, down to some in which but a single man came. They row with a thing like a baker's peel[6] and go wonderfully, and if they

---

[4] Tiny bells used in falconry; these had proved, along with other trifles, popular with African natives.

[5] Columbus accepted Aristotle's theory that people and things from the same latitude are similar.

[6] This was the first time that Europeans had seen canoe paddles.

capsize all begin to swim and right it and bail it out with calabashes[7] that they carry. They brought skeins of spun cotton, and parrots, and darts, and other trifles that would be tedious to describe, and give all for whatever is given to them. And I was attentive and worked hard to know if there was any gold, and saw that some of them wore a little piece hanging from a thing like a needle case which they have in the nose; and by signs I could understand that, going to the S, or doubling the island to the S, there was a king there who had great vessels of it and possessed a lot. I urged them to go there, and later saw that they were not inclined to the journey. I decided to wait until tomorrow afternoon and then depart to the SW, since, as many of them informed me, there should be land to the S, SW, and NW, and that they of the NW used to come to fight them many times; and so also to go to the SW to search for gold and precious stones. This island is very big[8] and very level; and the trees very green, and many bodies of water, and a very big lake in the middle, but no mountain, and the whole of it so green that it is a pleasure to gaze upon, and this people are very docile, and from their longing to have some of our things, and thinking that they will get nothing unless they give something, and not having it, they take what they can, and soon swim off. But all that they have, they give for whatever is given to them, even bartering for pieces of broken crockery and glass. I even saw 16 skeins of cotton given for three *ceitis* of Portugal, which is [equivalent to] a *blanca* of Castile,[9] and in them there was more than an *arroba*[10] of spun cotton. This I should have forbidden and would not have allowed anyone to take anything, except that I had ordered it all taken for Your Highnesses if there was any there in abundance. It is grown in this island; but from the short time I couldn't say for sure; and also here is found the gold that they wear hanging from the nose. But, to lose no time, I intend to go and see if I can find the Island of Çipango.[11] Now, as it was night, all went ashore in their dugouts.

[October 14, 1492]

Sunday, 14 October

"When day was breaking I ordered the ship's gig and the caravels' barges to be readied, and I went along the coast of the island to the NNE, to see the other side, which was the eastern side, what there was there, and also to see the villages; and soon I saw two or three, and the people who all came to the beach, shouting and giving thanks to God. Some brought us water, others, other things to eat. Others, when they saw that I didn't care to go ashore, plunged into the sea swimming, and came out, and we understood that they asked us if we had come from the sky. And one old man got into the boat, and others shouted in loud voices to all, men and women, 'Come and see the men who come from the sky, bring them food and drink.' Many came and many women, each with something, giving thanks to God, throwing themselves on the ground, they raised their hands to the sky, and then shouted to us to come ashore; but I was afraid to, from seeing a great reef of rocks which surrounded

---

[7] Gourds.
[8] About 16 nautical miles long and 7 wide.
[9] Fractions of a cent.
[10] About 25 pounds.

[11] Japan; following Marco Polo's report, Columbus thought the island of Japan was approximately 1,500 miles from the Asian continent.

the whole of this island, and inside it was deep water and a harbor to hold all the ships in Christendom, and the entrance of it very narrow. It's true that inside this reef there are some shoal spots, but the sea moves no more than within a well. In order to see all this I kept going this morning, that I might give an account of all to Your Highnesses, and also [to see] where there might be a fortress; and I saw a piece of land which is formed like an island, although it isn't one (and on it there are six houses), the which could in two days be made an island, although I don't see that it would be necessary, because these people are very unskilled in arms, as Your Highnesses will see from the seven that I caused to be taken to carry them off to learn our language and return; unless Your Highnesses should order them all to be taken to Castile or held captive in the same island, for with 50 men they could all be subjected and made to do all that one wished. And, moreover, next to said islet are groves of trees the most beautiful that I have seen, and as green and leafy as those of Castile in the months of April and May; and much water. I inspected all that harbor, and then returned to the ship and made sail, and saw so many islands that I could not decide where to go first; and those men whom I had captured made signs to me that they were so many that they could not be counted, and called by their names more than a hundred. Finally I looked for the biggest,[12] and decided to go there, and so I did, and it is probably distant from this island of San Salvador 5 leagues, and some of them more, some less. All are very level, without mountains, and very fertile, and all inhabited, and they make war on one another, although these are very simple people and very fine figures of men."

1492/1825

---

from Michele de Cuneo's Letter on Columbus's Second Voyage[*]

[October 28, 1495: The Cannibals]

In the name of Jesus and of his glorious mother Mary from whom all good things come. On the 25th of September, 1493, we left Cadiz under 17 sails and all in good order—15 square and 2 lateen sails—and on the 2nd of October we anchored at the Grand Canary Island; the following night we set sail and on the 5th we anchored at Gomera, one of the Canary Islands; and it would take too long to tell you about the glorious reception we were given, the rounds fired by cannons and flame-throwers, all ordered by the lady who governs the island and with whom our admiral was once somewhat in love.[1] Here we refreshed ourselves as much as we needed and on October

---

[12] Rum Cay.

[*] No official journal or abstract of the second voyage has survived. This account was written by Michele de Cuneo, an aristocratic friend who accompanied Columbus on the expedition. The translation here was prepared especially for this volume by Elissa Weaver.

[1] Although Cuneo is the only source of this information, Columbus apparently had fallen in love with the woman who ruled the island of Gomera.

10th we set out on our voyage, but due to unfavorable weather we stayed around the Canary Islands three days. On the morning of October 13th, a Sunday, we left the Island of Ferro [Hierro], the last of the Canaries and we headed southwest. On the 25th of October, the eve of Saints Simon and Jude, at approximately 1600 we hit a storm of such force you wouldn't believe it and we thought our time was up. It lasted all night and 'til day and was so bad we couldn't see one another; at the end, as it pleased God, we found each other, and on November 3rd, a Sunday, we sighted land—five unknown islands. Our admiral named the first Santo Domingo since it was discovered on the Lord's day; the second he called Santa Maria la Gallante out of love for his ship, which was called Maria la Gallante. These two were not very large islands; nevertheless the admiral mapped them. If I remember correctly, it took us 22 days to get from the Island of Ferro to Santa Maria la Gallante, but I think one could well make the trip in 16 days of good wind.

On the island of Santa Maria la Gallante we got water and wood. The island is uninhabited even though it's full of trees and plains. We set sail from there that day and arrived at a large island inhabited by Cannibals,[2] who fled immediately to the mountains when they saw us. We landed on this island and stayed about 6 days since eleven of our men, who had banded together in order to steal, went 5 or 6 miles into the deserted area by such a route that when they wanted to return, they were unable to find their way, even though they were all sailors and could follow the sun, which they couldn't see well for the thick and full woods. When the admiral saw that these men had not returned and were nowhere to be found, he sent 200 men divided into 4 squadrons with trumpets, horns and lanterns, but even they were unable to find the lost men, and there was a time when we were more worried about the 200 men than the others before them. But, as it pleased God, the 200 returned with great difficulty and greater hunger; we judged that the eleven had been eaten by the Cannibals as they are wont to do. However, after 5 or 6 days, the eleven men, as it pleased God, when there remained little hope of ever finding them, built a fire on a cape; seeing the fire, we judged it to be them and we sent a boat and in that way recovered them. Had it not been that an old woman showed them the way back with gestures they'd have been done for since we had planned to set sail on the following day.

On that island we took 12 very beautiful and fat females about 15 or 16 years old and 2 boys of the same age whose genital member had been cut off down to their belly; and we judged that this had been done to keep them from mixing with their women or at least to fatten them and then eat them. These boys and girls had been picked by the Cannibals for us to send to Spain to the king as an exhibit. The admiral named this island Santa Maria di Guadalupe.[3]

We set sail from this island of Santa Maria di Guadalupe, the Island of Cannibals, on November 10th and on the 14th we reached another beautiful and fertile island[4] of Cannibals and we came to a very beautiful port. When the Cannibals caught sight of us they fled, as the others had, to the mountains and abandoned their houses where

[2] In the original manuscript the word is *Camballi*; it means either 'Carib Indians" or "cannibals."

[3] Guadeloupe, named after the famous Spanish shrine.

[4] Now St. Croix.

we went and took what we liked. In these few days we found many islands where we didn't disembark, but others where we did—for the night. When we didn't leave the ship we kept it tied, and this we did so we wouldn't travel on and out of fear of running aground. Because these islands were closely adjoining, the admiral called them the Eleven Thousand Virgins,[5] and the previous one, Santa Croce.

We had anchored and gone ashore one day when we saw, coming from a cape, a canoe, that is, a boat, for so it is called in their speech, and it was beating oars as though it were a well-armed brigantine. On it there were three or four male Cannibals with two female Cannibals and two captured Indian slaves—so the Cannibals call their other neighbors from those other islands; they had also just cut off their genital member down to their belly and so they were still sick. Since we had the captain's boat ashore with us, when we saw this canoe we quickly jumped into the boat and gave chase to the canoe. As we approached it, the Cannibals shot hard at us with their bows, and if we had not had our Pavian shields[6] we would have been half destroyed. I must also tell you that a companion who had a shield in his hand got hit by an arrow which went through the shield and into his chest 3 inches causing him to die within a few days. We captured this canoe with all the men. One Cannibal was wounded by a lance-blow and thinking him dead we left him in the sea. Suddenly we saw him begin to swim away; therefore we caught him and with a long hook we pulled him aboard where we cut off his head with an axe. We sent the other Cannibals together with the two slaves to Spain. When I was in the boat, I took a beautiful Cannibal girl and the admiral gave her to me. Having her in my room and she being naked as is their custom, I began to want to amuse myself with her. Since I wanted to have my way with her and she was not willing, she worked me over so badly with her nails that I wished I had never begun. To get to the end of the story, seeing how things were going, I got a rope and tied her up so tightly that she made unheard of cries which you wouldn't have believed. At the end, we got along so well that, let me tell you, it seemed she had studied at a school for whores. The admiral named the cape on that island the Cape of the Arrow for the man who was killed by the arrow.

On the 14th of November we set sail from the island in bad weather. On the 19th we anchored at a large and beautiful island of Indians called, in their language, Boluchen, which the admiral named St. John the Baptist.[7] As we sailed these 5 days both on the right and on the left we saw many islands all of which the admiral has had clearly mapped. At the island mentioned above we stopped to refresh ourselves and on the 21st we sailed; on the 25th, in the name of God, we anchored at Hispaniola,[8] an island discovered earlier by the admiral, where we went ashore at an excellent port called Monte Christo. In these few days we had more bad weather and we saw about 10 islands. We judged the distance from the island of Santo Domingo to Monte Christo to be 300 leagues. We were not able to keep a straight course for the shallows.

[5] The Virgin Islands, named for the legend of St. Ursula and the 11,000 virgin martyrs of Cologne.

[6] Large, rectangular shields from the northern Italian city of Pavia.

[7] Now Puerto Rico.

[8] The large island that Columbus called Hispaniola is the present-day Haiti and the Dominican Republic.

On the 27th of November we set sail to go to Monte Santo where the admiral on his last voyage left 38 men, and that same night we anchored at that very place.[9] On the 28th we went ashore, where we found all of our above-mentioned men dead and still stretched out there on the ground; their eyes were gone and we judged they had been eaten since when the Cannibals decapitate someone they immediately take out his eyes and eat them. They could have been dead 15 to 20 days. We were with the ruler of the place whose name was Goachanari, who, with tears running down his chest, and his men likewise, told us that the ruler of the mountain area named Goacanaboa had come with 3 thousand men and killed them together with some of their own people and robbed them out of spite. We found none of the things the admiral had left there, and having heard this story, we took it to be true. We spent 10 days on this business and on the 8th of December we left the place since it was not healthful because of its swamps, and we went to another place on the same island to an excellent port where we went ashore. There we built 200 houses which are small, like the huts we build at home for hunting birds, and they are covered with grass.

When we had built the settlement[10] for ourselves, the inhabitants of the island, who lived between one and two leagues from us, came to visit, as though we were brothers, saying that we were men of God come down from the sky, and many stood in awe watching us. They brought us some of their food to eat and we gave them some of ours since they behaved like brothers. And here we arrive at the end of our voyage, although I will say more below of another voyage I made later with the admiral when he decided to find terra firma; but now we will speak of other things and first about the search for gold on the island of Hispaniola.

1495/1885

---

from Columbus's Letter to the Sovereigns on the Third Voyage*

[October 18, 1498: The Terrestrial Paradise]

When I sailed from Spain to the Indies I found immediately on passing 100 leagues west of the Azores a very considerable change in the sky and the stars, and in the temperature of the air and in the waters of the sea. I took great pains in putting this to the test. I found that, from north to south, passing the said islands by the said 100 leagues, the compass needles, which hitherto had varied northeasterly, now varied a full point to the NW. On reaching that line it was as if someone had transported a

---

[9] The fortress of Navidad, which Columbus had constructed on his first voyage.
[10] Isabella, the first European attempt at a permanent settlement in the New World.

* The first printed version of this text appeared in 1825. It was printed again in 1892–1894. The latter is the version used as the basis for this translation by Samuel Eliot Morison.

hill thither. Moreover, I found the sea full of a certain weed,[1] resembling little pin
branches and heavily laden with fruit like that of the mastic. It is so thick that o
the First Voyage I thought that it was a shoal and that the ship would run agroun
But until we reached this line we did not come upon a single branch. When we go
there, moreover, I found the sea very calm and smooth and although the wind wa
strong, it never got rough. Furthermore, beyond the said line, towards the west,
found the weather to be very mild and unchanging in character, winter or summer
When I was there I discovered that the North Star described a circle, with a diamete
of 5°, and when the Guards are in the Right [E] Arm, the star is at its lowest elevation
and it continues to rise until it reaches Left [W] Arm; then it has 5° [elevation]. From
that point it sinks until it once more returns to Right Arm.

On this [Third] Voyage . . . as soon as I succeeded in attaining this line [100 leagues
W of the Azores] I immediately found the temperature very mild, and the further
forward I went the more it increased; but I did not find the stars consistent with this.
I found that, as night fell, I observed the North Star at an altitude of 5°, and then
the Guards were at "head"; and afterwards at midnight I observed the Star 10° high,
and at daybreak at 15° with the Guards at "feet." I found the smoothness of the sea
conformed to this, but not the gulfweed. I was much amazed by this business of the
North Star, and hence for many nights I "shot" it with the quadrant very carefully.
But I always found that the plumb-bob and line hit the same point [on the scale].
I regard this as something new, and mayhap it will be concluded that in this little
space the sky changes so much.

I have always read that the world, both land and water, was spherical, as the
authority and researches of Ptolemy and all the others who have written on this
subject demonstrate and prove, as do the eclipses of the moon and other experiments
that are made from east to west, and the elevation of the North Star from north to
south. But I have seen this discrepancy, as I have said. I am compelled, therefore, to
come to this view of the world: I have found that it does not have the kind of
sphericity described by the authorities, but that it has the shape of a pear, which is
all very round, except at the stem, which is rather prominent, or that it is as if one
had a very round ball, on one part of which something like a woman's teat were
placed, this part with the stem being the uppermost and nearest to the sky, lying
below the equinoctial line in this ocean sea, at the end of the East. I mean by the
end of the East the point where its land and islands terminate. To confirm this I cite
all the arguments written above about the line which passes from north to south 100
leagues west of the Azores. For in crossing this to the westward the vessels keep
rising gradually toward the sky and then enjoy milder weather; and the needle
varied a point on account of this mildness. The farther and higher we went, the
more the needle varied towards the NW. This elevation is responsible for the variation of the circle which the North Star describes with the Guards. The closer one
comes to the equator, the higher they will rise and the greater the difference will
be in the said stars and their orbits.

Ptolemy and the other scholars who have written about this world believed it

[1] Gulfweed.

spherical, thinking that this hemisphere was round like that in which they lived and which has its center in the island of Aryn,[2] which is below the equinoctial line between the Arabian Gulf and the Persian Gulf; the circle passes over Cape St. Vincent in Portugal in the west and by Cangara and the Seres[3] in the east. In that hemisphere I see nothing that stands in the way of its being round, as they claim. But as for this other hemisphere I maintain that it is like a half of a very round pear which had a long stem, as I have said, or like a woman's teat on a round ball. So neither Ptolemy nor the others who wrote about the world had any information about this half, for it was altogether unknown. They merely based their opinion on the hemisphere in which they lived, which is round, as I have said above. And now that Your Highnesses have ordered navigation and search and discovery it is revealed very clearly. For during this voyage when I was 20 degrees N of the equinoctial line I was there in the latitude of Arguin[4] and those other lands, and the people there are black and the land thoroughly scorched. After I went to Cape Verde Islands [I noticed] that the people in those regions are much darker, and the farther south they are the closer they approach the extreme; so, on the parallel of Sierra Leone, where I was when the North Star at nightfall had an elevation of 5°, the people are extremely black, and, after I sailed westward there, [I met] extreme heat. Once the line of which I spoke was passed, I found the climate increasingly mild, to such a degree that when I made the island of Trinidad, where the North Star at nightfall also had an elevation of 5°, I found the temperature there and in the land of Gracia very mild, the ground and the trees being very green and as beautiful as the orchards of Valencia in April. The people there are of very handsome build and whiter than any others I have seen in the Indies. Their hair is very long and smooth. The people are more intelligent and have more ability, and they are not cowards. The sun was then in Virgo, above our heads and theirs.

All this comes from the very mild temperature which prevails there, and this in turn comes from its being the highest land in the world and the closest to the sky. I therefore assert that the world is not spherical but that it has this other shape which I have already described, and which is in the hemisphere where the Indies end and the Ocean Sea [begins], and its extremity is below the equator. And this view is greatly supported by the fact that the sun, when Our Lord first created it, was at the first point of the East,[5] and the first light was here in the Orient, here where the world is highest. Although Aristotle was of the opinion that the Antarctic pole or the land beneath it is the highest part of the world and nearest the sky, other wise men opposed him, saying that the highest part is beneath the Arctic pole. By this reasoning it appears that they believed that one part of the world must be higher and closer to the sky than the other, and they did not hit upon this view that it is beneath the equator, for the reason I have stated. This is not surprising, for no sound knowledge was available about this hemisphere, but only very vague information of uncertain character, for no one had ever gone, or been sent, to check on it until

[2] In ancient and medieval geography, a sacred Asian city thought to be the "umbilical" of the world; it divided East from West.

[3] Ancient name for China.
[4] Island off the west coast of Africa.
[5] Aryn. (See footnote 2.)

now, when Your Highnesses gave orders that the sea and land be explored and discovered.

Holy Scripture testifies that Our Lord created the Terrestrial Paradise and planted in it the tree of life, and that a fountain sprang up there, from which flow the four principal rivers of the world: the Ganges in India, the Tigris and the Euphrates in [blank], which cut through a mountain range and form Mesopotamia and flow into Persia, and the Nile, which rises in Ethiopia and empties into the sea at Alexandria. I do not find and have never found any Latin or Greek work which definitely locates the Terrestrial Paradise in this world,[6] nor have I seen it securely placed on any world map on the basis of proof. Some put it at the sources of the Nile in Ethiopia, but others have visited all these countries without finding evidence of it in the mildness of the sky, or in its height towards the sky, by which it might be understood that it was there, or that the waters of the flood, which had risen above, had penetrated to it. Some gentiles attempted to argue that it was in the Fortunate Islands, which are the Canaries, etc. St. Isidore, Bede, Strabo, the Master of Scholastic History, St. Ambrose, Scotus, and all dependable theologians, agree that the Terrestrial Paradise is in the east, etc.

I return to my discussion of the land of Gracia and the river and lake I found there, so large that it may better be called sea than lake; for a lake is a place containing water and if it is large it is called a sea, as in the case of the Sea of Galilee and the Dead Sea. I say that if this river does not originate in the Terrestrial Paradise, it comes and flows from a land of infinite size to the south, of which we have no knowledge as yet. But I am completely persuaded in my own mind that the Terrestrial Paradise is in the place I have described, and I rely upon the arguments and authorities above cited.

May it please Our Lord to grant Your Highnesses long life, health and leisure to be able to pursue this very noble Enterprise by which I think Our Lord is greatly served and Spain receives increase in dominion and all Christians are much consoled and pleased, for the name of Our Lord will here be preached. In all the lands which the vessels of Your Highnesses visit, and on every cape, I order a cross to be set up, and I inform all the people whom I find of the estate of Your Highnesses and how you are fixed in Spain. I tell them of our holy faith as best I can and of the dogma of our Holy Mother Church,[7] which has her members in the entire world: I tell them of the polity and nobility of all Christians, and of their faith in the Holy Trinity. May it please Our Lord to forgive the persons who reviled and do revile this most excellent Enterprise and who oppose and have opposed it so that it may not go forward, without considering how much honor and glory it is for the royal estate of Your Highnesses throughout the world. They know not what to say to malign it, except that it involves expense and that vessels have not

[6] Columbus had assimilated a great deal of medieval thought concerning the exact location of the biblical Garden of Eden (i.e., the "Terrestrial Paradise").

[7] I.e., the Catholic church.

een immediately dispatched laden with gold, without taking into account the hortness of time and the considerable difficulties that have been experienced ere. They do not consider that in Castile, in the household of Your Highnesses, here are persons who each of them annually earn greater sums than it is necessary to expend on this enterprise. They likewise fail to note that no princes of Spain ever gained territory outside their borders save now, when Your Highnesses have an Other World here, by which our holy faith can be so greatly advanced and from which such great wealth can be drawn . . .

　　　　　Thanks be to God.

1492/1825

Alvar Núñez Cabeza de Vaca
ca. 1490–ca. 1557

In 1528 Pánfilo de Narváez led an expedition to establish a conquistadorial regime on the west coast of Florida. Beaten by the Florida wilderness and the unyielding Apalachee Indians, the expedition—the first overland journey on future United States soil—tried to escape to Mexico, but a gulf storm wrecked the Spaniard's makeshift boats near Galveston Island, Texas. Starvation, exposure, disease, and exhaustion reduced the original party of three hundred to four men: Cabeza de Vaca, Alonzo del Castillo, Andrés Dorantes, and his Moroccan slave, Estevan (or Estevanico). For the next eight years they wandered the Gulf Coast, where they lived mainly on prickly pears and were periodically taken into captivity by various Indian tribes. The four apparently managed to survive by assuming the role—reluctantly at first—of medicine men or shamans and practicing faith healing. The grisly account of their journey is the subject of the first North American captivity tale, *The Narrative of Alvar Núñez Cabeza de Vaca* (1542).

Contemporary psychologists have observed that hostages may gradually come to identify with their captors. Because of his many favorable experiences, Cabeza de Vaca retained a sympathetic—though nonetheless politically superior—attitude to the Indians, which was far different from most other conquistadores. He argued that "to bring all these people to Christianity and subjection to Your Imperial Majesty, they must be won by kindness, the only certain way." At journey's end, Cabeza de Vaca assures the party of friendly Indians who had accompanied him to the Spanish outposts that they need fear no harm. He is deceived, and his profound disappointment with his own people results in a dramatic psychological event that will recur throughout the literature of the New World: A tough-minded European explorer adrift in a vast alien land must suddenly confront not a mere loss of direction but a far more disorienting loss of identity.

Further Reading:
M. Bishop, *The Odyssey of Cabeza de Vaca*, 1933.
H. Long, *The Power Within Us*, 1944.

Text:
Spanish Explorers in the Southern United States 1528–1543, ed. F. W. Hodge, trans. B. Smith, 1907.

from The Narrative of Alvar Núñez Cabeza de Vaca[*]

[The Faith Healers]

That same night of our arrival,[1] some Indians came to Castillo and told him that they had great pain in the head, begging him to cure them. After he made over them the sign of the cross, and commended them to God, they instantly said that all the pain had left, and went to their houses bringing us prickly pears,[2] with a piece of venison, a thing to us little known. As the report of Castillo's performances spread, many came to us that night sick, that we should heal them, each bringing a piece of venison, until the quantity became so great we knew not where to dispose of it. We gave many thanks to God, for every day went on increasing his compassion and his gifts. After the sick were attended to, they began to dance and sing, making themselves festive, until sunrise; and because of our arrival, the rejoicing was continued for three days.

When these were ended, we asked the Indians about the country farther on, the people we should find in it, and of the subsistence there. They answered us, that throughout all the region prickly-pear plants abounded; but the fruit was now gathered and all the people had gone back to their houses. They said the country was very cold, and there were few skins. Reflecting on this, and that it was already winter, we resolved to pass the season with these Indians.

Five days after our arrival, all the Indians went off, taking us with them to gather more prickly pears, where there were other peoples speaking different tongues. After walking five days in great hunger, since on the way was no manner of fruit, we came to a river[3] and put up our houses. We then went to seek the product of certain trees, which is like peas. As there are no paths in the country, I was detained some time. The others returned, and coming to look for them in the dark I got lost. Thank God I found a burning tree, and in the warmth of it I passed the cold of that night. In the morning, loading myself with sticks, and taking two brands with me, I returned to seek them. In this manner I wandered five days, ever with my fire and load; for if the wood had failed me where none could be found, as many parts are without any, though I might have sought sticks elsewhere, there would have been no fire to kindle them. This was all the protection I had against cold, while walking naked as I was born. Going to the low woods near the rivers, I prepared myself for the night, stopping in them before sunset. I made a hole in the ground and threw in fuel which the trees abundantly afforded, collected in good quantity from those that were fallen and dry. About the whole I made four fires, in the form of a cross, which I watched and made up from time to time. I also gathered some bundles of the coarse straw that there abounds, with which I covered myself in the hole. In this way I was sheltered at night from cold. On one occasion while I slept, the fire fell upon the straw, when it began to blaze so rapidly that notwithstanding the haste I made to get out of it,

---

[*] Cabeza de Vaca composed his narrative in 1536, after reaching Mexico; it was first published in Spain in 1542.
[1] In 1534.

[2] The spiny, edible fruit of the flat-stemmed cactus.
[3] Probably the San Antonio.

carried some marks on my hair of the danger to which I was exposed. All this while tasted not a mouthful, nor did I find anything I could eat. My feet were bare and led a good deal. Through the mercy of God, the wind did not blow from the north n all this time, otherwise I should have died.

At the end of the fifth day I arrived on the margin of a river,[4] where I found the Indians, who with the Christians, had considered me dead, supposing that I had been stung by a viper. All were rejoiced to see me, and most so were my companions. They said that up to that time they had struggled with great hunger, which was the cause of their not having sought me. At night, all gave me of their prickly pears, and the next morning we set out for a place where they were in large quantity, with which we satisfied our great craving, the Christians rendering thanks to our Lord that He had ever given us His aid. . . .

The next day morning, many Indians came, and brought five persons who had cramps and were very unwell. They came that Castillo might cure them. Each offered his bow and arrows, which Castillo received. At sunset he blessed them, commending them to God our Lord, and we all prayed to Him the best we could to send health; for that He knew there was no other means, than through Him, by which this people would aid us, so we could come forth from this unhappy existence. He bestowed it so mercifully, that, the morning having come, all got up well and sound, and were as strong as though they never had a disorder. It caused great admiration, and inclined us to render many thanks to God our Lord, whose goodness we now clearly beheld, giving us firm hopes that He would liberate and bring us to where we might serve Him. For myself I can say that I ever had trust in His providence that He would lead me out from that captivity, and thus I always spoke of it to my companions.

The Indians having gone and taken their friends with them in health, we departed for a place at which others were eating prickly pears. These people are called Cuthalchuches[5] and Malicones, who speak different tongues. Adjoining them were others called Coayos and Susolas, who were on the opposite side, others called Atayos, who were at war with the Susolas, exchanging arrow shots daily. As through all the country they talked only of the wonders which God our Lord worked through us, persons came from many parts to seek us that we might cure them. At the end of the second day after our arrival, some of the Susolas came to us and besought Castillo that he would go to cure one wounded and others sick, and they said that among them was one very near his end. Castillo was a timid practitioner, most so in serious and dangerous cases, believing that his sins would weigh, and some day hinder him in performing cures. The Indians told me to go and heal them, as they liked me; they remembered that I had ministered to them in the walnut grove when they gave us nuts and skins, which occurred when I first joined the Christians. So I had to go with them, and Dorantes accompanied me with Estevanico. Coming near their huts, I perceived that the sick man we went to heal was dead. Many persons were around him weeping, and his house was prostrate, a sign that the one who dwelt in it is no more. When I arrived I found his eyes rolled up, and the pulse gone, he having all the appearances of death, as they seemed to me and as Dorantes said. I removed a mat with which he was covered, and supplicated our Lord as fervently as I could, that He would be pleased to give health to him, and to the rest that might have need of

---

[4] Presumably, the same river where they had set up shelters.

[5] These two groups were apparently south Texas Indians.

it. After he had been blessed and breathed upon many times, they brought me his bow and gave me a basket of pounded prickly pears.

The natives took me to cure many others who were sick of a stupor, and presented me two more baskets of prickly pears, which I gave to the Indians who accompanied us. We then went back to our lodgings. Those to whom we gave the fruit tarried and returned at night to their houses, reporting that he who had been dead and for whom I wrought before them, had got up whole and walked, had eaten and spoken with them and that all to whom I had ministered were well and much pleased. This caused great wonder and fear, and throughout the land the people talked of nothing else. All to whom the fame of it reached, came to seek us that we should cure them and bless their children.

When the Cuthalchuches, who were in company with our Indians, were about to return to their own country, they left us all the prickly pears they had, without keeping one: they gave us flints of very high value there, a palm and a half in length, with which they cut. They begged that we would remember them and pray to God that they might always be well, and we promised to do so. They left, the most satisfied beings in the world, having given us the best of all they had.

We remained with the Avavares eight months, reckoned by the number of moons. In all this time people came to seek us from many parts, and they said that most truly we were children of the sun. Dorantes and the negro[6] to this time had not attempted to practise; but because of the great solicitation made by those coming from different parts to find us, we all became physicians, although in being venturous and bold to attempt the performance of any cure, I was the most remarkable. No one whom we treated, but told us he was left well; and so great was the confidence that they would become healed if we administered to them, they even believed that whilst we remained none of them could die. These and the rest of the people behind, related an extraordinary circumstance, and by the way they counted, there appeared to be fifteen or sixteen years since it occurred.

They said that a man wandered through the country whom they called Badthing; he was small of body and wore beard, and they never distinctly saw his features. When he came to the house where they lived, their hair stood up and they trembled. Presently a blazing torch shone at the door, when he entered and seized whom he chose, and giving him three great gashes in the side with a very sharp flint, the width of the hand and two palms in length, he put his hand through them, drawing forth the entrails, from one of which he would cut off a portion more or less, the length of a palm, and throw it on the embers. Then he would give three gashes to an arm, the second cut on the inside of an elbow, and would sever the limb. A little after this, he would begin to unite it, and putting his hands on the wounds, these would instantly become healed. They said that frequently in the dance he appeared among them, sometimes in the dress of a woman, at others in that of a man; that when it pleased him he would take a buhío, or house, and lifting it high, after a little he would come down with it in a heavy fall. They also stated that many times they offered him victuals, but that he never ate: they asked him whence he came and where was his abiding place, and he showed them a fissure in the earth and said that his house was there below. These things they told us of, we much laughed at and ridiculed; and they seeing our incredulity, brought to us many of those they said he had seized; and we

[6] Estevan, or Estevanico, mentioned previously.

saw the marks of the gashes made in the places according to the manner they had described. We told them he was an evil one, and in the best way we could, gave them to understand, that if they would believe in God our Lord, and become Christians like us, they need have no fear of him, nor would he dare to come and inflict those injuries, and they might be certain he would not venture to appear while we remained in the land. At this they were delighted and lost much of their dread. They told us that they had seen the Asturian and Figueroa with people farther along the coast, whom we had called those of the figs.

They are all ignorant of time, either by the sun or moon, nor do they reckon by the month or year; they better know and understand the differences of the seasons, when the fruits come to ripen, where the fish resort, and the position of the stars, at which they are ready and practised. By these we were ever well treated. We dug our own food and brought our loads of wood and water. Their houses and also the things we ate, are like those of the nation from which we came, but they suffer far greater want, having neither maize, acorns, nor nuts. We always went naked like them, and covered ourselves at night with deer-skins.

Of the eight months we were among this people, six we supported in great want, for fish are not to be found where they are. At the expiration of the time, the prickly pears began to ripen,[7] and I and the negro went, without these Indians knowing it, to others farther on, a day's journey distant, called Maliacones. At the end of three days, I sent him to bring Castillo and Dorantes, and they having arrived, we all set out with the Indians who were going to get the small fruit of certain trees on which they support themselves ten or twelve days whilst the prickly pears are maturing. They joined others called Arbadaos, whom we found to be very weak, lank, and swollen, so much so as to cause us great astonishment. We told those with whom we came, that we wished to stop with these people, at which they showed regret and went back by the way they came; so we remained in the field near the houses of the Indians, which when they observed, after talking among themselves they came up together, and each of them taking one of us by the hand, led us to their dwellings. Among them we underwent greater hunger than with the others; we ate daily not more than two handfuls of the prickly pears, which were green and so milky they burned our mouths. As there was lack of water, those who ate suffered great thirst. In our extreme want we bought two dogs, giving in exchange some nets, with other things, and a skin I used to cover myself.

I have already stated that throughout all this country we went naked, and as we were unaccustomed to being so, twice a year we cast our skins like serpents. The sun and air produced great sores on our breasts and shoulders, giving us sharp pain; and the large loads we had, being very heavy, caused the cords to cut into our arms. The country is so broken and thickset, that often after getting our wood in the forests, the blood flowed from us in many places, caused by the obstruction of thorns and shrubs that tore our flesh wherever we went. At times, when my turn came to get wood, after it had cost me much blood, I could not bring it out either on my back or by dragging. In these labors my only solace and relief were in thinking of the sufferings of our Redeemer, Jesus Christ, and in the blood He shed for me, in considering how much greater must have been the torment He sustained from the thorns, than that I there received.

[7] I.e., in the summer of 1535.

I bartered with these Indians in combs that I made for them and in bows, arrows, and nets. We made mats, which are their houses, that they have great necessity for; and although they know how to make them, they wish to give their full time to getting food, since when otherwise employed they are pinched with hunger. Sometimes the Indians would set me to scraping and softening skins; and the days of my greatest prosperity there, were those in which they gave me skins to dress. I would scrape them a very great deal and eat the scraps, which would sustain me two or three days. When it happened among these people, as it had likewise among others whom we left behind, that a piece of meat was given us, we ate it raw; for if we had put it to roast, the first native that should come along would have taken it off and devoured it; and it appeared to us not well to expose it to this risk; besides we were in such condition it would have given us pain to eat it roasted, and we could not have digested it so well as raw. Such was the life we spent there; and the meagre subsistence we earned by the matters of traffic which were the work of our hands.

1536/1542

Pedro de Casteñeda
ca. 1510–ca. 1570

One of the earliest overland expeditions into the North American interior was conducted by a man who was neither European, Christian, white, nor free. Estevan (or, as he was called informally, Estevanico), a Moor from Morocco, accompanied his Spanish master, Andrés Dorante, to the New World as a member of the disastrous Narváez expedition that tried to take Florida in 1528. Nothing is known of Estevan's past, and had not the Narváez expedition failed, his life would have undoubtedly been lived out in the anonymity of slavery. But Estevan was one of the expedition's four survivors (see "The Narrative of Alvar Núñez Cabeza de Vaca"); after eight years of wandering and intermittent captivity, he managed to find his way to Mexico City.

As the four men crossed Texas, they heard stories about "populous towns" to the north. Spanish explorers, continually motivated by the fabulous, were already on the lookout for the mythic Seven Cities of Cíbola, and when the towns were brought to the attention of the viceroy of Mexico, he immediately planned a military expedition that would try to duplicate the riches Pizarro had wrested from the Incas during his conquest of Peru in 1533. In 1539 the viceroy sent an adventurous Italian friar, Marcos de Nizza, on a scouting mission to map out a route and gather information for a major expedition that Francisco de Coronado would undertake the following year. To lead the scouting party, the viceroy appointed Estevan, who knew the region and had presumably acquired skills in translation and diplomacy. Estevan and Marcos, however, made poor traveling companions; the friar disliked the Moor's arrogance and resented the caravan of Indian women Estevan had accumulated along the way. To ease tensions, Estevan went on ahead to the first of the reputed seven cities, Hawikuh, near the present

New Mexico–Arizona border. There it seems that Estevan offended the Zuñi rulers, for he was put to death one May morning in 1539.

A terrified Marcos returned to Mexico with a handful of Indian survivors. His lavish descriptions of large and wealthy towns, however, encouraged Coronado's expedition in 1540 to the Colorado River region and the Great Plains. Though Coronado failed to find any precious metals and the most populous city turned out to be a village of a thousand inhabitants, his journey was the most extensive early foray into the interior of the present-day United States.

"The Death of the Negro Estevan" and "Coronado Discovers the Seven Cities of Gold" are recounted by a member of Coronado's army, Pedro de Casteñeda, in his memoirs, *The Narrative of the Expedition of Coronado* (ca. 1565).

Further Reading:
W. Lowery, *The Spanish Settlements Within the Present Limits of the United States*, 1901.
H. E. Bolton, *Coronado, Knight of Pueblos and Plains*, 1949.
J. U. Terrell, *Estevanico the Black*, 1968.

Text:
Spanish Explorers in the United States, 1528–1543, ed. F. Hodge, trans. G. P. Winship, 1907.

---

from The Narrative of the Expedition of Coronado[*]

[The Death of the Negro Estevan]

After Estevan had left the friars, he thought he could get all the reputation and honor himself, and that if he should discover those settlements with such famous high houses, alone, he would be considered bold and courageous. So he proceeded with the people who had followed him, and attempted to cross the wilderness which lies between the country he had passed through and Cibola. He was so far ahead of the friars that, when these reached Chichilticalli,[1] which is on the edge of the wilderness, he was already at Cibola, which is eighty leagues beyond. It is 220 leagues from Culiacan[2] to the edge of the wilderness, and eighty across the desert, which makes 300, or perhaps ten more or less. As I said, Estevan reached Cibola loaded with the large quantity of turquoises they had given him and some beautiful women whom the Indians who followed him and carried his things were taking with them and had given him. These had followed him from all the settlements he had passed, believing that under his protection they could traverse the whole world without any danger. But as the people in this country were more intelligent than those who followed Estevan, they lodged him in a little hut they had outside their village, and the older men and the governors heard his story and took steps to find out the reason he had come to that country. For three days

---

[*] Casteñeda accompanied Coronado between 1540 and 1542 on his expeditions, and some 20 years later he recorded the *Narrative*. The earliest existing manuscript bears the date 1596.
[1] "Red house," so identified by the Aztec Indians because of its color. Probably located on or near the Rio Gila, near present-day Solomsville in southern Arizona.
[2] San Miguel Culiacan in central Sinaloa.

they made inquiries about him and held a council. The account which the negro gave them of two white men who were following him, sent by a great lord, who knew about the things in the sky, and how these were coming to instruct them in divine matters, made them think that he must be a spy or a guide from some nations who wished to come and conquer them, because it seemed to them unreasonable to say that the people were white in the country from which he came and that he was sent by them, he being black. Besides these other reasons, they thought it was hard of him to ask them for turquoises and women, and so they decided to kill him. They did this, but they did not kill any of those who went with him, although they kept some young fellows and let the others, about sixty persons, return freely to their own country. As these, who were badly scared, were returning in flight, they happened to come upon the friars in the desert sixty leagues from Cibola, and told them the sad news, which frightened them so much that they would not even trust these folks who had been with the negro, but opened the packs they were carrying and gave away everything they had except the holy vestments for saying mass. They returned from here by double marches, prepared for anything, without seeing any more of the country except what the Indians told them.

[Coronado Discovers the Seven Cities of Gold]

. . .After the general had crossed the inhabited region and came to Chichilticalli, where the wilderness begins, and saw nothing favorable, he could not help feeling somewhat downhearted, for, although the reports were very fine about what was ahead, there was nobody who had seen it except the Indians who went with the negro, and these had already been caught in some lies. Besides all this, he was much affected by seeing that the fame of Chichilticalli was summed up in one tumbledown house without any roof, although it appeared to have been a strong place at some former time when it was inhabited, and it was very plain that it had been built by a civilized and warlike race of strangers who had come from a distance. This building was made of red earth. From here they went on through the wilderness, and in fifteen days came to a river about eight leagues from Cibola which they called Red River,[3] because its waters were muddy and reddish. In this river they found mullets like those of Spain. The first Indians from that country were seen here—two of them, who ran away to give the news. During the night following the next day, about two leagues from the village, some Indians in a safe place yelled so that, although the men were ready for anything, some were so excited that they put their saddles on hind-side before; but these were the new fellows. When the veterans had mounted and ridden round the camp, the Indians fled. None of them could be caught because they knew the country.

The next day they entered the settled country in good order, and when they saw the first village, which was Cibola, such were the curses that some hurled at Friar Marcos that I pray God may protect him from them.

It is a little, crowded village,[4] looking as if it had been crumpled all up together. There are haciendas[5] in New Spain which make a better appearance at a distance. It

---

[3] Present-day Zuñi River in Arizona.
[4] Hawikuh, located 15 miles southwest of present-day Zuñi near the Zuñi River in New

Mexico; probably the village where Estevan lost his life.
[5] Large estates or farms.

is a village of about two hundred warriors, is three and four stories high, with the houses small and having only a few rooms, and without a courtyard. One yard serves for each section. The people of the whole district had collected here, for there are seven villages in the province, and some of the others are even larger and stronger than Cibola. These folks waited for the army, drawn up by divisions in front of the village. When they refused to have peace on the terms the interpreters extended to them, but appeared defiant, the Santiago[6] was given, and they were at once put to flight. The Spaniards then attacked the village, which was taken with not a little difficulty, since they held the narrow and crooked entrance. During the attack they knocked the general down with a large stone, and would have killed him but for Don Garcia Lopez de Cardenas and Hernando de Alvarado, who threw themselves above him and drew him away, receiving the blows of the stones, which were not few. But the first fury of the Spaniards could not be resisted, and in less than an hour they entered the village and captured it. They discovered food there, which was the thing they were most in need of. After this the whole province was at peace.

ca. 1565/1596

Richard Hakluyt
ca. 1552–1616

California, like the Florida of Ponce de Leon, existed mythically long before it became a reliable designation on maps of the New World. According to the sixteenth-century Spanish historian António de Herrera, the conquistador who discovered California, Hernando Cortes, named it after an imaginary island of black Amazons he had read about in a popular chivalric romance, *Las Sergas del Virtuoso Cavallero Esplandian* (The adventures of the virtuous cavalier Esplandian). Explorers were familiar, too, with ancient legends concerning a western island inhabited solely by women. Cortes probably grafted these fictions together to fabricate yet another rich, exotic, and eminently exploitable kingdom.

Cortes, however, did not travel far beyond his immediate discovery; he explored only a small section of the Baja peninsula. It was left to later Spanish explorers, most notably Juan Rodriguez Cabrillo, to conduct charting expeditions and landings farther north along the coast. Gradually, the Spanish, starting from Mexico, began organizing inland marches into the southern areas. But though Spanish vessels had reached the coastal waters of northern California, it was not until 1579, when the English navigator Sir Francis Drake dropped anchor apparently in what is now Drake's Bay,[1] that Europeans made their first contact with the region.

Drake and his crew, who had just given up their search for the Northwest Passage, stayed in northern California five weeks, preparing their weather-torn

---

[6] War cry or "loud invocation addressed to Saint James before engaging in battle with the Infidels" (from Captain John Stevens's *Dictionary*).

[1] A great deal of controversy exists concerning the precise location of Drake's landing. One of the best authorities on the history of navigation, Samuel Eliot Morison, is "positive" Drake's Bay is the site, though others have made claims for Bodega Bay and San Francisco Bay.

ship, the *Golden Hinde,* for the rest of its historic journey around the globe. The beautiful white cliffs along the bay reminded Drake of his native land, and envisioning a future English colony, he called the region "Nova Albion." (It was the first "New England.") Albion, the ancient name for the island of Britain, has been translated as "white land," a name the Romans thought referred to the famous white cliffs of Dover.

The following encounter between Drake's crew and the coastal Miwok Indians was reported in Richard Hakluyt's *The Principal Navigations, Voyages, Traffiques and Discoveries of the English Nation* (second edition, 1598–1600). A geographer, parson, and archivist, Hakluyt (pronounced "Haklet") served tirelessly as the unofficial publicist for early British navigation. He edited, translated, and compiled a mass of firsthand documents pertaining to the discovery, exploration, and colonization of the New World. His first book, *Divers Voyages Touching the Discovery of America,* dedicated to Sir Philip Sidney, was published in 1582. His major work, *The Principal Navigations,* which first appeared in 1589, has been called "the prose epic of [the] modern English nation." Based on several eyewitness reports, Hakluyt's account of Drake's circumnavigation figured prominently in his collection, but a need for secrecy kept it out of the first edition. A full-length account of Drake's voyage did not appear until 1628.

Further Reading:
H. R. Wagner, *Sir Francis Drake's Voyage Around the World: Its Aims and Achievements,* 1926.
R. F. Heizer, *Francis Drake and the California Indians,* 1947.
D. Wilson, *The World Encompassed: Francis Drake and His Great Voyage,* 1977.

Text:
The Principal Navigations, Voyages, Traffiques and Discoveries of the English Nation, 1598–1600, 2d ed., abridged and ed. J. Beeching, 1972.

---

from The Famous Voyage of Sir Francis Drake[1]

[*The First "New England"*]

The 5 day of June,[2] being in 43 degrees towards the pole Arctic, we found the air so cold, that our men being grievously pinched with the same, complained of the extremity thereof, and the further we went, the more the cold increased upon us. Whereupon we thought it best for that time to seek the land, and did so, finding it not mountainous, but low plain land, till we came within 38 degrees, it pleased God to send us into a fair and good bay, with a good wind to enter the same.

In this bay we anchored, and the people of the country having their houses close

---

[1] The complete title of Hakluyt's account is *The Famous Voyage of Sir Francis Drake into the South Sea, and There Hence About the Whole Globe of the Earth, Begun in the Year of Our Lord, 1577.*
[2] In 1579.

by the water s side, showed themselves unto us, and sent a present to our general.

When they came unto us, they greatly wondered at the things that we brought, but our general (according to his natural and accustomed humanity) courteously entreated them, and liberally bestowed on them necessary things to cover their nakedness, whereupon they supposed us to be gods, and would not be persuaded to the contrary.

Their houses are digged round about with earth, and have clefts of wood set upon them, joining close together at the top like a spire steeple, which by reason of that closeness are very warm.

Their beds is the ground with rushes strewed on it, and lying about the house, have the fire in the midst. The men go naked, the women take bulrushes, and comb them after the manner of hemp, and thereof make their loose garments, which being knit about their middles, hang down about their hips, having also about their shoulders a skin of deer with the hair upon it. These women are very obedient and serviceable to their husbands.

After they were departed from us, they came and visited us the second time, and brought with them feathers and bags of tobacco for presents: and when they came to the top of the hill (at the bottom whereof we had pitched our tents) they stayed themselves: where one appointed for speaker wearied himself with making a long oration, which done, they left their bows upon the hill, and came down with their presents.

In the meantime the women remaining on the hill, tormented themselves lamentably, tearing their flesh from their cheeks,[3] whereby we perceived that they were about a sacrifice. In the meantime our general with his company went to prayer, and to reading of the Scriptures, at which exercise they were attentive, and seemed greatly to be affected with it.

The news of our being there spread through the country, the people that inhabited round about came down, and amongst them the king himself, a man of a goodly stature, and comely personage.

In the forefront was a man, who bore the sceptre or mace before the king, whereupon hanged two crowns, a lesser and a bigger, with three chains of a marvellous length: the crowns were made of knit work wrought artificially with feathers of divers colours: the chains were made of a bony substance, and few be the persons among them that are admitted to wear them. Next unto him, was the king himself, with his guard about his person, clad with coney skins, and other skins: after them followed the naked common sort of people, every one having his face painted, some with white, some with black, and other colours.

In the meantime our general gathered his men together, and marched within his fenced place, making against their approaching a very war-like show.

In coming towards our bulwarks and tents, the sceptre-bearer began a song observing his measures in a dance, and that with a stately countenance, whom the king with his guard, and every degree of persons following, did in like manner sing and dance, saving only the women, which danced and kept silence. The general permitted them to enter within our bulwark, where they continued their song and dance a reasonable

[3] The significance of this self-laceration still puzzles ethnographers.

time. They made signs to our general to sit down, to whom the king, and divers others made supplications, that he would take their province into his hand, and become their king, making signs that they would resign unto him their right and title of the whole land, and become his subjects.[4] In which, to persuade us the better, the king and the rest, with one consent, and with great reverence, joyfully singing a song, did set the crown upon his head, enriched his neck with all their chains: which thing our general thought not meet to reject, because he knew not what honour and profit it might be to our country. Wherefore in the name, and to the use of Her Majesty he took the sceptre, crown, and dignity of the said country into his hands.

Our necessary business being ended, our general with his company travelled up into the country to their villages, where we found herds of deer by 1,000 in a company, being most large, and fat of body.

Our general called this country Nova Albion, and that for two causes: the one in respect of the white cliffs, which lie towards the sea: and the other, because it might have some affinity with our country in name, which sometime was so called.

There is no part of earth here to be taken up, wherein there is not some probable show of gold or silver.

At our departure hence our general set up a monument of our being there, as also of Her Majesty's right and title to the same, namely a plate, nailed upon a fair great post, whereupon was engraved Her Majesty's name, the day and year of our arrival there, with the free giving up of the province and people into Her Majesty's hands, together with Her Highness' picture and arms, in a piece of six pence of current English money under the plate,[5] where under was also written the name of our general.

ca. 1589/1598–1600

Captain John Smith
1580–1631

Captain John Smith entered the arena of North American exploration at a time when the romantic age of buccaneers and seadogs was giving way to the new, financially cautious policies of seventeenth-century colonization. Born into a moderately prosperous Lincolnshire family, Smith received a solid English grammar school education and, after a brief apprenticeship to a prominent merchant, enlisted at the age of fifteen to fight in the Netherlands. For ten years Smith pursued an adventurous military career that took him to Hungary, France, Germany, Spain, Austria, Rumania, Transylvania, Turkey, and North Africa. Toward the end of his life he wrote about these experiences in a brief

---

[4] Or so Drake interpreted the signs.
[5] This plate was "found" in Marin County, California, in 1936 and was at the time authenticated by experts. It is now displayed at the entrance to the Bancroft Library at Berkeley. Other experts, however, including Samuel Eliot Morison, consider it a fake.

autobiography, *The True Travels, Adventures, and Observations of Captain John Smith* (1630).

Upon his return to England, Smith—always eager for new adventures—joined the expedition that founded the Jamestown colony in 1607. An iron-willed disciplinarian, he tried almost single-handedly to keep a quarrelsome, inept, and frequently dissatisfied party intact. In his reports to his superiors Smith deplored the lack of skilled labor, complaining that too many of the colonists were "gentlemen" who found "not English cities, nor such fair houses, nor at their own wishes any of their accustomed dainties, with feather beds and down pillows, taverns and alehouses in every breathing place . . . For the country was to them a misery, a ruin, a death, a hell."

While at Jamestown, Smith conducted several short exploratory trips into the interior. During one of these journeys he was captured by Chesapeake Indians, who brought him to their king, Powhatan. As Smith many years later recounted the incident, he was condemned to death and then saved at the last minute by the timely intercession of Powhatan's favorite daughter, Pocahontas. Smith's failure to mention this dramatic episode in his first account of the Virginia expedition led a number of historians (beginning with Henry Adams) to consider the Pocahontas incident as mere fabricated afterthought. Yet, given Smith's promotional purposes at the time, it is quite possible that he wanted to omit any material that might scare off potential colonists. Whether true report or tall tale, Captain Smith's brief captivity and his hairbreadth escape has become one of the best-known passages in the literature of North American exploration.

Smith stayed on at Jamestown until the fall of 1609, when it was becoming clear that his efforts to bring effective management to the colony were futile. In 1614 he made another trip to North America, this time mapping out the coast of New England, a region he not only named but also fell so in love with that he ardently promoted its colonization in two important books, *A Description of New England* (1614) and *Advertisements for the Unexperienced Planters of New England, or Anywhere* (1631). The *Advertisements,* a list of "experienced memorandums" offering practical advice and theoretical suggestions on colonization, was addressed to the Puritan leaders who founded the Massachusetts Bay Colony in 1630. It was Smith's last work, and given the way he had been neglected during his final years, he would not have been surprised to find that most of his admonitions went unheeded.

Further Reading:
H. Adams, "Captain John Smith: Sometime Governour in Virginia and Admirall of New England," *North American Review,* January 1867.
B. Smith, *Captain John Smith: His Life and Legend,* 1953.
P. L. Barbour, *The Three Worlds of Captain John Smith,* 1964.
E. H. Emerson, *Captain John Smith,* 1971.
A. T. Vaughan, *American Genesis: Captain John Smith and the Founding of Virginia,* 1975.
F. Mossiker, *Pocahontas: The Life and Legend,* 1976.

Text:
Travels and Works of Captain John Smith, ed. E. Arber, 1884; reprinted with an introduction by A. G. Bradley, 2 vols., 1910. Spelling and punctuation have been changed to conform to modern usage.

from The Generall Historie of Virginia,
New England, and the Summer Isles

from **Book III**

from *Chapter II: [Captain Smith's Captivity]*

But our comedies never endured long without a tragedy; some idle exceptions being muttered against Captain Smith[1] for not discovering the head of [the] Chickahominy river and [being] taxed by the Council to be too slow in so worthy an attempt. The next voyage he proceeded so far that with much labor by cutting of trees asunder he made his passage; but when his barge could pass no farther, he left her in a broad bay out of danger of shot, commanding none should go ashore till his return; himself with two English and two savages went up higher in a canoe. But he was not long absent but his men went ashore, whose want of government[2] gave both occasion and opportunity to the savages to surprise one George Cassen, whom they slew, and much failed not to have cut off the boat and all the rest.

Smith little dreaming of that accident, being got to the marshes at the river's head twenty miles in the desert,[3] had his two men slain (as is supposed) sleeping by the canoe, while himself by fowling sought them victual; who finding he was beset with 200 savages, two of them he slew, still defending himself with the aid of a savage his guide, whom he bound to his arm with his garters and used him as a buckler,[4] yet he[5] was shot in his thigh a little, and had many arrows that stuck in his clothes but no great hurt, till at last they took him prisoner.

When this news came to Jamestown, much was their sorrow for his loss, few expecting what ensued.

Six or seven weeks[6] those barbarians kept him prisoner, many strange triumphs and conjurations they made of him, yet he so demeaned[7] himself amongst them as he not only diverted them from surprising the fort, but procured his own liberty, and got himself and his company such estimation amongst them, that those savages admired him more than their own *Quiyoughkasoucks.*[8]

The manner how they used and delivered him, is as follows.

The savages having drawn from George Cassen whither Captain Smith was gone, prosecuting that opportunity they followed him with 300 bowmen, conducted by the King of Pamunkey, who in divisions searching the turnings of the river found Robinson and Emry by the fireside; those they shot full of arrows and

---

[1] The narrative is written in the third person. Smith often incorporated the official reports of others into his history; this section was written by Smith and several members of his party.
[2] Discipline.
[3] Wilderness.
[4] Shield.
[5] Smith.

[6] Actually, approximately the three weeks from December 16, 1607, to January 8, 1608.
[7] Behaved; conducted.
[8] In Smith's own glossary of Indian words, the term is defined as "petty Gods, and their affinities."

slew. Then finding the Captain, as is said, who used the savage that was his guide as his shield (three of them being slain and divers others so galled[9]) all the rest would not come near him. Thinking thus to have returned to his boat, regarding them, as he marched, more than his way, [he] slipped up to the middle in an oozy creek and his savage with him, yet durst they not come to him, till being near dead with cold, he threw away his arms. Then according to their composition[10] they drew him forth and led him to the fire where his men were slain. Diligently they chafed his benumbed limbs.

He demanding for their captain, they showed him Opechancanough, King of Pamunkey, to whom he gave a round ivory double compass dial. Much they marvelled at the playing of the fly[11] and needle, which they could see so plainly and yet not touch it because of the glass that covered them. But when he demonstrated by that globe-like jewel the roundness of the earth and skies, the sphere of the sun, moon, and stars, and how the sun did chase the night round about the world continually, the greatness of the land and sea, the diversity of nations, variety of complexions, and how we were to them antipodes,[12] and many other such like matters, they all stood as amazed with admiration.

Notwithstanding, within an hour after, they tied him to a tree, and as many as could stand about him prepared to shoot him; but the King holding up the compass in his hand, they all laid down their bows and arrows and in a triumphant manner led him to Orapakes,[13] where he was after their manner kindly feasted and well used.

Their order in conducting him was thus: Drawing themselves all in a file, the King in the midst had all their pieces and swords borne before him. Captain Smith was led after him by three great savages holding him fast by each arm, and on each side six went in file with their arrows nocked.[14] But arriving at the town (which was but only thirty or forty hunting houses made of mats, which they remove as they please, as we our tents) all the women and children staring to behold him, the soldiers first all in file performed the form of a *bissone*[15] so well as could be, and on each flank, officers as sergeants to see them keep their orders. A good time they continued this exercise and then cast themselves in a ring, dancing in such several postures and singing and yelling out such hellish notes and screeches; being strangely painted, every one his quiver of arrows and at his back a club, on his arm a fox or an otter's skin or some such matter for his vambrace;[16] their heads and shoulders painted red with oil and pocones[17] mingled together, which scarlet-like color made an exceeding handsome show; each had his bow in his hand and the skin of a bird with her wings spread abroad,[18] dried, tied on his head, a piece of copper, a white shell, a long feather, with a small rattle growing at the tails of their snakes tied to it, or some such like toy.

All this while Smith and the King stood in the midst guarded, as before is said,

[9] Harassed; annoyed.
[10] Habits.
[11] Compass face, indicating directional points.
[12] Opposite poles.
[13] An Indian village.

[14] Readied.
[15] A military maneuver.
[16] Forearm armor.
[17] Bloodroot.
[18] Spread out.

and after three dances they all departed. Smith they conducted to a long house where thirty or forty tall fellows did guard him, and ere long more bread and venison was brought him than would have served twenty men. I think his stomach at that time was not very good; what he left they put in baskets and tied over his head. About midnight they set the meat again before him; all this time not one of them would eat a bit with him, till the next morning they brought him as much more, and then did they eat all the old and reserved the new as they had done the other, which made him think they would fat him to eat him. Yet in this desperate estate, to defend him from the cold, one Maocassater brought him his gown in requital of some beads and toys Smith had given him at his first arrival in Virginia.

Two days after, a man would have slain him (but that the guard prevented it) for the death of his son, to whom they conducted him to recover the poor man then breathing his last. Smith told them that at Jamestown he had a water[19] would do it, if they would let him fetch it, but they would not permit that, but made all the preparations they could to assault Jamestown, craving his advice, and for recompense he should have, life, liberty, land, and women. In part of a table book[20] he wrote his mind to them at the fort, what was intended, how they should follow that direction to affright the messengers, and without fail send him such things as he wrote for, and an inventory with them. The difficulty and danger he told the savages of, the mines, great guns, and other engines, exceedingly affrighted them, yet according to his request they went to Jamestown in as bitter weather as could be of frost and snow, and within three days returned with an answer.

But when they came to Jamestown, seeing men sally out as he had told them they would, they fled; yet in the night they came again to the same place where he had told them they should receive an answer and such things as he had promised them, which they found accordingly and with which they returned with no small expedition, to the wonder of them all that heard it, that he could either divine[21] or the paper could speak.

Then they led him to the Youghtanunds, the Mattapanients, the Payankatanks, the Nantaughtacunds, and Onawmanients upon the rivers of Rappahannock and Potomac, over all those rivers and back again by divers other several nations to the King's habitation at Pamunkey, where they entertained him with most strange and fearful conjurations:

As if near led to hell,
Amongst the devils to dwell.

Not long after, early in a morning, a great fire was made in a long house and a mat spread on the one side as on the other; on the one they caused him to sit, and all the guard went out of the house, and presently came skipping in a great grim fellow all painted over with coal mingled with oil, and many snakes' and weasels' skins stuffed with moss, and all their tails tied together so as they met on the crown of his head

---

[19] A distilled alcoholic liquor, used medicinally.   [21] Prophesy.
[20] Notebook; tablet.

in a tassel, and round about the tassel was a coronet of feathers, the skins hanging round about his head, back, and shoulders and in a manner covered his face, with a hellish voice, and a rattle in his hand. With most strange gestures and passions he began his invocation and environed the fire with a circle of meal; which done, three more such like devils came rushing in with the like antique[22] tricks, painted half black, half red, but all their eyes were painted white and some red strokes like Mutchatos[23] along their cheeks; round about him those fiends danced a pretty while, and then came in three more as ugly as the rest, with red eyes and white strokes over their black faces; at last they all sat down right against him, three of them on the one hand of the chief priest and three on the other. Then all with their rattles began a song; which ended, the chief priest laid down five wheat corns; then, straining his arms and hands with such violence that he sweat and his veins swelled, he began a short oration; at the conclusion they all gave a short groan and then laid down three grains more. After that, began their song again, and then another oration, ever laying down so many corns as before till they had twice encircled the fire; that done, they took a bunch of little sticks prepared for that purpose, continuing still their devotion, and at the end of every song and oration they laid down a stick betwixt the divisions of corn. Till night, neither he nor they did either eat or drink, and then they feasted merrily with the best provisions they could make. Three days they used this ceremony; the meaning whereof, they told him, was to know if he intended them well or no. The circle of meal signified their country, the circles of corn the bounds of the sea, and the sticks his country. They imagined the world to be flat and round, like a trencher,[24] and they in the midst.

After this they brought him a bag of gunpowder, which they carefully preserved till the next spring, to plant as they did their corn, because they would be acquainted with the nature of that seed.

Opitchapam, the King's brother, invited him to his house, where, with as many platters of bread, fowl, and wild beasts as did environ him, he bid him welcome, but not any of them would eat a bit with him but put up all the remainder in baskets.

At his return to Opechancanough's, all the King's women and their children flocked about him for their parts,[25] as a due by custom, to be merry with such fragments.

> But his waking mind in hideous dreams did
> oft see wondrous shapes
>
> Of bodies strange, and huge in growth, and
> of stupendous makes.

At last they brought him to Werowocomoco,[26] where was Powhatan, their Emperor. Here more than two hundred of those grim courtiers stood wondering at

---

[22] Ancient.
[23] Mustaches.
[24] Platter.
[25] Gifts.

[26] Chief's Town, Powhatan's home on the York River. This was on January 5, 1608.

him, as [if] he had been a monster, till Powhatan and his train had put themselves in their greatest braveries.[27] Before a fire, upon a seat like a bedstead, he sat covered with a great robe made of Rarowcun[28] skins and all the tails hanging by. On either hand did sit a young wench of sixteen or eighteen years and along each side [of] the house, two rows of men and behind them as many women, with all their heads and shoulders painted red, many of their heads bedecked with the white down of birds; but every one with something, and a great chain of white beads about their necks.

At his entrance before the King, all the people gave a great shout. The Queen of Appomattoc[29] was appointed to bring him water to wash his hands, and another brought him a bunch of feathers, instead of a towel, to dry them; having feasted him after their best barbarous manner they could, a long consultation was held, but the conclusion was, two great stones were brought before Powhatan; then as many as could laid hands on him, dragged him to them, and thereon laid his head, and being ready with their clubs, to beat out his brains. Pocohontas, the King's dearest daughter, when no entreaty could prevail, got his head in her arms and laid her own upon his to save him from death,[30] whereat the Emperor was contented he should live to make him hatchets, and her bells, beads, and copper, for they thought him as well[31] of all occupations as themselves. For the King himself will make his own robes, shoes, bows, arrows, pots; plant, hunt, or do anything so well as the rest.

> They say he bore a pleasant show,
> But sure his heart was sad.
> For who can pleasant be, and rest,
> That lives in fear and dread:
> And having life suspected, doth
> It still suspected lead.

Two days after,[32] Powhatan, having disguised himself in the most fearfulest manner he could, caused Captain Smith to be brought forth to a great house in the woods and there upon a mat by the fire to be left alone. Not long after, from behind a mat that divided the house, was made the most dolefulest noise he ever heard; then Powhatan, more like a devil than a man, with some two hundred more as black as himself, came unto him and told him now they were friends, and presently he should go to Jamestown to send him two great guns and a grindstone for which he would give him the country of Capahowasick[33] and forever esteem him as his son Nantaquond.

So to Jamestown with twelve guides Powhatan sent him. That night they quartered in the woods, he still expecting (as he had done all this long time of his imprisonment) every hour to be put to one death or other, for all their feasting. But almighty God (by His divine providence) had mollified the hearts of those stern barbarians with compassion. The next morning betimes they came to the fort, where Smith having

---

[27] Costumes.
[28] Raccoon.
[29] Powhatan tribe on the James River.
[30] This may have been a custom among Indian women, who then had a claim over the person they rescued.
[31] Capable.
[32] On January 7, 1608.
[33] A neighboring tribe.

used the savages with what kindness he could, he showed Rawhunt, Powhatan's trusty servant, two demiculverins[34] and a millstone to carry [to] Powhatan; they found them somewhat too heavy, but when they did see him discharge them, being loaded with stones, among the boughs of a great tree loaded with icicles, the ice and branches came so tumbling down that the poor savages ran away half dead with fear. But at last we regained some conference with them and gave them such toys and sent to Powhatan, his women, and children such presents as gave them in general full content.

1624

[34] Nine-foot cannon.

Unknown artist,
Alice Mason,
oil on canvas, 1670.
Adams National Historic Site,
Quincy, Massachusetts.

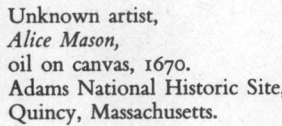

John Hesselius,
Charles Calvert,
oil on canvas, 1761.
The Baltimore Museum of Art.
Gift of Alfred R. and Henry G. Riggs
in memory of General Lawson Riggs

The Literature of
Colonial America
1620-1776

A "Citty upon a Hill"—New England

 In the seventeenth century a voluminous literature
came from the New England colonists who first
settled a rocky, sandy coastline that reaches into the
Atlantic like a grappling hook. These Pilgrim and
Puritan colonists aspired to be a "citty upon a hill,"
as the Massachusetts Puritan governor John Winthrop
put it. Ideal city notwithstanding, they coped at first
with primitive conditions. In the 1600s they
"forsooke a fruitful land, stately buildings, goodly
gardens, orchards, dear friends, and near relations" to
seek God's way in the "desert wilderness" of the
New World. In doing so, they also withdrew from
the bitter religious controversy that threatened their
livelihoods and their sense of spiritual and
psychological well-being in England. In effect, King
James I had carried out his threat against these
religious dissenters: "I shall make them conform or I
shall harry them out of the land."

The writings of the early explorers are
multinational, but the literature of colonial America,
north and south, is principally English, much of it
motivated by religious commitment and the need to
justify the radical act of uprooting households,
voyaging over three thousand miles of heaving
ocean, and starting life anew on a crudely mapped
continent whose very existence had been verified
only a century earlier. Much of the literature of
colonial America can be traced directly to distress in
the English families of such figures as William

Bradford, John Winthrop, and Anne Bradstreet. Their lives were entwined in the tumultuous religious Reformation begun by Martin Luther (1483–1546) and spurred by the teachings of the French theologian John Calvin (1509–1564).

The Religious Background

In fact, important origins of our nation's literature lie in the Protestant Reformation, a part of the Renaissance that essentially changed the direction and definition of all forms of European and English culture, including music, visual arts, literature, philosophy, in the fourteenth and fifteenth centuries.

This ferment extended to religion. By the late Middle Ages numerous Christians felt that the vital center of human life, the church, had strayed from its original mission and become corrupt. To a humanist like Erasmus the New Testament teachings of the Gospel seemed to have become secondary to concern for elaborate ritual and to church hierarchy and politics. Such Protestant reformers as William Tyndale argued that Scripture, not an institution or its trappings, was the essence of the Christian life. The authority of the Pope came into question, and in 1543 King Henry VIII formed the Church of England, a Protestant national church independent of Roman Catholicism and the Pope. By English law citizens were required to obey its rules and observe its practices.

A fundamental issue in this period of religious struggle was disagreement over authority. In Roman Catholicism the Pope was the highest temporal authority; the state was subject to the church he led. Henry VIII reversed that relationship when he formed the Church of England. Thereafter the monarch became the temporal authority with the church subject to the state. Conformity—or nonconformity—to established authority was a hallmark of this struggle. Nonconformists, all of whom accepted biblical authority as ultimate, put either the believing community or the individual in charge of making crucial religious decisions. It is from this strain that developed a great individualist literature that characterizes America, north and south.

English religious controversy continued after Henry VIII formed the Church of England, for some people felt that the national church still held a "Romish taint." Eventually, through the reigns of Queens Mary (1553–1558) and Elizabeth (1558–1603) the controversy focused on whether such matters as ceremony, vestments, ornament, and church governance represented godly tradition or human and demonic corruption. Conservatives defended their use, while the nonconformists who worked to rid the church of them were called, scornfully at first, Puritans, for their efforts at purification. Some others, notably the Bradford group who migrated to Plymouth, Massachusetts, despaired of successful reforms and separated from the Church of England altogether. They took direction from the Bible (2 Corinthians): "Come out from among them and be ye separate, saith the Lord."

Meanwhile, Anglican Church officials and agents of King James I (1566–1625) and of Charles I (1625–1649) made life difficult for all dissenters. "Nothing but the wide ocean and savage deserts," wrote the poet John Milton, "could hide and shelter . . . numbers of faithful and freeborn Englishmen . . . from the fury of the bishops."

One such group of "faithful and freeborn Englishmen" were the Plymouth Pilgrims, who represented a new kind of resident in America. Unlike the Jamestown colonists, the Pilgrims had no ambitions for riches. And they knew better than to try subsisting as an Indian trading post or seasonal fishing camp. They understood that a successful colony needed a sound financial basis, that it had to feed and sustain itself and be able to conduct trade. Since 1608 the Bradford group had lived in Holland, which afforded them religious freedom but "Dutchified" their lives. Fearing the loss of their cultural identity and religious intensity, they persuaded the Virginia Company of London to finance their American colony and, despite delays and mishaps, set sail on the *Mayflower* on September 15, 1620, with 149 aboard, forty-seven of them crewmen and officers. Their grim toll in that first American winter, when half of them died, can be traced in part to the two-month voyage on a diet deficient in fresh produce and to the cold and barren land where they settled.

Americans cherish the Pilgrims of the tiny Plymouth colony largely because of William Bradford's compelling account of it in *Of Plymouth Plantation* (1856), which he may have written in one of three "carved chairs" left in his will and doubtless transported on the *Mayflower*. Much more of our colonial literature, however, comes from the far less radical Puritan immigrants who arrived in a so-called Great Migration to the Massachusetts Bay Colony (1628–1643). They clustered in towns around current-day Boston and then extended into Connecticut and other parts of New England. Wherever they went, they and their descendants kept records of their experience in prose and verse.

The Puritans, like all immigrants to America, hoped to build a better life, one they defined largely in spiritual terms. Deploring the intractable corruption of the Church of England, they decided to build a church as pure as was humanly possible in New England. God seemed to direct them to do so through providential signs of catastrophe in their native land. King Charles I ascended to the English throne in 1625, a year in which the plague threatened London. He pressured Parliament to impose new, heavy taxes in a time of general high inflation and, in some trades, depression. In 1629 the king dissolved Parliament, stripping the populace of legislative representation.

Puritans like John Winthrop of Suffolk experienced these events personally. An attorney and landholder of high principles, he was dismayed by dishonesty at court and, though previously successful in his family's cloth trade, saw it sink in depression as prices rose and heavier taxes loomed. Mysteriously, he lost his attorney's license (perhaps for Puritan beliefs) and saw two friends imprisoned for tax resistance. Winthrop, a landholder with acreage planted in wheat, rye, and barley, was also a landlord responsible for his tenants and household servants, and a husband and father of seven children. He read God's message in this convergence of dire events and took drastic action. Within a year he arranged to transport his household and family to America to help build the spiritually exemplary "citty upon a hill."

The Voyage; the Landfall

At first these colonial immigrants lived in squalor brightened spiritually by their religious devotion and physically by the furnishings they managed to ship with the Winthrop fleet at the cost of four English pounds sterling per ton (in addition to the passage cost of five pounds per adult). Items like William Bradford's "six leather chairs," "great beer bowle," court cupboard, pewter dishes, and "red Turkey grogram suit of clothes" took up space below decks with the colony's supplies of firearms and ammunition, tools and farming implements. In the Winthrop party, livestock (240 cattle, "about sixty horses") traveled in separate ships topside in open pens. Many animals died in the early-spring Atlantic storms that made the colonists' shipboard lives miserable as well.

The sea voyage was a grim initiation for colonial living, especially for Puritan immigrants like the poet Anne Dudley Bradstreet, who was accustomed to certain middle-class comforts of the day. For three tempestuous months she—and the women and children like her—slept in the stuffy "between-decks" area, with the main deck their roof, the ceiling of the cargo hold their floor. Bradstreet's husband and father, like the other men, slept in hammocks slung everywhere. The only heat came from the cooking stove, and because the threat of fire prevented the use of candles or lanterns, each day ended at sundown, when the passengers took to their beds. The "great cabin" in the ship's stern provided space for religious worship. Doubtless John Winthrop preached his sermon "A Model of Christian Charity" there, having written it and begun his diary in these stressful onboard conditions punctuated by monotonous meals of salt meat or fish, hard "biscuit," and the beer or "syder" that were at least drinkable. The hardship of the voyage and landing has engaged the imagination of twentieth-century American writers.

Landfall presented its own complications. The *Arbella,* the flagship of the fleet, dropped anchor off the tiny, year-old settlement of Salem, Massachusetts, on June 12, 1630. "Some gentlemen and some of the women" were rowed ashore in shallops, and the scene before them must have looked like their own bleak futures. For Salem Plantation had, at most, forty dwellings, of which about a dozen were recognizable houses framed in oak and covered with pine boards roughly sawed or hewn with axes. Others were thatch-roofed cottages of one or two rooms with chimneys of logs or of wattle and daub (woven twigs and plaster) and windows of greased paper. The one "faire house," that of the Salem governor, had four rooms and an attic, a great central chimney of brick and fieldstone, a shingled roof, and probably small leaded windows of hand-blown, diamond-shaped panes of colored glass brought from England. Civilization itself was doubtless symbolized in that one house.

Yet the poet Anne Bradstreet, the diarist (and governor) Winthrop, and the writer of a notable historical letter, Thomas Dudley, could only have been sobered to see the wretched hovels of the less prosperous Salem colonists who lived in hillside excavations or in "English wigwams," described by one minister as "verie little and homely, made with small poles prick't into the ground and so bended and fastened at the tops and on the side, they are matted with boughs and

Homage to Mistress Bradstreet

By the week we landed we were, most, used up.
Strange ships across us, after a fortnight's winds
unfavouring, frightened us;
bone-sad cold, sleet, scurvy; so were ill
many as one day we could have no sermons;
broils, quelled; a fatherless child unkennelled; vermin
crowding & waiting: waiting.

. . . .

How long with nothing in the ruinous heat,
clams & acorns stomaching, distinction perishing,
at which my heart rose,
with brackish water, we would sing.
When whispers knew the Governor's last bread
was browning in his oven, we were discourag'd.
The Lady Arbella dying—
dyings—at which my heart rose, but I did submit.

John Berryman (1953)

covered with sedge and old mats." From Salem colonists who honored the newcomers with "a good venison pasty and good beer" came a grim story of overcrowding, of provisions in short supply, of such household necessities as soap produced by hand in the crudest fashion. No matter how spiritually elevated these Puritan writers and their fellow colonists felt, they knew the "citty upon a hill" needed to do better. It was one thing for southern colonial writers a century later to satirize colonists for "belly-aches" from eating unripe fruit or to poke fun at their rustic lives in which "conversation's lost, and manners drowned." But Massachusetts Bay colonists intending to build a new Jerusalem hardly found such matters to be the grounds for humor. Salem, as Dudley confided, "pleased us not."

For the first years, nonetheless, living conditions remained primitive. Dudley, who was Anne Bradstreet's father, offers a valuable glimpse of the colonial writer at work. "In the throng of domestic [and public] business" he wrote a newsletter to the Lady Bridget, Countess of Lincoln, in March 1631 apologizing for written work that he suspected might suffer from interruption, distraction, and crude surroundings. "I have yet," he reported, "no table, nor other room to write in than by the fireside upon my knee, in this sharp winter; to which my family must have leave to resort, though they break good manners, and make me many times forget what I would say, and say what I would not." Dudley was not the only colonial writer to observe that as he wrote, the ink froze in his well.

Puritan Beliefs

What specific beliefs, we ask, could motivate these New England colonists in tasks so discouraging? What thoughts sustained them and moved so many to write the histories and verses, the sermons and autobiographies that went far to shape the national identity of the people and the place that became the United States of America?

These Puritans and Pilgrims held in common one set of unshakable beliefs, most of which sound perplexing and harsh to modern Americans. They believed, first, that because Adam and Eve disobeyed God and fell from grace, all their heirs were also fallen and predestined to eternal punishment—except for an elect group redeemed by the sufferings of Jesus Christ and chosen to be recipients of God's grace. They spoke of their doctrine in terms of covenants, the binding and solemn agreements made between two parties. In the Bible they discerned, first, a covenant of works made between God and Adam, who was to enjoy perpetual life in the Garden of Eden in return for total obedience to God. When Adam disobeyed, he committed the first or original sin, broke the covenant, fell from grace, and, together with Eve, was cast out of the Garden forever to toil in the world.

Later God made a second covenant, one of grace, with Abraham, whose children he promised to save unconditionally. The Puritans considered themselves descendants of Abraham, redeemed by Jesus Christ who was sent by God to show His mercy. These saved souls, an indeterminate but limited number called the elect, were to be brought to a full consciousness of their condition by the ministry of the biblical word. God extended His irresistible grace to them. Ultimately these elect souls would dwell with God in eternity.

No Puritan, however, felt that any action of one's own could change the unalterable will of God. All Puritans knew that their innate human depravity prevented them from "earning" salvation through good works or deeds or generous thoughts or any number of prayers or devotions. Yet every Puritan or Pilgrim worked to live an industrious, upright life in a useful trade or profession. The saints, as the regenerate Puritans called themselves, tried to love their neighbors and to obey their civil magistrates, as Cotton Mather's *Bonifacius* (1710) reveals. And they strove daily to open their hearts in order to ascertain God's disposition toward them. Those convinced they were favored with grace were considered reborn or regenerate. The phenomenon was, as a Puritan synod or council agreed, "evidently a supernatural work, most powerful and at the same time most delightful, astonishing, mysterious, and ineffable . . . so that all in whose hearts God works in this marvellous manner are . . . regenerated, and do actually believe."

The experience of saving grace, however, was not usually swift or instantaneous, but slow and agonizing. The soul first came into consciousness of its sin and worthlessness, often with the help of a minister's sermon, which some writers spoke of as verbal arrows piercing sin-hardened hearts. In sermons Puritan writers worked always for a simplicity and directness of style so that hearers could understand immediately and, they hoped, be moved. But an awareness did not necessarily come in a church or meetinghouse. One New England immigrant, Thomas Shepard, got "dead drunk" on a Saturday night at college, awoke late "that Sabbath" with a hangover, and then "in shame and confusion . . . went out into the cornfields . . . where the Lord . . . did meet me with much sadness of heart and troubled my soul."

Shepard, like all regenerate Puritans, made a slow and tortuous way to the conviction that he was sanctified in God's grace. Even years later as a prominent, influential minister in New England, he confided to his journal the haunting pangs of envy, anger, and vanity. "I saw," he wrote, "how apt my heart was to be like the sea. . . . It's blown with any wind. . . . If God's spirit breathes, it follows that; if Satan, it follows that."

From one day to the next no Puritan could relax from vigilant perseverance in faith. Absolute certainty of election was regarded as prideful, and thus a sin, so Puritans always felt a certain anxiety about their spiritual state even as they examined the conscience and recorded the findings in a diary or journal or, like the poet Edward Taylor, embodied them in poems. Even the most spiritually persevering of Puritans ran the risk of self-delusion and thus of hypocrisy, possibilities that were humbling in themselves. And some souls in quest of union with Christ never, in good conscience, felt the stirrings of His grace. A Mrs. Sparhawk "came to the [immigrant] ship thinking to get God" but in New England found her spiritual state unchanged. She "saw herself far from humiliation [God's humbling] and thought it was a shame." It is no exaggeration to say that a voluminous colonial literature arose from the private need to examine the inner life. The spiritual struggles—in essence the search for integrity —among so many individuals could only naturally lead to the public necessity to justify and explain the formation of Puritan society as a whole. These struggles have captured the interest of some twentieth-century American poets.

It is extremely difficult for modern readers to appreciate the attraction of such life and to understand why by 1642 some twenty thousand people had immigrated to New England to enter into colonial life dominated by Puritan practices. It is helpful, perhaps, to be reminded that in England Puritanism reformulated the terms of society. On the basis of biblical (which is to say God's) authority, Puritanism found one person to be as good as another, no matter what that person's earthly social station. Aristocracy might rule England, at least for the present, but Puritanism argued that the average man or woman might be one of God's elect and thus a spiritual aristocrat destined to inherit the heavens and the earth.

This message was conveyed in the early 1600s by a new breed of minister quite different from the merely custodial clergy from aristocratic English families. The new Puritan ministers, from middle-class or impoverished backgrounds and trained in certain colleges at Cambridge University, were idealistic, energetic, intellectual, and pastoral or caring. They reached out to a small but warmly responsive public. Some, like John Cotton, were so powerfully persuasive that large numbers of their congregations came with them to America.

Mr. Edwards and the Spider

I saw the spiders marching through the air,
Swimming from tree to tree that mildewed day
   In latter August when the hay
   Came creaking to the barn. But where
     The wind is westerly,
Where gnarled November makes the spiders fly
Into the apparitions of the sky,
They purpose nothing but their ease and die
Urgently beating east to sunrise and the sea;

What are we in the hands of the great God?
It was in vain you set up thorn and briar
   In battle array against the fire
   And treason crackling in your blood;
     For the wild thorns grow tame
And will do nothing to oppose the flame;
Your lacerations tell the losing game
You play against a sickness past your cure.
How will the hands be strong? How will the heart endure?

A very little thing, a little worm,
Or hourglass-blazoned spider, it is said,
   Can kill a tiger. Will the dead
   Hold up his mirror and affirm
     To the four winds the smell
And flash of his authority? It's well
If God who holds you to the pit of hell,
Much as one holds a spider, will destroy,
Baffle and dissipate your soul. As a small boy

On Windsor Marsh, I saw the spider die
When thrown into the bowels of fierce fire:
   There's no long struggle, no desire
   To get up on its feet and fly—
     It stretches out its feet
And dies. This is the sinner's last retreat;
Yes, and no strength exerted on the heat
Then sinews the abolished will, when sick
And full of burning, it will whistle on a brick.

. . . .

Robert Lowell (1946)

These Puritans were not an other-worldly people. One article of faith especially connected their spiritual life to the work of colonization. Writings from William Bradford to Cotton Mather and beyond show the conviction that the apocalyptic prophecy of the New Testament Book of Revelation was about to be fulfilled. Within the scheme of Christian history, the Puritans believed, the final events of earthly time were coming to a close. They had a method for determining this. Martin Luther had shown them how. Luther argued that historical events on earth matched the symbols in Revelation. These symbols thus became guides to the past and to the future. The difficulty lay in correlating biblical and earthly events accurately. In theological study the ministers were trained to interpret such biblical symbols as the ten-horned beast, the grapes of wrath, the seven vials, and to apply their meaning to such worldly events as war, plague, and royal oppression. To do so accurately was to know God's own timetable for the final events of human history. For according to Scripture, there would occur a period of severe earthly tumult and dissension, after which the Messiah, the Christ, would return to earth. At that point God would bind up Satan for one thousand years, the duration of the peaceful and harmonious Millennium, to be followed by one final great battle that signified the end of the world and the eternal peace of the elect with God.

The subject of apocalypse recurs repeatedly in the literature of New England. The ideal of the peaceable kingdom of the millennium set a very high standard for the city on the hill. The new Jerusalem in America—as Cotton Mather put it, the *Theopolis Americana*—would have to be objectified in colonial life just as it was proclaimed in literature. Colonization itself, from felling trees to writing poems, was site preparation for the Christian millennium. Though the definition may have varied over the years, that may have been the first and deepest "American dream."

Colonial Life

That dream absorbed the daily energy of settlement, whose activities, terminology, and values also found their way into literature. What were those activities? How did these people live? As middle-class husbandmen and tradesmen, they brought English conventions to America, including belief in the great value of a permanent house and enclosed lands that kept the chaos of the dreaded wilderness out. During the first years of New England settlement, scouting parties of leading men surveyed inland areas for good soil, ample fresh water, timberlands, and natural meadows vital for feeding livestock. Returning to the coast, they got permission from the General Court (the legislature) to settle the area of their choice, then in good weather led their families, associates, and animals to it. Setting out in spring, they had at most eight months to settle before winter closed in.

On site a committee planned the house lots and fields based on English agriculture familiar to everyone. Each farmer needed several fields immediately— one for grain crops, another for pasture, and a third for meadow to yield hay for the winter feeding of livestock. No colonist had the time to clear picture-perfect fields. The charming stone fences of New England arose from the necessity to clear rocky fields so they could be tilled and planted, for the growing season was short and the harsh winters long. Well after the American Revolution, European travelers deplored the unsightly, scraggly fields in which crops grew among tall, charred stumps. But such visitors mistook necessity for slovenliness.

Providing shelter was a major undertaking. Northern colonists built heavy-timbered houses that began with the felling of entire trees whose trunks, intended for main supports, were hand-hewed and notched, then dragged with draft animals to the building site. Neighbors arrived on "raising day" to help push and fasten the structural timbers. The assembly was dangerous, its success a cause for prayers of thanks and celebration with food and perhaps "strong waters." The siding, usually of milled clapboards, and all the interior finishing were left to the occupant's family.

The colonial farmhouse in which many writers worked was divided into three areas: bedrooms, the hall or parlor for ceremonial occasions, and a kitchen, which became the center of activity. There the housewife, aided by older children and perhaps a serving girl or even a slave, smoked meats, dried herbs, put up fruits and vegetables, and ground grains. There she processed dairy products, dressed poultry, made soap from ashes, and carded and spun flax, wool, and cotton. Just outside, in the kitchen garden, she tended vegetables and a seasonal herb garden that was virtually the family's medicine chest. Chicory, for instance, soothed irritated eyes, mint aided women in childbirth, and thyme cured toothache. Anne Bradstreet would have known this lore and superintended these time-consuming tasks. Edward Taylor's "Huswifery" and other poems acknowledge his consciousness of them.

We must surmise that most colonial writers worked by candlelight after their very large households quieted down for the night. Those who were ministers doubtless had a certain family consent to withdraw to a quiet corner or, if they were city dwellers like Cotton Mather, to write sermons, verses, and diary entries in a private study off the streets "full of girls and boys sporting up and down," streets "full of good shops well furnished with all kinds of merchandise" and increasingly crowded with the specialized crafts and trades characteristic of the city.

The character of colonial New England life, however, was mainly rural. As each inland or coastal town was settled, the planning of house lots was crucial, since they were the tight nucleus of the society, which invited or "called" a minister and erected the all-important meetinghouse at the earliest opportunity. All roads radiated from the meetinghouse like the spokes of a wheel, for it was the hub of community life, attracting all but the sick for Sunday and Thursday sermons and, when death occurred, drawing the townspeople for funerals and burial in the graveyard adjacent to it. A few houses, including the parsonage, would be situated near the meetinghouse, in addition to a field sometimes called an artillery garden because the husbandmen-farmers gathered there regularly for militia exercises. Town magistrates were selected from the men of the community.

The meetinghouse, used for town meetings as well as for religious services, showed the Puritan congregation's fondness for color. As the center of religious and social life, townspeople contributed to its painting long before they could spare the expense of coloring their own houses. Favored shades were orange and chocolate, yellow, green, red, sky blue, and white. Such an accumulation might sound chaotic now, but at the time these colors signified a godly civil order in the wilderness.

Not surprisingly, some American innovation in agriculture proved necessary almost immediately. Predators and fierce winters forced colonists to build livestock shelters, and because native grasses were unsuited to grazing and haying, the settlers had to seed meadows in English grasses, which thrived. The ideal of the town as a corporation or commonwealth—an ideal recurrent in the literature —was objectified in cooperative "public works" projects such as bridges and livestock pounds, which required the hard work of fencing but kept the animals out of the arable fields. Stray livestock were a serious point of contention. In poems Anne Bradstreet lamented the absence of her husband on public business, but some of that business concerned lawsuits when, for example, a swine uprooted a farmer's field; once the Bradstreets' own mare was attacked by dogs and killed while eating hay on a neighbor's property.

Every New England housewife working to grind corn or wheat in a small hand mill looked forward to the day when her town had a miller. Every husbandman whose iron or steel tools needed repair anticipated the arrival of a blacksmith. Towns tried to lure these skilled craftsmen with promises of choice acreage and of a monopoly, for the mill and forge were considered public utilities. The sawmills, especially, proved welcome to colonists who dreaded the wilderness long before they saw it. These were people who brought to the New World a centuries-long European folkloric tradition that said that the unshaped land, or wilderness, was inhabited by unspeakable beasts. The sawmills that produced lumber for colonists' houses, and for export to Europe and the West Indies, also drove back the terrifying forest wilderness that harbored feral animals and satanic Indians.

Puritan Literature

From the beginnings of settlement the Puritan and Pilgrim writers labored to justify American innovations to an English audience. Men like Thomas Dudley and women like his daughter Anne did not have much leisure to sit writing before the fire, even with makeshift lapboards in the icy depths of winter. Their literary record reflects ideals and hardships. Historical literature like *Of Plymouth Plantation* (1856) and Winthrop's *Journal* (1853) and such sermons as Jonathan Edwards's "Sinners in the Hands of an Angry God" (1741) testify to the New Englanders' urgent justification of socioreligious practices.

Colonial writers also found ample subject matter in personal relations and in family life. To read the biographies of these writers is to see how vulnerable the women were to death in childbirth and how susceptible the children (and adults, for that matter) to mortal illness. Puritan writers' multiple marriages reflect the precariousness of colonial life and testify to their high regard for the sanctity of marriage, which they believed to be an ordinance of God.

The family and marriage, accordingly, became an important literary concern. It is evident, for example, in Cotton Mather's *Bonifacius, an Essay Upon the Good,*

1710, which deals with appropriate relations among family, neighbors, and community. Samuel Sewall's *Diary* shows a parent's anguish and joy, as does Anne Bradstreet's prose and verse. Marital love, too, found expression in Bradstreet.

The American experience provided colonial writers with some disquieting subject matter. Chattel slavery, customarily associated with the South, existed in New England and mocked Puritan aspirations; in the late 1600s the worldly Puritan diarist Samuel Sewall wrote an antislavery tract. The native Americans became another recurrent topic in colonial writing. Rhode Islander Roger Williams wrote a series of verses in which he used Indian traits to point up English barbarities. But orthodox Puritan writers could not regard Indians with objective interest, since a stated goal of colonization was the conversion of these heathen to Christianity. Squanto's help to the Pilgrims seemed to be God's providence at work in the initial encounter between the English and the Indians. But the "heathen" soon became alarmed by settlers' relentless encroachment on their lands, and two uprisings occurred, the Pequot War (1635–1636), which Puritans considered God's test of their mettle, and the severe King Philip's War (1675), which seriously threatened English settlement and suggested to some that their city on a hill was failing.

Internal trials and dissension were another important concern to the colonial writers, who felt that God tried them even as Satan worked to subvert them. It was one thing to decree an orderly society based, as Winthrop said, on "justice and mercy" but another to organize and sustain it. Puritan-Pilgrim culture was prone to superstition and intolerant of dissent, and by our later standards it did not handle either well. Witchcraft and heresy were investigated and punished and were considered a legitimate preoccupation of writers seeking, in Puritan terms, to justify the ways of God to men, as Cotton Mather does within his biography of Sir William Phips, which includes episodes on the witch trials of the early 1690s.

New England literature shows Puritan intolerance of religious sects eager to coexist in the colony. Some Quakers learned this when they persisted in reentering the Puritan's jurisdiction after repeated expulsions. The Massachusetts Bay colonists denounced the "ranters and quakers," cropped the ears of three men, and hanged two men and one woman who returned to the Bay Colony repeatedly under penalty of death. The town of New Haven ruled that the "cursed sect of heretics" could finally be punished by imprisonment, whipping, forced labor, branding, and having "their tongues bored through with a hot iron."

Other troublesome dissidents were, so to speak, deported. When the Englishman Thomas Morton settled in Mount Wollaston (now Quincy, Massachusetts) in 1625 to sell the Indians guns and to frolic with an assortment of traders, Indian maids, and former servants, Plymouth's Governor Bradford denounced the "riotous prodigallitie and profuse excess." Within three years several New England communities ousted the self-styled "Mine-Host of Merrymount," shipping him back to England. Morton's *New English Canaan* (1637) presents his side of the story, Bradford's *Of Plymouth Plantation* the other.

In the American Grain

The result of that brave setting out of the Pilgrims has been an atavism that thwarts and destroys. The agonized spirit, that has followed like an idiot with undeveloped brain, governs with its great muscles, babbling in a text of the dead years. Here souls perish miserably, or, escaping, are bent into grotesque designs of violence and despair. It is an added strength thrown to a continent already too powerful for men. One had not expected that this seed of England would come to impersonate, and to marry, the very primitive itself; to creep into the very intestines of the settlers and turn them against themselves, to befoul the New World.

It has become "the most lawless country in the civilized world," a panorama of murders, perversions, a terrific ungoverned strength, excusable only because of the horrid beauty of its great machines. To-day it is a generation of gross know-nothingism, of blackened churches where hymns groan like chants from stupefied jungles, a generation universally eager to barter permanent values (the hope of an aristocracy) in return for opportunist material advantages, a generation hating those whom it obeys.

What prevented the normal growth? Was it England, the northern strain, the soil they landed on? It was, of course, the whole weight of the wild continent that made their condition of mind advantageous, forcing it to reproduce its own likeness, and no more.

William Carlos Williams (1925)

It is helpful to recall that the pluralistic America of the twentieth century was unlike anything the Puritans could have envisioned or desired. New Englanders fled a society they thought corrupted in spirit and circumstance and made tremendous personal sacrifices to live under what they understood to be God's direction. From their viewpoint, strict laws and orthodox practices were proper godly vigilance, not brutality, though it is understandable that a modern American might react negatively to them.

The colonists of the Great Migration and thereafter worked exhaustively to build their agricultural New Jerusalem. Some twenty years after the Winthrop group looked at Salem in dismay, one colonist could boast that "this remote, rocky, barren, bushy, wild-woody wilderness . . . now through the mercy of Christ [has] become a second England for fertilness. In so short a space," he added, "that is indeed the wonder of the world."

A "Vale of Plenty": The South

Southern colonists did not come to America to found a city upon a hill. Their American dream was quite different. Captain John Smith's expression "vale of plenty" captured the essence of the southern response to America. The vale or valley of plenty signified a fruitful garden, even a paradise, that could be attained with human effort. Two centuries of southern colonial writers saw their land as a natural paradise, not a howling wilderness. The Puritan might write of hardship on an improvised lapboard in winter, but the southerner reports no such discomfort. In 1665 Sir Robert Moray wrote an epistle describing life in the Carolinas:

> None can know the sweetness of it but he that tasts it. One ocular [visual] inspection, one aromatick smel of our woods, one hearing of the consert of our birds in those woods would affect them more than 1000 reported stories let the authors be never so readible.

Southern colonists conceived of the good life in terms of a fertile valley that, industriously cultivated, could realistically become an American dream come true —as Robert Beverley put it, a "paradise improved." These colonists came from English villages and from cities like London and Bristol. But they brought to America an ideal of English farm life and the Renaissance commitment to exploration and knowledge.

The colonial South included cultures of the Chesapeake Bay, Virginia, the Carolinas, and, in the eighteenth century, Georgia. The early southern writers were planters, merchants, artisans, and ministers, and they wrote in many forms, among them letters, personal journals, autobiographies, poems, sermons, and translations. Colonial southern writing enriched the national literature with satire, song, storytelling, and a spirit of exploration inherent in the English Renaissance. The southern ideal, expressed in literature and the fine arts, was that of country life. It was modeled on English farm life but intended to surpass it in the sylvan New World. Thus southern writers like Smith and William Byrd II elaborated the idea of America as a Canaan, a "vale" of plenty.

Southern colonists suffered the same shipboard travails as their counterparts in New England. Their justification for taking the land was similar to that of the Puritans. "We chanced in a lande," wrote Smith, "even as God made it, where we found only an idle, improvident, scattered people." Through two centuries the southerners negotiated treaties with that "scattered people" as they penetrated inland, cultivating the tobacco crop that depleted the richest soil, and which induced them to move on and to recruit workers—at first whites, then black slaves—for field cultivation. Southern colonists learned to expect killing winter frosts but knew they could look forward to very long summers whose growing season averaged six to nine months. Daily life could be conducted in the outdoors in forms not possible in the North.

The southern colonists, like those in the North, first constructed dwellings of wattle and daub, though even in 1608 or 1609 a visitor to Jamestown noticed that beautifully woven Indian mats decorated colonists' walls. In Maryland, as elsewhere, early colonists ate and slept on shipboard while they constructed a framed timber fort and built cottages onshore. By the 1660s brick kilns were in use in Jamestown and Henrico, Virginia, and bricklayers were at work constructing houses. Later in that century, and throughout the next, brickwork became decorative in checkerboard and diagonal patterns that were popular throughout the South. The simple, versatile, quickly constructed log house, which was introduced to Englishmen by Germans and Scandinavians, probably first appeared in America in the Carolinas. By the end of the colonial period southern frontiersmen in western Virginia lived in it, as did some black slaves in "quarters" set at a distance from the main house.

Gardens complemented southern colonial houses at every socioeconomic level. They ranged from quadrangles of shrubs, flowers, and herbs to elaborate arrangements of terraces, mounds, ponds, and lakes modeled on English precedent but adapted to the new environment. Often decorative, edible, and medicinal vegetation was mixed together as ornamental gardens merged with the kitchen garden. And for some men and women interested in botany, medicine, and landscaping the ornamental garden was a nursery and experiment station.

The legend of southern gracious living persists in twentieth-century movies and in the remaining eighteenth-century plantation houses and grounds open to tourists. Colonial texts document this quality of southern life as early as 1686, when a French traveler commented on his visit to Colonel William Fitzhugh's estate near Manannas, Virginia: "The Colonel's accommodations were . . . so ample that this company [of twenty] gave him no trouble at all; we were all supplied with beds. . . . Col. Fitzhugh showed us the largest hospitality. He had store of good wine and other things to drink, and a frolic ensued." Philip Fithian's *Journal* nearly a century later tells a comparable story. "The Ladies dined first," Fithian reports of a private ball in mid-1770s Virginia.

> When they rose, each nimblest Fellow dined. . . . For drink, there were several sorts of Wine, good Lemon Punch, Toddy, Cyder, Porter, &c—About Seven the Ladies & Gentlemen begun to dance in the Ball-Room—first Minuets one Round; Second Giggs; third Reels; And last of All Country-Dances. . . . The Ladies were Dressed Gay, and splendid, & when dancing, their Skirts & Brocades rustled and trailed behind them.

Though Fithian observes the wealthy at play, it must be remembered that good music and the fine arts were a part of life for many southerners, including yeoman farmers, apprentices, and merchants.

Southern colonial life assumed its own social forms. If it lacked the visible community focal point of the meetinghouse, southerners were nonetheless joined together by waterways and rounds of visits. The men mustered for militia exercises at appointed times and places and attended sessions of court. Many families sojourned to Anglican and other church services, and the roads themselves were at times the scene of social life, as owners raced horses on them and wagered on the outcome. "There are races at Williamsburg twice a year," wrote an Englishman named J. D. F. Smith, who visited the colonies in 1772, "also matches and sweepstakes very often, the inhabitants, almost to a man, being quite devoted to the diversion of horse-racing."

Yet most southern colonists, whether of modest holdings or vast acreage, were farmers vitally interested in weather, soil, seeds, crops, livestock, and the trades and crafts necessary to agrarian life. The cultivation of the principal money crop, tobacco, points up the degree of work required for the "vale of plenty." By 1618 tobacco was entrenched as a profitable crop, but colonial farmers worked hard to bring it to market. They first chose a site where the forest mold was virgin and in midwinter burned a pile of brush and logs to enrich the soil with ash and to clear it of potential weeds. The minuscule tobacco seeds (ten thousand to a teaspoon) were sown before winter's end. By late spring the seedlings were transplanted to prepared fields. In dry weather the crusts of mud had to be broken, and when the plants began to bud, the tops had to be nipped so that the leaves would grow desirably large. Insects and worms were, of course, removed by hand. At harvest time the leaves were finally cut, hung to dry in a protective enclosure, and finally packed in a barrel through which an axle was driven so it could be wheeled, sometimes many miles, to a shipping point on a tidewater wharf.

Southern colonial intellectual life in this agrarian culture was both broad and deep in spite of dispersed settlement patterns. Indian missionary work was one educational incentive, which John Brinsley, a Virginian, recognized in 1622 when he wrote that God had "ordained schooles of learning to be a principal means to reduce a barbarous people to civilitie." Formal education became a concern throughout the colonies. There were Jesuit schools in Catholic Maryland, a school for orphans founded in Georgia by the preacher George Whitefield, and a variety of private, parish, and tutorial schools elsewhere. The College of William and Mary, which Thomas Jefferson attended, was founded in 1693.

Schoolteachers were sometimes recruited like laborers and skilled craftsmen. As John Harrower confided to his diary in 1774, "This day I being reduced to the last shilling I hade was obliged to engage to go [from London] to Virginia for four years as a schoolmaster for Bedd, Board, washing and five pound during the whole time." Harrower was hired by a Colonel Dangerfield of "Belvedere," near Fredericksburg ("This morning about 8 A M the Colonel delivered his three sons to my Charge to teach them to read, write, and figure. His oldest son Edwin, 10 years of age, intred into two syllables in the spelling book, Bathurst his second son six years of age in the Alphabete and William his third son 4 years of age does not know the letters"). Indications are that tutors like Harrower often ran plantation schools for pupils numbering twenty or thirty. Students like his, the sons of wealthy southern colonists, were sometimes sent abroad to England for higher education, as William Byrd II was. The Virginian Hugh Jones complained in 1724 that in England such young men were kept "drudging on in what is of least use to them, in pedantick methods, too tedious for their volatile genius." Such young men, however, were able to enjoy the London cultural scene, including the drama, which Puritans abhorred but which the southern colonies appreciated and supported. This colonial linkage to the mother country has held the attention of the modern writer, who deliberately displays the stylistic richness of the southern colonial.

Religious life was richly varied in the colonial South. During the seventeenth century the Anglican church (the Church of England) predominated, but Roman Catholics were appearing in all five southern colonies, as were other dissenters, including a few Puritans. With Lord Baltimore's founding of Maryland in 1634, Catholics had a colonial center. And Quaker missionaries were at work in Virginia in the mid-seventeenth century. After 1700, French and German Protestants, Lutherans, Baptists, and evangelical Presbyterians gained increasing religious influence in the South. They coexisted uneasily with the Anglican clergy, who overlooked the power of their evangelical fervor and so failed to take part in the religious movement known as the Great Awakening, a phenomenon in South and North alike.

The Sot-Weed Factor

In the last years of the seventeenth century there was to be found among the fops and fools of the London coffee-houses one rangy, gangling flitch called Ebenezer Cooke, more ambitious than talented, and yet more talented than prudent, who, like his friends-in-folly, all of whom were supposed to be educating at Oxford or Cambridge, had found the sound of Mother English more fun to game with than her sense to labor over, and so rather than applying himself to the pains of scholarship, had learned the knack of versifying, and ground out quires of couplets after the fashion of the day, afroth with Joves and Jupiters, aclang with jarring rhymes, and string-taut with similes stretched to the snapping-point. . . .

[This] was his origin: Ebenezer was born American, though he'd not seen his birthplace since earliest childhood. His father, Andrew Cooke 2nd, of the Parish of St. Giles in the Fields, County of Middlesex—a red-faced, white-chopped, stout-winded old lecher with flinty eye and withered arm—had spent his youth in Maryland as agent for a British manufacturer, as had his father before him, and having a sharp eye for goods and a sharper for men, had added to the Cooke estate by the time he was thirty some one thousand acres of good wood and arable land on the Choptank River. The point on which this land lay he called Cooke's Point, and the small manor-house he built there, Malden. He married late in life and conceived twin children, Ebenezer and his sister Anna, whose mother (as if such an inordinate casting had cracked the mold) died bearing them. When the twins were but four Andrew returned to England, leaving Malden in the hands of an overseer, and thenceforth employed himself as a merchant, sending his own factors to the plantations. His affairs prospered, and the children were well provided for.

John Barth (1960)

Colonial writers of the South, like their northern counterparts, wrote much literature that was deliberately useful or purposeful. Such texts as Indian treaties, promotion tracts, sermons, and treatises on education or science or technology were intentionally utilitarian even though they all had aesthetic qualities. Yet an abundance of verse (elegies, pastoral poems, satires, ballads) and of journals, diaries, letters, essays, and autobiographies shows the powerful belletristic strain in writings of the region. It must be remembered as well that a literary tradition was in the making in the slave quarters. A growing population of black African slaves sang songs and kept alive the African folklore which, mingled with the slaves' experience in the New World, would eventually find its way into formal writing in the twentieth century. Though some slaves learned to read and write (using these very skills in the eighteenth century to petition for their freedom), slaves by law were kept illiterate in the South and therefore had no opportunity in the colonial era to give written expression to their oral traditions. That flowering would have to wait two hundred years. The record of extant southern literature of the seventeenth and eighteenth centuries is one of white writers.

It is a record of a complex and sophisticated intellectual and literary life. The

Puritan Cotton Mather, an avid book collector, would have been surprised to learn that the only colonial American library larger than his own belonged to the Virginian aristocrat William Byrd II, a man of whom Mather could only have disapproved as licentious and ungodly. Ultimately the descendants of both men would join to unite the colonies in protest against British policy and, finally, in revolution. The Continental Congress and Declaration of Independence (1776) indicated the convergence of very different ways of life in the two regions. Southerners like William Byrd II were raconteurs and sharp observers of the American environment. When they joined their northern counterparts, the subjects congenial to them both were politics and the future of the colonies.

Toward the Revolution: The Eighteenth Century

In 1726 the English bishop, George Berkeley, wrote a verse which American colonists, including Benjamin Franklin, liked to quote because it nourished confidence in the growth of American culture:

> Westward the course of empire takes its way;
> The first four acts already past,
> A fifth shall close the drama with the day;
> Time's noblest offspring is the last.

Berkeley's "Verses on the Prospect of Planting Arts and Learning in America" expressed the patriotic idea of a progressively westward-moving culture. Through the eighteenth century the idea of westward empire began to coincide with the concept of nationhood. The European movement known as the Enlightenment began to transform American thought and writing and to make possible the political and literary unification of the thirteen very different colonies.

The Enlightenment

In the eighteenth century scientists and philosophers posed serious challenge to the seventeenth-century mind. Sir Isaac Newton (1642–1727) formulated the laws of gravity and motion, and John Locke (1633–1704) advanced the theory that knowledge is gained only by sensory perception. Newtonian thought embraced a pattern of ideas: that the universe is governed by immutable natural laws, that these laws constitute a harmonious system reflecting a benevolent and wise higher power, and that humankind desires to bring about a correspondingly harmonious, benevolent life on earth. Newton, a Christian, saw God as a cosmic geometrician. In so doing he inadvertently fostered the Enlightenment idea of Deism, which weakened the power of traditional religious authority.

The Deists, among them Benjamin Franklin, deduced the existence of God from the structure of the universe, not from the Bible. Surveying the numerous sects, each with its claims to unique divine revelation, they rejected revealed religion and looked instead to the "simplicity of nature," which signified the "established order, and course of natural things." The scientist Robert Boyle, a follower of Newton, wrote that mathematical and mechanical principles were "the alphabet in which God wrote the world." By implication, human beings could comprehend the laws of the universe and, by the application of reason, arrange human affairs in a correspondingly rational benevolent way. The Deists were less interested in theology than in the application of human reason to earthly problems. Concerns over human nature took precedence over such religious doctrines as the fall of man and the incarnation of Jesus Christ. John Locke reinforced this position by emphasizing that individuals are not born with innate ideas on good or evil but that each is a blank slate or *tabula rasa* upon which experience is inscribed to form character and personality. In eighteenth-century America, such Enlightenment ideas as the inevitability of progress, the efficacy of reason, and the perfectibility of man marked a distinct change in our literature. Concurrently, American writings were influenced by popular literary forms, including newspapers, and by social and religious patterns as well.

Living Conditions and Literacy

Living conditions in the colonies continued to vary in the eighteenth century. One Maryland colonist, a Dr. Hamilton, dined with a Susquehanna, Pennsylvania, family who had "neither knife, fork, spoon, plate, or napkin" and simply dug into a dirty wood dish, though in 1744 he observed that a New York City family owned such "superfluous things" as a "looking glass with a painted frame, half a dozen pewter spoons and as many plates, a set of stone tea dishes, and a tea pot." Such a family would be likely to read colonial newspapers, twenty-six of which had been published weekly by 1765. They were literary, attempting to imitate the sophisticated style of English periodicals, especially the essays of Joseph Addison and Richard Steele. William Park's *Virginia Gazette,* launched in Williamsburg in 1736, illustrates the compositional range of a successful early colonial newspaper. It contained a fair measure of poetry, a few mathematical puzzles, and a scattering of social announcements. It also featured serialized satirical pieces whose authors disguised their identity under such pen names as Miss Arabella Sly, Miss Amoret, and Miss Penelope Leer. Papers like the *Virginia Gazette* or Thomas Fleet's *Boston Evening Post* reached audiences of the gentry and professionals, as well as independent farmers, artisans, and schoolteachers. By the outbreak of the Revolutionary War, however, more papers began to adopt the principle of Isaiah Thomas, the Worcester, Massachusetts, editor-publisher who urged that journalism become a "popular" expression of "common sense in a common language."

Eighteenth-century booksellers, like many newspaper editors, depended on the professional classes for the bulk of their sales because books were terribly expensive. Personal libraries rarely exceeded twenty-five volumes and were dominated by what Cotton Mather called "devout and useful books," including the Bible, *The Pilgrim's Progress* (1678), sermons and tracts, almanacs, medical books, and practical and scientific treatises like *The Farmer's Companion* (1754) or Jared Eliot's *Essay on Field Husbandry* (1762).

Because the literacy rate was high (among white males, at least) in the South, the middle colonies, and especially New England, literary taste itself gradually

became a value in colonial eighteenth-century America. Writers looked to the
mother country for models, including those provided by Addison and Steele,
John Dryden, Dr. Samuel Johnson, Jonathan Swift, and especially Alexander
Pope, whose *Essay on Man* (1733–1734) went through forty-five American
printings before the end of the century. Benjamin Franklin took full advantage of
the exemplary lessons of these English figures. From an early age he equated
good writing with a successful career, for Franklin sought the approval of the
American reading public. His journalism, almanac wit, satirical essays, political
pamphlets, scientific papers, and prolific correspondence cover virtually the full
range of colonial writing, and do so in a crisp style that none of his American
contemporaries could match.

Franklin exemplifies the secular concerns of a Deist in the American
Enlightenment. His maxims ("Waste not, want not," for example) indicate paths
toward self-improvement, and his numerous essays address human foibles, vices
and virtues, and systematic programs by which the individual and society can be
improved. Underlying much of his writing is a utilitarian premise. "I believe
there is one supreme, most perfect Being, Author and Father of the Gods
themselves," wrote Franklin, who went on to say that only the virtuous man
could be happy. Consistently, his work addressed the subject of that virtue in a
secular realm.

Jonathan Edwards and the Great Awakening

Religious life continued to be crucial to the colonial experience through the
eighteenth century. Franklin's generation gave rise to a formidable theologian and
metaphysician, Jonathan Edwards, whose thought and temperament so differed
from Franklin's that it has become customary to view their careers as antithetical
parts of the colonial mind. Both men originated in Puritan New England and
were deeply influenced by the scientific and philosophical writing of Newton and
Locke. In Franklin those influences found expression in a progress-oriented,
public-spirited ideology based on the religious assumptions of Deism, the
Newtonian view of a God who did not participate directly in human affairs. In
Edwards, however, Enlightenment thought led to a reformulation of Puritanism,
with emphasis on the authenticity of feelings or affections as indices of God's
disposition toward the individual. Love, said Edwards, "is not only one of the
affections but it is the first and chief . . . and the fountain of all the affections."

Edwards's stirring sermons placed him at the center of a series of religious
revivals known as the Great Awakening, which was in large part a reaction
against Deism and Newtonian science. Begun in the 1740s, this evangelical
movement occurred in all colonies. It affected the Pennsylvania German Pietists,
the Methodists, and the Baptists, Quakers, and Scotch-Irish Presbyterians in North
Carolina, New Jersey, Connecticut, and Virginia. In several trips up and down
the coast, the Methodist itinerant preacher George Whitefield (1714–1770) prayed
that "grace in every heart might dwell," as the black versifier Phyllis Wheatley
wrote in her elegy "On the Death of the Rev. Mr. George Whitefield, 1770":
"Thy sermons in unequaled accents flowed, / And every bosom with devotion
glowed." Whitefield was just one of the itinerant ministers who evoked

evangelical religious feeling in the revival meetings. The Grand Itinerants, as Whitefield and his cohorts were called, made their way into remote settlements and released fervent emotional energies throughout the colonies.

In 1740 Whitefield brought his evangelistic energies to New England, traveling west from Boston to Jonathan Edwards's Northhampton, where he stayed with the Edwards family and preached in the parish church, moving Edwards to tears. Soon Edwards's own congregation—indeed the entire Holyoke Valley—was swept into the movement. Jonathan Edwards became its exponent. As a reader of John Locke in his student days, he understood the English philosopher's empiricism; but as a Puritan who had experienced the presence of God's grace in his early teens, Edwards felt that Locke's theories served to confine human life to the senses, even reduce it to the sensory level of beasts.

Yet Edwards saw in Lockean thought a potential antidote to the cold religiosity of reason, which he felt had gradually corrupted the Puritan mission in the eighteenth century. He used Lockean thought to reaffirm Puritan doctrine, especially that of predestination. Lockean psychology enabled Edwards to argue that the sovereignty of God is a phenomenon delightful to the senses. "I am bold to assert," he wrote in *A Treatise Concerning Religious Affections* (1746), "that there never was any considerable change wrought in the mind or conversation of any person, by any thing of a religious nature . . . who had not his affections moved," among them the "fear, hope, love, hatred, desire, joy, sorrow, gratitude, compassion, and zeal," all of which he thought were sanctioned in Scripture but neglected in a Deistic era.

The work of Edwards—in fact of all who participated in the Great Awakening—had significant implications for the American Revolution. The movement emphasized liberation from traditional authority and, in political terms, anticipated the eventual severance from England. Politically the Great Awakening can be read as a struggle between the values of a distant, established authority and those of individuals in remote communities. It bred intercolonial communications and fostered collective resistance toward distant, more orthodox opponents.

Settlers and Skirmishes

The eighteenth century saw marked demographic changes in the American colonies, deriving from the Treaty of Utrecht (1713) in which the monarchies of England, France, Spain, and Holland agreed to renounce claims to each other's thrones and entered into commercial pacts. Temporarily these pacts suppressed French and Spanish territorial designs and created a relatively stable Atlantic environment in which the colonies could undertake political and economic initiatives.

It is helpful to notice who lived where in the decades before the Revolution. In 1713 English colonists comprised ninety percent of the population. During the next fifty years that proportion declined to less than sixty percent even as the total colonial population increased fourfold. European colonists ventured to settle in the New World at a rate proportionally higher than at any previous time in American history. Germans found their way into Pennsylvania, western Maryland,

Virginia, the Carolinas, and Georgia. Scotch-Irish settled from Maine to South Carolina in border areas, providing a buffer zone between settled habitations and the Indian-filled wilderness. By 1749 they accounted for nearly one quarter of Pennsylvania's population. The French Protestants, the Huguenots, settled in the southern and middle colonies, while the Dutch established elaborate feudal estates in New York's Hudson valley and controlled much of the colony's mercantile activity.

One-third to one-half of all white settlers who entered the New World before the Revolution arrived under contract ("indenture") for four to seven years' service in exchange for the costs of their transportation, food, clothing, and shelter. Most of these individuals and families fulfilled their contracts through work as field hands or household servants, though a few became artisans or teachers. A high mortality rate threatened this group, but they were, technically at least, "free," their period of bondage limited by a legally binding contract. Not so the increasing slave population, which rose to upwards of one-half million by 1770, ninety percent in the southern colonies. By the eve of the Revolution black slavery had developed into the "peculiar institution," with a century-long history of court cases that grappled with the contradictory views of slaves as property and as people. The virtues of freedom and of the freeholding of land in a pluralistic society entered American literature in the writings of Franklin and, after the Revolution, in Michel Guillaume Jean de Crèvecoeur's *Letters from an American Farmer*.

Intercolonial affairs did not proceed smoothly. The decades leading to the Revolution were fraught with tensions, even violence among the colonies and among ethnic and religious groups. For instance, fighting erupted between Connecticut and Pennsylvania in the 1750s over rival claims to Susquehanna land. And cities with large slave populations, like Charleston and New York, lived in continuous dread of riots and arson. Occasional labor insurrections, like that of the Greek and Italian immigrants in Florida in 1769, led to the virtual extinction of newly formed communities of the indentured. And Indian raids were a constant threat, especially during the French-Indian War (1756–1763).

The succession of wars against the French in North America established the British hegemony in North America and had far-reaching political and military consequences for the English colonists, including George Washington, who learned guerila-type forest warfare and recognized that the British army was not invincible. When the French and Indians defeated General Braddock near Fort Duquesne (now Pittsburgh), Franklin noted that "the whole transaction gave us Americans the first suspicion that our exalted ideas of the prowess of British regulars had not been well founded."

In the decades leading up to the Revolutionary War, Britain found the colonists increasingly resistant to its policies, which often seemed capricious even to moderates. The Hat Act of 1732 and the Molasses Act of 1733, both unpopular measures to control colonial trade, had been countered with smuggling and commercial chicanery. The Stamp Act of 1765 met violent opposition. Tradesmen, artisans, and laborers joined in mass protests against the rather high tax levied on colonial newspapers, almanacs, advertisements, single-sheet or broadside publications, pamphlets, and legal documents. Colonial merchants agreed to boycott English goods, and the dissident "Sons of Liberty" intimidated or attacked British officials and destroyed their property.

Though Parliament repealed the Stamp Act within a year, the damage had been done. After 1765 newspapers scrutinized colonial affairs and assumed a major role in shaping anti-British sentiment, as did the more than two thousand pamphlets published between 1763 and 1776. Their authors were men like John Dickinson and Samuel and John Adams, whose names became synonymous with the literature of the Revolution. The pamphlets were a brilliant propaganda strategy, inexpensive to print and purchase, and both portable and durable. In the hands of a skilled rhetorician like Thomas Paine, the political pamphlet was a powerful armament for the colonists. It stirred sentiment and gave eloquent formal expression to strong feelings. Pamphlet literature reached colonists receptive to the contentious prose of political controversy and to an Enlightenment vocabulary of natural rights. Pamphlets hastened the formation of a revolutionary ideology. To overthrow British rule, one pamphlet declared, "nothing is wanted but your own Resolution, for great is the Authority and Power of the People."

Such sentiments were put to the test. When Parliament passed the Tea Act of 1773, colonial seaports united to prevent the unloading and sale of tea which, taxed by Britain, would still have been inexpensive to buy. The principle of unfair taxation, not the price of tea, was at issue when Samuel Adams's band of patriots disguised as Mohawks raided the British ships and dumped the tea chests into Boston Harbor. Immediately other colonies applauded the gesture and decided to stage "tea parties" of their own. By the following year, 1774, colonial relations with England had not improved, and the first of two Continental Congresses convened at Philadelphia. The colonists would soon hear rhetoric like Thomas Paine's: In January 1776 he wrote, "Of more worth is one honest man to society, and in the sight of God, than all the crowned ruffians that ever lived."

Within months Thomas Jefferson would codify those sentiments in the Declaration of Independence, a document thematically characteristic of a new body of American literature. In one sense the ideals of "life, liberty, and the pursuit of happiness" were characteristic of the American Enlightenment and so place Jefferson and the signers of the declaration fully in their contemporary moment.

Yet the ideology of the American Revolution has a long foreground in colonial American literature. Specific to its own cultural and historical moment, indebted to Enlightenment science and religion, the last and latest writings of the American colonists also hark back as far as Captain John Smith's Jamestown and William Bradford's Plymouth. Writings from the "vale of plenty" and from the Puritan "citty upon a hill" anticipate the literature of the American Revolution. Individual rights and the entitlement to liberty were values inscribed in the earliest colonial literature. If the "pursuit of happiness" is most congenial to the southern "vale of plenty" and if "liberty" itself required careful definition on the part of the Puritan, libertarian values nonetheless cut across geographic regions in writings dating from the early seventeenth century. Those values were embodied in a dazzling array of forms and genres, and they span the entire colonial period in literature, codifying the breadth and intensity of the American experience.

Two centuries of colonial writing prepared the way for a subsequent literature of a libertarian nation-state. Thus Charles Pinckney of South Carolina could envision the "new country" of post-Revolutionary America when he said, "There will be few poor and few dependent" and "more equality of rank and fortune than in any other country in the world." Those ideals had their origins in the lives and writings of colonial America.

Further Reading:

S. Ahlstrom, *A Religious History of the American People,* 1972.

L. Ziff, *Puritanism in America: New Culture in a New World,* 1973.

H. May, *The Enlightenment in America,* 1976.

E. Emerson, *Puritanism in America, 1620–1750,* 1977.

S. Bercovitch, *The American Jeremiad,* 1978.

R. Davis, *The Intellectual Life of the Colonial South,* 3 vols., 1978.

J. Stilgoe, *Common Landscape of America, 1580 to 1845,* 1982.

William Bradford
1590–1657

William Bradford is the writer synonymous with the Pilgrims, the *Mayflower,* the first Thanksgiving. As a colonist, he was a governor engaged for over thirty years in religious, social, and economic problems. Yet he coauthored a geographical survey and wrote more than one thousand lines of verse. His history of the New England pilgrims, *Of Plymouth Plantation,* stands as one of the major works of colonial literature. In it Bradford recorded the struggles of the Plymouth, Massachusetts, Pilgrims in language he called "a plain style, with singular regard unto the simple truth in all things." Bradford's history tells its readers of the mutual love and affection of the *Mayflower* group. It commends the heroism of individuals and laments the inevitable weaknesses of bad judgment, cowardice, and greed. Central to the work is the very question of the colonists' survival in the New World.

Bradford called himself "a man of sorrows" and in retrospect may seem an unlikely candidate for a literary life. He was born in Austerfield, Yorkshire, of modestly prosperous parents. But after the boy's father died, Bradford's mother remarried, and William was raised by uncles and grandparents who taught him agriculture and animal husbandry. Unlike the numerous university-trained Puritan writers who moved in intellectual circles, Bradford prepared to become a farmer.

His plans changed in William's mid-teens, when he heard the sermons of Richard Clyfton, a nonconformist minister of a small congregation that met secretly at the home of William Brewster in Nottinghamshire. Bradford was so stirred by Clyfton's sermons that, to the dismay of his family and the "scoff" of his neighbors, he left home to join the Brewster group. As he put it in verse, "In dayes of Youth, / God did make known to me his Truth, / And call'd me from my Native place."

At the height of the Reformation, numerous groups like the one Bradford joined were gathering throughout England. But the Scrooby Pilgrims differed from most others on one crucial point. They believed that the Church of England was so thoroughly corrupted that they had no alternative but to separate from it. To reform or purify it, as the Puritans wished to do, seemed out of the question. The Scrooby group proposed instead to establish a "particular" church based on a formal covenant or pact agreed upon by the members, who swore allegiance to it in perpetuity. Their model was the Old Testament covenant made first with Adam and then with Abraham, in addition to the New Testament redemption of Christ. Scripture, in short, was their highest authority. But the Scrooby congregation broke English law when they separated from the national church. They committed treason and were thereafter an outlaw band.

The Scrooby Pilgrims' sojourn in the Netherlands may seem to be a detour on the way to America. In fact, they planned in 1607 to move to the Low Countries in order to find "freedom of religion for all men." Bradford went with them to Amsterdam in 1608 and on to Leyden in the following year. There they worshiped "God amongst themselves" while Bradford earned his living as a weaver and studied several languages, including Dutch, French, Latin, and Greek. But the Scrooby Pilgrims became disappointed that other English nonconformists did not join them, preferring "prisons in England rather than this liberty in Holland." Ten years passed, and the group saw itself aging and thinned by death. Fearful of dispersal, impoverished, and worried about the encroachment of Dutch ways into their lives and those of their children, the group decided to move again. "Weighty and solid reasons" prevailed over "newfangledness" or "giddy humour," Bradford assures us. But two conditions had to be met before the group could become colonists. They needed a charter from England authorizing them to settle on American land owned by the Virginia Company of London, and they needed financing, obtained when a group of "merchant adventurers" agreed to underwrite their expenses in exchange for return shipments of fish, furs, and minerals.

The Bradford party sailed on the *Mayflower* in September 1620 and reached Cape Cod, Massachusetts, after a two-month voyage in crowded conditions and stormy weather. At landfall they were considerably distant from the northernmost boundary of the Virginia territory, which extended approximately to the present site of New York City. But the Pilgrims were exhausted and reluctant to continue a wintry voyage. They decided to stay in New England. Because they lacked royal title to its land, however, they were vulnerable to charges that their officials lacked legal authority. The point was critical because a majority of the colonists were not Pilgrims but "strangers," fellow voyagers eager to remake their lives but uncommitted to church fellowship. The Bradford group thus formulated the Mayflower Compact, legitimating the "Civil Body Politick." It was the first New World document on democratic government. Bradford was one of the signers and soon became a colonial leader. Upon the death of John Carver, the Pilgrim governor, Bradford was elected to that office; he was reelected thirty times between 1621 and 1656.

When Bradford began, in 1630, to write *Of Plymouth Plantation,* the population of the Plymouth colony stood at some three hundred, three times its original number at landfall. Yet the census was less important to him than the quality of the spiritual life among the colonists he first called Pilgrims. They were more concerned for their spiritual wealth than their material expectations in America, which Bradford called a "roost" or "resting place." At several points he linked the Plymouth group to the Old Testament Israelites led by Moses. The Pilgrims, too, were a chosen people journeying through the wilderness in search of the promised land. They, like the Massachusetts Bay Puritans, anticipated the commencement of the Christian millennium, the harvest of the Lord characterized by "the Spirit of God and His grace" on earth. They understood the millennium to be a state of spiritual community and not a materialistic utopia. In this sense the "weather-beaten face" of a "wild and savage" Cape Cod landscape was relatively unimportant. But Bradford lived to see piety decline, worldly interests rise, and "wickedness . . . break forth." He thus wrote *Of Plymouth Plantation* to record God's providential work among the colonists and to remind readers that the Pilgrims must once again return to their original religious mission. Bradford's readers would surely have heard the language of Scripture in the rhythms and the references of his prose, for the Bible was his manual of style and rhetoric, as well as the record of God's truth.

Bradford began his history in 1630, leaving off in 1647. The manuscript was well known to other colonial historians, who used it as source material. In printed form, however, it was available only in the much-edited *New England's Memoriall,* prepared by Bradford's nephew. The original manuscript disappeared and was presumed lost after the Revolution but was discovered in the house of the bishop of London and published for the first time in 1856. It was returned to this country in 1897 and deposited in the Massachusetts State House in Boston. *Of Plymouth Plantation* remains vital because it is very much a human story embodied in a political and religious testament.

Further Reading:
S. E. Morison, *Builders of the Bay Colony,* 1930, 1958.
B. Smith, *Bradford of Plymouth,* 1951.
G. Langdon, *Pilgrim Colony,* 1966.
K. Caffrey, *The Mayflower,* 1974.

Text:
Of Plymouth Plantation, ed. S. E. Morison, 1952, 1959.

from Of Plymouth Plantation

And first of the occasion and inducements thereunto; the which, that I may truly unfold, I must begin at the very root and rise of the same. The which I shall endeavour to manifest in a plain style, with singular regard unto the simple truth in all things; at least as near as my slender judgment can attain the same.

Chapter IX: Of Their Voyage, and How They Passed the Sea; and of Their Safe Arrival at Cape Cod

September 6. These troubles being blown over, and now all being compact together in one ship, they put to sea again with a prosperous wind, which continued divers days together, which was some encouragement unto them; yet, according to the usual manner, many were afflicted with seasickness. And I may not omit here a special work of God's providence. There was a proud and very profane young man, one of the seamen, of a lusty, able body, which made him the more haughty; he would always be contemning the poor people in their sickness and cursing them daily with grievous execrations; and did not let to tell them that he hoped to help to cast half of them overboard before they came to their journey's end, and to make merry with what they had; and if he were by any gently reproved, he would curse and swear most bitterly. But it pleased God before they came half seas over, to smite this young man with a grievous disease, of which he died in a desperate manner, and so was himself the first that was thrown overboard. Thus his curses light on his own head, and it was an astonishment to all his fellows for they noted it to be the just hand of God upon him.

After they had enjoyed fair winds and weather for a season, they were encountered many times with cross winds and met with many fierce storms with which the ship was shroudly shaken, and her upper works made very leaky; and one of the main beams in the midships was bowed and cracked, which put them in some fear that the ship could not be able to perform the voyage. So some of the chief of the company, perceiving the mariners to fear the sufficiency of the ship as appeared by their mutterings, they entered into serious consultation with the master and other officers of the ship, to consider in time of the danger, and rather to return than to cast themselves into a desperate and inevitable peril. And truly there was great distraction and difference of opinion amongst the mariners themselves; fain would they do what could be done for their wages' sake (being now near half the seas over) and on the other hand they were loath to hazard their lives too desperately. But in examining of all opinions, the master and others affirmed they knew the ship to be strong and firm under water; and for the buckling of the main beam, there was a great iron screw the passengers brought out of Holland, which would raise the beam into his place; the which being done, the carpenter and master affirmed that with a post put under it, set firm in the lower deck and otherways bound, he would make it sufficient. And as for the decks and upper works, they would caulk them as well as they could, and though with the working of the ship they would not long keep staunch, yet there would otherwise be no great danger, if they did not overpress her with sails. So they committed themselves to the will of God and resolved to proceed.

In sundry of these storms the winds were so fierce and the seas so high, as they could not bear a knot of sail, but were forced to hull[1] for divers days together. And in one of them, as they thus lay at hull in a mighty storm, a lusty young man called John Howland, coming upon some occasion above the gratings was, with a seele[2] of

---

[1] To drift with the wind under short sail, typically in a storm.   [2] A roll or a pitch.

the ship, thrown into sea; but it pleased God that he caught hold of the topsail halyards which hung overboard and ran out at length. Yet he held his hold (though he was sundry fathoms under water) till he was hauled up by the same rope to the brim of the water, and then with a boat hook and other means got into the ship again and his life saved. And though he was something ill with it, yet he lived many years after and became a profitable member both in church and commonwealth. In all this voyage there died but one of the passengers, which was William Butten, a youth, servant to Samuel Fuller, when they drew near the coast.

But to omit other things (that I may be brief) after long beating at sea they fell with that land which is called Cape Cod; the which being made and certainly known to be it, they were not a little joyful. After some deliberation had amongst themselves and with the master of the ship, they tacked about and resolved to stand for the southward (the wind and weather being fair) to find some place about Hudson's River for their habitation.[3] But after they had sailed that course about half the day, they fell amongst dangerous shoals and roaring breakers, and they were so far entangled therewith as they conceived themselves in great danger; and the wind shrinking upon them withal, they resolved to bear up again for the Cape and thought themselves happy to get out of those dangers before night overtook them, as by God's good providence they did. And the next day they got into the Cape Harbor where they rid in safety.

A word or two by the way of this cape. It was thus first named by Captain Gosnold and his company, Anno 1602, and after by Captain Smith was called Cape James; but it retains the former name amongst seamen. Also, that point which first showed those dangerous shoals unto them they called Point Care, and Tucker's Terrour; but the French and Dutch to this day call it Malabar by reason of those perilous shoals and the losses they have suffered there.

Being thus arrived in a good harbor, and brought safe to land, they fell upon their knees and blessed the God of Heaven who had brought them over the vast and furious ocean, and delivered them from all the perils and miseries thereof, again to set their feet on the firm and stable earth, their proper element. And no marvel if they were thus joyful, seeing wise Seneca[4] was so affected with sailing a few miles on the coast of his own Italy, as he affirmed, that he had rather remain twenty years on his way by land than pass by sea to any place in a short time, so tedious and dreadful was the same unto him.

But here I cannot but stay and make a pause, and stand half amazed at this poor people's present condition; and so I think will the reader, too, when he well considers the same. Being thus passed the vast ocean, and a sea of troubles before in their preparation (as may be remembered by that which went before), they had now no friends to welcome them nor inns to entertain or refresh their weatherbeaten bodies; no houses or much less towns to repair to, to seek for succour. It is recorded in Scripture as a mercy to the Apostle and his shipwrecked company, that the barbarians showed them no small kindness in refreshing them, but these savage barbarians, when they met with them (as after will appear) were readier to fill their sides full of arrows

---

[3] The English were aware of Dutch claims to the area but did not honor those claims. The Pilgrims hoped to be the first to colonize the area, which the Dutch did not settle until six years later.

[4] Lucius Annaeus Seneca (ca. 4 B.C.–A.D. 65), Roman statesman and philosopher.

than otherwise. And for the season it was winter, and they that know the winters of that country know them to be sharp and violent, and subject to cruel and fierce storms, dangerous to travel to known places, much more to search an unknown coast. Besides, what could they see but a hideous and desolate wilderness, full of wild beasts and wild men—and what multitudes there might be of them they knew not. Neither could they, as it were, go up to the top of Pisgah[5] to view from this wilderness a more goodly country to feed their hopes; for which way soever they turned their eyes (save upward to the heavens) they could have little solace or content in respect of any outward objects. For summer being done, all things stand upon them with a weatherbeaten face, and the whole country, full of woods and thickets, represented a wild and savage hue. If they looked behind them, there was the mighty ocean which they had passed and was now as a main bar and gulf to separate them from all the civil parts of the world. If it be said they had a ship to succour them, it is true; but what heard they daily from the master and company? But that with speed they should look out a place (with their shallop) where they would be, at some near distance; for the season was such as he would not stir from thence till a safe harbor was discovered by them, where they would be, and he might go without danger; and that victuals consumed apace but he must and would keep sufficient for themselves and their return. Yea, it was muttered by some that if they got not a place in time, they would turn them and their goods ashore and leave them. Let it also be considered what weak hopes of supply and succour they left behind them, that might bear up their minds in this sad condition and trials they were under; and they could not but be very small. It is true, indeed, the affections and love of their brethren at Leyden was cordial and entire towards them, but they had little power to help them or themselves; and how the case stood between them and the merchants at their coming away hath already been declared.

What could now sustain them but the Spirit of God and His grace? May not and ought not the children of these fathers rightly say: "Our fathers were Englishmen which came over this great ocean, and were ready to perish in this wilderness; but they cried unto the Lord, and He heard their voice and looked on their adversity,"[6] etc. "Let them therefore praise the Lord, because He is good: and His mercies endure forever." "Yea, let them which have been redeemed of the Lord, shew how He hath delivered them from the hand of the oppressor. When they wandered in the desert wilderness out of the way, and found no city to dwell in, both hungry and thirsty, their soul was overwhelmed in them. Let them confess before the Lord His loving-kindness and His wonderful works before the sons of men."[7]

Chapter X: Showing How They Sought Out a Place of Habitation; and What Befell Them Thereabout

Being thus arrived at Cape Cod the 11th of November, and necessity calling them to look out a place for habitation (as well as the master's and mariners' importunity); they having brought a large shallop with them out of England, stowed in quarters

---

[5] Deuteronomy 33:34: "And Moses went up . . . to the top of Pisgah . . . and the Lord showed him all the land of Gilead . . . unto the utmost sea."

[6] Deuteronomy 26:5, 7.

[7] Psalm 107:1–5, 8.

in the ship, they now got her out and set their carpenters to work to trim her up; but being much bruised and shattered in the ship with foul weather, they saw she would be long in mending. Whereupon a few of them tendered themselves to go by land and discover those nearest places, whilst the shallop was in mending; and the rather because as they went into that harbor there seemed to be an opening some two or three leagues off, which the master judged to be a river. It was conceived there might be some danger in the attempt, yet seeing them resolute, they were permitted to go, being sixteen of them well armed under the conduct of Captain Standish, having such instructions given them as was thought meet.

They set forth the 15th of November; and when they had marched about the space of a mile by the seaside, they espied five or six persons with a dog coming towards them, who were savages; but they fled from them and ran up into the woods, and the English followed them, partly to see if they could speak with them, and partly to discover if there might not be more of them lying in ambush. But the Indians seeing themselves thus followed, they again forsook the woods and ran away on the sands as hard as they could, so as they could not come near them but followed them by the track of their feet sundry miles and saw that they had come the same way. So, night coming on, they made their rendezvous and set out their sentinels, and rested in quiet that night; and the next morning followed their track till they had headed a great creek and so left the sands, and turned another way into the woods. But they still followed them by guess, hoping to find their dwellings; but they soon lost both them and themselves, falling into such thickets as were ready to tear their clothes and armor in pieces; but were most distressed for want of drink. But at length they found water and refreshed themselves, being the first New England water they drunk of, and was now in great thirst as pleasant unto them as wine or beer had been in foretimes.

Afterwards they directed their course to come to the other shore, for they knew it was a neck of land they were to cross over, and so at length got to the seaside and marched to this supposed river, and by the way found a pond of clear, fresh water, and shortly after a good quantity of clear ground where the Indians had formerly set corn, and some of their graves. And proceeding further they saw new stubble where corn had been set the same year; also they found where lately a house had been, where some planks and a great kettle was remaining, and heaps of sand newly paddled with their hands. Which, they digging up, found in them divers fair Indian baskets filled with corn, and some in ears, fair and good, of divers colours, which seemed to them a very goodly sight (having never seen any such before). This was near the place of that supposed river they came to seek, unto which they went and found it to open itself into two arms with a high cliff of sand in the entrance but more like to be creeks of salt water than any fresh, for aught they saw; and that there was good harborage for their shallop, leaving it further to be discovered by their shallop, when she was ready. So, their time limited them being expired, they returned to the ship lest they should be in fear of their safety; and took with them part of the corn and buried up the rest. And so, like the men from Eshcol, carried with them of the fruits of the land and showed their brethren; of which, and their return, they were marvelously glad and their hearts encouraged.

After this, the shallop being got ready, they set out again for the better discovery of this place, and the master of the ship desired to go himself. So there went some thirty men but found it to be no harbor for ships but only for boats. There was also found two of their houses covered with mats, and sundry of their implements in them, but the people were run away and could not be seen. Also there was found more of their corn and of their beans of various colours; the corn and beans they brought away, purposing to give them full satisfaction when they should meet with any of them as, about some six months afterward they did, to their good content.

And here is to be noted a special providence of God, and a great mercy to this poor people, that here they got seed to plant them corn the next year, or else they might have starved, for they had none nor any likelihood to get any till the season had been past, as the sequel did manifest. Neither is it likely they had had this, if the first voyage had not been made, for the ground was now all covered with snow and hard frozen; but the Lord is never wanting unto His in their greatest needs; let His holy name have all the praise.

The month of November being spent in these affairs, and much foul weather falling in, the 6th of December they sent out their shallop again with ten of their principal men and some seamen, upon further discovery, intending to circulate that deep bay of Cape Cod. The weather was very cold and it froze so hard as the spray of the sea lighting on their coats, they were as if they had been glazed. Yet that night betimes they got down into the bottom of the bay, and as they drew near the shore they saw some ten or twelve Indians very busy about something. They landed about a league or two from them, and had much ado to put ashore anywhere—it lay so full of flats. Being landed, it grew late and they made themselves a barricado with logs and boughs as well as they could in the time, and set out their sentinel and betook them to rest, and saw the smoke of the fire the savages made that night. When morning was come they divided their company, some to coast along the shore in the boat, and the rest marched through the woods to see the land, if any fit place might be for their dwelling. They came also to the place where they saw the Indians the night before, and found they had been cutting up a great fish like a grampus,[8] being some two inches thick of fat like a hog, some pieces whereof they had left by the way. And the shallop found two more of these fishes dead on the sands, a thing usual after storms in that place, by reason of the great flats of sand[9] that lie off.

So they ranged up and down all that day, but found no people, nor any place they liked. When the sun grew low, they hasted out of the woods to meet with their shallop, to whom they made signs to come to them into a creek hard by, the which they did at high water; of which they were very glad, for they had not seen each other all that day since the morning. So they made them a barricado as usually they did every night, with logs, stakes and thick pine boughs, the height of a man, leaving it open to leeward, partly to shelter them from the cold and wind (making their fire in the middle and lying round about it) and partly to defend them from any sudden assaults of the savages, if they should surround them; so being very weary, they betook them to rest. But about midnight they heard a hideous and great cry, and their sentinel called "Arm! arm!" So they bestirred them and stood to their arms and shot off a couple of muskets, and then the noise ceased. They concluded it was a company of wolves or such like wild beasts, for one of the seamen told them he had often heard such a noise in Newfoundland.

So they rested till about five of the clock in the morning; for the tide, and their

---

[8] Large sea mammal related to whales, dolphins, and porpoises.   [9] I.e., sand bars.

purpose to go from thence, made them be stirring betimes. So after prayer they prepared for breakfast, and it being day dawning it was thought best to be carrying things down to the boat. But some said it was not best to carry the arms down, others said they would be the readier, for they had lapped them up in their coats from the dew; but some three or four would not carry theirs till they went themselves. Yet as it fell out, the water being not high enough, they laid them down on the bank side and came up to breakfast.

But presently, all on the sudden, they heard a great and strange cry, which they knew to be the same voices they heard in the night, though they varied their notes; and one of their company being abroad came running in and cried, "Men, Indians! Indians!" And withal, their arrows came flying amongst them. Their men ran with all speed to recover their arms, as by the good providence of God they did. In the meantime, of those that were there ready, two muskets were discharged at them, and two more stood ready in the entrance of their rendezvous but were commanded not to shoot till they could take full aim at them. And the other two charged again with all speed, for there were only four had arms there, and defended the barricado, which was first assaulted. The cry of the Indians was dreadful, especially when they saw their men run out of the rendezvous toward the shallop to recover their arms, the Indians wheeling about upon them. But some running out with coats of mail on, and cutlasses in their hands, they soon got their arms and let fly amongst them and quickly stopped their violence. Yet there was a lusty man, and no less valiant, stood behind a tree within half a musket shot, and let his arrows fly at them; he was seen [to] shoot three arrows, which were all avoided. He stood three shots of a musket, till one taking full aim at him and made the bark or splinters of the tree fly about his ears, after which he gave an extraordinary shriek and away they went, all of them. They left some to keep the shallop and followed them about a quarter of a mile and shouted once or twice, and shot off two or three pieces, and so returned. This they did that they might conceive that they were not afraid of them or any way discouraged.

Thus it pleased God to vanquish their enemies and give them deliverance; and by His special providence so to dispose that not any one of them were either hurt or hit, though their arrows came close by them and on every side [of] them; and sundry of their coats, which hung up in the barricado, were shot through and through. After-wards they gave God solemn thanks and praise for their deliverance, and gathered up a bundle of their arrows and sent them into England afterward by the master of the ship, and called that place the First Encounter.

From hence they departed and coasted all along but discerned no place likely for harbor; and therefore hasted to a place that their pilot (one Mr. Coppin who had been in the country before) did assure them was a good harbor, which he had been in, and they might fetch it before night; of which they were glad for it began to be foul weather.

After some hours' sailing it began to snow and rain, and about the middle of the afternoon the wind increased and the sea became very rough, and they broke their rudder, and it was as much as two men could do to steer her with a couple of oars. But their pilot bade them be of good cheer for he saw the harbor; but the storm increasing, and night drawing on, they bore what sail they could to get in, while they could see. But herewith they broke their mast in three pieces and their sail fell overboard in a very grown sea, so as they had like to have been cast away. Yet by

God's mercy they recovered themselves, and having the flood with them, struck into the harbor. But when it came to, the pilot was deceived in the place, and said the Lord be merciful unto them for his eyes never saw that place before; and he and the master's mate would have run her ashore in a cove full of breakers before the wind. But a lusty seaman which steered bade those which rowed, if they were men, about with her or else they were all cast away; the which they did with speed. So he bid them be of good cheer and row lustily, for there was a fair sound before them, and he doubted not but they should find one place or other where they might ride in safety. And though it was very dark and rained sore, yet in the end they got under the lee of a small island and remained there all that night in safety. But they knew not this to be an island till morning, but were divided in their minds; some would keep the boat for fear they might be amongst the Indians, others were so wet and cold they could not endure but got ashore, and with much ado got fire (all things being so wet); and the rest were glad to come to them, for after midnight the wind shifted to the northwest and it froze hard.

But though this had been a day and night of much trouble and danger unto them, yet God gave them a morning of comfort and refreshing (as usually He doth to His children) for the next day was a fair, sunshining day, and they found themselves to be on an island secure from the Indians, where they might dry their stuff, fix their pieces and rest themselves; and gave God thanks for His mercies in their manifold deliverances. And this being the last day of the week, they prepared there to keep the Sabbath.

On Monday they sounded the harbor and found it fit for shipping, and marched into the land and found divers cornfields and little running brooks, a place (as they supposed) fit for situation. At least it was the best they could find, and the season and their present necessity made them glad to accept of it. So they returned to their ship again with this news to the rest of their people, which did much comfort their hearts.

On the 15th of December they weighed anchor to go to the place they had discovered, and came within two leagues of it, but were fain to bear up again; but the 16th day, the wind came fair, and they arrived safe in this harbor. And afterwards took better view of the place, and resolved where to pitch their dwelling; and the 25th day began to erect the first house for common use to receive them and their goods.

from **Chapter XI: The Remainder of Anno 1620**

[The Mayflower Compact]

I shall a little return back, and begin with a combination made by them before they came ashore; being the first foundation of their government in this place. Occasioned partly by the discontented and mutinous speeches that some of the strangers amongst them had let fall from them in the ship: That when they came ashore they would use their own liberty, for none had power to command them, the patent they had being for Virginia and not for New England, which belonged to another government, with which the Virginia Company had nothing to do. And partly that such an act by them done, this their condition considered, might be as firm as any patent, and in some respects more sure.

The form was as followeth:

IN THE NAME OF GOD, AMEN.

We whose names are underwritten, the loyal subjects of our dread Sovereign Lord King James, by the Grace of God of Great Britain, France, and Ireland King, Defender of the Faith, etc.

Having undertaken, for the Glory of God and advancement of the Christian Faith and Honour of our King and Country, a Voyage to plant the First Colony in the Northern Parts of Virginia, do by these presents solemnly and mutually in the presence of God and one of another, Covenant and Combine ourselves together into a Civil Body Politic, for our better ordering and preservation and furtherance of the ends aforesaid; and by virtue hereof to enact, constitute and frame such just and equal Laws, Ordinances, Acts, Constitutions and Offices, from time to time, as shall be thought most meet and convenient for the general good of the Colony, unto which we promise all due submission and obedience. In witness whereof we have hereunder subscribed our names at Cape Cod, the 11th of November, in the year of the reign of our Sovereign Lord King James, of England, France and Ireland the eighteenth, and of Scotland the fifty-fourth. Anno Domini 1620.

After this they chose, or rather confirmed, Mr. John Carver (a man godly and well approved amongst them) their Governor for that year. And after they had provided a place for their goods, or common store (which were long in unlading for want of boats, foulness of the winter weather and sickness of divers) and begun some small cottages for their habitation; as time would admit, they met and consulted of laws and orders, both for their civil and military government as the necessity of their condition did require, still adding thereunto as urgent occasion in several times, and as cases did require.

In these hard and difficult beginnings they found some discontents and murmurings arise amongst some, and mutinous speeches and carriages in other; but they were soon quelled and overcome by the wisdom, patience, and just and equal carriage of things, by the Governor and better part, which clave faithfully together in the main.

[The Starving Time]

But that which was most sad and lamentable was, that in two or three months' time half of their company died, especially in January and February, being the depth of winter, and wanting houses and other comforts; being infected with the scurvy and other diseases which this long voyage and their inaccommodate condition had brought upon them. So as there died some times two or three of a day in the foresaid time, that of 100 and odd persons, scarce fifty remained. And of these, in the time of most distress, there was but six or seven sound persons who to their great commendations, be it spoken, spared no pains night nor day, but with abundance of toil and hazard of their own health, fetched them wood, made them fires, dressed them meat, made their beds, washed their loathsome clothes, clothed and unclothed them. In a word, did all the homely and necessary offices for them which dainty and queasy stomachs cannot endure to hear named; and all this willingly and cheerfully, without any grudging in the least, showing herein their true love unto their friends and brethren; a rare example and worthy to be remembered. Two of these seven were Mr. William Brewster, their reverend Elder, and Myles Standish, their Captain and military commander, unto whom myself and many others were much beholden in our low and sick condition. And yet the Lord so upheld these persons as in this general calamity they were not at all infected either with sickness or lameness. And what I have said of these I may say of many others who died in this general visitation, and others yet living; that whilst they had health, yea, or any strength continuing, they were not wanting to any that had need of them. And I doubt not but their recompense is with the Lord.

But I may not here pass by another remarkable passage not to be forgotten. As this calamity fell among the passengers that were to be left here to plant, and were hasted ashore and made to drink water that the seamen might have the more beer, and one in his sickness desiring but a small can of beer, it was answered that if he were their own father he should have none. The disease began to fall amongst them also, so as almost half of their company died before they went away, and many of their officers and lustiest men, as the boatswain, gunner, three quartermasters, the cook and others. At which the Master was something strucken and sent to the sick ashore and told the Governor he should send for beer for them that had need of it, though he drunk water homeward bound.

But now amongst his company there was far another kind of carriage in this misery than amongst the passengers. For they that before had been boon companions in drinking and jollity in the time of their health and welfare, began now to desert one another in this calamity, saying they would not hazard their lives for them, they should be infected by coming to help them in their cabins; and so, after they came to lie by it, would do little or nothing for them but, "if they died, let them die." But such of the passengers as were yet aboard showed them what mercy they could, which made some of their hearts relent, as the boatswain (and some others) who was a proud young man and would often curse and scoff at the passengers. But when he grew weak, they had compassion on him and helped him; then he confessed he did not deserve it at their hands, he had abused them in word and deed. "Oh!" (saith he) "you, I now see, show your love like Christians indeed one to another, but we let one another lie and die like dogs." Another lay cursing his wife, saying if it had not been for her he had never come this unlucky voyage, and anon cursing his fellows, saying he had done this and that for some of them; he had spent so much and so much amongst them, and they were now weary of him and did not help him, having need. Another gave his companion all he had, if he died, to help him in his weakness; he went and got a little spice and made him a mess of meat once or twice. And because he died not so soon as he expected, he went amongst his fellows and swore the rogue would cozen him, he would see him choked before he made him any more meat; and yet the poor fellow died before morning.

[Indian Relations]

All this while the Indians came skulking about them, and would sometimes show themselves aloof off, but when any approached near them, they would run away; and once they stole away their tools where they had been at work and were gone to dinner.

But about the 16th of March, a certain Indian came boldly amongst them and spoke to them in broken English, which they could well understand but marveled at it. At length they understood by discourse with him, that he was not of these parts, but belonged to the eastern parts where some English ships came to fish, with whom he was acquainted and could name sundry of them by their names, amongst whom he had got his language. He became profitable to them in acquainting them with many things concerning the state of the country in the east parts where he lived, which was afterwards profitable unto them; as also of the people here, of their names, number and strength, of their situation and distance from this place, and who was chief amongst them. His name was Samoset. He told them also of another Indian whose name was Squanto, a native of this place, who had been in England and could speak better English than himself.

Being, after some time of entertainment and gifts dismissed, a while after he came again, and five more with him, and they brought again all the tools that were stolen away before, and made way for the coming of their great Sachem, called Massasoit. Who, about four or five days after, came with the chief of his friends and other attendance, with the aforesaid Squanto. With whom, after friendly entertainment and some gifts given him, they made a peace with him (which hath now continued this 24 years) in these terms:

1. That neither he nor any of his should injure or do hurt to any of their people.
2. That if any of his did hurt to any of theirs, he should send the offender, that they might punish him.
3. That if anything were taken away from any of theirs, he should cause it to be restored; and they should do the like to his.
4. If any did unjustly war against him, they would aid him; if any did war against them, he should aid them.
5. He should send to his neighbours confederates to certify them of this, that they might not wrong them, but might be likewise comprised in the conditions of peace.
6. That when their men came to them, they should leave their bows and arrows behind them.

After these things he returned to his place called Sowams, some 40 miles from this place, but Squanto continued with them and was their interpreter and was a special instrument sent of God for their good beyond their expectation. He directed them how to set their corn, where to take fish, and to procure other commodities, and was also their pilot to bring them to unknown places for their profit, and never left them till he died. He was a native of this place, and scarce any left alive besides himself. He was carried away with divers others by one Hunt, a master of a ship, who thought to sell them for slaves in Spain. But he got away for England and was entertained by a merchant in London, and employed to Newfoundland and other parts, and lastly brought hither into these parts by one Mr. Dermer, a gentleman employed by Sir Ferdinando Gorges and others for discovery and other designs in these parts. Of whom I shall say something, because it is mentioned in a book set forth Anno 1622 by the President and Council for New England, that he made the peace between the savages of these parts and the English, of which this plantation, as it is intimated, had the benefit; but what a peace it was may appear by what befell him and his men.

This Mr. Dermer was here the same year that these people came, as appears by a relation written by him and given me by a friend, bearing date June 30, Anno 1620. And they came in November following, so there was but four months difference. In which relation to his honoured friend, he hath these passages of this very place:

I will first begin (saith he) with that place from whence Squanto or Tisquantum, was taken away; which in Captain Smith's map is called Plymouth; and I would that Plymouth had the like commodities. I would that the first plantation might here be seated, if there come to the number of 50 persons, or upward. Otherwise, Charlton, because there the savages are less to be feared. The Pocanockets, which live to the west of Plymouth, bear an inveterate malice to the English, and are of more strength than all the savages from thence to Penobscot. Their desire of revenge was occasioned by an Englishman, who having many of them on board, made a greater slaughter with their murderers and small shot when as (they say) they offered no injury on their parts. Whether they were English or no it may be doubted; yet they believe they were, for the French have so possessed them. For which cause Squanto cannot deny but they would have killed me when I was at Namasket, had he not entreated hard for me.

The soil of the borders of this great bay may be compared to most of the plantations which I have seen in Virginia. The land is of divers sorts, for Patuxet is a hardy but strong soil; Nauset and Satucket are for the most part a blackish and deep mould much like that where groweth the best tobacco in Virginia. In the bottom of that great bay is store of cod and bass or mullet, etc. But above all he commends Pocanocket for the richest soil, and much open ground fit for English grain, etc.

Massachusetts is about nine leagues from Plymouth, and situated in the midst between both, is full of islands and peninsulas, very fertile for the most part.

With sundry such relations which I forbear to transcribe, being now better known than they were to him.

He was taken prisoner by the Indians at Manamoyick, a place not far from hence, now well known. He gave them what they demanded for his liberty, but when they had got what they desired, they kept him still, and endeavoured to kill his men. But he was freed by seizing on some of them and kept them bound till they gave him a canoe's load of corn. Of which, see *Purchas*, lib. 9, fol. 1778. But this was Anno 1619.

After the writing of the former relation, he came to the Isle of Capawack (which lies south of this place in the way to Virginia) and the aforesaid Squanto with him, where he going ashore amongst the Indians to trade, as he used to do, was betrayed and assaulted by them, and all his men slain, but one that kept the boat. But himself got aboard very sore wounded, and they had cut off his head upon the cuddy of the boat, had not the man rescued him with a sword. And so they got away and made shift to get into Virginia where he died, whether of his wounds or the diseases of the country, or both together, is uncertain. By all which it may appear how far these people were from peace, and with what danger this plantation was begun, save as the powerful hand of the Lord did protect them.

These things were partly the reason why they kept aloof and were so long before they came to the English. Another reason as after themselves made known was how about three years before, a French ship was cast away at Cape Cod, but the men got ashore and saved their lives, and much of their victuals and other goods. But after the Indians heard of it, they gathered together from these parts and never left watching and dogging them till they got advantage and killed them all but three or four which they kept, and sent from one sachem to another to make sport with, and used them worse than slaves. Of which the aforesaid Mr. Dermer redeemed two of them; and they conceived this ship was now come to revenge it.

Also, as after was made known, before they came to the English to make friendship, they got all the Powachs[10] of the country, for three days together in a horrid and devilish manner, to curse and execrate them with their conjurations, which assembly and service they held in a dark and dismal swamp.

But to return. The spring now approaching, it pleased God the mortality began to cease amongst them, and the sick and lame recovered apace, which put as [it] were new life into them, though they had borne their sad affliction with much patience and contentedness as I think any people could do. But it was the Lord which upheld them, and had beforehand prepared them; many having long borne the yoke, yea from their youth. Many other smaller matters I omit, sundry of them having been already published in a journal made by one of the company, and some other passages of journeys and relations already published, to which I refer those that are willing to know them more particularly.

And being now come to the 25th of March, I shall begin the year 1621. . . .

1856

John Winthrop
1588–1649

By birth and breeding, John Winthrop seems a man destined to have been a leader in Puritan colonial life. The son of an English country gentleman, Winthrop was at eighteen a married man acting as steward and justice of the peace on his father's estate at Groton, to which he had returned after two years of legal studies at Trinity College, Cambridge University. The Winthrops were Puritans, and though John wrote of his "wild and dissolute youth," he found "some peace and comfort in God and his wayes" in his late teens, and thereafter his faith strengthened by degrees.

Winthrop began to consider emigration to the New World when political and religious conditions worsened in England. Under the reign of Archbishop Laud, ministers who refused strict adherence to all Anglican practices fell under suspicion or were silenced. Openly a Puritan, Winthrop lost his attorneyship.

[10] Medicine men.

Everywhere the dreaded Roman Catholicism seemed on the rise. By spring 1629, Winthrop feared that "God will bringe some heavye Affliction upon this lande" in the form of political reprisals or natural disasters such as the plague. Yet he trusted that the Lord would "provide a shelter & a hidinge place for us and others."

The Lord's instrument seemed to be the new Massachusetts Bay Company, which elected Winthrop its first governor in 1629. He sailed for America the following year on the *Arbella,* the flagship vessel of a fleet carrying some seven hundred persons in a "Great Migration" that would soon bring twenty thousand settlers to New England. At sea on board the *Arbella* Winthrop preached a now-classic sermon on the ideals of Christian charity that he felt must govern the colony in all its affairs. It was imperative, he argued, that the settlers form a commonwealth for the mutual benefit of all and that their society be able to withstand the scrutiny of a watchful world. In the Massachusetts Bay Winthrop acted as governor or deputy governor for nearly twenty years, upholding the standards set in his "Model of Christian Charity." In practice his leadership was sought in trials of settlement, trade, property disputes, economic hard times, Indian wars, and the religious controversies that threatened to split the colony into warring camps. Winthrop's *Journal* was the record of these events and became, over time, a record by which to measure how close colonial New England came to being that model "citty upon a hill."

One sequence of *Journal* entries outlines a grave internal threat to the colony. The so-called antinomian controversy came to a head in the trials of Mistress Anne Hutchinson, a woman whom subsequent generations have identified as a martyr to the cause of religious freedom and women's rights. Hutchinson, a housewife and the mother of twelve children, had been a parishioner of the Reverend John Cotton in Boston, England. One year after Cotton's departure for America, the Hutchinson family followed him. Mistress Hutchinson soon established herself as a valued nurse and midwife. In addition, as a devout and intellectually gifted woman she attracted a circle of some sixty women and men to "private conferences" on Mr. Cotton's sermons. Soon she broadened her discussions to include critical analyses of the teachings of other ministers.

As a partisan of Cotton and a sharp critic of his colleagues, Hutchinson put herself at the center of a theological controversy that concerned the part human beings could play in preparing their hearts to receive God's saving grace. The debate had already pitted Cotton against other powerful ministers, and the widespread publicity of Anne Hutchinson's meetings made her the focus of dissension.

Finally brought to trial on charges of sedition, Hutchinson testified that she had received special divine revelation. In Puritan theology this was heresy and carried political implications as well. The individual who received divine guidance directly from God would not need the teaching of the scriptural word (in Latin, *nomen*) from the ministers. Nor would public officials like Winthrop retain their authority, since they claimed that their power came from biblical injunctions. Hutchinson implicitly challenged the power of both church and state. Her minister, Cotton, joined all the others in condemning her.

She was banished by the Massachusetts General Court in November 1637 and moved to Rhode Island with a small band of her followers. When Hutchinson delivered a malformed infant, Winthrop described it in the *Journal* in excruciating detail, interpreting the deformity as a sign of God's judgment on the heretic and, of course, as the implicit vindication of Puritan governmental action. Yet Hutchinson remained in the American imagination. She was a major source for Hawthorne's character Hester in *The Scarlet Letter*. And her intellectual power anticipates that of Margaret Fuller, the mid-nineteenth century writer and great conversationalist who was sometimes as disturbing to Ralph Waldo Emerson as Anne Hutchinson was to John Winthrop.

Winthrop's *Journal* contains accounts of major Puritan controversies like that surrounding Hutchinson. It presents sharp glimpses of colonial life, like that of a townsman who lost his way "and wandered in the woods and swamps three days and two nights without taking any food" and "had torn his legs." Throughout, it emphasizes the working of God's providence in Puritan affairs. (God brought the disoriented townsman to the community of Scituate when he was "near spent" or exhausted.)

From an aesthetic viewpoint it is regrettable that Winthrop did not reshape the *Journal* into a finished narrative, as he intended to do. Yet it stands as a text revealing the Puritan commitment to contemporary history, which they believed would justify the ways of God to man.

Further Reading:
R. Winthrop, *Life and Letters of John Winthrop*, 1864–1867.
S. E. Morison, *Builders of the Bay Colony*, 1930.
E. Morgan, *The Puritan Dilemma*, 1958.
D. Rutman, *Winthrop's Boston*, 1965.
S. Bercovitch, *Puritan Origins of the American Self*, 1975.

Texts:
"A Model of Christian Charity," *The Winthrop Papers*, ed. A. Forbes, 5 vols., 1929–1947.

---

from A Model of Christian Charity

Christian Charitie

A Modell Hereof

God Almightie in his most holy and wise providence hath soe disposed of the Condicion of mankinde, as in all times some must be rich some poore, some high and eminent in power and dignitie; others meane and in subjection.

The Reason Hereof

1. REAS: *First,* to hold conformity with the rest of his workes, being delighted to shewe forth the glory of his wisdome in the variety and differance of the Creatures and the glory of his power, in ordering all these differences for the preservacion and

good of the whole, and the glory of his greatnes that as it is the glory of princes to have many officers, soe this great King will have many Stewards counting himselfe more honoured in dispencing his gifts to man by man, than if hee did it by his owne immediate hand.

2. REAS: *Secondly,* That he might have the more occasion to manifest the worke of his Spirit: first, upon the wicked in moderating and restraining them: soe that the riche and mighty should not eate up the poore, nor the poore, and despised rise up against their superiours, and shake off their yoake; 2ly in the regenerate in exercising His graces in them, as in the greate ones, their love mercy, gentlenes, temperance etc., in the poore and inferiour sorte, their faithe patience, obedience etc:

3. REAS: Thirdly, That every man might have need of other, and from hence they might be all knitt more nearly together in the Bond of brotherly affection: from hence it appeares plainely that noe man is made more honourable than another or more wealthy etc., out of any particuler and singular respect to himselfe but for the glory of his Creator and the Common good of the Creature, Man; Therefore God still reserves the property of these gifts to himselfe as Ezek: 16. 17.[1] he there calls wealthe his gold and his silver etc. Prov: 3. 9.[2] he claimes their service as his due honour the Lord with thy riches etc. All men being thus (by divine providence) ranked into two sortes, riche and poore; under the first, are comprehended all such as are able to live comfortably by their owne meanes duly improved; and all others are poore according to the former distribution. There are two rules whereby wee are to walke one towards another: JUSTICE and MERCY. These are allways distinguished in their Act and in their obiect, yet may they both concurre in the same Subject in each respect; as sometimes there may be an occasion of shewing mercy to a rich man, in some sudden danger of distresse, and allso doing of meere Justice to a poor man in regard of some particuler contract etc. There is likewise a double Lawe by which wee are regulated in our conversacion one towardes another: in both the former respects, the lawe of nature and the lawe of grace, or the morrall lawe or the lawe of the gospell, to omit the rule of Justice as not properly belonging to this purpose otherwise then it may fall into consideracion in some particuler Cases: By the first of these lawes man as he was enabled soe withall is commaunded to love his neighbour as himselfe;[3] upon this ground stands all the precepts of the morrall lawe, which concernes our dealings with men. To apply this to the works of mercy this lawe requires two things: first that every man afford his help to another in every want or distresse; Secondly, That hee performe this out of the same affection, which makes him carefull of his owne good according to that of our Saviour (Math:[4] Whatsoever ye would that men should doe to you). This was practised by Abraham and Lott in entertaining the Angells and the old man of Gibea.[5]

The Lawe of Grace or the Gospell hath some differance from the former as in these

---

[1] "Thou hast also taken thy fair jewels given thee, and madest to thyself images of my gold and of my silver, which I had of men, and didst commit whoredom with them."

[2] "Honor the Lord with thy substance, and with the first fruits of all thine increase: So shall thy barns be filled with plenty, and thy presses burst out with new wine."

[3] Matthew 5:43; 19:19.

[4] Matthew 7:12.

[5] Abraham entertains the angels in Genesis 18:1–2. In Judges 19:16–21 an elderly man of Gilbeah shelters a Levite, a traveling priest, and defends him from enemies from a nearby city.

respectes: first the lawe of nature was given to man in the estate of innocency; this of the gospell in the estate of regeneracy:[6] 2ly, the former propounds one man to another, as the same flesh and Image of God, this as a brother in Christ allso, and in the Communion of the same spirit and soe teacheth us to put a difference betweene Christians and others. Do good to all especially to the household of faith; upon this ground the Israelites were to put a difference betweene the brethren of such as were strangers though not of the Canaanites.[7] 3ly. The Lawe of nature could give noe rules for dealing with enemies for all are to be considered as friends in the estate of innocency, but the Gospell commaunds love to an enemy. Proofe. If thine Enemie hunger feede him; Love your Enemies, doe good to them that hate you (Math: 5. 44).

This Lawe of the Gospell propoundes likewise a difference of seasons and occasions; there is a time when a christian must sell all and give to the poore as they did in the Apostles times.[8] There is a tyme allso when a christian (though they give not all yet) must give beyond their abillity, as they of Macedonia. Cor: 2. 6.[9] Likewise community of perills calls for extraordinary liberallity and soe doth Community in some speciall service for the Churche. Lastly, when there is noe other meanes whereby our Christian brother may be relieved in this distresse, wee must help him beyond our ability, rather than tempt God, in putting him upon help by miraculous or extraordinary meanes. . . .

It rests now to make some applicacion of this discourse by the present design which gave the occasion of writing of it. Herein are 4 things to be propounded: first the persons, 2ly, the worke, 3ly, the end, 4ly the meanes.

1. For the persons, wee are a Company professing our selves fellow members of Christ, In which respect only though wee were absent from eache other many miles, and had our imploymentes as farr distant, yet wee ought to account our selves knit together by this bond of love, and live in the excercise of it, if wee would have comforte of our being in Christ; this was notorious in the practise of the Christians in former times, as is testified of the Waldenses[10] from the mouth of one of the adversaries Aeneas Syluius,[11] mutuo penè antequam norint, they use to love any of their owne religion even before they were acquainted with them.

2ly. for the worke wee have in hand, it is by a mutuall consent through a speciall overruling providence, and a more then an ordinary approbation of the Churches of Christ to seeke out a place of Cohabitation and Consorteship under a due forme of Goverment both civill and ecclesiasticall. In such cases as this the care of the public must oversway all private respects, by which not only conscience, but meer Civill pollicy doth binde us; for it is a true rule that particuler estates cannot subsist in the ruine of the public.

---

[6] Mankind is here held to have fallen to an unregenerate state after Adam and Eve sinned. Christ redeemed mankind through his suffering and crucifixion, and thereafter those who believe in him are saved or regenerate.
[7] Those who lived in the Promised Land, Canaan.
[8] Luke 18:22: "Sell all that thou hast, and distribute unto the poor, and thou shalt have treasure in heaven."
[9] Actually 2 Corinthians 8:1–4.
[10] Followers of Pater Valdes, who rejected the authority of the pope and taught that the Bible was the sole authority in religion.
[11] Pope Pius II (1458–1464).

3ly. The end is to improve our lives to doe more service to the Lord the comforte and encrease of the body of christe whereof wee are members that our selves and posterity may be the better preserved from the Common corruptions of this evill world to serve the Lord and worke out our Salvacion under the power and purity of his holy Ordinances.

4ly for the meanes whereby this must be effected, they are 2fold: a Conformity with the worke and end wee aime at. These wee see are extraordinary, therefore wee must not content our selves with usuall ordinary meanes whatsoever wee did or ought to have done when wee lived in England, the same must wee do and more allso where wee goe: That which the most in their Churches maintain as a truth in profession only, wee must bring into familiar and constant practise, as in this duty of love wee must love brotherly without dissimulation, wee must love one another with a pure hearte fervently, wee must beare one anothers burthens, wee must not looke only on our owne things, but allso on the things of our brethren; neither must wee think that the lord will beare with such failings at our hands as hee dothe from those among whome wee have lived, and that for 3 Reasons.

1. In regard of the more neare bond of mariage, betweene him and us, wherein he hath taken us to be his after a most strickt and peculiar manner which will make him the more Jealous of our love and obedience, soe he tells the people of Israell, you only have I knowne of all the families of the Earthe, therefore will I punish you for your Transgressions.

2ly, because the lord will be sanctified in them that come neare him. Wee know that there were many that corrupted the service of the Lord, some setting up Alters before his owne, others offering both strange fire and strange Sacrifices allso; yet there came noe fire from heaven, or other sudden Judgement upon them as did upon Nadab and Abihu,[12] who yet wee may thinke did not sinn presumptuously.

3ly When God gives a speciall Commission he lookes to have it stricktly observed in every Article; when hee gave Saule a Commission to destroy Amaleck[13] hee indented with him upon certaine Articles, and because hee failed in one of the least, and that upon a faire pretence, it lost him the kingdome, which should have beene his reward, if hee had observed his Commission: Thus stands the cause betweene God and us, wee are entered into Covenant[14] with him for this worke, wee have taken out a Commission, the Lord hath given us leave to drawe our owne Articles, wee have professed to enterprise these Actions upon these and these ends, wee have hereupon besought him of favour and blessing: Now if the Lord shall please to heare us, and bring us in peace to the place wee desire, then hath hee ratified this Covenant and sealed our Commission, and will expect a strickt performance of the Articles contained in it, but if wee shall neglect the observacion of these Articles which are the ends wee have propounded, and dissembling with our God, shall fall to embrace this present world and prosecute our carnall intencions, seeking great things for our selves and

---

[12] See Leviticus 10:1–2.
[13] In 1 Samuel 15:1–34, God instructed Saul to destroy the Amalekites and all their possessions. Because he spared their sheep and oxen, Saul disobeyed God.

[14] A legal contract in which God extends protection to the faithful, who promise to abide by his word.

our posterity, the Lord will surely break out in wrathe against us be revenged of such a perjured people and make us know the price of the breach of such a Covenant.

Now the only way to avoide this shipwracke and to provide for our posterity is to followe the Counsell of Micah,[15] to doe Justly, to love mercy, to walke humbly with our God; for this end, wee must be knit together in this worke as one man, wee must entertaine each other in brotherly Affection, wee must be willing to abridge our selves of our superfluities for the supply of others necessities, wee must uphold a familiar Commerce together in all meekness, gentleness, patience and liberallity, wee must delight in each other, make others Condicions our owne, rejoice together, mourne together, labour, and suffer together, allways haveing before our eyes our Commission and Community in the worke, our Community as members of the same body. Soe shall wee keepe the unity of the spirit in the bond of peace, the Lord will be our God and delight to dwell among us, as his owne people and will command a blessing upon us in all our ways, soe that wee shall see much more of his wisdom power goodnes and truth than formerly wee have beene acquainted with; wee shall finde that the God of Israell is among us, when ten of us shall be able to resist a thousand of our enemies, when hee shall make us a praise and glory, that men shall say of succeeding plantations: the lord make it like that of New England: for wee must Consider that wee shall be as a Citty upon a Hill,[16] the eyes of all people are uppon us; soe that if wee shall deale falsely with our god in this worke wee have undertaken and soe cause him to withdrawe his present help from us, wee shall be made a story and a by-word through the world, wee shall open the mouths of enemies to speake evill of the ways of god and all professours for Gods sake; wee shall shame the faces of many of gods worthy servants, and cause their prayers to be turned into Cursses upon us till wee be consumed out of the good land whether wee are going: And to shutt up this discourse with that exhortation of Moses that faithfull servant of the Lord in his last farewell to Israell (Deut. 30):[17] Beloved there is now set before us life, and good, death and evill in that wee are Commaunded this day to love the Lord our God, and to love one another to walk in his ways and to keepe his Commaundements and his Ordinance, and his lawes, and the Articles of our Covenant with him that wee may live and be multiplied, and that the Lord our God may blesse us in the land whether wee go to possesse it: But if our heartes shall turne away soe that wee will not obey, but shall be seduced and worship other Gods our pleasures, and proffitts, and serve them; it is propounded unto us this day, wee shall surely perish out of the good Land whither wee passe over this vast Sea to possess it;

---

[15] Micah 6:8: ". . .and what doth the Lord require of thee, but to do justly, and to love mercy, and to walk humbly with thy God?"

[16] Matthew 5:14–15: "Ye are the light of the world. A city that is set on a hill cannot be hid. Neither do men light a candle, and put it under a bushel, but on a candlestick; and it giveth light unto all that are in the house."

[17] Deuteronomy 30:1–3: "And it shall come to pass, when all these things are come upon thee, the blessing and the curse, which I have set before thee, and thou shalt call them to mind among all the nations, whither the Lord thy God hath driven thee, And shalt return unto the Lord thy God, and shalt obey his voice according to all that I command thee this day, thou and thy children, with all thine heart, and with all thy soul; That then the Lord thy God will turn thy captivity, and have compassion upon thee, and will return and gather thee from all the nations, whither the Lord thy God hath scattered thee."

Therefore lett us choose life,[18]
> that wee, and our Seede,
> may live; by obeyeing his
voice, and cleaving to him,
> for hee is our life, and
> our prosperity.

1838

Anne Bradstreet
ca. 1612–1672

Anne Bradstreet was an English gentlewoman whose heart "rose" in revulsion at the sight of the New World. Yet she became the first significant poet in American literature precisely by capturing the essence of life as a Puritan and as a woman under colonial conditions. She "submitted," as she put it, to the "new world and new manners," though the transition was undeniably wrenching.

Anne Dudley was born in Northampton, England. Her father, Thomas, was then a financial officer in the household of the Earl of Lincoln. Anne called him her "guide," her "instructor," and "a magazine of history." Dudley evidently took unusual care with the education of his daughter, perhaps following one educator's advice to teach the "Abcie and primer" while "playing with [the little children] at dinners and suppers, or as they sit by the fire." Anne reported that at about age six or seven she was reading the Scriptures.

Young Anne Bradstreet's era was intellectually lively, as was her immediate environment in the household of the nobleman whose library was probably accessible to her. She evidently knew Sir Walter Raleigh's *History of the World* (1614), a study of the ancient kingdoms and dynasties emphasizing God's authority through every historical cycle. And she knew the poetry of Sir Philip Sidney, Edmund Spenser, and Michael Drayton, in addition to Robert Burton's *Anatomy of Melancholy* and Francis Bacon's *Essays*. She had probably read some Shakespeare, and she openly admired Joshua Sylvester's translation of Guillaume du Bartas's *Divine Weeks and Works*. In addition, Anne knew John Foxe's *Actes and Monuments,* a Protestant martyrology, and countless contemporary Puritan tracts and pamphlets. But the girl's education came only in part from books. Her mind was doubtless sharpened from listening to the household debate and discussion of a distinguished company of Puritan intellectuals in the thick of a religious controversy unequaled in intensity since that time.

In the late 1620s political conditions worsened for the Dudley family, Puritan

---

[18] Deuteronomy 30:19: ". . . I have set before you life and death, blessing and cursing: therefore, choose life, that both thou and thy seed may live. . . ."

employees of a Puritan nobleman increasingly in the king's disfavor. Charles I began to prosecute retainers of Lord Lincoln, and Anne's father fell under suspicion of harboring a fugitive. In 1630 the Dudley family sailed with the Winthrop party to Massachusetts.

Anne, at sixteen, voyaged not only as Dudley's daughter but also as the wife of Simon Bradstreet, a graduate of Emmanuel College, Cambridge, a university center of nonconformity. Anne had married the twenty-five-year-old steward, her father's assistant, about two years earlier. At the time of her wedding Anne was recuperating from smallpox; her convalescence was perhaps lengthened by her earlier childhood bouts of rheumatic fever, and for the remainder of her life Anne Bradstreet's health was tenuous. She was subject to lameness, fever, and fainting in a land rife with disease and death. It is understandable that the dominant images in her poems concern the human body, illness, and mortality.

The Bradstreets began Massachusetts life in Salem, then a settlement of forty dwellings, most no more than huts. Almost immediately the couple relocated in Charlestown, close to Boston's inner harbor. In a letter Anne's father wrote, "They who had health to labor fell to building, wherein many were interrupted with sickness, and many died weekly, yea, almost daily." Because Charlestown lacked an adequate water supply, the Bradstreets and their neighbors cast about once again for a suitable home and, in spring 1631, resettled in Newtown, now Cambridge, where both the Dudleys and the Bradstreets built sturdy houses. But following an acrimonious term as governor, father Dudley decided to move to Agawam (Ipswich), a remote settlement of the Bay Colony that "aboundeth with fish, and flesh of fowls and beasts, . . . plowing grounds, many good rivers and harbours and no rattle snakes."

The Bradstreets and their new infant son moved with the Dudleys to this town, which was settled by remarkably accomplished families. These Ipswich settlers in part transcended the horrific wilderness conditions by sustaining a vigorous cultural and intellectual life. It was here that Anne Bradstreet began to write Christian epic poetry. She reached her permanent home, however, only in 1645–1646, when her husband moved the family fifteen miles west to (North) Andover, a farming settlement surrounded on every side by dense virgin woodland. (At the time the Bradstreets took up residence, Andover offered a generous bounty for wolves, and "25 wolf-hooks" were among Simon Bradstreet's possessions.) Town officials allotted the Bradstreets twenty acres, and they probably lived in a three-story, central-chimney saltbox house. At this point they had five of what would be eight children.

During the years of their marriage, Simon Bradstreet was often absent on colonial business. He was secretary to the Bay Company, its deputy governor, and in 1645 its governor. In 1661, with the restoration of the monarchy in England, he traveled there to renegotiate the charter of the Bay Company. Bradstreet's absences increased his wife's burdens.

Given her circumstances, it is astonishing that Anne Bradstreet could make time to write poetry and prose. The household relocations, the eight births and years of child rearing, domestic and social obligations, the sicknesses, cramped quarters, and the disapproval (as she recorded in one poem) of "each carping tongue / who says my hand a needle better fits"—any or all would have silenced a writer who was less driven than she. Yet she called poetry a "room of my own," and she worked at it until her death.

Bradstreet's writings fall into two groups. One is scholarly and monumental and concerns such subjects as the four elements and four humors (named for the ancient Greeks' belief that the world was composed of earth, air, fire, and water and that the human temperament was formed of warmth, cold, wet, and dry). Bradstreet likewise searched for cosmic themes when she wrote poetry of historical cycles she called the ages of man and the four monarchies. This work was both imitative and derivative of her reading. It caused a stir when, without her knowledge, Bradstreet's brother-in-law took some of these poems to England and had them published under the title *The Tenth Muse Lately Sprung Up in America . . .* (1650). The printer's errors embarrassed Mistress Bradstreet, but the work had historical distinction as the first published volume of poetry to be written by a New England colonist. In these four-part poems Anne Bradstreet most fully reveals her ambition to take her place among the English and French poets, all of them men.

Ironically, the second group of "domestic" poems and the *Contemplations* stand as Bradstreet's literary achievement. She is now most appreciated for the writings that convey her personal feelings about New England and family life. As a mother she writes of her "eight birds hatcht in one nest" and as a wife inscribes her love for Simon ("If ever man were lov'd by wife, then thee"). Her tone ranges from light irony, as when she calls the error-ridden text of *The Tenth Muse* an "ill-form'd offspring of my feeble brain," to the poignance of the poem occasioned by the burning of the Bradstreet house in 1666. Her elegies on the death of her grandchildren convey a deep sense of loss even as they evoke the solace of her religion. These poems exploit the tension between the individual's wishes and desires and the need to submit to God's will. Many of the poems were published in 1678, six years after her death.

Some modern readers appreciate Bradstreet as a covertly secular poet, but Puritanism is a rigorous constant in her work. In early childhood she wrote, "I began to make conscience of my wayes, and what I knew was sinful. . . . I could not rest 'till by prayer I had confest unto God." In later life, sensitive to the natural world that surrounded her in Andover, she used motifs of nature to express her struggle en route to the heavenly kingdom. She attempted to view all nature as expressive of God's glory, and in affliction she turned to her Puritan God for solace and direction. She observed poignantly that "buds" like her granddaughter are "new blown to have so short a date" but affirmed that it is "His hand alone that guides nature and fate."

Further Reading:
J. Piercy, *Anne Bradstreet*, 1965.
E. White, *Anne Bradstreet: The Tenth Muse*, 1971.
A. Stanford, *Anne Bradstreet: The Worldly Puritan*, 1974.
W. Martin, *An American Triptych*, 1984.

Text:
The Works of Anne Bradstreet, ed. J. Hensley, 1967.

The Prologue

1

To sing of wars, of captains, and of kings,
Of cities founded, commonwealths begun,
For my mean pen are too superior things:
Or how they all, or each their dates have run
Let poets and historians set these forth,   5
My obscure lines shall not so dim their worth.

2

But when my wond'ring eyes and envious heart
Great Bartas'[1] sugared lines do but read o'er,
Fool I do grudge the Muses did not part
'Twixt him and me that overfluent store;   10
A Bartas can do what a Bartas will
But simple I according to my skill.

3

From schoolboy's tongue no rhet'ric we expect,
Nor yet a sweet consort from broken strings,
Nor perfect beauty where's a main defect: 15
My foolish, broken, blemished Muse so sings,
And this to mend, alas, no art is able,
'Cause nature made it so irreparable.

4

Nor can I, like that fluent sweet tongued Greek,[2]
Who lisped at first, in future times speak plain.   20
By art he gladly found what he did seek,
A full requital of his striving pain.
Art can do much, but this maxim's most sure:
A weak or wounded brain admits no cure.

5

I am obnoxious to each carping tongue   25
Who says my hand a needle better fits,

---

[1] Guillaume du Bartas (1544–1590), French poet.   [2] Demosthenes (385?–322 B.C.), Athenian orator.

A poet's pen all scorn I should thus wrong,
For such despite they cast on female wits:
If what I do prove well, it won't advance,
They'll say it's stol'n, or else it was by chance.   30

6

But sure the antique Greeks were far more mild
Else of our sex, why feigned they those nine
And poesy made Calliope's[3] own child;
So 'mongst the rest they placed the arts divine:
But this weak knot they will full soon untie,   35
The Greeks did nought, but play the fools and lie.

7

Let Greeks be Greeks, and women what they are
Men have precedency and still excel,
It is but vain unjustly to wage war;
Men can do best, and women know it well.   40
Preeminence in all and each is yours;
Yet grant some small acknowledgement of ours.

8

And oh ye high flown quills that soar the skies,
And ever with your prey still catch your praise,
If e'er you deign these lowly lines your eyes,   45
Give thyme or parsley wreath, I ask no bays;[4]
This mean and unrefined ore of mine
Will make your glist'ring gold but more to shine.

1650

The Author to Her Book

Thou ill-formed offspring of my feeble brain,
Who after birth didst by my side remain,
Till snatched from thence by friends, less wise
          than true,

---

[3] Calliope, the Muse of heroic poetry, was one of   [4] Laurels.
the nine Muses who presided over the arts and
sciences.

Who thee abroad, exposed to public view,
Made thee in rags, halting to th' press to trudge,   5
Where errors were not lessened (all may judge).
At thy return my blushing was not small,
My rambling brat (in print) should mother call,
I cast thee by as one unfit for light,
Thy visage was so irksome in my sight;   10
Yet being mine own, at length affection would
Thy blemishes amend, if so I could:
I washed thy face, but more defects I saw,
And rubbing off a spot still made a flaw.
I stretched thy joints to make thee even feet,   15
Yet still thou run'st more hobbling than is meet;
In better dress to trim thee was my mind,
But nought save homespun cloth i' th' house I find.
In this array 'mongst vulgars may'st thou roam.
In critic's hands beware thou dost not come,   20
And take thy way where yet thou art not known;
If for thy father asked, say thou hadst none;
And for thy mother, she alas is poor,
Which caused her thus to send thee out of door.

1678

Before the Birth of One of Her Children

All things within this fading world hath end,
Adversity doth still our joys attend;
No ties so strong, no friends so dear and sweet,
But with death's parting blow is sure to meet.
The sentence past is most irrevocable,   5
A common thing, yet oh, inevitable.
How soon, my Dear, death may my steps attend,
How soon't may be thy lot to lose thy friend,
We both are ignorant, yet love bids me
These farewell lines to recommend to thee,   10
That when that knot's untied that made us one,
I may seem thine, who in effect am none.
And if I see not half my days that's due,
What nature would, God grant to yours and you;
The many faults that well you know I have   15

Let be interred in my oblivious grave;
If any worth or virtue were in me,
Let that live freshly in thy memory
And when thou feel'st no grief, as I no harms,
Yet love thy dead, who long lay in thine arms.   20
And when thy loss shall be repaid with gains
Look to my little babes, my dear remains.
And if thou love thyself, or loved'st me,
These O protect from step-dame's injury.
And if chance to thine eyes shall bring this verse,   25
With some sad sighs honour my absent hearse;
And kiss this paper for thy love's dear sake,
Who with salt tears this last farewell did take.
1867

To My Dear and Loving Husband

If ever two were one, then surely we.
If ever man were loved by wife, then thee;
If ever wife was happy in a man,
Compare with me, ye women, if you can.
I prize thy love more than whole mines of gold   5
Or all the riches that the East doth hold.
My love is such that rivers cannot quench,
Nor ought but love from thee, give recompense.
Thy love is such I can no way repay,
The heavens reward thee manifold, I pray.   10
Then while we live, in love let's so persevere
That when we live no more, we may live ever.
1867

A Letter to Her Husband, Absent upon Public Employment

My head, my heart, mine eyes, my life, nay, more,
My joy, my magazine of earthly store,
If two be one, as surely thou and I,
How stayest thou there, whilst I at Ipswich lie?

So many steps, head from the heart to sever,
If but a neck, soon should we be together.
I, like the Earth this season, mourn in black,
My Sun is gone so far in's zodiac,
Whom whilst I 'joyed, nor storms, nor frost I felt,
His warmth such frigid colds did cause to melt,
My chilled limbs now numbed lie forlorn;
Return, return, sweet Sol, from Capricorn;[1]
In this dead time, alas, what can I more
Than view those fruits which through thy heat I
  bore?
Which sweet contentment yield me for a space,
True living pictures of their father's face.
O strange effect! now thou art southward gone,
I weary grow the tedious day so long;
But when thou northward to me shalt return,
I wish my Sun may never set, but burn
Within the Cancer[2] of my glowing breast,
The welcome house of him my dearest guest.
Where ever, ever stay, and go not thence,
Till nature's sad decree shall call thee hence;
Flesh of thy flesh, bone of thy bone,
I here, thou there, yet both but one.

1867

Another [Letter to Her Husband, Absent upon Public Employment]

Phoebus make haste, the day's too long, be gone,
The silent night's the fittest time for moan;
But stay this once, unto my suit give ear,
And tell my griefs in either hemisphere.
(And if the whirling of thy wheels don't drown'd)   5
The woeful accents of my doleful sound,
If in thy swift carrier thou canst make stay,
I crave this boon, this errand by the way,
Commend me to the man more loved than life,
Show him the sorrows of his widowed wife;   10
My dumpish thoughts, my groans, my brakish tears

---

[1] I.e., Winter.
[2] I.e., Summer.

My sobs, my longing hopes, my doubting fears,
And if he love, how can he there abide?
My interest's more than all the world beside.
He that can tell the stars or ocean sand,   15
Or all the grass that in the meads do stand,
The leaves in th' woods, the hail, or drops of rain,
Or in a corn-field number every grain,
Or every mote that in the sunshine hops,
May count my sighs, and number all my drops.   20
Tell him the countless steps that thou dost trace,
That once a day thy spouse thou may'st embrace;
And when thou canst not treat by loving mouth,
Thy rays afar salute her from the south.
But for one month I see no day (poor soul)   25
Like those far situate under the pole,
Which day by day long wait for thy arise,
O how they joy when thou dost light the skies.
O Phoebus, hadst thou but thus long from thine
Restrained the beams of thy beloved shine,   30
At thy return, if so thou could'st or durst,
Behold a Chaos blacker than the first.
Tell him here's worse than a confused matter,
His little world's a fathom under water.
Nought but the fervor of his ardent beams   35
Hath power to dry the torrent of these streams.
Tell him I would say more, but cannot well,
Oppressed minds abruptest tales do tell.
Now post with double speed, mark what I say,
By all our loves conjure him not to stay.   40

1867

In Memory of My Dear Grandchild Elizabeth Bradstreet, Who Deceased August, 1665, Being a Year and Half Old

[1]

Farewell dear babe, my heart's too much content,
Farewell sweet babe, the pleasure of mine eye,
Farewell fair flower that for a space was lent,
Then ta'en away unto eternity.

Blest babe, why should I once bewail thy fate,   5
Or sigh thy days so soon were terminate,
Sith thou art settled in an everlasting state.

2

By nature trees do rot when they are grown,
And plums and apples thoroughly ripe do fall,
And corn and grass are in their season mown,   10
And time brings down what is both strong and tall.
But plants new set to be eradicate,
And buds new blown to have so short a date,
Is by His hand alone that guides nature and fate.

1867

Here Follows Some Verses
upon the Burning of Our House
July 10th, 1666

Copied Out of a Loose Paper

In silent night when rest I took
For sorrow near I did not look
I wakened was with thund'ring noise
And piteous shrieks of dreadful voice.
That fearful sound of "Fire!" and "Fire!"   5
Let no man know is my desire.
I, starting up, the light did spy,
And to my God my heart did cry
To strengthen me in my distress
And not to leave me succorless.   10
Then, coming out, beheld a space
The flame consume my dwelling place.
And when I could no longer look,
I blest His name that gave and took,
That laid my goods now in the dust.   15
Yea, so it was, and so 'twas just.
It was His own, it was not mine,
Far be it that I should repine;
He might of all justly bereft
But yet sufficient for us left.   20
When by the ruins oft I past

My sorrowing eyes aside did cast,
And here and there the places spy
Where oft I sat and long did lie:
Here stood that trunk, and there that chest,   25
There lay that store I counted best.
My pleasant things in ashes lie,
And them behold no more shall I.
Under thy roof no guest shall sit,
Nor at thy table eat a bit.   30
No pleasant tale shall e'er be told,
Nor things recounted done of old.
No candle e'er shall shine in thee,
Nor bridegroom's voice e'er heard shall be.
In silence ever shall thou lie,   35
Adieu, Adieu, all's vanity.
Then straight I 'gin my heart to chide,
And did thy wealth on earth abide?
Didst fix thy hope on mold'ring dust?
The arm of flesh didst make thy trust?   40
Raise up thy thoughts above the sky
That dunghill mists away may fly.
Thou hast an house on high erect,
Framed by that mighty Architect,
With glory richly furnished,   45
Stands permanent though this be fled.
It's purchased and paid for too
By Him who hath enough to do.
A price so vast as is unknown
Yet by His gift is made thine own;   50
There's wealth enough, I need no more,
Farewell, my pelf,[1] farewell my store.
The world no longer let me love,
My hope and treasure lies above.
1867

Edward Taylor
ca. 1642–1729

Edward Taylor's poems were virtually hidden in a manuscript book for more
than two centuries. Their discovery and publication in 1939 brought Taylor to
light as colonial America's foremost poet, though information about his life
remains incomplete.

[1] Disparaging term for money or riches.

Taylor was born in Sketchley, England, near Leicestershire, during the turmoil of the English Civil War. As a farmer's son educated by a nonconformist schoolmaster, he grew up during the rise of Oliver Cromwell, the defeat of the armies of King Charles I, who was put to death, and the establishment of the Puritan Holy Commonwealth. It is possible that Taylor attended Cambridge University for a time, though official records are lacking. Taylor became a schoolmaster, but his career was cut short by the restoration of the English monarch in 1660: Taylor's unwillingness to comply with the Act of Uniformity, which required annual acceptance of communion at the Anglican ceremony, forced him to forfeit his position. In 1668 Taylor sailed for America.

He brought letters of introduction to several prominent Puritans of the Massachusetts Bay Colony, including Increase Mather, the wealthy mintmaster John Hull, and President Chauncy of Harvard. Taylor was admitted to the college with advanced standing in the class of 1671. The roommate of the diarist Samuel Sewall, Taylor prepared for the ministry. On commencement day he declaimed, in verse, before the president and fellows of the college on the virtues of English over the classical languages and Hebrew.

Though Taylor considered remaining at Harvard for additional study, he accepted a call to the sparsely settled western Massachusetts community of Westfield. In 1671 it took him eight days on horseback to travel the one hundred miles southwest from Boston across the Connecticut River to the settlement, where he spent the remainder of his life and wrote the poetry his readers have admired.

Three years after arriving at Westfield, Taylor married the daughter of a Connecticut clergyman and, when she died, remarried. Altogether Taylor fathered fourteen children, five of whom he buried in infancy or early childhood. "Five babes thou tookst from me," he wrote, addressing the God who had taken Taylor's wife and the mother of those "babes" as well. "Thine arrows . . . do strike and stob me in the very heart," he said, seeking comfort in God's mercy.

The Indian attacks known as "King Philip's War" (1675–1676) delayed Taylor's ordination and the gathering of his church. Instead, Westfield prepared for assault like other outlying settlements such as Lancaster, from which Mary Rowlandson was abducted. As a frontier minister, Taylor doubtless provided leadership during the crisis. In times of peace he would necessarily raise crops and tend livestock. He also prepared two weekly sermons and sustained the scholarly life to which he was so deeply committed. His library contained over two hundred books and tracts, many copied by hand because he could not afford to buy them. Taylor also served as the community physician, and it is not surprising to find images of medicinal plants and herbs in his poems.

By 1679 Taylor had "gathered" his church in a ceremony that conferred membership only on those who could attest to the presence of God's saving grace in their souls. Weekly the minister offered members the sacrament of communion, which represented the redemption of Christ through God's grace. None of Taylor's parishioners, however, knew that their minister's spiritual preparation had taken an unusual turn. At age forty-two Taylor embarked on a series of intensely private poems, the *Preparatory Meditations,* each one an integral part of his preparation to receive and to administer the sacrament of communion.

Though Taylor wrote over forty thousand lines of poetry during his life, these poems are considered to be his finest, in part because they show the tensions of a mind simultaneously feeling and thinking out the human relationship to the Creator in vivid figures of speech.

The literary origins of the *Preparatory Meditations* have become clear to modern readers. Though the only volume of poetry in Taylor's library was that of fellow New England poet Anne Bradstreet, he evidently was familiar with—and used—the metaphysical tradition of such poets as George Herbert, Francis Quarles, and the Catholic poet Richard Crashaw. Their work showed the forging of wit and passion. It emphasized playful language, such as puns, and elaborate imagery. For Taylor and other Puritans, God's messages could be divined in such wordplay. Taylor's poetic images come from several sources, first among them the Bible, especially the sensuous Song of Songs. But Taylor also used poetic figures from the activities of everyday life, such as the weaving and farming he knew from his English boyhood, and from the conditions of western Massachusetts, where, he wrote, "little save Rusticity is." Taylor's poetry has been called "wilderness baroque," bringing elements of the unexpected into an ordered and formal structure that elicits an "earthly enjoyment of things divine."

Apart from the *Preparatory Meditations,* Taylor wrote miscellaneous occasional poems whose images reveal his apprehension of detail and whose themes are those of an orthodox Puritan. His interest in natural science is evident in "Upon a Spider Catching a Fly," in which he carefully traces the movement of the satanic spider. Taylor's best-known long poem bears the lengthy title *Gods Determinations touching his Elect: and the Elects Combat in their Conversion and coming up to God in Christ together with the Comfortable Effects thereof.* Known simply as *Gods Determinations,* the poem is based in the medieval debate literature, including the morality plays that Taylor might have seen in boyhood. Taylor's divine drama opposes good and evil in military terms familiar to the poet from the Bible and from his youth amid events of the English Civil War. Although the work is uneven, parts of it represent Taylor at his best.

Taylor served as minister at Westfield until 1729, taking time away only to return to Harvard College at the age of seventy-eight for the conferral of his master's degree. He died in his eighty-eighth year, requesting his heirs not to publish his poetry. That request was honored, but in 1937 Taylor's leather manuscript book, containing some four hundred pages, was found in the Yale University Library. The publication of a substantial selection from that book in 1939 established Taylor, the poet of "wilderness baroque," as a major figure in colonial American literature.

Further Reading:
N. Grabo, *Edward Taylor,* 1962.
D. Stanford, *Edward Taylor,* 1965.
W. Scheick, *The Will and the Word: The Poetry of Edward Taylor,* 1974.
K. Keller, *The Example of Edward Taylor,* 1975.

Text:
The Poems of Edward Taylor, ed. D. Stanford, 1960.
See also *Edward Taylor's Christographia,* ed. N. Grabo, 1962.
The Diary of Edward Taylor, ed. F. Murphy, 1964.

from Preparatory Meditations

Meditation 6 (First Series):
[Am I thy Gold? Or Purse, Lord,
for thy Wealth]

Am I thy Gold? Or Purse, Lord, for thy Wealth;
  Whether in mine, or mint refinde for thee?
Ime counted so, but count me o're thyselfe,
  Lest gold washt face, and brass in Heart I bee.
I Feare my Touchstone¹ touches when I try   5
Mee, and my Counted Gold too overly.

Am I new minted by thy Stamp indeed?
  Mine Eyes are dim; I cannot clearly see.
Be thou my Spectacles that I may read
  Thine Image, and Inscription stampt on mee.   10
If thy bright Image do upon me stand
I am a Golden Angell² in thy hand.

Lord, make my Soule thy Plate: thine Image bright
  Within the Circle of the same enfoile.
And on its brims in golden Letters write   15
  Thy Superscription in an Holy style.
Then I shall be thy Money, thou my Hord:
Let me thy Angell bee, bee thou my Lord.

1939

Meditation 8 (First Series):
[I kening through Astronomy Divine]

*Joh. 6.51. I am the
Living Bread.*

I kening³ through Astronomy Divine
  The World's bright Battlement, wherein I spy
A Golden Path my Pensill cannot line,
  From that bright Throne unto my Threshold ly.
And while my puzzled thoughts about it pore   5
I finde the Bread of Life in't at my doore.

When that this Bird of Paradise put in
  This Wicker Cage (my Corps) to tweedle praise

---

¹ Used to test the purity of gold and silver by
the color of the streak produced on it by
rubbing it with either metal.

² Gold coin.
³ Discovering.

Had peckt the Fruite forbad: and so did fling
    Away its Food; and lost its golden dayes;   10
    It fell into Celestiall Famine sore:
    And never could attain a morsell more.

Alas! alas! Poore Bird, what wilt thou doe?
    The Creatures field no food for Souls e're gave.
And if thou knock at Angells dores they show   15
    An Empty Barrell: they no soul bread have.
    Alas! Poore Bird, the Worlds White Loafe is done.
    And cannot yield thee here the smallest Crumb.

In this sad state, Gods Tender Bowells[4] run
    Out streams of Grace: And he to end all strife   20
The Purest Wheate in Heaven, his deare–dear Son
    Grinds, and kneads up into this Bread of Life.
    Which Bread of Life from Heaven down came and stands
    Disht on thy Table up by Angells Hands.

Did God mould up this Bread in Heaven, and bake,   25
    Which from his Table came, and to thine goeth?
Doth he bespeake thee thus, This Soule Bread take.
    Come Eate thy fill of this thy God's White Loafe?
    Its Food too fine for Angells, yet come, take
    And Eate thy fill. Its Heavens Sugar Cake.   30

What Grace is this knead in this Loafe? This thing
    Souls are but petty things it to admire.
Yee Angells, help: This fill would to the brim
    Heav'ns whelm'd–down Chrystall meele Bowle, yea and higher.
    This Bread of Life dropt in thy mouth, doth Cry.   35
    Eate, Eate me, Soul, and thou shalt never dy.

1939

Meditation 29 (First Series): [My shattred Phancy stole away from mee]

*Joh. 20.17. My Father,
and your Father, to my God,
and your God.*

My shattred Phancy stole away from mee,
    (Wits run a Wooling[5] over Edens Parke)
And in Gods Garden saw a golden Tree,
    Whose Heart was All Divine, and gold its barke.

---

[4] The bowels were supposedly the seat of pity   [5] Daydreaming.
and tenderness.

Whose glorious limbs and fruitfull branches strong   5
With Saints, and Angells bright are richly hung.

Thou! thou! my Deare-Deare Lord, art this rich Tree
    The Tree of Life Within Gods Paradise.
I am a Withred Twig, dri'de fit to bee
    A Chat[6] Cast in thy fire, Writh[7] off by Vice.   10
    Yet if thy Milke white-Gracious Hand will take mee
    And grafft mee in this golden stock, thou'lt make mee.

Thou'lt make me then its Fruite, and Branch to spring.
    And though a nipping Eastwinde blow, and all
Hells Nymps[8] with spite their Dog's sticks thereat ding[9]   15
    To Dash the Grafft off, and it's fruits to fall,
    Yet I shall stand thy Grafft, and Fruits that are
    Fruits of the Tree of Life thy Grafft shall beare.

I being grafft in thee there up do stand
    In us Relations all that mutuall are.   20
I am thy Patient, Pupill, Servant, and
    Thy Sister, Mother, Doove, Spouse, Son, and Heire.
    Thou art my Priest, Physician, Prophet, King,
    Lord, Brother, Bridegroom, Father, Ev'ry thing.

I being grafft in thee am graffted here   25
    Into thy Family, and kindred Claim
To all in Heaven, God, Saints, and Angells there.
    I thy Relations my Relations name.
    Thy Father's mine, thy God my God, and I
    With Saints, and Angells draw Affinity.   30

My Lord, what is it that thou dost bestow?
    The Praise on this account fills up, and throngs
Eternity brimfull, doth overflow
    The Heavens vast with rich Angelick Songs.
    How should I blush? how Tremble at this thing,   35
    Not having yet my Gam-Ut,[10] learnd to sing.
But, Lord, as burnish't Sun Beams forth out fly
    Let Angell-Shine forth in my Life out flame,
That I may grace thy gracefull Family
    And not to thy Relations be a Shame.   40
    Make mee thy Grafft, be thou my Golden Stock.
    Thy Glory then I'le make my fruits and Crop.

1939

---

[6] Piece of kindling.   [9] Strike.
[7] Wrenched.   [10] Musical scale.
[8] Imps.

Meditation 39 (First Series):
[My Sin! my Sin, My God, these Cursed Dregs]

1 Joh. 2.1. If any
man sin, we have an Advocate.

My Sin! my Sin, My God, these Cursed Dregs,
    Green, Yellow, Blew streakt Poyson hellish, ranck,
Bubs[11] hatcht in natures nest on Serpents Eggs,
    Yelp, Cherp and Cry; they set my Soule a Cramp.
    I frown, Chide, strik and fight them, mourn and Cry   5
    To Conquour them, but cannot them destroy.

I cannot kill nor Coop them up: my Curb
    'S less than a Snaffle in their mouth: my Rains
They as a twine thrid,[12] snap: by hell they're spurd:
    And load my Soule with swagging loads of pains.   10
    Black Imps, young Divells, snap, bite, drag to bring
    And pick mee headlong hells dread Whirle Poole in.

Lord, hold thy hand: for handle mee thou may'st
    In Wrath: but, oh, a twinckling Ray of hope
Methinks I spie thou graciously display'st.   15
    There is an Advocate: a doore is ope.
    Sin's poyson swell my heart would till it burst,
    Did not a hope hence creep in't thus, and nurse't.

Joy, joy, Gods Son's the Sinners Advocate
    Doth plead the Sinner guiltless, and a Saint.   20
But yet Atturnies pleas spring from the State
    The Case is in: if bad its bad in plaint.
    My Papers do contain no pleas that do
    Secure mee from, but knock me down to, woe.

I have no plea mine Advocate to give: 25
    What now? He'l anvill Arguments greate Store
Out of his Flesh and Blood to make thee live.
    O Deare bought Arguments: Good pleas therefore.
    Nails made of heavenly Steel, more Choice than gold
    Drove home, Well Clencht, eternally will hold.   30

Oh! Dear bought Plea, Deare Lord, what buy't so deare?
    What with thy blood purchase thy plea for me?
Take Argument out of thy Grave t'appeare
    And plead my Case with, me from Guilt to free.
    These maule both Sins, and Divells, and amaze   35
    Both Saints, and Angells; Wreath their mouths with praise.

---

[11] Pustules.   [12] Thread.

What shall I doe, my Lord? what do, that I
    May have thee plead my Case? I fee thee will
With Faith, Repentance, and obediently
    Thy Service gainst Satanick Sins fulfill.
    I'l fight thy fields while Live I do, although
    I should be hackt in pieces by thy foe.

Make me thy Friend, Lord, be my Surety: I
    Will be thy Client, be my Advocate:
My Sins make thine, thy Pleas make mine hereby.
    Thou wilt mee save, I will thee Celebrate.
    Thou'lt kill my Sins that cut my heart within:
    And my rough Feet shall thy smooth praises sing.

1954

Meditation 83 (Second Series): [A Garden, yea a Paradise indeed]

*Can. 5.1. I am come into
my Garden, etc.*

A Garden, yea a Paradise indeed,
    Of all Delightfull Beauteous flowers and sweet,
(A Cloud of rich perfume hence did proceed
    From sweet breathd plants,) first Adam was to keep.
    But sinning here he's from this Farm exilde,
    And th'Farm, Lord, thou camst to, 's a Garden stylde

A Garden-Church, set with Choice Herbs and Flowers.
    Here Lign-Aloes. And th'Tree of Life.
Here trees of Frankincense and Myrrh up towers.
    Here's Sharons Rose and Lillie: Beauties Strife.
    Here's Cassia, Cinnamon, Cloves, Nut Megs, Mace.
    Sweet Calamus: and all Heavens herbs of Grace.[13]

Here's Order Choice, Beds, Allies[14] all in print.
    Here bud sweet blushing Blossoms, sparkling brave
And Beautifull rich, spangled Flowers bepinckt
    Which White, Red, Blushie, Cherry Cheek't Smiles have,
    Making Celestiall aire their Civit[15] Box
    Of Aromatick Vapors: Spirituall Drops.

This Garden, Lord, thy Church, this Paradise
    Thou comst into, with thy Choice Spirits Gales

[13] See Song of Solomon 1–8.
[14] Garden walkways; here, "avenues" to biblical
imagery in the Old and New Testaments.

[15] Perfume from the civit cat.

Making all Plants of Grace gust out like Spice
   Their sweet perfumed breath that us assailes.
   And sacrifice their Spirits sweet upon
   Their Beauties Altar to thee, Holy One.

This Garden too's the Soule, of thy Redeem'd: 25
   When thou thy Spirits plants therein hast set
In their Conversion now most Choicely 'steemd
   Embeautified with Graces bracelet.
   If that my Soule thy Paradise once bee:
   Thou wilt emparadise it e're with thee.   30

Make mee thy Garden; Lord, thy Grace my plant:
   Make mee thy Vineyard, and my plants thy Vine:
Then come into thy Garden: View each ranck:
   And make my Grape bleed in thy Cup rich wine.
   When thou comest in, My Garden flowers will smile   35
   And blossom Aromatick Praise the while.

1960

---

from God's Determinations

The Preface

   Infinity, when all things it beheld
   In Nothing, and of Nothing all did build,
   Upon what Base was fixt the Lath, wherein
   He turn'd this Globe, and riggalld[1] it so trim?
   Who blew the Bellows of his Furnace Vast?   5
   Or held the Mould wherein the world was Cast?
   Who laid its Corner Stone? Or whose Command?
   Where stand the Pillars upon which it stands?
   Who Lac'de and Fillitted the earth so fine,
   With Rivers like green Ribbons Smaragdine?   10
   Who made the Sea's its Selvedge,[2] and it locks
   Like a Quilt Ball within a Silver Box?
   Who Spread its Canopy? Or Curtains Spun?
   Who in this Bowling Alley bowld the Sun?
   Who made it always when it rises set   15
   To go at once both down, and up to get?
   Who th'Curtain rods made for this Tapistry?
   Who hung the twinckling Lanthorns in the Sky?

[1] Made ringed marks.   [2] Border.

Who? who did this? or who is he? Why, know
Its Onely Might Almighty this did doe.   20
His hand hath made this noble worke which Stands
His Glorious Handywork not made by hands.
Who spake all things from nothing; and with ease
Can speake all things to nothing, if he please.
Whose Little finger at his pleasure Can   25
Out mete ten thousand worlds with halfe a Span:
Whose Might Almighty can by half a looks
Root up the rocks and rock the hills by th'roots.
Can take this mighty World up in his hande,
And shake it like a Squitchen[3] or a Wand.   30
Whose single Frown will make the Heavens shake
Like as an aspen leafe the Winde makes quake.
Oh! what a might is this Whose single frown
Doth shake the world as it would shake it down?
Which All from Nothing fet,[4] from Nothing, All: 35
Hath All on Nothing set, lets Nothing fall.
Gave All to nothing Man indeed, whereby
Through nothing man all might him Glorify.
In Nothing then imbosst the brightest Gem
More pretious than all pretiousness in them.   40
But Nothing man did throw down all by Sin:
And darkened that lightsom Gem in him.
      That now his Brightest Diamond is grown
      Darker by far than any Coalpit Stone.

1939

Huswifery

Make me, O Lord, thy Spining Wheele compleate.
      Thy Holy Worde my Distaff[1] make for mee.
Make mine Affections[2] thy Swift Flyers neate
      And make my Soule thy holy Spoole to bee.
My Conversation make to be thy Reele   5
And reele the yarn thereon spun of thy
                        Wheele.

[3] A slip of branch cut for grafting.
[4] Fetched.
[1] The distaff holds the fibers of wool, which are
twisted into threads by the revolving flyers and
then wound onto the spool.
[2] Religious feelings.

Make me thy Loome then, knit therein this Twine:
    And make thy Holy Spirit, Lord, winde quills:[3]
Then weave the Web thyselfe. The yarn is fine.
    Thine Ordinances make my Fulling Mills.[4]   10
Then dy the same in Heavenly Colours
    Choice,
    All pinkt[5] with Varnisht[6] Flowers of Paradise.

Then cloath therewith mine Understanding, Will,
    Affections, Judgment, Conscience, Memory
My Words, and Actions, that their shine may fill   15
    My wayes with glory and thee glorify.
Then mine apparell shall display before yee
    That I am Cloathd in Holy robes for glory.

1937

Upon a Wasp Child[1] with Cold

The Bare[2] that breaths the Northern blast
Did numb, Torpedo like,[3] a Wasp
Whose stiffend limbs encrampt, lay bathing
In Sol's warm breath and shine as saving,
Which with her hands she chafes and stands   5
Rubbing her Legs, Shanks, Thighs, and hands.
Her petty toes, and fingers ends
Nipt with this breath, she out extends
Unto the Sun, in greate desire
To warm her digits at that fire.   10
Doth hold her Temples in this state
Where pulse doth beate, and head doth ake.
Doth turn, and stretch her body small,
Doth Comb her velvet Capitall.[4]
As if her little brain pan were   15
A Volume of Choice precepts cleare.
As if her sattin jacket hot
Contained Apothecaries Shop
Of Natures recepts,[5] that prevails

---

[3] Bobbins to hold the thread.
[4] Mills in which cloth is cleansed and stiffened.
[5] Decorated.
[6] Shining.
[1] Chilled.

[2] Ursa Major and Ursa Minor, northern
    constellations.
[3] Like the torpedo fish, which stuns its victims.
[4] Head.
[5] Recipes.

To remedy all her sad ailes,
As if her velvet helmet high
Did turret[6] rationality.
She fans her wing up to the Winde
As if her Pettycoate were lin'de,
With reasons fleece, and hoises sails
And hu'ming flies in thankfull gails
Unto her dun Curld[7] palace Hall
Her warm thanks offering for all.

    Lord cleare my misted sight that I
May hence view thy Divinity.
Some sparkes whereof thou up dost hasp[8]
Within this little downy Wasp
In whose small Corporation[9] wee
A school and a schoolmaster see
Where we may learn, and easily finde
A nimble Spirit bravely minde
Her worke in e'ry limb: and lace
It up neate with a vitall grace,
Acting each part though ne'er so small
Here of this Fustian[10] animall.
Till I enravisht Climb into
The Godhead on this Lather doe.
Where all my pipes inspir'de upraise
An Heavenly musick furrd[11] with praise.

1943

Samuel Sewall
1652–1730

Until his *Diary* was published late in the nineteenth century, Judge Samuel Sewall was known as the hanging judge of the infamous Salem witchcraft trials of 1692. Yet history has redeemed him, in part because Sewall publicly recanted his part in the witchcraft proceedings (taking "the Blame and Shame of it") and also because he wrote one of the earliest American antislavery tracts, *The Selling of Joseph* (1710). But the work that sympathetically documents Sewall's life is the *Diary,* a rich potpourri of Puritan colonial social history. The *Diary* firmly establishes Sewall as the recording secretary of colonial Boston and its environs, inhabited by six thousand souls between 1674 and 1727.

[6] Enclose.
[7] Dark, curved.
[8] Close.

[9] Body.
[10] Cloth similar to corduroy.
[11] Trimmed.

Sewall came from a well-to-do English family who provisioned themselves most comfortably in New England, to which Samuel was brought as a nine-year-old. Later, at Harvard, his roommate was the poet Edward Taylor, and as a ministerial student he met Hannah Hull, his future wife and the daughter of the colony's treasurer and mintmaster, who "set her affections" on him. Alliance by marriage with the Hull family virtually determined his future as a merchant, exporter, and magistrate.

An orthodox Puritan, Sewall was a conservative who gave money and land to his alma mater and sponsored missionary work among the Indians, whose land he felt was unfairly wrested from them. In 1683 he was elected to the Massachusetts General Court and served as a member of the Governor's Council. When the colonial charter was revoked and then restored at the time of the "Glorious Revolution" in the late 1680s, Sewall traveled to England to represent the interests of Massachusetts before Parliament. As a figure at the center of all Massachusetts affairs, Sewall perhaps inevitably became a judge in the witchcraft trials. Of the seven judges, only he repented sending twenty persons to their deaths largely on the strength of "spectral" evidence, or evidence of ghostly phenomena.

Sewall's *Diary* is not solely one of the psychological, spiritual introspection characteristic of the Puritan mind. It freely, even indiscriminately, mixes worldly with spiritual affairs, often with an abruptness that startles the modern reader but did not trouble a man convinced of the essential unity of God's cosmos.

Several Samuel Sewalls emerge in the fifty years covered by the *Diary*. There is always the orthodox Puritan horrified by signs of Roman Catholic "popery" and scornful of Anglicans and Quakers alike. There is the sensuous Sewall relishing seasonal fruits, good wines, and a well-laid table even as he scans the heavens for God's message inscribed in clouds, a comet's path, hailstones, or the earth in a chicken-yard allegory. There is the colonist mindful of the precariousness of life as he attended the countless funerals whose pageantry he enhanced with the elegies he wrote and had printed for the occasion, fastening them to the coffins as the mourners received souvenir rings or scarves. And there is the cost-conscious widower courting a succession of women in late midlife, enticing them with "almonds and reasons" as he calculated the financial status of two merged estates. Sprinkled throughout the *Diary* are the names of so many friends and acquaintances that a reader feels the entire population of Boston is registered at some point over the half century. Above all, this *Diary* shows Samuel Sewall as a family man, proud and often in spiritual doubt, but caring deeply about his children. He grieved terribly when his little son Henry died and forever worried about the happiness of his troubled son Samuel, Jr. It is this paternal Sewall who is represented in the following selection.

Further Reading:
O. Winslow, *Samuel Sewall of Boston,* 1964.
T. Strandness, *Samuel Sewall: A Puritan Portrait,*
1967.

Text:
The Diary of Samuel Sewall, ed. M. Thomas,
1973.
See also *The Diary of Samuel Sewall,* ed.
H. Wish, 1967.

from The Diary of Samuel Sewall

[January 13, 1677]

Jan. 13, 1676/7. Giving my chickens meat, it came to my mind that I gave them nothing save Indian corn and water, and yet they eat it and thrived very well, and that that food was necessary for them, how mean soever, which much affected me and convinced what need I stood in of spiritual food, and that I should not nauseat[1] daily duties of Prayer, &c.

[May 8, 1685]

Friday May 8th—past 6, even, Walk with the honored Governour [*Bradstreet*] up Hoar's Lane, so to the Alms House; then down the length of the Common to Mr. Dean's Pasture, then through Cowel's Lane to the New Garden, then to our House, then to our Pasture by Engs's, then I waited on his Honour to his Gate and so home. This day our old Red Cow is kill'd, and we have a new black one brought in the room, of about four years old and better, marked with a Crop and slit in the Left Ear, and a Crop off the right Ear, with a little hollowing in. As came with his Honour through Cowell's Lane, Sam. came running and call'd out a pretty way off and cried out the Cow was dead and by the Heels, meaning hang'd up by the Butcher. At which I was much startled, understanding him she had been dead upon a Hill or cast with her heels upward, and so had lost her; for I was then looking for her and 't was unexpected, Mother having partly bargained and the Butcher fetcht her away in the Night unknown. Had served this family above Ten years, above Nine since my dwelling in it.

[December 20, 1685]

Sabbath-day, Dec. 20. Send Notes to Mr. Willard and Mr. Moodey to pray for my Child Henry.

Monday, about four in the Morn the faint and moaning noise of my child forces me up to pray for it.

[December 21, 1685]

21. Monday even Mr. Moodey calls. I get him to go up and Pray with my extream sick Son.

[December 22, 1685]

Tuesday Morn, Dec. 22. Child makes no noise save by a kind of snoaring as it breathed, and as it were slept.

Read the 16th of the first Chron. in the family. Having read to my Wife and Nurse

---

[1] Feel disgusted by.

out of John: the fourteenth Chapter fell now in course, which I read and went to Prayer: By that time had done, could hear little Breathing, and so about Sun-rise, or little after, he fell asleep, I hope in Jesus, and that a Mansion was ready for him in the Father's House. Died in Nurse Hill's Lap. . . .

[December 24, 1685]

Thursday, Decr 24th 1685. We follow Little Henry to his Grave. . . .

[January 2, 1686]

Satterday, Jany 2^d Last night had a very unusual Dream; viz. That our Saviour in the dayes of his Flesh when upon Earth, came to Boston and abode here sometime, and moreover that He Lodged in that time at Father Hull's; upon which in my Dream had two Reflections, One was how much more Boston had to say than Rome boasting of Peter's being there. The other a sense of great Respect that I ought to have shewed Father Hull since Christ chose when in Town, to take up His Quarters at his House. Admired the goodness and Wisdom of Christ in coming hither and spending some part of His short Life here.

[September 13, 1686]

Monday, Septr 13, 1686. Mr. Cotton Mather preaches the Election Sermon for the Artillery, at Charlestown, from Ps. 144. 1. made a very good Discourse. President and Deputy President there. As I went in the morn I had Sam. to the Latin School, which is the first time. Mr. Chiever received him gladly.[2] . . .

[September 15, 1688]

Sept. 15, 1688. Corrected Sam. for breach of the 9th Commandment, saying he had been at the Writing School, when he had not.

[January 12, 1690]

Sabbath, Jan. 12. Richard Dummer, a flourishing youth of 9 years old, dies of the Small Pocks. I tell Sam. of it and what need he had to prepare for Death, and therefore to endeavour really to pray when he said over the Lord's Prayer: He seem'd not much to mind, eating an Apple; but when he came to say, Our father, he burst out into a bitter Cry, and when I askt what was the matter and he could speak, he burst out

[2] Samuel Sewall, Jr., was nine. Before long it must have been apparent to (the schoolmaster) Ezekiel Cheever, that Sam was not going to follow in his father's footsteps, for we find May 14, 1688 that he had been put to Eliezer Moody to learn to write. Sam's adolescence was a difficult period and the family prayed more than once for guidance as to his calling. He finally became a bookseller. In 1702 he married Rebecca, daughter of Governor Joseph Dudley, and later built a house at Muddy River (Brookline), where he engaged in farming. [This footnote and the following three footnotes are from M. Halsey Thomas, ed., *The Diary of Samuel Sewall* (New York: Farrar, Straus, & Giroux, 1973), and are reprinted by permission.]

into a bitter Cry and said he was afraid he should die. I pray'd with him, and read Scriptures comforting against death, as, O death where is thy sting, &c. All things yours. Life and Immortality brought to light by Christ, &c. 'Twas at noon.

[from May 9, 1690]

May 9. Friday, Rid to Dedham and there refresh'd, so home by 12. or thereabouts. . . .

Found my Family all well, save Sam's sore in his neck, and Hannah droops as though would have the Small Pocks. *Note.* I have had great heaviness on my Spirit before, and in this journey; and I resolved that if it pleas'd God to bring me to my family again, I would endeavour to serve Him better in Self-denial, Fruitfullness, Not pleasing Men, open Conversation, not being solicitous to seem in some indifferent things what I was not, or at least to conceal what I was; Endeavouring to goe and come at God's call and not otherwise; Labouring more constantly and throwly to Examin my self before sitting down to the Lord's Table. Now the good Lord God of his infinite Grace help me to perform my Vows, and give me a filial Fear of Himself, and save me from the fear of Man that brings a Snare.

[May 28, 1690]

May 28. Small Pocks appear.

[June 11, 1690]

Wednesday, June 11ᵗʰ. We put Sam. to Bed, having the Small Pocks come out upon him, as the Physician and we judge. Betty is so well as to Goe into Mother Hull's Chamber, and keep Jane Company, between 9 and 10. mane.

[June 17, 1690]

June 17ᵗʰ Tuesday. Sam. rises and sits up a good while very hearty and strong. Blessed be God.

[October 28, 1691]

Wednesday, Oct. 28, 1691. My wife is brought to Bed of a Daughter about 8. in the morning; Elisabeth Weeden, Midwife. Rose about 4. m.

[November 19, 1961]

Thursday, Nov. 19ᵗʰ 1691. Sam. goes to Cambridge with Mr. Henry Newman, who is to carry him to morrow Nov. 20. to Mr. Neh. Hobart's at New Cambridge.

[December 7, 1691]

Monday, Dec. 7 ^th^. I ride to New-Cambridge to see Sam. He could hardly speak to me, his affections were so mov'd, having not seen me for above a fortnight; his Cough is still very bad, much increas'd by his going to Cambridge on foot in the night.

[April 29, 1695]

Monday, April 29, 1695. The morning is very warm and Sunshiny; in the Afternoon there is Thunder and Lightening, and about 2 P.M. a very extraordinary Storm of Hail, so that the ground was made white with it, as with the blossoms when fallen; 'twas as bigg as pistoll and Musquet Bullets; It broke of the Glass of the new House about 480 Quarrels [squares] of the Front; of Mr. Sergeant's about as much; Col. Shrimpton, Major General, Govr Bradstreet, New Meetinghouse, Mr. Willard, &c. Mr. Cotton Mather dined with us, and was with me in the new Kitchen when this was; He had just been mentioning that more Ministers Houses than others proportionably had been smitten with Lightening; enquiring what the meaning of God should be in it. Many Hail-Stones broke throw the Glass and flew to the middle of the Room, or farther: People afterward Gazed upon the House to see its Ruins. I got Mr. Mather to pray with us after this awfull Providence; He told God He had broken the brittle part of our house, and prayd that we might be ready for the time when our Clay-Tabernacles should be broken. Twas a sorrowfull thing to me to see the house so far undon again before t'was finish'd. It seems at Milton on the one hand, and at Lewis's [the ordinary at Lynn] on the other, there was no Hail.

[July 15, 1695]

July 15. I discourse Capt. Sam Checkly about his taking Sam. to be his Prentice. He seems to incline to it; and in a manner all I mention it to encourage me. The good Lord direct and prosper.

[February 7, 1696]

Sixth-day, Feb. 7 ^th^. Mrs. Alden is buried. Bearers were Mr. Chiever, Capt. Hill, Capt. Williams, Mr. Walley, Mr. Ballentine.

Capt. Frary was pass'd by, though there, which several took notice of. *Note.* Last night Sam. could not sleep because of my Brother's speaking to him of removing to some other place, mentioning Mr. Usher's. I put him to get up a little wood, and he even fainted, at which Brother was much startled, and advis'd to remove him forthwith and place him somewhere else, or send him to Salem and he would doe the best he could for him. Since, I have express'd doubtfullness to Sam. as to his staying there.

He mention'd to me Mr. Wadsworth's Sermon against Idleness, which was an Affliction to him. He said his was an idle Calling, and that he did more at home than there, take one day with another. And he mention'd Mr. Stoddard's words to me, that should place him with a good Master, and where had fullness of Imployment. It seems Sam. overheard him, and now alleged these words against his being where he was because of his idleness. Mention'd also the difficulty of the imployment by reason of the numerousness of Goods and hard to distinguish them, many not being marked; whereas Books, the price of them was set down, and so could sell them readily. I spake to Capt. Checkly again and again, and he gave me no encouragement that his being there would be to Sam's profit; and Mrs. Checkly always discouraging.

Mr. Willard's Sermon from those Words. What doest thou here Elijah? was an Occasion to hasten the Removal.

[October 16, 1696]

October 16. Pray for Sam. and my daughters Hannah and Eliza. and others of my Children.

[April 14, 1700]

Sabbath, Apr. 14. I saw and heard the Swallows proclaim the Spring.

[April 29, 1700]

Monday, Apr. 29, 1700. Sam. Sewall, Josiah Willard Jn° Bayly, Sam. Gaskill, and [blank] Mountfort goe into the Harbour a fishing in a small Boat. Seeing Rich⁴ Fifield coming in, some would needs meet the ship and see who it was: Ship had fresh way with a fair wind; when came neare, Capt. call'd to them to beware, order'd what they should doe. But they did the clear contrary, fell foul on the ship, which broke their Mast short off, fill'd the Boat with water, threw Willard and Gaskill into the River. Both which were very near drown'd; especially Gaskill, who could not swim. It pleas'd God Fifield's Boat was out, so he presently man'd it and took them in. Gaskill was under water, but discover'd by his Hat that swam atop as a Buoy. Sam, Jn° Bayly and Mountfort caught hold of the Ship and climbed on board in a miserable fright as having stared death in the face. This is the second time Sam has been near drown'd with Josiah Willard. Mother was against his going, and prevented Joseph, who pleaded earnestly to go. He sensibly acknowledged the Good Providence in his staying at home, when he saw the issue.

[June 19, 1700]

Fourth-day, June, 19. 1700. Having been long and much dissatisfied with the Trade of fetching Negros from Guinea; at last I had a strong Inclination to Write something about it; but it wore off. At last reading Bayne, Ephes.³ about servants, who mentions Blackamoors; I began to be uneasy that I had so long neglected doing any thing. When I was thus thinking, in came Broʳ Belknap to shew me a Petition he intended to present to the Gen Court for the freeing a Negro and his wife, who were unjustly held in Bondage. And there is a Motion by a Boston Committee to get a Law that all

³ Paul Baynes, *A Commentarie Vpon The First Chapter of the Epistle of Saint Pavl, written to the Ephesians* (London, 1618).

Importers of Negros shall pay 40^s *per* head, to discourage the bringing of them. And Mr. C. Mather resolves to publish a sheet to exhort Masters to labour their Conversion. Which makes me hope that I was call'd of God to Write this Apology for them; Let his Blessing accompany the same.[4]

[July 20, 1702]

July, 20. Sam. visits Mrs. Rebecka Dudley.

[September 15, 1702]

Septr 15. Mr. Nehemiah Walter marries Mr. Sam Sewall and Mrs. Rebekah Dudley, in the Dining Room Chamber about 8 aclock. Mr. Willard concluded with prayer, Sung the last part of the 103 Psalm.

[June 18, 1703]

Friday, June, 18. 1703. My sons House was Raised at Muddy-River;[5] The day very comfortable because dry, cloudy, windy, cool.

[December 25, 1704]

Decr 25.. Monday, a Storm of Snow, yet many Sleds come to Town, with Wood, Hoops, Coal &c as is usual.

[December 30, 1704]

Decr 30. Satterday, Daughter Sewall of Brooklin is brought to Bed of a Daughter, Rebeka. 31. is baptised.

[June 16, 1707]

June. 16. My House was broken open in two places, and about Twenty pounds worth of Plate stolen away, and some Linen; My Spoon, and Knife, and Neckcloth was taken: I said, Is not this an Answer of Prayer? Jane came up, and gave us the Alarm betime in the morn. I was helped to submit to Christ's stroke, and say, Wellcome CHRIST!

[October 1, 1707]

Octob^r 1. 1707. I went to Brooklin, and chose some Apple-trees from which my Son is to send me Apples: Din'd with my Son and Daughter and little Grand-daughter;

---

[4] Here Sewall is referring to his anti-slavery tract, "The Selling of Joseph," which was printed June 24, 1700.

[5] On November 21, 1702, the General Court passed Private Act (No. 14), An Act to Enable Samuel Sewall Esq. and Hannah his wife, to Settle Certain Lands at Muddy River in the County of Suffolke upon Samuel Sewall their Eldest Son (*Acts and Resolves*, VI, 43–44). This tract contained about three hundred acres.

[November 23, 1707]

Nov' 23. 1707. My Son Samuel has his Son Samuel Baptised by Mr. Walter at Roxbury.

[August 3, 1710]

Fifth-day, Aug' 3. 1710. Our little Grand-Daughter Rebekah Sewall, born xr. 30. 1704. at Brooklin, died about Eight or Nine this morn. We knew not of her being Sick, till Dr. Noyes, as he returned, told us she was dead. The Lord effectually awaken us by these awfull Surprising Providences. My son and daughter got thither before their Child dyed, and had Mr. Walter to pray with her. She was sensible to the last, catching her breath till she quite lost it.

[August 18, 1717]

Friday, 8' 18. My wife grows worse and exceedingly Restless. Pray'd God to look upon her. Ask'd not after my going to bed. Had the advice of Mr. Williams and Dr. Cutler.

[August 19, 1717]

7ᵗʰ day, 8' 19. Call'd Dr. C. Mather to pray, which he did excellently in the Dining Room, having Suggested good Thoughts to my wife before he went down. After, Mr. Wadsworth pray'd in the Chamber when 'twas suppos'd my wife took little notice. About a quarter of an hour past four, my dear Wife expired in the Afternoon, whereby the Chamber was fill'd with a Flood of Tears. God is teaching me a new Lesson; to live a Widower's Life. Lord help me to Learn; and be a Sun and Shield to me, now so much of my Comfort and Defense are taken away.

[October 19, 1728]

October, 19. 1728. Seeing this to be the same day of the week and Moneth that the Wife of my youth expired Eleven years agoe, it much affected me. I writ to my dear Son Mr. Joseph Sewall of it, desiring him to come and dine with me: or however that he would call some time to join my Condolence. He came about Noon and made an excellent Prayer in the East Chamber. *Laus Deo.*

1878–1882

Cotton Mather
1663–1728

Honor and duty were thrust upon Cotton Mather from earliest childhood. He was the grandson of the illustrious Massachusetts Bay founders Richard Mather and John Cotton, the apparent prince regent of a Puritan dynasty. Mather accepted the responsibility of his lineage. He wrote in filial piety of the founders and in anxiety lest their backsliding descendants evade his efforts to revitalize the waning Puritan mission.

The Boston-born Mather was the eldest of twelve children. He was intellectually and spiritually precocious, at fourteen fasting to bring himself closer to God by bodily discipline and at sixteen joining his father's church, convinced that he had experienced God's saving grace and was therefore one of the elect. Before his teens the carefully tutored Mather had learned Hebrew and classical languages, and he entered Harvard at twelve. His youth and the prominence of his family made him vulnerable to the taunts of his classmates, who made his life miserable. When a stutter jeopardized his plans to enter the ministry, Mather decided instead to study medicine. Though the speech impediment abated and permitted the young man to resume his ministerial plans, Cotton Mather never lost interest in medicine and in scientific developments, as can be seen in his pioneering support of smallpox inoculation.

Mather was active in secular as well as religious affairs. He graduated from Harvard with distinction and remained for a master's degree in 1681. He served for the next forty years as his father's assistant in Boston's Old North Church, in whose tower Paul Revere would later look for his signal. Mather prepared up to five sermons per week while also working for reforms, including improved jail conditions, adequate and guaranteed schooling for children, and the religious education (and eventual emancipation) of slaves. Though Mather never left New England, he corresponded with religious leaders and scientists worldwide. He was elected a fellow of the Royal Society of London and awarded an honorary doctorate of divinity by the University of Glasgow in 1710. He had the largest scholarly library in New England.

Mather's personal life, never disclosed in his writings, was an "uneasy Wilderness." At twenty-three he married "a lovely and worthy young gentlewoman." She was the first of two beloved wives who died. His third wife went insane. Mather was evidently a most affectionate parent, but of his fifteen children only two survived him. He suffered embarrassing financial difficulties and lived to see his detractors name their slaves after him.

Though he worked to strengthen Puritanism, Cotton Mather's writings reflect its decline and, to some degree, a new spirit of ecumenicism. His major work, the *Magnalia Christi Americana* (1702), combines history and biography to commemorate the dedication and exemplary piety of such New England founders as Governor William Bradford, who stands in the *Magnalia* as an allegorical figure of Puritan sainthood.

The ecumenical side of Mather emerges in *Bonifacius, an Essay upon the Good,* written in 1710. This most popular of his writings transcended Puritan sectarianism as Mather sought to guide individuals, families, neighbors, communities, even nations in their proper relations with one another. These "essays to do good" hearken to the Puritan community ideals set forth seventy years earlier in John Winthrop's image of the shining city on a hill. Love, trust, fairness, and mutual responsibility are the recurrent themes of *Bonifacius.* Perhaps subconsciously Mather worked to transform his "uneasy Wilderness" of parental and domestic pain, and public humiliation, into an idealized realm of communal love and respect. In a growing population of practical-minded people, *Bonifacius* was a manual for self-improvement and remained in print in various editions until the mid-nineteenth century.

Mather intended his writings to glorify God and to revive Puritan zeal, hoping that America would become the millennial city, the *Theopolis Americana* of which he writes in rhapsodic prose. Historically the times were against him, and in certain ways his writings testify to a waning era, which Mather in part understood. He wrote in the *Magnalia*, "Whether New-England may live anywhere else or not, it must live in our history." If he sounds like the spiritual archivist of a passing age, Mather is nonetheless precocious in his epic vision of the American experience. In the *Magnalia* and elsewhere, Mather unfolds and asserts the meaning of the new yet predestined American nation in its comprehensiveness and multiplicity. In literature he thus anticipates the work of Walt Whitman and William Carlos Williams, figures of succeeding centuries who built upon the tradition he helped to found.

Further Reading:
B. Wendell, *Cotton Mather, The Puritan Priest,* 1891, 1963.
R. Middlekauff, *The Mathers: Three Generations of Puritan Intellectuals,* 1971.
S. Bercovitch, *The Puritan Origins of the American Self,* 1975.
D. Levin, *Cotton Mather,* 1978.
K. Silverman, *The Life and Times of Cotton Mather,* 1984.

Texts:
Theopolis Americana, 1710.
Bonifacius, an Essay upon the Good, ed. D. Levin, 1966.

---

from Theopolis Americana

. . . I happen this very Day, among certain Papers in my Study, to take up a copy of a Letter sent from a Worthy Person here, to one in *England,* about Seventy years ago, in which Letter there is this remarkable *Passage: Here is a Temple built, more glorious than* Solomons; *not of Dead Stones, but Living Saints; which may tempt the greatest Queen of Sheba, to come and see, and allure, even Kings from far to come and Worship in.*
————We may allow for the *Rhetorick* of the passage, and yet say, The *Golden Work* of God in these His Churches, if we may *Mend* any part, in which we should go on to more of the *Kingdom* of *Heaven,* let us Humbly do it. But, Sirs, Do not *Spoil* it. Oh! *Destroy it not; There is a Blessing in it.*

PEOPLE of GOD, May these be your Cares. Then there will be fulfilled unto us that Word, Isa. 1:26: *Thou shalt be called, The City of Righteousness, The Faithful City.* A CITY of such a GOLDEN STREET, will be a *Strong City;* God will *appoint Salvation for Walls and bulwarks* unto it; while none but a *Righteous Nation, which keeps the Truth,* inhabits it. O NEW ENGLAND, Keep such a STREET, and *Sweep* it where it wants to be better kept. Then, there *will be no breaking in or going out;* there will be *no Complaining in our Street*. No, we shall be an *Happy People,* I say, *an Happy people,* for the LORD will be OUR GOD. I will say unto you, Joel 2.21: *Fear not, O Land, be glad, and rejoyce, for the* LORD *will do great things.* God will make our *Enimies* to be found *Lyars* and *Losers;* Our *Coast* will be under His Protection. There will none dare go up against the *Land of Unwalled Villages.* Our God will incline the Government of our Nation also, to Remember what a *Loyal People* we have always approv'd our selves, and to cherish these *Colonies* as *Daughters* to be highly accounted of. Yea, O *Holy City;* Thou shalt *Lay up Gold as Dust,* and *the Gold of Potosi*[1] *as the Stones of the Brooks: The Almighty shall be thy Defence, and thou shalt have a Plenty* of all that thou desirest.

I have been Surprised at the Reading of a Passage in a Pagen Writer, who flourished more than Fifteen Hundred years ago. Tis Ælian,[2] a Grecian Writer, who says that in Times long preceding his, there was a Tradition that *Europe* and *Asia* and *Africa* were encompassed by the Ocean. But without and beyond the Ocean there was a *great Island,* as big as *They.* And in that Other World, there was an huge CITY, called Ενσεβνς, THE GODLY CITY. In that CITY, sayes he, they enjoy all possible *Peace* and *Health,* and *Plenty;* And, he Sayes, *They are without Controversy a very Righteous People*—So *Righteous,* that they have God marvellously coming down among them. I know not what well to make of a Tradition so very *Ancient,* and yet having Such an *American* Face upon it. All I will say, is thus much: There are many Arguments to perswade us, that our glorious LORD will have an HOLY CITY in AMERICA, a *City,* the STREET whereof will be *Pure* GOLD. We cannot imagine that the brave Countries and Gardens which fill the *American Hemisphere* were made for nothing but a *Place for Dragons.* We may not imagine that when the *Kingdom of God is come,* and His *Will is done on Earth as it is done in Heaven,* which we have never been taught to Pray for, if it must not one day be accomplished, a *Ballancing Half of the Globe* shall remain in the Hands of the *Devil,* who is then to be *Chained up* from *deceiving the Nations.* Has it not been promised unto our Great Saviour? Psalm 2.8: *I will give thee the uttermost parts of the Earth for thy Possession.* And, Psal. 86.9: *All Nations whom thou hast made shall come and worship before thee, O Lord, and shall glorify thy Name. And has it not been promised?* Mal. 1.11: *From the Rising of the Sun even unto the going down of the same, my Name shall be great among the Gentiles.* AMERICA is Legible in these Promises. But if it be not here plainly enough expressed, what can be more plain than the Prophecy concerning the Kingdom of our Saviour? Dan. 2.44: *It shall break in pieces, and consume all these Kingdoms, and it shall stand for ever.* The Kingdom of our Saviour becoming *a Great Mountain, that must fill the* WHOLE EARTH, does particularly fill and Change and Bless those Countries, which belong to the *Ten Kingdoms of the Roman Empire,* in the Papal and Final Edition of it. Now, the *American* Countries do belong to some of those *Ten Kingdoms;* are become a considerable part of their *Dominions;* And therefore, tis most certain, the *Glorious Holy Mountain* will some of it stand in these Countries as well as in the *European.* There have been MARTYRS OF CHRIST in *America.* The Blood of the *Martyrs* here is an Omen that the Truths for which they Suffered are to Rise, and

[1] City in Bolivia.
[2] Claudius Ælian (fl. A.D. 200), author of *Historical Miscellanies.*

Live, and carry all before them in the Land that has been so *Marked* for the Lord. Such men as they will doubtless have some Glorious *Power over the Nations* where they have been such *Overcomers;* They that are to *Shine as the Stars,* will *turn many unto Righteousness;* bring many to believe on the *Sun of Righteousness,* in these *Goings down of the Sun.* Tho' *Austin* knew nothing of *America,* yet no *American* could have made a better Descant on the Mystery of our Lord's *Garments, made of Four Parts, to every Souldier a Part,* than his *Quadripartita Vestis Domini Jesu, quadripartitam figuravit Ejus Ecclesiam, toto Scilicet, qui quatuor partibus constat, terrarum Orbe diffisam.*[3] The World, sayes he, which does *consist of Four Parts,* will have the *Church* of our Lord JESUS in every Part. But O AMERICA, will no Share of the Lord's *Garments* and *Glories* and the *Righteousness of the Saints* fall to thee, who art a Part of the World singly almost as great as the *Other Three?* Yea, the Day is at hand when that Voice will be heard concerning *shee. Put on thy beautiful Garments,* O America, *the Holy City!* Certainly, It was never intended that the Church of our Lord should be confined always within the Dimensions of *Scrabo's* Cloak, and that *all the World* should always be no more than it was when *Augustus* taxed it. We are Sorry, we are Troubled, That the *Good Seed* of the WORD, falling on the other *Three Soyls,* has brought forst so little *Good Fruit,* and for so little a while. But our Glorious LORD will order that *Good Seed* ere long to be cast upon the Fertile Regions of *America,*[4] and it shall here find a *Good Ground* where it shall bring forth *Fruit* unto Astonishments, and unto Perpetuity! When our Lord uttered the Parable to which I have now alluded, we read, *He went into a Ship,* and from thence instructed the *Multitude that stood on the Shore.* I will believe that in this very *Action* there was a *Parable* and a *Prophesy.* By *Navigation* there will be brought the Word of a Glorious CHRIST unto a Multitude afar off, and as the *Ships cover the Sea, the Earth,* and thou, AMERICA, too, *Shall be filled with the knowledge of the glorious Lord.* The Fall of Old Pagan *Babylon* was brought about by the Diversion of her *Euphrates* from her. The Fall of the New Popish *Babylon* will be accompanied with the Loss of her *American* Interest; but when 'tis diverted from her, certainly it will then serve the *City of God.* I will add this: When we critically Examine the *Accomplishment of the Prophecies* in the Judgments of the *Seven Trumpets,* whereof *Six* have done sounding, we shall find that by the SEA was meant *Portugal* and *Spain* and *France,* with the adjoyning *Islands* from the *Rhine* and the *Rhosne* to the Western Ocean, and the Peninsula of *Italy,* all which are almost wholly Encompassed with the *sea,* and mighty Rivers. I conceive we are now entring into the Dispensation of the *Seven Vials,*[5] one of the First whereof is *Poured out upon the Sea, and it becomes as the Blood of a Dead Man and every Living Soul dies in the Sea.* The most Obvious Application of it is to be trembled at!—But it is easy to draw Some *American* consequences. I wave them and only say, Tis thought by Some that *America* might be intended as a Place where the Worshippers of the Glorious JESUS may be Sheltered, while fearful Things are doing in the *European* World, and (as 'tis foretold it shall be!) *The Land shall be fearfully Emptied and Spoiled; The Curse will devour the Earth, and they that dwell therein will be desolate; the Inhabitants of the Earth will be burned, and few men will be left* (See the XXIV. of *Isaiah*). Whether it shall be so or no, we

---

[3] According to St. Augustine (354–430), one of the early Church Fathers, the garments of Jesus were divided into four parts, prefiguring the four-part division of the Christian church.

[4] See the parable of the sower in Matthew 13:1–17 and Luke 8:11–15.

[5] Reference to forthcoming Judgment Day. See Revelation 15:1–8; 16:2–21.

are sure there is a Day at hand, *When the Lord of Hosts will Reign among His Ancient People Gloriously.* In that Day, it will be impossible for the *Holy* People and the *Teachers* and *Rulers* of the *Reformed World* in the other *Hemisphere* to leave *America* unvisited. It will be impossible for a People so inspired from Heaven for the Propagation of true Christianity as will then be the *Stars* of that *Hemisphere,* to be unconcerned about *America,* and *all the Ends of the World that are to turn unto the Lord; all the Kindreds of the Nations that are to Worship before Him.* It will be impossible that the *Effect* of the Essayes used by Men filled with the SPIRIT of CHRIST, and able to do more than all that was done in the Primitive Times (For, *When He gives the Word, Great will be the Army of them that so Publish it!*), Should not be a conquest of *America,* ten thousand times more glorious than all that ever any *Cortez*[6] pretended unto. The *Kingdom* here will be *the Lord's,* and The Lord will be *Governour among the Nations.* When the Holy SPIRIT of God, that *River,* the *Streams* whereof are to *Make glad the City of God,* shall, as He will, Run down into and thorough the World, and make the World become a *Watered Garden* and an *Eden* for the *Lord from Heaven,* and *God shall dwell with men* by His Holy *Spirit* marvellously Possessing, and purifying, and Enlightening of them. Can you think that *America* shall be nothing but *Miery Places and Marshes, given to Salt?* By no means. O wide *Atlantick,* Thou shalt not stand in the way as any Hindrance of those Communications!

Verily, Our Glorious LORD will have Dominion from *Sea to Sea.* In those Days will the *Righteous flourish.* Then they who *dwell in the Wilderness* and even in *this* also *Shall bow before Him. They that are of the city* shall have something to do here for Him. O NEW ENGLAND, There is Room to hope That thou also shalt belong to the CITY. Thou hast already made a *Seihn* [sign] of *America,* on behalf of the Glorious LORD. It is in some sort His *Primier Seihn* [sign]. The *Seihn* [sign] *in Fact,* which the Son of GOD has taken of these *American* Territories is, we hope a *Seihn* [sign] *in Law* for all the rest. And certainly, Thou shalt not be cast off when He comes into the *Actual Possession* of all the rest. Thy Name shall then be *Jehovah Shammah,* THE LORD IS THERE. And, *As we have heard, so shall we see, in the City of the Lord of Hosts, in the City of our God:* GOD *will establish it* for ever more.

The Design of my SERMON is To bespeak all possible *Anticipations* of this Felicity!

1710

---

from Bonifacius, an Essay upon the Good

[from Chapter Three: Relative to Home and Neighborhood]

11. The *useful man* may now with a very good grace, extend and enlarge the *sphere* of his consideration. My next PROPOSAL now shall be: Let every man consider the RELATION, wherein the Sovereign God has placed him, and let him *devise what good*

---

[6] Hernando Cortes (1485–1547), Spanish explorer and conqueror of Mexico.

he may do, that may render his *relatives,* the better for him. One great way to prove ourselves *really good,* is to be *relatively* good. By this, more than by anything in the world, it is, that we *adorn the doctrine of God our Saviour.* It would be an *excellent wisdom* in a man, to make the *interest* he has in the good opinion and affection of *anyone,* an *advantage* to do good service for God upon them: He that *has a friend* will show himself indeed *friendly,* if he thinks, "Such an one loves me, and will hearken to me; what good shall I take advantage hence to persuade him to?"

This will take place more particularly, where the endearing ties of *natural relation* do give us an *interest.* Let us call over our several *relations,* and let us have devices of something that may be called *heroical goodness,* in our discharging of them. Why should we not, at least once or twice in a *week,* make this *relational goodness,* the subject of our *inquiries,* and our *purposes?* Particularly, let us begin with our *domestic relations,* and *provide for those of our own house,* lest we deny some glorious rules and hopes of our Christian faith, in our negligence.

First, in the CONJUGAL RELATION, how agreeably may the *consorts* think on those words: "What knowest thou, O wife, whether thou shalt save thy husband?" Or, "How knowest thou, O man, whether thou shalt save thy wife?"

The HUSBAND will do well to think: "What shall I do, that my wife may have cause forever to bless God, for bringing her unto me?" And, "What shall I do that in my carriage towards my wife, the kindness of the blessed JESUS towards His Church, may be followed and resembled?" That this question may be the more perfectly answered, Sir, sometimes ask her to help you in the answer; ask her to tell you, what she would have you to do.

But then, the WIFE also will do well to think: "Wherein may I be to my husband, a wife of that character: she will do him good, and not evil, all the days of his life?" . . . .

With my married people, I will particularly leave a good note, which I find in the Memorials of *Gervase Disney,* Esq. "Family passions, cloud faith, disturb duty, darken comfort." You'll do the more good unto one another, the more this note is thought upon. When the *husband* and *wife* are always contriving to be blessings unto one another, I will say with *Tertullian, Unde sufficiam ad enarrandam faelicitatem ejus matrimonii!*[1] O happy marriage!

PARENTS, Oh! how much ought you to be continually *devising,* and even *travailing,* for the *good* of your *children.* Often *devise:* how to make them *wise children;* how to carry on a desirable *education* for them; an *education* that shall render them desirable; how to render them lovely, and polite creatures, and *serviceable* in their generation. Often *devise,* how to enrich their minds with valuable *knowledge;* how to instill generous, and gracious, and heavenly *principles* into their minds; how to restrain and rescue them from the *paths of the Destroyer,* and fortify them against their *special temptations.* There is a world of *good,* that you have to do for them. You are without *bowels,* Oh! be not such *monsters!* if you are not in a continual agony to do for them all the *good* that ever you can. It was no mistake of *Pacatus Drepanius* in his panegyric to *Theodosius: Instituente natura plus fere filios quam nosmetipsos diligimus.*[2]

I will prosecute this matter, by transcribing a copy of PARENTAL RESOLUTIONS, which I have somewhere met withal.

---

[1] Latin: "How can I find words to describe the happiness of their marriage!"

[2] Latin: "Nature teaches us to love our children as ourselves."

I. "At the birth of my children, I would use all *explicit solemnity* in the *baptismal* dedication and consecration of them unto the LORD. I would present them to the BAPTISM of the Lord, not as a mere formality; but wondering at the grace of the infinite GOD, who will accept my children, as *His,* I would resolve to do all I can that they may be His. I would now actually give them up unto God; entreating, that the child may be a *child* of God the *Father,* a *subject* of God the *Son,* a temple of God the *Spirit,* and be rescued from the condition of a *child of wrath,* and be possessed and employed by the Lord as an everlasting instrument of His glory.

II. "My children are no sooner grown capable of minding the admonitions, but I would often, often admonish them to be sensible of their *baptismal engagements* to be the Lord's. Often tell them, of their *baptism,* and of what it binds 'em to: oftener far, and more times than there were *drops of water,* that were cast on the infant, upon that occasion!

"Often say to them, 'Child, you have been baptized; you were washed in the name of the great God; now you must not sin against Him; to sin is to do a dirty, a filthy thing.' Say, 'Child, you must every day cry to God that He would be your Father, and your Saviour, and your Leader; in your baptism He promised that He would be so, if you sought unto Him.' Say, 'Child, you must renounce the service of Satan, you must not follow the vanities of this world, you must lead a life of serious religion; in your baptism you were bound unto the service of your only Saviour.' Tell the child: 'What is your name; you must sooner forget this name, that was given you in your baptism, than forget that you are a servant of a glorious Christ whose name was put upon you in your baptism.'

III. "Let my *prayers* for my *children* be daily, with constancy, with fervency, with agony; yea, *by name* let me mention each one of them, every day before the Lord. I would importunately beg for all suitable blessings to be bestowed upon them: that God would *give them grace, and give them glory, and withhold no good thing from them; that God would smile on their education, and give His good angels the charge over them, and keep them from evil, that it may not grieve them;* that when *their father and mother shall forsake them, the Lord may take them up.* With importunity I would plead that promise on their behalf: *the Heavenly Father will give the Holy Spirit unto them that ask Him.* Oh! happy children, if by *asking* I may obtain the *Holy Spirit* for them!

IV. "I would betimes entertain the children, with delightful *stories* out of the Bible. In the talk of the *table,* I would go through the *Bible,* when the *olive-plants about my table* are capable of being so *watered.* But I would always conclude the *stories* with some *lessons* of piety, to be inferred from them. . . .

VIII. "I would betimes do what I can, to beget a *temper of benignity* in my *children,* both towards one another, and towards all other people. I will instruct them how ready they should be to *communicate unto others,* a part of what they have; and they shall see, my encouragements, when they discover a *loving,* a *courteous,* an *helpful* disposition. I will give them now and then a piece of money, for them with their own little hands to dispense unto the poor. Yea, if any one has *hurt* them, or *vexed* them, I will not only forbid them all *revenge,* but also oblige them to do a *kindness* as soon as may be to the *vexatious* person. All *coarseness* of *language* or *carriage* in them, I will discountenance it.

IX. "I would be solicitous to have my *children* expert, not only at reading handsomely, but also at writing a fair hand. I will then assign them such *books* to *read,* as I may judge most agreeable and profitable; obliging them to give me some account of what they *read;* but keep a strict eye upon them, that they don't stumble on *the Devil's library,* and poison themselves with foolish *romances,* or *novels,* or *plays,* or *songs,* or *jests that are not convenient.* I will set them also, to *write* out such things, as may be of the greatest benefit unto them; and they shall have their blank books, neatly kept on purpose, to enter such passages as I advise them to. I will particularly require them now and then, to *write* a *prayer* of their own composing, and bring it unto me; that so I may discern, what sense they have of their own everlasting interests.

X. "I wish that my *children* may as soon as may be, feel the principles of *reason* and *honor,* working in them, and that I may carry on their education, very much upon those principles. Therefore, first, I will wholly avoid, that harsh, fierce, crabbed usage of the children, that would make them tremble, and abhor to come into my presence. I will so use them, that they shall *fear* to offend me, and yet mightily *love* to see me, and be glad of my coming home, if I have been abroad at any time. I would have it looked upon as a severe and awful *punishment* for a crime in the family, to be *forbidden for awhile to come into my presence.* I would raise in them, an high opinion of their father's *love* to them, and of his being *better able* to judge what is good for them, than they are for themselves. I would bring them to believe, *'tis best for them to be and do as I would have them.* Hereupon I would continually magnify the matter to them, what a brave thing 'tis to *know* the things that are excellent; and more brave to *do* the things that are virtuous. I would have them to propose it as a *reward* of their well-doing at any time, *I will now go to my father, and he will teach me something that I was never taught before.* I would have them afraid of doing any *base* thing, from an horror of the *baseness* in it. My first animadversion on a lesser fault in them, shall be a *surprise,* a *wonder,* vehemently expressed before them, that ever they should be guilty of doing so foolishly; a vehement *belief,* that they will never do the like again; a weeping resolution in them, that they will not. I will never dispense a *blow,* except it be for an atrocious crime, or for a lesser fault obstinately persisted in; either for an enormity, or for an *obstinacy.* I would ever *proportion* chastisements unto miscarriages; not smite bitterly for a very small piece of *childishness,* and only frown a little for some real *wickedness.* Nor shall my *chatisements* ever be dispensed in a *passion* and a *fury;* but with them, I will first show them the command of GOD, by transgressing whereof they have displeased me. The slavish, raving, fighting way of education too commonly used, I look upon it, as a considerable article in the wrath and curse of GOD, upon a miserable world.

XI. "As soon as we can, we'll get up to yet *higher principles.* I will often tell the *children,* what cause they have to *love* a glorious CHRIST, who has *died* for them. And, how much He will be *well-pleased* with their *well-doing.* And, what a noble thing, 'tis to follow His *example;* which *example* I will describe unto them. I will often tell them, that the *eye of God* is upon them; the great GOD knows all they do, and hears all they speak. I will often tell them, that there will be a time, when they must appear before the *Judgment-Seat* of the holy LORD; and they must *now* do nothing, that may *then* be a grief and shame unto them. I will set before them, the delights of that *Heaven* that is prepared for pious children; and the torments of that *Hell* that is prepared of old, for naughty ones. I will inform them, of the *good offices* which the *good angels* do for *little ones* that have the fear of God, and are afraid of sin. And, how the *devils* tempt them to do ill things; how they hearken to the *devils,* and are like *them,* when they do such things; and what mischiefs the *devils* may get leave to do them in this world, and what a sad thing 'twill be, to be among the devils in the *Place of Dragons*. I will cry to God, that He *will make them feel the power of these principles.*

XII. "When the *children* are of a fit age for it, I will sometimes *closet* them; have them with me *alone;* talk with them about the state of their souls; their *experiences,* their *proficiencies,* their *temptations;* obtain their declared consent unto every stroke in the *Covenant of Grace;* and then pray with them, and weep unto the Lord for His *grace,* to be bestowed upon them, and make them witnesses of the agony with which I am *travailing* to see the image of CHRIST formed in them. Certainly, they'll never forget such actions!

XIII. "I would be very watchful and cautious, about the *companions* of my *children.* I will be very inquisitive, what *company* they keep; if they are in hazard of being ensnared by any *vicious company,* I will earnestly pull them out of it, as *brands out of the burning.* I will find out, and procure, *laudable companions* for them.

XIV. "As in *catechizing* the children, so in the *repetition* of the public sermons, I would use this method. I will put every *truth* into a *question,* to be answered still, with *Yes,* or *No.* By this method, I hope to awaken their *attention* as well as enlighten their *understanding.* And thus I shall have an opportunity to ask, 'Do you desire such or such a grace of God?' and the like. Yea, I may have opportunity to demand, and perhaps to *obtain* their early, and frequent, and why not *sincere?,* consent unto the glorious articles of the *New Covenant.* The *Spirit of Grace* may fall upon them in this action; and they may be seized by Him, and held as His *temples,* through eternal ages.

XV. "When a Day of *Humiliation* arrives, I will make them know the *meaning* of the Day. And after time given them to consider of it, I will order them to tell me: *what special afflictions they have met withal?* And, *what good they hope to get by those afflictions?* On a Day of *Thanksgiving,* they shall also be made to know the *intent* of the Day. And after consideration, they shall tell me, *what mercies of God unto them they take special notice of:* And, *what duties to God, they confess and resolve, under such obligations?* Indeed, for something of this importance, to be pursued in my conversation with the children, I would not confine myself unto the *solemn Days,* which may occur too seldom for it. Very particularly, when the *birthdays* of the children anniversarily arrive to any of them, I would then take them aside, and mind them of the age, which *having obtained help from God* they are come unto; how *thankful* they should be for the mercies of God, which they have hitherto lived upon; how *fruitful* they should be in all goodness, that so they may still enjoy their mercies. And I would inquire of them, whether they have ever yet begun to mind the *work* which God sent them into the world upon; how far they understand the work; and what good strokes they have struck at it; and, how they design to spend the rest of their time, if God still continue them in the world.

XVI. "When the *children* are in any *trouble,* as, if they be *sick,* or *pained,* I will take advantage therefrom, to set before them the evil of *sin,* which brings all our *trouble;* and how fearful a thing it will be to be cast among the damned, who are in easeless and endless *trouble.* I will set before them the benefit of an interest in a CHRIST, by which their *trouble* will be sanctified unto them, and they will be prepared for *death,* and for fullness of joy in an happy eternity after *death.*

XVII. "I incline, that among all the points of a polite education which I would endeavor for my *children,* they may each of them, the *daughters* as well as the *sons,* have so much insight into some *skill*, which lies in the way of *gain* (the *limners'*, or the *scriveners'*, or the *apothecaries'*, or some other *mystery*, to which their own inclination may most carry them) that they may be able to subsist themselves, and get something of a livelihood, in case the Providence of God should bring them into necessities. Why not they as well as *Paul the Tent-Maker!* The *children* of the best fashion, may have occasion to bless the parents, that make such a provision for them! The Jews have a saying; 'tis worth my remembering it: *Quicunque filium suum non docet opificium, perinde est ac si eum doceret latrocinium.* [3]

XVIII. "As soon as ever I can, I would make my children apprehensive of the main END, for which they are to *live;* that so they may as soon as may be, *begin to live;* and their *youth* not be nothing but *vanity.* I would show them, that their main END must be, *to acknowledge the great* GOD, *and His glorious* CHRIST; *and bring others to acknowledge Him:* and that they are never *wise* nor *well,* but when they are doing so. I would show them, what the *acknowledgments* are, and how they are to be made. I would make them able to answer the grand question, *why they live; and what is the end of the actions that fill their lives?* Teach them, how their *Creator* and *Redeemer* is to be obeyed in everything; and, how everything is to be done in *obedience* to Him; teach them, how even their *diversions,* and their *ornaments,* and the *tasks* of their education, must all be to fit them for the *further service* of Him, to whom I have devoted them; and how in these also, His commandments must be the rule of all they do. I would sometimes therefore surprise them with an inquiry, 'Child, what is this for? Give me a good account, why you do it?' How comfortably shall I see them *walking in the light,* if I may bring them *wisely* to answer this inquiry; and what *children of the light?*

XIX. "I would oblige the *children,* to retire sometimes, and ponder on that question: 'What shall I wish to have done, if I were now a-dying?' And report unto me, their *own answer* to the question; of which I would then take advantage, to inculcate the *lessons of godliness* upon them. I would also direct them and oblige them, at a proper time for it, seriously to realize, their own appearance before the awful *Judgment-Seat* of the Lord JESUS CHRIST, and consider, *what they have to plead, that they may not be sent away into everlasting punishment; what they have to plead, that they may be admitted into the Holy City.* I would instruct them, what *plea* to prepare; first, show them, how to get a part in the *righteousness* of Him that is to be their *Judge;* by receiving it with a thankful *faith,* as the *gift* of infinite grace unto the distressed and unworthy sinner: then, show them how to prove that their *faith* is not a counterfeit, by their continual endeavor to please Him in all things, who is to be their *Judge,* and to serve His Kingdom and interest in the world. And I would charge them, to make this preparation.

XX. "If I live to see the children *marriageable,* I would, before I consult with Heaven and earth for their best accommodation in the *married state,* endeavor the *espousal* of their souls unto their only *Saviour.* I would as plainly, and as fully as I can, propose unto them, the terms on which the glorious Redeemer would *espouse* them to Himself, *in righteousness and judgment, and favor, and mercies forever;* and solicit their consent unto His proposals and overtures. Then would I go on, to do what may be expected from a tender parent for them, in their *temporal circumstances.* . . .

[3] Latin: "He who does not teach his son a craft, teaches him theft."

MASTERS, yea, and MISTRESSES too, must have their *devices, how to do good unto their servants;* how to make them the *servants* of Christ, and the *children* of God. God whom you must remember to be *your Master in Heaven,* has brought them, and put them into your hands. Who can tell what *good* He has brought them for? How if they should be the *elect* of God, fetched from *Africa,* or the *Indies,* and brought into your families, on purpose, that by the means of their being *there,* they may be brought home unto the *Shepherd of Souls?* Oh! that the *souls* of our *slaves,* were of more account with us! that we gave a better demonstration that we *despise not our own souls,* by doing what we can for the *souls* of our *slaves,* and not using them as if they had no *souls!* that the poor *slaves* and *blacks,* which live with us, may by our means be made the *candidates* of the Heavenly life! How can we pretend unto *Christianity,* when we do no more to *Christianize* our *slaves!* Verily, you must give an *account* unto God, concerning *them.* If they be lost, through your negligence, what answer can you make unto *God the Judge of all!* Methinks, common principles of gratitude should incline you, to study the happiness of those, by whose obsequious labors, your lives are so much accommodated. Certainly, they would be the *better servants* to you, the more faithful, the more honest, the more industrious, and submissive *servants* to you, for your bringing them into the service of your *common Lord.*

But if any servant of God, may be so honored by Him, as to be made the successful instrument, of obtaining from a *British* Parliament, *an act for the Christianizing of the slaves in the Plantations;* then it may be hoped, something more may be done, than has yet been done, that the *blood of souls* may not be found in the *skirts* of our nation: a *controversy* of Heaven with our Colonies may be removed, and *prosperity* may be restored; or, however the honorable instrument, will have unspeakable *peace* and *joy,* in the remembrance of his endeavors. In the meantime, the *slave-trade* is a spectacle that shocks *humanity.*

> The harmless natives basely they trepan,
> And barter baubles for the *souls of men.*
> The wretches they to Christian climes bring o'er
> To serve worse heathens than they did before.

12. Methinks, this excellent zeal should be carried into our *neighborhood. Neighbors,* you stand *related* unto one another; and you should be full of *devices,* that all the *neighbors* may have cause to be glad of your being in the *neighborhood.* We read, "The righteous is more excellent than his neighbor." But we shall scarce own him so, except he be *more excellent* AS *a neighbor.* He must *excel* in the duties of *good neighborhood.* Let that man be *better* than his *neighbor,* who labors to be a *better neighbor;* to do most *good* unto his *neighbor.*

And here, first, the *poor* people that lie *wounded,* must have *wine* and *oil* poured into their *wounds.* It was a charming stroke in the character with [which?] a modern prince had given to him, *To be in distress, is to deserve his favor.* O good neighbor, put on that princely, that more than royal quality. See who in the neighborhood may *deserve thy favor.* We are told, *This is pure religion and undefiled* (a jewel, that neither is a counterfeit, nor has any flaws in it): *to visit the fatherless and widows in their affliction.* The *orphans* and the *widows,* and so all the children of *affliction* in the neighborhood, must be *visited,* and relieved with all agreeable kindnesses.

Neighbors, be concerned, that the *orphans* and *widows* in your neighborhood, may be well provided for. *They* meet with grievous difficulties; with unknown temptations. While their next *relatives* were yet living, they were, perhaps, but meanly provided for. What must they now be in their more solitary condition? Their condition should be considered: and the result of the consideration should be that: *I delivered the orphan, that had no helper, and I caused the heart of the widow to sing for joy.*

By consequence, all the afflicted in the neighborhood, are to be thought upon. Sirs, would it be too much for you, at least *once in a week,* to think, "What neighbor is reduced into a pinching and painful poverty? Or in any degree impoverished with heavy losses?" Think, "What neighbor is languishing with sickness; especially if sick with sore maladies, and of some continuance?" Think, "What neighbor is heartbroken with sad bereavements; bereaved of desirable relatives?" And think: "What neighbor has a soul buffeted, and buried with violent assaults of the Wicked one?" But then think, "What shall be done for such neighbors?"

First, you will *pity* them. The evangelical precept is, *Have compassion one of another, be pitiful.* It was of old, and ever will be, the just expectation, *To him that is afflicted, pity should be shown.* And let our *pity* to them, flame out in our *prayer* for them. It were a very lovely practice for you, in the *daily prayer* of your *closet* every evening, to think, "What miserable object have I seen today, that I may do well now to mention for the mercies of the Lord?"

But this is not all. 'Tis possible, 'tis probable, you may do well to *visit* them; and when you *visit* them, *comfort* them. Carry them some *good word,* which may raise a *gladness,* in an *heart stooping with heaviness.*

And lastly. Give them all the *assistances* that may answer their *occasions:* assist them with *advice* to them; assist them with *address* to others for them. And if it be needful, bestow your ALMS upon them; *deal thy bread to the hungry; bring to thy house the poor that are cast out; when thou seest the naked, cover him.* . . .

In moving for the *devices of good neighborhood,* a principal motion which I have to make, is, that you consult the *spiritual* interests of your neighborhood, as well as the *temporal.* Be concerned, lest the *deceitfulness of sin* undo any of the neighbors. If there be any *idle persons* among them, I beseech you, cure them of their *idleness;* don't nourish 'em and harden 'em in that; but find *employment* for them. Find 'em *work;* set 'em to *work;* keep 'em to *work. Then,* as much of your other bounty to them, as you please.

If any *children* in the neighborhood, are under no education, don't allow 'em to continue so. Let care be taken, that they may be better educated; and be taught to read; and be taught their *Catechism;* and the truths and ways of their only Saviour.

Once more. If any in the neighborhood, are taking to *bad courses,* lovingly and faithfully admonish them. If any in the neighborhood are enemies to their own welfare, or their families; prudently dispense your admonitions unto them. If there are any *prayerless families,* never leave off entreating and exhorting of them, till you have persuaded them, to set up the *worship* of God. If there be any *service* of God, or of His people, to which any one may need to be excited, give him a tender excitation. Whatever *snare* you see any one in, be so kind, as to tell him of his danger to be *ensnared,* and save him from it. By putting of *good books* into the hands of your neighbors, and gaining of them a promise to *read the books,* who can tell what good you may do unto them! It is possible, you may in this way, with ingenuity, and with efficacy, administer those *reproofs,* which you may owe unto such neighbors, as are to be *reproved* for their miscarriages. The *books* will balk nothing, that is to be said, on the subjects, that you would have the neighbors advised upon.

Finally. If there be any *base houses,* which threaten to debauch, and poison, and confound the neighborhood, let your charity to your neighbors make you do all you can for the suppression of them.

That my PROPOSAL *To Do Good in the Neighborhood, and as a Neighbor,* may be more fully formed and followed; I will conclude it, with minding you, that a world of *self-denial* is to be exercised in the execution of it. You must be armed against *selfishness,* all *selfish* and *squinting* intentions, in your generous resolutions. . . .
1710

William Byrd II
1674–1744

William Byrd II was a witty sophisticate who thoroughly enjoyed his life as a Virginia aristocrat. Wealthy and well read, Byrd moved as easily in the drawing rooms of Georgian England as he did on the tobacco docks of his colonial plantation. He was a literary man within the tradition of the urbane dilettante and had a library of over 22,000 volumes, the largest in the American colonies.

Byrd's father inherited substantial Virginia acreage and profited from the Indian fur trade. He enlarged his estate through marriage and sent his four children to England for education suitable to a prosperous family with connections to the English gentry. At age seven William attended an Essex grammar school notable for the strength of its classical education, which Byrd clearly appreciated. He kept lifelong habits of reading classical authors upon waking. ("I rose about 6 o'clock and read two chapters in Hebrew and some Greek in Lucian. I said my prayers and ate boiled milk for breakfast.")

Byrd's father insisted that the boy learn the business practices necessary for plantation management and so installed him in the offices of the family's London tobacco merchant. In addition, young Byrd studied law at the Middle Temple, one of the Inns of Court that harbored writers and intellectuals as well as barristers. There Byrd made the acquaintance of the dramatists William Congreve and William Wycherly, as well as Nicholas Rowe, the biographer and editor of Shakespeare. Evidently Byrd had sufficient interest in science to use his connections to gain admission to the Royal Society. Throughout his fifteen years in England, Byrd gradually took his place as a gentleman and gallant in sophisticated London society.

Byrd readily readapted to Virginia plantation life, however, when his father called him home in 1696. He became active in Virginia politics and, because of his London connections, traveled back and forth several times. At his father's death in 1704 Byrd assumed full responsibility for the estate, which totaled more than 26,000 acres of land, including the present site of Richmond. Byrd married in 1706 and remarried several years after the death of his wife, all the while increasing the size of his estate until he held 179,000 acres, which he left, along with Westover, the manor house he built in brick for permanence, to his son.

Byrd's literary reputation is based on several writings. His diary is a miscellany of dietary practices, religious devotions, social and business intercourse, and sexual escapades that resemble the plays of his dramatist friends. ("Then I went to visit Mrs. A—l—n and committed uncleanness with the maid because the mistress was not at home. However when the mistress came I rogered her and about 12 o'clock went home and ate a plum cake for supper. I neglected my prayers, for which God forgive me.")

In 1728 Byrd accepted a commission to survey the disputed boundary between Virginia and North Carolina. He later developed the diary of that undertaking into his *History of the Dividing Line,* which circulated among his friends before finally being published in 1841. The *History* is anecdotal, at points ironic and sardonic. Byrd's voice is that of the observer-participant who never fails to be interested in all phenomena of the American environment. As a planter, he saw himself as "one of the patriarchs" in a secular colonial Canaan.

Further Reading:
R. Beatty, *William Byrd of Westover*, 1932.
P. Marambaud, *William Byrd of Westover,*
1674–1744, 1971.
*The Correspondence of the Three William Byrds
of Westover, Virginia, 1684–1776*, 2 vols., ed.
M. Tinling, 1977.

Text:
The Prose Works of William Byrd of Westover,
ed. L. Wright, 1966.

---

from The History of the Dividing Line

[The Great Dismal Swamp]

7. This morning the surveyors began to run the dividing line from the cedar post we had driven into the sand, allowing near three degrees for the variation. Without making this just allowance, we should not have obeyed His Majesty's order in running a due-west line. It seems the former commissioners had not been so exact, which gave our friends of Carolina but too just an exception to their proceedings. The line cut Dosier's Island, consisting only of a flat sand with here and there an humble shrub growing upon it. From thence it crossed over a narrow arm of the sound into Knott's Island and there split a plantation belonging to William Harding.

The day being far spent, we encamped in this man's pasture, though it lay very low and the season now inclined people to aguish distempers. He suffered us to cut cedar branches for our enclosure and other wood for firing, to correct the moist air and drive away the damps. Our landlady, in the days of her youth, it seems, had been a laundress in the Temple and talked over her adventures in that station with as much pleasure as an old soldier talks over his battles and distempers and, I believe, with as many additions to the truth.

The soil is good in many places of this island, and the extent of it pretty large. It lies in the form of a wedge: the south end of it is several miles over, but toward the north it sharpens into a point. It is a plentiful place for stock by reason of the wide marshes adjacent to it and because of its warm situation. But the inhabitants pay a little dear for this convenience by losing as much blood in the summer season by the infinite number of mosquitoes as all their beef and pork can recruit in the winter.

The sheep are as large as in Lincolnshire,[1] because they are never pinched by cold or hunger. The whole island was hitherto reckoned to lie in Virginia, but now our line has given the greater part of it to Carolina. The principal freeholder here is Mr. White, who keeps open house for all travelers that either debt or shipwreck happens to cast in his way.

8. By break of day we sent away our largest piragua[2] with the baggage round the south end of Knott's Island, with orders to the men to wait for us in the mouth of North River. Soon after, we embarked ourselves on board the smaller vessel, with intent, if possible, to find a passage round the north end of the island.

We found this navigation very difficult by reason of the continued shoals and often stuck fast aground; for though the sound spreads many miles, yet it is in most places extremely shallow and requires a skillful pilot to steer even a canoe safe over it. It was almost as hard to keep our temper as to keep the channel in this provoking situation. But the most impatient amongst us stroked down their choler[3] and swallowed their curses, lest, if they suffered them to break out, they might sound like complaining, which was expressly forbid as the first step to sedition.

At a distance we descried several islands to the northward of us, the largest of which goes by the name of Cedar Island. Our piragua stuck so often that we had a fair chance to be benighted in this wide water, which must certainly have been our fate had we not luckily spied a canoe that was giving a fortuneteller a cast from Princess Anne County over to North Carolina. But, as conjurers are sometimes mistaken, the man mistrusted we were officers of justice in pursuit of a young wench he had carried off along with him. We gave the canoe chase for more than an hour and when we came up with her threatened to make them all prisoners unless they would direct us into the right channel. By the pilotage of these people we rowed up an arm of the sound called the Back Bay till we came to the head of it. There we were stopped by a miry pocosin[4] full half a mile in breadth, through which we were obliged to daggle on foot, plunging now and then, though we picked our way, up to the knees in mud. At the end of this charming walk we gained the terra firma of Princess Anne County. In that dirty condition we were afterwards obliged to foot it two miles as far as John Heath's plantation, where we expected to meet the surveyors and the men who waited upon them.

While we were performing this tedious voyage, they had carried the line through the firm land of Knott's Island, where it was no more than half a mile wide. After that they traversed a large marsh, that was exceeding miry and extended to an arm of the Back Bay. They crossed that water in a canoe which we had ordered round for that purpose and then waded over another marsh that reached quite to the high land of Princess Anne. Both these marshes together make a breadth of five miles, in which the men frequently sank up to the middle without muttering the least complaint. On the contrary, they turned all these disasters into merriment.

[1] In England.
[2] Canoe.
[3] Anger.
[4] Swamp.

It was discovered by this day's work that Knott's Island was improperly so called, being in truth no more than a peninsula. The northwest side of it is only divided from the main by the great marsh above-mentioned, which is seldom totally overflowed. Instead of that, it might by the labor of a few trenches be drained into firm meadow, capable of grazing as many cattle as Job in his best estate was master of. In the miry condition it now lies, it feeds great numbers in the winter, though when the weather grows warm they are driven from thence by the mighty armies of mosquitoes, which are the plague of the lower part of Carolina as much as the flies were formerly of Egypt (and some rabbis think those flies were no other than mosquitoes).

All the people in the neighborhood flocked to John Heath's to behold such rarities as they fancied us to be. The men left their beloved chimney corners, the good women their spinning wheels, and some, of more curiosity than ordinary, rose out of their sick beds to come and stare at us. They looked upon us as a troop of knights-errant who were running this great risk of our lives, as they imagined, for the public weal; and some of the gravest of them questioned much whether we were not all criminals condemned to this dirty work for offenses against the state. What puzzled them most was what could make our men so very light-hearted under such intolerable drudgery. "Ye have little reason to be merry, my masters," said one of them, with a very solemn face. "I fancy the pocosin you must struggle with tomorrow will make you change your note and try what metal you are made of. Ye are, to be sure, the first of human race that ever had the boldness to attempt it, and I dare say will be the last. If, therefore, you have any worldly goods to dispose of, my advice is that you make your wills this very night, for fear you die intestate tomorrow." But, alas, these frightful tales were so far from disheartening the men that they served only to whet their resolution.

9. The surveyors entered early upon their business this morning and ran the line through Mr. Eyland's plantation, as far as the banks of North River. They passed over it in the piragua and landed in Gibbs's marsh, which was a mile in breadth and tolerably firm. They trudged through this marsh without much difficulty as far as the high land, which promised more fertility than any they had seen in these lower parts. But this firm land lasted not long before they came upon the dreadful pocosin they had been threatened with. Nor did they find it one jot better than it had been painted to them. The beavers and otters had rendered it quite impassable for any creatures but themselves.

Our poor fellows had much ado to drag their legs after them in this quagmire, but, disdaining to be balked, they could hardly be persuaded from pressing forward by the surveyors, who found it absolutely necessary to make a traverse in the deepest place to prevent their sticking fast in the mire and becoming a certain prey to the turkey buzzards.

This horrible day's work ended two miles to the northward of Mr. Merchant's plantation, divided from Northwest River by a narrow swamp which is causewayed over. We took up our quarters in the open field not far from the house, correcting by a fire as large as a Roman funeral pile the aguish exhalations arising from the sunken grounds that surrounded us.

The neck of land included betwixt North River and Northwest River, with the adjacent marsh, belonged formerly to Governor Gibbs[5] but since his decrease to Colonel Bladen, in right of his first lady, who was Mr. Gibbs's daughter. It would be a valuable tract of land in any country but North Carolina, where, for want of navigation and commerce, the best estate affords little more than a coarse subsistence.

10. The Sabbath happened very opportunely, to give some ease to our jaded people, who rested religiously from every work but that of cooking the kettle. We observed very few cornfields in our walks and those very small, which seemed the stranger to us because we could see no other tokens of husbandry or improvement. But upon further inquiry we were given to understand people only made corn for themselves and not for their stocks, which know very well how to get their own living. Both cattle and hogs ramble into the neighboring marshes and swamps, where they maintain themselves the whole winter long and are not fetched home till the spring. Thus these indolent wretches during one half of the year lose the advantage of the milk of their cattle, as well as their dung, and many of the poor creatures perish in the mire, into the bargain, by this ill management. Some who pique themselves more upon industry than their neighbors will now and then, in compliment to their cattle, cut down a tree whose limbs are loaded with the moss afore-mentioned. The trouble would be too great to climb the tree in order to gather this provender, but the shortest way (which in this country is always counted the best) is to fell it, just like the lazy Indians, who do the same by such trees as bear fruit and so make one harvest for all. By this bad husbandry milk is so scarce in the winter season that were a big-bellied woman to long for it she would tax her longing. And, in truth, I believe this is often the case, and at the same time a very good reason why so many people in this province are marked with a custard complexion.

The only business here is raising of hogs, which is managed with the least trouble and affords the diet they are most fond of. The truth of it is, the inhabitants of North Carolina devour so much swine's flesh that it fills them full of gross humors. For want, too, of a constant supply of salt, they are commonly obliged to eat it fresh, and that begets the highest taint of scurvy. Thus, whenever a severe cold happens to constitutions thus vitiated, 'tis apt to improve into the yaws,[6] called there very justly the country distemper. This has all the symptoms of the pox, with this aggravation, that no preparation of mercury will touch it. First it seizes the throat, next the palate, and lastly shows its spite to the poor nose, of which 'tis apt in a small time treacherously to undermine the foundation. This calamity is so common and familiar here that it ceases to be a scandal, and in the disputes that happen about beauty the noses have in some companies much ado to carry it. Nay, 'tis said that once, after three good pork years, a motion had like to have been made in the House of Burgesses that a man with a nose should be incapable of holding any place of profit in the province; which extraordinary motion could never have been intended without some hopes of a majority.

Thus, considering the foul and pernicious effects of eating swine's flesh in a hot country, it was wisely forbid and made an abomination to the Jews, who lived much in the same latitude with Carolina.

---

[5] Although Philip Ludwell was appointed governor of North Carolina, John Gibbs claimed the title and refused to acknowledge the appointee's authority. Gibbs's heir, Martin Bladen, was married to Gibbs's daughter Mary. [6] A skin disease.

11. We ordered the surveyors early to their business, who were blessed with pretty dry grounds for three miles together. But they paid dear for it in the next two, consisting of one continued frightful pocosin, which no creatures but those of the amphibious kind ever had ventured into before. This filthy quagmire did in earnest put the men's courage to a trial, and though I can't say it made them lose their patience, yet they lost their humor for joking. They kept their gravity like so many Spaniards, so that a man might then have taken his opportunity to plunge up to the chin without danger of being laughed at. However, this unusual composure of countenance could not fairly be called complaining.

Their day's work ended at the mouth of Northern's Creek, which empties itself into Northwest River; though we chose to quarter a little higher up the river near Mossy Point. This we did for the convenience of an old house to shelter our persons and baggage from the rain, which threatened us hard. We judged the thing right, for there fell an heavy shower in the night that drove the most hardy of us into the house. Though indeed our case was not much mended by retreating thither, because, that tenement having not long before been used as a pork store, the moisture of the air dissolved the salt that lay scattered on the floor and made it as wet withindoors as without. However, the swamps and marshes we were lately accustomed to had made such beavers and otters of us that nobody caught the least cold.

We had encamped so early that we found time in the evening to walk near half a mile into the woods. There we came upon a family of mulattoes that called themselves free, though by the shyness of the master of the house, who took care to keep least in sight, their freedom seemed a little doubtful. It is certain many slaves shelter themselves in this obscure part of the world, nor will any of their righteous neighbors discover them. On the contrary, they find their account in settling such fugitives on some out-of-the-way corner of their land to raise stocks for a mean and inconsiderable share, well knowing their condition makes it necessary for them to submit to any terms. Nor were these worthy borderers content to shelter runaway slaves, but debtors and criminals have often met with the like indulgence. But if the government of North Carolina have encouraged this unneighborly policy in order to increase their people, it is no more than what ancient Rome did before them, which was made a city of refuge for all debtors and fugitives and from that wretched beginning grew up in time to be mistress of great part of the world. And, considering how Fortune delights in bringing great things out of small, who knows but Carolina may, one time or other, come to be the seat of some other great empire?

12. Everything had been so soaked with the rain that we were obliged to lie by a good part of the morning and dry them. However, that time was not lost, because it gave the surveyors an opportunity of platting off their work and taking the course of the river. It likewise helped to recruit the spirits of the men, who had been a little harassed with yesterday's march. Notwithstanding all this, we crossed the river before noon and advanced our line three miles. It was not possible to make more of it by reason good part of the way was either marsh or pocosin. The line cut two or three plantations, leaving part of them in Virginia and part of them in Carolina. This was a case that happened frequently, to the great inconvenience of the owners, who were therefore obliged to take out two patents and pay for a new survey in each government.

In the evening we took up our quarters in Mr. Ballance's pasture, a little above the bridge built over Northwest River. There we discharged the two piraguas, which in truth had been very serviceable in transporting us over the many waters in that dirty and difficult part of our business. Our landlord had a tolerable good house and clean furniture, and yet we could not be tempted to lodge in it. We chose rather to lie in the open field, for fear of growing too tender. A clear sky, spangled with stars, was our canopy, which, being the last thing we saw before we fell asleep, gave us magnificent dreams. The truth of it is, we took so much pleasure in that natural kind of lodging that I think at the foot of the account mankind are great losers by the luxury of feather beds and warm apartments.

The curiosity of beholding so new and withal so sweet a method of encamping brought one of the Senators of North Carolina to make us a midnight visit. But he was so very clamorous in his commendations of it that the sentinel, not seeing his quality either through his habit or behavior, had like to have treated him roughly. After excusing the unseasonableness of his visit and letting us know he was a parliament man, he swore he was so taken with our lodging that he would set fire to his house as soon as he got home and teach his wife and children to lie like us in the open field.

13. Early this morning our chaplain repaired to us with the men we had left at Mr. Wilson's. We had sent for them the evening before to relieve those who had the labor oar from Currituck Inlet. But to our great surprise, they petitioned not to be relieved, hoping to gain immortal reputation by being the first of mankind that ventured through the Great Dismal.[7] But the rest being equally ambitious of the same honor, it was but fair to decide their pretensions by lot. After Fortune had declared herself, those which she had excluded offered money to the happy persons to go in their stead. But Hercules would have as soon sold the glory of cleansing the Augean stables,[8] which was pretty near the same sort of work. No sooner was the controversy at an end but we sent those unfortunate fellows back to their quarters whom chance had condemned to remain upon firm land and sleep in a whole skin. In the meanwhile, the surveyors carried the line three miles, which was no contemptible day's work, considering how cruelly they were entangled with briers and gallbushes. The leaf of this last shrub bespeaks it to be of the alaternus family.

Our work ended within a quarter of a mile of the Dismal above-mentioned, where the ground began to be already full of sunken holes and slashes, which had, here and there, some few reeds growing in them. 'Tis hardly credible how little the bordering inhabitants were acquainted with this mighty swamp, notwithstanding they had lived their whole lives within smell of it. Yet, as great strangers as they were to it, they pretended to be very exact in their account of its dimensions and were positive it could not be above seven or eight miles wide, but knew no more of the matter than stargazers know of the distance of the fixed stars. At the same time, they were simple enough to amuse our men with idle stories of the lions, panthers, and alligators they were likely to encounter in that dreadful place. In short, we saw plainly there was no intelligence of this *Terra Incognita*[9] to be got but from our own experience. For that reason it was resolved to make the requisite dispositions to enter it next morning.

[7] I.e., the Great Dismal Swamp along the eastern boundary between Virginia and North Carolina.
[8] As one of twelve labors, each one an exercise in humility, Hercules was required to clean in one day the stables where the enormous herds of cattle owned by the King of Elis were housed.
[9] Latin: "Unexplored land."

We allotted every one of the surveyors for this painful enterprise, with twelve men to attend them. Fewer than that could not be employed in clearing the way, carrying the chain, marking the trees, and bearing the necessary bedding and provisions. Nor would the commissioners themselves have spared their persons on this occasion but for fear of adding to the poor men's burden, while they were certain they could add nothing to their resolution.

We quartered with our friend and fellow traveler, William Wilkins, who had been our faithful pilot to Currituck and lived about a mile from the place where the line ended. Everything looked so very clean and the furniture so neat that we were tempted to lodge withindoors. But the novelty of being shut up so close quite spoiled our rest, nor did we breathe so free by abundance as when we lay in the open air.

14. Before nine of the clock this morning the provisions, bedding, and other necessaries were made up into packs for the men to carry on their shoulders into the Dismal. They were victualed for eight days at full allowance, nobody doubting but that would be abundantly sufficient to carry them through that inhospitable place; nor indeed was it possible for the poor fellows to stagger under more. As it was, their loads weighed from sixty to seventy pounds, in just proportion to the strength of those who were to bear them. 'Twould have been unconscionable to have saddled them with burdens heavier than that, when they were to lug them through a filthy bog which was hardly practicable with no burden at all. Besides this luggage at their backs, they were obliged to measure the distance, mark the trees, and clear the way for the surveyors every step they went. It was really a pleasure to see with how much cheerfulness they undertook and with how much spirit they went through all this drudgery. For their greater safety, the commissioners took care to furnish them with Peruvian bark,[10] rhubarb, and ipecacuanha, in case they might happen, in that wet journey, to be taken with fevers or fluxes.

Although there was no need of example to inflame persons already so cheerful, yet to enter the people with the better grace, the author and two more of the commissioners accompanied them half a mile into the Dismal. The skirts of it were thinly planted with dwarf reeds and gallbushes, but when we got into the Dismal itself we found the reeds grew there much taller and closer and, to mend the matter, were so interlaced with bamboo briers that there was no scuffling through them without the help of pioneers. At the same time we found the ground moist and trembling under our feet like a quagmire, insomuch that it was an easy matter to run a ten-foot pole up to the head in it without exerting any uncommon strength to do it. Two of the men whose burdens were the least cumbersome had orders to march before with their tomahawks and clear the way in order to make an opening for the surveyors. By their assistance we made a shift to push the line half a mile in three hours and then reached a small piece of firm land about a hundred yards wide, standing up above the rest like an island. Here the people were glad to lay down their loads and take a little refreshment, while the happy man whose lot it was to carry the jug of rum began already, like Aesop's bread carriers, to find it grow a good deal lighter.

After reposing about an hour, the commissioners recommended vigor and constancy to their fellow travelers, by whom they were answered with three cheerful huzzas, in token of obedience. This ceremony was no sooner over but they took up

---

[10] Purported remedy for fever, especially malaria.

their burdens and attended the motion of the surveyors, who, though they worked with all their might, could reach but one mile farther, the same obstacles still attending them which they had met with in the morning. However small this distance may seem to such as are used to travel at their ease, yet our poor men, who were obliged to work with an unwieldy load at their backs, had reason to think it a long way; especially in a bog where they had no firm footing but every step made a deep impression which was instantly filled with water. At the same time they were laboring with their hands to cut down the reeds, which were ten feet high, their legs were hampered with briers. Besides, the weather happened to be warm, and the tallness of the reeds kept off every friendly breeze from coming to refresh them. And indeed it was a little provoking to hear the wind whistling among the branches of the white cedars, which grew here and there amongst the reeds, and at the same time not to have the comfort to feel the least breath of it.

In the meantime the three commissioners returned out of the Dismal the same way they went in and, having joined their brethren, proceeded that night as far as Mr. Wilson's. This worthy person lives within sight of the Dismal, in the skirts whereof his stocks range and maintain themselves all the winter, and yet he knew as little of it as he did of *Terra Australis Incognita.*[11] He told us a Canterbury tale of a North Briton whose curiosity spurred him a long way into this great desert, as he called it, near twenty years ago, but he, having no compass nor seeing the sun for several days together, wandered about till he was almost famished; but at last he bethought himself of a secret his countrymen make use of to pilot themselves in a dark day. He took a fat louse out of his collar and exposed it to the open day on a piece of white paper, which he brought along with him for his journal. The poor insect, having no eyelids, turned himself about till he found the darkest part of the heavens and so made the best of his way toward the North. By this direction he steered himself safe out and gave such a frightful account of the monsters he saw and the distresses he underwent that no mortal since has been hardy enough to go upon the like dangerous discovery.

15. The surveyors pursued their work with all diligence but still found the soil of the Dismal so spongy that the water oozed up into every footstep they took. To their sorrow, too, they found the reeds and briers more firmly interwoven than they did the day before. But the greatest grievance was from large cypresses which the wind had blown down and heaped upon one another. On the limbs of most of them grew sharp snags, pointing every way like so many pikes, that required much pains and caution to avoid. These trees, being evergreens and shooting their large tops very high, are easily overset by every gust of wind, because there is no firm earth to steady their roots. Thus many of them were laid prostrate, to the great encumbrance of the way. Such variety of difficulties made the business go on heavily, insomuch that from morning till night the line could advance no farther than one mile and thirty-one poles.

Never was rum, that cordial of life, found more necessary than it was in this dirty place. It did not only recruit the people's spirits, now almost jaded with fatigue, but served to correct the badness of the water and at the same time to resist the malignity of the air. Whenever the men wanted to drink, which was very often, they had

[11] Latin: "Unexplored land of Australia."

nothing more to do but make a hole and the water bubbled up in a moment. But it was far from being either clear or well tasted and had, besides, a physical effect from the tincture it received from the roots of the shrubs and trees that grew in the neighborhood.

While the surveyors were thus painfully employed, the commissioners discharged the long score they had with Mr. Wilson for the men and horses which had been quartered upon him during our expedition to Currituck. From thence we marched in good order along the east side of the Dismal and passed the long bridge that lies over the south branch of Elizabeth River. At the end of eighteen miles we reached Timothy Ivy's plantation, where we pitched our tent for the first time and were furnished with everything the place afforded. We perceived the happy effects of industry in this family, in which every one looked tidy and clean and carried in their countenances the cheerful marks of plenty. We saw no drones there, which are but too common, alas, in that part of the world. Though, in truth, the distemper of laziness seizes the men oftener much than the women. These last spin, weave, and knit, all with their own hands, while their husbands, depending on the bounty of the climate, are slothful in everything but getting of children, and in that only instance make themselves useful members of an infant colony.

There is but little wool in that province, though cotton grows very kindly and, so far south, is seldom nipped by the frost. The good women mix this with their wool for their outer garments; though, for want of fulling, that kind of manufacture is open and sleazy. Flax likewise thrives there extremely, being perhaps as fine as any in the world, and I question not might with a little care and pains be brought to rival that of Egypt; and yet the men are here so intolerably lazy they seldom take the trouble to propagate it.

16. The line was this day carried one mile and an half and sixteen poles. The soil continued soft and miry but fuller of trees, especially white cedars. Many of these, too, were thrown down and piled in heaps, high enough for a good Muscovite fortification. The worst of it was, the poor fellows began now to be troubled with fluxes, occasioned by bad water and moist lodging, but chewing of rhubarb kept that malady within bounds.

In the meantime, the commissioners decamped early in the morning and made a march of twenty-five miles, as far as Mr. Andrew Meade's, who lives upon Nansemond River. They were no sooner got under the shelter of that hospitable roof but it began to rain hard and continued so to do great part of the night. This gave them much pain for their friends in the Dismal, whose sufferings spoiled their taste for the good cheer wherewith they were entertained themselves. However, late that evening these poor men had the fortune to come upon another terra firma, which was the luckier for them because the lower ground, by the rain that fell, was made a fitter lodging for tadpoles than men. In our journey we remarked that the north side of this great swamp lies higher than either the east or the west, nor were the approaches to it so full of sunken grounds.

We passed by no less than two Quaker meetinghouses, one of which had an awkward ornament on the west end of it that seemed to ape a steeple. I must own I expected no such piece of foppery from a sect of so much outside simplicity. That persuasion prevails much in the lower end of Nansemond County, for want of ministers to pilot the people a decenter way to Heaven. The ill reputation of tobacco planted in those lower parishes makes the clergy unwilling to accept of them, unless it be such whose abilities are as mean as their pay. Thus, whether the churches be quite void or but indifferently filled, the Quakers will have an opportunity of gaining proselytes. 'Tis a wonder no popish missionaries are sent from Maryland to labor in this neglected vineyard, who we know have zeal enough to traverse sea and land on the meritorious errand of making converts. Nor is it less strange that some wolf in sheep's clothing arrives not from New England to lead astray a flock that has no shepherd. People uninstructed in any religion are ready to embrace the first that offers. 'Tis natural for helpless man to adore his Maker in some form or other, and were there any exception to this rule, I should suspect it to be among the Hottentots[12] of the Cape of Good Hope and of North Carolina.

There fell a great deal of rain in the night, accompanied with a strong wind. The fellow feeling we had for the poor Dismalites, on account of this unkind weather, rendered the down we laid upon uneasy. We fancied them half-drowned in their wet lodging, with the trees blowing down about their ears. These were the gloomy images our fears suggested, though 'twas so much uneasiness clear gains. They happened to come off much better, by being luckily encamped on the dry piece of ground afore-mentioned.

1841

Jonathan Edwards
1703–1758

Jonathan Edwards was a soft-spoken Puritan mystic and intellectual who ranged boldly in thought and writing; he is best known for a sermon that depicts sinners dangling by a spider's filament over "hell's wide gaping mouth." Edwards was born in East Windsor, Connecticut, the sole son among ten daughters of the Reverend Timothy Edwards and Esther Stoddard, herself the daughter of the renowned Puritan minister Solomon Stoddard. Tutored at home by his gifted parents, Edwards entered Yale at the age of thirteen. As his college diary shows, Edwards, like Benjamin Franklin, was determined to improve himself and "never to lose one moment of time." He graduated in 1720 and remained in New Haven for two additional years of theological study. Licensed to preach in 1722, Edwards served in a New York Presbyterian Church for two years, then returned to New Haven as a Yale tutor. The private writings of these student days show his youthful idealism, his deep concern for empirically gathered data, and his passionate involvement in religious experience.

In 1727, in his midtwenties, Edwards became his grandfather's assistant minister at the church in Northampton, Massachusetts. That July he married Sarah Pierrepont, the granddaughter of the illustrious Puritan minister Thomas Hooker. The young man doubtless looked forward to several years of a clerical apprenticeship, but Stoddard's death within two years left young Edwards the

---

[12] Natives of South Africa.

sole pastor of an important congregation. Situated at the northern part of the Connecticut River valley, Northampton was the home of many of the "river Gods," leading merchants and political figures of the valley who had grown accustomed to a liberal theology. Edwards's grandfather had presided over his congregation with a sense of the value of compromise.

Edwards proved to be very different from his predecessor, though initially he carried out his duties quietly. In 1731 he traveled to Boston to deliver an important lecture before an audience of prestigious ministers. Well aware of the contemporary ecumenical spirit of things, Edwards asserted that these newer "reasonable" moderations of Puritan doctrine were "repugnant to the design and tenor of the gospel." Edwards championed the orthodox Puritanism of the founders in the face of the new "free and catholick" temper of the times. His Northampton sermons and other writings over the next few years fortified that position. Above all, Edwards wished to move his congregation beyond a mere cerebral grasp of doctrine. His reading of the philosopher John Locke reinforced his belief that intellectual comprehension of religious ideas was insufficient. Instead, the individual must be moved actually to experience the doctrinal truth. It was the difference, Edwards wrote, between knowing the word *fire* and being burned. Edwards worked to make his Northampton congregation appreciate that difference and to yearn for religious experience. As Edwards wrote, "People do not need to have their heads stored so much as their hearts touched."

From 1735 the hearts of the Northampton congregation were indeed touched in an unusual religious revival in which Edwards played a vital part. The people of the town, he wrote, "seemed to be seized with a deep concern about their eternal salvation . . . in a truly wonderful and astonishing manner." Soon the revival spread throughout the Connecticut River valley, bringing much word-of-mouth attention to Edwards and his congregation. Though their revival ran its course in two years, the evangelical fervor of the Northampton awakening anticipated the much larger Great Awakening which preoccupied the American colonies from New England to Georgia in the 1740s.

Edwards grew increasingly interested in the psychology of religious conversion. He was familiar with the newer theories of sensate knowledge espoused by Locke and by the English philosopher George Berkeley, though his belief in the tenets of Puritanism was unshakable. Exploring the nature of religious experience, Edwards sought to reconcile his inherited Puritanism with the new theories, arguing that knowledge was acquired from sensory experience, not from innate powers of mind. His major work on this subject became *A Treatise Concerning Religious Affections* (1746). Edwards concluded that God's grace was experienced through the "affections," which were not merely emotions but the force that moved the individual toward affirmative possession or to repudiation. In Edwards's scheme of thought, love "is not only one of the affections but it is the first and chief . . . and the fountain of all the affections."

In large part Edwards's religious beliefs were the outcome of his mystical conversion experience in his youth. He later described it in his *Personal Narrative,* in terms so appreciative of the natural world that he sounds to some like a Romantic writer. Believing, however, in the absolute supremacy of God, Edwards saw revivalism as an opportunity to authenticate his faith and to restore

Puritanism to its original strength. To this end he delivered the sulphurous sermon titled "Sinners in the Hands of an Angry God," which remains the best-known sermon in American history. It was designed specifically to awaken the congregation to a sense of their sinfulness. In Puritan theology this intense, personal experience of depravity was the necessary first step toward conversion. "Sinners in the Hands of an Angry God" was just one of a handful of imprecatory sermons among the thousand extant from Edwards's twenty-four years at Northampton and from his years elsewhere, but it bears the stamp of his major concerns: that raised affections are visible signs, that mere human efforts to achieve salvation are futile, and that God alone is the omnipotent judge.

Edwards made Northampton a renowned center of orthodoxy and revived spirituality, but by the mid-1740s affairs between the minister and his congregation were moving toward crisis. A backlash developed over the excesses of the Great Awakening and its itinerant preachers, whose "beastly brayings" Edwards himself deplored. Yet some concurred with Edwards's ministerial opponent, Charles Chauncy, that Edwards was a "visionary enthusiast, and not to be minded." There was further squabbling over Edwards's propensity to trade with Boston merchants. There was trouble, too, when Edwards attempted to discipline some children of prominent families for circulating "bad books" (meaning a manual for midwives) and when Joseph Hawley, the son of a man who committed suicide during the Northampton revivals, rallied a faction against him. At last Edwards was forced to resign. Without public rancor he preached his farewell sermon in 1750.

In the following year Edwards assumed the duties of a frontier minister to whites and Indians in Stockbridge, a remote western Massachusetts mission. There Edwards wrote his greatest philosophical works, including *Freedom of the Will* (1754), *The Doctrine of Original Sin Defended* (1758), and *The Nature of True Virtue* (1765). These works examine the nature and place of free will in a predetermined universe and explore the relation between virtue and religious affections. The publication of these works brought Edwards renewed attention from scholars and intellectuals, who invited him to become the president of Princeton University. He arrived with his family amid an outbreak of smallpox. In 1758, after less than two months in office, Edwards died from an adverse reaction to a smallpox inoculation, for which he had volunteered. He is revered as an American philosopher of originality and a literary stylist of subtlety and power.

Further Reading:
T. H. Johnson, *The Printed Writings of Jonathan Edwards, 1703–1758,* 1940, 1970.
O. Winslow, *Jonathan Edwards,* 1940.
P. Miller, *Jonathan Edwards,* 1949.
A. Aldridge, *Jonathan Edwards,* 1964.
C. Cherry, *The Theology of Jonathan Edwards,* 1966.
E. Griffin, *Jonathan Edwards,* 1971.

Text:
The Works of President Edwards, 10 vols., ed. S. Dwight, 1829–1830.

Personal Narrative

I had a variety of concerns and exercises about my soul from my childhood; but had two more remarkable seasons of awakening,[1] before I met with that change by which I was brought to those new dispositions, and that new sense of things, that I have since had. The first time was when I was a boy, some years before I went to college, at a time of remarkable awakening in my father's congregation. I was then very much affected for many months, and concerned about the things of religion, and my soul's salvation; and was abundant in duties. I used to pray five times a day in secret, and to spend much time in religious talk with other boys; and used to meet with them to pray together. I experienced I know not what kind of delight in religion. My mind was much engaged in it, and had much self-righteous pleasure; and it was my delight to abound in religious duties. I with some of my schoolmates joined together, and built a booth in a swamp, in a very retired spot, for a place of prayer. And besides, I had particular secret places of my own in the woods, where I used to retire by myself; and was from time to time much affected. My affections[2] seemed to be lively and easily moved, and I seemed to be in my element when engaged in religious duties. And I am ready to think, many are deceived with such affections, and such a kind of delight as I then had in religion, and mistake it for grace.

But in process of time, my convictions and affections wore off; and I entirely lost all those affections and delights and left off secret prayer, at least as to any constant performance of it; and returned like a dog to his vomit,[3] and went on in the ways of sin. Indeed I was at times very uneasy, especially towards the latter part of my time at college, when it pleased God to seize me with the pleurisy, in which He brought me nigh to the grave, and shook me over the pit of hell. And yet, it was not long after my recovery, before I fell again into my old ways of sin. But God would not suffer me to go on with any quietness; I had great and violent inward struggles, till, after many conflicts with wicked inclinations, repeated resolutions, and bonds that I laid myself under by a kind of vows to God, I was brought wholly to break off all former wicked ways, and all ways of known outward sin; and to apply myself to seek salvation, and practice many religious duties; but without that kind of affection and delight which I had formerly experienced. My concern now wrought more by inward struggles and conflicts, and self-reflections. I made seeking my salvation the main business of my life. But yet, it seems to me I sought after a miserable manner; which has made me sometimes since to question, whether ever it issued in that which was saving; being ready to doubt, whether such miserable seeking ever succeeded. I was indeed brought to seek salvation in a manner that I never was before; I felt a spirit to part with all things in the world, for an interest in Christ. My concern continued and prevailed, with many exercising thoughts and inward struggles; but yet it never seemed to be proper to express that concern by the name of terror.

From my childhood up, my mind had been full of objections against the doctrine

---

[1] Religious enlivening.
[2] Religious feelings.

[3] See Proverbs 26:11.

of God's sovereignty, in choosing whom He would to eternal life, and rejecting whom He pleased; leaving them eternally to perish, and be everlastingly tormented in hell. It used to appear like a horrible doctrine to me. But I remember the time very well, when I seemed to be convinced, and fully satisfied, as to this sovereignty of God, and His justice in thus eternally disposing of men, according to His sovereign pleasure. But I never could give an account how, or by what means, I was thus convinced, not in the least imagining at the time, nor a long time after, that there was any extraordinary influence of God's Spirit in it; but only that now I saw further, and my reason apprehended the justice and reasonableness of it. However, my mind rested in it; and it put an end to all those cavils and objections. And there has been a wonderful alteration in my mind, with respect to the doctrine of God's sovereignty, from that day to this; so that I scarce ever have found so much as the rising of an objection against it, in the most absolute sense, in God's showing mercy to whom He will show mercy, and hardening whom He will.[4] God's absolute sovereignty and justice, with respect to salvation and damnation, is what my mind seems to rest assured of, as much as of anything that I see with my eyes; at least it is so at times. But I have often, since that first conviction, had quite another kind of sense of God's sovereignty than I had then. I have often since had not only a conviction, but a delightful conviction. The doctrine has very often appeared exceeding pleasant, bright, and sweet. Absolute sovereignty is what I love to ascribe to God. But my first conviction was not so.

The first instance that I remember of that sort of inward, sweet delight in God and divine things that I have lived much in since, was on reading those words, 1 Timothy 1:17, *Now unto the King eternal, immortal, invisible, the only wise God, be honor and glory forever and ever, Amen.* As I read the words, there came into my soul, and was as it were diffused through it, a sense of the glory of the Divine Being; a new sense, quite different from anything I ever experienced before. Never any words of Scripture seemed to me as these words did. I thought within myself, how excellent a Being that was, and how happy I should be, if I might enjoy that God, and be rapt[5] up to him in heaven, and be as it were swallowed up in him forever! I kept saying, and as it were singing over these words of Scripture to myself; and went to pray to God that I might enjoy Him, and prayed in a manner quite different from what I used to do; with a new sort of affection. But it never came into my thought that there was anything spiritual, or of a saving nature, in this.

From about that time, I began to have a new kind of apprehensions and ideas of Christ, and the work of redemption, and the glorious way of salvation by Him. An inward, sweet sense of these things, at times, came into my heart; and my soul was led away in pleasant views and contemplations of them. And my mind was greatly engaged to spend my time in reading and meditating on Christ, on the beauty and excellency of His person, and the lovely way of salvation by free grace in Him. I found no books so delightful to me, as those that treated of these subjects. Those words, Canticles[6] 2:1, used to be abundantly with me, *I am the Rose of Sharon, and the lily of the valleys.* The words seemed to me sweetly to represent the loveliness and beauty of Jesus Christ. The whole book of Canticles used to be pleasant to me, and I used

---

[4] See Romans 9:18.
[5] Lifted.
[6] The biblical Song of Solomon.

to be much in reading it, about that time; and found, from time to time, an inward sweetness, that would carry me away, in my contemplations. This I know not how to express otherwise, than by a calm, sweet abstraction of soul from all the concerns of this world; and sometimes a kind of vision, or fixed ideas and imaginations, of being alone in the mountains, or some solitary wilderness, far from all mankind, sweetly conversing with Christ, and wrapped and swallowed up in God. The sense I had of divine things would often of a sudden kindle up, as it were, a sweet burning in my heart; an ardor of soul, that I know not how to express.

Not long after I first began to experience these things, I gave an account to my father of some things that had passed in my mind. I was pretty much affected by the discourse we had together; and when the discourse was ended, I walked abroad alone, in a solitary place in my father's pasture, for contemplation. And as I was walking there, and looking up on the sky and clouds, there came into my mind so sweet a sense of the glorious *majesty* and *grace* of God, that I know not how to express. I seemed to see them both in a sweet conjunction; majesty and meekness joined together; it was a sweet and gentle, and holy majesty; and also a majestic meekness; an awful sweetness; a high, and great, and holy gentleness.

After this my sense of divine things gradually increased, and became more and more lively, and had more of that inward sweetness. The appearance of every thing was altered; there seemed to be, as it were, a calm, sweet cast, or appearance of divine glory, in almost everything. God's excellency, His wisdom, His purity and love, seemed to appear in every thing; in the sun, and moon, and stars; in the clouds and blue sky; in the grass, flowers, trees; in the water, and all nature; which used greatly to fix my mind. I often used to sit and view the moon for a long time; and in the day spent much time in viewing the clouds and sky, to behold the sweet glory of God in these things; in the meantime, singing forth, with a low voice, my contemplations of the Creator and Redeemer. And scarce anything, among all the works of nature, was so sweet to me as thunder and lightning; formerly, nothing had been so terrible to me. Before, I used to be uncommonly terrified with thunder, and to be struck with terror when I saw a thunder storm rising; but now, on the contrary, it rejoiced me. I felt God, so to speak, at the first appearance of a thunder storm; and used to take the opportunity, at such times, to fix myself in order to view the clouds, and see the lightnings play, and hear the majestic and awful voice of God's thunder, which oftentimes was exceedingly entertaining, leading me to sweet contemplations of my great and glorious God. While thus engaged, it always seemed natural to me to sing, or chant forth my meditations; or, to speak my thoughts in soliloquies with a singing voice.

I felt then great satisfaction, as to my good state; but that did not content me. I had vehement longings of soul after God and Christ, and after more holiness, where-with my heart seemed to be full, and ready to break; which often brought to my mind the words of the Psalmist, Psalms 119:20: *My soul breaketh for the longing that it hath.* I often felt a mourning and lamenting in my heart, that I had not turned to God sooner, that I might have had more time to grow in grace. My mind was greatly fixed on divine things; almost perpetually in the contemplation of them. I spent most of my time in thinking of divine things, year after year; often walking alone in the woods, and solitary places, for meditation, soliloquy, and prayer, and converse with God; and it was always my manner, at such times, to sing forth my contemplations.

I was almost constantly in ejaculatory prayer, wherever I was. Prayer seemed to be natural to me, as the breath by which the inward burnings of my heart had vent. The delights which I now felt in the things of religion, were of an exceeding different kind from those before mentioned, that I had when a boy; and what I then had no more notion of, than one born blind has of pleasant and beautiful colors. They were of a more inward, pure, soul-animating and refreshing nature. Those former delights never reached the heart; and did not arise from any sight of the divine excellency of the things of God; or any taste of the soul-satisfying and life-giving good there is in them.

My sense of divine things seemed gradually to increase, until I went to preach at New York,[7] which was about a year and a half after they[8] began; and while I was there, I felt them, very sensibly, in a higher degree than I had done before. My longings after God and holiness were much increased. Pure and humble, holy and heavenly Christianity appeared exceedingly amiable to me. I felt a burning desire to be in everything a complete Christian; and conformed to the blessed image of Christ; and that I might live, in all things, according to the pure, sweet and blessed rules of the gospel. I had an eager thirsting after progress in these things; which put me upon pursuing and pressing after them. It was my continual strife day and night, and constant inquiry, how I should *be* more holy, and *live* more holily, and more becoming a child of God, and a disciple of Christ. I now sought an increase of grace and holiness, and a holy life, with much more earnestness, than ever I sought grace before I had it. I used to be continually examining myself, and studying and contriving for likely ways and means, how I should live holily, with far greater diligence and earnestness, than ever I pursued anything in my life; but yet with too great a dependence on my own strength; which afterwards proved a great damage to me. My experience had not then taught me, as it has done since, my extreme feebleness and impotence, every manner of way; and the bottomless depths of secret corruption and deceit there was in my heart. However, I went on with my eager pursuit after more holiness, and conformity to Christ.

The heaven I desired was a heaven of holiness; to be with God, and to spend my eternity in divine love, and holy communion with Christ. My mind was very much taken up with contemplations on heaven, and the enjoyments there; and living there in perfect holiness, humility, and love; and it used at that time to appear a great part of the happiness of heaven, that there the saints could express their love to Christ. It appeared to me a great clog and burden, that what I felt within, I could not express as I desired. The inward ardor of my soul seemed to be hindered and pent up, and could not freely flame out as it would. I used often to think, how in heaven this principle should freely and fully vent and express itself. Heaven appeared exceedingly delightful, as a world of love; and that all happiness consisted in living in pure, humble, heavenly, divine love.

I remember the thoughts I used then to have of holiness; and said sometimes to myself, "I do certainly know that I love holiness, such as the gospel prescribes." It appeared to me, that there was nothing in it but what was ravishingly lovely; the highest beauty and amiableness—a *divine* beauty; far purer than anything here upon

---

[7] Edwards was minister of a church in New York City from August 1722 to May 1723.

[8] I.e., his sense of divine things.

earth; and that everything else was like mire and defilement, in comparison of it.

Holiness, as I then wrote down some of my contemplations on it, appeared to me to be of a sweet, pleasant, charming, serene, calm nature; which brought an inexpressible purity, brightness, peacefulness and ravishment to the soul. In other words, that it made the soul like a field or garden of God, with all manner of pleasant flowers; all pleasant, delightful, and undisturbed; enjoying a sweet calm, and the gentle vivifying beams of the sun. The soul of a true Christian, as I then wrote my meditations, appeared like such a little white flower as we see in the spring of the year; low and humble on the ground, opening its bosom to receive the pleasant beams of the sun's glory; rejoicing as it were in a calm rapture; diffusing around a sweet fragrancy; standing peacefully and lovingly, in the midst of other flowers round about; all in like manner opening their bosoms, to drink in the light of the sun. There was no part of creature holiness, that I had so great a sense of its loveliness, as humility, brokenness of heart, and poverty of spirit; and there was nothing that I so earnestly longed for. My heart panted after this, to lie low before God, as in the dust; that I might be nothing, and that God might be ALL, that I might become as a little child.[9]

While at New York, I was sometimes much affected with reflections on my past life, considering how late it was before I began to be truly religious; and how wickedly I had lived till then; and once so as to weep abundantly, and for a considerable time together.

On *January* 12, 1723, I made a solemn dedication of myself to God, and wrote it down; giving up myself and all that I had to God; to be for the future, in no respect my own; to act as one that had no right to himself in any respect. And solemnly vowed to take God for my whole portion and felicity; looking on nothing else as any part of my happiness, nor acting as if it were; and His law for the constant rule of my obedience; engaging to fight with all my might, against the world, the flesh, and the devil,[10] to the end of my life. But I have reason to be infinitely humbled, when I consider how much I have failed of answering my obligation.

I had then abundance of sweet religious conversation in the family where I lived, with Mr. John Smith and his pious mother. My heart was knit in affection to those in whom were appearances of true piety; and I could bear the thoughts of no other companions but such as were holy, and the disciples of the blessed Jesus. I had great longings for the advancement of Christ's kingdom in the world; and my secret prayer used to be, in great part, taken up in praying for it. If I heard the least hint of anything that happened, in any part of the world, that appeared, in some respect or other, to have a favorable aspect on the interests of Christ's kingdom, my soul eagerly catched at it; and it would much animate and refresh me. I used to be eager to read public news letters, mainly for that end; to see if I could not find some news favorable to the interest of religion in the world.

I very frequently used to retire into a solitary place, on the banks of Hudson's river, at some distance from the city, for contemplation on divine things, and secret converse with God; and had many sweet hours there. Sometimes Mr. Smith and I walked there

---

[9] Mark 10:15: "Whosoever shall not receive the kingdom of God as a little child, he shall not enter therein."

[10] From the Litany in the Anglican Book of Common Prayer.

together, to converse on the things of God; and our conversation used to turn much on the advancement of Christ's kingdom in the world, and the glorious things that God would accomplish for his church in the latter days. I had then, and at other times, the greatest delight in the holy Scriptures, of any book whatsoever. Oftentimes in reading it, every word seemed to touch my heart. I felt a harmony between something in my heart, and those sweet and powerful words. I seemed often to see so much light exhibited by every sentence, and such a refreshing food communicated, that I could not get along in reading; often dwelling long on one sentence, to see the wonders contained in it; and yet almost every sentence seemed to be full of wonders.

I came away from New York in the month of April, 1723, and had a most bitter parting with Madam Smith and her son. My heart seemed to sink within me at leaving the family and city, where I had enjoyed so many sweet and pleasant days. I went from New York to Wethersfield,[11] by water, and as I sailed away, I kept sight of the city as long as I could. However, that night, after this sorrowful parting, I was greatly comforted in God at Westchester,[12] where we went ashore to lodge; and had a pleasant time of it all the voyage to Saybrook.[13] It was sweet to me to think of meeting dear Christians in heaven, where we should never part more. At Saybrook we went ashore to lodge, on Saturday, and there kept the Sabbath; where I had a sweet and refreshing season, walking alone in the fields.

After I came home to Windsor,[14] I remained much in a like frame of mind, as when at New York; only sometimes I felt my heart ready to sink with the thoughts of my friends at New York. My support was in contemplations on the heavenly state; as I find in my diary of May 1, 1723. It was a comfort to think of that state, where there is fulness of joy; where reigns heavenly, calm, and delightful love, without alloy; where there are continually the dearest expressions of love; where is the enjoyment of the persons loved, without ever parting; where those persons who appear so lovely in this world, will really be inexpressibly more lovely and full of love to us. And how sweetly will the mutual lovers join together to sing the praises of God and the Lamb![15] How will it fill us with joy to think, that this enjoyment, these sweet exercises will never cease, but will last to all eternity! I continued much in the same frame, in the general, as when at New York, till I went to New Haven as tutor to the college;[16] particularly once at Bolton,[17] on a journey from Boston, while walking out alone in the fields. After I went to New Haven I sunk in religion; my mind being diverted from my eager pursuits after holiness, by some affairs that greatly perplexed and distracted my thoughts.

In September, 1725, I was taken ill at New Haven, and while endeavoring to go home to Windsor, was so ill at the North Village, that I could go no further; where I lay sick for about a quarter of a year. In this sickness, God was pleased to visit me again with the sweet influences of His Spirit. My mind was greatly engaged there in divine, pleasant contemplations, and longings of soul. I observed that those who watched with me, would often be looking out wishfully for the morning; which

[11] In Connecticut.
[12] Westchester County, near New York City.
[13] In Connecticut.
[14] In Connecticut.
[15] I.e., the Lamb of God, the symbol of Christ (Revelation 15:3).

[16] Yale College, where Edwards became a tutor in 1724.
[17] In Connecticut.

brought to my mind those words of the Psalmist, and which my soul with delight made its own language, *My soul waiteth for the Lord, more than they that watch for the morning, I say, more than they that watch for the morning;*[18] and when the light of the day came in at the windows, it refreshed my soul from one morning to another. It seemed to be some image of the light of God's glory.

I remember, about that time, I used greatly to long for the conversion of some that I was concerned with; I could gladly honor them, and with delight be a servant to them, and lie at their feet, if they were but truly holy. But, some time after this, I was again greatly diverted in my mind with some temporal concerns that exceedingly took up my thoughts, greatly to the wounding of my soul; and went on through various exercises, that it would be tedious to relate, which gave me much more experience of my own heart, than ever I had before.

Since I came to this town,[19] I have often had sweet complacency in God, in views of His glorious perfections and the excellency of Jesus Christ. God has appeared to me a glorious and lovely Being, chiefly on the account of His holiness. The holiness of God has always appeared to me the most lovely of all His attributes. The doctrines of God's absolute sovereignty, and free grace, in showing mercy to whom He would show mercy; and man's absolute dependence on the operations of God's Holy Spirit, have very often appeared to me as sweet and glorious doctrines. These doctrines have been much my delight. God's sovereignty has ever appeared to me, a great part of His glory. It has often been my delight to approach God, and adore Him as a sovereign God, and ask sovereign mercy of Him.

I have loved the doctrines of the gospel; they have been to my soul like green pastures. The gospel has seemed to me the richest treasure; the treasure that I have most desired, and long that it might dwell richly in me. The way of salvation by Christ has appeared, in a general way, glorious and excellent, most pleasant and most beautiful. It has often seemed to me, that it would in a great measure spoil heaven, to receive it in any other way. That text has often been affecting and delightful to me. Isaiah 32:2, *A man shall be an hiding place from the wind, and a covert from the tempest,* &c.

It has often appeared to me delightful, to be united to Christ; to have Him for my head, and to be a member of His body; also to have Christ for my teacher and prophet. I very often think with sweetness, and longings, and pantings of soul, of being, a little child, taking hold of Christ, to be led by Him through the wilderness of this world. That text, Matthew 18:3, has often been sweet to me, *Except ye be converted and become as little children,* &c. I love to think of coming to Christ, to receive salvation of Him, poor in spirit, and quite empty of self, humbly exalting Him alone; cut off entirely from my own root, in order to grow into, and out of Christ; to have God in Christ to be all in all; and to live by faith on the son of God, a life of humble, unfeigned confidence in Him. That scripture has often been sweet to me, Psalms 115:1. *Not unto us, O Lord, not unto us, but unto thy name give glory, for thy mercy, and for thy truth's sake.* And those words of Christ, Luke 10:21. *In that hour Jesus rejoiced in spirit, and said, I thank thee, O Father, Lord of heaven and earth, that thou hast hid these things*

---

[18] See Psalm 130:6.
[19] Northampton, Massachusetts. In 1727 Edwards was appointed assistant minister there.

from the wise and prudent, and has revealed them unto babes: even so, Father; for so it seemed good in thy sight. That sovereignty of God which Christ rejoiced in, seemed to me worthy of such joy; and that rejoicing seemed to show the excellency of Christ, and of what spirit He was.

Sometimes, only mentioning a single word caused my heart to burn within me; or only seeing the name of Christ, or the name of some attribute of God. And God has appeared glorious to me, on account of the Trinity. It has made me have exalting thoughts of God, that He subsists in three persons; Father, Son, and Holy Ghost. The sweetest joys and delights I have experienced, have not been those that have arisen from a hope of my own good estate; but in a direct view of the glorious things of the gospel. When I enjoy this sweetness, it seems to carry me above the thoughts of my own estate; it seems at such times a loss that I cannot bear, to take off my eye from the glorious pleasant object I behold without me, to turn my eye in upon myself, and my own good estate.

My heart has been much on the advancement of Christ's kingdom in the world. The histories of the past advancement of Christ's kingdom have been sweet to me. When I have read histories of past ages, the pleasantest thing in all my reading has been, to read of the kingdom of Christ being promoted. And when I have expected, in my reading, to come to any such thing, I have rejoiced in the prospect, all the way as I read. And my mind has been much entertained and delighted with the Scripture promises and prophecies, which relate to the future glorious advancement of Christ's kingdom upon earth.

I have sometimes had a sense of the excellent fulness of Christ, and His meetness and suitableness as a Saviour, whereby He has appeared to me, far above all, the chief of ten thousands.[20] His blood and atonement have appeared sweet, and His righteousness sweet; which was always accompanied with ardency of spirit; and inward strugglings, and breathings, and groanings that cannot be uttered to be emptied of myself, and swallowed up in Christ.

Once as I rode out into the woods for my health, in 1737, having alighted from my horse in a retired place, as my manner commonly has been, to walk for divine contemplation and prayer, I had a view that for me was extraordinary, of the glory of the Son of God, as Mediator between God and man, and His wonderful, great, full, pure and sweet grace and love, and meek and gentle condescension. This grace that appeared so calm and sweet, appeared also great above the heavens. The person of Christ appeared ineffably excellent, with an excellency great enough to swallow up all thought and conception—which continued, as near as I can judge, about an hour; which kept me the greater part of the time in a flood of tears, and weeping aloud. I felt an ardency of soul to be, what I know not otherwise how to express, emptied and annihilated; to lie in the dust, and to be full of Christ alone; to love Him with a holy and pure love; to trust in Him; to live upon Him; to serve and follow Him; and to be perfectly sanctified and made pure, with a divine and heavenly purity. I have, several other times, had views very much of the same nature, and which have had the same effects.

I have many times had a sense of the glory of the third person in the Trinity, in

[20] Song of Solomon 5:10: "My beloved is . . .
chiefest among ten thousand."

His office of sanctifier; in His holy operations, communicating divine light and life to the soul. God, in the communications of His Holy Spirit, has appeared as an infinite fountain of divine glory and sweetness; being full, and sufficient to fill and satisfy the soul; pouring forth itself in sweet communications; like the sun in its glory, sweetly and pleasantly diffusing light and life. And I have sometimes had an affecting sense of the excellency of the word of God, as the word of life; as the light of life; a sweet, excellent, life-giving word; accompanied with a thirsting after that word, that it might dwell richly in my heart.

Often, since I lived in this town, I have had very affecting views of my own sinfulness and vileness; very frequently to such a degree as to hold me in a kind of loud weeping, sometimes for a considerable time together; so that I have often been forced to shut myself up. I have had a vastly greater sense of my own wickedness, and the badness of my own heart, than ever I had before my conversion. It has often appeared to me, that if God should mark iniquity against me, I should appear the very worst of all mankind; of all that have been since the beginning of the world to this time; and that I should have by far the lowest place in hell. When others, that have come to talk with me about their soul concerns, have expressed the sense they have had of their own wickedness, by saying that it seemed to them, that they were as bad as the devil himself; I thought their expressions seemed exceedingly faint and feeble, to represent my wickedness.

My wickedness, as I am in myself, has long appeared to me perfectly ineffable, and swallowing up all thought and imagination; like an infinite deluge, or mountains over my head. I know not how to express better what my sins appear to me to be, than by heaping infinite upon infinite, and multiplying infinite by infinite. Very often, for these many years, these expressions are in my mind and in my mouth, "Infinite upon infinite—Infinite upon infinite!" When I look into my heart, and take a view of my wickedness, it looks like an abyss infinitely deeper than hell. And it appears to me, that were it not for free grace, exalted and raised up to the infinite height of all the fulness and glory of the great Jehovah, and the arm of His power and grace stretched forth in all the majesty of His power, and in all the glory of His sovereignty, I should appear sunk down in my sins below hell itself; far beyond the sight of everything, but the eye of sovereign grace, that can pierce even down to such a depth. And yet it seems to me that my conviction of sin is exceedingly small and faint; it is enough to amaze me, that I have no more sense of my sin. I know certainly, that I have very little sense of my sinfulness. When I have had turns of weeping for my sins, I thought I knew at the time that my repentance was nothing to my sin.

I have greatly longed of late, for a broken heart, and to lie low before God; and, when I ask for humility, I cannot bear the thoughts of being no more humble than other Christians. It seems to me, that though their degrees of humility may be suitable for them, yet it would be a vile self-exaltation in me, not to be the lowest in humility of all mankind. Others speak of their longing to be "humbled to the dust"; that may be a proper expression for them, but I always think of myself, that I ought, and it is an expression that has long been natural for me to use in prayer, "to lie infinitely low before God." And it is affecting to think, how ignorant I was, when a young Christian, of the bottomless, infinite depths of wickedness, pride, hypocrisy, and deceit, left in my heart.

I have a much greater sense of my universal, exceeding dependence on God's grace and strength and mere good pleasure, of late, than I used formerly to have; and have experienced more of an abhorrence of my own righteousness. The very thought of any joy arising in me, on any consideration of my own amiableness, performances, or experiences, or any goodness of heart or life, is nauseous and detestable to me. And yet I am greatly afflicted with a proud and self-righteous spirit, much more sensibly than I used to be formerly. I see that serpent rising and putting forth its head continually, everywhere, all around me.

Though it seems to me, that, in some respects, I was a far better Christian, for two or three years after my first conversion, than I am now; and lived in a more constant delight and pleasure; yet, of late years, I have had a more full and constant sense of the absolute sovereignty of God, and a delight in that sovereignty; and have had more of a sense of the glory of Christ, as a Mediator revealed in the gospel. On one Saturday night, in particular, I had such a discovery of the excellency of the gospel above all other doctrines, that I could not but say to myself, "This is my chosen light, my chosen doctrine;" and of Christ, "This is my chosen Prophet." It appeared sweet, beyond all expression, to follow Christ, and to be taught, and enlightened, and instructed by Him; to learn of Him, and live to Him. Another Saturday night, (*January,* 1739) I had such a sense, how sweet and blessed a thing it was to walk in the way of duty; to do that which was right and meet to be done, and agreeable to the holy mind of God; that it caused me to break forth into a kind of loud weeping, which held me some time, so that I was forced to shut myself up, and fasten the doors. I could not but, as it were, cry out, "How happy are they which do that which is right in the sight of God! They are blessed indeed, they are the happy ones!" I had, at the same time, a very affecting sense, how meet and suitable it was that God should govern the world, and order all things according to His own pleasure; and I rejoiced in it, that God reigned, and that His will was done.

1765

Sinners in the Hands of an Angry God

Their foot shall slide in due time.

Deuteronomy 32:35

In this verse is threatened the vengeance of God on the wicked unbelieving Israelites, that were God's visible people, and lived under means of grace;[1] and that notwithstanding all God's wonderful works that He had wrought towards that people, yet remained, as is expressed verse 28, void of counsel, having no understanding in them;

---

[1] According to God's covenant with Abraham (Genesis 17–18), the chosen people would receive God's grace and be saved. In Puritan thought Jesus' atonement fulfilled the covenant with Abraham, which restored the possibility of salvation previously lost through the sin of Adam and Eve.

and that, under all the cultivations of heaven, brought forth bitter and poisonous fruit; as in the two verses next preceding the text.

The expression that I have chosen for my text, *their foot shall slide in due time*, seems to imply the following things relating to the punishment and destruction that these wicked Israelites were exposed to.

1. That they are always exposed to *destruction*, as one that stands or walks in slippery places is always exposed to fall. This is implied in the manner of their destruction's coming upon them, being represented by their foot's sliding. The same is expressed, Psalm 73:18: "Surely thou didst set them in slippery places: thou castedst them down into destruction."

2. It implies that they were always exposed to sudden, unexpected destruction. As he that walks in slippery places is every moment liable to fall, he cannot foresee one moment whether he shall stand or fall the next; and when he does fall, he falls at once, without warning, which is also expressed in that Psalm 73:18–19: "Surely thou didst set them in slippery places: thou castedst them down into destruction. How are they brought into desolation as in a moment."

3. Another thing implied is that they are liable to fall of *themselves*, without being thrown down by the hand of another, as he that stands or walks on slippery ground needs nothing but his own weight to throw him down.

4. That the reason why they are not fallen already, and do not fall now, is only that God's appointed time is not come. For it is said that when that due time or appointed time comes, *their foot shall slide.* Then they shall be left to fall, as they are inclined by their own weight. God will not hold them up in these slippery places any longer but will let them go; and then, at that very instant, they shall fall into destruction; as he that stands on such slippery declining ground on the edge of a pit that he cannot stand alone, when he is let go he immediately falls and is lost.

The observation from the words that I would now insist upon is this.

There is nothing that keeps wicked men at any one moment out of hell, but the mere pleasure of God.

By the *mere* pleasure of God, I mean His *sovereign* pleasure, His arbitrary will, restrained by no obligation, hindered by no manner of difficulty, any more than if nothing else but God's mere will had in the least degree, or in any respect whatsoever, any hand in the preservation of wicked men one moment.

The truth of this observation may appear by the following considerations.

1. There is no want of *power* in God to cast wicked men into hell at any moment. Men's hands cannot be strong when God rises up: the strongest have no power to resist Him, nor can any deliver out of His hands.

He is not only able to cast wicked men into hell, but He can most easily do it. Sometimes an earthly prince meets with a great deal of difficulty to subdue a rebel that has found means to fortify himself and has made himself strong by the number of his followers. But it is not so with God. There is no fortress that is any defence against the power of God. Though hand join in hand, and vast multitudes of God's enemies combine and associate themselves, they are easily broken in pieces; they are as great heaps of light chaff before the whirlwind, or large quantities of dry stubble before devouring flames. We find it easy to tread on and crush a worm that we see crawling on the earth; so it is easy for us to cut or singe a slender thread that any thing hangs by; thus easy is it for God, when He pleases, to cast his enemies down to hell. What are we, that we should think to stand before Him, at whose rebuke the earth trembles and before Whom the rocks are thrown down!

2. They *deserve* to be cast into hell; so that divine justice never stands in the way, it makes no objection against God's using His power at any moment to destroy them. Yea, on the contrary, justice calls aloud for an infinite punishment of their sins. Divine justice says of the tree that brings forth such grapes of Sodom, "Cut it down, why cumbereth it the ground?" Luke 13:7. The sword of divine justice is every moment brandished over their heads, and it is nothing but the hand of arbitrary mercy, and God's mere will, that holds it back.

3. They are already under a sentence of *condemnation* to hell. They do not only justly deserve to be cast down thither, but the sentence of the law of God, that eternal and immutable rule of righteousness that God has fixed between Him and mankind, is gone out against them and stands against them, so that they are bound over already to hell: John 3:18, "He that believeth not is condemned already." So that every unconverted man properly belongs to hell; that is his place; from thence he is: John 8:23, "Ye are from beneath," and thither he is bound; it is the place that justice, and God's word, and the sentence of his unchangeable law, assign to him.

4. They are now the objects of that very same *anger* and wrath of God, that is expressed in the torments of hell; and the reason why they do not go down to hell at each moment, is not because God, in whose power they are, is not then very angry with them, as angry as He is with many of those miserable creatures that He is now tormenting in hell, and do there feel and bear the fierceness of His wrath. Yea, God is a great deal more angry with great numbers that are now on earth, yea, doubtless, with many that are now in this congregation, that, it may be, are at ease and quiet, than He is with many of those that are now in the flames of hell.

So that it is not because God is unmindful of their wickedness, and does not resent it, that He does not let loose his hand and cut them off. God is not altogether such a one as themselves, though they may imagine Him to be so. The wrath of God burns against them; their damnation does not slumber; the pit is prepared; the fire is made ready; the furnace is now hot, ready to receive them; the flames do now rage and glow. The glittering sword is whet,[2] and held over them, and the pit hath opened its mouth under them.

5. The *devil* stands ready to fall upon them, and seize them as his own, at what moment God shall permit him. They belong to him; he has their souls in his possession, and under his dominion. The Scripture represents them as his goods, Luke 11:21. The devils watch them; they are ever by them, at their right hand; they stand waiting for them, like greedy hungry lions that see their prey, and expect to have it, but are for the present kept back; if God should withdraw His hand, by which they are restrained, they would in one moment fly upon their poor souls. The old serpent is gaping for them; hell opens its mouth wide to receive them; and if God should permit it, they would be hastily swallowed up and lost.

6. There are in the souls of wicked men those hellish *principles* reigning, that would presently kindle and flame out into hell-fire, if it were not for God's restraints. There is laid in the very nature of carnal men, a foundation for the torments of hell; there are those corrupt principles, in reigning power in them, and in full possession of them,

---

[2] Sharpened.

that are the beginnings of hell-fire. These principles are active and powerful, exceeding violent in their nature, and if it were not for the restraining hand of God upon them, they would soon break out; they would flame out after the same manner as the same corruptions, the same enmity does in the hearts of damned souls, and would beget the same torments in them as they do in them. The souls of the wicked are in Scripture compared to the troubled sea, Isaiah 57:20. For the present, God restrains their wickedness by His mighty power, as He does the raging waves of the troubled sea, saying, "Hitherto shalt thou come, but no further;"[3] but if God should withdraw that restraining power, it would soon carry all before it. Sin is the ruin and misery of the soul; it is destructive in its nature; and if God should leave it without restraint, there would need nothing else to make the soul perfectly miserable. The corruption of the heart of man is a thing that is immoderate and boundless in its fury; and while wicked men live here, it is like fire pent up by God's restraints; whereas if it were let loose, it would set on fire the course of nature; and as the heart is now a sink of sin, so, if sin was not restrained, it would immediately turn the soul into a fiery oven or a furnace of fire and brimstone.

7. It is no security to wicked men for one moment, that there are no visible means of death at hand. It is no security to a natural man, that he is now in health, and that he does not see which way he should now immediately go out of the world by any accident, and that there is no visible danger in any respect in his circumstances. The manifold and continual experience of the world in all ages shows that this is no evidence that a man is not on the very brink of eternity and that the next step will not be into another world. The unseen, unthought of ways and means of persons going suddenly out of the world are innumerable and inconceivable. Unconverted men walk over the pit of hell on a rotten covering, and there are innumerable places in this covering so weak that they will not bear their weight, and these places are not seen. The arrows of death fly unseen at noonday;[4] the sharpest sight cannot discern them. God has so many different, unsearchable ways of taking wicked men out of the world and sending them to hell, that there is nothing to make it appear that God had need to be at the expense of a miracle, or go out of the ordinary course of His providence, to destroy any wicked man, at any moment. All the means that there are of sinners going out of the world, are so in God's hands and so absolutely subject to His power and determination, that it does not depend at all less on the mere will of God, whether sinners shall at any moment go to hell, than if means were never made use of or at all concerned in the case.

8. Natural men's *prudence* and *care* to preserve their own lives, or the care of others to preserve them, do not secure them a moment. This, divine providence and universal experience do also bear testimony to. There is this clear evidence that men's own wisdom is no security to them from death, that if it were otherwise we should see some difference between the wise and politic men of the world and others, with regard to their liableness to early and unexpected death; but how is it in fact? Ecclesiastes 2:16, "How dieth the wise man? As the fool."

9. All wicked men's *pains* and *contrivance* they use to escape hell, while they continue to reject Christ and so remain wicked men, do not secure them from hell

---

[3] Job 38:11.
[4] Psalm 91:5: "Thou shalt not be afraid for the terror by night; nor for the arrow that flieth by day."

one moment. Almost every natural man that hears of hell, flatters himself that he shall escape it; he depends upon himself for his own security; he flatters himself in what he has done, in what he is now doing, or what he intends to do; everyone lays out matters in his own mind how he shall avoid damnation and flatters himself that he contrives well for himself, and that his schemes will not fail. They hear indeed that there are but few saved and that the bigger part of men that have died heretofore are gone to hell; but each one imagines that he lays out matters better for his own escape than others have done; he does not intend to come to that place of torment; he says within himself that he intends to take care that shall be effectual and to order matters so for himself as not to fail.

But the foolish children of men do miserably delude themselves in their own schemes and in their confidence in their own strength and wisdom; they trust to nothing but a shadow. The greater part of those that heretofore have lived under the same means of grace, and are now dead, are undoubtedly gone to hell; and it was not because they were not as wise as those that are now alive; it was not because they did not lay out matters as well for themselves to secure their own escape. If it were so that we could come to speak with them, and could inquire of them, one by one, whether they expected, when alive, and when they used to hear about hell, ever to be subjects of that misery, we, doubtless, should hear one and another reply, "No, I never intended to come here; I had laid out matters otherwise in my mind; I thought I should contrive well for myself; I thought my scheme good; I intended to take effectual care; but it came upon me unexpectedly; I did not look for it at that time, and in that manner; it came as a thief; death outwitted me; God's wrath was too quick for me; O my cursed foolishness! I was flattering myself and pleasing myself with vain dreams of what I would do hereafter; and when I was saying, peace and safety, then sudden destruction came upon me."

10. God has laid Himself under *no obligation,* by any promise, to keep any natural man out of hell one moment; God certainly has made no promises either of eternal life, or of any deliverance or preservation from eternal death, but what are contained in the covenant of grace, the promises that are given in Christ, in whom all the promises are yea and amen. But surely they have no interest in the promises of the covenant of grace that are not the children of the covenant, and that do not believe in any of the promises of the covenant, and have no interest in the Mediator of the covenant.

So that, whatever some have imagined and pretended about promises made to natural men's earnest seeking and knocking, it is plain and manifest that whatever pains a natural man takes in religion, whatever prayers he makes, till he believes in Christ, God is under no manner of obligation to keep him a moment from eternal destruction.

So that thus it is, that natural men are held in the hand of God, over the pit of hell; they have deserved the fiery pit and are already sentenced to it; and God is dreadfully provoked; His anger is as great towards them as to those that are actually suffering the executions of the fierceness of His wrath in hell, and they have done nothing in the least to appease or abate that anger; neither is God in the least bound by any promise to hold them up one moment; the devil is waiting for them; hell is gaping for them; the flames gather and flash about them, and would fain lay hold on them and swallow them up; the fire pent up in their own hearts is struggling to break out; and they have no interest in any Mediator; there are no means within reach that can be any security to them. In short, they have no refuge, nothing to take hold of; all that preserves them every moment is the mere arbitrary will and uncovenanted, unobliged forbearance of an incensed God.

Application

The use of this awful subject may be of awakening unconverted persons in this congregation. This that you have heard is the case of every one of you that are out of Christ. That world of mercy, that lake of burning brimstone, is extended abroad under you. There is the dreadful pit of the glowing flames of the wrath of God; there is hell's wide gaping mouth open; and you have nothing to stand upon, nor any thing to take hold of. There is nothing between you and hell but the air; it is only the power and mere pleasure of God that holds you up.

You probably are not sensible of this; you find you are kept out of hell but do not see the hand of God in it; but look at other things, as the good state of your bodily constitution, your care of your own life, and the means you use for your own preservation. But indeed these things are nothing; if God should withdraw His hand, they would avail no more to keep you from falling than the thin air to hold up a person that is suspended in it.

Your wickedness makes you, as it were, heavy as lead and to tend downwards with great weight and pressure towards hell; and if God should let you go, you would immediately sink and swiftly descend and plunge into the bottomless gulf, and your healthy constitution, and your own care and prudence, and best contrivance, and all your righteousness, would have no more influence to uphold you and keep you out of hell, than a spider's web would have to stop a falling rock. Were it not that so is the sovereign pleasure of God, the earth would not bear you one moment; for you are a burden to it; the creation groans with you; the creature is made subject to the bondage of your corruption, not willingly; the sun does not willingly shine upon you to give you light to serve sin and Satan; the earth does not willingly yield her increase to satisfy your lusts; nor is it willingly a stage for your wickedness to be acted upon; the air does not willingly serve you for breath to maintain the flame of life in your vitals while you spend your life in the service of God's enemies. God's creatures are good, and were made for men to serve God with, and do not willingly subserve to any other purpose, and groan when they are abused to purposes so directly contrary to their nature and end. And the world would spew you out, were it not for the sovereign hand of Him who hath subjected it in hope. There are the black clouds of God's wrath now hanging directly over your heads, full of the dreadful storm and big with thunder; and were it not for the restraining hand of God, it would immediately burst forth upon you. The sovereign pleasure of God, for the present, stays His rough wind; otherwise it would come with fury, and your destruction would come like a whirlwind, and you would be like the chaff of the summer threshing floor.

The wrath of God is like great waters that are dammed for the present; they increase more and more, and rise higher and higher, till an outlet is given; and the longer the stream is stopped, the more rapid and mighty is its course when once it is let loose. It is true that judgment against your evil works has not been executed hitherto; the floods of God's vengeance have been withheld; but your guilt in the meantime is constantly increasing, and you are every day treasuring up more wrath, the waters are continually rising and waxing more and more mighty; and there is nothing but the mere pleasure of God that holds the waters back that are unwilling to be stopped and press hard to go forward. If God should only withdraw His hand from the floodgate, it would immediately fly open, and the fiery floods of the fierceness and wrath of God would rush forth with inconceivable fury and would come upon you with omnipotent power; and if your strength were ten thousand times greater than it is, yea, ten thousand times greater than the strength of the stoutest, sturdiest devil in hell, it would be nothing to withstand or endure it.

The bow of God's wrath is bent, and the arrow made ready on the string, and justice bends the arrow at your heart and strains the bow, and it is nothing but the mere pleasure of God, and that of an angry God, without any promise or obligation at all, that keeps the arrow one moment from being made drunk with your blood.

Thus are all you that never passed under a great change of heart, by the mighty power of the Spirit of God upon your souls; all that were never born again, and made new creatures, and raised from being dead in sin, to a state of new, and before altogether unexperienced light and life (however you may have reformed your life in many things, and may have had religious affections, and may keep up a form of religion in your families, and closets, and in the houses of God, and may be strict in it), you are thus in the hands of an angry God; it is nothing but His mere pleasure that keeps you from being this moment swallowed up in everlasting destruction.

However unconvinced you may now be of the truth of what you hear, by and by you will be fully convinced of it. Those that are gone from being in the like circumstances with you, see that it was so with them; for destruction came suddenly upon most of them, when they expected nothing of it and while they were saying, "Peace and safety;" now they see that those things that they depended on for peace and safety were nothing but thin air and empty shadows.

The God that holds you over the pit of hell, much as one holds a spider, or some loathsome insect, over the fire, abhors you and is dreadfully provoked; His wrath towards you burns like fire; He looks upon you as worthy of nothing else but to be cast into the fire; He is of purer eyes than to bear to have you in His sight; you are ten thousand times more abominable in His eyes than the most hateful and venomous serpent is in ours. You have offended Him infinitely more than ever a stubborn rebel did his prince; and yet it is nothing but His hand that holds you from falling into the fire every moment; it is to be ascribed to nothing else, that you did not go to hell the last night, that you were suffered to awake again in this world, after you closed your eyes to sleep; and there is no other reason to be given, why you have not dropped into hell since you arose in the morning, but that God's hand has held you up; there is no other reason to be given why you have not gone to hell, since you have sat here in the house of God, provoking His pure eyes by your sinful, wicked manner of attending His solemn worship; yea, there is nothing else that is to be given as a reason why you do not this very moment drop down into hell.

O sinner! consider the fearful danger you are in; it is a great furnace of wrath, a wide and bottomless pit, full of the fire of wrath, that you are held over in the hand of that God, whose wrath is provoked and incensed as much against you, as against many of the damned in hell; you hang by a slender thread, with the flames of divine wrath flashing about it and ready every moment to singe it and burn it asunder; and you have no interest in any Mediator and nothing to lay hold of to save yourself, nothing to keep off the flames of wrath, nothing of your own, nothing that you ever have done, nothing that you can do to induce God to spare you one moment.

And consider here more particularly several things concerning that wrath that you are in such danger of.

1. *Whose* wrath it is. It is the wrath of the infinite God. If it were only the wrath of man, though it were of the most potent prince, it would be comparatively little to be regarded. The wrath of kings is very much dreaded, especially of absolute monarchs that have the possessions and lives of their subjects wholly in their power, to be disposed of at their mere will. Proverbs 20:2, "The fear of a king is as the roaring of a lion: whoso provoketh him to anger sinneth against his own soul." The subject that very much enrages an arbitrary prince is liable to suffer the most extreme torments that human art can invent or human power can inflict. But the greatest earthly potentates, in their greatest majesty and strength, and when clothed in their greatest terrors, are but feeble, despicable worms of the dust, in comparison of the great and almighty Creator and King of heaven and earth; it is but little that they can do, when most enraged and when they have exerted the utmost of their fury. All the kings of the earth, before God, are as grasshoppers; they are nothing and less than nothing; both their love and their hatred is to be despised. The wrath of the great King of kings is as much more terrible than theirs, as His majesty is greater. Luke 12:4–5, "And I say unto you, my friends, Be not afraid of them that kill the body, and after that, have no more that they can do. But I will forewarn you whom ye shall fear: Fear him, which after he hath killed, hath power to cast into hell; yea, I say unto you, Fear him."

2. It is the *fierceness* of His wrath that you are exposed to. We often read of the fury of God; as in Isaiah 59:18: "According to their deeds, accordingly he will repay fury to his adversaries." So Isaiah 66:15, "For behold, the Lord will come with fire, and with his chariots like a whirlwind, to render his anger with fury, and his rebuke with flames of fire." And so in many other places. So Revelation 19:15. There we read of "the winepress of the fierceness and wrath of Almighty God." The words are exceedingly terrible; if it had only been said, "the wrath of God," the words would have implied that which is infinitely dreadful; but it is not only said so, but "the fierceness and wrath of God," the fury of God! the fierceness of Jehovah! Oh how dreadful must that be! Who can utter or conceive what such expressions carry in them! But it is also "the fierceness and wrath of Almighty God." As though there would be a very great manifestation of His almighty power in what the fierceness of His wrath should inflict, as though omnipotence should be, as it were, enraged and exerted, as men are wont to exert their strength in the fierceness of their wrath. Oh! then, what will be the consequence! What will become of the poor worm that shall suffer it! Whose hands can be strong! And whose heart endure! To what a dreadful, inexpressible, inconceivable depth of misery must the poor creature be sunk who shall be the subject of this!

Consider this, you that are here present, that yet remain in an unregenerate state. That God will execute the fierceness of His anger, implies that He will inflict wrath without any pity; when God beholds the ineffable extremity of your case, and sees your torment so vastly disproportioned to your strength, and sees how your poor soul is crushed and sinks down, as it were, into an infinite gloom, He will have no compassion upon you; He will not forbear the executions of his wrath or in the least lighten His hand; there shall be no moderation or mercy, nor will God then at all stay His rough wind; He will have no regard to your welfare, nor be at all careful lest you should suffer too much in any other sense, than only that you should not suffer beyond what strict justice requires; nothing shall be withheld because it is so hard for you to bear. Ezekiel 8:18, "Therefore will I also deal in fury: mine eye shall not spare, neither will I have pity: and though they cry in mine ears with a loud voice, yet will I not hear them." Now God stands ready to pity you; this is a day of mercy; you may cry now with some encouragement of obtaining mercy; but when once the day of mercy is past, your most lamentable and dolorous cries and shrieks will be in vain; you will be wholly lost and thrown away of God, as to any regard to your welfare; God will have no other use to put you to but to suffer misery; you shall be continued in being to no other end; for you will be a vessel of wrath fitted to destruction; and there will be no other use of this vessel but to be filled full of wrath; God will be so far from pitying you when you cry to him, that it is said he will only "laugh and mock," Proverbs 1:25–26, &c.

How awful are those words, Isaiah 63:3, which are the words of the great God: "I will tread them in mine anger, and trample them in my fury; and their blood shall be sprinkled upon my garments, and I will stain all my raiment." It is perhaps impossible to conceive of words that carry in them greater manifestations of these three things, viz., contempt, and hatred, and fierceness of indignation. If you cry to God to pity you, He will be so far from pitying you in your doleful case, or showing you the least regard or favor, that instead of that He will only tread you under foot; and though He will know that you cannot bear the weight of omnipotence treading upon you, He will not regard that, but He will crush you under His feet without mercy; He will crush out your blood and make it fly, and it shall be sprinkled on His garments, so as to stain all His raiment. He will not only hate you, but He will have you in the utmost contempt; no place shall be thought fit for you but under His feet, to be trodden down as the mire in the streets.

3. The *misery* you are exposed to is that which God will inflict to that end, that He might show what that wrath of Jehovah is. God hath had it on His heart to show to angels and men both how excellent His love is and also how terrible His wrath is. Sometimes earthly kings have a mind to show how terrible their wrath is, by the extreme punishments they would execute on those that provoke them. Nebuchadnezzar, that mighty and haughty monarch of the Chaldean empire, was willing to show his wrath when enraged with Shadrach, Meshech, and Abednego[5] and accordingly gave order that the burning fiery furnace should be heated seven times hotter than it was before; doubtless, it was raised to the utmost degree of fierceness that human art could raise it; but the great God is also willing to show His wrath and magnify His awful Majesty and mighty power in the extreme sufferings of His enemies. Romans 9:22, "What if God, willing to show his wrath, and to make his power known, endured with much long-suffering, the vessels of wrath fitted to destruction?" And seeing this is His design, and what He has determined, to show how terrible the unmixed, unrestrained wrath, the fury, and fierceness of Jehovah is, He will do it to effect. There will be something accomplished and brought to pass that will be dreadful

---

[5] As described in Daniel 3:1–30.

with a witness. When the great and angry God hath risen up and executed His awful vengeance on the poor sinner and the wretch is actually suffering the infinite weight and power of his indignation, then will God call upon the whole universe to behold that awful majesty and mighty power that is to be seen in it. Isaiah 33:12–14, "And the people shall be as the burnings of lime: as thorns cut up shall they be burnt in the fire. Hear, ye that are afar off, what I have done; and ye that are near, acknowledge my might. The sinners in Zion are afraid; fearfulness hath surprised the hypocrites," &c.

Thus it will be with you that are in an unconverted state, if you continue in it; the infinite might, and majesty, and terribleness of the Omnipotent God shall be magnified upon you in the ineffable strength of your torments; you shall be tormented in the presence of holy angels, and in the presence of the Lamb; and when you shall be in this state of suffering, the glorious inhabitants of heaven shall go forth and look on the awful spectacle, that they may see what the wrath and fierceness of the Almighty is; and when they have seen it, they will fall down and adore that great power and majesty. Isaiah 66:23–24, "And it shall come to pass, that from one new moon to another, and from one Sabbath to another, shall all flesh come to worship before me, saith the Lord. And they shall go forth and look upon the carcasses of the men that have transgressed against me; for their worm shall not die, neither shall their fire be quenched; and they shall be an abhorring unto all flesh."

4. It is everlasting wrath. It would be dreadful to suffer this fierceness and wrath of Almighty God one moment; but you must suffer it to all eternity. There will be no end to this exquisite horrible misery. When you look forward, you shall see a long forever, a boundless duration before you, which will swallow up your thoughts, and amaze your soul; and you will absolutely despair of ever having any deliverance, any end, any mitigation, any rest at all. You will know certainly that you must wear out long ages, millions of millions of ages, in wrestling and conflicting with this almighty merciless vengeance; and then when you have so done, when so many ages have actually been spent by you in this manner, you will know that all is but a point to what remains. So that your punishment will indeed be infinite. Oh, who can express what the state of a soul in such circumstances is! All that we can possibly say about it gives but a very feeble, faint representation of it; it is inexpressible and inconceivable: For "who knows the power of God's anger?"[6]

How dreadful is the state of those that are daily and hourly in the danger of this great wrath and infinite misery! But this is the dismal case of every soul in this congregation that has not been born again, however moral and strict, sober and religious, they may otherwise be. Oh that you would consider it, whether you be young or old! There is reason to think that there are many in this congregation now hearing this discourse that will actually be the subjects of this very misery to all eternity. We know not who they are, or in what seats they sit, or what thoughts they now have. It may be they are now at ease, and hear all these things without much disturbance, and are now flattering themselves that they are not the persons, promising themselves that they shall escape. If they knew that there was one person, and but one, in the whole congregation, that was to be the subject of this misery, what an awful thing would it be to think of! If we knew who it was, what an awful sight would

---

[6] Psalm 90:11.

it be to see such a person! How might all the rest of the congregation lift up a lamentable and bitter cry over him! But, alas! instead of one, how many is it likely will remember this discourse in hell? And it would be a wonder, if some that are now present should not be in hell in a very short time, even before this year is out. And it would be no wonder if some persons, that now sit here, in some seats of this meetinghouse, in health, quiet and secure, should be there before tomorrow morning. Those of you that finally continue in a natural condition, that shall keep out of hell longest will be there in a little time! your damnation does not slumber; it will come swiftly, and, in all probability, very suddenly upon many of you. You have reason to wonder that you are not already in hell. It is doubtless the case of some whom you have seen and known, that never deserved hell more than you, and that heretofore appeared as likely to have been now alive as you. Their case is past all hope; they are crying in extreme misery and perfect despair; but here you are in the land of the living and in the house of God, and have an opportunity to obtain salvation. What would not those poor damned hopeless souls give for one day's opportunity such as you now enjoy!

And now you have an extraordinary opportunity, a day wherein Christ has thrown the door of mercy wide open, and stands in calling and crying with a loud voice to poor sinners; a day wherein many are flocking to Him, and pressing into the kingdom of God. Many are daily coming from the east, west, north and south; many that were very lately in the same miserable condition that you are in, are now in a happy state, with their hearts filled with love to Him who has loved them and washed them from their sins in His own blood, and rejoicing in hope of the glory of God. How awful it is to be left behind at such a day! To see so many others feasting, while you are pining and perishing! To see so many rejoicing and singing for joy of heart, while you have cause to mourn for sorrow of heart and howl for vexation of spirit! How can you rest one moment in such a condition? Are not your souls as precious as the souls of the people at Suffield,[7] where they are flocking from day to day to Christ?

Are there not many here who have lived long in the world, and are not to this day born again? and so are aliens from the commonwealth of Israel, and have done nothing ever since they have lived, but treasure up wrath against the day of wrath? Oh, sirs, your case, in an especial manner, is extremely dangerous. Your guilt and hardness of heart is extremely great. Do you not see how generally persons of your years are passed over and left, in the present remarkable and wonderful dispensation of God's mercy? You had need to consider yourselves and awake thoroughly out of sleep. You cannot bear the fierceness and wrath of the infinite God. And you, young men and young women, will you neglect this precious season which you now enjoy, when so many others of your age are renouncing all youthful vanities and flocking to Christ? You especially have now an extraordinary opportunity; but if you neglect it, it will soon be with you as with those persons who spent all the precious days of youth in sin and are now come to such a dreadful pass in blindness and hardness. And you, children, who are unconverted, do not you know that you are going down to hell, to bear the dreadful wrath of that God who is now angry with you every day and every night? Will you be content to be the children of the devil, when so many

---

[7] Edwards's note: "A town in the neighborhood."

other children in the land are converted and are become the holy and happy children of the King of kings?

And let every one that is yet of Christ, and hanging over the pit of hell, whether they be old men and women, or middle aged, or young people, or little children, now hearken to the loud calls of God's word and providence. This acceptable year of the Lord, a day of such great favors to some, will doubtless be a day of as remarkable vengeance to others. Men's hearts harden, and their guilt increases apace at such a day as this, if they neglect their souls; and never was there so great danger of such persons being given up to hardness of heart and blindness of mind. God seems now to be hastily gathering in His elect in all parts of the land; and probably the greater part of adult persons that ever shall be saved will be brought in now in a little time and that it will be as it was on the great out-pouring of the Spirit upon the Jews in the apostles' days; the election will obtain, and the rest will be blinded. If this should be the case with you, you will eternally curse this day, and will curse the day that ever you were born to see such a season of the pouring out of God's Spirit, and will wish that you had died and gone to hell before you had seen it. Now undoubtedly it is, as it was in the days of John the Baptist, the axe is in an extraordinary manner laid at the root of the trees, that every tree which brings not forth good fruit may be hewn down and cast into the fire.[8]

Therefore, let every one that is out of Christ, now awake and fly from the wrath to come. The wrath of Almighty God is now undoubtedly hanging over a great part of this congregation: Let every one fly out of Sodom: "Haste and escape for your lives, look not behind you, escape to the mountain, lest you be consumed."[9]

1741

Benjamin Franklin
1706–1790

Eighteenth-century America produced a number of towering, versatile personalities, but none with the creative range of Benjamin Franklin. A summary of his career reads like one of Walt Whitman's catalogs of occupations: printer, publisher, journalist, essayist, scientist, philosopher, merchant, educator, inventor, politician, diplomat. "Everything," remarked Herman Melville ironically, "but a poet." Franklin possessed the kind of energy that wishes to improve nearly every aspect of life, and he combined that energy with a restless, empirical, pragmatic mode of thinking that would in time become stereotypical of the national character. That he also raised himself, as he says in the opening paragraph of his *Autobiography*, from "poverty and obscurity" to "a state of affluence and some degree of celebrity in the world" further enhances the distinctive American quality of his astounding career.

Franklin was born in Boston in 1706, the fifteenth child of a soap and candle maker. The early "poverty" in which he claims to have been raised may be more

[8] Luke 3:9.   [9] Genesis 19:17.

accurate than the "obscurity." As a respected member of the Boston community and the prestigious Old South Church, Josiah Franklin numbered among his friends many leading Boston figures, including the illustrious Samuel Sewall, whom young Franklin met at home prayer meetings. Showing signs of precocity, Franklin was sent to the Boston Grammar School, where he characteristically rose to the head of his class. The expenses of the large Franklin family, however, prevented his continuing in a college preparatory curriculum, and he was removed to a private school established to teach future tradesmen the necessary skills of "writing and arithmetic." At ten Franklin left school altogether to help in the family business, but disliking it, was officially apprenticed two years later to his half brother James, who had recently set up a printing shop in Boston. Franklin made, as he says, "great progress" in this trade and particularly enjoyed the access it gave him to books and booksellers.

Although Franklin may have turned out to be "everything but a poet," he nevertheless began his literary career with "two occasional ballads" that he single-handedly penned, printed, and peddled. But after his father ridiculed these performances and informed him that "verse makers" were generally "beggars," Franklin prudently turned his efforts to the development of a prose style that he claims in his *Autobiography* "has been of great use to me in the course of my life and was a principal means of my advancement." In 1722, the year after his brother founded the iconoclastic *New England Courant*—a newspaper Sewall characterized as "impudent"—Franklin wrote a series of humorous essays in the vein of Addison and Steele's popular *Spectator Papers* and submitted them to the *Courant* under a pseudonym. The essays appeared over the name of a "Mrs. Silence Dogood," a play on Cotton Mather's popular *Bonifacius, an Essay upon the Good* (1710), a book whose solid moral advice Franklin later admitted influenced his career. After the fourteenth "Dogood" paper, Franklin let his brother in on the author's identity, but this disclosure added to a growing tension between master and apprentice. The relationship ended bitterly the next year; Franklin violated the terms of indenture and ran off to begin a new life in Philadelphia.

He found work in Samuel Keimer's small, ill-equipped printing shop but did not stay for long. The governor of Pennsylvania, Sir William Keith, at the suggestion of Franklin's brother-in-law, decided to assist the young printer by sponsoring a trip to London, where he could master the trade, buy the latest equipment, and make important business contacts—all necessary if he were ever to run his own shop. When he reached London, Franklin learned that he could not rely on Keith's promises. Undiscouraged, he quickly found employment in a famous London printing house, where by day he perfected his craft and by evening made the acquaintance of some noted writers, scientists, and philosophers, including Hans Sloane and Bernard Mandeville. During this period he also wrote a brief metaphysical treatise, "A Dissertation on Liberty and Necessity, Pleasure and Pain." No Jonathan Edwards when it came to finely drawn speculation on freedom of the will, Franklin promptly disowned the work and later referred to it as one of the "errata" of his life.

Franklin returned to Philadelphia in 1726 and began working as a merchant's clerk. When his employer died the following year, he had little choice than go back to Keimer's printing shop. He determined to make a success of himself by adhering to a meticulous schedule of work and self-improvement and by methodically attending to every detail of daily existence with a rigor that would have pleased his Puritan forebears. Over the next three years Franklin purchased and revitalized a newspaper *(The Pennsylvania Gazette),* opened a stationer's shop, and was appointed public printer of Pennsylvania. In 1730 he married Deborah Read, whom he had first noticed the day he made his awkward entrance into Philadelphia as a runaway apprentice. Between 1733 and 1744 he founded a fire company, established America's first circulating library, was appointed deputy postmaster general of the colonies, launched a magazine, organized the American Philosophical Society, invented the popular Franklin stove, and drew up a proposal for what would become the University of Pennsylvania.

In 1732 Franklin began *Poor Richard's Almanac,* a somewhat parodic annual compendium of weather predictions, folk wisdom, poetic snippets, recipes, medical advice, proverbs, moral anecdotes, and useful information on how to make money and save time for people who had little of either. Franklin lifted domestic cost accounting to new heights: He worked unceasingly, always demanding of himself what he required in 1725 of the members of his "junto" for mutual improvement—that they "be serviceable to *mankind,* to their country, to their friends, or to themselves." Such a philosophy prompted D. H. Lawrence's famous reproach of Franklin's career: "All the qualities of a great man, and never more than a great citizen."

By 1748 Franklin had made enough money to leave the management of his various businesses in other hands so that he could concentrate his energies in two areas, science and politics, each of which earned for him an international reputation. He had begun conducting experiments in electricity in 1746, and five years later the first of many editions of *Experiments and Observations on Electricity* was published in London. Franklin had an eye for the theatrical side of science; in the summer of 1752 he performed his highly publicized kite experiments, which established the electrical nature of lightning and ensured his election to the Royal Society of London. Not one to ignore the practical application of a theoretical insight, Franklin recommended in 1753 that "pointed rods" be used on buildings to prevent damage from lightning, a suggestion soon implemented throughout the world. For painters and poets of the late eighteenth century, the bolt of lightning served as an image of political liberty. As a result of his experiments, Franklin became the embodiment of human enlightenment. To Philip Freneau, Franklin was a revolutionary philosopher "Who seized from kings their sceptred pride, / And turned the lightning's darts aside."

From his proposal for colonial unification at the Albany Congress in 1754 to his stirring speech at the Constitutional Convention in 1787, Franklin played a pivotal role in the struggle for colonial independence and the building of a new nation. In 1755 and 1756 he lent his business skills to help General Braddock obtain transportation and supplies during the French and Indian War. As a colonel of militia, he supervised the construction of forts in Pennsylvania. Between 1757 and 1762 he served as agent for the Province of Pennsylvania in London. Upon Franklin's leaving England, the philosopher David Hume wrote:

"I am very sorry that you intend soon to leave our hemisphere. America has sent us many good things,—gold, silver, sugar, tobacco, indigo, and so forth; but you are the first great man of letters, for whom we are beholden to her." Within two years Franklin was back in London—this time representing the colonies before the House of Commons to protest the Stamp Act.

Franklin returned to Philadelphia in 1775 to serve as a delegate to the Second Continental Congress and as a member of the committee appointed to draft the Declaration of Independence. Jefferson reportedly explained that Franklin was not asked to write the document because he could not have resisted the urge to include a few jokes. In 1776 Franklin sailed for Paris as a congressional minister to the Court of Louis XVI, where he secured crucial support for his homeland. He charmed Parisian society with his wit and warmth, unsuccessfully proposed marriage to Mme. Helvetius, a prominent widow (Franklin's wife had died in 1774), and printed on his small private press a series of graceful, amusing "bagatelles."

In 1781 Franklin was sent to France to negotiate a peace treaty with Great Britain, which he signed, with John Jay and John Adams, two years later. While in Paris he resumed his interest in science: He investigated the claims of Mesmer's experiments in animal magnetism, wrote *Maritime Observations* and *On the Causes and Cure of Smokey Chimneys,* and enthusiastically looked into the Montgolfier balloon ascensions. He resigned his diplomatic post in 1785 and returned to Philadelphia, where he served in the state government before being elected president of the Pennsylvanian Society for the Abolition of Slavery and a delegate to the Constitutional Convention. In 1788, "afflicted with almost constant and grievous pain," he retired altogether from public life.

On his second visit to England, during a leisurely week in August 1771, Franklin began his memoirs. He got as far as his marriage in 1730 when political responsibilities forced him to discontinue. He did not resume the task until urged by friends during his stay at Passy, a Paris suburb, to complete what one friend thought would be an "efficacious advertisement" for a new nation. Franklin complied, but this time he did not, (as he had in the opening section of the memoirs) address his writing to his son William, who had since taken up the Loyalist cause. Instead, he omitted family anecdotes and concentrated on his public career and the regimen he devised to ensure success and happiness. In 1788, back in Philadelphia, he completed another large installment and, just a few weeks before he died, added yet a fourth section, taking his career up until 1759. The uncompleted *Autobiography* passed through a number of unauthorized and unreliable editions until the original manuscript was discovered in France in 1868. Cotton Mather's "Life of Sir William Phips" (1697) had earlier used the paradigm of the self-made man in America, but Franklin's *Autobiography* transformed the rags-to-riches theme into world myth.

John Bunyan had always been one of Franklin's favorite authors, and it is not difficult to see his *Autobiography* as a kind of *Pilgrim's Progress* of the Enlightenment—a predominantly moral tale in which a "career" replaces a "calling." A secular pilgrim who never entirely relinquished his New England heritage, Franklin nevertheless permanently altered the meaning of *progress*.

Further Reading:
M. Twain, "The Late Benjamin Franklin,"
Galaxy, 1870.
C. Van Doren, *Benjamin Franklin*, 1938, 1973.
Benjamin Franklin and the American Character,
ed. C. G. Sanford, 1955.
I. Cohen, *Franklin and Newton*, 1956.
A. O. Aldridge, *Franklin and His French
Contemporaries*, 1957.
B. Granger, *Benjamin Franklin: An American
Man of Letters*, 1964.
R. F. Sayre, *The Examined Life*, 1964.
A. O. Aldridge, *Benjamin Franklin: Philosopher
and Man*, 1965.
R. Burlingame, *Benjamin Franklin: Envoy
Extraordinary*, 1967.
C. Lopez and E. W. Herbert, *The Private
Franklin: The Man and His Family*, 1975.
A. B. Tourtellot, *Benjamin Franklin: The Boston
Years*, 1977.

Texts:
The Autobiography of Benjamin Franklin, ed.
L. W. Labaree et al., 1964.
Other selections prior to 1773 are from *The
Papers of Benjamin Franklin*, ed. L. W. Labaree
et al., 21 vols., 1959–1978.
All remaining selections are from *The Writings
of Benjamin Franklin*, ed. A. H. Smyth, 10 vols.,
1905–1907.
(Some inconsistencies in spelling have been
silently corrected.)

---

from The Autobiography

from **Part One**

[The Runaway Apprentice]

Twyford, at the Bishop of St. Asaph's 1771.

. . . My Brother had in 1720 or 21, begun to print a Newspaper. It was the second
that appear'd in America, and was called *The New England Courant*. The only one
before it, was *the Boston News Letter*.[1] I remember his being dissuaded by some of his
Friends from the Undertaking, as not likely to succeed, one Newspaper being in their
Judgment enough for America. At this time 1771 there are not less than five and
twenty. He went on however with the Undertaking, and after having work'd in
composing the Types and printing off the Sheets I was employ'd to carry the Papers
thro' the Streets to the Customers. He had some ingenious Men among his Friends
who amus'd themselves by writing little Pieces for this Paper, which gain'd it Credit,
and made it more in Demand; and these Gentlemen often visited us. Hearing their
Conversations, and their Accounts of the Approbation their Papers were receiv'd with,
I was excited to try my Hand among them. But being still a Boy, and suspecting that
my Brother would object to printing any Thing of mine in his Paper if he knew it
to be mine, I contriv'd to disguise my Hand, and writing an anonymous Paper I put
it in at Night under the Door of the Printing House. It was found in the Morning
and communicated to his Writing Friends when they call'd in as usual. They read it,

---

[1] *The New England Courant* was the fourth. *The
Boston News Letter*, established April 24, 1704,
was the first continuously published newspaper

in the colonies. The earliest newspaper to
appear, *Publick Occurrences* (September 25,
1690), lasted only one issue.

commented on it in my Hearing, and I had the exquisite Pleasure, of finding it met with their Approbation, and that in their different Guesses at the Author none were named but Men of some Character among us for Learning and Ingenuity.

I suppose now that I was rather lucky in my Judges: And that perhaps they were not really so very good ones as I then esteem'd them. Encourag'd however by this, I wrote and convey'd in the same Way to the Press several more Papers,[2] which were equally approv'd, and I kept my Secret till my small Fund of Sense for such Performances was pretty well exhausted, and then I discovered it; when I began to be considered a little more by my Brother's Acquaintance, and in a manner that did not quite please him, as he thought, probably with reason, that it tended to make me too vain. And perhaps this might be one Occasion of the Differences that we frequently had about this Time. Tho' a Brother, he considered himself as my Master, and me as his Apprentice; and accordingly expected the same Services from me as he would from another; while I thought he demean'd me too much in some he requir'd of me, who from a Brother expected more Indulgence. Our Disputes were often brought before our Father, and I fancy I was either generally in the right, or else a better Pleader, because the Judgment was generally in my favour: But my Brother was passionate and had often beaten me, which I took extreamly amiss; and thinking my Apprenticeship very tedious, I was continually wishing for some Opportunity of shortening it, which at length offered in a manner unexpected.[3]

One of the Pieces in our News-Paper, on some political Point which I have now forgotten, gave Offence to the Assembly. He was taken up, censur'd and imprison'd for a Month by the Speaker's Warrant, I suppose because he would not discover his Author. I too was taken up and examin'd before the Council; but tho' I did not give them any Satisfaction, they contented themselves with admonishing me, and dismiss'd me; considering me perhaps as an Apprentice who was bound to keep his Master's Secrets. During my Brother's Confinement, which I resented a good deal, notwithstanding our private Differences, I had the Management of the Paper, and I made bold to give our Rulers some Rubs in it, which my Brother took very kindly, while others began to consider me in an unfavourable Light, as a young Genius that had a Turn for Libelling and Satyr. My Brother's Discharge was accompany'd with an Order of the House, (a very odd one) *that James Franklin should no longer print the Paper called the New England Courant.* There was a Consultation held in our Printing House among his Friends what he should do in this Case. Some propos'd to evade the Order by changing the Name of the Paper; but my Brother seeing Inconveniences in that, it was finally concluded on as a better Way, to let it be printed for the future under the Name of *Benjamin Franklin.* And to avoid the Censure of the Assembly that might fall on him, as still printing it by his Apprentice, the Contrivance was, that my old Indenture should be return'd to me with a full Discharge on the Back of it, to be shown on Occasion; but to secure to him the Benefit of my Service I was to sign new Indentures for the Remainder of the Term, which were to be kept private. A very flimsy Scheme it was, but however it was immediately executed, and the Paper went

---

[2] Franklin's 14 letters, published under the pseudonym "Silence Dogood" in *The New England Courant* between April 12 and October 8, 1722.

[3] Franklin's note: "I fancy his harsh and tyrannical Treatment of me, might be a means of impressing me with that Aversion to arbitrary Power that has stuck to me thro' my whole Life."

on accordingly under my Name for several Months. At length a fresh Difference arising between my Brother and me, I took upon me to assert my Freedom, presuming that he would not venture to produce the new Indentures. It was not fair in me to take this Advantage, and this I therefore reckon one of the first Errata[4] of my Life: But the Unfairness of it weigh'd little with me, when under the Impressions of Resentment, for the Blows his Passion too often urg'd him to bestow upon me. Tho' he was otherwise not an ill-natur'd Man: Perhaps I was too saucy and provoking.

When he found I would leave him, he took care to prevent my getting Employment in any other Printing-House of the Town, by going round and speaking to every Master, who accordingly refus'd to give me Work. I then thought of going to New York as the nearest Place where there was a Printer: and I was the rather inclin'd to leave Boston, when I reflected that I had already made myself a little obnoxious to the governing Party; and from the arbitrary Proceedings of the Assembly in my Brother's Case it was likely I might if I stay'd soon bring myself into Scrapes; and farther that my indiscrete Disputations about Religion began to make me pointed at with Horror by good People, as an Infidel or Atheist. I determin'd on the Point: but my Father now siding with my Brother, I was sensible that if I attempted to go openly, Means would be used to prevent me. My Friend Collins therefore undertook to manage a little for me. He agreed with the Captain of a New York Sloop for my Passage, under the Notion of my being a young Acquaintance of his that had got a naughty Girl with Child, whose Friends would compel me to marry her, and therefore I could not appear or come away publickly. So I sold some of my Books to raise a little Money, Was taken on board privately, and as we had a fair Wind in three Days I found my self in New York near 300 Miles from home, a Boy of but 17, without the least Recommendation to or Knowledge of any Person in the Place, and with very little Money in my Pocket.

My Inclinations for the Sea, were by this time worne out, or I might now have gratify'd them. But having a Trade, and supposing my self a pretty good Workman, I offer'd my Service to the Printer of the Place, old Mr. Wm. Bradford,[5] (who had been the first Printer in Pensilvania, but remov'd from thence upon the Quarrel of Geo. Keith).[6] He could give me no Employment, having little to do, and Help enough already: But, says he, my Son[7] at Philadelphia has lately lost his principal Hand, Aquila Rose, by Death. If you go thither I believe he may employ you. Philadelphia was 100 Miles farther. I set out, however, in a Boat for Amboy, leaving my Chest and Things to follow me round by Sea. In crossing the Bay we met with a Squall that tore our rotten Sails to pieces, prevented our getting into the Kill,[8] and drove us upon Long Island. In our Way a drunken Dutchman, who was a Passenger too, fell over board; when he was sinking I reach'd thro' the Water to his shock Pate and drew him up so that we got him in again. His Ducking sober'd him a little, and he went to sleep, taking first out of his Pocket a Book which he desir'd I would dry for him. It prov'd to be my old favourite Author Bunyan's Pilgrim's Progress in Dutch, finely printed on good Paper with copper Cuts, a Dress better than I had ever seen it wear

---

[4] Plural of Latin *erratum*: "errors."
[5] William Bradford (1663–1752), one of the chief printers in the colonies at the time.
[6] George Keith (1638–1716), a controversial Quaker leader.
[7] Andrew Bradford (1686–1742), who in 1719 published *The American Mercury,* the first newspaper printed in Pennsylvania.
[8] Narrow channel separating Staten Island, New York, from New Jersey.

in its own Language. I have since found that it has been translated into most of the Languages of Europe, and suppose it has been more generally read than any other Book except perhaps the Bible. Honest John was the first that I know of who mix'd Narration and Dialogue, a Method of Writing very engaging to the Reader, who in the most interesting Parts finds himself as it were brought into the Company, and present at the Discourse. Defoe in his Cruso, his Moll Flanders, Religious Courtship, Family Instructor, and other Pieces, has imitated it with Success. And Richardson has done the same in his Pamela, &c.[9]

When we drew near the Island we found it was at a Place where there could be no Landing, there being a great Surff on the stony Beach. So we dropt Anchor and swung round towards the Shore. Some People came down to the Water Edge and hallow'd to us, as we did to them. But the Wind was so high and the Surff so loud, that we could not hear so as to understand each other. There were Canoes on the Shore, and we made Signs and hallow'd that they should fetch us, but they either did not understand us, or thought it impracticable. So they went away, and Night coming on, we had no Remedy but to wait till the Wind should abate, and in the mean time the Boatman and I concluded to sleep if we could, and so crouded into the Scuttle with the Dutchman who was still wet, and the Spray beating over the Head of our Boat, leak'd thro' to us, so that we were soon almost as wet as he. In this Manner we lay all Night with very little Rest. But the Wind abating the next Day, we made a Shift to reach Amboy before Night, having been 30 Hours on the Water without Victuals, or any Drink but a Bottle of filthy Rum: The Water we sail'd on being salt.

In the Evening I found my self very feverish, and went in to Bed. But having read somewhere that cold Water drank plentifully was good for a Fever, I follow'd the Prescription, sweat plentifully most of the Night, my Fever left me, and in the Morning crossing the Ferry, I proceeded on my Journey, on foot, having 50 Miles to Burlington,[10] where I was told I should find Boats that would carry me the rest of the Way to Philadelphia.

It rain'd very hard all the Day, I was thoroughly soak'd and by Noon a good deal tir'd, so I stopt at a poor Inn, where I staid all Night, beginning now to wish I had never left home. I cut so miserable a Figure too, that I found by the Questions ask'd me I was suspected to be some runaway Servant, and in danger of being taken up on that Suspicion. However I proceeded the next Day, and got in the Evening to an Inn within 8 or 10 Miles of Burlington, kept by one Dr. Brown.

He entred into Conversation with me while I took some Refreshment, and finding I had read a little, became very sociable and friendly. Our Acquaintance continu'd as long as he liv'd. He had been, I imagine, an itinerant Doctor, for there was no Town in England, or Country in Europe, of which he could not give a very particular Account. He had some Letters, and was ingenious, but much of an Unbeliever, and wickedly undertook some Years after to travesty the Bible in doggrel Verse as Cotton[11] had done Virgil. By this means he set many of the Facts in a very ridiculous

[9] Samuel Richardson's *Pamela, or Virtue Rewarded* (1740) became the first novel published in the Colonies when Franklin reprinted it in 1744.

[10] Town in western New Jersey.

[11] Charles Cotton (1630–1687), author of *Scarronides, or the First Book of Virgil Travestie* (1664).

Light, and might have hurt weak minds if his Work had been publish'd: but it never was. At his House I lay that Night, and the next Morning reach'd Burlington. But had the Mortification to find that the regular Boats were gone, a little before my coming, and no other expected to go till Tuesday, this being Saturday. Wherefore I return'd to an old Woman in the Town of whom I had bought Gingerbread to eat on the Water, and ask'd her Advice; she invited me to lodge at her House till a Passage by Water should offer: and being tired with my foot Travelling, I accepted the Invitation. She understanding I was a Printer, would have had me stay at that Town and follow my Business, being ignorant of the Stock necessary to begin with. She was very hospitable, gave me a Dinner of Ox Cheek with great Goodwill, accepting only of a Pot of Ale in return. And I tho't my self fix'd till Tuesday should come. However walking in the Evening by the Side of the River a Boat came by, which I found was going towards Philadelphia, with several People in her. They took me in, and as there was no Wind, we row'd all the Way; and about Midnight not having yet seen the City, some of the Company were confident we must have pass'd it, and would row no farther, the others knew not where we were, so we put towards the Shore, got into a Creek, landed near an old Fence with the Rails of which we made a Fire, the Night being cold, in October, and there we remain'd till Daylight. Then one of the Company knew the Place to be Cooper's Creek a little above Philadelphia, which we saw as soon as we got out of the Creek, and arriv'd there about 8 or 9 a Clock, on the Sunday morning, and landed at the Market street Wharff.[12]

I have been the more particular in this Description of my Journey, and shall be so of my first Entry into that City, that you may in your Mind compare such unlikely Beginnings with the Figure I have since made there. I was in my Working Dress, my best Cloaths being to come round by Sea. I was dirty from my Journey; my Pockets were stuff'd out with Shirts and Stockings; I knew no Soul, nor where to look for Lodging. I was fatigu'd with Travelling, Rowing and Want of Rest. I was very hungry, and my whole Stock of Cash consisted of a Dutch Dollar and about a Shilling in Copper. The latter I gave the People of the Boat for my Passage, who at first refus'd it on Account of my Rowing; but I insisted on their taking it, a Man being sometimes more generous when he has but a little Money than when he has plenty, perhaps thro' Fear of being thought to have but little.

Then I walk'd up the Street, gazing about, till near the Market House I met a Boy with Bread. I had made many a Meal on Bread, and inquiring where he got it, I went immediately to the Baker's he directed me to in second Street; and ask'd for Bisket, intending such as we had in Boston, but they it seems were not made in Philadelphia, then I ask'd for a threepenny Loaf, and was told they had none such: so not considering or knowing the Difference of Money and the greater Cheapness nor the Names of his Bread, I bad him give me three penny worth of any sort. He gave me accordingly three great Puffy Rolls. I was surpriz'd at the Quantity, but took it, and having no room in my Pockets, walk'd off, with a Roll under each Arm, and eating the other. Thus I went up Market Street as far as fourth Street, passing by the Door of Mr. Read, my future Wife's Father, when she standing at the Door saw me, and thought I made as I certainly did a most awkward ridiculous Appearance. Then I turn'd and went

[12] The landing took place sometime in October 1723.

down Chestnut Street and part of Walnut Street, eating my Roll all the Way, and coming round found my self again at Market Street Wharff, near the Boat I came in, to which I went for a Draught of the River Water, and being fill'd with one of my Rolls, gave the other two to a Woman and her Child that came down the River in the Boat with us and were waiting to go farther. Thus refresh'd I walk'd again up the Street, which by this time had many clean dress'd People in it who were all walking the same Way; I join'd them, and thereby was led into the great Meeting House of the Quakers near the Market. I sat down among them, and after looking round a while and hearing nothing said, being very drowzy thro' Labour and want of Rest the preceding Night, I fell fast asleep, and continu'd so till the Meeting broke up, when one was kind enough to rouse me. This was therefore the first House I was in or slept in, in Philadelphia.

Walking again down towards the River, and looking in the Faces of People, I met a young Quaker Man whose Countenance I lik'd, and accosting him requested he would tell me where a Stranger could get Lodging. We were then near the Sign of the Three Mariners. Here, says he, is one Place that entertains Strangers, but it is not a reputable House; if thee wilt walk with me, I'll show thee a better. He brought me to the Crooked Billet in Water-Street. Here I got a Dinner. And while I was eating it, several sly Questions were ask'd me, as it seem'd to be suspected from my youth and Appearance, that I might be some Runaway. After Dinner my Sleepiness return'd: and being shown to a Bed, I lay down without undressing, and slept till Six in the Evening; was call'd to Supper; went to Bed again very early and slept soundly till the next Morning. Then I made my self as tidy as I could, and went to Andrew Bradford the Printer's. I found in the Shop the old Man his Father, whom I had seen at New York, and who travelling on horse back had got to Philadelphia before me. He introduc'd me to his Son, who receiv'd me civilly, gave me a Breakfast, but told me he did not at present want a Hand, being lately supply'd with one. But there was another Printer in town lately set up, one Keimer,[13] who perhaps might employ me; if not, I should be welcome to lodge at his House, and he would give me a little Work to do now and then till fuller Business should offer.

The old Gentleman said, he would go with me to the new Printer: and when we found him, Neighbour, says Bradford, I have brought to see you a young Man of your Business, perhaps you may want such a One. He ask'd me a few Questions, put a Composing Stick in my Hand to see how I work'd, and then said he would employ me soon, tho' he had just then nothing for me to do. And taking old Bradford whom he had never seen before, to be one of the Towns People that had a Good Will for him, enter'd into a Conversation on his present Undertaking and Prospects; while Bradford not discovering[14] that he was the other Printer's Father, on Keimer's saying he expected soon to get the greatest Part of the Business into his own Hands, drew him on by artful Questions and starting little Doubts, to explain all his Views, what interest he rely'd on, and in what manner he intended to proceed. I who stood by and heard all, saw immediately that one of them was a crafty old Sophister, and the

---

[13] Samuel Keimer (ca. 1688–1742) had deserted his wife in London and come to Philadelphia the year before in order to establish himself as a printer. At the time Franklin met him, Keimer was in his mid-thirties. After failing at the printer's trade, he left Philadelphia in 1730.
[14] Disclosing.

other a mere Novice. Bradford left me with Keimer, who was greatly surpriz'd when I told him who the old Man was.

Keimer's Printing House I found, consisted of an old shatter'd Press, and one small worn-out Fount of English,[15] which he was then using himself, composing in it an Elegy on Aquila Rose before-mentioned, an ingenious young Man of excellent Character much respected in the Town, Clerk of the Assembly, and a pretty Poet. Keimer made Verses, too, but very indifferently. He could not be said to write them, for his Manner was to compose them in the Types directly out of his Head; so there being no Copy, but one Pair of Cases, and the Elegy likely to require all the Letter, no one could help him. I endeavour'd to put his Press (which he had not yet us'd, and of which he understood nothing) into Order fit to be work'd with; and promising to come and print off his Elegy as soon as he should have got it ready, I return'd to Bradford's who gave me a little job to do for the present, and there I lodged and dieted. A few Days after Keimer sent for me to print off the Elegy.[16] And now he had got another Pair of Cases,[17] and a Pamphlet to reprint, on which he set me to work.

These two Printers I found poorly qualified for their Business. Bradford had not been bred to it, and was very illiterate; and Keimer tho' something of a Scholar, was a mere Compositor, knowing nothing of Presswork. He had been one of the French Prophets[18] and could act their enthusiastic Agitations. At this time he did not profess any particular Religion, but something of all on occasion; was very ignorant of the World, and had, as I afterwards found, a good deal of the Knave in his Composition. He did not like my Lodging at Bradford's while I work'd with him. He had a House indeed, but without Furniture, so he could not lodge me: But he got me a Lodging at Mr. Read's before-mentioned, who was the Owner of his House. And my Chest and Clothes being come by this time, I made rather a more respectable Appearance in the Eyes of Miss Read, than I had done when she first happen'd to see me eating my Roll in the Street. . . .

from Part Two: Continuation of the Account of My Life.

[The Project for Moral Perfection]

Begun at Passy[19] 1784

. . . I had been religiously educated as a Presbyterian; and tho' some of the Dogmas of that Persuasion, such as the Eternal Decrees of God, Election, Reprobation, &c. appear'd to me unintelligible, others doubtful, and I early absented myself from the Public Assemblies of the Sect, Sunday being my Studying-Day, I never was without some religious Principles; I never doubted, for instance, the Existance of the Deity,

---

[15] A "fount," or font, of type contains the complete alphabet of single letters cast in the same size and design. "English" was an oversized, and hence cumbersome, typeface.

[16] A single-leaf broadside, sold by Keimer for twopence.

[17] Trays of type.

[18] Sect of French Protestant refugees in England in 1706. Subject to trances and revelations, its members proclaimed the imminent coming of a messianic kingdom.

[19] Suburb of Paris where Franklin stayed while serving as negotiator for the United States during the writing of the Treaty of Paris.

that he made the World, and govern'd it by his Providence; that the most acceptable Service of God was the doing Good to Man; that our Souls are immortal; and that all Crime will be punished and Virtue rewarded either here or hereafter; these I esteem'd the Essentials of every Religion, and being to be found in all the Religions we had in our Country I respected them all, tho' with different degrees of Respect as I found them more or less mix'd with other Articles which without any Tendency to inspire, promote or confirm Morality, serv'd principally to divide us and make us unfriendly to one another. This Respect to all, with an Opinion that the worst had some good Effects, induc'd me to avoid all Discourse that might tend to lessen the good Opinion another might have of his own Religion; and as our Province increas'd in People and new Places of worship were continually wanted, and generally erected by voluntary Contribution, my Mite for such purpose, whatever might be the Sect, was never refused.[20]

Tho' I seldom attended any Public Worship, I had still an Opinion of its Propriety, and of its Utility when rightly conducted, and I regularly paid my annual Subscription for the Support of the only Presbyterian Minister or Meeting we had in Philadelphia. He us'd to visit me sometimes as a Friend, and admonish me to attend his Administrations, and I was now and then prevail'd on to do so, once for five Sundays successively. Had he been, *in my Opinion,* a good Preacher perhaps I might have continued, notwithstanding the occasion I had for the Sunday's Leisure in my Course of Study: but his Discourses were chiefly either polemic Arguments, or Explications of the Peculiar Doctrines of our Sect, and were all to me very dry, uninteresting and unedifying, since not a single moral Principle was inculcated or enforc'd, their Aim seeming to be rather to make us Presbyterians than good Citizens. At length he took for his Text that Verse of the 4th Chapter of Philippians, *Finally, Brethren, Whatsoever Things are true, honest, just, pure, lovely, or of good report, if there be any virtue, or any praise, think on these Things;*[21] and I imagin'd in a Sermon on such a Text, we could not miss of having some Morality: but he confin'd himself to five Points only as meant by the Apostle, viz. 1. Keeping holy the Sabbath Day. 2. Being diligent in Reading the Holy Scriptures. 3. Attending duly the Publick Worship. 4. Partaking of the Sacrament. 5. Paying a due Respect to God's Ministers. These might be all good Things, but as they were not the kind of good Things that I expected from that Text, I despaired of ever meeting with them from any other, was disgusted, and attended his Preaching no more. I had some Years before compos'd a little Liturgy or Form of Prayer for my own private Use, viz, in 1728. entitled, *Articles of Belief and Acts of Religion.* I return'd to the Use of this, and went no more to the public Assemblies. My Conduct might be blameable, but I leave it without attempting farther to excuse it, my present purpose being to relate Facts, and not to make Apologies for them.

It was about this time that I conceiv'd the bold and arduous Project of arriving at moral Perfection.[22] I wish'd to live without committing any Fault at any time; I would conquer all that either Natural Inclination, Custom, or Company might lead me into. As I knew, or thought I knew, what was right and wrong, I did not see why

[20] In 1788 Franklin was one of the largest donors to the erection of a synagogue for the Jewish population of Philadelphia.

[21] Philippians 4:8.

[22] Franklin had at one time planned to write a book on moral improvement.

I might not *always* do the one and avoid the other. But I soon found I had undertaken a Task of more Difficulty than I had imagined. While my *Attention was taken up* in guarding against one Fault, I was often surpriz'd by another. Habit took the Advantage of Inattention. Inclination was sometimes too strong for Reason. I concluded at length, that the mere speculative Conviction that it was our Interest to be compleatly virtuous, was not sufficient to prevent our Slipping, and that the contrary Habits must be broken and good ones acquired and established, before we can have any Dependance on a steady uniform Rectitude of Conduct. For this purpose I therefore contriv'd the following Method.

In the various Enumerations of the moral Virtues I had met with in my Reading, I found the Catalogue more or less numerous, as different Writers included more or fewer Ideas under the same Name. Temperance, for Example, was by some confin'd to Eating and Drinking, while by others it was extended to mean the moderating every other Pleasure, Appetite, Inclination or Passion, bodily or mental, even to our Avarice and Ambition. I propos'd to myself, for the sake of Clearness, to use rather more Names with fewer Ideas annex'd to each, than a few Names with more Ideas; and I included under Thirteen Names of Virtues all that at that time occurr'd to me as necessary or desirable, and annex'd to each a short Precept, which fully express'd the Extent I gave to its Meaning.

These Names of Virtues with their Precepts were

1. TEMPERANCE.

Eat not to Dulness. Drink not to Elevation.

2. SILENCE.

Speak not but what may benefit others or yourself. Avoid trifling Conversation.

3. ORDER.

Let all your Things have their Places. Let each Part of your Business have its Time.

4. RESOLUTION.

Resolve to perform what you ought. Perform without fail what you resolve.

5. FRUGALITY.

Make no Expence but to do good to others or yourself: i.e. Waste nothing.

6. INDUSTRY.

Lose no Time. Be always employ'd in something useful. Cut off all unnecessary Actions.

7. SINCERITY.

Use no hurtful Deceit. Think innocently and justly; and, if you speak, speak accordingly.

8. JUSTICE.

Wrong none, by doing Injuries or omitting the Benefits that are your Duty.

9. MODERATION.

Avoid Extreams. Forbear resenting Injuries so much as you think they deserve.

10. CLEANLINESS.

Tolerate no Uncleanness in Body, Cloaths or Habitation.

11. TRANQUILITY.

Be not disturbed at Trifles, or at Accidents common or unavoidable.

12. CHASTITY.

Rarely use Venery but for Health or Offspring; Never to Dulness, Weakness, or the Injury of your own or another's Peace or Reputation.

13. HUMILITY.

Imitate Jesus and Socrates.

My Intention being to acquire the *Habitude* of all these Virtues, I judg'd it would be well not to distract my Attention by attempting the whole at once, but to fix it on one of them at a time, and when I should be Master of that, then to proceed to another, and so on till I should have gone thro' the thirteen. And as the previous Acquisition of some might facilitate the Acquisition of certain others, I arrang'd them with that View as they stand above. *Temperance* first, as it tends to procure that Coolness and Clearness of Head, which is so necessary where constant Vigilance was to be kept up, and Guard maintained, against the unremitting Attraction of ancient Habits, and the Force of perpetual Temptations. This being acquir'd and establish'd, *Silence* would be more easy, and my Desire being to gain Knowledge at the same time that I improv'd in Virtue, and considering that in Conversation it was obtain'd rather by the use of the Ears than of the Tongue, and therefore wishing to break a Habit I was getting into of Prattling, Punning and Joking, which only made me acceptable to trifling Company, I gave *Silence* the second Place. This, and the next, *Order,* I expected would allow me more Time for attending to my Project and my Studies; RESOLUTION, once become habitual, would keep me firm in my Endeavours to obtain all the subsequent Virtues; *Frugality* and *Industry,* by freeing me from my remaining Debt, and producing Affluence and Independance, would make more easy the Practice of *Sincerity* and *Justice, &c. &c.* Conceiving then that agreable to the Advice of Pythagoras[23] in his Golden Verses daily Examination would be necessary, I contriv'd the following Method for conducting that Examination.

I made a little Book in which I allotted a Page for each of the Virtues. I rul'd each Page with red Ink, so as to have seven Columns, one for each Day of the Week, marking each Column with a Letter for the Day. I cross'd these Columns with thirteen red Lines, marking the Beginning of each Line with the first Letter of one of the Virtues, on which Line and in its proper Column I might mark by a little black Spot every Fault I found upon Examination to have been committed respecting that Virtue upon that Day.

I determined to give a Week's strict Attention to each of the Virtues successively. Thus in the first Week my great Guard was to avoid every the least Offence against Temperance, leaving the other Virtues to their ordinary Chance, only marking every Evening the Faults of the Day. Thus if in the first Week I could keep my first Line marked T clear of Spots, I suppos'd the Habit of that Virtue so much strengthen'd and its opposite weaken'd, that I might venture extending my Attention to include the next, and for the following Week keep both Lines clear of Spots. Proceeding thus to the last, I could go thro' a Course compleat in Thirteen Weeks, and four Courses in a Year. And like him who having a Garden to weed, does not attempt to eradicate all the bad Herbs at once, which would exceed his Reach and his Strength, but works on one of the Beds at a time, and having accomplish'd the first proceeds to a Second; so I should have, (I hoped) the encouraging Pleasure of seeing on my Pages the Progress I made in Virtue, by clearing successively my Lines of their Spots, till in the End by a Number of Courses, I should be happy in viewing a clean Book after a thirteen Weeks daily Examination.

Form of the Pages

		S	M	T	W	T	F	S
TEMPERANCE								
Eat not to Dulness. *Drink not to Elevation.*								
T								
S		••	•		•		•	
O		•	•	•		•	•	•
R			•			•		
F			•			•		
I					•			
S								
J								
M								
Cl.								
T								
Ch.								
H								

[23] Greek philosopher and mathematician (sixth century B.C.). Franklin intended to insert the appropriate verse: "Let sleep not close your eyes till you have thrice examined the transactions of the day: where have I strayed, what have I done, what good have I omitted?"

This my little Book had for its Motto these Lines from Addison's *Cato;*

Here will I hold: If there is a Pow'r above us,
(And that there is, all Nature cries aloud
Thro' all her Works) he must delight in Virtue,
And that which he delights in must be happy.[24]

Another from Cicero.

O Vitœ Philosophia Dux! O Virtutum indagatrix, expultrixcue vitiorum!
Unus dies bene, et ex preceptis tuis actus, peccanti immortalitati est anteponen-
dus.[25]

Another from the Proverbs of Solomon speaking of Wisdom or Virtue;

Length of Days is in her right hand, and in her Left Hand Riches and
Honours; Her Ways are Ways of Pleasantness, and all her Paths are Peace.
                                                            III, 16, 17.

And conceiving God to be the Fountain of Wisdom, I thought it right and
necessary to solicit his Assistance for obtaining it; to this End I form'd the following
little Prayer, which was prefix'd to my Tables of Examination; for daily Use.

O Powerful Goodness! bountiful Father! merciful Guide! Increase in me that
Wisdom which discovers my truest Interests; Strengthen my Resolutions to
perform what that Wisdom dictates. Accept my kind Offices to thy other
Children, as the only Return in my Power for thy continual Favours to me.

I us'd also sometimes a little Prayer which I took from Thomson's Poems. viz

Father of Light and Life, thou Good supreme,
O teach me what is good, teach me thy self!
Save me from Folly, Vanity and Vice,
From every low Pursuit, and fill my Soul
With Knowledge, conscious Peace, and Virtue pure,
Sacred, substantial, neverfading Bliss![26]

The Precept of *Order* requiring that *every Part of my Business should have its allotted
Time,* one Page in my little Book contain'd the following Scheme of Employment
for the Twenty-four Hours of a natural Day,

[24] Joseph Addison, *Cato, a Tragedy* (1713), Act V,
Sc. i, ll. 15–18.
[25] Marcus Tullius Cicero, *Tusculan Disputations,* V,
ii, 5: "O philosophy, guide of life! O seeker
out of virtues and expeller of vices! [Here
Franklin omitted several lines from the

original.] One day lived well, and according to
thy precepts, is to be preferred to an eternity of
sin."
[26] James Thomson, *The Seasons* (1726), "Winter,"
ll. 218–223.

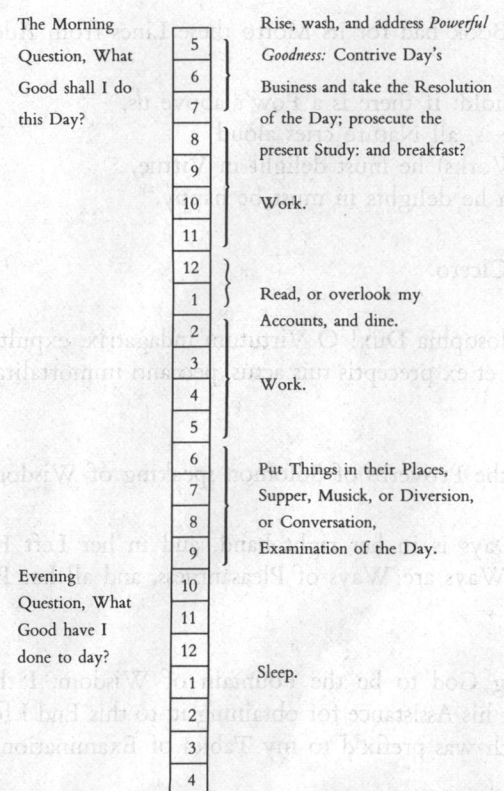

The Morning	5	Rise, wash, and address *Powerful*
Question, What		*Goodness:* Contrive Day's
Good shall I do	6	Business and take the Resolution
this Day?	7	of the Day; prosecute the
	8	present Study: and breakfast?
	9	
	10	Work.
	11	
	12	
	1	Read, or overlook my
	2	Accounts, and dine.
	3	Work.
	4	
	5	
	6	Put Things in their Places,
	7	Supper, Musick, or Diversion,
	8	or Conversation,
	9	Examination of the Day.
Evening	10	
Question, What	11	
Good have I	12	
done to day?	1	Sleep.
	2	
	3	
	4	

I enter'd upon the Execution of this Plan for Self Examination, and continu'd it with occasional Intermissions for some time. I was surpriz'd to find myself so much fuller of Faults than I had imagined, but I had the Satisfaction of seeing them diminish. To avoid the Trouble of renewing now and then my little Book, which by scraping out the Marks on the Paper of old Faults to make room for new Ones in a new Course, became full of Holes: I transferr'd my Tables and Precepts to the Ivory Leaves of a Memorandum Book, on which the Lines were drawn with red Ink that made a durable Stain, and on those Lines I mark'd my Faults with a black Lead Pencil, which Marks I could easily wipe out with a wet Sponge. After a while I went thro' one Course only in a year, and afterwards only one in several Years, till at length I omitted them entirely, being employ'd in Voyages and Business abroad with a Multiplicity of Affairs, that interfered, but I always carried my little Book with me.

My Scheme of ORDER, gave me the most Trouble, and I found, that tho' it might be practicable where a Man's Business was such as to leave him the Disposition of his Time, that of a Journey-Man Printer for instance, it was not possible to be exactly observ'd by a Master, who must mix with the World, and often receive People of Business at their own Hours. *Order* too, with regard to Places for Things, Papers, &c. I found extreamly difficult to acquire. I had not been early accustomed to *Method,* and having an exceeding good Memory, I was not so sensible of the

Inconvenience attending Want of Method. This Article therefore cost me so much painful Attention and my Faults in it vex'd me so much, and I made so little Progress in Amendment, and had such frequent Relapses, that I was almost ready to give up the Attempt, and content my self with a faulty Character in that respect. Like the Man who in buying an Ax of a Smith my neighbour, desired to have the whole of its Surface as bright as the Edge; the Smith consented to grind it bright for him if he would turn the Wheel. He turn'd while the Smith press'd the broad Face of the Ax hard and heavily on the Stone, which made the Turning of it very fatiguing. The Man came every now and then from the Wheel to see how the Work went on; and at length would take his Ax as it was without farther Grinding. No, says the Smith, Turn on, turn on; we shall have it bright by and by; as yet 'tis only speckled. Yes, says the Man; but—*I think I like a speckled Ax best.* And I believe this may have been the Case with many who having for want of some such Means as I employ'd found the Difficulty of obtaining good, and breaking bad Habits, in other Points of Vice and Virtue, have given up the Struggle, and concluded that *a speckled Ax was best.* For something that pretended to be Reason was every now and then suggesting to me, that such extream Nicety as I exacted of my self might be a kind of Foppery in Morals, which if it were known would make me ridiculous; that a perfect Character might be attended with the Inconvenience of being envied and hated; and that a benevolent Man should allow a few Faults in himself, to keep his Friends in Countenance.

In truth I found myself incorrigible with respect to *Order;* and now I am grown old, and my Memory bad, I feel very sensibly the want of it. But on the whole, tho' I never arrived at the Perfection I had been so ambitious of obtaining, but fell far short of it, yet I was by the Endeavour a better and a happier Man than I otherwise should have been, if I had not attempted it; As those who aim at perfect Writing by imitating the engraved Copies, tho' they never reach the wish'd for Excellence of those Copies, their Hand is mended by the Endeavour, and is tolerable while it continues fair and legible.

And it may be well my Posterity should be informed, that to this little Artifice, with the Blessing of God, their Ancestor ow'd the constant Felicity of his Life down to his 79th Year in which this is written. What Reverses may attend the Remainder is in the Hand of Providence: But if they arrive the Reflection on past Happiness enjoy'd ought to help his Bearing them with more Resignation. To *Temperance* he ascribes his long-continu'd Health, and what is still left to him of a good Constitution. To *Industry* and *Frugality* the early Easiness of his Circumstances, and Acquisition of his Fortune, with all that Knowledge which enabled him to be an useful Citizen, and obtain'd for him some Degree of Reputation among the Learned. To *Sincerity* and *Justice* the Confidence of his Country, and the honourable Employs it conferr'd upon him. And to the joint Influence of the whole Mass of the Virtues, even in the imperfect State he was able to acquire them, all that Evenness of Temper, and that Chearfulness in Conversation which makes his Company still sought for, and agreable even to his *younger Acquaintance. I hope therefore that some of my Descendants may follow the Example and reap the Benefit.*

It will be remark'd that, tho' my Scheme was not wholly without Religion there was in it no Mark of any of the distinguishing Tenets of any particular Sect. I had purposely avoided them; for being fully persuaded of the Utility and Excellency of my Method, and that it might be serviceable to People in all Religions, and intending some time or other to publish it, I would not have any thing in it that should prejudice any one of any Sect against it. I purposed writing a little Comment on each Virtue, in which I would have shown the Advantages of possessing it, and the Mischiefs attending its opposite Vice; and I should have called my Book the ART *of Virtue,* because it would have shown the *Means* and *Manner* of obtaining Virtue, which would have distinguish'd it from the mere Exhortation to be good, that does not instruct and indicate the Means; but is like the Apostle's Man of verbal Charity, who only, without showing to the Naked and the Hungry *how* or where they might get Cloaths or Victuals, exhorted them to be fed and clothed. *James* II, 15, 16.

But it so happened that my Intention of writing and publishing this Comment was never fulfilled. I did indeed, from time to time put down short Hints of the Sentiments, Reasonings, &c. to be made use of in it; some of which I have still by me: But the necessary close Attention to private Business in the earlier part of Life, and public Business since, have occasioned my postponing it. For it being connected in my Mind with a *great and extensive Project* that required the whole Man to execute, and which an unforeseen Succession of Employs prevented my attending to, it has hitherto remain'd unfinish'd.

In this Piece it was my Design to explain and enforce this Doctrine, that vicious Actions are not hurtful because they are forbidden, but forbidden because they are hurtful, the Nature of Man alone consider'd: That it was therefore every one's Interest to be virtuous, who wish'd to be happy even in this World. And I should from this Circumstance, there being always in the World a Number of rich Merchants, Nobility, States and Princes, who have need of honest Instruments for the Management of their Affairs, and such being so rare have endeavoured to convince young Persons, that no Qualities were so likely to make a poor Man's Fortune as those of Probity and Integrity.

My List of Virtues contain'd at first but twelve: But a Quaker Friend having kindly inform'd me that I was generally thought proud; that my Pride show'd itself frequently in Conversation; that I was not content with being in the right when discussing any Point, but was overbearing and rather insolent; of which he convinc'd me by mentioning several Instances; I determined endeavouring to cure myself if I could of this Vice or Folly among the rest, and I added *Humility* to my List, giving an extensive Meaning to the Word. I cannot boast of much Success in acquiring the *Reality* of this Virtue; but I had a good deal with regard to the *Appearance* of it. I made it a Rule to forbear all direct Contradiction to the Sentiments of others, and all positive Assertion of my own. I even forbid my self agreable to the old Laws of our Junto, the Use of every Word or Expression in the Language that imported a fix'd Opinion; such as *certainly, undoubtedly,* &c. and I adopted instead of them, *I conceive, I apprehend,* or *I imagine* a thing to be so or so, or it so appears to me at present. When another asserted something, that I thought an Error, I deny'd my self the Pleasure of contradicting him abruptly, and of showing immediately some Absurdity in his Proposition; and in answering I began by observing that in certain Cases or Circumstances his Opinion would be right, but that in the present case there *appear'd* or *seem'd* to me some Difference, &c. I soon found the Advantage of this Change in my Manners. The Conversations I engag'd in went on more pleasantly.

The modest way in which I propos'd my Opinions, procur'd them a readier Reception and less Contradiction; I had less Mortification when I was found to be in the wrong, and I more easily prevail'd with others to give up their Mistakes and join with me when I happen'd to be in the right. And this Mode, which I at first put on, with some violence to natural Inclination, became at length so easy and so habitual to me, that perhaps for these Fifty Years past no one has ever heard a dogmatical Expression escape me. And to this Habit (after my Character of Integrity) I think it principally owing, that I had early so much Weight with my Fellow Citizens, when I proposed new Institutions, or Alterations in the old; and so much Influence in public Councils when I became a Member. For I was but a bad Speaker, never eloquent, subject to much Hesitation in my choice of Words, hardly correct in Language, and yet I generally carried my Points.

In reality there is perhaps no one of our natural Passions so hard to subdue as *Pride*. Disguise it, struggle with it, beat it down, stifle it, mortify it as much as one pleases, it is still alive, and will every now and then peep out and show itself. You will see it perhaps often in this History. For even if I could conceive that I had compleatly overcome it, I should probably by [be] proud of my Humility.

Thus far written at Passy 1784

1784/1818

Silence Dogood, No. 7[*]

Give me the Muse, whose generous Force,
Impatient of the Reins,
Pursues an unattempted Course,
Breaks all the Criticks Iron Chains.
Watts[1]

To the Author of the *New-England Courant.*

Sir,

It has been the Complaint of many Ingenious Foreigners, who have travell'd amongst us, *That good Poetry is not to be expected in New-England.* I am apt to Fancy, the Reason is, not because our Countreymen are altogether void of a Poetical Genius, nor yet because we have not those Advantages of Education which other Countries have, but purely because we do not afford that Praise and Encouragement which is merited, when any thing extraordinary of this Kind is produc'd among us: Upon which Consideration I have determined, when I meet with a Good Piece of New-England Poetry, to give it a suitable Encomium, and thereby endeavour to discover to the World some of its Beautys, in order to encourage the Author to go on, and bless the World with more, and more Excellent Productions.

[*] Published in *The New England Courant,* June 25, 1722.   [1] Isaac Watts, *The Adventurous Muse* (1709).

There has lately appear'd among us a most Excellent Piece of Poetry, entituled, *An Elegy upon the much Lamented Death of Mrs. Mehitebell Kitel, Wife of Mr. John Kitel of Salem, &c.* It may justly be said in its Praise, without Flattery to the Author, that it is the most Extraordinary Piece that ever was wrote in New-England. The Language is so soft and Easy, the Expression so moving and pathetick, but above all, the Verse and Numbers so Charming and Natural, that it is almost beyond Comparison,

> The Muse disdains
>   Those Links and Chains,
>   Measures and Rules of vulgar Strains,
> And o'er the Laws of Harmony a Sovereign Queen she reigns.[2]

I find no English Author, Ancient or Modern, whose Elegies may be compar'd with this, in respect to the Elegance of Stile, or Smoothness of Rhime; and for the affecting Part, I will leave your Readers to judge, if ever they read any Lines, that would sooner make them *draw their Breath* and Sigh, if not shed Tears, than these following.

> Come let us mourn, for we have lost a Wife, a Daughter, and a Sister,
> Who has lately taken Flight, and greatly we have mist her.

In another Place,

> *Some little Time* before she yielded up her Breath,
> She said, I ne'er shall hear one Sermon more on Earth.
> She kist her Husband *some little Time* before she expir'd,
> Then lean'd her Head the Pillow on, just out of Breath and tir'd.

But the Threefold Appellation in the first Line

> a Wife, a Daughter, and a Sister,

must not pass unobserved. That Line in the celebrated Watts,

> *GUNSTON* the Just, the Generous, and the Young,

is nothing Comparable to it. The latter only mentions three Qualifications of *one* Person who was deceased, which therefore could raise Grief and Compassion but for *One*. Whereas the former, *(our most excellent Poet)* gives his Reader a Sort of an Idea of the Death of *Three Persons,* viz.

> a Wife, a Daughter, and a Sister,

which is *Three Times* as great a Loss as the Death of *One,* and consequently must raise *Three Times* as much Grief and Compassion in the Reader.

I should be very much straitned for Room, if I should attempt to discover even

---

[2] Watts, *The Adventurous Muse.*

half the Excellencies of this Elegy which are obvious to me. Yet I cannot omit one Observation, which is, that the Author has (to his Honour) invented a new Species of Poetry, which wants a Name, and was never before known. His Muse scorns to be confin'd to the old Measures and Limits, or to observe the dull Rules of Criticks;

> Nor Rapin gives her Rules to fly, nor Purcell Notes to sing. *Watts.*

Now 'tis Pity that such an Excellent Piece should not be dignify'd with a particular Name; and seeing it cannot justly be called, either *Epic, Sapphic, Lyric,* or *Pindaric,* nor any other Name yet invented, I presume it may, (in Honour and Remembrance of the Dead) be called the KITELIC. Thus much in the Praise of *Kitelic Poetry.*

It is certain, that those Elegies which are of our own Growth, (and our Soil seldom produces any other sort of Poetry) are by far the greatest part, wretchedly Dull and Ridiculous. Now since it is imagin'd by many, that our Poets are honest, well-meaning Fellows, who do their best, and that if they had but some Instructions how to govern Fancy with Judgment, they would make indifferent good Elegies; I shall here subjoin a Receipt for that purpose, which was left me as a Legacy, (among other valuable Rarities) by my Reverent Husband. It is as follows,

A RECEIPT to make a New-England Funeral ELEGY.

For the Title of your Elegy. Of these you may have enough ready made to your Hands; but if you should chuse to make it your self, you must be sure not to omit the Words *Aetatis Suae,*[3] which will Beautify it exceedingly.

For the Subject of your Elegy. Take one of your Neighbours who has lately departed this Life; it is no great matter at what Age the Party dy'd, but it will be best if he went away suddenly, being *Kill'd, Drown'd,* or *Froze to Death.*

Having chose the Person, take all his Virtues, Excellencies, &c. and if he have not enough, you may borrow some to make up a sufficient Quantity: To these add his last Words, dying Expressions, &c. if they are to be had; mix all these together, and be sure you strain them well. Then season all with a Handful or two of Melancholly Expressions, such as, *Dreadful, Deadly, cruel cold Death, unhappy Fate, weeping Eyes,* &c. Have mixed all these Ingredients well, put them into the empty Scull of some *young Harvard;* (but in Case you have ne'er a One at Hand, you may use your own,) there let them Ferment for the Space of a Fortnight, and by that Time they will be incorporated into a Body, which take out, and having prepared a sufficient Quantity of double Rhimes, such as, *Power, Flower; Quiver, Shiver; Grieve us, Leave us; tell you, excel you; Expeditions, Physicians; Fatigue him, Intrigue him;* &c. you must spread all upon Paper, and if you can procure a Scrap of Latin to put at the End, it will garnish it mightily; then having affixed your Name at the Bottom, with a *Mæstus Composuit,*[4] you will have an Excellent Elegy.

N.B. This Receipt will serve when a Female is the Subject of your Elegy, provided you borrow a greater Quantity of Virtues, Excellencies, &c. Sir, Your Servant,

SILENCE DOGOOD

1722/1722

---

[3] Latin: "Of His Age," a convention of Puritan elegies, usually abbreviated *Aet.*

[4] Latin: "Sorrowfully Composed," another elegaic convention.

On Literary Style*

To the Printer of the *Gazette*.

There are few Men, of Capacity for making any considerable Figure in Life, who have not frequent Occasion to communicate their Thoughts to others in *Writing;* if not sometimes publickly as Authors, yet continually in the Management of their private Affairs, both of Business and Friendship: and since, when ill-express'd, the most proper Sentiments and justest Reasoning lose much of their native Force and Beauty, it seems to me that there is scarce any Accomplishment more necessary to a Man of Sense, than that of *Writing well* in his Mother Tongue: But as most other polite Acquirements, make a greater Appearance in a Man's Character, this however useful, is generally neglected or forgotten.

I believe there is no better Means of learning to write well, than this of attempting to entertain the Publick now and then in one of your Papers. When the Writer conceals himself, he has the Advantage of hearing the Censure both of Friends and Enemies, express'd with more Impartiality. And since, in some degree, it concerns the Credit of the Province, that such Things as are printed be performed tolerably well, mutual Improvement seems to be the Duty of all Lovers of Writing: I shall therefore frankly communicate the Observations I have made or collected on this Subject, and request those of others in Return.

I have thought in general, that whoever would write so as not to displease good Judges, should have particular Regard to these Three things, viz. That his Performance be *smooth, clear,* and *short:* For the contrary Qualities are apt to offend, either the Ear, the Understanding, or the Patience.

'Tis an Observation of Dr. Swift,[1] that modern Writers injure the Smoothness of our Tongue, by omitting Vowels wherever it is possible, and joining the harshest Consonants together with only an Apostrophe between; thus for *judged,* in it self not the smoothest of Words, they say *judg'd;* for *disturbed, disturb'd,* &c. It may be added to this, says another, that by changing *eth* into *s,* they have shortned one Syllable in a multitude of Words, and have thereby encreased, not only the *Hissing,* too offensive before, but also the great Number of Monosyllables, of which, without great Difficulty, a smooth Sentence cannot be composed. The Smoothness of a Period is also often Hurt by Parentheses, and therefore the best Writers endeavour to avoid them.

To write *clearly,* not only the most expressive, but the plainest Words should be chosen. In this, as well as in every other Particular requisite to Clearness,

* Published in the *Pennsylvania Gazette,* August 2, 1733. Franklin in 1727 "form'd most of [his] ingenious Acquaintances into a Club for mutual Improvement, which [they] called the Junto." The rules, as Franklin states in his *Autobiography,* "requir'd that every Member in his Turn should produce one or more Queries on any Point of Morals, Politics or Natural Philosophy, to be discuss'd by the Company, and once in three Months pronounce and read an Essay of his own Writing on any Subject he pleased." "On Literary Style" was one of Franklin's many contributions to the Junto Club.

1 Jonathan Swift (1667–1745), Irish-born satirist and poet, who advocated a clear and cogent style of writing.

Dr. Tillotson[2] is an excellent Example. The Fondness of some Writers for such Words as carry with them an Air of Learning, renders them unintelligible to more than half their Countrymen. If a Man would that his Writings have an Effect on the Generality of Readers, he had better imitate that Gentleman, who would use no Word in his Works that was not well understood by his Cook-maid.

A too frequent Use of Phrases ought likewise to be avoided by him that would write clearly. They trouble the Language, not only rendring it extreamly difficult to Foreigners, but make the Meaning obscure to a great number of English Readers. Phrases, like learned Words, are seldom used without Affectation; when, with all true Judges, the simplest Stile is the most beautiful.

But supposing the most proper Words and Expressions chosen, the Performance may yet be weak and obscure, if it has not *Method*. If a Writer would *persuade,* he should proceed gradually from Things already allow'd, to those from which Assent is yet with-held, and make their Connection manifest. If he would *inform,* he must advance regularly from Things known to things unknown, distinctly without Confusion, and the lower he begins the better. It is a common Fault in Writers, to allow their Readers too much Knowledge: They begin with that which should be the Middle, and skipping backwards and forwards, 'tis impossible for any one but he who is perfect in the Subject before, to understand their Work, and such an one has no Occasion to read it. Perhaps a Habit of using good Method, cannot be better acquired, than by learning a little Geometry or Algebra.

Amplification, or the Art of saying Little in Much, should only be allowed to Speakers. If they preach, a Discourse of considerable Length is expected from them, upon every Subject they undertake, and perhaps they are not stock'd with naked Thoughts sufficient to furnish it out. If they plead in the Courts, it is of Use to speak abundance, tho' they reason little; for the Ignorant in a Jury, can scarcely believe it possible that a Man can talk so much and so long without being in the Right. Let them have the Liberty then, of repeating the same Sentences in other Words; let them put an Adjective to every Substantive, and double every Substantive with a Synonima; for this is more agreeable than hauking, spitting, taking Snuff, or any other Means of concealing Hesitation. Let them multiply Definitions, Comparisons, Similitudes and Examples. Permit them to make a Detail of Causes and Effects, enumerate all the Consequences, and express one Half by Metaphor and Circumlocution: Nay, allow the Preacher to tell us whatever a Thing is negatively, before he begins to tell us what it is affirmatively; and suffer him to divide and subdivide as far as *Two and fiftiethly.* All this is not intolerable while it is not written. But when a Discourse is to be bound down upon Paper, and subjected to the calm leisurely Examination of nice Judgment, every Thing that is needless gives Offence; and therefore all should be retrenched, that does not directly conduce to the End design'd. Had this been always done, many large and tiresome Folio's would have shrunk into Pamphlets, and many a Pamphlet into a single Period. However, tho' a multitude of Words obscure the Sense, and 'tis necessary to abridge a verbose Author in order to understand him; yet a Writer should take especial Care on the other Hand, that his Brevity doth not hurt his Perspicuity.

[2] John Tillotson (1630–1694), English archbishop, whose *Sermons* were collected between 1695 and 1704.

After all, if the Author does not intend his Piece for general Reading, he must exactly suit his Stile and Manner to the particular Taste of those he proposes for his Readers. Every one observes, the different Ways of Writing and Expression used by the different Sects of Religion; and can readily enough pronounce, that it is improper to use some of these Stiles in common, or to use the common Stile, when we address some of these Sects in particular.

To conclude, I shall venture to lay it down as a Maxim, *that no Piece can properly be called good, and well written, which is void of any Tendency to benefit the Reader, either by improving his Virtue or his Knowledge.* This Principle every Writer would do well to have in View, whenever he undertakes to write. All Performances done for meer Ostentation of Parts, are really contemptible; and withal far more subject to the Severity of Criticism, than those more meanly written, wherein the Author appears to have aimed at the Good of others. For when 'tis visible to every one, that a Man writes to show his Wit only, all his Expressions are sifted, and his Sense examined, in the nicest and most ill-natur'd manner; and every one is glad of an Opportunity to mortify him. But, what a vast Destruction would there be of Books, if they were to be saved or condemned on a Tryal by this Rule!

Besides, Pieces meerly humorous, are of all Sorts the hardest to succeed in. If they are not natural, they are stark naught; and there can be no real Humour in an Affectation of Humour.

Perhaps it may be said, that an ill Man is able to write an ill Thing well; that is, having an ill Design, and considering who are to be his Readers, he may use the properest Stile and Arguments to attain his Point. In this Sense, that is best wrote, which is best adapted to the Purpose of the Writer.

I am apprehensive, dear Readers, lest in this Piece, I should be guilty of every Fault I condemn, and deficient in every Thing I recommend; so much easier it is to offer Rules than to practise them. I am sure, however, of this, that I am Your very sincere Friend and Servant.

1733

---

from Poor Richard Improved, 1758[*]

[Father Abraham's Speech; or The Way to Wealth]

Courteous Reader,

I have heard that nothing gives an Author so great Pleasure, as to find his Works respectfully quoted by other learned Authors. This Pleasure I have seldom enjoyed; for tho' I have been, if I may say it without Vanity, an *eminent Author* of Almanacks

[*] Franklin's note from the *Autobiography*, Part III: "In 1732 I first published my Almanack, under the Name of *Richard Saunders;* it was continu'd by me about 25 Years, commonly call'd *Poor Richard's* Almanack. I endeavour'd to make it both entertaining and useful, and it accordingly came to be in such Demand that I reap'd considerable Profit from it, vending annually near ten Thousand. And observing that it was generally read, scarce any Neighbourhood in the

(continued)

annually now a full Quarter of a Century, my Brother Authors in the same Way, for what Reason I know not, have ever been very sparing in their Applauses; and no other Author has taken the least Notice of me, so that did not my Writings produce me some solid *Pudding,* the great Deficiency of *Praise* would have quite discouraged me.

I concluded at length, that the People were the best Judges of my Merit; for they buy my Works; and besides, in my Rambles, where I am not personally known, I have frequently heard one or other of my Adages repeated, with, *as Poor Richard says,* at the End on't; this gave me some Satisfaction, as it showed not only that my Instructions were regarded, but discovered likewise some Respect for my Authority; and I own, that to encourage the Practice of remembering and repeating those wise Sentences, I have sometimes *quoted myself* with great Gravity.

Judge then how much I must have been gratified by an Incident I am going to relate to you. I stopt my Horse lately where a great Number of People were collected at a Vendue of Merchant Goods. The Hour of Sale not being come, they were conversing on the Badness of the Times, and one of the Company call'd to a plain clean old Man, with white Locks, *Pray, Father Abraham, what think you of the Times? Won't these heavy Taxes quite ruin the Country? How shall we be ever able to pay them? What would you advise us to?*—Father Abraham stood up, and reply'd, If you'd have my Advice, I'll give it you in short, for a *Word to the Wise is enough,* and *many Words won't fill a Bushel,* as *Poor Richard says.* They join'd in desiring him to speak his Mind, and gathering round him, he proceeded as follows;

"Friends, says he, and Neighbours, the Taxes are indeed very heavy, and if those laid on by the Government were the only Ones we had to pay, we might more easily discharge them; but we have many others, and much more grievous to some of us. We are taxed twice as much by our *Idleness,* three times as much by our *Pride,* and four times as much by our *Folly,* and from these Taxes the Commissioners cannot ease or deliver us by allowing an Abatement. However let us hearken to good Advice,

Province being without it, I consider'd it as a proper Vehicle for conveying Instruction among the common People, who bought scarce any other Books. I therefore filled all the little Spaces that occurr'd between the Remarkable Days in the Calendar, with Proverbial Sentences, chiefly such as inculcated Industry and Frugality, as the Means of procuring Wealth and thereby securing Virtue, it being more difficult for a Man in Want to act always honestly, as (to use here one of those Proverbs) *it is hard for an empty Sack to stand upright.* These Proverbs, which contained the Wisdom of many Ages and Nations, I assembled and form'd into a connected Discourse prefix'd to the Almanack of 1757, as the Harangue of a wise old Man to the People attending an Auction. The bringing all these scatter'd Counsels thus into a Focus, enabled them to make greater Impression. The Piece being universally approved was copied in all the Newspapers of the Continent, reprinted in Britain on a Broadside to be stuck up in

Houses, two Translations were made of it in French, and great Numbers bought by the Clergy and Gentry to distribute gratis among their poor Parishioners and Tenants. In Pennsylvania, as it discouraged useless Expence in foreign Superfluities, some thought it had its share of Influence in producing that growing Plenty of Money which was observable for several Years after its Publication. . . ."

In 1748 Franklin enlarged his successful *Poor Richard's Almanack* and changed its title to *Poor Richard Improved.* For the 1758 edition, the twenty-sixth and last prepared under his supervision, Franklin invented the character Father Abraham, "a plain clean old Man, with white Locks," who in a long speech distills all of the aphoristic wisdom relating to hard work, prudence, and thrift contained in the earlier versions of the *Almanack.* This enormously popular preface, variously known as *Father Abraham's Speech* and *The Way to Wealth,* went through at least 145 printings before the end of the eighteenth century.

and something may be done for us; *God helps them that help themselves,* as Poor Richard says, in his Almanack of 1733.

It would be thought a hard Government that should tax its People one tenth Part of their *Time,* to be employed in its Service. But *Idleness* taxes many of us much more, if we reckon all that is spent in absolute *Sloth,* or doing of nothing, with that which is spent in idle Employments or Amusements, that amount to nothing. *Sloth,* by bringing on Diseases, absolutely shortens Life. *Sloth, like Rust, consumes faster than Labour wears, while the used Key is always bright,* as Poor Richard says. But *dost thou love Life, then do not squander Time, for that's the Stuff Life is made of,* as Poor Richard says. How much more than is necessary do we spend in Sleep! forgetting that *The sleeping Fox catches no Poultry,* and that *there will be sleeping enough in the Grave,* as Poor Richard says. If Time be of all Things the most precious, *wasting Time* must be, as Poor Richard says, *the greatest Prodigality,* since, as he elsewhere tells us, *Lost Time is never found again;* and what we call *Time-enough, always proves little enough:* Let us then be up and be doing, and doing to the Purpose; so by Diligence shall we do more with less Perplexity. *Sloth makes all Things difficult, but Industry all easy,* as Poor Richard says; and *He that riseth late, must trot all Day, and shall scarce overtake his Business at Night.* While *Laziness travels so slowly, that Poverty soon overtakes him,* as we read in Poor Richard, who adds, *Drive thy Business, let not that drive thee;* and *Early to Bed, and early to rise, makes a Man healthy, wealthy and wise.*

So what signifies *wishing* and *hoping* for better Times. We may make these Times better if we bestir ourselves. *Industry need not wish,* as Poor Richard says, and *He that lives upon Hope will die fasting. There are no Gains, without Pains;* then *Help Hands, for I have no Lands,* or if I have, they are smartly taxed. And, as Poor Richard likewise observes, *He that hath a Trade hath an Estate,* and *He that hath a Calling hath an Office of Profit and Honour;* but then the *Trade* must be worked at, and the *Calling* well followed, or neither the *Estate,* nor the *Office,* will enable us to pay our Taxes. If we are industrious we shall never starve; for, as Poor Richard says, *At the working Man's House Hunger looks in, but dares not enter.* Nor will the Bailiff nor the Constable enter, for *Industry pays Debts, while Despair encreaseth them,* says Poor Richard. What though you have found no Treasure, nor has any rich Relation left you a Legacy, *Diligence is the Mother of Good luck,* as Poor Richard says, and *God gives all Things to Industry.* Then *plough deep, while Sluggards sleep, and you shall have Corn to sell and to keep,* says Poor Dick. Work while it is called To-day, for you know not how much you may be hindered To-morrow, which makes Poor Richard say, *One To-day is worth two To-morrows;* and farther, *Have you somewhat to do To-morrow, do it To-day.* If you were a Servant, would you not be ashamed that a good Master should catch you idle? Are you then your own Master, *be ashamed to catch yourself idle,* as Poor Dick says. When there is so much to be done for yourself, your Family, your Country, and your gracious King, be up by Peep of Day; *Let not the Sun look down and say, Inglorious here he lies.* Handle your Tools without Mittens; remember that *the Cat in Gloves catches no Mice,* as Poor Richard says. 'Tis true there is much to be done, and perhaps you are weak handed, but stick to it steadily, and you will see great Effects, for *constant Dropping wears away Stones,* and by *Diligence and Patience the Mouse ate in two the Cable;* and *little Strokes fell great Oaks,* as Poor Richard says in his Almanack, the Year I cannot just now remember.

Methinks I hear some of you say, *Must a Man afford himself no Leisure?* I will tell thee, my Friend, what Poor Richard says, *Employ thy Time well if thou meanest to gain Leisure;* and, *since thou art not sure of a Minute, throw not away an Hour.* Leisure, is Time for doing something useful; this Leisure the diligent Man will obtain, but the lazy Man never; so that, as Poor Richard says, a *Life of Leisure and a Life of Laziness are two Things.* Do you imagine that Sloth will afford you more Comfort than Labour? No, for as Poor Richard says, *Trouble springs from Idleness, and grievous Toil from needless Ease.* Many without Labour, would live by their WITS only, but they break for want of Stock. Whereas Industry gives Comfort, and Plenty, and Respect: *Fly Pleasures, and they'll follow you.* The diligent Spinner has a large Shift;[1] and *now I have a Sheep and a Cow, every Body bids me Good morrow;* all which is well said by Poor Richard.

But with our Industry, we must likewise be *steady, settled* and *careful,* and oversee our own Affairs *with our own Eyes,* and not trust too much to others; for, as Poor Richard says,

> I never saw an oft removed Tree,
> Nor yet an oft removed Family,
> That throve so well as those that settled be.

And again, *Three Removes*[2] *is as bad as a Fire;* and again, *Keep thy Shop, and thy Shop will keep thee;* and again, *If you would have your Business done, go; If not, send.* And again,

> He that by the Plough would thrive,
> Himself must either hold or drive.

And again, *The Eye of a Master will do more Work than both his Hands;* and again, *Want of Care does us more Damage than Want of Knowledge;* and again, *Not to oversee Workmen, is to leave them your Purse open.* Trusting too much to others Care is the Ruin of many; for, as the Almanack says, *In the Affairs of this World, Men are saved, not by Faith, but by the Want of it;* but a Man's own Care is profitable; for, saith Poor Dick, *Learning is to the Studious,* and *Riches to the Careful,* as well as *Power to the Bold,* and *Heaven to the Virtuous.* And farther, *If you would have a faithful Servant, and one that you like, serve yourself.* And again, he adviseth to Circumspection and Care, even in the smallest Matters, because sometimes *a little Neglect may breed great Mischief;* adding, *For want of a Nail the Shoe was lost; for want of a Shoe the Horse was lost; and for want of a Horse the Rider was lost,* being overtaken and slain by the Enemy, all for want of Care about a Horse-shoe Nail.

So much for Industry, my Friends, and Attention to one's own Business; but to these we must add *Frugality,* if we would make our *Industry* more certainly successful. A Man may, if he knows not how to save as he gets, *keep his Nose all his Life to the Grindstone,* and die not worth a *Groat*[3] at last. *A fat Kitchen makes a lean Will,* as Poor Richard says; and,

---

[1] Wardrobe.
[2] Moves.

[3] About four pence.

Many Estates are spent in the Getting,
Since Women for Tea forsook Spinning and Knitting,
And Men for Punch forsook Hewing and Splitting.

If you would be wealthy, says he, in another Almanack, *think of Saving as well as of Getting: the Indies have not made Spain rich, because her* Outgoes *are greater than her* Incomes. Away then with your expensive Follies, and you will not have so much Cause to complain of hard Times, heavy Taxes, and chargeable Families; for, as Poor Dick says,

Women and Wine, Game and Deceit,
Make the Wealth small, and the Wants great.

And farther, *What maintains one Vice, would bring up two Children.* You may think perhaps, That a *little* Tea, or a *little* Punch now and then, Diet a *little* more costly, Clothes a *little* finer, and a *little* Entertainment now and then, can be no *great* Matter; but remember what Poor Richard says, *Many* a Little *makes a Mickle;*[4] and farther, *Beware of* little Expences; *a small Leak will sink a great Ship;* and again, *Who Dainties love, shall Beggars prove;* and moreover, *Fools make Feasts, and wise Men eat them.*

Here you are all got together at this Vendue of *Fineries* and *Knicknacks.* You call them *Goods,* but if you do not take Care, they will prove *Evils* to some of you. You expect they will be sold *cheap,* and perhaps they may for less than they cost; but if you have no Occasion for them, they must be *dear* to you. Remember what Poor Richard says, *Buy what thou hast no Need of, and ere long thou shalt sell thy Necessaries.* And again, *At a great Pennyworth pause a while:* He means, that perhaps the Cheapness is *apparent* only, and not *real;* or the Bargain, by straitning thee in thy Business, may do thee more Harm than Good. For in another Place he says, *Many have been ruined by buying good Pennyworths.* Again, Poor Richard says, *'Tis foolish to lay out Money in a Purchase of Repentance;* and yet this Folly is practised every Day at Vendues, for want of minding the Almanack. *Wise Men,* as Poor Dick says, *learn by others Harms, Fools scarcely by their own;* but, *Felix quem faciunt aliena Pericula cautum.*[5] Many a one, for the Sake of Finery on the Back, have gone with a hungry Belly, and half starved their Families; *Silks and Sattins, Scarlet and Velvets,* as Poor Richard says, *put out the Kitchen Fire.* These are not the *Necessaries* of Life; they can scarcely be called the *Conveniencies,* and yet only because they look pretty, how many *want* to *have* them. The *artificial* Wants of Mankind thus become more numerous than the *natural;* and, as Poor Dick says, *For one* poor *Person, there are an hundred* indigent. By these, and other Extravagancies, the Genteel are reduced to Poverty, and forced to borrow of those whom they formerly despised, but who through *Industry* and *Frugality* have maintained their Standing; in which Case it appears plainly, that a *Ploughman on his Legs is higher than a Gentleman on his Knees,* as Poor Richard says. Perhaps they have had a small Estate left them, which they knew not the Getting of; they think *'tis Day, and will never be Night;* that a little to be spent out of *so much,* is not worth minding; *(a Child and a Fool,* as Poor Richard says, *imagine Twenty Shillings and Twenty Years*

---

[4] Lot.
[5] Latin: "They are fortunate who have been made wary by the misfortunes of others."

can never be spent) but, *always taking out of the Meal-tub, and never putting in, soon comes to the Bottom;* then, as Poor Dick says, *When the Well's dry, they know the Worth of Water.* But this they might have known before, if they had taken his Advice; *If you would know the Value of Money, go and try to borrow some;* for, *he that goes a borrowing goes a sorrowing;* and indeed so does he that lends to such People, when he goes *to get it in again.* Poor Dick farther advises, and says,

Fond *Pride of Dress,* is sure a very Curse;
E'er *Fancy* you consult, consult your Purse.

And again, *Pride is as loud a Beggar as Want, and a great deal more saucy.* When you have bought one fine Thing you must buy ten more, that your Appearance may be all of a Piece; but Poor Dick says, *'Tis easier to* suppress *the first Desire, than to* satisfy *all that follow it.* And 'tis as truly Folly for the Poor to ape the Rich, as for the Frog to swell, in order to equal the Ox.

Great Estates may venture more,
But little Boats should keep near Shore.

'Tis however a Folly soon punished; for *Pride that dines on Vanity sups on Contempt,* as Poor Richard says. And in another Place, *Pride breakfasted with Plenty, dined with Poverty, and supped with Infamy.* And after all, of what Use is this *Pride of Appearance,* for which so much is risked, so much is suffered? It cannot promote Health, or ease Pain; it makes no Increase of Merit in the Person, it creates Envy, it hastens Misfortune.

What is a Butterfly? At best
He's but a Caterpillar drest.
The saucy Fop's his Picture just,

as Poor Richard says.

But what Madness must it be to *run in Debt* for these Superfluities! We are offered, by the Terms of this Vendue, *Six Months Credit;* and that perhaps has induced some of us to attend it, because we cannot spare the ready Money, and hope now to be fine without it. But, ah, think what you do when you run in Debt; *You give to another Power over your Liberty.* If you cannot pay at the Time, you will be ashamed to see your Creditor; you will be in Fear when you speak to him; you will make poor pitiful sneaking Excuses, and by Degrees come to lose your Veracity, and sink into base downright lying; for, as Poor Richard says, *The second Vice is Lying, the first is running in Debt.* And again, to the same Purpose, *Lying rides upon Debt's Back.* Whereas a freeborn Englishman ought not to be ashamed or afraid to see or speak to any Man living. But Poverty often deprives a Man of all Spirit and Virtue: *'Tis hard for an empty Bag to stand upright,* as Poor Richard truly says. What would you think of that Prince, or that Government, who should issue an Edict forbidding you to dress like a Gentleman or a Gentlewoman, on Pain of Imprisonment or Servitude? Would you not say, that you are free, have a Right to dress as you please, and that such an Edict would be a Breach of your Privileges, and such a Government tyrannical? And yet you are about to put yourself under that Tyranny when you run in Debt for such

Dress! Your Creditor has Authority at his Pleasure to deprive you of your Liberty, by confining you in Goal for Life, or to sell you for a Servant, if you should not be able to pay him! When you have got your Bargain, you may, perhaps, think little of Payment; but *Creditors,* Poor Richard tells us, *have better Memories than Debtors;* and in another Place says, *Creditors are a superstitious Sect, great Observers of set Days and Times.* The Day comes round before you are aware, and the Demand is made before you are prepared to satisfy it. Or if you bear your Debt in Mind, the Term which at first seemed so long, will, as it lessens, appear extreamly short. *Time* will seem to have added Wings to his Heels as well as Shoulders. *Those have a short Lent,* saith Poor Richard, *who owe Money to be paid at Easter.* Then since, as he says, *The Borrower is a Slave to the Lender, and the Debtor to the Creditor,* disdain the Chain, preserve your Freedom; and maintain your Independency: Be *industrious* and *free;* be *frugal* and *free.* At present, perhaps, you may think yourself in thriving Circumstances, and that you can bear a little Extravagance without Injury; but,

> For Age and Want, save while you may;
> No Morning Sun lasts a whole Day,

as Poor Richard says. Gain may be temporary and uncertain, but ever while you live, Expence is constant and certain; and *'tis easier to build two Chimnies than to keep one in Fuel,* as Poor Richard says. So *rather go to Bed supperless than rise in Debt.*

> Get what you can, and what you get hold;
> 'Tis the Stone that will turn all your Lead into Gold,

as Poor Richard says. And when you have got the Philosopher's Stone,[6] sure you will no longer complain of bad Times, or the Difficulty of paying Taxes.

This Doctrine, my Friends, is *Reason* and *Wisdom;* but after all, do not depend too much upon your own *Industry,* and *Frugality,* and *Prudence,* though excellent Things, for they may all be blasted without the Blessing of Heaven; and therefore ask that Blessing humbly, and be not uncharitable to those that at present seem to want it, but comfort and help them. Remember Job suffered, and was afterwards prosperous.

And now to conclude, *Experience keeps a dear School, but Fools will learn in no other, and scarce in that;* for it is true, *we may give Advice, but we cannot give Conduct,* as Poor Richard says: However, remember this, *They that won't be counselled, can't be helped,* as Poor Richard says: And farther, That *if you will not hear Reason, she'll surely rap your Knuckles.*

Thus the old Gentleman ended his Harangue. The People heard it, and approved the Doctrine, and immediately practised the contrary, just as if it had been a common Sermon; for the Vendue opened, and they began to buy extravagantly, notwithstanding all his Cautions, and their own Fear of Taxes. I found the good Man had thoroughly studied my Almanacks, and digested all I had dropt on those Topicks during the Course of Five-and-twenty Years. The frequent Mention he made of me must have tired any one else, but my Vanity was wonderfully delighted with it,

---

[6] In alchemy, the substance that was thought to turn base metals into gold.

though I was conscious that not a tenth Part of the Wisdom was my own which he ascribed to me, but rather the *Gleanings* I had made of the Sense of all Ages and Nations. However, I resolved to be the better for the Echo of it; and though I had at first determined to buy Stuff for a new Coat, I went away resolved to wear my old One a little longer. *Reader,* if thou wilt do the same, thy Profit will be as great as mine. I am, as ever, Thine to serve thee,   RICHARD SAUNDERS.[7]
July 7, 1757.

1757/1758

The Sale of the Hessians*

From the Count de Schaumbergh to the Baron Hohendorf, commanding the Hessian troops in America.

Rome, February 18, 1777.

MONSIEUR LE BARON:—On my return from Naples, I received at Rome your letter of the 27th December of last year. I have learned with unspeakable pleasure the courage our troops exhibited at Trenton,[1] and you cannot imagine my joy on being told that of the 1,950 Hessians engaged in the fight, but 345 escaped. There were just 1,605 men killed, and I cannot sufficiently commend your prudence in sending an exact list of the dead to my minister in London. This precaution was the more necessary, as the report sent to the English ministry does not give but 1,455 dead. This would make 483,450 florins instead of 643,500 which I am entitled to demand under our convention. You will comprehend the prejudice which such an error would work in my finances, and I do not doubt you will take the necessary pains to prove that Lord North's[2] list is false and yours correct.

The court of London objects that there were a hundred wounded who ought not to be included in the list, nor paid for as dead; but I trust you will not overlook my

---

[7] Franklin used the name of a well-known seventeenth century London almanac writer.
* The date and place of the initial publication of this essay, one of Franklin's most successful burlesques, are not known. According to Moses Coit Tyler in *The Literary History of the American Revolution, 1763–1783:* "The Count de Schaumbergh's letter of instructions, seems to have been written by Franklin not long after his arrival in France in the latter part of 1776, and was intended to hold up to the execration of the civilized world both parties in the transaction by which the King of England bought of certain petty princes in Germany the troops with which to butcher his late American subjects. In some respects, this is the most

powerful of all the satirical writings of Franklin. More, perhaps, than is the case with any other work of his, it displays, with marvelous subtlety and wit, that sort of genius which can reproduce with minute and perfect verisimilitude the psychological processes of some monstrous crime against human nature,—a crime which it thus portrays both to the horror and the derision of mankind."
[1] On Christmas night in 1776, Washington defeated a force of twelve hundred Hessians in the Battle of Trenton. Franklin exaggerates the report of Hessian casualties.
[2] Frederick North, British prime minister (1770–1782).

instructions to you on quitting Cassel, and that you will not have tried by human succor to recall the life of the unfortunates whose days could not be lengthened but by the loss of a leg or an arm. That would be making them a pernicious present, and I am sure they would rather die than live in a condition no longer fit for my service. I do not mean by this that you should assassinate them; we should be humane, my dear Baron, but you may insinuate to the surgeons with entire propriety that a crippled man is a reproach to their profession, and that there is no wiser course than to let every one of them die when he ceases to be fit to fight.

I am about to send to you some new recruits. Don't economize them. Remember glory before all things. Glory is true wealth. There is nothing degrades the soldier like the love of money. He must care only for honour and reputation, but this reputation must be acquired in the midst of dangers. A battle gained without costing the conqueror any blood is an inglorious success, while the conquered cover themselves with glory by perishing with their arms in their hands. Do you remember that of the 300 Lacedæmonians who defended the defile of Thermopylæ, not one returned? How happy should I be could I say the same of my brave Hessians!

It is true that their king, Leonidas, perished with them: but things have changed, and it is no longer the custom for princes of the empire to go and fight in America for a cause with which they have no concern. And besides, to whom should they pay the thirty guineas per man if I did not stay in Europe to receive them? Then, it is necessary also that I be ready to send recruits to replace the men you lose. For this purpose I must return to Hesse. It is true, grown men are becoming scarce there, but I will send you boys. Besides, the scarcer the commodity the higher the price. I am assured that the women and little girls have begun to till our lands, and they get on not badly. You did right to send back to Europe that Dr. Crumerus who was so successful in curing dysentery. Don't bother with a man who is subject to looseness of the bowels. That disease makes bad soldiers. One coward will do more mischief in an engagement than ten brave men will do good. Better that they burst in their barracks than fly in a battle, and tarnish the glory of our arms. Besides, you know that they pay me as killed for all who die from disease, and I don't get a farthing for runaways. My trip to Italy, which has cost me enormously, makes it desirable that there should be a great mortality among them. You will therefore promise promotion to all who expose themselves; you will exhort them to seek glory in the midst of dangers; you will say to Major Maundorff that I am not at all content with his saving the 345 men who escaped the massacre of Trenton. Through the whole campaign he has not had ten men killed in consequence of his orders. Finally, let it be your principal object to prolong the war and avoid a decisive engagement on either side, for I have made arrangements for a grand Italian opera, and I do not wish to be obliged to give it up. Meantime I pray God, my dear Baron de Hohendorf, to have you in his holy and gracious keeping.

n.d.

from Information to Those Who Would Remove to America[*]

Many Persons in Europe, having directly or by Letters, express'd to the Writer of this, who is well acquainted with North America, their Desire of transporting and establishing themselves in that Country; but who appear to have formed, thro' Ignorance, mistaken Ideas and Expectations of what is to be obtained there; he thinks it may be useful, and prevent inconvenient, expensive, and fruitless Removals and Voyages of improper Persons, if he gives some clearer and truer Notions of that part of the World, than appear to have hitherto prevailed.

He finds it is imagined by Numbers, that the Inhabitants of North America are rich, capable of rewarding, and dispos'd to reward, all sorts of Ingenuity; that they are at the same time ignorant of all the Sciences, and, consequently, that Strangers, possessing Talents in the Belles-Lettres, fine Arts, &c., must be highly esteemed, and so well paid, as to become easily rich themselves; that there are also abundance of profitable Offices to be disposed of, which the Natives are not qualified to fill; and that, having few Persons of Family among them, Strangers of Birth must be greatly respected, and of course easily obtain the best of those Offices, which will make all their Fortunes; that the Governments too, to encourage Emigrations from Europe, not only pay the Expence of personal Transportation, but give Lands gratis to Strangers, with Negroes to work for them, Utensils of Husbandry, and Stocks of Cattle. These are all wild Imaginations; and those who go to America with Expectations founded upon them will surely find themselves disappointed.

The Truth is, that though there are in that Country few People so miserable as the Poor of Europe, there are also very few that in Europe would be called rich; it is rather a general happy Mediocrity that prevails. There are few great Proprietors of the Soil, and few Tenants; most People cultivate their own Lands, or follow some Handicraft or Merchandise; very few rich enough to live idly upon their Rents or Incomes, or to pay the high Prices given in Europe for Paintings, Statues, Architecture, and the other Works of Art, that are more curious than useful. Hence the natural Geniuses, that have arisen in America with such Talents, have uniformly quitted that Country for Europe, where they can be more suitably rewarded. It is true, that Letters and Mathematical Knowledge are in Esteem there, but they are at the same time more common than is apprehended; there being already existing nine Colleges or Universities, viz. four in New England, and one in each of the Provinces of New York, New Jersey, Pensilvania, Maryland, and Virginia, all furnish'd with learned Professors; besides a number of smaller Academies; these educate many of their Youth in the Languages, and those Sciences that qualify men for the Professions of Divinity, Law, or Physick. Strangers indeed are by no means excluded from exercising those Professions; and the quick Increase of Inhabitants everywhere gives them a Chance of

---

[*] Title of pirated edition published in 1784. Franklin later that year published the pamphlet   under the title *Advice to Such as Would Remove to America.*

Employ, which they have in common with the Natives. Of civil Offices, or Employments, there are few; no superfluous Ones, as in Europe; and it is a Rule establish'd in some of the States, that no Office should be so profitable as to make it desirable. The 36th Article of the Constitution of Pennsilvania, runs expressly in these Words; "As every Freeman, to preserve his Independence, (if he has not a sufficient Estate) ought to have some Profession, Calling, Trade, or Farm, whereby he may honestly subsist, there can be no Necessity for, nor Use in, establishing Offices of Profit; the usual Effects of which are Dependance and Servility, unbecoming Freemen, in the Possessors and Expectants; Faction, Contention, Corruption, and Disorder among the People. Wherefore, whenever an Office, thro' Increase of Fees or otherwise, becomes so profitable, as to occasion many to apply for it, the Profits ought to be lessened by the Legislature."

These Ideas prevailing more or less in all the United States, it cannot be worth any Man's while, who has a means of Living at home, to expatriate himself, in hopes of obtaining a profitable civil Office in America; and, as to military Offices, they are at an End with the War, the Armies being disbanded. Much less is it adviseable for a Person to go thither, who has no other Quality to recommend him but his Birth. In Europe it has indeed its Value; but it is a Commodity that cannot be carried to a worse Market than that of America, where people do not inquire concerning a Stranger, *What is he?* but, *What can he do?* If he has any useful Art, he is welcome; and if he exercises it, and behaves well, he will be respected by all that know him; but a mere Man of Quality, who, on that Account, wants to live upon the Public, by some Office or Salary, will be despis'd and disregarded. The Husbandman is in honor there, and even the Mechanic, because their Employments are useful. The People have a saying, that God Almighty is himself a Mechanic, the greatest in the Univers; and he is respected and admired more for the Variety, Ingenuity, and Utility of his Handy-works, than for the Antiquity of his Family. They are pleas'd with the Observation of a Negro, and frequently mention it, that *Boccarorra* (meaning the White men) *make de black man workee, make de Horse workee, make de Ox workee, make ebery ting workee; only de Hog. He, de hog, no workee; he eat, he drink, he walk about, he go to sleep when he please, he libb like a Gentleman.* According to these Opinions of the Americans, one of them would think himself more oblig'd to a Genealogist, who could prove for him that his Ancestors and Relations for ten Generations had been Ploughmen, Smiths, Carpenters, Turners, Weavers, Tanners, or even Shoemakers, and consequently that they were useful Members of Society; than if he could only prove that they were Gentlemen, doing nothing of Value, but living idly on the Labour of others, mere *fruges consumere nati,*[1] and otherwise *good for nothing,* till by their Death their Estates, like the Carcass of the Negro's Gentleman-Hog, come to be *cut up.*

With regard to Encouragements for Strangers from Government, they are really only what are derived from good Laws and Liberty. Strangers are welcome, because there is room enough for them all, and therefore the old Inhabitants are not jealous of them; the Laws protect them sufficiently, so that they have no need of the Patronage of Great Men; and every one will enjoy securely the Profits of his Industry. But, if he does not bring a Fortune with him, he must work and be industrious to live. One

---

[1] Franklin's note: "Born Merely to eat up the corn.—Watts"

or two Years' residence gives him all the Rights of a Citizen; but the government does not at present, whatever it may have done in former times, hire People to become Settlers, by Paying their Passages, giving Land, Negroes, Utensils, Stock, or any other kind of Emolument whatsoever. In short, America is the Land of Labour, and by no means what the English call *Lubberland,* and the French *Pays de Cocagne,* where the streets are said to be pav'd with half-peck Loaves, the Houses til'd with Pancakes, and where the Fowls fly about ready roasted, crying, *Come eat me!*[2] . . .

1784

Letters to Peter Collinson

[October 19, 1752: The Kite Experiment][*]

Philadelphia, October 19

As frequent Mention is made in the News Papers from Europe, of the Success of the Philadelphia Experiment for drawing the Electric Fire from Clouds by Means of pointed Rods of Iron erected on high buildings, &c. it may be agreeable to the Curious to be inform'd, that the same Experiment has succeeded in Philadelphia, tho' made in a different and more easy Manner, which any one may try, as follows.

Make a small Cross of two light Strips of Cedar, the Arms so long as to reach to the four Corners of a large thin Silk Handkerchief when extended; tie the Corners of the Handkerchief to the Extremities of the Cross, so you have the Body of a Kite; which being properly accommodated with a Tail, Loop and String, will rise in the Air, like those made of Paper; but this being of Silk is fitter to bear the Wet and Wind of a Thunder Gust without tearing.[1] To the Top of the upright Stick of the Cross is to be fixed a very sharp pointed Wire, rising a Foot or more above the Wood. To the End of the Twine, next the Hand, is to be tied a silk Ribbon, and where the Twine and the silk join, a Key may be fastened. This Kite is to be raised when a Thunder Gust appears to be coming on, and the Person who holds the String must stand within a Door, or Window, or under some Cover, so that the Silk Ribbon may

[2] The text continues with a description of "the kind of Persons to whom an Emigration to America may be advantageous."

[*] Published in the *Pennsylvania Gazette,* October 19, 1752. Reprinted in Joseph Priestley, *The History and Present State of Electricity, with Original Experiments* (London, 1767). This statement was sent to Franklin's friend Peter Collinson (1694–1768) and was read to the Royal Society on December 21, 1752. Collinson, an English Quaker, merchant, and noted botanist, maintained a long correspondence with Franklin and published Franklin's *Experiments and Observations on Electricity* (1751).

[1] This was not the first time that Franklin had experimented with kites. In a letter to Barbeu

Dubourg (1773), Franklin nostalgically recalls a moment of childhood invention: "When I was a boy, I amused myself one day with flying a paper kite; and approaching the bank of a pond, which was near a mile broad, I tied the string to a stake, and the kite ascended to a very considerable height above the pond, while I was swimming. In a little time, being desirous of amusing myself with my kite, and enjoying at the same time the pleasure of swimming, I returned; and, loosing from the stake the string with the little stick which was fastened to it, went again into the water, where I found, that, lying on my back and holding the stick in my hands, I was drawn along the surface of the water in a very agreeable manner."

not be wet; and Care must be taken that the Twine does not touch the Frame of the Door or Window. As soon as any of the Thunder Clouds come over the Kite, the pointed Wire will draw the Electric Fire from them, and the Kite, with all the Twine, will be electrified, and the loose Filaments of the Twine will stand out every Way, and be attracted by an approaching Finger. And when the Rain has wet the Kite and Twine, so that it can conduct the Electric Fire freely, you will find it stream out plentifully from the Key on the Approach of your Knuckle. At this Key the Phial may be charg'd; and from Electric Fire thus obtain'd, Spirits may be kindled, and all the other Electric Experiments be perform'd, which are usually done by the Help of a rubbed Glass Globe or Tube; and thereby the *Sameness* of the Electric Matter with that of Lightning compleatly demonstrated.

B. FRANKLIN

1752/1752

[August 25, 1755: Whirlwinds]

Dear Sir,   Philadelphia, Aug. 25, 1755.

As you have my former papers on Whirlwinds, &c. I now send you an account[2] of one which I had lately an opportunity of seeing and examining myself.

Being in Maryland, riding with Col. Tasker, and some other gentlemen to his country-seat, where I and my son were entertained by that amiable and worthy man, with great hospitality and kindness, we saw in the vale below us, a small whirlwind beginning in the road, and shewing itself by the dust it raised and contained. It appeared in the form of a sugar-loaf, spinning on its point, moving up the hill towards us, and enlarging as it came forward. When it passed by us, its smaller part near the ground, appeared not bigger than a common barrel, but widening upwards, it seemed, at 40 or 50 feet high, to be 20 or 30 feet in diameter. The rest of the company stood looking after it, but my curiosity being stronger, I followed it, riding close by its side, and observed its licking up, in its progress, all the dust that was under its smaller part. As it is a common opinion that a shot, fired through a water-spout, will break it, I tried to break this little whirlwind, by striking my whip frequently through it, but without any effect. Soon after, it quitted the road and took into the woods, growing every moment larger and stronger, raising, instead of dust, the old dry leaves with which the ground was thick covered, and making a great noise with them and the branches of the trees, bending some tall trees round in a circle swiftly and very surprizingly, though the progressive motion of the whirl was not so swift but that a man on foot might have kept pace with it, but the circular motion was amazingly rapid. By the leaves it was now filled with, I could plainly perceive that the current of air they were driven by, moved upwards in a spiral line; and when I saw the trunks and bodies of large trees invelop'd in the passing whirl, which continued intire after it had left them, I no longer wondered that my whip had no effect on it in its smaller state. I accompanied it about three quarters of a mile, till some limbs of dead trees,

---

[2] The incident Franklin recounts most likely occurred in April 1755 during a trip to Maryland. Along with his famous kite experiment, Franklin's "attack" on the whirlwind shows the combination of his scientific curiosity and his characteristic bravado in the face of dangerous natural phenomena.

broken off by the whirl, flying about, and falling near me, made me more apprehensive of danger; and then I stopped, looking at the top of it as it went on, which was visible, by means of the leaves contained in it, for a very great height above the trees. Many of the leaves, as they got loose from the upper and widest part, were scattered in the wind; but so great was their height in the air, that they appeared no bigger than flies. My son, who was, by this time, come up with me, followed the whirlwind till it left the woods, and crossed an old tobacco-field, where, finding neither dust nor leaves to take up, it gradually became invisible below as it went away over that field. The course of the general wind then blowing was along with us as we travelled, and the progressive motion of the whirlwind was in a direction nearly opposite, though it did not keep a strait line, nor was its progressive motion uniform, it making little sallies on either hand as it went, proceeding sometimes faster, and sometimes slower, and seeming sometimes for a few seconds almost stationary, then starting forwards pretty fast again. When we rejoined the company, they were admiring the vast height of the leaves, now brought by the common wind, over our heads. These leaves accompanied us as we travelled, some falling now and then round about us, and some not reaching the ground till we had gone near three miles from the place where we first saw the whirlwind begin. Upon my asking Col. Tasker if such whirlwinds were common in Maryland, he answered pleasantly, *No, not at all common; but we got this on purpose to treat Mr. Franklin.* And a very high treat it was, to Dear Sir, Your affectionate friend, and humble servant   B. F.
1755/1769

Letter to Ezra Stiles[1]

Philad[a], March 9. 1790.

REVEREND AND DEAR SIR,

I received your kind Letter of Jan'y 28, and am glad you have at length received the portrait of Gov'r Yale[2] from his Family, and deposited it in the College Library. He was a great and good Man, and had the Merit of doing infinite Service to your Country by his Munificence to that Institution. The Honour you propose doing me by placing mine in the same Room with his, is much too great for my Deserts; but you always had a Partiality for me, and to that it must be ascribed. I am however too much obliged to Yale College, the first learned Society that took Notice of me and adorned me with its Honours,[3] to refuse a Request that comes from it thro' so esteemed a Friend. But I do not think any one of the Portraits you mention, as in my Possession, worthy of the Place and Company you propose to place it in. You

---

[1] Grandson of the Puritan poet Edward Taylor and president of Yale College, Stiles (1727–1795) had written Franklin for information about his religious "sentiments."

[2] Elihu Yale (1649–1721), for whom Yale College was named.

[3] Yale awarded Franklin an honorary degree in 1753.

have an excellent Artist lately arrived. If he will undertake to make one for you, I shall cheerfully pay the Expence; but he must not delay setting about it, or I may slip thro' his fingers, for I am now in my eighty-fifth year, and very infirm.[4]

I send with this a very learned Work, as it seems to me, on the antient Samaritan Coins, lately printed in Spain, and at least curious for the Beauty of the Impression. Please to accept it for your College Library. I have subscribed for the Encyclopædia[5] now printing here, with the Intention of presenting it to the College. I shall probably depart before the Work is finished, but shall leave Directions for its Continuance to the End. With this you will receive some of the first numbers.

You desire to know something of my Religion. It is the first time I have been questioned upon it. But I cannot take your Curiosity amiss, and shall endeavour in a few Words to gratify it. Here is my Creed. I believe in one God, Creator of the Universe. That he governs it by his Providence. That he ought to be worshipped. That the most acceptable Service we render to him is doing good to his other Children. That the soul of Man is immortal, and will be treated with Justice in another Life respecting its Conduct in this. These I take to be the fundamental Principles of all sound Religion, and I regard them as you do in whatever Sect I meet with them.

As to Jesus of Nazareth, my Opinion of whom you particularly desire, I think the System of Morals and his Religion, as he left them to us, the best the World ever saw or is likely to see; but I apprehend it has received various corrupting Changes, and I have, with most of the present Dissenters in England, some Doubts as to his Divinity; tho' it is a question I do not dogmatize upon, having never studied it, and think it needless to busy myself with it now, when I expect soon an Opportunity of knowing the Truth with less Trouble. I see no harm, however, in its being believed, if that Belief has the good Consequence, as probably it has, of making his Doctrines more respected and better observed; especially as I do not perceive, that the Supreme takes it amiss, by distinguishing the Unbelievers in his Government of the World with any peculiar Marks of his Displeasure.

I shall only add, respecting myself, that, having experienced the Goodness of that Being in conducting me prosperously thro' a long life, I have no doubt of its Continuance in the next, though without the smallest Conceit of meriting such Goodness. My Sentiments on this Head you will see in the Copy of an old Letter enclosed,[6] which I wrote in answer to one from a zealous Religionist, whom I had relieved in a paralytic case by electricity, and who, being afraid I should grow proud upon it, sent me his serious though rather impertinent Caution. I send you also the Copy of another Letter, which will shew something of my Disposition relating to Religion. With great and sincere Esteem and Affection, I am, Your obliged old Friend and most obedient humble Servant   B. FRANKLIN.

1790/1907

---

[4] Franklin died a month later, on April 17.

[5] Franklin refers here to the third edition of the *Encyclopedia Britannica,* which was being printed in America for the first time.

[6] Probably written to Thomas Paine.

Phillis Wheatley
ca. 1754–1784

A frail but precious child who "had no other covering than a quantity of dirty carpet about her" stood among the "small Negroes" offered for sale in the following advertisement printed in the August 3, 1761, edition of the Boston *Evening Post:*

To Be Sold

A parcel of likely Negroes, imported from Africa, cheap for cash, or short credit; Enquire of John Avery, at his house next Door to the White-Horse, or at a Store adjoining to said Avery's Distill House, at the South End, near the South Market; Also, if any Persons have any Negro Men, strong and hearty, tho' not of the best moral character, which are proper Subjects for Transportation, may have an exchange for small Negroes.

Susannah Wheatley, the wife of a prosperous Boston tailor, purchased this young girl "for a trifle" and gave her, as was the custom, a Christian first name. Although her roots are obscure, Phillis Wheatley was judged "from the circumstance of shedding her front teeth" to be approximately seven years of age at the time of her sale, and more certainly to be the kidnap victim of slave traders who used northern cities to dispose of those Africans who remained after the "strong and hearty" were sold at more lucrative southern markets.

Phillis Wheatley quickly revealed "uncommon intelligence" and within sixteen months at the Wheatley house had mastered English, astronomy, geography, and history, as well as the most knotty passages from the Scriptures. The Wheatley family encouraged Phillis's formidable talents, tutored her in classical languages and literatures, exempted her from the usual domestic labors, removed her from the company of other blacks, and gradually turned her into a curiosity in New England's intellectual circles. A brilliant conversationalist, she frequently accompanied her owners on their social rounds of Boston but invariably declined "the seat offered her at their board, and, requesting that a side-table might be laid for her, dined modestly apart from the rest of the company." Given such circumstances, Phillis Wheatley spent most of her life complaisantly isolated from both blacks and whites, enthralled only by the companionship of British poetry, most notably Alexander Pope's heroic couplets.

Writing "originally for the Amusement of the Author," she filled all her leisure moments with poetry, published her first verse at thirteen, and soon won the praise of such prominent figures as Dr. Benjamin Rush and Thomas Hutchinson, the last colonial governor of Massachusetts. Fame followed the publication in 1770 of her widely reprinted broadside poem on the death of "the celebrated Divine, and eminent Servant of Jesus Christ, the late Reverend, and Pious George Whitefield," the preacher-missionary whose remarkable popularity during the Great Awakening Samuel Johnson attributed to the "peculiarity of his manner. He would be followed by crowds were he to wear a night-cap in the pulpit, or were he to preach from a tree."

In her nineteenth year, Phillis Wheatley crossed the Atlantic once more, but this time as a celebrated writer bound for London and a meeting with the Countess of Huntingdon, Whitefield's patron. This "sooty prodigy" from Boston soon became the "Sable Muse" of London. Voltaire acclaimed her, Franklin visited her, and the Lord Mayor of London and the Earl of Dartmouth honored her with special editions of *Paradise Lost* and Smollett's translation of *Don Quixote*. But in the midst of plans to present her to King George III, Phillis had to return to America to care for her sickly mistress. When she left London, Phillis Wheatley carried with her copies of her recently printed *Poems on Various Subjects, Religious and Moral* (1773), the first published volume by a black American. The circulation of a book of poems by a nineteen-year-old slave was regarded as so unusual that Wheatley's work, dedicated to the Countess of Huntingdon, had to be prefaced by the testimony of eighteen prestigious Bostonians, including John Hancock and the Reverend Mather Byles, certifying the poems' authenticity.

Written for a white audience and imitative of the prevailing Augustan poetic fashion, Wheatley's occasional verse reveals little of the self-consciousness that distinguishes much of later Afro-American literature. Yet, as Richard Wright, the twentieth-century black American novelist, reminds us, "Before the webs of slavery had so tightened as to snare nearly all Negroes in our land, one was freed by accident to give in clear, bell-like limpid cadence the hope of freedom in the New World."

At the onset of the American Revolution, Phillis fled with the Wheatley family to Providence, where she addressed a letter and poem "To His Excellency George Washington." Responding four months later, Washington apologized for the delay by citing "important occurrences, continually interposing to distract the mind and withdraw the attention." He hailed "this new instance" of Wheatley's "genius" and, at the risk of "imputation of vanity," sent the poem to Thomas Paine to be published in his *Pennsylvania Magazine*.

In the years following, Phillis Wheatley gained her freedom upon the death of the Wheatleys, married a free black, John Peters, and bore three children, all of whom died in childhood. Destitute, in failing health, and suffering from the unaccustomed burdens of menial work at "a common negro boarding-house," Wheatley tried to reverse her misfortune by advertising a three-hundred-page volume of "Poems & Letters on various subjects, dedicated to the Right Hon. Benjamin Franklin Esq." For want of subscribers, the project never appeared, and Phillis Wheatley, once the best-known colonial poet in England, died in obscurity in 1784.

Further Reading:
M. M. Odell, *Memoir*, 1834.
W. D. Jordan, *White over Black: American Attitude Toward the Negro, 1550–1812*, 1968.
S. Graham, *The Story of Phillis Wheatley*, 1969.
M. A. Richmond, *Bid the Vassal Soar*, 1974.
W. Robinson, *Phillis Wheatley*, 1975.

Text:
The Poems of Phillis Wheatley, ed. J. D. Mason, 1966.

On the Death of the Rev. Mr. George Whitefield.[1] 1770

Hail, happy saint, on thine immortal throne,
Possest of glory, life, and bliss unknown;
We hear no more the music of thy tongue,
Thy wonted auditories cease to throng.
Thy sermons in unequall'd accents flow'd,   5
And ev'ry bosom with devotion glow'd;
Thou didst in strains of eloquence refin'd
Inflame the heart, and captivate the mind.
Unhappy we the setting sun deplore,
So glorious once, but ah! it shines no more.   10

   Behold the prophet in his tow'ring flight!
He leaves the earth for heav'n's unmeasur'd height,
And worlds unknown receive him from our sight.
There *Whitefield* wings with rapid course his way,
And sails to *Zion*[2] through vast seas of day.   15
Thy pray'rs, great saint, and thine incessant cries
Have pierc'd the bosom of thy native skies.
Thou moon hast seen, and all the stars of light,
How he has wrestled with his God by night.
He pray'd that grace in ev'ry heart might dwell,   20
He long'd to see *America* excel;
He charg'd its youth that ev'ry grace divine
Should with full lustre in their conduct shine;
That Saviour, which his soul did first receive,
The greatest gift that ev'n a God can give,   25
He freely offer'd to the num'rous throng,
That on his lips with list'ning pleasure hung.

   "Take him, ye wretched, for your only good,
"Take him ye starving sinners, for your food;
"Ye thirsty, come to this life-giving stream,   30
"Ye preachers, take him for your joyful theme;
"Take him my dear *Americans,* he said,
"Be your complaints on his kind bosom laid:

[1] Whitefield (1714–1770), an English disciple of John Wesley, was the most popular revivalist of the eighteenth century. Whitefield, who frequently visited the United States, died in Massachusetts. This, Wheatley's first published poem, brought her international acclaim.
[2] God's heavenly city.

"Take him, ye *Africans,* he longs for you,
"*Impartial Saviour* is his title due: 35
"Wash'd in the fountain of redeeming blood,
"You shall be sons, and kings, and priests to God."

Great *Countess,*[3] we *Americans* revere
Thy name, and mingle in thy grief sincere;
New England deeply feels, the *Orphans* mourn,   40
Their more than father will no more return.

But, though arrested by the hand of death,
Whitefield no more exerts his lab'ring breath,
Yet let us view him in th' eternal skies,
Let ev'ry heart to this bright vision rise;   45
While the tomb safe retains its sacred trust,
Till life divine re-animates his dust.

1770/1773

On Being Brought from Africa to America

'Twas mercy brought me from my *Pagan* land,
Taught my benighted soul to understand
That there's a God, that there's a *Saviour* too:
Once I redemption neither sought nor knew.
Some view our sable race with scornful eye,   5
"Their colour is a diabolic die."
Remember, *Christians, Negroes,* black as *Cain,*[1]
May be refin'd, and join th' angelic train.

1773/1773

[3] Selina Shirley Hastings (1707–1791), whom
Phillis Wheatley visited in 1773, was George
Whitefield's patron and an ardent member of
the Methodist church.

[1] Cain slew his brother, Abel, and for doing so
was marked by God (Genesis 4:1–15). This
mark is sometimes interpreted as the origin of
the Negro.

To S. M.[1] A Young African Painter, on Seeing His Works

To show the lab'ring bosom's deep intent,
And thought in living characters to paint,
When first thy pencil did those beauties give,
And breathing figures learnt from thee to live,
How did those prospects give my soul delight,   5
A new creation rushing on my sight?
Still, wond'rous youth! each noble path pursue,
On deathless glories fix thine ardent view:
Still may the painter's and the poet's fire
To aid thy pencil, and thy verse conspire!   10
And may the charms of each seraphic theme
Conduct thy footsteps to immortal fame!
High to the blissful wonders of the skies
Elate thy soul, and raise thy wishful eyes.
Thrice happy, when exalted to survey   15
That splendid city, crown'd with endless day,
Whose twice six gates[2] on radiant hinges ring:
Celestial *Salem*[3] blooms in endless spring.

Calm and serene thy moments glide along,
And may the muse inspire each future song!   20
Still, with the sweets of contemplation bless'd,
May peace with balmy wings your soul invest!
But when these shades of time are chas'd away,
And darkness ends in everlasting day,
On what seraphic pinions shall we move,   25
And view the landscapes in the realms above?
There shall thy tongue in heav'nly murmurs flow,
And there my muse with heav'nly transport glow:
No more to tell of *Damon's*[4] tender sighs,
Or rising radiance of *Aurora's*[5] eyes,   30
For nobler themes demand a nobler strain,
And purer language on th' ethereal plain.
Cease, gentle muse! the solemn gloom of night
Now seals the fair creation from my sight.

1773

[1] Probably Scipio Moorhead, a Boston slave of the Reverend John Moorhead.
[2] Revelation 21:12 represents the walls of heavenly Jerusalem by 12 gates.
[3] Jerusalem (in heaven).
[4] Damon: in classical mythology, a shepherd singer who pledged his life for his condemned friend Pythias.
[5] Aurora: goddess of the dawn in Roman myth.

Washington Allston,
The Poor Author and the Rich Bookseller,
oil on canvas, 1811.
Courtesy, Museum of Fine Arts, Boston.
Bequest of Charles Sprague Sargent, 1927.

The Literature of the New Republic 1776–1836

The Declaration of Independence proclaimed the political freedom of the American colonies and launched their self-conscious quest for a national identity. Americans quickly found themselves grappling with many momentous issues, not the least of them being, to borrow the title of St. Jean de Crèvecoeur's celebrated essay, "What is an American?" Along with that overarching question came several other related issues that were debated for the next century: Did America possess a unique, distinctive culture? Was there such a thing as an American language? Did an authentic American literature exist? That such issues were debated is not at all surprising given the colonies' newly won independence from England, but what is surprising is that they continued to be public concerns for many decades after the new nation had been founded.

The founding of the American republic hardly seemed auspicious in literary terms. Most literary historians have tended to dismiss the period between 1776 and 1836, as one put it, "as a sort of blank space between the Revolution and the mature work of Irving, Bryant and Cooper." Another judged the writers of the new republic "blind sailors navigating the Dead Sea of Federalist Pessimism." Yet important literary accomplishments *do* mark the period between 1776 and 1836. American writers expressed the essential features of a distinctive national literature during these years. For the first time, they consciously, though anxiously, asserted their autonomy, sought workable alternatives to servile imitation of English neoclassical models, and abandoned the traditional literary expressions of Enlightenment social consciousness in favor of greater individuality in more spontaneous forms commensurate with the powerful presence of the American landscape. This period also saw produced the early writings of such notable American literary figures as Edgar Allan Poe, Nathaniel Hawthorne, and Ralph Waldo Emerson, as well as the major works of Washington Irving, James Fenimore Cooper, and William Cullen Bryant.

More important, however, American writers in the years between 1776 and 1836 articulated the literary values that would define much of subsequent American literary history—indigenous values that would find their fullest expression in the years after 1836. The literature of the new republic constitutes this nation's first comprehensive attempt to establish an independent literary identity. Controversy, anxiety, false starts, numerous obstacles, and impressive accomplishments characterize this quest.

The Literature of Persuasion

"America must be as independent in *literature,*" wrote Noah Webster, "as she is in politics." Because the new nation had not yet created a literature free of English influence, Americans remained, to use Webster's phrase, "mental colonists." Just as the Revolution had fulfilled the nation's sense of political destiny, a distinctively national literature would express and fulfill America's cultural destiny. In this respect literature took on in the early years of the new republic both practical and almost religious functions. Once political independence had been achieved, developing an indigenous American literary tradition would be the next phase of America's quest to establish what the Puritans had called "a city on a hill." Yet establishing—and exercising— America's literary independence would take far longer than asserting it. Virtually every interested citizen recognized that the problems facing the new nation in its quest for literary autonomy were formidable; to some they appeared insurmountable. Patriotism could prove no substitute for talent and vision.

When the American colonists' grievances against British rule erupted into the Revolutionary War, the most widely circulated forms of colonial literature were travel narratives, religious journals, and political tracts, as well as poetry and occasional essays highly derivative in their structures and themes from British models. To be sure, a growing number of young writers sought to express what Philip Freneau and Hugh Henry Brackenridge called, in their 1771 Princeton University commencement ode, "the Rising Glory of America." Yet these same writers postponed their literary ambitions and put their pens in the service of securing political independence. As the notable literary historian Moses Coit Tyler explained, the Revolutionary War "drove out the tranquil forms of literature and encouraged more aggressive and partisan literary efforts." Forms of public discourse better suited to more topical subjects quickly gained prominence. Freneau described the literary mood of the period most succinctly when he wrote: "An age employ'd in steel, / Can no poetic rapture feel."

Writers seemed to be everywhere, aggressively addressing the pressing issues of the time. In no other period of American literary history would writers so passionately involve themselves with so strong a sense of public responsibility in such crucial public debates. As Thomas Paine noted in *The American Crisis,* writers had the power "to make a world happy—to teach mankind the art of being so—to exhibit, on the theater of the universe, a character hitherto unknown—and to have, as it were, a new creation entrusted to our hands." And with that power came a sense of moral leadership. American writers posted their patriotic ballads and broadsides in the streets and recited or sang them in local taverns and meeting halls. Their satires on the political controversies and caricatures of the leading personalities on both sides of the Atlantic contended for the shrinking space in newspapers whose pulp and rag content had increasingly been diverted to support the escalating war.

The popular literature of the American Revolution consisted principally of first-hand narratives of legendary campaigns, of a raw recruit's heroic life at the end of a gun barrel or in a prisoner-of-war camp. Modeled to a large extent on the Indian captivity narratives popular in the late seventeenth and early eighteenth centuries, these often harrowing battle accounts invariably substituted patriotic lessons for the moral conclusions of their predecessors. Religious writing, especially sermons both from the pulpit and later in print, also played an important role in mustering resistance to the British. The influence of the clergy in the revolutionary cause became noticeable enough to prompt those loyal to the crown to label the ministers who supported the Revolution "the Black Regiment."

Ethan Allen Captures Fort Ticonderoga

The garrison being asleep, except the sentries, we gave them three huzzas, which greatly surprised them. One of the sentries made a pass at one of my officers with a charged bayonet, and slightly wounded him. My first thought was to kill him with my sword; but, in an instant, I altered the design and fury of the blow to a slight cut on the side of the head, upon which he dropped his gun, and asked quarter, which I readily granted him. . . . I ordered the commander, Captain de la Place, to come forth instantly, or I would sacrifice the whole garrison; at which the Captain came immediately to the door, with his breeches in his hand, when I ordered him to deliver me the fort instantly; he asked me by what authority I demanded it: I answered him, *"In the name of the great Jehovah and the Continental Congress."* The authority of the Congress being very little known at that time, he began to speak again; but I interrupted him, and with my drawn sword over his head, again demanded an immediate surrender of the garrison; with which he then complied. . . . This surprise was carried into execution in the gray of the morning of the 10th of May, 1775. The sun seemed to rise that morning with a superior lustre, and Ticonderoga and its dependencies smiled to its conquerors, who tossed about the flowing bowl, and wished success to Congress, and the liberty and freedom of America.

Ethan Allen, *Narrative of Captivity* (1779)

The most pervasive and influential form of writing during the Revolutionary period was the political pamphlet, and its master the redoubtable Thomas Paine. Political pamphlets and essays were so widely distributed that American writing immediately before, during, and after the war might well be called "the literature of persuasion." Pamphlets, however, gradually yielded to the increasing number of newspapers and magazines that appeared at the turn of the century, only to resurface in the mid-nineteenth century during the heated public debate over slavery and secession.

Making Thirteen Clocks Tick Together

Developing a distinctively American literary tradition was irrevocably tied in the early years of the new republic to efforts to establish a *national* political identity. But securing such an identity remained complicated by such formidable obstacles as economic and cultural dependency on England as well as domestic diversity and conflict. In the aftermath of America's Declaration of Independence and its defeat of the British in the Revolutionary War, many former colonists became extremely concerned about whether the newly formed confederation of thirteen states could ever properly be called a nation. Little *national* sentiment was evident among the "united" states. State allegiances seemed more important in determining self-identity than the notion of being an "American." Many years and a bloody civil war would pass before Americans developed the habit of saying "the United States is" rather than "the United States are."

By and large, for both rich and poor, to live in the newly formed United States was to live in an economically and culturally "underdeveloped" country, whose standards of living and cultural taste depended almost exclusively on British goods and styles—whether in business, clothing, household furnishings, painting, architecture, periodicals, or heroic couplets. Independently minded Americans repeatedly complained about the new nation's economic and cultural subservience. St. Jean de Crèvecoeur, the French aristocrat successfully transplanted to the American frontier, complained about the number of shops stocked with British products and calculated that at least "one fifth of all our labors every year is laid out in English commodities." Thomas Jefferson, even more bitterly, regarded his fellow Virginia planters as little more than "a species of property annexed to certain mercantile houses in London." In economic terms, the original thirteen states remained for many years more closely tied to England than to each other. The lure of materialism frequently tested America's commitment to idealistic principles. In matters of goods and services, most Americans subscribed, however reluctantly, to the notion that British is better.

Socially, the new nation could hardly be described as a homogeneous democracy replete with egalitarian impulses. A slowly emerging economic and social hierarchy was increasingly evident—in classes ranging from quasi-aristocratic landholders to slaves and indentured servants, and from artisans and merchants boosting profits in coastal commercial centers to resolutely self-sufficient men and women pushing the wilderness farther southward and westward. Sectional rivalries and prejudices also abounded. In 1813 John Adams wrote disconsolately to a friend, "How shall we cure that distemper of State vanity?" The difficulties of traveling from one region to another gradually transformed lack of information into misperception.

No religion or national system of education unified the citizenry. The variety of religious affiliations (including, among other sects, Catholics, Hugenots, Unitarians, Presbyterians, and Lutherans) only increased factionalism among Americans. Virtually every religious sect had chosen sides in the conflict between the traditional authority of the Protestant church and faith in natural rights and individual reason. In this predominantly Newtonian view of religion, known as Deism, God exists but does not participate directly in human affairs.

Opposing political tendencies, regional interests, cultural diversity, and broad-based philosophical and religious tensions characterized much of the public life in the new nation. Nowhere were these traits more amply evident than in the debate over the function and powers of a central government. There was considerable concern about whether there would—or could—be an effective national government. As an expression of this crucial debate over whether a strong central government was at once indispensable to the new nation's survival as well as compatible with individual liberty, *The Federalist* constitutes the United States' first classic literary text.

"The Intellectual Soil of America Is Sterile"

The causes, indeed, why the intellectual soil of America is so comparatively sterile are obvious. We do not cultivate it; nor, while we can resort to foreign fields, from whence all our wants are so easily and readily supplied, and which have been cultivated for ages, do we find sufficient inducement to labour in our own. We are united by language, manners, and taste, by the bonds of peace and commercial intercourse, with an enlightened nation, the centre of whose arts and population may be considered as much *our* centre, as much the fountain whence *we* draw light and knowledge through books, as that of the inhabitants of Wales and Cumberland. In relation to the British capital as the centre of English literature, arts, and science, the situation of *New* and *Old York* may be regarded as the same. It is only the gradual influence of time, that, by increasing our numbers and furnishing a ready market for the works of domestic hands and heads, will at length generate and continue a race of artists and authors, purely indigenous, and who may vie with those of Europe.

Charles Brockden Brown, Preface to *The American Review and Literary Journal* (1801)

In 1787 the thirteen states, some quite reluctantly, sent delegates to take up the matter of a constitution, a document that would define the fundamental principles of the new nation, determine the powers and duties of the government, guarantee certain rights to the people, and codify the laws of the land. Draft in hand, these representatives returned home to weigh public support for ratification. Many Americans could see no point in abandoning the Articles of Confederation—which had entrusted nearly total sovereignty to the states and claimed no political authority over individuals. An equally large number of Americans, having fought to free themselves from the restraints of one powerful central authority, were wary of establishing another of their own.

To promote the Constitution in New York and in other reluctant states, Alexander Hamilton of New York, James Madison of Virginia, and John Jay of New York published a series of eighty-five letters in a New York newspaper in 1787 and 1788 under the collective pseudonym "Publius." These letters, given the title *The Federalist* when they were first collected in a volume in 1788, endorsed the principle of an indivisible union of states coordinated by a strong central government. *The Federalist* served as a tough-minded argument that gave meaning and justification to the Constitution and helped ensure its adoption. Yet, in another sense, *The Federalist* also contributed significantly to developing a national literature. In its discussion of the distinctions between "federal" and "national" and its predisposition to expect the worst and demand the best from human nature, *The Federalist* also helped define the polarities of the American character, establishing themes and a tone central to much of later American literature.

Cultivating New Meanings

The debate over the nature and extent of a federal government's powers reverberated in virtually every aspect of American culture. One important example can be found in the concerted effort, led by the young Noah Webster, to purify and standardize the American language. Webster envisioned an America "peopled with a hundred millions of men, *all speaking the same language,*" and his *Dissertations on the English Language* (1789) attempted to establish a uniform set of principles "for the rules of pronunciation in our language," just as his speller had done so much to regularize American orthography. Webster hoped, in effect, to do for the English language what the Puritan experiment in the New World had attempted to do for religion—to set an American example for purifying what had become corrupt in Europe. "On examining the language, and comparing the practice of speaking among the yeomanry of this country, with the stile of Shakespear and Addison," Webster observed, "I am constrained to declare that the people of America, in particular the English descendants, speak the most pure English now known in the world. There is hardly a foreign idiom in their language; by which I mean, a phrase that has not been used by the best English writers from the time of Chaucer." As this passage suggests, Webster's interest in linguistic reform was decidedly conservative. "In the few instances in which I write words a little differently from the present usage," he explained, "I do *not* innovate, but *reject innovation.* When I write *fether, lether,* and *mold,* I do nothing more than reduce the words to their original orthography, no other being used in our earliest English books." Searching for what he called a "primitive etymological orthography" that would "call back the language to the purity of former times," Webster envisioned a language spoken and written in America that would set the standard for enlightened discourse at home and abroad.

Linguistic uniformity had already become one of the hallmarks of the new nation in the wake of the Revolution. As John Witherspoon, the Scottish-born president of Princeton University, noted, Americans spoke with greater uniformity than people in England "for a very obvious reason, viz. that being much more unsettled, and moving frequently from place to place, they are not so liable to local peculiarities either in accent or phraseology. There is a greater difference in dialect between one county and another in Britain, than there is between one state and another in America." American mobility, the absence of sharply drawn geographic and class boundaries, and what James Fenimore Cooper called "the inexhaustible activity of the population" were creating a democratic base for developing a language common to all the American people.

In his quest for linguistic purity and uniformity, Webster had seriously miscalculated the influence on the American vocabulary of territorial expansion (into the polyglot Louisiana and Northwest territories) as well as frontier life and immigration. In addition, as H. L. Mencken later noted in his classic three-volume study *The American Language* (1919; 1974), more "Americanisms" (a word coined by John Witherspoon in 1781) entered the language between the American Revolution and 1800 than at any other time before the mid-nineteenth century rush to the West. When Webster published his *American Dictionary of the English Language* in 1828, he had not fundamentally changed his position on the purity of the American language, but he had softened it considerably. He recognized that differences between American and British English were traceable less to local variations than to basic differences in the respective institutions and customs of each nation. In drawing on numerous examples from American writers for his definitions, Webster apparently had become satisfied with explaining such distinctions with the skill of a lexicographer rather than continuing to call for reforms in spelling and usage.

Yet the issues Webster had raised about orthography would persist in American literature well into the twentieth century, stretching well beyond his search for etymological purity to Walt Whitman's unusual spellings and usages, as well as to Emily Dickinson's pronunciation (implied by her rhyme schemes) and Ezra Pound's abbreviations ("sd" and "thro," for example). In a curious way, the efforts of these three writers proved consistent with Webster's original purpose: to make words look more like they were spoken, to emphasize, in effect, the *voice* in American literature. And each writer also helped define, as did Webster, the distinctive nature of an American literary voice.

Literature and Commerce

The spirit of our people is *commercial*. It has been said, and perhaps with some justice, that the *love of gain* peculiarly characterizes the inhabitants of the United States. The tendency of this spirit to discourage literature is obvious. In such a state of Society, men will not only be apt to bend their whole attention to the acquirement of property and neglect the cultivation of their minds as an affair of secondary moment, but letters and science will seldom be found in high estimation; the amount of wealth will be the principal test of influence; the learned will experience but little reward either of honour or emolument; and, of course, superficial education will be the prevailing character.

Samuel Miller, *A Brief Retrospect of the Eighteenth Century* (1803)

The Quest for Literary Independence

The treaties of Paris (1783) and Ghent (1814) may have freed the new nation politically, but Americans remained extremely insecure both intellectually and culturally. The new nation's reliance on the English language and a lingering attraction to the cultural tradition deflated the initial and widespread expectation among Americans that their political freedom would result in an equally independent literary and cultural identity. Several other factors heightened the new nation's collective anxiety about its cultural identity both in the present and in the future. One highly controversial proposition, promoted by the French naturalist and theologian Georges Louis Le Clerc de Buffon (1707–1788), asserted that the human race had degenerated in the Western Hemisphere, an assertion rebuked by Thomas Jefferson in his *Notes on the State of Virginia* (1785) and attacked in a March 1787 editorial in *American Museum* magazine. The United States, the editors advised, ought "to explode the European creed, that we are infantile in our acquisitions, and savage in our manners, because we are inhabitants of a new world, lately occupied by a race of savages." More widespread—and accurate—was the conviction among many American writers that they could not establish an indigenous identity until they had developed both the language and the intellectual structures adequate to express the distinctive qualities of American experience.

Much of the nation's creative energy in its earliest years focused on securing economic and political stability. John Quincy Adams spoke for the vast majority when he noted how difficult it was "to be a man of business and a man of rime." More important, the United States lacked an audience sizable and interested enough to support writers and artists. Philip Freneau advised the would-be writer to "graft his authorship upon some other calling." Few writers in the early years of the new republic had the financial resources to devote themselves full-time to cultivating their art. Many, like Freneau and William Cullen Bryant, wrote for and edited newspapers; some practiced law or turned to teaching, lecturing, and training for the ministry. In 1816 John Pickering noted that books were written primarily "by men, who were obliged to depend upon other employments for their support, and who could devote to literary pursuits those few moments only, which their thirst for learning, stimulated them to snatch from their daily avocations." Several years later, Henry Wadsworth Longfellow's father urged his son to explore another calling because "there is not wealth and munificence enough in this country to afford sufficient encouragement and patronage to merely literary men." The sense of public responsibility and moral leadership that American writers had so vigorously exercised during the earliest years of the new nation was gradually yielding in the early decades of the nineteenth century to a sense of isolation, if not alienation. In this respect, the period between 1776 and 1836 reflects a growing anti-intellectual strain in American society that ever since has traditionally set writers apart from their fellow citizens.

Aspiring writers faced difficulties that loomed larger than personal sacrifice and distracted audiences. Cultural, political, and legal obstacles discouraged all but the resolute. Many cultivated citizens feared that the principles of democracy would reduce cultural standards to the least common denominator, thereby producing, in the reigning logic of the time, a mediocre literary tradition—a concern the influential magazine *Boston Anthology* bellowed in an 1807 editorial: "The spirit of democracy blasts everything beautiful in nature and corrodes everything in art." The lack of an adequate copyright law also discouraged native literary talent. Without enforceable protection for writers, American printers found it far easier to reprint, at far greater profit, already successful British books than to publish—at far greater risk—the works of American authors. John Adams remarked, for example, that American readers were "disposed to encourage a thousand foolish republications from Europe rather than one useful work of their own growth."

With American bookstores filled with English and continental models well into the second decade of the nineteenth century, American writers in the new republic continued to feel the pressure to imitate the prevailing forms of literary expression rather than to invent new ones to accommodate what was gradually being recognized as the unrelenting originality of American experience. The most notable writers during the first decades of the new nation—especially Joel Barlow, Timothy Dwight, and John Trumbull, who came to be known as the "Connecticut Wits"—adapted the major features of imported neoclassical forms to American subjects. In their shared interest in preserving literary decorum and restraint, working within traditional literary forms, especially those with epic and satiric purposes, and associating America with classical Greece and Rome, these writers strove to demonstrate that America was capable of inspiring its own versions of literary grandeur.

The predominance of neoclassical elements in the literature of the new republic also reflects both a lingering sense of American cultural inferiority among these writers and a concern that cultural anarchy might be a legacy of the American Revolution. Their reverence for tradition, their interest in learned rather than spontaneous forms of literary expression, and their readiness to conform artistically suggest that writers were quite willing—and prepared—to legislate national standards for both the new nation's political and literary experiences. They were eager advocates of an *orderly* search for national cultural identity and would willingly have assumed the role of moral monitors of the new nation's progress.

Given these predilections, these writers might seem at first to be anomalies in what eventually became the tradition of American literature that defined its essential features in the works of such later, and less predictable, figures as Emerson, Whitman, Dickinson, and Twain. Yet the Federalist writers' sense of moral superiority links them to the abolitionists and Transcendentalists of the next period, just as their interest in satire and social conservativism connects them to such writers as Longfellow, Thoreau, Whittier, and Lowell. And what places them in the mainstream of American literary tradition is their resolute belief in what the American historian Henry Adams, a descendant of a family more practiced in making history than in writing about it, called "the omnivorous ambition" of that time. Leaders like Thomas Jefferson, Adams observed, "might without extravagance count upon a coming time when diffused ease and education should bring the masses into familiar contact with higher forms of human achievement, and their vast creative power, turned toward a nobler culture, might rise to the level of that democratic genius which found expression in the Parthenon."

Westward the Course of Empire

At the center of American cultural development in the first few decades following the Revolution was a powerful, optimistic idea: the course of empire was inexorably moving westward. Many years after independence had been declared, John Adams could recall the pervasiveness of this cultural belief:

> There is nothing . . . more ancient in my memory than the observation that the arts, sciences, and empire had travelled westward; and in conversation it was always added since I was a child, that their next leap would be over the Atlantic and in to America.

At the back of Adams's mind, no doubt, were the stately lines of George Berkeley's "Verses on the Prospect of Planting Arts and Learning in America." Written in 1726, the poem both commemorated Berkeley's plans to establish a college in America and celebrated the next geographic "leap" in a centuries-old European concept:

> Westward the course of empire takes its way;
>   The first four acts already past,
> A fifth shall close the drama of the day;
>   Time's noblest offspring is the last.

Berkeley's poem went through a remarkable number of printings after its first appearance in America in 1752 and helped nourish confidence in the growth of an indigenous American culture. The patriotic idea of a progressively westward-moving culture would reverberate through virtually every aspect of the cultural life of the new nation.

When Yale president Ezra Stiles reiterated in 1783 the notion that "all the arts may be transplanted from Europe and Asia and flourish in America with an augmented lustre," he was thinking not only of the ennobling, humanistic disciplines (the "culture") Berkeley tried to cultivate in colonial America but also of the more utilitarian "arts" that would accelerate the new nation's growth and expansion. But there was little of an achieved "culture" that Stiles proudly could point to in 1783.

By any standard, the applied and imaginative arts in the early years of the new republic would have struck most cultivated Europeans as impoverished. From the English point of view, the United States could boast of no Addison and Steele; no Pope, Swift, Richardson, Johnson, Burke, or Hume; no Byron, Keats, or Shelley, who were the admired young writers of that time. Writing in his later years, Benjamin Franklin wondered why a "petty island" like England "should enjoy in every Neighbourhood, more sensible, virtuous, and elegant Minds, than we can collect in ranging one hundred Leagues in our vast Forests." Yet Franklin at least had patriotic convention on his side when he added: "But, 'tis said, the Arts delight to travel Westward." He did not dwell on the fact, however, that as the arts headed westward, a large percentage of American artistic and professional talent—painters, musicians, physicians, lawyers, and ministers—headed eastward to England and the continent for study and training. The two finest painters of the period, John Singleton Copley (1738–1815) and Benjamin West (1738–1820), both traveled from colonial America to England to secure their professional reputations.

Professional prospects seemed as dim for drama, playwrights, and actors in post-Revolutionary America. The first play written by an American and acted by a professional American company, Thomas Godfrey's *Prince of Parthia*, was not staged until 1767. Long afterward, New England still continued to legislate against plays as "dangerous to the soul" and as a "great and unnecessary" expense, a diversion that discouraged industry and frugality, and an entertainment which increased "immorality, impiety, and a contempt for religion." Actors discovered more receptive audiences in the southern states, where a few resident companies managed to earn a modest living in the more densely populated cities. And while a few English touring companies performed Shakespeare and Restoration drama for appreciative southern audiences, the population in most areas remained too scattered in the late eighteenth century to support residential theatrical groups.

What little American drama there was in the new nation consisted primarily of adaptations of European models reworked to satisfy American thematic interests. Royall Tyler's *The Contrast* (1787) is the best-known American play of this period. Its focus on the distinctions between native dignity and foreign affectation earned it a special place in the limited repertoire of American theater companies. Later, such writers as William Dunlap (1766–1839) and John Howard Payne (1791–1852) dramatized historical subjects and nationalistic sentiments to small but appreciative audiences, Dunlap in *André* (1798) and Payne in *Brutus* (1818). In the early decades of the new republic, the theater faced popular indifference and lacked institutional support.

Printing and the Reading Public

As a major industrial art, printing served as one of the clearest indications of the cultural lag that characterized the relationship of American and British arts, crafts, and trades into the early years of the nineteenth century. In 1776 well over one hundred printing presses were at work throughout the new nation. Yet a printing press in itself represented the merest beginning of a trade. It was in the best interests of British suppliers to continue the colonial policy of keeping Americans dependent on run-down, secondhand equipment and materials. Type, always difficult to obtain, remained prohibitively expensive after the Revolutionary War. Better quality paper and ink had never been available to the American colonists in sufficient amounts, and the Revolution did little to change that fact. The inadequacies of American printing were widely known and lamented. In 1779 the elderly Benjamin Franklin, serving as the American representative at the French court, wryly observed when sent a batch of Boston newspapers that the paper and typography were of such poor quality that "if you should ever have any secrets that you should wish to be well kept, get them printed in these papers."

In the first several decades following the Revolution, newspapers continued as the staple of the American printing trade. As such, their cultural content continued to reflect the economic and literary dependencies of their printer-publishers. American newspapers tried to reproduce a sophisticated, English literary tone, one that remained directly imported from the enormously successful periodical essays of Addison and Steele. American newspaper editors in the new republic seemed determined to sound as polite, chatty, and witty as their British models. And the contents of most American newspapers left little doubt that a relatively small, affluent class of readers determined the papers' interests, style, tone, and subscription base.

The Contrast

Exult each patriotic heart!—this night is shewn
A piece, which we may fairly call our own;
Where the proud titles of "My Lord! Your Grace!"
To humble Mr and plain Sir give place.
Our Author pictures not from foreign climes
The fashions, or the follies of the times;
But has confin'd the subject of his work
To the gay scenes—the circles of New-York.
On native themes his Muse displays her pow'rs;
If ours the faults, the virtues too are ours.
Why should our thoughts to distant countries roam,
When each refinement may be found at home?

Royall Tyler, from the prologue to The Contrast (1787)

Since newspapers provided one of the major outlets for the new republic's literary efforts, the space accorded literature in those pages was one reliable measure of their importance to the general public in the new nation. Newspapers contained a fair measure of poetry, a few occasional essays, and a scattering of literary reviews and notices. Yet newspaper columns in the new republic featured more profitable, less intellectually demanding enterprises: a scattering of social announcements, a generous sampling of political reports from local and congressional sources as well as foreign dispatches, a wealth of advertisements and lists of cargo arrivals, along with editorial commentary and thinly disguised satire. From their odes to their ads, most newspapers in the new republic were addressed to social groupings roughly designated in those presociology days as "the better sort" (the gentry and the upper ranks of professional classes) and "the middle sort" (independent farmers, artisans, schoolteachers, and the lower ranks of the professions). "The meaner sort" (laborers, seamen, and indentured servants), those whom Alexander Hamilton called "the great beast," did not find a place in the network of public communications until the introduction of the so-called "Penny Press" in the late 1820s and early 1830s.

After the Revolutionary War, more papers gradually began to adopt the principle advocated by Massachusetts printer Isaiah Thomas—that journalism ought to be "popular" and written in a style that would express "common sense in common language." Thomas promoted his own *Massachusetts Spy* (founded in 1770) as one that could be read by "mechanics and other classes of people who had not much time to spare from business." Thomas's confidence that newspapers could reach "the meaner sort" had been bolstered by an upward trend in reading and writing skills that moved closer to nearly universal literacy among American white males by the beginning of the nineteenth century. In New England the legacy of Calvinism, the policy of compulsory education, and the ideology of self-improvement resulted in the highest rate of literacy in the new republic. In the middle and southern colonies, the relatively high literacy rate among European immigrants counterbalanced the lower percentage of literate native white males and helped extend reading and writing skills beyond only the wealthy and socially prominent. Yet the spread of these "popular" forms of journalism reduced even further the number of ready outlets for publishing American writers.

The market for American newspapers developed rapidly in the early decades of the new republic. In 1785 approximately seventy-five newspapers were being printed in the United States. Five years later, that number had climbed to nearly one hundred. By 1820 technical improvements and the beginnings of industrialization had helped increase the total to 508. By 1830, such developments as steam and cylinder presses helped to more than double that number. Nearly every town in America—and several fairly remote frontier settlements—could boast of its own printing press. It seemed that Americans had become addicted to newsprint. But the ever-increasing number of newspapers in print was offset by the limited circulation of each. Even taking into account the rather high reader-per-copy ratio (estimated in the early years of the new nation to be well over twenty), the reading public for newspapers still represented in post-Revolutionary America a surprisingly small portion of the total reading public. The new nation was demonstrating a consistent cultural feature of modern societies: populations grow literate faster than they develop the habit of reading.

In many respects, the book market presented even greater problems for American printers than did newspaper circulations. Given the technical difficulties and production costs they continued to face after the Revolution, American printers could only occasionally afford to tie up their presses with books, and even then the quality of their products could hardly compete with the handsome editions routinely manufactured in England. But whether domestic or imported, books remained too expensive for most Americans' modest standard of living. A single volume of any writer's work would have cost an American laborer a sizable portion of a week's wages. Even for the fairly affluent, books were regarded as luxuries. With the introduction of such mechanical improvements as the Columbia iron press in 1807 and other more efficient printing methods, cheaper printed matter eventually found its way into the homes of the poor, but even then, as James Fenimore Cooper observed, such reading material usually consisted of little more than "a fragment of a Bible, *Pilgrim's Progress,* and an almanac that was four years old."

Regardless of their size and owner's profession, personal libraries in the first few decades following the Revolution were still dominated by the Puritan legacy of what Cotton Mather had called "devout and useful Books." The Bible, *Pilgrim's Progress, The Book of Common Prayer,* sermons, theological tracts, and such didactic staples as *The Practice of Piety* and *The Whole Duty of Man* lined many of the shelves in the growing number of bookshops squeezed into the bustling commercial districts of coastal cities. While Americans still seemed absorbed in reflection about their own spiritual welfare, they also seemed increasingly interested in broadening their experiences and cultivating the vast amount of untilled land that stretched farther and farther westward.

Frontiers of Literature

When Thomas Jefferson's purchase of the Louisiana Territory in 1803 doubled the area of the United States and opened the prospect of expansion to the Pacific, countless Americans were drawn by the large stretches of land available to anyone who wanted them. Not everyone, of course, could afford to develop this land or even, in some areas, to get to it; but many of those who could did so.

Successive waves of pioneers, settlers, farmers, speculators, townspeople, and managers of commerce explored the remote regions of the country in the first half of the nineteenth century. Eagerly they pursued visions of adventure, ownership, and economic self-sufficiency in settlements whose names expressed the new nation's collective hopes: Canaan, Valhalla, Arcadia, Paradise, El Dorado, Beulah. Yet these and other frontier settlements also quickly began to duplicate the distinguishing characteristics of the places the settlers had left. In effect, the American frontier would become the site for a cultural version of Eli Whitney's theory of interchangeable parts. With such names as Rome, Athens, Cambridge, Essex, and Plymouth, many American frontier towns would increasingly be built to reflect eastern and European specifications. Standardized building materials and prefabricated structures followed by the mid-nineteenth century. America's fascination with mobility and duplicative experience had begun to take on cultural as well as social and economic significance in American life and literature. Seen from a European perspective, America appeared to be, to use Thomas Babington Macaulay's phrase, "all sail and no anchor."

Despite the uncertainty that characterized much of American life in the early nineteenth century, reflected in its as yet undetermined geographical and experiential boundaries, Americans found it relatively easy to be optimistic about the future of their new nation. With so much of its territory unsettled, and with a population so rich in individual and collective spontaneity, vision, and energy, the United States promised to be, to use the literary historian Perry Miller's phrase, "nature's nation." Space was rapidly replacing time as the single most crucial factor in American life, and it would soon dominate American literature as well. The land itself had become the new nation's most precious commodity and its greatest source for literary subjects and locations. The land, and the sense of "place" it engendered, had come to serve as the locus for American vision and aspiration.

The Backwoodsman

The people in the Atlantic states have not yet recovered from the horror inspired by the term "backwoodsman." This prejudice is particularly strong in New England, and is more or less felt from Maine to Georgia. . . . But the backwoodsman of the west, as I have seen him, is generally an amiable and virtuous man. His general motive for coming here is to be a freeholder, to have plenty of rich land, and to be able to settle his children about him. It is a most virtuous motive. And I fully believe that nine in ten of the emigrants have come here with no other motive. You find, in truth, that he has vices and barbarisms peculiar to his situation. His manners are rough. He wears, it may be, a long beard. He has a great quantity of bear- and deerskins wrought into his household establishment, his furniture and dress. He carries a knife or a dirk in his bosom, and when in the woods has a rifle on his back and a pack of dogs at his heels. An Atlantic stranger, transferred directly from one of our cities to his door, would recoil from an encounter with him. But remember that his rifle and his dogs are among his chief means of support and profit. Remember that all his first days here were passed in the dread of the savages. Remember that he still encounters them, still meets bears and panthers. Enter his door and tell him you are benighted and wish the shelter of his cabin for the night. The welcome is indeed seemingly ungracious: "I reckon you can stay," or "I suppose we must let you stay." But this apparent ungraciousness is the harbinger of every kindness that he can bestow and every comfort that his cabin can afford. Good coffee, corn bread and butter, venison, pork, wild and tame fowls, are set before you. His wife, timid, silent, reserved, but constantly attentive to your comfort, does not sit at the table with you, but, like the wives of the patriarchs, stands and attends on you. You are shown to the best bed which the house can afford. When this kind of hospitality has been afforded you as long as you choose to stay, and when you depart and speak about your bill, you are most commonly told with some slight mark of resentment that they do not keep tavern.

Timothy Flint, *Recollections of the Last Ten Years* (1826)

Davy Crockett's Legendary Shooting Match with Mike Fink

Mike was a boatman on the Mississip, but he had a little cabbin on the head of the Cumberland, and a horrid handsome wife, that loved him the wickedest that ever you see. Mike only worked enough to find his wife in rags, and himself in powder, and lead, and whiskey, and the rest of the time he spent in nocking over bar and turkeys, and bouncing deer, and sometimes drawing a lead on an injun. So one night I fell in with him in the woods, where him and his wife shook down a blanket for me in his wigwam. In the morning sez Mike to me, "I've got the handsomest wife, and the fastest horse, and the sharpest shooting iron in all Kentuck, and if any man dare doubt it, I'll be in his hair quicker than hell could scorch a feather." This put my dander up, and sez I, "I've nothing to say agin your wife, Mike, for it can't be denied she's a shocking handesome woman, and Mrs. Crockett's in Tennessee, and I've got no horses. Mike, I don't exactly like to tell you you lie about what you say about your rifle, but I'm d——d if you speak the truth, and I'll prove it. Do you see that are cat sitting on the top rail of your potato patch, about a hundred and fifty yards off? If she ever hears agin, I'll be shot if it shan't be without ears."

Sketches and Eccentricities of Col. David Crockett, of West Tennessee (1833)

Scores of early nineteenth century pioneer diaries and journals, most to this day without public recognition, recorded the dramatic nature of unprecedented experiences along the ever-expanding southern and western frontiers. Gradually, however, as settlers transformed freshly cut clearings into towns, Americans with more literary aspirations began to turn out with increasing frequency a newly appropriate subject for literature—personal accounts of life west of the Alleghenies. Widely publicized literary excursions, including those of Washington Irving and James Fenimore Cooper, drew even greater attention to the American frontier, especially among readers in coastal cities. Broadening the nation's literary horizon had become a fact of cultural life in the new republic.

As new populations cleared more land and pushed the frontier farther southward and westward, the settlers' interest in the literature of the frontier remained secondary to their need for practical books. Guides to virtually every aspect of frontier life began to compete vigorously with political and religious titles. Backwoods peddlers had to create more places among their assorted wares for copies of various guides to farming and everyday life along the frontier. As white settlers pushed back the wilderness and displaced greater numbers of Native Americans, books about Indians also appeared with greater frequency, with such self-explanatory titles as *The American Savage: How He May Be Tamed by the Weapons of Civilization.* Yet at the same time that white settlers drove more and more Native Americans from their land and appropriated their knowledge of agriculture and medicine, the broader

American reading public continued to be fascinated with what were known as captivity narratives—harrowing accounts of the narrator's capture, imprisonment, torture, and inevitable escape from Indian captors. Eventually these narratives gave way to the equally heroic exploits of such legendary frontier figures as Daniel Boone and Davy Crockett. The popularity of these frontier stories gave rise to what became the even more celebrated tradition of the tall tale and local color fiction in late nineteenth century American literature.

Since land was now the new nation's principal commodity, and its cultivation a chief occupation, ownership disputes proved inevitable. Books on law were accordingly carted out to frontier settlements, where doctors, ministers, and occasionally the settlers themselves had to compensate for the shortage of lawyers in adjudicating conflicting claims. Even more specialized books dealing with, for example, medicine, agriculture, or horsemanship could be found nestled among the piles of outdated almanacs in backwoods cabins. The almanac undisputedly reigned as the new nation's best-seller and served as the chief instrument for reaching what one writer called "the solitary dwellings of the poor and illiterate, where the studied ingenuity of the learned writers never comes." Combined with the increasing sales of guides to domesticating the frontier, the almanac set what is still an enduring standard for America's dedication to self-made success.

Often there were not enough books to satisfy the American public's interest in self-improvement. Even if there were, many Americans could not afford them. The spread of subscription libraries offered one ingenious solution to this predicament. Beginning in 1731 when Benjamin Franklin organized the Library Company of Philadelphia, subscription libraries recruited members who paid fees to be put toward the purchase of books, which then circulated among the subscribers. At the outbreak of the Revolution, sixty-four subscription libraries, dedicated to "the promotion of knowledge and virtue," had been established, with the borrowing time sensibly determined by the length of the book, the user's distance from the library, and the fee charged. In the years following the Revolution, public circulating libraries flourished and exerted considerable influence on the cultural life of the new republic. In the preface to his novel *The Algerine Captive* (1797), Royall Tyler describes the libraries' impact on the changing literary consciousness of the nation:

> In our inland towns of consequence, social libraries had been constituted, composed of books designed to amuse rather than to instruct, and country book-shelves, fostering the new born taste of the people, had filled the whole land with modern Travels and Novels almost as incredible. The diffusion of a taste for any species of writing through all ranks, in so short a time, would appear impracticable to a European.

Reading was gradually becoming a democratic practice, no longer an activity restricted by virtue of education to the upper class in urban settings.

William Sidney Mount, The Long Story (Tough Story), *oil on panel, 1837 (© in the collection of The Corcoran Gallery of Art, Washington, D.C.).*

The Prospects of an American Literature

Despite a formidable list of circumstances and problems that had impaired the development of a truly distinctive American literature, writers and readers in the early nineteenth century could find several reasons to be encouraged about the cultural prospects of the new republic. In his monumental nine-volume study of the period, *History of the United States of America During the Administrations of Jefferson and Madison* (1889), Henry Adams observed:

> The average American was more intelligent than the average European, and was becoming every year still more active-minded as the new movement of society caught him up and swept him through a life of more varied experiences. On all sides the national mind responded to its stimulants. Deficient as the American was in the machinery of higher instruction; remote and poor, unable by any exertion to acquire the training, the capital, or even the elementary textbooks he needed for a fair development of his natural powers—his native energy and ambition already responded to the spur applied to them.

An American Education

The education we got was solid enough in some respects, and very superficial in others. In arithmetic, geometry, surveying, mechanics, and such solid and practical matters, we were earnest students, but our geography was chiefly American, and the United States was larger than all the universe beside. In the same way our history was American history, brief but glorious. We despised monarchial countries and governments too thoroughly to care much about their histories; and if we studied them, it was that we might contrast their despotisms with our own free and happy institutions. We were taught every day and in every way that ours was the freest, the happiest, and soon to be the greatest and most powerful country in the world. This is the religious faith of every American. He learns it in his infancy, and he can never forget it. . . .

Our education was adapted to intensify our self-esteem, and to make us believe that we were the most intelligent, the most enlightened, the freest, most Christian, and greatest people the sun ever shone upon. Ours was the model Government of the world; our institutions were the model institutions, our country the model Republic. I do not in the least exaggerate. We read it in our books and newspapers, heard it in sermons, speeches, and orations, thanked God for it in our prayers, and devoutly believed it always.

Thomas Low Nichols, *Forty Years of American Life* (1864)

Nowhere were these "varied experiences" and "native energy and ambition" more amply evident than in the scores of new magazines that appeared in the first few decades of the new republic. Frank Luther Mott, a respected historian of the trade, estimates that no fewer than seventy-one periodicals began publishing between 1785 and 1800, with "several hundred more" appearing between 1800 and 1830. Most were relatively brief (few exceeded sixty-four pages in length), and nearly all relied initially on material reprinted from British sources to fill their pages inexpensively. Yet their subtitles reveal the scope of their interests: the *Massachusetts Magazine* billed itself as a *Monthly Museum of Knowledge and Rational Entertainment. Containing, Poetry, Musick, Biography, History, Physick, Geography, Morality, Criticism, Philosophy, Mathematicks, Agriculture, Architecture, Chymistry, Novels, Tales, Romances, Translations, News, Marriages, Deaths, Meteorological Observations, &c.,&c.*

In addition to being compendiums, as one publication put it, of "useful knowledge of every kind," American periodicals also served as the principal forum for the debate over the prospects of developing a truly indigenous American literature. Each issue of the *North American Review*, founded in 1815 as the first American journal devoted exclusively to printing American material, resounded with calls for American writers to stop imitating British and continental literary models. The most vocal advocates of a distinctively national literature—including William Tudor, Walter Channing, and James Kirke Paulding—criticized the still prevailing preference among American writers for neoclassical forms and standards. These critics argued that American writers ought to concentrate instead on more immediate subjects and less studied forms for literary expression. Condeming what Channing called "the Literary Delinquency of America," these critics recognized in American scenery, history, and social relations suitable and untapped resources for literary distinction. Other critics, including R. H. Dana, Sr., and Francis Calley Gray, encouraged American literary independence, but at a much slower pace and without either excluding foreign examples or sacrificing literary standards.

James Kirke Paulding remained the most eloquent and hopeful voice among the periodical essayists' campaign for literary independence. In his essay "National Literature" (1819–1820), he noted that American writers had "debased the genius of this new world by making it the ape and the tributary of that of the old" and observed that the new nation had overlooked its own "rich resources, and sponged upon the exhausted treasury of our impoverished neighbors." American literary independence, Paulding claimed, would not be secure until the American writer freed himself

> from a habit of servile imitation; by daring to think and feel, and express his feelings; by dwelling on scenes and events connected with our pride and affections; by indulging in those little peculiarities of thought, feeling and expression which belong to every nation; by borrowing from nature, and not from those who disfigure or burlesque her. . . . These causes lead to the final establishment of a national literature. . . . This country is not destined to be always behind in the race of literary glory. The time will assuredly come, when that same freedom of thought and action which has given such a spur to our genius in other respects, will achieve similar wonders in literature.

American Language and Literature

The whole external character of our country is totally unlike that of England. Our descriptions, of course, which must, if we ever have a poetry, be made in the language of another country, can never be distinctive. They can never possess the peculiar claims which those of native individuality teem with; which are more beautiful to a foreigner because he is willing in reading them to heighten the beauties of an obscure passage by lending it the aid of his own imagination. How tame will his language sound who would describe Niagara in language fitted for the falls at London bridge, or attempt the majesty of the Mississippi in that which was made for the Thames?

Walter Channing (1815)

With its attention to "those little peculiarities of thought, feeling, and expression which belong to every nation," its emphasis on an "air and character of originality," and its promotion of American history and nature as suitable literary subjects, Paulding's remarks anticipate the major themes of Ralph Waldo Emerson's celebrated essay "The American Scholar." The message was clear: American writers must fathom their own distinctive experiences before they could create a national literature equal to expressing those experiences in indigenous terms.

The Makings of American Literature

The basic ingredients of an independent national literature were in place: ambitious writers, suitable subjects, and an increasing number of printing presses, newspapers, magazines, book shops, schools, and libraries. All that remained was to make that literature distinctively American. "It does not follow because many books are written by persons born in America," Margaret Fuller cautioned several years later, "that there exists an American literature. Books which imitate or represent the thought and life of Europe do not constitute an American literature. Before such can exist, an original idea must animate this nation and fresh currents must call into life fresh thoughts along its shores."

By the late 1820s, Americans could point with pride to the publication of, among other notable works, Washington Irving's *Sketch Book* (1819–1820), William Cullen Bryant's *Poems* (1821), three of James Fenimore Cooper's "Leather-Stocking Tales" (*The Pioneers,* 1823; *The Last of the Mohicans,* 1826; and *The Prairie,* 1827), Edgar Allan Poe's *Tamerlane and Other Poems* (1827), and Noah Webster's *American Dictionary* (1828). Ample evidence of America's literary progress could also be seen in the increasing number of writers who devoted themselves exclusively to their craft as well as in the growing interest in literary theory and controversy. The prominence of the so-called Knickerbocker School, the most famous group of writers in the early decades of the new republic, added luster to the American literary scene and helped turn New York into the literary matrix of the early nineteenth century, outshining Philadelphia, just as that city had in turn overshadowed Boston. However, the writers identified with the Knickerbocker group—including, among others, James Kirke Paulding, Fitz-Greene Halleck, John Howard Payne, Washington Irving, and, for a time, William Cullen Bryant and James Fenimore Cooper—were closer geographically than in aesthetic principle. Yet however loosely associated, these writers did avow the same interest in exploring American subjects and themes.

Yet none of these responses would have met Paulding's and Fuller's challenge to create an independent national literature. As their remarks underscore, the most persistent problem facing writers who aspired to create a national literature in the early nineteenth century was the inadequacy—or, better, the inappropriateness—of European forms to express states of consciousness that were specifically American. The issue was not the lack of American material suitable for literary purposes but the resistance of that material to European methods of expression. Intent on being *American,* writers in the new republic had yet to discover how to do so.

Self-consciousness about the irrepressible novelty of American experience proved to be the new nation's greatest literary resource. With, as Timothy Dwight observed, no "ancient castles, ruined abbeys, and fine pictures" to re-create in literature, American writers sought new modes and styles to express their nation's unprecedented experiences in the natural world. The land and the limitless experiences it generated had become an "experiment," a word first used in an American context. "Men are like plants," Crèvecoeur observed; they are as different as "the peculiar soil and exposition in which they grow." And with no sense of failure to inhibit them, Americans in the early decades of the new republic were free to explore their indigenous experience. The extraordinary discoveries in botany recorded in William Bartram's *Travels Through North and South Carolina, Georgia, East and West Florida* (1791), for example, not only increased the nation's understanding of the natural world but also provided many prominent American poets of the time (including Philip Freneau and William Cullen Bryant) with reliable yet exotic views of American nature.

Novelty and experimentation, which were everywhere apparent in daily American experience, surfaced at first only intermittently in the nation's characteristic literary forms. Imitating imported literary methods still dominated poetic expression throughout the period, including the works of its two major poets, Philip Freneau and William Cullen Bryant. Both Freneau and the renowned Bryant, who vehemently denounced those who "do not praise a thing until [they] see the seal of transatlantic approbation upon it," found it far easier to admire indigenous American subjects than to render them in distinctively American terms. In this respect, their stately and powerful poetic voices seem more harbingers of than precedents for such fiercely original poetic imaginations as those of Walt Whitman and Emily Dickinson later in the nineteenth century.

The familiar essay met much the same fate as poetry in the hands of American writers during the early republic. Most newspapers featured essay series, many written under such delightful pseudonyms as "The Prompter" (Noah Webster), "Tomo Cheeki" and "Robert Slender" (Philip Freneau), "Oliver Oldstyle" (Joseph Dennie), and "Jonathan Oldstyle" (from the pen of the master of the genre, Washington Irving). Despite the essay's use as the principal means to decry British influence on American literature, most American writers regularly invoked Addison and Steele as their literary precedent, just as American reviewers relied on their English counterparts to set the standard for witty and incisive commentary on cultural and social affairs.

During this same period, however, two groups that had rarely posited their voices in colonial American literature began to express their individual and collective interests and sensibilities. Women and blacks made significant gains as writers and readers during the years between 1776 and 1836. For blacks, a class deliberately kept uneducated in the new republic, learning to read and write was largely a matter of fortitude, luck, or subterfuge. But in March 1827, John B. Russwurm, the first black American college graduate (Bowdoin, 1826), and Samuel Cornish founded *Freedom's Journal* in New York City. This, the nation's first newspaper owned and edited by blacks, aimed to serve both to inform "our brethren in the different states of this great confederacy" and to

On Female Education

In calling on my patriotic countrymen, to effect so noble an object, the consideration of national glory, should not be overlooked. Ages have rolled away;—barbarians have trodden the weaker sex beneath their feet;—tyrants have robbed us of the present light of heaven, and fain would take its future also. Nations, calling themselves polite, have made us the fancied idols of ridiculous worship, and we have repaid them with ruin for their folly. But where is that wise and heroic country, which has considered, that our rights are sacred, though we cannot defend them? that tho' a weaker, we are an essential part of the body politic, whose corruption or improvement must affect the whole? and which, having thus considered, has sought to give us by education, that rank in the scale of being, to which our importance entitles us? History shows not that country. It shows many, whose legislatures have sought to improve their various vegetable productions, and their breeds of useful brutes; but none, whose public councils have made it an object of their deliberations, to improve the character of their women. Yet though history lifts not her finger to such a one, anticipation does. She points to a nation, which having thrown off the shackles of authority and precedent, shrinks not from schemes of improvement, because other nations have never attempted them; but, which, in its pride of independance, would rather lead than follow, in the march of human improvement: a nation, wise and magnanimous to plan, enterprising to undertake, and rich in resources to execute. Does not every American exult that this country is his own? And who knows how great and good a race of men, may yet arise from the forming hand of mothers, enlightened by the bounty of that beloved country, to defend her liberties, to plan her future improvement, and to raise her to unparalleled glory.

> Emma Willard, "An Address to . . . the Legislature of New York Proposing a Plan for Improving Female Education" (1819)

conciliate what the editors hoped would be a large white audience. In its attention to "useful knowledge of every kind," "moral and religious improvement," and "civil rights," *Freedom's Journal* succeeded admirably in its announced purpose: "to plead our own cause." It also contributed to the nature of the debate over abolition.

Women had from childhood on traditionally been discriminated against educationally in colonial America, and despite the urgings of Abigail Adams and other prominent women, the Revolution and its aftermath did little to improve their lot. For women in the new nation, literacy continued to be determined principally by their class. Those who read, did, and mainly fiction. The development of the American novel depended to a large extent on a female readership.

Sentimental novels were among the most popular forms of fiction in the new republic. Highly didactic, these novels featured an epistolary style derived primarily from Samuel Richardson. Other popular fictional forms of the time were the historical romances influenced primarily by Sir Walter Scott and the satiric novel. The American writer must "examine objects with his own eyes," exhorted Charles Brockden Brown, whose Gothic novels enjoyed wide readership. He must "employ European models merely for the improvement of his taste" and draw on "all that is genuine and peculiar in the scene before him" to create literature equivalent to his sources. The irony of Brown's work, like that of each of the other novelists in the new republic, is its dependence on English and continental sources. Yet these fictional forms also introduce characters, settings, and themes that would be developed more elaborately in the later fiction of Irving, Cooper, Poe, Hawthorne, and Melville.

European Models and the American Landscape

The careers of Washington Irving and James Fenimore Cooper span the period of America's self-conscious quest for an independent literary identity, and their writings most clearly illustrate the major tension in the literature of the new

---

"A Fitting Place to Speak of God"

Perhaps the most impressive characteristic of American scenery is its wildness.

It is the most distinctive because in civilized Europe the primitive features of scenery have long since been destroyed or modified—the extensive forests that once overshadowed a great part of it have been felled—rugged mountains have been smoothed, and impetuous rivers turned from their courses to accommodate the tastes and necessities of a dense population—the once tangled wood is now a grassy lawn; the turbulent brook a navigable stream—crags that could not be removed have been crowned with towers, and the rudest valleys tamed by the plough.

And to this cultivated state our western world is fast approaching; but nature is still predominant, and there are those who regret that with the improvements of cultivation the sublimity of the wilderness should pass away: for those scenes of solitude from which the hand of nature has never been lifted, affect the mind with a more deep toned emotion than aught which the hand of man has touched. Amid them the consequent associations are of God the creator—they are his undefiled works, and the mind is cast into the contemplation of eternal things.

Thomas Cole, "Essay on American Scenery" (1835)

republic: eager but anxious responses to the lure of literary nationalism set off against assurances of working within traditional European models. Their writings also underscore the principal literary issues in the new republic: the writer's identity in a society preoccupied with material progress; the literary consequences of America's absorption in the present and the future and its neglect of the past; and, above all, the writer's need to create an *American* time and place where the imagination could flourish. For Irving this would be colonial Sleepy Hollow. For Cooper it was the unspoiled, dense woods of the frontier as well as the open stretches of the sea, the same regions depicted in the new American landscape painting led by Thomas Cole. Later writers, including Hawthorne, Thoreau, Twain, Crane, and Faulkner, created their own distinctive versions of a specifically American historical context, but Irving and Cooper first grappled with the issue in a way that made the nature of both the literary problem and its solution luminously clear.

Irving helped American writers discover the literary potential of the past by adapting Europe's rich cultural heritage to American settings. Cooper shared Irving's interest in the literary possibilities of history and opened two additional prospects for American literature: the frontier and life at sea. Cooper's

John Quidor, The Return of Rip Van Winkle, oil on canvas, 1829 (National Gallery of Art, Washington, D.C., Andrew W. Mellon Collection).

"Leather-Stocking Tales" played a significant role in establishing the frontier as the principal shaping influence on nineteenth century and much of twentieth century American literature and turned Natty Bumppo into the American archetype of individual freedom and self-reliance. Cooper's backwoodsman served as the fictional forerunner of countless legendary mountain men and cowboys, America's purest examples of self-expression in the wilderness.

The irony of Cooper's and Irving's accomplishments is that in both cases they were nurtured principally during the authors' extended stays in Europe. Irving's and Cooper's familiar essays, stories, novels, and social criticism, adapted largely from European sources, form a compendium of American literary taste in the first half of the nineteenth century—moving in Irving's case from neoclassical wit and satire to Romantic interest in atmosphere and sentiment, and in the case of Cooper from an interest in the traditional novel of manners to the broader brushstrokes of painting mythic American landscapes populated with legendary characters. The diversity (their willingness to explore multiple aspects of experience), the dynamism (their constant growth as writers), and the organic unity of their writings (their interest in the whole as much as the part), along with their commitment to extolling a strong sense of individuality, independence, and introspection in the face of the powerful rawness of the American landscape, place Irving and Cooper at the beginning of what would become a long tradition of Romantic writing in American literature, a tradition that would have its fullest expression in the great flowering of the American Renaissance. At the end of "The American Scholar" (1837), Ralph Waldo Emerson proclaimed that Americans "will walk on our own feet; we will work with our own hands; we will speak our own minds." The writers of the new republic laid the foundation that enabled Emerson to declare the symbolic birth of a truly distinctive American literature with such confidence.

Further Reading:

H. Adams, *The History of the United States of America During the Administrations of Jefferson and Madison*, 8 vols., 1884–1901.

M. Ellis, *Joseph Dennie and His Circle*, 1915.

V. W. Brooks, *The Flowering of New England*, 1936.

L. Howard, *The Connecticut Wits*, 1943.

H. M. Jones, *O Strange New World: American Culture, the Formative Years*, 1952.

H. H. Clark, *Transitions in American Literary History*, 1953.

B. T. Spencer, *The Quest for Nationality*, 1957.

D. Boorstin, *The Americans: The Colonial Experience*, 1958.

M. Cunliffe, *The Nation Takes Shape*, 1959.

R. B. Nye, *The Cultural Life of the New Nation*, 1960.

L. P. Simpson, *The Federalist Literary Mind*, 1962.

C. L. Sanford, *Quest for America 1810–1824*, 1964.

D. Boorstin, *The Americans: The National Experience*, 1965.

G. Dangerfield, *The Awakening of American Nationalism, 1815–1828*, 1965.

W. Hedges, *Washington Irving: An American Study, 1802–1832*, 1965.

J. T. Main, *The Social Structure of Revolutionary America*, 1965.

P. Miller, *The Life of the Mind in America: From the Revolution to the Civil War*, 1965.

R. E. Spiller, *The American Literary Revolution*, 1967.

W. Charvat, *The Profession of Authorship in America, 1800–1870*, ed. M. J. Bruccoli, 1968.

H. Petter, *The Early American Novel*, 1971.

L. Simpson, *The Man of Letters in New England and the South*, 1973.

L. J. Friedman, *Inventors of the Promised Land*, 1975.

H. F. May, *The Enlightenment in America*, 1976.

K. Silverman, *Cultural History of the American Revolution*, 1976.

S. Bercovitch, *The Puritan Origins of the American Self*, 1978.

M. Kammen, *A Season of Youth: The American Revolution and the Historical Imagination*, 1978.

J. Ellis, *After the Revolution*, 1979.

E. Elliott, *Revolutionary Writers: Literature and Authority in the New Republic, 1725–1810*, 1982.

J. Fliegelman, *Prodigals and Pilgrims: The American Revolution Against Patriarchal Authority*, 1982.

R. Ferguson, *Law and Letters in American*

Culture, 1984.

R. H. Wiebe, *The Opening of American Society*, 1984.

L. Buell, *New England Literary Culture: From Revolution Through Renaissance*, 1986.

Thomas Jefferson
1743–1826

Thomas Jefferson's literary life is intertwined with his life as diplomat, statesman, architect, environmental planner, scientist, politician, and theorist of education. The versatile Jefferson is an awesome figure to later generations who proclaim the value and necessity of specialization. Jefferson embodies the eighteenth-century ideal of a gentleman, a "man of parts" who is worldly, learned, and proficient in numerous endeavors. Jefferson lived that ideal. More, he became an American paradox, an aristocrat who was also a democrat.

Jefferson was born in central Virginia near the future sites of Monticello and the University of Virginia. His father's estate, Shadwell, was at that time near the frontier, and Peter Jefferson, a farmer and surveyor, taught his son Indian lore and mapmaking, perhaps the basis for Jefferson's eventual interests in anthropological study and in design. At age five Jefferson was sent to an English school some fifty miles distant and at ten was enrolled in a Latin school for training in classical language and literature. In 1760 he entered the College of William and Mary, where he had the "great good fortune," as he put it, "to be instructed by Dr. William Small, then Professor of Mathematics, a man profound in most of the useful branches of science, with a happy talent of communication, correct and gentlemanly manners, and an enlarged and liberal mind." This teacher, Jefferson wrote, "probably fixed the destinies of my life."

Upon graduation in 1762, and with Small's guidance, Jefferson began to study law. Once again he found a mentor—George Wythe, a prominent attorney who also became Jefferson's "most affectionate friend through life." Under the influence of Small and Wythe, Jefferson gradually imbibed the principles of republicanism. He shed the orthodox, conservative Anglican heritage and embraced Deism, which provided the model of the Creator to be emulated in building a new republic. Through Dr. Small he became aware of the Scottish Common Sense school, from which he came to believe that the moral sense is one's highest faculty and is equally present to all, a view later expressed in the Declaration of Independence, which he drafted.

Jefferson was admitted to the bar in 1767 and practiced law while taking advantage of the cultural opportunities of Williamsburg, which was a colonial capital as well as a college town. He learned the violin, sometimes playing in string quartets with Governor Francis Fauquier, himself a member of the Royal Society and another of the father figures in the young man's life. Jefferson also attended theatrical performances and began collecting the books that proliferated into a library of about ten thousand volumes that later became the basis for the

Library of Congress. He doubtless learned to participate in the polished, urbane conversation of the colonial aristocracy, though Jefferson never was skilled in public speaking.

Jefferson entered Virginia politics in 1769, when he was elected to the legislative House of Burgesses. In those years he also began the construction of Monticello (the estate would not be complete for some forty years). Jefferson was acutely sensitive to style and proportion in architecture. He thought the buildings of his college, William and Mary, "misshapen," like "brick-kilns," and the Williamsburg governor's palace "not handsome." The design for Monticello was Jefferson's own, and has been called classical with American elements. Jefferson's interest in design continued into his Presidential years, when he took part in the plan for the nation's Capitol, and into his so-called retirement, when he designed the campus and buildings (and the curriculum) of the University of Virginia at Charlottesville.

In 1772 Jefferson married Martha Wayles Skelton, a wealthy, slaveholding widow. Within a year their first child, a daughter, was born. The couple had six children, including a son, but only two daughters lived to adulthood. Jefferson was deeply bereaved when his wife died after ten years of marriage. His daughter wrote, "In those melancholy rambles [on horseback], I was his constant companion— a solitary witness to many a burst of grief." Jefferson never remarried.

Pre-Revolutionary politics proved irresistible. In 1773 Jefferson attended a meeting of the Virginia Committee of Correspondence, an intercolonial group that promoted the exchange of letters in opposition to harsh and arbitrary British policies. In 1774 Jefferson attended the newly formed Continental Congress and won respect for his clear style and moderate tone in a pamphlet that defended colonial rights, A Summary View of the Rights of British America. By 1776, with events of the Revolution moving swiftly, Jefferson was one of a committee appointed to draft a document announcing the severance of the colonies from England. Though the committee and the congress edited the draft, the Declaration of Independence was Jefferson's. His remarks on the Declaration are revealing. "I turned to neither book nor pamphlet while writing it," he said. "I did not consider it as any part of my charge to invent new ideas, but to place before mankind the common sense of the subject." He considered the Declaration of Independence "an expression of the American mind." The ideals of the Declaration were compatible with Jefferson's work in Virginia to establish religious freedom by law and thus to separate church and state. These two achievements meant so much to him that he included them, together with his fathering of the University of Virginia, in the epitaph he wrote and left behind at his death.

During the Revolutionary War years, Jefferson served as governor of Virginia, narrowly escaping British capture. In 1783 he was elected to Congress and became minister to France, where he served for five years. He was a member of Washington's Cabinet, Vice-President under John Adams, and then President for two terms beginning in 1801. Jefferson envisioned the United States as a self-sufficient, agrarian nation and enacted his vision of its future in the Louisiana Purchase (1803), persuading Congress to sponsor the expedition of Meriwether Lewis and William Clark to explore and map the new territory. Jefferson's Presidency marked the beginning of the democratic plain style in politics. The

Chief Executive lived at a boardinghouse, rejected all outward signs of wealth or pomp (including ornamental shoe buckles), and was known to receive visitors in his slippers. After his Presidency he withdrew from public life. ("I am retired to Monticello, where, in the bosom of my family, and surrounded by my books, I enjoy a repose to which I have long been a stranger.")

Evidence suggests that the "bosom" of Jefferson's family included a thirty-eight-year relationship with a slave woman, Sally Hemings, who was a quadroon, the half sister of Jefferson's deceased wife. Social attitudes of the time would have made marital legitimation of the relationship impossible, no matter how much both parties might have wished otherwise. The affair, together with Jefferson's keeping of slaves, has raised charges of hypocrisy against him and has remained troubling to scholars and analysts. It must be pointed out, however, that Jefferson attempted to outlaw slavery in his original draft of the Declaration of Independence and that as President he worked successfully for the enactment of a law banning the further importation of slaves.

Jefferson's literary achievement is a part of his public life. His *Notes on Virginia* (1785), a work of natural science, was occasioned by a query by the Marquis de Barbé-Marois, who posed a set of questions concerning the geography, social history, and ecology of Virginia. Jefferson took the opportunity not only to respond to the questions but also to rebut the widely held European view that America was an unhealthy place that was causing the degeneration of its species. Jefferson's book won him the apology of the famous French naturalist Georges Louis Leclerc de Buffon.

In the years of his so-called retirement, Jefferson kept up a large correspondence. Fortunately, he had reconciled with his New England counterpart, former President John Adams, after a political rift of several years. The two resumed their friendship, and the letters on both sides deepened in reflection and outspokenness. Jefferson died within hours of his old friend Adams on the jubilee of the promulgation of the Declaration of Independence, July 4, 1826. He said, "I find friendship to be like wine, raw when new, ripened with age, the true old man's milk and restorative cordial."

Jefferson's splendid political legacy tends to obscure his achievement in literature. His style, however, and the rhetorical strategies evident in *Notes on Virginia*, in letters, and in the declaration evince the belletristic strain in Jefferson's intellect. His genres—from letters to political documents and geography—remind us that literature embraces wide-ranging forms that remain vital in the hands of a masterful practitioner.

Further Reading:
A. Koch, *The Philosophy of Thomas Jefferson*, 1943.
D. Malone, *Jefferson and His Time*, 5 vols., 1948–1974.
D. Boorstin, *The Lost World of Thomas Jefferson*, 1948.
M. Peterson, *Thomas Jefferson and the New Nation*, 1970.
F. Brodie, *Thomas Jefferson: An Intimate History*, 1974.
G. Wills, *Inventing America*, 1978.
W. Bottorff, *Thomas Jefferson*, 1979.

Texts:
"The Declaration of Independence," *Papers of Thomas Jefferson*, 18 vols., ed. J. Boyd., 1950–1971.
Notes on the State of Virginia, ed. W. Peden, 1955.
See also *Writings of Thomas Jefferson*, 10 vols., ed. P. Ford, 1892–1899.

The Declaration of Independence
as Adopted by Congress
In Congress July 4, 1776

The Unanimous Declaration
of the Thirteen United States
of America

When in the Course of human events, it becomes necessary for one people to dissolve
the political bands which have connected them with another, and to assume among
the powers of the earth, the separate and equal station to which the Laws of Nature
and of Nature's God entitle them, a decent respect to the opinions of mankind requires
that they should declare the causes which impel them to the separation. We hold these
truths to be self-evident, that all men are created equal, that they are endowed by their
Creator with certain unalienable Rights, that among these are Life, Liberty and the
pursuit of Happiness. That to secure these rights, Governments are instituted among
Men, deriving their just powers from the consent of the governed, That whenever
any Form of Government becomes destructive of these ends, it is the Right of the
People to alter or to abolish it, and to institute new Government, laying its foundation
on such principles and organizing its powers in such form, as to them shall seem most
likely to effect their Safety and Happiness. Prudence, indeed, will dictate that Governments long established should not be changed for light and transient causes; and
accordingly all experience hath shewn, that mankind are more disposed to suffer, while
evils are sufferable, than to right themselves by abolishing the forms to which they
are accustomed. But when a long train of abuses and usurpations, pursuing invariably
the same Object evinces a design to reduce them under absolute Despotism, it is their
right, it is their duty, to throw off such Government, and to provide new Guards for
their future security. Such has been the patient sufferance of these Colonies; and such
is now the necessity which constrains them to alter their former Systems of Government. The history of the present King of Great Britain is a history of repeated injuries
and usurpations, all having in direct object the establishment of an absolute Tyranny
over these States. To prove this, let Facts be submitted to a candid world. He has
refused his Assent to Laws, the most wholesome and necessary for the public good.
He has forbidden his Governors to pass Laws of immediate and pressing importance,
unless suspended in their operation till his Assent should be obtained; and when so
suspended, he has utterly neglected to attend to them. He has refused to pass other
Laws for the accommodation of large districts of people, unless those people would
relinquish the right of Representation in the Legislature, a right inestimable to them
and formidable to tyrants only. He has called together legislative bodies at places
unusual, uncomfortable, and distant from the depository of their public Records, for
the sole purpose of fatiguing them into compliance with his measures. He has dissolved
Representative Houses repeatedly, for opposing with manly firmness his invasions on
the rights of the people. He has refused for a long time, after such dissolutions, to
cause others to be elected; whereby the Legislative powers, incapable of Annihilation,
have returned to the People at large for their exercise; the State remaining in the mean
time exposed to all the dangers of invasion from without, and convulsions within.

He has endeavoured to prevent the population of these States; for that purpose obstructing the Laws for Naturalization of Foreigners; refusing to pass others to encourage their migrations hither, and raising the conditions of new Appropriations of Lands. He has obstructed the Administration of Justice, by refusing his Assent to Laws for establishing Judiciary powers. He has made Judges dependent on his Will alone, for the tenure of their offices, and the amount and payment of their salaries. He has erected a multitude of New Offices, and sent hither swarms of Officers to harrass our people, and eat out their substance. He has kept among us, in times of peace, standing Armies without the Consent of our legislatures. He has affected to render the Military independent of and superior to the Civil power. He has combined with others to subject us to a jurisdiction foreign to our constitution, and unacknowledged by our laws; giving his Assent to their Acts of pretended Legislation: For Quartering large bodies of armed troops among us: For protecting them, by a mock Trial, from punishment for any Murders which they should commit on the Inhabitants of these States: For cutting off our Trade with all parts of the world: For imposing Taxes on us without our Consent: For depriving us in many cases of the benefits of Trial by Jury: For transporting us beyond Seas to be tried for pretended offences: For abolishing the free System of English Laws in a neighbouring Province, establishing therein an Arbitrary government, and enlarging its Boundaries so as to render it at once an example and fit instrument for introducing the same absolute rule into these Colonies: For taking away our Charters, abolishing our most valuable Laws, and altering fundamentally the Forms of our Governments: For suspending our own Legislatures, and declaring themselves invested with power to legislate for us in all cases whatsoever. He has abdicated Government here, by declaring us out of his Protection and waging War against us. He has plundered our seas, ravaged our Coasts, burnt our towns, and destroyed the Lives of our people. He is at this time transporting large Armies of foreign Mercenaries to compleat the works of death, desolation and tyranny, already begun with circumstances of Cruelty & perfidy scarcely paralleled in the most barbarous ages, and totally unworthy the Head of a civilized nation. He has constrained our fellow Citizens taken Captive on the high Seas to bear Arms against their Country, to become the executioners of their friends and Brethren, or to fall themselves by their Hands. He has excited domestic insurrections amongst us, and has endeavoured to bring on the inhabitants of our frontiers, the merciless Indian Savages, whose known rule of warfare, is an undistinguished destruction of all ages, sexes and conditions. In every stage of these Oppressions We have Petitioned for Redress in the most humble terms: Our repeated Petitions have been answered only by repeated injury. A Prince, whose character is thus marked by every act which may define a Tyrant, is unfit to be the ruler of a free people. Nor have We been wanting in attentions to our Brittish brethren. We have warned them from time to time of attempts by their legislature to extend an unwarrantable jurisdiction over us. We have reminded them of the circumstances of our emigration and settlement here. We have appealed to their native justice and magnanimity, and we have conjured them by the ties of our common kindred to disavow these usurpations, which, would inevitably interrupt our connections and correspondence. They too have been deaf to the voice of justice and of consanguinity. We must, therefore, acquiesce in the necessity, which denounces our Separation, and hold them, as we hold the rest of mankind, Enemies in War, in Peace Friends.

We, therefore, the Representatives of the united States of America, in General

Congress, Assembled, appealing to the Supreme Judge of the world for the rectitude of our intentions, do, in the Name, and by Authority of the good People of these Colonies, solemnly publish and declare, That these United Colonies are, and of Right ought to be Free and Independent States; that they are Absolved from all Allegiance to the British Crown, and that all political connection between them and the State of Great Britain, is and ought to be totally dissolved; and that as Free and Independent States, they have full Power to levy War, conclude Peace, contract Alliances, establish Commerce, and to do all other Acts and Things which Independent States may of right do. And for the support of this Declaration, with a firm reliance on the protection of divine Providence, we mutually pledge to each other our Lives, our Fortunes and our sacred Honor.

1776

---

from Notes on the State of Virginia

from **Query IV: Mountains**

[Confluence of the Shenandoah and Potomac Rivers]

It is worthy notice, that our mountains are not solitary and scattered confusedly over the face of the country; but that they commence at about 150 miles from the sea-coast, are disposed in ridges one behind another, running nearly parallel with the sea-coast, though rather approaching it as they advance north-eastwardly. To the south-west, as the tract of country between the sea-coast and the Mississipi becomes narrower, the mountains converge into a single ridge, which, as it approaches the Gulph of Mexico, subsides into plain country, and gives rise to some of the waters of that Gulph, and particularly to a river called the Apalachicola, probably from the Apalachies, an Indian nation formerly residing on it. Hence the mountains giving rise to that river, and seen from its various parts, were called the Apalachian mountains, being in fact the end or termination only of the great ridges passing through the continent. European geographers however extended the name northwardly as far as the mountains extended; some giving it, after their separation into different ridges, to the Blue ridge, others to the North mountain, others to the Alleghaney, others to the Laurel ridge, as may be seen in their different maps. But the fact I believe is, that none of these ridges were ever known by that name to the inhabitants, either native or emigrant, but as they saw them so called in European maps. In the same direction generally are the veins of lime-stone, coal and other minerals hitherto discovered: and so range the falls of our great rivers. But the courses of the great rivers are at right angles with these. James and Patowmac penetrate through all the ridges of mountains eastward of the Alleghaney; that is broken by no watercourse. It is in fact the spine of the country between the Atlantic on one side, and the Mississipi and St. Laurence on the other. The passage of the Patowmac through the Blue ridge is perhaps one of the most stupendous scenes in nature. You stand on a very high point of land. On your right comes up the Shenandoah, having ranged along the foot of the mountain an hundred miles to seek a vent. On your left approaches the Patowmac, in quest of a passage also. In the moment of their junction they rush together against the mountain, rend it asunder, and pass off to the sea. The first glance of this scene hurries our senses into the opinion, that this earth has been created in time, that the mountains were formed first, that the rivers began to flow afterwards, that in this place particularly they have been dammed up by the Blue ridge of mountains, and have formed an ocean which filled the whole valley; that continuing to rise they have at length broken over at this spot, and have torn the mountain down from its summit to its base. The piles of rock on each hand, but particularly on the Shenandoah, the evident marks of their disrupture and avulsion from their beds by the most powerful agents of nature, corroborate the impression. But the distant finishing which nature has given to the picture is of a very different character. It is a true contrast to the fore-ground. It is as placid and delightful, as that is wild and tremendous. For the mountain being cloven asunder, she presents to your eye, through the cleft, a small catch of smooth blue horizon, at an infinite distance in the plain country, inviting you, as it were, from the riot and tumult roaring around, to pass through the breach and participate of the calm below. Here the eye ultimately composes itself; and that way too the road happens actually to lead. You cross the Patowmac above the junction, pass along its side through the base of the mountain for three miles, its terrible precipices hanging in fragments over you, and within about 20 miles reach Frederic town and the fine country around that. This scene is worth a voyage across the Atlantic. Yet here, as in the neighbourhood of the natural bridge, are people who have passed their lives within half a dozen miles, and have never been to survey these monuments of a war between rivers and mountains, which must have shaken the earth itself to its center. . . .

from **Query V: Cascades**

[Natural Bridge]

The *Natural bridge,* the most sublime of Nature's works, though not comprehended under the present head, must not be pretermitted.[1] It is on the ascent of a hill, which seems to have been cloven through its length by some great convulsion. The fissure, just at the bridge, is, by some admeasurements, 270 feet deep, by others only 205. It is about 45 feet wide at the bottom, and 90 feet at the top; this of course determines the length of the bridge, and its height from the water. Its breadth in the middle, is about 60 feet, but more at the ends, and the thickness of the mass at the summit of the arch, about 40 feet. A part of this thickness is constituted by a coat of earth, which gives growth to many large trees. The residue, with the hill on both sides, is one solid rock of limestone. The arch approaches the Semi-elliptical form; but the larger axis of the ellipsis, which would be the cord of the arch, is many times longer than the (semi-axis which gives its height.) Though the sides of this bridge are provided in some parts with a parapet of fixed rocks, yet few men have resolution to walk to them

[1] I.e., although not a cascade, the natural bridge must not be omitted.

and look over into the abyss. You involuntarily fall on your hands and feet, creep to the parapet and peep over it. Looking down from this height about a minute, gave me a violent head ach. (This painful sensation is relieved by a short, but pleasing view of the Blue ridge along the fissure downwards, and upwards by that of the Short hills, which, with the Purgatory mountain is a divergence from the North ridge; and, descending then to the valley below, the sensation becomes delightful in the extreme. It is impossible for the emotions, arising from the sublime, to be felt beyond what they are here: so beautiful an arch, so elevated, so light, and springing, as it were, up to heaven, the rapture of the Spectator is really indiscribable! The fissure continues deep and narrow and, following the margin of the stream upwards about three eights of a mile you arrive at a limestone cavern, less remarkable, however, for height and extent than those before described. Its entrance into the hill is but a few feet above the bed of the stream.) This bridge is in the county of Rockbridge, to which it has given name, and affords a public and commodious passage over a valley, which cannot be crossed elsewhere for a considerable distance. The stream passing under it is called Cedar creek. It is a water of James river, and sufficient in the driest seasons to turn a grist-mill, though its fountain is not more than two miles above.

from *Query VI: Productions Mineral, Vegetable and Animal*

[Rebuttal to Count Buffon]

The opinion advanced by the Count de Buffon,[2] is 1. That the animals common both to the old and new world, are smaller in the latter. 2. That those peculiar to the new, are on a smaller scale. 3. That those which have been domesticated in both, have degenerated in America: and 4. That on the whole it exhibits fewer species. And the reason he thinks is, that the heats of America are less; that more waters are spread over its surface by nature, and fewer of these drained off by the hand of man. In other words, that heat is friendly, and moisture adverse to the production and developement of large quadrupeds. . . .

Hitherto I have considered this hypothesis as applied to brute animals only, and not in its extension to the man of America, whether aboriginal or transplated. It is the opinion of Mons. de Buffon that the former furnishes no exception to it: "Although the savage of the new world is about the same height as man in our world, this does not suffice for him to constitute an exception to the general fact that all living nature has become smaller on that continent. The savage is feeble, and has small organs of generation; he has neither hair nor beard, and no ardor whatever for his female; although swifter than the European because he is better accustomed to running, he is, on the other hand, less strong in body; he is also less sensitive, and yet more timid and cowardly; he has no vivacity, no activity of mind; the activity of his body is less an exercise, a voluntary motion, than a necessary action caused by want; relieve him of hunger and thirst, and you deprive him of the active principle of all his movements;

[2] Georges Louis Leclerc de Buffon (1707–1788), French author of the multivolume *Natural History,* which argued that the American environment was conducive to the degeneration of species and thus unsuited to civilized life.

he will rest stupidly upon his legs or lying down entire days. There is no need for seeking further the cause of the isolated mode of life of these savages and their repugnance for society: the most precious spark of the fire of nature has been refused to them; they lack ardor for their females, and consequently have no love for their fellow men; not knowing this strongest and most tender of all affections, their other feelings are also cold and languid; they love their parents and children but little; the most intimate of all ties, the family connection, binds them therefore but loosely together; between family and family there is no tie at all; hence they have no communion, no commonwealth, no state of society. Physical love constitues their only morality; their heart is icy, their society cold, and their rule harsh. They look upon their wives only as servants for all work, or as beasts of burden, which they load without consideration with the burden of their hunting, and which they compel without mercy, without gratitude, to perform tasks which are often beyond their strength. They have only few children, and they take little care of them. Everywhere the original defect appears: they are indifferent because they have little sexual capacity, and this indifference to the other sex is the fundamental defect which weakens their nature, prevents its development, and—destroying the very germs of life—uproots society at the same time. Man is here no exception to the general rule. Nature, by refusing him the power of love, has treated him worse and lowered him deeper than any animal." An afflicting picture indeed, which, for the honor of human nature, I am glad to believe has no original. Of the Indian of South America I know nothing; for I would not honor with the appelation of knowledge, what I derive from the fables published of them. These I believe to be just as true as the fables of Æsop. This belief is founded on what I have seen of man, white, red, and black, and what has been written of him by authors, enlightened themselves, and writing amidst an enlightened people. The Indian of North America being more within our reach, I can speak of him somewhat from my own knowledge, but more from the information of others better acquainted with him, and on whose truth and judgment I can rely. From these sources I am able to say, in contradiction to this representation, that he is neither more defective in ardor, nor more impotent with his female, than the white reduced to the same diet and exercise: that he is brave, when an enterprize depends on bravery; education with him making the point of honor consist in the destruction of an enemy by stratagem, and in the preservation of his own person free from injury; or perhaps this is nature; while it is education which teaches us to honor force more than finesse; that he will defend himself against an host of enemies, always chusing to be killed, rather than to surrender, though it be to the whites, who he knows will treat him well: that in other situations also he meets death with more deliberation, and endures tortures with a firmness unknown almost to religious enthusiasm with us: that he is affectionate to his children, careful of them, and indulgent in the extreme: that his affections comprehend his other connections, weakening, as with us, from circle to circle, as they recede from the center: that his friendships are strong and faithful to the uttermost extremity: that his sensibility is keen, even the warriors weeping most bitterly on the loss of their children, though in general they endeavour to appear superior to human events: that his vivacity and activity of mind is equal to ours in the same situation; hence his eagerness for hunting, and for games of chance. The women are submitted to unjust drudgery. This I believe is the case with every barbarous people. With such, force is law. The stronger sex therefore imposes on the weaker. It is civilization alone which replaces women in the enjoyment of their natural equality. That first teaches us to subdue the selfish passions, and to respect those rights in others which we value in ourselves. Were we in equal barbarism, our females would be equal drudges. The man with them is less strong than with us, but their woman stronger than ours; and both for the same obvious reason; because our man and their woman is habituated to labour, and formed by it. With both races the sex which is indulged with ease is least athletic. An Indian man is small in the hand and wrist for the same reason for which a sailor is large and strong in the arms and shoulders, and a porter in the legs and thighs.—They raise fewer children than we do. The causes of this are to be found, not in a difference of nature, but of circumstance. The women very frequently attending the men in their parties of war and of hunting, child-bearing becomes extremely inconvenient to them. It is said, therefore, that they have learnt the practice of procuring abortion by the use of some vegetable; and that it even extends to prevent conception for a considerable time after. During these parties they are exposed to numerous hazards, to excessive exertions, to the greatest extremities of hunger. Even at their homes the nation depends for food, through a certain part of every year, on the gleanings of the forest: that is, they experience a famine once in every year. With all animals, if the female be badly fed, or not fed at all, her young perish: and if both male and female be reduced to like want, generation becomes less active, less productive. To the obstacles then of want and hazard, which nature has opposed to the multiplication of wild animals, for the purpose of restraining their numbers within certain bounds, those of labour and of voluntary abortion are added with the Indian. No wonder then if they multiply less than we do. Where food is regularly supplied, a single farm will shew more of cattle, than a whole country of forests can of buffaloes. The same Indian women, when married to white traders, who feed them and their children plentifully and regularly, who exempt them from excessive drudgery, who keep them stationary and unexposed to accident, produce and raise as many children as the white women. Instances are known, under these circumstances, of their rearing a dozen children. . . .

Before we condemn the Indians of this continent as wanting genius,[3] we must consider that letters[4] have not yet been introduced among them. Were we to compare them in their present state with the Europeans North of the Alps, when the Roman arms and arts first crossed those mountains, the comparison would be unequal, because, at that time, those parts of Europe were swarming with numbers; because numbers produce emulation, and multiply the chances of improvement, and one improvement begets another. Yet I may safely ask, How many good poets, how many able mathematicians, how many great inventors in arts or sciences, had Europe North of the Alps then produced? And it was sixteen centuries after this before a Newton could be formed. I do not mean to deny, that there are varieties in the race of man, distinguished by their powers both of body and mind. I believe there are, as I see to be the case in the races of other animals. I only mean to suggest a doubt, whether the bulk and faculties of animals depend on the side of the Atlantic on which their food happens to grow, or which furnishes the elements of which they are compounded? Whether nature has enlisted herself as a Cis[5] or Trans-Atlantic partisan? I

[3] Mental capacity and ability.
[4] Learning or knowledge.
[5] On the near side (i.e., European).

am induced to suspect, there has been more eloquence than sound reasoning displayed in support of this theory; that it is one of those cases where the judgment has been seduced by a glowing pen: and whilst I render every tribute of honor and esteem to the celebrated Zoologist, who has added, and is still adding, so many precious things to the treasures of science, I must doubt whether in this instance he has not cherished error also, by lending her for a moment his vivid imagination and bewitching language.

So far the Count de Buffon has carried this new theory of the tendency of nature to belittle her productions on this side of the Atlantic. Its application to the race of whites, transplanted from Europe, remained for the Abbé Raynal.[6] "One must be astonished (he says) that America has not yet produced one good poet, one able mathematician, one man of genius in a single art or a single science." "America has not yet produced one good poet." When we shall have existed as a people as long as the Greeks did before they produced a Homer, the Romans a Virgil, the French a Racine and Voltaire, the English a Shakespeare and Milton, should this reproach be still true, we will enquire from what unfriendly causes it has proceeded, that the other countries of Europe and quarters of the earth shall not have inscribed any name in the roll of poets. But neither has America produced "one able mathematician, one man of genius in a single art or a single science." In war we have produced a Washington, whose memory will be adored while liberty shall have votaries, whose name will triumph over time, and will in future ages assume its just station among the most celebrated worthies of the world, when that wretched philosophy shall be forgotten which would have arranged him among the degeneracies of nature. In physics we have produced a Franklin, than whom no one of the present age has made more important discoveries, nor has enriched philosophy with more, or more ingenious solutions of the phænomena of nature. We have supposed Mr. Rittenhouse[7] second to no astronomer living: that in genius he must be the first, because he is self-taught. As an artist he has exhibited as great a proof of mechanical genius as the world has ever produced. He has not indeed made a world; but he has by imitation approached nearer its Maker than any man who has lived from the creation to this day. As in philosophy and war, so in government, in oratory, in painting, in the plastic art, we might shew that America, though but a child of yesterday, has already given hopeful proofs of genius, as well of the nobler kinds, which arouse the best feelings of man, which call him into action, which substantiate his freedom, and conduct him to happiness, as of the subordinate, which serve to amuse him only. We therefore suppose, that this reproach is as unjust as it is unkind; and that, of the geniuses which adorn the present age, America contributes its full share. For comparing it with those countries, where genius is most cultivated, where are the most excellent models for art, and scaffoldings for the attainment of science, as France and England for instance, we calculate thus. The United States contain three millions of inhabitants; France twenty millions; and the British islands ten. We produce a Washington, a Franklin, a Rittenhouse. France then

---

[6] Guillaume Thomas François Raynal (1713–1796), French writer who concurred with Buffon that the American environment was degenerative.

[7] David Rittenhouse (1732–1796), American astronomer who built orreries, or models of the solar system.

should have half a dozen in each of these lines, and Great-Britain half that number, equally eminent. It may be true, that France has: we are but just becoming acquainted with her, and our acquaintance so far gives us high ideas of the genius of her inhabitants. It would be injuring too many of them to name particularly a Voltaire, a Buffon, the constellation of Encyclopedists,[8] the Abbé Raynal himself, &c. &c. We therefore have reason to believe she can produce her full quota of genius. The present war having so long cut off all communication with Great-Britain, we are not able to make a fair estimate of the state of science in that country. The spirit in which she wages war is the only sample before our eyes, and that does not seem the legitimate offspring either of science or of civilization. The sun of her glory is fast descending to the horizon. Her philosophy has crossed the Channel, her freedom the Atlantic, and herself seems passing to that awful dissolution, whose issue is not given human foresight to scan.

from **Query XVIII: Manners**

[On Slavery]

It is difficult to determine on the standard by which the manners of a nation may be tried, whether *catholic,*[9] or *particular.* It is more difficult for a native to bring to that standard the manners of his own nation, familiarized to him by habit. There must doubtless be an unhappy influence on the manners of our people produced by the existence of slavery among us. The whole commerce between master and slave is a perpetual exercise of the most boisterous passions, the most unremitting despotism on the one part, and degrading submissions on the other. Our children see this, and learn to imitate it; for man is an imitative animal. This quality is the germ of all education in him. From his cradle to his grave he is learning to do what he sees others do. If a parent could find no motive either in his philanthropy or his self-love, for restraining the intemperance of passion towards his slave, it should always be a sufficient one that his child is present. But generally it is not sufficient. The parent storms, the child looks on, catches the lineaments of wrath, puts on the same airs in the circle of smaller slaves, gives a loose to his worst of passions, and thus nursed, educated, and daily exercised in tyranny, cannot but be stamped by it with odious peculiarities. The man must be a prodigy who can retain his manners and morals undepraved by such circumstances. And with what execration should the statesman be loaded, who permitting one half the citizens thus to trample on the rights of the other, transforms those into despots, and these into enemies, destroys the morals of the one part, and the amor patriæ[10] of the other. For if a slave can have a country in this world, it must be any other in preference to that in which he is born to live and labour for another: in which he must lock up the faculties of his nature, contribute as far as depends on his individual endeavours to the evanishment[11] of the human race, or entail[12] his own miserable condition on the endless generations proceeding from him. With the morals of the

---

[8] Such figures as Denis Diderot (1713–1784), who contributed to the French *Encyclopédie* (1751–1771).
[9] Universal.

[10] Love of country; patriotism.
[11] Disappearance.
[12] Impose.

people, their industry also is destroyed. For in a warm climate, no man will labour for himself who can make another labour for him. This is so true, that of the proprietors of slaves a very small proportion indeed are ever seen to labour. And can the liberties of a nation be thought secure when we have removed their only firm basis, a conviction in the minds of the people that these liberties are of the gift of God? That they are not to be violated but with his wrath? Indeed I tremble for my country when I reflect that God is just: that his justice cannot sleep for ever: that considering numbers, nature and natural means only, a revolution of the wheel of fortune, an exchange of situation, is among possible events: that it may become probable by supernatural interference! The Almighty has no attribute which can take side with us in such a contest.—But it is impossible to be temperate and to pursue this subject through the various considerations of policy, of morals, of history natural and civil. We must be contented to hope they will force their way into every one's mind. I think a change already perceptible, since the origin of the present revolution. The spirit of the master is abating, that of the slave rising from the dust, his condition mollifying, the way I hope preparing, under the auspices of heaven, for a total emancipation, and that this is disposed, in the order of events, to be with the consent of the masters, rather than by their extirpation.

from Query XIX: Manufactures

[American Agrarianism]

The political œconomists of Europe have established it as a principle that every state should endeavour to manufacture for itself: and this principle, like many others, we transfer to America, without calculating the difference of circumstance which should often produce a difference of result. In Europe the lands are either cultivated, or locked up against the cultivator. Manufacture must therefore be resorted to of necessity not of choice, to support the surplus of their people. But we have an immensity of land courting the industry of the husbandman. Is it best then that all our citizens should be employed in its improvement, or that one half should be called off from that to exercise manufactures and handicraft arts for the other? Those who labour in the earth are the chosen people of God, if ever he had a chosen people, whose breasts he has made his peculiar deposit for substantial and genuine virtue. It is the focus in which he keeps alive that sacred fire, which otherwise might escape from the face of the earth. Corruption of morals in the mass of cultivators is a phænomenon of which no age nor nation has furnished an example. It is the mark set on those, who not looking up to heaven, to their own soil and industry, as does the husbandman, for their subsistance, depend for it on the casualties and caprice of customers. Dependance begets subservience and venality, suffocates the germ of virtue, and prepares fit tools for the designs of ambition. This, the natural progress and consequence of the arts, has sometimes perhaps been retarded by accidental circumstances: but, generally speaking, the proportion which the aggregate of the other classes of citizens bears in any state to that of its husbandmen, is the proportion of its unsound to its healthy parts, and is a good-enough barometer whereby to measure its degree of corruption. While we have land to labour then, let us never wish to see our citizens occupied at a workbench, or twirling a distaff.[13] Carpenters, masons, smiths, are wanting[14] in husbandry: but, for the general operations of manufacture, let our work-shops remain in Europe. It is better to carry provisions and materials to workmen there, than bring them to the provisions and materials, and with them their manners and principles. The loss by the transportation of commodities across the Atlantic will be made up in happiness and permanence of government. The mobs of great cities add just so much to the support of pure government, as sores do to the strength of the human body. It is the manners and spirit of a people which preserve a republic in vigour. A degeneracy in these is a canker which soon eats to the heart of its laws and constitution.

1785

Abigail Adams
1744–1818

Abigail Smith Adams, in failing health and retired from a rigorous public life, reflected on her married life in a letter to her granddaughter dated October 26, 1814:

> Yesterday completes half a century since I entered the married state, then just your age. I have great cause of thankfulness, that I have lived so long and enjoyed so large a portion of happiness as has been my lot. The greatest source of unhappiness I have known in that period has arisen from the long and cruel separations which I was called, in a time of war and with a young family around me, to submit to.

These "long and cruel separations" attended her husband John's many years of public service: as a Massachusetts delegate to the Continental Congresses, as a negotiator of the Treaty of Paris, as the American joint commissioner at the court of France, as the nation's first vice-president, and as the second president of the United States. John Adams's frequent and prolonged absences resulted not only in Abigail's uncommon self-sufficiency but also in her voluminous, rich correspondence with her husband; with her son John Quincy, who later served as sixth president of the United States; and with numerous political leaders in the new republic. These letters constitute one of the most incisive private commentaries on the public events that crowded the new nation's history.

Abigail Smith Adams was the second of three daughters born to Reverend William Smith and Elizabeth Quincy, parents who could trace their distinguished lineages back through the pages of Cotton Mather's *Magnalia Christi Americana*. She entered, as did all eighteenth-century women, a world indifferent to the education of females. In a letter dated 1817, she observed:

---

[13] Spinning-wheel attachment.   [14] Lacking.

My early education did not partake of the opportunities which the present days offer, and which even our common country schools now afford. I never was sent to any school. I was always sick. Female education, in the best families, went no further than writing and arithmetic; in some few and rare instances, music and dancing.

Under the tutelage of her grandmother, who offered a "happy method of mixing instruction and amusement," young Abigail became a practiced letter writer early on and read widely among English poets and essayists, developing an especially high regard for Addison and Steele's *Spectator* papers.

In 1764 she married John Adams, despite some resistance from her family, who regarded this lawyer son of a small farmer as beneath their own social and professional standing. Within the next decade, Abigail Adams bore a daughter, Abby, and three sons, John Quincy, Thomas, and Charles. As her husband traveled more frequently to participate in the political controversies that led to the American Revolution, Abigail endured the prolonged silences of late eighteenth-century mail and took on increasingly more responsibility for her family's well-being. Her letters to John during this period reveal her many talents: cultivating a farm, managing the finances, ordering and selling goods from abroad, discussing current prices, and arguing over local and national politics.

Armed with an independent and imaginative intelligence, she vigorously expressed her ideas on a wide range of subjects, most particularly on women's rights. Her letters reveal her longing for an American declaration of independence, and she was one of the first Americans to perceive the implications of the Revolution for blacks and women. A lifelong advocate of black emancipation and education, Abigail Adams also repeatedly argued that women should be better educated than their colonial ancestors. She also insisted that wives ought to be freed from the absolute legal authority husbands held over their lives: "If particular care and attention is not paid to the ladies, we are determined to foment a rebellion, and will not hold ourselves bound by any laws in which we have no voice or representation." Abigail Adams remained steadfast in the counsel she offered her husband: She was determined to strengthen women's roles in American culture and politics. She once admonished her husband, "If you complain of education in sons, what shall I say in regard to daughters who every day experience the want of it? . . . If we mean to have heroes, statesmen, and philosophers, we should have learned women." Her own wide reading is evident in the many literary and biblical allusions that punctuate her correspondence, especially in her letters detailing the progress of the Revolutionary War while her husband was abroad. In this respect, she may well have been of more assistance to him than he to her.

Soon after the war, Abigail Adams joined her husband in Europe for the American trade negotiations. Her correspondence during this period is filled with trenchant observations on European manners and customs as well as revealing glimpses of the social behavior of some of the leading American representatives, including Benjamin Franklin and Thomas Jefferson. The Adams family returned to the United States in 1788 and to John Adams's election as vice-president. The presidency followed in 1797, and it was not until 1801 that the family settled permanently in their home at Braintree (now Quincy), Massachusetts, where Abigail lived in retirement until her death from typhoid fever in 1818.

Abigail Adams's letters document the personal costs of supporting public needs. Not until Franklin and Eleanor Roosevelt would America once again witness such a celebrated union of such dynamic individuals. Yet no marriage of such visible figures in American life has so successfully wed public and private lives for so long.

Further Reading:
J. Whitney, *Abigail Adams*, 1947.
L. Withey, *Dearest Friend: A Life of Abigail Adams*, 1981.

Texts:
Letters of Mrs. Adams, the Wife of John Adams, ed. C. F. Adams, 2 vols., 1840.
Familiar Letters of John Adams and His Wife Abigail Adams, During the Revolution, ed. C. F. Adams, 1876.
The Book of Abigail and John: Selected Letters of the Adams Family, 1762–1784, ed. L. H. Butterfield et al., 1975.
See also *New Letters, 1788–1801*, ed. S. Mitchell, 1947.

Letters to John Adams

[March 31, 1776]

Braintree March 31 1776

I wish you would ever write me a Letter half as long as I write you; and tell me if you may where your Fleet are gone? What sort of Defence Virginia can make against our common Enemy? Whether it is so situated as to make an able Defence? Are not the Gentery Lords and the common people vassals, are they not like the uncivilized Natives Brittain represents us to be? I hope their Riffel Men who have shewen themselves very savage and even Blood thirsty; are not a specimen of the Generality of the people.

I am willing to allow the Colony great merrit for having produced a Washington but they have been shamefully duped by a Dunmore.[1]

I have sometimes been ready to think that the passion for Liberty cannot be Eaquelly Strong in the Breasts of those who have been accustomed to deprive their fellow Creatures of theirs. Of this I am certain that it is not founded upon that generous and christian principal of doing to others as we would that others should do unto us.

Do not you want to see Boston; I am fearfull of the small pox, or I should have been in before this time. I got Mr. Crane[2] to go to our House and see what state it

---

[1] John, earl of Dunmore and colonial governor of Virginia, who favored the Loyalist cause. He later seized the supplies of the colonial arsenal at Williamsburg.

[2] Abigail Adams's agent in Boston.

was in. I find it has been occupied by one of the Doctors of a Regiment, very dirty, but no other damage has been done to it. The few things which were left in it are all gone. Cranch[3] has the key which he never deliverd up. I have wrote to him for it and am determined to get it cleand as soon as possible and shut it up. I look upon it a new acquisition of property, a property which one month ago I did not value at a single Shilling, and could with pleasure have seen it in flames.

The Town in General is left in a better state than we expected, more oweing to a percipitate flight than any Regard to the inhabitants, tho some individuals discovered a sense of honour and justice and have left the rent of the Houses in which they were, for the owners and the furniture unhurt, or if damaged suffcent to make it good.

Others have committed abominable Ravages. The Mansion House of your President is safe and the furniture unhurt whilst both the House and Furniture of the Solisiter General have fallen a prey to their own merciless party. Surely the very Fiends feel a Reverential awe for Virtue and patriotism, whilst they Detest the paricide and traitor.

I feel very differently at the approach of spring to what I did a month ago. We knew not then whether we could plant or sow with safety, whether when we had toild we could reap the fruits of our own industery, whether we could rest in our own Cottages, or whether we should not be driven from the sea coasts to seek shelter in the wilderness, but now we feel as if we might sit under our own vine and eat the good of the land.

I feel a gaieti de Coar[4] to which before I was a stranger. I think the Sun looks brighter, the Birds sing more melodiously, and Nature puts on a more chearfull countanance. We feel a temporary peace, and the poor fugitives are returning to their deserted habitations.

Tho we felicitate ourselves, we sympathize with those who are trembling least the Lot of Boston should be theirs. But they cannot be in similar circumstances unless pusilanimity and cowardise should take possession of them. They have time and warning given them to see the Evil and shun it.—I long to hear that you have declared an independancy—and by the way in the new Code of Laws[5] which I suppose it will be necessary for you to make I desire you would Remember the Ladies, and be more generous and favourable to them than your ancestors. Do not put such unlimited power into the hands of the Husbands. Remember all Men would be tyrants if they could. If perticuliar care and attention is not paid to the Laidies we are determined to foment a Rebelion, and will not hold ourselves bound by any Laws in which we have no voice, or Representation.

That your Sex are Naturally Tyrannical is a Truth so thoroughly established as to admit of no dispute, but such of you as wish to be happy willingly give up the harsh title of Master for the more tender and endearing one of Friend. Why then, not put it out of the power of the vicious and the Lawless to use us with cruelty and indignity with impunity. Men of Sense in all Ages abhor those customs which treat us only as the vassals of your Sex. Regard us then as Beings placed by providence under your

[3] Most likely a slip of the pen that should read "Crane." Richard Cranch was Abigail's brother-in-law.

[4] *Gaieté du coeur,* French for "lightheartedness."

[5] Abigail Adams's eager anticipation of what would become the Declaration of Independence and the Constitution.

protection and in immitation of the Supreem Being make use of that power only for our happiness.

1776/1876

[August 14, 1776]

August 14 1776

I wrote you to day by Mr. Smith[6] but as I suppose this will reach you sooner, I omitted mentioning any thing of my family in it.

Nabby[7] has enough of the small Pox for all the family beside. She is pretty well coverd, not a spot but what is so soar that she can neither walk sit stand or lay with any comfort. She is as patient as one can expect, but they are a very soar sort. If it was a disorder to which we could be subject more than once I would go as far as it was possible to avoid it. She is sweld a good deal. You will receive a perticuliar account before this reaches you of the uncommon manner in which the small Pox acts, it bafels the skill of the most Experience'd here. Billy Cranch[8] is now out with about 40, and so well as not to be detaind at Home an hour for it. Charlly[9] remains in the same state he did.

Your Letter of August 3 came by this days Post. I find it very conveniant to be so handy. I can receive a Letter at Night, sit down and reply to it, and send it of in the morning.

You remark upon the deficiency of Education in your Countrymen. It never I believe was in a worse state, at least for many years. The Colledge is not in the state one could wish, the Schollars complain that their professer in Philosophy is taken of by publick Business to their great detriment. In this Town I never saw so great a neglect of Education. The poorer sort of children are wholly neglected, and left to range the Streets without Schools, without Buisness, given up to all Evil. The Town is not as formerly divided into Wards. There is either too much Buisness left upon the hands of a few, or too little care to do it. We daily see the Necessity of a regular Government.—You speak of our Worthy Brother.[10] I often lament it that a Man so peculiarly formed for the Education of youth, and so well qualified as he is in many Branches of Litrature, excelling in Philosiphy and the Mathematicks, should not be imploid in some publick Station. I know not the person who would make half so good a Successor to Dr. Winthrope.[11] He has a peculiar easy manner of communicating his Ideas to Youth, and the Goodness of his Heart, and the purity of his morrals without an affected austerity must have a happy Effect upon the minds of Pupils.

If you complain of neglect of Education in sons, What shall I say with regard to daughters, who every day experience the want of it. With regard to the Education of my own children, I find myself soon out of my depth, and destitute and deficient in every part of Education.

[6] Mr. B. Smith, a visitor from South Carolina.
[7] The Adamses' daughter Abigail.
[8] William Cranch, son of Richard and Mary Cranch.
[9] The Adamses' son Charles.
[10] Probably Richard Cranch, who became a judge of the Court of the Common Pleas in Massachusetts.
[11] Dr. John Winthrope (d. 1779), Hollis Professor of Mathematics and Natural Philosophy at Harvard College.

I most sincerely wish that some more liberal plan might be laid and executed for the Benefit of the rising Generation, and that our new constitution may be distinguished for Learning and Virtue. If we mean to have Heroes, Statesmen and Philosophers, we should have learned women. The world perhaps would laugh at me, and accuse me of vanity, But you I know have a mind too enlarged and liberal to disregard the Sentiment. If much depends as is allowed upon the early Education of youth and the first principals which are instilld take the deepest root, great benifit must arise from litirary accomplishments in women.

Excuse me my pen has run away with me. I have no thoughts of comeing to P[hiladelphi]a. The length of time I have [and] shall be detaind here would have prevented me, even if you had no thoughts of returning till December, but I live in daily Expectation of seeing you here. Your Health I think requires your immediate return. I expected Mr. Gerry[12] would have set off before now, but he finds it perhaps very hard to leave his Mistress[13]—I won't say harder than some do to leave their wives. Mr. Gerry stood very high in my Esteem—what is meat for one is not for an other —no accounting for fancy. She is a queer dame and leads people wild dances.

But hush—Post, dont betray your trust and loose my Letter.

Nabby is poorly this morning. The pock are near the turn, 6 or 7 hundred boils are no agreable feeling. You and I know not what a feeling it is. Miss Katy can tell. I had but 3 they were very clever and fill'd nicely. The Town instead of being clear of this distemper are now in the height of it, hundreds having it in the natural way through the deceitfulness of innoculation.

Adieu ever yours. Breakfast waits.

Portia[14]

1776/1876

[April 10, 1782]

April 10th. 1782

My dearest Friend

How great was my joy to see the well known Signature of my Friend after a Melancholy Solicitude of many months in which my hopes and fears alternately preponderated.

It was January when Charles arrived. By him I expected Letters, but found not a line; instead of which the heavy tidings of your illness reachd me. I then found my Friends had been no strangers of what they carefully conceald from me. Your Letter to Charles dated in November was the only consolation I had; by that I found that the most dargerous period of your illness was pass'd, and that you considerd yourself as recovering tho feeble. My anxiety and apprehensions from that day untill your

[12] Elbridge Gerry (1744–1814), a signer of the Declaration of Independence, delegate to the Continental Congress in Philadelphia (1776–1781), and later vice-president of the United States (1813–1814).

[13] Catherine Hunt, whom Gerry did not marry because she had not been educated in reading or

writing and subsequently could not respond to his letters.

[14] A signature Abigail adopted after marriage. The character Portia, in Shakespeare's *The Merchant of Venice* (1596–1597), aids her lover's best friend by her clever negotiations.

Letters arrived, which was near 3 months, conspired to render me unhappy. Capt. Trowbridge in the Fire Brand[15] arrived with your favours of October and December and in some measure dispeld the Gloom which hung heavy at my heart. How did it leap for joy to find I was not the misirable Being I sometimes feared I was. I felt that Gratitude to Heaven which great deliverences both demand and inspire. I will not distrust the providential Care of the supreem disposer of events, from whose Hand I have so frequently received distinguished favours. Such I call the preservation of my dear Friend and children from the uncertain Element upon which they have frequently embarked; their preservation from the hands of their enimies I have reason to consider in the same view, especially when I reflect upon the cruel and inhumane treatment experienced by a Gentleman of Mr. Laurences[16] age and respectable character.

The restoration of my dearest Friend from so dangerous a Sickness, demands all my gratitude, whilst I fail not to supplicate Heaven for the continuance of a Life upon which my temporal happiness rests, and deprived of which my own existance would become a burden. Often has the Question which you say staggerd your philosophy occured to me, nor have I felt so misirable upon account of my own personal Situation, when I considerd that according to the common course of Nature, more than half my days were allready passt, as for those in whom our days are renewed. Their hopes and prospects would vanish, their best prospects, those of Education, would be greatly diminished—but I will not anticipate those miseries which I would shun. Hope is my best Friend and kindest comforter; she assures me that the pure unabated affection, which neither time or absence can allay or abate, shall e'er long be crowned with the completion of its fondest wishes, in the safe return of the beloved object; the age of romance has long ago past, but the affection of almost Infant years has matured and strengthend untill it has become a vital principle, nor has the world any thing to bestow which could in the smallest degree compensate for the loss. Desire and Sorrow were denounced upon our Sex; as a punishment for the transgression of Eve. I have sometimes thought that we are formed to experience more exquisite Sensations than is the Lot of your Sex. More tender and susceptable by Nature of those impression[s] which create happiness or misiry, we Suffer and enjoy in a higher degree. I never wonderd at the philosopher who thanked the Gods that he was created a Man rather than a Woman.

I cannot say, but that I was dissapointed when I found that your return to your native land was a still distant Idea. I think your Situation cannot be so dissagreable as I feared it was, yet that dreadfull climate is my terror.—You mortify me indeed when you talk of sending Charles to Colledge, who it is not probable will be fit under three or four years. Surely my dear Friend fleeting as time is I cannot reconcile myself to the Idea of living in this cruel State of Seperation for [4?] or even three years to come. Eight years have already past, since you could call yourself an Inhabitant of this State. I shall assume the Signature of Penelope,[17] for my dear Ulysses[18] has already been a wanderer from me near half the term of years that, that Hero was encountering

---

[15] Captain Trowbridge commanded the merchant ship *Firebrand*.

[16] John Laurance (1750–1810), a judge who later served in the U. S. Senate (1797–1800).

[17] Devoted wife of Odysseus (Latin: "Ulysses") in Homer's *Odyssey* (sixth century B.C.). Penelope was a model of domestic fidelity who endured twenty years of anxiety and grief during her husband's absence.

[18] In the *Odyssey,* king of Ithaca and Greek leader in the Trojan War who journeyed for ten years after the war before returning home.

Neptune, Calipso, the Circes and Syrens.[19] In the poetical Language of Penelope I shall address you

> "Oh! haste to me! A Little longer Stay
> Will ev'ry grace, each fancy'd charm decay:
> Increasing cares, and times resistless rage
> Will waste my bloom, and wither it to age."[20]

You will ask me I suppose what is become of my patriotick virtue? It is that which most ardently calls for your return. I greatly fear that the climate in which you now reside will prove fatal to your Life, whilst your Life and usefullness might be many years of Service to your Country in a more Healthy climate. If the Essentials of her political system are safe, as I would fain hope they are, yet the impositions and injuries, to which she is hourly liable, and daily suffering, call for the exertions of her wisest and ablest citizens. You know by many years experience what it is to struggle with difficulties—with wickedness in high places—from thence you are led to covet a private Station as the post of Honour, but should such an Idea generally prevail, who would be left to stem the torrent?

Should we at this day possess those invaluable Blessings transmitted us by our venerable Ancestors, if they had not inforced by their example, what they taught by their precepts?

> "While pride, oppression and injustice reign
> the World will still demand her Catos[21] presence."[22]

Why should I indulge an Idea, that whilst the active powers of my Friend remain, they will not be devoted to the Service of his country?

Can I believe that the Man who fears neither poverty or dangers, who sees not charms sufficient either in Riches, power or places to tempt him in the least to swerve from the purest Sentiments of Honour and Delicacy; will retire, unnoticed, Fameless to a Rustick cottage there by dint of Labour to earn his Bread. I need not much examination of my Heart to say I would not willing[ly] consent to it.

Have not Cincinnatus and Regulus[23] been handed down to posterity, with immortal honour?

Without fortune it is more than probable we shall end our days, but let the well earned Fame of having Sacrificed those prospects, from a principal of universal

---

[19] Neptune: Roman god of the sea; Calipso: the divine nymph with whom Odysseus lived for seven years after his ship foundered and he washed ashore on her island; Circe: a sorceress who changed Odysseus' men to swine but was forced by Odysseus to change them back; Syrens: Greek mythic female creatures who lured mariners onto the rocks around their island with their singing.

[20] Abigail Adams's own verse.

[21] Probably either Cato the Elder (234–149 B.C.) or Cato the Younger (95–46 B.C.), Roman statesman and philosopher, respectively.

[22] The source of these lines is unknown.

[23] Cincinnatus was appointed Roman dictator in 458 B.C. and was dispatched to rescue Minucius from the seige of Aequu. He freed Minucius, resigned his dictatorship, and returned to his farm beyond the Tiber. Regulus was in command of Roman troops on an African expedition when he was defeated and captured in Carthage. He was sent in 250 B.C. to Rome on parole to arrange an exchange of prisoners; he then voluntarily returned to Carthage, where he was purportedly tortured to death.

Benevolence and good will to Man, descend as an inheritance to our ofspring. The Luxery of Foreign Nations may possibly infect them but they have not before them an example of it, so far as respects their domestick life. They are not Bred up with an Idea of possessing Hereditary Riches or Grandeur. Retired from the Capital, they see little of the extravagance or dissipation, which prevails there, and at the close of day, in lieu of the Card table, some usefull Book employs their leisure hours. These habits early fixed, and daily inculcated, will I hope render them usefull and ornamental Members of Society.—But we cannot see into futurity.—With Regard to politicks, it is rather a dull season for them, we are recruiting for the Army.

The Enemy make sad Havock with our Navigation. Mr. Lovell[24] is appointed continental Receiver of taxes and is on his way to this State.

It is difficult to get Gentlemen of abilities and Integrity to serve in congress, few very few are willing to Sacrifice their Interest as others have done before them.

Your favour of december 18th came by way of Philadelphia, but all those Letters sent by Capt. Reeler[25] were lost, thrown over Board. Our Friends are well and desire to be rememberd to you. Charles will write if he is able to, before the vessel sails, but he is sick at present, threatned I fear with a fever. I received one Letter from my young Russian to whom I shall write—and 2 from Mr. Thaxter.[26] If the vessel gives me time I shall write. We wait impatiently for the result of your demand. These slow slugish wheels move not in unison with our feelings.

Adieu my dear Friend. How gladly would I visit you and partake of your Labours and cares, sooth you to rest, and alleviate your anxieties were it given me to visit you even by moon Light, as the faries are fabled to do.

I cheer my Heart with the distant prospect. All that I can hope for at present, is to hear of your welfare which of all things lies nearest the Heart of Your ever affectionate

Portia

1782/1973

Thomas Paine
1737–1809

Thomas Paine sailed to Philadelphia on the eve of the American Revolution, buoyed by a letter of introduction from Benjamin Franklin extolling his ingenuity and recommending his employment as "a clerk, or as assistant tutor in a school, or assistant surveyor." At the age of thirty-seven, Paine was determined to reverse his misfortune as a member of the English commercial class.

The son of a Thetford corsetmaker, Paine had twice fled the Quaker environment of his youth before settling in London, resuming his father's trade,

---

[24] James Lovell (1737–1814), a delegate from Massachusetts to the General Congress.
[25] The Adamses' friend and commander of a merchant ship.

[26] John Thaxter, Abigail Adams's cousin and tutor to their son John Quincy Adams.

and filling himself with all the science and political philosophy his considerable intellectual curiosity could gather. In 1760 Paine experienced the first in a series of adversities: the death of his wife in childbirth during the first year of their marriage. He was later fired twice from his job collecting excise taxes, worked briefly—and unhappily—as a teacher in Kensington, married someone with whom he apparently never lived, and took over her father's failing business. Before long, Paine was reduced to posting the following announcement in the local British newspaper:

> To be sold by auction, on Thursday the 14th of April, and following day, all the household furniture, stock in trade and other effects of Thomas Pain, grocer and tobacconist, near the West Gate in Lewes: Also a horse tobacco snuff mill, with all the utensils for cutting tobacco and grinding snuff; and two unopened crates of cream colored stoneware.

Such indignities would pursue Thomas Paine all his life. His own repeated misfortunes make more appreciable his fundamental commitment "to meliorate the situation of mankind."

Within six months of his arrival in America, Paine could proudly report to Franklin that, despite never having "published a syllable" in England, his numerous topical essays on slavery, unhappy marriages, dueling, inventions, and the rights of the "Female Sex" had helped nearly triple the circulation of the *Pennsylvania Magazine, or American Museum,* the journal he edited and gradually converted into an important popular advocate of independence. He had entered a new world of political turmoil, yet the populace's attachment to Britain was, as he noted, "obstinate." Like the majority of Americans, Paine regarded the dispute with England "as a kind of law suit, in which I supposed, the parties would find a way either to decide or settle it. I had no thoughts of independence or arms." But these sentiments shifted radically with the outbreak of hostilities at Lexington and Concord:

> The world could not then have persuaded me that I should be either a soldier or an author. If I had any talents for either, they were buried in me, and might ever have continued so, had not the necessity of the times dragged and driven them into action. I had formed my plan of life, and conceiving myself happy, wished everybody else so. But when the country into which I had just set foot, was set on fire about my ears, it was time to stir. Those who had been long settled had something to defend; those who had just come had something to pursue; and the call was equal and universal.

On January 10, 1776, at the encouragement of Dr. Benjamin Rush, Paine published *Common Sense.* Within three months, the pamphlet had sold more than one hundred thousand copies, an extraordinary number in an age when most works were published by subscription, with sales averaging well below one thousand. Paine drew on the conversational idioms of taverns, coffeehouses, and street-corner oratory to create an incisive commentary on the source and function of government. His bold and simple argument rallied a scattered citizenry to the cause of freedom and exerted considerable influence on the new nation's emerging political philosophy.

Paine's conviction that "those who expect to reap the blessings of freedom must . . . undergo the fatigue of supporting it" led him to enlist in the Revolutionary forces, serving as aide-de-camp to General Nathanael Greene. Witnessing the loss of New York and joining the retreat to Newark, Paine wrote the first of the *American Crisis* letter-pamphlets ("These are the times that try men's souls"), a text that George Washington ordered read to all the troops. Over the next seven years, Paine published thirteen essays in the series, along with three supplementary pieces. Each helped bolster the sagging spirits of the ill-fitted troops and firm the resolve of an occasionally diffident population.

After a brief stint in western Pennsylvania soliciting the support of the Indians in the Revolutionary cause, Paine was elected secretary of the Congressional Committee on Foreign Affairs in April 1777. He held this post until disclosing secret information he knew would save Congress the expense of profiteering loans from France. Once again beset by dwindling finances, Paine drifted in and out of various jobs and causes. He supported Robert Morris's efforts to start what is now the Bank of America; he traveled to France to secure additional relief for the Continental Army; he drafted the first legislative act of emancipation while serving as clerk of the Pennsylvania Assembly. In 1783 he moved to Bordentown, New Jersey, and devoted himself to invention. He produced, among other items, a smokeless candle and developed a model for an iron bridge without piers. But in 1787, when he could not muster enough capital to finance his projects, he once again left for France.

Paine traveled frequently to England over the next few years and oversaw the construction of the first bridge built under the patent the British government had awarded him. He visited Paris in 1790 to observe the French Revolution and quickly became enmeshed in the political debate it inspired. In 1791 he drafted the first part of *The Rights of Man* as a defense of the French cause in response to Edmund Burke's *Reflections on the Late Revolution in France.* Paine defended what he called the "natural rights" of national independence, free discussion, personal freedom, and franchise. He also reaffirmed the belief Roger Williams had posited nearly one hundred years earlier—that these rights must be confirmed by each generation. In Paine's view, "every age and generation must be free to act for itself *in all cases* as the ages and generations which preceded it. The vanity and presumption of governing beyond the grave is the most ridiculous and insolent of all tyrannies." Charged with sedition in England, Paine fled to France in 1792, where he was made an honorary citizen, represented Calais at the French Convention, and helped draft that nation's constitution. But his opposition to the execution of Louis XVI landed him in prison for ten months. Before being led away, Paine gave to Joel Barlow, the American poet and journalist, the first part of *The Age of Reason,* a Deist tract that attacked Christianity and praised the virtues of both an impersonal God and the common people.

Paine was released from prison through the efforts of James Monroe, the American ambassador, in whose home Paine lived for the next eighteen months.

In ill health and bitter about his neglect while in prison, Paine wrote the second part of *The Age of Reason*, published numerous essays denouncing the Federalists in America, and formulated "agrarian justice," a radical proposal for the democratization of wealth. Banished from England, imprisoned in France, and branded an "infidel" in America, Paine could take some solace in an earlier declaration:

> I speak an open and disinterested language, dictated by no passion but that of humanity. . . . Independence is my happiness, and I view things as they are, without regard to place or purpose; my country is the world, and my religion is to do good.

His altruistic sense of the world included humanitarian views of capital punishment, labor reform, and pensions. His vision culminated in the prospect of a league of nations to foster disarmament.

Thomas Paine returned to the United States in 1802 and spent his last seven years adjusting to new political and social circumstances. Insulted and harassed because of his religious writings, Paine suffered one final round of ignominy: He was not allowed to vote; he was humiliated on his deathbed by the local clergy and barred from burial in a Quaker cemetery. Ten years after his death, Paine's body was exhumed and returned to England to be displayed as a symbol of social reform. His bones, which eventually disappeared, were reported to have been auctioned off as a curiosity.

Paine's criticism of the Bible (Theodore Roosevelt called him a "filthy little atheist") long distracted readers from recognizing Paine's importance as a writer. His humanitarian impulses shaped much of the new nation's thinking about tyranny, justice, equality, and the natural rights of the individual. And his determination to offer a willing audience a plain, simple, vigorous, and forthright version of eighteenth-century liberal thought made Paine one of the most persuasive writers in America's struggle for independence.

Further Reading:
M. D. Conway, *The Life of Thomas Paine*, 2 vols., 1892.
J. Dos Passos, *The Living Thoughts of Thomas Paine*, 1940.
L. Gurko, *Tom Paine, Freedom's Apostle*, 1957.
A. O. Aldridge, *Man of Reason: The Life of Thomas Paine*, 1959.
D. Hawke, *Paine*, 1974.

Text:
The Writings of Thomas Paine, ed. M. D. Conway, 4 vols., 1894–1896.

from Common Sense*

Introduction

Perhaps the sentiments contained in the following pages, are not *yet* sufficiently fashionable to procure them general Favor; a long Habit of not thinking a Thing *wrong,* gives it a superficial appearance of being *right,* and raises at first a formidable outcry in defence of Custom. But the Tumult soon subsides. Time makes more Converts than Reason.

As a long and violent abuse of power is generally the means of calling the right of it in question, (and in matters too which might never have been thought of, had not the sufferers been aggravated into the inquiry,) and as the King of England hath undertaken in his *own right,* to support the Parliament in what he calls *Theirs,* and as the good People of this Country are grievously oppressed by the Combination, they have an undoubted privilege to enquire into the Pretensions of both, and equally to reject the Usurpation of *either.*

In the following Sheets, the Author hath studiously avoided every thing which is personal among ourselves. Compliments as well as censure to individuals make no part thereof. The wise and the worthy need not the triumph of a Pamphlet; and those whose sentiments are injudicious or unfriendly will cease of themselves, unless too much pains is bestowed upon their conversions.

The cause of America is in a great measure the cause of all mankind. Many circumstances have, and will arise, which are not local, but universal, and through which the principles of all lovers of mankind are affected, and in the event of which their affections are interested. The laying a country desolate with fire and sword, declaring war against the natural rights of all mankind, and extirpating the defenders thereof from the face of the earth, is the concern of every man to whom nature hath given the power of feeling; of which class, regardless of party censure, is

THE AUTHOR.

Thoughts on the Present State of American Affairs

In the following pages I offer nothing more than simple facts, plain arguments, and common sense: and have no other preliminaries to settle with the reader, than that he will divest himself of prejudice and prepossession, and suffer his reason and his feelings to determine for themselves: that he will put on, or rather that he will not put off, the true character of a man, and generously enlarge his views beyond the present day.

Volumes have been written on the subject of the struggle between England and America. Men of all ranks have embarked in the controversy, from different motives,

---

* The complete title is *Common Sense: Addressed to the Inhabitants of America on the Following Interesting Subjects: viz.: I. Of the origin and design of government in general; with concise remarks on the English constitution. II. of* monarchy and hereditary succession. III. Thoughts on the present state of American affairs. IV. Of the present ability of America; with some miscellaneous reflections.*

and with various designs; but all have been ineffectual, and the period of debate is closed. Arms as the last resource decide the contest; the appeal was the choice of the King, and the Continent has accepted the challenge.

It hath been reported of the late Mr. Pelham[1] (who tho' an able minister was not without his faults) that on his being attacked in the House of Commons on the score that his measures were only of a temporary kind, replied, *"they will last my time."* Should a thought so fatal and unmanly possess the Colonies in the present contest, the name of ancestors will be remembered by future generations with detestation.

The Sun never shined on a cause of greater worth. 'Tis not the affair of a City, a County, a Province, or a Kingdom; but of a Continent—of at least one eighth part of the habitable Globe. 'Tis not the concern of a day, a year, or an age; posterity are virtually involved in the contest, and will be more or less affected even to the end of time, by the proceedings now. Now is the seed-time of Continental union, faith and honour. The least fracture now will be like a name engraved with the point of a pin on the tender rind of a young oak; the wound would enlarge with the tree, and posterity read it in full grown characters.

By referring the matter from argument to arms, a new æra for politics is struck —a new method of thinking hath arisen. All plans, proposals, &c. prior to the nineteenth of April, *i.e.* to the commencement of hostilities,[2] are like the almanacks of the last year; which tho' proper then, are superceded and useless now. Whatever was advanced by the advocates on either side of the question then, terminated in one and the same point, viz. a union with Great Britain; the only difference between the parties was the method of effecting it; the one proposing force, the other friendship; but it hath so far happened that the first hath failed, and the second hath withdrawn her influence.

As much hath been said of the advantages of reconciliation, which, like an agreeable dream, hath passed away and left us as we were, it is but right that we should examine the contrary side of the argument, and enquire into some of the many material injuries which these Colonies sustain, and always will sustain, by being connected with and dependent on Great-Britain. To examine that connection and dependence, on the principles of nature and common sense, to see what we have to trust to, if separated, and what we are to expect, if dependant.

I have heard it asserted by some, that as America has flourished under her former connection with Great-Britain, the same connection is necessary towards her future happiness, and will always have the same effect. Nothing can be more fallacious than this kind of argument. We may as well assert that because a child has thrived upon milk, that it is never to have meat, or that the first twenty years of our lives is to become a precedent for the next twenty. But even this is admitting more than is true; for I answer roundly, that America would have flourished as much, and probably much more, had no European power taken any notice of her. The commerce by which she hath enriched herself are the necessaries of life, and will always have a market while eating is the custom of Europe.

But she has protected us, say some. That she hath engrossed us is true, and defended

---

[1] British prime minister (1743–1754).
[2] At Lexington, Massachusetts, the first armed conflict of the American Revolution began as the "minutemen" defended their ammunition stores against the British on April 19, 1775.

the Continent at our expense as well as her own, is admitted; and she would have defended Turkey from the same motive, *viz.* for the sake of trade and dominion.

Alas! we have been long led away by ancient prejudices and made large sacrifices to superstition. We have boasted the protection of Great Britain, without considering, that her motive was *interest* not *attachment;* and that she did not protect us from *our enemies* on *our account;* but from *her enemies* on *her own account,* from those who had no quarrel with us on any *other account,* and who will always be our enemies on the *same account.* Let Britain waive her pretensions to the Continent, or the Continent throw off the dependance, and we should be at peace with France and Spain, were they at war with Britain. The miseries of Hanover[3] last war ought to warn us against connections.

It hath lately been asserted in parliament, that the Colonies have no relation to each other but through the Parent Country, *i.e.* that Pennsylvania and the Jerseys,[4] and so on for the rest, are sister Colonies by the way of England; this is certainly a very roundabout way of proving relationship, but it is the nearest and only true way of proving enmity (or enemyship, if I may so call it.) France and Spain never were, nor perhaps ever will be, our enemies as *Americans,* but as our being the *subjects of Great Britain.*

But Britain is the parent country, say some. Then the more shame upon her conduct. Even brutes do not devour their young, nor savages make war upon their families; Wherefore, the assertion, if true, turns to her reproach; but it happens not to be true, or only partly so, and the phrase *parent* or *mother country* hath been jesuitically adopted by the King and his parasites, with a low papistical design of gaining an unfair bias on the credulous weakness of our minds. Europe, and not England, is the parent country of America. This new World hath been the asylum for the persecuted lovers of civil and religious liberty from *every part* of Europe. Hither have they fled, not from the tender embraces of the mother, but from the cruelty of the monster; and it is so far true of England, that the same tyranny which drove the first emigrants from home, pursues their descendants still.

In this extensive quarter of the globe, we forget the narrow limits of three hundred and sixty miles (the extent of England) and carry our friendship on a larger scale; we claim brotherhood with every European Christian, and triumph in the generosity of the sentiment.

It is pleasant to observe by what regular gradations we surmount the force of local prejudices, as we enlarge our acquaintance with the World. A man born in any town in England divided into parishes, will naturally associate most with his fellow parishioners (because their interests in many cases will be common) and distinguish him by the name of *neighbour;* if he meet him but a few miles from home, he drops the narrow idea of a street, and salutes him by the name of *townsman;* if he travel out of the county and meet him in any other, he forgets the minor divisions of street and town, and calls him *countryman, i.e. countyman:* but if in their foreign excursions they should associate in France, or any other part of *Europe,* their local remembrance would be

---

[3] Britain's King George III was a descendant of the Prussian House of Hanover; here Paine refers to the Seven Years' War (1756–1763), which originally engaged Prussia and Austria and expanded to include all major European powers. Although Britain was favored in the war settlement, American losses in the French and Indian campaigns were severe.

[4] At the time the colony was sectioned into East and West Jersey.

enlarged into that of *Englishmen*. And by a just parity of reasoning, all Europeans meeting in America, or any other quarter of the globe, are *countrymen;* for England, Holland, Germany, or Sweden, when compared with the whole, stand in the same places on the larger scale, which the divisions of street, town, and county do on the smaller ones; Distinctions too limited for Continental minds. Not one third of the inhabitants, even of this province[5] are of English descent. Wherefore, I reprobate the phrase of Parent or Mother Country applied to England only, as being false, selfish, narrow and ungenerous.

But, admitting that we were all of English descent, what does it amount to? Nothing. Britain, being now an open enemy, extinguishes every other name and title: and to say that reconciliation is our duty, is truly farcical. The first king of England, of the present line (William the Conqueror) was a Frenchman, and half the peers of England are descendants from the same country; wherefore, by the same method of reasoning, England ought to be governed by France.

Much hath been said of the united strength of Britain and the Colonies, that in conjunction they might bid defiance to the world: But this is mere presumption; the fate of war is uncertain, neither do the expressions mean any thing; for this continent would never suffer itself to be drained of inhabitants, to support the British arms in either Asia, Africa, or Europe.

Besides, what have we to do with setting the world at defiance? Our plan is commerce, and that, well attended to, will secure us the peace and friendship of all Europe; because it is the interest of all Europe to have America a free port. Her trade will always be a protection, and her barrenness of gold and silver secure her from invaders.

I challenge the warmest advocate for reconciliation to show a single advantage that this continent can reap by being connected with Great Britain. I repeat the challenge; not a single advantage is derived. Our corn will fetch its price in any market in Europe, and our imported goods must be paid for by them where we will.

But the injuries and disadvantages which we sustain by that connection, are without number; and our duty to mankind at large, as well as to ourselves, instruct us to renounce the alliance: because, any submission to, or dependance on, Great Britain, tends directly to involve this Continent in European wars and quarrels, and set us at variance with nations who would otherwise seek our friendship, and against whom we have neither anger nor complaint. As Europe is our market for trade, we ought to form no partial connection with any part of it. It is the true interest of America to steer clear of European contentions, which she never can do, while, by her dependance on Britain, she is made the makeweight in the scale of British politics.

Europe is too thickly planted with Kingdoms to be long at peace, and whenever a war breaks out between England and any foreign power, the trade of America goes to ruin, *because of her connection with Britain.* The next war may not turn out like the last,[6] and should it not, the advocates for reconciliation now will be wishing for separation then, because neutrality in that case would be a safer convoy than a man of war. Everything that is right or reasonable pleads for separation. The blood of the

[5] Pennsylvania.
[6] At the conclusion of the Seven Years' War, Britain was given all the French territory in North America through the Treaty of Paris (1763).

slain, the weeping voice of nature cries. 'TIS TIME TO PART. Even the distance at which the Almighty hath placed England and America is a strong and natural proof that the authority of the one over the other, was never the design of Heaven. The time likewise at which the Continent was discovered, adds weight to the argument, and the manner in which it was peopled, encreases the force of it. The Reformation was preceded by the discovery of America: As if the Almighty graciously meant to open a sanctuary to the persecuted in future years, when home should afford neither friendship nor safety.

The authority of Great Britain over this continent, is a form of government, which sooner or later must have an end: And a serious mind can draw no true pleasure by looking forward, under the painful and positive conviction that what he calls "the present constitution" is merely temporary. As parents, we can have no joy, knowing that this government is not sufficiently lasting to ensure any thing which we may bequeath to posterity: And by a plain method of argument, as we are running the next generation into debt, we ought to do the work of it, otherwise we use them meanly and pitifully. In order to discover the line of our duty rightly, we should take our children in our hand, and fix our station a few years farther into life; that eminence will present a prospect which a few present fears and prejudices conceal from our sight.

Though I would carefully avoid giving unnecessary offence, yet I am inclined to believe, that all those who espouse the doctrine of reconciliation, may be included within the following descriptions.

Interested men, who are not to be trusted, weak men who *cannot* see, prejudiced men who will not see, and a certain set of moderate men who think better of the European world than it deserves; and this last class, by an ill-judged deliberation, will be the cause of more calamities to this Continent than all the other three.

It is the good fortune of many to live distant from the scene of present sorrow; the evil is not sufficiently brought to their doors to make them feel the precariousness with which all American property is possessed. But let our imaginations transport us a few moments to Boston; that seat of wretchedness will teach us wisdom, and instruct us for ever to renounce a power in whom we can have no trust.[7] The inhabitants of that unfortunate city who but a few months ago were in ease and affluence, have now no other alternative than to stay and starve, or turn out to beg. Endangered by the fire of their friends if they continue within the city, and plundered by the soldiery if they leave it, in their present situation they are prisoners without the hope of redemption, and in a general attack for their relief they would be exposed to the fury of both armies.

Men of passive tempers look somewhat lightly over the offences of Great Britain, and, still hoping for the best, are apt to call out, *Come, come, we shall be friends again for all this.* But examine the passions and feelings of mankind: bring the doctrine of reconciliation to the touchstone of nature, and then tell me whether you can hereafter love, honour, and faithfully serve the power that hath carried fire and sword into your land? If you cannot do all these, then are you only deceiving yourselves, and by your delay bringing ruin upon posterity. Your future connection with Britain, whom you can neither love nor honour, will be forced and unnatural, and being formed only

---

[7] Boston was blockaded for six months under British military occupation.

on the plan of present convenience, will in a little time fall into a relapse more wretched than the first. But if you say, you can still pass the violations over, then I ask, hath your house been burnt? Hath your property been destroyed before your face? Are your wife and children destitute of a bed to lie on, or bread to live on? Have you lost a parent or a child by their hands, and yourself the ruined and wretched survivor? If you have not, then you are not a judge of those who have. But if you have, and can still shake hands with the murderers, then are you unworthy the name of husband, father, friend, or lover, and whatever may be your rank or title in life, you have the heart of a coward, and the spirit of a sycophant.

This is not inflaming or exaggerating matters, but trying them by those feelings and affections which nature justifies, and without which we should be incapable of discharging the social duties of life, or enjoying the felicities of it. I mean not to exhibit horror for the purpose of provoking revenge, but to awaken us from fatal and unmanly slumbers, that we may pursue determinately some fixed object. 'Tis not in the power of Britain or of Europe to conquer America, if she doth not conquer herself by delay and timidity. The present winter is worth an age if rightly employed, but if lost or neglected the whole Continent will partake of the misfortune; and there is no punishment which that man doth not deserve, be he who, or what, or where he will, that may be the means of sacrificing a season so precious and useful.

'Tis repugnant to reason, to the universal order of things, to all examples from former ages, to suppose that this Continent can long remain subject to any external power. The most sanguine in Britain doth not think so. The utmost stretch of human wisdom cannot, at this time, compass a plan, short of separation, which can promise the continent even a year's security. Reconciliation is *now* a fallacious dream. Nature hath deserted the connection, and art cannot supply her place. For, as Milton wisely expresses, "never can true reconcilement grow where wounds of deadly hate have pierced so deep."[8]

A government of our own is our natural right: and when a man seriously reflects on the precariousness of human affairs, he will become convinced, that it is infinitely wiser and safer, to form a constitution of our own in a cool deliberate manner, while we have it in our power, than to trust such an interesting event to time and chance. If we omit it now, some Massanello[9] may hereafter arise, who, laying hold of popular disquietudes, may collect together the desperate and the discontented, and by assuming to themselves the powers of government, finally sweep away the liberties of the Continent like a deluge. Should the government of America return again into the hands of Britain, the tottering situation of things will be a temptation for some desperate adventurer to try his fortune; and in such a case, what relief can Britain give? Ere she could hear the news, the fatal business might be done; and ourselves suffering like the wretched Britons under the oppression of the Conqueror. Ye that oppose independance now, ye know not what ye do: ye are opening a door to eternal tyranny, by keeping vacant the seat of government. There are thousands and tens of thousands, who would think it glorious to expel from the Continent, that barbarous and hellish

[8] John Milton, *Paradise Lost*, IV, 98–99.
[9] Paine's note: "Thomas Anello, otherwise Massanello, a fisherman of Naples who after spiriting up his countrymen in the public marketplace, against the oppression of the Spaniards, to whom the place was then subject, prompted them to revolt, and in the space of a day became King."

power, which hath stirred up the Indians and the Negroes to destroy us; the cruelty hath a double guilt, it is dealing brutally by us, and treacherously by them.

To talk of friendship with those in whom our reason forbids us to have faith, and our affections wounded thro' a thousand pores instruct us to detest, is madness and folly. Every day wears out the little remains of kindred between us and them; and can there be any reason to hope, that as the relationship expires, the affection will encrease, or that we shall agree better when we have ten times more and greater concerns to quarrel over than ever?

Ye that tell us of harmony and reconciliation, can ye restore to us the time that is past? Can ye give to prostitution its former innocence? neither can ye reconcile Britain and America. The last cord now is broken, the people of England are presenting addresses against us. There are injuries which nature cannot forgive; she would cease to be nature if she did. As well can the lover forgive the ravisher of his mistress, as the Continent forgive the murders of Britain. The Almighty hath implanted in us these unextinguishable feelings for good and wise purposes. They are the Guardians of his Image in our hearts. They distinguish us from the herd of common animals. The social compact would dissolve, and justice be extirpated from the earth, or have only a casual existence were we callous to the touches of affection. The robber and the murderer would often escape unpunished, did not the injuries which our tempers sustain, provoke us into justice.

O! ye that love mankind! Ye that dare oppose not only the tyranny but the tyrant, stand forth! Every spot of the old world is overrun with oppression. Freedom hath been hunted round the Globe. Asia and Africa have long expelled her. Europe regards her like a stranger, and England hath given her warning to depart. O! receive the fugitive, and prepare in time an asylum for mankind.

1776

---

from # The American Crisis

Number 1

These are the times that try men's souls. The summer soldier and the sunshine patriot will, in this crisis, shrink from the service of their country; but he that stands it *now,* deserves the love and thanks of man and woman. Tyranny, like hell, is not easily conquered; yet we have this consolation with us, that the harder the conflict, the more glorious the triumph. What we obtain too cheap, we esteem too lightly: it is dearness only that gives every thing its value. Heaven knows how to put a proper price upon its goods; and it would be strange indeed if so celestial an article as FREEDOM should not be highly rated. Britain, with an army to enforce her tyranny, has declared that she has a right (*not only to* TAX) but "to BIND *us in* ALL CASES WHATSOEVER,"[1] and if being *bound in that manner,* is not slavery, then is there not such a thing as slavery

---

[1] The quotation is from an English parliamentary act of 1776.

upon earth. Even the expression is impious; for so unlimited a power can belong only to God.

Whether the independence of the continent was declared too soon, or delayed too long, I will not now enter into as an argument; my own simple opinion is, that had it been eight months earlier, it would have been much better. We did not make a proper use of last winter, neither could we, while we were in a dependant state. However, the fault, if it were one, was all our own;[2] we have none to blame but ourselves. But no great deal is lost yet. All that Howe[3] has been doing for this month past, is rather a ravage than a conquest, which the spirit of the Jerseys,[4] a year ago, would have quickly repulsed, and which time and a little resolution will soon recover.

I have as little superstition in me as any man living, but my secret opinion has ever been, and still is, that God Almighty will not give up a people to military destruction, or leave them unsupportedly to perish, who have so earnestly and so repeatedly sought to avoid the calamities of war, by every decent method which wisdom could invent. Neither have I so much of the infidel in me, as to suppose that He has relinquished the government of the world, and given us up to the care of devils; and as I do not, I cannot see on what grounds the king of Britain can look up to heaven for help against us: a common murderer, a highwayman, or a house-breaker, has as good a pretence as he.

'Tis surprising to see how rapidly a panic will sometimes run through a country. All nations and ages have been subject to them: Britain has trembled like an ague at the report of a French fleet of flat bottomed boats; and in the fourteenth century[5] the whole English army, after ravaging the kingdom of France, was driven back like men petrified with fear; and this brave exploit was performed by a few broken forces collected and headed by a woman, Joan of Arc. Would that heaven might inspire some Jersey maid to spirit up her countrymen, and save her fair fellow sufferers from ravage and ravishment! Yet panics, in some cases, have their uses; they produce as much good as hurt. Their duration is always short; the mind soon grows through them, and acquires a firmer habit than before. But their peculiar advantage is, that they are the touchstones of sincerity and hypocrisy, and bring things and men to light, which might otherwise have lain forever undiscovered. In fact, they have the same effect on secret traitors, which an imaginary apparition would have upon a private murderer. They sift out the hidden thoughts of man, and hold them up in public to the world. Many a disguised tory has lately shown his head, that shall penitentially solemnize with curses the day on which Howe arrived upon the Delaware.

As I was with the troops at Fort Lee, and marched with them to the edge of Pennsylvania, I am well acquainted with many circumstances, which those who live at a distance know but little or nothing of. Our situation there was exceedingly cramped, the place being a narrow neck of land between the North River[6] and the

---

[2] Paine's note, a quotation from his *Common Sense* (1776): "The present winter is worth an age, if rightly employed; but if lost or neglected, the whole continent will partake of the evil; and there is no punishment that man does not deserve, be he who, or what, or where he will, that may be the means of sacrificing a season so precious and useful."

[3] British general.

[4] The colony was composed of East Jersey and West Jersey.

[5] Actually the fifteenth century.

[6] The Hudson.

Hackensack. Our force was inconsiderable, being not one fourth so great as Howe could bring against us. We had no army at hand to have relieved the garrison, had we shut ourselves up and stood on our defence. Our ammunition, light artillery, and the best part of our stores, had been removed, on the apprehension that Howe would endeavor to penetrate the Jerseys, in which case Fort Lee could be of no use to us; for it must occur to every thinking man, whether in the army or not, that these kind of field forts are only for temporary purposes, and last in use no longer than the enemy directs his force against the particular object, which such forts are raised to defend. Such was our situation and condition at Fort Lee on the morning of the 20th of November, when an officer arrived with information that the enemy with 200 boats had landed about seven miles above: Major General [Nathaniel] Green, who commanded the garrison, immediately ordered them under arms, and sent express to General Washington at the town of Hackensack, distant by the way of the ferry = six miles. Our first object was to secure the bridge over the Hackensack, which laid up the river between the enemy and us, about six miles from us, and three from them. General Washington arrived in about three quarters of an hour, and marched at the head of the troops towards the bridge, which place I expected we should have a brush for; however, they did not choose to dispute it with us, and the greatest part of our troops went over the bridge, the rest over the ferry, except some which passed at a mill on a small creek, between the bridge and the ferry, and made their way through some marshy grounds up to the town of Hackensack, and there passed the river. We brought off as much baggage as the wagons could contain, the rest was lost. The simple object was to bring off the garrison, and march them on till they could be strengthened by the Jersey or Pennsylvania militia, so as to be enabled to make a stand. We staid four days at Newark, collected our out-posts with some of the Jersey militia, and marched out twice to meet the enemy, on being informed that they were advancing, though our numbers were greatly inferior to theirs. Howe, in my little opinion, committed a great error in generalship in not throwing a body of forces off from Staten Island through Amboy, by which means he might have seized all our stores at Brunswick, and intercepted our march into Pennsylvania; but if we believe the power of hell to be limited, we must likewise believe that their agents are under some providential controul.

I shall not now attempt to give all the particulars of our retreat to the Delaware; suffice it for the present to say, that both officers and men, though greatly harassed and fatigued, frequently without rest, covering, or provision, the inevitable consequences of a long retreat, bore it with a manly and martial spirit. All their wishes centered in one, which was, that the country would turn out and help them to drive the enemy back. Voltaire has remarked that king William[7] never appeared to full advantage but in difficulties and in action; the same remark may be made on General Washington, for the character fits him. There is a natural firmness in some minds which cannot be unlocked by trifles, but which, when unlocked, discovers a cabinet of fortitude; and I reckon it among those kind of public blessings, which we do not immediately see, that God hath blessed him with uninterrupted health, and given him a mind that can even flourish upon care.

[7] William III, king of England from 1689 to 1702.

I shall conclude this paper with some miscellaneous remarks on the state of our affairs; and shall begin with asking the following question, Why is it that the enemy have left the New-England provinces, and made these middle ones the seat of war? The answer is easy: New-England is not infested with tories, and we are. I have been tender in raising the cry against these men, and used numberless arguments to show them their danger, but it will not do to sacrifice a world either to their folly or their baseness. The period is now arrived, in which either they or we must change our sentiments, or one or both must fall. And what is a tory? Good God! what is he? I should not be afraid to go with a hundred whigs against a thousand tories, were they to attempt to get into arms. Every tory is a coward; for servile, slavish, self-interested fear is the foundation of toryism; and a man under such influence, though he may be cruel, never can be brave.

But, before the line of irrecoverable separation be drawn between us, let us reason the matter together: Your conduct is an invitation to the enemy, yet not one in a thousand of you has heart enough to join him. Howe is as much deceived by you as the American cause is injured by you. He expects you will all take up arms, and flock to his standard, with muskets on your shoulders. Your opinions are of no use to him, unless you support him personally, for 'tis soldiers, and not tories, that he wants.

I once felt all that kind of anger, which a man ought to feel, against the mean principles that are held by the tories: a noted one, who kept a tavern at Amboy, was standing at his door, with as pretty a child in his hand, about eight or nine years old, as I ever saw, and after speaking his mind as freely as he thought was prudent, finished with this unfatherly expression, *"Well! give me peace in my day."* Not a man lives on the continent but fully believes that a separation must some time or other finally take place, and a generous parent should have said, *"If there must be trouble, let it be in my day, that my child may have peace;"* and this single reflection, well applied, is sufficient to awaken every man to duty. Not a place upon earth might be so happy as America. Her situation is remote from all the wrangling world, and she has nothing to do but to trade with them. A man can distinguish himself between temper and principle, and I am as confident, as I am that God governs the world, that America will never be happy till she gets clear of foreign dominion. Wars, without ceasing, will break out till that period arrives, and the continent must in the end be conqueror; for though the flame of liberty may sometimes cease to shine, the coal can never expire.

America did not, nor does not want force; but she wanted a proper application of that force. Wisdom is not the purchase of a day, and it is no wonder that we should err at the first setting off. From an excess of tenderness, we were unwilling to raise an army, and trusted our cause to the temporary defence of a well-meaning militia. A summer's experience has now taught us better; yet with those troops, while they were collected, we were able to set bounds to the progress of the enemy, and, thank God! they are again assembling. I always considered militia as the best troops in the world for a sudden exertion, but they will not do for a long campaign. Howe, it is probable, will make an attempt on this city;[8] should he fail on this side the Delaware, he is ruined: if he succeeds, our cause is not ruined. He stakes all on his side against a part on ours; admitting he succeeds, the consequence will be, that armies from both

[8] Philadelphia.

ends of the continent will march to assist their suffering friends in the middle states; for he cannot go everywhere, it is impossible. I consider Howe as the greatest enemy the tories have; he is bringing a war into their country, which, had it not been for him and partly for themselves, they had been clear of. Should he now be expelled, I wish with all the devotion of a Christian, that the names of whig and tory may never more be mentioned; but should the tories give him encouragement to come, or assistance if he come, I as sincerely wish that our next year's arms may expel them from the continent, and the congress appropriate their possessions to the relief of those who have suffered in well-doing. A single successful battle next year will settle the whole. America could carry on a two years war by the confiscation of the property of disaffected persons, and be made happy by their expulsion. Say not that this is revenge, call it rather the soft resentment of a suffering people, who, having no object in view but the *good* of *all,* have staked their *own all* upon a seemingly doubtful event. Yet it is folly to argue against determined hardness; eloquence may strike the ear, and the language of sorrow draw forth the tear of compassion, but nothing can reach the heart that is steeled with prejudice.

Quitting this class of men, I turn with the warm ardor of a friend to those who have nobly stood, and are yet determined to stand the matter out: I call not upon a few, but upon all: not on *this* state or *that* state, but on *every* state: up and help us; lay your shoulders to the wheel; better have too much force than too little, when so great an object is at stake. Let it be told to the future world, that in the depth of winter, when nothing but hope and virtue could survive, that the city and the country, alarmed at one common danger, came forth to meet and to repulse it. Say not that thousands are gone, turn out your tens of thousands; throw not the burden of the day upon Providence, but *"show your faith by your works,"*[9] that God may bless you. It matters not where you live, or what rank of life you hold, the evil or the blessing will reach you all. The far and the near, the home counties and the back, the rich and the poor, will suffer or rejoice alike. The heart that feels not now, is dead: the blood of his children will curse his cowardice, who shrinks back at a time when a little might have saved the whole, and made *them* happy. I love the man that can smile in trouble, that can gather strength from distress, and grow brave by reflection. 'Tis the business of little minds to shrink; but he whose heart is firm, and whose conscience approves his conduct, will pursue his principles unto death. My own line of reasoning is to myself as straight and clear as a ray of light. Not all the treasures of the world, so far as I believe, could have induced me to support an offensive war, for I think it murder; but if a thief breaks into my house, burns and destroys my property, and kills or threatens to kill me, or those that are in it, and to *"bind me in all cases whatsoever"*[10] to his absolute will, am I to suffer it? What signifies it to me, whether he who does it is a king or a common man; my countryman or not my countryman; whether it be done by an individual villain, or an army of them? If we reason to the root of things we shall find no difference; neither can any just cause be assigned why we should punish in the one case and pardon in the other. Let them call me rebel, and welcome, I feel no concern from it; but I should suffer the misery of devils, were

[9] James 2:18.   [10] See footnote 1.

I to make a whore of my soul by swearing allegiance to one whose character is that of a sottish, stupid, stubborn, worthless, brutish man. I conceive likewise a horrid idea in receiving mercy from a being, who at the last day shall be shrieking to the rocks and mountains to cover him, and fleeing with terror from the orphan, the widow, and the slain of America.

There are cases which cannot be overdone by language, and this is one. There are persons, too, who see not the full extent of the evil which threatens them; they solace themselves with hopes that the enemy, if he succeed, will be merciful. It is the madness of folly, to expect mercy from those who have refused to do justice; and even mercy, where conquest is the object, is only a trick of war; the cunning of the fox is as murderous as the violence of the wolf, and we ought to guard equally against both. Howe's first object is, partly by threats and partly by promises, to terrify or seduce the people to deliver up their arms and receive mercy. The ministry recommended the same plan to Gage,[11] and this is what the tories call making their peace, *"a peace which passeth all understanding" indeed!*[12] A peace which would be the immediate forerunner of a worse ruin than any we have yet thought of. Ye men of Pennsylvania, do reason upon these things! Were the back counties to give up their arms, they would fall an easy prey to the Indians, who are all armed: this perhaps is what some tories would not be sorry for. Were the home counties to deliver up their arms, they would be exposed to the resentment of the back counties, who would then have it in their power to chastise their defection at pleasure. And were any one state to give up its arms, *that* state must be garrisoned by all Howe's army of Britons and Hessians to preserve it from the anger of the rest. Mutual fear is the principal link in the chain of mutual love, and woe be to that state that breaks the compact. Howe is mercifully inviting you to barbarous destruction, and men must be either rogues or fools that will not see it. I dwell not upon the vapours of imagination; I bring reason to your ears, and, in language as plain as A, B, C, hold up truth to your eyes.

I thank God, that I fear not. I see no real cause for fear. I know our situation well, and can see the way out of it. While our army was collected, Howe dared not risk a battle; and it is no credit to him that he decamped from the White Plains, and waited a mean opportunity to ravage the defenceless Jerseys; but it is great credit to us, that, with a handful of men, we sustained an orderly retreat for near an hundred miles, brought off our ammunition, all our field pieces, the greatest part of our stores, and had four rivers to pass. None can say that our retreat was precipitate, for we were near three weeks in performing it, that the country[13] might have time to come in. Twice we marched back to meet the enemy, and remained out till dark. The sign of fear was not seen in our camp, and had not some of the cowardly and disaffected inhabitants spread false alarms through the country, the Jerseys had never been ravaged. Once more we are again collected and collecting; our new army at both ends of the continent is recruiting fast, and we shall be able to open the next campaign with sixty thousand men, well armed and clothed. This is our situation, and who will

11 A commander of British forces from 1763 to 1775.

12 A play on Philippians 4:7.

13 I.e., local volunteers.

may know it. By perseverance and fortitude we have the prospect of a glorious issue; by cowardice and submission, the sad choice of a variety of evils—a ravaged country —a depopulated city—habitations without safety, and slavery without hope—our homes turned into barracks and bawdy-houses for Hessians, and a future race to provide for, whose fathers we shall doubt of. Look on this picture and weep over it! and if there yet remains one thoughtless wretch who believes it not, let him suffer it unlamented.

COMMON SENSE.

1776

St. Jean de Crèvecoeur
1735–1813

"What then is the American, this new man?" With that question a Jesuit-trained, English-educated, aristocratic Frenchman who had adopted New York as his native ground began one of the earliest inquiries into a relatively new psychosocial phenomenon, the American identity.

The question suited the personality of the man who asked it. Himself an amalgam of identities, Michel-Guillaume Jean de Crèvecoeur was born near Caen, in Normandy, in 1735. He received a Jesuit education, completed his studies in England, and then, at nineteen, left for Canada, where he served as an officer and cartographer under General Montcalm. After Wolfe defeated the French at Quebec in 1759, Crèvecoeur resigned his commission and traveled extensively through the British colonies. He finally settled down in New York, where in 1765 he took out citizenship papers, purchased a large farm in Orange County, married a woman from Yonkers, had three children, and immersed himself physically and philosophically in the role of "a simple American farmer." Presumably to assure himself of his new identity, he decided to go by the English name Hector St. John, though he was never consistent about what he called himself: "J. Hector St. John (a *Pennsylvanian* farmer)" appears on the title page of his first book, and throughout his career he used various combinations of his real and assumed names.

The American Revolution interrupted a pattern of life that Crèvecoeur rhapsodically described as one of idyllic agrarian self-sufficiency. Partisans are not noted for their tolerance of mixed identities during times of political crisis, and Crèvecoeur, who attempted to remain neutral, found himself suspected by both sides. His rural tranquility shattered by the war, his life in danger, he resolved to leave the country. After months of anxious waiting and a few more months in a British prison in New York City, Crèvecoeur obtained permission in 1780 to sail with one of his children for Europe. He took with him manuscripts he had worked on during his early travels and his farming days. In 1782 a London publisher brought out *Letters from an American Farmer,* a series of twelve epistolary essays, all but one of which Crèvecoeur had composed before the

Revolution. The *Letters* were an immediate success, and Crèvecoeur became a popular figure in Parisian literary circles, where, according to the fashionable primitivism of the time, he was referred to as "an American savage." An advertisement appended to the *Letters* promised a second series, but in 1783 Crèvecoeur accepted a position in New York City as French consul to New York, Connecticut, and New Jersey. The second series of letters remained unpublished until the 1920s, when they were rediscovered and brought out as *Sketches of Eighteenth-Century America.* Revealing more clearly than in previous writings his Tory leanings and advocating highly restrictive trade policies, the sequel of letters had probably been suppressed once Crèvecoeur had assumed his new diplomatic position.

When Crèvecoeur returned to America in 1783, he found his wife dead, his farm destroyed by an allied attack of Loyalists and Indians, and his children in the care of a Boston family. Recovering his children, he moved to New York City, where he established headquarters and worked at continuing friendly diplomatic relations between his two countries. He also contributed medical and agricultural articles to journals and is credited with having introduced alfalfa to the United States. He made another trip to Paris to prepare a second edition of the *Letters,* then, after serving as consul for three more years, left America permanently in 1790. In 1801 he published in French a three-volume travel book on America, *Le Voyage dans la haute Pennsylvanie et dans l'état de New-York,* which he camouflaged as merely his edited translation of an anonymous, deteriorated English manuscript discovered in Copenhagen. Crèvecoeur died in Normandy in 1813.

Like many late-eighteenth-century writers, Crèvecoeur wrote glowingly of nature and the values of an agrarian economy. His enticing descriptions of a simple rural life based on a domestic economy of "ample subsistence" had the unfortunate promotional effect of luring many people into frontier conditions that little resembled the author's Orange County plantation. "I used to admire my head off," said D. H. Lawrence of Crèvecoeur's world, "before I tiptoed into the Wilds and saw the shacks of the Homesteaders." But if Crèvecoeur sometimes cheats on the side of sentimentality when it comes to providing an accurate account of rural benefits and New World opportunities, he could, as *Sketches of Eighteenth-Century America* shows, also write quite convincingly of rural hardships and the ordinary tasks of agricultural life. The set of sketches collected as "Thoughts of an American Farmer on Various Rural Subjects" offers one of the most vivid accounts we have of everyday life in a small, late-eighteenth-century farm community.

Although Crèvecoeur wrote most effectively when he was being least promotional and least theoretical, he nevertheless remains best known for his investigations into the American character. He concludes his most famous essay *with a case study* (omitted here) of a single immigrant whose history answers the essay's central question, "What is an American?" Given Crèvecoeur's versatility, his pragmatic buoyancy, his capacity for multiple loyalties, and his self-reliance and self-inventiveness, he might just as well have appended his own biography as the answer to that still intriguing question.

Further Reading:
J. P. Mitchell, *St. Jean de Crèvecoeur*, 1916.
Thomas Philbrick, *St. John de Crèvecoeur*, 1970.

Texts:
Letters from an American Farmer, ed. W. B. Trent, 1904.
See also *Crèvecoeur's 18th-Century Travels in Pennsylvania and New York*, ed. P. G. Adams, 1962.
Letters from an American Farmer, ed. A. E. Stone, 1963.
Journey into Northern Pennsylvania and the State of New York, ed. C. S. Bostelmann, 1964.

---

from Letters from an American Farmer

from Letter III: What Is an American?

I wish I could be acquainted with the feelings and thoughts which must agitate the heart and present themselves to the mind of an enlightened Englishman, when he first lands on this continent. He must greatly rejoice that he lived at a time to see this fair country discovered and settled; he must necessarily feel a share of national pride, when he views the chain of settlements which embellishes these extended shores. When he says to himself, this is the work of my countrymen, who, when convulsed by factions, afflicted by a variety of miseries and wants, restless and impatient, took refuge here. They brought along with them their national genius, to which they principally owe what liberty they enjoy, and what substance they possess. Here he sees the industry of his native country displayed in a new manner, and traces in their works the embrios of all the arts, sciences, and ingenuity which flourish in Europe. Here he beholds fair cities, substantial villages, extensive fields, an immense country filled with decent houses, good roads, orchards, meadows, and bridges, where an hundred years ago all was wild, woody and uncultivated! What a train of pleasing ideas this fair spectacle must suggest; it is a prospect which must inspire a good citizen with the most heartfelt pleasure. The difficulty consists in the manner of viewing so extensive a scene. He is arrived on a new continent; a modern society offers itself to his contemplation, different from what he had hitherto seen. It is not composed, as in Europe, of great lords who possess every thing, and of a herd of people who have nothing. Here are no aristocratical families, no courts, no kings, no bishops, no ecclesiastical dominion, no invisible power giving to a few a very visible one; no great manufacturers employing thousands, no great refinements of luxury. The rich and the poor are not so far removed from each other as they are in Europe. Some few towns excepted, we are all tillers of the earth, from Nova Scotia to West Florida. We are a people of cultivators, scattered over an immense territory, communicating with each other by means of good roads and navigable rivers, united by the silken bands of mild government, all respecting the laws, without dreading their power, because they are equitable. We are all animated with the spirit of an industry which is unfettered and unrestrained, because each person works for himself. If he travels through our rural districts he views not the hostile castle, and the haughty mansion, contrasted with the clay-built hut and miserable cabbin, where cattle and men help to keep each other warm, and dwell in meanness, smoke, and indigence. A pleasing uniformity of decent competence appears throughout our habitations. The meanest of our log-houses is a dry and comfortable habitation. Lawyer or merchant are the fairest titles our towns afford; that of a farmer is the only appellation of the rural inhabitants of our country. It must take some time ere he can reconcile himself to our dictionary, which is but short in words of dignity, and names of honour. There, on a Sunday, he sees a congregation of respectable farmers and their wives, all clad in neat homespun, well mounted, or riding in their own humble waggons. There is not among them an esquire, saving the unlettered magistrate. There he sees a parson as simple as his flock, a farmer who does not riot on the labour of others. We have no princes, for whom we toil, starve, and bleed: we are the most perfect society now existing in the world. Here man is free as he ought to be; nor is this pleasing equality so transitory as many others are. Many ages will not see the shores of our great lakes replenished with inland nations, nor the unknown bounds of North America entirely peopled. Who can tell how far it extends? Who can tell the millions of men whom it will feed and contain? for no European foot has as yet travelled half the extent of this mighty continent!

The next wish of this traveller will be to know whence came all these people? they are a mixture of English, Scotch, Irish, French, Dutch, Germans, and Swedes. From this promiscuous breed, that race now called Americans have arisen. The eastern provinces must indeed be excepted, as being the unmixed descendents of Englishmen. I have heard many wish that they had been more intermixed also: for my part, I am no wisher, and think it much better as it has happened. They exhibit a most conspicuous figure in this great and variegated picture; they too enter for a great share in the pleasing perspective displayed in these thirteen provinces. I know it is fashionable to reflect on them, but I respect them for what they have done; for the accuracy and wisdom with which they have settled their territory; for the decency of their manners; for their early love of letters; their ancient college,[1] the first in this hemisphere; for their industry; which to me who am but a farmer, is the criterion of everything. There never was a people, situated as they are, who with so ungrateful a soil have done more in so short a time. Do you think that the monarchical ingredients which are more prevalent in other governments, have purged them from all foul stains? Their histories assert the contrary.

In this great American asylum, the poor of Europe have by some means met together, and in consequence of various causes; to what purpose should they ask one another what countrymen they are? Alas, two thirds of them had no country. Can a wretch who wanders about, who works and starves, whose life is a continual scene of sore affliction or pinching penury; can that man call England or any other kingdom his country? A country that had no bread for him, whose fields procured him no harvest, who met with nothing but the frowns of the rich, the severity of the laws, with jails and punishments; who owned not a single foot of the extensive surface of this planet? No! urged by a variety of motives, here they came. Every thing has tended to regenerate them; new laws, a new mode of living, a new social system; here they are become men: in Europe they were as so many useless plants, wanting vegetative mould, and refreshing showers; they withered, and were mowed down by want, hunger, and war; but now by the power of transplantation, like all other plants they

[1] Harvard, founded in 1636.

have taken root and flourished! Formerly they were not numbered in any civil lists of their country, except in those of the poor; here they rank as citizens. By what invisible power has the surprising metamorphosis been performed? By that of the laws and that of their industry. The laws, the indulgent laws, protect them as they arrive, stamping on them the symbol of adoption; they receive ample rewards for their labours; these accumulated rewards procure them lands; those lands confer on them the title of freemen, and to that title every benefit is affixed which men can possibly require. This is the great operation daily performed by our laws. From whence proceed these laws? From our government. Whence the government? It is derived from the original genius and strong desire of the people ratified and confirmed by the crown. This is the great chain which links us all, this is the picture which every province exhibits, Nova Scotia excepted. There the crown has done all;[2] either there were no people who had genius, or it was not much attended to: the consequence is, that the province is very thinly inhabited indeed; the power of the crown in conjunction with the musketos has prevented men from settling there. Yet some parts of it flourished once, and it contained a mild harmless set of people. But for the fault of a few leaders, the whole were banished. The greatest political error the crown ever committed in America, was to cut off men from a country which wanted nothing but men!

What attachment can a poor European emigrant have for a country where he had nothing? The knowledge of the language, the love of a few kindred as poor as himself, were the only cords that tied him: his country is now that which gives him land, bread, protection, and consequence: *Ubi panis ibi patria,*[3] is the motto of all emigrants. What then is the American, this new man? He is either an European, or the descendant of an European, hence that strange mixture of blood, which you will find in no other country. I could point out to you a family whose grandfather was an Englishmen, whose wife was Dutch, whose son married a French woman, and whose present four sons have now four wives of different nations. *He* is an American, who leaving behind him all his ancient prejudices and manners, receives new ones from the new mode of life he has embraced, the new government he obeys, and the new rank he holds. He becomes an American by being received in the broad lap of our great *Alma Mater.* Here individuals of all nations are melted into a new race of men, whose labours and posterity will one day cause great changes in the world. Americans are the western pilgrims, who are carrying along with them that great mass of arts, sciences, vigour, and industry which began long since in the east; they will finish the great circle. The Americans were once scattered all over Europe; here they are incorporated into one of the finest systems of population which has ever appeared, and which will hereafter become distinct by the power of the different climates they inhabit. The American ought therefore to love this country much better than that wherein either he or his forefathers were born. Here the rewards of his industry follow with equal steps the progress of his labour; his labour is founded on the basis of nature, *self-interest;* can it want a stronger allurement? Wives and children, who before in vain demanded of him a morsel of bread, now, fat and frolicsome, gladly help their father to clear those fields whence exuberant crops are to arise to feed and to clothe them all; without any

[2] In 1755 the English banished thousands of French settlers from Nova Scotia.

[3] Latin: "Where bread is, there is one's country."

part being claimed, either by a despotic prince, a rich abbot, or a mighty lord. Here religion demands but little of him; a small voluntary salary to the minister, and gratitude to God; can he refuse these? The American is a new man, who acts upon new principles; he must therefore entertain new ideas, and form new opinions. From involuntary idleness, servile dependence, penury, and useless labour, he has passed to toils of a very different nature, rewarded by ample subsistence.—This is an American.

British America is divided into many provinces, forming a large association, scattered along a coast 1500 miles extent and about 200 wide. This society I would fain examine, at least such as it appears in the middle provinces; if it does not afford that variety of tinges and gradations which may be observed in Europe, we have colours peculiar to ourselves. For instance, it is natural to conceive that those who live near the sea, must be very different from those who live in the woods; the intermediate space will afford a separate and distinct class.

Men are like plants; the goodness and flavour of the fruit proceeds from the peculiar soil and exposition in which they grow. We are nothing but what we derive from the air we breathe, the climate we inhabit, the government we obey, the system of religion we profess, and the nature of our employment. Here you will find but few crimes; these have acquired as yet no root among us. I wish I were able to trace all my ideas; if my ignorance prevents me from describing them properly, I hope I shall be able to delineate a few of the outlines, which are all I propose.

Those who live near the sea, feed more on fish than on flesh, and often encounter that boisterous element. This renders them more bold and enterprising; this leads them to neglect the confined occupations of the land. They see and converse with a variety of people; their intercourse with mankind becomes extensive. The sea inspires them with a love of traffic, a desire of transporting produce from one place to another; and leads them to a variety of resources which supply the place of labour. Those who inhabit the middle settlements, by far the most numerous, must be very different; the simple cultivation of the earth purifies them, but the indulgences of the government, the soft remonstrances of religion, the rank of independent freeholders, must necessarily inspire them with sentiments, very little known in Europe among people of the same class. What do I say? Europe has no such class of men; the early knowledge they acquire, the early bargains they make, give them a great degree of sagacity. As freemen they will be litigious; pride and obstinacy are often the cause of law suits; the nature of our laws and governments may be another. As citizens it is easy to imagine, that they will carefully read the newspapers, enter into every political disquisition, freely blame or censure governors and others. As farmers they will be careful and anxious to get as much as they can, because what they get is their own. As northern men they will love the chearful cup. As Christians, religion curbs them not in their opinions; the general indulgence leaves every one to think for themselves in spiritual matters; the laws inspect our actions, our thoughts are left to God. Industry, good living, selfishness, litigiousness, country politics, the pride of freemen, religious indifference, are their characteristics. If you recede still farther from the sea, you will come into more modern settlements; they exhibit the same strong lineaments, in a ruder appearance. Religion seems to have still less influence, and their manners are less improved.

Now we arrive near the great woods, near the last inhabited districts; there men seem to be placed still farther beyond the reach of government, which in some measure leaves them to themselves. How can it pervade every corner; as they were driven there by misfortunes, necessity of beginnings, desire of acquiring large tracks of land, idleness, frequent want of economy, ancient debts; the re-union of such people does not afford a very pleasing spectacle. When discord, want of unity and friendship; when either drunkenness or idleness prevail in such remote districts; contention, inactivity, and wretchedness must ensue. There are not the same remedies to these evils as in a long established community. The few magistrates they have, are in general little better than the rest; they are often in a perfect state of war; that of man against man, sometimes decided by blows, sometimes by means of the law; that of man against every wild inhabitant of these venerable woods, of which they are come to dispossess them. There men appear to be no better than carnivorous animals of a superior rank, living on the flesh of wild animals when they can catch them, and when they are not able, they subsist on grain. He who would wish to see America in its proper light, and have a true idea of its feeble beginnings and barbarous rudiments, must visit our extended line of frontiers where the last settlers dwell, and where he may see the first labours of settlement, the mode of clearing the earth, in all their different appearances; where men are wholly left dependent on their native tempers, and on the spur of uncertain industry, which often fails when not sanctified by the efficacy of a few moral rules. There, remote from the power of example, and check of shame, many families exhibit the most hideous parts of our society. They are a kind of forlorn hope, preceding by ten or twelve years the most respectable army of veterans which come after them. In that space, prosperity will polish some, vice and the law will drive off the rest, who uniting again with others like themselves will recede still farther; making room for more industrious people, who will finish their improvements, convert the loghouse into a convenient habitation, and rejoicing that the first heavy labours are finished, will change in a few years that hitherto barbarous country into a fine fertile, well regulated district. Such is our progress, such is the march of the Europeans toward the interior parts of this continent. In all societies there are off-casts; this impure part serves as our precursors or pioneers; my father himself was one of that class, but he came upon honest principles, and was therefore one of the few who held fast; by good conduct and temperance, he transmitted to me his fair inheritance, when not above one in fourteen of his contemporaries had the same good fortune.[4]

Forty years ago this smiling country was thus inhabited; it is now purged, a general decency of manners prevails throughout, and such has been the fate of our best countries.

Exclusive of those general characteristics, each province has its own, founded on the government, climate, mode of husbandry, customs, and peculiarity of circumstances. Europeans submit insensibly to these great powers, and become, in the course of a few generations, not only Americans in general, but either Pennsylvanians, Virginians, or provincials under some other name. Whoever traverses the continent must easily observe those strong differences, which will grow more evident in time. The inhabitants of Canada, Massachuset, the middle provinces, the southern ones will be as different as their climates; their only points of unity will be those of religion and language.

As I have endeavoured to shew you how Europeans become Americans; it may

---

[4] Part of Crèvecoeur's disguise; his father had
never been to America.

not be disagreeable to shew you likewise how the various Christian sects introduced, wear out, and how religious indifference becomes prevalent. When any considerable number of a particular sect happen to dwell contiguous to each other, they immediately erect a temple, and there worship the Divinity agreeably to their own peculiar ideas. Nobody disturbs them. If any new sect springs up in Europe, it may happen that many of its professors will come and settle in America. As they bring their zeal with them, they are at liberty to make proselytes if they can, and to build a meeting and to follow the dictates of their consciences; for neither the government nor any other power interferes. If they are peaceable subjects, and are industrious, what is it to their neighbours how and in what manner they think fit to address their prayers to the Supreme Being? But if the sectaries are not settled close together, if they are mixed with other denominations, their zeal will cool for want of fuel, and will be extinguished in a little time. Then the Americans become as to religion, what they are as to country, allied to all. In them the name of Englishman, Frenchman, and European is lost, and in like manner, the strict modes of Christianity as practised in Europe are lost also. This effect will extend itself still farther hereafter, and though this may appear to you as a strange idea, yet it is a very true one. I shall be able perhaps hereafter to explain myself better, in the meanwhile, let the following example serve as my first justification.

Let us suppose you and I to be travelling; we observe that in this house, to the right, lives a Catholic, who prays to God as he has been taught, and believes in transubstantiation; he works and raises wheat, he has a large family of children, all hale and robust; his belief, his prayers offend nobody. About one mile farther on the same road, his next neighbour may be a good honest plodding German Lutheran, who addresses himself to the same God, the God of all, agreeably to the modes he has been educated in, and believes in consubstantiation; by so doing he scandalizes nobody; he also works in his fields, embellishes the earth, clears swamps, &c. What has the world to do with his Lutheran principles? He persecutes nobody, and nobody persecutes him, he visits his neighbours, and his neighbours visit him. Next to him lives a seceder, the most enthusiastic of all sectaries; his zeal is hot and fiery, but separated as he is from others of the same complexion, he has no congregation of his own to resort to, where he might cabal and mingle religious pride with worldly obstinacy. He likewise raises good crops, his house is handsomely painted, his orchard is one of the fairest in the neighbourhood. How does it concern the welfare of the country, or of the province at large, what this man's religious sentiments are, or really whether he has any at all? He is a good farmer, he is a sober, peaceable, good citizen: William Penn himself would not wish for more. This is the visible character, the invisible one is only guessed at, and is nobody's business. Next again lives a Low Dutchman, who implicitly believes the rules laid down by the synod of Dort. He conceives no other idea of a clergyman than that of a hired man; if he does his work well he will pay him the stipulated sum; if not he will dismiss him, and do without his sermons, and let his church be shut up for years. But notwithstanding this coarse idea, you will find his house and farm to be the neatest in all the country; and you will judge by his waggon and fat horses, that he thinks more of the affairs of this world than of those of the next. He is sober and laborious, therefore he is all he ought to be as to the affairs of this life; as for those of the next, he must trust to the great Creator. Each of these people instruct their children as well as they can, but these instructions are feeble compared to those which are given to the youth of the poorest class in Europe. Their children will therefore grow up less zealous and more indifferent in matters of religion than their parents. The foolish vanity, or rather the fury of making Proselytes, is unknown here; they have no time, the seasons call for all their attention, and thus in a few years, this mixed neighbourhood will exhibit a strange religious medley, that will be neither pure Catholicism nor pure Calvinism. A very perceptible indifference even in the first generation, will become apparent; and it may happen that the daughter of the Catholic will marry the son of the seceder, and settle by themselves at a distance from their parents. What religious education will they give their children? A very imperfect one. If there happens to be in the neighbourhood any place of worship, we will suppose a Quaker's meeting; rather than not shew their fine clothes, they will go to it, and some of them may perhaps attach themselves to that society. Others will remain in a perfect state of indifference; the children of these zealous parents will not be able to tell what their religious principles are, and their grandchildren still less. The neighbourhood of a place of worship generally leads them to it, and the action of going thither, is the strongest evidence they can give of their attachment to any sect. The Quakers are the only people who retain a fondness for their own mode of worship; for be they ever so far separated from each other, they hold a sort of communion with the society, and seldom depart from its rules, at least in this country. Thus all sects are mixed as well as all nations; thus religious indifference is imperceptibly disseminated from one end of the continent to the other; which is at present one of the strongest characteristics of the Americans. Where this will reach no one can tell, perhaps it may leave a vacuum fit to receive other systems. Persecution, religious pride, the love of contradiction, are the food of what the world commonly calls religion. These motives have ceased here: zeal in Europe is confined; here it evaporates in the great distance it has to travel; there it is a grain of powder inclosed, here it burns away in the open air, and consumes without effect.

But to return to our back settlers. I must tell you, that there is something in the proximity of the woods, which is very singular. It is with men as it is with the plants and animals that grow and live in the forests; they are entirely different from those that live in the plains. I will candidly tell you all my thoughts but you are not to expect that I shall advance any reasons. By living in or near the woods, their actions are regulated by the wildness of the neighbourhood. The deer often come to eat their grain, the wolves to destroy their sheep, the bears to kill their hogs, the foxes to catch their poultry. This surrounding hostility, immediately puts the gun into their hands; they watch these animals, they kill some; and thus by defending their property, they soon become professed hunters; this is the progress; once hunters, farewell to the plough. The chase renders them ferocious, gloomy, and unsociable; a hunter wants no neighbour, he rather hates them, because he dreads the competition. In a little time their success in the woods makes them neglect their tillage. They trust to the natural fecundity of the earth, and therefore do little; carelessness in fencing, often exposes what little they sow to destruction; they are not at home to watch; in order therefore to make up the deficiency, they go oftener to the woods. That new mode of life brings along with it a new set of manners, which I cannot easily describe. These new manners being grafted on the old stock, produce a strange sort of lawless profligacy, the impressions of which are indelible. The manners of the Indian natives are respectable, compared with this European medley. Their wives and children live in sloth and inactivity; and having no proper pursuits, you may judge what education the latter receive. Their tender minds have nothing else to contemplate but the example of their parents; like them they grow up a mongrel breed, half civilized, half savage, except nature stamps on them some constitutional propensities. That rich, that voluptuous sentiment is gone that struck them so forcibly; the possession of their freeholds no longer conveys to their minds the same pleasure and pride. To all these reasons you must add, their lonely situation, and you cannot imagine what an effect on manners the great distances they live from each other has! Consider one of the last settlements in it's first view: of what is it composed? Europeans who have not that sufficient share of knowledge they ought to have, in order to prosper; people who have suddenly passed from oppression, dread of government, and fear of laws, into the unlimited freedom of the woods. This sudden change must have a very great effect on most men, and on that class particularly. Eating of wild meat, whatever you may think, tends to alter their temper; though all the proof I can adduce, is, that I have seen it: and having no place of worship to resort to, what little society this might afford, is denied them. The Sunday meetings, exclusive of religious benefits, were the only social bonds that might have inspired them with some degree of emulation in neatness. Is it then surprising to see men thus situated, immersed in great and heavy labours, degenerate a little? It is rather a wonder the effect is not more diffusive. The Moravians and the Quakers are the only instances in exception to what I have advanced. The first never settle singly, it is a colony of the society which emigrates; they carry with them their forms, worship, rules, and decency: the others never begin so hard, they are always able to buy improvements, in which there is a great advantage, for by that time the country is recovered from its first barbarity. Thus our bad people are those who are half cultivators and half hunters; and the worst of them are those who have degenerated altogether into the hunting state. As old ploughmen and new men of the woods, as Europeans and new made Indians, they contract the vices of both; they adopt the moroseness and ferocity of a native, without his mildness, or even his industry at home. If manners are not refined, at least they are rendered simple and inoffensive by tilling the earth; all our wants are supplied by it, our time is divided between labour and rest, and leaves none for the commission of great misdeeds. As hunters it is divided between the toil of the chase, the idleness of repose, or the indulgence of inebriation. Hunting is but a licentious idle life, and if it does not always pervert good dispositions; yet, when it is united with bad luck, it leads to want: want stimulates that propensity to rapacity and injustice, too natural to needy men, which is the fatal gradation. After this explanation of the effects which follow by living in the woods, shall we yet vainly flatter ourselves with the hope of converting the Indians? We should rather begin with converting our back-settlers; and now if I dare mention the name of religion, its sweet accents would be lost in the immensity of these woods. Men thus placed, are not fit either to receive or remember its mild instructions; they want temples and ministers, but as soon as men cease to remain at home, and begin to lead an erratic life, let them be either tawny or white, they cease to be its disciples.

Thus have I faintly and imperfectly endeavoured to trace our society from the sea to our woods! yet you must not imagine that every person who moves back, acts upon the same principles, or falls into the same degeneracy. Many families carry with them all their decency of conduct, purity of morals, and respect of religion; but these are scarce, the power of example is sometimes irresistible. Even among these back-settlers, their depravity is greater or less, according to what nation or province they belong. Were I to adduce proofs of this, I might be accused of partiality. If there happens to be some rich intervals, some fertile bottoms, in those remote districts, the people will there prefer tilling the land to hunting, and will attach themselves to it; but even on these fertile spots you may plainly perceive the inhabitants to acquire a great degree of rusticity and selfishness.

It is in consequence of this straggling situation, and the astonishing power it has on manners, that the back-settlers of both the Carolinas, Virginia, and many other parts, have been long a set of lawless people; it has been even dangerous to travel among them. Government can do nothing in so extensive a country, better it should wink at these irregularities, than that it should use means inconsistent with its usual mildness. Time will efface those stains: in proportion as the great body of population approaches them they will reform, and become polished and subordinate. Whatever has been said of the four New England provinces, no such degeneracy of manners has ever tarnished their annals; their back-settlers have been kept within the bounds of decency, and government, by means of wise laws, and by the influence of religion. What a detestable idea such people must have given to the natives of the Europeans! They trade with them, the worst of people are permitted to do that which none but persons of the best characters should be employed in. They get drunk with them, and often defraud the Indians. Their avarice, removed from the eyes of their superiors, knows no bounds; and aided by a little superiority of knowledge, these traders deceive them, and even sometimes shed blood. Hence those shocking violations, those sudden devastations which have so often stained our frontiers, when hundreds of innocent people have been sacrificed for the crimes of a few. It was in consequence of such behaviour, that the Indians took the hatchet against the Virginians in 1774. Thus are our first steps trod, thus are our first trees felled, in general, by the most vicious of our people; and thus the path is opened for the arrival of a second and better class, the true American freeholders; the most respectable set of people in this part of the world: respectable for their industry, their happy independence, the great share of freedom they possess, the good regulation of their families, and for extending the trade and the dominion of our mother country.

Europe contains hardly any other distinctions but lords and tenants; this fair country alone is settled by freeholders, the possessors of the soil they cultivate, members of the government they obey, and the framers of their own laws, by means of their representatives. This is a thought which you have taught me to cherish; our difference from Europe, far from diminishing, rather adds to our usefulness and consequence as men and subjects. Had our forefathers remained there, they would only have crouded it, and perhaps prolonged those convulsions which had shook it so long. Every industrious European who transports himself here, may be compared to a sprout growing at the foot of a great tree; it enjoys and draws but a little portion of sap; wrench it from the parent roots, transplant it, and it will become a tree bearing fruit also. Colonists are therefore entitled to the consideration due to the most useful subjects; a hundred families barely existing in some parts of Scotland, will here in six years, cause an annual exportation of 10,000 bushels of wheat: 100 bushels being but a common quantity for an industrious family to sell, if they cultivate good land. It is here then that the idle may be employed, the useless become useful, and the poor become rich; but by riches I do not mean gold and silver, we have but little of those metals; I mean a better sort of wealth, cleared lands, cattle, good houses, good cloaths, and an increase of people to enjoy them.

There is no wonder that this country has so many charms, and presents to Europeans so many temptations to remain in it. A traveller in Europe becomes a stranger as soon as he quits his own kingdom; but it is otherwise here. We know, properly speaking, no strangers; this is every person's country; the variety of our soils, situations, climates, governments, and produce, hath something which must please every body. No sooner does an European arrive, no matter of what condition, than his eyes are opened upon the fair prospect; he hears his language spoke, he retraces many of his own country manners, he perpetually hears the names of families and towns with which he is acquainted; he sees happiness and prosperity in all places disseminated; he meets with hospitality, kindness, and plenty every where; he beholds hardly any poor, he seldom hears of punishments and executions; and he wonders at the elegance of our towns, those miracles of industry and freedom. He cannot admire enough our rural districts, our convenient roads, good taverns, and our many accommodations; he involuntarily loves a country where every thing is so lovely. When in England, he was a mere Englishman; here he stands on a larger portion of the globe, not less than its fourth part, and may see the productions of the north, in iron and naval stores; the provisions of Ireland, the grain of Egypt, the indigo, the rice of China. He does not find, as in Europe, a crouded society, where every place is over-stocked; he does not feel that perpetual collision of parties, that difficulty of beginning, that contention which oversets so many. There is room for every body in America; has he any particular talent, or industry? he exerts it in order to procure a livelihood, and it succeeds. Is he a merchant? the avenues of trade are infinite; is he eminent in any respect? he will be employed and respected. Does he love a country life? pleasant farms present themselves; he may purchase what he wants, and thereby become an American farmer. Is he a labourer, sober and industrious? he need not go many miles, nor receive many informations before he will be hired, well fed at the table of his employer, and paid four or five times more than he can get in Europe. Does he want uncultivated lands? thousands of acres present themselves, which he may purchase cheap. Whatever be his talents or inclinations, if they are moderate, he may satisfy them. I do not mean that every one who comes will grow rich in a little time; no, but he may procure an easy, decent maintenance, by his industry. Instead of starving he will be fed, instead of being idle he will have employment; and these are riches enough for such men as come over here. The rich stay in Europe, it is only the middling and the poor that emigrate. Would you wish to travel in independent idleness, from north to south, you will find easy access, and the most chearful reception at every house; society without ostentation, good cheer without pride, and every decent diversion which the country affords, with little expence. It is no wonder that the European who has lived here a few years, is desirous to remain; Europe with all its pomp, is not to be compared to this continent, for men of middle stations, or labourers.

An European, when he first arrives, seems limited in his intentions, as well as in his views; but he very suddenly alters his scale; two hundred miles formerly appeared a very great distance, it is now but a trifle; he no sooner breathes our air than he forms schemes, and embarks in designs he never would have thought of in his own country.

There the plenitude of society confines many useful ideas, and often extinguishes the most laudable schemes which here ripen into maturity. Thus Europeans become Americans.

But how is this accomplished in that croud of low, indigent people, who flock here every year from all parts of Europe? I will tell you; they no sooner arrive than they immediately feel the good effects of that plenty of provisions we possess: they fare on our best food, and are kindly entertained; their talents, character, and peculiar industry are immediately inquired into; they find countrymen every where disseminated, let them come from whatever part of Europe. Let me select one as an epitome of the rest; he is hired, he goes to work, and works moderately; instead of being employed by a haughty person, he finds himself with his equal, placed at the substantial table of the farmer, or else at an inferior one as good; his wages are high, his bed is not like that bed of sorrow on which he used to lie: if he behaves with propriety, and is faithful, he is caressed, and becomes as it were a member of the family. He begins to feel the effects of a sort of resurrection; hitherto he had not lived, but simply vegetated; he now feels himself a man, because he is treated as such; the laws of his own country had overlooked him in his insignificancy; the laws of this cover him with their mantle. Judge what an alteration there must arise in the mind and thoughts of this man; he begins to forget his former servitude and dependence, his heart involuntarily swells and glows; this first swell inspires him with those new thoughts which constitute an American. What love can he entertain for a country where his existence was a burthen to him; if he is a generous good man, the love of this new adoptive parent will sink deep into his heart. He looks around, and sees many a prosperous person, who but a few years before was as poor as himself. This encourages him much, he begins to form some little scheme, the first, alas, he ever formed in his life. If he is wise he thus spends two or three years, in which time he acquires knowledge, the use of tools, the modes of working the lands, felling trees, &c. This prepares the foundation of a good name, the most useful acquisition he can make. He is encouraged, he has gained friends; he is advised and directed, he feels bold, he purchases some land; he gives all the money he has brought over, as well as what he has earned, and trusts to the God of harvests for the discharge of the rest. His good name procures him credit. He is now possessed of the deed, conveying to him and his posterity the fee simple[5] and absolute property of two hundred acres of land, situated on such a river. What an epocha in this man's life! He is become a freeholder, from perhaps a German boor—he is now an American, a Pennsylvanian, an English subject. He is naturalized, his name is enrolled with those of the other citizens of the province. Instead of being a vagrant, he has a place of residence; he is called the inhabitant of such a county, or of such a district, and for the first time in his life counts for something; for hitherto he has been a cypher. I only repeat what I have heard many say, and no wonder their hearts should glow, and be agitated with a multitude of feelings, not easy to describe. From nothing to start into being; from a servant to the rank of a master; from being the slave of some despotic prince, to become a free man, invested with lands, to which every municipal blessing is annexed! What a change indeed! It is in consequence of that change that he becomes an American. This great metamorphosis has a double effect, it extinguishes all his European prejudices, he

[5] Full legal possession.

forgets that mechanism of subordination, that servility of disposition which poverty had taught him; and sometimes he is apt to forget too much, often passing from one extreme to the other. If he is a good man, he forms schemes of future prosperity, he proposes to educate his children better than he has been educated himself; he thinks of future modes of conduct, feels an ardor to labour he never felt before. Pride steps in and leads him to every thing that the laws do not forbid: he respects them; with a heart-felt gratitude he looks toward the east, toward that insular government from whose wisdom all his new felicity is derived, and under whose wings and protection he now lives. These reflections constitute him the good man and the good subject. Ye poor Europeans, ye, who sweat, and work for the great—ye, who are obliged to give so many sheaves to the church, so many to your lords, so many to your government, and have hardly any left for yourselves—ye, who are held in less estimation than favourite hunters or useless lap dogs—ye, who only breathe the air of nature, because it cannot be withheld from you; it is here that ye can conceive the possibility of those feelings I have been describing; it is here the laws of naturalization invite every one to partake of our great labours and felicity, to till unrented, untaxed lands! Many, corrupted beyond the power of amendment, have brought with them all their vices, and disregarding the advantages held to them, have gone on in their former career of iniquity, until they have been overtaken and punished by our laws. It is not every emigrant who succeeds; no, it is only the sober, the honest, and industrious: happy those to whom this transition has served as a powerful spur to labour, to prosperity, and to the good establishment of children, born in the days of their poverty; and who had no other portion to expect but the rags of their parents, had it not been for their happy emigration. Others again, have been led astray by this enchanting scene; their new pride, instead of leading them to the fields, has kept them in idleness; the idea of possessing lands is all that satisfies them—though surrounded with fertility, they have mouldered away their time in inactivity, misinformed husbandry, and ineffectual endeavours. How much wiser, in general, the honest Germans than almost all other Europeans; they hire themselves to some of their wealthy landsmen, and in that apprenticeship learn every thing that is necessary. They attentively consider the prosperous industry of others, which imprints in their minds a strong desire of possessing the same advantages. This forcible idea never quits them, they launch forth, and by dint of sobriety, rigid parsimony, and the most persevering industry, they commonly succeed. Their astonishment at their first arrival from Germany is very great—it is to them a dream; the contrast must be powerful indeed; they observe their countrymen flourishing in every place; they travel through whole counties where not a word of English is spoken; and in the names and the language of the people, they retrace Germany. They have been an useful acquisition to this continent, and to Pennsylvania in particular; to them it owes some share of its prosperity: to their mechanical knowledge and patience, it owes the finest mills in all America, the best teams of horses, and many other advantages. The recollection of their former poverty and slavery never quits them as long as they live.

The Scotch and the Irish might have lived in their own country perhaps as poor, but enjoying more civil advantages, the effects of their new situation do not strike them so forcibly, nor has it so lasting an effect. From whence the difference arises I know not, but out of twelve families of emigrants of each country, generally seven Scotch will succeed, nine German, and four Irish. The Scotch are frugal and laborious, but their wives cannot work so hard as German women, who on the contrary vie with their husbands, and often share with them the most severe toils of the field, which they understand better. They have therefore nothing to struggle against, but the common casualties of nature. The Irish do not prosper so well; they love to drink and to quarrel; they are litigious, and soon take to the gun, which is the ruin of every thing; they seem beside to labour under a greater degree of ignorance in husbandry than the others; perhaps it is that their industry had less scope, and was less exercised at home. I have heard many relate, how the land was parcelled out in that kingdom; their ancient conquest has been a great detriment to them, by over-setting their landed property. The lands possessed by a few, are leased down *ad infinitum,* and the occupiers often pay five guineas an acre. The poor are worse lodged there than any where else in Europe; their potatoes, which are easily raised, are perhaps an inducement to laziness: their wages are too low and their whisky too cheap.

There is no tracing observations of this kind, without making at the same time very great allowances, as there are every where to be found, a great many exceptions. The Irish themselves, from different parts of that kingdom, are very different. It is difficult to account for this surprising locality, one would think on so small an island an Irishman must be an Irishman: yet it is not so, they are different in their aptitude to, and in their love of labour.

The Scotch on the contrary are all industrious and saving; they want nothing more than a field to exert themselves in, and they are commonly sure of succeeding. The only difficulty they labour under is, that technical American knowledge which requires some time to obtain; it is not easy for those who seldom saw a tree, to conceive how it is to be felled, cut up, and split into rails and posts.

As I am fond of seeing and talking of prosperous families, I intend to finish this letter by relating to you the history of an honest Scotch Hebridean, who came here in 1774, which will shew you in epitome, what the Scotch can do, wherever they have room for the exertion of their industry. Whenever I hear of any new settlement, I pay it a visit once or twice a year, on purpose to observe the different steps each settler takes, the gradual improvements, the different tempers of each family, on which their prosperity in a great nature depends; their different modifications of industry, their ingenuity, and contrivance; for being all poor, their life requires sagacity and prudence. In an evening I love to hear them tell their stories, they furnish me with new ideas; I sit still and listen to their ancient misfortunes, observing in many of them a strong degree of gratitude to God, and the government. Many a well meant sermon have I preached to some of them. When I found laziness and inattention to prevail, who could refrain from wishing well to these new countrymen; after having undergone so many fatigues. Who could withhold good advice? What a happy change it must be, to descend from the high, sterile, bleak lands of Scotland, where every thing is barren and cold, to rest on some fertile farms in these middle provinces! Such a transition must have afforded the most pleasing satisfaction.

The following dialogue passed at an out-settlement, where I lately paid a visit:

Well, friend, how do you do now; I am come fifty odd miles on purpose to see you; how do you go on with your new cutting and slashing? Very well, good Sir, we learn the use of the axe bravely, we shall make it out; we have a belly full of victuals every day, our cows run about, and come home full of milk, our hogs get fat of themselves in the woods: Oh, this is a good country! God bless the king, and

William Penn; we shall do very well by and by, if we keep our healths. Your loghouse looks neat and light, where did you get these shingles? One of our neighbours is a New-England man, and he shewed us how to split them out of chestnut-trees. Now for a barn, but all in good time, here are fine trees to build with. Who is to frame it, sure you don't understand that work yet? A countryman of ours who has been in America these ten years, offers to wait for his money until the second crop is lodged in it. What did you give for your land? Thirty-five shillings per acre, payable in seven years. How many acres have you got? An hundred and fifty. That is enough to begin with; is not your land pretty hard to clear? Yes, Sir, hard enough, but it would be harder still if it was ready cleared, for then we should have no timber, and I love the woods much: the land is nothing without them. Have not you found out any bees yet? No, Sir; and if we had we should not know what to do with them. I will tell you by and by. You are very kind. Farewell, honest man, God prosper you; whenever you travel toward ————, enquire for J.S. he will entertain you kindly, provided you bring him good tidings from your family and farm. In this manner I often visit them, and carefully examine their houses, their modes of ingenuity, their different ways; and make them all relate all they know, and describe all they feel. These are scenes which I believe you would willingly share with me. I well remember your philanthropic turn of mind. Is it not better to contemplate under these humble roofs, the rudiments of future wealth and population, than to behold the accumulated bundles of litigious papers in the office of a lawyer? To examine how the world is gradually settled, how the howling swamp is converted into a pleasing meadow, the rough ridge into a fine field; and to hear the chearful whistling, the rural song, where there was no sound heard before save the yell of the savage, the screech of the owl, or the hissing of the snake? Here an European, fatigued with luxury, riches, and pleasures, may find a sweet relaxation in a series of interesting scenes, as affecting as they are new. England, which now contains so many domes, so many castles, was once like this; a place woody and marshy; its inhabitants, now the favourite nation for arts and commerce, were once painted like our neighbours. The country will flourish in its turn, and the same observations will be made which I have just delineated. Posterity will look back with avidity and pleasure, to trace, if possible, the area of this or that particular settlement.

Pray, what is the reason that the Scots are in general more religious, more faithful, more honest, and industrious than the Irish? I do not mean to insinuate national reflections, God forbid! It ill becomes any man, and much less an American; but as I know men are nothing of themselves, and that they owe all their different modifications either to government or other local circumstances, there must be some powerful causes which constitute this great national difference.

Agreeable to the account which severale Scotchmen have given me of the north of Britain, of the Orkneys, and the Hebride Islands, they seem, on many accounts, to be unfit for the habitation of men; they appear to be calculated only for great sheep pastures. Who then can blame the inhabitants of these countries for transporting themselves hither? This great continent must in time absorb the poorest part of Europe; and this will happen in proportion as it becomes better known; and as war, taxation, oppression, and misery increase there. The Hebrides appear to be fit only for the residence of malefactors, and it would be much better to send felons there than either to Virginia or Maryland. What a strange compliment has our mother country paid to two of the finest provinces in America! England has entertained in that respect very mistaken ideas; what was intended as a punishment, is become the good fortune of several; many of those who have been transported as felons, are now rich, and strangers to the stings of those wants that urged them to violations of the law: they are become industrious, exemplary, and useful citizens. The English government should purchase the most northern and barren of those islands; it should send over to us the honest, primitive Hebrideans, settle them here on good lands, as a reward for their virtue and ancient poverty; and replace them with a colony of her wicked sons. The severity of the climate, the inclemency of the seasons, the sterility of the soil, the tempestuousness of the sea, would afflict and punish enough. Could there be found a spot better adapted to retaliate the injury it had received by their crimes? Some of those islands might be considered as the hell of Great Britain, where all evil spirits should be sent. Two essential ends would be answered by this simple operation. The good people, by emigration, would be rendered happier; the bad ones would be placed where they ought to be. In a few years the dread of being sent to that wintry region would have a much stronger effect, than that of transportation.—This is no place of punishment; were I a poor hopeless, breadless Englishman, and not restrained by the power of shame, I should be very thankful for the passage. It is of very little importance how, and in what manner an indigent man arrives; for if he is but sober, honest, and industrious, he has nothing more to ask of heaven. Let him go to work, he will have opportunities enough to earn a comfortable support, and even the means of procuring some land; which ought to be the utmost wish of every person who has health and hands to work. I knew a man who came to this country, in the literal sense of the expression, stark naked; I think he was a Frenchman, and a sailor on board an English man of war. Being discontented, he had stripped himself and swam ashore; where finding clothes and friends, he settled afterwards at Maraneck, in the county of Chester, in the province of New-York: he married and left a good farm to each of his sons. I knew another person who was but twelve years old when he was taken on the frontiers of Canada, by the Indians; at his arrival at Albany he was purchased by a gentleman, who generously bound him apprentice to a taylor. He lived to the age of ninety, and left behind him a fine estate and a numerous family, all well settled; many of them I am acquainted with.—Where is then the industrious European who ought to despair?

After a foreigner from any part of Europe is arrived, and become a citizen; let him devoutly listen to the voice of our great parent, which says to him, "Welcome to my shores, distressed European; bless the hour in which thou didst see my verdant fields, my fair navigable rivers, and my green mountains!—If thou wilt work, I have bread for thee; if thou wilt be honest, sober, and industrious, I have greater rewards to confer on thee—ease and independence. I will give thee fields to feed and cloath thee; a comfortable fire-side to sit by, and tell thy children by what means thou has prospered; and a decent bed to repose on. I shall endow thee beside with the immunities of a freeman. If thou wilt carefully educate thy children, teach them gratitude to God, and reverence to that government, that philanthropic government, which has collected here so many men and made them happy. I will also provide for thy progeny; and to every good man this ought to be the most holy, the most powerful, the most earnest wish he can possibly form, as well as the most consolatory prospect when he dies. Go thou and work and till; thou shalt prosper, provided thou be just, grateful and industrious." . . .

The Federalist

On October 27, 1787, a month after the Federal Convention presented for individual state ratification a new constitution to replace the six-year-old Articles of Confederation, the first of a series of eighty-five incisively argued political essays defending the new document appeared in a New York newspaper. Signed "Publius" and explicitly addressed "to the People of New York," the essay, written by Alexander Hamilton (1757–1804), established immediately the topic and tone of the series: to persuade the citizens of New York by means of careful "deliberation" that their personal liberty and security as well as the future prosperity of the entire country depended on a strong central government, which only the immediate adoption of the proposed Constitution could provide. Although the Constitution required only the approval of nine states for ratification, its supporters felt that anything short of unanimity would cause a serious breach among the states, one that would inevitably lead to dangerous alliances among themselves and with foreign nations. Hamilton especially felt that New York, led by its governor, George Clinton, a powerful advocate of local sovereignty, represented a key state in the impending battle for ratification.

"Publius" became a collective pseudonym shortly after the first essay as Hamilton enlisted the help of two other partisans: John Jay (1745–1829), the affluent, conservative New York attorney who eventually served as a Supreme Court Justice and later as governor of New York, and the young though politically seasoned Virginian, James Madison (1751–1836), who, more than any other delegate to the convention, had been responsible for the overall design of the Constitution and who would later serve as fourth president of the United States. Since Jay had held the office of secretary of foreign affairs under the Articles of Confederation and had helped negotiate the Treaty of Paris, his diplomatic experiences lent impressive support to his essays on international relations. Because of poor health, however, Jay was able to contribute only five essays to the series; after the fifth paper it became, with one exception, exclusively the labor of Hamilton and Madison.

A native of the West Indies, Alexander Hamilton completed his studies at Columbia (then called King's College), served on Washington's staff during the Revolution, and afterward established a highly successful law practice in New York City. At the Constitutional Convention, which he attended sporadically, Hamilton argued strenuously for an energetic central government headed by a powerful executive. An outspoken proponent of business interests and industrialization, Hamilton, as the first secretary of the Treasury, brilliantly engineered a fiscal policy that gave the floundering new nation the foreign credibility and domestic assurance it needed to survive. When in January 1790, only a year and a half after the final *Federalist* essay went to press, Hamilton submitted to Congress his "Report on the Public Credit," his chief political opponent had become Publius's other half, James Madison. By then, the Constitution ratified and the machinery of the new administration in operation,

Madison was thinking and acting more sectionally as a Virginian and less, as Hamilton liked to put it, "continentally" as an American.

But in 1787 Publius's "split personality" could be seen only in a few inconsistencies and disparate emphases, tensions forgivable and easily overlooked in the steadily accumulating output of penetrating political analysis. Composed hastily and under too much pressure, the papers could hardly offer systematic coverage of all the principles of constitutional government. Nevertheless, given the strains of collaboration and deadlines, Publius achieved a remarkably high-minded level of political discourse and an admirable degree of theoretical complexity. The man who would in a few years become Hamilton's fiercest enemy, Thomas Jefferson, considered *The Federalist* "the best commentary on the principles of government, which ever was written" and later made the book required reading for all students at the University of Virginia. What was conceived primarily as a popular series of campaign tracts to influence a relatively small group of voters eventually became, by virtue of its articulation and political discernment, one of the central documents of American government, a necessary supplement to all historical and judicial interpretation of the Constitution.

At the center of Publius's argument, as the opening paper makes clear, is the desire for a strong Union and the belief that a new constitution must supersede the totally inadequate Articles of Confederation. What may seem obvious today, it is important to remember, was not so obvious then. A country that had recently gone through a debilitating war to shake off the political and economic impositions of one strong government was hardly eager to adopt another to replace it. Many Americans naturally equated a strong central government with monarchy. They saw, furthermore, the Articles of Confederation as a perfectly respectable document that guaranteed nearly complete sovereignty to the separate states and, even better, claimed no political authority over individuals. And as Hamilton noted in the first paper, people holding positions in state government would understandably be reluctant to support any new confederation, loose or strong, that threatened the continuation of their offices or promised to diminish their authority. The Constitutional Convention itself, moreover, was viewed by many citizens (especially in New York and Virginia) as unauthorized and extralegal, a fairly open conspiracy among a small group of reactionary, propertied people who, in their enthusiasm to "form a more perfect union," would undoubtedly perpetuate an aristocracy of the wealthy and influential.

Another objection that serious, well-informed citizens raised against the Constitution was that no republic, certainly no democracy, could be maintained in a country as geographically diverse and extensive as their own. In general, objections to the Constitution varied according to the degree of local suspicions and local power. The main task Publius faced throughout the papers was to convince a skeptical public that a strong central government was not only possible and indispensable for security and survival but also that, more important, it was compatible with individual liberty.

In Publius's papers, as in all significant political discourse, definitions and distinctions play a crucial role. In fact, the very title given to the series after the individual essays had been collected in May 1788, *The Federalist,* caused considerable confusion. Those who supported the Articles of Confederation argued that *they* were the real Federalists and contended that Publius had coopted the term to disguise what was essentially a nationalist program. *National,* an explosive political word at the time, had been conscientiously eliminated from the Constitution. The term appears throughout the papers, especially in the thirty-ninth letter, where Madison, always apprehensive about nomenclature, maintains a delicately balanced argument as he moves back and forth between federal and national definitions, continually refining his distinctions as he demonstrates the inevitable interpenetration of both forms in the total operations of government. (Though neither Hamilton nor Madison seems nervous with the word, it is interesting that one of the most decisive reasons that could be offered today for the existence of a national state—a common cultural identity—is rarely appealed to as an argument for union.) In an earlier paper Madison had confronted another result of the "confusion of names," the important distinctions between a republic and a democracy. Language, he acknowledges in yet another paper, is a "cloudy medium" in which the science of politics and the complex institutions it attempts to delineate are continually being trapped in "obscurity."

For Hamilton and Madison, the intellectual confusions brought about by vague and inaccurate definitions and the emotional confusions resulting from "intemperance of expression" presented formidable obstacles to both good government and good writing. Political and literary style was best preserved by adhering to "cool and deliberate" thinking; Publius seldom indulges in rhetorical flourishes. In fact, the vocabulary of "passion" (one of the key words of *The Federalist*) is throughout the series closely associated with the "animosity," "violence," and "disease" generated by the "factions" that Madison examines in the celebrated tenth paper. Hamilton, in particular, was wary of political emotions and believed that the papers would help protect the public from "every sudden breeze of passion or every transient impulse." In their exacting style and dispassionate designs, Publius's essays, always lucid, often ironic, tough-mindedly predisposed to expect the worst and demand the best from human nature, represent the consummate expression of one of America's most consequential political programs and philosophies.

Further Reading:
G. Dietze, *The Federalist: A Classic on Federalism and Free Government,* 1960.
J. C. Miller, *The Federalist Era,* 1960.

Text:
The Federalist, ed. J. E. Cooke, 1961.

from **The Federalist**

No. 10 [James Madison]

November 22, 1787

To the People of the State of New York.

Among the numerous advantages promised by a well constructed Union, none deserves to be more accurately developed than its tendency to break and control the violence of faction. The friend of popular governments, never finds himself so much alarmed for their character and fate, as when he contemplates their propensity to this dangerous vice. He will not fail therefore to set a due value on any plan which, without violating the principles to which he is attached, provides a proper cure for it. The instability, injustice and confusion introduced into the public councils, have in truth been the mortal diseases under which popular governments have every where perished; as they continue to be the favorite and fruitful topics from which the adversaries to liberty derive their most specious declamations. The valuable improvements made by the American Constitutions on the popular models, both ancient and modern, cannot certainly be too much admired; but it would be an unwarrantable partiality, to contend that they have as effectually obviated the danger on this side as was wished and expected. Complaints are every where heard from our most considerate and virtuous citizens, equally the friends of public and private faith, and of public and personal liberty; that our governments are too unstable; that the public good is disregarded in the conflicts of rival parties; and that measures are too often decided, not according to the rules of justice, and the rights of the minor party; but by the superior force of an interested and over-bearing majority. However anxiously we may wish that these complaints had no foundation, the evidence of known facts will not permit us to deny that they are in some degree true. It will be found indeed, on a candid review of our situation, that some of the distresses under which we labor, have been erroneously charged on the operation of our governments; but it will be found, at the same time, that other causes will not alone account for many of our heaviest misfortunes; and particularly, for that prevailing and increasing distrust of public engagements, and alarm for private rights, which are echoed from one end of the continent to the other. These must be chiefly, if not wholly, effects of the unsteadiness and injustice, with which a factious spirit has tainted our public administrations.

By a faction I understand a number of citizens, whether amounting to a majority or minority of the whole, who are united and actuated by some common impulse of passion, or of interest, adverse to the rights of other citizens, or to the permanent and aggregate interests of the community.

There are two methods of curing the mischiefs of faction: the one, by removing its causes; the other, by controling its effects.

There are again two methods of removing the causes of faction: the one by destroying the liberty which is essential to its existence; the other, by giving to every citizen the same opinions, the same passions, and the same interests.

It could never be more truly said than of the first remedy, that it is worse than the disease. Liberty is to faction, what air is to fire, an aliment[1] without which it instantly expires. But it could not be a less folly to abolish liberty, which is essential to political life, because it nourishes faction, than it would be to wish the annihilation of air, which is essential to animal life, because it imparts to fire its destructive agency.

The second expedient is as impracticable, as the first would be unwise. As long as the reason of man continues fallible, and he is at liberty to exercise it, different opinions will be formed. As long as the connection subsists between his reason and his self-love, his opinions and his passions will have a reciprocal influence on each other; and the former will be objects to which the latter will attach themselves. The diversity in the faculties of men from which the rights of property originate, is not less an insuperable obstacle to a uniformity of interests. The protection of these faculties is the first object of Government. From the protection of different and unequal faculties of acquiring property, the possession of different degrees and kinds of property immediately results: and from the influence of these on the sentiments and views of the respective proprietors, ensues a division of the society into different interests and parties.

The latent causes of faction are thus sown in the nature of man; and we see them every where brought into different degrees of activity, according to the different circumstances of civil society. A zeal for different opinions concerning religion, concerning Government and many other points, as well of speculation as of practice; an attachment to different leaders ambitiously contending for pre-eminence and power; or to persons of other descriptions whose fortunes have been interesting to the human passions, have in turn divided mankind into parties, inflamed them with mutual animosity, and rendered them much more disposed to vex and oppress each other, than to co-operate for their common good. So strong is this propensity of mankind to fall into mutual animosities, that where no substantial occasion presents itself, the most frivolous and fanciful distinctions have been sufficient to kindle their unfriendly passions, and excite their most violent conflicts. But the most common and durable source of factions, has been the various and unequal distribution of property. Those who hold, and those who are without property, have ever formed distinct interests in society. Those who are creditors, and those who are debtors, fall under a like discrimination. A landed interest, a manufacturing interest, a mercantile interest, a monied interest, with many lesser interests, grow up of necessity in civilized nations, and divide them into different classes, actuated by different sentiments and views. The regulation of these various and interfering interests forms the principal task of modern Legislation, and involves the spirit of party and faction in the necessary and ordinary operations of Government.

No man is allowed to be a judge in his own cause; because his interest would certainly bias his judgment, and, not improbably, corrupt his integrity. With equal, nay with greater reason, a body of men, are unfit to be both judges and parties, at the same time; yet, what are many of the most important acts of legislation, but so many judicial determinations, not indeed concerning the rights of single persons, but concerning the rights of large bodies of citizens; and what are the different classes of legislators, but advocates and parties to the causes which they determine? Is a law proposed concerning private debts? It is a question to which the creditors are parties

---

[1] Nutriment.

on one side, and the debtors on the other. Justice ought to hold the balance between them. Yet the parties are and must be themselves the judges; and the most numerous party, or, in other words, the most powerful faction must be expected to prevail. Shall domestic manufactures be encouraged, and in what degree, by restrictions on foreign manufactures? are questions which would be differently decided by the landed and the manufacturing classes; and probably by neither, with a sole regard to justice and the public good. The apportionment of taxes on the various descriptions of property, is an act which seems to require the most exact impartiality; yet, there is perhaps no legislative act in which greater opportunity and temptation are given to a predominant party, to trample on the rules of justice. Every shilling with which they over-burden the inferior number, is a shilling saved to their own pockets.

It is in vain to say, that enlightened statesmen will be able to adjust these clashing interests, and render them all subservient to the public good. Enlightened statesmen will not always be at the helm: Nor, in many cases, can such an adjustment be made at all, without taking into view indirect and remote considerations, which will rarely prevail over the immediate interest which one party may find in disregarding the rights of another, or the good of the whole.

The inference to which we are brought, is, that the *causes* of faction cannot be removed; and that relief is only to be sought in the means of controling its *effects*.

If a faction consists of less than a majority, relief is supplied by the republican principle, which enables the majority to defeat its sinister views by regular vote: It may clog the administration, it may convulse the society; but it will be unable to execute and mask its violence under the forms of the Constitution. When a majority is included in a faction, the form of popular government on the other hand enables it to sacrifice to its ruling passion or interest, both the public good and the rights of other citizens. To secure the public good, and private rights, against the danger of such a faction, and at the same time to preserve the spirit and the form of popular government, is then the great object to which our enquiries are directed: Let me add that it is the great desideratum,[2] by which alone this form of government can be rescued from the opprobrium under which it has so long labored, and be recommended to the esteem and adoption of mankind.

By what means is this object attainable? Evidently by one of two only. Either the existence of the same passion or interest in a majority at the same time, must be prevented; or the majority, having such co-existent passion or interest, must be rendered, by their number and local situation, unable to concert and carry into effect schemes of oppression. If the impulse and the opportunity be suffered to coincide, we well know that neither moral nor religious motives can be relied on as an adequate control. They are not found to be such on the injustice and violence of individuals, and lose their efficacy in proportion to the number combined together; that is, in proportion as their efficacy becomes needful.

From this view of the subject, it may be concluded, that a pure Democracy, by which I mean, a Society, consisting of a small number of citizens, who assemble and administer the Government in person, can admit of no cure for the mischiefs of faction. A common passion or interest will, in almost every case, be felt by a majority of the whole; a communication and concert results from the form of Government

[2] Necessary goal.

itself; and there is nothing to check the inducements to sacrifice the weaker party, or an obnoxious individual. Hence it is, that such Democracies have ever been spectacles of turbulence and contention; have ever been found incompatible with personal security, or the rights of property; and have in general been as short in their lives, as they have been violent in their deaths. Theoretic politicians, who have patronized this species of Government, have erroneously supposed, that by reducing mankind to a perfect equality in their political rights, they would, at the same time, be perfectly equalized and assimilated in their possessions, their opinions, and their passions.

A Republic, by which I mean a Government in which the scheme of representation takes place, opens a different prospect, and promises the cure for which we are seeking. Let us examine the points in which it varies from pure Democracy, and we shall comprehend both the nature of the cure, and the efficacy which it must derive from the Union.

The two great points of difference between a Democracy and a Republic are, first, the delegation of the Government, in the latter, to a small number of citizens elected by the rest: secondly, the greater number of citizens, and greater sphere of country, over which the latter may be extended.

The effect of the first difference is, on the one hand to refine and enlarge the public views, by passing them through the medium of a chosen body of citizens, whose wisdom may best discern the true interest of their country, and whose patriotism and love of justice, will be least likely to sacrifice it to temporary or partial considerations. Under such a regulation, it may well happen that the public voice pronounced by the representatives of the people, will be more consonant to the public good, than if pronounced by the people themselves convened for the purpose. On the other hand, the effect may be inverted. Men of factious tempers, of local prejudices, or of sinister designs, may by intrigue, by corruption or by other means, first obtain the suffrages,[3] and then betray the interests of the people. The question resulting is, whether small or extensive Republics are most favorable to the election of proper guardians of the public weal:[4] and it is clearly decided in favor of the latter by two obvious considerations.

In the first place it is to be remarked that however small the Republic may be, the Representatives must be raised to a certain number, in order to guard against the cabals of a few; and that however large it may be, they must be limited to a certain number, in order to guard against the confusion of a multitude. Hence the number of Representatives in the two cases, not being in proportion to that of the Constituents, and being proportionally greatest in the small Republic, it follows, that if the proportion of fit characters, be not less, in the large than in the small Republic, the former will present a greater option, and consequently a greater probability of a fit choice.

In the next place, as each Representative will be chosen by a greater number of citizens in the large than in the small Republic, it will be more difficult for unworthy candidates to practise with success the vicious arts, by which elections are too often carried; and the suffrages of the people being more free, will be more likely to centre on men who possess the most attractive merit, and the most diffusive and established characters.

[3] Support of the voters.   [4] Well-being.

It must be confessed, that in this, as in most other cases, there is a mean, on both sides of which inconveniences will be found to lie. By enlarging too much the number of electors, you render the representative too little acquainted with all their local circumstances and lesser interests; as by reducing it too much, you render him unduly attached to these, and too little fit to comprehend and pursue great and national objects. The Federal Constitution forms a happy combination in this respect; the great and aggregate interests being referred to the national, the local and particular, to the state legislatures.

The other point of difference is, the greater number of citizens and extent of territory which may be brought within the compass of Republican, than of Democratic Government; and it is this circumstance principally which renders factious combinations less to be dreaded in the former, than in the latter. The smaller the society, the fewer probably will be the distinct parties and interests composing it; the fewer the distinct parties and interests, the more frequently will a majority be found of the same party; and the smaller the number of individuals composing a majority, and the smaller the compass within which they are placed, the more easily will they concert and execute their plans of oppression. Extend the sphere, and you take in a greater variety of parties and interests; you make it less probable that a majority of the whole will have a common motive to invade the rights of other citizens; or if such a common motive exists, it will be more difficult for all who feel it to discover their own strength, and to act in unison with each other. Besides other impediments, it may be remarked, that where there is a consciousness of unjust or dishonorable purposes, communication is always checked by distrust, in proportion to the number whose concurrence is necessary.

Hence it clearly appears, that the same advantage, which a Republic has over a Democracy, in controling the effects of faction, is enjoyed by a large over a small Republic—is enjoyed by the Union over the States composing it. Does this advantage consist in the substitution of Representatives, whose enlightened views and virtuous sentiments render them superior to local prejudices, and to schemes of injustice? It will not be denied, that the Representation of the Union will be most likely to possess these requisite endowments. Does it consist in the greater security afforded by a greater variety of parties, against the event of any one party being able to outnumber and oppress the rest? In an equal degree does the encreased variety of parties, comprised within the Union, encrease this security. Does it, in fine, consist in the greater obstacles opposed to the concert and accomplishment of the secret wishes of an unjust and interested majority? Here, again, the extent of the Union gives it the most palpable advantage.

The influence of factious leaders may kindle a flame within their particular States, but will be unable to spread a general conflagration through the other States: a religious sect, may degenerate into a political faction in a part of the Confederacy: but the variety of sects dispersed over the entire face of it, must secure the national Councils against any danger from that source: a rage for paper money, for an abolition of debts, for an equal division of property, or for any other improper or wicked project, will be less apt to pervade the whole body of the Union, than a particular member of it; in the same proportion as such a malady is more likely to taint a particular county or district, than an entire State.

In the extent and proper structure of the Union, therefore, we behold a Republican

remedy for the diseases most incident to Republican Government. And according to
the degree of pleasure and pride, we feel in being Republicans, ought to be our zeal
in cherishing the spirit, and supporting the character of Federalists.

PUBLIUS.[5]

1787/1787

Philip Freneau
1752–1832

When Philip Freneau died in 1832 on the side of a snow-swept road in the rural
stretches of New Jersey, he was far removed from the center of the political and
ideological controversies that dominated the earliest years of the new republic. He
had once been heralded as the most forceful literary voice in the American
Revolution. Later he was considered too radical for many political tastes and was
finally regarded as simply unfashionable. With no appreciable audience for his
acerbic wit and arcadian visions, Freneau could only lament: "To write was my
sad destiny, / The worst of trades, we all agree." His disillusionment with the
course of American politics and the drift of his own career ferried him back and
forth between satire and solitude.

The son of a prosperous woman of Scottish ancestry and a French Hugenot
émigré, Philip Freneau was born into comfortable circumstances in New York
City on January 2, 1752. The eldest of five children, Freneau stayed behind to
study the classics and the English poets when the family moved to Mount
Pleasant, a thousand-acre tract in New Jersey modeled on an elaborate southern
plantation and the site to which Freneau would intermittently retreat from
economic misfortune and political combat. At the urging of his father, Freneau
prepared for the ministry, and at the age of sixteen he enrolled as a second-year
student at the College of New Jersey (later Princeton), where he was a classmate
of James Madison and Hugh Henry Brackenridge and a friend of Aaron Burr.
While there, Freneau alternately inveighed against the British program of
colonial taxation and wrote fanciful, grandiloquent verses on such historical
subjects as "The Prophet Jonah," "The Pyramids of Egypt," and "The Monument
of Phaon." He also collaborated with Brackenridge on an unfinished novel, *Father
Bombo's Pilgrimage to Mecca in Arabia,* and on "A Poem on the Rising Glory of
America," read as the commencement ode in 1771. Freneau's commitment to a
vision of America's future inspired him to record indigenous experiences,
although ones that, at least for his generation, were best expressed in the forms of
"heav'nly Pope" and "godlike Addison."

After college, Freneau worked first at education. He spent thirteen remarkably
long days on Long Island teaching the children of "some bullies, some merchants,

---

[5] "Publius" was the pseudonym of the writers of
the *Federalist* and was known to be such by
most eighteenth-century readers.

and other scoundrels." He later served for less than a year as Brackenridge's assistant at the Somerset Academy in Maryland. Commenting in a letter to Madison that teaching "by no means suits my 'giddy wandring brain,' " Freneau proceeded to study theology for two years before gravitating to New York, where he wrote a series of popular attacks on the British presence in the colonies. Discouraged by the political controversy his poetry had occasioned, Freneau left New York in 1776 for a two-year stay in the West Indies, during which he produced a fitting number of idyllic poems. But the increasing tempo of Revolutionary activities drew him home. He was captured and released by the British en route and joined the New Jersey militia when he reached the United States.

Freneau devoted himself completely to the Revolutionary cause. He ran supplies through British naval blockades and contributed patriotic verse to Brackenridge's newly formed United States Magazine. In 1780 Freneau was again captured at sea, but this time he was imprisoned aboard British ships in New York harbor. Within a year of his release, Freneau published "The Prison Ship," a popular broadside recording his mistreatment at the hands of his captors. He then traveled to Philadelphia to help edit the strongly anti-British Freeman's Journal.

After a brief stint as a postal clerk at the end of the war and a new round of disheartening squabbles in Pennsylvania politics, Freneau withdrew to the seclusion of nearly seven years of work at sea. He served as the captain of coastal vessels and published a great deal of satirical, fanciful, and humorous verse in the newspapers of the ports he plied. The growing popularity of his poetry lured him ashore, and in 1790 he settled in New York. There he helped edit the Daily Advertiser, married Eleanor Forman, and served as a translator for the State Department under Thomas Jefferson.

Inspired by the politics of Jefferson and the other prominent Republicans of the time, Freneau established the National Gazette in Philadelphia as a virulent response to the Federalist political and economic policies of Alexander Hamilton and John Adams. While Jefferson judged that Freneau had saved a nation "which was galloping fast into monarchy," George Washington had only scorn for "that rascal Freneau." Yale president Timothy Dwight regarded him as a "mere incendiary, or rather as a despicable tool of bigger incendiaries," and branded Freneau's newspaper "a public nuisance."

A yellow fever epidemic, poor advertising revenue, and unbridled attacks on his Republican editorials drove Freneau from Philadelphia in 1793. He retired to Mount Pleasant for nearly a year but returned to public life as publisher of another newspaper, the Jersey Chronicle. When that venture failed, he launched yet another, the Time-Piece and Literary Companion, which focused, he announced, on "literary amusements and an abridgement of the most interesting intelligence foreign and domestic." Despite an unusually large number of female contributors who "gave freely of their sentimental lyrics and sprightly letters," the journal overplayed Freneau's public-spirited but sneering editorials on the federal government and fell victim to the sedition law. Retreating once again to Mount Pleasant, Freneau penned a series of humorous essays for the Philadelphia Aurora in the guise of Robert Slender, a rustic sage far removed from political controversy. By 1800 Freneau had settled into discreet obscurity and returned to a life at sea. He surfaced again at the outbreak of the War of 1812, but with much of his vituperative energy drained.

Freneau published five volumes of poetry in his lifetime. In each, the intensity of his poems on the splendor of the American landscape often competed with self-conscious political satires on British subjects. Yet Freneau always maintained his commitment to explore native themes in colloquial terms. "The Wild Honeysuckle" (1786) and "The Indian Burying Ground" (1788), printed more than a decade before Wordsworth and Coleridge's *Lyrical Ballads,* are perhaps the best testaments to that interest.

The unpretentious characters that populate Freneau's essays and journalism ("The Pilgrim," "Tomo-Cheeki, the Creek Indian," and "Hezakiah Salem," the defrocked Yankee deacon) express his sensitivity to the philosophical, social, and economic issues that preoccupied American society in the first decades of the new nation. Freneau anticipated William Cullen Bryant's preoccupation with lush poetic landscapes, Ralph Waldo Emerson's insistent individualism, and Walt Whitman's embrace of the commonplace in America. Freneau's writing helped expand the field for American writers and introduced complexities into native themes.

Freneau's passion for the Revolution, when combined with his own career frustrations and his gradual alienation from the political management of the early republic, no doubt impelled him to construct mythopoetic versions of order and tranquillity, which ultimately reveal as much about Freneau's own consciousness as they do about the currents of political life in late-eighteenth-century America. Freneau turned politics into an image of himself, and he became the final victim of his own imagination.

Further Reading:
L. Leary, *That Rascal Freneau: A Study in Literary Failure,* 1941, 1964.
N. F. Adkins, *Philip Freneau and Cosmic Enigma: The Religious and Philosophical Speculations of an American Poet,* 1949.
J. Axelrad, *Philip Freneau: Champion of Democracy,* 1967.
P. Marsh, *The Works of Philip Freneau: A Critical Study,* 1968.
M. Bowden, *Philip Freneau,* 1976.
R. Vitzthum, *Land and Sea: The Lyric Poetry of Philip Freneau,* 1978.

Texts:
"On Mr. Paine's Rights of Man" from *Poems of Freneau,* ed. H. H. Clark, 1929.
All others from *The Poems of Philip Freneau,* ed. F. L. Pattee, 3 vols., 1902–1907.

On the Emigration to America
And Peopling the Western Country

To western woods, and lonely plains,
Palemon[1] from the crowd departs,
Where Nature's wildest genius reigns,
To tame the soil, and plant the arts—
What wonders there shall freedom show,   5
What mighty states successive grow!

From Europe's proud, despotic shores
Hither the stranger takes his way,
And in our new found world explores
A happier soil, a milder sway,   10
Where no proud despot holds him down,
No slaves insult him with a crown.

What charming scenes attract the eye,
On wild Ohio's savage stream!
There Nature reigns, whose works outvie   15
The boldest pattern art can frame;
There ages past have rolled away,
And forests bloomed but to decay.

From these fair plains, these rural seats,
So long concealed, so lately known,   20
The unsocial Indian far retreats,
To make some other clime his own,
When other streams, less pleasing, flow,
And darker forests round him grow.

Great Sire[2] of floods! whose varied wave   25
Through climes and countries takes its way,
To whom creating Nature gave
Ten thousand streams to swell thy sway!
No longer shall they useless prove,
Nor idly through the forests rove;   30

Nor longer shall your princely flood
From distant lakes be swelled in vain,
Nor longer through a darksome wood

---

[1] Character in Chaucer's "Knight's Tale" (in *The Canterbury Tales*) who has come to represent any person setting out on a journey.

[2] Freneau's note: "Mississippi."

Advance, unnoticed, to the main,
Far other ends, the heavens decree—   35
And commerce plans new freights for thee.

While virtue warms the generous breast,
There heaven-born freedom shall reside,
Nor shall the voice of war molest,
Nor Europe's all-aspiring pride—   40
There Reason shall new laws devise,
And order from confusion rise.

Forsaking kings and regal state,
With all their pomp and fancied bliss,
The traveller owns, convinced though late,   45
No realm so free, so blest as this—
The east is half to slaves consigned,
Where kings and priests enchain the mind.

O come the time, and haste the day,
When man shall man no longer crush,   50
When Reason shall enforce her sway,
Nor these fair regions raise our blush,
Where still the African complains,
And mourns his yet unbroken chains.

Far brighter scenes a future age,   55
The muse predicts, these States will hail,
Whose genius may the world engage,
Whose deeds may over death prevail,
And happier systems bring to view,
Than all the eastern sages knew.   60
1784/1785

The Wild Honey Suckle

Fair flower, that dost so comely grow,
Hid in this silent, dull retreat,
Untouched thy honied blossoms blow,
Unseen thy little branches greet:
        No roving foot shall crush thee here,   5
        No busy hand provoke a tear.

By Nature's self in white arrayed,
    She bade thee shun the vulgar eye,
And planted here the guardian shade,
    And sent soft waters murmuring by;   10
      Thus quietly thy summer goes,
      Thy days declining to repose.

Smit with those charms, that must decay,
    I grieve to see your future doom;
They died—nor were those flowers more gay,   15
    The flowers that did in Eden bloom;
      Unpitying frosts, and Autumn's power
      Shall leave no vestige of this flower.

From morning suns and evening dews
    At first thy little being came: 20
If nothing once, you nothing lose,
    For when you die you are the same;
      The space between, is but an hour,
      The frail duration of a flower.

1786

The Indian Burying Ground

In spite of all the learned have said,
    I still my old opinion keep;
The posture, that we give the dead,
    Points out the soul's eternal sleep.

Not so the ancients of these lands—   5
    The Indian, when from life released,
Again is seated with his friends,
    And shares again the joyous feast.[1]

His imaged birds, and painted bowl,
    And venison, for a journey dressed,   10

[1] Freneau's note: "The North American Indians bury their dead in a sitting posture; decorating the corpse with wampum, the images of birds, quadrupeds, &c: And (if that of a warrior) with bows, arrows, tomhawks [sic], and other military weapons."

Bespeak the nature of the soul,
    Activity, that knows no rest.

His bow, for action ready bent,
    And arrows, with a head of stone,
Can only mean that life is spent,   15
    And not the old ideas gone.

Thou, stranger, that shalt come this way,
    No fraud upon the dead commit—
Observe the swelling turf, and say
    They do not lie, but here they sit.   20

Here still a lofty rock remains,
    On which the curious eye may trace
(Now wasted, half, by wearing rains)
    The fancies of a ruder race.

Here still an aged elm aspires,   25
    Beneath whose far-projecting shade
(And which the shepherd still admires)
    The children of the forest played!

There oft a restless Indian queen
    (Pale Shebah,[2] with her braided hair)   30
And many a barbarous form is seen
    To chide the man that lingers there.

By midnight moons, o'er moistening dews;
    In habit for the chase arrayed,
The hunter still the deer pursues,   35
    The hunter and the deer, a shade!

And long shall timorous fancy see
    The painted chief, and pointed spear,
And Reason's self shall bow the knee
    To shadows and delusions here.   40

1787

---

[2] The Queen of Sheba, legendary for her beauty
and wisdom. (See 1 Kings 10 and 2 Chronicles
9.)

On Mr. Paine's Rights of Man[*]

Thus briefly sketched the sacred RIGHTS OF MAN,
How inconsistent with the ROYAL PLAN!
Which for itself exclusive honour craves,
Where some are masters born, and millions slaves.
With what contempt must every eye look down   5
On that base, childish bauble called a *crown,*
The gilded bait, that lures the crowd, to come,
Bow down their necks, and meet a slavish doom;
The source of half the miseries men endure,
The quack that kills them, while it seems to cure.   10
   Roused by the REASON of his manly page,
Once more shall PAINE a listening world engage:
From Reason's source, a bold reform he brings,
In raising up *mankind,* he pulls down *kings,*
Who, source of discord, patrons of all wrong,   15
On blood and murder have been fed too long:
Hid from the world, and tutored to be base,
The curse, the scourge, the ruin of our race,
Their's was the task, a dull designing few,
To shackle beings that they scarcely knew,   20
Who made this globe the residence of slaves,
And built their thrones on systems formed by
   knaves
—Advance, bright years, to work their final fall,
And haste the period that shall crush them all.
   Who, that has read and scann'd the historic page 25
But glows, at every line, with kindling rage,
To see by them the rights of men aspersed,
Freedom restrain'd, and Nature's law reversed,
Men, ranked with beasts, by monarchs *will'd* away,
And bound young fools, or madmen to obey: 30
Now driven to wars, and now oppressed at home,
Compelled in crowds o'er distant seas to roam,
From India's climes the plundered prize to bring
To glad the strumpet, or to glut the king.
   COLUMBIA,[1] hail! immortal be thy reign: 35
Without a king, we till the smiling plain;
Without a king, we trace the unbounded sea,

[*] Thomas Paine (1737–1809) had supported the French Revolution in *The Rights of Man* (1791).

[1] America.

And traffic round the globe, through each degree;
Each foreign clime our honour'd flag reveres,
Which asks no monarch, to support the STARS: 40
Without a *king,* the laws maintain their sway,
While honour bids each generous heart obey.
Be ours the task the ambitious to restrain,
And this great lesson teach—that kings are vain;
That warring realms to certain ruin haste,   45
That kings subsist by war, and wars are waste:
So shall our nation, form'd on Virtue's plan,
Remain the guardian of the Rights of Man,
A vast Republic, famed through every clime,
Without a king, to see the end of time.   50

1791

On a Honey Bee

Drinking from a glass of wine and drowned therein

Thou, born to sip the lake or spring,
Or quaff the waters of the stream,
Why hither come on vagrant wing?—
Does Bacchus tempting seem—
Did he, for you, this glass prepare?—   5
Will I admit you to a share?

Did storms harass or foes perplex,
Did wasps or king-birds bring dismay—
Did wars distress, or labours vex,
Or did you miss your way?—   10
A better seat you could not take
Than on the margin of this lake.

Welcome!—I hail you to my glass:
All welcome, here, you find;
Here, let the cloud of trouble pass,   15
Here, be all care resigned.—
This fluid never fails to please,
And drown the griefs of men or bees.

What forced you here, we cannot know,
And you will scarcely tell—   20
But cheery we would have you go

And bid a glad farewell:
On lighter wings we bid you fly,
Your dart will now all foes defy.

Yet take not, oh! too deep a drink,   2
And in this ocean die;
Here bigger bees than you might sink,
Even bees full six feet high.
Like Pharaoh,[1] then, you would be said
To perish in a sea of red.   3c

Do as you please, your will is mine;
Enjoy it without fear—
And your grave will be this glass of wine,
Your epitaph—a tear—
Go, take your seat in Charon's boat,   35
We'll tell the hive, you died afloat.

1797

Native American Literature

In *Studies in Classic American Literature,* D. H. Lawrence points to the haunting presence of Native Americans in the nation's cultural consciousness: "A curious thing about the Spirit of Place is the fact that no place exerts its full influence upon a new-comer until the old inhabitant is dead or absorbed. So America." In the nearly five centuries that have passed since Christopher Columbus accidentally discovered America and opened unbounded vistas for the literature of the New World, the response of European emigrants to America to the people they found there has fluctuated greatly, often moving rapidly between the extremes of trying ruthlessly to eliminate or mindlessly to glorify the Native American population. Within these extremes, the colonists persisted in their efforts to assimilate each Native American group within their nation's cultural heritage.

Europeans found Columbus's discovery of the New World as bewildering as it was unexpected. Samuel Eliot Morison, the distinguished biographer of Columbus, notes that "when discovered it [America] was not wanted, and most of the exploration for the next fifty years was done in the hope of getting through or around it." Columbus's reports on his voyages, for example, underscore his conviction that he had accomplished what he had set out to do: discover a shorter route to the East Indies. And because he could not adjust his expectations to the reality he confronted in the New World, Columbus insisted on calling the people he found there Indians, as though they were the people of the Near East he had sailed west to find. Columbus had discovered America, but not its people.

[1] Pharaoh's army drowned in the Red Sea while pursuing the Israelites. (See Exodus 14:1–27.)

Generations of European explorers and colonists repeated Columbus's efforts to reinvent America and its inhabitants. Europeans dealt with the unrelenting novelty of their experiences with this newfound land and the people who inhabited it by reconstituting those experiences according to a more readily accessible and familiar cultural framework. As the historian Edmundo O'Gorman has noted, "The native cultures of the newly found lands could not be recognized and respected in their own right, as an original way of realizing human ideals and values, but only for the meaning they might have in relation to Christian European culture." America was invented, O'Gorman suggests, "in the image of its inventor," by those who could not free themselves from inherited European cultural perspectives and values. As a result, the distinctive nature of Native American culture was, to use William Carlos Williams's terms (from *In the American Grain*), "lost in chaos of borrowed titles, many of them inappropriate, under which the true character lies hid." The pages that follow try to present Native American literature in its own terms, to draw, as Williams notes, "from every source one thing, the strange phosphorus of the life, nameless under an old misappellation."

The most striking fact about Native American literature is the cultural diversity that it represents. At the time of Columbus's voyages, more than 350 distinct, mutually unintelligible Native American languages were spoken in the area that is now the United States—and nearly half of these languages are still spoken in contemporary America. Literally thousands of distinct political and social groups were spread across the land. Given this range of identities, no single image of the Native American people can accurately capture the complexity of their culture. Yet historically, convenient stereotypes have dominated the nation's view of Native Americans: naked, mysterious, gullible creatures or noble savages; cigar-store props and dime-novel caricatures on the warpath or resilient, loyal companions of white-horsed heroes; and, more recently, soft-spoken wise men with drug-induced access to fundamental knowledge. Over the course of five centuries, Native Americans have come to be isolated geographically and culturally, relegated to the lowly status of the "other," with relatively few opportunities to posit the richness and complexity of their individual and collective voices in the cultural consciousness of the nation within whose boundaries they live.

The literature of Native Americans has been transmitted primarily through the oral tradition. Skills in oratory are highly valued, in part because most North American tribes govern themselves through participatory democracy. Research conducted since the late nineteenth century reveals a number of highly developed oral literary forms—including ceremonial and popular songs, prayers, incantations, and mythic narratives—each with its own characteristic style and art in each Native American language. Yet because this literature is based on Native American cultural assumptions, it has traditionally been regarded as the province of anthropology rather than literary studies, much like Puritan sermons and explorers' narratives—texts that while culturally interesting have not been considered part of the belles lettres tradition. Closer examination suggests that the literary features of these Native American texts are consistent with the stylistic qualities, including repetition and rhythmic patterning, of the great oral tradition of European literature dating back to classical antiquity. Like its European counterpart, the Native American literary oral tradition has articulated important states of individual consciousness while helping to reinforce a sense of community within each language group.

The confrontation between European and Native American cultures in the New World is amply reported from colonial points of view. Spanish, English, and French explorers and missionaries have left graphic narratives of their efforts to "civilize" and convert the New World's population. Relatively few voices remain, however, to represent reliably the Native American perspective on these same events. Most eyewitness accounts survive through secondhand and thirdhand translations. Many suffer to an indeterminate extent by being "screened" by a colonial sensibility. The surviving text may well reflect more what their white audiences thought, or hoped, Native Americans had said than what they did in fact say. In other instances, such as Mayan responses to the Spanish conquest, Native American authors had to master the language of their conquerors in order to preserve the anguish of their people.

Since the late nineteenth century, an increasing amount of indigenous oral literature has been transcribed by Native Americans in their own languages as well as in English and is increasingly available to be read. As a result, accurate texts of Native American literature can be included in the American literary tradition with greater confidence and frequency. The texts presented here illustrate the varying forms of literature that distinguished the conquered from the conqueror in the New World. These texts help us appreciate not only how each side discovered the "other" that neither knew but also how vibrant the Native American oral tradition has remained.

Further Reading:
For comprehensive studies of the history and literature of Native Americans, see H. E. Driver, *Indians of North America*, 1961. W. T. Hagan, *American Indians*, 1961. R. H. Pearce, *The Savages of America: A Study of the Indian and the Idea of Civilization*, 2nd ed., 1965. D. McNickle, *Native American Tribalism*, 1973. W. E. Washburn, *The Indian in America*, 1975. *Handbook of North American Indians*, ed. W. C. Sturtevant, 20 vols. planned, 1978–. D. Hymes, *In Vain I Tried to Tell You: Essays in Native American Ethnopoetics*, 1981. K. Kroeber, *American Indian Literature: Texts and Interpretations*, 1981.

A. Rosenstiel, *Red and White: Indian Views of the White Man, 1492–1982*, 1983. *Studies in American Indian Literature*, ed. Paula Gunn Allen, 1983. For Native American material in "The Literature of the New World," see E. O'Gorman, *The Invention of America*, 1961. D. Tedlock, *The Spoken Word and the Work of Interpretation*, 1983. T. Todorov, *The Conquest of America*, 1984. D. Buhane, *The Navajo Creation Story*, 1985.

A Bering Strait Eskimo Creation Myth

All Native American groups possess a body of narratives that can be called myths because of the central role they play in articulating religious experience and organizing ethical, moral, and social behavior. The myths also relate to Native

American rituals and ceremonies. Just as the Christian mass or communion service reenacts a critical section of the Gospel (the Last Supper) and the Jewish Passover seder recalls central acts in the book of Exodus, Native American rituals and ceremonies frequently refer to and reenact important sections of myths.

Myths also had—and continue to have—an educational function, much as Bible stories are the basis of moral instruction in Christian Sunday schools. (In Native American societies, children's instruction took place primarily in the home, usually at night, and often during the winter season.)

In all their roles, Native American myths might best be understood as resembling dramatic performances. Virtually every component of the narrative includes direct speech, sometimes without apparent reason. In actual performance, the narrator would enact the scene, taking on different voices and gestures for different characters. Such a well-formed oral narrative may seem slow or awkward when written down in the form usually reserved for fiction, but in performance it would be absorbing. Moreover, like theater, the performance of oral literature can be expected to vary with the narrator, audience, setting, and time period.

Printed here are the beginning episodes of a Bering Strait Eskimo creation myth collected in Alaska between 1877 and 1881 by Edward William Nelson. The elderly man who told the tale remembered having learned the text from an old man who came from the Bering Strait. Nelson's source also remembered that when the man from Bering Strait "finished the tales on the third evening, he would pour a cup of water on the floor and say: 'Drink well, spirits of those of whom I have told.'"

The Bering Sea Eskimos occupy the lowland regions of western Alaska, between the Bering Straits and the Aleutian Islands. Unlike the Native Americans of the eastern Arctic and Greenland, Bering Strait Eskimos live in large, permanent villages with sizable log and sod houses during the winter and in plank houses during the summer. They eat a diet of stored fish, game, and berries, much like their Indian neighbors to the south on the Northwest coast. During the winter months they hold large festivals and dramatized ceremonies with masks and elaborate theatrical effects, the primary purpose of which is "to propitiate the spirits controlling the universe and bring success in hunting."

In their elegantly illustrated description of Bering Sea Eskimo life, William W. Fitzhugh and Susan A. Kaplan offer the following explanation of the cultural and religious importance of the Raven: "Spiritual transformation, symbolized by Man's first encounter with his maker, Raven, was at the heart of Bering Sea Eskimo life and culture. When an animal died its *inua* inhabited the form of an unborn animal of the same or similar species. Therefore, man needed to deal respectfully with animals and objects so as not to displease their *inuas*."

Further Reading:
W. W. Fitzhugh and S. A. Kaplan, *Inua: Spirit World of the Bering Sea Eskimos,* 1982.
Handbook of North American Indians, gen. ed.
W. C. Sturtevant, vol. 5, *Arctic,* ed. D. Damas, 1984.

Text:
18th Annual Report, Part 1, Bureau of American Ethnology, 1896–1897.

from The Time When There Were No People on the Earth Plain

It was in the time when there were no people on the earth plain. During four days the first man lay coiled up in the pod of a beach-pea. On the fifth day he stretched out his feet and burst the pod, falling to the ground, where he stood up, a full-grown man. He looked about him, and then moved his hands and arms, his neck and legs, and examined himself curiously. Looking back, he saw the pod from which he had fallen, still hanging to the vine, with a hole in the lower end, out of which he had dropped. Then he looked about him again and saw that he was getting farther away from his starting place, and that the ground moved up and down under his feet and seemed very soft. After a while he had an unpleasant feeling in his stomach, and he stooped down to take some water into his mouth from a small pool at his feet. The water ran down into his stomach and he felt better. When he looked up again he saw approaching, with a waving motion, a dark object which came on until just in front of him, when it stopped, and, standing on the ground, looked at him. This was a raven, and, as soon as it stopped, it raised one of its wings, pushed up its beak, like a mask, to the top of its head, and changed at once into a man. Before he raised his mask Raven had stared at the man, and after it was raised he stared more than ever, moving about from side to side to obtain a better view. At last he said: "What are you? Whence did you come? I have never seen anything like you." Then Raven looked at Man, and was still more surprised to find that this strange new being was so much like himself in shape.

Then he told Man to walk away a few steps, and in astonishment exclaimed again: "When did you come? I have never seen anything like you before." To this Man replied: "I came from the pea-pod." And he pointed to the plant from which he came. "Ah!" exclaimed Raven, "I made that vine, but did not know that anything like you would ever come from it. Come with me to the high ground over there; this ground I made later, and it is still soft and thin, but it is thicker and harder there."

In a short time they came to the higher land, which was firm under their feet. Then Raven asked Man if he had eaten anything. The latter answered that he had taken some soft stuff into him at one of the pools. "Ah!" said Raven, "you drank some water. Now wait for me here."

Then he drew down the mask over his face, changing again into a bird, and flew far up into the sky where he disappeared. Man waited where he had been left until the fourth day, when Raven returned, bringing four berries in his claws. Pushing up his mask, Raven became a man again and held out two salmonberries and two hearthberries, saying, "Here is what I have made for you to eat. I also wish them to be plentiful over the earth. Now eat them." Man took the berries and placed them in his mouth one after the other and they satisfied his hunger, which had made him feel uncomfortable. Raven then led Man to a small creek near by and left him while he went to the water's edge and molded a couple of pieces of clay into the form of a pair of mountain sheep, which he held in his hand, and when they became dry he called Man to show him what he had done. Man thought they were very pretty, and Raven told him to close his eyes. As soon as Man's eyes were closed Raven drew down his mask and waved his wings four times over the images, when they became endowed with life and bounded away as full-grown mountain sheep. Raven then raised his mask and told Man to look. When Man saw the sheep moving away, full of life, he cried out with pleasure. Seeing how pleased Man was, Raven said, "If these animals are numerous, perhaps people will wish very much to get them." And Man said he thought they would. "Well," said Raven, "it will be better for them to have their home among the high cliffs, so that every one can not kill them, and there only shall they be found."

Then Raven made two animals of clay which he endowed with life as before, but as they were dry only in spots when they were given life, they remained brown and white, and so originated the tame reindeer with mottled coat. Man thought these were very handsome, and Raven told him that they would be very scarce. In the same way a pair of wild reindeer were made and permitted to get dry and white only on their bellies, then they were given life; in consequence, to this day the belly of the wild reindeer is the only white part about it. Raven told Man that these animals would be very common, and people would kill many of them.

"You will be very lonely by yourself," said Raven. "I will make you a companion." He then went to a spot some distance from where he had made the animals, and looking now and then at Man, made an image very much like him. Then he fastened a lot of fine water grass on the back of the head for hair, and after the image had dried in his hands, he waved his wings over it as before and a beautiful young woman arose and stood beside Man. "There," cried Raven, "is a companion for you," and he led them back to a small knoll near by.

In those days there were no mountains far or near, and the sun never ceased shining brightly; no rain ever fell and no winds blew. When they came to the knoll, Raven showed the pair how to make a bed in the dry moss, and they slept there very warmly; Raven drew down his mask and slept near by in the form of a bird. Waking before the others, Raven went back to the creek and made a pair each of sticklebacks, graylings, and blackfish. When these were swimming about in the water, he called Man to see them. When the latter looked at them and saw the sticklebacks swim up the stream with a wriggling motion he was so surprised that he raised his hand suddenly and the fish darted away. Raven then showed him the graylings and told him that they would be found in clear mountain streams, while the sticklebacks would live along the seacoast and that both would be good for food. Next the shrew-mouse was made, Raven saying that it would not be good for food but would enliven the ground and prevent it from seeming barren and cheerless.

In this way Raven continued for several days making birds, fishes, and animals, showing them to Man, and explaining their uses. . . .

1899

Seneca and Cherokee Oral History

No sooner had Europeans encountered coastal-dwelling Native Americans than many Indian people quickly ceased to exist. Within twenty years of Columbus's first having sighted America on October 12, 1492, the entire native population of Hispaniola (now Santo Domingo) was eliminated. Powhatan's Algonquin Confederacy had disappeared within fifty years of his speech to Captain John Smith.

Native American groups living considerably inland, such as the Iroquois, the Cherokee, and the Creek, were far more fortunate. Several generations passed before the number of European emigrants on the coast became so large that the adventurous were encouraged to strike out for the frontier. During this period of colonial expansion, several large inland groups of Native Americans had the opportunity to adjust physically to the new diseases the Europeans had carried with them (such as measles, smallpox, and whooping cough) as well as to adjust culturally, economically, and socially to the implications of permanent white settlement in North America. In addition, interior groups such as the Iroquois, the Cherokee, and the Creek were able to maintain a far more independent stance in response to the different European factions competing for dominance in the region. These Native Americans were able to play off the various European powers, especially the French and the English, against each other.

While the coastal Indians were alternately fighting off and trying to make peace with various European colonial groups, the inland tribes continued to be preoccupied with intertribal relations. But the introduction of European goods complicated matters. The Indians found themselves increasingly caught up in the fur trade in order to satisfy their initial desire, and subsequent need, for those goods. For example, the northern Iroquois tribes of the Five Nations, in what is now northern New York State, not only participated in the fur trade as primary suppliers but also served increasingly as brokers between neighboring Indian groups and the Europeans. They maintained this position through the political and military power of the Iroquois League. Before 1680 they had conquered all of the tribes on their immediate borders and aimed their military prowess against the more distant Illinois, Catawba, and Cherokee tribes. For nearly one hundred years the Iroquois and Cherokee continued to conduct small-scale raids on each other. As James Mooney notes in *Myths of the Cherokee,* "The great object of every Iroquois boy [was] to go against the Cherokee as soon as he was old enough to take the war path."

The journey from Iroquois country to the Cherokee frontier took more than five days "for a rapidly traveling war party" from what is now western New York State along "the Great Indian War Path" to Virginia, Kentucky, northern Tennessee, and North Carolina and on to the Creek territory in what is now Alabama. Mooney observes that "as the distance was too great for large expeditions, the war consisted chiefly of a series of individual exploits, a single Cherokee often going hundreds of miles to strike a blow, which was surely to be retaliated by the warriors to the north." The two narratives printed here offer different perspectives on such skirmishes and reveal something of the Native American ritual and folklore that surround war. The first selection represents Senecan oral history, the second Cherokee.

Cherokee oral tradition reports that the war was finally brought to an end by an Iroquois delegation sent to the Cherokee to propose a general alliance of southern and western tribes. A formal peace treaty was arranged by Sir William Johnson, the British agent for the Mohawk, in 1768.

Further Reading:
A. F. C. Wallace, *The Death and Rebirth of the Seneca*, 1970.
Handbook of North American Indians, gen. ed. W. C. Sturtevant, vol. 15, *Northeast*, ed. B. G. Trigger, 1978.

Text:
J. Mooney, *Myths of the Cherokees, 19th Annual Report of the Bureau of American Ethnology, Part 1, 1897–98*, 1900.

The Unseen Helpers

Ganogwioeoñ, a war chief of the Seneca, led a party against the Cherokee. When they came near the first town he left his men outside and went in alone. At the first house he found an old woman and her granddaughter. They did not see him, and he went into the house and hid himself under some wood. When darkness came on he heard the old woman say, "Maybe Ganogwioeoñ is near; I'll close the door." After a while he heard them going to bed. When he thought they were asleep he went into the house. The fire had burned down low, but the girl was still awake and saw him. She was about to scream, when he said, "I am Ganogwioeoñ. If you scream I'll kill you. If you keep quiet I'll not hurt you." They talked together, and he told her that in the morning she must bring the chief's daughter to him. She promised to do it, and told her where he should wait. Just before daylight he left the house.

In the morning the girl went to the chief's house and said to his daughter, "Let's go out together for wood." The chief's daughter got ready and went with her, and when they came to the place where Ganogwioeoñ was hiding he sprang out and killed her,[1] but did not hurt the other girl. He pulled off the scalp and gave such a loud scalp yell that all the warriors in the town heard it and came running out after him. He shook the scalp at them and then turned and ran. He killed the first one that came up, but when he tried to shoot the next one the bow broke and the Cherokee got him.

They tied him and carried him to the two women of the tribe who had the power to decide what should be done with him. Each of these women had two snakes tattooed on her lips, with their heads opposite each other, in such a way that when

---

[1] The Iroquois believed that killing a woman required greater courage because the attacker had to penetrate a village to do so.

she opened her mouth the two snakes opened their mouths also. They decided to burn the soles of his feet until they were blistered, then to put grains of corn under the skin and to chase him with clubs until they had beaten him to death.

They stripped him and burnt his feet. Then they tied a bark rope around his waist, with an old man to hold the other end, and made him run between two lines of people, and with clubs in their hands. When they gave the word to start Ganogwioeoñ pulled the rope away from the old man and broke through the line and ran until he had left them all out of sight. When night came he crawled into a hollow log. He was naked and unarmed, with his feet in a pitiful condition, and thought he could never get away.

He heard footsteps on the leaves outside and thought his enemies were upon him. The footsteps came up to the log and some one said to another, "This is our friend." Then the stranger said to Ganogwioeoñ, "You think you are the same as dead, but it is not so. We will take care of you. Stick out your feet." He put out his feet from the log and felt something licking them. After a while the voice said, "I think we have licked his feet enough. Now we must crawl inside the log and lie on each side of him to keep him warm." They crawled in beside him. In the morning they crawled out and told him to stick out his feet again. They licked them again and then said to him, "Now we have done all we can do this time. Go on until you come to the place where you made a bark shelter a long time ago, and under the bark you will find something to help you." Ganogwioeoñ crawled out of the log, but they were gone. His feet were better now and he could walk comfortably. He went on until about noon, when he came to the bark shelter, and under it he found a knife, an awl, and a flint, that his men had hidden there two years before. He took them and started on again.

Toward evening he looked around until he found another hollow tree and crawled into it to sleep. At night he heard the footsteps and voices again. When he put out his feet again, as the strangers told him to do, they licked his feet as before and then crawled in and lay down on each side of him to keep him warm. Still he could not see them. In the morning after they went out they licked his feet again and said to him, "At noon you will find food." Then they went away.

Ganogwioeoñ crawled out of the tree and went on. At noon he came to a burning log, and near it was a dead bear, which was still warm, as if it had been killed only a short time before. He skinned the bear and found it very fat. He cut up the meat and roasted as much as he could eat or carry. While it was roasting he scraped the skin and rubbed rotten wood dust on it to clean it until he was tired. When night came he lay down to sleep. He heard the steps and the voices again and one said, "Well, our friend is lying down. He has plenty to eat, and it does not seem as if he is going to die. Let us lick his feet again." When they had finished they said to him, "You need not worry any more now. You will get home all right." Before it was day they left him.

When morning came he put the bearskin around him like a shirt, with the hair outside, and started on again, taking as much of the meat as he could carry. That night his friends came to him again. They said, "Your feet are well, but you will be cold," so they lay again on each side of him. Before daylight they left, saying, "About noon you will find something to wear." He went on and about midday he came to two young bears just killed. He skinned them and dressed the skins, then roasted as much meat as he wanted, and lay down to sleep. In the morning he made leggings of the skins, took some of the meat, and started on.

His friends came again the next night and told him that in the morning he would come upon something else to wear. As they said, about noon he found two fawns just killed. He turned the skins and made himself a pair of moccasins, then cut some of the meat, and traveled on until evening, when he made a fire and had supper.

That night again he heard the steps and voices, and one said, "My friend, very soon now you will reach home safely and find your friends all well. Now we will tell you why we have helped you. Whenever you went hunting you always gave the best part of the meat to us and kept only the smallest part for yourself. For that we are thankful and help you. In the morning you will see us and know who we are."[2]

In the morning when he woke up they were still there—two men as he thought —but after he had said the last words to them and started on, he turned again to look, and one was a white wolf and the other a black wolf. That day he reached home.

1900

Hemp-Carrier

On the southern slope of the ridge, along the trail from Robbinsville to Valley river, in Cherokee county, North Carolina, are the remains of a number of stone cairns. The piles are leveled now, but thirty years ago the stones were still heaped up into pyramids, to which every Cherokee who passed added a stone. According to the tradition these piles marked the graves of a number of women and children of the tribe who were surprised and killed on the spot by a raiding party of the Iroquois shortly before the final peace between the two Nations. As soon as the news was brought to the settlements on Hiwassee and Cheowa[1] a party was made under Tâle'tanigi'skĭ, "Hemp-carrier," to follow and take vengeance on the enemy. Among others of the party was the father of the noted chief Tsunu'lǎhûñ'skĭ, or Junaluska, who died on Cheowa about 1855.

For days they followed the trail of the Iroquois across the Great Smoky mountains, through forests and over rivers, until they finally tracked them to their very town in the far northern Seneca country. On the way they met another war party headed for the south, and the Cherokee killed them all and took their scalps. When they came near the Seneca town it was almost night, and they heard shouts in the townhouse, where the women were dancing over the fresh Cherokee scalps. The avengers hid themselves near the spring, and as the dancers came down to drink the Cherokee

---

[2] Ganogwioeoñ is apparently a member of the wolf clan, whose totemic figure protects him here. The Iroquois always left a portion of their hunting for their totemic animal. Thus the wolf protects him here.

[1] Rivers running through Tennessee and North Carolina.

silently killed one and another until they had counted as many scalps as had been taken on Cheowa, and still the dancers in the townhouse never thought that enemies were near. Then said the Cherokee leader, "We have covered the scalps of our women and children. Shall we go home now like cowards, or shall we raise the war whoop and let the Seneca know that we are men?" "Let them come, if they will," said his men; and they raised the scalp yell of the Cherokee. At once there was an answering shout from the townhouse, and the dance came to a sudden stop. The Seneca warriors swarmed out with ready gun and hatchet, but the nimble Cherokee were off and away. There was a hot pursuit in the darkness, but the Cherokee knew the trails and were light and active runners, and managed to get away with the loss of only a single man. The rest got home safely, and the people were so well pleased with Hemp-carrier's bravery and success that they gave him seven wives.[2]

1900

William Ralganal Benson
ca. 1863–1936

There are few reliable accounts of what actually transpired during the early years of contact between Native Americans and western settlers. Official government documents usually branded Native American resistance to the settlers' occupation of their lands an uprising or massacre whenever settlers' lives were lost. So too, most early white efforts to defend Native American behavior depended on sentimental distortions of the Indians' beliefs, rights, and culture. William Ralganal Benson's account of the Stone and Kelsey "massacre" on the shores of northern California's Clear Lake in 1849 is limited by neither predisposition. As an informant and interpreter of Native American experience and lore for the anthropologists who worked in the Clear Lake region in the early twentieth century, Benson was well known for his integrity. From all indications, his narrative is at once one of the most reliable reports of the early conflicts between white settlers and Native Americans and one of the most insightful and compelling views of Native American attitudes toward the settlers who eventually crowded them off their lands.

William Ralganal Benson was born about 1863 in what were then still the remote stretches of Lake County, California. His mother was descended from a long line of Pomo chiefs; his father, a white settler named Addison Benson, had renounced his former life and taken up permanent residence among the Pomo tribe. He died when his son was fairly young, leaving Ralganal, the Pomo word for "wampum gatherer," with little knowledge of English. Over the years, William Ralganal Benson taught himself to read and write mostly by ear, and much of the text printed here reflects his practice with phonetic spelling. Benson also taught himself to type, and the unusual punctuation in this text reflects his deliberate efforts to preserve the oral tradition of retelling his story. Each period,

[2] Seven is the Cherokee ritual number.

for example, is meant to indicate an emphasis or a fairly long pause in the narrative.

Benson's story serves to counterbalance the official versions of the incident recorded in local histories. One such account of the "massacre" consists of the following brief entry:

> In the fall of 1849, when Stone and Kelsey were away with the vaqueros, attending to their cattle one day, Augustine's squaw poured water into their guns. The next morning some of the Indians made a charge on the house. Kelsey was killed outright with an arrow shot through the window. Stone escaped upstairs and on the Indians rushing up against him, jumped out of an upper window, ran to the creek and hid in a clump of willows. . . . An old Indian found him and killed him with a blow of a rock on the head.

But even these "official" renditions of what happened at Kelseyville acknowledge, in the words of another report, that "the consensus of opinion is that the deed was justified by the harsh and unjust treatment given the Indians by these two frontiersmen."

Benson's narrative does fuse events that took place nearly a year apart. Stone and Kelsey were killed in the fall of 1849, after gold had been discovered and Kelsey had impressed several of the Pomo tribe into joining his failed search for instant wealth. The second episode, the retaliatory raid against the Pomo tribe, occurred almost a year later. Although not an eyewitness, Benson nonetheless takes us closer to the state of mind of the Native Americans who were no longer willing to endure the abuses of greedy settlers.

Further Reading:
The official versions of what occurred at Kelseyville may be found in C. A. Menifee, *Historical and Descriptive Sketch Book of Napa, Sonoma, Lake and Mendocino Counties*, 1879, *History of Napa and Lake Counties*, 1881, and A. O. Carpenter and P. H. Millberry, *History of Mendocino and Lake Counties*, 1910.

Text:
California Historical Society Quarterly, 1932.

The Stone and Kelsey "Massacre"

The Facts Of Stone and Kelsey Massacre. in Lake County California.[1] As it was stated to me by the five indians who went to stone and kelseys house purpose to kill the two white men. after debateing all night. Shuk and Xasis.[2] these two men were the

---

[1] Located in northern California.
[2] Members of the Pomo tribe, as are the other Indian names that follow.

instigators of the massacre. it was not because Shuk and Xasis had any Ill feeling torge the two white men. there were two indian villages. one on west side and one on the east side.[3] the indians in both of these camps were starveing, stone or kelsey would not let them go out hunting or fishing. Shuk and Xasis was stone and kelsey headriders looking out for stock. cattle horses and hogs. the horses and cattle were all along the lake on the west side and some in bachelors valley. also in upper lake. so it took 18 indian herdsman to look after the stock in these places. Shuk and Xasis was foremans for the herds. and only those herds got anything to eat. each one of these herders got 4 cups of wheat for a days work. this cup would hold about one and ahalf pint of water. the wheat was boiled before it was given to the herders. and the herders shire with thir famlys. the herders who had large famlys were also starveing. about 20 old people died during the winter from starvetion. from severe whipping 4 died. a nephew of an indian lady who were liveing with stone was shoot to deth by stone. the mother of this young man was sick and starveing. this sick woman told her son to go over to stones wife or the sick womans sister. tell your aunt that iam starveing and sick tell her that i would like to have a handfull of wheat. the young man lost no time going to stones house. the young man told the aunt what his mother said. the lady then gave the young man 5 cups of wheat and tied it up in her apron and the young man started for the camp. stone came about that time and called the young man back. the young man stoped stone who was horse back. rode up to the young man took the wheat from him and then shoot him. the young man died two days after. such as whipping and tieing their hands togather with rope, the rope then thrown over a limb of a tree and then drawn up untell the indians toes barly touchs the ground and let them hang there for hours. this was common punishment. when a father or mother of young girl. was asked to bring the girl to his house. by stone or kelsey. if this order was not obeyed. he or her would be whipped or hung by the hands. such punishment occurred two or three times a week. and many of the old men and woman died from fear and starvetion.

these two white men had the indians to build a high fence around thir villages. and the head riders were to see that no indian went out side of this fence after dark. if any one was caught out side of this fence after dark was taken to stones and kelseys house and there was tied both hands and feet and placed in a room and kept there all night. the next day was taken to a tree and was tied down. then the strongs man was chosen to whippe the prisoner. the village on the west side was the Qu-Lah-Na-Poh[4] tribes the village on the east side. Xa-Bah-Na-Poh.[5] tribes.

the starvetion of the indians was the cause of the massacre of stone and kelsey. the indians who was starving hired a man by the name of Shuk and a nother man by the name of Xasis. to kill a beef for them. Shuk and Xasis agreed to go out and kill a beef for them. the two men then plan to go out that nigth and kill a beef for them. thir plan then was to take the best horsses in the barn. stones horse which was the best lasso horse. so between the two men. they agreed to take both stones and kelseys

---

[3] I.e., of Clear Lake.
[4] One of the two pre-contact villages (Quuhlá-Naapó in contemporary Eastern Pomo practical orthography) in Big Valley; it was located on the west side of Clear Lake in northern California.

[5] The second of the two Pomo villages (Xaabé-Naapó in contemporary Eastern Pomo practical orthography), this one located on the eastern side of Clear Lake.

horses. so the two men went to stone and kelseys house to see if they had went to bed. it was raining a little. moonligth now and then they found stone and kelsey had went to bed so they went to the barn and took stone and kelseys horses and saddles. Shuk wanted to do the job in the day time but Xasis said stone or kelsey would sure find them and would kill the both of them. Shuk said then somebody is going to get killed on this job so any how they went out west they knew where a larg band was feeding they soon rounded the band up and Shuk was to make the first lasso Xasis was good on lassing the foot of anox so he was to do the foot lassing. Shuk said to Xasis get recy i see large one hear hurry and come on. Shuk got a chance and threwed the rope on the large or Xasis came as quick as he could the band then begin to stampede. the ox also started with the band. the ground was wet and slippery and raining. and before Xasis could get his rope on. Shuks horse fell to the ground. the horse and the ox got away. Xasis tried to lass the horse but could not get near it to throw the rope on. the horse soon found the other horses and it was then much harder to get the horse. so the chase was given up. the two went back to the camp and reported to the people who hired them. told them the bad luck they had. Xasis then took the horse he had back to the barn which was kelseys horse. all the men who hired Shuk and Xasis was gathered in Xasiss house, here they debated all night. Shuk and Xasis wanted to kill stone and kelsey. they said stone and kelsey would kill them as soon as they would find out that the horses was taken with out them known; one man got up and suggested that the tribe give stone and kelsey forty sticks of beades which means 16000 beads or 100 dollars. no one agreed. another man suggested that he or Shuk. tell stoneor kelsey that the horse was stolen. no one agreed, and another man suggested that the other horse should be turned out and tell stone and kelsey both horses were stlen. no one agreed. every thing looks bad for Shuk and Xasis. no one agreed with Shuk and Xasis to kill the two white men. at daylight one man agreed to go with Shuk and Xasis. his indian name. Ba-Tus, was known by the whites as Busi. and alittle while later Kra-nas agreed. and as the four men started out another man joined the Shuk and Xasis band: Ma-Laxa-Qe-Tu. while this Debateing was going on the hired or servants boys and girls of stones and kelseys were told by Shuk and Xasis to carrie out allthe guns. bows and arrows. knives and every thing like weapon was taken out of the house by these girls and boys so the two white men was helpless in defense. so Shuk and Xasis knew the white man, did not have any thing to defen themselfs with and they were sure of their victims. so the five men went to the house where stone and kelsey were liveing. at daylight were to the place where stone always built a fire under a large pot in which he boiled wheat for the indian herders.about 16 of them. these five men waited around this pot untell stone came out to build the fire. Stone came out with pot full of fire which was taken from the fireplace. and said to the indians. whats the matter boys you came Early this morning. some thing rong; the indians said. O nothing me hungry thats all. Qka-Nas: or cayote Jim as he was known by the whites: Qka-Nas said to the men. I thought you men came to kill this man; give me these arrows and bow. He jerk the bow and the arrows away from Shuk and drew it and as he did.Stone rose quickly and turned to Qka-Nas and said what are you trying to do Jim, and as Stone said it. the indian cut loose. the arrow. struck the victimpith of the stomach. the victim mediately pull the arrow out and ran for the house. fighting his way. he broke one mans arm with the pot he had. and succeeded in geting in the house and locked the door after him.

little later Kelsey came and opened the door and noticed the blood on the doorstep. the indians advanced. Kelsey seen that the indians ment business. he said to them. no matar kelsey. kelsey bueno hombre para vosotros.[6] the indians charged and two of the indians caught kelsey and the fight began. in this fight kelsey was stabed twice in the back. kelsey managed to brake loose. he ran for the creek and the indians after him. a man by the name of Xa-sis or blind Jose, as he was known by the whites. who was in pursuit. shot kelsey in the back. kelsey manage to pull the arrow out jest as he got to the creek and jumped in the water and dove under and came out on the other side of the creek. where several indians were waiting. there was one man kelsey knew well. he thought who would save him. this man was Joe sefeis, indian name. Ju-Luh. he beged Joe to save him. Joe he could not save him from being killed. Joe said to kelsey. its too late kelsey; if I attempt to save you. I allso will be killed. I can not save you kelsey; kelsey was geting weak from loss of blood. Big Jim and Joe had kelsey by the arms. Big Jim said to his wife. this is a man who killed our son. take this spear. now you have the chance to take revenge. Big Jim's wife took the spear and stabed the white man in the hart. this womans name was Da-Pi-Tauo. the body was left laying there for the cayotes. this hapend on the east side of the creek. while this was going on. Xasis and Qra-Nas was trailing the blood up stairs and for a hour allmost. Qra-Nas said they crawled up stairs breathless thinking that stone was yet alive. they opend the door of a wheat bend and saw stones foot Qra-Nas drew his arrow across the bow. redy to cut loose. for a moment they watch the lifeless body. Xa-sis discovered that the body was dead. they then took the body and threw it out the window. and then they called all the people to come and take what wheat and corn they could pack and go to-a hiding place. where they could not be found by the whites. so the indian of both villages came and took all the wheat and corn they could gather in the place. and then went to hide themselfs. some went to Fishels point and somewent to scotts valley. the men went out to kill cattle for their use and every man who was able to ride caught himself a horse. in around the valley and upper lake and bachelor valley. there was about one thousand head of horses. and about four thousand head of cattles. so the indians lived fat for a while. Qra-Nas and Ma-Laq-Qe-Tou was chosen to watch the trail that came in from lower lake. and Shuk and Xasis was watching the trail on the west side of the valley. yom-mey-nah and ge-we-leh were watching the trail that came from eight mile valley. two—or three weeks had pass. no white man were seen on eather trail. one day. Qra-nas and ma-Laq-Qe-Tou seen two white men on horse back came over the hill. they stoped on top of the hill. they saw nothing staring around stone and kelseys place. no indians in the village. Qra-nas and Ma-Laq-Tou. went around behind a small hill to cut the white man off. the white man saw the indians trying to go around behind them. the whites turned and went back before the indians got in back of them. so three or four days went by. no more white man was seen. one day the lake watchers saw a boat came around the point. som news coming. they said to each others. two of the men went to the landing. to see what the news were. they were told that the white warriors had came to kill all the indians around the lake. so hide the best you can. the whites are making boats and with that they are coming up the lake. so we are told by the people down there. so they had two men go up on top of uncle sam mountain. the north peak. from there they watch the lower lake.for three days they watch the lake. one morning they saw a long boat came up the lake with pole on the bow with red cloth. and several of them came. every one of the boats had ten to fifteen men. the smoke signal was given by the two watchmen. every indian around the lake knew the soldiers were coming up the lake. and how many of them. and those who were watching the trail saw the infantrys coming over the hill from lower lake. these two men were watching from ash hill. they went to stones and kelseys house.from there the horsemen went down torge the lake and the soldiers went across the valley torge lakeport. they went on to scotts valley. shoot afew shoots with their big gun and went on to upper lake and camped on Emmerson hill. from there they saw the indian camp on the island. the next morning the white warriors went across in their long dugouts. the indians said they would met them in peace.so when the whites landed the indians went to wellcom them.but the white man was determined to kill them. Ge-Wi-Lih said he threw up his hands and said no harm me good man. but the white man fired and shoot him in the arm and another shoot came and hit a man staning along side of him and was killed.so they had to run and fight back; as they ran back in the tules and hed under the water; four or five of them gave alittle battle and another man was shoot in the shoulder. some of them jumped in the water and hed in the tuleys. many women and children were killed on around this island. one old lady a (indian) told about what she saw while hiding under abank,in under aover hanging tuleys. She said she saw two white man coming with their guns up in the air and on their guns hung a little girl. they brought it to the creek and threw it in the water. and alittle while later, two more men came in the same manner. this time they had a little boy on the end of their guns and also threw it in the water. alittle ways from her she, said layed awoman shoot through the shoulder. she held her little baby in her arms. two white men came running torge the woman and baby, they stabed the woman and the baby and, and threw both of them over the bank in to the water. she said she heared the woman say, O my baby; she said when they gathered the dead, they found all the little ones were killed by being stabed, and many of the woman were also killed stabing. she said it took them four or five days to gather up the dead. and the dead were all burnt on the east side by the creek. they called it the sailand creek. (Ba-Don-Bi-Da-Meh). this old lady also told about the whites hung aman on Emerson sailand this indian was met by the soldiers while marching from scotts valley to upper lake. the indian was hung and alarge fire built under the hanging indian. and another indian was caught near Emerson hill. this one was tied to atree and burnt to death.

the next morning the soldiers started for mendocino county.[7] and there killed many indians. the camp was on the ranch now known as Ed Howell ranch. the solders made camp a little ways below, bout one half mile from the indian camp. the indians wanted to surrender, but the solders did not give them time, the solders went in the camp and shoot them down as tho if they were dogs. som of them escaped by going down a little creek leading to the river. and som of them hed in the brush. and those who hed in the brush most of them were killed. and those who hed in the water was over looked. they killed mostly woman and children.

the solders caught two boys age about 14 or 15. the solders took them to lower lake, and then turned them loose, when the solders started the two boys back, they

<hr>

[7] County north of San Francisco.

loded them with meat and hard bread, one said as soon as they got out of site, they threw the meat away and som of the bread also. he said they went on a dog trot for dear life. thinking all the time that the solders would follow them and kill them. he said they would side tract once and awhile and get up on a high peak to see if the solders were coming he said when they got back that night they could nothing but crying. he said all the dead had been taken across to a large dance house had been and was cremated. wetness, Bo-Dom, or Jeo Beatti, and Krao Lah, indian-name.an old lady said her further dug a large hole in abank of the river and they hed in the hole. one old man said that he was aboy at the time he said the solders shoot his mother, she fell to the ground with her baby in her arms, he said his mother told him to climb high up in the tree.so he did and from there he said he could see the solders running about the camp and shooting the men and woman and stabing boys and girls. he said mother was not yet dead and was telling him to keep quit. two of the solders heard her talking and ran up to her and stabed her and child. and a little ways from his mother, he said laid a man dieing, holding his boy in his arms the solders also stabed him, but did not kill the boy, they took the boy to the camp, crying, they gave it every thing they could find in camp but the little boy did not quit crying. it was aboy about three years of age, when the solders were geting redy to move camp, they raped the boy up in ablanket and lief the little boy seting by the fire raped up in a blanket and was stell crying, and that boy is live today, his name is bill ball, now lives in Boonville; One Old man told me about the solders killing the indiuns in this same camp. he said young man.from the description he gave. he must have been about 18 or 20 years of age. he said he and another boy about the same age was taken by the soldurs and.he said there were two solders in charge of them. one would walk ahead and one behind them. he said the solders took him and the other boy. they both were bearfooted he said when they begin to climb the mountain between mendocino and lake country. he said they were made to keep up with the solders. thir feet were geting sore but they had to keep up with the solders. when they were climbing over the bottlerock mountain.thir feet were cutup by the rocks and thir feet were bleeding and they could not walk up with the solders. the man behind would jab them with the sharp knife fixed on the end of the gun. he said one of the solders came and looked at thir feet and went to abox opened it took a cup and diped something out of asack and brought it to them and told them both of them to hold their foots on a log near by. the solder took ahand full of the stuff and rubed it in the cuts on the bottom of their feet. he said he noticed that the stuff the solder put on their feet look like salt. sureenough it was salt. the solder tied clouth over their feet and told them not to take them off.he said the tears were roling down his cheeks. he said all the solders came and stood around them laughing. he said they roled and twested for about two hours. and they also rubed salt in the wounds on their seats and backs wher they jabed them with the solders big knife.as he call it. two or three days later the chife solder told them they could go back. they was then gaven meat and bread, all they could pack. he said they started on thir back journey. he said it was all most difficult for them to walk but raped alot of cloth around thir feet and by doing so made thir way all right. he said the meat and bread got too heavy for fast traveling so they threw the meat and some of the bread away. looking back all the time thinking that the solders would follow them and kill them. now and then they would side tract. and look back to see if the solders were following them. after seen no solders following them they would start out for another run. he said they traveled in such manner untell they got to thir home. he said to himself. hear Iam not to see my mother and sister but to see thir blood scattered over the ground like water and thir bodys for coyotes to devour. he said he sat down under a tree and cryed all day.

1932

Seattle
1786–1866

Few Native Americans have had as enduring a presence in ordinary American life as Seattle, chief of the Suquamish and Dewamish tribes. The Pacific Northwest's largest city is named in his honor. He and his predecessors maintained amiable relations with white settlers and traders for several generations—relations that were strengthened by Seattle's conversion to Christianity in the 1830s. Intent on minimizing the possible conflicts between his people and the American government, Seattle was the first Native American to sign the Treaty of Port Elliott in 1855. That agreement provided Seattle's tribe with a reservation in what is now Washington State. In many respects, Seattle's public identity encapsulated the cumulative image white Americans had found it useful to cultivate—a trustworthy, noble "savage" who had been "civilized" by Christianity and the American government's "generosity."

In 1853 the Washington Territory was organized, and a plan for the city of Seattle was prepared. Two years later, Isaac Stevens, the governor of the territory, visited the city, seeking a pledge of cooperation from the Native Americans. Seattle willingly offered that, but his response to Stevens, printed here, sought assurances that his people would be treated humanely and that their cultural differences with the white settlers would be recognized and respected. The speech was recorded by Henry Smith, a physician fluent in the tribal languages. But the existing text appears to be corrupt; white American interpolations ("pale-face," "Happy Hunting Ground," and the like) suggest that Seattle's speech has been edited to make it conform to the settlers' highly romanticized, stereotypical view of Native Americans.

Further Reading:
E. G. Anderson, *Chief Seattle*, 1943.
W. C. Vanderwerth, *Indian Oratory*, 1971.
A. Rosenteil, *Red and White: Indian Views of the White Man*, 1983.

Text:
The Washington Historical Quarterly, 1931.

"Our People Are Ebbing Away Like a Rapidly Receding Tide"[*]

Yonder sky that has wept tears of compassion upon my people for centuries untold, and which to us appears changeless and eternal, may change. Today is fair. Tomorrow it may be overcast with clouds. My words are like the stars that never change. Whatever Seattle says the great chief at Washington[1] can rely upon with as much certainty as he can upon the return of the sun or the seasons. The White Chief says that Big Chief at Washington sends us greetings of friendship and good will. This is kind of him for we know he has little need of our friendship in return. His people are many. They are like the grass that covers vast prairies. My people are few. They resemble the scattering trees of a storm-swept plain. The Great—and I presume—good White Chief sends us word that he wishes to buy our lands but is willing to allow us enough to live comfortably. This indeed appears just, even generous, for the Red Man no longer has rights that he need respect, and the offer may be wise also, as we are no longer in need of an extensive country.

There was a time when our people covered the land as the waves of a wind-ruffled sea cover its shell-paved floor, but that time long since passed away with the greatness of tribes that are now but a mournful memory. I will not dwell on, nor mourn over, our untimely decay, nor reproach my pale face brothers with hastening it as we too may have been somewhat to blame.

Youth is impulsive. When our young men grow angry at some real or imaginary wrong, and disfigure their faces with black paint, it denotes that their hearts are black —and then they are often cruel and relentless, and our old men and old women are unable to restrain them. Thus it has ever been. Thus it was when the white man first began to push our forefathers westward. But let us hope that the hostilities between us may never return. We would have everything to lose and nothing to gain. Revenge by young braves is considered gain, even at the cost of their own lives, but old men who stay at home in times of war, and mothers who have sons to lose, know better.

Our good father at Washington—for I presume he is now our father as well as yours, since King George[2] has moved his boundaries further north—our great and good father, I say, sends us word that if we do as he desires he will protect us. His brave warriors will be to us a bristling wall of strength, and his wonderful ships of war will fill our harbors so that our ancient enemies far to the northward—the Hidas and Timpsions,[3] will cease to frighten our women, children and old men. Then in reality will he be our father and we his children. But can that ever be? Your God is not our God! Your God loves your people and hates mine. He folds his strong protecting arms lovingly about the pale face and leads him by the hand as a father

---

[*] Speech delivered to Governor Isaac Stevens of the Oregon Territory, 1855.
[1] President Franklin Pierce.
[2] King of England during the American Revolution.
[3] I.e., the Haidas and Tsimshian, two Northwest Coast Indian groups living in what is now British Columbia, Canada.

leads his infant son—but He has forsaken His red children—if they are really His. Our God, the Great Spirit, seems also to have forsaken us. Your God makes your people wax strong every day. Soon they will fill all the land. Our people are ebbing away like a rapidly receding tide that will never return. The white man's God can not love our people or He would protect them. They seem to be orphans who can look nowhere for help. How then can we be brothers? How can your God become our God and renew our prosperity and awaken in us dreams of returning greatness. If we have a common Heavenly Father He must be partial—for He came to His pale-face[4] children. We never saw Him. He gave you laws but had no word for His red children whose teeming multitudes once filled this vast continent as stars fill the firmament. No. We are two distinct races with separate origins and separate destinies. There is little in common between us.

To us the ashes of our ancestors are sacred and their resting place is hallowed ground. You wander far from the graves of your ancestors and seemingly without regret. Your religion was written on tables of stone by the iron finger of your God so that you could not forget. The Red Man could never comprehend nor remember it. Our religion is the traditions of our ancestors—the dreams of our old men, given them in the solemn hours of night by the Great Spirit; and the visions of our sachems, and is written in the hearts of our people.

Your dead cease to love you and the land of their nativity as soon as they pass the portals of the tomb and wander away beyond the stars. They are soon forgotten and never return. Our dead never forget the beautiful world that gave them being. They still love its verdant valleys, its murmuring rivers, its magnificent mountains, sequestered vales and verdant-lined lakes and bays, and ever yearn in tender, fond affection over the lonely hearted living, and often return from the Happy Hunting Ground to visit, guide, console and comfort them.

Day and night can not dwell together. The Red Man has ever fled the approach of the White Man as the morning mist flees before the rising sun.

However, your proposition seems fair, and I think that my folks will accept it and will retire to the reservation you offer them. Then we will dwell apart in peace for the words of the Great White Chief seem to be the voice of Nature speaking to my people out of dense darkness.

It matters little where we pass the remnant of our days. They will not be many. The Indian's night promises to be dark. Not a single star of hope hovers above his horizon. Sad-voiced winds moan in the distance. Grim Nemesis[5] seems to be on the Red Man's trail, and wherever he goes he will hear the approaching footsteps of his fell destroyer and prepare to stolidly meet his doom, as does the wounded doe that hears the approaching footsteps of the hunter.

A few more moons. A few more winters—and not one of the descendants of the mighty hosts that once moved over this broad land or lived in happy homes, protected by the Great Spirit, will remain to mourn over the graves of a people—once more powerful and hopeful than yours. But why should I mourn at the untimely fate of my people? Tribe follows tribe, and nation follows nation, like the waves of the sea.

---

[4] This and terms that follow, such as "Happy Hunting Ground" and "a few more moons," suggest that the text has been heavily edited by

white Americans to conform to stereotypes of Indian speech.

[5] Retribution.

It is the order of nature, and regret is useless. Your time of decay may be distant—but it will surely come, for even the White Man whose God walked and talked with him as friend with friend, can not be exempt from the common destiny. We may be brothers after all. We will see.

We will ponder your proposition and when we decide we will let you know. But should we accept it, I here and now make this condition—that we will not be denied the privilege without molestation, of visiting at any time the tombs of our ancestors, friends and children. Every part of this soil is sacred, in the estimation of my people. Every hillside, every valley, every plain and grove, has been hallowed by some sad or happy event in days long vanished. Even the rocks, which seem to be dumb and dead as they swelter in the sun along the silent shore thrill with memories of stirring events connected with the lives of my people, and the very dust upon which you now stand responds more lovingly to their footsteps than to yours, because it is rich with the dust of our ancestors and our bare feet are conscious of the sympathetic touch. Our departed braves, fond mothers, glad, happy-hearted maidens, and even the little children who lived here and rejoiced here for a brief season, still love these sombre solitudes and at eventide they grow shadowy of returning spirits. And when the last Red Man shall have perished, and the memory of my tribe shall have become a myth among the white man, these shores will swarm with the invisible dead of my tribe, and when your children's children think themselves alone in the field, the store, the shop, upon the highway, or in the silence of the pathless woods, they will not be alone. In all the earth there is no place dedicated to solitude. At night when the streets of your cities and villages are silent and you think them deserted, they will throng with the returning hosts that once filled them and still love this beautiful land. The White Man will never be alone.

Let him be just and deal kindly with my people, for the dead are not powerless. Dead—I say? There is no death. Only a change of worlds.

1855/1931

Alexander Lawrence Posey
1873–1908

One of the best-known Native American humorists and journalists, Alexander Posey also wrote some of the most compelling Native American poetry in the late nineteenth and early twentieth centuries. Alexander Posey was born in what is now McIntosh County, Oklahoma, on August 3, 1873, the son of a Creek mother and a part-Creek, part–Scots-Irish father. Alexander Posey learned English at the age of twelve from a private teacher whom he later described as "a dried-up, hard-up, weazen-faced, irritable fellow." Posey began publishing essays on Indian affairs while studying at the Indian University in what was then the Oklahoma Territory. He entered public life in 1895 when he was elected to the Creek Nation's House of Warriors. His fluency in both Creek and English as well as his honesty and sense of responsibility earned him membership on virtually every important tribal council until his death in 1908 from drowning.

In 1896 Posey served as superintendent of the Creek Orphan Asylum and, beginning in 1897, as superintendent of public instruction for the Creek Nation. In 1902 Posey started a two-year stint as editor of the still-publishing *Indian Journal,* where he printed a series of political satires under the heading "Fus Fixico Letters" (meaning "bird with no heart") and became a strong advocate of statehood for Oklahoma, which he proposed calling Sequoyah. During this same period Posey also wrote a great deal of poetry, much of which was printed over the pseudonym "Chinnubbie Harjo," an evil genius in Creek myth. "All of my people are poets," Posey proclaimed, "natural-born poets, gifted with wonderful imaginative power and the ability to express in sonorous, musical phrases their impressions of life and nature." In the poems printed here, Posey applies those skills to commemorating two Creeks who articulated and defended their nation's rights.

Further Reading:
D. Challacombe, "Alexander Lawrence Posey," *Chronicles of Oklahoma,* 1933.
L. G. Barnett, "Este Cate Emunkv: Red Man Always," *Chronicles of Oklahoma,* 1968.

Text:
The Poems of Alexander Lawrence Posey, ed. with "Memoir" by W. E. Connelly, 1910. See also "Journal of Alexander Lawrence Posey with Annotations, January 1–September 4, 1897," ed. E. E. Dale, *Chronicles of Oklahoma,* 1967–1968.

Ode to Sequoyah[1]

The names of Waitie and Boudinot[2]—
   The valiant warrior and gifted sage—
And other Cherokees, may be forgot,
   But thy name shall descend to every age;
The mysteries enshrouding Cadmus'[3] name   5
Cannot obscure thy claim to fame.

The people's language cannot perish—nay,
   When from the face of this great continent
Inevitable doom hath swept away
   The last memorial—the last fragment   10
Of tribes,—some scholar learned shall pore
Upon thy letters, seeking ancient lore.

[1] Posey's note: "SEQUOYAH—The Cherokee who invented the Cherokee alphabet."
[2] Elias Boudinot, founder of the *Cherokee Phœnix* newspaper and advocate of Cherokee culture and human rights.
[3] Cadmus: perhaps the Phoenician prince who killed a dragon and sowed its teeth, from which sprang up an army of men who fought one another until only five survived; with these Cadmus founded the city of Thebes.

Some bard shall lift a voice in praise of thee,
In moving numbers tell the world how men
Scoffed thee, hissed thee, charged with lunacy!   15
And who could not give 'nough honor when
At length, in spite of jeers, of want and need,
Thy genius shaped a dream into a deed.

By cloud-capped summits in the boundless west,[4]
Or mighty river rolling to the sea,   20
Where'er thy footsteps led thee on that quest,
Unknown, rest thee, illustrious Cherokee!

1910

On the Capture and Imprisonment of Crazy Snake[1]

January, 1900

Down with him! chain him! bind him fast!
Slam to the iron door and turn the key!
The one true Creek, perhaps the last
To dare declare, "You have wronged me!"
Defiant, stoical, silent,   5
Suffers imprisonment!

Such coarse black hair! such eagle eye!
Such stately mien!—how arrow-straight!
Such will! such courage to defy
The powerful makers of his fate!   10
A traitor, outlaw,—what you will,
He is the noble red man still.

Condemn him and his kind to shame!
I bow to him, exalt his name!   15

1910

---

[4] Posey's note: "Sequoyah wandered away from his tribe, and died somewhere in the southwest part of the United States or in Mexico."
[1] Posey's note: "CRAZY SNAKE—Chitto Harjo. The leader of a band of Creeks who oppose the abolishment of their tribal rights. Several times Harjo has been imprisoned because of his defying the United States authorities."

Washington Irving
1783–1859

Washington Irving's life spans virtually all of American history and culture from the Revolution to the Civil War. Celebrated both at home and abroad as the dean of American letters, Irving lived to see his writings translated into twelve languages and printed in more than fifty different editions. His essays and sketches earned the respect of Europe's leading intellectuals and the praise of such prominent English writers as Coleridge, Byron, Scott, and Dickens. The influential London *Athenaeum* credited Irving with having declared America's literary independence. He was universally regarded, in the words of the Victorian novelist William Makepeace Thackeray, as "the first Ambassador whom the New World of Letters sent to the Old." Irving's immense popularity reflected his mastery of the leading aesthetic assumptions of the times. The Neoclassical wit and satire of his early essays and the Romantic interest in atmosphere and sentiment of his later sketches constitute a compendium of American literary taste in the first half of the nineteenth century. His anxieties as a writer offer an enlightening introduction to the cultural preoccupations of the new republic, and his accomplishments remain a harbinger of the literary achievements of the American Renaissance.

Washington Irving was born in New York's lower Manhattan in April 1783, a few days before Congress ratified the preliminary treaty ending the Revolutionary War; he was named after the war's most prominent hero. The youngest of eleven children, Irving grew up in a home bristling with Federalist sentiments and Calvinist principles; his father, a Scottish hardware merchant, is said to have "led the children to believe all pleasures were wicked." Although the New York of Irving's youth was hardly the bustling metropolis Walt Whitman would celebrate in *Leaves of Grass* (1855), the city's abundant supply of Dutch and British cultural traditions did provide this frail child with a great deal of fascinating folklore to explore. His relatively brief formal schooling took place in the city's private academies, but his more enduring education occurred along the city's streets and piers listening to merchants and seamen weave homespun tales of adventure and romance.

Washington Irving took a very early interest in writing and, much like Benjamin Franklin before him, modeled his first work on the familiar essays of Addison and Steele's *Spectator,* also publishing them under a pseudonym in the newspaper his brother edited. His first published writing, a series of nine essays written at the age of nineteen and printed over the signature "Jonathan, Oldstyle, Gent.," lightly satirizes American political, social, and literary provincialism and earned Irving modest critical attention. The pseudonym Irving used in these essays —a combination of the British nickname for American patriots and the name of the calendar abandoned by England and the colonies in 1752—reflects the lifelong tension he felt between the lure of literary nationalism and a reliance on European cultural forms.

Irving had studied law, but in 1803 he eagerly interrupted his work as a law clerk (he assisted the judge who had tried Aaron Burr for treason) to travel through the frontier of upper New York State and eastern Canada. The threat of tuberculosis prompted Irving's family to send him to Europe in 1804. In Rome he met the American painter Washington Allston and flirted with the idea of taking up art. His notebooks from this two-year tour reveal a burgeoning interest in writing and contain a wealth of material to be used later in his essays and sketches. He returned to the United States not only in better health but also with greater sensitivity to American provincialism. He was admitted to the New York bar in 1806, but, like such later distinguished American literary figures as James Russell Lowell and Sidney Lanier, Irving practiced in a desultory fashion, preferring to spend his time cultivating his interests in current political and cultural affairs and nurturing his friendships with several like-minded young professionals. This group, loosely assembled under such names as the Nine Worthies, the Ancient Club of New York, and (Irving's own favorite) the Lads of Kilkenny, consisted of well-to-do and well-read bachelors intent on displaying their wit and sophistication in New York's taverns and literary circles.

The spirit of this group is best represented in Irving's first major literary venture, *Salmagundi; or, the Whim-Whams and Opinions of Launcelot Langstaff, Esq., and Others* (1807–1808). Published in collaboration with his brother William and James Kirke Paulding, this series of twenty pocket-sized pamphlets was lightheartedly addressed to "critics, amateurs, dilettanti, and cognoscenti" and intended "to instruct the young, reform the old, correct the town, and castigate the age." They named their magazine after a spicy hash and developed it into a delightful intellectual potpourri of social criticism, literary reviews, and lampoons of the latest trends in politics and the theater. Yet each issue also contained a healthy measure of self-parody; the editors recognized they could be as naive and sentimental about progress as the people they ridiculed.

The immediate success of *Salmagundi* drew the attention of numerous writers. It quickly became the gravitational center of a literary circle that eventually became known as the Knickerbocker school. This group included such writers as Fitz-Greene Halleck, Joseph Rodman Drake, Samuel Woodworth, and the authors of such American popular classics as "Home, Sweet Home" (John Howard Payne) and "A Visit from St. Nicholas" (Clement Clark Moore). William Cullen Bryant and James Fenimore Cooper were also identified with this "school." In virtually every case, however, the association of these writers was more geographic than aesthetic. But as soon as Washington Irving had published Diedrich Knickerbocker's *History of New York* (1809), the label would prove hard to escape.

A History of New York, from the Beginning of the World to the End of the Dutch Dynasty, by Diedrich Knickerbocker was intended as a burlesque of the methods of contemporary historians, more particularly those of Dr. Samuel Mitchell in his *Pictures of New York; or the Traveller's Guide through the Commercial Metropolis of the United States* (1807). The eight books of Irving's *History* provide a caustic view of New York's Dutch colonial history, interspersed with satiric portraits of current politics and literature, including Thomas Jefferson's vision of democracy and Joel Barlow's and Timothy Dwight's efforts to create epic poetry for the new republic. The book brought Irving extraordinary financial success, earning several thousand dollars in royalties at a time when nearly all authors had to underwrite the costs of publishing their work. Irving also enjoyed international acclaim; Sir Walter Scott praised the work in what undoubtedly were then extravagant terms: "I have never read anything so closely resembling the style of Dean Swift, as the annals of Diedrich Knickerbocker."

Irving remained a Federalist in politics and culture throughout his life. His critics accused him of being a dandy and an Anglophile whose American identity as a writer was more a matter of birth than sensibility. Yet Irving's early work had dealt directly—and most often satirically—with the issue most central to an American writer's identity, the absence of a native cultural tradition. Having exhausted what he saw as the possibilities of cultural satire, Irving lapsed into nearly a ten-year lull as a writer.

His prolonged literary silence is generally attributed to the psychological malaise that attended the death of his young fiancée, Matilda Hoffman, but more particularly it well may be the lingering result of what he viewed as the cultural vacuum in America. Irving filled these ten years with numerous, although irregular, activities. He traveled among the social circles of New York, Philadelphia, and Washington; he signed on as a partner in a brother's cutlery firm; he saw brief service as a staff adjutant in the War of 1812; he edited— anonymously—Philadelphia's *Analectic* magazine, in which he printed both excerpts from British periodicals and commissioned occasional essays.

What might be called the second phase of Irving's career began in 1815 with his second trip to Europe. He remained there for the next seventeen years. Ostensibly, Irving had traveled to Europe to help manage the Liverpool office of his family's importing business, but he may also have been seeking circumstances more conducive to his literary interests. Within three years, the family business had collapsed into bankruptcy and Irving had decided to gamble on making a living as a writer.

Irving's years in Europe regenerated his creative energies. Encouraged by Scott, Irving discovered the literary potential of the English countryside in the works of the Romantic poets. He resolved to adapt Europe's rich cultural heritage to American settings. The principal expression of this interest was *The Sketch Book* (1819–1820), a compendium of gracefully written familiar essays nostalgically surveying the traditions of English life ("The Christmas Dinner," "A Sunday in London," "Westminster Abbey"), along with six chapters on American scenes, including two Americanized renditions of European folktales, among them "Rip Van Winkle." Published in several installments, *The Sketch Book* captured unprecedented attention for an American work. Irving had become the first American to command an international audience. As Geoffrey Crayon, the pseudonym he used in writing *The Sketch Book,* Irving had also become a literary celebrity. Although he was viewed slightly condescendingly by the English (as an American who writes as though he were English), he was lionized as a figure of national pride in the United States. *The Sketch Book* had answered one British critic's challenge: "In the four quarters of the globe, who reads an American book?"

Irving's accomplishments in *The Sketch Book* transcend his use of picturesque Hudson Valley local color to create a realistic context for stories adapted from

European sources. "Rip Van Winkle" also highlights concerns fundamental to appreciating American literary history: the role of the imagination in a society devoted to material progress, the marginal identity of the artist in American life, the sense of loss implicit in America's commitment to the present and future while neglecting the past, and the urgent need to establish a specifically American historical context. At the same time, *The Sketch Book* expresses the American writer's need to create what the critic Richard Poirier has called "a world elsewhere," a place (in this case Sleepy Hollow) where and a time (colonial America) when the imagination might flourish. Later American writers would locate this "world" in colonial Salem (Nathaniel Hawthorne), Walden Pond (Henry David Thoreau), the boundless ocean (Herman Melville), the splendid Mississippi (Mark Twain), and Yoknapatawpha County (William Faulkner), to name but a few.

Washington Irving spent the early 1820s searching the Continent for additional literary material, all the while enjoying the the literary status afforded him in London, Paris, Dresden, and Vienna. His next work, *Bracebridge Hall* (1822), an account of life in preindustrial England, contained little of the thematic focus and the stylistic energy of *The Sketch Book,* but it was equally well received. After collaborating with J. H. Payne on writing and producing several plays in France, Irving published—to uniformly discouraging reviews—*Tales of a Traveller* (1824), an unsuccessful blend of German and American folklore. Two unproductive years followed in France before he served as a diplomatic attaché in Spain (1826–1829). There he began translating Martin Fernández de Navarette's life of Columbus, recognizing in Columbus's life a predicament quite similar to his own as a figure torn between the Old World and the New. He soon abandoned the translation, immersed himself in archival records, and produced an erudite but popular *History of the Life and Voyages of Christopher Columbus* (1828), followed by *A Chronicle of the Conquest of Granada* (1829) and *The Alhambra* (1832), which the American historian William Hickling Prescott judged "a beautiful Spanish Sketch-Book."* Before returning to the United States in 1832, Irving served for nearly three years as secretary to the American legation in London.

When challenged to explain whether his protracted absence from the United States indicated that he had renounced his native land, Irving replied, "I am endeavouring to serve my country. Whatever I have written has been written with the feelings and published as the writing of an American. Is that renouncing my country? How else am I to serve my country—by coming home and begging an office of it: which I should not have the kind of talent or the business habits requisite to fill?—If I can do any good in this world it is with my pen." Irving's sense of dislocation, if not alienation, during his seventeen years in Europe anticipates the experiences of later American writers, including Henry James and the prominent figures in what has come to be known as the "Lost Generation": Ezra Pound, T. S. Eliot, Gertrude Stein, and Ernest Hemingway.

The final phase of Irving's career began with his triumphant return to the United States. He brought with him an honorary degree from Oxford, the medal of the Royal Society of Literature, and an international reputation unprecedented for an American writer. Soon after his arrival, he set out for a tour of the American South and West. The diary of his adventurous experiences on the

Oklahoma frontier formed the basis for his autobiographical narrative *A Tour of the Prairies,* printed as the first volume of *The Crayon Miscellany* (1835). The book marks another significant shift in Irving's work, from the detached cynicism of Jonathan Oldstyle and the reserve of Geoffrey Crayon to direct authorial participation in *A Tour.* As Irving moves farther into the Plains, he gradually sheds his storyteller's distance and interest in romance and recounts each successive primitive incident with far less ironic detachment. The later portions of *A Tour* may be seen as Irving's own dramatic initiation into what are often the violent rituals of establishing a distinctively American identity.

Irving settled in New York for the decade following his western tour. He published two additional books based on this trip: *Astoria* (1836), an account of John Jacob Astor's fur-trading empire, and *The Adventures of Captain Bonneville, U.S.A.* (1837). He also cultivated his interests in antiquarian subjects and American biography. He declined invitations to run for election as mayor of New York City and later to serve as secretary of the navy under President Van Buren. But Irving did return to Europe in 1842 as minister to Spain, the first in a line of literary figures—including James Russell Lowell, Nathaniel Hawthorne, Bret Harte, and William Dean Howells—to serve their country as foreign ministers. After three years in Spain, Irving spent a year in London negotiating a diplomatic resolution to the Oregon question. He returned to the United States in 1846 and spent his last years at Sunnyside, his country retreat near Tarrytown, New York, to enjoy his literary preeminence and to continue writing.

Preoccupied with biography during his final years, Irving published a study of the English writer Oliver Goldsmith in 1840 and the two-volume *Mahomet and His Successors* in 1849 and 1850. In 1859, the year he died, Irving completed a massive five-volume biography of George Washington. He planned the biography as early as 1825 and had been absorbed in the details of Washington's life ever since. He recognized in Washington's life the instructive paradigm for the American experience that he judged the new nation needed. He regarded the project as something of a prose epic and as an opportunity for America to re-create a distinguished past for itself worthy of its imagined future greatness.

Washington Irving's career as a writer paralleled the new nation's as a culture. His literary career reflects both the cultural anxiety of the new republic and its growing self-assurance in the years immediately preceding the Civil War. In this respect, Irving's work illustrates with striking clarity the early struggle of American culture to establish its autonomy. Many prominent American writers in the nineteenth century, from James Fenimore Cooper to Henry James, claimed that America lacked subject matter suitable for literature. Yet, as Irving's work suggests, the problem was not as much the paucity of American experience as it was that such experience was resistant to the European forms imposed on it. As Irving eventually discovered, the literary models available to American writers in the early decades of the nineteenth century were inappropriate—or inadequate— to the experiences they were expected to transform. This problem often left the literature of the new republic either fragmented or derivative. Irving's struggles with this problem illustrate rather than resolve America's efforts to establish cultural independence. Years before James Fenimore Cooper, Nathaniel Hawthorne, and Henry James investigated the nature of the American identity,

Washington Irving recognized the artistic problems implicit in forging a distinctively new American prespective from inherited English traditions. Despite the derivative nature of a good deal of Irving's writing, he helped develop the American short story and secured the legitimacy of American authorship. Irving's work remains not only a hallmark of the new nation's literary tastes but also a projection of new patterns of vision responsive to a new cultural context.

Further Reading:
V. W. Brooks, *The World of Washington Irving*, 1950.
S. T. Williams, *The Life of Washington Irving*, 1935.
E. Wagenknecht, *Washington Irving: Moderation Displayed*, 1962.
L. Leary, *Irving*, 1963.
W. L. Hedges, *Washington Irving: An American Study, 1802–1832*, 1965.
D. Ringe, *The Pictorial Mode: Space and Time in the Art of Bryant, Irving, and Cooper*, 1971.
A. B. Myer, *Washington Irving: A Tribute*, 1972.
M. Roth, *Comedy and America: The Lost World of Washington Irving*, 1976.
A. B. Myer, *A Century of Commentary on the Works of Washington Irving*, 1976.
H. Springer, *Washington Irving: A Reference Guide*, 1976.

Text:
The Works of Washington Irving, 1860.
A definitive edition of Washington Irving's writing, under the general editorship of Richard Dilworth Rust, is scheduled for completion in 1986.

---

from The Sketch Book*

The Author's Account of Himself

> *"I am of this mind with Homer, that as the snaile that crept out of her shel was turned eftsoons into a toad, and thereby was forced to make a stoole to sit on; so the traveller that stragleth from his owne country is in a short time transformed into so monstrous a shape, that he is faine to alter his mansion with his manners, and to live where he can, not where he would."*
>
> Lyly's *Euphues*[1]

I was always fond of visiting new scenes, and observing strange characters and manners. Even when a mere child I began my travels, and made many tours of discovery into foreign parts and unknown regions of my native city, to the frequent alarm of my parents, and the emolument of the town-crier. As I grew into boyhood, I extended the range of my observations. My holiday afternoons were spent in rambles about the surrounding country. I made myself familiar with all its places famous in

---

* This essay and two others were originally published in 1819–1820 as *The Sketch Book of Geoffrey Crayon, Gent*, which incorporates an adopted pseudonym for Irving. The *Sketch Book* was later revised and expanded to include 32 tales and sketches.
[1] From *Euphues and his England* (1580), a prose romance by John Lyly (1554?–1606).

history or fable. I knew every spot where a murder or robbery had been committed, or a ghost seen. I visited the neighboring villages, and added greatly to my stock of knowledge, by noting their habits and customs, and conversing with their sages and great men. I even journeyed one long summer's day to the summit of the most distant hill, whence I stretched my eye over many a mile of terra incognita,[2] and was astonished to find how vast a globe I inhabited.

This rambling propensity strengthened with my years. Books of voyages and travels became my passion, and in devouring their contents, I neglected the regular exercises of the school. How wistfully would I wander about the pierheads in fine weather, and watch the parting ships, bound to distant climes—with what longing eyes would I gaze after their lessening sails, and waft myself in imagination to the ends of the earth!

Further reading and thinking, though they brought this vague inclination into more reasonable bounds, only served to make it more decided. I visited various parts of my own country; and had I been merely a lover of fine scenery, I should have felt little desire to seek elsewhere its gratification, for on no country have the charms of nature been more prodigally lavished. Her mighty lakes, like oceans of liquid silver; her mountains, with their bright aerial tints; her valleys, teeming with wild fertility; her tremendous cataracts, thundering in their solitudes; her boundless plains, waving with spontaneous verdure; her broad deep rivers, rolling in solemn silence to the ocean; her trackless forests, where vegetation puts forth all its magnificence; her skies, kindling with the magic of summer clouds and glorious sunshine;—no, never need an American look beyond his own country for the sublime and beautiful of natural scenery.

But Europe held forth the charms of storied and poetical association. There were to be seen the masterpiece of art, the refinements of highly-cultivated society, the quaint peculiarities of ancient and local custom. My native country was full of youthful promise: Europe was rich in the accumulated treasures of age. Her very ruins told the history of times gone by, and every mouldering stone was a chronicle. I longed to wander over the scenes of renowned achievement—to tread, as it were, in the footsteps of antiquity—to loiter about the ruined castle—to meditate on the falling tower—to escape, in short, from the common-place realities of the present, and lose myself among the shadowy grandeurs of the past.

I had, beside all this, an earnest desire to see the great men of the earth. We have, it is true, our great men in America: not a city but has an ample share of them. I have mingled among them in my time, and been almost withered by the shade into which they cast me; for there is nothing so baleful to a small man as the shade of a great one, particularly the great man of a city. But I was anxious to see the great men of Europe; for I had read in the works of various philosophers, that all animals degenerated in America, and man among the number.[3] A great man of Europe, thought I, must therefore be as superior to a great man of America, as a peak of the Alps to a highland of the Hudson; and in this idea I was confirmed, by observing the comparative importance and swelling magnitude of many English travellers

---

[2] Latin: "unknown land."
[3] Georges Louis Leclerc de Buffon (1707–1788), a French naturalist, concluded that the American environment would cause the physical degeneration of European emigrants.

among us, who, I was assured, were very little people in their own country. I will visit this land of wonders, thought I, and see the gigantic race from which I am degenerated.

It has been either my good or evil lot to have my roving passion gratified. I have wandered through different countries, and witnessed many of the shifting scenes of life. I cannot say that I have studied them with the eye of a philosopher; but rather with the sauntering gaze with which humble lovers of the picturesque stroll from the window of one print-shop to another; caught sometimes by the delineations of beauty, sometimes by the distortions of caricature, and sometimes by the loveliness of landscape. As it is the fashion for modern tourists to travel pencil in hand, and bring home their portfolios filled with sketches, I am disposed to get up a few for the entertainment of my friends. When, however, I look over the hints and memorandums I have taken down for the purpose, my heart almost fails me at finding how my idle humor has led me aside from the great objects studied by every regular traveller who would make a book. I fear I shall give equal disappointment with an unlucky landscape painter, who had travelled on the continent, but, following the bent of his vagrant inclination, had sketched in nooks, and corners, and by-places. His sketch-book was accordingly crowded with cottages, and landscapes, and obscure ruins; but he had neglected to paint St. Peter's, or the Coliseum; the cascade of Terni,[4] or the bay of Naples; and had not a single glacier or volcano in his whole collection.

Rip Van Winkle[5]

A posthumous writing of Diedrich Knickerbocker

By Woden,[6] God of Sacons,
From whence comes Wensday, that is Wodensday.
Truth is a thing that ever I will keep
Unto thylke day in which I creep into
My sepulchre—
                    Cartwright[7]

[The following Tale was found among the papers of the late Diedrich Knickerbocker, an old gentleman of New York, who was very curious in the Dutch history of the province, and the manners of the descendants from its primitive settlers. His historical researches, however, did not lie so much among books as among men; for the former are lamentably scanty on his favorite topics; whereas he found the old burghers, and still more their wives, rich in that legendary lore, so invaluable to true history. Whenever, therefore, he happened upon a genuine Dutch family, snugly shut up in its low-roofed farmhouse, under a spreading sycamore, he looked upon it as a little clasped volume of black-letter,[8] and studied it with the zeal of a book-worm.

The result of all these researches was a history of the province during the reign

---

[4] Famous waterfalls in central Italy.
[5] "Rip Van Winkle" and "The Legend of Sleepy Hollow" are adaptations of German folk legends.
[6] In Norse mythology, supreme god and creator.

[7] From *The Ordinary* (1651) by English playwright William Cartwright (1611–1643).
[8] Typeface used in early printed books, now called Gothic or Old English.

of the Dutch governors, which he published some years since. There have been various opinions as to the literary character of his work, and, to tell the truth, it is not a whit better than it should be. Its chief merit is its scrupulous accuracy, which indeed was a little questioned on its first appearance, but has since been completely established; and it is now admitted into all historical collections, as a book of unquestionable authority.

The old gentleman died shortly after the publication of his work, and now that he is dead and gone, it cannot do much harm to his memory to say that his time might have been much better employed in weightier labors. He, however, was apt to ride his hobby his own way; and though it did now and then kick up the dust a little in the eyes of his neighbors, and grieve the spirit of some friends, for whom he felt the truest deference and affection; yet his errors and follies are remembered "more in sorrow than in anger,"[9] and it begins to be suspected, that he never intended to injure or offend. But however his memory may be appreciated by critics, it is still held dear by many folk, whose good opinion is well worth having; particularly by certain biscuit-bakers, who have gone so far as to imprint his likeness on their new-year cakes; and have thus given him a chance for immortality, almost equal to the being stamped on a Waterloo Medal,[10] or a Queen Anne's Farthing.][11]

Whoever has made a voyage up the Hudson must remember the Kaatskill[12] mountains. They are a dismembered branch of the great Appalachian family, and are seen away to the west of the river, swelling up to a noble height, and lording it over the surrounding country. Every change of season, every change of weather, indeed, every hour of the day, produces some change in the magical hues and shapes of these mountains, and they are regarded by all the good wives, far and near, as perfect barometers. When the weather is fair and settled, they are clothed in blue and purple, and print their bold outlines on the clear evening sky; but, sometimes, when the rest of the landscape is cloudless, they will gather a hood of gray vapors about their summits, which, in the last rays of the setting sun, will glow and light up like a crown of glory.

At the foot of these fairy mountains, the voyager may have descried the light smoke curling up from a village, whose shingle-roofs gleam among the trees, just where the blue tints of the upland melt away into the fresh green of the nearer landscape. It is a little village, of great antiquity, having been founded by some of the Dutch colonists, in the early times of the province, just about the beginning of the government of the good Peter Stuyvesant,[13] (may he rest in peace!) and there were some of the houses of the original settlers standing within a few years, built of small yellow bricks brought from Holland, having latticed windows and gable fronts, surmounted with weather-cocks.

In that same village, and in one of these very houses (which, to tell the precise truth, was sadly time-worn and weather-beaten), there lived many years since, while the country was yet a province of Great Britain, a simple good-natured fellow, of the name of Rip Van Winkle. He was a descendant of the Van Winkles who

---

[9] Shakespeare's *Hamlet*, Act I, Sc. ii, l. 232.
[10] The Waterloo Medal was minted after the British defeat of Napoleon in 1815.
[11] Farthing: English coin of small value.

[12] The Catskills in southeastern New York.
[13] Last governor of the Dutch province of New Netherlands (1647–1664).

figured so gallantly in the chivalrous days of Peter Stuyvesant, and accompanied him to the siege of Fort Christina.[14] He inherited, however, but little of the martial character of his ancestors. I have observed that he was a simple good-natured man; he was, moreover, a kind neighbor, and an obedient hen-pecked husband. Indeed, to the latter circumstance might be owing that meekness of spirit which gained him such universal popularity; for those men are most apt to be obsequious and conciliating abroad, who are under the discipline of shrews at home. Their tempers, doubtless, are rendered pliant and malleable in the fiery furnace of domestic tribulation; and a curtain lecture[15] is worth all the sermons in the world for teaching the virtues of patience and long-suffering. A termagant wife may, therefore, in some respects, be considered a tolerable blessing; and if so, Rip Van Winkle was thrice blessed.

Certain it is, that he was a great favorite among all the good wives of the village, who, as usual, with the amiable sex, took his part in all family squabbles; and never failed, whenever they talked those matters over in their evening gossipings, to lay all the blame on Dame Van Winkle. The children of the village, too, would shout with joy whenever he approached. He assisted at their sports, made their playthings, taught them to fly kites and shoot marbles, and told them long stories of ghosts, witches, and Indians. Whenever he went dodging about the village, he was surrounded by a troop of them, hanging on his skirts, clambering on his back, and playing a thousand tricks on him with impunity; and not a dog would bark at him throughout the neighborhood.

The great error in Rip's composition was an insuperable aversion to all kinds of profitable labor. It could not be from the want of assiduity or perseverance; for he would sit on a wet rock, with a rod as long and heavy as a Tartar's lance, and fish all day without a murmur, even though he should not be encouraged by a single nibble. He would carry a fowling-piece on his shoulder for hours together, trudging through woods and swamps, and up hill and down dale, to shoot a few squirrels or wild pigeons. He would never refuse to assist a neighbor even in the roughest toil, and was a foremost man at all country frolics for husking Indian corn, or building stone-fences; the women of the village, too, used to employ him to run their errands, and to do such little odd jobs as their less obliging husbands would not do for them. In a word Rip was ready to attend to anybody's business but his own; but as to doing family duty, and keeping his farm in order, he found it impossible.

In fact, he declared it was of no use to work on his farm; it was the most pestilent little piece of ground in the whole country; every thing about it went wrong, and would go wrong, in spite of him. His fences were continually falling to pieces; his cow would either go astray, or get among the cabbages; weeds were sure to grow quicker in his fields than anywhere else; the rain always made a point of setting in just as he had some out-door work to do; so that though his patrimonial estate had dwindled away under his management, acre by acre, until there was little more left than a mere patch of Indian corn and potatoes, yet it was the worst conditioned farm in the neighborhood.

[14] Peter Stuyvesant (1592–1672) led Dutch forces in defeating the Swedish colonists at Fort Christina on the Delaware in 1655.

[15] Tirade delivered by an angry wife from behind her bed curtains.

His children, too, were as ragged and wild as if they belonged to nobody. His son Rip, an urchin begotten in his own likeness, promised to inherit the habits, with the old clothes of his father. He was generally seen trooping like a colt at his mother's heels, equipped in a pair of his father's cast-off galligaskins, which he had much ado to hold up with one hand, as a fine lady does her train in bad weather.

Rip Van Winkle, however, was one of those happy mortals, of foolish, well-oiled dispositions, who take the world easy, eat white bread or brown, whichever can be got with least thought or trouble, and would rather starve on a penny than work for a pound. If left to himself, he would have whistled life away in perfect contentment; but his wife kept continually dinning in his ears about his idleness, his carelessness, and the ruin he was bringing on his family. Morning, noon, and night, her tongue was incessantly going, and every thing he said or did was sure to produce a torrent of household eloquence. Rip had but one way of replying to all lectures of the kind, and that, by frequent use, had grown into a habit. He shrugged his shoulders, shook his head, cast up his eyes, but said nothing. This, however, always provoked a fresh volley from his wife; so that he was fain to draw off his forces, and take to the outside of the house—the only side which, in truth, belongs to a hen-pecked husband.

Rip's sole domestic adherent was his dog Wolf, who was as much hen-pecked as his master; for Dame Van Winkle regarded them as companions in idleness, and even looked upon Wolf with an evil eye, as the cause of his master's going so often astray. True it is, in all points of spirit befitting an honorable dog, he was as courageous an animal as ever scoured the woods—but what courage can withstand the everduring and all-besetting terrors of a woman's tongue? The moment Wolf entered the house his crest fell, his tail drooped to the ground, or curled between his legs, he sneaked about with a gallows air, casting many a sidelong glance at Dame Van Winkle, and at the least flourish of a broomstick or ladle, he would fly to the door with yelping precipitation.

Times grew worse and worse with Rip Van Winkle as years of matrimony rolled on; a tart temper never mellows with age, and a sharp tongue is the only edged tool that grows keener with constant use. For a long while he used to console himself, when driven from home, by frequenting a kind of perpetual club of the sages, philosophers, and other idle personages of the village; which held its sessions on a bench before a small inn, designated by a rubicund portrait of His Majesty George the Third. Here they used to sit in the shade through a long lazy summer's day, talking listlessly over village gossip, or telling endless sleepy stories about nothing. But it would have been worth any statesman's money to have heard the profound discussions that sometimes took place, when by chance an old newspaper fell into their hands from some passing traveller. How solemnly they would listen to the contents, as drawled out by Derrick Van Bummel, the schoolmaster, a dapper learned little man, who was not to be daunted by the most gigantic word in the dictionary; and how sagely they would deliberate upon public events some months after they had taken place.

The opinions of this junto[16] were completely controlled by Nicholas Vedder, a patriarch of the village, and landlord of the inn, at the door of which he took his seat from morning till night, just moving sufficiently to avoid the sun and keep in the shade of a large tree; so that the neighbors could tell the hour by his movements

[16] Committee or caucus.

as accurately as by a sun-dial. It is true he was rarely heard to speak, but smoked his pipe incessantly. His adherents, however (for every great man has his adherents), perfectly understood him, and knew how to gather his opinions. When any thing that was read or related displeased him, he was observed to smoke his pipe vehemently, and to send forth short, frequent and angry puffs; but when pleased, he would inhale the smoke slowly and tranquilly, and emit it in light and placid clouds; and sometimes, taking the pipe from his mouth, and letting the fragrant vapor curl about his nose, would gravely nod his head in token of perfect approbation.

From even this stronghold the unlucky Rip was at length routed by his termagant wife, who would suddenly break in upon the tranquillity of the assemblage and call the members all to naught; nor was that august personage, Nicholas Vedder himself, sacred from the daring tongue of this terrible virago, who charged him outright with encouraging her husband in habits of idleness.

Poor Rip was at last reduced almost to despair; and his only alternative, to escape from the labor of the farm and clamor of his wife, was to take gun in hand and stroll away into the woods. Here he would sometimes seat himself at the foot of a tree, and share the contents of his wallet[17] with Wolf, with whom he sympathized as a fellow-sufferer in persecution. "Poor Wolf," he would say, "thy mistress leads thee a dog's life of it; but never mind, my lad, whilst I live thou shalt never want a friend to stand by thee!" Wolf would wag his tail, look wistfully in his master's face, and if dogs can feel pity I verily believe he reciprocated the sentiment with all his heart.

In a long ramble of the kind on a fine autumnal day, Rip had unconsciously scrambled to one of the highest parts of the Kaatskill mountains. He was after his favorite sport of squirrel shooting, and the still solitudes had echoed and reechoed with the reports of his gun. Panting and fatigued, he threw himself, late in the afternoon, on a green knoll, covered with mountain herbage, that crowned the brow of a precipice. From an opening between the trees he could overlook all the lower country for many a mile of rich woodland. He saw at a distance the lordly Hudson, far, far below him, moving on its silent but majestic course, with the reflection of a purple cloud, or the sail of a lagging bark, here and there sleeping on its glassy bosom, and at last losing itself in the blue highlands.

On the other side he looked down into a deep mountain glen, wild, lonely, and shagged, the bottom filled with fragments from the impending cliffs, and scarcely lighted by the reflected rays of the setting sun. For some time Rip lay musing on this scene; evening was gradually advancing; the mountains began to throw their long blue shadows over the valleys; he saw that it would be dark long before he could reach the village, and he heaved a heavy sigh when he thought of encountering the terrors of Dame Van Winkle.

As he was about to descend, he heard a voice from a distance, hallooing, "Rip Van Winkle! Rip Van Winkle!" He looked round, but could see nothing but a crow winging its solitary flight across the mountain. He thought his fancy must have deceived him, and turned again to descend, when he heard the same cry ring through the still evening air; "Rip Van Winkle! Rip Van Winkle!"—at the same time Wolf bristled up his back, and giving a low growl, skulked to his master's side, looking fearfully down into the glen. Rip now felt a vague apprehension stealing over him;

[17] Here, knapsack.

he looked anxiously in the same direction, and perceived a strange figure slowly toiling up the rocks, and bending under the weight of something he carried on his back. He was surprised to see any human being in this lonely and unfrequented place, but supposing it to be some one of the neighborhood in need of his assistance, he hastened down to yield it.

On nearer approach he was still more surprised at the singularity of the stranger's appearance. He was a short square-built old fellow, with thick bushy hair, and a grizzled beard. His dress was of the antique Dutch fashion—a cloth jerkin strapped round the waist—several pair of breeches, the outer one of ample volume, decorated with rows of buttons down the sides, and bunches at the knees. He bore on his shoulder a stout keg, that seemed full of liquor, and made signs for Rip to approach and assist him with the load. Though rather shy and distrustful of this new acquaintance, Rip complied with his usual alacrity; and mutually relieving one another, they clambered up a narrow gully, apparently the dry bed of a mountain torrent. As they ascended, Rip every now and then heard long rolling peals, like distant thunder, that seemed to issue out of a deep ravine, or rather cleft, between lofty rocks, toward which their rugged path conducted. He paused for an instant, but supposing it to be the muttering of one of those transient thunder-showers which often take place in mountain heights, he proceeded. Passing through the ravine, they came to a hollow, like a small amphitheatre surrounded by perpendicular precipices, over the brinks of which impending trees shot their branches, so that you only caught glimpses of the azure sky and the bright evening cloud. During the whole time Rip and his companion had labored on in silence; for though the former marvelled greatly what could be the object of carrying a keg of liquor up this wild mountain, yet there was something strange and incomprehensible about the unknown, that inspired awe and checked familiarity.

On entering the amphitheatre, new objects of wonder presented themselves. On a level spot in the centre was a company of odd-looking personages playing at nine-pins. They were dressed in a quaint outlandish fashion; some wore short doublets, others jerkins, with long knives in their belts, and most of them had enormous breeches, of similar style with that of the guide's. Their visages, too, were peculiar: one had a large beard, broad face, and small piggish eyes: the face of another seemed to consist entirely of nose, and was surmounted by a white sugar-loaf hat, set off with a little red cock's tail. They all had beards, of various shapes and colors. There was one who seemed to be the commander. He was a stout old gentleman, with a weather-beaten countenance; he wore a laced doublet, broad belt and hanger,[18] high crowned hat and feather, red stockings, and high-heeled shoes, with roses[19] in them. The whole group reminded Rip of the figures in an old Flemish painting, in the parlor of Dominic[20] Van Shaick, the village parson, and which had been brought over from Holland at the time of the settlement.

What seemed particularly odd to Rip was, that though these folks were evidently amusing themselves, yet they maintained the gravest faces, the most mysterious silence, and were, withal, the most melancholy party of pleasure he had ever witnessed. Nothing interrupted the stillness of the scene but the noise of the balls, which,

---

[18] Short, curved sword worn at the side.
[19] Rosettes.

[20] Pastor.

whenever they were rolled, echoed along the mountains like rumbling peals of thunder.

As Rip and his companion approached them, they suddenly desisted from their play, and stared at him with such fixed statue-like gaze, and such strange, uncouth, lack-lustre countenances, that his heart turned within him, and his knees smote together. His companion now emptied the contents of the keg into large flagons, and made signs to him to wait upon the company. He obeyed with fear and trembling; they quaffed the liquor in profound silence, and then returned to their game.

By degrees Rip's awe and apprehension subsided. He even ventured, when no eye was fixed upon him, to taste the beverage, which he found had much of the flavor of excellent Hollands.[21] He was naturally a thirsty soul, and was soon tempted to repeat the draught. One taste provoked another; and he reiterated his visits to the flagon so often that at length his senses were overpowered, his eyes swam in his head, his head gradually declined, and he fell into a deep sleep.

On waking, he found himself on the green knoll whence he had first seen the old man of the glen. He rubbed his eyes—it was a bright sunny morning. The birds were hopping and twittering among the bushes, and the eagle was wheeling aloft, and breasting the pure mountain breeze. "Surely," thought Rip, "I have not slept here all night." He recalled the occurrences before he fell asleep. The strange man with a keg of liquor—the mountain ravine—the wild retreat among the rocks—the wobegone party at nine-pins—the flagon—"Oh! that flagon! that wicked flagon!" thought Rip—"what excuse shall I make to Dame Van Winkle!"

He looked round for his gun, but in place of the clean well-oiled fowling-piece, he found an old firelock lying by him, the barrel incrusted with rust, the lock falling off, and the stock worm-eaten. He now suspected that the grave roysters of the mountain had put a trick upon him, and, having dosed him with liquor, had robbed him of his gun. Wolf, too, had disappeared, but he might have strayed away after a squirrel or partridge. He whistled after him and shouted his name, but all in vain; the echoes repeated his whistle and shout, but no dog was to be seen.

He determined to revisit the scene of the last evening's gambol, and if he met with any of the party, to demand his dog and gun. As he rose to walk, he found himself stiff in the joints, and wanting in his usual activity. "These mountain beds do not agree with me," thought Rip, "and if this frolic should lay me up with a fit of the rheumatism, I shall have a blessed time with Dame Van Winkle." With some difficulty he got down into the glen: he found the gully up which he and his companion had ascended the preceding evening; but to his astonishment a mountain stream was now foaming down it, leaping from rock to rock, and filling the glen with babbling murmurs. He, however, made shift to scramble up its sides, working his toilsome way through thickets of birch, sassafras, and witch-hazel, and sometimes tripped up or entangled by the wild grapevines that twisted their coils or tendrils from tree to tree, and spread a kind of network in his path.

At length he reached to where the ravine had opened through the cliffs to the amphitheatre; but no traces of such opening remained. The rocks presented a high

[21] Dutch gin.

impenetrable wall over which the torrent came tumbling in a sheet of feathery foam, and fell into a broad deep basin, black from the shadows of the surrounding forest. Here, then, poor Rip was brought to a stand. He again called and whistled after his dog; he was only answered by the cawing of a flock of idle crows, sporting high in air about a dry tree that overhung a sunny precipice; and who, secure in their elevation, seemed to look down and scoff at the poor man's perplexities. What was to be done? the morning was passing away, and Rip felt famished for want of his breakfast. He grieved to give up his dog and gun; he dreaded to meet his wife; but it would not do to starve among the mountains. He shook his head, shouldered the rusty firelock, and, with a heart full of trouble and anxiety, turned his steps homeward.

As he approached the village he met a number of people, but none whom he knew, which somewhat surprised him, for he had thought himself acquainted with every one in the country round. Their dress, too, was of a different fashion from that to which he was accustomed. They all stared at him with equal marks of surprise, and whenever they cast their eyes upon him, invariably stroked their chins. The constant recurrence of this gesture induced Rip, involuntarily, to do the same, when, to his astonishment, he found his beard had grown a foot long!

He had now entered the skirts of the village. A troop of strange children ran at his heels, hooting after him, and pointing at his gray beard. The dogs, too, not one of which he recognized for an old acquaintance, barked at him as he passed. The very village was altered; it was larger and more populous. There were rows of houses which he had never seen before, and those which had been his familiar haunts had disappeared. Strange names were over the doors—strange faces at the windows—every thing was strange. His mind now misgave him; he began to doubt whether both he and the world around him were not bewitched. Surely this was his native village, which he had left but the day before. There stood the Kaatskill mountains—there ran the silver Hudson at a distance—there was every hill and dale precisely as it had always been—Rip was sorely perplexed—"That flagon last night," thought he, "has addled my poor head sadly!"

It was with some difficulty that he found the way to his own house, which he approached with silent awe, expecting every moment to hear the shrill voice of Dame Van Winkle. He found the house gone to decay—the roof fallen in, the windows shattered, and the doors off the hinges. A half-starved dog that looked like Wolf was sulking about it. Rip called him by name, but the cur snarled, showed his teeth, and passed on. This was an unkind cut indeed—"My very dog," sighed poor Rip, "has forgotten me!"

He entered the house, which, to tell the truth, Dame Van Winkle had always kept in neat order. It was empty, forlorn, and apparently abandoned. This desolateness overcame all his connubial fears—he called loudly for his wife and children—the lonely chambers rang for a moment with his voice, and then all again was silence.

He now hurried forth, and hastened to his old resort, the village inn—but it too was gone. A large rickety wooden building stood in its place, with great gaping windows, some of them broken and mended with old hats and petticoats, and over the door was painted, "the Union Hotel, by Jonathan Doolittle." Instead of the great tree that used to shelter the quiet little Dutch inn of yore, there now was reared a tall naked pole, with something on the top that looked like a red night-cap, and from it was fluttering a flag, on which was a singular assemblage of stars and stripes—all this was strange and incomprehensible.[22] He recognized on the sign, however, the ruby face of King George, under which he had smoked so many a peaceful pipe; but even this was singularly metamorphosed. The red coat was changed for one of blue and buff,[23] a sword was held in the hand instead of a sceptre, the head was decorated with a cocked hat, and underneath was painted in large characters, GENERAL WASHINGTON.

There was, as usual, a crowd of folk about the door, but none that Rip recollected. The very character of the people seemed changed. There was a busy, bustling, disputatious tone about it, instead of the accustomed phlegm and drowsy tranquillity. He looked in vain for the sage Nicholas Vedder, with his broad face, double chin, and fair long pipe, uttering clouds of tobacco-smoke instead of idle speeches; or Van Bummel, the schoolmaster, doling forth the contents of an ancient newspaper. In place of these, a lean, bilious-looking fellow, with his pockets full of handbills, was haranguing vehemently about rights of citizens—elections—members of congress— liberty—Bunker's Hill—heroes of seventy-six—and other words, which were a perfect Babylonish jargon[24] to the bewildered Van Winkle.

The appearance of Rip, with his long grizzled beard, his rusty fowling-piece, his uncouth dress, and an army of women and children at his heels, soon attracted the attention of the tavern politicians. They crowded around him, eyeing him from head to foot with great curiosity. The orator bustled up to him, and, drawing him partly aside, inquired "on which side he voted?" Rip stared in vacant stupidity. Another short but busy little fellow pulled him by the arm, and, rising on tiptoe, inquired in his ear, "Whether he was Federal or Democrat?"[25] Rip was equally at a loss to comprehend the question; when a knowing, self-important old gentleman, in a sharp cocked hat, made his way through the crowd, putting them to the right and left with his elbows as he passed, and planting himself before Van Winkle, with one arm akimbo, the other resting on his cane, his keen eyes and sharp hat penetrating, as it were, into his very soul, demanded in an austere tone, "what brought him to the election with a gun on his shoulder, and a mob at his heels, and whether he meant to breed a riot in the village?"—"Alas! gentlemen," cried Rip, somewhat dismayed, "I am a poor quiet man, a native of the place, and a loyal subject of the king, God bless him!"

Here a general shout burst from the by-standers—"A tory! a tory! a spy! a refugee! hustle him! away with him!" It was with great difficulty that the self-important man in the cocked hat restored order; and, having assumed a tenfold austerity of brow, demanded again of the unknown culprit, what he came there for, and whom he was seeking? The poor man humbly assured him that he meant no harm, but merely came there in search of some of his neighbors, who used to keep about the tavern.

"Well—who are they?—name them."

Rip bethought himself a moment, and inquired, "Where's Nicholas Vedder?"

There was a silence for a little while, when an old man replied, in a thin piping voice, "Nicholas Vedder! why, he is dead and gone these eighteen years! There was

[22] The liberty cap and liberty pole were adopted as symbols of freedom during the French and American revolutions.
[23] Colors of the American army uniforms.

[24] Reference to the "Confusion of Tongues" at the Tower of Babel (Genesis 11:1–9).
[25] Political parties of early America, respectively conservative and liberal.

a wooden tombstone in the church-yard that used to tell all about him, but that's rotten and gone too."

"Where's Brom Dutcher?"

"Oh, he went off to the army in the beginning of the war; some say he was killed at the storming of Stony Point—others say he was drowned in a squall at the foot of Antony's Nose.[26] I don't know—he never came back again."

"Where's Van Bummel, the schoolmaster?"

"He went off to the wars too, was a great militia general, and is now in congress."

Rip's heart died away at hearing of these sad changes in his home and friends, and finding himself thus alone in the world. Every answer puzzled him too, by treating of such enormous lapses of time, and of matters which he could not understand: war —congress—Stony Point;—he had no courage to ask after any more friends, but cried out in despair, "Does nobody here know Rip Van Winkle?"

"Oh, Rip Van Winkle!" exclaimed two or three, "Oh, to be sure! that's Rip Van Winkle yonder, leaning against the tree."

Rip looked, and beheld a precise counterpart of himself, as he went up to the mountain: apparently as lazy, and certainly as ragged. The poor fellow was now completely confounded. He doubted his own identity, and whether he was himself or another man. In the midst of his bewilderment, the man in the cocked hat demanded who he was, and what was his name?

"God knows," exclaimed he, at his wit's end; "I'm not myself—I'm somebody else —that's me yonder—no—that's somebody else got into my shoes—I was myself last night, but I fell asleep on the mountain, and they've changed my gun, and every thing's changed, and I'm changed, and I can't tell what's my name, or who I am!"

The by-standers began now to look at each other, nod, wink significantly, and tap their fingers against their foreheads. There was a whisper, also, about securing the gun, and keeping the old fellow from doing mischief, at the very suggestion of which the self-important man in the cocked hat retired with some precipitation. At this critical moment a fresh comely woman pressed through the throng to get a peep at the gray-bearded man. She had a chubby child in her arms, which, frightened at his looks, began to cry. "Hush, Rip," cried she, "hush, you little fool; the old man won't hurt you." The name of the child, the air of the mother, the tone of her voice, all awakened a train of recollections in his mind. "What is your name, my good woman?" asked he.

"Judith Gardenier."

"And your father's name?"

"Ah, poor man, Rip Van Winkle was his name, but it's twenty years since he went away from home with his gun, and never has been heard of since—his dog came home without him; but whether he shot himself, or was carried away by the Indians, nobody can tell. I was then but a little girl."

Rip had but one question more to ask; but he put it with a faltering voice:

"Where's your mother?"

"Oh, she too had died but a short time since; she broke a blood-vessel in a fit of passion at a New-England peddler."

There was a drop of comfort, at least, in this intelligence. The honest man could

[26] Mountain near West Point on the Hudson River.

contain himself no longer. He caught his daughter and her child in his arms. "I am your father!" cried he—"Young Rip Van Winkle once—old Rip Van Winkle now! —Does nobody know poor Rip Van Winkle?"

All stood amazed, until an old woman, tottering out from among the crowd, put her hand to her brow, and peering under it in his face for a moment, exclaimed, "Sure enough! it is Rip Van Winkle—it is himself! Welcome home again, old neighbor —Why, where have you been these twenty long years?"

Rip's story was soon told, for the whole twenty years had been to him but as one night. The neighbors stared when they heard it; some were seen to wink at each other, and put their tongues in their cheeks: and the self-important man in the cocked hat, who, when the alarm was over, had returned to the field, screwed down the corners of his mouth, and shook his head—upon which there was a general shaking of the head throughout the assemblage.

It was determined, however, to take the opinion of old Peter Vanderdonk, who was seen slowly advancing up the road. He was a descendant of the historian of that name,[27] who wrote one of the earliest accounts of the province. Peter was the most ancient inhabitant of the village, and well versed in all the wonderful events and traditions of the neighborhood. He recollected Rip at once, and corroborated his story in the most satisfactory manner. He assured the company that it was a fact, handed down from his ancestor the historian, that the Kaatskill mountains had always been haunted by strange beings. That it was affirmed that the great Hendrick Hudson,[28] the first discoverer of the river and country, kept a kind of vigil there every twenty years, with his crew of the Half-moon; being permitted in this way to revisit the scenes of his enterprise, and keep a guardian eye upon the river, and the great city called by his name.[29] That his father had once seen them in their old Dutch dresses playing at nine-pins in a hollow of the mountain; and that he himself had heard, one summer afternoon, the sound of their balls, like distant peals of thunder.

To make a long story short, the company broke up, and returned to the more important concerns of the election. Rip's daughter took him home to live with her; she had a snug, well-furnished house, and a stout cheery farmer for a husband, whom Rip recollected for one of the urchins that used to climb upon his back. As to Rip's son and heir, who was the ditto of himself, seen leaning against the tree, he was employed to work on the farm; but evinced an hereditary disposition to attend to any thing else but his business.

Rip now resumed his old walks and habits; he soon found many of his former cronies, though all rather the worse for the wear and tear of time; and preferred making friends among the rising generation, with whom he soon grew into great favor.

Having nothing to do at home, and being arrived at that happy age when a man can be idle with impunity, he took his place once more on the bench at the inn door, and was reverenced as one of the patriarchs of the village, and a chronicle of the old times "before the war." It was some time before he could get into the regular track

---

[27] Adriaen Van Der Donck (1620?–1655), Dutch lawyer and author of a history of New Netherlands (Amsterdam, 1655).
[28] English navigator Henry Hudson (d. 1611), employed by the Dutch to explore the river that now bears his name.
[29] The town of Hudson, New York.

of gossip, or could be made to comprehend the strange events that had taken place during his torpor. How that there had been a revolutionary war—that the country had thrown off the yoke of old England—and that, instead of being a subject of his Majesty George the Third, he was now a free citizen of the United States. Rip, in fact, was no politician; the changes of states and empires made but little impression on him; but there was one species of despotism under which he had long groaned, and that was—petticoat government. Happily that was at an end; he had got his neck out of the yoke of matrimony, and could go in and out whenever he pleased, without dreading the tyranny of Dame Van Winkle. Whenever her name was mentioned, however, he shook his head, shrugged his shoulders, and cast up his eyes; which might pass either for an expression of resignation to his fate, or joy at his deliverance.

He used to tell his story to every stranger that arrived at Mr. Doolittle's hotel. He was observed, at first, to vary on some points every time he told it, which was, doubtless, owing to his having so recently awaked. It at last settled down precisely to the tale I have related, and not a man, woman, or child in the neighborhood, but knew it by heart. Some always pretended to doubt the reality of it, and insisted that Rip had been out of his head, and that this was one point on which he always remained flighty. The old Dutch inhabitants, however, almost universally gave it full credit. Even to this day they never hear a thunderstorm of a summer afternoon about the Kaatskill, but they say Hendrick Hudson and his crew are at their game of nine-pins; and it is a common wish of all henpecked husbands in the neighborhood, when life hangs heavy on their hands, that they might have a quieting draught out of Rip Van Winkle's flagon.

Note

The foregoing Tale, one would suspect, had been suggested to Mr. Knickerbocker by a little German superstition about the Emperor Frederick *der Rothbart*,[30] and the Kypphaüser mountain: the subjoined note, however, which he had appended to the tale, shows that it is an absolute fact, narrated with his usual fidelity:

"The story of Rip Van Winkle may seem incredible to many, but nevertheless I give it my full belief, for I know the vicinity of our old Dutch settlements to have been very subject to marvellous events and appearances. Indeed, I have heard many stranger stories than this, in the villages along the Hudson; all of which were too well authenticated to admit of a doubt. I have even talked with Rip Van Winkle myself, who, when last I saw him, was a very venerable old man, and so perfectly rational and consistent on every other point, that I think no conscientious person could refuse to take this into the bargain; nay, I have seen a certificate on the subject taken before a country justice and signed with a cross, in the justice's own handwriting. The story, therefore, is beyond the possibility of doubt.

D.K."

1819–1820

[30] Frederick Barbarossa (1123–1190), emperor of the Holy Roman Empire (1152–1190). Legend maintains that he is resting in a cave in the Kyffhauser Mountain in Germany until his country needs his rule. (*Barbarossa* and *der Rothbart* mean "red beard" in Latin and German, respectively.)

from **A History of the Life and Voyages
of Christopher Columbus**

from **Book IV**

Chapter I: First Landing of Columbus in the New World

It was on Friday morning, the 12th of October, that Columbus first beheld the New World. As the day dawned he saw before him a level island, several leagues in extent, and covered with trees like a continual orchard. Though apparently uncultivated, it was populous, for the inhabitants were seen issuing from all parts of the woods and running to the shore. They were perfectly naked, and, as they stood gazing at the ships, appeared by their attitudes and gestures to be lost in astonishment. Columbus made signal for the ships to cast anchor, and the boats to be manned and armed. He entered his own boat, richly attired in scarlet, and holding the royal standard; whilst Martin Alonzo Pinzon, and Vincent Jañez his brother, put off in company in their boats; each with a banner of the enterprise emblazoned with a green cross, having on either side the letters F. and Y., the initials of the Castilian monarchs Fernando and Ysabel, surmounted by crowns.

As he approached the shore, Columbus, who was disposed for all kinds of agreeable impressions, was delighted with the purity and suavity of the atmosphere, the crystal transparency of the sea, and the extraordinary beauty of the vegetation. He beheld, also, fruits of an unknown kind upon the trees which overhung the shores. On landing he threw himself on his knees, kissed the earth, and returned thanks to God with tears of joy. His example was followed by the rest, whose hearts indeed overflowed with the same feelings of gratitude. Columbus then rising drew his sword, displayed the royal standard, and assembling round him the two captains, with Rodrigo de Escobedo, notary of the armament, Rodrigo Sanchez, and the rest who had landed, he took solemn possession in the name of the Castilian sovereigns, giving the island the name of San Salvador. Having complied with the requisite forms and ceremonies, he called upon all present to take the oath of obedience to him, as admiral and viceroy, representing the persons of the sovereigns.

The feelings of the crew now burst forth in the most extravagant transports. They had recently considered themselves devoted men, hurrying forward to destruction; they now looked upon themselves as favorites of fortune, and gave themselves up to the most unbounded joy. They thronged around the admiral with overflowing zeal, some embracing him, others kissing his hands. Those who had been most mutinous and turbulent during the voyage, were now most devoted and enthusiastic. Some begged favors of him, as if he had already wealth and honors in his gift. Many abject spirits, who had outraged him by their insolence, now crouched at his feet, begging pardon for all the trouble they had caused him, and promising the blindest obedience for the future.

The natives of the island, when, at the dawn of day, they had beheld the ships hovering on their coast, had supposed them monsters which had issued from the deep during the night. They had crowded to the beach, and watched their movements with awful anxiety. Their veering about, apparently without effort, and the shifting and furling of their sails, resembling huge wings, filled them with astonishment. When they beheld their boats approach the shore, and a number of strange beings clad in glittering steel, or raiment of various colors, landing upon the beach, they fled in affright to the woods. Finding, however, that there was no attempt to pursue nor molest them, they gradually recovered from their terror, and approached the Spaniards with great awe; frequently prostrating themselves on the earth, and making signs of adoration. During the ceremonies of taking possession, they remained gazing in timid admiration at the complexion, the beards, the shining armor, and splendid dress of the Spaniards. The admiral particularly attracted their attention, from his commanding height, his air of authority, his dress of scarlet, and the deference which was paid him by his companions; all which pointed him out to be the commander. When they had still further recovered from their fears, they approached the Spaniards, touched their beards, and examined their hands and faces, admiring their whiteness. Columbus was pleased with their gentleness and confiding simplicity, and suffered their scrutiny with perfect acquiescence, winning them by his benignity. They now supposed that the ships had sailed out of the crystal firmament which bounded their horizon, or had descended from above on their ample wings, and that these marvelous beings were inhabitants of the skies.

The natives of the island were no less objects of curiosity to the Spaniards, differing, as they did, from any race of men they had ever seen. Their appearance gave no promise of either wealth or civilization, for they were entirely naked, and painted with a variety of colors. With some it was confined merely to a part of the face, the nose, or around the eyes; with others it extended to the whole body, and gave them a wild and fantastic appearance. Their complexion was of a tawny or copper hue, and they were entirely destitute of beards. Their hair was not crisped, like the recently-discovered tribes of the African coast, under the same latitude, but straight and coarse, partly cut short above the ears, but some locks were left long behind and falling upon their shoulders. Their features, though obscured and disfigured by paint, were agreeable; they had lofty foreheads and remarkably fine eyes. They were of moderate stature and well-shaped; most of them appeared to be under thirty years of age: there was but one female with them, quite young, naked like her companions, and beautifully formed.

As Columbus supposed himself to have landed on an island at the extremity of India, he called the natives by the general appellation of Indians, which was universally adopted before the true nature of his discovery was known, and has since been extended to all the aboriginals of the New World.

The islanders were friendly and gentle. Their only arms were lances, hardened at the end by fire, or pointed with a flint, or the teeth or bone of a fish. There was no iron to be seen, nor did they appear acquainted with its properties; for, when a drawn sword was presented to them, they unguardedly took it by the edge.

Columbus distributed among them colored caps, glass beads, hawks' bells, and other trifles, such as the Portuguese were accustomed to trade with among the nations of the gold coast of Africa. They received them eagerly, hung the beads round their necks, and were wonderfully pleased with their finery, and with the sound of the bells. The Spaniards remained all day on shore refreshing themselves after their anxious voyage amidst the beautiful groves of the island; and returned on board late in the evening, delighted with all they had seen.

On the following morning, at break of day, the shore was thronged with the natives; some swam off to the ships, others came in light barks which they called canoes, formed of a single tree, hollowed, and capable of holding from one man to the number of forty or fifty. These they managed dextrously with paddles, and, if overturned, swam about in the water with perfect unconcern, as if in their natural element, righting their canoes with great facility, and baling them with calabashes.[1]

They were eager to procure more toys and trinkets, not, apparently, from any idea of their intrinsic value, but because every thing from the hands of the strangers possessed a supernatural virtue in their eyes, as having been brought from heaven; they even picked up fragments of glass and earthenware as valuable prizes. They had but few objects to offer in return, except parrots, of which great numbers were domesticated among them, and cotton yarn, of which they had abundance, and would exchange large balls of five and twenty pounds' weight for the merest trifle. They brought also cakes of a kind of bread called cassava,[2] which constituted a principal part of their food, and was afterwards an important article of provisions with the Spaniards. It was formed from a great root called yuca, which they cultivated in fields. This they cut into small morsels, which they grated or scraped, and strained in a press, making a broad thin cake, which was afterwards dried hard, and would keep for a long time, being steeped in water when eaten. It was insipid, but nourishing, though the water strained from it in the preparation was a deadly poison. There was another kind of yuca destitute of this poisonous quality, which was eaten in the root, either boiled or roasted.

The avarice of the discoverers was quickly excited by the sight of small ornaments of gold, worn by some of the natives in their noses. These the latter gladly exchanged for glass beads and hawks' bells; and both parties exulted in the bargain, no doubt admiring each other's simplicity. As gold, however, was an object of royal monopoly in all enterprises of discovery, Columbus forbade any traffic in it without his express sanction; and he put the same prohibition on the traffic for cotton, reserving to the crown all trade for it, wherever it should be found in any quantity.

He inquired of the natives where this gold was procured. They answered him by signs, pointing to the south, where, he understood them, dwelt a king of such wealth that he was served in vessels of wrought gold. He understood, also, that there was land to the south, the southwest, and the northwest; and that the people from the last mentioned quarter frequently proceeded to the southwest in quest of gold and precious stones, making in their way descents upon the islands, and carrying off the inhabitants. Several of the natives showed him scars of wounds received in battles with these invaders. It is evident that a great part of this fancied intelligence was self-delusion on the part of Columbus; for he was under a spell of the imagination, which gave its own shapes and colors to every object. He was persuaded that he had arrived among the islands described by Marco Polo, as lying opposite Cathay, in the Chinese sea, and

[1] Gourds that served as containers.
[2] The fleshy rootstocks of the cassava plant yielded a nutritious starch or flour.

he construed every thing to accord with the account given of those opulent regions. Thus the enemies which the natives spoke of as coming from the northwest, he concluded to be the people of the mainland of Asia, the subjects of the great Khan of Tartary, who were represented by the Venetian traveler as accustomed to make war upon the islands, and to enslave their inhabitants. The country to the south, abounding in gold, could be no other than the famous island of Cipango; and the king who was served out of vessels of gold, must be the monarch whose magnificent city and gorgeous palace, covered with plates of gold, had been extolled in such splendid terms by Marco Polo.

The island where Columbus had thus, for the first time, set his foot upon the New World, was called by the natives, Guanahanè. It still retains the name of San Salvador, which he gave to it, though called by the English, Cat Island. The light which he had seen the evening previous to his making land, may have been on Watling's Island, which lies a few leagues to the east. San Salvador is one of the great cluster of the Lucayos, or Bahama Islands, which stretch southeast and northwest, from the coast of Florida to Hispaniola, covering the northern coast of Cuba.

On the morning of the 14th of October, the admiral set off at daybreak with the boats of the ships to reconnoitre the island, directing his course to the northeast. The coast was surrounded by a reef of rocks, within which there was depth of water and sufficient harbor to receive all the ships in Christendom. The entrance was very narrow; within there were several sand-banks, but the water was as still as in a pool.

The island appeared throughout to be well wooded, with streams of water, and a large lake in the centre. As the boats proceeded, they passed two or three villages, the inhabitants of which, men as well as women, ran to the shores, throwing themselves on the ground, lifting up their hands and eyes, either giving thanks to Heaven, or worshiping the Spaniards as supernatural beings. They ran along parallel to the boats, calling after the Spaniards, and inviting them by signs to land, offering them various fruits and vessels of water. Finding, however, that the boats continued on their course, many threw themselves into the sea and swam after them, and others followed in canoes. The admiral received them all with kindness, giving them glass beads and other trifles, which were received with transport as celestial presents, for the invariable idea of the savages was, that the white men had come from the skies.

In this way they pursued their course, until they came to a small peninsula, which with two or three days' labor might be separated from the main-land and surrounded with water, and was therefore specified by Columbus as an excellent situation for a fortress. On this were six Indian cabins, surrounded by groves and gardens as beautiful as those of Castile. The sailors being wearied with rowing, and the island not appearing to the admiral of sufficient importance to induce colonization, he returned to the ships, taking seven of the natives with him, that they might acquire the Spanish language and serve as interpreters.

Having taken in a supply of wood and water, they left the island of San Salvador the same evening, the admiral being impatient to arrive at the wealthy country to the south, which he flattered himself would prove the famous island of Cipango.

1828

James Fenimore Cooper
1789–1851

James Fenimore Cooper's life spans America's cultural transformation—from the new nation's anxious efforts to establish a distinctive cultural identity to its confident expression of a truly distinguished literary tradition in the mid-nineteenth-century "renaissance." In 1789, the year of Cooper's birth, American writers self-consciously struggled with the lag between the new republic's political and cultural independence. "The first was accomplished in about seven years," Philip Freneau wrote half humorously; "the latter will not be completely effected, perhaps, in as many centuries." In 1851, the year of Cooper's death, American readers had already seen the publication of most of Ralph Waldo Emerson's essays and poems, Edgar Allan Poe's tales and verse, Nathaniel Hawthorne's *The Scarlet Letter* (1850) and *House of the Seven Gables* (1851), and Herman Melville's *Moby Dick* (1851). Henry David Thoreau's *Walden* (1854) and Walt Whitman's *Leaves of Grass* (1855) would follow within a few years of Cooper's death.

James Fenimore Cooper played a primary role in America's early literary development. Writing in 1831 as an author celebrated both in the United States and abroad, Cooper proposed a literary ambition that he had little difficulty satisfying: America's "mental independence is my object, and if I can go down to the grave with the reflection that I have done a little towards it, I shall have the consolation of knowing that I have not been useless in my generation." Cooper's accomplishments far exceeded his literary aims. He was the first American novelist to explore and define native themes, settings, and characters. He launched several distinct genres in American fiction: the American novel of manners, the sea novel, the European-American novel, and, in the "Leather-Stocking" series, the novel of the mythic frontier. Cooper also helped establish what has become the American writer's traditional role as a social and cultural critic.

Within fourteen months of their son's birth in Burlington, New Jersey, in 1789, Cooper's parents moved their family to the several-thousand-acre tract they owned on the shores of Otsego Lake in central New York State. Cooperstown, founded and named by his father, provided both the setting for much of Cooper's childhood and the source for his aristocratic view of the frontier and its inhabitants. Cooper's father, Judge William Cooper, a prominent political leader (a two-term member of Congress) as well as a wealthy merchant and landowner, passed on his ardent Federalist beliefs to his son. Trained from birth to be a country gentleman, James Cooper prepared for college by studying with an English tutor. He entered Yale at age thirteen, steeped in Shakespeare and the major eighteenth-century English poets. Within two years, Cooper had been summarily dismissed by Timothy Dwight, then the president, for rowdy behavior and dangerous pranks. Family tradition has it that young Cooper had set off a small explosion in another student's room by jamming a rag full of powder into the keyhole and igniting it.

Sent to sea by his father after his dismissal from Yale, Cooper served for two years as a deckhand on a merchant ship before being commissioned a midshipman in the navy, where he labored—without distinction or disruption—for the next three years. He resigned his commission in 1811 shortly after his marriage to Susan Augusta De Lancey, the daughter of a wealthy New York family with lingering Tory sentiments. His father died soon after—from a blow to the head received during a political dispute. Cooper's inheritance included more than fifty thousand dollars as well as his father's political and social conservatism. Quickly settled into a life as a country gentleman, Cooper revealed little initial interest in pursuing a career as a writer.

Cooper never freed himself completely from the legacy of his accomplished and strong-willed father. Their relationship in many respects previews the persistent tension evident both in Cooper's writing and in his nation's culture—the conflicting lures of the desire for personal and cultural originality and the attraction toward established forms and inherited contexts. This dual anxiety is most readily felt in Cooper's—and his nation's—attitudes toward the future: at once a celebratory anticipation and an overarching fear that undisciplined originality would lead to chaos. These contradictory impulses took on greater importance as the amount of Cooper's inheritance steadily dwindled.

Cooper plunged into a literary career at age thirty, when his wife urged him to act on his claim that he could write a better novel than the sentimental tale of rural English life he had been reading aloud to her. In her *Family Memoirs,* Cooper's daughter Susan recounts the episode that changed the course of her father's life:

> My mother was not well, she was lying on the sofa, and he was reading this newly imported novel to her; it must have been very trashy; after a chapter or two he threw it aside exclaiming, "I could write you a better book myself." Our mother laughed at the idea as at the height of absurdity—he who disliked writing even a letter, that he should write a book! He persisted in his declarations, however, and almost immediately wrote the first pages of a tale not yet named, the scene laid in England as a matter of course.

Impatient with his own efforts, Cooper destroyed those first pages but soon completed a full-length manuscript, *Precaution* (1820). A novel of manners in the tradition of Jane Austen, *Precaution* proved his point and left him with a lifelong urge to write.

Cooper's second novel, *The Spy: A Tale of the Neutral Ground* (1821), was yet another—although not immediate—product of that family incident. As Cooper later explained in *A Letter to His Countrymen* (1834):

> Accident first made me a writer, and the same accident gave a direction to my pen. Ashamed to have fallen into the track of imitation, I endeavored to repair the wrong done to my own views, by producing a work that should be purely American, and of which love of country should be the theme.

With the Revolutionary War as a backdrop, *The Spy* demonstrated Cooper's belief that American history could be a suitable setting for fiction. The novel quickly became a best-seller in the United States and in Europe. Within a year, it was reprinted in several editions, turned into a play, and translated into several languages. Cooper had suddenly become the most popular American writer in Europe.

The frontier of his childhood provided the setting for his third novel, *The Pioneers; or, The Sources of the Susquehanna*. Set in the Otsego Lake region during the decade following the Revolutionary War, *The Pioneers* also became an immediate best-seller and the first in what would become a series of five "Leather-Stocking Tales": *The Pioneers* (1823), *The Last of the Mohicans* (1826), *The Prairie* (1827), *The Pathfinder* (1840), and *The Deerslayer* (1841). (In relation to plot, the sequence is *The Deerslayer, The Last of the Mohicans, The Pathfinder, The Pioneers,* and *The Prairie*.) Deriving their collective title from their hero's nickname (based on his habit of wearing long deerskin leggings), the "Leather-Stocking Tales" trace the life, adventures, and death of Natty Bumppo and his Indian companions, most notably the chieftain Chingachgook. A simple character whose love of the wilderness and dislike of civilization's restraints remain consistent—and uncompromised—throughout the series, Natty Bumppo possesses the moral resolve, generosity, and resourcefulness that set the standard for American fictional heroes well into the twentieth century.

Following the publication of *The Pioneers,* Cooper's attention to American settings and characters promptly shifted from the wilderness to the sea. In *The Pilot* (1823), he set out to prove that he could draw on his own experience to create a more accurate and appealing rendition of life at sea than the English novelist Walter Scott had provided in his novel *The Pirate* (1823). The first of what would be Cooper's eleven sea novels, *The Pilot* blended technical detail, memorable characters (such as Long Tom Coffin), and patriotic appeal to create yet another enormously successful novel—a fictional precedent whose influence Herman Melville and Joseph Conrad would later generously acknowledge.

In the short span of three years, Cooper had opened three new territories for American fiction: the nation's past, its frontier, and its life at sea. The three settings of Cooper's fiction—and the characters who populated them—became the precursors of everything from the renegade heroes in the novels of such classic American writers as Melville, Twain, and Faulkner to the rugged western stereotypes in American dime novels and their celluloid counterparts in popular films and television.

By the mid-1820s, James Fenimore Cooper (he added his mother's maiden name in 1826) had established a formidable reputation in American literary circles. He moved to New York City, where he founded the Bread and Cheese Club, which included such notable literary figures as the poets Fitz-Greene Halleck and William Cullen Bryant and such celebrated painters as Asher Durand and Samuel F. B. Morse. To commemorate each of the thirteen original states and to strengthen his reputation as America's leading novelist, Cooper projected a series of novels on national themes. He completed only *Lionel Lincoln* (1825), a romantic tale of Boston during the Revolution.

The success of *The Pioneers* prompted Cooper to resume his account of the adventures of the frontier scout Natty Bumppo in *The Last of the Mohicans* (1826) and *The Prairie* (1827), completing the latter while traveling in Europe. Initially drawn to the Continent because of his own poor health, his interest in introducing his daughters to Italian and French culture, and his eagerness to protect his royalties abroad, Cooper spent the next seven years there, based primarily in Lyons, where he served, often rather casually, as the American consul. During this period he also wrote several more novels, three of which—*The Red Rover* (1827), *The Wept of Wishton-Wish* (1829), and *The Water Witch* (1830)—focus on American history and life at sea.

While abroad, Cooper unhesitatingly defended American culture and democracy from attacks by cynical British commentators. Cooper responded to these critics in *Notions of the Americans* (1828), a series of fictional letters from a sophisticated European traveler to a member of a geographic society. The book, however, pleased neither the Americans, who were increasingly alienated both by Cooper's long absence and by his association with European aristocracy, nor the English, who preferred the America depicted in *The Pioneers*. Cooper returned to fiction in *The Bravo* (1831), *The Heidenmauer* (1832), and *The Headsman* (1833). This trilogy, published as a response to Sir Walter Scott's idealized treatment of medieval England, focused on the limits of European social standards by tracing their development out of feudal abuses. Cooper's seven years in Europe also marked a serious shift in his writing—from his early, largely optimistic writing to his later, more broad-ranging and highly critical work. The moral champion of American life would soon become one of its fiercest critics. And literature would become his means for proposing social reforms.

Cooper had set out for Europe during the presidency of John Quincy Adams. He returned to a far different place, Jacksonian America. Repulsed by what he regarded as President Jackson's vulgar and narrow version of frontier democracy, Cooper argued strenuously for a return to American life led by an elite minority, principally the Christian agrarian gentlemen of his youth. He was quickly judged a reactionary by the same Americans he had idealized while living abroad; he received neither the warm reception nor the privileged treatment afforded Washington Irving when he had returned from Europe the year before. Sorely disappointed by what he considered the mediocrity of Jacksonian democracy, Cooper launched a series of polemic salvos at American behavior and belief. *A Letter to His Countrymen* (1834), *The Monikins* (1835), four volumes of *Gleanings in Europe* (1837–1838), and *The American Democrat* (1838) express his social and political criticism as well as his aristocratic ideals. *Homeward Bound* (1838) and *Home as Found* (1838) render these same concerns in fictional terms.

Cooper's repudiation of the faults of the American society he returned to was neither cranky nor negative but reformist in character and intention. He returned to America hoping that he would find an independent culture equal to any in Europe; what he discovered was a nation whose excesses in the name of democracy were exacerbated by the mediocrity of its lowest-common-denominator approach to national issues and values. During what had become a fractious period in American history, Cooper hoped to unify American social and cultural principles and opinions. "It is high time," he wrote in *Gleanings in Europe*, "not only for the respectability, but for the *safety* of the American people, that they should promulgate a set of principles that are more in harmony with their facts." Cooper's purpose in writing had become as much to exert moral leadership as to set aesthetic standards.

Cooper envisioned an America in which democratic gentlemen would provide the leadership necessary to explore the full potential of the New World. These paragons would combine a respect for tradition with a commitment to democratic values and reasoned change. Their position would be achieved by merit rather than birth, by manifest quality rather than privilege. For Cooper, moderation and balance were cardinal virtues. In his vision, America would embody neither the common excesses of frontier democracy nor the traditional arrogance of European aristocracy. America would mature into a democracy in which the access afforded by social mobility would elevate the best people to positions of power. Yet if Cooper had served as the progenitor of American social criticism, he would also eventually become its victim.

There is both a hopeful exuberance and a mounting sadness in Cooper's social criticism. *Notions of the Americans* expressed his belief in his nation's unbounded possibilities, yet he steadily lost that faith as he realized that power in America had become the province of those he regarded as demagogues rather than of the Jeffersonian gentry like himself. Cooper feared the mediocrity that conformity inevitably produced.

Charged by the press with being a Tory renegade, Cooper spent a good deal of the rest of his life defending himself in public and suing his detractors for libel. More often than not, he won. He spent a good portion of each year in Cooperstown, where he enjoyed the companionship and support of his daughter Susan, who also served as his amanuensis. But he eventually became embroiled in controversy there as well. He sided with the rural landlords in their disputes with tenant farmers, a debate that erupted into violence in the "Anti-rent War" of the 1840s. The trilogy known as "The Littlepage Manuscripts"—*Satanstoe* (1845), *The Chainbearer* (1845), and *The Redskins* (1846)—traces three generations of the Littlepage family through the decades that led to the Anti-rent War.

During these years, Cooper's prodigious talents had also produced a controversial *History of the Navy* (1839), several biographies of naval officers and a former shipmate, and a book, *Mercedes of Castile* (1840), focusing on Columbus's first voyage to the New World. Other notable works included *Wyandotte* (1843), on the early days of the Revolution in New York; *Le Mouchoir* (1843), reissued as *Autobiography of a Pocket-Handkerchief*, a brief romantic sketch of New York's class distinctions; *Afloat and Ashore* (1844) and a sequel, *Miles Wallingford* (1844), which contains Cooper's fictional self-portrait; *The Crater* (1848), a utopian social allegory; and *Jack Tier* (1848), *The Oak Openings* (1848), and *Sea Lions* (1848), each a fast-paced historical romance. *The Ways of the Hour* (1850), Cooper's last novel, helped refine the nature of the mystery tale.

Despite the extraordinary range of his literary interests and accomplishments, Cooper's fame in his own day and his importance in American cultural history depended primarily, he realized, on the reception of his "Leather-Stocking Tales." He resumed the series with the publication of the fourth volume, *The Pathfinder*, in 1840 and concluded his treatment of Natty Bumppo in *The Deerslayer* (1841), which recounts the earliest exploits of his mythic hero in the years before the French and Indian Wars. The popularity of the "Leather-Stocking" series, their articulation of an American mythos, their movement from old age to youth (what D. H. Lawrence called "the true myth of America"), their progressive departure from overt social engagement, and their definition of the frontier as the primary fact of American history truly distinguished these novels as classics in American literature. Yet later generations of American writers, most notably Mark Twain in his widely read essay "Fenimore Cooper's Literary Offenses," ridiculed Cooper's handling of language, syntax, dialogue, plot, narrative pace, and characterization—especially his portrayal of women. As James Russell Lowell wryly noted in *A Fable for Critics* (1848): "The women he draws from one model don't vary, / All sappy as maples and flat as a prairie." Such criticism reduced the "Leather-Stocking" series to the status of elementary school texts by the turn of the twentieth century. Renewed attention to Cooper's social criticism in the 1920s gradually led to a reassessment of the "Leather-Stocking" novels.

Although Cooper did have considerable difficulty developing a style to express adequately the distinctiveness of his American subject matter in the "Leather-Stocking Tales," he did unfold several themes that quickly took on mythic importance in American literary history. Cooper used some of the major thematic concerns of the series—advancing a sense of both temporal order and the past's continued presence—to help give shape to American history at a time when our nation's historical consciousness seemed precarious and ephemeral. The "Leather-Stocking" series also helped define the American preoccupation with the landscape. Cooper had recognized quite early that space was—and remains—*the* fundamental reality of American life. And his depiction of the American land— and more particularly his ability to envision personal freedom in the unencumbered space stretching beyond the confines of institutional life—enabled his "Leather-Stocking Tales" to transcend the creakiness of his plots and the clumsiness of his language. As a cultural mediator between civilization and the wilderness, Natty Bumppo served as the metaphor for all that Cooper achieved— an image of an ideal, balanced existence that receded ceaselessly into the past. As Cooper explained in his preface to the "Leather-Stocking Tales," Natty Bumppo was "a fit subject to represent the better qualities of both conditions, without pushing either to extremes." As such, Natty Bumppo is a prototypical American hero, an antecedent of, for example, Melville's Ishmael, Twain's Huck Finn, Faulkner's Ike McCaslin, and Hemingway's protagonists.

The sense of loss that increasingly dominates each of the "Leather-Stocking" novels illustrated—much like Cooper's social criticism—the shifting national views on America's direction and destiny in the first half of the nineteenth century. The pervasive melancholy of late-eighteenth- and early-nineteenth-century literature, which essentially shaped Cooper's writing, ceased to be merely a borrowed rhetorical device in the course of the "Leather-Stocking" series and became instead a way to conceptualize a recurring image in American writing—a gradual diminution of an impossible vision of the land, one that nonetheless remained a powerful *imagined* alternative to material progress.

James Fenimore Cooper died on September 14, 1851, in Cooperstown, New York. Less than two weeks later a memorial service was held in New York City, at which Washington Irving presided and Daniel Webster and William Cullen Bryant spoke. In his eulogy, Bryant praised Cooper's achievements and noted:

> He wrote not for the fastidious, the over-refined, the morbidly delicate . . . but he wrote . . . for men and women in the ordinary healthful state of feeling— and in their admiration he found his reward. It is for this class that public

libraries are obliged to provide themselves with an extraordinary number of copies of his works. . . . Hence it is that he has earned a fame wider, I think, than any author of modern times.

Cooper's life and work had already taken on mythic dimensions. The breadth of his interests and the range of his accomplishments set the standards for nineteenth-century American writers. He was the first American novelist to create an extensive body of work. His social criticism helped define issues central to American identity—qualities of leadership, standards of excellence, measures for minority and majority voices, and the like. In this respect, Cooper might be regarded, to use D. H. Lawrence's phrase, as a saint with a gun. And just as the "Leather-Stocking Tales" had returned American culture to a pristine origin that defined all that was to follow, so too did Cooper's writing create a foundation for the careers of later writers and the directions of our nation's literary canon.

Cooper's primacy in American literary history, then, is not as much a matter of historical accident as it is the result of his visionary power. He articulated a compelling sense of the literary potential of American history—of the possibilities implicit in its past, of the tensions and contradictions inherent in its present, of the pressures exerted by its uncertain and unprecedented future. Cooper helped accelerate America's literary development by formulating thematic patterns, narrative structures, and prototypical characters and situations that later writers would return to again and again in their own efforts to come to terms with America's distinctive cultural identity.

Further Reading:
W. C. Bryant, "Discourse on the Life and Genius of Cooper," in *Memorial of James Fenimore Cooper*, 1852.
S. F. Cooper, *The Cooper Gallery*, 1865.
D. H. Lawrence, *Studies in Classic American Literature*, 1923.
H. W. Boynton, *James Fenimore Cooper*, 1931.
R. E. Spiller, *Fenimore Cooper: Critic of His Times*, 1931.
V. W. Brooks, *The World of Washington Irving*, 1950.
J. Grossman, *James Fenimore Cooper*, 1947, 1967.
H. N. Smith, *The Virgin Land*, 1957.
M. Bewley, *The Eccentric Design*, 1959.
D. A. Ringe, *James Fenimore Cooper*, 1962.
L. Fiedler, *Love and Death in the American Novel*, 1966.
R. Slotkin, *Regeneration Through Violence: The Mythology of the American Frontier, 1600–1860*, 1973.
H. D. Peck, *A World by Itself: The Pastoral Moment in Cooper's Fiction*, 1977.
S. Railton, *Fenimore Cooper: A Study of His Life and Imagination*, 1979.
W. Franklin, *The New World of James Fenimore Cooper*, 1982.
W. P. Kelly, *Plotting America's Past: Fenimore Cooper and the Leatherstocking Tales*, 1984.

Texts:
Cooper's Novels, 1859–1861.
A 48-volume edition of the works of James Fenimore Cooper is being prepared by the State University of New York Press.
See also *The Letters and Journals of James Fenimore Cooper*, ed. J. F. Beard, 6 vols., 1960–1968.

Preface to *The Leather-Stocking Tales* *

This series of Stories, which has obtained the name of "The Leather-Stocking Tales," has been written in a very desultory and inartificial manner. The order in which the several books appeared was essentially different from that in which they would have been presented to the world, had the regular course of their incidents been consulted. In "The Pioneers," the first of the series written, the Leather-Stocking is represented as already old, and driven from his early haunts in the forest, by the sound of the axe and the smoke of the settler. "The Last of the Mohicans," the next book in the order of publication, carried the readers back to a much earlier period in the history of our hero, representing him as middle-aged, and in the fullest vigor of manhood. In "The Prairie," his career terminates, and he is laid in his grave. There, it was originally the intention to leave him, in the expectation that, as in the case of the human mass, he would soon be forgotten. But a latent regard for this character induced the author to resuscitate him in "The Pathfinder," a book that was not long after succeeded by "The Deerslayer," thus completing the series as it now exists.

While the five books that have been written were originally published in the order just mentioned, that of the incidents insomuch as they are connected with the career of their principal character, is, as has been stated, very different. Taking the life of the Leather-Stocking as a guide, "The Deerslayer" should have been the opening book, for in that work he is seen just emerging into manhood; to be succeeded by "The Last of the Mohicans," "The Pathfinder," "The Pioneers," and "The Prairie." This arrangement embraces the order of events, though far from being that in which the books at first appeared. "The Pioneers" was published in 1822;[1] "The Deerslayer" in 1841; making the interval between them nineteen years. Whether these progressive years have had a tendency to lessen the value of the last-named book, by lessening the native fire of its author, or of adding somewhat in the way of improved taste and a more matured judgment, is for others to decide.

If anything from the pen of the writer of these romances is at all to outlive himself, it is, unquestionably, the series of "The Leather-Stocking Tales." To say this is not to predict a very lasting reputation for the series itself, but simply to express the belief it will outlast any, or all, of the works from the same hand.

It is undeniable that the desultory manner in which "The Leather-Stocking Tales" were written has, in a measure, impaired their harmony, and otherwise lessened their interest. This is proved by the fate of the two books last published, though probably the two most worthy an enlightened and cultivated reader's notice. If the facts could be ascertained, it is probable the result would show that of all those (in America, in particular) who have read the three first books of the series, not one in ten has a

---

* Written especially for a complete edition of *The Leather-Stocking Tales* that appeared in 1850.

[1] *The Pioneers* did not appear until February 1823.

knowledge of the existence even of the two last. Several causes have tended to produce this result. The long interval of time between the appearance of "The Prairie" and that of "The Pathfinder" was itself a reason why the later books of the series should be overlooked. There was no longer novelty to attract attention, and the interest was materially impaired by the manner in which events were necessarily anticipated, in laying the last of the series first before the world. With the generation that is now coming on the stage this fault will be partially removed by the edition contained in the present work, in which the several tales will be arranged solely in reference to their connection with each other.

The author has often been asked if he had any original in his mind, for the character of Leather-Stocking. In a physical sense, different individuals known to the writer in early life certainly presented themselves as models, through his recollections; but in a moral sense this man of the forest is purely a creation. The idea of delineating a character that possessed little of civilization but its highest principles as they are exhibited in the uneducated, and all of savage life that is not incompatible with these great rules of conduct, is perhaps natural to the situation in which Natty was placed. He is too proud of his origin to sink into the condition of the wild Indian, and too much a man of the woods not to imbibe as much as was at all desirable from his friends and companions. In a moral point of view it was the intention to illustrate the effect of seed scattered by the wayside. To use his own language, his "gifts" were "white gifts," and he was not disposed to bring on them discredit. On the other hand, removed from nearly all the temptations of civilized life, placed in the best associations of that which is deemed savage, and favorably disposed by nature to improve such advantages, it appeared to the writer that his hero was a fit subject to represent the better qualities of both conditions, without pushing either to extremes.

There was no violent stretch of the imagination, perhaps, in supposing one of civilized associations in childhood retaining many of his earliest lessons amid the scenes of the forest. Had these early impressions, however, not been sustained by continued though casual connection with men of his own color, if not of his own caste, all our information goes to show he would soon have lost every trace of his origin. It is believed that sufficient attention was paid to the particular circumstances in which this individual was placed, to justify the picture of his qualities that has been drawn. The Delawares early attracted the attention of the missionaries, and were a tribe unusually influenced by their precepts and example. In many instances they became Christians, and cases occurred in which their subsequent lives gave proof of the efficacy of the great moral changes that had taken place within them.

A leading character in a work of fiction has a fair right to the aid which can be obtained from a poetical view of the subject. It is in this view, rather than in one more strictly circumstantial, that Leather-Stocking has been drawn. The imagination has no great task in portraying to itself a being removed from the every-day inducements to err which abound in civilized life, while he retains the best and simplest of his early impressions; who sees God in the forest; hears him in the winds; bows to him in the firmament that o'ercanopies all; submits to his sway in a humble belief of his justice and mercy—in a word, a being who finds the impress of the Deity in all the works of nature, without any of the blots produced by the expedients, and passion, and mistakes of man. This is the most that has been attempted in the character of Leather-Stocking. Had this been done without any of the drawbacks of humanity, the picture would have been, in all probability, more pleasing than just. In order to preserve the *vraisemblable,*[2] therefore, traits derived from the prejudices, tastes, and even the weaknesses of his youth, have been mixed up with these higher qualities and longings, in a way, it is hoped, to represent a reasonable picture of human nature, without offering to the spectator a "monster of goodness."

It has been objected to these books that they give a more favorable picture of the red man than he deserves. The writer apprehends that much of this objection arises from the habits of those who have made it. One of his critics, on the appearance of the first work in which Indian character was portrayed, objected that its "characters were Indians of the school of Heckewelder,[3] rather than of the school of nature." These words quite probably contain the substance of the true answer to the objection. Heckewelder was an ardent, benevolent missionary, bent on the good of the red man, and seeing in him one who had the soul, reason, and characteristics of a fellow-being. The critic is understood to have been a very distinguished agent of the government, one very familiar with Indians, as they are seen at the councils to treat for the sale of their lands, where little or none of their domestic qualities come in play, and where, indeed, their evil passions are known to have the fullest scope. As just would it be to draw conclusions of the general state of American society from the scenes of the capital, as to suppose that the negotiating of one of these treaties is a fair picture of Indian life.

It is the privilege of all writers of fiction, more particularly when their works aspire to the elevation of romances, to present the *beau-idéal*[4] of their characters to the reader. This it is which constitutes poetry, and to suppose that the red man is to be represented only in the squalid misery or in the degraded moral state that certainly more or less belongs to his condition, is, we apprehend, taking a very narrow view of an author's privileges. Such criticism would have deprived the world of even Homer.

1850

---

[2] French: "verisimilitude." In a literary sense, realism.

[3] John Gottlieb Heckewelder (1743–1823), pioneer Moravian missionary among the Indians.

[4] French: "highest form of beauty."

from The Deerslayer

Chapter VII

"Clear, placid Leman! Thy contrasted lake
With the wild world I dwelt in, is a thing
Which warns me, with its stillness, to forsake
Earth's troubled waters for a purer spring.
This quiet sail is as a noiseless wing
To waft me from distraction: once I loved
Torn ocean's roar, but thy soft murmuring
Sounds sweet as if a sister's voice reproved,
*   That I with stern delights should e'er have been so*
moved."[1]
                    Byron.

Day had fairly dawned before the young man, whom we have left in the situation described in the last chapter, again opened his eyes. This was no sooner done than he started up and looked about him with the eagerness of one who suddenly felt the importance of accurately ascertaining his precise position. His rest had been deep and undisturbed; and when he awoke, it was with a clearness of intellect and a readiness of resources that were much needed at that particular moment. The sun had not risen, it is true, but the vault of heaven was rich with the winning softness that "brings and shuts the day," while the whole air was filled with the carols of birds, the hymns of the feathered tribe. These sounds first told Deerslayer the risks he ran. The air—for wind it could scarce be called—was still light, it is true, but it had increased a little in the course of the night, and as the canoes were mere feathers on the water, they had drifted twice the expected distance; and, what was still more dangerous, had approached so near the base of the mountain, that here rose precipitously from the eastern shore, as to render the carols of the birds plainly audible. This was not the worst. The third canoe had taken the same direction, and was slowly drifting toward a point where it must inevitably touch, unless turned aside by a shift of wind or human hands. In other respects, nothing presented itself to attract attention or to awaken alarm. The castle stood on its shoal, nearly abreast of the canoes, for the drift had amounted to miles in the course of the night, and the ark lay fastened to its piles, as both had been left so many hours before.

As a matter of course, Deerslayer's attention was first given to the canoe ahead. It was already quite near the point, and a very few strokes of the paddle sufficed to tell him that it must touch before he could possibly overtake it. Just at this moment, too, the wind inopportunely freshened, rendering the drift of the light craft much more rapid and certain. Feeling the impossibility of preventing a contact with the land, the young man wisely determined not to heat himself with unnecessary exertions; but first looking to the priming of his piece, he proceeded slowly and warily toward the point, taking care to make a little circuit, that he might be exposed on only one side as he approached.

[1] *Childe Harold's Pilgrimage* (Canto III, stanza 85),
by George Gordon, Lord Byron (1788–1824).

The canoe adrift, being directed by no such intelligence, pursued its proper way and grounded on a small sunken rock, at the distance of three or four yards from the shore. Just at that moment, Deerslayer had got abreast of the point and turned the bows of his own boat to the land; first casting loose his tow, that his movements might be unencumbered. The canoe hung an instant on the rock; then it rose a hair's-breadth on an almost imperceptible swell of the water, swung round, floated clear, and reached the strand. All this the young man noted, but it neither quickened his pulses nor hastened his hand. If any one had been lying in wait for the arrival of the waif, he must be seen, and the utmost caution in approaching the shore became indispensable; if no one was in ambush, hurry was unnecessary. The point being nearly diagonally opposite to the Indian encampment, he hoped the last, though the former was not only possible, but probable; for the savages were prompt in adopting all the expedients of their particular modes of warfare, and quite likely had many scouts searching the shores for craft to carry them off to the castle. As a glance at the lake from any height or projection would expose the smallest object on its surface, there was little hope that either of the canoes could pass unseen; and Indian sagacity needed no instruction to tell which way a boat or a log would drift, when the direction of the wind was known. As Deerslayer drew nearer and nearer to the land, the stroke of his paddle grew slower, his eye became more watchful, and his ears and nostrils almost dilated with the effort to detect any lurking danger. 'Twas a trying moment for a novice, nor was there the encouragement which even the timid sometimes feel, when conscious of being observed and commended. He was entirely alone, thrown on his own resources, and was cheered by no friendly eye, emboldened by no encouraging voice. Notwithstanding all these circumstances, the most experienced veteran in forest warfare could not have behaved better. Equally free from recklessness and hesitation, his advance was marked by a sort of philosophical prudence, that appeared to render him superior to all motives but those which were best calculated to effect his purpose. Such was the commencement of a career in forest exploits, that afterward rendered this man, in his way, and under the limits of his habits and opportunities, as renowned as many a hero whose name has adorned the pages of works more celebrated than legends simple as ours can ever become.

When about a hundred yards from the shore, Deerslayer rose in the canoe, gave three or four vigorous strokes with the paddle, sufficient of themselves to impel the bark to land, and then quickly laying aside the instrument of labor, he seized that of war. He was in the very act of raising the rifle, when a sharp report was followed by the buzz of a bullet that passed so near his body as to cause him involuntarily to start. The next instant Deerslayer staggered and fell his whole length in the bottom of the canoe. A yell—it came from a single voice—followed, and an Indian leaped from the bushes upon the open area of the point, bounding toward the canoe. This was the moment the young man desired. He rose on the instant and levelled his own rifle at his uncovered foe; but his finger hesitated about pulling the trigger on one whom he held at such a disadvantage. This little delay, probably, saved the life of the Indian, who bounded back into the cover as swiftly as he had broken out of it. In the mean time Deerslayer had been swiftly approaching the land, and his own canoe reached the point just as his enemy disappeared. As its movements had not been directed, it touched the shore a few yards from the other boat; and though the rifle of his foe had to be loaded, there was not time to secure his prize and to carry it beyond danger before he would be exposed to another shot. Under the circumstances, therefore, he did not pause an instant, but dashed into the woods and sought a cover.

On the immediate point there was a small open area, partly in native grass and partly beach, but a dense fringe of bushes lined its upper side. This narrow belt of dwarf vegetation passed, one issued immediately into the high and gloomy vaults of the forest. The land was tolerably level for a few hundred feet, and then it rose precipitously in a mountain-side. The trees were tall, large, and so free from underbrush that they resembled vast columns, irregularly scattered, upholding a dome of leaves. Although they stood tolerably close together, for their ages and size, the eye could penetrate to considerable distances; and bodies of men, even, might have engaged beneath their cover with concert and intelligence.

Deerslayer knew that his adversary must be employed in reloading, unless he had fled. The former proved to be the case, for the young man had no sooner placed himself behind a tree than he caught a glimpse of the arm of the Indian, his body being concealed by an oak, in the very act of forcing the leathered bullet home. Nothing would have been easier than to spring forward and decide the affair by a close assault on his unprepared foe; but every feeling of Deerslayer revolted at such a step, although his own life had just been attempted from a cover. He was yet unpractised in the ruthless expedients of savage warfare, of which he knew nothing except by tradition and theory, and it struck him as an unfair advantage to assail an unarmed foe. His color had heightened, his eye frowned, his lips were compressed, and all his energies were collected and ready; but, instead of advancing to fire, he dropped his rifle to the usual position of a sportsman in readiness to catch his aim, and muttered to himself, unconscious that he was speaking:

"No, no—that may be red-skin warfare, but it's not a Christian's gifts. Let the miscreant charge, and then we'll take it out like men; for the canoe he *must* not and *shall* not have. No, no; let him have time to load, and God will take care of the right!"

All this time the Indian had been so intent on his own movements that he was even ignorant that his enemy was in the wood. His only apprehension was, that the canoe would be recovered and carried away before he might be in readiness to prevent it. He had sought the cover from habit, but was within a few feet of the fringe of bushes, and could be at the margin of the forest in readiness to fire in a moment. The distance between him and his enemy was about fifty yards, and the trees were so arranged by nature that the line of sight was not interrupted, except by the particular trees behind which each party stood.

His rifle was no sooner loaded than the savage glanced around him, and advanced incautiously as regarded the real, but stealthily as respected the fancied position of his enemy, until he was fairly exposed. Then Deerslayer stepped from behind his own cover and hailed him.

"This-a-way, red-skin; this-a-way, if you're looking for me," he called out. "I'm young in war, but not so young as to stand on an open beach to be shot down like an owl by daylight. It rests on yourself whether it's peace or war atween us; for my gifts are white gifts, and I'm not one of them that thinks it valiant to slay human mortals singly in the woods."

The savage was a good deal startled by this sudden discovery of the danger he ran. He had a little knowledge of English, however, and caught the drift of the other's meaning. He was also too well schooled to betray alarm, but, dropping the butt of his rifle to the earth with an air of confidence, he made a gesture of lofty courtesy. All this was done with the ease and self-possession of one accustomed to consider no man his superior. In the midst of this consummate acting, however, the volcano that raged within caused his eyes to glare and his nostrils to dilate like those of some wild beast that is suddenly prevented from taking the fatal leap.

"Two canoe," he said, in the deep guttural tones of his race, holding up the number of fingers he mentioned, by way of preventing mistakes; "one for you—one for me."

"No, no, Mingo,² that will never do. You own neither; and neither shall you have, as long as I can prevent it. I know it's war atween your people and mine, but that's no reason why human mortals should slay each other like savage creatur's that meet in the woods; go your way, then, and leave me to go mine. The world is large enough for us both; and when we meet fairly in battle, why, the Lord will order the fate of each of us."

"Good!" exclaimed the Indian; "my brother missionary—great talk; all about Manitou."³

"Not so—not so, warrior. I'm not good enough for the Moravians,⁴ and am too good for most of the other vagabonds that preach about in the woods. No, no, I'm only a hunter, as yet, though afore the peace is made, 'tis like enough there'll be occasion to strike a blow at some of your people. Still, I wish it to be done in fair fight, and not in a quarrel about the ownership of a miserable canoe."

"Good! My brother very young—but he very wise. Little warrior—great talker. Chief, sometimes, in council."

"I don't know this, nor do I say it, Injin," returned Deerslayer, coloring a little at the ill-concealed sarcasm of the other's manner; "I look forward to a life in the woods, and I only hope it may be a peaceable one. All young men must go on the war-path when there's occasion, but war isn't needfully massacre. I've seen enough of the last, this very night, to know that Providence frowns on it; and I now invite you to go your own way, while I go mine; and hope that we may part fri'nds."

"Good! My brother has two scalp—grey hair under t'other. Old wisdom—young tongue."

Here the savage advanced with confidence, his hand extended, his face smiling, and his whole bearing denoting amity and respect. Deerslayer met his offered friendship in a proper spirit, and they shook hands cordially, each endeavoring to assure the other of his sincerity and desire to be at peace.

"All have his own," said the Indian; "my canoe, mine; your canoe, your'n. Go look; if your'n, you keep; if mine, I keep."

"That's just, red-skin; though you must be wrong in thinking the canoe your property. Howsever, seein' is believin', and we'll go down to the shore, where you may look with your own eyes; for it's likely you'll object to trustin' altogether to mine."

The Indian uttered his favorite exclamation of "good!" and then they walked side by side toward the shore. There was no apparent distrust in the manner of either, the Indian moving in advance, as if he wished to show his companion that he did not fear turning his back to him. As they reached the open ground the former pointed toward Deerslayer's boat, and said emphatically:

---

² Slang term for an Iroquois or Sioux brave.
³ One of the great spirits that rule nature.

⁴ Early sect of devout European missionaries who preached among the Indians.

"No mine—pale-face canoe. *This* red-man's. No want other man's canoe—want his own."

"You're wrong, red-skin, you're altogether wrong. This canoe was left in old Hutter's keeping, and is his'n according to all law, red or white, till its owner comes to claim it. Here's the seats and the stitching of the bark to speak for themselves. No man ever know'd an Injin to turn off such work."

"Good! My brother little ole—big wisdom. Injin no make him. White man's work."

"I'm glad you think so, for holding out to the contrary might have made ill blood atween us; every one having a right to take possession of his own. I'll just shove the canoe out of reach of dispute at once, as the quickest way of settling difficulties."

While Deerslayer was speaking he put a foot against the end of the light boat, and giving a vigorous shove, he sent it out into the lake a hundred feet or more, where, taking the true current, it would necessarily float past the point and be in no further danger of coming ashore. The savage started at this ready and decided expedient, and his companion saw that he cast a hurried and fierce glance at his own canoe, or that which contained the paddles. The change of manner, however, was but momentary, and then the Iroquois resumed his air of friendliness and a smile of satisfaction.

"Good!" he repeated, with stronger emphasis than ever. "Young head, old mind. Know how to settle quarrel. Farewell, brother. He go to house in water—muskrat house—Injin go to camp; tell chiefs no find canoe."

Deerslayer was not sorry to hear this proposal, for he felt anxious to join the females, and he took the offered hand of the Indian very willingly. The parting words were friendly, and, while the red-man walked calmly toward the wood, with the rifle in the hollow of his arm, without once looking back in uneasiness or distrust, the white man moved toward the remaining canoe, carrying his piece in the same pacific manner, it is true, but keeping his eyes fastened on the movements of the other. This distrust, however, seemed to be altogether uncalled for, and as if ashamed to have entertained it, the young man averted his look and stepped carelessly up to his boat. Here he began to push the canoe from the shore and to make his other preparations for departing. He might have been thus employed a minute, when, happening to turn his face toward the land, his quick and certain eye told him at a glance the imminent jeopardy in which his life was placed. The black, ferocious eyes of the savage were glancing on him, like those of the crouching tiger, through a small opening in the bushes, and the muzzle of his rifle seemed already to be opening in a line with his own body.

Then, indeed, the long practice of Deerslayer, as a hunter, did him good service. Accustomed to fire with the deer on the bound, and often when the precise position of the animal's body had in a manner to be guessed at, he used the same expedients here. To cock and poise his rifle were the acts of a single moment and a single motion; then, aiming almost without sighting, he fired into the bushes where he knew a body ought to be, in order to sustain the appalling countenance which alone was visible. There was not time to raise the piece any higher or to take a more deliberate aim. So rapid were his movements that both parties discharged their pieces at the same instant, the concussions mingling in one report. The mountains, indeed, gave back but a single echo. Deerslayer dropped his piece and stood, with head erect, steady as one of the pines in the calm of a June morning, watching the result; while the savage gave the yell that has become historical for its appalling influence leaped through the bushes and came bounding across the open ground, flourishing a tomahawk. Still Deerslayer moved not, but stood with his unloaded rifle fallen against his shoulders, while, with a hunter's habits, his hands were mechanically feeling for the powder-horn and charger. When about forty feet from his enemy, the savage hurled his keen weapon; but it was with an eye so vacant and a hand so unsteady and feeble that the young man caught it by the handle as it was flying past him. At that instant the Indian staggered and fell his whole length on the ground.

"I know'd it—I know'd it!" exclaimed Deerslayer, who was already preparing to force a fresh bullet into his rifle; "I know'd it must come to this, as soon as I had got the range from the creatur's eyes. A man sights suddenly and fires quick when his own life's in danger; yes, I know'd it would come to this. I was about the hundredth part of a second too quick for him, or it might have been bad for me! The riptyle's bullet has just grazed my side—but, say what you will for or ag'in 'em, a red-skin is by no means as sartain with powder and ball as a white man. Their gifts don't seem to lie that-a-way. Even Chingachgook,[5] great as he is in other matters, isn't downright deadly with the rifle."

By this time the piece was reloaded, and Deerslayer, after tossing the tomahawk into the canoe, advanced to his victim, and stood over him, leaning on his rifle, in melancholy attention. It was the first instance in which he had seen a man fall in battle —it was the first fellow-creature against whom he had ever seriously raised his own hand. The sensations were novel; and regret, with the freshness of our better feelings, mingled with his triumph. The Indian was not dead, though shot directly through the body. He lay on his back motionless, but his eyes, now full of consciousness, watched each action of his victor—as the fallen bird regards the fowler—jealous of every movement. The man probably expected the fatal blow which was to precede the loss of his scalp; or perhaps he anticipated that this latter act of cruelty would precede his death. Deerslayer read his thoughts; and he found a melancholy satisfaction in relieving the apprehensions of the helpless savage.

"No, no, red-skin," he said; "you've nothing more to fear from me. I am of a Christian stock, and scalping is not of my gifts. I'll just make sartain of your rifle and then come back and do you what service I can. Though here I can't stay much longer, as the crack of three rifles will be apt to bring some of your devils down upon me."

The close of this was said in a sort of a soliloquy, as the young man went in quest of the fallen rifle. The piece was found where its owner had dropped it, and was immediately put into the canoe. Laying his own rifle at its side, Deerslayer then returned and stood over the Indian again.

"All inmity atween you and me's at an ind, red-skin," he said; "and you may set your heart at rest on the score of the scalp or any further injury. My gifts are white, as I've told you; and I hope my conduct will be white also!"

Could looks have conveyed all they meant, it is probable Deerslayer's innocent vanity on the subject of color would have been rebuked a little; but he comprehended the gratitude that was expressed in the eyes of the dying savage, without in the least detecting the bitter sarcasm that struggled with the better feeling.

---

[5] A young Mohican chief of the larger Delaware tribe, he is also Deerslayer's Indian "blood-brother." Natty Bumppo was orphaned at an early age and was partially raised by the Delaware Indians. Chingachgook plays a significant role in both The Deerslayer and The Last of the Mohicans.

"Water!" ejaculated the thirsty and unfortunate creature; "give poor Injun water."

"Aye, water you shall have, if you drink the lake dry. I'll just carry you down to it, that you may take your fill. This is the way, they tell me, with all wounded people—water is their greatest comfort and delight."

So saying, Deerslayer raised the Indian in his arms, and carried him to the lake. Here he first helped him to take an attitude in which he could appease his burning thirst; after which he seated himself on a stone and took the head of his wounded adversary in his own lap and endeavored to soothe his anguish in the best manner he could.

"It would be sinful in me to tell you your time hadn't come, warrior," he commenced, "and therefore I'll not say it. You've passed the middle age already, and, considerin' the sort of lives ye lead, your days have been pretty well filled. The principal thing now is to look forward to what comes next. Neither red-skin nor pale-face, on the whole, calculates much on sleepin' forever; but both expect to live in another world. Each has his gifts, and will be judged by 'em, and, I suppose, you've thought these matters over enough, not to stand in need of sarmons when the trial comes. You'll find your happy hunting-grounds, if you've been a just Injin; if an onjust, you'll meet your desarts in another way. I've my own idees about these things; but you're too old and exper'enced to need any explanations from one as young as I."

"Good!" ejaculated the Indian, whose voice retained its depth even as life ebbed away; "young head—ole wisdom!"

"It's sometimes a consolation, when the ind comes, to know that them we've harmed, or *tried* to harm, forgive us. I suppose natur' seeks this relief, by way of getting a pardon on 'arth; as we never can know whether He pardons, who is all in all, till judgment itself comes. It's soothing to know that *any* pardon at such times; and that, I conclude, is the secret. Now, as for myself, I overlook altogether your designs ag'in my life; first, because no harm came of 'em; next, because it's your gifts and natur' and trainin', and I ought not to have trusted you at all; and, finally and chiefly, because I can bear no ill-will to a dying man, whether heathen or Christian. So put your heart at ease, so far as I'm consarned; you know best what other matters ought to trouble you, or what ought to give you satisfaction in so trying a moment."

It is probable that the Indian had some of the fearful glimpses of the unknown state of being which God in mercy seems at times to afford to all the human race; but they were necessarily in conformity with his habits and prejudices. Like most of his people, and like too many of our own, he thought more of dying in a way to gain applause among those he left than to secure a better state of existence hereafter. While Deerslayer was speaking, his mind was a little bewildered, though he felt that the intention was good; and when he had done, a regret passed over his spirit that none of his own tribe were present to witness his stoicism under extreme bodily suffering, and the firmness with which he met his end. With the high innate courtesy that so often distinguishes the Indian warrior before he becomes corrupted by too much intercourse with the worst class of the white men, he endeavored to express his thankfulness for the other's good intentions, and to let him understand that they were appreciated.

"Good!" he repeated, for this was an English word much used by the savages—"good—young head; young *heart,* too. *Old* heart tough; no shed tear. Hear Indian when he die, and no want to lie—what he call him?"

"Deerslayer is the name I bear now, though the Delawares have said that when I get back from this war-path, I shall have a more manly title, provided I can 'arn one."

"That good name for boy—poor name for warrior. He get better quick. No fear *there* "—the savage had strength sufficient, under the strong excitement he felt, to raise a hand and tap the young man on his breast—"eye sartain—finger lightning—aim, death—great warrior soon. No Deerslayer—Hawkeye—Hawkeye—Hawkeye. Shake hand."

Deerslayer—or Hawkeye, as the youth was then first named, for in after years he bore the appellation throughout all that region—Deerslayer took the hand of the savage, whose last breath was drawn in that attitude, gazing in admiration at the countenance of a stranger, who had shown so much readiness, skill, and firmness, in a scene that was equally trying and novel. When the reader remembers it is the highest gratification an Indian can receive to see his enemy betray weakness, he will be better able to appreciate the conduct which had extorted so great a concession at such a moment.

"His spirit has fled!" said Deerslayer, in a suppressed, melancholy voice. "Ah's me! Well, to this we must all come, sooner or later; and he is happiest, let his skin be of what color it may, who is best fitted to meet it. Here lies the body of no doubt a brave warrior, and the soul is already flying toward its heaven or hell, whether that be a happy hunting-ground, a place scant of game; regions of glory, according to Moravian doctrine, or flames of fire! So it happens, too, as regards other matters! Here have old Hutter and Hurry Harry got themselves into difficulty, if they hav'n't got themselves into torment and death, and all for a bounty that luck offers to me in what many would think a lawful and suitable manner. But not a farthing of such money shall cross my hand. White I was born, and white will I die; clinging to color to the last, even though the King's Majesty, his governors, and all his councils, both at home and in the Colonies, forget from what they come, and where they hope to go, and all for a little advantage in warfare. No, no—warrior, hand of mine shall never molest your scalp, and so your soul may rest in peace on the p'int of making a decent appearance, when the body comes to join it, in your own land of spirits."

Deerslayer arose as soon as he had spoken. Then he placed the body of the dead man in a sitting posture, with its back against the little rock, taking the necessary care to prevent it from falling or in any way settling into an attitude that might be thought unseemly by the sensitive, though wild, notions of a savage. When this duty was performed, the young man stood gazing at the grim countenance of his fallen foe, in a sort of melancholy abstraction. As was his practice, however, a habit gained by living so much alone in the forest, he then began again to give utterance to his thoughts and feelings aloud.

"I didn't wish your life, red-skin," he said, "but you left me no choice atween killing or being killed. Each party acted according to his gifts, I suppose, and blame can light on neither. You were treacherous, according to your natur' in war, and I was a little oversightful, as I'm apt to be in trusting others. Well, this is my first battle with a human mortal, though it's not likely to be the last. I have fou't most of the creatur's of the forest, such as bears, wolves, painters,[6] and catamounts,[7] but this is the beginning with the red-skins. If I was Injin born, now, I might tell of this, or carry

---

[6] Panthers.   [7] Lynxes or cougars.

in the scalp, and boast of the expl'ite afore the whole tribe; or, if my inimy had only been even a bear, 'twould have been nat'ral and proper to let everybody know what had happened; but I don't well see how I'm to let even Chingachgook into this secret, so long as it can be done only by boasting with a white tongue. And why should I wish to boast of it a'ter all? It's slaying a human, although he was a savage; and how do I know that he was a just Injin; and that he has not been taken away suddenly to anything but happy hunting-grounds. When it's onsartain whether good or evil has been done, the wisest way is not to be boastful—still, I *should* like Chingachgook to know that I haven't discredited the Delawares or my training!"

Part of this was uttered aloud, while part was merely muttered between the speaker's teeth; his more confident opinions enjoying the first advantage, while his doubts were expressed in the latter mode. Soliloquy and reflection received a startling interruption, however, by the sudden appearance of a second Indian on the lake shore, a few hundred yards from the point. This man, evidently another scout, who had probably been drawn to the place by the reports of the rifles, broke out of the forest with so little caution that Deerslayer caught a view of his person before he was himself discovered. When the latter event did occur, as was the case a moment later, the savage gave a loud yell, which was answered by a dozen voices from different parts of the mountain-side. There was no longer any time for delay; in another minute the boat was quitting the shore under long and steady sweeps of the paddle.

As soon as Deerslayer believed himself to be at a safe distance, he ceased his efforts, permitting the little bark to drift, while he leisurely took a survey of the state of things. The canoe first sent adrift was floating before the air, quite a quarter of a mile above him, and a little nearer to the shore than he wished, now that he knew more of the savages were so near at hand. The canoe shoved from the point was within a few yards of him, he having directed his own course toward it on quitting the land. The dead Indian lay in grim quiet where he had left him, the warrior who had shown himself from the forest had already vanished, and the woods themselves were as silent and seemingly deserted as the day they came fresh from the hands of their great Creator. This profound stillness, however, lasted but a moment. When time had been given to the scouts of the enemy to reconnoitre, they burst out of the thicket upon the naked point, filling the air with yells of fury at discovering the death of their companion. These cries were immediately succeeded by shouts of delight when they reached the body and clustered eagerly around it. Deerslayer was a sufficient adept in the usages of the natives to understand the reason of the change. The yell was the customary lamentation at the loss of a warrior, the shout a sign of rejoicing that the conqueror had not been able to secure the scalp; the trophy without which a victory is never considered complete. The distance at which the canoes lay probably prevented any attempts to injure the conqueror, the American Indian, like the panther of his own woods, seldom making any effort against his foe unless tolerably certain it is under circumstances that may be expected to prove effective.

As the young man had no longer any motive to remain near the point, he prepared to collect his canoes, in order to tow them off to the castle. That nearest was soon in tow, when he proceeded in quest of the other, which was all this time floating up the lake. The eye of Deerslayer was no sooner fastened on this last boat, than it struck him that it was nearer to the shore than it would have been had it merely followed the course of the gentle current of air. He began to suspect the influence of some unseen current in the water, and he quickened his exertions, in order to regain possession of it before it could drift into a dangerous proximity to the woods. On getting nearer, he thought that the canoe had a perceptible motion through the water, and, as it lay broadside to the air, that this motion was taking it toward the land. A few vigorous strokes of the paddle carried him still nearer, when the mystery was explained. Something was evidently in motion on the off-side of the canoe or that which was furthest from himself, and closer scrutiny showed that it was a naked human arm. An Indian was lying in the bottom of the canoe, and was propelling it slowly, but certainly, to the shore, using his hand as a paddle. Deerslayer understood the whole artifice at a glance. A savage had swum off to the boat while he was occupied with his enemy on the point, got possession, and was using these means to urge it to the shore.

Satisfied that the man in the canoe could have no arms, Deerslayer did not hesitate to dash close alongside of the retiring boat, without deeming it necessary to raise his own rifle. As soon as the wash of the water, which he made in approaching, became audible to the prostrate savage, the latter sprang to his feet, and uttered an exclamation that proved how completely he was taken by surprise.

"If you've enj'yed yourself enough in that canoe, redskin," Deerslayer coolly observed, stopping his own career in sufficient time to prevent an absolute collision between the two boats—"if you've enj'yed yourself enough in that canoe, you'll do a prudent act by taking to the lake ag'in. I'm reasonable in these matters, and don't crave your blood, though there's them about that would look upon you more as a due-bill for the bounty than a human mortal.[8] Take to the lake this minute, afore we get to hot words."

The savage was one of those who did not understand a word of English, and he was indebted to the gestures of Deerslayer, and to the expression of an eye that did not often deceive, for an imperfect comprehension of his meaning. Perhaps, too, the sight of the rifle that lay so near the hand of the white man quickened his decision. At all events, he crouched like a tiger about to take his leap, uttered a yell, and the next instant his naked body disappeared in the water. When he rose to take breath, it was at the distance of several yards from the canoe, and the hasty glance he threw behind him denoted how much he feared the arrival of a fatal messenger from the rifle of his foe. But the young man made no indication of any hostile intention. Deliberately securing the canoe to the others, he began to paddle from the shore; and by the time the Indian reached the land, and had shaken himself, like a spaniel on quitting the water, his dreaded enemy was already beyond rifle-shot on his way to the castle. As was so much his practice, Deerslayer did not fail to soliloquize on what had just occurred, while steadily pursuing his course toward the point of destination.

"Well, well"—he commenced—" 'twould have been wrong to kill a human mortal without an object. Scalps are of no account with me, and life is sweet, and ought not to be taken marcilessly by them that have white gifts. The savage was a Mingo, it's true; and I make no doubt he is, and will be as long as he lives, a ra'al

---

[8] At the time, the British were offering an attractive premium for Indian scalps.

riptyle and vagabond; but that's no reason I should forget my gifts and color. No, no—let him go; if ever we meet ag'in, rifle in hand, why then 'twill be seen which has the stoutest heart and the quickest eye. Hawkeye! That's not a bad name for a warrior, sounding much more manful and valiant than Deerslayer! 'Twouldn't be a bad title to begin with, and it has been fairly 'arned. If 'twas Chingachgook, now, he might go home and boast of his deeds, and the chiefs would name him Hawkeye in a minute; but it don't become white blood to brag, and 'tisn't easy to see how the matter can be known unless I do. Well, well—everything is in the hands of Providence; this affair as well as another; I'll trust to that for getting my desarts in all things."

Having thus betrayed what might be termed his weak spot, the young man continued to paddle in silence, making his way diligently, and as fast as his tows would allow him, toward the castle. By this time the sun had not only risen, but it had appeared over the eastern mountains, and was shedding a flood of glorious light on this as yet unchristened sheet of water. The whole scene was radiant with beauty; and no one unaccustomed to the ordinary history of the woods would fancy it had so lately witnessed incidents so ruthless and barbarous. As he approached the building of old Hutter, Deerslayer thought, or rather *felt,* that its appearance was in singular harmony with all the rest of the scene. Although nothing had been consulted but strength and security, the rude, massive logs, covered with their rough bark, the projecting roof, and the form, would contribute to render the building picturesque in almost any situation, while its actual position added novelty and piquancy to its other points of interest.

When Deerslayer drew nearer to the castle, however, objects of interest presented themselves that at once eclipsed any beauties that might have distinguished the scenery of the lake, and the site of the singular edifice. Judith and Hetty stood on the platform before the door, Hurry's door-yard, awaiting his approach with manifest anxiety; the former, from time to time, taking a survey of his person and of the canoes through the old ship's spy-glass that has been already mentioned. Never probably did this girl seem more brilliantly beautiful than at that moment; the flush of anxiety and alarm increasing her color to its richest tints, while the softness of her eyes, a charm that even poor Hetty shared with her, was deepened by intense concern. Such, at least, without pausing or pretending to analyze motives, or to draw any other very nice distinctions between cause and effect, were the opinions of the young man, as his canoes reached the side of the ark, where he carefully fastened all three before he put his foot on the platform.

1841

from The Last of the Mohicans

Chapter XIII

"I'll seek a readier path."
Parnell

The route taken by Hawk-eye lay across those sandy plains, relieved by occasional valleys and swells of land, which had been traversed by their party on the morning of the same day, with the baffled Magua for their guide. The sun had now fallen low toward the distant mountains; and as their journey lay through the interminable forest, the heat was no longer oppressive. Their progress, in consequence, was proportionate; and long before the twilight gathered about them, they had made good many toilsome miles on their return.

The hunter, like the savage whose place he filled, seemed to select among the blind signs of their wild route, with a species of instinct, seldom abating his speed, and never pausing to deliberate. A rapid and oblique glance at the moss on the trees, with an occasional upward gaze toward the setting sun, or a steady but passing look at the direction of the numerous watercourses, through which he waded, were sufficient to determine his path, and remove his greatest difficulties. In the mean time, the forest began to change its hues, losing that lively green which had embellished its arches, in the graver light which is the usual precursor of the close of day.

While the eyes of the sisters were endeavoring to catch glimpses through the trees of the flood of golden glory which formed a glittering halo around the sun, tingeing here and there with ruby streaks, or bordering with narrow edgings of shining yellow, a mass of clouds that lay piled at no great distance above the western hills, Hawk-eye turned suddenly, and pointing upward toward the gorgeous heavens, he spoke—

"Yonder is the signal given to man to seek his food and natural rest," he said; "better and wiser would it be, if he could understand the signs of nature, and take a lesson from the fowls of the air, and the beasts of the fields! Our night, however, will soon be over; for, with the moon, we must be up and moving again. I remember to have fou't the Maquas, hereaways, in the first war in which I ever drew blood from man; and we threw up a work of blocks, to keep the ravenous varments from handling our scalps. If my marks do not fail me, we shall find the place a few rods further to our left."

Without waiting for an assent, or, indeed, for any reply, the sturdy hunter moved boldly into a dense thicket of young chestnuts, shoving aside the branches of the exuberant shoots which nearly covered the ground, like a man who expected, at each step, to discover some object he had formerly known. The recollection of the scout did not deceive him. After penetrating through the brush, matted as it was with briers, for a few hundred feet, he entered an open space, that surrounded a low, green hillock,

[1] From the poem "A Night-Piece on Death" by
Thomas Parnell (1679–1718).

which was crowned by the decayed block-house in question. This rude and neglected building was one of those deserted works, which, having been thrown up on an emergency, had been abandoned with the disappearance of danger, and was now quietly crumbling in the solitude of the forest, neglected, and nearly forgotten, like the circumstances which had caused it to be reared. Such memorials of the passage and struggles of man are yet frequent throughout the broad barrier of wilderness which once separated the hostile provinces, and form a species of ruins that are intimately associated with the recollections of colonial history, and which are in appropriate keeping with the gloomy character of the surrounding scenery. The roof of bark had long since fallen, and mingled with the soil; but the huge logs of pine, which had been hastily thrown together, still preserved their relative positions, though one angle of the work had given way under the pressure, and threatened a speedy downfall to the remainder of the rustic edifice. While Heyward and his companions hesitated to approach a building so decayed, Hawk-eye and the Indians entered within the low walls, not only without fear, but with obvious interest. While the former surveyed the ruins, both internally and externally, with the curiosity of one whose recollections were reviving at each moment, Chingachgook related to his son, in the language of the Delawares, and with the pride of a conqueror, the brief history of the skirmish which had been fought, in his youth, in that secluded spot. A strain of melancholy, however, blended with his triumph, rendering his voice, as usual, soft and musical.

In the mean time, the sisters gladly dismounted, and prepared to enjoy their halt in the coolness of the evening, and in a security which they believed nothing but the beasts of the forest could invade.

"Would not our resting-place have been more retired, my worthy friend," demanded the more vigilant Duncan, perceiving that the scout had already finished his short survey, "had we chosen a spot less known, and one more rarely visited than this?"

"Few live who know the block-house was ever raised," was the slow and musing answer, " 'tis not often that books are made, and narratives written, of such a skrimmage as was here fou't atween the Mohicans and the Mohawks,[2] in a war of their own waging. I was then a younker, and went out with the Delawares, because I know'd they were a scandalized and wronged race. Forty days and forty nights did the imps crave our blood around this pile of logs, which I designed and partly reared, being, as you'll remember, no Indian myself, but a man without a cross. The Delawares lent themselves to the work, and we made it good, ten to twenty, until our numbers were nearly equal, and then we sallied out upon the hounds, and not a man of them ever got back to tell the fate of his party. Yes, yes; I was then young, and new to the sight of blood; and not relishing the thought that creatures who had spirits like myself should lay on the naked ground, to be torn asunder by beasts, or to bleach in the rains, I buried the dead with my own hands, under that very little hillock where you have placed yourselves; and no bad seat does it make neither, though it be raised by the bones of mortal men."

Heyward and the sisters arose, on the instant, from the grassy sepulchre; nor could

---

[2] The Mohicans and Mohawks were rival groups within the Algonquin tribe. The Mohicans, a considerably smaller group occupying the upper Hudson River area, were eventually eliminated by the Mohawks.

the two latter, notwithstanding the terrific scenes they had so recently passed through, entirely suppress an emotion of natural horror, when they found themselves in such familiar contact with the grave of the dead Mohawks. The gray light, the gloomy little area of dark grass, surrounded by its border of brush, beyond which the pines rose, in breathing silence, apparently, into the very clouds, and the deathlike stillness of the vast forest, were all in unison to deepen such a sensation.

"They are gone, and they are harmless," continued Hawk-eye, waving his hand, with a melancholy smile, at their manifest alarm: "they'll never shout the war-whoop nor strike a blow with the tomahawk again! And of all those who aided in placing them where they lie, Chingachgook and I only are living. The brothers and family of the Mohican formed our war-party; and you see before you all that are now left of his race."

The eyes of the listeners involuntarily sought the forms of the Indians, with a compassionate interest in their desolate fortune. Their dark persons were still to be seen within the shadows of the block-house, the son listening to the relation of his father with that sort of intenseness which would be created by a narrative that redounded so much to the honor of those whose names he had long revered for their courage and savage virtues.

"I had thought the Delawares a pacific people," said Duncan, "and that they never waged war in person; trusting the defence of their lands to those very Mohawks that you slew!"

" 'Tis true in part," returned the scout, "and yet, at the bottom, 'tis a wicked lie. Such a treaty was made in ages gone by, through the deviltries of the Dutchers, who wished to disarm the natives that had the best right to the country, where they had settled themselves. The Mohicans, though a part of the same nation having to deal with the English, never entered into the silly bargain, but kept to their manhood; as in truth did the Delawares, when their eyes were opened to their folly. You see before you a chief of the great Mohican Sagamores! Once his family could chase their deer over tracts of country wider than that which belongs to the Albany Patteroon, without crossing brook or hill that was not their own; but what is left to their descendant! He may find his six feet of earth when God chooses, and keep it in peace perhaps, if he has a friend who will take the pains to sink his head so low, that the ploughshares cannot reach it!"

"Enough!" said Heyward, apprehensive that the subject might lead to a discussion that would interrupt the harmony so necessary to the preservation of his fair companions: "we have journeyed far, and few among us are blessed with forms like that of yours, which seems to know neither fatigue nor weakness."

"The sinews and bones of a man carry me through it all," said the hunter, surveying his muscular limbs with a simplicity that betrayed the honest pleasure the compliment afforded him: "there are larger and heavier men to be found in the settlements, but you might travel many days in a city before you could meet one able to walk fifty miles without stopping to take breath, or who has kept the hounds within hearing during a chase of hours. However, as flesh and blood are not always the same, it is quite reasonable to suppose that the gentle ones are willing to rest, after all they have seen and done this day. Uncas, clear out the spring, while your father and I make a cover for their tender heads of these chestnut shoots, and a bed of grass and leaves."

The dialogue ceased, while the hunter and his companions busied themselves in preparations for the comfort and protection of those they guided. A spring, which many long years before had induced the natives to select the place for their temporary fortification, was soon cleared of leaves, and a fountain of crystal gushed from the bed, diffusing its waters over the verdant hillock. A corner of the building was then roofed in such a manner as to exclude the heavy dew of the climate, and piles of sweet shrubs and dried leaves were laid beneath it for the sisters to repose on.

While the diligent woodsmen were employed in this manner, Cora and Alice partook of that refreshment which duty required much more than inclination prompted them to accept. They then retired within the walls, and first offering up their thanksgivings for past mercies, and petitioning for a continuance of the Divine favor throughout the coming night, they laid their tender forms on the fragrant couch, and in spite of recollections and forebodings, soon sank into those slumbers which nature so imperiously demanded, and which were sweetened by hopes for the morrow. Duncan had prepared himself to pass the night in watchfulness near them, just without the ruin, but the scout, perceiving his intention, pointed toward Chingachgook, as he cooly disposed his own person on the grass, and said—

"The eyes of a white man are too heavy and too blind for such a watch as this! The Mohican will be our sentinel, therefore let us sleep."

"I proved myself a sluggard on my post during the past night," said Heyward, "and have less need of repose than you, who did more credit to the character of a soldier. Let all the party seek their rest, then, while I hold the guard."

"If we lay among the white tents of the 60th, and in front of an enemy like the French, I could not ask for a better watchman," returned the scout; "but in the darkness and among the signs of the wilderness your judgment would be like the folly of a child, and your vigilance thrown away. Do then, like Uncas and myself, sleep, and sleep in safety."

Heyward perceived, in truth, that the younger Indian had thrown his form on the side of the hillock while they were talking, like one who sought to make the most of the time allotted to rest, and that his example had been followed by David, whose voice literally "clove to his jaws" with the fever of his wound, heightened, as it was, by their toilsome march. Unwilling to prolong a useless discussion, the young man affected to comply, by posting his back against the logs of the block-house, in a half-recumbent posture, though resolutely determined, in his own mind, not to close an eye until he had delivered his precious charge into the arms of Munro himself. Hawk-eye, believing he had prevailed, soon fell asleep, and a silence as deep as the solitude in which they had found it pervaded the retired spot.

For many minutes Duncan succeeded in keeping his senses on the alert, and alive to every moaning sound that arose from the forest. His vision became more acute as the shades of evening settled on the place; and even after the stars were glimmering above his head, he was able to distinguish the recumbent forms of his companions, as they lay stretched on the grass, and to note the person of Chingachgook, who sat upright and motionless as one of the trees which formed the dark barrier on every side of them. He still heard the gentle breathings of the sisters, who lay within a few feet of him, and not a leaf was ruffled by the passing air, of which his ear did not detect the whispering sound. At length, however, the mournful notes of a whip-poor-will became blended with the moanings of an owl; his heavy eyes occasionally sought the bright rays of the stars, and then he fancied he saw them through the fallen lids. At instants of momentary wakefulness he mistook a bush for his associate sentinel; his head next sank upon his shoulder, which, in its turn, sought the support of the ground; and, finally, his whole person became relaxed and pliant, and the young man sank into a deep sleep, dreaming that he was a knight of ancient chivalry, holding his midnight vigils before the tent of a recaptured princess, whose favor he did not despair of gaining, by such a proof of devotion and watchfulness.

How long the tired Duncan lay in this insensible state he never knew himself, but his slumbering visions had been long lost in total forgetfulness, when he was awakened by a light tap on the shoulder. Aroused by this signal, slight as it was, he sprang upon his feet with a confused recollection of the self-imposed duty he had assumed with the commencement of the night—

"Who comes?" he demanded, feeling for his sword, at the place where it was usually suspended. "Speak! friend or enemy?"

"Friend," replied the low voice of Chingachgook; who, pointing upward at the luminary which was shedding its mild light through the opening in the trees, directly on their bivouac, immediately added, in his rude English, "moon comes, and white man's fort far—far off; time to move, when sleep shuts both eyes of the Frenchman!"

"You say true! call up your friends, and bridle the horses, while I prepare my own companions for the march!"

"We are awake, Duncan," said the soft, silvery tones of Alice within the building, "and ready to travel very fast, after so refreshing a sleep; but you have watched through the tedious night in our behalf, after having endured so much fatigue the livelong day!"

"Say, rather, I would have watched, but my treacherous eyes betrayed me; twice have I proved myself unfit for the trust I bear."

"Nay, Duncan, deny it not," interrupted the smiling Alice, issuing from the shadows of the building into the light of the moon, in all the loveliness of her freshened beauty; "I know you to be a heedless one, when self is the object of your care, and but too vigilant in favor of others. Can we not tarry here a little longer, while you find the rest you need? Cheerfully, most cheerfully, will Cora and I keep the vigils, while you, and all these brave men, endeavor to snatch a little sleep!"

"If shame could cure me of my drowsiness, I should never close an eye again," said the uneasy youth, gazing at the ingenuous countenance of Alice, where, however, in its sweet solicitude, he read nothing to confirm his half-awakened suspicion. "It is but too true, that after heading you into danger by my heedlessness, I have not even the merit of guarding your pillows as should become a soldier."

"No one but Duncan himself should accuse Duncan of such a weakness. Go, then, and sleep; believe me, neither of us, weak girls as we are, will betray our watch."

The young man was relieved from the awkwardness of making any further protestations of his own demerits, by an exclamation from Chingachgook, and the attitude of riveted attention assumed by his son.

"The Mohicans hear an enemy!" whispered Hawk-eye, who, by this time, in common with the whole party, was awake and stirring. "They scent danger in the wind!"

"God forbid!" exclaimed Heyward. "Surely we have had enough of bloodshed."

While he spoke, however, the young soldier seized his rifle, and advancing toward the front, prepared to atone for his venial remissness, by freely exposing his life in defence of those he attended.

" 'Tis some creature of the forest prowling around us in quest of food," he said, in a whisper, as soon as the low, and apparently distant sounds, which had startled the Mohicans, reached his own ears.

"Hist!" returned the attentive scout; "'tis man; even I can now tell his tread, poor as my senses are when compared to an Indian's! That scampering Huron has fallen in with one of Montcalm's outlying parties, and they have struck upon our trail. I shouldn't like, myself, to spill more human blood in this spot," he added, looking around with anxiety in his features, at the dim objects by which he was surrounded; "but what must be, must! Lead the horses into the block-house, Uncas; and, friends, do you follow to the same shelter. Poor and old as it is, it offers a cover, and has rung with the crack of a rifle afore to-night!"

He was instantly obeyed, the Mohicans leading the Narragansets within the ruin, whither the whole party repaired, with the most guarded silence.

The sounds of approaching footsteps were now too distinctly audible, to leave any doubts as to the nature of the interruption. They were soon mingled with voices calling to each other in an Indian dialect, which the hunter, in a whisper, affirmed to Heyward was the language of the Hurons. When the party reached the point where the horses had entered the thicket which surrounded the block-house, they were evidently at fault, having lost those marks which, until that moment, had directed their pursuit.

It would seem by the voices that twenty men were soon collected at that one spot, mingling their different opinions and advice in noisy clamor.

"The knaves know our weakness," whispered Hawk-eye, who stood by the side of Heyward, in deep shade, looking through an opening in the logs, "or they wouldn't indulge their idleness in such a squaw's march. Listen to the reptiles! each man among them seems to have two tongues, and but a single leg."

Duncan, brave as he was in the combat, could not, in such a moment of painful suspense, make any reply to the cool and characteristic remark of the scout. He only grasped his rifle more firmly, and fastened his eyes upon the narrow opening, through which he gazed upon the moonlight view with increasing anxiety. The deeper tones of one who spoke as having authority were next heard, amid a silence that denoted the respect with which his orders, or rather advice, was received. After which, by the rustling of leaves, and cracking of dried twigs, it was apparent the savages were separating in pursuit of the lost trail. Fortunately for the pursued, the light of the moon, while it shed a flood of mild lustre upon the little area around the ruin, was not sufficiently strong to penetrate the deep arches of the forest, where the objects still lay in deceptive shadow. The search proved fruitless; for so short and sudden had been the passage from the faint path the travellers had journeyed into the thicket, that every trace of their footsteps was lost in the obscurity of the woods.

It was not long, however, before the restless savages were heard beating the brush, and gradually approaching the inner edge of that dense border of young chestnuts which encircled the little area.

"They are coming," muttered Heyward, endeavoring to thrust his rifle through the chink in the logs; "let us fire on their approach."

"Keep everything in the shade," returned the scout; "the snapping of a flint, or even the smell of a single karnel of the brimstone, would bring the hungry varlets upon us in a body. Should it please God that we must give battle for the scalps, trust to the experience of men who know the ways of the savages, and who are not often backward when the war-whoop is howled."

Duncan cast his eyes behind him, and saw that the trembling sisters were cowering in the far corner of the building, while the Mohicans stood in the shadow, like two upright posts, ready, and apparently willing, to strike, when the blow should be needed. Curbing his impatience, he again looked out upon the area, and awaited the result in silence. At that instant the thicket opened, and a tall and armed Huron advanced a few paces into the open space. As he gazed upon the silent block-house, the moon fell full upon his swarthy countenance, and betrayed its surprise and curiosity. He made the exclamation which usually accompanies the former emotion in an Indian, and, calling in a low voice, soon drew a companion to his side.

These children of the woods stood together for several moments pointing at the crumbling edifice, and conversing in the unintelligible language of their tribe. They then approached, though with slow and cautious steps, pausing every instant to look at the building, like startled deer, whose curiosity struggled powerfully with their awakened apprehensions for the mastery. The foot of one of them suddenly rested on the mound, and he stopped to examine its nature. At this moment, Heyward observed that the scout loosened his knife in its sheath, and lowered the muzzle of his rifle. Imitating these movements, the young man prepared himself for the struggle, which now seemed inevitable.

The savages were so near, that the least motion in one of the horses, or even a breath louder than common, would have betrayed the fugitives. But, in discovering the character of the mound, the attention of the Hurons appeared directed to a different object. They spoke together, and the sounds of their voices were low and solemn, as if influenced by a reverence that was deeply blended with awe. Then they drew wearily back, keeping their eyes riveted on the ruin, as if they expected to see the apparitions of the dead issue from its silent walls, until having reached the boundary of the area, they moved slowly into the thicket, and disappeared.

Hawk-eye dropped the breech of his rifle to the earth, and drawing a long, free breath, exclaimed in an audible whisper—

"Ay! they respect the dead, and it has this time saved their own lives, and it may be, the lives of better men too."

Heyward lent his attention, for a single moment, to his companion, but without replying, he again turned toward those who just then interested him more. He heard the two Hurons leave the bushes, and it was soon plain that all the pursuers were gathered about them, in deep attention to their report. After a few minutes of earnest and solemn dialogue, altogether different from the noisy clamor with which they had first collected about the spot, the sounds grew fainter and more distant, and finally were lost in the depths of the forest.

Hawk-eye waited until a signal from the listening Chingachgook assured him that every sound from the retiring party was completely swallowed by the distance, when he motioned to Heyward to lead forth the horses, and to assist the sisters into their saddles. The instant this was done, they issued through the broken gateway, and stealing out by a direction opposite to the one by which they had entered, they quitted the spot, the sisters casting furtive glances at the silent grave and crumbling ruin, as they left the soft light of the moon, to bury themselves in the gloom of the woods.

1826

from The Pathfinder

Chapter XVIII

It is to be all made of sighs and tears;—
It is to be all made of faith and service:—
It is to be all made of fantasy—
All made of passion, and all made of wishes:
All adoration, duty, an observance;
All humbleness, all patience, and impatience,
All purity, all trial, all observance."[1]

Shakespeare

It was near noon when the gale broke; and then its force abated as suddenly as its violence had arisen. In less than two hours after the wind fell, the surface of the lake, though still agitated, was no longer glittering with foam; and in double that time the entire sheet presented the ordinary scene of disturbed water, that was unbroken by the violence of a tempest. Still the waves came rolling incessantly toward the shore, and the lines of breakers remained, though the spray had ceased to fly: the combing of the swells was more moderate, and all that there was of violence proceeded from the impulsion of wind that had abated.

As it was impossible to make head against the sea that was still up, with the light opposing air that blew from the eastward, all thoughts of getting under way that afternoon were abandoned. Jasper, who had now quietly resumed the command of the Scud, busied himself, however, in heaving up to the anchors, which were lifted in succession. The kedges that backed them were weighed, and everything was got in readiness for a prompt departure, as soon as the state of the weather would allow. In the mean time, they who had no concern with those duties sought such means of amusement as their peculiar circumstances allowed.

As is common with those who are unused to the confinement of a vessel, Mabel cast wistful eyes toward the shore; nor was it long before she expressed a wish that it were possible to land. The Pathfinder was near her at the time, and he assured her that nothing would be easier, as they had a bark canoe on deck, which was the best possible mode of conveyance to go through a surf. After the usual doubts and misgivings, the sergeant was appealed to: his opinion proved to be favorable, and preparations to carry the whim into effect were immediately made.

The party that was to land consisted of Sergeant Dunham, his daughter, and the Pathfinder. Accustomed to the canoe, Mabel took her seat in the centre with great steadiness, her father was placed in the bows, while the guide assumed the office of conductor, by steering in the stern. There was little need of impelling the canoe by means of the paddle, for the rollers sent it forward, at moments, with a violence that set every effort to govern its movements at defiance. More than once, ere the shore was reached, Mabel repented of her temerity, but Pathfinder encouraged her, and really manifested so much self-possession, coolness, and strength of arm himself that even a female might have hesitated about owning all her apprehensions. Our heroine

[1] *As You Like It*, Act V, Sc. ii, ll. 83, 88, 93–97.

was no coward, and while she felt the novelty of her situation, she also experienced a fair proportion of its wild delight. At moments, indeed, her heart was in her mouth, as the bubble of a boat floated on the very crest of a foaming breaker, appearing to skim the water like a swallow, and then she flushed and laughed, as, left by the glancing element, they appeared to linger behind, ashamed of having been outdone in the headlong race. A few minutes sufficed for this excitement, for, though the distance between the cutter and the land considerably exceeded a quarter of a mile, the intermediate space was passed in a very few minutes.

On landing, the sergeant kissed his daughter kindly, for he was so much of a soldier as always to feel more at home on terra-firma[2] than when afloat, and, taking his gun, he announced his intention to pass an hour in quest of game.

"Pathfinder will remain near you, girl, and no doubt he will tell you some of the traditions of this part of the world or some of his own experiences with the Mingos."

The guide laughed, promised to have a care of Mabel, and in a few minutes the father had ascended a steep acclivity, and disappeared in the forest. The others took another direction, which, after a few minutes of sharp ascent also, brought them to a small naked point on the promontory, where the eye overlooked an extensive and very peculiar panorama. Here Mabel seated herself on a fragment of fallen rock, to recover her breath and strength, while her companion, on whose sinews no personal exertion seemed to make any impression, stood at her side, leaning in his own and not ungraceful manner on his long rifle. Several minutes passed, and neither spoke; Mabel, in particular, being lost in admiration of the view.

The position the two had attained was sufficiently elevated to command a wide reach of the lake, which stretched away toward the northeast in a boundless sheet, glittering beneath the rays of an afternoon's sun, and yet betraying the remains of that agitation which it had endured while tossed by the late tempest. The land set bounds to its limits, in a huge crescent, disappearing in distance toward the southeast and the north. Far as the eye could reach, nothing but forest was visible, not even a solitary sign of civilization breaking in upon the uniform and grand magnificence of nature. The gale had driven the Scud beyond the line of those forts with which the French were then endeavoring to gird the English North American possessions; for, following the channels of communication between the great lakes, their posts were on the banks of the Niagara, while our adventurers had reached a point many leagues westward of that celebrated strait. The cutter rode at single anchor, without the breakers, resembling some well-imagined and accurately executed toy, that was intended rather for a glass case than for the struggles with the elements which she had so lately gone through; while the canoe lay on the narrow beach, just out of reach of the waves that came booming upon the land, a speck upon the shingles.

"We are very far, here, from human habitations!" exclaimed Mabel, when, after a long and musing survey of the scene, its principal peculiarities forced themselves on her active and ever-brilliant imagination: "this is, indeed, being on a frontier!"

"Have they more sightly scenes than this nearer the sea, and around their large towns?" demanded Pathfinder, with an interest he was apt to discover in such a subject.

"I will not say that; there is more to remind one of his fellow-beings there than here; less, perhaps, to remind one of God."

---

[2] Latin: "solid ground."

"Ay, Mabel, that is what my own feelings say. I am but a poor hunter, I know; untaught and unl'arned; but God is as near me, in this my home, as he is near the king in his royal palace."

"Who can doubt it?" returned Mabel, looking from the view up into the hard-featured but honest face of her companion, though not without surprise at the energy of his manner. "One feels nearer to God, in such a spot, I think, than when the mind is distracted by the objects of the towns."

"You say all I wish to say myself, Mabel, but in so much plainer speech that you make me ashamed of wishing to let others know what I feel on such matters. I have coasted this lake in s'arch of skins, afore the war, and have been here already; not at this very spot, for we landed yonder, where you may see the blasted oak that stands above the cluster of hemlocks—"

"How! Pathfinder, can you remember all these trifles so accurately?"

"These are our streets and houses; our churches and palaces. Remember them, indeed! I once made an appointment with the Big Sarpent, to meet at twelve o'clock at noon near the foot of a certain pine, at the end of six months, when neither of us was within three hundred miles of the spot. The tree stood and stands still, unless the judgment of Providence has lighted on that too, in the midst of the forest, fifty miles from any settlement, but in a most extraordinary neighborhood for beaver."

"And did you meet at that very spot and hour?"

"Does the sun rise and set? When I reached the tree, I found the Sarpent leaning against its trunk, with torn leggings and muddied moccasins. The Delaware had got into a swamp, and it worried him not a little to find his way out of it; but, as the sun which comes over the eastern hills in the morning goes down behind the western at night, so was he true to time and place. No fear of Chingachgook when there is either a friend or an enemy in the case. He is equally sartain with each."

"And where is the Delaware now—why is he not with us to-day?"

"He is scouting on the Mingo trail, where I ought to have been too, but for a great human infirmity."

"You seem above, beyond, superior to all infirmity, Pathfinder; I never yet met with a man who appeared to be so little liable to the weaknesses of nature."

"If you mean in the way of health and strength, Mabel, Providence has been kind to me; though I fancy the open air, long hunts, active scoutings, forest fare, and the sleep of a good conscience may always keep the doctors at a distance. But I am human arter all; yes, I find I'm very human in some of my feelin's."

Mabel looked surprised, and it would be no more than delineating the character of her sex if we added that her sweet countenance expressed a good deal of curiosity, too, though her tongue was more discreet.

"There is something bewitching in this wild life of yours, Pathfinder," she exclaimed, a tinge of enthusiasm mantling her cheeks. "I find I'm fast getting to be a frontier girl, and am coming to love all this grand silence of the woods. The towns seem tame to me; and, as my father will probably pass the remainder of his days here, where he has already lived so long, I begin to feel that I should be happy to continue with him, and not return to the seashore."

"The woods are never silent, Mabel, to such as understand their meaning. Days at a time have I travelled them alone, without feeling the want of company; and, as for conversation, for such as can comprehend their language, there is no want of rational and instructive discourse."

"I believe you are happier when alone, Pathfinder, than when mingling with your fellow-creatures."

"I will not say that—I will not say exactly that! I have seen the time when I have thought that God was sufficient for me in the forest, and that I craved no more than his bounty and his care. But other feelin's have got uppermost, and I suppose natur' will have its way. All other creatur's mate, Mabel, and it was intended man should do so, too."

"And have you never bethought you of seeking a wife, Pathfinder, to share your fortunes?" inquired the girl, with the directness and simplicity that the pure of heart and the undesigning are the most apt to manifest, and with that feeling of affection which is inbred in her sex. "To me, it seems, you only want a home to return to, from your wanderings, to render your life completely happy. Were I a man, it would be my delight to roam through these forests at will or to sail over this beautiful lake."

"I understand you, Mabel; and God bless you for thinking of the welfare of men as humble as we are. We have our pleasures, it is true, as well as our gifts, but we might be happier; yes, I do think we might be happier."

"Happier! in what way, Pathfinder? In this pure air, with these cool and shaded forests to wander through, this lovely lake to gaze at and sail upon, with clear consciences, and abundance for all the real wants, men ought to be nothing less than as perfectly happy as their infirmities will allow."

"Every creatur' has its gifts, Mabel, and men have theirn," answered the guide, looking stealthily at his beautiful companion, whose cheeks had flushed and eyes brightened under the ardor of feelings excited by the novelty of her striking situation; "and all must obey them. Do you see yonder pigeon that is just alightin' on the beech, —here in a line with the fallen chestnut?"

"Certainly; it is the only thing stirring with life in it, besides ourselves, that is to be seen in this vast solitude."

"Not so, Mabel, not so; Providence makes nothing that lives to live quite alone. Here is its mate, just rising on the wing; it has been feedin' near the other beech, but it will not long be separated from its companion."

"I understand you, Pathfinder," returned Mabel, smiling sweetly, though as calmly as if the discourse was with her father. "But a hunter may find a mate, even in this wild region. The Indian girls are affectionate and true, I know, for such was the wife of Arrowhead, to a husband who oftener frowned than smiled."

"That would never do, Mabel, and good would never come of it. Kind must cling to kind, and country to country, if one would find happiness. If, indeed, I could meet with one like you, who would consent to be a hunter's wife, and who would not scorn my ignorance and rudeness, then, indeed, would all the toil of the past appear like the sporting of the young deer, and all the future like sunshine!"

"One like me!—A girl of my years and indiscretion would hardly make a fit companion for the boldest scout and surest hunter on the lines!"

"Ah! Mabel, I fear me that I have been improving a red-skin's gifts with a pale-face's natur'! Such a character would insure a wife, in an Injin village."

"Surely, surely, Pathfinder, you would not think of choosing one as ignorant, as frivolous, as vain, and as inexperienced as I, for your wife!" Mabel would have added, "and as young," but an instinctive feeling of delicacy repressed the words.

"And why not, Mabel? If you are ignorant of frontier usages, you know more than all of us of pleasant anecdotes and town customs; as for frivolous, I know not what it means, but if it signifies beauty, ah's me! I fear it is no fault in my eyes. Vain you are not, as is seen by the kind manner in which you listen to all my idle tales about scoutings and trails; and as for experience, that will come with years. Besides, Mabel, I fear men think little of these matters, when they are about to take wives, I do."

"Pathfinder—your words—your looks—surely all this is meant in trifling—you speak in pleasantry!"

"To me it is always agreeable to be near you, Mabel, and I should sleep sounder this blessed night than I have done for a week past, could I think that you find such discourse as pleasant as I do."

We shall not say that Mabel Dunham had not believed herself a favorite with the guide. This her quick feminine sagacity had early discovered, and perhaps she had occasionally thought there had mingled with his regard and friendship some of that manly tenderness which the ruder sex must be coarse indeed not to show, on occasions, to the gentler; but the idea that he seriously sought her for his wife had never before crossed the mind of the spirited and ingenuous girl. Now, however, a gleam of something like the truth broke in upon her imagination, less induced by the words of her companion, perhaps, than by his manner. Looking earnestly into the rugged, honest countenance of the scout, Mabel's own features became concerned and grave, and when she spoke again, it was with a gentleness of manner that attracted him to her even more powerfully than the words themselves were calculated to repel.

"You and I should understand each other, Pathfinder," she said, with an earnest sincerity, "nor should there be any cloud between us. You are too upright and frank to meet with anything but sincerity and frankness in return. Surely—surely, all this means nothing—has no other connection with your feelings than such a friendship as one of your wisdom and character would naturally feel for a girl like me!"

"I believe it's all as nat'ral, Mabel; yes, I do; the sergeant tells me he had such feelings toward your own mother, and I think I've seen something like it in the young people I have, from time to time, guided through the wilderness. Yes, yes—I dare say it's all nat'ral enough, and that makes it come so easy, and is a great comfort to me."

"Pathfinder, your words make me uneasy! Speak plainer, or change the subject forever. You do not—cannot mean that—you—cannot wish me to understand—" Even the tongue of the spirited Mabel faltered, and she shrank with maiden shame from adding what she wished so earnestly to say. Rallying her courage, however, and determined to know all as soon and as plainly as possible, after a moment's hesitation she continued: "I mean, Pathfinder, that you do not wish me to understand that you seriously think of me as a wife?"

"I do, Mabel; that's it—that's just it, and you have put the matter in a much better point of view than I, with my forest gifts and frontier ways, would ever be able to do. The sargeant and I have concluded on the matter, if it is agreeable to you, as he thinks is likely will be the case, though I doubt my own power to please one who deserves the best husband America can produce."

Mabel's countenance changed from uneasiness to surprise, and then, by a transition still quicker, from surprise to pain.

"My father!" she exclaimed. "My dear father has thought of my becoming your wife, Pathfinder!"

"Yes, he has, Mabel; he has indeed. He has even thought such a thing might be agreeable to you, and has almost encouraged me to fancy it might be true."

"But you, yourself—you certainly can care nothing whether this singular expectation shall ever be realized or not?"

"Anan?"

"I mean, Pathfinder, that you have talked of this match more to oblige my father than anything else; that your feelings are no way concerned, let my answer be what it may?"

The scout looked earnestly into the beautiful face of Mabel, which had flushed with the ardor and novelty of her sensations, and it was impossible to mistake the intense admiration that betrayed itself in every lineament of his ingenuous countenance.

"I have often thought myself happy, Mabel, when ranging the woods, on a successful hunt, breathing the pure air of the hills, and filled with vigor and health, but I now feel that it has all been idleness and vanity compared with the delight it would give me to know that you thought better of me than you think of most others."

"Better of you!—I do indeed think better of you, Pathfinder, than of most others —I am not certain that I do not think better of you than of any other; for your truth, honesty, simplicity, justice, and courage are scarcely equalled by any of earth."

"Ah! Mabel!—These are sweet and encouraging words from you, and the sargeant, a'ter all, was not as near wrong as I feared."

"Nay, Pathfinder—in the name of all that is sacred and just, do not let us misunderstand each other, in a matter of so much importance. While I esteem, respect—nay, reverence you, almost as much as I reverence my own dear father, it is impossible that I should ever become your wife—that I—"

The change in her companion's countenance was so sudden and so great that the moment the effect of what she had uttered became visible in the face of the Pathfinder Mabel arrested her own words, notwithstanding her strong desire to be explicit, the reluctance with which she could at any time cause pain being sufficient of itself to induce the pause. Neither spoke for some time, the shade of disappointment that crossed the rugged lineaments of the hunter amounting so nearly to anguish as to frighten his companion, while the sensation of choking became so strong in the Pathfinder that he fairly griped his throat, like one who sought physical relief for physical suffering. The convulsive manner in which his fingers worked actually struck the alarmed girl with a feeling of awe.

"Nay, Pathfinder," Mabel eagerly added, the instant she could command her voice —"I may have said more than I mean, for all things of this nature are possible, and women, they say, are never sure of their own minds. What I wish you to understand is, that it is not likely that you and I should ever think of each other as man and wife ought to think of each other."

"I do not—I shall never think in that way again, Mabel," gasped forth the Pathfinder, who appeared to utter his words like one just raised above the pressure of some suffocating substance. "No—no—I shall never think of you, or any one else, again, in that way."

"Pathfinder—dear Pathfinder—understand me—do not attach more meaning to my words than I do myself—a match like that would be unwise—unnatural, perhaps."

"Yes, unnat'ral—ag'in natur'; and so I told the sargeant, but he *would* have it otherwise."

"Pathfinder!—Oh! this is worse than I could have imagined—take my hand, excellent Pathfinder, and let me see that you do not hate me. For God's sake, smile upon me again!"

"Hate you, Mabel!—Smile upon you!—Ah's me!"

"Nay, give me your hand; your hardy, true, and manly hand—both, both, Pathfinder, for I shall not be easy until I feel certain that we are friends again, and that all this has been a mistake."

"Mabel," said the guide, looking wistfully into the face of the generous and impetuous girl, as she held his two hard and sunburnt hands in her own pretty and delicate fingers, and laughing in his own silent and peculiar manner, while anguish gleamed over lineaments which seemed incapable of deception, even while agitated with emotions so conflicting, "Mabel, the sargeant was wrong!"

The pent-up feelings could endure no more, and the tears rolled down the cheeks of the scout like rain. His fingers again worked convulsively at his throat, and his breast heaved, as if it possessed a tenant of which it would be rid, by any effort, however desperate.

"Pathfinder!—Pathfinder!" Mabel almost shrieked,—"anything but this—anything but this. Speak to me, Pathfinder,—smile again—say one kind word—anything to prove you can forgive me."

"The sargeant was wrong!" exclaimed the guide, laughing amid his agony, in a way to terrify his companion by the unnatural mixture of anguish and light-heartedness. "I knew it—I knew it, and said it; yes, the sargeant was wrong, a'ter all."

"We can be friends, though we cannot be man and wife," continued Mabel, almost as much disturbed as her companion, scarce knowing what she said; "we can always be friends, and always will."

"I thought the sargeant was mistaken," resumed the Pathfinder, when a great effort had enabled him to command himself, "for I did not think my gifts were such as would please the fancy of a town-bred gal. It would have been better, Mabel, had he not over-persuaded me into a different notion; and it might have been better, too, had you not been so pleasant and friendly, like; yes, it would."

"If I thought any error of mine had raised false expectations in you, Pathfinder, however unintentionally on my part, I should never forgive myself; for, believe me, I would rather endure pain in my own feelings than you should suffer."

"That's just it, Mabel; that's just it. These speeches and opinions, spoken in so soft a voice, and in a way I'm so unused to in the woods, have done the mischief. But I now see plainly, and begin to understand the difference between us better, and will strive to keep down thought, and to go abroad ag'in as I used to do, looking for the game and the inimy. Ah's me! Mabel, I have indeed been on a false trail since we met!"

"But you will now travel on the true one. In a little while you will forget all this, and think of me as a friend who owes you her life."

"This may be the way in the towns, but I doubt if it's nat'ral to the woods. With us, when the eye sees a lovely sight, it is apt to keep it long in view, or when the mind takes in an upright and proper feeling, it is loath to part with it."

"But it is not a proper feeling that you should love me, nor am I a lovely sight. You will forget it all, when you come seriously to recollect that I am altogether unsuited to be your wife."

"So I told the sargeant—but he would have it otherwise. I knew you was too young and beautiful for one of middle age, like myself, and who never was comely to look at, even in youth; and then your ways have not been my ways, nor would a hunter's cabin be a fitting place for one who was edicated among chiefs, as it were. If I were younger and comelier, though, like Jasper Eau-douce—"

"Never mind Jasper Eau-douce," interrupted Mabel, impatiently; "we can talk of something else."

"Jasper is a worthy lad, Mabel; ay, and a comely," returned the guileless guide, looking earnestly at the girl, as if he distrusted her judgment in speaking slightingly of his friend. "Were I only half as comely as Jasper Western, my misgivings in this affair would not have been so great, and they might not have been so true."

"We will not talk of Jasper Western," repeated Mabel, the color mounting to her temples; "he may be good enough in a gale or on the lake, but he is not good enough to talk of here."

"I fear me, Mabel, he is better than the man who is likely to be your husband, though the sargeant says that never can take place. But the sargeant was wrong once, and he may be wrong twice."

"And who is likely to be my husband, Pathfinder? This is scarcely less strange than what has just passed between us!"

"I know it is nat'ral for like to seek like, and for them that have consorted much with officers' ladies to wish to be officers' ladies themselves. But, Mabel, I may speak plainly to you, I know, and I hope my words will not give you pain, for, now I understand what it is to be disappointed in such feelings, I wouldn't wish to cause even a Mingo sorrow on this head. But happiness is not always to be found in a marquee, any more than in a tent; and though the officers' quarters may look more tempting than the rest of the barracks, there is often great misery between husband and wife inside of their doors."

"I do not doubt it in the least, Pathfinder; and did it rest with me to decide, I would sooner follow you to some cabin in the woods, and share your fortune, whether it might be better or worse, than go inside the door of any officer I know, with an intention of remaining there as its master's wife."

"Mabel, this is not what Lundie hopes or Lundie thinks!"

"And what care I for Lundie? He is major of the 55th, and may command his men to wheel and march about as he pleases, but he cannot compel me to wed the greatest or the meanest of his mess: besides, what can you know of Lundie's wishes on such a subject?"

"From Lundie's own mouth. The sargeant had told him that he wished me for a son-in-law; and the major being an old and a true friend, conversed with me on the subject: he put it to me plainly, whether it would not be more ginerous in me to let an officer succeed than to strive to make you share a hunter's fortune. I owned the truth, I did; and that was that I thought it might; but when he told me that the quartermaster would be his choice, I would not abide by the conditions. No—no— Mabel; I know Davy Muir well, and though he may make you a lady, he can never make you a happy woman, or himself a gentleman. I say this honestly, I do; for I now plainly see that the sargeant has been wrong."

"My father has been very wrong if he has said or done aught to cause you sorrow, Pathfinder; and so great is my respect for you, so sincere my friendship, that were it not for one—I mean that no person need fear Lieutenant Muir's influence with me.

I would rather remain as I am to my dying day than become a lady at the cost of being his wife."

"I do not think you would say that which you do not feel, Mabel," returned Pathfinder, earnestly.

"Not at such a moment, on such a subject, and least of all to you. No; Lieutenant Muir may find wives where he can—my name shall never be on his catalogue."

"Thank you—thank you for that, Mabel; for though there is no longer any hope for me, I could never be happy were you to take to the quartermaster. I feared the commission might count for something, I did, and I know the man. It is not jealousy that makes me speak in this manner, but truth, for I know the man. Now, were you to fancy a desarving youth, one like Jasper Western, for instance—"

"Why always mention Jasper Eau-douce, Pathfinder? he can have no concern with our friendship; let us talk of yourself, and of the manner in which you intend to pass the winter."

"Ah's me!—I'm little worth at the best, Mabel, unless it may be on a trail, or with the rifle; and less worth now that I've discovered the sargeant's mistake. There is no need, therefore, of talking of me. It has been very pleasant to me to be near you so long, and even to fancy that the sargeant was right, but that is all over now. I shall go down the lake with Jasper, and then there will be business to occupy us, and that will keep useless thoughts out of the mind."

"And you will forget this—forget me—no, not forget me either, Pathfinder; but you will resume your old pursuits, and cease to think a girl of sufficient importance to disturb your peace?"

"I never know'd it afore, Mabel, but girls, as you call them, though gals is the name I've been taught to use, are of more account in this life than I could have believed. Now, afore I know'd you, the new-born babe did not sleep more sweetly than I used to could; my head was no sooner on the root, or the stone, or mayhap on the skin, than all was lost to the senses, unless it might be to go over in the night the business of the day, in a dream like; and there I lay till the moment came to be stirring, and the swallows were not more certain to be on the wing with the light than I to be afoot at the moment I wished to be. All this seemed a gift, and might be calculated on, even in the midst of a Mingo camp; for I've been outlying, in my time, in the very villages of the vagabonds."

"And all this will return to you, Pathfinder; for one so upright and sincere will never waste his happiness on a mere fancy. You will dream again of your hunts, of the deer you have slain, and of the beaver you have taken."

"Ah's me, Mabel, I wish never to dream again! Before we met I had a sort of pleasure in following up the hounds, in fancy, as it might be; and even in striking a trail of the Iroquois—nay, I've been in skrimmages and ambushments in thought, like, and found satisfaction in it according to my gifts; but all those things have lost their charms since I've made acquaintance with you. Now, I think no longer of anything rude in my dreams, but the very last night we stayed in the garrison I imagined I had a cabin in a grove of sugar maples, and at the root of every tree was a Mabel Dunham, while the birds that were among the branches sang ballads, instead of the notes that natur' gave, and even the deer stopped to listen. I tried to shoot a fa'an, but Killdeer missed fire, and the creatur' laughed in my face, as pleasantly as a young girl laughs in her merriment, and then it bounded away, looking back as if expecting me to follow."

"No more of this, Pathfinder—we'll talk no more of these things," said Mabel, dashing the tears from her eyes; for the simple, earnest manner in which this hardy woodsman betrayed the deep hold she had taken of his feelings nearly proved too much for her own generous heart. "Now let us look for my father; he cannot be distant, as I heard his gun quite near."

"The sargeant was wrong—yes, he was wrong, and it's of no use to attempt to make the dove consort with the wolf."

"Here comes my dear father," interrupted Mabel; "let us look cheerful and happy, Pathfinder, as such good friends ought to look, and keep each other's secrets."

A pause succeeded; the sargeant's foot was heard crushing the dried twigs hard by, and then his form appeared shoving aside the bushes of a copse quite near. As he issued into the open ground the old soldier scrutinized his daughter and her companion, and speaking good-naturedly, he said:

"Mabel, child, you are young and light of foot—look for a bird I've shot that fell just beyond the thicket of young hemlocks on the shore; and as Jasper is showing signs of an intention of getting under way, you need not take the trouble to clamber up this hill again, but we will meet you on the beach in a few minutes."

Mabel obeyed, bounding down the hill with the elastic step of youth and health. But, notwithstanding the lightness of her steps, the heart of the girl was heavy, and no sooner was she hid from observation by the thicket than she threw herself on the root of a tree and wept as if her heart would break. The sargeant watched her until she disappeared, with a father's pride, and then turned to his companion with a smile as kind and as familiar as his habits would allow him to use toward any.

"She has her mother's lightness and activity, my friend, with somewhat of her father's force," he said. "Her mother was not quite as handsome, I think myself; but the Dunhams were always thought comely, whether men or women. Well, Pathfinder, I take it for granted you've not overlooked the opportunity, but have spoken plainly to the girl? Women like frankness in matters of this sort."

"I believe Mabel and I understand each other, at last, sargeant," returned the other, looking another way to avoid the soldier's face.

"So much the better. Some people fancy that a little doubt and uncertainty make love all the livelier, but I am one of those who think the plainer the tongue speaks the easier the mind will comprehend. Was Mabel surprised?"

"I fear she was, sargeant; I fear she was taken quite by surprise—yes, I do."

"Well, well, surprises in love are like an ambush in war, and quite as lawful; though it is not as easy to tell when a woman is surprised as to tell when it happens to an enemy. Mabel did not run away, my worthy friend, did she?"

"No, sargeant, Mabel did not try to escape; that I can say with a clear conscience."

"I hope the girl was not too willing, neither! Her mother was shy and coy for a month, at least—but frankness, after all, is a recommendation in man or woman."

"That it is—that it is—and judgment, too."

"You are not to look for too much judgment in a young creature of twenty,

Pathfinder, but it will come with experience. A mistake in you, or in me, for instance, might not be so easily overlooked, but in a girl of Mabel's years one is not to strain at a gnat lest they swallow a camel."

The muscles of the listener's face twitched as the sargeant was thus delivering his sentiments, though the former had now recovered a portion of that stoicism which formed so large a part of his character, and which he had probably imbibed from long association with the Indians. His eyes rose and fell, and once a gleam shot athwart his hard features, as if he were about to indulge in his peculiar laugh; but the joyous feeling, if it really existed, was as quickly lost in a look allied to anguish. It was this unusual mixture of wild and keen mental agony with native, simple joyousness that had most struck Mabel, who, in the interview just related, had a dozen times been on the point of believing that her suitor's heart was only lightly touched, as images of happiness and humor gleamed over a mind that was almost infantine in its simplicity and nature; an impression, however, that was soon driven away by the discovery of emotions so painful and so deep that they seemed to harrow the very soul. Indeed, in this respect, the Pathfinder was a mere child: unpractised in the ways of the world, he had no idea of concealing a thought of any kind, and his mind received and reflected each emotion with the pliability and readiness of that period of life; the infant scarcely yielding its wayward imagination to the passing impression with greater facility than this man, so simple in all his personal feelings, so stern, stoical, masculine, and severe in all that touched his ordinary pursuits.

"You say true, sargeant," Pathfinder answered—"a mistake in one like you is a more serious matter."

"You will find Mabel sincere and honest in the end, give her but a little time."

"Ah's me, sargeant!"

"A man of your merits would make an impression on a rock, give him time, Pathfinder."

"Sargeant Dunham, we are old fellow-campaigners—that is, as campaigns are carried on here in the wilderness; and we have done so many kind acts to each other that we can afford to be candid—what has caused you to believe that a girl like Mabel could ever fancy one as rude as I am?"

"What?—why, a variety of reasons, and good reasons, too, my friend. Those same acts of kindness, perhaps, and the campaigns you mention; moreover, you are my sworn and tried comrade."

"All this sounds well, so far as you and I be consarned, but they do not touch the case of your pretty da'ghter. She may think these very campaigns have destroyed the little comeliness I may once have had, and I am not quite sartain that being an old friend of her father would lead any young maiden's mind into a particular affection for a suitor. Like loves like, I tell you, sargeant, and my gifts are not altogether the gifts of Mabel Dunham."

"These are some of your old modest qualms, Pathfinder, and will do you no credit with the girl. Women distrust men who distrust themselves, and take to men who distrust nothing. Modesty is a capital thing in a recruit, I grant you, or in a young subaltern who has just joined, for it prevents his railing at the non-commissioned officers before he knows what to rail at; I'm not sure it is out of place in a commissary or a parson, but it's the devil and all when it gets possession of either a real soldier or a lover. Have as little to do with it as possible, if you would win a woman's heart.

As for your doctrine that like loves like, it is as wrong as possible in matters of this sort. If like loved like women would love one another, and men also. No—no—like loves dislike." the sargeant was merely a scholar of the camp, "and you have nothing to fear from Mabel on that score. Look at Lieutenant Muir; the man has had five wives already, they tell me, and there is no more modest in him than there is in a cat-o'-nine-tails."[3]

"Lieutenant Muir will never be the husband of Mabel Dunham, let him ruffle his feathers as much as he may."

"That is a sensible remark of yours, Pathfinder, for my mind is made up that you shall be my son-in-law. If I were an officer myself, Mr. Muir might have some chance; but time has placed one door between my child and myself, and I don't intend there shall be that of a marquee also."

"Sargeant, we must let Mabel follow her own fancy; she is young and light of heart, and God forbid that any wish of mine should lay the weight of a feather on a mind that is all gayety now, or take one note of happiness from her laughter."

"Have you conversed freely with the girl?" the sergeant demanded quickly, and with some asperity of manner.

Pathfinder was too honest to deny a truth plain as that which the answer required, and yet too honorable to betray Mabel and expose her to the resentment of one whom he well knew to be stern in his anger.

"We have laid open our minds," he said, "and though Mabel's is one that any man might love to look at, I find little there, sargeant, to make me think any better of myself."

"The girl has not dared to refuse you—to refuse her father's best friend?"

Pathfinder turned his face away to conceal the look of anguish that consciousness told him was passing athwart it, but he continued the discourse in his own quiet, manly tones.

"Mabel is too kind to refuse anything, or to utter harsh words to a dog. I have not put the question in a way to be downright refused, sargeant."

"And did you expect my daughter to jump into your arms before you asked her? She would not have been her mother's child had she done any such thing, nor do I think she would have been mine. The Dunhams like plain dealing as well as the king's majesty, but they are no jumpers. Leave me to manage this matter for you, Pathfinder, and there shall be no unnecessary delay. I'll speak to Mabel myself this very evening, using your name as principal in the affair."

"I'd rather not—I'd rather not, sargeant. Leave the matter to Mabel and me, and I think all will come right in the ind. Young gals be like timorsome birds, they do not over-relish being hurried or spoken harshly to, neither. Leave the matter to Mabel and me."

"On one condition I will, my friend; and that is, that you promise me on the honor of a scout that you will put the matter plainly to Mabel, the first suitable opportunity, and no mincing of words."

"I will ask her, sargeant—yes, I will ask her, on condition that you promise not to meddle in the affair—yes, I will promise to ask Mabel the question whether she

[3] Whip of nine knotted cords used for punishing criminals.

will marry me, even though she laugh in my face at my doing so, on that condition."

Sergeant Dunham gave the desired promise very cheerfully, for he had completely wrought himself up into the belief that the man he so much esteemed and respected himself must be acceptable to his daughter. He had married a woman much younger than himself, and he saw no unfitness in the respective years of the intended couple. Mabel was educated so much above him, too, that he was not aware of the difference which actually existed between the parent and child, in this respect; for it is one of the most unpleasant features in the intercourse between knowledge and ignorance, taste and unsophistication, refinement and vulgarity, that the higher qualities are often necessarily subjected to the judgments of those who have absolutely no perception of their existence. It followed that Sargeant Dunham was not altogether qualified to appreciate his daughter's tastes, or to form a very probable conjecture of the direction taken by those feelings which oftener depend on impulses and passion than on reason. Still, the worthy soldier was not so wrong in his estimate of the Pathfinder's chances as might at first appear. Knowing, as he well did, all the sterling qualities of the man, his truth, integrity of purpose, courage, self-devotion, disinterestedness, it was far from unreasonable to suppose that qualities like these would produce a deep impression on any female heart, where there was an opportunity to acquire a knowledge of their existence; and the father erred principally in fancying that the daughter might know, as it might be, by intuition, what he himself had acquired by years of intercourse and adventure.

As Pathfinder and his military friend descended the hill to the shore of the lake, the discourse did not flag. The latter continued to persuade the former that his diffidence alone prevented complete success with Mabel, and that he had only to persevere in order to prevail. Pathfinder was much too modest by nature, and had been too plainly, though so delicately, discouraged, in the recent interview, to believe all he heard; still the father used so many arguments that seemed plausible, and it was so grateful to fancy that the daughter might yet be his, the reader is not to be surprised when he is told that this unsophisticated being did not view Mabel's recent conduct in precisely the light in which he may be inclined to view it himself. He did not credit all that the sergeant told him, it is true; but he began to think virgin coyness, and ignorance of her own feelings, might have induced Mabel to use the language she had.

"The quartermaster is no favorite," said Pathfinder, in answer to one of his companion's remarks. "Mabel will never look on him as more than one who has had four or five wives already."

"Which is more than his share. A man may marry twice, without offence to good morals and decency, I allow, but four times is an aggravation."

"I should think even marrying once what Master Cap calls a circumstance," put in Pathfinder, laughing in his quiet way, for by this time his spirits had recovered some of their buoyancy.

"It is indeed, my friend, and a most solemn circumstance too. If it were not that Mabel is to be your wife, I would advise you to remain single. But here is the girl herself, and discretion is the word."

"Ah's me! sergeant, I fear you are mistaken!"

1840

from **The Pioneers**

Chapter XXXIII

Fetch here the stocks, ho!
You stubborn ancient knave, you reverend braggart,
We'll teach you![1]
Lear

The long days and early sun of July allowed time for a gathering of the interested, before the little bell of the academy announced that the appointed hour had arrived for administering right to the wronged, and punishment to the guilty. Ever since the dawn of day, the highways and woodpaths that, issuing from the forests, and winding along the sides of the mountains, centered in Templeton, had been thronged with equestrians and footmen, bound to the haven of justice. There was to be seen a well-clad yeoman, mounted on a sleek, switch-tailed steed, ambling along the highway, with his red face elevated in a manner that said, "I have paid for my land, and fear no man:" while his bosom was swelling with the pride of being one of the grand inquest for the county. At his side rode a companion, his equal in independence of feeling, perhaps, but his inferior in thrift, as in property and consideration. This was a professed dealer in lawsuits,—a man whose name appeared in every calendar,— whose substance, gained in the multifarious expedients of a settler's changeable habits, was wasted in feeding the harpies[2] of the courts. He was endeavoring to impress the mind of the grand juror with the merits of a cause now at issue. Along with these was a pedestrian, who, having thrown a rifle frock over his shirt, and placed his best wool hat above his sunburnt visage, had issued from his retreat in the woods by a footpath, and was striving to keep company with the others, on his way to hear and to decide the disputes of his neighbors, as a petit juror.[3] Fifty similar little knots of countrymen might have been seen, on that morning, journeying toward the shire-town on the same errand.

By ten o'clock the streets of the village were filled with busy faces; some talking of their private concerns, some listening to a popular expounder of political creeds; and others gaping in at the open stores, admiring the finery, or examining scythes, axes, and such other manufactures as attracted their curiosity or excited their admiration. A few women were in the crowd, most carrying infants, and followed, at a lounging, listless gait, by their rustic lords and masters. There was one young couple, in whom connubial love was yet fresh, walking at a respectful distance from each other; while the swain directed the timid steps of his bride, by a gallant offering of a thumb!

At the first stroke of the bell, Richard issued from the door of the "Bold Dragoon," flourishing a sheathed sword, that he was fond of saying his ancestors had carried in one of Cromwell's victories, and crying, in an authoritative tone, to "clear the way

---

[1] Shakespeare's *King Lear,* Act II, Sc. ii, ll. 129-131.
[2] Mythological predatory monsters having the heads and torsos of women and the tails, wings, and talons of birds.
[3] Member of a civil jury.

for the court." The order was obeyed promptly, though not servilely, the members of the crowd nodding familiarly to the members of the procession as it passed. A party of constables with their staves followed the Sheriff, preceding Marmaduke, and four plain, grave-looking yeomen, who were his associates on the bench. There was nothing to distinguish these subordinate judges from the better part of the spectators, except gravity, which they affected a little more than common, and that one of their number was attired in an old-fashioned military coat, with skirts that reached no lower than the middle of his thighs, and bearing two little silver epaulettes, not half so big as a modern pair of shoulder-knots. This gentleman was a colonel of the militia, in attendance on a courtmartial, who found leisure to steal a moment from his military to attend to his civil jurisdiction; but this incongruity excited neither notice nor comment. Three or four clean-shaved lawyers followed, as meekly as if they were lambs going to the slaughter. One or two of their number had contrived to obtain an air of scholastic gravity by wearing spectacles. The rear was brought up by another posse of constables, and the mob followed the whole into the room where the court held its sittings.

The edifice was composed of a basement of squared logs, perforated here and there with small grated windows, through which a few wistful faces were gazing at the crowd without. Among the captives were the guilty, downcast countenances of the counterfeiters, and the simple but honest features of the Leather-stocking. The dungeons were to be distinguished, externally, from the debtors' apartments only by the size of the apertures, the thickness of the grates, and by the heads of the spikes that were driven into the logs as a protection against the illegal use of edge-tools. The upper story was of framework, regularly covered with boards, and contained one room decently fitted up for the purposes of justice. A bench, raised on a narrow platform to the height of a man above the floor, and protected in front by a light railing, ran along one of its sides. In the centre was a seat, furnished with rude arms, that was always filled by the presiding judge. In front, on a level with the floor of the room, was a large table covered with green baize, and surrounded by benches; and at either of its ends were rows of seats, rising one over the other, for jury boxes. Each of these divisions was surrounded by a railing. The remainder of the room was an open square, appropriated to the spectators.

When the judges were seated, the lawyers had taken possession of the table, and the noise of moving feet had ceased in the area, the proclamations were made in the usual form, the jurors were sworn, the charge was given, and the court proceeded to hear the business before them.

We shall not detain the reader with a description of the captious discussions that occupied the court for the first two hours. Judge Temple had impressed on the jury, in his charge, the necessity for despatch on their part, recommending to their notice, from motives of humanity, the prisoners in the jail, as the first objects of their attention. Accordingly, after the period we have mentioned had elapsed, the cry of the officer to "clear the way for the grand jury," announced the entrance of that body. The usual forms were observed, when the foreman handed up to the bench two bills, on both of which the Judge observed, at the first glance of his eye, the name of Nathaniel Bumppo. It was a leisure moment with the court; some low whispering passed between the bench and the Sheriff, who gave a signal to his officers, and in a very few minutes the silence that prevailed was interrupted by a general movement in the outer crowd; when presently the Leather-Stocking made his appearance, ushered into the criminal's bar under the custody of two constables. The hum ceased, the people closed into the open space again, and the silence soon became so deep, that the hard breathing of the prisoner was audible.

Natty was dressed in his buckskin garments, without his coat, in place of which he wore only a shirt of coarse linen-check, fastened at his throat by the sinew of a deer, leaving his red neck and weather-beaten face exposed and bare. It was the first time that he had ever crossed the threshold of a court of justice, and curiosity seemed to be strongly blended with his personal feelings. He raised his eyes to the bench, thence to the jury-boxes, the bar, and the crowd without, meeting everywhere looks fastened on himself. After surveying his own person, as searching the cause of this unusual attraction, he once more turned his face around the assemblage, and opened his mouth in one of his silent and remarkable laughs.

"Prisoner, remove your cap," said Judge Temple.

The order was either unheard or unheeded.

"Nathaniel Bumppo, be uncovered," repeated the Judge.

Natty started at the sound of his name, and raising his face earnestly toward the bench, he said—

"Anan!"

Mr. Lippet arose from his seat at the table, and whispered in the ear of the prisoner; when Natty gave him a nod of assent, and took the deerskin covering from his head.

"Mr. District Attorney," said the Judge, "the prisoner is ready; we wait for the indictment."

The duties of public prosecutor were discharged by Dirck Van der School, who adjusted his spectacles, cast a cautious look around him at his brethren of the bar, which he ended by throwing his head aside so as to catch one glance over the glasses, when he proceeded to read the bill aloud. It was the usual charge for an assault and battery on the person of Hiram Doolittle, and was couched in the ancient language of such instruments, especial care having been taken by the scribe not to omit the name of a single offensive weapon known to the law. When he had done, Mr. Van der School removed his spectacles, which he closed and placed in his pocket, seemingly for the pleasure of again opening and replacing them on his nose. After this revolution was repeated once or twice, he handed the bill over to Mr. Lippet, with a cavalier air, that said as much as "Pick a hole in that if you can."

Natty listened to the charge with great attention, leaning forward toward the reader with an earnestness that denoted his interest; and when it was ended, he raised his tall body to the utmost, and drew a long sigh. All eyes were turned to the prisoner, whose voice was vainly expected to break the stillness of the room.

"You have heard the presentment that the grand jury have made, Nathaniel Bumppo," said the Judge; "what do you plead to the charge?"

The old man dropped his head for a moment in a reflecting attitude, and then raising it, he laughed before he answered—

"That I handled the man a little rough or so, is not to be denied; but that there was occasion to make use of all the things that the gentleman has spoken of, is downright untrue. I am not much of a wrestler, seeing that I'm getting old; but I was out among the Scotch-Irishers[4]—let me see—it must have been as long ago as the first year of the old war—"

"Mr. Lippet, if you are retained for the prisoner," interrupted Judge Temple, "instruct your client how to plead; if not, the court will assign him counsel."

Aroused from studying the indictment by this appeal, the attorney got up, and after a short dialogue with the hunter in a low voice, he informed the court that they were ready to proceed.

"Do you plead guilty or not guilty?" said the Judge.

"I may say not guilty with a clean conscience," returned Natty; "for there's no guilt in doing what's right; and I'd rather died on the spot, than had him put foot in the hut at that moment."

Richard started at this declaration, and bent his eyes significantly on Hiram, who returned the look with a slight movement of his eyebrows.

"Proceed to open the cause, Mr. District Attorney," continued the Judge. "Mr. Clerk, enter the plea of not guilty."

After a short opening address from Mr. Van der School, Hiram was summoned to the bar to give his testimony. It was delivered to the letter, perhaps, but with all that moral coloring which can be conveyed under such expressions as, "thinking no harm," "feeling it my bounden duty as a magistrate," and "seeing that the constable was back'ard in the business." When he had done, and the district attorney declined putting any further interrogatories, Mr. Lippet arose, with an air of keen investigation, and asked the following questions:

"Are you a constable of this county, sir?"

"No, sir," said Hiram, "I'm only a justice-peace."

"I ask you, Mr. Doolittle, in the face of this court, putting it to your conscience and your knowledge of the law, whether you had any right to enter that man's dwelling?"

"Hem!" said Hiram, undergoing a violent struggle between his desire for vengeance and his love of legal fame; "I do suppose—that in—that is—strict law—that supposing—maybe I hadn't a real—lawful right;—but as the case was—and Billy was so back'ard—I thought I might come for'ard in the business."

"I ask you again, sir," continued the lawyer, following up his success, "whether this old, this friendless old man, did or did not repeatedly forbid your entrance?"

"Why, I must say," said Hiram, "that he was considerable cross-grained; not what I call clever, seeing that it was only one neighbor wanting to go into the house of another."

"Oh! then you own it was only meant for a neighborly visit on your part, and without the sanction of law. Remember, gentlemen, the words of the witness, 'one neighbor wanting to enter the house of another.' Now, sir, I ask you if Nathaniel Bumppo did not again and again order you not to enter?"

"There was some words passed between us," said Hiram, "but I read the warrant to him aloud."

"I repeat my question; did he tell you not to enter his habitation?"

<hr>

[4] Group of early settlers of mixed Scottish and Irish lineage who fought in the British-Indian wars.

"There was a good deal passed betwixt us—but I've the warrant in my pocket; maybe the court would wish to see it?"

"Witness," said Judge Temple, "answer the question directly; did or did not the prisoner forbid your entering his hut?"

"Why, I some think—"

"Answer without equivocation," continued the Judge, sternly.

"He did."

"And did you attempt to enter after this order?"

"I did; but the warrant was in my hand."

"Proceed, Mr. Lippet, with your examination."

But the attorney saw that the impression was in favor of his client, and, waving his hand with a supercilious manner, as if unwilling to insult the understanding of the jury with any further defence, he replied—

"No, sir; I leave it for your honor to charge; I rest my case here."

"Mr. District Attorney," said the Judge, "have you anything to say?"

Mr. Van der School removed his spectacles, folded them, and replacing them once more on his nose, eyed the other bill which he held in his hand, and then said, looking at the bar over the top of his glasses—

"I shall rest the prosecution here, if the court please."

Judge Temple arose and began the charge.

"Gentlemen of the jury," he said, "you have heard the testimony, and I shall detain you but a moment. If an officer meet with resistance in the execution of a process he has an undoubted right to call any citizen to his assistance; and the acts of such assistant come within the protection of the law. I shall leave you to judge, gentlemen, from the testimony, how far the witness in this prosecution can be so considered, feeling less reluctance to submit the case thus informally to your decision, because there is yet another indictment to be tried, which involves heavier charges against the unfortunate prisoner."

The tone of Marmaduke was mild and insinuating, and as his sentiments were given with such apparent impartiality, they did not fail of carrying due weight with the jury. The grave-looking yeomen who composed this tribunal, laid their heads together for a few minutes, without leaving the box, when the foreman arose, and after the forms of the court were duly observed, he pronounced the prisoner to be—

"Not guilty."

"You are acquitted of this charge, Nathaniel Bumppo," said the Judge.

"Anan!" said Natty.

"You are found not guilty of striking and assaulting Mr. Doolittle."

"No, no, I'll not deny but that I took him a little roughly by the shoulders," said Natty, looking about him with great simplicity, "and that I—"

"You are acquitted," interrupted the Judge, "and there is nothing further to be said or done in the matter."

A look of joy lighted up the features of the old man, who now comprehended the case, and placing his cap eagerly on his head again, he threw up the bar of his little prison, and said feelingly—

"I must say this for you, Judge Temple, that the law has not been so hard on me as I dreaded. I hope God will bless you for the kind things you've done to me this day."

But the staff of the constable was opposed to his egress, and Mr. Lippet whispered a few words in his ear, when the aged hunter sank back into his place, and, removing his cap, stroked down the remnants of his gray and sandy locks, with an air of mortification mingled with submission.

"Mr. District Attorney," said Judge Temple, affecting to busy himself with his minutes, "proceed with the second indictment."

Mr. Van der School took great care that no part of the presentment, which he now read, should be lost on his auditors. It accused the prisoner of resisting the execution of a search-warrant, by force of arms, and particularized, in the vague language of the law, among a variety of other weapons, the use of the rifle. This was indeed a more serious charge than an ordinary assault and battery, and a corresponding degree of interest was manifested by the spectators in its result. The prisoner was duly arraigned, and his plea again demanded. Mr. Lippet had anticipated the answers of Natty, and in a whisper advised him how to lead. But the feelings of the old hunter were awakened by some of the expressions of the indictment, and, forgetful of his caution, he exclaimed—

"'Tis a wicked untruth; I crave no man's blood. Them thieves, the Iroquois, won't say it to my face, that I ever thirsted after man's blood. I have fou't as a soldier that feared his Maker and his officer, but I never pulled trigger on any but a warrior that was up and awake. No man can say that I ever struck even a Mingo in his blanket. I believe there's some who thinks there's no God in a wilderness!"

"Attend to your plea, Bumppo," said the Judge; "you hear that you are accused of using your rifle against an officer of justice? are you guilty or not guilty?"

By this time the irritated feelings of Natty had found vent; and he rested on the bar for a moment, in a musing posture, when he lifted his face, with his silent laugh, and, pointing to where the wood-chopper stood, he said—

"Would Billy Kirby be standing there, d'ye think, if I had used the rifle?"

"Then you deny it," said Mr. Lippet; "you plead not guilty?"

"Sartain," said Natty; "Billy knows that I never fired at all. Billy, do you remember the turkey last winter? ah! me! that was better than common firing; but I can't shoot as I used to could."

"Enter the plea of not guilty," said Judge Temple, strongly affected by the simplicity of the prisoner.

Hiram was again sworn, and his testimony given on the second charge. He had discovered his former error, and proceeded more cautiously than before. He related very distinctly, and for the man, with amazing terseness, the suspicion against the hunter, the complaint, the issuing of the warrant, and the swearing in of Kirby; all of which, he affirmed, were done in due form of law. He then added the manner in which the constable had been received; and stated distinctly, that Natty had pointed the rifle at Kirby, and threatened his life, if he attempted to execute his duty. All this was confirmed by Jotham, who was observed to adhere closely to the story of the magistrate. Mr. Lippet conducted an artful cross-examination of these two witnesses, but after consuming much time, was compelled to relinquish the attempt to obtain any advantage, in despair.

At length the district attorney called the wood-chopper to the bar. Billy gave an extremely confused account of the whole affair, although he evidently aimed at the truth, until Mr. Van der School aided him, by asking some direct questions:—

"It appears from examining the papers, that you demanded admission into the hut legally; so you were put in bodily fear by his rifle and threats?"

"I didn't mind them that, man," said Billy, snapping his fingers; "I should be a poor stick to mind old Leather-Stocking."

"But I understood you to say (referring to your previous words (as delivered here in court) in the commencement of your testimony) that you thought he meant to shoot you?"

"To be sure I did; and so would you too, squire, if you had seen the chap dropping a muzzle that never misses, and cocking an eye that has a natural squint by long practice. I thought there would be a dust on't, and my back was up at once; but Leather-Stocking gi'n up the skin, and so the matter ended."

"Ah! Billy," said Natty, shaking his head, "'twas a lucky thought in me to throw out the hide, or there might have been blood spilt; and I'm sure, if it had been yourn, I should have mourn'd it sorely the little while I have to stay."

"Well, Leather-Stocking," returned Billy, facing the prisoner with a freedom and familiarity that utterly disregarded the presence of the court, "as you are on the subject, it may be that you've no—"

"Go on with your examination, Mr. District Attorney."

That gentleman eyed the familiarity between his witness and the prisoner with manifest disgust, and indicated to the court that he was done.

"Then you didn't feel frightened, Mr. Kirby?" said the counsel for the prisoner.

"Me! no," said Billy, casting his eyes over his own huge frame with evident self-satisfaction; "I'm not to be skeared so easy."

"You look like a hardy man; where were you born, sir?"

"Varmount state; 'tis a mountaynious place, but there's a stiff soil, and it's pretty much wooded with beech and maple."

"I have always heard so," said Mr. Lippet, soothingly. "You have been used to the rifle yourself, in that country?"

"I pull the second best trigger in this county. I knock under to Natty Bumppo there, sin' he shot the pigeon."

Leather-Stocking raised his head, and laughed again, when he abruptly thrust out a wrinkled hand, and said—

"You're young yet, Billy, and hav'n't seen the matches that I have; but here's my hand; I bear no malice to you, I don't."

Mr. Lippet allowed this conciliatory offering to be accepted, and judiciously paused, while the spirit of peace was exercising its influence over the two; but the Judge interposed his authority.

"This is an improper place for such dialogues," he said.

"Proceed with your examination of this witness, Mr. Lippet, or I shall order the next."

The attorney started, as if unconscious of any impropriety, and continued—

"So you settled the matter with Natty amicably on the spot, did you?"

"He gi'n me the skin, and I didn't want to quarrel with an old man; for my part, I see no such mighty matter in shooting a buck!"

"And you parted friends? and you would never have thought of bringing the business up before a court, hadn't you been subpœnaed?"

"I don't think I should; he gi'n the skin, and I didn't feel a hard thought, though Squire Doolittle got some affronted."

"I have done, sir," said Mr. Lippet, probably relying on the charge of the Judge, as he again seated himself, with the air of a man who felt that his success was certain.

When Mr. Van der School arose to address the jury, he commenced by saying—
"Gentlemen of the jury, I should have interrupted the leading questions put by the prisoner's counsel (by leading questions I mean telling him what to say), did I not feel confident that the law of the land was superior to any advantages (I mean legal advantages) which he might obtain by his art. The counsel for the prisoner, gentlemen, has endeavored to persuade you, in opposition to your own good sense, to believe that pointing a rifle at a constable (elected or deputed) is a very innocent affair; and that society (I mean the commonwealth, gentlemen) shall not be endangered thereby. But let me claim your attention, while we look over the particulars of this heinous offence." Here Mr. Van der School favored the jury with an abridgment of the testimony, recounted in such a manner as utterly to confuse the faculties of his worthy listeners. After this exhibition he closed as follows:—"And now, gentlemen, having thus made plain to your senses the crime of which this unfortunate man has been guilty (unfortunate both on account of his ignorance and his guilt), I shall leave you to your own consciences; not in the least doubting that you will see the importance (notwithstanding the prisoner's counsel (doubtless relying on your former verdict) wishes to appear so confident of success) of punishing the offender, and asserting the dignity of the laws."

It was now the duty of the Judge to deliver his charge. It consisted of a short, comprehensive summary of the testimony, laying bare the artifice of the prisoner's counsel, and placing the facts in so obvious a light, that they could not well be misunderstood. "Living as we do, gentlemen," he concluded, "on the skirts of society, it becomes doubly necessary to protect the ministers of the law. If you believe the witnesses, in their construction of the acts of the prisoner, it is your duty to convict him; but if you believe that the old man, who this day appears before you, meant not to harm the constable, but was acting more under the influence of habit than by the instigations of malice, it will be your duty to judge him, but to do it with lenity."

As before, the jury did not leave their box; but, after a consultation of some little time, their foreman arose, and pronounced the prisoner—
"Guilty."

There was but little surprise manifested in the court room at this verdict, as the testimony, the greater part of which we have omitted, was too clear and direct to be passed over. The judges seemed to have anticipated this sentiment, for a consultation was passing among them also, during the deliberation of the jury, and the preparatory movements of the "bench" announced the coming sentence.

"Nathaniel Bumppo," commenced the Judge, making the customary pause.

The old hunter, who had been musing again, with his head on the bar, raised himself, and cried, with a prompt, military tone—
"Here."

The Judge waved his hand for silence, and proceeded—
"In forming their sentence, the court have been governed as much by the consideration of your ignorance of the laws, as by a strict sense of the importance of punishing such outrages as this of which you have been found guilty. They have therefore passed over the obvious punishment of whipping on the bare back, in mercy to your years; but as the dignity of the law requires an open exhibition of the consequences of your crime, it is ordered, that you be conveyed from this room to the public stocks, where you are to be confined for one hour; that you pay a fine to the state of one hundred

dollars; and that you be imprisoned in the jail of this county for one calendar month, and furthermore, that your imprisonment do not cease until the said fine shall be paid. I feel it my duty, Nathaniel Bumppo—"

"And where should I get the money?" interrupted the Leather-Stocking, eagerly; "where should I get the money? you'll take away the bounty on the painters,[5] because I cut the throat of a deer; and how is an old man to find so much gold or silver in the woods? No, no, judge: think better of it, and don't talk of shutting me up in a jail for the little time I have to stay."

"If you have anything to urge against the passing of the sentence, the court will yet hear you," said the Judge, mildly.

"I have enough to say ag'in it," cried Natty, grasping the bar on which his fingers were working with a convulsed motion. "Where am I to get the money? Let me out into the woods and hills, where I've been used to breathe the clear air, and though I'm threescore and ten, if you've left game enough in the country, I'll travel night and day but I'll make you up the sum afore the season is over. Yes, yes—you see the reason of the thing, and the wickedness of shutting up an old man, that has spent his days, as one may say, where he could always look into the windows of heaven."

"I must be governed by the law—"

"Talk not to me of law, Marmaduke Temple," interrupted the hunter. "Did the beast of the forest mind your laws, when it was thirsty and hungering for the blood of your own child! She was kneeling to her God for a greater favor than I ask, and he heard her; and if you now say no to my prayers, do you think he will be deaf?"

"My private feelings must not enter into—"

"Hear me, Marmaduke Temple," interrupted the old man, with melancholy earnestness, "and hear reason. I've travelled these mountains when you was no judge, but an infant in your mother's arms; and I feel as if I had a right and a privilege to travel them ag'in afore I die. Have you forgot the time that you come on to the lake-shore, when there wasn't even a jail to lodge in; and didn't I give you my own bear-skin to sleep on, and the fat of a noble buck to satisfy the cravings of your hunger? Yes, yes—you thought it no sin then to kill a deer! And this I did, though I had no reason to love you, for you had never done anything but harm to them that loved and sheltered me. And now, will you shut me up in your dungeons to pay me for my kindness? A hundred dollars! where should I get the money? No, no—there's them that says hard things of you, Marmaduke Temple, but you an't so bad as to wish to see an old man die in a prison, because he stood up for the right. Come, friend, let me pass; it's long sin' I've been used to such crowds, and I crave to be in the woods ag'in. Don't fear me, Judge—I bid you not to fear me; for if there's beaver enough left on the streams, or the buckskins will sell for a shilling a-piece, you shall have the last penny of the fine. Where are ye, pups! come away, dogs! come away! we have a grievous toil to do for our years, but it shall be done—yes, yes, I've promised it, and it shall be done!"

It is unnecessary to say, that the movement of the Leather-Stocking was again intercepted by the constable; but before he had time to speak, a bustling in the crowd, and a loud hem, drew all eyes to another part of the room.

Benjamin had succeeded in edging his way through the people, and was now seen

[5] Panthers.

balancing his short body, with one foot in a window and the other on a railing of the jurybox. To the amazement of the whole court, the steward was evidently preparing to speak. After a good deal of difficulty, he succeeded in drawing from his pocket a small bag, and then found utterance.

"If-so-be," he said, "that your honor is agreeable to trust the poor fellow out on another cruise among the beasts, here's a small matter that will help to bring down the risk, seeing that there's just thirty-five of your Spaniards[6] in it; and I wish, from the bottom of my heart, that they was raal British guineas,[7] for the sake of the old boy. But 'tis as it is; and if Squire Dickens will just be so good as to overhaul this small bit of an account, and take enough from the bag to settle the same, he's welcome to hold on upon the rest, till such time as the Leather-Stocking can grapple with them said beaver, or, for that matter, forever, and no thanks asked."

As Benjamin concluded, he thrust out the wooden register of his arrears to the "Bold Dragon" with one hand, while he offered his bag of dollars with the other. Astonishment at this singular interruption produced a profound stillness in the room, which was only interrupted by the Sheriff, who struck his sword on the table, and cried—

"Silence!"

"There must be an end to this," said the Judge, struggling to overcome his feelings. "Constable, lead the prisoner to the stocks. Mr. Clerk, what stands next on the calendar?"

Natty seemed to yield to his destiny, for he sank his head on his chest, and followed the officer from the court-room in silence. The crowd moved back for the passage of the prisoner, and when his tall form was seen descending from the outer door, a rush of the people to the scene of his disgrace followed.

1823

---

from The Prairie

Chapter XXXIV

—Methought I heard a voice.[1]
Shakespeare

The watercourses were at their height, and the boat went down the swift current like a bird. The passage proved prosperous and speedy. In less than a third of the time that would have been necessary for the same journey by land, it was accomplished by the favor of those rapid rivers. Issuing from one stream into another, as the veins of the human body communicate with the larger channels of life, they soon entered the grand artery of the western waters, and landed safely at the very door of the father of Inez.

---

[6] Spanish dollars.
[7] Guinea: British coin worth about £1.

[1] *Macbeth*, Act II, Sc. ii, 1. 35.

The joy of Don Augustin, and the embarrassment of the worthy father Ignatius, may be imagined. The former wept and returned thanks to Heaven; the latter returned thanks and did not weep. The mild provincials were too happy to raise any questions on the character of so joyful a restoration; and, by a sort of general consent, it soon became to be an admitted opinion that the bride of Middleton had been kidnapped by a villain, and that she was restored to her friends by human agency. There were, as respects this belief, certainly a few sceptics, but then they enjoyed their doubts in private, with that species of sublimated and solitary gratification that a miser finds in gazing at his growing, but useless hoards.

In order to give the worthy priest something to employ his mind, Middleton made him the instrument of uniting Paul and Ellen. The former consented to the ceremony, because he found that all his friends laid great stress on the matter; but shortly after, he led his bride into the plains of Kentucky, under the pretence of paying certain customary visits to sundry members of the family of Hover. While there, he took occasion to have the marriage properly solemnized by a justice of the peace of his acquaintance, in whose ability to forge the nuptial chain he had much more faith than in that of all the gownsmen[2] within the pale of Rome. Ellen, who appeared conscious that some extraordinary preventives might prove necessary to keep one of so erratic a temper as her partner, within the proper matrimonial boundaries, raised no objections to these double knots, and all parties were content.

The local importance Middleton had acquired, by his union with the daughter of so affluent a proprietor as Don Augustin, united to his personal merit, attracted the attention of the government. He was soon employed in various situations of responsibility and confidence, which both served to elevate his character in the public estimation, and to afford the means of patronage. The bee-hunter was among the first of those to whom he saw fit to extend his favor. It was far from difficult to find situations suited to the abilities of Paul, in the state of society that existed three-and-twenty years ago in those regions. The efforts of Middleton and Inez, in behalf of her husband, were warmly and sagaciously seconded by Ellen, and they succeeded, in process of time, in working a great and beneficial change in his character. He soon became a landholder, then a prosperous cultivator of the soil, and shortly after a town-officer. By that progressive change in fortunes, which in the republic is often seen to be so singularly accompanied by a corresponding improvement in knowledge and self-respect, he went on, from step to step, until his wife enjoyed the maternal delight of seeing her children placed far beyond the danger of returning to that state from which both their parents had issued. Paul is actually at this moment a member of the lower branch of the legislature of the State where he has long resided; and he is even notorious for making speeches that have a tendency to put that deliberative body in good humor, and which, as they are based on great practical knowledge suited to the condition of the country, possess a merit that is much wanted in many more subtle and fine-spun theories, that are daily heard in similar assemblies, to issue from the lips of certain instinctive politicians. But all these happy fruits were the results of much care, and of a long period of time. Middleton, who fills, with a credit better suited to the difference in their educations, a seat in a far higher branch of legislative authority, is the source from which we have derived most of the intelligence necessary

[2] I.e., ministers or priests.

to compose our legend. In addition to what he has related of Paul, and of his own continued happiness, he has added a short narrative of what took place on a subsequent visit to the prairies, with which, as we conceive it a suitable termination to what has gone before, we shall judge it wise to conclude our labors.

In the autumn of the year that succeeded the season in which the preceding events occurred, the young man, still in the military service, found himself on the waters of the Missouri, at a point not far remote from the Pawnee towns. Released from any immediate calls of duty, and strongly urged to the measure by Paul, who was in his company, he determined to take horse, and cross the country to visit the partisan, and to inquire into the fate of his friend the trapper. As his train was suited to his functions and rank, the journey was effected, with the privations and hardships that are the accompaniments to all travelling in a wild, but without any of those dangers and alarms that marked his former passage through the same regions. When within a proper distance, he despatched an Indian runner, belonging to a friendly tribe, to announce the approach of himself and party, continuing his route at a deliberate pace, in order that the intelligence might, as was customary, precede his arrival. To the surprise of the travellers, their message was unanswered. Hour succeeded hour, and mile after mile was passed, without bringing either the signs of an honorable reception, or the more simple assurances of a friendly welcome. At length the cavalcade, at whose head rode Middleton and Paul, descended from the elevated plain, on which they had long been journeying, to a luxuriant bottom, that brought them to the level of the village of the Loups. The sun was beginning to fall, and a sheet of golden light was spread over the placid plain, lending to its even surface those glorious tints and hues, that the human imagination is apt to conceive, form the embellishment of still more imposing scenes. The verdure of the year yet remained, and herds of horses and mules were grazing peacefully in the vast natural pasture, under the keeping of vigilant Pawnee boys. Paul pointed out among them the well-known form of Asinus, sleek, fat, and luxuriating in the fulness of content, as he stood with reclining ears and closed eyelids, seemingly musing on the exquisite nature of his present indolent enjoyment.

The route of the party led them at no great distance from one of those watchful youths who was charged with a trust heavy as the principal wealth of his tribe. He heard the trampling of the horses, and cast his eye aside, but instead of manifesting curiosity or alarm, his look instantly returned whence it had been withdrawn, to the spot where the village was known to stand.

"There is something remarkable in all this," muttered Middleton, half offended at what he conceived to be not only a slight to his rank, but offensive to himself personally; "yonder boy has heard of our approach, or he would not fail to notify his tribe; and yet he scarcely deigns to favor us with a glance. Look to your arms, men; it may be necessary to let these savages feel our strength."

"Therein, Captain, I think you're in an error," returned Paul: "if honesty is to be met on the prairies at all, you will find it in our old friend Hard-Heart; neither is an Indian to be judged of by the rules of a white. See! we are not altogether slighted, for here comes a party at last to meet us, though it is a little pitiful as to show and numbers."

Paul was right in both particulars. A group of horsemen were at length seen wheeling round a little copse, and advancing across the plain directly toward them.

The advance of this party was slow and dignified. As it drew nigh, the partisan of the Loups was seen at its head, followed by a dozen younger warriors of his tribe. They were all unarmed, nor did they even wear any of those ornaments or feathers, which are considered testimonials of respect to the guest an Indian receives, as well as evidence of his own importance.

The meeting was friendly, though a little restrained on both sides. Middleton, jealous of his own consideration, no less than of the authority of his government, suspected some undue influence on the part of the agents of the Canadas; and, as he was determined to maintain the authority of which he was the representative, he felt himself constrained to manifest a hauteur[3] that he was far from feeling. It was not so easy to penetrate the motives of the Pawnees. Calm, dignified, and yet far from repulsive, they set an example of courtesy, blended with reserve, that many a diplomatist of the most polished court might have striven in vain to imitate.

In this manner the two parties continued their course to the town. Middleton had time during the remainder of the ride, to revolve in his mind all the probable reasons which his ingenuity could suggest for this strange reception. Although he was accompanied by a regular interpreter, the chiefs made their salutations in a manner that dispensed with his services. Twenty times the Captain turned his glance on his former friend, endeavoring to read the expression of his rigid features. But every effort and all conjectures proved equally futile. The eye of Hard-Heart was fixed, composed, and a little anxious; but as to every other emotion, impenetrable. He neither spoke himself, nor seemed willing to invite discourse in his visitors: it was therefore necessary for Middleton to adopt the patient manners of his companions, and to await the issue for the explanation.

When they entered the town, its inhabitants were seen collected in an open space, where they were arranged with the customary deference to age and rank. The whole formed a large circle, in the centre of which were perhaps a dozen of the principal chiefs. Hard-Heart waved his hand as he approached, and, as the mass of bodies opened he rode through, followed by his companions. Here they dismounted; and as the beasts were led apart, the strangers found themselves environed by a thousand grave, composed, but solicitous faces.

Middleton gazed about him in growing concern, for no cry, no song, no shout welcomed him among a people, from whom he had so lately parted with regret. His uneasiness, not to say apprehensions, was shared by all his followers. Determination and stern resolution began to assume the place of anxiety in every eye, as each man silently felt for his arms, and assured himself that his several weapons were in a state for service. But there was no answering symptom of hostility on the part of their hosts. Hard-Heart beckoned for Middleton and Paul to follow, leading the way toward the cluster of forms that occupied the centre of the circle. Here the visitors found a solution of all the movements which had given them so much reason for apprehension.

The trapper was placed on a rude seat, which had been made, with studied care, to support his frame in an upright and easy attitude. The first glance of the eye told his former friends, that the old man was at length called upon to pay the last tribute of nature. His eye was glazed, and apparently as devoid of sight as of expression. His features were a little more sunken and strongly marked than formerly; but there, all

---

[3] Haughtiness.

change, so far as exterior was concerned, might be said to have ceased. His approaching end was not to be ascribed to any positive disease, but had been a gradual and mild decay of the physical powers. Life, it is true, still lingered in his system; but it was as if at times entirely ready to depart, and then it would appear to reanimate the sinking form, reluctant to give up the possession of a tenement that had never been corrupted by vice or undermined by disease. It would have been no violent fancy to have imagined that the spirit fluttered about the placid lips of the old woodsman, reluctant to depart from a shell that had so long given it an honest and honorable shelter.

His body was placed so as to let the light of the setting sun fall full upon the solemn features. His head was bare, the long, thin locks of gray fluttering lightly in the evening breeze. His rifle lay upon his knee, and the other accoutrements of the chase were placed at his side, within reach of his hand. Between his feet lay the figure of a hound, with its head crouching to the earth, as if it slumbered; and so perfectly easy and natural was its position, that a second glance was necessary to tell Middleton he saw only the skin of Hector, stuffed, by Indian tenderness and ingenuity, in a manner to represent the living animal. His own dog was playing at a distance with the child of Tachechana and Mahtoree. The mother herself stood at hand, holding in her arms a second offspring, that might boast of a parentage no less honorable than that which belonged to the son of Hard-Heart. Le Balafré was seated nigh the dying trapper, with every mark about his person that the hour of his own departure was not far distant. The rest of those immediately in the centre were aged men, who had apparently drawn near in order to observe the manner in which a just and fearless warrior would depart on the greatest of his journeys.

The old man was reaping the rewards of a life remarkable for temperance and activity, in a tranquil and placid death. His vigor in a manner endured to the very last. Decay, when it did occur, was rapid, but free from pain. He had hunted with the tribe in the spring, and even throughout most of the summer; when his limbs suddenly refused to perform their customary offices. A sympathizing weakness took possession of all his faculties; and the Pawnees believed that they were going to lose, in this unexpected manner, a sage and counsellor whom they had begun both to love and respect. But, as we have already said, the immortal occupant seemed unwilling to desert its tenement. The lamp of life flickered, without becoming extinguished. On the morning of the day on which Middleton arrived, there was a general reviving of the powers of the whole man. His tongue was again heard in wholesome maxims, and his eye from time to time recognized the persons of his friends. It merely proved to be a brief and final intercourse with the world, on the part of one who had already been considered, as to mental communion, to have taken his leave of it forever.

When he had placed his guests in front of the dying man, Hard-Heart, after a pause, that proceeded as much from sorrow as decorum, leaned a little forward, and demanded—

"Does my father hear the words of his son?"

"Speak," returned the trapper, in tones that issued from his chest, but which were rendered awfully distinct by the stillness that reigned in the place. "I am about to depart from the village of the Loups, and shortly shall be beyond the reach of your voice."

"Let the wise chief have no cares for his journey," continued Hard-Heart, with an earnest solicitude that led him to forget, for the moment, that others were waiting to address his adopted parent; "a hundred Loups shall clear his path from briers."

"Pawnee, I die, as I have lived, a Christian man!" resumed the trapper, with a force of voice that had the same startling effect on his hearers as is produced by the trumpet, when its blast rises suddenly and freely on the air, after its obstructed sounds have been heard struggling in the distance: "as I came into life so will I leave it. Horses and arms are not needed to stand in the presence of the Great Spirit of my people. He knows my color, and according to my gifts will He judge my deeds."

"My father will tell my young men how many Mingoes he has struck, and what acts of valor and justice he has done, that they may know how to imitate him."

"A boastful tongue is not heard in the heaven of a white man!" solemnly returned the old man. "What I have done He has seen. His eyes are always open. That which has been well done will He remember; wherein I have been wrong will He not forget to chastise, though He will do the same in mercy. No, my son; a Pale-face may not sing his own praises, and hope to have them acceptable before his God!"

A little disappointed, the young partisan stepped modestly back, making way for the recent comers to approach. Middleton took one of the meagre hands of the trapper, and struggling to command his voice, he succeeded in announcing his presence.

The old man listened like one whose thoughts were dwelling on a very different subject; but when the other had succeeded in making him understand that he was present, an expression of joyful recognition passed over his faded features.

"I hope you have not so soon forgotten those whom you so materially served!" Middleton concluded. "It would pain me to think my hold on your memory was so light."

"Little that I have ever seen is forgotten," returned the trapper; "I am at the close of many weary days, but there is not one among them all that I could wish to overlook. I remember you, with the whole of your company; ay, and your gran'ther, that went before you. I am glad that you have come back upon these plains, for I had need of one who speaks the English, since little faith can be put in the traders of these regions. Will you do a favor to an old and dying man?"

"Name it," said Middleton; "it shall be done."

"It is a far journey to send such trifles," resumed the old man, who spoke at short intervals, as strength and breath permitted, "a far and weary journey is the same; but kindnesses and friendships are things not to be forgotten. There is a settlement among the Otsego hills—"

"I know the place," interrupted Middleton, observing that he spoke with increasing difficulty; "proceed to tell me what you would have done."

"Take this rifle, and pouch, and horn, and send them to the person whose name is graven on the plates of the stock,—a trader cut the letters with his knife,—for it is long that I have intended to send him such a token of my love!"

"It shall be so. Is there more that you could wish?"

"Little else have I to bestow. My traps I give to my Indian son; for honestly and kindly has he kept his faith. Let him stand before me."

Middleton explained to the chief what the trapper had said, and relinquished his own place to the other.

"Pawnee," continued the old man, always changing his language to suit the person he addressed, and not unfrequently according to the ideas he expressed, "it is a custom of my people for the father to leave his blessing with the son before he shuts his eyes forever. This blessing I give to you; take it; for the prayers of a Christian man will never make the path of a just warrior to the blessed prairies either longer or more tangled. May the God of a white man look on your deeds with friendly eyes, and may you never commit an act that shall cause Him to darken His face. I know not whether we shall ever meet again. There are many traditions concerning the place of Good Spirits. It is not for one like me, old and experienced though I am, to set up my opinion against a nation's. You believe in the blessed prairies, and I have faith in the sayings of my fathers. If both are true our parting will be final; but if it should prove that the same meaning is hid under different words, we shall yet stand together, Pawnee, before the face of your Wahcondah, who will then be no other than my God. There is much to be said in favor of both religions, for each seems suited to its own people, and no doubt it was so intended. I fear I have not altogether followed the gifts of my color, inasmuch as I find it a little painful to give up forever the use of the rifle, and the comforts of the chase. But then the fault has been my own, seeing that it could not have been His. Ay, Hector," he continued, leaning forward a little, and feeling for the ears of the hound, "our parting has come at last, dog, and it will be a long hunt. You have been an honest, and a bold, and a faithful hound. Pawnee, you cannot slay the pup on my grave, for where a Christian dog falls there he lies forever; but you can be kind to him after I am gone, for the love you bear his master."

"The words of my father are in my ears," returned the young partisan, making a grave and respectful gesture of assent.

"Do you hear what the chief has promised, dog?" demanded the trapper, making an effort to attract the notice of the insensible effigy of his hound. Receiving no answering look, nor hearing any friendly whine, the old man felt for the mouth, and endeavored to force his hand between the cold lips. The truth then flashed upon him, although he was far from perceiving the whole extent of the deception. Falling back in his seat, he hung his head, like one who felt a severe and unexpected shock. Profiting by this momentary forgetfulness, two young Indians removed the skin with the same delicacy of feeling that had induced them to attempt the pious fraud.

"The dog is dead!" muttered the trapper, after a pause of many minutes; "a hound has his time as well as a man; and well has he filled his days! Captain," he added, making an effort to wave his hand for Middleton, "I am glad you have come; for though kind, and well meaning according to the gifts of their color, these Indians are not the men to lay the head of a white man in his grave. I have been thinking, too, of this dog at my feet; it will not do to set forth the opinion that a Christian can expect to meet his hound again; still there can be little harm in placing what is left of so faithful a servant nigh the bones of his master."

"It shall be as you desire."

"I'm glad you think with me in this matter. In order, then, to save labor, lay the pup at my feet; or for that matter, put him side by side. A hunter need never be ashamed to be found in company with his dog!"

"I charge myself with your wish."

The old man made a long, and apparently a musing pause. At times he raised his eyes wistfully, as if he would again address Middleton, but some innate feeling appeared always to suppress his words. The other, who observed his hesitation, inquired in a way most likely to encourage him to proceed whether there was aught else that he could wish to have done.

"I am without kith or kin in the wide world!" the trapper answered: "when I am gone there will be an end of my race. We have never been chiefs; but honest, and useful in our way I hope it cannot be denied we have always proved ourselves. My father lies buried near the sea, and the bones of his son will whiten on the prairie—"

"Name the spot, and your remains shall be placed by the side of your father," interrupted Middleton.

"Not so, not so, Captain. Let me sleep where I have lived—beyond the din of the settlements! Still I see no need why the grave of an honest man should be hid, like a Red-skin in his ambushment. I paid a man in the settlements to make and put a graven stone at the head of my father's resting-place. It was of the value of twelve beaverskins, and cunningly and curiously was it carved! Then it told to all comers that the body of such a Christian lay beneath; and it spoke of his manner of life, of his years, and of his honesty. When we had done with the Frenchers in the old war I made a journey to the spot, in order to see that all was rightly performed, and glad I am to say, the workman had not forgotten his faith."

"And such a stone you would have at your grave?"

"I! no, no, I have no son but Hard-Heart, and it is little that an Indian knows of white fashions and usages. Besides, I am his debtor already, seeing it is so little I have done since I have lived in his tribe. The rifle might bring the value of such a thing —but then I know it will give the boy pleasure to hang the piece in his hall, for many is the deer and the bird that he has seen it destroy. No, no, the gun must be sent to him whose name is graven on the lock!"

"But there is one who would gladly prove his affection in the way you wish; he who owes you not only his own deliverance from so many dangers, but who inherits a heavy debt of gratitude from his ancestors. The stone shall be put at the head of your grave."

The old man extended his emaciated hand, and gave the other a squeeze of thanks.

"I thought you might be willing to do it, but I was backward in asking the favor," he said, "seeing that you are not of my kin. Put no boastful words on the same, but just the name, the age, and the time of the death, with something from the holy book; no more, no more. My name will then not be altogether lost on 'arth; I need no more."

Middleton intimated his assent, and then followed a pause that was only broken by distant and broken sentences from the dying man. He appeared now to have closed his accounts with the world, and to await merely for the final summons to quit it. Middleton and Hard-Heart placed themselves on the opposite sides of his seat, and watched with melancholy solicitude, the variations of his countenance. For two hours there was no very sensible alteration. The expression of his faded and time-worn features was that of a calm and dignified repose. From time to time he spoke, uttering some brief sentence in the way of advice, or asking some simple questions concerning those in whose fortunes he took a friendly interest. During the whole of that solemn and anxious period each individual of the tribe kept his place, in the most self-restrained patience. When the old man spoke, all bent their heads to listen; and when his words were uttered, they seemed to ponder on their wisdom and usefulness.

As the flame drew nigher to the socket his voice was hushed, and there were moments when his attendants doubted whether he still belonged to the living. Middleton, who watched each wavering expression of his weather-beaten visage, with the interest of a keen observer of human nature, softened by the tenderness of personal regard, fancied he could read the workings of the old man's soul in the strong lineaments of his countenance. Perhaps what the enlightened soldier took for the delusion of mistaken opinion did actually occur—for who has returned from that unknown world to explain by what forms, and in what manner, he was introduced into its awful precincts? Without pretending to explain what must ever be a mystery to the quick, we shall simply relate facts as they occurred.

The trapper had remained nearly motionless for an hour. His eyes alone had occasionally opened and shut. When opened, his gaze seemed fastened on the clouds which hung around the western horizon, reflecting the bright colors, and giving form and loveliness to the glorious tints of an American sunset. The hour—the calm beauty of the season—the occasion, all conspired to fill the spectators with solemn awe. Suddenly, while musing on the remarkable position in which he was placed, Middleton felt the hand which he held grasp his own with incredible power, and the old man, supported on either side by his friends, rose upright to his feet. For a moment he looked about him, as if to invite all in presence to listen (the lingering remnant of human frailty), and then, with a fine military elevation of the head, and with a voice that might be heard in every part of that numerous assembly, he pronounced the word—

"Here!"

A movement so entirely unexpected, and the air of grandeur and humility which were so remarkably united in the mien of the trapper, together with the clear and uncommon force of his utterance, produced a short period of confusion in the faculties of all present. When Middleton and Hard-Heart, each of whom had involuntarily extended a hand to support the form of the old man, turned to him again, they found that the subject of their interest was removed forever beyond the necessity of their care. They mournfully placed the body in its seat, and Le Balafré arose to announce the termination of the scene to the tribe. The voice of the old Indian seemed a sort of echo from that invisible world to which the meek spirit of the trapper had just departed.

"A valiant, a just, and a wise warrior, has gone on the path which will lead him to the blessed grounds of his people!" he said. "When the voice of the Wahcondah called him, he was ready to answer. Go, my children; remember the just chief of the Pale-faces, and clear your own tracks from briers!"

The grave was made beneath the shade of some noble oaks. It has been carefully watched to the present hour by the Pawnees of the Loup, and is often shown to the traveller and the trader as a spot where a just white man sleeps. In due time the stone was placed at its head, with the simple inscription which the trapper had himself requested. The only liberty taken by Middleton was to add—*"May no wanton hand ever disturb his remains!"*

1827

William Cullen Bryant
1794–1878

William Cullen Bryant's popular image haunts his poetry. The classroom portrait of this legendary patriarch of American verse, with a chiseled old face and deep-set eyes peering out from behind bushy eyebrows and a long, flowing white beard, solemnly oversaw generations of American schoolchildren dutifully reciting "Thanatopsis" and "To a Waterfowl." Not until Robert Frost in the mid-twentieth century would there be another American poet with as venerable a public reputation.

Few American writers have had longer—or more visible—literary careers than Bryant. His publications span the administrations of seventeen presidents, from Thomas Jefferson to Rutherford B. Hayes. Yet the definitive edition of Bryant's poems consists of but two relatively small volumes. And few American poets have expressed a more consistent vision of the world: meditative, restrained, full of dignified serenity and pleasure in nature. Bryant's early work reveals few youthful flaws, his last efforts few signs of his eighty-three years.

William Cullen Bryant was born in Cummington, a small town in western Massachusetts's Berkshire Mountains. His mother, a hardy Calvinist descendant of the Pilgrim John Alden, made the following brief entry in her diary for November 3, 1794: "Stormy, wind N.E. Churned. Seven in the evening a son was born." His father, a doctor, encouraged him to read widely in the family's modest but well-chosen library of English and classical literature. The following passage from Bryant's fragment of an autobiography recalls the importance of his youth:

> I was always from my earliest years a delighted observer of external nature—the splendors of a winter daybreak over the wide waste of snow seen from our windows, the glories of the autumnal woods, the gloomy approaches of the thunderstorm, and its departure amid sunshine and rainbows, the return of spring, with its flowers, and the first snowfall of winter. The poets fostered this taste in me, and though at the time I rarely heard such things spoken of, it was none the less cherished in my secret mind.

Privately educated by country ministers, as was the custom in rural New England, Bryant began writing poetry at eight years of age and, supported by his father, had his first work published as an anonymous "Youth of Thirteen." *The Embargo; or, Sketches of the Times* (1808) is a Federalist satire on the policies of President Jefferson, whom Bryant came to admire years later. The poem's vitriolic couplets testify both to Bryant's youthful poetic tendencies and to the still reigning influence of Alexander Pope on American verse. At fifteen, Bryant entered Williams College as a sophomore, but financial difficulties prevented him from transferring to Yale for his junior year. He studied law privately instead and was admitted to the Massachusetts bar in 1814. He wrote a great deal of poetry during those early years of practicing law, and he also served as town clerk of Great Barrington, where in 1821 he married Fanny Fairchild. His *Poems* were published in the same year. Bryant was eager to settle in Boston, but his father discouraged him, noting that there were too many lawyers there already. Poetry provided no alternative as a livelihood. Four years after the publication of his poems, the volume had earned him a meager $14.21.

In 1825 Bryant moved to New York, where he edited a magazine, the *New York Review,* and became part of a literary group that came to be known as the Knickerbocker School and included Washington Irving and James Fenimore Cooper. In 1826 he signed on as the assistant editor of the New York *Evening Post,* and from 1829 to his death in 1878 he served as its editor in chief. An inveterate traveler, Bryant made several trips to Europe and the American frontier (to visit his pioneer brothers) and lengthy visits to Canada, Mexico, and the Caribbean. But New York remained his home and writing his central activity for the rest of his life.

Although Bryant spent more than fifty years there, New York seems to have had little impact on either his character or his poetry. Never quite as urbane as Washington Irving, Bryant maintained the austerity of a New England winter in his life and work. He rarely allowed himself, as he notes in "The Poet," the luxury of "burning words" or "impassioned thought." One early biographer claimed that this predilection may have stemmed from "the fact that when he was a child his parents, becoming alarmed at the unnaturally large size of his head, used to soak it in cold water, sometimes breaking the ice to do so. Bryant never quite got this chill out of his style." A less apocryphal explanation might be Bryant's lifelong interest in the classics and his familiarity with the leading eighteenth-century Neoclassical English poets who wrote on nature and melancholy, especially those in the "Graveyard school," most notably Thomson, Blair, Young, and Gray. This influence is never more apparent than in "Thanatopsis," first published in the newly established *North American Review* in 1817. Recalling the circumstances, one of the editors, Richard Henry Dana, Sr., later wrote:

> Going into town one day while assisting E. T. Channing (now Professor) in the *North American Review* [1817], he read to me a couple of pieces of poetry which had just been sent to the *Review*—the "Thanatopsis" and "The Inscription for the Entrance to a Wood." While C—— was reading one of them, I broke out, saying, "That was never written on this side of the water"—and naturally enough, considering what American poetry had been up to that moment.

Bryant, like many of his contemporaries, was absorbed in the issues surrounding American literary nationalism. He vigorously opposed the lingering tendency of many Americans who "do not praise a thing until [they] see the seal of transatlantic approbation upon it." He insisted that America was "a rich and varied field for literature." Yet, like his counterparts in the art world, particularly his "kindred spirits" in what came to be known as the Hudson River school, Bryant was more successful at introducing indigenous American subjects than in treating them in distinctively American terms.

His literary criticism, however, stands as one of the earliest efforts in the new nation to study poetry systematically. From his *Lectures on Poetry* (delivered in 1825 but published posthumously in 1884) to his essay "Poets and Poetry of the English Language" (printed as the introduction to his anthology, *A Library of Poetry and Song,* in 1871), Bryant consistently focused on the original, imaginative, moral, and didactic properties of poetry. Bryant sought "a luminous style" in his verse, and in reading him we ought to keep in mind his own guidelines for writing it:

> The elements of poetry lie in natural objects, in the vicissitudes of human life, in the emotions of the human heart, and the relations of man to man. He who can present them in combinations and lights which at once affect the mind with a deep sense of their truth and beauty is the poet for his own age and the ages that succeed him. . . . The metaphysician, the subtle thinker, the dealer in abstruse speculations, whatever his skill in versification, misapplies it when he abandons the more convenient form of prose, and perplexes himself with the attempt to express his ideas in poetic numbers.

More than two-thirds of Bryant's poems focus on the natural world. In this respect, his repeated reading of Wordsworth as a youth had a profound impact on his verse. Dana describes the nature of the influence:

> I never shall forget with what feeling my friend Bryant, some years ago, described to me the effect produced upon him by his meeting for the first time with Wordsworth's ballads. He said that, upon opening the book, a thousand springs seemed to gush up at once in his heart, and the face of Nature, of a sudden, to change into a strange freshness and life.

Bryant's enthusiasm for Wordsworth's verse had waned noticeably by the time they finally met in England in 1845. Yet Bryant's vision of nature, like Wordsworth's, remains stately; both write with considerable self-control, emotional distance, and purity of line. And, revealing the influence of Wordsworth, Bryant is the first major American poet to celebrate what would soon become the Romantic tradition of recognizing divine splendor in nature's beauty and taking personal solace from it. In this respect, Bryant spent much of his life using nature and poetry as tools to create a religion to sustain himself. Yet Bryant's calm and powerful poetic voice remains a harbinger rather than an example of the more daring and fiercely independent literary imaginations that would soon demand the attention of mid-nineteenth-century audiences.

Nearly all of Bryant's poetry that claims our attention was written before 1840, when the pressures of editing a major newspaper in one of the nation's largest cities allowed him little time to write verse. Responding to his friend Dana's urging that he leave more time for poetry, Bryant wistfully noted:

> I should be glad of an opportunity to attempt something in the way I like best, and am, perhaps, fittest for; but here I am a draught-horser, harnessed to a daily drag. I have so much to do with my legs and hoofs, struggling and pulling and

kicking, that, if there is anything of the Pegasus in me, I am too much exhausted to use my wings.

Bryant knew that there was but a small audience for poetry in the early decades of nineteenth-century America and that, as he told Dana, "no man makes money by it. . . . The taste for it is something old-fashioned; the march of the age is in another direction; mankind are occupied with politics, railroads, and steamboats." Not surprisingly, Bryant's became one of the most respected voices in nineteenth-century American journalism, and his incisive editorials tackled virtually every important issue of the the time. His opinions counted in every public cause, and his presence was felt in innumerable acts of community planning and service.

Bryant's literary efforts in his last few decades focused primarily on translating the *Iliad* (1870) and the *Odyssey* (1872), editing Shakespeare, celebrating American history and literature, and eulogizing the deaths of the nation's leading writers. The most revealing appraisal of Bryant's later life and work is implicit in Nathaniel Hawthorne's description of meeting him in Italy in 1858:

> There was a weary look in his face, as if he were tired of seeing things and doing things, though with certainly enough still to do and see. . . . His manners and whole aspect are particularly plain, though not affectedly so; but it seems as if in the decline of life, and the security of his position, he had put off whatever artificial polish he may heretofore have had, and resumed the simpler habits and deportment of his early New England breeding. . . . He is a man of refinement, who has seen the world, and is well aware of his own place in it.

Bryant remained an extremely popular poet, despite the long intervals between his volumes. By the time of his death in 1878, Bryant had become such a prominent figure in New York intellectual and political circles that the city's flags flew at half mast, its shops draped in black.

Bryant's importance in American literature can be considered in the appraisals of his more distinguished contemporaries. Edgar Allan Poe called Bryant "full of the aristocracy of intellect." Ralph Waldo Emerson praised Bryant as "always original—a true painter of the face of the country, and of the sentiment of his own people. . . . It is his proper praise that he first, and he only, made known to mankind our northern landscape—its summer splendor, its autumn russet, its winter lights and glooms." But it is Walt Whitman who offers the most expansive version of Bryant's achievement:

> Bryant pulsing the first interior verse-throbs of a mighty world—bard of the river and the wood, ever conveying a taste of open air . . . always lurkingly fond of threnodies—beginning and ending his long career with chants of death . . . touching the highest universal truth, enthusiasms, duties—morals as grim and eternal, if not as stormy and fateful, as anything in Aeschylus.

Further Reading:
P. Godwin, *The Life and Works of William Cullen Bryant*, 2 vols., 1883.
J. Bigelow, *William Cullen Bryant*, 1890.
W. A. Bradley, *William Cullen Bryant*, 1905.
A. Nevins, *The Evening Post: A Century of Journalism*, 1922.
T. McDowell, *Bryant*, 1935.
H. H. Peckham, *Gotham Yankee: A Biography of William Cullen Bryant*, 1950.
C. S. Johnson, *Politics and a Bellyful: The Journalistic Career of William Cullen Bryant*, 1962.
A. McLean, *William Cullen Bryant*, 1964.
C. Brown, *William Cullen Bryant*, 1972.

Text:
The Poetical Works of William Cullen Bryant, ed. P. Godwin, 2 vols., 1883.

Thanatopsis[1]

To him who in the love of Nature holds
Communion with her visible forms, she speaks
A various language; for his gayer hours
She has a voice of gladness, and a smile
And eloquence of beauty, and she glides   5
Into his darker musings, with a mild
And healing sympathy, that steals away
Their sharpness, ere he is aware. When thoughts
Of the last bitter hour come like a blight
Over thy spirit, and sad images   10
Of the stern agony, and shroud, and pall,
And breathless darkness, and the narrow house,
Make thee to shudder, and grow sick at heart;—
Go forth, under the open sky, and list
To Nature's teachings, while from all around—   15
Earth and her waters, and the depths of air—
Comes a still voice.—

      Yet a few days, and thee
The all-beholding sun shall see no more
In all his course; nor yet in the cold ground,
Where thy pale form was laid, with many tears,   20
Nor in the embrace of ocean, shall exist

[1] Greek: "Meditation on Death."

Thy image. Earth, that nourished thee, shall claim
Thy growth, to be resolved to earth again,
And, lost each human trace, surrendering up
Thine individual being, shalt thou go   25
To mix for ever with the elements,
To be a brother to the insensible rock
And to the sluggish clod, which the rude swain
Turns with his share,[2] and treads upon. The oak
Shall send his roots abroad, and pierce thy mould.   30

 Yet not to thine eternal resting-place
Shalt thou retire alone, nor couldst thou wish
Couch more magnificent. Thou shalt lie down
With patriarchs of the infant world—with kings,
The powerful of the earth—the wise, the good,   35
Fair forms, and hoary seers of ages past,
All in one mighty sepulchre. The hills
Rock-ribbed and ancient as the sun,—the vales
Stretching in pensive quietness between;
The venerable woods—rivers that move   40
In majesty, and the complaining brooks
That make the meadows green; and, poured round all,
Old Ocean's gray and melancholy waste,—
Are but the solemn decorations all
Of the great tomb of man. The golden sun,   45
The planets, all the infinite host of heaven,
Are shining on the sad abodes of death,
Through the still lapse of ages. All that tread
The globe are but a handful to the tribes
That slumber in its bosom.—Take the wings   50
Of morning, pierce the Barcan wilderness,[3]
Or lose thyself in the continuous woods
Where rolls the Oregon,[4] and hears no sound,
Save his own dashings—yet the dead are there:
And millions in those solitudes, since first   55
The flight of years began, have laid them down
In their last sleep—the dead reign there alone.
So shalt thou rest, and what if thou withdraw
In silence from the living, and no friend
Take note of thy departure? All that breathe   60
Will share thy destiny. The gay will laugh
When thou art gone, the solemn brood of care
Plod on, and each one as before will chase
His favorite phantom; yet all these shall leave

---

[2] Plowshare.
[3] The desert of Barca in northeast Libya.

[4] Indian name for what is now the Columbia River.

Their mirth and their employments, and shall come   65
And make their bed with thee. As the long train
Of ages glides away, the sons of men,
The youth in life's fresh spring, and he who goes
In the full strength of years, matron and maid,
The speechless babe, and the gray-headed man—   70
Shall one by one be gathered to thy side,
By those, who in their turn shall follow them.

So live, that when thy summons comes to join
The innumerable caravan, which moves
To that mysterious realm, where each shall take   75
His chamber in the silent halls of death,
Thou go not, like the quarry-slave at night,
Scourged to his dungeon, but, sustained and soothed
By an unfaltering trust, approach thy grave,
Like one who wraps the drapery of his couch   80
About him, and lies down to pleasant dreams.

ca. 1814/1817; 1821

Inscription for the Entrance to a Wood

Stranger, if thou hast learned a truth which needs
No school of long experience, that the world
Is full of guilt and misery, and hast seen
Enough of all its sorrows, crimes, and cares,
To tire thee of it, enter this wild wood   5
And view the haunts of Nature. The calm shade
Shall bring a kindred calm, and the sweet breeze
That makes the green leaves dance, shall waft a balm
To thy sick heart. Thou wilt find nothing here
Of all that pained thee in the haunts of men,   10
And made thee loathe thy life. The primal curse[1]
Fell, it is true, upon the unsinning earth,
But not in vengeance. God hath yoked to guilt
Her pale tormentor, misery. Hence, these shades
Are still the abodes of gladness; the thick roof   15

[1] The curse of God placed on all creatures of the
earth upon the exile of Adam and Eve from
the Garden of Eden. (See Genesis 3.)

Of green and stirring branches is alive
And musical with birds, that sing and sport
In wantonness of spirit; while below
The squirrel, with raised paws and form erect,
Chirps merrily. Throngs of insects in the shade   20
Try their thin wings and dance in the warm beam
That waked them into life. Even the green trees
Partake the deep contentment; as they bend
To the soft winds, the sun from the blue sky
Looks in and sheds a blessing on the scene.   25
Scarce less the cleft-born wild-flower seems to enjoy
Existence than the wingèd plunderer
That sucks its sweets. The mossy rocks themselves,
And the old and ponderous trunks of prostrate trees
That lead from knoll to knoll a causey[2] rude   30
Or bridge the sunken brook, and their dark roots,
With all their earth upon them, twisting high,
Breathe fixed tranquillity. The rivulet
Sends forth glad sounds, and tripping o'er its bed
Of pebbly sands, or leaping down the rocks,   35
Seems, with continuous laughter, to rejoice
In its own being. Softly tread the marge,[3]
Lest from her midway perch thou scare the wren
That dips her bill in water. The cool wind,
That stirs the stream in play, shall come to thee,   40
Like one that loves thee nor will let thee pass
Ungreeted, and shall give its light embrace.

1817

To a Waterfowl

Whither, midst falling dew,
    While glow the heavens with the last steps of day,
Far, through their rosy depths, dost thou pursue
    Thy solitary way?

    Vainly the fowler's eye   5
Might mark thy distant flight to do thee wrong,
As, darkly painted on the crimson sky,
    Thy figure floats along.

---

[2] Obsolete term for causeway.   [3] Archaic: border or edge.

Seek'st thou the plashy brink
Of weedy lake, or marge of river wide,   10
Or where the rocking billows rise and sink
    On the chafed ocean-side?

There is a Power whose care
Teaches thy way along that pathless coast—
The desert and illimitable air—   15
    Lone wandering, but not lost.

All day thy wings have fanned,
At that far height, the cold, thin atmosphere,
Yet stoop not, weary, to the welcome land,
    Though the dark night is near.   20

And soon that toil shall end;
Soon shalt thou find a summer home, and rest,
And scream among thy fellows; reeds shall bend,
    Soon, o'er thy sheltered nest.

Thou'rt gone, the abyss of heaven   25
Hath swallowed up thy form; yet, on my heart
Deeply has sunk the lesson thou hast given,
    And shall not soon depart.

He who, from zone to zone,
Guides through the boundless sky thy certain flight,   30
In the long way that I must tread alone,
    Will lead my steps aright.

1815/1818; 1821

The Yellow Violet

When beechen buds begin to swell,
    And woods the blue-bird's warble know,
The yellow violet's modest bell
    Peeps from the last year's leaves below.

Ere russet fields their green resume,   5
    Sweet flower, I love, in forest bare,
To meet thee, when thy faint perfume
    Alone is in the virgin air.

Of all her train, the hands of Spring
    First plant thee in the watery mould,   10
And I have seen thee blossoming
    Beside the snow-bank's edges cold.

Thy parent sun, who bade thee view
    Pale skies, and chilling moisture sip,
Has bathed thee in his own bright hue,   15
    And streaked with jet thy glowing lip.

Yet slight thy form, and low thy seat,
    And earthward bent thy gentle eye,
Unapt the passing view to meet,
    When loftier flowers are flaunting nigh.   20

Oft, in the sunless April day,
    Thy early smile has stayed my walk;
But midst the gorgeous blooms of May,
    I passed thee on thy humble stalk.

So they, who climb to wealth, forget   25
    The friends in darker fortunes tried.
I copied them—but I regret
    That I should ape the ways of pride.

And when again the genial hour
    Awakes the painted tribes of light.   30
I'll not o'erlook the modest flower
    That made the woods of April bright.

1814/1821

To Cole, the Painter, Departing for Europe*

Thine eyes shall see the light of distant skies;
    Yet, COLE! thy heart shall bear to Europe's strand
    A living image of our own bright land,
Such as upon thy glorious canvas lies;

* Addressed to Bryant's friend Thomas Cole
(1801–1848), English-born painter of naturalist
American landscapes.

Lone lakes—savannas where the bison roves—   5
   Rocks rich with summer garlands—solemn streams—
   Skies, where the desert eagle wheels and screams—
Spring bloom and autumn blaze of boundless groves.
Fair scenes shall greet thee where thou goest—fair,
   But different—everywhere the trace of men,   10
   Paths, homes, graves, ruins, from the lowest glen
To where life shrinks from the fierce Alpine air.
   Gaze on them, till the tears shall dim thy sight,
   But keep that earlier, wilder image bright.

1829/1830

To the Fringed Gentian

Thou blossom bright with autumn dew,
And colored with the heaven's own blue,
That openest when the quiet light
Succeeds the keen and frosty night.

Thou comest not when violets lean   5
O'er wandering brooks and springs unseen,
Or columbines, in purple dressed,
Nod o'er the ground-bird's hidden nest.

Thou waitest late and com'st alone,
When woods are bare and birds are flown,   10
And frosts and shortening days portend
The aged year is near his end.

Then doth thy sweet and quiet eye
Look through its fringes to the sky,
Blue—blue—as if that sky let fall   15
A flower from its cerulean wall.

I would that thus, when I shall see
The hour of death draw near to me,
Hope, blossoming within my heart,
May look to heaven as I depart.   20

1829/1832

George Caleb Bingham,
Daniel Boone Escorting Settlers Through the Cumberland Gap,
oil on canvas, 1851–1852.
Collection, Washington University Gallery of Art, St. Louis.

The Literature of the American Renaissance 1836–1865

"Who Reads an American Book?"

Could literature and art, as defined by colonial standards, thrive in the new nation? Were they at all appropriate to the special political, social, and economic conditions Americans found and in turn created? How could the language and literary models of England be naturalized to these conditions? Was there a cultural counterpart to political independence? These were some of the issues confronting the men and women who became the writers of the American Renaissance.

"We have no distinct class of literati in our country," Thomas Jefferson had noted. "Every man is engaged in some industrious pursuit. . . . Few therefore of those who are qualified have leisure to write." Former President John Quincy Adams declared "that literature was, and in its nature must always be, aristocratic; that democracy of numbers and literature were self-contradictory." Democratic nations, said Alexis de Tocqueville after visiting Jacksonian America in 1831, "will habitually prefer the useful to the beautiful, and they will require that the beautiful should be useful." Americans were newspaper readers, he said, and they relied on newspapers to "maintain civilization." "The universal equality of conditions spreads a monotonous tint over all society," said his traveling companion, the novelist Gustave de Beaumont; he warned Europeans not to "look for poetry, literature, or fine arts in this country." When one of the proprietors of the *North*

American Review first read young William Cullen Bryant's blank verse, Wordsworthian "Thanatopsis" (1817), a poem subsequently hailed as the finest yet written in America, he assumed the author was British: "No one on this side of the Atlantic is capable of writing such verse."

Washington Irving and James Fenimore Cooper, both successful professional men of letters, believed they had overcome cultural and economic obstacles likely to discourage other native writers. Americans were supposedly too busy making money and taming the wilderness to have leisure for literary reading, but with a few notable exceptions, chiefly the work of Irving and Cooper, most of the books they did read were written in England. This was partly due to a shortsighted Copyright Act, passed by the First Congress in 1790, that granted protection only to citizens or residents of the United States. All others were fair game for "pirates," publishers of unauthorized editions. The act's implicit rejection of international copyright encouraged American book, magazine, and newspaper publishers to favor foreign authors, whose work they could get for nothing and bring out cheaply, thereby neglecting or exploiting native authors, to whom they had to pay royalties or fees. ("Who will give two dollars a volume for Prescott," asked the author of *The Conquest of Peru,* "when they can buy Macaulay for seventy-five cents?") Established authors like Irving and Cooper brought out their own books and paid publishers a commission to distribute them, while untested American authors simply took their chances. Harper & Brothers paid Richard Henry Dana, Jr., a total of $250 for the copyright on his *Two Years Before the Mast* (1840), a best-seller that earned them about $50,000 before their license ran out. Outspoken opponents of international copyright, Harper & Brothers soon became the largest publisher in the world, with over fifteen hundred titles in print by midcentury.

After 1836 Charles Dickens succeeded Sir Walter Scott as the most popular author of both hemispheres and, consequently, chief victim of the pirates. "Dickens' *American Notes* were received by us at eight o'clock on Sunday evening," the publishers of the weekly *New World* announced on November 12, 1842. "We printed them complete in a double extra number . . . and issued them at one o'clock on Monday—being precisely seventeen hours from the time 'the copy was put in hand.' " They predicted a sale of 400,000 copies, not one of which would earn Dickens a penny. "There must be an international copyright agreement," he had argued on his visit to the United States earlier that year. "It becomes the character of a great country; firstly, because it is justice; secondly, because without it you can never have, and keep, a literature of your own." (Half a century later an International Copyright Law finally stood on the statute books.)

As yet without the annals, traditions, and associations that nurtured Old World writers, the United States offered its own a "poverty of materials," Cooper said. "The weakest hand can extract a spark from the flint, but it would baffle the strength of a giant to attempt kindling a flame with a pudding-stone." Yet Cooper had a shrewd sense of the future. "The literature of the United States is a subject of the highest interest to the civilized world," he wrote, "for when it does begin to be felt, it will be felt with a force, a directness, and a common sense in its application, that has never yet been known. . . . I think the time for the experiment is getting near."

John L. O'Sullivan launched his grandly titled *United States Magazine and Democratic Review* in 1837 with a declaration of purpose: "The vital principle of our literature must be democracy. . . . All history is to be rewritten; political science and the whole scope of moral truth have to be reconsidered in the light of the democratic principle." Following its "manifest destiny," a resounding slogan that O'Sullivan coined, messianic "Young America" was "to overspread the continent allotted by Providence for the free development of our yearly multiplying millions" and also lead the world to salvation by the road of republicanism. In ideology as well as religion this was an evangelical age. "We Americans are the peculiar, chosen people—the Israel of our times," Herman Melville wrote in 1850. "We bear the ark of the liberties of the world. . . . In our youth is our strength; in our inexperience, our wisdom." Writing in praise of Hawthorne's *Mosses from an Old Manse,* he declared that "men not very much inferior to Shakespeare are this day being born on the banks of the Ohio."

Similar spread-eagle sentiments were voiced all through the period. They were undoubtedly good for morale, but they were not necessarily good for literature and criticism. "It is now the fashion to extol everything American," Cooper observed. "The country is filled, today, with the most profound provincial self-admiration." "We are becoming boisterous and arrogant in the pride of a too speedily assumed literary freedom," said Poe. "We get up a hue and cry about the necessity of encouraging native writers of merit—we blindly fancy that we can accomplish this by indiscriminate puffing of good, bad, and indifferent . . . and thus often find ourselves involved in the gross paradox of liking a stupid book the better, because, sure enough, its stupidity is American." Poe was a universalist rather than a nationalist. He developed a body of literary theory that drew upon many European sources, and he enjoyed a considerable reputation in England and Europe, particularly among Charles Baudelaire and the French Symbolists. As editor he anticipated the great magazine-reading audience that arrived in full force only after the Civil War. As poet and fiction writer he courted the public's favor—and from time to time won it to a spectacular degree. During the later 1840s Poe's raven, the dusky phantom of his most popular poem, was so celebrated that it vied with the eagle for the title of national bird.

In *Kavanagh: A Tale* (1849), Longfellow satirized the rant of the "Young America" movement. "We want a national literature commensurate with our mountains and rivers," one of his characters announces. "We want a national literature altogether shaggy and unshorn, that shall shake the earth, like a herd of buffaloes, thundering over the prairies!" It was clear that something more than bluster and false analogies was called for if the country were to have a culture in keeping with its political character. "It does not follow because many books are written by persons born in America that there exists an American literature," Margaret Fuller wrote in 1846. "Before such can exist, an original idea must animate this nation and fresh currents of life must call into life fresh thoughts along its shores."

There were several main issues in this ongoing discussion. One, whether America provided a favorable cultural climate for writers, artists, and intellectuals, was to be debated again and again, after the Civil War and especially during the 1920s. But a second issue, whether America was capable of making a literature of its own fit to stand with the literatures of the Old World, simply ceased to exist. In retrospect one has only to point to two native poetic geniuses flourishing around midcentury, Walt Whitman and Emily Dickinson (her poems, written mainly during the early 1860s, were not published until several years after her death in 1886). As for broad popularity, Harriet Beecher Stowe and Henry Wadsworth Longfellow alone offered a sufficient rejoinder to the English wit Sydney Smith's gibe, "In the four quarters of the globe, who reads an American book?" London bookshops in 1852 displayed twenty different editions of *Uncle Tom's Cabin*. By 1856 this novel had sold nearly a million copies in the British Isles, had been translated into every European language, and was on its way to achieving a global popularity second only to that of the Bible. As for Longfellow, "No other poet has anything like your vogue," Hawthorne wrote to him from England in 1855, when Longfellow brought out *The Song of Hiawatha*, a long poem dealing with a native theme but treating it in accordance with the conventions of Norse epic. On publication day in 1858, Londoners bought some ten thousand copies of Longfellow's *The Courtship of Miles Standish*, another excursion into national legend. His reputation collapsed in the twentieth century, but his sculptured portrait, installed in the Poets' Corner at Westminster Abbey in 1884, two years after his death, continues to keep company with Chaucer, Spenser, and Shakespeare.

A wondrous half decade, 1850–1855, saw the publication of Hawthorne's *The Scarlet Letter* and *The House of the Seven Gables*, Melville's *Moby-Dick* and *Pierre*, Thoreau's *Walden*, and Whitman's *Leaves of Grass*. Together their short-term sales may not have exceeded that of any single now-forgotten domestic novel of the 1850s (Susan Warner's *The Wide, Wide World*, for example, or Mrs. E. D. E. N. Southworth's *The Curse of Clifton*). Most of these American classics, as they are now seen to be, did not begin to receive their full due until the 1920s. Like all significant and lasting art, they are autonomous, self-contained, self-justifying, and even to some extent self-generated. Still, neither Hawthorne's books nor those of Melville, Thoreau, and Whitman could have emerged from any other country in any other century, nor did they happen overnight or in a vacuum. "It takes a great deal of history to produce a little literature," Henry James was to say. "It needs a complex social machinery to set a writer in motion."

"The Infinitude of the Private Man"

"There are always two parties," Emerson wrote, "the party of the Past and the party of the Future; the Establishment and the Movement." He and the Reverend Theodore Parker, another prominent spokesman for Transcendentalism, claimed it was not a concerted party or movement at all but a loose confederation of compatible souls. Having imbibed a distillate of Kant, Goethe, Coleridge, Wordsworth, Carlyle, and other philosophical and literary idealists, the Transcendentalists set about their business in a characteristically self-reliant way. Embroiled in a doctrinal controversy over Holy Communion, Emerson went through a personal crisis and resigned from the Unitarian ministry to follow a career as writer and lecturer. Parker continued in the ministry but exhausted himself in debates and reforms. Margaret Fuller published the first major

American feminist treatise, *Woman in the Nineteenth Century,* in 1845; the following year she went to Europe as foreign correspondent for Horace Greeley's *New York Tribune* and committed herself to the cause of Italian nationalism. Thoreau built his hut at Walden Pond, was jailed for refusing to pay a poll tax, and preached civil disobedience.

Transcendentalism had only a scant organizational existence. It began as an informal "club," first convened in 1836. It generated *The Dial,* a quarterly journal of "literature, philosophy, and religion," edited by Fuller and Emerson, which lasted only four years (1840–1844), never reached a circulation of over three hundred, and was frequently ridiculed for unballasted flights into the empyrean. And it inspired two experiments in cooperative living and high thinking near Boston: Brook Farm (1841–1847) and Fruitlands (1843). Yet, out of all proportion to these evidences, Transcendentalism, especially as channeled through Emerson, generated a significant reexamination of values even in those who derided it. Reversing the European historical order, the Transcendental "reformation," announcing a gospel of spiritual self-sufficiency, came before the literary "renaissance," an awakening, maturation, and release of radical energies.

The Transcendentalists set themselves against what they considered to be the materialism, rationalism, conformity, and played-out liberalism of American religion and society. The social reformer William Henry Channing recalled the movement as inspiring "a vague yet exalting conception of the godlike nature of the human spirit" and "a pilgrimage from the idolatrous world of creeds and rituals to the temple of the Living God in the soul." Ideas of God, right and wrong, and immortality were not matters of doctrine or theology but, according to Parker, "facts of consciousness given by the instinctive action of human nature itself." The Transcendentalists contemplated the actualities of life in the street, the mill, the farmhouse, and the marketplace and aimed to restore to the humblest persons and pursuits a measure of poetry, religious impulse, mystery, surprise, joy, and dread and a sense of wonder and oneness with the universe. "I have taught

---

Letter to the Church in Purchase Street

There is a class of persons who desire a reform in the prevailing philosophy of the day. These are called Transcendentalists, because they believe in an order of truths which transcends the sphere of the external sense. Their leading idea is the supremacy of mind over matter. Hence they maintain that the truth of religion does not depend on tradition, nor historical facts, but has an unerring witness in the soul. There is a light, they believe, which enlighteneth every man that cometh into the world; there is a faculty in all—the most degraded, the most ignorant, the most obscure—to perceive spiritual truth when distinctly presented; and the ultimate appeal on all moral questions is not to a jury of scholars, a hierarchy of divines, or the prescriptions of a creed, but to the common sense of the human race.

George Ripley (1840)

one doctrine," Emerson said, "the infinitude of the private man." "All Souls' Day" had dawned: Each and every person was at once priest, church, and Bible, "a part of eternity and immensity, a god walking in flesh." "So we saunter toward the Holy Land," Thoreau wrote, "till one day the sun shall shine more brightly than ever he has done, shall perchance shine into our minds and hearts, and light up our whole lives with a great awakening light, as warm and serene and golden as on a bankside in autumn."

Transcendentalism arrived as social and religious protest. The conservative theologian Andrews Norton denounced it as "the latest form of infidelity," an unassisted and therefore arrogant attempt to attain assurance "concerning the unseen, the eternal, the great objects of religion." By the 1870s much of Transcendentalism's radical force had become diluted, dissipated, and factional. Emerson's particular brand ended up buttressing the cult of success. "Money is, in its effects and laws, as beautiful as roses," he said. "Property keeps the accounts of the world, and is always moral." After the Civil War, princes of industry and finance quoted his advice, "Hitch your wagon to a star," and installed him in the pantheon of American practical philosophers along with Benjamin Franklin. But Transcendentalism, as Emerson articulated it during the 1830s and 1840s, deplored materialism. A religious, ethical, and aesthetic response to nationalism, a homegrown counterpart of European romanticism with elements drawn from Eastern philosophy, this "latest form of infidelity" proved to be the animating force without which, as Margaret Fuller said, there could be no "American literature."

Responses to *The American Scholar*

Out of the West comes a clear utterance, clearly recognizable as a *man's* voice, and I *have* a kinsman and brother: God be thanked for it! I could have *wept* to read that speech; the clear high melody of it went tingling through my heart. . . . My brave Emerson!

Thomas Carlyle (1837)

This grand oration was our intellectual Declaration of Independence. . . . No listener ever forgot that Address, and among all the noble utterances of the speaker it may be questioned if one ever contained more truth in language more like that of immediate inspiration.

Oliver Wendell Holmes (1885)

We were socially and intellectually moored to English thought, till Emerson cut the cable and gave us a chance at the dangers and glories of blue water. . . . His oration before the Phi Beta Kappa Society at Cambridge, some thirty years ago, was an event without any former parallel in our literary annals.

James Russell Lowell (1871)

> It is good to be shifty in a new country.
>
> J. J. Hooper, *Some Adventures of Captain Simon Suggs, Late of the Tallapoosa Volunteers* (1845)

Three decisive Emerson statements—*Nature* (1836), *The American Scholar* (1837), and his 1838 address to the Harvard Divinity School—served as a Declaration of Independence for the spirit, intellect, and imagination. The homeliest trifle bristled with the polarity of material and spiritual truth; the writer was seer and sayer, "eye" and "I"; language was the hinge of the seen and the unseen, and all the world was a text to be read, studied, and rewritten. "Oregon and Texas are yet unsung," said Emerson. He awaited the arrival of native geniuses possessing "nerve and dagger" and a "tyrannous" command of "our incomparable materials." "America is a poem in our eyes; its ample geography dazzles the imagination, and it will not wait long for metres." Eventually Whitman had the last word in the debate over nationalism and culture. "The United States themselves," he announced in 1855, "are essentially the greatest poem."

In major respects, the literature of the American Renaissance was "a language experiment," as Whitman once described *Leaves of Grass,* a grappling with the transcendency of words. But it was also a series of inspired explorations of the theme of solitude and, correspondingly, of society. Tocqueville had warned, "Not only does democracy make each man forget his ancestors, but it hides his descendants and separates his contemporaries from them; it throws him back upon himself alone and threatens in the end to confine him entirely within the solitude of his own heart." "Instead of the social existence which all shared, was now separation," Emerson said. "Every one for himself; driven to find all his resources, hopes, rewards, society and deity within himself." This was as true of Thoreau in his cabin at Walden as it was of Melville's Ishmael aboard the *Pequod.* As Poe recognized, solitude also generated claustrophobia.

"Incomparable Materials"

The period of the American Renaissance is framed by two upheavals, the Panic of 1837 and the Civil War, and by two political leaders, Andrew Jackson and Abraham Lincoln, each of whom was widely perceived as representing the will of the people and the spirit of the frontier. The saturnalia of Jackson's first inauguration in 1829, a riot of drunkenness, bloody noses, and broken crystal and china, seemed to mark an end to patrician Presidency. The "great democratic God," Melville wrote in *Moby-Dick,* had plucked Old Hickory from the backwoods of Tennessee, hurled him upon a warhorse, and thundered him "higher than a throne." Yet for all the swirl, boil, and social ferment associated with Jacksonian democracy, to some contemporary observers the 1830s seemed peculiarly prosaic, a falling-off from the heroic age of the founders. A revolutionary nation was becoming middle-class. "Public and private avarice make the air we breathe thick and fat," Emerson said. "The mind of this country, taught to aim at low objects, eats upon itself." The celebrated "age of the common man" saw growing concentrations of wealth in the hands of a tiny percentage of the population. It was also an age of urban slums, wage slavery, and other inequities connected with the shift from an agrarian to an industrial economy. At New Orleans in 1815, Jackson defeated the British. In the White House two decades later, the first of the log-cabin Presidents, he defeated the Eastern banking interests only to see the country plunge into business failures and unemployment. The Panic of 1837 initiated the worst depression the United States had yet known.

Abraham Lincoln exercised unprecedented executive authority during a civil war far bloodier and longer than anyone had foreseen. Midway through the war, Whitman described Lincoln:

> He has a face like a hoosier Michael Angelo, so awful ugly it becomes beautiful, with its strange mouth, its deep cut, cris-cross lines, and its doughnut complexion. . . . He has shown, I sometimes think, an almost supernatural tact in keeping the ship afloat at all, with head steady, not only not going down, and now certain not to, but with proud and resolute spirit, and flag flying in sight of the world, menacing and high as ever.

Lincoln's "idiomatic western genius," as Whitman called it, was above all conspicuous in his spoken and written prose, a supple middle style that was lofty and colloquial, beautiful and homely, and always got to the point. Lincoln's prose showed that the basic forms of American humor, including the tall tale and the anecdote, were appropriate in statecraft as well as in literature. For the thirty-year-old Mark Twain, Lincoln's "With malice toward none" address proved that simplicity was one of the secrets of eloquence.

In the years between these two Presidencies, the face, form, and fiber of the United States underwent enormous change. Pushed by poverty and overcrowding at home and pulled by the promise of limitless opportunity in America, great waves of newcomers arrived from Ireland, Western Europe, and Scandinavia to settle in the cities, clear the wilderness, work the farms, build the canals and railroads. They created new opportunities and new labor needs that in turn attracted other immigrants. Meanwhile, especially in New York and New England in the 1840s and after, a riptide of movement from the country to the city, from the barn to the mill, drained villages and townships. Farmhouses stood empty, cleared land reverted to forest, and some regions, as Melville noted, looked as if they had been "depopulated by plague and war." When Jackson left office in 1837 the population was sixteen million. By 1865 it was thirty-six million, having grown by about thirty-five percent each decade. (Had that growth rate continued, the population of the United States today would be greater than China's.) What sorts of readers would these new millions be, and what sorts of writers could meet their needs? Whitman believed that "to have great poets, there must be great audiences, too."

"Self-made or Never Made"

The abolition of slavery was the most vigorous and portentous reform issue of the period. It drew militant support from other reform causes, notably the women's rights movement, given official identity in 1848 at the Seneca Falls (New York) Convention. The Quaker poet John Greenleaf Whittier told his fellow abolitionists, the southerners Sarah and Angelina Grimké, he feared "the cause of the poor and miserable slave" was being weakened by its association with women's rights, which he described as "a selfish crusade against some paltry grievance of your own." Nevertheless, the alliance was powerful evidence of an improving spirit that affected nearly every aspect of American life, from the care of the blind, the deaf, and the insane to municipal sanitation, the prevention of drunkenness, and the salvation of souls.

In 1837, the year of a great financial panic, Massachusetts established America's first state board of education and appointed as its secretary Horace Mann. He believed that the public elementary school, "the greatest discovery ever made by man," could prevent life in the open society from becoming a series of "gladiatorial contests." Under Mann and other reformers in the field, public education, a democratic dream that had appeared to be fading because it was expensive to provide as a service and humiliating to receive as a charity, became a significant cause. Until the results of normal-school training made themselves felt, elementary education remained largely a matter of the three R's administered by amateurs. One thrifty pedagogical system, devised by an English Quaker, Joseph Lancaster, employed hierarchies of student monitors to distribute rote learning along with fundamental moral precepts. In principle Lancaster's system separated children from ignorance the way Eli Whitney's cotton gin separated fibers from seeds. Standard school texts, William H. McGuffey's six *Eclectic Readers* (1836–1857), provided the same emphasis on the moral education of the young, morality here being understood as a worldly, materialistic, and thoroughly middle-class amalgam of religious principles and laissez-faire capitalism. The McGuffey *Readers,* which sold an estimated 122 million copies during the century, established canons of standard authors and literary decorum.

By midcentury, attendance in public systems that went from the infant grades through high school was growing faster than the population as a whole. Higher education, however, remained beyond the reach of all but a relative few (the estimated college enrollment was 27,000 in 1850, 56,000 in 1860). Along with a literacy rate significantly higher that that of the British Isles came a familiarity with certain basic texts (the Bible, Shakespeare, Dickens, and John Bunyan's *Pilgrim's Progress,* for example) that would seem quite remarkable today. Even the Mississippi valley "lunkheads" Mark Twain portrayed in *Huckleberry Finn* felt comfortable with the Bard's "histrionic muse" and possessed a considerable vocabulary of allusion.

The Teacher's Manual

We have been told of a teacher, who frequently relaxed discipline to such a degree, that the whole school was in an uproar. Awakened thus from his stupor, he would seize his cane, and belabor all round, till order was completely restored. This state of quiet, however, would last but a short time. The universal silence would soon be broken by a low whispering, which, remaining unnoticed, gradually increased in intensity, ending, finally, in loud talk, laughter, and jumping across the benches, which, of course, brought about the same round of general whipping, universal silence, &c. This picture is probably highly exaggerated; but there are few, who have not seen schools managed, more or less, on the same principles.

Thomas H. Palmer (1840)

For the developing readership of the period, the debating society and the lyceum were available, potent agencies of higher education. Benjamin Franklin's Junto Club, organized at Philadelphia in 1727, was the first of many debating and social societies that were to serve Americans as gymnasiums for mental exercise. Debaters in cities, towns, and villages addressed themselves to such topics as the pros and cons of slavery, capital punishment, and unrestricted immigration; the role of the arts and sciences in a democracy and of genetic and social factors in the formation of character; the achievements of Napoleon Bonaparte; and the relative merits of Queen Elizabeth and Mary, Queen of Scots. Tocqueville noted that the habit of public argument acquired in these societies left its mark on the native character: "An American cannot converse, but he can discuss. He speaks to you as if he was addressing a meeting."

The New Englander Josiah Holbrook described the lyceum system (which he founded in 1826) as a national network of "associations of Adults for Mutual Education." Arriving in remote settlements with the locomotive and the depot, lyceum lecture courses took their place in the civic order alongside the church, the schoolhouse, the courtroom, the saloon, and the jail. Citizens bought series or single tickets to hear evening talks on the North American Indian, the lives of Mohammed and Oliver Cromwell, the productive cycle of the honeybee, causes of the American Revolution, the sun, the education of children, and the capacity of the human mind for culture and improvement. "There was the real impression," Edward Everett Hale recalled, "that the kingdom of heaven was to be brought in by teaching people what were the relations of acids to alkalies, and what was the derivation of the word 'cordwainer.' If only we knew enough, it was thought, we should be wise enough to keep out of the fire, and we should not be burned." Lyceum lectures also served a social purpose in towns that lacked other secular entertainments: They enabled young men and women to mingle in semidarkened halls.

Emerson the Lecturer

In what other country, on sleety winter nights, would provincial and bucolic populations have gone forth in hundreds for the cold comfort of a literary discourse? The distillation anywhere else would certainly have appeared too thin, the appeal too special. But for many years the American people of the middle regions, outside of a few cities, had in the most rigorous seasons no other recreation. A gentleman, grave or gay, in a bare room, with a manuscript, before a desk, offered the reward of toil, the refreshment of pleasure, to the young, the middle-aged and the old of both sexes.

Henry James, *Partial Portraits* (1888)

By the end of the Civil War period, Holbrook's high-minded scheme began to give way to entertainment, box office, and the star system. But during its heyday as a distinctive institution of American life, the lyceum educated a generation and a half of readers, offered a forum for debate on such important reform issues as women's rights, temperance, and the abolition of slavery, and also provided writers and intellectuals with a source of income. For over thirty years Emerson, a preeminently popular figure on the lyceum circuit, endured the hardships of winter travel and made his living from lecture fees.

An era of self-trust, self-improvement, and perfectionism in general offered many other attractive ways of bringing in the kingdom of heaven. In the nineteenth as well as the twentieth century, the United States was world haven not only for immigrants and refugees from European oppression but also for schemes promising social and individual happiness, among them phrenology, or the science of mind, a European import. One of its founders, Johann Kaspar Spurzheim, was hailed as a messiah when he arrived in America in 1832 and was mourned accordingly when he was buried there the same year. His truth, such as it was, marched on for three decades.

In the phrenological scheme of things, each intellectual faculty had a specific location in the brain and could be measured by corresponding bumps on the skull; "secretiveness," "amativeness," "benevolence," and other traits were as palpable and distinct as onions, turnips, and potatoes in a sack. These homely propositions had an electrifying corollary. In the words of Orson Squire Fowler, the leading American popularizer of phrenology, "the exercise of particular mental faculties . . . causes the exercise, and consequent enlargement, of corresponding portions of the brain." One could "elevate" faculties that had been diagnosed deficient, "depress" those that were too prominent, and presumably arrive near, if not at, a state of perfection in personality, temperament, and ability. Fowler's motto was "self-made or never made."

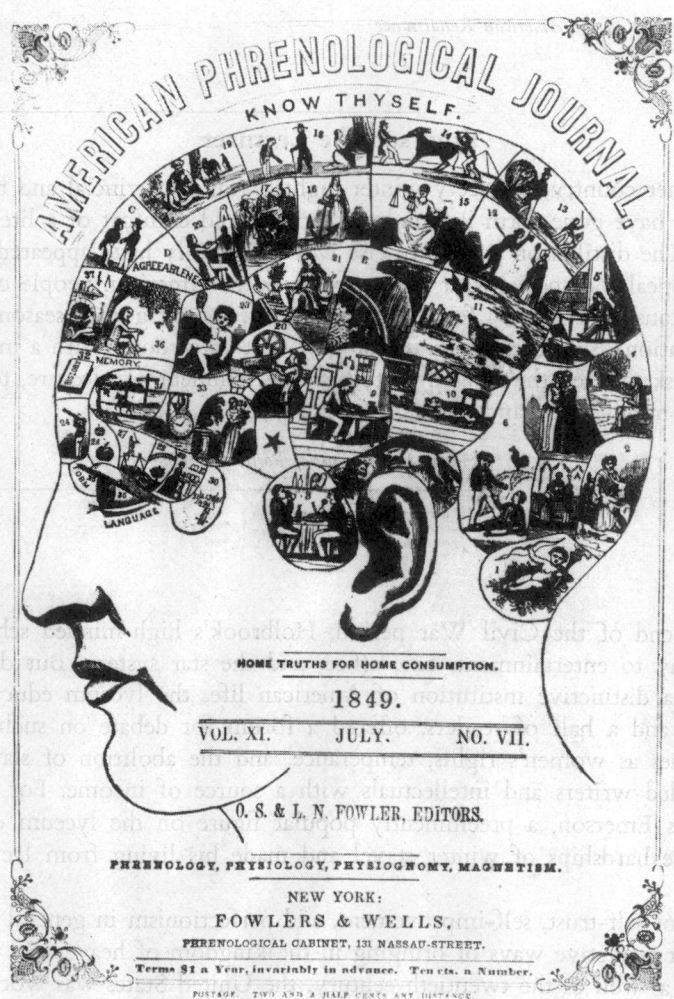

American Phrenological Journal (July 1949). Photograph courtesy of the Harvard College Library.

"The Peripatetic Phrenologist"

One of the most frequent arrivals in our village of Hannibal was the peripatetic phrenologist and he was popular and always welcome. . . . It is not at all likely, I think, that the traveling expert ever got any villager's character quite right, but it is a safe guess that he was always wise enough to furnish his clients character-charts that would compare favorably with George Washington's. It was a long time ago and I think I still remember that no phrenologist ever came across a skull in our town that fell much short of the Washington standard. This general and close approach to perfection ought to have roused suspicion, perhaps, but I do not remember that it did. It is my impression that the people admired phrenology and believed in it and that the voice of the doubter was not heard in the land.

Mark Twain (1906)

Phrenology turned out to be a benevolent, infinitely attractive fantasy, with no footing in either fact or theory, and in the hands of shabby practitioners plying their trade along the frontier it eventually declined into simple quackery. But when faith was strong the great science of mind offered the promise, Theodore Parker said, of "leading men to study the constitution of man more wisely than before." Poe claimed phrenology had achieved "the majesty of a science, and as a science ranks among the most important which can engage the attention of thinking beings." Horace Mann, as wholly serious as when confronting slavery, ignorance, profanity, or drunkenness, said phrenology was "the guide of philosophy, and the handmaid of Christianity," an opinion shared by Horace Greeley, William Cullen Bryant, Henry Ward Beecher, and others of comparable eminence. Emerson and Webster had their bumps read; so did Whitman, who was thereby confirmed in his mission to become the poet of America. Even in his old age he said, "I probably have not got by the phrenology stage yet."

In its heyday phrenology also energized a variety of other approaches to self-improvement and well-being. "Hydropathy," or water cure, offered an avenue to sobriety, moderation, personal cleanliness, and relief from bodily ills. Holistic regimens like those of Sylvester Graham, known then as the "Peristaltic Persuader" and memorialized now in the cracker that bears his name, prescribed unsifted whole-wheat flour, boiled vegetables, doses of cold water, and sexual abstinence. Mesmerists dealt in "animal magnetism," an "irradiating power" that worked on principles supposedly resembling those of the magnetic telegraph and accounted for telepathy, clairvoyance, and two-way communication with the dead. Spiritualism, epidemic after 1848 when the Fox sisters reported mysterious rappings and knockings in their upstate New York cottage, appeared to make heaven as democratic and accessible as the county courthouse. Among millions of believers in animal magnetism and related phenomena were Cooper, Irving, Poe, Hawthorne, Longfellow, Whittier, Greeley, and the Reverend Thomas Wentworth Higginson, who said that the discovery of "spiritual electricity" was as momentous as that of steam.

The word *spiritual* had deeper and more far-reaching meanings in a period of religious revivalism, another Great Awakening and evangelical renewal of faith. Especially along the frontier, the characteristic expression of this awakening was the camp meeting, a great outdoor assembly of the faithful and the repentant who came to pray and to be exhorted. "There is no country in the world where the Christian religion retains a greater influence over the souls of men than in America," Tocqueville wrote, adding that, despite the constitutional principle of separation of church and state, "the sovereign authority is religious." In certain sectors the religious revival tended to scant what might be seen as the moral contradiction of Christianity and slavery; it provoked outbreaks of virulent nativism and anti-Catholicism, and it resulted in an extraordinary proliferation of schisms and sectarian rivalries, as Emerson noted in his account of the Chardon Street Convention in Boston (1840–1841), an ad hoc ecumenical congress: "If the assembly was disorderly, it was picturesque. Madmen, madwomen, men with beards, Dunkers, Muggletonians, Come-outers, Groaners, Agrarians, Seventh-day Baptists, Quakers, Abolitionists, Calvinists, Unitarians, and Philosophers,—all came successively to the top, and seized their moment, if not their *hour,* wherein to chide, or pray, or preach, or protest." It seemed almost that the entire country was one vast camp meeting dedicated to the final eradication of sin and the redemption of the individual and scheduled to remain in session until the Second Coming. The same indigenous spiritual boil that generated Transcendentalism, Emersonian idealism, and much of the literature of the American Renaissance also generated two world religions, Joseph Smith's Church of Jesus Christ of Latter-Day Saints (1830) and Mary Baker Eddy's Church of Christ, Scientist (1879). Emily Dickinson wrote in hymn meters; Whitman's free verse was shaped by biblical cadences, and he envisioned the poet's role as that of prophet and priest.

Gold Rush

Between 1840 and 1860, expansion, conquest, and purchase increased the land area of the United States from 1.8 million to 3 million square miles. The Treaty of Guadalupe Hidalgo, concluding the war with Mexico in 1848, added the areas of present-day Texas, California, Arizona, New Mexico, and Utah, along with parts of Colorado and Wyoming—altogether an acquisition of over 500,000 square miles that was second in size only to the Louisiana Purchase. Five years later, the Gadsden Purchase completed the continental boundaries of the United States. Nevertheless, as Whitman wrote after the Civil War, expansionists continued to "reach north for Canada and south for Cuba." Their imaginations fired by explorers' reports like those of John C. Frémont, the most effective publicist of the trans-Mississippi West, thousands of young men left city and farm jobs, packed up their families, and set out along the Santa Fe, Oregon, and California trails.

Continental space, seemingly limitless, shaped the vision of writers and artists by demanding corresponding qualities of amplitude, grandeur, and reverence. But the fulfillment of manifest destiny also raised questions about where America was going. Whitman said, "It is as if we were somehow being endow'd with a vast and more and more thoroughly-appointed body, and then left with little or no soul." Reflecting on the war with Mexico, the New York diarist Philip Hone said that "Annexation is now the greatest word in the American vocabulary. 'Veni-vidi-vici!' is inscribed on the banners of every Caesar who leads a straggling band of American adventurers across the prairies, over the mountains, up the rivers, and into the chaparral of a territory which an unprovoked war has given them the right to invade."

"Great Deeds Away out Yonder"

I fancied I could see Frémont's men, hauling the cannon up the savage battlements of the Rocky Mountains, flags in the air, Frémont at the head, waving his sword, his horse neighing wildly in the mountain wind, with unknown and unnamed empires on every hand. . . . I began to be inflamed with a love for action, adventure, glory, and great deeds away out yonder under the path of the setting sun.

Joaquin Miller, Overland in a Covered Wagon: An Autobiography (1930)

"The Abundance of Gold"

It was known that mines of the precious metals existed to a considerable extent in California at the time of its acquisition. Recent discoveries render it probable that these mines are more extensive and valuable than was anticipated. The accounts of the abundance of gold in that territory are of such an extraordinary character as would scarcely command belief, were they not corroborated by the authentic reports of officers in the public service, who have visited the mineral district, and derived the facts which they detail from personal observation. . . . The effects produced by the discovery of these rich mineral deposits, and the success which has attended the labours of those who have resorted to them, have produced a surprising change in the state of affairs in California. Labour commands a most exorbitant price, and all other pursuits but that of searching for the precious metal are abandoned. Nearly the whole of the male population of the country have gone to the gold districts. Ships arriving on the coast are deserted by their crews, and their voyages suspended for want of sailors.

President James K. Polk, message to Congress
(December 5, 1848)

The discovery of California gold in January 1848, just nine days before the signing of the Treaty of Guadalupe Hidalgo, appeared to many patriots to be something more than Yankee luck. It was a providential event, a confirmation of national grace and mission. Although this gold lay under their feet and ready to their hands, patriotic logic ran, it had not been revealed to the Indians, Spaniards, and Mexicans who occupied the land for two centuries before it became a part of Protestant America. ("In the hands of an enterprising people," Dana had said of California in 1840, "what a country this might be!") Now the existence of a great treasure had been discovered, quite accidentally, by a man from New Jersey, James Marshall, overseeing the construction of a sawmill on the south fork of the American River. "My eye was caught by something shining in the bottom of a ditch. . . . I reached my hand down and picked it up; it made my heart thump, for I was certain it was gold. The piece was about half the size and shape of a pea. Then I saw another." After President Polk verified the extent of the finds in his 1848 message to Congress, California gold fever supplanted the "Oregon fever" of a few years earlier, and a new wave of emigrants traveled west by way of Cape Horn (a fifteen-thousand-mile voyage), the Isthmus of Panama, and the overland trails. Many of them believed, as a paper in Ithaca, New York, reported, that all they had to do when they reached the Sacramento valley was "select a suitable location, erect cabins, and proceed to rake in the dust."

"Instead of being rich, I am ruined," said John Sutter, on whose property Marshall made his find. Marauders and squatters killed Sutter's cattle; his workers ran off to become prospectors while his wheat rotted in the fields and his tannery and mills stood idle; strangers preempted his mining claims. "By this sudden discovery of the gold, all my great plans were destroyed. Had I succeeded with my mills and manufactories for a few years before the gold was discovered, I should have been the richest citizen on the Pacific shore; but it had to be different." Marshall was another casualty and ended up working as a gardener. For him and Sutter, as well as for the many thousand prospectors who never struck it rich and were happy just to return home alive, the Gold Rush (like B. Traven's novel and John Huston's film, *The Treasure of the Sierra Madre*) proved to be a native version of Chaucer's tale about three revelers who quarreled over gold and killed one another. But the Gold Rush was also a peculiarly apt fable of America in transition. "I know of no more startling development of the morality of trade and all the modes of getting a living than the rush to California affords," Thoreau wrote in his journal. "Of what significance is . . . a world that will rush to the lottery of California gold-digging—to live by luck, to get the means of commanding the labor of others less lucky, *i.e.* slaveholding, without contributing any value to society? . . . Going to California. It is only three thousand miles nearer to hell." "The Californian rush for wealth in '49," Mark Twain was to recall, "introduced the change and begot the lust for money which is the rule of life to-day, and the hardness and cynicism which is the spirit of to-day." "And where are they now?" he wondered about the forty-niners. "Scattered to the ends of the earth—or prematurely aged and decrepit—or shot or stabbed in street affrays—or dead of disappointed hopes and broken hearts—all gone, or nearly all—victims devoted upon the altar of the golden calf."

Railroad Iron

California promoters had invoked the preclassical example of Jason's Argonauts and the Golden Fleece to suggest that the Gold Rush was a return to an Arcadian age of adventure. Thoreau, Mark Twain, and other social critics thought of the Gold Rush as a dividing line between America's own Arcadian age—in idealized retrospect a time of pastoral peace, agrarian self-sufficiency, and communal rectitude—and the industrial age of cities and machines, steam, electricity, steel, and big business. Gone was what the English journalist Harriet Martineau had called "a sweet temper diffused like sunshine over the land." For a glorious year and a half (April 1860–October 1861) Pony Express riders, buckskin-clad heroes armed with Colt six-shooters and eighteen-inch knives, carried mail nearly two thousand miles in eight days between Sacramento, California, and St. Joseph, Missouri, but the entire venture was little more than a romantic rear-guard action, "a flash of unreal fantasy," in Mark Twain's words. Outmoded by the telegraph and steam locomotive, the age's most conspicuous symbols and agencies of change, the Pony Express passed into American folklore. By the end of the 1860s, travelers rode coast-to-coast in the sleeping and dining luxury of George Pullman's Palace Cars.

"Railroad iron is a magician's rod in its power to evoke the sleeping energies of land and water," Emerson said. "Readers of poetry see the factory-village and the railway, and fancy that the poetry of the landscape is broken up by these; for these works of art are not yet consecrated in their reading; but the poet sees them fall within the great Order not less than the beehive or the spider's geometrical web." By the end of the period, the number of miles of track in operation

(35,000) had grown by a factor of twenty-six, and the prairies were opened for agricultural use; railroading was America's first billion-dollar industry and the pattern for other gigantic concentrations of capital. Literature and the facts of industry may have been compatible, as Emerson claimed, but what did these facts mean?

"Railroad iron" opened the wilderness but also preserved it by putting up obstacles to agriculture along the right-of-way. "Punctual as a Star," the locomotive was, in Emily Dickinson's words, both "docile and omnipotent"; its "horrid, hooting stanza" broke the primal silence, interrupted meditation, and itself became the subject of meditation. Hawthorne described the locomotive as looking "much more like a sort of mechanical demon, that would hurry us to the infernal regions, than a laudable contrivance for smoothing our way to the Celestial City." "I will not have my eyes put out and my ears spoiled by its smoke and steam and hissing," Thoreau wrote in Concord. Even on the empty Pacific, sailing toward his destruction while his country sailed toward civil war, Captain Ahab read his fate in the landscape of the steam locomotive: "The path to my fixed purpose is laid with iron rails, whereon my soul is grooved to run. Over unsounded gorges, through the rifled hearts of mountains, under torrents' beds, unerringly I rush! Naught's an obstacle, naught's an angle to the iron way!"

Impending Crisis

Whether the new industrial age represented progress or destruction was one of several ambiguities writers of the period had to confront. They were as divided here as they were in their responses to the other contradictions—social, economic, political, and moral—of American life around the middle of the century. The freest nation on earth, inspired by dreams of a just and perfect society, maintained the institution of slavery, denied women the vote and other legal rights, and harried its aboriginal population toward extinction through chicanery, forced removals, and broken treaties.

Torn between humanitarian and expedient principles, many Americans detested slavery but at the same time despaired of finding a fair or peaceful way of putting an end to it. Frederick Law Olmsted, travel writer, landscape architect, and subsequently designer (with architect Calvert Vaux) of New York's Central Park, journeyed extensively through the South during the 1850s. In *The Cotton Kingdom* (1861), a collection of his travel writings, he presented what is still respected as an informed picture of the wretchedness of slavery and slaveholding society. But for the most part, the writers of New England and the Middle States had as muddled a comprehension of the South, based on little or no firsthand experience, as their southern counterparts had of the North. Each group accused the other of fanaticism and monomania and fell back on unexamined stereotypes: The South was a violent, backward, culturally barren region ruled by King Cotton and his Lords of the Lash, while the North was culturally tyrannical, obsessed with trade and stirring up blood violence between slaves and masters. Moreover, within each loosely defined opposed faction there were, in turn, differences almost as extreme as those existing between the factions themselves.

At one end of the northern spectrum stood the abolitionist poet John Greenleaf Whittier. His single-mindedness was tempered by Quaker pacifism, while William Lloyd Garrison's abolitionist zeal—he denounced the U.S. Constitution as a "Covenant with Death and an Agreement with Hell"—made him as ardent a secessionist as the most fire-eating southerner. During the 1830s and 1840s, Emerson remained evasive on the great issue of the day: "What right have I to speak of slavery? Are we not *all* slaves?" (This meshed with the antiabolitionist argument that the white wage slaves—the indentured servants—of the North and industrialized England were infinitely worse off than the black chattel slaves of the Cotton Kingdom.) Hawthorne and Melville (despite the marked sympathy for blacks the latter showed in his novels) shunned reform causes and mass initiatives in general. Not a joiner either, Thoreau, before the Mexican War and the passage of the Fugitive Slave Law, nevertheless wrote in support of the antislavery movement and held an abolitionist meeting at Walden. Longfellow withdrew into genial isolation.

The historian Francis Parkman represented the other extreme of northern opinion and spoke for many southerners as well: "For my part, I would see every slave knocked on the head before I would see the Union go to pieces, and would include in the sacrifice as many abolitionists as could be conveniently brought together." This was the fundamental position that Lowell, a hot abolitionist earlier, arrived at just before the war and that Whitman, self-annointed bard of the Union and democracy, maintained even during the war.

Writers in the South, less visible as a group, in part because of their dependence on northern readers and publishing outlets, were also less vocal as a group, but they were spread along the same broad spectrum of opinion. The Charleston romancer William Gilmore Simms, the most prolific and popular writer of the South, and James De Bow, professor of political economy at the University of Louisiana, shared the familiar antebellum dream that a great civilization, like that of ancient Greece, could be raised on a foundation of human bondage. "The negro slaves of the South are the happiest, and in some sense, the freest people in the world," wrote the Virginia lawyer George Fitzhugh, author of *Sociology for the South; or, The Failure of Free Society* (1854) and *Cannibals All! or, Slaves Without Masters* (1857). "The children and the aged and infirm work not at all, and yet have all the comforts and necessities of life provided for them. They enjoy liberty, because they are oppressed neither by care nor labor. . . . Free laborers have not a thousandth part of the rights and liberties of negro slaves. Indeed, they have not a single right or a single liberty, unless it be the right or liberty to die." Neither a racist nor a secessionist, Fitzhugh believed that in a wicked world southern slavery was not quite so wicked as northern capitalism.

Meanwhile, Hinton Rowan Helper of North Carolina, a failed prospector in the Gold Rush who had become an out-and-out negrophobe, was urging abolition on the grounds that black slavery depressed the market for white labor and kept the South poor and backward. His populist, superficially progressive, but bitterly racist tract, *The Impending Crisis of the South* (1857), suppressed in some slave states and widely circulated by abolitionists in the North, may have been as effective in arousing sectional antagonism as *Uncle Tom's Cabin*. Fierce and uncompromising, the fire-eating Simms tried to promote his antithetic gospel of slavery to northern lecture audiences in 1856. Another Charlestonian, the poet Henry Timrod, was an apologist for slavery and "the laureate of the Confederacy" only with the utmost reluctance—he had tried to stay above sectional issues. Maryland novelist and politician John Pendleton Kennedy, Poe's friend and patron, wrote and lectured against secession. Like that of the North, the southern literary and intellectual community did not speak with one voice on the underlying issues of the Civil War.

The Missouri Compromise (1820), an attempt to establish geographical and political balance between free states and slave states, had offered the promise of domestic tranquillity while evading the basic moral issue involved. Nevertheless, Jefferson heard in its terms "a fire-bell" tolling "the knell of the Union." After half a generation of silence this bell began to toll again with increasing frequency. In November 1837, two months after Emerson called on "the American scholar" to speak his own mind and look to self-trust, a mob in Alton, Illinois, murdered Elijah Lovejoy, editor of the *Observer*, an abolitionist newspaper. The antislavery cause had its first martyr in a line that would end with Captain John Brown. Wendell Phillips's tribute to Lovejoy at a public meeting in Boston's Faneuil Hall belonged in a tradition of abolitionist oratory that eventually included Theodore Parker, Senator Charles Sumner, the Reverend Henry Ward Beecher, Frederick Douglass, and Henry Thoreau. The slavery issue surfaced again in the Mexican war, "essentially a war of false pretenses," Lowell said at the time, which would result in "widening the boundaries and so prolonging the life of slavery." "I call it murder," said Lowell's cracker-barrel Yankee, Hosea Biglow:

> They jest want this Californy
> So's to lug new slave-States in
> To abuse ye, an' to scorn ye,
> An' to plunder ye like sin. . . .
> Chaps that make black slaves o' niggers
> Want to make wite slaves o' you.

The Impending Crisis of the South: How to Meet It

The causes which have impeded the progress and prosperity of the South, which have dwindled our commerce, and other similar pursuits, into the most contemptible insignificance; sunk a large majority of our people in galling poverty and ignorance, rendered a small minority conceited and tyrannical, and driven the rest away from their homes; entailed upon us a humiliating dependence on the Free States; disgraced us in the recesses of our own souls, and brought us under reproach in the eyes of all civilized and enlightened nations— may all be traced to one common source, and there find solution in the most hateful and horrible word, that was ever incorporated into the vocabulary of human economy—*Slavery!*

Hinton Rowan Helper (1857)

The Wilmot Proviso (1846), an attempt to outlaw slavery in any territory acquired from Mexico, revealed the peculiarly complex and contradictory makeup of the Free Soil movement, an amalgam of conscience, self-interest, and racism. "As if by magic," said a Whig paper in Boston, "it brought to a head the great question which is about to divide the American people." The author of the proviso, David Wilmot, a hitherto inconspicuous Democratic member of Congress from Pennsylvania, had "no morbid sympathy for the slave," he said, only a desire to protect white men from "the disgrace which association with negro slavery brings upon free labor." His position scarcely differed from Helper's.

On these issues Whitman exemplifies the hesitancies that afflicted other writers of the period. An ardent Free-Soiler, editor and publisher of the Brooklyn *Freeman,* a weekly newspaper dedicated to opposing "under all circumstances the addition to the Union, in future, of a single inch of *slave land,"* Whitman denounced abolitionism because it was fanatical, defied the law of the land, and, at a time when "United States" was still a plural noun, as in "these United States," jeopardized the sacred constitutional pact. (When the war came, Whitman maintained, as Lincoln did, that it was fought over the issue of the Union, not slavery, although without slavery the war might not have been fought at all.) Like Emerson, Thoreau, Parker, and many other writers (with the conspicuous exception of Melville) who accepted "scientific" doctrines of the day, Whitman also believed that blacks were genetically unsuited for assimilation into American life. "Nature has set an impassable seal against it," he declared in an 1850s editorial. His day-to-day social policy and conduct were no different from those of most northerners, abolitionists included, who deplored slavery but at the same time denied free blacks the most rudimentary civil rights. "You loathe them as you would a snake or a toad, yet you are indignant at their wrongs," St. Clare, a Louisiana planter, says to his New England cousin in Harriet Beecher Stowe's novel, *Uncle Tom's Cabin.* "You would not have them abused; but you don't want to have anything to do with them yourselves. You would send them to Africa, out of your sight and smell, and then send a missionary or two to do up all the self-denial of elevating them compendiously." Like her brother Henry Ward Beecher, Theodore Parker, and other antislavery radicals, Mrs. Stowe believed that the ultimate solution to an intolerable race problem was black colonization in a more tropical part of the world than the North American continent.

Bitter congressional debates over Henry Clay's "Omnibus Bill" (1850) and the Kansas-Nebraska Act (1854) created further dismay and confusion for northern liberals. Among their deposed heroes was Daniel Webster, a man of outstanding intellect and character; according to the phrenologists, his skull (twenty-five inches around) was to common skulls "what the great dome of St. Peter's is to the small cupolas at its side." On the Senate floor in March 1850, Webster, faced, as he believed, with the momentous choice of preserving the Union or countenancing secession, threw his support to Clay's compromise resolutions. In the bitter aftermath of Webster's speech, Parker said, "There is no such life of crime long enough to prepare a man for such a pitch of depravity." "When faith is lost, when honor dies, / The man is dead": In Whittier's poem, Webster is the biblical Ichabod, a name meaning, "the glory is departed."

"I Would Save the Union"

I would save the Union. I would save it the shortest way under the Constitution. The sooner the national authority can be restored; the nearer the Union will be "the Union as it was." If there be those who would not save the Union, unless they could at the same time *save* slavery, I do not agree with them. If there be those who would not save the Union unless they could at the same time *destroy* slavery, I do not agree with them. My paramount object in this struggle *is* to save the Union, and is *not* either to save or destroy slavery.

Abraham Lincoln, letter to Horace Greeley (August 22, 1862)

    The most inflammatory of the compromise measures that Webster supported, the Fugitive Slave Law made the federal government the enforcing agency of southern property claims and created a corps of federal slave catchers to penetrate the asylums and underground railroads of the North. "This filthy enactment," Emerson wrote in his journal, "was made in the nineteenth century by men who could read and write. I will not obey it, by God." The Fugitive Slave Law triggered Mrs. Stowe's famous novel. President Franklin Pierce dispatched a government cutter and federal troops, armed with loaded rifles and fixed bayonets, to Boston in June 1854 to ensure the return of Anthony Burns, a runaway slave, to his owner in Virginia. The rendition of Burns left Thoreau "with the sense of having suffered a vast and indefinite loss," he said in his July 4 address, *Slavery in Massachusetts.* "I did not know at first what ailed me. At last it occurred to me that what I had lost was a country. . . . We have used up all our inherited freedom. If we would save our lives, we must fight for them." This was his version of the same "higher law" that Captain John Brown invoked in October 1859 when, hoping to raise a black insurrection in Virginia, he led his attack on the federal arsenal at Harpers Ferry and again, a month and a half later, when he mounted the scaffold to die "for God's eternal truth." Devoutly antislavery northerners believed, as Emerson put it, that Brown made "the gallows glorious like the Cross." "He is not Old Brown any longer," Thoreau said; "he is an angel of light." For Melville and Whitman, Brown's execution was also a "meteor" that aroused "forebodings," "portent" of a cataclysmic four-year civil war.

    "I saw an open field," Ulysses Grant was to write of the Battle of Shiloh (April 6–7, 1862), "over which the Confederates had made repeated charges the day before, so covered with dead that it would have been possible to walk across the clearing, in any direction, without a foot touching the ground." Until Shiloh, Grant, "as well as thousands of other citizens, believed that the rebellion against the Government would collapse suddenly and soon."

Further Reading:

V. Brooks, *The Flowering of New England,*
1815–1865, 1936.
F. O. Matthiessen, *American Renaissance,* 1941.
V. Brooks, *The Times of Melville and Whitman,*
1947.
The Transcendentalists, ed. P. Miller, 1950.
H. N. Smith, *Virgin Land,* 1950.
R. W. B. Lewis, *The American Adam,* 1955.
C. Bode, *The Anatomy of Popular Culture,*
1840–1861, 1959.
E. Wilson, *Patriotic Gore,* 1962.
L. Marx, *The Machine in the Garden,* 1964.
D. Boorstin, *The Americans: The National
Experience,* 1965.
J. A. Hawgood, *America's Western Frontiers,*

1967.
D. Aaron, *The Unwritten War,* 1973.
L. Buell, *Literary Transcendentalism,* 1973.
P. Miller, *The Raven and the Whale,* 1973.
R. B. Nye, *Society and Culture in America,*
1830–1860, 1974.
G. B. Forgie, *Patricide in the House Divided,*
1979.
B. Novak, *Nature and Culture: American
Landscape and Painting, 1825–1875,* 1980.
J. S. Holliday, *The World Rushed In: The
California Gold Rush Experience,* 1981.
L. Ziff, *Literary Democracy,* 1981.
J. R. Stilgoe, *Metropolitan Corridor,* 1983.
A. Kazin, *An American Procession,* 1984.

Ralph Waldo Emerson
1803–1882

Ralph Waldo Emerson has been such an original and pervasive presence in nineteenth- and twentieth-century American culture that most Americans know something about the spirit and substance of his writing, even if they have never deliberately read a line of his work. In voluminous journals, lectures, essays, and poems, Emerson articulated principles that have become central to defining traditional American values: self-reliance, individual authority and responsibility, a resolute optimism, moral idealism, the veneration of experience, and a worshipful return to nature. Emerson's expression of these fundamental principles in America's collective identity has been quoted, endorsed, and adapted by so many generations of writers and public figures that their familiarity may well reduce our appreciation of just how original these ideas were when Emerson expressed them. As the inheritors of a literary legacy nourished on a schoolroom diet of Emerson's most epigrammatic lines, contemporary readers must rediscover the range, freshness, complexity, and elasticity of his writing. The challenge in reading Emerson is to recover the originality of his now-familiar ideas.

From all accounts, Ralph Waldo Emerson was an intellectual radical who led a private and public life imbued with tradition and convention. Emerson was born in 1803 and grew up in a family whose heritage included nine successive generations of notable New England ministers. Religious custom and social ritual pervaded his life both at home and in Boston. His father, a well-known Unitarian preacher, died when Waldo was eight, leaving him, his mother, and four brothers with little more than pride in a family name that filled several chapters in local church history. With the encouragement of his resilient and inventive mother, Ruth Haskins, the support of his Puritanical step-grandfather, the Reverend Ezra Ripley, and the stern guidance of his strong-willed aunt, Mary Moody Emerson, Waldo entered Harvard at the age of 14. There he began keeping what quickly became extensive journals. In one early entry he succinctly summarized his childhood: "My recollections of early life are not very pleasant."

Emerson's performance at Harvard was not particularly distinguished. He graduated in 1821, thirty-ninth in a class of fifty-nine. After several unsettling years teaching, Emerson enrolled in the Harvard Divinity School and prepared to carry on the family tradition by studying to be a Unitarian minister. A liberal movement that first flourished in the eighteenth century as a rejection of the Calvinist legacy of Jonathan Edwards and the Great Awakening, Unitarianism shifted the emphasis in religious experience from the individual's depravity to one's moral capabilities and prospects for salvation. In effect, Unitarian belief substituted the principle of a moral democracy for the Puritan concept of a moral aristocracy. But by the time Emerson was "approbated to preach" in 1826, Unitarianism had taken on all of the trappings of the reigning orthodoxy at the Harvard Divinity School. Emerson's studies, interrupted by spells of weak eyesight and his own unconventional thinking, proceeded slowly. As he dispassionately noted some years later, "Had they examined me, they would never have passed me."

Within a few years, however, Emerson had married an aspiring poet, Ellen Tucker, and had settled into a successful life as the pastor of Boston's Second Church, where Increase and Cotton Mather had preached more than a century earlier. There he attracted considerable attention for his eloquent and unorthodox sermons. This period of what he called "uninterrupted prosperity" included an honorary membership in Phi Beta Kappa, appointment as chaplain of the Massachusetts Senate, and election to the Boston School Committee. But this period of contentment was short-lived. By 1831 his wife had died, his brother Edward's health had deteriorated rapidly, and his doubts about his own ministry had increased greatly. Impatient with the ceremonial rituals and institutional structures and pressures of the church, Emerson began to seek more direct and immediate access to religious experience. His journal entry for June 1832 summarizes his state of mind: "I have sometimes thought that in order to be a good minister it was necessary to leave the ministry. The profession is antiquated. In an altered age, we worship the dead forms of our forefathers." In Emerson's view, the Unitarian church had become far too negative and rational— "corpse-cold," as he called it. Advocating greater attention to the emotional and subjective elements of faith, Emerson sought more intuitive, personally revelatory religious experiences. In late October 1832 Emerson resigned his pastorate, having decided that he could no longer in good conscience administer Communion. "I find this amazing revelation of my immediate relation to God a solution to all the doubts that oppressed me," he wrote.

On Christmas Day in 1832 Emerson sailed for Europe and spent the next 10 months on the Continent and in England reading, recovering his health, and meeting such influential writers as William Wordsworth, Samuel Taylor Coleridge, and Thomas Carlyle, the latter of whom became a lifelong friend. Emerson returned to Massachusetts in 1833 and began a lecture series in Boston and its surrounding communities with such titles as "Human Life," "The Present Age," and "Human Culture." While his reputation as an orator earned him considerable attention, his $1,200 annual income from Ellen Tucker's estate—

approximately two-thirds of his earnings as a minister—freed him from the financial concerns that had afflicted him and his family since childhood. After the death of his brother Edward in 1834, Emerson moved to Concord, Massachusetts, where he briefly took up residence at the "Old Manse," the home of his Puritan ancestors and later of Nathaniel Hawthorne.

After a brief courtship filled with the "most agreeable recollections," Emerson married Lydia Jackson in 1835 and settled into a comfortable life in a large plain white frame house ("Coolidge Castle," or "Bush," as it came to be known), where they remained until fire destroyed it in 1872. Soon after their marriage, Emerson began a lifelong practice of calling his wife "Lidian," to avoid the New England pronunciation that slips an r sound between words that end and begin with a vowel. Nestled in the domestic quiet of a town filled with Revolutionary history, Emerson cultivated the simple pleasures of country living and worked on his writing. Occasionally, he traveled in the Northeast and out to the western frontier to lecture.

Only rarely did Emerson draw the same large crowds that came to hear the most popular politicians, reformers, phrenologists, and mesmerists of the mid-nineteenth century. Yet he always cut an imposing figure behind the lectern. He was tall, but years of poor health had worn at his body, sloped his shoulders, and made him appear slightly gaunt. Emerson had a chiseled look—a long, narrow, weathered face beneath a furrowed brow and thick brown hair, with deeply recessed blue eyes set off by a prominent nose and an angular chin. He had a broad mouth, but one unaccustomed to laughter. There was always something highly serious, almost lofty, even ethereal, about him. The calm dignity of his voice exuded the polished cadences of an eloquent preacher, and the practiced rhythm of his intonation created an air of oracular authority for his provocative statements.

Emerson the lecturer was as ambitious as he was dynamic. "A lecture is a new literature," he noted in his journals, "which leaves aside all tradition, time, place, circumstance, & addresses an assembly as mere human beings. . . . It has never been done well. It is an organ of sublime power." Emerson prepared rigorously for his lectures. He drew primarily on his extensive journals (his "savings bank," as he called them) for both subjects and phrasing. Although he did not make daily entries, his journals did serve as an invaluable compendium of his comments on the controversies of the time; descriptions of friends, neighbors, and public figures; musings about himself, his family, and his community; and reports on his reading, along with notes on the issues provoked by it. Once Emerson had settled on a subject for a lecture, he would work through his journals (he created an index for easier reference) in search of appropriate entries. Characteristically, he then rewrote these entries and blended them into a final draft. He later recast the most successful of his lectures into essays. In effect, Emerson used his lectures to field-test his ideas before committing them to print.

Emerson's first major publication was Nature (1836). The sizable first printing (1,500 copies) sold out within a few months, earning him a modest profit and considerable attention in the United States and abroad. Nature provides the theoretical underpinnings for developing what became an indigenous American literature in the nineteenth century. The essay is Emerson's most dramatic effort to reject the Old World and build anew: "Embosomed for a season in nature, whose floods of life stream around and through us, . . . why should we grope among the dry bones of the past?" Emerson determined that the imagination, set loose in the natural world, offered the best prospects to discover, as he declared, "an original relation to the universe."

Emerson's efforts to define the word *nature* remain far more than an exercise in semantics or philosophical speculation. He builds into his essay a strikingly bold proposition: to substitute nature for what was generally regarded to be the new nation's lack of a distinctive cultural heritage. In Emerson's view, nature— the land itself—should be the source for articulating and developing a unique American cultural identity. He would have nature become the gravitational field for defining American experience. Like his counterparts in art—most notably the painter Thomas Cole, who figured so prominently in the Hudson River school— Emerson revered nature and saw in America the finest expression of what has been called "Nature's nation." In contrast to the many Americans who viewed nature as something to exploit in their relentless push westward, Emerson and Cole venerated nature not for the economic but for the spiritual and artistic opportunities inherent in it. For Emerson and Cole, nature would replace the Bible as the greatest spiritual text, capable of being read by anyone. As Emerson noted in a later essay, "Circles": "We can never see christianity from the catechism;—from the pasture, from a boat in the pond, from amidst the songs of wood-birds we possibly may." Or, as he put it even more succinctly in a journal entry dated a few months before the publication of *Nature:* "Make your own Bible."

Emerson returned to Harvard in 1837 as the keynote speaker on Phi Beta Kappa Day. His address on that occasion, "The American Scholar," urged his audience to break with the past and to concentrate on recognizing and developing the enormous cultural potential of their own experience. Emerson hoped to formulate a set of distinctive principles for American experience, a forward-looking philosophy based on spontaneous action, creative intuition, and self-reliance. Like most of his writing, "The American Scholar" is explicitly inspirational. To be the representative American, the scholar must be self-reliant —full enough of self-trust to be open to any experience and patient enough to "relinquish display and immediate fame." The "true scholar," Emerson declared, doesn't lead a repetitive, derivative life but looks insistently and carefully at the present; refusing to be cut off from the world of action, the scholar relies on the creative power of intuition rather than on the treatises of others to map out the "resounding tumult" of experience.

Toward the end of "The American Scholar," Emerson underscored his revolutionary call for distinctively American experience and culture:

> I ask not for the great, the remote, the romantic, what is doing in Italy or Arabia; what is Greek art, or Provencal ministrelsy; I embrace the common, I explore and sit at the feet of the familiar, the low. Give me insight into to-day, and you may have the antique and future worlds.

It is through experience, the instincts, and "things near" that we may discover the unity of the world—the "one design," he noted, that "unites and animates the farthest pinnacle and the lowest trench." Emerson closed by proclaiming America's literary independence: "We have listened too long to the courtly muses of Europe. . . . We shall walk on our own feet, we will work with our own hands, we will speak our own minds."

"The American Scholar" produced, according to Emerson's close friend Bronson Alcott, a mixture of "confusion, consternation, surprise, and wonder." For Oliver Wendell Holmes, then a prominent young physician, the address represented nothing less than America's "intellectual Declaration of Independence." The distinguished literary critic James Russell Lowell, recalling his undergraduate days at Harvard, offered perhaps the most comprehensive view of the lecture's significance:

> The Puritan revolt had made us ecclesiastically and the Revolution politically independent, but we were socially and intellectually moored to English thought, till Emerson cut the cable and gave us a chance at the dangers and glories of blue water. . . . His oration before the Phi Beta Kappa Society at Cambridge, some thirty years ago, was an event without any former parallel in our literary annals.

Emerson broadened the nation's cultural horizons by encouraging the scholar to explore the aesthetic potential of what had previously been ignored—to recognize the potential majesty in the immediate, to see the ultimate lurking in the ordinary. No longer, Emerson asserted, would there be a hierarchy of meaning. No longer would "quality" be abstract. For Emerson, quality resided in the texture of experience. The scholar's—everyone's—task, then, would be to explore the implicitness of experience. In this respect, much of late-nineteenth- and twentieth-century literature, art, and popular culture can be said to have its symbolic birth in "The American Scholar." Consider, for example, Emerson's influence on the work of such divergent figures as Walt Whitman, William James, Robert Frost, William Carlos Williams, F. Scott Fitzgerald, Willa Cather, Gertrude Stein, A. R. Ammons, Frederick Law Olmsted, Louis Sullivan, Frank Lloyd Wright, and innumerable others.

Emerson's increasing reputation as a lecturer put him at the center of a small group of disaffected intellectuals who met frequently—though not on any regular schedule—to exchange ideas. Dubbed the "Transcendentalists" by their detractors (principally because they were reported to have spent so much time discussing Immanuel Kant's "transcendental" philosophy), the group included, among others, Margaret Fuller, Theodore Parker, Orestes Brownson, Bronson Alcott, Elizabeth Peabody, George Ripley, Frederic Henry Hedge, and Christopher Cranch. Mostly young and Boston bred, these feisty radical thinkers tackled the most pressing issues of the time and endorsed, with varying degrees of zeal, the major efforts at moral reform—most notably abolition, the temperance movement, and women's rights.

The first gathering of the Transcendentalists took place in September 1836, a few days after Emerson's *Nature* was published. The most appreciable public result of their discussions was *The Dial*, an intellectual miscellany published between 1840 and 1844 and edited at various times by Margaret Fuller, George

Ripley, and Emerson. Although *The Dial* had a relatively small circulation, it called attention to the Transcendentalists and gave them a public forum for expressing their characteristically liberal views of religious and social matters.

Because more than half the participants in the Transcendentalists' conversations had trained for the Unitarian ministry, their discussions naturally drifted toward the religious controversies of the day. These occasions invariably provided Emerson with frequent opportunities to test his own ideas about religion. Emerson firmly believed that the individual could experience God firsthand and was unequivocally opposed to the forms and ceremonies of any church. During one of these meetings, Emerson is known to have said:

> The Puritans came here in revolt against forms. Why should they have kept any, then? . . . Is *any* form necessary? Do we need any gift or foreign force? Can we not be self-sustaining? See this divinity of daisies around us. Can we not be level to them? What need is there of miracles? That Jesus lived purely was his strong argument.

These are substantially the same points that Emerson developed in a controversial address to the senior class at the Harvard Divinity School in the summer of 1838, a lecture that dramatically affected the remainder of his life.

The Divinity School address argued that religion is practiced by America's ministers "as if God were dead." Emerson challenged the church's assumption that "the age of inspiration is dead." He identified Jesus and the prophets as "holy bards," discounted the importance of miracles, redefined *good* and *evil,* and urged these fledgling ministers to cast aside conformity, to free themselves from the authority of the church. They must help their parishioners "to love God without mediator or veil." Hoping to stir these ministers to recognize that their preaching had to be "rammed with life," Emerson instead was roundly condemned as a heretic by the Divinity School faculty and effectively banned from speaking at Harvard for the next 30 years. In a journal entry dated April 1840, Emerson recalled the lecture and the furor it had caused:

> In all my lectures, I have taught one doctrine, namely, the infinitude of the private man. This the people accept readily enough, and even with loud commendation, as long as I call the lecture Art, or Politics, or Literature, or the Household; but the moment I call it Religion, they are shocked, though it only be the application of the same truth which they receive everywhere else, to a new class of facts.

The Divinity School address made Emerson a public figure of considerable importance. Some said it made him infamous. But perhaps Bronson Alcott's observation best summarizes this phase of Emerson's life: "Emerson's church consists of one member—himself."

Emerson's two volumes of essays, published in 1841 and 1844, respectively, provide ample evidence with which to trace his distinctively American mind. Yet his ideas grew and changed over the span of nearly fifty years of lecturing and writing. He often modified his thinking and occasionally shifted it dramatically. In his later years, for example, he tempered much of his earlier, occasionally extravagant optimism. Recursive in his early essays, his thinking tended to be linear in later ones. Throughout his essays, however, Emerson steadfastly resisted the complacency of attaching himself to any single, narrow, categorical view of experience; "to define is to confine," he noted. His thinking is characteristically provisional. It has a democratic ring to it—open to any influence, receptive to change and growth. Emerson's ideas can develop over the course of a single essay or over the length of his career precisely because he resists fixing or even limiting the significance of a thought. In this respect, reading Emerson may well be akin to listening to someone think aloud. Flashes of truth and moments of insight encourage a sense of surprise and intellectual discovery in his readers.

Emerson envisions an ideal for himself as a thinker and a writer wherein he can approximate in his essays the fluidity he ascribes to nature. He seeks to make the movement of thought in each of his sentences and paragraphs analogous to the flow of the natural world—to the point where the mind "insures an order of expression which is the order of nature itself." Thinking and writing are organic for Emerson; his essays characteristically proceed by association rather than by logic. They reflect the way his mind actually works: moving from impression to impression, from association to association, always enlarging the context and broadening the range of experience. Ideas often spiral out in many directions, usually without being drawn together in some sort of unifying statement or conclusion. As Emerson's mind moves in a tangled web of observation, discovery, allusion, aphorism, and quotation, his essays become aggregates of sentences and paragraphs—a collection of insights. In this respect, a sentence in Emerson's essays generally carries the weight of what in other writers would be a paragraph. Often he seems to leap from one sentence to the next with little regard for transitions. Like nineteenth-century American culture itself, Emerson's essays seem to have little patience with a single idea. Emerson recognized the need to create at least a provisional order for writing. "The maker of a sentence," he notes, "launches out into the infinite and builds a road into chaos and old night, and is followed by those who hear him with something of a wild creative delight." But Emerson's road is rarely either straight or narrow.

By the mid-1840s Emerson was spending more and more of his time on the road as one of the most respected members of what was known as the Lyceum movement, an association formed to offer general instruction to adults through a network of lectures and concerts. He was by no means successful everywhere he lectured. In the West, especially, he found difficult traveling conditions, primitive lodgings, and cantankerous and occasionally rowdy audiences more accustomed to humorous tall tales than to intellectual speculation. Yet Emerson's lectures, despite occasionally confused or unflattering responses, drew large audiences virtually everywhere. And his addresses on democratic self-reliance, repeated in nearly every section of the nation, became an unofficial national anthem for the integrity of the individual mind. The moral and personal values Emerson advocated—

especially the basic belief that each individual has "a greater possibility"—had enormous appeal to the average American in the 1840s.

Emerson lectured extensively in England in 1847 and 1848, spent more time with his friend Carlyle, and took copious notes for what became *Representative Men* (1850) and *English Traits* (1856), the latter a detailed, witty, insightful, and occasionally startled look at British culture. These works suggest just how empirical and skeptical Emerson had grown in the years following his first two collections of essays. The death of his six-year-old son, Waldo, in 1842 had deeply affected him, and although he had tried to "justify" the child's death in his essay "Experience" and in the poem "Threnody," Emerson clearly had begun to moderate his optimism. By the late 1840s he seemed willing to accept the painful realities of particular places, times, and events. He had also become slightly more aristocratic, even fateful, about the average American's potential. By the time he published *English Traits,* Emerson's style had become more factual and reportorial. He now observed the world from a more detached point of view.

A renowned international figure by the 1850s, Emerson spent much of his time resisting involvement in the public controversies of the day. "I do not often speak to public questions," he announced. "They are odious and hurtful, and it seems like meddling or leaving your work." He preferred to cultivate the interior landscape of what Thoreau called "home cosmography." There were exceptions, of course: He opposed racial and social injustice, slavery, the removal of the Cherokee Nation from Georgia in the late 1830s, United States involvement in the Mexican War, and the Fugitive Slave Law. The epigraph to his journal for 1837 puts his views on public issues most succinctly: "I write the laws, / Not plead a cause."

The Emerson house in Concord became a port of call for virtually every major American writer of the time. His last years were devoted to being "the representative American." Too old to participate in the Civil War, Emerson became absorbed in the rhetoric surrounding it and wrote movingly about the Emancipation Proclamation and the death of Lincoln. Regarded as a sage in the United States and abroad, Emerson spent much of his time lecturing and trying to compensate for what he believed was America's "bad name for superficialness." In the years following the Civil War he grew increasingly impatient with his own failing health and eventually needed the help of both his daughter, Ellen, and James Cabot, his authorized biographer and literary executor, to see him through his lecturing and publishing commitments. It may well have been the accidental burning of "Coolidge House" in 1872 that precipitated Emerson's decline. Facing the loss of important papers and the disarray of so many others, he began to lose his memory and slipped into senility. His memory gone and his ability to perform publicly irreparably impaired, Emerson slowly settled into dying. On April 27, 1882, Concord's church bells rang 79 times, proclaiming his life and announcing his death.

Perhaps the most appropriate epitaph for Emerson's life had been offered unceremoniously years before his death. In the early summer of 1848, near the end of his very successful—and controversial—lecture tour of Great Britain, a letter from a disconsolate reader appeared in a London newspaper, requesting that the admission price of Emerson's lectures be reduced so that the poorer classes could hear him speak. "Emerson," the letter writer observed, "is a phenomenon whose like is not in the world, and to miss him is to lose an important part of the Nineteenth century."

Further Reading:
O. W. Holmes, *Ralph Waldo Emerson*, 1885.
J. Cabot, *A Memoir of Ralph Waldo Emerson*, 2 vols., 1887.
V. W. Brooks, *The Life of Emerson*, 1932.
R. Rusk, *The Life of Ralph Waldo Emerson*, 1949, 1957.
V. Hopkins, *Spires of Form*, 1951.
S. Paul, *Emerson's Angle of Vision*, 1952.
F. Carpenter, *The Emerson Handbook*, 1953.
S. Whicher, *Freedom and Fate*, 1953, 1959.
Emerson's Workshop: An Analysis of His Reading in Periodicals Through 1836, ed. K. W. Cameron, 1964.
R. Poirier, *A World Elsewhere*, 1966.
Emerson Among His Contemporaries, ed. K. W. Cameron, 1967.
W. Harding, *Emerson's Library*, 1967.
J. Porte, *Emerson and Thoreau: Transcendentalists in Conflict*, 1967.
L. Buell, *Literary Transcendentalism*, 1973.
H. H. Waggoner, *Emerson as Poet*, 1974.
S. Bercovitch, *The Puritan Origin of the American Self*, 1975.
D. Porter, *Emerson and Literary Change*, 1978.
R. A. Yoder, *Emerson and the Orphic Poet in America*, 1978.
J. Porte, *Representative Man: Ralph Waldo Emerson in His Time*, 1979.
G. W. Allen, *Waldo Emerson*, 1981.
B. Packer, *Emerson's Fall*, 1982.
D. Robinson, *Apostle of Culture: Emerson as Preacher and Lecturer*, 1982.
D. Yannela, *Ralph Waldo Emerson*, 1982.
J. McAleer, *Ralph Waldo Emerson: Days of Encounter*, 1984.

Texts:
"Nature," "The American Scholar," the Divinity School address, and "Self-reliance" from *The Collected Works of Ralph Waldo Emerson*, vol. 1, ed. R. E. Spiller and A. R. Ferguson, 1971, and vol. 2, ed. J. Slater, A. R. Ferguson, and J. F. Carr, 1979.
See also *The Early Lectures of Ralph Waldo Emerson*, 3 vols., ed. S. Whicher et al., 1959–1971.
"The Poet" from *Essays, Second Series*, 1844.
All poetry from *The Complete Works of Ralph Waldo Emerson*, ed. E. W. Emerson, 1903–1904.
Journal entries from *Emerson in His Journals*, ed. J. Porte, 1982.
See also *The Journals of Ralph Waldo Emerson*, 10 vols., ed. E. W. Emerson and W. Forbes, 1909–1914, and *The Journals and Miscellaneous Notebooks of Ralph Waldo Emerson*, ed. W. Gilman, 16 vols., 1960–1982.
Emerson's Literary Criticism, ed. E. W. Carlson, 1979.

Nature*

A subtle chain of countless rings
The next unto the farthest brings;
The eye reads omens where it goes,
And speaks all languages the rose;
And, striving to be man, the worm
Mounts through all the spires of form.[1]

Introduction

Our age is retrospective. It builds the sepulchres of the fathers. It writes biographies, histories, and criticism. The foregoing generations beheld God and nature face to face; we, through their eyes. Why should not we also enjoy an original relation to the universe? Why should not we have a poetry and philosophy of insight and not of tradition, and a religion by revelation to us, and not the history of theirs? Embosomed for a season in nature, whose floods of life stream around and through us, and invite us, by the powers they supply, to action proportioned to nature, why should we grope among the dry bones of the past, or put the living generation into masquerade out of its faded wardrobe? The sun shines to-day also. There is more wool and flax in the fields. There are new lands, new men, new thoughts. Let us demand our own works and laws and worship.

Undoubtedly we have no questions to ask which are unanswerable. We must trust the perfection of the creation so far as to believe that whatever curiosity the order of things has awakened in our minds, the order of things can satisfy. Every man's condition is a solution in hieroglyphic to those inquiries he would put. He acts it as life, before he apprehends it as truth. In like manner, nature is already, in its forms and tendencies, describing its own design. Let us interrogate the great apparition that shines so peacefully around us. Let us inquire, to what end is nature?

All science has one aim, namely, to find a theory of nature. We have theories of races and of functions, but scarcely yet a remote approach to an idea of creation. We are now so far from the road to truth, that religious teachers dispute and hate each other, and speculative men are esteemed unsound and frivolous. But to a sound judgment, the most abstract truth is the most practical. Whenever a true theory appears, it will be its own evidence. Its test is, that it will explain all phenomena. Now many are thought not only unexplained but inexplicable; as language, sleep, madness, dreams, beasts, sex.

Philosophically considered, the universe is composed of Nature and the Soul. Strictly speaking, therefore, all that is separate from us, all which Philosophy distinguishes as the NOT ME, that is, both nature and art, all other men and my own body,

---

* Emerson's first major work and the first proclamation of New England Transcendentalism.

[1] The first edition of "Nature" in 1836 had as its motto a quote from the Roman philosopher Plotinus: "Nature is but an image or imitation of wisdom, the last thing of the soul; nature being a thing which doth only do, but not know." In the 1849 edition, Emerson's epigraphic poem was substituted, supporting Darwin's concept of evolutionary progress.

must be ranked under this name, NATURE. In enumerating the values of nature and casting up their sum, I shall use the word in both senses—in its common and in its philosophical import. In inquiries so general as our present one, the inaccuracy is not material; no confusion of thought will occur. *Nature,* in the common sense, refers to essences unchanged by man; space, the air, the river, the leaf. *Art* is applied to the mixture of his will with the same things, as in a house, a canal, a statue, a picture. But his operations taken together are so insignificant, a little chipping, baking, patching, and washing, that in an impression so grand as that of the world on the human mind, they do not vary the result.

I

To go into solitude, a man needs to retire as much from his chamber as from society. I am not solitary whilst I read and write, though nobody is with me. But if a man would be alone, let him look at the stars. The rays that come from those heavenly worlds will separate between him and what he touches. One might think the atmosphere was made transparent with this design, to give man, in the heavenly bodies, the perpetual presence of the sublime. Seen in the streets of cities, how great they are! If the stars should appear one night in a thousand years, how would men believe and adore; and preserve for many generations the remembrance of the city of God which had been shown! But every night come out these envoys of beauty, and light the universe with their admonishing smile.

The stars awaken a certain reverence, because though always present, they are inaccessible; but all natural objects make a kindred impression, when the mind is open to their influence. Nature never wears a mean appearance. Neither does the wisest man extort her secret, and lose his curiosity by finding out all her perfection. Nature never became a toy to a wise spirit. The flowers, the animals, the mountains, reflected the wisdom of his best hour, as much as they had delighted the simplicity of his childhood.

When we speak of nature in this manner, we have a distinct but most poetical sense in the mind. We mean the integrity of impression made by manifold natural objects. It is this which distinguishes the stick of timber of the wood-cutter from the tree of the poet. The charming landscape which I saw this morning is indubitably made up of some twenty or thirty farms. Miller owns this field, Locke that, and Manning the woodland beyond. But none of them owns the landscape. There is a property in the horizon which no man has but he whose eye can integrate all the parts, that is, the poet. This is the best part of these men's farms, yet to this their warranty-deeds give no title.

To speak truly, few adult persons can see nature. Most persons do not see the sun. At least they have a very superficial seeing. The sun illuminates only the eye of the man, but shines into the eye and the heart of the child. The lover of nature is he whose inward and outward senses are still truly adjusted to each other; who has retained the spirit of infancy even into the era of manhood. His intercourse with heaven and earth becomes part of his daily food. In the presence of nature a wild delight runs through the man, in spite of real sorrows. Nature says—he is my creature, and maugre all his impertinent griefs, he shall be glad with me. Not the sun or the summer alone, but every hour and season yields its tribute of delight; for every hour and change corresponds to and authorizes a different state of the mind, from breathless noon to grimmest midnight. Nature is a setting that fits equally well a comic or a mourning piece. In good health, the air is a cordial of incredible virtue. Crossing a bare common, in snow puddles, at twilight, under a clouded sky, without having in my thoughts any occurrence of special good fortune, I have enjoyed a perfect exhilaration. I am glad to the brink of fear. In the woods, too, a man casts off his years, as the snake his slough, and at what period soever of life is always a child. In the woods is perpetual youth. Within these plantations of God, a decorum and sanctity reign, a perennial festival is dressed, and the guest sees not how he should tire of them in a thousand years. In the woods, we return to reason and faith. There I feel that nothing can befall me in life—no disgrace, no calamity (leaving me my eyes), which nature cannot repair. Standing on the bare ground—my head bathed by the blithe air and uplifted into infinite space—all mean egotism vanishes. I become a transparent eyeball; I am nothing; I see all; the currents of the Universal Being circulate through me; I am part or parcel of God. The name of the nearest friend sounds then foreign and accidental: to be brothers, to be acquaintances, master or servant, is then a trifle and a disturbance. I am the lover of uncontained and immortal beauty. In the wilderness, I find something more dear and connate than in streets or villages. In the tranquil landscape, and especially in the distant line of the horizon, man beholds somewhat as beautiful as his own nature.

The greatest delight which the fields and woods minister is the suggestion of an occult relation between man and the vegetable. I am not alone and unacknowledged. They nod to me, and I to them. The waving of the boughs in the storm is new to me and old. It takes me by surprise, and yet is not unknown. Its effect is like that of a higher thought or a better emotion coming over me, when I deemed I was thinking justly or doing right.

Yet it is certain that the power to produce this delight does not reside in nature, but in man, or in a harmony of both. It is necessary to use these pleasures with great temperance. For nature is not always tricked[2] in holiday attire, but the same scene which yesterday breathed perfume and glittered as for the frolic of the nymphs is overspread with melancholy to-day. Nature always wears the colors of the spirit. To a man laboring under calamity, the heat of his own fire hath sadness in it. Then there is a kind of contempt of the landscape felt by him who has just lost by death a dear friend. The sky is less grand as it shuts down over less worth in the population.

II: Commodity

Whoever considers the final cause of the world will discern a multitude of uses that enter as parts into that result. They all admit of being thrown into one of the following classes: Commodity; Beauty; Language; and Discipline.

Under the general name of commodity, I rank all those advantages which our senses owe to nature. This, of course, is a benefit which is temporary and mediate,[3] not ultimate, like its service to the soul. Yet although low, it is perfect in its kind, and is the only use of nature which all men apprehend. The misery of man appears like childish petulance, when we explore the steady and prodigal provision that has been

---

[2] Clad.   [3] In between.

made for his support and delight on this green ball which floats him through the heavens. What angels invented these splendid ornaments, these rich conveniences, this ocean of air above, this ocean of water beneath, this firmament of earth between? this zodiac of lights, this tent of dropping clouds, this striped coat of climates, this fourfold year? Beasts, fire, water, stones, and corn serve him. The field is at once his floor, his work-yard, his play-ground, his garden, and his bed.

> "More servants wait on man
> Than he'll take notice of."[4]

Nature, in its ministry to man, is not only the material, but is also the process and the result. All the parts incessantly work into each other's hands for the profit of man. The wind sows the seed; the sun evaporates the sea; the wind blows the vapor to the field; the ice, on the other side of the planet, condenses rain on this; the rain feeds the plant; the plant feeds the animal; and thus the endless circulations of the divine charity nourish man.

The useful arts are reproductions or new combinations by the wit of man, of the same natural benefactors. He no longer waits for favoring gales, but by means of steam, he realizes the fable of Aeolus's bag,[5] and carries the two and thirty winds in the boiler of his boat. To diminish friction, he paves the road with iron bars,[6] and, mounting a coach with a ship-load of men, animals, and merchandise behind him, he darts through the country; from town to town, like an eagle or a swallow through the air. By the aggregate of these aids, how is the face of the world changed, from the era of Noah to that of Napoleon! The private poor man hath cities, ships, canals, bridges, built for him. He goes to the post-office, and the human race run on his errands; to the book-shop, and the human race read and write of all that happens for him; to the court-house, and nations repair his wrongs. He sets his house upon the road, and the human race go forth every morning, and shovel out the snow, and cut a path for him.

But there is no need of specifying particulars in this class of uses. The catalogue is endless, and the examples so obvious, that I shall leave them to the reader's reflection, with the general remark, that this mercenary benefit is one which has respect to a farther good. A man is fed, not that he may be fed, but that he may work.

III: Beauty

A nobler want of man is served by nature, namely, the love of Beauty.

The ancient Greeks called the world χόσμος,[7] beauty. Such is the constitution of all things, or such the plastic power of the human eye, that the primary forms, as the sky, the mountain, the tree, the animal, give us a delight *in and for themselves;* a pleasure arising from outline, color, motion, and grouping. This seems partly owing to the eye itself. The eye is the best of artists. By the mutual action of its structure

[4] From "Man" by the English poet George Herbert (1593–1633).
[5] Aeolus, a god in Homer's *Odyssey,* gave Odysseus "a mighty bag" of bottled winds. Inquisitive sailors opened this bag and released a tumultuous storm.
[6] Railroad tracks.
[7] Greek: "beauty" in the sense of the complexity of the universe expressed as orderly and harmonious.

and of the laws of light, perspective is produced, which integrates every mass of objects, of what character soever, into a well colored and shaded globe, so that where the particular objects are mean and unaffecting, the landscape which they compose is round and symmetrical. And as the eye is the best composer, so light is the first of painters. There is no object so foul that intense light will not make beautiful. And the stimulus it affords to the sense, and a sort of infinitude which it hath, like space and time, make all matter gay. Even the corpse has its own beauty. But besides this general grace diffused over nature, almost all the individual forms are agreeable to the eye, as is proved by our endless imitations of some of them, as the acorn, the grape, the pine-cone, the wheat-ear, the egg, the wings and forms of most birds, the lion's claw, the serpent, the butterfly, sea-shells, flames, clouds, buds, leaves, and the forms of many trees, as the palm.

For better consideration, we may distribute the aspects of Beauty in a threefold manner.

1. First, the simple perception of natural forms is a delight. The influence of the forms and actions in nature is so needful to man, that, in its lowest functions, it seems to lie on the confines of commodity and beauty. To the body and mind which have been cramped by noxious work or company, nature is medicinal and restores their tone. The tradesman, the attorney comes out of the din and craft of the street and sees the sky and the woods, and is a man again. In their eternal calm, he finds himself. The health of the eye seems to demand a horizon. We are never tired, so long as we can see far enough.

But in other hours, Nature satisfies by its loveliness, and without any mixture of corporeal benefit. I see the spectacle of morning from the hilltop over against my house, from daybreak to sunrise, with emotions which an angel might share. The long slender bars of cloud float like fishes in the sea of crimson light. From the earth, as a shore, I look out into that silent sea. I seem to partake its rapid transformations; the active enchantment reaches my dust, and I dilate and conspire with the morning wind. How does Nature deify us with a few and cheap elements! Give me health and a day, and I will make the pomp of emperors ridiculous. The dawn is my Assyria;[8] the sunset and moonrise my Paphos,[9] and unimaginable realms of faerie; broad noon shall be my England of the senses and the understanding; the night shall be my Germany of mystic philosophy and dreams.[10]

Not less excellent, except for our less susceptibility in the afternoon, was the charm, last evening, of a January sunset. The western clouds divided and subdivided themselves into pink flakes modulated with tints of unspeakable softness, and the air had so much life and sweetness that it was a pain to come within doors. What was it that nature would say? Was there no meaning in the live repose of the valley behind the mill, and which Homer or Shakspeare could not re-form for me in words? The leafless trees become spires of flame in the sunset, with the blue east for their background, and the stars of the dead calices[11] of flowers, and every withered stem and stubble rimed with frost, contribute something to the mute music.

The inhabitants of cities suppose that the country landscape is pleasant only half

---

[8] Ancient Near Eastern empire, emblematic of magnificence.
[9] Ancient city of Cyprus, distinguished for its worship of Aphrodite, Greek goddess of love and beauty.

[10] The rational empiricism of English philosophers, such as Hume, and the "common sense" school of thought are contrasted to the idealism of German philosophers, such as Kant.
[11] External, leafy parts of flowers.

the year. I please myself with the graces of the winter scenery, and believe that we are as much touched by it as by the genial influences of summer. To the attentive eye, each moment of the year has its own beauty, and in the same field, it beholds, every hour, a picture which was never seen before and which shall never be seen again. The heavens change every moment, and reflect their glory or gloom on the plains beneath. The state of the crop in the surrounding farms alters the expression of the earth from week to week. The succession of native plants in the pastures and roadsides, which make the silent clock by which time tells the summer hours, will make even the divisions of the day sensible to a keen observer. The tribes of birds and insects, like the plants punctual to their time, follow each other, and the year has room for all. By watercourses, the variety is greater. In July, the blue pontederia or pickerel-weed blooms in large beds in the shallow parts of our pleasant river,[12] and swarms with yellow butterflies in continual motion. Art cannot rival this pomp of purple and gold. Indeed the river is a perpetual gala, and boasts each month a new ornament.

But this beauty of Nature which is seen and felt as beauty, is the least part. The shows of day, the dewy morning, the rainbow, mountains, orchards in blossom, stars, moonlight, shadows in still water, and the like, if too eagerly hunted, become shows merely, and mock us with their unreality. Go out of the house to see the moon, and 't is mere tinsel; it will not please as when its light shines upon your necessary journey. The beauty that shimmers in the yellow afternoons of October, who ever could clutch it? Go forth to find it, and it is gone; 't is only a mirage as you look from the windows of diligence.

2.   The presence of a higher, namely, of the spiritual element is essential to its perfection. The high and divine beauty which can be loved without effeminacy, is that which is found in combination with the human will. Beauty is the mark God sets upon virtue. Every natural action is graceful. Every heroic act is also decent, and causes the place and the bystanders to shine. We are taught by great actions that the universe is the property of every individual in it. Every rational creature has all nature for his dowry and estate. It is his, if he will. He may divest himself of it; he may creep into a corner, and abdicate his kingdom, as most men do, but he is entitled to the world by his constitution. In proportion to the energy of his thought and will, he takes up the world into himself. "All those things for which men plough, build, or sail, obey virtue;" said Sallust.[13] "The winds and waves," said Gibbon, "are always on the side of the ablest navigators."[14] So are the sun and moon and all the stars of heaven. When a noble act is done—perchance in a scene of great natural beauty; when Leonidas[15] and his three hundred martyrs consume one day in dying, and the sun and moon come each and look at them once in the steep defile of Thermopylae; when Arnold Winkelried,[16] in the high Alps, under the shadow of the avalanche, gathers in his side a sheaf of Austrian spears to break the line for his comrades; are not these heroes entitled to add the beauty of the scene to the beauty of the deed? When the

[12] The Concord River.

[13] From *The Conspiracy of Catiline* by the Roman historian Gaius Sallustius Crispus (86–35 B.C.).

[14] From *The Decline and Fall of the Roman Empire* (1788) by Edward Gibbon (1737–1794), English historian.

[15] King Leonidas and 300 fellow Spartans died

while defending the pass at Thermopylae against the Persian army in 480 B.C.

[16] Swiss hero who exposed himself to the spears of the Austrians in the Battle of Sempach (1386). When the Austrians had exhausted their supply, Winkelried defeated them and proclaimed Swiss independence.

bark of Columbus nears the shore of America; before it the beach lined with savages, fleeing out of all their huts of cane; the sea behind; and the purple mountains of the Indian Archipelago around, can we separate the man from the living picture? Does not the New World clothe his form with her palm-groves and savannahs as fit drapery? Ever does natural beauty steal in like air, and envelop great actions. When Sir Harry Vane[17] was dragged up the Tower-hill,[18] sitting on a sled, to suffer death as the champion of the English laws, one of the multitude cried out to him, "You never sate on so glorious a seat!" Charles II, to intimidate the citizens of London, caused the patriot Lord Russell[19] to be drawn in an open coach through the principal streets of the city on his way to the scaffold. "But," his biographer says, "the multitude imagined they saw liberty and virtue sitting by his side." In private places, among sordid objects, an act of truth or heroism seems at once to draw to itself the sky as its temple, the sun as its candle. Nature stretches out her arms to embrace man, only let his thoughts be of equal greatness. Willingly does she follow his steps with the rose and the violet, and bend her lines of grandeur and grace to the decoration of her darling child. Only let his thoughts be of equal scope, and the frame will suit the picture. A virtuous man is in unison with her works, and makes the central figure of the visible sphere. Homer, Pindar, Socrates, Phocion,[20] associate themselves fitly in our memory with the geography and climate of Greece. The visible heavens and earth sympathize with Jesus. And in common life whosoever has seen a person of powerful character and happy genius, will have remarked how easily he took all things along with him—the persons, the opinions, and the day, and nature became ancillary to a man.

3.   There is still another aspect under which the beauty of the world may be viewed, namely, as it becomes an object of the intellect. Beside the relation of things to virtue, they have a relation to thought. The intellect searches out the absolute order of things as they stand in the mind of God, and without the colors of affection. The intellectual and the active powers seem to succeed each other, and the exclusive activity of the one generates the exclusive activity of the other. There is something unfriendly in each to the other, but they are like the alternate periods of feeding and working in animals; each prepares and will be followed by the other. Therefore does beauty, which, in relation to actions, as we have seen, comes unsought, and comes because it is unsought, remain for the apprehension and pursuit of the intellect; and then again, in its turn, of the active power. Nothing divine dies. All good is eternally reproductive. The beauty of nature re-forms itself in the mind, and not for barren contemplation, but for new creation.

All men are in some degree impressed by the face of the world; some men even to delight. This love of beauty is Taste. Others have the same love in such excess, that, not content with admiring, they seek to embody it in new forms. The creation of beauty is Art.

---

[17] *English Puritan (1613–1662) executed for opposing the restoration of Charles II.*
[18] Hill next to the Tower of London where executions for treason took place.
[19] William Russell (1639–1683), executed for cooperating with a plot to overthrow Charles II.

[20] Homer: Greek epic poet (fl. 850? B.C.); Pindar: Greek poet (522?–443 B.C.); Socrates: Greek philosopher (470?–399 B.C.); Phocion: Athenian general and statesman (402?–317 B.C.).

The production of a work of art throws a light upon the mystery of humanity. A work of art is an abstract or epitome of the world. It is the result or expression of nature, in miniature. For although the works of nature are innumerable and all different, the result or the expression of them all is similar and single. Nature is a sea of forms radically alike and even unique. A leaf, a sunbeam, a landscape, the ocean, make an analogous impression on the mind. What is common to them all—that perfectness and harmony, is beauty. The standard of beauty is the entire circuit of natural forms—the totality of nature; which the Italians expressed by defining beauty "il più nell' uno."[21] Nothing is quite beautiful alone; nothing but is beautiful in the whole. A single object is only so far beautiful as it suggests this universal grace. The poet, the painter, the sculptor, the musician, the architect, seek each to concentrate this radiance of the world on one point, and each in his several work to satisfy the love of beauty which stimulates him to produce. Thus is Art a nature passed through the alembic of man. Thus in art does Nature work through the will of a man filled with the beauty of her first works.

The world thus exists to the soul to satisfy the desire of beauty. This element I call an ultimate end. No reason can be asked or given why the soul seeks beauty. Beauty, in its largest and profoundest sense, is one expression for the universe. God is the all-fair. Truth, and goodness, and beauty, are but different faces of the same All. But beauty in nature is not ultimate. It is the herald of inward and eternal beauty, and is not alone a solid and satisfactory good. It must stand as a part, and not as yet the last or highest expression of the final cause of Nature.

IV: Language

Language is a third use which Nature subserves to man. Nature is the vehicle of thought, and in a simple, double, and three-fold degree.

1.   Words are signs of natural facts.
2.   Particular natural facts are symbols of particular spiritual facts.
3.   Nature is the symbol of spirit.

1.   Words are signs of natural facts. The use of natural history is to give us aid in supernatural history; the use of the outer creation, to give us language for the beings and changes of the inward creation. Every word which is used to express a moral or intellectual fact, if traced to its root, is found to be borrowed from some material appearance. *Right* means *straight; wrong* means *twisted; Spirit* primarily means *wind; transgression,* the crossing of a *line; supercilious,* the *raising of the eyebrow.* We say the *heart* to express emotion, the *head* to denote thought; and *thought* and *emotion* are words borrowed from sensible things, and now appropriated to spiritual nature. Most of the process by which this transformation is made, is hidden from us in the remote time when language was framed; but the same tendency may be daily observed in children. Children and savages use only nouns or names of things, which they convert into verbs, and apply to analogous mental acts.

2.   But this origin of all words that convey a spiritual import—so conspicuous a fact in the history of language—is our least debt to nature. It is not words only that are emblematic; it is things which are emblematic. Every natural fact is a symbol of some spiritual fact. Every appearance in nature corresponds to some state of the

[21] Italian: "the many in one."

mind, and that state of the mind can only be described by presenting that natural appearance as its picture. An enraged man is a lion, a cunning man is a fox, a firm man is a rock, a learned man is a torch. A lamb is innocence; a snake is subtle spite; flowers express to us the delicate affections. Light and darkness are our familiar expression for knowledge and ignorance; and heat for love. Visible distance behind and before us, is respectively our image of memory and hope.

Who looks upon a river in a meditative hour and is not reminded of the flux of all things? Throw a stone into the stream, and the circles that propagate themselves are the beautiful type of all influence. Man is conscious of a universal soul within or behind his individual life, wherein, as in a firmament, the natures of Justice, Truth, Love, Freedom, arise and shine. This universal soul he calls Reason: it is not mine, or thine, or his, but we are its; we are its property and men. And the blue sky in which the private earth is buried, the sky with its eternal calm, and full of everlasting orbs, is the type of Reason. That which intellectually considered we call Reason, considered in relation to nature, we call Spirit. Spirit is the Creator. Spirit hath life in itself. And man in all ages and countries embodies it in his language as the FATHER.

It is easily seen that there is nothing lucky or capricious in these analogies, but that they are constant, and pervade nature. These are not the dreams of a few poets, here and there, but man is an analogist, and studies relations in all objects. He is placed in the centre of beings, and a ray of relation passes from every other being to him. And neither can man be understood without these objects, nor these objects without man. All the facts in natural history taken by themselves, have no value, but are barren, like a single sex. But marry it to human history, and it is full of life. Whole floras, all Linnæus' and Buffon's[22] volumes, are dry catalogues of facts; but the most trivial of these facts, the habit of a plant, the organs, or work, or noise of an insect, applied to the illustration of a fact in intellectual philosophy, or in any way associated to human nature, affects us in the most lively and agreeable manner. The seed of a plant —to what affecting analogies in the nature of man is that little fruit made use of, in all discourse, up to the voice of Paul, who calls the human corpse a seed—"It is sown a natural body; it is raised a spiritual body."[23] The motion of the earth round its axis and round the sun, makes the day and the year. These are certain amounts of brute light and heat. But is there no intent of an analogy between man's life and the seasons? And do the seasons gain no grandeur or pathos from that analogy? The instincts of the ant are very unimportant considered as the ant's; but the moment a ray of relation is seen to extend from it to man, and the little drudge is seen to be a monitor, a little body with a mighty heart, then all its habits, even that said to be recently observed, that it never sleeps, become sublime.

Because of this radical correspondence between visible things and human thoughts, savages, who have only what is necessary, converse in figures. As we go back in history, language becomes more picturesque, until its infancy, when it is all poetry; or all spiritual facts are represented by natural symbols. The same symbols are found to make the original elements of all languages. It has moreover been observed, that the idioms of all languages approach each other in passages of the greatest eloquence

---

[22] Linnæus: Carolus Linnæus (1707–1778), Swedish   [23] See 1 Corinthians 15:44.
botanist; Buffon: Georges Louis Leclerc, comte
de Buffon (1707–1788), French naturalist.

and power. And as this is the first language, so is it the last. This immediate dependence of language upon nature, this conversion of an outward phenomenon into a type of somewhat in human life, never loses its power to affect us. It is this which gives that piquancy to the conversation of a strong-natured farmer or backwoodsman, which all men relish.

A man's power to connect his thought with its proper symbol, and so to utter it, depends on the simplicity of his character, that is, upon his love of truth and his desire to communicate it without loss. The corruption of man is followed by the corruption of language. When simplicity of character and the sovereignty of ideas is broken up by the prevalence of secondary desires—the desire of riches, of pleasure, of power, and of praise—and duplicity and falsehood take place of simplicity and truth, the power over nature as an interpreter of the will is in a degree lost; new imagery ceases to be created, and old words are perverted to stand for things which are not; a paper currency is employed, when there is no bullion in the vaults. In due time the fraud is manifest, and words lose all power to stimulate the understanding or the affections. Hundreds of writers may be found in every long-civilized nation who for a short time believe and make others believe that they see and utter truths, who do not of themselves clothe one thought in its natural garment, but who feed unconsciously on the language created by the primary writers of the country, those, namely, who hold primarily on nature.

But wise men pierce this rotten diction and fasten words again to visible things; so that picturesque language is at once a commanding certificate that he who employs it is a man in alliance with truth and God. The moment our discourse rises above the ground line of familiar facts and is inflamed with passion or exalted by thought, it clothes itself in images. A man conversing in earnest, if he watch his intellectual processes, will find that a material image more or less luminous arises in his mind, contemporaneous with every thought, which furnishes the vestment of the thought. Hence, good writing and brilliant discourse are perpetual allegories. This imagery is spontaneous. It is the blending of experience with the present action of the mind. It is proper creation. It is the working of the Original Cause through the instruments he has already made.

These facts may suggest the advantage which the country-life possesses, for a powerful mind, over the artificial and curtailed life of cities. We know more from nature than we can at will communicate. Its light flows into the mind evermore, and we forget its presence. The poet, the orator, bred in the woods, whose senses have been nourished by their fair and appeasing changes, year after year, without design and without heed—shall not lose their lesson altogether, in the roar of cities or the broil of politics. Long hereafter, amidst agitation and terror in national councils— in the hour of revolution—these solemn images shall reappear in their morning lustre, as fit symbols and words of the thoughts which the passing events shall awaken. At the call of a noble sentiment, again the woods wave, the pines murmur, the river rolls and shines, and the cattle low upon the mountains, as he saw and heard them in his infancy. And with these forms, the spells of persuasion, the keys of power are put into his hands.

3.   We are thus assisted by natural objects in the expression of particular meanings. But how great a language to convey such pepper-corn[24] informations! Did it need

---

[24] Unimportant.

such noble races of creatures, this profusion of forms, this host of orbs in heaven, to furnish man with the dictionary and grammar of his municipal speech? Whilst we use this grand cipher to expedite the affairs of our pot and kettle, we feel that we have not yet put it to its use, neither are able. We are like travellers using the cinders of a volcano to roast their eggs. Whilst we see that it always stands ready to clothe what we would say, we cannot avoid the question whether the characters are not significant of themselves. Have mountains, and waves, and skies, no significance but what we consciously give them when we employ them as emblems of our thoughts? The world is emblematic. Parts of speech are metaphors, because the whole of nature is a metaphor of the human mind. The laws of moral nature answer to those of matter as face to face in a glass. "The visible world and the relation of its parts, is the dial plate of the invisible."[25] The axioms of physics translate the laws of ethics. Thus, "the whole is greater than its part;" "reaction is equal to action;" "the smallest weight may be made to lift the greatest, the difference of weight being compensated by time;" and many the like propositions, which have an ethical as well as physical sense. These propositions have a much more extensive and universal sense when applied to human life, than when confined to technical use.

In like manner, the memorable words of history and the proverbs of nations consist usually of a natural fact, selected as a picture or parable of a moral truth. Thus: A rolling stone gathers no moss; A bird in the hand is worth two in the bush; A cripple in the right way will beat a racer in the wrong; Make hay while the sun shines; 'T is hard to carry a full cup even; Vinegar is the son of wine; The last ounce broke the camel's back; Long-lived trees make roots first—and the like. In their primary sense these are trivial facts, but we repeat them for the value of their analogical import. What is true of proverbs, is true of all fables, parables, and allegories.

This relation between the mind and matter is not fancied by some poet, but stands in the will of God, and so is free to be known by all men. It appears to men, or it does not appear. When in fortunate hours we ponder this miracle, the wise man doubts if at all other times he is not blind and deaf;

> "Can such things be,
> And overcome us like a summer's cloud,
> Without our special wonder?"[26]

for the universe becomes transparent, and the light of higher laws than its own shines through it. It is the standing problem which has exercised the wonder and the study of every fine genius since the world began; from the era of the Egyptians and the Brahmins to that of Pythagoras, of Plato, of Bacon, of Leibnitz, of Swedenborg.[27] There sits the Sphinx[28] at the road-side, and from age to age, as each prophet comes

---

[25] Quoted from the philosopher Emanuel Swedenborg (1688–1772) (see note 27 below).

[26] Shakespeare's *Macbeth*, Act III, Sc. iv, ll. 110–112.

[27] Teachings that influenced Emerson's interpretations of the universe. Egyptian and Brahmin mystics taught transmigration of the soul. Pythagoras (sixth century B.C.) believed in the infinite recurrence of phenomena. Plato (428–347 B.C.) fostered the idealism of Western

philosophy. Francis Bacon (1561–1626), British founder of inductive science, believed in religious mysticism. Gottfried Wilhelm von Leibnitz (1646–1716) was a German mathematician and idealist philosopher. Emanuel Swedenborg (1688–1772) was the Swedish religious mentor whom Emerson characterized as "the mystic" in *Representative Men*.

[28] According to Greek mythology, this monster killed anyone who failed to answer her riddle.

by, he tries his fortune at reading her riddle. There seems to be a necessity in spirit to manifest itself in material forms; and day and night, river and storm, beast and bird, acid and alkali, preëxist in necessary Ideas in the mind of God, and are what they are by virtue of preceding affections in the world of spirit. A Fact is the end or last issue of spirit. The visible creation is the terminus or the circumference of the invisible world. "Material objects," said a French philosopher,[29] "are necessarily kinds of scoriæ [30] of the substantial thoughts of the Creator, which must always preserve an exact relation to their first origin; in other words, visible nature must have a spiritual and moral side."

This doctrine is abstruse, and though the images of "garment," "scoriæ," "mirror," etc., may stimulate the fancy, we must summon the aid of subtler and more vital expositors to make it plain. "Every scripture is to be interpreted by the same spirit which gave it forth,"[31] is the fundamental law of criticism. A life in harmony with Nature, the love of truth and of virtue, will purge the eyes to understand her text. By degrees we may come to know the primitive sense of the permanent objects of nature, so that the world shall be to us an open book, and every form significant of its hidden life and final cause.

A new interest surprises us, whilst, under the view now suggested, we contemplate the fearful extent and multitude of objects; since "every object rightly seen, unlocks a new faculty of the soul."[32] That which was unconscious truth, becomes, when interpreted and defined in an object, a part of the domain of knowledge—a new weapon in the magazine of power.

V: Discipline

In view of the significance of nature, we arrive at once at a new fact, that nature is a discipline. This use of the world includes the preceding uses, as parts of itself.

Space, time, society, labor, climate, food, locomotion, the animals, the mechanical forces, give us sincerest lessons, day by day, whose meaning is unlimited. They educate both the Understanding and the Reason. Every property of matter is a school for the understanding—its solidity or resistance, its inertia, its extension, its figure, its divisibility. The understanding adds, divides, combines, measures, and finds nutriment and room for its activity in this worthy scene. Meantime, Reason transfers all these lessons into its own world of thought, by perceiving the analogy that marries Matter and Mind.

1. Nature is a discipline of the understanding in intellectual truths. Our dealing with sensible objects is a constant exercise in the necessary lessons of difference, of likeness, of order, of being and seeming, of progressive arrangement; of ascent from particular to general; of combination to one end of manifold forces. Proportioned to the importance of the organ to be formed, is the extreme care with which its tuition is provided—a care pretermitted in no single case. What tedious training, day after day, year after year, never ending, to form the common sense; what continual reproduction of annoyances, inconveniences, dilemmas; what rejoicing over us of little

---

[29] Guillaume Oegger in The True Messiah (1829).
[30] Slag from the melting of metals.
[31] Quoted from the English Quaker George Fox (1624–1691).

[32] From a compendium of literary criticism and philosophy, Aids to Reflection (1825), by Samuel Taylor Coleridge (1772–1834).

men; what disputing of prices, what reckonings of interest—and all to form the Hand of the mind—to instruct us that "good thoughts are no better than good dreams, unless they be executed!"[33]

The same good office is performed by Property and its filial systems of debt and credit. Debt, grinding debt, whose iron face the widow, the orphan, and the sons of genius fear and hate—debt, which consumes so much time, which so cripples and disheartens a great spirit with cares that seem so base, is a preceptor whose lessons cannot be foregone, and is needed most by those who suffer from it most. Moreover, property, which has been well compared to snow—"if it fall level to-day, it will be blown into drifts to-morrow," is the surface action of internal machinery, like the index on the face of a clock. Whilst now it is the gymnastics of the understanding, it is hiving, in the foresight of the spirit, experience in profounder laws.

The whole character and fortune of the individual are affected by the least inequalities in the culture of the understanding; for example, in the perception of differences. Therefore is Space, and therefore Time, that man may know that things are not huddled and lumped, but sundered and individual. A bell and a plough have each their use, and neither can do the office of the other. Water is good to drink, coal to burn, wool to wear; but wool cannot be drunk, nor water spun, nor coal eaten. The wise man shows his wisdom in separation, in gradation, and his scale of creatures and of merits is as wide as nature. The foolish have no range in their scale, but suppose every man is as every other man. What is not good they call the worst, and what is not hateful, they call the best.

In like manner, what good heed Nature forms in us! She pardons no mistakes. Her yea is yea, and her nay, nay.

The first steps in Agriculture, Astronomy, Zoölogy (those first steps which the farmer, the hunter, and the sailor take), teach that Nature's dice are always loaded; that in her heaps and rubbish are concealed sure and useful results.

How calmly and genially the mind apprehends one after another the laws of physics! What noble emotions dilate the mortal as he enters into the councils of the creation, and feels by knowledge the privilege to BE! His insight refines him. The beauty of nature shines in his own breast. Man is greater that he can see this, and the universe less, because Time and Space relations vanish as laws are known.

Here again we are impressed and even daunted by the immense Universe to be explored. "What we know is a point to what we do not know."[34] Open any recent journal of science, and weigh the problems suggested concerning Light, Heat, Electricity, Magnetism, Physiology, Geology, and judge whether the interest of natural science is likely to be soon exhausted.

Passing by many particulars of the discipline of nature, we must not omit to specify two.

The exercise of the Will, or the lesson of power, is taught in every event. From the child's successive possession of his several senses up to the hour when he saith, "Thy will be done!"[35] he is learning the secret that he can reduce under his will not only

---

[33] From "Of Great Place" in the *Essays* (1625) of Sir Francis Bacon (1561–1626).
[34] Quotation attributed to English theologian and moralist Bishop Joseph Butler (1692–1752).
[35] Matthew 6:10; 26:42.

particular events but great classes, nay, the whole series of events, and so conform all facts to his character. Nature is thoroughly mediate. It is made to serve. It receives the dominion of man as meekly as the ass on which the Saviour rode.[36] It offers all its kingdoms to man as the raw material which he may mould into what is useful. Man is never weary of working it up. He forges the subtile and delicate air into wise and melodious words, and gives them wing as angels of persuasion and command. One after another his victorious thought comes up with and reduces all things, until the world becomes at last only a realized will—the double of the man.

2. Sensible objects conform to the premonitions of Reason and reflect the conscience. All things are moral; and in their boundless changes have an unceasing reference to spiritual nature. Therefore is nature glorious with form, color, and motion; that every globe in the remotest heaven, every chemical change from the rudest crystal up to the laws of life, every change of vegetation from the first principle of growth in the eye of a leaf, to the tropical forest and antediluvian coal-mine, every animal function from the sponge up to Hercules, shall hint or thunder to man the laws of right and wrong, and echo the Ten Commandments. Therefore is Nature ever the ally of Religion: lends all her pomp and riches to the religious sentiment. Prophet and priest, David, Isaiah, Jesus, have drawn deeply from this source. This ethical character so penetrates the bone and marrow of nature, as to seem the end for which it was made. Whatever private purpose is answered by any member or part, this is its public and universal function, and is never omitted. Nothing in nature is exhausted in its first use. When a thing has served an end to the uttermost, it is wholly new for an ulterior service. In God, every end is converted into a new means. Thus the use of commodity, regarded by itself, is mean and squalid. But it is to the mind an education in the doctrine of Use, namely, that a thing is good only so far as it serves; that a conspiring of parts and efforts to the production of an end is essential to any being. The first and gross manifestation of this truth is our inevitable and hated training in values and wants, in corn and meat.

It has already been illustrated, that every natural process is a version of a moral sentence. The moral law lies at the centre of nature and radiates to the circumference. It is the pith and marrow of every substance, every relation, and every process. All things with which we deal, preach to us. What is a farm but a mute gospel? The chaff and the wheat, weeds and plants, blight, rain, insects, sun—it is a sacred emblem from the first furrow of spring to the last stack which the snow of winter overtakes in the fields. But the sailor, the shepherd, the miner, the merchant, in their several resorts, have each an experience precisely parallel, and leading to the same conclusion: because all organizations are radically alike. Nor can it be doubted that this moral sentiment which thus scents the air, grows in the grain, and impregnates the waters of the world, is caught by man and sinks into his soul. The moral influence of nature upon every individual is that amount of truth which it illustrates to him. Who can estimate this? Who can guess how much firmness the sea-beaten rock has taught the fisherman? How much tranquillity has been reflected to man from the azure sky, over whose unspotted deeps the winds forevermore drive flocks of stormy clouds, and leave no wrinkle or stain? How much industry and providence and affection we have caught from the

[36] Matthew 21:5: "Behold thy king cometh unto thee, meek, and sitting upon an ass."

pantomime of brutes? What a searching preacher of self-command is the varying phenomenon of Health!

Herein is especially apprehended the unity of Nature—the unity in variety—which meets us everywhere. All the endless variety of things make an identical impression. Xenophanes[37] complained in his old age, that, look where he would, all things hastened back to Unity. He was weary of seeing the same entity in the tedious variety of forms. The fable of Proteus[38] has a cordial truth. A leaf, a drop, a crystal, a moment of time, is related to the whole, and partakes of the perfection of the whole. Each particle is a microcosm, and faithfully renders the likeness of the world.

Not only resemblances exist in things whose analogy is obvious, as when we detect the type of the human hand in the flipper of the fossil saurus,[39] but also in objects wherein there is great superficial unlikeness. Thus architecture is called "frozen music," by De Staël and Goethe.[40] Vitruvius[41] thought an architect should be a musician. "A Gothic church," said Coleridge,[42] "is a petrified religion." Michael Angelo maintained, that, to an architect, a knowledge of anatomy is essential. In Haydn's oratorios,[43] the notes present to the imagination not only motions, as of the snake, the stag, and the elephant, but colors also; as the green grass. The law of harmonic sounds reappears in the harmonic colors. The granite is differenced in its laws only by the more or less of heat from the river that wears it away. The river, as it flows, resembles the air that flows over it; the air resembles the light which traverses it with more subtle currents; the light resembles the heat which rides with it through Space. Each creature is only a modification of the other; the likeness in them is more than the difference, and their radical law is one and the same. A rule of one art, or a law of one organization, holds true throughout nature. So intimate is this Unity, that, it is easily seen, it lies under the undermost garment of Nature, and betrays its source in Universal Spirit. For it pervades Thought also. Every universal truth which we express in words, implies or supposes every other truth. *Omne verum vero consonat.*[44] It is like a great circle on a sphere, comprising all possible circles; which, however, may be drawn and comprise it in like manner. Every such truth is the absolute Ens[45] seen from one side. But it has innumerable sides.

The central Unity is still more conspicuous in actions. Words are finite organs of the infinite mind. They cannot cover the dimensions of what is in truth. They break, chop, and impoverish it. An action is the perfection and publication of thought. A right action seems to fill the eye, and to be related to all nature. "The wise man, in doing one thing, does all; or, in the one thing he does rightly, he sees the likeness of all which is done rightly."[46]

Words and actions are not the attributes of brute nature. They introduce us to the

---

[37] Greek philosopher of the sixth century B.C.
[38] God of Greek fable who could assume various forms.
[39] Extinct reptiles.
[40] De Staël: French writer Anne Louise Germaine (1766–1817), baronne de Staël; Goethe: German poet Johann Wolfgang von Goethe (1749–1832).
[41] Roman architect Marcus Vitruvius Pollio (first century B.C.).
[42] From "A Lecture on the General Characteristics

of the Gothic Mind in the Middle Ages" in *Literary Remains* (1836) by Samuel Taylor Coleridge.
[43] Choral music of Austrian composer Franz Joseph Haydn (1732–1809).
[44] Latin: "Every truth agrees with every other truth."
[45] A name for "abstract being" in Latin philosophy.
[46] Quote from Goethe's *Wilhelm Meister's Travels* (1821, 1829).

human form, of which all other organizations appear to be degradations. When this appears among so many that surround it, the spirit prefers it to all others. It says, "From such as this have I drawn joy and knowledge; in such as this have I found and beheld myself; I will speak to it; it can speak again; it can yield me thought already formed and alive." In fact, the eye—the mind—is always accompanied by these forms, male and female; and these are incomparably the richest informations of the power and order that lie at the heart of things. Unfortunately every one of them bears the marks as of some injury; is marred and superficially defective. Nevertheless, far different from the deaf and dumb nature around them, these all rest like fountain-pipes on the unfathomed sea of thought and virtue whereto they alone, of all organizations, are the entrances.

It were a pleasant inquiry to follow into detail their ministry to our education, but where would it stop? We are associated in adolescent and adult life with some friends, who, like skies and waters, are coextensive with our idea; who, answering each to a certain affection of the soul, satisfy our desire on that side; whom we lack power to put at such focal distance from us, that we can mend or even analyze them. We cannot choose but love them. When much intercourse with a friend has supplied us with a standard of excellence, and has increased our respect for the resources of God who thus sends a real person to outgo our ideal; when he has, moreover, become an object of thought, and, whilst his character retains all its unconscious effect, is converted in the mind into solid and sweet wisdom—it is a sign to us that his office is closing, and he is commonly withdrawn from our sight in a short time.

VI: Idealism

Thus is the unspeakable but intelligible and practicable meaning of the world conveyed to man, the immortal pupil, in every object of sense. To this one end of Discipline, all parts of nature conspire.

A noble doubt perpetually suggests itself—whether this end be not the Final Cause of the Universe; and whether nature outwardly exists. It is a sufficient account of that Appearance we call the World, that God will teach a human mind, and so makes it the receiver of a certain number of congruent sensations, which we call sun and moon, man and woman, house and trade. In my utter impotence to test the authenticity of the report of my senses, to know whether the impressions they make on me correspond with outlying objects, what difference does it make, whether Orion[47] is up there in heaven, or some god paints the image in the firmament of the soul? The relations of parts and the end of the whole remaining the same, what is the difference, whether land and sea interact, and worlds revolve and intermingle without number or end— deep yawning under deep, and galaxy balancing galaxy, throughout absolute space —or whether, without relations of time and space, the same appearances are inscribed in the constant faith of man? Whether nature enjoy a substantial existence without, or is only in the apocalypse of the mind, it is alike useful and alike venerable to me. Be it what it may, it is ideal to me so long as I cannot try the accuracy of my senses.

The frivolous make themselves merry with the Ideal theory, as if its consequences were burlesque; as if it affected the stability of nature. It surely does not. God never

[47] Constellation of stars.

jests with us, and will not compromise the end of nature by permitting any inconsequence in its procession. Any distrust of the permanence of laws would paralyze the faculties of man. Their permanence is sacredly respected, and his faith therein is perfect. The wheels and springs of man are all set to the hypothesis of the permanence of nature. We are not built like a ship to be tossed, but like a house to stand. It is a natural consequence of this structure, that so long as the active powers predominate over the reflective, we resist with indignation any hint that nature is more short-lived or mutable than spirit. The broker, the wheelwright, the carpenter, the tollman, are much displeased at the intimation.

But whilst we acquiesce entirely in the permanence of natural laws, the question of the absolute existence of nature still remains open. It is the uniform effect of culture on the human mind, not to shake our faith in the stability of particular phenomena, as of heat, water, azote; but to lead us to regard nature as phenomenon, not a substance; to attribute necessary existence to spirit; to esteem nature as an accident and an effect.

To the senses and the unrenewed understanding, belongs a sort of instinctive belief in the absolute existence of nature. In their view man and nature are indissolubly joined. Things are ultimates, and they never look beyond their sphere. The presence of Reason mars this faith. The first effort of thought tends to relax this despotism of the senses which binds us to nature as if we were a part of it, and shows us nature aloof, and, as it were, afloat. Until this higher agency intervened, the animal eye sees, with wonderful accuracy, sharp outlines and colored surfaces. When the eye of Reason opens, to outline and surface are at once added grace and expression. These proceed from imagination and affection, and abate somewhat of the angular distinctness of objects. If the Reason be stimulated to more earnest vision, outlines and surfaces become transparent, and are no longer seen; causes and spirits are seen through them. The best moments of life are these delicious awakenings of the higher powers, and the reverential withdrawing of nature before its God.

Let us proceed to indicate the effects of culture.

1. Our first institution in the Ideal philosophy is a hint from Nature herself.

Nature is made to conspire with spirit to emancipate us. Certain mechanical changes, a small alteration in our local position, apprizes us of a dualism. We are strangely affected by seeing the shore from a moving ship, from a balloon, or through the tints of an unusual sky. The least change in our point of view gives the whole world a pictorial air. A man who seldom rides, needs only to get into a coach and traverse his own town, to turn the street into a puppet-show. The men, the women —talking, running, bartering, fighting—the earnest mechanic, the lounger, the beggar, the boys, the dogs, are unrealized at once, or, at least, wholly detached from all relation to the observer, and seen as apparent, not substantial beings. What new thoughts are suggested by seeing a face of country quite familiar, in the rapid movement of the railroad car! Nay, the most wonted objects (make a very slight change in the point of vision), please us most. In a camera obscura,[48] the butcher's cart, and the figure of one of our own family amuse us. So a portrait of a well-known face gratifies us. Turn the eyes upside down, by looking at the landscape through your

[48] Chamber into which an image is projected onto a wall; forerunner of the modern camera.

legs, and how agreeable is the picture, though you have seen it any time these twenty years!

In these cases, by mechanical means, is suggested the difference between the observer and the spectacle—between man and nature. Hence arises a pleasure mixed with awe; I may say, a low degree of the sublime is felt, from the fact, probably, that man is hereby apprized that whilst the world is a spectacle, something in himself is stable.

2. In a higher manner the poet communicates the same pleasure. By a few strokes he delineates, as on air, the sun, the mountain, the camp, the city, the hero, the maiden, not different from what we know them, but only lifted from the ground and afloat before the eye. He unfixes the land and the sea, makes them revolve around the axis of his primary thought, and disposes them anew. Possessed himself by a heroic passion, he uses matter as symbols of it. The sensual man conforms thoughts to things; the poet conforms things to his thoughts. The one esteems nature as rooted and fast; the other, as fluid, and impresses his being thereon. To him, the refractory world is ductile and flexible; he invests dust and stones with humanity, and makes them the words of the Reason. The Imagination may be defined to be the use which the Reason makes of the material world. Shakspeare possesses the power of subordinating nature for the purposes of expression, beyond all poets. His imperial muse tosses the creation like a bauble from hand to hand, and uses it to embody any caprice of thought that is uppermost in his mind. The remotest spaces of nature are visited, and the farthest sundered things are brought together, by a subtile spiritual connection. We are made aware that magnitude of material things is relative, and all objects shrink and expand to serve the passion of the poet. Thus in his sonnets, the lays of birds, the scents and dyes of flowers he finds to be the *shadow* of his beloved; time, which keeps her from him, is his *chest;* the suspicion she has awakened, is her *ornament;*

> The ornament of beauty is Suspect,
> A crow which flies in heaven's sweetest air.[49]

His passion is not the fruit of chance; it swells, as he speaks, to a city, or a state.

> No, it was builded far from accident;
> It suffers not in smiling pomp, nor falls
> Under the brow of thralling discontent;
> It fears not policy, that heretic,
> That works on leases of short numbered hours,
> But all alone stands hugely politic.[50]

In the strength of his constancy, the Pyramids seem to him recent and transitory. The freshness of youth and love dazzles him with its resemblance to morning;

> Take those lips away
> Which so sweetly were forsworn;
> And those eyes,—the break of day,
> Lights that do mislead the morn.[51]

---

[49] Shakespeare, *Sonnets,* LXX, ll. 3–4.
[50] Shakespeare, *Sonnets,* CXXIV, ll. 5–11.
[51] Shakespeare, *Measure for Measure,* Act IV, Sc. i, ll. 1–4.

The wild beauty of this hyperbole, I may say in passing, it would not be easy to match in literature.

This transfiguration which all material objects undergo through the passion of the poet—this power which he exerts to dwarf the great, to magnify the small—might be illustrated by a thousand examples from his Plays. I have before me the Tempest, and will cite only these few lines.

> ARIEL. The strong based promontory
> Have I made shake, and by the spurs plucked up
> The pine and cedar.

Prospero calls for music to soothe the frantic Alonzo, and his companions;

> A solemn air, and the best comforter
> To an unsettled fancy, cure thy brains
> Now useless, boiled within thy skull.

Again;

> The charm dissolves apace,
> And, as the morning steals upon the night,
> Melting the darkness, so their rising senses
> Begin to chase the ignorant fumes that mantle
> Their clearer reason.
> Their understanding
> Begins to swell: and the approaching tide
> Will shortly fill the reasonable shores
> That now lie foul and muddy.[52]

The perception of real affinities between events (that is to say, of *ideal* affinities, for those only are real), enables the poet thus to make free with the most imposing forms and phenomena of the world, and to assert the predominance of the soul.

3.   Whilst thus the poet animates nature with his own thoughts, he differs from the philosopher only herein, that the one proposes Beauty as his main end; the other Truth. But the philosopher, not less than the poet, postpones the apparent order and relations of things to the empire of thought. "The problem of philosophy," according to Plato, "is, for all that exists conditionally, to find a ground unconditioned and absolute."[53] It proceeds on the faith that a law determines all phenomena, which being known, the phenomena can be predicted. That law, when in the mind, is an idea. Its beauty is infinite. The true philosopher and the true poet are one, and a beauty, which is truth, and a truth, which is beauty, is the aim of both. Is not the charm of one of Plato's or Aristotle's definitions strictly like that of the Antigone of Sophocles? It is, in both cases, that a spiritual life has been imparted to nature; that the solid seeming

---

[52] Shakespeare, *The Tempest,* Act V, Sc. i, ll. 46–48, 58–60, 64–68, 79–82. Prospero, not Ariel, speaks the opening lines.

[53] Quotation from Plato's *Republic,* Book V. Emerson uses an abridged rendering from Coleridge's *The Friend* (1818).

block of matter has been pervaded and dissolved by a thought; that this feeble human being has penetrated the vast masses of nature with an informing soul, and recognized itself in their harmony, that is, seized their law. In physics, when this is attained, the memory disburthens itself of its cumbrous catalogues of particulars, and carries centuries of observation in a single formula.

Thus even in physics, the material is degraded before the spiritual. The astronomer, the geometer, rely on their irrefragable analysis, and disdain the results of observation. The sublime remark of Euler[54] on his law of arches, "This will be found contrary to all experience, yet is true;" had already transferred nature into the mind, and left matter like an outcast corpse.

4. Intellectual science has been observed to beget invariably a doubt of the existence of matter. Turgot[55] said, "He that has never doubted the existence of matter, may be assured he has no aptitude for metaphysical inquiries." It fastens the attention upon immortal necessary uncreated natures, that is, upon Ideas; and in their presence we feel that the outward circumstance is a dream and a shade. Whilst we wait in this Olympus of gods, we think of nature as an appendix to the soul. We ascend into their region, and know that these are the thoughts of the Supreme Being. "These are they who were set up from everlasting, from the beginning, or ever the earth was. When he prepared the heavens, they were there; when he established the clouds above, when he strengthened the fountains of the deep. Then they were by him, as one brought up with him. Of them took he counsel."[56]

Their influence is proportionate. As objects of science they are accessible to few men. Yet all men are capable of being raised by piety or by passion, into their region. And no man touches these divine natures, without becoming, in some degree, himself divine. Like a new soul, they renew the body. We become physically nimble and lightsome; we tread on air; life is no longer irksome, and we think it will never be so. No man fears age or misfortune or death in their serene company, for he is transported out of the district of change. Whilst we behold unveiled the nature of Justice and Truth, we learn the difference between the absolute and the conditional or relative. We apprehend the absolute. As it were, for the first time, *we exist.* We become immortal, for we learn that time and space are relations of matter; that with a perception of truth or a virtuous will they have no affinity.

5. Finally, religion and ethics, which may be fitly called the practice of ideas, or the introduction of ideas into life, have an analogous effect with all lower culture, in degrading nature and suggesting its dependence on spirit. Ethics and religion differ herein; that the one is the system of human duties commencing from man; the other, from God. Religion includes the personality of God; Ethics does not. They are one to our present design. They both put nature under foot. The first and last lesson of religion is, "The things that are seen, are temporal; the things that are unseen, are eternal."[57] It puts an affront upon nature. It does that for the unschooled, which

---

[54] Swiss mathematician Leonhard Euler (1707–1783).
[55] French statesman and economist Robert Jacques Turgot (1727–1781).

[56] Abbreviated version of Proverbs 8:23, 27, 28, 30.
[57] See 2 Corinthians 4:18.

philosophy does for Berkeley and Viasa.[58] The uniform language that may be heard in the churches of the most ignorant sects is—"Contemn the unsubstantial shows of the world; they are vanities, dreams, shadows, unrealities; seek the realities of religion." The devotee flouts nature. Some theosophists have arrived at a certain hostility and indignation towards matter, as the Manichean[59] and Plotinus.[60] They distrusted in themselves any looking back to these flesh-pots of Egypt.[61] Plotinus was ashamed of his body. In short, they might all say of matter, what Michael Angelo said of external beauty, "It is the frail and weary weed, in which God dresses the soul which he has called into time."[62]

It appears that motion, poetry, physical and intellectual science, and religion, all tend to affect our convictions of the reality of the external world. But I own there is something ungrateful in expanding too curiously the particulars of the general proposition, that all culture tends to imbue us with idealism. I have no hostility to nature, but a child's love to it. I expand and live in the warm day like corn and melons. Let us speak her fair. I do not wish to fling stones at my beautiful mother, nor soil my gentle nest. I only wish to indicate the true position of nature in regard to man, wherein to establish man all right education tends; as the ground which to attain is the object of human life, that is, of man's connection with nature. Culture inverts the vulgar view of nature, and brings the mind to call that apparent which it uses to call real, and that real which it uses to call visionary. Children, it is true, believe in the external world. The belief that it appears only, is an afterthought, but with culture this faith will as surely arise on the mind as did the first.

The advantage of the ideal theory over the popular faith is this, that it presents the world in precisely that view which is most desirable to the mind. It is, in fact, the view which Reason, both speculative and practical, that is, philosophy and virtue, take. For seen in the light of thought, the world always is phenomenal; and virtue subordinates it to the mind. Idealism sees the world in God. It beholds the whole circle of persons and things, of actions and events, of country and religion, not as painfully accumulated, atom after atom, act after act, in an aged creeping Past, but as one vast picture which God paints on the instant eternity for the contemplation of the soul. Therefore the soul holds itself off from a too trivial and microscopic study of the universal tablet. It respects the end too much to immerse itself in the means. It sees something more important in Christianity than the scandals of ecclesiastical history or the niceties of criticism; and, very incurious concerning persons or miracles, and not at all disturbed by chasms of historical evidence, it accepts from God the phenomenon, as it finds it, as the pure and awful form of religion in the world. It is not hot and passionate at the appearance of what it calls its own good or bad fortune, at the union or opposition of other persons. No man is its enemy. It accepts whatsoever befalls, as part of its lesson. It is a watcher more than a doer, and it is a doer, only that it may the better watch.

---

[58] Berkeley: George Berkeley (1685–1753), English churchman and philosophical idealist; Viyasa: proverbial Hindu philosopher.

[59] A disciple of Manes, third-century Christian sage who theorized that the evil of the body exists in duality with the goodness of the soul.

[60] Roman Neoplatonic philosopher (205?–?270).

[61] See Exodus 16:2–3.

[62] Michelangelo, *Sonnet* 51.

VII: Spirit

It is essential to a true theory of nature and of man, that it should contain[63] somewhat progressive. Uses that are exhausted or that may be, and facts that end in the statement, cannot be all that is true of this brave lodging wherein man is harbored, and wherein all his faculties find appropriate and endless exercise. And all the uses of nature admit of being summed in one, which yields the activity of man an infinite scope. Through all its kingdoms, to the suburbs and outskirts of things, it is faithful to the cause whence it had its origin. It always speaks of Spirit. It suggests the absolute. It is a perpetual effect. It is a great shadow pointing always to the sun behind us.

The aspect of Nature is devout. Like the figure of Jesus, she stands with bended head, and hands folded upon the breast. The happiest man is he who learns from nature the lesson of worship.

Of that ineffable essence which we call Spirit, he that thinks most, will say least. We can foresee God in the coarse, and, as it were, distant phenomena of matter; but when we try to define and describe himself, both language and thought desert us, and we are as helpless as fools and savages. That essence refuses to be recorded in propositions, but when man has worshipped him intellectually, the noblest ministry of nature is to stand as the apparition of God. It is the organ through which the universal spirit speaks to the individual, and strives to lead back the individual to it.

When we consider Spirit, we see that the views already presented do not include the whole circumference of man. We must add some related thoughts.

Three problems are put by nature to the mind: What is matter? Whence is it? and Whereto? The first of these questions only, the ideal theory answers. Idealism saith: matter is a phenomenon, not a substance. Idealism acquaints us with the total disparity between the evidence of our own being and the evidence of the world's being. The one is perfect; the other, incapable of any assurance; the mind is a part of the nature of things; the world is a divine dream, from which we may presently awake to the glories and certainties of day. Idealism is a hypothesis to account for nature by other principles than those of carpentry and chemistry. Yet, if it only deny the existence of matter, it does not satisfy the demands of the spirit. It leaves God out of me. It leaves me in the splendid labyrinth of my perceptions, to wander without end. Then the heart resists it, because it balks the affections in denying substantive being to men and women. Nature is so pervaded with human life that there is something of humanity in all and in every particular. But this theory makes nature foreign to me, and does not account for that consanguinity which we acknowledge to it.

Let it stand then, in the present state of our knowledge, merely as a useful introductory hypothesis, serving to apprize us of the eternal distinction between the soul and the world.

But when, following the invisible steps of thoughts, we come to inquire, Whence is matter? and Whereto? many truths arise to us out of the recesses of consciousness. We learn that the highest is present to the soul of man; that the dread universal essence, which is not wisdom, or love, or beauty, or power, but all in one, and each entirely, is that for which all things exist, and that by which they are; that spirit creates; that behind nature, throughout nature, spirit is present; one and not compound it does not

---

[63] Remain.

act upon us from without, that is, in space and time, but spiritually, or through ourselves: therefore, that spirit, that is, the Supreme Being, does not build up nature around us, but puts it forth through us, as the life of the tree puts forth new branches and leaves through the pores of the old. As a plant upon the earth, so a man rests upon the bosom of God; he is nourished by unfailing fountains, and draws at his need inexhaustible power. Who can set bounds to the possibilities of man? Once inhale the upper air, being admitted to behold the absolute natures of justice and truth, and we learn that man has access to the entire mind of the Creator, is himself the creator in the finite. This view, which admonishes me where the sources of wisdom and power lie, and points to virtue as to

"The golden key
Which opes the palace of eternity,"[64]

carries upon its face the highest certificate of truth, because it animates me to create my own world through the purification of my soul.

The world proceeds from the same spirit as the body of man. It is a remoter and inferior incarnation of God, a projection of God in the unconscious. But it differs from the body in one important respect. It is not, like that, now subjected to the human will. Its serene order is inviolable by us. It is, therefore, to us, the present expositor of the divine mind. It is a fixed point whereby we may measure our departure. As we degenerate, the contrast between us and our house is more evident. We are as much strangers in nature as we are aliens from God. We do not understand the notes of birds. The fox and the deer run away from us; the bear and tiger rend us. We do not know the uses of more than a few plants, as corn and the apple, the potato and the vine. Is not the landscape, every glimpse of which hath a grandeur, a face of him? Yet this may show us what discord is between man and nature, for you cannot freely admire a noble landscape if laborers are digging in the field hard by. The poet finds something ridiculous in his delight until he is out of the sight of men.

VIII: Prospects

In inquiries respecting the laws of the world and the frame of things, the highest reason is always the truest. That which seems faintly possible, it is so refined, is often faint and dim because it is deepest seated in the mind among the eternal verities. Empirical science is apt to cloud the sight, and by the very knowledge of functions and processes to bereave the student of the manly contemplation of the whole. The savant becomes unpoetic. But the best read naturalist who lends an entire and devout attention to truth, will see that there remains much to learn of his relation to the world, and that it is not to be learned by any addition or subtraction or other comparison of known quantities, but is arrived at by untaught sallies of the spirit, by a continual self-recovery, and by entire humility. He will perceive that there are far more excellent qualities in the student than preciseness and infallibility; that a guess is often more fruitful than an indisputable affirmation, and that a dream may let us deeper into the secret of nature than a hundred concerted experiments.

[64] John Milton, *Comus*, ll. 13–14.

For the problems to be solved are precisely those which the physiologist and the naturalist omit to state. It is not so pertinent to man to know all the individuals of the animal kingdom, as it is to know whence and whereto is this tyrannizing unity in his constitution, which evermore separates and classifies things, endeavoring to reduce the most diverse to one form. When I behold a rich landscape, it is less to my purpose to recite correctly the order and superposition of the strata, than to know why all thought of multitude is lost in a tranquil sense of unity. I cannot greatly honor minuteness in details, so long as there is no hint to explain the relation between things and thoughts; no ray upon the *metaphysics* of conchology, of botany, of the arts, to show the relation of the forms of flowers, shells, animals, architecture, to the mind, and build science upon ideas. In a cabinet of natural history,[65] we become sensible of a certain occult recognition and sympathy in regard to the most unwieldy and eccentric form of beast, fish, and insect. The American who has been confined, in his own country, to the sight of buildings designed after foreign models, is surprised on entering York Minster[66] or St. Peter's at Rome, by the feeling that these structures are imitations also—faint copies of an invisible archetype. Nor has science sufficient humanity, so long as the naturalist overlooks that wonderful congruity which subsists between man and the world; of which he is lord, not because he is the most subtile inhabitant, but because he is its head and heart, and finds something of himself in every great and small thing, in every mountain stratum, in every new law of color, fact of astronomy, or atmospheric influence which observation or analysis lays open. A perception of this mystery inspires the muse of George Herbert, the beautiful psalmist of the seventeenth century. The following lines are part of his little poem on Man.

Man is all symmetry,
Full of proportions, one limb to another,
And all to all the world besides.
Each part may call the farthest, brother;
For head with foot hath private amity,
And both with moons and tides.

Nothing hath got so far
But man hath caught and kept it as his prey;
His eyes dismount the highest star:
He is in little all the sphere.
Herbs gladly cure our flesh, because that they
Find their acquaintance there.

For us, the winds do blow,
The earth doth rest, heaven move, and fountains flow;
Nothing we see, but means our good,
As our delight, or as our treasure;
The whole is either our cupboard of food,
Or cabinet of pleasure.

[65] I.e., display case of biological specimens.   [66] Stately cathedral at York, England.

> The stars have us to bed:
> Night draws the curtain; which the sun withdraws.
> Music and light attend our head.
> All things unto our flesh are kind,
> In their descent and being; to our mind,
> In their ascent and cause.
>
> More servants wait on man
> Than he'll take notice of. In every path,
> He treads down that which doth befriend him
> When sickness makes him pale and wan.
> Oh mighty love! Man is one world, and hath
> Another to attend him.[67]

The perception of this class of truths makes the attraction which draws men to science, but the end is lost sight of in attention to the means. In view of this half-sight of science, we accept the sentence of Plato, that "poetry comes nearer to vital truth than history." Every surmise and vaticination of the mind is entitled to a certain respect, and we learn to prefer imperfect theories, and sentences which contain glimpses of truth, to digested systems which have no one valuable suggestion. A wise writer will feel that the ends of study and composition are best answered by announcing undiscovered regions of thought, and so communicating, through hope, new activity to the torpid spirit.

I shall therefore conclude this essay with some traditions of man and nature, which a certain poet[68] sang to me; and which, as they have always been in the world, and perhaps reappear to every bard, may be both history and prophecy.

"The foundations of man are not in matter, but in spirit. But the element of spirit is eternity. To it, therefore, the longest series of events, the oldest chronologies are young and recent. In the cycle of the universal man, from whom the known individuals proceed, centuries are points, and all history is but the epoch of one degradation.

"We distrust and deny inwardly our sympathy with nature. We own and disown our relation to it, by turns. We are like Nebuchadnezzar, dethroned, bereft of reason, and eating grass like an ox.[69] But who can set limits to the remedial force of spirit?

"A man is a god in ruin. When men are innocent, life shall be longer, and shall pass into the immortal as gently as we awake from dreams. Now, the world would be insane and rabid, if these disorganizations should last for hundreds of years. It is kept in check by death and infancy. Infancy is the perpetual Messiah, which comes into the arms of fallen men, and pleads with them to return to paradise.

"Man is the dwarf of himself. Once he was permeated and dissolved by spirit. He filled nature with his overflowing currents. Out from him sprang the sun and moon; from man the sun, from woman the moon. The laws of his mind, the periods of his actions externized themselves into day and night, into the year and the seasons. But,

---

[67] Stanzas 1–4 and 6 of "Man" (1633) by George Herbert (1593–1633), English poet.
[68] Perhaps Emerson himself, or Bronson Alcott (1799–1888), New England Transcendentalist and author of *Orphic Sayings* (1840).

[69] See Daniel 4:24–33. Nebuchadnezzar became irrational, "was driven from men, and did eat grass as oxen."

having made for himself this huge shell, his waters retired; he no longer fills the veins and veinlets; he is shrunk to a drop. He sees that the structure still fits him, but fits him colossally. Say, rather, once it fitted him, now it corresponds to him from far and on high. He adores timidly his own work. Now is man the follower of the sun, and woman the follower of the moon. Yet sometimes he starts in his slumber, and wonders at himself and his house, and muses strangely at the resemblance betwixt him and it. He perceives that if his law is still paramount, if still he have elemental power, if his word is sterling yet in nature, it is not conscious power, it is not inferior but superior to his will. It is instinct." Thus my Orphic[70] poet sang.

At present, man applies to nature but half his force. He works on the world with his understanding alone. He lives in it and masters it by a penny-wisdom; and he that works most in it is but a half-man, and whilst his arms are strong and his digestion good, his mind is imbruted, and he is a selfish savage. His relation to nature, his power over it, is through the understanding, as by manure; the economic use of fire, wind, water, and the mariner's needle; steam, coal, chemical agriculture; the repairs of the human body by the dentist and the surgeon. This is such a resumption of power as if a banished king should buy his territories inch by inch, instead of vaulting at once into his throne. Meantime, in the thick darkness, there are not wanting gleams of a better light—occasional examples of the action of man upon nature with his entire force—with reason as well as understanding. Such examples are, the traditions of miracles in the earliest antiquity of all nations; the history of Jesus Christ; the achievements of a principle, as in religious and political revolutions, and in the abolition of the slave-trade; the miracles of enthusiasm,[71] as those reported of Swedenborg, Hohenlohe, and the Shakers;[72] many obscure and yet contested facts, now arranged under the name of Animal Magnetism;[73] prayer; eloquence; self-healing; and the wisdom of children. These are examples of Reason's momentary grasp of the sceptre; the exertions of a power which exists not in time or space, but an instantaneous in-streaming causing power. The difference between the actual and the ideal force of man is happily figured by the schoolmen, in saying, that the knowledge of man is an evening knowledge, *vespertina cognitio,* but that of God is a morning knowledge, *matutina cognitio.*[74]

The problem of restoring to the world original and eternal beauty is solved by the redemption of the soul. The ruin or the blank that we see when we look at nature, is in our own eye. The axis of vision is not coincident with the axis of things, and so they appear not transparent but opaque. The reason why the world lacks unity, and lies broken and in heaps, is because man is disunited with himself. He cannot be a naturalist until he satisfies all the demands of the spirit. Love is as much its demand as perception. Indeed, neither can be perfect without the other. In the uttermost

---

[70] I.e., characteristic of mystic doctrines ascribed to Orpheus, poet of Greek mythology.
[71] Divine hysteria.
[72] Swedenborg: see note 27 above; Hohenlohe: Leopold Emmerich, German prince of Hohenlohe-Waldenberg-Schillingfurst (1794–1849), Catholic bishop and writer; Shakers: those affiliated with the millenial

church, which had its inception in England in 1747 and which was renowned for its frenzied dancing and prophetic manifestations in services.
[73] Hypnosis.
[74] Latin phrases attributable to academic philosophers of the Middle Ages, particularly St. Augustine and St. Thomas Aquinas.

meaning of the words thought is devout, and devotion is thought. Deep calls unto deep.[75] But in actual life, the marriage is not celebrated. There are innocent men who worship God after the tradition of their fathers, but their sense of duty has not yet extended to the use of all their faculties. And there are patient naturalists, but they freeze their subject under the wintry light of the understanding. Is not prayer also a study of truth—a sally of the soul into the unfound infinite? No man ever prayed heartily without learning something. But when a faithful thinker, resolute to detach every object from personal relations and see it in the light of thought, shall, at the same time, kindle science with the fire of the holiest affections, then will God go forth anew into the creation.

It will not need, when the mind is prepared for study, to search for objects. The invariable mark of wisdom is to see the miraculous in the common. What is a day? What is a year? What is summer? What is woman? What is a child? What is sleep? To our blindness, these things seem unaffecting. We make fables to hide the baldness of the fact and conform it, as we say, to the higher law of the mind. But when the fact is seen under the light of an idea, the gaudy fable fades and shrivels. We behold the real higher law. To the wise, therefore, a fact is true poetry, and the most beautiful of fables. These wonders are brought to our own door. You also are a man. Man and woman and their social life, poverty, labor, sleep, fear, fortune, are known to you. Learn that none of these things is superficial, but that each phenomenon has its roots in the faculties and affections of the mind. Whilst the abstract question occupies your intellect, nature brings it in the concrete to be solved by your hands. It were a wise inquiry for the closet, to compare, point by point, especially at remarkable crises in life, our daily history with the rise and progress of ideas in the mind.

So shall we come to look at the world with new eyes. It shall answer the endless inquiry of the intellect—What is truth? and of the affections—What is good? by yielding itself passive to the educated Will. Then shall come to pass what my poet said: "Nature is not fixed but fluid. Spirit alters, moulds, makes it. The immobility or bruteness of nature is the absence of spirit; to pure spirit it is fluid, it is volatile, it is obedient. Every spirit builds itself a house, and beyond its house a world, and beyond its world a heaven. Know then that the world exists for you. For you is the phenomenon perfect. What we are, that only can we see. All that Adam had, all that Cæsar could, you have and can do. Adam called his house, heaven and earth; Cæsar called his house, Rome; you perhaps call yours, a cobbler's trade; a hundred acres of ploughed land; or a scholar's garret. Yet line for line and point for point your dominion is as great as theirs, though without fine names. Build therefore your own world. As fast as you conform your life to the pure idea in your mind, that will unfold its great proportions. A correspondent revolution in things will attend the influx of the spirit. So fast will disagreeable appearances, swine, spiders, snakes, pests, mad-houses, prisons, enemies, vanish; they are temporary and shall be no more seen. The sordor and filths of nature, the sun shall dry up and the wind exhale. As when the summer comes from the south the snow-banks melt and the face of the earth becomes green before it, so shall the advancing spirit create its ornaments along its path, and carry with it the beauty it visits and the song which enchants it; it shall draw beautiful

[75] Psalm 42:7.

faces, warm hearts, wise discourse, and heroic acts, around its way, until evil is no more seen. The kingdom of man over nature, which cometh not with observation —a dominion such as now is beyond his dream of God—he shall enter without more wonder than the blind man feels who is gradually restored to sight."

1836

The American Scholar[*]

MR. PRESIDENT AND GENTLEMEN:

I greet you on the recommencement of our literary year.[1] Our anniversary is one of hope, and, perhaps, not enough of labor. We do not meet for games of strength or skill, for the recitation of histories, tragedies, and odes, like the ancient Greeks; for parliaments of love and poesy, like the Troubadours;[2] nor for the advancement of science, like our contemporaries in the British and European capitals. Thus far, our holiday has been simply a friendly sign of the survival of the love of letters amongst a people too busy to give to letters any more. As such it is precious as the sign of an indestructible instinct. Perhaps the time is already come when it ought to be, and will be, something else; when the sluggard intellect of this continent will look from under its iron lids and fill the postponed expectation of the world with something better than the exertions of mechanical skill. Our day of dependence, our long apprenticeship to the learning of other lands, draws to a close. The millions that around us are rushing into life, cannot always be fed on the sere remains of foreign harvests. Events, actions arise, that must be sung, that will sing themselves. Who can doubt that poetry will revive and lead in a new age, as the star in the constellation Harp,[3] which now flames in our zenith, astronomers announce, shall one day be the polestar[4] for a thousand years?

In this hope I accept the topic which not only usage but the nature of our association seem to prescribe to this day—the AMERICAN SCHOLAR. Year by year we come up hither to read one more chapter of his biography. Let us inquire what light new days and events have thrown on his character and his hopes.

It is one of those fables which out of an unknown antiquity convey an unlooked-for wisdom, that the gods, in the beginning, divided Man into men, that he might be more helpful to himself;[5] just as the hand was divided into fingers, the better to answer its end.

---

[*] This essay was first printed as a pamphlet entitled *Man Thinking: An Oration Delivered Before the Phi Beta Kappa Society, at Cambridge, August 31, 1837.* Emerson retitled it "The American Scholar" in *Essays* (1841) in order to address all students and anyone else committed to thought.
[1] The customary college year, beginning in September.

[2] Courtly poets of southern France in the twelfth and thirteenth centuries.
[3] The constellation referred to is Lyra, which includes the bright star Vega.
[4] The earth's axis points toward the North Star.
[5] The fable recalled by Emerson is from Plato's *Symposium.*

The old fable covers a doctrine ever new and sublime; that there is One Man—present to all particular men only partially, or through one faculty; and that you must take the whole society to find the whole man. Man is not a farmer, or a professor, or an engineer, but he is all. Man is priest, and scholar, and statesman, and producer, and soldier. In the *divided* or social state these functions are parcelled out to individuals, each of whom aims to do his stint of the joint work, whilst each other performs his. The fable implies that the individual, to possess himself, must sometimes return from his own labor to embrace all the other laborers. But, unfortunately, this original unit, this fountain of power, has been so distributed to multitudes, has been so minutely subdivided and peddled out, that it is spilled into drops, and cannot be gathered. The state of society is one in which the members have suffered amputation from the trunk, and strut about so many walking monsters—a good finger, a neck, a stomach, an elbow, but never a man.

Man is thus metamorphosed into a thing, into many things. The planter, who is Man sent out into the field to gather food, is seldom cheered by any idea of the true dignity of his ministry. He sees his bushel and his cart, and nothing beyond, and sinks into the farmer, instead of Man on the farm. The tradesman scarcely ever gives an ideal worth to his work, but is ridden by the routine of his craft, and the soul is subject to dollars. The priest becomes a form; the attorney a statute-book; the mechanic a machine; the sailor a rope of the ship.

In this distribution of functions the scholar is the delegated intellect. In the right state he is *Man Thinking.* In the degenerate state, when the victim of society, he tends to become a mere thinker, or still worse, the parrot of other men's thinking.

In this view of him, as Man Thinking, the theory of his office is contained. Him Nature solicits with all her placid, all her monitory pictures; him the past instructs; him the future invites. Is not indeed every man a student, and do not all things exist for the student's behoof? And, finally, is not the true scholar the only true master? But the old oracle said, "All things have two handles: beware of the wrong one." In life, too often, the scholar errs with mankind and forfeits his privilege. Let us see him in his school, and consider him in reference to the main influences he receives.

I.   The first in time and the first in importance of the influences upon the mind is that of nature. Every day, the sun; and, after sunset, Night and her stars. Ever the winds blow; ever the grass grows. Every day, men and women, conversing—beholding and beholden. The scholar is he of all men whom this spectacle most engages. He must settle its value in his mind. What is nature to him? There is never a beginning, there is never an end, to the inexplicable continuity of this web of God, but always circular power returning into itself. Therein it resembles his own spirit, whose beginning, whose ending, he never can find—so entire, so boundless. Far too as her splendors shine, system on system shooting like rays, upward, downward, without centre, without circumference—in the mass and in the particle, Nature hastens to render account of herself to the mind. Classification begins. To the young mind every thing is individual, stands by itself. By and by, it finds how to join two things and see in them one nature; then three, then three thousand; and so, tyrannized over by its own unifying instinct, it goes on tying things together, diminishing anomalies, discovering roots running under ground whereby contrary and remote things cohere and flower out from one stem. It presently learns that since the dawn of history there has been a constant accumulation and classifying of facts. But what is classification but the perceiving that these objects are not chaotic, and are not foreign, but have a law which is also a law of the human mind? The astronomer discovers that geometry, a pure abstraction of the human mind, is the measure of planetary motion. The chemist finds proportions and intelligible method throughout matter; and science is nothing but the finding of analogy, identity, in the most remote parts. The ambitious soul sits down before each refractory fact; one after another reduces all strange constitutions, all new powers, to their class and their law, and goes on forever to animate the last fibre of organization, the outskirts of nature, by insight.

Thus to him, to this schoolboy under the bending dome of day, is suggested that he and it proceed from one root; one is leaf and one is flower; relation, sympathy, stirring in every vein. And what is that root? Is not that the soul of his soul? A thought too bold; a dream too wild. Yet when this spiritual light shall have revealed the law of more earthly natures—when he has learned to worship the soul, and to see that the natural philosophy that now is, is only the first gropings of its gigantic hand, he shall look forward to an ever expanding knowledge as to a becoming creator. He shall see that nature is the opposite of the soul, answering to it part for part. One is seal and one is print. Its beauty is the beauty of his own mind. Its laws are the laws of his own mind. Nature then becomes to him the measure of his attainments. So much of nature as he is ignorant of, so much of his own mind does he not yet possess. And, in fine, the ancient precept, "Know thyself," and the modern precept, "Study nature," become at last one maxim.

II. The next great influence[6] into the spirit of the scholar is the mind of the Past —in whatever form, whether of literature, of art, of institutions, that mind is inscribed. Books are the best type of the influence of the past, and perhaps we shall get at the truth—learn the amount of this influence more conveniently—by considering their value alone.

The theory of books is noble. The scholar of the first age received into him the world around; brooded thereon; gave it the new arrangement of his own mind, and uttered it again. It came into him life; it went out from him truth. It came to him shortlived actions; it went out from him immortal thoughts. It came to him business; it went from him poetry. It was dead fact; now, it is quick[7] thought. It can stand, and it can go. It now endures, it now flies, it now inspires. Precisely in proportion to the depth of mind from which it issued, so high does it soar, so long does it sing.

Or, I might say, it depends on how far the process had gone, of transmuting life into truth. In proportion to the completeness of the distillation, so will the purity and imperishableness of the product be. But none is quite perfect. As no air-pump can by any means make a perfect vacuum, so neither can any artist entirely exclude the conventional, the local, the perishable from his book, or write a book of pure thought, that shall be as efficient, in all respects, to a remote posterity, as to contemporaries, or rather to the second age. Each age, it is found, must write its own books; or rather, each generation for the next succeeding. The books of an older period will not fit this.

Yet hence arises a grave mischief. The sacredness which attaches to the act of creation, the act of thought, is transferred to the record. The poet chanting was felt

---

[6] Inflowing, from the Latin verb *influere*.   [7] Active or living.

to be a divine man: henceforth the chant is divine also. The writer was a just and wise spirit: henceforward it is settled the book is perfect; as love of the hero corrupts into worship of his statue. Instantly the book becomes noxious: the guide is a tyrant. The sluggish and perverted mind of the multitude, slow to open to the incursions of Reason, having once so opened, having once received this book, stands upon it, and makes an outcry if it is disparaged. Colleges are built on it. Books are written on it by thinkers, not by Man Thinking; by men of talent, that is, who start wrong, who set out from accepted dogmas, not from their own sight of principles. Meek young men grow up in libraries, believing it their duty to accept the views which Cicero, which Locke, which Bacon[8] have given; forgetful that Cicero, Locke, and Bacon were only young men in libraries when they wrote these books.

Hence, instead of Man Thinking, we have the bookworm. Hence the book-learned class, who value books, as such; not as related to nature and the human constitution, but as making a sort of Third Estate[9] with the world and the soul. Hence the restorers of readings, the emendators, the bibliomaniacs of all degrees.

Books are the best of things, well used; abused, among the worst. What is the right use? What is the one end which all means go to effect? They are for nothing but to inspire. I had better never see a book than to be warped by its attraction clean out of my own orbit, and made a satellite instead of a system. The one thing in the world, of value, is the active soul. This every man is entitled to; this every man contains within him, although in almost all men obstructed and as yet unborn. The soul active sees absolute truth and utters truth, or creates. In this action it is genius; not the privilege of here and there a favorite, but the sound estate of every man. In its essence it is progressive. The book, the college, the school of art, the institution of any kind, stop with some past utterance of genius. This is good, say they—let us hold by this. They pin me down. They look backward and not forward. But genius looks forward: the eyes of man are set in his forehead, not in his hindhead: man hopes: genius creates. Whatever talents may be, if the man create not, the pure efflux of the Deity is not his; cinders and smoke there may be, but not yet flame. There are creative manners, there are creative actions, and creative words; manners, actions, words, that is, indicative of no custom or authority, but springing spontaneous from the mind's own sense of good and fair.

On the other part, instead of being its own seer, let it receive from another mind its truth, though it were in torrents of light, without periods of solitude, inquest, and self-recovery, and a fatal disservice is done. Genius is always sufficiently the enemy of genius by over-influence. The literature of every nation bears me witness. The English dramatic poets have Shakspearized now for two hundred years.

Undoubtedly there is a right way of reading, so it be sternly subordinated. Man Thinking must not be subdued by his instruments. Books are for the scholar's idle times. When he can read God directly, the hour is too precious to be wasted in other men's transcripts of their readings. But when the intervals of darkness come, as come

---

[8] Cicero: Marcus Tullius Cicero (106–43 B.C.), Roman statesman and orator; Locke: John Locke (1632–1704), English philosopher and political thinker; Bacon: Sir Francis Bacon (1561–1626), English statesman and pioneer of inductive science.

[9] Analogous to the third of three separate estates or classes that feudal Europe acknowledged: the clergy, the nobility, and the common people.

they must—when the sun is hid and the stars withdraw their shining—we repair to the lamps which were kindled by their ray, to guide our steps to the East again, where the dawn is. We hear, that we may speak. The Arabian proverb says, "A fig tree, looking on a fig tree, becometh fruitful."

It is remarkable, the character of the pleasure we derive from the best books. They impress us with the conviction that one nature wrote and the same reads. We read the verses of one of the great English poets, of Chaucer, of Marvell, of Dryden, with the most modern joy—with a pleasure, I mean, which is in great part caused by the abstraction of all *time* from their verses. There is some awe mixed with the joy of our surprise, when this poet, who lived in some past world, two or three hundred years ago, says that which lies close to my own soul, that which I also had well-nigh thought and said. But for the evidence thence afforded to the philosophical doctrine of the identity of all minds, we should suppose some preëstablished harmony, some foresight of souls that were to be, and some preparation of stores for their future wants, like the fact observed in insects, who lay up food before death for the young grub they shall never see.

I would not be hurried by any love of system, by any exaggeration of instincts, to underrate the Book. We all know, that as the human body can be nourished on any food, though it were boiled grass and the broth of shoes, so the human mind can be fed by any knowledge. And great and heroic men have existed who had almost no other information than by the printed page. I only would say that it needs a strong head to bear that diet. One must be an inventor to read well. As the proverb says, "He that would bring home the wealth of the Indies, must carry out the wealth of the Indies." There is then creative reading as well as creative writing. When the mind is braced by labor and invention, the page of whatever book we read becomes luminous with manifold allusion. Every sentence is doubly significant, and the sense of our author is as broad as the world. We then see, what is always true, that as the seer's hour of vision is short and rare among heavy days and months, so is its record, perchance, the least part of his volume. The discerning will read, in his Plato or Shakspeare, only that least part—only the authentic utterances of the oracles; all the rest he rejects, were it never so many times Plato's and Shakspeare's.

Of course there is a portion of reading quite indispensable to a wise man. History and exact science he must learn by laborious reading. Colleges, in like manner, have their indispensable office—to teach elements. But they can only highly serve us when they aim not to drill, but to create; when they gather from far every ray of various genius to their hospitable halls, and by the concentrated fires, set the hearts of their youth on flame. Thought and knowledge are natures in which apparatus and pretension avail nothing. Gowns and pecuniary foundations, though of towns of gold, can never countervail the least sentence or syllable of wit. Forget this, and our American colleges will recede in their public importance, whilst they grow richer every year.

III. There goes in the world a notion that the scholar should be a recluse, a valetudinarian—as unfit for any handiwork or public labor as a penknife for an axe. The so-called "practical men" sneer at speculative men, as if, because they speculate or *see,* they could do nothing. I have heard it said that the clergy—who are always, more universally than any other class, the scholars of their day—are addressed as women; that the rough, spontaneous conversation of men they do not hear, but only a mincing and diluted speech. They are often virtually disfranchised; and indeed there are advocates for their celibacy. As far as this is true of the studious classes, it is not just and wise. Action is with the scholar subordinate, but it is essential. Without it he is not yet man. Without it thought can never ripen into truth. Whilst the world hangs before the eye as a cloud of beauty, we cannot even see its beauty. Inaction is cowardice, but there can be no scholar without the heroic mind. The preamble of thought, the transition through which it passes from the unconscious to the conscious, is action. Only so much do I know, as I have lived. Instantly we know whose words are loaded with life, and whose not.

The world—this shadow of the soul, or *other me*—lies wide around. Its attractions are the keys which unlock my thoughts and make me acquainted with myself. I run eagerly into this resounding tumult. I grasp the hands of those next me, and take my place in the ring to suffer and to work, taught by an instinct that so shall the dumb abyss be vocal with speech. I pierce its order; I dissipate its fear; I dispose of it within the circuit of my expanding life. So much only of life as I know by experience, so much of the wilderness have I vanquished and planted, or so far have I extended my being, my dominion. I do not see how any man can afford, for the sake of his nerves and his nap, to spare any action in which he can partake. It is pearls and rubies to his discourse. Drudgery, calamity, exasperation, want, are instructors in eloquence and wisdom. The true scholar grudges every opportunity of action past by, as a loss of power. It is the raw material out of which the intellect moulds her splendid products. A strange process too, this by which experience is converted into thought, as a mulberry leaf is converted into satin.[10] The manufacture goes forward at all hours.

The actions and events of our childhood and youth are now matters of calmest observation. They lie like fair pictures in the air. Not so with our recent actions—with the business which we now have in hand. On this we are quite unable to speculate. Our affections as yet circulate through it. We no more feel or know it than we feel the feet, or the hand, or the brain of our body. The new deed is yet a part of life—remains for a time immersed in our unconscious life. In some contemplative hour it detaches itself from the life like a ripe fruit, to become a thought of the mind. Instantly it is raised, transfigured; the corruptible has put on incorruption.[11] Henceforth it is an object of beauty, however base its origin and neighborhood. Observe too the impossibility of antedating this act. In its grub state, it cannot fly, it cannot shine, it is a dull grub. But suddenly, without observation, the selfsame thing unfurls beautiful wings, and is an angel of wisdom. So is there no fact, no event, in our private history, which shall not, sooner or later, lose its adhesive, inert form, and astonish us by soaring from our body into the empyrean. Cradle and infancy, school and playground, the fear of boys, and dogs, and ferrules, the love of little maids and berries, and many another fact that once filled the whole sky, are gone already; friend and relative, profession and party, town and country, nation and world, must also soar and sing.

Of course, he who has put forth his total strength in fit actions has the richest return of wisdom. I will not shut myself out of this globe of action, and transplant an oak into a flowerpot, there to hunger and pine; nor trust the revenue of some single faculty, and exhaust one vein of thought, much like those Savoyards,[12] who, getting

---

[10] I.e., silk, which is produced by silkworms feeding on mulberry leaves.

[11] 1 Corinthians 15:53: "For this corruptible must put on incorruption, and this mortal must put on immortality."

[12] Residents of Savoy, now a province of France.

their livelihood by carving shepherds, shepherdesses, and smoking Dutchmen,[13] for all Europe, went out one day to the mountain to find stock, and discovered that they had whittled up the last of their pine trees. Authors we have, in numbers, who have written out their vein, and who, moved by a commendable prudence, sail for Greece or Palestine, follow the trapper into the prairie, or ramble round Algiers, to replenish their merchantable stock.

If it were only for a vocabulary, the scholar would be covetous of action. Life is our dictionary. Years are well spent in country labors; in town; in the insight into trades and manufactures; in frank intercourse with many men and women; in science; in art; to the one end of mastering in all their facts a language by which to illustrate and embody our perceptions. I learn immediately from any speaker how much he has already lived, through the poverty or the splendor of his speech. Life lies behind us as the quarry from whence we get tiles and copestones for the masonry of to-day. This is the way to learn grammar. Colleges and books only copy the language which the field and the work-yard made.

But the final value of action, like that of books, and better than books, is that it is a resource. That great principle of Undulation in nature, that shows itself in the inspiring and expiring of the breath; in desire and satiety; in the ebb and flow of the sea; in day and night; in heat and cold; and, as yet more deeply ingrained in every atom and every fluid, is known to us under the name of Polarity—these "fits of easy transmission and reflection," as Newton[14] called them, are the law of nature because they are the law of spirit.

The mind now thinks, now acts, and each fit reproduces the other. When the artist has exhausted his materials, when the fancy no longer paints, when thoughts are no longer apprehended and books are a weariness—he has always the resources to *live*. Character is higher than intellect. Thinking is the function. Living is the functionary. The stream retreats to its source. A great soul will be strong to live, as well as strong to think. Does he lack organ or medium to impart his truths? He can still fall back on this elemental force of living them. This is a total act. Thinking is a partial act. Let the grandeur of justice shine in his affairs. Let the beauty of affection cheer his lowly roof. Those "far from fame," who dwell and act with him, will feel the force of his constitution in the doings and passages of the day better than it can be measured by any public and designed display. Time shall teach him that the scholar loses no hour which the man lives. Herein he unfolds the sacred germ of his instinct, screened from influence. What is lost in seemliness is gained in strength. Not out of those on whom systems of education have exhausted their culture, comes the helpful giant to destroy the old or to build the new, but out of unhandselled[15] savage nature; out of terrible Druids and Berserkers[16] come at last Alfred[17] and Shakspeare.

I hear therefore with joy whatever is beginning to be said of the dignity and necessity of labor to every citizen. There is virtue yet in the hoe and the spade, for learned as well as for unlearned hands. And labor is everywhere welcome; always we

---

[13] I.e., pipes.
[14] From *Optics* by Sir Isaac Newton (1642–1727), English mathematician and philosopher.
[15] Ungrateful.
[16] Respectively, barbaric Celts and uncivilized warriors of Norse mythology.

[17] Alfred (849–901), king of the West Saxons, who instituted English laws and fostered literacy.

are invited to work; only be this limitation observed, that a man shall not for the sake of wider activity sacrifice any opinion to the popular judgments and modes of action.

I have now spoken of the education of the scholar by nature, by books, and by action. It remains to say somewhat of his duties.

They are such as become Man Thinking. They may all be comprised in self-trust. The office of the scholar is to cheer, to raise, and to guide men by showing them facts amidst appearances. He plies the slow, unhonored, and unpaid task of observation. Flamsteed and Herschel,[18] in their glazed observatories, may catalogue the stars with the praise of all men, and the results being splendid and useful, honor is sure. But he, in his private observatory, cataloguing obscure and nebulous stars of the human mind, which as yet no man has thought of as such—watching days and months sometimes for a few facts; correcting still his old records; must relinquish display and immediate fame. In the long period of his preparation he must betray often an ignorance and shiftlessness in popular arts, incurring the disdain of the able who shoulder him aside. Long he must stammer in his speech; often forego the living for the dead. Worse yet, he must accept—how often!—poverty and solitude. For the ease and pleasure of treading the old road, accepting the fashions, the education, the religion of society, he takes the cross of making his own, and, of course, the self-accusation, the faint heart, the frequent uncertainty and loss of time, which are the nettles and tangling vines in the way of the self-relying and self-directed; and the state of virtual hostility in which he seems to stand to society, and especially to educated society. For all this loss and scorn, what offset? He is to find consolation in exercising the highest functions of human nature. He is one who raises himself from private considerations and breathes and lives on public and illustrious thoughts. He is the world's eye. He is the world's heart. He is to resist the vulgar prosperity that retrogrades ever to barbarism, by preserving and communicating heroic sentiments, noble biographies, melodious verse, and the conclusions of history. Whatsoever oracles the human heart, in all emergencies, in all solemn hours, has uttered as its commentary on the world of actions—these he shall receive and impart. And whatsoever new verdict Reason from her inviolable seat pronounces on the passing men and events of to-day—this he shall hear and promulgate.

These being his functions, it becomes him to feel all confidence in himself, and to defer never to the popular cry. He and he only knows the world. The world of any moment is the merest appearance. Some great decorum, some fetish of a government, some ephemeral trade, or war, or man, is cried up by half mankind and cried down by the other half, as if all depended on this particular up or down. The odds are that the whole question is not worth the poorest thought which the scholar has lost in listening to the controversy. Let him not quit his belief that a popgun is a popgun, though the ancient and honorable of the earth affirm it to be the crack of doom. In silence, in steadiness, in severe abstraction, let him hold by himself; add observation to observation, patient of neglect, patient of reproach, and bide his own time—happy enough if he can satisfy himself alone that this day he has seen something truly. Success

[18] John Flamsteed (1646–1719) and Sir Frederick William Herschel (1738–1822), prominent English astronomers.

treads on every right step. For the instinct is sure, that prompts him to tell his brother what he thinks. He then learns that in going down into the secrets of his own mind he has descended into the secrets of all minds. He learns that he who has mastered any law in his private thoughts, is master to that extent of all men whose language he speaks, and of all into whose language his own can be translated. The poet, in utter solitude remembering his spontaneous thoughts and recording them, is found to have recorded that which men in crowded cities find true for them also. The orator distrusts at first the fitness of his frank confessions, his want of knowledge of the persons he addresses, until he finds that he is the complement of his hearers; that they drink his words because he fulfils for them their own nature; the deeper he dives into his privatest, secretest presentiment, to his wonder he finds this is the most acceptable, most public, and universally true. The people delight in it; the better part of every man feels, This is my music; this is myself.

In self-trust all the virtues are comprehended. Free should the scholar be—free and brave. Free even to the definition of freedom, "without any hindrance that does not arise out of his own constitution." Brave; for fear is a thing which a scholar by his very function puts behind him. Fear always springs from ignorance. It is a shame to him if his tranquillity, amid dangerous times, arise from the presumption that like children and women his is a protected class; or if he seek a temporary peace by the diversion of his thoughts from politics or vexed questions, hiding his head like an ostrich in the flowering bushes, peeping into microscopes, and turning rhymes, as a boy whistles to keep his courage up. So is the danger a danger still; so is the fear worse. Manlike let him turn and face it. Let him look into its eye and search its nature, inspect its origin—see the whelping of this lion—which lies no great way back; he will then find in himself a perfect comprehension of its nature and extent; he will have made his hands meet on the other side, and can henceforth defy it and pass on superior. The world is his who can see through its pretension. What deafness, what stone-blind custom, what overgrown error you behold is there only by sufferance—by your sufferance. See it to be a lie, and you have already dealt it its mortal blow.

Yes, we are the cowed—we the trustless. It is a mischievous notion that we are come late into nature; that the world was finished a long time ago. As the world was plastic and fluid in the hands of God, so it is ever to so much of his attributes as we bring to it. To ignorance and sin, it is flint. They adapt themselves to it as they may; but in proportion as a man has any thing in him divine, the firmament flows before him and takes his signet and form. Not he is great who can alter matter, but he who can alter my state of mind. They are the kings of the world who give the color of their present thought to all nature and all art, and persuade men by the cheerful serenity of their carrying the matter, that this thing which they do is the apple which the ages have desired to pluck, now at last ripe, and inviting nations to the harvest. The great man makes the great thing. Wherever Macdonald sits, there is the head of the table.[19] Linnaeus makes botany the most alluring of studies, and wins it from the farmer and the herb-woman; Davy, chemistry; and Cuvier,[20] fossils. The day is always his who works in it with serenity and great aims. The unstable estimates of men crowd

---

[19] Emerson's version of a proverb of the time.
[20] Linnaeus: Swedish botanist Carolus Linnaeus (1707–1778); Davy: English chemist Sir

Humphrey Davy (1778–1829); Cuvier: French naturalist Georges Cuvier (1769–1832).

to him whose mind is filled with a truth, as the heaped waves of the Atlantic follow the moon.

For this self-trust, the reason is deeper than can be fathomed—darker than can be enlightened. I might not carry with me the feeling of my audience in stating my own belief. But I have already shown the ground of my hope, in adverting to the doctrine that man is one. I believe man has been wronged; he has wronged himself. He has almost lost the light that can lead him back to his prerogatives. Men are become of no account. Men in history, men in the world of to-day, are bugs, are spawn, and are called "the mass" and "the herd." In a century, in a millennium, one or two men; that is to say, one or two approximations to the right state of every man. All the rest behold in the hero or the poet their own green and crude being—ripened; yes, and are content to be less, so *that* may attain to its full stature. What a testimony, full of grandeur, full of pity, is borne to the demands of his own nature, by the poor clansman, the poor partisan, who rejoices in the glory of his chief. The poor and the low find some amends to their immense moral capacity, for their acquiescence in a political and social inferiority. They are content to be brushed like flies from the path of a great person, so that justice shall be done by him to that common nature which it is the dearest desire of all to see enlarged and glorified. They sun themselves in the great man's light, and feel it to be their own element. They cast the dignity of man from their downtrod selves upon the shoulders of a hero, and will perish to add one drop of blood to make that great heart beat, those giant sinews combat and conquer. He lives for us, and we live in him.

Men, such as they are, very naturally seek money or power; and power because it is as good as money—the "spoils," so called, "of office." And why not? for they aspire to the highest, and this, in their sleep-walking, they dream is highest. Wake them and they shall quit the false good and leap to the true, and leave governments to clerks and desks. This revolution is to be wrought by the gradual domestication of the idea of Culture. The main enterprise of the world for splendor, for extent, is the upbuilding of a man. Here are the materials strewn along the ground. The private life of one man shall be a more illustrious monarchy, more formidable to its enemy, more sweet and serene in its influence to its friend, than any kingdom in history. For a man, rightly viewed, comprehendeth the particular natures of all men. Each philosopher, each bard, each actor has only done for me, as by a delegate, what one day I can do for myself. The books which once we valued more than the apple of the eye, we have quite exhausted. What is that but saying that we have come up with the point of view which the universal mind took through the eyes of one scribe; we have been that man, and have passed on. First, one, then another, we drain all cisterns, and waxing greater by all these supplies, we crave a better and more abundant food. The man has never lived that can feed us ever. The human mind cannot be enshrined in a person who shall set a barrier on any one side to this unbounded, unboundable empire. It is one central fire, which, flaming now out of the lips of Etna,[21] lightens the capes of Sicily, and now out of the throat of Vesuvius,[22] illuminates the towers and vineyards of Naples. It is one light which beams out of a thousand stars. It is one soul which animates all men.

But I have dwelt perhaps tediously upon this abstraction of the Scholar. I ought

---

[21] Active volcano in Sicily.   [22] Volcano in Italy.

not to delay longer to add what I have to say of nearer reference to the time and to this country.

Historically, there is thought to be a difference in the ideas which predominate over successive epochs, and there are data for marking the genius of the Classic, of the Romantic, and now of the Reflective or Philosophical age. With the views I have intimated of the oneness or the identity of the mind through all individuals, I do not much dwell on these differences. In fact, I believe each individual passes through all three. The boy is a Greek; the youth, romantic; the adult, reflective. I deny not, however, that a revolution in the leading idea may be distinctly enough traced.

Our age is bewailed as the age of Introversion. Must that needs be evil? We, it seems, are critical; we are embarrassed with second thoughts; we cannot enjoy any thing for hankering to know whereof the pleasure consists; we are lined with eyes; we see with our feet; the time is infected with Hamlet's unhappiness—

"Sicklied o'er with the pale cast of thought."[23]

It is so bad then? Sight is the last thing to be pitied. Would we be blind? Do we fear lest we should outsee nature and God, and drink truth dry? I look upon the discontent of the literary class as a mere announcement of the fact that they find themselves not in the state of mind of their fathers, and regret the coming state as untried; as a boy dreads the water before he has learned that he can swim. If there is any period one would desire to be born in, is it not the age of Revolution; when the old and the new stand side by side and admit of being compared; when the energies of all men are searched by fear and by hope; when the historic glories of the old can be compensated by the rich possibilities of the new era? This time, like all times, is a very good one, if we but know what to do with it.

I read with some joy of the auspicious signs of the coming days, as they glimmer already through poetry and art, through philosophy and science, through church and state.

One of these signs is the fact that the same movement which effected the elevation of what was called the lowest class in the state, assumed in literature a very marked and as benign an aspect. Instead of the sublime and beautiful, the near, the low, the common, was explored and poetized. That which had been negligently trodden under foot by those who were harnessing and provisioning themselves for long journeys into far countries, is suddenly found to be richer than all foreign parts. The literature of the poor, the feelings of the child, the philosophy of the street, the meaning of household life, are the topics of the time. It is a great stride. It is a sign—is it not? —of new vigor when the extremities are made active, when currents of warm life run into the hands and the feet. I ask not for the great, the remote, the romantic; what is doing in Italy or Arabia; what is Greek art, or Provencal minstrelsy;[24] I embrace the common, I explore and sit at the feet of the familiar, the low. Give me insight into to-day, and you may have the antique and future worlds. What would we really know the meaning of? The meal in the firkin; the milk in the pan; the ballad in the

---

[23] Shakespeare's *Hamlet*, Act III, Sc. i, l. 85.
[24] The troubadors of the late Middle Ages

established Provence in southeast France as a cultural center.

street; the news of the boat; the glance of the eye; the form and the gait of the body; show me the ultimate reason of these matters; show me the sublime presence of the highest spiritual cause lurking, as always it does lurk, in these suburbs and extremities of nature; let me see every trifle bristling with the polarity that ranges it instantly on an eternal law; and the shop, the plough, and the ledger referred to the like cause by which light undulates and poets sing; and the world lies no longer a dull miscellany and lumber-room,[25] but has form and order; there is no trifle, there is no puzzle, but one design unites and animates the farthest pinnacle and the lowest trench.

This idea has inspired the genius of Goldsmith, Burns, Cowper, and, in a newer time, of Goethe, Wordsworth, and Carlyle. This idea they have differently followed and with various success. In contrast with their writing, the style of Pope, of Johnson, of Gibbon, looks cold and pedantic. This writing is blood-warm. Man is surprised to find that things near are not less beautiful and wondrous than things remote. The near explains the far. The drop is a small ocean. A man is related to all nature. This perception of the worth of the vulgar is fruitful in discoveries. Goethe, in this very thing the most modern of the moderns, has shown us, as none ever did, the genius of the ancients.

There is one man of genius who has done much for this philosophy of life, whose literary value has never yet been rightly estimated; I mean Emanuel Swedenborg.[26] The most imaginative of men, yet writing with the precision of a mathematician, he endeavored to engraft a purely philosophical Ethics on the popular Christianity of his time. Such an attempt of course must have difficulty which no genius could surmount. But he saw and showed the connection between nature and the affections of the soul. He pierced the emblematic or spiritual character of the visible, audible, tangible word. Especially did his shade-loving muse hover over and interpret the lower parts of nature; he showed the mysterious bond that allies moral evil to the foul material forms, and has given in epical parables a theory of insanity, of beasts, of unclean and fearful things.

Another sign of our times, also marked by an analogous political movement, is the new importance given to the single person. Every thing that tends to insulate the individual—to surround him with barriers of natural respect, so that each man shall feel the world is his, and man shall treat with man as a sovereign state with a sovereign state—tends to true union as well as greatness. "I learned," said the melancholy Pestalozzi,[27] "that no man in God's wide earth is either willing or able to help any other man." Help must come from the bosom alone. The scholar is that man who must take up into himself all the ability of the time, all the contributions of the past, all the hopes of the future. He must be an university of knowledges. If there be one lesson more than another which should pierce his ear, it is, The world is nothing, the man is all; in yourself is the law of all nature, and you know not yet how a globule of sap ascends; in yourself slumbers the whole of Reason; it is for you to know all; it is for you to dare all. Mr. President and Gentlemen, this confidence in the unsearched might of man belongs, by all motives, by all prophecy, by all preparation, to the American Scholar. We have listened too long to the courtly muses of Europe. The spirit of the American free-man is already suspected to be timid, imitative, tame.

---

[25] Room for storage.
[26] Swedish scientist and theologian (1688–1772).

[27] Swiss educational theorist Johann Heinrich Pestalozzi (1746–1826).

Public and private avarice make the air we breathe thick and fat. The scholar is decent, indolent, complaisant. See already the tragic consequence. The mind of this country, taught to aim at low objects, eats upon itself. There is no work for any but the decorous and the complaisant. Young men of the fairest promise, who begin life upon our shores, inflated by the mountain winds, shined upon by all the stars of God, find the earth below not in unison with these, but are hindered from action by the disgust which the principles on which business is managed inspire, and turn drudges, or die of disgust, some of them suicides. What is the remedy? They did not yet see, and thousands of young men as hopeful now crowding to the barriers for the career do not yet see, that if the single man plant himself indomitably on his instincts, and there abide, the huge world will come round to him. Patience—patience; with the shades of all the good and great for company; and for solace the perspective of your own infinite life; and for work the study and the communication of principles, the making those instincts prevalent, the conversion of the world. Is it not the chief disgrace in the world, not to be an unit; not to be reckoned one character; not to yield that peculiar fruit which each man was created to bear, but to be reckoned in the gross, in the hundred, or the thousand, of the party, the section, to which we belong; and our opinion predicted geographically, as the north, or the south? Not so, brothers and friends—please God, ours shall not be so. We will walk on our own feet; we will work with our own hands; we will speak our own minds. The study of letters shall be no longer a name for pity, for doubt, and for sensual indulgence. The dread of man and the love of man shall be a wall of defence and a wreath of joy around all. A nation of men will for the first time exist, because each believes himself inspired by the Divine Soul which also inspires all men.

1837

An Address*

In this refulgent summer, it has been a luxury to draw the breath of life. The grass grows, the buds burst, the meadow is spotted with fire and gold in the tint of flowers. The air is full of birds, and sweet with the breath of the pine, the balm-of-Gilead,[1] and the new hay. Night brings no gloom to the heart with its welcome shade. Through the transparent darkness the stars pour their almost spiritual rays. Man under them seems a young child, and his huge globe a toy. The cool night bathes the world as with a river, and prepares his eyes again for the crimson dawn. The mystery of nature was never displayed more happily. The corn and the wine have been freely dealt to all creatures, and the never-broken silence with which the old bounty goes forward

---

* Soon after it was delivered, Emerson's lecture was published as *An Address Delivered Before the Senior Class in Divinity College, Cambridge, Sunday Evening 15 July 1838.* His criticism of traditional Christianity so offended the religious establishment at Harvard that he was not invited to speak there again for 30 years.

[1] Fragrant evergreen tree.

has not yielded yet one word of explanation. One is constrained to respect the perfection of this world in which our senses converse. How wide; how rich; what invitation from every property it gives to every faculty of man! In its fruitful soils; in its navigable sea; in its mountains of metal and stone; in its forests of all woods; in its animals; in its chemical ingredients; in the powers and path of light, heat, attraction and life, it is well worth the pith and heart of great men to subdue and enjoy it. The planters, the mechanics, the inventors, the astronomers, the builders of cities, and the captains, history delights to honor.

But when the mind opens and reveals the laws which traverse the universe and make things what they are, then shrinks the great world at once into a mere illustration and fable of this mind. What am I? and What is? asks the human spirit with a curiosity new-kindled, but never to be quenched. Behold these outrunning laws, which our imperfect apprehension can see tend this way and that, but not come full circle. Behold these infinite relations, so like, so unlike; many, yet one. I would study, I would know, I would admire forever. These works of thought have been the entertainments of the human spirit in all ages.

A more secret, sweet, and overpowering beauty appears to man when his heart and mind open to the sentiment of virtue. Then he is instructed in what is above him. He learns that his being is without bound; that to the good, to the perfect, he is born, low as he now lies in evil and weakness. That which he venerates is still his own, though he has not realized it yet. *He ought.* He knows the sense of that grand word, though his analysis fails to render account of it. When in innocency or when by intellectual perception he attains to say—"I love the Right; Truth is beautiful within and without for evermore. Virtue, I am thine; save me; use me; thee will I serve, day and night, in great, in small, that I may be not virtuous, but virtue;" then is the end of the creation answered, and God is well pleased.

The sentiment of virtue is a reverence and delight in the presence of certain divine laws. It perceives that this homely game of life we play, covers, under what seem foolish details, principles that astonish. The child amidst his baubles is learning the action of light, motion, gravity, muscular force; and in the game of human life, love, fear, justice, appetite, man, and God, interact. These laws refuse to be adequately stated. They will not be written out on paper, or spoken by the tongue. They elude our persevering thought; yet we read them hourly in each other's faces, in each other's actions, in our own remorse. The moral traits which are all globed into every virtuous act and thought—in speech we must sever, and describe or suggest by painful enumeration of many particulars. Yet, as this sentiment is the essence of all religion, let me guide your eye to the precise objects of the sentiment, by an enumeration of some of those classes of facts in which this element is conspicuous.

The intuition of the moral sentiment is an insight of the perfection of the laws of the soul. These laws execute themselves. They are out of time, out of space, and not subject to circumstance. Thus in the soul of man there is a justice whose retributions are instant and entire. He who does a good deed is instantly ennobled. He who does a mean deed is by the action itself contracted. He who puts off impurity, thereby puts on purity. If a man is at heart just, then in so far is he God; the safety of God, the immortality of God, the majesty of God do enter into that man with justice. If a man dissemble, deceive, he deceives himself, and goes out of acquaintance with his own being. A man in the view of absolute goodness, adores, with total humility.

Every step so downward, is a step upward. The man who renounces himself, comes to himself.

See how this rapid intrinsic energy worketh everywhere, righting wrongs, correcting appearances, and bringing up facts to a harmony with thoughts. Its operation in life, though slow to the senses, is at last as sure as in the soul. By it a man is made the Providence to himself, dispensing good to his goodness, and evil to his sin. Character is always known. Thefts never enrich; alms never impoverish; murder will speak out of stone walls. The least admixture of a lie—for example, the taint of vanity, any attempt to make a good impression, a favorable appearance—will instantly vitiate the effect. But speak the truth, and all nature and all spirits help you with unexpected furtherance. Speak the truth, and all things alive or brute are vouchers, and the very roots of the grass underground there do seem to stir and move to bear you witness. See again the perfection of the Law as it applies itself to the affections, and becomes the law of society. As we are, so we associate. The good, by affinity, seek the good; the vile, by affinity, the vile. Thus of their own volition, souls proceed into heaven, into hell.

These facts have always suggested to man the sublime creed that the world is not the product of manifold power, but of one will, of one mind; and that one mind is everywhere active, in each ray of the star, in each wavelet of the pool; and whatever opposes that will is everywhere balked and baffled, because things are made so, and not otherwise. Good is positive. Evil is merely privative, not absolute: it is like cold, which is the privation of heat. All evil is so much death or nonentity. Benevolence is absolute and real. So much benevolence as a man hath, so much life hath he. For all things proceed out of this same spirit, which is differently named love, justice, temperance, in its different applications, just as the ocean receives different names on the several shores which it washes. All things proceed out of the same spirit, and all things conspire with it. Whilst a man seeks good ends, he is strong by the whole strength of nature. In so far as he roves from these ends, he bereaves himself of power, or auxiliaries; his being shrinks out of all remote channels, he becomes less and less, a mote, a point, until absolute badness is absolute death.

The perception of this law of laws awakens in the mind a sentiment which we call the religious sentiment, and which makes our highest happiness. Wonderful is its power to charm and to command. It is a mountain air. It is the embalmer of the world. It is myrrh and storax, and chlorine and rosemary. It makes the sky and the hills sublime, and the silent song of the stars is it. By it is the universe made safe and habitable, not by science or power. Thought may work cold and intransitive in things, and find no end or unity; but the dawn of the sentiment of virtue on the heart, gives and is the assurance that Law is sovereign over all natures; and the worlds, time, space, eternity, do seem to break out into joy.

This sentiment is divine and deifying. It is the beatitude of man. It makes him illimitable. Through it, the soul first knows itself. It corrects the capital mistake of the infant man, who seeks to be great by following the great, and hopes to derive advantages *from another*—by showing the fountain of all good to be in himself, and that he, equally with every man, is an inlet into the deeps of Reason. When he says, "I ought;" when love warms him; when he chooses, warned from on high, the good and great deed; then, deep melodies wander through his soul from Supreme Wisdom. Then he can worship, and be enlarged by his worship; for he can never go behind this sentiment. In the sublimest flights of the soul, rectitude is never surmounted, love is never outgrown.

This sentiment lies at the foundation of society, and successively creates all forms of worship. The principle of veneration never dies out. Man fallen into superstition, into sensuality, is never quite without the visions of the moral sentiment. In like manner, all the expressions of this sentiment are sacred and permanent in proportion to their purity. The expressions of this sentiment affect us more than all other compositions. The sentences of the oldest time, which ejaculate this piety, are still fresh and fragrant. This thought dwelled always deepest in the minds of men in the devout and contemplative East; not alone in Palestine, where it reached its purest expression, but in Egypt, in Persia, in India, in China. Europe has always owed to oriental genius its divine impulses. What these holy bards said, all sane men found agreeable and true. And the unique impression of Jesus upon mankind, whose name is not so much written as ploughed into the history of this world, is proof of the subtle virtue of this infusion.

Meantime, whilst the doors of the temple stand open, night and day, before every man, and the oracles of this truth cease never, it is guarded by one stern condition; this, namely. it is an intuition. It cannot be received at second hand. Truly speaking, it is not instruction, but provocation, that I can receive from another soul. What he announces, I must find true in me, or reject; and on his word, or as his second, be he who he may, I can accept nothing. On the contrary, the absence of this primary faith is the presence of degradation. As is the flood, so is the ebb. Let this faith depart, and the very words it spake and the things it made become false and hurtful. Then falls the church, the state, art, letters, life. The doctrine of the divine nature being forgotten, a sickness infects and dwarfs the constitution. Once man was all; now he is an appendage, a nuisance. And because the indwelling Supreme Spirit cannot wholly be got rid of, the doctrine of it suffers this perversion, that the divine nature is attributed to one or two persons, and denied to all the rest, and denied with fury. The doctrine of inspiration is lost; the base doctrine of the majority of voices usurps the place of the doctrine of the soul. Miracles, prophecy, poetry, the ideal life, the holy life, exist as ancient history merely; they are not in the belief, nor in the aspiration of society; but, when suggested, seem ridiculous. Life is comic or pitiful as soon as the high ends of being fade out of sight, and man becomes near-sighted, and can only attend to what addresses the senses.

These general views, which, whilst they are general, none will contest, find abundant illustration in the history of religion, and especially in the history of the Christian church. In that, all of us have had our birth and nurture. The truth contained in that, you, my young friends, are now setting forth to teach. As the Cultus, or established worship of the civilized world, it has great historical interest for us. Of its blessed words, which have been the consolation of humanity, you need not that I should speak. I shall endeavor to discharge my duty to you on this occasion, by pointing out two errors in its administration, which daily appear more gross from the point of view we have just now taken.

Jesus Christ belonged to the true race of prophets. He saw with open eye the mystery of the soul. Drawn by its severe harmony, ravished with its beauty, he lived in it, and had his being there. Alone in all history he estimated the greatness of man. One man was true to what is in you and me. He saw that God incarnates himself in man, and evermore goes forth anew to take possession of his World. He said, in this jubilee of sublime emotion, 'I am divine. Through me, God acts; through me, speaks. Would you see God, see me; or see thee, when thou also thinkest as I now think.' But what a distortion did his doctrine and memory suffer in the same, in the next, and the following ages! There is no doctrine of the Reason which will bear to be taught by the Understanding.[2] The understanding caught this high chant from the poet's lips, and said, in the next age, 'This was Jehovah come down out of heaven. I will kill you, if you say he was a man.' The idioms of his language and the figures of his rhetoric have usurped the place of his truth; and churches are not built on his principles, but on his tropes. Christianity became a Mythus,[3] as the poetic teaching of Greece and of Egypt, before. He spoke of miracles; for he felt that man's life was a miracle, and all that man doth, and he knew that this daily miracle shines as the character ascends. But the word Miracle, as pronounced by Christian churches, gives a false impression; it is Monster. It is not one with the blowing clover and the falling rain.

He felt respect for Moses and the prophets, but no unfit tenderness at postponing their initial revelations to the hour and the man that now is; to the eternal revelation in the heart. Thus was he a true man. Having seen that the law in us is commanding, he would not suffer it to be commanded. Boldly, with hand, and heart, and life, he declared it was God. Thus is he, as I think, the only soul in history who has appreciated the worth of man.

1. In this point of view we become sensible of the first defect of historical Christianity. Historical Christianity has fallen into the error that corrupts all attempts to communicate religion. As it appears to us, and as it has appeared for ages, it is not the doctrine of the soul, but an exaggeration of the personal, the positive, the ritual. It has dwelt, it dwells, with noxious exaggeration about the *person* of Jesus. The soul knows no persons. It invites every man to expand to the full circle of the universe, and will have no preferences but those of spontaneous love. But by this eastern monarchy of a Christianity, which indolence and fear have built, the friend of man is made the injurer of man. The manner in which his name is surrounded with expressions which were once sallies of admiration and love, but are now petrified into official titles, kills all generous sympathy and liking. All who hear me, feel that the language that describes Christ to Europe and America is not the style of friendship and enthusiasm to a good and noble heart, but is appropriated and formal—paints a demigod, as the Orientals or the Greeks would describe Osiris or Apollo.[4] Accept the injurious impositions of our early catechetical instruction,[5] and even honesty and self-denial were but splendid sins, if they did not wear the Christian name. One would rather be

"A pagan, suckled in a creed outworn,"[6]

[2] Throughout his works, Emerson uses "Reason" to mean knowledge derived from intuition and "Understanding" to mean knowledge derived from logic.

[3] Deliberately promoted cult.

[4] Osiris: Egyptian fertility god; Apollo: Greek god of the sun.

[5] Technique of religious instruction employing dogmatic questions and answers.

[6] From the sonnet "The World Is Too Much with Us" (1807) by William Wordsworth (1770–1850).

than to be defrauded of his manly right in coming into nature and finding not names and places, not land and professions, but even virtue and truth foreclosed and monopolized. You shall not be a man even. You shall not own the world; you shall not dare and live after the infinite Law that is in you, and in company with the infinite Beauty which heaven and earth reflect to you in all lovely forms; but you must subordinate your nature to Christ's nature; you must accept our interpretations, and take his portrait as the vulgar draw it.

That is always best which gives me to myself. The sublime is excited in me by the great stoical doctrine, Obey thyself. That which shows God in me, fortifies me. That which shows God out of me, makes me a wart and a wen. There is no longer a necessary reason for my being. Already the long shadows of untimely oblivion creep over me, and I shall decrease forever.

The divine bards are the friends of my virtue, of my intellect, of my strength. They admonish me that the gleams which flash across my mind are not mine, but God's; that they had the like, and were not disobedient to the heavenly vision.[7] So I love them. Noble provocations go out from them, inviting me to resist evil; to subdue the world; and to Be. And thus, by his holy thoughts, Jesus serves us, and thus only. To aim to convert a man by miracles is a profanation of the soul. A true conversion, a true Christ, is now, as always, to be made by the reception of beautiful sentiments. It is true that a great and rich soul, like his, falling among the simple, does so preponderate, that, as his did, it names the world. The world seems to them to exist for him, and they have not yet drunk so deeply of his sense as to see that only by coming again to themselves, or to God in themselves, can they grow for evermore. It is a low benefit to give me something; it is a high benefit to enable me to do somewhat of myself. The time is coming when all men will see that the gift of God to the soul is not a vaunting, overpowering, excluding sanctity, but a sweet, natural goodness, a goodness like thine and mine, and that so invites thine and mine to be and to grow.

The injustice of the vulgar tone of preaching is not less flagrant to Jesus than to the souls which it profanes. The preachers do not see that they make his gospel not glad, and shear him of the locks of beauty and the attributes of heaven. When I see a majestic Epaminondas,[8] or Washington; when I see among my contemporaries a true orator, an upright judge, a dear friend; when I vibrate to the melody and fancy of a poem; I see beauty that is to be desired. And so lovely, and with yet more entire consent of my human being, sounds in my ear the severe music of the bards that have sung of the true God in all ages. Now do not degrade the life and dialogues of Christ out of the circle of this charm, by insulation and peculiarity. Let them lie as they befell, alive and warm, part of human life and the landscape and the cheerful day.

2. The second defect of the traditionary and limited way of using the mind of Christ is a consequence of the first; this, namely; that the Moral Nature, that Law of laws whose revelations introduce greatness—yea, God himself—into the open soul, is not explored as the fountain of the established teaching in society. Men have come to speak of the revelation as somewhat long ago given and done, as if God were dead.

---

[7] See Acts 26:19: "I was not disobedient unto the heavenly vision."

[8] Greek statesman and general instrumental in ending Sparta's dominance in Greece.

The injury to faith throttles the preacher; and the goodliest of institutions becomes an uncertain and inarticulate voice.

It is very certain that it is the effect of conversation with the beauty of the soul, to beget a desire and need to impart to others the same knowledge and love. If utterance is denied, the thought lies like a burden on the man. Always the seer is a sayer. Somehow his dream is told; somehow he publishes it with solemn joy: sometimes with pencil on canvas, sometimes with chisel on stone, sometimes in towers and aisles of granite, his soul's worship is builded; sometimes in anthems of indefinite music; but clearest and most permanent, in words.

The man enamored of this excellency becomes its priest or poet. The office is coeval with the world. But observe the condition, the spiritual limitation of the office. The spirit only can teach. Not any profane man, not any sensual, not any liar, not any slave can teach, but only he can give, who has; he only can create, who is. The man on whom the soul descends, through whom the soul speaks, alone can teach. Courage, piety, love, wisdom, can teach; and every man can open his door to these angels, and they shall bring him the gift of tongues. But the man who aims to speak as books enable, as synods use, as the fashion guides, and as interest commands, babbles. Let him hush.

To this holy office you propose to devote yourselves. I wish you may feel your call in throbs of desire and hope. The office is the first in the world. It is of that reality that it cannot suffer the deduction of any falsehood. And it is my duty to say to you that the need was never greater of new revelation than now. From the views I have already expressed, you will infer the sad conviction, which I share, I believe, with numbers, of the universal decay and now almost death of faith in society. The soul is not preached. The Church seems to totter to its fall, almost all life extinct. On this occasion, any complaisance would be criminal which told you, whose hope and commission it is to preach the faith of Christ, that the faith of Christ is preached.

It is time that this ill-suppressed murmur of all thoughtful men against the famine of our churches; this moaning of the heart because it is bereaved of the consolation, the hope, the grandeur that come alone out of the culture of the moral nature—should be heard through the sleep of indolence, and over the din of routine. This great and perpetual office of the preacher is not discharged. Preaching is the expression of the moral sentiment in application to the duties of life. In how many churches, by how many prophets, tell me, is man made sensible that he is an infinite Soul; that the earth and heavens are passing into his mind; that he is drinking forever the soul of God? Where now sounds the persuasion, that by its very melody imparadises my heart, and so affirms its own origin in heaven? Where shall I hear words such as in elder ages drew men to leave all and follow—father and mother, house and land, wife and child?[9] Where shall I hear these august laws of moral being so pronounced as to fill my ear, and I feel ennobled by the offer of my uttermost action and passion? The test of the true faith, certainly, should be its power to charm and command the soul, as the laws of nature control the activity of the hands—so commanding that we find pleasure and honor in obeying. The faith should blend with the light of rising and of setting suns,

---

[9] See Matthew 19:28–29: "And Jesus said unto them, . . . every one that hath forsaken houses, or brethren, or sisters, or father, or mother, or wife, or children, or lands, for my name's sake, shall receive an hundredfold, and shall inherit everlasting life."

with the flying cloud, the singing bird, and the breath of flowers. But now the priest's Sabbath has lost the splendor of nature; it is unlovely; we are glad when it is done; we can make, we do make, even sitting in our pews, a far better, holier, sweeter, for ourselves.

Whenever the pulpit is usurped by a formalist, then is the worshipper defrauded and disconsolate. We shrink as soon as the prayers begin, which do not uplift, but smite and offend us. We are fain to wrap our cloaks about us, and secure, as best we can, a solitude that hears not. I once heard a preacher who sorely tempted me to say I would go to church no more. Men go, thought I, where they are wont to go, else had no soul entered the temple in the afternoon. A snow-storm was falling around us. The snow-storm was real, the preacher merely spectral, and the eye felt the sad contrast in looking at him, and then out of the window behind him into the beautiful meteor of the snow. He had lived in vain. He had no one word intimating that he had laughed or wept, was married or in love, had been commended, or cheated, or chagrined. If he had ever lived and acted, we were none the wiser for it. The capital secret of his profession, namely, to convert life into truth, he had not learned. Not one fact in all his experience had he yet imported into his doctrine. This man had ploughed and planted and talked and bought and sold; he had read books; he had eaten and drunken; his head aches, his heart throbs; he smiles and suffers; yet was there not a surmise, a hint, in all the discourse, that he had ever lived at all. Not a line did he draw out of real history. The true preacher can be known by this, that he deals out to the people his life—life passed through the fire of thought. But of the bad preacher, it could not be told from his sermon what age of the world he fell in; whether he had a father or a child; whether he was a freeholder or a pauper; whether he was a citizen or a countryman; or any other fact of his biography. It seemed strange that the people should come to church. It seemed as if their houses were very unentertaining, that they should prefer this thoughtless clamor. It shows that there is a commanding attraction in the moral sentiment, that can lend a faint tint of light to dulness and ignorance coming in its name and place. The good hearer is sure he has been touched sometimes; is sure there is somewhat to be reached, and some word that can reach it. When he listens to these vain words, he comforts himself by their relation to his remembrance of better hours, and so they clatter and echo unchallenged.

I am not ignorant that when we preach unworthily, it is not always quite in vain. There is a good ear, in some men, that draws supplies to virtue out of very indifferent nutriment. There is poetic truth concealed in all the commonplaces of prayer and of sermons, and though foolishly spoken, they may be wisely heard; for each is some select expression that broke out in a moment of piety from some stricken or jubilant soul, and its excellency made it remembered. The prayers and even the dogmas of our church are like the zodiac of Denderah[10] and the astronomical monuments of the Hindoos, wholly insulated from anything now extant in the life and business of the people. They mark the height to which the waters once rose. But this docility is a check upon the mischief from the good and devout. In a large portion of the community, the religious service gives rise to quite other thoughts and emotions. We

---

[10] Ancient city in Egypt and place of worship of the goddess Hathor, where a zodiacal table is displayed in an ancient ruined temple.

need not chide the negligent servant. We are struck with pity, rather, at the swift retribution of his sloth. Alas for the unhappy man that is called to stand in the pulpit, and *not* give bread of life. Everything that befalls, accuses him. Would he ask contributions for the missions, foreign or domestic? Instantly his face is suffused with shame, to propose to his parish that they should send money a hundred or a thousand miles, to furnish such poor fare as they have at home and would do well to go the hundred or the thousand miles to escape. Would he urge people to a godly way of living; and can he ask a fellow-creature to come to Sabbath meetings, when he and they all know what is the poor uttermost they can hope for therein? Will he invite them privately to the Lord's Supper?[11] He dares not. If no heart warm this rite, the hollow, dry, creaking formality is too plain, than that he can face a man of wit and energy and put the invitation without terror. In the street, what has he to say to the bold village blasphemer? The village blasphemer sees fear in the face, form, and gait of the minister.

Let me not taint the sincerity of this plea by any oversight of the claims of good men. I know and honor the purity and strict conscience of numbers of the clergy. What life the public worship retains, it owes to the scattered company of pious men, who minister here and there in the churches, and who, sometimes accepting with too great tenderness the tenet of the elders, have not accepted from others, but from their own heart, the genuine impulses of virtue, and so still command our love and awe, to the sanctity of character. Moreover, the exceptions are not so much to be found in a few eminent preachers, as in the better hours, the truer inspirations of all—nay, in the sincere moments of every man. But, with whatever exception, it is still true that tradition characterizes the preaching of this country; that it comes out of the memory, and not out of the soul; that it aims at what is usual, and not at what is necessary and eternal; that thus historical Christianity destroys the power of preaching, by withdrawing it from the exploration of the moral nature of man; where the sublime is, where are the resources of astonishment and power. What a cruel injustice it is to that Law, the joy of the whole earth, which alone can make thought dear and rich; that Law whose fatal sureness the astronomical orbits poorly emulate; that it is travestied and depreciated, that it is behooted and behowled, and not a trait, not a word of it articulated. The pulpit in losing sight of this Law, loses its reason, and gropes after it knows not what. And for want of this culture the soul of the community is sick and faithless. It wants nothing so much as a stern, high, stoical, Christian discipline, to make it know itself and the divinity that speaks through it. Now man is ashamed of himself; he skulks and sneaks through the world, to be tolerated, to be pitied, and scarcely in a thousand years does any man dare to be wise and good, and so draw after him the tears and blessings of his kind.

Certainly there have been periods when, from the inactivity of the intellect on certain truths, a greater faith was possible in names and persons. The Puritans in England and America found in the Christ of the Catholic Church and in the dogmas inherited from Rome, scope for their austere piety and their longings for civil freedom. But their creed is passing away, and none arises in its room. I think no man can go with his thoughts about him into one of our churches, without feeling that

[11] In 1832 Emerson decided to resign as minister of the Second Church of Boston after losing faith in the special graces of the sacrament of Holy Communion.

what hold the public worship had on men is gone, or going. It has lost its grasp on the affection of the good and the fear of the bad. In the country, neighborhoods, half parishes are *signing off*, to use the local term. It is already beginning to indicate character and religion to withdraw from the religious meetings. I have heard a devout person, who prized the Sabbath, say in bitterness of heart, "On Sundays, it seems wicked to go to church." And the motive that holds the best there is now only a hope and a waiting. What was once a mere circumstance, that the best and the worst men in the parish, the poor and the rich, the learned and the ignorant, young and old, should meet one day as fellows in one house, in sign of an equal right in the soul, has come to be a paramount motive for going thither.

My friends, in these two errors, I think, I find the causes of a decaying church and a wasting unbelief. And what greater calamity can fall upon a nation than the loss of worship? Then all things go to decay. Genius leaves the temple to haunt the senate or the market. Literature becomes frivolous. Science is cold. The eye of youth is not lighted by the hope of other worlds, and age is without honor. Society lives to trifles, and when men die we do not mention them.

And now, my brothers, you will ask, What in these desponding days can be done by us? The remedy is already declared in the ground of our complaint of the Church. We have contrasted the Church with the Soul. In the soul then let the redemption be sought. Wherever a man comes, there comes revolution. The old is for slaves. When a man comes, all books are legible, all things transparent, all religions are forms. He is religious. Man is the wonderworker. He is seen amid miracles. All men bless and curse. He saith yea and nay, only. The stationariness of religion; the assumption that the age of inspiration is past, that the Bible is closed; the fear of degrading the character of Jesus by representing him as a man; indicate with sufficient clearness the falsehood of our theology. It is the office of a true teacher to show us that God is, not was; that He speaketh, not spake. The true Christianity—a faith like Christ's in the infinitude of men—is lost. None believeth in the soul of man, but only in some man or person old and departed. Ah me! no man goeth alone. All men go in flocks to this saint or that poet, avoiding the God who seeth in secret. They cannot see in secret; they love to be blind in public. They think society wiser than their soul, and know not that one soul, and their soul, is wiser than the whole world. See how nations and races flit by on the sea of time and leave no ripple to tell where they floated or sunk, and one good soul shall make the name of Moses, or of Zeno, or of Zoroaster,[12] reverend forever. None assayeth the stern ambition to be the Self of the nation and of nature, but each would be an easy secondary to some Christian scheme, or sectarian connection, or some eminent man. Once leave your own knowledge of God, your own sentiment, and take secondary knowledge, as St. Paul's, or George Fox's, or Swedenborg's,[13] and you get wide from God with every year this secondary form lasts, and if, as now, for centuries—the chasm yawns to that breadth, that men can scarcely be convinced there is in them anything divine.

Let me admonish you, first of all, to go alone; to refuse the good models, even

---

[12] Zeno: Greek philosopher Zeno of Citium (ca. 334–262 B.C.), founder of Stoicism; Zoroaster: religious reformer of ancient Persia (ca. 628–552 B.C.) and founder of Zoroastrianism.

[13] George Fox: English founder (1624–1691), of the Society of Friends (Quakers); Swedenborg: Emanuel Swedenborg (1688–1722), Swedish philosopher and theologian.

those which are sacred in the imagination of men, and dare to love God without mediator or veil. Friends enough you shall find who will hold up to your emulation Wesleys and Oberlins,[14] Saints and Prophets. Thank God for these good men, but say, 'I also am a man.' Imitation cannot go above its model. The imitator dooms himself to hopeless mediocrity. The inventor did it because it was natural to him, and so in him it has a charm. In the imitator something else is natural, and he bereaves himself of his own beauty, to come short of another man's.

Yourself a newborn bard of the Holy Ghost, cast behind you all conformity, and acquaint men at first hand with Deity. Look to it first and only, that fashion, custom, authority, pleasure, and money, are nothing to you—are not bandages over your eyes, that you cannot see—but live with the privilege of the immeasurable mind. Not too anxious to visit periodically all families and each family in your parish connection —when you meet one of these men or women, be to them a divine man; be to them thought and virtue; let their timid aspirations find in you a friend; let their trampled instincts be genially tempted out in your atmosphere; let their doubts know that you have doubted, and their wonder feel that you have wondered. By trusting your own heart, you shall gain more confidence in other men. For all our penny-wisdom, for all our soul-destroying slavery to habit, it is not to be doubted that all men have sublime thoughts; that all men value the few real hours of life; they love to be heard; they love to be caught up into the vision of principles. We mark with light in the memory the few interviews we have had, in the dreary years of routine and of sin, with souls that made our souls wiser; that spoke what we thought; that told us what we knew; that gave us leave to be what we inly were. Discharge to men the priestly office, and, present or absent, you shall be followed with their love as by an angel.

And, to this end, let us not aim at common degrees of merit. Can we not leave, to such as love it, the virtue that glitters for the commendation of society, and ourselves pierce the deep solitudes of absolute ability and worth? We easily come up to the standard of goodness in society. Society's praise can be cheaply secured, and almost all men are content with those easy merits; but the instant effect of conversing with God will be to put them away. There are persons who are not actors, not speakers, but influences; persons too great for fame, for display; who disdain eloquence; to whom all we call art and artist, seems too nearly allied to show and by-ends, to the exaggeration of the finite and selfish, and loss of the universal. The orators, the poets, the commanders encroach on us only as fair women do, by our allowance and homage. Slight them by preoccupation of mind, slight them, as you can well afford to do, by high and universal aims, and they instantly feel that you have right, and that it is in lower places that they must shine. They also feel your right; for they with you are open to the influx of the all-knowing Spirit, which annihilates before its broad noon the little shades and gradations of intelligence in the compositions we call wiser and wisest.

In such high communion let us study the grand strokes of rectitude: a bold benevolence, an independence of friends, so that not the unjust wishes of those who love us shall impair our freedom, but we shall resist for truth's sake the freest flow

---

[14] Wesley: English preacher John Wesley (1703–1791) or his brother Charles (1707–1788), founders of Methodism; Oberlin: Lutheran preacher Jean Frederic Oberlin (1740–1826), innovator in children's education.

of kindness, and appeal to sympathies far in advance; and—what is the highest form in which we know this beautiful element—a certain solidity of merit, that has nothing to do with opinion, and which is so essentially and manifestly virtue, that it is taken for granted that the right, the brave, the generous step will be taken by it, and nobody thinks of commending it. You would compliment a coxcomb doing a good act, but you would not praise an angel. The silence that accepts merit as the most natural thing in the world, is the highest applause. Such souls, when they appear, are the Imperial Guard of Virtue, the perpetual reserve, the dictators of fortune. One needs not praise their courage—they are the heart and soul of nature. O my friends, there are resources in us on which we have not drawn. There are men who rise refreshed on hearing a threat; men to whom a crisis which intimidates and paralyzes the majority—demanding not the faculties of prudence and thrift but comprehension, immovableness, the readiness of sacrifice—comes graceful and beloved as a bride. Napoleon said of Massena,[15] that he was not himself until the battle began to go against him; then, when the dead began to fall in ranks around him, awoke his powers of combination, and he put on terror and victory as a robe. So it is in rugged crises, in unweariable endurance, and in aims which put sympathy out of question that the angel is shown. But these are heights that we can scarce remember and look up to without contrition and shame. Let us thank God that such things exist.

And now let us do what we can to rekindle the smouldering, nigh quenched fire on the altar. The evils of the church that now is are manifest. The question returns, What shall we do? I confess, all attempts to project and establish a Cultus with new rites and forms, seem to me vain. Faith makes us, and not we it, and faith makes its own forms. All attempts to contrive a system are as cold as the new worship introduced by the French to the goddess of Reason—to-day, pasteboard and filigree, and ending to-morrow in madness and murder. Rather let the breath of new life be breathed by you through the forms already existing. For if once you are alive, you shall find they shall become plastic and new. The remedy to their deformity is first, soul, and second, soul, and evermore, soul. A whole popedom[16] of forms one pulsation of virtue can uplift and vivify. Two inestimable advantages Christianity has given us; first the Sabbath, the jubilee of the whole world, whose light dawns welcome alike into the closet of the philosopher, into the garret of toil, and into prison-cells, and everywhere suggests, even to the vile, the dignity of spiritual being. Let it stand forevermore, a temple, which new love, new faith, new sight shall restore to more than its first splendor to mankind. And secondly, the institution of preaching—the speech of man to men—essentially the most flexible of all organs, of all forms. What hinders that now, everywhere, in pulpits, in lecture-rooms, in houses, in fields, wherever the invitation of men or your own occasions lead you, you speak the very truth, as your life and conscience teach it, and cheer the waiting, fainting hearts of men with new hope and new revelation?

I look for the hour when that supreme Beauty which ravished the souls of those Eastern men, and chiefly of those Hebrews, and through their lips spoke oracles to all time, shall speak in the West also. The Hebrew and Greek Scriptures contain

[15] André Massena (1758–1817), marshal of Napoleon's empire.

[16] I.e., inflexible hierarchy.

immortal sentences, that have been bread of life to millions. But they have no epical integrity; are fragmentary; are not shown in their order to the intellect. I look for the new Teacher that shall follow so far those shining laws that he shall see them come full circle; shall see their rounding complete grace; shall see the world to be the mirror of the soul; shall see the identity of the law of gravitation with purity of heart; and shall show that the Ought, that Duty, is one thing with Science, with Beauty, and with Joy.

1838

Self-Reliance

"Ne te quæsiveris extra."[1]

"Man is his own star; and the soul that can
Render an honest and a perfect man,
Commands all light, all influence, all fate;
Nothing to him falls early or too late.
Our acts our angels are, or good or ill,
Our fatal shadows that walk by us still."
Epilogue to Beaumont and Fletcher's
Honest Man's Fortune[2]

Cast the bantling[3] *on the rocks,*
Suckle him with the she-wolf's teat;
Wintered with the hawk and fox,
Power and speed be hands and feet.[4]

I read the other day some verses written by an eminent painter[5] which were original and not conventional. The soul always hears an admonition in such lines, let the subject be what it may. The sentiment they instil is of more value than any thought they may contain. To believe your own thought, to believe that what is true for you in your private heart, is true for all men,—that is genius. Speak your latent conviction and it shall be the universal sense; for the inmost in due time becomes the outmost, —and our first thought is rendered back to us by the trumpets of the Last Judgment. Familiar as the voice of the mind is to each, the highest merit we ascribe to Moses, Plato, and Milton, is that they set at naught books and traditions, and spoke not what men wrote but what they thought. A man should learn to detect and watch that gleam of light which flashes across his mind from within, more than the lustre of the firmament of bards and sages. Yet he dismisses without notice his thought, because it is his. In every work of genius we recognize our own rejected thoughts: they come back to us with a certain alienated majesty. Great works of art have no more affecting lesson for us than this. They teach us to abide by our spontaneous impression with

---

[1] Latin: "Do not seek outside yourself."
[2] Elizabethan playwrights Francis Beaumont (1584–1616) and John Fletcher (1579–1625) were authors of *Honest Man's Fortune* (1647).

[3] Infant.
[4] Emerson's own verses.
[5] Most likely the American painter and poet Washington Allston (1779–1843).

good-humored inflexibility then most when the whole cry of voices is on the other side. Else, to-morrow a stranger will say with masterly good sense precisely what we have thought and felt all the time, and we shall be forced to take with shame our own opinion from another.

There is a time in every man's education when he arrives at the conviction that envy is ignorance; that imitation is suicide; that he must take himself for better, for worse, as his portion; that though the wide universe is full of good, no kernel of nourishing corn can come to him but through his toil bestowed on that plot of ground which is given to him to till. The power which resides in him is new in nature, and none but he knows what that is which he can do, nor does he know until he has tried. Not for nothing one face, one character, one fact makes much impression on him, and another none. This sculpture in the memory is not without preëstablished harmony. The eye was placed where one ray should fall, that it might testify of that particular ray. We but half express ourselves, and are ashamed of that divine idea which each of us represents. It may be safely trusted as proportionate and of good issues, so it be faithfully imparted, but God will not have his work made manifest by cowards. A man is relieved and gay when he has put his heart into his work and done his best; but what he has said or done otherwise, shall give him no peace. It is a deliverance which does not deliver. In the attempt his genius deserts him; no muse befriends; no invention, no hope.

Trust thyself: every heart vibrates to that iron string. Accept the place the divine Providence has found for you; the society of your contemporaries, the connexion of events. Great men have always done so and confided themselves childlike to the genius of their age, betraying their perception that the absolutely trustworthy was seated at their heart, working through their hands, predominating in all their being. And we are now men, and must accept in the highest mind the same transcendent destiny; and not minors and invalids in a protected corner, not cowards fleeing before a revolution, but guides, redeemers, and benefactors, obeying the Almighty effort, and advancing on Chaos and the Dark.

What pretty oracles nature yields us on this text in the face and behavior of children, babes and even brutes. That divided and rebel mind, that distrust of a sentiment because our arithmetic has computed the strength and means opposed to our purpose, these have not. Their mind being whole, their eye is as yet unconquered, and when we look in their faces, we are disconcerted. Infancy conforms to nobody: all conform to it, so that one babe commonly makes four or five out of the adults who prattle and play to it. So God has armed youth and puberty and manhood no less with its own piquancy and charm, and made it enviable and gracious and its claims not to be put by, if it will stand by itself. Do not think the youth has no force because he cannot speak to you and me. Hark! in the next room his voice is sufficiently clear and emphatic. It seems he knows how to speak to his contemporaries. Bashful or bold, then, he will know how to make us seniors very unnecessary.

The nonchalance of boys who are sure of a dinner, and would disdain as much as a lord to do or say aught to conciliate one, is the healthy attitude of human nature. A boy is in the parlour what the pit[6] is in the playhouse; independent, irre-

---

[6] Least expensive section of older theaters, where the audience was often clamorous and unrestrained.

sponsible, looking out from his corner on such people and facts as pass by, he tries and sentences them on their merits, in the swift summary way of boys, as good, bad, interesting, silly, eloquent, troublesome. He cumbers himself never about consequences, about interests: he gives an independent, genuine verdict. You must court him: he does not court you. But the man is, as it were, clapped into jail by his consciousness. As soon as he has once acted or spoken with eclat, he is a committed person, watched by the sympathy or the hatred of hundreds whose affections must now enter into his account. There is no Lethe[7] for this. Ah, that he could pass again into his neutrality! Who can thus avoid all pledges, and having observed, observe again from the same unaffected, unbiassed, unbribable, unaffrighted innocence, must always be formidable. He would utter opinions on all passing affairs, which being seen to be not private but necessary, would sink like darts into the ear of men, and put them in fear.

These are the voices which we hear in solitude, but they grow faint and inaudible as we enter into the world. Society everywhere is in conspiracy against the manhood of every one of its members. Society is a joint-stock company in which the members agree for the better securing of his bread to each shareholder, to surrender the liberty and culture of the eater. The virtue in most request is conformity. Self-reliance is its aversion. It loves not realities and creators, but names and customs.

Whoso would be a man must be a nonconformist. He who would gather immortal palms must not be hindered by the name of goodness, but must explore if it be goodness. Nothing is at last sacred but the integrity of your own mind. Absolve you to yourself, and you shall have the suffrage of the world. I remember an answer which when quite young I was prompted to make to a valued adviser who was wont to importune me with the dear old doctrines of the church. On my saying, What have I to do with the sacredness of traditions, if I live wholly from within? my friend suggested—"But these impulses may be from below, not from above." I replied, "They do not seem to me to be such; but if I am the Devil's child, I will live then from the Devil." No law can be sacred to me but that of my nature. Good and bad are but names very readily transferable to that or this; the only right is what is after my constitution, the only wrong what is against it. A man is to carry himself in the presence of all opposition as if everything were titular and ephemeral but he. I am ashamed to think how easily we capitulate to badges and names, to large societies and dead institutions. Every decent and well-spoken individual affects and sways me more than is right. I ought to go upright and vital, and speak the rude truth in all ways. If malice and vanity wear the coat of philanthropy, shall that pass? If an angry bigot assumes this bountiful cause of Abolition, and comes to me with his last news from Barbadoes,[8] why should I not say to him, "Go love thy infant; love thy wood-chopper: be good-natured and modest: have that grace; and never varnish your hard, uncharitable ambition with this incredible tenderness for black folk a thousand miles off. Thy love afar is spite at home." Rough and graceless would be such greeting, but truth is handsomer than the affectation of love. Your goodness must have some edge to it —else it is none. The doctrine of hatred must be preached as the counteraction of the doctrine of love when that pules and whines. I shun father and mother and wife and

---

[7] River in Greek mythology that causes forgetfulness.

[8] In 1834 slavery was officially abolished on this island (Barbados) in the British West Indies.

brother, when my genius calls me. I would write on the lintels of the door-post, *Whim.*[9] I hope it is somewhat better than whim at last, but we cannot spend the day in explanation. Expect me not to show cause why I seek or why I exclude company. Then, again, do not tell me, as a good man did to-day, of my obligation to put all poor men in good situations. Are they *my* poor? I tell thee, thou foolish philanthropist, that I grudge the dollar, the dime, the cent I give to such men as do not belong to me and to whom I do not belong. There is a class of persons to whom by all spiritual affinity I am bought and sold; for them I will go to prison, if need be; but your miscellaneous popular charities; the education at college of fools; the building of meeting-houses to the vain end to which many now stand; alms to sots; and the thousandfold Relief Societies;—though I confess with shame I sometimes succumb and give the dollar, it is a wicked dollar which by and by I shall have the manhood to withhold.

Virtues are in the popular estimate rather the exception than the rule. There is the man *and* his virtues. Men do what is called a good action, as some piece of courage or charity, much as they would pay a fine in expiation of daily non-appearance on parade. Their works are done as an apology or extenuation of their living in the world, —as invalids and the insane pay a high board. Their virtues are penances. I do not wish to expiate, but to live. My life is for itself and not for a spectacle. I much prefer that it should be of a lower strain, so it be genuine and equal, than that it should be glittering and unsteady. I wish it to be sound and sweet, and not to need diet and bleeding.[10] I ask primary evidence that you are a man, and refuse this appeal from the man to his actions. I know that for myself it makes no difference whether I do or forbear those actions which are reckoned excellent. I cannot consent to pay for a privilege where I have intrinsic right. Few and mean as my gifts may be, I actually am, and do not need for my own assurance or the assurance of my fellows any secondary testimony.

What I must do, is all that concerns me, not what the people think. This rule, equally arduous in actual and in intellectual life, may serve for the whole distinction between greatness and meanness. It is the harder, because you will always find those who think they know what is your duty better than you know it. It is easy in the world to live after the world's opinion; it is easy in solitude to live after our own; but the great man is he who in the midst of the crowd keeps with perfect sweetness the independence of solitude.

The objection to conforming to usages that have become dead to you, is, that it scatters your force. It loses your time and blurs the impression of your character. If you maintain a dead church, contribute to a dead Bible-Society, vote with a great party either for the Government or against it, spread your table like base housekeepers, —under all these screens, I have difficulty to detect the precise man you are. And, of course, so much force is withdrawn from your proper life. But do your work, and I shall know you. Do your work, and you shall reinforce yourself. A man must consider what a blindman's-buff is this game of conformity. If I know your sect, I

[9] I.e., for rejecting a family in order to obey a divine command (Matthew 10:34–37). See Exodus 12:17, in which God tells Moses to mark the "upper door post" and "two side posts" with blood so that God would not include those inside when he came to "smite all the firstborn in the land of Egypt, both man and beast."
[10] Bloodletting.

anticipate your argument. I hear a preacher announce for his text and topic the expediency of one of the institutions of his church. Do I not know beforehand that not possibly can he say a new and spontaneous word? Do I not know that with all this ostentation of examining the grounds of the institution, he will do no such thing? Do I not know that he is pledged to himself not to look but at one side,—the permitted side, not as a man, but as a parish minister? He is a retained attorney, and these airs of the bench are the emptiest affectation. Well, most men have bound their eyes with one or another handkerchief, and attached themselves to some one of these communities of opinion. This conformity makes them not false in a few particulars, authors of a few lies, but false in all particulars. Their every truth is not quite true. Their two is not the real two, their four not the real four: so that every word they say chagrins us, and we know not where to begin to set them right. Meantime nature is not slow to equip us in the prison-uniform of the party to which we adhere. We come to wear one cut of face and figure, and acquire by degrees the gentlest asinine expression. There is a mortifying experience in particular which does not fail to wreck itself also in the general history; I mean "the foolish face of praise,"[11] the forced smile which we put on in company where we do not feel at ease in answer to conversation which does not interest us. The muscles, not spontaneously moved, but moved by a low usurping wilfulness, grow tight about the outline of the face with the most disagreeable sensation.

For nonconformity the world whips you with its displeasure. And therefore a man must know how to estimate a sour face. The bystanders look askance on him in the public street or in the friend's parlor. If this aversation had its origin in contempt and resistance like his own, he might well go home with a sad countenance; but the sour faces of the multitude, like their sweet faces, have no deep cause, but are put on and off as the wind blows, and a newspaper directs. Yet is the discontent of the multitude more formidable than that of the senate and the college. It is easy enough for a firm man who knows the world to brook the rage of the cultivated classes. Their rage is decorous and prudent, for they are timid as being very vulnerable themselves. But when to their feminine rage the indignation of the people is added, when the ignorant and the poor are aroused, when the unintelligent brute force that lies at the bottom of society is made to growl and mow,[12] it needs the habit of magnanimity and religion to treat it godlike as a trifle of no concernment.

The other terror that scares us from self-trust is our consistency; a reverence for our past act or word, because the eyes of others have no other data for computing our orbit than our past acts, and we are loath to disappoint them.

But why should you keep your head over your shoulder? Why drag about this corpse of your memory, lest you contradict somewhat you have stated in this or that public place? Suppose you should contradict yourself; what then? It seems to be a rule of wisdom never to rely on your memory alone, scarcely even in acts of pure memory, but to bring the past for judgment into the thousand-eyed present, and live ever in a new day. In your metaphysics you have denied personality to the Deity: yet when

---

[11] Alexander Pope, "Epistle to Dr. Arbuthnot," l. 212.   [12] Archaic for "grimace."

the devout motions of the soul come, yield to them heart and life, though they should clothe God with shape and color. Leave your theory as Joseph his coat in the hand of the harlot,[13] and flee.

A foolish consistency is the hobgoblin of little minds, adored by little statesmen and philosophers and divines. With consistency a great soul has simply nothing to do. He may as well concern himself with his shadow on the wall. Speak what you think now in hard words, and to-morrow speak what to-morrow thinks in hard words again, though it contradict every thing you said to-day.—'Ah, so you shall be sure to be misunderstood.'—Is it so bad then to be misunderstood? Pythagoras[14] was misunderstood, and Socrates, and Jesus, and Luther, and Copernicus,[15] and Galileo,[16] and Newton, and every pure and wise spirit that ever took flesh. To be great is to be misunderstood.

I suppose no man can violate his nature. All the sallies of his will are rounded in by the last of his being as the inequalities of Andes and Himmaleh[17] are insignificant in the curve of the sphere. Nor does it matter how you gauge and try him. A character is like an acrostic or Alexandrian stanza;[18]—read it forward, backward, or across, it still spells the same thing. In this pleasing contrite wood-life which God allows me, let me record day by day my honest thought without prospect or retrospect, and, I cannot doubt, it will be found symmetrical, though I mean it not, and see it not. My book should smell of pines and resound with the hum of insects. The swallow over my window should interweave that thread or straw he carried in his bill into my web also. We pass for what we are. Character teaches above our wills. Men imagine that they communicate their virtue or vice only by overt actions and do not see that virtue or vice emit a breath every moment.

There will be an agreement in whatever variety of actions, so they be each honest and natural in their hour. For of one will, the actions will be harmonious, however unlike they seem. These varieties are lost sight of at a little distance, at a little height of thought. One tendency unites them all. The voyage of the best ship is a zigzag line of a hundred tacks. See the line from a sufficient distance, and it straightens itself to the average tendency. Your genuine action will explain itself and will explain your other genuine actions. Your conformity explains nothing. Act singly, and what you have already done singly, will justify you now. Greatness appeals to the future. If I can be firm enough to-day to do right and scorn eyes, I must have done so much right before, as to defend me now. Be it how it will, do right now. Always scorn appearances, and you always may. The force of character is cumulative. All the foregone days of virtue work their health into this. What makes the majesty of the heroes of the senate and the field, which so fills the imagination? The consciousness of a train of great days and victories behind. They shed an united light on the

[13] In Genesis 39:12, Potiphar's wife tempted Joseph by grabbing his garment and asking him to sleep with her, whereupon Joseph fled, leaving the garment behind.
[14] Greek mathematician (sixth century B.C.) and mystic philosopher.
[15] Polish astronomer (1473–1543) who proposed the current theory of the solar system, which was rejected in his lifetime.
[16] Galileo Galilei (1564–1642), Italian astronomer and physicist who endorsed Copernicus's theories and as a result was tried by the Inquisition of the Catholic church.
[17] Mountains in Asia bordering China and India (now Himalayas).
[18] Palindrome, or statement that can be read the same forward and backward.

advancing actor. He is attended as by a visible escort of angels. That is it which throws thunder into Chatham's[19] voice, and dignity into Washington's[20] port,[21] and America into Adams's[22] eye. Honor is venerable to us because it is no ephemeris. It is always ancient virtue. We worship it to-day, because it is not of to-day. We love it and pay it homage, because it is not a trap for our love and homage, but is self-dependent, self-derived, and therefore of an old immaculate pedigree, even if shown in a young person.

I hope in these days we have heard the last of conformity and consistency. Let the words be gazetted[23] and ridiculous henceforward. Instead of the gong for dinner, let us hear a whistle from the Spartan fife.[24] Let us never bow and apologize more. A great man is coming to eat at my house. I do not wish to please him: I wish that he should wish to please me. I will stand here for humanity, and though I would make it kind, I would make it true. Let us affront and reprimand the smooth mediocrity and squalid contentment of the times, and hurl in the face of custom, and trade, and office, the fact which is the upshot of all history, that there is a great responsible Thinker and Actor working wherever a man works; that a true man belongs to no other time or place, but is the centre of things. Where he is, there is nature. He measures you, and all men, and all events. Ordinarily every body in society reminds us of somewhat else or of some other person. Character, reality, reminds you of nothing else; it takes place of the whole creation. The man must be so much that he must make all circumstances indifferent. Every true man is a cause, a country, and an age; requires infinite spaces and numbers and time fully to accomplish his design; —and posterity seem to follow his steps as a train of clients. A man Cæsar is born, and for ages after, we have a Roman Empire. Christ is born, and millions of minds so grow and cleave to his genius, that he is confounded with virtue and the possible of man. An institution is the lengthened shadow of one man; as, Monachism, of the Hermit Antony; the Reformation, of Luther; Quakerism of Fox; Methodism, of Wesley; Abolition, of Clarkson.[25] Scipio,[26] Milton called "the height of Rome;" and all history resolves itself very easily into the biography of a few stout and earnest persons.

Let a man then know his worth, and keep things under his feet. Let him not peep or steal, or skulk up and down with the air of a charity-boy, a bastard, or an interloper, in the world which exists for him. But the man in the street finding no worth in himself which corresponds to the force which built a tower or sculptured a marble god, feels poor when he looks on these. To him a palace, a statue, or a costly book have an alien and forbidding air, much like a gay equipage, and seem to say like that, "Who are you, sir?" Yet they all are his, suitors for his notice, petitioners to his

---

[19] Chatham: William Pitt (1708–1778), earl of Chatham, English orator and statesman.
[20] Washington: George Washington (1732–1799), first American president.
[21] Demeanor.
[22] Adams: Revolutionary War patriot Samuel Adams (1722–1803); John Adams (1735–1826), second president; John Quincy Adams (1767–1848), sixth president.
[23] I.e., let an announcement be made of their public dismissal.

[24] The Spartans were noted for their strict discipline.
[25] Antony: St. Anthony (ca. 250–350) originated Christian monasticism; Fox: George Fox (1624–1691) founded the Society of Friends in England; Wesley: John Wesley (1703–1791) fostered Methodism; Clarkson: Thomas Clarkson (1760–1846) advocated abolition in England.
[26] Roman general (237–183 B.C.) who conquered Carthage.

faculties that they will come out and take possession. The picture waits for my verdict: it is not to command me, but I am to settle its claims to praise. That popular fable of the sot who was picked up dead drunk in the street, carried to the duke's house, washed and dressed and laid in the duke's bed, and, on his waking, treated with all obsequious ceremony like the duke, and assured that he had been insane, owes its popularity to the fact, that it symbolizes so well the state of man, who is in the world a sort of sot, but now and then wakes up, exercises his reason, and finds himself a true prince.

Our reading is mendicant and sycophantic. In history, our imagination plays us false. Kingdom and lordship, power and estate are a gaudier vocabulary than private John and Edward in a small house and common day's work: but the things of life are the same to both: the sum total of both is the same. Why all this deference to Alfred, and Scanderbeg, and Gustavus?[27] Suppose they were virtuous: did they wear out virtue? As great a stake depends on your private act to-day, as followed their public and renowned steps. When private men shall act with original views, the lustre will be transferred from the actions of kings to those of gentlemen.

The world has been instructed by its kings, who have so magnetized the eyes of nations. It has been taught by this colossal symbol the mutual reverence that is due from man to man. The joyful loyalty with which men have everywhere suffered the king, the noble, or the great proprietor to walk among them by a law of his own, make his own scale of men and things, and reverse theirs, pay for benefits not with money but with honor, and represent the Law in his person, was the hieroglyphic by which they obscurely signified their consciousness of their own right and comeliness, the right of every man.

The magnetism which all original action exerts is explained when we inquire the reason of self-trust. Who is the Trustee? What is the aboriginal Self on which a universal reliance may be grounded? What is the nature and power of that science-baffling star, without parallax,[28] without calculable elements, which shoots a ray of beauty even into trivial and impure actions, if the least mark of independence appear? The inquiry leads us to that source, at once the essence of genius, of virtue, and of life, which we call Spontaneity or Instinct. We denote this primary wisdom as Intuition, whilst all later teachings are tuitions. In that deep force, the last fact behind which analysis cannot go, all things find their common origin. For the sense of being which in calm hours rises, we know not how, in the soul, is not diverse from things, from space, from light, from time, from man, but one with them, and proceeds obviously from the same source whence their life and being also proceed. We first share the life by which things exist, and afterwards see them as appearances in nature, and forget that we have shared their cause. Here is the fountain of action and of thought. Here are the lungs of that inspiration which giveth man wisdom, and which cannot be denied without impiety and atheism. We lie in the lap of immense intelligence, which makes us receivers of its truth and organs of its activity. When we discern justice, when we discern truth, we do nothing of ourselves, but allow a

---

[27] Alfred: Alfred the Great (849–899), king of England; Scanderbeg: national hero of Albania (1403?–1468); Gustavus: Gustavus Adolphus (1594–1632), king of Sweden.
[28] Apparent change in the direction of an object caused by a change in the position from which it is seen. Emerson may well be using "without parallax" to mean "without an observational position."

passage to its beams. If we ask whence this comes, if we seek to pry into the soul that causes, all philosophy is at fault. Its presence or its absence is all we can affirm. Every man discriminates between the voluntary acts of his mind, and his involuntary perceptions, and knows that to his involuntary perceptions a perfect faith is due. He may err in the expression of them, but he knows that these things are so, like day and night, not to be disputed. My wilful actions and acquisitions are but roving;— the idlest reverie, the faintest native emotion, command my curiosity and respect. Thoughtless people contradict as readily the statement of perceptions as of opinions, or rather much more readily; for, they do not distinguish between perception and notion. They fancy that I choose to see this or that thing. But perception is not whimsical, but fatal. If I see a trait, my children will see it after me, and in course of time, all mankind,—although it may chance that no one has seen it before me. For my perception of it is as much a fact as the sun.

The relations of the soul to the divine spirit are so pure that it is profane to seek to interpose helps. It must be that when God speaketh, he should communicate not one thing, but all things; should fill the world with his voice; should scatter forth light, nature, time, souls, from the centre of the present thought; and new date and new create the whole. Whenever a mind is simple, and receives a divine wisdom, old things pass away,—means, teachers, texts, temples fall; it lives now and absorbs past and future into the present hour. All things are made sacred by relation to it,—one as much as another. All things are dissolved to their centre by their cause, and in the universal miracle petty and particular miracles disappear. If, therefore, a man claims to know and speak of God, and carries you backward to the phraseology of some old moul-dered nation in another country, in another world, believe him not. Is the acorn better than the oak which is its fullness and completion? Is the parent better than the child into whom he has cast his ripened being? Whence then this worship of the past? The centuries are conspirators against the sanity and authority of the soul. Time and space are but physiological colors which the eye makes, but the soul is light; where it is, is day; where it was, is night; and history is an impertinence and an injury, if it be anything more than a cheerful apologue or parable of my being and becoming.

Man is timid and apologetic; he is no longer upright; he dares not say 'I think,' 'I am,' but quotes some saint or sage. He is ashamed before the blade of grass or the blowing rose. These roses under my window make no reference to former roses or to better ones; they are for what they are; they exist with God to-day. There is no time to them. There is simply the rose; it is perfect in every moment of its existence. Before a leaf-bud has burst, its whole life acts; in the full-blown flower, there is no more; in the leafless root, there is no less. Its nature is satisfied, and it satisfies nature, in all moments alike. But man postpones or remembers; he does not live in the present, but with reverted eye laments the past, or, heedless of the riches that surround him, stands on tiptoe to foresee the future. He cannot be happy and strong until he too lives with nature in the present, above time.

This should be plain enough. Yet see what strong intellects dare not yet hear God himself, unless he speak the phraseology of I know not what David, or Jeremiah, or Paul.[29] We shall not always set so great a price on a few texts, on a few lives. We are like children who repeat by rote the sentences of grandames and tutors, and, as

[29] The three biblical authors.

they grow older, of the men of talents and character they chance to see,—painfully recollecting the exact words they spoke; afterwards, when they come into the point of view which those had who uttered these sayings, they understand them, and are willing to let the words go; for, at any time, they can use words as good, when occasion comes. If we live truly, we shall see truly. It is as easy for the strong man to be strong, as it is for the weak to be weak. When we have new perception, we shall gladly disburden the memory of its hoarded treasures as old rubbish. When a man lives with God, his voice shall be as sweet as the murmur of the brook and the rustle of the corn.

And now at last the highest truth on this subject remains unsaid; probably, cannot be said; for all that we say is the far off remembering of the intuition. That thought, by what I can now nearest approach to say it, is this. When good is near you, when you have life in yourself, it is not by any known or accustomed way; you shall not discern the foot-prints of any other; you shall not see the face of man; you shall not hear any name;—the way, the thought, the good shall be wholly strange and new. It shall exclude example and experience. You take the way from man, not to man. All persons that ever existed are its forgotten ministers. Fear and hope are alike beneath it. There is somewhat low even in hope. In the hour of vision, there is nothing that can be called gratitude, nor properly joy. The soul raised over passion beholds identity and eternal causation, perceives the self-existence of Truth and Right, and calms itself with knowing that all things go well. Vast spaces of nature, the Atlantic Ocean, the South Sea,—long intervals of time, years, centuries,—are of no account. This which I think and feel underlay every former state of life and circumstances, as it does underlie my present, and what is called life, and what is called death.

Life only avails, not the having lived. Power ceases in the instant of repose; it resides in the moment of transition from a past to a new state, in the shooting of the gulf, in the darting to an aim. This one fact the world hates, that the soul *becomes;* for, that forever degrades the past, turns all riches to poverty, all reputation to a shame, confounds the saint with the rogue, shoves Jesus and Judas equally aside. Why then do we prate of self-reliance? Inasmuch as the soul is present, there will be power not confident but agent. To talk of reliance, is a poor external way of speaking. Speak rather of that which relies, because it works and is. Who has more obedience than I, masters me, though he should not raise his finger. Round him I must revolve by the gravitation of spirits. We fancy it rhetoric when we speak of eminent virtue. We do not yet see that virtue is Height, and that a man or a company of men plastic and permeable to principles, by the law of nature must overpower and ride all cities, nations, kings, rich men, poets, who are not.

This is the ultimate fact which we so quickly reach on this as on every topic, the resolution of all into the ever blessed ONE. Self-existence is the attribute of the Supreme Cause, and it constitutes the measure of good by the degree in which it enters into all lower forms. All things real are so by so much virtue as they contain. Commerce, husbandry, hunting, whaling, war, eloquence, personal weight, are somewhat, and engage my respect as examples of its presence and impure action. I see the same law working in nature for conservation and growth. Power is in nature the essential measure of right. Nature suffers nothing to remain in her kingdoms which cannot help itself. The genesis and maturation of a planet, its poise and orbit, the bended tree recovering itself from the strong wind, the vital resources of every animal and vegetable, are demonstrations of the self-sufficing, and therefore self-relying soul.

Thus all concentrates; let us not rove; let us sit at home with the cause. Let us stun and astonish the intruding rabble of men and books and institutions by a simple declaration of the divine fact. Bid the invaders take the shoes from off their feet, for God is here within.[30] Let our simplicity judge them, and our docility to our own law demonstrate the poverty of nature and fortune beside our native riches.

But now we are a mob. Man does not stand in awe of man, nor is his genius admonished to stay at home, to put itself in communication with the internal ocean, but it goes abroad to beg a cup of water of the urns of other men. We must go alone. I like the silent church before the service begins, better than any preaching. How far off, how cool, how chaste the persons look, begirt each one with a precinct or sanctuary. So let us always sit. Why should we assume the faults of our friend, or wife, or father, or child, because they sit around our hearth, or are said to have the same blood? All men have my blood, and I have all men's. Not for that will I adopt their petulance or folly, even to the extent of being ashamed of it. But your isolation must not be mechanical, but spiritual, that is, must be elevation. At times the whole world seems to be in conspiracy to importune you with emphatic trifles. Friend, client, child, sickness, fear, want, charity, all knock at once at thy closet door and say,— "Come out unto us." But keep thy state; come not into their confusion. The power men possess to annoy me, I give them by a weak curiosity. No man can come near me but through my act. "What we love that we have, but by desire we bereave ourselves of the love."

If we cannot at once rise to the sanctities of obedience and faith, let us at least resist our temptations; let us enter into the state of war, and wake Thor and Woden,[31] courage and constancy, in our Saxon breasts. This is to be done in our smooth times by speaking the truth. Check this lying hospitality and lying affection. Live no longer to the expectation of these deceived and deceiving people with whom we converse. Say to them, O father, O mother, O wife, O brother, O friend, I have lived with you after appearances hitherto. Henceforward I am the truth's. Be it known unto you that henceforward I obey no law less than the eternal law. I will have no covenants but proximities. I shall endeavor to nourish my parents, to support my family, to be the chaste husband of one wife,—but these relations I must fill after a new and unprecedented way. I appeal from your customs. I must be myself. I cannot break myself any longer for you, or you. If you can love me for what I am, we shall be the happier. If you cannot, I will still seek to deserve that you should. I will not hide my tastes or aversions. I will so trust that what is deep is holy, that I will do strongly before the sun and moon whatever inly rejoices me, and the heart appoints. If you are noble, I will love you; if you are not, I will not hurt you and myself by hypocritical attentions. If you are true, but not in the same truth with me, cleave to your companions; I will seek my own. I do this not selfishly, but humbly and truly. It is alike your interest and mine and all men's, however long we have dwelt in lies, to live in truth. Does this sound harsh to-day? You will soon love what is dictated by your nature as well as mine, and if we follow the truth, it will bring us out safe at last.—But so you may give these friends pain. Yes, but I cannot sell my liberty

---

[30] See Exodus 3:5, in which God says to Moses: "Put off thy shoes from off thy feet, for the place whereon thou standest is holy ground."

[31] Thor and Woden (Odin) are gods of preeminent power in Norse mythology.

and my power, to save their sensibility. Besides, all persons have their moments of reason when they look out into the region of absolute truth; then will they justify me and do the same thing.

The populace think that your rejection of popular standards is a rejection of all standard, and mere antinomianism;[32] and the bold sensualist will use the name of philosophy to gild his crimes. But the law of consciousness abides. There are two confessionals, in one or the other of which we must be shriven. You may fulfil your round of duties by clearing yourself in the *direct,* or, in the *reflex* way. Consider whether you have satisfied your relations to father, mother, cousin, neighbor, town, cat, and dog; whether any of these can upbraid you. But I may also neglect this reflex standard, and absolve me to myself. I have my own stern claims and perfect circle. It denies the name of duty to many offices that are called duties. But if I can discharge its debts, it enables me to dispense with the popular code. If any one imagines that this law is lax, let him keep its commandment one day.

And truly it demands something godlike in him who has cast off the common motives of humanity, and has ventured to trust himself for a taskmaster. High be his heart, faithful his will, clear his sight, that he may in good earnest be doctrine, society, law to himself, that a simple purpose may be to him as strong as iron necessity is to others.

If any man consider the present aspects of what is called by distinction *society,* he will see the need of these ethics. The sinew and heart of man seem to be drawn out, and we are become timorous desponding whimperers. We are afraid of truth, afraid of fortune, afraid of death, and afraid of each other. Our age yields no great and perfect persons. We want men and women who shall renovate life and our social state, but we see that most natures are insolvent, cannot satisfy their own wants, have an ambition out of all proportion to their practical force, and do lean and beg day and night continually. Our housekeeping is mendicant, our arts, our occupations, our marriages, our religion we have not chosen, but society has chosen for us. We are parlor soldiers. We shun the rugged battle of fate, where strength is born.

If our young men miscarry in their first enterprizes, they lose all heart. If the young merchant fails, men say he is *ruined.* If the finest genius studies at one of our colleges, and is not installed in an office within one year afterwards in the cities or suburbs of Boston or New York, it seems to his friends and to himself that he is right in being disheartened and in complaining the rest of his life. A sturdy lad from New Hampshire or Vermont, who in turn tries all the professions, who *teams it, farms it, peddles,* keeps a school, preaches, edits a newspaper, goes to Congress, buys a township, and so forth, in successive years, and always, like a cat, falls on his feet, is worth a hundred of these city dolls. He walks abreast with his days, and feels no shame in not 'studying a profession,' for he does not postpone his life, but lives already. He has not one chance, but a hundred chances. Let a Stoic[33] open the resources of man, and tell men they are not leaning willows, but can and must detach themselves; that with the exercise of self-trust, new powers shall appear; that a man is the word made flesh,[34] born to shed

---

[32] Resistance to religious and moral laws.

[33] Ancient Greek philosophers who professed passionless independence and submission to natural law.

[34] John 1:14: "And the word was made flesh, and dwelt among us . . . full of grace and truth."

healing to the nations, that he should be ashamed of our compassion, and that the moment he acts from himself, tossing the laws, the books, idolatries, and customs out of the window, we pity him no more but thank and revere him,—and that teacher shall restore the life of man to splendor, and make his name dear to all History.

It is easy to see that a greater self-reliance must work a revolution in all the offices and relations of men; in their religion; in their education; in their pursuits; their modes of living; their association; in their property; in their speculative views.

1. In what prayers do men allow themselves! That which they call a holy office, is not so much as brave and manly. Prayer looks abroad and asks for some foreign addition to come through some foreign virtue, and loses itself in endless mazes of natural and supernatural, and mediatorial and miraculous. Prayer that craves a particular commodity,—any thing less than all good,—is vicious. Prayer is the contemplation of the facts of life from the highest point of view. It is the soliloquy of a beholding and jubilant soul. It is the spirit of God pronouncing his works good.[35] But prayer as a means to effect a private end, is meanness and theft. It supposes dualism and not unity in nature and consciousness. As soon as the man is at one with God, he will not beg. He will then see prayer in all action. The prayer of the farmer kneeling in his field to weed it, the prayer of the rower kneeling with the stroke of his oar, are true prayers heard throughout nature, though for cheap ends. Caratach, in Fletcher's Bonduca,[36] when admonished to inquire the mind of the god Audate, replies,—

"His hidden meaning lies in our endeavors,
Our valors are our best gods."

Another sort of false prayers are our regrets. Discontent is the want of self-reliance: it is infirmity of will. Regret calamities, if you can thereby help the sufferer; if not, attend your own work, and already the evil begins to be repaired. Our sympathy is just as base. We come to them who weep foolishly, and sit down and cry for company, instead of imparting to them truth and health in rough electric shocks, putting them once more in communication with their own reason. The secret of fortune is joy in our hands. Welcome evermore to gods and men is the self-helping man. For him all doors are flung wide: him all tongues greet, all honors crown, all eyes follow with desire. Our love goes out to him and embraces him, because he did not need it. We solicitously and apologetically caress and celebrate him, because he held on his way and scorned our disapprobation. The gods love him because men hated him. "To the persevering mortal," said Zoroaster,[37] "the blessed Immortals are swift."

As men's prayers are a disease of the will, so are their creeds a disease of the intellect. They say with those foolish Israelites, "Let not God speak to us, lest we die. Speak thou, speak any man with us, and we will obey."[38] Everywhere I am hindered of meeting God in my brother, because he has shut his own temple doors, and recites fables merely of his brother's, or his brother's brother's God. Every new mind is a new classification. If it prove a mind of uncommon activity and power, a Locke, a

---

[35] Genesis 1:31: "And God saw everything that he had made, and, behold, *it was* very good."

[36] Drama by Elizabethan playwright John Fletcher (1579–1625). The lines Emerson cites are slightly misquoted.

[37] Persian prophet of the sixth century B.C.

[38] Anxious words of the Hebrews to Moses, after God had given him the Ten Commandments. (See Exodus 20:19.)

Lavoisier, a Hutton, a Bentham, a Fourier,[39] it imposes its classification on other men, and lo! a new system. In proportion to the depth of the thought, and so to the number of the objects it touches and brings within reach of the pupil, is his complacency. But chiefly is this apparent in creeds and churches, which are also classifications of some powerful mind acting on the elemental thought of Duty, and man's relation to the Highest. Such is Calvinism, Quakerism, Swedenborgianism. The pupil takes the same delight in subordinating every thing to the new terminology, as a girl who has just learned botany in seeing a new earth and new seasons thereby. It will happen for a time, that the pupil will find his intellectual power has grown by the study of his master's mind. But in all unbalanced minds, the classification is idolized, passes for the end, and not for a speedily exhaustible means, so that the walls of the system blend to their eye in the remote horizon with the walls of the universe; the luminaries of heaven seem to them hung on the arch their master built. They cannot imagine how you aliens have any right to see,—how you can see; "It must be somehow that you stole the light from us." They do not yet perceive, that light, unsystematic, indomitable, will break into any cabin, even into theirs. Let them chirp awhile and call it their own. If they are honest and do well, presently their neat new pinfold[40] will be too strait and low, will crack, will lean, will rot and vanish, and the immortal light, all young and joyful, million-orbed, million-colored, will beam over the universe as on the first morning.

2. It is for want of self-culture that the superstition of Travelling, whose idols are Italy, England, Egypt, retains its fascination for all educated Americans. They who made England, Italy, or Greece venerable in the imagination, did so by sticking fast where they were, like an axis of the earth. In manly hours, we feel that duty is our place. The soul is no traveller: the wise man stays at home, and when his necessities, his duties, on any occasion call him from his house, or into foreign lands, he is at home still, and shall make men sensible by the expression of his countenance, that he goes the missionary of wisdom and virtue, and visits cities and men like a sovereign, and not like an interloper or a valet.

I have no churlish objection to the circumnavigation of the globe, for the purposes of art, of study, and benevolence, so that the man is first domesticated, or does not go abroad with the hope of finding somewhat greater than he knows. He who travels to be amused, or to get somewhat which he does not carry, travels away from himself, and grows old even in youth among old things. In Thebes, in Palmyra,[41] his will and mind have become old and dilapidated as they. He carries ruins to ruins.

Travelling is a fool's paradise. Our first journeys discover to us the indifference of places. At home I dream that at Naples, at Rome, I can be intoxicated with beauty, and lose my sadness. I pack my trunk, embrace my friends, embark on the sea, and at last wake up in Naples, and there beside me is the stern Fact, the sad self, unrelenting, identical, that I fled from. I seek the Vatican, and the palaces. I affect to be intoxicated

[39] Locke: John Locke (1632–1704), English philosopher who heralded a theory of knowledge; Lavoisier: Antoine Laurent Lavoisier (1743–1794), who initiated advances in chemistry; Hutton: James Hutton (1726–1797), pioneer in geology; Bentham: Jeremy Bentham (1748–1832), who originated practical doctrines for law and government; Fourier: François Marie Charles Fourier (1772–1837), who pioneered in sociology.
[40] Fenced yard for holding animals.
[41] Thebes; Palmyra: ancient cities in Egypt and Syria, respectively.

with sights and suggestions, but I am not intoxicated. My giant goes with me wherever I go.

3. But the rage of travelling is a symptom of a deeper unsoundness affecting the whole intellectual action. The intellect is vagabond, and our system of education fosters restlessness. Our minds travel when our bodies are forced to stay at home. We imitate; and what is imitation but the travelling of the mind? Our houses are built with foreign taste; our shelves are garnished with foreign ornaments; our opinions, our tastes, our faculties, lean, and follow the Past and the Distant. The soul created the arts wherever they have flourished. It was in his own mind that the artist sought his model. It was an application of his own thought to the thing to be done and the conditions to be observed. And why need we copy the Doric or the Gothic model? Beauty, convenience, grandeur of thought, and quaint expression are as near to us as to any, and if the American artist will study with hope and love the precise thing to be done by him, considering the climate, the soil, the length of the day, the wants of the people, the habit and form of the government, he will create a house in which all these will find themselves fitted, and taste and sentiment will be satisfied also.

Insist on yourself; never imitate. Your own gift you can present every moment with the cumulative force of a whole life's cultivation; but of the adopted talent of another, you have only an extemporaneous, half possession. That which each can do best, none but his Maker can teach him. No man yet knows what it is, nor can, till that person has exhibited it. Where is the master who could have taught Shakspeare? Where is the master who could have instructed Franklin, or Washington, or Bacon, or Newton? Every great man is a unique. The Scipionism[42] of Scipio is precisely that part he could not borrow. Shakspeare will never be made by the study of Shakspeare. Do that which is assigned you, and you cannot hope too much or dare too much. There is at this moment for you an utterance brave and grand as that of the colossal chisel of Phidias,[43] or trowel of the Egyptians, or the pen of Moses, or Dante, but different from all these. Not possibly will the soul all rich, all eloquent, with thousand-cloven tongue, deign to repeat itself; but if you can hear what these patriarchs say, surely you can reply to them in the same pitch of voice: for the ear and the tongue are two organs of one nature. Abide in the simple and noble regions of thy life, obey thy heart, and thou shalt reproduce the Foreworld again.

4. As our Religion, our Education, our Art look abroad, so does our spirit of society. All men plume themselves on the improvement of society, and no man improves.

Society never advances. It recedes as fast on one side as it gains on the other. It undergoes continual changes: it is barbarous, it is civilized, it is christianized, it is rich, it is scientific; but this change is not amelioration. For every thing that is given, something is taken. Society acquires new arts and loses old instincts. What a contrast between the well-clad, reading, writing, thinking American, with a watch, a pencil, and a bill of exchange in his pocket, and the naked New Zealander, whose property is a club, a spear, a mat, and an undivided twentieth of a shed to sleep under. But compare the health of the two men, and you shall see that the white man has lost

---

[42] I.e., Scipio's essence.
[43] Renowned Greek sculptor of the fifth century B.C.

his aboriginal strength. If the traveller tell us truly, strike the savage with a broad axe, and in a day or two the flesh shall unite and heal as if you struck the blow into soft pitch, and the same blow shall send the white to his grave.

The civilized man has built a coach, but has lost the use of his feet. He is supported on crutches, but lacks so much support of muscle. He has a fine Geneva watch, but he fails of the skill to tell the hour by the sun. A Greenwich nautical almanac he has, and so being sure of the information when he wants it, the man in the street does not know a star in the sky. The solstice he does not observe; the equinox he knows as little; and the whole bright calendar of the year is without a dial in his mind. His note-books impair his memory; his libraries overload his wit; the insurance office increases the number of accidents; and it may be a question whether machinery does not encumber; whether we have not lost by refinement some energy, by a christianity entrenched in establishments and forms, some vigor of wild virtue. For every stoic was a stoic; but in Christendom where is the Christian?

There is no more deviation in the moral standard than in the standard of height or bulk. No greater men are now than ever were. A singular equality may be observed between the great men of the first and of the last ages; nor can all the science, art, religion and philosophy of the nineteenth century avail to educate greater men than Plutarch's[44] heroes, three or four and twenty centuries ago. Not in time is the race progressive. Phocion, Socrates, Anaxagoras, Diogenes, are great men, but they leave no class.[45] He who is really of their class will not be called by their name, but will be his own man, and, in his turn the founder of a sect. The arts and inventions of each period are only its costume, and do not invigorate men. The harm of the improved machinery may compensate its good. Hudson and Behring accomplished so much in their fishing-boats, as to astonish Parry and Franklin, whose equipment exhausted the resources of science and art.[46] Galileo, with an opera-glass, discovered a more splendid series of celestial phenomena than any one since. Columbus found the New World in an undecked boat. It is curious to see the periodical disuse and perishing of means and machinery which were introduced with loud laudation, a few years or centuries before. The great genius returns to essential man. We reckoned the improvements of the art of war among the triumphs of science, and yet Napoleon conquered Europe by the Bivouac, which consisted of falling back on naked valor, and disencumbering it of all aids. The Emperor held it impossible to make a perfect army, says Las Cases,[47] "without abolishing our arms, magazines, commissaries, and carriages, until in imitation of the Roman custom, the soldier should receive his supply of corn, grind it in his hand-mill, and bake his bread himself."

Society is a wave. The wave moves onward, but the water of which it is composed, does not. The same particle does not rise from the valley to the ridge. Its unity is only phenomenal. The persons who make up a nation to-day, next year die, and their experience with them.

---

44 Plutarch: Greek biographer (46?–?120) who recorded the lives of famous Romans and Greeks.
45 All "great men" cited here were Greek philosophers of the third and fourth centuries B.C.
46 Hudson: English navigator Henry Hudson

(d. 1611); Behring: Dutch navigator Vitus Jonassen Bering (1680–1741); Parry and Franklin: English arctic explorers Sir William Edward Parry (1790–1855) and Sir John Franklin (1786–1847).
47 French historian Comte Emmanuel Augustin de las Cases (1766–1842).

And so the reliance on Property, including the reliance on governments which protect it, is the want of self-reliance. Men have looked away from themselves and at things so long, that they have come to esteem the religious, learned, and civil institutions, as guards of property, and they deprecate assaults on these, because they feel them to be assaults on property. They measure their esteem of each other, by what each has, and not by what each is. But a cultivated man becomes ashamed of his property, out of new respect for his nature. Especially he hates what he has, if he see that it is accidental,—came to him by inheritance, or gift, or crime; then he feels that it is not having; it does not belong to him, has no root in him, and merely lies there, because no revolution or no robber takes it away. But that which a man is, does always by necessity acquire, and what the man acquires is living property, which does not wait the beck of rulers, or mobs, or revolutions, or fire, or storm, or bankruptcies, but perpetually renews itself wherever the man breathes. "Thy lot or portion of life," said the Caliph Ali,[48] "is seeking after thee; therefore be at rest from seeking after it." Our dependence on these foreign goods leads us to our slavish respect for numbers. The political parties meet in numerous conventions; the greater the concourse, and with each new uproar of announcement, The delegation from Essex![49] The Democrats from New Hampshire! The Whigs of Maine! the young patriot feels himself stronger than before by a new thousand of eyes and arms. In like manner the reformers summon conventions, and vote and resolve in multitude. Not so, O friends! will the God deign to enter and inhabit you, but by a method precisely the reverse. It is only as a man puts off all foreign support, and stands alone, that I see him to be strong and to prevail. He is weaker by every recruit to his banner. Is not a man better than a town? Ask nothing of men, and in the endless mutation, thou only firm column must presently appear the upholder of all that surrounds thee. He who knows that power is inborn, that he is weak because he has looked for good out of him and elsewhere, and so perceiving, throws himself unhesitatingly on his thought, instantly rights himself, stands in the erect position, commands his limbs, works miracles; just as a man who stands on his feet is stronger than a man who stands on his head.

So use all that is called Fortune. Most men gamble with her, and gain all, and lose all, as her wheel rolls. But do thou leave as unlawful these winnings, and deal with Cause and Effect, the chancellors of God. In the Will work and acquire, and thou hast chained the wheel of Chance, and shalt sit hereafter out of fear from her rotations. A political victory, a rise of rents, the recovery of your sick, or the return of your absent friend, or some other favorable event, raises your spirits, and you think good days are preparing for you. Do not believe it. Nothing can bring you peace but yourself. Nothing can bring you peace but the triumph of principles.

1841

---

[48] Ali-ibn-abn-Talib (600?–661), fourth Moslem caliph of Mecca.
[49] County in Massachusetts.

The Poet

A moody child and wildly wise
Pursued the game with joyful eyes,
Which chose, like meteors, their way,
And rived the dark with private ray:
They overleapt the horizon's edge,
Searched with Apollo's privilege;
Through man, and woman, and sea, and star,
Saw the dance of nature forward far;
Through worlds, and races, and terms, and times,
Saw musical order, and pairing rhymes. [1]

Olympian bards who sung
Divine ideas below,
Which always find us young,
And always keep us so. [2]

Those who are esteemed umpires of taste, are often persons who have acquired some knowledge of admired pictures or sculptures, and have an inclination for whatever is elegant; but if you inquire whether they are beautiful souls, and whether their own acts are like fair pictures, you learn that they are selfish and sensual. Their cultivation is local, as if you should rub a log of dry wood in one spot to produce fire, all the rest remaining cold. Their knowledge of the fine arts is some study of rules and particulars, or some limited judgment of color or form, which is exercised for amusement or for show. It is a proof of the shallowness of the doctrine of beauty, as it lies in the minds of our amateurs, that men seem to have lost the perception of the instant dependence of form upon soul. There is no doctrine of forms in our philosophy. We were put into our bodies, as fire is put into a pan, to be carried about; but there is no accurate adjustment between the spirit and the organ, much less is the latter the germination of the former. So in regard to other forms, the intellectual men do not believe in any essential dependence of the material world on thought and volition. Theologians think it a pretty air-castle to talk of the spiritual meaning of a ship or a cloud, of a city or a contract, but they prefer to come again to the solid ground of historical evidence; and even the poets are contented with a civil and conformed manner of living, and to write poems from the fancy, at a safe distance from their own experience. But the highest minds of the world have never ceased to explore the double meaning, or, shall I say, the quadruple, or the centuple, or much more manifold meaning, of every sensuous fact: Orpheus, Empedocles, Heraclitus, Plato, Plutarch, Dante, Swedenborg,[3] and the masters of sculpture, picture, and poetry. For we are not pans and barrows, nor even porters of the fire and torch-bearers, but children of the fire, made of it, and only the same divinity transmuted, and at two or three removes, when we know least about it. And this hidden truth, that the

---

[1] From Emerson's unfinished poem "The Poet," published posthumously.
[2] From Emerson's "Ode to Beauty."
[3] Emerson refers here, respectively, to a mythical Greek poet, Greek philosophers of the fifth, sixth, and fourth centuries B.C., a Greek biographer of the first century, an Italian poet of the Middle Ages, and a Swedish mystical scientist of the eighteenth century.

fountains when all this river of Time, and its creatures, floweth, are intrinsically ideal and beautiful, draws us to the consideration of the nature and functions of the Poet, or the man of Beauty, to the means and materials he uses, and to the general aspect of the art in the present time.

The breadth of the problem is great, for the poet is representative. He stands among partial men for the complete man, and apprises us not of his wealth, but of the commonwealth. The young man reveres men of genius, because, to speak truly, they are more himself than he is. They receive of the soul as he also receives, but they more. Nature enhances her beauty, to the eye of loving men, from their belief that the poet is beholding her shows at the same time. He is isolated among his contemporaries, by truth and by his art, but with this consolation in his pursuits, that they will draw all men sooner or later. For all men live by truth, and stand in need of expression. In love, in art, in avarice, in politics, in labor, in games, we study to utter our painful secret. The man is only half himself, the other half is his expression.

Notwithstanding this necessity to be published, adequate expression is rare. I know not how it is that we need an interpreter; but the great majority of men seem to be minors, who have not yet come into possession of their own, or mutes, who cannot report the conversation they have had with nature. There is no man who does not anticipate a supersensual utility in the sun, and stars, earth, and water. These stand and wait to render him a peculiar service. But there is some obstruction, or some excess of phlegm in our constitution, which does not suffer them to yield the due effect. Too feeble fall the impressions of nature on us to make us artists. Every touch should thrill. Every man should be so much an artist, that he could report in conversation what had befallen him. Yet, in our experience, the rays or appulses[4] have sufficient force to arrive at the senses, but not enough to reach the quick, and compel the reproduction of themselves in speech. The poet is the person in whom these powers are in balance, the man without impediment, who sees and handles that which others dream of, traverses the whole scale of experience, and its representatives of man, in virtue of being the largest power to receive and to impart.

For the Universe has three children, born at one time, which reappear, under different names, in every system of thought, whether they be called cause, operation, and effect; or, more poetically, Jove, Pluto, Neptune; or, theologically, the Father, the Spirit, and the Son; but which we will call here, the Knower, the Doer, and the Sayer. These stand respectively for the love of truth, for the love of good, and for the love of beauty. These three are equal. Each is that which he is essentially, so that he cannot be surmounted or analyzed, and each of these three has the power of the others latent in him, and his own patent.

The poet is the sayer, the namer, and represents beauty. He is a sovereign, and stands on the centre. For the world is not painted, or adorned, but is from the beginning beautiful; and God has not made some beautiful things, but Beauty is the creator of the universe. Therefore the poet is not any permissive potentate, but is emperor in his own right. Criticism is infested with a cant of materialism, which assumes that manual skill and activity is the first merit of all men, and disparages such as say and do not, overlooking the fact, that some men, namely, poets, are natural sayers, sent into the world to the end of expression, and confounds them with those whose province is action, but who quit it to imitate the sayers. But Homer's words are as

---

[4] Potent energies.

costly and admirable to Homer, as Agamemnon's victories are to Agamemnon. The poet does not wait for the hero or the sage, but, as they act and think primarily, so he writes primarily what will and must be spoken, reckoning the others, though primaries also, yet, in respect to him, secondaries and servants; as sitters or models in the studio of a painter, or as assistants who bring building materials to an architect.

For poetry was all written before time was, and whenever we are so finely organized that we can penetrate into that region where the air is music, we hear those primal warblings, and attempt to write them down, but we lose ever and anon a word, or a verse, and substitute something of our own, and thus miswrite the poem. The men of more delicate ear write down these cadences more faithfully, and these transcripts, though imperfect, become the songs of the nations. For nature is as truly beautiful as it is good, or as it is reasonable, and must as much appear, as it must be done, or be known. Words and deeds are quite indifferent modes of the divine energy. Words are also actions, and actions are a kind of words.

The sign and credentials of the poet are, that he announces that which no man foretold. He is the true and only doctor;[5] he knows and tells; he is the only teller of news, for he was present and privy to the appearance which he describes. He is a beholder of ideas, and an utterer of the necessary and causal. For we do not speak now of men of poetical talents, or of industry and skill in metre, but of the true poet. I took part in a conversation the other day, concerning a recent writer of lyrics, a man of subtle mind, whose head appeared to be a music-box of delicate tunes and rhythms, and whose skill, and command of language, we could not sufficiently praise. But when the question arose, whether he was not only a lyrist, but a poet, we were obliged to confess that he is plainly a contemporary, not an eternal man. He does not stand out of our low limitations, like a Chimborazo[6] under the line, running up from the torrid base through all the climates of the globe, with belts of the herbage of every latitude on its high and mottled sides; but this genius is the landscape-garden of a modern house, adorned with fountains and statues, with well-bred men and women standing and sitting in the walks and terraces. We hear, through all the varied music, the ground-tone of conventional life. Our poets are men of talents who sing, and not the children of music. The argument is secondary, the finish of the verses is primary.

For it is not metres, but a metre-making argument, that makes a poem,—a thought so passionate and alive, that, like the spirit of a plant or an animal, it has an architecture of its own, and adorns nature with a new thing. The thought and the form are equal in the order of time, but in the order of genesis the thought is prior to the form. The poet has a new thought: he has a whole new experience to unfold; he will tell us how it was with him, and all men will be the richer in his fortune. For, the experience of each new age requires a new confession, and the world seems always waiting for its poet. I remember, when I was young, how much I was moved one morning by tidings that genius had appeared in a youth who sat near me at table. He had left his work, and gone rambling none knew whither, and had written hundreds of lines, but could not tell whether that which was in him was therein told: he could tell nothing but that all was changed,—man, beast, heaven, earth, and sea. How gladly we listened! how credulous! Society seemed to be compromised. We sat in the aurora of a sunrise

---

[5] In the traditional Latin sense, teacher.
[6] Mountain in Ecuador located below the equator.

which was to put out all the stars. Boston seemed to be at twice the distance it had the night before, or was much farther than that. Rome,—what was Rome? Plutarch and Shakspeare were in the yellow leaf,[7] and Homer no more should be heard of. It is much to know that poetry has been written this very day, under this very roof, by your side. What! that wonderful spirit has not expired! these stony moments are still sparkling and animated! I had fancied that the oracles were all silent, and nature had spent her fires, and behold! all night, from every pore, these fine auroras have been streaming. Every one has some interest in the advent of the poet, and no one knows how much it may concern him. We know that the secret of the world is profound, but who or what shall be our interpreter, we know not. A mountain ramble, a new style of face, a new person, may put the key into our hands. Of course, the value of genius to us is in the veracity of its report. Talent may frolic and juggle; genius realizes and adds. Mankind, in good earnest, have availed so far in understanding themselves and their work, that the foremost watchman on the peak announces his news. It is the truest word ever spoken, and the phrase will be the fittest, most musical, and the unerring voice of the world for that time.

All that we call sacred history attests that the birth of a poet is the principal event in chronology. Man, never so often deceived, still watches for the arrival of a brother who can hold him steady to a truth, until he has made it his own. With what joy I begin to read a poem, which I confide in as an inspiration! And now my chains are to be broken; I shall mount above these clouds and opaque airs in which I live,—opaque, though they seem transparent,—and from the heaven of truth I shall see and comprehend my relations. That will reconcile me to life, and renovate nature, to see trifles animated by a tendency, and to know what I am doing. Life will no more be a noise; now I shall see men and women, and know the signs by which they may be discerned from fools and satans. This day shall be better than my birth-day: then I became an animal: now I am invited into the science of the real. Such is the hope, but the fruition is postponed. Oftener it falls, that this winged man, who will carry me into the heaven, whirls me into the clouds, then leaps and frisks about with me from cloud to cloud, still affirming that he is bound heavenward; and I, being myself a novice, am slow in perceiving that he does not know the way into the heavens, and is merely bent that I should admire his skill to rise, like a fowl or a flying fish, a little way from the ground or the water; but the all-piercing, all-feeding, and ocular air of heaven, that man shall never inhabit. I tumble down again soon into my old nooks, and lead the life of exaggerations as before, and have lost my faith in the possibility of any guide who can lead me thither where I would be.

But leaving these victims of vanity, let us, with new hope, observe how nature, by worthier impulses, has ensured the poet's fidelity to his office of announcement and affirming, namely, by the beauty of things, which becomes a new, and higher beauty, when expressed. Nature offers all her creatures to him as a picture-language. Being used as a type, a second wonderful value appears in the object, far better than its old value, as the carpenter's stretched cord, if you hold your ear close enough, is musical in the breeze. "Things more excellent than every image," says Jamblichus,[8] "are expressed through images." Things admit of being used as symbols, because nature

---

[7] *Macbeth,* Act V, Sc. iii, ll. 22–23: "I have lived long enough. My way of life is fallen into the sere, the yellow leaf."

[8] Philosopher of the fourth century who advocated Neoplatonism, a religious mysticism drawing on elements of Greek philosophy.

is a symbol, in the whole, and in every part. Every line we can draw in the sand, has expression; and there is no body without its spirit or genius. All form is an effect of character; all condition, of the quality of the life; all harmony, of health; (and, for this reason, a perception of beauty should be sympathetic, or proper only to the good.) The beautiful rests on the foundations of the necessary. The soul makes the body, as the wise Spenser teaches:—

> "So every spirit, as it is most pure,
> And hath in it the more of heavenly light,
> So it the fairer body doth procure
> To habit in, and it more fairly dight,
> With cheerful grace and amiable sight.
> For, of the soul, the body form doth take,
> For soul is form, and doth the body make."[9]

Here we find ourselves, suddenly, not in a critical speculation, but in a holy place, and should go very warily and reverently. We stand before the secret of the world, there where Being passes into Appearance, and Unity into Variety.

The Universe is the externisation of the soul. Wherever the life is, that bursts into appearance around it. Our science is sensual, and therefore superficial. The earth, and the heavenly bodies, physics, and chemistry, we sensually treat, as if they were self-existent; but these are the retinue of that Being we have. "The mighty heaven," said Proclus,[10] "exhibits, in its transfigurations, clear images of the splendor of intellectual perceptions; being moved in conjunction with the unapparent periods of intellectual natures." Therefore, science always goes abreast with the just elevation of the man, keeping step with religion and metaphysics; or, the state of science is an index of our self-knowledge. Since everything in nature answers to a moral power, if any phenomenon remains brute and dark, it is that the corresponding faculty in the observer is not yet active.

No wonder, then, if these waters be so deep, that we hover over them with a religious regard. The beauty of the fable proves the importance of the sense; to the poet, and to all others; or, if you please, every man is so far a poet as to be susceptible of these enchantments of nature: for all men have the thoughts whereof the universe is the celebration. I find that the fascination resides in the symbol. Who loves nature? Who does not? Is it only poets, and men of leisure and cultivation, who live with her? No; but also hunters, farmers, grooms, and butchers, though they express their affection in their choice of life, and not in their choice of words. The writer wonders what the coachman or the hunter values in riding, in horses, and dogs. It is not superficial qualities. When you talk with him, he holds these at as slight a rate as you. His worship is sympathetic; he has no definitions, but he is commanded in nature, by the living power which he feels to be there present. No imitation, or playing of these things, would content him; he loves the earnest of the northwind, of rain, of stone, and wood, and iron. A beauty not explicable, is dearer than a beauty which we can see to the end of. It is nature the symbol, nature certifying the supernatural, body overflowed by life, which he worships, with coarse, but sincere rites.

---

[9] From "An Hymn in Honor of Beauty" (1596)   [10] Greek Neoplatonic philosopher (411–485).
by English poet Edmund Spenser (1552?–1599).

The inwardness, and mystery, of this attachment, drives men of every class to the use of emblems. The schools of poets, and philosophers, are not more intoxicated with their symbols, than the populace with theirs. In our political parties, compute the power of badges and emblems. See the great ball which they roll from Baltimore to Bunker hill![11] In the political processions, Lowell goes in a loom, and Lynn in a shoe, and Salem in a ship.[12] Witness the cider-barrel, the log-cabin, the hickory-stick, the palmetto, and all the cognizances of party. See the power of national emblems. Some stars, lilies, leopards, a crescent, a lion, an eagle, or other figure, which came into credit God knows how, on an old rag of bunting, blowing in the wind, on a fort, at the ends of the earth, shall make the blood tingle under the rudest, or the most conventional exterior. The people fancy they hate poetry, and they are all poets and mystics!

Beyond this universality of the symbolic language, we are apprised of the divineness of this superior use of things, whereby the world is a temple, whose walls are covered with emblems, pictures, and commandments of the Deity, in this, that there is no fact in nature which does not carry the whole sense of nature; and the distinctions which we make in events, and in affairs, of low and high, honest and base, disappear when nature is used as a symbol. Thought makes every thing fit for use. The vocabulary of an omniscient man would embrace words and images excluded from polite conversation. What would be base, or even obscene, to the obscene, becomes illustrious, spoken in a new connexion of thought. The piety of the Hebrew prophets purges their grossness. The circumcision is an example of the power of poetry to raise the low and offensive. Small and mean things serve as well as great symbols. The meaner the type by which a law is expressed, the more pungent it is, and the more lasting in the memories of men: just as we choose the smallest box, or case, in which any needful utensil can be carried. Bare lists of words are found suggestive, to an imaginative and excited mind; as it is related of Lord Chatham,[13] that he was accustomed to read in Bailey's Dictionary, when he was preparing to speak in Parliament. The poorest experience is rich enough for all the purposes of expressing thought. Why covet a knowledge of new facts? Day and night, house and garden, a few books, a few actions, serve us as well as would all trades and all spectacles. We are far from having exhausted the significance of the few symbols we use. We can come to use them yet with a terrible simplicity. It does not need that a poem should be long. Every word was once a poem. Every new relation is a new word. Also, we use defects and deformities to a sacred purpose, so expressing our sense that the evils of the world are such only to the evil eye. In the old mythology, mythologists observe, defects are ascribed to divine natures, as lameness to Vulcan, blindness to Cupid, and the like, to signify exuberances.

For, as it is dislocation and detachment from the life of God, that makes things ugly, the poet, who re-attaches things to nature and the Whole,—re-attaching even artificial things, and violations of nature, to nature, by a deeper insight,—disposes very easily of the most disagreeable facts. Readers of poetry see the factory-village, and the railway, and fancy that the poetry of the landscape is broken up by these; for these works of art are not yet consecrated in their reading; but the poet sees them fall within

---

[11] Allusion to a political gimmick used by the 1840 campaign supporters of W. H. Harrison: "Keep the ball a-rolling."

[12] The towns of Lowell, Lynn, and Salem,

Massachusetts, are represented by their major products.

[13] William Pitt (1708–1778), earl of Chatham, was a powerfully eloquent English statesman.

the great Order not less than the bee-hive, or the spider's geometrical web. Nature adopts them very fast into her vital circles, and the gliding train of cars she loves like her own. Besides, in a centred mind, it signifies nothing how many mechanical inventions you exhibit. Though you add millions, and never so surprising, the fact of mechanics has not gained a grain's weight. The spiritual fact remains unalterable, by many or by few particulars; as no mountain is of any appreciable height to break the curve of the sphere. A shrewd country-boy goes to the city for the first time, and the complacent citizen is not satisfied with his little wonder. It is not that he does not see all the fine houses, and know that he never saw such before, but he disposes of them as easily as the poet finds place for the railway. The chief value of the new fact, is to enhance the great and constant fact of Life, which can dwarf any and every circumstance, and to which the belt of wampum, and the commerce of America, are alike.

The world being thus put under the mind for verb and noun, the poet is he who can articulate it. For, though life is great, and fascinates, and absorbs,—and though all men are intelligent of the symbols through which it is named,—yet they cannot originally use them. We are symbols, and inhabit symbols; workman, work, and tools, words and things, birth and death, all are emblems; but we sympathize with the symbols, and, being infatuated with the economical uses of things, we do not know that they are thoughts. The poet, by an ulterior intellectual perception, gives them a power which makes their old use forgotten, and puts eyes, and a tongue, into every dumb and inanimate object. He perceives the independence of the thought on the symbol, the stability of the thought, the accidency and fugacity of the symbol. As the eyes of Lyncæus[14] were said to see through the earth, so the poet turns the world to glass, and shows us all things in their right series and procession. For, through that better perception, he stands one step nearer to things, and sees the flowing or metamorphosis; perceives that thought is multiform; that within the form of every creature is a force impelling it to ascend into a higher form; and, following with his eyes the life, uses the forms which express that life, and so his speech flows with the flowing of nature. All the facts of the animal economy, sex, nutriment, gestation, birth, growth, are symbols of the passage of the world into the soul of man, to suffer there a change, and reappear, a new and higher fact. He uses forms according to the life, and not according to the form. This is true science. The poet alone knows astronomy, chemistry, vegetation, and animation, for he does not stop at these facts, but employs them as signs. He knows why the plain, or meadow of space, was strown with these flowers we call suns, and moons, and stars; why the great deep is adorned with animals, with men, and gods; for, in every word he speaks he rides on them as the horses of thought.

By virtue of this science the poet is the Namer, or Language-maker, naming things sometimes after their appearance, sometimes after their essence, and giving to every one its own name and not another's, thereby rejoicing the intellect, which delights in detachment or boundary. The poets made all the words, and therefore language is the archives of history, and, if we must say it, a sort of tomb of the muses. For, though the origin of most of our words is forgotten, each word was at first a stroke of genius, and obtained currency, because for the moment it symbolized the world to the first speaker and to the hearer. The etymologist finds the deadest word to have

---

[14] In Greek myth, the sailor with the keenest eye.

been once a brilliant picture. Language is fossil poetry. As the limestone of the continent consists of infinite masses of the shells of animalcules, so language is made up of images, or tropes, which now, in their secondary use, have long ceased to remind us of their poetic origin. But the poet names the thing because he sees it, or comes one step nearer to it than any other. This expression, or naming, is not art, but a second nature, grown out of the first, as a leaf out of a tree. What we call nature, is a certain self-regulated motion, or change; and nature does all things by her own hands, and does not leave another to baptise her, but baptises herself; and this through the metamorphosis again. I remember that a certain poet[15] described it to me thus:

Genius is the activity which repairs the decays of things, whether wholly or partly of a material and finite kind. Nature, through all her kingdoms, insures herself. Nobody cares for planting the poor fungus: so she shakes down from the gills of one agaric countless spores, any one of which, being preserved, transmits new billions of spores to-morrow or next day. The new agaric of this hour has a chance which the old one had not. This atom of seed is thrown into a new place, not subject to the accidents which destroyed its parent two rods off. She makes a man; and having brought him to ripe age, she will no longer run the risk of losing this wonder at a blow, but she detaches from him a new self, that the kind may be safe from accidents to which the individual is exposed. So when the soul of the poet has come to ripeness of thought, she detaches and sends away from it its poems or songs,—a fearless, sleepless, deathless progeny, which is not exposed to the accidents of the weary kingdom of time: a fearless, vivacious offspring, clad with wings (such was the virtue of the soul out of which they came), which carry them fast and far, and infix them irrecoverably into the hearts of men. These wings are the beauty of the poet's soul. The songs, thus flying immortal from their mortal parent, are pursued by clamorous flights of censures, which swarm in far greater numbers, and threaten to devour them; but these last are not winged. At the end of a very short leap they fall plump down, and rot, having received from the souls out of which they came no beautiful wings. But the melodies of the poet ascend, and leap, and pierce into the deeps of infinite time.

So far the bard taught me, using his freer speech. But nature has a higher end, in the production of new individuals, than security, namely, *ascension,* or, the passage of the soul into higher forms. I knew, in my younger days, the sculptor who made the statue of the youth which stands in the public garden. He was, as I remember, unable to tell directly, what made him happy, or unhappy, but by wonderful indirections he could tell. He rose one day, according to his habit, before the dawn, and saw the morning break, grand as the eternity out of which it came, and, for many days after, he strove to express this tranquillity, and, lo! his chisel had fashioned out of marble the form of a beautiful youth, Phosphorus,[16] whose aspect is such, that, it is said, all persons who look on it become silent. The poet also resigns himself to his mood, and that thought which agitated him is expressed, but

---

[15] Presumably this is a droll reference to Emerson himself.   [16] "Light-bearing," a mythical Greek god associated with the morning star.

alter idem, [17] in a manner totally new. The expression is organic, or, the new type which things themselves take when liberated. As, in the sun, objects paint their images on the retina of the eye, so they, sharing the aspiration of the whole universe, tend to paint a far more delicate copy of their essence in his mind. Like the metamorphosis of things into higher organic forms, is their change into melodies. Over everything stands its dæmon, or soul, and, as the form of the thing is reflected by the eye, so the soul of the thing is reflected by a melody. The sea, the mountain-ridge, Niagara, and every flower-bed, pre-exist, or super-exist, in pre-cantations, [18] which sail like odors in the air, and when any man goes by with an ear sufficiently fine, he overhears them, and endeavors to write down the notes, without diluting or depraving them. And herein is the legitimation of criticism, in the mind's faith, that the poems are a corrupt version of some text in nature, with which they ought to be made to tally. A rhyme in one of our sonnets should not be less pleasing than the iterated nodes of a sea-shell, or the resembling difference of a group of flowers. The pairing of the birds is an idyl, not tedious as our idyls are; a tempest is a rough ode, without falsehood or rant: a summer, with its harvest sown, reaped, and stored, is an epic song, subordinating how many admirably executed parts. Why should not the symmetry and truth that modulate these, glide into our spirits, and we participate the invention of nature?

This insight, which expresses itself by what is called Imagination, is a very high sort of seeing, which does not come by study, but by the intellect being where and what it sees, by sharing the path, or circuit of things through forms, and so making them translucid to others. The path of things is silent. Will they suffer a speaker to go with them? A spy they will not suffer; a lover, a poet, is the transcendency of their own nature,—him they will suffer. The condition of true naming, on the poet's part, is his resigning himself to the divine aura which breathes through forms, and accompanying that.

It is a secret which every intellectual man quickly learns, that, beyond the energy of his possessed and conscious intellect, he is capable of a new energy (as of an intellect doubled on itself), by abandonment to the nature of things; that, beside his privacy of power as an individual man, there is a great public power, on which he can draw, by unlocking, at all risks, his human doors, and suffering the ethereal tides to roll and circulate through him: then he is caught up into the life of the Universe, his speech is thunder, his thought is law, and his words are universally intelligible as the plants and animals. The poet knows that he speaks adequately, then, only when he speaks somewhat wildly, or, "with the flower of the mind;" not with the intellect, used as an organ, but with the intellect released from all service, and suffered to take its direction from its celestial life; or, as the ancients were wont to express themselves, not with intellect alone, but with the intellect inebriated by nectar. As the traveller who has lost his way, throws his reins on his horse's neck, and trusts to the instinct of the animal to find his road, so must we do with the divine animal who carries us through this world. For if in any manner we can stimulate this instinct, new passages are opened for us into nature, the mind flows into and through things hardest and highest, and the metamorphosis is possible.

This is the reason why bards love wine, mead, narcotics, coffee, tea, opium, the fumes of sandal-wood and tobacco, or whatever other species of animal exhilaration.

[17] Latin: "the same yet not identical."   [18] Incantations that are foretelling.

All men avail themselves of such means as they can, to add this extraordinary power to their normal powers; and to this end they prize conversation, music, pictures, sculpture, dancing, theatres, travelling, war, mobs, fires, gaming, politics, or love, or science, or animal intoxication, which are several coarser or finer *quasi*-mechanical substitutes for the true nectar, which is the ravishment of the intellect by coming nearer to the fact. These are auxiliaries to the centrifugal tendency of a man, to his passage out into free space, and they help him to escape the custody of that body in which he is pent up, and of that jail-yard of individual relations in which he is enclosed. Hence a great number of such as were professionally expressors of Beauty, as painters, poets, musicians, and actors, have been more than others wont to lead a life of pleasure and indulgence; all but the few who received the true nectar; and, as it was a spurious mode of attaining freedom, as it was an emancipation not into the heavens, but into the freedom of baser places, they were punished for that advantage they won, by a dissipation and deterioration. But never can any advantage be taken of nature by a trick. The spirit of the world, the great calm presence of the creator, comes not forth to the sorceries of opium or of wine. The sublime vision comes to the pure and simple soul in a clean and chaste body. That is not an inspiration which we owe to narcotics, but some counterfeit excitement and fury. Milton says, that the lyric poet may drink wine and live generously, but the epic poet, he who shall sing of the gods, and their descent unto men, must drink water out of a wooden bowl.[19] For poetry is not 'Devil's wine,' but God's wine. It is with this as it is with toys. We fill the hands and nurseries of our children with all manner of dolls, drums, and horses, withdrawing their eyes from the plain face and sufficing objects of nature, the sun, and moon, the animals, the water, and stones, which should be their toys. So the poet's habit of living should be set on a key so low and plain, that the common influences should delight him. His cheerfulness should be the gift of the sunlight; the air should suffice for his inspiration, and he should be tipsy with water. That spirit which suffices quiet hearts, which seems to come forth to such from every dry knoll of sere grass, from every pine-stump, and half-imbedded stone, on which the dull March sun shines, comes forth to the poor and hungry, and such as are of simple taste. If thou fill thy brain with Boston and New York, with fashion and covetousness, and wilt stimulate thy jaded senses with wine and French coffee, thou shalt find no radiance of wisdom in the lonely waste of the pinewoods.

If the imagination intoxicates the poet, it is not inactive in other men. The metamorphosis excites in the beholder an emotion of joy. The use of symbols has a certain power of emancipation and exhilaration for all men. We seem to be touched by a wand, which makes us dance and run about happily, like children. We are like persons who come out of a cave or cellar into the open air. This is the effect on us of tropes, fables, oracles, and all poetic forms. Poets are thus liberating gods. Men have really got a new sense, and found within their world, another world, or nest of worlds; for, the metamorphosis once seen, we divine that it does not stop. I will not now consider how much this makes the charm of algebra and the mathematics, which also have their tropes, but it is felt in every definition; as, when Aristotle defines *space* to be an immovable vessel, in which things are contained;—or, when Plato defines a *line* to be a flowing point; or, *figure* to be bound of solid; and many the like. What

[19] Restated from "Sixth Latin Elegy," a poem by John Milton.

a joyful sense of freedom we have, when Vitruvius[20] announces the old opinion of artists, that no architect can build any house well, who does not know something of anatomy. When Socrates, in Charmides,[21] tells us that the soul is cured of its maladies by certain incantations, and that these incantations are beautiful reasons, from which temperance is generated in souls; when Plato calls the world an animal; and Timæus[22] affirms that the plants also are animals; or affirms a man to be a heavenly tree, growing with his root, which is his head, upward; and, as George Chapman, following him, writes,—

> "So in our tree of man, whose nervie root
> Springs in his top;"[23]

when Orpheus speaks of hoariness as "that white flower which marks extreme old age;" when Proclus calls the universe the statue of the intellect; when Chaucer, in his praise of "Gentilesse,"[24] compares good blood in mean condition to fire, which, though carried to the darkest house betwixt this and the mount of Caucasus, will yet hold its natural office, and burn as bright as if twenty thousand men did it behold, when John saw, in the apocalypse, the ruin of the world through evil, and the stars fall from heaven, as the figtree casteth her untimely fruit;[25] when Æsop reports the whole catalogue of common daily relations through the masquerade of birds and beasts;—we take the cheerful hint of the immortality of our essence, and its versatile habit and escapes, as when the gypsies say, "it is in vain to hang them, they cannot die."

The poets are thus liberating gods. The ancient British bards had for the title of their order, "Those who are free throughout the world." They are free, and they make free. An imaginative book renders us much more service at first, by stimulating us through its tropes, than afterward, when we arrive at the precise sense of the author. I think nothing is of any value in books, excepting the transcendental and extraordinary. If a man is inflamed and carried away by his thought, to that degree that he forgets the authors and the public, and heeds only this one dream, which holds him like an insanity, let me read his paper, and you may have all the arguments and histories and criticism. All the value which attaches to Pythagoras, Paracelsus, Cornelius Agrippa, Cardan, Kepler, Swedenborg, Schelling, Oken,[26] or any other who introduces questionable facts into his cosmogony, as angels, devils, magic, astrology, palmistry, mesmerism, and so on, is the certificate we have of departure from routine, and that here is a new witness. That also is the best success in conversation, the magic of liberty, which puts the world, like a ball, in our hands. How cheap even the liberty then seems; how mean to study, when an emotion communicates to the intellect the power to sap and upheave nature: how great the perspective! nations, times, systems,

---

[20] Roman architect and writer.
[21] Dialogue of Plato.
[22] Another dialogue of Plato.
[23] Excerpt from George Chapman's (1559?–?1634) dedication to his translation of Homer.
[24] In "The Wife of Bath's Tale" by Geoffrey Chaucer.
[25] See Revelation 6:13.
[26] All of the following were dedicated to theoretical speculation. Pythagoras: Greek mathematician and mystic philosopher (sixth

century B.C.); Paracelsus: Swiss alchemist Philippus Paracelsus (1493–1541); Cornelius Agrippa: German physician (1486?–1535); Cardan: Italian mathematician Jerome Cardan (1501–1576); Kepler: German astronomer Johannes Kepler (1571–1630); Swedenborg: Swedish philosopher and religious writer Emanuel Swedenborg (1688–1772); Schelling: German philosopher Freidrich von Schelling (1775–1854); Oken: German naturalist Lorenz Oken (1779–1851).

enter and disappear, like threads in tapestry of large figure and many colors; dream delivers us to dream, and, while the drunkenness lasts, we will sell our bed, our philosophy, our religion, in our opulence.

There is good reason why we should prize this liberation. The fate of the poor shepherd, who, blinded and lost in the snowstorm, perishes in a drift within a few feet of his cottage door, is an emblem of the state of man. On the brink of the waters of life and truth, we are miserably dying. The inaccessibleness of every thought but that we are in, is wonderful. What if you come near to it,—you are as remote, when you are nearest, as when you are farthest. Every thought is also a prison; every heaven is also a prison. Therefore we love the poet, the inventor, who in any form, whether in an ode, or in an action, or in looks and behavior, has yielded us a new thought. He unlocks our chains, and admits us to a new scene.

This emancipation is dear to all men, and the power to impart it, as it must come from greater depth and scope of thought, is a measure of intellect. Therefore all books of the imagination endure, all which ascend to that truth, that the writer sees nature beneath him, and uses it as his exponent. Every verse or sentence, possessing this virtue, will take care of its own immortality. The religions of the world are the ejaculations of a few imaginative men.

But the quality of the imagination is to flow, and not to freeze. The poet did not stop at the color, or the form, but read their meaning; neither may he rest in this meaning, but he makes the same objects exponents of his new thought. Here is the difference betwixt the poet and the mystic, that the last nails a symbol to one sense, which was a true sense for a moment, but soon becomes old and false. For all symbols are fluxional; all language is vehicular and transitive, and is good, as ferries and horses are, for conveyance, not as farms and houses are, for homestead. Mysticism consists in the mistake of an accidental and individual symbol for an universal one. The morning-redness happens to be the favorite meteor to the eyes of Jacob Behmen,[27] and comes to stand to him for truth and faith; and he believes should stand for the same realities to every reader. But the first reader prefers as naturally the symbol of a mother and child, or a gardener and his bulb, or a jeweller polishing a gem. Either of these, or of a myriad more, are equally good to the person to whom they are significant. Only they must be held lightly, and be very willingly translated into the equivalent terms which others use. And the mystic must be steadily told,—All that you say is just as true without the tedious use of that symbol as with it. Let us have a little algebra, instead of this trite rhetoric,—universal signs, instead of these village symbols, —and we shall both be gainers. The history of hierarchies seems to show, that all religious error consisted in making the symbol too stark and solid, and, at last, nothing but an excess of the organ of language.

Swedenborg, of all men in the recent ages, stands eminently for the translator of nature into thought. I do not know the man in history to whom things stood so uniformly for words. Before him the metamorphosis continually plays. Everything on which his eye rests, obeys the impulses of moral nature. The figs become grapes whilst he eats them. When some of his angels affirmed a truth, the laurel twig which they held blossomed in their hands. The noise which, at a distance, appeared like gnashing and thumping, on coming nearer was found to be the voice of disputants. The men, in one of his visions, seen in heavenly light, appeared like dragons, and

[27] German theosophist and mystic (1575–1624).

seemed in darkness; but, to each other, they appeared as men, and, when the light from heaven shone into their cabin, they complained of the darkness, and were compelled to shut the window that they might see.

There was this perception in him, which makes the poet or seer, an object of awe and terror, namely, that the same man, or society of men, may wear one aspect to themselves and their companions, and a different aspect to higher intelligences. Certain priests, whom he describes as conversing very learnedly together, appeared to the children, who were at some distance, like dead horses: and many the like misappearances. And instantly the mind inquires, whether these fishes under the bridge, yonder oxen in the pasture, those dogs in the yard, are immutably fishes, oxen, and dogs, or only so appear to me, and perchance to themselves appear upright men; and whether I appear as a man to all eyes. The Bramins and Pythagoras propounded the same question, and if any poet has witnessed the transformation, he doubtless found it in harmony with various experiences. We have all seen changes as considerable in wheat and caterpillars. He is the poet, and shall draw us with love and terror, who sees, through the flowing vest, the firm nature, and can declare it.

I look in vain for the poet whom I describe. We do not, with sufficient plainness, or sufficient profoundness, address ourselves to life, nor dare we chaunt our own times and social circumstance. If we filled the day with bravery, we should not shrink from celebrating it. Time and nature yield us many gifts, but not yet the timely man, the new religion, the reconciler, whom all things await. Dante's praise is, that he dared to write his autobiography in colossal cipher, or into universality. We have yet had no genius in America, with tyrannous eye, which knew the value of our incomparable materials, and saw, in the barbarism and materialism of the times, another carnival of the same gods whose picture he so much admires in Homer; then in the middle age; then in Calvinism. Banks and tariffs, the newspaper and caucus, methodism and unitarianism, are flat and dull to dull people, but rest on the same foundations of wonder as the town of Troy, and the temple of Delphos, and are as swiftly passing away. Our logrolling, our stumps[28] and their politics, our fisheries, our Negroes, and Indians, our boats, and our repudiations, the wrath of rogues, and the pusillanimity of honest men, the northern trade, the southern planting, the western clearing, Oregon, and Texas, are yet unsung. Yet America is a poem in our eyes; its ample geography dazzles the imagination, and it will not wait long for metres. If I have not found that excellent combination of gifts in my countrymen which I seek, neither could I aid myself to fix the idea of the poet by reading now and then in Chalmers's[29] collection of five centuries of English poets. These are wits, more than poets, though there have been poets among them. But when we adhere to the ideal of the poet, we have our difficulties even with Milton and Homer. Milton is too literary, and Homer too literal and historical.

But I am not wise enough for a national criticism, and must use the old largeness a little longer, to discharge my errand from the muse to the poet concerning his art.

Art is the path of the creator to his work. The paths, or methods, are ideal and eternal, though few men ever see them, not the artist himself for years, or for a lifetime, unless he come into the conditions. The painter, the sculptor, the composer, the epic rhapsodist, the orator, all partake one desire, namely, to express themselves

---

[28] Political deceptions; public speaking.
[29] Scottish journalist and biographer Alexander

Chalmers (1759–1834) compiled an extensive collection of English poetry (1810).

symmetrically and abundantly, not dwarfishly and fragmentarily. They found or put themselves in certain conditions, as, the painter and sculptor before some impressive human figures; the orator, into the assembly of the people; and the others, in such scenes as each has found exciting to his intellect; and each presently feels the new desire. He hears a voice, he sees a beckoning. Then he is apprised, with wonder, what herds of dæmons hem him in. He can no more rest; he says, with the old painter, "By God, it is in me, and must go forth of me." He pursues a beauty, half seen, which flies before him. The poet pours out verses in every solitude. Most of the things he says are conventional, no doubt; but by and by he says something which is original and beautiful. That charms him. He would say nothing else but such things. In our way of talking, we say, "That is yours, this is mine;" but the poet knows well that it is not his; that it is as strange and beautiful to him as to you; he would fain hear the like eloquence at length. Once having tasted this immortal ichor, he cannot have enough of it, and, as an admirable creative power exists in these intellections, it is of the last importance that these things get spoken. What a little of all we know is said! What drops of all the sea of our science are baled up! and by what accident it is that these are exposed, when so many secrets sleep in nature! Hence the necessity of speech and song; hence these throbs and heart-beatings in the orator, at the door of the assembly, to the end, namely, that thought may be ejaculated as Logos, or Word.

Doubt not, O poet, but persist. Say, "It is in me, and shall out." Stand there, baulked and dumb, stuttering and stammering, hissed and hooted, stand and strive, until, at last, rage draw out of thee that *dream*-power which every night shows thee is thine own; a power transcending all limit and privacy, and by virtue of which a man is the conductor of the whole river of electricity. Nothing walks, or creeps, or grows, or exists, which must not in turn arise and walk before him as exponent of his meaning. Comes he to that power, his genius is no longer exhaustible. All the creatures, by pairs and by tribes, pour into his mind as into a Noah's ark, to come forth again to people a new world. This is like the stock of air for our respiration, or for the combustion of our fireplace, not a measure of gallons, but the entire atmosphere if wanted. And therefore the rich poets, as Homer, Chaucer, Shakspeare, and Raphael, have obviously no limits to their works, except the limits of their lifetime, and resemble a mirror carried through the street, ready to render an image of every created thing.

O poet! a new nobility is conferred in groves and pastures, and not in castles, or by the sword-blade, any longer. The conditions are hard, but equal. Thou shalt leave the world, and know the muse only. Thou shalt not know any longer the times, customs, graces, politics, or opinions of men, but shalt take all from the muse. For the time of towns is tolled from the world by funereal chimes, but in nature the universal hours are counted by succeeding tribes of animals and plants, and by growth of joy on joy. God wills also that thou abdicate a manifold and duplex life, and that thou be content that others speak for thee. Others shall be thy gentlemen, and shall represent all courtesy and worldly life for thee; others shall do the great and resounding actions also. Thou shalt lie close hid with nature, and canst not be afforded to the Capitol or the Exchange. The world is full of renunciations and apprenticeships, and this is thine: thou must pass for a fool and a churl for a long season. This is the screen and sheath in which Pan[30] has protected his well-beloved flower, and thou shalt

---

[30] God of the woods and fields in Greek mythology.

be known only to thine own, and they shall console thee with tenderest love. And thou shalt not be able to rehearse the names of thy friends in thy verse, for an old shame before the holy ideal. And this is the reward: that the ideal shall be real to thee, and the impressions of the actual world shall fall like summer rain, copious, but not troublesome, to thy invulnerable essence. Thou shalt have the whole land for thy park and manor, the sea for thy bath and navigation, without tax and without envy; the woods and the rivers thou shalt own; and thou shalt possess that wherein others are only tenants and boarders. Thou true land-lord! sea-lord! air-lord! Wherever snow falls, or water flows, or birds fly, wherever day and night meet in twilight, wherever the blue heaven is hung by clouds, or sown with stars, wherever are forms with transparent boundaries, wherever are outlets into celestial space, wherever is danger, and awe, and love, there is Beauty, plenteous as rain, shed for thee, and though thou shouldest walk the world over, thou shalt not be able to find a condition inopportune or ignoble.

1844

Concord Hymn[*]

Sung at the completion of the Battle Monument,
July 4, 1837

By the rude bridge that arched the flood,
 Their flag to April's breeze unfurled,
Here once the embattled farmers stood
 And fired the shot heard round the world.

The foe long since in silence slept;   5
 Alike the conqueror silent sleeps;
And Time the ruined bridge has swept
 Down the dark stream which seaward creeps.

On this green bank, by this soft stream,
 We set to-day a votive stone;   10
That memory may their deed redeem,
 When, like our sires, our sons are gone.

Spirit, that made those heroes dare
 To die, and leave their children free,
Bid Time and Nature gently spare   15
 The shaft we raise to them and thee.

1837

[*] This poem was first printed in a pamphlet distributed at the dedication of the monument commemorating the battles of Lexington and Concord (April 19, 1775) in the American Revolutionary War.

The Rhodora[1]

On being asked, whence is the flower?

In May, when sea-winds pierced our solitudes,
I found the fresh Rhodora in the woods,
Spreading its leafless blooms in a damp nook,
To please the desert and the sluggish brook.
The purple petals, fallen in the pool,   5
Made the black water with their beauty gay;
Here might the red-bird come his plumes to cool,
And court the flower that cheapens his array.
Rhodora! if the sages ask thee why
This charm is wasted on the earth and sky,   10
Tell them, dear, that if eyes were made for seeing,
Then Beauty is its own excuse for being:
Why thou wert there, O rival of the rose!
I never thought to ask, I never knew:
But, in my simple ignorance, suppose   15
The self-same Power that brought me there brought you.

1834/1839

Each and All

Little thinks, in the field, yon red-cloaked clown[1]
Of thee from the hill-top looking down;
The heifer that lows in the upland farm,
Far-heard, lows not thine ear to charm;
The sexton, tolling his bell at noon,   5
Deems not that great Napoleon
Stops his horse, and lists with delight,
Whilst his files sweep round yon Alpine height;
Nor knowest thou what argument
Thy life to thy neighbor's creed has lent.   10
All are needed by each one;
Nothing is fair or good alone.
I thought the sparrow's note from heaven,

---

[1] Shrub similar to the rhododendron found in
New England.

[1] Rustic; peasant.

Singing at dawn on the alder bough;
I brought him home, in his nest, at even;   15
He sings the song, but it cheers not now,
For I did not bring home the river and sky;—
He sang to my ear,—they sang to my eye.
The delicate shells lay on the shore;
The bubbles of the latest wave   20
Fresh pearls to their enamel gave,
And the bellowing of the savage sea
Greeted their safe escape to me.
I wiped away the weeds and foam,
I fetched my sea-born treasures home;   25
But the poor, unsightly, noisome things
Had left their beauty on the shore
With the sun and the sand and the wild uproar.
The lover watched his graceful maid,
As 'mid the virgin train she strayed,   30
Nor knew her beauty's best attire
Was woven still by the snow-white choir.
At last she came to his hermitage,
Like the bird from the woodlands to the cage;—
The gay enchantment was undone,   35
A gentle wife, but fairy none.
Then I said, 'I covet truth;
Beauty is unripe childhood's cheat;
I leave it behind with the games of youth:'—
As I spoke, beneath my feet   40
The ground-pine curled its pretty wreath,
Running over the club-moss burrs;
I inhaled the violet's breath;
Around me stood the oaks and firs;
Pine-cones and acorns lay on the ground;   45
Over me soared the eternal sky,
Full of light and of deity;
Again I saw, again I heard,
The rolling river, the morning bird;—
Beauty through my senses stole;   50
I yielded myself to the perfect whole.

1839

The Problem

I like a church; I like a cowl;
I love a prophet of the soul;
And on my heart monastic aisles
Fall like sweet strains, or pensive smiles;
Yet not for all his faith can see   5
Would I that cowlèd churchman be.

Why should the vest[1] on him allure,
Which I could not on me endure?

Not from a vain or shallow thought
His awful Jove young Phidias[2] brought;   10
Never from lips of cunning fell
The thrilling Delphic oracle;[3]
Out from the heart of nature rolled
The burdens of the Bible old;
The litanies of nations came,   15
Like the volcano's tongue of flame,
Up from the burning core below,—
The canticles of love and woe:
The hand[4] that rounded Peter's dome
And groined the aisles of Christian Rome   20
Wrought in a sad sincerity;
Himself from God he could not free;
He builded better than he knew;—
The conscious stone to beauty grew.

Know'st thou what wove yon woodbird's nest   25
Of leaves, and feathers from her breast?
Or how the fish outbuilt her shell,
Painting with morn each annual cell?
Or how the sacred pine-tree adds
To her old leaves new myriads?   30
Such and so grew these holy piles,
Whilst love and terror laid the tiles.
Earth proudly wears the Parthenon,
As the best gem upon her zone,

[1] Vestment.
[2] Greek sculptor, fifth century B.C.
[3] Prophetess at the Temple of Apollo at Delphos in ancient Greece.

[4] Reference to Michelangelo (1475–1564), who became the principal architect of St. Peter's Cathedral in Rome.

And Morning opes with haste her lids   35
To gaze upon the Pyramids;
O'er England's abbeys bends the sky,
As on its friends, with kindred eye;
For out of Thought's interior sphere
These wonders rose to upper air;   40
And Nature gladly gave them place,
Adopted them into her race,
And granted them an equal date
With Andes and with Ararat.[5]

These temples grew as grows the grass;   45
Art might obey, but not surpass.
The passive Master lent his hand
To the vast soul that o'er him planned;
And the same power that reared the shrine
Bestrode the tribes that knelt within.   50
Ever the fiery Pentecost[6]
Girds with one flame the countless host,
Trances the heart through chanting choirs,
And through the priest the mind inspires.
The word unto the prophet spoken   55
Was writ on tables yet unbroken;
The word by seers or sibyls told,
In groves of oak, or fanes[7] of gold,
Still floats upon the morning wind,
Still whispers to the willing mind.   60
One accent of the Holy Ghost
The heedless world hath never lost.
I know what say the fathers wise,—
The Book itself before me lies,
Old *Chrysostom*,[8] best Augustine,[9]   65
And he who blent both in his line,
The younger *Golden Lips* or mines,
Taylor,[10] the Shakspeare of divines.
His words are music in my ear,
I see his cowlèd portrait dear;   70
And yet, for all his faith could see,
I would not the good bishop be.

1840

---

[5] Andes: mountain range in South America; Ararat: mountain in Asia Minor where Noah's ark landed after the flood.

[6] The Holy Spirit, who descended upon the apostles. (See Acts 2.)

[7] Temples.

[8] St. John of Antioch (A.D. 345?–407), called "Golden Lips" (Greek: *Chrysostom*) for his eloquence.

[9] St. Augustine (A.D. 354–430), author of *Confessions* and *The City of God*.

[10] Jeremy Taylor (1613–1667). English theologian.

The Snow-storm

Announced by all the trumpets of the sky,
Arrives the snow, and, driving o'er the fields,
Seems nowhere to alight: the whited air
Hides hills and woods, the river, and the heaven,
And veils the farm-house at the garden's end.   5
The sled and traveller stopped, the courier's feet
Delayed, all friends shut out, the housemates sit
Around the radiant fireplace, enclosed
In a tumultuous privacy of storm.

Come see the north wind's masonry.   10
Out of an unseen quarry evermore
Furnished with tile, the fierce artificer
Curves his white bastions with projected roof
Round every windward stake, or tree, or door.
Speeding, the myriad-handed, his wild work   15
So fanciful, so savage, nought cares he
For number or proportion. Mockingly,
On coop or kennel he hangs Parian[1] wreaths;
A swan-like form invests the hidden thorn;
Fills up the farmer's lane from wall to wall,   20
Maugre the farmer's sighs; and at the gate
A tapering turret overtops the work.
And when his hours are numbered, and the world
Is all his own, retiring, as he were not,
Leaves, when the sun appears, astonished Art   25
To mimic in slow structures, stone by stone,
Built in an age, the mad wind's night-work,
The frolic architecture of the snow.

1835/1841

---

[1] I.e., like white marble quarried from the island
Paros, used by Greek sculptors.

Uriel[1]

It fell in the ancient periods
   Which the brooding soul surveys,
Or ever the wild Time coined itself
   Into calendar months and days.

This was the lapse of Uriel,   5
Which in Paradise befell.
Once, among the Pleiads[2] walking,
Seyd[3] overheard the young gods talking;
And the treason, too long pent,
To his ears was evident.   10
The young deities discussed
Laws of form, and metre just,
Orb, quintessence, and sunbeams,
What subsisteth, and what seems.
One, with low tones that decide,   15
And doubt and reverend use defied,
With a look that solved the sphere,
And stirred the devils everywhere,
Gave his sentiment divine
Against the being of a line.   20
'Line in nature is not found;
Unit and universe are round;
In vain produced, all rays return;
Evil will bless, and ice will burn.'
As Uriel spoke with piercing eye,   25
A shudder ran around the sky;
The stern old war-gods shook their heads,
The seraphs frowned from myrtle-beds;
Seemed to the holy festival
The rash word boded ill to all;   30
The balance-beam of Fate was bent;
The bounds of good and ill were rent;
Strong Hades[4] could not keep his own,
But all slid to confusion.

A sad self-knowledge, withering, fell   35
On the beauty of Uriel;

---

[1] Name ascribed to the god of light in John Milton's *Paradise Lost* (1667).
[2] Cluster of seven stars named for the seven daughters of Atlas and Pleione in Greek myth.
[3] The thirteenth-century Persian poet Saadi.
[4] Another name for Pluto, ruler of the underworld in Greek myth.

In heaven once eminent, the god
Withdrew, that hour, into his cloud;
Whether doomed to long gyration
In the sea of generation,   40
Or by knowledge grown too bright
To hit the nerve of feebler sight.
Straightway, a forgetting wind
Stole over the celestial kind,
And their lips the secret kept,   45
If in ashes the fire-seed slept.
But now and then, truth-speaking things
Shamed the angels' veiling wings;
And, shrilling from the solar course,
Or from fruit of chemic force,   50
Procession of a soul in matter,
Or the speeding change of water,
Or out of the good of evil born,
Came Uriel's voice of cherub scorn,
And a blush tinged the upper sky,   55
And the gods shook, they knew not why.
1847

Hamatreya[1]

Bulkeley, Hunt, Willard, Hosmer, Meriam, Flint,[2]
Possessed the land which rendered to their toil
Hay, corn, roots, hemp, flax, apples, wool and wood.
Each of these landlords walked amidst his farm,
Saying, ' 'T is mine, my children's and my name's.   5
How sweet the west wind sounds in my own trees!
How graceful climb those shadows on my hill!
I fancy these pure waters and the flags[3]
Know me, as does my dog: we sympathize;
And, I affirm, my actions smack of the soil.'   10

Where are these men? Asleep beneath their grounds:
And strangers, fond as they, their furrows plough.
Earth laughs in flowers, to see her boastful boys
Earth-proud, proud of the earth which is not theirs;

---

[1] A derivation of *Maitreya*, the Hindu god named
in the sacred *Vishnu Purana*. Also possibly a
Greek interpretation of "earth-mother."

[2] Family names of the first settlers of Concord,
Massachusetts.
[3] Wild irises.

Who steer the plough, but cannot steer their feet   15
Clear of the grave.
They added ridge to valley, brook to pond,
And sighed for all that bounded their domain;
'This suits me for a pasture; that's my park;
We must have clay, lime, gravel, granite-ledge,   20
And misty lowland, where to go for peat.
The land is well,—lies fairly to the south.
'T is good, when you have crossed the sea and back,
To find the sitfast acres where you left them.'
Ah! the hot owner sees not Death, who adds   25
Him to his land, a lump of mould the more.
Hear what the Earth says:—

EARTH-SONG

'Mine and yours;
Mine, not yours.
Earth endures;   30
Stars abide—
Shine down in the old sea;
Old are the shores;
But where are old men?
I who have seen much,   35
Such have I never seen.

'The lawyer's deed
Ran sure,
In tail.[4]
To them, and to their heirs   40
Who shall succeed,
Without fail,
Forevermore.

'Here is the land,
Shaggy with wood,   45
With its old valley,
Mound and flood.
But the heritors?—

Fled like the flood's foam.
The lawyer, and the laws,   50
And the kingdom,
Clean swept herefrom.

---

[4] As in *entail*, the legal designation of an
inheritance to specific descendants.

'They called me theirs,
Who so controlled me;
Yet every one
Wished to stay, and is gone,
How am I theirs,
If they cannot hold me,
But I hold them?'

When I heard the Earth-song
I was no longer brave;
My avarice cooled
Like lust in the chill of the grave.

1847

Ode

Inscribed to W. H. Channing[1]

Though loath to grieve
The evil time's sole patriot,
I cannot leave
My honied thought
For the priest's cant,   5
Or statesman's rant.

If I refuse
My study for their politique,
Which at the best is trick,
The angry Muse   10
Puts confusion in my brain.

But who is he that prates
Of the culture of mankind,
Of better arts and life?
Go, blindworm, go,   15
Behold the famous States
Harrying Mexico
With rifle and with knife![2]

Or who, with accent bolder,
Dare praise the freedom-loving mountaineer?   20

---

[1] William Henry Channing (1810–1884),
Unitarian clergyman, Transcendentalist,
abolitionist, and nephew of William Ellery
Channing (1780–1842), Unitarian leader.

[2] Emerson opposed the Mexican War
(1846–1848), which he regarded as an effort to
extend slavery.

I found by thee, O rushing Contoocook![3]
And in thy valleys, Agiochook![4]
The jackals of the negro-holder.

The God who made New Hampshire   25
Taunted the lofty land
With little men;
Small bat and wren
House in the oak:
If earth-fire cleave
The upheaved land, and bury the folk,   30
The southern crocodile would grieve.
Virtue palters; Right is hence;
Freedom praised, but hid;
Funeral eloquence
Rattles the coffin-lid.   35

What boots thy zeal,
O glowing friend,
That would indignant rend
The northland from the south?
Wherefore? to what good end?   40
Boston Bay and Bunker Hill
Would serve things still;
Things are of the snake.

The horseman serves the horse,
The neatherd[5] serves the neat,   45
The merchant serves the purse,
The eater serves his meat;
'T is the day of the chattel,
Web to weave, and corn to grind;
Things are in the saddle,   50
And ride mankind.

There are two laws discrete,
Not reconciled—
Law for man, and law for thing;
The last builds town and fleet,   55
But it runs wild,
And doth the man unking.

'T is fit the forest fall,
The steep be graded,

---

[3] River in New Hampshire.   [5] Cowherd.
[4] The White Mountains of New Hampshire, a
state that had voted the Democratic, or
proslavery, ticket at the time.

The mountain tunnelled,
The sand shaded,
The orchard planted,
The glebe[6] tilled,
The prairie granted,
The stamer built.   6

Let man serve law for man;
Live for friendship, live for love,
For truth's and harmony's behoof;
The state may follow how it can,
As Olympus follows Jove.[7]   70

Yet do not I implore
The wrinkled shopman to my sounding woods,
Nor bid the unwilling senator
Ask votes of thrushes in the solitudes.
Every one to his chosen work;   75
Foolish hands may mix and mar;
Wise and sure the issues are.
Round they roll till dark is light,
Sex to sex, and even to odd;
The over-god   80
Who marries Right to Might,
Who peoples, unpeoples,
He who exterminates
Races by stronger races,
Black by white faces,   85
Knows to bring honey
Out of the lion;[8]
Grafts gentlest scion
On pirate and Turk.

The Cossack eats Poland,[9]   90
Like stolen fruit;
Her last noble is ruined,
Her last poet mute:
Straight, into double band
The victors divide;   95
Half for freedom strike and stand;
The astonished Muse finds thousands at her side.
1847

---

6 Soil.
7 Another name for Zeus, or Jupiter, father of the
Olympian deities in Greek myth.
8 See Judges 14:8. Samson found the carcass of a
lion in which bees had made honey: "Out of

the eater came forth meat, and out of the
strong came forth sweetness."
9 Poland had been divided three times in the late
eighteenth century, with Russia ("the Cossack")
getting the most territory.

Give All to Love

Give all to love;
Obey thy heart;
Friends, kindred, days,
Estate, good-fame,
Plans, credit and the Muse,—   5
Nothing refuse.

'T is a brave master;
Let it have scope:
Follow it utterly,
Hope beyond hope: 10
High and more high
It dives into noon,
With wing unspent,
Untold intent;
But it is a god,   15
Knows its own path
And the outlets of the sky.

It was never for the mean;
It requireth courage stout.
Souls above doubt,   20
Valor unbending,
It will reward,—
They shall return
More than they were,
And ever ascending.   25

Leave all for love;
Yet, hear me, yet,
One word more thy heart behoved,
One pulse more of firm endeavor,—
Keep thee to-day,   30
To-morrow, forever,
Free as an Arab
Of thy beloved.

Cling with life to the maid;
But when the surprise,   35
First vague shadow of surmise
Flits across her bosom young,
Of a joy apart from thee,

Free be she, fancy-free;
Nor thou detain her vesture's hem,   40
Nor the palest rose she flung
From her summer diadem.

Though thou loved her as thyself,
As a self of purer clay,
Though her parting dims the day,   45
Stealing grace from all alive;
Heartily know,
When half-gods go,
The gods arrive.
1847

Days

Daughters of Time, the hypocritic Days,
Muffled and dumb like barefoot dervishes,
And marching single in an endless file,
Bring diadems and fagots in their hands.
To each they offer gifts after his will,   5
Bread, kingdoms, stars, and sky that holds them all.
I, in my pleached garden, watched the pomp,
Forgot my morning wishes, hastily
Took a few herbs and apples, and the Day
Turned and departed silent. I, too late,   10
Under her solemn fillet saw the scorn.
1857

Brahma[1]

If the red slayer[2] think he slays,
   Or if the slain think he is slain,
They know not well the subtle ways
   I keep, and pass, and turn again,

[1] In Hindu belief, the supreme spirit of the   [2] Death.
universe.

> Far or forgot to me is near;   5
> Shadow and sunlight are the same;
> The vanished gods to me appear;
> And one to me are shame and fame.
>
> They reckon ill who leave me out;
> When me they fly, I am the wings;   10
> I am the doubter and the doubt,
> And I the hymn the Brahmin sings.
>
> The strong gods³ pine for my abode,
> And pine in vain the sacred Seven;⁴
> But thou, meek lover of the good!   15
> Find me, and turn thy back on heaven.
>
> *1856/1857*

from Journals

[June 2, 1832]

I have sometimes thought that in order to be a good minister it was necessary to leave the ministry. The profession is antiquated. In an altered age, we worship in the dead forms of our forefathers. Were not a Socratic paganism better than an effete super-annuated Christianity?

[September 1, 1833, Liverpool]

I thank the great God who has led me through this European scene, this last school-room in which he has pleased to instruct me from Malta's isle, thro' Sicily, thro' Italy, thro' Switzerland, thro' France, thro' England, thro' Scotland, in safety & pleasure & has now brought me to the shore & the ship that steers westward. He has shown me the men I wished to see—Landor, Coleridge, Carlyle, Wordsworth¹—he has thereby comforted & confirmed me in my convictions. Many things I owe to the sight of these men. I shall judge more justly, less timidly, of wise men forevermore. To be sure not one of these is a mind of the very first class, but what the intercourse with each of these suggests is true of intercourse with better men, that they never *fill the ear*—fill the mind—no, it is an *idealized* portrait which always we draw of them. Upon an intelligent man, wholly a stranger to their names, they would make in conversation no deep impression—none of a world-filling fame—they would be

---

³ Agni, god of fire; Indra, god of the sky; and Yama, god of death.
⁴ The seven high saints of Hinduism.
¹ English poets and essayists Walter Savage

Landor (1775–1864), Samuel Taylor Coleridge (1772–1834), Thomas Carlyle (1795–1881), and William Wordsworth (1770–1850).

remembered as sensible well read earnest men—not more. Especially are they all deficient all these four—in different degrees but all deficient—in insight into religious truth. They have no idea of that species of moral truth which I call the first philosophy. (Peter Hunt[2] is as wise a talker as either of these men. Don't laugh.)

The comfort of meeting men of genius such as these is that they talk sincerely. They feel themselves to be so rich that they are above the meanness of pretending to knowledge which they have not & they frankly tell you what puzzles them. But Carlyle. Carlyle is so amiable that I love him. But I am very glad my travelling is done. A man not old feels himself too old to be a vagabond. The people at their work, the people whose avocations I interrupt by my letters of introduction accuse me by their looks for leaving my business to hinder theirs.

These men make you feel that fame is a conventional thing & that man is a sadly 'limitary' spirit. You speak to them as to children or persons of inferior capacity whom it is necessary to humor; adapting our tone & remarks to their known prejudices & not to our knowledge of the truth.

I believe in my heart it is better to admire too rashly, as I do, than to be admired too rashly as the great men of this day are. They miss by their premature canonization a great deal of necessary knowledge, & one of these days must begin the world again (as to their surprize they will find needful) poor. I speak now in general & not of these individuals. God save a great man from a little circle of flatterers. I know it is sweet, very sweet, rats bane.

[September 6, 1833]

Fair fine wind, still in the Channel—off the coast of Ireland but not in sight of land. This morning 37 sail in sight.

I like my book about nature & wish I knew where & how I ought to live. God will show me. I am glad to be on my way home yet not so glad as others & my way to the bottom I could find perchance with less regret for I think it would not hurt me, that is the ducking or drowning.

[November–December 1833]

This Book is my Savings Bank. I grow richer because I have somewhere to deposit my earnings; and fractions are worth more to me because corresponding fractions are waiting here that shall be made integers by their addition.

[May 26, 1837]

Who shall define to me an Individual? I behold with awe & delight many illustrations of the One Universal Mind. I see my being imbedded in it. As a plant in the earth so I grow in God. I am only a form of him. He is the soul of Me. I can even with a mountainous aspiring say, *I am God,* by transferring my *Me* out of the flimsy & unclean precincts of my body, my fortunes, my private will, & meekly retiring upon

[2] Student of Emerson's in 1825.

the holy austerities of the Just & the Loving—upon the secret fountains of Nature. That thin & difficult ether, I also can breathe. The mortal lungs & nostrils burst & shrivel, but the soul itself needeth no organs—it is all element & all organ. Yet why not always so? How came the Individual thus armed & impassioned to parricide, thus murderously inclined ever to traverse & kill the divine life? Ah wicked Manichee![3] Into that dim problem I cannot enter. A believer in Unity, a seer of Unity, I yet behold two.

I behold; I bask in beauty; I await; I wonder; Where is my Godhead now? This is the Male & Female principle in Nature. One Man, male & female created he him. Hard as it is to describe God, it is harder to describe the Individual.

A certain wandering light comes to me which I instantly perceive to be the Cause of Causes. It transcends all proving. It is itself the ground of being; and I see that it is not one & I another, but this is the life of my life. That is one fact, then; that in certain moments I have known that I existed directly from God, and am, as it were, his organ. And in my ultimate consciousness Am He. Then, secondly, the contradictory fact is familiar, that I am a surprised spectator & learner of all my life. This is the habitual posture of the mind—beholding. But whenever the day dawns, the great day of truth on the soul, it comes with awful invitation to me to accept it, to blend with its aurora.

Cannot I conceive the Universe without a contradiction?

[August 31, 1838]

Yesterday a ΦBK[4] anniversary. Steady, steady. I am convinced that if a man will be a true scholar, he shall have perfect freedom. The young people & the mature hint at odium, & aversion of faces to be presently encountered in society. I say no: I fear it not. No scholar need fear it. For if it be true that he is merely an observer, a dispassionate reporter, no partisan, a singer merely for the love of music, his is a position of perfect immunity: to him no disgusts can attach; he is invulnerable. The vulgar think he would found a sect & would be installed & made much of. He knows better & much prefers his melons & his woods. Society has no bribe for me, neither in politics, nor church, nor college, nor city. My resources are far from exhausted. If they will not hear me lecture, I shall have leisure for my book which wants me. Beside, it is an universal maxim worthy of all acceptation that a man may have that allowance which he takes. Take the place & attitude to which you see your unquestionable right, & all men acquiesce. Who are these murmurers, these haters, these revilers? Men of no knowledge, & therefore no stability. The scholar on the contrary is sure of his point, is fast-rooted, & can securely predict the hour when all this roaring multitude shall roar *for* him. Analyze the chiding opposition & it is made up of such timidities, uncertainties, & no opinions, that it is not worth dispersing.

It is one of the blessings of old friends that you can afford to be stupid with them.

[3] Manichean: one who follows the dualistic religious philosophy taught by the Persian prophet Manes (ca. third century B.C.).
[4] Phi Beta Kappa, the national honor society of college students and graduates chosen on the basis of high academic standing. (See Emerson's essay "The American Scholar.")

[from **October 26, 1838]**

Every word, every striking word that occurs in the pages of an original genius will provoke attack & be the subject of twenty pamphlets & a hundred paragraphs. Should he be so duped as to stop & listen? Rather, let him know that the page he writes today will contain a new subject for the pamphleteers, & that which he writes tomorrow, more. Let him not be misled to give it any more than the notice due from him, viz. just that which it had in his first page, before the controversy. The exaggeration of the notice is right for them, false for him. Every word that he quite naturally writes is as prodigious & offensive. So write on, & by & by will come a reader and an age that will justify all your context. Do not even look behind. Leave that bone for them to pick & welcome.

Let me study & work contentedly & faithfully, I do not remember my critics. I forget them—I depart from them by every step I take. If I think then of them, it is a bad sign. . . .

[May **28, 1839]**

There is no history: There is only Biography. The attempt to perpetuate, to fix a thought or principle, fails continually. You can only live for yourself: Your action is good only whilst it is alive—whilst it is in you. The awkward imitation of it by your child or your disciple, is not a repetition of it, is not the same thing but another thing. The new individual must work out the whole problem of science, letters, & theology for himself, can owe his fathers nothing. There is no history; only biography.

[from **September 14–17, 1839]**

. . . The mob are always interesting. We hate editors, preachers, & all manner of scholars, and fashionists. A blacksmith, a truckman, a farmer we follow into the barroom & watch with eagerness what they shall say, for such as they, do not speak because they are expected to, but because they have somewhat to say.

It seems as if the present age of words should naturally be followed by an age of silence when men shall speak only through facts & so regain their health. We die of words. We are hanged, drawn, & quartered by dictionaries. We walk in the vale of shadows. It is an age of hobgoblins. Public Opinion is a hobgoblin, Christianity a hobgoblin, the God of popular worship a hobgoblin. When shall we attain to be real & be born into the new heaven & earth of nature & truth? . . .

[October **17, 1840]**

Yesterday George & Sophia Ripley, Margaret Fuller & Alcott[5] discussed here the new social plans.[6] I wished to be convinced, to be thawed, to be made nobly mad by the

---

[5] George Ripley (1802–1880), his wife Sophia, Margaret Fuller (1810–1850), and Amos Bronson Alcott (1799–1888).

[6] I.e., plans for Brook Farm, a utopian community.

kindlings before my eye of a new dawn of human piety. But this scheme was arithmetic & comfort; this was a hint borrowed from the Tremont House & U.S. Hotel;[7] a rage in our poverty & politics to live rich & gentlemanlike, an anchor to leeward against a change of weather; a prudent forecast on the probable issue of the great questions of pauperism & property. And not once could I be inflamed—but sat aloof & thoughtless, my voice faltered & fell. It was not the cave of persecution which is the palace of spiritual power, but only a room in the Astor House hired for the Transcendentalists. I do not wish to remove from my present prison to a prison a little larger. I wish to break all prisons. I have not yet conquered my own house. It irks & repents me. Shall I raise the siege of this hencoop & march baffled away to a pretended siege of Babylon? It seems to me that so to do were to dodge the problem I am set to solve, & to hide my impotency in the thick of a crowd. I can see too afar that I should not find myself more than now—no, not so much, in that select, but not by me selected, fraternity. Moreover to join this body would be to traverse all my long trumpeted theory, and the instinct which spoke from it, that one man is a counterpoise to a city—that a man is stronger than a city, that his solitude is more prevalent & beneficent than the concert of crowds.

[September(?) 1841]

I told H.T.[8] that his freedom is in the form, but he does not disclose new matter. I am very familiar with all his thoughts—they are my own quite originally drest. But if the question be, what new ideas has he thrown into circulation, he has not yet told what that is which he was created to say. I said to him what I often feel, I only know three persons who seem to me fully to see this law of reciprocity or compensation —himself, Alcott,[9] & myself: and 'tis odd that we should all be neighbors, for in the wide land or the wide earth I do not know another who seems to have it as deeply & originally as these three Gothamites.[10]

[from July–October 1851]

H. T.[11] will not stick—he is not practically renovator. He is a boy, & will be an old boy. Pounding beans is good to the end of pounding Empires, but not, if at the end of years, it is only beans.

I fancy it an inexcusable fault in him that he is insignificant here in the town. He speaks at Lyceum or other meeting but somebody else speaks & his speech falls dead & is forgotten. He rails at the town doings & ought to correct & inspire them.

America is the idea of emancipation.

Abolish kingcraft, Slavery, feudalism, blackletter monopoly, pull down gallows, explode priestcraft, tariff, open the doors of the sea to all emigrants. Extemporize government, California, Texas, Lynch Law. All this covers selfgovernment. All

---

[7] The Tremont House (opened in 1829) and the U.S. Hotel (opened in 1840) were famous hotels in Boston. The Astor House (opened in 1836) was a famous luxury hotel in New York.
[8] Henry David Thoreau (1817–1862), then

Emerson's neighbor and a resident at Walden Pond.
[9] Amos Bronson Alcott.
[10] City dwellers.
[11] Henry David Thoreau.

proceeds on the belief that as the people have made a govt. they can make another, that their Union & law is not in their memory but in their blood. If they unmake the law they can easily make it again. . . .

[from June 1863]

In reading Henry Thoreau's Journal, I am very sensible of the vigor of his constitution. That oaken strength which I noted whenever he walked or worked or surveyed wood lots, the same unhesitating hand with which a field-laborer accosts a piece of work which I should shun as a waste of strength, Henry shows in his literary task. He has muscle, & ventures on & performs feats which I am forced to decline. In reading him, I find the same thought, the same spirit that is in me, but he takes a step beyond, & illustrates by excellent images that which I should have conveyed in a sleepy generality. 'Tis as if I went into a gymnasium, & saw youths leap, climb, & swing with a force unapproachable—though their feats are only continuations of my initial grapplings & jumps.

[from May 24, 1864]

Yesterday, 23 May, we buried Hawthorne in Sleepy Hollow, in a pomp of sunshine & verdure, & gentle winds. James F. Clarke[12] read the service in the Church & at the grave. Longfellow, Lowell, Holmes, Agassiz, Hoar, Dwight, Whipple, Norton, Alcott, Hillard, Fields, Judge Thomas, & I, attended the hearse as pall bearers.[13] Franklin Pierce[14] was with the family. The church was copiously decorated with white flowers delicately arranged. The corpse was unwillingly shown—only a few moments to this company of his friends. But it was noble & serene in its aspect—nothing amiss —a calm & powerful head. A large company filled the church, & the grounds of the cemetery. All was so bright & quiet, that pain or mourning was hardly suggested, & Holmes said to me, that it looked like a happy meeting. . . .

1824–1870s(?)/1909

[12] James Freeman Clarke (1810–1888), who had officiated at Nathaniel Hawthorne's marriage to Sophia Peabody.

[13] Many of the pallbearers at Hawthorne's funeral were, along with Emerson, members of the Saturday Club, which gathered the last Saturday of each month at the Parker House in Boston. Henry Wadsworth Longfellow (1807–1882), and James Russell Lowell (1819–1891), prominent poets; Oliver Wendell Holmes (1809–1894), physician and author; Louis Agassiz (1807–1873), Swiss immigrant and scientist at Harvard; Ebenezer Rockwood Hoar

(1816–1895), brother of Charles Emerson's fiancee Elizabeth Hoar; John S. Dwight (1813–1893), music critic; Edwin Percy Whipple (1819–1886), literary critic; Charles Eliot Norton (1827–1908), writer; Amos Bronson Alcott (1799–1888), educator and Transcendentalist; George Hillard (1808–1879), writer and lawyer; James T. Fields (1817–1881), Hawthorne's publisher; and B. F. Thomas (1813–1878), Boston judge.

[14] Franklin Pierce (1804–1869) had served as president of the United States from 1853 to 1857.

Margaret Fuller
1810–1850

Margaret Fuller's life and work transcended virtually every stereotype American women had to endure in the first half of the nineteenth century. She matured intellectually at a very early age yet married very late. She was a feminist pioneer in East Coast literary circles at a time when women pioneers were more apt to be leading wagon trains to the West Coast. She wrote first-rate—and controversial—journalism as well as social and literary criticism when women were expected to be preoccupied with insuring domestic tranquillity. She read the leading writers of her time and was vilified by many of them. Nine years after her death, Nathaniel Hawthorne poured out his dislike of her in his notebooks. He called her a "great humbug," a woman with a "strong, heavy, unpliable, and in many respects defective and evil nature." Even her friend, the English poet Elizabeth Barrett Browning, who knew her when both were living in Italy, cautioned potential readers: "If I wished anyone to do her justice, I should say, as I have said, 'Never read what she has written.'" Henry James concluded early on that Margaret Fuller had "left nothing behind her, her written utterance being naught." Yet recent scholarship suggests that Margaret Fuller did produce an impressive body of work. An accomplished teacher, translator, editor, columnist, poet, critic, and feminist theorist and advocate, as well as a social and political activist, Fuller became an articulate and influential voice in America's struggle to come to terms with its literary identity and social conscience.

Sarah Margaret Fuller was born in Cambridgeport, Massachusetts, on May 23, 1810, the first of Margaret and Timothy Fuller's five children. Her mother, having to contend with poor health, struggled continually to raise the family. Her father, a Harvard-trained lawyer and member of Congress, compensated for his wife's frailty by dominating the children's lives with an almost ruthless passion that apparently he alone considered affection. Recognizing young Margaret's intellectual bent, he decided to cultivate it as quickly and as fully as possible by designing a highly rigorous education for her. He was, as she later explained, "a severe teacher, both from his habits of mind and his ambitions for me." A stern disciplinarian and a dogmatic educational theorist, Timothy Fuller trained his daughter to read the classics by age six, Shakespeare by eight. Thereafter, he schooled her in modern languages, especially German, as well as in ancient and modern history, biblical scholarship, and English literature.

Reading and writing served as the principal activities of Margaret Fuller's early years. A prodigious letter writer, she repeatedly punctuated her youthful correspondence with the anxious intellectual ranklings of one who had been denied the pleasures of a peaceful childhood. Her father's intense and deliberate tutelage resulted, as she later noted, in a "premature development of the brain, that made me a 'youthful prodigy' by day, and by night a victim of spectral illusions," the most recurrent of which was a nightmare in which horses galloped across her head. The intellectual independence her father demanded of her prompted Margaret Fuller to regard herself as clearly out of place in a society that established homemaking and etiquette as high priorities in the training of young women.

After an unsettling year attending the Misses Prescott's school in rural Groton, Massachusetts (where for a time she sat next to Oliver Wendell Holmes), Margaret Fuller returned home in 1824 and resumed the course of study her father had so carefully laid out for her. For nearly the next decade she led a rather isolated, although intellectually high-charged, life. From all accounts, her education was far more rigorous than the instruction nearby Harvard University still denied to women of that time. Only occasionally did she venture out into the elite, male conversational world to which her father introduced her. Of the daring young liberal clergymen and writers she met during the late 1820s and early 1830s, Margaret Fuller developed lasting friendships with but a few, most notably James Freeman Clarke and W. H. Channing, who, along with Ralph Waldo Emerson, would prepare her *Memoirs* after her death. Yet even these few opportunities for intellectual companionship were denied her in 1833 when she moved with her family to Groton, where she was expected to concentrate on educating the four younger children in the family.

When Margaret Fuller's father died unexpectedly in 1835, responsibility for supporting the family fell to her. She did this principally through teaching at various schools for several years, including Boston's experimental Temple School, directed by the Transcendentalist Bronson Alcott. During this same period she intensified her study of German with the assistance of Dr. William Ellery Channing, the longtime minister at Boston's Federal Street Church. Reading Goethe would influence the course of both her thinking and teaching and prepare her for her first two book-length publications, translations titled *Eckermann's Conversations with Goethe* (1839) and *Correspondence of Franklin Günderode with Bettina von Arnim* (1842). Within a few years after her father's death, Margaret Fuller had expanded her once meager conversational network to include such soon-to-be celebrated cultural figures as Ralph Waldo Emerson (whom she first had visited in Concord in 1836), Henry David Thoreau, Frederic Henry Hedge, and most of the other liberal thinkers who came to be known as the Transcendentalists. In a letter dated November 16, 1837, to Caroline Sturgis, the intellectually energetic daughter of a Boston merchant, Fuller presented her own particularly insightful, if somewhat defensive and ironic, view of her own association with Transcendentalism:

> As to transcendentalism and the nonsense which is talked by so many about it—I do not know what is meant. For myself, I should say that if it is meant that I have an active mind frequently busy with large topics, I hope it is so— if it is meant that I am honoured by the friendship of Mr. Emerson, Mr. Ripley, or Mr. Alcott, I hope it is so—but if it is meant that I cherish any opinions which interfere with domestic duties, cheerful carriage and judgment in the practical affairs of life, I challenge any or all in the little world which knows me to prove such deficiency from any acts of mine since I came to woman's estate.

Her "active mind" would indeed be "busy with large topics" in the years to come, both in her participation in the occasional meetings of the Transcendentalist Club and in her more frequent gatherings of Boston's most distinguished women.

Margaret Fuller assembled Boston's most intellectually powerful women at weekly "Conversations" at the home of the eminent teacher Elizabeth Peabody. Fuller orchestrated discussions of topics in such wide-ranging fields as mythology, education, philosophy, theology, and the fine arts, and she encouraged the group to consider contemporary social and ethical issues. Her intellectual leadership at these meetings was rarely challenged, and many sessions were reported to have ended when she lapsed into trancelike silences, broken only by the occasional rumbling of some indecipherable words. Her prominence in Boston's intellectual life seemed assured, if rather flamboyant.

In 1840 Fuller agreed to serve as the unsalaried editor of *The Dial,* the principal journal of Transcendentalist thought, and in July of that year she saw the first issue into print. For the next two years, she energetically tried to fulfill her hopes for this quarterly publication, described in a March 1840 letter to her friend W. H. Channing:

> A perfectly free organ is to be offered for the expression of individual thought and character. There are no party measures to be carried, no particular standard to be set up. A fair calm tone, I hope will pervade the essays in every form[.] I hope there will neither be a spirit of dogmatism nor of compromise. That this periodical will not aim at leading public opinion, but at stimulating each man to think for himself, to think more deeply and nobly by letting them see how some minds are keep alive by wise self-trust.

In addition to her literary reviews, which helped promote European Romanticism among America's young intellectuals, Fuller contributed several essays to *The Dial,* the most important of which was her important statement on women's rights, "The Great Lawsuit: Man Versus Men. Woman Versus Women." This essay established Fuller as a pioneer in women's rights. During the fall of 1844 she expanded the essay to book-length form and published it in 1845 under the title *Woman in the Nineteenth Century.* The original *Dial* essay is a more tightly argued and powerful version of her hortatory invocation to free men and women from the social roles in which they have been trapped, although it lacks many of the book's scholarly allusions to women in history, mythology, and poetry. In both versions, however, Fuller uses what was even then the conventional analogy between the woman and the slave. At a time when the moral fervor surrounding abolition had increased dramatically, such rhetorical strategies proved particularly effective, if also controversial. Fuller's writing on women's issues helped inspire the reforms and clarify the agenda for political action proposed at the Seneca Falls conference on that subject in 1848.

Fuller resigned as the sole editor of *The Dial* after the July 1842 issue, but she continued to help Emerson edit the journal until it ceased publication in April 1844. Fuller's increasingly ambivalent attitude toward what she regarded as the inconsistent positions of the Transcendentalists was reflected in her changing attitude toward Emerson. Despite her considerable affection for him, she came to realize, for example, that his commitment to developing the self should have led him to be more interested in current social and political issues. And while she praised Emerson's "high tendency, absolute purity," and his seemingly effortless ability to "summon the freedom and infinite graces of an intellect cultivated much beyond any I had known," she also recognized the limitations of their relationship. "I was, indeed, always called on to be worthy," she said. "He absolutely distrusted me in every region of my life with which he was unacquainted. The same trait I detected in his relations with others. He had faith in the Universal, but not in the Individual Man; he met men, not as a brother, but as a critic."

Emerson's view of their relationship was equally ambivalent. He wrote of his "strange, cold-warm, attractive-repelling" conversations with her. And while he respected the intelligence and conviction that distinguished her life, he also groused, as he reports in the *Memoirs* of her life he helped prepare, that "she looked upon herself as a living statue, which should always stand on a polished pedestal, with rich accessories, and under the most fitting lights." Emerson apparently could not free himself from the female archetype he saw in her, at once an emotionally charged and intellectually arrogant woman.

Her contemporaries contempuously referred to her "mountainous me," a phrase derived from Emerson's well-circulated (and perhaps apocryphal) account of her own self-estimate: "I now know all the people worth knowing in America, and I find no intellect comparable to my own." Emerson, like many of his contemporaries, failed to remember that Margaret Fuller was a brilliant, feisty woman struggling for intellectual recognition in the male-dominated literary world of mid-nineteenth-century America. At a time when women were hardly encouraged to develop an active role in the new nation's culture, she was repeatedly made to think that the problem was hers and not the culture's.

Margaret Fuller's perspective on American culture broadened considerably when she accompanied her friend James Freeman Clarke and his wife, Sarah, on a trip to the Midwest in 1843. Her journal entries during that excursion form the basis for *Summer on the Lakes* (1844). The book is an intellectual miscellany, consisting of sketches, poetry, and brief translations, as well as excerpts from the books she had been reading, along with a critical commentary on each. The book's commercial failure was somewhat offset by the modest praise it earned. The newspaper publisher and editor Horace Greeley called it "one of the best works in the department ever issued from the American press." It also provided Henry David Thoreau with a convenient model for a similar compilation, *A Week on the Concord and Merrimack Rivers* (1849).

Horace Greeley's appreciation of *Summer on the Lakes* prompted him to offer Fuller a job as the literary critic for his newspaper, the *New York Tribune*. In December 1844 Fuller moved to New York to work as the first female writer on that prominent newspaper's staff. The reflective pace of editing *The Dial* quickly yielded to daily deadlines, and the small circle of readers who debated the contents of the Boston quarterly were subsumed within the collective identity of the masses who read the *Tribune*. Yet Fuller took great pleasure in her work; it provided her, she noted, with "a more various view of life than any I ever before was in."

Fuller wrote literary criticism distinguished by her breadth of learning and her uncompromising standards. Her unfavorable reviews of such figures as James Russell Lowell and Henry Wadsworth Longfellow offended Boston's literary Brahmins and caused Lowell to satirize her severely in "A Fable for Critics." Yet her essays on the most durable features of the literature of that time gained her the respect of most other writers and readers, including Edgar Allan Poe, who praised her intellectual rigor and freedom from partisanship, although he, like many others, criticized her syntactic and stylistic faults. As more of Fuller's literary criticism has been reprinted, she has come to be increasingly ranked with Poe as one of America's first two major literary critics.

The focus of her work gradually shifted from literary reviews to social criticism. Fuller tackled controversial public issues with great verve, exposing, for example, official neglect of such mid-nineteenth-century misfits as the blind and the insane; she also called attention to the abuses of female prisoners in New York. In 1846 she published *Papers on Literature and Art*, a collection of essays hastily assembled in the weeks preceding her eagerly anticipated departure for Europe, where she would serve as a foreign correspondent for Greeley's *Tribune*.

Soon after her arrival in Europe, Fuller met Thomas Carlyle, the renowned English writer, who judged her in a journal entry "a strange, lilting, lean old maid, not nearly such a bore as I expected." Carlyle added that Fuller's was "a truly heroic mind, altogether unique, so far as I know among the writing women of this generation." Before leaving London, Fuller also met Giuseppe Mazzini, the Italian patriot and republican revolutionary, who sparked her interest in political action. In Paris she met the novelist George Sand and Adam Mickiewicz, a Polish émigré writer who espoused revolutionary causes. Attracted to the revolutionary ferment sweeping across Europe, Fuller traveled in 1847 to Italy, then a very unsteady alignment of independent as well as papal and Austrian-controlled states. She regularly dispatched reports to the *Tribune* on the unification efforts of Mazzini and Giuseppe Garibaldi.

In the midst of this fast-paced period in Italy, Margaret Fuller met—and eventually married—Giovanni Angelo Ossoli, an aristocratic Italian (a marquis) sympathetic to the revolutionary effort. Ossoli seemed to prefer the elegant tempo of Rome's local cafés to the intense discussions of social and political issues from which his wife gained so much intellectual sustenance. She gave birth to a son, Angelo, in September 1848, but her writing and political action continued unabated.

By her own account, Fuller's stay in Europe helped her recognize the limitations of her liberal social conscience. At the same time that the *Communist Manifesto* was being published in London, Fuller was acting on her newly articulated belief that socialism would change the world and fulfill the promise of American democracy. Within a few months of Garibaldi's arrival in Rome and his declaration of the Roman Republic, France lay siege to the city on behalf of papal interests. Fuller served as the director of a hospital on an island in the Tiber River. When Rome fell to the French on July 4, 1849, she led her family to Florence, where, with the encouragement of Robert and Elizabeth Barrett

Browning, Fuller began gathering information and anecdotes and drafting a history of the Italian revolution. That work was never completed. In dire need of money, Margaret Fuller, her husband, and son boarded a ship bound for the United States. On July 19, 1850, that ship sank off the Long Island coast at Fire Island, and all three perished.

Margaret Fuller's life and work offer ample evidence of the "cost," to use Thoreau's term, of being a productive woman in mid-nineteenth-century America. Unable to control what Hawthorne had described as her "unpliable" nature when she was among them, Fuller's friends reinterpreted her life in her *Memoirs*. The highly bowdlerized life recreated by James Freeman Clarke, W. H. Channing, and Ralph Waldo Emerson buried the aspects of her past that they regarded as radical. Only recently has scholarship begun to recover the complexities of her identity and work. She faced, for example, the conflict between being a woman and a writer at a time when American culture had not reconciled the two identities. She talked of the anguish of being regarded as "either a genius or a character. . . . I love but to be a woman; but womanhood is at present too strait-bounded to give me scope. At hours, I live truly as a woman; at others, I should stifle; as, on the other hand, I should palsy, when I would play the artist." One of the ironies of Margaret Fuller's life is that she did not discover herself fully as either an American woman or a writer until she moved to Europe.

Her work expresses one of the nation's most articulate early views of women's rights, and her literary criticism helped identify and clarify the strengths and weaknesses of American writing of her time. Hers was an original and influential voice in American literature. Soon after her death, Emerson confided to his journal that "I have lost in her my audience." Henry James acknowledged in his later years that Margaret Fuller "still unmistakably walks the passages" of his novels. And, given the recent interest in her prose, the real extent of her influence may well surface in the next generations of writers who read her work.

Further Reading:
W. H. Channing, J. F. Clarke, and R. W. Emerson, *Memoirs of Margaret Fuller Ossoli*, 1852.
M. Wade, *Margaret Fuller, Whetstone of Genius*, 1940.
M. B. Stern, *The Life of Margaret Fuller*, 1942.
J. J. Deiss, *The Roman Years of Margaret Fuller*, 1969.
B. G. Chevigny, *The Woman and the Myth: Margaret Fuller's Life and Writings*, 1976.
J. Myerson, *Margaret Fuller: An Annotated Bibliography*, 1977.
M. V. Allen, *The Achievement of Margaret Fuller*, 1979.
M. O. Urbanski, *Margaret Fuller's* Woman of the Nineteenth Century: *A Literary Study of Form and Content, of Sources and Influences*, 1980.
J. Myerson, *Critical Essays on Margaret Fuller*, 1980.

Texts:
"American Literature. Its Position in the Present Time, and Prospects for the Future" from *Papers on Literature and Art*, 1846.
See also *Letters of Margaret Fuller*, ed. R. N. Hudspeth, 1983–.

American Literature

Its Position in the Present Time,
and Prospects for the Future

Some thinkers may object to this essay, that we are about to write of that which has as yet no existence.

For it does not follow because many books are written by persons born in America that there exists an American literature. Books which imitate or represent the thoughts and life of Europe do not constitute an American literature. Before such can exist, an original idea must animate this nation and fresh currents of life must call into life fresh thoughts along its shores.

We have no sympathy with national vanity. We are not anxious to prove that there is as yet much American literature. Of those who think and write among us in the methods and of the thoughts of Europe, we are not impatient; if their minds are still best adapted to such food and such action. If their books express life of mind and character in graceful forms, they are good and we like them. We consider them as colonists and useful schoolmasters to our people in a transition state; which lasts rather longer than is occupied in passing bodily the ocean which separates the New from the Old World.

We have been accused of an undue attachment to foreign continental literature, and it is true that in childhood we had well nigh "forgotten our English" while constantly reading in other languages. Still what we loved in the literature of continental Europe was the range and force of ideal manifestation in forms of national and individual greatness. A model was before us in the great Latins of simple masculine minds seizing upon life with unbroken power. The stamp both of nationality and individuality was very strong upon them; their lives and thoughts stood out in clear and bold relief. The English character has the iron force of the Latins, but not the frankness and expansion. Like their fruits, they need a summer sky to give them more sweetness and a richer flavor. This does not apply to Shakespeare, who has all the fine side of English genius, with the rich coloring and more fluent life of the Catholic countries. Other poets of England also are expansive more or less, and soar freely to seek the blue sky, but take it as a whole, there is in English literature, as in English character, a reminiscence of walls and ceilings, a tendency to the arbitrary and conventional that repels a mind trained in admiration of the antique spirit. It is only in later days that we are learning to prize the peculiar greatness which a thousand times outweighs this fault, and which has enabled English genius to go forth from its insular position and conquer such vast dominion in the realms both of matter and of mind.

Yet there is often between child and parent a reaction from excessive influence having been exerted, and such a one we have experienced in behalf of our country against England. We use her language and receive in torrents the influence of her thought, yet it is in many respects uncongenial and injurious to our constitution. What suits Great Britain, with her insular position and consequent need to concentrate and intensify her life, her limited monarchy and spirit of trade, does not suit a mixed race continually enriched with new blood from other stocks the most unlike that of our first descent, with ample field and verge enough to range in and leave every impulse free, and abundant opportunity to develop a genius wide and full as our rivers, flowery, luxuriant, and impassioned as our vast prairies, rooted in strength as the rocks on which the Puritan fathers landed.

That such a genius is to rise and work in this hemisphere we are confident; equally so that scarce the first faint streaks of that day's dawn are yet visible. It is sad for those that foresee, to know they may not live to share its glories, yet it is sweet, too, to know that every act and word uttered in the light of that foresight may tend to hasten or ennoble its fulfillment.

That day will not rise till the fusion of races among us is more complete. It will not rise till this nation shall attain sufficient moral and intellectual dignity to prize moral and intellectual no less highly than political freedom, not till the physical resources of the country being explored, all its regions studded with towns, broken by the plow, netted together by railways and telegraph lines, talent shall be left at leisure to turn its energies upon the higher department of man's existence. Nor then shall it be seen till from the leisurely and yearning soul of that riper time national ideas shall take birth, ideas craving to be clothed in a thousand fresh and original forms.

Without such ideas all attempts to construct a national literature must end in abortions like the monster of Frankenstein, things with forms and the instincts of forms, but soulless and therefore revolting. We cannot have expression till there is something to be expressed.

The symptoms of such a birth may be seen in a longing felt here and there for the sustenance of such ideas. At present it shows itself, where felt, in sympathy with the prevalent tone of society by attempts at external action, such as are classed under the head of social reform. But it needs to go deeper before we can have poets, needs to penetrate beneath the springs of action, to stir and remake the soil as by the action of fire.

Another symptom is the need felt by individuals of being even sternly sincere. This is the one great means by which alone progress can be essentially furthered. Truth is the nursing mother of genius. No man can be absolutely true to himself, eschewing cant, compromise, servile imitation, and complaisance, without becoming original, for there is in every creature a fountain of life which, if not choked back by stones and other dead rubbish, will create a fresh atmosphere and bring to life fresh beauty. And it is the same with the nation as with the individual man.

The best work we do for the future is by such truth. By use of that in whatever way, we harrow the soil and lay it open to the sun and air. The winds from all quarters of the globe bring seed enough, and there is nothing wanting but preparation of the soil and freedom in the atmosphere, for ripening of a new and golden harvest.

We are sad that we cannot be present at the gathering-in of this harvest. And yet we are joyous too, when we think that though our name may not be writ on the pillar of our country's fame, we can really do far more towards rearing it than those who come at a later period and to a seemingly fairer task. *Now,* the humblest effort, made in a noble spirit and with religious hope, cannot fail to be even infinitely useful.

Whether we introduce some noble model from another time and clime to encourage aspiration in our own, or cheer into blossom the simplest wood-flower that ever rose from the earth, moved by the genuine impulse to grow, independent of the lures of money or celebrity; whether we speak boldly when fear or doubt keep others silent, or refuse to swell the popular cry upon an unworthy occasion, the spirit of truth, purely worshiped, shall turn our acts and forbearances alike to profit, informing them with oracles which the latest time shall bless.

Under present circumstances the amount of talent and labor given to writing ought to surprise us. Literature is in this dim and struggling state, and its pecuniary results exceedingly pitiful. From many well-known causes it is impossible for ninety-nine out of the hundred who wish to use the pen to ransom by its use the time they need. This state of things will have to be changed in some way. No man of genius writes for money; but it is essential to the free use of his powers that he should be able to disembarrass his life from care and perplexity. This is very difficult here; and the state of things gets worse and worse, as less and less is offered in pecuniary meed for works demanding great devotion of time and labor (to say nothing of the ether engaged) and the publisher, obliged to regard the transaction as a matter of business, demands of the author to give him only what will find an immediate market, for he cannot afford to take anything else. This will not do! When an immortal poet was secure only of a few copyists to circulate his works, there were princes and nobles to patronize literature and the arts. Here is only the public, and the public must learn how to cherish the nobler and rarer plants, and to plant the aloe, able to wait a hundred years for its bloom, or its garden will contain presently nothing but potatoes and pot-herbs. We shall have in the course of the next two or three years a convention of authors to inquire into the causes of this state of things and propose measures for its remedy. Some have already been thought of that look promising, but we shall not announce them till the time be ripe; that date is not distant, for the difficulties increase from day to day in consequence of the system of cheap publication on a great scale.

The ranks that led the way in the first half century of this republic were far better situated than we, in this respect. The country was not so deluged with the dingy page reprinted from Europe, and patriotic vanity was on the alert to answer the question, "Who reads an American book?" And many were the books written as worthy to be read as any out of the first class in England. They were, most of them, except in their subject matter, English books.

The list is large, and in making some cursory comments we do not wish to be understood as designating *all* who are worthy of notice, but only those who present themselves to our minds with some special claims.

In the department of ethics and philosophy we may inscribe two names as likely to live and be blessed and honored in the later time. These are the names of Channing[1] and of Emerson.

Dr. Channing had several leading thoughts which corresponded with the wants of his time, and have made him in it a father of thought. His leading idea of the "dignity of human nature" is one of vast results, and the peculiar form in which he

---

[1] William Ellery Channing (1780–1842), clergyman and founder of Unitarianism.

advocated it had a great work to do in this new world. The spiritual beauty of his writings is very great; they are all distinguished for sweetness, elevation, candor, and a severe devotion to truth. On great questions he took middle ground and sought a panoramic view; he wished also to stand high, yet never forgot what was above more than what was around and beneath him. He was not well acquainted with man on the impulsive and passionate side of his nature, so that his view of character was sometimes narrow, but it was always noble. He exercised an expansive and purifying power on the atmosphere, and stands a godfather at the baptism of this country.

The Sage of Concord[2] has a very different mind, in everything except that he has the same disinterestedness and dignity of purpose, the same purity of spirit. He is a profound thinker. He is a man of ideas, and deals with causes rather than effects. His ideas are illustrated from a wide range of literary culture and refined observation, and embodied in a style whose melody and subtle fragrance enchant those who stand stupefied before the thoughts themselves, because their utmost depths do not enable them to sound his shallows. His influence does not yet extend over a wide space; he is too far beyond his place and his time to be felt at once or in full, but it searches deep, and yearly widens its circles. He is a harbinger of the better day. His beautiful elocution has been a great aid to him in opening the way for the reception of his written word.

In that large department of literature which includes descriptive sketches, whether of character or scenery, we are already rich. Irving,[3] a genial and fair nature, just what he ought to be and would have been at any time of the world, has drawn the scenes amid which his youth was spent in their primitive lineaments, with all the charms of his graceful jocund humor. He has his niche and need never be deposed; it is not one that another could occupy.

The first enthusiasm about Cooper[4] having subsided, we remember more his faults

---

[2] Title bestowed on Ralph Waldo Emerson as a resident of Concord, Massachusetts.

[3] Washington Irving (1783–1859), American writer.

[4] James Fenimore Cooper (1789–1851). The following is Fuller's note: "Since writing the above we have read some excellent remarks by Mr. W.G. Simms on the writings of Cooper. We think the reasons are given for the powerful interest excited by Hawkeye and the Pilot, with great discrimination and force. 'They both think and feel, with a highly individual nature, that has been taught, by constant contemplation, in scenes of solitude. The vast unbroken ranges of forest to its one lonely occupant press upon the mind with the same sort of solemnity which one feels condemned to a life of partial isolation upon the ocean. Both are permitted that degree of commerce with their fellow beings, which suffices to maintain in strength the sweet and sacred sources of their humanity. . . . The very isolation to which, in the most successful of his stories, Mr. Cooper subjects his favorite personages, is, alone, a proof of his strength and genius. While the ordinary writer, the man of mere talent, is compelled to look around him among masses for his material, he contents himself with one man, and flings him upon the wilderness. The picture, then, which follows, must be one of intense individuality. Out of this one man's nature, his moods and fortunes, he spins his story. The agencie and dependencies are few. With self-reliance which is only found in true genius, he goes forward into the wilderness, whether of land or ocean; and the vicissitudes of either region, acting upon the natural resources of one man's mind, furnish the whole material of his work-shop. This mode of performance is highly dramatic, and thus it is that his scout, his trapper, his hunter, his pilot, all live to our eyes and thoughts, the perfect ideals of moral individuality.' "

than his merits. His ready resentment and way of showing it in cases which it is the wont of gentlemen to pass by in silence or meet with a good-humored smile have caused unpleasant associations with his name, and his fellow-citizens, in danger of being tormented by suits for libel if they spoke freely of him, have ceased to speak of him at all. But neither these causes, nor the baldness of his plots, shallowness of thought, and poverty in the presentation of character, should make us forget the grandeur and originality of his sea-sketches, nor the redemption from oblivion of our forest-scenery, and the noble romance of the hunter-pioneer's life. Already, but for him, this fine page of life's romance would be almost forgotten. He has done much to redeem these irrevocable beauties from the corrosive acid of a semi-civilized invasion.

What shall we say of the poets? The list is scanty; amazingly so, for there is nothing in the causes that paralyze other kinds of literature that could affect lyrical and narrative poetry. Men's hearts beat, hope, and suffer always, and they must crave such means to vent them; yet of the myriad leaves garnished with smooth, stereotyped rhymes that issue yearly from our press, you will not find, one time in a million, a little piece written from any such impulse or with the least sincerity or sweetness of tone. They are written for the press in the spirit of imitation or vanity, the paltriest offspring of the human brain, for the heart disclaims, as the ear is shut against them. This is the kind of verse which is cherished by the magazines as a correspondent to the tawdry pictures of smiling milliners' dolls in the frontispiece. Like these they are only a fashion, a fashion based on no reality of love or beauty. The inducement to write them consists in a little money, or more frequently the charm of seeing an anonymous name printed at the top in capitals.

At their head Mr. Bryant[5] stands alone. His range is not great, nor his genius fertile. But his poetry is purely the language of his inmost nature, and the simple lovely garb in which his thoughts are arranged, a direct gift from the Muse. He has written nothing that is not excellent, and the atmosphere of his verse refreshes and composes the mind, like leaving the highway to enter some green lovely fragrant wood.

Longfellow[6] is artificial and imitative. He borrows incessantly, and mixes what he borrows, so that it does not appear to the best advantage. He is very faulty in using broken or mixed metaphors. The ethical part of his writing has a hollow, secondhand sound. He has, however, elegance, a love of the beautiful, and a fancy for what is large and manly, if not a full sympathy with it. His verse breathes at times much sweetness; and if not allowed to supersede what is better, may promote a taste for good poetry. Though imitative, he is not mechanical.

We cannot say as much for Lowell,[7] who, we must declare it, though to the grief of some friends and the disgust of more, is absolutely wanting in the true spirit and tone of poesy. His interest in the moral questions of the day has supplied the want of vitality in himself; his great facility at versification has enabled him to fill the ear with a copious stream of pleasant sound. But his verse is stereotyped; his thought sounds no depth; and posterity will not remember him.

---

[5] William Cullen Bryant (1794–1878).
[6] Henry Wadsworth Longfellow (1807–1882).

[7] James Russell Lowell (1819–1891).

R. W. Emerson, in melody, in subtle beauty of thought and expression, takes the highest rank upon this list. But his poems are mostly philosophical, which is not the truest kind of poetry. They want the simple force of nature and passion, and while they charm the ear and interest the mind, fail to wake far-off echoes in the heart. The imagery wears a symbolical air, and serves rather as illustration than to delight us by fresh and glowing forms of life.

Meanwhile the most important part of our literature, while the work of diffusion is still going on, lies in the journals which monthly, weekly, daily send their messages to every corner of this great land, and form at present the only efficient instrument for the general education of the people.

Among these, the magazines take the lowest rank. Their object is principally to cater for the amusement of vacant hours, and as there is not a great deal of wit and light talent in this country, they do not even this to much advantage. More wit, grace, and elegant trifling embellish the annals of literature in one day of France than in a year of America.

The reviews are more able. If they cannot compare on equal terms with those of France, England, and Germany, where if genius be rare, at least a vast amount of talent and culture is brought to bear upon all the departments of knowledge, they are yet very creditable to a new country where so large a portion of manly ability must be bent on making laws, making speeches, making railroads and canals. They are, however, much injured by a partisan spirit and the fear of censure from their own public. This last is always slow death to a journal; its natural and only safe position is to *lead;* if instead it bows to the will of the multitude, it will find the ostracism of democracy far more dangerous than the worst censure of a tyranny could be. It is not half so dangerous to a man to be immured in a dungeon alone with God and his own clear conscience as to walk the streets fearing the scrutiny of a thousand eyes, ready to veil with anxious care whatever may not suit the many-headed monster in its momentary mood. Gentleness is dignified but caution is debasing; only a noble fearlessness can give wings to the mind, with which to soar beyond the common ken and learn what may be of use to the crowd below. Writers have nothing to do but to love truth fervently, seek justice according to their ability, and then express what is in the mind; they have nothing to do with consequences, God will take care of those. The want of such noble courage, such faith in the power of truth and good desire, paralyzes mind greatly in this country. Publishers are afraid; authors are afraid; and if a worthy resistance is not made by religious souls, there is danger that all the light will soon be put under bushels, lest some wind should waft from it a spark that may kindle dangerous fire.

For want of such faith, and the catholic spirit that flows from it, we have no great leading review. The *North American* was once the best. While under the care of Edward Everett,[8] himself a host in extensive knowledge, grace and adroitness in applying it, and the power of enforcing grave meanings by a light and flexible satire that tickled while it wounded, it boasted more force, more life, a finer scope of power.

[8] Everett (1794–1865) was editor of *The North American Review* (1815–1821).

But now though still exhibiting ability and information upon special points, it is entirely deficient in great leadings and the *vivida vis*,[9] but ambles and jogs at an old gentlemanly pace along a beaten path that leads to no important goal.

Several other journals have more life, energy, and directness than this, but there is none which occupies a truly great and commanding position, a beacon-light to all who sail that way. In order to do this, a journal must know how to cast aside all local and temporary considerations when new convictions command, and allow free range in its columns to all kinds of ability and all ways of viewing subjects. That would give it a life rich, bold, various.

The life of intellect is becoming more and more determined to the weekly and daily papers, whose light leaves fly so rapidly and profusely over the land. Speculations are afloat as to the influence of the electric telegraph upon their destiny, and it seems obvious that it should raise their character by taking from them in some measure the office of gathering and dispersing the news, and requiring of them rather to arrange and interpret it.

This mode of communication is susceptible of great excellence in the way of condensed essay, narrative, criticism, and is the natural receptacle for the lyrics of the day. That so few good ones deck the poet's corner, is because the indifference or unfitness of editors as to choosing and refusing makes this place at present undesirable to the poet. It might be otherwise.

The means which this organ affords of diffusing knowledge and sowing the seeds of thought where they may hardly fail of an infinite harvest, cannot be too highly prized by the discerning and benevolent. Minds of the first class are generally indisposed to this kind of writing; what must be done on the spur of the occasion and cast into the world so incomplete, as the hurried offspring of a day or hour's labor must generally be, cannot satisfy their judgment or do justice to their powers. But he who looks to the benefit of others and sees with what rapidity and ease instruction and thought are assimilated by men, when they come thus as it were on the wings of the wind, may be content, as an unhonored servant to the grand purposes of Destiny, to work in such a way at the Pantheon[10] which the ages shall complete, on which his name may not be inscribed but which will breathe the life of his soul.

The confidence in uprightness of intent and the safety of truth is still more needed here than in the more elaborate kinds of writing, as meanings cannot be fully explained nor expressions revised. Newspaper-writing is next door to conversation, and should be conducted on the same principles. It has this advantage: we address not our neighbor, who forces us to remember his limitations and prejudices, but the ideal presence of human nature as we feel it ought to be and trust it will be. We address America rather than Americans.

We see we have omitted honored names in this essay. We have not spoken of Brown,[11] as a novelist by far our first in point of genius and instruction as to the soul of things. Yet his works have fallen almost out of print. It is their dark deep gloom that prevents their being popular, for their very beauties are grave and sad.

---

[9] Latin: "living force."
[10] Greek or Roman temple of the gods.

[11] Charles Brockden Brown (1771–1810), American novelist.

But we see that *Ormond* is being republished at this moment. The picture of Roman character, of the life and resources of a single noble creature, of Constantia alone, should make that book an object of reverence. All these novels should be republished; if not favorites, they should at least not be lost sight of, for there will always be some who find in such powers of mental analysis the only response to their desires.

We have not spoken of Hawthorne,[12] the best writer of the day, in a similar range with Irving, only touching many more points and discerning far more deeply. But we have omitted many things in this slight sketch, for the subject even in this stage lies as a volume in our mind, and cannot be unrolled in completeness unless time and space were more abundant. Our object was to show that although by a thousand signs the existence is foreshown of those forces which are to animate an American literature, that faith, those hopes are not yet alive which shall usher it into a homogeneous or fully organized state of being. The future is glorious with certainties for those who do their duty in the present, and larklike, seeking the sun, challenge its eagles to an earthward flight, where their nests may be built in our mountains, and their young raise their cry of triumph unchecked by dullness in the echoes.

1846

Henry David Thoreau
1817–1862

Thoreau was a determined man. He may not have always recognized exactly what form his life would take, but he knew that he was meant to serve. As an avid student of what words signify once one cuts through the surface, he responded fully to the demands placed on him by "vocation"—the voice that calls someone out of the crowd to perform a sacred duty to the world.

To trace Thoreau's life and his writing career is to realize what "growing up in Concord" meant in the fertile, fervid years prior to the Civil War, particularly to one of the young people who had been born, as Emerson put it, with "knives in their brains." Thoreau spent his forty-four years listening to the sounds of the voice that led him toward his destiny. This attentiveness made him kin to a number of his New England contemporaries, especially those loosely grouped under the label Transcendentalists. But Thoreau felt compelled to follow a somewhat different drummer than the one followed by Ralph Waldo Emerson, Bronson Alcott, William Ellery Channing, or Margaret Fuller.

Any review of the checkered annals of Thoreau's aspirations, disappointments, and achievements makes clear how this man failed in the sight of many of his contemporaries, those relative few who had even heard of him. Such a review of his life also suggests why he is now considered one of America's major literary figures; it indicates that the myth of the man in the woods—the lonely rebel of

---

[12] Nathaniel Hawthorne (1804–1864).

Walden Pond—is less interesting and provocative than the reality that lies behind that misty cult figure.

Thoreau was born and raised in Concord, Massachusetts, the only hometown boy among the band of men and women later associated with that small but enormously influential New England village. In the parlance of the success stories that have piqued the American imagination since Benjamin Franklin's *Autobiography*, the Thoreau family was "poor but honest." One of the ways the Thoreaus got along was by making lead pencils in a family-circle factory, the kind of work that was being eased out of existence by the Industrial Revolution. The talent for entrepreneurship that made Thoreau an adroit maker of good pencils gave him pause once when he realized how easy it would be for him to corner the local cranberry market and become not so poor or so honest. His experiences in basic economics helped spur him to try other experiments in spiritual coinage. It became urgent for him to discover alternatives to the habits of buying and selling that he believed would ruin the American character.

But first Thoreau had to educate himself. Like Benjamin Franklin, Herman Melville, and Mark Twain (to name a few of the self-educated men of American literature), Thoreau learned that true education meant immersion in the world, whether or not he always liked what he found there. Thoreau started out, however, as a Harvard man. At the age of sixteen, he became one of the poor but diligent young men who, like Emerson a few years before, worked their way through the college. Thoreau's student essays are dutiful and a bit plodding, but they show early signs of his talent for seeing things from his distinctive point of view, one that would continue to puzzle conventional minds throughout his lifetime. Upon graduation in 1837, he returned to Concord—as he always did after forays away from home. He taught briefly but soon resigned that post rather than do what was expected of local schoolmasters: inflict bodily punishment on erring students. Four years of running a private school with his older brother John followed. John's illness and death put an end to Thoreau's interest in teaching in the institutional sense. He would remain a teacher all his days, but he had to find other ways to instruct, just as he had to find other means of working so that he could live well, rather than living wretchedly in order to work.

Emerson's house and mind were good places for Thoreau to continue his tutelage in the demands of the spirit. Between 1841 and 1843 he lived with the Emerson family as a handyman. He also lived with the ideas Emerson provided the Transcendentalist Club, a group that met to talk about social and personal reforms. However, the most crucial event in Thoreau's life occurred in 1845, the year he moved two miles out of Concord to live in a one-room hut erected beside Walden Pond on land Emerson had loaned him. But experiences other than Harvard and the Emersons had been readying Thoreau for that maturing time by the pond. They helped him to decide which voices he must use to persuade his listeners to the message of challenge and joy he felt compelled to declare.

Speaking in a classroom had not sufficed for Thoreau. His contemporaries found ready audiences for their ideas by lecturing before local groups, so he began to try his hand at this popular form of public address. Thoreau's audiences wanted either to be instructed with the kind of nature lore he drew from the walks in the woods he had been making since he was a child or to be amused by familiar Yankee wit, the kind that was simultaneously exaggeration and understatement. Thoreau provided both the lore and the wit in his lectures, but also something more, and this was not so readily accepted. His audiences did not care to be told that they were fools for having resigned themselves to living stupid, wasted lives, but this was precisely what Thoreau most wanted to tell them. Somehow he had to find ways to make his often harsh home truths palatable to the people he most wished to affect.

By the mid-1840s Thoreau had found a means to win over his audiences. He told them of his travels through the New England landscape, offered them brief essays on a life lived honestly and close to the nub, shucked free of the unnecessary "thingness" that weighed down their materialistic society. Out of a two-week canoe excursion that Thoreau and his brother had taken in 1839 came the experiences of the book *A Week on the Concord and Merrimack Rivers*. Thoreau's only previous experience at writing had been the essays and poems that Emerson printed in *The Dial*, the journal that he and Margaret Fuller edited, along with a piece placed in a Boston journal and two essays sold to New York editors during his brief stay on Staten Island in 1843 while tutoring the children of Emerson's brother. These events came in quick succession, and the early 1840s were busy and instructive years for Thoreau's career. Just at this point, Thoreau walked out of Concord to the hut by Walden Pond and set up housekeeping; it was a day he considered symbolically apt for his first major undertaking as a writer: Independence Day, 1845.

Thoreau went into the woods to live the Walden life; while there, he stored up thoughts and experiences he would use when he left the pond in the early autumn of 1847 to begin the long process of writing his masterwork, *Walden*. But the initial reason he settled into the hut was to write *A Week on the Concord and Merrimack Rivers*. Framed by the narrated events of a seven-day river trip, *A Week* is a mélange of nature observations, histories of the region through which the brothers pass in their little boat, and glimpses of contemporary scenes where the natural inhabitants are sometimes seen in abrasive contact with the human encroachments of factories and mills lining the banks. But Thoreau brought to *A Week* more than the notes he took in 1839 and the observations he had been keeping in journals since his college days; he brought into the narrative all his bookishness—the intellectual equipment common to well-read aspirants to literary fame in Thoreau's generation. Of the thousand copies of the book Thoreau had printed in 1849, approximately two hundred were sold. Writing *A Week* at Walden Pond was a failed experiment in the most obvious sense. But what Thoreau learned about addressing his audience from that failure was of the utmost value when it came time to write his next full-length book.

Walden: or, Life in the Woods, published in 1854, is what we remember best about Thoreau. The book was slow in coming into its final form. Thoreau spent five years reworking the material he had gathered into his journals during the

Walden years of 1845 to 1847. He tinkered and copied, rewrote and recopied. With extreme consciousness of effort, he mastered a language of spontaneity. With great seriousness, he pointed up the wit of his observations concerning the absurdities of the country's social conditions. When at last the book was published, his friends responded to its several levels of mysticism and social theory. Too many took Thoreau's remarks too literally. *Walden* was liked, but not greatly and it received relatively little critical attention. Thoreau's masterwork, so many years in the making, had to wait almost eighty years more—until the 1930s—before people recognized how advanced his program for the good life was.

Thoreau left Walden Pond in 1847 because he had "several more lives to live and could not spare any more for that one." Those other lives, of involvement with social and literary matters, together with "that one" of the man "on vacation" at Walden, resulted in the activities that occupied him through the fifteen years he had yet to live, giving him the ideas and energies he expended on the writing that lay ahead.

Thoreau said he scorned the need to travel far. Unlike the young Richard Henry Dana, Herman Melville, or the men who were just then setting out for the California gold fields, Thoreau insisted that the best traveling is done while staying home, exploring the cosmography of the imagination. Yet Thoreau made three forays into Maine, where he encountered forests and mountains far rawer than anything he could see in the gentler areas around Concord. Parts of the Maine experiences with Indians, moose, and mountains were published in magazines during his lifetime. *The Maine Woods,* the book version, appeared in 1864. Four trips to Cape Cod, one to Canada, and a long trip to Minnesota the year before his death also occurred during the years after he left Walden Pond. (Like many of the Transcendentalists, he was not averse to contradicting himself at times. Journeys to California were despicable; trips north or to Minnesota were worthy endeavors.) Each of these excursions, except the Minnesota trip, resulted in a book published posthumously: *Cape Cod* (1865) and *A Yankee in Canada* (1866).

Thoreau dealt with the life of the spirit, but he also kept close account of events that were shaking the American social and political system to its foundation: the Fugitive Slave Act, utopian reform plans for communal living and socialistic societies, the Mexican–American War, John Brown's raid on the Harpers Ferry arsenal, the underground railroad, the effects of the new telegraph and increased newspaper circulation, the coming to New England of the Irish immigrants and the changes in the landscape caused by the railroads they were hired to construct, the marketing of everything from blocks of pond ice for chilling the drinks of urban Bostonians to the wild berries whose flavor vanished the moment they were picked for shipment from their native hillsides. Thoreau took note of these events, wrote about them all, and participated directly in several: calling his neighbors together after John Brown's capture to read them his lecture in praise of the man's heroic acts on behalf of the slaves, conveying blacks over the underground railroad on their run toward freedom, and refusing to pay local taxes that supported the Mexican-American War effort.

Thoreau said he was happiest alone, yet he was frequently in contact with the Concord-Boston group that included Emerson, Fuller, Hawthorne, Alcott, and Ellery Channing. He made a special trip to New Jersey to meet Walt Whitman; he visited with others on his walks through the woods and to the surrounding farms, such as the Canadian woodcutter Alek Therion. He spent many hours as "servant to Admetus" (an allusion to the Greek myth of the poet-god Apollo, who lived among mortals by doing menial tasks for a local ruler), and he earned the wealth of his observations. Thoreau was also in touch with newspaper editors and book publishers whom he tried to interest in his works, as well as with the men who arranged his lecturing engagements that took him as far afield as Philadelphia and Bangor. Thoreau lived so busy a life, filled with so many activities that kept him in almost constant give-and-take with the everyday world, that it might seem surprising he had time for solitary meditations on the simplified life dedicated to contemplating eternal and universal truths.

Thoreau's health began to decline as early as 1855. By May 1862 he was dead of tuberculosis. Emerson stood over his grave outside Concord and delivered a eulogy that praised Thoreau's exceptional character but also lamented that he had failed to be all he should have been. These comments were based on Emerson's own expectations, colored by the on-again, off-again relationship of admiration and disappointment shared by the older man and his prickly younger friend. That scene by Thoreau's graveside represents what continued to happen in the years following his death as his status was taken under consideration by some of the more influential reputation makers of the period. John Greenleaf Whittier, Oliver Wendell Holmes, and James Russell Lowell, among others, sniped at Thoreau for having been surly, self-conscious, antagonistic, and without humor; that is, for personality traits that assumed more importance in their minds than the form his life's work as a writer had taken.

Thoreau's personal force had not been totally ignored during his lifetime, either as a writer or a thinker. The abrasive urgency of his self-appointed role as prophet and the pawky intelligence of his writing style made it impossible for his essays to be met altogether by silence or dismissal. Immediately after his death, however, it was easier to give approval to Thoreau by taming him, by reducing him to the pupil who had stood in the shadow cast by Emerson. Some tried to convert him into a nature writer who provided nice descriptions of woodland walks. Others turned him into the anecdotist of quaint bits of New England history. By the end of the century, however, Thoreau was taken up as a social reformer by the English Fabians and by Mahatma Ghandi in India, who focused on the same lessons in passive resistance that Martin Luther King, Jr., was to use in the American civil rights struggles. By the 1960s and 1970s Thoreau's image had been reshaped yet again. Many elected to make him the defiant loner and social anarchist, the mindless nature boy, or the dedicated environmentalist. The general effect of these manipulations continued to be reductive. Those who used

Thoreau for their own purposes were often incapable of recognizing the critical
eye and the sharp tongue he would have turned on their own slack minds and
wayward doings.

Recent scholarship has reassessed the quality of Thoreau's prose style and
analyzed the conscious adjustments he made in his writing so that what he
wanted to say could be brought into line with what his audiences wanted to
read. Older and continuing views of Thoreau as naturalist, social philosopher,
and—inevitably—grist for psychobiographies are now being supplemented by
appraisals of his forceful literary imagination. Hitherto neglected writings—
including the journals—are the subject of the appraisals they deserve.

None of these newer evaluations threatens the place of *Walden*. It remains
secure as one of the American masterworks. What is gained, however, in going
beyond the conventional views of Thoreau is a better appreciation of how
exactly he responded to the "voice" that pointed him toward his special vocation
as a writer. The recent emphasis in the criticism points up the literary means he
used to present the fact that we live perilously and paradoxically between heaven
and earth—between "the higher laws" and "brute neighbors."

The many discrepancies Thoreau found in the world parallel his own nature.
Both as a man and as a writer, he tried to convert the jagged connections of the
world of human society into the seamless cosmic whole of nature's universe. He
portrayed the aspirations of our dual selves, which go to the bottom of ponds
and to the heights of stars. Thoreau realized the hazardous terms by which our
duality comes into conjunction with the universe. We are instructed to live in
the exact nick of time, lest we fall outside the fateful rhythms set up for our
lives. We must be fully awake in order to escape the seep of the spirit into the
dead weight of an exclusively material system. We have to simplify the acts of
our daily doings while relishing the array of meanings that lie in the sacred
"texts" found in the natural world. We are encouraged to go to inner frontiers
where facts are "confronted"—traveling far while staying home.

But if Thoreau discovered means that save the soul, he did not fully know
how to bring his discoveries to bear upon his own existence, or—most crucial to
him as a writer—exactly how to make convincing contact with readers who are
indifferent to the dangers surrounding them. However, in *Walden* and other
works, we find Thoreau working hard to convert into a confident prose style the
anxieties we all feel in the face of universal paradoxes. Thoreau's writings
provide a list of all the things he believed we must be concerned with because
they were what mattered the most to him: how, without "marriage," to have the
perfect friendship between one person and another or between the dual selves that
lie within each person's nature; how to evoke the sense of social crisis without
singing an ode of dejection; how to appeal to religious sensibilities while keeping
free of the accepted Christian conventions of doctrine; how to achieve self-pride
in the midst of self-doubts; how to attempt to live a model life without
appearing to be an egoist and how to write in the autobiographical mode even
when the facts make one seem the village fool; how to balance the carnal,
"woodchuck" needs of our physical nature with a desire for chastity of spirit;

how to insist on the primacy of the present and the value of the future; how to replace the past while using the wisdom of ancient scriptures; how to convey common sense by the uncommon means of language; and, most of all, how to celebrate the unique attributes of the true American democrat who must aspire to live in the heavens yet acknowledge the muddy depths and demands of the everyday world.

Further Reading:

J. Atkinson, *Henry Thoreau, The Cosmic Yankee,* 1927.

H. Canby, *Thoreau,* 1939, 1968.

J. Krutch, *Henry David Thoreau,* 1948.

R. Cook, *Passage to Walden,* 1949.

H. Hough, *Thoreau of Walden,* 1956.

Thoreau: A Century of Criticism, ed. W. Harding, 1954.

L. Shanley, *The Making of Walden,* 1957.

S. Paul, *The Shores of America: Thoreau's Inward Exploration,* 1958.

W. Harding, *Thoreau Handbook,* 1959, revised 1980.

A. Derluth, *Concord Rebel: A Life of Henry David Thoreau,* 1962.

W. Harding and M. Meltzer, *A Thoreau Profile,* 1962.

Thoreau: A Collection of Critical Essays, ed. S. Paul, 1962.

W. Harding, *The Days of Henry Thoreau,* 1965.

J. Porte, *Emerson and Thoreau, Transcendentalists in Conflict,* 1966.

C. Anderson, *The Magic Circle of Walden,* 1968.

J. G. Murray, *Henry David Thoreau,* 1968.

R. F. Stowell, *A Thoreau Gazetteer,* 1970, 1974.

S. Cavell, *The Senses of Walden,* 1972.

J. McIntosh, *Thoreau as Romantic Naturalist,* 1974.

R. C. Tuerk, *Central Still,* 1975.

M. Meyer, *Several More Lives to Live,* 1977.

F. Garber, *Thoreau's Redemptive Imagination,* 1977.

R. Lebeaux, *Young Man Thoreau,* 1977.

R. F. Sayre, *Thoreau and the American Indians,* 1977.

M. E. Moller, *Thoreau in the Human Community,* 1980.

R. Bridgman, *Dark Thoreau,* 1982.

W. Howarth, *The Book of Concord,* 1982.

Thoreau's Psychology, ed. R. D. Gozzi, 1983.

R. Lebeaux, *Thoreau's Seasons,* 1984.

Texts:

Walden and "Resistance to Civil Government" from *The Writings of Henry D. Thoreau,* 25 vols. projected, ed. W. Harding, 1971–.

The journals from *The Writings of Henry David Thoreau* (Walden edition), 20 vols., 1906.

See also *Collected Poems of Henry Thoreau,* ed. C. Bode, 1943, 1964, 1974.

Consciousness in Concord: Thoreau's Lost Journal (1840–1841), ed. P. Miller, 1958.

The Journal of Henry D. Thoreau, 2 vols., 1962.

from Walden*

Economy

When I wrote the following pages, or rather the bulk of them, I lived alone, in the woods, a mile from any neighbor, in a house which I had built myself, on the shore of Walden Pond, in Concord, Massachusetts, and earned my living by the labor of my hands only. I lived there two years and two months. At present I am a sojourner in civilized life again.

I should not obtrude my affairs so much on the notice of my readers if very particular inquiries had not been made by my townsmen concerning my mode of life, which some would call impertinent, though they do not appear to me at all impertinent, but, considering the circumstances, very natural and pertinent. Some have asked what I got to eat; if I did not feel lonesome; if I was not afraid; and the like. Others have been curious to learn what portion of my income I devoted to charitable purposes; and some, who have large families, how many poor children I maintained. I will therefore ask those of my readers who feel no particular interest in me to pardon me if I undertake to answer some of these questions in this book. In most books, the *I*, or first person, is omitted; in this it will be retained; that, in respect to egotism, is the main difference. We commonly do not remember that it is, after all, always the first person that is speaking. I should not talk so much about myself if there were any body else whom I knew as well. Unfortunately, I am confined to this theme by the narrowness of my experience. Moreover, I, on my side, require of every writer, first or last, a simple and sincere account of his own life, and not merely what he has heard of other men's lives; some such account as he would send to his kindred from a distant land; for if he has lived sincerely, it must have been in a distant land to me. Perhaps these pages are more particularly addressed to poor students. As for the rest of my readers, they will accept such portions as apply to them. I trust that none will stretch the seams in putting on the coat, for it may do good service to him whom it fits.

I would fain say something, not so much concerning the Chinese and Sandwich Islanders[1] as you who read these pages, who are said to live in New England; something about your condition, especially your outward condition or circumstances in this world, in this town, what it is, whether it is necessary that it be as bad as it is, whether it cannot be improved as well as not. I have travelled a good deal in Concord; and every where, in shops, and offices, and fields, the inhabitants have appeared to me to be doing penance in a thousand remarkable ways. What I have heard of Brahmins[2] sitting exposed to four fires and looking in the face of the sun; or hanging suspended, with their heads downward, over flames; or looking at the heavens over their shoulders "until it becomes impossible for them to resume their natural position, while from the twist of the neck nothing but liquids can pass into

---

* *Walden* was published in 1854, seven years after Thoreau left his hut by the pond. While living at Walden Pond, Thoreau wrote *A Week on the Concord and Merrimack Rivers* and portions of

Walden. He continued revising the latter between 1849 and 1854.
[1] Natives of what are now the Hawaiian Islands.
[2] Hindus of the highest caste.

the stomach;" or dwelling, chained for life, at the foot of a tree; or measuring with their bodies, like caterpillars, the breadth of vast empires; or standing on one leg on the tops of pillars,—even these forms of conscious penance are hardly more incredible and astonishing than the scenes which I daily witness. The twelve labors of Hercules[3] were trifling in comparison with those which my neighbors have undertaken; for they were only twelve, and had an end; but I could never see that these men slew or captured any monster or finished any labor. They have no friend Iolas to burn with a hot iron the root of the hydra's head, but as soon as one head is crushed, two spring up.

I see young men, my townsmen, whose misfortune it is to have inherited farms, houses, barns, cattle, and farming tools; for these are more easily acquired than got rid of. Better if they had been born in the open pasture and suckled by a wolf, that they might have seen with clearer eyes what field they were called to labor in. Who made them serfs of the soil? Why should they eat their sixty acres, when man is condemned to eat only his peck of dirt? Why should they begin digging their graves as soon as they are born? They have got to live a man's life, pushing all these things before them, and get on as well as they can. How many a poor immortal soul have I met well nigh crushed and smothered under its load, creeping down the road of life, pushing before it a barn seventy-five feet by forty, its Augean stables[4] never cleansed, and one hundred acres of land, tillage, mowing, pasture, and wood-lot! The portionless, who struggle with no such unnecessary inherited encumbrances, find it labor enough to subdue and cultivate a few cubic feet of flesh.

But men labor under a mistake. The better part of the man is soon ploughed into the soil for compost. By a seeming fate, commonly called necessity, they are employed, as it says in an old book, laying up treasures which moth and rust will corrupt and thieves break through and steal.[5] It is a fool's life, as they will find when they get to the end of it, if not before. It is said that Deucalion and Pyrrha[6] created men by throwing stones over their heads behind them:—

> Inde genus durum sumus, experiensque laborum,
>   Et documenta damus quâ simus origine nati.[7]

Or, as Raleigh rhymes it in his sonorous way,—

> "From thence our kind hard-hearted is, enduring pain and care,
>   Approving that our bodies of a stony nature are."[8]

---

[3] In classic myth, the hero Hercules was set to perform twelve arduous tasks. Among these was the slaying of the nine-headed monster Hydra, which he was able to do with the help of his companion Iolas. Iolas seared the stumps of each of Hydra's heads as Hercules cut them off, so they could not grow back.

[4] Stables in which 3,000 oxen had been kept for 30 years by King Augeas; it was one of Hercules' labors to clean them.

[5] Thoreau paraphrases from Matthew 6:19, from "the old book (the Bible)."

[6] Survivors of a great flood, Deucalion and Pyrrha in classic myth repopulated the earth by throwing stones over their shoulders which were transformed into men and women.

[7] *Metamorphoses*, Book I, by Ovid (43 B.C.–A.D. 17?).

[8] From *The History of the World* (1614) by Sir Walter Raleigh (1552?–1618), English explorer, historian, poet, and courtier.

So much for a blind obedience to a blundering oracle, throwing the stones over their heads behind them, and not seeing where they fell.

Most men, even in this comparatively free country, through mere ignorance and mistake, are so occupied with the factitious cares and superfluously coarse labors of life that its finer fruits cannot be plucked by them. Their fingers, from excessive toil, are too clumsy and tremble too much for that. Actually, the laboring man has not leisure for a true integrity day by day; he cannot afford to sustain the manliest relations to men; his labor would be depreciated in the market. He has no time to be any thing but a machine. How can he remember well his ignorance—which his growth requires —who has so often to use his knowledge? We should feed and clothe him gratuitously sometimes, and recruit him with our cordials, before we judge of him. The finest qualities of our nature, like the bloom on fruits, can be preserved only by the most delicate handling. Yet we do not treat ourselves nor one another thus tenderly.

Some of you, we all know, are poor, find it hard to live, are sometimes, as it were, gasping for breath. I have no doubt that some of you who read this book are unable to pay for all the dinners which you have actually eaten, or for the coats and shoes which are fast wearing or are already worn out, and have come to this page to spend borrowed or stolen time, robbing your creditors of an hour. It is very evident what mean and sneaking lives many of you live, for my sight has been whetted by experience; always on the limits,[9] trying to get into business and trying to get out of debt, a very ancient slough, called by the Latins, *æs alienum*, another's brass,[10] for some of their coins were made of brass; still living, and dying, and buried by this other's brass; always promising to pay, promising to pay, to-morrow, and dying to-day, insolvent; seeking to curry favor, to get custom, by how many modes, only not state-prison offences; lying, flattering, voting, contracting yourselves into a nutshell of civility, or dilating into an atmosphere of thin and vaporous generosity, that you may persuade your neighbor to let you make his shoes, or his hat, or his coat, or his carriage, or import his groceries for him; making yourselves sick, that you may lay up something against a sick day, something to be tucked away in an old chest, or in a stocking behind the plastering, or, more safely, in the brick bank; no matter where, no matter how much or how little.

I sometimes wonder that we can be so frivolous, I may almost say, as to attend to the gross but somewhat foreign form of servitude called Negro Slavery, there are so many keen and subtle masters that enslave both north and south. It is hard to have a southern overseer; it is worse to have a northern one; but worst of all when you are the slave-driver of yourself. Talk of a divinity in man! Look at the teamster on the highway, wending to market by day or night; does any divinity stir within him? His highest duty to fodder and water his horses! What is his destiny to him compared with the shipping interests? Does not he drive for Squire Make-a-stir? How godlike, how immortal, is he? See how he cowers and sneaks, how vaguely all the day he fears, not being immortal nor divine, but the slave and prisoner of his own opinion of himself, a fame won by his own deeds. Public opinion is a weak tyrant compared with our own private opinion. What a man thinks of himself, that it is which determines, or rather indicates, his fate. Self-emancipation even in the West Indian provinces of

[9] In matters of credit.
[10] Someone else's money.

the fancy and imagination,—what Wilberforce[11] is there to bring that about? Think, also, of the ladies of the land weaving toilet[12] cushions against the last day, not to betray too green an interest in their fates! As if you could kill time without injuring eternity.

The mass of men lead lives of quiet desperation. What is called resignation is confirmed desperation. From the desperate city you go into the desperate country, and have to console yourself with the bravery of minks and muskrats. A stereotyped but unconscious despair is concealed even under what are called the games and amusements of mankind. There is no play in them, for this comes after work. But it is a characteristic of wisdom not to do desperate things.

When we consider what, to use the words of the catechism,[13] is the chief end of man, and what are the true necessaries and means of life, it appears as if men had deliberately chosen the common mode of living because they preferred it to any other. Yet they honestly think there is no choice left. But alert and healthy natures remember that the sun rose clear. It is never too late to give up our prejudices. No way of thinking or doing, however ancient, can be trusted without proof. What every body echoes or in silence passes by as true to-day may turn out to be falsehood to-morrow, mere smoke of opinion, which some had trusted for a cloud that would sprinkle fertilizing rain on their fields. What old people say you cannot do you try and find that you can. Old deeds for old people, and new deeds for new. Old people did not know enough once, perchance, to fetch fresh fuel to keep the fire a-going; new people put a little dry wood under a pot,[14] and are whirled round the globe with the speed of birds, in a way to kill old people, as the phrase is. Age is no better, hardly so well, qualified for an instructor as youth, for it has not profited so much as it has lost. One may almost doubt if the wisest man has learned any thing of absolute value by living. Practically, the old have no very important advice to give the young, their own experience has been so partial, and their lives have been such miserable failures, for private reasons, as they must believe; and it may be that they have some faith left which belies that experience, and they are only less young than they were. I have lived some thirty years on this planet, and I have yet to hear the first syllable of valuable or even earnest advice from my seniors. They have told me nothing, and probably cannot tell me any thing, to the purpose. Here is life, an experiment to a great extent untried by me; but it does not avail me that they have tried it. If I have any experience which I think valuable, I am sure to reflect that this my Mentors said nothing about.

One farmer says to me, "You cannot live on vegetable food solely, for it furnishes nothing to make bones with;" and so he religiously devotes a part of his day to supplying his system with the raw material of bones; walking all the while he talks behind his oxen, which, with vegetable-made bones, jerk him and his lumbering plough along in spite of every obstacle. Some things are really necessaries of life in some circles, the most helpless and diseased, which in others are luxuries merely, and in others still are entirely unknown.

[11] William Wilberforce (1759–1833), English philanthropist and abolitionist.
[12] Boudoir, dressing room.
[13] The Westminster Catechism, printed in the *New England Primer,* the book of instruction for children in the New England colonies, stated that the chief purpose of human existence "is to glorify God and to enjoy him forever."
[14] Locomotive steam boiler.

The whole ground of human life seems to some to have been gone over by their predecessors, both the heights and the valleys, and all things to have been cared for. According to Evelyn,[15] "the wise Solomon prescribed ordinances for the very distances of trees; and the Roman prætors have decided how often you may go into your neighbor's land to gather the acorns which fall on it without trespass, and what share belongs to that neighbor." Hippocrates[16] has even left directions how we should cut our nails; that is, even with the ends of the fingers, neither shorter nor longer. Undoubtedly the very tedium and ennui which presume to have exhausted the variety and the joys of life are as old as Adam. But man's capacities have never been measured; nor are we to judge of what he can do by any precedents, so little has been tried. Whatever have been thy failures hitherto, "be not afflicted, my child, for who shall assign to thee what thou hast left undone?"[17]

We might try our lives by a thousand simple tests; as, for instance, that the same sun which ripens my beans illumines at once a system of earths like ours. If I had remembered this it would have prevented some mistakes. This was not the light in which I hoed them. The stars are the apexes of what wonderful triangles! What distant and different beings in the various mansions of the universe are contemplating the same one at the same moment! Nature and human life are as various as our several constitutions. Who shall say what prospect life offers to another? Could a greater miracle take place than for us to look through each other's eyes for an instant? We should live in all the ages of the world in an hour; ay, in all the worlds of the ages. History, Poetry, Mythology!—I know of no reading of another's experience so startling and informing as this would be.

The greater part of what my neighbors call good I believe in my soul to be bad, and if I repent of any thing, it is very likely to be my good behavior. What demon possessed me that I behaved so well? You may say the wisest thing you can, old man, —you who have lived seventy years, not without honor of a kind,—I hear an irresistible voice which invites me away from all that. One generation abandons the enterprises of another like stranded vessels.

I think that we may safely trust a good deal more than we do. We may waive just so much care of ourselves as we honestly bestow elsewhere. Nature is as well adapted to our weakness as to our strength. The incessant anxiety and strain of some is a well nigh incurable form of disease. We are made to exaggerate the importance of what work we do; and yet how much is not done by us! or, what if we had been taken sick? How vigilant we are! determined not to live by faith if we can avoid it; all the day long on the alert, at night we unwillingly say our prayers and commit ourselves to uncertainties. So thoroughly and sincerely are we compelled to live, reverencing our life, and denying the possibility of change. This is the only way, we say; but there are as many ways as there can be drawn radii from one centre. All change is a miracle to contemplate; but it is a miracle which is taking place every instant. Confucius[18] said, "To know that we know what we know, and that we do not know

---

[15] John Evelyn (1620–1706), best known for his diaries, but also the author of *Sylva* (1644), a book on the growing of trees.
[16] Greek physician (460?–377 B.C.).

[17] From the *Vishnu Purana,* a Hindu sacred text.
[18] From *The Analects,* II, 17, by the Chinese philosopher Confucius (ca. 551–479 B.C.).

what we do not know, that is true knowledge." When one man has reduced a fact of the imagination to be a fact to his understanding, I foresee that all men will at length establish their lives on that basis.

Let us consider for a moment what most of the trouble and anxiety which I have referred to is about, and how much it is necessary that we be troubled or, at least, careful. It would be some advantage to live a primitive and frontier life, though in the midst of an outward civilization, if only to learn what are the gross necessaries of life and what methods have been taken to obtain them; or even to look over the old daybooks of the merchants, to see what it was that men most commonly bought at the stores, what they stored, that is, what are the grossest groceries. For the improvements of ages have had but little influence on the essential laws of man's existence; as our skeletons, probably, are not to be distinguished from those of our ancestors.

By the words, *necessary of life*, I mean whatever, of all that man obtains by his own exertions, has been from the first, or from long use has become, so important to human life that few, if any, whether from savageness, or poverty, or philosophy, ever attempt to do without it. To many creatures there is in this sense but one necessary of life, Food. To the bison of the prairie it is a few inches of palatable grass, with water to drink; unless he seeks the Shelter of the forest or the mountain's shadow. None of the brute creation requires more than Food and Shelter. The necessaries of life for man in this climate may, accurately enough, be distributed under the several heads of Food, Shelter, Clothing, and Fuel; for not till we have secured these are we prepared to entertain the true problems of life with freedom and a prospect of success. Man has invented, not only houses, but clothes and cooked food; and possibly from the accidental discovery of the warmth of fire, and the consequent use of it, at first a luxury, arose the present necessity to sit by it. We observe cats and dogs acquiring the same second nature. By proper Shelter and Clothing we legitimately retain our own internal heat; but with an excess of these, or of Fuel, that is, with an external heat greater than our own internal, may not cookery properly be said to begin? Darwin, the naturalist, says of the inhabitants of Tierra del Fuego,[19] that while his own party, who were well clothed and sitting close to a fire, were far from too warm, these naked savages, who were farther off, were observed, to his great surprise, "to be streaming with perspiration at undergoing such a roasting." So, we are told, the New Hollander[20] goes naked with impunity, while the European shivers in his clothes. Is it impossible to combine the hardiness of these savages with the intellectualness of the civilized man? According to Liebig,[21] man's body is a stove, and food the fuel which keeps up the internal combustion in the lungs. In cold weather we eat more, in warm less. The animal heat is the result of a slow combustion, and disease and death take place when this is too rapid; or for want of fuel, or from some defect in the draught, the fire goes out. Of course the vital heat is not to be confounded with fire; but so much for analogy. It appears, therefore, from the above list, that the expression,

[19] Charles Darwin (1809–1882) described this archipelago near the southern tip of South America in his *Journal of Researches* (1839).

[20] Aboriginal Australian.

[21] The German chemist Justus von Liebig (1803–1873).

animal life, is nearly synonymous with the expression, *animal heat;* for while Food may be regarded as the Fuel which keeps up the fire within us,—and Fuel serves only to prepare that Food or to increase the warmth of our bodies by addition from without, —Shelter and Clothing also serve only to retain the *heat* thus generated and absorbed.

The grand necessity, then, for our bodies, is to keep warm, to keep the vital heat in us. What pains we accordingly take, not only with our Food, and Clothing, and Shelter, but with our beds, which are our night-clothes, robbing the nests and breasts of birds to prepare this shelter within a shelter, as the mole has its bed of grass and leaves at the end of its burrow! The poor man is wont to complain that this is a cold world; and to cold, no less physical than social, we refer directly a great part of our ails. The summer, in some climates, makes possible to man a sort of Elysian life.[22] Fuel, except to cook his Food, is then unnecessary; the sun is his fire, and many of the fruits are sufficiently cooked by its rays; while Food generally is more various, and more easily obtained, and Clothing and Shelter are wholly or half unnecessary. At the present day, and in this country, as I find by my own experience, a few implements, a knife, an axe, a spade, a wheelbarrow, & c., and for the studious, lamplight, stationery, and access to a few books, rank next to necessaries, and can all be obtained at a trifling cost. Yet some, not wise, go to the other side of the globe, to barbarous and unhealthy regions, and devote themselves to trade for ten or twenty years, in order that they may live,—that is, keep comfortably warm,—and die in New England at last. The luxuriously rich are not simply kept comfortably warm, but unnaturally hot;[23] as I implied before, they are cooked, of course *à la mode.*[24]

Most of the luxuries, and many of the so called comforts of life, are not only not indispensable, but positive hinderances to the elevation of mankind. With respect to luxuries and comforts, the wisest have ever lived a more simple and meager life than the poor. The ancient philosophers, Chinese, Hindoo, Persian, and Greek, were a class than which none has been poorer in outward riches, none so rich in inward. We know not much about them. It is remarkable that *we* know so much of them as we do. The same is true of the more modern reformers and benefactors of their race. None can be an impartial or wise observer of human life but from the vantage ground of what *we* should call voluntary poverty. Of a life of luxury the fruit is luxury, whether in agriculture, or commerce, or literature, or art. There are nowadays professors of philosophy, but not philosophers. Yet it is admirable to profess because it was once admirable to live. To be a philosopher is not merely to have subtle thoughts, nor even to found a school, but so to love wisdom as to live according to its dictates, a life of simplicity, independence, magnanimity, and trust. It is to solve some of the problems of life, not only theoretically, but practically. The success of great scholars and thinkers is commonly a courtier-like success, not kingly, not manly. They make shift to live merely by conformity, practically as their fathers did, and are in no sense the progenitors of a nobler race of men. But why do men degenerate ever? What makes families run out? What is the nature of the luxury which enervates and destroys nations? Are we sure that there is none of it in our own lives? The philosopher is in

[22] I.e., as fine a life as that enjoyed by the inhabitants of the paradise described in Greek myth.

[23] With central heating.

[24] In high style.

advance of his age even in the outward form of his life. He is not fed, sheltered, clothed, warmed, like his contemporaries. How can a man be a philosopher and not maintain his vital heat by better methods than other men?

When a man is warmed by the several modes which I have described, what does he want next? Surely not more warmth of the same kind, as more and richer food, larger and more splendid houses, finer and more abundant clothing, more numerous incessant and hotter fires, and the like. When he has obtained those things which are necessary to life, there is another alternative than to obtain the superfluities; and that is, to adventure on life now, his vacation from humbler toil having commenced. The soil, it appears, is suited to the seed, for it has sent its radicle[25] downward, and it may now send its shoot upward also with confidence. Why has man rooted himself thus firmly in the earth, but that he may rise in the same proportion into the heavens above? —for the nobler plants are valued for the fruit they bear at last in the air and light, far from the ground, and are not treated like the humbler esculents, which, though they may be biennials, are cultivated only till they have perfected their root, and often cut down at top for this purpose, so that most would not know them in their flowering season.

I do not mean to prescribe rules to strong and valiant natures, who will mind their own affairs whether in heaven or hell, and perchance build more magnificently and spend more lavishly than the richest, without ever impoverishing themselves, not knowing how they live,—if, indeed, there are any such, as has been dreamed; nor to those who find their encouragement and inspiration in precisely the present condition of things, and cherish it with the fondness and enthusiasm of lovers,—and, to some extent, I reckon myself in this number; I do not speak to those who are well employed, in whatever circumstances, and they know whether they are well employed or not; —but mainly to the mass of men who are discontented, and idly complaining of the hardness of their lot or of the times, when they might improve them. There are some who complain most energetically and inconsolably of any, because they are, as they say, doing their duty. I also have in my mind that seemingly wealthy, but most terribly impoverished class of all, who have accumulated dross, but know not how to use it, or get rid of it, and thus have forged their own golden or silver fetters.

If I should attempt to tell how I have desired to spend my life in years past, it would probably surprise those of my readers who are somewhat acquainted with its actual history; it would certainly astonish those who know nothing about it. I will only hint at some of the enterprises which I have cherished.

In any weather, at any hour of the day or night, I have been anxious to improve the nick of time, and notch it on my stick too; to stand on the meeting of two eternities, the past and future, which is precisely the present moment; to toe that line. You will pardon some obscurities, for there are more secrets in my trade than in most men's, and yet not voluntarily kept, but inseparable from its very nature. I would gladly tell all that I know about it, and never paint "No Admittance" on my gate.

I long ago lost a hound, a bay horse, and a turtledove, and am still on their trail. Many are the travellers I have spoken concerning them, describing their tracks and what calls they answered to. I have met one or two who had heard the hound, and

[25] Root.

the tramp of the horse, and even seen the dove disappear behind a cloud, and they seemed as anxious to recover them as if they had lost them themselves.

To anticipate, not the sunrise and the dawn merely, but, if possible, Nature herself! How many mornings, summer and winter, before yet any neighbor was stirring about his business, have I been about mine! No doubt, many of my townsmen have met me returning from this enterprise, farmers starting for Boston in the twilight, or woodchoppers going to their work. It is true, I never assisted the sun materially in his rising, but, doubt not, it was of the last importance only to be present at it.

So many autumn, ay, and winter days, spent outside the town, trying to hear what was in the wind, to hear and carry it express! I well-nigh sunk all my capital in it, and lost my own breath into the bargain, running in the face of it. If it had concerned either of the political parties, depend upon it, it would have appeared in the Gazette[26] with the earliest intelligence.[27] At other times watching from the observatory of some cliff or tree, to telegraph any new arrival; or waiting at evening on the hill-tops for the sky to fall, that I might catch something, though I never caught much, and that, manna-wise,[28] would dissolve again in the sun.

For a long time I was reporter to a journal,[29] of no very wide circulation, whose editor has never yet seen fit to print the bulk of my contributions, and, as is too common with writers, I got only my labor for my pains. However, in this case my pains were their own reward.

For many years I was self-appointed inspector of snow storms and rain storms, and did my duty faithfully; surveyor, if not of highways, then of forest paths and all across-lot routes, keeping them open, and ravines bridged and passable at all seasons, where the public heel had testified to their utility.

I have looked after the wild stock of the town, which give a faithful herdsman a good deal of trouble by leaping fences; and I have had an eye to the unfrequented nooks and corners of the farm; though I did not always know whether Jonas or Solomon worked in a particular field to-day; that was none of my business. I have watered the red huckleberry, the sand cherry and the nettle tree, the red pine and the black ash, the white grape and the yellow violet, which might have withered else in dry seasons.

In short, I went on thus for a long time, I may say it without boasting, faithfully minding my business, till it became more and more evident that my townsmen would not after all admit me into the list of town officers, nor make my place a sinecure with a moderate allowance. My accounts, which I can swear to have kept faithfully, I have, indeed, never got audited, still less accepted, still less paid and settled. However, I have not set my heart on that.

Not long since, a strolling Indian went to sell baskets at the house of a well-known lawyer in my neighborhood. "Do you wish to buy any baskets?" he asked. "No, we do not want any," was the reply. "What!" exclaimed the Indian as he went out the gate, "do you mean to starve us?" Having seen his industrious white neighbors so well off,—that the lawyer had only to weave arguments, and by some magic wealth and

---

[26] The weekly newspaper of Concord.
[27] News.
[28] Exodus 16 recounts the time that manna, a food given to the Israelites on their journey out of Egypt, melted in the sun.

[29] Thoreau wrote on different occasions for *The Dial, The Democratic Review,* and other magazines, and at all times faithfully "reported" his activities and thoughts to his own journals.

standing followed, he had said to himself; I will go into business; I will weave baskets; it is a thing which I can do. Thinking that when he had made the baskets he would have done his part, and then it would be the white man's to buy them. He had not discovered that it was necessary for him to make it worth the other's while to buy them, or at least make him think that it was so, or to make something else which it would be worth his while to buy. I too had woven a kind of basket of a delicate texture, but I had not made it worth any one's while to buy them. Yet not the less, in my case, did I think it worth my while to weave them, and instead of studying how to make it worth men's while to buy my baskets, I studied rather how to avoid the necessity of selling them. The life which men praise and regard as successful is but one kind. Why should we exaggerate any one kind at the expense of the others?

Finding that my fellow-citizens were not likely to offer me any room in the court house, or any curacy or living any where else, but I must shift for myself, I turned my face more exclusively than ever to the woods, where I was better known. I determined to go into business at once, and not wait to acquire the usual capital, using such slender means as I had already got. My purpose in going to Walden Pond was not to live cheaply nor to live dearly there, but to transact some private business[30] with the fewest obstacles; to be hindered from accomplishing which for want of a little common sense, a little enterprise and business talent, appeared not so sad as foolish.

I have always endeavored to acquire strict business habits; they are indispensable to every man. If your trade is with the Celestial Empire,[31] then some small counting house on the coast, in some Salem harbor, will be fixture enough. You will export such articles as the country affords, purely native products, much ice and pine timber and a little granite, always in native bottoms. These will be good ventures. To oversee all the details yourself in person; to be at once pilot and captain, and owner and underwriter; to buy and sell and keep the accounts; to read every letter received, and write or read every letter sent; to superintend the discharge of imports night and day; to be upon many parts of the coast almost at the same time;—often the richest freight will be discharged upon a Jersey shore;[32]—to be your own telegraph, unweariedly sweeping the horizon, speaking all passing vessels bound coastwise; to keep up a steady despatch of commodities, for the supply of such a distant and exorbitant market; to keep yourself informed of the state of the markets, prospects of war and peace every where, and anticipate the tendencies of trade and civilization,—taking advantage of the results of all exploring expeditions, using new passages and all improvements in navigation;—charts to be studied, the position of reefs and new lights and buoys to be ascertained, and ever, and ever, the logarithmic tables to be corrected, for by the error of some calculator the vessel often splits upon a rock that should have reached a friendly pier,—there is the untold fate of La Perouse;[33]—universal science to be kept pace with, studying the lives of all great discoverers and navigators, great adventurers and merchants, from Hanno and the Phœnicians[34] down to our day; in fine, account of stock to be taken from time to time, to know how you stand. It is a labor to task

[30] To complete his first book, *A Week on the Concord and Merrimack Rivers* (1849).
[31] China.
[32] New Jersey.
[33] Jean François de Gallup, count de la Perouse (1741–1788), French explorer lost somewhere in the South Pacific.
[34] Hanno was a Carthaginian explorer of the fifth century B.C.; the ancient Phoenicians were also famous for their voyages into uncharted waters.

the faculties of a man,—such problems of profit and loss, of interest, of tare and tret,[35] and gauging of all kinds in it, as demand a universal knowledge.

I have thought that Walden Pond would be a good place for business, not solely on account of the railroad and the ice trade; it offers advantages which it may not be good policy to divulge; it is a good port and a good foundation. No Neva[36] marshes to be filled; though you must every where build on piles of your own driving. It is said that a flood-tide, with a westerly wind, and ice in the Neva, would sweep St. Petersburg from the face of the earth.

As this business was to be entered into without the usual capital, it may not be easy to conjecture where those means, that will still be indispensable to every such undertaking, were to be obtained. As for Clothing, to come at once to the practical part of the question, perhaps we are led oftener by the love of novelty, and a regard for the opinions of men, in procuring it, than by a true utility. Let him who has work to do recollect that the object of clothing is, first, to retain the vital heat, and secondly, in this state of society, to cover nakedness, and he may judge how much of any necessary or important work may be accomplished without adding to his wardrobe. Kings and queens who wear a suit but once, though made by some tailor or dressmaker to their majesties, cannot know the comfort of wearing a suit that fits. They are no better than wooden horses to hang the clean clothes on. Every day our garments become more assimilated to ourselves, receiving the impress of the wearer's character, until we hesitate to lay them aside, without such delay and medical appliances and some such solemnity even as our bodies. No man ever stood the lower in my estimation for having a patch in his clothes; yet I am sure that there is greater anxiety, commonly, to have fashionable, or at least clean and unpatched clothes, than to have a sound conscience. But even if the rent is not mended, perhaps the worst vice betrayed is improvidence. I sometimes try my acquaintances by such tests as this;—who could wear a patch, or two extra seams only, over the knee? Most behave as if they believed that their prospects for life would be ruined if they should do it. It would be easier for them to hobble to town with a broken leg than with a broken pantaloon. Often if an accident happens to a gentleman's legs, they can be mended; but if a similar accident happens to the legs of his pantaloons, there is no help for it; for he considers, not what is truly respectable, but what is respected. We know but few men, a great many coats and breeches. Dress a scarecrow in your last shift, you standing shiftless by, who would not soonest salute the scarecrow? Passing a cornfield the other day, close by a hat and coat on a stake, I recognized the owner of the farm. He was only a little more weather-beaten than when I saw him last. I have heard of a dog that barked at every stranger who approached his master's premises with clothes on, but was easily quieted by a naked thief. It is an interesting question how far men would retain their relative rank if they were divested of their clothes. Could you, in such a case, tell surely of any company of civilized men, which belonged to the most *respected class?* When Madam Pfeiffer,[37] in her adventurous travels round the world, from east to west, had got so near home as Asiatic Russia, she says that she felt the

---

[35] Calculations of weight.
[36] River in Russia near the site of St. Petersburg, now Leningrad.

[37] Ida Reyer Pfeiffer (1797–1358), Austrian writer of travel books, such as *A Woman's Journey Round the World* (1852).

necessity of wearing other than a travelling dress, when she went to meet the authorities, for she "was now in a civilized country, where —— people are judged of by their clothes." Even in our democratic New England towns the accidental possession of wealth, and its manifestation in dress and equipage alone, obtain for the possessor almost universal respect. But they who yield such respect, numerous as they are, are so far heathen, and need to have a missionary sent to them. Beside, clothes introduced sewing, a kind of work which you may call endless; a woman's dress, at least, is never done.

A man who has at length found something to do will not need to get a new suit to do it in; for him the old will do, that has lain dusty in the garret for an indeterminate period. Old shoes will serve a hero longer than they have served his valet,—if a hero ever has a valet—bare feet are older than shoes, and he can make them do. Only they who go to soirées and legislative halls must have new coats, coats to change as often as the man changes in them. But if my jacket and trousers, my hat and shoes, are fit to worship God in, they will do; will they not? Who ever saw his old clothes,—his old coat, actually worn out, resolved into its primitive elements, so that it was not a deed of charity to bestow it on some poor boy, by him perchance to be bestowed on some poorer still, or shall we say richer, who could do with less? I say, beware of all enterprises that require new clothes, and not rather a new wearer of clothes. If there is not a new man, how can the new clothes be made to fit? If you have any enterprise before you, try it in your old clothes. All men want, not something to *do with,* but something to *do,* or rather something to *be.* Perhaps we should never procure a new suit, however ragged or dirty the old, until we have so conducted, so enterprised or sailed in some way, that we feel like new men in the old, and that to retain it would be like keeping new wine in old bottles.[38] Our moulting season, like that of the fowls, must be a crisis in our lives. The loon retires to solitary ponds to spend it. Thus also the snake casts its slough, and the caterpillar its wormy coat, by an internal industry and expansion; for clothes are but our outmost cuticle and mortal coil. Otherwise we shall be found sailing under false colors, and be inevitably cashiered at last by our own opinion, as well as that of mankind.

We don garment after garment, as if we grew like exogenous plants by addition without. Our outside and often thin and fanciful clothes are our epidermis or false skin, which partakes not of our life, and may be stripped off here and there without fatal injury; our thicker garments, constantly worn, are our cellular integument, or cortex; but our shirts are our liber or true bark, which cannot be removed without girdling and so destroying the man. I believe that all races at some seasons wear something equivalent to the shirt. It is desirable that a man be clad so simply that he can lay his hands on himself in the dark, and that he live in all respects so compactly and preparedly, that, if an enemy take the town, he can, like the old philosopher, walk out the gate empty-handed without anxiety. While one thick garment is, for most purposes, as good as three thin ones, and cheap clothing can be obtained at prices really to suit customers; while a thick coat can be bought for five dollars, which will last as many years, thick pantaloons for two dollars, cowhide boots for a dollar and a half a pair, a summer hat for a quarter of a dollar, and a winter cap for sixty-two and a half cents, or a better be made at home at a nominal cost, where is he so poor that,

[38] Allusion to Matthew 9:17.

clad in such a suit, *of his own earning,* there will not be found wise men to do him reverence?

When I ask for a garment of a particular form, my tailoress tells me gravely, "They do not make them so now," not emphasizing the "They" at all, as if she quoted an authority as impersonal as the Fates,[39] and I find it difficult to get made what I want, simply because she cannot believe that I mean what I say, that I am so rash. When I hear this oracular sentence, I am for a moment absorbed in thought, emphasizing to myself each word separately that I may come at the meaning of it, that I may find out by what degree of consanguinity *They* are related to *me,* and what authority they may have in an affair which affects me so nearly; and, finally, I am inclined to answer her with equal mystery, and without any more emphasis of the "they,"—"It is true, they did not make them so recently, but they do now." Of what use this measuring of me if she does not measure my character, but only the breadth of my shoulders, as it were a peg to hang the coat on? We worship not the Graces,[40] nor the Parcæ,[41] but Fashion. She spins and weaves and cuts with full authority. The head monkey[42] at Paris puts on a traveller's cap, and all the monkeys in America do the same. I sometimes despair of getting any thing quite simple and honest done in this world by the help of men. They would have to be passed through a powerful press first, to squeeze their old notions out of them, so that they would not soon get upon their legs again, and then there would be some one in the company with a maggot in his head, hatched from an egg deposited there nobody knows when, for not even fire kills these things, and you would have lost your labor. Nevertheless, we will not forget that some Egyptian wheat is said to have been handed down to us by a mummy.[43]

On the whole, I think that it cannot be maintained that dressing has in this or any country risen to the dignity of an art. At present men make shift to wear what they can get. Like shipwrecked sailors, they put on what they can find on the beach, and at a little distance, whether of space or time, laugh at each other's masquerade. Every generation laughs at the old fashions, but follows religiously the new. We are amused at beholding the costume of Henry VIII., or Queen Elizabeth,[44] as much as if it was that of the King and Queen of the Cannibal Islands. All costume off a man is pitiful or grotesque. It is only the serious eye peering from and the sincere life passed within it, which restrain laughter and consecrate the costume of any people. Let Harlequin be taken with a fit of the colic and his trappings will have to serve that mood too. When the soldier is hit by a cannon ball rags are as becoming as purple.

The childish and savage taste of men and women for new patterns keeps how many shaking and squinting through kaleidoscopes that they may discover the particular figure which this generation requires to-day. The manufacturers have learned that this taste is merely whimsical. Of two patterns which differ only by a few threads more or less of a particular color, the one will be sold readily, the other lie on the shelf, though it frequently happens that after the lapse of a season the latter becomes the most fashionable. Comparatively, tattooing is not the hid-

---

[39] In classic myth, the goddesses who determine men's destinies.

[40] Greek deities of beauty, happiness, and brilliance.

[41] Roman goddesses of destiny.

[42] Dictator of fashion.

[43] I.e., sprung from seeds sealed within an Egyptian tomb.

[44] Tudor king (1509–1547) and queen (1558–1603) of England.

eous custom which it is called. It is not barbarous merely because the printing is skin-deep and unalterable.

I cannot believe that our factory system is the best mode by which men may get clothing. The condition of the operatives is becoming every day more like that of the English; and it cannot be wondered at, since, as far as I have heard or observed, the principal object is, not that mankind may be well and honestly clad, but, unquestionably, that the corporations may be enriched. In the long run men hit only what they aim at. Therefore, though they should fail immediately, they had better aim at something high.

As for a Shelter, I will not deny that this is now a necessary of life, though there are instances of men having done without it for long periods in colder countries than this. Samuel Laing[45] says that "The Laplander in his skin dress, and in a skin bag which he puts over his head and shoulders, will sleep night after night on the snow——in a degree of cold which would extinguish the life of one exposed to it in any woollen clothing." He had seen them asleep thus. Yet he adds, "They are not hardier than other people." But, probably, man did not live long on the earth without discovering the convenience which there is in a house, the domestic comforts, which phrase may have originally signified the satisfactions of the house more than of the family; though these must be extremely partial and occasional in those climates where the house is associated in our thoughts with winter or the rainy season chiefly, and two thirds of the year, except for a parasol, is unnecessary. In our climate, in the summer, it was formerly almost solely a covering at night. In the Indian gazettes a wigwam was the symbol of a day's march, and a row of them cut or painted on the bark of a tree signified that so many times they had camped. Man was not made so large limbed and robust but that he must seek to narrow his world, and wall in a space such as fitted him. He was at first bare and out of doors; but though this was pleasant enough in serene and warm weather, by daylight, the rainy season and the winter, to say nothing of the torrid sun, would perhaps have nipped his race in the bud if he had not made haste to clothe himself with the shelter of a house. Adam and Eve, according to the fable, wore the bower before other clothes. Man wanted a home, a place of warmth, or comfort, first of physical warmth, then the warmth of the affections.

We may imagine a time when, in the infancy of the human race, some enterprising mortal crept into a hollow in a rock for shelter. Every child begins the world again, to some extent, and loves to stay out doors, even in wet and cold. It plays house, as well as horse, having an instinct for it. Who does not remember the interest with which when young he looked at shelving rocks, or any approach to a cave? It was the natural yearning of that portion of our most primitive ancestor which still survived in us. From the cave we have advanced to roofs of palm leaves, of bark and boughs, of linen woven and stretched, of grass and straw, of boards and shingles, of stones and tiles. At last, we know not what it is to live in the open air, and our lives are domestic in more senses than we think. From the hearth to the field is a great distance. It would be well perhaps if we were to spend more of our days and nights

[45] In his book *Journal of a Residence in Norway* (1837).

without any obstruction between us and the celestial bodies, if the poet did not speak so much from under a roof, or the saint dwell there so long. Birds do not sing in caves, nor do doves cherish their innocence in dovecots.

However, if one designs to construct a dwelling house, it behooves him to exercise a little Yankee shrewdness, lest after all he find himself in a workhouse, a labyrinth without a clew, a museum, an almshouse, a prison, or a splendid mausoleum instead. Consider first how slight a shelter is absolutely necessary. I have seen Penobscot Indians,[46] in this town, living in tents of thin cotton cloth, while the snow was nearly a foot deep around them, and I thought that they would be glad to have it deeper to keep out the wind. Formerly, when how to get my living honestly, with freedom left for my proper pursuits, was a question which vexed me even more than it does now, for unfortunately I am become somewhat callous, I used to see a large box by the railroad, six feet long by three wide, in which the laborers locked up their tools at night, and it suggested to me that every man who was hard pushed might get such a one for a dollar, and, having bored a few auger holes in it, to admit the air at least, get into it when it rained and at night, and hook down the lid, and so have freedom in his love, and in his soul be free. This did not appear the worst, nor by any means a despicable alternative. You could sit up as late as you pleased, and, whenever you got up, go abroad without any landlord or house-lord dogging you for rent. Many a man is harassed to death to pay the rent of a larger and more luxurious box who would not have frozen to death in such a box as this. I am far from jesting. Economy is a subject which admits of being treated with levity, but it cannot so be disposed of. A comfortable house for a rude and hardy race, that lived mostly out of doors, was once made here almost entirely of such materials as Nature furnished ready to their hands. Gookin,[47] who was superintendent of the Indians subject to the Massachusetts Colony, writing in 1674, says, "The best of their houses are covered very neatly, tight and warm, with barks of trees, slipped from their bodies at those seasons when the sap is up and made into great flakes, with pressure of weighty timber, when they are green. . . . The meaner sort are covered with mats which they make of a kind of bulrush, and are also indifferently tight and warm, but not so good as the former. . . . Some I have seen, sixty or a hundred feet long and thirty feet broad. . . . I have often lodged in their wigwams, and found them as warm as the best English houses." He adds, that they were commonly carpeted and lined within with well-wrought embroidered mats, and were furnished with various utensils. The Indians had advanced so far as to regulate the effect of the wind by a mat suspended over the hole in the roof and moved by a string. Such a lodge was in the first instance constructed in a day or two at most, and taken down and put up in a few hours; and every family owned one, or its apartment in one.

In the savage state every family owns a shelter as good as the best, and sufficient for its coarser and simpler wants; but I think that I speak within bounds when I say that, though the birds of the air have their nests, and the foxes their holes,[48] and the savages their wigwams, in modern civilized society not more than one half the families own a shelter. In the large towns and cities, where civilization especially prevails, the

[46] Thoreau visited northern Maine and became acquainted with members of the Penobscot tribe at that time.

[47] Daniel Gookin (1612–1687) wrote *Historical Collections of the Indians in New England*.
[48] Reference to Matthew 8:20.

number of those who own a shelter is a very small fraction of the whole. The rest pay an annual tax for this outside garment of all, become indispensable summer and winter, which would buy a village of Indian wigwams, but now helps to keep them poor as long as they live. I do not mean to insist here on the disadvantage of hiring compared with owning, but it is evident that the savage owns his shelter because it costs so little, while the civilized man hires his commonly because he cannot afford to own it; nor can he, in the long run, any better afford to hire. But, answers one, by merely paying this tax the poor civilized man secures an abode which is a palace compared with the savage's. An annual rent of from twenty-five to a hundred dollars, these are the country rates, entitles him to the benefit of the improvements of centuries, spacious apartments, clean paint and paper, Rumford fireplace,[49] back plastering,[50] Venetian blinds, copper pump, spring lock, a commodious cellar, and many other things. But how happens it that he who is said to enjoy these things is so commonly a *poor* civilized man, while the savage, who has them not, is rich as a savage? If it is asserted that civilization is a real advance in the condition of man,—and I think that it is, though only the wise improve their advantages,—it must be shown that it has produced better dwellings without making them more costly; and the cost of a thing is the amount of what I will call life which is required to be exchanged for it, immediately or in the long run. An average house in this neighborhood costs perhaps eight hundred dollars, and to lay up this sum will take from ten to fifteen years of the laborer's life, even if he is not encumbered with a family;—estimating the pecuniary value of every man's labor at one dollar a day, for if some receive more, others receive less;—so that he must have spent more than half his life commonly before *his* wigwam will be earned. If we suppose him to pay a rent instead, this is but a doubtful choice of evils. Would the savage have been wise to exchange his wigwam for a palace on these terms?

It may be guessed that I reduce almost the whole advantage of holding this superfluous property as a fund in store against the future, so far as the individual is concerned, mainly to the defraying of funeral expenses. But perhaps a man is not required to bury himself. Nevertheless this points to an important distinction between the civilized man and the savage; and, no doubt, they have designs on us for our benefit, in making the life of a civilized people an *institution,* in which the life of the individual is to a great extent absorbed, in order to preserve and perfect that of the race. But I wish to show at what a sacrifice this advantage is at present obtained, and to suggest that we may possibly so live as to secure all the advantage without suffering any of the disadvantage. What mean ye by saying that the poor ye have always with you, or that the fathers have eaten sour grapes, and the children's teeth are set on edge?[51]

"As I live, saith the Lord God, ye shall not have occasion any more to use this proverb in Israel."

"Behold all souls are mine; as the soul of the father, so also the soul of the son is mine: the soul that sinneth it shall die."[52]

---

[49] Smokeless stove invented by Count Rumford (1753–1814).

[50] Insulation.

[51] Reference to John 12:8 and Ezekiel 18:2.

[52] Ezekiel 18:3–4.

When I consider my neighbors, the farmers of Concord, who are at least as well off as the other classes, I find that for the most part they have been toiling twenty, thirty, or forty years, that they may become the real owners of their farms, which commonly they have inherited with encumbrances, or else bought with hired money, —and we may regard one third of that toil as the cost of their houses,—but commonly they have not paid for them yet. It is true, the encumbrances sometimes outweigh the value of the farm, so that the farm itself becomes one great encumbrance, and still a man is found to inherit it, being well acquainted with it, as he says. On applying to the assessors, I am surprised to learn that they cannot at once name a dozen in the town who own their farms free and clear. If you would know the history of these homesteads, inquire at the bank where they are mortgaged. The man who has actually paid for his farm with labor on it is so rare that every neighbor can point to him. I doubt if there are three such men in Concord. What has been said of the merchants, that a very large majority, even ninety-seven in a hundred, are sure to fail, is equally true of the farmers. With regard to the merchants, however, one of them says pertinently that a great part of their failures are not genuine pecuniary failures, but merely failures to fulfil their engagements, because it is inconvenient; that is, it is the moral character that breaks down. But this puts an infinitely worse face on the matter, and suggests, beside, that probably not even the other three succeed in saving their souls, but are perchance bankrupt in a worse sense than they who fail honestly. Bankruptcy and repudiation are the spring-boards from which much of our civilization vaults and turns its somersets, but the savage stands on the unelastic plank of famine. Yet the Middlesex Cattle Show[53] goes off here with *éclat* annually, as if all the joints of the agricultural machine were suent.[54]

The farmer is endeavoring to solve the problem of livelihood by a formula more complicated than the problem itself. To get his shoestrings he speculates in herds of cattle. With consummate skill he has set his trap with a hair spring to catch comfort and independence, and then, as he turned away, got his own leg into it. This is the reason he is poor; and for a similar reason we are all poor in respect to a thousand savage comforts, though surrounded by luxuries. As Chapman sings,—

"The false society of men—
  —for earthly greatness
All heavenly comforts rarefies to air."[55]

And when the farmer has got his house, he may not be the richer but the poorer for it, and it be the house that has got him. As I understand it, that was a valid objection urged by Momus[56] against the house which Minerva[57] made, that she "had not made it movable, by which means a bad neighborhood might be avoided;" and it may still be urged, for our houses are such unwieldy property that we are often imprisoned rather than housed in them; and the bad neighborhood to be avoided is

---

[53] Annual agricultural fair held in Concord.
[54] Properly functioning.
[55] From *Caesar and Pompey* (1631), Act V, Sc. i, ll. 210, 212–213, by George Chapman, English poet, dramatist, and translator (1559?–1634).

[56] God of mockery in classic myth.
[57] Handicrafts was one of the skills for which the Greek goddess acted as patron.

our own scurvy selves. I know one or two families, at least, in this town, who, for nearly a generation, have been wishing to sell their houses in the outskirts and move into the village, but have not been able to accomplish it, and only death will set them free.

Granted that the *majority* are able at last either to own or hire the modern house with all its improvements. While civilization has been improving our houses, it has not equally improved the men who are to inhabit them. It has created palaces, but it was not so easy to create noblemen and kings. And *if the civilized man's pursuits are no worthier than the savage's, if he is employed the greater part of his life in obtaining gross necessaries and comforts merely, why should he have a better dwelling than the former?*

But how do the poor *minority* fare? Perhaps it will be found, that just in proportion as some have been placed in outward circumstances above the savage, others have been degraded below him. The luxury of one class is counterbalanced by the indigence of another. On the one side is the palace, on the other are the almshouse and "silent poor."[58] The myriads who built the pyramids to be the tombs of the Pharaohs were fed on garlic, and it may be were not decently buried themselves. The mason who finishes the cornice of the palace returns at night perchance to a hut not so good as a wigwam. It is a mistake to suppose that, in a country where the usual evidences of civilization exist, the condition of a very large body of the inhabitants may not be as degraded as that of savages. I refer to the degraded poor, not now to the degraded rich. To know this I should not need to look farther than to the shanties which every where border our railroads, that last improvement in civilization; where I see in my daily walks human beings living in sties, and all winter with an open door, for the sake of light, without any visible, often imaginable, wood pile, and the forms of both old and young are permanently contracted by the long habit of shrinking from cold and misery, and the development of all their limbs and faculties is checked. It certainly is fair to look at that class by whose labor the works which distinguish this generation are accomplished. Such too, to a greater or less extent, is the condition of the operatives of every denomination in England, which is the great workhouse of the world. Or I could refer you to Ireland,[59] which is marked as one of the white or enlightened spots on the map. Contrast the physical condition of the Irish with that of the North American Indian, or the South Sea Islander, or any other savage race before it was degraded by contact with the civilized man. Yet I have no doubt that that people's rulers are as wise as the average of civilized rulers. Their condition only proves what squalidness may consist with civilization. I hardly need refer now to the laborers in our Southern States who produce the staple exports of this country, and are themselves a staple production of the South. But to confine myself to those who are said to be in *moderate* circumstances.

Most men appear never to have considered what a house is, and are actually though needlessly poor all their lives because they think that they must have such a one as their neighbors have. As if one were to wear any sort of coat which the tailor might cut out for him, or, gradually leaving off palmleaf hat or cap of woodchuck skin, complain of hard times because he could not afford to buy him a crown! It is possible

[58] Those who conceal their poverty.
[59] That is, Ireland in the grip of the potato famine of the 1840s.

to invent a house still more convenient and luxurious than we have, which yet all would admit that man could not afford to pay for. Shall we always study to obtain more of these things, and not sometimes to be content with less? Shall the respectable citizen thus gravely teach, by precept and example, the necessity of the young man's providing a certain number of superfluous glow-shoes,[60] and umbrellas, and empty guest chambers for empty guests, before he dies? Why should not our furniture be as simple as the Arab's or the Indian's? When I think of the benefactors of the race, whom we have apotheosized as messengers from heaven, bearers of divine gifts to man, I do not see in my mind any retinue at their heels, any car-load of fashionable furniture. Or what if I were to allow—would it not be a singular allowance?—that our furniture should be more complex than the Arab's, in proportion as we are morally and intellectually his superiors! At present our houses are cluttered and defiled with it, and a good housewife would sweep out the greater part into the dust hole, and not leave her morning's work undone. Morning work! By the blushes of Aurora[61] and the music of Memnon,[62] what should be man's *morning work* in this world? I had three pieces of limestone on my desk, but I was terrified to find that they required to be dusted daily, when the furniture of my mind was all undusted still, and I threw them out the window in disgust. How, then, could I have a furnished house? I would rather sit in the open air, for no dust gathers on the grass, unless where man has broken ground.

It is the luxurious and dissipated who set the fashions which the herd so diligently follow. The traveller who stops at the best houses, so called, soon discovers this, for the publicans presume him to be a Sardanapalus,[63] and if he resigned himself to their tender mercies he would soon be completely emasculated. I think that in the railroad car we are inclined to spend more on luxury than on safety and convenience, and it threatens without attaining these to become no better than a modern drawing room, with its divans, and ottomans, and sunshades, and a hundred other oriental things, which we are taking west with us, invented for the ladies of the harem and the effeminate natives of the Celestial Empire, which Jonathan[64] should be ashamed to know the names of. I would rather sit on a pumpkin and have it all to myself, than be crowded on a velvet cushion. I would rather ride on earth in an ox cart with a free circulation, than go to heaven in the fancy car of an excursion train and breathe a *malaria* all the way.

The very simplicity and nakedness of man's life in the primitive ages imply this advantage at least, that they left him still but a sojourner in nature. When he was refreshed with food and sleep he contemplated his journey again. He dwelt, as it were, in a tent in this world, and was either threading the valleys, or crossing the plains, or climbing the mountain tops. But lo! men have become the tools of their tools. The man who independently plucked the fruits when he was hungry is become a farmer; and he who stood under a tree for shelter, a housekeeper. We now no longer camp as for a night, but have settled down on earth and forgotten heaven. We have adopted Christianity merely as an improved method of *agri-*culture. We have built for this

---

[60] Overshoes.
[61] Goddess of dawn in classic myth.
[62] Gigantic statue of an ancient Egyptian king that emitted musical sounds when struck by the morning light.

[63] Ruler of Assyria, whose kingdom was destroyed in the ninth century B.C.; known for his immorality and decadent behavior.
[64] A Yankee or American.

world a family mansion, and for the next a family tomb. The best works of art are the expression of man's struggle to free himself from this condition, but the effect of our art is merely to make this low state comfortable and that higher state to be forgotten. There is actually no place in this village for a work of *fine* art, if any had come down to us, to stand, for our lives, our houses and streets, furnish no proper pedestal for it. There is not a nail to hang a picture on, nor a shelf to receive the bust of a hero or a saint. When I consider how our houses are built and paid for, or not paid for, and their internal economy managed and sustained, I wonder that the floor does not give way under the visitor while he is admiring the gewgaws upon the mantel-piece, and let him through into the cellar, to some solid and honest though earthy foundation. I cannot but perceive that this so called rich and refined life is a thing jumped at, and I do not get on in the enjoyment of the *fine* arts which adorn it, my attention being wholly occupied with the jump; for I remember that the greatest genuine leap, due to human muscles alone, on record, is that of certain wandering Arabs, who are said to have cleared twenty-five feet on level ground. Without factitious support, man is sure to come to earth again beyond that distance. The first question which I am tempted to put to the proprietor of such great impropriety is, Who bolsters you? Are you one of the ninety-seven who fail? or of the three who succeed? Answer me these questions, and then perhaps I may look at your bawbles and find them ornamental. The cart before the horse is neither beautiful nor useful. Before we can adorn our houses with beautiful objects the walls must be stripped, and our lives must be stripped, and beautiful housekeeping and beautiful living be laid for a foundation: now, a taste for the beautiful is most cultivated out of doors, where there is no house and no housekeeper.

Old Johnson,[65] in his "Wonder-Working Providence," speaking of the first settlers of this town, with whom he was contemporary, tells us that "they burrow themselves in the earth for their first shelter under some hillside, and, casting the soil aloft upon timber, they make a smoky fire against the earth, at the highest side." They did not "provide them houses," says he, "till the earth, by the Lord's blessing, brought forth bread to feed them," and the first year's crop was so light that "they were forced to cut their bread very thin for a long season." The secretary of the Province of New Netherland,[66] writing Dutch, in 1650, for the information of those who wished to take up land there, states more particularly, that "those in New Netherland, and especially in New England, who have no means to build farm houses at first according to their wishes, dig a square pit in the ground, cellar fashion, six or seven feet deep, as long and as broad as they think proper, case the earth inside with wood all round the wall, and line the wood with the bark of trees or something else to prevent the caving in of the earth; floor this cellar with plank, and wainscot it overhead for a ceiling, raise a roof of spars clear up, and cover the spars with bark or green sods, so that they can live dry and warm in these houses with their entire families for two, three, and four years, it being understood that partitions are run through those cellars which are adapted to the size of the family. The wealthy and principal men in New England,

---

[65] Edward Johnson (1598–1672), author of *Wonder-Working Providence of Sion's Saviour in New England* (1654), account of early Puritan settlement.

[66] Later the colony of New York. The quotation that follows is taken from *The Documentary History of the State of New York* (1951).

in the beginning of the colonies, commenced their first dwelling houses in this fashion for two reasons; firstly, in order not to waste time in building, and not to want food the next season; secondly, in order not to discourage poor laboring people whom they brought over in numbers from Fatherland. In the course of three or four years when the country became adapted to agriculture, they built themselves handsome houses, spending on them several thousands."

In this course which our ancestors took there was a show of prudence at least, as if their principle were to satisfy the more pressing wants first. But are the more pressing wants satisfied now? When I think of acquiring for myself one of our luxurious dwellings, I am deterred, for, so to speak, the country is not yet adapted to *human* culture, and we are still forced to cut our *spiritual* bread far thinner than our forefathers did their wheaten. Not that all architectural ornament is to be neglected even in the rudest periods; but let our houses first be lined with beauty, where they come in contact with our lives, like the tenement of the shellfish, and not overlaid with it. But, alas! I have been inside one or two of them, and know what they are lined with.

Though we are not so degenerate but that we might possibly live in a cave or a wigwam or wear skins today, it certainly is better to accept the advantages, though so dearly bought, which the invention and industry of mankind offer. In such a neighborhood as this, boards and shingles, lime and bricks, are cheaper and more easily obtained than suitable caves, or whole logs, or bark in sufficient quantities, or even well-tempered clay or flat stones. I speak understandingly on this subject, for I have made myself acquainted with it both theoretically and practically. With a little more wit we might use these materials so as to become richer than the richest now are, and make our civilization a blessing. The civilized man is a more experienced and wiser savage. But to make haste to my own experiment.

Near the end of March, 1845, I borrowed an axe and went down to the woods by Walden Pond, nearest to where I intended to build my house, and began to cut down some tall arrowy white pines, still in their youth, for timber. It is difficult to begin without borrowing, but perhaps it is the most generous course thus to permit your fellow-men to have an interest in your enterprise. The owner of the axe, as he released his hold on it, said that it was the apple of his eye; but I returned it sharper than I received it. It was a pleasant hillside where I worked, covered with pine woods, through which I looked out on the pond, and a small open field in the woods where pines and hickories were springing up. The ice in the pond was not yet dissolved, though there were some open spaces, and it was all dark colored and saturated with water. There were some slight flurries of snow during the days that I worked there; but for the most part when I came out on to the railroad, on my way home, its yellow sand heap stretched away gleaming in the hazy atmosphere, and the rails shone in the spring sun, and I heard the lark and pewee and other birds already come to commence another year with us. They were pleasant spring days, in which the winter of man's discontent[67] was thawing as well as the earth, and the life that had lain torpid began to stretch itself. One day, when my axe had come off and I had cut a green hickory

---

[67] Paraphrase from *Richard III,* Act I, Sc. i, l. 1,
Shakespeare's history play.

for a wedge, driving it with a stone, and had placed the whole to soak in a pond hole in order to swell the wood, I saw a striped snake run into the water, and he lay on the bottom, apparently without inconvenience, as long as I staid there, or more than a quarter of an hour; perhaps because he had not yet fairly come out of the torpid state. It appeared to me that for a like reason men remain in their present low and primitive condition; but if they should feel the influence of the spring of springs arousing them, they would of necessity rise to a higher and more ethereal life. I had previously seen the snakes in frosty mornings in my path with portions of their bodies still numb and inflexible, waiting for the sun to thaw them. On the 1st of April it rained and melted the ice, and in the early part of the day, which was very foggy, I heard a stray goose groping about over the pond and cackling as if lost, or like the spirit of the fog.

So I went on for some days cutting and hewing timber, and also studs and rafters, all with my narrow axe, not having many communicable or scholar-like thoughts, singing to myself,—

> Men say they know many things;
> But lo! they have taken wings,—
> The arts and sciences,
> And a thousand appliances;
> The wind that blows
> Is all that any body knows.[68]

I hewed the main timbers six inches square, most of the studs on two sides only, and the rafters and floor timbers on one side, leaving the rest of the bark on, so that they were just as straight and much stronger than sawed ones. Each stick was carefully mortised or tenoned by its stump, for I had borrowed other tools by this time. My days in the woods were not very long ones; yet I usually carried my dinner of bread and butter, and read the newspaper in which it was wrapped, at noon, sitting amid the green pine boughs which I had cut off, and to my bread was imparted some of their fragrance, for my hands were covered with a thick coat of pitch. Before I had done I was more the friend than the foe of the pine tree, though I had cut down some of them, having become better acquainted with it. Sometimes a rambler in the wood was attracted by the sound of my axe, and we chatted pleasantly over the chips which I had made.

By the middle of April, for I made no haste in my work, but rather made the most of it, my house was framed and ready for the raising. I had already bought the shanty of James Collins, an Irishman who worked on the Fitchburg Railroad, for boards. James Collins' shanty was considered an uncommonly fine one. When I called to see it he was not at home. I walked about the outside, at first unobserved from within, the window was so deep and high. It was of small dimensions, with a peaked cottage roof, and not much else to be seen, the dirt being raised five feet all around as if it were a compost heap. The roof was the soundest part, though a good deal warped and made brittle by the sun. Door-sill there was none, but a perennial passage for the hens under the door board. Mrs. C. came to the door and asked me to view it from

---

[68] Thoreau's own verses.

the inside. The hens were driven in by my approach. It was dark, and had a dirt floor for the most part, dank, clammy, and aguish, only here a board and there a board which would not bear removal. She lighted a lamp to show me the inside of the roof and the walls, and also that the board floor extended under the bed, warning me not to step into the cellar, a sort of dust hole two feet deep. In her own words, they were "good boards overhead, good boards all around, and a good window,"—of two whole squares originally, only the cat had passed out that way lately. There was a stove, a bed, and a place to sit, an infant in the house where it was born, a silk parasol, gilt-framed looking-glass, and a patent new coffee mill nailed to an oak sapling, all told. The bargain was soon concluded, for James had in the mean while returned. I to pay four dollars and twenty-five cents to-night, he to vacate at five tomorrow morning, selling to nobody else meanwhile: I to take possession at six. It were well, he said, to be there early, and anticipate certain indistinct but wholly unjust claims on the score of ground rent and fuel. This he assured me was the only encumbrance. At six I passed him and his family on the road. One large bundle held their all,— bed, coffee-mill, looking-glass, hens,—all but the cat, she took to the woods and became a wild cat, and, as I learned afterward, trod in a trap set for woodchucks, and so became a dead cat at last.

I took down this dwelling the same morning, drawing the nails, and removed it to the pond side by small cartloads, spreading the boards on the grass there to bleach and warp back again in the sun. One early thrush gave me a note or two as I drove along the woodland path. I was informed treacherously by a young Patrick[69] that neighbor Seeley, an Irishman, in the intervals of the carting, transferred the still tolerable, straight, and drivable nails, staples, and spikes to his pocket, and then stood when I came back to pass the time of day, and look freshly up, unconcerned, with spring thoughts, at the devastation; there being a dearth of work, as he said. He was there to represent spectatordom, and help make this seemingly insignificant event one with the removal of the gods of Troy.[70]

I dug my cellar in the side of a hill sloping to the south, where a woodchuck had formerly dug his burrow, down through sumach and blackberry roots, and the lowest stain of vegetation, six feet square by seven deep, to a fine sand where potatoes would not freeze in any winter. The sides were left shelving, and not stoned; but the sun having never shone on them, the sand still keeps its place. It was but two hours' work. I took particular pleasure in this breaking of ground, for in almost all latitudes men dig into the earth for an equable temperature. Under the most splendid house in the city is still to be found the cellar where they store their roots as of old, and long after the superstructure has disappeared posterity remark its dent in the earth. The house is still but a sort of porch at the entrance of a burrow.

At length, in the beginning of May, with the help of some of my acquaintances, rather to improve so good an occasion for neighborliness than from any necessity, I set up the frame of my house. No man was ever more honored in the character of his raisers than I. They are destined, I trust, to assist at the raising of loftier structures one day. I began to occupy my house on the 4th of July, as soon as it was boarded

---

[69] Irishman.
[70] In Greek legend, Troy was safe as long as the statue of the goddess Pallas Athena remained in her temple; during the Trojan War the Greeks stole the statue, supposedly making their later victory possible.

and roofed, for the boards were carefully feather-edged and lapped, so that it was perfectly impervious to rain; but before boarding I laid the foundation of a chimney at one end, bringing two cartloads of stones up the hill from the pond in my arms. I built the chimney after my hoeing in the fall, before a fire became necessary for warmth, doing my cooking in the mean while out of doors on the ground, early in the morning: which mode I still think is in some respects more convenient and agreeable than the usual one. When it stormed before my bread was baked, I fixed a few boards over the fire, and sat under them to watch my loaf, and passed some pleasant hours in that way. In those days, when my hands were much employed, I read but little, but the least scraps of paper which lay on the ground, my holder, or tablecloth, afforded me as much entertainment, in fact answered the same purpose as the Iliad.[71]

It would be worth the while to build still more deliberately than I did, considering, for instance, what foundation a door, a window, a cellar, a garret, have in the nature of man, and perchance never raising any superstructure until we found a better reason for it than our temporal necessities even. There is some of the same fitness in a man's building his own house that there is in a bird's building its own nest. Who knows but if men constructed their dwellings with their own hands, and provided food for themselves and families simply and honestly enough, the poetic faculty would be universally developed, as birds universally sing when they are so engaged? But alas! we do like cowbirds and cuckoos, which lay their eggs in nests which other birds have built, and cheer no traveller with their chattering and unmusical notes. Shall we forever resign the pleasure of construction to the carpenter? What does architecture amount to in the experience of the mass of men? I never in all my walks came across a man engaged in so simple and natural an occupation as building his house. We belong to the community. It is not the tailor alone who is the ninth part of a man;[72] it is as much the preacher, and the merchant, and the farmer. Where is this division of labor to end? and what object does it finally serve? No doubt another *may* also think for me; but it is not therefore desirable that he should do so to the exclusion of my thinking for myself.

True, there are architects so called in this country, and I have heard of one at least possessed with the idea of making architectural ornaments have a core of truth, a necessity, and hence a beauty, as if it were a revelation to him. All very well perhaps from his point of view, but only a little better than the common dilettantism. A sentimental reformer in architecture, he began at the cornice, not at the foundation. It was only how to put a core of truth within the ornaments, that every sugar plum in fact might have an almond or caraway seed in it,—though I hold that almonds are most wholesome without the sugar,—and not how the inhabitant, the indweller, might build truly within and without, and let the ornaments take care of themselves. What reasonable man ever supposed that ornaments were something outward and in the skin merely,—that the tortoise got his spotted shell, or the shellfish its mother-o'-pearl tints, by such a contract as the inhabitants of Broadway their Trinity

[71] Homer's epic poem about the fall of Troy.
[72] According to the old saying, which recognizes that those who make our clothes contribute to our being.

Church?[73] But a man has no more to do with the style of architecture of his house than a tortoise with that of its shell: nor need the soldier be so idle as to try to paint the precise color of his virtue on his standard. The enemy will find it out. He may turn pale when the trial comes. This man seemed to me to lean over the cornice and timidly whisper his half truth to the rude occupants who really knew it better than he. What of architectural beauty I now see, I know has gradually grown from within outward, out of the necessities and character of the indweller, who is the only builder, —out of some unconscious truthfulness, and nobleness, without ever a thought for the appearance; and whatever additional beauty of this kind is destined to be produced will be preceded by a like unconscious beauty of life. The most interesting dwellings in this country, as the painter knows, are the most unpretending, humble log huts and cottages of the poor commonly; it is the life of the inhabitants whose shells they are, and not any peculiarity in their surfaces merely, which makes them *picturesque;* and equally interesting will be the citizen's suburban box, when his life shall be as simple and as agreeable to the imagination, and there is as little straining after effect in the style of his dwelling. A great proportion of architectural ornaments are literally hollow, and a September gale would strip them off, like borrowed plumes, without injury to the substantials. They can do without *architecture* who have no olives nor wines in the cellar. What if an equal ado were made about the ornaments of style in literature, and the architects of our bibles spent as much time about their cornices as the architects of our churches do? So are made the *belles-lettres* and the *beaux-arts* and their professors. Much it concerns a man, forsooth, how a few sticks are slanted over him or under him, and what colors are daubed upon his box. It would signify somewhat, if, in any earnest sense, *he* slanted them and daubed it; but the spirit having departed out of the tenant, it is of a piece with constructing his own coffin,—the architecture of the grave, and "carpenter" is but another name for "coffin-maker." One man says, in his despair or indifference to life, take up a handful of the earth at your feet, and paint your house that color. Is he thinking of his last and narrow house?[74] Toss up a copper[75] for it as well. What an abundance of leisure he must have! Why do you take up a handful of dirt? Better paint your house your own complexion; let it turn pale or blush for you. An enterprise to improve the style of cottage architecture! When you have got my ornaments ready I will wear them.

Before winter I built a chimney, and shingled the sides of my house, which were already impervious to rain, with imperfect and sappy shingles made of the first slice of the log, whose edges I was obliged to straighten with a plane.

I have thus a tight shingled and plastered house, ten feet wide by fifteen long, and eight-feet posts, with a garret and a closet, a large window on each side, two trap doors, one door at the end, and a brick fireplace opposite. The exact cost of my house, paying the usual price for such materials as I used, but not counting the work, all of which was done by myself, was as follows; and I give the details because very few are able to tell exactly what their houses cost, and fewer still, if any, the separate cost of the various materials which compose them:—

---

[73] Ornate Gothic-style church built in New York City (1839–1846).
[74] I.e., coffin.

[75] Coin used in payment to Charon, who ferried the dead across the river Styx in classic myth.

Boards, ...	$8 03 1/2,	mostly shanty boards.
Refuse shingles for roof and sides, ...	4 00	
Laths, ...	1 25	
Two second-hand windows with glass, ...	2 43	
One thousand old brick, ...	4 00	
Two casks of lime, ...	2 40	That was high.
Hair, ...	0 31	More than I needed.
Mantle-tree iron, ...	0 15	
Nails, ...	3 90	
Hinges and screws, ...	0 14	
Latch, ...	0 10	
Chalk, ...	0 01	
Transportation, ...	1 40	} I carried a good part on my back.
In all, ...	$28 12 1/2	

These are all the materials excepting the timber stones and sand, which I claimed by squatter's right. I have also a small wood-shed adjoining, made chiefly of the stuff which was left after building the house.

I intend to build me a house which will surpass any on the main street in Concord in grandeur and luxury, as soon as it pleases me as much and will cost me no more than my present one.

I thus found that the student who wishes for a shelter can obtain one for a lifetime at an expense not greater than the rent which he now pays annually. If I seem to boast more than is becoming, my excuse is that I brag for humanity rather than for myself; and my shortcomings and inconsistencies do not affect the truth of my statement. Notwithstanding much cant and hypocrisy,—chaff which I find it difficult to separate from my wheat, but for which I am as sorry as any man,—I will breathe freely and stretch myself in this respect, it is such a relief to both the moral and physical system; and I am resolved that I will not through humility become the devil's attorney.[76] I will endeavor to speak a good word for the truth. At Cambridge College[77] the mere rent of a student's room, which is only a little larger than my own, is thirty dollars each year, though the corporation had the advantage of building thirty-two side by side and under one roof, and the occupant suffers the inconvenience of many and noisy neighbors, and perhaps a residence in the fourth story. I cannot but think that if we had more true wisdom in these respects, not only less education would be needed, because, forsooth, more would already have been acquired, but the pecuniary expense of getting an education would in a great measure vanish. Those conveniences which

[76] Official appointed to Roman Catholic courts to probe any weaknesses in the cases of persons put forward for sainthood.

[77] Harvard College; Thoreau was a graduate in 1837.

the student requires at Cambridge or elsewhere cost him or somebody else ten times as great a sacrifice of life as they would with proper management on both sides. Those things for which the most money is demanded are never the things which the student most wants. Tuition, for instance, is an important item in the term bill, while for the far more valuable education which he gets by associating with the most cultivated of his contemporaries no charge is made. The mode of founding a college is, commonly, to get up a subscription of dollars and cents, and then following blindly the principles of a division of labor to its extreme, a principle which should never be followed but with circumspection,—to call in a contractor who makes this a subject of speculation, and he employs Irishmen or other operatives actually to lay the foundations, while the students that are to be are said to be fitting themselves for it; and for these oversights successive generations have to pay. I think that it would be *better than this,* for the students, or those who desire to be benefited by it, even to lay the foundation themselves. The student who secures his coveted leisure and retirement by systematically shirking any labor necessary to man obtains but an ignoble and unprofitable leisure, defrauding himself of the experience which alone can make leisure fruitful. "But," says one, "you do not mean that the students should go to work with their hands instead of their heads?" I do not mean that exactly, but I mean something which he might think a good deal like that; I mean that they should not *play* life, or *study* it merely, while the community supports them at this expensive game, but earnestly *live* it from beginning to end. How could youths better learn to live than by at once trying the experiment of living? Methinks this would exercise their minds as much as mathematics. If I wished a boy to know something about the arts and sciences, for instance, I would not pursue the common course, which is merely to send him into the neighborhood of some professor, where any thing is professed and practised but the art of life;—to survey the world through a telescope or a microscope, and never with his natural eye; to study chemistry, and not learn how his bread is made, or mechanics, and not learn how it is earned; to discover new satellites to Neptune, and not detect the motes in his eyes, or to what vagabond he is a satellite himself; or to be devoured by the monsters that swarm all around him, while contemplating the monsters in a drop of vinegar. Which would have advanced the most at the end of a month,—the boy who had made his own jack-knife from the ore which he had dug and smelted, reading as much as would be necessary for this,—or the boy who had attended the lectures on metallurgy at the Institute in the mean while, and had received a Rodgers' penknife[78] from his father? Which would be most likely to cut his fingers?—To my astonishment I was informed on leaving college that I had studied navigation!—why, if I had taken one turn down the harbor I should have known more about it. Even the *poor* student studies and is taught only *political* economy, while that economy of living which is synonymous with philosophy is not even sincerely professed in our colleges. The consequence is, that while he is reading Adam Smith, Ricardo, and Say,[79] he runs his father in debt irretrievably.

As with our colleges, so with a hundred "modern improvements"; there is an illusion about them; there is not always a positive advance. The devil goes on

---

[78] Made by Joseph Rodgers, cutlery maker from Sheffield, England.

[79] Adam Smith, David Ricardo, and Jean Baptiste Léon Say, eighteenth-century economists.

exacting compound interest to the last for his early share and numerous succeeding investments in them. Our inventions are wont to be pretty toys, which distract our attention from serious things. They are but improved means to an unimproved end, an end which it was already but too easy to arrive at; as railroads lead to Boston or New York. We are in great haste to construct a magnetic telegraph from Maine to Texas; but Maine and Texas, it may be, have nothing important to communicate. Either is in such a predicament as the man who was earnest to be introduced to a distinguished deaf woman, but when he was presented, and one end of her ear trumpet was put into his hand, had nothing to say. As if the main object were to talk fast and not to talk sensibly. We are eager to tunnel under the Atlantic and bring the old world some weeks nearer to the new; but perchance the first news that will leak through into the broad, flapping American ear will be that the Princess Adelaide[80] has the whooping cough. After all, the man whose horse trots a mile in a minute does not carry the most important messages; he is not an evangelist, nor does he come round eating locusts and wild honey.[81] I doubt if Flying Childers[82] ever carried a peck of corn to mill.

One says to me, "I wonder that you do not lay up money; you love to travel; you might take the cars and go to Fitchburg[83] to-day and see the country." But I am wiser than that. I have learned that the swiftest traveller is he that goes afoot. I say to my friend, Suppose we try who will get there first. The distance is thirty miles; the fare ninety cents. That is almost a day's wages. I remember when wages were sixty cents a day for laborers on this very road. Well, I start now on foot, and get there before night; I have travelled at that rate by the week together. You will in the mean while have earned your fare, and arrive there some time to-morrow, or possibly this evening, if you are lucky enough to get a job in season. Instead of going to Fitchburg, you will be working here the greater part of the day. And so, if the railroad reached round the world, I think that I should keep ahead of you; and as for seeing the country and getting experience of that kind, I should have to cut your acquaintance altogether.

Such is the universal law, which no man can ever outwit, and with regard to the railroad even we may say it is as broad as it is long. To make a railroad round the world available to all mankind is equivalent to grading the whole surface of the planet. Men have an indistinct notion that if they keep up this activity of joint stocks and spades long enough all will at length ride somewhere, in next to no time, and for nothing; but though a crowd rushes to the depot, and the conductor shouts "All aboard!" when the smoke is blown away and the vapor condensed, it will be perceived that a few are riding, but the rest are run over,—and it will be called, and will be, "A melancholy accident." No doubt they can ride at last who shall have earned their fare, that is, if they survive so long, but they will probably have lost their elasticity and desire to travel by that time. This spending of the best part of one's life earning money in order to enjoy a questionable liberty during the least valuable part of it, reminds me of the Englishman who went to India to make a fortune first, in order that he might return to England and live the life of a poet. He should have gone up

---

[80] Sister of Louis-Phillipe, king of France, she lived 1771–1847.
[81] What sustained John the Baptist while living in the wilderness (Matthew 3:4).
[82] Well-known racehorse of the eighteenth century.
[83] Small town near Concord; end of the railroad line that passed by Walden Pond.

garret at once. "What!" exclaim a million Irishmen starting up from all the shanties in the land, "is not this railroad which we have built a good thing?" Yes, I answer, *comparatively* good, that is, you might have done worse; but I wish, as you are brothers of mine, that you could have spent your time better than digging in this dirt.

Before I finished my house, wishing to earn ten or twelve dollars by some honest and agreeable method, in order to meet my unusual expenses, I planted about two acres and a half of light and sandy soil near it chiefly with beans, but also a small part with potatoes, corn, peas, and turnips. The whole lot contains eleven acres, mostly growing up to pines and hickories, and was sold the preceding season for eight dollars and eight cents an acre. One farmer said that it was "good for nothing but to raise cheeping squirrels on." I put no manure on this land, not being the owner, but merely a squatter, and not expecting to cultivate so much again, and I did not quite hoe it all once. I got out several cords of stumps in ploughing, which supplied me with fuel for a long time, and left small circles of virgin mould, easily distinguishable through the summer by the greater luxuriance of the beans there. The dead and for the most part unmerchantable wood behind my house, and the driftwood from the pond, have supplied the remainder of my fuel. I was obliged to hire a team and a man for the ploughing, though I held the plough myself. My farm outgoes for the first season were, for implements, seed, work, &c., $14 72 1/2. The seed corn was given me. This never costs any thing to speak of, unless you plant more than enough. I got twelve bushels of beans, and eighteen bushels of potatoes, beside some peas and sweet corn. The yellow corn and turnips were too late to come to any thing. My whole income from the farm was

$23 44.

Deducting the outgoes, ... 14 72 1/2

there are left, ... $ 8 71 1/2,

beside produce consumed and on hand at the time this estimate was made of the value of $4 50,—the amount on hand much more than balancing a little grass which I did not raise. All things considered, that is, considering the importance of a man's soul and of to-day, notwithstanding the short time occupied by my experiment, nay, partly even because of its transient character, I believe that that was doing better than any farmer in Concord did that year.

The next year I did better still, for I spaded up all the land which I required, about a third of an acre, and I learned from the experience of both years, not being in the least awed by many celebrated works on husbandry, Arthur Young[84] among the rest, that if one would live simply and eat only the crop which he raised, and raise no more than he ate, and not exchange it for an insufficient quantity of more luxurious and expensive things, he would need to cultivate only a few rods of ground, and that it would be cheaper to spade up that than to use oxen to plough it, and to select a fresh spot from time to time than to manure the old, and he could do all his necessary farm work as it were with his left hand at odd hours in the summer; and thus he would not be tied to an ox, or horse, or cow, or pig, as at present. I desire to speak impartially

---

[84] English author (1741–1820) of works on husbandry.

on this point, and as one not interested in the success or failure of the present economical and social arrangements. I was more independent than any farmer in Concord, for I was not anchored to a house or farm, but could follow the bent of my genius, which is a very crooked one, every moment. Beside being better off than they already, if my house had been burned or my crops had failed, I should have been nearly as well off as before.

I am wont to think that men are not so much the keepers of herds as herds are the keepers of the men, the former are so much the freer. Men and oxen exchange work; but if we consider necessary work only, the oxen will be seen to have greatly the advantage, their farm is so much the larger. Man does some of his part of the exchange work in his six weeks of haying, and it is no boy's play. Certainly no nation that lived simply in all respects, that is, no nation of philosophers, would commit so great a blunder as to use the labor of animals. True, there never was and is not likely soon to be a nation of philosophers, nor am I certain it is desirable that there should be. However, *I* should never have broken a horse or bull and taken him to board for any work he might do for me, for fear I should become a horse-man or a herds-man merely; and if society seems to be the gainer by so doing, are we certain that what is one man's gain is not another's loss, and that the stable-boy has equal cause with his master to be satisfied? Granted that some public works would not have been constructed without this aid, and let man share the glory of such with the ox and horse; does it follow that he could not have accomplished works yet more worthy of himself in that case? When men begin to do, not merely unnecessary or artistic, but luxurious and idle work, with their assistance, it is inevitable that a few do all the exchange work with the oxen, or, in other words, become the slaves of the strongest. Man thus not only works for the animal within him, but, for a symbol of this, he works for the animal without him. Though we have many substantial houses of brick or stone, the prosperity of the farmer is still measured by the degree to which the barn overshadows the house. This town is said to have the largest houses for oxen cows and horses hereabouts, and it is not behindhand in its public buildings; but there are very few halls for free worship or free speech in this county. It should not be by their architecture, but why not even by their power of abstract thought, that nations should seek to commemorate themselves? How much more admirable the Bhagvat-Geeta[85] than all the ruins of the East! Towers and temples are the luxury of princes. A simple and independent mind does not toil at the bidding of any prince. Genius is not a retainer to any emperor, nor is its material silver, or gold, or marble, except to a trifling extent. To what end, pray, is so much stone hammered? In Arcadia,[86] when I was there, I did not see any hammering stone. Nations are possessed with an insane ambition to perpetuate the memory of themselves by the amount of hammered stone they leave. What if equal pains were taken to smooth and polish their manners? One piece of good sense would be more memorable than a monument as high as the moon. I love better to see stones in place. The grandeur of Thebes was a vulgar grandeur. More sensible is a rod of stone wall that bounds an honest man's field than a hundred-gated Thebes[87] that has wandered farther from the true end of life. The

[85] A sacred text of the Hindus, the *Bhagavad Gita*.
[86] Region in Greek myth where men supposedly lived in pastoral happiness. (Thoreau visited it only by means of his imagination.)

[87] City in ancient Egypt whose walls had 100 gates.

religion and civilization which are barbaric and heathenish build splendid temples; but what you might call Christianity does not. Most of the stone a nation hammers goes toward its tomb only. It buries itself alive. As for the Pyramids, there is nothing to wonder at in them so much as the fact that so many men could be found degraded enough to spend their lives constructing a tomb for some ambitious booby, whom it would have been wiser and manlier to have drowned in the Nile, and then given his body to the dogs. I might possibly invent some excuse for them and him, but I have no time for it. As for the religion and love of art of the builders, it is much the same all the world over, whether the building be an Egyptian temple or the United States Bank. It costs more than it comes to. The mainspring is vanity, assisted by the love of garlic and bread and butter. Mr. Balcom, a promising young architect, designs it on the back of his Vitruvius,[88] with hard pencil and ruler, and the job is let out to Dobson & Sons, stonecutters. When the thirty centuries begin to look down on it, mankind begin to look up at it. As for your high towers and monuments, there was a crazy fellow once in this town who undertook to dig through to China, and he got so far that, as he said, he heard the Chinese pots and kettles rattle; but I think that I shall not go out of my way to admire the hole which he made. Many are concerned about the monuments of the West and the East,—to know who built them. For my part, I should like to know who in those days did not build them,—who were above such trifling. But to proceed with my statistics.

By surveying, carpentry, and day-labor of various other kinds in the village in the mean while, for I have as many trades as fingers, I had earned $13 34. The expense of food for eight months, namely, from July 4th to March 1st, the time when these estimates were made, though I lived there more than two years,—not counting potatoes, a little green corn, and some peas, which I had raised, nor considering the value of what was on hand at the last date, was

Rice,	$1 73 1/2	
Molasses,	1 73	Cheapest form of the saccharine.
Rye meal,	1 04 3/4	
Indian meal,	0 99 3/4	Cheaper than rye.
Pork,	0 22	
Flour	0 88	} Costs more than Indian meal, both money and trouble.
Sugar,	0 80	
Lard,	0 65	
Apples,	0 25	
Dried apple,	0 22	
Sweet potatoes,	0 10	
One pumpkin,	0 6	
One watermelon,	0 2	
Salt,	0 3	

All experiments which failed.

[88] Roman writings on architecture by Vitruvius (first century E.C.).

Yes, I did eat $8 74, all told; but I should not thus unblushingly publish my guilt, if I did not know that most of my readers were equally guilty with myself, and that their deeds would look no better in print. The next year I sometimes caught a mess of fish for my dinner, and once I went so far as to slaughter a woodchuck which ravaged my bean-field,—effect his transmigration, as a Tartar[89] would say,—and devour him, partly for experiment's sake; but though it afforded me a momentary enjoyment, notwithstanding a musky flavor, I saw that the longest use would not make that a good practice, however it might seem to have your woodchucks ready dressed by the village butcher.

Clothing and some incidental expenses within the same dates, though little can be inferred from this item, amounted to

$8 40 3/4

Oil and some household utensils, ... 2 00

So that all the pecuniary outgoes, excepting for washing and mending, which for the most part were done out of the house, and their bills have not yet been received, —and these are all and more than all the ways by which money necessarily goes out in this part of the world,—were

House, ... $28 12 1/2
Farm one year, ... 14 72 1/2
Food eight months, ... 8 74
Clothing, &c., eight months, ... 8 40 3/4
Oil, &c., eight months, ... 2 00
                                                   ─────────
In all, ... $61 99 3/4

I address myself now to those of my readers who have a living to get. And to meet this I have for farm produce sold

                                                   $23 44
Earned by day-labor, ... 13 34
                                                   ─────────
In all, ... $36 78,

which subtracted from the sum of the outgoes leaves a balance of $25 21 3/4 on the one side,—this being very nearly the means with which I started, and the measure of expenses to be incurred,—and on the other, beside the leisure and independence and health thus secured, a comfortable house for me as long as I choose to occupy it.

These statistics, however accidental and therefore uninstructive they may appear, as they have a certain completeness, have a certain value also. Nothing was given me of which I have not rendered some account. It appears from the above estimate, that

[89] Native of Russian Asia; the Tartars held that after death their souls passed into other bodies.

my food alone cost me in money about twenty-seven cents a week. It was, for nearly two years after this, rye and Indian meal without yeast, potatoes, rice, a very little salt pork, molasses, and salt, and my drink water. It was fit that I should live on rice, mainly, who loved so well the philosophy of India. To meet the objections of some inveterate cavillers, I may as well state, that if I dined out occasionally, as I always had done, and I trust shall have opportunities to do again, it was frequently to the detriment of my domestic arrangements. But the dining out, being, as I have stated, a constant element, does not in the least affect a comparative statement like this.

I learned from my two years' experience that it would cost incredibly little trouble to obtain one's necessary food, even in this latitude; that a man may use as simple a diet as the animals, and yet retain health and strength. I have made a satisfactory dinner, satisfactory on several accounts, simply off a dish of purslane *(Portulaca oleracea)* which I gathered in my cornfield, boiled and salted. I give the Latin on account of the savoriness of the trivial name. And pray what more can a reasonable man desire, in peaceful times, in ordinary noons, than a sufficient number of ears of green sweet-corn boiled, with the addition of salt? Even the little variety which I used was a yielding to the demands of appetite, and not of health. Yet men have come to such a pass that they frequently starve, not for want of necessaries, but for want of luxuries; and I know a good woman who thinks that her son lost his life because he took to drinking water only.

The reader will perceive that I am treating the subject rather from an economic than a dietetic point of view, and he will not venture to put my abstemiousness to the test unless he has a well-stocked larder.

Bread I at first made of pure Indian meal and salt, genuine hoe-cakes, which I baked before my fire out of doors on a shingle or the end of a stick of timber sawed off in building my house; but it was wont to get smoked and to have a piny flavor. I tried flour also; but have at last found a mixture of rye and Indian meal most convenient and agreeable. In cold weather it was no little amusement to bake several small loaves of this in succession, tending and turning them as carefully as an Egyptian his hatching eggs. They were a real cereal fruit which I ripened, and they had to my senses a fragrance like that of other noble fruits, which I kept in as long as possible by wrapping them in cloths. I made a study of the ancient and indispensable art of bread-making, consulting such authorities as offered, going back to the primitive days and first invention of the unleavened kind, when from the wildness of nuts and meats men first reached the mildness and refinement of this diet, and travelling gradually down in my studies through that accidental souring of the dough which, it is supposed, taught the leavening process, and through the various fermentations thereafter, till I came to "good, sweet, wholesome bread," the staff of life. Leaven, which some deem the soul of bread, the *spiritus*[90] which fills its cellular tissue, which is religiously preserved like the vestal fire,[91]—some precious bottle-full, I suppose, first brought over in the May-flower, did the business for America, and its influence is still rising, swelling, spreading, in cerealian[92] billows over the land,—this seed I regularly and faithfully procured from the village, till at length one morning I forgot the rules, and scalded my yeast; by which accident I discovered that even this was not indispensable,

---

[90] Latin: "breath of life."
[91] Sacred flame of the ancient Romans.
[92] Wordplay in reference to *cerulean,* the color blue.

—for my discoveries were not by the synthetic but analytic process,—and I have gladly omitted it since, though most housewives earnestly assured me that safe and wholesome bread without yeast might not be, and elderly people prophesied a speedy decay of the vital forces. Yet I find it not to be an essential ingredient, and after going without it for a year am still in the land of the living; and I am glad to escape the trivialness of carrying a bottle-full in my pocket, which would sometimes pop and discharge its contents to my discomfiture. It is simpler and more respectable to omit it. Man is an animal who more than any other can adapt himself to all climates and circumstances. Neither did I put any sal soda, or other acid or alkali, into my bread. It would seem that I made it according to the recipe which Marcus Porcius Cato[93] gave about two centuries before Christ. "Panem depsticium sic facito. Manus mortari-umque bene lavato. Farinam in mortarium indito, aquæ paulatim addito, subigitoque pulchre. Ubi bene subegeris, defingito, coquitoque sub testu." Which I take to mean —"Make kneaded bread thus. Wash your hands and trough well. Put the meal into the trough, add water gradually, and knead it thoroughly. When you have kneaded it well, mould it, and bake it under a cover," that is, in a baking-kettle. Not a word about leaven. But I did not always use this staff of life. At one time, owing to the emptiness of my purse, I saw none of it for more than a month.

Every New Englander might easily raise all his own breadstuffs in this land of rye and Indian corn, and not depend on distant and fluctuating markets for them. Yet so far are we from simplicity and independence that, in Concord, fresh and sweet meal is rarely sold in the shops, and hominy and corn in a still coarser form are hardly used by any. For the most part the farmer gives to his cattle and hogs the grain of his own producing, and buys flour, which is at least no more wholesome, at a greater cost, at the store. I saw that I could easily raise my bushel or two of rye and Indian corn, for the former will grow on the poorest land, and the latter does not require the best, and grind them in a hand-mill, and so do without rice and pork; and if I must have some concentrated sweet, I found by experiment that I could make a very good molasses either of pumpkins or beets, and I knew that I needed only to set out a few maples to obtain it more easily still, and while these were growing I could use various substitutes beside those which I have named, "For," as the Forefathers sang,—

"we can make liquor to sweeten our lips
Of pumpkins and parsnips and walnut-tree chips."

Finally, as for salt, that grossest of groceries, to obtain this might be a fit occasion for a visit to the seashore, or, if I did without it altogether, I should probably drink the less water. I do not learn that the Indians ever troubled themselves to go after it.

Thus I could avoid all trade and barter, so far as my food was concerned, and having a shelter already, it would only remain to get clothing and fuel. The pantaloons which I now wear were woven in a farmer's family,—thank Heaven there is so much virtue still in man; for I think the fall from the farmer to the operative as great and memorable as that from the man to the farmer;—and in a new country fuel is an

[93] Roman statesman (234–149 B.C.), from whose
De Agricultura the recipe is taken.

encumbrance. As for a habitat, if I were not permitted still to squat, I might purchase one acre at the same price for which the land I cultivated was sold—namely, eight dollars and eight cents. But as it was, I considered that I enhanced the value of the land by squatting on it.

There is a certain class of unbelievers who sometimes ask me such questions as, if I think that I can live on vegetable food alone; and to strike at the root of the matter at once,—for the root is faith,—I am accustomed to answer such, that I can live on board nails. If they cannot understand that, they cannot understand much that I have to say. For my part, I am glad to hear of experiments of this kind being tried; as that a young man tried for a fortnight to live on hard, raw corn on the ear, using his teeth for all mortar. The squirrel tribe tried the same and succeeded. The human race is interested in these experiments, though a few old women who are incapacitated for them, or who own their thirds in mills,[94] may be alarmed.

My furniture, part of which I made myself, and the rest cost me nothing of which I have not rendered an account, consisted of a bed, a table, a desk, three chairs, a looking-glass three inches in diameter, a pair of tongs and andirons, a kettle, a skillet, and a frying-pan, a dipper, a wash-bowl, two knives and forks, three plates, one cup, one spoon, a jug for oil, a jug for molasses, and a japanned lamp. None is so poor that he need sit on a pumpkin. That is shiftlessness. There is a plenty of such chairs as I like best in the village garrets to be had for taking them away. Furniture! Thank God, I can sit and I can stand without the aid of a furniture warehouse. What man but a philosopher would not be ashamed to see his furniture packed in a cart and going up country exposed to the light of heaven and the eyes of men, a beggarly account of empty boxes? That is Spaulding's furniture. I could never tell from inspecting such a load whether it belonged to a so called rich man or a poor one; the owner always seemed poverty-stricken. Indeed, the more you have of such things the poorer you are. Each load looks as if it contained the contents of a dozen shanties; and if one shanty is poor, this is a dozen times as poor. Pray, for what do we *move* ever but to get rid of our furniture, our *exuviæ;*[95] at last to go from this world to another newly furnished, and leave this to be burned? It is the same as if all these traps were buckled to a man's belt, and he could not move over the rough country where our lines are cast without dragging them,—dragging his trap. He was a lucky fox that left his tail in the trap. The muskrat will gnaw his third leg off to be free. No wonder man has lost his elasticity. How often he is at a dead set![96] "Sir, if I may be so bold, what do you mean by a dead set?" If you are a seer, whenever you meet a man you will see all that he owns, ay, and much that he pretends to disown, behind him, even to his kitchen furniture and all the trumpery which he saves and will not burn, and he will appear to be harnessed to it and making what headway he can. I think that the man is at a dead set who has got through a knot hole or gateway where his sledge load of furniture cannot follow him. I cannot but feel compassion when I hear some trig,[97] compact-looking man, seemingly free, all girded and ready, speak of his "furniture,"

---

[94] Toothless old women or those who own the traditional third of the estate left them upon their husbands' deaths and have invested in mills that do their grinding for them.

[95] Latin: "discards."
[96] At a dead end; immobile.
[97] Spruce.

as whether it is insured or not. "But what shall I do with my furniture?" My gay butterfly is entangled in a spider's web then. Even those who seem for a long while not to have any, if you inquire more narrowly you will find have some stored in somebody's barn. I look upon England to-day as an old gentleman who is travelling with a great deal of baggage, trumpery which has accumulated from long housekeeping, which he has not the courage to burn; great trunk, little trunk, bandbox and bundle. Throw away the first three at least. It would surpass the powers of a well man nowadays to take up his bed and walk, and I should certainly advise a sick one to lay down his bed and run. When I have met an immigrant tottering under a bundle which contained his all,—looking like an enormous wen which had grown out of the nape of his neck,—I have pitied him, not because that was his all, but because he had all *that* to carry. If I have got to drag my trap, I will take care that it be a light one and do not nip me in a vital part. But perchance it would be wisest never to put one's paw into it.

I would observe, by the way, that it costs me nothing for curtains, for I have no gazers to shut out but the sun and moon, and I am willing that they should look in. The moon will not sour milk nor taint meat of mine, nor will the sun injure my furniture or fade my carpet, and if he is sometimes too warm a friend, I find it still better economy to retreat behind some curtain which nature has provided, than to add a single item to the details of housekeeping. A lady once offered me a mat, but as I had no room to spare within the house, nor time to spare within or without to shake it, I declined it, preferring to wipe my feet on the sod before my door. It is best to avoid the beginnings of evil.

Not long since I was present at the auction of a deacon's effects, for his life had not been ineffectual:—

"The evil that men do lives after them."[98]

As usual, a great proportion was trumpery which had begun to accumulate in his father's day. Among the rest was a dried tapeworm. And now, after lying half a century in his garret and other dust holes, these things were not burned; instead of a *bonfire*, or purifying destruction of them, there was an *auction*,[99] or increasing of them. The neighbors eagerly collected to view them, bought them all, and carefully transported them to their garrets and dust holes, to lie there till their estates are settled, when they will start again. When a man dies he kicks the dust.

The customs of some savage nations might, perchance, be profitably imitated by us, for they at least go through the semblance of casting their slough annually; they have the idea of the thing, whether they have the reality or not. Would it not be well if we were to celebrate such a "busk," or "feast of first fruits," as Bartram[100] describes to have been the custom of the Mucclasse Indians? "When a town celebrates the busk," says he, "having previously provided themselves with new clothes, new pots, pans, and other household utensils and furniture, they collect all their worn out

---

[98] From Shakespeare's *Julius Caesar*, Act III, Sc. ii, l. 81.

[99] The original Latin meant "an increase"; modern usage applies to the raising of the cost of an item by bidding.

[100] William Bartram (1739–1823), American naturalist and travel writer.

clothes and other despicable things, sweep and cleanse their houses, squares, and the whole town, of their filth, which with all the remaining grain and other old provisions they cast together into one common heap, and consume it with fire. After having taken medicine, and fasted for three days, all the fire in the town is extinguished. During this fast they abstain from the gratification of every appetite and passion whatever. A general amnesty is proclaimed; all malefactors may return to their town.—"

"On the fourth morning, the high priest, by rubbing dry wood together, produces new fire in the public square, from whence every habitation in the town is supplied with the new and pure flame."

They then feast on the new corn and fruits and dance and sing for three days, "and the four following days they receive visits and rejoice with their friends from neighboring towns who have in like manner purified and prepared themselves."

The Mexicans also practised a similar purification at the end of every fifty-two years, in the belief that it was time for the world to come to an end.

I have scarcely heard of a truer sacrament, that is, as the dictionary defines it, "outward and visible sign of an inward and spiritual grace," than this, and I have no doubt that they were originally inspired directly from Heaven to do thus, though they have no biblical record of the revelation.

For more than five years I maintained myself thus solely by the labor of my hands, and I found, that by working about six weeks in a year, I could meet all the expenses of living. The whole of my winters, as well as most of my summers, I had free and clear for study. I have thoroughly tried school-keeping, and found that my expenses were in proportion, or rather out of proportion, to my income, for I was obliged to dress and train, not to say think and believe, accordingly, and I lost my time into the bargain. As I did not teach for the good of my fellow-men, but simply for a livelihood, this was a failure. I have tried trade; but I found that it would take ten years to get under way in that, and that then I should probably be on my way to the devil. I was actually afraid that I might by that time be doing what is called a good business. When formerly I was looking about to see what I could do for a living, some sad experience in conforming to the wishes of friends being fresh in my mind to tax my ingenuity, I thought often and seriously of picking huckleberries; that surely I could do, and its small profits might suffice,—for my greatest skill has been to want but little,—so little capital it required, so little distraction from my wonted moods, I foolishly thought. While my acquaintances went unhesitatingly into trade or the professions, I contemplated this occupation as most like theirs; ranging the hills all summer to pick the berries which came in my way, and thereafter carelessly dispose of them; so, to keep the flocks of Admetus.[101] I also dreamed that I might gather the wild herbs, or carry evergreens to such villagers as loved to be reminded of the woods, even to the city, by hay-cart loads. But I have since learned that trade curses every thing it handles; and though you trade in messages from heaven, the whole curse of trade attaches to the business.

As I preferred some things to others, and especially valued my freedom, as I could fare hard and yet succeed well, I did not wish to spend my time in earning rich carpets

---

[101] To pass a time of servitude, as the god Apollo once did in the service of King Admetus.

or other fine furniture, or delicate cookery, or a house in the Grecian or the Gothic style just yet. If there are any to whom it is no interruption to acquire these things, and who know how to use them when acquired, I relinquish to them the pursuit. Some are "industrious," and appear to love labor for its own sake, or perhaps because it keeps them out of worse mischief; to such I have at present nothing to say. Those who would not know what to do with more leisure than they now enjoy, I might advise to work twice as hard as they do,—work till they pay for themselves, and get their free papers.[102] For myself I found that the occupation of a day-laborer was the most independent of any, especially as it required only thirty or forty days in a year to support one. The laborer's day ends with the going down of the sun, and he is then free to devote himself to his chosen pursuit, independent of his labor; but his employer, who speculates from month to month, has no respite from one end of the year to the other.

In short, I am convinced, both by faith and experience, that to maintain one's self on this earth is not a hardship but a pastime, if we will live simply and wisely; as the pursuits of the simpler nations are still the sports of the more artificial. It is not necessary that a man should earn his living by the sweat of his brow, unless he sweats easier than I do.

One young man of my acquaintance, who has inherited some acres, told me that he thought he should live as I did, *if he had the means.* I would not have any one adopt *my* mode of living on any account; for, beside that before he has fairly learned it I may have found out another for myself, I desire that there may be as many different persons in the world as possible; but I would have each one be very careful to find out and pursue *his own* way, and not his father's or his mother's or his neighbor's instead. The youth may build or plant or sail, only let him not be hindered from doing that which he tells me he would like to do. It is by a mathematical point only that we are wise, as the sailor or the fugitive slave keeps the polestar[103] in his eye; but that is sufficient guidance for all our life. We may not arrive at our port within a calculable period, but we would preserve the true course.

Undoubtedly, in this case, what is true for one is truer still for a thousand, as a large house is not more expensive than a small one in proportion to its size, since one roof may cover, one cellar underlie, and one wall separate several apartments. But for my part, I preferred the solitary dwelling. Moreover, it will commonly be cheaper to build the whole yourself than to convince another of the advantage of the common wall; and when you have done this, the common partition, to be much cheaper, must be a thin one, and that other may prove a bad neighbor, and also not keep his side in repair. The only coöperation which is commonly possible is exceedingly partial and superficial; and what little true coöperation there is, is as if it were not, being a harmony inaudible to men. If a man has faith he will coöperate with equal faith every where; if he has not faith, he will continue to live like the rest of the world, whatever company he is joined to. To coöperate, in the highest as well as the lowest sense, means *to get our living together.* I heard it proposed lately that two young men should travel together over the world, the one without money, earning his means as he went, before the mast and behind the plough, the other carrying a bill of exchange

---

[102] To end their period of indenturedness by working off their debts.

[103] The North Star, which guides him toward freedom in Canada.

in his pocket. It was easy to see that they could not long be companions or coöperate, since one would not *operate* at all. They would part at the first interesting crisis in their adventures. Above all, as I have implied, the man who goes alone can start today; but he who travels with another must wait till that other is ready, and it may be a long time before they get off.

But all this is very selfish, I have heard some of my townsmen say. I confess that I have hitherto indulged very little in philanthropic enterprises. I have made some sacrifices to a sense of duty, and among others have sacrificed this pleasure also. There are those who have used all their arts to persuade me to undertake the support of some poor family in the town; and if I had nothing to do,—for the devil finds employment for the idle,—I might try my hand at some such pastime as that. However, when I have thought to indulge myself in this respect, and lay their Heaven under an obligation by maintaining certain poor persons in all respects as comfortably as I maintain myself, and have even ventured so far as to make them the offer, they have one and all unhesitatingly preferred to remain poor. While my townsmen and women are devoted in so many ways to the good of their fellows, I trust that one at least may be spared to other and less humane pursuits. You must have a genius for charity as well as for any thing else. As for Doing-good, that is one of the professions which are full. Moreover, I have tried it fairly, and, strange as it may seem, am satisfied that it does not agree with my constitution. Probably I should not consciously and deliberately forsake my particular calling to do the good which society demands of me, to save the universe from annihilation; and I believe that a like but infinitely greater steadfastness elsewhere is all that now preserves it. But I would not stand between any man and his genius; and to him who does this work, which I decline, with his whole heart and soul and life, I would say, Persevere, even if the world call it doing evil, as it is most likely they will.

I am far from supposing that my case is a peculiar one; no doubt many of my readers would make a similar defence. At doing something,—I will not engage that my neighbors shall pronounce it good,—I do not hesitate to say that I should be a capital fellow to hire; but what that is, it is for my employer to find out. What *good* I do, in the common sense of that word, must be aside from my main path, and for the most part wholly unintended. Men say, practically, Begin where you are and such as you are, without aiming mainly to become of more worth, and with kindness aforethought go about doing good. If I were to preach at all in this strain, I should say rather, Set about being good. As if the sun should stop when he had kindled his fires up to the splendor of a moon or a star of the sixth magnitude, and go about like a Robin Goodfellow,[104] peeping in at every cottage window, inspiring lunatics, and tainting meats, and making darkness visible, instead of steadily increasing his genial heat and beneficence till he is of such brightness that no mortal can look him in the face, and then, and in the mean while too, going about the world in his own orbit, doing it good, or rather, as a truer philosophy has discovered, the world going about him getting good. When Phaeton,[105] wishing to prove his heavenly birth by his beneficence, had the sun's chariot but one day, and drove out of the beaten track,

[104] In folklore, the elf who plays tricks; associated with Puck. [105] Apollo's son, and thereby the son of the Sun.

he burned several blocks of houses in the lower streets of heaven, and scorched the surface of the earth, and dried up every spring, and made the great desert of Sahara, till at length Jupiter hurled him headlong to the earth with a thunderbolt, and the sun, through grief at his death, did not shine for a year.

There is no odor so bad as that which arises from goodness tainted. It is human, it is divine, carrion. If I knew for a certainty that a man was coming to my house with the conscious design of doing me good, I should run for my life, as from that dry and parching wind of the African deserts called the simoom, which fills the mouth and nose and ears and eyes with dust till you are suffocated, for fear that I should get some of his good done to me,—some of its virus mingled with my blood. No, —in this case I would rather suffer evil the natural way. A man is not a good *man* to me because he will feed me if I should be starving, or warm me if I should be freezing, or pull me out of a ditch if I should ever fall into one. I can find you a Newfoundland dog that will do as much. Philanthropy is not love for one's fellow-man in the broadest sense. Howard[106] was no doubt an exceedingly kind and worthy man in his way, and has his reward; but, comparatively speaking, what are a hundred Howards to *us,* if their philanthropy do not help *us* in our best estate, when we are most worthy to be helped? I never heard of a philanthropic meeting in which it was sincerely proposed to do any good to me, or the like of me.

The Jesuits[107] were quite balked by those Indians who, being burned at the stake, suggested new modes of torture to their tormentors. Being superior to physical suffering, it sometimes chanced that they were superior to any consolation which the missionaries could offer; and the law to do as you would be done by fell with less persuasiveness on the ears of those, who, for their part, did not care how they were done by, who loved their enemies after a new fashion, and came very near freely forgiving them all they did.

Be sure that you give the poor the aid they most need, though it be your example which leaves them far behind. If you give money, spend yourself with it, and do not merely abandon it to them. We make curious mistakes sometimes. Often the poor man is not so cold and hungry as he is dirty and ragged and gross. It is partly his taste, and not merely his misfortune. If you give him money, he will perhaps buy more rags with it. I was wont to pity the clumsy Irish laborers who cut ice on the pond, in such mean and ragged clothes, while I shivered in my more tidy and somewhat more fashionable garments, till, one bitter cold day, one who had slipped into the water came to my house to warm him, and I saw him strip off three pairs of pants and two pairs of stockings ere he got down to the skin, though they were dirty and ragged enough, it is true, and that he could afford to refuse the *extra* garments which I offered him, he had so many *intra* ones.[108] This ducking was the very thing he needed. Then I began to pity myself, and I saw that it would be a greater charity to bestow on me a flannel shirt than a whole slop-shop on him. There are a thousand hacking at the branches of evil to one who is striking at the root, and it may be that he who bestows the largest amount of time and money on the needy is doing the most by his mode of life to produce that misery which he strives in vain to relieve. It is the pious slave-breeder devoting the proceeds of every tenth

[106] John Howard (1726?–1790), English leader in prison reform.
[107] Roman Catholic religious order, the Society of Jesus; one of its concerns was to convert Indians to Christianity.
[108] *Extra:* "outer"; *intra:* "inner."

slave[109] to buy a Sunday's liberty for the rest. Some show their kindness to the poor by employing them in their kitchens. Would they not be kinder if they employed themselves there? You boast of spending a tenth part of your income in charity; may be you should spend the nine tenths so, and done with it. Society recovers only a tenth part of the property then. Is this owing to the generosity of him in whose possession it is found, or to the remissness of the officers of justice?

Philanthropy is almost the only virtue which is sufficiently appreciated by mankind. Nay, it is greatly overrated; and it is our selfishness which overrates it. A robust poor man, one sunny day here in Concord, praised a fellow-townsman to me, because, as he said, he was kind to the poor; meaning himself. The kind uncles and aunts of the race are more esteemed than its true spiritual fathers and mothers. I once heard a reverend lecturer on England, a man of learning and intelligence, after enumerating her scientific, literary, and political worthies, Shakspeare, Bacon, Cromwell, Milton, Newton, and others, speak next of her Christian heroes, whom, as if his profession required it of him, he elevated to a place far above all the rest, as the greatest of the great. They were Penn, Howard, and Mrs. Fry.[110] Every one must feel the falsehood and cant of this. The last were not England's best men and women; only, perhaps, her best philanthropists.

I would not subtract any thing from the praise that is due to philanthropy, but merely demand justice for all who by their lives and works are a blessing to mankind. I do not value chiefly a man's uprightness and benevolence, which are, as it were, his stem and leaves. Those plants of whose greenness withered we make herb tea for the sick, serve but a humble use, and are most employed by quacks. I want the flower and fruit of a man; that some fragrance be wafted over from him to me, and some ripeness flavor our intercourse. His goodness must not be a partial and transitory act, but a constant superfluity, which costs him nothing and of which he is unconscious. This is a charity that hides a multitude of sins. The philanthropist too often surrounds mankind with the remembrance of his own cast-off griefs as an atmosphere, and calls it sympathy. We should impart our courage, and not our despair, our health and ease, and not our disease, and take care that this does not spread by contagion. From what southern plains[111] comes up the voice of wailing? Under what latitudes reside the heathen to whom we would send light? Who is that intemperate and brutal man whom we would redeem? If any thing ail a man, so that he does not perform his functions, if he have a pain in his bowels even,—for that is the seat of sympathy,[112] —he forthwith sets about reforming—the world. Being a microcosm himself, he discovers, and it is a true discovery, and he is the man to make it,—that the world has been eating green apples; to his eyes, in fact, the globe itself is a great green apple, which there is danger awful to think of that the children of men will nibble before it is ripe; and straightway his drastic philanthropy seeks out the Esquimaux[113] and the Patagonian,[114] and embraces the populous Indian and Chinese villages; and thus, by a few years of philanthropic activity, the powers in the mean while using him for their own ends, no doubt, he cures himself of his dyspepsia, the globe acquires a faint

---

[109] In the custom of the tithe, churchgoers give one tenth of their income to support the church's good works.

[110] Like John Howard, the Quakers William Penn (1644–1718) and Elizabeth Fry (1780–1845) were active reformers of social ills.

[111] Slave states.

[112] That compassion found its source in the bowels was an age-old notion.

[113] Eskimo.

[114] From the nethermost region of South America.

blush on one or both of its cheeks, as if it were beginning to be ripe, and life loses its crudity and is once more sweet and wholesome to live. I never dreamed of any enormity greater than I have committed. I never knew, and never shall know, a worse man than myself.

I believe that what so saddens the reformer is not his sympathy with his fellows in distress, but, though he be the holiest son of God, is his private ail. Let this be righted, let the spring come to him, the morning rise over his couch, and he will forsake his generous companions without apology. My excuse for not lecturing against the use of tobacco is, that I never chewed it; that is a penalty which reformed tobacco-chewers have to pay; though there are things enough I have chewed, which I could lecture against. If you should ever be betrayed into any of these philanthropies, do not let your left hand know what your right hand does, for it is not worth knowing.[115] Rescue the drowning and tie your shoe-strings. Take your time, and set about some free labor.

Our manners have been corrupted by communication with the saints. Our hymn-books resound with a melodious cursing of God and enduring him forever. One would say that even the prophets and redeemers had rather consoled the fears than confirmed the hopes of man. There is nowhere recorded a simple and irrepressible satisfaction with the gift of life, any memorable praise of God. All health and success does me good, however far off and withdrawn it may appear; all disease and failure helps to make me sad and does me evil, however much sympathy it may have with me or I with it. If, then, we would indeed restore mankind by truly Indian, botanic, magnetic, or natural means, let us first be as simple and well as Nature ourselves, dispel the clouds which hang over our own brows, and take up a little life into our pores. Do not stay to be an overseer of the poor, but endeavor to become one of the worthies of the world.

I read in the Gulistan, or Flower Garden, of Sheik Sadi of Shiraz,[116] that "They asked a wise man, saying; Of the many celebrated trees which the Most High God has created lofty and umbrageous, they call none azad, or free, excepting the cypress, which bears no fruit; what mystery is there in this? He replied; Each has its appropriate produce, and appointed season, during the continuance of which it is fresh and blooming, and during their absence dry and withered; to neither of which states is the cypress exposed, being always flourishing; and of this nature are the azads, or religious independents.—Fix not thy heart on that which is transitory; for the Dijlah, or Tigris, will continue to flow through Bagdad after the race of caliphs is extinct: if thy hand has plenty, be liberal as the date tree; but if it affords nothing to give away, be an azad, or free man, like the cypress."

Complemental Verses

The Pretensions of Poverty[117]

"Thou dost presume too much, poor needy wretch,
    To claim a station in the firmament,

---

[115] See Matthew 6:3.
[116] Persian poet of the thirteenth century.
[117] The English poet Thomas Carew (1595?–1645)

wrote this poem, which was included in *Coelum Brittannicum* (1661). Thoreau added the title.

Because thy humble cottage, or thy tub,
Nurses some lazy or pedantic virtue
In the cheap sunshine or by shady springs,
With roots and pot-herbs; where thy right hand,
Tearing those humane passions from the mind,
Upon whose stocks fair blooming virtues flourish,
Degradeth nature, and benumbeth sense,
And, Gorgon-like, turns active men to stone.
We not require the dull society
Of your necessitated temperance,
Or that unnatural stupidity
That knows nor joy nor sorrow; nor your forc'd
Falsely exalted passive fortitude
Above the active. This low abject brood,
That fix their seats in mediocrity,
Become your servile minds; but we advance
Such virtues only as admit excess,
Brave, bounteous acts, regal magnificence,
All-seeing prudence, magnanimity
That knows no bound, and that heroic virtue
For which antiquity hath left no name,
But patterns only, such as Hercules,
Achilles, Theseus. Back to thy loath'd cell;
And when thou seest the new enlightened sphere,
Study to know but what those worthies were."

T. CAREW

Where I Lived, and What I Lived For

At a certain season of our life we are accustomed to consider every spot as the possible site of a house. I have thus surveyed the country on every side within a dozen miles of where I live. In imagination I have bought all the farms in succession, for all were to be bought, and I knew their price. I walked over each farmer's premises, tasted his wild apples, discoursed on husbandry with him, took his farm at his price, at any price, mortgaging it to him in my mind; even put a higher price on it,—took every thing but a deed of it,—took his word for his deed, for I dearly love to talk,—cultivated it, and him too to some extent, I trust, and withdrew when I had enjoyed it long enough, leaving him to carry it on. This experience entitled me to be regarded as a sort of real-estate broker by my friends. Wherever I sat, there I might live, and the landscape radiated from me accordingly. What is a house but a *sedes,* a seat?—better if a country seat. I discovered many a site for a house not likely to be soon improved, which some might have thought too far from the village, but to my eyes the village was too far from it. Well, there I might live, I said; and there I did live, for an hour, a summer and a winter life; saw how I could let the years run off, buffet the winter through, and see the spring come in. The future inhabitants of this region, wherever they may place their houses, may be sure that they have been anticipated. An afternoon sufficed to lay out the land into orchard woodlot and pasture, and to decide what fine oaks or pines should be left to stand before the door, and whence each blasted tree could be seen to the best advantage; and then I let it lie, fallow perchance, for a man is rich in proportion to the number of things which he can afford to let alone.

My imagination carried me so far that I even had the refusal of several farms,— the refusal was all I wanted,—but I never got my fingers burned by actual possession. The nearest that I came to actual possession was when I bought the Hollowell Place, and had begun to sort my seeds, and collected materials with which to make a wheelbarrow to carry it on or off with; but before the owner gave me a deed of it, his wife—every man has such a wife—changed her mind and wished to keep it, and he offered me ten dollars to release him. Now, to speak the truth, I had but ten cents in the world, and it surpassed my arithmetic to tell, if I was that man who had ten cents, or who had a farm, or ten dollars, or all together. However, I let him keep the ten dollars and the farm too, for I had carried it far enough; or rather, to be generous, I sold him the farm for just what I gave for it, and, as he was not a rich man, made him a present of ten dollars, and still had my ten cents, and seeds, and materials for a wheelbarrow left. I found thus that I had been a rich man without any damage to my poverty. But I retained the landscape, and I have since annually carried off what it yielded without a wheelbarrow. With respect to landscapes,—

"I am monarch of all I *survey*,
  My right there is none to dispute."[118]

I have frequently seen a poet withdraw, having enjoyed the most valuable part of a farm, while the crusty farmer supposed that he had got a few wild apples only. Why, the owner does not know it for many years when a poet has put his farm in rhyme, the most admirable kind of invisible fence, has fairly impounded it, milked it, skimmed it, and got all the cream, and left the farmer only the skimmed milk.

The real attractions of the Hollowell farm, to me, were; its complete retirement, being about two miles from the village, half a mile from the nearest neighbor, and separated from the highway by a broad field; its bounding on the river, which the owner said protected it by its fogs from frosts in the spring, though that was nothing to me; the gray color and ruinous state of the house and barn, and the dilapidated fences, which put such an interval between me and the last occupant; the hollow and lichen-covered apple trees, gnawed by rabbits, showing what kind of neighbors I should have; but above all, the recollection I had of it from my earliest voyages up the river, when the house was concealed behind a dense grove of red maples, through which I heard the house-dog bark. I was in haste to buy it, before the proprietor finished getting out some rocks, cutting down the hollow apple trees, and grubbing up some young birches which had sprung up in the pasture, or, in short, had made any more of his improvements. To enjoy these advantages I was ready to carry it on; like Atlas,[119] to take the world on my shoulders,—I never heard what compensation

---

[118] Thoreau, a part-time surveyor, chose to emphasize the word *survey* when quoting from "Verses Supposed to be Written by Alexander Selkirk" by William Cowper (1731–1800).

[119] In classic myth, the giant who bore the world on his shoulders.

he received for that,—and do all those things which had no other motive or excuse but that I might pay for it and be unmolested in my possession of it; for I knew all the while that it would yield the most abundant crop of the kind I wanted if I could only afford to let it alone. But it turned out as I have said.

All that I could say, then, with respect to farming on a large scale, (I have always cultivated a garden,) was, that I had had my seeds ready. Many think that seeds improve with age. I have no doubt that time discriminates between the good and the bad; and when at last I shall plant, I shall be less likely to be disappointed. But I would say to my fellows, once for all, As long as possible live free and uncommitted. It makes but little difference whether you are committed to a farm or the county jail.

Old Cato, whose "De Re Rusticâ"[120] is my "Cultivator," says, and the only translation I have seen makes sheer nonsense of the passage, "When you think of getting a farm, turn it thus in your mind, not to buy greedily; nor spare your pains to look at it, and do not think it enough to go round it once. The oftener you go there the more it will please you, if it is good." I think I shall not buy greedily, but go round and round it as long as I live, and be buried in it first, that it may please me the more at last.

The present was my next experiment of this kind, which I purpose to describe more at length; for convenience, putting the experience of two years into one. As I have said, I do not propose to write an ode to dejection, but to brag as lustily as chanticleer in the morning, standing on his roost, if only to wake my neighbors up.

When first I took up my abode in the woods, that is, began to spend my nights as well as days there, which, by accident, was on Independence Day, or the fourth of July, 1845, my house was not finished for winter, but was merely a defence against the rain, without plastering or chimney, the walls being of rough weather-stained boards, with wide chinks, which made it cool at night. The upright white hewn studs and freshly planed door and window casings gave it a clean and airy look, especially in the morning, when its timbers were saturated with dew, so that I fancied that by noon some sweet gum would exude from them. To my imagination it retained throughout the day more or less of this auroral character, reminding me of a certain house on a mountain which I had visited the year before. This was an airy and unplastered cabin, fit to entertain a travelling god, and where a goddess might trail her garments. The winds which passed over my dwelling were such as sweep over the ridges of mountains, bearing the broken strains, or celestial parts only, of terrestrial music. The morning wind forever blows, the poem of creation is uninterrupted; but few are the ears that hear it. Olympus[121] is but the outside of the earth every where.

The only house I had been the owner of before, if I except a boat, was a tent, which I used occasionally when making excursions in the summer, and this is still rolled up in my garret; but the boat, after passing from hand to hand, has gone down the stream of time. With this more substantial shelter about me, I had made some progress toward settling in the world. This frame, so slightly clad, was a sort of crystallization around me, and reacted on the builder. It was suggestive somewhat as a picture in outlines. I did not need to go out doors to take the air, for the atmosphere within had lost

[120] Marcus Porcius Cato (234–149 B.C.), author of a [121] Mountain abode of the Greek gods.
work on agriculture (160? B.C.) that is
sometimes given this name.

none of its freshness. It was not so much within doors as behind a door where I sat, even in the rainiest weather. The Harivansa[122] says, "An abode without birds is like a meat without seasoning." Such was not my abode, for I found myself suddenly neighbor to the birds; not by having imprisoned one, but having caged myself near them. I was not only nearer to some of those which commonly frequent the garden and the orchard, but to those wilder and more thrilling songsters of the forest which never, or rarely, serenade a villager,—the wood-thrush, the veery, the scarlet tanager, the field-sparrow, the whippoorwill, and many others.

I was seated by the shore of a small pond, about a mile and a half south of the village of Concord and somewhat higher than it, in the midst of an extensive wood between that town and Lincoln, and about two miles south of that our only field known to fame, Concord Battle Ground;[123] but I was so low in the woods that the opposite shore, half a mile off, like the rest, covered with wood, was my most distant horizon. For the first week, whenever I looked out on the pond it impressed me like a tarn high up on the side of a mountain, its bottom far above the surface of other lakes, and, as the sun arose, I saw it throwing off its nightly clothing of mist, and here and there, by degrees, its soft ripples, or its smooth reflecting surface was revealed, while the mists, like ghosts, were stealthily withdrawing in every direction into the woods, as at the breaking up of some nocturnal conventicle. The very dew seemed to hang upon the trees later into the day than usual, as on the sides of mountains.

This small lake was of most value as a neighbor in the intervals of a gentle rain storm in August, when, both air and water being perfectly still, but the sky overcast, mid-afternoon had all the serenity of evening, and the wood-thrush sang around, and was heard from shore to shore. A lake like this is never smoother than at such a time; and the clear portion of the air above it being shallow and darkened by clouds, the water, full of light and reflections, becomes a lower heaven itself so much the more important. From a hill top near by, where the wood had been recently cut off, there was a pleasing vista southward across the pond, through a wide indentation in the hills which form the shore there, where their opposite sides sloping toward each other suggested a stream flowing out in that direction through a wooded valley, but stream there was none. That way I looked between and over the near green hills to some distant and higher ones in the horizon, tinged with blue. Indeed, by standing on tiptoe I could catch a glimpse of some of the peaks of the still bluer and more distant mountain ranges in the north-west, those true-blue coins from heaven's own mint, and also of some portion of the village. But in other directions, even from this point, I could not see over or beyond the woods which surrounded me. It is well to have some water in your neighborhood, to give buoyancy to and float the earth. One value even of the smallest well is, that when you look into it you see that earth is not continent but insular. This is as important as that it keeps butter cool. When I looked across the pond from this peak toward the Sudbury meadows, which in time of flood I distinguished elevated perhaps by a mirage in their seething valley, like a coin in a basin, all the earth beyond the pond appeared like a thin crust insulated and floated even by this small sheet of intervening water, and I was reminded that this on which I dwelt was but *dry land*.

---

[122] Fifth century Hindu religious epic.
[123] Where one of the opening battles of the

American Revolution was fought, on April 19, 1775.

Though the view from my door was still more contracted, I did not feel crowded or confined in the least. There was pasture enough for my imagination. The low shrub-oak plateau to which the opposite shore arose, stretched away toward the prairies of the West and the steppes of Tartary,[124] affording ample room for all the roving families of men. "There are none happy in the world but beings who enjoy freely a vast horizon,"—said Damodara,[125] when his herds required new and larger pastures.

Both place and time were changed, and I dwelt nearer to those parts of the universe and to those eras in history which had most attracted me. Where I lived was as far off as many a region viewed nightly by astronomers. We are wont to imagine rare and delectable places in some remote and more celestial corner of the system, behind the constellation of Cassiopeia's Chair, far from noise and disturbance. I discovered that my house actually had its site in such a withdrawn, but forever new and unprofaned, part of the universe. If it were worth the while to settle in those parts near to the Pleiades or the Hyades, to Aldebaran or Altair,[126] then I was really there, or at an equal remoteness from the life which I had left behind, dwindled and twinkling with as fine a ray to my nearest neighbor, and to be seen only in moonless nights by him. Such was that part of creation where I had squatted;—

"There was a shepherd that did live,
    And held his thoughts as high
  As were the mounts whereon his flocks
    Did hourly feed him by."

What should we think of the shepherd's life if his flocks always wandered to higher pastures than his thoughts?

Every morning was a cheerful invitation to make my life of equal simplicity, and I may say innocence, with Nature herself. I have been as sincere a worshipper of Aurora[127] as the Greeks. I got up early and bathed in the pond; that was a religious exercise, and one of the best things which I did. They say that characters were engraven on the bathing tub of king Tching-thang[128] to this effect: "Renew thyself completely each day; do it again, and again, and forever again." I can understand that. Morning brings back the heroic ages. I was as much affected by the faint hum of a mosquito making its invisible and unimaginable tour through my apartment at earliest dawn, when I was sitting with door and windows open, as I could be by any trumpet that ever sang of fame. It was Homer's requiem; itself an Iliad and Odyssey in the air, singing its own wrath and wanderings. There was something cosmical about it; a standing advertisement, till forbidden, of the everlasting vigor and fertility of the world. The morning, which is the most memorable season of the day, is the awakening hour. Then there is least somnolence in us; and for an hour, at least, some part of us

---

124 In Russian Asia.
125 Hindu god mentioned in the *Harivansa;* another name for Krishna.
126 Stars and constellations.
127 Although Thoreau refers to Aurora as a Greek goddess (of the dawn), that was the Roman name for her.

128 The lines, taken from the tub of the Chinese monarch who founded the Shang dynasty (1766–1122 B.C.), are from a gloss of Confucius' *The Great Learning.*

awakes which slumbers all the rest of the day and night. Little is to be expected of that day, if it can be called a day, to which we are not awakened by our Genius, but by the mechanical nudgings of some servitor, are not awakened by our own newly-acquired force and aspirations from within, accompanied by the undulations of celestial music, instead of factory bells, and a fragrance filling the air—to a higher life than we fell asleep from; and thus the darkness bear its fruit, and prove itself to be good, no less than the light. That man who does not believe that each day contains an earlier, more sacred, and auroral hour than he has yet profaned, has despaired of life, and is pursuing a descending and darkening way. After a partial cessation of his sensuous life, the soul of man, or its organs rather, are reinvigorated each day, and his Genius[129] tries again what noble life it can make. All memorable events, I should say, transpire in morning time and in a morning atmosphere. The Vedas[130] say, "All intelligences awake with the morning." Poetry and art, and the fairest and most memorable of the actions of men, date from such an hour. All poets and heroes, like Memnon, are the children of Aurora, and emit their music at sunrise. To him whose elastic and vigorous thought keeps pace with the sun, the day is a perpetual morning. It matters not what the clocks say or the attitudes and labors of men. Morning is when I am awake and there is a dawn in me. Moral reform is the effort to throw off sleep. Why is it that men give so poor an account of their day if they have not been slumbering? They are not such poor calculators. If they had not been overcome with drowsiness they would have performed something. The millions are awake enough for physical labor; but only one in a million is awake enough for effective intellectual exertion, only one in a hundred millions to a poetic or divine life. To be awake is to be alive. I have never yet met a man who was quite awake. How could I have looked him in the face?

We must learn to reawaken and keep ourselves awake, not by mechanical aids, but by an infinite expectation of the dawn, which does not forsake us in our soundest sleep. I know of no more encouraging fact than the unquestionable ability of man to elevate his life by a conscious endeavor. It is something to be able to paint a particular picture, or to carve a statue, and so to make a few objects beautiful; but it is far more glorious to carve and paint the very atmosphere and medium through which we look, which morally we can do. To affect the quality of the day, that is the highest of arts. Every man is tasked to make his life, even in its details, worthy of the contemplation of his most elevated and critical hour. If we refused, or rather used up, such paltry information as we get, the oracles would distinctly inform us how this might be done.

I went to the woods because I wished to live deliberately, to front only the essential facts of life, and see if I could not learn what it had to teach, and not, when I came to die, discover that I had not lived. I did not wish to live what was not life, living is so dear; nor did I wish to practise resignation, unless it was quite necessary. I wanted to live deep and suck out all the marrow of life, to live so sturdily and Spartanlike as to put to rout all that was not life, to cut a broad swath and shave close, to drive life into a corner, and reduce it to its lowest terms, and, if it proved to be mean, why then to get the whole and genuine meanness of it, and publish its meanness to the world; or if it were sublime, to know it by experience, and be able to give a true account of it in my next excursion. For most men, it appears to me, are in a strange

---

[129] Guardian spirit.   [130] Religious text of the Hindus.

uncertainty about it, whether it is of the devil or of God, and have *somewhat hastily* concluded that it is the chief end of man here to "glorify God and enjoy him forever."

Still we live meanly, like ants; though the fable tells us that we were long ago changed into men;[131] like pygmies we fight with cranes;[132] it is error upon error, and clout upon clout, and our best virtue has for its occasion a superfluous and evitable wretchedness. Our life is frittered away by detail. An honest man has hardly need to count more than his ten fingers, or in extreme cases he may add his ten toes, and lump the rest. Simplicity, simplicity, simplicity! I say, let your affairs be as two or three, and not a hundred or a thousand; instead of a million count half a dozen, and keep your accounts on your thumb nail. In the midst of this chopping sea of civilized life, such are the clouds and storms and quicksands and thousand-and-one items to be allowed for, that a man has to live, if he would not founder and go to the bottom and not make his port at all, by dead reckoning,[133] and he must be a great calculator indeed who succeeds. Simplify, simplify. Instead of three meals a day, if it be necessary eat but one; instead of a hundred dishes, five; and reduce other things in proportion. Our life is like a German Confederacy,[134] made up of petty states, with its boundary forever fluctuating, so that even a German cannot tell you how it is bounded at any moment. The nation itself, with all its so called internal improvements, which, by the way, are all external and superficial, is just such an unwieldy and overgrown establishment, cluttered with furniture and tripped up by its own traps, ruined by luxury and heedless expense, by want of calculation and a worthy aim, as the million households in the land; and the only cure for it as for them is in a rigid economy, a stern and more than Spartan simplicity of life and elevation of purpose. It lives too fast. Men think that it is essential that the *Nation* have commerce, and export ice, and talk through a telegraph, and ride thirty miles an hour, without a doubt, whether *they* do or not; but whether we should live like baboons or like men, is a little uncertain. If we do not get our sleepers,[135] and forge rails, and devote days and nights to the work, but go to tinkering upon our *lives* to improve *them,* who will build railroads? And if railroads are not built, how shall we get to heaven in season? But if we stay at home and mind our business, who will want railroads? We do not ride on the railroad; it rides upon us. Did you ever think what those sleepers are that underlie the railroad? Each one is a man, an Irish-man, or a Yankee man. The rails are laid on them, and they are covered with sand, and the cars run smoothly over them. They are sound sleepers, I assure you. And every few years a new lot is laid down and run over; so that, if some have the pleasure of riding on a rail, others have the misfortune to be ridden upon. And when they run over a man that is walking in his sleep, a supernumerary sleeper in the wrong position, and wake him up, they suddenly stop the cars, and make a hue and cry about it, as if this were an exception. I am glad to know that it takes a gang of men for every five miles to keep the sleepers down and level in their beds as it is, for this is a sign that they may sometime get up again.

[131] In a classic myth Zeus transformed ants into men for the purpose of repopulating a plague-devastated land.
[132] The Trojans were likened to cranes that fought with pygmies in the *Iliad,* Book III.
[133] A system for navigating a ship at sea without the aid of the sun and stars.

[134] Germany, as Thoreau knew it during his lifetime, was an unstable grouping of states; only in 1871 was it brought together into a national unit by Bismarck.
[135] Railroad ties.

Why should we live with such hurry and waste of life? We are determined to be starved before we are hungry. Men say that a stitch in time saves nine, and so they take a thousand stitches to-day to save nine to-morrow. As for *work,* we haven't any of any consequence. We have the Saint Vitus' dance, and cannot possibly keep our heads still. If I should only give a few pulls at the parish bell-rope, as for a fire, that is, without setting the bell,[136] there is hardly a man on his farm in the outskirts of Concord, notwithstanding that press of engagements which was his excuse so many times this morning, nor a boy, nor a woman, I might almost say, but would forsake all and follow that sound, not mainly to save property from the flames, but, if we will confess the truth, much more to see it burn, since burn it must, and we, be it known, did not set it on fire,—or to see it put out, and have a hand in it, if that is done as handsomely; yes, even if it were the parish church itself. Hardly a man takes a half hour's nap after dinner, but when he wakes he holds up his head and asks, "What's the news?" as if the rest of mankind had stood his sentinels. Some give directions to be waked every half hour, doubtless for no other purpose; and then, to pay for it, they tell what they have dreamed. After a night's sleep the news is as indispensable as the breakfast. "Pray tell me any thing new that has happened to a man any where on this globe,"—and he reads it over his coffee and rolls, that a man has had his eyes gouged out this morning on the Wachito River;[137] never dreaming the while that he lives in the dark unfathomed mammoth cave of this world, and has but the rudiment of an eye himself.

For my part, I could easily do without the post-office. I think that there are very few important communications made through it. To speak critically, I never received more than one or two letters in my life—I wrote this some years ago—that were worth the postage. The penny-post is, commonly, an institution through which you seriously offer a man that penny for his thoughts which is so often safely offered in jest. And I am sure that I never read any memorable news in a newspaper. If we read of one man robbed, or murdered, or killed by accident, or one house burned, or one vessel wrecked, or one steamboat blown up, or one cow run over on the Western Railroad, or one mad dog killed, or one lot of grasshoppers in the winter,—we never need read of another. One is enough. If you are acquainted with the principle, what do you care for a myriad instances and applications? To a philosopher all *news,* as it is called, is gossip, and they who edit and read it are old women over their tea. Yet not a few are greedy after this gossip. There was such a rush, as I hear, the other day at one of the offices to learn the foreign news by the last arrival, that several large squares of plate glass belonging to the establishment were broken by the pressure,— news which I seriously think a ready wit might write a twelvemonth or twelve years beforehand with sufficient accuracy. As for Spain, for instance, if you know how to throw in Don Carlos and the Infanta, and Don Pedro[138] and Seville and Granada, from time to time in the right proportions,—they may have changed the names a little since I saw the papers,—and serve up a bull-fight when other entertainments fail, it will be true to the letter, and give us as good an idea of the exact state or ruin of things in Spain as the most succinct and lucid reports under this head in the newspapers: and as for England, almost the last significant scrap of news from that quarter was the

---

[136] Inverting the bell by pulling it too hard.
[137] Tributary of the Red River in Arkansas.

[138] Members of the Spanish nobility.

revolution of 1649;[139] and if you have learned the history of her crops for an average year, you never need attend to that thing again, unless your speculations are of a merely pecuniary character. If one may judge who rarely looks into the newspapers, nothing new does ever happen in foreign parts, a French revolution not excepted.

What news! how much more important to know what that is which was never old! "Kieou-pe-yu (great dignitary of the state of Wei) sent a man to Khoung-tseu[140] to know his news. Khoung-tseu caused the messenger to be seated near him, and questioned him in these terms: What is your master doing? The messenger answered with respect: My master desires to diminish the number of his faults, but he cannot accomplish it. The messenger being gone, the philosopher remarked: What a worthy messenger! What a worthy messenger!" The preacher, instead of vexing the ears of drowsy farmers on their day of rest at the end of the week,—for Sunday is the fit conclusion of an ill-spent week, and not the fresh and brave beginning of a new one,—with this one other draggle-tail of a sermon, should shout with thundering voice,—"Pause! Avast! Why so seeming fast, but deadly slow?"

Shams and delusions are esteemed for soundest truths, while reality is fabulous. If men would steadily observe realities only, and not allow themselves to be deluded, life, to compare it with such things as we know, would be like a fairy tale and the Arabian Nights' Entertainments. If we respected only what is inevitable and has a right to be, music and poetry would resound along the streets. When we are unhurried and wise, we perceive that only great and worthy things have any permanent and absolute existence,—that petty fears and petty pleasures are but the shadow of the reality. This is always exhilarating and sublime. By closing the eyes and slumbering, and consenting to be deceived by shows, men establish and confirm their daily life of routine and habit every where, which still is built on purely illusory foundations. Children, who play life, discern its true law and relations more clearly than men, who fail to live it worthily, but who think that they are wiser by experience, that is, by failure. I have read in a Hindoo book, that "there was a king's son, who, being expelled in infancy from his native city, was brought up by a forester, and, growing up to maturity in that state, imagined himself to belong to the barbarous race with which he lived. One of his father's ministers having discovered him, revealed to him what he was, and the misconception of his character was removed, and he knew himself to be a prince. So soul," continues the Hindoo philosopher, "from the circumstances in which it is placed, mistakes its own character, until the truth is revealed to it by some holy teacher, and then it knows itself to be *Brahme*."[141] I perceive that we inhabitants of New England live this mean life that we do because our vision does not penetrate the surface of things. We think that that is which *appears* to be. If a man should walk through this town and see only the reality, where, think you, would the "Mill-dam"[142] go to? If he should give us an account of the realities he beheld there, we should not recognize the place in his description. Look at a meeting-house, or a court-house, or a jail, or a shop, or a dwelling-house, and say what that thing really is before a true gaze, and they would all go to pieces in your account of them. Men esteem truth

---

[139] The end of the British monarchy at the hands of the Puritan Commonwealth.

[140] Confucius. The incident is described in *The Analects*, XIV, 26.

[141] The foremost god in the Hindu hierarchy.

[142] Concord's town center, meeting place for idle chatter.

remote, in the outskirts of the system, behind the farthest star, before Adam and after the last man. In eternity there is indeed something true and sublime. But all these times and places and occasions are now and here. God himself culminates in the present moment, and will never be more divine in the lapse of all the ages. And we are enabled to apprehend at all what is sublime and noble only by the perpetual instilling and drenching of the reality which surrounds us. The universe constantly and obediently answers to our conceptions; whether we travel fast or slow, the track is laid for us. Let us spend our lives in conceiving then. The poet or the artist never yet had so fair and noble a design but some of his posterity at least could accomplish it.

Let us spend one day as deliberately as Nature, and not be thrown off the track by every nutshell and mosquito's wing that falls on the rails. Let us rise early and fast, or break fast, gently and without perturbation; let company come and let company go, let the bells ring and the children cry,—determined to make a day of it. Why should we knock under and go with the stream? Let us not be upset and overwhelmed in that terrible rapid and whirlpool called a dinner, situated in the meridian shallows. Weather this danger and you are safe, for the rest of the way is down hill. With unrelaxed nerves, with morning vigor, sail by it, looking another way, tied to the mast like Ulysses.[143] If the engine whistles, let it whistle till it is hoarse for its pains. If the bell rings, why should we run? We will consider what kind of music they are like. Let us settle ourselves, and work and wedge our feet downward through the mud and slush of opinion, and prejudice, and tradition, and delusion, and appearance, that alluvion which covers the globe, through Paris and London, through New York and Boston and Concord, through church and state, through poetry and philosophy and religion, till we come to a hard bottom and rocks in place, which we can call *reality*, and say, This is, and no mistake; and then begin, having a *point d'appui*, below freshet and frost and fire, a place where you might found a wall or a state, or set a lamp-post safely, or perhaps a gauge, not a Nilometer, but a Realometer, that future ages might know how deep a freshet of shams and appearances had gathered from time to time. If you stand right fronting and face to face to a fact, you will see the sun glimmer on both its surfaces, as if it were a cimeter,[144] and feel its sweet edge dividing you through the heart and marrow, and so you will happily conclude your mortal career. Be it life or death, we crave only reality. If we are really dying, let us hear the rattle in our throats and feel cold in the extremities; if we are alive, let us go about our business.

Time is but the stream I go a-fishing in. I drink at it; but while I drink I see the sandy bottom and detect how shallow it is. Its thin current slides away, but eternity remains. I would drink deeper; fish in the sky, whose bottom is pebbly with stars. I cannot count one. I know not the first letter of the alphabet. I have always been regretting that I was not as wise as the day I was born. The intellect is a cleaver; it discerns and rifts its way into the secret of things. I do not wish to be any more busy with my hands than is necessary. My head is hands and feet. I feel all my best faculties concentrated in it. My instinct tells me that my head is an organ for burrowing, as

[143] I.e., be able to move past dangers in safety, like   [144] Scimitar.
Ulysses in the *Odyssey*, who had himself bound
to the ship's mast so that he could both listen
to the Sirens' song and resist their fatal call.

some creatures use their snout and fore-paws, and with it I would mine and burrow my way through these hills. I think that the richest vein is somewhere hereabouts; so by the divining rod and thin rising vapors I judge; and here I will begin to mine.

Brute Neighbors

Sometimes I had a companion[145] in my fishing, who came through the village to my house from the other side of the town, and the catching of the dinner was as much a social exercise as the eating of it.

Hermit. I wonder what the world is doing now. I have not heard so much as a locust over the sweet-fern these three hours. The pigeons are all asleep upon their roosts,—no flutter from them. Was that a farmer's noon horn which sounded from beyond the woods just now? The hands are coming in to boiled salt beef and cider and Indian bread. Why will men worry themselves so? He that does not eat need not work. I wonder how much they have reaped. Who would live there where a body can never think for the barking of Bose?[146] And O, the housekeeping! to keep bright the devil's door-knobs, and scour his tubs this bright day! Better not keep a house. Say, some hollow tree; and then for morning calls and dinner-parties! Only a woodpecker tapping. O, they swarm; the sun is too warm there; they are born too far into life for me. I have water from the spring, and a loaf of brown bread on the shelf.—Hark! I hear a rustling of the leaves. Is it some ill-fed village hound yielding to the instinct of the chase? or the lost pig which is said to be in these woods, whose tracks I saw after the rain? It comes on apace; my sumachs and sweet-briars tremble.—Eh, Mr. Poet, is it you? How do you like the world to-day?

Poet. See those clouds; how they hang! That's the greatest thing I have seen to-day. There's nothing like it in old paintings, nothing like it in foreign lands,—unless when we were off the coast of Spain. That's a true Mediterranean sky. I thought, as I have my living to get, and have not eaten to-day, that I might go a-fishing. That's the true industry for poets. It is the only trade I have learned. Come, let's along.

Hermit. I cannot resist. My brown bread will soon be gone. I will go with you gladly soon, but I am just concluding a serious meditation. I think that I am near the end of it. Leave me alone, then, for a while. But that we may not be delayed, you shall be digging the bait meanwhile. Angle-worms are rarely to be met with in these parts, where the soil was never fattened with manure; the race is nearly extinct. The sport of digging the bait is nearly equal to that of catching the fish, when one's appetite is not too keen; and this you may have all to yourself today. I would advise you to set in the spade down yonder among the ground-nuts, where you see the johnswort waving. I think that I may warrant you one worm to every three sods you turn up, if you look well in among the roots of the grass, as if you were weeding. Or, if you choose to go farther, it will not be unwise, for I have found the increase of fair bait to be very nearly as the squares of the distances.

Hermit alone. Let me see; where was I? Methinks I was nearly in this frame of

---

[145] William Ellery Channing the younger.
[146] Like Fido, a common name for a dog in Thoreau's time.

mind; the world lay about at this angle. Shall I go to heaven or a-fishing? If I should soon bring this meditation to an end, would another so sweet occasion be likely to offer? I was as near being resolved into the essence of things as ever I was in my life. I fear my thoughts will not come back to me. If it would do any good, I would whistle for them. When they make us an offer, is it wise to say, We will think of it? My thoughts have left no track, and I cannot find the path again. What was it that I was thinking of? It was a very hazy day. I will just try these three sentences of Con-fut-see;[147] they may fetch that state about again. I know not whether it was the dumps or a budding ecstasy. Mem.[148] There never is but one opportunity of a kind.

Poet. How now, Hermit, is it too soon? I have got just thirteen whole ones, beside several which are imperfect or undersized; but they will do for the smaller fry; they do not cover up the hook so much. Those village worms are quite too large; a shiner may make a meal off one without finding the skewer.

Hermit. Well, then, let's be off. Shall we to the Concord? There's good sport there if the water be not too high.

Why do precisely these objects which we behold make a world? Why has man just these species of animals for his neighbors; as if nothing but a mouse could have filled this crevice? I suspect that Pilpay & Co.[149] have put animals to their best use, for they are all beasts of burden, in a sense, made to carry some portion of our thoughts.

The mice which haunted my house were not the common ones, which are said to have been introduced into the country, but a wild native kind (*Mus leucopus*) not found in the village. I sent one to a distinguished naturalist, and it interested him much. When I was building, one of these had its nest underneath the house, and before I had laid the second floor, and swept out the shavings, would come out regularly at lunch time and pick up the crumbs at my feet. It probably had never seen a man before; and it soon became quite familiar, and would run over my shoes and up my clothes. It could readily ascend the sides of the room by short impulses, like a squirrel, which it resembled in its motions. At length, as I leaned with my elbow on the bench one day, it ran up my clothes, and along my sleeve, and round and round the paper which held my dinner, while I kept the latter close, and dodged and played at bo-peep with it; and when at last I held still a piece of cheese between my thumb and finger, it came and nibbled it, sitting in my hand, and afterward cleaned its face and paws, like a fly, and walked away.

A phœbe soon built in my shed, and a robin for protection in a pine which grew against the house. In June the partridge, (*Tetrao umbellus*,) which is so shy a bird, led her brood past my windows, from the woods in the rear to the front of my house, clucking and calling to them like a hen, and in all her behavior proving herself the hen of the woods. The young suddenly disperse on your approach, at a signal from the mother, as if a whirlwind had swept them away, and they so exactly resemble the dried leaves and twigs that many a traveller has placed his foot in the midst of a brood, and heard the whir of the old bird as she flew off, and her anxious calls and

[147] Confucius.
[148] Memorandum.

[149] Makers of tales, in reference to the teller of ancient Sanskrit fables.

mewing, or seen her trail her wings to attract his attention, without suspecting their neighborhood. The parent will sometimes roll and spin round before you in such a dishabille, that you cannot, for a few moments, detect what kind of creature it is. The young squat still and flat, often running their heads under a leaf, and mind only their mother's directions given from a distance, nor will your approach make them run again and betray themselves. You may even tread on them, or have your eyes on them for a minute, without discovering them. I have held them in my open hand at such a time, and still their only care, obedient to their mother and their instinct, was to squat there without fear or trembling. So perfect is this instinct, that once, when I had laid them on the leaves again, and one accidentally fell on its side, it was found with the rest in exactly the same position ten minutes afterward. They are not callow like the young of most birds, but more perfectly developed and precocious even than chickens. The remarkably adult yet innocent expression of their open and serene eyes is very memorable. All intelligence seems reflected in them. They suggest not merely the purity of infancy, but a wisdom clarified by experience. Such an eye was not born when the bird was, but is coeval with the sky it reflects. The woods do not yield another such a gem. The traveller does not often look into such a limpid well. The ignorant or reckless sportsman often shoots the parent at such a time, and leaves these innocents to fall a prey to some prowling beast or bird, or gradually mingle with the decaying leaves which they so much resemble. It is said that when hatched by a hen they will directly disperse on some alarm, and so are lost, for they never hear the mother's call which gathers them again. These were my hens and chickens.

It is remarkable how many creatures live wild and free though secret in the woods, and still sustain themselves in the neighborhood of towns, suspected by hunters only. How retired the otter manages to live here! He grows to be four feet long, as big as a small boy, perhaps without any human being getting a glimpse of him. I formerly saw the raccoon in the woods behind where my house is built, and probably still heard their whinnering[150] at night. Commonly I rested an hour or two in the shade at noon, after planting, and ate my lunch, and read a little by a spring which was the source of a swamp and of a brook, oozing from under Brister's Hill, half a mile from my field. The approach to this was through a succession of descending grassy hollows, full of young pitch-pines, into a larger wood about the swamp. There, in a very secluded and shaded spot, under a spreading white-pine, there was yet a clean firm sward to sit on. I had dug out the spring and made a well of clear gray water, where I could dip up a pailful without roiling it, and thither I went for this purpose almost every day in midsummer, when the pond was warmest. Thither too the wood-cock led her brood, to probe the mud for worms, flying but a foot above them down the bank, while they ran in a troop beneath; but at last, spying me, she would leave her young and circle round and round me, nearer and nearer, till within four or five feet, pretending broken wings and legs, to attract my attention and get off her young, who would already have taken up their march, with faint wiry peep, single file through the swamp, as she directed. Or I heard the peep of the young when I could not see the parent bird. There too the turtle-doves sat over the spring, or fluttered from bough to bough of the soft white-pines over my head; or the red squirrel, coursing down the nearest bough, was particularly familiar and inquisitive. You only need sit still

[150] A sound like whining.

long enough in some attractive spot in the woods that all its inhabitants may exhibit themselves to you by turns.

I was witness to events of a less peaceful character. One day when I went out to my wood-pile, or rather my pile of stumps, I observed two large ants, the one red, the other much larger, nearly half an inch long, and black, fiercely contending with one another. Having once got hold they never let go, but struggled and wrestled and rolled on the chips incessantly. Looking farther, I was surprised to find that the chips were covered with such combatants, that it was not a *duellum,* but a *bellum,*[151] a war between two races of ants, the red always pitted against the black, and frequently two red ones to one black. The legion of these Myrmidons[152] covered all the hills and vales in my wood-yard, and the ground was already strewn with the dead and dying, both red and black. It was the only battle which I have ever witnessed, the only battle-field I ever trod while the battle was raging; internecine war; the red republicans on the one hand, and the black imperialists on the other. On every side they were engaged in deadly combat, yet without any noise that I could hear, and human soldiers never fought so resolutely. I watched a couple that were fast locked in each other's embraces, in a little sunny valley amid the chips, now at noon-day prepared to fight till the sun went down, or life went out. The smaller red champion had fastened himself like a vice to his adversary's front, and through all the tumblings on that field never for an instant ceased to gnaw at one of his feelers near the root, having already caused the other to go by the board; while the stronger black one dashed him from side to side, and, as I saw on looking nearer, had already divested him of several of his members. They fought with more pertinacity than bull-dogs. Neither manifested the least disposition to retreat. It was evident that their battle-cry was Conquer or die. In the mean while there came along a single red ant on the hill-side of this valley, evidently full of excitement, who either had despatched his foe, or had not yet taken part in the battle; probably the latter, for he had lost none of his limbs; whose mother had charged him to return with his shield or upon it. Or perchance he was some Achilles, who had nourished his wrath apart, and had now come to avenge or rescue his Patroclus.[153] He saw this unequal combat from afar,—for the blacks were nearly twice the size of the red,—he drew near with rapid pace till he stood on his guard within half an inch of the combatants; then, watching his opportunity, he sprang upon the black warrior, and commenced his operations near the root of his right fore-leg, leaving the foe to select among his own members; and so there were three united for life, as if a new kind of attraction had been invented which put all other locks and cements to shame. I should not have wondered by this time to find that they had their respective musical bands stationed on some eminent chip, and playing their national airs the while, to excite the slow and cheer the dying combatants. I was myself excited somewhat even as if they had been men. The more you think of it, the less the difference. And certainly there is not the fight recorded in Concord history, at least,

---

[151] I.e., not a duel, but a war.
[152] Since *myrmex* is the Greek word for "ant," Thoreau is able to link the battle of the ants with the fighting done by the Myrmidons, the troops of Achilles in the Trojan War, as told in the *Iliad.*

[153] Patroclus was Achilles' friend; when he was slain, Achilles out of wrath threw himself into the war against the Trojans.

if in the history of America, that will bear a moment's comparison with this, whether for the numbers engaged in it, or for the patriotism and heroism displayed. For numbers and for carnage it was an Austerlitz or Dresden.[154] Concord Fight![155] Two killed on the patriots' side, and Luther Blanchard wounded! Why here every ant was a Buttrick,—"Fire! for God's sake fire!"—and thousands shared the fate of Davis and Hosmer. There was not one hireling[156] there. I have no doubt that it was a principle they fought for, as much as our ancestors, and not to avoid a three-penny tax on their tea; and the results of this battle will be as important and memorable to those whom it concerns as those of the battle of Bunker Hill, at least.

I took up the chip on which the three I have particularly described were struggling, carried it into my house, and placed it under a tumbler on my windowsill, in order to see the issue. Holding a microscope to the first-mentioned red ant, I saw that though he was assiduously gnawing at the near fore-leg of his enemy, having severed his remaining feeler, his own breast was all torn away, exposing what vitals he had there to the jaws of the black warrior, whose breast-plate was apparently too thick for him to pierce; and the dark carbuncles of the sufferer's eyes shone with ferocity such as war only could excite. They struggled half an hour longer under the tumbler, and when I looked again the black soldier had severed the heads of his foes from their bodies, and the still living heads were hanging on either side of him like ghastly trophies at his saddle-bow, still apparently as firmly fastened as ever, and he was endeavoring with feeble struggles, being without feelers and with only the remnant of a leg, and I know not how many other wounds, to divest himself of them; which at length, after half an hour more, he accomplished. I raised the glass, and he went off over the window-sill in that crippled state. Whether he finally survived that combat, and spent the remainder of his days in some Hotel des Invalides,[157] I do not know; but I thought that his industry would not be worth much thereafter. I never learned which party was victorious, nor the cause of the war; but I felt for the rest of that day as if I had had my feelings excited and harrowed by witnessing the struggle, the ferocity and carnage, of a human battle before my door.

Kirby and Spence tell us that the battles of ants have long been celebrated and the date of them recorded, though they say that Huber[158] is the only modern author who appears to have witnessed them. "Æneas Sylvius,"[159] say they, "after giving a very circumstantial account of one contested with great obstinacy by a great and small species on the trunk of a pear tree," adds that " 'This action was fought in the pontificate of Eugenius the Fourth,[160] in the presence of Nicholas Pistoriensis, an eminent lawyer, who related the whole history of the battle with the greatest fidelity.' A similar engagement between great and small ants is recorded by Olaus Magnus,[161] in which the small ones, being victorious, are said to have buried the bodies of their own soldiers, but left those of their giant enemies a prey to the birds. This event

---

[154] Battles fought during the wars of Napoleon.
[155] Battle of April 1775, the opening engagement of the American Revolution. The names and remarks that follow refer to that conflict.
[156] Mercenary.
[157] Veterans' hospital in Paris.
[158] Kirby and Spence's book on entomology includes the description of a battle among ants, taken from Huber's study of 1810.
[159] Name used by Pope Pius II (1405–1464) for his writings.
[160] Pope between 1431 and 1447.
[161] Swedish historian and churchman (1490–1557).

happened previous to the expulsion of the tyrant Christiern the Second from Sweden."[162] The battle which I witnessed took place in the Presidency of Polk, five years before the passage of Webster's Fugitive-Slave Bill.[163]

Many a village Bose, fit only to course a mud-turtle in a victualling cellar, sported his heavy quarters in the woods, without the knowledge of his master, and ineffectually smelled at old fox burrows and woodchucks' holes; led perchance by some slight cur which nimbly threaded the wood, and might still inspire a natural terror in its denizens;—now far behind his guide, barking like a canine bull toward some small squirrel which had treed itself for scrutiny, then, cantering off, bending the bushes with his weight, imagining that he is on the track of some stray member of the gerbille family. Once I was surprised to see a cat walking along the stony shore of the pond, for they rarely wander so far from home. The surprise was mutual. Nevertheless the most domestic cat, which has lain on a rug all her days, appears quite at home in the woods, and, by her sly and stealthy behavior, proves herself more native there than the regular inhabitants. Once, when berrying, I met with a cat with young kittens in the woods, quite wild, and they all, like their mother, had their backs up and were fiercely spitting at me. A few years before I lived in the woods there was what was called a "winged cat" in one of the farm-houses in Lincoln nearest the pond, Mr. Gilian Baker's. When I called to see her in June, 1842, she was gone a-hunting in the woods, as was her wont. (I am not sure, whether it was a male or female, and so use the more common pronoun,) but her mistress told me that she came into the neighborhood a little more than a year before, in April, and was finally taken into their house; that she was of a dark brownish-gray color, with a white spot on her throat, and white feet, and had a large bushy tail like a fox; that in the winter the fur grew thick and flattened out along her sides, forming strips ten or twelve inches long by two and a half wide, and under her chin like a muff, the upper side loose, the under matted like felt, and in the spring these appendages dropped off. They gave me a pair of her "wings," which I keep still. There is no appearance of a membrane about them. Some thought it was part flying-squirrel or some other wild animal, which is not impossible, for, according to naturalists, prolific hybrids have been produced by the union of the marten and domestic cat. This would have been the right kind of cat for me to keep, if I had kept any; for why should not a poet's cat be winged as well as his horse?[164]

In the fall the loon (*Colymbus glacialis*) came, as usual, to moult and bathe in the pond, making the woods ring with his wild laughter before I had risen. At rumor of his arrival all the Mill-dam sportsmen are on the alert, in gigs[165] and on foot, two by two and three by three, with patent rifles and conical balls and spy-glasses. They come rustling through the woods like autumn leaves, at least ten men to one loon. Some station themselves on this side of the pond, some on that, for the poor bird cannot be omnipresent; if he dive here he must come up there. But now the kind October wind rises, rustling the leaves and rippling the surface of the water, so that no loon can be heard or seen, though his foes sweep the pond with spy-glasses, and

---

[162] Sixteenth-century king.
[163] Fugitive Slave Law (1850) supported by Daniel Webster, Massachusetts senator. James K. Polk was president between 1845 and 1849.

[164] Reference to Pegasus, the winged horse ridden by poets in classic myth.
[165] Light, one-horse carriages.

make the woods resound with their discharges. The waves generously rise and dash angrily, taking sides with all waterfowl, and our sportsmen must beat a retreat to town and shop and unfinished jobs. But they were too often successful. When I went to get a pail of water early in the morning I frequently saw this stately bird sailing out of my cove within a few rods. If I endeavored to overtake him in a boat, in order to see how he would manœuvre, he would dive and be completely lost, so that I did not discover him again, sometimes, till the latter part of the day. But I was more than a match for him on the surface. He commonly went off in a rain.

As I was paddling along the north shore one very calm October afternoon, for such days especially they settle on to the lakes, like the milkweed down, having looked in vain over the pond for a loon, suddenly one, sailing out from the shore toward the middle a few rods in front of me, set up his wild laugh and betrayed himself. I pursued with a paddle and he dived, but when he came up I was nearer than before. He dived again, but I miscalculated the direction he would take, and we were fifty rods apart when he came to the surface this time, for I had helped to widen the interval; and again he laughed long and loud, and with more reason than before. He manœuvred so cunningly that I could not get within half a dozen rods of him. Each time, when he came to the surface, turning his head this way and that, he coolly surveyed the water and the land, and apparently chose his course so that he might come up where there was the widest expanse of water and at the greatest distance from the boat. It was surprising how quickly he made up his mind and put his resolve into execution. He led me at once to the widest part of the pond, and could not be driven from it. While he was thinking one thing in his brain, I was endeavoring to divine his thought in mine. It was a pretty game, played on the smooth surface of the pond, a man against a loon. Suddenly your adversary's checker disappears beneath the board, and the problem is to place yours nearest to where his will appear again. Sometimes he would come up unexpectedly on the opposite side of me, having apparently passed directly under the boat. So long-winded was he and so unweariable, that when he had swum farthest he would immediately plunge again, nevertheless; and then no wit could divine where in the deep pond, beneath the smooth surface, he might be speeding his way like a fish, for he had time and ability to visit the bottom of the pond in its deepest part. It is said that loons have been caught in the New York lakes eighty feet beneath the surface, with hooks set for trout,—though Walden is deeper than that. How surprised must the fishes be to see this ungainly visitor from another sphere speeding his way amid their schools! Yet he appeared to know his course as surely under water as on the surface, and swam much faster there. Once or twice I saw a ripple where he approached the surface, just put his head out to reconnoitre, and instantly dived again. I found that it was as well for me to rest on my oars and wait his reappearing as to endeavor to calculate where he would rise; for again and again, when I was straining my eyes over the surface one way, I would suddenly be startled by his unearthly laugh behind me. But why, after displaying so much cunning, did he invariably betray himself the moment he came up by that loud laugh? Did not his white breast enough betray him? He was indeed a silly loon, I thought. I could commonly hear the plash of the water when he came up, and so also detected him. But after an hour he seemed as fresh as ever, dived as willingly and swam yet farther than at first. It was surprising to see how serenely he sailed off with unruffled breast when he came to the surface, doing all the work with his webbed feet beneath. His usual note was this demoniac laughter, yet somewhat like that of a water-fowl; but occasionally, when he had balked me most successfully and come up a long way off, he uttered a long-drawn unearthly howl, probably more like that of a wolf than any bird; as when a beast puts his muzzle to the ground and deliberately howls. This was his looning,—perhaps the wildest sound that is ever heard here, making the woods ring far and wide. I concluded that he laughed in derision of my efforts, confident of his own resources. Though the sky was by this time overcast, the pond was so smooth that I could see when he broke the surface when I did not hear him. His white breast, the stillness of the air, and the smoothness of the water were all against him. At length, having come up fifty rods off, he uttered one of those prolonged howls, as if calling on the god of loons to aid him, and immediately there came a wind from the east and rippled the surface, and filled the whole air with misty rain, and I was impressed as if it were the prayer of the loon answered, and his god was angry with me; and so I left him disappearing far away on the tumultuous surface.

For hours, in fall days, I watched the ducks cunningly tack and veer and hold the middle of the pond, far from the sportsman; tricks which they will have less need to practise in Louisiana bayous. When compelled to rise they would sometimes circle round and round and over the pond at a considerable height, from which they could easily see to other ponds and the river, like black motes in the sky; and, when I thought they had gone off thither long since, they would settle down by a slanting flight of a quarter of a mile on to a distant part which was left free; but what beside safety they got by sailing in the middle of Walden I do not know, unless they love its water for the same reason that I do.

Spring

The opening of large tracts by the ice-cutters commonly causes a pond to break up earlier; for the water, agitated by the wind, even in cold weather, wears away the surrounding ice. But such was not the effect on Walden that year, for she had soon got a thick new garment to take the place of the old. This pond never breaks up so soon as the others in this neighborhood, on account both of its greater depth and its having no stream passing through it to melt or wear away the ice. I never knew it to open in the course of a winter, not excepting that of '52–3, which gave the ponds so severe a trial. It commonly opens about the first of April, a week or ten days later than Flint's Pond and Fair-Haven, beginning to melt on the north side and in the shallower parts where it began to freeze. It indicates better than any water hereabouts the absolute progress of the season, being least affected by transient changes of temperature. A severe cold of a few days' duration in March may very much retard the opening of the former ponds, while the temperature of Walden increases almost uninterruptedly. A thermometer thrust into the middle of Walden on the 6th of March, 1847, stood at 32°, or freezing point; near the shore at 33°; in the middle of Flint's Pond, the same day, at 32 1/2°; at a dozen rods from the shore, in shallow water, under ice a foot thick, at 36°. This difference of three and a half degrees between the temperature of the deep water and the shallow in the latter pond, and the fact that a great proportion of it is comparatively shallow, show why it should break up so much sooner than Walden. The ice in the shallowest part was at this time several inches thinner than in the middle. In mid-winter the middle had been the warmest and the ice thinnes: there. So, also, every one who has waded about the shores of a pond in summer must have perceived how much warmer the water is close to the shore, where only three or four inches deep, than a little distance out, and on the surface where it is deep, than near the bottom. In spring the sun not only exerts an influence through the increased temperature of the air and earth, but its heat passes through ice a foot or more thick, and is reflected from the bottom in shallow water, and so also warms the water and melts the under side of the ice, at the same time that it is melting it more directly above, making it uneven, and causing the air bubbles which it contains to extend themselves upward and downward until it is completely honeycombed, and at last disappears suddenly in a single spring rain. Ice has its grain as well as wood, and when a cake begins to rot or "comb," that is, assume the appearance of honey-comb, whatever may be its position, the air cells are at right angles with what was the water surface. Where there is a rock or a log rising near to the surface the ice over it is much thinner, and is frequently quite dissolved by this reflected heat; and I have been told that in the experiment at Cambridge to freeze water in a shallow wooden pond, though the cold air circulated underneath, and so had access to both sides, the reflection of the sun from the bottom more than counterbalanced this advantage. When a warm rain in the middle of the winter melts off the snow-ice from Walden, and leaves a hard dark or transparent ice on the middle, there will be a strip of rotten though thicker white ice, a rod or more wide, about the shores, created by this reflected heat. Also, as I have said, the bubbles themselves within the ice operate as burning glasses to melt the ice beneath.

The phenomena of the year take place every day in a pond on a small scale. Every morning, generally speaking, the shallow water is being warmed more rapidly than the deep, though it may not be made so warm after all, and every evening it is being cooled more rapidly until the morning. The day is an epitome of the year. The night is the winter, the morning and evening are the spring and fall, and the noon is the summer. The cracking and booming of the ice indicate a change of temperature. One pleasant morning after a cold night, February 24th, 1850, having gone to Flint's Pond to spend the day, I noticed with surprise, that when I struck the ice with the head of my axe, it resounded like a gong for many rods around, or as if I had struck on a tight drum-head. The pond began to boom about an hour after sunrise, when it felt the influence of the sun's rays slanted upon it from over the hills; it stretched itself and yawned like a waking man with a gradually increasing tumult, which was kept up three or four hours. It took a short siesta at noon, and boomed once more toward night, as the sun was withdrawing his influence. In the right state of the weather a pond fires its evening gun with great regularity. But in the middle of the day, being full of cracks, and the air also being less elastic, it had completely lost its resonance, and probably fishes and muskrats could not then have been stunned by a blow on it. The fishermen say that the "thundering of the pond" scares the fishes and prevents their biting. The pond does not thunder every evening, and I cannot tell surely when to expect its thundering; but though I may perceive no difference in the weather, it does. Who would have suspected so large and cold and thick-skinned a thing to be so sensitive? Yet it has its law to which it thunders obedience when it should as surely as the buds expand in the spring. The earth is all alive and covered with papillæ. The largest pond is as sensitive to atmospheric changes as the globule of mercury in its tube.

One attraction in coming to the woods to live was that I should have leisure and opportunity to see the spring come in. The ice in the pond at length begins to be honey-combed, and I can set my heel in it as I walk. Fogs and rains and warmer suns are gradually melting the snow; the days have grown sensibly longer; and I see how I shall get through the winter without adding to my wood-pile, for large fires are no longer necessary. I am on the alert for the first signs of spring, to hear the chance note of some arriving bird, or the striped squirrel's chirp, for his stores must be now nearly exhausted, or see the woodchuck venture out of his winter quarters. On the 13th of March, after I had heard the bluebird, song-sparrow, and red-wing, the ice was still nearly a foot thick. As the weather grew warmer, it was not sensibly worn away by the water, nor broken up and floated off as in rivers, but, though it was completely melted for half a rod in width about the shore, the middle was merely honey-combed and saturated with water, so that you could put your foot through it when six inches thick; but by the next day evening, perhaps, after a warm rain followed by fog, it would have wholly disappeared, all gone off with the fog, spirited away. One year I went across the middle only five days before it disappeared entirely. In 1845 Walden was first completely open on the 1st of April; in '46, the 25th of March; in '47, the 8th of April; in '51, the 28th of March; in '52, the 18th of April, in '53, the 23d of March; in '54, about the 7th of April.

Every incident connected with the breaking up of the rivers and ponds and the settling of the weather is particularly interesting to us who live in a climate of so great extremes. When the warmer days come, they who dwell near the river hear the ice crack at night with a startling whoop as loud as artillery, as if its icy fetters were rent from end to end, and within a few days see it rapidly going out. So the alligator comes out of the mud with quakings of the earth. One old man, who has been a close observer of Nature, and seems as thoroughly wise in regard to all her operations as if she had been put upon the stocks when he was a boy, and he had helped to lay her keel,—who has come to his growth, and can hardly acquire more of natural lore if he should live to the age of Methuselah,[166]—told me, and I was surprised to hear him express wonder at any of Nature's operations, for I thought that there were no secrets between them, that one spring day he took his gun and boat, and thought that he would have a little sport with the ducks. There was ice still on the meadows, but it was all gone out of the river, and he dropped down without obstruction from Sudbury, where he lived, to Fair-Haven Pond, which he found, unexpectedly, covered for the most part with a firm field of ice. It was a warm day, and he was surprised to see so great a body of ice remaining. Not seeing any ducks, he hid his boat on the north or back side of an island in the pond, and then concealed himself in the bushes on the south side, to await them. The ice was melted for three or four rods from the shore, and there was a smooth and warm sheet of water, with a muddy bottom, such as the ducks love, within, and he thought it likely that some would be along pretty soon. After he had lain still there about an hour he heard a low and seemingly very distant sound, but singularly grand and impressive, unlike any thing he had ever heard,

[166] He lived 969 years (Genesis 5:27).

gradually swelling and increasing as if it would have a universal and memorable ending, a sullen rush and roar, which seemed to him all at once like the sound of a vast body of fowl coming in to settle there, and, seizing his gun, he started up in haste and excited; but he found, to his surprise, that the whole body of the ice had started while he lay there, and drifted in to the shore, and the sound he had heard was made by its edge grating on the shore,—at first gently nibbled and crumbled off, but at length heaving up and scattering its wrecks along the island to a considerable height before it came to a stand still.

At length the sun's rays have attained the right angle, and warm winds blow up mist and rain and melt the snow banks, and the sun dispersing the mist smiles on a checkered landscape of russet and white smoking with incense, through which the traveller picks his way from islet to islet, cheered by the music of a thousand tinkling rills and rivulets whose veins are filled with the blood of winter which they are bearing off.

Few phenomena gave me more delight than to observe the forms which thawing sand and clay assume in flowing down the sides of a deep cut on the railroad through which I passed on my way to the village, a phenomenon not very common on so large a scale, though the number of freshly exposed banks of the right material must have been greatly multiplied since railroads were invented. The material was sand of every degree of fineness and of various rich colors, commonly mixed with a little clay. When the frost comes out in the spring, and even in a thawing day in the winter, the sand begins to flow down the slopes like lava, sometimes bursting out through the snow and overflowing it where no sand was to be seen before. Innumerable little streams overlap and interlace one with another, exhibiting a sort of hybrid product, which obeys half way the law of currents, and half way that of vegetation. As it flows it takes the forms of sappy leaves or vines, making heaps of pulpy sprays a foot or more in depth, and resembling, as you look down on them, the laciniated lobed and imbricated thalluses of some lichens; or you are reminded of coral, of leopards' paws or birds' feet, of brains or lungs or bowels, and excrements of all kinds. It is a truly *grotesque* vegetation, whose forms and color we see imitated in bronze, a sort of architectural foliage more ancient and typical than acanthus, chiccory, ivy, vine, or any vegetable leaves; destined perhaps, under some circumstances, to become a puzzle to future geologists. The whole cut impressed me as if it were a cave with its stalactites laid open to the light. The various shades of the sand are singularly rich and agreeable, embracing the different iron colors, brown, gray, yellowish, and reddish. When the flowing mass reaches the drain at the foot of the bank it spreads out flatter into *strands,* the separate streams losing their semi-cylindrical form and gradually becoming more flat and broad, running together as they are more moist, till they form an almost flat *sand,* still variously and beautifully shaded, but in which you can trace the original forms of vegetation; till at length, in the water itself, they are converted into *banks,* like those formed off the mouths of rivers, and the forms of vegetation are lost in the ripple marks on the bottom.

The whole bank, which is from twenty to forty feet high, is sometimes overlaid with a mass of this kind of foliage, or sandy rupture, for a quarter of a mile on one or both sides, the produce of one spring day. What makes this sand foliage remarkable is its springing into existence thus suddenly. When I see on the one side the inert bank, —for the sun acts on one side first,—and on the other this luxuriant foliage, the creation of an hour, I am affected as if in a peculiar sense I stood in the laboratory of the Artist who made the world and me,—had come to where he was still at work, sporting on this bank, and with excess of energy strewing his fresh designs about. I feel as if I were nearer to the vitals of the globe, for this sandy overflow is something such a foliaceous mass as the vitals of the animal body. You find thus in the very sands an anticipation of the vegetable leaf. No wonder that the earth expresses itself outwardly in leaves, it so labors with the idea inwardly. The atoms have already learned this law, and are pregnant by it. The overhanging leaf sees here its prototype. *Internally,* whether in the globe or animal body, it is a moist thick *lobe,* a word especially applicable to the liver and lungs and the *leaves* of fat, (λείβω, *labor, lapsus,* to flow or slip downward, a lapsing; λοβος, *globus,* lobe, globe; also lap, flap, and many other words,) *externally* a dry thin *leaf,* even as the *f* and *v* are a pressed and dried *b.* The radicals of lobe are *lb,* the soft mass of the *b* (single lobed, or B, double lobed,) with a liquid *l* behind it pressing it forward. In globe, *glb,* the guttural *g* adds to the meaning the capacity of the throat. The feathers and wings of birds are still drier and thinner leaves. Thus, also, you pass from the lumpish grub in the earth to the airy and fluttering butterfly. The very globe continually transcends and translates itself, and becomes winged in its orbit. Even ice begins with delicate crystal leaves, as if it had flowed into moulds which the fronds of water plants have impressed on the watery mirror. The whole tree itself is but one leaf, and rivers are still vaster leaves whose pulp is intervening earth, and towns and cities are the ova of insects in their axils.

When the sun withdraws the sand ceases to flow, but in the morning the streams will start once more and branch and branch again into a myriad of others. You here see perchance how blood vessels are formed. If you look closely you observe that first there pushes forward from the thawing mass a stream of softened sand with a drop-like point, like the ball of the finger, feeling its way slowly and blindly downward, until at last with more heat and moisture, as the sun gets higher, the most fluid portion, in its effort to obey the law to which the most inert also yields, separates from the latter and forms for itself a meandering channel or artery within that, in which is seen a little silvery stream glancing like lightning from one stage of pulpy leaves or branches to another, and ever and anon swallowed up in the sand. It is wonderful how rapidly yet perfectly the sand organizes itself as it flows, using the best material its mass affords to form the sharp edges of its channel. Such are the sources of rivers. In the silicious matter which the water deposits is perhaps the bony system, and in the still finer soil and organic matter the fleshy fibre or cellular tissue. What is man but a mass of thawing clay? The ball of the human finger is but a drop congealed. The fingers and toes flow to their extent from the thawing mass of the body. Who knows what the human body would expand and flow out to under a more genial heaven? Is not the hand a spreading *palm* leaf with its lobes and veins? The ear may be regarded, fancifully, as a lichen, *umbilicaria,* on the side of the head, with its lobe or drop. The lip (*labium* from *labor* (?)) laps or lapses from the sides of the cavernous mouth. The nose is a manifest congealed drop or stalactite. The chin is a still larger drop, the confluent dripping of the face. The cheeks are a slide from the brows into the valley of the face, opposed and diffused by the cheek bones. Each rounded lobe of the vegetable leaf, too, is a thick and now loitering drop, larger or smaller; the lobes are the fingers of the leaf; and as many lobes as it has, in so many directions it tends to flow, and more heat or other genial influences would have caused it to flow yet farther.

Thus it seemed that this one hillside illustrated the principle of all the operations of Nature. The Maker of this earth but patented a leaf. What Champollion[167] will decipher this hieroglyphic for us, that we may turn over a new leaf at last? This phenomenon is more exhilarating to me than the luxuriance and fertility of vineyards. True, it is somewhat excrementitious in its character, and there is no end to the heaps of liver lights and bowels, as if the globe were turned wrong side outward; but this suggests at least that Nature has some bowels, and there again is mother of humanity. This is the frost coming out of the ground; this is Spring. It precedes the green and flowery spring, as mythology precedes regular poetry. I know of nothing more purgative of winter fumes and indigestions. It convinces me that Earth is still in her swaddling clothes, and stretches forth baby fingers on every side. Fresh curls spring from the baldest brow. There is nothing inorganic. These foliaceous heaps lie along the bank like the slag of a furnace, showing that Nature is "in full blast" within. The earth is not a mere fragment of dead history, stratum upon stratum like the leaves of a book, to be studied by geologists and antiquaries chiefly, but living poetry like the leaves of a tree, which precede flowers and fruit,—not a fossil earth, but a living earth; compared with whose great central life all animal and vegetable life is merely parasitic. Its throes will heave our exuviæ from their graves. You may melt your metals and cast them into the most beautiful moulds you can; they will never excite me like the forms which this molten earth flows out into. And not only it, but the institutions upon it, are plastic like clay in the hands of the potter.

Ere long, not only on these banks, but on every hill and plain and in every hollow, the frost comes out of the ground like a dormant quadruped from its burrow, and seeks the sea with music, or migrates to other climes in clouds. Thaw with his gentle persuasion is more powerful than Thor[168] with his hammer. The one melts, the other but breaks in pieces.

When the ground was partially bare of snow, and a few warm days had dried its surface somewhat, it was pleasant to compare the first tender signs of the infant year just peeping forth with stately beauty of the withered vegetation which had withstood the winter,—life-everlasting, golden-rods, pinweeds, and graceful wild grasses, more obvious and interesting frequently than in summer even, as if their beauty was not ripe till then; even cotton-grass, cat-tails, mulleins, johnswort, hard-hack, meadow-sweet, and other strong stemmed plants, those unexhausted granaries which entertain the earliest birds,—decent weeds, at least, which widowed Nature wears. I am particularly attracted by the arching and sheaf-like top of the wool-grass; it brings back the summer to our winter memories, and is among the forms which art loves to copy, and which, in the vegetable kingdom, have the same relation to types already in the mind of man that astronomy has. It is an antique style older than Greek or Egyptian. Many of the phenomena of Winter are suggestive of an inexpressible tenderness and

---

[167] Jean François Champollion (1790–1832), Frenchman who deciphered the hieroglyphics inscribed on the Rosetta Stone and thus opened up ancient Egyptian culture to contemporary knowledge.

[168] Norse god of thunder, whose name Thoreau liked to associate with his own.

fragile delicacy. We are accustomed to hear this king described as a rude and boisterous tyrant; but with the gentleness of a lover he adorns the tresses of Summer.

At the approach of spring the red-squirrels got under my house, two at a time, directly under my feet as I sat reading or writing, and kept up the queerest chuckling and chirruping and vocal pirouetting and gurgling sounds that ever were heard; and when I stamped they only chirruped the louder, as if past all fear and respect in their mad pranks, defying humanity to stop them. No you don't—chickaree—chickaree. They were wholly deaf to my arguments, or failed to perceive their force, and fell into a strain of invective that was irresistible.

The first sparrow of spring! The year beginning with younger hope than ever! The faint silvery warblings heard over the partially bare and moist fields from the blue-bird, the song-sparrow, and the red-wing, as if the last flakes of winter tinkled as they fell! What at such a time are histories, chronologies, traditions, and all written revelations? The brooks sing carols and glees to the spring. The marsh-hawk sailing low over the meadow is already seeking the first slimy life that awakes. The sinking sound of melting snow is heard in all dells, and the ice dissolves apace in the ponds. The grass flames up on the hillsides like a spring fire,—"et primitus oritur herba imbribus primoribus evocata,"[169]—as if the earth sent forth an inward heat to greet the returning sun; not yellow but green is the color of its flame;—the symbol of perpetual youth, the grass-blade, like a long green ribbon, streams from the sod into the summer, checked indeed by the frost, but anon pushing on again, lifting its spear of last year's hay with the fresh life below. It grows as steadily as the rill oozes out of the ground. It is almost identical with that, for in the growing days of June, when the rills are dry, the grass blades are their channels, and from year to year the herds drink at this perennial green stream, and the mower draws from it betimes their winter supply. So our human life but dies down to its root, and still puts forth its green blade to eternity.

Walden is melting apace. There is a canal two rods wide along the northerly and westerly sides, and wider still at the east end. A great field of ice has cracked off from the main body. I hear a song-sparrow singing from the bushes on the shore,—*olit, olit, olit,—chip, chip, chip, che char,—che wiss, wiss, wiss.* He too is helping to crack it. How handsome the great sweeping curves in the edge of the ice, answering somewhat to those of the shore, but more regular! It is unusually hard, owing to the recent severe but transient cold, and all watered or waved like a palace floor. But the wind slides eastward over its opaque surface in vain, till it reaches the living surface beyond. It is glorious to behold this ribbon of water sparkling in the sun, the bare face of the pond full of glee and youth, as if it spoke the joy of the fishes within it, and of the sands on its shore,—a silvery sheen as from the scales of a *leuciscus*,[170] as it were all one active fish. Such is the contrast between winter and spring. Walden was dead and is alive again.[171] But this spring it broke up more steadily, as I have said.

The change from storm and winter to serene and mild weather, from dark and sluggish hours to bright and elastic ones, is a memorable crisis which all things proclaim. It is seemingly instantaneous at last. Suddenly an influx of light filled my

---

[169] Latin: "and summonded by the early rains, the grass starts to grow." From *De Re Rustica* by Varro (116–27 B.C.).

[170] Freshwater fish.

[171] Here Thoreau echoes the language of the New Testament in the parable of the Prodigal Son, with perhaps also an allusion to Christ's resurrection.

house, though the evening was at hand, and the clouds of winter still overhung it, and the eaves were dripping with sleety rain. I looked out the window, and lo! where yesterday was cold gray ice there lay the transparent pond already calm and full of hope as on a summer evening, reflecting a summer evening sky in its bosom, though none was visible overhead, as if it had intelligence with some remote horizon. I heard a robin in the distance, the first I had heard for many a thousand years, methought, whose note I shall not forget for many a thousand more,—the same sweet and powerful song of yore. O the evening robin, at the end of a New England summer day! If I could ever find the twig he sits upon! I mean *he;* I mean *the twig*. This at least is not the *Turdus migratorius*. [172] The pitch-pines and shrub-oaks about my house, which had so long drooped, suddenly resumed their several characters, looked brighter, greener, and more erect and alive, as if effectually cleansed and restored by the rain. I knew that it would not rain any more. You may tell by looking at any twig of the forest, ay, at your very wood-pile, whether its winter is past or not. As it grew darker, I was startled by the *honking* of geese flying low over the woods, like weary travellers getting in late from southern lakes, and indulging at last in unrestrained complaint and mutual consolation. Standing at my door, I could hear the rush of their wings; when, driving toward my house, they suddenly spied my light, and with hushed clamor wheeled and settled in the pond. So I came in, and shut the door, and passed my first spring night in the woods.

In the morning I watched the geese from the door through the mist, sailing in the middle of the pond, fifty rods off, so large and tumultuous that Walden appeared like an artificial pond for their amusement. But when I stood on the shore they at once rose up with a great flapping of wings at the signal of their commander, and when they had got into rank circled about over my head, twenty-nine of them, and then steered straight to Canada, with a regular *honk* from the leader at intervals, trusting to break their fast in muddier pools. A "plump"[173] of ducks rose at the same time and took the route to the north in the wake of their noisier cousins.

For a week I heard the circling groping clangor of some solitary goose in the foggy mornings, seeking its companion, and still peopling the woods with the sound of a larger life than they could sustain. In April the pigeons were seen again flying express in small flocks, and in due time I heard the martins twittering over my clearing, though it had not seemed that the township contained so many that it could afford me any, and I fancied that they were peculiarly of the ancient race that dwelt in hollow trees ere white men came. In almost all climes the tortoise and the frog are among the precursors and heralds of this season, and birds fly with song and glancing plumage, and plants spring and bloom, and winds blow, to correct this slight oscillation of the poles and preserve the equilibrium of Nature.

As every season seems best to us in its turn, so the coming in of spring is like the creation of Cosmos out of Chaos and the realization of the Golden Age.—

"Eurus ad Auroram, Nabathæaque regna recessit,
    Persidaque, et radiis juga subdita matutinis."

"The East-Wind withdrew to Aurora and the
    Nabathæan kingdom,

---

[172] American robin.   [173] Flock.

And the Persian, and the ridges placed under
　　the morning rays.

*　　　　　*　　　　　*

Man was born. Whether that Artificer of things,
The origin of a better world, made him from
　　the divine seed;
Or the earth being recent and lately sundered
　　from the high
Ether, retained some seeds of cognate heaven."[174]

A single gentle rain makes the grass many shades greener. So our prospects brighten on the influx of better thoughts. We should be blessed if we lived in the present always, and took advantage of every accident that befell us, like the grass which confesses the influence of the slightest dew that falls on it; and did not spend our time in atoning for the neglect of past opportunities, which we call doing our duty. We loiter in winter while it is already spring. In a pleasant spring morning all men's sins are forgiven. Such a day is a truce to vice. While such a sun holds out to burn, the vilest sinner may return. Through our own recovered innocence we discern the innocence of our neighbors. You may have known your neighbor yesterday for a thief, a drunkard, or a sensualist, and merely pitied or despised him, and despaired of the world; but the sun shines bright and warm this first spring morning, re-creating the world, and you meet him at some serene work, and see how his exhausted and debauched veins expand with still joy and bless the new day, feel the spring influence with the innocence of infancy, and all his faults are forgotten. There is not only an atmosphere of good will about him, but even a savor of holiness groping for expression, blindly and ineffectually perhaps, like a new-born instinct, and for a short hour the south hill-side echoes to no vulgar jest. You see some innocent fair shoots preparing to burst from his gnarled rind and try another year's life, tender and fresh as the youngest plant. Even he has entered into the joy of his Lord. Why the jailer does not leave open his prison doors,—why the judge does not dismiss his case,— why the preacher does not dismiss his congregation! It is because they do not obey the hint which God gives them, nor accept the pardon which he freely offers to all.

"A return to goodness produced each day in the tranquil and beneficent breath of the morning, causes that in respect to the love of virtue and the hatred of vice, one approaches a little the primitive nature of man, as the sprouts of the forest which has been felled. In like manner the evil which one does in the interval of a day prevents the germs of virtues which began to spring up again from developing themselves and destroys them.

"After the germs of virtue have thus been prevented many times from developing themselves, then the beneficent breath of evening does not suffice to preserve them. As soon as the breath of evening does not suffice longer to preserve them, then the nature of man does not differ much from that of the brute. Men seeing the nature of this man like that of the brute, think that he has never possessed the innate faculty of reason. Are those the true and natural sentiments of man?"[175]

[174] From Ovid's *Metamorphoses*, Book I.
[175] From *The Book of Mencius*. The lines that
follow are again from *Metamorphoses*, Book I.

> "The Golden Age was first created, which without
>   any avenger
> Spontaneously without law cherished fidelity and
>   rectitude.
> Punishment and fear were not; nor were threaten-
>   ing words read
> On suspended brass; nor did the suppliant crowd
>   fear
> The words of their judge; but were safe without
>   an avenger.
> Not yet the pine felled on its mountains had de-
>   scended
> To the liquid waves that it might see a foreign
>   world,
> And mortals knew no shores but their own.
>   *   *   *
> There was eternal spring, and placid zephyrs with
>   warm
> Blasts soothed the flowers born without seed."

On the 29th of April, as I was fishing from the bank of the river near the Nine-Acre-Corner bridge, standing on the quaking grass and willow roots, where the muskrats lurk, I heard a singular rattling sound, somewhat like that of the sticks which boys play with their fingers, when, looking up, I observed a very slight and graceful hawk, like a night-hawk, alternately soaring like a ripple and tumbling a rod or two over and over, showing the underside of its wings, which gleamed like a satin ribbon in the sun, or like the pearly inside of a shell. This sight reminded me of falconry and what nobleness and poetry are associated with that sport. The Merlin it seemed to me it might be called: but I care not for its name. It was the most ethereal flight I had ever witnessed. It did not simply flutter like a butterfly, nor soar like the larger hawks, but it sported with proud reliance in the fields of air; mounting again and again with its strange chuckle, it repeated its free and beautiful fall, turning over and over like a kite, and then recovering from its lofty tumbling, as if it had never set its foot on *terra firma*. It appeared to have no companion in the universe,—sporting there alone,—and to need none but the morning and the ether with which it played. It was not lonely, but made all the earth lonely beneath it. Where was the parent which hatched it, its kindred, and its father in the heavens? The tenant of the air, it seemed related to the earth but by an egg hatched some time in the crevice of a crag;—or was its native nest made in the angle of a cloud, woven of the rainbow's trimmings and the sunset sky, and lined with some soft midsummer haze caught up from earth? Its eyry[176] now some cliffy cloud.

Beside this I got a rare mess of golden and silver and bright cupreous fishes, which looked like a string of jewels. Ah! I have penetrated to those meadows on the morning of many a first spring day, jumping from hummock to hummock, from willow root to willow root, when the wild river valley and the woods were bathed in so pure and bright a light as would have waked the dead, if they had been slumbering in their

[176] Bird's nest.

graves, as some suppose. There needs no stronger proof of immortality. All things must live in such a light. O Death, where was thy sting? O Grave, where was thy victory, then?[177]

Our village life would stagnate if it were not for the unexplored forests and meadows which surround it. We need the tonic of wildness,—to wade sometimes in marshes where the bittern and the meadow-hen lurk, and hear the booming of the snipe; to smell the whispering sedge where only some wilder and more solitary fowl builds her nest, and the mink crawls with its belly close to the ground. At the same time that we are earnest to explore and learn all things, we require that all things be mysterious and unexplorable, that land and sea be infinitely wild, unsurveyed and unfathomed by us because unfathomable. We can never have enough of Nature. We must be refreshed by the sight of inexhaustible vigor, vast and Titanic features, the sea-coast with its wrecks, the wilderness with its living and its decaying trees, the thunder cloud, and the rain which lasts three weeks and produces freshets. We need to witness our own limits transgressed, and some life pasturing freely where we never wander. We are cheered when we observe the vulture feeding on the carrion which disgusts and disheartens us and deriving health and strength from the repast. There was a dead horse in the hollow by the path to my house, which compelled me sometimes to go out of my way, especially in the night when the air was heavy, but the assurance it gave me of the strong appetite and inviolable health of Nature was my compensation for this. I love to see that Nature is so rife with life that myriads can be afforded to be sacrificed and suffered to prey on one another; that tender organizations can be so serenely squashed out of existence like pulp,—tadpoles which herons gobble up, and tortoises and toads run over in the road; and that sometimes it has rained flesh and blood! With the liability to accident, we must see how little account is to be made of it. The impression made on a wise man is that of universal innocence. Poison is not poisonous after all, nor are any wounds fatal. Compassion is a very untenable ground. It must be expeditious. Its pleadings will not bear to be stereotyped.

Early in May, the oaks, hickories, maples, and other trees, just putting out amidst the pine woods around the pond, imparted a brightness like sunshine to the landscape, especially in cloudy days, as if the sun were breaking through mists and shining faintly on the hill-sides here and there. On the third or fourth of May I saw a loon in the pond, and during the first week of the month I heard the whippoorwill, the brown-thrasher, the veery, the wood-pewee, the chewink, and other birds. I had heard the wood-thrush long before. The phoebe had already come once more and looked in at my door and window, to see if my house was cavern-like enough for her, sustaining herself on humming wings with clinched talons, as if she held by the air, while she surveyed the premises. The sulphur-like pollen of the pitch-pine soon covered the pond and the stones and rotten wood along the shore, so that you could have collected a barrel-ful. This is the "sulphur showers" we hear of. Even in Calidas' drama of Sacontala,[178] we read of "rills dyed yellow with the golden dust of the lotus." And so the seasons went rolling on into summer, as one rambles into higher and higher grass.

[177] Allusion to 1 Corinthians 15:55.
[178] The Sanskrit drama *Sakuntala* by the fifth-century Hindu poet Kalidasa.

Thus was my first year's life in the woods completed; and the second year was similar to it. I finally left Walden September 6th, 1847.

Conclusion

To the sick the doctors wisely recommend a change of air and scenery. Thank Heaven, here is not all the world. The buck-eye does not grow in New England, and the mocking-bird is rarely heard here. The wild-goose is more of a cosmopolite than we; he breaks his fast in Canada, takes a luncheon in the Ohio, and plumes himself for the night in a southern bayou. Even the bison, to some extent, keeps pace with the seasons, cropping the pastures of the Colorado only till a greener and sweeter grass awaits him by the Yellowstone. Yet we think that if rail-fences are pulled down, and stone-walls piled up on our farms, bounds are henceforth set to our lives and our fates decided. If you are chosen town-clerk, forsooth, you cannot go to Tierra del Fuego this summer: but you may go to the land of infernal fire nevertheless. The universe is wider than our views of it.

Yet we should oftener look over the tafferel[179] of our craft, like curious passengers, and not make the voyage like stupid sailors picking oakum. The other side of the globe is but the home of our correspondent. Our voyaging is only great-circle sailing,[180] and the doctors prescribe for diseases of the skin merely. One hastens to Southern Africa to chase the giraffe; but surely that is not the game he would be after. How long, pray, would a man hunt giraffes if he could? Snipes and woodcocks also may afford rare sport; but I trust it would be nobler game to shoot one's self.—

> "Direct your eye sight inward, and you'll find
> A thousand regions in your mind
> Yet undiscovered. Travel them, and be
> Expert in home-cosmography."[181]

What does Africa,—what does the West stand for? Is not our own interior white on the chart?[182] black though it may prove, like the coast, when discovered. Is it the source of the Nile, or the Niger, or the Mississippi, or a North-West Passage around this continent, that we would find? Are these the problems which most concern mankind? Is Franklin[183] the only man who is lost, that his wife should be so earnest to find him? Does Mr. Grinnell[184] know where he himself is? Be rather the Mungo Park, the Lewis and Clarke and Frobisher,[185] of your own streams and oceans; explore your own higher latitudes,—with shiploads of preserved meats to support you, if they be necessary; and pile the empty cans sky-high for a sign.[186] Were preserved meats invented to preserve meat merely? Nay, be a Columbus to whole new continents and worlds within you, opening new channels, not of trade, but of thought. Every man is the lord of a realm

[179] Rail at the ship's stern.
[180] Traveling by direct route.
[181] From "To My Honoured Friend, Sir Ed. P. Knight" by William Habington (1605–1654).
[182] Not yet mapped, because unexplored.
[183] Sir John Franklin (1786–1847), British explorer lost on expedition to discover open route between the Atlantic and the Pacific.
[184] Henry Grinnell (1799–1874), American who sponsored a rescue mission to find Franklin.
[185] Leaders of various explorations: Africa (Park), the American Northwest (Lewis and Clark), and Canada (Sir Martin Frobisher).
[186] A stack of cans marked one of the camps deserted by the Franklin expedition.

beside which the earthly empire of the Czar[187] is but a petty state, a hummock left by the ice. Yet some can be patriotic who have no self-respect, and sacrifice the greater to the less. They love the soil which makes their graves, but have no sympathy with the spirit which may still animate their clay. Patriotism is a maggot in their heads. What was the meaning of that South-Sea Exploring Expedition,[188] with all its parade and expense, but an indirect recognition of the fact, that there are continents and seas in the moral world, to which every man is an isthmus or an inlet, yet unexplored by him, but that it is easier to sail many thousand miles through cold and storm and cannibals, in a government ship, with five hundred men and boys to assist one, than it is to explore the private sea, the Atlantic and Pacific Ocean of one's being alone.—

> "Erret, et extremos alter scrutetur Iberos.
> Plus habet hic vitæ, plus habet ille viæ."

> Let them wander and scrutinize the outlandish
>   Australians.
> I have more of God, they more of the road.[189]

It is not worth the while to go round the world to count the cats in Zanzibar. Yet do this even till you can do better, and you may perhaps find some "Symmes' Hole"[190] by which to get at the inside at last. England and France, Spain and Portugal, Gold Coast and Slave Coast, all front on this private sea; but no bark from them has ventured out of sight of land, though it is without doubt the direct way to India. If you would learn to speak all tongues and conform to the customs of all nations, if you would travel farther than all travellers, be naturalized in all climes, and cause the Sphinx to dash her head against a stone,[191] even obey the precept of the old philosopher, and Explore thyself. Herein are demanded the eye and the nerve. Only the defeated and deserters go to the wars, cowards that run away and enlist. Start now on that farthest western way, which does not pause at the Mississippi or the Pacific, nor conduct toward a worn-out China or Japan, but leads on direct a tangent to this sphere, summer and winter, day and night, sun down, moon down, and at last earth down too.

It is said that Mirabeau[192] took to highway robbery "to ascertain what degree of resolution was necessary in order to place one's self in formal opposition to the most sacred laws of society." He declared that "a soldier who fights in the ranks does not require half so much courage as a foot-pad,"—"that honor and religion have never stood in the way of a well-considered and a firm resolve." This was manly, as the world goes; and yet it was idle, if not desperate. A saner man would have found himself often enough "in formal opposition" to what are deemed "the most sacred

---

[187] During Thoreau's lifetime Czarist Russia was the largest country.

[188] Antarctic expedition (1838–1842) led by the American Charles Wilkes.

[189] From lines by the Roman poet Claudian, with "Australians" and "of God" replacing the original words.

[190] John Symmes (1780–1829) fostered a theory that the globe was hollow, habitable, and open at either end.

[191] In frustration over Oedipus' solving the riddle she posed to him, the Sphinx killed herself.

[192] Count de Mirabeau (1749–1791), French diplomat.

laws of society," through obedience to yet more sacred laws, and so have tested his resolution without going out of his way. It is not for a man to put himself in such an attitude to society, but to maintain himself in whatever attitude he find himself through obedience to the laws of his being, which will never be one of opposition to a just government, if he should chance to meet with such.

I left the woods for as good a reason as I went there. Perhaps it seemed to me that I had several more lives to live, and could not spare any more time for that one. It is remarkable how easily and insensibly we fall into a particular route, and make a beaten track for ourselves. I had not lived there a week before my feet wore a path from my door to the pond-side; and though it is five or six years since I trod it, it is still quite distinct. It is true, I fear that others may have fallen into it, and so helped to keep it open. The surface of the earth is soft and impressible by the feet of men; and so with the paths which the mind travels. How worn and dusty, then, must be the highways of the world, how deep the ruts of tradition and conformity! I did not wish to take a cabin passage, but rather to go before the mast and on the deck of the world, for there I could best see the moonlight amid the mountains. I do not wish to go below now.

I learned this, at least, by my experiment; that if one advances confidently in the direction of his dreams, and endeavors to live the life which he has imagined, he will meet with a success unexpected in common hours. He will put some things behind, will pass an invisible boundary; new, universal, and more liberal laws will begin to establish themselves around and within him; or the old laws be expanded, and interpreted in his favor in a more liberal sense, and he will live with the license of a higher order of beings. In proportion as he simplifies his life, the laws of the universe will appear less complex, and solitude will not be solitude, nor poverty poverty, nor weakness weakness. If you have built castles in the air, your work need not be lost; that is where they should be. Now put the foundations under them.

It is a ridiculous demand which England and America make, that you shall speak so that they can understand you. Neither men nor toad-stools grow so. As if that were important, and there were not enough to understand you without them. As if Nature could support but one order of understandings, could not sustain birds as well as quadrupeds, flying as well as creeping things, and *hush* and *who*,[193] which Bright can understand, were the best English. As if there were safety in stupidity alone. I fear chiefly lest my expression may not be *extra-vagant* enough, may not wander far enough beyond the narrow limits of my daily experience, so as to be adequate to the truth of which I have been convinced. *Extra vagance!* it depends on how you are yarded. The migrating buffalo, which seeks new pastures in another latitude, is not extravagant like the cow which kicks over the pail, leaps the cow-yard fence, and runs after her calf, in milking time. I desire to speak somewhere *without* bounds; like a man in a waking moment, to men in their waking moments; for I am convinced that I cannot exaggerate enough even to lay the foundation of a true expression. Who that has heard a strain of music feared then lest he should speak extravagantly any more forever? In view of the future or possible, we should live quite laxly and undefined in front, our outlines dim and misty on that side; as our shadows reveal an insensible

---

[193] *Hush* and *whc*: commands to an ox ("Bright")
for "go" and "stop," respectively.

perspiration toward the sun. The volatile truth of our words should continually betray the inadequacy of the residual statement. Their truth is instantly *translated;* its literal monument alone remains. The words which express our faith and piety are not definite; yet they are significant and fragrant like frankincense to superior natures.

Why level downward to our dullest perception always, and praise that as common sense? The commonest sense is the sense of men asleep, which they express by snoring. Sometimes we are inclined to class those who are once-and-a-half witted with the half-witted, because we appreciate only a third part of their wit. Some would find fault with the morning-red, if they ever got up early enough. "They pretend," as I hear, "that the verses of Kabir[194] have four different senses; illusion, spirit, intellect, and the exoteric doctrine of the Vedas;" but in this part of the world it is considered a ground for complaint if a man's writings admit of more than one interpretation. While England endeavors to cure the potato-rot, will not any endeavor to cure the brain-rot, which prevails so much more widely and fatally?

I do not suppose that I have attained to obscurity, but I should be proud if no more fatal fault were found with my pages on this score than was found with the Walden ice. Southern customers objected to its blue color, which is the evidence of its purity, as if it were muddy, and preferred the Cambridge ice, which is white, but tastes of weeds. The purity men love is like the mists which envelop the earth, and not like the azure ether beyond.

Some are dinning in our ears that we Americans, and moderns generally, are intellectual dwarfs compared with the ancients, or even the Elizabethan men. But what is that to the purpose? A living dog is better than a dead lion. Shall a man go and hang himself because he belongs to the race of pygmies, and not be the biggest pygmy that he can? Let every one mind his own business, and endeavor to be what he was made.

Why should we be in such desperate haste to succeed, and in such desperate enterprises? If a man does not keep pace with his companions, perhaps it is because he hears a different drummer. Let him step to the music which he hears, however measured or far away. It is not important that he should mature as soon as an apple-tree or an oak. Shall he turn his spring into summer? If the condition of things which we were made for is not yet, what were any reality which we can substitute? We will not be shipwrecked on a vain reality. Shall we with pains erect a heaven of blue glass over ourselves, though when it is done we shall be sure to gaze still at the true ethereal heaven far above, as if the former were not?

There was an artist in the city of Kouroo[195] who was disposed to strive after perfection. One day it came into his mind to make a staff. Having considered that in an imperfect work time is an ingredient, but into a perfect work time does not enter, he said to himself, It shall be perfect in all respects, though I should do nothing else in my life. He proceeded instantly to the forest for wood, being resolved that it should not be made of unsuitable material; and as he searched for and rejected stick after stick, his friends gradually deserted him, for they grew old in their works and died, but he grew not older by a moment. His singleness of purpose and resolution, and his elevated piety, endowed him, without his knowledge, with perennial youth. As he made no compromise with Time, Time kept out of his way, and only sighed

---

[194] Hindu mystic.   [195] This fable is most likely Thoreau's fabrication.

at a distance because he could not overcome him. Before he had found a stock in all respects suitable the city of Kouroo was a hoary ruin, and he sat on one of its mounds to peel the stick. Before he had given it the proper shape the dynasty of the Candahars was at an end, and with the point of the stick he wrote the name of the last of that race in the sand, and then resumed his work. By the time he had smoothed and polished the staff Kalpa was no longer the pole-star; and ere he had put on the ferrule and the head adorned with precious stones, Brahma had awoke and slumbered many times. But why do I stay to mention these things? When the finishing stroke was put to his work, it suddenly expanded before the eyes of the astonished artist into the fairest of all the creations of Brahma. He had made a new system in making a staff, a world with full and fair proportions; in which, though the old cities and dynasties had passed away, fairer and more glorious ones had taken their places. And now he saw by the heap of shavings still fresh at his feet, that, for him and his work, the former lapse of time had been an illusion, and that no more time had elapsed than is required for a single scintillation from the brain of Brahma to fall on and inflame the tinder of a mortal brain. The material was pure, and his art was pure; how could the result be other than wonderful?

No face which we can give to a matter will stead us so well at last as the truth. This alone wears well. For the most part, we are not where we are, but in a false position. Through an infirmity of our natures, we suppose a case, and put ourselves into it, and hence are in two cases at the same time, and it is doubly difficult to get out. In sane moments we regard only the facts, the case that is. Say what you have to say, not what you ought. Any truth is better than make-believe. Tom Hyde, the tinker, standing on the gallows, was asked if he had any thing to say. "Tell the tailors," said he, "to remember to make a knot in their thread before they take the first stitch." His companion's prayer is forgotten.

However mean your life is, meet it and live it; do not shun it and call it hard names. It is not so bad as you are. It looks poorest when you are richest. The fault-finder will find faults even in paradise. Love your life, poor as it is. You may perhaps have some pleasant, thrilling, glorious hours, even in a poorhouse. The setting sun is reflected from the windows of the alms-house as brightly as from the rich man's abode; the snow melts before its door as early in the spring. I do not see but a quiet mind may live as contentedly there, and have as cheering thoughts, as in a palace. The town's poor seem to me often to live the most independent lives of any. May be they are simply great enough to receive without misgiving. Most think that they are above being supported by the town; but it oftener happens that they are not above supporting themselves by dishonest means, which should be more disreputable. Cultivate poverty like a garden herb, like sage. Do not trouble yourself much to get new things, whether clothes or friends. Turn the old; return to them. Things do not change; we change. Sell your clothes and keep your thoughts. God will see that you do not want society. If I were confined to a corner of a garret all my days, like a spider, the world would be just as large to me while I had my thoughts about me. The philosopher said: "From an army of three divisions one can take away its general, and put it in disorder; from the man the most abject and vulgar one cannot take away his thought." Do not seek so anxiously to be developed, to subject yourself to many influences to be played on; it is all dissipation. Humility like darkness reveals the heavenly lights. The shadows of poverty and meanness gather around us, "and lo! creation widens to our view." We are often reminded that if there were bestowed on us the wealth of Crœsus,[196] our aims must still be the same, and our means essentially the same. Moreover, if you are restricted in your range by poverty, if you cannot buy books and newspapers, for instance, you are but confined to the most significant and vital experiences; you are compelled to deal with the material which yields the most sugar and the most starch. It is life near the bone where it is sweetest. You are defended from being a trifler. No man loses ever on a lower level by magnanimity on a higher. Superfluous wealth can buy superfluities only. Money is not required to buy one necessary of the soul.

I live in the angle of a leaden wall, into whose composition was poured a little alloy of bell metal. Often, in the repose of my mid-day, there reaches my ears a confused *tintinnabulum* from without. It is the noise of my contemporaries. My neighbors tell me of their adventures with famous gentlemen and ladies, what notabilities they met at the dinner-table; but I am no more interested in such things than in the contents of the Daily Times. The interest and the conversation are about costume and manners chiefly; but a goose is a goose still, dress it as you will. They tell me of California and Texas, of England and the Indies, of the Hon. Mr. ———— of Georgia or of Massachusetts, all transient and fleeting phenomena, till I am ready to leap from their court-yard like the Mameluke bey.[197] I delight to come to my bearings, —not walk in procession with pomp and parade, in a conspicuous place, but to walk even with the Builder of the universe, if I may,—not to live in this restless, nervous, bustling, trivial Nineteenth Century, but stand or sit thoughtfully while it goes by. What are men celebrating? They are all on a committee of arrangements, and hourly expect a speech from somebody. God is only the president of the day, and Webster is his orator.[198] I love to weigh, to settle, to gravitate toward that which most strongly and rightfully attracts me;—not hang by the beam of the scale and try to weigh less, —not suppose a case, but take the case that is; to travel the only path I can, and that on which no power can resist me. It affords me no satisfaction to commence to spring an arch before I have got a solid foundation. Let us not play at kittly-benders.[199] There is a solid bottom every where. We read that the traveller asked the boy if the swamp before him had a hard bottom. The boy replied that it had. But presently the traveller's horse sank in up to the girths, and he observed to the boy, "I thought you said that this bog had a hard bottom." "So it has," answered the latter, "but you have not got half way to it yet." So it is with the bogs and quicksands of society; but he is an old boy that knows it. Only what is thought said or done at a certain rare coincidence is good. I would not be one of those who will foolishly drive a nail into mere lath and plastering; such a deed would keep me awake nights. Give me a hammer, and let me feel for the furring.[200] Do not depend on the putty. Drive a nail home and clinch it so faithfully that you can wake up in the night and think of your work with satisfaction,—a work at which you would not be ashamed to invoke the Muse. So will help you God, and so only. Every nail driven should be as another rivet in the machine of the universe, you carrying on the work.

[196] Legendary king who was accounted the wealthiest man of all time.

[197] The way one of the Mamelukes, a member of the Egyptian army clique, escaped being massacred in Cairo in 1811.

[198] Daniel Webster, a contemporary of Thoreau, was considered the foremost speaker on the American political scene.

[199] Running across thin ice.

[200] Wall studs.

Rather than love, than money, than fame, give me truth. I sat at a table where were rich food and wine in abundance, and obsequious attendance, but sincerity and truth were not; and I went away hungry from the inhospitable board. The hospitality was as cold as the ices. I thought that there was no need of ice to freeze them. They talked to me of the age of the wine and the fame of the vintage; but I thought of an older, a newer, and purer wine, of a more glorious vintage, which they had not got, and could not buy. The style, the house and grounds and "entertainment" pass for nothing with me. I called on the king, but he made me wait in his hall, and conducted like a man incapacitated for hospitality. There was a man in my neighborhood who lived in a hollow tree. His manners were truly regal. I should have done better had I called on him.

How long shall we sit in our porticoes practising idle and musty virtues, which any work would make impertinent? As if one were to begin the day with long-suffering, and hire a man to hoe his potatoes; and in the afternoon go forth to practise Christian meekness and charity with goodness aforethought! Consider the China pride and stagnant self-complacency of mankind. This generation reclines a little to congratulate itself on being the last of an illustrious line; and in Boston and London and Paris and Rome, thinking of its long descent, it speaks of its progress in art and science and literature with satisfaction. There are the Records of the Philosophical Societies, and the public Eulogies of *Great Men!* It is the good Adam contemplating his own virtue. "Yes, we have done great deeds, and sung divine songs, which shall never die," —that is, as long as *we* can remember them. The learned societies and great men of Assyria,—where are they? What youthful philosophers and experimentalists we are! There is not one of my readers who has yet lived a whole human life. These may be but the spring months in the life of the race. If we have had the seven-years' itch, we have not seen the seventeen-year locust yet in Concord. We are acquainted with a mere pellicle of the globe on which we live. Most have not delved six feet beneath the surface, nor leaped as many above it. We know not where we are. Beside, we are sound asleep nearly half our time. Yet we esteem ourselves wise, and have an established order on the surface. Truly, we are deep thinkers, we are ambitious spirits! As I stand over the insect crawling amid the pine needles on the forest floor, and endeavoring to conceal itself from my sight, and ask myself why it will cherish those humble thoughts, and hide its head from me who might perhaps be its benefactor, and impart to its race some cheering information, I am reminded of the greater Benefactor and Intelligence that stands over me the human insect.

There is an incessant influx of novelty into the world, and yet we tolerate incredible dulness. I need only suggest what kind of sermons are still listened to in the most enlightened countries. There are such words as joy and sorrow, but they are only the burden of a psalm, sung with a nasal twang, while we believe in the ordinary and mean. We think that we can change our clothes only. It is said that the British Empire is very large and respectable, and that the United States are a first-rate power. We do not believe that a tide rises and falls behind every man which can float the British Empire like a chip, if he should ever harbor it in his mind. Who knows what sort of seventeen-year locust will next come out of the ground? The government of the world I live in was not framed, like that of Britain, in after-dinner conversations over the wine.

The life in us is like the water in the river. It may rise this year higher than man has ever known it, and flood the parched uplands; even this may be the eventful year, which will drown out all our muskrats. It was not always dry land where we dwell. I see far inland the banks which the stream anciently washed, before science began to record its freshets. Every one has heard the story which has gone the rounds of New England, of a strong and beautiful bug which came out of the dry leaf of an old table of apple-tree wood, which had stood in a farmer's kitchen for sixty years, first in Connecticut, and afterward in Massachusetts,—from an egg deposited in the living tree many years earlier still, as appeared by counting the annual layers beyond it; which was heard gnawing out for several weeks, hatched perchance by the heat of an urn. Who does not feel his faith in a resurrection and immortality strengthened by hearing of this? Who knows what beautiful and winged life, whose egg has been buried for ages under many concentric layers of woodenness in the dead dry life of society, deposited at first in the alburnum of the green and living tree, which has been gradually converted into the semblance of its well-seasoned tomb,—heard perchance gnawing out now for years by the astonished family of man, as they sat round the festive board,—may unexpectedly come forth from amidst society's most trivial and handselled furniture, to enjoy its perfect summer life at last!

I do not say that John or Jonathan[201] will realize all this; but such is the character of that morrow which mere lapse of time can never make to dawn. The light which puts out our eyes is darkness to us. Only that day dawns to which we are awake. There is more day to dawn. The sun is but a morning star.

1846/1854

Resistance to Civil Government

I heartily accept the motto,—"That government is best which governs least;"[1] and I should like to see it acted up to more rapidly and systematically. Carried out, it finally amounts to this, which also I believe,—"That government is best which governs not at all;" and when men are prepared for it, that will be the kind of government which they will have. Government is at best but an expedient; but most governments are usually, and all governments are sometimes, inexpedient. The objections which have been brought against a standing army, and they are many and weighty, and deserve to prevail, may also at last be brought against a standing government. The standing army is only an arm of the standing government. The government itself, which is only the mode which the people have chosen to execute their will, is equally liable to be

[201] Common terms for a Britisher ("John Bull") and an American ("Brother Jonathan"), respectively.

[1] Motto displayed on the masthead of the *Democratic Review*, a New York journal which, with these words, continued to support a sentiment widely upheld from the time of Thomas Jefferson.

abused and perverted before the people can act through it. Witness the present Mexican war,[2] the work of comparatively a few individuals using the standing government as their tool; for, in the outset, the people would not have consented to this measure.

This American government,—what is it but a tradition, though a recent one, endeavoring to transmit itself unimpaired to posterity, but each instant losing some of its integrity? It has not the vitality and force of a single living man; for a single man can bend it to his will. It is a sort of wooden gun to the people themselves; and, if ever they should use it in earnest as a real one against each other, it will surely split. But it is not the less necessary for this; for the people must have some complicated machinery or other, and hear its din, to satisfy that idea of government which they have. Governments show thus how successfully men can be imposed on, even impose on themselves, for their own advantage. It is excellent, we must all allow; yet this government never of itself furthered any enterprise, but by the alacrity with which it got out of its way. *It* does not keep the country free. *It* does not settle the West. *It* does not educate. The character inherent in the American people has done all that has been accomplished; and it would have done somewhat more, if the government had not sometimes got in its way. For government is an expedient by which men would fain succeed in letting one another alone; and, as has been said, when it is most expedient, the governed are most let alone by it. Trade and commerce, if they were not made of India rubber, would never manage to bounce over the obstacles which legislators are continually putting in their way; and, if one were to judge these men wholly by the effects of their actions, and not partly by their intentions, they would deserve to be classed and punished with those mischievous persons who put obstructions on the railroads.

But, to speak practically and as a citizen, unlike those who call themselves no-government men, I ask for, not at once no government, but at *once* a better government. Let every man make known what kind of government would command his respect, and that will be one step toward obtaining it.

After all, the practical reason why, when the power is once in the hands of the people, a majority are permitted, and for a long period continue, to rule, is not because they are most likely to be in the right, nor because this seems fairest to the minority, but because they are physically the strongest. But a government in which the majority rule in all cases cannot be based on justice, even as far as men understand it. Can there not be a government in which majorities do not virtually decide right and wrong, but conscience?—in which majorities decide only those questions to which the rule of expediency is applicable? Must the citizen ever for a moment, or in the least degree, resign his conscience to the legislator? Why has every man a conscience, then? I think that we should be men first, and subjects afterward. It is not desirable to cultivate a respect for the law, so much as for the right. The only obligation which I have a right to assume, is to do at any time what I think right. It is truly enough said, that a

---

[2] Thoreau first delivered this essay in the form of a lecture on January 26, 1848, during the height of the controversy over the Mexican War (1846–1848), which was seen by many in the North as a plan by Southern slave owners to extend the slavery system to the West.

corporation has no conscience; but a corporation of conscientious men is a corporation *with* a conscience. Law never made men a whit more just; and, by means of their respect for it, even the well-disposed are daily made the agents of injustice. A common and natural result of an undue respect for law is, that you may see a file of soldiers, colonel, captain, corporal, privates, powder-monkeys and all, marching in admirable order over hill and dale to the wars, against their wills, aye, against their common sense and consciences, which makes it very steep marching indeed, and produces a palpitation of the heart. They have no doubt that it is a damnable business in which they are concerned; they are all peaceably inclined. Now, what are they? Men at all? or small moveable forts and magazines, at the service of some unscrupulous man in power? Visit the Navy Yard, and behold a marine, such a man an American government can make, or such as it can make a man with its black arts, a mere shadow and reminiscence of humanity, a man laid out alive and standing, and already, as one may say, buried under arms with funeral accompaniments, though it may be

"Not a drum was heard, not a funeral note,
    As his corse to the rampart we hurried;
Not a soldier discharged his farewell shot
    O'er the grave where our hero we buried."[3]

The mass of men serve the State thus, not as men mainly, but as machines, with their bodies. They are the standing army, and the militia, jailers, constables, *posse comitatus,*[4] &c. In most cases there is no free exercise whatever of the judgment or of the moral sense; but they put themselves on a level with wood and earth and stones, and wooden men can perhaps be manufactured that will serve the purpose as well. Such command no more respect than men of straw, or a lump of dirt. They have the same sort of worth only as horses and dogs. Yet such as these even are commonly esteemed good citizens. Others, as most legislators, politicians, lawyers, ministers, and officeholders, serve the State chiefly with their heads; and, as they rarely make any moral distinctions, they are as likely to serve the devil, without intending it, as God. A very few, as heroes, patriots, martyrs, reformers in the great sense, and *men,* serve the State with their consciences also, and so necessarily resist it for the most part; and they are commonly treated by it as enemies. A wise man will only be useful as a man, and will not submit to be "clay," and "stop a hole to keep the wind away,"[5] but leave that office to his dust at least:—

"I am too high-born to be propertied,
    To be a secondary at control,
    Or useful serving-man and instrument
    To any sovereign state throughout the world."[6]

<hr />

[3] Song based on "The Burial of Sir John Moore at Corunna" (1817) by Charles Wolfe (1791–1823).

[4] The Latin phrase from which the term "sheriff's posse" is derived.

[5] *Hamlet,* Act V, Sc. i, ll. 236–237.

[6] *King John,* Act V, Sc. ii, ll. 79–82.

He who gives himself entirely to his fellow-men appears to them useless and selfish; but he who gives himself partially to them is pronounced a benefactor and philanthropist.

How does it become a man to behave toward this American government to-day? I answer that he cannot without disgrace be associated with it. I cannot for an instant recognize that political organization as *my* government which is the *slave's* government also.

All men recognize the right of revolution; that is, the right to refuse allegiance to and to resist the government, when its tyranny or its inefficiency are great and unendurable. But almost all say that such is not the case now. But such was the case, they think, in the Revolution of '75.[7] If one were to tell me that this was a bad government because it taxed certain foreign commodities brought to its ports, it is most probable that I should not make an ado about it, for I can do without them: all machines have their friction; and possibly this does enough good to counterbalance the evil. At any rate, it is a great evil to make a stir about it. But when the friction comes to have its machine, and oppression and robbery are organized, I say, let us not have such a machine any longer. In other words, when a sixth of the population of a nation which has undertaken to be the refuge of liberty are slaves, and a whole country is unjustly overrun and conquered by a foreign army, and subjected to military law, I think that it is not too soon for honest men to rebel and revolutionize. What makes this duty the more urgent is the fact, that the country so overrun is not our own, but ours is the invading army.

Paley, a common authority with many on moral questions, in his chapter on the "Duty of Submission to Civil Government,"[8] resolves all civil obligation into expediency; and he proceeds to say, "that so long as the interest of the whole society requires it, that is, so long as the established government cannot be resisted or changed without public inconveniency, it is the will of God that the established government be obeyed, and no longer." . . . "This principle being admitted, the justice of every particular case of resistance is reduced to a computation of the quantity of the danger and grievance on the one side, and of the probability and expense of redressing it on the other." Of this, he says, every man shall judge for himself. But Paley appears never to have contemplated those cases to which the rule of expediency does not apply, in which a people, as well as an individual, must do justice, cost what it may. If I have unjustly wrested a plank from a drowning man, I must restore it to him though I drown myself. This, according to Paley, would be inconvenient. But he that would save his life, in such a case, shall lose it.[9] This people must cease to hold slaves, and to make war on Mexico, though it cost them their existence as a people.

In their practice, nations agree with Paley; but does any one think that Massachusetts does exactly what is right at the present crisis?

---

[7] The American Revolution (1775–1783).

[8] From *Principles of Moral and Political Philosophy* (1785) by William Paley (1743–1805), English theologian.

[9] Example of Thoreau's constant use of scriptural references; here, from Luke 9:24.

"A drab of state, a cloth-o'-silver slut,
   To have her train borne up, and her soul trail in the dirt."[10]

Practically speaking, the opponents to a reform in Massachusetts are not a hundred thousand politicians at the South, but a hundred thousand merchants and farmers here, who are more interested in commerce and agriculture than they are in humanity, and are not prepared to do justice to the slave and to Mexico, *cost what it may*. I quarrel not with far-off foes, but with those who, near at home, co-operate with, and do the bidding of those far away, and without whom the latter would be harmless. We are accustomed to say, that the mass of men are unprepared; but improvement is slow, because the few are not materially wiser or better than the many. It is not so important that many should be as good as you, as that there be some absolute goodness somewhere; for that will leaven the whole lump.[11] There are thousands who are *in opinion* opposed to slavery and to the war, who yet in effect do nothing to put an end to them; who, esteeming themselves children of Washington and Franklin, sit down with their hands in their pockets, and say that they know not what to do, and do nothing; who even postpone the question of freedom to the question of free-trade, and quietly read the prices-current along with the latest advices[12] from Mexico, after dinner, and, it may be, fall asleep over them both. What is the price-current of an honest man and patriot to-day? They hesitate, and they regret, and sometimes they petition; but they do nothing in earnest and with effect. They will wait, well-disposed, for others to remedy the evil, that they may no longer have it to regret. At most, they give only a cheap vote, and a feeble countenance and God-speed, to the right, as it goes by them. There are nine hundred and ninety-nine patrons of virtue to one virtuous man; but it is easier to deal with the real possessor of a thing than with the temporary guardian of it.

All voting is a sort of gaming, like chequers or backgammon, with a slight moral tinge to it, a playing with right and wrong, with moral questions; and betting naturally accompanies it. The character of the voters is not staked. I cast my vote, perchance, as I think right; but I am not vitally concerned that that right should prevail. I am willing to leave it to the majority. Its obligation, therefore, never exceeds that of expediency. Even voting *for the right* is *doing* nothing for it. It is only expressing to men feebly your desire that it should prevail. A wise man will not leave the right to the mercy of chance, nor wish it to prevail through the power of the majority. There is but little virtue in the action of masses of men. When the majority shall at length vote for the abolition of slavery, it will be because they are indifferent to slavery, or because there is but little slavery left to be abolished by their vote. *They* will then be the only slaves. Only *his* vote can hasten the abolition of slavery who asserts his own freedom by his vote.

I hear of a convention to be held at Baltimore, or elsewhere, for the selection of a candidate for the Presidency, made up chiefly of editors, and men who are politicians by profession; but I think, what is it to any independent, intelligent, and respectable man what decision they may come to, shall we not have the advantage

---

[10] *The Revenger's Tragedy* (1607), Act IV, Sc. iv, ll. 70–72, attributed to Cyril Tourneur (1575?–1629).

[11] Paraphrase of 1 Corinthians 5:6.
[12] News dispatches.

of his wisdom and honesty, nevertheless? Can we not count upon some independent votes? Are there not many individuals in the country who do not attend conventions? But no: I find that the respectable man, so called, has immediately drifted from his position, and despairs of his country, when his country has more reason to despair of him. He forthwith adopts one of the candidates thus selected as the only *available* one, thus proving that he is himself *available* for any purposes of the demagogue. His vote is of no more worth than that of any unprincipled foreigner or hireling native, who may have been bought. Oh for a man who is a *man,* and, as my neighbor says, has a bone in his back which you cannot pass your hand through! Our statistics are at fault: the population has been returned too large. How many *men* are there to a square thousand miles in this country? Hardly one. Does not America offer any inducement for men to settle here? The American has dwindled into an Odd Fellow,[13]—one who may be known by the development of his organ of gregariousness,[14] and a manifest lack of intellect and cheerful self-reliance; whose first and chief concern, on coming into the world, is to see that the almshouses are in good repair; and, before yet he has lawfully donned the virile garb,[15] to collect a fund for the support of the widows and orphans that may be; who, in short, ventures to live only by the aid of the mutual insurance company, which has promised to bury him decently.

It is not a man's duty, as a matter of course, to devote himself to the eradication of any, even the most enormous wrong; he may still properly have other concerns to engage him; but it is his duty, at least, to wash his hands of it, and, if he gives it no thought longer, not to give it practically his support. If I devote myself to other pursuits and contemplations, I must first see, at least, that I do not pursue them sitting upon another man's shoulders. I must get off him first, that he may pursue his contemplations too. See what gross inconsistency is tolerated. I have heard some of my townsmen say, "I should like to have them order me out to help put down an insurrection of the slaves, or to march to Mexico,—see if I would go;" and yet these very men have each, directly by their allegiance, and so indirectly, at least, by their money, furnished a substitute. The soldier is applauded who refuses to serve in an unjust war by those who do not refuse to sustain the unjust government which makes the war; is applauded by those whose own act and authority he disregards and sets at nought; as if the State were penitent to that degree that it hired one to scourge it while it sinned, but not to that degree that it left off sinning for a moment. Thus, under the name of order and civil government, we are all made at last to pay homage to and support our own meanness. After the first blush of sin, comes its indifference and from immoral it becomes, as it were, *un*moral, and not quite unnecessary to that life which we have made.

The broadest and most prevalent error requires the most disinterested virtue to sustain it. The slight reproach to which the virtue of patriotism is commonly liable, the noble are most likely to incur. Those who, while they disapprove of the character and measures of a government, yield to it their allegiance and support, are undoubt-

---

[13] Satiric reference to members of a secret fraternal society, the Independent Order of Odd Fellows, as part of Thoreau's argument that most Americans had fallen away from independent self-sufficiency into conformism.

[14] Phrenological term applied to persons who prefer belonging to the group.

[15] Attire that acknowledged that a Roman boy had attained adulthood.

edly its most conscientious supporters, and so frequently the most serious obstacles to reform. Some are petitioning the State to dissolve the Union, to disregard the requisitions of the President.[16] Why do they not dissolve it themselves,—the union between themselves and the State,—and refuse to pay their quota into its treasury? Do not they stand in the same relation to the State, that the State does to the Union? And have not the same reasons prevented the State from resisting the Union, which have prevented them from resisting the State?

How can a man be satisfied to entertain an opinion merely, and enjoy *it?* Is there any enjoyment in it, if his opinion is that he is aggrieved? If you are cheated out of a single dollar by your neighbor, you do not rest satisfied with knowing that you are cheated, or with saying that you are cheated, or even with petitioning him to pay you your due; but you take effectual steps at once to obtain the full amount, and see that you are never cheated again. Action from principle,—the perception and the performance of right,—changes things and relations; it is essentially revolutionary, and does not consist wholly with any thing which was. It not only divides states and churches, it divides families; aye, it divides the *individual,* separating the diabolical in him from the divine.

Unjust laws exist: shall we be content to obey them, or shall we endeavor to amend them, and obey them until we have succeeded, or shall we transgress them at once? Men generally, under such a government as this, think that they ought to wait until they have persuaded the majority to alter them. They think that, if they should resist, the remedy would be worse than the evil. But it is the fault of the government itself that the remedy *is* worse than the evil. *It* makes it worse. Why is it not more apt to anticipate and provide for reform? Why does it not cherish its wise minority? Why does it cry and resist before it is hurt? Why does it not encourage its citizens to be on the alert to point out its faults, and *do* better than it would have them? Why does it always crucify Christ, and excommunicate Copernicus and Luther,[17] and pronounce Washington and Franklin rebels?

One would think, that a deliberate and practical denial of its authority was the only offence never contemplated by government; else, why has it not assigned its definite, its suitable and proportionate penalty? If a man who has no property refuses but once to earn nine shillings[18] for the State, he is put in prison for a period unlimited by any law that I know, and determined only by the discretion of those who placed him there; but if he should steal ninety times nine shillings from the State, he is soon permitted to go at large again.

If the injustice is part of the necessary friction of the machine of government, let it go, let it go: perchance it will wear smooth,—certainly the machine will wear out. If the injustice has a spring, or a pulley, or a rope, or a crank, exclusively for itself, then perhaps you may consider whether the remedy will not be worse than the evil; but if it is of such a nature that it requires you to be the agent of injustice to another,

[16] President James K. Polk sought money and troops for the Mexican conflict over the objections of certain New England radicals who proposed breaking away from the Union in order to further their aims as abolitionists.
[17] Both the Polish astronomer Copernicus (1473–1543) and the German head of the Protestant reformation, Martin Luther (1483–1546), were considered heretics by the Roman church. The former in fact died before he could be excommunicated.
[18] The amount of some $2, which Thoreau refused to pay in taxes.

then, I say, break the law. Let your life be a counter friction to stop the machine. What I have to do is to see, at any rate, that I do not lend myself to the wrong which I condemn.

As for adopting the ways which the State has provided for remedying the evil, I know not of such ways. They take too much time, and a man's life will be gone. I have other affairs to attend to. I came into this world, not chiefly to make this a good place to live in, but to live in it, be it good or bad. A man has not every thing to do, but something; and because he cannot do *every thing,* it is not necessary that he should do *something* wrong. It is not my business to be petitioning the governor or the legislature any more than it is theirs to petition me; and, if they should not hear my petition, what should I do then? But in this case the State has provided no way: its very Constitution is the evil. This may seem to be harsh and stubborn and unconciliatory; but it is to treat with the utmost kindness and consideration the only spirit that can appreciate or deserves it. So is all change for the better, like birth and death which convulse the body.

I do not hesitate to say, that those who call themselves abolitionists should at once effectually withdraw their support, both in person and property, from the government of Massachusetts, and not wait till they constitute a majority of one, before they suffer the right to prevail through them. I think that it is enough if they have God on their side, without waiting for that other one. Moreover, any man more right than his neighbors, constitutes a majority of one already.

I meet this American government, or its representative the State government, directly, and face to face, once a year, no more, in the person of its tax-gatherer; this is the only mode in which a man situated as I am necessarily meets it; and it then says distinctly, Recognize me; and the simplest, the most effectual, and, in the present posture of affairs, the indispensablest mode of treating with it on this head, of expressing your little satisfaction with and love for it, is to deny it then. My civil neighbor, the tax-gatherer, is the very man I have to deal with,—for it is, after all, with men and not with parchment that I quarrel,—and he has voluntarily chosen to be an agent of the government. How shall he ever know well what he is and does as an officer of the government, or as a man, until he is obliged to consider whether he shall treat me, his neighbor, for whom he has respect, as a neighbor and well-disposed man, or as a maniac and disturber of the peace, and see if he can get over this obstruction to his neighborliness without a ruder and more impetuous thought or speech corresponding with his action? I know this well, that if one thousand, if one hundred, if ten men whom I could name,—if ten *honest* men only,—aye, if *one* HONEST man, in this State of Massachusetts, *ceasing to hold slaves,* were actually to withdraw from this copartnership, and be locked up in the county jail therefor, it would be the abolition of slavery in America. For it matters not how small the beginning may seem to be: what is once well done is done for ever. But we love better to talk about it: that we say is our mission. Reform keeps many scores of newspapers in its service, but not one man. If my esteemed neighbor, the State's ambassador,[19] who

---

[19] Samuel Hoar (1778–1856) of Concord was sent by the State of Massachusetts (which he represented as senator) to South Carolina in an attempt to aid black sailors who had been taken from Massachusetts ships in Southern ports. His efforts were frustrated when he was expelled from Charleston by legal action.

will devote his days to the settlement of the question of human rights in the Council Chamber, instead of being threatened with the prisons of Carolina, were to sit down the prisoner of Massachusetts, that State which is so anxious to foist the sin of slavery upon her sister,—though at present she can discover only an act of inhospitality to be the ground of a quarrel with her,—the Legislature would not wholly waive the subject the following winter.

Under a government which imprisons any unjustly, the true place for a just man is also a prison. The proper place to-day, the only place which Massachusetts has provided for her freer and less desponding spirits, is in her prisons, to be put out and locked out of the State by her own act, as they have already put themselves out by their principles. It is there that the fugitive slave, and the Mexican prisoner on parole, and the Indian come to plead the wrongs of his race, should find them; on that separate, but more free and honorable ground, where the State places those who are not *with* her but *against* her,—the only house in a slave-state in which a free man can abide with honor. If any think that their influence would be lost there, and their voices no longer afflict the ear of the State, that they would not be as an enemy within its walls, they do not know by how much truth is stronger than error, nor how much more eloquently and effectively he can combat injustice who has experienced a little in his own person. Cast your whole vote, not a strip of paper merely, but your whole influence. A minority is powerless while it conforms to the majority; it is not even a minority then; but it is irresistible when it clogs by its whole weight. If the alternative is to keep all just men in prison, or give up war and slavery, the State will not hesitate which to choose. If a thousand men were not to pay their tax-bills this year, that would not be a violent and bloody measure, as it would be to pay them, and enable the State to commit violence and shed innocent blood. This is, in fact, the definition of a peaceable revolution, if any such is possible. If the tax-gatherer, or any other public officer, asks me, as one has done, "But what shall I do?" my answer is, "If you really wish to do any thing, resign your office." When the subject has refused allegiance, and the officer has resigned his office, then the revolution is accomplished. But even suppose blood should flow. Is there not a sort of blood shed when the conscience is wounded? Through this wound a man's real manhood and immortality flow out, and he bleeds to an everlasting death. I see this blood flowing now.

I have contemplated the imprisonment of the offender, rather than the seizure of his goods,—though both will serve the same purpose,—because they who assert the purest right, and consequently are most dangerous to a corrupt State, commonly have not spent much time in accumulating property. To such the State renders comparatively small service, and a slight tax is wont to appear exorbitant, particularly if they are obliged to earn it by special labor with their hands. If there were one who lived wholly without the use of money, the State itself would hesitate to demand it of him. But the rich man—not to make any invidious comparison—is always sold to the institution which makes him rich. Absolutely speaking, the more money, the less virtue; for money comes between a man and his objects, and obtains them for him; and it was certainly no great virtue to obtain it. It puts to rest many questions which he would otherwise be taxed to answer; while the only new question which it puts is the hard but superfluous one, how to spend it. Thus his moral ground is taken from under his feet. The opportunities of living are diminished in proportion as what are called the "means" are increased. The best thing a man can do for his culture when he is rich is to endeavour to carry out those schemes which he entertained when he was poor. Christ answered the Herodians according to their condition. "Show me the tribute-money," said he;—and one took a penny out of his pocket;—If you use money which has the image of Cæsar on it, and which he has made current and valuable, that is, *if you are men of the State,* and gladly enjoy the advantages of Cæsar's government, then pay him back some of his own when he demands it; "Render therefore to Cæsar that which is Cæsar's, and to God those things which are God's,"[20] —leaving them no wiser than before as to which was which; for they did not wish to know.

When I converse with the freest of my neighbors, I perceive that, whatever they may say about the magnitude and seriousness of the question, and their regard for the public tranquillity, the long and the short of the matter is, that they cannot spare the protection of the existing government, and they dread the consequences of disobedience to it to their property and families. For my own part, I should not like to think that I ever rely on the protection of the State. But, if I deny the authority of the State when it presents its tax-bill, it will soon take and waste all my property, and so harass me and my children without end. This is hard. This makes it impossible for a man to live honestly and at the same time comfortably in outward respects. It will not be worth the while to accumulate property; that would be sure to go again. You must hire or squat somewhere, and raise but a small crop, and eat that soon. You must live within yourself, and depend upon yourself, always tucked up and ready for a start, and not have many affairs. A man may grow rich in Turkey even, if he will be in all respects a good subject of the Turkish government. Confucius said.—"If a State is governed by the principles of reason, poverty and misery are subjects of shame; if a State is not governed by the principles of reason, riches and honors are the subjects of shame."[21] No: until I want the protection of Massachusetts to be extended to me in some distant southern port, where my liberty is endangered, or until I am bent solely on building up an estate at home by peaceful enterprise, I can afford to refuse allegiance to Massachusetts, and her right to my property and life. It costs me less in every sense to incur the penalty of disobedience to the State, than it would to obey. I should feel as if I were worth less in that case.

Some years ago, the State met me in behalf of the church, and commanded me to pay a certain sum toward the support of a clergyman whose preaching my father attended, but never I myself. "Pay it," it said, "or be locked up in the jail." I declined to pay. But, unfortunately, another man saw fit to pay it. I did not see why the schoolmaster should be taxed to support the priest, and not the priest the schoolmaster; for I was not the State's schoolmaster, but I supported myself by voluntary subscription. I did not see why the lyceum should not present its tax-bill, and have the State to back its demand, as well as the church. However, at the request of the selectmen, I condescended to make some such statement as this in writing:—"Know all men by these presents, that I, Henry Thoreau, do not wish to be regarded as a member of any incorporated society which I have not joined." This I gave to the town-clerk; and he has it. The State, having thus learned that I did not wish to be regarded as a member

[20] See Matthew 22:16–22.
[21] From *The Analects* by the Chinese philosopher Confucius (ca. 551–479 B.C.).

of that church, has never made a like demand on me since; though it said that it must adhere to its original presumption that time. If I had known how to name them, I should then have signed off in detail from all the societies which I never signed on to; but I did not know where to find a complete list.

I have paid no poll-tax for six years. I was put into a jail once on this account, for one night;[22] and, as I stood considering the walls of solid stone, two or three feet thick, the door of wood and iron, a foot thick, and the iron grating which strained the light, I could not help being struck with the foolishness of that institution which treated me as if I were mere flesh and blood and bones, to be locked up. I wondered that it should have concluded at length that this was the best use it could put me to, and had never thought to avail itself of my services in some way. I saw that, if there was a wall of stone between me and my townsmen, there was a still more difficult one to climb or break through, before they could get to be as free as I was. I did not for a moment feel confined, and the walls seemed a great waste of stone and mortar. I felt as if I alone of all my townsmen had paid my tax. They plainly did not know how to treat me, but behaved like persons who are underbred. In every threat and in every compliment there was a blunder; for they thought that my chief desire was to stand the other side of that stone wall. I could not but smile to see how industriously they locked the door on my meditations, which followed them out again without let or hinderance, and *they* were really all that was dangerous. As they could not reach me, they had resolved to punish my body; just as boys, if they cannot come at some person against whom they have a spite, will abuse his dog. I saw that the State was half-witted, that it was timid as a lone woman with her silver spoons, and that it did not know its friends from its foes, and I lost all my remaining respect for it, and pitied it.

Thus the State never intentionally confronts a man's sense, intellectual or moral, but only his body, his senses. It is not armed with superior wit or honesty, but with superior physical strength. I was not born to be forced. I will breathe after my own fashion. Let us see who is the strongest. What force has a multitude? They only can force me who obey a higher law than I. They force me to become like themselves. I do not hear of *men* being *forced* to live this way or that by masses of men. What sort of life were that to live? When I meet a government which says to me, "Your money or your life," why should I be in haste to give it my money? It may be in a great strait, and not know what to do: I cannot help that. It must help itself; do as I do. It is not worth the while to snivel about it. I am not responsible for the successful working of the machinery of society. I am not the son of the engineer. I perceive that, when an acorn and a chestnut fall side by side, the one does not remain inert to make way for the other, but both obey their own laws, and spring and grow and flourish as best they can, till one, perchance, overshadows and destroys the other. If a plant cannot live according to its nature, it dies; and so a man.

The night in prison was novel and interesting enough. The prisoners in their shirt-sleeves were enjoying a chat and the evening air in the door-way, when I entered. But the jailer said, "Come, boys, it is time to lock up;" and so they dispersed, and I heard the sound of their steps returning into the hollow

[22] July 23 or 24, 1846.

apartments. My roommate was introduced to me by the jailer, as "a first-rate fellow and a clever[23] man." When the door was locked, he showed me where to hang my hat, and how he managed matters there. The rooms were white-washed once a month; and this one, at least, was the whitest, most simply furnished, and probably the neatest apartment in the town. He naturally wanted to know where I came from, and what brought me there; and, when I had told him, I asked him in my turn how he came there, presuming him to be an honest man, of course; and, as the world goes, I believe he was. "Why," said he, "they accuse me of burning a barn; but I never did it." As near as I could discover, he had probably gone to bed in a barn when drunk, and smoked his pipe there; and so a barn was burnt. He had the reputation of being a clever man, had been there some three months waiting for his trial to come on, and would have to wait as much longer; but he was quite domesticated and contented, since he got his board for nothing, and thought that he was well treated.

He occupied one window, and I the other; and I saw, that, if one stayed there long, his principal business would be to look out the window. I had soon read all the tracts that were left there, and examined where former prisoners had broken out, and where a grate had been sawed off, and heard the history of the various occupants of that room; for I found that even here there was a history and a gossip which never circulated beyond the walls of the jail. Probably this is the only house in the town where verses are composed, which are afterward printed in a circular form, but not published. I was shown quite a long list of verses which were composed by some young men who had been detected in a attempt to escape, who avenged themselves by singing them.

I pumped my fellow-prisoner as dry as I could, for fear I should never see him again; but at length he showed me which was my bed, and left me to blow out the lamp.

It was like travelling into a far country, such as I had never expected to behold, to lie there for one night. It seemed to me that I never had heard the town-clock strike before, nor the evening sounds of the village; for we slept with the windows open, which were inside the grating. It was to see my native village in the light of the middle ages, and our Concord was turned into a Rhine stream, and visions of knights and castles passed before me. They were the voices of old burghers that I heard in the streets. I was an involuntary spectator and auditor of whatever was done and said in the kitchen of the adjacent village-inn, —a wholly new and rare experience to me. It was a closer view of my native town. I was fairly inside of it. I never had seen its institutions before. This is one of its peculiar institutions; for it is a shire town.[24] I began to comprehend what its inhabitants were about.

In the morning, our breakfasts were put through the hole in the door, in small oblong-square tin pans, made to fit, and holding a pint of chocolate, with brown bread, and an iron spoon. When they called for the vessels again, I was green enough to return what bread I had left; but my comrade seized it, and said that I should lay that up for lunch or dinner. Soon after, he was let out to work at haying in a neighboring field, whither he went every day, and would not

[23] Honest.   [24] Country seat.

be back till noon; so he bade me good-day, saying that he doubted if he should seen me again.

When I came out of prison,—for some one interfered, and paid the tax,— I did not perceive that great changes had taken place on the common, such as he observed who went in a youth, and emerged a tottering and grayheaded man; and yet a change had to my eyes come over the scene,—the town, and State, and country,—greater than any that mere time could effect. I saw yet more distinctly the State in which I lived. I saw to what extent the people among whom I lived could be trusted as good neighbors and friends; that their friendship was for summer weather only; that they did not greatly purpose to do right; that they were a distinct race from me by their prejudices and superstitions, as the Chinamen and Malays are; that, in their sacrifices to humanity, they ran no risks, not even to their property; that, after all, they were not so noble but they treated the thief as he had treated them, and hoped, by a certain outward observance and a few prayers, and by walking in a particular straight though useless path from time to time, to save their souls. This may be to judge my neighbors harshly; for I believe that most of them are not aware that they have such an institution as the jail in their village.

It was formerly the custom in our village, when a poor debtor came out of jail, for his acquaintances to salute him, looking through their fingers, which were crossed to represent the grating of a jail window, "How do ye do?" My neighbors did not thus salute me, but first looked at me, and then at one another, as if I had returned from a long journey. I was put into jail as I was going to the shoemaker's to get a shoe which was mended. When I was let out the next morning, I proceeded to finish my errand, and, having put on my mended shoe, joined a huckleberry party, who were impatient to put themselves under my conduct; and in half an hour,—for the horse was soon tackled,—was in the midst of a huckleberry field, on one of our highest hills, two miles off; and then the State was nowhere to be seen.

This is the whole history of "My Prisons."[25]

I have never declined paying the highway tax, because I am as desirous of being a good neighbor as I am of being a bad subject; and, as for supporting schools, I am doing my part to educate my fellow-countrymen now. It is for no particular item in the tax-bill that I refuse to pay it. I simply wish to refuse allegiance to the State, to withdraw and stand aloof from it effectually. I do not care to trace the course of my dollar, if I could, till it buys a man, or a musket to shoot one with,—the dollar is innocent,—but I am concerned to trace the effects of my allegiance. In fact, I quietly declare war with the State, after my fashion, though I will still make what use and get what advantage of her I can, as is usual in such cases.

If others pay the tax which is demanded of me, from a sympathy with the State, they do but what they have already done in their own case, or rather they abet injustice to a greater extent than the State requires. If they pay the tax from a mistaken interest

[25] Reference to a book of that title published in 1832 by Silvio Pellico, an Italian poet imprisoned by the Austrians for his revolutionary activities against their occupation of Italy.

in the individual taxed, to save his property or prevent his going to jail, it is because they have not considered wisely how far they let their private feelings interfere with the public good.

This, then, is my position at present. But one cannot be too much on his guard in such a case, lest his action be biassed by obstinacy, or an undue regard for the opinions of men. Let him see that he does only what belongs to himself and to the hour.

I think sometimes, Why, this people mean well; they are only ignorant; they would do better if they knew how: why give your neighbors this pain to treat you as they are not inclined to? But I think, again, this is no reason why I should do as they do, or permit others to suffer much greater pain of a different kind. Again, I sometimes say to myself, When many millions of men, without heat, without ill-will, without personal feeling of any kind, demand of you a few shillings only, without the possibility, such is their constitution, of retracting or altering their present demand, and without the possibility, on your side, of appeal to any other millions, why expose yourself to this overwhelming brute force? You do not resist cold and hunger, the winds and the waves, thus obstinately; you quietly submit to a thousand similar necessities. You do not put your head into the fire. But just in proportion as I regard this as not wholly a brute force, but partly a human force, and consider that I have relations to those millions as to so many millions of men, and not of mere brute or inanimate things, I see that appeal is possible, first and instantaneously, from them to the Maker of them, and, secondly, from them to themselves. But, if I put my head deliberately into the fire, there is no appeal to fire or to the Maker of fire, and I have only myself to blame. If I could convince myself that I have any right to be satisfied with men as they are, and to treat them accordingly, and not according, in some respects, to my requisitions and expectations of what they and I ought to be, then, like a good Mussulman[26] and fatalist, I should endeavor to be satisfied with things as they are, and say it is the will of God. And, above all, there is this difference between resisting this and a purely brute or natural force, that I can resist this with some effect; but I cannot expect, like Orpheus,[27] to change the nature of the rocks and trees and beasts.

I do not wish to quarrel with any man or nation. I do not wish to split hairs, to make fine distinctions, or set myself up as better than my neighbors. I seek rather, I may say, even an excuse for conforming to the laws of the land. I am but too ready to conform to them. Indeed I have reason to suspect myself on this head; and each year, as the tax-gatherer comes round, I find myself disposed to review the acts and position of the general and state governments, and the spirit of the people, to discover a pretext for conformity. I believe that the State will soon be able to take all my work of this sort out of my hands, and then I shall be no better a patriot than my fellow-countrymen. Seen from a lower point of view, the Constitution, with all its faults, is very good; the law and the courts are very respectable; even this State and this American government are, in many respects, very admirable and rare things, to be thankful for, such as a great many have described them; but seen from a point of view a little higher, they are what I have described them; seen from a higher still,

[26] Mohammedan
[27] The poet-musician of classic myth whose powers of song were so great that he could throw a spell over beasts and natural objects.

and the highest, who shall say what they are, or that they are worth looking at or thinking of at all?

However, the government does not concern me much, and I shall bestow the fewest possible thoughts on it. It is not many moments that I live under a government, even in this world. If a man is thought-free, fancy-free, imagination-free, that which is *not* never for a long time appearing *to be* to him, unwise rulers or reformers cannot fatally interrupt him.

I know that most men think differently from myself; but those whose lives are by profession devoted to the study of these or kindred subjects, content me as little as any. Statesmen and legislators, standing so completely within the institution, never distinctly and nakedly behold it. They speak of moving society; but have no resting-place without it. They may be men of a certain experience and discrimination, and have no doubt invented ingenious and even useful systems, for which we sincerely thank them; but all their wit and usefulness lie within certain not very wide limits. They are wont to forget that the world is not governed by policy and expediency. Webster[28] never goes behind government, and so cannot speak with authority about it. His words are wisdom to those legislators who contemplate no essential reform in the existing government; but for thinkers, and those who legislate for all time, he never once glances at the subject. I know of those whose serene and wise speculations on this theme would soon reveal the limits of his mind's range and hospitality. Yet, compared with the cheap professions of most reformers, and the still cheaper wisdom and eloquence of politicians in general, his are almost the only sensible and valuable words, and we thank Heaven for him. Comparatively, he is always strong, original, and, above all, practical. Still his quality is not wisdom, but prudence. The lawyer's truth is not Truth, but consistency, or a consistent expediency. Truth is always in harmony with herself, and is not concerned chiefly to reveal the justice that may consist with wrong-doing. He well deserves to be called, as he has been called, the Defender of the Constitution. There are really no blows to be given by him but defensive ones. He is not a leader, but a follower. His leaders are the men of '87.[29] "I have never made an effort," he says, "and never propose to make an effort; I have never countenanced an effort, and never mean to countenance an effort, to disturb the arrangement as originally made, by which the various States came into the Union."[30] Still thinking of the sanction which the Constitution gives to slavery, he says, "Because it was a part of the original compact, —let it stand." Notwithstanding his special acuteness and ability, he is unable to take a fact out of its merely political relations, and behold it as it lies absolutely to be disposed of by the intellect,—what, for instance, it behoves a man to do here in America to-day with regard to slavery,—but ventures, or is driven, to make some such desperate answer as the following, while professing to speak absolutely, and as a private man,—from which what new and singular code of social duties might be inferred?—"The manner," says he, "in which the governments of those States where

[28] Daniel Webster (1782–1852), influential senator from Massachusetts who was felt by the abolitionists to be a betrayer of their principles when he supported the Fugitive Slave Law, which made it possible to return slaves who had escaped to the North to their Southern masters.

[29] Drafters of the Constitution in 1787.
[30] Both here and below, lines quoted from speeches delivered by Webster in 1845 and 1848. These extracts were added by Thoreau after he gave his lecture, a fact he noted when preparing the printed text of his essay.

slavery exists are to regulate it, is for their own consideration, under their responsibility to their constituents, to the general laws of propriety, humanity, and justice, and to God. Associations formed elsewhere, springing from a feeling of humanity, or any other cause, have nothing whatever to do with it. They have never received any encouragement from me, and they never will."

They who know of no purer sources of truth, who have traced up its stream no higher, stand, and wisely stand, by the Bible and the Constitution, and drink at it there with reverence and humility; but they who behold where it comes trickling into this lake or that pool, gird up their loins once more, and continue their pilgrimage toward its fountain-head.

No man with a genius for legislation has appeared in America. They are rare in the history of the world. There are orators, politicians, and eloquent men, by the thousand; but the speaker has not yet opened his mouth to speak, who is capable of settling the much-vexed questions of the day. We love eloquence for its own sake, and not for any truth which it may utter, or any heroism it may inspire. Our legislators have not yet learned the comparative value of free-trade and of freedom, of union, and of rectitude, to a nation. They have no genius or talent for comparatively humble questions of taxation and finance, commerce and manufactures and agriculture. If we were left solely to the wordy wit of legislators in Congress for our guidance, uncorrected by the seasonable experience and the effectual complaints of the people, America would not long retain her rank among the nations. For eighteen hundred years, though perchance I have no right to say it, the New Testament has been written; yet where is the legislator who has wisdom and practical talent enough to avail himself of the light which it sheds on the science of legislation?

The authority of government, even such as I am willing to submit to,—for I will cheerfully obey those who know and can do better than I, and in many things even those who neither know nor can do so well,—is still an impure one: to be strictly just, it must have the sanction and consent of the governed. It can have no pure right over my person and property but what I concede to it. The progress from an absolute to a limited monarchy, from a limited monarchy to a democracy, is a progress toward a true respect for the individual. Is a democracy, such as we know it, the last improvement possible in government? Is it not possible to take a step further towards recognizing and organizing the rights of man? There will never be a really free and enlightened State, until the State comes to recognize the individual as a higher and independent power, from which all its own power and authority are derived, and treats him accordingly. I please myself with imagining a State at last which can afford to be just to all men, and to treat the individual with respect as a neighbor; which even would not think it inconsistent with its own repose, if a few were to live aloof from it, not meddling with it, nor embraced by it, who fulfilled all the duties of neighbors and fellow-men. A State which bore this kind of fruit, and suffered it to drop off as fast as it ripened, would prepare the way for a still more perfect and glorious State, which also I have imagined, but not yet anywhere seen.

1849

from The Journal

[April 4, 1839]

April 4. The atmosphere of morning gives a healthy hue to our prospects. Disease is a sluggard that overtakes, never encounters, us. We have the start each day, and may fairly distance him before the dew is off; but if we recline in the bowers of noon, he will come up with us after all. The morning dew breeds no cold. We enjoy a diurnal reprieve in the beginning of each day's creation. In the morning we do not believe in expediency; we will start afresh, and have no patching, no temporary fixtures. The afternoon man has an interest in the past; his eye is divided, and he sees indifferently well either way.

Drifting in a sultry day on the sluggish waters of the pond, I almost cease to live and begin to be. A boatman stretched on the deck of his craft and dallying with the noon would be as apt an emblem of eternity for me as the serpent with his tail in his mouth. I am never so prone to lose my identity. I am dissolved in the haze.

[November 13, 1839]

Nov. 13. Make the most of your regrets; never smother your sorrow, but tend and cherish it till it comes to have a separate and integral interest. To regret deeply is to live afresh. By so doing you will be astonished to find yourself restored once more to all your emoluments.

[November 14, 1839]

Nov. 14. There is nowhere any apology for despondency. Always there is life which, rightly lived, implies a divine satisfaction. I am soothed by the rain-drops on the door-sill; every globule that pitches thus confidently from the eaves to the ground is my life insurance. Disease and a rain-drop cannot coexist. The east wind is not itself consumptive, but has enjoyed a rare health from of old. If a fork or brand stand erect, *good* is portended by it. They are the warrant of universal innocence.

[from March 21, 1840]*

March 21. The world is a fit theatre to-day in which any part may be acted. There is this moment proposed to me every kind of life that men lead anywhere, or that imagination can paint. By another spring I may be a mail-carrier in Peru, or a South African planter, or a Siberian exile, or a Greenland whaler, or a settler on the Columbia River, or a Canton merchant, or a soldier in Florida, or a mackerel-fisher off Cape Sable, or a Robinson Crusoe[1] in the Pacific, or a silent navigator of any sea. So wide is the choice of parts, what a pity if the part of Hamlet be left out!

I am freer than any planet; no complaint reaches round the world. I can move away

---

[1] Shipwrecked hero of Daniel Defoe's novel (1719). (Cape Sable is in Nova Scotia.)

from public opinion, from government, from religion, from education, from society. Shall I be reckoned a ratable poll[2] in the county of Middlesex, or be rated at one spear under the palm trees of Guinea? Shall I raise corn and potatoes in Massachusetts, or figs and olives in Asia Minor? sit out the day in my office in State Street, or ride it out on the steppes of Tartary? For my Brobdingnag[3] I may sail to Patagonia; for my Lilliput, to Lapland. In Arabia and Persia, my day's adventures may surpass the Arabian Nights' Entertainments. I may be a logger on the head waters of the Penobscot, to be recorded in fable hereafter as an amphibious river-god, by as sounding a name as Triton or Proteus;[4] carry furs from Nootka to China, and so be more renowned than Jason[5] and his golden fleece; or go on a South Sea exploring expedition, to be hereafter recounted along with the periplus of Hanno.[6] I may repeat the adventures of Marco Polo or Mandeville.[7]

These are but few of my chances, and how many more things may I do with which there are none to be compared! . . .

[April 26, 1841]

April 26. Monday. At R. W. E.'s.[8]

The charm of the Indian to me is that he stands free and unconstrained in Nature, is her inhabitant and not her guest, and wears her easily and gracefully. But the civilized man has the habits of the house. His house is a prison, in which he finds himself oppressed and confined, not sheltered and protected. He walks as if he sustained the roof; he carries his arms as if the walls would fall in and crush him, and his feet remember the cellar beneath. His muscles are never relaxed. It is rare that he overcomes the house, and learns to sit at home in it, and roof and floor and walls support themselves, as the sky and trees and earth.

It is a great art to saunter.

[February 21, 1842]

Feb. 21. I must confess there is nothing so strange to me as my own body. I love any other piece of nature, almost, better.

I was always conscious of sounds in nature which my ears could never hear,—that I caught but the prelude to a strain. She always retreats as I advance. Away behind and behind is she and her meaning. Will not this faith and expectation make to itself ears at length? I never saw to the end, nor heard to the end; but the best part was unseen and unheard.

I am like a feather floating in the atmosphere; on every side is depth unfathomable.

I feel as if years had been crowded into the last month, and yet the regularity of

[2] Taxable voter.
[3] Land of giants in *Gulliver's Travels.* (Patagonia is in southern Chile and Argentina.)
[4] I.e., a name as fine sounding as those of river-gods in Greek myths. (The Penobscot River runs through Maine.)
[5] Greek hero of classic myth who sailed forth to find the fabled golden fleece. (Nootka Sound is a Pacific inlet in British Columbia.)
[6] The written record of the voyages of Hanno, Carthaginian navigator of ca. 500 B.C.
[7] Marco Polo: Venetian adventurer (1254?–1324?) who traveled extensively in China; Sir John Mandeville, fictitious writer of a fourteenth-century account of journeys in exotic lands.
[8] R. W. E.: Ralph Waldo Emerson.

what we call time has been so far preserved as that I ... will be welcome in the present. I have lived ill for the most part because too near myself. I have tripped myself up, so that there was no progress for my own narrowness. I cannot walk conveniently and pleasantly but when I hold myself far off in the horizon. And the soul dilutes the body and makes it passable. My soul and body have tottered along together of late, tripping and hindering one another like unpracticed Siamese twins. They two should walk as one, that no obstacle may be nearer than the firmament.

There must be some narrowness in the soul that compels one to have secrets.

[July 5, 1845]

July 5. Saturday. Walden.—Yesterday I came here to live. My house makes me think of some mountain houses I have seen, which seemed to have a fresher auroral atmosphere about them, as I fancy of the halls of Olympus. I lodged at the house of a saw-miller last summer, on the Caatskill Mountains, high up as Pine Orchard, in the blueberry and raspberry region, where the quiet and cleanliness and coolness seemed to be all one,—which had their ambrosial character. He was the miller of the Kaaterskill Falls. They were a clean and wholesome family, inside and out, like their house. The latter was not plastered, only lathed, and the inner doors were not hung. The house seemed high-placed, airy, and perfumed, fit to entertain a travelling god. It was so high, indeed, that all the music, the broken strains, the waifs and accompaniments of tunes, that swept over the ridge of the Caatskills, passed through its aisles. Could not man be man in such an abode? And would he ever find out this grovelling life? It was the very light and atmosphere in which the works of Grecian art were composed, and in which they rest. They have appropriated to themselves a loftier hall than mortals ever occupy, at least on a level with the mountain-brows of the world. There was wanting a little of the glare of the lower vales, and in its place a pure twilight as became the precincts of heaven. Yet so equable and calm was the season there that you could not tell whether it was morning or noon or evening. Always there was the sound of the morning cricket.

[July 6, 1845]

July 6. I wish to meet the facts of life—the vital facts, which are the phenomena or actuality the gods meant to show us—face to face, and so I came down here. Life! who knows what it is, what it does? If I am not quite right here, I am less wrong than before; and now let us see what they will have. The preacher, instead of vexing the ears of drowsy farmers on their day of rest, at the end of the week,—for Sunday always seemed to me like a fit conclusion of an ill-spent week and not the fresh and brave beginning of a new one,—with this one other draggletail and postponed affair of a sermon, from thirdly to fifteenthly, should teach them with a thundering voice pause and simplicity. "Stop! Avast! Why so fast?" In all studies we go not forward but rather backward with redoubled pauses. We always study *antiques* with silence and reflection. Even time has a depth, and below its surface the waves do not lapse and roar. I wonder men can be so frivolous almost as to attend to the gross form of negro slavery, there are so many keen and subtle masters who subject us both. Self-emancipation in the West Indies of a man's thinking and imagining provinces, which should be more than his island territory,—one emancipated heart and intellect!

[from 1850]

. . . Getting into Patchogue late one night in an oyster-boat, there was a drunken Dutchman aboard whose wit reminded me of Shakespeare. When we came to leave the beach, our boat was aground, and we were detained three hours waiting for the tide. In the meanwhile two of the fishermen took an extra dram at the beach house. Then they stretched themselves on the seaweed by the shore in the sun to sleep off the effects of their debauch. One was an inconceivably broad-faced young Dutchman, —but oh! of such a peculiar breadth and heavy look, I should not know whether to call it more ridiculous or sublime. You would say that he had humbled himself so much that he was beginning to be exalted. An indescribable mynheerish[9] stupidity. I was less disgusted by their filthiness and vulgarity, because I was compelled to look on them as animals, as swine in their sty. For the whole voyage they lay flat on their backs on the bottom of the boat in the bilge-water and wet with each bailing, half insensible and wallowing in their vomit. But ever and anon, when aroused by the rude kicks or curses of the skipper, the Dutchman, who never lost his wit nor equanimity, though snoring and rolling in the vomit produced by his debauch, blurted forth some happy repartee like an illuminated swine. It was the earthiest, slimiest wit I ever heard. The countenance was one of a million. It was unmistakable Dutch. In the midst of a million faces of other races it could not be mistaken. It told of Amsterdam. I kept racking my brains to conceive how he could have been born in America, how lonely he must feel, what he did for fellowship. When we were groping up the narrow creek of Patchogue at ten o'clock at night, keeping our boat off, now from this bank, now from that, with a pole, the two inebriates roused themselves betimes. For in spite of their low estate they seemed to have all their wits as much about them as ever, aye, and all the self-respect they ever had. And the Dutchman gave wise directions to the steerer, which were not heeded. Suddenly rousing himself up where the sharpest-eyed might be bewildered in the darkness, he leaned over the side of the boat and pointed straight down into the creek, averring that that identical hole was a first-rate place for eels. And again he roused himself at the right time and declared what luck he had once had with his pots (not his cups) in another place, which we were floating over in the dark. At last he suddenly stepped on to another boat which was moored to the shore, with a divine ease and sureness, saying, "Well, good-night, take care of yourselves, I can't be with you any longer." He was one of the few remarkable men whom I have met. I have been impressed by one or two men in their cups. There was really a divinity stirred within them, so that in their case I have reverenced the drunken, as savages the insane, man. So stupid that he could never be intoxicated. When I said, "You have had a hard time of it to-day," he answered with indescribable good humor out of the very midst of his debauch, with watery eyes, "Well, it does

[9] Supposedly characteristic of natives of the Netherlands, where males are addressed as "Mynheer."

n't happen every day." It was happening then. He had taken me aboard on his back, the boat lying a rod from the shore, before I knew his condition. In the darkness our skipper steered with a pole on the bottom, for an oysterman knows the bottom of his bay as well as the shores, and can tell where he is by the soundings. . . .

[February 15, 1851]

Feb. 15. Fatal is the discovery that our friend is fallible, that he has prejudices. He is, then, only prejudiced in our favor. What is the value of his esteem who does not justly esteem another?

Alas! Alas! when my friend begins to deal in confessions, breaks silence, makes a theme of friendship (which then is always something past), and descends to merely human relations! As long as there is a spark of love remaining, cherish that alone. Only *that* can be kindled into a flame. I thought that friendship, that love was still possible between [us]. I thought that we had not withdrawn very far asunder. But now that my friend rashly, thoughtlessly, profanely speaks, *recognizing* the distance between us, that distance seems infinitely increased.

Of our friends we do not incline to speak, to complain, to others; we would not disturb the foundations of confidence that may still be.

Why should we not still continue to live with the intensity and rapidity of infants? Is not the world, are not the heavens, as unfathomed as ever? Have we exhausted any joy, any sentiment?

[July 6, 1851]

There is some advantage in being the humblest, cheapest, least dignified man in the village, so that the very stable boys shall damn you. Methinks I enjoy that advantage to an unusual extent. There is many a coarsely well-meaning fellow, who knows only the skin of me, who addresses me familiarly by my Christian name. I get the whole good of him and lose nothing myself. There is "Sam," the jailer,—whom I never call Sam, however,—who exclaimed last evening: "Thoreau, are you going up the street pretty soon? Well, just take a couple of these handbills along and drop one in at Hoar's piazza[10] and one at Holbrook's, and I'll do as much for you another time." I am not above being used, aye abused, sometimes.

[July 19, 1851]

July 19. Here I am thirty-four years old, and yet my life is almost wholly unexpanded. How much is in the germ! There is such an interval between my ideal and the actual in many instances that I may say I am unborn. There is the instinct for society, but no society. Life is not long enough for one success. Within another thirty-four years that miracle can hardly take place. Methinks my seasons revolve more slowly than those of nature; I am differently timed. I am contented. This rapid revolution of nature, even of nature in me, why should it hurry me? Let a man step to the music

---

[10] Large covered veranda.

which he hears, however measured. Is it important that I should mature as soon as an apple tree? aye, as soon as an oak? May not my life in nature, in proportion as it is supernatural, be only the spring and infantile portion of my spirit's life? Shall I turn my spring to summer? May I not sacrifice a hasty and petty completeness here to entireness there? If my curve is large, why bend it to a smaller circle? My spirit's unfolding observes not the pace of nature. The society which I was made for is not here. Shall I, then, substitute for the anticipation of that this poor reality? I would [rather] have the unmixed expectation of that than this reality. If life is a waiting, so be it. I will not be shipwrecked on a vain reality. What were any reality which I can substitute? Shall I with pains erect a heaven of blue glass over myself, though when it is done I shall be sure to gaze still on the true ethereal heaven far above, as if the former were not,—that still distant sky o'er-arching that blue expressive eye of heaven? I am enamored of the blue-eyed arch of heaven.

I did not *make* this demand for a more thorough sympathy. This is not my idiosyncrasy or disease. He that made the demand will answer the demand.

My blood flows as slowly as the waves of my native Musketaquid; yet they reach the ocean sooner, perchance, than those of the Nashua.

Already the goldenrod is budded, but I can make no haste for that.

[October 1, 1851]

Oct. 1. 5 P.M.—Just put a fugitive slave, who has taken the name of Henry Williams, into the cars[11] for Canada. He escaped from Stafford County, Virginia, to Boston last October; has been in Shadrach's place at the Cornhill Coffee-House; had been corresponding through an agent with his master, who is his father, about buying himself, his master asking $600, but he having been able to raise only $500. Heard that there were writs out for two Williamses, fugitives, and was informed by his fellow-servants and employer that Augerhole Burns and others of the police had called for him when he was out. Accordingly fled to Concord last night on foot, bringing a letter to our family from Mr. Lovejoy of Cambridge and another which Garrison[12] had formerly given him on another occasion. He lodged with us, and waited in the house till funds were collected with which to forward him. Intended to dispatch him at noon through to Burlington, but when I went to buy his ticket, saw one at the depot who looked and behaved so much like a Boston policeman that I did not venture that time. An intelligent and very well-behaved man, a mulatto.

[November 9, 1851]

I, too, would fain set down something beside facts. Facts should only be as the frame to my pictures; they should be material to the mythology which I am writing; not facts to assist men to make money, farmers to farm profitably, in any common sense; facts to tell who I am, and where I have been or what I have thought: as now the bell rings for evening meeting, and its volumes of sound, like smoke which rises from

---

[11] Railway cars.
[12] William Lloyd Garrison (1805–1879), leader of the Abolitionists in New England.

where a cannon is fired, make the tent in which I dwell. My facts shall be falsehoods to the common sense. I would so state facts that they shall be significant, shall be myths or mythologic. Facts which the mind perceived, thoughts which the body thought, —with these I deal. I, too, cherish vague and misty forms, vaguest when the cloud at which I gaze is dissipated quite and naught but the skyey depths are seen.

[January 30, 1852]

Nature allows of no universal secrets. The more carefully a secret is kept on one side of the globe, the larger the type it is printed in on the other. Nothing is too pointed, too personal, too immodest, for her to blazon. The relations of sex, transferred to flowers, become the study of ladies in the drawing-room. While men wear fig leaves, she grows the *Phallus impudicus* and *P. caninus* and other phallus-like fungi.

The rhymes which I used to see on the walls of privies, scribbled by boys, I have lately seen, word for word the same; in spite [of] whitewash and brick walls and admonitions they survive. They are no doubt older than Orpheus,[13] and have come down from an antiquity as remote as mythology or fable. So, too, no doubt corporations have ever struggled in vain to obtain cleanliness in those provinces. Filth and impurity are as old as cleanliness and purity. To correspond to man completely, Nature is even perhaps unchaste herself. Or perchance man's impurity begets a monster somewhere, to proclaim his sin. The poetry of the jakes,[14]—it flows as perennially as the gutter.

[April 23, 1857]

April 23. I saw at Ricketson's a young woman, Miss Kate Brady, twenty years old, her father an Irishman, a worthless fellow, her mother a smart Yankee. The daughter formerly did sewing, but now keeps school for a livelihood. She was born at the Brady house, I think in Freetown, where she lived till twelve years old and helped her father in the field. There she rode horse to plow and was knocked off the horse by apple tree boughs, kept sheep, caught fish, etc., etc. I never heard a girl or woman express so strong a love for nature. She purposes to return to that lonely ruin, and dwell there alone, since her mother and sister will not accompany her; says that she knows all about farming and keeping sheep and spinning and weaving, though it would puzzle her to shingle the old house. There she thinks she can "live free." I was pleased to hear of her plans, because they were quite cheerful and original, not professedly reformatory, but growing out of her love for "Squire's Brook and the Middleborough ponds." A strong love for outward nature is singularly rare among both men and women. The scenery immediately about her homestead is quite ordinary, yet she appreciates and can use that part of the universe as no other being can. Her own sex, so tamely bred, only jeer at her for entertaining such an idea, but she has a strong head and a love for good reading, which may carry her through. I would by no means discourage, nor yet particularly encourage her, for I would have her so strong as to succeed in spite of all ordinary discouragements.

1837–1859/1906

---

[13] Poet-musician in classic myth.

[14] I.e., the graffiti found in outdoor privies.

Edgar Allan Poe
1809–1849

There seems to be enough of Edgar Allan Poe to go around to please, or to exasperate, almost everyone. The title of Daniel Hoffman's recent study of the writer visually represents this fact: *Poe, Poe, Poe, Poe, Poe, Poe, Poe.* As Hoffman observes, there emerges from the writings "a surrogate for all of Poe's readers"—the private "I" that each of us adds to, and discovers in, the shadows cast by the tales and the poems. There is the Poe whose horror stories scared us when we were fourteen and whom we are supposed to grow away from in our maturity; but there is also the Poe whose thoughts on personal epistemologies (what we know) and cosmic ontologies (what is real) awe us with their seeming profundity. There is the dissolute wastrel portrayed by Poe's first biographers—and in part by Poe himself, in the stories he spread. There is also the helpless genius who needed lots of mothering, as put forward in the swooning remembrances of the various maternal figures with which he filled his life. There is the truth sayer on the absolutes of poetry and beauty, and the diddler who took his revenge on the stupidity of his contemporaries by making fools of them for falling for his cunningly wrought hoaxes. There is the creator of the detective Dupin, whom American mystery buffs claim as the originator of "their kind" of story, the poet whom the French appropriate as the true representative of Gallic culture, and the Gothicist whom the South likes to have share its own exile from mainstream Yankee literature. Poe comes to us as drug-sodden madman or as the cool possessor of a computerlike brain that would today move him into the executive suites of IBM. He is the anarchist self we flaunt, to the extent of welcoming death when wanting to rebel against the boring routines that limit the soul. But he is also the person who sits in his dull little office as dutiful editor and reviewer, moving all his papers into the out basket. He is Poe the incomplete poet, or the precursor of the French Symbolists. He is the cheap comedown from "good" writing, or the St. John the Baptist who announces the arrival of the modern short story and short poem.

Perhaps only two warnings are in order when we approach Poe's writings, which we tend to turn into litmus tests for our own multiple selves: not to make Poe too dull (coming to him through pedantry) and not to make him too exciting (getting at him through pathology, since even the act of sensationalizing his life and writings makes them collapse boringly in on themselves).

Neat little résumés are difficult to produce when it comes to the facts of Poe's life and the development of his career as poet, writer of tales, editor, and literary critic. Too many biographers have intervened since he was found near death in a Baltimore street on an October night in 1849. But certain details have been sorted out from the slanders that attack and the legends that extol. Even so, every "normal" fact—such as his birth in Boston on January 19, 1809—is matched by something unsettling. His parents were wandering actors, members of a disreputable profession; his drunkard father decamped and his mother died by the time the child was two. Elizabeth Arnold Poe happened to die while on tour in Richmond, and when the infant Edgar and an older brother were placed with whoever would agree to care for them, a well-to-do merchant of the city, John Allan, took charge of Edgar Poe. All went well enough for the first twenty years. Although never legally adopted by the Allans, their young ward accompanied them on their travels to England (where Poe attended school) and back again to the upper-class education and social expectations of a well-bred Richmond family. But Poe's status in the Allan household was an uncertain one. He was unable to forget how shameful his antecedents were. Friction developed between Poe and John Allan—perhaps as the result of Allan's jealousy over his wife's fondness for the boy or of Poe's reluctance to go into Allan's tobacco export business. Then again, it could have been his precociously romantic involvements with several young women of his set or the gambling debts he accumulated during his year at the University of Virginia that set him at odds with his guardian.

By 1827 the tensions were too great to bear. Poe left Richmond and went to Boston, where he published with his own funds his first collection, *Tamerlane and Other Poems,* signed simply "A Bostonian." Then he vanished for a short period into the army under the pseudonym Edgar A. Perry. A brief truce between Poe and John Allan led to his discharge from the regulars and an appointment to West Point in July 1830, less than a year after the appearance of his second volume, *Al Aaraaf, Tamerlane, and Minor Poems.* Poe did not stay at West Point long. He found that he disliked the regimen and lacked the necessary allowance from John Allan that would let him live like both an officer and a gentleman. Deliberately flaunting rules about class attendance, he encouraged his own dismissal.

Meanwhile matters had again become ugly at home. The young man wished to have his position as a "son" clarified, and John Allan refused to give him that satisfaction. Allan's first wife died, and he remarried. The new wife bore him twin sons, then became pregnant again almost immediately. By the time Poe left West Point after seven months at the Academy, he realized there was no chance for him ever to be named the Allan heir; the break was complete. He was totally on his own at the age of twenty-two.

In May 1831, Poe's friends at West Point provided him with the money he needed to publish *Poems,* dedicated to "the U.S. Corps of Cadets." This collection included revisions of earlier poems and the addition of two poems, including the first and best version of "To Helen." Poe decided that writing would obviously have to be the way he would earn his living and to make a "name" for himself, now that he had been denied the name Allan and the social identity of a Virginia gentleman and West Point officer. But writing poems that appeared in "little collections" was an avocation for men of independent means, not the way to lift a poor man set adrift in the shark-rich seas of an American society more interested in rewarding tobacco merchants than brilliant young poets.

Poe launched himself as an editor, a career that would sustain him, but not very well, until his death eighteen years later. He first went to Baltimore, where he lived between 1831 and 1835 with relatives from his father's side of the family. Foremost among these were his aunt, who became one of a series of "mothers" he needed to offset his lack of true "fathers," and his aunt's young daughter Virginia, whom Poe married by 1836, when she was fourteen. This threesome lived together in poverty, with Poe working with exceptional vigor.

Five of his first stories appeared in a Philadelphia newspaper during 1832. In 1833 "MS Found in a Bottle" won first prize in a story contest run by a Baltimore paper. Tales written for publication in the popular press in those days were governed by the particular demands of newspaper space and the need to achieve immediate impact; these were formulas Poe mastered quickly. By 1835, at twenty-six, he had sufficient reputation as a writer of popular fiction to win the assistant editorship of the *Southern Literary Messenger* in Richmond, but he did not keep the job long. He performed his editorial duties brilliantly, but emotionally he could not stay the course or keep his peace with the owners. The same sarcasm that gained welcome notoriety for the magazine from the reviews he wrote did not endear him to his associates. Bouts of drinking recommenced. He was fired. He had to move quickly.

He spent a few months in New York, where Harper's published his novel *The Narrative of Arthur Gordon Pym* in 1838, to no financial or critical advantage. He moved to Philadelphia in 1839. Living for a time on a diet of bread and molasses and constantly on the edge of total discouragement, Poe worked on. "Ligeia" was only the first of the major stories he wrote in 1839. It appeared, with other stories and poems, in the *American Museum* of Baltimore. Over the next few years, Poe became connected with three different magazines: *Burton's Gentleman's Magazine* (where he was coeditor from 1839 to 1840, until fired for drinking), *Graham's Magazine* (where he went in 1841 after being recommended by his former employer), and the Philadelphia weekly *Saturday Museum* in 1843. In 1842 Virginia sickened with tuberculosis (she would die at twenty-five), and Poe tried —unsuccessfully—to start a magazine of his own. But his reputation was advancing. Few readers could overlook the quality—or quantity—of his editorial writing, his critical reviews, his poems, and his stories of great impact. *Tales of the Grotesque and Arabesque* were collected in two volumes in 1840, and "The Gold Bug" won fame and the top prize of one hundred dollars in a contest sponsored by a Philadelphia newspaper.

In 1844 Poe took Virginia and his faithful aunt with him to New York, where they subsisted on the fees he earned from work on various papers and magazines. His drinking increased, gossip circulated about his eccentric behavior with various sentimental ladies who encouraged his attentions, and his sniping attacks on the literary follies he found everywhere in American letters made him the target of further vilification. Yet 1845 was a vintage year for Poe's literary career. "The Raven" appeared, and the stir it caused resulted in his giving lectures on poetry, being named the lead reviewer for the *Broadway Journal,* and being mentioned favorably by James Russell Lowell, the foremost critic of the period. Poe said proudly of "The Raven" (referring to the prize "The Gold Bug" had won him), "The bird beat the bug . . . all hollow." He made influential literary friends, and this led to the publication of *The Raven and Other Poems* by the prestigious publishing house of Wiley and Putnam. He purchased the *Broadway Journal* on credit, with the hope that the lift brought by his recent fame would bring financial success. However, by early 1846 the *Journal* had gone under, and by January 1847 Virginia was dead. What had never been a steady life now became an accelerating series of personal crises and professional disappointments.

Writing still, as ever under the compulsion to get down everything that filled his brain, Poe overextended himself even more. He attempted several editorial schemes, entered upon some fervid romances (culminating in an engagement to an old sweetheart, while writing excited letters to yet another woman), drank even more and became physically debilitated by what may have been a brain lesion. Somehow in the midst of this turmoil, enough to have unsettled a stolid man of regular habits, Poe wrote the poems "Ulalume" and "Annabel Lee," commenced the long prose poem *Eureka* in which he declared he would explain the nature of the universe, and completed the story "Hop-Frog." Despair over the loss of one's beloved, revenge on one's enemies, and exaltation over the final unification of consciousness with the cosmos—these were the themes Poe worked over in these final pieces. By now his activities were frenetic. He told tales of attempted suicides and of murder plots against his life; he gave lectures and readings of his work; he signed into a temperance group; he revisited the Richmond of his childhood. Suddenly it was over in October of 1849. On his way to Philadelphia for an editing job, he got off the train in Baltimore. He was found unconscious a few days later in the street. He died in a hospital on October 7 and was buried in Baltimore.

Poe was hardly in his grave before his biographers began to "create" a life for him. (That grave, incidently, remained unmarked for twenty-six years; when in 1875 a tombstone was placed there, the only literary representative present was Walt Whitman.) Two days after Poe's death, his literary executor and supposed friend, Rufus Griswold, attacked him in a newspaper obituary. The next year the introduction supplied by Griswold for the published collection of Poe's work contained an "exposé" of Poe's depravity—the "facts" for which Griswold obtained by falsifying Poe's letters. Griswold clearly benefited from these actions. Book sales were greatly helped by the sensationalism attending these slanders. Even Poe's aunt and Virginia's mother, Mrs. Clemm, was able to turn a profit selling copies of the edition that damned her "dear Eddie." From then on, critics, editors, and biographers have continued re-creating Poe after the images that most satisfied their own imaginations. But whether Poe was seen as a demon or as a misunderstood genius, the effect was to serve up one version or other of the Byronic hero—the most serviceable romantic image of the poet that lay at hand. It was the old story of a writer's life being substituted for his literary works as the source of the reader's interest and of having the writings evaluated according to whether one approves or disapproves of the writer. T. S. Eliot's admonition that poetry should be our "escape from personality" is not always followed. Certainly to look at the poem and not at the poet (especially if the latter happens to be Poe) can be difficult.

Critics and poets as sophisticated as Baudelaire, Mallarmé, and Valéry transformed Poe into an "honorary" Frenchman and symbolist poet, thereby accomplishing a double task: an attack on the bourgeois mentality of their own countrymen for its insensitivity to the poetic soul and an excoriation of the philistine qualities they associated with the American democratic system. In his own country, Poe was as much chastised for his literary failings as for his personal life. Emerson emerged long enough from the mental fog of his later years to characterize Poe as "the jingle man." In his memoirs, Henry James vividly recalled the excitement he and his brother William felt as boys waiting to snatch from the postman the latest issues of the magazines that contained Poe's horror tales. But James also registered his disapproval of adults who continued to take pleasure in a man whose writings were not sufficiently "about something." James knew from his own experience what Daniel Hoffman has expressed—that Poe's stories "can frighten a boy out of his pajamas." But James asked more of Poe than Poe would give. Mark Twain, D. H. Lawrence, and T. S. Eliot were also less than charitable about Poe's literary achievements. Yet through it all, Poe has been read and absorbed by almost everyone in this country, on the Continent, and in England. The roster of well-known poets and writers of fiction who have admitted the ways in which Poe's writing has colored their own imaginations is impressive. Critics of every literary persuasion find his works an inexhaustible field for cultivation. Most of all, people read Poe and respond to him with an enthusiasm that has little to do with the rise and fall of his critical status.

Poe biographies are now undergoing "domestication." The current emphasis is on a Poe snugly at home with Virginia and Aunt Clemm rather than on the drunk wandering the streets. The focus is on the orphan, not the outlaw, as one biographer, John Carl Miller, has noted. It is less on Poe's oedipal and necrophiliac fantasies than on the hours he spent at the office turning out copy for the printers. This turnabout seems sound, but it is still unwise to suggest that anyone has, or ever will, truly know Poe the man.

What seems clearer these days is the nature of Poe's literary contributions. With a total of only forty-eight poems (many of them turned out at the jingle level that Emerson referred to), Poe pointed the way toward a new kind of symbolist poetry, verses that evoke mood rather than meaning, that call attention to their own technique, and that celebrate experimentation for its own sake.

With his horror tales, Poe took over—and, in some of his best examples, transcended—the Gothic formula that had been supplying thrills to readers of popular literature for some time. Poe is credited with inventing the detective story, a form that juxtaposes the threat of anarchy (outrageous crimes whose violence and unfathomable causes upset the stability of society) with a mix of the rational (mental coolness and the application of mathematical logic) and the intuitive (emotional reactions to the illogicality of events). Poe's stories of trips to the moon, as well as his musings about the evolution and consummation of the cosmos (whether taken straight or as hoax), extended the possibilities of science fiction. Psychological literature got a boost by his tales of alter egos and outlawed urges that stalk his characters' minds. He had inherited the tradition of the romance that located terror in outward places; he relocated it, as he announced, in the soul.

In a country young in literary experience, where critical theory and the analysis of literary techniques were rude or nonexistent, Poe's reviews and essays on poetic principles set an example that would eventually bring Americans to sophistication in the arts of reading and writing. The stand Poe took against the didacticism that evaluates literary worth according to the moral truths a story demonstrates has led American literature to participate in that particular strain of Romanticism that seeks out intensity of feeling and the pleasures of beauty, not moralisms. His strictures on the merits of brevity hardly kept Walt Whitman or Hart Crane from attempting long epic poems or William Faulkner and Henry James from exploring the extended novel form, but Poe gave the American short story form the base from which it moved toward true accomplishment.

Difficulties abound, however, in the interpretation given both to the meaning of Poe's individual works and to his literary intentions. It is difficult to know whether a particular poem or story originated from an excess of feverish emotion or from calculated designs on the reader's imagination, whether it was done as a hoax or offered in sober earnestness. Much of Poe's work exists teasingly between two poles, as both *Eureka* and *The Narrative of Arthur Gordon Pym* suggest. Critics who like to tidy things up are frustrated when they find it impossible to say whether "The Fall of the House of Usher" is a bona fide tale of horror or the parody of one, or whether the decor in the tower room in "Ligeia" is intentionally vulgar or the result of the innate verbal kitsch of a man whose own tastes were deplorably déclassé. We know that Poe could work with extreme calculation to arouse his readers' feelings. His essays "How to Write a *Blackwood's* Article" and "The Philosophy of Composition" reveal the clever means by which the writer can manipulate responses. But then, perhaps these essays are at the same time exercises in leg-pulling, ways of disguising the urgency Poe felt to express his strongest passions about his literary craft.

What we finally retain from an immersion in the often nightmarish world of Poe's writings is the sense that our secret fears and desires have been touched upon: the fear of being buried alive, of being destroyed by perverse instincts that overturn the rational measures by which we protect ourselves; desires imaged in acts of revenge, cannibalism, incest, and the quest for death. It was Poe's greatest discovery that we want and yet avoid self-examination and self-knowledge. To know the secrets of the universe would be to possess will, to have power and control over our fates. Knowledge, will, power—these appear to be at the heart of Poe's authority over our imaginations. He affects us by force, not clarity. It is a lesson taken to heart by masters of the gothic romance and of the modern literary work. The example of Poe is apparent in both.

Further Reading:

G. Woodberry, *The Life of Edgar Allan Poe,
Personal and Literary*, 2 vols., 1885, 1909.
H. Allen, *Israfel—The Life and Times of Edgar
Allan Poe*, 2 vols., 1926, 1934.
J. Krutch, *Edgar Allan Poe*, 1926.
K. Campbell, *The Mind of Poe and Other
Studies*, 1933.
A. Quinn, *Edgar Allan Poe*, 1941, 1966.
M. Bonaparte, *The Life and Works of Edgar
Allan Poe: A Psycho-Analytic Interpretation*, 1949,
1971.
N. Fagin, *The Histrionic Mr. Poe*, 1949.
E. Davidson, *Poe: A Critical Study*, 1957.
V. Buranelli, *Edgar Allan Poe*, 1961, 1977.
S. Moss, *Poe's Literary Battles: The Critic in the
Context of His Literary Milieu*, 1963.
E. Wagenknecht, *Edgar Allan Poe: The Man
Behind the Legend*, 1963.
E. Parks, *Edgar Allan Poe*, 1967.
F. Stovall, *Edgar Allan Poe the Poet*, 1969.
R. L. Gale, *Plots and Characters in the Fiction
and Poetry of Edgar Allan Poe*, 1970.
D. Hoffman, *Poe, Poe, Poe, Poe, Poe, Poe, Poe*,
1972.
Critics on Poe, ed. D. Kesterson, 1973.
J. M. Dillon, *Edgar Allan Poe: His Genius and
Character*, 1974.
Poe at Work: Seven Textual Studies, ed.
B. Fisher, 1978.
J. Symons, *The Tell-Tale Heart*, 1978.
D. Ketterer, *The Rationale of Deception in Poe*,
1979.
E. Phillips, *Edgar Allan Poe: An American
Imagination*, 1979.
B. R. Pollin, *Poe, Creator of Words*, 1980.

Texts:

"Ligeia," "The Fall of the House of Usher,"
"Nathaniel Hawthorne's 'Twice-Told Tales,' "
and "The Philosophy of Composition" from
The Complete Works of Edgar Allan Poe, 17
vols., ed. J. Harrison, 1902. "The Purloined
Letter," "The Cask of Amontillado," and poems
from *Collected Works of Edgar Allan Poe*, 3
vols., ed. T. Mabbott, 1969–1978.
See also *The Works of Edgar Allan Poe*, 10 vols.,
ed. E. Stedman and G. Woodberry, 1894–1895,
1914.
*The Complete Poems and Stories of Edgar Allan
Poe*, 2 vols., ed. A. Quinn and E. O'Neill,
1946.
The Letters of Edgar Allan Poe, 2 vols., ed.
J. Ostrom, 1948, 1966.

Ligeia

*And the will therein lieth, which dieth not. Who knoweth the mysteries
of the will, with its vigor? For God is but a great will pervading all
things by nature of its intentness. Man doth not yield himself to the
angels, nor unto death utterly, save only through the weakness of his
feeble will.*

Joseph Glanvill[1]

I cannot, for my soul, remember how, when, or even precisely where, I first became
acquainted with the lady Ligeia. Long years have since elapsed, and my memory is
feeble through much suffering. Or, perhaps, I cannot *now* bring these points to mind,

---

[1] Joseph Glanville (1636–1680), one of the
Cambridge Platonists who attempted to
reconcile seventeenth-century scientific thought
with Christian teachings. This quotation is
apparently a fabrication by Poe to suit the
purposes of the narrative.

because, in truth, the character of my beloved, her rare learning, her singular yet placid cast of beauty, and the thrilling and enthralling eloquence of her low musical language, made their way into my heart by paces so steadily and stealthily progressive that they have been unnoticed and unknown. Yet I believe that I met her first and most frequently in some large, old, decaying city near the Rhine. Of her family— I have surely heard her speak. That it is of a remotely ancient date cannot be doubted. Ligeia! Ligeia! Buried in studies of a nature more than all else adapted to deaden impressions of the outward world, it is by that sweet word alone—by Ligeia—that I bring before mine eyes in fancy the image of her who is no more. And now, while I write, a recollection flashes upon me that I have *never known* the paternal name of her who was my friend and my betrothed, and who became the partner of my studies, and finally the wife of my bosom. Was it a playful charge on the part of my Ligeia? or was it a test of my strength of affection, that I should institute no inquiries upon this point? or was it rather a caprice of my own—a wildly romantic offering on the shrine of the most passionate devotion? I but indistinctly recall the fact itself—what wonder that I have utterly forgotten the circumstances which originated or attended it? And, indeed, if ever that spirit which is entitled *Romance*—if ever she, the wan and the misty-winged *Ashtophet*[2] of idolatrous Egypt, presided, as they tell, over marriages ill-omened, then most surely she presided over mine.

There is one dear topic, however, on which my memory fails me not. It is the *person* of Ligeia. In stature she was tall, somewhat slender, and, in her latter days, even emaciated. I would in vain attempt to portray the majesty, the quiet ease, of her demeanor, or the incomprehensible lightness and elasticity of her footfall. She came and departed as a shadow. I was never made aware of her entrance into my closed study save by the dear music of her low sweet voice, as she placed her marble hand upon my shoulder. In beauty of face no maiden ever equalled her. It was the radiance of an opium-dream—an airy and spirit-lifting vision more wildly divine than the phantasies which hovered about the slumbering souls of the daughters of Delos.[3] Yet her features were not of that regular mould which we have been falsely taught to worship in the classical labors of the heathen. "There is no exquisite[4] beauty," says Bacon, Lord Verulam, speaking truly of all the forms and *genera* of beauty, "without some *strangeness* in the proportion." Yet, although I saw that the features of Ligeia were not of a classic regularity—although I perceived that her loveliness was indeed "exquisite," and felt that there was much of "strangeness" pervading it, yet I have tried in vain to detect the irregularity and to trace home my own perception of "the strange." I examined the contour of the lofty and pale forehead—it was faultless— how cold indeed that word when applied to a majesty so divine!—the skin rivalling the purest ivory, the commanding extent and repose, the gentle prominence of the regions above the temples; and then the raven-black, the glossy, the luxuriant and naturally-curling tresses, setting forth the full force of the Homeric epithet, "hyacin-

[2] Fertility goddess.
[3] Aegean island frequently mentioned in classic myth.
[4] *In his essay "Of Beauty" (1625), Francis Bacon, baron Verulam (1561–1626), used the word* "excellent"; Poe substituted "exquisite." In the next line, *genera* is the Latin word for "races" or "kinds"; here it is used broadly for "species" (plural).

thine!"[5] I looked at the delicate outlines of the nose—and nowhere but in the graceful medallions of the Hebrews had I beheld a similar perfection. There were the same luxurious smoothness of surface, the same scarcely perceptible tendency to the aquiline, the same harmoniously curved nostrils speaking the free spirit. I regarded the sweet mouth. Here was indeed the triumph of all things heavenly—the magnificent turn of the short upper lip—the soft, voluptuous slumber of the under—the dimples which sported, and the color which spoke—the teeth glancing back, with a brilliancy almost startling, every ray of the holy light which fell upon them in her serene and placid, yet most exultingly radiant of all smiles. I scrutinized the formation of the chin—and here, too, I found the gentleness of breadth, the softness and the majesty, the fullness and the spirituality, of the Greek—the contour which the god Apollo revealed but in a dream, to Cleomenes,[6] the son of the Athenian. And then I peered into the large eyes of Ligeia.

For eyes we have no models in the remotely antique. It might have been, too, that in these eyes of my beloved lay the secret to which Lord Verulam alludes. They were, I must believe, far larger than the ordinary eyes of our own race. They were even fuller than the fullest of the gazelle eyes of the tribe of the valley of Nourjahad.[7] Yet it was only at intervals—in moments of intense excitement—that this peculiarity became more than slightly noticeable in Ligeia. And at such moments was her beauty —in my heated fancy thus it appeared perhaps—the beauty of beings either above or apart from the earth—the beauty of the fabulous Houri[8] of the Turk. The hue of the orbs was the most brilliant of black, and, far over them, hung jetty lashes of great length. The brows, slightly irregular in outline, had the same tint. The "strangeness," however, which I found in the eyes, was of a nature distinct from the formation, or the color, or the brilliancy of the features, and must, after all, be referred to the *expression*. Ah, word of no meaning! behind whose vast latitude of mere sound we intrench our ignorance of so much of the spiritual. The expression of the eyes of Ligeia! How for long hours have I pondered upon it! How have I, through the whole of a midsummer night, struggled to fathom it! What *was* it—that something more profound than the well of Democritus[9]—which lay far within the pupils of my beloved? What was it? I was possessed with a passion to discover. Those eyes! those large, those shining, those divine orbs! they became to me twin stars of Leda,[10] and I to them devoutest of astrologers.

There is no point, among the many incomprehensible anomalies of the science of mind, more thrillingly exciting than the fact—never, I believe, noticed in the schools —that, in our endeavors to recall to memory something long forgotten, we often find ourselves *upon the very verge* of remembrance, without being able, in the end, to

---

[5] Homer's epic poem the *Odyssey* likens the curly hair of its hero to the hyacinth.

[6] Athenian sculptor said to have created the original version of the famous statue known as the Medici Venus, inspired by Apollo, god of the arts.

[7] Virgins who await the faithful in Mohammedan paradise, as described in *The History of Nourjahad* (1767) by Frances Sheridan.

[8] Another reference to the beauteous women of the Moslem paradise.

[9] Greek philosopher (fifth century B.C.) who observed that truth is to be found at the bottom of a well.

[10] In the constellation Gemini; named after the twin sons of Leda, who were born of her rape by Zeus.

remember. And thus how frequently, in my intense scrutiny of Ligeia's eyes, have I felt approaching the full knowledge of their expression—felt it approaching—yet not quite be mine—and so at length entirely depart! And (strange, oh strangest mystery of all!) I found, in the commonest objects of the universe, a circle of analogies to that expression. I mean to say that, subsequently to the period when Ligeia's beauty passed into my spirit, there dwelling as in a shrine, I derived, from many existences in the material world, a sentiment such as I felt always aroused within me by her large and luminous orbs. Yet not the more could I define that sentiment, or analyze, or even steadily view it. I recognized it, let me repeat, sometimes in the survey of a rapidly-growing vine—in the contemplation of a moth, a butterfly, a chrysalis, a stream of running water. I have felt it in the ocean; in the falling of a meteor. I have felt it in the glances of unusually aged people. And there are one or two stars in heaven—(one especially, a star of the sixth magnitude, double and changeable, to be found near the large star in Lyra[11]) in a telescopic scrutiny of which I have been made aware of the feeling. I have been filled with it by certain sounds from stringed instruments, and not unfrequently by passages from books. Among innumerable other instances, I well remember something in a volume of Joseph Glanvill, which (perhaps merely from its quaintness—who shall say?) never failed to inspire me with the sentiment;—"And the will therein lieth, which dieth not. Who knoweth the mysteries of the will, with its vigor? For God is but a great will pervading all things by nature of its intentness. Man doth not yield him to the angels, nor unto death utterly, save only through the weakness of his feeble will."

Length of years, and subsequent reflection, have enabled me to trace, indeed, some remote connection between this passage in the English moralist and a portion of the character of Ligeia. An *intensity* in thought, action, or speech, was possibly, in her, a result, or at least an index, of that gigantic volition which, during our long intercourse, failed to give other and more immediate evidence of its existence. Of all the women whom I have ever known, she, the outwardly calm, the ever-placid Ligeia, was the most violently a prey to the tumultuous vultures of stern passion. And of such passion I could form no estimate, save by the miraculous expansion of those eyes which at once so delighted and appalled me—by the almost magical melody, modulation, distinctness and placidity of her very low voice—and by the fierce energy (rendered doubly effective by contrast with her manner of utterance) of the wild words which she habitually uttered.

I have spoken of the learning of Ligeia: it was immense—such as I have never known in woman. In the classical tongues was she deeply proficient, and as far as my own acquaintance extended in regard to the modern dialects of Europe, I have never known her at fault. Indeed upon any theme of the most admired, because simply the most abstruse of the boasted erudition of the academy, have I *ever* found Ligeia at fault? How singularly—how thrillingly, this one point in the nature of my wife has forced itself, at this late period only, upon my attention! I said her knowledge was such as I have never known in woman—but where breathes the man who has traversed, and successfully, *all* the wide areas of moral, physical, and mathematical science? I saw not then what I now clearly perceive, that the acquisitions of Ligeia

[11] Constellation with the brilliant star Vega.

were gigantic, were astounding; yet I was sufficiently aware of her infinite supremacy to resign myself, with a child-like confidence, to her guidance through the chaotic world of metaphysical investigation at which I was most busily occupied during the earlier years of our marriage. With how vast a triumph—with how vivid a delight —with how much of all that is ethereal in hope—did I *feel*, as she bent over me in studies but little sought—but less known—that delicious vista by slow degrees expanding before me, down whose long, gorgeous, and all untrodden path, I might at length pass onward to the goal of a wisdom too divinely precious not to be forbidden!

How poignant, then, must have been the grief with which, after some years, I beheld my well-grounded expectations take wings to themselves and fly away! Without Ligeia I was but as a child groping benighted. Her presence, her readings alone, rendered vividly luminous the many mysteries of the transcendentalism in which we were immersed. Wanting the radiant lustre of her eyes, letters, lambent and golden, grew duller than Saturnian lead.[12] And now those eyes shone less and less frequently upon the pages over which I pored. Ligeia grew ill. The wild eyes blazed with a too—too glorious effulgence; the pale fingers became of the transparent waxen hue of the grave, and the blue veins upon the lofty forehead swelled and sank impetuously with the tides of the most gentle emotion. I saw that she must die—and I struggled desperately in spirit with the grim Azrael.[13] And the struggles of the passionate wife were, to my astonishment, even more energetic than my own. There had been much in her stern nature to impress me with the belief that, to her, death would have come without its terrors;—but not so. Words are impotent to convey any just idea of the fierceness of resistance with which she wrestled with the Shadow. I groaned in anguish at the pitiable spectacle. I would have soothed—I would have reasoned; but, in the intensity of her wild desire for life,—for life—*but* for life— solace and reason were alike the uttermost of folly. Yet not until the last instance, amid the most convulsive writhings of her fierce spirit, was shaken the external placidity of her demeanor. Her voice grew more gentle—grew more low—yet I would not wish to dwell upon the wild meaning of the quietly uttered words. My brain reeled as I hearkened entranced, to a melody more than mortal—to assumptions and aspirations which mortality had never before known.

That she loved me I should not have doubted; and I might have been easily aware that, in a bosom such as hers, love would have reigned no ordinary passion. But in death only, was I fully impressed with the strength of her affection. For long hours, detaining my hand, would she pour out before me the overflowing of a heart whose more than passionate devotion amounted to idolatry. How had I deserved to be so blessed by such confessions?—how had I deserved to be so cursed with the removal of my beloved in the hour of her making them? But upon this subject I cannot bear to dilate. Let me say only, that in Ligeia's more than womanly aban- donment to a love, alas! all unmerited, all unworthily bestowed, I at length recog- nized the principle of her longing with so wildly earnest a desire for the life which

---

[12] According to astrological lore the influence of Saturn (the alchemical term for lead) turns one gloomy and listless.

[13] In both Jewish and Moslem legend, the Angel of Death.

was now fleeing so rapidly away. It is this wild longing—it is this eager vehemence of desire for life—*but* for life—that I have no power to portray—no utterance capable of expressing.

At high noon of the night in which she departed, beckoning me, peremptorily, to her side, she bade me repeat certain verses composed by herself not many days before. I obeyed her.—They were these:

> Lo! 't is a gala night
>   Within the lonesome latter years!
> An angel throng, bewinged, bedight
>   In veils, and drowned in tears,
> Sit in a theatre, to see
>   A play of hopes and fears,
> While the orchestra breathes fitfully
>   The music of the spheres.
>
> Mimes, in the form of God on high,
>   Mutter and mumble low,
> And hither and thither fly—
>   Mere puppets they, who come and go
> At bidding of vast formless things
>   That shift the scenery to and fro,
> Flapping from out their Condor wings
>   Invisible Wo!
>
> That motley drama!—oh, be sure
>   It shall not be forgot!
> With its Phantom chased forever more,
>   By a crowd that seize it not,
> Through a circle that ever returneth in
>   To the self-same spot,
> And much of Madness and more of Sin
>   And Horror the soul of the plot.
>
> But see, amid the mimic rout,
>   A crawling shape intrude!
> A blood-red thing that writhes from out
>   The scenic solitude!
> It writhes!—it writhes!—with mortal pangs
>   The mimes become its food,
> And the seraphs sob at vermin fangs
>   In human gore imbued.
>
> Out—out are the lights—out all!
>   And over each quivering form,
> The curtain, a funeral pall,
>   Comes down with the rush of a storm,

And the angels, all pallid and wan,
Uprising, unveiling, affirm
That the play is the tragedy, "Man,"
And its hero the Conqueror Worm.

"Oh God!" half shrieked Ligeia, leaping to her feet and extending her arms aloft
with a spasmodic movement, as I made an end of these lines—"O God! O Divine
Father!—shall these things be undeviatingly so?—shall this Conqueror be not once
conquered? Are we not part and parcel in Thee? Who—who knoweth the mysteries
of the will with its vigor? Man doth not yield him to the angels, *nor unto death utterly,*
save only through the weakness of his feeble will."

And now, as if exhausted with emotion, she suffered her white arms to fall, and
returned solemnly to her bed of death. And as she breathed her last sighs, there came
mingled with them a low murmur from her lips. I bent to them my ear and
distinguished, again, the concluding words of the passage in Glanvill—*"Man doth not
yield him to the angels, nor unto death utterly, save only through the weakness of his feeble
will."*

She died;—and I, crushed into the very dust with sorrow, could no longer endure
the lonely desolation of my dwelling in the dim and decaying city by the Rhine. I
had no lack of what the world calls wealth. Ligeia had brought me far more, very
far more than ordinarily falls to the lot of mortals. After a few months, therefore,
of weary and aimless wandering, I purchased, and put in some repair, an abbey, which
I shall not name, in one of the wildest and least frequented portions of fair England.
The gloomy and dreary grandeur of the building, the almost savage aspect of the
domain, the many melancholy and time-honored memories connected with both, had
much in unison with the feelings of utter abandonment which had driven me into
that remote and unsocial region of the country. Yet although the external abbey, with
its verdant decay hanging about it, suffered but little alteration, I gave way, with a
child-like perversity, and perchance with a faint hope of alleviating my sorrows, to
a display of more than regal magnificence within.—For such follies, even in childhood, I had imbibed a taste and now they came back to me as if in the dotage of
grief. Alas, I feel how much even of incipient madness might have been discovered
in the gorgeous and fantastic draperies, in the solemn carvings of Egypt, in the wild
cornices and furniture, in the Bedlam[14] patterns of the carpets of tufted gold! I had
become a bounden slave in the trammels of opium, and my labors and my orders had
taken a coloring from my dreams. But these absurdities I must not pause to detail.
Let me speak only of that one chamber, ever accursed, whither in a moment of mental
alienation, I led from the altar as my bride—as the successor of the unforgotten Ligeia
—the fair-haired and blue-eyed Lady Rowena Trevanion, of Tremaine.

There is no individual portion of the architecture and decoration of that bridal
chamber which is not now visibly before me. Where were the souls of the haughty
family of the bride, when, through thirst of gold, they permitted to pass the threshold
of an apartment *so* bedecked, a maiden and a daughter so beloved? I have said that

---

[14] Crazed. The London lunatic asylum Bethlehem
Hospital was known as "Bedlam," a contraction
of the name.

I minutely remember the details of the chamber—yet I am sadly forgetful on topics of deep moment—and here there was no system, no keeping, in the fantastic display, to take hold upon the memory. The room lay in a high turret of the castellated abbey, was pentagonal in shape, and of capacious size. Occupying the whole southern face of the pentagon was the sole window—an immense sheet of unbroken glass from Venice—a single pane, and tinted of a leaden hue, so that the rays of either the sun or moon, passing through it, fell with a ghastly lustre on the objects within. Over the upper portion of this huge window, extended the trellice-work of an aged vine, which clambered up the massy walls of the turret. The ceiling, of gloomy-looking oak, was excessively lofty, vaulted, and elaborately fretted with the wildest and most grotesque specimens of a semi-Gothic, semi-Druidical[15] device. From out the most central recess of this melancholy vaulting, depended, by a single chain of gold with long links, a huge censer of the same metal, Saracenic[16] in pattern, and with many perforations so contrived that there writhed in and out of them, as if endued with a serpent vitality, a continual succession of parti-colored fires.

Some few ottomans and golden candelabra, of Eastern figure, were in various stations about—and there was the couch, too—the bridal couch—of an Indian model, and low, and sculptured of solid ebony, with a pall-like canopy above. In each of the angles of the chamber stood on end a gigantic sarcophagus of black granite, from the tombs of the kings over against Luxor,[17] with their aged lids full of immemorial sculpture. But in the draping of the apartment lay, alas! the chief phantasy of all. The lofty walls, gigantic in height—even unproportionably so—were hung from summit to foot, in vast folds, with a heavy and massive-looking tapestry—tapestry of a material which was found alike as a carpet on the floor, as a covering for the ottomans and the ebony bed, as a canopy for the bed, and as the gorgeous volutes of the curtains which partially shaded the window. The material was the richest cloth of gold. It was spotted all over, at irregular intervals, with arabesque figures, about a foot in diameter, and wrought upon the cloth in patterns of the most jetty black. But these figures partook of the true character of the arabesque only when regarded from a single point of view. By a contrivance now common, and indeed traceable to a very remote period of antiquity, they were made changeable in aspect. To one entering the room, they bore the appearance of simple monstrosities; but upon a farther advance, this appearance gradually departed; and step by step, as the visiter moved his station in the chamber, he saw himself surrounded by an endless succession of the ghastly forms which belong to the superstition of the Norman,[18] or arise in the guilty slumbers of the monk. The phantasmagoric effect was vastly heightened by the artificial introduction of a strong continual current of wind behind the draperies—giving a hideous and uneasy animation to the whole.

In halls such as these—in a bridal chamber such as this—I passed, with the Lady of Tremaine, the unhallowed hours of the first month of our marriage—passed them with but little disquietude. That my wife dreaded the fierce moodiness of my temper —that she shunned me and loved me but little—I could not help perceiving; but it

[15] In the style of the Druids, the priestly class of Celtic Britain.
[16] Arabic.
[17] City in ancient Egypt.

[18] The Vikings who came from the North in conquest of that area of the European continent later known as French Normandy. Their crafts are noted for their intricate designs.

gave me rather pleasure than otherwise. I loathed her with a hatred belonging more to demon than to man. My memory flew back, (oh, with what intensity of regret!) to Ligeia, the beloved, the august, the beautiful, the entombed. I revelled in recollections of her purity, of her wisdom, of her lofty, her ethereal nature, of her passionate, her idolatrous love. Now, then, did my spirit fully and freely burn with more than all the fires of her own. In the excitement of my opium dreams (for I was habitually fettered in the shackles of the drug) I would call aloud upon her name, during the silence of the night, or among the sheltered recesses of the glens by day, as if, through the wild eagerness, the solemn passion, the consuming ardor of my longing for the departed, I could restore her to the pathway she had abandoned—ah, *could* it be forever?—upon the earth.

About the commencement of the second month of the marriage, the Lady Rowena was attacked with sudden illness, from which her recovery was slow. The fever which consumed her rendered her nights uneasy; and in her perturbed state of half-slumber, she spoke of sounds, and of motions, in and about the chamber of the turret, which I concluded had no origin save in the distemper of her fancy, or perhaps in the phantasmagoric influences of the chamber itself. She became at length convalescent—finally well. Yet but a brief period elapsed, ere a second more violent disorder again threw her upon a bed of suffering; and from this attack her frame, at all times feeble, never altogether recovered. Her illnesses were, after this epoch, of alarming character, and of more alarming recurrence, defying alike the knowledge and the great exertions of her physicians. With the increase of the chronic disease which had thus, apparently, taken too sure hold upon her constitution to be eradicated by human means, I could not fail to observe a similar increase in the nervous irritation of her temperament, and in her excitability by trivial causes of fear. She spoke again, and now more frequently and pertinaciously, of the sounds—of the slight sounds—and of the unusual motions among the tapestries, to which she had formerly alluded.

One night, near the closing in of September, she pressed this distressing subject with more than usual emphasis upon my attention. She had just awakened from an unquiet slumber, and I had been watching, with feelings half of anxiety, half of vague terror, the workings of her emaciated countenance. I sat by the side of her ebony bed, upon one of the ottomans of India. She partly arose, and spoke, in an earnest low whisper, of sounds which she *then* heard, but which I could not hear—of motions which she *then* saw, but which I could not perceive. The wind was rushing hurriedly behind the tapestries, and I wished to show her (what, let me confess it, I could not *all* believe) that those almost inarticulate breathings, and those very gentle variations of the figures upon the wall, were but the natural effects of that customary rushing of the wind. But a deadly pallor, overspreading her face, had proved to me that my exertions to reassure her would be fruitless. She appeared to be fainting, and no attendants were within call. I remembered where was deposited a decanter of light wine which had been ordered by her physicians, and hastened across the chamber to procure it. But, as I stepped beneath the light of the censer, two circumstances of a startling nature attracted my attention. I had felt that some palpable although invisible object had passed lightly by my person; and I saw that there lay upon the golden carpet, in the very middle of the rich lustre thrown from the censer, a shadow—a faint, indefinite shadow of angelic aspect—such as might be fancied for the shadow of a shade. But I was wild with the excitement of an immoderate dose of opium, and heeded these things but little, nor spoke of them to Rowena. Having found the wine, I recrossed the chamber, and poured out a goblet-ful, which I held to the lips of the fainting lady. She had now partially recovered, however, and took the vessel herself, while I sank upon an ottoman near me, with my eyes fastened upon her person. It was then that I became distinctly aware of a gentle foot-fall upon the carpet, and near the couch; and in a second thereafter, as Rowena was in the act of raising the wine to her lips, I saw, or may have dreamed that I saw, fall within the goblet, as if from some invisible spring in the atmosphere of the room, three or four large drops of a brilliant and ruby colored fluid. If this I saw—not so Rowena. She swallowed the wine unhesitatingly, and I forbore to speak to her of a circumstance which must, after all, I considered, have been but the suggestion of a vivid imagination, rendered morbidly active by the terror of the lady, by the opium, and by the hour.

Yet I cannot conceal it from my own perception that, immediately subsequent to the fall of the ruby-drops, a rapid change for the worse took place in the disorder of my wife; so that, on the third subsequent night, the hands of her menials prepared her for the tomb, and on the fourth, I sat alone, with her shrouded body, in that fantastic chamber which had received her as my bride.—Wild visions, opium-engendered, flitted, shadowlike, before me. I gazed with unquiet eye upon the sarcophagi in the angles of the room, upon the varying figures of the drapery, and upon the writhing of the parti-colored fires in the censer overhead. My eyes then fell, as I called to mind the circumstances of a former night, to the spot beneath the glare of the censer where I had seen the faint traces of the shadow. It was there, however, no longer; and breathing with greater freedom, I turned my glances to the pallid and rigid figure upon the bed. Then rushed upon me a thousand memories of Ligeia—and then came back upon my heart, with the turbulent violence of a flood, the whole of that unutterable wo with which I had regarded *her* thus enshrouded. The night waned; and still, with a bosom full of bitter thoughts of the one only and supremely beloved, I remained gazing upon the body of Rowena.

It might have been midnight, or perhaps earlier, or later, for I had taken no note of time, when a sob, low, gentle, but very distinct, startled me from my revery.—I *felt* that it came from the bed of ebony—the bed of death. I listened in an agony of superstitious terror—but there was no repetition of the sound. I strained my vision to detect any motion in the corpse—but there was not the slightest perceptible. Yet I could not have been deceived. I *had* heard the noise, however faint, and my soul was awakened within me. I resolutely and perseveringly kept my attention riveted upon the body. Many minutes elapsed before any circumstance occurred tending to throw light upon the mystery. At length it became evident that a slight, a very feeble, and barely noticeable tinge of color had flushed up within the cheeks, and along the sunken small veins of the eyelids. Through a species of unutterable horror and awe, for which the language of mortality has no sufficiently energetic expression, I felt my heart cease to beat, my limbs grow rigid where I sat. Yet a sense of duty finally operated to restore my self-possession. I could no longer doubt that we had been precipitate in our preparations—that Rowena still lived. It was necessary that some immediate exertion be made; yet the turret was altogether apart from the portion of the abbey tenanted by the servants—there were none within call—I had no means of summoning them to my aid without leaving the room for many minutes—and this I could not venture to do. I therefore struggled alone in my endeavors to call back the spirit still hovering. In a short period it was certain, however, that a relapse had taken place; the color disappeared from both eyelid and cheek, leaving a wanness even more than that of marble; the lips became doubly shrivelled and pinched up in the ghastly expression of death; a repulsive clamminess and coldness overspread rapidly the surface of the body; and all the usual rigorous stiffness immediately supervened. I fell back with a shudder upon the couch from which I had been so startlingly aroused, and again gave myself up to passionate waking visions of Ligeia.

An hour thus elapsed when (could it be possible?) I was a second time aware of some vague sound issuing from the region of the bed. I listened—in extremity of horror. The sound came again—it was a sigh. Rushing to the corpse, I saw—distinctly saw—a tremor upon the lips. In a minute afterward they relaxed, disclosing a bright line of the pearly teeth. Amazement now struggled in my bosom with the profound awe which had hitherto reigned there alone. I felt that my vision grew dim, that my reason wandered; and it was only by a violent effort that I at length succeeded in nerving myself to the task which duty thus once more had pointed out. There was now a partial glow upon the forehead and upon the cheek and throat; a perceptible warmth pervaded the whole frame; there was even a slight pulsation at the heart. The lady *lived;* and with redoubled ardor I betook myself to the task of restoration. I chafed and bathed the temples and the hands, and used every exertion which experience, and no little medical reading, could suggest. But in vain. Suddenly, the color fled, the pulsation ceased, the lips resumed the expression of the dead, and, in an instant afterward, the whole body took upon itself the icy chilliness, the livid hue, the intense rigidity, the sunken outline, and all the loathsome peculiarities of that which has been, for many days, a tenant of the tomb.

And again I sunk into visions of Ligeia—and again, (what marvel that I shudder while I write?) *again* there reached my ears a low sob from the region of the ebony bed. But why shall I minutely detail the unspeakable horrors of that night? Why shall I pause to relate how, time after time, until near the period of the gray dawn, this hideous drama of revification was repeated; how each terrific relapse was only into a sterner and apparently more irredeemable death; how each agony wore the aspect of a struggle with some invisible foe; and how each struggle was succeeded by I know not what of wild change in the personal appearance of the corpse? Let me hurry to a conclusion.

The greater part of the fearful night had worn away, and she who had been dead, once again stirred—and now more vigorously than hitherto, although arousing from a dissolution more appalling in its utter hopelessness than any. I had long ceased to struggle or to move, and remained sitting rigidly upon the ottoman, a helpless prey to a whirl of violent emotions, of which extreme awe was perhaps the least terrible, the least consuming. The corpse, I repeat, stirred, and now more vigorously than before. The hues of life flushed up with unwonted energy into the countenance— the limbs relaxed—and, save that the eyelids were yet pressed heavily together, and that the bandages and draperies of the grave still imparted their charnel character to the figure, I might have dreamed that Rowena had indeed shaken off, utterly, the fetters of Death. But if this idea was not, even then, altogether adopted, I could at least doubt no longer, when, arising from the bed, tottering, with feeble steps, with closed eyes, and with the manner of one bewildered in a dream, the thing that was enshrouded advanced boldly and palpably into the middle of the apartment.

I trembled not—I stirred not—for a crowd of unutterable fancies connected with the air, the stature, the demeanor of the figure, rushing hurriedly through my brain, had paralyzed—had chilled me into stone. I stirred not—but gazed upon the apparition. There was a mad disorder in my thoughts—a tumult unappeasable. Could it, indeed, be the *living* Rowena who confronted me? Could it indeed by Rowena *at all*—the fair-haired, the blue-eyed Lady Rowena Trevanion of Tremaine? Why, *why* should I doubt it? The bandage lay heavily about the mouth—but then might it not be the mouth of the breathing Lady of Tremaine? And the cheeks—there were the roses as in her noon of life—yes, these might indeed be the fair cheeks of the living Lady of Tremaine. And the chin, with its dimples, as in health, might it not be hers? —but *had she then grown taller since her malady?* What inexpressible madness seized me with that thought? One bound, and I had reached her feet! Shrinking from my touch, she let fall from her head, unloosened, the ghastly cerements which had confined it, and there streamed forth, into the rushing atmosphere of the chamber, huge masses of long and dishevelled hair; *it was blacker than the raven wings of the midnight!* And now slowly opened *the eyes* of the figure which stood before me. "Here, then, at least," I shrieked aloud, "can I never—can I never be mistaken—these are the full, and the black, and the wild eyes—of my lost love—of the lady—of the LADY LIGEIA."

1838

The Fall of the House of Usher

Son cœur est un luth suspendu;
Sitôt qu'on le touche il résonne.
De Béranger[1]

During the whole of a dull, dark, and soundless day in the autumn of the year, when the clouds hung oppressively low in the heavens, I had been passing alone, on horseback, through a singularly dreary tract of country; and at length found myself, as the shades of the evening drew on, within view of the melancholy House of Usher. I know not how it was—but, with the first glimpse of the building, a sense of insufferable gloom pervaded my spirit. I say insufferable; for the feeling was unrelieved by any of that half-pleasurable, because poetic, sentiment, with which the mind usually receives even the sternest natural images of the desolate or terrible. I looked upon the scene before me—upon the mere house, and the simple landscape features of the domain—upon the bleak walls—upon the vacant eye-like windows —upon a few rank sedges—and upon a few white trunks of decayed trees—with an utter depression of soul which I can compare to no earthly sensation more properly

---

[1] From "Le Refus" (1831) by the French poet Pierre-Jean de Béranger (1780–1857). The lines, which Poe partly altered to read "his heart" rather than "my heart," translate as "His heart is a lute, tightly strung; / The instant one touches it, it resounds."

than to the after-dream of the reveller upon opium—the bitter lapse into every-day life—the hideous dropping off of the veil. There was an iciness, a sinking, a sickening of the heart—an unredeemed dreariness of thought which no goading of the imagination could torture into aught of the sublime. What was it—I paused to think—what was it that so unnerved me in the contemplation of the House of Usher? It was a mystery all insoluble; nor could I grapple with the shadowy fancies that crowded upon me as I pondered. I was forced to fall back upon the unsatisfactory conclusion, that while, beyond doubt, there *are* combinations of very simple natural objects which have the power of thus affecting us, still the analysis of this power lies among considerations beyond our depth. It was possible, I reflected, that a mere different arrangement of the particulars of the scene, of the details of the picture, would be sufficient to modify, or perhaps to annihilate its capacity for sorrowful impression; and, acting upon this idea, I reined my horse to the precipitous brink of a black and lurid tarn[2] that lay in unruffled lustre by the dwelling, and gazed down—but with a shudder even more thrilling than before—upon the remodelled and inverted images of the gray sedge, and the ghastly tree-stems, and the vacant and eye-like windows.

Nevertheless, in this mansion of gloom I now proposed to myself a sojourn of some weeks. Its proprietor, Roderick Usher, had been one of my boon companions in boyhood; but many years had elapsed since our last meeting. A letter, however, had lately reached me in a distant part of the country—a letter from him—which, in its wildly importunate nature, had admitted of no other than a personal reply. The MS. gave evidence of nervous agitation. The writer spoke of acute bodily illness—of a mental disorder which oppressed him—and of an earnest desire to see me, as his best, and indeed his only personal friend, with a view of attempting, by the cheerfulness of my society, some alleviation of his malady. It was the manner in which all this, and much more, was said—it was the apparent *heart* that went with his request— which allowed me no room for hesitation; and I accordingly obeyed forthwith what I still considered a very singular summons.

Although, as boys, we had been even intimate associates, yet I really knew little of my friend. His reserve had been always excessive and habitual. I was aware, however, that his very ancient family had been noted, time out of mind, for a peculiar sensibility of temperament, displaying itself, through long ages, in many works of exalted art, and manifested, of late, in repeated deeds of munificent yet unobtrusive charity, as well as in a passionate devotion to the intricacies, perhaps even more than to the orthodox and easily recognisable beauties, of musical science. I had learned, too, the very remarkable fact, that the stem of the Usher race, all time-honoured as it was, had put forth, at no period, any enduring branch; in other words, that the entire family lay in the direct line of descent, and had always, with very trifling and very temporary variation, so lain. It was this deficiency, I considered, while running over in thought the perfect keeping of the character of the premises with the accredited character of the people, and while speculating upon the possible influence which the one, in the long lapse of centuries, might have exercised upon the other—it was this deficiency, perhaps, of collateral issue, and the consequent undeviating transmission, from sire to son, of the patrimony with the name, which had, at length, so identified the two as to merge the original title of the estate in the quaint and equivocal appellation of the

[2] Small mountain lake.

"House of Usher"—an appellation which seemed to include, in the minds of the peasantry who used it, both the family and the family mansion.

I have said that the sole effect of my somewhat childish experiment—that of looking down within the tarn—had been to deepen the first singular impression. There can be no doubt that the consciousness of the rapid increase of my superstition —for why should I not so term it?—served mainly to accelerate the increase itself. Such, I have long known, is the paradoxical law of all sentiments having terror as a basis. And it might have been for this reason only, that, when I again uplifted my eyes to the house itself, from its image in the pool, there grew in my mind a strange fancy—a fancy so ridiculous, indeed, that I but mention it to show the vivid force of the sensations which oppressed me. I had so worked upon my imagination as really to believe that about the whole mansion and domain there hung an atmosphere peculiar to themselves and their immediate vicinity—an atmosphere which had no affinity with the air of heaven, but which had reeked up from the decayed trees, and the gray wall, and the silent tarn—a pestilent and mystic vapour, dull, sluggish, faintly discernible, and leaden-hued.

Shaking off from my spirit what *must* have been a dream, I scanned more narrowly the real aspect of the building. Its principal feature seemed to be that of an excessive antiquity. The discoloration of ages had been great. Minute fungi overspread the whole exterior, hanging in a fine tangled web-work from the eaves. Yet all this was apart from any extraordinary dilapidation. No portion of the masonry had fallen; and there appeared to be a wild inconsistency between its still perfect adaptation of parts, and the crumbling condition of the individual stones. In this there was much that reminded me of the specious totality of old wood-work which has rotted for long years in some neglected vault, with no disturbance from the breath of the external air. Beyond this indication of extensive decay, however, the fabric gave little token of instability. Perhaps the eye of a scrutinising observer might have discovered a barely perceptible fissure, which, extending from the roof of the building in front, made its way down the wall in a zigzag direction, until it became lost in the sullen waters of the tarn.

Noticing these things, I rode over a short causeway to the house. A servant in waiting took my horse, and I entered the Gothic archway of the hall. A valet, of stealthy step, thence conducted me, in silence, through many dark and intricate passages in my progress to the *studio* of his master. Much that I encountered on the way contributed, I know not how, to heighten the vague sentiments of which I have already spoken. While the objects around me—while the carvings of the ceilings, the sombre tapestries of the walls, the ebon blackness of the floors, and the phantasmagoric armorial trophies which rattled as I strode, were but matters to which, or to such as which, I had been accustomed from my infancy—while I hesitated not to acknowledge how familiar was all this—I still wondered to find how unfamiliar were the fancies which ordinary images were stirring up. On one of the staircases, I met the physician of the family. His countenance, I thought, wore a mingled expression of low cunning and perplexity. He accosted me with trepidation and passed on. The valet now threw open a door and ushered me into the presence of his master.

The room in which I found myself was very large and lofty. The windows were long, narrow, and pointed, and at so vast a distance from the black oaken floor as to be altogether inaccessible from within. Feeble gleams of encrimsoned light made their way through the trellised panes, and served to render sufficiently distinct the more prominent objects around; the eye, however, struggled in vain to reach the remoter angles of the chamber, or the recesses of the vaulted and fretted ceiling. Dark draperies hung upon the walls. The general furniture was profuse, comfortless, antique, and tattered. Many books and musical instruments lay scattered about, but failed to give any vitality to the scene. I felt that I breathed an atmosphere of sorrow. An air of stern, deep, and irredeemable gloom hung over and pervaded all.

Upon my entrance, Usher arose from a sofa on which he had been lying at full length, and greeted me with a vivacious warmth which had much in it, I at first thought, of an overdone cordiality—of the constrained effort of the *ennuyé*[3] man of the world. A glance, however, at his countenance, convinced me of his perfect sincerity. We sat down; and for some moments, while he spoke not, I gazed upon him with a feeling half of pity, half of awe. Surely, man had never before so terribly altered, in so brief a period, as had Roderick Usher! It was with difficulty that I could bring myself to admit the identity of the wan being before me with the companion of my early boyhood. Yet the character of his face had been at all times remarkable. A cadaverousness of complexion; an eye large, liquid, and luminous beyond comparison; lips somewhat thin and very pallid, but of a surpassingly beautiful curve; a nose of a delicate Hebrew model, but with a breadth of nostril unusual in similar formations; a finely moulded chin, speaking, in its want of prominence, of a want of moral energy; hair of a more than web-like softness and tenuity; these features, with an inordinate expansion above the regions of the temple, made up altogether a countenance not easily to be forgotten. And now in the mere exaggeration of the prevailing character of these features, and of the expression they were wont to convey, lay so much of change that I doubted to whom I spoke. The now ghastly pallor of the skin, and the now miraculous lustre of the eye, above all things startled and even awed me. The silken hair, too, had been suffered to grow all unheeded, and as, in its wild gossamer texture, it floated rather than fell about the face, I could not, even with effort, connect its Arabesque[4] expression with any idea of simple humanity.

In the manner of my friend I was at once struck with an incoherence—an inconsistency; and I soon found this to arise from a series of feeble and futile struggles to overcome an habitual trepidancy—an excessive nervous agitation. For something of this nature I had indeed been prepared, no less by his letter, than by reminiscences of certain boyish traits, and by conclusions deduced from his peculiar physical conformation and temperament. His action was alternately vivacious and sullen. His voice varied rapidly from a tremulous indecision (when the animal spirits seemed utterly in abeyance) to that species of energetic concision—that abrupt, weighty, unhurried, and hollow-sounding enunciation—that leaden, self-balanced and perfectly modulated guttural utterance, which may be observed in the lost drunkard, or the irreclaimable eater of opium, during the periods of his most intense excitement.

It was thus that he spoke of the object of my visit, of his earnest desire to see me, and of the solace he expected me to afford him. He entered, at some length, into what he conceived to be the nature of his malady. It was, he said, a constitutional and a family evil, and one for which he despaired to find a remedy—a mere nervous affection, he immediately added, which would undoubtedly soon pass off. It displayed

---

[3] French: "bored."

[4] Fantastic, complex.

itself in a host of unnatural sensations. Some of these, as he detailed them, interested and bewildered me; although, perhaps, the terms and the general manner of the narration had their weight. He suffered much from a morbid acuteness of the senses; the most insipid food was alone endurable; he could wear only garments of certain texture; the odours of all flowers were oppressive; his eyes were tortured by even a faint light; and there were but peculiar sounds, and these from stringed instruments, which did not inspire him with horror.

To an anomalous species of terror I found him a bounden slave. "I shall perish," said he, "I *must* perish in this deplorable folly. Thus, thus, and not otherwise, shall I be lost. I dread the events of the future, not in themselves, but in their results. I shudder at the thought of any, even the most trivial, incident, which may operate upon this intolerable agitation of soul. I have, indeed, no abhorrence of danger, except in its absolute effect—in terror. In this unnerved—in this pitiable condition—I feel that the period will sooner or later arrive when I must abandon life and reason together, in some struggle with the grim phantasm, FEAR."

I learned, moreover, at intervals, and through broken and equivocal hints, another singular feature of his mental condition. He was enchained by certain superstitious impressions in regard to the dwelling which he tenanted, and whence, for many years, he had never ventured forth—in regard to an influence whose suppositious force was conveyed in terms too shadowy here to be re-stated—an influence which some peculiarities in the mere form and substance of his family mansion, had, by dint of long sufferance, he said, obtained over his spirit—an effect which the *physique* of the gray walls and turrets, and of the dim tarn into which they all looked down, had, at length, brought about upon the *morale* of his existence.

He admitted, however, although with hesitation, that much of the peculiar gloom which thus afflicted him could be traced to a more natural and far more palpable origin —to the severe and long-continued illness—indeed to the evidently approaching dissolution—of a tenderly beloved sister—his sole companion for long years—his last and only relative on earth. "Her decease," he said, with a bitterness which I can never forget, "would leave him (him the hopeless and the frail) the last of the ancient race of the Ushers." While he spoke, the lady Madeline (for so was she called) passed slowly through a remote portion of the apartment, and, without having noticed my presence, disappeared. I regarded her with an utter astonishment not unmingled with dread—and yet I found it impossible to account for such feelings. A sensation of stupor oppressed me, as my eyes followed her retreating steps. When a door, at length, closed upon her, my glance sought instinctively and eagerly the countenance of the brother—but he had buried his face in his hands, and I could only perceive that a far more than ordinary wanness had overspread the emaciated fingers through which trickled many passionate tears.

The disease of the lady Madeline had long baffled the skill of her physicians. A settled apathy, a gradual wasting away of the person, and frequent although transient affections of a partially cataleptical character, were the unusual diagnosis. Hitherto she had steadily borne up against the pressure of her malady, and had not betaken herself finally to bed; but, on the closing in of the evening of my arrival at the house, she succumbed (as her brother told me at night with inexpressible agitation) to the prostrating power of the destroyer; and I learned that the glimpse I had obtained of her person would thus probably be the last I should obtain—that the lady, at least while living, would be seen by me no more.

For several days ensuing, her name was unmentioned by either Usher or myself: and during this period I was busied in earnest endeavours to alleviate the melancholy of my friend. We painted and read together; or I listened, as if in a dream, to the wild improvisations of his speaking guitar. And thus, as a closer and still closer intimacy admitted me more unreservedly into the recesses of his spirit, the more bitterly did I perceive the futility of all attempt at cheering a mind from which darkness, as if an inherent positive quality, poured forth upon all objects of the moral and physical universe, in one unceasing radiation of gloom.

I shall ever bear about me a memory of the many solemn hours I thus spent alone with the master of the House of Usher. Yet I should fail in any attempt to convey an idea of the exact character of the studies, or of the occupations, in which he involved me, or led me the way. An excited and highly distempered ideality threw a sulphureous lustre over all. His long improvised dirges will ring forever in my ears. Among other things, I hold painfully in mind a certain singular perversion and amplification of the wild air of the last waltz of Von Weber.[5] From the paintings over which his elaborate fancy brooded, and which grew, touch by touch, into vaguenesses at which I shuddered the more thrillingly, because I shuddered knowing not why;—from these paintings (vivid as their images now are before me) I would in vain endeavour to educe more than a small portion which should lie within the compass of merely written words. By the utter simplicity, by the nakedness of his designs, he arrested and overawed attention. If ever mortal painted an idea, that mortal was Roderick Usher. For me at least—in the circumstances then surrounding me— these arose out of the pure abstractions which the hypochondriac contrived to throw upon his canvas, an intensity of intolerable awe, no shadow of which felt I ever yet in the contemplation of the certainly glowing yet too concrete reveries of Fuseli.[6]

One of the phantasmagoric conceptions of my friend, partaking not so rigidly of the spirit of abstraction, may be shadowed forth, although feebly, in words. A small picture presented the interior of an immensely long and rectangular vault or tunnel, with low walls, smooth, white, and without interruption or device. Certain accessory points of the design served well to convey the idea that this excavation lay at an exceeding depth below the surface of the earth. No outlet was observed in any portion of its vast extent, and no torch, or other artificial source of light was discernible; yet a flood of intense rays rolled throughout, and bathed the whole in a ghastly and inappropriate splendour.

I have just spoken of that morbid condition of the auditory nerve which rendered all music intolerable to the sufferer, with the exception of certain effects of stringed instruments. It was, perhaps, the narrow limits to which he thus confined himself upon the guitar, which gave birth, in great measure, to the fantastic character of his performances. But the fervid *facility* of his *impromptus* could not be so accounted for.

---

[5] Karl Maria von Weber (1786–1826), German Romantic composer, who was honored by "The Last Waltz of Von Weber," written by Karl Gottlieb Reissiger (1798–1859).

[6] Henry Fuseli (1742–1825), Swiss-born artist with a long career in England, whose paintings manifest the more nightmarish side of Romanticism.

They must have been, and were, in the notes, as well as in the words of his wild fantasias (for he not unfrequently accompanied himself with rhymed verbal improvisations), the result of that intense mental collectedness and concentration to which I have previously alluded as observable only in particular moments of the highest artificial excitement. The words of one of these rhapsodies I have easily remembered. I was, perhaps, the more forcibly impressed with it, as he gave it, because in the under or mystic current of its meaning, I fancied that I perceived, and for the first time, a full consciousness on the part of Usher, of the tottering of his lofty reason upon her throne. The verses, which were entitled "The Haunted Palace," ran very nearly, if not accurately, thus:

I.

In the greenest of our valleys,
    By good angels tenanted,
Once a fair and stately palace—
    Radiant palace—reared its head.
In the monarch Thought's dominion—
    It stood there!
Never seraph spread a pinion
    Over fabric half so fair.

II.

Banners yellow, glorious, golden,
    On its roof did float and flow;
(This—all this—was in the olden
    Time long ago)
And every gentle air that dallied,
    In that sweet day,
Along the ramparts plumed and pallid,
    A winged odour went away.

III.

Wanderers in that happy valley
    Through two luminous windows saw
Spirits moving musically
    To a lute's well-tunèd law,
Round about a throne, where sitting
    (Porphyrogene!)[7]
In state his glory well befitting,
    The ruler of the realm was seen.

---

[7] "Born to the purple"; that is, of royal lineage.

IV.

And all with pearl and ruby glowing
    Was the fair palace door,
Through which came flowing, flowing, flowing
    And sparkling evermore,
A troop of Echoes whose sweet duty
    Was but to sing,
In voices of surpassing beauty,
    The wit and wisdom of their king.

V.

But evil things, in robes of sorrow,
    Assailed the monarch's high estate;
(Ah, let us mourn, for never morrow
    Shall dawn upon him, desolate!)
And, round about his home, the glory
    That blushed and bloomed
Is but a dim-remembered story
    Of the old time entombed.

VI.

And travellers now within that valley,
    Through the red-litten windows, see
Vast forms that move fantastically
    To a discordant melody;
While, like a rapid ghastly river,
    Through the pale door,
A hideous throng rush out forever,
    And laugh—but smile no more.

I well remember that suggestions arising from this ballad, led us into a train of thought wherein there became manifest an opinion of Usher's which I mention not so much on account of its novelty, (for other men[8] have thought thus,) as on account of the pertinacity with which he maintained it. This opinion, in its general form, was that of the sentience of all vegetable things. But, in his disordered fancy, the idea had assumed a more daring character, and trespassed, under certain conditions, upon the kingdom of inorganization. I lack words to express the full extent, or the earnest

[8] Poe's note: "Watson, Dr. Percival, Spallanzani, and especially the Bishop of Landaff.—See 'Chemical Essays,' vol. v." That is, Richard Watson (1737–1816), bishop of Llandaff, English theologian, chemist, and author of *Chemical Essays*; Robert Percival (1756–1839), English physician and student of chemistry; Lazzaro Spallanzani (1739–1799), Italian physiologist.

abandon of his persuasion. The belief, however, was connected (as I have previously hinted) with the gray stones of the home of his forefathers. The conditions of the sentience had been here, he imagined, fulfilled in the method of collocation of these stones—in the order of their arrangement, as well as in that of the many *fungi* which overspread them, and of the decayed trees which stood around—above all, in the long undisturbed endurance of this arrangement, and in its reduplication in the still waters of the tarn. Its evidence—the evidence of the sentience—was to be seen, he said, (and I here started as he spoke,) in the gradual yet certain condensation of an atmosphere of their own about the waters and the walls. The result was discoverable, he added, in that silent, yet importunate and terrible influence which for centuries had moulded the destinies of his family, and which made *him* what I now saw him—what he was. Such opinions need no comment, and I will make none.

Our books—the books which, for years, had formed no small portion of the mental existence of the invalid—were, as might be supposed, in strict keeping with this character of phantasm. We poured together over such works as the Ververt et Chartreuse of Gresset; the Belphegor of Machiavelli; the Heaven and Hell of Swedenborg; the Subterranean Voyage of Nicholas Klimm by Holberg; the Chiromancy of Robert Flud, of Jean D'Indaginé, and of De la Chambre; the Journey into the Blue Distance of Tieck; and the City of the Sun of Campanella.[9] One favourite volume was a small octavo edition of the *Directorium Inquisitorum,* by the Dominican Eymeric de Gironne;[10] and there were passages in Pomponius Mela,[11] about the old African Satyrs and Ægipans, over which Usher would sit dreaming for hours. His chief delight, however, was found in the perusal of an exceedingly rare and curious book in quarto Gothic—the manual of a forgotten church—the *Vigiliæ Mortuorum secundum Chorum Ecclesiæ Maguntinæ.*[12]

I could not help thinking of the wild ritual of this work, and of its probable influence upon the hypochondriac, when, one evening, having informed me abruptly that the lady Madeline was no more, he stated his intention of preserving her corpse for a fortnight, (previously to its final interment,) in one of the numerous vaults within the main walls of the building. The worldly reason, however, assigned for this singular proceeding, was one which I did not feel at liberty to dispute. The brother had been led to his resolution (so he told me) by consideration of the unusual character of the malady of the deceased, of certain obtrusive and eager inquiries on the part of her medical men, and of the remote and exposed situation of the burial-ground of the family. I will not deny that when I called to mind the sinister countenance

[9] Usher's collection of occult lore contains actual works by a number of European and British authors spanning centuries of interest in the supernatural. His holdings include titles by Louis Gresset (1709–1777); Niccolò Machiavelli (1469–1527); Emanuel Swedenborg (1688–1772); Ludwig Holberg (1684–1754); Robert Fludd (1574–1637); Joannes Indaginé (early sixteenth century); Martin Cureau de la Chambre (1594–1669); Ludwig Tieck (1773–1853); Tommaso Campanella (1568–1639).

[10] Nicholas Eymeric de Gironne (1320?–1399), the Dominican who wrote on the tortures of the Inquisition.

[11] The Roman author, Pomponious Mela, who peopled his geography of the ancient world with fabulous beasts, including tales of satyrs and the goat-god Pan (the "Aegipan").

[12] Book written around 1500, known as *Vigils for the Dead, according to the Choir of the Church of Mayence.*

of the person whom I met upon the staircase, on the day of my arrival at the house, I had no desire to oppose what I regarded as at best but a harmless, and by no means an unnatural, precaution.[13]

At the request of Usher, I personally aided him in the arrangements for the temporary entombment. The body having been encoffined, we two alone bore it to its rest. The vault in which we placed it (and which had been so long unopened that our torches, half smothered in its oppressive atmosphere, gave us little opportunity for investigation) was small, damp, and entirely without means of admission for light; lying, at great depth, immediately beneath that portion of the building in which was my own sleeping apartment. It had been used, apparently, in remote feudal times, for the worst purposes of a donjon-keep, and, in later days, as a place of deposit for powder, or some other highly combustible substance, as a portion of its floor, and the whole interior of a long archway through which we reached it, were carefully sheathed with copper. The door, of massive iron, had been, also, similarly protected. Its immense weight caused an unusually sharp grating sound, as it moved upon its hinges.

Having deposited our mournful burden upon tressels within this region of horror, we partially turned aside the yet unscrewed lid of the coffin, and looked upon the face of the tenant. A striking similitude between the brother and sister now first arrested my attention; and Usher, divining, perhaps, my thoughts, murmured out some few words from which I learned that the deceased and himself had been twins, and that sympathies of a scarcely intelligible nature had always existed between them. Our glances, however, rested not long upon the dead—for we could not regard her unawed. The disease which had thus entombed the lady in the maturity of youth, had left, as usual in all maladies of a strictly cataleptical character, the mockery of a faint blush upon the bosom and the face, and that suspiciously lingering smile upon the lip which is so terrible in death. We replaced and screwed down the lid, and, having secured the door of iron, made our way, with toil, into the scarcely less gloomy apartments of the upper portion of the house.

And now, some days of bitter grief having elapsed, an observable change came over the features of the mental disorder of my friend. His ordinary manner had vanished. His ordinary occupations were neglected or forgotten. He roamed from chamber to chamber with hurried, unequal, and objectless step. The pallor of his countenance had assumed, if possible, a more ghastly hue—but the luminousness of his eye had utterly gone out. The once occasional huskiness of his tone was heard no more; and a tremulous quaver, as if of extreme terror, habitually characterized his utterance. There were times, indeed, when I thought his unceasingly agitated mind was labouring with some oppressive secret, to divulge which he struggled for the necessary courage. At times, again, I was obliged to resolve all into the mere inexplicable vagaries of madness, for I beheld him gazing upon vacancy for long hours, in an attitude of the profoundest attention as if listening to some imaginary sound. It was no wonder that his condition terrified—that it infected me. I felt creeping upon me, by slow yet

[13] To prevent Madeline's body from being stolen from its grave and sold for medical experiments, a real possibility in those days of illicit traffic in corpses.

certain degrees, the wild influences of his own fantastic yet impressive superstitions.

It was, especially, upon retiring to bed late in the night of the seventh or eighth day after the placing of the lady Madeline within the donjon, that I experienced the full power of such feelings. Sleep came not near my couch—while the hours waned and waned away. I struggled to reason off the nervousness which had dominion over me. I endeavoured to believe that much, if not all of what I felt, was due to the bewildering influence of the gloomy furniture of the room—of the dark and tattered draperies, which, tortured into motion by the breath of a rising tempest, swayed fitfully to and fro upon the walls, and rustled uneasily about the decorations of the bed. But my efforts were fruitless. An irrepressible tremour gradually pervaded my frame; and, at length, there sat upon my very heart an incubus of utterly causeless alarm. Shaking this off with a gasp and a struggle, I uplifted myself upon the pillows, and, peering earnestly within the intense darkness of the chamber, hearkened—I know not why, except that an instinctive spirit prompted me—to certain low and indefinite sounds which came, through the pauses of the storm, at long intervals, I knew not whence. Overpowered by an intense sentiment of horror, unaccountable yet unendurable, I threw on my clothes with haste (for I felt that I should sleep no more during the night), and endeavoured to arouse myself from the pitiable condition into which I had fallen, by pacing rapidly to and fro through the apartment.

I had taken but few turns in this manner, when a light step on an adjoining staircase arrested my attention. I presently recognised it as that of Usher. In an instant afterward he rapped, with a gentle touch, at my door, and entered, bearing a lamp. His countenance was, as usual, cadaverously wan—but, moreover, there was a species of mad hilarity in his eyes—an evidently restrained *hysteria* in his whole demeanour. His air appalled me—but anything was preferable to the solitude which I had so long endured, and I even welcomed his presence as a relief.

"And you have not seen it?" he said abruptly, after having stared about him for some moments in silence—"you have not then seen it?—but, stay! you shall." Thus speaking, and having carefully shaded his lamp, he hurried to one of the casements, and threw it freely open to the storm.

The impetuous fury of the entering gust nearly lifted us from our feet. It was, indeed, a tempestuous yet sternly beautiful night, and one wildly singular in its terror and its beauty. A whirlwind had apparently collected its force in our vicinity; for there were frequent and violent alterations in the direction of the wind; and the exceeding density of the clouds (which hung so low as to press upon the turrets of the house) did not prevent our perceiving the life-like velocity with which they flew careering from all points against each other, without passing away into the distance. I say that even their exceeding density did not prevent our perceiving this—yet we had no glimpse of the moon or stars—nor was there any flashing forth of the lightning. But the under surfaces of the huge masses of agitated vapour, as well as all terrestrial objects immediately around us, were glowing in the unnatural light of a faintly luminous and distinctly visible gaseous exhalation which hung about and enshrouded the mansion.

"You must not—you shall not behold this!" said I, shudderingly, to Usher, as I led him, with a gentle violence, from the window to a seat. "These appearances, which bewilder you, are merely electrical phenomena not uncommon—or it may be that they have their ghastly origin in the rank miasma of the tarn. Let us close this casement;

—the air is chilling and dangerous to your frame. Here is one of your favourite romances. I will read, and you shall listen;—and so we will pass away this terrible night together."

The antique volume which I had taken up was the "Mad Trist"[14] of Sir Launcelot Canning; but I had called it a favourite of Usher's more in sad jest than in earnest; for, in truth, there is little in its uncouth and unimaginative prolixity which could have had interest for the lofty and spiritual ideality of my friend. It was, however, the only book immediately at hand; and I indulged a vague hope that the excitement which now agitated the hypochondriac, might find relief (for the history of mental disorder is full of similar anomalies) even in the extremeness of the folly which I should read. Could I have judged, indeed, by the wild over-strained air of vivacity with which he hearkened, or apparently hearkened, to the words of the tale, I might well have congratulated myself upon the success of my design.

I had arrived at that well-known portion of the story where Ethelred, the hero of the Trist, having sought in vain for peaceable admission into the dwelling of the hermit, proceeds to make good an entrance by force. Here, it will be remembered, the words of the narrative run thus:

"And Ethelred, who was by nature of a doughty heart, and who was now mighty withal, on account of the powerfulness of the wine which he had drunken, waited no longer to hold parley with the hermit, who, in sooth, was of an obstinate and maliceful turn, but, feeling the rain upon his shoulders, and fearing the rising of the tempest, uplifted his mace outright, and, with blows, made quickly room in the plankings of the door for his gauntleted hand; and now pulling therewith sturdily, he so cracked, and ripped, and tore all asunder, that the noise of the dry and hollow-sounding wood alarumed and reverberated throughout the forest."

At the termination of this sentence I started, and for a moment, paused; for it appeared to me (although I at once concluded that my excited fancy had deceived me)—it appeared to me that, from some very remote portion of the mansion, there came, indistinctly, to my ears, what might have been, in its exact similarity of character, the echo (but a stifled and dull one certainly) of the very cracking and ripping sound which Sir Launcelot had so particularly described. It was, beyond doubt, the coincidence alone which had arrested my attention; for, amid the rattling of the sashes of the casements, and the ordinary commingled noises of the still increasing storm, the sound, in itself, had nothing, surely, which should have interested or disturbed me. I continued the story:

"But the good champion Ethelred, now entering within the door, was sore enraged and amazed to perceive no signal of the maliceful hermit; but, in the stead thereof, a dragon of a scaly and prodigious demeanour, and of a fiery tongue, which sate in guard before a palace of gold, with a floor of silver; and upon the wall there hung a shield of shining brass with this legend enwritten—

Who entereth herein, a conqueror hath bin;
Who slayeth the dragon, the shield he shall win;

[14] A title and narrative fabricated by Poe. "Trist" (for *tryst*) is used in the sense of an appointed meeting.

And Ethelred uplifted his mace, and struck upon the head of the dragon, which fell before him, and gave up his pesty breath, with a shriek so horrid and harsh, and withal so piercing, that Ethelred had fain to close his ears with his hands against the dreadful noise of it, the like whereof was never before heard."

Here again I paused abruptly, and now with a feeling of wild amazement—for there could be no doubt whatever that, in this instance, I did actually hear (although from what direction it proceeded I found it impossible to say) a low and apparently distant, but harsh, protracted, and most unusual screaming or grating sound—the exact counterpart of what my fancy had already conjured up for the dragon's unnatural shriek as described by the romancer.

Oppressed, as I certainly was, upon the occurrence of the second and most extraordinary coincidence, by a thousand conflicting sensations, in which wonder and extreme terror were predominant, I still retained sufficient presence of mind to avoid exciting, by any observation, the sensitive nervousness of my companion. I was by no means certain that he had noticed the sounds in question; although, assuredly, a strange alteration had, during the last few minutes, taken place in his demeanour. From a position fronting my own, he had gradually brought round his chair, so as to sit with his face to the door of the chamber; and thus I could but partially perceive his features, although I saw that his lips trembled as if he were murmuring inaudibly. His head had dropped upon his breast—yet I knew that he was not asleep, from the wide and rigid opening of the eye as I caught a glance of it in profile. The motion of his body, too, was at variance with this idea—for he rocked from side to side with a gentle yet constant and uniform sway. Having rapidly taken notice of all this, I resumed the narrative of Sir Launcelot, which thus proceeded:

"And now, the champion, having escaped from the terrible fury of the dragon, bethinking himself of the brazen shield, and of the breaking up of the enchantment which was upon it, removed the carcass from out of the way before him, and approached valorously over the silver pavement of the castle to where the shield was upon the wall; which in sooth tarried not for his full coming, but fell down at his feet upon the silver floor, with a mighty great and terrible ringing sound."

No sooner had these syllables passed my lips, than—as if a shield of brass had indeed, at the moment, fallen heavily upon a floor of silver—I became aware of a distinct, hollow, metallic, and clangorous, yet apparently muffled reverberation. Completely unnerved, I leaped to my feet; but the measured rocking movement of Usher was undisturbed. I rushed to the chair in which he sat. His eyes were bent fixedly before him, and throughout his whole countenance there reigned a stony rigidity. But, as I placed my hand upon his shoulder, there came a strong shudder over his whole person; a sickly smile quivered about his lips; and I saw that he spoke in a low, hurried, and gibbering murmur, as if unconscious of my presence. Bending closely over him, I at length drank in the hideous import of his words.

"Not hear it?—yes, I hear it, and *have* heard it. Long—long—long—many minutes, many hours, many days, have I heard it—yet I dared not—oh, pity me, miserable wretch that I am!—I dared not—I *dared* not speak! *We have put her living in the tomb!* Said I not that my senses were acute? I *now* tell you that I heard her first feeble movements in the hollow coffin. I heard them—many, many days ago—yet I dared not—*I dared not speak!* And now—to-night—Ethelred—ha! ha!—the breaking of the hermit's door, and the death-cry of the dragon, and the clangour of the shield! say, rather, the rending of her coffin, and the grating of the iron hinges of her prison, and her struggles within the coppered archway of the vault! Oh whither shall I fly? Will she not be here anon? Is she not hurrying to upbraid me for my haste? Have I not heard her footstep on the stair? Do I not distinguish that heavy and horrible beating of her heart? MADMAN!" here he sprang furiously to his feet, and shrieked out his syllables, as if in the effort he were giving up his soul—"MADMAN! I TELL YOU THAT SHE NOW STANDS WITHOUT THE DOOR!"

As if in the superhuman energy of his utterance there had been found the potency of a spell—the huge antique panels to which the speaker pointed, threw slowly back, upon the instant, their ponderous and ebony jaws. It was the work of the rushing gust —but then without those doors there did stand the lofty and enshrouded figure of the lady Madeline of Usher. There was blood upon her white robes, and the evidence of some bitter struggle upon every portion of her emaciated frame. For a moment she remained trembling and reeling to and fro upon the threshold, then, with a low moaning cry, fell heavily inward upon the person of her brother, and in her violent and now final death-agonies, bore him to the floor a corpse, and a victim to the terrors he had anticipated.

From that chamber, and from that mansion, I fled aghast. The storm was still abroad in all its wrath as I found myself crossing the old causeway. Suddenly there shot along the path a wild light, and I turned to see whence a gleam so unusual could have issued; for the vast house and its shadows were alone behind me. The radiance was that of the full, setting, and blood-red moon which now shone vividly through that once barely-discernible fissure of which I have before spoken as extending from the roof of the building, in a zigzag direction, to the base. While I gazed, this fissure rapidly widened—there came a fierce breath of the whirlwind—the entire orb of the satellite burst at once upon my sight—my brain reeled as I saw the mighty walls rushing asunder—there was a long tumultuous shouting sound like the voice of a thousand waters—and the deep and dank tarn at my feet closed sullenly and silently over the fragments of the "HOUSE OF USHER."

1839

---

from Nathaniel Hawthorne's *Twice-Told Tales**

We said a few hurried words about Mr. Hawthorne in our last number, with the design of speaking more fully in the present. We are still, however, pressed for room, and must necessarily discuss his volumes more briefly and more at random than their high merits deserve.

---

* In the April 1842 issue of *Graham's Magazine*, Poe briefly noted Hawthorne's collection of tales. He followed in May with a more extensive examination of Hawthorne's writings, the review from which this selection is extracted.

The book professes to be a collection of *tales,* yet is, in two respects, misnamed. These pieces are now in their third publication, and, of course, are thrice-told.[1] Moreover, they are by no means *all* tales, either in the ordinary or in the legitimate understanding of the term. Many of them are pure essays; for example, "Sights from a Steeple," "Sunday at Home," "Little Annie's Ramble," "A Rill from the Town Pump," "The Toll-Gatherer's Day," "The Haunted Mind," "The Sister Years," "Snow-Flakes," "Night-Sketches," and "Foot-Prints on the Sea-Shore." We mention these matters chiefly on account of their discrepancy with that marked precision and finish by which the body of the work is distinguished.

Of the essays just named, we must be content to speak in brief. They are each and all beautiful, without being characterised by the polish and adaptation so visible in the tales proper. A painter would at once note their leading or predominant feature, and style it *repose.* There is no attempt at effect. All is quiet, thoughtful, subdued. Yet this repose may exist simultaneously with high originality of thought; and Mr. Hawthorne has demonstrated the fact. At every turn we meet with novel combinations; yet these combinations never surpass the limits of the quiet. We are soothed as we read; and withal is a calm astonishment that ideas so apparently obvious have never occurred or been presented to us before. Herein our author differs materially from Lamb or Hunt or Hazlitt[2]—who, with vivid originality of manner and expression, have less of the true novelty of thought than is generally supposed, and whose originality, at best, has an uneasy and meretricious quaintness, replete with startling effects unfounded in nature, and inducing trains of reflection which lead to no satisfactory result. The Essays of Hawthorne have much of the character of Irving,[3] with more of originality, and less of finish; while, compared with the Spectator,[4] they have a vast superiority at all points. The Spectator, Mr. Irving, and Mr. Hawthorne have in common that tranquil and subdued manner which we have chosen to denominate *repose;* but, in the case of the two former, this repose is attained rather by the absence of novel combination, or of originality, than otherwise, and consists chiefly in the calm, quiet, unostentatious expression of commonplace thoughts, in an unambitious, unadulterated Saxon. In them, by strong effort, we are made to conceive the absence of all. In the essays before us the absence of effort is too obvious to be mistaken, and a strong undercurrent of *suggestion* runs continuously beneath the upper stream of the tranquil thesis. In short, these effusions of Mr. Hawthorne are the product of a truly imaginative intellect, restrained, and in some measure repressed, by fastidiousness of taste, by constitutional melancholy and by indolence.

But it is of his tales that we desire principally to speak. The tale proper, in our opinion, affords unquestionably the fairest field for the exercise of the loftiest talent, which can be afforded by the wide domains of mere prose. Were we bidden to say

---

[1] Poe here notes that Hawthorne's tales had first appeared in various magazines, were then collected and published in a volume in 1837, and were published again in an 1842 edition (the "thrice-told" version that he is reviewing).

[2] Three English essayists: Charles Lamb (1775–1834), Leigh Hunt (1784–1859), and William Hazlitt (1778–1830).

[3] Washington Irving (1783–1859), whose *Tales of a Traveller* (1824) had been compared with Hawthorne's tales in Poe's April review.

[4] That is, with material that appeared in the eighteenth-century English magazine *Spectator,* edited by Richard Steele (1672–1729) and Joseph Addison (1672–1719).

how the highest genius could be most advantageously employed for the best display of its own powers, we should answer, without hesitation—in the composition of a rhymed poem, not to exceed in length what might be perused in an hour. Within this limit alone can the highest order of true poetry exist. We need only here say, upon this topic, that, in almost all classes of composition, the unity of effect or impression is a point of the greatest importance. It is clear, moreover, that this unity cannot be thoroughly preserved in productions whose perusal cannot be completed at one sitting. We may continue the reading of a prose composition, from the very nature of prose itself, much longer than we can persevere, to any good purpose, in the perusal of a poem. This latter, if truly fulfilling the demands of the poetic sentiment, induces an exaltation of the soul which cannot be long sustained. All high excitements are necessarily transient. Thus a long poem is a paradox. And, without unity of impression, the deepest effects cannot be brought about. Epics were the offspring of an imperfect sense of Art, and their reign is no more. A poem *too* brief may produce a vivid, but never an intense or enduring impression. Without a certain continuity of effort—without a certain duration or repetition of purpose—the soul is never deeply moved. There must be the dropping of the water upon the rock. De Béranger[5] has wrought brilliant things—pungent and spirit-stirring—but, like all immassive[6] bodies, they lack *momentum,* and thus fail to satisfy the Poetic Sentiment. They sparkle and excite, but, from want of continuity, fail deeply to impress. Extreme brevity will degenerate into epigrammatism; but the sin of extreme length is even more unpardonable. *In medio tutissimus ibis.*[7]

Were we called upon, however, to designate that class of composition which, next to such a poem as we have suggested, should best fulfill the demands of high genius —should offer it the most advantageous field of exertion—we should unhesitatingly speak of the prose tale, as Mr. Hawthorne has here exemplified it. We allude to the short prose narrative, requiring from a half-hour to one or two hours in its perusal. The ordinary novel is objectionable, from its length, for reasons already stated in substance. As it cannot be read at one sitting, it deprives itself, of course, of the immense force derivable from *totality.* Worldly interests intervening during the pauses of perusal, modify, annul, or counteract, in a greater or less degree, the impressions of the book. But simple cessation in reading, would, of itself, be sufficient to destroy the true unity. In the brief tale, however, the author is enabled to carry out the fulness of his intention, be it what it may. During the hour of perusal the soul of the reader is at the writer's control. There are no external or extrinsic influences—resulting from weariness or interruption.

A skilful literary artist has constructed a tale. If wise, he has not fashioned his thoughts to accommodate his incidents; but having conceived, with deliberate care, a certain unique or single *effect* to be wrought out, he then invents such incidents— he then combines such events as may best aid him in establishing this preconceived effect. If his very initial sentence tend not to the outbringing of this effect, then he has failed in his first step. In the whole composition there should be no word written, of which the tendency, direct or indirect, is not to the one pre-established design. And

---

[5] French poet Pierre-Jean de Béranger (1780–1857).
[6] Without mass.

[7] Latin: "You will go most safely in the middle way."

by such means, with such care and skill, a picture is at length painted which leaves in the mind of him who contemplates it with a kindred art, a sense of the fullest satisfaction. The idea of the tale has been presented unblemished, because undisturbed; and this is an end unattainable by the novel. Undue brevity is just as exceptionable here as in the poem; but undue length is yet more to be avoided.

We have said that the tale has a point of superiority even over the poem. In fact, while the *rhythm* of this latter is an essential aid in the development of the poet's highest idea—the idea of the Beautiful—the artificialities of this rhythm are an inseparable bar to the development of all points of thought or expression which have their basis in *Truth*. But Truth is often, and in very great degree, the aim of the tale. Some of the finest tales are tales of ratiocination. Thus the field of this species of composition, if not in so elevated a region on the mountain of Mind, is a table-land of far vaster extent than the domain of the mere poem. Its products are never so rich, but infinitely more numerous, and more appreciable by the mass of mankind. The writer of the prose tale, in short, may bring to his theme a vast variety of modes or inflections of thought and expression—(the ratiocinative, for example, the sarcastic, or the humorous) which are not only antagonistical to the nature of the poem, but absolutely forbidden by one of its most peculiar and indispensable adjuncts; we allude, of course, to rhythm. It may be added here, *par parenthèse*,[8] that the author who aims at the purely beautiful in a prose tale is laboring at great disadvantage. For Beauty can be better treated in the poem. Not so with terror, or passion, or horror, or a multitude of such other points. And here it will be seen how full of prejudice are the usual animadversions against those *tales of effect,* many fine examples of which were found in the earlier numbers of Blackwood.[9] The impressions produced were wrought in a legitimate sphere of action, and constituted a legitimate although sometimes an exaggerated interest. They were relished by every man of genius: although there were found many men of genius who condemned them without just ground. The true critic will but demand that the design intended be accomplished, to the fullest extent, by the means most advantageously applicable.

We have very few American tales of real merit—we may say, indeed, none, with the exception of "The Tales of a Traveller" of Washington Irving, and these "Twice-Told Tales" of Mr. Hawthorne. Some of the pieces of Mr. John Neal[10] abound in vigor and originality; but in general, his compositions of this class are excessively diffuse, extravagant, and indicative of an imperfect sentiment of Art. Articles at random are, now and then, met with in our periodicals which might be advantageously compared with the best effusions of the British Magazines; but, upon the whole, we are far behind our progenitors in this department of literature.

Of Mr. Hawthorne's Tales we would say, emphatically, that they belong to the highest region of Art—an Art subservient to genius of a very lofty order. We had supposed, with good reason for so supposing, that he had been thrust into his present position by one of the impudent *cliques* which beset our literature, and whose pretensions it is our full purpose to expose at the earliest opportunity; but we have been most agreeably mistaken. We know of few compositions which the critic can

---

[8] French: "parenthetically."
[9] Blackwood's *Edinburgh Magazine,* a British monthly, made a speciality of the gothic tale.
[10] American writer (1793–1876).

more honestly commend than these "Twice-Told Tales." As Americans, we felt proud of the book.

Mr. Hawthorne's distinctive trait is invention, creation, imagination, originality—a trait which, in the literature of fiction, is positively worth all the rest. But the nature of originality, so far as regards its manifestation in letters, is but imperfectly understood. The inventive or original mind as frequently displays itself in novelty of *tone* as in novelty of matter. Mr. Hawthorne is original at *all* points. . . .

In the way of objection we have scarcely a word to say of these tales. There is, perhaps, a somewhat too general or prevalent *tone*—a tone of melancholy and mysticism. The subjects are insufficiently varied. There is not so much of *versatility* evinced as we might well be warranted in expecting from the high powers of Mr. Hawthorne. But beyond these trivial exceptions we have really none to make. The style is purity itself. Force abounds. High imagination gleams from every page. Mr. Hawthorne is a man of the truest genius. We only regret that the limits of our Magazine will not permit us to pay him that full tribute of commendation, which, under other circumstances, we should be so eager to pay.

1842

The Purloined Letter

At Paris, just after dark one gusty evening in the autumn of 18——, I was enjoying the twofold luxury of meditation and a meerschaum, in company with my friend C. Auguste Dupin, in his little back library, or book-closet, *au troisième,*[1] *No. 33, Rue Dunôt, Faubourg St. Germain.* For one hour at least we had maintained a profound silence; while each, to any casual observer, might have seemed intently and exclusively occupied with the curling eddies of smoke that oppressed the atmosphere of the chamber. For myself, however, I was mentally discussing certain topics which had formed matter for conversation between us at an earlier period of the evening; I mean the affair of the Rue Morgue, and the mystery attending the murder of Marie Rogêt.[2] I looked upon it, therefore, as something of a coincidence, when the door of our apartment was thrown open and admitted our old acquaintance, Monsieur G——, the Prefect of the Parisian police.

We gave him a hearty welcome; for there was nearly half as much of the entertaining as of the contemptible about the man, and we had not seen him for several years. We had been sitting in the dark, and Dupin now arose for the purpose of lighting a lamp, but sat down again, without doing so, upon G.'s saying that he had called

---

[1] "On the third floor" (not counting the ground floor) in French; thus, on what we call the fourth floor.

[2] Two earlier cases solved by Dupin.

to consult us, or rather to ask the opinion of my friend, about some official business which had occasioned a great deal of trouble.

"If it is any point requiring reflection," observed Dupin, as he forebore to enkindle the wick, "we shall examine it to better purpose in the dark."

"That is another of your odd notions," said the Prefect, who had a fashion of calling every thing "odd" that was beyond his comprehension, and thus lived amid an absolute legion of "oddities."

"Very true," said Dupin, as he supplied his visiter with a pipe, and rolled towards him a comfortable chair.

"And what is the difficulty now?" I asked. "Nothing more in the assassination way, I hope?"

"Oh no; nothing of that nature. The fact is, the business is *very* simple indeed, and I make no doubt that we can manage it sufficiently well ourselves; but then I thought Dupin would like to hear the details of it, because it is so excessively *odd.*"

"Simple and odd," said Dupin.

"Why, yes; and not exactly that, either. The fact is, we have all been a good deal puzzled because the affair is so simple, and yet baffles us altogether."

"Perhaps it is the very simplicity of the thing which puts you at fault," said my friend.

"What nonsense you *do* talk!" replied the Prefect, laughing heartily.

"Perhaps the mystery is a little *too* plain," said Dupin.

"Oh, good heavens! who ever heard of such an idea?"

"A little *too* self-evident."

"Ha! ha! ha!—ha! ha! ha!—ho! ho! ho!" roared our visiter, profoundly amused, "oh, Dupin, you will be the death of me yet!"

"And what, after all, *is* the matter on hand?" I asked.

"Why, I will tell you," replied the Prefect, as he gave a long, steady, and contemplative puff, and settled himself in his chair. "I will tell you in a few words; but, before I begin, let me caution you that this is an affair demanding the greatest secrecy, and that I should most probably lose the position I now hold, were it known that I confided it to any one."

"Proceed," said I.

"Or not," said Dupin.

"Well, then; I have received personal information, from a very high quarter, that a certain document of the last importance, has been purloined from the royal apartments. The individual who purloined it is known; this beyond a doubt; he was seen to take it. It is known, also, that it still remains in his possession."

"How is this known?" asked Dupin.

"It is clearly inferred," replied the Prefect, "from the nature of the document, and from the non-appearance of certain results which would at once arise from its passing *out* of the robber's possession;—that is to say, from his employing it as he must design in the end to employ it."

"Be a little more explicit," I said.

"Well, I may venture so far as to say that the paper gives its holder a certain power in a certain quarter where such power is immensely valuable." The Prefect was fond of the cant of diplomacy.

"Still I do not quite understand," said Dupin.

"No? Well; the disclosure of the document to a third person, who shall be nameless, would bring in question the honor of a personage of most exalted station; and this fact gives the holder of the document an ascendancy over the illustrious personage whose honor and peace are so jeopardized."

"But this ascendancy," I interposed, "would depend upon the robber's knowledge of the loser's knowledge of the robber. Who would dare—"

"The thief," said G., "is the Minister D——, who dares all things, those unbecoming as well as those becoming a man. The method of the theft was not less ingenious than bold. The document in question—a letter, to be frank—had been received by the personage robbed while alone in the royal *boudoir*. During its perusal she was suddenly interrupted by the entrance of the other exalted personage from whom especially it was her wish to conceal it. After a hurried and vain endeavor to thrust it in a drawer, she was forced to place it, open as it was, upon a table. The address, however, was uppermost, and, the contents thus unexposed, the letter escaped notice. At this juncture enters the Minister D——. His lynx eye immediately perceives the paper, recognises the handwriting of the address, observes the confusion of the personage addressed, and fathoms her secret. After some business transactions, hurried through in his ordinary manner, he produces a letter somewhat similar to the one in question, opens it, pretends to read it, and then places it in close juxtaposition to the other. Again he converses, for some fifteen minutes, upon the public affairs. At length, in taking leave, he takes also from the table the letter to which he had no claim. Its rightful owner saw, but, of course, dared not call attention to the act, in the presence of the third personage who stood at her elbow. The minister decamped; leaving his own letter—one of no importance—upon the table."

"Here, then," said Dupin to me, "you have precisely what you demand to make the ascendancy complete—the robber's knowledge of the loser's knowledge of the robber."

"Yes," replied the Prefect; "and the power thus attained has, for some months past, been wielded, for political purposes, to a very dangerous extent. The personage robbed is more thoroughly convinced, every day, of the necessity of reclaiming her letter. But this, of course, cannot be done openly. In fine, driven to despair, she has committed the matter to me."

"Than whom," said Dupin, amid a perfect whirlwind of smoke, "no more sagacious agent could, I suppose, be desired, or even imagined."

"You flatter me," replied the Prefect; "but it is possible that some such opinion may have been entertained."

"It is clear," said I, "as you observe, that the letter is still in possession of the minister; since it is this possession, and not any employment of the letter, which bestows the power. With the employment the power departs."

"True," said G.; "and upon this conviction I proceeded. My first care was to make thorough search of the minister's hotel;[3] and here my chief embarrassment lay in the necessity of searching without his knowledge. Beyond all things, I have been warned of the danger which would result from giving him reason to suspect our design."

"But," said I, "you are quite *au fait*[4] in these investigations. The Parisian police have done this thing often before."

---

[3] Large private residence.   [4] French: "accomplished."

"O yes; and for this reason I did not despair. The habits of the minister gave me, too, a great advantage. He is frequently absent from home all night. His servants are by no means numerous. They sleep at a distance from their master's apartment, and, being chiefly Neapolitans, are readily made drunk. I have keys, as you know, with which I can open any chamber or cabinet in Paris. For three months a night has not passed, during the greater part of which I have not been engaged, personally, in ransacking the D—— Hotel. My honor is interested, and, to mention a great secret, the reward is enormous. So I did not abandon the search until I had become fully satisfied that the thief is a more astute man than myself. I fancy that I have investigated every nook and corner of the premises in which it is possible that the paper can be concealed."

"But is it not possible," I suggested, "that although the letter may be in possession of the minister, as it unquestionably is, he may have concealed it elsewhere than upon his own premises?"

"This is barely possible," said Dupin. "The present peculiar condition of affairs at court, and especially of those intrigues in which D—— is known to be involved, would render the instant availability of the document—its susceptibility of being produced at a moment's notice—a point of nearly equal importance with its possession."

"Its susceptibility of being produced?" said I.

"That is to say, of being *destroyed*," said Dupin.

"True," I observed; "the paper is clearly then upon the premises. As for its being upon the person of the minister, we may consider that as out of the question."

"Entirely," said the Prefect. "He has been twice waylaid, as if by footpads, and his person rigorously searched under my own inspection."

"You might have spared yourself this trouble," said Dupin. "D——, I presume, is not altogether a fool, and, if not, must have anticipated these waylayings, as a matter of course."

"Not *altogether* a fool," said G., "but then he's a poet, which I take to be only one remove from a fool."

"True," said Dupin, after a long and thoughtful whiff from his meerschaum, "although I have been guilty of certain doggrel myself."

"Suppose you detail," said I, "the particulars of your search."

"Why the fact is, we took our time, and we searched *every where*. I have had long experience in these affairs. I took the entire building, room by room; devoting the nights of a whole week to each. We examined, first, the furniture of each apartment. We opened every possible drawer; and I presume you know that, to a properly trained police agent, such a thing as a *secret* drawer is impossible. Any man is a dolt who permits a 'secret' drawer to escape him in a search of this kind. The thing is *so* plain. There is a certain amount of bulk—of space—to be accounted for in every cabinet. Then we have accurate rules. The fiftieth part of a line could not escape us. After the cabinets we took the chairs. The cushions we probed with fine long needles you have seen me employ. From the tables we removed the tops."

"Why so?"

"Sometimes the top of a table, or other similarly arranged piece of furniture, is removed by the person wishing to conceal an article; then the leg is excavated, the article deposited within the cavity, and the top replaced. The bottoms and tops of bedposts are employed in the same way."

"But could not the cavity be detected by sounding?" I asked.

"By no means, if, when the article is deposited, a sufficient wadding of cotton be placed around it. Besides, in our case, we were obliged to proceed without noise."

"But you could not have removed—you could not have taken to pieces *all* articles of furniture in which it would have been possible to make a deposit in the manner you mention. A letter may be compressed into a thin spiral roll, not differing much in shape or bulk from a large knitting-needle, and in this form it might be inserted into the rung of a chair, for example, You did not take to pieces all the chairs?"

"Certainly not; but we did better—we examined the rungs of every chair in the hotel, and, indeed, the jointings of every description of furniture, by the aid of a most powerful microscope.[5] Had there been any traces of recent disturbance we should not have failed to detect it instantly. A single grain of gimlet-dust, for example, would have been as obvious as an apple. Any disorder in the glueing—any unusual gaping in the joints—would have sufficed to insure detection."

"I presume you looked to the mirrors, between the boards and the plates, and you probed the beds and the bed-clothes, as well as the curtains and carpets."

"That of course; and when we had absolutely completed every particle of the furniture in this way, then we examined the house itself. We divided its entire surface into compartments, which we numbered, so that none might be missed; then we scrutinized each individual square inch throughout the premises, including the two houses immediately adjoining, with the microscope, as before."

"The two houses adjoining!" I exclaimed; "you must have had a great deal of trouble."

"We had; but the reward offered is prodigious."

"You include the *grounds* about the houses?"

"All the grounds are paved with brick. They gave us comparatively little trouble. We examined the moss between the bricks, and found it undisturbed."

"You looked among D——'s papers, of course, and into the books of the library?"

"Certainly; we opened every package and parcel; we not only opened every book, but we turned over every leaf in each volume, not contenting ourselves with a mere shake, according to the fashion of some of our police officers. We also measured the thickness of every book-*cover*, with the most accurate admeasurement, and applied to each the most jealous scrutiny of the microscope. Had any of the bindings been recently meddled with, it would have been utterly impossible that the fact should have escaped observation. Some five or six volumes, just from the hand of the binder, we carefully probed, longitudinally, with the needles."

"You explored the floors beneath the carpets?"

"Beyond doubt. We removed every carpet, and examined the boards with the microscope."

"And the paper on the walls?"

"Yes."

"You looked into the cellars?"

[5] Magnifying glass.

"We did."

"Then," I said, "you have been making a miscalculation, and the letter is *not* upon the premises, as you suppose."

"I fear you are right there," said the Prefect. "And now, Dupin, what would you advise me to do?"

"To make a thorough re-search of the premises."

"That is absolutely needless," replied G——. "I am not more sure that I breathe than I am that the letter is not at the Hotel."

"I have no better advice to give you," said Dupin. "You have, of course, an accurate description of the letter?"

"Oh yes!"—And here the Prefect, producing a memorandum-book, proceeded to read aloud a minute account of the internal, and especially of the external appearance of the missing document. Soon after finishing the perusal of this description, he took his departure, more entirely depressed in spirits than I had ever known the good gentleman before.

In about a month afterwards he paid us another visit, and found us occupied very nearly as before. He took a pipe and a chair and entered into some ordinary conversation. At length I said,—

"Well, but G——, what of the purloined letter? I presume you have at last made up your mind that there is no such thing as overreaching the Minister?"

"Confound him, say I—yes; I made the re-examination, however, as Dupin suggested—but it was all labor lost, as I knew it would be."

"How much was the reward offered, did you say?" asked Dupin.

"Why a very great deal—a *very* liberal reward—I don't like to say how much, precisely; but one thing I *will* say, that I wouldn't mind giving my individual check for fifty thousand francs to any one who could obtain me that letter. The fact is, it is becoming of more and more importance every day; and the reward has been lately doubled. If it were trebled, however, I could do no more than I have done."

"Why, yes," said Dupin, drawlingly, between the whiffs of his meerschaum, "I really—think, G——, you have not exerted yourself—to the utmost in this matter. You might—do a little more, I think, eh?"

"How?—in what way?"

"Why—puff, puff—you might—puff, puff—employ counsel in the matter, eh? —puff, puff, puff. Do you remember the story they tell of Abernethy?"[6]

"No; hang Abernethy!"

"To be sure! hang him and welcome. But, once upon a time, a certain rich miser conceived the design of spunging upon this Abernethy for a medical opinion. Getting up, for this purpose, an ordinary conversation in a private company, he insinuated his case to the physician, as that of an imaginary individual.

"'We will suppose,' said the miser, 'that his symptoms are such and such; now, doctor, what would *you* have directed him to take?'

"'Take!' said Abernethy, 'why, take *advice,* to be sure.'"

"But," said the Prefect, a little discomposed, "I am *perfectly* willing to take advice, and to pay for it. I would *really* give fifty thousand francs to any one who would aid me in the matter."

[6] John Abernethy, English surgeon (1764–1831).

"In that case," replied Dupin, opening a drawer, and producing a check-book, "you may as well fill me up a check for the amount mentioned. When you have signed it, I will hand you the letter."

I was astounded. The Prefect appeared absolutely thunder-stricken. For some minutes he remained speechless and motionless, looking incredulously at my friend with open mouth, and eyes that seemed starting from their sockets; then, apparently recovering himself in some measure, he seized a pen, and after several pauses and vacant stares, finally filled up and signed a check for fifty thousand francs, and handed it across the table to Dupin. The latter examined it carefully and deposited it in his pocketbook; then, unlocking an *escritoire*,[7] took thence a letter and gave it to the Prefect. This functionary grasped it in a perfect agony of joy, opened it with a trembling hand, cast a rapid glance at its contents, and then, scrambling and struggling to the door, rushed at length unceremoniously from the room and from the house, without having uttered a syllable since Dupin had requested him to fill up the check.

When he had gone, my friend entered into some explanations.

"The Parisian police," he said, "are exceedingly able in their way. They are persevering, ingenious, cunning, and thoroughly versed in the knowledge which their duties seem chiefly to demand. Thus, when G—— detailed to us his mode of searching the premises at the Hotel D——, I felt entire confidence in his having made a satisfactory investigation—so far as his labors extended."

"So far as his labors extended?" said I.

"Yes," said Dupin. "The measures adopted were not only the best of their kind, but carried out to absolute perfection. Had the letter been deposited within the range of their search, these fellows would, beyond a question, have found it."

I merely laughed—but he seemed quite serious in all that he said.

"The measures, then," he continued, "were good in their kind, and well executed; their defect lay in their being inapplicable to the case, and to the man. A certain set of highly ingenious resources are, with the Prefect, a sort of Procrustean bed,[8] to which he forcibly adapts his designs. But he perpetually errs by being too deep or too shallow, for the matter in hand; and many a school-boy is a better reasoner than he. I knew one about eight years of age, whose success at guessing in the game of 'even and odd' attracted universal admiration. This game is simple, and is played with marbles. One player holds in his hand a number of these toys, and demands of another whether that number is even or odd. If the guess is right, the guesser wins one; if wrong, he loses one. The boy to whom I allude won all the marbles of the school. Of course he had some principle of guessing; and this lay in mere observation and admeasurement of the astuteness of his opponents. For example, an arrant simpleton is his opponent, and, holding up his closed hand, asks, 'are they even or odd?' Our schoolboy replies, 'odd,' and loses; but upon the second trial he wins, for he then says to himself, "the simpleton had them even upon the first trial, and his amount of cunning is just sufficient to make him have them odd upon the second; I will therefore guess odd;—he guesses odd, and wins. Now, with a simpleton a degree above the first, he would have reasoned thus: 'This fellow finds that in the first instance I guessed odd,

---

[7] French: "writing desk."
[8] I.e., an unyielding system. Procrustes, robber in classic myth, forced his victims to fit the bed to which he tied them by cutting off their legs if they were too long or by stretching them if too short.

and, in the second, he will propose to himself, upon the first impulse, a simple variation from even to odd, as did the first simpleton; but then a second thought will suggest that this is too simple a variation, and finally he will decide upon putting it even as before. I will therefore guess even;'—he guesses even, and wins. Now this mode of reasoning in the schoolboy, whom his fellows termed 'lucky,'—what, in its last analysis, is it?"

"It is merely," I said, "an identification of the reasoner's intellect with that of his opponent."

"It is," said Dupin; "and, upon inquiring of the boy by what means he effected the *thorough* identification in which his success consisted, I received answer as follows: 'When I wish to find out how wise, or how stupid, or how good, or how wicked is any one, or what are his thoughts at the moment, I fashion the expression of my face, as accurately as possible, in accordance with the expression of his, and then wait to see what thoughts or sentiments arise in my mind or heart, as if to match or correspond with the expression.' This response of the schoolboy lies at the bottom of all the spurious profundity which has been attributed to Rochefoucault, to La Bruyère, to Machiavelli, and to Campanella."[9]

"And the identification," I said, "of the reasoner's intellect with that of his opponent, depends, if I understand you aright, upon the accuracy with which the opponent's intellect is admeasured."

"For its practical value it depends upon this," replied Dupin; "and the Prefect and his cohort fail so frequently, first, by default of this identification, and, secondly, by ill-admeasurement, or rather through non-admeasurement, of the intellect with which they are engaged. They consider only their *own* ideas of ingenuity; and, in searching for anything hidden, advert only to the modes in which *they* would have hidden it. They are right in this much—that their own ingenuity is a faithful representative of that of *the mass;* but when the cunning of the individual felon is diverse in character from their own, the felon foils them, of course. This always happens when it is above their own, and very usually when it is below. They have no variation of principle in their investigations; at best, when urged by some unusual emergency—by some extraordinary reward—they extend or exaggerate their old modes of *practice,* without touching their principles. What, for example, in this case of D——, has been done to vary the principle of action? What is all this boring, and probing, and sounding, and scrutinizing with the microscope, and dividing the surface of the building into registered square inches—what is it all but an exaggeration *of the application* of the one principle or set of principles of search, which are based upon the one set of notions regarding human ingenuity, to which the Prefect, in the long routine of his duty, has been accustomed? Do you not see he has taken it for granted that *all* men proceed to conceal a letter,—not exactly in a gimlet-hole bored in a chair-leg—but, at least, in *some* out-of-the-way hole or corner suggested by the same tenor of thought which would urge a man to secrete a letter in a gimlet-hole bored in a chair-leg? And do you not see also, that such *recherchés*[10] nooks for concealment are adapted only for ordinary occasions, and would be adopted only by ordinary intellects; for, in all cases of concealment, a disposal of the article concealed—a disposal of it in this *recherché*

[9] French and Italian moralists and philosophers of the fifteenth to seventeenth centuries.   [10] French: "unusual."

manner,—is, in the very first instance, presumable and presumed; and thus its discovery depends, not at all upon the acumen, but altogether upon the mere care, patience, and determination of the seekers; and where the case is of importance—or, what amounts to the same thing in the policial eyes, when the reward is of magnitude,— the qualities in question have *never* been known to fail. You will now understand what I meant in suggesting that, had the purloined letter been hidden any where within the limits of the Prefect's examination—in other words, had the principle of its concealment been comprehended within the principles of the Prefect—its discovery would have been a matter altogether beyond question. This functionary, however, has been thoroughly mystified; and the remote source of his defeat lies in the supposition that the Minister is a fool, because he has acquired renown as a poet. All fools are poets; this the Prefect *feels;* and he is merely guilty of a *non distributio medii* [11] in thence inferring that all poets are fools."

"But is this really the poet?" I asked. "There are two brothers, I know; and both have attained reputation in letters. The Minister I believe has written learnedly on the Differential Calculus. He is a mathematician, and no poet."

"You are mistaken; I know him well; he is both. As poet *and* mathematician, he would reason well; as mere mathematician, he could not have reasoned at all, and thus would have been at the mercy of the Prefect."

"You surprise me," I said, "by these opinions, which have been contradicted by the voice of the world. You do not mean to set at naught the well-digested idea of centuries. The mathematical reason has long been regarded as *the* reason *par excellence.*" [12]

"*'Il y a à parier,'* " replied Dupin, quoting from Chamfort, " *'que toute idée publique, toute convention reçue, est une sottise, car elle a convenu au plus grand nombre.'* [13] The mathematicians, I grant you, have done their best to promulgate the popular error to which you allude, and which is none the less an error for its promulgation as truth. With an art worthy a better cause, for example, they have insinuated the term 'analysis' into application to algebra. The French are the originators of this particular deception; but if a term is of any importance—if words derive any value from applicability—then 'analysis' conveys 'algebra' about as much as, in Latin, *'ambitus'* implies 'ambition,' *'religio'* 'religion,' or *'homines honesti,'* a set of *honorable* men."

"You have a quarrel on hand, I see," said I, "with some of the algebraists of Paris; but proceed."

"I dispute the availability, and thus the value, of that reason which is cultivated in any especial form other than the abstractly logical. I dispute, in particular, the reason educed by mathematical study. The mathematics are the science of form and quantity; mathematical reasoning is merely logic applied to observation upon form and quantity. The great error lies in supposing that even the truths of what is called *pure* algebra, are abstract or general truths. And this error is so egregious that I am confounded at the universality with which it has been received. Mathematical axioms are *not* axioms of general truth. What is true of *relation*—of form and quantity—

[11] Latin: "undistributed middle." A term in logic that indicates faulty reasoning.
[12] French: "the very best."
[13] A maxim from the eighteenth-century French moralist Sebastien Chamfort: "There's a good chance that every generally accepted notion, every commonly received convention, is nonsense, exactly because it pleased the majority view."

is often grossly false in regard to morals, for example. In this latter science it is very usually *un*true that the aggregated parts are equal to the whole. In chemistry also the axiom fails. In the consideration of motive it fails; for two motives, each of a given value, have not, necessarily, a value when united, equal to the sum of their values apart. There are numerous other mathematical truths which are only truths within the limits of *relation*. But the mathematician argues, from his *finite truths*, through habit, as if they were of an absolutely general applicability—as the world indeed imagines them to be. Bryant,[14] in his very learned 'Mythology,' mentions an analogous source of error, when he says that 'although the Pagan fables are not believed, yet we forget ourselves continually, and make inferences from them as existing realities.' With the algebraists, however, who are Pagans themselves, the 'Pagan fables' *are* believed, and the inferences are made, not so much through lapse of memory, as through an unaccountable addling of the brains. In short, I never yet encountered the mere mathematician who could be trusted out of equal roots, or one who did not clandestinely hold it as a point of his faith that x^2+px was absolutely and unconditionally equal to q. Say to one of these gentlemen, by way of experiment, if you please, that you believe occasions may occur where x^2+px is *not* altogether equal to q, and, having made him understand what you mean, get out of his reach as speedily as convenient, for, beyond doubt, he will endeavor to knock you down.

"I mean to say," continued Dupin, while I merely laughed at his last observations, "that if the Minister had been no more than a mathematician, the Prefect would have been under no necessity of giving me this check. I knew him, however, as both mathematician and poet, and my measures were adapted to his capacity, with reference to the circumstances by which he was surrounded. I knew him as a courtier, too, and as a bold *intriguant*.[15] Such a man, I considered, could not fail to be aware of the ordinary policial modes of action. He could not have failed to anticipate—and events have proved that he did not fail to anticipate—the waylayings to which he was subjected. He must have foreseen, I reflected, the secret investigations of his premises. His frequent absences from home at night, which were hailed by the Prefect as certain aids to his success, I regarded only as *ruses*, to afford opportunity for thorough search to the police, and thus the sooner to impress them with the conviction to which G——, in fact, did finally arrive—the conviction that the letter was not upon the premises. I felt, also, that the whole train of thought, which I was at some pains in detailing to you just now, concerning the invariable principle of policial action in searches for articles concealed—I felt that this whole train of thought would necessarily pass through the mind of the Minister. It would imperatively lead him to despise all the ordinary *nooks* of concealment. *He* could not, I reflected, be so weak as not to see that the most intricate and remote recess of his hotel would be as open as his commonest closets to the eyes, to the probes, to the gimlets, and to the microscopes of the Prefect. I saw, in fine, that he would be driven, as a matter of course, to *simplicity*, if not deliberately induced to it as a matter of choice. You will remember, perhaps, how desperately the Prefect laughed when I suggested, upon our first inter-

---

[14] Jacob Bryant (1715–1804), whose *A New System, or an Analysis of Antient Mythology* was published between 1774 and 1776.

[15] French: "conniver."

view, that it was just possible this mystery troubled him so much on account of its being so *very* self-evident."

"Yes," said I, "I remember his merriment well. I really thought he would have fallen into convulsions."

"The material world," continued Dupin, "abounds with very strict analogies to the immaterial; and thus some color of truth has been given to the rhetorical dogma, that metaphor, or simile, may be made to strengthen an argument, as well as to embellish a description. The principle of the *vis inertiæ*,[16] for example, seems to be identical in physics and metaphysics. It is not more true in the former, that a large body is with more difficulty set in motion than a smaller one, and that its subsequent *momentum* is commensurate with this difficulty, than it is, in the latter, that intellects of the vaster capacity, while more forcible, more constant, and more eventful in their movements than those of inferior grade, are yet the less readily moved, and more embarrassed and full of hesitation in the first few steps of their progress. Again: have you ever noticed which of the street signs, over the shop-doors, are the most attractive of attention?"

"I have never given the matter a thought," I said.

"There is a game of puzzles," he resumed, "which is played upon a map. One party playing requires another to find a given word—the name of town, river, state or empire—any word, in short, upon the motley and perplexed surface of the chart. A novice in the game generally seeks to embarrass his opponents by giving them the most minutely lettered names; but the adept selects such words as stretch, in large characters, from one end of the chart to the other. These, like the over-largely lettered signs and placards of the street, escape observation by dint of being excessively obvious; and here the physical oversight is precisely analogous with the moral inapprehension by which the intellect suffers to pass unnoticed those considerations which are too obtrusively and too palpably self-evident. But this is a point, it appears, somewhat above or beneath the understanding of the Prefect. He never once thought it probable, or possible, that the Minister had deposited the letter immediately beneath the nose of the whole world, by way of best preventing any portion of that world from perceiving it.

"But the more I reflected upon the daring, dashing, and discriminating ingenuity of D——; upon the fact that the document must always have been *at hand*, if he intended to use it to good purpose; and upon the decisive evidence, obtained by the Prefect, that it was not hidden within the limits of that dignitary's ordinary search —the more satisfied I became that, to conceal this letter, the Minister had resorted to the comprehensive and sagacious expedient of not attempting to conceal it at all.

"Full of these ideas, I prepared myself with a pair of green spectacles, and called one fine morning, quite by accident at the Ministerial hotel. I found D—— at home, yawning, lounging, and dawdling, as usual, and pretending to be in the last extremity of *ennui*. He is, perhaps, the most really energetic human being now alive—but that is only when nobody sees him.

"To be even with him, I complained of my weak eyes, and lamented the necessity of the spectacles, under cover of which I cautiously and thoroughly surveyed the apartment, while seemingly intent only upon the conversation of my host.

---

[16] Latin: "power of inertia."

"I paid especial attention to a large writing-table near which he sat, and upon which lay confusedly, some miscellaneous letters and other papers, with one or two musical instruments and a few books. Here, however, after a long and very deliberate scrutiny, I saw nothing to excite particular suspicion.

"At length my eyes, in going the circuit of the room, fell upon a trumpery fillagree card-rack of pasteboard, that hung dangling by a dirty blue ribbon from a little brass knob just beneath the middle of the mantel-piece. In this rack, which had three or four compartments, were five or six visiting cards and a solitary letter. This last was much soiled and crumpled. It was torn nearly in two, across the middle—as if a design, in the first instance, to tear it entirely up as worthless, had been altered, or stayed, in the second. It had a large black seal, bearing the D—— cipher *very* conspicuously, and was addressed, in a diminutive female hand, to D——, the minister, himself. It was thrust carelessly, and even, as it seemed, contemptuously, into one of the upper divisions of the rack.

"No sooner had I glanced at this letter, than I concluded it to be that of which I was in search. To be sure, it was, to all appearance, radically different from the one of which the Prefect had read us so minute a description Here the seal was large and black, with the D—— cipher; there it was small and red, with the ducal arms of the S—— family. Here, the address, to the Minister, was diminutive and feminine; there the superscription, to a certain royal personage, was markedly bold and decided; the size alone formed a point of correspondence. But, then, the *radicalness* of these differences, which was excessive; the dirt; the soiled and torn condition of the paper, so inconsistent with the *true* methodical habits of D——, and so suggestive of a design to delude the beholder into an idea of the worthlessness of the document; these things, together with the hyperobtrusive situation of this document, full in the view of every visiter, and thus exactly in accordance with the conclusions to which I had previously arrived; these things, I say, were strongly corroborative of suspicion, in one who came with the intention to suspect.

"I protracted my visit as long as possible, and, while I maintained a most animated discussion with the Minister, on a topic which I knew well had never failed to interest and excite him, I kept my attention really riveted upon the letter. In this examination, I committed to memory its external appearance and arrangement in the rack; and also fell, at length, upon a discovery which set at rest whatever trivial doubt I might have entertained. In scrutinizing the edges of the paper, I observed them to be more *chafed* than seemed necessary. They presented the *broken* appearance which is manifested when a stiff paper, having been once folded and pressed with a folder, is refolded in a reversed direction, in the same creases or edges which had formed the original fold. This discovery was sufficient. It was clear to me that the letter had been turned, as a glove, inside out, re-directed, and re-sealed. I bade the Minister good morning, and took my departure at once, leaving a gold snuff-box upon the table.

"The next morning I called for the snuff-box, when we resumed, quite eagerly, the conversation of the preceding day. While thus engaged, however, a loud report, as if of a pistol, was heard immediately beneath the windows of the hotel, and was succeeded by a series of fearful screams, and the shoutings of a mob. D—— rushed to a casement, threw it open, and looked out. In the meantime, I stepped to the card-rack, took the letter, put it in my pocket, and replaced it by a *fac-simile,* (so far as regards externals,) which I had carefully prepared at my lodgings; imitating the D—— cipher, very readily, by means of a seal formed of bread.

"The disturbance in the street had been occasioned by the frantic behavior of a man with a musket. He had fired it among a crowd of women and children. It proved, however, to have been without ball, and the fellow was suffered to go his way as a lunatic or a drunkard. When he had gone, D—— came from the window, whither I had followed him immediately upon securing the object in view. Soon afterwards I bade him farewell. The pretended lunatic was a man in my own pay."

"But what purpose had you," I asked, "in replacing the letter by a *fac-simile?* Would it not have been better, at the first visit, to have seized it openly, and departed?"

"D——," replied Dupin, "is a desperate man, and a man of nerve. His hotel, too, is not without attendants devoted to his interests. Had I made the wild attempt you suggest, I might never have left the Ministerial presence alive. The good people of Paris might have heard of me no more. But I had an object apart from these considerations. You know my political prepossessions. In this matter, I act as a partisan of the lady concerned. For eighteen months the Minister has had her in his power. She has now him in hers; since, being unaware that the letter is not in his possession, he will proceed with his exactions as if it was. Thus will he inevitably commit himself, at once, to his political destruction. His downfall, too, will not be more precipitate than awkward. It is all very well to talk about the *facilis descensus Averni;*[17] but in all kinds of climbing, as Catalani[18] said of singing, it is far more easy to get up than to come down. In the present instance I have no sympathy—at least no pity—for him who descends. He is that *monstrum horrendum,*[19] an unprincipled man of genius. I confess, however, that I should like very well to know the precise character of his thoughts, when, being defied by her whom the Prefect terms 'a certain personage,' he is reduced to opening the letter which I left for him in the card-rack."

"How? did you put any thing particular in it?"

"Why—it did not seem altogether right to leave the interior blank—that would have been insulting. D——, at Vienna once, did me an evil turn, which I told him, quite good-humoredly, that I should remember. So, as I knew he would feel some curiosity in regard to the identity of the person who had outwitted him, I thought it a pity not to give him a clue. He is well acquainted with my MS., and I just copied into the middle of the blank sheet the words—

——Un dessein si funeste,
S'il n'est digne d'Atrée, est digne de Thyeste.

They are to be found in Crébillon's 'Atrée.' "[20]

1844

[17] Paraphrase from Virgil's *Aeneid:* "The way down to Hell is easy."

[18] Angelica Catalani (1780–1849), Italian soprano.

[19] "Latin: "hideous monstrosity."

[20] The drama *Atrée et Thyeste* (1770) by Prosper de Crébillon (1674–1762), based on the classic myth of the revenge of Atreus. Having seduced Atreus' wife, Thyestes is served a feast prepared from the bodies of his sons, whom Atreus has murdered. The quotation states: "So dire a scheme, / Though unworthy of Atreus, is worthy of Thyestes."

The Cask of Amontillado

The thousand injuries of Fortunato I had borne as I best could; but when he ventured upon insult, I vowed revenge. You, who so well know the nature of my soul, will not suppose, however, that I gave utterance to a threat. *At length* I would be avenged; this was a point definitively settled—but the very definitiveness with which it was resolved precluded the idea of risk. I must not only punish, but punish with impunity. A wrong is unredressed when retribution overtakes its redresser. It is equally unredressed when the avenger fails to make himself felt as such to him who has done the wrong.

It must be understood that neither by word nor deed had I given Fortunato cause to doubt my good will. I continued, as was my wont, to smile in his face, and he did not perceive that my smile *now* was at the thought of his immolation.

He had a weak point—this Fortunato—although in other regards he was a man to be respected and even feared. He prided himself on his connoisseurship in wine. Few Italians have the true virtuoso spirit. For the most part their enthusiasm is adopted to suit the time and opportunity—to practice imposture upon the British and Austrian *millionaires*. In painting and gemmary[1] Fortunato, like his countrymen, was a quack —but in the matter of old wines he was sincere. In this respect I did not differ from him materially; I was skilful in the Italian vintages myself, and bought largely whenever I could.

It was about dusk, one evening during the supreme madness of the carnival season, that I encountered my friend. He accosted me with excessive warmth, for he had been drinking much. The man wore motley. He had on a tight-fitting parti-striped dress, and his head was surmounted by the conical cap and bells. I was so pleased to see him that I thought I should never have done wringing his hand.

I said to him—"My dear Fortunato, you are luckily met. How remarkably well you are looking to-day! But I have received a pipe of what passes for Amontillado, and I have my doubts."

"How?" said he. "Amontillado? A pipe? Impossible! And in the middle of the carnival!"

"I have my doubts," I replied; "and I was silly enough to pay the full Amontillado price without consulting you in the matter. You were not to be found, and I was fearful of losing a bargain."

"Amontillado!"

"I have my doubts."

"Amontillado!"

"And I must satisfy them."

"Amontillado!"

"As you are engaged, I am on my way to Luchesi. If any one has a critical turn, it is he. He will tell me—"

"Luchesi cannot tell Amontillado from Sherry."

[1] Knowledge of precious gems.

"And yet some fools will have it that his taste is a match for your own."

"Come, let us go."

"Whither?"

"To your vaults."

"My friend, no; I will not impose upon your good nature. I perceive you have an engagement. Luchesi—"

"I have no engagement;—come."

"My friend, no. It is not the engagement, but the severe cold with which I perceive you are afflicted. The vaults are insufferably damp. They are encrusted with nitre."

"Let us go, nevertheless. The cold is merely nothing. Amontillado! You have been imposed upon. And as for Luchesi, he cannot distinguish Sherry from Amontillado."

Thus speaking, Fortunato possessed himself of my arm. Putting on a mask of black silk, and drawing a *roquelaire* closely about my person, I suffered him to hurry me to my palazzo.[2]

There were no attendants at home; they had absconded to make merry in honor of the time. I had told them that I should not return until the morning, and had given them explicit orders not to stir from the house. These orders were sufficient, I well knew, to insure their immediate disappearance, one and all, as soon as my back was turned.

I took from their sconces two flambeaux, and giving one to Fortunato, bowed him through several suites of rooms to the archway that led into the vaults. I passed down a long and winding staircase, requesting him to be cautious as he followed. We came at length to the foot of the descent, and stood together on the damp ground of the catacombs of the Montresors.

The gait of my friend was unsteady, and the bells upon his cap jingled as he strode.

"The pipe," said he.

"It is farther on," said I; "but observe the white web-work which gleams from these cavern walls."

He turned towards me, and looked into my eyes with two filmy orbs that distilled the rheum of intoxication.

"Nitre?" he asked, at length.

"Nitre," I replied. "How long have you had that cough?"

"Ugh! ugh! ugh!—ugh! ugh! ugh!—ugh! ugh! ugh!—ugh! ugh! ugh!—ugh! ugh! ugh!"

My poor friend found it impossible to reply for many minutes.

"It is nothing," he said, at last.

"Come," I said, with decision, "we will go back; your health is precious. You are rich, respected, admired, beloved; you are happy, as once I was. You are a man to be missed. For me it is no matter. We will go back; you will be ill, and I cannot be responsible. Besides, there is Luchesi—"

"Enough," he said; "the cough is a mere nothing; it will not kill me. I shall not die of a cough."

"True—true," I replied; "and, indeed, I had no intention of alarming you unnecessarily—but you should use all proper caution. A draught of this Medoc will defend us from the damps."

[2] Large residence.

Here I knocked off the neck of a bottle which I drew from a long row of its fellows that lay upon the mould.

"Drink" I said, presenting him the wine.

He raised it to his lips with a leer. He paused and nodded to me familiarly, while his bells jingled.

"I drink," he said, "to the buried that repose around us."

"And I to your long life."

He again took my arm, and we proceeded.

"These vaults," he said, "are extensive."

"The Montresors," I replied, "were a great and numerous family."

"I forget your arms."

"A huge human foot d'or, in a field azure;³ the foot crushes a serpent rampant whose fangs are imbedded in the heel."

"And the motto?"

"Nemo me impune lacessit."⁴

"Good!" he said.

The wine sparkled in his eyes and the bells jingled. My own fancy grew warm with the Medoc. We had passed through walls of piled bones, with casks and puncheons intermingling, into the inmost recesses of the catacombs. I paused again, and this time I made bold to seize Fortunato by an arm above the elbow.

"The nitre!" I said; "see, it increases. It hangs like moss upon the vaults. We are below the river's bed. The drops of moisture trickle among the bones. Come, we will go back ere it is too late. Your cough—"

"It is nothing," he said; "let us go on. But first, another draught of the Medoc."

I broke and reached him a flaçon of De Grâve.⁵ He emptied it at a breath. His eyes flashed with a fierce light. He laughed and threw the bottle upwards with a gesticulation I did not understand.

I looked at him in surprise. He repeated the movement—a grotesque one.

"You do not comprehend?" he said.

"Not I," I replied.

"Then you are not of the brotherhood."

"How?"

"You are not of the masons."

"Yes, yes," I said, "yes, yes."

"You? Impossible! A mason?"

"A mason," I replied.

"A sign," he said.

"It is this," I answered, producing a trowel from beneath the folds of my *roquelaire*.

"You jest," he exclaimed, recoiling a few paces. "But let us proceed to the Amontillado."

---

³ Heraldic terms describing a golden foot laid upon a blue background.

⁴ "No one may insult me without fearing punishment."

⁵ White wine from Bordeaux.

"Be it so," I said, replacing the tool beneath the cloak, and again offering him my arm. He leaned upon it heavily. We continued our route in search of the Amontillado. We passed through a range of low arches, descended, passed on, and descending again, arrived at a deep crypt, in which the foulness of the air caused our flambeaux rather to glow than flame.

At the most remote end of the crypt there appeared another less spacious. Its walls had been lined with human remains, piled to the vault overhead, in the fashion of the great catacombs of Paris. Three sides of this interior crypt were still ornamented in this manner. From the fourth the bones had been thrown down, and lay promiscuously upon the earth, forming at one point a mound of some size. Within the wall thus exposed by the displacing of the bones, we perceived a still interior recess, in depth about four feet, in width three, in height six or seven. It seemed to have been constructed for no especial use within itself, but formed merely the interval between two of the colossal supports of the roof of the catacombs, and was backed by one of their circumscribing walls of solid granite.

It was in vain that Fortunato, uplifting his dull torch, endeavored to pry into the depth of the recess. Its termination the feeble light did not enable us to see.

"Proceed," I said; "herein is the Amontillado. As for Luchesi—"

"He is an ignoramus," interrupted my friend, as he stepped unsteadily forward, while I followed immediately at his heels. In an instant he had reached the extremity of the niche, and finding his progress arrested by the rock, stood stupidly bewildered. A moment more and I had fettered him to the granite. In its surface were two iron staples, distant from each other about two feet, horizontally. From one of these depended a short chain, from the other a padlock. Throwing the links about his waist, it was but the work of a few seconds to secure it. He was too much astounded to resist. Withdrawing the key I stepped back from the recess.

"Pass your hand," I said, "over the wall; you cannot help feeling the nitre. Indeed it is *very* damp. Once more let me *implore* you to return. No? Then I must positively leave you. But I must first render you all the little attentions in my power."

"The Amontillado!" ejaculated my friend, not yet recovered from his astonishment.

"True," I replied; "the Amontillado."

As I said these words I busied myself among the pile of bones of which I have before spoken. Throwing them aside, I soon uncovered a quantity of building stone and mortar. With these materials and with the aid of my trowel, I began vigorously to wall up the entrance of the niche.

I had scarcely laid the first tier of the masonry when I discovered that the intoxication of Fortunato had in a great measure worn off. The earliest indication I had of this was a low moaning cry from the depth of the recess. It was *not* the cry of a drunken man. There was then a long and obstinate silence. I laid the second tier, and the third, and the fourth; and then I heard the furious vibrations of the chain. The noise lasted for several minutes, during which, that I might hearken to it with the more satisfaction, I ceased my labors and sat down upon the bones. When at last the clanking subsided, I resumed the trowel, and finished without interruption the fifth, the sixth, and the seventh tier. The wall was now nearly upon a level with my breast. I again paused, and holding the flambeaux over the mason-work, threw a few feeble rays upon the figure within.

A succession of loud and shrill screams, bursting suddenly from the throat of the chained form, seemed to thrust me violently back. For a brief moment I hesitated—I trembled. Unsheathing my rapier, I began to grope with it about the recess: but the thought of an instant reassured me. I placed my hand upon the solid fabric of the catacombs, and felt satisfied. I reapproached the wall. I replied to the yells of him who clamored. I re-echoed—I aided—I surpassed them in volume and in strength. I did this, and the clamorer grew still.

It was now midnight, and my task was drawing to a close. I had completed the eighth, the ninth, and the tenth tier. I had finished a portion of the last and the eleventh; there remained but a single stone to be fitted and plastered in. I struggled with its weight; I placed it partially in its destined position. But now there came from out the niche a low laugh that erected the hairs upon my head. It was succeeded by a sad voice, which I had difficulty in recognising as that of the noble Fortunato. The voice said—

"Ha! ha? ha?—he! he!—a very good joke indeed—an excellent jest. We will have many a rich laugh about it at the palazzo—he! he! he!—over our wine—he! he! he!"

"The Amontillado!" I said.

"He! he! he!—he! he! he!—yes, the Amontillado. But is it not getting late? Will not they be awaiting us at the palazzo, the Lady Fortunato and the rest? Let us be gone."

"Yes," I said, "let us be gone."

"*For the love of God, Montresor!*"

"Yes," I said, "for the love of God!"

But to these words I hearkened in vain for a reply. I grew impatient. I called aloud—

"Fortunato!"

No answer. I called again—

"Fortunato!"

No answer still. I thrust a torch through the remaining aperture and let it fall within. There came forth in return only a jingling of the bells. My heart grew sick —on account of the dampness of the catacombs. I hastened to make an end of my labor. I forced the last stone into its position; I plastered it up. Against the new masonry I re-erected the old rampart of bones. For the half of a century no mortal has disturbed them. *In pàce requiescat!*[6]

1846

---

[6] "Rest in peace!"

The Philosophy of Composition

Charles Dickens, in a note now lying before me, alluding to an examination I once made of the mechanism of "Barnaby Rudge,"[1] says—"By the way, are you aware that Godwin wrote his 'Caleb Williams' backwards?[2] He first involved his hero in a web of difficulties, forming the second volume and then, for the first, cast about him for some mode of accounting for what had been done."

I cannot think this the *precise* mode of procedure on the part of Godwin—and indeed what he himself acknowledges, is not altogether in accordance with Mr. Dickens' idea—but the author of "Caleb Williams" was too good an artist not to perceive the advantage derivable from at least a somewhat similar process. Nothing is more clear than that every plot, worth the name, must be elaborated to its *dénouement* before anything be attempted with the pen. It is only with the *dénouement* constantly in view that we can give a plot its indispensable air of consequence, or causation, by making the incidents, and especially the tone at all points, tend to the development of the intention.

There is a radical error, I think, in the usual mode of constructing a story. Either history affords a thesis—or one is suggested by an incident of the day—or, at best, the author sets himself to work in the combination of striking events to form merely the basis of his narrative—designing, generally, to fill in with description, dialogue, or autorial comment, whatever crevices of fact, or action, may, from page to page, render themselves apparent.

I prefer commencing with the consideration of an *effect*. Keeping originality *always* in view—for he is false to himself who ventures to dispense with so obvious and so easily attainable a source of interest—I say to myself, in the first place, "Of the innumerable effects, or impressions, of which the heart, the intellect, or (more generally) the soul is susceptible, what one shall I, on the present occasion, select?" Having chosen a novel, first, and secondly a vivid effect, I consider whether it can be best wrought by incident or tone—whether by ordinary incidents and peculiar tone, or the converse, or by peculiarity both of incident and tone—afterward looking about me (or rather within) for such combinations of event, or tone, as shall best aid me in the construction of the effect.

I have often thought how interesting a magazine paper might be written by any author who would—that is to say who could—detail, step by step, the processes by which any one of his compositions attained its ultimate point of completion. Why such a paper has never been given to the world, I am much at a loss to say—but, perhaps, the autorial vanity has had more to do with the omission that any one other cause. Most writers—poets in especial—prefer having it understood that they compose by a species of fine frenzy—an ecstatic intuition—and would positively shudder

---

[1] While the opening chapters of Dickens's novel were appearing in serialized form during 1841, Poe wrote an essay in which he conjectured about the conclusion to the extent of correctly naming the murderer.

[2] The 1832 preface which William Godwin wrote for his novel, first published in 1794, makes the assertion that he wrote it from end to beginning.

at letting the public take a peep behind the scenes, at the elaborate and vacillating crudities of thought—at the true purposes seized only at the last moment—at the innumerable glimpses of idea that arrived not at the maturity of full view—at the fully matured fancies discarded in despair as unmanageable—at the cautious selections and rejections—at the painful erasures and interpolations—in a word, at the wheels and pinions—the tackle for scene-shifting—the step-ladders and demon-traps—the cock's feathers, the red paint and the black patches, which, in ninety-nine cases out of the hundred, constitute the properties of the literary *histrio*.[3]

I am aware, on the other hand, that the case is by no means common, in which an author is at all in condition to retrace the steps by which his conclusions have been attained. In general, suggestions, having arisen pell-mell, are pursued and forgotten in a similar manner.

For my own part, I have neither sympathy with the repugnance alluded to, nor, at any time the least difficulty in recalling to mind the progressive steps of any of my compositions; and, since the interest of an analysis, or reconstruction, such as I have considered a *desideratum,* is quite independent of any real or fancied interest in the thing analyzed, it will not be regarded as a breach of decorum on my part to show the *modus operandi* by which some one of my own works was put together. I select "The Raven," as most generally known. It is my design to render it manifest that no one point in its composition is referrible either to accident or intuition—that the work proceeded, step by step, to its completion with the precision and rigid conse- quence of a mathematical problem.

Let us dismiss, as irrelevant to the poem, *per se,* the circumstance—or say the necessity—which, in the first place, gave rise to the intention of composing a poem that should suit at once the popular and the critical taste.

We commence, then, with this intention.

The initial consideration was that of extent. If any literary work is too long to be read at one sitting, we must be content to dispense with the immensely important effect derivable from unity of impression—for, if two sittings be required, the affairs of the world interfere, and every thing like totality is at once destroyed. But since, *ceteris paribus,*[4] no poet can afford to dispense with *any thing* that may advance his design, it but remains to be seen whether there is, in extent, any advantage to counterbalance the loss of unity which attends it. Here I say no, at once. What we term a long poem is, in fact, merely a succession of brief ones—that is to say, of brief poetical effects. It is needless to demonstrate that a poem is such, only inasmuch as it intensely excites, by elevating, the soul; and all intense excitements are, through a psychal[5] necessity, brief. For this reason, at least one half of the "Paradise Lost"[6] is essentially prose—a succession of poetical excitements interspersed, *inevitably,* with corresponding depressions—the whole being deprived, through the extremeness of its length, of the vastly important artistic element, totality, or unity, of effect.

It appears evident, then, that there is a distinct limit, as regards length, to all works

[3] Performer.
[4] Latin: "other things being equal."
[5] Emotional or spiritual.

[6] This epic poem by John Milton is an example of the extreme length Poe sought to reject.

of literary art—the limit of a single sitting—and that, although in certain classes of prose composition, such as "Robinson Crusoe,"[7] (demanding no unity,) this limit may be advantageously overpassed, it can never properly be overpassed in a poem. Within this limit, the extent of a poem may be made to bear mathematical relation to its merit —in other words, to the excitement or elevation—again in other words, to the degree of the true poetical effect which it is capable of inducing; for it is clear that the brevity must be in direct ratio of the intensity of the intended effect:—this, with one proviso —that a certain degree of duration is absolutely requisite for the production of any effect at all.

Holding in view these considerations, as well as that degree of excitement which I deemed not above the popular, while not below the critical, taste, I reached at once what I conceived the proper *length* for my intended poem—a length of about one hundred lines. It is, in fact, a hundred and eight.

My next thought concerned the choice of an impression, or effect, to be conveyed: and here I may as well observe that, throughout the construction, I kept steadily in view the design of rendering the work *universally* appreciable. I should be carried too far out of my immediate topic were I to demonstrate a point upon which I have repeatedly insisted, and which, with the poetical, stands not in the slightest need of demonstration—the point, I mean, that Beauty is the sole legitimate province of the poem. A few words, however, in elucidation of my real meaning, which some of my friends have evinced a disposition to misrepresent. That pleasure which is at once the most intense, the most elevating, and the most pure, is, I believe, found in the contemplation of the beautiful. When, indeed, men speak of Beauty, they mean, precisely, not a quality, as is supposed, but an effect—they refer, in short, just to that intense and pure elevation of *soul*—*not* of intellect, or of heart—upon which I have commented, and which is experienced in consequence of contemplating "the beauti- ful." Now I designate Beauty as the province of the poem, merely because it is an obvious rule of Art that effects should be made to spring from direct causes—that objects should be attained through means best adapted for their attainment—no one as yet having been weak enough to deny that the peculiar elevation alluded to is *most readily* attained in the poem. Now the object, Truth, or the satisfaction of the intellect, and the object Passion, or the excitement of the heart, are, although attainable, to a certain extent, in poetry, far more readily attainable in prose. Truth, in fact, demands a precision, and Passion a *homeliness* (the truly passionate will comprehend me) which are absolutely antagonistic to that Beauty which, I maintain, is the excitement, or pleasurable elevation, of the soul. It by no means follows from any thing here said, that passion, or even truth, may not be introduced, and even profitably introduced, into a poem—for they may serve in elucidation, or aid the general effect, as do discords in music, by contrast—but the true artist will always contrive, first, to tone them into proper subservience to the predominant aim, and, secondly, to enveil them, as far as possible, in that Beauty which is the atmosphere and the essence of the poem.

Regarding, then, Beauty as my province, my next question referred to the *tone*

[7] Lengthy novel by Daniel Defoe, published in 1719.

of its highest manifestation—and all experience has shown that this tone is one of *sadness*. Beauty of whatever kind, in its supreme development, invariably excites the sensitive soul to tears. Melancholy is thus the most legitimate of all the poetical tones.

The length, the province, and the tone, being thus determined, I betook myself to ordinary induction, with the view of obtaining some artistic piquancy which might serve me as a key-note in the construction of the poem—some pivot upon which the whole structure might turn. In carefully thinking over all the usual artistic effects— or more properly *points,* in the theatrical sense—I did not fail to perceive immediately that no one had been so universally employed as that of the *refrain.* The universality of its employment sufficed to assure me of its intrinsic value, and spared me the necessity of submitting it to analysis. I considered it, however, with regard to its susceptibility of improvement, and soon saw it to be in a primitive condition. As commonly used, the *refrain,* or burden, not only is limited to lyric verse, but depends for its impression upon the force of monotone—both in sound and thought. The pleasure is deduced solely from the sense of identity—of repetition. I resolved to diversify, and so heighten, the effect, by adhering, in general, to the monotone of sound, while I continually varied that of thought: that is to say, I determined to produce continuously novel effects, by the variation *of the application* of the *refrain* —the *refrain* itself remaining, for the most part, unvaried.

These points being settled, I next bethought me of the *nature* of my *refrain.* Since its application was to be repeatedly varied, it was clear that the *refrain* itself must be brief, for there would have been an insurmountable difficulty in frequent variations of application in any sentence of length. In proportion to the brevity of the sentence, would, of course, be the facility of the variation. This led me at once to a single word as the best *refrain.*

The question now arose as to the *character* of the word. Having made up my mind to a *refrain,* the division of the poem into stanzas was, of course, a corollary: the *refrain* forming the close of each stanza. That such a close, to have force, must be sonorous and susceptible of protracted emphasis, admitted no doubt: and these considerations inevitably led me to the long *o* as the most sonorous vowel, in connection with *r* as the most producible consonant.

The sound of the *refrain* being thus determined, it became necessary to select a word embodying this sound, and at the same time in the fullest possible keeping with that melancholy which I had predetermined as the tone of the poem. In such a search it would have been absolutely impossible to overlook the word "Nevermore." In fact, it was the very first which presented itself.

The next *desideratum* was a pretext for the continuous use of the word "nevermore." In observing the difficulty which I at once found in inventing a sufficiently plausible reason for its continuous repetition, I did not fail to perceive that this difficulty arose solely from the pre-assumption that the word was to be so continuously or monotonously spoken by a *human* being—I did not fail to perceive, in short, that the difficulty lay in the reconciliation of this monotony with the exercise of reason on the part of the creature repeating the word. Here, then, immediately arose the idea of a *non-*reasoning creature capable of speech; and, very naturally, a parrot, in the first instance, suggested itself, but was superseded forthwith by a Raven, as equally capable of speech, and infinitely more in keeping with the intended *tone.*

I had now gone so far as the conception of a Raven—the bird of ill omen—

monotonously repeating the one word, "Nevermore," at the conclusion of each stanza, in a poem of melancholy tone, and in length about one hundred lines. Now, never losing sight of the object *supremeness,* or perfection, at all points, I asked myself— "Of all melancholy topics, what, according to the *universal* understanding of mankind, is the *most* melancholy?" Death—was the obvious reply. "And when," I said, "is this most melancholy of topics most poetical?" From what I have already explained at some length, the answer, here also, is obvious—"When it most closely allies itself to *Beauty:* the death, then, of a beautiful woman is, unquestionably, the most poetical topic in the world—and equally is it beyond doubt that the lips best suited for such topic are those of a bereaved lover."

I had now to combine the two ideas, of a lover lamenting his deceased mistress and a Raven continuously repeating the word "Nevermore."—I had to combine these, bearing in mind my design of varying, at every turn, the *application* of the word repeated; but the only intelligible mode of such combination is that of imagining the Raven employing the word in answer to the queries of the lover. And here it was that I saw at once the opportunity afforded for the effect on which I had been depending—that is to say, the effect of the *variation of application.* I saw that I could make the first query propounded by the lover—the first query to which the Raven should reply "Nevermore"—that I could make this first query a commonplace one —the second less so—the third still less, and so on—until at length the lover, startled from his original *nonchalance* by the melancholy character of the word itself—by its frequent repetition—and by a consideration of the ominous reputation of the fowl that uttered it—is at length excited to superstition, and wildly propounds queries of a far different character—queries whose solution he has passionately at heart— propounds them half in superstition and half in that species of despair which delights in self-torture—propounds them not altogether because he believes in the prophetic or demoniac character of the bird (which, reason assures him, is merely repeating a lesson learned by rote) but because he experiences a phrenzied pleasure in so modeling his questions as to receive from the *expected* "Nevermore" the most delicious because the most intolerable of sorrow. Perceiving the opportunity thus afforded me—or, more strictly, thus forced upon me in the progress of the construction—I first established in mind the climax, or concluding query—that query to which "Nevermore" should be in the last place an answer—that in reply to which this word "Nevermore" should involve the utmost conceivable amount of sorrow and despair.

Here then the poem may be said to have its beginning—at the end, where all works of art should begin—for it was here, at this point of my preconsiderations, that I first put pen to paper in the composition of the stanza:

"Prophet," said I, "thing of evil! prophet still if bird or devil!
By that heaven that bends above us—by that God we both adore,
Tell this soul with sorrow laden, if within the distant Aidenn,
It shall clasp a sainted maiden whom the angels name Lenore—
Clasp a rare and radiant maiden whom the angels name Lenore."
    Quoth the raven "Nevermore."

I composed this stanza, at this point, first that, by establishing the climax, I might the better vary and graduate, as regards seriousness and importance, the preceding queries of the lover—and, secondly, that I might definitely settle the rhythm, the metre, and the length and general arrangement of the stanza—as well as graduate the stanzas which were to precede, so that none of them might surpass this in rhythmical effect. Had I been able, in the subsequent composition, to construct more vigorous stanzas, I should, without scruple, have purposely enfeebled them, so as not to interfere with the climacteric effect.

And here I may as well say a few words of the versification. My first object (as usual) was originality. The extent to which this has been neglected, in versification, is one of the most unaccountable things in the world. Admitting that there is little possibility of variety in mere *rhythm,* it is still clear that the possible varieties of metre and stanza are absolutely infinite—and yet, *for centuries, no man, in verse, has ever done, or ever seemed to think of doing, an original thing.* The fact is, that originality (unless in minds of very unusual force) is by no means a matter, as some suppose, of impulse or intuition. In general, to be found, it must be elaborately sought, and although a positive merit of the highest class, demands in its attainment less of invention than negation.

Of course, I pretend to no originality in either the rhythm or metre of the "Raven." The former is trochaic—the latter is octameter acatalectic, alternating with heptameter catalectic repeated in the *refrain* of the fifth verse, and terminating with tetrameter catalectic. Less pedantically—the feet employed throughout (trochees) consist of a long syllable followed by a short: the first line of the stanza consists of eight of these feet—the second of seven and a half (in effect two-thirds)—the third of eight—the fourth of seven and a half—the fifth the same—the sixth three and a half. Now, each of these lines, taken individually, has been employed before, and what originality the "Raven" has, is in their *combination into stanza;* nothing even remotely approaching this combination has ever been attempted. The effect of this originality of combination is aided by other unusual, and some altogether novel effects, arising from an extension of the application of the principles of rhyme and alliteration.

The next point to be considered was the mode of bringing together the lover and the Raven—and the first branch of this consideration was the *locale.* For this the most natural suggestion might seem to be a forest, or the fields—but it has always appeared to me that a close *circumscription of space* is absolutely necessary to the effect of insulated incident:—it has the force of a frame to a picture. It has an indisputable moral power in keeping concentrated the attention, and, of course, must not be confounded with mere unity of place.

I determined, then, to place the lover in his chamber—in a chamber rendered sacred to him by memories of her who had frequented it. The room is represented as richly furnished—this in mere pursuance of the ideas I have already explained on the subject of Beauty, as the sole true poetical thesis.

The *locale* being thus determined, I had now to introduce the bird—and the thought of introducing him through the window, was inevitable. The idea of making the lover suppose, in the first instance, that the flapping of the wings of the bird against the shutter, is a "tapping" at the door, originated in a wish to increase, by prolonging, the reader's curiosity, and in a desire to admit the incidental effect arising from the lover's throwing open the door, finding all dark, and thence adopting the half-fancy that it was the spirit of his mistress that knocked.

I made the night tempestuous, first, to account for the Raven's seeking admission, and secondly, for the effect of contrast with the (physical) serenity within the chamber.

I made the bird alight on the bust of Pallas,[8] also for the effect of contrast between the marble and the plumage—it being understood that the bust was absolutely *suggested* by the bird—the bust of *Pallas* being chosen, first, as most in keeping with the scholarship of the lover, and, secondly, for the sonorousness of the word, Pallas, itself.

About the middle of the poem, also, I have availed myself of the force of contrast, with a view of deepening the ultimate impression. For example, an air of the fantastic —approaching as nearly to the ludicrous as was admissible—is given to the Raven's entrance. He comes in "with many a flirt and flutter."

Not the *least obeisance made he*—not a moment stopped or stayed he,
But with *mien of lord or lady,* perched above my chamber door.

In the two stanzas which follow, the design is more obviously carried out:—

Then this ebony bird beguiling my sad fancy into smiling
By the *grave and stern decorum of the countenance it wore,*
"Though *thy crest be shorn and shaven* thou," I said, "art sure no craven,
Ghastly grim and ancient Raven wandering from the nightly shore—
Tell me what thy lordly name is on the Night's Plutonian shore?"
        Quoth the Raven "Nevermore."

Much I marvelled *this ungainly fowl* to hear discourse so plainly
Though its answer little meaning—little relevancy bore;
For we cannot help agreeing that no living human being
Ever yet was blessed with seeing bird above his chamber door—
Bird or beast upon the sculptured bust above his chamber door,
        With such name as "Nevermore."

The effect of the *dénouement* being thus provided for, I immediately drop the fantastic for a tone of the most profound seriousness:—this tone commencing in the stanza directly following the one last quoted, with the line,

But the Raven, sitting lonely on that placid bust, spoke only, etc.

From this epoch the lover no longer jests—no longer sees any thing even of the fantastic in the Raven's demeanor. He speaks of him as a "grim, ungainly, ghastly, gaunt, and ominous bird of yore," and feels the "fiery eyes" burning into his "bosom's core." This revolution of thought, or fancy, on the lover's part, is intended to induce a similar one on the part of the reader—to bring the mind into a proper frame for the *dénouement*—which is now brought about as rapidly and as *directly* as possible.

[8] Marble bust of Pallas Athena, goddess of wisdom in classic myth.

With the *dénouement* proper—with the Raven's reply, "Nevermore," to the lover's final demand if he shall meet his mistress in another world—the poem, in its obvious phase, that of a simple narrative, may be said to have its completion. So far, every thing is within the limits of the accountable—of the real. A raven, having learned by rote the single word "Nevermore," and having escaped from the custody of its owner, is driven at midnight, through the violence of a storm, to seek admission at a window from which a light still gleams—the chamber-window of a student, occupied half in pouring over a volume, half in dreaming of a beloved mistress deceased. The casement being thrown open at the fluttering of the bird's wings, the bird itself perches on the most convenient seat out of the immediate reach of the student, who, amused by the incident and the oddity of the visitor's demeanor, demands of it, in jest and without looking for a reply, its name. The raven addressed, answers with its customary word, "Nevermore"—a word which finds immediate echo in the melancholy heart of the student, who, giving utterance aloud to certain thoughts suggested by the occasion, is again startled by the fowl's repetition of "Nevermore." The student now guesses the state of the case, but is impelled, as I have before explained, by the human thirst for self-torture, and in part by superstition, to propound such queries to the bird as will bring him, the lover, the most of the luxury of sorrow, through the anticipated answer "Nevermore." With the indulgence, to the extreme, of this self-torture, the narration, in what I have termed its first or obvious phase, has a natural termination, and so far there has been no overstepping of the limits of the real.

But in subjects so handled, however skilfully, or with however vivid an array of incident, there is always a certain hardness or nakedness, which repels the artistical eye. Two things are invariably required—first, some amount of complexity, or more properly, adaptation; and, secondly, some amount of suggestiveness—some under-current, however indefinite, of meaning. It is this latter, in especial, which imparts to a work of art so much of that *richness* (to borrow from colloquy a forcible term) which we are too fond of confounding with *the ideal*. It is the *excess* of the suggested meaning—it is the rendering this the upper instead of the under current of the theme—which turns into prose (and that of the very flattest kind) the so called poetry of the so called transcendentalists.

Holding these opinions, I have added the two concluding stanzas of the poem—their suggestiveness being thus made to pervade all the narrative which has preceded them. The under-current of meaning is rendered first apparent in the lines—

> "Take thy beak from out *my heart,* and take thy form from off
>   my door!"
>
>   Quoth the Raven "Nevermore!"

It will be observed that the words, "from out my heart," involve the first meta-phorical expression in the poem. They, with the answer, "Nevermore," dispose the mind to seek a moral in all that has been previously narrated. The reader begins now to regard the Raven as emblematical—but it is not until the very last line of the very last stanza, that the intention of making him emblematical of *Mournful and Never-ending Remembrance* is permitted distinctly to be seen:

And the Raven, never flitting, still is sitting, still is sitting,
On the pallid bust of Pallas, just above my chamber door;
And his eyes have all the seeming of a demon's that is dreaming,
And the lamplight o'er him streaming throws his shadow on the floor;
And my soul *from out that shadow* that lies floating on the floor
        Shall be lifted—nevermore.

1846

Sonnet—to Science

Science! true daughter of Old Time thou art!
  Who alterest all things with thy peering eyes.
Why preyest thou thus upon the poet's heart,
  Vulture, whose wings are dull realities?
How should he love thee? or how deem thee wise.   5
  Who wouldst not leave him in his wandering
To seek for treasure in the jewelled skies.
  Albeit he soared with an undaunted wing?
Hast thou not dragged Diana from her car?
  And driven the Hamadryad from the wood   10
To seek a shelter in some happier star?
  Hast thou not torn the Naiad from her flood,
The Elfin from the green grass, and from me
The summer dream beneath the tamarind tree?

1829

The City in the Sea[*]

Lo! Death has reared himself a throne
In a strange city lying alone
Far down within the dim West,
Where the good and the bad and the worst and the best

[*] This poem was first published as "The Doomed
City," in 1831. It was revised and retitled in
1845.

Have gone to their eternal rest.
There shrines and palaces and towers
(Time-eaten towers that tremble not!)
Resemble nothing that is ours.
Around, by lifting winds forgot,
Resignedly beneath the sky
The melancholy waters lie.

No rays from the holy heaven come down
On the long night-time of that town;
But light from out the lurid sea
Streams up the turrets silently—
Gleams up the pinnacles far and free
Up domes—up spires—up kingly halls—
Up fanes—up Babylon-like' walls—
Up shadowy long-forgotten bowers
Of sculptured ivy and stone flowers—
Up many and many a marvellous shrine
Whose wreathéd friezes intertwine
The viol, the violet, and the vine.

Resignedly beneath the sky
The melancholy waters lie.
So blend the turrets and shadows there
That all seem pendulous in air,
While from a proud tower in the town
Death looks gigantically down.

There open fanes and gaping graves
Yawn level with the luminous waves;
But not the riches there that lie
In each idol's diamond eye—
Not the gaily-jewelled dead
Tempt the waters from their bed;
For no ripples curl, alas!
Along that wilderness of glass—
No swellings tell that winds may be
Upon some far-off happier sea—
No heavings hint that winds have been
On seas less hideously serene.

But lo, a stir is in the air!
The wave—there is a movement there!
As if the towers had thrust aside,

' The city of ancient Babylon was famous for its
immense towers and walls.

In slightly sinking, the dull tide—
As if their tops had feebly given
A void within the filmy Heaven.
The waves have now a redder glow—
The hours are breathing faint and low— 50
And when, amid no earthly moans,
Down, down that town shall settle hence,
Hell, rising from a thousand thrones,
Shall do it reverence.

1831–1845

To Helen*

Helen,¹ thy beauty is to me
    Like those Nicéan² barks of yore,
That gently, o'er a perfumed sea,
    The weary, way-worn wanderer bore
        To his own native shore.   5

On desperate seas long wont to roam,
    Thy hyacinth³ hair, thy classic face,
Thy Naiad⁴ airs have brought me home
    To the glory that was Greece,
    And the grandeur that was Rome.   10

Lo! in yon brilliant window-niche
    How statue-like I see thee stand,
The agate lamp within thy hand!
    Ah, Psyche,⁵ from the regions which
        Are Holy-Land!⁶   15

1831–1843

---

* This poem first appeared in 1831 but was rewritten over the next 12 years. This version was included in the 1845 edition of *The Raven and Other Poems.*

¹ Helen of Troy, considered the most beautiful woman of ancient times, was celebrated in the Homeric epic the *Iliad.* She was considered the cause of the Trojan War.

² Probably derived from Nike, the Greek goddess of Victory; thus, "victorious."

³ Lustrous, curling hair.

⁴ Water nymph.

⁵ Greek word for soul.

⁶ If Palestine is a religious holy land, Greece is the sacred place of art.

The Raven[*]

Once upon a midnight dreary, while I pondered, weak and weary,
Over many a quaint and curious volume of forgotten lore—
While I nodded, nearly napping, suddenly there came a tapping,
As of some one gently rapping, rapping at my chamber door—
" 'Tis some visiter," I muttered, "tapping at my chamber door—   5
      Only this and nothing more."

Ah, distinctly I remember it was in the bleak December;
And each separate dying ember wrought its ghost upon the floor.
Eagerly I wished the morrow;—vainly I had sought to borrow
From my books surcease of sorrow—sorrow for the lost Lenore—   10
For the rare and radiant maiden whom the angels name Lenore—
      Nameless *here* for evermore.

And the silken, sad, uncertain rustling of each purple curtain
Thrilled me—filled me with fantastic terrors never felt before;
So that now, to still the beating of my heart, I stood repeating   15
" 'Tis some visiter entreating entrance at my chamber door—
Some late visiter entreating entrance at my chamber door;—
      This it is and nothing more."

Presently my soul grew stronger; hesitating then no longer,
"Sir," said I, "or Madam, truly your forgiveness I implore;   20
But the fact is I was napping, and so gently you came rapping,
And so faintly you came tapping, tapping at my chamber door,
That I scarce was sure I heard you"—here I opened wide the door;——
      Darkness there and nothing more.

Deep into that darkness peering, long I stood there wondering, fearing,   25
Doubting, dreaming dreams no mortal ever dared to dream before;
But the silence was unbroken, and the stillness gave no token,
And the only word there spoken was the whispered word, "Lenore?"
This I whispered, and an echo murmured back the word, "Lenore!"
      Merely this and nothing more.   30

Back into the chamber turning, all my soul within me burning,
Soon again I heard a tapping somewhat louder than before.
"Surely," said I, "surely that is something at my window lattice;

[*] This poem was probably written during 1844. It
was first published in January 1845. This version
was published in September 1849.

Let me see, then, what thereat is, and this mystery explore—
Let my heart be still a moment and this mystery explore;—   35
      'Tis the wind and nothing more!"

Open here I flung the shutter, when with many a flirt and flutter,
In there stepped a stately Raven of the saintly days of yore;
Not the least obeisance made he; not a minute stopped or stayed he;
But, with mien of lord or lady, perched above my chamber door—   40
Perched upon a bust of Pallas¹ just above my chamber door—
      Perched, and sat, and nothing more.

Then this ebony bird beguiling my sad fancy into smiling,
By the grave and stern decorum of the countenance it wore,
"Though thy crest be shorn and shaven, thou," I said, "art sure no craven,   45
Ghastly grim and ancient Raven wandering from the Nightly shore—
Tell me what thy lordly name is on the Night's Plutonian² shore!"
      Quoth the Raven "Nevermore."

Much I marvelled this ungainly fowl to hear discourse so plainly,
Though its answer little meaning—little relevancy bore;   50
For we cannot help agreeing that no living human being
Ever yet was blessed with seeing bird above his chamber door—
Bird or beast upon the sculptured bust above his chamber door,
      With such name as "Nevermore."

But the Raven, sitting lonely on the placid bust, spoke only   55
That one word, as if his soul in that one word he did outpour.
Nothing farther then he uttered—not a feather then he fluttered—
Till I scarcely more than muttered "Other friends have flown before—
On the morrow *he* will leave me, as my Hopes have flown before."
      Then the bird said "Nevermore."   60

Startled at the stillness broken by reply so aptly spoken,
"Doubtless," said I, "what it utters is its only stock and store
Caught from some unhappy master whom unmerciful Disaster
Followed fast and followed faster till his songs one burden bore—
Till the dirges of his Hope that melancholy burden bore   65
      Of 'Never—nevermore.' "

But the Raven still beguiling my sad fancy into smiling,
Straight I wheeled a cushioned seat in front of bird, and bust and door;
Then, upon the velvet sinking, I betook myself to linking
Fancy unto fancy, thinking what this ominous bird of yore—   70

---

¹ Athena, in classic myth the goddess of wisdom.
² I.e., as black as the region of the underworld
ruled over by Pluto in mythology.

What this grim, ungainly, ghastly, gaunt, and ominous bird of yore
　　　Meant in croaking "Nevermore."

This I sat engaged in guessing, but no syllable expressing
To the fowl whose fiery eyes now burned into my bosom's core;
This and more I sat divining, with my head at ease reclining   75
On the cushion's velvet lining that the lamp-light gloated[3] o'er,
But whose velvet-violet lining with the lamp-light gloating o'er,
　　　She shall press, ah, nevermore!

Then, methought, the air grew denser, perfumed from an unseen censer
Swung by seraphim whose foot-falls tinkled on the tufted floor.   80
"Wretch," I cried, "thy God hath lent thee—by these angels he hath sent
　　thee
Respite—respite and nepenthe from thy memories of Lenore;
Quaff, oh quaff this kind nepenthe and forget this lost Lenore!"
　　　Quoth the Raven "Nevermore."

"Prophet!" said I, "thing of evil!—prophet still, if bird, or devil!—   85
Whether Tempter sent, or whether tempest tossed thee here ashore,
Desolate yet all undaunted, on this desert land enchanted—
On this home by Horror haunted—tell me truly, I implore—
Is there—*is* there balm in Gilead?[4]—tell me—tell me, I implore!"
　　　Quoth the Raven "Nevermore."   90

"Prophet!" said I, "thing of evil!—prophet still, if bird or devil!
By that Heaven that bends above us—by that God we both adore—
Tell this soul with sorrow laden if, within the distant Aidenn,[5]
It shall clasp a sainted maiden whom the angels name Lenore—
Clasp a rare and radiant maiden whom the angels name Lenore."   95
　　　Quoth the Raven "Nevermore."

"Be that word our sign of parting, bird or fiend!" I shrieked, upstarting—
"Get thee back into the tempest and the Night's Plutonian shore!
Leave no black plume as a token of that lie thy soul hath spoken!
Leave my loneliness unbroken!—quit the bust above my door!   100
Take thy beak from out my heart, and take thy form from off my door!"
　　　Quoth the Raven "Nevermore."

And the Raven, never flitting, still is sitting, *still* is sitting
On the pallid bust of Pallas just above my chamber door;

---

[3] Here meaning both glowed and relished with
malicious pleasure.
[4] Reference to lines from Jeremiah 8:22, which
speak ironically of the healing medicinal resin

taken from evergreen trees in the region of
Gilead in Jordan.
[5] Of Arabic derivation, suggesting Eden.

And his eyes have all the seeming of a demon's that is dreaming,   105
And the lamp-light o'er him streaming throws his shadow on the floor;
And my soul from out that shadow that lies floating on the floor
      Shall be lifted—nevermore!

1844–1849

Ulalume—a Ballad[*]

  The skies they were ashen and sober;
    The leaves they were crispéd and sere—
    The leaves they were withering and sere:
  It was night, in the lonesome October
    Of my most immemorial[1] year: 5
  It was hard by the dim lake of Auber,
    In the misty mid region of Weir:—
  It was down by the dank tarn[2] of Auber,
    In the ghoul-haunted woodland of Weir.

  Here once, through an alley Titanic,   10
    Of cypress, I roamed with my Soul—
    Of cypress, with Psyche, my Soul.
  These were days when my heart was volcanic
    As the scoriac[3] rivers that roll—
    As the lavas that restlessly roll   15
  Their sulphurous currents down Yaanek,
    In the ultimate climes of the Pole[4]—
  That groan as they roll down Mount Yaanek,
    In the realms of the Boreal[5] Pole.

  Our talk had been serious and sober.   20
    By our thoughts they were palsied and sere—
    Our memories were treacherous and sere;
  For we knew not the month was October,
    And we marked not the night of the year—
    (Ah, night of all nights in the year!)[6]   25
  We noted not the dim lake of Auber,
    (Though once we had journeyed down here)

---

[*] This poem was first written and published in 1847. This version is from a revision written in 1849.
[1] Memorable.
[2] Mountain lake.

[3] Lavalike.
[4] The South Pole.
[5] Here, the direction of the south magnetic pole.
[6] All Saints' Eve.

We remembered not the dank tarn of Auber,
Nor the ghoul-haunted woodland of Weir.

And now, as the night was senescent,   3
  And star-dials pointed to morn—
  As the star-dials hinted of morn—
At the end of our path a liquescent
  And nebulous lustre was born,
Out of which a miraculous crescent   35
  Arose with a duplicate horn—
Astarte's[7] bediamonded crescent,
  Distinct with its duplicate horn.

And I said—"She is warmer than Dian;[8]
  She rolls through an ether of sighs—   40
  She revels in a region of sighs.
She has seen that the tears are not dry on
  These cheeks where the worm never dies,
And has come past the stars of the Lion,[9]
  To point us the path to the skies—   45
  To the Lethean[10] peace of the skies—
Come up, in despite of the Lion,
  To shine on us with her bright eyes—
Come up, through the lair of the Lion,
  With love in her luminous eyes."   50

But Psyche, uplifting her finger,
  Said—"Sadly this star I mistrust—
  Her pallor I strangely mistrust—
Ah, hasten!—ah, let us not linger!
  Ah, fly!—let us fly!—for we must."   55
In terror she spoke; letting sink her
  Wings till they trailed in the dust—
In agony sobbed; letting sink her
  Plumes till they trailed in the dust—
  Till they sorrowfully trailed in the dust.   60

I replied—"This is nothing but dreaming.
  Let us on, by this tremulous light!
  Let us bathe in this crystalline light!
Its Sibyllio[11] splendor is beaming
  With Hope and in Beauty to-night—   65

[7] Astarte: Phoenician fertility goddess, patroness of carnal love.

[8] Diana, virgin goddess of the moon.

[9] The constellation Leo, sign of uneasy love.

[10] Forgetfulness, caused by drinking from the river Lethe in Hades.

[11] In classic myth, the Sibyls prophesied the future.

See!—it flickers up the sky through the night!
Ah, we safely may trust to its gleaming
    And be sure it will lead us aright—
We surely may trust to a gleaming
    That cannot but guide us aright   70
Since it flickers up to Heaven through the night."

Thus I pacified Psyche and kissed her,
    And tempted her out of her gloom—
    And conquered her scruples and gloom;
And we passed to the end of the vista—   75
    But were stopped by the door of a tomb—
    By the door of a legended tomb:—
And I said—"What is written, sweet sister.
    On the door of this legended tomb?"
She replied—"Ulalume—Ulalume!—   80
    'Tis the vault of thy lost Ulalume!"

Then my heart it grew ashen and sober
    As the leaves that were crispéd and sere—
    As the leaves that were withering and sere—
And I cried—"It was surely October,   85
    On *this* very night of last year,
    That I journeyed—I journeyed down here!—
    That I brought a dread burden down here—
    On this night, of all nights in the year,
    Ah, what demon hath tempted me here?   90
Well I know, now, this dim lake of Auber—
    This misty mid region of Weir:—
Well I know, now, this dank tarn of Auber—
    This ghoul-haunted woodland of Weir."

Said we, then—the two, then—"Ah, can it   95
    Have been that the woodlandish ghouls—
    The pitiful, the merciful ghouls,
To bar up our way and to ban it
    From the secret that lies in these wolds—
    From the thing that lies hidden in these wolds—   100
Have drawn up the spectre of a planet
    From the limbo[12] of lunary souls—

This sinfully scintillant planet
    From the Hell of the planetary souls?"

1847–1849

[12] The resting place of the unbaptized on the
fringes of hell.

A Dream Within a Dream

Take this kiss upon the brow!
And, in parting from you now,
Thus much let me avow—
You are not wrong, who deem
That my days have been a dream;   5
Yet if hope has flown away
In a night, or in a day,

In a vision, or in none,
Is it therefore the less *gone?*
All that we see or seem   10
Is but a dream within a dream.

I stand amid the roar
Of a surf-tormented shore,
And I hold within my hand
Grains of the golden sand—   15
How few! yet how they creep
Through my fingers to the deep,
While I weep—while I weep!
O God! can I not grasp
Them with a tighter clasp?   20
O God! can I not save
One from the pitiless wave?
Is *all* that we see or seem
But a dream within a dream?
                                            1849

Annabel Lee

It was many and many a year ago,
    In a kingdom by the sea,
That a maiden there lived whom you may know
    By the name of Annabel Lee;—
And this maiden she lived with no other thought   5
    Than to love and be loved by me.

I was a child and *she* was a child,
  In this kingdom by the sea;
But we loved with a love that was more than love—
  I and my Annabel Lee—   10
With a love that the wingéd seraphs in Heaven
  Coveted her and me.

And this was the reason that, long ago,
  In this kingdom by the sea,
A wind blew out of a cloud, chilling   15
  My beautiful Annabel Lee;
So that her high-born kinsmen came
  And bore her away from me,
To shut her up in a sepulchre,
  In this kingdom by the sea.   20

The angels, not half so happy in Heaven,
  Went envying her and me—
Yes!—that was the reason (as all men know,
  In this kingdom by the sea)
That the wind came out of the cloud by night,   25
  Chilling and killing my Annabel Lee.

But our love it was stronger by far than the love
  Of those who were older than we—
  Of many far wiser than we—
And neither the angels in Heaven above,   30
  Nor the demons down under the sea,
Can ever dissever my soul from the soul
  Of the beautiful Annabel Lee:—

For the moon never beams, without bringing me dreams
  Of the beautiful Annabel Lee;   35
And the stars never rise, but I feel the bright eyes
  Of the beautiful Annabel Lee:—
And so, all the night-tide, I lie down by the side
Of my darling—my darling—my life and my bride,
  In her sepulchre there by the sea—   40
  In her tomb by the sounding sea.

1849

Nathaniel Hawthorne
1804–1864

Nathaniel Hawthorne rarely seemed at ease with himself, his work, or his place in American literary history. The author of America's most famous novel of religious conscience, he nevertheless professed to be unmoved by any form of religion. He characterized his regularly enforced attendance at the services at Salem's Meeting House, where his ancestors had worshiped for nearly two centuries, as "the frozen purgatory of my childhood." A writer who spent twelve years in self-imposed retirement from the world, ensconced in the literary solitude of a small room tucked under the eaves of the family house in Salem, he nevertheless yearned to participate in what he called "the opaque substance of today." Consider the letter he wrote to his sister Louisa shortly before his graduation from college. In it, Hawthorne solemnly announced: "I have thought much upon the subject and have finally come to the conclusion that I shall never make a distinguished figure in the world, and all I hope or wish is to plod along with the multitude."

This constant struggle between the private and public self, the real and the imagined self, also marked Hawthorne's attitude toward his writing. He seemed interested in creating a literary world abstracted from reality, yet he also noted that "the most desirable mode of existence might be that of a spiritualized Paul Pry, hovering invisible round men and women, witnessing their deeds, searching their hearts, borrowing brightness from their felicity and shade from their sorrow, and retaining no emotion peculiar to himself." Henry James, in his celebrated study of the writer, perceptively identified this as Hawthorne's paradoxical mixture of "evasive and inquisitive tendencies."

Hawthorne's literary ambition was often at odds with what he regarded as his accomplishments. He criticized himself, for example, for not having transcribed the reality of Puritan New England accurately enough, yet his genius transformed it into what later readers called classic fiction. Hawthorne drew his strength as a writer from his ample reserves of self-doubt. And while the circumstances of his life may appear uneventful, the drama in his life—much like the conflict in his fiction—took place in the private moral and psychic recesses of this complex individual.

Nathaniel Hawthorne was born on July 4, 1804, in Salem, Massachusetts. His Puritan ancestors were among the first settlers in the state and included two prominent judges, one active in the persecution of the Quakers in the 1650s, the other in the witch trials of the 1690s. By Hawthorne's time, however, the family had receded from public eminence. Both his father and his grandfather were captains of merchant ships. In 1808 his father died of yellow fever in Dutch Guiana (now Surinam), leaving his widow with three children: Nathaniel; an older sister, Elizabeth; and a younger sister, Louisa. Taking the customs of Puritan bereavement to an unusual extreme, the mother moved with her children back into the household of her parents and rarely left her room for the 40 remaining years of her life, eating nearly all her meals alone. Her grief, Hawthorne later noted, "outlasted its vitality, and grew to be merely a torpid habit."

Hawthorne attended school in Salem but at the age of nine was hurt playing ball. Partially lame for three years, he was tutored at home, where his devotion to reading Spenser, Shakespeare, Milton, Thomson, and Bunyan's *The Pilgrim's Progress* first showed itself. (The first book he bought with his own money was *The Faerie Queene.*) He did not remain entirely inactive, however. His mother's family owned some land and houses in Raymond, Maine, a settlement in the middle of dense and broad forests. Hawthorne made several lengthy visits there, one lasting a year. "I lived in Maine like a bird of the air, so perfect was the freedom I enjoyed. But it was there I first got my cursed habits of solitude."

In 1821 he entered Bowdoin College in Maine, and some aspects of his career there suggest that his habits of solitude were temporarily modified. He joined, for example, a literary society, a card-playing club, and a student militia led by his friend Franklin Pierce, who was to become the fourteenth president of the United States. Hawthorne described himself during this period as an "idle student," one who was "negligent of college rules and the Procrustean details of academic life, rather choosing to nurse my own fancies than to dig into Greek roots." He took up tobacco chewing and, like many of his fellow undergraduates, was fined on more than one occasion for drinking and gambling. An unusually handsome and charming young man, he participated in social activities; yet full of self-effacement and reserve, he avoided drawing attention to himself. His classmates described him as aloof when in company, and one remarked at the time: "I love Hawthorne; I admire him; but I do not know him. He lives in a mysterious world of thought and imagination which he never permits me to enter." Hawthorne graduated in 1825, an undistinguished eighteenth in a class of 38.

Returning to Salem, he lived with his mother and sisters and settled once again into a solitary way of life. With no immediate need to work for pay, he was able to read widely, showing a special interest in the history of Puritan New England, in Gothic romances, and in the great novelists of the eighteenth century, especially Fielding, Smollett, and Richardson. He also took long walks along the seashore and, after dark, through town. But he was also at work writing. In 1828 his first novel, *Fanshawe,* was published anonymously. The story, set in a rural American college (said to resemble the Bowdoin of Hawthorne's day) is one of abduction: A villain enters the scene and makes off with the ward of the college president. She is rescued by Fanshawe, described as a handsome, brave, yet reclusive student, someone "unconnected with the world, unconnected in its feelings, and uninfluenced by it in any of his pursuits. In this respect he probably deceived himself. If his inmost heart could have been laid open, there would have been discovered that dream of undying fame, which dream as it is, is more powerful than a thousand realities." She is willing to marry her rescuer, but Fanshawe declines the opportunity and, being "a hard scholar," reads himself into an early grave. Though generally regarded as a minor work, *Fanshawe* is an accomplished performance for a twenty-four-year-old author, one that reflected the styles of Fielding and Scott. However, the novel did not sell many copies, and Hawthorne soon became dissatisfied with it himself. He never later acknowledged it as his work.

Hawthorne's first short stories were published in the early 1830s. They appeared in "gift-books," a kind of magazine published annually that printed poems, stories, and essays, usually with no attribution to the author. In such stories as "Young Goodman Brown," a strong narrative voice presents mysterious or puzzling incidents. Yet, as the stories unfold, Hawthorne often suppresses that narrative voice to achieve a dramatic mode that frequently leaves the puzzles unresolved. During this period, he also worked for six months in Boston as the editor of *The American Magazine of Useful and Entertaining Knowledge,* for which he and his sister Elizabeth wrote nearly all the material. When a fire pushed the magazine to the brink of bankruptcy, Hawthorne resigned and wrote a history of the world for children. The volume sold well over a million copies, yet Hawthorne had signed a contract that earned him only a $100 fee.

In 1837 *Twice-Told Tales,* his first acknowledged book, was published. Of it, Hawthorne reported in a letter to Henry Wadsworth Longfellow, a former fellow student at Bowdoin, "I have . . . great difficulty in the lack of materials, for I have seen so little of the world that I have nothing but thin air to concoct my stories of, and it is not easy to give a life-like semblance to such shadowy stuff." Hawthorne began to address this problem in one way by keeping a notebook and filling it with telling observations of daily life—many of which were incorporated into his fiction. *Twice-Told Tales* contained about half of his stories that had appeared by that time. The collection received favorable reviews and sold steadily for many months, gradually earning him a considerable reputation, if not Fanshawe's secretly desired "undying fame."

At the same time, Hawthorne began to mix in the society of Salem, most notably with the Peabody family. Sophia Peabody, seven years younger, was a well-educated, talented artist and a near invalid. Their love grew quickly, and by the end of 1838 they were secretly engaged. Looking forward to supporting a family, Hawthorne turned to work that would be more remunerative than writing stories for magazines. In 1839, through the political influence of old friends, he obtained a position as an inspector at the Boston Custom House, weighing and measuring the goods shipped in and out of the harbor. He composed some short tales for children in these years, but he was distracted from doing any more substantial literary work. Increasingly displeased by the working conditions at the port, Hawthorne was glad to be relieved of the job when the political administration changed in 1841.

He moved almost immediately to the Brook Farm Institute of Agriculture and Education, a communal experiment founded by a group of writers and thinkers associated with Transcendentalism. There he intended to "establish a mode of life which shall combine the enchantments of poetry with the facts of daily experience." He worked conscientiously on the farm but gradually judged the chores disagreeable and his fellow workers troublesome and intrusive. He left after eight months. "I can best attain the higher ends of my life by retaining the ordinary relation to society," he announced in a letter at the time.

Yet Hawthorne's life-style after Brook Farm seems only slightly more ordinary. He married Sophia Peabody in 1842, and soon afterward they took up residence at Concord in the Old Manse, a house built by Ralph Waldo Emerson's grandfather. He gardened, took on many of the housekeeping chores, boated on the river in summer, and skated in the winter. Occasionally, he wrote. He also mixed, sometimes, with such illustrious neighbors as Emerson, Margaret Fuller, Ellery Channing, Amos Bronson Alcott, and Henry David Thoreau. His conversations with Emerson and Fuller were awkward at best. Emerson, Hawthorne noted, was "a great searcher for facts; but they seem to melt away and become unsubstantial in his grasp." (Henry James explained the incompatibility from a more distant and generous perspective: "Emerson, as a spiritual sun-worshipper, could have attached but a moderate value to Hawthorne's catlike faculty of seeing in the dark.") Hawthorne seemed unable— perhaps finally unwilling—to share Emerson's cosmic optimism and his Transcendentalist belief in the salvific qualities of experience. The young Herman Melville, in reviewing *Mosses from an Old Manse,* had also recognized Hawthorne's "Calvinistic sense of Innate Depravity and Original Sin, from whose visitations . . . no deeply thinking mind is always and wholly free."

Despite this social awkwardness and the fact that during their stay at the Old Manse Nathaniel and Sophia Hawthorne lived rather meagerly on their savings and on the small payments Hawthorne received for his writing, they always referred to these years as an extremely happy period of their lives. The birth of their first child, a daughter named Una, in 1844 only augmented the spiritual self-sufficiency of their household.

Eventually, however, the family needed more income. In 1846 Hawthorne moved his family back into his mother's house and began a three-year stint as surveyor of customs, under conditions he described fully in the essay "The Custom-House," printed as a preface to *The Scarlet Letter.* Although he published very little during this time, an extraordinary period of creative work was to follow. As before, Hawthorne's job had been a political appointment, and he lost it when the presidential administration changed in 1849. Soon after, his mother died. Through the summer and autumn of that year, his family living on money Sophia had saved and from unsolicited loans from friends, Hawthorne composed *The Scarlet Letter,* generally considered his greatest work.

The central idea of the novel—a woman sentenced to wear a lettered badge as punishment for adultery—had been conceived by Hawthorne more than a decade earlier in his short story "Endicott and the Red Cross" (1838). Usually rather desultory in his writing habits, Hawthorne threw himself into drafting *The Scarlet Letter,* writing "immensely," as his wife said—up to nine hours a day. He had originally planned it to be a tale, somewhat longer than usual, to be included in his next collection. But his publisher, James T. Fields, read the manuscript, praised it highly, and urged him to expand the work and issue it as a single volume. He did so, completing it in February 1850.

Hawthorne judged the book to be "positively a hell-fired story, into which I found it almost impossible to throw a cheering light," and he feared it would not be well received. He described in his notebook his experience as he read the final scene aloud to his wife—or "tried to read it, rather, for my voice swelled and heaved, as if I were tossed up and down on an ocean as it subsided after a storm. But I was in a very nervous state, then, having gone through a great diversity and severity of emotion, for many months past." His anxiety was short lived. On the day following the incident he was able to write to a friend in a very different tone to describe his wife's experience: "It broke her heart and sent her to bed with a grievous headache—which I look upon as a triumphant success! Judging from its effects on her and the publisher, I may calculate on what bowlers call a ten-strike!" He had calculated correctly, for the first edition sold out in ten days, and reviewers variously classed him with Alexander Pope, Sir Walter Scott, Charles Lamb, and Charles Dickens.

In the spring of 1850, Hawthorne moved with his wife and children (a son, Julian, had been born in 1846) to Lenox, Massachussetts, at the time a rural community where many literary people spent the summer. Characteristically, Hawthorne was found by many to be an aloof, even reluctant member of the community. During this time, he and Melville saw each other often, usually at Melville's suggestion. With the success of *The Scarlet Letter,* Hawthorne began work on a new romance, *The House of the Seven Gables,* which he intended to be more varied in tone and less uniformly somber than *The Scarlet Letter.* He finished the new book in 1851, and, against his expectations, it proved to be as popular as its predecessor. Other new work included another volume of stories for children, *Tanglewood Tales for Boys and Girls* (1851), a new edition of *Twice-Told Tales* (1851), and another collection of stories, *The Snow-Image, and Other Twice-Told Tales* (1851). For the first time Hawthorne was earning enough from his writing to support his family. (A daughter, Rose, was born in 1852.) Looking for a less rustic environment than Lenox, the family moved to West Newton, a suburb of Boston. Here Hawthorne began *The Blithedale Romance* (1852), a book satirizing the pretensions and delusions of social reformers.

Acclaimed in both America and Britain as one of the preeminent writers of the day, Hawthorne could finally afford to buy a permanent home for his family. In 1852 he bought The Wayside, the former house of Bronson Alcott in Concord, and once again entered the neighborhood of Emerson, Fuller, Channing, and Thoreau. Here he worked on a final volume of children's stories as well as on a campaign biography of his college friend Franklin Pierce, who had been unexpectedly chosen the Democratic candidate for president. Soon after Pierce's election, he appointed Hawthorne American consul at Liverpool, England.

Hawthorne served as consul from 1853 to 1857. Following the pattern he had established at the customhouses in Boston and Salem, Hawthorne soon grew to dislike the job. Once again he composed no fiction while employed, but he wrote copiously in his notebooks. And though he traveled widely through the English countryside, he did not seek out the company of literary people. As the title of his published recollections of this time, *Our Old Home,* suggests, he felt a certain hereditary connection to the culture of England. Yet as an American he felt a more immediate link to the increasingly distinct culture of America. England for Hawthorne was "our *old* home," not simply "our home."

Hawthorne's relation to America in the years immediately preceding the Civil War was, however, still uneasy. "It sickens me to look back at America," he wrote in a letter from England. "I am sick to death of the continual fuss and tumult and excitement and bad blood which we keep up about political topics."

It is easy to imagine how the intensely factional climate at home would have repulsed Hawthorne, a naturally reserved man who, largely for reasons of friendship rather than ideology, supported Pierce, then being villified as a proslavery leader.

When Hawthorne left the consulate in 1857, he moved his family to Italy. They settled eventually in the countryside near Florence, not far from Robert and Elizabeth Barrett Browning, with whom they had become friendly. Here Hawthorne began work, slowly, on his last completed romance, *The Marble Faun*, which treats the conflict between American and Old World values. He remained in Italy two years, writing and visiting the American and British artists residing there. On the journey home the family stopped again in England, where Hawthorne finished *The Marble Faun*. He returned to The Wayside in June 1860.

Though he supported the Union during the Civil War, Hawthorne maintained a fairly evenhanded view of the conflict. He shared little of the abolitionist zeal of many of his neighbors in New England. (On the occasion of John Brown's execution, Hawthorne remarked, "Nobody was ever more justly hanged.") During this period, he felt increasingly out of touch with the nation that had gone to war with itself. Henry James, Sr., the novelist's father, described Hawthorne at the time as having the look "of a rogue who suddenly finds himself in the company of detectives." Hawthorne continued to work, revising his English notebooks for publication and sketching new romances, but he found it difficult to complete these drafts, and finally he abandoned them.

By the spring of 1864, Hawthorne's health had mysteriously and rapidly declined. Though mentally alert, he was quite feeble. He could hardly hold the pen as he wrote. Oliver Wendell Holmes, visiting him at the time, inferred that he had a brain tumor. Pierce proposed to take him on a trip to the seacoast of Maine, hoping this might revive his health and spirit. But on May 19, soon after they reached Plymouth, New Hampshire, Hawthorne died quietly in his sleep. His body was returned to Concord, where he was buried at Sleepy Hollow cemetery.

At a time when, as Emerson said, "things are in the saddle," Hawthorne devoted himself to a more aesthetic purpose—to explore the territory "where the Actual and the Imaginary might meet." And the setting Hawthorne most often chose for this encounter was Puritan New England, a place of "dark necessity," as he called it, an overbearing, threatening world where the responsibility for moral order remained with individuals who were themselves seriously flawed. His interests were humanistic and literary. He drew on Puritan orthodoxy not to study theology but to examine individual and collective consciousness under the pressures of anguish and suffering. He sought to dramatize the relation between society and powerful individuals; to probe such themes as the individual's relation to sin, guilt, and retribution; to explore the mysteries of the human heart; to examine characters caught in the grip of the past or in the need for greater experience and knowledge. His writing is marked by its introspective depth, by its urge to get inside the characters he created. In this respect, Hawthorne is one of the first major American writers of fiction to focus on the interior lives of his characters, to explore what Henry James would later call "the deeper psychology of art."

More generally, the compelling energy of Hawthorne's fiction derives from his fascination with the interplay of characters living in extremes and absolutes—be they a community of Puritans obsessed with uncovering sin or a scientist, artist, or idealist preoccupied with perfecting the world by pressing beyond the boundaries of mortal action. Hawthorne's work suggests that the imagination might reconcile such extremes and establish a more balanced, less dehumanized view of individual action and moral responsibility. But he was not always confident that this was possible. He leaves us with a fictional world in which, as in reality, the consequences of trying to transcend the mortal and the moral remain all too painfully apparent.

Hawthorne never stopped studying his own techniques as a writer. Perhaps this is one reason so many other major writers were so attracted to his work. Poe admired him, as did Henry James, Thomas Hardy, and D. H. Lawrence. And Herman Melville dedicated *Moby-Dick* to Hawthorne "in token of my admiration for his genius." And yet it may be most fitting to turn to one of Hawthorne's own early sketches for a projection of his contribution to an indigenous American literature. In "A Select Party," Hawthorne creates a character, not unlike himself in appearance, manner, and aspiration, who is "as yet unhonored" by those around him but "for whom our country is looking anxiously into the mist of Time, as destined to fulfill the great mission of creating an American literature, as it were, out of our intellectual quarries." The enduring strength of Hawthorne's writing suggests that he accomplished that mission.

Further Reading:

H. James, *Hawthorne*, 1879.

J. Hawthorne, *Nathaniel Hawthorne and His Wife*, 2 vols., 1884, 1968.

G. Woodberry, *Nathaniel Hawthorne*, 1902.

D. H. Lawrence, *Studies in Classic American Literature*, 1923.

F. A. O. Matthiessen, *The American Renaissance*, 1941.

H. Levin, *The Power of Blackness*, 1958, 1980.

A. Turner, *Nathaniel Hawthorne. An Introduction and Interpretation*, 1961.

Hawthorne Centenary Essays, ed. R. H. Pearce, 1964.

F. Crews, *The Sins of the Fathers, Hawthorne's Psychological Themes*, 1966.

Hawthorne: A Collection of Critical Essays, ed. A. Kaul, 1966.

Hawthorne Among His Contemporaries, ed. K. Cameron, 1968.

J. C. Stubbs, *The Pursuit of Form: A Study of Hawthorne and the Romance*, 1970.

N. F. Doubleday, *Hawthorne's Early Tales: A Critical Study*, 1972.

R. H. Brodhead, *Hawthorne, Melville, and the Novel*, 1976.

A. Turner, *Nathaniel Hawthorne: A Biography*, 1980.

J. Mellows, *Nathaniel Hawthorne in His Times*, 1980.

T. Martin, *Nathaniel Hawthorne*, 1983.

Texts:

The Complete Works of Nathaniel Hawthorne, 12 vols., 1883.

See also *Nathaniel Hawthorne: Tales and Sketches*, ed. R. H. Pearce, 1982.

Nathaniel Hawthorne: Novels, ed. M. Bell, 1983.

My Kinsman, Major Molineux

After the kings of Great Britain had assumed the right of appointing the colonial governors,[1] the measures of the latter seldom met with the ready and general approbation which had been paid to those of their predecessors, under the original charters. The people looked with most jealous scrutiny to the exercise of power which did not emanate from themselves, and they usually rewarded their rulers with slender gratitude for the compliances by which, in softening their instructions from beyond the sea, they had incurred the reprehension of those who gave them. The annals of Massachusetts Bay will inform us, that of six governors in the space of about forty years from the surrender of the old charter, under James II., two were imprisoned by a popular insurrection; a third, as Hutchinson[2] inclines to believe, was driven from the province by the whizzing of a musket-ball; a fourth, in the opinion of the same historian, was hastened to his grave by continual bickerings with the House of Representatives; and the remaining two, as well as their successors, till the Revolution, were favored with few and brief intervals of peaceful sway. The inferior members of the court party,[3] in times of high political excitement, led scarcely a more desirable life. These remarks may serve as a preface to the following adventures, which chanced upon a summer night, not far from a hundred years ago. The reader, in order to avoid a long and dry detail of colonial affairs, is requested to dispense with an account of the train of circumstances that had caused much temporary inflammation of the popular mind.

It was near nine o'clock of a moonlight evening, when a boat crossed the ferry with a single passenger, who had obtained his conveyance at that unusual hour by the promise of an extra fare. While he stood on the landing-place, searching in either pocket for the means of fulfilling his agreement, the ferryman lifted a lantern, by the aid of which, and the newly risen moon, he took a very accurate survey of the stranger's figure. He was a youth of barely eighteen years, evidently country-bred, and now, as it should seem, upon his first visit to town. He was clad in a coarse gray coat, well worn, but in excellent repair; his under garments were durably constructed of leather, and fitted tight to a pair of serviceable and well-shaped limbs; his stockings of blue yarn were the incontrovertible work of a mother or a sister; and on his head was a three-cornered hat, which in its better days had perhaps sheltered the graver brow of the lad's father. Under his left arm was a heavy cudgel formed of an oak sapling, and retaining a part of the hardened root; and his equipment was completed by a wallet,[4] not so abundantly stocked as to incommode the vigorous shoulders on which it hung. Brown, curly hair, well-shaped features, and bright, cheerful eyes were nature's gifts, and worth all that art could have done for his adornment.

The youth, one of whose names was Robin, finally drew from his pocket the half

---

[1] The first royal governor of Massachusetts was appointed in 1685 by James II, after the Massachusetts Charter had been annulled.

[2] Thomas Hutchinson (1711–1780), the last royal governor of Massachusetts, was also a historian

and author of *The History of the Colony and Province of Massachusetts-Bay* (1764, 1767).

[3] The pro-royal party.

[4] Knapsack.

of a little province bill[5] of five shillings, which, in the depreciation in that sort of currency, did but satisfy the ferryman's demand, with the surplus of a sexangular piece of parchment, valued at three pence. He then walked forward into the town, with as light a step as if his day's journey had not already exceeded thirty miles, and with as eager an eye as if he were entering London city, instead of the little metropolis of a New England colony. Before Robin had proceeded far, however, it occurred to him that he knew not whither to direct his steps; so he paused, and looked up and down the narrow street, scrutinizing the small and mean wooden buildings that were scattered on either side.

"This low hovel cannot be my kinsman's dwelling," thought he, "nor yonder old house, where the moonlight enters at the broken casement; and truly I see none hereabouts that might be worthy of him. It would have been wise to inquire my way of the ferryman, and doubtless he would have gone with me, and earned a shilling from the Major for his pains. But the next man I meet will do as well."

He resumed his walk, and was glad to perceive that the street now became wider, and the houses more respectable in their appearance. He soon discerned a figure moving on moderately in advance, and hastened his steps to overtake it. As Robin drew nigh, he saw that the passenger was a man in years, with a full periwig of gray hair, a wide-skirted coat of dark cloth, and silk stockings rolled above his knees. He carried a long and polished cane, which he struck down perpendicularly before him at every step; and at regular intervals he uttered two successive hems, of a peculiarly solemn and sepulchral intonation. Having made these observations, Robin laid hold of the skirt of the old man's coat, just when the light from the open door and windows of a barber's shop fell upon both their figures.

"Good evening to you," honored sir, said he, making a low bow, and still retaining his hold of the skirt. "I pray you tell me whereabouts is the dwelling of my kinsman, Major Molineux."

The youth's question was uttered very loudly; and one of the barbers, whose razor was descending on a well-soaped chin, and another who was dressing a Ramillies wig,[6] left their occupations, and came to the door. The citizen, in the mean time, turned a long-favored countenance upon Robin, and answered him in a tone of excessive anger and annoyance. His two sepulchral hems, however, broke into the very centre of his rebuke, with most singular effect, like a thought of the cold grave obtruding among wrathful passions.

"Let go my garment, fellow! I tell you, I know not the man you speak of. What! I have authority, I have—hem, hem—authority; and if this be the respect you show for your betters, your feet shall be brought acquainted with the stocks[7] by daylight, tomorrow morning!"

Robin released the old man's skirt, and hastened away, pursued by an ill-mannered roar of laughter from the barber's shop. He was at first considerably surprised by the result of his question, but, being a shrewd youth, soon thought himself able to account for the mystery.

"This is some country representative," was his conclusion, "who has never seen the

---

[5] Colonial paper money.
[6] Elaborately braided wig named for a British victory at Ramillies, Belgium.

[7] Heavy wooden instruments, used for public punishment, that lock around the ankles and sometimes the wrists.

inside of my kinsman's door, and lacks the breeding to answer a stranger civilly. The man is old, or verily—I might be tempted to turn back and smite him on the nose. Ah, Robin, Robin! even the barber's boys laugh at you for choosing such a guide! You will be wiser in time, friend Robin."

He now became entangled in a succession of crooked and narrow streets, which crossed each other, and meandered at no great distance from the water-side. The smell of tar was obvious to his nostrils, the masts of vessels pierced the moonlight above the tops of the buildings, and the numerous signs, which Robin paused to read, informed him that he was near the centre of business. But the streets were empty, the shops were closed, and lights were visible only in the second stories of a few dwelling-houses. At length, on the corner of a narrow lane, through which he was passing, he beheld the broad countenance of a British hero swinging before the door[8] of an inn, whence proceeded the voices of many guests. The casement of one of the lower windows was thrown back, and a very thin curtain permitted Robin to distinguish a party at supper, round a well-furnished table. The fragrance of the good cheer steamed forth into the outer air, and the youth could not fail to recollect that the last remnant of his travelling stock of provision had yielded to his morning appetite, and that noon had found and left him dinnerless.

"Oh, that a parchment three-penny might give me a right to sit down at yonder table!" said Robin, with a sigh. "But the Major will make me welcome to the best of his victuals; so I will even step boldly in, and inquire my way to his dwelling."

He entered the tavern, and was guided by the murmur of voices and the fumes of tobacco to the public-room. It was a long and low apartment, with oaken walls, grown dark in the continual smoke, and a floor which was thickly sanded, but of no immaculate purity. A number of persons—the larger part of whom appeared to be mariners, or in some way connected with the sea—occupied the wooden benches, or leather-bottomed chairs, conversing on various matters, and occasionally lending their attention to some topic of general interest. Three or four little groups were draining as many bowls of punch, which the West India trade had long since made a familiar drink in the colony. Others, who had the appearance of men who lived by regular and laborious handicraft, preferred the insulated bliss of an unshared potation, and became more taciturn under its influence. Nearly all, in short, evinced a predilection for the Good Creature[9] in some of its various shapes, for this is a vice to which, as Fast Day[10] sermons of a hundred years ago will testify, we have a long hereditary claim. The only guests to whom Robin's sympathies inclined him were two or three sheepish countrymen, who were using the inn somewhat after the fashion of a Turkish caravansary,[11] they had gotten themselves into the darkest corner of the room, and heedless of the Nicotian[12] atmosphere, were supping on the bread of their own ovens, and the bacon cured in their own chimney-smoke. But though Robin felt a sort of brotherhood with these strangers, his eyes were attracted from them to a person who stood near the door, holding whispered conversation with a group of ill-dressed associates. His features were separately striking almost to grotesqueness, and the whole

[8] I.e., on a signboard.
[9] See 1 Timothy 4:4: "For every creature of God is good and nothing to be refused, if it be received with Thanksgiving."
[10] A day for public penitence.

[11] Inn built to accommodate caravans.
[12] Smoke-filled from tobacco. Jean Nicot (hence "nicotine") brought the first tobacco to France from Lisbon.

face left a deep impression on the memory. The forehead bulged out into a double prominence, with a vale between; the nose came boldly forth in an irregular curve, and its bridge was of more than a finger's breadth; the eyebrows were deep and shaggy, and the eyes glowed beneath them like fire in a cave.

While Robin deliberated of whom to inquire respecting his kinsman's dwelling, he was accosted by the innkeeper, a little man in a stained white apron, who had come to pay his professional welcome to the stranger. Being in the second generation from a French Protestant, he seemed to have inherited the courtesy of his parent nation; but no variety of circumstances was ever known to change his voice from the one shrill note in which he now addressed Robin.

"From the country, I presume, sir?" said he, with a profound bow. "Beg leave to congratulate you on your arrival, and trust you intend a long stay with us. Fine town here, sir, beautiful buildings, and much that may interest a stranger. May I hope for the honor of your commands in respect to supper?"

"The man sees a family likeness! the rogue has guessed that I am related to the Major!" thought Robin, who had hitherto experienced little superfluous civility.

All eyes were now turned on the country lad, standing at the door, in his worn three-cornered hat, gray coat, leather breeches, and blue yarn stockings, leaning on an oaken cudgel, and bearing a wallet on his back.

Robin replied to the courteous innkeeper, with such an assumption of confidence as befitted the Major's relative. "My honest friend," he said, "I shall make it a point to patronize your house on some occasion, when"—here he could not help lowering his voice—"when I may have more than a parchment three-pence in my pocket. My present business," continued he, speaking with lofty confidence, "is merely to inquire my way to the dwelling of my kinsman, Major Molineux."

There was a sudden and general movement in the room, which Robin interpreted as expressing the eagerness of each individual to become his guide. But the innkeeper turned his eyes to a written paper on the wall, which he read, or seemed to read, with occasional recurrences to the young man's figure.

"What have we here?" said he, breaking his speech into little dry fragments. " 'Left the house of the subscriber, bounden servant,[13] Hezekiah Mudge,—had on, when he went away, gray coat, leather breeches, master's third-best hat. One pound currency reward to whosoever shall lodge him in any jail of the province.' Better trudge, boy; better trudge!"

Robin had begun to draw his hand towards the lighter end of the oak cudgel, but a strange hostility in every countenance induced him to relinquish his purpose of breaking the courteous innkeeper's head. As he turned to leave the room, he encountered a sneering glance from the bold-featured personage whom he had before noticed; and no sooner was he beyond the door, than he heard a general laugh, in which the innkeeper's voice might be distinguished, like the dropping of small stones into a kettle.

"Now, is it not strange," thought Robin, with his usual shrewdness,—"is it not strange that the confession of an empty pocket should outweigh the name of my kinsman, Major Molineux? Oh, if I had one of those grinning rascals in the woods,

[13] Person bound to servitude (indentured) for a specific period, usually in exchange for transportation to the colonies.

where I and my oak sapling grew up together, I would teach him that my arm is heavy though my purse be light!"

On turning the corner of the narrow lane, Robin found himself in a spacious street, with an unbroken line of lofty houses on each side, and a steepled building at the upper end, whence the ringing of a bell announced the hour of nine. The light of the moon, and the lamps from the numerous shop-windows, discovered people promenading on the pavement, and amongst them Robin hoped to recognize his hitherto inscrutable relative. The result of his former inquiries made him unwilling to hazard another, in a scene of such publicity, and he determined to walk slowly and silently up the street, thrusting his face close to that of every elderly gentleman, in search of the Major's lineaments. In his progress, Robin encountered many gay and gallant figures. Embroidered garments of showy colors, enormous periwigs, gold-laced hats, and silver-hilted swords glided past him and dazzled his optics. Travelled youths, imitators of the European fine gentlemen of the period, trod jauntily along, half dancing to the fashionable tunes which they hummed, and making poor Robin ashamed of his quiet and natural gait. At length, after many pauses to examine the gorgeous display of goods in the shop-windows, and after suffering some rebukes for the impertinence of his scrutiny into people's faces, the Major's kinsman found himself near the steepled building, still unsuccessful in his search. As yet, however, he had seen only one side of the thronged street; so Robin crossed, and continued the same sort of inquisition down the opposite pavement, with stronger hopes than the philosopher seeking an honest man,[14] but with no better fortune. He had arrived about midway towards the lower end, from which his course began, when he overheard the approach of some one who struck down a cane on the flag-stones at every step, uttering, at regular intervals, two sepulchral hems.

"Mercy on us!" quoth Robin, recognizing the sound.

Turning a corner, which chanced to be close at his right hand, he hastened to pursue his researches in some other part of the town. His patience now was wearing low, and he seemed to feel more fatigue from his rambles since he crossed the ferry, than from his journey of several days on the other side. Hunger also pleaded loudly within him, and Robin began to balance the propriety of demanding, violently, and with lifted cudgel, the necessary guidance from the first solitary passenger whom he should meet. While a resolution to this effect was gaining strength, he entered a street of mean appearance, on either side of which a row of ill-built houses was straggling towards the harbor. The moonlight fell upon no passenger along the whole extent, but in the third domicile which Robin passed there was a half-opened door, and his keen glance detected a woman's garment within.

"My luck may be better here," said he to himself.

Accordingly, he approached the door, and beheld it shut closer as he did so; yet an open space remained, sufficing for the fair occupant to observe the stranger, without a corresponding display on her part. All that Robin could discern was a strip of scarlet petticoat, and the occasional sparkle of an eye, as if the moon-beams were trembling on some bright thing.

"Pretty mistress," for I may call her so with a good conscience, thought the shrewd

[14] Diogenes, Greek Cynic philosopher (412?–323 B.C.), supposedly roamed the world in search of an honest man.

youth, since I know nothing to the contrary,—"my sweet pretty mistress, will you be kind enough to tell me whereabouts I must seek the dwelling of my kinsman, Major Molineux?"

Robin's voice was plaintive and winning, and the female, seeing nothing to be shunned in the handsome country youth, thrust open the door, and came forth into the moonlight. She was a dainty little figure, with a white neck, round arms, and a slender waist, at the extremity of which her scarlet petticoat jutted out over a hoop, as if she were standing in a balloon. Moreover, her face was oval and pretty, her hair dark beneath the little cap, and her bright eyes possessed a sly freedom, which triumphed over those of Robin.

"Major Molineux dwells here," said this fair woman.

Now, her voice was the sweetest Robin had heard that night, the airy counterpart of a stream of melted silver; yet he could not help doubting whether that sweet voice spoke Gospel truth. He looked up and down the mean street, and then surveyed the house before which they stood. It was a small, dark edifice of two stories, the second of which projected over the lower floor, and the front apartment had the aspect of a shop for petty commodities.

"Now, truly, I am in luck," replied Robin, cunningly, "and so indeed is my kinsman, the Major, in having so pretty a housekeeper. But I prithee trouble him to step to the door; I will deliver him a message from his friends in the country, and then go back to my lodgings at the inn."

"Nay, the Major has been abed this hour or more," said the lady of the scarlet petticoat; "and it would be to little purpose to disturb him to-night, seeing his evening draught was of the strongest. But he is a kind-hearted man, and it would be as much as my life's worth to let a kinsman of his turn away from the door. You are the good old gentleman's very picture, and I could swear that was his rainy-weather hat. Also he has garments very much resembling those leather small-clothes. But come in, I pray, for I bid you hearty welcome in his name."

So saying, the fair and hospitable dame took our hero by the hand; and the touch was light, and the force was gentleness, and though Robin read in her eyes what he did not hear in her words, yet the slender-waisted woman in the scarlet petticoat proved stronger than the athletic country youth. She had drawn his half-willing footsteps nearly to the threshold, when the opening of a door in the neighborhood startled the Major's housekeeper, and, leaving the Major's kinsman, she vanished speedily into her own domicile. A heavy yawn preceded the appearance of a man, who, like the Moonshine of Pyramus and Thisbe,[15] carried a lantern, needlessly aiding his sister luminary in the heavens. As he walked sleepily up the street, he turned his broad, dull face on Robin, and displayed a long staff, spiked at the end.

"Home, vagabond, home!" said the watchman, in accents that seemed to fall asleep as soon as they were uttered. "Home, or we'll set you in the stocks by peep of day!"

"This is the second hint of the kind," thought Robin. "I wish they would end my difficulties, by setting me there to-night."

Nevertheless, the youth felt an instinctive antipathy towards the guardian of midnight order, which at first prevented him from asking his usual question. But just

[15] Moonshine appears in a bumbling enactment of the story of Pyramus and Thisbe by characters in Shakespeare's play *A Midsummer Night's Dream*.

when the man was about to vanish behind the corner, Robin resolved not to lose the opportunity, and shouted lustily after him,—

"I say, friend! will you guide me to the house of my kinsman, Major Molineux?"

The watchman made no reply, but turned the corner and was gone; yet Robin seemed to hear the sound of drowsy laughter stealing along the solitary street. At that moment, also, a pleasant titter saluted him from the open window above his head; he looked up, and caught the sparkle of a saucy eye; a round arm beckoned to him, and next he heard light footsteps descending the staircase within. But Robin, being of the household of a New England clergyman, was a good youth, as well as a shrewd one; so he resisted temptation, and fled away.

He now roamed desperately, and at random, through the town, almost ready to believe that a spell was on him, like that by which a wizard of his country had once kept three pursuers wandering, a whole winter night, within twenty paces of the cottage which they sought. The streets lay before him, strange and desolate, and the lights were extinguished in almost every house. Twice, however, little parties of men, among whom Robin distinguished individuals in outlandish attire, came hurrying along; but, though on both occasions they paused to address him, such intercourse did not at all enlighten his perplexity. They did but utter a few words in some language of which Robin knew nothing, and perceiving his inability to answer, bestowed a curse upon him in plain English and hastened away. Finally, the lad determined to knock at the door of every mansion that might appear worthy to be occupied by his kinsman, trusting that perseverance would overcome the fatality that had hitherto thwarted him. Firm in this resolve, he was passing beneath the walls of a church, which formed the corner of two streets, when, as he turned into the shade of its steeple, he encountered a bulky stranger, muffled in a cloak. The man was proceeding with the speed of earnest business, but Robin planted himself full before him, holding the oak cudgel with both hands across his body as a bar to further passage.

"Halt, honest man, and answer me a question," said he, very resolutely. "Tell me, this instant, whereabouts is the dwelling of my kinsman, Major Molineux!"

"Keep your tongue between your teeth, fool, and let me pass!" said a deep, gruff voice, which Robin partly remembered. "Let me pass, I say, or I'll strike you to the earth!"

"No, no, neighbor!" cried Robin, flourishing his cudgel, and then thrusting its larger end close to the man's muffled face. "No, no, I'm not the fool you take me for, nor do you pass till I have an answer to my question. Whereabouts is the dwelling of my kinsman, Major Molineux?"

The stranger, instead of attempting to force his passage, stepped back into the moonlight, unmuffled his face, and stared full into that of Robin.

"Watch here an hour, and Major Molineux will pass by," said he.

Robin gazed with dismay and astonishment on the unprecedented physiognomy of the speaker. The forehead with its double prominence, the broad hooked nose, the shaggy eyebrows, and fiery eyes were those which he had noticed at the inn, but the man's complexion had undergone a singular, or, more properly, a twofold change. One side of the face blazed an intense red, while the other was black as midnight, the division line being in the broad bridge of the nose; and a mouth which seemed to extend from ear to ear was black or red, in contrast to the color of the cheek. The effect was as if two individual devils, a fiend of fire and a fiend of darkness, had united themselves to form this infernal visage. The stranger grinned in Robin's face, muffled his party-colored features, and was out of sight in a moment.

"Strange things we travellers see!" ejaculated Robin.

He seated himself, however, upon the steps of the church-door, resolving to wait the appointed time for his kinsman. A few moments were consumed in philosophical speculations upon the species of man who had just left him; but having settled this point shrewdly, rationally, and satisfactorily, he was compelled to look elsewhere for his amusement. And first he threw his eyes along the street. It was of more respectable appearance than most of those into which he had wandered; and the moon, creating, like the imaginative power, a beautiful strangeness in familiar objects, gave something of romance to a scene that might not have possessed it in the light of day. The irregular and often quaint architecture of the houses, some of whose roofs were broken into numerous little peaks, while others ascended, steep and narrow, into a single point, and others again were square; the pure snow-white of some of their complexions, the aged darkness of others, and the thousand sparklings, reflected from bright substances in the walls of many; these matters engaged Robin's attention for a while, and then began to grow wearisome. Next he endeavored to define the forms of distant objects, starting away, with almost ghostly indistinctness, just as his eye appeared to grasp them; and finally he took a minute survey of an edifice which stood on the opposite side of the street, directly in front of the church-door, where he was stationed. It was a large, square mansion, distinguished from its neighbors by a balcony, which rested on tall pillars, and by an elaborate Gothic window, communicating therewith.

"Perhaps this is the very house I have been seeking," thought Robin.

Then he strove to speed away the time, by listening to a murmur which swept continually along the street, yet was scarcely audible, except to an unaccustomed ear like his; it was a low, dull, dreamy sound, compounded of many noises, each of which was at too great a distance to be separately heard. Robin marvelled at this snore of a sleeping town, and marvelled more whenever its continuity was broken by now and then a distant shout, apparently loud where it originated. But altogether it was a sleep-inspiring sound, and, to shake off its drowsy influence, Robin arose, and climbed a window-frame, that he might view the interior of the church. There the moonbeams came trembling in, and fell down upon the deserted pews, and extended along the quiet aisles. A fainter yet more awful radiance was hovering around the pulpit, and one solitary ray had dared to rest upon the open page of the great Bible. Had nature, in that deep hour, become a worshipper in the house which man had builded? Or was that heavenly light the visible sanctity of the place,—visible because no earthly and impure feet were within the walls? The scene made Robin's heart shiver with a sensation of loneliness stronger than he had ever felt in the remotest depths of his native woods; so he turned away and sat down again before the door. There were graves around the church, and now an uneasy thought obtruded into Robin's breast. What if the object of his search, which had been so often and so strangely thwarted, were all the time mouldering in his shroud? What if his kinsman should glide through yonder gate, and nod and smile to him in dimly passing by?

"Oh that any breathing thing were here with me!" said Robin.

Recalling his thoughts from this uncomfortable track, he sent them over forest, hill, and stream, and attempted to imagine how that evening of ambiguity and weariness had been spent by his father's household. He pictured them assembled at the door, beneath the tree, the great old tree, which had been spared for its huge twisted trunk and venerable shade, when a thousand leafy brethren fell. There, at the going down of the summer sun, it was his father's custom to perform domestic worship, that the neighbors might come and join with him like brothers of the family, and that the wayfaring man might pause to drink at that fountain, and keep his heart pure by freshening the memory of home. Robin distinguished the seat of every individual of the little audience; he saw the good man in the midst, holding the Scriptures in the golden light that fell from the western clouds; he beheld him close the book and all rise up to pray. He heard the old thanksgivings for daily mercies, the old supplications for their continuance, to which he had so often listened in weariness, but which were now among his dear remembrances. He perceived the slight inequality of his father's voice when he came to speak of the absent one; he noted how his mother turned her face to the broad and knotted trunk; how his elder brother scorned, because the beard was rough upon his upper lip, to permit his features to be moved; how the younger sister drew down a low hanging branch before her eyes; and how the little one of all, whose sports had hitherto broken the decorum of the scene, understood the prayer for her playmate, and burst into clamorous grief. Then he saw them go in at the door; and when Robin would have entered also, the latch tinkled into its place, and he was excluded from his home.

"Am I here, or there?" cried Robin, starting; for all at once, when his thoughts had become visible and audible in a dream, the long, wide, solitary street shone out before him.

He aroused himself, and endeavored to fix his attention steadily upon the large edifice which he had surveyed before. But still his mind kept vibrating between fancy and reality; by turns, the pillars of the balcony lengthened into the tall, bare stems of pines, dwindled down to human figures, settled again into their true shape and size, and then commenced a new succession of changes. For a single moment, when he deemed himself awake, he could have sworn that a visage—one which he seemed to remember, yet could not absolutely name as his kinsman's—was looking towards him from the Gothic window. A deeper sleep wrestled with and nearly overcame him, but fled at the sound of footsteps along the opposite pavement. Robin rubbed his eyes, discerned a man passing at the foot of the balcony, and addressed him in a loud, peevish, and lamentable cry.

"Hallo, friend! must I wait here all night for my kinsman, Major Molineux?"

The sleeping echoes awoke, and answered the voice; and the passenger, barely able to discern a figure sitting in the oblique shade of the steeple, traversed the street to obtain a nearer view. He was himself a gentleman in his prime, of open, intelligent, cheerful, and altogether prepossessing countenance. Perceiving a country youth, apparently homeless and without friends, he accosted him in a tone of real kindness, which had become strange to Robin's ears.

"Well, my good lad, who are you sitting here?" inquired he. "Can I be of service to you in any way?"

"I am afraid not, sir," replied Robin, despondingly; "yet I shall take it kindly, if you'll answer me a single question. I've been searching, half the night, for one Major Molineux; now, sir, is there really such a person in these parts, or am I dreaming?"

"Major Molineux! The name is not altogether strange to me," said the gentleman, smiling. "Have you any objection to telling me the nature of your business with him?"

Then Robin briefly related that his father was a clergyman, settled on a small salary, at a long distance back in the country, and that he and Major Molineux were brothers' children. The Major, having inherited riches, and acquired civil and military rank, had visited his cousin, in great pomp, a year or two before; had manifested much interest in Robin and an elder brother, and, being childless himself, had thrown out hints respecting the future establishment of one of them in life. The elder brother was destined to succeed to the farm which his father cultivated in the interval of sacred duties; it was therefore determined that Robin should profit by his kinsman's generous intentions, especially as he seemed to be rather the favorite, and was thought to possess other necessary endowments.

"For I have the name of being a shrewd youth," observed Robin, in this part of his story.

"I doubt not you deserve it," replied his new friend, good-naturedly; "but pray proceed."

"Well, sir, being nearly eighteen years old, and well grown, as you see," continued Robin, drawing himself up to his full height, "I thought it high time to begin the world. So my mother and sister put me in handsome trim, and my father gave me half the remnant of his last year's salary, and five days ago I started for this place, to pay the Major a visit. But, would you believe it, sir! I crossed the ferry a little after dark, and have yet found nobody that would show me the way to his dwelling; only, an hour or two since, I was told to wait here, and Major Molineux would pass by."

"Can you describe the man who told you this?" inquired the gentleman.

"Oh, he was a very ill-favored fellow, sir," replied Robin, "with two great bumps on his forehead, a hook nose, fiery eyes; and, what struck me as the strangest, his face was of two different colors. Do you happen to know such a man, sir?"

"Not intimately," answered the stranger, "but I chanced to meet him a little time previous to your stopping me. I believe you may trust his word, and that the Major will very shortly pass through this street. In the mean time, as I have a singular curiosity to witness your meeting, I will sit down here upon the steps and bear you company."

He seated himself accordingly, and soon engaged his companion in animated discourse. It was but of brief continuance, however, for a noise of shouting, which had long been remotely audible, drew so much nearer that Robin inquired its cause.

"What may be the meaning of this uproar?" asked he. "Truly, if your town be always as noisy, I shall find little sleep while I am an inhabitant."

"Why, indeed, friend Robin, there do appear to be three or four riotous fellows abroad to-night," replied the gentleman. "You must not expect all the stillness of your native woods here in our streets. But the watch will shortly be at the heels of these lads and"—

"Ay, and set them in the stocks by peep of day," interrupted Robin, recollecting his own encounter with the drowsy lantern-bearer. "But, dear sir, if I may trust my ears, an army of watchmen would never make head against such a multitude of rioters. There were at least a thousand voices went up to make that one shout."

"May not a man have several voices, Robin, as well as two complexions?" said his friend.

"Perhaps a man may; but Heaven forbid that a woman should!" responded the shrewd youth, thinking of the seductive tones of the Major's housekeeper.

The sounds of a trumpet in some neighboring street now became so evident and continual, that Robin's curiosity was strongly excited. In addition to the shouts, he heard frequent bursts from many instruments of discord, and a wild and confused laughter filled up the intervals. Robin rose from the steps, and looked wistfully towards a point whither people seemed to be hastening.

"Surely some prodigious merry-making is going on," exclaimed he. "I have laughed very little since I left home, sir, and should be sorry to lose an opportunity. Shall we step round the corner by that darkish house, and take our share of the fun?"

"Sit down again, sit down, good Robin," replied the gentleman, laying his hand on the skirt of the gray coat. "You forget that we must wait here for your kinsman; and there is reason to believe that he will pass by, in the course of a very few moments."

The near approach of the uproar had now disturbed the neighborhood; windows flew open on all sides: and many heads, in the attire of the pillow, and confused by sleep suddenly broken, were protruded to the gaze of whoever had leisure to observe them. Eager voices hailed each other from house to house, all demanding the explanation, which not a soul could give. Half-dressed men hurried towards the unknown commotion, stumbling as they went over the stone steps that thrust themselves into the narrow foot-walk. The shouts, the laughter, and the tuneless bray, the antipodes of music, came onwards with increasing din, till scattered individuals, and then denser bodies, began to appear round a corner at the distance of a hundred yards.

"Will you recognize your kinsman, if he passes in this crowd?" inquired the gentleman.

"Indeed, I can't warrant it, sir; but I'll take my stand here, and keep a bright lookout," answered Robin, descending to the outer edge of the pavement.

A mighty stream of people now emptied into the street, and came rolling slowly towards the church. A single horseman wheeled the corner in the midst of them, and close behind him came a band of fearful wind-instruments, sending forth a fresher discord now that no intervening buildings kept it from the ear. Then a redder light disturbed the moonbeams, and a dense multitude of torches shone along the street, concealing, by their glare, whatever object they illuminated. The single horseman, clad in a military dress, and bearing a drawn sword, rode onward as the leader, and, by his fierce and variegated countenance, appeared like war personified; the red of one cheek was an emblem of fire and sword; the blackness of the other betokened the mourning that attends them. In his train were wild figures in the Indian dress, and many fantastic shapes without a model, giving the whole march a visionary air, as if a dream had broken forth from some feverish brain, and were sweeping visibly through the midnight streets. A mass of people, inactive, except as applauding spectators, hemmed the procession in; and several women ran along the sidewalk, piercing the confusion of heavier sounds with their shrill voices of mirth or terror.

"The double-faced fellow has his eye upon me," muttered Robin, with an indefinite but an uncomfortable idea that he was himself to bear a part in the pageantry.

The leader turned himself in the saddle, and fixed his glance full upon the country youth, as the steed went slowly by. When Robin had freed his eyes from those fiery ones, the musicians were passing before him, and the torches were close at hand; but the unsteady brightness of the latter formed a veil which he could not penetrate. The rattling of wheels over the stones sometimes found its way to his ear, and confused traces of a human form appeared at intervals, and then melted into the vivid light.

A moment more, and the leader thundered a command to halt: the trumpets vomited a horrid breath, and then held their peace; the shouts and laughter of the people died away, and there remained only a universal hum, allied to silence. Right before Robin's eyes was an uncovered cart. There the torches blazed the brightest, there the moon shone out like day, and there, in tar-and-feathery dignity, sat his kinsman, Major Molineux!

He was an elderly man, of large and majestic person, and strong, square features, betokening a steady soul; but steady as it was, his enemies had found means to shake it. His face was pale as death, and far more ghastly; the broad forehead was contracted in his agony, so that his eyebrows formed one grizzled line; his eyes were red and wild, and the foam hung white upon his quivering lip. His whole frame was agitated by a quick and continual tremor, which his pride strove to quell, even in those circumstances of overwhelming humiliation. But perhaps the bitterest pang of all was when his eyes met those of Robin; for he evidently knew him on the instant, as the youth stood witnessing the foul disgrace of a head grown gray in honor. They stared at each other in silence, and Robin's knees shook, and his hair bristled, with a mixture of pity and terror. Soon, however, a bewildering excitement began to seize upon his mind; the preceding adventures of the night, the unexpected appearance of the crowd, the torches, the confused din and the hush that followed, the spectre of his kinsman reviled by that great multitude,—all this, and, more than all, a perception of tremendous ridicule in the whole scene, affected him with a sort of mental inebrity. At that moment a voice of sluggish merriment saluted Robin's ears; he turned instinctively, and just behind the corner of the church stood the lantern-bearer, rubbing his eyes, and drowsily enjoying the lad's amazement. Then he heard a peal of laughter like the ringing of silvery bells; a woman twitched his arm, a saucy eye met his, and he saw the lady of the scarlet petticoat. A sharp, dry cachinnation[16] appealed to his memory, and, standing on tiptoe in the crowd, with his white apron over his head, he beheld the courteous little innkeeper. And lastly, there sailed over the heads of the multitude a great, broad laugh, broken in the midst by two sepulchral hems; thus, "Haw, haw, haw,—hem, hem,—haw, haw, haw, haw!"

The sound proceeded from the balcony of the opposite edifice, and thither Robin turned his eyes. In front of the Gothic window stood the old citizen, wrapped in a wide gown, his gray periwig exchanged for a nightcap, which was thrust back from his forehead, and his silk stockings hanging about his legs. He supported himself on his polished cane in a fit of convulsive merriment, which manifested itself on his solemn old features like a funny inscription on a tomb-stone. Then Robin seemed to hear the voices of the barbers, of the guests of the inn, and of all who had made sport of him that night. The contagion was spreading among the multitude, when all at once, it seized upon Robin, and he sent forth a shout of laughter that echoed through the street,—every man shook his sides, every man emptied his lungs, but Robin's shout was the loudest there. The cloud-spirits peeped from their silvery islands, as the congregated mirth went roaring up the sky! The Man in the Moon heard the far bellow. "Oho," quoth he, "the old earth is frolicsome to-night!"

When there was a momentary calm in that tempestuous sea of sound, the leader gave the sign, the procession resumed its march. On they went, like fiends that throng in mockery around some dead potentate, mighty no more, but majestic still in his

---

[16] Laugh.

agony. On they went, in counterfeited pomp, in senseless uproar, in frenzied merriment, trampling all on an old man's heart. On swept the tumult, and left a silent street behind. . . .

"Well, Robin, are you dreaming?" inquired the gentleman, laying his hand on the youth's shoulder.

Robin started, and withdrew his arm from the stone post to which he had instinctively clung, as the living stream rolled by him. His cheek was somewhat pale, and his eye not quite as lively as in the earlier part of the evening.

"Will you be kind enough to show me the way to the ferry?" said he, after a moment's pause.

"You have, then, adopted a new subject of inquiry?" observed his companion, with a smile.

"Why, yes, sir," replied Robin, rather dryly. "Thanks to you, and to my other friends, I have at last met my kinsman, and he will scarce desire to see my face again. I begin to grow weary of a town life, sir. Will you show me the way to the ferry?"

"No, my good friend Robin,—not to-night, at least," said the gentleman. "Some few days hence, if you wish it, I will speed you on your journey. Or, if you prefer to remain with us, perhaps, as you are a shrewd youth, you may rise in the world without the help of your kinsman, Major Molineux."

1832

Young Goodman Brown

Young Goodman[1] Brown came forth at sunset into the street at Salem village; but put his head back, after crossing the threshold, to exchange a parting kiss with his young wife. And Faith, as the wife was aptly named, thrust her own pretty head into the street, letting the wind play with the pink ribbons of her cap while she called to Goodman Brown.

"Dearest heart," whispered she, softly and rather sadly, when her lips were close to his ear, "prithee put off your journey until sunrise and sleep in your own bed to-night. A lone woman is troubled with such dreams and such thoughts that she's afeard of herself sometimes. Pray tarry with me this night, dear husband, of all nights in the year."

"My love and my Faith," replied young Goodman Brown, "of all nights in the year, this one night must I tarry away from thee. My journey, as thou callest it, forth and back again, must needs be done 'twixt now and sunrise. What, my sweet, pretty wife, dost thou doubt me already, and we but three months married?"

"Then God bless you!" said Faith, with the pink ribbons; "and may you find all well when you come back."

---

[1] Polite term of address for a man of humble standing.

"Amen!" cried Goodman Brown. "Say thy prayers, dear Faith, and go to bed at dusk, and no harm will come to thee."

So they parted; and the young man pursued his way until, being about to turn the corner by the meeting-house, he looked back and saw the head of Faith still peeping after him with a melancholy air, in spite of her pink ribbons.

"Poor little Faith!" thought he, for his heart smote him. "What a wretch am I to leave her on such an errand! She talks of dreams, too. Methought as she spoke there was trouble in her face, as if a dream had warned her what work is to be done tonight. But no, no; 't would kill her to think it. Well, she's a blessed angel on earth; and after this one night I'll cling to her skirts and follow her to heaven."

With this excellent resolve for the future, Goodman Brown felt himself justified in making more haste on his present evil purpose. He had taken a dreary road, darkened by all the gloomiest trees of the forest, which barely stood aside to let the narrow path creep through, and closed immediately behind. It was all as lonely as could be; and there is this peculiarity in such a solitude, that the traveller knows not who may be concealed by the innumerable trunks and the thick boughs overhead; so that with lonely footsteps he may yet be passing through an unseen multitude.

"There may be a devilish Indian behind every tree," said Goodman Brown to himself; and he glanced fearfully behind him as he added, "What if the devil himself should be at my very elbow!"

His head being turned back, he passed a crook of the road, and, looking forward again, beheld the figure of a man, in grave and decent attire, seated at the foot of an old tree. He arose at Goodman Brown's approach and walked onward side by side with him.

"You are late, Goodman Brown," said he. "The clock of the Old South[2] was striking as I came through Boston, and that is full fifteen minutes agone."

"Faith kept me back a while," replied the young man, with a tremor in his voice, caused by the sudden appearance of his companion, though not wholly unexpected.

It was now deep dusk in the forest, and deepest in that part of it where these two were journeying. As nearly as could be discerned, the second traveller was about fifty years old, apparently in the same rank of life as Goodman Brown, and bearing a considerable resemblance to him, though perhaps more in expression than features. Still they might have been taken for father and son. And yet, though the elder person was as simply clad as the younger, and as simple in manner too, he had an indescribable air of one who knew the world, and who would not have felt abashed at the governor's dinner table or in King William's[3] court, were it possible that his affairs should call him thither. But the only thing about him that could be fixed upon as remarkable was his staff, which bore the likeness of a great black snake, so curiously wrought that it might almost be seen to twist and wriggle itself like a living serpent. This, of course, must have been an ocular deception, assisted by the uncertain light.

"Come, Goodman Brown," cried his fellow-traveller, "this is a dull pace for the beginning of a journey. Take my staff, if you are so soon weary."

---

[2] Famous church in Boston.
[3] William III ruled England jointly with Queen Mary II from 1689 to 1702.

"Friend," said the other, exchanging his slow pace for a full stop, "having kept covenant by meeting thee here, it is my purpose now to return whence I came. I have scruples touching the matter thou wot'st[4] of."

"Sayest thou so?" replied he of the serpent, smiling apart. "Let us walk on, nevertheless, reasoning as we go; and if I convince thee not thou shalt turn back. We are but a little way in the forest yet."

"Too far! too far!" exclaimed the goodman, unconsciously resuming his walk. "My father never went into the woods on such an errand, nor his father before him. We have been a race of honest men and good Christians since the days of the martyrs;[5] and shall I be the first of the name of Brown that ever took this path and kept"—

"Such company, thou wouldst say," observed the elder person, interpreting his pause. "Well said, Goodman Brown! I have been as well acquainted with your family as with ever a one among the Puritans; and that's no trifle to say. I helped your grandfather, the constable, when he lashed the Quaker woman so smartly through the streets of Salem; and it was I that brought your father a pitch-pine knot, kindled at my own hearth, to set fire to an Indian village, in King Philip's war.[6] They were my good friends, both; and many a pleasant walk have we had along this path, and returned merrily after midnight. I would fain be friends with you for their sake."

"If it be as thou sayest," replied Goodman Brown, "I marvel they never spoke of these matters; or, verily, I marvel not, seeing that the least rumor of the sort would have driven them from New England. We are a people of prayer, and good works to boot, and abide no such wickedness."

"Wickedness or not," said the traveller with the twisted staff, "I have a very general acquaintance here in New England. The deacons of many a church have drunk the communion wine with me; the selectmen of divers towns make me their chairman; and a majority of the Great and General Court[7] are firm supporters of my interest. The governor and I, too—But these are state secrets."

"Can this be so?" cried Goodman Brown, with a stare of amazement at his undisturbed companion. "Howbeit, I have nothing to do with the governor and council; they have their own ways, and are no rule for a simple husbandman[8] like me. But, were I to go on with thee, how should I meet the eye of that good old man, our minister, at Salem village? Oh, his voice would make me tremble both Sabbath day and lecture day."[9]

Thus far the elder traveller had listened with due gravity; but now burst into a fit of irrepressible mirth, shaking himself so violently that his snake-like staff actually seemed to wriggle in sympathy.

"Ha! ha! ha!" shouted he again and again; then composing himself, "Well, go on, Goodman Brown, go on; but, prithee, don't kill me with laughing."

"Well, then, to end the matter at once," said Goodman Brown, considerably

---

[4] Knowest.
[5] Allusion to the treatment of Protestants in England under the Catholic monarch Mary Tudor (1553–1558).
[6] War waged (1675–1676) against the New England colonists by the Indian leader Metacomset, also known as "King Philip."

[7] Legislature of the Puritan colony.
[8] Most often a farmer, but here a man of ordinary standing.
[9] Midweek sermon day, either Wednesday or Thursday.

nettled, "there is my wife, Faith. It would break her dear little heart; and I'd rather break my own."

"Nay, if that be the case," answered the other, "e'en go thy ways, Goodman Brown. I would not for twenty old women like the one hobbling before us that Faith should come to any harm."

As he spoke he pointed his staff at a female figure on the path, in whom Goodman Brown recognized a very pious and exemplary dame, who had taught him his catechism in youth, and was still his moral and spiritual adviser, jointly with the minister and Deacon Gookin.

"A marvel, truly, that Goody[10] Cloyse[11] should be so far in the wilderness at nightfall," said he. "But with your leave, friend, I shall take a cut through the woods until we have left this Christian woman behind. Being a stranger to you, she might ask whom I was consorting with and whither I was going."

"Be it so," said his fellow-traveller. "Betake you to the woods, and let me keep the path."

Accordingly the young man turned aside, but took care to watch his companion, who advanced softly along the road until he had come within a staff's length of the old dame. She, meanwhile, was making the best of her way, with singular speed for so aged a woman, and mumbling some indistinct words—a prayer, doubtless—as she went. The traveller put forth his staff and touched her withered neck with what seemed the serpent's tail.

"The devil!" screamed the pious old lady.

"Then Goody Cloyse knows her old friend?" observed the traveller, confronting her and leaning on his writhing stick.

"Ah, forsooth, and is it your worship indeed?" cried the good dame. "Yea, truly is it, and in the very image of my old gossip, Goodman Brown, the grandfather of the silly fellow that now is. But—would your worship believe it?—my broomstick hath strangely disappeared, stolen, as I suspect, by that unhanged witch, Goody Cory, and that, too, when I was all anointed with the juice of smallage, and cinquefoil, and wolf's bane"[12]—

"Mingled with fine wheat and the fat of a new-born babe," said the shape of old Goodman Brown.

"Ah, your worship knows the recipe," cried the old lady, cackling aloud. "So, as I was saying, being all ready for the meeting, and no horse to ride on, I made up my mind to foot it; for they tell me there is a nice young man to be taken into communion to-night. But now your good worship will lend me your arm, and we shall be there in a twinkling."

"That can hardly be," answered her friend. "I may not spare you my arm, Goody Cloyse; but here is my staff, if you will."

So saying, he threw it down at her feet, where, perhaps, it assumed life, being one of the rods which its owner had formerly lent to the Egyptian magi.[13] Of this fact, however, Goodman Brown could not take cognizance. He had cast up his eyes in

[10] Contraction of "goodwife" and a polite term for a married woman of humble standing.
[11] Hawthorne uses given names (such as Cloyse and Cory) of people involved in the Salem witch trials.
[12] The plants mentioned here were associated with magic and witchcraft.
[13] See Exodus 7 for a description of the Egyptian magicians who turned their rods into serpents.

astonishment, and, looking down again, beheld neither Goody Cloyse nor the serpentine staff, but his fellow-traveller alone, who waited for him as calmly as if nothing had happened.

"That old woman taught me my catechism," said the young man; and there was a world of meaning in this simple comment.

They continued to walk onward, while the elder traveller exhorted his companion to make good speed and persevere in the path, discoursing so aptly that his arguments seemed rather to spring up in the bosom of his auditor than to be suggested by himself. As they went, he plucked a branch of maple to serve for a walking stick, and began to strip it of the twigs and little boughs, which were wet with evening dew. The moment his fingers touched them they became strangely withered and dried up as with a week's sunshine. Thus the pair proceeded, at a good free pace, until suddenly, in a gloomy hollow of the road, Goodman Brown sat himself down on the stump of a tree and refused to go any farther.

"Friend," said he, stubbornly, "my mind is made up. Not another step will I budge on this errand. What if a wretched old woman do choose to go to the devil when I thought she was going to heaven: is that any reason why I should quit my dear Faith and go after her?"

"You will think better of this by and by," said his acquaintance, composedly. "Sit here and rest yourself a while; and when you feel like moving again, there is my staff to help you along."

Without more words, he threw his companion the maple stick, and was as speedily out of sight as if he had vanished into the deepening gloom. The young man sat a few moments by the roadside, applauding himself greatly, and thinking with how clear a conscience he should meet the minister in his morning walk, nor shrink from the eye of good old Deacon Gookin. And what calm sleep would be his that very night, which was to have been spent so wickedly, but so purely and sweetly now, in the arms of Faith! Amidst these pleasant and praiseworthy meditations, Goodman Brown heard the tramp of horses along the road, and deemed it advisable to conceal himself within the verge of the forest, conscious of the guilty purpose that had brought him thither, though now so happily turned from it.

On came the hoof tramps and the voices of the riders, two grave old voices, conversing soberly as they drew near. These mingled sounds appeared to pass along the road, within a few yards of the young man's hiding-place; but, owing doubtless to the depth of the gloom at that particular spot, neither the travellers nor their steeds were visible. Though their figures brushed the small boughs by the wayside, it could not be seen that they intercepted, even for a moment, the faint gleam from the strip of bright sky athwart which they must have passed. Goodman Brown alternately crouched and stood on tiptoe, pulling aside the branches and thrusting forth his head as far as he durst without discerning so much as a shadow. It vexed him the more, because he could have sworn, were such a thing possible, that he recognized the voices of the minister and Deacon Gookin, jogging along quietly, as they were wont to do, when bound to some ordination or ecclesiastical council. While yet within hearing, one of the riders stopped to pluck a switch.

"Of the two, reverend sir," said the voice like the deacon's, "I had rather miss an ordination dinner than to-night's meeting. They tell me that some of our community are to be here from Falmouth[14] and beyond, and others from Connecticut and Rhode Island, besides several of the Indian powwows,[15] who, after their fashion, know almost as much deviltry as the best of us. Moreover, there is a goodly young woman to be taken into communion."

"Mighty well, Deacon Gookin!" replied the solemn old tones of the minister. "Spur up, or we shall be late. Nothing can be done, you know, until I get on the ground."

The hoofs clattered again; and the voices, talking so strangely in the empty air, passed on through the forest, where no church had ever been gathered or solitary Christian prayed. Whither, then, could these holy men be journeying so deep into the heathen wilderness? Young Goodman Brown caught hold of a tree for support, being ready to sink down on the ground, faint and overburdened with the heavy sickness of his heart. He looked up to the sky, doubting whether there really was a heaven above him. Yet there was the blue arch, and the stars brightening in it.

"With heaven above and Faith below, I will yet stand firm against the devil!" cried Goodman Brown.

While he still gazed upward into the deep arch of the firmament and had lifted his hands to pray, a cloud, though no wind was stirring, hurried across the zenith and hid the brightening stars. The blue sky was still visible, except directly overhead, where this black mass of cloud was sweeping swiftly northward. Aloft in the air, as if from the depths of the cloud, came a confused and doubtful sound of voices. Once the listener fancied that he could distinguish the accents of towns-people of his own, men and women, both pious and ungodly, many of whom he had met at the communion table, and had seen others rioting at the tavern. The next moment, so indistinct were the sounds, he doubted whether he had heard aught but the murmur of the old forest, whispering without a wind. Then came a stronger swell of those familiar tones, heard daily in the sunshine at Salem village, but never until now from a cloud of night. There was one voice, of a young woman, uttering lamentations, yet with an uncertain sorrow, and entreating for some favor, which, perhaps, it would grieve her to obtain; and all the unseen multitude, both saints and sinners, seemed to encourage her onward.

"Faith!" shouted Goodman Brown, in a voice of agony and desperation; and the echoes of the forest mocked him, crying, "Faith! Faith!" as if bewildered wretches were seeking her all through the wilderness.

The cry of grief, rage, and terror was yet piercing the night, when the unhappy husband held his breath for a response. There was a scream, drowned immediately in a louder murmur of voices, fading into far-off laughter, as the dark cloud swept away, leaving the clear and silent sky above Goodman Brown. But something fluttered lightly down through the air and caught on the branch of a tree. The young man seized it, and beheld a pink ribbon.

"My Faith is gone!" cried he, after one stupefied moment. "There is no good on earth; and sin is but a name. Come, devil; for to thee is this world given."

And, maddened with despair, so that he laughed loud and long, did Goodman

---

[14] Town on Cape Cod, 70 miles from Salem, Massachusetts.   [15] Medicine men.

Brown grasp his staff and set forth again, at such a rate that he seemed to fly along the forest path rather than to walk or run. The road grew wilder and drearier and more faintly traced, and vanished at length, leaving him in the heart of the dark wilderness, still rushing onward with the instinct that guides mortal man to evil. The whole forest was peopled with frightful sounds—the creaking of the trees, the howling of wild beasts, and the yell of Indians; while sometimes the wind tolled like a distant church bell, and sometimes gave a broad roar around the traveller, as if all Nature were laughing him to scorn. But he was himself the chief horror of the scene, and shrank not from its other horrors.

"Ha! ha! ha!" roared Goodman Brown when the wind laughed at him. "Let us hear which will laugh loudest. Think not to frighten me with your deviltry. Come witch, come wizard, come Indian powwow, come devil himself, and here comes Goodman Brown. You may as well fear him as he fear you."

In truth, all through the haunted forest there could be nothing more frightful than the figure of Goodman Brown. On he flew among the black pines, brandishing his staff with frenzied gestures, now giving vent to an inspiration of horrid blasphemy, and now shouting forth such laughter as set all the echoes of the forest laughing like demons around him. The fiend in his own shape is less hideous than when he rages in the breast of man. Thus sped the demoniac on his course, until, quivering among the trees, he saw a red light before him, as when the felled trunks and branches of a clearing have been set on fire, and throw up their lurid blaze against the sky, at the hour of midnight. He paused, in a lull of the tempest that had driven him onward, and heard the swell of what seemed a hymn, rolling solemnly from a distance with the weight of many voices. He knew the tune; it was a familiar one in the choir of the village meeting-house. The verse died heavily away, and was lengthened by a chorus, not of human voices, but of all the sounds of the benighted wilderness pealing in awful harmony together. Goodman Brown cried out, and his cry was lost to his own ear by its unison with the cry of the desert.

In the interval of silence he stole forward until the light glared full upon his eyes. At one extremity of an open space, hemmed in by the dark wall of the forest, arose a rock, bearing some rude, natural resemblance either to an altar or a pulpit, and surrounded by four blazing pines, their tops aflame, their stems untouched, like candles at an evening meeting. The mass of foliage that had overgrown the summit of the rock was all on fire, blazing high into the night and fitfully illuminating the whole field. Each pendent twig and leafy festoon was in a blaze. As the red light arose and fell, a numerous congregation alternately shone forth, then disappeared in shadow, and again grew, as it were, out of the darkness, peopling the heart of the solitary woods at once.

"A grave and dark-clad company," quoth Goodman Brown.

In truth they were such. Among them, quivering to and fro between gloom and splendor, appeared faces that would be seen next day at the council board of the province, and others which, Sabbath after Sabbath, looked devoutly heavenward, and benignantly over the crowded pews, from the holiest pulpits in the land. Some affirm that the lady of the governor was there. At least there were high dames well known to her, and wives of honored husbands, and widows, a great multitude, and ancient maidens, all of excellent repute, and fair young girls, who trembled lest their mothers should espy them. Either the sudden gleams of light flashing over the obscure field bedazzled Goodman Brown, or he recognized a score of the church members of Salem village famous for their especial sanctity. Good old Deacon Gookin had arrived, and waited at the skirts of that venerable saint, his revered pastor. But, irreverently consorting with these grave, reputable, and pious people, these elders of the church, these chaste dames and dewy virgins, there were men of dissolute lives and women of spotted fame, wretches given over to all mean and filthy vice, and suspected even of horrid crimes. It was strange to see that the good shrank not from the wicked, nor were the sinners abashed by the saints. Scattered also among their pale-faced enemies were the Indian priests, or powwows, who had often scared their native forest with more hideous incantations than any known to English witchcraft.

"But where is Faith?" thought Goodman Brown; and, as hope came into his heart, he trembled.

Another verse of the hymn arose, a slow and mournful strain, such as the pious love, but joined to words which expressed all that our nature can conceive of sin, and darkly hinted at far more. Unfathomable to mere mortals is the lore of fiends. Verse after verse was sung; and still the chorus of the desert swelled between like the deepest tone of a mighty organ; and with the final peal of that dreadful anthem there came a sound, as if the roaring wind, the rushing streams, the howling beasts, and every other voice of the unconcerted wilderness were mingling and according with the voice of guilty man in homage to the prince of all. The four blazing pines threw up a loftier flame, and obscurely discovered shapes and visages of horror on the smoke wreaths above the impious assembly. At the same moment the fire on the rock shot redly forth and formed a glowing arch above its base, where now appeared a figure. With reverence be it spoken, the figure bore no slight similitude, both in garb and manner, to some grave divine of the New England churches.

"Bring forth the converts!" cried a voice that echoed through the field and rolled into the forest.

At the word, Goodman Brown stepped forth from the shadow of the trees and approached the congregation, with whom he felt a loathful brotherhood by the sympathy of all that was wicked in his heart. He could have well-nigh sworn that the shape of his own dead father beckoned him to advance, looking downward from a smoke wreath, while a woman, with dim features of despair, threw out her hand to warn him back. Was it his mother? But he had no power to retreat one step, nor to resist, even in thought, when the minister and good old Deacon Gookin seized his arms and led him to the blazing rock. Thither came also the slender form of a veiled female, led between Goody Cloyse, that pious teacher of the catechism, and Martha Carrier,[16] who had received the devil's promise to be queen of hell. A rampant hag was she. And there stood the proselytes beneath the canopy of fire.

"Welcome, my children," said the dark figure, "to the communion of your race. You have found thus young your nature and your destiny. My children, look behind you!"

They turned; and flashing forth, as it were, in a sheet of flame, the fiend worshippers were seen; the smile of welcome gleamed darkly on every visage.

"There," resumed the sable form, "are all whom ye have reverenced from youth.

[16] Woman hanged in Salem in 1697 for claiming the devil had appointed her queen of hell.

Ye deemed them holier than yourselves, and shrank from your own sin, contrasting it with their lives of righteousness and prayerful aspirations heavenward. Yet here are they all in my worshipping assembly. This night it shall be granted you to know their secret deeds: how hoary-bearded elders of the church have whispered wanton words to the young maids of their households; how many a woman, eager for widows' weeds, has given her husband a drink at bedtime and let him sleep his last sleep in her bosom; how beardless youths have made haste to inherit their fathers' wealth; and how fair damsels—blush not, sweet ones—have dug little graves in the garden, and bidden me, the sole guest, to an infant's funeral. By the sympathy of your human hearts for sin ye shall scent out all the places—whether in church, bed-chamber, street, field, or forest—where crime has been committed, and shall exult to behold the whole earth one stain of guilt, one mighty blood spot. Far more than this. It shall be yours to penetrate, in every bosom, the deep mystery of sin, the fountain of all wicked arts, and which inexhaustibly supplies more evil impulses than human power—than my power at its utmost—can make manifest in deeds. And now, my children, look upon each other."

They did so; and, by the blaze of the hell-kindled torches, the wretched man beheld his Faith, and the wife her husband, trembling before that unhallowed altar.

"Lo, there ye stand, my children," said the figure, in a deep and solemn tone, almost sad with its despairing awfulness, as if his once angelic nature could yet mourn for our miserable race. "Depending upon one another's hearts, ye had still hoped that virtue were not all a dream. Now are ye undeceived. Evil is the nature of mankind. Evil must be your only happiness. Welcome again, my children, to the communion of your race."

"Welcome," repeated the fiend worshippers, in one cry of despair and triumph.

And there they stood, the only pair, as it seemed, who were yet hesitating on the verge of wickedness in this dark world. A basin was hollowed, naturally, in the rock. Did it contain water, reddened by the lurid light? or was it blood? or, perchance, a liquid flame? Herein did the shape of evil dip his hand and prepare to lay the mark of baptism upon their foreheads, that they might be partakers of the mystery of sin, more conscious of the secret guilt of others, both in deed and thought, than they could now be of their own. The husband cast one look at his pale wife, and Faith at him. What polluted wretches would the next glance show them to each other, shuddering alike at what they disclosed and what they saw!

"Faith! Faith!" cried the husband, "look up to heaven, and resist the wicked one."

Whether Faith obeyed he knew not. Hardly had he spoken when he found himself amid calm night and solitude, listening to a roar of the wind which died heavily away through the forest. He staggered against the rock, and felt it chill and damp; while a hanging twig, that had been all on fire, besprinkled his cheek with the coldest dew.

The next morning young Goodman Brown came slowly into the street of Salem village, staring around him like a bewildered man. The good old minister was taking a walk along the graveyard to get an appetite for breakfast and meditate his sermon, and bestowed a blessing, as he passed, on Goodman Brown. He shrank from the venerable saint as if to avoid an anathema. Old Deacon Gookin was at domestic worship, and the holy words of his prayer were heard through the open window. "What God doth the wizard pray to?" quoth Goodman Brown. Goody Cloyse, that excellent old Christian, stood in the early sunshine at her own lattice, catechizing a little girl who had brought her a pint of morning's milk. Goodman Brown snatched away the child as from the grasp of the fiend himself. Turning the corner by the meeting-house, he spied the head of Faith, with the pink ribbons, gazing anxiously forth, and bursting into such joy at sight of him that she skipped along the street and almost kissed her husband before the whole village. But Goodman Brown looked sternly and sadly into her face, and passed on without a greeting.

Had Goodman Brown fallen asleep in the forest and only dreamed a wild dream of a witch-meeting?

Be it so if you will; but, alas! it was a dream of evil omen for young Goodman Brown. A stern, a sad, a darkly meditative, a distrustful, if not a desperate man did he become from the night of that fearful dream. On the Sabbath day, when the congregation were singing a holy psalm, he could not listen because an anthem of sin rushed loudly upon his ear and drowned all the blessed strain. When the minister spoke from the pulpit with power and fervid eloquence, and, with his hand on the open Bible, of the sacred truths of our religion, and of saint-like lives and triumphant deaths, and of future bliss or misery unutterable, then did Goodman Brown turn pale, dreading lest the roof should thunder down upon the gray blasphemer and his hearers. Often, awaking suddenly at midnight, he shrank from the bosom of Faith; and at morning or eventide, when the family knelt down at prayer, he scowled and muttered to himself, and gazed sternly at his wife, and turned away. And when he had lived long, and was borne to his grave a hoary corpse, followed by Faith, an aged woman, and children and grandchildren, a goodly procession, besides neighbors not a few, they carved no hopeful verse upon his tombstone, for his dying hour was gloom.

1835

The Maypole of Merry Mount[1]

There is an admirable foundation for a philosophic romance in the curious history of the early settlement of Mount Wollaston, or Merry Mount. In the slight sketch here attempted, the facts, recorded on the grave pages of our New England annalists, have wrought themselves, almost spontaneously, into a sort of allegory. The masques, mummeries, and festive customs, described in the text, are in accordance with the manners of the age. Authority on these points may be found in Strutt's Book of English Sports and Pastimes.[2]

Bright were the days at Merry Mount, when the Maypole[3] was the banner staff of that gay colony! They who reared it, should their banner be triumphant, were to pour sunshine over New England's rugged hills, and scatter flower seeds throughout the soil. Jollity and gloom were contending for an empire. Midsummer eve[4] had come, bringing deep verdure to the forest, and roses in her lap, of a more vivid hue than

---

[1] For additional information on the colony of Merry Mount, see William Bradford's *Of Plymouth Plantation*.

[2] Joseph Strutt, *The Sports and Pastimes of the People of England* (1801).

[3] The tall, flower-wreathed pole that is the chief symbol of May Day. Participants in May Day celebrations dressed in outlandish paganlike costumes and wore animal masks; the Puritans condemned these activities as licentious.

[4] The evening before Midsummer Day (June 24), which is the celebration of the nativity of John the Baptist.

the tender buds of Spring. But May, or her mirthful spirit, dwelt all the year round at Merry Mount, sporting with the Summer months, and revelling with Autumn, and basking in the glow of Winter's fireside. Through a world of toil and care she flitted with a dreamlike smile, and came hither to find a home among the lightsome hearts of Merry Mount.

Never had the Maypole been so gayly decked as at sunset on midsummer eve. This venerated emblem was a pine-tree, which had preserved the slender grace of youth, while it equalled the loftiest height of the old wood monarchs. From its top streamed a silken banner, colored like the rainbow. Down nearly to the ground the pole was dressed with birchen boughs, and others of the liveliest green, and some with silvery leaves, fastened by ribbons that fluttered in fantastic knots of twenty different colors, but no sad ones. Garden flowers, and blossoms of the wilderness, laughed gladly forth amid the verdure, so fresh and dewy that they must have grown by magic on that happy pinetree. Where this green and flowery splendor terminated, the shaft of the Maypole was stained with the seven brilliant hues of the banner at its top. On the lowest green bough hung an abundant wreath of roses, some that had been gathered in the sunniest spots of the forest, and others, of still richer blush, which the colonists had reared from English seed. O, people of the Golden Age, the chief of your husbandry was to raise flowers!

But what was the wild throng that stood hand in hand about the Maypole? It could not be that the fauns and nymphs, when driven from their classic groves and homes of ancient fable, had sought refuge, as all the persecuted did, in the fresh woods of the West. These were Gothic monsters, though perhaps of Grecian ancestry. On the shoulders of a comely youth uprose the head and branching antlers of a stag; a second, human in all other points, had the grim visage of a wolf; a third, still with the trunk and limbs of a mortal man, showed the beard and horns of a venerable he-goat. There was the likeness of a bear erect, brute in all but his hind legs, which were adorned with pink silk stockings. And here again, almost as wondrous, stood a real bear of the dark forest, lending each of his fore paws to the grasp of a human hand, and as ready for the dance as any in that circle. His inferior nature rose half way, to meet his companions as they stooped. Other faces wore the similitude of man or woman, but distorted or extravagant, with red noses pendulous before their mouths, which seemed of awful depth, and stretched from ear to ear in an eternal fit of laughter. Here might be seen the Salvage Man,[5] well known in heraldry, hairy as a baboon, and girdled with green leaves. By his side, a noble figure, but still a counterfeit, appeared an Indian hunter, with feathery crest and wampum belt. Many of this strange company wore foolscaps, and had little bells appended to their garments, tinkling with a silvery sound, responsive to the inaudible music of their gleesome spirits. Some youths and maidens were of soberer garb, yet well maintained their places in the irregular throng by the expression of wild revelry upon their features. Such were the colonists of Merry Mount, as they stood in the broad smile of sunset round their venerated Maypole.

Had a wanderer, bewildered in the melancholy forest, heard their mirth, and stolen a half-affrighted glance, he might have fancied them the crew of Comus,[6] some already transformed to brutes, some midway between man and beast, and the others rioting in the flow of tipsy jollity that foreran the change. But a band of Puritans, who

[5] Someone dressed in foliage to represent a savage.

[6] The classical god of merrymaking, here associated with John Milton's poem "Comus."

watched the scene, invisible themselves, compared the masques to those devils and ruined souls with whom their superstition peopled the black wilderness.

Within the ring of monsters appeared the two airiest forms that had ever trodden on any more solid footing than a purple and golden cloud. One was a youth in glistening apparel, with a scarf of the rainbow pattern crosswise on his breast. His right hand held a gilded staff, the ensign[7] of high dignity among the revellers, and his left grasped the slender fingers of a fair maiden, not less gayly decorated than himself. Bright roses glowed in contrast with the dark and glossy curls of each, and were scattered round their feet, or had sprung up spontaneously there. Behind this lightsome couple, so close to the Maypole that its boughs shaded his jovial face, stood the figure of an English priest, canonically dressed, yet decked with flowers, in heathen fashion, and wearing a chaplet[8] of the native vine leaves. By the riot of his rolling eye, and the pagan decorations of his holy garb, he seemed the wildest monster there, and the very Comus of the crew.

"Votaries[9] of the Maypole," cried the flower-decked priest, "merrily, all day long, have the woods echoed to your mirth. But be this your merriest hour, my hearts! Lo, here stand the Lord and Lady of the May, whom I, a clerk[10] of Oxford, and high priest of Merry Mount, am presently to join in holy matrimony. Up with your nimble spirits, ye morris-dancers, green men, and glee maidens,[11] bears and wolves, and horned gentlemen! Come; a chorus now, rich with the old mirth of Merry England, and the wilder glee of this fresh forest; and then a dance, to show the youthful pair what life is made of, and how airily they should go through it! All ye that love the Maypole, lend your voices to the nuptial song of the Lord and Lady of the May!"

This wedlock was more serious than most affairs of Merry Mount, where jest and delusion, trick and fantasy, kept up a continual carnival. The Lord and Lady of the May, though their titles must be laid down at sunset, were really and truly to be partners for the dance of life, beginning the measure that same bright eve. The wreath of roses, that hung from the lowest green bough of the Maypole, had been twined for them, and would be thrown over both their heads, in symbol of their flowery union. When the priest had spoken, therefore, a riotous uproar burst from the rout of monstrous figures.

"Begin you the stave,[12] reverend Sir," cried they all; "and never did the woods ring to such a merry peal as we of the Maypole shall send up!"

Immediately a prelude of pipe, cithern,[13] and viol, touched with practised min-strelsy, began to play from a neighboring thicket, in such a mirthful cadence that the boughs of the Maypole quivered to the sound. But the May Lord, he of the gilded staff, chancing to look into his Lady's eyes, was wonder struck at the almost pensive glance that met his own.

"Edith, sweet Lady of the May," whispered he reproachfully, "is yon wreath of roses a garland to hang above our graves, that you look so sad? O, Edith, this is our golden time! Tarnish it not by any pensive shadow of the mind; for it may be that nothing of futurity will be brighter than the mere remembrance of what is now passing."

[7] Symbolic emblem or flag.
[8] Wreath.
[9] Devotees.
[10] One who assists the clergyman.
[11] Morris dancers, green men, and glee maidens

were all part of the traditional May Day celebrations.
[12] Stanza.
[13] Cittern or lute.

"That was the very thought that saddened me! How came it in your mind too?" said Edith, in a still lower tone than he, for it was high treason to be sad at Merry Mount. "Therefore do I sigh amid this festive music. And besides, dear Edgar, I struggle as with a dream, and fancy that these shapes of our jovial friends are visionary, and their mirth unreal, and that we are no true Lord and Lady of the May. What is the mystery in my heart?"

Just then, as if a spell had loosened them, down came a little shower of withering rose leaves from the Maypole. Alas, for the young lovers! No sooner had their hearts glowed with real passion than they were sensible of something vague and unsubstantial in their former pleasures, and felt a dreary presentiment of inevitable change. From the moment that they truly loved, they had subjected themselves to earth's doom of care and sorrow, and troubled joy, and had no more a home at Merry Mount. That was Edith's mystery. Now leave we the priest to marry them, and the masquers to sport round the Maypole, till the last sunbeam be withdrawn from its summit, and the shadows of the forest mingle gloomily in the dance. Meanwhile, we may discover who these gay people were.

Two hundred years ago, and more, the old world and its inhabitants became mutually weary of each other. Men voyaged by thousands to the West: some to barter glass beads, and such like jewels, for the furs of the Indian hunter; some to conquer virgin empires; and one stern band to pray. But none of these motives had much weight with the colonists of Merry Mount. Their leaders were men who had sported so long with life, that when Thought and Wisdom came, even these unwelcome guests were led astray by the crowd of vanities which they should have put to flight. Erring Thought and perverted Wisdom were made to put on masques, and play the fool. The men of whom we speak, after losing the heart's fresh gayety, imagined a wild philosophy of pleasure, and came hither to act out their latest day-dream. They gathered followers from all that giddy tribe whose whole life is like the festal[14] days of soberer men. In their train were minstrels, not unknown in London streets: wandering players, whose theatres had been the halls of noblemen; mummers,[15] rope-dancers, and mountebanks,[16] who would long be missed at wakes, church ales, and fairs; in a word, mirth makers of every sort, such as abounded in that age, but now began to be discountenanced by the rapid growth of Puritanism. Light had their footsteps been on land, and as lightly they came across the sea. Many had been maddened by their previous troubles into a gay despair; others were as madly gay in the flush of youth, like the May Lord and his Lady; but whatever might be the quality of their mirth, old and young were gay at Merry Mount. The young deemed themselves happy. The elder spirits, if they knew that mirth was but the counterfeit of happiness, yet followed the false shadow wilfully, because at least her garments glittered brightest. Sworn triflers of a lifetime, they would not venture among the sober truths of life not even to be truly blest.

All the hereditary pastimes of Old England were transplanted hither. The King of Christmas was duly crowned, and the Lord of Misrule[17] bore potent sway. On the Eve of St. John,[18] they felled whole acres of the forest to make bonfires, and danced by the blaze all night, crowned with garlands, and throwing flowers into

---

[14] Festive.
[15] Costumed revelers.
[16] Street venders who peddle quack medicines.

[17] Leader of Christmas revelry.
[18] June 23, Midsummer's Eve.

the flame. At harvest time, though their crop was of the smallest, they made an image with the sheaves of Indian corn, and wreathed it with autumnal garlands, and bore it home triumphantly. But what chiefly characterized the colonists of Merry Mount was their veneration for the Maypole. It has made their true history a poet's tale. Spring decked the hallowed emblem with young blossoms and fresh green boughs; Summer brought roses of the deepest blush, and the perfected foliage of the forest; Autumn enriched it with that red and yellow gorgeousness which converts each wildwood leaf into a painted flower; and Winter silvered it with sleet, and hung it round with icicles, till it flashed in the cold sunshine, itself a frozen sunbeam. Thus each alternate season did homage to the Maypole, and paid it a tribute of its own richest splendor. Its votaries danced round it, once, at least, in every month; sometimes they called it their religion, or their altar; but always, it was the banner staff of Merry Mount.

Unfortunately, there were men in the new world of a sterner faith than these Maypole worshippers. Not far from Merry Mount was a settlement of Puritans, most dismal wretches, who said their prayers before daylight, and then wrought in the forest or the cornfield till evening made it prayer time again. Their weapons were always at hand to shoot down the straggling savage. When they met in conclave, it was never to keep up the old English mirth, but to hear sermons three hours long, or to proclaim bounties on the heads of wolves and the scalps of Indians. Their festivals were fast days, and their chief pastime the singing of psalms. Woe to the youth or maiden who did but dream of a dance! The selectman nodded to the constable; and there sat the light-heeled reprobate in the stocks; or if he danced, it was round the whipping-post, which might be termed the Puritan Maypole.

A party of these grim Puritans, toiling through the difficult woods, each with a horseload of iron armor to burden his footsteps, would sometimes draw near the sunny precincts of Merry Mount. There were the silken colonists, sporting round their Maypole; perhaps teaching a bear to dance, or striving to communicate their mirth to the grave Indian; or masquerading in the skins of deer and wolves, which they had hunted for that especial purpose. Often, the whole colony were playing at blindman's buff, magistrates and all, with their eyes bandaged, except a single scapegoat, whom the blinded sinners pursued by the tinkling of the bells at his garments. Once, it is said, they were seen following a flower-decked corpse, with merriment and festive music, to his grave. But did the dead man laugh? In their quietest times, they sang ballads and told tales, for the edification of their pious visitors; or perplexed them with juggling tricks; or grinned at them through horse collars; and when sport itself grew wearisome, they made game of their own stupidity, and began a yawning match. At the very least of these enormities, the men of iron shook their heads and frowned so darkly that the revellers looked up, imagining that a momentary cloud had overcast the sunshine, which was to be perpetual there. On the other hand, the Puritans affirmed that, when a psalm was pealing from their place of worship, the echo which the forest sent them back seemed often like the chorus of a jolly catch, closing with a roar of laughter. Who but the fiend, and his bond slaves, the crew of Merry Mount, had thus disturbed them? In due time, a feud arose, stern and bitter on one side, and as serious on the other as anything could be among such light spirits as had sworn allegiance to the Maypole. The future complexion of New England was involved in this important quarrel. Should the grizzly saints establish their jurisdiction over the gay sinners, then would their spirits darken all the clime, and make it a land of clouded visages, of hard toil, of sermon and psalm forever. But should the banner staff of Merry Mount be fortunate, sunshine would break upon the hills, and flowers would beautify the forest, and late posterity do homage to the Maypole.

After these authentic passages from history, we return to the nuptials of the Lord and Lady of the May. Alas! we have delayed too long, and must darken our tale too suddenly. As we glance again at the Maypole, a solitary sunbeam is fading from the summit, and leaves only a faint, golden tinge blended with the hues of the rainbow banner. Even that dim light is now withdrawn, relinquishing the whole domain of Merry Mount to the evening gloom, which has rushed so instantaneously from the black surrounding woods. But some of these black shadows have rushed forth in human shape.

Yes, with the setting sun, the last day of mirth had passed from Merry Mount. The ring of gay masquers was disordered and broken; the stag lowered his antlers in dismay; the wolf grew weaker than a lamb; the bells of the morris-dancers tinkled with tremulous affright. The Puritans had played a characteristic part in the Maypole mummeries. Their darksome figures were intermixed with the wild shapes of their foes, and made the scene a picture of the moment, when waking thoughts start up amid the scattered fantasies of a dream. The leader of the hostile party stood in the centre of the circle, while the route of monsters cowered around him, like evil spirits in the presence of a dread magician. No fantastic foolery could look him in the face. So stern was the energy of his aspect, that the whole man, visage, frame, and soul, seemed wrought of iron, gifted with life and thought, yet all of one substance with his headpiece and breastplate. It was the Puritan of Puritans; it was Endicott[19] himself!

"Stand off, priest of Baal!"[20] said he, with a grim frown, and laying no reverent hand upon the surplice. "I know thee, Blackstone![21] Thou art the man who couldst not abide the rule even of thine own corrupted church,[22] and hast come hither to preach iniquity, and to give example of it in thy life. But now shall it be seen that the Lord hath sanctified this wilderness for his peculiar people. Woe unto them that would defile it! And first, for this flower-decked abomination, the altar of thy worship!"

And with his keen sword Endicott assaulted the hallowed Maypole. Nor long did it resist his arm. It groaned with a dismal sound; it showered leaves and rosebuds upon the remorseless enthusiast; and finally, with all its green boughs and ribbons and flowers, symbolic of departed pleasures, down fell the banner staff of Merry Mount. As it sank, tradition says, the evening sky grew darker, and the woods threw forth a more sombre shadow.

"There," cried Endicott, looking triumphantly on his work, "there lies the only Maypole in New England! The thought is strong within me that, by its fall, is shadowed forth the fate of light and idle mirth makers, amongst us and our posterity. Amen, saith John Endicott."

[19] John Endicott (1589–1665), governor of the colony of Massachusetts.
[20] Fertility god (see 1 Kings 18).
[21] Hawthorne's note: "Did Governor Endicott speak less positively, we should suspect a mistake here. The Reverend Blackstone, though an eccentric, is not known to have been an immoral man. We rather doubt his identity with the priest of Merry Mount."
[22] I.e., the Church of England.

"Amen!" echoed his followers.

But the votaries of the Maypole gave one groan for their idol. At the sound, the Puritan leader glanced at the crew of Comus, each a figure of broad mirth, yet, at this moment, strangely expressive of sorrow and dismay.

"Valiant captain," quoth Peter Palfrey, the Ancient[23] of the band, "what order shall be taken with the prisoners?"

"I thought not to repent me of cutting down a Maypole," replied Endicott, "yet now I could find in my heart to plant it again, and give each of these bestial pagans one other dance round their idol. It would have served rarely for a whipping-post!"

"But there are pine-trees enow," suggested the lieutenant.

"True, good Ancient," said the leader. "Wherefore, bind the heathen crew, and bestow on them a small matter of stripes apiece, as earnest of our future justice. Set some of the rogues in the stocks to rest themselves, so soon as Providence shall bring us to one of our own well-ordered settlements, where such accommodations may be found. Further penalties, such as branding and cropping of ears, shall be thought of hereafter."

"How many stripes for the priest?" inquired Ancient Palfrey.

"None as yet," answered Endicott, bending his iron frown upon the culprit. "It must be for the Great and General Court to determine, whether stripes and long imprisonment, and other grievous penalty, may atone for his transgressions. Let him look to himself! For such as violate our civil order, it may be permitted us to show mercy. But woe to the wretch that troubleth our religion!"

"And this dancing bear," resumed the officer. "Must he share the stripes of his fellows?"

"Shoot him through the head!" said the energetic Puritan. "I suspect witchcraft in the beast."

"Here be a couple of shining ones," continued Peter Palfrey, pointing his weapon at the Lord and Lady of the May. "They seem to be of high station among these misdoers. Methinks their dignity will not be fitted with less than a double share of stripes."

Endicott rested on his sword, and closely surveyed the dress and aspect of the hapless pair. There they stood, pale, downcast, and apprehensive. Yet there was an air of mutual support, and of pure affection, seeking aid and giving it, that showed them to be man and wife, with the sanction of a priest upon their love. The youth, in the peril of the moment, had dropped his gilded staff, and thrown his arm about the Lady of the May, who leaned against his breast, too lightly to burden him, but with weight enough to express that their destinies were linked together, for good or evil. They looked first at each other, and then into the grim captain's face. There they stood, in the first hour of wedlock, while the idle pleasures, of which their companions were the emblems, had given place to the sternest cares of life, personified by the dark Puritans. But never had their youthful beauty seemed so pure and high as when its glow was chastened by adversity.

"Youth," said Endicott, "ye stand in an evil case thou and thy maiden wife. Make

---

[23] Bearer of an emblem or flag.

ready presently, for I am minded that ye shall both have a token to remember your wedding day!"

"Stern man," cried the May Lord, "how can I move thee? Were the means at hand, I would resist to the death. Being powerless, I entreat! Do with me as thou wilt, but let Edith go untouched!"

"Not so," replied the immitigable zealot. "We are not wont to show an idle courtesy to that sex, which requireth the stricter discipline. What sayest thou, maid? Shall thy silken bridegroom suffer thy share of the penalty, besides his own?"

"Be it death," said Edith, "and lay it all on me!"

Truly, as Endicott had said, the poor lovers stood in a woful case. Their foes were triumphant, their friends captive and abased, their home desolate, the benighted wilderness around them, and a rigorous destiny, in the shape of the Puritan leader, their only guide. Yet the deepening twilight could not altogether conceal that the iron man was softened; he smiled at the fair spectacle of early love; he almost sighed for the inevitable blight of early hopes.

"The troubles of life have come hastily on this young couple," observed Endicott. "We will see how they comport themselves under their present trials ere we burden them with greater. If, among the spoil, there be any garments of a more decent fashion, let them be put upon this May Lord and his Lady, instead of their glistening vanities. Look to it, some of you."

"And shall not the youth's hair be cut?" asked Peter Palfrey, looking with abhorrence at the lovelock and long glossy curls of the young man.

"Crop it forthwith, and that in the true pumpkin-shell[24] fashion," answered the captain. "Then bring them along with us, but more gently than their fellows. There be qualities in the youth, which may make him valiant to fight, and sober to toil, and pious to pray; and in the maiden, that may fit her to become a mother in our Israel,[25] bringing up babes in better nurture than her own hath been. Nor think ye, young ones, that they are the happiest, even in our lifetime of a moment, who misspend it in dancing round a Maypole!"

And Endicott, the severest Puritan of all who laid the rock foundation of New England, lifted the wreath of roses from the ruin of the Maypole, and threw it, with his own gauntleted hand, over the heads of the Lord and Lady of the May. It was a deed of prophecy. As the moral gloom of the world overpowers all systematic gayety, even so was their home of wild mirth made desolate amid the sad forest. They returned to it no more. But as their flowery garland was wreathed of the brightest roses that had grown there, so, in the tie that united them, were intertwined all the purest and best of their early joys. They went heavenward, supporting each other along the difficult path which it was their lot to tread, and never wasted one regretful thought on the vanities of Merry Mount.

1836

---

[24] The Puritan style of closely cropped hair.
[25] Puritan name for the promised land, envisioned as America.

The Minister's Black Veil

A Parable[1]

The sexton stood in the porch of Milford meeting house, pulling busily at the bell-rope. The old people of the village came stooping along the street. Children, with bright faces, tripped merrily beside their parents, or mimicked a graver gait, in the conscious dignity of their Sunday clothes. Spruce bachelors looked sidelong at the pretty maidens, and fancied that the Sabbath sunshine made them prettier than on week days. When the throng had mostly streamed into the porch, the sexton began to toll the bell, keeping his eye on the Reverend Mr. Hooper's door. The first glimpse of the clergyman's figure was the signal for the bell to cease its summons.

"But what has good Parson Hooper got upon his face?" cried the sexton in astonishment.

All within hearing immediately turned about, and beheld the semblance of Mr. Hooper, pacing slowly his meditative way towards the meeting-house. With one accord they started, expressing more wonder than if some strange minister were coming to dust the cushions of Mr. Hooper's pulpit.

"Are you sure it is our parson?" inquired Goodman Gray of the sexton.

"Of a certainty it is good Mr. Hooper," replied the sexton. "He was to have exchanged pulpits with Parson Shute, of Westbury; but Parson Shute sent to excuse himself yesterday, being to preach a funeral sermon."

The cause of so much amazement may appear sufficiently slight. Mr. Hooper, a gentlemanly person, of about thirty, though still a bachelor, was dressed with due clerical neatness, as if a careful wife had starched his band, and brushed the weekly dust from his Sunday's garb. There was but one thing remarkable in his appearance. Swathed about his forehead, and hanging down over his face, so low as to be shaken by his breath, Mr. Hooper had on a black veil. On a nearer view it seemed to consist of two folds of crape, which entirely concealed his features, except the mouth and chin, but probably did not intercept his sight, further than to give a darkened aspect to all living and inanimate things. With this gloomy shade before him, good Mr. Hooper walked onward, at a slow and quiet pace, stooping somewhat, and looking on the ground, as is customary with abstracted men, yet nodding kindly to those of his parishioners who still waited on the meeting-house steps. But so wonder-struck were they that his greeting hardly met with a return.

"I can't really feel as if good Mr. Hooper's face was behind that piece of crape," said the sexton.

"I don't like it," muttered an old woman, as she hobbled into the meeting-house. "He has changed himself into something awful, only by hiding his face."

"Our parson has gone mad!" cried Goodman Gray, following him across the threshold.

[1] Hawthorne's note: "Another clergyman in New England, Mr. Joseph Moody, of York, Maine, who died about eighty years since made himself remarkable by the same eccentricity that is here related of the Reverend Mr. Hooper. In this case, however, the symbol had a different import. In early life he had accidentally killed a beloved friend; and from that day till the hour of his own death, he hid his face from men."

A rumor of some unaccountable phenomenon had preceded Mr. Hooper into the meeting-house, and set all the congregation astir. Few could refrain from twisting their heads towards the door; many stood upright, and turned directly about; while several little boys clambered upon the seats, and came down again with a terrible racket. There was a general bustle, a rustling of the women's gowns and shuffling of the men's feet, greatly at variance with that hushed repose which should attend the entrance of the minister. But Mr. Hooper appeared not to notice the perturbation of his people. He entered with an almost noiseless step, bent his head mildly to the pews on each side, and bowed as he passed his oldest parishioner, a white-haired great-grandsire, who occupied an arm-chair in the centre of the aisle. It was strange to observe how slowly this venerable man became conscious of something singular in the appearance of his pastor. He seemed not fully to partake of the prevailing wonder, till Mr. Hooper had ascended the stairs, and showed himself in the pulpit, face to face with his congregation, except for the black veil. That mysterious emblem was never once withdrawn. It shook with his measured breath, as he gave out the psalm; it threw its obscurity between him and the holy page, as he read the Scriptures; and while he prayed, the veil lay heavily on his uplifted countenance. Did he seek to hide it from the dread Being whom he was addressing?

Such was the effect of this simple piece of crape, that more than one woman of delicate nerves was forced to leave the meeting-house. Yet perhaps the pale-faced congregation was almost as fearful a sight to the minister, as his black veil to them.

Mr. Hooper had the reputation of a good preacher, but not an energetic one: he strove to win his people heavenward by mild, persuasive influences, rather than to drive them thither by the thunders of the Word. The sermon which he now delivered was marked by the same characteristics of style and manner as the general series of his pulpit oratory. But there was something, either in the sentiment of the discourse itself, or in the imagination of the auditors, which made it greatly the most powerful effort that they had ever heard from their pastor's lips. It was tinged, rather more darkly than usual, with the gentle gloom of Mr. Hooper's temperament. The subject had reference to secret sin, and those sad mysteries which we hide from our nearest and dearest, and would fain conceal from our own consciousness, even forgetting that the Omniscient can detect them. A subtle power was breathed into his words. Each member of the congregation, the most innocent girl, and the man of hardened breast, felt as if the preacher had crept upon them, behind his awful veil, and discovered their hoarded iniquity of deed or thought. Many spread their clasped hands on their bosoms. There was nothing terrible in what Mr. Hooper said, at least, no violence; and yet, with every tremor of his melancholy voice, the hearers quaked. An unsought pathos came hand in hand with awe. So sensible were the audience of some unwonted attribute in their minister, that they longed for a breath of wind to blow aside the veil, almost believing that a stranger's visage would be discovered, though the form, gesture, and voice were those of Mr. Hooper.

At the close of the services, the people hurried out with indecorous confusion, eager to communicate their pent-up amazement, and conscious of lighter spirits the moment they lost sight of the black veil. Some gathered in little circles, huddled closely together, with their mouths all whispering in the centre; some went homeward alone, wrapt in silent meditation; some talked loudly, and profaned the Sabbath day with ostentatious laughter. A few shook their sagacious heads, intimating that they could penetrate the mystery; while one or two affirmed that there was no mystery at all, but only that Mr. Hooper's eyes were so weakened by the midnight lamp, as to require a shade. After a brief interval, forth came good Mr. Hooper also, in the rear of his flock. Turning his veiled face from one group to another, he paid due reverence to the hoary heads, saluted the middle aged with kind dignity as their friend and spiritual guide, greeted the young with mingled authority and love, and laid his hands on the little children's heads to bless them. Such was always his custom on the Sabbath day. Strange and bewildered looks repaid him for his courtesy. None, as on former occasions, aspired to the honor of walking by their pastor's side. Old Squire Saunders, doubtless by an accidental lapse of memory, neglected to invite Mr. Hooper to his table, where the good clergyman had been wont to bless the food, almost every Sunday since his settlement. He returned, therefore, to the parsonage, and, at the moment of closing the door, was observed to look back upon the people, all of whom had their eyes fixed upon the minister. A sad smile gleamed faintly from beneath the black veil, and flickered about his mouth, glimmering as he disappeared.

"How strange," said a lady, "that a simple black veil, such as any woman might wear on her bonnet, should become such a terrible thing on Mr. Hooper's face!"

"Something must surely be amiss with Mr. Hooper's intellects," observed her husband, the physician of the village. "But the strangest part of the affair is the effect of this vagary, even on a sober-minded man like myself. The black veil, though it covers only our pastor's face, throws its influence over his whole person, and makes him ghostlike from head to foot. Do you not feel it so?"

"Truly do I," replied the lady; "and I would not be alone with him for the world. I wonder he is not afraid to be alone with himself!"

"Men sometimes are so," said her husband.

The afternoon service was attended with similar circumstances. At its conclusion, the bell tolled for the funeral of a young lady. The relatives and friends were assembled in the house, and the more distant acquaintances stood about the door, speaking of the good qualities of the deceased, when their talk was interrupted by the appearance of Mr. Hooper, still covered with his black veil. It was now an appropriate emblem. The clergyman stepped into the room where the corpse was laid, and bent over the coffin, to take a last farewell of his deceased parishioner. As he stooped, the veil hung straight down from his forehead, so that, if her eyelids had not been closed forever, the dead maiden might have seen his face. Could Mr. Hooper be fearful of her glance, that he so hastily caught back the black veil? A person who watched the interview between the dead and living, scrupled not to affirm, that, at the instant when the clergyman's features were disclosed, the corpse had slightly shuddered, rustling the shroud and muslin cap, though the countenance retained the composure of death. A superstitious old woman was the only witness of this prodigy. From the coffin Mr. Hooper passed into the chamber of the mourners, and thence to the head of the staircase, to make the funeral prayer. It was a tender and heart-dissolving prayer, full of sorrow, yet so imbued with celestial hopes, that the music of a heavenly harp, swept by the fingers of the dead, seemed faintly to be heard among the saddest accents of the minister. The people trembled, though they but darkly understood him when he prayed that they, and himself, and all of mortal race, might be ready, as he trusted this young maiden had been, for the dreadful hour that should snatch the veil from their faces. The bearers went heavily forth, and the mourners followed, saddening all the street, with the dead before them, and Mr. Hooper in his black veil behind.

"Why do you look back?" said one in the procession to his partner.

"I had a fancy," replied she, "that the minister and the maiden's spirit were walking hand in hand."

"And so had I, at the same moment," said the other.

That night, the handsomest couple in Milford village were to be joined in wedlock. Though reckoned a melancholy man, Mr. Hooper had a placid cheerfulness for such occasions, which often excited a sympathetic smile where livelier merriment would have been thrown away. There was no quality of his disposition which made him more beloved than this. The company at the wedding awaited his arrival with impatience, trusting that the strange awe, which had gathered over him throughout the day, would now be dispelled. But such was not the result. When Mr. Hooper came, the first thing that their eyes rested on was the same horrible black veil, which had added deeper gloom to the funeral, and could portend nothing but evil to the wedding. Such was its immediate effect on the guests that a cloud seemed to have rolled duskily from beneath the black crape, and dimmed the light of the candles. The bridal pair stood up before the minister. But the bride's cold fingers quivered in the tremulous hand of the bridegroom, and her deathlike paleness caused a whisper that the maiden who had been buried a few hours before was come from her grave to be married. If ever another wedding were so dismal, it was that famous one where they tolled the wedding knell. After performing the ceremony, Mr. Hooper raised a glass of wine to his lips, wishing happiness to the new-married couple in a strain of mild pleasantry that ought to have brightened the features of the guests, like a cheerful gleam from the hearth. At that instant, catching a glimpse of his figure in the looking-glass, the black veil involved his own spirit in the horror with which it overwhelmed all others. His frame shuddered, his lips grew white, he spilt the untasted wine upon the carpet, and rushed forth into the darkness. For the Earth, too, had on her Black Veil.

The next day, the whole village of Milford talked of little else than Parson Hooper's black veil. That, and the mystery concealed behind it, supplied a topic for discussion between acquaintances meeting in the street, and good women gossiping at their open windows. It was the first item of news that the tavernkeeper told to his guests. The children babbled of it on their way to school. One imitative little imp covered his face with an old black handkerchief, thereby so affrighting his playmates that the panic seized himself, and he well-nigh lost his wits by his own waggery.

It was remarkable that of all the busybodies and impertinent people in the parish, not one ventured to put the plain question to Mr. Hooper, wherefore he did this thing. Hitherto, whenever there appeared the slightest call for such interference, he had never lacked advisers, nor shown himself averse to be guided by their judgment. If he erred at all, it was by so painful a degree of self-distrust, that even the mildest censure would lead him to consider an indifferent action as a crime. Yet, though so well acquainted with this amiable weakness, no individual among his parishioners chose to make the black veil a subject of friendly remonstrance. There was a feeling of dread, neither plainly confessed nor carefully concealed, which caused each to shift the responsibility upon another, till at length it was found expedient to send a deputation of the church, in order to deal with Mr. Hooper about the mystery, before it should grow into a scandal. Never did an embassy so ill discharge its duties. The minister received them with friendly courtesy, but became silent, after they were seated, leaving to his visitors the whole burden of introducing their important business. The topic, it might be supposed, was obvious enough. There was the black veil swathed round Mr. Hooper's forehead, and concealing every feature above his placid mouth, on which, at times, they could perceive the glimmering of a melancholy smile. But that piece of crape, to their imagination, seemed to hang down before his heart, the symbol of a fearful secret between him and them. Were the veil but cast aside, they might speak freely of it, but not till then. Thus they sat a considerable time, speechless, confused, and shrinking uneasily from Mr. Hooper's eye, which they felt to be fixed upon them with an invisible glance. Finally, the deputies returned abashed to their constituents, pronouncing the matter too weighty to be handled, except by a council of the churches, if, indeed, it might not require a general synod.

But there was one person in the village unappalled by the awe with which the black veil had impressed all beside herself. When the deputies returned without an explanation, or even venturing to demand one, she, with the calm energy of her character, determined to chase away the strange cloud that appeared to be settling round Mr. Hooper, every moment more darkly than before. As his plighted wife, it should be her privilege to know what the black veil concealed. At the minister's first visit, therefore, she entered upon the subject with a direct simplicity, which made the task easier both for him and her. After he had seated himself, she fixed her eyes steadfastly upon the veil, but could discern nothing of the dreadful gloom that had so overawed the multitude: it was but a double fold of crape, hanging down from his forehead to his mouth, and slightly stirring with his breath.

"No," said she aloud, and smiling, "there is nothing terrible in this piece of crape, except that it hides a face which I am always glad to look upon. Come, good sir, let the sun shine from behind the cloud. First lay aside your black veil: then tell me why you put it on."

Mr. Hooper's smile glimmered faintly.

"There is an hour to come," said he, "when all of us shall cast aside our veils. Take it not amiss, beloved friend, if I wear this piece of crape till then."

"Your words are a mystery, too," returned the young lady. "Take away the veil from them, at least."

"Elizabeth, I will," said he, "so far as my vow may suffer me. Know, then, this veil is a type and a symbol, and I am bound to wear it ever, both in light and darkness, in solitude and before the gaze of multitudes, and as with strangers, so with my familiar friends. No mortal eye will see it withdrawn. This dismal shade must separate me from the world: even you, Elizabeth, can never come behind it!"

"What grievous affliction hath befallen you," she earnestly inquired, "that you should thus darken your eyes forever?"

"If it be a sign of mourning," replied Mr. Hooper, "I, perhaps, like most other mortals, have sorrows dark enough to be typified by a black veil."

"But what if the world will not believe that it is the type of an innocent sorrow?" urged Elizabeth. "Beloved and respected as you are, there may be whispers that you hide your face under the consciousness of secret sin. For the sake of your holy office, do away this scandal!"

The color rose into her cheeks as she intimated the nature of the rumors that were already abroad in the village. But Mr. Hooper's mildness did not forsake him. He even smiled again—that same sad smile, which always appeared like a faint glimmering of light, proceeding from the obscurity beneath the veil.

"If I hide my face for sorrow, there is cause enough," he merely replied; "and if I cover it for secret sin, what mortal might not do the same?"

And with this gentle, but unconquerable obstinacy did he resist all her entreaties. At length Elizabeth sat silent. For a few moments she appeared lost in thought, considering, probably, what new methods might be tried to withdraw her lover from so dark a fantasy, which, if it had no other meaning, was perhaps a symptom of mental disease. Though of a firmer character than his own, the tears rolled down her cheeks. But, in an instant, as it were, a new feeling took the place of sorrow: her eyes were fixed insensibly on the black veil, when, like a sudden twilight in the air, its terrors fell around her. She arose, and stood trembling before him.

"And do you feel it then, at last?" said he mournfully.

She made no reply, but covered her eyes with her hand, and turned to leave the room. He rushed forward and caught her arm.

"Have patience with me, Elizabeth!" cried he, passionately. "Do not desert me, though this veil must be between us here on earth. Be mine, and hereafter there shall be no veil over my face, no darkness between our souls! It is but a mortal veil—it is not for eternity! O! you know not how lonely I am, and how frightened, to be alone behind my black veil. Do not leave me in this miserable obscurity forever!"

"Lift the veil but once, and look me in the face," said she.

"Never! It cannot be!" replied Mr. Hooper.

"Then farewell!" said Elizabeth.

She withdrew her arm from his grasp, and slowly departed, pausing at the door, to give one long shuddering gaze, that seemed almost to penetrate the mystery of the black veil. But, even amid his grief, Mr. Hooper smiled to think that only a material emblem had separated him from happiness, though the horrors, which it shadowed forth, must be drawn darkly between the fondest of lovers.

From that time no attempts were made to remove Mr. Hooper's black veil, or, by a direct appeal, to discover the secret which it was supposed to hide. By persons who claimed a superiority to popular prejudice, it was reckoned merely an eccentric whim, such as often mingles with the sober actions of men otherwise rational, and tinges them all with its own semblance of insanity. But with the multitude, good Mr. Hooper was irreparably a bugbear. He could not walk the street with any peace of mind, so conscious was he that the gentle and timid would turn aside to avoid him, and that others would make it a point of hardihood to throw themselves in his way. The impertinence of the latter class compelled him to give up his customary walk at sunset to the burial ground; for when he leaned pensively over the gate, there would always be faces behind the gravestones, peeping at his black veil. A fable went the rounds that the stare of the dead people drove him thence. It grieved him, to the very depth of his kind heart, to observe how the children fled from his approach, breaking up their merriest sports, while his melancholy figure was yet afar off. Their instinctive dread caused him to feel more strongly than aught else, that a preternatural horror was interwoven with the threads of the black crape. In truth, his own antipathy to the veil was known to be so great, that he never willingly passed before a mirror, nor stooped to drink at a still fountain, lest, in its peaceful bosom, he should be affrighted by himself. This was what gave plausibility to the whispers, that Mr. Hooper's conscience tortured him for some great crime too horrible to be entirely concealed, or otherwise than so obscurely intimated. Thus, from beneath the black veil, there rolled a cloud into the sunshine, an ambiguity of sin or sorrow, which enveloped the poor minister, so that love or sympathy could never reach him. It was said that ghost and fiend consorted with him there. With self-shudderings and outward terrors, he walked continually in its shadow, groping darkly within his own soul, or gazing through a medium that saddened the whole world. Even the lawless wind, it was believed, respected his dreadful secret, and never blew aside the veil. But still good Mr. Hooper sadly smiled at the pale visages of the worldly throng as he passed by.

Among all its bad influences, the black veil had the one desirable effect, of making its wearer a very efficient clergyman. By the aid of his mysterious emblem—for there was no other apparent cause—he became a man of awful power over souls that were in agony for sin. His converts always regarded him with a dread peculiar to themselves, affirming, though but figuratively, that, before he brought them to celestial light, they had been with him behind the black veil. Its gloom, indeed, enabled him to sympathize with all dark affections. Dying sinners cried aloud for Mr. Hooper, and would not yield their breath till he appeared; though ever, as he stooped to whisper consolation, they shuddered at the veiled face so near their own. Such were the terrors of the black veil, even when Death had bared his visage! Strangers came long distances to attend service at his church, with the mere idle purpose of gazing at his figure, because it was forbidden them to behold his face. But many were made to quake ere they departed! Once, during Governor Belcher's administration,[2] Mr. Hooper was appointed to preach the election sermon.[3] Covered with his black veil, he stood before the chief magistrate, the council, and the representatives, and wrought so deep an impression, that the legislative measures of that year were characterized by all the gloom and piety of our earliest ancestral sway.

In this manner Mr. Hooper spent a long life, irreproachable in outward act, yet shrouded in dismal suspicions; kind and loving, though unloved, and dimly feared; a man apart from men, shunned in their health and joy, but ever summoned to their aid in mortal anguish. As years wore on, shedding their snows above his sable veil, he acquired a name throughout the New England churches, and they called him Father Hooper. Nearly all his parishioners, who were of mature age when he was settled, had been borne away by many a funeral: he had one congregation in the church, and a more crowded one in the churchyard; and having wrought so late into the evening, and done his work so well, it was now good Father Hooper's turn to rest.

Several persons were visible by the shaded candlelight, in the death chamber of the old clergyman. Natural connections he had none. But there was the decorously grave, though unmoved physician, seeking only to mitigate the last pangs of the patient whom he could not save. There were the deacons, and other eminently pious members of his church. There, also, was the Reverend Mr. Clark, of Westbury, a young and zealous divine, who had ridden in haste to pray by the bedside of the expiring minister.

[2] Jonathan Belcher (1682–1757) was governor of Massachusetts and New Hampshire from 1730 to 1741.

[3] It was an honor to be chosen to preach the special sermon at the inauguration of a new governor.

There was the nurse, no hired handmaiden of death, but one whose calm affection had endured thus long in secrecy, in solitude, amid the chill of age, and would not perish, even at the dying hour. Who, but Elizabeth! And there lay the hoary head of good Father Hooper upon the death pillow, with the black veil still swathed about his brow, and reaching down over his face, so that each more difficult gasp of his faint breath caused it to stir. All through life that piece of crape had hung between him and the world: it had separated him from cheerful brotherhood and woman's love, and kept him in that saddest of all prisons, his own heart; and still it lay upon his face, as if to deepen the gloom of his darksome chamber, and shade him from the sunshine of eternity.

For some time previous, his mind had been confused, wavering doubtfully between the past and the present, and hovering forward, as it were, at intervals, into the indistinctness of the world to come. There had been feverish turns, which tossed him from side to side, and wore away what little strength he had. But in his most convulsive struggles, and in the wildest vagaries of his intellect, when no other thought retained its sober influence, he still showed an awful solicitude lest the black veil should slip aside. Even if his bewildered soul could have forgotten, there was a faithful woman at his pillow, who, with averted eyes, would have covered that aged face, which she had last beheld in the comeliness of manhood. At length the death-stricken old man lay quietly in the torpor of mental and bodily exhaustion, with an imperceptible pulse, and breath that grew fainter and fainter, except when a long, deep, and irregular inspiration seemed to prelude the flight of his spirit.

The minister of Westbury approached the bedside.

"Venerable Father Hooper," said he, "the moment of your release is at hand. Are you ready for the lifting of the veil that shuts in time from eternity?"

Father Hooper at first replied merely by a feeble motion of his head; then, apprehensive, perhaps, that his meaning might be doubtful, he exerted himself to speak.

"Yea," said he, in faint accents, "my soul hath a patient weariness until that veil be lifted."

"And is it fitting," resumed the Reverend Mr. Clark, "that a man so given to prayer, of such a blameless example, holy in deed and thought, so far as mortal judgment may pronounce; is it fitting that a father in the church should leave a shadow on his memory, that may seem to blacken a life so pure? I pray you, my venerable brother, let not this thing be! Suffer us to be gladdened by your triumphant aspect as you go to your reward. Before the veil of eternity be lifted, let me cast aside this black veil from your face!"

And thus speaking, the Reverend Mr. Clark bent forward to reveal the mystery of so many years. But, exerting a sudden energy, that made all the beholders stand aghast, Father Hooper snatched both his hands from beneath the bedclothes, and pressed them strongly on the black veil, resolute to struggle, if the minister of Westbury would contend with a dying man.

"Never!" cried the veiled clergyman. "On earth, never!"

"Dark old man!" exclaimed the affrighted minister, "with what horrible crime upon your soul are you now passing to the judgment?"

Father Hooper's breath heaved; it rattled in his throat; but, with a mighty effort, grasping forward with his hands, he caught hold of life, and held it back till he should speak. He even raised himself in bed; and there he sat, shivering with the arms of death around him, while the black veil hung down, awful, at that last moment, in the gathered terrors of a lifetime. And yet the faint, sad smile, so often there, now seemed to glimmer from its obscurity, and linger on Father Hooper's lips.

"Why do you tremble at me alone?" cried he, turning his veiled face round the circle of pale spectators. "Tremble also at each other! Have men avoided me, and women shown no pity, and children screamed and fled, only for my black veil? What, but the mystery which it obscurely typifies, has made this piece of crape so awful? When the friend shows his inmost heart to his friend; the lover to his best beloved; when man does not vainly shrink from the eye of his Creator, loathsomely treasuring up the secret of his sin; then deem me a monster, for the symbol beneath which I have lived, and die! I look around me, and, lo! on every visage a Black Veil!"

While his auditors shrank from one another, in mutual affright, Father Hooper fell back upon his pillow, a veiled corpse, with a faint smile lingering on the lips. Still veiled, they laid him in his coffin, and a veiled corpse they bore him to the grave. The grass of many years has sprung up and withered on that grave, the burial stone is moss-grown, and good Mr. Hooper's face is dust; but awful is still the thought that it mouldered beneath the Black Veil!

1836

Rappaccini's Daughter

(From the writings of Aubépine.[1])

We do not remember to have seen any translated specimens of the productions of M. de l'Aubépine—a fact the less to be wondered at, as his very name is unknown to many of his own countrymen as well as to the student of foreign literature. As a writer, he seems to occupy an unfortunate position between the Transcendentalists (who, under one name or another, have their share in all the current literature of the world) and the great body of pen-and-ink men who address the intellect and sympathies of the multitude. If not too refined, at all events too remote, too shadowy, and unsubstantial in his modes of development to suit the taste of the latter class, and yet too popular to satisfy the spiritual or metaphysical requisitions of the former, he must necessarily find himself without an audience, except here and there an individual or possibly an isolated clique. His writings, to do them justice, are not altogether destitute of fancy and originality; they might have won him greater reputation but for an inveterate love of allegory, which is apt to invest his plots and characters with the aspect of scenery and people in the clouds, and to steal away the human warmth out of his conceptions. His fictions are sometimes historical, sometimes of the present day, and sometimes, so far as can be discovered, have little or no reference either to time or space. In any case, he generally contents himself with a very slight embroidery of

[1] French: "Hawthorne."

outward manners,—the faintest possible counterfeit of real life,—and endeavors to create an interest by some less obvious peculiarity of the subject. Occasionally a breath of Nature, a raindrop of pathos and tenderness, or a gleam of humor, will find its way into the midst of his fantastic imagery, and make us feel as if, after all, we were yet within the limits of our native earth. We will only add to this very cursory notice that M. de l'Aubépine's productions, if the reader chance to take them in precisely the proper point of view, may amuse a leisure hour as well as those of a brighter man; if otherwise, they can hardly fail to look excessively like nonsense.

Our author is voluminous; he continues to write and publish with as much praiseworthy and indefatigable prolixity as if his efforts were crowned with the brilliant success that so justly attends those of Eugene Sue.[2] His first appearance was by a collection of stories in a long series of volumes entitled "Contes deux fois racontées."[3] The titles of some of his more recent works (we quote from memory) are as follows: "Le Voyage Céleste à Chemin de Fer," 3 tom., 1838; "Le nouveau Père Adam et la nouvelle Mère Eve," 2 tom., 1839; "Roderic; ou le Serpent à l'estomac," 2 tom., 1840; "Le Culte du Feu," a folio volume of ponderous research into the religion and ritual of the old Persian Ghebers, published in 1841; "La Soirée du Chateau en Espagne," 1 tom., 8vo, 1842; and "L'Artiste du Beau; ou le Papillon Mécanique," 5 tom., 4to, 1843.[4] Our somewhat wearisome perusal of this startling catalogue of volumes has left behind it a certain personal affection and sympathy, though by no means admiration, for M. de l'Aubépine; and we would fain do the little in our power towards introducing him favorably to the American public. The ensuing tale is a translation of his "Beatrice; ou la Belle Empoisonneuse," recently published in "La Revue Anti-Aristocratique." This journal, edited by the Comte de Bearhaven,[5] has for some years past led the defence of liberal principles and popular rights with a faithfulness and ability worthy of all praise.

A young man, named Giovanni Guasconti, came, very long ago, from the more southern region of Italy, to pursue his studies at the University of Padua. Giovanni, who had but a scanty supply of gold ducats in his pocket, took lodgings in a high and gloomy chamber of an old edifice which looked not unworthy to have been the palace of a Paduan noble, and which, in fact, exhibited over its entrance the armorial bearings of a family long since extinct. The young stranger, who was not unstudied in the great poem of his country, recollected that one of the ancestors of this family, and perhaps an occupant of this very mansion, had been pictured by Dante as a partaker of the immortal agonies of his Inferno. These reminiscences and associations, together with the tendency to heartbreak natural to a young man for the first time out of his native sphere, caused Giovanni to sigh heavily as he looked around the desolate and ill-furnished apartment.

"Holy Virgin, signor!" cried old Dame Lisabetta, who, won by the youth's remarkable beauty of person, was kindly endeavoring to give the chamber a habitable air, "what a sigh was that to come out of a young man's heart! Do you find this old

---

[2] Popular French novelist (1804–1857).
[3] I.e., Hawthorne's *Twice-Told Tales* (1837).
[4] Mock bibliographic references, including the supposed volume ("tom"), octavo ("8vo"), and quarto ("4to") of each work.

[5] John O'Sullivan, editor of *The Democractic Review*.

mansion gloomy? For the love of Heaven, then, put your head out of the window, and you will see as bright sunshine as you have left in Naples."

Guasconti mechanically did as the old woman advised, but could not quite agree with her that the Paduan sunshine was as cheerful as that of southern Italy. Such as it was, however, it fell upon a garden beneath the window and expended its fostering influences on a variety of plants, which seemed to have been cultivated with exceeding care.

"Does this garden belong to the house?" asked Giovanni.

"Heaven forbid, signor, unless it were fruitful of better pot herbs than any that grow there now," answered old Lisabetta. "No; that garden is cultivated by the own hands of Signor Giacomo Rappaccini, the famous doctor, who, I warrant him, has been heard of as far as Naples. It is said that he distils these plants into medicines that are as potent as a charm. Oftentimes you may see the signor doctor at work, and perchance the signora, his daughter, too, gathering the strange flowers that grow in the garden."

The old woman had now done what she could for the aspect of the chamber; and, commending the young man to the protection of the saints, took her departure.

Giovanni still found no better occupation than to look down into the garden beneath his window. From its appearance, he judged it to be one of those botanic gardens which were of earlier date in Padua than elsewhere in Italy or in the world. Or, not improbably, it might once have been the pleasure-place of an opulent family; for there was the ruin of a marble fountain in the centre, sculptured with rare art, but so wofully shattered that it was impossible to trace the original design from the chaos of remaining fragments. The water, however, continued to gush and sparkle into the sunbeams as cheerfully as ever. A little gurgling sound ascended to the young man's window, and made him feel as if the fountain were an immortal spirit that sung its song unceasingly and without heeding the vicissitudes around it, while one century imbodied it in marble and another scattered the perishable garniture on the soil. All about the pool into which the water subsided grew various plants, that seemed to require a plentiful supply of moisture for the nourishment of gigantic leaves, and, in some instances, flowers gorgeously magnificent. There was one shrub in particular, set in a marble vase in the midst of the pool, that bore a profusion of purple blossoms, each of which had the lustre and richness of a gem; and the whole together made a show so resplendent that it seemed enough to illuminate the garden, even had there been no sunshine. Every portion of the soil was peopled with plants and herbs, which, if less beautiful, still bore tokens of assiduous care, as if all had their individual virtues, known to the scientific mind that fostered them. Some were placed in urns, rich with old carving, and others in common garden pots; some crept serpent-like along the ground or climbed on high, using whatever means of ascent was offered them. One plant had wreathed itself round a statue of Vertumnus,[6] which was thus quite veiled and shrouded in a drapery of hanging foliage, so happily arranged that it might have served a sculptor for a study.

While Giovanni stood at the window he heard a rustling behind a screen of leaves, and became aware that a person was at work in the garden. His figure soon emerged

[6] Mythic god who controlled plant growth by presiding over the seasons.

into view, and showed itself to be that of no common laborer, but a tall, emaciated, sallow, and sickly-looking man, dressed in a scholar's garb of black. He was beyond the middle term of life, with gray hair, a thin, gray beard, and a face singularly marked with intellect and cultivation, but which could never, even in his more youthful days, have expressed much warmth of heart.

Nothing could exceed the intentness with which this scientific gardener examined every shrub which grew in his path: it seemed as if he was looking into their inmost nature, making observations in regard to their creative essence, and discovering why one leaf grew in this shape and another in that, and wherefore such and such flowers differed among themselves in hue and perfume. Nevertheless, in spite of this deep intelligence on his part, there was no approach to intimacy between himself and these vegetable existences. On the contrary, he avoided their actual touch or the direct inhaling of their odors with a caution that impressed Giovanni most disagreeably; for the man's demeanor was that of one walking among malignant influences, such as savage beasts, or deadly snakes, or evil spirits, which, should he allow them one moment of license, would wreak upon him some terrible fatality. It was strangely frightful to the young man's imagination to see this air of insecurity in a person cultivating a garden, that most simple and innocent of human toils, and which had been alike the joy and labor of the unfallen parents of the race. Was this garden, then, the Eden of the present world? And this man, with such a perception of harm in what his own hands caused to grow,—was he the Adam?

The distrustful gardener, while plucking away the dead leaves or pruning the too luxuriant growth of the shrubs, defended his hands with a pair of thick gloves. Nor were these his only armor. When, in his walk through the garden, he came to the magnificent plant that hung its purple gems beside the marble fountain, he placed a kind of mask over his mouth and nostrils, as if all this beauty did but conceal a deadlier malice; but, finding his task still too dangerous, he drew back, removed the mask, and called loudly, but in the infirm voice of a person affected with inward disease,—

"Beatrice! Beatrice!"

"Here am I, my father. What would you?" cried a rich and youthful voice from the window of the opposite house—a voice as rich as a tropical sunset, and which made Giovanni, though he knew not why, think of deep hues of purple or crimson and of perfumes heavily delectable. "Are you in the garden?"

"Yes, Beatrice," answered the gardener, "and I need your help."

Soon there emerged from under a sculptured portal the figure of a young girl, arrayed with as much richness of taste as the most splendid of the flowers, beautiful as the day, and with a bloom so deep and vivid that one shade more would have been too much. She looked redundant with life, health, and energy; all of which attributes were bound down and compressed, as it were, and girdled tensely, in their luxuriance, by her virgin zone.[7] Yet Giovanni's fancy must have grown morbid while he looked down into the garden; for the impression which the fair stranger made upon him was as if here were another flower, the human sister of those vegetable ones, as beautiful as they, more beautiful than the richest of them, but still to be touched only with a glove, nor to be approached without a mask. As Beatrice came down the garden

[7] Belt or girdle customarily worn by unmarried women.

path, it was observable that she handled and inhaled the odor of several of the plants which her father had most sedulously avoided.

"Here, Beatrice," said the latter, "see how many needful offices require to be done to our chief treasure. Yet, shattered as I am, my life might pay the penalty of approaching it so closely as circumstances demand. Henceforth, I fear, this plant must be consigned to your sole charge."

"And gladly will I undertake it," cried again the rich tones of the young lady, as she bent towards the magnificent plant and opened her arms as if to embrace it. "Yes, my sister, my splendor, it shall be Beatrice's task to nurse and serve thee; and thou shalt reward her with thy kisses and perfumed breath, which to her is as the breath of life."

Then, with all the tenderness in her manner that was so strikingly expressed in her words, she busied herself with such attentions as the plant seemed to require; and Giovanni, at his lofty window, rubbed his eyes and almost doubted whether it were a girl tending her favorite flower, or one sister performing the duties of affection to another. The scene soon terminated. Whether Dr. Rappaccini had finished his labors in the garden, or that his watchful eye had caught the stranger's face, he now took his daughter's arm and retired. Night was already closing in; oppressive exhalations seemed to proceed from the plants and steal upward past the open window; and Giovanni, closing the lattice, went to his couch and dreamed of a rich flower and beautiful girl. Flower and maiden were different, and yet the same, and fraught with some strange peril in either shape.

But there is an influence in the light of morning that tends to rectify whatever errors of fancy, or even of judgment, we may have incurred during the sun's decline, or among the shadows of the night, or in the less wholesome glow of moonshine. Giovanni's first movement, on starting from sleep, was to throw open the window and gaze down into the garden which his dreams had made so fertile of mysteries. He was surprised and a little ashamed to find how real and matter-of-fact an affair it proved to be, in the first rays of the sun which gilded the dew-drops that hung upon leaf and blossom, and, while giving a brighter beauty to each rare flower, brought everything within the limits of ordinary experience. The young man rejoiced that, in the heart of the barren city, he had the privilege of overlooking this spot of lovely and luxuriant vegetation. It would serve, he said to himself, as a symbolic language to keep him in communion with Nature. Neither the sickly and thought-worn Dr. Giacomo Rappaccini, it is true, nor his brilliant daughter, were now visible; so that Giovanni could not determine how much of the singularity which he attributed to both was due to their own qualities and how much to his wonder-working fancy; but he was inclined to take a most rational view of the whole matter.

In the course of the day he paid his respects to Signor Pietro Baglioni, professor of medicine in the university, a physician of eminent repute, to whom Giovanni had brought a letter of introduction. The professor was an elderly personage, apparently of genial nature, and habits that might almost be called jovial. He kept the young man to dinner, and made himself very agreeable by the freedom and liveliness of his conversation, especially when warmed by a flask or two of Tuscan wine. Giovanni, conceiving that men of science, inhabitants of the same city, must needs be on familiar terms with one another, took an opportunity to mention the name of Dr. Rappaccini. But the professor did not respond with so much cordiality as he had anticipated.

"Ill would it become a teacher of the divine art of medicine," said Professor Pietro Baglioni, in answer to a question of Giovanni, "to withhold due and well-considered praise of a physician so eminently skilled as Rappaccini; but, on the other hand, I should answer it but scantily to my conscience were I to permit a worthy youth like yourself, Signor Giovanni, the son of an ancient friend, to imbibe erroneous ideas respecting a man who might hereafter chance to hold your life and death in his hands. The truth is, our worshipful Dr. Rappaccini has as much science as any member of the faculty—with perhaps one single exception—in Padua, or all Italy; but there are certain grave objections to his professional character."

"And what are they?" asked the young man.

"Has my friend Giovanni any disease of body or heart, that he is so inquisitive about physicians?" said the professor, with a smile. "But as for Rappaccini, it is said of him—and I, who know the man well, can answer for its truth—that he cares infinitely more for science than for mankind. His patients are interesting to him only as subjects for some new experiment. He would sacrifice human life, his own among the rest, or whatever else was dearest to him, for the sake of adding so much as a grain of mustard seed to the great heap of his accumulated knowledge."

"Methinks he is an awful man indeed," remarked Guasconti, mentally recalling the cold and purely intellectual aspect of Rappaccini. "And yet, worshipful professor, is it not a noble spirit? Are there many men capable of so spiritual a love of science?"

"God forbid," answered the professor, somewhat testily; "at least, unless they take sounder views of the healing art than those adopted by Rappaccini. It is his theory that all medicinal virtues are comprised within those substances which we term vegetable poisons. These he cultivates with his own hands, and is said even to have produced new varieties of poison, more horribly deleterious than Nature, without the assistance of this learned person, would ever have plagued the world withal. That the signor doctor does less mischief than might be expected with such dangerous substances is undeniable. Now and then, it must be owned, he has effected, or seemed to effect, a marvellous cure; but, to tell you my private mind, Signor Giovanni, he should receive little credit for such instances of success,—they being probably the work of chance,—but should be held strictly accountable for his failures, which may justly be considered his own work."

The youth might have taken Baglioni's opinions with many grains of allowance had he known that there was a professional warfare of long continuance between him and Dr. Rappaccini, in which the latter was generally thought to have gained the advantage. If the reader be inclined to judge for himself, we refer him to certain black-letter tracts on both sides, preserved in the medical department of the University of Padua.

"I know not, most learned professor," returned Giovanni, after musing on what had been said of Rappaccini's exclusive zeal for science,—"I know not how dearly this physician may love his art; but surely there is one object more dear to him. He has a daughter."

"Aha!" cried the professor, with a laugh. "So now our friend Giovanni's secret is out. You have heard of this daughter, whom all the young men in Padua are wild about, though not half a dozen have ever had the good hap to see her face. I know little of the Signora Beatrice save that Rappaccini is said to have instructed her deeply in his science, and that, young and beautiful as fame reports her, she is already qualified to fill a professor's chair. Perchance her father destines her for mine! Other absurd rumors there be, not worth talking about or listening to. So now, Signor Giovanni, drink off your glass of lachryma."[8]

Guasconti returned to his lodgings somewhat heated with the wine he had quaffed, and which caused his brain to swim with strange fantasies in reference to Dr. Rappaccini and the beautiful Beatrice. On his way, happening to pass by a florist's, he bought a fresh bouquet of flowers.

Ascending to his chamber, he seated himself near the window, but within the shadow thrown by the depth of the wall, so that he could look down into the garden with little risk of being discovered. All beneath his eye was a solitude. The strange plants were basking in the sunshine, and now and then nodding gently to one another, as if in acknowledgment of sympathy and kindred. In the midst, by the shattered fountain, grew the magnificent shrub, with its purple gems clustering all over it; they glowed in the air, and gleamed back again out of the depths of the pool, which thus seemed to overflow with colored radiance from the rich reflection that was steeped in it. At first, as we have said, the garden was a solitude. Soon, however,—as Giovanni had half hoped, half feared, would be the case,—a figure appeared beneath the antique sculptured portal, and came down between the rows of plants, inhaling their various perfumes as if she were one of those beings of old classic fable that lived upon sweet odors. On again beholding Beatrice, the young man was even startled to perceive how much her beauty exceeded his recollection of it; so brilliant, so vivid, was its character, that she glowed amid the sunlight, and, as Giovanni whispered to himself, positively illuminated the more shadowy intervals of the garden path. Her face being now more revealed than on the former occasion, he was struck by its expression of simplicity and sweetness,—qualities that had not entered into his idea of her character, and which made him ask anew what manner of mortal she might be. Nor did he fail again to observe, or imagine, an analogy between the beautiful girl and the gorgeous shrub that hung its gemlike flowers over the fountain,—a resemblance which Beatrice seemed to have indulged a fantastic humor in heightening, both by the arrangement of her dress and the selection of its hues.

Approaching the shrub, she threw open her arms, as with a passionate ardor, and drew its branches into an intimate embrace—so intimate that her features were hidden in its leafy bosom and her glistening ringlets all intermingled with the flowers.

"Give me thy breath, my sister," exclaimed Beatrice; "for I am faint with common air. And give me this flower of thine, which I separate with gentlest fingers from the stem and place it close beside my heart."

With these words the beautiful daughter of Rappaccini plucked one of the richest blossoms of the shrub, and was about to fasten it in her bosom. But now, unless Giovanni's draughts of wine had bewildered his senses, a singular incident occurred. A small orange-colored reptile, of the lizard or chameleon species, chanced to be

[8] I.e., Lachryma Christi ("Tears of Christ"), an
Italian wine produced near Vesuvius.

creeping along the path, just at the feet of Beatrice. It appeared to Giovanni,—but, at the distance from which he gazed, he could scarcely have seen anything so minute, —it appeared to him, however, that a drop or two of moisture from the broken stem of the flower descended upon the lizard's head. For an instant the reptile contorted itself violently, and then lay motionless in the sunshine. Beatrice observed this remarkable phenomenon, and crossed herself, sadly, but without surprise; nor did she therefore hesitate to arrange the fatal flower in her bosom. There it blushed, and almost glimmered with the dazzling effect of a precious stone, adding to her dress and aspect the one appropriate charm which nothing else in the world could have supplied. But Giovanni, out of the shadow of his window, bent forward and shrank back, and murmured and trembled.

"Am I awake? Have I my senses?" said he to himself. "What is this being? Beautiful shall I call her, or inexpressibly terrible?"

Beatrice now strayed carelessly through the garden, approaching closer beneath Giovanni's window, so that he was compelled to thrust his head quite out of its concealment in order to gratify the intense and painful curiosity which she excited. At this moment there came a beautiful insect over the garden wall; it had, perhaps, wandered through the city, and found no flowers or verdure among those antique haunts of men until the heavy perfumes of Dr. Rappaccini's shrubs had lured it from afar. Without alighting on the flowers, this winged brightness seemed to be attracted by Beatrice, and lingered in the air and fluttered about her head. Now, here it could not be but that Giovanni Guasconti's eyes deceived him. Be that as it might, he fancied that, while Beatrice was gazing at the insect with childish delight, it grew faint and fell at her feet; its bright wings shivered; it was dead—from no cause that he could discern, unless it were the atmosphere of her breath. Again Beatrice crossed herself and sighed heavily as she bent over the dead insect.

An impulsive movement of Giovanni drew her eyes to the window. There she beheld the beautiful head of the young man—rather a Grecian than an Italian head, with fair, regular features, and a glistening of gold among his ringlets—gazing down upon her like a being that hovered in mid air. Scarcely knowing what he did, Giovanni threw down the bouquet which he had hitherto held in his hand.

"Signora," said he, "there are pure and healthful flowers. Wear them for the sake of Giovanni Guasconti."

"Thanks, signor," replied Beatrice, with her rich voice, that came forth as it were like a gush of music, and with a mirthful expression half childish and half woman-like. "I accept your gift, and would fain recompense it with this precious purple flower; but if I toss it into the air it will not reach you. So Signor Guasconti must even content himself with my thanks."

She lifted the bouquet from the ground, and then, as if inwardly ashamed at having stepped aside from her maidenly reserve to respond to a stranger's greeting, passed swiftly homeward through the garden. But few as the moments were, it seemed to Giovanni, when she was on the point of vanishing beneath the sculptured portal, that his beautiful bouquet was already beginning to wither in her grasp. It was an idle thought; there could be no possibility of distinguishing a faded flower from a fresh one at so great a distance.

For many days after this incident the young man avoided the window that looked into Dr. Rappaccini's garden, as if something ugly and monstrous would have blasted his eyesight had he been betrayed into a glance. He felt conscious of having put himself, to a certain extent, within the influence of an unintelligible power by the communication which he had opened with Beatrice. The wisest course would have been, if his heart were in any real danger, to quit his lodgings and Padua itself at once; the next wiser, to have accustomed himself, as far as possible, to the familiar and daylight view of Beatrice—thus bringing her rigidly and systematically within the limits of ordinary experience. Least of all, while avoiding her sight, ought Giovanni to have remained so near this extraordinary being that the proximity and possibility even of intercourse should give a kind of substance and reality to the wild vagaries which his imagination ran riot continually in producing. Guasconti had not a deep heart—or, at all events, its depths were not sounded now; but he had a quick fancy, and an ardent southern temperament, which rose every instant to a higher fever pitch. Whether or no Beatrice possessed those terrible attributes, that fatal breath, the affinity with those so beautiful and deadly flowers which were indicated by what Giovanni had witnessed, she had at least instilled a fierce and subtle poison into his system. It was not love, although her rich beauty was a madness to him; nor horror, even while he fancied her spirit to be imbued with the same baneful essence that seemed to pervade her physical frame; but a wild offspring of both love and horror that had each parent in it, and burned like one and shivered like the other. Giovanni knew not what to dread; still less did he know what to hope; yet hope and dread kept a continual warfare in his breast, alternately vanquishing one another and starting up afresh to renew the contest. Blessed are all simple emotions, be they dark or bright! It is the lurid intermixture of the two that produces the illuminating blaze of the infernal regions.

Sometimes he endeavored to assuage the fever of his spirit by a rapid walk through the streets of Padua or beyond its gates: his footsteps kept time with the throbbings of his brain, so that the walk was apt to accelerate itself to a race. One day he found himself arrested; his arm was seized by a portly personage, who had turned back on recognizing the young man and expended much breath in overtaking him.

"Signor Giovanni! Stay, my young friend!" cried he. "Have you forgotten me? That might well be the case if I were as much altered as yourself."

It was Baglioni, whom Giovanni had avoided ever since their first meeting, from a doubt that the professor's sagacity would look too deeply into his secrets. Endeavoring to recover himself, he stared forth wildly from his inner world into the outer one and spoke like a man in a dream.

"Yes; I am Giovanni Guasconti. You are Professor Pietro Baglioni. Now let me pass!"

"Not yet, not yet, Signor Giovanni Guasconti," said the professor, smiling, but at the same time scrutinizing the youth with an earnest glance. "What! did I grow up side by side with your father? and shall his son pass me like a stranger in these old streets of Padua? Stand still, Signor Giovanni; for we must have a word or two before we part."

"Speedily, then, most worshipful professor, speedily," said Giovanni, with feverish impatience. "Does not your worship see that I am in haste?"

Now, while he was speaking there came a man in black along the street, stooping and moving feebly like a person in inferior health. His face was all overspread with a most sickly and sallow hue, but yet so pervaded with an expression of piercing and active intellect that an observer might easily have overlooked the merely physical attributes and have seen only this wonderful energy. As he passed, this person exchanged a cold and distant salutation with Baglioni, but fixed his eyes upon Giovanni with an intentness that seemed to bring out whatever was within him worthy of notice. Nevertheless, there was a peculiar quietness in the look, as if taking merely a speculative, not a human, interest in the young man.

"It is Dr. Rappaccini!" whispered the professor when the stranger had passed. "Has he ever seen your face before?"

"Not that I know," answered Giovanni, starting at the name.

"He *has* seen you! he must have seen you!" said Baglioni, hastily. "For some purpose or other, this man of science is making a study of you. I know that look of his! It is the same that coldly illuminates his face as he bends over a bird, a mouse, or a butterfly, which, in pursuance of some experiment, he has killed by the perfume of a flower; a look as deep as Nature itself, but without Nature's warmth of love. Signor Giovanni, I will stake my life upon it, you are the subject of one of Rappaccini's experiments!"

"Will you make a fool of me?" cried Giovanni, passionately. "*That,* signor professor, were an untoward experiment."

"Patience! patience!" replied the imperturbable professor. "I tell thee, my poor Giovanni, that Rappaccini has a scientific interest in thee. Thou hast fallen into fearful hands! And the Signora Beatrice,—what part does she act in this mystery?"

But Guasconti, finding Baglioni's pertinacity intolerable, here broke away, and was gone before the professor could again seize his arm. He looked after the young man intently and shook his head.

"This must not be," said Baglioni to himself. "The youth is the son of my old friend, and shall not come to any harm from which the arcana of medical science can preserve him. Besides, it is too insufferable an impertinence in Rappaccini, thus to snatch the lad out of my own hands, as I may say, and make use of him for his infernal experiments. This daughter of his! It shall be looked to. Perchance, most learned Rappaccini, I may foil you where you little dream of it!"

Meanwhile Giovanni had pursued a circuitous route, and at length found himself at the door of his lodgings. As he crossed the threshold he was met by old Lisabetta, who smirked and smiled, and was evidently desirous to attract his attention; vainly, however, as the ebullition of his feelings had momentarily subsided into a cold and dull vacuity. He turned his eyes full upon the withered face that was puckering itself into a smile, but seemed to behold it not. The old dame, therefore, laid her grasp upon his cloak.

"Signor! signor!" whispered she, still with a smile over the whole breadth of her visage, so that it looked not unlike a grotesque carving in wood, darkened by centuries. "Listen, signor! There is a private entrance into the garden!"

"What do you say?" exclaimed Giovanni, turning quickly about, as if an inanimate thing should start into feverish life. "A private entrance into Dr. Rappaccini's garden?"

"Hush! hush! not so loud!" whispered Lisabetta, putting her hand over his mouth. "Yes; into the worshipful doctor's garden, where you may see all his fine shrubbery. Many a young man in Padua would give gold to be admitted among those flowers."

Giovanni put a piece of gold into her hand.

"Show me the way," said he.

A surmise, probably excited by his conversation with Baglioni, crossed his mind, that this interposition of old Lisabetta might perchance be connected with the intrigue, whatever were its nature, in which the professor seemed to suppose that Dr. Rappaccini was involving him. But such a suspicion, though it disturbed Giovanni, was inadequate to restrain him. The instant that he was aware of the possibility of approaching Beatrice, it seemed an absolute necessity of his existence to do so. It mattered not whether she were angel or demon; he was irrevocably within her sphere, and must obey the law that whirled him onward, in ever-lessening circles, towards a result which he did not attempt to foreshadow; and yet, strange to say, there came across him a sudden doubt whether this intense interest on his part were not delusory; whether it were really of so deep and positive a nature as to justify him in now thrusting himself into an incalculable position; whether it were not merely the fantasy of a young man's brain, only slightly or not at all connected with his heart.

He paused, hesitated, turned half about, but again went on. His withered guide led him along several obscure passages, and finally undid a door, through which, as it was opened, there came the sight and sound of rustling leaves, with the broken sunshine glimmering among them. Giovanni stepped forth, and, forcing himself through the entanglement of a shrub that wreathed its tendrils over the hidden entrance, stood beneath his own window in the open area of Dr. Rappaccini's garden.

How often is it the case that, when impossibilities have come to pass and dreams have condensed their misty substance into tangible realities, we find ourselves calm, and even coldly self-possessed, amid circumstances which it would have been a delirium of joy or agony to anticipate! Fate delights to thwart us thus. Passion will choose his own time to rush upon the scene, and lingers sluggishly behind when an appropriate adjustment of events would seem to summon his appearance. So was it now with Giovanni. Day after day his pulses had throbbed with feverish blood at the improbable idea of an interview with Beatrice, and of standing with her, face to face, in this very garden, basking in the Oriental sunshine of her beauty, and snatching from her full gaze the mystery which he deemed the riddle of his own existence. But now there was a singular and untimely equanimity within his breast. He threw a glance around the garden to discover if Beatrice or her father were present, and, perceiving that he was alone, began a critical observation of the plants.

The aspect of one and all of them dissatisfied him; their gorgeousness seemed fierce, passionate, and even unnatural. There was hardly an individual shrub which a wanderer, straying by himself through a forest, would not have been startled to find growing wild, as if an unearthly face had glared at him out of the thicket. Several also would have shocked a delicate instinct by an appearance of artificialness indicating that there had been such commixture, and, as it were, adultery, of various vegetable species, that the production was no longer of God's making, but the monstrous offspring of man's depraved fancy, glowing with only an evil mockery of beauty. They were probably the result of experiment, which in one or two cases had succeeded in mingling plants individually lovely into a compound possessing the questionable and ominous character that distinguished the whole growth of the garden. In fine, Giovanni recognized but two or three plants in the collection, and those of a kind that he well knew to be poisonous. While busy with these contemplations he heard the rustling of a silken garment, and, turning, beheld Beatrice emerging from beneath the sculptured portal.

Giovanni had not considered with himself what should be his deportment; whether he should apologize for his intrusion into the garden, or assume that he was there with the privity at least, if not by the desire, of Dr. Rappaccini or his daughter; but Beatrice's manner placed him at his ease, though leaving him still in doubt by what agency he had gained admittance. She came lightly along the path and met him near the broken fountain. There was surprise in her face, but brightened by a simple and kind expression of pleasure.

"You are a connoisseur in flowers, signor," said Beatrice, with a smile, alluding to the bouquet which he had flung her from the window. "It is no marvel, therefore, if the sight of my father's rare collection has tempted you to take a nearer view. If he were here, he could tell you many strange and interesting facts as to the nature and habits of these shrubs; for he has spent a lifetime in such studies, and this garden is his world."

"And yourself, lady," observed Giovanni, "if fame says true,—you likewise are deeply skilled in the virtues indicated by these rich blossoms and these spicy perfumes. Would you deign to be my instructress, I should prove an apter scholar than if taught by Signor Rappaccini himself."

"Are there such idle rumors?" asked Beatrice, with the music of a pleasant laugh. "Do people say that I am skilled in my father's science of plants? What a jest is there! No; though I have grown up among these flowers, I know no more of them than their hues and perfume; and sometimes methinks I would fain rid myself of even that small knowledge. There are many flowers here, and those not the least brilliant, that shock and offend me when they meet my eye. But pray, signor, do not believe these stories about my science. Believe nothing of me save what you see with your own eyes."

"And must I believe all that I have seen with my own eyes?" asked Giovanni, pointedly, while the recollection of former scenes made him shrink. "No, signora; you demand too little of me. Bid me believe nothing save what comes from your own lips."

It would appear that Beatrice understood him. There came a deep flush to her cheek; but she looked full into Giovanni's eyes, and responded to his gaze of uneasy suspicion with a queenlike haughtiness.

"I do so bid you, signor," she replied. "Forget whatever you may have fancied in regard to me. If true to the outward senses, still it may be false in its essence; but the words of Beatrice Rappaccini's lips are true from the depths of the heart outward. Those you may believe."

A fervor glowed in her whole aspect and beamed upon Giovanni's consciousness like the light of truth itself; but while she spoke there was a fragrance in the atmosphere around her, rich and delightful, though evanescent, yet which the young man, from an indefinable reluctance, scarcely dared to draw into his lungs. It might be the odor of the flowers. Could it be Beatrice's breath which thus embalmed her words with a strange richness, as if by steeping them in her heart? A faintness passed like a shadow over Giovanni and flitted away; he seemed to gaze through the beautiful girl's eyes into her transparent soul, and felt no more doubt or fear.

The tinge of passion that had colored Beatrice's manner vanished; she became gay, and appeared to derive a pure delight from her communion with the youth not unlike what the maiden of a lonely island might have felt conversing with a voyager from the civilized world. Evidently her experience of life had been confined within the limits of that garden. She talked now about matters as simple as the daylight or summer clouds, and now asked questions in reference to the city, or Giovanni's distant home, his friends, his mother, and his sisters—questions indicating such seclusion, and such lack of familiarity with modes and forms, that Giovanni responded as if to an infant. Her spirit gushed out before him like a fresh rill that was just catching its first glimpse of the sunlight and wondering at the reflections of earth and sky which were flung into its bosom. There came thoughts, too, from a deep source, and fantasies of a gemlike brilliancy, as if diamonds and rubies sparkled upward among the bubbles of the fountain. Ever and anon there gleamed across the young man's mind a sense of wonder that he should be walking side by side with the being who had so wrought upon his imagination, whom he had idealized in such hues of terror, in whom he had positively witnessed such manifestations of dreadful attributes,—that he should be conversing with Beatrice like a brother, and should find her so human and so maidenlike. But such reflections were only momentary; the effect of her character was too real not to make itself familiar at once.

In this free intercourse they had strayed through the garden, and now, after many turns among its avenues, were come to the shattered fountain, beside which grew the magnificent shrub, with its treasury of glowing blossoms. A fragrance was diffused from it which Giovanni recognized as identical with that which he had attributed to Beatrice's breath, but incomparably more powerful. As her eyes fell upon it, Giovanni beheld her press her hand to her bosom as if her heart were throbbing suddenly and painfully.

"For the first time in my life," murmured she, addressing the shrub, "I had forgotten thee."

"I remember, signora," said Giovanni, "that you once promised to reward me with one of these living gems for the bouquet which I had the happy boldness to fling to your feet. Permit me now to pluck it as a memorial of this interview."

He made a step towards the shrub with extended hand; but Beatrice darted forward, uttering a shriek that went through his heart like a dagger. She caught his hand and drew it back with the whole force of her slender figure. Giovanni felt her touch thrilling through his fibers.

"Touch it not!" exclaimed she, in a voice of agony. "Not for thy life! It is fatal!"

Then, hiding her face, she fled from him and vanished beneath the sculptured portal. As Giovanni followed her with his eyes, he beheld the emaciated figure and pale intelligence of Dr. Rappaccini, who had been watching the scene, he knew not how long, within the shadow of the entrance.

No sooner was Guasconti alone in his chamber than the image of Beatrice came back to his passionate musings, invested with all the witchery that had been gathering around it ever since his first glimpse of her, and now likewise imbued with a tender warmth of girlish womanhood. She was human; her nature was endowed with all gentle and feminine qualities; she was worthiest to be worshipped; she was capable, surely, on her part, of the height and heroism of love. Those tokens which he had hitherto considered as proofs of a frightful peculiarity in her physical and moral system were now either forgotten, or, by the subtle sophistry of passion transmitted into a golden crown of enchantment, rendering Beatrice the more admirable by so much as she was the more unique. Whatever had looked ugly was now beautiful; or, if incapable of such a change, it stole away and hid itself among those shapeless half ideas which throng the dim region beyond the daylight of our perfect consciousness. Thus did he spend the night, nor fell asleep until the dawn had begun to awake the slumbering flowers in Dr. Rappaccini's garden, whither Giovanni's dreams doubtless led him. Up rose the sun in his due season, and, flinging his beams upon the young man's eyelids, awoke him to a sense of pain. When thoroughly aroused, he became sensible of a burning and tingling agony in his hand—in his right hand—the very hand which Beatrice had grasped in her own when he was on the point of plucking one of the gemlike flowers. On the back of that hand there was now a purple print like that of four small fingers, and the likeness of a slender thumb upon his wrist.

Oh, how stubbornly does love,—or even that cunning semblance of love which flourishes in the imagination, but strikes no depth of root into the heart,—how stubbornly does it hold its faith until the moment comes when it is doomed to vanish into thin mist! Giovanni wrapped a handkerchief about his hand and wondered what evil thing had stung him, and soon forgot his pain in a reverie of Beatrice.

After the first interview, a second was in the inevitable course of what we call fate. A third; a fourth; and a meeting with Beatrice in the garden was no longer an incident in Giovanni's daily life, but the whole space in which he might be said to live; for the anticipation and memory of that ecstatic hour made up the remainder. Nor was it otherwise with the daughter of Rappaccini. She watched for the youth's appearance, and flew to his side with confidence as unreserved as if they had been playmates from early infancy—as if they were such playmates still. If, by any unwonted chance, he failed to come at the appointed moment, she stood beneath the window and sent up the rich sweetness of her tones to float around him in his chamber and echo and reverberate throughout his heart: "Giovanni! Giovanni! Why tarriest thou? Come down!" And down he hastened into that Eden of poisonous flowers.

But, with all this intimate familiarity, there was still a reserve in Beatrice's demeanor, so rigidly and invariably sustained that the idea of infringing it scarcely occurred to his imagination. By all appreciable signs, they loved; they had looked love with eyes that conveyed the holy secret from the depths of one soul into the depths of the other, as if it were too sacred to be whispered by the way; they had even spoken love in those gushes of passion when their spirits darted forth in articulated breath like tongues of long-hidden flame; and yet there had been no seal of lips, no clasp of hands, nor any slightest caress such as love claims and hallows. He had never touched one of the gleaming ringlets of her hair; her garment—so marked was the physical barrier between them—had never been waved against him by a breeze. On the few occasions when Giovanni had seemed tempted to overstep the limit, Beatrice grew so sad, so stern, and withal wore such a look of desolate separation, shuddering at itself, that not a spoken word was requisite to repel him. At such times he was startled at the horrible suspicions that rose, monster-like, out of the caverns of his heart and stared him in the face; his love grew thin and faint as the morning mist, his doubts alone had substance. But, when Beatrice's face brightened again after the momentary shadow, she was transformed at once from the mysterious, questionable being whom he had watched with so much awe and horror; she was now the beautiful and unsophisticated girl whom he felt that his spirit knew with a certainty beyond all other knowledge.

A considerable time had now passed since Giovanni's last meeting with Baglioni. One morning, however, he was disagreeably surprised by a visit from the professor, whom he had scarcely thought of for whole weeks, and would willingly have forgotten still longer. Given up as he had long been to a pervading excitement, he could tolerate no companions except upon condition of their perfect sympathy with his present state of feeling. Such sympathy was not to be expected from Professor Baglioni.

The visitor chatted carelessly for a few moments about the gossip of the city and the university, and then took up another topic.

"I have been reading an old classic author lately," said he, "and met with a story[9] that strangely interested me. Possibly you may remember it. It is of an Indian prince, who sent a beautiful woman as a present to Alexander the Great. She was as lovely as the dawn and gorgeous as the sunset; but what especially distinguished her was a certain rich perfume in her breath—richer than a garden of Persian roses. Alexander, as was natural to a youthful conqueror, fell in love at first sight with this magnificent stranger; but a certain sage physician, happening to be present, discovered a terrible secret in regard to her."

"And what was that?" asked Giovanni, turning his eyes downward to avoid those of the professor.

"That this lovely woman," continued Baglioni, with emphasis, "had been nourished with poisons from her birth upward, until her whole nature was so imbued with them that she herself had become the deadliest poison in existence. Poison was her element of life. With that rich perfume of her breath she blasted the very air. Her love would have been poison—her embrace death. Is not this a marvellous tale?"

"A childish fable," answered Giovanni, nervously starting from his chair. "I marvel how your worship finds time to read such nonsense among your graver studies."

"By the by," said the professor, looking uneasily about him, "what singular fragrance is this in your apartment? Is it the perfume of your gloves? It is faint, but delicious; and yet, after all, by no means agreeable. Were I to breathe it long, methinks it would make me ill. It is like the breath of a flower; but I see no flowers in the chamber."

"Nor are there any," replied Giovanni, who had turned pale as the professor spoke; "nor, I think, is there any fragrance except in your worship's imagination. Odors, being a sort of element combined of the sensual and the spiritual, are apt to deceive us in this manner. The recollection of a perfume, the bare idea of it, may easily be mistaken for a present reality."

"Ay; but my sober imagination does not often play such tricks," said Baglioni; "and, were I to fancy any kind of odor, it would be that of some vile apothecary drug, wherewith my fingers are likely enough to be imbued. Our worshipful friend Rappaccini, as I have heard, tinctures his medicaments with odors richer than those of Araby. Doubtless, likewise, the fair and learned Signora Beatrice would minister to her patients with draughts as sweet as a maiden's breath; but woe to him that sips them!"

Giovanni's face evinced many contending emotions. The tone in which the professor alluded to the pure and lovely daughter of Rappaccini was a torture to his soul; and yet the intimation of a view of her character, opposite to his own, gave instantaneous distinctness to a thousand dim suspicions, which now grinned at him like so

[9] See *Vulgar Errors* (1646) by Sir Thomas Browne (1605–1682), English physician and author.

many demons. But he strove hard to quell them and to respond to Baglioni with a true lover's perfect faith.

"Signor professor," said he, "you were my father's friend; perchance, too, it is your purpose to act a friendly part towards his son. I would fain feel nothing towards you save respect and deference; but I pray you to observe, signor, that there is one subject on which we must not speak. You know not the Signora Beatrice. You cannot, therefore, estimate the wrong—the blasphemy, I may even say—that is offered to her character by a light or injurious word."

"Giovanni! my poor Giovanni!" answered the professor, with a calm expression of pity, "I know this wretched girl far better than yourself. You shall hear the truth in respect to the poisoner Rappaccini and his poisonous daughter; yes, poisonous as she is beautiful. Listen; for, even should you do violence to my gray hairs, it shall not silence me. That old fable of the Indian woman has become a truth by the deep and deadly science of Rappaccini and in the person of the lovely Beatrice."

Giovanni groaned and hid his face.

"Her father," continued Baglioni, "was not restrained by natural affection from offering up his child in this horrible manner as the victim of his insane zeal for science; for, let us do him justice, he is as true a man of science as ever distilled his own heart in an alembic.[10] What, then, will be your fate? Beyond a doubt you are selected as the material of some new experiment. Perhaps the result is to be death; perhaps a fate more awful still. Rappaccini, with what he calls the interest of science before his eyes, will hesitate at nothing."

"It is a dream," muttered Giovanni to himself; "surely it is a dream."

"But," resumed the professor, "be of good cheer, son of my friend. It is not yet too late for the rescue. Possibly we may even succeed in bringing back this miserable child within the limits of ordinary nature, from which her father's madness has estranged her. Behold this little silver vase! It was wrought by the hands of the renowned Benvenuto Cellini,[11] and is well worthy to be a love gift to the fairest dame in Italy. But its contents are invaluable. One little sip of this antidote would have rendered the most virulent poisons of the Borgias[12] innocuous. Doubt not that it will be as efficacious against those of Rappaccini. Bestow the vase, and the precious liquid within it, on your Beatrice, and hopefully await the result."

Baglioni laid a small, exquisitely wrought silver vial on the table and withdrew, leaving what he had said to produce its effect upon the young man's mind.

"We will thwart Rappaccini yet," thought he, chuckling to himself, as he descended the stairs; "but, let us confess the truth of him, he is a wonderful man—a wonderful man indeed; a vile empiric, however, in his practice, and therefore not to be tolerated by those who respect the good old rules of the medical profession."

Throughout Giovanni's whole acquaintance with Beatrice, he had occasionally, as we have said, been haunted by dark surmises as to her character; yet so thoroughly had she made herself felt by him as a simple, natural, most affectionate, and guileless creature, that the image now held up by Professor Baglioni looked as strange and incredible as if it were not in accordance with his own original conception. True, there

[10] Laboratory device for distillation of substances.
[11] Italian artisan, artist, and writer Benvenuto Cellini (1500–1571).

[12] Aristocratic Italian family influential in Renaissance religion and politics, and notorious for its cruelty and licentiousness.

were ugly recollections connected with his first glimpses of the beautiful girl; he could not quite forget the bouquet that withered in her grasp, and the insect that perished amid the sunny air, by no ostensible agency save the fragrance of her breath. These incidents, however, dissolving in the pure light of her character, had no longer the efficacy of facts, but were acknowledged as mistaken fantasies, by whatever testimony of the senses they might appear to be substantiated. There is something truer and more real than what we can see with the eyes and touch with the finger. On such better evidence had Giovanni founded his confidence in Beatrice, though rather by the necessary force of her high attributes than by any deep and generous faith on his part. But now his spirit was incapable of sustaining itself at the height to which the early enthusiasm of passion had exalted it; he fell down, grovelling among earthly doubts, and defiled therewith the pure whiteness of Beatrice's image. Not that he gave her up; he did but distrust. He resolved to institute some decisive test that should satisfy him, once for all, whether there were those dreadful peculiarities in her physical nature which could not be supposed to exist without some corresponding monstrosity of soul. His eyes, gazing down afar, might have deceived him as to the lizard, the insect, and the flowers; but if he could witness, at the distance of a few paces, the sudden blight of one fresh and healthful flower in Beatrice's hand, there would be room for no further question. With this idea he hastened to the florist's and purchased a bouquet that was still gemmed with the morning dew-drops.

It was now the customary hour of his daily interview with Beatrice. Before descending into the garden, Giovanni failed not to look at his figure in the mirror, —a vanity to be expected in a beautiful young man, yet, as displaying itself at that troubled and feverish moment, the token of a certain shallowness of feeling and insincerity of character. He did gaze, however, and said to himself that his features had never before possessed so rich a grace, nor his eyes such vivacity, nor his cheeks so warm a hue of super-abundant life.

"At least," thought he, "her poison has not yet insinuated itself into my system. I am no flower to perish in her grasp."

With that thought he turned his eyes on the bouquet, which he had never once laid aside from his hand. A thrill of indefinable horror shot through his frame on perceiving that those dewy flowers were already beginning to droop; they wore the aspect of things that had been fresh and lovely yesterday. Giovanni grew white as marble, and stood motionless before the mirror, staring at his own reflection there as at the likeness of something frightful. He remembered Baglioni's remark about the fragrance that seemed to pervade the chamber. It must have been the poison in his breath! Then he shuddered—shuddered at himself. Recovering from his stupor, he began to watch with curious eye a spider that was busily at work hanging its web from the antique cornice of the apartment, crossing and recrossing the artful system of interwoven lines—as vigorous and active a spider as ever dangled from an old ceiling. Giovanni bent towards the insect, and emitted a deep, long breath. The spider suddenly ceased its toil; the web vibrated with a tremor originating in the body of the small artisan. Again Giovanni sent forth a breath, deeper, longer, and imbued with a venomous feeling out of his heart: he knew not whether he were wicked, or only desperate. The spider made a convulsive gripe with his limbs and hung dead across the window.

"Accursed! accursed!" muttered Giovanni, addressing himself. "Hast thou grown so poisonous that this deadly insect perishes by thy breath?"

At that moment a rich, sweet voice came floating up from the garden.

"Giovanni! Giovanni! It is past the hour! Why tarriest thou? Come down!"

"Yes," muttered Giovanni again. "She is the only being whom my breath may not slay! Would that it might!"

He rushed down, and in an instant was standing before the bright and loving eyes of Beatrice. A moment ago his wrath and despair had been so fierce that he could have desired nothing so much as to wither her by a glance; but with her actual presence there came influences which had too real an existence to be at once shaken off: recollections of the delicate and benign power of her feminine nature, which had so often enveloped him in a religious calm; recollections of many a holy and passionate outgush of her heart, when the pure fountain had been unsealed from its depths and made visible in its transparency to his mental eye; recollections which, had Giovanni known how to estimate them, would have assured him that all this ugly mystery was but an earthly illusion, and that, whatever mist of evil might seem to have gathered over her, the real Beatrice was a heavenly angel. Incapable as he was of such high faith, still her presence had not utterly lost its magic. Giovanni's rage was quelled into an aspect of sullen insensibility. Beatrice, with a quick spiritual sense, immediately felt that there was a gulf of blackness between them which neither he nor she could pass. They walked on together, sad and silent, and came thus to the marble fountain and to its pool of water on the ground, in the midst of which grew the shrub that bore gem-like blossoms. Giovanni was affrighted at the eager enjoyment—the appetite, as it were—with which he found himself inhaling the fragrance of the flowers.

"Beatrice," asked he, abruptly, "whence came this shrub?"

"My father created it," answered she, with simplicity.

"Created it! created it!" repeated Giovanni. "What mean you, Beatrice?"

"He is a man fearfully acquainted with the secrets of Nature," replied Beatrice; "and, at the hour when I first drew breath, this plant sprang from the soil, the offspring of his science, of his intellect, while I was but his earthly child. Approach it not!" continued she, observing with terror that Giovanni was drawing nearer to the shrub. "It has qualities that you little dream of. But I, dearest Giovanni,—I grew up and blossomed with the plant and was nourished with its breath. It was my sister, and I loved it with a human affection; for, alas!—hast thou not suspected it?—there was an awful doom."

Here Giovanni frowned so darkly upon her that Beatrice paused and trembled. But her faith in his tenderness reassured her, and made her blush that she had doubted for an instant.

"There was an awful doom," she continued, "the effect of my father's fatal love of science, which estranged me from all society of my kind. Until Heaven sent thee, dearest Giovanni, oh, how lonely was thy poor Beatrice!"

"Was it a hard doom?" asked Giovanni, fixing his eyes upon her.

"Only of late have I known how hard it was," answered she, tenderly. "Oh, yes; but my heart was torpid, and therefore quiet."

Giovanni's rage broke forth from his sullen gloom like a lightning flash out of a dark cloud.

"Accursed one!" cried he, with venomous scorn and anger. "And, finding thy solitude wearisome, thou hast severed me likewise from all the warmth of life and enticed me into thy region of unspeakable horror!"

"Giovanni!" exclaimed Beatrice, turning her large bright eyes upon his face. The force of his words had not found its way into her mind; she was merely thunderstruck.

"Yes, poisonous thing!" repeated Giovanni, beside himself with passion. "Thou hast done it! Thou hast blasted me! Thou hast filled my veins with poison! Thou hast made me as hateful, as ugly, as loathsome and deadly a creature as thyself—a world's wonder of hideous monstrosity! Now, if our breath be happily as fatal to ourselves as to all others, let us join our lips in one kiss of unutterable hatred, and so die!"

"What has befallen me?" murmured Beatrice, with a low moan out of her heart. "Holy Virgin, pity me, a poor heart-broken child!"

"Thou,—dost thou pray?" cried Giovanni, still with the same fiendish scorn. "Thy very prayers, as they come from thy lips, taint the atmosphere with death. Yes, yes; let us pray! Let us to church and dip our fingers in the holy water at the portal! They that come after us will perish as by a pestilence! Let us sign crosses in the air! It will be scattering curses abroad in the likeness of holy symbols!"

"Giovanni," said Beatrice, calmly, for her grief was beyond passion, "why dost thou join thyself with me thus in those terrible words? I, it is true, am the horrible thing thou namest me. But thou,—what hast thou to do, save with one other shudder at my hideous misery to go forth out of the garden and mingle with thy race, and forget that there ever crawled on earth such a monster as poor Beatrice?"

"Dost thou pretend ignorance?" asked Giovanni, scowling upon her. "Behold! this power have I gained from the pure daughter of Rappaccini."

There was a swarm of summer insects flitting through the air in search of the food promised by the flower odors of the fatal garden. They circled round Giovanni's head, and were evidently attracted towards him by the same influence which had drawn them for an instant within the sphere of several of the shrubs. He sent forth a breath among them, and smiled bitterly at Beatrice as at least a score of the insects fell dead upon the ground.

"I see it! I see it!" shrieked Beatrice. "It is my father's fatal science! No, no, Giovanni; it was not I! Never! never! I dreamed only to love thee and be with thee a little time, and so to let thee pass away, leaving but thine image in mine heart; for, Giovanni, believe it, though my body be nourished with poison, my spirit is God's creature, and craves love as its daily food. But my father,—he has united us in this fearful sympathy. Yes; spurn me, tread upon me, kill me! Oh, what is death after such words as thine? But it was not I. Not for a world of bliss would I have done it."

Giovanni's passion had exhausted itself in its outburst from his lips. There now came across him a sense, mournful, and not without tenderness, of the intimate and peculiar relationship between Beatrice and himself. They stood, as it were, in an utter solitude, which would be made none the less solitary by the densest throng of human life. Ought not, then, the desert of humanity around them to press this insulated pair closer together? If they should be cruel to one another, who was there to be kind to them? Besides, thought Giovanni, might there not still be a hope of his returning within the limits of ordinary nature, and leading Beatrice, the redeemed Beatrice, by the hand? O, weak, and selfish, and unworthy spirit, that could dream of an earthly union and earthly happiness as possible, after such deep love had been so bitterly wronged as was Beatrice's love by Giovanni's blighting words! No, no; there could be no such hope. She must pass heavily, with that broken heart, across the borders of Time—she must bathe her hurts in some fount of paradise, and forget her grief in the light of immortality, and *there* be well.

But Giovanni did not know it.

"Dear Beatrice," said he, approaching her, while she shrank away as always at his approach, but now with a different impulse, "dearest Beatrice, our fate is not yet so desperate. Behold! there is a medicine, potent, as a wise physician has assured me, and almost divine in its efficacy. It is composed of ingredients the most opposite to those by which thy awful father has brought this calamity upon thee and me. It is distilled of blessed herbs. Shall we not quaff it together, and thus be purified from evil?"

"Give it me!" said Beatrice, extending her hand to receive the little silver vial which Giovanni took from his bosom. She added, with a peculiar emphasis, "I will drink; but do thou await the result."

She put Baglioni's antidote to her lips; and, at the same moment, the figure of Rappaccini emerged from the portal and came slowly towards the marble fountain. As he drew near, the pale man of science seemed to gaze with a triumphant expression at the beautiful youth and maiden, as might an artist who should spend his life in achieving a picture or a group of statuary and finally be satisfied with his success. He paused; his bent form grew erect with conscious power; he spread out his hands over them in the attitude of a father imploring a blessing upon his children; but those were the same hands that had thrown poison into the stream of their lives. Giovanni trembled. Beatrice shuddered nervously, and pressed her hand upon her heart.

"My daughter," said Rappaccini, "thou art no longer lonely in the world. Pluck one of those precious gems from thy sister shrub and bid thy bridegroom wear it in his bosom. It will not harm him now. My science and the sympathy between thee and him have so wrought within his system that he now stands apart from common men, as thou dost, daughter of my pride and triumph, from ordinary women. Pass on, then, through the world, most dear to one another and dreadful to all besides!"

"My father," said Beatrice, feebly,—and still as she spoke she kept her hand upon her heart,—"wherefore didst thou inflict this miserable doom upon thy child?"

"Miserable!" exclaimed Rappaccini. "What mean you, foolish girl? Dost thou deem it misery to be endowed with marvellous gifts against which no power nor strength could avail an enemy—misery, to be able to quell the mightiest with a breath—misery, to be as terrible as thou art beautiful? Wouldst thou, then, have preferred the condition of a weak woman, exposed to all evil and capable of none?"

"I would fain have been loved, not feared," murmured Beatrice, sinking down upon the ground. "But now it matters not. I am going, father, where the evil which thou hast striven to mingle with my being will pass away like a dream—like the fragrance of these poisonous flowers, which will no longer taint my breath among the flowers of Eden. Farewell, Giovanni! Thy words of hatred are like lead within my heart; but they, too, will fall away as I ascend. Oh, was there not, from the first, more poison in thy nature than in mine?"

To Beatrice,—so radically had her earthly part been wrought upon by Rappaccini's skill,—as poison had been life, so the powerful antidote was death; and thus the poor victim of man's ingenuity and of thwarted nature, and of the fatality that attends all such efforts of perverted wisdom, perished there, at the feet of her father and Giovanni. Just at that moment Professor Pietro Baglioni looked forth from the window, and called loudly, in a tone of triumph mixed with horror, to the thunderstricken man of science,—

"Rappaccini! Rappaccini! and is *this* the upshot of your experiment!"

1844

Ethan Brand

A Chapter from an Abortive Romance

Bartram the lime-burner,[1] a rough, heavy-looking man, begrimed with charcoal, sat watching his kiln at nightfall, while his little son played at building houses with the scattered fragments of marble, when, on the hill-side below them, they heard a roar of laughter, not mirthful, but slow, and even solemn, like a wind shaking the boughs of the forest.

"Father, what is that?" asked the little boy, leaving his play, and pressing betwixt his father's knees.

"Oh, some drunken man, I suppose," answered the lime-burner; "some merry fellow from the bar-room in the village, who dared not laugh loud enough within doors lest he should blow the roof of the house off. So here he is, shaking his jolly sides at the foot of Graylock."[2]

"But, father," said the child, more sensitive than the obtuse, middle-aged clown, "he does not laugh like a man that is glad. So the noise frightens me!"

"Don't be a fool, child!" cried his father, gruffly. "You will never make a man, I do believe; there is too much of your mother in you. I have known the rustling of a leaf startle you. Hark! Here comes the merry fellow now. You shall see that there is no harm in him."

Bartram and his little son, while they were talking thus, sat watching the same lime-kiln that had been the scene of Ethan Brand's solitary and meditative life, before he began his search for the Unpardonable Sin. Many years, as we have seen, had now elapsed, since that portentous night when the IDEA was first developed. The kiln, however, on the mountain-side, stood unimpaired, and was in nothing changed since he had thrown his dark thoughts into the intense glow of its furnace, and melted them, as it were, into the one thought that took possession of his life. It was a rude, round, tower-like structure about twenty feet high, heavily built of rough stones, and with a hillock of earth heaped about the larger part of its circumference; so that the blocks and fragments of marble might be drawn by cart-loads, and thrown in at the top. There was an opening at the bottom of the tower, like an oven-mouth, but large enough to admit a man in a stooping posture, and provided with a massive iron door. With the smoke and jets of flame issuing from the chinks and crevices of this door, which seemed to give admittance into the hill-side, it resembled nothing so much as the private entrance to the infernal regions, which the shepherds of the Delectable Mountains were accustomed to show to pilgrims.[3]

There are many such lime-kilns in that tract of country, for the purpose of burning the white marble which composes a large part of the substance of the hills. Some of them, built years ago, and long deserted, with weeds growing in the vacant round of the interior, which is open to the sky, and grass and wildflowers rooting themselves

---

[1] One who burns limestone in the making of cement.

[2] Mt. Graylock in the Berkshires has the highest elevation in the state of Massachusetts.

[3] In John Bunyan's novel *The Pilgrim's Progress* (1678, 1684), the pilgrims were taken to the top of the Delectable Mountains to view the gates of both Heaven and Hell.

into the chinks of the stones, look already like relics of antiquity, and may yet be overspread with the lichens of centuries to come. Others, where the lime-burner still feeds his daily and night-long fire, afford points of interest to the wanderer among the hills, who seats himself on a log of wood or a fragment of marble, to hold a chat with the solitary man. It is a lonesome, and, when the character is inclined to thought, may be an intensely thoughtful occupation; as it proved in the case of Ethan Brand, who had mused to such strange purpose, in days gone by, while the fire in this very kiln was burning.

The man who now watched the fire was of a different order, and troubled himself with no thoughts save the very few that were requisite to his business. At frequent intervals, he flung back the clashing weight of the iron door, and, turning his face from the insufferable glare, thrust in huge logs of oak, or stirred the immense brands with a long pole. Within the furnace were seen the curling and riotous flames, and the burning marble, almost molten with the intensity of heat; while without, the reflection of the fire quivered on the dark intricacy of the surrounding forest, and showed in the foreground a bright and ruddy little picture of the hut, the spring beside its door, the athletic and coal-begrimed figure of the lime-burner, and the half-frightened child, shrinking into the protection of his father's shadow. And when, again, the iron door was closed, then reappeared the tender light of the half-full moon, which vainly strove to trace out the indistinct shapes of the neighboring mountains; and, in the upper sky, there was a flitting congregation of clouds, still faintly tinged with the rosy sunset, though thus far down into the valley the sunshine had vanished long and long ago.

The little boy now crept still closer to his father, as footsteps were heard ascending the hill-side, and a human form thrust aside the bushes that clustered beneath the trees.

"Halloo! who is it?" cried the lime-burner, vexed at his son's timidity, yet half infected by it. "Come forward, and show yourself, like a man, or I'll fling this chunk of marble at your head!"

"You offer me a rough welcome," said a gloomy voice, as the unknown man drew nigh. "Yet I neither claim nor desire a kinder one, even at my own fireside."

To obtain a distincter view, Bartram threw open the iron door of the kiln, whence immediately issued a gush of fierce light, that smote full upon the stranger's face and figure. To a careless eye there appeared nothing very remarkable in his aspect, which was that of a man in a coarse, brown, country-made suit of clothes, tall and thin, with the staff and heavy shoes of a wayfarer. As he advanced, he fixed his eyes—which were very bright—intently upon the brightness of the furnace, as if he beheld, or expected to behold, some object worthy of note within it.

"Good evening, stranger," said the lime-burner; "whence come you, so late in the day?"

"I come from my search," answered the wayfarer; "for, at last, it is finished."

"Drunk!—or crazy!" muttered Bartram to himself. "I shall have trouble with the fellow. The sooner I drive him away, the better."

The little boy, all in a tremble, whispered to his father, and begged him to shut the door of the kiln, so that there might not be so much light; for that there was something in the man's face which he was afraid to look at, yet could not look away from. And, indeed, even the lime-burner's dull and torpid sense began to be impressed by an indescribable something in that thin, rugged, thoughtful visage, with the grizzled hair hanging wildly about it, and those deeply sunken eyes, which gleamed like fires within the entrance of a mysterious cavern. But, as he closed the door, the stranger turned towards him, and spoke in a quiet, familiar way, that made Bartram feel as if he were a sane and sensible man, after all.

"Your task draws to an end, I see," said he. "This marble has already been burning three days. A few hours more will convert the stone to lime."

"Why, who are you?" exclaimed the lime-burner. "You seem as well acquainted with my business as I am myself."

"And well I may be," said the stranger; "for I followed the same craft many a long year, and here, too, on this very spot. But you are a new-comer in these parts. Did you never hear of Ethan Brand?"

"The man that went in search of the Unpardonable Sin?" asked Bartram, with a laugh.

"The same," answered the stranger. "He has found what he sought, and therefore he comes back again."

"What! then you are Ethan Brand himself?" cried the lime-burner, in amazement. "I am a new-comer here, as you say, and they call it eighteen years since you left the foot of Graylock. But, I can tell you, the good folks still talk about Ethan Brand, in the village yonder, and what a strange errand took him away from his lime-kiln. Well, and so you have found the Unpardonable Sin?"

"Even so!" said the stranger, calmly.

"If the question is a fair one," proceeded Bartram, "where might it be?"

Ethan Brand laid his finger on his own heart.

"Here!" replied he.

And then, without mirth in his countenance, but as if moved by an involuntary recognition of the infinite absurdity of seeking throughout the world for what was the closest of all things to himself, and looking into every heart, save his own, for what was hidden in no other breast, he broke into a laugh of scorn. It was the same slow, heavy laugh, that had almost appalled the lime-burner when it heralded the wayfarer's approach.

The solitary mountain-side was made dismal by it. Laughter, when out of place, mistimed, or bursting forth from a disordered state of feeling, may be the most terrible modulation of the human voice. The laughter of one asleep, even if it be a little child, —the madman's laugh,—the wild, screaming laugh of a born idiot,—are sounds that we sometimes tremble to hear, and would always willingly forget. Poets have imagined no utterance of fiends or hobgoblins so fearfully appropriate as a laugh. And even the obtuse lime-burner felt his nerves shaken, as this strange man looked inward at his own heart, and burst into laughter that rolled away into the night, and was indistinctly reverberated among the hills.

"Joe," said he to his little son, "scamper down to the tavern in the village, and tell the jolly fellows there that Ethan Brand has come back, and that he has found the Unpardonable Sin!"

The boy darted away on his errand, to which Ethan Brand made no objection, nor seemed hardly to notice it. He sat on a log of wood, looking steadfastly at the iron door of the kiln. When the child was out of sight, and his swift and light footsteps ceased to be heard treading first on the fallen leaves and then on the rocky mountain-path, the lime-burner began to regret his departure. He felt that the little fellow's presence had been a barrier between his guest and himself, and that he must now deal, heart to heart, with a man who, on his own confession, had committed the one only crime for which Heaven could afford no mercy. That crime, in its indistinct blackness, seemed to overshadow him. The lime-burner's own sins rose up within him, and made his memory riotous with a throng of evil shapes that asserted their kindred with the Master Sin, whatever it might be, which it was within the scope of man's corrupted nature to conceive and cherish. They were all of one family; they went to and fro between his breast and Ethan Brand's, and carried dark greetings from one to the other.

Then Bartram remembered the stories which had grown traditionary in reference to this strange man, who had come upon him like a shadow of the night, and was making himself at home in his old place, after so long absence, that the dead people, dead and buried for years, would have had more right to be at home, in any familiar spot, than he. Ethan Brand, it was said, had conversed with Satan himself in the lurid blaze of this very kiln. The legend had been matter of mirth heretofore, but looked grisly now. According to this tale, before Ethan Brand departed on his search, he had been accustomed to evoke a fiend from the hot furnace of the lime-kiln, night after night, in order to confer with him about the Unpardonable Sin; the man and the fiend each laboring to frame the image of some mode of guilt which could neither be atoned for nor forgiven. And, with the first gleam of light upon the mountain-top, the fiend crept in at the iron door, there to abide the intensest element of fire until again summoned forth to share in the dreadful task of extending man's possible guilt beyond the scope of Heaven's else infinite mercy.

While the lime-burner was struggling with the horror of these thoughts, Ethan Brand rose from the log, and flung open the door of the kiln. The action was in such accordance with the idea in Bartram's mind, that he almost expected to see the Evil One issue forth, red-hot, from the raging furnace.

"Hold! hold!" cried he, with a tremulous attempt to laugh; for he was ashamed of his fears, although they overmastered him. "Don't, for mercy's sake, bring out your Devil now!"

"Man!" sternly replied Ethan Brand, "what need have I of the Devil? I have left him behind me, on my track. It is with such half-way sinners as you that he busies himself. Fear not, because I open the door. I do but act by old custom, and am going to trim your fire, like a lime-burner, as I was once."

He stirred the vast coals, thrust in more wood, and bent forward to gaze into the hollow prison-house of the fire, regardless of the fierce glow that reddened upon his face. The lime-burner sat watching him, and half suspected this strange guest of a purpose, if not to evoke a fiend, at least to plunge bodily into the flames, and thus vanish from the sight of man. Ethan Brand, however, drew quietly back, and closed the door of the kiln.

"I have looked," said he, "into many a human heart that was seven times hotter with sinful passions than yonder furnace is with fire. But I found not there what I sought. No, not the Unpardonable Sin!"

"What is the Unpardonable Sin?" asked the lime-burner; and then he shrank farther from his companion, trembling lest his question should be answered.

"It is a sin that grew within my own breast," replied Ethan Brand, standing erect, with a pride that distinguishes all enthusiasts of his stamp. "A sin that grew nowhere else! The sin of an intellect that triumphed over the sense of brotherhood with man and reverence for God, and sacrificed everything to its own mighty claims! The only sin that deserves a recompense of immortal agony! Freely, were it to do again, would I incur the guilt. Unshrinkingly I accept the retribution!"

"The man's head is turned," muttered the lime-burner to himself. "He may be a sinner like the rest of us,—nothing more likely,—but, I'll be sworn, he is a madman too."

Nevertheless, he felt uncomfortable at his situation, alone with Ethan Brand on the wild mountain-side, and was right glad to hear the rough murmur of tongues, and the footsteps of what seemed a pretty numerous party, stumbling over the stones and rustling through the underbrush. Soon appeared the whole lazy regiment that was wont to infest the village tavern, comprehending three or four individuals who had drunk flip[4] beside the bar-room fire through all the winters, and smoked their pipes beneath the stoop through all the summers, since Ethan Brand's departure. Laughing boisterously, and mingling all their voices together in unceremonious talk, they now burst into the moonshine and narrow streaks of firelight that illuminated the open space before the lime-kiln. Bartram set the door ajar again, flooding the spot with light, that the whole company might get a fair view of Ethan Brand, and he of them.

There, among other old acquaintances, was a once ubiquitous man, now almost extinct, but whom we were formerly sure to encounter at the hotel of every thriving village throughout the country. It was the stage-agent. The present specimen of the genus was a wilted and smoke-dried man, wrinkled and red-nosed, in a smartly cut, brown, bobtailed coat, with brass buttons, who, for a length of time unknown, had kept his desk and corner in the bar-room, and was still puffing what seemed to be the same cigar that he had lighted twenty years before. He had great fame as a dry joker, though, perhaps, less on account of any intrinsic humor than from a certain flavor of brandy-toddy and tobacco-smoke, which impregnated all his ideas and expressions, as well as his person. Another well-remembered, though strangely altered, face was that of Lawyer Giles, as people still called him in courtesy; an elderly ragamuffin, in his soiled shirt-sleeves and tow-cloth[5] trousers. This poor fellow had been an attorney, in what he called his better days, a sharp practitioner, and in great vogue among the village litigants; but flip, and sling, and toddy, and cocktails, imbibed at all hours, morning, noon, and night, had caused him to slide from intellectual to various kinds and degrees of bodily labor, till at last, to adopt his own phrase, he slid into a soap-vat. In other words, Giles was now a soap-boiler, in a small way. He had come to be but the fragment of a human being, a part of one foot having been chopped off by an axe, and an entire hand torn away by the devilish grip of a steam-engine. Yet, though the corporeal hand was gone, a spiritual member remained; for, stretching forth the stump, Giles steadfastly averred that he felt an invisible thumb and fingers with as vivid a sensation as before the real ones were amputated. A maimed and miserable wretch he was; but one, nevertheless, whom the world could not trample on, and had no right to scorn, either in this or any previous stage of his misfortunes, since he had still kept up the courage and spirit of a man, asked nothing in charity, and with his one hand—and that the left one—fought a stern battle against want and hostile circumstances.

---

[4] A spicy, sweet beer or ale.   [5] Coarse fabric.

Among the throng, too, came another personage, who, with certain points of similarity to Lawyer Giles, had many more of difference. It was the village doctor; a man of some fifty years, whom, at an earlier period of his life, we introduced as paying a professional visit to Ethan Brand during the latter's supposed insanity. He was now a purple-visaged, rude, and brutal, yet half-gentlemanly figure, with something wild, ruined, and desperate in his talk, and in all the details of his gesture and manners. Brandy possessed this man like an evil spirit, and made him as surly and savage as a wild beast, and as miserable as a lost soul; but there was supposed to be in him such wonderful skill, such native gifts of healing, beyond any which medical science could impart, that society caught hold of him, and would not let him sink out of its reach. So, swaying to and fro upon his horse, and grumbling thick accents at the bedside, he visited all the sick-chambers for miles about among the mountain towns, and sometimes raised a dying man, as it were; by miracle, or quite as often, no doubt, sent his patient to a grave that was dug many a year too soon. The doctor had an everlasting pipe in his mouth, and, as somebody said, in allusion to his habit of swearing, it was always alight with hell-fire.

These three worthies pressed forward, and greeted Ethan Brand each after his own fashion, earnestly inviting him to partake of the contents of a certain black bottle, in which, as they averred, he would find something far better worth seeking for than the Unpardonable Sin. No mind, which has wrought itself by intense and solitary meditation into a high state of enthusiasm, can endure the kind of contact with low and vulgar modes of thought and feeling to which Ethan Brand was now subjected. It made him doubt—and, strange to say, it was a painful doubt—whether he had indeed found the Unpardonable Sin, and found it within himself. The whole question on which he had exhausted life, and more than life, looked like a delusion.

"Leave me," he said bitterly, "ye brute beasts, that have made yourselves so, shrivelling up your souls with fiery liquors! I have done with you. Years and years ago, I groped into your hearts and found nothing there for my purpose. Get ye gone!"

"Why, you uncivil scoundrel," cried the fierce doctor, "is that the way you respond to the kindness of your best friends? Then let me tell you the truth. You have no more found the Unpardonable Sin than yonder boy Joe has. You are but a crazy fellow,—I told you so twenty years ago,—neither better nor worse than a crazy fellow, and the fit companion of old Humphrey, here!"

He pointed to an old man, shabbily dressed, with long white hair, thin visage, and unsteady eyes. For some years past this aged person had been wandering about among the hills, inquiring of all travellers whom he met for his daughter. The girl, it seemed, had gone off with a company of circus-performers, and occasionally tidings of her came to the village, and fine stories were told of her glittering appearance as she rode on horseback in the ring, or performed marvellous feats on the tight-rope.

The white-haired father now approached Ethan Brand, and gazed unsteadily into his face.

"They tell me you have been all over the earth," said he, wringing his hands with earnestness. "You must have seen my daughter, for she makes a grand figure in the world, and everybody goes to see her. Did she send any word to her old father, or say when she was coming back?"

Ethan Brand's eye quailed beneath the old man's. That daughter, from whom he so earnestly desired a word of greeting, was the Esther of our tale, the very girl whom, with such cold and remorseless purpose, Ethan Brand had made the subject of a psychological experiment, and wasted, absorbed, and perhaps annihilated her soul, in the process.

"Yes," murmured he, turning away from the hoary wanderer, "it is no delusion. There is an Unpardonable Sin!"

While these things were passing, a merry scene was going forward in the area of cheerful light, beside the spring and before the door of the hut. A number of the youth of the village, young men and girls, had hurried up the hill-side, impelled by curiosity to see Ethan Brand, the hero of so many a legend familiar to their childhood. Finding nothing, however, very remarkable in his aspect,—nothing but a sunburnt wayfarer, in plain garb and dusty shoes, who sat looking into the fire as if he fancied pictures among the coals,—these young people speedily grew tired of observing him. As it happened, there was other amusement at hand. An old German Jew travelling with a diorama[6] on his back, was passing down the mountain-road towards the village just as the party turned aside from it, and, in hopes of eking out the profits of the day, the showman had kept them company to the lime-kiln.

"Come, old Dutchman," cried one of the young men, "let us see your pictures, if you can swear they are worth looking at!"

"Oh yes, Captain," answered the Jew,—whether as a matter of courtesy or craft, he styled everybody Captain,—"I shall show you, indeed, some very superb pictures!"

So, placing his box in a proper position, he invited the young men and girls to look through the glass orifices of the machine, and proceeded to exhibit a series of the most outrageous scratchings and daubings, as specimens of the fine arts, that ever an itinerant showman had the face to impose upon his circle of spectators. The pictures were worn out, moreover, tattered, full of cracks and wrinkles, dingy with tobacco-smoke, and otherwise in a most pitiable condition. Some purported to be cities, public edifices, and ruined castles in Europe; others represented Napoleon's battles and Nelson's[7] sea-fights; and in the midst of these would be seen a gigantic, brown, hairy hand,—which might have been mistaken for the Hand of Destiny, though, in truth, it was only the showman's,—pointing its forefinger to various scenes of the conflict, while its owner gave historical illustrations. When, with much merriment at its abominable deficiency of merit, the exhibition was concluded, the German bade little Joe put his head into the box. Viewed through the magnifying-glasses, the boy's round, rosy visage assumed the strangest imaginable aspect of an immense Titanic child, the mouth grinning broadly, and the eyes and every other feature overflowing with fun at the joke. Suddenly, however, that merry face turned pale, and its expression changed to horror, for this easily impressed and excitable child had become sensible that the eye of Ethan Brand was fixed upon him through the glass.

"You make the little man to be afraid, Captain," said the German Jew, turning up the dark and strong outline of his visage from his stooping posture. "But look again, and, by chance, I shall cause you to see somewhat that is very fine, upon my word!"

Ethan Brand gazed into the box for an instant, and then starting back, looked fixedly at the German. What had he seen? Nothing, apparently; for a curious youth,

---

[6] Box or chamber used for viewing inserted pictures.

[7] Horatio Nelson (1758–1805), British admiral.

who had peeped in almost at the same moment, beheld only a vacant space of canvas.

"I remember you now," muttered Ethan Brand to the showman.

"Ah, Captain, whispered the Jew of Nuremburg, with a dark smile, "I find it to be a heavy matter in my show-box,—this Unpardonable Sin! By my faith, Captain, it has wearied my shoulders, this long day, to carry it over the mountain."

"Peace," answered Ethan Brand, sternly, "or get thee into the furnace yonder!"

The Jew's exhibition had scarcely concluded, when a great, elderly dog—who seemed to be his own master, as no person in the company laid claim to him—saw fit to render himself the object of public notice. Hitherto, he had shown himself a very quiet, well-disposed old dog, going round from one to another, and, by way of being sociable, offering his rough head to be patted by any kindly hand that would take so much trouble. But now, all of a sudden, this grave and venerable quadruped, of his own mere motion, and without the slightest suggestion from anybody else, began to run round after his tail, which, to heighten the absurdity of the proceeding, was a great deal shorter than it should have been. Never was seen such headlong eagerness in pursuit of an object that could not possibly be attained; never was heard such a tremendous outbreak of growling, snarling, barking, and snapping,—as if one end of the ridiculous brute's body were at deadly and most unforgivable enmity with the other. Faster and faster, round about went the cur; and faster and still faster fled the unapproachable brevity of his tail; and louder and fiercer grew his yells of rage and animosity; until, utterly exhausted, and as far from the goal as ever, the foolish old dog ceased his performance as suddenly as he had begun it. The next moment he was as mild, quiet, sensible, and respectable in his deportment, as when he first scraped acquaintance with the company.

As may be supposed, the exhibition was greeted with universal laughter, clapping of hands, and shouts of encore, to which the canine performer responded by wagging all that there was to wag of his tail, but appeared totally unable to repeat his very successful effort to amuse the spectators.

Meanwhile, Ethan Brand had resumed his seat upon the log, and moved, it might be, by a perception of some remote analogy between his own case and that of this self-pursuing cur, he broke into the awful laugh, which, more than any other token, expressed the condition of his inward being. From that moment, the merriment of the party was at an end; they stood aghast, dreading lest the inauspicious sound should be reverberated around the horizon, and that mountain would thunder it to mountain, and so the horror be prolonged upon their ears. Then, whispering one to another that it was late,—that the moon was almost down,—that the August night was growing chill,—they hurried homewards, leaving the lime-burner and little Joe to deal as they might with their unwelcome guest. Save for these three human beings, the open space on the hill-side was a solitude, set in a vast gloom of forest. Beyond that darksome verge, the firelight glimmered on the stately trunks and almost black foliage of pines, intermixed with the lighter verdure of sapling oaks, maples, and poplars, while here and there lay the gigantic corpses of dead trees, decaying on the leaf-strewn soil. And it seemed to little Joe—a timorous and imaginative child—that the silent forest was holding its breath until some fearful thing should happen.

Ethan Brand thrust more wood into the fire, and closed the door of the kiln; then looking over his shoulder at the lime-burner and his son, he bade, rather than advised, them to retire to rest.

"For myself, I cannot sleep," said he. "I have matters that it concerns me to meditate upon. I will watch the fire, as I used to do in the old time."

"And call the Devil out of the furnace to keep you company, I suppose," muttered Bartram, who had been making intimate acquaintance with the black bottle above mentioned. "But watch, if you like, and call as many devils as you like! For my part, I shall be all the better for a snooze. Come, Joe!"

As the boy followed his father into the hut, he looked back at the wayfarer, and the tears came into his eyes, for his tender spirit had an intuition of the bleak and terrible loneliness in which this man had enveloped himself.

When they had gone, Ethan Brand sat listening to the crackling of the kindled wood, and looking at the little spirts of fire that issued through the chinks of the door. These trifles, however, once so familiar, had but the slightest hold of his attention, while deep within his mind he was reviewing the gradual but marvelous change that had been wrought upon him by the search to which he had devoted himself. He remembered how the night dew had fallen upon him,—how the dark forest had whispered to him,—how the stars had gleamed upon him,—a simple and loving man, watching his fire in the years gone by, and ever musing as it burned. He remembered with what tenderness, with what love and sympathy for mankind, and what pity for human guilt and woe, he had first begun to contemplate those ideas which afterwards became the inspiration of his life; with what reverence he had then looked into the heart of man, viewing it as a temple originally divine, and, however desecrated, still to be held sacred by a brother; with what awful fear he had deprecated the success of his pursuit, and prayed that the Unpardonable Sin might never be revealed to him. Then ensued that vast intellectual development, which, in its progress, disturbed the counterpoise between his mind and heart. The Idea that possessed his life had operated as a means of education; it had gone on cultivating his powers to the highest point of which they were susceptible; it had raised him from the level of an unlettered laborer to stand on a star-lit eminence, whither the philosophers of the earth, laden with the lore of universities, might vainly strive to clamber after him. So much for the intellect! But where was the heart? That, indeed, had withered,—had contracted, —had hardened,—had perished! It had ceased to partake of the universal throb. He had lost his hold of the magnetic chain of humanity. He was no longer a brother-man, opening the chambers or the dungeons of our common nature by the key of holy sympathy, which gave him a right to share in all its secrets; he was now a cold observer, looking on mankind as the subject of his experiment, and, at length, converting man and woman to be his puppets, and pulling the wires that moved them to such degrees of crime as were demanded for his study.

Thus Ethan Brand became a fiend. He began to be so from the moment that his moral nature had ceased to keep the pace of improvement with his intellect. And now, as his highest effort and inevitable development,—as the bright and gorgeous flower, and rich, delicious fruit of his life's labor,—he had produced the Unpardonable Sin!

"What more have I to seek? what more to achieve?" said Ethan Brand to himself. "My task is done, and well done!"

Starting from the log with a certain alacrity in his gait and ascending the hillock of earth that was raised against the stone circumference of the lime-kiln, he thus reached the top of the structure. It was a space of perhaps ten feet across, from edge to edge, presenting a view of the upper surface of the immense mass of broken marble with which the kiln was heaped. All these innumerable blocks and fragments of marble were red-hot and vividly on fire, sending up great spouts of blue flame, which quivered aloft and danced madly, as within a magic circle, and sank and rose again, with continual and multitudinous activity. As the lonely man bent forward over this terrible body of fire, the blasting heat smote up against his person with a breath that, it might be supposed, would have scorched and shrivelled him up in a moment.

Ethan Brand stood erect, and raised his arms on high. The blue flames played upon his face, and imparted the wild and ghastly light which alone could have suited its expression; it was that of a fiend on the verge of plunging into his gulf of intensest torment.

"O Mother Earth," cried he, "who art no more my Mother, and into whose bosom this frame shall never be resolved! O mankind, whose brotherhood I have cast off, and trampled thy great heart beneath my feet! O stars of heaven, that shone on me of old, as if to light me onward and upward!—farewell all, and forever. Come, deadly element of Fire,—henceforth my familiar friend! Embrace me, as I do thee!"

That night the sound of a fearful peal of laughter rolled heavily through the sleep of the lime-burner and his little son; dim shapes of horror and anguish haunted their dreams, and seemed still present in the rude hovel, when they opened their eyes to the day-light.

"Up, boy, up!" cried the lime-burner, staring about him. "Thank Heaven, the night is gone, at last; and rather than pass such another, I would watch my lime-kiln, wide awake, for a twelvemonth. This Ethan Brand, with his humbug of an Unpardonable Sin, has done me no such mighty favor, in taking my place!"

He issued from the hut, followed by little Joe, who kept fast hold of his father's hand. The early sunshine was already pouring its gold upon the mountaintops, and though the valleys were still in shadow, they smiled cheerfully in the promise of the bright day that was hastening onward. The village, completely shut in by hills, which swelled away gently about it, looked as if it had rested peacefully in the hollow of the great hand of Providence. Every dwelling was distinctly visible; the little spires of the two churches pointed upwards, and caught a fore-glimmering of brightness from the sun-gilt skies upon their gilded weather-cocks. The tavern was astir, and the figure of the old, smoke-dried stage-agent, cigar in mouth, was seen beneath the stoop. Old Graylock was glorified with a golden cloud upon his head. Scattered likewise over the breasts of the surrounding mountains, there were heaps of hoary mist, in fantastic shapes, some of them far down into the valley, others high up towards the summits, and still others, of the same family of mist or cloud, hovering in the gold radiance of the upper atmosphere. Stepping from one to another of the clouds that rested on the hills, and thence to the loftier brotherhood that sailed in air, it seemed almost as if a mortal man might thus ascend into the heavenly regions. Earth was so mingled with sky that it was a day-dream to look at it.

To supply that charm of the familiar and homely, which Nature so readily adopts into a scene like this, the stage-coach was rattling down the mountain-road, and the driver sounded his horn, while Echo[8] caught up the notes, and intertwined them into

---

[8] In classical mythology, the nymph Echo was turned into a voice that could only repeat what was said to her.

a rich and varied and elaborate harmony, of which the original performer could lay claim to little share. The great hills played a concert among themselves, each contributing a strain of airy sweetness.

Little Joe's face brightened at once.

"Dear father," cried he, skipping cheerily to and fro, "that strange man is gone, and the sky and the mountains all seem glad of it!"

"Yes," growled the lime-burner, with an oath, "but he has let the fire go down, and no thanks to him if five hundred bushels of lime are not spoiled. If I catch the fellow hereabouts again, I shall feel like tossing him into the furnace!"

With his long pole in his hand, he ascended to the top of the kiln. After a moment's pause, he called to his son.

"Come up here, Joe!" said he.

So little Joe ran up the hillock, and stood by his father's side. The marble was all burnt into perfect, snow-white lime. But on its surface, in the midst of the circle,— snow-white too, and thoroughly converted into lime,—lay a human skeleton, in the attitude of a person who, after long toil, lies down to long repose. Within the ribs —strange to say—was the shape of a human heart.

"Was the fellow's heart made of marble?" cried Bartram, in some perplexity at this phenomenon. "At any rate, it is burnt into what looks like special good lime; and, taking all the bones together, my kiln is half a bushel the richer for him."

So saying, the rude lime-burner lifted his pole, and, letting it fall upon the skeleton, the relics of Ethan Brand were crumbled into fragments.

1850

Preface to *Twice-Told Tales*

The Author of "Twice-Told Tales" has a claim to one distinction, which, as none of his literary brethren will care about disputing it with him, he need not be afraid to mention. He was, for a good many years, the obscurest man of letters in America.

These stories were published in magazines and annuals, extending over a period of ten or twelve years, and comprising the whole of the writer's young manhood, without making (so far as he has ever been aware) the slightest impression on the public. One or two among them, the "Rill from the Town Pump," in perhaps a greater degree than any other, had a pretty wide newspaper circulation; as for the rest, he had no grounds for supposing that, on their first appearance, they met with the good or evil fortune to be read by anybody. Throughout the time above specified, he had no incitement to literary effort in a reasonable prospect of reputation or profit, nothing but the pleasure itself of composition—an enjoyment not at all amiss in its way, and perhaps essential to the merit of the work in hand, but which, in the long run, will hardly keep the chill out of a writer's heart, or the numbness out of his fingers. To this total lack of sympathy, at the age when his mind would naturally have been most effervescent, the public owe it (and it is certainly an effect not to be regretted on either part) that the Author can show nothing for the thought and industry of that portion of his life, save the forty sketches, or thereabouts, included in these volumes.

Much more, indeed, he wrote; and some very small part of it might yet be rummaged out (but it would not be worth the trouble) among the dingy pages of fifteen-or-twenty-year-old periodicals, or within the shabby morocco covers of faded souvenirs. The remainder of the works alluded to had a very brief existence, but, on the score of brilliancy, enjoyed a fate vastly superior to that of their brotherhood, which succeeded in getting through the press. In a word, the Author burned them without mercy or remorse, and, moreover, without any subsequent regret, and had more than one occasion to marvel that such very dull stuff, as he knew his condemned manuscripts to be, should yet have possessed inflammability enough to set the chimney on fire!

After a long while the first collected volume of the "Tales" was published. By this time, if the Author had ever been greatly tormented by literary ambition (which he does not remember or believe to have been the case), it must have perished, beyond resuscitation, in the dearth of nutriment. This was fortunate; for the success of the volume was not such as would have gratified a craving desire for notoriety. A moderate edition was "got rid of" (to use the publisher's very significant phrase) within a reasonable time, but apparently without rendering the writer or his productions much more generally known than before. The great bulk of the reading public probably ignored the book altogether. A few persons read it, and liked it better than it deserved. At an interval of three or four years, the second volume was published, and encountered much the same sort of kindly, but calm, and very limited reception. The circulation of the two volumes was chiefly confined to New England; nor was it until long after this period, if it even yet be the case, that the Author could regard himself as addressing the American public, or, indeed, any public at all. He was merely writing to his known or unknown friends.

As he glances over these long-forgotten pages, and considers his way of life while composing them, the Author can very clearly discern why all this was so. After so many sober years, he would have reason to be ashamed if he could not criticize his own work as fairly as another man's; and, though it is little his business, and perhaps still less his interest, he can hardly resist a temptation to achieve something of the sort. If writers were allowed to do so, and would perform the task with perfect sincerity and unreserve, their opinions of their own productions would often be more valuable and instructive than the works themselves.

At all events, there can be no harm in the Author's remarking that he rather wonders how the "Twice-Told Tales" should have gained what vogue they did than that it was so little and so gradual. They have the pale tint of flowers that blossomed in too retired a shade,—the coolness of a meditative habit, which diffuses itself through the feeling and observation of every sketch. Instead of passion there is sentiment; and, even in what purport to be pictures of actual life, we have allegory, not always so warmly dressed in its habiliments of flesh and blood as to be taken into the reader's mind without a shiver. Whether from lack of power, or an unconquerable reserve, the Author's touches have often an effect of tameness; the merriest man can hardly contrive to laugh at his broadest humor; the tenderest woman, one would suppose, will hardly shed warm tears at his deepest pathos. The book, if you would see anything in it, requires to be read in the clear, brown, twilight atmosphere in which it was written; if opened in the sunshine, it is apt to look exceedingly like a volume of blank pages.

With the foregoing characteristics, proper to the production of a person in retirement (which happened to be the Author's category at the time), the book is devoid of others that we should quite as naturally look for. The sketches are not, it is hardly necessary to say, profound; but it is rather more remarkable that they seldom, if ever, show any design on the writer's part to make them so. They have none of the abstruseness of idea, or obscurity of expression, which mark the written communications of a solitary mind with itself. They never need translation. It is, in fact, the style of a man of society. Every sentence, so far as it embodies thought or sensibility, may be understood and felt by anybody who will give himself the trouble to read it, and will take up the book in a proper mood.

This statement of apparently opposite peculiarities leads us to a perception of what the sketches truly are. They are not the talk of a secluded man with his own mind and heart (had it been so, they could hardly have failed to be more deeply and permanently valuable), but his attempts, and very imperfectly successful ones, to open an intercourse with the world.

The Author would regret to be understood as speaking sourly or querulously of the slight mark made by his earlier literary efforts on the Public at large. It is so far the contrary, that he has been moved to write this Preface chiefly as affording him an opportunity to express how much enjoyment he has owed to these volumes, both before and since their publication. They are the memorials of very tranquil and not unhappy years. They failed, it is true,—nor could it have been otherwise,—in winning an extensive popularity. Occasionally, however, when he deemed them entirely forgotten, a paragraph or an article, from a native or foreign critic, would gratify his instincts of authorship with unexpected praise,—too generous praise, indeed, and too little alloyed with censure, which, therefore, he learned the better to inflict upon himself. And, by the by, it is a very suspicious symptom of a deficiency of the popular element in a book when it calls forth no harsh criticism. This has been particularly the fortune of the "TWICE-TOLD TALES." They made no enemies, and were so little known and talked about that those who read, and chanced to like them, were apt to conceive the sort of kindness for the book which a person naturally feels for a discovery of his own.

This kindly feeling (in some cases, at least) extended to the Author, who, on the internal evidence of his sketches, came to be regarded as a mild, shy, gentle, melancholic, exceedingly sensitive, and not very forcible man, hiding his blushes under an assumed name, the quaintness of which was supposed, somehow or other, to symbolize his personal and literary traits. He is by no means certain that some of his subsequent productions have not been influenced and modified by a natural desire to fill up so amiable an outline, and to act in consonance with the character assigned to him; nor, even now, could he forfeit it without a few tears of tender sensibility. To conclude, however: these volumes have opened the way to most agreeable associations, and to the formation of imperishable friendships; and there are many golden threads interwoven with his present happiness, which he can follow up more or less directly, until he finds their commencement here; so that his pleasant pathway among realities seems to proceed out of the Dreamland of his youth, and to be bordered with just enough of its shadowy foliage to shelter him from the heat of the day. He is therefore satisfied with what the "TWICE-TOLD TALES" have done for him and feels it to be far better than fame.

LENOX, *January* 11, 1851.

1851/1851

---

from The House of the Seven Gables

Preface

When a writer calls his work a Romance, it need hardly be observed that he wishes to claim a certain latitude, both as to its fashion and material, which he would not have felt himself entitled to assume had he professed to be writing a Novel. The latter form of composition is presumed to aim at a very minute fidelity, not merely to the possible, but to the probable and ordinary course of man's experience. The former —while, as a work of art, it must rigidly subject itself to laws, and while it sins unpardonably so far as it may swerve aside from the truth of the human heart—has fairly a right to present that truth under circumstances, to a great extent, of the writer's own choosing or creation. If he think fit, also, he may so manage his atmospherical medium as to bring out or mellow the lights and deepen and enrich the shadows of the picture. He will be wise, no doubt, to make a very moderate use of the privileges here stated, and, especially, to mingle the Marvellous rather as a slight, delicate, and evanescent flavor, than as any portion of the actual substance of the dish offered to the public. He can hardly be said, however, to commit a literary crime even if he disregard this caution.

In the present work, the author has proposed to himself—but with what success, fortunately, it is not for him to judge—to keep undeviatingly within his immunities. The point of view in which this tale comes under the Romantic definition lies in the attempt to connect a bygone time with the very present that is flitting away from us. It is a legend prolonging itself, from an epoch now gray in the distance, down into our own broad daylight, and bringing along with it some of its legendary mist, which the reader, according to his pleasure, may either disregard, or allow it to float almost imperceptibly about the characters and events for the sake of a picturesque effect. The narrative, it may be, is woven of so humble a texture as to require this advantage, and, at the same time, to render it the more difficult of attainment.

Many writers lay very great stress upon some definite moral purpose, at which they profess to aim their works. Not to be deficient in this particular, the author has provided himself with a moral,—the truth, namely, that the wrong-doing of one generation lives into the successive ones, and, divesting itself of every temporary advantage, becomes a pure and uncontrollable mischief; and he would feel it a singular gratification if this romance might effectually convince mankind—or, indeed, any one man—of the folly of tumbling down an avalanche of ill-gotten gold, or real estate, on the heads of an unfortunate posterity, thereby to maim and crush them, until the accumulated mass shall be scattered abroad in its original atoms. In good faith, however, he is not sufficiently imaginative to flatter himself with the slightest hope of this kind. When romances do really teach anything, or produce any effective operation, it is usually through a far more subtle process than the ostensible one. The author has considered it hardly worth his while, therefore, relentlessly to impale the story with its moral as with an iron rod,—or, rather, as by sticking a pin through a butterfly,—thus at once depriving it of life, and causing it to stiffen in an ungainly and unnatural attitude. A high truth, indeed, fairly, finely, and skilfully wrought out, brightening at every step, and crowning the final development of a work of fiction, may add an artistic glory, but is never any truer, and seldom any more evident, at the last page than at the first.

The reader may perhaps choose to assign an actual locality to the imaginary events of this narrative. If permitted by the historical connection,—which, though slight, was essential to his plan,—the author would very willingly have avoided anything of this nature. Not to speak of other objections, it exposes the romance to an inflexible and exceedingly dangerous species of criticism, by bringing his fancy-pictures almost into positive contact with the realities of the moment. It has been no part of his object, however, to describe local manners, nor in any way to meddle with the characteristics of a community for whom he cherishes a proper respect and a natural regard. He trusts not to be considered as unpardonably offending by laying out a street that infringes upon nobody's private rights, and appropriating a lot of land which had no visible owner, and building a house of materials long in use for constructing castles in the air. The personages of the tale—though they give themselves out to be of ancient stability and considerable prominence—are really of the author's own making, or, at all events, of his own mixing; their virtues can shed no lustre, nor their defects redound, in the remotest degree, to the discredit of the venerable town[1] of which they profess to be inhabitants. He would be glad, therefore, if—especially in the quarter to which he alludes—the book may be read strictly as a Romance, having a great deal more to do with the clouds over head than with any portion of the actual soil of the County of Essex.

LENOX, January 27, 1851.

1851/1851

Herman Melville
1819–1891

The twentieth century recognizes Herman Melville as a major American writer, but in his lifetime Melville was regarded only as an exciting and once-popular travel writer whose strange fiction cast doubt on his sanity. Melville traced his ancestry to two Revolutionary War figures. His mother was the daughter of

---

[1] Salem, Massachusetts.

Albany's wealthy General Peter Gansvoort, and his father, Allan, was a New York City merchant-importer. The family took pride in its ties to American history. Typical of their educated, merchant class, they enrolled Herman, the third child of eight, at the New York Male High School at the age of seven. Evidently his parents foresaw a career in business for him, perhaps the very business that enabled the Melville family to prosper. That situation changed drastically in 1830, however, when the overextended business of young Herman's father collapsed, forcing him into bankruptcy. The family moved to Albany, where for a time Allan Melville recovered financially. Herman and his two brothers attended the Albany Academy, where the boy saw his older brother, Gansvoort, distinguish himself in prestigious classical subjects while young Herman pursued the commercial course. But once again Allan Melville suffered business reverses, which led to the mental and physical breakdown that preceded his death in 1832. These family experiences would ultimately emerge in *Pierre*.

Melville's next years were a scramble for a career. Forced to leave school, he became successively a bank clerk, a farmhand on the western Massachusetts acreage of his uncle Thomas, a store clerk and bookkeeper for his successful older brother Gansvoort, and, when Gansvoort's business failed, a country schoolmaster. In 1838 the family moved to Lansingburgh, in upstate New York, where they lived thriftily with aid from a wealthy relative. Hoping—in vain, as it turned out—for work on the new Erie Canal, Melville enrolled in a course in engineering and surveying at the local academy. When no job materialized, Melville looked downstate, toward New York City, where a packet to Liverpool had a berth for him. Melville later developed that maritime experience into the novel *Redburn*. Back in the United States in 1840, the young man traveled West to Illinois. Though his trip included a Mississippi riverboat ride later crucial to the novel *The Confidence-Man*, it yielded no immediate career prospects. Early the next year, doubtless feeling desperate, Melville shipped out from New Bedford, Massachusetts, on the whaling ship *Acushnet*, bound for the South Pacific.

Melville's maritime adventures have been well documented. The *Acushnet* killed few whales, and morale sank as dissension mounted between the captain and the officers. With a shipmate, Melville jumped ship in summer 1842 and lived with a native tribe in the Marquesas for several weeks. Picked up by an Australian whaler, he participated in a revolt that landed him in a Tahiti prison along with a physician-companion, who later helped him explore the flora and fauna of Tahiti and Eimeo, where Melville shipped aboard a Nantucket whaler. Discharged at Honolulu, Melville stayed in Hawaii for a few months as a beachcomber, then signed onto the frigate *United States*. That ship's captain of the maintop, John J. ("Jack") Chase, proved to be a Melvillian hero. (He appears as a character in *White-Jacket*, a novel on the severity of maritime discipline, and *Billy Budd* is dedicated to him.) The *United States* toured the Pacific before sailing for Boston, arriving in autumn 1844, when Melville was twenty-five years old and, after drawing his pay, an unemployed sailor.

A few months later, again living at home, Melville began sorting out the meaning of his adventures and his life. His introspection led to the psychological unfolding he graphed in all his writings. "Until I was twenty-five," he later wrote to his friend and fellow writer, Nathaniel Hawthorne, "I had no development at all. From my twenty-fifth year I date my life."

Melville's self-styled birth occurred when he wrote fictionalized versions of his South Sea adventures. *Typee* (1846) and *Omoo* (1847) were popular successes with American and English readers eager for tales of exotic places. Some close readers were offended by Melville's critique of the missionaries who "evangelized" and "civilized" the islanders into "draft horses" or "beasts of burden," but prospects were generally bright for the young author. Washington Irving, American literature's patriarchal figure, thought *Typee* brilliant, and even at the end of the century the writer Henry Adams consulted it in preparation for his South Sea voyage.

Largely on the strength of his prospects as a professional author, Melville married Elizabeth Shaw and settled in New York City in a house that also accommodated his younger brother Allan and Allan's new bride, Melville's mother, and his unmarried sisters. He soon took his place in the New York literary life dominated by the prominent editor and writer Evert Duyckinck, for whose *Literary World* Melville wrote reviews. Unknown to the young author, his career was about to reach a critical point. Had he continued to write adventure stories in the mold of his early books, he might have been a financially successful "pen-and-ink man" and a footnote in literary history. Instead, Melville's third novel, *Mardi,* took a radical midway departure into philosophy, satire, fantasy, and allegory. The young writer had discovered the works of Robert Burton, Sir Thomas Browne, Francois Rabelais, and others and, encouraged by their example, broke the bounds of conventional form. He was taken aback when the public spurned his effort and reviewers urged him to resume the style and structure of his adventure narratives.

Melville now faced the terrible problem common to American writers from the eighteenth century into the twentieth. To earn a living from the sale of his books, he needed to win the very readers whose professed values and beliefs he attacked. How could he possibly find favor with a public that wished only to be entertained, when he offered probing, experimental, critical writings in the face of social complacency? The issue was especially pressing because Melville now had an infant son, Malcolm, to support. Chastened, he wrote two novels intended to satisfy popular taste, *Redburn* (1849) and *White-Jacket* (1850), based respectively on his youthful Liverpool voyage and on his South Pacific tour. The style of both is gently ironic, though Melville felt constrained by both efforts and called them the literary equivalent of "sawing wood." Determined to realize maximal profits from his literary slave labor, Melville carried proofs of *White-Jacket* to England personally to arrange terms with his London publisher. After brief visits to France and Germany, he returned home, pleased when his books earned critical acclaim and sold well.

A newly confident Melville now began his whaling book. Initially he may have intended once again to write an adventure story based on his experience on whaling ships. But Melville had been rereading Shakespeare and the works of Thomas Carlyle. He also had made the acquaintance of Nathaniel Hawthorne, whom he would soon call an American Shakespeare in a review-essay entitled "Hawthorne and His Mosses," a survey of the state of American writers in the

English-speaking world. In *Moby-Dick,* Melville continued to unfold his psyche, and the style and structure of the new work embodied the change. He was relentlessly speculative, posing challenge to the literary and social status quo, probing society's hypocrisies, its complacency, its contradictions.

Meanwhile, the crowded conditions of the New York City household made it necessary for Melville to move his family. Western Massachusetts had become a summer resort for American writers, who picnicked together in an occasional "pleasure party." Doubtless anticipating the seasonal literary comradeship, Melville moved his family in autumn 1850 to a 160-acre farm called Arrowhead, purchased in part with a loan from the formidable Judge Lemuel Shaw, Melville's father-in-law. By winter Melville had completed his book on whaling, which he revised in the study whose window looked out upon Mt. Greylock, its peak shaped rather like the outline of a whale. Customarily Melville wrote into the afternoon, then read and gathered materials in the evening and at night. His meals were sometimes served on trays left at his study door. Beyond the door and walls he could hear all household noises.

Moby-Dick (1851) was published to a mixed reception, and sales were disappointing. This masculine, experimental novel did not appeal to a novel-reading public principally comprising women. By now Melville was financially pressed, in debt to his publisher, Harper, for advances, and responsible for a household that included his mother, his sisters, one small child, and a pregnant wife. Once again he attempted to capture a popular audience, this time with a deliberately sentimental gothic novel. Melville promised "a rural bowl of milk" in *Pierre,* the story of a young landed gentleman. Instead the novel became a dark exploration of sexuality, identity, depravity, tragic and inevitable destruction, and, covertly, the plight of the American artist. The manuscript was long, and Harper offered poor royalties. The reception of the book was hostile. Reviewers attacked Melville personally. Everett Duyckinck, a reviewer who had thought *Moby-Dick* immoral, was scandalized and concluded that Melville had gone insane.

Under severe strain, Melville managed to keep apace of his farm work, though the family feared that his health was in jeopardy. And financial problems were less important that the public's repudiation of his work. With the election of Franklin Pierce, Melville's well-connected relatives (as well as Pierce's onetime classmate Hawthorne) tried to secure him a political appointment, but their efforts were unsuccessful. Thereafter Melville turned to short fiction (such as "Bartleby, the Scrivener"), which he wrote for such magazines as *Harper's* and *Putnam's,* and cast in a style intended to be accessible to a large readership. The short novel *Israel Potter* was written along such lines. A fire at Harper's destroyed an inventory of Melville's work, and to meet his obligations, including debts to the publisher, he continued to write stories and sketches into the mid-1850s.

In April 1856, Melville sold half of his farm. He saw *The Piazza Tales* published in that year, and he also prepared for publication a new novel, *The Confidence-Man* (1857), which criticized American culture and its corrupt language. The work satirized several American writers, including Ralph Waldo Emerson and Henry David Thoreau. But it lacked conventional action and plot, and sales were dismal. Melville, now thirty-seven, was tired and frustrated. The writings he most cared about were met with public indifference, while his potboilers brought meager returns. He needed to find another occupation.

Melville went abroad alone in 1856 for his health under the financial sponsorship of his family. He toured Scotland, then went on to Liverpool, England, where he renewed his friendship with Hawthorne, the U.S. consul. In the Mediterranean, Melville visited Malta, Greece, and Egypt. In 1857, he toured the Holy Land, which became the setting for his long poem *Clarel*. After hasty tours of Italy, Switzerland, Germany, and the Netherlands, he returned to England and sailed for home. For two seasons Melville earned a living of sorts by giving lectures on topics like "Statues in Rome" and "The South Seas." In 1860 he traveled again briefly, to San Francisco. The death of his father-in-law and the inheritance of a portion of the estate enabled Melville to move to New York City. In 1866 Harper published his Civil War poems, *Battle-Pieces,* though that work, too, was soon forgotten. Melville seemed destined, as he once observed to Hawthorne, to be known as "the man who lived among the cannibals." Considered a failure by his in-laws, Melville at last obtained a political job in 1866 as deputy inspector of customs in New York City. Through the 1860s and 1870s he worked on *Clarel,* which became an eighteen-thousand-line poem in which this "pondering man," as Melville called himself, explored the relation between religious faith and skepticism in the age of Darwinian theory.

Melville's last years were tragic and ironic. Several bequests left him and his wife materially comfortable, but his first child, Malcolm, had committed suicide in 1867, and his second, Stanwix, had become a drifter; Stanwyx died in San Francisco in 1886. One of his daughters, Bessie, was severely arthritic, and the second, Frances, felt only bitterness toward her father. In the late 1880s Melville wrote *Billy Budd,* a work perhaps motivated by the suicide of his son and found nearly complete among his papers after his death. *Billy Budd* was published in 1924 and stands as a major achievement in American literature. When Melville died, a newspaper obituary speculated that "his own generation has long thought him dead." Hawthorne had already offered a fitting epitaph: "He has a very high and noble nature, and better worth immortality than most of us."

Further Reading:
R. Chase, *Herman Melville: A Critical Study,* 1949.
N. Arvin, *Herman Melville,* 1950, 1957.
J. Leyda, *The Melville Log,* 2 vols., 1951, 1969.
L. Howard, *Herman Melville,* 1951, 1958.
The Letters of Herman Melville, ed. M. Davis and W. Gilman, 1960.
E. Dryden, *Melville's Thematics of Form,* 1969.
J. Seelye, *Melville: The Ironic Diagram,* 1970.
R. B. Bickley, *The Method of Melville's Short Fiction,* 1975.
T. Herbert, *Marquesan Encounters,* 1981.

Texts:
"Bartleby" from *The Piazza Tales,* ed. E. Oliver, 1962.
Billy Budd, Sailor, ed. H. Hayford and M. Sealts, 1962.
Battle Pieces and Aspects of the War, 1866.
Remaining selections from *The Collected Poems,* ed. H. P. Vincent, 1948, 1981.
See also *The Works of Herman Melville,* 16 vols., 1922–1924, 1963.
Complete Works of Herman Melville, 14 vols. projected, 7 published, ed. H. Vincent, 1947–1969, superseded by the ongoing *Writings of Herman Melville,* 16 vols. projected, ed. H. Hayford, 1968–.
Selected Poems of Herman Melville, ed. H. Cohen, 1964.

Bartleby, the Scrivener

I am a rather elderly man. The nature of my avocations, for the last thirty years, has brought me into more than ordinary contact with what would seem an interesting and somewhat singular set of men, of whom, as yet, nothing, that I know of, has ever been written—I mean, the law-copyists, or scriveners. I have known very many of them, professionally and privately, and, if I pleased, could relate divers histories, at which good-natured gentlemen might smile, and sentimental souls might weep. But I waive the biographies of all other scriveners, for a few passages in the life of Bartleby, who was a scrivener, the strangest I ever saw, or heard of. While, of other law-copyists, I might write the complete life, of Bartleby nothing of that sort can be done. I believe that no materials exist, for a full and satisfactory biography of this man. It is an irreparable loss to literature. Bartleby was one of those beings of whom nothing is ascertainable, except from the original sources, and, in his case, those are very small. What my own astonished eyes saw of Bartleby, *that* is all I know of him, except, indeed, one vague report, which will appear in the sequel.

Ere introducing the scrivener, as he first appeared to me, it is fit I make some mention of myself, my *employés,* my business, my chambers, and general surroundings; because some such description is indispensable to an adequate understanding of the chief character about to be presented. Imprimis: I am a man who, from his youth upwards, has been filled with a profound conviction that the easiest way of life is the best. Hence, though I belong to a profession proverbially energetic and nervous, even to turbulence, at times, yet nothing of that sort have I ever suffered to invade my peace. I am one of those unambitious lawyers who never addresses a jury, or in any way draws down public applause; but, in the cool tranquillity of a snug retreat, do a snug business among rich men's bonds, and mortgages, and title-deeds. All who know me, consider me an eminently *safe* man. The late John Jacob Astor, a personage little given to poetic enthusiasm, had no hesitation in pronouncing my first grand point to be prudence; my next, method. I do not speak it in vanity, but simply record the fact, that I was not unemployed in my profession by the late John Jacob Astor; a name which, I admit, I love to repeat; for it hath a rounded and orbicular sound to it, and rings like unto bullion. I will freely add, that I was not insensible to the late John Jacob Astor's good opinion.

Some time prior to the period at which this little history begins, my avocations had been largely increased. The good old office, now extinct in the State of New York, of a Master in Chancery, had been conferred upon me. It was not a very arduous office, but very pleasantly remunerative. I seldom lose my temper; much more seldom indulge in dangerous indignation at wrongs and outrages; but, I must be permitted to be rash here, and declare, that I consider the sudden and violent abrogation of the office of Master in Chancery, by the new Constitution, as a—premature act; inasmuch as I had counted upon a life-lease of the profits, whereas I only received those of a few short years. But this is by the way.

My chambers were up stairs, at No. ———— Wall Street. At one end, they looked upon the white wall of the interior of a spacious sky-light shaft, penetrating the building from top to bottom.

This view might have been considered rather tame than otherwise, deficient in what landscape painters call "life." But, if so, the view from the other end of my chambers offered, at least, a contrast, if nothing more. In that direction, my windows commanded an unobstructed view of a lofty brick wall, black by age and everlasting shade; which wall required no spy-glass to bring out its lurking beauties, but, for the benefit of all near-sighted spectators, was pushed up to within ten feet of my window panes. Owing to the great height of the surrounding buildings, and my chambers being on the second floor, the interval between this wall and mine not a little resembled a huge square cistern.

At the period just preceding the advent of Bartleby, I had two persons as copyists in my employment, and a promising lad as an office-boy. First, Turkey; second, Nippers; third, Ginger Nut. These may seem names, the like of which are not usually found in the Directory. In truth, they were nicknames, mutually conferred upon each other by my three clerks, and were deemed expressive of their respective persons or characters. Turkey was a short, pursy[1] Englishman, of about my own age—that is, somewhere not far from sixty. In the morning, one might say, his face was of a fine florid hue, but after twelve o'clock, meridian—his dinner hour—it blazed like a grate full of Christmas coals; and continued blazing—but, as it were, with a gradual wane —till six o'clock, P.M., or thereabouts; after which, I saw no more of the proprietor of the face, which, gaining its meridian with the sun, seemed to set with it, to rise, culminate, and decline the following day, with the like regularity and undiminished glory. There are many singular coincidences I have known in the course of my life, not the least among which was the fact, that, exactly when Turkey displayed his fullest beams from his red and radiant countenance, just then, too, at that critical moment, began the daily period when I considered his business capacities as seriously disturbed for the remainder of the twenty-four hours. Not that he was absolutely idle, or averse to business, then; far from it. The difficulty was, he was apt to be altogether too energetic. There was a strange, inflamed, flurried, flighty recklessness of activity about him. He would be incautious in dipping his pen into his inkstand. All his blots upon my documents were dropped there after twelve o'clock, meridian. Indeed, not only would he be reckless, and sadly given to making blots in the afternoon, but, some days, he went further, and was rather noisy. At such times, too, his face flamed with augmented blazonry, as if cannel coal had been heaped on anthracite. He made an unpleasant racket with his chair; spilled his sand-box; in mending his pens, impatiently split them all to pieces, and threw them on the floor in a sudden passion; stood up, and leaned over his table, boxing his papers about in a most indecorous manner, very sad to behold in an elderly man like him. Nevertheless, as he was in many ways a most valuable person to me, and all the time before twelve o'clock, meridian, was the quickest, steadiest creature, too, accomplishing a great deal of work in a style not easily to be matched—for these reasons, I was willing to overlook his eccentricities, though, indeed, occasionally, I remonstrated with him. I did this very gently, however, because, though the civilest, nay, the blandest and most reverential of men in

[1] Short-winded, especially from fatness.

the morning, yet, in the afternoon, he was disposed, upon provocation, to be slightly rash with his tongue—in fact, insolent. Now, valuing his morning services as I did, and resolved not to lose them—yet, at the same time, made uncomfortable by his inflamed ways after twelve o'clock—and being a man of peace, unwilling by my admonitions to call forth unseemly retorts from him, I took upon me, one Saturday noon (he was always worse on Saturdays) to hint to him, very kindly, that, perhaps, now that he was growing old, it might be well to abridge his labors; in short, he need not come to my chambers after twelve o'clock, but, dinner over, had best go home to his lodgings, and rest himself till tea-time. But no; he insisted upon his afternoon devotions. His countenance became intolerably fervid, as he oratorically assured me —gesticulating with a long ruler at the other end of the room—that if his services in the morning were useful, how indispensable, then, in the afternoon?

"With submission, sir," said Turkey, on this occasion, "I consider myself your right-hand man. In the morning I but marshal and deploy my columns; but in the afternoon I put myself at their head, and gallantly charge the foe, thus"—and he made a violent thrust with the ruler.

"But the blots, Turkey," intimated I.

"True; but, with submission, sir, behold these hairs! I am getting old. Surely, sir, a blot or two of a warm afternoon is not to be severely urged against gray hairs. Old age—even if it blot the page—is honorable. With submission, sir, we *both* are getting old."

This appeal to my fellow-feeling was hardly to be resisted. At all events, I saw that go he would not. So, I made up my mind to let him stay, resolving, nevertheless, to see to it that, during the afternoon, he had to do with my less important papers.

Nippers, the second on my list, was a whiskered, sallow, and, upon the whole, rather piratical-looking young man, of about five and twenty. I always deemed him the victim of two evil powers—ambition and indigestion. The ambition was evinced by a certain impatience of the duties of a mere copyist, an unwarrantable usurpation of strictly professional affairs, such as the original drawing up of legal documents. The indigestion seemed betokened in an occasional nervous testiness and grinning irritability, causing the teeth to audibly grind together over mistakes committed in copying; unnecessary maledictions, hissed, rather than spoken, in the heat of business; and especially by a continual discontent with the height of the table where he worked. Though of a very ingenious mechanical turn, Nippers could never get this table to suit him. He put chips under it, blocks of various sorts, bits of pasteboard, and at last went so far as to attempt an exquisite adjustment, by final pieces of folded blotting-paper. But no invention would answer. If, for the sake of easing his back, he brought the table lid at a sharp angle well up towards his chin, and wrote there like a man using the steep roof of a Dutch house for his desk, then he declared that it stopped the circulation in his arms. If now he lowered the table to his waistbands, and stooped over it in writing, then there was a sore aching in his back. In short, the truth of the matter was, Nippers knew not what he wanted. Or, if he wanted anything, it was to be rid of a scrivener's table altogether. Among the manifestations of his diseased ambition was a fondness he had for receiving visits from certain ambiguous-looking fellows in seedy coats, whom he called his clients. Indeed, I was aware that not only was he, at times, considerable of a ward-politician, but he occasionally did a little business at the Justices' courts, and was not unknown on the steps of the Tombs. I have good reason to believe, however, that one individual who called upon him at my chambers, and who, with a grand air, he insisted was his client, was no other than a dun,[2] and the alleged title-deed, a bill. But, with all his failings, and the annoyances he caused me, Nippers, like his compatriot Turkey, was a very useful man to me; wrote a neat, swift hand; and, when he chose, was not deficient in a gentlemanly sort of deportment. Added to this, he always dressed in a gentlemanly sort of way; and so, incidentally, reflected credit upon my chambers. Whereas, with respect to Turkey, I had much ado to keep him from being a reproach to me. His clothes were apt to look oily, and smell of eating-houses. He wore his pantaloons very loose and baggy in summer. His coats were execrable; his hat not to be handled. But while the hat was a thing of indifference to me, inasmuch as his natural civility and deference, as a dependent Englishman, always led him to doff it the moment he entered the room, yet his coat was another matter. Concerning his coats, I reasoned with him; but with no effect. The truth was, I suppose, that a man with so small an income could not afford to sport such a lustrous face and a lustrous coat at one and the same time. As Nippers once observed, Turkey's money went chiefly for red ink. One winter day, I presented Turkey with a highly respectable-looking coat of my own—a padded gray coat, of a most comfortable warmth, and which buttoned straight up from the knee to the neck. I thought Turkey would appreciate the favor, and abate his rashness and obstreperousness of afternoons. But no; I verily believe that buttoning himself up in so downy and blanket-like a coat had a pernicious effect upon him—upon the same principle that too much oats are bad for horses. In fact, precisely as a rash, restive horse is said to feel his oats, so Turkey felt his coat. It made him insolent. He was a man whom prosperity harmed.

Though, concerning the self-indulgent habits of Turkey, I had my own private surmises, yet, touching Nippers, I was well persuaded that, whatever might be his faults in other respects, he was, at least, a temperate young man. But, indeed, nature herself seemed to have been his vintner, and, at his birth, charged him so thoroughly with an irritable, brandy-like disposition, that all subsequent potations were needless. When I consider how, amid the stillness of my chambers, Nippers would sometimes impatiently rise from his seat, and stooping over his table, spread his arms wide apart, seize the whole desk, and move it, and jerk it, with a grim, grinding motion on the floor, as if the table were a perverse voluntary agent, intent on thwarting and vexing him, I plainly perceive that, for Nippers, brandy-and-water were altogether superfluous.

It was fortunate for me that, owing to its peculiar cause—indigestion—the irritability and consequent nervousness of Nippers were mainly observable in the morning, while in the afternoon he was comparatively mild. So that, Turkey's paroxysms only coming on about twelve o'clock, I never had to do with their eccentricities at one time. Their fits relieved each other, like guards. When Nippers's was on, Turkey's was off; and *vice versa*. This was a good natural arrangement, under the circumstances.

Ginger Nut, the third on my list, was a lad, some twelve years old. His father was a car-man, ambitious of seeing his son on the bench instead of a cart, before he died. So he sent him to my office, as student at law, errand-boy, cleaner and sweeper, at the rate of one dollar a week. He had a little desk to himself, but he did not use it

[2] Bill collector.

much. Upon inspection, the drawer exhibited a great array of the shells of various sorts of nuts. Indeed, to this quick-witted youth, the whole noble science of the law was contained in a nutshell. Not the least among the employments of Ginger Nut, as well as one which he discharged with the most alacrity, was his duty as cake and apple purveyor for Turkey and Nippers. Copying law-papers being proverbially a dry, husky sort of business, my two scriveners were fain to moisten their mouths very often with Spitzenbergs,[3] to be had at the numerous stalls nigh the Custom House and Post Office. Also, they sent Ginger Nut very frequently for that peculiar cake —small, flat, round, and very spicy—after which he had been named by them. Of a cold morning, when business was but dull, Turkey would gobble up scores of these cakes, as if they were mere wafers—indeed, they sell them at the rate of six or eight for a penny—the scrape of his pen blending with the crunching of the crisp particles in his mouth. Of all the fiery afternoon blunders and flurried rashnesses of Turkey, was his once moistening a ginger-cake between his lips, and clapping it on to a mortgage, for a seal. I came within an ace of dismissing him then. But he mollified me by making an oriental bow, and saying—

"With submission, sir, it was generous of me to find you in stationery on my own account."

Now my original business—that of a conveyancer and title hunter, and drawer-up of recondite documents of all sorts[4]—was considerably increased by receiving the master's office. There was now great work for scriveners. Not only must I push the clerks already with me, but I must have additional help.

In answer to my advertisement, a motionless young man one morning stood upon my office threshold, the door being open, for it was summer. I can see that figure now —pallidly neat, pitiably respectable, incurably forlorn! It was Bartleby.

After a few words touching his qualifications, I engaged him, glad to have among my corps of copyists a man of so singularly sedate an aspect, which I thought might operate beneficially upon the flighty temper of Turkey, and the fiery one of Nippers.

I should have stated before that ground glass folding-doors divided my premises into two parts, one of which was occupied by my scriveners, the other by myself. According to my humor, I threw open these doors, or closed them. I resolved to assign Bartleby a corner by the folding-doors, but on my side of them, so as to have this quiet man within easy call, in case any trifling thing was to be done. I placed his desk close up to a small side-window in that part of the room, a window which originally had afforded a lateral view of certain grimy back-yards and bricks, but which, owing to subsequent erections, commanded at present no view at all, though it gave some light. Within three feet of the panes was a wall, and the light came down from far above, between two lofty buildings, as from a very small opening in a dome. Still further to a satisfactory arrangement, I procured a high green folding screen, which might entirely isolate Bartleby from my sight, though not remove him from my voice. And thus, in a manner, privacy and society were conjoined.

At first, Bartleby did an extraordinary quantity of writing. As if long famishing for something to copy, he seemed to gorge himself on my documents. There was no

---

[3] Apples.
[4] Legal work beyond ordinary knowledge, such as drawing up deeds for property transfers or checking records to ascertain that there are no prior claims on property to be transferred.

pause for digestion. He ran a day and night line, copying by sun-light and by candle-light. I should have been quite delighted with his application, had he been cheerfully industrious. But he wrote on silently, palely, mechanically.

It is, of course, an indispensable part of a scrivener's business to verify the accuracy of his copy, word by word. Where there are two or more scriveners in an office, they assist each other in this examination, one reading from the copy, the other holding the original. It is a very dull, wearisome, and lethargic affair. I can readily imagine that, to some sanguine temperaments, it would be altogether intolerable. For example, I cannot credit that the mettlesome poet, Byron, would have contentedly sat down with Bartleby to examine a law document of, say five hundred pages, closely written in a crimpy hand.

Now and then, in the haste of business, it had been my habit to assist in comparing some brief document myself, calling Turkey or Nippers for this purpose. One object I had, in placing Bartleby so handy to me behind the screen, was, to avail myself of his services on such trivial occasions. It was on the third day, I think, of his being with me, and before any necessity had arisen for having his own writing examined, that, being much hurried to complete a small affair I had in hand, I abruptly called to Bartleby. In my haste and natural expectancy of instant compliance, I sat with my head bent over the original on my desk, and my right hand sideways, and somewhat nervously extended with the copy, so that, immediately upon emerging from his retreat, Bartleby might snatch it and proceed to business without the least delay.

In this very attitude did I sit when I called to him, rapidly stating what it was I wanted him to do—namely, to examine a small paper with me. Imagine my surprise, nay, my consternation, when, without moving from his privacy, Bartleby, in a singularly mild, firm voice, replied, "I would prefer not to."

I sat awhile in perfect silence, rallying my stunned faculties. Immediately it occurred to me that my ears had deceived me, or Bartleby had entirely misunderstood my meaning. I repeated my request in the clearest tone I could assume; but in quite as clear a one came the previous reply, "I would prefer not to."

"Prefer not to," echoed I, rising in high excitement, and crossing the room with a stride. "What do you mean? Are you moon-struck? I want you to help me compare this sheet here—take it," and I thrust it towards him.

"I would prefer not to," said he.

I looked at him steadfastly. His face was leanly composed; his gray eye dimly calm. Not a wrinkle of agitation rippled him. Had there been the least uneasiness, anger, impatience or impertinence in his manner; in other words, had there been any thing ordinarily human about him, doubtless I should have violently dismissed him from the premises. But as it was, I should have as soon thought of turning my pale plaster-of-paris bust of Cicero[5] out of doors. I stood gazing at him awhile, as he went on with his own writing, and then reseated myself at my desk. This is very strange, thought I. What had one best do? But my business hurried me. I concluded to forget the matter for the present, reserving it for my future leisure. So calling Nippers from the other room, the paper was speedly examined.

A few days after this, Bartleby concluded four lengthy documents, being quadru-

[5] Roman statesman and orator (106–42 B.C.).

plicates of a week's testimony taken before me in my High Court of Chancery. It became necessary to examine them. It was an important suit, and great accuracy was imperative. Having all things arranged, I called Turkey, Nippers, and Ginger Nut, from the next room, meaning to place the four copies in the hands of my four clerks, while I should read from the original. Accordingly, Turkey, Nippers, and Ginger Nut had taken their seats in a row, each with his document in his hand, when I called to Bartleby to join this interesting group.

"Bartleby! quick, I am waiting."

I heard a slow scrape of his chair legs on the uncarpeted floor, and soon he appeared standing at the entrance of his hermitage.

"What is wanted?" said he, mildly.

"The copies, the copies," said I, hurriedly. "We are going to examine them. There"—and I held towards him the fourth quadruplicate.

"I would prefer not to," he said, and gently disappeared behind the screen.

For a few moments I was turned into a pillar of salt,[6] standing at the head of my seated column of clerks. Recovering myself, I advanced towards the screen, and demanded the reason for such extraordinary conduct.

"*Why* do you refuse?"

"I would prefer not to."

With any other man I should have flown outright into a dreadful passion, scorned all further words, and thrust him ignominiously from my presence. But there was something about Bartleby that not only strangely disarmed me, but, in a wonderful manner, touched and disconcerted me. I began to reason with him.

"These are your own copies we are about to examine. It is labor saving to you, because one examination will answer for your four papers. It is common usage. Every copyist is bound to help examine his copy. Is it not so? Will you not speak? Answer!"

"I prefer not to," he replied in a flutelike tone. It seemed to me that, while I had been addressing him, he carefully revolved every statement that I made; fully comprehended the meaning; could not gainsay the irresistible conclusion; but, at the same time, some paramount consideration prevailed with him to reply as he did.

"You are decided, then, not to comply with my request—a request made according to common usage and common sense?"

He briefly gave me to understand, that on that point my judgment was sound. Yes: his decision was irreversible.

It is not seldom the case that, when a man is browbeaten in some unprecedented and violently unreasonable way, he begins to stagger in his own plainest faith. He begins, as it were, vaguely to surmise that, wonderful as it may be, all the justice and all the reason is on the other side. Accordingly, if any disinterested persons are present, he turns to them for some reinforcement of his own faltering mind.

"Turkey," said I, "what do you think of this? Am I not right?"

"With submission, sir," said Turkey, in his blandest tone, "I think that you are."

"Nippers," said I, "what do *you* think of it?"

"I think I should kick him out of the office."

(The reader, of nice perceptions, will here perceive that, it being morning, Turkey's

---

[6] Like Lot's disobedient wife (Genesis 19:26).

answer is couched in polite and tranquil terms, but Nippers replies in ill-tempered ones. Or, to repeat a previous sentence, Nippers's ugly mood was on duty, and Turkey's off.)

"Ginger Nut," said I, willing to enlist the smallest suffrage in my behalf, "what do *you* think of it?"

"I think, sir, he's a little *luny,*" replied Ginger Nut, with a grin.

"You hear what they say," said I, turning towards the screen, "come forth and do your duty."

But he vouchsafed no reply. I pondered a moment in sore perplexity. But once more business hurried me. I determined again to postpone the consideration of this dilemma to my future leisure. With a little trouble we made out to examine the papers without Bartleby, though at every page or two Turkey deferentially dropped his opinion, that this proceeding was quite out of the common; while Nippers, twitching in his chair with a dyspeptic nervousness, ground out, between his set teeth, occasional hissing maledictions against the stubborn oaf behind the screen. And for his (Nippers's) part, this was the first and the last time he would do another man's business without pay.

Meanwhile Bartleby sat in his hermitage, oblivious to everything but his own peculiar business there.

Some days passed, the scrivener being employed upon another lengthy work. His late remarkable conduct led me to regard his ways narrowly. I observed that he never went to dinner; indeed, that he never went anywhere. As yet I had never, of my personal knowledge, known him to be outside of my office. He was a perpetual sentry in the corner. At about eleven o'clock though, in the morning, I noticed that Ginger Nut would advance toward the opening in Bartleby's screen, as if silently beckoned thither by a gesture invisible to me where I sat. The boy would then leave the office, jingling a few pence, and reappear with a handful of ginger-nuts, which he delivered in the hermitage, receiving two of the cakes for his trouble.

He lives, then, on ginger-nuts, thought I; never eats a dinner, properly speaking; he must be a vegetarian, then; but no; he never eats even vegetables, he eats nothing but ginger-nuts. My mind then ran on in reveries concerning the probable effects upon the human constitution of living entirely on ginger-nuts. Ginger-nuts are so called, because they contain ginger as one of their peculiar constituents, and the final flavoring one. Now, what was ginger? A hot, spicy thing. Was Bartleby hot and spicy? Not at all. Ginger, then, had no effect upon Bartleby. Probably he preferred it should have none.

Nothing so aggravates an earnest person as a passive resistance. If the individual so resisted be of a not inhumane temper, and the resisting one perfectly harmless in his passivity, then, in the better moods of the former, he will endeavor charitably to construe to his imagination what proves impossible to be solved by his judgment. Even so, for the most part, I regarded Bartleby and his ways. Poor fellow! thought I, he means no mischief; it is plain he intends no insolence; his aspect sufficiently evinces that his eccentricities are involuntary. He is useful to me. I can get along with him. If I turn him away, the chances are he will fall in with some less-indulgent employer, and then he will be rudely treated, and perhaps driven forth miserably to starve. Yes. Here I can cheaply purchase a delicious self-approval. To befriend Bartleby; to humor him in his strange willfulness, will cost me little or nothing, while I lay up in my soul what will eventually prove a sweet morsel for my conscience. But this mood was not invariable with me. The passiveness of Bartleby sometimes irritated me. I felt strangely goaded on to encounter him in new opposition—to elicit some angry spark from him answerable to my own. But, indeed, I might as well have essayed to strike fire with my knuckles against a bit of Windsor soap. But one afternoon the evil impulse in me mastered me, and the following little scene ensued:

"Bartleby," said I, "when those papers are all copied, I will compare them with you."

"I would prefer not to."

"How? Surely you do not mean to persist in that mulish vagary?"

No answer.

I threw open the folding-doors near by, and, turning upon Turkey and Nippers, exclaimed:

"Bartleby a second time says, he won't examine his papers. What do you think of it, Turkey?"

It was afternoon, be it remembered. Turkey sat glowing like a brass boiler; his bald head steaming; his hands reeling among his blotted papers.

"Think of it?" roared Turkey; "I think I'll just step behind his screen, and black his eyes for him!"

So saying, Turkey rose to his feet and threw his arms into a pugilistic position. He was hurrying away to make good his promise, when I detained him, alarmed at the effect of incautiously rousing Turkey's combativeness after dinner.

"Sit down, Turkey," said I, "and hear what Nippers has to say. What do you think of it, Nippers? Would I not be justified in immediately dismissing Bartleby?"

"Excuse me, that is for you to decide, sir. I think his conduct quite unusual, and, indeed, unjust, as regards Turkey and myself. But it may only be a passing whim."

"Ah," exclaimed I, "you have strangely changed your mind, then—you speak very gently of him now."

"All beer," cried Turkey; "gentleness is effects of beer—Nippers and I dined together to-day. You see how gentle *I* am, sir. Shall I go and black his eyes?"

"You refer to Bartleby, I suppose. No, not to-day, Turkey," I replied; "pray, put up your fists."

I closed the doors, and again advanced towards Bartleby. I felt additional incentives tempting me to my fate. I burned to be rebelled against again. I remembered that Bartleby never left the office.

"Bartleby," said I, "Ginger Nut is away; just step around to the Post Office, won't you? (it was but a three minutes' walk), and see if there is anything for me."

"I would prefer not to."

"You *will* not?"

"I *prefer* not."

I staggered to my desk, and sat there in a deep study. My blind inveteracy returned. Was there any other thing in which I could procure myself to be ignominiously repulsed by this lean, penniless wight?—my hired clerk? What added thing is there, perfectly reasonable, that he will be sure to refuse to do?

"Bartleby!"

No answer.

"Bartleby," in a louder tone.

No answer.

"Bartleby," I roared.

Like a very ghost, agreeably to the laws of magical invocation, at the third summons, he appeared at the entrance of his hermitage.

"Go to the next room, and tell Nippers to come to me."

"I prefer not to," he respectfully and slowly said, and mildly disappeared.

"Very good, Bartleby," said I, in a quiet sort of serenely-severe self-possessed tone, intimating the unalterable purpose of some terrible retribution very close at hand. At the moment I half intended something of the kind. But upon the whole, as it was drawing towards my dinner-hour, I thought it best to put on my hat and walk home for the day, suffering much from perplexity and distress of mind.

Shall I acknowledge it? The conclusion of this whole business was, that it soon became a fixed fact of my chambers, that a pale young scrivener, by the name of Bartleby, had a desk there; that he copied for me at the usual rate of four cents a folio (one hundred words); but he was permanently exempt from examining the work done by him, that duty being transferred to Turkey and Nippers, out of compliment, doubtless, to their superior acuteness; moreover, said Bartleby was never, on any account, to be dispatched on the most trivial errand of any sort; and that even if entreated to take upon him such a matter, it was generally understood that he would "prefer not to"—in other words, that he would refuse point-blank.

As days passed on, I became considerably reconciled to Bartleby. His steadiness, his freedom from all dissipation, his incessant industry (except when he chose to throw himself into a standing revery behind his screen), his great stillness, his unalterableness of demeanor under all circumstances, made him a valuable acquisition. One prime thing was this—*he was always there*—first in the morning, continually through the day, and the last at night. I had a singular confidence in his honesty. I felt my most precious papers perfectly safe in his hands. Sometimes, to be sure, I could not, for the very soul of me, avoid falling into sudden spasmodic passions with him. For it was exceeding difficult to bear in mind all the time those strange peculiarities, privileges, and unheard of exemptions, forming the tacit stipulations on Bartleby's part under which he remained in my office. Now and then, in the eagerness of dispatching pressing business, I would inadvertently summon Bartleby, in a short, rapid tone, to put his finger, say, on the incipient tie of a bit of red tape with which I was about compressing some papers. Of course, from behind the screen the usual answer, "I prefer not to," was sure to come; and then, how could a human creature, with the common infirmities of our nature, refrain from bitterly exclaiming upon such perverseness— such unreasonableness. However, every added repulse of this sort which I received only tended to lessen the probability of my repeating the inadvertence.

Here it must be said, that according to the custom of most legal gentlemen occupying chambers in densely-populated law buildings, there were several keys to my door. One was kept by a woman residing in the attic, which person weekly scrubbed and daily swept and dusted my apartments. Another was kept by Turkey for convenience sake. The third I sometimes carried in my own pocket. The fourth I knew not who had.

Now, one Sunday morning I happened to go to Trinity Church, to hear a celebrated preacher, and finding myself rather early on the ground I thought I would walk around to my chambers for a while. Luckily I had my key with me; but upon applying it to the lock, I found it resisted by something inserted from the inside. Quite surprised, I called out; when to my consternation a key was turned from within; and thrusting his lean visage at me, and holding the door ajar, the apparition of Bartleby appeared, in his shirt sleeves, and otherwise in a strangely tattered deshabille, saying quietly that he was sorry, but he was deeply engaged just then, and—preferred not admitting me at present. In a brief word or two, he moreover added, that perhaps I had better walk around the block two or three times, and by that time he would probably have concluded his affairs.

Now, the utterly unsurmised appearance of Bartleby, tenanting my law-chambers of a Sunday morning, with his cadaverously gentlemanly *nonchalance,* yet withal firm and self-possessed, had such a strange effect upon me, that incontinently I slunk away from my own door, and did as desired. But not without sundry twinges of impotent rebellion against the mild effrontery of this unaccountable scrivener. Indeed, it was his wonderful mildness chiefly, which not only disarmed me, but unmanned me as it were. For I consider that one, for the time, is a sort of unmanned when he tranquilly permits his hired clerk to dictate to him, and order him away from his own premises. Furthermore, I was full of uneasiness as to what Bartleby could possibly be doing in my office in his shirt sleeves, and in an otherwise dismantled condition of a Sunday morning. Was anything amiss going on? Nay, that was out of the question. It was not to be thought of for a moment that Bartleby was an immoral person. But what could he be doing there?—copying? Nay again, whatever might be his eccentricities, Bartleby was an eminently decorous person. He would be the last man to sit down to his desk in any state approaching to nudity. Besides, it was Sunday; and there was something about Bartleby that forbade the supposition that he would by any secular occupation violate the proprieties of the day.

Nevertheless, my mind was not pacified; and full of a restless curiosity, at last I returned to the door. Without hindrance I inserted my key, opened it, and entered. Bartleby was not to be seen. I looked round anxiously, peeped behind his screen; but it was very plain that he was gone. Upon more closely examining the place, I surmised that for an indefinite period Bartleby must have ate, dressed, and slept in my office, and that, too without plate, mirror, or bed. The cushioned seat of a ricketty old sofa in one corner bore the faint impress of a lean, reclining form. Rolled away under his desk, I found a blanket; under the empty grate, a blacking box and brush; on a chair, a tin basin, with soap and a ragged towel; in a newspaper a few crumbs of ginger-nuts and a morsel of cheese. Yes, thought I, it is evident enough that Bartleby has been making his home here, keeping bachelor's hall all by himself. Immediately then the thought came sweeping across me, what miserable friendlessness and loneliness are here revealed! His poverty is great; but his solitude, how horrible! Think of it. Of a Sunday, Wall Street is deserted as Petra;[7] and every night of every day it is an emptiness. This building, too, which of week-days hums with industry and life, at nightfall echoes with sheer vacancy, and all through Sunday is forlorn. And here Bartleby makes his home; sole spectator of a solitude which he has seen all populous —a sort of innocent and transformed Marius brooding among the ruins of Carthage![8]

For the first time in my life a feeling of over-powering stinging melancholy seized

---

[7] Ruins of ancient city on Mt. Hor, Jordan.
[8] Marius: Gaius Marius (157–86 B.C.), Roman general; Carthage: commercial empire destroyed by Rome in the Third Punic War.

me. Before, I had never experienced aught but a not unpleasing sadness. The bond of a common humanity now drew me irresistibly to gloom. A fraternal melancholy! For both I and Bartleby were sons of Adam. I remembered the bright silks and sparkling faces I had seen that day, in gala trim, swan-like sailing down the Mississippi of Broadway; and I contrasted them with the pallid copyist, and thought to myself, Ah, happiness courts the light, so we deem the world is gay; but misery hides aloof, so we deem that misery there is none. These sad fancyings—chimeras, doubtless, of a sick and silly brain—led on to other and more special thoughts, concerning the eccentricities of Bartleby. Presentiments of strange discoveries hovered round me. The scrivener's pale form appeared to me laid out, among uncaring strangers, in its shivering winding sheet.

Suddenly I was attracted by Bartleby's closed desk, the key in open sight left in the lock.

I mean no mischief, seek the gratification of no heartless curiosity, thought I; besides, the desk is mine, and its contents, too, so I will make bold to look within. Everything was methodically arranged, the papers smoothly placed. The pigeon holes were deep, and removing the files of documents, I groped into their recesses. Presently I felt something there, and dragged it out. It was an old bandanna handkerchief, heavy and knotted. I opened it, and saw it was a savings's bank.

I now recalled all the quiet mysteries which I had noted in the man. I remembered that he never spoke but to answer; that, though at intervals he had considerable time to himself, yet I had never seen him reading—no, not even a newspaper; that for long periods he would stand looking out, at his pale window behind the screen, upon the dead brick wall; I was quite sure he never visited any refectory or eating house; while his pale face clearly indicated that he never drank beer like Turkey, or tea and coffee even, like other men; that he never went anywhere in particular that I could learn; never went out for a walk, unless, indeed, that was the case at present; that he had declined telling who he was, or whence he came, or whether he had any relatives in the world; that though so thin and pale, he never complained of ill health. And more than all, I remembered a certain unconscious air of pallid—how shall I call it?—of pallid haughtiness, say, or rather an austere reserve about him, which had positively awed me into my tame compliance with his eccentricities, when I had feared to ask him to do the slightest incidental thing for me, even though I might know, from his long-continued motionlessness, that behind his screen he must be standing in one of those dead-wall reveries of his.

Revolving all these things, and coupling them with the recently discovered fact, that he made my office his constant abiding place and home, and not forgetful of his morbid moodiness; revolving all these things, a prudential feeling began to steal over me. My first emotions had been those of pure melancholy and sincerest pity; but just in proportion as the forlornness of Bartleby grew and grew to my imagination, did that same melancholy merge into fear, that pity into repulsion. So true it is, and so terrible, took that up to a certain point the thought or sight of misery enlists our best affections; but, in certain special cases, beyond that point it does not. They err who would assert that invariably this is owing to the inherent selfishness of the human heart. It rather proceeds from a certain hopelessness of remedying excessive and organic ill. To a sensitive being, pity is not seldom pain. And when at last it is perceived that such pity cannot lead to effectual succor, common sense bids the soul be rid of it. What I saw that morning persuaded me that the scrivener was the victim of innate and incurable disorder. I might give alms to his body; but his body did not pain him; it was his soul that suffered, and his soul I could not reach.

I did not accomplish the purpose of going to Trinity Church that morning. Somehow, the things I had seen disqualified me for the time from church-going. I walked homeward, thinking what I would do with Bartleby. Finally, I resolved upon this—I would put certain calm questions to him the next morning, touching his history, etc., and if he declined to answer them openly and unreservedly (and I supposed he would prefer not), then to give him a twenty dollar bill over and above whatever I might owe him, and tell him his services were no longer required; but that if in any other way I could assist him, I would be happy to do so, especially if he desired to return to his native place, wherever that might be, I would willingly help to defray the expenses. Moreover, if, after reaching home, he found himself at any time in want of aid, a letter from him would be sure of a reply.

The next morning came.

"Bartleby," said I, gently calling to him behind his screen.

No reply.

"Bartleby," said I, in a still gentler tone, "come here; I am not going to ask you to do anything you would prefer not to do—I simply wish to speak to you."

Upon this he noiselessly slid into view.

"Will you tell me, Bartleby, where you were born?"

"I would prefer not to."

"Will you tell me *anything* about yourself?"

"I would prefer not to."

"But what reasonable objection can you have to speak to me? I feel friendly towards you."

He did not look at me while I spoke, but kept his glance fixed upon my bust of Cicero, which, as I then sat, was directly behind me, some six inches above my head.

"What is your answer, Bartleby," said I, after waiting a considerable time for a reply, during which his countenance remained immovable, only there was the faintest conceivable tremor of the white attenuated mouth.

"At present I prefer to give no answer," he said, and retired into his hermitage.

It was rather weak in me I confess, but his manner, on this occasion, nettled me. Not only did there seem to lurk in it a certain calm disdain, but his perverseness seemed ungrateful, considering the undeniable good usage and indulgence he had received from me.

Again I sat ruminating what I should do. Mortified as I was at his behavior, and resolved as I had been to dismiss him when I entered my office, nevertheless I strangely felt something superstitious knocking at my heart, and forbidding me to carry out my purpose, and denouncing me for a villain if I dared to breathe one bitter word against this forlornest of mankind. At last, familiarly drawing my chair behind his screen, I sat down and said: "Bartleby, never mind, then, about revealing your history; but let me entreat you, as a friend, to comply as far as may be with the usages of this office. Say now, you will help to examine papers to-morrow or next day: in short, say now, that in a day or two you will begin to be a little reasonable:—say so, Bartleby."

"At present I would prefer not to be a little reasonable," was his mildly cadaverous reply.

Just then the folding-doors opened, and Nippers approached. He seemed suffering from an unusually bad night's rest, induced by severer indigestion than common. He overheard those final words of Bartleby.

"*Prefer not*, eh?" gritted Nippers—"I'd *prefer* him, if I were you, sir," addressing me—"I'd *prefer* him; I'd give him preferences, the stubborn mule! What is it, sir, pray, that he *prefers* not to do now?"

Bartleby moved not a limb.

"Mr. Nippers," said I, "I'd prefer that you would withdraw for the present."

Somehow, of late, I had got into the way of involuntarily using this word "prefer" upon all sorts of not exactly suitable occasions. And I trembled to think that my contact with the scrivener had already and seriously affected me in a mental way. And what further and deeper aberration might it not yet produce? This apprehension had not been without efficacy in determining me to summary measures.

As Nippers, looking very sour and sulky, was departing, Turkey blandly and deferentially approached.

"With submission, sir," said he, "yesterday I was thinking about Bartleby here, and I think that if he would but prefer to take a quart of good ale every day, it would do much towards mending him, and enabling him to assist in examining his papers."

"So you have got the word, too," said I, slightly excited.

"With submission, what word, sir," asked Turkey, respectfully crowding himself into the contracted space behind the screen, and by so doing, making me jostle the scrivener. "What word, sir?"

"I would prefer to be left alone here," said Bartleby, as if offended at being mobbed in his privacy.

"*That's* the word, Turkey," said I—"*that's* it."

"Oh, *prefer*? oh yes—queer word. I never use it myself. But, sir, as I was saying, if he would but prefer—"

"Turkey," interrupted I, "you will please withdraw."

"Oh, certainly, sir, if you prefer that I should."

As he opened the folding-door to retire, Nippers at his desk caught a glimpse of me, and asked whether I would prefer to have a certain paper copied on blue paper or white. He did not in the least roguishly accent the word prefer. It was plain that it involuntarily rolled from his tongue. I thought to myself, surely I must get rid of a demented man, who already has in some degree turned the tongues, if not the heads of myself and clerks. But I thought it prudent not to break the dismission at once.

The next day I noticed that Bartleby did nothing but stand at his window in his dead-wall revery. Upon asking him why he did not write, he said that he had decided upon doing no more writing.

"Why, how now? what next?" exclaimed I, "do no more writing?"

"No more."

"And what is the reason?"

"Do you not see the reason for yourself," he indifferently replied.

I looked steadfastly at him, and perceived that his eyes looked dull and glazed. Instantly it occurred to me, that his unexampled diligence in copying by his dim window for the first few weeks of his stay with me might have temporarily impaired his vision.

I was touched. I said something in condolence with him. I hinted that of course he did wisely in abstaining from writing for a while; and urged him to embrace that opportunity of taking wholesome exercise in the open air. This, however, he did not do. A few days after this, my other clerks being absent, and being in a great hurry to dispatch certain letters by the mail, I thought that, having nothing else earthly to do, Bartleby would surely be less inflexible than usual, and carry these letters to the post-office. But he blankly declined. So, much to my inconvenience, I went myself.

Still added days went by. Whether Bartleby's eyes improved or not, I could not say. To all appearance, I thought they did. But when I asked him if they did, he vouchsafed no answer. At all events, he would do no copying. At last, in reply to my urgings, he informed me that he had permanently given up copying.

"What!" exclaimed I; "suppose your eyes should get entirely well—better than ever before—would you not copy then?"

"I have given up copying," he answered, and slid aside.

He remained as ever, a fixture in my chamber. Nay—if that were possible—he became still more of a fixture than before. What was to be done? He would do nothing in the office; why should he stay there? In plain fact, he had now become a millstone to me, not only useless as a necklace, but afflictive to bear. Yet I was sorry for him. I speak less than truth when I say that, on his own account, he occasioned me uneasiness. If he would but have named a single relative or friend, I would instantly have written, and urged their taking the poor fellow away to some convenient retreat. But he seemed alone, absolutely alone in the universe. A bit of wreck in the mid Atlantic. At length, necessities connected with my business tyrannized over all other considerations. Decently as I could, I told Bartleby that in six days time he must unconditionally leave the office. I warned him to take measures, in the interval, for procuring some other abode. I offered to assist him in this endeavor, if he himself would but take the first step towards a removal. "And when you finally quit me, Bartleby," added I, "I shall see that you go not away entirely unprovided. Six days from this hour, remember."

At the expiration of that period, I peeped behind the screen, and lo! Bartleby was there.

I buttoned up my coat, balanced myself; advanced slowly towards him, touched his shoulder, and said, "The time has come; you must quit this place; I am sorry for you; here is money; but you must go."

"I would prefer not," he replied, with his back still towards me.

"You *must.*"

He remained silent.

Now I had an unbounded confidence in this man's common honesty. He had frequently restored to me sixpences and shillings carelessly dropped upon the floor, for I am apt to be very reckless in such shirt-button affairs. The proceeding, then, which followed will not be deemed extraordinary.

"Bartleby," said I, "I owe you twelve dollars on account; here are thirty-two; the odd twenty are yours—Will you take it?" and I handed the bills towards him.

But he made no motion.

"I will leave them here, then," putting them under a weight on the table. Then taking my hat and cane and going to the door, I tranquilly turned and added—"After you have removed your things from these offices, Bartleby, you will of course lock the door—since every one is now gone for the day but you—and if you please, slip your key underneath the mat, so that I may have it in the morning. I shall not see you again; so good-by to you. If, hereafter, in your new place of abode, I can be of any service to you, do not fail to advise me by letter. Good-by, Bartleby, and fare you well."

But he answered not a word; like the last column of some ruined temple, he remained standing mute and solitary in the middle of the otherwise deserted room.

As I walked home in a pensive mood, my vanity got the better of my pity. I could not but highly plume myself on my masterly management in getting rid of Bartleby. Masterly I call it, and such it must appear to any dispassionate thinker. The beauty of my procedure seemed to consist in its perfect quietness. There was no vulgar bullying, no bravado of any sort, no choleric hectoring, and striding to and fro across the apartment, jerking out vehement commands for Bartleby to bundle himself off with his beggarly traps. Nothing of the kind. Without loudly bidding Bartleby depart —as an inferior genius might have done—I *assumed* the ground that depart he must; and upon that assumption built all I had to say. The more I thought over my procedure, the more I was charmed with it. Nevertheless, next morning, upon awakening, I had my doubts—I had somehow slept off the fumes of vanity. One of the coolest and wisest hours a man has, is just after he awakes in the morning. My procedure seemed as sagacious as ever—but only in theory. How it would prove in practice—there was the rub. It was truly a beautiful thought to have assumed Bartleby's departure; but, after all, that assumption was simply my own, and none of Bartleby's. The great point was, not whether I had assumed that he would quit me, but whether he would prefer so to do. He was more a man of preferences than assumptions.

After breakfast, I walked down town, arguing the probabilities *pro* and *con*. One moment I thought it would prove a miserable failure, and Bartleby would be found all alive at my office as usual; the next moment it seemed certain that I should find his chair empty. And so I kept veering about. At the corner of Broadway and Canal Street, I saw quite an excited group of people standing in earnest conversation.

"I'll take odds he doesn't," said a voice as I passed.

"Doesn't go?—done!" said I, "put up your money."

I was instinctively putting my hand in my pocket to produce my own, when I remembered that this was an election day. The words I had overheard bore no reference to Bartleby, but to the success or non-success of some candidate for the mayoralty. In my intent frame of mind, I had, as it were, imagined that all Broadway shared in my excitement, and were debating the same question with me. I passed on, very thankful that the uproar of the street screened my momentary absent-mindedness.

As I had intended, I was earlier than usual at my office door. I stood listening for a moment. All was still. He must be gone. I tried the knob. The door was locked. Yes, my procedure had worked to a charm; he indeed must be vanished. Yet a certain melancholy mixed with this: I was almost sorry for my brilliant success. I was fumbling under the door mat for the key, which Bartleby was to have left there for me, when accidentally my knee knocked against a panel, producing a summoning sound, and in response a voice came to me from within—"Not yet; I am occupied."

It was Bartleby.

I was thunderstruck. For an instant I stood like the man who, pipe in mouth, was killed one cloudless afternoon long ago in Virginia, by summer lightning; at his own warm open window he was killed, and remained leaning out there upon the dreamy afternoon, till some one touched him, when he fell.

"Not gone!" I murmured at last. But again obeying that wondrous ascendancy which the inscrutable scrivener had over me, and from which ascendancy, for all my chafing, I could not completely escape, I slowly went down stairs and out into the street, and while walking round the block, considered what I should next do in this unheard-of perplexity. Turn the man out by an actual thrusting I could not; to drive him away by calling him hard names would not do; calling in the police was an unpleasant idea; and yet, permit him to enjoy his cadaverous triumph over me—this, too, I could not think of. What was to be done? or, if nothing could be done, was there anything further that I could *assume* in the matter? Yes, as before I had prospectively assumed that Bartleby would depart, so now I might retrospectively assume that departed he was. In the legitimate carrying out of this assumption, I might enter my office in a great hurry, and pretending not to see Bartleby at all, walk straight against him as if he were air. Such a proceeding would in a singular degree have the appearance of a home-thrust. It was hardly possible that Bartleby could withstand such an application of the doctrine of assumptions. But upon second thoughts the success of the plan seemed rather dubious. I resolved to argue the matter over with him again.

"Bartleby," said I, entering the office, with a quietly severe expression, "I am seriously displeased. I am pained, Bartleby. I had thought better of you. I had imagined you of such a gentlemanly organization, that in any delicate dilemma a slight hint would suffice—in short, an assumption. But it appears I am deceived. Why," I added, unaffectedly starting, "you have not even touched that money yet," pointing to it, just where I had left it the evening previous.

He answered nothing.

"Will you, or will you not, quit me?" I now demanded in a sudden passion, advancing close to him.

"I would prefer *not* to quit you," he replied, gently emphasizing the *not.*

"What earthly right have you to stay here? Do you pay any rent? Do you pay my taxes? Or is this property yours?"

He answered nothing.

"Are you ready to go on and write now? Are your eyes recovered? Could you copy a small paper for me this morning? or help examine a few lines? or step round to the post-office? In a word, will you do anything at all, to give a coloring to your refusal to depart the premises?"

He silently retired into his hermitage.

I was now in such a state of nervous resentment that I thought it but prudent to check myself at present from further demonstrations. Bartleby and I were alone. I remembered the tragedy of the unfortunate Adams and the still more unfortunate Colt in the solitary office of the latter; and how poor Colt, being dreadfully incensed by Adams, and imprudently permitting himself to get wildly excited, was at unawares hurried into his fatal act—an act which certainly no man could possibly deplore more than the actor himself.[9] Often it had occurred to me in my ponderings upon the subject, that had that altercation taken place in the public street, or at a private residence, it would not have terminated as it did. It was the circumstance of being alone in a solitary office, up stairs, of a building entirely unhallowed by humanizing domestic associations—an uncarpeted office, doubtless, of a dusty, haggard sort of appearance—this it must have been, which greatly helped to enhance the irritable desperation of the hapless Colt.

But when this old Adam of resentment rose in me and tempted me concerning Bartleby, I grappled him and threw him. How? Why, simply by recalling the divine injunction: "A new commandment give I unto you, that ye love one another." Yes, this it was that saved me. Aside from higher considerations, charity often operates as a vastly wise and prudent principle—a great safeguard to its possessor. Men have committed murder for jealousy's sake, and anger's sake, and hatred's sake, and selfishness' sake, and spiritual pride's sake; but no man, that ever I heard of, ever committed a diabolical murder for sweet charity's sake. Mere self-interest, then, if no better motive can be enlisted, should, especially with high-tempered men, prompt all beings to charity and philanthropy. At any rate, upon the occasion in question, I strove to drown my exasperated feelings towards the scrivener by benevolently construing his conduct. Poor fellow, poor fellow! thought I, he don't mean anything; and besides, he has seen hard times, and ought to be indulged.

I endeavored, also, immediately to occupy myself, and at the same time to comfort my despondency. I tried to fancy, that in the course of the morning, at such time as might prove agreeable to him, Bartleby, of his own free accord, would emerge from his hermitage and take up some decided line of march in the direction of the door. But no. Half-past twelve o'clock came; Turkey began to glow in the face, overturn his inkstand, and become generally obstreperous; Nippers abated down into quietude and courtesy; Ginger Nut munched his noon apple; and Bartleby remained standing at his window in one of his profoundest dead-wall reveries. Will it be credited? Ought I to acknowledge it? That afternoon I left the office without saying one further word to him.

Some days now passed, during which, at leisure intervals I looked a little into "Edwards on the Will," and "Priestly on Necessity."[10] Under the circumstances, those books induced a salutary feeling. Gradually I slid into the persuasion that these troubles of mine, touching the scrivener, had been all predestinated from eternity, and Bartleby was billeted upon me for some mysterious purpose of an allwise Providence, which it was not for a mere mortal like me to fathom. Yes, Bartleby, stay there behind your screen, thought I; I shall persecute you no more; you are harmless and noiseless as any of these old chairs; in short, I never feel so private as when I know you are here. At

---

[9] In 1841 John C. Colt axe-murdered his creditor, Samuel Adams, and committed suicide following his conviction for the crime, which was widely publicized.

[10] Both the Puritan theologian Jonathan Edwards and the English scientist Joseph Priestly concluded that the will is not free.

last I see it, I feel it; I penetrate to the predestinated purpose of my life. I am content. Others may have loftier parts to enact; but my mission in this world, Bartleby, is to furnish you with office-room for such period as you may see fit to remain.

I believe that this wise and blessed frame of mind would have continued with me, had it not been for the unsolicited and uncharitable remarks obtruded upon me by my professional friends who visited the rooms. But thus it often is, that the constant friction of illiberal minds wears out at last the best resolves of the more generous. Though to be sure, when I reflected upon it, it was not strange that people entering my office should be struck by the peculiar aspect of the unaccountable Bartleby, and so be tempted to throw out some sinister observations concerning him. Sometimes an attorney, having business with me, and calling at my office, and finding no one but the scrivener there, would undertake to obtain some sort of precise information from him touching my whereabouts; but without heeding his idle talk, Bartleby would remain standing immovable in the middle of the room. So after contemplating him in that position for a time, the attorney would depart, no wiser than he came.

Also, when a reference[11] was going on, and the room full of lawyers and witnesses, and business driving fast, some deeply-occupied legal gentleman present, seeing Bartleby wholly unemployed, would request him to run round to his (the legal gentleman's) office and fetch some papers for him. Thereupon, Bartleby would tranquilly decline, and yet remain idle as before. Then the lawyer would give a great stare, and turn to me. And what could I say? At last I was made aware that all through the circle of my professional acquaintance, a whisper of wonder was running round, having reference to the strange creature I kept at my office. This worried me very much. And as the idea came upon me of his possibly turning out a long-lived man, and keep occupying my chambers, and denying my authority; and perplexing my visitors; and scandalizing my professional reputation; and casting a general gloom over the premises; keeping soul and body together to the last upon his savings (for doubtless he spent but half a dime a day), and in the end perhaps outlive me, and claim possession of my office by right of his perpetual occupancy: as all these dark anticipations crowded upon me more and more, and my friends continually intruded their relentless remarks upon the apparition in my room; a great change was wrought in me. I resolved to gather all my faculties together, and forever rid me of this intolerable incubus.

Ere revolving any complicated project, however, adapted to this end, I first simply suggested to Bartleby the propriety of his permanent departure. In a calm and serious tone, I commended the idea to his careful and mature consideration. But, having taken three days to meditate upon it, he apprised me, that his original determination remained the same; in short, that he still preferred to abide with me.

What shall I do? I now said to myself, buttoning up my coat to the last button. What shall I do? what ought I to do? what does conscience say I _should_ do with this man, or, rather, ghost. Rid myself of him, I must; go, he shall. But how? You will not thrust him, the poor, pale, passive mortal—you will not thrust such a helpless creature out of your door? you will not dishonor yourself by such cruelty? No, I will not, I cannot do that. Rather would I let him live and die here, and then mason up his remains in the wall. What, then, will you do? For all your coaxing, he will not

[11] The referring of disputes to arbitrators.

budge. Bribes he leaves under your own paper-weight on your table; in short, it is quite plain that he prefers to cling to you.

Then something severe, something unusual must be done. What! surely you will not have him collared by a constable, and commit his innocent pallor to the common jail? And upon what ground could you procure such a thing to be done?—a vagrant, is he? What! he a vagrant, a wanderer, who refuses to budge? It is because he will *not* be a vagrant, then, that you seek to count him *as* a vagrant. That is too absurd. No visible means of support: there I have him. Wrong again: for indubitably he *does* support himself, and that is the only unanswerable proof that any man can show of his possessing the means so to do. No more, then. Since he will not quit me, I must quit him. I will change my offices; I will move elsewhere, and give him fair notice, that if I find him on my new premises I will then proceed against him as a common trespasser.

Acting accordingly, next day I thus addressed him: "I find these chambers too far from the City Hall; the air is unwholesome. In a word, I propose to remove my offices next week, and shall no longer require your services. I tell you this now, in order that you may seek another place."

He made no reply, and nothing more was said.

On the appointed day I engaged carts and men, proceeded to my chambers, and, having but little furniture, everything was removed in a few hours. Throughout, the scrivener remained standing behind the screen, which I directed to be removed the last thing. It was withdrawn; and, being folded up like a huge folio, left him the motion-less occupant of a naked room. I stood in the entry watching him a moment, while something from within me upbraided me.

I re-entered, with my hand in my pocket—and—and my heart in my mouth.

"Good-by, Bartleby; I am going—good-by, and God some way bless you; and take that," slipping something in his hand. But it dropped upon the floor, and then— strange to say—I tore myself from him whom I had so longed to be rid of.

Established in my new quarters, for a day or two I kept the door locked, and started at every footfall in the passages. When I returned to my rooms, after any little absence, I would pause at the threshold for an instant, and attentively listen, ere applying my key. But these fears were needless. Bartleby never came nigh me.

I thought all was going well, when a perturbed-looking stranger visited me, inquiring whether I was the person who had recently occupied rooms at No. ———— Wall Street.

Full of forebodings, I replied that I was.

"Then, sir," said the stranger, who proved a lawyer, "you are responsible for the man you left there. He refuses to do any copying; he refuses to do anything; he says he prefers not to; and he refuses to quit the premises."

"I am very sorry, sir," said I, with assumed tranquillity, but an inward tremor, "but, really, the man you allude to is nothing to me—he is no relation or apprentice of mine, that you should hold me responsible for him."

"In mercy's name, who is he?"

"I certainly cannot inform you. I know nothing about him. Formerly I employed him as a copyist; but he has done nothing for me now for some time past."

"I shall settle him, then—good morning, sir."

Several days passed, and I heard nothing more; and, though I often felt a charitable prompting to call at the place and see poor Bartleby, yet a certain squeamishness, of I know not what, withheld me.

All is over with him, by this time, thought I, at last, when, through another week, no further intelligence reached me. But, coming to my room the day after, I found several persons waiting at my door in a high state of nervous excitement.

"That's the man—here he comes," cried the foremost one, whom I recognized as the lawyer who had previously called upon me alone.

"You must take him away, sir, at once," cried a portly person among them, advancing upon me, and whom I knew to be the landlord of No. ———— Wall Street. "These gentlemen, my tenants, cannot stand it any longer; Mr. B——," pointing to the lawyer, "has turned him out of his room, and he now persists in haunting the building generally, sitting upon the banisters of the stairs by day, and sleeping in the entry by night. Everybody is concerned; clients are leaving the offices; some fears are entertained of a mob; something you must do, and that without delay."

Aghast at this torrent, I fell back before it, and would fain have locked myself in my new quarters. In vain I persisted that Bartleby was nothing to me—no more than to any one else. In vain—I was the last person known to have anything to do with him, and they held me to the terrible account. Fearful, then, of being exposed in the papers (as one person present obscurely threatened), I considered the matter, and, at length, said, that if the lawyer would give me a confidential interview with the scrivener, in his (the lawyer's) own room, I would, that afternoon, strive my best to rid them of the nuisance they complained of.

Going up stairs to my old haunt, there was Bartleby silently sitting upon the banister at the landing.

"What are you doing here, Bartleby?" said I.

"Sitting upon the banister," he mildly replied.

I motioned him into the lawyer's room, who then left us.

"Bartleby," said I, "are you aware that you are the cause of great tribulation to me, by persisting in occupying the entry after being dismissed from the office?"

No answer.

"Now one of two things must take place. Either you must do something, or something must be done to you. Now what sort of business would you like to engage in? Would you like to re-engage in copying for some one?"

"No; I would prefer not to make any change."

"Would you like a clerkship in a dry-goods store?"

"There is too much confinement about that. No, I would not like a clerkship; but I am not particular."

"Too much confinement," I cried, "why you keep yourself confined all the time!"

"I would prefer not to take a clerkship," he rejoined, as if to settle that little item at once.

"How would a bar-tender's business suit you? There is no trying of the eye-sight in that."

"I would not like it at all; though, as I said before, I am not particular."

His unwonted wordiness inspirited me. I returned to the charge.

"Well, then, would you like to travel through the country collecting bills for the merchants? That would improve your health."

"No, I would prefer to be doing something else."

"How, then, would going as a companion to Europe, to entertain some young gentleman with your conversation—how would that suit you?"

"Not at all. It does not strike me that there is anything definite about that. I like to be stationary. But I am not particular."

"Stationary you shall be, then," I cried, now losing all patience, and, for the first time in all my exasperating connection with him, fairly flying into a passion. "If you do not go away from these premises before night, I shall feel bound—indeed, I *am* bound—to—to—to quit the premises myself!" I rather absurdly concluded, knowing not with what possible threat to try to frighten his immobility into compliance. Despairing of all further efforts, I was precipitately leaving him, when a final thought occurred to me—one which had not been wholly unindulged before.

"Bartleby," said I, in the kindest tone I could assume under such exciting circumstances, "will you go home with me now—not to my office, but my dwelling—and remain there till we can conclude upon some convenient arrangement for you at our leisure? Come, let us start now, right away."

"No: at present I would prefer not to make any change at all."

I answered nothing; but, effectually dodging every one by the suddenness and rapidity of my flight, rushed from the building, ran up Wall Street towards Broadway, and, jumping into the first omnibus, was soon removed from pursuit. As soon as tranquillity returned, I distinctly perceived that I had now done all that I possibly could, both in respect to the demands of the landlord and his tenants, and with regard to my own desire and sense of duty, to benefit Bartleby, and shield him from rude persecution. I now strove to be entirely care-free and quiescent; and my conscience justified me in the attempt; though, indeed, it was not so successful as I could have wished. So fearful was I of being again hunted out by the incensed landlord and his exasperated tenants, that, surrendering my business to Nippers, for a few days, I drove about the upper part of the town and through the suburbs, in my rockaway;[12] crossed over to Jersey City and Hoboken, and paid fugitive visits to Manhattanville and Astoria. In fact, I almost lived in my rockaway for the time.

When again I entered my office, lo, a note from the landlord lay upon the desk. I opened it with trembling hands. It informed me that the writer had sent to the police, and had Bartleby removed to the Tombs as a vagrant. Moreover, since I knew more about him than any one else, he wished me to appear at that place, and make a suitable statement of the facts. These tidings had a conflicting effect upon me. At first I was indignant; but, at last, almost approved. The landlord's energetic, summary disposition, had led him to adopt a procedure which I do not think I would have decided upon myself; and yet, as a last resort, under such peculiar circumstances, it seemed the only plan.

As I afterwards learned, the poor scrivener, when told that he must be conducted to the Tombs, offered not the slightest obstacle; but, in his pale, unmoving way, silently acquiesced.

Some of the compassionate and curious bystanders joined the party; and headed by one of the constables arm in arm with Bartleby, the silent procession filed its way through all the noise, and heat, and joy of the roaring thoroughfares at noon.

[12] Carriage.

The same day I received the note, I went to the Tombs, or, to speak more properly, the Halls of Justice. Seeking the right officer, I stated the purpose of my call, and was informed that the individual I described was, indeed, within. I then assured the functionary that Bartleby was a perfectly honest man, and greatly to be compassionated, however unaccountably eccentric. I narrated all I knew, and closed by suggesting the idea of letting him remain in as indulgent confinement as possible, till something less harsh might be done—though, indeed, I hardly knew what. At all events, if nothing else could be decided upon, the alms-house must receive him. I then begged to have an interview.

Being under no disgraceful charge, and quite serene and harmless in all his ways, they had permitted him freely to wander about the prison, and, especially, in the inclosed grass-platted yards thereof. And so I found him there, standing all alone in the quietest of the yards, his face towards a high wall, while all around, from the narrow slits of the jail windows, I thought I saw peering out upon him the eyes of murderers and thieves.

"Bartleby"

"I know you," he said, without looking around—"and I want nothing to say to you."

"It was not I that brought you here, Bartleby," said I, keenly pained at his implied suspicion. "And to you, this should not be so vile a place. Nothing reproachful attaches to you by being here. And see, it is not so sad a place as one might think. Look, there is the sky, and here is the grass."

"I know where I am," he replied, but would say nothing more, and so I left him.

As I entered the corridor again, a broad meat-like man, in an apron, accosted me, and, jerking his thumb over his shoulder, said—"Is that your friend?"

"Yes."

"Does he want to starve? If he does, let him live on the prison fare, that's all."

"Who are you?" asked I, not knowing what to make of such an unofficially speaking person in such a place.

"I am the grub-man. Such gentlemen as have friends here, hire me to provide them with something good to eat."

"Is this so?" said I, turning to the turnkey.

He said it was.

"Well, then," said I, slipping some silver into the grub-man's hands (for so they called him), 'I want you to give particular attention to my friend there; let him have the best dinner you can get. And you must be as polite to him as possible."

"Introduce me, will you?" said the grub-man, looking at me with an expression which seemed to say he was all impatience for an opportunity to give a specimen of his breeding.

Thinking it would prove of benefit to the scrivener, I acquiesced; and, asking the grub-man his name, went up with him to Bartleby.

"Bartleby, this is a friend; you will find him very useful to you."

"Your sarvant, sir, your sarvant," said the grub-man, making a low salutation behind his apron. "Hope you find it pleasant here, sir; nice grounds—cool apartments—hope you'll stay with us sometime—try to make it agreeable. What will you have for dinner to-day?"

"I prefer not to dine to-day," said Bartleby, turning away. "It would disagree with me; I am unused to dinners." So saying, he slowly moved to the other side of the inclosure, and took up a position fronting the dead-wall.

"How's this?" said the grub-man, addressing me with a stare of astonishment. "He's odd, ain't he?"

"I think he is a little deranged," said I, sadly.

"Deranged? deranged is it? Well, now, upon my word, I thought that friend of yourn was a gentleman forger; they are always pale and genteel-like, them forgers. I can't help pity 'em—can't help it, sir. Did you know Monroe Edwards?"[13] he added, touchingly, and paused. Then, laying his hand piteously on my shoulder, sighed, "he died of consumption at Sing-Sing. So you weren't acquainted with Monroe?"

"No, I was never socially acquainted with any forgers. But I cannot stop longer. Look to my friend yonder. You will not lose by it. I will see you again."

Some few days after this, I again obtained admission to the Tombs, and went through the corridors in quest of Bartleby; but without finding him.

"I saw him coming from his cell not long ago," said a turnkey, "may be he's gone to loiter in the yards."

So I went in that direction.

"Are you looking for the silent man?" said another turnkey, passing me. "Yonder he lies—sleeping in the yard there. 'Tis not twenty minutes since I saw him lie down."

The yard was entirely quiet. It was not accessible to the common prisoners. The surrounding walls, of amazing thickness, kept off all sounds behind them. The Egyptian character of the masonry weighed upon me with its gloom. But a soft imprisoned turf grew under foot. The heart of the eternal pyramids, it seemed, wherein, by some strange magic, through the clefts, grass-seed, dropped by birds, had sprung.

Strangely huddled at the base of the wall, his knees drawn up, and lying on his side, his head touching the cold stones, I saw the wasted Bartleby. But nothing stirred. I paused; then went close up to him; stooped over, and saw that his dim eyes were open; otherwise he seemed profoundly sleeping. Something prompted me to touch him. I felt his hand, when a tingling shiver ran up my arm and down my spine to my feet.

The round face of the grub-man peered upon me now. "His dinner is ready. Won't he dine to-day, either? Or does he live without dining?"

"Lives without dining," said I, and closed the eyes.

"Eh!—He's asleep, ain't he?"

"With kings and counselors,"[14] murmured I.

There would seem little need for proceeding further in this history. Imagination will readily supply the meagre recital of poor Bartleby's interment. But, ere parting with the reader, let me say, that if this little narrative has sufficiently interested him, to awaken curiosity as to who Bartleby was, and what manner of life he led prior to the present narrator's making his acquaintance, I can only reply, that in such curiosity I fully share, but am wholly unable to gratify it. Yet here I hardly know whether I should divulge one little item of rumor, which came to my ear a few months after the scrivener's decease. Upon what basis it rested, I could never ascertain; and hence, how true it is I cannot now tell. But, inasmuch as this vague report has not

---

[13] Financier convicted in 1842 of forgery and swindle.

[14] Job 3:14.

been without a certain suggestive interest to me, however sad, it may prove the same with some others; and so I will briefly mention it. The report was this: that Bartleby had been a subordinate clerk in the Dead Letter Office at Washington, from which he had been suddenly removed by a change in the administration. When I think over this rumor, hardly can I express the emotions which seize me. Dead letters! does it not sound like dead men? Conceive a man by nature and misfortune prone to a pallid hopelessness, can any business seem more fitted to heighten it than that of continually handling these dead letters, and assorting them for the flames? For by the cart-load they are annually burned. Sometimes from out the folded paper the pale clerk takes a ring—the finger it was meant for, perhaps, moulders in the grave; a bank-note sent in swiftest charity—he whom it would relieve, nor eats nor hungers any more; pardon for those who died despairing; hope for those who died unhoping; good tidings for those who died stifled by unrelieved calamities. On errands of life, these letters speed to death.

Ah, Bartleby! Ah, humanity!

1853/1856

Billy Budd, Sailor
(An Inside Narrative)*

Dedicated
to
JACK CHASE
Englishman
Wherever that great heart may now be
Here on Earth or harbored in Paradise.
Captain of the Maintop
in the year 1843
in the U.S. Frigate
United States[1]

1

In the time before steamships, or then more frequently than now, a stroller along the docks of any considerable seaport would occasionally have his attention arrested by a group of bronzed mariners, man-of-war's men or merchant sailors in holiday attire,

---

* Melville's mysterious phrase has been interpreted in several ways. Historically *Billy Budd* is based upon a 1797 mutiny in the British Navy, yet it also is the insider's version of an 1842 mutiny on the *Somers,* an American naval ship. Psychologically, *Billy Budd,* may represent Melville's private, inner life. And the narrative, which on one level is an adventure story, also yields deeper, "inside" meanings. *Billy Budd* was written in the late 1880s, then found in manuscript among Melville's belongings after his death, and finally published in 1924.

[1] Jack Chase, Melville's shipmate on the *United States,* appeared in Melville's novel *White-Jacket* (1850) as the leader of the skilled crew assigned to the top of the mainmast.

ashore on liberty. In certain instances they would flank, or like a bodyguard quite surround, some superior figure of their own class, moving along with them like Aldebaran[2] among the lesser lights of his constellation. That signal object was the "Handsome Sailor" of the less prosaic time alike of the military and merchant navies. With no perceptible trace of the vain-glorious about him, rather with the offhand unaffectedness of natural regality, he seemed to accept the spontaneous homage of his shipmates.

A somewhat remarkable instance recurs to me. In Liverpool, now half a century ago, I saw under the shadow of the great dingy street-wall of Prince's Dock (an obstruction long since removed) a common sailor so intensely black that he must needs have been a native African of the unadulterate blood of Ham[3]—a symmetric figure much above the average height. The two ends of a gay silk handkerchief thrown loose about the neck danced upon the displayed ebony of his chest, in his ears were big hoops of gold, and a Highland bonnet with a tartan band set off his shapely head. It was a hot noon in July; and his face, lustrous with perspiration, beamed with barbaric good humor. In jovial sallies right and left, his white teeth flashing into view, he rollicked along, the center of a company of his shipmates. These were made up of such an assortment of tribes and complexions as would have well fitted them to be marched up by Anacharsis Cloots[4] before the bar of the first French Assembly as Representatives of the Human Race. At each spontaneous tribute rendered by the wayfarers to this black pagod[5] of a fellow—the tribute of a pause and stare, and less frequently an exclamation—the motley retinue showed that they took that sort of pride in the evoker of it which the Assyrian priests doubtless showed for their grand sculptured Bull when the faithful prostrated themselves.

To return. If in some cases a bit of a nautical Murat[6] in setting forth his person ashore, the Handsome Sailor of the period in question evinced nothing of the dandified Billy-be-Dam, an amusing character all but extinct now, but occasionally to be encountered, and in a form yet more amusing than the original, at the tiller of the boats on the tempestuous Erie Canal or, more likely, vaporing in the groggeries along the towpath.[7] Invariably a proficient in his perilous calling, he was also more or less of a mighty boxer or wrestler. It was strength and beauty. Tales of his prowess were recited. Ashore he was the champion; afloat the spokesman; on every suitable occasion always foremost. Close-reefing topsails in a gale, there he was, astride the weather yardarm-end, foot in the Flemish horse as stirrup,[8] both hands tugging at the earing as at a bridle, in very much the attitude of young Alexander curbing the fiery Bucephalus.[9] A superb figure, tossed up as by the horns of Taurus against the thunderous sky, cheerily hallooing to the strenuous file along the spar.

The moral nature was seldom out of keeping with the physical make. Indeed,

[2] The brightest star and "eye" of the constellation Taurus, the Bull.

[3] Noah's curse on his son Ham, in Genesis 9:22–25, was assumed to result in black skin in Ham's descendants.

[4] Revolutionary Prussian (1755–1794) who demonstrated the variety and unity of mankind by parading men of different classes and nationalities before the French National Assembly.

[5] Idol.

[6] Joachim Murat (1767–1815), a dandy and king of Naples.

[7] I.e., boasting in the saloons, the placid Erie Canal being hardly tempestuous.

[8] I.e., he was lowering sails and fastening them to a yardarm or spar while braced in the foot rope on the end of the yardarm on the windward side.

[9] Horse of Alexander the Great (356–323 B.C.).

except as toned by the former, the comeliness and power, always attractive in masculine conjunction, hardly could have drawn the sort of honest homage the Handsome
Sailor in some examples received from his less gifted associates.

Such a cynosure, at least in aspect, and something such too in nature, though with
important variations made apparent as the story proceeds, was welkin-eyed[10] Billy
Budd—or Baby Budd, as more familiarly, under circumstances hereafter to be given,
he at last came to be called—aged twenty-one, a foretopman[11] of the British fleet
toward the close of the last decade of the eighteenth century. It was not very long
prior to the time of the narration that follows that he had entered the King's service,
having been impressed on the Narrow Seas[12] from a homeward-bound English merchantman into a seventy-four[13] outward bound, H.M.S. *Bellipotent;* which ship, as was
not unusual in those hurried days, having been obliged to put to sea short of her proper
complement of men. Plump upon Billy at first sight in the gangway the boarding
officer, Lieutenant Ratcliffe, pounced, even before the merchantman's crew was
formally mustered on the quarter-deck for his deliberate inspection. And him only
he elected. For whether it was because the other men when ranged before him showed
to ill advantage after Billy, or whether he had some scruples in view of the merchantman's being rather short-handed, however it might be, the officer contented himself
with his first spontaneous choice. To the surprise of the ship's company, though much
to the lieutenant's satisfaction, Billy made no demur. But, indeed, any demur would
have been as idle as the protest of a goldfinch popped into a cage.

Noting this uncomplaining acquiescence, all but cheerful, one might say, the
shipmaster turned a surprised glance of silent reproach at the sailor. The shipmaster
was one of those worthy mortals found in every vocation, even the humbler ones—
the sort of person whom everybody agrees in calling "a respectable man." And—nor
so strange to report as it may appear to be—though a ploughman of the troubled
waters, lifelong contending with the intractable elements, there was nothing this
honest soul at heart loved better than simple peace and quiet. For the rest, he was fifty
or thereabouts, a little inclined to corpulence, a prepossessing face, unwhiskered, and
of an agreeable color—a rather full face, humanely intelligent in expression. On a
fair day with a fair wind and all going well, a certain musical chime in his voice
seemed to be the veritable unobstructed outcome of the innermost man. He had much
prudence, much conscientiousness, and there were occasions when these virtues were
the cause of overmuch disquietude in him. On a passage, so long as his craft was in
any proximity to land, no sleep for Captain Graveling. He took to heart those serious
responsibilities not so heavily borne by some shipmasters.

Now while Billy Budd was down in the forecastle[14] getting his kit together, the
Bellipotent's lieutenant, burly and bluff, nowise disconcerted by Captain Graveling's
omitting to proffer the customary hospitalities on an occasion so unwelcome to him,
an omission simply caused by preoccupation of thought, unceremoniously invited
himself into the cabin, and also to a flask from the spirit locker, a receptacle which
his experienced eye instantly discovered. In fact he was one of those sea dogs in whom

all the hardship and peril of naval life in the great prolonged wars of his time never impaired the natural instinct for sensuous enjoyment. His duty he always faithfully did; but duty is sometimes a dry obligation, and he was for irrigating its aridity, whensoever possible, with a fertilizing decoction of strong waters. For the cabin's proprietor there was nothing left but to play the part of the enforced host with whatever grace and alacrity were practicable. As necessary adjuncts to the flask, he silently placed tumbler and water jug before the irrepressible guest. But excusing himself from partaking just then, he dismally watched the unembarrassed officer deliberately diluting his grog a little, then tossing it off in three swallows, pushing the empty tumbler away, yet not so far as to be beyond easy reach, at the same time settling himself in his seat and smacking his lips with high satisfaction, looking straight at the host.

These proceedings over, the master broke the silence; and there lurked a rueful reproach in the tone of his voice: "Lieutenant, you are going to take my best man from me, the jewel of 'em."

"Yes, I know," rejoined the other, immediately drawing back the tumbler preliminary to a replenishing. "Yes, I know. Sorry."

"Beg pardon, but you don't understand, Lieutenant. See here, now. Before I shipped that young fellow, my forecastle was a rat-pit of quarrels. It was black times, I tell you, aboard the *Rights* here. I was worried to that degree my pipe had no comfort for me. But Billy came; and it was like a Catholic priest striking peace in an Irish shindy.[15] Not that he preached to them or said or did anything in particular; but a virtue went out of him, sugaring the sour ones. They took to him like hornets to treacle; all but the buffer[16] of the gang, the big shaggy chap with the fire-red whiskers. He indeed, out of envy, perhaps, of the newcomer, and thinking such a "sweet and pleasant fellow," as he mockingly designated him to the others, could hardly have the spirit of a gamecock, must needs bestir himself in trying to get up an ugly row with him. Billy forebore with him and reasoned with him in a pleasant way—he is something like myself, Lieutenant, to whom aught like a quarrel is hateful —but nothing served. So, in the second dogwatch one day, the Red Whiskers in presence of the others, under pretense of showing Billy just whence a sirloin steak was cut—for the fellow had once been a butcher—insultingly gave him a dig under the ribs. Quick as lightning Billy let fly his arm. I dare say he never meant to do quite as much as he did, but anyhow he gave the burly fool a terrible drubbing. It took about half a minute, I should think. And, lord bless you, the lubber was astonished at the celerity. And will you believe it, Lieutenant, the Red Whiskers now really loves Billy—loves him, or is the biggest hypocrite that ever I heard of. But they all love him. Some of 'em do his washing, darn his old trousers for him; the carpenter is at odd times making a pretty little chest of drawers for him. Anybody will do anything for Billy Budd; and it's the happy family here. But now, Lieutenant, if that young fellow goes—I know how it will be aboard the *Rights*. Not again very soon shall I, coming up from dinner, lean over the capstan smoking a quiet pipe—no, not very soon again, I think. Ay, Lieutenant, you are going to take away the jewel of 'em; you are going to take away my peacemaker!" And with that the good soul had really some ado in checking a rising sob.

[15] Brawl.   [16] Bully.

"Well," said the lieutenant, who had listened with amused interest to all this and now was waxing merry with his tipple; "well, blessed are the peacemakers, especially the fighting peacemakers. And such are the seventy-four beauties some of which you see poking their noses out of the portholes of yonder warship lying to for me," pointing through the cabin window at the *Bellipotent*. "But courage! Don't look so downhearted, man. Why, I pledge you in advance the royal approbation. Rest assured that His Majesty will be delighted to know that in a time when his hardtack is not sought for by sailors with such avidity as should be, a time also when some shipmasters privily resent the borrowing from them a tar or two for the service; His Majesty, I say, will be delighted to learn that *one* shipmaster at least cheerfully surrenders to the King the flower of his flock, a sailor who with equal loyalty makes no dissent.——But where's my beauty? Ah," looking through the cabin's open door, "here he comes; and, by Jove, lugging along his chest—Apollo with his portmanteau!—My man," stepping out to him, "you can't take that big box aboard a warship. The boxes there are mostly shot boxes. Put your duds in a bag, lad. Boot and saddle for the cavalryman, bag and hammock for the man-of-war's man."

The transfer from chest to bag was made. And, after seeing his man into the cutter and then following him down, the lieutenant pushed off from the *Rights-of-Man*.[17] That was the merchant ship's name, though by her master and crew abbreviated in sailor fashion into the *Rights*. The hardheaded Dundee owner[18] was a staunch admirer of Thomas Paine, whose book in rejoinder to Burke's arraignment of the French Revolution had then been published for some time and had gone everywhere. In christening his vessel after the title of Paine's volume the man of Dundee was something like his contemporary shipowner, Stephen Girard[19] of Philadelphia, whose sympathies, alike with his native land and its liberal philosophers, he evinced by naming his ships after Voltaire, Diderot, and so forth.

But now, when the boat swept under the merchantman's stern, and officer and oarsmen were noting—some bitterly and others with a grin—the name emblazoned there; just then it was that the new recruit jumped up from the bow where the coxswain[20] had directed him to sit, and waving hat to his silent shipmates sorrowfully looking over at him from the taffrail,[21] bade the lads a genial good-bye. Then, making a salutation as to the ship herself, "And good-bye to you too, old *Rights-of-Man*."

"Down, sir!" roared the lieutenant, instantly assuming all the rigor of his rank, though with difficulty repressing a smile.

To be sure, Billy's action was a terrible breach of naval decorum. But in that decorum he had never been instructed; in consideration of which the lieutenant would hardly have been so energetic in reproof but for the concluding farewell to the ship. This he rather took as meant to convey a covert sally on the new recruit's part, a sly slur at impressment in general, and that of himself in especial. And yet, more likely, if satire it was in effect, it was hardly so by intention, for Billy, though happily endowed with the gaiety of high health, youth, and a free heart, was yet by no means

[17] Thomas Paine's *The Rights of Man* (1791–1792) argued for individual human rights. It was a direct response to Edmund Burke's *Reflections on the Revolution in France* (1790), which stated that human rights are best preserved through strong social and political institutions.

[18] Scotsman from the seaport of Dundee.
[19] Merchant and shipper who admired the views of the French philosophers Voltaire (1694–1778) and Denis Diderot (1713–1784).
[20] Boat steersman.
[21] Rail at ship's rear or stern.

of a satirical turn. The will to it and the sinister dexterity were alike wanting. To deal in double meanings and insinuations of any sort was quite foreign to his nature.

As to his enforced enlistment, that he seemed to take pretty much as he was wont to take any vicissitude of weather. Like the animals, though no philosopher, he was, without knowing it, practically a fatalist. And it may be that he rather liked this adventurous turn in his affairs, which promised an opening into novel scenes and martial excitements.

Aboard the *Bellipotent* our merchant sailor was forthwith rated as an able seaman and assigned to the starboard watch of the foretop. He was soon at home in the service, not at all disliked for his unpretentious good looks and a sort of genial happy-go-lucky air. No merrier man in his mess: in marked contrast to certain other individuals included like himself among the impressed portion of the ship's company; for these when not actively employed were sometimes, and more particularly in the last dogwatch[22] when the drawing near of twilight induced revery, apt to fall into a saddish mood which in some partook of sullenness. But they were not so young as our foretopman, and no few of them must have known a hearth of some sort, others may have had wives and children left, too probably, in uncertain circumstances, and hardly any but must have had acknowledged kith and kin, while for Billy, as will shortly be seen, his entire family was practically invested in himself.

2

Though our new-made foretopman was well received in the top and on the gun decks, hardly here was he that cynosure he had previously been among those minor ship's companies of the merchant marine, with which companies only had he hitherto consorted.

He was young; and despite his all but fully developed frame, in aspect looked even younger than he really was, owing to a lingering adolescent expression in the as yet smooth face all but feminine in purity of natural complexion but where, thanks to his seagoing, the lily was quite suppressed and the rose had some ado visibly to flush through the tan.

To one essentially such a novice in the complexities of factitious life, the abrupt transition from his former and simpler sphere to the ampler and more knowing world of a great warship; this might well have abashed him had there been any conceit or vanity in his composition. Among her miscellaneous multitude, the *Bellipotent* mustered several individuals who however inferior in grade were of no common natural stamp, sailors more signally susceptive of that air which continuous martial discipline and repeated presence in battle can in some degree impart even to the average man. As the Handsome Sailor, Billy Budd's position aboard the seventy-four was something analogous to that of a rustic beauty transplanted from the provinces and brought into competition with the highborn dames of the court. But this change of circumstances he scarce noted. As little did he observe that something about him provoked an ambiguous smile in one or two harder faces among the blue jackets. Nor less unaware

[22] A two-hour watch between 4 and 8 P.M. Billy's assignment as foretopman and rating as an able-bodied seaman indicate his skills as a sailor.

was he of the peculiar favorable effect his person and demeanor had upon the more intelligent gentlemen of the quarter-deck.[23] Nor could this well have been otherwise. Cast in a mold peculiar to the finest physical examples of those Englishmen in whom the Saxon strain would seem not at all to partake of any Norman or other admixture, he showed in face that humane look of reposeful good nature which the Greek sculptor in some instances gave to his heroic strong man, Hercules. But this again was subtly modified by another and pervasive quality. The ear, small and shapely, the arch of the foot, the curve in mouth and nostril, even the indurated hand dyed to the orange-tawny of the toucan's bill, a hand telling alike of the halyards and tar bucket; but, above all, something in the mobile expression, and every chance attitude and movement, something suggestive of a mother eminently favored by Love and the Graces; all this strangely indicated a lineage in direct contradiction to his lot. The mysteriousness here became less mysterious through a matter of fact elicited when Billy at the capstan was being formally mustered into the service. Asked by the officer, a small, brisk little gentleman as it chanced, among other questions, his place of birth, he replied, "Please, sir, I don't know."

"Don't know where you were born? Who was your father?"

"God knows, sir."

Struck by the straightforward simplicity of these replies, the officer next asked, "Do you know anything about your beginning?"

"No, sir. But I have heard that I was found in a pretty silk-lined basket hanging one morning from the knocker of a good man's door in Bristol."

"*Found,* say you? Well," throwing back his head and looking up and down the new recruit; "well, it turns out to have been a pretty good find. Hope they'll find some more like you, my man; the fleet sadly needs them."

Yes, Billy Budd was a foundling, a presumable by-blow,[24] and, evidently, no ignoble one. Noble descent was as evident in him as in a blood horse.

For the rest, with little or no sharpness of faculty or any trace of the wisdom of the serpent, nor yet quite a dove,[25] he possessed that kind and degree of intelligence going along with the unconventional rectitude of a sound human creature, one to whom not yet has been proffered the questionable apple of knowledge. He was illiterate; he could not read, but he could sing, and like the illiterate nightingale was sometimes the composer of his own song.

Of self-consciousness he seemed to have little or none, or about as much as we may reasonably impute to a dog of Saint Bernard's breed.

Habitually living with the elements and knowing little more of the land than as a beach, or, rather, that portion of the terraqueous globe providentially set apart for dance-houses, doxies, and tapsters, in short what sailors call a "fiddler's green,"[26] his simple nature remained unsophisticated by those moral obliquities which are not in every case incompatible with that manufacturable thing known as respectability. But are sailors, frequenters of fiddlers' greens, without vices? No; but less often than with landsmen do their vices, so called, partake of crookedness of heart, seeming less to

[23] Rear section of the main deck, customarily reserved for officers.

[24] Bastard.

[25] Matthew 10:16: "Behold, I send you forth as sheep in the midst of wolves; be ye therefore wise as serpents and harmless as doves."

[26] Doxies: wenches; tapsters: bartenders; "fiddler's green": a sailors' pleasureground.

proceed from viciousness than exuberance of vitality after long constraint: frank manifestations in accordance with natural law. By his original constitution aided by the co-operating influences of his lot, Billy in many respects was little more than a sort of upright barbarian, much such perhaps as Adam presumably might have been ere the urbane Serpent wriggled himself into his company.

And here be it submitted that apparently going to corroborate the doctrine of man's Fall,[27] a doctrine now popularly ignored, it is observable that where certain virtues pristine and unadulterate peculiarly characterize anybody in the external uniform of civilization, they will upon scrutiny seem not to be derived from custom or convention, but rather to be out of keeping with these, as if indeed exceptionally transmitted from a period prior to Cain's city[28] and citified man. The character marked by such qualities has to an unvitiated taste an untampered-with flavor like that of berries, while the man thoroughly civilized, even in a fair specimen of the breed, has to the same moral palate a questionable smack as of a compounded wine. To any stray inheritor of these primitive qualities found, like Caspar Hauser,[29] wandering dazed in any Christian capital of our time, the good-natured poet's famous invocation, near two thousand years ago, of the good rustic out of his latitude in the Rome of the Caesars, still appropriately holds:

> Honest and poor, faithful in word and thought,
> What hath thee, Fabian, to the city brought?[30]

Though our Handsome Sailor had as much of masculine beauty as one can expect anywhere to see; nevertheless, like the beautiful woman in one of Hawthorne's minor tales,[31] there was just one thing amiss in him. No visible blemish indeed, as with the lady; no, but an occasional liability to a vocal defect. Though in the hour of elemental uproar or peril he was everything that a sailor should be, yet under sudden provocation of strong heart-feeling his voice, otherwise singularly musical, as if expressive of the harmony within, was apt to develop an organic hesitancy, in fact more or less of a stutter or even worse. In this particular Billy was a striking instance that the arch interferer, the envious marplot of Eden, still has more or less to do with every human consignment to this planet of Earth. In every case, one way or another he is sure to slip in his little card, as much as to remind us—I too have a hand here.

The avowal of such an imperfection in the Handsome Sailor should be evidence not alone that he is not presented as a conventional hero, but also that the story in which he is the main figure is no romance.

3

At the time of Billy Budd's arbitrary enlistment into the *Bellipotent* that ship was on her way to join the Mediterranean fleet. No long time elapsed before the junction was effected. As one of that fleet the seventy-four participated in its movements, though at times on account of her superior sailing qualities, in the absence of frigates,

---

[27] Human downfall caused by Adam and Eve's sin.

[28] See Genesis 4:16–17. Cain killed his brother, Abel, and then "went out from the presence of the Lord. . . . And he builded a city."

[29] German boy (1812?–1833) of mysterious origins, supposed to be of noble birth and to exhibit an innocent nature.

[30] Martial, *Epigrams,* I, iv.

[31] Hawthorne's "The Birthmark."

dispatched on separate duty as a scout and at times on less temporary service. But with all this the story has little concernment, restricted as it is to the inner life of one particular ship and the career of an individual sailor.

It was the summer of 1797. In the April of that year had occurred the commotion at Spithead followed in May by a second and yet more serious outbreak in the fleet at the Nore.[32] The latter is known, and without exaggeration in the epithet, as "the Great Mutiny." It was indeed a demonstration more menacing to England than the contemporary manifestoes and conquering and proselyting armies of the French Directory.[33] To the British Empire the Nore Mutiny was what a strike in the fire brigade would be to London threatened by general arson. In a crisis when the kingdom might well have anticipated the famous signal[34] that some years later published along the naval line of battle what it was that upon occasion England expected of Englishmen; *that* was the time when at the mastheads of the three-deckers and seventy-fours moored in her own roadstead—a fleet the right arm of a Power then all but the sole free conservative one of the Old World—the bluejackets, to be numbered by thousands, ran up with huzzas the British colors with the union and cross wiped out; by that cancellation transmuting the flag of founded law and freedom defined, into the enemy's red meteor of unbridled and unbounded revolt. Reasonable discontent growing out of practical grievances in the fleet had been ignited into irrational combustion as by live cinders blown across the Channel from France in flames.

The event converted into irony for a time those spirited strains of Dibdin[35]—as a song-writer no mean auxiliary to the English government at that European conjuncture—strains celebrating, among other things, the patriotic devotion of the British tar: "And as for my life, 'tis the King's!"

Such an episode in the Island's grand naval story her naval historians naturally abridge, one of them (William James) candidly acknowledging that fain would he pass it over did not "impartiality forbid fastidiousness." And yet his mention is less a narration than a reference, having to do hardly at all with details. Nor are these readily to be found in the libraries. Like some other events in every age befalling states everywhere, including America, the Great Mutiny was of such character that national pride along with views of policy would fain shade it off into the historical background. Such events cannot be ignored, but there is a considerate way of historically treating them. If a well-constituted individual refrains from blazoning aught amiss or calamitous in his family, a nation in the like circumstance may without reproach be equally discreet.

Though after parleyings between government and the ringleaders, and concessions by the former as to some glaring abuses, the first uprising—that at Spithead—with difficulty was put down, or matters for the time pacified; yet at the Nore the unforeseen renewal of insurrection on a yet larger scale, and emphasized in the conferences that ensued by demands deemed by the authorities not only inadmissible but aggressively insolent, indicated—if the Red Flag[36] did not sufficiently do so— what was the spirit animating the men. Final suppression, however, there was; but only

---

[32] Spithead and Nore were locations in which British seamen mutinied.
[33] Post-Revolutionary French governing body (1795–1799).
[34] Reference to British Admiral Nelson's famous

signal, "England expects every man to do his duty," prior to the Battle of Trafalgar (1805).
[35] Charles Dibdin (1745–1815), English writer of patriotic songs.
[36] Traditional banner of revolution.

made possible perhaps by the unswerving loyalty of the marine corps[37] and a voluntary resumption of loyalty among influential sections of the crews.

To some extent the Nore Mutiny may be regarded as analogous to the distempering irruption of contagious fever in a frame constitutionally sound, and which anon throws it off.

At all events, of these thousands of mutineers were some of the tars who not so very long afterwards—whether wholly prompted thereto by patriotism, or pugnacious instinct, or by both—helped to win a coronet for Nelson at the Nile, and the naval crown of crowns for him at Trafalgar. To the mutineers, those battles and especially Trafalgar were a plenary absolution and a grand one. For all that goes to make up scenic naval display and heroic magnificence in arms, those battles, especially Trafalgar, stand unmatched in human annals.

4

In this matter of writing, resolve as one may to keep to the main road, some bypaths have an enticement not readily to be withstood. I am going to err into such a bypath. If the reader will keep me company I shall be glad. At the least, we can promise ourselves that pleasure which is wickedly said to be in sinning, for a literary sin the divergence will be.

Very likely it is no new remark that the inventions of our time have at last brought about a change in sea warfare in degree corresponding to the revolution in all warfare effected by the original introduction from China into Europe of gunpowder. The first European firearm, a clumsy contrivance, was, as is well known, scouted by no few of the knights as a base implement, good enough peradventure for weavers too craven to stand up crossing steel with steel in frank fight. But as ashore knightly valor, though shorn of its blazonry, did not cease with the knights, neither on the seas—though nowadays in encounters there a certain kind of displayed gallantry be fallen out of date as hardly applicable under changed circumstances—did the nobler qualities of such naval magnates as Don John of Austria, Doria, Van Tromp, Jean Bart, the long line of British admirals, and the American Decaturs of 1812 become obsolete with their wooden walls.[38]

Nevertheless, to anybody who can hold the Present at its worth without being inappreciative of the Past, it may be forgiven, if to such an one the solitary old hulk at Portsmouth, Nelson's *Victory,* seems to float there, not alone as the decaying monument of a fame incorruptible, but also as a poetic reproach, softened by its picturesqueness, to the *Monitors* and yet mightier hulls of the European ironclads.[39] And this not altogether because such craft are unsightly, unavoidably lacking the symmetry and grand lines of the old battleships, but equally for other reasons.

There are some, perhaps, who while not altogether inaccessible to that poetic

---

[37] Marines were stationed on men-of-war and often had an antagonistic relation to the crew.

[38] Don Juan of Austria (1547–1578) led a fleet to defeat Turkey (1571); Andrea Doria (1466–1560) was renowned as admiral of the Genoese and French fleet; Maarten Van Tromp (1597–1653) commanded Dutch fleets against Britain and Spain; Jean Bart (1651?–1702) led French privateers against the Dutch; Stephen Decatur (1779–1820) led American naval ships against Tripoli pirates and against Britain in the War of 1812.

[39] The *Victory* was Nelson's flagship at Trafalgar, where he died; the iron-clad Union *Monitor* defeated the Confederate *Merrimac* in the American Civil War.

reproach just alluded to, may yet on behalf of the new order be disposed to parry it; and this to the extent of iconoclasm, if need be. For example, prompted by the sight of the star inserted in the *Victory*'s quarter-deck designating the spot where the Great Sailor fell, these martial utilitarians may suggest considerations implying that Nelson's ornate publication of his person in battle was not only unnecessary, but not military, nay, savored of foolhardiness and vanity. They may add, too, that at Trafalgar it was in effect nothing less than a challenge to death; and death came; and that but for his bravado the victorious admiral might possibly have survived the battle, and so, instead of having his sagacious dying injunctions overruled by his immediate successor in command, he himself when the contest was decided might have brought his shattered fleet to anchor, a proceeding which might have averted the deplorable loss of life by shipwreck in the elemental tempest that followed the martial one.

Well, should we set aside the more than disputable point whether for various reasons it was possible to anchor the fleet, then plausibly enough the Benthamites[40] of war may urge the above. But the *might-have-been* is but boggy ground to build on. And, certainly, in foresight as to the larger issue of an encounter, and anxious preparations for it—buoying the deadly way and mapping it out, as at Copenhagen[41] —few commanders have been so painstakingly circumspect as this same reckless declarer of his person in fight.

Personal prudence, even when dictated by quite other than selfish considerations, surely is no special virtue in a military man; while an excessive love of glory, impassioning a less burning impulse, the honest sense of duty, is the first. If the name *Wellington* is not so much of a trumpet to the blood as the simpler name *Nelson,* the reason for this may perhaps be inferred from the above. Alfred[42] in his funeral ode on the victor of Waterloo ventures not to call him the greatest soldier of all time, though in the same ode he invokes Nelson as "the greatest sailor since our world began."

At Trafalgar Nelson on the brink of opening the fight sat down and wrote his last brief will and testament. If under the presentiment of the most magnificent of all victories to be crowned by his own glorious death, a sort of priestly motive led him to dress his person in the jewelled vouchers of his own shining deeds; if thus to have adorned himself for the altar and the sacrifice were indeed vainglory, then affectation and fustian is each more heroic line in the great epics and dramas, since in such lines the poet but embodies in verse those exaltations of sentiment that a nature like Nelson, the opportunity being given, vitalizes into acts.

5

Yes, the outbreak at the Nore was put down. But not every grievance was redressed. If the contractors, for example, were no longer permitted to ply some practices peculiar to their tribe everywhere, such as providing shoddy cloth, rations not sound, or false in the measure; not the less impressment, for one thing, went on. By custom sanctioned for centuries, and judicially maintained by a Lord Chancellor as late as

[40] Followers of Jeremy Bentham (1748–1832), English advocate of utilitarianism.
[41] Reference to Nelson's careful preparations for the Battle of Copenhagen (1801).

[42] Alfred, Lord Tennyson (1809–1892) commemorated the English victory over Napoleon at Waterloo (1815) in "Ode on the Death of the Duke of Wellington."

Mansfield,[43] that mode of manning the fleet, a mode now fallen into a sort of abeyance but never formally renounced, it was not practicable to give up in those years. Its abrogation would have crippled the indispensable fleet, one wholly under canvas, no steam power, its innumerable sails and thousands of cannon, everything in short, worked by muscle alone; a fleet the more insatiate in demand for men, because then multiplying its ships of all grades against contingencies present and to come of the convulsed Continent.

Discontent foreran the Two Mutinies, and more or less it lurkingly survived them. Hence it was not unreasonable to apprehend some return of trouble sporadic or general. One instance of such apprehensions: In the same year with this story, Nelson, then Rear Admiral Sir Horatio, being with the fleet off the Spanish coast, was directed by the admiral in command to shift his pennant from the *Captain* to the *Theseus;* and for this reason: that the latter ship having newly arrived on the station from home, where it had taken part in the Great Mutiny, danger was apprehended from the temper of the men; and it was thought that an officer like Nelson was the one, not indeed to terrorize the crew into base subjection, but to win them, by force of his mere presence and heroic personality, back to an allegiance if not as enthusiastic as his own yet as true.

So it was that for a time, on more than one quarter-deck, anxiety did exist. At sea, precautionary vigilance was strained against relapse. At short notice an engagement might come on. When it did, the lieutenants assigned to batteries felt it incumbent on them, in some instances, to stand with drawn swords behind the men working the guns.

6

But on board the seventy-four in which Billy now swung his hammock, very little in the manner of the men and nothing obvious in the demeanor of the officers would have suggested to an ordinary observer that the Great Mutiny was a recent event. In their general bearing and conduct the commissioned officers of a warship naturally take their tone from the commander, that is if he have that ascendancy of character that ought to be his.

Captain the Honorable Edward Fairfax Vere, to give his full title, was a bachelor of forty or thereabouts, a sailor of distinction even in a time prolific of renowned seamen. Though allied to the higher nobility, his advancement had not been altogether owing to influences connected with that circumstance. He had seen much service, been in various engagements, always acquitting himself as an officer mindful of the welfare of his men, but never tolerating an infraction of discipline; thoroughly versed in the science of his profession, and intrepid to the verge of temerity, though never injudiciously so. For his gallantry in the West Indian waters as flag lieutenant under Rodney in that admiral's crowning victory over De Grasse,[44] he was made a post captain.

Ashore, in the garb of a civilian, scarce anyone would have taken him for a sailor, more especially that he never garnished unprofessional talk with nautical terms, and grave in his bearing, evinced little appreciation of mere humor. It was not out of

[43] William Murray, the earl of Mansfield (1705–1793), authorized impressment, virtual kidnapping, to secure sailors for the naval fleet.

[44] British Admiral George Rodney (1719–1792) defeated French admiral François Paul DeGrasse (1722–1788) in the West Indies in 1782.

keeping with these traits that on a passage when nothing demanded his paramount action, he was the most undemonstrative of men. Any landsman observing this gentleman not conspicuous by his stature and wearing no pronounced insignia, emerging from his cabin to the open deck, and noting the silent deference of the officers retiring to leeward, might have taken him for the King's guest, a civilian aboard the King's ship, some highly honorable discreet envoy on his way to an important post. But in fact this unobtrusiveness of demeanor may have proceeded from a certain unaffected modesty of manhood sometimes accompanying a resolute nature, a modesty evinced at all times not calling for pronounced action, which shown in any rank of life suggests a virtue aristocratic in kind. As with some others engaged in various departments of the world's more heroic activities, Captain Vere though practical enough upon occasion would at times betray a certain dreaminess of mood. Standing alone on the weather side of the quarter-deck, one hand holding by the rigging, he would absently gaze off at the black sea. At the presentation to him then of some minor matter interrupting the current of his thoughts, he would show more or less irascibility; but instantly he would control it.

In the navy he was popularly known by the appellation "Starry Vere." How such a designation happened to fall upon one who whatever his sterling qualities was without any brilliant ones, was in this wise: A favorite kinsman, Lord Denton, a freehearted fellow, had been the first to meet and congratulate him upon his return to England from his West Indian cruise; and but the day previous turning over a copy of Andrew Marvell's poems had lighted, not for the first time, however, upon the lines entitled "Appleton House," the name of one of the seats of their common ancestor, a hero in the German wars of the seventeenth century, in which poem occur the lines:

This 'tis to have been from the first
In a domestic heaven nursed,
Under the discipline severe
Of Fairfax and the starry Vere.[45]

And so, upon embracing his cousin fresh from Rodney's great victory wherein he had played so gallant a part, brimming over with just family pride in the sailor of their house, he exuberantly exclaimed, "Give ye joy, Ed; give ye joy, my starry Vere!" This got currency, and the novel prefix serving in familiar parlance readily to distinguish the *Bellipotent*'s captain from another Vere his senior, a distant relative, an officer of like rank in the navy, it remained permanently attached to the surname.

7

In view of the part that the commander of the *Bellipotent* plays in scenes shortly to follow, it may be well to fill out that sketch of him outlined in the previous chapter.

Aside from his qualities as a sea officer Captain Vere was an exceptional character. Unlike no few of England's renowned sailors, long and arduous service with signal devotion to it had not resulted in absorbing and *salting* the entire man. He had a

[45] The poet Andrew Marvell's lines refer to Ann Vere, wife of Lord Fairfax (1612–1671);   Melville adapts the material to his own fictional uses here.

marked leaning toward everything intellectual. He loved books, never going to sea without a newly replenished library, compact but of the best. The isolated leisure, in some cases so wearisome, falling at intervals to commanders even during a war cruise, never was tedious to Captain Vere. With nothing of that literary taste which less heeds the thing conveyed than the vehicle, his bias was toward those books to which every serious mind of superior order occupying any active post of authority in the world naturally inclines: books treating of actual men and events no matter of what era— history, biography, and unconventional writers like Montaigue, who, free from cant and convention, honestly and in the spirit of common sense philosophize upon realities. In this line of reading he found confirmation of his own more reserved thoughts—confirmation which he had vainly sought in social converse, so that as touching most fundamental topics, there had got to be established in him some positive convictions which he forefelt would abide in him essentially unmodified so long as his intelligent part remained unimpaired. In view of the troubled period in which his lot was cast, this was well for him. His settled convictions were as a dike against those invading waters of novel opinion social, political, and otherwise, which carried away as in a torrent no few minds in those days, minds by nature not inferior to his own. While other members of that aristocracy to which by birth he belonged were incensed at the innovators mainly because their theories were inimical to the privileged classes, Captain Vere disinterestedly opposed them not alone because they seemed to him insusceptible of embodiment in lasting institutions, but at war with the peace of the world and the true welfare of mankind.

With minds less stored than his and less earnest, some officers of his rank, with whom at times he would necessarily consort, found him lacking in the companionable quality, a dry and bookish gentleman, as they deemed. Upon any chance withdrawal from their company one would be apt to say to another something like this: "Vere is a noble fellow, Starry Vere. 'Spite the gazettes,[46] Sir Horatio" (meaning him who became Lord Nelson) "is at bottom scarce a better seaman or fighter. But between you and me now, don't you think there is a queer streak of the pedantic running through him? Yes, like the King's yarn[47] in a coil of navy rope?"

Some apparent ground there was for this sort of confidential criticism; since not only did the captain's discourse never fall into the jocosely familiar, but in illustrating of any point touching the stirring personages and events of the time he would be as apt to cite some historic character or incident of antiquity as he would be to cite from the moderns. He seemed unmindful of the circumstance that to his bluff company such remote allusions, however pertinent they might really be, were altogether alien to men whose reading was mainly confined to the journals. But considerateness in such matters is not easy to natures constituted like Captain Vere's. Their honesty prescribes to them directness, sometimes far-reaching like that of a migratory fowl that in its flight never heeds when it crosses a frontier.

8

The lieutenants and other commissioned gentlemen forming Captain Vere's staff it is not necessary here to particularize, nor needs it to make any mention of any of the

---

[46] Despite newspaper reports.   [47] Noticeable thread in a length of rope.

warrant officers. But among the petty officers was one who, having much to do with the story, may as well be forthwith introduced. His portrait I essay, but shall never hit it. This was John Claggart, the master-at-arms. But that sea title may to landsmen seem somewhat equivocal. Originally, doubtless, that petty officer's function was the instruction of the men in the use of arms, sword or cutlass. But very long ago, owing to the advance in gunnery making hand-to-hand encounters less frequent and giving to niter and sulphur the pre-eminence over steel,[48] that function ceased; the master-at-arms of a great warship becoming a sort of chief of police charged among other matters with the duty of preserving order on the populous lower gun decks.

Claggart was a man about five-and-thirty, somewhat spare and tall, yet of no ill figure upon the whole. His hand was too small and shapely to have been accustomed to hard toil. The face was a notable one, the features all except the chin cleanly cut as those on a Greek medallion; yet the chin, beardless as Tecumseh's,[49] had something of strange protuberant broadness in its make that recalled the prints of the Reverend Dr. Titus Oates, the historic deponent with the clerical drawl in the time of Charles II and the fraud of the alleged Popish Plot.[50] It served Claggart in his office that his eye could cast a tutoring glance. His brow was of the sort phrenologically associated with more than average intellect; silken jet curls partly clustering over it, making a foil to the pallor below, a pallor tinged with a faint shade of amber akin to the hue of time-tinted marbles of old. This complexion, singularly contrasting with the red or deeply bronzed visages of the sailors, and in part the result of his official seclusion from the sunlight, though it was not exactly displeasing, nevertheless seemed to hint of something defective or abnormal in the constitution and blood. But his general aspect and manner were so suggestive of an education and career incongruous with his naval function that when not actively engaged in it he looked like a man of high quality, social and moral, who for reasons of his own was keeping incog.[51] Nothing was known of his former life. It might be that he was an Englishman; and yet there lurked a bit of accent in his speech suggesting that possibly he was not such by birth, but through naturalization in early childhood. Among certain grizzled sea gossips of the gun decks and forecastle went a rumor perdue that the master-at-arms was a *chevalier*[52] who had volunteered into the King's navy by way of compounding for some mysterious swindle whereof he had been arraigned at the King's Bench.[53] The fact that nobody could substantiate this report was, of course, nothing against its secret currency. Such a rumor once started on the gun decks in reference to almost anyone below the rank of a commissioned officer would, during the period assigned to this narrative, have seemed not altogether wanting in credibility to the tarry old wiseacres of a man-of-war crew. And indeed a man of Claggart's accomplishments, without prior nautical experience entering the navy at mature life, as he did, and necessarily allotted at the start to the lowest grade in it; a man too who never made allusion to his previous life ashore; these were circumstances which in the dearth of exact knowledge as to his true antecedents opened to the invidious a vague field for unfavorable surmise.

[48] Gunpowder formed by mixture of charcoal, sulphur, and potassium nitrate.
[49] Tecumseh: Shawnee Indian chief (1768?–1813).
[50] The perjurer Oates (1649–1705) accused Catholics of plotting to murder English Protestants and King Charles II, and to burn London.
[51] Incognito.
[52] Adventurer.
[53] Court of law.

But the sailors' dogwatch gossip concerning him derived a vague plausibility from the fact that now for some period the British navy could so little afford to be squeamish in the matter of keeping up the muster rolls, that not only were press gangs notoriously abroad both afloat and ashore, but there was little or no secret about another matter, namely, that the London police were at liberty to capture any able-bodied suspect, any questionable fellow at large, and summarily ship him to the dockyard or fleet. Furthermore, even among voluntary enlistments there were instances where the motive thereto partook neither of patriotic impulse nor yet of a random desire to experience a bit of sea life and martial adventure. Insolvent debtors of minor grade, together with the promiscuous lame ducks of morality, found in the navy a convenient and secure refuge, secure because, once enlisted aboard a King's ship, they were as much in sanctuary as the transgressor of the Middle Ages harboring himself under the shadow of the altar. Such sanctioned irregularities, which for obvious reasons the government would hardly think to parade at the time and which consequently, and as affecting the least influential class of mankind, have all but dropped into oblivion, lend color to something for the truth whereof I do not vouch, and hence have some scruple in stating; something I remember having seen in print though the book I cannot recall; but the same thing was personally communicated to me now more than forty years ago by an old pensioner in a cocked hat with whom I had a most interesting talk on the terrace at Greenwich, a Baltimore Negro, a Trafalgar man. It was to this effect: In the case of a warship short of hands whose speedy sailing was imperative, the deficient quota, in lack of any other way of making it good, would be eked out by drafts culled direct from the jails. For reasons previously suggested it would not perhaps be easy at the present day directly to prove or disprove the allegation. But allowed as a verity, how significant would it be of England's straits at the time confronted by those wars[54] which like a flight of harpies rose shrieking from the din and dust of the fallen Bastille. That era appears measurably clear to us who look back at it, and but read of it. But to the grandfathers of us graybeards, the more thoughtful of them, the genius of it presented an aspect like that of Camoëns'[55] Spirit of the Cape, an eclipsing menace mysterious and prodigious. Not America was exempt from apprehension. At the height of Napoleon's unexampled conquests, there were Americans who had fought at Bunker Hill who looked forward to the possibility that the Atlantic might prove no barrier against the ultimate schemes of this French portentous upstart from the revolutionary chaos who seemed in act of fulfilling judgment prefigured in the Apocalypse.

But the less credence was to be given to the gun-deck talk touching Claggart, seeing that no man holding his office in a man-of-war can ever hope to be popular with the crew. Besides, in derogatory comments upon anyone against whom they have a grudge, or for any reason or no reason mislike, sailors are much like landsmen: they are apt to exaggerate or romance it.

About as much was really known to the Bellipotent's tars of the master-at-arms' career before entering the service as an astronomer knows about a comet's travels prior to its first observable appearance in the sky. The verdict of the sea quidnuncs[56] has

---

[54] I.e., the Napoleonic wars (1796–1815).
[55] Luis de Camoëns (1524–1580), Portuguese epic poet of Vasco da Gama's voyage to India via the treacherous Cape of Good Hope.

[56] Gossips.

been cited only by way of showing what sort of moral impression the man made upon rude uncultivated natures whose conceptions of human wickedness were necessarily of the narrowest, limited to ideas of vulgar rascality—a thief among the swinging hammocks during a night watch, or the man-brokers and land-sharks of the seaports.

It was no gossip, however, but fact that though, as before hinted, Claggart upon his entrance into the navy was, as a novice, assigned to the least honorable section of a man-of-war's crew, embracing the drudgery, he did not long remain there. The superior capacity he immediately evinced, his constitutional sobriety, an ingratiating deference to superiors, together with a peculiar ferreting genius manifested on a singular occasion; all this, capped by a certain austere patriotism, abruptly advanced him to the position of master-at-arms.

Of this maritime chief of police the ship's corporals, so called, were the immediate subordinates, and compliant ones; and this, as is to be noted in some business departments ashore, almost to a degree inconsistent with entire moral volition. His place put various converging wires of underground influence under the chief's control, capable when astutely worked through his understrappers of operating to the mysterious discomfort, if nothing worse, of any of the sea commonalty.

9

Life in the foretop well agreed with Billy Budd. There, when not actually engaged on the yards yet higher aloft, the topmen, who as such had been picked out for youth and activity, constituted an aerial club lounging at ease against the smaller stun'sails rolled up into cushions, spinning yarns like the lazy gods, and frequently amused with what was going on in the busy world of the decks below. No wonder then that a young fellow of Billy's disposition was well content in such society. Giving no cause of offense to anybody, he was always alert at a call. So in the merchant service it had been with him. But now such a punctiliousness in duty was shown that his topmates would sometimes good-naturedly laugh at him for it. This heightened alacrity had its cause, namely, the impression made upon him by the first formal gangway-punishment he had ever witnessed, which befell the day following his impressment. It had been incurred by a little fellow, young, a novice afterguardsman absent from his assigned post when the ship was being put about; a dereliction resulting in a rather serious hitch to that maneuver, one demanding instantaneous promptitude in letting go and making fast. When Billy saw the culprit's naked back under the scourge, gridironed with red welts and worse, when he marked the dire expression in the liberated man's face as with his woolen shirt flung over him by the executioner he rushed forward from the spot to bury himself in the crowd, Billy was horrified. He resolved that never through remissness would he make himself liable to such a visitation or do or omit aught that might merit even verbal reproof. What then was his surprise and concern when ultimately he found himself getting into petty trouble occasionally about such matters as the stowage of his bag or something amiss in his hammock, matters under the police oversight of the ship's corporals of the lower decks, and which brought down on him a vague threat from one of them.

So heedful in all things as he was, how could this be? He could not understand it, and it more than vexed him. When he spoke to his young topmates about it they were either lightly incredulous or found something comical in his unconcealed anxiety. "Is it your bag, Billy?" said one. "Well, sew yourself up in it, bully boy, and then you'll be sure to know if anybody meddles with it."

Now there was a veteran aboard who because his years began to disqualify him for more active work had been recently assigned duty as mainmastman in his watch, looking to the gear belayed at the rail roundabout that great spar near the deck. At off-times the foretopman had picked up some acquaintance with him, and now in his trouble it occurred to him that he might be the sort of person to go to for wise counsel. He was an old Dansker[57] long anglicized in the service, of few words, many wrinkles, and some honorable scars. His wizened face, time-tinted and weather-stained to the complexion of an antique parchment, was here and there peppered blue by the chance explosion of a gun cartridge in action.

He was an *Agamemnon* man, some two years prior to the time of this story having served under Nelson when still captain in that ship immortal in naval memory, which dismantled and in part broken up to her bare ribs is seen a grand skeleton in Haden's etching.[58] As one of a boarding party from the *Agamemnon* he had received a cut slantwise along one temple and cheek leaving a long pale scar like a streak of dawn's light falling athwart the dark visage. It was on account of that scar and the affair in which it was known that he had received it, as well as from his blue-peppered complexion, that the Dansker went among the *Bellipotent's* crew by the name of "Board-Her-in-the-Smoke."

Now the first time that his small weasel eyes happened to light on Billy Budd, a certain grim internal merriment set all his ancient wrinkles into antic play. Was it that his eccentric unsentimental old sapience, primitive in its kind, saw or thought it saw something which in contrast with the warship's environment looked oddly incongruous in the Handsome Sailor? But after slyly studying him at intervals, the old Merlin's[59] equivocal merriment was modified; for now when the twain would meet, it would start in his face a quizzing sort of look, but it would be but momentary and sometimes replaced by an expression of speculative query as to what might eventually befall a nature like that, dropped into a world not without some mantraps and against whose subtleties simple courage lacking experience and address, and without any touch of defensive ugliness, is of little avail; and where such innocence as man is capable of does yet in a moral emergency not always sharpen the faculties or enlighten the will.

However it was, the Dansker in his ascetic way rather took to Billy. Nor was this only because of a certain philosophic interest in such a character. There was another cause. While the old man's eccentricities, sometimes bordering on the ursine, repelled the juniors, Billy, undeterred thereby, revering him as a salt hero, would make advances, never passing the old *Agamemnon* man without a salutation marked by that respect which is seldom lost on the aged, however crabbed at times or whatever their station in life.

There was a vein of dry humor, or what not, in the mastman; and, whether in freak of patriarchal irony touching Billy's youth and athletic frame, or for some other and more recondite reason, from the first in addressing him he always substituted *Baby*

<hr />

[57] Dane.
[58] Francis Seymour Haden's (1818–1910) popular etching *The Breaking Up of Ole Agamemnon* (1870).

[59] Merlin: Magician in the legends of King Arthur.

for Billy, the Dansker in fact being the originator of the name by which the foretopman eventually became known aboard ship.

Well then, in his mysterious little difficulty going in quest of the wrinkled one, Billy found him off duty in a dogwatch ruminating by himself, seated on a shot box of the upper gun deck, now and then surveying with a somewhat cynical regard certain of the more swaggering promenaders there. Billy recounted his trouble, again wondering how it all happened. The salt seer attentively listened, accompanying the foretopman's recital with queer twitchings of his wrinkles and problematical little sparkles of his small ferret eyes. Making an end of his story, the foretopman asked, "And now, Dansker, do tell me what you think of it."

The old man, shoving up the front of his tarpaulin[60] and deliberately rubbing the long slant scar at the point where it entered the thin hair, laconically said, "Baby Budd, *Jemmy Legs*" (meaning the master-at-arms) "is down on you."

"*Jemmy Legs!*" ejaculated Billy, his welkin eyes expanding. "What for? Why, he calls me 'the sweet and pleasant young fellow,' they tell me."

"Does he so?" grinned the grizzled one; then said, "Ay, Baby had, a sweet voice has Jemmy Legs."

"No, not always. But to me he has. I seldom pass him but there comes a pleasant word."

"And that's because he's down upon you, Baby Budd."

Such reiteration, along with the manner of it, incomprehensible to a novice, disturbed Billy almost as much as the mystery for which he had sought explanation. Something less unpleasingly oracular he tried to extract; but the old sea Chiron,[61] thinking perhaps that for the nonce he had sufficiently instructed his young Achilles, pursed his lips, gathered all his wrinkles together, and would commit himself to nothing further.

Years, and those experiences which befall certain shrewder men subordinated lifelong to the will of superiors, all this had developed in the Dansker the pithy guarded cynicism that was his leading characteristic.

10

The next day an incident served to confirm Billy Budd in his incredulity as to the Dansker's strange summing up of the case submitted. The ship at noon, going large before the wind, was rolling on her course, and he below at dinner and engaged in some sportful talk with the members of his mess, chanced in a sudden lurch to spill the entire contents of his soup pan upon the new-scrubbed deck. Claggart, the master-at-arms, official rattan[62] in hand, happened to be passing along the battery in a bay of which the mess was lodged, and the greasy liquid streamed just across his path. Stepping over it, he was proceeding on his way without comment, since the matter was nothing to take notice of under the circumstances, when he happened to observe who it was that had done the spilling. His countenance changed. Pausing, he was about to ejaculate something hasty at the sailor, but checked himself, and pointing down to the streaming soup, playfully tapped him from behind with his rattan, saying in a low musical voice peculiar to him at times, "Handsomely done, my lad! And

---

[60] Waterproof hat.
[61] Teacher of Achilles in Greek myth.

[62] Cane.

handsome is as handsome did it, too!" And with that passed on. Not noted by Billy as not coming within his view was the involuntary smile, or rather grimace, that accompanied Claggart's equivocal words. Aridly it drew down the thin corners of his shapely mouth. But everybody taking his remark as meant for humorous, and at which therefore as coming from a superior they were bound to laugh "with counter-feited glee,"[63] acted accordingly; and Billy, tickled, it may be, by the allusion to his being the Handsome Sailor, merrily joined in; then addressing his messmates ex-claimed, "There now, who says that Jemmy Legs is down on me!"

"And who said he was, Beauty?" demanded one Donald with some surprise. Whereat the foretopman looked a little foolish, recalling that it was only one person, Board-Her-in-the-Smoke, who had suggested what to him was the smoky idea that this master-at-arms was in any peculiar way hostile to him. Meantime that function-ary, resuming his path, must have momentarily worn some expression less guarded than that of the bitter smile, usurping the face from the heart—some distorting expression perhaps, for a drummer-boy heedlessly frolicking along from the opposite direction and chancing to come into light collision with his person was strangely disconcerted by his aspect. Nor was the impression lessened when the official, impetu-ously giving him a sharp cut with the rattan, vehemently exclaimed, "Look where you go!"

11

What was the matter with the master-at-arms? And, be the matter what it might, how could it have direct relation to Billy Budd, with whom prior to the affair of the spilled soup he had never come into any special contact official or otherwise? What indeed could the trouble have to do with one so little inclined to give offense as the merchant-ship's "peacemaker," even him who in Claggart's own phrase was "the sweet and pleasant young fellow"? Yes, why should Jemmy Legs, to borrow the Dansker's expression, be "down" on the Handsome Sailor? But, at heart and not for nothing, as the late chance encounter may indicate to the discerning, down on him, secretly down on him, he assuredly was.

Now to invent something touching the more private career of Claggart, something involving Billy Budd, of which something the latter should be wholly ignorant, some romantic incident implying that Claggart's knowledge of the young blue-jacket began at some period anterior to catching sight of him on board the seventy-four—all this, not so difficult to do, might avail in a way more or less interesting to account for whatever of enigma may appear to lurk in the case. But in fact there was nothing of the sort. And yet the cause necessarily to be assumed as the sole one assignable is in its very realism as much charged with that prime element of Radcliffian romance, the mysterious, as any that the ingenuity of the author of The Mysteries of Udolpho could devise.[64] For what can more partake of the mysterious than an antipathy spontaneous and profound such as is evoked in certain exceptional mortals by the mere

---

[63] In Oliver Goldsmith's poem "The Deserted Village" (1770), the school children laugh "with counterfeited glee" at the jokes of the tyrannical schoolmaster.

[64] Ann Radcliffe (1764–1823) wrote The Mysteries of Udolpho (1794) and other gothic novels.

aspect of some other mortal, however harmless he may be, if not called forth by this very harmlessness itself?

Now there can exist no irritating juxtaposition of dissimilar personalities comparable to that which is possible aboard a great warship fully manned and at sea. There, every day among all ranks, almost every man comes into more or less of contact with almost every other man. Wholly there to avoid even the sight of an aggravating object one must needs give it Jonah's toss[65] or jump overboard himself. Imagine how all this might eventually operate on some peculiar human creature the direct reverse of a saint!

But for the adequate comprehending of Claggart by a normal nature these hints are insufficient. To pass from a normal nature to him one must cross "the deadly space between." And this is best done by indirection.

Long ago an honest scholar, my senior, said to me in reference to one who like himself is now no more, a man so unimpeachably respectable that against him nothing was ever openly said though among the few something was whispered, "Yes, X—— is a nut not to be cracked by the tap of a lady's fan. You are aware that I am the adherent of no organized religion, much less of any philosophy built into a system. Well, for all that, I think that to try and get into X——, enter his labyrinth and get out again, without a clue derived from some source other than what is known as 'knowledge of the world'—that were hardly possible, at least for me."

"Why," said I, "X——, however singular a study to some, is yet human, and knowledge of the world assuredly implies the knowledge of human nature, and in most of its varieties."

"Yes, but a superficial knowledge of it, serving ordinary purposes. But for anything deeper, I am not certain whether to know the world and to know human nature be not two distinct branches of knowledge, which while they may coexist in the same heart, yet either may exist with little or nothing of the other. Nay, in an average man of the world, his constant rubbing with it blunts that finer spiritual insight indispensable to the understanding of the essential in certain exceptional characters, whether evil ones or good. In a matter of some importance I have seen a girl wind an old lawyer about her little finger. Nor was it the dotage of senile love. Nothing of the sort. But he knew law better than he knew the girl's heart. Coke and Blackstone[66] hardly shed so much light into obscure spiritual places as the Hebrew prophets. And who were they? Mostly recluses."

At the time, my inexperience was such that I did not quite see the drift of all this. It may be that I see it now. And, indeed, if that lexicon which is based on Holy Writ were any longer popular, one might with less difficulty define and denominate certain phenomenal men. As it is, one must turn to some authority not liable to the charge of being tinctured with the biblical element.

In a list of definitions included in the authentic translation of Plato, a list attributed to him, occurs this: "Natural Depravity: a depravity according to nature," a definition

---

[65] Jonah 1:15: "So they took up Jonah, and cast him forth into the sea" (i.e., threw him overboard).

[66] Sir Edward Coke (1552–1634) and Sir William

Blackstone (1723–1780) were renowned British jurists.

which, though savoring of Calvinism, by no means involves Calvin's dogma as to total mankind.[67] Evidently its intent makes it applicable but to individuals. Not many are the examples of this depravity which the gallows and jail supply. At any rate, for notable instances, since these have no vulgar alloy of the brute in them, but invariably are dominated by intellectuality, one must go elsewhere. Civilization, especially if of the austerer sort, is suspicious to it. It folds itself in the mantle of respectability. It has its certain negative virtues serving as silent auxiliaries. It never allows wine to get within its guard. It is not going too far to say that it is without vices or small sins. There is a phenomenal pride in it that excludes them. It is never mercenary or avaricious. In short, the depravity here meant partakes nothing of the sordid or sensual. It is serious, but free from acerbity. Though no flatterer of mankind it never speaks ill of it.

But the thing which in eminent instances signalizes so exceptional a nature is this: Though the man's even temper and discreet bearing would seem to intimate a mind peculiarly subject to the law of reason, not the less in heart he would seem to riot in complete exemption from that law, having apparently little to do with reason further than to employ it as an ambidexter implement for effecting the irrational. That is to say: Toward the accomplishment of an aim which in wantonness of atrocity would seem to partake of the insane, he will direct a cool judgment sagacious and sound. These men are madmen, and of the most dangerous sort, for their lunacy is not continuous, but occasional, evoked by some special object; it is protectively secretive, which is as much as to say it is self-contained, so that when, moreover, most active it is to the average mind not distinguishable from sanity, and for the reason above suggested: that whatever its aims may be—and the aim is never declared—the method and the outward proceeding are always perfectly rational.

Now something such an one was Claggart, in whom was the mania of an evil nature, not engendered by vicious training or corrupting books or licentious living, but born with him and innate, in short "a depravity according to nature."

Dark sayings are these, some will say. But why? Is it because they somewhat savor of Holy Writ in its phrase "mystery of iniquity?"[68] If they do, such savor was far enough from being intended, for little will it commend these pages to many a reader of today.

The point of the present story turning on the hidden nature of the master-at-arms has necessitated this chapter. With an added hint or two in connection with the incident at the mess, the resumed narrative must be left to vindicate, as it may, its own credibility.

12

That Claggart's figure was not amiss, and his face, save the chin, well molded, has already been said. Of these favorable points he seemed not insensible, for he was not only neat but careful in his dress. But the form of Billy Budd was heroic; and if his

---

[67] The theologian John Calvin (1509–1564) emphasized that all mankind is born depraved as a consequence of the sin of Adam and Eve.

[68] See 2 Thessalonians 2:7: ". . . the mystery of iniquity doth already work."

face was without the intellectual look of the pallid Claggart's, not the less was it lit, like his, from within, though from a different source. The bonfire in his heart made luminous the rose-tan in his cheek.

In view of the marked contrast between the persons of the twain, it is more than probable that when the master-at-arms in the scene last given applied to the sailor the proverb "Handsome is as handsome does," he there let escape an ironic inkling, not caught by the young sailors who heard it, as to what it was that had first moved him against Billy, namely, his significant personal beauty.

Now envy and antipathy, passions irreconcilable in reason, nevertheless in fact may spring conjoined like Chang and Eng[69] in one birth. Is Envy then such a monster? Well, though many an arraigned mortal has in hopes of mitigated penalty pleaded guilty to horrible actions, did ever anybody seriously confess to envy? Something there is in it universally felt to be more shameful than even felonious crime. And not only does everybody disown it, but the better sort are inclined to incredulity when it is in earnest imputed to an intelligent man. But since its lodgment is in the heart not the brain, no degree of intellect supplies a guarantee against it. But Claggart's was no vulgar form of the passion. Nor, as directed toward Billy Budd, did it partake of that streak of apprehensive jealousy that marred Saul's visage perturbedly brooding on the comely young David.[70] Claggart's envy struck deeper. If askance he eyed the good looks, cheery health, and frank enjoyment of young life in Billy Budd, it was because these went along with a nature that, as Claggart magnetically felt, had in its simplicity never willed malice or experienced the reactionary bite of that serpent. To him, the spirit lodged within Billy, and looking out from his welkin eyes as from windows, that ineffability it was which made the dimple in his dyed cheek, suppled his joints, and dancing in his yellow curls made him pre-eminently the Handsome Sailor. One person excepted, the master-at-arms was perhaps the only man in the ship intellectually capable of adequately appreciating the moral phenomenon presented in Billy Budd. And the insight but intensified his passion, which assuming various secret forms within him, at times assumed that of cynic disdain, disdain of innocence—to be nothing more than innocent! Yet in an aesthetic way he saw the charm of it, the courageous free-and-easy temper of it, and fain would have shared it, but he despaired of it.

With no power to annul the elemental evil in him, though readily enough he could hide it; apprehending the good, but powerless to be it; a nature like Claggart's, surcharged with energy as such natures almost invariably are, what recourse is left to it but to recoil upon itself and, like the scorpion for which the Creator alone is responsible, act out to the end the part allotted it.

13

Passion, and passion in its profoundest, is not a thing demanding a palatial stage whereon to play its part. Down among the groundlings, among the beggars and rakers of the garbage, profound passion is enacted. And the circumstances that provoke it,

---

[69] Famous Siamese twins displayed by P. T. Barnum in the United States.

[70] Saul's jealousy of David, recounted in 1 Samuel 16, 18.

however trivial or mean, are no measure of its power. In the present instance the stage is a scrubbed gun deck, and one of the external provocations a man-of-war's man's spilled soup.

Now when the master-at-arms noticed whence came that greasy fluid streaming before his feet, he must have taken it—to some extent wilfully, perhaps—not for the mere accident it assuredly was, but for the sly escape of a spontaneous feeling on Billy's part more or less answering to the antipathy on his own. In effect a foolish demonstration, he must have thought, and very harmless, like the futile kick of a heifer, which yet were the heifer a shod stallion would not be so harmless. Even so was it that into the gall of Claggart's envy he infused the vitriol of his contempt. But the incident confirmed to him certain telltale reports purveyed to his ear by "Squeak," one of his more cunning corporals, a grizzled little man, so nicknamed by the sailors on account of his squeaky voice and sharp visage ferreting about the dark corners of the lower decks after interlopers, satirically suggesting to them the idea of a rat in a cellar.

From his chief's employing him as an implicit tool in laying little traps for the worriment of the foretopman—for it was from the master-at-arms that the petty persecutions heretofore adverted to had proceeded—the corporal, having naturally enough concluded that his master could have no love for the sailor, made it his business, faithful understrapper that he was, to foment the ill blood by perverting to his chief certain innocent frolics of the good-natured foretopman, besides inventing for his mouth sundry contumelious epithets he claimed to have overheard him let fall. The master-at-arms never suspected the veracity of these reports, more especially as to the epithets, for he well knew how secretly unpopular may become a master-at-arms, at least a master-at-arms of those days, zealous in his function, and how the bluejackets shoot at him in private their raillery and wit; the nickname by which he goes among them (Jemmy Legs) implying under the form of merriment their cherished disrespect and dislike. But in view of the greediness of hate for pabulum[71] it hardly needed a purveyor to feed Claggart's passion.

An uncommon prudence is habitual with the subtler depravity, for it has everything to hide. And in case of an injury but suspected, its secretiveness voluntarily cuts it off from enlightenment or disillusion; and, not unreluctantly, action is taken upon surmise as upon certainty. And the retaliation is apt to be in monstrous disproportion to the supposed offense; for when in anybody was revenge in its exactions aught else but an inordinate usurer? But how with Claggart's conscience? For though consciences are unlike as foreheads, every intelligence, not excluding the scriptural devils who "believe and tremble,"[72] has one. But Claggart's conscience being but the lawyer to his will, made ogres of trifles, probably arguing that the motive imputed to Billy in spilling the soup just when he did, together with the epithets alleged, these, if nothing more, made a strong case against him; nay, justified animosity into a sort of retributive righteousness. The Pharisee is the Guy Fawkes[73] prowling in the hid chambers underlying some natures like Claggart's. And they can really form no conception of an unreciprocated malice. Probably the master-at-arms' clandestine persecution of Billy was started to try the temper of the man; but it had not developed any quality in him that enmity could make official use of or even pervert into plausible self-

[71] Food.
[72] James 2:19.
[73] Conspirator in the Gunpowder Plot to blow up Parliament.

justification; so that the occurrence at the mess, petty if it were, was a welcome one to that peculiar conscience assigned to be the private mentor of Claggart; and, for the rest, not improbably it put him upon new experiments.

14

Not many days after the last incident narrated, something befell Billy Budd that more graveled him than aught that had previously occurred.

It was a warm night for the latitude; and the foretopman, whose watch at the time was properly below, was dozing on the uppermost deck whither he had ascended from his hot hammock, one of hundreds suspended so closely wedged together over a lower gun deck that there was little or no swing to them. He lay as in the shadow of a hillside, stretched under the lee of the booms, a piled ridge of spare spars amidships between foremast and mainmast among which the ship's largest boat, the launch, was stowed. Alongside of three other slumberers from below, he lay near that end of the booms which approaches the foremast; his station aloft on duty as a foretopman being just over the deck-station of the forecastlemen, entitling him according to usage to make himself more or less at home in that neighborhood.

Presently he was stirred into semiconsciousness by somebody, who must have previously sounded the sleep of the others, touching his shoulder, and then, as the foretopman raised his head, breathing into his ear in a quick whisper, "Slip into the lee forechains, Billy; there is something in the wind. Don't speak. Quick, I will meet you there," and disappearing.

Now Billy, like sundry other essentially good-natured ones, had some of the weaknesses inseparable from essential good nature; and among these was a reluctance, almost an incapacity of plumply saying *no* to an abrupt proposition not obviously absurd on the face of it, nor obviously unfriendly, nor iniquitous. And being of warm blood, he had not the phlegm[74] tacitly to negative any proposition by unresponsive inaction. Like his sense of fear, his apprehension as to aught outside of the honest and natural was seldom very quick. Besides, upon the present occasion, the drowse from his sleep still hung upon him.

However it was, he mechanically rose and, sleepily wondering what could be in the wind, betook himself to the designated place, a narrow platform, one of six, outside of the high bulwarks and screened by the great deadeyes and multiple co-lumned lanyards of the shrouds and backstays; and, in a great warship of that time, of dimensions commensurate to the hull's magnitude; a tarry balcony in short, over-hanging the sea, and so secluded that one mariner of the *Bellipotent,* a Nonconformist old tar of a serious turn, made it even in daytime his private oratory.[75]

In this retired nook the stranger soon joined Billy Budd. There was no moon as yet; a haze obscured the starlight. He could not distinctly see the stranger's face. Yet from something in the outline and carriage, Billy took him, and correctly, for one of the afterguard.

"Hist! Billy," said the man, in the same quick cautionary whisper as before. "You were impressed, weren't you? Well, so was I"; and he paused, as to mark the effect. But Billy, not knowing exactly what to make of this, said nothing. Then the other:

---

[74] Cool self-control.   [75] Place for prayer.

"We are not the only impressed ones, Billy. There's a gang of us.——Couldn't you——help——at a pinch?"

"What do you mean?" demanded Billy, here thoroughly shaking off his drowse.

"Hist, hist!" the hurried whisper now growing husky. "See here," and the man held up two small objects faintly twinkling in the night-light; "see, they are yours, Billy, if you'll only——"

But Billy broke in, and in his resentful eagerness to deliver himself his vocal infirmity somewhat intruded. "D——d——damme, I don't know what you are d——d——driving at, or what you mean, but you had better g——g——go where you belong!" For the moment the fellow, as confounded, did not stir; and Billy, springing to his feet, said, "If you d——don't start, I'll t——t——toss you back over the r——rail!" There was no mistaking this, and the mysterious emissary decamped, disappearing in the direction of the mainmast in the shadow of the booms.[76]

"Hallo, what's the matter?" here came growling from a forecastleman awakened from his deck-doze by Billy's raised voice. And as the foretopman reappeared and was recognized by him: "Ah, Beauty, is it you? Well, something must have been the matter, for you st——st——stuttered."

"Oh," rejoined Billy, now mastering the impediment, "I found an afterguardsman in our part of the ship here, and I bid him be off where he belongs."

"And is that all you did about it, Foretopman?" gruffly demanded another, an irascible old fellow of brick-colored visage and hair who was known to his associate forecastlemen as "Red Pepper." "Such sneaks I should like to marry to the gunner's daughter!"——by that expression meaning that he would like to subject them to disciplinary castigation over a gun.

However, Billy's rendering of the matter satisfactorily accounted to these inquirers for the brief commotion, since of all the sections of a ship's company the forecastlemen, veterans for the most part and bigoted in their sea prejudices, are the most jealous in resenting territorial encroachments, especially on the part of any of the afterguard, of whom they have but a sorry opinion——chiefly landsmen, never going aloft except to reef or furl the mainsail, and in no wise competent to handle a marlinspike or turn in a deadeye,[77] say.

15

This incident sorely puzzled Billy Budd. It was an entirely new experience, the first time in his life that he had ever been personally approached in underhand intriguing fashion. Prior to this encounter he had known nothing of the afterguardsman, the two men being stationed wide apart, one forward and aloft during his watch, the other on deck and aft.

What could it mean? And could they really be guineas, those two glittering objects the interloper had held up to his (Billy's) eyes? Where could the fellow get guineas? Why, even spare buttons are not so plentiful at sea. The more he turned the matter over, the more he was nonplussed, and made uneasy and discomfited. In his disgustful

---

[76] Horizontal poles for extending the feet or bottoms of sails.

[77] I.e., to use a rope-splicing tool or a rope-threaded wood block as a pulley.

recoil from an overture which, though he but ill comprehended, he instinctively knew must involve evil of some sort, Billy Budd was like a young horse fresh from the pasture suddenly inhaling a vile whiff from some chemical factory, and by repeated snortings trying to get it out of his nostrils and lungs. This frame of mind barred all desire of holding further parley with the fellow, even were it but for the purpose of gaining some enlightenment as to his design in approaching him. And yet he was not without natural curiosity to see how such a visitor in the dark would look in broad day.

He espied him the following afternoon in his first dogwatch below, one of the smokers on that forward part of the upper gun deck allotted to the pipe. He recognized him by his general cut and build more than by his round freckled face and glassy eyes of pale blue, veiled with lashes all but white. And yet Billy was a bit uncertain whether indeed it were he—yonder chap about his own age chatting and laughing in freehearted way, leaning against a gun; a genial young fellow enough to look at, and something of a rattlebrain, to all appearance. Rather chubby too for a sailor, even an afterguardsman. In short, the last man in the world, one would think, to be overburdened with thoughts, especially those perilous thoughts that must needs belong to a conspirator in any serious project, or even to the underling of such a conspirator.

Although Billy was not aware of it, the fellow, with a sidelong watchful glance, had perceived Billy first, and then noting that Billy was looking at him, thereupon nodded a familiar sort of friendly recognition as to an old acquaintance, without interrupting the talk he was engaged in with the group of smokers. A day or two afterwards, chancing in the evening promenade on a gun deck to pass Billy, he offered a flying word of good-fellowship, as it were, which by its unexpectedness, and equivocalness under the circumstances, so embarrassed Billy that he knew not how to respond to it, and let it go unnoticed.

Billy was now left more at a loss than before. The ineffectual speculations into which he was led were so disturbingly alien to him that he did his best to smother them. It never entered his mind that here was a matter which, from its extreme questionableness, it was his duty as a loyal bluejacket to report in the proper quarter. And, probably, had such a step been suggested to him, he would have been deterred from taking it by the thought, one of novice magnanimity, that it would savor overmuch of the dirty work of a telltale. He kept the thing to himself. Yet upon one occasion he could not forbear a little disburdening himself to the old Dansker, tempted thereto perhaps by the influence of a balmy night when the ship lay becalmed; the twain, silent for the most part, sitting together on deck, their heads propped against the bulwarks. But it was only a partial and anonymous account that Billy gave, the unfounded scruples above referred to preventing full disclosure to anybody. Upon hearing Billy's version, the sage Dansker seemed to divine more than he was told; and after a little meditation, during which his wrinkles were pursed as into a point, quite effacing for the time that quizzing expression his face sometimes wore: "Didn't I say so, Baby Budd?"

"Say what?" demanded Billy.

"Why, *Jemmy Legs* is *down* on you."

"And what," rejoined Billy in amazement, "has *Jemmy Legs* to do with that cracked afterguardsman?"

"Ho, it was an afterguardsman, then. A cat's-paw, a cat's-paw!" And with that exclamation, whether it had reference to a light puff of air just then coming over the calm sea, or a subtler relation to the afterguardsman, there is no telling, the old Merlin gave a twisting wrench with his black teeth at his plug of tobacco, vouchsafing no reply to Billy's impetuous question, though now repeated, for it was his wont to relapse into grim silence when interrogated in skeptical sort as to any of his sententious oracles, not always very clear ones, rather partaking of that obscurity which invests most Delphic deliverances[78] from any quarter.

Long experience had very likely brought this old man to that bitter prudence which never interferes in aught and never gives advice.

16

Yes, despite the Dansker's pithy insistence as to the master-at-arms being at the bottom of these strange experiences of Billy on board the *Bellipotent*, the young sailor was ready to ascribe them to almost anybody but the man who, to use Billy's own expression, "always had a pleasant word for him." This is to be wondered at. Yet not so much to be wondered at. In certain matters, some sailors even in mature life remain unsophisticated enough. But a young seafarer of the disposition of our athletic foretopman is much of a child-man. And yet a child's utter innocence is but its blank ignorance, and the innocence more or less wanes as intelligence waxes. But in Billy Budd intelligence, such as it was, had advanced while yet his simple-mindedness remained for the most part unaffected. Experience is a teacher indeed; yet did Billy's years make his experience small. Besides, he had none of that intuitive knowledge of the bad which in natures not good or incompletely so foreruns experience, and therefore may pertain, as in some instances it too clearly does pertain, even to youth.

And what could Billy know of man except of man as a mere sailor? And the old-fashioned sailor, the veritable man before the mast, the sailor from boyhood up, he, though indeed of the same species as a landsman, is in some respects singularly distinct from him. The sailor is frankness, the landsman is finesse. Life is not a game with the sailor, demanding the long head—no intricate game of chess where few moves are made in straightforwardness and ends are attained by indirection, an oblique, tedious, barren game hardly worth that poor candle burnt out in playing it.

Yes, as a class, sailors are in character a juvenile race. Even their deviations are marked by juvenility, this more especially holding true with the sailors of Billy's time. Then too, certain things which apply to all sailors do more pointedly operate here and there upon the junior one. Every sailor, too, is accustomed to obey orders without debating them; his life afloat is externally ruled for him; he is not brought into that promiscuous commerce with mankind where unobstructed free agency on equal terms —equal superficially, at least—soon teaches one that unless upon occasion he exercise a distrust keen in proportion to the fairness of the appearance, some foul turn may be served him. A ruled undemonstrative distrustfulness is so habitual, not with businessmen so much as with men who know their kind in less shallow relations than business, namely, certain men of the world, that they come at last to employ it all

[78] Prophesies of the priests at the shrine of Apollo
at Delphi in Greece.

but unconsciously; and some of them would very likely feel real surprise at being charged with it as one of their general characteristics.

17

But after the little matter at the mess Billy Budd no more found himself in strange trouble at times about his hammock or his clothes bag or what not. As to that smile that occasionally sunned him, and the pleasant passing word, these were, if not more frequent, yet if anything more pronounced than before.

But for all that, there were certain other demonstrations now. When Claggart's unobserved glance happened to light on belted Billy rolling along the upper gun deck in the leisure of the second dogwatch, exchanging passing broadsides of fun with other young promenaders in the crowd, that glance would follow the cheerful sea Hyperion[79] with a settled meditative and melancholy expression, his eyes strangely suffused with incipient feverish tears. Then would Claggart look like the man of sorrows.[80] Yes, and sometimes the melancholy expression would have in it a touch of soft yearning, as if Claggart could even have loved Billy but for fate and ban. But this was an evanescence, and quickly repented of, as it were, by an immitigable look, pinching and shriveling the visage into the momentary semblance of a wrinkled walnut. But sometimes catching sight in advance of the foretopman coming in his direction, he would, upon their nearing, step aside a little to let him pass, dwelling upon Billy for the moment with the glittering dental satire of a Guise.[81] But upon any abrupt unforeseen encounter a red light would flash forth from his eye like a spark from an anvil in a dusk smithy. That quick, fierce light was a strange one, darted from orbs which in repose were of a color nearest approaching a deeper violet, the softest of shades.

Though some of these caprices of the pit could not but be observed by their object, yet were they beyond the construing of such a nature. And the thews of Billy were hardly compatible with that sort of sensitive spiritual organization which in some cases instinctively conveys to ignorant innocence an admonition of the proximity of the malign. He thought the master-at-arms acted in a manner rather queer at times. That was all. But the occasional frank air and pleasant word went for what they purported to be, the young sailor never having heard as yet of the "too fair-spoken man."

Had the foretopman been conscious of having done or said anything to provoke the ill will of the official, it would have been different with him, and his sight might have been purged if not sharpened. As it was, innocence was his blinder.

So was it with him in yet another matter. Two minor officers, the armorer and captain of the hold, with whom he had never exchanged a word, his position in the ship not bringing him into contact with them, these men now for the first began to cast upon Billy, when they chanced to encounter him, that peculiar glance which evidences that the man from whom it comes has been some way tampered with, and to the prejudice of him upon whom the glance lights. Never did it occur to Billy as a thing to be noted or a thing suspicious, though he well knew the fact, that the armorer and captain of the hold, with the ship's yeoman, apothecary, and others of

---

[79] Titan in Greek myth.
[80] See Isaiah 53:3.

[81] French family known for villainies masked by smiles.

that grade, were by naval usage messmates of the master-at-arms, men with ears convenient to his confidential tongue.

But the general popularity that came from our Handsome Sailor's manly forwardness upon occasion and irresistible good nature, indicating no mental superiority tending to excite an invidious feeling, this good will on the part of most of his shipmates made him the less to concern himself about such mute aspects toward him as those whereto allusion has just been made, aspects he could not so fathom as to infer their whole import.

As to the afterguardsman, though Billy for reasons already given necessarily saw little of him, yet when the two did happen to meet, invariably came the fellow's offhand cheerful recognition, sometimes accompanied by a passing pleasant word or two. Whatever that equivocal young person's original design may really have been, or the design of which he might have been the deputy, certain it was from his manner upon these occasions that he had wholly dropped it.

It was as if his precocity of crookedness (and every vulgar villain is precocious) had for once deceived him, and the man he had sought to entrap as a simpleton had through his very simplicity ignominiously baffled him.

But shrewd ones may opine that it was hardly possible for Billy to refrain from going up to the afterguardsman and bluntly demanding to know his purpose in the initial interview so abruptly closed in the forechains. Shrewd ones may also think it but natural in Billy to set about sounding some of the other impressed men of the ship in order to discover what basis, if any, there was for the emissary's obscure suggestions as to plotting disaffection abroad. Yes, shrewd ones may so think. But something more, or rather something else than mere shrewdness is perhaps needful for the due understanding of such a character as Billy Budd's.

As to Claggart, the monomania in the man—if that indeed it were—as involuntarily disclosed by starts in the manifestations detailed, yet in general covered over by his self-contained and rational demeanor; this, like a subterranean fire, was eating its way deeper and deeper in him. Something decisive must come of it.

18

After the mysterious interview in the forechains, the one so abruptly ended there by Billy, nothing especially germane to the story occurred until the events now about to be narrated.

Elsewhere it has been said that in the lack of frigates (of course better sailers than line-of-battleships) in the English squadron up the Straits at that period, the *Bellipotent 74* was occasionally employed not only as an available substitute for a scout, but at times on detached service of more important kind. This was not alone because of her sailing qualities, not common in a ship of her rate, but quite as much, probably, that the character of her commander, it was thought, specially adapted him for any duty where under unforeseen difficulties a prompt initiative might have to be taken in some matter demanding knowledge and ability in addition to those qualities implied in good seamanship. It was on an expedition of the latter sort, a somewhat distant one, and when the *Bellipotent* was almost at her furthest remove from the fleet, that in the latter part of an afternoon watch she unexpectedly came in sight of a ship of the enemy. It proved to be a frigate. The latter, perceiving through the glass that the weight of men and metal would be heavily against her, invoking her light heels crowded sail to get away. After a chase urged almost against hope and lasting until about the middle of the first dogwatch, she signally succeeded in effecting her escape.

Not long after the pursuit had been given up, and ere the excitement incident thereto had altogether waned away, the master-at-arms, ascending from his cavernous sphere, made his appearance cap in hand by the mainmast respectfully waiting the notice of Captain Vere, then solitary walking the weather side of the quarter-deck, doubtless somewhat chafed at the failure of the pursuit. The spot where Claggart stood was the place allotted to men of lesser grades seeking some more particular interview either with the officer of the deck or the captain himself. But from the latter it was not often that a sailor or petty officer of those days would seek a hearing; only some exceptional cause would, according to established custom, have warranted that.

Presently, just as the commander, absorbed in his reflections, was on the point of turning aft in his promenade, he became sensible of Claggart's presence, and saw the doffed cap held in deferential expectancy. Here be it said that Captain Vere's personal knowledge of this petty officer had only begun at the time of the ship's last sailing from home, Claggart then for the first, in transfer from a ship detained for repairs, supplying on board the *Bellipotent* the place of a previous master-at-arms disabled and ashore.

No sooner did the commander observe who it was that now deferentially stood awaiting his notice than a peculiar expression came over him. It was not unlike that which uncontrollably will flit across the countenance of one at unawares encountering a person who, though known to him indeed, has hardly been long enough known for thorough knowledge, but something in whose aspect nevertheless now for the first provokes a vaguely repellent distaste. But coming to a stand and resuming much of his wonted official manner, save that a sort of impatience lurked in the intonation of the opening word, he said "Well? What is it, Master-at-arms?"

With the air of a subordinate grieved at the necessity of being a messenger of ill tidings, and while conscientiously determined to be frank yet equally resolved upon shunning overstatement, Claggart at this invitation, or rather summons to disburden, spoke up. What he said, conveyed in the language of no uneducated man, was to the effect following, if not altogether in these words, namely, that during the chase and preparations for the possible encounter he had seen enough to convince him that at least one sailor aboard was a dangerous character in a ship mustering some who not only had taken a guilty part in the late serious troubles, but others also who, like the man in question, had entered His Majesty's service under another form than enlistment.

At this point Captain Vere with some impatience interrupted him: "Be direct, man; say *impressed men*."

Claggart made a gesture of subservience, and proceeded. Quite lately he (Claggart) had begun to suspect that on the gun decks some sort of movement prompted by the sailor in question was covertly going on, but he had not thought himself warranted in reporting the suspicion so long as it remained indistinct. But from what he had that afternoon observed in the man referred to, the suspicion of something clandestine going on had advanced to a point less removed from certainty. He deeply felt, he added, the serious responsibility assumed in making a report involving such possible consequences to the individual mainly concerned, besides tending to augment those natural anxieties which every naval commander must feel in view of extraordinary outbreaks so recent as those which, he sorrowfully said it, it needed not to name.

Now at the first broaching of the matter Captain Vere, taken by surprise, could not wholly dissemble his disquietude. But as Claggart went on, the former's aspect changed into restiveness under something in the testifier's manner in giving his testimony. However, he refrained from interrupting him. And Claggart, continuing, concluded with this: "God forbid, your honor, that the *Bellipotent*'s should be the experience of the——"

"Never mind that!" here peremptorily broke in the superior, his face altering with anger, instinctively divining the ship that the other was about to name, one in which the Nore Mutiny had assumed a singularly tragical character that for a time jeopardized the life of its commander. Under the circumstances he was indignant at the purposed allusion. When the commissioned officers themselves were on all occasions very heedful how they referred to the recent events in the fleet, for a petty officer unnecessarily to allude to them in the presence of his captain, this struck him as a most immodest presumption. Besides, to his quick sense of self-respect it even looked under the circumstances something like an attempt to alarm him. Nor at first was he without some surprise that one who so far as he had hitherto come under his notice had shown considerable tact in his function should in this particular evince such lack of it.

But these thoughts and kindred dubious ones flitting across his mind were suddenly replaced by an intuitional surmise which, though as yet obscure in form, served practically to affect his reception of the ill tidings. Certain it is that, long versed in everything pertaining to the complicated gun-deck life, which like every other form of life has its secret mines and dubious side, the side popularly disclaimed, Captain Vere did not permit himself to be unduly disturbed by the general tenor of his subordinate's report.

Furthermore, if in view of recent events prompt action should be taken at the first palpable sign of recurring insubordination, for all that, not judicious would it be, he thought, to keep the idea of lingering disaffection alive by undue forwardness in crediting an informer, even if his own subordinate and charged among other things with police surveillance of the crew. This feeling would not perhaps have so prevailed with him were it not that upon a prior occasion that patriotic zeal officially evinced by Claggart had somewhat irritated him as appearing rather supersensible and strained. Furthermore, something even in the official's self-possessed and somewhat ostentatious manner in making his specifications strangely reminded him of a bandsman, a perjurous witness in a capital case before a court-martial ashore of which when a lieutenant he (Captain Vere) had been a member.

Now the peremptory check given to Claggart in the matter of the arrested allusion was quickly followed up by this: "You say that there is at least one dangerous man aboard. Name him."

"William Budd, a foretopman, your honor."

"William Budd!" repeated Captain Vere with unfeigned astonishment. "And mean you the man that Lieutenant Ratcliffe took from the merchantman not very long ago, the young fellow who seems to be so popular with the men—Billy, the Handsome Sailor, as they call him?"

"The same, your honor; but for all his youth and good looks, a deep one. Not for nothing does he insinuate himself into the good will of his shipmates, since at the least they will at a pinch say—all hands will—a good word for him, and at all hazards. Did Lieutenant Ratcliffe happen to tell your honor of that adroit fling of Budd's, jumping up in the cutter's bow under the merchantman's stern when he was being taken off? It is even masked by that sort of good-humored air that at heart he resents his impressment. You have but noted his fair cheek. A mantrap may be under the ruddy-tipped daisies."

Now the Handsome Sailor as a signal figure among the crew had naturally enough attracted the captain's attention from the first. Though in general not very demonstrative to his officers, he had congratulated Lieutenant Ratcliffe upon his good fortune in lighting on such a fine specimen of the *genus homo,* who in the nude might have posed for a statue of young Adam before the Fall. As to Billy's adieu to the ship *Rights-of-Man,* which the boarding lieutenant had indeed reported to him, but, in a deferential way, more as a good story than aught else, Captain Vere, though mistakenly understanding it as a satiric sally, had but thought so much the better of the impressed man for it; as a military sailor, admiring the spirit that could take an arbitrary enlistment so merrily and sensibly. The foretopman's conduct, too, so far as it had fallen under the captain's notice, had confirmed the first happy augury, while the new recruit's qualities as a "sailor-man" seemed to be such that he had thought of recommending him to the executive officer for promotion to a place that would more frequently bring him under his own observation, namely, the captaincy of the mizzentop, replacing there in the starboard watch a man not so young whom partly for that reason he deemed less fitted for the post. Be it parenthesized here that since the mizzentopmen have not to handle such breadths of heavy canvas as the lower sails on the mainmast and foremast, a young man if of the right stuff not only seems best adapted to duty there, but in fact is generally selected for the captaincy of that top, and the company under him are light hands and often but striplings. In sum, Captain Vere had from the beginning deemed Billy Budd to be what in the naval parlance of the time was called a "King's bargain": that is to say, for His Britannic Majesty's navy a capital investment at small outlay or none at all.

After a brief pause, during which the reminiscences above mentioned passed vividly through his mind and he weighed the import of Claggart's last suggestion conveyed in the phrase "mantrap under the daisies," and the more he weighed it the less reliance he felt in the informer's good faith, suddenly he turned upon him and in a low voice demanded: "Do you come to me, Master-at-arms, with so foggy a tale? As to Budd, cite me an act or spoken word of his confirmatory of what you in general charge against him. Stay," drawing nearer to him; "heed what you speak. Just now, and in a case like this, there is a yardarm-end[82] for the false witness."

"Ah, your honor!" sighed Claggart, mildly shaking his shapely head as in sad depreciation of such unmerited severity of tone. Then, bridling—erecting himself as in virtuous self-assertion—he circumstantially alleged certain words and acts which collectively, if credited, led to presumptions mortally inculpating Budd. And for some of these averments, he added, substantiating proof was not far.

With gray eyes impatient and distrustful essaying to fathom to the bottom Claggart's calm violet ones, Captain Vere again heard him out; then for the moment stood

[82] I.e., hanging.

ruminating. The mood he evinced, Claggart—himself for the time liberated from the other's scrutiny—steadily regarded with a look difficult to render: a look curious of the operation of his tactics, a look such as might have been that of the spokesman of the envious children of Jacob deceptively imposing upon the troubled patriarch the blood-dyed coat of young Joseph.[83]

Though something exceptional in the moral quality of Captain Vere made him, in earnest encounter with a fellow man, a veritable touchstone of that man's essential nature, yet now as to Claggart and what was really going on in him his feeling partook less of intuitional conviction than of strong suspicion clogged by strange dubieties. The perplexity he evinced proceeded less from aught touching the man informed against—as Claggart doubtless opined—than from considerations how best to act in regard to the informer. At first, indeed, he was naturally for summoning that substantiation of his allegations which Claggart said was at hand. But such a proceeding would result in the matter at once getting abroad, which in the present stage of it, he thought, might undesirably affect the ship's company. If Claggart was a false witness—that closed the affair. And therefore, before trying the accusation, he would first practically test the accuser; and he thought this could be done in a quiet, undemonstrative way.

The measure he determined upon involved a shifting of the scene, a transfer to a place less exposed to observation than the broad quarter-deck. For although the few gun-room officers there at the time had, in due observance of naval etiquette, withdrawn to leeward the moment Captain Vere had begun his promenade on the deck's weather side; and though during the colloquy with Claggart they of course ventured not to diminish the distance; and though throughout the interview Captain Vere's voice was far from high, and Claggart's silvery and low; and the wind in the cordage and the wash of the sea helped the more to put them beyond earshot; nevertheless, the interview's continuance already had attracted observation from some topmen aloft and other sailors in the waist or further forward.

Having determined upon his measures, Captain Vere forthwith took action. Abruptly turning to Claggart, he asked, "Master-at-arms, is it now Budd's watch aloft?"

"No, your honor."

Whereupon, "Mr. Wilkes!" summoning the nearest midshipman. "Tell Albert to come to me." Albert was the captain's hammock-boy, a sort of sea valet in whose discretion and fidelity his master had much confidence. The lad appeared.

"You know Budd, the foretopman?"

"I do, sir."

"Go find him. It is his watch off. Manage to tell him out of earshot that he is wanted aft. Contrive it that he speaks to nobody. Keep him in talk yourself. And not till you get well aft here, not till then let him know that the place where he is wanted is my cabin. You understand. Go.—Master-at-arms, show yourself on the decks below, and when you think it time for Albert to be coming with his man, stand by quietly to follow the sailor in."

[83] In Genesis 37:31–32, Joseph's brothers use the coat, stained with a goat's blood, to convince their father, Jacob, that Joseph is dead.

19

Now when the foretopman found himself in the cabin, closeted there, as it were, with the captain and Claggart, he was surprised enough. But it was a surprise unaccompanied by apprehension or distrust. To an immature nature essentially honest and humane, forewarning intimations of subtler danger from one's kind come tardily if at all. The only thing that took shape in the young sailor's mind was this: Yes, the captain, I have always thought, looks kindly upon me. Wonder if he's going to make me his coxswain.[84] I should like that. And may be now he is going to ask the master-at-arms about me.

"Shut the door there, sentry," said the commander; "stand without, and let nobody come in.—Now, Master-at-arms, tell this man to his face what you told of him to me," and stood prepared to scrutinize the mutually confronting visages.

With the measured step and calm collected air of an asylum physician approaching in the public hall some patient beginning to show indications of a coming paroxysm, Claggart deliberately advanced within short range of Billy and, mesmerically looking him in the eye, briefly recapitulated the accusation.

Not at first did Billy take it in. When he did, the rose-tan of his cheek looked struck as by white leprosy. He stood like one impaled and gagged. Meanwhile the accuser's eyes, removing not as yet from the blue dilated ones, underwent a phenomenal change, their wonted rich violet color blurring into a muddy purple. Those lights of human intelligence, losing human expression, were gelidly protruding like the alien eyes of certain uncatalogued creatures of the deep. The first mesmeristic glance was one of serpent fascination; the last was as the paralyzing lurch of the torpedo fish.[85]

"Speak, man!" said Captain Vere to the transfixed one, struck by his aspect even more than by Claggart's. "Speak! Defend yourself!" Which appeal caused but a strange dumb gesturing and gurgling in Billy; amazement at such an accusation so suddenly sprung on inexperienced nonage; this, and, it may be, horror of the accuser's eyes, serving to bring out his lurking defect and in this instance for the time intensifying it into a convulsed tongue-tie; while the intent head and entire form straining forward in an agony of ineffectual eagerness to obey the injunction to speak and defend himself, gave an expression to the face like that of a condemned vestal priestess in the moment of being buried alive, and in the first struggle against suffocation.

Though at the time Captain Vere was quite ignorant of Billy's liability to vocal impediment, he now immediately divined it, since vividly Billy's aspect recalled to him that of a bright young schoolmate of his whom he had once seen struck by much the same startling impotence in the act of eagerly rising in the class to be foremost in response to a testing question put to it by the master. Going close up to the young sailor, and laying a soothing hand on his shoulder, he said, "There is no hurry, my boy. Take your time, take your time." Contrary to the effect intended, these words so fatherly in tone, doubtless touching Billy's heart to the quick, prompted yet more violent efforts at utterance—efforts soon ending for the time in confirming the paralysis, and bringing to his face an expression which was as a crucifixion to behold. The next instant, quick as the flame from a discharged cannon at night, his right arm

---

[84] Steerer and crew leader of the captain's own boat.

[85] Fish that stuns its prey with electrical shocks.

shot out, and Claggart dropped to the deck. Whether intentionally or but owing to the young athlete's superior height, the blow had taken effect full upon the forehead, so shapely and intellectual-looking a feature in the master-at-arms; so that the body fell over lengthwise, like a heavy plank tilted from erectness. A gasp or two, and he lay motionless.

"Fated boy," breathed Captain Vere in tone so low as to be almost a whisper, "what have you done! But here, help me."

The twain raised the felled one from the loins up into a sitting position. The spare form flexibly acquiesced, but inertly. It was like handling a dead snake. They lowered it back. Regaining erectness, Captain Vere with one hand covering his face stood to all appearance as impassive as the object at his feet. Was he absorbed in taking in all the bearings of the event and what was best not only now at once to be done, but also in the sequel? Slowly he uncovered his face; and the effect was as if the moon emerging from eclipse should reappear with quite another aspect than that which had gone into hiding. The father in him, manifested towards Billy thus far in the scene, was replaced by the military disciplinarian. In his official tone he bade the foretopman retire to a stateroom aft (pointing it out), and there remain till thence summoned. This order Billy in silence mechanically obeyed. Then going to the cabin door where it opened on the quarter-deck, Captain Vere said to the sentry without, "Tell somebody to send Albert here." When the lad appeared, his master so contrived it that he should not catch sight of the prone one. "Albert," he said to him, "tell the surgeon I wish to see him. You need not come back till called."

When the surgeon entered—a self-poised character of that grave sense and experience that hardly anything could take him aback—Captain Vere advanced to meet him, thus unconsciously intercepting his view of Claggart, and, interrupting the other's wonted cermonious salutation, said, "Nay. Tell me how it is with yonder man," directing his attention to the prostrate one.

The surgeon looked, and for all his self-command somewhat started at the abrupt revelation. On Claggart's always pallid complexion, thick black blood was now oozing from nostril and ear. To the gazer's professional eye it was unmistakably no living man that he saw.

"Is it so, then?" said Captain Vere, intently watching him. "I thought it. But verify it." Whereupon the customary tests confirmed the surgeon's first glance, who now, looking up in unfeigned concern, cast a look of intense inquisitiveness upon his superior. But Captain Vere, with one hand to his brow, was standing motionless. Suddenly, catching the surgeon's arm convulsively, he exclaimed, pointing down to the body, "It is the divine judgment on Ananias![86] Look!"

Disturbed by the excited manner he had never before observed in the *Bellipotent*'s captain, and as yet wholly ignorant of the affair, the prudent surgeon nevertheless held his peace, only again looking an earnest interrogatory as to what it was that had resulted in such a tragedy.

But Captain Vere was now again motionless, standing absorbed in thought. Again starting, he vehemently exclaimed, "Struck dead by an angel of God! Yet the angel must hang!"

---

[86] According to Acts 5:3–5, Ananias dropped dead when told he had lied to God.

At these passionate interjections, mere incoherences to the listener as yet unapprised of the antecedents, the surgeon was profoundly discomposed. But now, as recollecting himself, Captain Vere in less passionate tone briefly related the circumstances leading up to the event. "But come; we must dispatch," he added. "Help me to remove him" (meaning the body) "to yonder compartment," designating one opposite that where the foretopman remained immured. Anew disturbed by a request that, as implying a desire for secrecy, seemed unaccountably strange to him, there was nothing for the subordinate to do but comply.

"Go now," said Captain Vere with something of his wonted manner. "Go now. I presently shall call a drumhead court.[87] Tell the lieutenants what has happened, and tell Mr. Mordant" (meaning the captain of marines), "and charge them to keep the matter to themselves."

20

Full of disquietude and misgiving, the surgeon left the cabin. Was Captain Vere suddenly affected in his mind, or was it but a transient excitement, brought about by so strange and extraordinary a tragedy? As to the drumhead court, it struck the surgeon as impolitic, if nothing more. The thing to do, he thought, was to place Billy Budd in confinement, and in a way dictated by usage, and postpone further action in so extraordinary a case to such time as they should rejoin the squadron, and then refer it to the admiral. He recalled the unwonted agitation of Captain Vere and his excited exclamations, so at variance with his normal manner. Was he unhinged?

But assuming that he is, it is not so susceptible of proof. What then can the surgeon do? No more trying situation is conceivable than that of an officer subordinate under a captain whom he suspects to be not mad, indeed, but yet not quite unaffected in his intellects. To argue his order to him would be insolence. To resist him would be mutiny.

In obedience to Captain Vere, he communicated what had happened to the lieutenants and captain of marines, saying nothing as to the captain's state. They fully shared his own surprise and concern. Like him too, they seemed to think that such a matter should be referred to the admiral.

21

Who in the rainbow can draw the line where the violet tint ends and the orange tint begins? Distinctly we see the difference of the colors, but where exactly does the one first blendingly enter into the other? So with sanity and insanity. In pronounced cases there is no question about them. But in some supposed cases, in various degrees supposedly less pronounced, to draw the exact line of demarcation few will undertake, though for a fee becoming considerate some professional experts will. There is nothing namable but that some men will, or undertake to, do it for pay.

Whether Captain Vere, as the surgeon professionally and privately surmised, was really the sudden victim of any degree of aberration, every one must determine for himself by such light as this narrative may afford.

[87] Court-martial.

That the unhappy event which has been narrated could not have happened at a worse juncture was but too true. For it was close on the heel of the suppressed insurrections, an aftertime very critical to naval authority, demanding from every English sea commander two qualities not readily interfusable—prudence and rigor. Moreover, there was something crucial in the case.

In the jugglery of circumstances preceding and attending the event on board the *Bellipotent,* and in the light of that martial code whereby it was formally to be judged, innocence and guilt personified in Claggart and Budd in effect changed places. In a legal view the apparent victim of the tragedy was he who had sought to victimize a man blameless; and the indisputable deed of the latter, navally regarded, constituted the most heinous of military crimes. Yet more. The essential right and wrong involved in the matter, the clearer that might be, so much the worse for the responsibility of a loyal sea commander, inasmuch as he was not authorized to determine the matter on that primitive basis.

Small wonder then that the *Bellipotent*'s captain, though in general a man of rapid decision, felt that circumspectness not less than promptitude was necessary. Until he could decide upon his course, and in each detail; and not only so, but until the concluding measure was upon the point of being enacted, he deemed it advisable, in view of all the circumstances, to guard as much as possible against publicity. Here he may or may not have erred. Certain it is, however, that subsequently in the confidential talk of more than one or two gun rooms and cabins he was not a little criticized by some officers, a fact imputed by his friends and vehemently by his cousin Jack Denton to professional jealousy of Starry Vere. Some imaginative ground for invidious comment there was. The maintenance of secrecy in the matter, the confining all knowledge of it for a time to the place where the homicide occurred, the quarter-deck cabin; in these particulars lurked some resemblance to the policy adopted in those tragedies of the palace which have occurred more than once in the capital founded by Peter the Barbarian.[88]

The case indeed was such that fain would the *Bellipotent*'s captain have deferred taking any action whatever respecting it further than to keep the foretopman a close prisoner till the ship rejoined the squadron and then submitting the matter to the judgment of his admiral.

But a true military officer is in one particular like a true monk. Not with more of self-abnegation will the latter keep his vows of monastic obedience than the former his vows of allegiance to martial duty.

Feeling that unless quick action was taken on it, the deed of the foretopman, so soon as it should be known on the gun decks, would tend to awaken any slumbering embers of the Nore among the crew, a sense of the urgency of the case overruled in Captain Vere every other consideration. But though a conscientious disciplinarian, he was no lover of authority for mere authority's sake. Very far was he from embracing opportunities for monopolizing to himself the perils of moral responsibility, none at least that could properly be referred to an official superior or shared with him by his official equals or even subordinates. So thinking, he was glad it would not be at variance with usage to turn the matter over to a summary court of his own officers,

[88] Peter the Great of Russia (1672–1725), founder of St. Petersburg (now Leningrad).

reserving to himself, as the one on whom the ultimate accountability would rest, the right of maintaining a supervision of it, or formally or informally interposing at need. Accordingly a drumhead court was summarily convened, he electing the individuals composing it: the first lieutenant, the captain of marines, and the sailing master.

In associating an officer of marines with the sea lieutenant and the sailing master in a case having to do with a sailor, the commander perhaps deviated from general custom. He was prompted thereto by the circumstance that he took that soldier to be a judicious person, thoughtful, and not altogether incapable of grappling with a difficult case unprecedented in his prior experience. Yet even as to him he was not without some latent misgiving, for withal he was an extremely good-natured man, an enjoyer of his dinner, a sound sleeper, and inclined to obesity—a man who though he would always maintain his manhood in battle might not prove altogether reliable in a moral dilemma involving aught of the tragic. As to the first lieutenant and the sailing master, Captain Vere could not but be aware that though honest natures, of approved gallantry upon occasion, their intelligence was mostly confined to the matter of active seamanship and the fighting demands of their profession.

The court was held in the same cabin where the unfortunate affair had taken place. This cabin, the commander's, embraced the entire area under the poop deck. Aft, and on either side, was a small stateroom, the one now temporarily a jail and the other a dead-house, and a yet smaller compartment, leaving a space between expanding forward into a goodly oblong of length coinciding with the ship's beam. A skylight of moderate dimension was overhead, and at each end of the oblong space were two sashed porthole windows easily convertible back into embrasures for short carronades.[89]

All being quickly in readiness, Billy Budd was arraigned, Captain Vere necessarily appearing as the sole witness in the case, and as such temporarily sinking his rank, though singularly maintaining it in a matter apparently trivial, namely, that he testified from the ship's weather side, with that object having caused the court to sit on the lee side. Concisely he narrated all that had led up to the catastrophe, omitting nothing in Claggart's accusation and deposing as to the manner in which the prisoner had received it. At this testimony the three officers glanced with no little surprise at Billy Budd, the last man they would have suspected either of the mutinous design alleged by Claggart or the undeniable deed he himself had done. The first lieutenant, taking judicial primacy and turning toward the prisoner, said, "Captain Vere has spoken. Is it or is it not as Captain Vere says?"

In response came syllables not so much impeded in the utterance as might have been anticipated. They were these: "Captain Vere tells the truth. It is just as Captain Vere says, but it is not as the master-at-arms said. I have eaten the King's bread and I am true to the King."

"I believe you, my man," said the witness, his voice indicating a suppressed emotion not otherwise betrayed.

"God will bless you for that, your honor!" not without stammering said Billy, and all but broke down. But immediately he was recalled to self-control by another question, to which with the same emotional difficulty of utterance he said, "No, there was no malice between us. I never bore malice against the master-at-arms. I am sorry

[89] Cannon.

that he is dead. I did not mean to kill him. Could I have used my tongue I would not have struck him. But he foully lied to my face and in presence of my captain, and I had to say something, and I could only say it with a blow, God help me!"

In the impulsive aboveboard manner of the frank one the court saw confirmed all that was implied in words that just previously had perplexed them, coming as they did from the testifier to the tragedy and promptly following Billy's impassioned disclaimer of mutinous intent—Captain Vere's words, "I believe you, my man."

Next it was asked of him whether he knew of or suspected aught savoring of incipient trouble (meaning mutiny, though the explicit term was avoided) going on in any section of the ship's company.

The reply lingered. This was naturally imputed by the court to the same vocal embarrassment which had retarded or obstructed previous answers. But in main it was otherwise here, the question immediately recalling to Billy's mind the interview with the afterguardsman in the forechains. But an innate repugnance to playing a part at all approaching that of an informer against one's own shipmates—the same erring sense of uninstructed honor which had stood in the way of his reporting the matter at the time, though as a loyal man-of-war's man it was incumbent on him, and failure so to do, if charged against him and proven, would have subjected him to the heaviest of penalties; this, with the blind feeling now his that nothing really was being hatched, prevailed with him. When the answer came it was a negative.

"One question more," said the officer of marines, now first speaking and with a troubled earnestness. "You tell us that what the master-at-arms said against you was a lie. Now why should he have so lied, so maliciously lied, since you declare there was no malice between you?"

At that question, unintentionally touching on a spiritual sphere wholly obscure to Billy's thoughts, he was nonplussed, evincing a confusion indeed that some observers, such as can readily be imagined, would have construed into involuntary evidence of hidden guilt. Nevertheless, he strove some way to answer, but all at once relinquished the vain endeavor, at the same time turning an appealing glance towards Captain Vere as deeming him his best helper and friend. Captain Vere, who had been seated for a time, rose to his feet, addressing the interrogator. "The question you put to him comes naturally enough. But how can he rightly answer it?—or anybody else, unless indeed it be he who lies within there," designating the compartment where lay the corpse. "But the prone one there will not rise to our summons. In effect, though, as it seems to me, the point you make is hardly material. Quite aside from any conceivable motive actuating the master-at-arms, and irrespective of the provocation to the blow, a martial court must needs in the present case confine its attention to the blow's consequence, which consequence justly is to be deemed not otherwise than as the striker's deed."

This utterance, the full significance of which it was not at all likely that Billy took in, nevertheless caused him to turn a wistful interrogative look toward the speaker, a look in its dumb expressiveness not unlike that which a dog of generous breed might turn upon his master, seeking in his face some elucidation of a previous gesture ambiguous to the canine intelligence. Nor was the same utterance without marked effect upon the three officers, more especially the soldier. Couched in it seemed to them a meaning unanticipated, involving a prejudgment on the speaker's part. It served to augment a mental disturbance previously evident enough.

The soldier once more spoke, in a tone of suggestive dubiety addressing at once his associates and Captain Vere: "Nobody is present—none of the ship's company, I mean—who might shed lateral light, if any is to be had, upon what remains mysterious in this matter."

"That is thoughtfully put," said Captain Vere; "I see your drift. Ay, there is a mystery; but, to use a scriptural phrase, it is a 'mystery of iniquity,' a matter for psychologic theologians to discuss. But what has a military court to do with it? Not to add that for us any possible investigation of it is cut off by the lasting tongue-tie of—him—in yonder," again designating the mortuary sateroom. "The prisoner's deed —with that alone we have to do."

To this, and particularly the closing reiteration, the marine soldier, knowing not how aptly to reply, sadly abstained from saying aught. The first lieutenant, who at the outset had not unnaturally assumed primacy in the court, now overrulingly instructed by a glance from Captain Vere, a glance more effective than words, resumed that primacy. Turning to the prisoner, "Budd," he said, and scarce in equable tones, "Budd, if you have aught further to say for yourself, say it now."

Upon this the young sailor turned another quick glance toward Captain Vere; then, as taking a hint from that aspect, a hint confirming his own instinct that silence was now best, replied to the lieutenant, "I have said all, sir."

The marine—the same who had been the sentinel without the cabin door at the time that the foretopman, followed by the master-at-arms, entered it—he, standing by the sailor throughout these judicial proceedings, was now directed to take him back to the after compartment originally assigned to the prisoner and his custodian. As the twain disappeared from view, the three officers, as partially liberated from some inward constraint associated with Billy's mere presence, simultaneously stirred in their seats. They exchanged looks of troubled indecision, yet feeling that decide they must and without long delay. For Captain Vere, he for the time stood—unconsciously with his back toward them, apparently in one of his absent fits—gazing out from a sashed porthole to windward upon the monotonous blank of the twilight sea. But the court's silence continuing, broken only at moments by brief consultations, in low earnest tones, this served to arouse him and energize him. Turning, he to-and-fro paced the cabin athwart; in the returning ascent to windward climbing the slant deck in the ship's lee roll, without knowing it symbolizing thus in his action a mind resolute to surmount difficulties even if against primitive instincts strong as the wind and the sea. Presently he came to a stand before the three. After scanning their faces he stood less as mustering his thoughts for expression than as one inly deliberating how best to put them to well-meaning men not intellectually mature, men with whom it was necessary to demonstrate certain principles that were axioms to himself. Similar impatience as to talking is perhaps one reason that deters some minds from addressing any popular assemblies.

When speak he did, something, both in the substance of what he said and his manner of saying it, showed the influence of unshared studies modifying and tempering the practical training of an active career. This, along with his phraseology, now and then was suggestive of the grounds whereon rested that imputation of a certain pedantry socially alleged against him by certain naval men of wholly practical cast, captains who nevertheless would frankly concede that His Majesty's navy mustered no more efficient officer of their grade than Starry Vere.

What he said was to this effect: "Hitherto I have been but the witness, little more; and I should hardly think now to take another tone, that of your coadjutor for the time, did I not perceive in you—at the crisis too—a troubled hesitancy, proceeding, I doubt not, from the clash of military duty with moral scruple—scruple vitalized by compassion. For the compassion, how can I otherwise than share it? But, mindful of paramount obligations, I strive against scruples that may tend to enervate decision. Not, gentlemen, that I hide from myself that the case is an exceptional one. Speculatively regarded, it well might be referred to a jury of casuists. But for us here, acting not as casuists or moralists, it is a case practical, and under martial law practically to be dealt with.

"But your scruples: do they move as in a dusk? Challenge them. Make them advance and declare themselves. Come now; do they import something like this: If, mindless of palliating circumstances, we are bound to regard the death of the master-at-arms as the prisoner's deed, then does that deed constitute a capital crime whereof the penalty is a mortal one. But in natural justice is nothing but the prisoner's overt act to be considered? How can we adjudge to summary and shameful death a fellow creature innocent before God, and whom we feel to be so?—Does that state it aright? You sign sad assent. Well, I too feel that, the full force of that. It is Nature. But do these buttons that we wear attest that our allegiance is to Nature? No, to the King. Though the ocean, which is inviolate Nature primeval, though this be the element where we move and have our being as sailors, yet as the King's officers lies our duty in a sphere correspondingly natural? So little is that true, that in receiving our commissions we in the most important regards ceased to be natural free agents. When war is declared are we the commissioned fighters previously consulted? We fight at command. If our judgments approve the war, that is but coincidence. So in other particulars. So now. For suppose condemnation to follow these present proceedings. Would it be so much we ourselves that would condemn as it would be martial law operating through us? For that law and the rigor of it, we are not responsible. Our vowed responsibility is in this: That however pitilessly that law may operate in any instances, we nevertheless adhere to it and administer it.

"But the exceptional in the matter moves the hearts within you. Even so too is mine moved. But let not warm hearts betray heads that should be cool. Ashore in a criminal case, will an upright judge allow himself off the bench to be waylaid by some tender kinswoman of the accused seeking to touch him with her tearful plea? Well, the heart here, sometimes the feminine in man, is as that piteous woman, and hard though it be, she must here be ruled out."

He paused, earnestly studying them for a moment; then resumed.

"But something in your aspect seems to urge that it is not solely the heart that moves in you, but also the conscience, the private conscience. But tell me whether or not, occupying the position we do, private conscience should not yield to that imperial one formulated in the code under which alone we officially proceed?"

Here the three men moved in their seats, less convinced than agitated by the course of an argument troubling but the more the spontaneous conflict within.

Perceiving which, the speaker paused for a moment; then abruptly changing his tone, went on.

"To steady us a bit, let us recur to the facts.—In wartime at sea a man-of-war's man strikes his superior in grade, and the blow kills. Apart from its effect the blow itself is, according to the Articles of War, a capital crime. Furthermore—"

"Ay, sir," emotionally broke in the officer of marines, "in one sense it was. But surely Budd purposed neither mutiny nor homicide."

"Surely not, my good man. And before a court less arbitrary and more merciful than a martial one, that plea would largely extenuate. At the Last Assizes[90] it shall acquit. But how here? We proceed under the law of the Mutiny Act. In feature no child can resemble his father more than that Act resembles in spirit the thing from which it derives—War. In His Majesty's service—in this ship, indeed—there are Englishmen forced to fight for the King against their will. Against their conscience, for aught we know. Though as their fellow creatures some of us may appreciate their position, yet as navy officers what reck we of it? Still less recks the enemy. Our impressed men he would fain cut down in the same swath with our volunteers. As regards the enemy's naval conscripts, some of whom may even share our own abhorrence of the regicidal French Directory, it is the same on our side. War looks but to the frontage, the appearance. And the Mutiny Act, War's child, takes after the father. Budd's intent or non-intent is nothing to the purpose.

"But while, put to it by those anxieties in you which I cannot but respect, I only repeat myself—while thus strangely we prolong proceedings that should be summary —the enemy may be sighted and an engagement result. We must do; and one of two things must we do—condemn or let go."

"Can we not convict and yet mitigate the penalty?" asked the sailing master, here speaking, and falteringly, for the first.

"Gentlemen, were that clearly lawful for us under the circumstances, consider the consequences of such clemency. The people" (meaning the ship's company) "have native sense; most of them are familiar with our naval usage and tradition; and how would they take it? Even could you explain to them—which our official position forbids—they, long molded by arbitrary discipline, have not that kind of intelligent responsiveness that might qualify them to comprehend and discriminate. No, to the people the foretopman's deed, however it be worded in the announcement, will be plain homicide committed in a flagrant act of mutiny. What penalty for that should follow, they know. But it does not follow. *Why?* they will ruminate. You know what sailors are. Will they not revert to the recent outbreak at the Nore? Ay. They know the well-founded alarm—the panic it struck throughout England. Your clement sentence they would account pusillanimous. They would think that we flinch, that we are afraid of them—afraid of practicing a lawful rigor singularly demanded at this juncture, lest it should provoke new troubles. What shame to us such a conjecture on their part, and how deadly to discipline. You see then, whither, prompted by duty and the law, I steadfastly drive. But I beseech you, my friends, do not take me amiss. I feel as you do for this unfortunate boy. But did he know our hearts, I take him to be of that generous nature that he would feel even for us on whom in this military necessity so heavy a compulsion is laid."

[90] On Judgment Day.

With that, crossing the deck he resumed his place by the sashed porthole, tacitly leaving the three to come to a decision. On the cabin's opposite side the troubled court sat silent. Loyal lieges, plain and practical, though at bottom they dissented from some points Captain Vere had put to them, they were without the faculty, hardly had the inclination, to gainsay one whom they felt to be an earnest man, one too not less their superior in mind than in naval rank. But it is not improbable that even such of his words as were not without influence over them, less came home to them than his closing appeal to their instinct as sea officers: in the forethought he threw out as to the practical consequences to discipline, considering the unconfirmed tone of the fleet at the time, should a man-of-war's man's violent killing at sea of a superior in grade be allowed to pass for aught else than a capital crime demanding prompt infliction of the penalty.

Not unlikely they were brought to something more or less akin to that harassed frame of mind which in the year 1842 actuated the commander of the U.S. brig-of-war *Somers* to resolve, under the so-called Articles of War, Articles modeled upon the English Mutiny Act, to resolve upon the execution at sea of a midshipman and two sailors as mutineers designing the seizure of the brig. Which resolution was carried out though in a time of peace and within not many days' sail of home. An act vindicated by a naval court of inquiry subsequently convened ashore. History, and here cited without comment. True, the circumstances on board the *Somers* were different from those on board the *Bellipotent*. But the urgency felt, well-warranted or otherwise, was much the same.

Says a writer whom few know,[91] "Forty years after a battle it is easy for a noncombatant to reason about how it ought to have been fought. It is another thing personally and under fire to have to direct the fighting while involved in the obscuring smoke of it. Much so with respect to other emergencies involving considerations both practical and moral, and when it is imperative promptly to act. The greater the fog the more it imperils the steamer, and speed is put on though at the hazard of running somebody down. Little ween[92] the snug card players in the cabin of the responsibilities of the sleepless man on the bridge."

In brief, Billy Budd was formally convicted and sentenced to be hung at the yardarm in the early morning watch, it being now night. Otherwise, as is customary in such cases, the sentence would forthwith have been carried out. In wartime on the field or in the fleet, a mortal punishment decreed by a drumhead court—on the field sometimes decreed by but a nod from the general—follows without delay on the heel of conviction, without appeal.

22

It was Captain Vere himself who of his own motion communicated the finding of the court to the prisoner, for that purpose going to the compartment where he was in custody and bidding the marine there to withdraw for the time.

Beyond the communication of the sentence, what took place at this interview was never known. But in view of the character of the twain briefly closeted in that stateroom, each radically sharing in the rarer qualities of our nature—so rare indeed

---

[91] Melville is perhaps referring to himself. [92] Think.

as to be all but incredible to average minds however much cultivated—some conjectures may be ventured.

It would have been in consonance with the spirit of Captain Vere should he on this occasion have concealed nothing from the condemned one—should he indeed have frankly disclosed to him the part he himself had played in bringing about the decision, at the same time revealing his actuating motives. On Billy's side it is not improbable that such a confession would have been received in much the same spirit that prompted it. Not without a sort of joy, indeed, he might have appreciated the brave opinion of him implied in his captain's making such a confidant of him. Nor, as to the sentence itself, could he have been insensible that it was imparted to him as to one not afraid to die. Even more may have been. Captain Vere in end may have developed the passion sometimes latent under an exterior stoical or indifferent. He was old enough to have been Billy's father. The austere devotee of military duty, letting himself melt back into what remains primeval in our formalized humanity, may in end have caught Billy to his heart, even as Abraham may have caught young Isaac on the brink of resolutely offering him up in obedience to the exacting behest.[93] But there is no telling the sacrament, seldom if in any case revealed to the gadding world, wherever under circumstances at all akin to those here attempted to be set forth two of great Nature's nobler order embrace. There is privacy at the time, inviolable to the survivor; and holy oblivion, the sequel to each diviner magnanimity, providentially covers all at last.

The first to encounter Captain Vere in act of leaving the compartment was the senior lieutenant. The face he beheld, for the moment one expressive of the agony of the strong, was to that officer, though a man of fifty, a startling revelation. That the condemned one suffered less than he who mainly had effected the condemnation was apparently indicated by the former's exclamation in the scene soon perforce to be touched upon.

23

Of a series of incidents within a brief term rapidly following each other, the adequate narration may take up a term less brief, especially if explanation or comment here and there seem requisite to the better understanding of such incidents. Between the entrance into the cabin of him who never left it alive, and him who when he did leave it left it as one condemned to die; between this and the closeted interview just given, less than an hour and a half had elapsed. It was an interval long enough, however, to awaken speculations among no few of the ship's company as to what it was that could be detaining in the cabin the master-at-arms and the sailor; for a rumor that both of them had been seen to enter it and neither of them had been seen to emerge, this rumor had got abroad upon the gun decks and in the tops, the people of a great warship being in one respect like villagers, taking microscopic note of every outward movement or non-movement going on. When therefore, in weather not at all tempestuous, all hands were called in the second dogwatch, a summons under such circumstances not usual in those hours, the crew were not wholly unprepared for some

---

[93] See Genesis 22:1–18. God tested Abraham by commanding him to sacrifice his son Isaac. At the moment of sacrifice, God withdrew the command.

announcement extraordinary, one having connection too with the continued absence of the two men from their wonted haunts.

There was a moderate sea at the time; and the moon, newly risen and near to being at its full, silvered the white spar deck wherever not blotted by the clear-cut shadows horizontally thrown of fixtures and moving men. On either side the quarterdeck the marine guard under arms was drawn up; and Captain Vere, standing in his place surrounded by all the wardroom officers, addressed his men. In so doing, his manner showed neither more nor less than that properly pertaining to his supreme position aboard his own ship. In clear terms and concise he told them what had taken place in the cabin: that the master-at-arms was dead, that he who had killed him had been already tried by a summary court and condemned to death, and that the execution would take place in the early morning watch. The word *mutiny* was not named in what he said. He refrained too from making the occasion an opportunity for any preachment as to the maintenance of discipline, thinking perhaps that under existing circumstances in the navy the consequence of violating discipline should be made to speak for itself.

Their captain's announcement was listened to by the throng of standing sailors in a dumbness like that of a seated congregation of believers in hell listening to the clergyman's announcement of his Calvinistic text.

At the close, however, a confused murmur went up. It began to wax. All but instantly, then, at a sign, it was pierced and suppressed by shrill whistles of the boatswain and his mates. The word was given to about ship.

To be prepared for burial Claggart's body was delivered to certain petty officers of his mess. And here, not to clog the sequel with lateral matters, it may be added that at a suitable hour, the master-at-arms was committed to the sea with every funeral honor properly belonging to his naval grade.

In this proceeding as in every public one growing out of the tragedy strict adherence to usage was observed. Nor in any point could it have been at all deviated from, either with respect to Claggart or Billy Budd, without begetting undesirable speculations in the ship's company, sailors, and more particularly men-of-war's men, being of all men the greatest sticklers for usage. For similar cause, all communication between Captain Vere and the condemned one ended with the closeted interview already given, the latter being now surrendered to the ordinary routine preliminary to the end. His transfer under guard from the captain's quarters was effected without unusual precautions—at least no visible ones. If possible, not to let the men so much as surmise that their officers anticipate aught amiss from them is the tacit rule in a military ship. And the more that some sort of trouble should really be apprehended, the more do the officers keep that apprehension to themselves, though not the less unostentatious vigilance may be augmented. In the present instance, the sentry placed over the prisoner had strict orders to let no one have communication with him but the chaplain. And certain unobtrusive measures were taken absolutely to insure this point.

24

In a seventy-four of the old order the deck known as the upper gun deck was the one covered over by the spar deck, which last, though not without its armament, was for the most part exposed to the weather. In general it was at all hours free from hammocks; those of the crew swinging on the lower gun deck and berth deck, the latter being not only a dormitory but also the place for the stowing of the sailors' bags, and on both sides lined with the large chests or movable pantries of the many messes of the men.

On the starboard side of the *Bellipotent*'s upper gun deck, behold Billy Budd under sentry lying prone in irons in one of the bays formed by the regular spacing of the guns comprising the batteries on either side. All these pieces were of the heavier caliber of that period. Mounted on lumbering wooden carriages, they were hampered with cumbersome harness of breeching and strong side-tackles for running them out. Guns and carriages, together with the long rammers and shorter linstocks[94] lodged in loops overhead—all these, as customary, were painted black; and the heavy hempen breechings, tarred to the same tint, wore the like livery of the undertakers. In contrast with the funereal hue of these surroundings, the prone sailor's exterior apparel, white jumper and white duck trousers, each more or less soiled, dimly glimmered in the obscure light of the bay like a patch of discolored snow in early April lingering at some upland cave's black mouth. In effect he is already in his shroud, or the garments that shall serve him in lieu of one. Over him but scarce illuminating him, two battle lanterns swing from two massive beams of the deck above. Fed with the oil supplied by the war contractors (whose gains, honest or otherwise, are in every land an anticipated portion of the harvest of death), with flickering splashes of dirty yellow light they pollute the pale moonshine all but ineffectually struggling in obstructed flecks through the open ports from which the tampioned[95] cannon protrude. Other lanterns at intervals serve but to bring out somewhat the obscurer bays which, like small confessionals or side-chapels in a cathedral, branch from the long dim-vistaed broad aisle between the two batteries of that covered tier.

Such was the deck where now lay the Handsome Sailor. Through the rose-tan of his complexion no pallor could have shown. It would have taken days of sequestration from the winds and the sun to have brought about the effacement of that. But the skeleton in the cheekbone at the point of its angle was just beginning delicately to be defined under the warm-tinted skin. In fervid hearts self-contained, some brief experiences devour our human tissue as secret fire in a ship's hold consumes cotton in the bale.

But now lying between the two guns, as nipped in the vice of fate, Billy's agony, mainly proceeding from a generous young heart's virgin experience of the diabolical incarnate and effective in some men—the tension of that agony was over now. It survived not the something healing in the closeted interview with Captain Vere. Without movement, he lay as in a trance, that adolescent expression previously noted as his taking on something akin to the look of a slumbering child in the cradle when the warm hearth-glow of the still chamber at night plays on the dimples that at whiles mysteriously form in the cheek, silently coming and going there. For now and then in the gyved[96] one's trance a serene happy light born of some wandering reminiscence or dream would diffuse itself over his face, and then wane away only anew to return.

The chaplain, coming to see him and finding him thus, and perceiving no sign that

---

[94] Sticks that hold the match used to fire cannon.   [96] Shackled.
[95] Plugged.

he was conscious of his presence, attentively regarded him for a space, then slipping aside, withdrew for the time, peradventure feeling that even he, the minister of Christ though receiving his stipend from Mars, had no consolation to proffer which could result in a peace transcending that which he beheld. But in the small hours he came again. And the prisoner, now awake to his surroundings, noticed his approach, and civilly, all but cheerfully, welcomed him. But it was to little purpose that in the interview following, the good man sought to bring Billy Budd to some godly understanding that he must die, and at dawn. True, Billy himself freely referred to his death as a thing close at hand; but it was something in the way that children will refer to death in general, who yet among their other sports will play a funeral with hearse and mourners.

Not that like children Billy was incapable of conceiving what death really is. No, but he was wholly without irrational fear of it, a fear more prevalent in highly civilized communities than those so-called barbarous ones which in all respects stand nearer to unadulterate Nature. And, as elsewhere said, a barbarian Billy radically was —as much so, for all the costume, as his countrymen the British captives, living trophies, made to march in the Roman triumph of Germanicus.[97] Quite as much so as those later barbarians, young men probably, and picked specimens among the earlier British converts to Christianity, at least nominally such, taken to Rome (as today converts from lesser isles of the sea may be taken to London), of whom the Pope[98] of that time, admiring the strangeness of their personal beauty so unlike the Italian stamp, their clear ruddy complexion and curled flaxen locks, exclaimed, "Angles" (meaning *English*, the modern derivative), "Angels, do you call them? And is it because they look so like angels?" Had it been later in time, one would think that the Pope had in mind Fra Angelico's[99] seraphs, some of whom, plucking apples in gardens of the Hesperides,[100] have the faint rosebud complexion of the more beautiful English girls.

If in vain the good chaplain sought to impress the young barbarian with ideas of death akin to those conveyed in the skull, dial, and crossbones on old tombstones, equally futile to all appearance were his efforts to bring home to him the thought of salvation and a Savior. Billy listened, but less out of awe or reverence, perhaps, than from a certain natural politeness, doubtless at bottom regarding all that in much the same way that most mariners of his class take any discourse abstract or out of the common tone of the workaday world. And this sailor way of taking clerical discourse is not wholly unlike the way in which the primer of Christianity, full of transcendent miracles, was received long ago on tropic isles by any superior *savage,* so called— a Tahitian, say, of Captain Cook's[101] time or shortly after that time. Out of natural courtesy he received, but did not appropriate. It was like a gift placed in the palm of an outreached hand upon which the fingers do not close.

But the *Bellipotent*'s chaplain was a discreet man possessing the good sense of a good heart. So he insisted not in his vocation here. At the instance of Captain Vere, a lieutenant had apprised him of pretty much everything as to Billy; and since he felt

---

[97] Germanicus Caesar (15 B.C.–A.D. 19), whose military victories were celebrated in Rome.
[98] Gregory the Great (540–604).
[99] Fra Angelico: Italian painter (1387–1455).

[100] In Greek myth, gardens in which golden apples grow.
[101] James Cook (1728–1779), English explorer of the Pacific.

that innocence was even a better thing than religion wherewith to go to Judgment, he reluctantly withdrew; but in his emotion not without first performing an act strange enough in an Englishman, and under the circumstances yet more so in any regular priest. Stooping over, he kissed on the fair cheek his fellow man, a felon in martial law, one whom though on the confines of death he felt he could never convert to a dogma; nor for all that did he fear for his future.

Marvel not that having been made acquainted with the young sailor's essential innocence the worthy man lifted not a finger to avert the doom of such a martyr to martial discipline. So to do would not only have been as idle as invoking the desert, but would also have been an audacious transgression of the bounds of his function, one as exactly prescribed to him by military law as that of the boatswain or any other naval officer. Bluntly put, a chaplain is the minister of the Prince of Peace serving in the host of the God of War—Mars. As such, he is as incongruous as a musket would be on the altar at Christmas. Why, then, is he there? Because he indirectly subserves the purpose attested by the cannon; because too he lends the sanction of the religion of the meek to that which practically is the abrogation of everything but brute Force.

25

The night so luminous on the spar deck, but otherwise on the cavernous ones below, levels so like the tiered galleries in a coal mine—the luminous night passed away. But like the prophet in the chariot disappearing in heaven and dropping his mantle to Elisha,[102] the withdrawing night transferred its pale robe to the breaking day. A meek, shy light appeared in the East, where stretched a diaphanous fleece of white furrowed vapor. That light slowly waxed. Suddenly *eight bells* was struck aft, responded to by one louder metallic stroke from forward. It was four o'clock in the morning. Instantly the silver whistles were heard summoning all hands to witness punishment. Up through the great hatchways rimmed with racks of heavy shot the watch below came pouring, overspreading with the watch already on deck the space between the mainmast and foremast including that occupied by the capacious launch and the black booms tiered on either side of it, boat and booms making a summit of observation for the powder-boys and younger tars. A different group comprising one watch of topmen leaned over the rail of that sea balcony, no small one in a seventy-four, looking down on the crowd below. Man or boy, none spake but in whisper, and few spake at all. Captain Vere—as before, the central figure among the assembled commissioned officers—stood nigh the break of the poop deck[103] facing forward. Just below him on the quarter-deck the marines in full equipment were drawn up much as at the scene of the promulgated sentence.

At sea in the old time, the execution by halter of a military sailor was generally from the foreyard. In the present instance, for special reasons the mainyard was assigned. Under an arm of that yard the prisoner was presently brought up, the chaplain attending him. It was noted at the time, and remarked upon afterwards, that in this final scene the good man evinced little or nothing of the perfunctory. Brief

---

[102] In 2 Kings 2:11–13, the prophet Elijah, ascending to heaven, drops his mantle, which Elisha then takes up.

[103] Raised deck at ship's stern.

speech indeed he had with the condemned one, but the genuine Gospel was less on his tongue than in his aspect and manner towards him. The final preparations personal to the latter being speedily brought to an end by two boatswain's mates, the consummation impended. Billy stood facing aft. At the penultimate moment, his words, his only ones, words wholly unobstructed in the utterance, were these: "God bless Captain Vere!" Syllables so unanticipated coming from one with the ignominious hemp about his neck—a conventional felon's benediction directed aft towards the quarters of honor; syllables too delivered in the clear melody of a singing bird on the point of launching from the twig—had a phenomenal effect, not unenhanced by the rare personal beauty of the young sailor, spiritualized now through late experiences so poignantly profound.

Without volition, as it were, as if indeed the ship's populace were but the vehicles of some vocal current electric, with one voice from alow and aloft came a resonant sympathetic echo: "God bless Captain Vere!" And yet at that instant Billy alone must have been in their hearts, even as in their eyes.

At the pronounced words and the spontaneous echo that voluminously rebounded them, Captain Vere, either through stoic self-control or a sort of momentary paralysis induced by emotional shock, stood erectly rigid as a musket in the ship-armorer's rack.

The hull, deliberately recovering from the periodic roll to leeward, was just regaining an even keel when the last signal, a preconcerted dumb one, was given. At the same moment it chanced that the vapory fleece hanging low in the East was shot through with a soft glory as of the fleece of the Lamb of God seen in mystical vision, and simultaneously therewith, watched by the wedged mass of upturned faces, Billy ascended; and, ascending, took the full rose of the dawn.

In the pinioned figure arrived at the yard-end, to the wonder of all no motion was apparent, none save that created by the slow roll of the hull in moderate weather, so majestic in a great ship ponderously cannoned.

26

When some days afterwards, in reference to the singularity just mentioned, the purser,[104] a rather ruddy, rotund person more accurate as an accountant than profound as a philosopher, said at mess to the surgeon, "What testimony to the force lodged in will power," the latter, saturnine, spare, and tall, one in whom a discreet causticity went along with a manner less genial than polite, replied, "Your pardon, Mr. Purser. In a hanging scientifically conducted—and under special orders I myself directed how Budd's was to be effected—any movement following the completed suspension and originating in the body suspended, such movement indicates mechanical spasm in the muscular system. Hence the absence of that is no more attributable to will power, as you call it, than to horsepower—begging your pardon."

"But this muscular spasm you speak of, is not that in a degree more or less invariable in these cases?"

"Assuredly so, Mr. Purser."

"How then, my good sir, do you account for its absence in this instance?"

"Mr. Purser, it is clear that your sense of the singularity in this matter equals not

[104] Ship's financial officer.

mine. You account for it by what you call will power—a term not yet included in the lexicon of science. For me, I do not, with my present knowledge, pretend to account for it at all. Even should we assume the hypothesis that at the first touch of the halyards the action of Budd's heart, intensified by extraordinary emotion at its climax, abruptly stopped—much like a watch when in carelessly winding it up you strain at the finish, thus snapping the chain—even under that hypothesis how account for the phenomenon that followed?"

"You admit, then, that the absence of spasmodic movement was phenomenal."

"It was phenomenal, Mr. Purser, in the sense that it was an appearance the cause of which is not immediately to be assigned."

"But tell me, my dear sir," pertinaciously continued the other, "was the man's death effected by the halter, or was it a species of euthanasia?"[105]

"*Euthanasia,* Mr. Purser, is something like your *will power:* I doubt its authenticity as a scientific term—begging your pardon again. It is at once imaginative and metaphysical—in short, Greek.—But," abruptly changing his tone, "there is a case in the sick bay that I do not care to leave to my assistants. Beg your pardon, but excuse me." And rising from the mess he formally withdrew.

27

The silence at the moment of execution and for a moment or two continuing thereafter, a silence but emphasized by the regular wash of the sea against the hull or the flutter of a sail caused by the helmsman's eyes being tempted astray, this emphasized silence was gradually disturbed by a sound not easily to be verbally rendered. Whoever has heard the freshet-wave of a torrent suddenly swelled by pouring showers in tropical mountains, showers not shared by the plain; whoever has heard the first muffled murmur of its sloping advance through precipitous woods may form some conception of the sound now heard. The seeming remoteness of its source was because of its murmurous indistinctness, since it came from close by, even from the men massed on the ship's open deck. Being inarticulate, it was dubious in significance further than it seemed to indicate some capricious revulsion of thought or feeling such as mobs ashore are liable to, in the present instance possibly implying a sullen revocation on the men's part of their involuntary echoing of Billy's benediction. But ere the murmur had time to wax into clamor it was met by a strategic command, the more telling that it came with abrupt unexpectedness: "Pipe down the starboard watch, Boatswain, and see that they go."

Shrill as the shriek of the sea hawk, the silver whistles of the boatswain and his mates pierced that ominous low sound, dissipating it; and yielding to the mechanism of discipline the throng was thinned by one-half. For the remainder, most of them were set to temporary employments connected with trimming the yards and so forth, business readily to be got up to serve occasion by any officer of the deck.

Now each proceeding that follows a mortal sentence pronounced at sea by a drumhead court is characterized by promptitude not perceptibly merging into hurry, though bordering that. The hammock, the one which had been Billy's bed when alive, having already been ballasted with shot and otherwise prepared to serve for his canvas

[105] Mercy-killing.

coffin, the last offices of the sea undertakers, the sailmaker's mates, were now speedily completed. When everything was in readiness a second call for all hands, made necessary by the strategic movement before mentioned, was sounded, now to witness burial.

The details of this closing formality it needs not to give. But when the tilted plank let slide its freight into the sea, a second strange human murmur was heard, blended now with another inarticulate sound proceeding from certain larger seafowl who, their attention having been attracted by the peculiar commotion in the water resulting from the heavy sloped dive of the shotted hammock into the sea, flew screaming to the spot. So near the hull did they come, that the stridor or bony creak of their gaunt double-jointed pinions was audible. As the ship under light airs passed on, leaving the burial spot astern, they still kept circling it low down with the moving shadow of their outstretched wings and the croaked requiem of their cries.

Upon sailors as superstitious as those of the age preceding ours, men-of-war's men too who had just beheld the prodigy of repose in the form suspended in air, and now foundering in the deeps; to such mariners the action of the seafowl, though dictated by mere animal greed for prey, was big with no prosaic significance. An uncertain movement began among them, in which some encroachment was made. It was tolerated but for a moment. For suddenly the drum beat to quarters, which familiar sound happening at least twice every day, had upon the present occasion a signal peremptoriness in it. True martial discipline long continued superinduces in average man a sort of impulse whose operation at the official word of command much resembles in its promptitude the effect of an instinct.

The drumbeat dissolved the multitude, distributing most of them along the batteries of the two covered gun decks. There, as wonted, the guns' crews stood by their respective cannon erect and silent. In due course the first officer, sword under arm and standing in his place on the quarter-deck, formally received the successive reports of the sworded lieutenants commanding the sections of batteries below; the last of which reports being made, the summed report he delivered with the customary salute to the commander. All this occupied time, which in the present case was the object in beating to quarters at an hour prior to the customary one. That such variance from usage was authorized by an officer like Captain Vere, a martinet as some deemed him, was evidence of the necessity for unusual action implied in what he deemed to be temporarily the mood of his men. "With mankind," he would say, "forms, measured forms, are everything; and that is the import couched in the story of Orpheus[106] with his lyre spellbinding the wild denizens of the wood." And this he once applied to the disruption of forms going on across the Channel and the consequences thereof.

At this unwonted muster at quarters, all proceeded as at the regular hour. The band on the quarter-deck played a sacred air, after which the chaplain went through the customary morning service. That done, the drum beat the retreat; and toned by music and religious rites subserving the discipline and purposes of war, the men in their wonted orderly manner dispersed to the places allotted them when not at the guns.

And now it was full day. The fleece of low-hanging vapor had vanished, licked up by the sun that late had so glorified it. And the circumambient air in the clearness

[106] In Greek myth, the poet whose music charmed wild beasts.

of its serenity was like smooth white marble in the polished block not yet removed from the marble-dealer's yard.

28

The symmetry of form attainable in pure fiction cannot so readily be achieved in a narration essentially having less to do with fable than with fact. Truth uncompromisingly told will always have its ragged edges; hence the conclusion of such a narration is apt to be less finished than an architectural finial.

How it fared with the Handsome Sailor during the year of the Great Mutiny has been faithfully given. But though properly the story ends with his life, something in way of sequel will not be amiss. Three brief chapters will suffice.

In the general rechristening under the Directory of the craft originally forming the navy of the French monarchy, the *St. Louis* line-of-battle ship was named the *Athée* (the *Atheist*). Such a name, like some other substituted ones in the Revolutionary fleet, while proclaiming the infidel audacity of the ruling power, was yet, though not so intended to be, the aptest name, if one consider it, ever given to a warship; far more so indeed than the *Devastation*, the *Erebus* (the *Hell*), and similar names bestowed upon fighting ships.

On the return passage to the English fleet from the detached cruise during which occurred the events already recorded, the *Bellipotent* fell in with the *Athée*. An engagement ensued, during which Captain Vere, in the act of putting his ship alongside the enemy with a view of throwing his boarders across her bulwarks, was hit by a musket ball from a porthole of the enemy's main cabin. More than disabled, he dropped to the deck and was carried below to the same cockpit where some of his men already lay. The senior lieutenant took command. Under him the enemy was finally captured, and though much crippled was by rare good fortune successfully taken into Gibraltar, an English port not very distant from the scene of the fight. There, Captain Vere with the rest of the wounded was put ashore. He lingered for some days, but the end came. Unhappily he was cut off too early for the Nile and Trafalgar.[107] The spirit that 'spite its philosophic austerity may yet have indulged in the most secret of all passions, ambition, never attained to the fulness of fame.

Not long before death, while lying under the influence of that magical drug which, soothing the physical frame, mysteriously operates on the subtler element in man, he was heard to murmur words inexplicable to his attendant: "Billy Budd, Billy Budd." That these were not the accents of remorse would seem clear from what the attendant said to the *Bellipotent*'s senior officer of marines, who, as the most reluctant to condemn of the members of the drumhead court, too well knew, though here he kept the knowledge to himself, who Billy Budd was.

29

Some few weeks after the execution, among other matters under the head of "News from the Mediterranean," there appeared in a naval chronicle of the time, an authorized weekly publication, an account of the affair. It was doubtless for the most part

---

[107] Subsequent battles (Nile, 1798; Trafalgar, 1805).

written in good faith, though the medium, partly rumor, through which the facts must have reached the writer served to deflect and in part falsify them. The account was as follows:

"On the tenth of the last month a deplorable occurrence took place on board H.M.S. *Bellipotent*. John Claggart, the ship's master-at-arms, discovering that some sort of plot was incipient among an inferior section of the ship's company, and that the ringleader was one William Budd; he, Claggart, in the act of arraigning the man before the captain, was vindictively stabbed to the heart by the suddenly drawn sheath knife of Budd.

"The deed and the implement employed sufficiently suggest that though mustered into the service under an English name the assassin was no Englishman, but one of those aliens adopting English cognomens whom the present extraordinary necessities of the service have caused to be admitted into it in considerable numbers.

"The enormity of the crime and the extreme depravity of the criminal appear the greater in view of the character of the victim, a middle-aged man respectable and discreet, belonging to that minor official grade, the petty officers, upon whom, as none know better than the commissioned gentlemen, the efficiency of His Majesty's navy so largely depends. His function was a responsible one, at once onerous and thankless; and his fidelity in it the greater because of his strong patriotic impulse. In this instance as in so many other instances in these days, the character of this unfortunate man signally refutes, if refutation were needed, that peevish saying attributed to the late Dr. Johnson,[108] that patriotism is the last refuge of a scoundrel.

"The criminal paid the penalty of his crime. The promptitude of the punishment has proved salutary. Nothing amiss is now apprehended aboard H.M.S. *Bellipotent*."

The above, appearing in a publication now long ago superannuated and forgotten, is all that hitherto has stood in human record to attest what manner of men respectively were John Claggart and Billy Budd.

30

Everything is for a term venerated in navies. Any tangible object associated with some striking incident of the service is converted into a monument. The spar from which the foretopman was suspended was for some few years kept trace of by the bluejackets. Their knowledges followed it from ship to dockyard and again from dockyard to ship, still pursuing it even when at last reduced to a mere dockyard boom. To them a chip of it was as a piece of the Cross. Ignorant though they were of the secret facts of the tragedy, and not thinking but that the penalty was somehow unavoidably inflicted from the naval point of view, for all that, they instinctively felt that Billy was a sort of man as incapable of mutiny as of wilful murder. They recalled the fresh young image of the Handsome Sailor, that face never deformed by a sneer or subtler vile freak of the heart within. This impression of him was doubtless deepened by the fact that he was gone, and in a measure mysteriously gone. On the gun decks of the *Bellipotent* the general estimate of his nature and its unconscious simplicity eventually found rude utterance from another foretopman, one of his own watch, gifted, as some

[108] The lexicographer Samuel Johnson (1709–1784).

sailors are, with an artless *poetic* temperament. The tarry hand made some lines which, after circulating among the shipboard crews for a while, finally got rudely printed at Portsmouth as a ballad. The title given to it was the sailor's.

BILLY IN THE DARBIES[109]

Good of the chaplain to enter Lone Bay
And down on his marrowbones here and pray
For the likes just o' me, Billy Budd.—But, look:
Through the port comes the moonshine astray!
It tips the guard's cutlass and silvers this nook;
But 'twill die in the dawning of Billy's last day.
A jewel-block they'll make of me tomorrow,
Pendant pearl from the yardarm-end
Like the eardrop I gave to Bristol Molly—
O, 'tis me, not the sentence they'll suspend.
Ay, ay, all is up; and I must up too,
Early in the morning, aloft from alow.
On an empty stomach now never it would do.
They'll give me a nibble—bit o' biscuit ere I go.
Sure, a messmate will reach me the last parting cup;
But, turning heads away from the hoist and the belay.
Heaven knows who will have the running of me up!
No pipe to those halyards.—But aren't it all sham?
A blur's in my eyes; it is dreaming that I am.
A hatchet to my hawser? All adrift to go?
The drum roll to grog, and Billy never know?
But Donald he has promised to stand by the plank;
So I'll shake a friendly hand ere I sink.
But—no! It is dead then I'll be, come to think.
I remember Taff the Welshman when he sank.
And his cheek it was like the budding pink.
But me they'll lash in hammock, drop me deep.
Fathoms down, fathoms down, how I'll dream fast asleep.
I feel it stealing now. Sentry, are you there?
Just ease these darbies at the wrist,
And roll me over fair!
I am sleepy, and the oozy weeds about me twist.

1924

---

[109] Handcuffs.

from Battle Pieces and Aspects of the War

The Portent

(1859)

Hanging from the beam,
    Slowly swaying (such the law),
Gaunt the shadow on your green,
    Shenandoah!
The cut is on the crown 5
    (Lo, John Brown),[1]
And the stabs shall heal no more.

Hidden in the cap[2]
    Is the anguish none can draw;
So your future veils its face, 10
    Shenandoah!
But the streaming beard is shown
    (Weird John Brown),
The meteor of the war.
1866

The March into Virginia
Ending in the First Manassas

(July, 1861)[3]

Did all the lets[4] and bars appear
    To every just or larger end,
Whence should come the trust and cheer?
    Youth must its ignorant impulse lend—
Age finds place in the rear. 5
    All wars are boyish, and are fought by boys,
The champions and enthusiasts of the state:
    Turbid ardors and vain joys
    Not barrenly abate—

---

[1] In 1859 the bearded abolitionist John Brown was hanged for treason after he had incited a slave rebellion and led an attack on a Federal arsenal at Harper's Ferry, Virginia. He had received a scalp wound when captured.
[2] Hood placed over the head of the condemned man.

[3] At Bull Run, near Manassas, Virginia, Confederate troops defeated Union forces in July 1861.
[4] Obstacles.

Stimulants to the power mature,   10
    Preparatives of fate.

Who here forecasteth the event?
What heart but spurns at precedent
And warnings of the wise,
Contemned foreclosures of surprise?   15
The banners play, the bugles call,
The air is blue and prodigal.
    No berrying party, pleasure-wooed,
No picnic party in the May,
Ever went less loth than they   20
    Into that leafy neighborhood.
In Bacchic glee[5] they file toward Fate,
Moloch's[6] uninitiate;
Expectancy, and glad surmise
Of battle's unknown mysteries.   25

All they feel is this: 'tis glory,
A rapture sharp, though transitory,
Yet lasting in belaureled story.
So they gayly go to fight,
Chatting left and laughing right.   30

But some who this blithe mood present,
    As on in lightsome files they fare,
Shall die experienced ere three days be spent—
    Perish, enlightened by the vollied glare;
Or shame survive, and, like to adamant,   35
    The throe of Second Manassas[7] share.

    1866

A Utilitarian View of the Monitor's Fight[8]

Plain be the phrase, yet apt the verse,
    More ponderous than nimble;
For since grimed War here laid aside
His Orient pomp, 'twould ill befit
    Overmuch to ply   5
    The rhyme's barbaric cymbal.

---

[5] Revels of the kind inspired by Bacchus, Roman god of wine.
[6] Moloch: Ancient Semitic god to whom worshippers sacrificed children.
[7] In the Second Battle of Manassas (August 1862), Union forces were once again defeated.

[8] One of the two ironclad vessels that battled in May 1862, at Hampton Roads, Virginia. The *Monitor* belonged to the Union navy, and its adversary was the Confederate *Merrimack*.

Hail to victory without the gaud
　　Of glory; zeal that needs no fans
Of banners; plain mechanic power
Plied cogently in War now placed—　　　　　　　　　10
　　Where War belongs—
　　Among the trades and artisans.

Yet this was battle, and intense—
　　Beyond the strife of fleets heroic;
Deadlier, closer, calm 'mid storm;　　　　　　　　　15
No passion; all went on by crank,
　　Pivot, and screw,
　　And calculations of caloric.

Needless to dwell; the story's known.
　　The ringing of those plates on plates　　　　　　20
Still ringeth round the world—
The clangor of that blacksmiths' fray.
　　The anvil-din
　　Resounds this message from the Fates:

War yet shall be, and to the end;　　　　　　　　　25
　　But war-paint shows the streaks of weather;
War yet shall be, but warriors
Are now but operatives;[9] War's made
　　Less grand than Peace,
　　And a singe runs through lace and feather.　　　30
1866

Shiloh[10]

A Requiem

(April, 1862)

Skimming lightly, wheeling still,
　　The swallows fly low
Over the field in clouded days,
　　The forest-field of Shiloh—
Over the field where April rain　　　　　　　　　5
Solaced the parched ones stretched in pain
Through the pause of night
That followed the Sunday fight
　　Around the church of Shiloh—
The church so lone, the log-built one,　　　　　　10

---

[9] Factory workers.
[10] Site of battle and Confederate victory over
Union forces in western Tennessee, April 1862.

That echoed to many a parting groan
And natural prayer
Of dying foemen mingled there—
Foemen at morn, but friends at eve—
Fame or country least their care: 15
(What like a bullet can undeceive!)
But now they lie low,
While over them the swallows skim,
And all is hushed at Shiloh.

1866

---

from John Marr and Other Sailors

The Tuft of Kelp

All dripping in tangles green,
    Cast up by a lonely sea
If purer for that, O Weed,
    Bitterer, too, are 'ye?

1888

The Maldive Shark

About the Shark, phlegmatical one,
Pale sot of the Maldive sea,[1]
The sleek little pilot-fish, azure and slim,
How alert in attendance be.
From his saw-pit of mouth, from his charnel of maw   5
They have nothing of harm to dread,
But liquidly glide on his ghastly flank
Or before his Gorgonian[2] head;
Or lurk in the port of serrated teeth
In white triple tiers of glittering gates,   10
And there find a haven when peril's abroad,
An asylum in jaws of the Fates!

They are friends; and friendly they guide him to prey,
Yet never partake of the treat—
Eyes and brains to the dotard lethargic and dull,   15
Pale ravener of horrible meat.

1888

[1] Indian Ocean near the Maldive Islands, southwest of the southern end of India.   [2] Able to turn the beholder to stone, as the Gorgon's head did in Greek mythology.

from Timoleon, Etc.

Monody[1]

To have known him, to have loved him
    After loneness long;
And then to be estranged in life,
    And neither in the wrong;
And now for death to set his seal—   5
    Ease me, a little ease, my song!

By wintry hills his hermit-mound
    The sheeted snow-drifts drape,
And houseless there the snow-bird flits
    Beneath the fir-trees' crape: 10
Glazed now with ice the cloistral vine
    That hid the shyest grape.

1891

Art

In placid hours well-pleased we dream
Of many a brave unbodied scheme.
But form to lend, pulsed life create,
What unlike things must meet and mate:
A flame to melt—a wind to freeze;   5
Sad patience—joyous energies;
Humility—yet pride and scorn;
Instinct and study; love and hate;
Audacity—reverence. These must mate,
And fuse with Jacob's[2] mystic heart,   10
To wrestle with the angel—Art.

1891

Greek Architecture

Not magnitude, not lavishness,
    But Form—the Site;
Not innovating wilfulness,
    But reverence for the Archetype.

1891

---

[1] Ode, elegy, or dirge sung by one voice. "Monody" is thought to be a lament for Melville's fellow writer, Nathaniel Hawthorne.

[2] According to Genesis 32:24–30, Jacob wrestled with an angel.

Henry Wadsworth Longfellow
1807–1882

Henry Wadsworth Longfellow belonged to the "New England triumvirate" of ruling poets, which included James Russell Lowell and John Greenleaf Whittier. Their works graced the Victorian parlors and the rude outland cabins of western frontier America. Longfellow proved that the poetry of an American could be hailed on both sides of the Atlantic: He was awarded an honorary doctoral degree by Oxford and Cambridge universities and honored with a bust in the Poets' Corner of Westminster Abbey. Longfellow symbolized the respectability, culture, and learning that signified a mature America. In the Revolutionary era John Adams had predicted that it would take three generations before citizens of the new nation could "give their children a right to study . . . Poetry." Longfellow's success meant that the time had come.

Longfellow was born in Portland, Maine, at the time a part of Massachusetts. His parents traced their ancestry to the *Mayflower.* Henry was a sports-minded boy who grew up with access to his father's library, which contained the works of Shakespeare, Milton, Pope, and classical authors. At the age of thirteen he saw his own verse published in the *Portland Gazette,* and in the following year he was admitted to Bowdoin College, though he waited another year before beginning his studies there. A classmate remembers Henry as "genial, sociable, and agreeable," "free from envy and every corroding passion and vice," and "always a gentleman in his deportment." Fortunately Longfellow, a classmate of Nathaniel Hawthorne, found a faculty mentor who guided his work in language and literature. He continued to write poems, placing some in reputable Boston and Philadelphia periodicals.

Opposed to his father's proposal that he study law, Henry argued for a career in publishing after graduate study in languages at Harvard, quoting the saying that "as many languages as a person acquires, so many times is he a man." In a happy convergence of circumstances, the young man had the opportunity to hold college positions in the then-new field of modern foreign languages, first at Bowdoin and then at Harvard, where he became a professor in 1836. Both colleges sent Longfellow abroad for intense study of languages. From 1826 to 1829 and again from 1835 to 1836 he sojourned in Europe, making the acquaintance of scholars and poets and acquiring habits of dress that made him a dandified figure back in America. In 1831 he married a Portland girl, Mary Storer Potter, who died just four years later. Longfellow referred obliquely to her death as "sorrow, and a care that almost killed."

Professor Longfellow taught responsibly but without great enthusiasm. He confided to his journal, "Perhaps the worst thing in a College Life is this having your mind constantly a play-mate for boys." He finally resigned from teaching in 1854. By then he had earned a considerable reputation for such poems as "Psalm of Life," which Whittier called the "moral enginery of an age of action." His first book of poems, *Voices of the Night* (1839), had sold an impressive 43,000 copies, and he later published *Ballads and Other Poems* (1841) and *Poems on*

Slavery (1842). Longfellow had also remarried. Frances Appleton was the daughter of one of Boston's wealthiest merchants, whose wedding gift was Craigie House, once General Washington's headquarters and now a literary landmark. In 1861 Frances Appleton Longfellow, the mother of four children, died in a house fire. "The Cross of Snow," one of Longfellow's most moving poems, was occasioned by her death and was found among the poet's personal effects after his own death.

Longfellow's genius lay in the expression of American values and yearnings. He mixed moral statement with hymns to the work ethic, family relationships, and nature. In a nation still primitive in material conditions he sought to "clothe the real with the ideal and make actual and common things radiant with poetic beauty."

In large part that clothing was a masterful prosody seldom equaled in American literature. Longfellow's metrics bear the closest scrutiny, and the variety of his verse forms, from ballad to sonnet, is astonishing. In an era that valued smoothly flowing rhythms, uplifting sentiment, and poetic statement close to the surface of each stanza, Longfellow's work became the standard against which poetry and poetic success were measured. In addition, in works like *Evangeline* (1847), *Hiawatha* (1855), and *The Courtship of Miles Standish* (1858), Longfellow gave Americans a poetry of "native materials." He also brought the long ago and far away to his nineteenth-century readers in such works as *The Belfry of Bruges and Other Poems* (1845) and *Tales of a Wayside Inn* (1863), modeled on *The Decameron,* a story collection of the Italian Renaissance poet Boccaccio. These works gratified Americans eager to believe in their nation's achievement in the fine arts, which many judged by European standards. Longfellow's work conferred the mantle of European legitimacy on America. The writer Henry James understood this, remarking that he found Longfellow engaging because his " 'European' culture and his native kept house together."

Further Reading:
S. Longfellow, *The Life of Henry Wadsworth Longfellow,* 3 vols., 1886.
L. Thompson, *Young Longfellow,* 1938.
N. Arvin, *Longfellow: His Life and Work,* 1963.
C. Williams, *Henry Wadsworth Longfellow,* 1964.
E. Wagenknecht, *Henry Wadsworth Longfellow: Portrait of an American Humanist,* 1966.

Text:
The Complete Poetical Works of Henry Wadsworth Longfellow, 1922.

A Psalm of Life

What the Heart of the Young Man Said to the Psalmist

Tell me not, in mournful numbers,
    Life is but an empty dream!——
For the soul is dead that slumbers,
    And things are not what they seem.

Life is real! Life is earnest!   5
    And the grave is not its goal;
Dust thou art, to dust returnest,
    Was not spoken of the soul.

Not enjoyment, and not sorrow,
    Is our destined end or way;   10
But to act, that each to-morrow
    Find us farther than to-day.

Art is long, and Time is fleeting,
    And our hearts, though stout and brave,
Still, like muffled drums, are beating   15
    Funeral marches to the grave.

In the world's broad field of battle,
    In the bivouac of Life,
Be not like dumb, driven cattle!
    Be a hero in the strife!   20

Trust no Future, howe'er pleasant!
    Let the dead Past bury its dead!
Act,—act in the living Present!
    Heart within, and God o'erhead!

Lives of great men all remind us   25
    We can make our lives sublime,
And, departing, leave behind us
    Footprints on the sands of time;

Footprints, that perhaps another,
    Sailing o'er life's solemn main,   30
A forlorn and shipwrecked brother,
    Seeing, shall take heart again.

Let us, then, be up and doing,
    With a heart for any fate;
Still achieving, still pursuing,   35
    Learn to labor and to wait.

1838

The Arsenal at Springfield

This is the Arsenal. From floor to ceiling,
    Like a huge organ, rise the burnished arms;
But from their silent pipes no anthem pealing
    Startles the villages with strange alarms.

Ah! what a sound will rise, how wild and dreary,   5
    When the death-angel touches those swift keys!
What loud lament and dismal Miserere
    Will mingle with their awful symphonies!

I hear even now the infinite fierce chorus,
    The cries of agony, the endless groan,   10
Which, through the ages that have gone before us,
    In long reverberations reach our own.

On helm and harness rings the Saxon hammer,
    Through Cimbric forest roars the Norseman's song,
And loud, amid the universal clamor,   15
    O'er distant deserts sounds the Tartar gong.

I hear the Florentine, who from his palace
    Wheels out his battle-bell with dreadful din,
And Aztec priests upon their teocallis¹
    Beat the wild war-drums made of serpent's skin;   20

The tumult of each sacked and burning village;
    The shout that every prayer for mercy drowns;
The soldiers' revels in the midst of pillage;
    The wail of famine in beleaguered towns;

The bursting shell, the gateway wrenched asunder,   25
    The rattling musketry, the clashing blade;
And ever and anon, in tones of thunder
    The diapason² of the cannonade.

Is it, O man, with such discordant noises,
    With such accursed instruments as these.   30
Thou drownest Nature's sweet and kindly voices,
    And jarrest the celestial harmonies?

¹ Low, terraced pyramid.
² Full tonal range.

Were half the power that fills the world with terror,
   Were half the wealth bestowed on camps and courts,
Given to redeem the human mind from error,   35
   There were no need of arsenals or forts:

The warrior's name would be a name abhorrèd!
   And every nation, that should lift again
Its hand against a brother, on its forehead
   Would wear forevermore the curse of Cain!   40

Down the dark future, through long generations,
   The echoing sounds grow fainter and then cease;
And like a bell, with solemn, sweet vibrations,
   I hear once more the voice of Christ say, "Peace!"

Peace! and no longer from its brazen portals   45
   The blast of War's great organ shakes the skies!
But beautiful as songs of the immortals,
   The holy melodies of love arise.
1844

The Fire of Drift-wood

Devereux Farm near Marblehead

We sat within the farm-house old,
   Whose windows, looking o'er the bay,
Gave to the sea-breeze damp and cold
   An easy entrance, night and day.

Not far away we saw the port,   5
   The strange, old-fashioned, silent town,
The lighthouse, the dismantled fort,
   The wooden houses, quaint and brown.

We sat and talked until the night,
   Descending, filled the little room;   10
Our faces faded from the sight,
   Our voices only broke the gloom.

We spake of many a vanished scene,
   Of what we once had thought and said,
Of what had been, and might have been,   15
   And who was changed, and who was dead;

And all that fills the hearts of friends,
  When first they feel, with secret pain,
Their lives thenceforth have separate ends,
  And never can be one again;   20

The first slight swerving of the heart,
  That words are powerless to express,
And leave it still unsaid in part,
  Or say it in too great excess.

The very tones in which we spake   25
  Had something strange, I could but mark;
The leaves of memory seemed to make
  A mournful rustling in the dark.

Oft died the words upon our lips,
  As suddenly, from out the fire   30
Built of the wreck of stranded ships,
  The flames would leap and then expire.

And, as their splendor flashed and failed,
  We thought of wrecks upon the main,
Of ships dismasted, that were hailed   35
  And sent no answer back again.

The windows, rattling in their frames,
  The ocean, roaring up the beach,
The gusty blast, the bickering flames,
  All mingled vaguely in our speech;   40

Until they made themselves a part
  Of fancies floating through the brain,
The long-lost ventures of the heart,
  That send no answers back again.

O flames that glowed! O hearts that yearned!   45
  They were indeed too much akin,
The drift-wood fire without that burned,
  The thoughts that burned and glowed within.
        1849

The Jewish Cemetery at Newport

How strange it seems! These Hebrews in their graves,
   Close by the street of this fair seaport town,
Silent beside the never-silent waves,
   At rest in all this moving up and down!

The trees are white with dust, that o'er their sleep   5
   Wave their broad curtains in the south-wind's breath,
While underneath these leafy tents they keep
   The long, mysterious Exodus of Death.

And these sepulchral stones, so old and brown,
   That pave with level flags their burial-place,   10
Seem like the tablets of the Law, thrown down
   And broken by Moses at the mountain's base.

The very names recorded here are strange,
   Of foreign accent, and of different climes;
Alvares and Rivera interchange   15
   With Abraham and Jacob of old times.

"Blessed be God, for he created Death!"
   The mourners said, "and Death is rest and peace";
Then added, in the certainty of faith,
   "And giveth Life that nevermore shall cease."   20

Closed are the portals of their Synagogue,
   No Psalms of David now the silence break,
No Rabbi reads the ancient Decalogue[1]
   In the grand dialect the Prophets spake.

Gone are the living, but the dead remain,   25
   And not neglected; for a hand unseen,
Scattering its bounty, like a summer rain,
   Still keeps their graves and their remembrance green.

How came they here? What burst of Christian hate,
   What persecution, merciless and blind,   30
Drove o'er the sea—that desert desolate—
   These Ishmaels and Hagars of mankind?

---

[1] The Ten Commandments (see Exodus 20:1–17).

They lived in narrow streets and lanes obscure,
    Ghetto and Judenstrass, in mirk and mire;
Taught in the school of patience to endure   35
    The life of anguish and the death of fire.

All their lives long, with the unleavened bread
    And bitter herbs of exile and its fears,
The wasting famine of the heart they fed,
    And slaked its thirst with marah[2] of their tears.   40

Anathema maranatha![3] was the cry
    That rang from town to town, from street to street:
At every gate the accursed Mordecai[4]
    Was mocked and jeered, and spurned by Christian feet.

Pride and humiliation hand in hand
    Walked with them through the world where'er they went;   45
Trampled and beaten were they as the sand,
    And yet unshaken as the continent.

For in the background figures vague and vast
    Of patriarchs and of prophets rose sublime,
And all the great traditions of the Past   50
    They saw reflected in the coming time.

And thus forever with reverted look
    The mystic volume of the world they read,
Spelling it backward, like a Hebrew book,
    Till life became a Legend of the Dead.   55

But ah! what once has been shall be no more!
    The groaning earth in travail and in pain
Brings forth its races, but does not restore,
And the dead nations never rise again.
1854   60

---

[2] Hebrew: "bitter."
[3] A vile curse of the early Christians applied to the Jews.

[4] Foster father of Esther, wife of the Persian king Xerxes.

Aftermath

When the summer fields are mown,
When the birds are fledged and flown,
And the dry leaves strew the path:
With the falling of the snow,
With the cawing of the crow,   5
Once again the fields we mow
And gather in the aftermath.

Not the sweet, new grass with flowers
Is this harvesting of ours;
Not the upland clover bloom;   10
But the rowen mixed with weeds,
Tangled tufts from marsh and meads,
Where the poppy drops its seeds
In the silence and the gloom.

1873

Chaucer

An old man in a lodge¹ within a park;
The chamber walls depicted all around
With portraitures of huntsman, hawk, and hound,
And the hurt deer. He listeneth to the lark,
Whose song comes with the sunshine through the dark   5
Of painted glass in leaden lattice bound;
He listeneth and he laugheth at the sound,
Then writeth in a book like any clerk.
He is the poet of the dawn, who wrote
The Canterbury Tales, and his old age   10
Made beautiful with song; and as I read
I hear the crowing cock, I hear the note
Of lark and linnet, and from every page
Rise odors of ploughed field or flowery mead.

1875

¹ I.e., a hunting lodge.

Milton

I pace the sounding sea-beach and behold
How the voluminous billows roll and run.
Upheaving and subsiding, while the sun
Shines through their sheeted emerald far unrolled,
And the ninth wave, slow gathering fold by fold   5
All its loose-flowing garments into one,
Plunges upon the shore, and floods the dun
Pale reach of sands, and changes them to gold.
So in majestic cadence rise and fall
The mighty undulations of thy song,   10
O sightless bard, England's Mæonides![1]
And ever and anon, high over all
Uplifted, a ninth wave superb and strong,
Floods all the soul with its melodious seas.
1875

Keats

The young Endymion sleeps Endymion's sleep;
The shepherd-boy whose tale was left half told!
The solemn grove uplifts its shield of gold
To the red rising moon, and loud and deep
The nightingale is singing from the steep;   5
It is midsummer, but the air is cold;
Can it be death? Alas, beside the fold
A shepherd's pipe lies shattered near his sheep.
Lo! in the moonlight gleams a marble white,
On which I read: "Here lieth one whose name   10
Was writ in water." And was this the meed
Of his sweet singing? Rather let me write:
"The smoking flax before it burst to flame
Was quenched by death, and broken the bruised reed."
1875

[1] Pseudonym for the Greek poet Homer.

Nature

As a fond mother, when the day is o'er,
  Leads by the hand her little child to bed,
  Half willing, half reluctant to be led,
  And leave his broken playthings on the floor,
Still gazing at them through the open door,   5
  Nor wholly reassured and comforted
  By promises of others in their stead,
  Which, though more splendid, may not please him more:
So Nature deals with us, and takes away
  Our playthings one by one, and by the hand   10
  Leads us to rest so gently, that we go
Scarce knowing if we wish to go or stay,
  Being too full of sleep to understand
  How far the unknown transcends the what we know.

1875

The Cross of Snow

In the long, sleepless watches of the night,
  A gentle face—the face of one long dead—
  Looks at me from the wall, where round its head
  The night-lamp casts a halo of pale light.
Here in this room she died; and soul more white   5
  Never through martyrdom of fire was led
  To its repose; nor can in books be read
  The legend of a life more benedight.[1]
There is a mountain in the distant West
  That, sun-defying, in its deep ravines   10
  Displays a cross of snow upon its side.
Such is the cross I wear upon my breast
  These eighteen years, through all the changing scenes
  And seasons, changeless since the day she died.

1886

[1] Blessed.

John Greenleaf Whittier
1807–1892

A century-old, hand-hewn oak cabin north of Boston, near the seacoast town of Haverhill, Massachusetts, provided the unassuming setting for John Greenleaf Whittier's birth in 1807. The son of devout and industrious Quaker farmers, Whittier was limited by his daily chores and frail health to irregular attendance at the local country school. There he was introduced to the works of Robert Burns, which he described as "about the first poetry I had ever read" and which "had a lasting influence upon me." Reflecting on the modest circumstances of his childhood, Whittier noted somewhat wistfully, "I had at that time a great thirst for knowledge and little means to gratify it. The beauty of outward nature early impressed me, and the moral and spiritual beauty of the holy lives I read of in the Bible and other books also affected me with a sense of my falling short and longing for a better life." Whittier quickly discovered in poetry an appropriate outlet for his idyllic vision of the American experience. His verse remains preindustrial America's most ardent expression of such rustic values as simplicity, independence, and moral certitude.

Whittier nourished his youthful "thirst for knowledge" both by reading the "few books within my reach," most notably such staples of the Quaker tradition as the Bible and Bunyan's *Pilgrim's Progress,* as well as by writing what he later called "wood hymns" devoted to nature and country folklore. His older sister, confident of his ability, sent several of these poems to local newspapers, one of which, the Newburyport *Free Press,* was edited by the youthful, but not yet zealous, abolitionist William Lloyd Garrison. Delighted with what he read, Garrison published the first of many of Whittier's poems in 1826 and soon traveled to the Whittier farm to encourage this young poet and to urge his father to provide his son with "every facility for the development of his remarkable genius"—to which the senior Whittier quickly replied, "Sir, poetry will not give him bread." An "over-wearied child," too slender for the heavy work required of him, Whittier enrolled, with his father's reluctant permission, at nearby Haverhill Academy and supported himself through two terms with odd jobs, including service as a cobbler. Unable to afford a college education, Whittier worked as a country journalist and editorial assistant at several minor newspapers in Boston and Hartford while continuing to circulate his verse. In the years that followed, the public recognition his poetry earned him was invariably offset by his poor health, which often forced him to resign his newspaper work and return to the family farm to recuperate.

As a young adult, Whittier suffered through several years of personal turmoil filled with depression, self-pity, and insomnia and marked by a series of unrequited loves. (He was to remain a lifelong bachelor.) During this period he began to gain considerable attention as his poetry reached a wider audience. Conscious of both what he called his own "slumbering powers" and of his neighbors' confidence in him, Whittier began to speak out on public issues and to participate in local politics. At the age of thirty, he was elected to the Massachusetts state legislature and reelected the following year. He declined another term, responding instead to Garrison's call that he devote his energies to the abolition of slavery: "The cause is worthy of Gabriel, yea, the God of hosts places himself at its head. Whittier enlist!—Your talents, zeal, influence—all are needed."

Resolving to knock "Pegasus on the head," Whittier began what would be a distinguished three-decade career as an abolitionist poet and editorialist when he published at his own expense a pamphlet entitled *Justice and Expediency* (1833). In that same year, he represented the state of Massachusetts at the first meeting of the American Anti-Slavery Society. He later declared that having drafted and then signed the resolutions of that convention meant more to him than having his name on any book he had written. Throughout these years, Whittier sustained himself as a full-time political activist and a part-time editor of several abolitionist newspapers, including the *Pennsylvania Freeman* and *The National Era*, which would later publish Harriet Beecher Stowe's *Uncle Tom's Cabin* as a serial. Whittier drew his abolitionist zeal primarily from his Quaker heritage, most eloquently expressed in the late-eighteenth-century work of John Woolman. But, as he explained in a letter to E. L. Godkin, then editor of *The Nation*, altruism, modesty, and a recognition of the personal "costs" of a literary life also reinforced his commitment to abolitionist causes: "I can not be sufficiently grateful to the Divine Providence that so early called my attention to the great interests of humanity, saving me from the poor ambitions and miserable jealousies of a selfish pursuit of literary reputation, the pain of disappointment and the temptation to envy." Nathaniel Hawthorne later noted, "Strictly speaking, Whittier did not care much for literature."

Whittier quickly became the most eloquent voice in the abolitionist movement by publishing in virtually every major newspaper and periodical sympathetic to the cause. He first gathered the work of this period in a volume entitled *Poems Written During the Progress of the Abolition Question* (1837). Subsequent volumes included *Lays of My Home* (1843), *Voices of Freedom* (1846), *Songs of Labor and Other Poems* (1850), *The Chapel of the Hermits and Other Poems* (1853), and *The Panorama and Other Poems* (1856). Describing himself as a "silent, shy, peace-loving man," Whittier was an early advocate of organized nonviolence and always hoped that reform rather than war could resolve the slavery issue. Yet Whittier eventually aligned himself, as did such writers as James Russell Lowell, with several of the more extreme positions of the abolitionists, including their willingness to see the Union dissolve if that were necessary to end the injustice of slavery. After the Civil War, Whittier wrote of his abolitionist verse, "They were written with no expectation that they would survive the occasions which called them forth: they were protests, alarm signals, trumpet-calls to actions, words wrung from the writer's heart, forged at white heat, and of course lacking the finish and careful word-selection which reflection and patient brooding might have given." Yet several of the poems of this period, including "Massachusetts to Virginia" and "Letter from a Missionary," contain a lyric vitality that carries them beyond the limitations of the specific political contexts in which they were written.

Whittier's prominence during his three-decade struggle to defeat slavery did not prevent him from quietly continuing to write reflective verse focusing on New England's rustic life. The first volume in this series, *Legends of New England*

(1831), consists of eleven poems and seven prose pieces on local country lore. Like Cooper, Longfellow, and Hawthorne, Whittier frequently turned to the New England past, an interest reflected in such volumes as *Moll Pitcher* (1832), *Mogg Megone* (1836), and a historical novel, *Leaves from Margaret Smith's Journal* (1849), a richly textured tale of Quaker life in colonial New England told in the form of a young girl's diary. He also published a collection of essays titled *Literary Recreations and Miscellanies* (1854). But it was not until 1857, when James Russell Lowell, the editor of the newly founded *Atlantic Monthly,* invited Whittier to contribute regularly to the magazine, that he enjoyed some measure of financial security.

Widespread recognition for the quality of Whittier's verse came late—when, after the Emancipation Proclamation, he could turn from engaging in polemic battles over slavery to devoting more time to cultivating his literary talents. In 1866, the same year that Herman Melville published *Battle-Pieces* in relative obscurity, Whittier published "Snow-Bound" to critical acclaim. "Snow-Bound" remains universally regarded as his most significant work. The poem offers in direct, simple, concrete, and sincere terms an idyllic vision of American life that the war-torn nation could take great comfort in. And as the nation became increasingly swept up in the rush toward industrialization in the decades that followed, new generations continued to find Whittier's Edenic view of village and farm life singularly appealing.

In the post–Civil War years, Whittier published several more volumes, including *Among the Hills and Other Poems* (1869) and *Ballads of New England* (1870), each replete with charming poetic renditions of local folklore and superstition. Whittier remained fascinated with childhood innocence, individualism, moral righteousness, social equality, and honest emotions throughout his career. Yet in his later years, his poetic interests broadened to include religious humanism; he became preoccupied as much with the possibility of moral perfection as with the prospect of political and social reform. His poems quickly became schoolroom classics. Venerated as a public figure, he celebrated his seventieth birthday at a public reception in the company of nearly every major American writer, from the elderly William Cullen Bryant to the feisty Mark Twain. Each came to sing his praises.

Whittier delighted in the public adulation. Like Walt Whitman, he began to manage his public image. He interviewed himself for publication; he wrote a flattering entry for himself in an encyclopedia of biography; he provided photographers with numerous opportunities to portray him in his favorite rural settings. In his later years, he rarely ventured from the family home that he had inherited. After years of illness, he died at home of a stroke in 1892, the same year as Whitman. Whittier's final volume, *At Sundown,* was published shortly before his death.

In the prelude to his volume *The Tent on the Beach and Other Poems* (1867), Whittier described himself as a "dreamer" who had "a mission to fulfill," a writer who had "left the Muses' haunts to turn / The crank of an opinion-mill, / Making his rustic reed of song / A weapon in the war with wrong." He readily recognized his own limitations as a poet. In a letter to Francis H. Underwood, who had begun work on Whittier's biography, the old poet endorsed James Russell Lowell's assessment of him in "A Fable for Critics": Whittier's was "a fervor of mind which knows no separation / 'Twixt simple excitement and pure inspiration." Yet the best of Whittier's poetry focuses on the place he knew best—rural New England. His lifelong interest in rendering the universal qualities of the everyday experiences of commonplace people remains an eloquent response to Ralph Waldo Emerson's plea in "The American Scholar" that American writers embrace "the near, the low, the common."

Further Reading:
S. T. Pickard, *The Life and Letters of John Greenleaf Whittier*, 2 vols., 1894, 1907.
A. Mordell, *Quaker Militant: John Greenleaf Whittier*, 1933.
W. T. Scott, "Poetry in America: A New Consideration of Whittier's Verse," *New England Quarterly* 7, 1934.
T. F. Currier, *A Bibliography of John Greenleaf Whittier*, 1937.
W. Bennett, *Whittier, Bard of Freedom*, 1941.
Whittier on Writers and Writing, ed. E. H. Cady and H. H. Clark, 1950.
G. Arms, *The Fields Were Green*, 1953.

J. B. Pickard, *John Greenleaf Whittier: An Introduction and Interpretation*, 1961.
L. Leary, *John Greenleaf Whittier*, 1961.
E. Wagenknecht, *John Greenleaf Whittier: A Portrait in Paradox*, 1967.
R. P. Warren, *John Greenleaf Whittier's Poetry: An Appraisal and a Selection*, 1971.
W. J. Linton, *Life of Whittier*, 1972.
D. C. Freeman, J. B. Pickard, and R. C. Woodwell, *Whittier and Whittierland: Portrait of a Poet and His World*, 1976.
Critical Essays on John Greenleaf Whittier, ed. J. K. Kribbs, 1980.

Text:
The Complete Poetical Works of John Greenleaf Whittier, ed. H. E. Scudder, 1892.

Massachusetts to Virginia*

The blast from Freedom's Northern hills, upon its Southern way,
Bears greeting to Virginia from Massachusetts Bay:
No word of haughty challenging, nor battle bugle's peal,
Nor steady tread of marching files, nor clang of horsemen's steel.

No trains of deep-mouthed cannon along our highways go;   5
Around our silent arsenals untrodden lies the snow;
And to the land-breeze of our ports, upon their errands far,
A thousand sails of commerce swell, but none are spread for war.

---

* Whittier's note: "Written on reading an account of the proceedings of the citizens of Norfolk, Va., in reference to George Latimer, the alleged fugitive slave, who was seized in Boston without warrant at the request of James B. Grey, of Norfolk, claiming to be his master. The case caused great excitement North and South, and led to the presentation of a petition to Congress, signed by more than fifty thousand citizens of Massachusetts, calling for such laws and proposed amendments to the Constitution as should relieve the Commonwealth from all further participation in the crime of oppression. George Latimer himself was finally given free papers for the sum of four hundred dollars."

We hear thy threats, Virginia! thy stormy words and high
Swell harshly on the Southern winds which melt along our sky;
Yet, not one brown, hard hand foregoes its honest labor here,
No hewer of our mountain oaks suspends his axe in fear.

Wild are the waves which lash the reefs along St. George's bank;[1]
Cold on the shores of Labrador the fog lies white and dank;
Through storm, and wave, and blinding mist, stout are the hearts which man   1
The fishing-smacks of Marblehead, the seaboats of Cape Ann.[2]

The cold north light and wintry sun glare on their icy forms,
Bent grimly o'er their straining lines or wrestling with the storms;
Free as the winds they drive before, rough as the waves they roam,
They laugh to scorn the slaver's threat against their rocky home.   20

What means the Old Dominion?[3] Hath she forgot the day
When o'er her conquered valleys swept the Briton's steel array?
How side by side, with sons of hers, the Massachusetts men
Encountered Tarleton's charge of fire, and stout Cornwallis,[4] then?

Forgets she how the Bay State,[5] in answer to the call   25
Of her old House of Burgesses,[6] spoke out from Faneuil Hall?[7]
When, echoing back her Henry's cry,[8] came pulsing on each breath
Of Northern winds the thrilling sounds of "Liberty or Death!"

What asks the Old Dominion? If now her sons have proved
False to their fathers' memory, false to the faith they loved;   30
If she can scoff at Freedom, and its great charter[9] spurn,
Must we of Massachusetts from truth and duty turn?

We hunt your bondmen,[10] flying from Slavery's hateful hell;
Our voices, at your bidding, take up the bloodhound's yell;
We gather, at your summons, above our fathers' graves,   35
From Freedom's holy altar-horns[11] to tear your wretched slaves!

Thank God! not yet so vilely can Massachusetts bow;
The spirit of her early time is with her even now;

[1] Off Newfoundland.
[2] On the Massachusetts coast.
[3] Nickname for the state of Virginia.
[4] General Charles Cornwallis (1738–1805), commander of British forces in Virginia during the American Revolution.
[5] Massachusetts.
[6] Lower house of Virginia's colonial legislature.
[7] Boston meeting hall.
[8] Reference to Patrick Henry's speech at the Virginia convention.
[9] I.e., the Declaration of Independence.
[10] The Northern states were required by the fugitive slave laws to capture and return escaped slaves to the South.
[11] Horns projecting from the corners of Hebrew altars offered sanctuary to fugitives. (See 1 Kings 1:50–53 and 2:28.)

Dream not because her Pilgrim blood moves slow and calm and cool,
She thus can stoop her chainless neck, a sister's slave and tool!   40

All that a sister State should do, all that a free State may,
Heart, hand, and purse we proffer, as in our early day;
But that one dark loathsome burden ye must stagger with alone,
And reap the bitter harvest which ye yourselves have sown!

Hold, while ye may, your struggling slaves, and burden God's free air   45
With woman's shriek beneath the lash, and manhood's wild despair;
Cling closer to the "cleaving curse"[12] that writes upon your plains
The blasting of Almighty wrath against a land of chains.

Still shame your gallant ancestry, the cavaliers of old,
By watching round the shambles[13] where human flesh is sold;   50
Gloat o'er the new-born child, and count his market value, when
The maddened mother's cry of woe shall pierce the slaver's den!

Lower than plummet[14] soundeth, sink the Virginia name;
Plant, if ye will, your fathers' graves with rankest weeds of shame;
Be, if ye will, the scandal of God's fair universe;   55
We wash our hands forever of your sin and shame and curse.

A voice from lips whereon the coal from Freedom's shrine hath been,[15]
Thrilled, as but yesterday, the hearts of Berkshire's[16] mountain men:
The echoes of that solemn voice are sadly lingering still
In all our sunny valleys, on every windswept hill.   60

And when the prowling man-thief[17] came hunting for his prey
Beneath the very shadow of Bunker's shaft[18] of gray,
How, through the free lips of the son, the father's warning spoke;
How, from its bonds of trade and sect, the Pilgrim city broke!

A hundred thousand right arms were lifted up on high,   65
A hundred thousand voices sent back their loud reply;
Through the thronged towns of Essex the startling summons rang,
And up from bench and loom and wheel her young mechanics sprang!

[12] Some slavery advocates asserted that as Cain's descendants blacks bore a curse "cleaving" them from the human race. (See Genesis 4:11–12.)

[13] Meat market and slaughterhouse.

[14] Lead weight for measuring depths (as in Shakespeare's *The Tempest*, Act III, Sc. iii, ll. 101–102: "I'll seek him deeper than the plummet soundeth / and with him there lie mudded").

[15] Isaiah 6:6–7: "Then flew one of the seraphims unto me, having a live coal in his hand, which he had taken with tongs from off the altar: And he laid it upon my mouth, and said, Lo, this hath touched thy lips; and thine iniquity is taken away, and thy sin purged."

[16] Berkshire: a county in Massachusetts, along with Essex, Middlesex, Norfolk, Plymouth, Worcester, Barnstable, Bristol, Hampden, and Hampshire in the lines that follow.

[17] Slave catcher.

[18] Monument commemorating the Battle of Bunker Hill in the American Revolution.

The voice of free, broad Middlesex, of thousands as of one,
The shaft of Bunker calling to that of Lexington;
From Norfolk's ancient villages, from Plymouth's rocky bound
To where Nantucket[19] feels the arms of ocean close her round;

7

From rich and rural Worcester, where through the calm repose
Of cultured vales and fringing woods the gentle Nashua flows,[20]
To where Wachuset's[21] wintry blasts the mountain larches stir,
Swelled up to Heaven the thrilling cry of "God save Latimer!"

7:

And sandy Barnstable rose up, wet with the salt sea spray;
And Bristol sent her answering shout down Narragansett Bay!
Along the broad Connecticut[22] old Hampden felt the thrill,
And the cheer of Hampshire's woodmen swept down from Holyoke Hill.

80

The voice of Massachusetts! Of her free sons and daughters,
Deep calling unto deep aloud, the sound of many waters![23]
Against the burden of that voice what tyrant power shall stand?
No fetters in the Bay State! No slave upon her land!

Look to it well, Virginians! In calmness, we have borne,
In answer to our faith and trust, your insult and your scorn;
You've spurned our kindest counsels; you've hunted for our lives;
And shaken round our hearths and homes your manacles and gyves!

85

We wage no war, we lift no arm, we fling no torch within
The fire-damps[24] of the quaking mine beneath your soil of sin;
We leave ye with your bondmen, to wrestle, while ye can,
With the strong upward tendencies and godlike soul of man!

90

But for us and for our children, the vow which we have given
For freedom and humanity is registered in heaven;
No slave-hunt in our borders,—no pirate on our strand!
No fetters in the Bay State,—no slave upon our land!

95

1843

---

[19] Island off the coast of Massachusetts.
[20] River in Massachusetts.
[21] Mountain in Massachusetts.
[22] River flowing through Massachusetts.

[23] Psalms 42:7: "Deep calleth unto deep at the noise of thy water spouts"; Ezekiel 43:2: "His voice was like a noise of many waters."
[24] Explosive gases formed in mines.

Ichabod*

So fallen! so lost! the light withdrawn
    Which once he wore!
The glory from his gray hairs gone
    Forevermore!

Revile him not, the Tempter hath   5
    A snare for all;
And pitying tears, not scorn and wrath,
    Befit his fall!

Oh, dumb be passion's stormy rage,
    When he who might   10
Have lighted up and led his age,
    Falls back in night.

Scorn! would the angels laugh, to mark
    A bright soul driven,
Fiend-goaded, down the endless dark,   15
    From hope and heaven!

Let not the land once proud of him
    Insult him now,
Nor brand with deeper shame his dim,
    Dishonored brow.   20

But let its humbled sons, instead,
    From sea to lake,

* The title is from 1 Samuel 4:21: "And she named the child Ichabod, saying the glory is departed from Israel." Whittier's note: "This poem was the outcome of the surprise and grief and forecast of evil consequences which I felt on reading the seventh of March speech of Daniel Webster in support of the 'compromise,' and the Fugitive Slave Law. No partisan or personal enmity dictated it. On the contrary my admiration of the splendid personality and intellectual power of the great Senator was never stronger than when I laid down his speech, and, in one of the saddest moments of my life, penned my protest. I saw, as I wrote, with painful clearness its sure results,—the Slave Power arrogant and defiant, strengthened and encouraged to carry out its scheme for the extension of its baleful system, or the dissolution of the Union, the guaranties of personal liberty in the free States broken down, and the whole country made the hunting-ground of slave-catchers. In the horror of such a vision, so soon fearfully fulfilled, if one spoke at all, he could only speak in tones of stern and sorrowful rebuke.

But death softens all resentments, and the consciousness of a common inheritance of frailty and weakness modifies the severity of judgment. Years after, in *The Lost Occasion*, I gave utterance to an almost universal regret that the great statesman did not live to see the flag which he loved trampled under the feet of Slavery, and, in view of this desecration, make his last days glorious in defence of 'Liberty and Union, one and inseparable.'"

A long lament, as for the dead,
  In sadness make.

Of all we loved and honored, naught   25
  Save power remains;
A fallen angel's pride of thought,
  Still strong in chains.

All else is gone; from those great eyes
  The soul has fled;   30
When faith is lost, when honor dies,
  The man is dead!

Then, pay the reverence of old days
  To his dead fame;
Walk backward, with averted gaze,   35
  And hide the shame!

1850

Skipper Ireson's Ride*

Of all the rides since the birth of time,
Told in story or sung in rhyme,—
On Apuleius's Golden Ass,[1]
Or one-eyed Calender's horse of brass,[2]
Witch astride of a human back,   5
Islam's prophet on Al-Borák,[3]—
The strangest ride that ever was sped
Was Ireson's, out from Marblehead![4]
  Old Floyd Ireson, for his hard heart,
  Tarred and feathered and carried in a cart   10
  By the women of Marblehead!

* Whittier claims that this ballad "was founded solely on a fragment of rhyme which I heard from one of my early schoolmates, a native of Marblehead." The fragment is presumably the refrain sung by either the women escorting Captain Ireson in his cart or by the skipper himself. This record of events is "pure fancy," as Whittier declared in his note for the 1888 edition, and not according to the facts about the case presented in *History of Marblehead* (1879) by Samuel Roads.

[1] Roman satirist Lucius Apuleius (second century B.C.) tells of the metamorphosis of Aman into an "excellent" ass in *The Golden Ass*.
[2] In the *Arabian Nights* tale, "the story of the third royal mendicant," a calender (or dervish) slew the owner of a horse of brass and later lost an eye.
[3] In one legend, Mohammed was carried to highest heaven by a supernatural winged animal.
[4] Massachusetts seaport.

Body of turkey, head of owl,
Wings a-droop like a rained-on fowl,
Feathered and ruffled in every part,
Skipper Ireson stood in the cart.   15
Scores of women, old and young,
Strong of muscle, and glib of tongue,
Pushed and pulled up the rocky lane.
Shouting and singing the shrill refrain:
  "Here's Flud Oirson, fur his horrd horrt,   20
  Torr'd an' futherr'd an' corr'd in a corrt
    By the women o' Morble'ead!"[5]

Wrinkled scolds with hands on hips,
Girls in bloom of cheek and lips,
Wild-eyed, free-limbed, such as chase   25
Bacchus[6] round some antique vase,
Brief of skirt, with ankles bare,
Loose of kerchief and loose of hair,
With conch-shells blowing and fish-horns'[7] twang,
Over and over the Mænads sang: 30
  "Here's Flud Oirson, fur his horrd horrt,
  Torr'd an' futherr'd an' corr'd in a corrt
    By the women o' Morble'ead!"

Small pity for him!—He sailed away
From a leaking ship in Chaleur Bay,[3]—   35
Sailed away from a sinking wreck,
With his own town's-people on her deck!
"Lay by! lay by!" they called to him.
Back he answered, "Sink or swim!
Brag of your catch of fish again!"   40
And off he sailed through the fog and rain!
  Old Floyd Ireson, for his hard heart,
  Tarred and feathered and carried in a cart
    By the women of Marblehead!

Fathoms deep in dark Chaleur   45
That wreck shall lie forevermore.
Mother and sister, wife and maid,
Looked from the rocks of Marblehead
Over the moaning and rainy sea,—
Looked for the coming that might not be!   50

What did the winds and the sea-birds say
Of the cruel captain who sailed away?—
Old Floyd Ireson, for his hard heart,
Tarred and feathered and carried in a cart
By the women of Marblehead! 55

Through the street, on either side,
Up flew windows, doors swung wide;
Sharp-tongued spinsters, old wives gray,
Treble lent the fish-horn's bray.
Sea-worn grandsires, cripple-bound, 60
Hulks of old sailors run aground,
Shook head, and fist, and hat, and cane,
And cracked with curses the hoarse refrain:
"Here's Flud Oirson, fur his horrd horrt,
Torr'd an' futherr'd an' corr'd in a corrt 65
By the women o' Morble'ead!"

Sweetly along the Salem road
Bloom of orchard and lilac showed.
Little the wicked skipper knew
Of the fields so green and the sky so blue. 70
Riding there in his sorry trim,
Like an Indian idol glum and grim,
Scarcely he seemed the sound to hear
Of voices shouting, far and near:
"Here's Flud Oirson, fur his horrd horrt, 75
Torr'd an' futherr'd an' corr'd in a corrt
By the women o' Morble'ead!"

"Hear me, neighbors!" at last he cried,—
"What to me is this noisy ride?
What is the shame that clothes the skin 80
To the nameless horror that lives within?
Waking or sleeping, I see a wreck,
And hear a cry from a reeling deck!
Hate me and curse me,—I only dread
The hand of God and the face of the dead!" 85
Said old Floyd Ireson, for his hard heart,
Tarred and feathered and carried in a cart
By the women of Marblehead!

Then the wife of the skipper lost at sea
Said, "God has touched him! why should we!" 90
Said an old wife mourning her only son,
"Cut the rogue's tether and let him run!"

So with soft relentings and rude excuse,
Half scorn, half pity, they cut him loose,
And gave him a cloak to hide him in,   95
And left him alone with his shame and sin.
   Poor Floyd Ireson, for his hard heart,
    Tarred and feathered and carried in a cart
     By the women of Marblehead!

1857

Telling the Bees[1]

Here is the place; right over the hill
  Runs the path I took;
You can see the gap in the old wall still,
  And the stepping-stones in the shallow brook.

There is the house, with the gate red-barred,
  And the poplars tall;   5
And the barn's brown length, and the cattle-yard,
  And the white horns tossing above the wall.

There are the beehives ranged in the sun;
  And down by the brink
Of the brook are her poor flowers, weed-o'errun,   10
  Pansy and daffodil, rose and pink.

A year has gone, as the tortoise goes,
  Heavy and slow;
And the same rose blows, and the same sun glows,   15
  And the same brook sings of a year ago.

There's the same sweet clover-smell in the breeze;
  And the June sun warm
Tangles his wings of fire in the trees,
  Setting, as then, over Fernside farm.   20

[1] Whittier's note: "A remarkable custom, brought from the Old Country, formerly prevailed in the rural districts of New England. On the death of a member of the family, the bees were at once informed of the event, and their hives dressed in mourning. This ceremonial was supposed to be necessary to prevent the swarms from leaving their hives and seeking a new home."

I mind me how with a lover's care
  From my Sunday coat
I brushed off the burrs, and smoothed my hair,
  And cooled at the brookside my brow and throat.

Since we parted, a month had passed,—   25
  To love, a year;
Down through the beeches I looked at last
  On the little red gate and the well-sweep near.

I can see it all now,—the slantwise rain
  Of light through the leaves,   30
The sundown's blaze on her window-pane,
  The bloom of her roses under the eaves.

Just the same as a month before,—
  The house and the trees,
The barn's brown gable, the vine by the door,—   35
  Nothing changed but the hives of bees.

Before them, under the garden wall,
  Forward and back,
Went drearily singing the chore-girl small,
  Draping each hive with a shred of black.   40

Trembling, I listened: the summer sun
  Had the chill of snow;
For I knew she was telling the bees of one
  Gone on the journey we all must go!

Then I said to myself, "My Mary weeps   45
  For the dead to-day:
Haply her blind old grandsire sleeps
  The fret and the pain of his age away."

But her dog whined low; on the doorway sill,
  With his cane to his chin,   50
The old man sat; and the chore-girl still
  Sung to the bees stealing out and in.

And the song she was singing ever since
  In my ear sounds on:—
"Stay at home, pretty bees, fly not hence!   55
  Mistress Mary is dead and gone!"
1858

Oliver Wendell Holmes
1809–1894

Dr. Oliver Wendell Holmes was born in 1809, exactly one hundred years after the major English literary figure Dr. Samuel Johnson—a coincidence Holmes enjoyed immensely, as he strived to emulate Johnson's Neoclassical approach to life. "It was for me," Holmes said of the bond he felt with Johnson, "a kind of unison between two instruments, both playing that old familiar air, 'Life'—one a bassoon . . . the other an oaten pipe. . . . At last the thinner thread of sound is heard by itself, and its deep accompaniment rolls out its thunder no more." Compared to Johnson's robust proportions, Holmes's five-foot two-inch slender frame made a thin pipe indeed. And his seemingly gentle, colloquial style matched his physique, just as Johnson's orotund style matched his. Yet Holmes's self-deprecation of both his intellectual and physical stature as well as his occasionally overly sentimental style belies the impregnable core of honesty at the center of his writing. That core enabled him to reject the Calvinist heritage of his father, the Reverend Abiel Holmes, an orthodox Congregationalist minister, just as his own son and namesake, Justice Oliver Wendell Holmes, would eventually reject his father's conservatism. Dr. Holmes's own self-criticisms to the contrary, such honesty in his poems, essays, novels, lectures, and conversations made him as eminent a man of letters in his time as Johnson was in his. Even more than Johnson, who was assuredly a dilettante in many intellectual spheres, Holmes spread his considerable talents far beyond his avocation for literature, making a name for himself as a prominent medical man, a scientist, an inventor, a teacher, a moralist, and finally as a kind of elder statesman for Boston, the town that he called home and that, in Holmes's provincial and patriotic estimation at least, he celebrated as "the hub of the solar system."

In the popular opinion of the time, Oliver Wendell Holmes was the brightest star of what was undeniably the cultural hub of the nation, if not quite the solar system. Holmes may seem today to have been eclipsed by his son, the Justice, but such a judgment is more the result of changing tastes and literary fashions than any actual intrinsic literary skill. Although many modern readers regard Holmes primarily as a writer of congenial occasional verse, his literary and moral influence was far vaster. Surrounded by a constellation of dazzling literary luminaries that included Ralph Waldo Emerson, Nathaniel Hawthorne, Henry Wadsworth Longfellow, James Russell Lowell, and William Dean Howells, Holmes's chief claim to literary fame was, as Dr. Johnson's had been, a remarkable conversational wit. That wit first achieved notoriety in 1831, when Holmes was only twenty-two and attending medical school. In a series of essays for the *New England Magazine* titled "The Autocrat of the Breakfast Table," Holmes displayed a virtuosity at monologue at once entertaining and acerbic. More than twenty-five years later, he resumed this series for the *Atlantic Monthly,* a periodical whose considerable reputation both here and abroad he helped establish and ensure. By this time Holmes did not merely hold his own among the literary giants of the Saturday Club when they met once a month. More often, he monopolized and mesmerized them with a verbal barrage so intense that he occasionally felt compelled to apologize: "I came to listen and then I talked too much again." Such enthusiasm proved equally Holmes's success and his undoing as he struggled with a wider and wider range of interests.

As a student at Harvard, Holmes excelled both academically and socially. Elected to Phi Beta Kappa, he also wrote less than genteel poetry for the satiric wits who belonged to the Hasty Pudding Club, along with several sophomoric satires of the faculty, thereby ingratiating himself with his fellow students. He was the class poet in 1829, the year he graduated. Holmes spent the following year studying law, only to discover himself apparently unsuited for the profession.

The year 1830 also brought Holmes literary recognition. His poetry achieved national prominence with the publication in the *Boston Daily Advertiser* of "Old Ironsides," an indignant, rousing poem patriotically protesting the scrapping of the frigate *Constitution,* a Boston-built ship that had served the nation well in many battles. Typically, the unassuming Holmes signed this poem simply "H." In favor of pursuing still another vocation, medicine, Holmes ignored the favorable critical reception of this early poem and another, "The Last Leaf," which Edgar Allan Poe pronounced "an excellent well conceived and well managed specimen of versification." Yet literature would remain Holmes's lifelong interest.

Religious beliefs, like vocational choices, created dilemmas for Holmes. Though he remained outwardly loyal to his father's preaching, privately he agreed with the more liberal members of his father's congregation, who eventually rejected Abiel Holmes's rather puritanical brand of Calvinism, forcing the minister to form a new parish. In a similar vein, Holmes remembered that as a young boy he had viewed John Bunyan's *Pilgrim's Progress* "more like the hunting of sinners with a pack of demons for the amusement of the lord of the terrestrial manor than like the tender care of a father for his offspring." This is, perhaps, the first inkling of what in later essays and lectures would stir considerable controversy. In these writings Holmes risked his moral reputation by claiming that the chief end of man could not be prescribed by religious dogma since that end varied with the individual.

Doubtless Holmes's own difficulty in settling on a chief end for himself helped prompt such liberal views. Yet he remained far more comfortable in the role of one of the most prominent cultural conservatives of his time. Finding the Romantically inspired thinking of his Transcendental contemporaries superfluous —and rather too difficult to understand—Holmes preferred the relative surety of science, keeping even his literary forays into the study of human conduct mainly within the realm of what he regarded as the practical.

Holmes had begun to study medicine in Boston in 1830, and in 1833 he left for Paris, where experimental techniques were revolutionizing the profession. He returned to Harvard in 1836, taking a degree in medicine a year after his first volume, *Poems,* was published. Holmes's three years of medical study in Paris gave him a clear and strong sense of purpose. Before he left, American doctors still relied on what were considered archaic remedies: leeches, blistering, and emetics. When he returned, Holmes helped change these primitive practices. After two years as professor of anatomy at Dartmouth (1838–1840), Holmes settled into private practice in Boston and married.

Teaching and medical writing gradually had become his chief professional interests. In *Homeopathy and Its Kindred Delusions* (1842) Holmes advocated a reduction in primitive medical treatments, and in *The Contagiousness of Puerperal Fever* (1843) he argued for cleanliness among doctors and midwives to inhibit the spread of infection at childbirth. In 1847 he was named Parkman Professor of Anatomy and Physiology at the Harvard Medical School, where he remained for nearly forty years. During his tenure there, Holmes introduced the microscopic study of tissues, advocated such radical practices as the use of anesthesia and antisepsis, and helped found the American Medical Association. Yet such devotion to science kept Holmes distant from the social causes of his time. He remained secure in his identity as a respectable citizen—a conservative culturally and a humanitarian professionally.

Writing was his favorite, steady avocation. He published volumes of poetry in 1846, 1849, 1852, and 1854. In 1857 he helped found the *Atlantic Monthly*, which he named. He helped set the distinctive tone of that magazine with the publication of his *Autocrat* essays, for which he soon earned national recognition. The first collected edition of these conversational essays was published in 1858 as *The Autocrat of the Breakfast Table*. Later volumes appeared as *The Professor of the Breakfast Table* (1860), *The Poet at the Breakfast Table* (1872), and *Over the Teacups* (1891). Over these same decades, Holmes continued to cultivate his interest in verse. Marked by a delightful mixture of urbane wit and comic sensibility, Holmes's reflective and occasional poems were published principally in the *Atlantic Monthly*. Several of these poems (including "Old Ironsides," "The Chambered Nautilus," and "The Deacon's Masterpiece, or 'The One-Hoss Shay' ") eventually became schoolroom classics.

Holmes's novels brought him far less attention and praise. *Elsie Venner: A Romance of Destiny* (1861), *The Guardian Angel* (1867), and *A Moral Antipathy* (1885) blend social commentary and character analysis but lack mastery of fictional technique and a strong narrative line. Self-styled "medicated" novels by Holmes, each traces a character's psychological reaction, as it would be called today, to the events that shaped his or her life. Holmes's point in these novels is less to demonstrate literary excellence than to explore alternatives to a strictly theological explanation for human behavior. In *Elsie Venner,* for instance, a pregnant woman is bitten by a rattlesnake. At birth, the child embodies the snakelike characteristics of that prenatal influence. Thus the novel remains, as Holmes recognized it would be, more a curious early psychological study than a first-rate literary effort. In their attention to such issues as moral responsibility, hereditary influence, and mental trauma, these novels anticipate a good deal of later, more technically sophisticated fiction.

Holmes was in great demand as a lecturer at medical meetings, and he wrote several treatises, along with three biographical studies, the most widely known of which focuses on his friend Ralph Waldo Emerson. Like his novels, Holmes's study of Emerson for the *American Men of Letters* series (1885) attempted to treat only those aspects of character and behavior Holmes felt sure he understood. He did not capture Emerson the literary theorist as well as he presented Emerson the person, the friend he knew from their meetings at the Saturday Club and from their mutual literary acquaintances.

By the 1870s, Holmes had became one of America's most respected public figures, renowned as a medical practitioner, a respected author of humorous witty essays and whimsical verse for special occasions, and as the late nineteenth century's most celebrated after-dinner speaker. Holmes's writing represented the epitome of what he dubbed the "Brahmin Caste of New England," the "harmless, inoffensive, untitled aristocracy" that is "merely the richer part of the community, that live in the tallest houses, drive real carriages (not 'kerridges') . . . and have a provokingly easy way of dressing, walking, talking, and nodding to people." For eighty-five years, Oliver Wendell Holmes practiced that easy way, to everyone's delight.

Further Reading:
Life and Letters of Oliver Wendell Holmes, ed. J. T. Morse, Jr., 2 vols., 1896.
M. A. D. Howe, *Holmes of the Breakfast Table*, 1939, 1972.
Oliver Wendell Holmes, ed. S. I. Hayakawa and H. M. Jones, 1939.
M. Tilton, *Amiable Autocrat: A Biography of Oliver Wendell Holmes*, 1947.
E. P. Hoyt, *The Improper Bostonian: Dr. Oliver Wendell Holmes*, 1979.

Text:
The Complete Poetical Works of Oliver Wendell Holmes, ed. H. E. Scudder, 1895.

The Last Leaf[*]

I saw him once before,
As he passed by the door,
    And again
The pavement stones resound,
As he totters o'er the ground
    With his cane.   5

They say that in his prime,
Ere the pruning-knife of Time
    Cut him down,

---

[*] Holmes's note: "This poem was suggested by the sight of a figure well known to Bostonians, that of Major Thomas Melville, 'the last of the cocked hats,' as he was often pointed at as one of the 'Indians' of the famous 'Boston Tea Party' of 1774. His aspect among the crowds of a late generation reminded me of a withered leaf which has held to its stem through the storms of autumn and winter, and finds itself still clinging to its bough while the new growths of spring are bursting their buds and spreading their foliage all around it." Major Thomas Melville was Herman Melville's grandfather.

Not a better man was found   10
By the Crier on his round
        Through the town.

But now he walks the streets,
And he looks at all he meets
        Sad and wan,   15
And he shakes his feeble head,
That it seems as if he said,
        "They are gone."

The mossy marbles rest
On the lips that he has prest   20
        In their bloom,
And the names he loved to hear
Have been carved for many a year
        On the tomb.

My grandmamma has said—   25
Poor old lady, she is dead
        Long ago—
That he had a Roman nose,
And his cheek was like a rose
        In the snow;   30

But now his nose is thin,
And it rests upon his chin
        Like a staff,
And a crook is in his back,
And a melancholy crack   35
        In his laugh.

I know it is a sin
For me to sit and grin
        At him here;
But the old three-cornered hat,   40
And the breeches, and all that,
        Are so queer!

And if I should live to be
The last leaf upon the tree
        In the spring,   45
Let them smile, as I do now,
At the old forsaken bough
        Where I cling.

                1831

My Aunt

My aunt! my dear unmarried aunt!
   Long years have o'er her flown;
Yet still she strains the aching clasp[1]
   That binds her virgin zone;
I know it hurts her,—though she looks   5
   As cheerful as she can;
Her waist is ampler than her life,
   For life is but a span.

My aunt! my poor deluded aunt!
   Her hair is almost gray;   10
Why will she train that winter curl
   In such a spring-like way?
How can she lay her glasses down,
   And say she reads as well,
When through a double convex lens   15
   She just makes out to spell?

Her father—grandpapa! forgive
   This erring lip its smiles—
Vowed she should make the finest girl
   Within a hundred miles;   20
He sent her to a stylish school;
   'T was in her thirteenth June;
And with her, as the rules required,
   "Two towels and a spoon."

They braced my aunt against a board,   25
   To make her straight and tall;
They laced her up, they starved her down,
   To make her light and small;
They pinched her feet, they singed her hair,
   They screwed it up with pins;—   30
Oh, never mortal suffered more
   In penance for her sins.

So, when my precious aunt was done,
   My grandsire brought her back;
(By daylight, lest some rabid youth   35
   Might follow on the track;)

[1] Broad ornamental belt.

"Ah!" said my grandsire, as he shook
    Some powder in his pan,[2]
"What could this lovely creature do
    Against a desperate man!"   40

Alas! nor chariot, nor barouche,[3]
    Nor bandit cavalcade,
Tore from the trembling father's arms
    His all-accomplished maid.
For her how happy had it been!   45
    And Heaven had spared to me
To see one sad, ungathered rose
    On my ancestral tree.

1831

The Chambered Nautilus[*]

This is the ship of pearl,[1] which, poets feign,
    Sails the unshadowed main,—
    The venturous bark that flings
On the sweet summer wind its purpled wings
In gulfs enchanted, where the Siren[2] sings,   5
    And coral reefs lie bare,
Where the cold sea-maids rise to sun their streaming hair.

Its webs of living gauze no more unfurl;
    Wrecked is the ship of pearl!
    And every chambered cell,   10
Where its dim dreaming life was wont to dwell,
As the frail tenant shaped his growing shell,
    Before thee lies revealed,—
Its irised ceiling rent, its sunless crypt unsealed!

Year after year beheld the silent toil   15
    That spread his lustrous coil;

[2] Hollow in the lock of a musket where priming powder was placed.
[3] Four-wheeled carriage fashionable at the time.
[*] This poem, published as part of *The Autocrat of the Breakfast-Table,* first appeared in the *Atlantic Monthly* in February 1858.
[1] The "chambered" or pearly nautilus is a South Pacific and Indian Ocean mollusk that builds a spiral shell by adding a compartment each year. The Greeks thought it capable of moving over the water using its membrane as a sail.
[2] Mythical sea nymph who lures sailors to destruction with her song.

Still, as the spiral grew,
He left the past year's dwelling for the new,
Stole with soft step its shining archway through,
    Built up its idle door,
Stretched in his last-found home, and knew the old no more.

Thanks for the heavenly message brought by thee,
    Child of the wandering sea,
    Cast from her lap, forlorn!
From thy dead lips a clearer note is born
Than ever Triton[3] blew from wreathèd horn!
    While on mine ear it rings,
Through the deep caves of thought I hear a voice that sings:—

Build thee more stately mansions, O my soul,
    As the swift seasons roll!
    Leave thy low-vaulted past!
Let each new temple, nobler than the last,
Shut thee from heaven with a dome more vast,
    Till thou at length art free,
Leaving thine outgrown shell by life's unresting sea!
1858

20

25

30

35

Harriet Beecher Stowe
1811–1896

Harriet Beecher Stowe was the daughter of a New England Congregational
preacher, the sister of five preachers, and the wife of another. Born in Litchfield,
Connecticut, on June 14, 1811, she was raised in a family whose members had
devoted themselves to Christian purpose, self-abnegation, and spiritual rebirth, "a
kind of moral heaven, replete with moral oxygen—fully charged with
intellectual electricity." She was educated at a local school for girls and in 1824
graduated from—and then taught at—the Hartford Female Seminary, founded by
her famous sister Catherine, a pioneer in women's education. When her father
accepted an appointment to head the Lane Theological Seminary in 1832, she
moved with her family to Cincinnati, a town at the border of North and South,
East and West and at the center of increasing antislavery sentiment. While
working at Catherine's newly founded Western Female Institute, Harriet Beecher
began writing sketches and stories for literary and evangelical periodicals. In 1836

[3] In Greek myth, the sea god who ruled the
waves with a conch-shell trumpet.

she married the Reverend Calvin Ellis Stowe, a preacher and a professor of biblical literature at Lane Theological Seminary. The demands of raising their seven children forced Mrs. Stowe to set aside the idea of a literary career. Yet during what would amount to nearly fifteen years, she wrote, when she could find the time, mostly to help support their large family. And she came to realize that she was a woman writer drawn to a provocative subject: the moral, political, and ethical issues surrounding the slavery question.

The moral principles that guided her life infused her thinking and writing. Her views on slavery derived from reading both slave narratives and abolitionist tracts, visiting slaveholding plantations in Kentucky, and feeling moral revulsion at the passage of the Fugitive Slave Law (1850), which legally obliged residents of free states to return fugitives to their "rightful owners." Her plans to write a moral "epic of negro bondage" crystallized in a vision of a slave's suffering and death she had in a church in Brunswick, Maine, where the family had moved in 1850. Years later, Stowe described her state of mind at the time: "My heart was bursting with the anguish excited by the cruelty and injustice our nation was showing to the slave, and praying to God to let me do a little and to cause my cry for them to be heard." Eventually, she came to believe that she was simply God's instrument for writing *Uncle Tom's Cabin,* a book she hoped would "make this whole nation feel what an accursed thing slavery is."

With an incomplete draft in hand, Stowe approached *The National Era,* a Washington, D.C., antislavery weekly, with plans to publish her novel in three or four installments. The success of this serial led in 1852 to the publication in two volumes of what was originally titled *Uncle Tom's Cabin, or The Man That Was a Thing.* It was a historic event in publishing: Ten thousand copies were sold in the first week, over three hundred thousand in the first year. By the outbreak of the Civil War that number had soared beyond three million. The book was translated into thirty-seven languages. Praise poured in from all over the world. Ralph Waldo Emerson spoke for many when he hailed Stowe's ability to create a book that at once could enjoy popular success, speak "to the universal heart," and be "read with equal interest to three audiences, namely, in the parlor, in the kitchen, and in the nursery of every house." Suddenly, Harriet Beecher Stowe found herself the most famous literary figure in America and an international celebrity. She toured England and met many of the leading literary figures there and on the Continent. Several years later, when the diminutive Stowe met the towering president, Lincoln is reported to have said, "So this is the little lady who made this big war!"

A powerful but controversial instrument of reform, *Uncle Tom's Cabin* had an extraordinary impact on the culture and politics of its time. Its publication helped change public opinion and sway political action. Its message—that the slave, the master, and their respective families are destroyed by slavery—stirred the nation. And its principal characters—Simon Legree, Eliza, Little Eva, and Uncle Tom—became archetypes in the national literary consciousness. The book not only inspired southern writers to respond in print but also sparked intense debates among politicians and readers on both sides of the Mason-Dixon line. In 1853

Stowe published *Key to Uncle Tom's Cabin,* in which she defended herself against widespread charges that she had distorted the reality of slave life. Stowe's reliance on slave narratives as her primary sources and her correspondence with Frederick Douglass to verify the accuracy of her presentation of Tom made *Uncle Tom's Cabin* a significant early example of black literature's influence on a mainstream American novel. In a similar manner, Stowe's second novel on slavery, *Dred* (1856), drew heavily on the widely circulated slave narrative *Confessions of Nat Turner* (1831) but enjoyed no comparable popular success.

Harriet Beecher Stowe applied her considerable literary skills to subjects other than the moral and social reform advocated in her novels about slavery. And whether it was a gripping potboiler or a polemic essay on domestic affairs, a sentimental romance or a delightful sketch of the rural New England she knew so well, a piece of journalism or a letter to a friend, Harriet Beecher Stowe wrote immensely readable prose. She had an excellent ear for local idiom and a practiced eye for telling details. Her local-color fiction constitutes, in the words of Edmund Wilson, the celebrated literary critic, "a kind of encyclopedia of old New England institutions, characters, customs and points of view." She wrote at least one book in each of the years between 1862 and 1884, and many—including *The Minister's Wooing* (1859), *The Pearl of Orr's Island* (1862), and *Oldtown Fireside Stories* (1872)—captured domestic life and local color and vividness. Stowe called *Oldtown Folks* (1869) "my résumé of the whole spirit and body of New England" and described her technique and purpose in these terms: "to make my mind as still and passive as a looking-glass, or a mountain lake, and then to give you merely the images reflected there." In this respect, her novels anticipate much of the local-color realism of Mary Wilkins Freeman and especially Sarah Orne Jewett, who acknowledged her indebtedness to Stowe.

Within Stowe's lifetime, the characters over whom half the world had anguished were gradually refashioned into stereotypes and burlesqued on stage and in literature. Aunt Chloe was transformed into Aunt Jemima, and Uncle Tom, once the focus of compassion, became an object of derision, a symbol of the foot-shuffling, servile black. An era of new sensibilities challenged the misconceptions of even the best-intentioned social reformers, activists, and writers. Yet there was little in Stowe's later years that turned out the way she would have preferred. One of her children died from alcoholism, another from drug addiction, a third from drowning, a fourth from cholera. She received none of the foreign and theatrical royalties due her for *Uncle Tom's Cabin,* and most of what she did receive was lost in mismanaged real estate investments. The adultery trial of her brother Henry Ward Beecher, one of the most famous preachers in the nineteenth century, greatly affected her. And her friendship with Lady Byron —and her exposé in the *Atlantic Monthly* of the Lord Byron–Augusta Leigh incest episode—cost the magazine nearly fifteen thousand subscribers and caused many readers of her fiction to regard her as a spiteful gossip. Stowe spent her later years in Hartford, the winters in Florida. She died in 1896, several years after senility had taken its toll. At her funeral her coffin was draped with a wreath from a group of Boston blacks. The note read, "The Children of Uncle Tom."

Further Reading:

The Life of Harriet Beecher Stowe from Her Letters and Journals, ed. C. E. Stowe, 1889.

F. Wilson, *Crusader in Crinoline: The Life of Harriet Beecher Stowe,* 1941.

J. Baldwin, "Everybody's Protest Novel," *Partisan Review* 16, 1949.

C. H. Foster, *The Rungless Ladder: Harriet Beecher Stowe and New England Puritanism,* 1954.

E. Wilson, *Patriotic Gore,* 1962.

J. R. Adams, *Harriet Beecher Stowe,* 1963.

E. Wagenknecht, *Harriet Beecher Stowe: The Known and the Unknown,* 1965.

A. Crozier, *The Novels of Harriet Beecher Stowe,* 1970.

E. B. Kirkham, *The Building of "Uncle Tom's Cabin,"* 1977.

Text:

The Writings of Harriet Beecher Stowe, 16 vols., 1896.

from Uncle Tom's Cabin;
Or, Life Among the Lowly

Chapter V: Showing the Feelings of Living Property on Changing Owners

Mr. and Mrs. Shelby had retired to their apartment for the night. He was lounging in a large easy-chair, looking over some letters that had come in the afternoon mail, and she was standing before her mirror, brushing out the complicated braids and curls in which Eliza had arranged her hair; for, noticing her pale cheeks and haggard eyes, she had excused her attendance that night, and ordered her to bed. The employment, naturally enough, suggested her conversation with the girl in the morning; and, turning to her husband, she said carelessly,—

"By the bye, Arthur, who was that low-bred fellow that you lugged in to our dinner-table to-day?"

"Haley is his name," said Shelby, turning himself rather uneasily in his chair, and continuing with his eyes fixed on a letter.

"Haley! Who is he, and what may be his business here, pray?"

"Well, he's a man that I transacted some business with, last time I was at Natchez," said Mr. Shelby.

"And he presumed on it to make himself quite at home, and call and dine here, ay?"

"Why, I invited him; I had some accounts with him," said Shelby.

"Is he a negro-trader?" said Mrs. Shelby, noticing a certain embarrassment in her husband's manner.

"Why, my dear, what put that into your head?" said Shelby, looking up.

"Nothing,—only Eliza came in here, after dinner, in a great worry, crying and taking on, and said you were talking with a trader, and that she heard him make an offer for her boy,—the ridiculous little goose!"

"She did, hey?" said Mr. Shelby, returning to his paper, which he seemed for a few moments quite intent upon, not perceiving that he was holding it bottom upwards.

"It will have to come out," said he mentally; "as well now as ever."

"I told Eliza," said Mrs. Shelby, as she continued brushing her hair, "that she was a little fool for her pains, and that you never had anything to do with that sort of persons. Of course, I knew you never meant to sell any of our people,—least of all, to such a fellow."

"Well, Emily," said her husband, "so I have always felt and said; but the fact is that my business lies so that I cannot get on without. I shall have to sell some of my hands."

"To that creature? Impossible! Mr. Shelby, you cannot be serious."

"I'm sorry to say that I am," said Mr. Shelby. "I've agreed to sell Tom."

"What! our Tom?—that good, faithful creature!—been your faithful servant from a boy! Oh, Mr. Shelby!—and you have promised him his freedom, too,—you and I have spoken to him a hundred times of it. Well, I can believe anything now,—I can believe *now* that you could sell little Harry, poor Eliza's only child!" said Mrs. Shelby, in a tone between grief and indignation.

"Well, since you must know all, it is so. I have agreed to sell Tom and Harry both; and I don't know why I am to be rated, as if I were a monster, for doing what every one does every day."

"But why, of all others, choose these?" said Mrs. Shelby. "Why sell them, of all on the place, if you must sell at all?"

"Because they will bring the highest sum of any,—that's why. I could choose another, if you say so. The fellow made me a high bid on Eliza, if that would suit you any better," said Mr. Shelby.

"The wretch!" said Mrs. Shelby vehemently.

"Well, I didn't listen to it, a moment,—out of regard to your feelings, I wouldn't; —so give me some credit."

"My dear," said Mrs. Shelby, recollecting herself, "forgive me; I have been hasty. I was surprised, and entirely unprepared for this;—but surely you will allow me to intercede for these poor creatures. Tom is a noble-hearted, faithful fellow, if he is black. I do believe, Mr. Shelby, that if he were put to it, he would lay down his life for you."

"I know it,—I dare say;—but what's the use of all this?—I can't help myself."

"Why not make a pecuniary sacrifice? I'm willing to bear my part of the inconvenience. Oh, Mr. Shelby, I have tried—tried most faithfully, as a Christian woman should—to do my duty to these poor, simple, dependent creatures. I have cared for them, instructed them, watched over them, and known all their little cares and joys, for years; and how can I ever hold up my head again among them if, for the sake of a little paltry gain, we sell such a faithful, excellent, confiding creature as poor Tom, and tear from him in a moment all we have taught him to love and value? I have taught them the duties of the family, of parent and child, and husband and wife; and how can I bear to have this open acknowledgment that we care for no tie, no duty, no relation, however sacred, compared with money? I have talked with Eliza about her boy,—her duty to him as a Christian mother, to watch over him, pray for him, and bring him up in a Christian way; and now what can I say, if you tear him away, and sell him, soul and body, to a profane, unprincipled man, just to save a little money? I have told her that one soul is worth more than all the money in the world; and how will she believe me when she sees us turn round and sell her child?—sell him, perhaps, to certain ruin of body and soul!"

"I'm sorry you feel so about it, Emily,—indeed I am," said Mr. Shelby; "and I respect your feelings, too, though I don't pretend to share them to their full extent; but I tell you now, solemnly, it's of no use,—I can't help myself. I didn't mean to tell you this, Emily; but in plain words, there is no choice between selling these two and selling everything. Either they must go, or *all* must. Haley has come into possession of a mortgage which, if I don't clear off with him directly, will take everything before it. I've raked, and scraped, and borrowed, and all but begged,— and the price of these two was needed to make up the balance, and I had to give them up. Haley fancied the child; he agreed to settle the matter that way and no other. I was in his power, and *had* to do it. If you feel so to have them sold, would it be any better to have *all* sold?"

Mrs. Shelby stood like one stricken. Finally, turning to her toilet, she rested her face in her hands, and gave a sort of groan.

"This is God's curse on slavery!—a bitter, bitter, most accursed thing!—a curse to the master and a curse to the slave! I was a fool to think I could make anything good out of such a deadly evil. It is a sin to hold a slave under laws like ours,—I always felt it was,—I always thought so when I was a girl,—I thought so still more after I joined the church; but I thought I could gild it over,—I thought, by kindness, and care, and instruction, I could make the condition of mine better than freedom, —fool that I was!"

"Why, wife, you are getting to be an abolitionist, quite."

"Abolitionist! if they knew all I know about slavery they *might* talk! We don't need them to tell us; you know I never thought that slavery was right,—never felt willing to own slaves."

"Well, therein you differ from many wise and pious men," said Mr. Shelby. "You remember Mr. B.'s sermon, the other day?"

"I don't want to hear such sermons; I never wish to hear Mr. B. in our church again. Ministers can't help the evil, perhaps,—can't cure it, any more than we can, — but defend it!—it always went against my common sense. And I think you did n't think much of that sermon, either."

"Well," said Shelby, "I must say these ministers sometimes carry matters further than we poor sinners would exactly dare to do. We men of the world must wink pretty hard at various things, and get used to a deal that is n't the exact thing. But we don't quite fancy, when women and ministers come out broad and square, and go beyond us in matters of either modesty or morals, that's a fact. But now, my dear, I trust you see the necessity of the thing, and you see that I have done the very best that circumstances would allow."

"Oh, yes, yes!" said Mrs. Shelby, hurriedly and abstractedly fingering her gold watch,—"I have n't any jewelry of any amount," she added thoughtfully; "but would not this watch do something?—it was an expensive one when it was bought. If I could only at least save Eliza's child, I would sacrifice anything I have."

"I'm sorry, very sorry, Emily," said Mr. Shelby. "I'm sorry this takes hold of you so; but it will do no good. The fact is, Emily, the thing's done; the bills of sale are already signed, and in Haley's hands; and you must be thankful it is no worse. That man has had it in his power to ruin us all,—and now he is fairly off. If you knew the man as I do, you'd think that we had had a narrow escape."

"Is he so hard, then?"

"Why, not a cruel man, exactly, but a man of leather,— a man alive to nothing but trade and profit,—cool, and unhesitating, and unrelenting, as death and the grave. He'd sell his own mother at a good percentage,—not wishing the old woman any harm, either."

"And this wretch owns that good, faithful Tom and Eliza's child!"

"Well, my dear, the fact is that this goes rather hard with me; it's a thing I hate to think of. Haley wants to drive matters, and take possession to-morrow. I'm going to get out my horse bright and early, and be off. I can't see Tom, that's a fact; and you had better arrange a drive somewhere, and carry Eliza off. Let the thing be done when she is out of sight."

"No, no," said Mrs. Shelby; "I'll be in no sense accomplice or help in this cruel business. I'll go and see poor old Tom, God help him, in his distress! They shall see, at any rate, that their mistress can feel for and with them. As to Eliza, I dare not think about it. The Lord forgive us! What have we done, that this cruel necessity should come on us?"

There was one listener to this conversation whom Mr. and Mrs. Shelby little suspected.

Communicating with their apartment was a large closet, opening by a door into the outer passage. When Mrs. Shelby had dismissed Eliza for the night, her feverish and excited mind had suggested the idea of this closet; and she had hidden herself there, and, with her ear pressed close against the crack of the door, had lost not a word of the conversation.

When the voices died into silence, she rose and crept stealthily away. Pale, shivering, with rigid features and compressed lips, she looked an entirely altered being from the soft and timid creature she had been hitherto. She moved cautiously along the entry, paused one moment at her mistress's door and raised her hands in mute appeal to Heaven, and then turned and glided into her own room. It was a quiet, neat apartment, on the same floor with her mistress. There was the pleasant sunny window, where she had often sat singing at her sewing; there, a little case of books, and various little fancy articles, ranged by them, the gifts of Christmas holidays; there was her simple wardrobe in the closet and in the drawers:—here was, in short, her home; and, on the whole, a happy one it had been to her. But there, on the bed, lay her slumbering boy, his long curls falling negligently around his unconscious face, his rosy mouth half open, his little fat hands thrown out over the bedclothes, and a smile spread like a sunbeam over his whole face.

"Poor boy! poor fellow!" said Eliza; "they have sold you! but your mother will save you yet!"

No tear dropped over that pillow; in such straits as these the heart has no tears to give,—it drops only blood, bleeding itself away in silence. She took a piece of paper and a pencil, and wrote hastily,—

"Oh, Missis! dear Missis! don't think me ungrateful,—don't think hard of me, anyway,—I heard all you and Master said to-night. I am going to try to save my boy,—you will not blame me! God bless and reward you for all your kindness!"

Hastily folding and directing this, she went to a drawer and made up a little package of clothing for her boy, which she tied with a handkerchief firmly round her waist; and, so fond is a mother's remembrance that, even in the terrors of that hour, she did not forget to put in the little package one or two of his favorite toys, reserving a gayly painted parrot to amuse him, when she should be called on to awaken him. It was some trouble to arouse the little sleeper; but, after some effort, he sat up, and was playing with his bird, while his mother was putting on her bonnet and shawl.

"Where are you going, mother?" said he, as she drew near the bed, with his little coat and cap.

His mother drew near, and looked so earnestly into his eyes that he at once divined that something unusual was the matter.

"Hush, Harry," she said; "mustn't speak loud, or they will hear us. A wicked man was coming to take little Harry away from his mother, and carry him 'way off in the dark; but mother won't let him,—she's going to put on her little boy's cap and coat, and run off with him, so the ugly man can't catch him."

Saying these words, she had tied and buttoned on the child's simple outfit, and, taking him in her arms, she whispered to him to be very still; and, opening a door in her room which led into the outer veranda, she glided noiselessly out.

It was a sparkling, frosty, starlight night, and the mother wrapped the shawl close round her child, as, perfectly quiet with vague terror, he clung round her neck.

Old Bruno, a great Newfoundland, who slept at the end of the porch, rose, with a low growl, as she came near. She gently spoke his name, and the animal, an old pet and playmate of hers, instantly, wagging his tail, prepared to follow her, though apparently revolving much, in his simple dog's head, what such an indiscreet midnight promenade might mean. Some dim ideas of imprudence or impropriety in the measure seemed to embarrass him considerably; for he often stopped, as Eliza glided forward, and looked wistfully, first at her and then at the house, and then, as if reassured by reflection, he pattered along after her again. A few minutes brought them to the window of Uncle Tom's cottage, and Eliza, stopping, tapped lightly on the window-pane.

The prayer-meeting at Uncle Tom's had, in the order of hymn-singing, been protracted to a very late hour; and, as Uncle Tom had indulged himself in a few lengthy solos afterwards, the consequence was that, although it was now between twelve and one o'clock, he and his worthy helpmeet were not yet asleep.

"Good Lord! what's that?" said Aunt Chloe, starting up and hastily drawing the curtain. "My sakes alive, if it ain't Lizy! Get on your clothes, old man, quick! —there's old Bruno, too, a-pawin' round. What on airth—I'm gwine to open the door."

And, suiting the action to the word, the door flew open, and the light of the tallow candle, which Tom had hastily lighted, fell on the haggard face and dark, wild eyes of the fugitive.

"Lord bless you!—I'm skeered to look at ye, Lizy! Are ye tuck sick, or what's come over ye?"

"I'm running away,—Uncle Tom and Aunt Chloe,—carrying off my child,— Master sold him!"

"Sold him?" echoed both, lifting up their hands in dismay.

"Yes, sold him!" said Eliza firmly. "I crept into the closet by Mistress's door to-night, and I heard Master tell Missis that he had sold my Harry, and you, Uncle Tom, both to a trader; and that he was going off this morning on his horse, and that the man was to take possession to-day."

Tom had stood, during the speech, with his hands raised, and his eyes dilated, like a man in a dream. Slowly and gradually, as its meaning came over him, he collapsed, rather than seated himself, on his old chair, and sunk his head down upon his knees.

"The good Lord have pity on us!" said Aunt Chloe. "Oh, it don't seem as if it was true! What has he done, that Mas'r should sell *him?*"

"He hasn't done anything,—it is n't for that. Master don't want to sell; and Missis, —she's always good. I heard her plead and beg for us; but he told her 't was no use; that he was in this man's debt, and that this man had got the power over him; and that if he didn't pay him off clear, it would end in his having to sell the place and all the people, and move off. Yes, I heard him say there was no choice between selling these two and selling all, the man was driving him so hard. Master said he was sorry; but oh, Missis,—you ought to have heard her talk! If she ain't a Christian and an angel, there never was one. I'm a wicked girl to leave her so; but, then, I can't help it. She said, herself, one soul was worth more than the world; and this boy has a soul, and if I let him be carried off, who knows what'll become of it? It must be right; but, if it ain't right, the Lord forgive me, for I can't help doing it!"

"Well, old man!" said Aunt Chloe, "why don't you go, too? Will you wait to be toted down river, where they kill niggers with hard work and starving? I'd a heap rather die than go there, any day! There's time for ye,—be off with Lizy,—you've got a pass to come and go any time. Come, bustle up, and I'll get your things together."

Tom slowly raised his head, and looked sorrowfully but quietly around, and said,—

"No, no,—I ain't going. Let Eliza go,—it's her right! I wouldn't be the one to say no,—'t ain't in *natur* for her to stay; but you heard what she said! If I must be sold, or all the people on the place, and everything go to rack, why, let me be sold. I s'pose I can b'ar it as well as any on 'em," he added, while something like a sob and a sigh shook his broad, rough chest convulsively. "Mas'r always found me on the spot,—he always will. I never have broke trust, nor used my pass noways contrary to my word, and I never will. It's better for me alone to go, than to break up the place and sell all. Mas'r ain't to blame, Chloe, and he'll take care of you and the poor"—

Here he turned to the rough trundle-bed full of little woolly heads, and broke fairly down. He leaned over the back of the chair, and covered his face with his large hands. Sobs, heavy, hoarse, and loud, shook the chair, and great tears fell through his fingers on the floor: just such tears, sir, as you dropped into the coffin where lay your firstborn son; such tears, woman, as you shed when you heard the cries of your dying babe. For, sir, he was a man,—and you are but another man. And, woman, though dressed in silk and jewels, you are but a woman, and, in life's great straits and mighty griefs, ye feel but one sorrow!

"And now," said Eliza, as she stood in the door, "I saw my husband only this afternoon, and I little knew then what was to come. They have pushed him to the very last standing-place, and he told me, to-day, that he was going to run away. Do try, if you can, to get word to him. Tell him how I went, and why I went; and tell him I'm going to try and find Canada. You must give my love to him, and tell him, if I never see him again,"—she turned away, and stood with her back to them for a moment, and then added, in a husky voice,—"tell him to be as good as he can, and try and meet me in the kingdom of heaven."

"Call Bruno in there," she added. "Shut the door on him, poor beast! He must n't go with me!"

A few last words and tears, a few simple adieus and blessings, and, clasping her wondering and affrighted child in her arms, she glided noiselessly away.

1851–1852

Thomas Bangs Thorpe
1815–1875

"Our eyes will be turned westward," Emerson wrote in 1843, "and a new and stronger tone in literature will be the result." Emerson was not thinking here of James Fenimore Cooper and Washington Irving, writers who had helped launch American literature's western movement yet who clearly felt more at home in European capitals than in frontier towns. Instead, Emerson envisioned a western American literature arising from a new generation of frontier writers whose work was steeped in an authentic idiom: "The Kentucky stump-oratory, the exploits of Boone and David Crockett, the journals of western pioneers, agriculturalists and socialists . . . are genuine growths, which are sought with avidity in Europe, where our European-like books are of no value." Daniel Boone's legendary adventures first appeared in print in 1784, and Davy—Emerson's own distance from the frontier is apparent in his use of "David"—Crockett's distinctive blend of backwoods humor and self-promotion made for exciting reading throughout the 1830s. By the next decade, a sizable body of writing from the Midwest and Old Southwest had begun to attract the attention of eastern writers and editors.

One of these editors was William T. Porter, a Vermonter who had moved to New York City and in 1831 founded *Spirit of the Times,* a racy "Chronicle of the Turf, Agriculture, Field Sports, Literature, and the Stage." With a nationwide circulation of over forty thousand, *Spirit of the Times* soon grew to be a leading organ of southwestern humor, printing such classics as the Sut Lovingood tales of George Washington Harris. In 1841 Porter published what would become one of the most famous tall tales of American frontier literature, Thomas Bangs Thorpe's "The Big Bear of Arkansas." Arkansas (known as the "Bear State" until 1923) had been admitted into the Union as the twenty-fifth state in 1836. Public interest in the region had been especially fueled by an enormously popular humor book, *The Arkansas Traveler* (1840). Thorpe's tale is as much a piece of self-conscious regional boosterism for "the creation state, the finishing-up country" as it is an enduring frontier myth about an "unhuntable bar."

Thomas Bangs Thorpe was born in Westfield, Massachusetts, on March 1, 1815. He grew up in New York City, where he studied painting with John

Quidor, a fine early American historical and figure painter who derived many of his themes from the work of Washington Irving. Thorpe attended Wesleyan University in Middletown, Connecticut, from 1834 to 1836 but because of ill health moved to Louisiana. He lived there from 1837 to 1853, painting portraits and landscapes as well as contributing tales and hunting sketches to Porter's *Spirit of the Times*. In 1846 Thorpe published a collection of his stories, *The Mysteries of the Backwoods,* and in the same year wrote and illustrated a book on the Mexican War, *Our Army on the Rio Grande.* Thorpe returned to New York City in 1854; he published a second collection of backwoods tales, *The Hive of "The Bee-Hunter"* (1854), and after Porter's death in 1858 took over *Spirit of the Times* until it folded in 1861. As a colonel in the Union army, Thorpe served as city administrator of New Orleans during the occupation. From 1869 until his death in 1878, he worked at the customs house in New York City and continued to write for various magazines. But never again did he capture the American literary imagination as he did with that one short sketch of Jim Doggett and his pursuit of the fabulous bear.

Further Reading:
W. Blair, "The Technique of 'The Big Bear of Arkansas,'" *Southwest Review,* Summer 1943.
M. Rickels, *Thomas Bangs Thorpe: Humorist of the Old Southwest,* 1962.

Text:
The Big Bear of Arkansas, and Other Sketches Illustrative of Characters and Incidents in the South and South-West, ed. W. T. Porter, 1845.

The Big Bear of Arkansas

As the author of "Tom Owen the Bee Hunter," and other tales and sketches, Mr. THORPE has acquired a distinguished reputation on both sides of the Atlantic. Though by profession a painter, his time for several years past has been about equally divided between the brush and the pen. He is now engaged in the publication of the "Concordia Intelligencer," a journal of unusual ability, issued weekly in the pleasant little village situated directly opposite the city of Natchez. The New York "Spirit of the Times" was the medium through which Mr. T. first appeared before the world of letters; and his inimitable delineations of South-western characters, incidents, and scenery, soon attracted attention. Now, wherever the language is spoken, he is deemed
—"Great in mouths of wisest censure."
It is understood to be his intention to publish, at an early day, a collection of his writings, original and selected, to be illustrated by himself. As he is alike felicitous in the use of crayon, brush, or pen, we anticipate a brace or two of volumes of the highest pictorial and literary interest. The story annexed will give the reader an idea of his peculiar style in hitting off the original "characters" frequently met with in the great valley of the Mississippi.

A steamboat on the Mississippi frequently, in making her regular trips, carries between places varying from one to two thousand miles apart; and as these boats advertise to land passengers and freight at "all intermediate landings," the heterogeneous character of the passengers of one of these up-country boats can scarcely be imagined by one who has never seen it with his own eyes. Starting from New Orleans in one of these boats, you will find yourself associated with men from every state in the Union, and from every portion of the globe; and a man of observation need not lack for amusement or instruction in such a crowd, if he will take the trouble to read the great book of character so favourably opened before him. Here may be seen jostling together the wealthy Southern planter, and the pedler of tin-ware from New England—the Northern merchant, and the Southern jockey—a venerable bishop, and a desperate gambler—the land speculator, and the honest farmer—professional men of all creeds and characters—Wolvereens, Suckers, Hoosiers, Buckeyes, and Corn-crackers,[1] beside a "plentiful sprinkling" of the half-horse and half-alligator species of men,[2] who are peculiar to "old Mississippi," and who appear to gain a livelihood simply by going up and down the river. In the pursuit of pleasure or business, I have frequently found myself in such a crowd.

On one occasion, when in New Orleans, I had occasion to take a trip of a few miles up the Mississippi, and I hurried on board the well-known "high-pressure-and-beat-every-thing" steamboat "Invincible," just as the last note of the last bell was sounding; and when the confusion and bustle that is natural to a boat's getting under way had subsided, I discovered that I was associated in as heterogeneous a crowd as was ever got together. As my trip was to be of a few hours' duration only, I made no endeavours to become acquainted with my fellow passengers, most of whom would be together many days. Instead of this, I took out of my pocket the "latest paper," and more critically than usual examined its contents; my fellow passengers at the same time disposed of themselves in little groups. While I was thus busily employed in reading, and my companions were more busily still employed in discussing such subjects as suited their humours best, we were startled most unexpectedly by a loud Indian whoop, uttered in the "social hall," that part of the cabin fitted off for a bar; then was to be heard a loud crowing, which would not have continued to have interested us—such sounds being quite common in that *place of spirits*—had not the hero of these windy accomplishments stuck his head into the cabin and hallooed out, "Hurra for the Big Bar of Arkansaw!" and then might be heard a confused hum of voices, unintelligible, save in such broken sentences as "horse," "screamer,"[3] "lightning is slow," &c. As might have been expected, this continued interruption attracted the attention of every one in the cabin; all conversation dropped, and in the midst of this surprise the "Big Bar" walked into the cabin, took a chair, put his feet on the stove, and looking back over his shoulder, passed the general and familiar salute of "Strangers, how are you?" He then expressed himself as much at home as if he had been at "the Forks of Cypress," and "prehaps a little more so." Some of the company at this familiarity looked a little angry, and some astonished; but in a moment every face

[1] Nicknames for the inhabitants of Michigan, Illinois, Indiana, Ohio, and Kentucky, respectively.

[2] Popular expression for the breed of noisy, boasting Mississippi River raftsmen and backwoodsmen. Washington Irving: "It is an old remark that persons of Indian mixture are half civilized, half savage, and half devil—a third half being provided for their particular convenience. It is for similar reasons, and probably with equal truth, that the backwoodsmen of Kentucky are styled half man, half horse, and half alligator, by the settlers on the Mississippi, and held accordingly in great respect and abhorrence."

[3] Slang expression for a burly, noisy, bragging backwoodsman; i.e., a "Kentucky Screamer."

was wreathed in a smile. There was something about the intruder that won the heart on sight. He appeared to be a man enjoying perfect health and contentment: his eyes were as sparkling as diamonds, and good-natured to simplicity. Then his perfect confidence in himself was irresistibly droll. "Prehaps," said he, "gentlemen," running on without a person speaking, "prehaps you have been to New Orleans often; I never made *the first visit before,* and I don't intend to make another in a crow's life. I am thrown away in that ar place, and useless, that ar a fact. Some of the gentlemen thar called me *green*—well, prehaps I am, said I, *but I arn't so at home;* and if I aint off my trail much, the heads of them perlite chaps themselves wern't much the hardest; for according to my notion, they were *real know-nothings,* green as a pumpkin-vine —could'nt, in farming, I'll bet, raise a crop of turnips: and as for shooting, they'd miss a barn if the door was swinging, and that, too, with the best rifle in the country. And then they talked to me 'bout hunting, and laughed at my calling the principal game in Arkansaw poker, and high-low-jack. 'Prehaps,' said I, 'you prefer, chickens and rolette;'[4] at this they laughed harder than ever, and asked me if I lived in the woods, and didn't know what *game* was? At this I rather think I laughed. 'Yes,' I roared, and says, 'Strangers, if you'd asked me *how we got our meat* in Arkansaw, I'd a told you at once, and given you a list of varmints that would make a caravan, beginning with the bar, and ending off with the cat; that's *meat* though, not game.' Game, indeed, that's what city folks call it; and with them it means chippen-birds and shite-pokes;[5] maybe such trash live in my diggins, but I arn't noticed them yet: a bird any way is too trifling. I never did shoot at but one, and I'd never forgiven myself for that, had it weighed less than forty pounds. I wouldn't draw a rifle on any thing less than that; and when I meet with another wild turkey of the same weight I will drap him."

"A wild turkey weighing forty pounds!" exclaimed twenty voices in the cabin at once.

"Yes, strangers, and wasn't it a whopper? You see, the thing was so fat that it couldn't fly far; and when he fell out of the tree, after I shot him, on striking the ground he bust open behind, and the way the pound gobs of tallow rolled out of the opening was perfectly beautiful."

"Where did all that happen?" asked a cynical-looking Hoosier.

"Happen! happened in Arkansaw: where else could it have happened, but in the creation state, the finishing-up country—a state where the *sile* runs down to the centre of the 'arth, and government gives you a title to every inch of it? Then its airs— just breathe them, and they will make you snort like a horse. It's a state without a fault, it is."

"Excepting mosquitoes," cried the Hoosier.

"Well, stranger, except them; for it ar a fact that they are rather *enormous,* and do push themselves in somewhat troublesome. But, stranger, they never stick twice in the same place; and give them a fair chance for a few months, and you will get as much above noticing them as an alligator. They can't hurt my feelings, for they lay under the skin; and I never knew but one case of injury resulting from them, and that was to a Yankee: and they take worse to foreigners, any how, than they do to natives.

---

[4] "Chickens" is probably a misprint for "checkers"; "rolette": roulette.

[5] Chirping sparrows and herons, respectively.

But the way they used that fellow up! first they punched him until he swelled up and busted; then he sup-per-a-ted, as the doctor called it, until he was as raw as beef; then he took the ager,[6] owing to the warm weather, and finally he took a steamboat and left the country. He was the only man that ever took mosquitoes at heart that I know of. But mosquitoes is natur, and I never find fault with her. If they ar large, Arkansaw is large, her varmints ar large, her trees ar large, her rivers ar large, and a small mosquitoe would be of no more use in Arkansaw than preaching in a cane-brake."

This knock-down argument in favour of big mosquitoes used the Hoosier up, and the logician started on a new track, to explain how numerous bear were in his "diggins," where he represented them to be "about as plenty as blackberries, and a little plentifuler."

Upon the utterance of this assertion, a timid little man near me inquired if the bear in Arkansaw ever attacked the settlers in numbers.

"No," said our hero, warming with the subject, "no, stranger, for you see it ain't the natur of bar to go in droves; but the way they squander about in pairs and single ones is edifying. And then the way I hunt them—the old black rascals know the crack of my gun as well as they know a pig's squealing. They grow thin in our parts, it frightens them so, and they do take the noise dreadfully, poor things. That gun of mine is a perfect *epidemic among bar:* if not watched closely, it will go off as quick on a warm scent as my dog Bowie-knife[7] will: and then that dog—whew! why the fellow thinks that the world is full of bar, he finds them so easy. It's lucky he don't talk as well as think; for with his natural modesty, if he should suddenly learn how much he is acknowledged to be ahead of all other dogs in the universe, he would be astonished to death in two minutes. Strangers, that dog knows a bar's way as well as a horse-jockey knows a woman's: he always barks at the right time, bites at the exact place, and whips without getting a scratch. I never could tell whether he was made expressly to hunt bar, or whether bar was made expressly for him to hunt: any way, I believe they were ordained to go together as naturally as Squire Jones says a man and woman is, when he moralizes in marrying a couple. In fact, Jones once said, said he, 'Marriage according to law is a civil contract of divine origin; it's common to all countries as well as Arkansaw, and people take to it as naturally as Jim Doggett's Bowie-knife takes to bar.'"

"What season of the year do your hunts take place?" inquired a gentlemanly foreigner, who, from some peculiarities of his baggage, I suspected to be an Englishman, on some hunting expedition, probably at the foot of the Rocky mountains.

"The season for bar hunting, stranger," said the man of Arkansaw, "is generally all the year round, and the hunts take place about as regular. I read in history that varmints have their fat season, and their lean season. That is not the case in Arkansaw, feeding as they do upon the *spontenacious* productions of the sile, they have one continued fat season the year round: though in winter things in this way is rather more greasy than in summer, I must admit. For that reason bar with us run in warm weather, but in winter they only waddle. Fat, fat! it's an enemy to speed; it tames every thing

---

[6] Fever and chills; ague.
[7] Famous knife named for the frontiersman and soldier James Bowie (1799–1836).

that has plenty of it. I have seen wild turkeys, from its influence, as gentle as chickens. Run a bar in this fat condition, and the way it improves the critter for eating is amazing; it sort of mixes the ile up with the meat, until you can't tell t'other from which. I've done this often. I recollect one perty morning in particular, of putting an old he fellow on the stretch, and considering the weight he carried, he run well. But the dogs soon tired him down, and when I came up with him wasn't he in a beautiful sweat—I might say fever; and then to see his tongue sticking out of his mouth a feet,[8] and his sides sinking and opening like a bellows, and his cheeks so fat he couldn't look cross. In this fix I blazed at him, and pitch me naked into a briar patch if the steam didn't come out of the bullet-hole ten foot in a straight line. The fellow, I reckon, was made on the high-pressure system, and the lead sort of bust his biler."

"That column of steam was rather curious, or else the bear must have been warm," observed the foreigner, with a laugh.

"Stranger, as you observe, that bar was WARM, and the blowing off of the steam show'd it, and also how hard the varmint had been run. I have no doubt if he had kept on two miles farther his insides would have been stewed; and I expect to meet with a varmint yet of extra bottom, who will run himself into a skinfull of bar's grease: it is possible; much onlikelier things have happened."

"Whereabouts are these bears so abundant?" inquired the foreigner, with increasing interest.

"Why, stranger, they inhabit the neighbourhood of my settlement, one of the prettiest places on old Mississippi—a perfect location, and no mistake; a place that had some defects until the river made the 'cut-off' at 'Shirt-tail bend,' and that remedied the evil, as it brought my cabin on the edge of the river—a great advantage in wet weather, I assure you, as you can now roll a barrel of whiskey into my yard in high water from a boat, as easy as falling off a log. It's a great improvement, as toting it by land in a jug, as I used to do, *evaporated* it too fast, and it became expensive. Just stop with me, stranger, a month or two, or a year if you like, and you will appreciate my place. I can give you plenty to eat; for beside hog and hominy, you can have bar-ham, and bar-sausages, and a mattrass of bar-skins to sleep on, and a wildcat-skin, pulled off hull, stuffed with corn-shucks, for a pillow. That bed would put you to sleep if you had the rheumatics in every joint in your body. I call that ar bed a *quietus.*[9] Then look at my land—the government ain't got another such a piece to dispose of. Such timber, and such bottom land, why you can't preserve any thing natural you plant in it unless you pick it young, things thar will grow out of shape so quick. I once planted in those diggins a few potatoes and beets: they took a fine start, and after that an ox team couldn't have kept them from growing. About that time I went off to old Kentuck on bisiness, and did not hear from them things in three months, when I accidentally stumbled on a fellow who had stopped at my place, with an idea of buying me out. 'How did you like things?' said I. 'Pretty well,' said he; 'the cabin is convenient, and the timber land is good; but that bottom land ain't worth the first red cent.' 'Why?' said I. ' 'Cause,' said he. ' 'Cause what?' said I. ' 'Cause it's full of cedar stumps and Indian mounds,' said he, 'and *it can't be cleared.*' 'Lord,' said I, 'them ar "cedar stumps" is beets, and them ar "Indian mounds" ar tater hills.' As I expected, the crop was overgrown and useless: the sile is too rich, *and*

---

[8] Probably misprint for "foot."　　　　[9] Final release from all cares; i.e., death.

planting in Arkansaw is dangerous. I had a good-sized sow killed in that same bottom land. The old thief stole an ear of corn, and took it down where she slept at night to eat. Well, she left a grain or two on the ground, and lay down on them: before morning the corn shot up, and the percussion killed her dead. I don't plant any more: natur intended Arkansaw for a hunting ground, and I go according to natur."

The questioner who thus elicited the description of our hero's settlement, seemed to be perfectly satisfied, and said no more; but the "Big Bar of Arkansaw" rambled on from one thing to another with a volubility perfectly astonishing, occasionally disputing with those around him, particularly with a "live Sucker" from Illinois, who had the daring to say that our Arkansaw friend's stories "smelt rather tall."

In this manner the evening was spent; but conscious that my own association with so singular a personage would probably end before morning, I asked him if he would not give me a description of some particular bear hunt; adding, that I took great interest in such things, though I was no sportsman. The desire seemed to please him, and he squared himself round towards me, saying, that he could give me an idea of a bar hunt that was never beat in this world, or in any other. His manner was so singular, that half of his story consisted in his excellent way of telling it, the great peculiarity of which was, the happy manner he had of emphasizing the prominent parts of his conversation. As near as I can recollect, I have italicized them, and given the story in his own words.

"Stranger," said he, "in bar hunts *I am numerous,* and which particular one, as you say, I shall tell, puzzles me. There was the old she devil I shot at the Hurricane last fall—then there was the old hog thief I popped over at the Bloody Crossing, and then—Yes, I have it! I will give you an idea of a hunt, in which the greatest bar was killed that ever lived, *none excepted;* about an old fellow that I hunted, more or less, for two or three years; and if that ain't a *particular bar hunt,* I ain't got one to tell. But in the first place, stranger, let me say, I am pleased with you, because you ain't ashamed to gain information by asking, and listening; and that's what I say to Countess's pups every day when I'm home; and I have got great hopes of them ar pups, because they are continually *nosing* about; and though they stick it sometimes in the wrong place, they gain experience any how, and may learn something useful to boot. Well, as I was saying about this big bar, you see when I and some more first settled in our region, we were drivin to hunting naturally; we soon liked it, and after that we found it an easy matter to make the thing our business. One old chap who had pioneered 'afore us, gave us to understand that we had settled in the right place. He dwelt upon its merits until it was affecting, and showed us, to prove his assertions, more marks on the sassafras trees than I ever saw on a tavern door 'lection time.[10] 'Who keeps that ar reckoning?' said I. 'The bar,' said he. 'What for?' said I. 'Can't tell,' said he; 'but so it is: the bar bite the bark and wood too, at the highest point from the ground they can reach, and you can tell, by the marks,' said he, 'the length of the bar to an inch.' 'Enough,' said I; 'I've learned something here a'ready, and I'll put it in practice.'

"Well, stranger, just one month from that time I killed a bar, and told its exact length before I measured it, by those very marks; and when I did that, I swelled up

[10] Drinking was notoriously heavy at election
time, and the reckonings of bills were marked
on the doors of taverns.

considerable—I've been a prouder man ever since. So I went on, larning something every day, until I was reckoned a buster," and allowed to be decidedly the best bar hunter in my district; and that is a reputation as much harder to earn than to be reckoned first man in Congress, as an iron ramrod is harder than a toad-stool. Did the varmints grow over-cunning by being fooled with by green-horn hunters, and by this means get troublesome, they send for me as a matter of course; and thus I do my own hunting, and most of my neighbours'. I walk into the varmints though, and it has become about as much the same to me as drinking. It is told in two sentences —a bar is started, and he is killed. The thing is somewhat monotonous now—I know just how much they will run, where they will tire, how much they will growl, and what a thundering time I will have in getting them home. I could give you this history of the chase with all the particulars at the commencement, I know the signs so well —*Stranger, I'm certain.* Once I met with a match though, and I will tell you about it; for a common hunt would not be worth relating.

"On a fine fall day, long time ago, I was trailing about for bar, and what should I see but fresh marks on the sassafras trees, about eight inches above any in the forests that I knew of. Says I, 'them marks is a hoax, or it indicates the d——t bar that was ever grown.' In fact, stranger, I couldn't believe it was real, and I went on. Again I saw the same marks, at the same height, and *I knew the thing lived.* That conviction came home to my soul like an earthquake. Says I, 'here is something a-purpose for me: that bar is mine, or I give up the hunting business.' The very next morning what should I see but a number of buzzards hovering over my corn-field. 'The rascal has been there,' said I, 'for that sign is certain:' and, sure enough, on examining, I found the bones of what had been as beautiful a hog the day before, as was ever raised by a Buckeye. Then I tracked the critter out of the field to the woods, and all the marks he left behind, showed me that he was *the bar.*

"Well, stranger, the first fair chase I ever had with that big critter, I saw him no less than three distinct times at a distance: the dogs run him over eighteen miles and broke down, my horse gave out, and I was as nearly used up as a man can be, made on *my* principle, *which is patent.* Before this adventure, such things were unknown to me as possible; but, strange as it was, that bar got me used to it before I was done with him; for he got so at last, that he would leave me on a long chase *quite easy.* How he did it, I never could understand. That a bar runs at all, is puzzling; but how this one could tire down and bust up a pack of hounds and a horse, that were used to overhauling everything they started after in no time, was past my understanding. Well, stranger, that bar finally got so sassy, that he used to help himself to a hog off my premises whenever he wanted one; the buzzards followed after what he left, and so, between *bar and buzzard,* I rather think I was *out of pork.*

"Well, missing that bar so often took hold of my vitals, and I wasted away. The thing had been carried too far, and it reduced me in flesh faster than an ager. I would see that bar in every thing I did: *he hunted me,* and that, too, like a devil, which I began to think he was. While in this fix, I made preparations to give him a last brush, and be done with it. Having completed every thing to my satisfaction, I started at sunrise, and to my great joy, I discovered from the way the dogs run, that they were near him; finding his trail was nothing, for that had become as

---

" Slang for a big, roaring fellow.

plain to the pack as a turnpike road. On we went, and coming to an open country, what should I see but the bar very leisurely ascending a hill, and the dogs close at his heels, either a match for him this time in speed, or else he did not care to get out of their way——I don't know which. But wasn't he a beauty, though? I loved him like a brother.

"On he went, until he came to a tree, the limbs of which formed a crotch about six feet from the ground. Into this crotch he got and seated himself, the dogs yelling all around it; and there he sat eyeing them as quiet as a pond in low water. A green-horn friend of mine, in company, reached shooting distance before me, and blazed away, hitting the critter in the centre of his forehead. The bar shook his head as the ball struck it, and then walked down from that tree as gently as a lady would from a carriage. 'Twas a beautiful sight to see him do that——he was in such a rage that he seemed to be as little afraid of the dogs as if they had been sucking pigs; and the dogs warn't slow in making a ring around him at a respectful distance, I tell you; even Bowie-knife, himself, stood off. Then the way his eyes flashed——why the fire of them would have singed a cat's hair; in fact that bar was in a *wrath all over*. Only one pup came near him, and he was brushed out so totally with the bar's left paw, that he entirely disappeared; and that made the old dogs more cautious still. In the mean time, I came up, and taking deliberate aim as a man should do, at his side, just back of his foreleg, if *my gun did not snap*,[12] call me a coward, and I won't take it personal. Yes, stranger, *it snapped,* and I could not find a cap[13] about my person. While in this predicament, I turned round to my fool friend——says I, 'Bill,' says I, 'you're an ass——you're a fool——you might as well have tried to kill that bar by barking the tree under his belly, as to have done it by hitting him in the head. Your shot has made a tiger of him, and blast me, if a dog gets killed or wounded when they come to blows, I will stick my knife into your liver, I will ————, my wrath was up. I had lost my caps, my gun had snapped, the fellow with me had fired at the bar's head, and I expected every moment to see him close in with the dogs, and kill a dozen of them at least. In this thing I was mistaken, for the bar leaped over the ring formed by the dogs, and giving a fierce growl, was off——the pack, of course, in full cry after him. The run this time was short, for coming to the edge of a lake the varmint jumped in, and swam to a little island in the lake, which it reached just a moment before the dogs. 'I'll have him now,' said I, for I had found my caps in the *lining of my coat*—— so, rolling a log into the lake, I paddled myself across to the island, just as the dogs had cornered the bar in a thicket. I rushed up and fired——at the same time the critter leaped over the dogs and came within three feet of me, running like mad; he jumped into the lake, and tried to mount the log I had just deserted, but every time he got half his body on it, it would roll over and send him under; the dogs, too, got around him, and pulled him about, and finally Bowie-knife clenched with him, and they sunk into the lake together. Stranger, about this time I was excited, and I stripped off my coat, drew my knife, and intended to have taken a part with Bowie-knife myself, when the bar rose to the surface. But the varmint staid under——Bowie-knife came up alone, more dead than alive, and with the pack came ashore. 'Thank God,' said I, 'the old villain has got his deserts at last.' Determined to have the body, I cut a grape-vine for a rope, and dove down where I could see the bar in the water, fastened

[12] Misfire.   [13] Percussion cap.

my queer rope to his leg, and fished him, with great difficulty, ashore. Stranger, may I be chawed to death by young alligators, if the thing I looked at wasn't a *she bar, and not the old critter after all.* The way matters got mixed on that island was onaccountably curious, and thinking of it made me more than ever convinced that I was hunting the devil himself. I went home that night and took to my bed—the thing was killing me. The entire team of Arkansaw in bar-hunting, acknowledged himself used up, and the fact sunk into my feelings like a snagged boat will in the Mississippi. I grew as cross as a bar with two cubs and a sore tail. The thing got out 'mong my neighbours, and I was asked how come on that individ-u-al that never lost a bar when once started? and if that same individ-u-al didn't wear telescopes when he turned a she bar, of ordinary size, into an old he one, a little larger than a horse? 'Prehaps,' said I, 'friends' —getting wrathy—'prehaps you want to call somebody a liar.' 'Oh, no,' said they, 'we only heard such things as being *rather common* of late, but we don't believe one word of it; oh, no,'—and then they would ride off and laugh like so many hyenas over a dead nigger. It was too much, and I determined to catch that bar, go to Texas, or die,—and I made my preparations accordin'. I had the pack shut up and rested. I took my rifle to pieces, and iled it. I put caps in every pocket about my person, *for fear of the lining.* I then told my neighbours, that on Monday morning—naming the day—I would start THAT BAR, and bring him home with me, or they might divide my settlement among them, the owner having disappeared. Well, stranger, on the morning previous to the great day of my hunting expedition, I went into the woods near my house, taking my gun and Bowie-knife along, just *from habit,* and there sitting down also from habit,[14] what should I see, getting over my fence, but *the bar!* Yes, the old varmint was within a hundred yards of me, and the way he walked over that fence—stranger, he loomed up like a *black mist,* he seemed so large, and he walked right towards me. I raised myself, took deliberate aim, and fired. Instantly the varmint wheeled, gave a yell, and *walked through the fence* like a falling tree would through a cobweb. I started after, but was tripped up by my inexpressibles,[15] which either from habit, or the excitement of the moment, were about my heels, and before I had really gathered myself up, I heard the old varmint groaning in a thicket near by, like a thousand sinners, and by the time I reached him he was a corpse. Stranger, it took five niggers and myself to put that carcase on a mule's back, and old long-ears waddled under his load, as if he was foundered in every leg of his body, and with a common whopper of a bar, he would have trotted off, and enjoyed himself. 'Twould astonish you to know how big he was: I made a *bed-spread of his skin,* and the way it used to cover my bar mattress, and leave several feet on each side to tuck up, would have delighted you. It was in fact a creation bar, and if it had lived in Samson's[16] time, and had met him, in a fair fight, it would have licked him in the twinkling of a dice-box. But, stranger, I never liked the way I hunted him, *and missed him.* There is something curious about it, I could never understand,—and I never was satisfied at his giving in so *easy at last.* Prehaps, he had heard of my preparations to hunt him the next day, so he jist come in, like Capt. Scott's coon,[17] to save his wind to grunt

---

[14] I.e., habitual morning bowel movement.
[15] Euphemism for trousers. Doggett had lowered them from "habit."
[16] Samson: Biblical hero famous for his great strength (Judges 13–16).

[17] Allusion to a popular anecdote in which a raccoon, seeing that it is about to be shot, wisely gives up.

with in dying; but that ain't likely. My private opinion is, that that bar was an *unhuntable bar, and died when his time come."*

When the story was ended, our hero sat some minutes with his auditors in a grave silence; I saw there was a mystery to him connected with the bear whose death he had just related, that had evidently made a strong impression on his mind. It was also evident that there was some superstitious awe connected with the affair,—a feeling common with all "children of the wood," when they meet with any thing out of their everyday experience. He was the first one, however, to break the silence, and jumping up, he asked all present to "liquor" before going to bed,—a thing which he did, with a number of companions, evidently to his heart's content.

Long before day, I was put ashore at my place of destination, and I can only follow with the reader, in imagination, our Arkansas friend, in his adventures at the "Forks of Cypress" on the Mississippi.

1841

Frederick Douglass
1817?–1895

This black man, who did not know his birthday or who his father was, who rarely saw his mother after he was taken from her as an infant, created a life for himself out of the nothingness his slave status had conferred upon him and his race. At twenty-one Frederick Bailey escaped from the Maryland plantation where he had spent most of his young life. He arrived in 1838 in New Bedford, Massachusetts, where he changed his name to Douglass, ostensibly to throw his pursuers off his trail but also to forge an identity for himself as a free man.

Douglass taught himself to read and write, then launched himself into the thick of the abolitionist movement. By 1841 he was recognized as one of the most eloquent speakers for the Massachusetts Anti-Slavery Society. Writing and lecturing took Douglass across the northern states and to England. Purchasing his freedom in 1847, he added editing to his other activities by founding the *North Star* and *Douglass' Monthly*. During the Civil War he recruited blacks for service in the Union Army. His active life included serving as a United States Marshal and an appointment as Consul General to the Haitian Republic as well as speaking out for women's rights, antilynching laws, and the betterment of the lives of poor tenant farmers in the postwar South.

It was natural for Douglass to thrust himself into the center of public attention on heated issues, but the ugliest kind of controversy surrounded him when he married a white woman and, later, when he was reputed to have supported John Brown's raid on the Harper's Ferry arsenal—a false accusation that caused him, prudently, to leave the country until the facts were made clear. But it was as a writer of autobiography that he achieved his greatest fame.

The first version of Douglass's memoirs appeared in 1845 under the title *Narrative of the Life of Frederick Douglass.* Later revisions and additions led to *My Bondage and My Freedom,* published in 1855. Two much later revisions resulted in the *Life and Times of Frederick Douglass,* brought out in 1881 and 1892. In these accounts, Douglass borrows, with irony, the autobiographical form of the young man on his way to fame and fortune that Benjamin Franklin made a central motif in American letters. Douglass joined it, however, to another literary tradition: slave narratives that recounted the oppression of a people who were not considered human enough to have the rights of autobiography. As the final title of his book indicates, Douglass's life is also a powerful examination of the times that he made and that made him. Douglass's autobiography now stands as one of the most memorable of the exemplary lives written by self-created Americans.

Further Reading:

C. Chesnutt, *Frederick Douglass,* 1899, 1970.
B. Washington, *Frederick Douglass,* 1906, 1969.
E. Fuller, *A Star Pointed North,* 1946.
S. Graham, *There Once Was a Slave,* 1947.
B. Quarles, *Frederick Douglass,* 1968.
J. Gregory, *Frederick Douglass, The Orator,* 1969.
F. Holland, *Frederick Douglass: The Colored Orator,* 1969.
C. Hoexter, *Black Crusader: Frederick Douglass,* 1970.
A. Bontemps, *Free at Last: The Life of Frederick Douglass,* 1971.

Frederick Douglass on Women's Rights, ed. P. Foner, 1976.
The Frederick Douglass Papers, 2 vols., ed. J. Blassingame, 1979.
N. I. Huggins, *Slave and Citizen: The Life of Frederick Douglass,* 1980.
D. Preston, *Young Frederick Douglass: The Maryland Years,* 1980.
W. E. Martin, Jr., *The Mind of Frederick Douglass,* 1985.
D. J. Preston, *Young Frederick Douglass: The Maryland Years,* 1985.

Text:
Life and Times of Frederick Douglass, 1892.

---

from Life and Times of Frederick Douglass[*]

Chapter XIII: Covey, the Negro-Breaker

In the region of the bay there was a farm renter named Edward Covey who was said to be a first-rate hand at breaking young Negroes. Mr. Covey had the most fiery farm helpers of the neighborhood at little cost to himself because he could be depended upon to return them to their owners well broken. While I could not look forward to going to him with pleasure I was glad to get away from St. Michaels. I believed I would get enough to eat at Covey's, even if I suffered in other respects.

Eight or ten years had now passed since I had been taken from my grandmother's cabin in Tuckahoe. For the most part I had spent these years in Baltimore where I was treated with comparative tenderness. I was now about to sound profounder depths of slave life.

[*] The full title of this 1892 version—the final and complete version—of Douglass's autobiography is *Life and Times of Frederick Douglass: his early life as a slave, his escape and* *bondage, and his complete history, written by himself.* Previous but markedly different versions of the autobiography had been published in 1845, 1855, and 1881.

The morning of January 1, 1834, found me on the road to Covey's. The chilling wind and pinching frost matched the winter of my own mind as I trudged along. At last I came in sight of a small wooden building about a mile from the main road. From the description I had received, I recognized it as my new home. The little house stood on the banks of Chesapeake Bay, which was now white with foam raised by a heavy northwest wind. The good clothes I had brought with me from Baltimore were now worn thin and had not been replaced. I was glad to find shelter of any kind, even with the dreaded Covey, and I hurried on to the house.

The family consisted of Mr. and Mrs. Covey; Mrs. Kemp (a broken-backed woman), sister to Mrs. Covey; William Hughes, cousin to Mr. Covey; Caroline, the cook; Bill Smith, a hired man; and myself. For the first time in my life I was now to be a field hand. Bill Smith, Bill Hughes, and I were the working force of the farm, which was three or four hundred acres in size.

I had been in my new home only three days before Mr. Covey gave me a bitter foretaste of what was in store for me. At daybreak I was ordered to get a load of wood from a forest about two miles from the house. To perform this work, Mr. Covey gave me a pair of unbroken oxen. He knew what I had yet to discover, that though tame and docile when well trained, oxen are the most sullen and intractable of animals when half broken to the yoke. Mr. Covey took a rope about ten feet long and one inch thick and placed one end of it around the horns of one of the oxen and gave the other end to me. He told me that if the oxen started to run away (as he knew they would) I must hold onto the rope and stop them. I afterwards learned that even Covey himself would not have taken the oxen to the woods without first driving them for some time in the open field. At the time, however, I had no directions other than the ones he had given me, and I started for the woods anxious to perform my first exploit in a creditable manner.

I had never driven oxen before, and I was as awkward a driver as it is possible to imagine. Yet the first mile, from the house to the gate at the woods, was passed over with little difficulty. The animals ran, but I was fast enough in the open field to keep up with them. On reaching the woods, my situation took a turn for the worse. The animals became frightened and started off ferociously. As I held the rope I expected every moment to be crushed between the cart and the huge trees. After running for several minutes, my oxen were finally brought to a halt by a tree. Wild and enraged, they dashed themselves against it with such violence that they became entangled in some young saplings. The body of the cart was flung in one direction and the wheels and tongue in another, all in the greatest confusion.

I stood a few minutes surveying the damage and wondering how best to put it all right again. I took one end of the cart body and by an extra outlay of strength succeeded in getting it in its place on the axle tree. The cart was provided with an ax, a tool which I had learned to use in the shipyard at Baltimore. With this I cut down the saplings and freed my oxen. I again pursued my journey with my heart in my mouth lest the beasts cut up another caper. On reaching the part of the forest where I had been chopping wood the day before, I filled the cart with a heavy load.

Half the day was gone, and I had not yet started home. I knew that such an apparent waste of time would not be overlooked by Covey, and I hurried back through the woods. On reaching the edge of the field, I let go the end of the rope to open the gate. Once the gate was opened in front of them, my oxen charged through full tilt. They caught the huge gate between the wheel and the cart body, crushing it to splinters and coming within a few inches of crushing me with it.

When I went to Covey to explain about the casualties of my trip, his sharp face became intensely ferocious.

"Go back to the woods again," he said, muttering something about wasting time.

I obeyed, and looking over my shoulder, I saw that he was following me. On reaching the woods, Covey told me that he would now teach me how to break gates and idle away my time. He went to a large black gum tree, the young shoots of which are generally used for ox goads because they are exceedingly tough. He cut off three of these goads, from four to six feet long, and trimmed them up with his large jackknife. This done, he ordered me to take off my clothes. I made no reply, but by ignoring his order I indicated my determination to do no such thing.

"If you beat me," I thought, "you shall do so over my clothes."

After many threats he rushed at me with the savage fierceness of a wolf, tore off the few thin clothes I had on, and proceeded to wear out on my back the heavy goads which he had cut from the gum tree.

This was the first of a series of floggings I received while at Covey's. It was less severe than many which came after it, and these for offenses far lighter than the gate-breaking. I remained with Mr. Covey one year, and during the first six months there I was whipped, either with sticks or a cowhide whip, every week. Aching bones and a sore back were my constant companions. From the dawn of day in the morning till complete darkness in the evening, I was kept hard at work in the field or the woods. He had in his life been an overseer, and he well understood the business of slave driving. There was no deceiving him. He knew just what a man or boy could do and he held both to strict account.

It was, however, scarcely necessary for Mr. Covey to be present in the field to have his work go on industriously. We never knew when we were being watched. He would creep in the gullies and hide behind bushes. We were never secure. He would sometimes mount his horse and make believe he was going to St. Michaels. But thirty minutes afterwards we might find his horse tied in the woods. A short distance away, Covey might be seen lying flat in the ditch with his head lifted above its edge, watching every movement of the slaves. He did not seem conscious that such spying had anything contemptible about it. It was part of an important system with him, essential to the relation of master and slave.

Mr. Edward Covey was a poor but ambitious man. He was just beginning to lay the foundation of his fortune, and in a slave state that meant owning human property. He had acquired one slave of his own, a woman named Caroline, whom he had bought "as a breeder." Covey and his wife were ecstatic with joy when twins were born at the end of the year. No one reproached the woman or found fault with the hired man, Bill Smith, the father of the children. Mr. Covey had locked the two up together every night to bring about this result.

If at any one time of my life more than another I was made to drink the bitterest dregs of slavery, that time was during the first six months of my stay with this man Covey. We worked all weathers. It was never too hot or too cold. It could never rain, blow, snow, or hail too hard for us to work in the field. Work, work, work was as much the order of the night as the order of the day. I had neither time to eat nor time to sleep. I was somewhat unmanageable at first, but a few months of Covey's discipline tamed me. He succeeded in breaking me in body, soul, and spirit. My natural elasticity was crushed, my intellect languished, the wish to read departed, and the dark night of slavery closed in upon me.

Sunday was my only leisure time. I spent this in a sort of beast-like stupor, between sleeping and waking, under some large tree. I was sometimes tempted to take my life and that of Covey but was prevented by a combination of hope and fear. My sufferings, as I remember them now, seem like a dream rather than a stern reality.

Chapter XIV: The Beginning of the End

One hot day in August of that year I was at work in what was called the "treading yard," where wheat was threshed from the straw by the horses' feet. The work required strength and activity rather than skill. Our force consisted of Bill Hughes, Bill Smith, and a slave by the name of Eli who had been hired for the occasion. I was bringing wheat to the "fan" while Bill Smith was feeding.

About three o'clock, while the sun poured down its burning rays and not a breeze stirred, I suddenly broke down. My strength failed me. I was seized with a violent headache, dizziness, and trembling. Knowing that it would never do to stop work, I nerved myself up and tried to stagger on. But at last I fell by the side of the wheat fan, bringing the entire work to a standstill. There was work for four. Each of us had his part to perform, and each part depended on the other; when one stopped, all were compelled to stop. Covey, who had become my dread, was at the house about a hundred yards from where we were working. Instantly, upon hearing the work cease, he came down to the treading yard. Bill Smith told him I was sick and that I was unable to bring wheat to the fan any longer.

By this time I had crawled to a place in the shade and was exceedingly ill. The intense heat of the sun, the heavy dust rising from the fan, and the continual stooping to take up the wheat from the yard had caused a rush of blood to my head. Covey stood over me and asked what was the matter. I told him as well as I could, for it was difficult for me to speak. He gave me a savage kick in the side which jarred my whole frame, and commanded me to get up. He had obtained complete control over me, and if he had commanded me to do any possible thing, I would have tried to obey. I made an effort to rise but fell back before getting to my feet. He gave me another heavy kick and again told me to rise. I again tried and succeeded in standing up. But when I stooped to get the tub with which I was feeding the fan I again staggered and fell to the ground. If I had been threatened with a hundred bullets I could not have gotten up.

"If you have got the headache, I'll cure you," he said.

He took up a hickory slab and with the edge of it dealt me a heavy blow on my head which made a large gash and caused the blood to run freely. He ordered me again to rise, but I made no effort to do so. I had now made up my mind that it was useless and the villain could do no worse than kill me and put me out of my misery.

Finding me unable to rise, or rather giving up hope of my doing so, Covey left to get on with the work without me. I was bleeding freely, and my face was soon covered with blood. Cruel as the blow was, the wound was a fortunate one for me. The pain in my head quickly abated, and I was soon able to rise. I asked myself if I should return to my work or should I find my way to St. Michaels, show Capt. Auld the results of Covey's cruelty, and beseech him to get me another master? Remembering Capt. Thomas Auld's behavior of the past, there was little ground to hope that he would receive me favorably. Nevertheless, I thought he might interfere on my behalf from selfish considerations.

"He cannot," I thought, "allow his property to be thus bruised and battered, marred, and defaced, and I will go to him about the matter."

In order to get to St. Michaels by the most direct road I had to walk seven miles, and this, in my sad condition, was no easy thing to do. However, I watched my chance while Covey was looking in another direction and started off across the field for St. Michaels. I was halfway across the field toward the woods when Covey saw me.

"Come back! Come back!" he shouted, with threats of what he would do if I did not return instantly.

But I disregarded his calls and threats and hurried on toward the woods as fast as my feeble state would allow. Seeing no signs of my stopping, he had his horse brought out and saddled as if he intended to pursue me. I reached the woods where I kept away from the road. If he followed me, I did not see or hear him.

I had not gone far among the trees before my strength failed me again and I was obliged to lie down. The blood was still oozing from the wound in my head, and for a time I suffered more than I can describe. I was afraid I might bleed to death. The thought of dying in the woods all alone and being torn to pieces by the buzzards was not a tolerable one. I was glad when the shade of the trees and the cool evening breeze stopped the flow of blood and I could again take up my journey to St. Michaels. I was five hours in going the seven or eight miles, partly because of the difficulties of the route I took and partly because of the feebleness induced by my illness, bruises, and loss of blood.

On reaching my master's, I found I had jumped from a sinking ship into the sea. I told him the circumstances as well as I could. At first Master Thomas walked the floor, agitated by my story and the spectacle I presented. But soon it was his turn to talk. He said that he had no doubt I deserved the treatment I had received from Covey. He did not believe I was sick but that I was only trying to get out of work. He asked what I wanted him to do. I told him I wished him to let me find a new master. I told him that I was sure if I went back again to live with Mr. Covey that I would be killed or, if not that, that I would be ruined for future service.

Master Thomas regarded this as "nonsense." He said that Mr. Covey was a good man, industrious and religious.

"Besides," he said, "if you leave Covey now with your year only half over, I will lose your wages for the entire year. You belong to Mr. Covey for one year, and you must go back to him come what will. You must not trouble me with any more stories. If you don't go back to Covey's house immediately, I'll give you a whipping myself."

"But sir," I said, "I am sick and tired, and I cannot get home tonight."

He finally allowed me to spend the night but made me swallow a huge dose of Epsom salts, which was about the only medicine ever administered to slaves.

Chapter XV: The Last Flogging

Sleep does not always come to the relief of the weary in body and broken in spirit. I remained, but did not sleep, all that Friday night at St. Michaels. In the morning I set off feeling that I had no friend on earth and doubting if I had one in heaven. I reached the field at Covey's house about nine o'clock. True to his snakish habits Covey darted out at me from a fence corner where he had hidden himself for the purpose of capturing me. He had a cowhide whip and a rope, and he evidently intended to tie me up and wreak his vengeance on me to the fullest extent. I would have been easy prey had he gotten his hands upon me. I had taken no food since noon the day before, and this, with the other trying circumstances, had greatly reduced my strength. However, I darted back into the woods before he could reach me and buried myself in a thicket. He was much chagrined that I escaped him, as I could see by his angry movements as he returned to the house.

I was alone in the woods, buried in somber gloom, shut in with nature, and I wanted to pray. But the sham religion which I saw everywhere made me doubt that my prayers would be of any help.

Night came. I was still in the woods and had not yet made up my mind whether to remain in the woods and starve or return to Covey and have my flesh torn off. I lay down in the leaves to rest. I had been watching for hunters all day, but not having seen them during the day, I expected no disturbance from them during the night. I had come to the conclusion that Covey believed I would be driven home by hunger, and in this I believe I was correct, for he made no effort to catch me after the morning.

During the night I heard the step of a man in the woods. He was coming toward the place where I lay. I hid myself in the leaves to prevent discovery. But as the stranger drew nearer, I found him to be a friend, not an enemy. He was a slave of Mr. William Groomes of Easton, a kindhearted fellow named "Sandy." Sandy lived with Mr. Kemp about four miles from St. Michaels. He, like myself, had been hired out that year, but not to be broken. He was the husband of a free woman who lived not far away and he was now on his way through the woods to spend Sunday with her.

As soon as I discovered that the intruder was the goodnatured Sandy I came out from my hiding place. I explained the circumstances of the past two days which had driven me to the woods, and he deeply sympathized with me. Sandy knew Covey well, for Mrs. Covey was the daughter of Mrs. Kemp. Sandy had heard of the barbarous treatment to which I had been subjected, and he wanted to do something for me. I did not ask him to shelter me. Had I been found in his slave quarters, he would have suffered thirty-nine lashes on his bare back, if not something worse. But Sandy was too generous to leave me to my fate. He took me with him to the home of his free wife, who owned her house and lot. It was about midnight, but his wife was called up, a fire was made, some Indian meal was mixed with salt and water, and an ash cake was baked to relieve my hunger. Since that night I have partaken of banquets. But my supper on ash cake and cold water with these two fine people was the meal of all my life most sweet to my taste and most vivid to my memory.

Both Sandy and his wife seemed to think it a privilege to help me. I was hated by Covey and by my master, but I was the only slave in that region who could read or write, and my knowledge was the pride of my brother slaves. No doubt Sandy felt something of the general interest in me on that account.

In Sandy at least I found an old adviser. He was not only a religious man but a genuine African and had inherited some of the so-called magical powers said to be possessed by those from the eastern nations. He told me that there was an herb which possessed all the powers required for my protection. He told me further that if I would take the root of the herb and wear it on my right side it would be impossible for a white man to whip me. He said he had carried it for years and that he had fully tested its virtues. He had never received a blow from a slaveholder since he carried it.

All this talk about the root was, to me, ridiculous, if not positively sinful. I did not propose to load up my pockets with "magic roots" and felt the whole notion was beneath my intelligence. But Sandy was more than a match for me.

"Your book learning," he said, "has not protected you from Covey." I confess this was a powerful argument just then. He entreated me to try the root. Sandy was so confident that, to please him, I took the roots and placed them in my right-hand pocket.

Sunday morning dawned, and Sandy woke me and urged me to hurry home. He advised me to walk up to the house as though nothing had happened. I started off toward Covey's, as directed. Just as I entered the yard gate I met Covey and his wife dressed in their Sunday best. Smiling like a pair of angels, they were on their way to church. Covey inquired how I was and told me that the pigs had got into the lot and he wished me to go drive them out. I was amazed to see the change in him, but I suspected that the Sabbath, not the root, was the real cause. His religion kept him from breaking the Sabbath but not from breaking my skin on any other day than Sunday.

Long before daylight on Monday I was called and told to go feed, rub, and curry the horses. I obeyed, for I had resolved to obey every order, however unreasonable. But I had made up my mind that if Mr. Covey tried to beat me in spite of my best efforts to please him, I would defend and protect myself to the best of my ability. A bitter but wonderful thing had happened to me. I was no longer afraid to die.

I went to the barn to get the horses ready for the field. But as I was climbing the ladder to the stable loft, Covey sneaked into the stable and seized me suddenly by the leg. He tried to slip a rope around my legs before I could draw up my feet. As soon as I found what he was up to I gave a sudden spring (my two days' rest had been of much help to me) and he brought me to the floor, giving my newly-mended body a terrible jar. He seemed to think he had me securely in his power. Two days before Covey could, with his slightest word, have made me tremble like a leaf in a storm, but no more. The fighting madness was upon me, and I found my strong fingers firmly attached to his throat, heedless of consequences. The color of the man was forgotten. I felt supple as a cat, ready for him at every turn. Every blow of his was parried, although I dealt no blows in return. I was determined to prevent him from injuring me. I flung him on the ground several times when he meant to have hurled me there. I held him so firmly by the throat that his blood followed my nails. He held me and I held him.

All was fair so far, and the contest was about equal. Covey was taken back by my unexpected resistance.

"Are you going to resist, you scoundrel?" said he.

"Yes, sir," I politely replied, steadily gazing him in the eye.

But the conflict did not long remain equal. Covey cried lustily for help, not because I was getting the best of him but because he was making no progress in getting the best of me. He called for his cousin, Bill Hughes, to come help him, and I saw the tide was about to turn against me. I was now compelled to give blows as well as ward them off. Since I expected to suffer anyway, because I was resisting, I felt that I might as well be hanged for an old sheep as a lamb. On his first approach, Hughes tried to catch and tie my right hand. I stopped him by giving him a kick which sent him staggering away in pain, all the while holding Covey with a firm hand.

Taken by surprise, Covey stood puffing for a moment, unable to deliver words or blows. When he saw Hughes half bent with pain he asked if I meant to continue to resist. I told him I did mean to resist, come what might. I said that I had been treated like a brute during the last six months and would stand it no longer. With that he gave me a shake and tried to drag me toward a stick of wood lying just outside the stable door. He meant to knock me down with it. Just as he leaned over to get the stick of wood, I seized him by the collar. With a vigorous and sudden snatch I threw him full length on the not over-clean ground of the cow yard. He picked the place for the fight, and I thought it was only right that he would enjoy its advantages, foul-smelling though those advantages might be.

By this time Bill, the hired man, came home. Covey and I had been fighting since before daybreak, and we were still at it. I could not see where the matter was to end. Covey called Bill to help him, and the scene became comical. Bill, who knew perfectly well what Covey wished him to do, pretended that he did not.

"What shall I do, Master Covey?" said Bill

"Take hold of him! Take hold of him!" cried Covey.

"Indeed, Master Covey, I want to go to work."

"This is your work," shouted Covey. "Take hold of him!"

"My master hired me here to work," Bill replied with spirit, "and not to help you whip Frederick."

It was my turn to speak. "Bill," said I, "don't put your hands on me."

"My God, Frederick," he whined. "I ain't goin' to tech ye," and he walked off, leaving Covey and myself to settle our differences as best we might.

My advantage was again threatened when I saw Caroline, the slave woman, coming to the cow yard to milk. She was a powerful woman and could overcome me easily, exhausted as I was.

As soon as she came near, Covey ordered her to help him. Strangely and fortunately, Caroline was in no humor to take a hand in any such sport. She answered Covey's command to take hold of me much as Bill had done. Caroline endangered herself more than Bill, however, for she was the slave of Covey and he could do what he pleased with her. It was not so with Bill, and Bill knew it. Samuel Harris, Bill's owner, did not allow his slaves to be beaten unless they were guilty of some crime which the law would punish. But poor Caroline, like myself, was at Covey's mercy. On this occasion, indeed, she did not escape the results of her refusal. Covey gave her several sharp blows.

At last, after two hours had gone by, Covey gave up. Letting go of me, puffing and blowing at a great rate, he said, "Now, you scoundrel, go to your work. I would not have whipped you half so hard if you had not resisted."

The fact was, he had not whipped me at all. I was the one who had drawn blood from him, not the other way around.

During the months I lived with Covey after this episode, he never again laid his finger on me in anger. Occasionally he would say he "did not want to have to get hold of me again," and I had no trouble believing this statement. I silently answered, "You had better not wished to get hold of me again because you will be likely to come off worse in a second fight than you did in the first."

This battle with Mr. Covey was the turning point in my life as a slave. I was a changed being after that fight. I was nothing before; I was a man now. It inspired me with a renewed determination to be a free man.

The reader may like to know why Mr. Covey did not turn me over to the authorities. I myself expected it. By the law of Maryland, at that time, a slave who resisted his master was sentenced to the gallows. The probable reason is that Covey was ashamed to have it known that he had lost a fight to a boy of sixteen. His reputation as a first-rate overseer and Negro-breaker enabled him to procure his farm hands cheaply and easily. His interest and his pride would both suggest the wisdom of silence.

I am not altogether proud to say that after this conflict I did, at times, purposely try to provoke him to attack me again by refusing to keep with the other hands in the field. But I could never bully him into another battle.

1892

Henry Timrod
1828–1867

It may at first seem odd that Henry Timrod, described by his contemporaries as at once "timid, reserved, unready if taken by surprise" and as someone who "shrank from noisy debate, and the wordy clash of argument," should serve as the poetic voice for the Confederacy during the Civil War. But to know the circumstances of Timrod's life is to recognize the connections between his career and the fate of the South during this nation's war with itself.

Henry Timrod was born in 1828 in Charleston, South Carolina, the son of a Scots-Irish bookbinder and a Swiss-English homemaker who imbued him with a love of nature. An ambitious, active, yet frail child, Henry Timrod attended Charleston's German Friendly Society School and later studied at the nearby Classical School of Christopher Cotes, where he developed a lifelong friendship with the writer Paul Hamilton Hayne.

In January 1845 Timrod entered the University of Georgia as a sophomore and diligently studied literature and the classics, only to withdraw a year later without taking a degree because of ill health and insufficient funds. But that year provided him with the opportunity to exercise his fledgling poetic talents. "A large part of my leisure at college was occupied in the composition of love verses, frantic or tender. Every pretty girl's face I met acted upon me like an inspiration!" Several of the wittiest of these poems were published in the

Charleston Evening News over the signature "T.W." From 1847 to 1849, while preparing himself for a university appointment teaching classics, Timrod worked in the law office of James L. Petigru, who judged him "too wholly a poet to keep company with so exacting a mistress as the law." During this period Timrod also began contributing to the *Southern Literary Messenger* under the psuedonym "Aglaus." With no professorship forthcoming, Timrod spent virtually the full decade of the 1850s working as a tutor on various plantations. During this period he returned as often as possible to Charleston to join the lively conversations of a small group of literary friends headed by the novelist William Gilmore Simms. From these "little suppers," as Timrod called them, came the impetus to found a new southern literary periodical, *Russell's Magazine* (1857–1860), in which Timrod published several literary essays and many of his best poems. In 1860 Ticknor and Fields, one of Boston's prestigious publishing houses, printed Timrod's small collection, *Poems,* which earned him favorable reviews in both the North and the South. But attention to the volume was quickly diverted by the rush of events leading to the Civil War.

Henry Timrod wrote movingly of both the impending hostilities and the outbreak of the war. His stirring series of war poems earned him an international audience and increasing acclaim; the popular press endorsed Alfred Lord Tennyson's suggestion that he be dubbed "the laureate of the South." Timrod spent the first year of the war in Charleston, tending to his poor health. In March 1862 he enlisted as a private in the Confederate Army and served as a clerk and then a war correspondent on the western front before being discharged that December because of ill health. Timrod reenlisted in July 1863, but a severe hemorrhage forced him to resign again, this time after a single day of service. Soon after, he worked as the assistant editor of the Charleston *Mercury,* leaving in January 1864 to become the associate editor of the Columbia *Daily South Carolinian.* He wrote most of that newspaper's editorials until the city was captured and burned by Union troops in February 1865. His livelihood destroyed, his infant son dead, his health weakened, Timrod summarized his misfortunes in a letter to his friend Hayne:

> I can embody it all in a few words: *beggary, starvation, death, bitter grief, utter want of hope....* We have lived for a long period, and are still living, on the proceeds of the gradual sale of furniture and plate.... I not only feel that I can write no more verse, but I am perfectly indifferent to the fate of what I have already composed. I would consign every line of it to eternal oblivion for—*one hundred dollars in hand.*

In the three remaining years of his life following the Civil War, Timrod struggled with his deteriorating health to work temporarily as a journalist, teacher, and part-time secretary to South Carolina governor J. L. Orr. Henry Timrod died on October 7, 1867, after yet another bout with tuberculosis, before seeing the bulk of his work in print. Paul Hamilton Hayne collected Timrod's poems and published them, along with a memoir, in 1873.

Despite the sickness, anguish, and violence that crowded his later years, Henry Timrod managed to write highly balanced and carefully controlled poetry.

These "classical" tendencies were nurtured by his wide reading among eighteenth-century English poets, but not at the expense of his fondness for those of the early nineteenth century, including Byron, Tennyson, Browning, and especially Wordsworth, whose influence is everywhere apparent in Timrod's poetry and literary criticism. His declamatory verse has remained most memorable. Its clear vision, vigorous imagery, irrepressible sincerity, and oratorical elegance expressed the collective hopes of the South during the Civil War and earned him the praise of his contemporaries as "the ablest poet the South has yet produced."

Further Reading:
G. P. Voigt, "New Light on Timrod's 'Memorial Ode,'" *American Literature,* January 1933.
J. B. Hubbell, *The Last Years of Henry Timrod,* 1941.
E. W. Parks, *Henry Timrod,* 1964.

Text:
Poems of Henry Timrod, 1899.
See also *The Uncollected Poems of Henry Timrod,* ed. G. A. Coldwell, Jr., 1942.

Charleston

Calm as that second summer which precedes
    The first fall of the snow,
In the broad sunlight of heroic deeds,
    The City bides the foe.

As yet, behind their ramparts stern and proud,   5
    Her bolted thunders sleep—
Dark Sumter, like a battlemented cloud,
    Looms o'er the solemn deep.

No Calpe[1] frowns from lofty cliff or scar
    To guard the holy strand;   10
But Moultrie[2] holds in leash her dogs of war
    Above the level sand.

And down the dunes a thousand guns lie couched,
    Unseen, beside the flood—
Like tigers in some Orient jungle crouched   15
    That wait and watch for blood.

[1] Gibraltar.
[2] Fort on Sullivan's Island named for General William Moultrie.

Meanwhile, through streets still echoing with trade,
    Walk grave and thoughtful men,
Whose hands may one day wield the patriot's blade
    As lightly as the pen.   20

And maidens, with such eyes as would grow dim
    Over a bleeding hound,
Seem each one to have caught the strength of him
    Whose sword she sadly bound.

Thus girt without and garrisoned at home,   25
    Day patient following day,
Old Charleston looks from roof, and spire, and dome,
    Across her tranquil bay.

Ships, through a hundred foes, from Saxon lands
    And spicy Indian ports,   30
Bring Saxon steel and iron to her hands,
    And Summer to her courts.

But still, along yon dim Atlantic line,
    The only hostile smoke
Creeps like a harmless mist above the brine,   35
    From some frail, floating oak.

Shall the Spring dawn, and she still clad in smiles,
    And with an unscathed brow,
Rest in the strong arms of her palm-crowned isles,
    As fair and free as now?   40

We know not; in the temple of the Fates
    God has inscribed her doom;
And, all untroubled in her faith, she waits
    The triumph or the tomb.

1862

Spring

            Spring, with that nameless pathos in the air
                Which dwells with all things fair,
            Spring, with her golden suns and silver rain,
                Is with us once again.

Out in the lonely woods the jasmine burns   5
Its fragrant lamps, and turns
Into a royal court with green festoons
The banks of dark lagoons.

In the deep heart of every forest tree
The blood is all aglee,   10
And there's a look about the leafless bowers
As if they dreamed of flowers.

Yet still on every side we trace the hand
Of Winter in the land,
Save where the maple reddens on the lawn,   15
Flushed by the season's dawn;

Or where, like those strange semblances we find
That age to childhood bind,
The elm puts on, as if in Nature's scorn,
The brown of Autumn corn.   20

As yet the turf is dark, although you know
That, not a span below,
A thousand germs are groping through the gloom,
And soon will burst their tomb.

Already, here and there, on frailest stems   25
Appear some azure gems,
Small as might deck, upon a gala day,
The forehead of a fay.

In gardens you may note amid the dearth
The crocus breaking earth;   30
And near the snowdrop's tender white and green,
The violet in its screen.

But many gleams and shadows need must pass
Along the budding grass,
And weeks go by, before the enamored South   35
Shall kiss the rose's mouth.

Still there's a sense of blossoms yet unborn
In the sweet airs of morn;
One almost looks to see the very street
Grow purple at his feet.   40

At times a fragrant breeze comes floating by,
And brings, you know not why,

A feeling as when eager crowds await
Before a palace gate

Some wondrous pageant; and you scarce would
    start,   45
If from a beech's heart,
A blue-eyed Dryad, stepping forth, should say,
"Behold me! I am May!"

Ah! who would couple thoughts of war and crime
With such a blessèd time!   50
Who in the west wind's aromatic breath
Could hear the call of Death!

Yet not more surely shall the Spring awake
The voice of wood and brake,
Than she shall rouse, for all her tranquil charms,   55
A million men to arms.

There shall be deeper hues upon her plains
Than all her sunlit rains,
And every gladdening influence around,
Can summon from the ground.   60

Oh! standing on this desecrated mould,
Methinks that I behold,
Lifting her bloody daisies up to God,
Spring kneeling on the sod,

And calling, with the voice of all her rills,   65
Upon the ancient hills
To fall and crush the tyrants and the slaves
Who turn her meads to graves.

1863

Ode

Sung on the occasion of decorating the graves of the
Confederate dead at Magnolia Cemetery, Charleston,
S. C., 1866

Sleep sweetly in your humble graves,
    Sleep, martyrs of a fallen cause!—
Though yet no marble column craves
    The pilgrim here to pause.

In seeds of laurels in the earth,   5
   The garlands of your fame are sown;
And, somewhere, waiting for its birth,
   The shaft is in the stone.

Meanwhile, your sisters for the years
   Which hold in trust your storied tombs,   10
Bring all they now can give you—tears,
   And these memorial blooms.

Small tributes, but your shades will smile
   As proudly on these wreaths to-day,
As when some cannon-moulded pile   15
   Shall overlook this Bay.

Stoop, angels, hither from the skies!
   There is no holier spot of ground,
Than where defeated valor lies
   By mourning beauty crowned.   20

1866

James Russell Lowell
1819–1891

The Lowells trace their New England heritage to 1639. Over the course of 350 years, this distinguished American family has produced an impressive number of eminent religious, political, business, and literary figures, including most recently the poets Amy and Robert Lowell. James Russell Lowell enhanced the reputation of this family, already renowned for its accomplishments and tradition. As a poet, critic, essayist, editor, linguist, teacher, reformer, and diplomat, he was was widely regarded as one of the most versatile and respected literary figures in America in the second half of the nineteenth century.

James Russell Lowell was born in 1819 at Elmwood, the family's large, pre-Revolutionary house prominently situated on a street called Tory Row near the Charles River in Cambridge. His background and education reflect what Oliver Wendell Holmes called the "Brahmin caste." His father maintained a large library, and Lowell very early developed a taste for literature, especially Spenser's *Faerie Queene* and the novels of Sir Walter Scott. In 1834 Lowell enrolled at Harvard, where, from at least an official point of view, he proved to be a rather weak student who habitually missed class and chapel exercises, preferring to immerse himself in classical, Renaissance, and modern literature—"nearly everything," he later noted, "except the books prescribed by the faculty." He also held two posts—secretary of the Hasty Pudding Club and editor of the college magazine—that afforded him the opportunity to publish his own writing. One measure of his success among this small audience was his election as class poet.

When Lowell graduated in 1838, he had not yet settled on a career. He had also experienced an unhappy love affair and for a considerable time lost the cheerfulness that characterized the rest of his life. "I remember in '39," he wrote some years later, "putting a cocked pistol to my forehead and being afraid to pull the trigger." With some misgivings, he studied law and obtained his degree in 1840. In that same year he became engaged to Maria White, the sister of a classmate. A poet herself, she was well educated and idealistic and introduced Lowell to "the Band," a group of young people committed to various humanitarian causes and social reforms. Lowell soon spoke out in favor of temperance and woman suffrage and became a strong, vocal, but not extreme, abolitionist. (He was not willing, for example, to see the Union dissolved in order to end slavery, as were such more ardent compatriots as William Lloyd Garrison and John Greenleaf Whittier.)

Lowell cultivated his interests in poetry and literary essays while practicing law. His first volume of verse, *A Year's Life* (1841), earned critical acclaim. Soon after, he abandoned his law practice to found and edit a literary magazine replete with Lowell's faith in the prospects for serious literature in America. Yet despite the best of intentions—and the contributions of Edgar Allan Poe, Hawthorne, and Whittier—Lowell could not keep *The Pioneer* in print beyond its first three issues. In 1843 he published *Poems,* which contained a great deal of topical verse on political and social issues and received uniformly favorable reviews. He and Maria White married in 1844, living in part by selling poems and essays to magazines and in part by writing blistering editorials for such abolitionist newspapers as the *Pennsylvania Freeman.* His literary essays and frequent contributions to antislavery periodicals brought him a good deal of attention. In 1845 he published a collection of critical essays, *Conversations on Some of the Old Poets,* before returning to Elmwood a celebrated author in 1846.

In that year Lowell published the first of *The Biglow Papers,* a newspaper series that eventually extended to nine numbers. The success of this satire depended as much on Lowell's literary skills as on his fierce opposition to the Mexican War, which he thought at least partially motivated by southern interests in extending the boundaries of slavery. Hosea Biglow's clever and amusing observations in these "letters" represent one of the earliest and most artful uses of local dialect and humor for satirical political purposes. An eager student of language, Lowell spoke of an American anxiety in the literature of the period to be formally correct, if not elegant, in the use of English. ("We use it," Lowell said, "not as if it belonged to us, but as if wished to prove that we belong to it.") In *The Biglow Papers,* from which "The Courtin' " is extracted, he attempted what he called a "Yankee pastoral," employing vernacular American speech for poetic ends.

The year 1848 was perhaps the most remarkable year in Lowell's literary career. He published what were to be his major works: *Poems: Second Series,* the collected two-volume edition of his verse; *The Vision of Sir Launfal,* a Christian allegory popular for many years in schools; the collected first series of *The Biglow Papers;* as well as his most famous work, *A Fable for Critics.* His *Fable* represents the best features of Lowell's writing throughout what became a long and highly respected career. Similar to his other light verse, *Fable* demonstrates his facility and wit in rhyming. And, similar to his later criticism and academic work, the poem is grounded in his thorough familiarity with works of classical and modern literature. Finally, similar to his criticism and even his later conduct as a diplomat, *Fable* expresses a supreme confidence in his own ability to evaluate the achievements and actions of others, to identify their strengths, and to expose their pretensions. Given its comic deflation of several distinguished American literary reputations, *A Fable for Critics* was also a rather bold poetic venture. Only a writer with Lowell's urbane wit, judicious taste, and quiet confidence could have carried it off as effectively as he did. Wisely, Lowell chose not to exempt himself from his own good-natured criticism; he presented himself in the poem as someone "Who's striving Parnassus to climb / With a whole bale of *isms* tied together with rhyme."

Lowell's lifelong success as a writer did not exempt him from misery. Between 1847 and 1853, his domestic life was ravaged by the deaths of three of his four children, his wife, and his mother. But after a trip to Europe he resumed his work, writing travel sketches and essays on his trip abroad as well as lecturing on the major English poets. In 1855 he was chosen to succeed Henry Wadsworth Longfellow as Smith Professor of Modern Languages and Literature at Harvard. Lowell prepared for this appointment by traveling for a year in Europe to strengthen his command of foreign languages and literature. Soon after his return, he married Frances Dunlap, the governess of his remaining child, and settled into sixteen years of what from all reports were dazzling lectures on literature at Harvard.

An eager conversationalist, Lowell became identified with several social groups, including the famous Saturday Club, that brought him into the company of the most distinguished writers in New England, including Ralph Waldo Emerson, Nathaniel Hawthorne, Henry Wadsworth Longfellow, John Greenleaf Whittier, Dr. Oliver Wendell Holmes, the geologist Louis Agassiz, and the historian William Hickling Prescott. (Henry David Thoreau is said to have refused to attend the Saturday Club because he could not tolerate their smoking at the meetings; Lowell would later criticize Thoreau as one who "watched Nature like a detective.") Lowell's prominence in Boston's most prestigious literary circles made him this group's choice for editor when they collectively launched the *Atlantic Monthly* in 1857. Lowell resigned this post after a few years, but in 1864 he took on the same responsibilities at the *North American Review.* But he had already helped set a standard for American literary journalism.

During the Civil War, Lowell promoted the northern cause through essays in the *Atlantic Monthly* and a second series of *Biglow Papers.* But his most celebrated writing about the Civil War was not composed until after it was over. In 1865 he was invited to contribute a poem to the memorial service held at Harvard for its graduates who were killed during the war, including three of Lowell's beloved nephews. The poem he read that day expresses his deep and unwavering belief in democratic principles and his opposition to slavery. His reputation as a poet and literary critic soon took on international dimensions; on a trip to England from 1872 to 1874 he was awarded honorary degrees from Oxford and Cambridge.

Various social and political issues—especially corruption in the civil service—continued to attract Lowell's attention in the decade after the Civil War. He attacked political bosses in print and wrote speeches for candidates who shared his zeal for reform. He also published two additional volumes of poetry, *Under the Willows* (1869) and *The Cathedral* (1869 but dated 1870), as well as two more collections of essays, *Among My Books* (1870) and *My Study Windows* (1871). In 1877 he was appointed ambassador to Spain (a post Washington Irving had also held), and in 1880 ambassador to England, where he lectured widely on American culture. "During my reign," Queen Victoria noted of Lowell, "no ambassador or minister has created so much interest or won so much regard." Returning to the United States in 1885, soon after the death of his second wife, Lowell spent his last years lecturing on literature and politics as well as collecting his essays and speeches for publication. He died at Elmwood on August 12, 1891.

A few years after Lowell's death, Henry James offered a judicious estimate of Lowell's importance in American literary history. Having reread his work, James noted: "He looms, in such a renewed impression, very large and ripe and sane. . . . He was strong without narrowness; he was wise without bitterness and bright without folly. That appears for the most part the clearest ideal of those who handle the English form, and he was altogether in the straight tradition."

Further Reading:
H. James, "James Russell Lowell," in *Essays in London and Elsewhere*, 1893.
W. D. Howells, "Studies of Lowell," in *Literary Friends and Acquaintances*, 1900.
H. E. Scudder, *James Russell Lowell: A Biography*, 2 vols., 1901.
F. Greenslet, *James Russell Lowell: His Life and Work*, 1905, 1969.
L. Howard, *Victorian Knight-Errant: A Study of the Early Literary Career of James Russell Lowell*, 1952.
M. Duberman, *James Russell Lowell*, 1966.
C. McGlinchee, *James Russell Lowell*, 1967.
E. Wagenknecht, *James Russell Lowell: A Portrait of a Many-Sided Man*, 1971.
C. David Heymann, *American Aristocracy: The Lives and Times of James Russell, Amy, & Robert Lowell*, 1980.

Text:
The Writings of James Russell Lowell, 10 vols., 1890.
See also *Letters of James Russell Lowell*, ed. C. E. Norton, 3 vols., 1894.
New Letters of James Russell Lowell, ed. M. A. D. Howe, 1932.
James Russell Lowell's The Biglow Papers, 1st series, ed. T. Wortham, 1977.

from A Fable for Critics

Reader! walk up at once (it will soon be too late),
and buy at a perfectly ruinous rate

A FABLE FOR CRITICS:

OR, BETTER,

(I LIKE, AS A THING THAT THE READER'S FIRST FANCY MAY STRIKE,

AN OLD-FASHIONED TITLE-PAGE,

SUCH AS PRESENTS A TABULAR VIEW OF THE VOLUME'S CONTENTS),

A GLANCE AT A FEW OF OUR LITERARY PROGENIES

(MRS. MALAPROP'S[1] WORD)

FROM THE TUB OF DIOGENES;[2]

A VOCAL AND MUSICAL MEDLEY,

THAT IS,

A SERIES OF JOKES

By A Wonderful Quiz,

WHO ACCOMPANIES HIMSELF WITH A RUB-A-DUB-DUB, FULL OF SPIRIT AND GRACE,
ON THE TOP OF THE TUB.

Set forth in October, the 31st day,
In the year '48, G. P. Putnam, Broadway.

It being the commonest mode of procedure, I premise a few candid remarks
To THE READER:—

This trifle, begun to please only myself and my own private fancy, was laid on
the shelf. But some friends, who had seen it, induced me, by dint of saying they liked

---

[1] Mrs. Malaprop, a character in Richard Brinsley
Sheridan's play *The Rivals* (1775), was noted
for her misuse of words.

[2] Greek philospher (412?–323 B.C.) who
purportedly lived in a tub and from there
criticized society.

it, to put it in print. That is, having come to that very conclusion, I asked their advice when 't would make no confusion. For though (in the gentlest of ways) they had hinted it was scarce worth the while, I should doubtless have printed it.

I began it, intending a Fable, a frail, slender thing, rhyme-ywinged, with a sting in its tail. But, by addings and alterings not previously planned, digressions chance-hatched, like birds' eggs in the sand, and dawdlings to suit every whimsey's demand (always freeing the bird which I held in my hand, for the two perched, perhaps out of reach, in the tree),—it grew by degrees to the size which you see. I was like the old woman that carried the calf, and my neighbors, like hers, no doubt, wonder and laugh; and when, my strained arms with their grown burthen full, I call it my Fable, they call it a bull.[3]

Having scrawled at full gallop (as far as that goes) in a style that is neither good verse nor bad prose, and being a person whom nobody knows, some people will say I am rather more free with my readers than it is becoming to be, that I seem to expect them to wait on my leisure in following wherever I wander at pleasure, that, in short, I take more than a young author's lawful ease, and laugh in a queer way so like Mephistopheles,[4] that the Public will doubt, as they grope through my rhythm, if in truth I am making fun *of* them or *with* them.

So the excellent Public is hereby assured that the sale of my book is already secured. For there is not a poet throughout the whole land but will purchase a copy or two out of hand, in the fond expectation of being amused in it, by seeing his betters cut up and abused in it. Now, I find, by a pretty exact calculation, there are something like ten thousand bards in the nation, of that special variety whom the Review and Magazine critics call *lofty* and *true,* and about thirty thousand (*this* tribe is increasing) of the kinds who are termed *full of promise* and *pleasing.* The Public will see by a glance at this schedule, that they cannot expect me to be over-sedulous about courting *them,* since it seems I have got enough fuel made sure of for boiling my pot.

As for such of our poets as find not their names mentioned once in my pages, with praises or blames, let them SEND IN THEIR CARDS, without further DELAY, to my friend G. P. PUTNAM, Esquire, in Broadway, where a LIST will be kept with the strictest regard to the day and the hour of receiving the card. Then, taking them up as I chance to have time (that is, if their names can be twisted in rhyme), I will honestly give each his PROPER POSITION, at the rate of ONE AUTHOR to each new EDITION. Thus a PREMIUM is offered sufficiently HIGH (as the magazines say when they tell their best lie) to induce bards to CLUB their resources and buy the balance of every edition, until they have all of them fairly been run through the mill.

One word to such readers (judicious and wise) as read books with something behind the mere eyes, of whom in the country, perhaps, there are two, including myself, gentle reader, and you. All the characters sketched in this slight *jeu d'esprit,*[5] though, it may be, they seem, here and there, rather free, and drawn from a somewhat too cynical standpoint, are *meant* to be faithful, for that is the grand point, and none but an owl would feel sore at a rub from a jester who tells you, without any subterfuge, that he sits in Diogenes' tub.

---

[3] Jest or linguistic blunder.
[4] One of the seven fallen archangels; Satan.

[5] French: "witty jest."

[from *Emerson*]

"There comes Emerson[6] first, whose rich words, every one,
Are like gold nails[7] in temples to hang trophies on,
Whose prose is grand verse, while his verse, the Lord knows,
Is some of it pr—— No, 't is not even prose;
I'm speaking of metres; some poems have welled   5
From those rare depths of soul that have ne'er been excelled;
They 're not epics, but that does n't matter a pin,
In creating, the only hard thing 's to begin;
A grass-blade 's no easier to make than an oak;
If you 've once found the way, you 've achieved the grand stroke;   10
In the worst of his poems are mines of rich matter,
But thrown in a heap with a crash and a clatter;
Now it is not one thing nor another alone
Makes a poem, but rather the general tone,
The something pervading, uniting the whole,   15
The before unconceived, unconceivable soul,
So that just in removing this trifle or that, you
Take away, as it were, a chief limb of the statue;
Roots, wood, bark, and leaves singly perfect may be,
But, clapt hodge-podge together, they don't make a tree.   20

"But, to come back to Emerson (whom, by the way,
I believe we left waiting),—his is, we may say,
A Greek head on right Yankee shoulders, whose range
Has Olympus for one pole, for t' other the Exchange;[8]
He seems, to my thinking (although I'm afraid   25
The comparison must, long ere this, have been made),
A Plotinus-Montaigne,[9] where the Egyptian's gold mist
And the Gascon's shrewd wit cheek-by-jowl coexist;
All admire, and yet scarcely six converts he's got
To I don't (nor they either) exactly know what;   30
For though he builds glorious temples, 't is odd
He leaves never a doorway to get in a god.
'T is refreshing to old-fashioned people like me
To meet such a primitive Pagan as he,
In whose mind all creation is duly respected   35
As parts of himself—just a little projected;
And who 's willing to worship the stars and the sun,
A convert to—nothing but Emerson.

[6] Ralph Waldo Emerson (1803–1882).
[7] Ecclesiastes 12:11: "The words of the wise are as goads, and as nails fastened by the masters of assemblies, which are given from one shepherd."
[8] Olympus: dwelling place of the Greek gods; Exchange: the stock exchange.

[9] Plotinus (205?–?270): Roman Neoplatonic philosopher born in Egypt; Michel de Montaigne (1533–1592): skeptical French essayist.

So perfect a balance there is in his head,
That he talks of things sometimes as if they were dead;   40
Life, nature, love, God, and affairs of that sort,
He looks at as merely ideas; in short,
As if they were fossils stuck round in a cabinet,
Of such vast extent that our earth's a mere dab in it;
Composed just as he is inclined to conjecture her,   45
Namely, one part pure earth, ninety-nine parts pure lecturer;
You are filled with delight at his clear demonstration,
Each figure, word, gesture, just fits the occasion,
With the quiet precision of science he 'll sort 'em,
But you can't help suspecting the whole a *post mortem*.   50

　"There are persons, mole-blind to the soul's make and style,
Who insist on a likeness 'twixt him and Carlyle;[10]
To compare him with Plato[11] would be vastly fairer,
Carlyle's the more burly, but E. is the rarer;
He sees fewer objects, but clearlier, truelier,   55
If C. 's as original, E. 's more peculiar;
That he 's more of a man you might say of the one,
Of the other he 's more of an Emerson;
C. 's the Titan,[12] as shaggy of mind as of limb,—
E. the clear-eyed Olympian, rapid and slim;   60
The one 's two thirds Norseman, the other half Greek,
Where the one 's most abounding, the other 's to seek;
C.'s generals require to be seen in the mass,—
E.'s specialties gain if enlarged by the glass;
C. gives nature and God his own fits of the blues,   65
And rims common-sense things with mystical hues,—
E. sits in a mystery calm and intense,
And looks coolly around him with sharp commonsense;
C. shows you how every-day matters unite
With the dim transdiurnal recesses of night,—   70
While E., in a plain, preternatural way,
Makes mysteries matters of mere every day;
C. draws all his characters quite *à la* Fuseli,[13]—
Not sketching their bundles of muscles and thews illy,
He paints with a brush so untamed and profuse,   75
They seem nothing but bundles of muscles and thews;
E. is rather like Flaxman,[14] lines strait and severe,
And a colorless outline, but full, round, and clear;—

---

[10] Thomas Carlyle (1795–1881), English essayist
and friend of Ralph Waldo Emerson.
[11] The Greek philosopher (427–347 B.C.).
[12] One of the primitive gods, the children of
heaven and earth, who were overthrown by the
Olympian gods.

[13] In the manner of Johann Heinrich Fuseli
(1741–1825), Swiss-born painter of extravagant,
distorted figures.
[14] John Flaxman (1755–1826), English sculptor and
illustrator, celebrated for his drawings of
Homer's and Dante's epics.

To the men he thinks worthy he frankly accords
The design of a white marble statue in words.   80
C. labors to get at the centre, and then
Take a reckoning from there of his actions and men;
E. calmly assumes the said centre as granted,
And, given himself, has whatever is wanted.

"He has imitators in scores, who omit   85
No part of the man but his wisdom and wit,—
Who go carefully o'er the sky-blue of his brain,
And when he has skimmed it once, skim it again;
If at all they resemble him, you may be sure it is
Because their shoals mirror his mists and obscurities,   90
As a mud-puddle seems deep as heaven for a minute,
While a cloud that floats o'er is reflected within it.

. . . .

1848

[from **Whittier**]

"There is Whittier,[15] whose swelling and vehement heart
Strains the strait-breasted drab of the Quaker apart,
And reveals the live Man, still supreme and erect,
Underneath the bemummying wrappers of sect;
There was ne'er a man born who had more of the swing   5
Of the true lyric bard and all that kind of thing;
And his failures arise (though he seem not to know it)
From the very same cause that has made him a poet,—
A fervor of mind which knows no separation
'Twixt simple excitement and pure inspiration,   10
As my Pythoness[16] erst sometimes erred from not knowing
If 't were I or mere wind through her tripod was blowing;
Let his mind once get head in its favorite direction
And the torrent of verse bursts the dams of reflection,
While, borne with the rush of the metre along,   15
The poet may chance to go right or go wrong,
Content with the whirl and delirium of song;
Then his grammar 's not always correct, nor his rhymes,
And he's prone to repeat his own lyrics sometimes,
Not his best, though, for those are struck off at white-heats   20
When the heart in his breast like a trip-hammer beats,

[15] John Greenleaf Whittier (1807–1892).
[16] Priestess of Apollo who delivered inspired
prophecies while seated on a tripod.

And can ne'er be repeated again any more
Than they could have been carefully plotted before:
Like old what's-his-name[17] there at the battle of Hastings
(Who, however, gave more than mere rhythmical bastings),   25
Our Quaker leads off metaphorical fights
For reform and whatever they call human rights,
Both singing and striking in front of the war,
And hitting his foes with the mallet of Thor;[18]
Anne haec, one exclaims, on beholding his knocks,   30
Vestis filii tui,[19] O leather-clad Fox?
Can that be thy son, in the battle's mid din,
Preaching brotherly love and then driving it in
To the brain of the tough old Goliath[20] of sin,
With the smoothest of pebbles from Castaly's spring[21]   35
Impressed on his hard moral sense with a sling?

   "All honor and praise to the right-hearted bard
Who was true to The Voice when such service was hard,
Who himself was so free he dared sing for the slave
When to look but a protest in silence was brave;   40
All honor and praise to the women and men
Who spoke out for the dumb and the down-trodden then!
It needs not to name them, already for each
I see History preparing the statue and niche;
They were harsh, but shall you be so shocked at hard words   45
Who have beaten your pruning-hooks up into swords,[22]
Whose rewards and hurrahs men are surer to gain
By the reaping of men and of women than grain?
Why should you stand aghast at their fierce wordy war, if
You scalp one another for Bank or for Tariff?[23]   50
Your calling them cut-throats and knaves all day long
Does n't prove that the use of hard language is wrong;
While the World's heart beats quicker to think of such men
As signed Tyranny's doom with a bloody steel-pen,
While on Fourth-of-Julys beardless orators fright one   55

---

[17] The minstrel Taillefer, who led the charge of
William the Conquerer's cavalry at the Battle
of Hastings (1066).
[18] Norse god of thunder.
[19] Latin translation of Genesis 37:32: "This we
have found: know now whether it be thy son's
coat or no." (Asked by Jacob's deceitful sons,
who show him a bloodied coat to suggest that
Joseph, his favorite son, is dead.) Fox: George
Fox (1624–1691), founder of the Quakers,
known for wearing leather breeches.

[20] The giant Goliath, slain by a rock from David's
slingshot. (See 1 Samuel 17.)
[21] Castaly's spring: tributary at the base of Mount
Parnassus from which poets drink for
inspiration.
[22] Allusion to mobilizing for the Mexican War.
[23] Two controversial issues of the time were the
creation of a national bank and whether to raise
or lower tariffs.

With hints at Harmodius and Aristogeiton,[24]
You need not look shy at your sisters and brothers
Who stab with sharp words for the freedom of others;—
No, a wreath, twine a wreath for the loyal and true
Who, for sake of the many, dared stand with the few,   6
Not of blood-spattered laurel for enemies braved,
But of broad, peaceful oak-leaves for citizens saved!

. . . .

1848

[from Hawthorne]

"There is Hawthorne,[25] with genius so shrinking and rare
That you hardly at first see the strength that is there;
A frame so robust, with a nature so sweet,
So earnest, so graceful, so lithe and so fleet,
Is worth a descent from Olympus to meet;   5
'Tis as if a rough oak that for ages had stood,
With his gnarled bony branches like ribs of the wood,
Should bloom, after cycles of struggle and scathe,
With a single anemone trembly and rathe;
His strength is so tender, his wildness so meek,   10
That a suitable parallel sets one to seek,—
He's a John Bunyan Fouqué, a Puritan Tieck;[26]
When Nature was shaping him, clay was not granted
For making so full-sized a man as she wanted,
So, to fill out her model, a little she spared   15
From some finer-grained stuff for a woman prepared,
And she could not have hit a more excellent plan
For making him fully and perfectly man.

. . . .

1848

[from Cooper]

"Here's Cooper,[27] who's written six volumes to show
He 's as good as a lord: well, let's grant that he's so;
If a person prefer that description of praise,
Why, a coronet 's certainly cheaper than bays;
But he need take no pains to convince us he 's not   5

[24] Greek assassins of the Athenian tyrant
Hipparchus in the sixth century B.C., regarded as
heroes after their execution.
[25] Nathaniel Hawthorne (1804–1864).
[26] I.e., Hawthorne is seen as both a Puritan and a
romantic: a combination of John Bunyan

(1628–1688), Puritan author of *The Pilgrim's
Progress* (1678); Friedrich Heinrich Karl La
Motte-Fouqué (1777–1843), German author of
the romantic *Undine* (1811); and Ludwig Tieck
(1773–1853), German romanticist.
[27] James Fenimore Cooper (1789–1851).

(As his enemies say) the American Scott.[28]
Choose any twelve men, and let C. read aloud
That one of his novels of which he's most proud,
And I 'd lay any bet that, without ever quitting
Their box,[29] they'd be all, to a man, for acquitting.   10
He has drawn you one character, though, that is new,
One wildflower he 's plucked that is wet with the dew
Of this fresh Western world, and, the thing not to mince,
He has done naught but copy it ill ever since;
His Indians, with proper respect be it said,   15
Are just Natty Bumppo,[30] daubed over with red,
And his very Long Toms[31] are the same useful Nat,
Rigged up in duck pants and a sou'wester hat
(Though once in a Coffin, a good chance was found
To have slipped the old fellow away underground).   20
All his other men-figures are clothes upon sticks,
The *dernière chemise*[32] of a man in a fix
(As a captain besieged, when his garrison 's small,
Sets up caps upon poles to be seen o'er the wall);
And the women he draws from one model don't vary,   25
All sappy as maples and flat as a prairie.
When a character 's wanted, he goes to the task
As a cooper would do in composing a cask;
He picks out the staves, of their qualities heedful,
Just hoops them together as tight as is needful,   30
And, if the best fortune should crown the attempt, he
Has made at the most something wooden and empty.

   "Don't suppose I would underrate Cooper's abilities;
If I thought you 'd do that, I should feel very ill at ease;
The men who have given to *one* character life   35
And objective existence are not very rife;
You may number them all, both prose-writers and singers,
Without overrunning the bounds of your fingers,
And Natty won't go to oblivion quicker
Than Adams the parson or Primrose the vicar.[33]   40

   "There is one thing in Cooper I like, too, and that is
That on manners he lectures his countrymen gratis;

---

[28] Sir Walter Scott (1771–1832), English novelist
after whom Cooper patterned some of his early
fiction.
[29] I.e., the jury box where jurors sit.
[30] Hero of Cooper's *Leather-Stocking Tales*.
[31] Long Tom Coffin, hero of Cooper's novel *The
Pilot* (1823).

[32] French: "last shirt."
[33] Adams: parson in Henry Fielding's *Joseph
Andrews* (1742); Primrose: Dr. Primrose in
Oliver Goldsmith's *The Vicar of Wakefield*
(1766).

Not precisely so either, because, for a rarity,
He is paid for his tickets in unpopularity.
Now he may overcharge his American pictures,   45
But you'll grant there 's a good deal of truth in his strictures;
And I honor the man who is willing to sink
Half his present repute for the freedom to think,
And, when he has thought, be his cause strong or weak,
Will risk t' other half for the freedom to speak,   50
Caring naught for what vengeance the mob has in store,
Let that mob be the upper ten thousand or lower.

"There are truths you Americans need to be told,
And it never 'll refute them to swagger and scold;
John Bull, looking o'er the Atlantic, in choler   55
At your aptness for trade, says you worship the dollar;
But to scorn such eye-dollar-try 's what very few do,
And John goes to that church as often as you do.
No matter what John says, don't try to outcrow him,
'T is enough to go quietly on and outgrow him;   60
Like most fathers, Bull hates to see Number One
Displacing himself in the mind of his son,
And detests the same faults in himself he 'd neglected
When he sees them again in his child's glass reflected;
To love one another you 're too like by half;   65
If he is a bull, you 're a pretty stout calf,
And tear your own pasture for naught but to show
What a nice pair of horns you 're beginning to grow.

"There are one or two things I should just like to hint,
For you don't often get the truth told you in print;   70
The most of you (this is what strikes all beholders)
Have a mental and physical stoop in the shoulders;
Though you ought to be free as the winds and the waves,
You 've the gait and the manners of runaway slaves;
Though you brag of your New World, you don't half believe in it; 75
And as much of the Old as is possible weave in it;
Your goddess of freedom, a tight, buxom girl,
With lips like a cherry and teeth like a pearl,
With eyes bold as Herë's,[34] and hair floating free,
And full of the sun as the spray of the sea,   80
Who can sing at a husking or romp at a shearing,
Who can trip through the forests alone without fearing,
Who can drive home the cows with a song through the grass,
Keeps glancing aside into Europe's cracked glass,

[34] Herë: Hera, Olympian goddess and wife of
Zeus.

Hides her red hands in gloves, pinches up her lithe waist,   85
And makes herself wretched with transmarine taste;
She loses her fresh country charm when she takes
Any mirror except her own rivers and lakes.

"You steal Englishmen's books[35] and think Englishmen's thought,
With their salt on her tail your wild eagle is caught;   90
Your literature suits its each whisper and motion
To what will be thought of it over the ocean;
The cast clothes of Europe your statesmanship tries
And mumbles again the old blarneys and lies;—
Forget Europe wholly, your veins throb with blood,   95
To which the dull current in hers is but mud;
Let her sneer, let her say your experiment fails,
In her voice there's a tremble e'en now while she rails,
And your shore will soon be in the nature of things
Covered thick with gilt drift-wood of castaway kings,   100
Where alone, as it were in a Longfellow's Waif,[36]
Her fugitive pieces will find themselves safe.
O my friends, thank your god, if you have one, that he
'Twixt the Old World and you set the gulf of a sea;
Be strong-backed, brown-handed, upright as your pines,   105
By the scale of a hemisphere shape your designs,
Be true to yourselves and this new nineteenth age,
As a statue by Powers, or a picture by Page,[37]
Plough, sail, forge, build, carve, paint, make all over new,
To your own New-World instincts contrive to be true,   110
Keep your ears open wide to the Future's first call,
Be whatever you will, but yourselves first of all,
Stand fronting the dawn on Toil's heaven-scaling peaks,
And become my new race of more practical Greeks.—   115
Hem! your likeness at present, I shudder to tell o't,
Is that you have your slaves, and the Greek had his helot."[38]

. . . .

1848

[from **Poe**]

"There comes Poe,[39] with his raven, like Barnaby Rudge,[40]
Three fifths of him genius and two fifths sheer fudge,

---

[35] Foreign authors could not copyright their
works in the United States at this time.
[36] Anthology of poetry published by Henry
Wadsworth Longfellow in 1845.
[37] Powers: Hiram Powers (1805–1873), sculptor of
such political figures as Calhoun and Jackson;
Page: William Page (1811–1885), painter of
American historical scenes.

[38] Spartan serf who, unlike the American slave,
could not be sold and could be freed by the
state.
[39] Edgar Allan Poe (1809–1849).
[40] Central character in Charles Dickens's novel
Barnaby Rudge (1841); Rudge owned a raven.

Who talks like a book of iambs and pentameters,
In a way to make people of common sense damn metres,
Who has written some things quite the best of their kind,   5
But the heart somehow seems all squeezed out by the mind.
Who—But hey-day! What's this? Messieurs Mathews[41] and Poe,
You must n't fling mud-balls at Longfellow so,
Does it make a man worse that his character 's such
As to make his friends love him (as you think) too much?   10
Why, there is not a bard at this moment alive
More willing than he that his fellows should thrive;
While you are abusing him thus, even now
He would help either one of you out of a slough;
You may say that he 's smooth and all that till you 're hoarse,   15
But remember that elegance also is force;
After polishing granite as much as you will,
The heart keeps its tough old persistency still;
Deduct all you can, *that* still keeps you at bay;
Why, he 'll live till men weary of Collins and Gray.[42]   20
I 'm not over-fond of Greek metres in English,[43]
To me rhyme's a gain, so it be not too jinglish,
And your modern hexameter verses are no more
Like Greek ones than sleek Mr. Pope is like Homer;[44]
As the roar of the sea to the coo of a pigeon is,   25
So, compared to your moderns, sounds old Melesigenes;
I may be too partial, the reason, perhaps, o't is
That I've heard the old blind man recite his own rhapsodies,
And my ear with that music impregnate may be,
Like the poor exiled shell with the soul of the sea,   30
Or as one can't bear Strauss when his nature is cloven
To its deeps within deeps by the stroke of Beethoven;[45]
But, set that aside, and 't is truth that I speak,
Had Theocritus[46] written in English, not Greek,
I believe that his exquisite sense would scarce change a line   35
In that rare, tender, virgin-like pastoral Evangeline.
That's not ancient nor modern, its place is apart
Where time has no sway, in the realm of pure Art,

---

[41] Cornelius Mathews (1817–1889), editor, novelist, and magazine writer who joined Poe in criticizing Longfellow's work.

[42] Collins: William Collins (1721–1759), English author of odes and elegies; Gray: Thomas Gray (1716–1771), English author of "Elegy Written in a Country Churchyard" (1751).

[43] Longfellow adapted the hexameter of Greek epic poetry in his *Evangeline, A Tale of Arcadie* (1847).

[44] Alexander Pope (1688–1744) translated Homer's *Iliad* and *Odyssey* into English heroic couplets. "Old Melesigenes," the "old blind man" below, is Homer, who was supposedly born in Melos.

[45] Strauss: Johann Strauss (1804–1849), Austrian composer famous for his waltzes; Beethoven: Ludwig van Beethoven (1770–1827), German composer.

[46] Greek pastoral poet of the third century B.C.

'Tis a shrine of retreat from Earth's hubbub and strife
As quiet and chaste as the author's own life.   40

. . . .

1848

[from **Irving**]

"What! Irving? thrice welcome, warm heart and fine brain,
You bring back the happiest spirit from Spain,[47]
And the gravest sweet humor, that ever were there
Since Cervantes[48] met death in his gentle despair;
Nay, don't be embarrassed, nor look so beseeching.   5
I sha'n't run directly against my own preaching,
And, having just laughed at their Raphaels and Dantes,
Go to setting you up beside matchless Cervantes;
But allow me to speak what I honestly feel,—
To a true poet-heart add the fun of Dick Steele,[49]   10
Throw in all of Addison, *minus* the chill,
With the whole of that partnership's stock and good-will,
Mix well, and while stirring, hum o'er, as a spell,
The fine *old* English Gentleman,[50] simmer it well,
Sweeten just to your own private liking, then strain,   15
That only the finest and clearest remain,
Let it stand out of doors till a soul it receives
From the warm lazy sun loitering down through green leaves,
And you 'll find a choice nature, not wholly deserving
A name either English or Yankee,—just Irving.   20

. . . .

1848

[from **Lowell**]

"There is Lowell, who's striving Parnassus to climb
With a whole bale of *isms* tied together with rhyme,
He might get on alone, spite of brambles and boulders,
But he can't with that bundle he has on his shoulders,
The top of the hill he will ne'er come nigh reaching   5
Till he learns the distinction 'twixt singing and preaching;
His lyre has some chords that would ring pretty well,

[47] Washington Irving (1783–1859) had served as minister to Spain in the early 1840s. He also had written a history of Granada (1829) and *The Legend of the Alhambra* (1832).
[48] Miguel de Cervantes Saavedra (1547–1616), author of *Don Quixote* (1605; 1615).

[49] Richard Steele (1672–1729). English essayist; collaborator with Joseph Addison (1672–1719) on the periodical *The Spectator*.
[50] Allusion to "The English Country Gentleman," an essay in Irving's *Bracebridge Hall* (1822).

But he 'd rather by half make a drum of the shell,
And rattle away till he 's old as Methusalem,[51]
At the head of a march to the last new Jerusalem.

. . . .

1848

---

from The Biglow Papers, Second Series

from **Introduction**

THE COURTIN'[*]

God makes sech nights, all white an' still
    Fur 'z you can look or listen,
Moonshine an' snow on field an' hill,
    All silence an' all glisten.

Zekle crep' up quite unbeknown   5
    An' peeked in thru' the winder,
An' there sot Huldy all alone,
    'ith no one nigh to hender.

A fireplace filled the room's one side
    With half a cord o' wood in—   10
There warn't no stoves (tell comfort died)
    To bake ye to a puddin'.

The wa'nut logs shot sparkles out
    Towards the pootiest, bless her,

---

[51] Methuselah is said to have lived 969 years. (See Genesis 5:27.)

[*] A brief version of 44 lines of the poem appeared in *The Biglow Papers, First Series* (1848). In the introduction to the *Second Series,* Lowell explains why and how he expanded it: "The only attempt I had ever made at anything like a pastoral (if that may be called an attempt which was the result almost of pure accident) was in 'The Courtin.'' While the Introduction to the First Series was going through the press, I received word from the printer that there was a blank page left which must be filled. I sat down at once and improvised another fictitious 'notice of the press,' in which, because verse would fill up space more cheaply than prose, I inserted an extract from a supposed ballad of Mr. Biglow. I kept no copy of it, and the printer, as directed, cut it off when the gap was filled. Presently I began to receive letters asking for the rest of it, sometimes for the *balance* of it. I had none, but to answer such demands, I patched a conclusion upon it in a later edition. Those who had only the first continued to importune me. Afterward, being asked to write it out as an autograph for the Baltimore Sanitary Commission Fair, I added other verses, into some of which I infused a little more sentiment in a homely way, and after a fashion completed it by sketching in the characters and making a connected story. Most likely I have spoiled it, but I shall put it at the end of this Introduction to answer once for all those kindly importunings."

An' leetle flames danced all about   15
    The chiny on the dresser.

Agin the chimbley crook-necks[1] hung,
    An' in amongst 'em rusted
The ole queen's-arm[2] thet gran'ther Young
    Fetched back f'om Concord busted.   20

The very room, coz she was in,
    Seemed warm f'om floor to ceilin',
An' she looked full ez rosy agin
    Ez the apples she was peelin'.

'T was kin' o' kingdom-come to look   25
    On sech a blessed cretur,
A dogrose blushin' to a brook
    Ain't modester nor sweeter.

He was six foot o' man, A 1,
    Clear grit an' human natur',   30
None could n't quicker pitch a ton
    Nor dror a furrer straighter.

He 'd sparked it with full twenty gals,
    Hed squired 'em, danced 'em, druv 'em,
Fust this one, an' then thet, by spells—   35
    All is, he could n't love 'em.

But long o' her his veins 'ould run
    All crinkly like curled maple,
The side she breshed felt full o' sun
    Ez a south slope in Ap'il.   40

She thought no v'ice hed sech a swing
    Ez hisn in the choir;
My! when he made Ole Hunderd[3] ring,
    She *knowed* the Lord was nigher.

An' she 'd blush scarlit, right in prayer,   45
    When her new meetin'-bunnet
Felt somehow thru' its crown a pair
    O' blue eyes sot upun it.

Thet night, I tell ye, she looked *some!*
    She seemed to 've gut a new soul,   50

[1] Gourds.
[2] Revolutionary War musket.
[3] I.e., Psalm 100. A psalm.

For she felt sartin-sure he 'd come,
  Down to her very shoe-sole.

She heered a foot, an' knowed it tu,
  A-raspin' on the scraper,—
All ways to once her feelins flew   55
  Like sparks in burnt-up paper.

He kin' o' l'itered on the mat,
  Some doubtfle o' the sekle,[4]
His heart kep' goin' pity-pat,
  But hern went pity Zekle.   60

An' yit she gin her cheer a jerk
  Ez though she wished him furder,
An' on her apples kep' to work,
  Parin' away like murder.

"You want to see my Pa, I s'pose?"   65
  "Wal . . . no . . . I come dasignin' "
"To see my Ma? She 's sprinklin' clo'es
  Agin to-morrer's i'nin'."

To say why gals acts so or so,
  Or don't, 'ould be presumin';   70
Mebby to mean *yes* an' say *no*
  Comes nateral to women.

He stood a spell on one foot fust,
  Then stood a spell on t' other,
An' on which one he felt the wust   75
  He could n't ha' told ye nuther.

Says he, "I'd better call agin";
  Says she, "Think likely, Mister":
Thet last word pricked him like a pin,
  An' . . . Wal, he up an' kist her.   80

When Ma bimeby upon 'em slips,
  Huldy sot pale ez ashes,
All kin' o' smily roun' the lips
  An' teary roun' the lashes.

For she was jes' the quiet kind   85
  Whose naturs never vary,
Like streams that keep a summer mind
  Snowhid in Jenooary.

---

[4] Sequel.

> The blood clost roun' her heart felt glued
>   Too tight for all expressin',   90
> Tell mother see how metters stood,
>   An' gin 'em both her blessin'.
>
> Then her red come back like the tide
>   Down to the Bay o' Fundy,
> An' all I know is they was cried   95
>   In meetin' come nex' Sunday.⁵

1848/1867

Abraham Lincoln
1809–1865

Abraham Lincoln came to the presidency from a successful law practice and exercised unprecedented executive authority during a civil war far bloodier and longer than anyone had foreseen. Midway through the war, Whitman described Lincoln:

> He has a face like a hoosier Michael Angelo, so awful ugly it becomes beautiful, with its strange mouth, its deep cut, cris-cross lines, and its doughnut complexion. . . . He has shown, I sometimes think, an almost supernatural tack in keeping the ship afloat at all, with head steady, not only not going down, and now certain not to, but with proud and resolute spirit, and flag flying in sight of the world, menacing and high as ever.

Lincoln's "idiomatic western genius," as Whitman called it, was above all conspicuous in his spoken and written prose, a supple middle style that was lofty and colloquial, beautiful and homely, and always got to the point. Lincoln's prose showed that the basic forms of American humor, including the tall tale and the anecdote, were appropriate in statecraft as well as literature. For the thirty-year-old Mark Twain, Lincoln's "With malice toward none" address proved that simplicity was one of the secrets of eloquence.

Only Andrew Jackson among the presidents was as true a child of the frontier as Lincoln, though many others claimed birth in a log cabin. Born in a clearing in Hardin County, Kentucky, to illiterate parents, Lincoln had a harsh father and a loving mother whom he lost when he was nine. Largely self-educated, Lincoln was deeply read in the few books he could find, including the Bible and Shakespeare, two major sources he drew on in preparing his public addresses.

It was Lincoln's destiny to lead the disunited states through the fire of a civil war that established the Union as we know it. His addresses have passed beyond literature into the heritage, character, and soul of the nation. The style was the

---

⁵ I.e., the wedding was announced in church the following Sunday.

man, a powerful genius of a politician joined to the mystical sensitivity of a poet.

Further Reading:
C. B. Strozier, *Lincoln's Quest for Union*, 1982.
S. B. Oates, *Abraham Lincoln: The Man Behind the Myths*, 1984.
G. Vidal, *Lincoln*, 1984.

Text:
R. P. Basler et al., *The Collected Works of Abraham Lincoln*, 9 vols., 1953.

Address Delivered at the Dedication of the Cemetery at Gettysburg*

November 19, 1863

Four score and seven years ago our fathers brought forth on this continent, a new nation, conceived in Liberty, and dedicated to the proposition that all men are created equal.

Now we are engaged in a great civil war, testing whether that nation, or any nation so conceived and so dedicated, can long endure. We are met on a great battle-field of that war. We have come to dedicate a portion of that field, as a final resting place for those who here gave their lives that that nation might live. It is altogether fitting and proper that we should do this.

But, in a larger sense, we can not dedicate—we can not consecrate—we can not hallow—this ground. The brave men, living and dead, who struggled here, have consecrated it, far above our poor power to add or detract. The world will little note, nor long remember what we say here, but it can never forget what they did here. It is for us the living, rather, to be dedicated here to the unfinished work which they who fought here have thus far so nobly advanced. It is rather for us to be here dedicated to the great task remaining before us—that from these honored dead we take increased devotion to that cause for which they gave the last full measure of devotion—that we here highly resolve that these dead shall not have died in vain—that this nation, under God, shall have a new birth of freedom—and that government of the people, by the people, for the people, shall not perish from the earth.

Abraham Lincoln.

November 19, 1863.

1863

---

* Only four months before Lincoln's address, Robert E. Lee, with 70,000 Southern troops, had engaged George Gordon Meade, with an army of 90,000, in a three-day battle resulting in over 6,000 deaths and many thousands of injuries. (Meade, to Lincoln's private disgust, failed to pursue the retreating Lee, who led his army safely back to Virginia.) The Union dead were buried on Cemetery Hill, where Lincoln spoke. Lee's defeat at Gettysburg, Pennsylvania, coming on the same day Ulysses Grant took Vicksburg, 1,000 miles to the southwest (and thus cutting the Confederacy in two), spelled the end of the South's realistic chances for world recognition as an independent country, ensured the preservation of the Union, and guaranteed the final abolition of slavery. These prospects notwithstanding, the war was to continue for nearly another two years.

Second Inaugural Address*

March 4, 1865

At this second appearing to take the oath of the presidential office, there is less occasion for an extended address than there was at the first. Then a statement, somewhat in detail, of a course to be pursued, seemed fitting and proper. Now, at the expiration of four years, during which public declarations have been constantly called forth on every point and phase of the great contest which still absorbs the attention, and engrosses the energies of the nation, little that is new could be presented. The progress of our arms, upon which all else chiefly depends, is as well known to the public as to myself; and it is, I trust, reasonably satisfactory and encouraging to all. With high hope for the future, no prediction in regard to it is ventured.

On the occasion corresponding to this four years ago, all thoughts were anxiously directed to an impending civil war. All dreaded it—all sought to avert it. While the inaugural address was being delivered from this place, devoted altogether to *saving* the Union without war, insurgent agents were in the city seeking to *destroy* it without war—seeking to dissolve the Union, and divide effects, by negotiation. Both parties deprecated war; but one of them would *make* war rather than let the nation survive; and the other would *accept* war rather than let it perish. And the war came.

One eighth of the whole population were colored slaves, not distributed generally over the Union, but localized in the Southern part of it. These slaves constituted a peculiar and powerful interest. All knew that this interest was, somehow, the cause of the war. To strengthen, perpetuate, and extend this interest was the object for which the insurgents would rend the Union, even by war; while the government claimed no right to do more than to restrict the territorial enlargement of it. Neither party expected for the war, the magnitude, or the duration, which it has already attained. Neither anticipated that the *cause* of the conflict might cease with, or even before, the conflict itself should cease. Each looked for an easier triumph, and a result less fundamental and astounding. Both read the same Bible, and pray to the same God and each invokes His aid against the other. It may seem strange that any men should dare to ask a just God's assistance in wringing their bread from the sweat of other men's faces; but let us judge not that we be not judged. The prayers of both could not be answered; that of neither has been answered fully. The Almighty has his own purposes. "Woe unto the world because of offences! for it must needs be that offences come; but woe to that man by whom the offence cometh!"[1] If we shall suppose that American Slavery is one of those offences which, in the providence of God, must needs come, but which, having continued through His appointed time, He now wills to remove, and that He gives to both North and South, this terrible war, as the woe due to those by whom the offence came, shall we discern therein any departure from those

---

* Delivered a month before the Union victories at Petersburg and Richmond (Virginia) and 35 days before the decisive surrender of General Robert E. Lee to the Union commander, Ulysses S. Grant, at Appomattox. On April 14, only weeks before the war ended, Lincoln was fatally shot; he died the following day. In its reason and compassion the Second Inaugural Address is considered to rank in world literature with Pericles' funeral oration to the Athenians.

[1] Matthew 18:7.

divine attributes which the believers in a Living God always ascribe to Him? Fondly do we hope—fervently do we pray—that this mighty scourge of war may speedily pass away. Yet, if God wills that it continue, until all the wealth piled by the bond-man's two hundred and fifty years of unrequited toil shall be sunk, and until every drop of blood drawn with the lash, shall be paid by another drawn with the sword, as was said three thousand years ago, so still it must be said "the judgments of the Lord, are true and righteous altogether."[2]

With malice toward none; with charity for all; with firmness in the right, as God gives us to see the right, let us strive on to finish the work we are in; to bind up the nation's wounds; to care for him who shall have borne the battle, and for his widow, and his orphan—to do all which may achieve and cherish a just and lasting peace, among ourselves, and with all nations.

1865

Walt Whitman
1819–1892

Whitman is the great bridge figure of nineteenth-century American literature. He links the era of Hawthorne and Thoreau to that of Mark Twain and Henry James. He fulfilled the promise of romanticism while pointing to the open road of modernist form, vision, and experiment. His powerful, imperial presence continues to assert itself in the work of Wallace Stevens, William Carlos Williams, Ezra Pound, Hart Crane, and the generation of Allen Ginsberg. Whitman once said that his leading trait was caution and that there was "something in my nature *furtive* like an old hen." Still, he worshiped boldness, contradiction, and change, shocked contemporaries with his candor about sexuality, and created a radical poetry voicing a radical consciousness: "For I confront peace, security, and all the settled laws, to unsettle them." He was the most ardent of nationalists and said that his book "could not possibly have emerged or been fashion'd or completed, from any other era than the latter half of the Nineteenth Century, nor from any other land than democratic America." Yet he was also America's chief poet of international standing, with followers in the British Isles, Europe, and Scandinavia. Today his work is read in Chinese, Japanese, Russian, and every other major tongue.

When Whitman was born in 1819, in a farmhouse on eastern Long Island, New York, the United States was rural and relatively isolated. The President, James Monroe, had fought in the Revolution and still wore knee breeches. When Whitman died in 1892, in a working-class neighborhood of Camden, New Jersey, a corporation lawyer, Benjamin Harrison, occupied the White House and the United States was a world power.

During the poet's early years, the Whitmans, descendants of early Dutch and English settlers, fell on hard times and moved from the country districts to

---

[2] Psalms 19:9.

Brooklyn, then a thriving, independent city. They were in psychic as well as economic disarray. A failure at farming and business, Walter Whitman, Sr., was "addicted to alcohol," according to his son, and frequently depressed. Of his eight children who survived infancy, four were disturbed or incompetent, but one went on to celebrate "physiology from top to toe . . . Life immense in passion, pulse, and power."

Walt Whitman's dependent childhood, along with all the formal schooling he was ever to have, came to an end when he was about twelve. Like Benjamin Franklin, Mark Twain, and William Dean Howells, he learned the printing trade and in the printing office, the poor-boy's college for many Americans, began to acquire a miscellaneous literary and intellectual culture. He worked in Brooklyn and New York and on Long Island as a typesetter, schoolteacher, newspaper editor, free-lance journalist, storekeeper, and housebuilder. During the 1840s he published a novel, *Franklin Evans,* about the evils of drink, at least sixteen conventional poems, and about two dozen stories and sketches, most of them imitative or hackwork, that nevertheless anticipate many of the themes and images of his mature work.

The poet, Whitman was to say, "must flood himself with the immediate age as with vast oceanic tides." He absorbed the Emersonian gospel of self-trust and the infinitude of the private man; oratory; the writings of George Sand and Thomas Carlyle; science, art, and philosophy; the Free-Soil movement; the vibrant life of Broadway and "million-footed Manhattan." He studied linguistics and the American vernacular, believing that "a perfect writer would make words sing, dance, kiss, do the male and female act, bear children . . . or do any thing that man or woman or the natural powers can do." Whitman's discovery of grand opera, which was then enjoying its first vogue in the United States, released his emotions, suggested poetic equivalents for recitative and aria, and helped free him from conventional forms and meters. Although he may have reasoned his way to the right conclusions by using the wrong data, phrenology and other pseudosciences and improving regimens revealed a creative potential within himself that he believed was as large as the American continent. He saw the continent itself and democratic vistas of city and wilderness in a five-thousand-mile journey he took in 1848 from New York to New Orleans and back. Egyptology and Eastern wisdom-writing opened up other vistas of time and space.

"I was simmering, simmering, simmering." In his early thirties Whitman at last found a supreme purpose, to be "a master after my own kind, making the poems of emotions, as they pass or stay, the poems of freedom, and the exposé of personality—singing in high tones democracy and the New World of it through These States." He intended *Leaves of Grass* to be nothing less than a "new Bible" for the new age of democracy and science. A pre-1855 verse fragment suggests the inner drama of Whitman's transformation: "I cannot be awake, for nothing looks to me as it did before, / Or else I am awake for the first time, and all before has been a mean sleep."

In July 1855, "after many MS. doings and undoings—(I had great trouble in leaving out the stock 'poetical' touches—but succeeded at last)," Whitman issued the first edition of *Leaves of Grass.* A slim volume, with its title stamped on the

Leaves

of

Grass.

Brooklyn, New York:
1855.

Photograph courtesy of the Library of Congress

cloth cover in tendriled letters, Whitman's ninety-six-page book opened with an uncaptioned frontispiece portrait of a bearded man wearing a broad-brimmed hat and an open-necked shirt. The facing title page did not give the author's name. An eccentrically punctuated prose preface, the most decisive of Whitman's critical manifestos, introduced twelve as yet untitled poems, at first glance clusters of prose sentences set up like Bible verses. Not until page twenty-nine did the author declare his identity: "Walt Whitman, An American, one of the roughs, a kosmos, / Disorderly, fleshy and sensual."

Leaves of Grass came into a largely indifferent world in 1855 not as a trial venture, not as a greatly "promising" book, but as a stylistically and substantively achieved masterpiece. "I find it the most extraordinary piece of wit and wisdom that America has yet contributed," Emerson wrote to the new poet. "I give you joy of your free and brave thought. I have great joy in it. I find incomparable things said incomparably well, as they must be. I find the courage of treatment which so delights us, and which large perception only can inspire. I greet you at the beginning of a great career, which yet must have had a long foreground somewhere, for such a start." Emerson's celebrated letter remains unequaled for the generosity, force, and simple justice of its understanding.

Leaves of Grass changed and grew over the next four decades. Whitman wished to endow it with the scope and structure of something monumental, a great tree with many growth rings, a cathedral, a modern city like his million-footed Manhattan. His second edition (1856) added twenty new poems, among them "Crossing Brooklyn Ferry"; his third (1860) added 146, including "Out of the Cradle Endlessly Rocking" and two cycles, or "clusters," "Calamus" (treating "manly love," or "the love of comrades") and "Children of Adam" (treating heterosexual love); his fourth (1867) added the Civil War cycle "Drum-Taps" and the majestic poem of mourning for Abraham Lincoln, "When Lilacs Last in the Dooryard Bloom'd." By the time Whitman issued his final ("deathbed" edition of 1891–1892, the original ninety-six printed pages of 1855 had grown to 438. After the late 1850s, a markedly tragic element tempered his early, lyric celebrations. Still later, his diction, once assertively American and vernacular, tended to become somewhat denatured, even transatlantic, and he vacillated between a poetry of precise observation and a poetry of ideas and large declarations.

"The proof of a poet," Whitman declared in his preface, "is that his country absorbs him as affectionately as he has absorbed it." Years later he was to concede, "I have not gain'd the acceptance of my time." While he lived, his most fervent readers as a group turned out to be not the working-class American men and women—the democratic leaven—he had hoped to reach but another class altogether, even another nationality: highly cultivated foreign writers and intellectuals like William Michael Rossetti, Oscar Wilde, Algernon Charles Swinburne, Robert Louis Stevenson, Gerard Manley Hopkins, poet laureate Alfred Tennyson, John Addington Symonds, and Professor Edward Dowden of Trinity College, Dublin. One English admirer, Anne Gilchrist, wrote an important appreciation, fell in love with Whitman, and came to America with the hope of marrying him. But aside from his attachments to semiliterate younger men, it was Whitman's book that remained his sole heart's companion, the center of his life. He was willing to go to any length to preserve, protect, and defend it.

Whitman's effective exploitation of Emerson's private letter (he circulated it without permission and used it as promotional material) distressed the Concord sage and his friends. But this episode only marked the beginning of Whitman's unremitting campaign to assure *Leaves of Grass* a breathing space in the world. Like Mark Twain a brilliant publicist, he reviewed his own book on several occasions, planted newspaper stories about his doings and whereabouts, interviewed himself, collaborated with the authors of biographies, polemics, and encomiums, and eagerly sat for hundreds of photographs and portraits that called attention to his trademark flowing beard and open-necked shirts. One unsigned article by Whitman, published in a Camden paper in 1876, touched off a noisy Anglo-American controversy over the extent to which he was allegedly neglected by his compatriots.

For a few years after 1855, Whitman made a living as a newspaper editor and free-lance journalist. During the Civil War, having vowed to live a "purged" and "cleansed" life, he turned his back on New York's literary and artistic bohemia and moved to beleaguered Washington. There, supporting himself by part-time clerking in the army paymaster's office, he served as volunteer nurse and comforter—"wound-dresser"—in the military hospitals. This caring for the sick, wounded, and dying may have been the most intense emotional experience of his middle and later years. In 1865 he was appointed to a full-time government clerkship, a job that paid him about $1,600 a year until 1874. By then he was an invalid, having suffered a paralytic stroke the year before, and had moved, permanently, from Washington to Camden. With the major exceptions of trips to Colorado and Canada in 1879 and 1880, he spent the rest of his life in Camden, first as a paying guest in his brother's house and finally as the owner of 328 Mickle Street, "a little old shanty of my own" that he bought for $1,750. Whitman managed to live in frugal comfort, and even build an imposing tomb, on money derived from royalties, direct sales of books, fees and honoraria, and gifts from admirers. His average annual income from 1876 to 1892 was $1,270. During those years, as for most of his career, he mainly isolated himself from professional literary people in New York, Philadelphia, and Boston, preferring the company of the small band of disciples that had formed around him and celebrated his birthdays with eucharistic feasts.

An important prose writer as well as a poet, Whitman published *Democratic Vistas* (1871), a searching essay on American society and ideals, and *Specimen Days* (1882), a loosely structured autobiography focusing on the Civil War period. His history after 1855, however, is largely the history of *Leaves of Grass* in its successive editions and collisions with guardians of public taste and morals. Despite Emerson's endorsement, early reviewers called Whitman's poetry "a mass of stupid filth" and its author a pig rooting "among a rotten garbage of licentious thoughts." In 1865 the secretary of the Interior fired Whitman from his clerkship on the grounds that *Leaves of Grass* violated "the rules of decorum and propriety prescribed by a Christian Civilization." Whitman was quickly transferred to an equivalent post in the attorney general's office, but in the hands of supporters like William Douglas O'Connor, Whitman's dismissal became a cause célèbre and served an important purpose in his developing reputation: No longer "one of the roughs," he was now, in O'Connor's words, "The Good Gray Poet," sage, martyr, and redeemer. Fifteen years later a district attorney in Boston found *Leaves of Grass* actionable under "the Public Statutes respecting obscene literature" and in effect forced Whitman's publishers there to withdraw the book. *Leaves of Grass* moved to Philadelphia for its final editions. Such "bruises" and "buffetings" did not discourage its author. Whitman believed that his book was "a candidate for the future" and that its value would be "decided by time."

Further Reading:

H. Traubel, *With Walt Whitman in Camden*, 6 vols., 1906–1982.
N. Arvin, *Whitman*, 1938.
H. S. Canby, *Walt Whitman, An American*, 1943.
R. D. Faner, *Walt Whitman and Opera*, 1951.
R. Chase, *Walt Whitman Reconsidered*, 1955.
Leaves of Grass One Hundred Years After, ed. M. Hindus, 1955.
J. E. Miller, Jr., *A Critical Guide to Leaves of Grass*, 1957.
R. Asselineau, *The Evolution of Walt Whitman*, 2 vols., 1960, 1962.
Whitman: A Collection of Critical Essays, ed. R. H. Pierce, 1962.
G. W. Allen, *The Solitary Singer*, 1967.
E. H. Miller, *Walt Whitman's Poetry: A Psychological Journey*, 1968.
G. W. Allen, *The New Walt Whitman Handbook*, 1975.
S. Black, *Whitman's Journey into Chaos*, 1975.
J. Kaplan, *Walt Whitman: A Life*, 1980.
P. Zweig, *Walt Whitman: The Making of the Poet*, 1984.

Texts:

Leaves of Grass, 1855, 1891–1892.
Collected Prose Works, 1892.
See also *The Collected Writings of Walt Whitman*, ed. G. W. Allen and S. Bradley, 1963–.

Leaves of Grass [1855]

[Preface][*]

America does not repel the past or what it has produced under its forms or amid other politics or the idea of castes or the old religions . . . . accepts the lesson with calmness . . . is not so impatient as has been supposed that the slough still sticks to opinions and manners and literature while the life which served its requirements has passed into the new life of the new forms . . . perceives that the corpse is slowly borne from the eating and sleeping rooms of the house . . . perceives that it waits a little while in the door . . . that it was fittest for its days . . . that its action has descended to the stalwart and wellshaped heir who approaches . . . and that he shall be fittest for his days.

The Americans of all nations at any time upon the earth have probably the fullest poetical nature. The United States themselves are essentially the greatest poem. In the history of the earth hitherto the largest and most stirring appear tame and orderly to their ampler largeness and stir. Here at last is something in the doings of man that corresponds with the broadcast doings of the day and night. Here is not merely a nation but a teeming nation of nations. Here is action untied from strings necessarily blind to particulars and details magnificently moving in vast masses. Here is the hospitality which forever indicates heroes . . . . Here are the roughs and beards and space and ruggedness and nonchalance that the soul loves. Here the performance disdaining the trivial unapproached in the tremendous audacity of its crowds and groupings and the push of its perspective spreads with crampless and flowing breadth and showers its prolific and splendid extravagance. One sees it must indeed own the riches of the summer and winter, and need never be bankrupt while corn grows from the ground or the orchards drop apples or the bays contain fish or men beget children upon women.

Other states indicate themselves in their deputies . . . . but the genius of the United States is not best or most in its executives or legislatures, nor in its ambassadors or authors or colleges or churches or parlors, nor even in its newspapers or inventors . . . but always most in the common people. Their manners speech dress friendships —the freshness and candor of their physiognomy—the picturesque looseness of their carriage . . . their deathless attachment to freedom—their aversion to anything indecorous or soft or mean—the practical acknowledgment of the citizens of one state by the citizens of all other states—the fierceness of their roused resentment—their curiosity and welcome of novelty—their self-esteem and wonderful sympathy—their susceptibility to a slight—the air they have of persons who never knew how it felt to stand in the presence of superiors—the fluency of their speech—their delight in music, the sure symptom of manly tenderness and native elegance of soul . . . their good temper and open-handedness—the terrible significance of their elections—the President's taking off his hat to them not they to him—these too are unrhymed poetry. It awaits the gigantic and generous treatment worthy of it.

[*] Untitled in 1855 and omitted from subsequent editions.

The largeness of nature or the nation were monstrous without a corresponding largeness and generosity of the spirit of the citizen. Not nature nor swarming states nor streets and steamships nor prosperous business nor farms nor capital nor learning may suffice for the ideal of man . . . nor suffice the poet. No reminiscences may suffice either. A live nation can always cut a deep mark and can have the best authority the cheapest . . . namely from its own soul. This is the sum of the profitable uses of individuals or states and of present action and grandeur and of the subjects of poets. —As if it were necessary to trot back generation after generation to the eastern records! As if the beauty and sacredness of the demonstrable must fall behind that of the mythical! As if men do not make their mark out of any times! As if the opening of the western continent by discovery and what has transpired since in North and South America were less than the small theatre of the antique or the aimless sleepwalking of the middle ages! The pride of the United States leaves the wealth and finesse of the cities and all returns of commerce and agriculture and all the magnitude of geography or shows of exterior victory to enjoy the breed of fullsized men or one fullsized man unconquerable and simple.

The American poets are to enclose old and new for America is the race of races. Of them a bard is to be commensurate with a people. To him the other continents arrive as contributions . . . he gives them reception for their sake and his own sake. His spirit responds to his country's spirit . . . . he incarnates its geography and natural life and rivers and lakes. Mississippi with annual freshets and changing chutes, Missouri and Columbia and Ohio and Saint Lawrence with the falls and beautiful masculine Hudson, do not embouchure where they spend themselves more than they embouchure into him. The blue breadth over the inland sea of Virginia and Maryland and the sea off Massachusetts and Maine and over Manhattan bay and over Champlain and Erie and over Ontario and Huron and Michigan and Superior, and over the Texan and Mexican and Floridian and Cuban seas and over the seas off California and Oregon, is not tallied by the blue breadth of the waters below more than the breadth of above and below is tallied by him. When the long Atlantic coast stretches longer and the Pacific coast stretches longer he easily stretches with them north or south. He spans between them also from east to west and reflects what is between them. On him rise solid growths that offset the growths of pine and cedar and hemlock and liveoak and locust and chestnut and cypress and hickory and limetree and cottonwood and tuliptree and cactus and wildvine and tamarind and persimmon . . . . and tangles as tangled as any canebrake or swamp . . . . and forests coated with transparent ice and icicles hanging from the boughs and crackling in the wind . . . . and sides and peaks of mountains . . . . and pasturage sweet and free as savannah or upland or prairie . . . . with flights and songs and screams that answer those of the wildpigeon and highhold and orchard-oriole and coot and surf-duck and redshouldered-hawk and fish-hawk and white-ibis and indian-hen and cat-owl and water-pheasant and qua-bird and piedsheldrake and blackbird and mockingbird and buzzard and condor and night-heron and eagle. To him the hereditary countenance descends both mother's and father's. To him enter the essences of the real things and past and present events— of the enormous diversity of temperature and agriculture and mines—the tribes of red aborigines—the weatherbeaten vessels entering new ports or making landings on rocky coasts—the first settlements north or south—the rapid stature and muscle—the haughty defiance of '76, and the war and peace and formation of the constitution . . . . the union always surrounded by blatherers and always calm and impregnable —the perpetual coming of immigrants—the wharfhem'd cities and superior marine —the unsurveyed interior—the loghouses and clearings and wild animals and hunters and trappers . . . . the free commerce—the fisheries and whaling and gold-digging —the endless gestation of new states—the convening of Congress every December, the members duly coming up from all climates and the uttermost parts . . . . the noble character of the young mechanics and of all free American workmen and workwomen . . . . the general ardor and friendliness and enterprise—the perfect equality of the female with the male . . . . the large amativeness—the fluid movement of the population—the factories and mercantile life and laborsaving machinery—the Yankee swap—the New-York firemen and the target excursion—the southern plantation life —the character of the northeast and of the northwest and southwest—slavery and the tremulous spreading of hands to protect it, and the stern opposition to it which shall never cease till it ceases or the speaking of tongues and the moving of lips cease. For such the expression of the American poet is to be transcendant and new. It is to be indirect and not direct or descriptive or epic. Its quality goes through these to much more. Let the age and wars of other nations be chanted and their eras and characters be illustrated and that finish the verse. Not so the great psalm of the republic. Here the theme is creative and has vista. Here comes one among the wellbeloved stonecut-ters and plans with decision and science and sees the solid and beautiful forms of the future where there are now no solid forms.

Of all nations the United States with veins full of poetical stuff most need poets and will doubtless have the greatest and use them the greatest. Their Presidents shall not be their common referee so much as their poets shall. Of all mankind the great poet is the equable man. Not in him but off from him things are grotesque or eccentric or fail of their sanity. Nothing out of its place is good and nothing in its place is bad. He bestows on every object or quality its fit proportions neither more nor less. He is the arbiter of the diverse and he is the key. He is the equalizer of his age and land . . . . he supplies what wants supplying and checks what wants checking. If peace is the routine out of him speaks the spirit of peace, large, rich, thrifty, building vast and populous cities, encouraging agriculture and the arts and commerce—lighting the study of man, the soul, immortality—federal, state or municipal government, mar-riage, health, freetrade, intertravel by land and sea . . . . nothing too close, nothing too far off . . . the stars not too far off. In war he is the most deadly force of the war. Who recruits him recruits horse and foot . . . he fetches parks of artillery the best that engineer ever knew. If the time becomes slothful and heavy he knows how to arouse it . . . he can make every word he speaks draw blood. Whatever stagnates in the flat of custom or obedience or legislation he never stagnates. Obedience does not master him, he masters it. High up out of reach he stands turning a concentrated light . . . he turns the pivot with his finger . . . . he baffles the swiftest runners as he stands and easily overtakes and envelops them. The time straying toward infidelity and confections and persiflage he withholds by his steady faith . . . he spreads out his dishes . . . . he offers the sweet firmfibred meat that grows men and women. His brain is the ultimate brain. He is no arguer . . . he is judgment. He judges not as the judge judges but as the sun falling around a helpless thing. As he sees the farthest he has the most faith. His thoughts are the hymns of the praise of things. In the talk on the soul and eternity and God off of his equal plane he is silent. He sees eternity less like a play with a prologue and denouement . . . . he sees eternity in men and women . . . he does not see men and women as dreams or dots. Faith is the antiseptic of the soul . . . it pervades the common people and preserves them . . . they never give up believing and expecting and trusting. There is that indescribable freshness and uncon-sciousness about an illiterate person that humbles and mocks the power of the noblest expressive genius. The poet sees for a certainty how one not a great artist may be just as sacred and perfect as the greatest artist. . . . . . The power to destroy or remould is freely used by him but never the power of attack. What is past is past. If he does not expose superior models and prove himself by every step he takes he is not what is wanted. The presence of the greatest poet conquers . . . not parleying or struggling or any prepared attempts. Now he has passed that way see after him! there is not left any vestige of despair or misanthropy or cunning or exclusiveness or the ignominy of a nativity or color or delusion of hell or the necessity of hell . . . . . and no man thenceforward shall be degraded for ignorance or weakness or sin.

The greatest poet hardly knows pettiness or triviality. If he breathes into any thing that was before thought small it dilates with the grandeur and life of the universe. He is a seer . . . . he is individual . . . he is complete in himself . . . . the others are as good as he, only he sees it and they do not. He is not one of the chorus . . . . he does not stop for any regulation . . . he is the president of regulation. What the eyesight does to the rest he does to the rest. Who knows the curious mystery of the eyesight? The other senses corroborate themselves, but this is removed from any proof but its own and foreruns the identities of the spiritual world. A single glance of it mocks all the investigations of man and all the instruments and books of the earth and all reasoning. What is marvellous? what is unlikely? what is impossible or baseless or vague? after you have once just opened the space of a peachpit and given audience to far and near and to the sunset and had all things enter with electric swiftness softly and duly without confusion or jostling or jam.

The land and sea, the animals fishes and birds, the sky of heaven and the orbs, the forests mountains and rivers, are not small themes . . . but folks expect of the poet to indicate more than the beauty and dignity which always attach to dumb real objects . . . . they expect him to indicate the path between reality and their souls. Men and women perceive the beauty well enough . . probably as well as he. The passionate tenacity of hunters, woodmen, early risers, cultivators of gardens and orchards and fields, the love of healthy women for the manly form, seafaring persons, drivers of horses, the passion for light and the open air, all is an old varied sign of the unfailing perception of beauty and of a residence of the poetic in outdoor people. They can never be assisted by poets to perceive . . . some may but they never can. The poetic quality is not marshalled in rhyme or uniformity or abstract addresses to things nor in melancholy complaints or good precepts, but is the life of these and much else and is in the soul. The profit of rhyme is that it drops seeds of a sweeter and more luxuriant rhyme, and of uniformity that it conveys itself into its own roots in the ground out of sight. The rhyme and uniformity of perfect poems show the free growth of metrical laws and bud from them as unerringly and loosely as lilacs or roses on a bush, and take shapes as compact as the shapes of chestnuts and oranges and melons and pears, and shed the perfume impalpable to form. The fluency and ornaments of the finest poems or music or orations or recitations are not independent but dependent. All beauty comes from beautiful blood and a beautiful brain. If the greatnesses are in conjunction in a man or woman it is enough . . . . the fact will prevail through the universe . . . . but the gaggery and gilt of a million years will not prevail. Who troubles himself about his ornaments or fluency is lost. This is what you shall do: Love the earth and sun and the animals, despise riches, give alms to every one that asks, stand up for the stupid and crazy, devote your income and labor to others, hate tyrants, argue not concerning God, have patience and indulgence toward the people, take off your hat to nothing known or unknown or to any man or number of men, go freely with powerful uneducated persons and with the young and with the mothers of families, read these leaves in the open air every season of every year of your life, re-examine all you have been told at school or church or in any book, dismiss whatever insults your own soul, and your very flesh shall be a great poem and have the richest fluency not only in its words but in the silent lines of its lips and face and between the lashes of your eyes and in every motion and joint of your body . . . . The poet shall not spend his time in unneeded work. He shall know that the ground is always ready ploughed and manured . . . . others may not know it but he shall. He shall go directly to the creation. His trust shall master the trust of everything he touches . . . . and shall master all attachment.

The known universe has one complete lover and that is the greatest poet. He consumes an eternal passion and is indifferent which chance happens and which possible contingency of fortune or misfortune and persuades daily and hourly his delicious pay. What balks or breaks others is fuel for his burning progress to contact and amorous joy. Other proportions of the reception of pleasure dwindle to nothing to his proportions. All expected from heaven or from the highest he is rapport with in the sight of the daybreak or a scene of the winter woods or the presence of children playing or with his arm round the neck of a man or woman. His love above all love has leisure and expanse . . . . he leaves room ahead of himself. He is no irresolute or suspicious lover . . . he is sure . . . he scorns intervals. His experience and the showers and thrills are not for nothing. Nothing can jar him . . . . suffering and darkness cannot —death and fear cannot. To him complaint and jealousy and envy are corpses buried and rotten in the earth . . . . he saw them buried. The sea is not surer of the shore or the shore of the sea than he is of the fruition of his love and of all perfection and beauty.

The fruition of beauty is no chance of hit or miss . . . it is inevitable as life . . . . it is exact and plumb as gravitation. From the eyesight proceeds another eyesight and from the hearing proceeds another hearing and from the voice proceeds another voice eternally curious of the harmony of things with man. To these respond perfections not only in the committees that were supposed to stand for the rest but in the rest themselves just the same. These understand the law of perfection in masses and floods . . . that its finish is to each for itself and onward from itself . . . that it is profuse and impartial . . . that there is not a minute of the light or dark nor an acre of the earth or sea without it—nor any direction of the sky nor any trade or employment nor any turn of events. This is the reason that about the proper expression of beauty there is precision and balance . . . one part does not need to be thrust above another. The best singer is not the one who has the most lithe and powerful organ . . . the pleasure of poems is not in them that take the handsomest measure and similes and sound.

Without effort and without exposing in the least how it is done the greatest poet brings the spirit of any or all events and passions and scenes and persons some more and some less to bear on your individual character as you hear or read. To do this well is to compete with the laws that pursue and follow time. What is the purpose must surely be there and the clue of it must be there . . . . and the faintest indication is the indication of the best and then becomes the clearest indication. Past and present and future are not disjoined but joined. The greatest poet forms the consistence of what is to be from what has been and is. He drags the dead out of their coffins and stands them again on their feet . . . . he says to the past, Rise and walk before me that I may realize you. He learns the lesson . . . . he places himself where the future becomes present. The greatest poet does not only dazzle his rays over character and scenes and passions . . . he finally ascends and finishes all . . . he exhibits the pinnacles that no man can tell what they are for or what is beyond . . . . he glows a moment on the extremest verge. He is most wonderful in his last half-hidden smile or frown . . . by that flash of the moment of parting the one that sees it shall be encouraged or terrified afterward for many years. The greatest poet does not moralize or make applications of morals . . . he knows the soul. The soul has that measureless pride which consists in never acknowledging any lessons but its own. But it has sympathy as measureless as its pride and the one balances the other and neither can stretch too far while it stretches in company with the other. The inmost secrets of art sleep with the twain. The greatest poet has lain close betwixt both and they are vital in his style and thoughts.

The art of art, the glory of expression and the sunshine of the light of letters is simplicity. Nothing is better than simplicity . . . . nothing can make up for excess or for the lack of definiteness. To carry on the heave of impulse and pierce intellectual depths and give all subjects their articulations are powers neither common nor very uncommon. But to speak in literature with the perfect rectitude and insousiance of the movements of animals and the unimpeachableness of the sentiment of trees in the woods and grass by the roadside is the flawless triumph of art. If you have looked on him who has achieved it you have looked on one of the masters of the artists of all nations and times. You shall not contemplate the flight of the graygull over the bay or the mettlesome action of the blood horse or the tall leaning of sunflowers on their stalk or the appearance of the sun journeying through heaven or the appearance of the moon afterward with any more satisfaction than you shall contemplate him. The greatest poet has less a marked style and is more the channel of thoughts and things without increase or diminution, and is the free channel of himself. He swears to his art, I will not be meddlesome, I will not have in my writing any elegance or effect or originality to hang in the way between me and the rest like curtains. I will have nothing hang in the way, not the richest curtains. What I tell I tell for precisely what it is. Let who may exalt or startle or fascinate or soothe I will have purposes as health or heat or snow has and be as regardless of observation. What I experience or portray shall go from my composition without a shred of my composition. You shall stand by my side and look in the mirror with me.

The old red blood and stainless gentility of great poets will be proved by their unconstraint. A heroic person walks at his ease through and out of that custom or precedent or authority that suits him not. Of the traits of the brotherhood of writers savans musicians inventors and artists nothing is finer than silent defiance advancing from new free forms. In the need of poems philosophy politics mechanism science behaviour, the craft of art, an appropriate native grand-opera, shipcraft, or any craft, he is greatest forever and forever who contributes the greatest original practical example. The cleanest expression is that which finds no sphere worthy of itself and makes one.

The messages of great poets to each man and woman are, Come to us on equal terms, Only then can you understand us, We are no better than you, What we enclose you enclose, What we enjoy you may enjoy. Did you suppose there could be only one Supreme? We affirm there can be unnumbered Supremes, and that one does not countervail another any more than one eyesight countervails another . . and that men can be good or grand only of the consciousness of their supremacy within them. What do you think is the grandeur of storms and dismemberments and the deadliest battles and wrecks and the wildest fury of the elements and the power of the sea and the motion of nature and of the throes of human desires and dignity and hate and love? It is that something in the soul which says, Rage on, Whirl on, I tread master here and everywhere, Master of the spasms of the sky and of the shatter of the sea, Master of nature and passion and death, And of all terror and all pain.

The American bards shall be marked for generosity and affection and for encouraging competitors . . They shall be kosmos . . without monopoly or secrecy . . glad to pass any thing to any one . . hungry for equals night and day. They shall not be careful of riches and privilege . . . . they shall be riches and privilege . . . . they shall perceive who the most affluent man is. The most affluent man is he that confronts all the shows he sees by equivalents out of the stronger wealth of himself. The American bard shall delineate no class of persons nor one or two out of the strata of interests nor love most nor truth most nor the soul most nor the body most . . . . . and not be for the eastern states more than the western or the northern states more than the southern.

Exact science and its practical movements are no checks on the greatest poet but always his encouragement and support. The outset and remembrance are there . . there the arms that lifted him first and brace him best . . . . there he returns after all his goings and comings. The sailor and traveler . . the anatomist chemist astronomer geologist phrenologist spiritualist mathematician historian and lexicographer are not poets, but they are the lawgivers of poets and their construction underlies the structure of every perfect poem. No matter what rises or is uttered they sent the seed of the conception of it . . . . of them and by them stand the visible proofs of souls . . . . . always of their fatherstuff must be begotten the sinewy races of bards. If there shall be love and content between the father and the son and if the greatness of the son is the exuding of the greatness of the father there shall be love between the poet and the man of demonstrable science. In the beauty of poems are the tuft and final applause of science.

Great is the faith of the flush of knowledge and of the investigation of the depths of qualities and things. Cleaving and circling here swells the soul of the poet yet is president of itself always. The depths are fathomless and therefore calm. The innocence and nakedness are resumed . . . they are neither modest nor immodest. The whole theory of the special and supernatural and all that was twined with it or educed out of it departs as a dream. What has ever happened . . . . what happens and whatever may or shall happen, the vital laws enclose all . . . . they are sufficient for any case and for all cases . . . none to be hurried or retarded . . . . any miracle of affairs or persons inadmissible in the vast clear scheme where every motion and every spear of grass and the frames and spirits of men and women and all that concerns them are unspeakably perfect miracles all referring to all and each distinct and in its place. It is also not consistent with the reality of the soul to admit that there is anything in the known universe more divine than men and women.

Men and women and the earth and all upon it are simply to be taken as they are, and the investigation of their past and present and future shall be unintermitted and shall be done with perfect candor. Upon this basis philosophy speculates ever looking toward the poet, ever regarding the eternal tendencies of all toward happiness never inconsistent with what is clear to the senses and to the soul. For the eternal tendencies of all toward happiness make the only point of sane philosophy. Whatever comprehends less than that . . . whatever is less than the laws of light and of astronomical motion . . . or less than the laws that follow the thief the liar the glutton and the drunkard through this life and doubtless afterward . . . . . . or less than vast stretches of time or the slow formation of density or the patient upheaving of strata—is of no account. Whatever would put God in a poem or system of philosophy as contending against some being or influence is also of no account. Sanity and ensemble characterise the great master . . . spoilt in one principle all is spoilt. The great master has nothing to do with miracles. He sees health for himself in being one of the mass . . . . he sees the hiatus in singular eminence. To the perfect shape comes common ground. To be under the general law is great for that is to correspond with it. The master knows that he is unspeakably great and that all are unspeakably great . . . . that nothing for instance is greater than to conceive children and bring them up well . . . that to be is just as great as to perceive or tell.

In the make of the great masters the idea of political liberty is indispensible. Liberty takes the adherence of heroes wherever men and women exist . . . . but never takes any adherence or welcome from the rest more than from poets. They are the voice and exposition of liberty. They out of ages are worthy the grand idea . . . . to them it is confided and they must sustain it. Nothing has precedence of it and nothing can warp or degrade it. The attitude of great poets is to cheer up slaves and horrify despots. The turn of their necks, the sound of their feet, the motions of their wrists, are full of hazard to the one and hope to the other. Come nigh them awhile and though they neither speak or advise you shall learn the faithful American lesson. Liberty is poorly served by men whose good intent is quelled from one failure or two failures or any number of failures, or from the casual indifference or ingratitude of the people, or from the sharp show of the tushes of power, or the bringing to bear soldiers and cannon or any penal statutes. Liberty relies upon itself, invites no one, promises nothing, sits in calmness and light, is positive and composed, and knows no discouragement. The battle rages with many a loud alarm and frequent advance and retreat .... the enemy triumphs .... the prison, the handcuffs, the iron necklace and anklet, the scaffold, garrote and leadballs do their work .... the cause is asleep .... the strong throats are choked with their own blood .... the young men drop their eyelashes toward the ground when they pass each other .... and is liberty gone out of that place? No never. When liberty goes it is not the first to go nor the second or third to go .. it waits for all the rest to go .. it is the last ... When the memories of the old martyrs are faded utterly away .... when the large names of patriots are laughed at in the public halls from the lips of the orators .... when the boys are no more christened after the same but christened after tyrants and traitors instead .... when the laws of the free are grudgingly permitted and laws for informers and bloodmoney are sweet to the taste of the people .... when I and you walk abroad upon the earth stung with compassion at the sight of numberless brothers answering our equal friendship and calling no man master—and when we are elated with noble joy at the sight of slaves .... when the soul retires in the cool communion of the night and surveys its experience and has much extasy over the word and deed that put back a helpless innocent person into the gripe of the gripers or into any cruel inferiority .... when those in all parts of these states who could easier realize the true American character but do not yet—when the swarms of cringers, suckers, doughfaces, lice of politics, planners of sly involutions for their own preferment to city offices or state legislatures or the judiciary or congress or the presidency, obtain a response of love and natural deference from the people whether they get the offices or no .... when it is better to be a bound booby and rogue in office at a high salary than the poorest free mechanic or farmer with his hat unmoved from his head and firm eyes and a candid and generous heart .... and when servility by town or state or the federal government or any oppression on a large scale or small scale can be tried on without its own punishment following duly after in exact proportion against the smallest chance of escape .... or rather when all life and all the souls of men and women are discharged from any part of the earth—then only shall the instinct of liberty be discharged from that part of the earth.

As the attributes of the poets of the kosmos concentre in the real body and soul and in the pleasure of things they possess the superiority of genuineness over all fiction and romance. As they emit themselves facts are showered over with light .... the daylight is lit with more volatile light .... also the deep between the setting and rising sun goes deeper many fold. Each precise object or condition or combination or process exhibits a beauty .... the multiplication table its—old age its—the carpenter's trade its—the grand-opera its .... the hugehulled cleanshaped New-York clipper at sea under steam or full sail gleams with unmatched beauty .... the American circles and large harmonies of government gleam with theirs .... and the commonest definite intentions and actions with theirs. The poets of the kosmos advance through all interpositions and coverings and turmoils and stratagems to first principles. They are of use .... they dissolve poverty from its need and riches from its conceit. You large proprietor they say shall not realize or perceive more than any one else. The owner of the library is not he who holds a legal title to it having bought and paid for it. Any one and every one is owner of the library who can read the same through all the varieties of tongues and subjects and styles, and in whom they enter with ease and take residence and force toward paternity and maternity, and make supple and powerful and rich and large. . . . . These American states strong and healthy and accomplished shall receive no pleasure from violations of natural models and must not permit them. In paintings or mouldings or carvings in mineral or wood, or in the illustrations of books or newspapers, or in any comic or tragic prints, or in the patterns of woven stuffs or any thing to beautify rooms or furniture or costumes, or to put upon cornices or monuments or on the prows or sterns of ships, or to put anywhere before the human eye indoors or out, that which distorts honest shapes or which creates unearthly beings or places or contingencies is a nuisance and revolt. Of the human form especially it is so great it must never be made ridiculous. Of ornaments to a work nothing outre can be allowed . . but those ornaments can be allowed that conform to the perfect facts of the open air and that flow out of the nature of the work and come irrepressibly from it and are necessary to the completion of the work. Most works are most beautiful without ornament. . . Exaggerations will be revenged in human physiology. Clean and vigorous children are jetted and conceived only in those communities where the models of natural forms are public every day. . . . . Great genius and the people of these states must never be demeaned to romances. As soon as histories are properly told there is no more need of romances.

The great poets are also to be known by the absence in them of tricks and by the justification of perfect personal candor. Then folks echo a new cheap joy and a divine voice leaping from their brains: How beautiful is candor! All faults may be forgiven of him who has perfect candor. Henceforth let no man of us lie, for we have seen that openness wins the inner and outer world and that there is no single exception, and that never since our earth gathered itself in a mass have deceit or subterfuge or prevarication attracted its smallest particle or the faintest tinge of a shade—and that through the enveloping wealth and rank of a state or the whole republic of states a sneak or sly person shall be discovered and despised . . . . and that the soul has never been once fooled and never can be fooled . . . . and thrift without the loving nod of the soul is only a fœtid puff . . . . and there never grew up in any of the continents of the globe nor upon any planet or satellite or star, nor upon the asteroids, nor in any part of ethereal space, nor in the midst of density, nor under the fluid wet of the sea, nor in that condition which precedes the birth of babes, nor at any time during the changes of life, nor in that condition that follows what we term death, nor in any stretch of abeyance or action afterward of vitality, nor in any process of formation or reformation anywhere, a being whose instinct hated the truth.

Extreme caution or prudence, the soundest organic health, large hope and comparison and fondness for women and children, large alimentiveness and destructiveness and causality, with a perfect sense of the oneness of nature and the propriety of the same spirit applied to human affairs . . these are called up of the float of the brain of the world to be parts of the greatest poet from his birth out of his mother's womb and from her birth out of her mother's. Caution seldom goes far enough. It has been thought that the prudent citizen was the citizen who applied himself to solid gains and did well for himself and his family and completed a lawful life without debt or crime. The greatest poet sees and admits these economies as he sees the economies of food and sleep, but has higher notions of prudence than to think he gives much when he gives a few slight attentions at the latch of the gate. The premises of the prudence of life are not the hospitality of it or the ripeness and harvest of it. Beyond the independence of a little sum laid aside for burial-money, and of a few clapboards around and shingles overhead on a lot of American soil owned, and the easy dollars that supply the year's plain clothing and meals, the melancholy prudence of the abandonment of such a great being as a man is to the toss and pallor of years of moneymaking with all their scorching days and icy nights and all their stifling deceits and underhanded dodgings, or infinitessimals of parlors, or shameless stuffing while others starve . . and all the loss of the bloom and odor of the earth and of the flowers and atmosphere and of the sea and of the true taste of the women and men you pass or have to do with in youth or middle age, and the issuing sickness and desperate revolt at the close of a life without elevation or naivete, and the ghastly chatter of a death without serenity or majesty, is the great fraud upon modern civilization and fore-thought, blotching the surface and system which civilization undeniably drafts, and moistening with tears the immense features it spreads and spreads with such velocity before the reached kisses of the soul. . . Still the right explanation remains to be made about prudence. The prudence of the mere wealth and respectability of the most esteemed life appears too faint for the eye to observe at all when little and large alike drop quietly aside at the thought of the prudence suitable for immortality. What is wisdom that fills the thinness of a year or seventy or eighty years to wisdom spaced out by ages and coming back at a certain time with strong reinforcements and rich presents and the clear faces of wedding-guests as far as you can look in every direction running gaily toward you? Only the soul is of itself . . . . all else has reference to what ensues. All that a person does or thinks is of consequence. Not a move can a man or woman make that affects him or her in a day or a month or any part of the direct lifetime or the hour of death but the same affects him or her onward afterward through the indirect lifetime. The indirect is always as great and real as the direct. The spirit receives from the body just as much as it gives to the body. Not one name of word or deed . . not of venereal sores or discolorations . . not the privacy of the onanist . . not of the putrid veins of gluttons or rumdrinkers . . . not peculation or cunning or betrayal or murder . . no serpentine poison of those that seduce women . . not the foolish yielding of women . . not prostitution . . not of any depravity of young men . . not of the attainment of gain by discreditable means . . not any nastiness of appetite . not any harshness of officers to men or judges to prisoners or fathers to sons or sons to fathers or of husbands to wives or bosses to their boys . . not of greedy looks or malignant wishes . . . nor any of the wiles practised by people upon themselves . . . ever is or ever can be stamped on the programme but it is duly realized and returned, and that returned in further performances . . . and they returned again. Nor can the push of charity or personal force ever be any thing else than the profoundest reason, whether it brings arguments to hand or no. No specification is necessary . . to add or subtract or divide is in vain. Little or big, learned or unlearned, white or black, legal or illegal, sick or well, from the first inspiration down the windpipe to the last expiration out of it, all that a male or female does that is vigorous and benevolent and clean is so much sure profit to him or her in the unshakable order of the universe and through the whole scope of it forever. If the savage or felon is wise it is well . . . . if the greatest poet or savan is wise it is simply the same . . if the President or chief justice is wise it is the same . . . if the young mechanic or farmer is wise it is no more or less . . if the prostitute is wise it is no more nor less. The interest will come round . . all will come round. All the best actions of war and peace . . . all help given to relatives and strangers and the poor and old and sorrowful and young children and widows and the sick, and to all shunned persons . . all furtherance of fugitives and of the escape of slaves . . all the self-denial that stood steady and aloof on wrecks and saw others take the seats of the boats . . . all offering of substance or life for the good old cause, or for a friend's sake or opinion's sake . . . all pains of enthusiasts scoffed at by their neighbors . . all the vast sweet love and precious suffering of mothers . . . all honest men baffled in strifes recorded or unrecorded . . . . all the grandeur and good of the few ancient nations whose fragments of annals we inherit . . and all the good of the hundreds of far mightier and more ancient nations unknown to us by name or date or location . . . . all that was ever manfully begun, whether it succeeded or no . . . . all that has at any time been well suggested out of the divine heart of man or by the divinity of his mouth or by the shaping of his great hands . . and all that is well thought or done this day on any part of the surface of the globe . . or on any of the wandering stars or fixed stars by those there as we are here . . or that is henceforth to be well thought or done by you whoever you are, or by any one—these singly and wholly inured at their time and inure now and will inure always to the identities from which they sprung or shall spring. . . Did you guess any of them lived only its moment? The world does not so exist . . no parts palpable or impalpable so exist . . . no result exists now without being from its long antecedent result, and that from its antecedent, and so backward without the farthest mentionable spot coming a bit nearer the beginning than any other spot. . . . . Whatever satisfies the soul is truth. The prudence of the greatest poet answers at last the craving and glut of the soul, is not contemptuous of less ways of prudence if they conform to its ways, puts off nothing, permits no let-up for its own case or any case, has no particular sabbath or judgment-day, divides not the living from the dead or the righteous from the unrighteous, is satisfied with the present, matches every thought or act by its correlative, knows no possible forgiveness or deputed atonement . . knows that the young man who composedly periled his life and lost it has done exceeding well for himself, while the man who has not periled his life and retains it to old age in riches and ease has perhaps achieved nothing for himself worth mentioning . . and that only that person has no great prudence to learn who has learnt to prefer real longlived things, and favors body and soul the same, and perceives the indirect assuredly following the direct, and what evil or good he does leaping onward and waiting to meet him again—and who in his spirit in any emergency whatever neither hurries or avoids death.

The direct trial of him who would be the greatest poet is today. If he does not flood himself with the immediate age as with vast oceanic tides . . . . . and if he does not attract his own land body and soul to himself and hang on its neck with incomparable love and plunge his semitic muscle into its merits and demerits . . . and if he be not himself the age transfigured . . . . and if to him is not opened the eternity which gives similitude to all periods and locations and processes and animate and inanimate forms, and which is the bond of time, and rises up from its inconceivable vagueness and infiniteness in the swimming shape of today, and is held by the ductile anchors of life, and makes the present spot the passage from what was to what shall be, and commits itself to the representation of this wave of an hour and this one of the sixty beautiful children of the wave—let him merge in the general run and wait his development. . . . . Still the final test of poems or any character or work remains. The prescient poet projects himself centuries ahead and judges performer or performance after the changes of time. Does it live through them? Does it still hold on untired? Will the same style and the direction of genius to similar points be satisfactory now? Has no new discovery in science or arrival at superior planes of thought and judgment and behaviour fixed him or his so that either can be looked down upon? Have the marches of tens and hundreds and thousands of years made willing detours to the right hand and the left hand for his sake? Is he beloved long and long after he is buried? Does the young man think often of him? and the young woman think often of him? and do the middleaged and the old think of him?

A great poem is for ages and ages in common and for all degrees and complexions and all departments and sects and for a woman as much as a man and a man as much as a woman. A great poem is no finish to a man or woman but rather a beginning. Has any one fancied he could sit at last under some due authority and rest satisfied with explanations and realize and be content and full? To no such terminus does the greatest poet bring . . . he brings neither cessation or sheltered fatness and ease. The touch of him tells in action. Whom he takes he takes with firm sure grasp into live regions previously unattained . . . . thenceforward is no rest . . . . they see the space and ineffable sheen that turn the old spots and lights into dead vacuums. The companion of him beholds the birth and progress of stars and learns one of the meanings. Now there shall be a man cohered out of tumult and chaos . . . . the elder encourages the younger and shows him how . . . they two shall launch off fearlessly together till the new world fits an orbit for itself and looks unabashed on the lesser orbits of the stars and sweeps through the ceaseless rings and shall never be quiet again.

There will soon be no more priests. Their work is done. They may wait awhile . . perhaps a generation or two . . dropping off by degrees. A superior breed shall take their place . . . . the gangs of kosmos and prophets en masse shall take their place. A new order shall arise and they shall be the priests of man, and every man shall be his own priest. The churches built under their umbrage shall be the churches of men and women. Through the divinity of themselves shall the kosmos and the new breed of poets be interpreters of men and women and of all events and things. They shall find their inspiration in real objects today, symptoms of the past and future . . . . They shall not deign to defend immortality or God or the perfection of things or liberty or the exquisite beauty and reality of the soul. They shall arise in America and be responded to from the remainder of the earth.

The English language befriends the grand American expression . . . . it is brawny enough and limber and full enough. On the tough stock of a race who through all change of circumstance was never without the idea of political liberty, which is the animus of all liberty, it has attracted the terms of daintier and gayer and subtler and more elegant tongues. It is the powerful language of resistance . . . it is the dialect of common sense. It is the speech of the proud and melancholy races and of all who aspire. It is the chosen tongue to express growth faith self-esteem freedom justice equality friendliness amplitude prudence decision and courage. It is the medium that shall well nigh express the inexpressible.

No great literature nor any like style of behaviour or oratory or social intercourse or household arrangements or public institutions or the treatment by bosses of employed people, nor executive detail or detail of the army or navy, nor spirit of legislation or courts or police or tuition or architecture or songs or amusements or the costumes of young men, can long elude the jealous and passionate instinct of American standards. Whether or no the sign appears from the mouths of the people, it throbs a live interrogation in every freeman's and freewoman's heart after that which passes by or this built to remain. Is it uniform with my country? Are its disposals without ignominious distinctions? Is it for the evergrowing communes of brothers and lovers, large, well-united, proud beyond the old models, generous beyond all models? Is it something grown fresh out of the fields or drawn from the sea for use to me today here? I know that what answers for me an American must answer for any individual or nation that serves for a part of my materials. Does this answer? or is it without reference to universal needs? or sprung of the needs of the less developed society of special ranks? or old needs of pleasure overlaid by modern science and forms? Does this acknowledge liberty with audible and absolute acknowledgement, and set slavery at nought for life and death? Will it help breed one goodshaped and wellhung man, and a woman to be his perfect and independent mate? Does it improve manners? Is it for the nursing of the young of the republic? Does it solve readily with the sweet milk of the nipples of the breasts of the mother of many children? Has it too the old ever-fresh forbearance and impartiality? Does it look with the same love on the last born and on those hardening toward stature, and on the errant, and on those who disdain all strength of assault outside of their own?

The poems distilled from other poems will probably pass away. The coward will surely pass away. The expectation of the vital and great can only be satisfied by the demeanor of the vital and great. The swarms of the polished deprecating and reflectors and the polite float off and leave no remembrance. America prepares with composure and goodwill for the visitors that have sent word. It is not intellect that is to be their warrant and welcome. The talented, the artist, the ingenious, the editor, the statesman, the erudite .. they are not unappreciated .. they fall in their place and do their work. The soul of the nation also does its work. No disguise can pass on it .. no disguise can conceal from it. It rejects none, it permits all. Only toward as good as itself and toward the like of itself will it advance half-way. An individual is as superb as a nation when he has the qualities which make a superb nation. The soul of the largest and wealthiest and proudest nation may well go half-way to meet that of its poets. The signs are effectual. There is no fear of mistake. If the one is true the other is true. The proof of a poet is that his country absorbs him as affectionately as he has absorbed it.

from Leaves of Grass [1891–1892]

from Inscriptions

One's-Self I Sing

One's-Self I sing, a simple separate person,
Yet utter the word Democratic, the word En-Masse.

Of physiology from top to toe I sing,
Not physiognomy alone nor brain alone is worthy for the Muse, I say the
   Form complete is worthier far,
The Female equally with the Male I sing.   5

Of Life immense in passion, pulse, and power,
Cheerful, for freest action form'd under the laws divine,
The Modern Man I sing.

1867

When I Read the Book

When I read the book, the biography famous,
And is this then (said I) what the author calls a man's life?
And so will some one when I am dead and gone write my life?
(As if any man really knew aught of my life,
Why even I myself I often think know little or nothing of my real life,   5
Only a few hints, a few diffused faint clews and indirections
I seek for my own use to trace out here.)

1867

Beginning My Studies

Beginning my studies the first step pleas'd me so much,
The mere fact consciousness, these forms, the power of motion,
The least insect or animal, the senses, eyesight, love,
The first step I say awed me and pleas'd me so much,
I have hardly gone and hardly wish'd to go any farther,   5
But stop and loiter all the time to sing it in ecstatic songs.

1865

I Hear America Singing

I hear America singing, the varied carols I hear,
Those of mechanics, each one singing his as it should be blithe and strong,
The carpenter singing his as he measures his plank or beam,
The mason singing his as he makes ready for work, or leaves off work,

The boatman singing what belongs to him in his boat, the deckhand singing on
    the steamboat deck,   5
The shoemaker singing as he sits on his bench, the hatter singing as he stands,
The wood-cutter's song, the ploughboy's on his way in the morning, or at noon
    intermission or at sundown,
The delicious singing of the mother, or of the young wife at work, or of the
    girl sewing or washing,
Each singing what belongs to him or her and to none else,
The day what belongs to the day—at night the party of young fellows, robust,
    friendly,   10
Singing with open mouths their strong melodious songs.

1860

Song of Myself*

1

I celebrate myself, and sing myself,
And what I assume you shall assume,
For every atom belonging to me as good belongs to you.

I loafe and invite my soul,
I lean and loafe at my ease observing a spear of summer grass.   5

My tongue, every atom of my blood, form'd from this soil, this air,
Born here of parents born here from parents the same, and their parents the
    same,
I, now thirty-seven years old in perfect health begin,
Hoping to cease not till death.

Creeds and schools in abeyance,   10
Retiring back a while sufficed at what they are, but never forgotten,
I harbor for good or bad, I permit to speak at every hazard,
Nature without check with original energy.

2

Houses and rooms are full of perfumes, the shelves are crowded with perfumes,
I breathe the fragrance myself and know it and like it,   15
The distillation would intoxicate me also, but I shall not let it.

---

* Untitled when first published in the 1855
edition of *Leaves of Grass*, "Song of Myself"
became "Poem of Walt Whitman, an
American" and then "Walt Whitman" before
being given its final title in 1881.

The atmosphere is not a perfume, it has no taste of the distillation, it is
    odorless,
It is for my mouth forever, I am in love with it,
I will go to the bank by the wood and become undisguised and naked,
I am mad for it to be in contact with me.   20

The smoke of my own breath,
Echoes, ripples, buzz'd whispers, love-root, silk-thread, crotch and vine,
My respiration and inspiration, the beating of my heart, the passing of blood
    and air through my lungs,
The sniff of green leaves and dry leaves, and of the shore and dark-color'd
    sea-rocks, and of hay in the barn,
The sound of the belch'd words of my voice loos'd to the eddies of the wind,   25
A few light kisses, a few embraces, a reaching around of arms,
The play of shine and shade on the trees as the supple boughs wag,
The delight alone or in the rush of the streets, or along the fields and hill-sides,
The feeling of health, the full-noon trill, the song of me rising from bed and
    meeting the sun.

Have you reckon'd a thousand acres much? have you reckon'd the earth much?   30
Have you practis'd so long to learn to read?
Have you felt so proud to get at the meaning of poems?

Stop this day and night with me and you shall possess the origin of all poems,
You shall possess the good of the earth and sun, (there are millions of suns left,)
You shall no longer take things at second or third hand, nor look through the
    eyes of the dead, nor feed on the spectres in books,   35
You shall not look through my eyes either, nor take things from me,
You shall listen to all sides and filter them from your self.

3

I have heard what the talkers were talking, the talk of the beginning and the
    end,
But I do not talk of the beginning or the end.

There was never any more inception than there is now,   40
Nor any more youth or age than there is now,
And will never be any more perfection than there is now,
Nor any more heaven or hell than there is now.

Urge and urge and urge,
Always the procreant urge of the world.   45

Out of the dimness opposite equals advance, always substance and increase,
  always sex,
Always a knit of identity, always distinction, always a breed of life.

To elaborate is no avail, learn'd and unlearn'd feeling that it is so.

Sure as the most certain sure, plumb in the uprights, well entretied,[1] braced in
  the beams,
Stout as a horse, affectionate, haughty, electrical,   5·
I and this mystery here we stand.

Clear and sweet is my soul, and clear and sweet is all that is not my soul.

Lack one lacks both, and the unseen is proved by the seen,
Till that becomes unseen and receives proof in its turn.

Showing the best and dividing it from the worst age vexes age,   55
Knowing the perfect fitness and equanimity of things, while they discuss I am
  silent, and go bathe and admire myself.

Welcome is every organ and attribute of me, and of any man hearty and clean,
Not an inch nor a particle of an inch is vile, and none shall be less familiar
  than the rest.

I am satisfied—I see, dance, laugh, sing;
As the hugging and loving bed-fellow sleeps at my side through the night, and
  withdraws at the peep of the day with stealthy tread,   60
Leaving me baskets cover'd with white towels swelling the house with their
  plenty,
Shall I postpone my acceptance and realization and scream at my eyes,
That they turn from gazing after and down the road,
And forthwith cipher and show me to a cent,
Exactly the value of one and exactly the value of two, and which is ahead?   65

4

Trippers and askers surround me,
People I meet, the effect upon me of my early life or the ward and city I live
  in, or the nation,
The latest dates, discoveries, inventions, societies, authors old and new,
My dinner, dress, associates, looks, compliments, dues,
The real or fancied indifference of some man or woman I love,   70
The sickness of one of my folks or of myself, or ill-doing or loss or lack of
  money, or depressions or exaltations,

---

[1] Cross-braced.

Battles, the horrors of fratricidal war, the fever of doubtful news, the fitful
    events;
These come to me days and nights and go from me again,
But they are not the Me myself.

Apart from the pulling and hauling stands what I am,   75
Stands amused, complacent, compassionating, idle, unitary,
Looks down, is erect, or bends an arm on an impalpable certain rest,
Looking with side-curved head curious what will come next,
Both in and out of the game and watching and wondering at it.
Backward I see in my own days where I sweated through fog with linguists
    and contenders,   80
I have no mockings or arguments, I witness and wait.

5

I believe in you my soul, the other I am must not abase itself to you,
And you must not be abased to the other.

Loafe with me on the grass, loose the stop from your throat,
Not words, not music or rhyme I want, not custom or lecture, not even the
    best,   85
Only the lull I like, the hum of your valvèd voice.

I mind how once we lay such a transparent summer morning,
How you settled your head athwart my hips and gently turn'd over upon me,
And parted the shirt from my bosom-bone, and plunged your tongue to my
    bare-stript heart,
And reach'd till you felt my beard, and reach'd till you held my feet.   90

Swiftly arose and spread around me the peace and knowledge that pass all the
    argument of the earth,
And I know that the hand of God is the promise of my own,
And I know that the spirit of God is the brother of my own,
And that all the men ever born are also my brothers, and the women my sisters
    and lovers,
And that a kelson[2] of the creation is love,   95
And limitless are leaves stiff or drooping in the fields,
And brown ants in the little wells beneath them,
And mossy scabs of the worm fence, heap'd stones, elder, mullein and
    poke-weed.

[2] Superstructure of a ship's keel.

6

A child said *What is the grass?* fetching it to me with full hands;
How could I answer the child? I do not know what it is any more than he.   10
I guess it must be the flag of my disposition, out of hopeful green stuff woven.

Or I guess it is the handkerchief of the Lord,
A scented gift and remembrancer designedly dropt,
Bearing the owner's name someway in the corners, that we may see and remark,
   and say *Whose?*

Or I guess the grass is itself a child, the produced babe of the vegetation.   105

Or I guess it is a uniform hieroglyphic,
And it means, Sprouting alike in broad zones and narrow zones,
Growing among black folks as among white,
Kanuck,[3] Tuckahoe,[4] Congressman, Cuff,[5] I give them the same, I receive them
   the same.

And now it seems to me the beautiful uncut hair of graves.   110

Tenderly will I use you curling grass,
It may be you transpire from the breasts of young men,
It may be if I had known them I would have loved them,
It may be you are from old people, or from offspring taken soon out of their
   mothers' laps,
And here you are the mothers' laps.   115

This grass is very dark to be from the white heads of old mothers,
Darker than the colorless beards of old men,
Dark to come from under the faint red roofs of mouths.

O I perceive after all so many uttering tongues,
And I perceive they do not come from the roofs of mouths for nothing.   120

I wish I could translate the hints about the dead young men and women,
And the hints about old men and mothers, and the offspring taken soon out of
   their laps.
What do you think has become of the young and old men?
And what do you think has become of the women and children?

They are alive and well somewhere,   125
The smallest sprout shows there is really no death,

---

[3] French Canadian.   [5] Black.
[4] Native of tidewater Virginia.

And if ever there was it led forward life, and does not wait at the end to arrest
    it,
And ceas'd the moment life appear'd.

All goes onward and outward, nothing collapses,
And to die is different from what any one supposed, and luckier.   130

7

Has any one supposed it lucky to be born?
I hasten to inform him or her it is just as lucky to die, and I know it.

I pass death with the dying and birth with the new-wash'd babe, and am not
    contain'd between my hat and boots,
And peruse manifold objects, no two alike and every one good,
The earth good and the stars good, and their adjuncts all good.   135

I am not an earth nor an adjunct of an earth,
I am the mate and companion of people, all just as immortal and fathomless as
    myself,
(They do not know how immortal, but I know.)

Every kind for itself and its own, for me mine male and female,
For me those that have been boys and that love women,   140
For me the man that is proud and feels how it stings to be slighted,
For me the sweet-heart and the old maid, for me mothers and the mothers of
    mothers,
For me lips that have smiled, eyes that have shed tears,
For me children and the begetters of children.
Undrape! you are not guilty to me, nor stale nor discarded,   145
I see through the broadcloth and gingham whether or no,
And am around, tenacious, acquisitive, tireless, and cannot be shaken away.

8

The little one sleeps in its cradle,
I lift the gauze and look a long time, and silently brush away flies with my
    hand.

The youngster and the red-faced girl turn aside up the bushy hill,   150
I peeringly view them from the top.

The suicide sprawls on the bloody floor of the bedroom,
I witness the corpse with its dabbled hair, I note where the pistol has fallen.

The blab of the pave, tires of carts, sluff of boot-soles, talk of the promenaders,
The heavy omnibus, the driver with his interrogating thumb, the clank of the
    shod horses on the granite floor,   155

The snow-sleighs, clinking, shouted jokes, pelts of snow-balls,
The hurrahs for popular favorites, the fury of rous'd mobs,
The flap of the curtain'd litter, a sick man inside borne to the hospital,
The meeting of enemies, the sudden oath, the blows and fall,
The excited crowd, the policeman with his star quickly working his passage to
    the centre of the crowd,
The impassive stones that receive and return so many echoes,
What groans of over-fed or half-starv'd who fall sunstruck or in fits,
What exclamations of women taken suddenly who hurry home and give birth
    to babes,
What living and buried speech is always vibrating here, what howls restrain'd
    by decorum,
Arrests of criminals, slights, adulterous offers made, acceptances, rejections with
    convex lips,
I mind them or the show or resonance of them—I come and I depart.

9

The big doors of the country barn stand open and ready,
The dried grass of the harvest-time loads the slow-drawn wagon,
The clear light plays on the brown gray and green intertinged,
The armfuls are pack'd to the sagging mow.

I am there, I help, I came stretch'd atop of the load,
I felt its soft jolts, one leg reclined on the other,
I jump from the cross-beams and seize the clover and timothy,
And roll head over heels and tangle my hair full of wisps.

10

Alone far in the wilds and mountains I hunt,
Wandering amazed at my own lightness and glee,
In the late afternoon choosing a safe spot to pass the night,
Kindling a fire and broiling the fresh-kill'd game,
Falling asleep on the gather'd leaves with my dog and gun by my side.

The Yankee clipper is under her sky-sails, she cuts the sparkle and scud,
My eyes settle the land, I bend at her prow or shout joyously from the deck.

The boatmen and clam-diggers arose early and stopt for me,
I tuck'd my trowser-ends in my boots and went and had a good time;
You should have been with us that day round the chowder-kettle.

I saw the marriage of the trapper in the open air in the far west, the bride was
    a red girl,
Her father and his friends sat near cross-legged and dumbly smoking, they had
    moccasins to their feet and large thick blankets hanging from their shoulders,
On a bank lounged the trapper, he was drest mostly in skins, his luxuriant
    beard and curls protected his neck, he held his bride by the hand,

She had long eyelashes, her head was bare, her coarse straight locks descended
   upon her voluptuous limbs and reach'd to her feet.

The runaway slave came to my house and stopt outside,
I heard his motions crackling the twigs of the woodpile,   190
Through the swung half-door of the kitchen I saw him limpsy and weak,
And went where he sat on a log and led him in and assured him,
And brought water and fill'd a tub for his sweated body and bruis'd feet,
And gave him a room that enter'd from my own, and gave him some coarse
   clean clothes,
And remember perfectly well his revolving eyes and his awkwardness,   195
And remember putting plasters on the galls of his neck and ankles;
He staid with me a week before he was recuperated and pass'd north,
I had him sit next me at table, my fire-lock lean'd in the corner.

11

Twenty-eight young men bathe by the shore,
Twenty-eight young men and all so friendly;   200
Twenty-eight years of womanly life and all so lonesome.

She owns the fine house by the rise of the bank,
She hides handsome and richly drest aft the blinds of the window.

Which of the young men does she like the best?
Ah the homeliest of them is beautiful to her.   205

Where are you off to, lady? for I see you,
You splash in the water there, yet stay stock still in your room.

Dancing and laughing along the beach came the twenty-ninth bather,
The rest did not see her, but she saw them and loved them.
The beards of the young men glisten'd with wet, it ran from their long hair,   210
Little streams pass'd all over their bodies.

An unseen hand also pass'd over their bodies,
It descended tremblingly from their temples and ribs.

The young men float on their backs, their white bellies bulge to the sun, they
   do not ask who seizes fast to them,
They do not know who puffs and declines with pendant and bending arch,   215
They do not think whom they souse with spray.

12

The butcher-boy puts off his killing-clothes, or sharpens his knife at the stall in
   the market,
I loiter enjoying his repartee and his shuffle[6] and break-down.[7]

---

[6] Slow dance.   [7] Rollicking dance.

Blacksmiths with grimed and hairy chests environ the anvil,
Each has his main-sledge, they are all out, there is a great heat in the fire.   2.

From the cinder-strew'd threshold I follow their movements,
The lithe sheer of their waists plays even with their massive arms,
Overhand the hammers swing, overhand so slow, overhand so sure,
They do not hasten, each man hits in his place.

13

The negro holds firmly the reins of his four horses, the block swags underneath
    on its tied-over chain,   22.
The negro that drives the long dray of the stone-yard, steady and tall he stands
    pois'd on one leg on the string-piece,[8]
His blue shirt exposes his ample neck and breast and loosens over his hip-band,
His glance is calm and commanding, he tosses the slouch of his hat away from
    his forehead,
The sun falls on his crispy hair and mustache, falls on the black of his polish'd
    and perfect limbs.
I behold the picturesque giant and love him, and I do not stop there,   230
I go with the team also.

In me the caresser of life wherever moving, backward as well as forward sluing,
To niches aside and junior bending, not a person or object missing,
Absorbing all to myself and for this song.

Oxen that rattle the yoke and chain or halt in the leafy shade, what is that you
    express in your eyes?   235
It seems to me more than all the print I have read in my life.

My tread scares the wood-drake and wood-duck on my distant and day-long
    ramble,
They rise together, they slowly circle around.

I believe in those wing'd purposes,
And acknowledge red, yellow, white, playing within me,   240
And consider green and violet and the tufted crown intentional,
And do not call the tortoise unworthy because she is not something else,
And the jay in the woods never studied the gamut, yet trills pretty well to me,
And the look of the bay mare shames silliness out of me.

14

The wild gander leads his flock through the cool night,   245
Ya-honk he says, and sounds it down to me like an invitation,

[8] Connective or supporting timber.

The pert may suppose it meaningless, but I listening close,
Find its purpose and place up there toward the wintry sky.

The sharp-hoof'd moose of the north, the cat on the house-sill, the chickadee,
    the prairie-dog,
The litter of the grunting sow as they tug at her teats,   250
The brood of the turkey-hen and she with her half-spread wings,
I see in them and myself the same old law.
The press of my foot to the earth springs a hundred affections,
They scorn the best I can do to relate them.

I am enamour'd of growing out-doors,   255
Of men that live among cattle or taste of the ocean or woods,
Of the builders and steerers of ships and the wielders of axes and mauls, and the
    drivers of horses,
I can eat and sleep with them week in and week out.

What is commonest, cheapest, nearest, easiest, is Me,
Me going in for my chances, spending for vast returns,   260
Adorning myself to bestow myself on the first that will take me,
Not asking the sky to come down to my good will,
Scattering it freely forever.

15

The pure contralto sings in the organ loft,
The carpenter dresses his plank, the tongue of his foreplane whistles its wild
    ascending lisp,   265
The married and unmarried children ride home to their Thanksgiving dinner,
The pilot seizes the king-pin, he heaves down with a strong arm,
The mate stands braced in the whale-boat, lance and harpoon are ready,
The duck-shooter walks by silent and cautious stretches,
The deacons are ordain'd with cross'd hands at the altar,   270
The spinning-girl retreats and advances to the hum of the big wheel,
The farmer stops by the bars as he walks on a First-day loafe and looks at the
    oats and rye,
The lunatic is carried at last to the asylum a confirm'd case,
(He will never sleep any more as he did in the cot in his mother's bed-room;)
The jour printer[9] with gray head and gaunt jaws works at his case,   275
He turns his quid of tobacco while his eyes blurr with the manuscript;
The malform'd limbs are tied to the surgeon's table,
What is removed drops horribly in a pail;
The quadroon girl is sold at the auction-stand, the drunkard nods by the
    bar-room stove,

[9] Journeyman or working printer (from French
jour: "day").

The machinist rolls up his sleeves, the policeman travels his beat, the gate-keeper
marks who pass,
The young fellow drives the express-wagon, (I love him, though I do not
know him;)
The half-breed straps on his light boots to compete in the race,
The western turkey-shooting draws old and young, some lean on their rifles,
some sit on logs,
Out from the crowd steps the marksman, takes his position, levels his piece;
The groups of newly-come immigrants cover the wharf or levee,
As the woolly-pates hoe in the sugar-field, the overseer views them from his
saddle,
The bugle calls in the ball-room, the gentlemen run for their partners, the
dancers bow to each other,
The youth lies awake in the cedar-roof'd garret and harks to the musical rain,
The Wolverine[10] sets traps on the creek that helps fill the Huron,
The squaw wrapt in her yellow-hemm'd cloth is offering moccasins and
bead-bags for sale,
The connoisseur peers along the exhibition-gallery with half-shut eyes bent
sideways,
As the deck-hands make fast the steamboat the plank is thrown for the
shore-going passengers,
The young sister holds out the skein while the elder sister winds it off in a ball,
and stops now and then for the knots,
The one-year wife is recovering and happy having a week ago borne her first
child,
The clean-hair'd Yankee girl works with her sewing-machine or in the factory
or mill,
The paving-man leans on his two-handed rammer, the reporter's lead flies
swiftly over the note-book, the sign-painter is lettering with blue and gold,
The canal boy trots on the tow-path, the book-keeper counts at his desk, the
shoemaker waxes his thread,
The conductor beats time for the band and all the performers follow him,
The child is baptized, the convert is making his first professions,
The regatta is spread on the bay, the race is begun, (how the white sails
sparkle!)
The drover watching his drove sings out to them that would stray,
The pedler sweats with his pack on his back, (the purchaser higgling about the
odd cent;)
The bride unrumples her white dress, the minute-hand of the clock moves
slowly,
The opium-eater reclines with rigid head and just-open'd lips,
The prostitute draggles her shawl, her bonnet bobs on her tipsy and pimpled
neck,
The crowd laugh at her blackguard oaths, the men jeer and wink to each
other,

[10] Native of Michigan.

(Miserable! I do not laugh at your oaths nor jeer you;)
The President holding a cabinet council is surrounded by the great Secretaries,
On the piazza walk three matrons stately and friendly with twined arms,
The crew of the fish-smack pack repeated layers of halibut in the hold,   310
The Missourian crosses the plains toting his wares and his cattle,
As the fare-collector goes through the train he gives notice by the jingling of
    loose change,
The floor-men are laying the floor, the tinners are tinning the roof, the masons
    are calling for mortar,
In single file each shouldering his hod pass onward the laborers;
Seasons pursuing each other the indescribable crowd is gather'd, it is the fourth
    of Seventh-month, (what salutes of cannon and small arms!)   315
Seasons pursuing each other the plougher ploughs, the mower mows, and the
    winter-grain falls in the ground;
Off on the lakes the pike-fisher watches and waits by the hole in the frozen
    surface,
The stumps stand thick round the clearing, the squatter strikes deep with his
    axe,
Flatboatmen make fast towards dusk near the cotton-wood or pecan-trees,
Coon-seekers go through the regions of the Red river or through those drain'd
    by the Tennessee, or through those of the Arkansas,   320
Torches shine in the dark that hangs on the Chattahooche or Altamahaw,
Patriarchs sit at supper with sons and grandsons and great-grandsons around
    them,
In walls of adobie, in canvas tents, rest hunters and trappers after their day's
    sport,
The city sleeps and the country sleeps,
The living sleep for their time, the dead sleep for their time,   325
The old husband sleeps by his wife and the young husband sleeps by his wife;
And these tend inward to me, and I tend outward to them,
And such as it is to be of these more or less I am,
And of these one and all I weave the song of myself.

16

I am of old and young, of the foolish as much as the wise,   330
Regardless of others, ever regardful of others,
Maternal as well as paternal, a child as well as a man,
Stuff'd with the stuff that is coarse and stuff'd with the stuff that is fine,
One of the Nation of many nations, the smallest the same and the largest the
    same,
A Southerner soon as a Northerner, a planter nonchalant and hospitable down
    by the Oconee I live,   335
A Yankee bound my own way ready for trade, my joints the limberest joints
    on earth and the sternest joints on earth,
A Kentuckian walking the vale of the Elkhorn in my deerskin leggings, a
    Louisianian or Georgian,

A boatman over lakes or bays or along coasts, a Hoosier, Badger, Buckeye;"
At home on Kanadian snow-shoes or up in the bush, or with fishermen off
    Newfoundland,
At home in the fleet of ice-boats, sailing with the rest and tacking,   34?
At home on the hills of Vermont or in the woods of Maine, or the Texan
    ranch,
Comrade of Californians, comrade of free North-Westerners, (loving their big
    proportions,)
Comrade of raftsmen and coalmen, comrade of all who shake hands and
    welcome to drink and meat,
A learner with the simplest, a teacher of the thoughtfullest,
A novice beginning yet experient of myriads of seasons,   34:
Of every hue and caste am I, of every rank and religion,
A farmer, mechanic, artist, gentleman, sailor, quaker,
Prisoner, fancy-man, rowdy, lawyer, physician, priest.

I resist any thing better than my own diversity,
Breathe the air but leave plenty after me,   350
And am not stuck up, and am in my place.

(The moth and the fish-eggs are in their place,
The bright suns I see and the dark suns I cannot see are in their place,
The palpable is in its place and the impalpable is in its place.)

17

These are really the thoughts of all men in all ages and lands, they are not
    original with me,
If they are not yours as much as mine they are nothing, or next to nothing,   355
If they are not the riddle and the untying of the riddle they are nothing,
If they are not just as close as they are distant they are nothing.

This is the grass that grows wherever the land is and the water is,
This the common air that bathes the globe.   360

18

With music strong I come, with my cornets and my drums,
I play not marches for accepted victors only, I play marches for conquer'd and
    slain persons.
Have you heard that it was good to gain the day?
I also say it is good to fall, battles are lost in the same spirit in which they are
    won.

" Hoosier; Badger; Buckeye: natives, respectively,
of Indiana, Wisconsin, and Ohio.

I beat and pound for the dead,   365
I blow through my embouchures[12] my loudest and gayest for them.

Vivas to those who have fail'd!
And to those whose war-vessels sank in the sea!
And to those themselves who sank in the sea!
And to all generals that lost engagements, and all overcome heroes!   370
And the numberless unknown heroes equal to the greatest heroes known!

19

This is the meal equally set, this the meat for natural hunger,
It is for the wicked just the same as the righteous, I make appointments with
      all,
I will not have a single person slighted or left away,
The kept-woman, sponger, thief, are hereby invited,   375
The heavy-lipp'd slave is invited, the venerealee is invited;
There shall be no difference between them and the rest.

This is the press of a bashful hand, this the float and odor of hair,
This the touch of my lips to yours, this the murmur of yearning,
This the far-off depth and height reflecting my own face,   380
This the thoughtful merge of myself, and the outlet again.

Do you guess I have some intricate purpose?
Well I have, for the Fourth-month showers have, and the mica on the side of a
      rock has.

Do you take it I would astonish?
Does the daylight astonish? does the early redstart twittering through the
      woods?   385
Do I astonish more than they?
This hour I tell things in confidence,
I might not tell everybody, but I will tell you.

20

Who goes there? hankering, gross, mystical, nude;
How is it I extract strength from the beef I eat?   390

What is a man anyhow? what am I? what are you?

All I mark as my own you shall offset it with your own,
Else it were time lost listening to me.

[12] Mouthpieces of wind instruments.

I do not snivel that snivel the world over,
That months are vacuums and the ground but wallow and filth. 3

Whimpering and truckling fold with powders for invalids, conformity goes to
    the fourth-remov'd,
I wear my hat as I please indoors or out.

Why should I pray? why should I venerate and be ceremonious?

Having pried through the strata, analyzed to a hair, counsel'd with doctors and
    calculated close,
I find no sweeter fat than sticks to my own bones. 40

In all people I see myself, none more and not one a barley-corn less,
And the good or bad I say of myself I say of them.

I know I am solid and sound,
To me the converging objects of the universe perpetually flow,
All are written to me, and I must get what the writing means. 40

I know I am deathless,
I know this orbit of mine cannot be swept by a carpenter's compass,
I know I shall not pass like a child's carlacue[13] cut with a burnt stick at night.
I know I am august,
I do not trouble my spirit to vindicate itself or be understood,
I see that the elementary laws never apologize,
(I reckon I behave no prouder than the level I plant my house by, after all.) 410

I exist as I am, that is enough,
If no other in the world be aware I sit content,
And if each and all be aware I sit content. 415

One world is aware and by far the largest to me, and that is myself,
And whether I come to my own to-day or in ten thousand or ten million
    years,
I can cheerfully take it now, or with equal cheerfulness I can wait.

My foothold is tenon'd and mortis'd in granite,
I laugh at what you call dissolution,
And I know the amplitude of time. 420

21

I am the poet of the Body and I am the poet of the Soul,
The pleasures of heaven are with me and the pains of hell are with me,
The first I graft and increase upon myself, the latter I translate into a new
    tongue.

[13] Curlicue.

I am the poet of the woman the same as the man,   425
And I say it is as great to be a woman as to be a man,
And I say there is nothing greater than the mother of men.

I chant the chant of dilation or pride,
We have had ducking and deprecating about enough,
I show that size is only development.   430

Have you outstript the rest? are you the President?
It is a trifle, they will more than arrive there every one, and still pass on.

I am he that walks with the tender and growing night,
I call to the earth and sea half-held by the night.

Press close bare-bosom'd night—press close magnetic nourishing night!   435
Night of south winds—night of the large few stars!
Still nodding night—mad naked summer night.

Smile O voluptuous cool-breath'd earth!
Earth of the slumbering and liquid trees!
Earth of departed sunset—earth of the mountains misty-topt!   440
Earth of the vitreous pour of the full moon just tinged with blue!
Earth of shine and dark mottling the tide of the river!
Earth of the limpid gray of clouds brighter and clearer for my sake!
Far-swooping elbow'd earth—rich apple-blossom'd earth!
Smile, for your lover comes.   445

Prodigal, you have given me love—therefore I to you give love!
O unspeakable passionate love.

22

You sea! I resign myself to you also—I guess what you mean,
I behold from the beach your crooked inviting fingers,
I believe you refuse to go back without feeling of me,   450
We must have a turn together, I undress, hurry me out of sight of the land,
Cushion me soft, rock me in billowy drowse,
Dash me with amorous wet, I can repay you.

Sea of stretch'd ground-swells,
Sea breathing broad and convulsive breaths,   455
Sea of the brine of life and of unshovell'd yet always-ready graves,
Howler and scooper of storms, capricious and dainty sea,
I am integral with you, I too am of one phase and of all phases.
Partaker of influx and efflux I, extoller of hate and conciliation,
Extoller of amies and those that sleep in each others' arms.   460

I am he attesting sympathy,
(Shall I make my list of things in the house and skip the house that supports
   them?)

I am not the poet of goodness only, I do not decline to be the poet of
   wickedness also.

What blurt is this about virtue and about vice?
Evil propels me and reform of evil propels me, I stand indifferent,   46
My gait is no fault-finder's or rejecter's gait,
I moisten the roots of all that has grown.

Did you fear some scrofula out of the unflagging pregnancy?
Did you guess the celestial laws are yet to be work'd over and rectified?

I find one side a balance and the antipodal side a balance,   47c
Soft doctrine as steady help as stable doctrine,
Thoughts and deeds of the present our rouse and early start.

This minute that comes to me over the past decillions,
There is no better than it and now.

What behaved well in the past or behaves well to-day is not such a wonder,   475
The wonder is always and always how there can be a mean man or an infidel.

23

Endless unfolding of words of ages!
And mine a word of the modern, the word En-Masse.

A word of the faith that never balks,
Here or henceforward it is all the same to me, I accept Time absolutely.   480
It alone is without flaw, it alone rounds and completes all,
That mystic baffling wonder alone completes all.

I accept Reality and dare not question it,
Materialism first and last imbuing.

Hurrah for positive science! long live exact demonstration!   485
Fetch stonecrop mixt with cedar and branches of lilac,
This is the lexicographer, this the chemist, this made a grammar of the old
   cartouches,
These mariners put the ship through dangerous unknown seas.
This is the geologist, this works with the scalpel, and this is a mathematician.

Gentlemen, to you the first honors always!   490
Your facts are useful, and yet they are not my dwelling,
I but enter by them to an area of my dwelling.

Less the reminders of properties told my words,
And more the reminders they of life untold, and of freedom and extrication,
And make short account of neuters and geldings, and favor men and women
    fully equipt,   495
And beat the gong of revolt, and stop with fugitives and them that plot and
    conspire.

24

Walt Whitman, a kosmos, of Manhattan the son,
Turbulent, fleshy, sensual, eating, drinking and breeding,
No sentimentalist, no stander above men and women or apart from them,
No more modest than immodest.   500

Unscrew the locks from the doors!
Unscrew the doors themselves from their jambs!

Whoever degrades another degrades me,
And whatever is done or said returns at last to me.
Through me the afflatus surging and surging, through me the current and index.   505

I speak the pass-word primeval, I give the sign of democracy,
By God! I will accept nothing which all cannot have their counterpart of on
    the same terms.

Through me many long dumb voices,
Voices of the interminable generations of prisoners and slaves,
Voices of the diseas'd and despairing and of thieves and dwarfs,   510
Voices of cycles of preparation and accretion,
And of the threads that connect the stars, and of wombs and of the father-stuff,
And of the rights of them the others are down upon,
Of the deform'd, trivial, flat, foolish, despised,
Fog in the air, beetles rolling balls of dung.   515

Through me forbidden voices,
Voices of sexes and lusts, voices veil'd and I remove the veil,
Voices indecent by me clarified and transfigur'd.

I do not press my fingers across my mouth,
I keep as delicate around the bowels as around the head and heart,   520
Copulation is no more rank to me than death is.

I believe in the flesh and the appetites,
Seeing, hearing, feeling, are miracles, and each part and tag of me is a miracle.

Divine am I inside and out, and I make holy whatever I touch or am touch'd
    from,

The scent of these arm-pits aroma finer than prayer,   52
This head more than churches, bibles, and all the creeds.

If I worship one thing more than another it shall be the spread of my own
    body, or any part of it,
Translucent mould of me it shall be you!
Shaded ledges and rests it shall be you!
Firm masculine colter it shall be you!   53(
Whatever goes to the tilth of me it shall be you!
You my rich blood! your milky stream pale strippings of my life!
Breast that presses against other breasts it shall be you!
My brain it shall be your occult convolutions!
Root of wash'd sweet-flag! timorous pond-snipe! nest of guarded duplicate
    eggs! it shall be you!   535
Mix'd tussled hay of head, beard, brawn, it shall be you!
Trickling sap of maple, fibre of manly wheat, it shall be you!
Sun so generous it shall be you!
Vapors lighting and shading my face it shall be you!
You sweaty brooks and dews it shall be you!   540
Winds whose soft-tickling genitals rub against me it shall be you!
Broad muscular fields, branches of live oak, loving lounger in my winding
    paths, it shall be you!
Hands I have taken, face I have kiss'd, mortal I have ever touch'd, it shall be
    you.

I dote on myself, there is that lot of me and all so luscious,
Each moment and whatever happens thrills me with joy,   545
I cannot tell how my ankles bend, nor whence the cause of my faintest wish,
Nor the cause of the friendship I emit, nor the cause of the friendship I take
    again.

That I walk up my stoop, I pause to consider if it really be,
A morning-glory at my window satisfies me more than the metaphysics of
    books.

To behold the day-break!   550
The little light fades the immense and diaphanous shadows,
The air tastes good to my palate.

Hefts of the moving world at innocent gambols silently rising freshly exuding,
Scooting obliquely high and low.

Something I cannot see puts upward libidinous prongs,   555
Seas of bright juice suffuse heaven.
The earth by the sky staid with, the daily close of their junction,
The heav'd challenge from the east that moment over my head,
The mocking taunt. See then whether you shall be master!

25

Dazzling and tremendous how quick the sun-rise would kill me,   560
If I could not now and always send sun-rise out of me.

We also ascend dazzling and tremendous as the sun,
We found our own O my soul in the calm and cool of the day-break.

My voice goes after what my eyes cannot reach,
With the twirl of my tongue I encompass worlds and volumes of worlds.   565

Speech is the twin of my vision, it is unequal to measure itself,
It provokes me forever, it says sarcastically,
Walt you contain enough, why don't you let it out then?

Come now I will not be tantalized, you conceive too much of articulation,
Do you not know O speech how the buds beneath you are folded?   570
Waiting in gloom, protected by frost,
The dirt receding before my prophetical screams,
I underlying causes to balance them at last,
My knowledge my live parts, it keeping tally with the meaning of all things,
Happiness, (which whoever hears me let him or her set out in search of this
   day.)   575

My final merit I refuse you, I refuse putting from me what I really am,
Encompass worlds, but never try to encompass me,
I crowd your sleekest and best by simply looking toward you.
Writing and talk do not prove me,
I carry the plenum of proof and every thing else in my face,   580
With the hush of my lips I wholly confound the skeptic.

26

Now I will do nothing but listen,
To accrue what I hear into this song, to let sounds contribute toward it.

I hear bravuras of birds, bustle of growing wheat, gossip of flames, clack of
   sticks cooking my meals,
I hear the sound I love, the sound of the human voice,   585
I hear all sounds running together, combined, fused or following,
Sounds of the city and sounds out of the city, sounds of the day and night,
Talkative young ones to those that like them, the loud laugh of work-people at
   their meals,
The angry base of disjointed friendship, the faint tones of the sick,
The judge with hands tight to the desk, his pallid lips pronouncing a
   death-sentence,   590
The heave'e'yo of stevedores unlading ships by the wharves, the refrain of the
   anchor-lifters,

The ring of alarm-bells, the cry of fire, the whirr of swift-streaking engines and
   hose-carts with premonitory tinkles and color'd lights,
The steam-whistle, the solid roll of the train of approaching cars,
The slow march play'd at the head of the association marching two and two,
(They go to guard some corpse, the flag-tops are draped with black muslin.)   59

I hear the violoncello, ('tis the young man's heart's complaint,)
I hear the key'd cornet, it glides quickly in through my ears,
It shakes mad-sweet pangs through my belly and breast.

I hear the chorus, it is a grand opera,
Ah this indeed is music—this suits me.   600
A tenor large and fresh as the creation fills me,
The orbic flex of his mouth is pouring and filling me full.

I hear the train'd soprano (what work with hers is this?)
The orchestra whirls me wider than Uranus flies,
It wrenches such ardors from me I did not know I possess'd them,   605
It sails me, I dab with bare feet, they are lick'd by the indolent waves,
I am cut by bitter and angry hail, I lose my breath,
Steep'd amid honey'd morphine, my windpipe throttled in fakes of death,
At length let up again to feel the puzzle of puzzles,
And that we call Being.   610

27

To be in any form, what is that?
(Round and round we go, all of us, and ever come back thither,)
If nothing lay more develop'd the quahaug in its callous shell were enough.

Mine is no callous shell,
I have instant conductors all over me whether I pass or stop,   615
They seize every object and lead it harmlessly through me.

I merely stir, press, feel with my fingers, and am happy,
To touch my person to some one else's is about as much as I can stand.

28

Is this then a touch? quivering me to a new identity,
Flames and ether making a rush for my veins,   620
Treacherous tip of me reaching and crowding to help them,
My flesh and blood playing out lightning to strike what is hardly different
   from myself,
On all sides prurient provokers stiffening my limbs,
Straining the udder of my heart for its withheld drip,
Behaving licentious toward me, taking no denial,   625

Depriving me of my best as for a purpose,
Unbuttoning my clothes, holding me by the bare waist,
Deluding my confusion with the calm of the sunlight and pasture-fields,
Immodestly sliding the fellow-senses away,
They bribed to swap off with touch and go and graze at the edges of me,   630
No consideration, no regard for my draining strength or my anger,
Fetching the rest of the herd around to enjoy them a while,
Then all uniting to stand on a headland and worry me.

The sentries desert every other part of me,
They have left me helpless to a red marauder,   635
They all come to the headland to witness and assist against me.

I am given up by traitors,
I talk wildly, I have lost my wits, I and nobody else am the greatest traitor,
I went myself first to the headland, my own hands carried me there.

You villain touch! what are you doing? my breath is tight in its throat,   640
Unclench your floodgates, you are too much for me.

29

Blind loving wrestling touch, sheath'd hooded sharp-tooth'd touch!
Did it make you ache so, leaving me?

Parting track'd by arriving, perpetual payment of perpetual loan,
Rich showering rain, and recompense richer afterward.   645

Sprouts take and accumulate, stand by the curb prolific and vital,
Landscapes projected masculine, full-sized and golden.

30

All truths wait in all things,
They neither hasten their own delivery nor resist it,
They do not need the obstetric forceps of the surgeon,   650
The insignificant is as big to me as any,
(What is less or more than a touch?)

Logic and sermons never convince,
The damp of the night drives deeper into my soul.

(Only what proves itself to every man and woman is so,   655
Only what nobody denies is so.)

A minute and a drop of me settle my brain,
I believe the soggy clods shall become lovers and lamps,

And a compend of compends is the meat of a man or woman,
And a summit and flower there is the feeling they have for each other,
And they are to branch boundlessly out of that lesson until it becomes omnific,
And until one and all shall delight us, and we them.

31

I believe a leaf of grass is no less than the journey-work of the stars,
And the pismire is equally perfect, and a grain of sand, and the egg of the
    wren,
And the tree-toad is a chef-d'œuvre for the highest,
And the running blackberry would adorn the parlors of heaven,
And the narrowest hinge in my hand puts to scorn all machinery,
And the cow crunching with depress'd head surpasses any statue,
And a mouse is miracle enough to stagger sextillions of infidels.

I find I incorporate gneiss, coal, long-threaded moss, fruits, grains, esculent
    roots,
And am stucco'd with quadrupeds and birds all over,
And have distanced what is behind me for good reasons,
But call any thing back again when I desire it.
In vain the speeding or shyness,
In vain the plutonic rocks send their old heat against my approach,
In vain the mastodon retreats beneath its own powder'd bones,
In vain objects stand leagues off and assume manifold shapes,
In vain the ocean settling in hollows and the great monsters lying low,
In vain the buzzard houses herself with the sky,
In vain the snake slides through the creepers and logs,
In vain the elk takes to the inner passes of the woods,
In vain the razor-bill'd auk sails far north to Labrador,
I follow quickly, I ascend to the nest in the fissure of the cliff.

32

I think I could turn and live with animals, they are so placid and self-contain'd,
I stand and look at them long and long.

They do not sweat and whine about their condition,
They do not lie awake in the dark and weep for their sins,
They do not make me sick discussing their duty to God,
Not one is dissatisfied, not one is demented with the mania of owning things,
Not one kneels to another, nor to his kind that lived thousands of years ago,
Not one is respectable or unhappy over the whole earth.

So they show their relations to me and I accept them,
They bring me tokens of myself, they evince them plainly in their possession.

I wonder where they get those tokens,
Did I pass that way huge times ago and negligently drop them?   695

Myself moving forward then and now and forever,
Gathering and showing more always and with velocity,
Infinite and omnigenous,[14] and the like of these among them,
Not too exclusive toward the reachers of my remembrancers,
Picking out here one that I love, and now go with him on brotherly terms.   700

A gigantic beauty of a stallion, fresh and responsive to my caresses,
Head high in the forehead, wide between the ears,
Limbs glossy and supple, tail dusting the ground,
Eyes full of sparkling wickedness, ears finely cut, flexibly moving.

His nostrils dilate as my heels embrace him,   705
His well-built limbs tremble with pleasure as we race around and return.

I but use you a minute, then I resign you, stallion,
Why do I need your paces when I myself out-gallop them?
Even as I stand or sit passing faster than you.

33

Space and Time! now I see it is true, what I guess'd at,   710
What I guess'd when I loaf'd on the grass,
What I guess'd while I lay alone in my bed,
And again as I walk'd the beach under the paling stars of the morning.

My ties and ballasts leave me, my elbows rest in sea-gaps,
I skirt sierras, my palms cover continents,   715
I am afoot with my vision.

By the city's quadrangular houses—in log huts, camping with lumbermen,
Along the ruts of the turnpike, along the dry gulch and rivulet bed,
Weeding my onion-patch or hoeing rows of carrots and parsnips, crossing
   savannas, trailing in forests,
Prospecting, gold-digging, girdling the trees of a new purchase,   720
Scorch'd ankle-deep by the hot sand, hauling my boat down the shallow river,
Where the panther walks to and fro on a limb overhead, where the buck turns
   furiously at the hunter,
Where the rattlesnake suns his flabby length on a rock, where the otter is
   feeding on fish,
Where the alligator in his tough pimples sleeps by the bayou,
Where the black bear is searching for roots or honey, where the beaver pats the
   mud with his paddle-shaped tail;   725

[14] Of all kinds.

Over the growing sugar, over the yellow-flower'd cotton plant, over the rice in its low moist field,

Over the sharp-peak'd farm house, with its scallop'd scum and slender shoots from the gutters,

Over the western persimmon, over the long-leav'd corn, over the delicate blue-flower flax,

Over the white and brown buckwheat, a hummer and buzzer there with the rest,

Over the dusky green of the rye as it ripples and shades in the breeze;   7

Scaling mountains, pulling myself cautiously up, holding on by low scragged limbs,

Walking the path worn in the grass and beat through the leaves of the brush,

Where the quail is whistling betwixt the woods and the wheat-lot,

Where the bat flies in the Seventh-month eve, where the great goldbug drops through the dark,

Where the brook puts out of the roots of the old tree and flows to the meadow,   73

Where cattle stand and shake away flies with the tremulous shuddering of their hides,

Where the cheese-cloth hangs in the kitchen, where andirons straddle the hearth-slab, where cobwebs fall in festoons from the rafters;

Where trip-hammers crash, where the press is whirling its cylinders,

Wherever the human heart beats with terrible throes under its ribs,

Where the pear-shaped balloon is floating aloft, (floating in it myself and looking composedly down,)   740

Where the life-car is drawn on the slip-noose, where the heat hatches pale-green eggs in the dented sand,

Where the she-whale swims with her calf and never forsakes it,

Where the steam-ship trails hind-ways its long pennant of smoke,

Where the fin of the shark cuts like a black chip out of the water,

Where the half-burn'd brig is riding on unknown currents,   745

Where shells grow to her slimy deck, where the dead are corrupting below;

Where the dense-starr'd flag is borne at the head of the regiments,

Approaching Manhattan up by the long-stretching island,

Under Niagara, the cataract falling like a veil over my countenance,

Upon a door-step, upon the horse-block of hard wood outside,   750

Upon the race-course, or enjoying picnics or jigs or a good game of base-ball,

At he-festivals, with blackguard gibes, ironical license, bull-dances, drinking, laughter,

At the cider-mill tasting the sweets of the brown mash, sucking the juice through a straw,

At apple-peelings wanting kisses for all the red fruit I find,

At musters, beach-parties, friendly bees, huskings, house-raisings;   755

Where the mocking-bird sounds his delicious gurgles, cackles, screams, weeps,

Where the hay-rick stands in the barn-yard, where the dry-stalks are scatter'd, where the brood-cow waits in the hovel,

Where the bull advances to do his masculine work, where the stud to the mare, where the cock is treading the hen,

Where the heifers browse, where geese nip their food with short jerks,
Where sun-down shadows lengthen over the limitless and lonesome prairie,   760
Where herds of buffalo make a crawling spread of the square miles far and
  near,
Where the humming-bird shimmers, where the neck of the long-lived swan is
  curving and winding,
Where the laughing-gull scoots by the shore, where she laughs her near-human
  laugh,
Where bee-hives range on a gray bench in the garden half hid by the high
  weeds,
Where band-neck'd partridges roost in a ring on the ground with their heads
  out,   765
Where burial coaches enter the arch'd gates of a cemetery,
Where winter wolves bark amid wastes of snow and icicled trees,
Where the yellow-crown'd heron comes to the edge of the marsh at night and
  feeds upon small crabs,
Where the splash of swimmers and divers cools the warm noon,
Where the katy-did works her chromatic reed on the walnut-tree over the
  well,   770
Through patches of citrons and cucumbers with silver-wired leaves,
Through the salt-lick or orange glade, or under conical firs,
Through the gymnasium, through the curtain'd saloon, through the office or
  public hall;
Pleas'd with the native and pleas'd with the foreign, pleas'd with the new and
  old,
Pleas'd with the homely woman as well as the handsome,   775
Pleas'd with the quakeress as she puts off her bonnet and talks melodiously,
Pleas'd with the tune of the choir of the whitewash'd church,
Pleas'd with the earnest words of the sweating Methodist preacher, impress'd
  seriously at the camp-meeting;
Looking in at the shop-windows of Broadway the whole forenoon, flatting the
  flesh of my nose on the thick plate glass,
Wandering the same afternoon with my face turn'd up to the clouds, or down
  a lane or along the beach,   780
My right and left arms round the sides of two friends, and I in the middle;
Coming home with the silent and dark-cheek'd bush-boy, (behind me he rides
  at the drape of the day,)
Far from the settlements studying the print of animals' feet, or the moccasin
  print,
By the cot in the hospital reaching lemonade to a feverish patient,
Nigh the coffin'd corpse when all is still, examining with a candle;   785
Voyaging to every port to dicker and adventure,
Hurrying with the modern crowd as eager and fickle as any,
Hot toward one I hate, ready in my madness to knife him,
Solitary at midnight in my back yard, my thoughts gone from me a long
  while,
Walking the old hills of Judæa with the beautiful gentle God by my side,   790
Speeding through space, speeding through heaven and the stars,

Speeding amid the seven satellites and the broad ring, and the diameter of
    eighty thousand miles,
Speeding with tail'd meteors, throwing fire-balls like the rest,
Carrying the crescent child that carries its own full mother in its belly,
Storming, enjoying, planning, loving, cautioning,   7
Backing and filling, appearing and disappearing,
I tread day and night such roads.

I visit the orchards of spheres and look at the product,
And look at quintillions ripen'd and look at quintillions green.

I fly those flights of a fluid and swallowing soul,   80
My course runs below the soundings of plummets.

I help myself to material and immaterial,
No guard can shut me off, no law prevent me.

I anchor my ship for a little while only,
My messengers continually cruise away or bring their returns to me.   80

I go hunting polar furs and the seal, leaping chasms with a pike-pointed staff,
    clinging to topples of brittle and blue.

I ascend to the foretruck,
I take my place late at night in the crow's-nest,
We sail the arctic sea, it is plenty light enough,
Through the clear atmosphere I stretch around on the wonderful beauty,   810
The enormous masses of ice pass me and I pass them, the scenery is plain in all
    directions,
The white-topt mountains show in the distance, I fling out my fancies toward
    them,
We are approaching some great battle-field in which we are soon to be
    engaged,
We pass the colossal outposts of the encampment, we pass with still feet and
    caution,
Or we are entering by the suburbs some vast and ruin'd city,   815
The blocks and fallen architecture more than all the living cities of the globe.

I am a free companion, I bivouac by invading watchfires,
I turn the bridegroom out of bed and stay with the bride myself,
I tighten her all night to my thighs and lips.

My voice is the wife's voice, the screech by the rail of the stairs,   820
They fetch my man's body up dripping and drown'd.

I understand the large hearts of heroes,
The courage of present times and all times,

How the skipper saw the crowded and rudderless wreck of the steam-ship, and
    Death chasing it up and down the storm,
How he knuckled tight and gave not back an inch, and was faithful of days
    and faithful of nights,   825
And chalk'd in large letters on a board, *Be of good cheer, we will not desert you;*
How he follow'd with them and tack'd with them three days and would not
    give it up,
How he saved the drifting company at last,
How the lank loose-gown'd women look'd when boated from the side of their
    prepared graves,
How the silent old-faced infants and the lifted sick, and the sharp-lipp'd
    unshaved men;   830
All this I swallow, it tastes good, I like it well, it becomes mine,
I am the man, I suffer'd, I was there.

The disdain and calmness of martyrs,
The mother of old, condemn'd for a witch, burnt with dry wood, her children
    gazing on,
The hounded slave that flags in the race, leans by the fence, blowing, cover'd
    with sweat,   835
The twinges that sting like needles his legs and neck, the murderous buckshot
    and the bullets,
All these I feel or am.

I am the hounded slave, I wince at the bite of the dogs,
Hell and despair are upon me, crack and again crack the marksmen,
I clutch the rails of the fence, my gore dribs, thinn'd with the ooze of my skin, 840
I fall on the weeds and stones,
The riders spur their unwilling horses, haul close,
Taunt my dizzy ears and beat me violently over the head with whip-stocks.

Agonies are one of my changes of garments,
I do not ask the wounded person how he feels, I myself become the wounded
    person,   845
My hurts turn livid upon me as I lean on a cane and observe.

I am the mash'd fireman with breast-bone broken,
Tumbling walls buried me in their debris,
Heat and smoke I inspired, I heard the yelling shouts of my comrades,
I heard the distant click of their picks and shovels,   850
They have clear'd the beams away, they tenderly lift me forth.

I lie in the night air in my red shirt, the pervading hush is for my sake,
Painless after all I lie exhausted but not so unhappy,
White and beautiful are the faces around me, the heads are bared of their
    fire-caps,
The kneeling crowd fades with the light of the torches.   855

Distant and dead resuscitate,
They show as the dial or move as the hands of me, I am the clock myself.

I am an old artillerist, I tell of my fort's bombardment,
I am there again.

Again the long roll of the drummers,   8c
Again the attacking cannon, mortars,
Again to my listening ears the cannon responsive.

I take part, I see and hear the whole,
The cries, curses, roar, the plaudits for well-aim'd shots,
The ambulanza[15] slowly passing trailing its red drip,   86
Workmen searching after damages, making indispensable repairs,
The fall of grenades through the rent roof, the fan-shaped explosion,
The whizz of limbs, heads, stone, wood, iron, high in the air.

Again gurgles the mouth of my dying general, he furiously waves with his
    hand,
He gasps through the clot *Mind not me—mind—the entrenchments.*   870

34

Now I tell what I knew in Texas in my early youth,
(I tell not the fall of Alamo,
Not one escaped to tell the fall of Alamo,
The hundred and fifty are dumb yet at Alamo,)
'Tis the tale of the murder in cold blood of four hundred and twelve young
    men.   875

Retreating they had form'd in a hollow square with their baggage for
    breastworks,
Nine hundred lives out of the surrounding enemy's, nine times their number,
    was the price they took in advance,
Their colonel was wounded and their ammunition gone,
They treated for an honorable capitulation, receiv'd writing and seal, gave up
    their arms and march'd back prisoners of war.

They were the glory of the race of rangers,   880
Matchless with horse, rifle, song, supper, courtship,
Large, turbulent, generous, handsome, proud, and affectionate,
Bearded, sunburnt, drest in the free costume of hunters,
Not a single one over thirty years of age.

---

[15] Italian: "ambulance."

The second First-day morning they were brought out in squads and massacred,
    it was beautiful early summer, 885
The work commenced about five o'clock and was over by eight.

None obey'd the command to kneel,
Some made a mad and helpless rush, some stood stark and straight,
A few fell at once, shot in the temple or heart, the living and dead lay
    together,
The maim'd and mangled dug in the dirt, the new-comers saw them there, 890
Some half-kill'd attempted to crawl away,
These were despatch'd with bayonets or batter'd with the blunts of muskets,
A youth not seventeen years old seiz'd his assassin till two more came to release
    him,
The three were all torn and cover'd with the boy's blood.

At eleven o'clock began the burning of the bodies; 895
That is the tale of the murder of the four hundred and twelve young men.

35

Would you hear of an old-time sea-fight?
Would you learn who won by the light of the moon and stars?
List to the yarn, as my grandmother's father the sailor told it to me.

Our foe was no skulk in his ship I tell you, (said he,) 900
His was the surly English pluck, and there is no tougher or truer, and never
    was, and never will be;
Along the lower'd eve he came horribly raking us.

We closed with him, the yards entangled, the cannon touch'd,
My captain lash'd fast with his own hands.

We had receiv'd some eighteen pound shots under the water, 905
On our lower-gun-deck two large pieces had burst at the first fire, killing all
    around and blowing up overhead.

Fighting at sun-down, fighting at dark,
Ten o'clock at night, the full moon well up, our leaks on the gain, and five
    feet of water reported,
The master-at-arms loosing the prisoners confined in the after-hold to give them
    a chance for themselves.

The transit to and from the magazine is now stopt by the sentinels, 910
They see so many strange faces they do not know whom to trust.

Our frigate takes fire,
The other asks if we demand quarter?
If our colors are struck and the fighting done?

Now I laugh content, for I hear the voice of my little captain, 9

We have not struck, he composedly cries, *we have just begun our part of the fighting.*

Only three guns are in use,

One is directed by the captain himself against the enemy's mainmast,

Two well serv'd with grape and canister silence his musketry and clear his decks.

The tops alone second the fire of this little battery, especially the main-top, 92

They hold out bravely during the whole of the action.

Not a moment's cease,

The leaks gain fast on the pumps, the fire eats toward the powder-magazine.

One of the pumps has been shot away, it is generally thought we are sinking.

Serene stands the little captain, 925

He is not hurried, his voice is neither high nor low,

His eyes give more light to us than our battle-lanterns.

Toward twelve there in the beams of the moon they surrender to us.

36

Stretch'd and still lies the midnight,

Two great hulls motionless on the breast of the darkness,

Our vessel riddled and slowly sinking, preparations to pass to the one we have 930

conquer'd,

The captain on the quarter-deck coldly giving his orders through a countenance white as a sheet,

Near by the corpse of the child that serv'd in the cabin,

The dead face of an old salt with long white hair and carefully curl'd whiskers,

The flames spite of all that can be done flickering aloft and below, 935

The husky voices of the two or three officers yet fit for duty,

Formless stacks of bodies and bodies by themselves, dabs of flesh upon the masts and spars,

Cut of cordage, dangle of rigging, slight shock of the soothe of waves,

Black and impassive guns, litter of powder-parcels, strong scent,

A few large stars overhead, silent and mournful shining, 940

Delicate sniffs of sea-breeze, smells of sedgy grass and fields by the shore, death-messages given in charge to survivors,

The hiss of the surgeon's knife, the gnawing teeth of his saw,

Wheeze, cluck, swash of falling blood, short wild scream, and long, dull, tapering groan,

These so, these irretrievable.

37

You laggards there on guard! look to your arms!   945
In at the conquer'd doors they crowd! I am possess'd!
Embody all presences outlaw'd or suffering,
See myself in prison shaped like another man,
And feel the dull unintermitted pain.

For me the keepers of convicts shoulder their carbines and keep watch,   950
It is I let out in the morning and barr'd at night.

Not a mutineer walks handcuff'd to jail but I am handcuff'd to him and walk
    by his side,
(I am less the jolly one there, and more the silent one with sweat on my
    twitching lips.)

Not a youngster is taken for larceny but I go up too, and am tried and
    sentenced.

Not a cholera patient lies at the last gasp but I also lie at the last gasp,   955
My face is ash-color'd, my sinews gnarl, away from me people retreat.

Askers embody themselves in me and I am embodied in them,
I project my hat, sit shame-faced, and beg.

38

Enough! enough! enough!
Somehow I have been stunn'd. Stand back!   960
Give me a little time beyond my cuff'd head, slumbers, dreams, gaping,
I discover myself on the verge of a usual mistake.
That I could forget the mockers and insults!
That I could forget the trickling tears and the blows of the bludgeons and
    hammers!
That I could look with a separate look on my own crucifixion and bloody
    crowning.   965

I remember now,
I resume the overstaid fraction,
The grave of rock multiplies what has been confided to it, or to any graves,
Corpses rise, gashes heal, fastenings roll from me.

I troop forth replenish'd with supreme power, one of an average unending
    procession,   970
Inland and sea-coast we go, and pass all boundary lines,
Our swift ordinances on their way over the whole earth,
The blossoms we wear in our hats the growth of thousands of years.

Eleves,[16] I salute you! come forward!
Continue your annotations, continue your questionings.

39

The friendly and flowing savage, who is he?
Is he waiting for civilization, or past it and mastering it?

Is he some Southwesterner rais'd out-doors? is he Kanadian?
Is he from the Mississippi country? Iowa, Oregon, California?
The mountains? prairie-life, bush-life? or sailor from the sea?

Wherever he goes men and women accept and desire him,
They desire he should like them, touch them, speak to them, stay with them.

Behavior lawless as snow-flakes, words simple as grass, uncomb'd head, laughter,
    and naivetè,
Slow-stepping feet, common features, common modes and emanations,
They descend in new forms from the tips of his fingers,
They are wafted with the odor of his body or breath, they fly out of the
    glance of his eyes.

40

Flaunt of the sunshine I need not your bask—lie over!
You light surfaces only, I force surfaces and depths also.

Earth! you seem to look for something at my hands,
Say, old top-knot,[17] what do you want?

Man or woman, I might tell how I like you, but cannot,
And might tell what it is in me and what it is in you, but cannot,
And might tell that pining I have, that pulse of my nights and days.

Behold, I do not give lectures or a little charity,
When I give I give myself.

You there, impotent, loose in the knees,
Open your scarf'd chops till I blow grit within you,
Spread your palms and lift the flaps of your pockets,
I am not to be denied, I compel, I have stores plenty and to spare,
And any thing I have I bestow.

---

[16] Pupils or disciples (from French *élève:*   [17] An Indian.
"student").

I do not ask who you are, that is not important to me,
You can do nothing and be nothing but what I will infold you.

To cotton-field drudge or cleaner of privies I lean,
On his right cheek I put the family kiss,
And in my soul I swear I never will deny him.   1005

On women fit for conception I start bigger and nimbler babes,
(This day I am jetting the stuff of far more arrogant republics.)

To any one dying, thither I speed and twist the knob of the door,
Turn the bed-clothes toward the foot of the bed,
Let the physician and the priest go home.   1010
I seize the descending man and raise him with resistless will,
O despairer, here is my neck,
By God, you shall not go down! hang your whole weight upon me.

I dilate you with tremendous breath, I buoy you up,
Every room of the house do I fill with an arm'd force,   1015
Lovers of me, bafflers of graves.

Sleep—I and they keep guard all night,
Not doubt, not decease shall dare to lay finger upon you,
I have embraced you, and henceforth possess you to myself,
And when you rise in the morning you will find what I tell you is so.   1020

41

I am he bringing help for the sick as they pant on their backs,
And for strong upright men I bring yet more needed help.

I heard what was said of the universe,
Heard it and heard it of several thousand years;
It is middling well as far as it goes—but is that all?   1025

Magnifying and applying come I,
Outbidding at the start the old cautious hucksters,
Taking myself the exact dimensions of Jehovah,
Lithographing Kronos, Zeus his son, and Hercules[18] his grandson,
Buying drafts of Osiris, Isis,[19] Belus, Brahma,[20] Buddha,[21]   1030
In my portfolio placing Manito[22] loose, Allah[23] on a leaf, the crucifix engraved,
With Odin[24] and the hideous-faced Mexitli[25] and every idol and image,

---

[18] Kronos; Zeus; Hercules: divinities in Greek
mythology.
[19] Osiris; Isis: Egyptian deities.
[20] Belus; Brahma: Hindu gods.
[21] Indian religious leader ("the Enlightened One").

[22] Algonquin Indian nature spirit.
[23] Moslem supreme being.
[24] Norse god of war.
[25] Aztec god of war.

Taking them all for what they are worth and not a cent more,
Admitting they were alive and did the work of their days,
(They bore mites as for unfledg'd birds who have now to rise and fly and sing
    for themselves,)
Accepting the rough deific sketches to fill out better in myself, bestowing them
    freely on each man and woman I see,
Discovering as much or more in a framer framing a house,
Putting higher claims for him there with his roll'd-up sleeves driving the mallet
    and chisel,
Not objecting to special revelations, considering a curl of smoke or a hair on
    the back of my hand just as curious as any revelation,
Lads ahold of fire-engines and hook-and-ladder ropes no less to me than the
    gods of the antique wars,
Minding their voices peal through the crash of destruction,
Their brawny limbs passing safe over charr'd laths, their white foreheads whole
    and unhurt out of the flames;
By the mechanic's wife with her babe at her nipple interceding for every person
    born,
Three scythes at harvest whizzing in a row from three lusty angels with shirts
    bagg'd out at their waists,
The snag-tooth'd hostler with red hair redeeming sins past and to come,
Selling all he possesses, traveling on foot to fee lawyers for his brother and sit
    by him while he is tried for forgery;
What was strewn in the amplest strewing the square rod about me, and not
    filling the square rod then,
The bull and the bug never worshipp'd half enough,
Dung and dirt more admirable than was dream'd,
The supernatural of no account, myself waiting my time to be one of the
    supremes,
The day getting ready for me when I shall do as much good as the best, and be
    as prodigious;
By my life-lumps! becoming already a creator,
Putting myself here and now to the ambush'd womb of the shadows.

42

A call in the midst of the crowd,
My own voice, orotund sweeping and final.

Come my children,
Come my boys and girls, my women, household and intimates,
Now the performer launches his nerve, he has pass'd his prelude on the reeds
    within.
Easily written loose-finger'd chords—I feel the thrum of your climax and close.

My head slues round on my neck,
Music rolls, but not from the organ,
Folks are around me, but they are no household of mine.

Ever the hard unsunk ground,
Ever the eaters and drinkers, ever the upward and downward sun, ever the air
    and the ceaseless tides,
Ever myself and my neighbors, refreshing, wicked, real,   1065
Ever the old inexplicable query, ever that thorn'd thumb, that breath of itches
    and thirsts,
Ever the vexer's *hoot! hoot!* till we find where the sly one hides and bring him
    forth,
Ever love, ever the sobbing liquid of life,
Ever the bandage under the chin, ever the trestles of death.

Here and there with dimes on the eyes walking,   1070
To feed the greed of the belly the brains liberally spooning,
Tickets buying, taking, selling, but in to the feast never once going.
Many sweating, ploughing, thrashing, and then the chaff for payment receiving,
A few idly owning, and they the wheat continually claiming.

This is the city and I am one of the citizens,   1075
Whatever interests the rest interests me, politics, wars, markets, newspapers,
    schools,
The mayor and councils, banks, tariffs, steamships, factories, stocks, stores, real
    estate and personal estate.

The little plentiful manikins skipping around in collars and tail'd coats,
I am aware who they are, (they are positively not worms or fleas,)
I acknowledge the duplicates of myself, the weakest and shallowest is deathless
    with me,   1080
What I do and say the same waits for them,
Every thought that flounders in me the same flounders in them.
I know perfectly well my own egotism,
Know my omnivorous lines and must not write any less,
And would fetch you whoever you are flush with myself.   1085

Not words of routine this song of mine,
But abruptly to question, to leap beyond yet nearer bring;
This printed and bound book—but the printer and the printing-office boy?
The well-taken photographs—but your wife or friend close and solid in your
    arms?
The black ship mail'd with iron, her mighty guns in her turrets—but the pluck
    of the captain and engineers?   1090
In the houses the dishes and fare and furniture—but the host and hostess, and
    the look out of their eyes?
The sky up there—yet here or next door, or across the way?
The saints and sages in history—but you yourself?
Sermons, creeds, theology—but the fathomless human brain,
And what is reason? and what is love? and what is life?   1095

43

I do not despise you priests, all time, the world over,
My faith is the greatest of faiths and the least of faiths,
Enclosing worship ancient and modern and all between ancient and modern,
Believing I shall come again upon the earth after five thousand years,
Waiting responses from oracles, honoring the gods, saluting the sun,   I
Making a fetich of the first rock or stump, powowing with sticks in the circle
  of obis,[26]
Helping the llama[27] or brahmin as he trims the lamps of the idols,
Dancing yet through the streets in a phallic procession, rapt and austere in the
  woods a gymnosophist,[28]
Drinking mead from the skull-cup, to Shastas[29] and Vedas admirant, minding
  the Koran,
Walking the teokallis,[30] spotted with gore from the stone and knife, beating the
  serpent-skin drum,   II
Accepting the Gospels, accepting him that was crucified, knowing assuredly that
  he is divine,
To the mass kneeling or the puritan's prayer rising, or sitting patiently in a
  pew,
Ranting and frothing in my insane crisis, or waiting deadlike till my spirit
  arouses me,
Looking forth on pavement and land, or outside of pavement and land,
Belonging to the winders of the circuit of circuits.   III

One of that centripetal and centrifugal gang I turn and talk like a man leaving
  charges before a journey.

Down-hearted doubters dull and excluded,
Frivolous, sullen, moping, angry, affected, dishearten'd, atheistical,
I know every one of you, I know the sea of torment, doubt, despair and
  unbelief.

How the flukes splash!   III5
How they contort rapid as lightning, with spasms and spouts of blood!

Be at peace bloody flukes of doubters and sullen mopers,
I take my place among you as much as among any,
The past is the push of you, me, all, precisely the same,
And what is yet untried and afterward is for you, me, all, precisely the same.   II20

I do not know what is untried and afterward,
But I know it will in its turn prove sufficient, and cannot fail.

[26] I.e., obeah, referring to West African witchcraft   [29] I.e., Shastras, Hindu sacred writings (cf. the
and sorcery.   Vedas).
[27] I.e., lama, a Buddhist monk.   [30] Aztec temples.
[28] Hindu ascetic.

Each who passes is consider'd, each who stops is consider'd, not a single one can
    it fail.

It cannot fail the young man who died and was buried,
Nor the young woman who died and was put by his side,   1125
Nor the little child that peep'd in at the door, and then drew back and was
    never seen again,
Nor the old man who has lived without purpose, and feels it with bitterness
    worse than gall,
Nor him in the poor house tubercled by rum and the bad disorder,
Nor the numberless slaughter'd and wreck'd, nor the brutish koboo[31] call'd the
    ordure of humanity,
Nor the sacs merely floating with open mouths for food to slip in,   1130
Nor any thing in the earth, or down in the oldest graves of the earth,
Nor any thing in the myriads of spheres, nor the myriads of myriads that
    inhabit them,
Nor the present, nor the least wisp that is known.

44

It is time to explain myself—let us stand up.

What is known I strip away,   1135
I launch all men and women forward with me into the Unknown.

The clock indicates the moment—but what does eternity indicate?

We have thus far exhausted trillions of winters and summers,
There are trillions ahead, and trillions ahead of them.

Births have brought us richness and variety,   1140
And other births will bring us richness and variety.

I do not call one greater and one smaller,
That which fills its period and place is equal to any.

Were mankind murderous or jealous upon you, my brother, my sister?
I am sorry for you, they are not murderous or jealous upon me,   1145
All has been gentle with me, I keep no account with lamentation,
(What have I to do with lamentation?)
I am an acme of things accomplish'd, and I an encloser of things to be.

My feet strike an apex of the apices of the stairs,
On every step bunches of ages, and larger bunches between the steps,   1150
All below duly travel'd, and still I mount and mount.

[31] Sumatran savage.

Rise after rise bow the phantoms behind me,
Afar down I see the huge first Nothing, I know I was even there,
I waited unseen and always, and slept through the lethargic mist,
And took my time, and took no hurt from the fetid carbon.

Long I was hugg'd close—long and long.

Immense have been the preparations for me,
Faithful and friendly the arms that have help'd me.

Cycles ferried my cradle, rowing and rowing like cheerful boatmen,
For room to me stars kept aside in their own rings,
They sent influences to look after what was to hold me.

Before I was born out of my mother generations guided me,
My embryo has never been torpid, nothing could overlay it.

For it the nebula cohered to an orb,
The long slow strata piled to rest it on,
Vast vegetables gave it sustenance,
Monstrous sauroids[32] transported it in their mouths and deposited it with care.

All forces have been steadily employ'd to complete and delight me,
Now on this spot I stand with my robust soul.

45

O span of youth! ever-push'd elasticity!
O manhood, balanced, florid and full.
My lovers suffocate me,
Crowding my lips, thick in the pores of my skin,
Jostling me through streets and public halls, coming naked to me at night,
Crying by day *Ahoy!* from the rocks of the river, swinging and chirping over
    my head,
Calling my name from flower-beds, vines, tangled underbrush.
Lighting on every moment of my life,
Bussing my body with soft balsamic busses,
Noiselessly passing handfuls out of their hearts and giving them to be mine.

Old age superbly rising! O welcome, ineffable grace of dying days!

Every condition promulges not only itself, it promulges[33] what grows after and
    out of itself,
And the dark hush promulges as much as any.

---

[32] Prehistoric reptiles.　　　　　[33] Promulgates.

I open my scuttle at night and see the far-sprinkled systems,
And all I see multiplied as high as I can cipher edge but the rim of the farther
  systems.

Wider and wider they spread, expanding, always expanding,   1185
Outward and outward and forever outward.

My sun has his sun and round him obediently wheels,
He joins with his partners a group of superior circuit,
And greater sets follow, making specks of the greatest inside them.

There is no stoppage and never can be stoppage,   1190
If I, you, and the worlds, and all beneath or upon their surfaces, were this
  moment reduced back to a pallid float, it would not avail in the long run,
We should surely bring up again where we now stand,
And surely go as much farther, and then farther and farther.

A few quadrillions of eras, a few octillions of cubic leagues, do not hazard the
  span or make it impatient,   1195
They are but parts, any thing is but a part.
See ever so far, there is limitless space outside of that,
Count ever so much, there is limitless time around that.

My rendezvous is appointed, it is certain,
The Lord will be there and wait till I come on perfect terms,   1200
The great Camerado, the lover true for whom I pine will be there.

46

I know I have the best of time and space, and was never measured and never
  will be measured.

I tramp a perpetual journey, (come listen all!)
My signs are a rain-proof coat, good shoes, and a staff cut from the woods,
No friend of mine takes his ease in my chair,   1205
I have no chair, no church, no philosophy,
I lead no man to a dinner-table, library, exchange,
But each man and each woman of you I lead upon a knoll,
My left hand hooking you round the waist,
My right hand pointing to landscapes of continents and the public road.   1210

Not I, not any one else can travel that road for you,
You must travel it for yourself.

It is not far, it is within reach,
Perhaps you have been on it since you were born and did not know,
Perhaps it is everywhere on water and on land.   1215

Shoulder your duds dear son, and I will mine, and let us hasten forth,
Wonderful cities and free nations we shall fetch as we go.

If you tire, give me both burdens, and rest the chuff[34] of your hand on my hip,
And in due time you shall repay the same service to me,
For after we start we never lie by again.
This day before dawn I ascended a hill and look'd at the crowded heaven,
And I said to my spirit *When we become the enfolders of those orbs, and the*
    pleasure and knowledge of every thing in them, shall we be fill'd and satisfied then?
And my spirit said *No, we but level that lift to pass and continue beyond.*

You are also asking me questions and I hear you,
I answer that I cannot answer, you must find out for yourself.

Sit a while dear son,
Here are biscuits to eat and here is milk to drink,
But as soon as you sleep and renew yourself in sweet clothes, I kiss you with a
    good-by kiss and open the gate for your egress hence.

Long enough have you dream'd contemptible dreams,
Now I wash the gum from your eyes,
You must habit yourself to the dazzle of the light and of every moment of
    your life.

Long have you timidly waded holding a plank by the shore,
Now I will you to be a bold swimmer,
To jump off in the midst of the sea, rise again, nod to me, shout, and
    laughingly dash with your hair.

47

I am the teacher of athletes,
He that by me spreads a wider breast than my own proves the width of my
    own,
He most honors my style who learns under it to destroy the teacher.

The boy I love, the same becomes a man not through derived power, but in his
    own right,
Wicked rather than virtuous out of conformity or fear,
Fond of his sweetheart, relishing well his steak,
Unrequited love or a slight cutting him worse than sharp steel cuts,
First-rate to ride, to fight, to hit the bull's eye, to sail a skiff, to sing a song or
    play on the banjo,
Preferring scars and the beard and faces pitted with smallpox over all latherers,
And those well-tann'd to those that keep out of the sun.

[34] Heel.

I teach straying from me, yet who can stray from me?   1245
I follow you whoever you are from the present hour
My words itch at your ears till you understand them.

I do not say these things for a dollar or to fill up the time while I wait for a
    boat,
(It is you talking just as much as myself, I act as the tongue of you,
Tied in your mouth, in mine it begins to be loosen'd.)   1250

I swear I will never again mention love or death inside a house,
And I swear I will never translate myself at all, only to him or her who
    privately stays with me in the open air.

If you would understand me go to the heights or water-shore,
The nearest gnat is an explanation, and a drop or motion of waves a key,
The maul, the oar, the hand-saw, second my words.   1255

No shutter'd room or school can commune with me,
But roughs and little children better than they.

The young mechanic is closest to me, he knows me well,
The woodman that takes his axe and jug with him shall take me with him all
    day,
The farm-boy ploughing in the field feels good at the sound of my voice,   1260
In vessels that sail my words sail, I go with fishermen and seamen and love
    them.

The soldier camp'd or upon the march is mine,
On the night ere the pending battle many seek me, and I do not fail them,
On that solemn night (it may be their last) those that know me seek me.
My face rubs to the hunter's face when he lies down alone in his blanket,   1265
The driver thinking of me does not mind the jolt of his wagon,
The young mother and old mother comprehend me,
The girl and the wife rest the needle a moment and forget where they are,
They and all would resume what I have told them.

48

I have said that the soul is not more than the body,   1270
And I have said that the body is not more than the soul,
And nothing, not God, is greater to one than one's self is,
And whoever walks a furlong without sympathy walks to his own funeral drest
    in his shroud,
And I or you pocketless of a dime may purchase the pick of the earth,
And to glance with an eye or show a bean in its pod confounds the learning of
    all times,   1275

And there is no trade or employment but the young man following it may
    become a hero,
And there is no object so soft but it makes a hub for the wheel'd universe,
And I say to any man or woman, Let your soul stand cool and composed
    before a million universes.

And I say to mankind, Be not curious about God,
For I who am curious about each am not curious about God,   I.
(No array of terms can say how much I am at peace about God and about
    death.)

I hear and behold God in every object, yet understand God not in the least,
Nor do I understand who there can be more wonderful than myself.

Why should I wish to see God better than this day?
I see something of God each hour of the twenty-four, and each moment then,   12
In the faces of men and women I see God, and in my own face in the glass,
I find letters from God dropt in the street, and every one is sign'd by God's
    name,
And I leave them where they are, for I know that wheresoe'er I go,
Others will punctually come for ever and ever.

49

And as to you Death, and you bitter hug of mortality, it is idle to try to alarm
    me.
                                                                                          129

To his work without flinching the accoucheur[35] comes,
I see the elder-hand pressing receiving supporting,
I recline by the sills of the exquisite flexible doors,
And mark the outlet, and mark the relief and escape.

And as to you Corpse I think you are good manure, but that does not offend
    me,
                                                                                          1295
I smell the white roses sweet-scented and growing,
I reach to the leafy lips, I reach to the polish'd breasts of melons.

And as to you Life I reckon you are the leavings of many deaths,
(No doubt I have died myself ten thousand times before.)

I hear you whispering there O stars of heaven,   1300
O suns—O grass of graves—O perpetual transfers and promotions,
If you do not say any thing how can I say any thing?

[35] Midwife.

Of the turbid pool that lies in the autumn forest,
Of the moon that descends the steeps of the soughing twilight,
Toss, sparkles of day and dusk—toss on the black stems that decay in the muck,
Toss to the moaning gibberish of the dry limbs.
I ascend from the moon, I ascend from the night,   1305
I perceive that the ghastly glimmer is noonday sunbeams reflected,
And debouch to the steady and central from the offspring great or small.

50

There is that in me—I do not know what it is—but I know it is in me.   1310

Wrench'd and sweaty—calm and cool then my body becomes,
I sleep—I sleep long.

I do not know it—it is without name—it is a word unsaid,
It is not in any dictionary, utterance, symbol.

Something it swings on more than the earth I swing on,   1315
To it the creation is the friend whose embracing awakes me.

Perhaps I might tell more. Outlines! I plead for my brothers and sisters.

Do you see O my brothers and sisters?
It is not chaos or death—it is form, union, plan—it is eternal life—it is
    Happiness.

51

The past and present wilt—I have fill'd them, emptied them,   1320
And proceed to fill my next fold of the future.

Listener up there! what have you to confide to me?
Look in my face while I snuff the sidle of evening,
(Talk honestly, no one else hears you, and I stay only a minute longer.)

Do I contradict myself?   1325
Very well then I contradict myself,
(I am large, I contain multitudes.)
I concentrate toward them that are nigh, I wait on the door-slab.

Who has done his day's work? who will soonest be through with his supper?
Who wishes to walk with me?   1330

Will you speak before I am gone? will you prove already too late?

52

The spotted hawk swoops by and accuses me, he complains of my gab and my
  loitering.

I too am not a bit tamed, I too am untranslatable,
I sound my barbaric yawp over the roofs of the world.

The last scud of day holds back for me,   133:
It flings my likeness after the rest and true as any on the shadow'd wilds,
It coaxes me to the vapor and the dusk.

I depart as air, I shake my white locks at the runaway sun,
I effuse my flesh in eddies, and drift it in lacy jags.

I bequeath myself to the dirt to grow from the grass I love,   134·
If you want me again look for me under your boot-soles.

You will hardly know who I am or what I mean,
But I shall be good health to you nevertheless,
And filter and fibre your blood.

Failing to fetch me at first keep encouraged,   1345
Missing me one place search another,
I stop somewhere waiting for you.
1855

from Children of Adam
I Sing the Body Electric

1

I sing the body electric,
The armies of those I love engirth me and I engirth them,
They will not let me off till I go with them, respond to them,
And discorrupt them, and charge them full with the charge of the soul.

Was it doubted that those who corrupt their own bodies conceal themselves?   5
And if those who defile the living are as bad as they who defile the dead?
And if the body does not do fully as much as the soul?
And if the body were not the soul, what is the soul?

2

The love of the body of man or woman balks account, the body itself balks
  account,
That of the male is perfect, and that of the female is perfect.   10

The expression of the face balks account,
But the expression of a well-made man appears not only in his face,
It is in his limbs and joints also, it is curiously in the joints of his hips and
    wrists,
It is in his walk, the carriage of his neck, the flex of his waist and knees, dress
    does not hide him,
The strong sweet quality he has strikes through the cotton and broadcloth,   15
To see him pass conveys as much as the best poem, perhaps more,
You linger to see his back, and the back of his neck and shoulder-side.

The sprawl and fulness of babes, the bosoms and heads of women, the folds of
    their dress, their style as we pass in the street, the contour of their shape
    downwards,
The swimmer naked in the swimming-bath, seen as he swims through the
    transparent green-shine, or lies with his face up and rolls silently to and fro
    in the heave of the water,
The bending forward and backward of rowers in row-boats, the horseman in his
    saddle,   20
Girls, mothers, house-keepers, in all their performances,
The group of laborers seated at noon-time with their open dinner-kettles, and
    their wives waiting,
The female soothing a child, the farmer's daughter in the garden or cow-yard,
The young fellow hoeing corn, the sleigh-driver driving his six horses through
    the crowd,
The wrestle of wrestlers, two apprentice-boys, quite grown, lusty, good-natured,
    native-born, out on the vacant lot at sundown after work,   25
The coats and caps thrown down, the embrace of love and resistance,
The upper-hold and under-hold, the hair rumpled over and blinding the eyes;
The march of firemen in their own costumes, the play of masculine muscle
    through clean-setting trowsers and waist-straps,
The slow return from the fire, the pause when the bell strikes suddenly again,
    and the listening on the alert,
The natural, perfect, varied attitudes, the bent head, the curv'd neck and the
    counting;   30
Such-like I love—I loosen myself, pass freely, am at the mother's breast with
    the little child,
Swim with the swimmers, wrestle with wrestlers, march in line with the
    firemen, and pause, listen, count.

3

I knew a man, a common farmer, the father of five sons,
And in them the fathers of sons, and in them the fathers of sons.
This man was of wonderful vigor, calmness, beauty of person,   35
The shape of his head, the pale yellow and white of his hair and beard, the

immeasurable meaning of his black eyes, the richness and breadth of his manners,

These I used to go and visit him to see, he was wise also,

He was six feet tall, he was over eighty years old, his sons were massive, clean, bearded, tan-faced, handsome,

They and his daughters loved him, all who saw him loved him,

They did not love him by allowance, they loved him with personal love,   40

He drank water only, the blood show'd like scarlet through the clear-brown skin of his face,

He was a frequent gunner and fisher, he sail'd his boat himself, he had a fine one presented to him by a ship-joiner, he had fowling-pieces presented to him by men that loved him,

When he went with his five sons and many grand-sons to hunt or fish, you would pick him out as the most beautiful and vigorous of the gang,

You would wish long and long to be with him, you would wish to sit by him in the boat that you and he might touch each other.

4

I have perceiv'd that to be with those I like is enough,   45

To stop in company with the rest at evening is enough,

To be surrounded by beautiful, curious, breathing, laughing flesh is enough,

To pass among them or touch any one, or rest my arm ever so lightly round his or her neck for a moment, what is this then?

I do not ask any more delight, I swim in it as in a sea.

There is something in staying close to men and women and looking on them, and in the contact and odor of them, that pleases the soul well,   50

All things please the soul, but these please the soul well.

5

This is the female form,

A divine nimbus exhales from it from head to foot,

It attracts with fierce undeniable attraction,

I am drawn by its breath as if I were no more than a helpless vapor, all falls aside but myself and it,   55

Books, art, religion, time, the visible and solid earth, and what was expected of heaven or fear'd of hell, are now consumed,

Mad filaments, ungovernable shoots play out of it, the response likewise ungovernable,

Hair, bosom, hips, bend of legs, negligent falling hands all diffused, mine too diffused,

Ebb stung by the flow and flow stung by the ebb, love-flesh swelling and deliciously aching,

Limitless limpid jets of love hot and enormous, quivering jelly of love, white-blow and delirious juice,   60

Bridegroom night of love working surely and softly into the prostrate dawn,
Undulating into the willing and yielding day,
Lost in the cleave of the clasping and sweet-flesh'd day.
This the nucleus—after the child is born of woman, man is born of woman,
This the bath of birth, this the merge of small and large, and the outlet again.   65

Be not ashamed women, your privilege encloses the rest, and is the exit of the
    rest,
You are the gates of the body, and you are the gates of the soul.

The female contains all qualities and tempers them,
She is in her place and moves with perfect balance,
She is all things duly veil'd, she is both passive and active,   70
She is to conceive daughters as well as sons, and sons as well as daughters.

As I see my soul reflected in Nature,
As I see through a mist, One with inexpressible completeness, sanity, beauty,
See the bent head and arms folded over the breast, the Female I see.

6

The male is not less the soul nor more, he too is in his place,   75
He too is all qualities, he is action and power,
The flush of the known universe is in him,
Scorn becomes him well, and appetite and defiance become him well,
The wildest largest passions, bliss that is utmost, sorrow that is utmost become
    him well, pride is for him,
The full-spread pride of man is calming and excellent to the soul,   80
Knowledge becomes him, he likes it always, he brings every thing to the test of
    himself,
Whatever the survey, whatever the sea and the sail he strikes soundings at last
    only here,
(Where else does he strike soundings except here?)

The man's body is sacred and the woman's body is sacred,
No matter who it is, it is sacred—is it the meanest one in the laborers' gang?   85
Is it one of the dull-faced immigrants just landed on the wharf?
Each belongs here or anywhere just as much as the well-off, just as much as
    you,
Each has his or her place in the procession.

(All is a procession,
The universe is a procession with measured and perfect motion.)   90

Do you know so much yourself that you call the meanest ignorant?
Do you suppose you have a right to a good sight, and he or she has no right
    to a sight?

Do you think matter has cohered together from its diffuse float, and the soil is
    on the surface, and water runs and vegetation sprouts,
For you only, and not for him and her?

7

A man's body at auction,   95
(For before the war I often go to the slave-mart and watch the sale,)
I help the auctioneer, the sloven does not half know his business.

Gentlemen look on this wonder,
Whatever the bids of the bidders they cannot be high enough for it,
For it the globe lay preparing quintillions of years without one animal or plant, 100
For it the revolving cycles truly and steadily roll'd.

In this head the all-baffling brain,
In it and below it the makings of heroes.

Examine these limbs, red, black, or white, they are cunning in tendon and
    nerve,
They shall be stript that you may see them.   105
Exquisite senses, life-lit eyes, pluck, volition,
Flakes of breast-muscle, pliant backbone and neck, flesh not flabby, good-sized
    arms and legs,
And wonders within there yet.

Within there runs blood,
The same old blood! the same red-running blood!   110
There swells and jets a heart, there all passions, desires, reachings, aspirations,
(Do you think they are not there because they are not express'd in parlors and
    lecture-rooms?)

This is not only one man, this the father of those who shall be fathers in their
    turns,
In him the start of populous states and rich republics,
Of him countless immortal lives with countless embodiments and enjoyments. 115

How do you know who shall come from the offspring of his offspring through
    the centuries?
(Who might you find you have come from yourself, if you could trace back
    through the centuries?)

8

A woman's body at auction,
She too is not only herself, she is the teeming mother of mothers,
She is the bearer of them that shall grow and be mates to the mothers.   120

Have you ever loved the body of a woman?
Have you ever loved the body of a man?
Do you not see that these are exactly the same to all in all nations and times all
   over the earth?

If any thing is sacred the human body is sacred,
And the glory and sweet of a man is the token of manhood untainted,   125
And in man or woman a clean, strong, firm-fibred body, is more beautiful than
   the most beautiful face.
Have you seen the fool that corrupted his own live body? or the fool that
   corrupted her own live body?
For they do not conceal themselves, and cannot conceal themselves.

9

O my body! I dare not desert the likes of you in other men and women, nor
   the likes of the parts of you,
I believe the likes of you are to stand or fall with the likes of the soul, (and
   that they are the soul,)   130
I believe the likes of you shall stand or fall with my poems, and that they are
   my poems,
Man's, woman's, child's, youth's, wife's, husband's, mother's, father's, young
   man's, young woman's poems,
Head, neck, hair, ears, drop and tympan of the ears,
Eyes, eye-fringes, iris of the eye, eyebrows, and the waking or sleeping of the
   lids,
Mouth, tongue, lips, teeth, roof of the mouth, jaws, and the jaw-hinges,   135
Nose, nostrils of the nose, and the partition,
Cheeks, temples, forehead, chin, throat, back of the neck, neck-slue,
Strong shoulders, manly beard, scapula, hind-shoulders, and the ample
   side-round of the chest,
Upper-arm, armpit, elbow-socket, lower-arm, arm-sinews, arm-bones,
Wrist and wrist-joints, hand, palm, knuckles, thumb, forefinger, finger-joints,
   finger-nails,   140
Broad breast-front, curling hair of the breast, breast-bone, breast-side,
Ribs, belly, backbone, joints of the backbone,
Hips, hip-sockets, hip-strength, inward and outward round, man-balls, man-root,
Strong set of thighs, well carrying the trunk above,
Leg-fibres, knee, knee-pan, upper-leg, under-leg,   145
Ankles, instep, foot-ball, toes, toe-joints, the heel;
All attitudes, all the shapeliness, all the belongings of my or your body or of
   any one's body, male or female,
The lung-sponges, the stomach-sac, the bowels sweet and clean,
The brain in its folds inside the skull-frame,
Sympathies, heart-valves, palate-valves, sexuality, maternity,   150
Womanhood, and all that is a woman, and the man that comes from woman,

The womb, the teats, nipples, breast-milk, tears, laughter, weeping, love-looks,
    love-perturbations and risings,
The voice, articulation, language, whispering, shouting aloud,
Food, drink, pulse, digestion, sweat, sleep, walking, swimming,
Poise on the hips, leaping, reclining, embracing, arm-curving and tightening,   15
The continual changes of the flex of the mouth, and around the eyes,
The skin, the sunburnt shade, freckles, hair,
The curious sympathy one feels when feeling with the hand the naked meat of
    the body,
The circling rivers the breath, and breathing it in and out,
The beauty of the waist, and thence of the hips, and thence downward toward
    the knees,   160
The thin red jellies within you or within me, the bones and the marrow in the
    bones,
The exquisite realization of health;
O I say these are not the parts and poems of the body only, but of the soul,
O I say now these are the soul!

1855

A Woman Waits for Me

A woman waits for me, she contains all, nothing is lacking,
Yet all were lacking if sex were lacking, or if the moisture of the right man
    were lacking.

Sex contains all, bodies, souls,
Meanings, proofs, purities, delicacies, results, promulgations,
Songs, commands, health, pride, the maternal mystery, the seminal milk,   5
All hopes, benefactions, bestowals, all the passions, loves, beauties, delights of
    the earth,
All the governments, judges, gods, follow'd persons of the earth,
These are contain'd in sex as parts of itself and justifications of itself.

Without shame the man I like knows and avows the deliciousness of his sex,
Without shame the woman I like knows and avows hers.   10

Now I will dismiss myself from impassive women,
I will go stay with her who waits for me, and with those women that are
    warm-blooded and sufficient for me,
I see that they understand me and do not deny me,
I see that they are worthy of me, I will be the robust husband of those women.

They are not one jot less than I am,   15
They are tann'd in the face by shining suns and blowing winds,
Their flesh has the old divine suppleness and strength,
They know how to swim, row, ride, wrestle, shoot, run, strike, retreat, advance,
    resist, defend themselves,

They are ultimate in their own right—they are calm, clear, well-possess'd of
    themselves.

I draw you close to me, you women,   20
I cannot let you go, I would do you good,
I am for you, and you are for me, not only for our own sake, but for others'
    sakes,
Envelop'd in you sleep greater heroes and bards,
They refuse to awake at the touch of any man but me.

It is I, you women, I make my way,   25
I am stern, acrid, large, undissuadable, but I love you,
I do not hurt you any more than is necessary for you,
I pour the stuff to start sons and daughters fit for these States, I press with slow
    rude muscle,
I brace myself effectually, I listen to no entreaties,
I dare not withdraw till I deposit what has so long accumulated within me.   30
Through you I drain the pent-up rivers of myself,
In you I wrap a thousand onward years,
On you I graft the grafts of the best-beloved of me and America,
The drops I distil upon you shall grow fierce and athletic girls, new artists,
    musicians, and singers,
The babes I beget upon you are to beget babes in their turn,   35
I shall demand perfect men and women out of my love-spendings,
I shall expect them to interpenetrate with others, as I and you interpenetrate
    now,
I shall count on the fruits of the gushing showers of them, as I count on the
    fruits of the gushing showers I give now,
I shall look for loving crops from the birth, life, death, immortality, I plant so
    lovingly now.

1856

Once I Pass'd Through a Populous City

Once I pass'd through a populous city imprinting my brain for future use with
    its shows, architecture, customs, traditions,
Yet now of all that city I remember only a woman I casually met there who
    detain'd me for love of me,
Day by day and night by night we were together—all else has long been
    forgotten by me,
I remember I say only that woman who passionately clung to me,
Again we wander, we love, we separate again,   5
Again she holds me by the hand, I must not go,
I see her close beside me with silent lips sad and tremulous.

1860

Facing West from California's Shores

Facing west from California's shores,
Inquiring, tireless, seeking what is yet unfound,
I, a child, very old, over waves, towards the house of maternity, the land of
    migrations, look afar,
Look off the shores of my Western sea, the circle almost circled;
For starting westward from Hindustan, from the vales of Kashmere,   5
From Asia, from the north, from the God, the sage, and the hero,
From the south, from the flowery peninsulas and the spice islands,
Long having wander'd since, round the earth having wander'd,
Now I face home again, very pleas'd and joyous,
(But where is what I started for so long ago?   10
And why is it yet unfound?)
1860

As Adam Early in the Morning

As Adam early in the morning,
Walking forth from the bower refresh'd with sleep,
Behold me where I pass, hear my voice, approach,
Touch me, touch the palm of your hand to my body as I pass,
Be not afraid of my body.   5
1861

from Calamus

Scented Herbage of My Breast

Scented herbage of my breast,
Leaves from you I glean, I write, to be perused best afterwards,
Tomb-leaves, body-leaves growing up above me above death,
Perennial roots, tall leaves, O the winter shall not freeze you delicate leaves,
Every year shall you bloom again, out from where you retired you shall
    emerge again;   5
O I do not know whether many passing by will discover you or inhale your
    faint odor, but I believe a few will;
O slender leaves! O blossoms of my blood! I permit you to tell in your own
    way of the heart that is under you,
O I do not know what you mean there underneath yourselves, you are not
    happiness,
You are often more bitter than I can bear, you burn and sting me,
Yet you are beautiful to me you faint tinged roots, you make me think of
    death,
Death is beautiful from you, (what indeed is finally beautiful except death and   10
    love?)
O I think it is not for life I am chanting here my chant of lovers, I think it
    must be for death,

For how calm, how solemn it grows to ascend to the atmosphere of lovers,
Death or life I am then indifferent, my soul declines to prefer,
(I am not sure but the high soul of lovers welcomes death most,)   15
Indeed O death, I think now these leaves mean precisely the same as you mean,
Grow up taller sweet leaves that I may see! grow up out of my breast!
Spring away from the conceal'd heart there!
Do not fold yourself so in your pink-tinged roots timid leaves!
Do not remain down there so ashamed, herbage of my breast!   20
Come I am determin'd to unbare this broad breast of mine, I have long enough
    stifled and choked;
Emblematic and capricious blades I leave you, now you serve me not,
I will say what I have to say by itself,
I will sound myself and comrades only, I will never again utter a call only
    their call,
I will raise with it immortal reverberations through the States,   25
I will give an example to lovers to take permanent shape and will through the
    States,
Through me shall the words be said to make death exhilarating,
Give me your tone therefore O death, that I may accord with it,
Give me yourself, for I see that you belong to me now above all, and are
    folded inseparably together, you love and death are,
Nor will I allow you to balk me any more with what I was calling life,   30
For now it is convey'd to me that you are the purports essential,
That you hide in these shifting forms of life, for reasons, and that they are
    mainly for you,
That you beyond them come forth to remain, the real reality,
That behind the mask of materials you patiently wait, no matter how long,
That you will one day perhaps take control of all,   35
That you will perhaps dissipate this entire show of appearance,
That may-be you are what it is all for, but it does not last so very long,
But you will last very long.

1860

Recorders Ages Hence

Recorders ages hence,
Come, I will take you down underneath this impassive exterior, I will tell you
    what to say of me,
Publish my name and hang up my picture as that of the tenderest lover,
The friend the lover's portrait, of whom his friend his lover was fondest,
Who was not proud of his songs, but of the measureless ocean of love within
    him, and freely pour'd it forth,   5
Who often walk'd lonesome walks thinking of his dear friends, his lovers,
Who pensive away from one he lov'd often lay sleepless and dissatisfied at
    night,
Who knew too well the sick, sick dread lest the one he lov'd might secretly be
    indifferent to him,

Whose happiest days were far away through fields, in woods, on hills, he and
    another wandering hand in hand, they twain apart from other men,
Who oft as he saunter'd the streets curv'd with his arm the shoulder of his
    friend, while the arm of his friend rested upon him also.   10

1860

When I Heard at the Close of the Day

When I heard at the close of the day how my name had been receiv'd with
    plaudits in the capitol, still it was not a happy night for me that follow'd,
And else when I carous'd, or when my plans were accomplish'd, still I was not
    happy,
But the day when I rose at dawn from the bed of perfect health, refresh'd,
    singing, inhaling the ripe breath of autumn,
When I saw the full moon in the west grow pale and disappear in the morning
    light,
When I wander'd alone over the beach, and undressing bathed, laughing with
    the cool waters, and saw the sun rise,   5
And when I thought how my dear friend my lover was on his way coming, O
    then I was happy,
O then each breath tasted sweeter, and all that day my food nourish'd me more,
    and the beautiful day pass'd well,
And the next came with equal joy, and with the next at evening came my
    friend,
And that night while all was still I heard the waters roll slowly continually up
    the shores,
I heard the hissing rustle of the liquid and sands as directed to me whispering to
    congratulate me,   10
For the one I love most lay sleeping by me under the same cover in the cool
    night,
In the stillness in the autumn moonbeams his face was inclined toward me,
And his arm lay lightly around my breast—and that night I was happy.

1860

I Saw in Louisiana a Live-Oak Growing

I saw in Louisiana a live-oak growing,
All alone stood it and the moss hung down from the branches,
Without any companion it grew there uttering joyous leaves of dark green,
And its look, rude, unbending, lusty, made me think of myself,
But I wonder'd how it could utter joyous leaves standing alone there without
    its friend near, for I knew I could not,   5
And I broke off a twig with a certain number of leaves upon it, and twined
    around it a little moss,
And brought it away, and I have placed it in sight in my room,
It is not needed to remind me as of my own dear friends,

(For I believe lately I think of little else than of them,)
Yet it remains to me a curious token, it makes me think of manly love;   10
For all that, and though the live-oak glistens there in Louisiana solitary in a
    wide flat space,
Uttering joyous leaves all its life without a friend a lover near,
I know very well I could not.

1860

Here the Frailest Leaves of Me

Here the frailest leaves of me and yet my strongest lasting,
Here I shade and expose my thoughts, I myself do not expose them,
And yet they expose me more than all my other poems.

1860

Crossing Brooklyn Ferry*

1

Flood-tide below me! I see you face to face!
Clouds of the west—sun there half an hour high—I see you also face to face.

Crowds of men and women attired in the usual costumes, how curious you are
    to me!
On the ferry-boats the hundreds and hundreds that cross, returning home, are
    more curious to me than you suppose,
And you that shall cross from shore to shore years hence are more to me, and
    more in my meditations, than you might suppose.   5

2

The impalpable sustenance of me from all things at all hours of the day,
The simple, compact, well-join'd scheme, myself disintegrated, every one
    disintegrated yet part of the scheme,
The similitudes of the past and those of the future,
The glories strung like beads on my smallest sights and hearings, on the walk in
    the street and the passage over the river,
The current rushing so swiftly and swimming with me far away,   10
The others that are to follow me, the ties between me and them,
The certainty of others, the life, love, sight, hearing of others.

Others will enter the gates of the ferry and cross from shore to shore,
Others will watch the run of the flood-tide,

---

* Titled "Sun-Down Poem" when first published
in 1856.

Others will see the shipping of Manhattan north and west, and the heights of
    Brooklyn to the south and east,   1
Others will see the islands large and small;
Fifty years hence, others will see them as they cross, the sun half an hour high,
A hundred years hence, or ever so many hundred years hence, others will see
    them,
Will enjoy the sunset, the pouring-in of the flood-tide, the falling-back to the
    sea of the ebb-tide.

3

It avails not, time nor place—distance avails not,   20
I am with you, you men and women of a generation, or ever so many
    generations hence,
Just as you feel when you look on the river and sky, so I felt,
Just as any of you is one of a living crowd, I was one of a crowd,
Just as you are refresh'd by the gladness of the river and the bright flow, I was
    refresh'd,
Just as you stand and lean on the rail, yet hurry with the swift current, I stood
    yet was hurried,   25
Just as you look on the numberless masts of ships and the thick-stemm'd pipes
    of steamboats, I look'd.

I too many and many a time cross'd the river of old,
Watched the Twelfth-month[36] sea-gulls, saw them high in the air floating with
    motionless wings, oscillating their bodies,
Saw how the glistening yellow lit up parts of their bodies and left the rest in
    strong shadow,
Saw the slow-wheeling circles and the gradual edging toward the south,   30
Saw the reflection of the summer sky in the water,
Had my eyes dazzled by the shimmering track of beams,
Look'd at the fine centrifugal spokes of light round the shape of my head in the
    sunlit water,
Look'd on the haze on the hills southward and southwestward,
Look'd on the vapor as it flew in fleeces tinged with violet,   35
Look'd toward the lower bay to notice the vessels arriving,
Saw their approach, saw aboard those that were near me,
Saw the white sails of schooners and sloops, saw the ships at anchor,
The sailors at work in the rigging or out astride the spars,
The round masts, the swinging motion of the hulls, the slender serpentine
    pennants,
                                                                                       40
The large and small steamers in motion, the pilots in their pilot-houses,
The white wake left by the passage, the quick tremulous whirl of the wheels,
The flags of all nations, the falling of them at sunset,

---

[36] December (Quaker style).

The scallop-edged waves in the twilight, the ladled cups, the frolicsome crests
    and glistening,
The stretch afar growing dimmer and dimmer, the gray walls of the granite
    storehouses by the docks,   45
On the river the shadowy group, the big steam-tug closely flank'd on each side
    by the barges, the hay-boat, the belated lighter,
On the neighboring shore the fires from the foundry chimneys burning high
    and glaringly into the night,
Casting their flicker of black contrasted with wild red and yellow light over
    the tops of houses, and down into the clefts of streets.

4

These and all else were to me the same as they are to you,
I loved well those cities, loved well the stately and rapid river,   50
The men and women I saw were all near to me,
Others the same—others who look back on me because I look'd forward to
    them,
(The time will come, though I stop here to-day and to-night.)

5

What is it then between us?
What is the count of the scores or hundreds of years between us?   55

Whatever it is, it avails not—distance avails not, and place avails not,
I too lived, Brooklyn of ample hills was mine,
I too walk'd the streets of Manhattan island, and bathed in the waters around it,
I too felt the curious abrupt questionings stir within me,
In the day among crowds of people sometimes they came upon me,   60
In my walks home late at night or as I lay in my bed they came upon me,
I too had been struck from the float forever held in solution,
I too had receiv'd identity by my body,
That I was I knew was of my body, and what I should be I knew I should be
    of my body.

6

It is not upon you alone the dark patches fall,   65
The dark threw its patches down upon me also,
The best I had done seem'd to me blank and suspicious,
My great thoughts as I supposed them, were they not in reality meagre?
Nor is it you alone who know what it is to be evil,
I am he who knew what it was to be evil,   70
I too knotted the old knot of contrariety,
Blabb'd, blush'd, resented, lied, stole, grudg'd,
Had guile, anger, lust, hot wishes I dared not speak,

Was wayward, vain, greedy, shallow, sly, cowardly, malignant,
The wolf, the snake, the hog, not wanting in me,   7
The cheating look, the frivolous word, the adulterous wish, not wanting,
Refusals, hates, postponements, meanness, laziness, none of these wanting,
Was one with the rest, the days and haps of the rest,
Was call'd by my nighest name by clear loud voices of young men as they saw
    me approaching or passing,
Felt their arms on my neck as I stood, or the negligent leaning of their flesh
    against me as I sat,   8c
Saw many I loved in the street or ferry-boat or public assembly, yet never told
    them a word,
Lived the same life with the rest, the same old laughing, gnawing, sleeping,
Play'd the part that still looks back on the actor or actress,
The same old role, the role that is what we make it, as great as we like,
Or as small as we like, or both great and small.   85

7

Closer yet I approach you,
What thought you have of me now, I had as much of you—I laid in my stores
    in advance,
I consider'd long and seriously of you before you were born.

Who was to know what should come home to me?
Who knows but I am enjoying this?   90
Who knows, for all the distance, but I am as good as looking at you now, for
    all you cannot see me?

8

Ah, what can ever be more stately and admirable to me than mast-hemm'd
    Manhattan?
River and sunset and scallop-edg'd waves of flood-tide?
The sea-gulls oscillating their bodies, the hat-boat in the twilight, and the
    belated lighter?
What gods can exceed these that clasp me by the hand, and with voices I love
    call me promptly and loudly by my nighest name as I approach?   95
What is more subtle than this which ties me to the woman or man that looks
    in my face?
Which fuses me into you now, and pours my meaning into you?

We understand then do we not?
What I promis'd without mentioning it, have you not accepted?
What the study could not teach—what the preaching could not accomplish is
    accomplish'd, is it not?   100

9

Flow on, river! flow with the flood-tide, and ebb with the ebb-tide!
Frolic on, crested and scallop-edg'd waves!
Gorgeous clouds of the sunset! drench with your splendor me, or the men and
    women generations after me!
Cross from shore to shore, countless crowds of passengers!
Stand up, tall masts of Mannahatta! stand up, beautiful hills of Brooklyn!   105
Throb, baffled and curious brain! throw out questions and answers!
Suspend here and everywhere, eternal float of solution!
Gaze, loving and thirsting eyes, in the house or street or public assembly!
Sound out, voices of young men! loudly and musically call me by my nighest
    name!
Live, old life! play the part that looks back on the actor or actress!   110
Play the old role, the role that is great or small according as one makes it!
Consider, you who peruse me, whether I may not in unknown ways be looking
    upon you;
Be firm, rail over the river, to support those who lean idly, yet haste with the
    hasting current;
Fly on, sea-birds! fly sideways, or wheel in large circles high in the air;
Receive the summer sky, you water, and faithfully hold it till all downcast eyes
    have time to take it from you!   115
Diverge, fine spokes of light, from the shape of my head, or any one's head, in
    the sunlit water!
Come on, ships from the lower bay! pass up or down, white-sail'd schooners,
    sloops, lighters!
Flaunt away, flags of all nations! be duly lower'd at sunset!
Burn high your fires, foundry chimneys! cast black shadows at nightfall! cast
    red and yellow light over the tops of the houses!
Appearances, now or henceforth, indicate what you are,   120
You necessary film, continue to envelop the soul,
About my body for me, and your body for you, be hung out divinest aromas,
Thrive, cities—bring your freight, bring your shows, ample and sufficient
    rivers,
Expand, being than which none else is perhaps more spiritual,
Keep your places, objects than which none else is more lasting.   125

You have waited, you always wait, you dumb, beautiful ministers,
We receive you with free sense at last, and are insatiate henceforward,
Not you any more shall be able to foil us, or withhold yourselves from us,
We use you, and do not cast you aside—we plant you permanently within us,
We fathom you not—we love you—there is perfection in you also,   130
You furnish your parts toward eternity,
Great or small, you furnish your parts toward the soul.

1856

from **Sea-Drift**

Out of the Cradle Endlessly Rocking

Out of the cradle endlessly rocking,
Out of the mocking-bird's throat, the musical shuttle,
Out of the Ninth-month[37] midnight,
Over the sterile sands and the fields beyond, where the child leaving his bed
    wander'd alone, bareheaded, barefoot,
Down from the shower'd halo, 5
Up from the mystic play of shadows twining and twisting as if they were alive,
Out from the patches of briers and blackberries,
From the memories of the bird that chanted to me,
From your memories sad brother, from the fitful risings and fallings I heard,
From under that yellow half-moon late-risen and swollen as if with tears, 10
From those beginning notes of yearning and love there in the mist,
From the thousand responses of my heart never to cease,
From the myriad thence-arous'd words,
From the word stronger and more delicious than any,
From such as now they start the scene revisiting, 15
As a flock, twittering, rising, or overhead passing,
Borne hither, ere all eludes me, hurriedly,
A man, yet by these tears a little boy again,
Throwing myself on the sand, confronting the waves,
I, chanter of pains and joys, uniter of here and hereafter, 20
Taking all hints to use them, but swiftly leaping beyond them,
A reminiscence sing.

Once Paumanok,[38]
When the lilac-scent was in the air and Fifth-month[39] grass was growing,
Up this seashore in some briers, 25
Two feather'd guests from Alabama, two together,
And their nest, and four light-green eggs spotted with brown,
And every day the he-bird to and fro near at hand,
And every day the she-bird crouch'd on her nest, silent, with bright eyes,
And every day I, a curious boy, never too close, never disturbing them, 30
Cautiously peering, absorbing, translating.

Shine! shine! shine!
Pour down your warmth, great sun!
While we bask, we two together.

Two together! 35
Winds blow south, or winds blow north,
Day come white, or night come black,

---

[37] September (Quaker style).   [39] May (Quaker style).
[38] Indian name for Long Island.

Home, or rivers and mountains from home,
Singing all time, minding no time,
While we two keep together.   40

Till of a sudden,
May-be kill'd, unknown to her mate,
One forenoon the she-bird crouch'd not on the nest,
Nor return'd that afternoon, nor the next,
Nor ever appear'd again.   45

And thenceforward all summer in the sound of the sea,
And at night under the full of the moon in calmer weather,
Over the hoarse surging of the sea,
Or flitting from brier to brier by day,
I saw, I heard at intervals the remaining one, the he-bird,   50
The solitary guest from Alabama.

Blow! blow! blow!
Blow up sea-winds along Paumanok's shore;
I wait and I wait till you blow my mate to me.

Yes, when the stars glisten'd,   55
All night long on the prong of a moss-scallop'd stake,
Down almost amid the slapping waves,
Sat the lone singer wonderful causing tears.

He call'd on his mate,
He pour'd forth the meanings which I of all men know.   60
Yes my brother I know,
The rest might not, but I have treasur'd every note,
For more than once dimly down to the beach gliding,
Silent, avoiding the moonbeams, blending myself with the shadows,
Recalling now the obscure shapes, the echoes, the sounds and sights after their
     sorts,   65
The white arms out in the breakers tirelessly tossing,
I, with bare feet, a child, the wind wafting my hair,
Listen'd long and long.

Listen'd to keep, to sing, now translating the notes,
Following you my brother.   70

Soothe! soothe! soothe!
Close on its wave soothes the wave behind,
And again another behind embracing and lapping, every one close,
But my love soothes not me, not me.

Low hangs the moon, it rose late,
It is lagging—O I think it is heavy with love, with love.   7

O madly the sea pushes upon the land,
With love, with love.

O night! do I not see my love fluttering out among the breakers?
What is that little black thing I see there in the white?   80

Loud! loud! loud!
Loud I call to you, my love!

High and clear I shoot my voice over the waves,
Surely you must know who is here, is here,
You must know who I am, my love.   85

Low-hanging moon!
What is that dusky spot in your brown yellow?
O it is the shape, the shape of my mate!
O moon do not keep her from me any longer.
Land! land! O land!   90
Whichever way I turn, O I think you could give me my mate back again if you only
     would,
For I am almost sure I see her dimly whichever way I look.

O rising stars!
Perhaps the one I want so much will rise, will rise with some of you.

O throat! O trembling throat!   95
Sound clearer through the atmosphere!
Pierce the woods, the earth,
Somewhere listening to catch you must be the one I want.

Shake out carols!
Solitary here, the night's carols!   100
Carols of lonesome love! death's carols!
Carols under that lagging, yellow, waning moon!
O under that moon where she droops almost down into the sea!
O reckless despairing carols.

But soft! sink low!   105
Soft! let me just murmur,
And do you wait a moment you husky-nois'd sea,
For somewhere I believe I heard my mate responding to me,

So faint, I must be still, be still to listen,
But not altogether still, for then she might not come immediately to me.　110

Hither my love!
Here I am! here!
With this just-sustain'd note I announce myself to you,
This gentle call is for you my love, for you.

Do not be decoy'd elsewhere,　115
That is the whistle of the wind, it is not my voice,
That is the fluttering, the fluttering of the spray,
Those are the shadows of leaves.

O darkness! O in vain!
O I am very sick and sorrowful.　120
O brown halo in the sky near the moon, drooping upon the sea!
O troubled reflection in the sea!
O throat! O throbbing heart!
And I singing uselessly, uselessly all the night.

O past! O happy life! O songs of joy!　125
In the air, in the woods, over fields,
Loved! loved! loved! loved! loved!
But my mate no more, no more with me!
We two together no more.

The aria sinking,　130
All else continuing, the stars shining,
The winds blowing, the notes of the bird continuous echoing,
With angry moans the fierce old mother incessantly moaning,
On the sands of Paumanok's shore gray and rustling,
The yellow half-moon enlarged, sagging down, drooping, the face of the sea
  almost touching,　135
The boy ecstatic, with his bare feet the waves, with his hair the atmosphere
  dallying,
The love in the heart long pent, now loose, now at last tumultuously bursting,
The aria's meaning, the ears, the soul, swiftly depositing,
The strange tears down the cheeks coursing,
The colloquy there, the trio, each uttering,　140
The undertone, the savage old mother incessantly crying,
To the boy's soul's questions sullenly timing, some drown'd secret hissing,
To the outsetting bard.

Demon or bird! (said the boy's soul,)
Is it indeed toward your mate you sing? or is it really to me?　145

For I, that was a child, my tongue's use sleeping, now I have heard you,
Now in a moment I know what I am for, I awake,
And already a thousand singers, a thousand songs, clearer, louder and more
    sorrowful than yours,
A thousand warbling echoes have started to life within me, never to die.
O you singer solitary, singing by yourself, projecting me,   15
O solitary me listening, never more shall I cease perpetuating you,
Never more shall I escape, never more the reverberations,
Never more the cries of unsatisfied love be absent from me,
Never again leave me to be the peaceful child I was before what there in the
    night,
By the sea under the yellow and sagging moon,   155
The messenger there arous'd, the fire, the sweet hell within,
The unknown want, the destiny of me.

O give me the clew! (it lurks in the night here somewhere,)
O if I am to have so much, let me have more!

A word then, (for I will conquer it,)   160
The word final, superior to all,
Subtle, sent up—what is it?—I listen;
Are you whispering it, and have been all the time, you seawaves?
Is that it from your liquid rims and wet sands?

Whereto answering, the sea,   165
Delaying not, hurrying not,
Whisper'd me through the night, and very plainly before daybreak,
Lisp'd to me the low and delicious word death,
And again death, death, death, death,
Hissing melodious, neither like the bird nor like my arous'd child's heart,   170
But edging near as privately for me rustling at my feet,
Creeping thence steadily up to my ears and laving me softly all over,
Death, death, death, death, death.

Which I do not forget,
But fuse the song of my dusky demon and brother,   175
That he sang to me in the moonlight on Paumanok's gray beach,
With the thousand responsive songs at random,
My own songs awaked from that hour,
And with them the key, the word up from the waves,
The word of the sweetest song and all songs,   180
That strong and delicious word which, creeping to my feet,
(Or like some old crone rocking the cradle, swathed in sweet garments, bending
    aside,)
The sea whisper'd me.

1859

As I Ebb'd with the Ocean of Life*

1

As I ebb'd with the ocean of life,
As I wended the shores I know,
As I walk'd where the ripples continually wash you Paumanok,
Where they rustle up hoarse and sibilant,
Where the fierce old mother endlessly cries for her castaways,   5
I musing late in the autumn day, gazing off southward,
Held by this electric self out of the pride of which I utter poems,
Was seiz'd by the spirit that trails in the lines underfoot,
The rim, the sediment that stands for all the water and all the land of the
    globe.

Fascinated, my eyes reverting from the south, dropt, to follow those slender
    windrows,   10
Chaff, straw, splinters of wood, weeds, and the sea-gluten,
Scum, scales from shining rocks, leaves of salt-lettuce, left by the tide,
Miles walking, the sound of breaking waves the other side of me,
Paumanok there and then as I thought the old thought of likenesses,
These you presented to me you fish-shaped island,   15
As I wended the shores I know,
As I walk'd with that electric self seeking types.

2

As I wend to the shores I know not,
As I list to the dirge, the voices of men and women wreck'd,
As I inhale the impalpable breezes that set in upon me,
As the ocean so mysterious rolls toward me closer and closer,   20
I too but signify at the utmost a little wash'd-up drift,
A few sands and dead leaves to gather,
Gather, and merge myself as part of the sands and drift.

O baffled, balk'd, bent to the very earth,   25
Oppress'd with myself that I have dared to open my mouth,
Aware now that amid all that blab whose echoes recoil upon me I have not
    once had the least idea who or what I am,
But that before all my arrogant poems the real Me stands yet untouch'd, untold,
    altogether unreach'd,
Withdrawn far, mocking me with mock-congratulatory signs and bows,
With peals of distant ironical laughter at every word I have written,   30
Pointing in silence to these songs, and then to the sand beneath.

---

* First published with the title "Bardic Symbols"
in the *Atlantic Monthly,* April 1860.

I perceive I have not really understood any thing, not a single object, and that
no man ever can,

Nature here in sight of the sea taking advantage of me to dart upon me and
sting me,

Because I have dared to open my mouth to sing at all.

3

You oceans both, I close with you,   35
We murmur alike reproachfully rolling sands and drift, knowing not why,
These little shreds indeed standing for you and me and all.

You friable shore with trails of debris,
You fish-shaped island, I take what is underfoot,
What is yours is mine my father.   40

I too Paumanok,
I too have bubbled up, floated the measureless float, and been wash'd on your
shores,
I too am but a trail of drift and debris,
I too leave little wrecks upon you, you fish-shaped island,
I throw myself upon your breast my father,   45
I cling to you so that you cannot unloose me,
I hold you so firm till you answer me something.

Kiss me my father,
Touch me with your lips as I touch those I love,
Breathe to me while I hold you close the secret of the murmuring I envy.   50

4

Ebb, ocean of life, (the flow will return,)
Cease not your moaning you fierce old mother,
Endlessly cry for your castaways, but fear not, deny not me,
Rustle not up so hoarse and angry against my feet as I touch you or gather
from you.

I mean tenderly by you and all,   55
I gather for myself and for this phantom looking down where we lead, and
following me and mine.

Me and mine, loose windrows, little corpses,
Froth, snowy white, and bubbles,
(See, from my dead lips the ooze exuding at last,   60
See, the prismatic colors glistening and rolling,)
Tufts of straw, sands, fragments,
Buoy'd hither from many moods, one contradicting another,

From the storm, the long calm, the darkness, the swell,
Musing, pondering, a breath, a briny tear, a dab of liquid or soil,   65
Up just as much out of fathomless workings fermented and thrown,
A limp blossom or two, torn, just as much over waves floating, drifted at
     random,
Just as much for us that sobbing dirge of Nature,
Just as much whence we come that blare of the cloud-trumpets,
We, capricious, brought hither we know not whence, spread out before you,
You up there walking or sitting,   70
Whoever you are, we too lie in drifts at your feet.
1860

On the Beach at Night Alone

On the beach at night alone,
As the old mother sways her to and fro singing her husky song,
As I watch the bright stars shining, I think a thought of the clef of the
     universes and of the future.

A vast similitude interlocks all,
All spheres grown, ungrown, small, large, suns, moons, planets,   5
All distances of place however wide,
All distances of time, all inanimate forms,
All souls, all living bodies though they be ever so different, or in different
     worlds,
All gaseous, watery, vegetable, mineral processes, the fishes, the brutes,
All nations, colors, barbarisms, civilizations, languages,   10
All identities that have existed or may exist on this globe, or any globe,
All lives and deaths, all of the past, present, future,
This vast similitude spans them, and always has spann'd,
And shall forever span them and compactly hold and enclose them.
1856

from By the Roadside

When I Heard the Learn'd Astronomer

When I heard the learn'd astronomer,
When the proofs, the figures, were ranged in columns before me,
When I was shown the charts and diagrams, to add, divide, and measure them,
When I sitting heard the astronomer where he lectured with much applause in
     the lecture-room,
How soon unaccountable I became tired and sick,   5
Till rising and gliding out I wander'd off by myself,
In the mystical moist night-air, and from time to time,
Look'd up in perfect silence at the stars.
1865

The Dalliance of the Eagles

Skirting the river road, (my forenoon walk, my rest,)
Skyward in air a sudden muffled sound, the dalliance of the eagles,
The rushing amorous contact high in space together,
The clinching interlocking claws, a living, fierce, gyrating wheel,
Four beating wings, two beaks, a swirling mass tight grappling,   5
In tumbling turning clustering loops, straight downward falling,
Till o'er the river pois'd, the twain yet one, a moment's lull,
A motionless still balance in the air, then parting, talons loosing,
Upward again on slow-firm pinions slanting, their separate diverse flight,
She hers, he his, pursuing.   10

1880

from Drum-Taps

Beat! Beat! Drums!

Beat! beat! drums!—blow! bugles! blow!
Through the windows—through doors—burst like a ruthless force,
Into the solemn church, and scatter the congregation,
Into the school where the scholar is studying;
Leave not the bridegroom quiet—no happiness must he have now with his
    bride,   5
Nor the peaceful farmer any peace, ploughing his field or gathering his grain,
So fierce you whirr and pound you drums—so shrill you bugles blow.

Beat! beat! drums!—blow! bugles! blow!
Over the traffic of cities—over the rumble of wheels in the streets;
Are beds prepared for sleepers at night in the houses? no sleepers must sleep in
    those beds,   10
No bargainers' bargains by day—no brokers or speculators—would they
    continue?
Would the talkers be talking? would the singer attempt to sing?
Would the lawyer rise in the court to state his case before the judge?
Then rattle quicker, heavier drums—you bugles wilder blow.

Beat! beat! drums!—blow! bugles! blow!   15
Make no parley—stop for no expostulation,
Mind not the timid—mind not the weeper or prayer,
Mind not the old man beseeching the young man,
Let not the child's voice be heard, nor the mother's entreaties,
Make even the trestles to shake the dead where they lie awaiting the hearses,   20
So strong you thump O terrible drums—so loud you bugles blow.

1861

Cavalry Crossing a Ford

A line in long array where they wind betwixt green islands,
They take a serpentine course, their arms flash in the sun—hark to the musical
  clank,
Behold the silvery river, in it the splashing horses loitering stop to drink,
Behold the brown-faced men, each group, each person a picture, the negligent
  rest on the saddles,
Some emerge on the opposite bank, others are just entering the ford—while,   5
Scarlet and blue and snowy white,
The guidon flags flutter gayly in the wind.

1865

Bivouac on a Mountain Side

I see before me now a traveling army halting,
Below a fertile valley spread, with barns and the orchards of summer,
Behind, the terraced sides of a mountain, abrupt, in places rising high,
Broken, with rocks, with clinging cedars, with tall shapes dingily seen,
The numerous camp-fires scatter'd near and far, some away up on the mountain, 5
The shadowy forms of men and horses, looming, large-sized, flickering,
And over all the sky—the sky! far, far out of reach, studded, breaking out, the
  eternal stars.

1865

Vigil Strange I Kept on the Field One Night

Vigil strange I kept on the field one night;
When you my son and my comrade dropt at my side that day,
One look I but gave which your dear eyes return'd with a look I shall never
  forget,
One touch of your hand to mine O boy, reach'd up as you lay on the ground,
Then onward I sped in the battle, the even-contested battle,   5
Till late in the night reliev'd to the place at last again I made my way,
Found you in death so cold dear comrade, found your body son of responding
  kisses, (never again on earth responding,)
Bared your face in the starlight, curious the scene, cool blew the moderate
  night-wind,
Long there and then in vigil I stood, dimly around me the battle-field
  spreading,
Vigil wondrous and vigil sweet there in the fragrant silent night,   10
But not a tear fell, not even a long-drawn sigh, long, long I gazed,
Then on the earth partially reclining sat by your side leaning my chin in my
  hands,

Passing sweet hours, immortal and mystic hours with you dearest comrade—not
    a tear, not a word,
Vigil of silence, love and death, vigil for you my son and my soldier,
As onward silently stars aloft, eastward new ones upward stole,   15
Vigil final for you brave boy, (I could not save you, swift was your death,
I faithfully loved you and cared for you living, I think we shall surely meet
    again,)
Till at latest lingering of the night, indeed just as the dawn appear'd,
My comrade I wrapt in his blanket, envelop'd well his form,
Folded the blanket well, tucking it carefully over head and carefully under feet,   20
And there and then and bathed by the rising sun, my son in his grave, in his
    rude-dug grave I deposited,
Ending my vigil strange with that, vigil of night and battlefield dim,
Vigil for boy of responding kisses, (never again on earth responding,)
Vigil for comrade swiftly slain, vigil I never forget, how as day brighten'd,
I rose from the chill ground and folded my soldier well in his blanket,   25
And buried him where he fell.

1865

A March in the Ranks Hard-Prest, and the Road Unknown

A march in the ranks hard-prest, and the road unknown,
A route through a heavy wood with muffled steps in the darkness,
Our army foil'd with loss severe, and the sullen remnant retreating,
Till after midnight glimmer upon us the lights of a dim-lighted building,
We come to an open space in the woods, and halt by the dim-lighted building,   5
'Tis a large old church at the crossing roads, now an impromptu hospital,
Entering but for a minute I see a sight beyond all the pictures and poems ever
    made,
Shadows of deepest, deepest black, just lit by moving candles and lamps,
And by one great pitchy torch stationary with wild red flame and clouds of
    smoke,
By these, crowds, groups of forms vaguely I see on the floor, some in the pews
    laid down,   10
At my feet more distinctly a soldier, a mere lad, in danger of bleeding to death,
    (he is shot in the abdomen,)
I stanch the blood temporarily, (the youngster's face is white as a lily,)
Then before I depart I sweep my eyes o'er the scene fain to absorb it all,
Faces, varieties, postures beyond description, most in obscurity, some of them
    dead,
Surgeons operating, attendants holding lights, the smell of ether, the odor of
    blood,   15
The crowd, O the crowd of the bloody forms, the yard outside also fill'd,
Some on the bare ground, some on planks or stretchers, some in the
    death-spasm sweating,
An occasional scream or cry, the doctor's shouted orders or calls,

The glisten of the little steel instruments catching the glint of the torches,
These I resume as I chant, I see again the forms, I smell the odor,   20
Then hear outside the orders given, *Fall in, my men, fall in;*
But first I bend to the dying lad, his eyes open, a half-smile gives he me,
Then the eyes close, calmly close, and I speed forth to the darkness,
Resuming, marching, ever in darkness marching, on in the ranks,
The unknown road still marching.   25

1865

A Sight in Camp in the Daybreak
Gray and Dim

A sight in camp in the daybreak gray and dim,
As from my tent I emerge so early sleepless,
As slow I walk in the cool fresh air the path near by the hospital tent,
Three forms I see on stretchers lying, brought out there untended lying,
Over each the blanket spread, ample brownish woolen blanket,   5
Gray and heavy blanket, folding, covering all.

Curious I halt and silent stand,
Then with light fingers I from the face of the nearest the first just lift the
    blanket;
Who are you elderly man so gaunt and grim, with well-gray'd hair, and flesh
    all sunken about the eyes?
Who are you my dear comrade?   10

Then to the second I step—and who are you my child and darling?
Who are you sweet boy with cheeks yet blooming?

Then to the third—a face nor child nor old, very calm, as of beautiful
    yellow-white ivory;
Young man I think I know you—I think this face is the face of the Christ
    himself,
Dead and divine and brother of all, and here again he lies.   15

1865

The Wound-Dresser

1

An old man bending I come among new faces,
Years looking backward resuming in answer to children,
Come tell us old man, as from young men and maidens that love me,
(Arous'd and angry, I'd thought to beat the alarum, and urge relentless war,
But soon my fingers fail'd me, my face droop'd and I resign'd myself,   5
To sit by the wounded and soothe them, or silently watch the dead;)

Years hence of these scenes, of these furious passions, these chances,
Of unsurpass'd heroes, (was one side so brave? the other was equally brave;)
Now be witness again, paint the mightiest armies of earth,
Of those armies so rapid so wondrous what saw you to tell us?   10
What stays with you latest and deepest? of curious panics,
Of hard-fought engagements or sieges tremendous what deepest remains?

2

O maidens and young men I love and that love me,
What you ask of my days those the strangest and sudden your talking recalls,
Soldier alert I arrive after a long march cover'd with sweat and dust,   15
In the nick of time I come, plunge in the fight, loudly shout in the rush of
     successful charge,
Enter the captur'd works—yet lo, like a swift-running river they fade,
Pass and are gone they fade—I dwell not on soldiers' perils or soldier's joys,
(Both I remember well—many the hardships, few the joys, yet I was content.)

But in silence, in dreams' projections,   20
While the world of gain and appearance and mirth goes on,
So soon what is over forgotten, and waves wash the imprints off the sand,
With hinged knees returning I enter the doors, (while for you up there,
Whoever you are, follow without noise and be of strong heart.)

Bearing the bandages, water and sponge,   25
Straight and swift to my wounded I go,
Where they lie on the ground after the battle brought in,
Where their priceless blood reddens the grass the ground,
Or to the rows of the hospital tent, or under the roof'd hospital,
To the long rows of cots up and down each side I return,   30
To each and all one after another I draw near, not one do I miss,
An attendant follows holding a tray, he carries a refuse pail,
Soon to be fill'd with clotted rags and blood, emptied, and fill'd again.

I onward go, I stop,
With hinged knees and steady hand to dress wounds,   35
I am firm with each, the pangs are sharp yet unavoidable,
One turns to me his appealing eyes—poor boy! I never knew you,
Yet I think I could not refuse this moment to die for you, if that would save
     you.

3

On, and I go, (open doors of time! open hospital doors!)
The crush'd head I dress, (poor crazed hand tear not the bandage away,)   40

The neck of the cavalry-man with the bullet through and through I examine,
Hard the breathing rattles, quite glazed already the eye, yet life struggles hard,
(Come sweet death! be persuaded O beautiful death!
In mercy come quickly.)

From the stump of the arm, the amputated hand,   45
I undo the clotted lint, remove the slough, wash off the matter and blood,
Back on his pillow the soldier bends with curv'd neck and side-falling head,
His eyes are closed, his face is pale, he dares not look on the bloody stump,
And has not yet look'd on it.
I dress a wound in the side, deep, deep,   50
But a day or two more, for see the frame all wasted and sinking,
And the yellow-blue countenance see.

I dress the perforated shoulder, the foot with the bullet-wound,
Cleanse the one with a gnawing and putrid gangrene, so sickening, so offensive,
While the attendant stands behind aside me holding the tray and pail.   55

I am faithful, I do not give out,
The fractur'd thigh, the knee, the wound in the abdomen,
These and more I dress with impassive hand, (yet deep in my breast a fire, a
     burning flame.)

4

Thus in silence in dreams' projections,
Returning, resuming, I thread my way through the hospitals,   60
The hurt and wounded I pacify with soothing hand,
I sit by the restless all the dark night, some are so young,
Some suffer so much, I recall the experience sweet and sad,
(Many a soldier's loving arms about this neck have cross'd and rested,
Many a soldier's kiss dwells on these bearded lips.)   65
1865

Reconciliation

Word over all, beautiful as the sky,
Beautiful that war and all its deeds of carnage must in time be utterly lost,
That the hands of the sisters Death and Night incessantly softly wash again, and
     ever again, this soil'd world;
For my enemy is dead, a man divine as myself is dead,
I look where he lies white-faced and still in the coffin—I draw near,   5
Bend down and touch lightly with my lips the white face in the coffin.

1865–1866

from Memories of President Lincoln
When Lilacs Last in the Dooryard Bloom'd

1

When lilacs last in the dooryard bloom'd,
And the great star[40] early droop'd in the western sky in the night,
I mourn'd, and yet shall mourn with ever-returning spring.

Ever-returning spring, trinity sure to me you bring,
Lilac blooming perennial and drooping star in the west,   5
And thought of him I love.

2

O powerful western fallen star!
O shades of night—O moody, tearful night!
O great star disappear'd—O the black murk that hides the star!
O cruel hands that hold me powerless—O helpless soul of me!   10
O harsh surrounding cloud that will not free my soul.

3

In the dooryard fronting an old farm-house near the white-wash'd palings,
Stands the lilac-bush tall-growing with heart-shaped leaves of rich green,
With many a pointed blossom rising delicate, with the perfume strong I love,
With every leaf a miracle—and from this bush in the dooryard,   15
With delicate-color'd blossoms and heart-shaped leaves of rich green,
A sprig with its flower I break.

4

In the swamp in secluded recesses,
A shy and hidden bird is warbling a song.

Solitary the thrush,   20
The hermit withdrawn to himself, avoiding the settlements,
Sings by himself a song.
Song of the bleeding throat,
Death's outlet song of life, (for well dear brother I know,
If thou wast not granted to sing thou would'st surely die.)   25

[40] I.e., the planet Venus.

5

Over the breast of the spring, the land, amid cities,
Amid lanes and through old woods, where lately the violets peep'd from the
    ground, spotting the gray debris,
Amid the grass in the fields each side of the lanes, passing the endless grass,
Passing the yellow-spear'd wheat, every grain from its shroud in the
    dark-brown fields uprisen,
Passing the apple-tree blows of white and pink in the orchards,   30
Carrying a corpse to where it shall rest in the grave,
Night and day journeys a coffin.

6

Coffin that passes through lanes and streets,
Through day and night with the great cloud darkening the land,
With the pomp of the inloop'd flags with the cities draped in black,   35
With the show of the States themselves as of crape-veil'd women standing,
With processions long and winding and the flambeaus of the night,
With the countless torches lit, with the silent sea of faces and the unbared
    heads,
With the waiting depot, the arriving coffin, and the sombre faces,
With dirges through the night, with the thousand voices rising strong and
    solemn,   40
With all the mournful voices of the dirges pour'd around the coffin,
The dim-lit churches and the shuddering organs—where amid these you
    journey,
With the tolling tolling bells' perpetual clang,
Here, coffin that slowly passes,
I give you my sprig of lilac.   45

7

(Nor for you, for one alone,
Blossoms and branches green to coffins all I bring,
For fresh as the morning, thus would I chant a song for you O sane and sacred
    death.

All over bouquets of roses,
O death, I cover you over with roses and early lilies,   50
But mostly and now the lilac that blooms the first,
Copious I break, I break the sprigs from the bushes,
With loaded arms I come, pouring for you,
For you and the coffins all of you O death.)

8

O western orb sailing the heaven,
Now I know what you must have meant as a month since I walk'd,
As I walk'd in silence the transparent shadowy night,
As I saw you had something to tell as you bent to me night after night,
As you droop'd from the sky low down as if to my side, (while the other stars
    all look'd on,)
As we wander'd together the solemn night, (for something I know not what
    kept me from sleep,)
As the night advanced, and I saw on the rim of the west how full you were of
    woe,
As I stood on the rising ground in the breeze in the cool transparent night,
As I watch'd where you pass'd and was lost in the netherward black of the
    night,
As my soul in its trouble dissatisfied sank, as where you sad orb,
Concluded, dropt in the night, and was gone.

9

Sing on there in the swamp,
O singer bashful and tender, I hear your notes, I hear your call,
I hear, I come presently, I understand you,
But a moment I linger, for the lustrous star has detain'd me,
The star my departing comrade holds and detains me.

10

O how shall I warble myself for the dead one there I loved?
And how shall I deck my song for the large sweet soul that has gone?
And what shall my perfume be for the grave of him I love?

Sea-winds blown from east and west,
Blown from the Eastern sea and blown from the Western sea, till there on the
    prairies meeting,
These and with these and the breath of my chant,
I'll perfume the grave of him I love.

11

O what shall I hang on the chamber walls?
And what shall the pictures be that I hang on the walls,
To adorn the burial-house of him I love?

Pictures of growing spring and farms and homes,
With the Fourth-month eve at sundown, and the gray smoke lucid and bright,

With floods of the yellow gold of the gorgeous, indolent, sinking sun, burning,
    expanding the air,
With the fresh sweet herbage under foot, and the pale green leaves of the trees
    prolific,
In the distance the flowing glaze, the breast of the river, with a wind-dapple
    here and there,   85
With ranging hills on the banks, with many a line against the sky, and
    shadows,
And the city at hand with dwellings so dense, and stacks of chimneys,
And all the scenes of life and the workshops, and the workmen homeward
    returning.

12

Lo, body and soul—this land,
My own Manhattan with spires, and the sparkling and hurrying tides, and the
    ships,   90
The varied and ample land, the South and the North in the light, Ohio's shores
    and flashing Missouri,
And ever the far-spreading prairies cover'd with grass and corn.

Lo, the most excellent sun so calm and haughty,
The violet and purple morn with just-felt breezes,
The gentle soft-born measureless light,   95
The miracle spreading bathing all, the fulfill'd noon,
The coming eve delicious, the welcome night and the stars,
Over my cities shining all, enveloping man and land.

13

Sing on, sing on you gray-brown bird,
Sing from the swamps, the recesses, pour your chant from the bushes,   100
Limitless out of the dusk, out of the cedars and pines.

Sing on dearest brother, warble your reedy song,
Loud human song, with voice of uttermost woe.

O liquid and free and tender!
O wild and loose to my soul—O wondrous singer!   105
You only I hear—yet the star holds me, (but will soon depart,)
Yet the lilac with mastering odor holds me.

14

Now while I sat in the day and look'd forth,
In the close of the day with its light and the fields of spring, and the farmers
    preparing their crops,

In the large unconscious scenery of my land with its lakes and forests,   110
In the heavenly aerial beauty, (after the perturb'd winds and the storms,)
Under the arching heavens of the afternoon swift passing, and the voices of
    children and women,
The many-moving sea-tides, and I saw the ships how they sail'd,
And the summer approaching with richness, and the fields all busy with labor,
And the infinite separate houses, how they all went on, each with its meals and
    minutia of daily usages,   115
And the streets how their throbbings throbb'd, and the cities pent—lo, then and
    there,
Falling upon them all and among them all, enveloping me with the rest,
Appear'd the cloud, appear'd the long black trail,
And I knew death, its thought, and the sacred knowledge of death.

Then with the knowledge of death as walking one side of me,   120
And the thought of death close-walking the other side of me,
And I in the middle as with companions, and as holding the hands of
    companions,
I fled forth to the hiding receiving night that talks not,
Down to the shores of the water, the path by the swamp in the dimness,
To the solemn shadowy cedars and ghostly pines so still.   125

And the singer so shy to the rest receiv'd me,
The gray-brown bird I know receiv'd us comrades three,
And he sang the carol of death, and a verse for him I love.

From deep secluded recesses,
From the fragrant cedars and the ghostly pines so still,   130
Came the carol of the bird.

And the charm of the carol rapt me,
As I held as if by their hands my comrades in the night,
And the voice of my spirit tallied the song of the bird.

Come lovely and soothing death,   135
Undulate round the world, serenely arriving, arriving,
In the day, in the night, to all, to each,
Sooner or later delicate death.

Prais'd be the fathomless universe,
For life and joy, and for objects and knowledge curious,   140
And for love, sweet love—but praise! praise! praise!
For the sure-enwinding arms of cool-enfolding death.

Dark mother always gliding near with soft feet,
Have none chanted for thee a chant of fullest welcome?
Then I chant it for thee, I glorify thee above all,   145
I bring thee a song that when thou must indeed come, come unfalteringly.

Approach strong deliveress,
When it is so, when thou hast taken them I joyously sing the dead,
Lost in the loving floating ocean of thee,
Laved in the flood of thy bliss O death.   150

From me to thee glad serenades,
Dances for thee I propose saluting thee, adornments and feastings for thee,
And the sights of the open landscape and the high-spread sky are fitting,
And life and the fields, and the huge and thoughtful night.

The night in silence under many a star,   155
The ocean shore and the husky whispering wave whose voice I know,
And the soul turning to thee O vast and well-veil'd death,
And the body gratefully nestling close to thee.

Over the tree-tops I float thee a song,
Over the rising and sinking waves, over the myriad fields and the prairies wide,   160
Over the dense-pack'd cities all and the teeming wharves and ways,
I float this carol with joy, with joy to thee O death.

15

To the tally of my soul,
Loud and strong kept up the gray-brown bird,
With pure deliberate notes spreading filling the night.   165

Loud in the pines and cedars dim,
Clear in the freshness moist and the swamp-perfume,
And I with my comrades there in the night.

While my sight that was bound in my eyes unclosed,
As to long panoramas of visions.   170
And I saw askant the armies,
I saw as in noiseless dreams hundreds of battle-flags,
Borne through the smoke of the battles and pierc'd with missiles I saw them,
And carried hither and yon through the smoke, and torn and bloody,
And at last but a few shreds left on the staffs, (and all in silence,)   175
And the staffs all splinter'd and broken.

I saw battle-corpses, myriads of them,
And the white skeletons of young men, I saw them,
I saw the debris and debris of all the slain soldiers of the war,
But I saw they were not as was thought,   180
They themselves were fully at rest, they suffer'd not,
The living remain'd and suffer'd, the mother suffer'd,
And the wife and the child and the musing comrade suffer'd,
And the armies that remain'd suffer'd.

16

Passing the visions, passing the night,
Passing, unloosing the hold of my comrades' hands,
Passing the song of the hermit bird and the tallying song of my soul,
Victorious song, death's outlet song, yet varying ever-altering song,
As low and wailing, yet clear the notes, rising and falling, flooding the night,
Sadly sinking and fainting, as warning and warning, and yet again bursting
    with joy,
Covering the earth and filling the spread of the heaven,
As that powerful psalm in the night I heard from recesses,
Passing, I leave thee lilac with heart-shaped leaves,
I leave thee there in the door-yard, blooming, returning with spring.

I cease from my song for thee,
From my gaze on thee in the west, fronting the west, communing with thee,
O comrade lustrous with silver face in the night.
Yet each to keep and all, retrievements out of the night,
The song, the wondrous chant of the gray-brown bird,
And the tallying chant, the echo arous'd in my soul,
With the lustrous and drooping star with the countenance full of woe,
With the holders holding my hand nearing the call of the bird,
Comrades mine and I in the midst, and their memory ever to keep, for the
    dead I loved so well,
For the sweetest, wisest soul of all my days and lands—and this for his dear
    sake,
Lilac and star and bird twined with the chant of my soul,
There in the fragrant pines and the cedars dusk and dim.

1865–1866

from Autumn Rivulets
There Was a Child Went Forth

There was a child went forth every day,
And the first object he look'd upon, that object he became,
And that object became part of him for the day or a certain part of the day,
Or for many years or stretching cycles of years.

The early lilacs became part of this child,
And grass and white and red morning-glories, and white and red clover, and
    the song of the phœbe-bird,
And the Third-month lambs and the sow's pink-faint litter, and the mare's foal
    and the cow's calf,
And the noisy brood of the barnyard or by the mire of the pond-side,
And the fish suspending themselves so curiously below there, and the beautiful
    curious liquid,
And the water-plants with their graceful flat heads, all became part of him.

The field-sprouts of Fourth-month and Fifth-month became part of him,
Winter-grain sprouts and those of the light-yellow corn, and the esculent roots
    of the garden,
And the apple-trees cover'd with blossoms and the fruit afterward, and
    wood-berries, and the commonest weeds by the road,
And the old drunkard staggering home from the outhouse of the tavern whence
    he had lately risen,
And the schoolmistress that pass'd on her way to the school,   15
And the friendly boys that pass'd, and the quarrelsome boys,
And the tidy and fresh-cheek'd girls, and the barefoot negro boy and girl,
And all the changes of city and country wherever he went.

His own parents, he that had father'd him and she that had conceiv'd him in
    her womb and birth'd him,
They gave this child more of themselves than that,   20
They gave him afterward every day, they became part of him.

The mother at home quietly placing the dishes on the supper-table,
The mother with mild words, clean her cap and gown, a wholesome odor
    falling off her person and clothes as she walks by,
The father, strong, self-sufficient, manly, mean, anger'd, unjust,
The blow, the quick loud word, the tight bargain, the crafty lure,   25
The family usages, the language, the company, the furniture, the yearning and
    swelling heart,
Affection that will not be gainsay'd, the sense of what is real, the thought if
    after all it should prove unreal,
The doubts of day-time and the doubts of night-time, the curious whether and
    how,
Whether that which appears so is so, or is it all flashes and specks?
Men and women crowding fast in the streets, if they are not flashes and specks
    what are they?   30
The streets themselves and the façades of houses, and goods in the windows,
Vehicles, teams, the heavy-plank'd wharves, the huge crossing at the ferries,
The village on the highland seen from afar at sunset, the river between,
Shadows, aureola and mist, the light falling on roofs and gables of white or
    brown two miles off,
The schooner near by sleepily dropping down the tide, the little boat
    slack-tow'd astern,   35
The hurrying tumbling waves, quick-broken crests, slapping,
The strata of color'd clouds, the long bar of maroon-tint away solitary by itself,
    the spread of purity it lies motionless in,
The horizon's edge, the flying sea-crow, the fragrance of salt marsh and shore
    mud,
These became part of that child who went forth every day, and who now goes,
    and will always go forth every day.

1855

This Compost

1

Something startles me where I thought I was safest,
I withdraw from the still woods I loved,
I will not go now on the pastures to walk,
I will not strip the clothes from my body to meet my lover the sea,
I will not touch my flesh to the earth as to other flesh to renew me.   5

O how can it be that the ground itself does not sicken?
How can you be alive you growths of spring?
How can you furnish health you blood of herbs, roots, orchards, grain?
Are they not continually putting distemper'd corpses within you?
Is not every continent work'd over and over with sour dead?   10

Where have you disposed of their carcasses?
Those drunkards and gluttons of so many generations?
Where have you drawn off all the foul liquid and meat?
I do not see any of it upon you to-day, or perhaps I am deceiv'd,
I will run a furrow with my plough, I will press my spade through the sod and
    turn it up underneath,   15
I am sure I shall expose some of the foul meat.

2

Behold this compost! behold it well!
Perhaps every mite has once form'd part of a sick person—yet behold!
The grass of spring covers the prairies,
The bean bursts noiselessly through the mould in the garden,   20
The delicate spear of the onion pierces upward,
The apple-buds cluster together on the apple-branches,
The resurrection of the wheat appears with pale visage out of its graves,
The tinge awakes over the willow-tree and the mulberry-tree,
The he-birds carol mornings and evenings while the she-birds sit on their nests,   25
The young of poultry break through the hatch'd eggs,
The new-born of animals appear, the calf is dropt from the cow, the colt from
    the mare,
Out of its little hill faithfully rise the potato's dark green leaves,
Out of its hill rises the yellow maize-stalk, the lilacs bloom in the dooryards,
The summer growth is innocent and disdainful above all those strata of sour
    dead.   30

What chemistry!
That the winds are really not infectious,

That this is no cheat, this transparent green-wash of the sea which is so amorous after me,
That it is safe to allow it to lick my naked body all over with its tongues,
That it will not endanger me with the fevers that have deposited themselves in it,   35
That all is clean forever and forever,
That the cool drink from the well tastes so good,
That blackberries are so flavorous and juicy,
That the fruits of the apple-orchard and the orange-orchard, that melons, grapes, peaches, plums, will none of them poison me,
That when I recline on the grass I do not catch any disease,   40
Though probably every spear of grass rises out of what was once a catching disease.

Now I am terrified at the Earth, it is that calm and patient,
It grows such sweet things out of such corruptions,
It turns harmless and stainless on its axis, with such endless successions of diseas'd corpses,
It distills such exquisite winds out of such infused fetor,   45
It renews with such unwitting looks its prodigal, annual, sumptuous crops,
It gives such divine materials to men, and accepts such leavings from them at last.

1856

Passage to India

1

Singing my days,
Singing the great achievements of the present,
Singing the strong light works of engineers,
Our modern wonders, (the antique ponderous Seven outvied,)
In the Old World the east the Suez canal,[41]   5
The New by its mighty railroad spann'd,
The seas inlaid with eloquent gentle wires;[42]
Yet first to sound, and ever sound, the cry with thee O soul,
The Past! the Past! the Past!

The Past—the dark unfathom'd retrospect!   10
The teeming gulf—the sleepers and the shadows!
The past—the infinite greatness of the past!
For what is the present after all but a growth out of the past?

---

[41] Opened in 1869.
[42] The transcontinental railroad link was

completed in 1869 and the Atlantic Cable successfully completed in 1866.

(As a projectile form'd, impell'd, passing a certain line, still keeps on,
So the present, utterly form'd, impell'd by the past.)   1[

2

Passage O soul to India!
Eclaircise[43] the myths Asiatic, the primitive fables.

Not you alone proud truths of the world,
Nor you alone ye facts of modern science,
But myths and fables of eld, Asia's, Africa's fables,   20
The far-darting beams of the spirit, the unloos'd dreams,
The deep diving bibles and legends,
The daring plots of the poets, the elder religions;
O you temples fairer than lilies pour'd over by the rising sun!
O you fables spurning the known, eluding the hold of the known, mounting to
     heaven!   25
You lofty and dazzling towers, pinnacled, red as roses, burnish'd with gold!
Towers of fables immortal fashion'd from mortal dreams!
You too I welcome and fully the same as the rest!
You too with joy I sing.
Passage to India!   30
Lo, soul, seest thou not God's purpose from the first?
The earth to be spann'd, connected by network,
The races, neighbors, to marry and be given in marriage,
The oceans to be cross'd, the distant brought near,
The lands to be welded together.   35

A worship new I sing,
You captains, voyagers, explorers, yours,
You engineers, you architects, machinists, yours,
You, not for trade or transportation only,
But in God's name, and for thy sake O soul.   40

3

Passage to India!
Lo soul for thee of tableaus twain,
I see in one the Suez canal initiated, open'd,
I see the procession of steamships, the Empress Eugenie's[44] leading the van,
I mark from on deck the strange landscape, the pure sky, the level sand in the
     distance,   45
I pass swiftly the picturesque groups, the workmen gather'd,
The gigantic dredging machines.

---

[43] French: "clarify."   [44] Empress Eugenie was the wife of Napoleon III.

In one again, different, (yet thine, all thine, O soul, the same,)
I see over my own continent the Pacific railroad surmounting every barrier,
I see continual trains of cars winding along the Platte carrying freight and
    passengers, 50
I hear the locomotives rushing and roaring, and the shrill steam-whistle,
I hear the echoes reverberate through the grandest scenery in the world,
I cross the Laramie plains, I note the rocks in grotesque shapes, the buttes,
I see the plentiful larkspur and wild onions, the barren, colorless, sage-deserts,
I see in glimpses afar or towering immediately above me the great mountains, I
    see the Wind river and the Wahsatch mountains, 55
I see the Monument mountain and the Eagle's Nest, I pass the Promontory, I
    ascend the Nevadas,
I scan the noble Elk mountain and wind around its base,
I see the Humboldt range, I thread the valley and cross the river,
I see the clear waters of lake Tahoe, I see forests of majestic pines,
Or crossing the great desert, the alkaline plains, I behold enchanting mirages of
    waters and meadows, 60
Marking through these and after all, in duplicate slender lines,
Bridging the three or four thousand miles of land travel,
Tying the Eastern to the Western sea,
The road between Europe and Asia.

(Ah Genoese[45] thy dream! thy dream! 65
Centuries after thou art laid in thy grave,
The shore thou foundest verifies thy dream.)

4

Passage to India!
Struggles of many a captain, tales of many a sailor dead,
Over my mood stealing and spreading they come, 70
Like clouds and cloudlets in the unreach'd sky.

Along all history, down the slopes,
As a rivulet running, sinking now, and now again to the surface rising,
A ceaseless thought, a varied train—lo, soul, to thee, thy sight, they rise,
The plans, the voyages again, the expeditions; 75
Again Vasco de Gama sails forth,
Again the knowledge gain'd, the mariner's compass,
Lands found and nations born, thou born America,
For purpose vast, man's long probation fill'd,
Thou rondure of the world at last accomplish'd. 80

[45] I.e., Christopher Columbus.

5

O vast Rondure, swimming in space,
Cover'd all over with visible power and beauty,
Alternate light and day and the teeming spiritual darkness,
Unspeakable high processions of sun and moon and countless stars above,
Below, the manifold grass and waters, animals, mountains, trees,   85
With inscrutable purpose, some hidden prophetic intention,
Now first it seems my thought begins to span thee.

Down from the gardens of Asia descending radiating,
Adam and Eve appear, then their myriad progeny after them,
Wandering, yearning, curious, with restless explorations,   90
With questionings, baffled, formless, feverish, with never-happy hearts,
With that sad incessant refrain, *Wherefore unsatisfied soul?* and *Whither O
    mocking life?*

Ah who shall soothe these feverish children?
Who justify these restless explorations?
Who speak the secret of impassive earth?   95
Who bind it to us? what is this separate Nature so unnatural?
What is this earth to our affections? (unloving earth, without a throb to answer
    ours,
Cold earth, the place of graves.)

Yet soul be sure the first intent remains, and shall be carried out,
Perhaps even now the time has arrived.   100

After the seas are all cross'd, (as they seem already cross'd,)
After the great captains and engineers have accomplish'd their work,
After the noble inventors, after the scientists, the chemist, the geologist,
    ethnologist,
Finally shall come the poet worthy that name,
The true son of God shall come singing his songs.   105

Then not your deeds only O voyagers, O scientists and inventors, shall be
    justified,
All these hearts as of fretted children shall be sooth'd,
All affection shall be fully responded to, the secret shall be told,
All these separations and gaps shall be taken up and hook'd and link'd together,
The whole earth, this cold, impassive, voiceless earth, shall be completely
    justified,   110
Trinitas divine shall be gloriously accomplish'd and compacted by the true son
    of God, the poet,
(He shall indeed pass the straits and conquer the mountains,

He shall double the cape of Good Hope to some purpose,)
Nature and Man shall be disjoin'd and diffused no more,
The true son of God shall absolutely fuse them.   115

6

Year at whose wide-flung door I sing!
Year of the purpose accomplish'd!
Year of the marriage of continents, climates and oceans!
(No mere doge of Venice now wedding the Adriatic,)
I see O year in you the vast terraqueous globe given and giving all,   120
Europe to Asia, Africa join'd, and they to the New World,
The lands, geographies, dancing before you, holding a festival garland,
As brides and bridegrooms hand in hand.

Passage to India!
Cooling airs from Caucasus far, soothing cradle of man,   125
The river Euphrates flowing, the past lit up again.

Lo soul, the retrospect brought forward,
The old, most populous, wealthiest of earth's lands,
The streams of the Indus and the Ganges and their many affluents,
(I my shores of America walking to-day behold, resuming all,)   130
The tale of Alexander[46] on his warlike marches suddenly dying,
On one side China and on the other side Persia and Arabia,
To the south the great seas and the bay of Bengal,
The flowing literatures, tremendous epics, religions, castes,
Old occult Brahma interminably far back, the tender and junior Buddha,   135
Central and southern empires and all their belongings, possessors,
The wars of Tamerlane, the reign of Aurungzebe,
The traders, rulers, explorers, Moslems, Venetians, Byzantium, the Arabs,
    Portuguese,
The first travelers famous yet, Marco Polo, Batouta the Moor,
Doubts to be solv'd, the map incognita, blanks to be fill'd,   140
The foot of man unstay'd, the hands never at rest,
Thyself O soul that will not brook a challenge.

The mediæval navigators rise before me,
The world of 1492, with its awaken'd enterprise,
Something swelling in humanity now like the sap of the earth in spring,   145
The sunset splendor of chivalry declining.

---

[46] Alexander the Great (356–323 B.C.).

And who art thou sad shade?
Gigantic, visionary, thyself a visionary,
With majestic limbs and pious beaming eyes,
Spreading around with every look of thine a golden world,   150
Enhuing it with gorgeous hues.

As the chief histrion,
Down to the footlights walks in some great scena,
Dominating the rest I see the Admiral himself,
(History's type of courage, action, faith,)   155
Behold him sail from Palos leading his little fleet,
His voyage behold, his return, his great fame,
His misfortunes, calumniators, behold him a prisoner, chain'd,
Behold his dejection, poverty, death.

(Curious in time I stand, noting the efforts of heroes,   160
Is the deferment long? bitter the slander, poverty, death?
Lies the seed unreck'd for centuries in the ground? lo, to God's due occasion,
Uprising in the night, it sprouts, blooms,
And fills the earth with use and beauty.)

7

Passage indeed O soul to primal thought,   165
Not lands and seas alone, thy own clear freshness,
The young maturity of brood and bloom,
To realms of budding bibles.

O soul, repressless, I with thee and thou with me,
Thy circumnavigation of the world begin,   170
Of man, the voyage of his mind's return,
To reason's early paradise,
Back, back to wisdom's birth, to innocent intuitions,
Again with fair creation.

8

O we can wait no longer,   175
We too take ship O soul,
Joyous we too launch out on trackless seas,
Fearless for unknown shores on waves of ecstasy to sail,
Amid the wafting winds, (thou pressing me to thee, I thee to me, O soul,)
Caroling free, singing our song of God,   180
Chanting our chant of pleasant exploration.

With laugh and many a kiss,
(Let others deprecate, let others weep for sin, remorse, humiliation,)
O soul thou pleasest me, I thee.

Ah more than any priest O soul we too believe in God,   185
But with the mystery of God we dare not dally.

O soul thou pleasest me, I thee,
Sailing these seas or on the hills, or waking in the night,
Thoughts, silent thoughts, of Time and Space and Death, like waters flowing,
Bear me indeed as through the regions infinite,   190
Whose air I breathe, whose ripples hear, lave me all over,
Bathe me O God in thee, mounting to thee,
I and my soul to range in range of thee.
O Thou transcendent,
Nameless, the fibre and the breath,   195
Light of the light, shedding forth universes, thou centre of them,
Thou mightier centre of the true, the good, the loving,
Thou moral, spiritual fountain—affection's source—thou reservoir,
(O pensive soul of me—O thirst unsatisfied—waitest not there?
Waitest not haply for us somewhere there the Comrade perfect?)   200
Thou pulse—thou motive of the stars, suns, systems,
That, circling, move in order, safe, harmonious,
Athwart the shapeless vastnesses of space,
How should I think, how breathe a single breath, how speak, if, out of myself,
I could not launch, to those, superior universes?   205

Swiftly I shrivel at the thought of God,
At Nature and its wonders, Time and Space and Death,
But that I, turning, call to thee O soul, thou actual Me,
And lo, thou gently masterest the orbs,
Thou matest Time, smilest content at Death,   210
And fillest, swellest full the vastnesses of Space.

Greater than stars or suns,
Bounding O soul thou journeyest forth;
What love than thine and ours could wider amplify?
What aspirations, wishes, outvie thine and ours O soul?   215
What dreams of the ideal? What plans of purity, perfection, strength?
What cheerful willingness for others' sake to give up all?
For others' sake to suffer all?

Reckoning ahead O soul, when thou, the time achiev'd,
The seas all cross'd, weather'd the capes, the voyage done,   220

Surrounded, copest, frontest God, yieldest, the aim attain'd,
As fill'd with friendship, love complete, the Elder Brother found,
The Younger melts in fondness in his arms.

9

Passage to more than India!
Are thy wings plumed indeed for such far flights?
O soul, voyagest thou indeed on voyages like those?
Disportest thou on waters such as those?
Soundest below the Sanscrit and the Vedas?
Then have thy bent unleash'd.

Passage to you, your shores, ye aged fierce enigmas!
Passage to you, to mastership of you, ye strangling problems!
You, strew'd with the wrecks of skeletons, that, living, never reach'd you.

Passage to more than India!
O secret of the earth and sky!
Of you O waters of the sea! O winding creeks and rivers!
Of you O woods and fields! of you strong mountains of my land!
Of you O prairies! of you gray rocks!
O morning red! O clouds! O rain and snows!
O day and night, passage to you!

O sun and moon and all you stars! Sirius and Jupiter!   240
Passage to you!

Passage, immediate passage! the blood burns in my veins!
Away O soul! hoist instantly the anchor!
Cut the hawsers—haul out—shake out every sail!
Have we not stood here like trees in the ground long enough?   245
Have we not grovel'd here long enough, eating and drinking like mere brutes?
Have we not darken'd and dazed ourselves with books long enough?

Sail forth—steer for the deep waters only,
Reckless O soul, exploring, I with thee, and thou with me,
For we are bound where mariner has not yet dared to go,   250
And we will risk the ship, ourselves and all.
O my brave soul!
O farther farther sail!
O daring joy, but safe! are they not all the seas of God?
O farther, farther, farther sail!   255
1871

The Sleepers

1

I wander all night in my vision,
Stepping with light feet, swiftly and noiselessly stepping and stopping,
Bending with open eyes over the shut eyes of sleepers,
Wandering and confused, lost to myself, ill-assorted, contradictory,
Pausing, gazing, bending, and stopping.   5

How solemn they look there, stretch'd and still,
How quiet they breathe, the little children in their cradles.

The wretched features of ennuyés,[47] the white features of corpses, the livid faces
    of drunkards, the sick-gray faces of onanists,
The gash'd bodies on battle-fields, the insane in their strong-door'd rooms, the
    sacred idiots, the new-born emerging from gates, and the dying emerging
    from gates,
The night pervades them and infolds them.   10
The married couple sleep calmly in their bed, he with his palm on the hip of
    the wife, and she with her palm on the hip of the husband,
The sisters sleep lovingly side by side in their bed,
The men sleep lovingly side by side in theirs,
And the mother sleeps with her little child carefully wrapt.

The blind sleep, and the deaf and dumb sleep,   15
The prisoner sleeps well in the prison, the runaway son sleeps,
The murderer that is to be hung next day, how does he sleep?
And the murder'd person, how does he sleep?

The female that loves unrequited sleeps,
And the male that loves unrequited sleeps,
The head of the money-maker that plotted all day sleeps,   20
And the enraged and treacherous dispositions, all, all sleep.

I stand in the dark with drooping eyes by the worst-suffering and the most
    restless,
I pass my hands soothingly to and fro a few inches from them,
The restless sink in their beds, they fitfully sleep.   25

Now I pierce the darkness, new beings appear,
The earth recedes from me into the night,
I saw that it was beautiful, and I see that what is not the earth is beautiful.

I go from bedside to bedside, I sleep close with the other sleepers each in turn,
I dream in my dream all the dreams of the other dreamers,   30
And I become the other dreamers.

---

[47] French: "bored persons."

I am a dance—play up there! the fit is whirling me fast!

I am the ever-laughing—it is new moon and twilight,
I see the hiding of douceurs,[48] I see nimble ghosts whichever way I look,
Cache[49] and cache again deep in the ground and sea, and where it is neither
     ground nor sea.   35
Well do they do their jobs those journeymen divine,
Only from me can they hide nothing, and would not if they could,
I reckon I am their boss and they make me a pet besides,
And surround me and lead me and run ahead when I walk,
To lift their cunning covers to signify me with stretch'd arms, and resume the
     way;   40
Onward we move, a gay gang of blackguards! with mirth-shouting music and
     wild-flapping pennants of joy!

I am the actor, the actress, the voter, the politician,
The emigrant and the exile, the criminal that stood in the box,
He who has been famous and he who shall be famous after to-day,
The stammerer, the well-form'd person, the wasted or feeble person.   45

I am she who adorn'd herself and folded her hair expectantly,
My truant lover has come, and it is dark.

Double yourself and receive me darkness,
Receive me and my lover too, he will not let me go without him.

I roll myself upon you as upon a bed, I resign myself to the dusk.   50

He whom I call answers me and takes the place of my lover,
He rises with me silently from the bed.

Darkness, you are gentler than my lover, his flesh was sweaty and panting,
I feel the hot moisture yet that he left me.

My hands are spread forth, I pass them in all directions,   55
I would sound up the shadowy shore to which you are journeying.

Be careful darkness! already what was it touch'd me?
I thought my lover had gone, else darkness and he are one,
I hear the heart-beat, I follow, I fade away.

2

I descend my western course, my sinews are flaccid,   60
Perfume and youth course through me and I am their wake.

---

[48] French: "delights."   [49] Hide (from French *cacher*: "to hide").

It is my face yellow and wrinkled instead of the old woman's,
I sit low in a straw-bottom chair and carefully darn my grandson's stockings.

It is I too, the sleepless widow looking out on the winter midnight,
I see the sparkles of starshine on the icy and pallid earth.   65

A shroud I see and I am the shroud, I wrap a body and lie in the coffin,
It is dark here under ground, it is not evil or pain here, it is blank here, for
   reasons.

(It seems to me that every thing in the light and air ought to be happy,
Whoever is not in his coffin and the dark grave let him know he has enough.)

3

I see a beautiful gigantic swimmer swimming naked through the eddies of the
   sea,   70
His brown hair lies close and even to his head, he strikes out with courageous
   arms, he urges himself with his legs,
I see his white body, I see his undaunted eyes,
I hate the swift-running eddies that would dash him head-foremost on the
   rocks.

What are you doing you ruffianly red-trickled waves?
Will you kill the courageous giant? will you kill him in the prime of his
   middle age?   75

Steady and long he struggles,
He is baffled, bang'd, bruis'd, he holds out while his strength holds out,
The slapping eddies are spotted with his blood, they bear him away, they roll
   him, swing him, turn him,
His beautiful body is borne in the circling eddies, it is continually bruis'd on
   rocks,
Swiftly and out of sight is borne the brave corpse.   80

4

I turn but do not extricate myself,
Confused, a past-reading, another, but with darkness yet.

The beach is cut by the razory ice-wind, the wreck-guns sound,
The tempest lulls, the moon comes floundering through the drifts.

I look where the ship helplessly heads end on, I hear the burst as she strikes, I
   hear the howls of dismay, they grow fainter and fainter.   85

I cannot aid with my wringing fingers,
I can but rush to the surf and let it drench me and freeze upon me.

I search with the crowd, not one of the company is wash'd to us alive,
In the morning I help pick up the dead and lay them in rows in a barn.

5

Now of the older war-days, the defeat at Brooklyn,[50]   90
Washington stands inside the lines, he stands on the intrench'd hills amid a
    crowd of officers,
His face is cold and damp, he cannot repress the weeping drops,
He lifts the glass perpetually to his eyes, the color is blanch'd from his cheeks,
He sees the slaughter of the southern braves confided to him by their parents.

The same at last and at last when peace is declared,   95
He stands in the room of the old tavern,[51] the well-belov'd soldiers all pass
    through,
The officers speechless and slow draw near in their turns,
The chief encircles their necks with his arm and kisses them on the cheek,
He kisses lightly the wet cheeks one after another, he shakes hands and bids
    good-by to the army.

6

Now what my mother told me one day as we sat at dinner together,   100
Of when she was a nearly grown girl living home with her parents on the old
    homestead.

A red squaw came one breakfast-time to the old homestead,
On her back she carried a bundle of rushes for rush-bottoming chairs,
Her hair, straight, shiny, coarse, black, profuse, half-envelop'd her face,
Her step was free and elastic, and her voice sounded exquisitely as she spoke. 105

My mother look'd in delight and amazement at the stranger,
She look'd at the freshness of her tall-borne face and full and pliant limbs,
The more she look'd upon her she loved her,
Never before had she seen such wonderful beauty and purity,
She made her sit on a bench by the jamb of the fireplace, she cook'd food for
    her,   110
She had no work to give her, but she gave her remembrance and fondness.

The red squaw staid all the forenoon, and toward the middle of the afternoon
    she went away,
O my mother was loth to have her go away,
All the week she thought of her, she watch'd for her many a month,
She remember'd her many a winter and many a summer,   115
But the red squaw never came nor was heard of there again.

[50] In the battle of Long Island, August 1776.   [51] Fraunces Tavern in New York City.

7

A show of the summer softness—a contact of something unseen—an amour of
    the light and air,
I am jealous and overwhelm'd with friendliness,
And will go gallivant with the light and air myself.

O love and summer, you are in the dreams and in me,   120
Autumn and winter are in the dreams, the farmer goes with his thrift,
The droves and crops increase, the barns are well-fill'd.

Elements merge in the night, ships make tacks in the dreams,
The sailor sails, the exile returns home,
The fugitive returns unharm'd, the immigrant is back beyond months and years, 125
The poor Irishman lives in the simple house of his childhood with the
    well-known neighbors and faces,
They warmly welcome him, he is barefoot again, he forgets he is well off,
The Dutchman voyages home, and the Scotchman and Welshman voyage home,
    and the native of the Mediterranean voyages home,
To every port of England, France, Spain, enter well-fill'd ships,
The Swiss foots it toward his hills, the Prussian goes his way, the Hungarian his
    way, and the Pole his way,   130
The Swede returns, and the Dane and Norwegian return.

The homeward bound and the outward bound,
The beautiful lost swimmer, the ennuyé, the onanist, the female that loves
    unrequited, the money-maker,
The actor and actress, those through with their parts and those waiting to
    commence,
The affectionate boy, the husband and wife, the voter, the nominee that is
    chosen and the nominee that has fail'd,   135
The great already known and the great any time after to-day,
The stammerer, the sick, the perfect-form'd, the homely,
The criminal that stood in the box, the judge that sat and sentenced him, the
    fluent lawyers, the jury, the audience,
The laugher and weeper, the dancer, the midnight widow, the red squaw,
The consumptive, the erysipalite, the idiot, he that is wrong'd,   140
The antipodes, and every one between this and them in the dark,
I swear they are averaged now—one is no better than the other,
The night and sleep have liken'd them and restored them.

I swear they are all beautiful,
Every one that sleeps is beautiful, every thing in the dim light is beautiful,   145
The wildest and bloodiest is over, and all is peace.

Peace is always beautiful,
The myth of heaven indicates peace and night.

The myth of heaven indicates the soul,
The soul is always beautiful, it appears more or it appears less, it comes or it
    lags behind,
It comes from its embower'd garden and looks pleasantly on itself and encloses
    the world,
Perfect and clean the genitals previously jetting, and perfect and clean the
    womb cohering,
The head well-grown proportion'd and plumb, and the bowels and joints
    proportion'd and plumb.

The soul is always beautiful,
The universe is duly in order, every thing is in its place,   15
What has arrived is in its place and what waits shall be in its place,
The twisted skull waits, the watery or rotten blood waits,
The child of the glutton or venerealee waits long, and the child of the
    drunkard waits long, and the drunkard himself waits long,
The sleepers that lived and died wait, the far advanced are to go on in their
    turns, and the far behind are to come on in their turns,
The diverse shall be no less diverse, but they shall flow and unite—they unite
    now.   160

8

The sleepers are very beautiful as they lie unclothed,
They flow hand in hand over the whole earth from east to west as they lie
    unclothed,
The Asiatic and African are hand in hand, the European and American are hand
    in hand,
Learn'd and unlearn'd are hand in hand, and male and female are hand in hand,
The bare arm of the girl crosses the bare breast of her lover, they press close
    without lust, his lips press her neck,   165
The father holds his grown or ungrown son in his arms with measureless love,
    and the son holds the father in his arms with measureless love,
The white hair of the mother shines on the white wrist of the daughter,
The breath of the boy goes with the breath of the man, friend is inarm'd by
    friend,
The scholar kisses the teacher and the teacher kisses the scholar, the wrong'd is
    made right,
The call of the slave is one with the master's call, and the master salutes the
    slave,   170
The felon steps forth from the prison, the insane becomes sane, the suffering of
    sick persons is reliev'd,
The sweatings and fevers stop, the throat that was unsound is sound, the lungs
    of the consumptive are resumed, the poor distress'd head is free,
The joints of the rheumatic move as smoothly as ever, and smoother than ever,
Stiflings and passages open, the paralyzed become supple,
The swell'd and convuls'd and congested awake to themselves in condition,   175

They pass the invigoration of the night and the chemistry of the night, and
    awake.

I too pass from the night,
I stay a while away O night, but I return to you again and love you.

Why should I be afraid to trust myself to you?
I am not afraid, I have been well brought forward by you,   180
I love the rich running day, but I do not desert her in whom I lay so long,
I know not how I came of you and I know not where I go with you, but I
    know I came well and shall go well.

I will stop only a time with the night, and rise betimes,
I will duly pass the day O my mother, and duly return to you.

1855

from Whispers of Heavenly Death

A Noiseless Patient Spider

A noiseless patient spider,
I mark'd where on a little promontory it stood isolated,
Mark'd how to explore the vacant vast surrounding,
It launch'd forth filament, filament, filament, out of itself,
Ever unreeling them, ever tirelessly speeding them.   5

And you O my soul where you stand,
Surrounded, detached, in measureless oceans of space,
Ceaselessly musing, venturing, throwing, seeking the spheres to connect them,
Till the bridge you will need be form'd, till the ductile anchor hold,
Till the gossamer thread you fling catch somewhere, O my soul.   10

1868

from From Noon to Starry Night

To a Locomotive in Winter

Thee for my recitative,
Thee in the driving storm even as now, the snow, the winter-day declining,
Thee in thy panoply, thy measur'd dual throbbing and thy beat convulsive,
Thy black cylindric body, golden brass and silvery steel,
Thy ponderous side-bars, parallel and connecting rods, gyrating, shuttling at thy
    sides,   5
Thy metrical, now swelling pant and roar, now tapering in the distance,
Thy great protruding head-light fix'd in front,
Thy long, pale, floating vapor-pennants, tinged with delicate purple,
The dense and murky clouds out-belching from thy smokestack,
Thy knitted frame, thy springs and valves, the tremulous twinkle of thy wheels,   10

Thy train of cars behind, obedient, merrily following,
Through gale or calm, now swift, now slack, yet steadily careering;
Type of the modern—emblem of motion and power—pulse of the continent,
For once come serve the Muse and merge in verse, even as here I see thee,
With storm and buffeting gusts of wind and falling snow,   1
By day thy warning ringing bell to sound its notes,
By night thy silent signal lamps to swing.

Fierce-throated beauty!
Roll through my chant with all thy lawless music, thy swinging lamps at night,
Thy madly-whistled laughter, echoing, rumbling like an earth-quake, rousing
    all,
    20
Law of thyself complete, thine own track firmly holding,
(No sweetness debonair of tearful harp or glib piano thine,)
Thy trills of shrieks by rocks and hills return'd,
Launch'd o'er the prairies wide, across the lakes,
To the free skies unpent and glad and strong.   25
1876

from **Songs of Parting**
So Long!

To conclude, I announce what comes after me.

I remember I said before my leaves sprang at all,
I would raise my voice jocund and strong with reference to consummations.

When America does what was promis'd,
When through these States walk a hundred millions of superb persons,   5
When the rest part away for superb persons and contribute to them,
When breeds of the most perfect mothers denote America,
Then to me and mine our due fruition.

I have press'd through in my own right,
I have sung the body and the soul, war and peace have I sung, and the songs of
    life and death,   10
And the songs of birth, and shown that there are many births.

I have offer'd my style to every one, I have journey'd with confident step;
While my pleasure is yet at the full I whisper *So long!*
And take the young woman's hand and the young man's hand for the last time.

I announce natural persons to arise,   15
I announce justice triumphant,
I announce uncompromising liberty and equality,
I announce the justification of candor and the justification of pride.

I announce that the identity of these States is a single identity only,
I announce the Union more and more compact, indissoluble,   20
I announce splendors and majesties to make all the previous politics of the earth
  insignificant.

I announce adhesiveness,⁵² I say it shall be limitless, unloosen'd,
I say you shall yet find the friend you were looking for.

I announce a man or woman coming, perhaps you are the one, (*So long!*)
I announce the great individual, fluid as Nature, chaste, affectionate,
  compassionate, fully arm'd.   25

I announce a life that shall be copious, vehement, spiritual, bold,
I announce an end that shall lightly and joyfully meet its translation.

I announce myriads of youths, beautiful, gigantic, sweetblooded,
I announce a race of splendid and savage old men.

O thicker and faster—(*So long!*)   30
O crowding too close upon me,
I foresee too much, it means more than I thought,
It appears to me I am dying.

Hasten throat and sound your last,
Salute me—salute the days once more. Peal the old cry once more.   35

Screaming electric, the atmosphere using,
At random glancing, each as I notice absorbing,
Swiftly on, but a little while alighting,
Curious envelop'd messages delivering,
Sparkles hot, seed ethereal down in the dirt dropping,   40
Myself unknowing, my commission obeying, to question it never daring,
To ages and ages yet the growth of the seed leaving,
To troops out of the war arising, they the tasks I have set promulging,
To women certain whispers of myself bequeathing, their affection me more
  clearly explaining,
To young men my problems offering—no dallier I—I the muscle of their
  brains trying,   45
So I pass, a little time vocal, visible, contrary,
Afterward a melodious echo, passionately bent for, (death making me really
  undying,)
The best of me then when no longer visible, for toward that I have been
  incessantly preparing.

⁵² In phrenology, friendship, or the love of
comrades, as distinguished from amativeness, or
sexual love.

What is there more, that I lag and pause and crouch extended with unshut
    mouth?
Is there a single final farewell?   50

My songs cease, I abandon them,
From behind the screen where I hid I advance personally solely to you.

Camerado, this is no book,
Who touches this touches a man,
(Is it night? are we here together alone?)   55
It is I you hold and who holds you,
I spring from the pages into your arms—decease calls me forth.

O how your fingers drowse me,
Your breath falls around me like dew, your pulse lulls the tympans of my ears,
I feel immerged from head to foot,   60
Delicious, enough.

Enough, O deed impromptu and secret,
Enough O gliding present—enough O summ'd-up past.

Dear friend whoever you are take this kiss,
I give it especially to you, do not forget me,   65
I feel like one who has done work for the day to retire awhile,
I receive now again of my many translations, from my avataras[53] ascending,
    while others doubtless await me,
An unknown sphere more real than I dream'd, more direct, darts awakening
    rays about me, *So long!*
Remember my words, I may again return,
I love you, I depart from materials,   70
I am as one disembodied, triumphant, dead.

1860

from First Annex: Sands at Seventy

Yonnondio

(The sense of the word is *Lament for the Aborigines.*
It is an Iroquois term; and has been used for a
personal name.)

A song, a poem of itself—the word itself a dirge,
Amid the wilds, the rocks, the storm and wintry night,
To me such misty, strange tableaux the syllables calling up;

---

[53] I.e., avatars: incarnations or manifestations.

Yonnondio—I see, far in the west or north, a limitless ravine, with plains and
    mountains dark,
I see swarms of stalwart chieftains, medicine-men, and warriors,   5
As flitting by like clouds of ghosts, they pass and are gone in the twilight,
(Race of the woods, the landscapes free, and the falls!
No picture, poem, statement, passing them to the future:)
Yonnondio! Yonnondio!—unlimn'd they disappear;
To-day gives place, and fades—the cities, farms, factories fade;   10
A muffled sonorous sound, a wailing word is borne through the air for a
    moment,
Then blank and gone and still, and utterly lost.

1887

A Prairie Sunset

Shot gold, maroon and violet, dazzling silver, emerald, fawn,
The earth's whole amplitude and Nature's multiform power consign'd for once
    to colors;
The light, the general air possess'd by them—colors till now unknown,
No limit, confine—not the Western sky alone—the high meridian—North,
    South, all,
Pure luminous color fighting the silent shadows to the last.   5

1888

After the Supper and Talk

After the supper and talk—after the day is done,
As a friend from friends his final withdrawal prolonging,
Good-bye and Good-bye with emotional lips repeating,
(So hard for his hand to release those hands—no more will they meet,
No more for communion of sorrow and joy, of old and young,   5
A far-stretching journey awaits him, to return no more,)
Shunning, postponing severance—seeking to ward off the last word ever so
    little,
E'en at the exit-door turning—charges superfluous calling back—e'en as he
    descends the steps,
Something to eke out a minute additional—shadows of nightfall deepening,
Farewells, messages lessening—dimmer the forthgoer's visage and form,   10
Soon to be lost for aye in the darkness—loth, O so loth to depart!
Garrulous to the very last.

1887

from Democratic Vistas

[from Democracy in America]

I say that democracy can never prove itself beyond cavil, until it founds and luxuriantly grows its own forms of art, poems, schools, theology, displacing all that exists, or that has been produced anywhere in the past, under opposite influences. It is curious to me that while so many voices, pens, minds, in the press, lecture-rooms, in our Congress, &c., are discussing intellectual topics, pecuniary dangers, legislative problems, the suffrage, tariff and labor questions, and the various business and benevolent needs of America, with propositions, remedies, often worth deep attention, there is one need, a hiatus the profoundest, that no eye seems to perceive, no voice to state. Our fundamental want to-day in the United States, with closest, amplest reference to present conditions, and to the future, is of a class, and the clear idea of a class, of native authors, literatures, far different, far higher in grade than any yet known, sacerdotal, modern, fit to cope with our occasions, lands, permeating the whole mass of American mentality, taste, belief, breathing into it a new breath of life, giving it decision, affecting politics far more than the popular superficial suffrage, with results inside and underneath the elections of Presidents or Congresses—radiating, begetting appropriate teachers, schools, manners, and, as its grandest result, accomplishing, (what neither the schools nor the churches and their clergy have hitherto accomplish'd, and without which this nation will no more stand, permanently, soundly, than a house will stand without a substratum,) a religious and moral character beneath the political and productive and intellectual bases of the States. For know you not, dear, earnest reader, that the people of our land may all read and write, and may all possess the right to vote—and yet the main things may be entirely lacking?—(and this to suggest them.)

View'd, to-day, from a point of view sufficiently over-arching, the problem of humanity all over the civilized world is social and religious, and is to be finally met and treated by literature. The priest departs, the divine literatus comes. Never was anything more wanted than, to-day, and here in the States, the poet of the modern is wanted, or the great literatus of the modern. At all times, perhaps, the central point in any nation, and that whence it is itself really sway'd the most, and whence it sways others, is its national literature, especially its archetypal poems. Above all previous lands, a great original literature is surely to become the justification and reliance, (in some respects the sole reliance,) of American democracy.

Few are aware how the great literature penetrates all, gives hue to all, shapes aggregates and individuals, and, after subtle ways, with irresistible power, constructs, sustains, demolishes at will. Why tower, in reminiscence, above all the nations of the earth, two special lands, petty in themselves, yet inexpressibly gigantic, beautiful, columnar? Immortal Judah lives, and Greece immortal lives, in a couple of poems.

Nearer than this. It is not generally realized, but it is true, as the genius of Greece, and all the sociology, personality, politics and religion of those wonderful states, resided in their literature or esthetics, that what was afterwards the main support of European chivalry, the feudal, ecclesiastical, dynastic world over there—forming its osseous structure, holding it together for hundreds, thousands of years, preserving its flesh and bloom, giving it form, decision, rounding it out, and so saturating it in the conscious and unconscious blood, breed, and belief, and intuitions of men, that it still prevails powerful to this day, in defiance of the mighty changes of time—was its literature, permeating to the very marrow, especially that major part, its enchanting songs, ballads, and poems.[1]

To the ostent of the senses and eyes, I know, the influences which stamp the world's history are wars, uprisings or downfalls of dynasties, changeful movements of trade, important inventions, navigation, military or civil governments, advent of powerful personalities, conquerors, &c. These of course play their part; yet, it may be, a single new thought, imagination, abstract principle, even literary style, fit for the time, put in shape by some great literatus, and projected among mankind, may duly cause changes, growths, removals, greater than the longest and bloodiest war, or the most stupendous merely political, dynastic, or commercial overturn.

In short, as, though it may not be realized, it is strictly true, that a few first-class poets, philosophs, and authors, have substantially settled and given status to the entire religion, education, law, sociology, &c., of the hitherto civilized world, by tinging and often creating the atmospheres out of which they have arisen, such also must stamp, and more than ever stamp, the interior and real democratic construction of this American continent, to-day, and days to come. Remember also this fact of difference, that, while through the antique and through the mediæval ages, highest thoughts and ideals realized themselves, and their expression made its way by other arts, as much as, or even more than by, technical literature, (not open to the mass of persons, or even to the majority of eminent persons,) such literature in our day and for current purposes, is not only more eligible than all the other arts put together, but has become the only general means of morally influencing the world. Painting, sculpture, and the dramatic theatre, it would seem, no longer play an indispensable or even important part in the workings and mediumship of intellect, utility, or even high esthetics. Architecture remains, doubtless with capacities, and a real future. Then music, the combiner, nothing more spiritual, nothing more sensuous, a god, yet completely human, advances, prevails, holds highest place; supplying in certain wants and quarters what nothing else could supply. Yet in the civilization of to-day it is undeniable that, over all the arts, literature dominates, serves beyond all—shapes the character of church and school—or, at any rate, is capable of doing so. Including the literature of science, its scope is indeed unparallel'd.

Before proceeding further, it were perhaps well to discriminate on certain points. Literature tills its crops in many fields, and some may flourish, while others lag. What I say in these Vistas has its main bearing on imaginative literature, especially poetry, the stock of all. In the department of science, and the specialty of journalism, there appear, in these States, promises, perhaps fulfilments, of highest earnestness, reality, and

[1] Whitman's note: "See, for hereditaments, specimens, Walter Scott's Border Minstrelsy, Percy's collection, Ellis's early English Metrical Romances, the European continental poems of Walter of Aquitania, and the Nibelungen, of pagan stock, but monkish-feudal redaction; the history of the Troubadours, by Fauriel; even the far-back cumbrous old Hindu epics, as indicating the Asian eggs out of which European chivalry was hatch'd; Ticknor's chapters on the Cid, and on the Spanish poems and poets of Calderon's time. Then always, and, of course, as the superbest poetic culmination-expression of feudalism, the Shaksperean dramas, in the attitudes, dialogue, characters, &c., of the princes, lords and gentlemen, the pervading atmosphere, the implied and express'd standard of manners, the high port and proud stomach, the regal embroidery of style, &c."

life. These, of course, are modern. But in the region of imaginative, spinal and essential attributes, something equivalent to creation is, for our age and lands, imperatively demanded. For not only is it not enough that the new blood, new frame of democracy shall be vivified and held together merely by political means, superficial suffrage, legislation, &c., but it is clear to me that, unless it goes deeper, gets at least as firm and as warm a hold in men's hearts, emotions and belief, as, in their days, feudalism or ecclesiasticism, and inaugurates its own perennial sources, welling from the centre forever, its strength will be defective, its growth doubtful, and its main charm wanting. I suggest, therefore, the possibility, should some two or three really original American poets, (perhaps artists or lecturers,) arise, mounting the horizon like planets, stars of the first magnitude, that, from their eminence, fusing contributions, races, far localities, &c., together they would give more compaction and more moral identity, (the quality to-day most needed,) to these States, than all its Constitutions, legislative and judicial ties, and all its hitherto political, warlike, or materialistic experiences. As, for instance, there could hardly happen anything that would more serve the States, with all their variety of origins, their diverse climes, cities, standards, &c., than possessing an aggregate of heroes, characters, exploits, sufferings, prosperity or misfortune, glory or disgrace, common to all, typical of all—no less, but even greater would it be to possess the aggregation of a cluster of mighty poets, artists, teachers, fit for us, national expressers, comprehending and effusing for the men and women of the States, what is universal, native, common to all, inland and seaboard, northern and southern. The historians say of ancient Greece, with her ever-jealous autonomies, cities, and states, that the only positive unity she ever own'd or receiv'd, was the sad unity of a common subjection, at the last, to foreign conquerors. Subjection, aggregation of that sort, is impossible to America; but the fear of conflicting and irreconcilable interiors, and the lack of a common skeleton, knitting all close, continually haunts me. Or, if it does not, nothing is plainer than the need, a long period to come, of a fusion of the States into the only reliable identity, the moral and artistic one. For, I say, the true nationality of the States, the genuine union, when we come to a mortal crisis, is, and is to be, after all, neither the written law, nor, (as is generally supposed,) either self-interest, or common pecuniary or material objects—but the fervid and tremendous IDEA, melting everything else with resistless heat, and solving all lesser and definite distinctions in vast, indefinite, spiritual, emotional power.

It may be claim'd, (and I admit the weight of the claim,) that common and general worldly prosperity, and a populace well-to-do, and with all life's material comforts, is the main thing, and is enough. It may be argued that our republic is, in performance, really enacting to-day the grandest arts, poems, &c., by beating up the wilderness into fertile farms, and in her railroads, ships, machinery, &c. And it may be ask'd, Are these not better, indeed, for America, than any utterances even of greatest rhapsode, artist, or literatus?

I too hail those achievements with pride and joy: then answer that the soul of man will not with such only—nay, not with such at all—be finally satisfied; but needs what, (standing on these and on all things, as the feet stand on the ground,) is address'd to the loftiest, to itself alone.

Out of such considerations, such truths, arises for treatment in these Vistas the important question of character, of an American stock-personality, with literatures and arts for outlets and return-expressions, and, of course, to correspond, within outlines common to all. To these, the main affair, the thinkers of the United States, in general so acute, have either given feeblest attention, or have remain'd, and remain, in a state of somnolence.

For my part, I would alarm and caution even the political and business reader, and to the utmost extent, against the prevailing delusion that the establishment of free political institutions, and plentiful intellectual smartness, with general good order, physical plenty, industry, &c., (desirable and precious advantages as they all are,) do, of themselves, determine and yield to our experiment of democracy the fruitage of success. With such advantages at present fully, or almost fully, possess'd—the Union just issued, victorious, from the struggle with the only foes it need ever fear, (namely, those within itself, the interior ones,) and with unprecedented materialistic advance-ment—society, in these States, is canker'd, crude, superstitious, and rotten. Political, or law-made society is, and private, or voluntary society, is also. In any vigor, the element of the moral conscience, the most important, the verteber to State or man, seems to me either entirely lacking, or seriously enfeebled or ungrown.

I say we had best look our times and lands searchingly in the face, like a physician diagnosing some deep disease. Never was there, perhaps, more hollowness at heart than at present, and here in the United States. Genuine belief seems to have left us. The underlying principles of the States are not honestly believ'd in, (for all this hectic glow, and these melo-dramatic screamings,) nor is humanity itself believ'd in. What penetrating eye does not everywhere see through the mask? The spectacle is appaling. We live in an atmosphere of hypocrisy throughout. The men believe not in the women, nor the women in the men. A scornful superciliousness rules in literature. The aim of all the *littérateurs* is to find something to make fun of. A lot of churches, sects, &c., the most dismal phantasms I know, usurp the name of religion. Conversation is a mass of badinage. From deceit in the spirit, the mother of all false deeds, the offspring is already incalculable. An acute and candid person, in the revenue department in Washington, who is led by the course of his employment to regularly visit the cities, north, south and west, to investigate frauds, has talk'd much with me about his discoveries. The depravity of the business classes of our country is not less than has been supposed, but infinitely greater. The official services of America, national, state, and municipal, in all their branches and departments, except the judiciary, are saturated in corruption, bribery, falsehood, mal-administration; and the judiciary is tainted. The great cities reek with respectable as much as non-respectable robbery and scoundrelism. In fashionable life, flippancy, tepid amours, weak infidelism, small aims, or no aims at all, only to kill time. In business, (this all-devouring modern word, business,) the one sole object is, by any means, pecuniary gain. The magician's serpent in the fable ate up all the other serpents; and money-making is our magician's serpent, remaining to-day sole master of the field. The best class we show, is but a mob of fashionably dress'd speculators and vulgarians. True, indeed, behind this fantastic farce, enacted on the visible stage of society, solid things and stupendous labors are to be discover'd, existing crudely and going on in the background, to advance and tell themselves in time. Yet the truths are none the less terrible. I say that our New World democracy, however great a success in uplifting the masses out of their sloughs, in materialistic development, products, and in a certain highly-deceptive superficial popular intellec-tuality, is, so far, an almost complete failure in its social aspects, and in really grand religious, moral, literary, and esthetic results. In vain do we march with unprecedented strides to empire so colossal, outvying the antique, beyond Alexander's, beyond the proudest sway of Rome. In vain have we annex'd Texas, California, Alaska, and reach north for Canada and south for Cuba. It is as if we were somehow being endow'd with a vast and more and more thoroughly-appointed body, and then left with little or no soul.

Let me illustrate further, as I write, with current observations, localities, &c. The subject is important, and will bear repetition. After an absence, I am now again (September, 1870) in New York city and Brooklyn, on a few weeks' vacation. The splendor, picturesqueness, and oceanic amplitude and rush of these great cities, the unsurpass'd situation, rivers and bay, sparkling sea-tides, costly and lofty new buildings, facades of marble and iron, of original grandeur and elegance of design, with the masses of gay color, the preponderance of white and blue, the flags flying, the endless ships, the tumultuous streets, Broadway, the heavy, low, musical roar, hardly ever intermitted, even at night; the jobbers' houses, the rich shops, the wharves, the great Central Park, and the Brooklyn Park of hills, (as I wander among them this beautiful fall weather, musing, watching, absorbing)—the assemblages of the citizens in their groups, conversations, trades, evening amusements, or along the by-quarters —these, I say, and the like of these, completely satisfy my senses of power, fulness, motion, &c., and give me, through such senses and appetites, and through my esthetic conscience, a continued exaltation and absolute fulfilment. Always and more and more, as I cross the East and North rivers, the ferries, or with the pilots in their pilot-houses, or pass an hour in Wall street, or the gold exchange, I realize, (if we must admit such partialisms,) that not Nature alone is great in her fields of freedom and the open air, in her storms, the shows of night and day, the mountains, forests, seas—but in the artificial, the work of man too is equally great—in this profusion of teeming humanity—in these ingenuities, streets, goods, houses, ships—these hurrying, feverish, electric crowds of men, their complicated business genius, (not least among the geniuses,) and all this mighty, many-threaded wealth and industry concentrated here.

But sternly discarding, shutting our eyes to the glow and grandeur of the general superficial effect, coming down to what is of the only real importance, Personalities, and examining minutely, we question, we ask, Are there, indeed, *men* here worthy the name? Are there athletes? Are there perfect women, to match the generous material luxuriance? Is there a pervading atmosphere of beautiful manners? Are there crops of fine youths, and majestic old persons? Are there arts worthy freedom and a rich people? Is there a great moral and religious civilization—the only justification of a great material one? Confess that to severe eyes, using the moral microscope upon humanity, a sort of dry and flat Sahara appears, these cities, crowded with petty grotesques, malformations, phantoms, playing meaningless antics. Confess that everywhere, in shop, street, church, theatre, bar-room, official chair, are pervading flippancy and vulgarity, low cunning, infidelity—everywhere the youth puny, impudent, foppish, prematurely ripe—everywhere an abnormal libidinousness, unhealthy forms, male, female, painted, padded, dyed, chignon'd, muddy complexions, bad blood, the capacity for good motherhood decreasing or decreas'd, shallow notions of beauty, with a range of manners, or rather lack of manners, (considering the advantages enjoy'd,) probably the meanest to be seen in the world.[2]

Of all this, and these lamentable conditions, to breathe into them the breath recuperative of sane and heroic life, I say a new founded literature, not merely to copy and reflect existing surfaces, or pander to what is called taste—not only to amuse, pass away time, celebrate the beautiful, the refined, the past, or exhibit technical, rhythmic, or grammatical dexterity—but a literature underlying life, religious, consistent with science, handling the elements and forces with competent power, teaching and training men—and, as perhaps the most precious of its results, achieving the entire redemption of woman out of these incredible holds and webs of silliness, millinery, and every kind of dyspeptic depletion—and thus insuring to the States a strong and sweet Female Race, a race of perfect Mothers—is what is needed.

And now, in the full conception of these facts and points, and all that they infer, pro and con—with yet unshaken faith in the elements of the American masses, the composites, of both sexes, and even consider'd as individuals—and ever recognizing in them the broadest bases of the best literary and esthetic appreciation—I proceed with my speculations, Vistas.

First, let us see what we can make out of a brief, general, sentimental consideration of political democracy, and whence it has arisen, with regard to some of its current features, as an aggregate, and as the basic structure of our future literature and authorship. We shall, it is true, quickly and continually find the origin-idea of the singleness of man, individualism, asserting itself, and cropping forth, even from the opposite ideas. But the mass, or lump character, for imperative reasons, is to be ever carefully weigh'd, borne in mind, and provided for. Only from it, and from its proper regulation and potency, comes the other, comes the chance of individualism. The two are contradictory, but our task is to reconcile them.[3]

The political history of the past may be summ'd up as having grown out of what underlies the words, order, safety, caste, and especially out of the need of some prompt deciding authority, and of cohesion at all cost. Leaping time, we come to the period within the memory of people now living, when, as from some lair where they had

---

[2] Whitman's note: "Of these rapidly-sketch'd hiatuses, the two which seem to me most serious are, for one, the condition, absence, or perhaps the singular abeyance, of moral conscientious fibre all through American society; and, for another, the appaling depletion of women in their powers of sane athletic maternity, their crowning attribute, and ever making the woman, in loftiest spheres, superior to the man.

I have sometimes thought, indeed, that the sole avenue and means of a reconstructed sociology depended, primarily, on a new birth, elevation, expansion, invigoration of woman, affording, for races to come, (as the conditions that antedate birth are indispensable,) a perfect motherhood. Great, great, indeed, far greater than they know, is the sphere of women. But

doubtless the question of such new sociology all goes together, includes many varied and complex influences and premises, and the man as well as the woman, and the woman as well as the man."

[3] Whitman's note: "The question hinted here is one which time only can answer. Must not the virtue of modern Individualism, continually enlarging, usurping all, seriously affect, perhaps keep down entirely, in America, the like of the ancient virtue of Patriotism, the fervid and absorbing love of general country? I have no doubt myself that the two will merge, and will mutually profit and brace each other, and that from them a greater product, a third, will arise. But I feel that at present they and their oppositions form a serious problem and paradox in the United States."

slumber'd long, accumulating wrath, sprang up and are yet active, (1790, and on even to the present, 1870,) those noisy eructations, destructive iconoclasms, a fierce sense of wrongs, amid which moves the form, well known in modern history, in the old world, stain'd with much blood, and mark'd by savage reactionary clamors and demands. These bear, mostly, as on one inclosing point of need.

For after the rest is said—after the many time-honor'd and really true things for subordination, experience, rights of property, &c., have been listen'd to and acquiesced in—after the valuable and well-settled statement of our duties and relations in society is thoroughly conn'd over and exhausted—it remains to bring forward and modify everything else with the idea of that Something a man is, (last precious consolation of the drudging poor,) standing apart from all else, divine in his own right, and a woman in hers, sole and untouchable by any canons of authority, or any rule derived from precedent, state-safety, the acts of legislatures, or even from what is called religion, modesty, or art. The radiation of this truth is the key of the most significant doings of our immediately preceding three centuries, and has been the political genesis and life of America. Advancing visibly, it still more advances invisibly. Underneath the fluctuations of the expressions of society, as well as the movements of the politics of the leading nations of the world, we see steadily pressing ahead and strengthening itself, even in the midst of immense tendencies toward aggregation, this image of completeness in separatism, of individual personal dignity, of a single person, either male or female, characterized in the main, not from extrinsic acquirements or position, but in the pride of himself or herself alone; and, as an eventual conclusion and summing up, (or else the entire scheme of things is aimless, a cheat, a crash,) the simple idea that the last, best dependence is to be upon humanity itself, and its own inherent, normal, full-grown qualities, without any superstitious support whatever. This idea of perfect individualism it is indeed that deepest tinges and gives character to the idea of the aggregate. For it is mainly or altogether to serve independent separatism that we favor a strong generalization, consolidation. As it is to give the best vitality and freedom to the rights of the States, (every bit as important as the right of nationality, the union,) that we insist on the identity of the Union at all hazards.

The purpose of democracy—supplanting old belief in the necessary absoluteness of establish'd dynastic rulership, temporal, ecclesiastical, and scholastic, as furnishing the only security against chaos, crime, and ignorance—is, through many transmigrations, and amid endless ridicules, arguments, and ostensible failures, to illustrate, at all hazards, this doctrine or theory that man, properly train'd in sanest, highest freedom, may and must become a law, and series of laws, unto himself, surrounding and providing for, not only his own personal control, but all his relations to other individuals, and to the State; and that, while other theories, as in the past histories of nations, have proved wise enough, and indispensable perhaps for their conditions, *this*, as matters now stand in our civilized world, is the only scheme worth working from, as warranting results like those of Nature's laws, reliable, when once establish'd, to carry on themselves.

The argument of the matter is extensive, and, we admit, by no means all on one side. What we shall offer will be far, far from sufficient. But while leaving unsaid much that should properly even prepare the way for the treatment of this many-sided question of political liberty, equality, or republicanism—leaving the whole history and consideration of the feudal plan and its products, embodying humanity, its politics and civilization, through the retrospect of past time, (which plan and products, indeed, make up all of the past, and a large part of the present)—leaving unanswer'd, at least by any specific and local answer, many a well-wrought argument and instance, and many a conscientious declamatory cry and warning—as, very lately, from an eminent and venerable person abroad[4]—things, problems, full of doubt, dread, suspense, (not new to me, but old occupiers of many an anxious hour in city's din, or night's silence,) we still may give a page or so, whose drift is opportune. Time alone can finally answer these things. But as a substitute in passing, let us, even if fragmentarily, throw forth a short direct or indirect suggestion of the premises of that other plan, in the new spirit, under the new forms, started here in our America.

As to the political section of Democracy, which introduces and breaks ground for further and vaster sections, few probably are the minds, even in these republican States, that fully comprehend the aptness of that phrase, "THE GOVERNMENT OF THE PEOPLE, BY THE PEOPLE, FOR THE PEOPLE," which we inherit from the lips of Abraham Lincoln; a formula whose verbal shape is homely wit, but whose scope includes both the totality and all minutiæ of the lesson.

The People! Like our huge earth itself, which, to ordinary scansion, is full of vulgar contradictions and offence, man, viewed in the lump, displeases, and is a constant puzzle and affront to the merely educated classes. The rare, cosmical, artist-mind, lit with the Infinite, alone confronts his manifold and oceanic qualities—but taste, intelligence and culture, (so-called,) have been against the masses, and remain so. There is plenty of glamour about the most damnable crimes and hoggish meannesses, special and general, of the feudal and dynastic world over there, with its *personnel* of lords and queens and courts, so well-dress'd and so handsome. But the People are ungrammatical, untidy, and their sins gaunt and ill-bred.

Literature, strictly consider'd, has never recognized the People, and, whatever may be said, does not to-day. Speaking generally, the tendencies of literature, as hitherto pursued, have been to make mostly critical and querulous men. It seems as if, so far, there were some natural repugnance between a literary and professional life, and the rude rank spirit of the democracies. There is, in later literature, a treatment of benevolence, a charity business, rife enough it is true; but I know nothing more rare, even in this country, than a fit scientific estimate and reverent appreciation of the People—of their measureless wealth of latent power and capacity, their vast, artistic contrasts of lights and shades—with, in America, their entire reliability in emergencies, and a certain breadth of historic grandeur, of peace or war, far surpassing all the vaunted samples of book-heroes, or any *haut-ton* coteries, in all the records of the world. . . .

[4] The English essayist and historian Thomas Carlyle (1795–1881) attacked democratic ideology and institutions in "Shooting Niagara" (1867). Whitman's note follows. " 'SHOOTING NIAGARA.'—I was at first roused to much anger and abuse by this essay from Mr. Carlyle, so insulting to the theory of America—but happening to think afterwards how I had more than once been in the like mood, during which his essay was evidently cast, and seen persons and things in the same light, (indeed some might say there are signs of the same feeling in these Vistas)—I have since read it again, not only as a study, expressing as it does certain judgments from the highest feudal point of view, but have read it with respect as coming from an earnest soul, and as contributing certain sharp-cutting metallic grains, which, if not gold or silver, may be good hard, honest iron."

[from A National Character]

So much contributed, to be conn'd well, to help prepare and brace our edifice, our plann'd Idea—we still proceed to give it in another of its aspects—perhaps the main, the high façade of all. For to democracy, the leveler, the unyielding principle of the average, is surely join'd another principle, equally unyielding, closely tracking the first, indispensable to it, opposite, (as the sexes are opposite,) and whose existence, confronting and ever modifying the other, often clashing, paradoxical, yet neither of highest avail without the other, plainly supplies to these grand cosmic politics of ours, and to the launch'd forth mortal dangers of republicanism, to-day or any day, the counterpart and offset whereby Nature restrains the deadly original relentlessness of all her first-class laws. This second principle is individuality, the pride and centripetal isolation of a human being in himself—identity—personalism. Whatever the name, its acceptance and thorough infusion through the organizations of political common-alty now shooting Aurora-like about the world, are of utmost importance, as the principle itself is needed for very life's sake. It forms, in a sort, or is to form, the compensating balance-wheel of the successful working machinery of aggregate America.

And, if we think of it, what does civilization itself rest upon—and what object has it, with its religions, arts, schools, &c., but rich, luxuriant, varied personalism? To that, all bends; and it is because toward such result democracy alone, on anything like Nature's scale, breaks up the limitless fallows of humankind, and plants the seed, and gives fair play, that its claims now precede the rest. The literature, songs, esthetics, &c., of a country are of importance principally because they furnish the materials and suggestions of personality for the women and men of that country, and enforce them in a thousand effective ways.[5] As the top-most claim of a strong consolidating of the nationality of these States, is, that only by such powerful compaction can the separate States secure that full and free swing within their spheres, which is becoming to them,

[5] Whitman's note: "After the rest is satiated, all interest culminates in the field of persons, and never flags there. Accordingly in this field have the great poets and literatuses signally toil'd. They too, in all ages, all lands, have been creators, fashioning, making types of men and women, as Adam and Eve are made in the divine fable. Behold, shaped, bred by orientalism, feudalism, through their long growth and culmination, and breeding back in return—(when shall we have an equal series, typical of democracy?)—behold, commencing in primal Asia, (apparently formulated, in what beginning we know, in the gods of the mythologies, and coming down thence,) a few samples out of the countless product, bequeath'd to the moderns, bequeath'd to America as studies. For the men, Yudishtura, Rama, Arjuna, Solomon, most of the Old and New Testament characters; Achilles, Ulysses, Theseus, Prometheus, Hercules, Æneas, Plutarch's heroes; the Merlin of Celtic bards; the Cid, Arthur and his knights, Siegfried and Hagen in the Nibelungen; Roland and Oliver; Roustam in the Shah-Nemah; and so on to Milton's Satan, Cervantes' Don Quixote, Shakspere's Hamlet, Richard II., Lear, Marc Antony, &c., and the modern Faust. These, I say, are models, combined, adjusted to other standards than America's, but of priceless value to her and hers.

Among women, the goddesses of the Egyptian, Indian and Greek mythologies, certain Bible characters, especially the Holy Mother; Cleopatra, Penelope; the portraits of Brunhelde and Chriemhilde in the Nibelungen; Oriana, Una, &c.; the modern Consuelo, Walter Scott's Jeanie and Effie Deans, &c., &c. (Yet woman portray'd or outlin'd at her best, or as perfect human mother, does not hitherto, it seems to me, fully appear in literature.)"

each after its kind, so will individuality, with unimpeded branchings, flourish best under imperial republican forms.

Assuming Democracy to be at present in its embryo condition, and that the only large and satisfactory justification of it resides in the future, mainly through the copious production of perfect characters among the people, and through the advent of a sane and pervading religiousness, it is with regard to the atmosphere and spaciousness fit for such characters, and of certain nutriment and cartoon-draftings proper for them, and indicating them for New World purposes, that I continue the present state-ment—an exploration, as of new ground, wherein, like other primitive surveyors, I must do the best I can, leaving it to those who come after me to do much better. (The service, in fact, if any, must be to break a sort of first path or track, no matter how rude and ungeometrical.)

We have frequently printed the word Democracy. Yet I cannot too often repeat that it is a word the real gist of which still sleeps, quite unawaken'd, notwithstanding the resonance and the many angry tempests out of which its syllables have come, from pen or tongue. It is a great word, whose history, I suppose, remains unwritten, because that history has yet to be enacted. It is, in some sort, younger brother of another great and often-used word, Nature, whose history also waits unwritten. As I perceive, the tendencies of our day, in the States, (and I entirely respect them,) are toward those vast and sweeping movements, influences, moral and physical, of humanity, now and always current over the planet, on the scale of the impulses of the elements. Then it is also good to reduce the whole matter to the consideration of a single self, a man, a woman, on permanent grounds. Even for the treatment of the universal, in politics, metaphysics, or anything, sooner or later we come down to one single, solitary soul.

There is, in sanest hours, a consciousness, a thought that rises, independent, lifted out from all else, calm, like the stars, shining eternal. This is the thought of identity—yours for you, whoever you are, as mine for me. Miracle of miracles, beyond statement, most spiritual and vaguest of earth's dreams, yet hardest basic fact, and only entrance to all facts. In such devout hours, in the midst of the significant wonders of heaven and earth, (significant only because of the Me in the centre,) creeds, conven-tions, fall away and become of no account before this simple idea. Under the luminousness of real vision, it alone takes possession, takes value. Like the shadowy dwarf in the fable, once liberated and look'd upon, it expands over the whole earth, and spreads to the roof of heaven.

The quality of BEING, in the object's self, according to its own central idea and purpose, and of growing therefrom and thereto—not criticism by other standards, and adjustments thereto—is the lesson of Nature. True, the full man wisely gathers, culls, absorbs; but if, engaged disproportionately in that, he slights or overlays the precious idiocrasy and special nativity and intention that he is, the man's self, the main thing, is a failure, however wide his general cultivation. Thus, in our times, refinement and delicatesse are not only attended to sufficiently, but threaten to eat us up, like a cancer. Already, the democratic genius watches, ill-pleased, these tendencies. Provision for a little healthy rudeness, savage virtue, justification of what one has in one's self, whatever it is, is demanded. Negative qualities, even deficiencies, would be a relief. Singleness and normal simplicity and separation, amid this more and more complex, more and more artificialized state of society—how pensively we yearn for them! how we would welcome their return!

In some such direction, then—at any rate enough to preserve the balance—we feel called upon to throw what weight we can, not for absolute reasons, but current ones. To prune, gather, trim, conform, and ever cram and stuff, and be genteel and proper, is the pressure of our days. While aware that much can be said even in behalf of all this, we perceive that we have not now to consider the question of what is demanded to serve a half-starved and barbarous nation, or set of nations, but what is most applicable, most pertinent, for numerous congeries of conventional, over-corpulent societies, already becoming stifled and rotten with flatulent, infidelistic literature, and polite conformity and art. In addition to establish'd sciences, we suggest a science as it were of healthy average personalism, on original-universal grounds, the object of which should be to raise up and supply through the States a copious race of superb American men and women, cheerful, religious, ahead of any yet known.

America has yet morally and artistically originated nothing. She seems singularly unaware that the models of persons, books, manners, &c., appropriate for former conditions and for European lands, are but exiles and exotics here. No current of her life, as shown on the surfaces of what is authoritatively called her society, accepts or runs into social or esthetic democracy; but all the currents set squarely against it. Never, in the Old World, was thoroughly upholster'd exterior appearance and show, mental and other, built entirely on the idea of caste, and on the sufficiency of mere outside acquisition—never were glibness, verbal intellect, more the test, the emulation—more loftily elevated as head and sample—than they are on the surface of our republican States this day. The writers of a time hint the mottoes of its gods. The word of the modern, say these voices, is the word Culture.

We find ourselves abruptly in close quarters with the enemy. This word Culture, or what it has come to represent, involves, by contrast, our whole theme, and has been, indeed, the spur, urging us to engagement. Certain questions arise. As now taught, accepted and carried out, are not the processes of culture rapidly creating a class of supercilious infidels, who believe in nothing? Shall a man lose himself in countless masses of adjustments, and be so shaped with reference to this, that, and the other, that the simply good and healthy and brave parts of him are reduced and clipp'd away, like the bordering of box in a garden? You can cultivate corn and roses and orchards—but who shall cultivate the mountain peaks, the ocean, and the tumbling gorgeousness of the clouds? Lastly—is the readily-given reply that culture only seeks to help, systematize, and put in attitude, the elements of fertility and power, a conclusive reply?

I do not so much object to the name, or word, but I should certainly insist, for the purposes of these States, on a radical change of category, in the distribution of precedence. I should demand a programme of culture, drawn out, not for a single class alone, or for the parlors or lecture-rooms, but with an eye to practical life, the west, the working-men, the facts of farms and jack-planes and engineers, and of the broad range of the women also of the middle and working strata, and with reference to the perfect equality of women, and of a grand and powerful motherhood. I should demand of this programme or theory a scope generous enough to include the widest human area. It must have for its spinal meaning the formation of a typical personality of character, eligible to the uses of the high average of men—and *not* restricted by conditions ineligible to the masses. The best culture will always be that of the manly and courageous instincts, and loving perceptions, and of self-respect—aiming to form, over this continent, an idiocrasy of universalism, which, true child of America, will bring joy to its mother, returning to her in her own spirit, recruiting myriads of offspring, able, natural, perceptive, tolerant, devout believers in her, America, and with some definite instinct why and for what she has arisen, most vast, most formidable of historic births, and is, now and here, with wonderful step, journeying through Time.

The problem, as it seems to me, presented to the New World, is, under permanent law and order, and after preserving cohesion, (ensemble-Individuality,) at all hazards, to vitalize man's free play of special Personalism, recognizing in it something that calls ever more to be consider'd, fed, and adopted as the substratum for the best that belongs to us, (government indeed is for it,) including the new esthetics of our future.

To formulate beyond this present vagueness—to help line and put before us the species, or a specimen of the species, of the democratic ethnology of the future, is a work toward which the genius of our land, with peculiar encouragement, invites her well-wishers. Already certain limnings, more or less grotesque, more or less fading and watery, have appear'd. We too, (repressing doubts and qualms,) will try our hand.

Attempting, then, however crudely, a basic model or portrait of personality for general use for the manliness of the States, (and doubtless that is most useful which is most simple and comprehensive for all, and toned low enough,) we should prepare the canvas well beforehand. Parentage must consider itself in advance. (Will the time hasten when fatherhood and motherhood shall become a science—and the noblest science?) To our model, a clear-blooded, strong-fibred physique, is indispensable; the questions of food, drink, air, exercise, assimilation, digestion, can never be intermitted. Out of these we descry a well-begotten selfhood—in youth, fresh, ardent, emotional, aspiring, full of adventure; at maturity, brave, perceptive, under control, neither too talkative nor too reticent, neither flippant nor sombre; of the bodily figure, the movements easy, the complexion showing the best blood, somewhat flush'd, breast expanded, an erect attitude, a voice whose sound outvies music, eyes of calm and steady gaze, yet capable also of flashing—and a general presence that holds its own in the company of the highest. (For it is native personality, and that alone, that endows a man to stand before presidents or generals, or in any distinguish'd collection, with *aplomb*—and *not* culture, or any knowledge or intellect whatever.)

With regard to the mental-educational part of our model, enlargement of intellect, stores of cephalic knowledge, &c., the concentration thitherward of all the customs of our age, especially in America, is so overweening, and provides so fully for that part, that, important and necessary as it is, it really needs nothing from us here—except, indeed, a phrase of warning and restraint. Manners, costumes, too, though important, we need not dwell upon here. Like beauty, grace of motion, &c., they are results. Causes, original things, being attended to, the right manners unerringly follow. Much is said, among artists, of "the grand style," as if it were a thing by itself. When a man, artist or whoever, has health, pride, acuteness, noble aspirations, he has the motive-elements of the grandest style. The rest is but manipulation, (yet that is no small matter.)

Leaving still unspecified several sterling parts of any model fit for the future personality of America, I must not fail, again and ever, to pronounce myself on one, probably the least attended to in modern times—a hiatus, indeed, threatening its gloomiest consequences after us. I mean the simple, unsophisticated Conscience, the primary moral element. If I were asked to specify in what quarter lie the grounds of darkest dread, respecting the America of our hopes, I should have to point to this particular. I should demand the invariable application to individuality, this day and any day, of that old, ever-true plumb-rule of persons, eras, nations. Our triumphant modern civilizee, with his all-schooling and his wondrous appliances, will still show himself but an amputation while this deficiency remains. Beyond, (assuming a more hopeful tone,) the vertebration of the manly and womanly personalism of our western world, can only be, and is, indeed, to be, (I hope,) its all penetrating Religiousness.

The ripeness of Religion is doubtless to be looked for in this field of individuality, and is a result that no organization or church can ever achieve. As history is poorly retain'd by what the technists call history, and is not given out from their pages, except the learner has in himself the sense of the well-wrapt, never yet written, perhaps impossible to be written, history—so Religion, although casually arrested, and, after a fashion, preserv'd in the churches and creeds, does not depend at all upon them, but is a part of the identified soul, which, when greatest, knows not bibles in the old way, but in new ways—the identified soul, which can really confront Religion when it extricates itself entirely from the churches, and not before.

Personalism fuses this, and favors it. I should say, indeed, that only in the perfect uncontamination and solitariness of individuality may the spirituality of religion positively come forth at all. Only here, and on such terms, the meditation, the devout ecstasy, the soaring flight. Only here, communion with the mysteries, the eternal problems, whence? whither? Alone, and identity, and the mood—and the soul emerges, and all statements, churches, sermons, melt away like vapors. Alone, and silent thought and awe, and aspiration—and then the interior consciousness, like a hitherto unseen inscription, in magic ink, beams out its wondrous lines to the sense. Bibles may convey, and priests expound, but it is exclusively for the noiseless operation of one's isolated Self, to enter the pure ether of veneration, reach the divine levels, and commune with the unutterable.

To practically enter into politics is an important part of American personalism. To every young man, north and south, earnestly studying these things, I should here, as an offset to what I have said in former pages, now also say, that may-be to views of very largest scope, after all, perhaps the political, (perhaps the literary and sociological,) America goes best about its development its own way—sometimes, to temporary sight, appaling enough. It is the fashion among dillettants and fops (perhaps I myself am not guiltless,) to decry the whole formulation of the active politics of America, as beyond redemption, and to be carefully kept away from. See you that you do not fall into this error. America, it may be, is doing very well upon the whole, notwithstanding these antics of the parties and their leaders, these half-brain'd nominees, the many ignorant ballots, and many elected failures and blatherers. It is the dillettants, and all who shirk their duty, who are not doing well. As for you, I advise you to enter more strongly yet into politics. I advise every young man to do so. Always inform yourself; always do the best you can; always vote. Disengage yourself from parties. They have been useful, and to some extent remain so; but the floating, uncommitted electors, farmers, clerks, mechanics, the masters of parties—watching aloof, including victory this side or that side—such are the ones most needed, present and future. For America, if eligible at all to downfall and ruin, is eligible within herself, not without; for I see clearly that the combined foreign world could not beat her down. But these savage, wolfish parties alarm me. Owning no law but their own will, more and more combative, less and less tolerant of the idea of ensemble and of equal brotherhood, the perfect equality of the States, the ever-overarching American ideas, it behooves you to convey yourself implicitly to no party, nor submit blindly to their dictators, but steadily hold yourself judge and master over all of them.

So much, (hastily toss'd together, and leaving far more unsaid,) for an ideal, or intimations of an ideal, toward American manhood. But the other sex, in our land, requires at least a basis of suggestion.

I have seen a young American woman, one of a large family of daughters, who, some years since, migrated from her meagre country home to one of the northern cities, to gain her own support. She soon became an expert seamstress, but finding the employment too confining for health and comfort, she went boldly to work for others, to house-keep, cook, clean, &c. After trying several places, she fell upon one where she was suited. She has told me that she finds nothing degrading in her position; it is not inconsistent with personal dignity, self-respect, and the respect of others. She confers benefits and receives them. She has good health; her presence itself is healthy and bracing; her character is unstain'd; she has made herself understood, and preserves her independence, and has been able to help her parents, and educate and get places for her sisters; and her course of life is not without opportunities for mental improvement, and of much quiet, uncosting happiness and love.

I have seen another woman who, from taste and necessity conjoin'd, has gone into practical affairs, carries on a mechanical business, partly works at it herself, dashes out more and more into real hardy life, is not abash'd by the coarseness of the contact, knows how to be firm and silent at the same time, holds her own with unvarying coolness and decorum, and will compare, any day, with superior carpenters, farmers, and even boatmen and drivers. For all that, she has not lost the charm of the womanly nature, but preserves and bears it fully, though through such rugged presentation.

Then there is the wife of a mechanic, mother of two children, a woman of merely passable English education, but of fine wit, with all her sex's grace and intuitions, who exhibits, indeed, such a noble female personality, that I am fain to record it here. Never abnegating her own proper independence, but always genially preserving it, and what belongs to it—cooking, washing, child-nursing, house-tending—she beams sunshine out of all these duties, and makes them illustrious. Physiologically sweet and sound, loving work, practical, she yet knows that there are intervals, however few, devoted to recreation, music, leisure, hospitality—and affords such intervals. Whatever she does, and wherever she is, that charm, that indescribable perfume of genuine womanhood attends her, goes with her, exhales from her, which belongs of right to all the sex, and is, or ought to be, the invariable atmosphere and common aureola of old as well as young.

My dear mother once described to me a resplendent person, down on Long Island, whom she knew in early days. She was known by the name of the Peacemaker. She was well toward eighty years old, of happy and sunny temperament, had always lived on a farm, and was very neighborly, sensible and discreet, an invariable and welcom'd favorite, especially with young married women. She had numerous children and grandchildren. She was uneducated, but possess'd a native dignity. She had come to be a tacitly agreed upon domestic regulator, judge, settler of difficulties, shepherdess, and reconciler in the land. She was a sight to draw near and look upon, with her large figure, her profuse snow-white hair, (uncoif'd by any head-dress or cap,) dark eyes, clear complexion, sweet breath, and peculiar personal magnetism.

The foregoing portraits, I admit, are frightfully out of line from these imported models of womanly personality—the stock feminine characters of the current novelists, or of the foreign court poems, (Ophelias, Enids, princesses, or ladies of one thing or another,) which fill the envying dreams of so many poor girls, and are accepted by our men, too, as supreme ideals of feminine excellence to be sought after. But I present mine just for a change.

Then there are mutterings, (we will not now stop to heed them here, but they must be heeded,) of something more revolutionary. The day is coming when the deep questions of woman's entrance amid the arenas of practical life, politics, the suffrage, &c., will not only be argued all around us, but may be put to decision, and real experiment.

Of course, in these States, for both man and woman, we must entirely recast the types of highest personality from what the oriental, feudal, ecclesiastical worlds bequeath us, and which yet possess the imaginative and esthetic fields of the United States, pictorial and melodramatic, not without use as studies, but making sad work, and forming a strange anachronism upon the scenes and exigencies around us. Of course, the old undying elements remain. The task is, to successfully adjust them to new combinations, our own days. Nor is this so incredible. I can conceive a community, to-day and here, in which, on a sufficient scale, the perfect personalities, without noise meet; say in some pleasant western settlement or town, where a couple of hundred best men and women, of ordinary worldly status, have by luck been drawn together, with nothing extra of genius or wealth, but virtuous, chaste, industrious, cheerful, resolute, friendly and devout. I can conceive such a community organized in running order, powers judiciously delegated—farming, building, trade, courts, mails, schools, elections, all attended to; and then the rest of life, the main thing, freely branching and blossoming in each individual, and bearing golden fruit. I can see there, in every young and old man, after his kind, and in every woman after hers, a true personality, develop'd, exercised proportionately in body, mind, and spirit. I can imagine this case as one not necessarily rare or difficult, but in buoyant accordance with the municipal and general requirements of our times. And I can realize in it the culmination of something better than any stereotyped *eclat* of history or poems. Perhaps, unsung, undramatized, unput in essays or biographies—perhaps even some such community already exists, in Ohio, Illinois, Missouri, or somewhere, practically fulfilling itself, and thus outvying, in cheapest vulgar life, all that has been hitherto shown in best ideal pictures.

In short, and to sum up, America, betaking herself to formative action, (as it is about time for more solid achievement, and less windy promise,) must, for her purposes, cease to recognize a theory of character grown of feudal aristocracies, or form'd by merely literary standards, or from any ultramarine, full-dress formulas of culture, polish, caste, &c., and must sternly promulgate her own new standard, yet old enough, and accepting the old, the perennial elements, and combining them into groups, unities, appropriate to the modern, the democratic, the west, and to the practical occasions and needs of our own cities, and of the agricultural regions. Ever the most precious in the common. Ever the fresh breeze of field, or hill, or lake, is more than any palpitation of fans, though of ivory, and redolent with perfume; and the air is more than the costliest perfumes. . . .

[from *A National Literature*]

Compared with the past, our modern science soars, and our journals serve—but ideal and even ordinary romantic literature, does not, I think, substantially advance. Behold the prolific brood of the contemporary novel, magazine-tale, theatre-play, &c. The same endless thread of tangled and superlative love-story, inherited, apparently from the Amadises and Palmerins of the 13th, 14th, and 15th centuries over there in Europe. The costumes and associations brought down to date, the seasoning hotter and more varied, the dragons and ogres left out—but the *thing,* I should say, has not advanced—is just as sensational, just as strain'd—remains about the same, nor more, nor less.

What is the reason our time, our lands, that we see no fresh local courage, sanity, of our own—the Mississippi, stalwart Western men, real mental and physical facts, Southerners, &c., in the body of our literature? especially the poetic part of it. But always, instead, a parcel of dandies and ennuyees, dapper little gentlemen from abroad, who flood us with their thin sentiment of parlors, parasols, piano-songs, tinkling rhymes, the five-hundredth importation—or whimpering and crying about something, chasing one aborted conceit after another, and forever occupied in dyspeptic amours with dyspeptic women. While, current and novel, the grandest events and revolutions, and stormiest passions of history, are crossing to-day with unparallel'd rapidity and magnificence over the stages of our own and all the continents, offering new materials, opening new vistas, with largest needs, inviting the daring launching forth of conceptions in literature, inspired by them, soaring in highest regions, serving art in its highest, (which is only the other name for serving God, and serving humanity,) where is the man of letters, where is the book, with any nobler aim than to follow in the old track, repeat what has been said before—and, as its utmost triumph, sell well, and be erudite or elegant?

Mark the roads, the processes, through which these States have arrived, standing easy, henceforth ever-equal, ever-compact, in their range to-day. European adventures? the most antique? Asiatic or African? old history—miracles—romances? Rather, our own unquestion'd facts. They hasten, incredible, blazing bright as fire. From the deeds and days of Columbus down to the present, and including the present—and especially the late Secession war—when I con them, I feel, every leaf, like stopping to see if I have not made a mistake, and fall'n on the splendid figments of some dream. But it is no dream. We stand, live, move, in the huge flow of our age's materialism—in its spirituality. We have had founded for us the most positive of lands. The founders have pass'd to other spheres—but what are these terrible duties they have left us?

Their politics the United States have, in my opinion, with all their faults, already substantially establish'd, for good, on their own native, sound, long-vista'd principles, never to be overturn'd, offering a sure basis for all the rest. With that, their future religious forms, sociology, literature, teachers, schools, costumes, &c., are of course to make a compact whole, uniform, on tallying principles. For how can we remain, divided, contradicting ourselves, this way?[6] I say we can only attain harmony and stability by consulting ensemble and the ethic purports, and faithfully building upon them. For the New World, indeed, after two grand stages of preparation-strata, I perceive that now a third stage, being ready for, (and without which the other two were useless,) with unmistakable signs appears. The First stage was the planning and putting on record the political foundation rights of immense masses of people—indeed all people—in the organization of republican National, State, and municipal governments, all constructed with reference to each, and each to all. This is the American programme, not for classes, but for universal man, and is embodied in the compacts of the Declaration of Independence, and, as it began and has now grown, with its amendments, the Federal Constitution—and in the State governments, with all their interiors, and with general suffrage; those having the sense not only of what is in themselves, but that their certain several things started, planted, hundreds of others in the same direction duly arise and follow. The Second stage relates to material prosperity, wealth, produce, labor-saving machines, iron, cotton, local, State and continental railways, intercommunication and trade with all lands, steamships, mining, general employment, organization of great cities, cheap appliances for comfort, numberless technical schools, books, newspapers, a currency for money circulation, &c. The Third stage, rising out of the previous ones, to make them and all illustrious, I, now, for one, promulge, announcing a native expression-spirit, getting into form, adult, and through mentality, for these States, self-contain'd, different from others, more expansive, more rich and free, to be evidenced by original authors and poets to come, by American personalities, plenty of them, male and female, traversing the States, none excepted—and by native superber tableaux and growths of language, songs, operas, orations, lectures, architecture—and by a sublime and serious Religious Democracy sternly taking command, dissolving the old, sloughing off surfaces, and from its own interior and vital principles, reconstructing, democratizing society.

[6] Whitman's note: "Note, to-day, an instructive, curious spectacle and conflict. Science, (twin, in its fields, of Democracy in its)—Science, testing absolutely all thoughts, all works, has already burst well upon the world—a sun, mounting, most illuminating, most glorious—surely never again to set. But against it, deeply entrench'd, holding possession, yet remains, (not only through the churches and schools, but by imaginative literature, and unregenerate poetry,) the fossil theology of the mythic-materialistic, superstitious, untaught and credulous, fable-loving, primitive ages of humanity."

For America, type of progress, and of essential faith in man, above all his errors and wickedness—few suspect how deep, how deep it really strikes. The world evidently supposes, and we have evidently supposed so too, that the States are merely to achieve the equal franchise, an elective government—to inaugurate the respectability of labor, and become a nation of practical operatives, law-abiding, orderly and well off. Yes, those are indeed parts of the task of America; but they not only do not exhaust the progressive conception, but rather arise, teeming with it, as the mediums of deeper, higher progress. Daughter of a physical revolution—mother of the true revolutions, which are of the interior life, and of the arts. For so long as the spirit is not changed, any change of appearance is of no avail.

The old men, I remember as a boy, were always talking of American independence. What is independence? Freedom from all laws or bonds except those of one's own being, control'd by the universal ones. To lands, to man, to woman, what is there at last to each, but the inherent soul, nativity, idiocrasy, free, highest-poised, soaring its own flight, following out itself?

At present, these States, in their theology and social standards, (of greater importance than their political institutions,) are entirely held possession of by foreign lands. We see the sons and daughters of the New World, ignorant of its genius, not yet inaugurating the native, the universal, and the near, still importing the distant, the partial, and the dead. We see London, Paris, Italy—not original, superb, as where they belong—but second-hand here, where they do not belong. We see the shreds of Hebrews, Romans, Greeks; but where, on her own soil, do we see, in any faithful, highest, proud expression, America herself? I sometimes question whether she has a corner in her own house.

Not but that in one sense, and a very grand one, good theology, good art, or good literature, has certain features shared in common. The combination fraternizes, ties the races—is, in many particulars, under laws applicable indifferently to all, irrespective of climate or date, and, from whatever source, appeals to emotions, pride, love, spirituality, common to humankind. Nevertheless, they touch a man closest, (perhaps only actually touch him,) even in these, in their expression through autochthonic lights and shades, flavors, fondnesses, aversions, specific incidents, illustrations, out of his own nationality, geography, surroundings, antecedents, &c. The spirit and the form are one, and depend far more on association, identity and place, than is supposed. Subtly interwoven with the materiality and personality of a land, a race—Teuton, Turk, Californian, or what not—there is always something—I can hardly tell what it is—history but describes the results of it—it is the same as the untellable look of some human faces. Nature, too, in her stolid forms, is full of it—but to most it is there a secret. This something is rooted in the invisible roots, the profoundest meanings of that place, race, or nationality; and to absorb and again effuse it, uttering words and products as from its midst, and carrying it into highest regions, is the work, or a main part of the work, of any country's true author, poet, historian, lecturer, and perhaps even priest and philosoph. Here, and here only, are the foundations for our really valuable and permanent verse, drama, &c.

But at present, (judged by any higher scale than that which finds the chief ends of existence to be to feverishly make money during one-half of it, and by some "amusement," or perhaps foreign travel, flippantly kill time, the other half,) and consider'd with reference to purposes of patriotism, health, a noble personality, religion, and the democratic adjustments, all these swarms of poems, literary magazines, dramatic plays, resultant so far from American intellect, and the formation of our best ideas, are useless and a mockery. They strengthen and nourish no one, express nothing characteristic, give decision and purpose to no one, and suffice only the lowest level of vacant minds.

Of what is called the drama, or dramatic presentation in the United States, as now put forth at the theatres, I should say it deserves to be treated with the same gravity, and on a par with the questions of ornamental confectionery at public dinners, or the arrangement of curtains and hangings in a ball-room—nor more, nor less. Of the other, I will not insult the reader's intelligence, (once really entering into the atmosphere of these Vistas,) by supposing it necessary to show, in detail, why the copious dribble, either of our little or well-known rhymesters, does not fulfil, in any respect, the needs and august occasions of this land. America demands a poetry that is bold, modern, and all-surrounding and kosmical, as she is herself. It must in no respect ignore science or the modern, but inspire itself with science and the modern. It must bend its vision toward the future, more than the past. Like America, it must extricate itself from even the greatest models of the past, and, while courteous to them, must have entire faith in itself, and the products of its own democratic spirit only. Like her, it must place in the van, and hold up at all hazards, the banner of the divine pride of man in himself, (the radical foundation of the new religion.) Long enough have the People been listening to poems in which common humanity, deferential, bends low, humiliated, acknowledging superiors. But America listens to no such poems. Erect, inflated, and fully self-esteeming be the chant; and then America will listen with pleased ears.

Nor may the genuine gold, the gems, when brought to light at last, be probably usher'd forth from any of the quarters currently counted on. To-day, doubtless, the infant genius of American poetic expression, (eluding those highly-refined imported and gilt-edged themes, and sentimental and butterfly flights, pleasant to orthodox publishers—causing tender spasms in the coteries, and warranted not to chafe the sensitive cuticle of the most exquisitely artificial gossamer delicacy,) lies sleeping far away, happily unrecognized and uninjur'd by the coteries, the art-writers, the talkers and critics of the saloons, or the lecturers in the colleges—lies sleeping, aside, unrecking itself, in some western idiom, or native Michigan or Tennessee repartee, or stump-speech—or in Kentucky or Georgia, or the Carolinas—or in some slang or local song or allusion of the Manhattan, Boston, Philadelphia or Baltimore mechanic —or up in the Maine woods—or off in the hut of the California miner, or crossing the Rocky mountains, or along the Pacific railroad—or on the breasts of the young farmers of the northwest, or Canada, or boatmen of the lakes. Rude and coarse nursing-beds, these; but only from such beginnings and stocks, indigenous here, may haply arrive, be grafted, and sprout, in time, flowers of genuine American aroma, and fruits truly and fully our own.

I say it were a standing disgrace to these States—I say it were a disgrace to any nation, distinguish'd above others by the variety and vastness of its territories, its materials, its inventive activity, and the splendid practicality of its people, not to rise and soar above others also in its original styles in literature and art, and its own supply of intellectual and esthetic masterpieces, archetypal, and consistent with itself. I know not a land except ours that has not, to some extent, however small, made its title clear. The Scotch have their born ballads, subtly expressing their past and present, and expressing character. The Irish have theirs. England, Italy, France, Spain, theirs. What has America? With exhaustless mines of the richest ore of epic, lyric, tale, tune, picture, &c., in the Four Years' War; with, indeed, I sometimes think, the richest masses of material ever afforded a nation, more variegated, and on a larger scale—the first sign of proportionate, native, imaginative Soul, and first-class works to match, is, (I cannot too often repeat), so far wanting.

Long ere the second centennial arrives, there will be some forty to fifty great States, among them Canada and Cuba. When the present century closes, our population will be sixty or seventy millions. The Pacific will be ours, and the Atlantic mainly ours. There will be daily electric communication with every part of the globe. What an age! What a land! Where, elsewhere, one so great? The individuality of one nation must then, as always, lead the world. Can there be any doubt who the leader ought to be? Bear in mind, though, that nothing less than the mightiest original non-subordinated SOUL has ever really, gloriously led, or ever can lead. (This Soul—its other name, in these Vistas, is LITERATURE.)

In fond fancy leaping those hundred years ahead, let us survey America's works, poems, philosophies, fulfilling prophecies, and giving form and decision to best ideals. Much that is now undream'd of, we might then perhaps see establish'd, lux-uriantly cropping forth, richness, vigor of letters and of artistic expression, in whose products character will be a main requirement, and not merely erudition or elegance.

Intense and loving comradeship, the personal and passionate attachment of man to man—which, hard to define, underlies the lessons and ideals of the profound saviours of every land and age, and which seems to promise, when thoroughly develop'd, cultivated and recognized in manners and literature, the most substantial hope and safety of the future of these States, will then be fully express'd.[7]

A strong-fibred joyousness and faith, and the sense of health *al fresco,* may well enter into the preparation of future noble American authorship. Part of the test of a great literatus shall be the absence in him of the idea of the covert, the lurid, the

[7] Whitman's note: "It is to the development, identification, and general prevalence of that fervid comradeship, (the adhesive love, at least rivaling the amative love hitherto possessing imaginative literature, if not going beyond it,) that I look for the counterbalance and offset of our materialistic and vulgar American democracy, and for the spiritualization thereof. Many will say it is a dream, and will not follow my inferences: but I confidently expect a time when there will be seen, running like a half-hid warp through all the myriad audible and visible worldly interests of America, threads of manly friendship, fond and loving, pure and sweet, strong and life-long, carried to degrees hitherto unknown—not only giving tone to individual character, and making it unprecedently emotional, muscular, heroic, and refined, but having the deepest relations to general politics. I say democracy infers such loving comradeship, as its most inevitable twin or counterpart, without which it will be incomplete, in vain, and incapable of perpetuating itself."

maleficent, the devil, the grim estimates inherited from the Puritans, hell, natural depravity, and the like. The great literatus will be known, among the rest, by his cheerful simplicity, his adherence to natural standards, his limitless faith in God, his reverence, and by the absence in him of doubt, ennui, burlesque, persiflage, or any strain'd and temporary fashion.

Nor must I fail, again and yet again, to clinch, reiterate more plainly still, (O that indeed such survey as we fancy, may show in time this part completed also!) the lofty aim, surely the proudest and the purest, in whose service the future literatus, of whatever field, may gladly labor. As we have intimated, offsetting the material civilization of our race, our nationality, its wealth, territories, factories, population, products, trade, and military and naval strength, and breathing breath of life into all these, and more, must be its moral civilization—the formulation, expression, and aidancy whereof, is the very highest height of literature. The climax of this loftiest range of civilization, rising above all the gorgeous shows and results of wealth, intellect, power, and art, as such—above even theology and religious fervor—is to be its development, from the eternal bases, and the fit expression, of absolute Conscience, moral soundness, Justice. Even in religious fervor there is a touch of animal heat. But moral conscientiousness, crystalline, without flaw, not Godlike only, entirely human, awes and enchants forever. Great is emotional love, even in the order of the rational universe. But, if we must make gradations, I am clear there is something greater. Power, love, veneration, products, genius, esthetics, tried by subtlest comparisons, analyses, and in serenest moods, somewhere fail, somehow become vain. Then noiseless, with flowing steps, the lord, the sun, the last ideal comes. By the names right, justice, truth, we suggest, but do not describe it. To the world of men it remains a dream, an idea as they call it. But no dream is it to the wise—but the proudest, almost only solid lasting thing of all. Its analogy in the material universe is what holds together this world, and every object upon it, and carries its dynamics on forever sure and safe. Its lack, and the persistent shirking of it, as in life, sociology, literature, politics, business, and even sermonizing, these times, or any times, still leaves the abysm, the mortal flaw and smutch, mocking civilization to-day, with all its unquestion'd triumphs, and all the civilization so far known.[8]

Present literature, while magnificently fulfilling certain popular demands, with

---

[8] Whitman's note: "I am reminded as I write that out of this very conscience, or idea of conscience, of intense moral right, and in its name and strain'd construction, the worst fanaticisms, wars, persecutions, murders, &c., have yet, in all lands, in the past, been broach'd, and have come to their devilish fruition. Much is to be said—but I may say here, and in response, that side by side with the unflagging stimulation of the elements of religion and conscience must henceforth move with equal sway, science, absolute reason, and the general proportionate development of the whole man. These scientific facts, deductions, are divine too —precious counted parts of moral civilization, and, with physical health, indispensable to it, to prevent fanaticism. For abstract religion, I perceive, is easily led astray, ever credulous, and is capable of devouring, remorseless, like fire and flame. Conscience, too, isolated from all else, and from the emotional nature, may but attain the beauty and purity of glacial, snowy ice. We want, for these States, for the general character, a cheerful, religious fervor, endued with the ever-present modifications of the human emotions, friendship, benevolence, with a fair field for scientific inquiry, the right of individual judgment, and always the cooling influences of material Nature."

plenteous knowledge and verbal smartness, is profoundly sophisticated, insane, and its very joy is morbid. It needs tally and express Nature, and the spirit of Nature, and to know and obey the standards. I say the question of Nature, largely consider'd, involves the questions of the esthetic, the emotional, and the religious—and involves happiness. A fitly born and bred race, growing up in right conditions of out-door as much as in-door harmony, activity and development, would probably, from and in those conditions, find it enough merely *to live*—and would, in their relations to the sky, air, water, trees, &c., and to the countless common shows, and in the fact of life itself, discover and achieve happiness—with Being suffused night and day by whole-some extasy, surpassing all the pleasures that wealth, amusement, and even gratified intellect, erudition, or the sense of art, can give.

In the prophetic literature of these States (the reader of my speculations will miss their principal stress unless he allows well for the point that a new Literature, perhaps a new Metaphysics, certainly a new Poetry, are to be, in my opinion, the only sure and worthy supports and expressions of the American Democracy,) Nature, true Nature, and the true idea of Nature, long absent, must, above all, become fully restored, enlarged, and must furnish the pervading atmosphere to poems, and the test of all high literary and esthetic compositions. I do not mean the smooth walks, trimm'd hedges, poseys and nightingales of the English poets, but the whole orb, with its geologic history, the kosmos, carrying fire and snow, that rolls through the illimitable areas, light as a feather, though weighing billions of tons. Furthermore, as by what we now partially call Nature is intended, at most, only what is entertainable by the physical conscience, the sense of matter, and of good animal health—on these it must be distinctly accumulated, incorporated, that man, comprehending these, has, in towering superaddition, the moral and spiritual consciences, indicating his destina-tion beyond the ostensible, the mortal.

To the heights of such estimate of Nature indeed ascending, we proceed to make observations for our Vistas, breathing rarest air. What is I believe called Idealism seems to me to suggest, (guarding against extravagance, and ever modified even by its opposite,) the course of inquiry and desert of favor for our New World metaphysics, their foundation of and in literature, giving hue to all.[9]

[9] Whitman's note: "The culmination and fruit of literary artistic expression, and its final fields of pleasure for the human soul, are in metaphysics, including the mysteries of the spiritual world, the soul itself, and the question of the immortal continuation of our identity. In all ages, the mind of man has brought up here—and always will. Here, at least, of whatever race or era, we stand on common ground. Applause, too, is unanimous, antique or modern. Those authors who work well in this field—though their reward, instead of a handsome percentage, or royalty, may be but simply the laurel-crown of the victors in the great Olympic games—will be dearest to humanity, and their works, however esthetically defective, will be treasur'd forever. The altitude of literature and poetry has always been religion—and always will be. The Indian Vedas, the Nackas of Zoroaster, the Talmud of the Jews, the Old Testament, the Gospel of Christ and his disciples, Plato's works, the Koran of Mohammed, the Edda of Snorro, and so on toward our own day, to Swedenborg, and to the invaluable contributions of Leibnitz, Kant and Hegel—these, with such poems only in which, (while singing well of persons and events, of the passions of man, and the shows of the material universe,) the religious tone, the consciousness of mystery, the recognition of the future, of the unknown, of Deity over and under all, and of the divine purpose, are never absent, but indirectly give tone to all—exhibit literature's real heights and elevations, towering up like the great mountains of the earth.

Standing on this ground—the last, the highest, only permanent ground—and sternly criticising, from it, all works, either of the

(continued)

The elevating and etherealizing ideas of the unknown and of unreality must be brought forward with authority, as they are the legitimate heirs of the known, and of reality, and at least as great as their parents. Fearless of scoffing, and of the ostent, let us take our stand, our ground, and never desert it, to confront the growing excess and arrogance of realism. To the cry, now victorious—the cry of sense, science, flesh, incomes, farms, merchandise, logic, intellect, demonstrations, solid perpetuities, buildings of brick and iron, or even the facts of the shows of trees, earth, rocks, &c., fear not, my brethren, my sisters, to sound out with equally determin'd voice, that conviction brooding within the recesses of every envision'd soul—illusions! apparitions! figments all! True, we must not condemn the show, neither absolutely deny it, for the indispensability of its meanings; but how clearly we see that, migrate in soul to what we can already conceive of superior and spiritual points of view, and, palpable as it seems under present relations, it all and several might, nay certainly would, fall apart and vanish.

I hail with joy the oceanic, variegated, intense practical energy, the demand for facts, even the business materialism of the current age, our States. But wo to the age or land in which these things, movements, stopping at themselves, do not tend to ideas. As fuel to flame, and flame to the heavens, so must wealth, science, materialism—even this democracy of which we make so much—unerringly feed the highest mind, the soul. Infinitude the flight: fathomless the mystery. Man, so diminutive, dilates beyond the sensible universe, competes with, outcopes space and time, meditating even one great idea. Thus, and thus only, does a human being, his spirit, ascend above, and justify, objective Nature, which, probably nothing in itself, is incredibly and divinely serviceable, indispensable, real, here. And as the purport of objective Nature is doubtless folded, hidden, somewhere here—as somewhere here is what this globe and its manifold forms, and the light of day, and night's darkness, and life itself, with all its experiences, are for—it is here the great literature, especially verse, must get its inspiration and throbbing blood. Then may we attain to a poetry worthy the immortal soul of man, and which, while absorb-

---

literary, or any art, we have peremptorily to dismiss every pretensive production, however fine its esthetic or intellectual points, which violates or ignores, or even does not celebrate, the central divine idea of All, suffusing universe, of eternal trains of purpose, in the development, by however slow degrees, of the physical, moral, and spiritual kosmos. I say he has studied, meditated to no profit, whatever may be his mere erudition, who has not absorb'd this simple consciousness and faith. It is not entirely new—but it is for Democracy to elaborate it, and look to build upon and expand from it, with uncompromising reliance. Above the doors of teaching the inscription is to appear, Though little or nothing can be absolutely known, perceiv'd, except from a point of view which is evanescent, yet we

know at least one permanency, that Time and Space, in the will of God, furnish successive chains, completions of material births and beginnings, solve all discrepancies, fears and doubts, and eventually fulfil happiness—and that the prophecy of those births, namely spiritual results, throws the true arch over all teaching, all science. The local considerations of sin, disease, deformity, ignorance, death, &c., and their measurement by the superficial mind, and ordinary legislation and theology, are to be met by science, boldly accepting, promulging this faith, and planting the seeds of superber laws—of the explication of the physical universe through the spiritual—and clearing the way for a religion, sweet and unimpugnable alike to little child or great savan."

ing materials, and, in their own sense, the shows of Nature, will, above all, have, both directly and indirectly, a freeing, fluidizing, expanding, religious character, exulting with science, fructifying the moral elements, and stimulating aspirations, and meditations on the unknown. . . .

1871

Alfred Stieglitz,
The Steerage,
photograph, 1907.
International Museum
of Photography
at George Eastman House.

Julius J. Stewart,
*The Yacht Namouna
in Venetian Waters,*
oil on canvas, 1890.
Courtesy, Wadsworth Atheneum,
Hartford.
The Ella Gallup Sumner and
Mary Catlin Sumner Collection.

The Literature of
an Expanding Nation
1865–1912

Reconciliation

 At a cost of over 600,000 lives, the Civil War put an end to chattel slavery, but not its heritage of social injustice, and vindicated the principle of Union. *United States* became a singular collective noun in postwar usage, instead of a plural one as before. The name now denoted a powerful young nation supposedly at peace with itself and dedicated to binding up its wounds. Whitman's image for the advent of peace was "Reconciliation . . . word over all, beautiful as the sky." But such sentiments, reflecting hopes rather than realities, belonged to what Emerson called "the optative mood" of American literature and spiritual history and found little support in the events of the period. Lincoln's martyrdom and "ascension" were followed in 1868 by impeachment proceedings against President Andrew Johnson for "high crimes and misdemeanors." Reconstruction politics tended to be a continuation of war by other means. For Whitman the democratic vistas of 1871 were marked by abandonment of principle, "hollowness of heart," "hypocrisy," "depravity," "robbery and scoundrelism": "What penetrating eye does not everywhere see through the mask? The spectacle is appalling." James Russell Lowell scanned "the festering news . . . of public scandal, private fraud" in "the Land of Broken Promise."

"There's millions in it," says Mark Twain's Colonel Beriah Sellers *(The Gilded Age)*. "I've got the biggest scheme on earth—and I'll take you in; I've taken in every friend I've got that's ever stood by me, for there's enough for all, and to spare." A dealer in schemes involving mules, corn, bottled eyewash, and an illusory rail line serving Slouchburg, Hallelujah, and Corruptionville, the fictional Sellers typifies the promoter, a distinctive occupation of the period. The joining of the Union Pacific and Central Pacific rail lines at Promontory Point, Utah, in 1869 was a promoter's triumph. It fulfilled vision, purpose, engineering genius, and venture capitalism; passengers and goods traveled in less than a week across a nation whose separate parts were now bound to each other by three thousand miles of steel. The promoters of the transcontinental railroad, it was soon learned, had set up a construction company, Crédit Mobilier, that bilked the investing public of more than $20 million and, to avoid exposure, bribed the vice-president of the United States, Schuyler Colfax, along with members of the House and Senate. The Crédit Mobilier affair, which unraveled just before the general election of 1872, was the Watergate of its day but not an isolated instance. On "Black Friday" in September 1869, the market collapsed after two sharpers, Jim Fisk and Jay Gould, tried to make a corner in gold. On "Black Friday" in 1873, an economy built on wildcat speculations fell on its face, ushering in the worst depression the United States had yet known. Crédit Mobilier was part of a cycle of abuses and reverses that darkened nearly every corner of national life.

The Reconstruction era had more than its share of memorably representative figures, among them Ulysses Grant, the North's supreme military hero. Men like General William Tecumseh Sherman had fought under Grant with "the faith a Christian has in his Savior." Grant's two terms in the White House, however, were notable for corruption, neglect, incompetence, and cronyism. (America had "reverted to the stone age," Henry Adams lamented. "The progress of evolution from President Washington to President Grant was alone evidence enough to upset Darwin.") In New York "Boss" William Tweed and his Tammany ring made off with somewhere between $30 million and $100 million in public funds.

The Revised Catechism

What is the chief end of man?—to get rich. In what way?—dishonestly if we must; honestly if we can. Who is God, the one only and true? Money is God. Gold and Greenbacks and Stock—father, son, and the ghost of same—three persons in one; these are the true and only God, mighty and supreme: and William Tweed is his prophet.

Mark Twain, in the *New York Tribune* (September 27, 1871)

Victoria Woodhull and her sister Tennessee Celeste Claflin, reformers and leaders in the suffragist movement, set themselves up as financial wizards on Wall Street and in 1872 precipitated what Victoria called "one of the most stupendous scandals which has ever occurred in any community." They accused Harriet Beecher Stowe's brother, Henry Ward Beecher, the most popular Protestant divine of his day, of carrying on an adulterous relationship with a parishioner. The charge was never proved, but "the Beecher horror," as Lowell called it, dragged on in the press and courts through the summer of 1875. By then Beecher's guilt was more or less taken for granted and accepted as further evidence, if any were needed, of wickedness in high places.

The tutelary spirit of the Reconstruction era was not Lincoln but Benjamin Franklin, stripped for the most part of his irony, sense of play, heterodoxy, and free-ranging intellectual curiosity. In 1864 one of his biographers, the popular historian James Parton, counted 136 American towns named after Franklin; Ohio alone had nineteen. "I think I adequately appreciate the greatness of Washington," said Horace Greeley, the powerful editor of the *New York Tribune,* "yet I must place Franklin above him as the consummate type and flowering of human nature under the skies of colonial America." But it was not until 1868 that Franklin's *Autobiography,* long established as obligatory reading for his compatriots, was first published from a complete and authentic manuscript instead of a corrupt, partial source. This prompted a rediscovery and consequently a reinterpretation of the man in line with some of the dominant values of the era. His humble origins, dedication to self-improvement, and genius for business set an example for "Self-Made Men" (the title of Greeley's popular lecture) determined to acquire what the master showman P. T. Barnum called "The Art of Money-Getting." Barnum's best-selling autobiography, *Struggles and Triumphs,* suggests not only that his chief model was Franklin but that he regarded himself as the Franklin of humbug, harnessing credulity instead of lightning. If there was "a sucker born every minute," as Barnum is supposed to have said, credulity was never in short supply.

"A Bread-Winner in the Family"

The eldest son of parents who were themselves poor, I had, fortunately, to begin to perform some useful work in the world while still very young in order to earn an honest livelihood, and was thus shown even in early boyhood that my duty was to assist my parents and like them become, as soon as possible, a bread-winner in the family. . . . It seems, nowadays, a matter of universal desire that poverty should be abolished. We should be quite willing to abolish luxury, but to abolish honest, industrious, self-denying poverty would be to destroy the soil upon which mankind produces the virtues which enable our race to reach a still higher civilization than it now possesses.

Andrew Carnegie, "How I Served My Apprenticeship," *Youth's Companion* (April 23, 1896)

Franklin's gospel of getting on in the world, as it was then interpreted at face value, merged with practical Christianity, Emersonian self-reliance, and social Darwinism, an application of evolutionary theories of natural selection and the survival of the fittest to the daily race for bread, money, and status. The results of the merger could be seen in Horatio Alger's Ragged Dick books (1867 and after), lecture performances such as Henry Ward Beecher's "The Ministry of Wealth" and Thomas Wentworth Higginson's "The Natural Aristocracy of the Dollar," and *Acres of Diamonds,* an inspirational address that Philadelphia Baptist clergyman Russell Conwell, founder of Temple University, delivered about six thousand times. "Opportunity is in your own backyard," Conwell said. "Money is power. Every good man and woman ought to strive for power, to do good with it when obtained."

The Gilded Age

The most enduring label for the period that followed Lee's surrender at Appomattox and Lincoln's death comes from the novel Mark Twain wrote in 1873 with his Hartford neighbor, Charles Dudley Warner: *The Gilded Age.* It connotes vulgarity, boom times, specious glitter, and superficial glow. Since then historians of the period have generated many other phrases that tend to scant the vitality and significant achievements of the times. A synoptic account compiled from book titles and verbal tags might read something like this: During a "tragic era" that was also an "age of negation," an "age of excess," and an "awkward age" and spanned several "brown decades," the American people, traveling "the road to reunion," were lured into "pragmatic acquiescence" and sedated by a bloodless "genteel tradition"; they created a cheap "chromo civilization" and watched complacently as "robber barons" devoured the nation's resources in a "great barbecue."

Labels aside, however, this was a dynamic era out of which emerged cultural and industrial maturity together with other lineaments of the United States in the coming century. Corruption and abuse brought on investigation and exposure; the beginnings of a reform, protest, and labor movement; and searching structural critiques such as Whitman's *Democratic Vistas* and Henry George's *Progress and Poverty* in the 1870s and, at the turn of the century, the economist and social theorist Thorstein Veblen's *The Theory of the Leisure Class.* Warring profiteers wasted money and labor, but the railroads were built all the same. During 1872 more miles of track (7,500) were put down than in any other year before or after; the combined systems grew from 35,000 miles in 1865 to 93,000 in 1880, by which time the refrigerator car had enabled Chicago to become Carl Sandburg's "Hog Butcher for the World." Parvenus and vulgarians set a pattern for what Veblen called the "conspicuous consumption of valuable goods," but they did so by virtue of a social and economic mobility that made everyone a potential tycoon. The tycoons amassed enormous fortunes, but some of them—Andrew Carnegie and John D. Rockefeller, for example—endowed universities and libraries and set up great private foundations dedicated to education, research, and public welfare.

"The Reaction Must Come"

In the United States it is clear that squalor and misery, and the vices and crimes that spring from them, everywhere increase as the village grows to the city, and the march of development brings the advantages of the improved methods of production and exchange. It is in the older and richer sections of the Union that pauperism and distress among the working classes are becoming most painfully apparent. . . . So long as all the increased wealth which modern progress brings goes but to build up great fortunes and make sharper the contrast between the House of Have and the House of Want, progress is not real and cannot be permanent. The reaction must come.

Henry George, *Progress and Poverty* (1879)

The year 1876, the hundredth anniversary of the Declaration of Independence, offers a fair sampling of the varieties and vicissitudes of American life in the Gilded Age. At Little Bighorn, Montana, Sioux Indians led by Chiefs Sitting Bull and Crazy Horse annihilated Lieutenant Colonel George Armstrong Custer and his expeditionary force. Jesse James, the American Robin Hood, reached the zenith of his career by robbing a stagecoach in Texas, a train in Missouri, and a bank in Minnesota. Evangelists Dwight Moody and Ira Sankey led a nationwide crusade to eradicate sin and reduce the future population of hell. President Grant's secretary of war and private secretary stood accused, respectively, of bribery and tax fraud. In a bitterly contested presidential election—its outcome was tainted at the polls and nearly decided at bayonet point—Rutherford B. Hayes of Ohio defeated Samuel J. Tilden of New York. Thomas Edison established his "invention factory" at Menlo Park, New Jersey. J. W. Draper took the first photographs of the solar spectrum. Alexander Graham Bell patented the telephone. Daniel Coit Gilman reorganized Johns Hopkins University and set national standards for graduate studies and advanced research. William James, then an instructor in physiology at Harvard, established the first American psychological laboratory. Professor Willard Gibbs of Yale published a paper on thermodynamics, "On the Equilibrium of Heterogeneous Substances," that remains one of the great creative achievements of nineteenth-century science. Mark Twain published *The Adventures of Tom Sawyer*.

Nearly eight million visitors, equal to a sixth of the national population, passed through the turnstiles of the Centennial Exhibition at Philadelphia. Most of them were impressed by how far the United States had come during its first one hundred years toward fulfilling its mission to be the driving force as well as the light of the world. Dominating the exhibition was a forty-foot-high Corliss steam engine, which supplied power to the eight thousand presses, pumps, gins, mills, and lathes chugging away in Machinery Hall. "Yes, it is still in these things of iron and steel," said William Dean Howells, "that the national genius most freely speaks." But the national genius also spoke, if perhaps less freely, in other things and with a degree of distinction and purpose that should have won over English skeptics such as Darwin's champion, T. H. Huxley, and the poet-critic

Matthew Arnold. Architect H. H. Richardson, painters Thomas Eakins, Winslow Homer, and Albert Pinkham Ryder, motion photography pioneer Eadweard Muybridge, and the Roeblings, father and son engineers and bridge builders, to name only a few, did their part in making what Lewis Mumford has called a "Buried Renaissance," "buried" because "the laval flow of industrialism after the war had swept over all the cities of the spirit, leaving here and there only an ashen ruin, standing erect in the crumbled landscape."

Labor unrest, on the rise since the Panic of 1873, peaked in 1877, a year of violence marked by riots and the use of federal troops to put down railroad strikes in West Virginia, Maryland, and Pennsylvania. In response, armories multiplied in cities all over America. Their crenellations, embrasures, and iron-studded sally ports suggested that the enemies of an economic society founded on steam, electricity, and dynamite were going to be repelled with crossbow, harquebus, and boiling oil. The age produced other public buildings that were anachronisms, eyesores, or swindles from their footings up. The Philadelphia city hall carried ornamentation about as far and as high as it could go. Tweed's Manhattan County Courthouse, a three-story iron-and-marble Palladian villa, cost taxpayers almost twice what Seward had paid for Alaska. Yet out of the same era came the Brooklyn Bridge, a structure of such purity and aspiration that it seemed to leap out of its century while fulfilling, at the same time, that century's passion for force and quantification. From the bridge's two majestic towers, together containing 85,159 cubic yards of masonry, hung four cables, each woven of 3,515 miles of wire and capable of supporting 24,621,780 pounds. The entire structure added up to an incomparably moving presence. "No one who has ever been upon it can ever forget it," said Mayor Seth Low of New York when the bridge was opened to traffic in 1883, thirteen years after construction began. "Not one shall see it and not feel prouder to be a man." In Hart Crane's epic celebration it was to be, quite simply, *The Bridge*.

"Civilization in the United States"

I cannot say that I am in the slightest degree impressed by your bigness, or your material resources, as such. Size is not grandeur, and territory does not make a nation. The great issue, about which hangs a true sublimity, and the terror of overhanging fate, is what are you going to do with all these things? What is to be the end to which these are to be the means?

T. H. Huxley, *American Addresses* (1877)

In truth, everything is against distinction in America, and against the sense of elevation to be gained through admiring and respecting it. The glorification of "the average man," who is quite a religion with statesmen and publicists there, is against it. The addiction to "the funny man," who is a national misfortune there, is against it. Above all, the newspapers are against it.

Matthew Arnold, "Civilization in the United States," *The Nineteenth Century* (April 1888)

The Old Order

"If the tone of the American world is in some respects provincial, it is in none more so than in this matter of the exaggerated homage rendered to authorship," Henry James wrote in *Hawthorne* (1879). "In the United States at present authorship is a pedestal and literature is the fashion." These were signs of waning vitality, even stagnation, and of the need once again for those fresh currents of life and thought Margaret Fuller had called for thirty years earlier. ("Instead of mighty and vital breezes," Whitman said of "the existing condition of poetry," "I find a few little silly fans languidly moved by shrunken fingers.")

By the centennial year, Whitman, Melville, and Lowell, all born in 1819, were lapsing, respectively, into self-imitation, silence, and public service. Emily Dickinson, with Whitman the most important American poet of the century, was active during the 1860s, 1870s, and 1880s but remained a largely invisible literary presence (only half a dozen fugitive verses appeared in print) until the 1890s, when three volumes of her work were published posthumously. Of the older writers, Poe, Hawthorne, and Thoreau were dead. Whittier, Holmes, Longfellow, and Emerson, the last slipping into senility, were figures in a pantheon, objects of quasi-religious veneration. What Emerson once called "the Movement" and "the party of the Future" had become "the Establishment" and "the party of the Past" and now served as guardians and high priests of an official culture. The critic Tony Tanner has described this as a "culture of forms, frozen on the surface, hollow within; prohibitant rather than enabling; a series of habits adhered to by the imaginatively somnolent."

Local colorists were already celebrating the regional ambience and folkways of the Maine forests, Louisiana bayous, and Western mining camps. Realism asserted itself in frontier tales and the novels of William Dean Howells and Henry James. Naturalist writers such as Frank Norris and Stephen Crane would portray characters who were victims of circumstance and natural law instead of the free creatures of the Romantic tradition. And a literature of social protest and of America's oppressed races was about to emerge. Meanwhile, during the late 1870s Mark Twain and Henry James figured separately in two public controversies that illuminate the conflict between representatives of the old literary order and the new.

Written almost thirty years after the event it describes, "The Story of a Speech" is Mark Twain's still-divided account of his performance at Whittier's seventieth-birthday dinner, sponsored by the *AtlanticMonthly,* in December 1877. He had recently published *Tom Sawyer* and begun the long composition of *Adventures of Huckleberry Finn,* a task that occupied him, intermittently, for nearly eight years. His tribute to Emerson ("a seedy little bit of a chap"), Holmes ("fat as a balloon"), and Longfellow ("built like a prize-fighter") asserted a spirit of travesty then considered alien to the occasion. He insinuated, although perhaps only in a subintentional way, that the three "gracious singers" might themselves be "impostors." Howells, the *Atlantic* editor in chief, a pilgrim from Ohio who had come to New England to worship at the feet of her great men, recalled his friend's after-dinner speech as an "amazing mistake," a "bewildering blunder," a "cruel catastrophe" that left Mark Twain "standing solitary amid his appalled and appalling listeners, with his joke dead on his hands." "Literary men in America, where so much is tolerated," one newspaper letter concluded, "ought to aim higher than the gutter, no matter what they have of talent, or even genius." Other published responses and reports agreed that "a wild Californian bull" in the "China shop" of polite letters had committed an unpardonable breach of taste, decorum, and morals. This was the same charge soon to be brought against *Huckleberry Finn,* a revolutionary work of realism and social satire that opened up new possibilities for the American writer.

Henry James's offense against official culture came from a different vantage and raised once again the question of whether America could nurture artists. James had taken up residence in England and consolidated his reputation there by seeing through the press, in the course of one year, 1879, no fewer than seven volumes of his work, including *The American, Daisy Miller,* and *Hawthorne,* the first book-length critical study of an American writer. The alleged condescension and European bias of James's *Hawthorne,* along with its comments on the narrowness of American experience and materials, stirred up a controversy that he tried to dismiss as "a very big tempest in a very small teapot," "the clucking of a brood of prairie hens." His outraged critics cast "a lurid light upon the state of American 'culture,'" he said, and supplied him further "evidence for calling American taste 'provincial.'" Issued in London, *Hawthorne* was also the first American subject among the twenty-nine volumes of John Morley's English Men of Letters series; in loyal response, Charles Dudley Warner and the publishing house of Houghton Mifflin launched their American Men of Letters series in 1881. Two related developments also suggest the degree (excessive, in James's understanding) to which the country had become aware of its home-grown writers: Princeton offered a college course on American literature as early as 1872; six years later Moses Coit Tyler published his scholarly, durable *History of American Literature During the Colonial Time.*

"Exquisitely and Consistently Provincial"

When I say inexperience, I mean that Hawthorne's experience had been narrow. His fifty years had been spent, for much the larger part, in small American towns—Salem, the Boston of forty years ago, Concord, Lenox, West Newton —and he had led exclusively what one may call a village life. . . . In other words, and to call things by their names, he was exquisitely and consistently provincial.

Henry James, *Hawthorne* (1879)

The Writer's Profession

Seemingly opposed figures except in their rejection of New England, James looked toward Europe and high art, while Mark Twain spoke for the vernacular West and what he called "the mighty mass of the uncultivated." It was clear in many other ways that the sources of continuing vitality were no longer located in and around Boston. A new class of professional writers, diverse in geographic and social origins and working under new professional conditions, emerged to make the nation's literature, a significant part of it regional in program and nature. Indicatively, William Dean Howells, the adoptive New Englander from the Midwest, was to leave the *Atlantic* to write for the *Century* and *Harper's*, both published in New York, where he eventually settled. But although this city became the nation's book and magazine publishing center, it was not necessarily where other writers chose to live and work. "Death to the spirit," Whitman said of New York, "a good market for the harvest but a bad place for farming." Among writers born during the three decades before the Civil War, Kate Chopin flourished in New Orleans; San Francisco counted Mark Twain among its celebrities. This dispersal of centers of literary creation from the eastern seaboard augured a later generation of writers of the Midwest (Willa Cather, Sherwood Anderson, Sinclair Lewis, F. Scott Fitzgerald, Ernest Hemingway) and of the South (Katherine Anne Porter, William Faulkner, Thomas Wolfe, Zora Neale Hurston, Richard Wright).

Post–Civil War book publishing had become a two-tiered, two-culture system that reached overlapping but distinguishable classes of readers. "Trade" publishers —centered in New York, Boston, and Philadelphia—sold their books in bookstores to a primarily urban and educated audience, enjoyed prestige, and in turn conferred it on their authors. "Subscription" publishers, on the other hand, were merchandisers who employed door-to-door salesmen, armed with alluring prospectuses and binders' dummies, to work the towns and country districts; a broad, nonliterary audience—often tradesmen, farmers, and their families— ordered in advance of publication works of history, moral philosophy, patriotism, medical advice, and occasionally humor and fiction. "Anything but subscription publishing is printing for private circulation," Mark Twain said. He showed fellow writers like Howells, Thomas Bailey Aldrich, and George Washington Cable yet other avenues to income: the lecture circuit (later, public "readings"), the magazines, and the theater, with dramatizations of his novels. The career of letters had become a matter of business as well as craft and during the 1880s began to require the professional services of literary agents.

The post–Civil War era opened up vistas of regret as well as opportunity for American writers. The world they inhabited, said Henry James, "was a more complicated place than it had hitherto seemed, the future more treacherous, success more difficult." Henry Adams, who lived into the twentieth century but thought of himself as a child of the eighteenth, felt like a ghost or revenant. Mark Twain's Connecticut Yankee mourns a "lost land . . . so fresh and new, so virgin" that progress and the industrial revolution had destroyed. Similarly, a significant number of writers attempted to preserve in fiction or memoir what seemed the idyllic simplicities of village life before the war and helped create a literary cult of childhood and innocence. Harriet Beecher Stowe's *Oldtown Folks,* Louisa May Alcott's *Little Women,* and Thomas Bailey Aldrich's *The Story of a Bad Boy* were all published in 1868 or 1869; *Tom Sawyer* was their counterpart for the 1870s and a likely model for Howells's *A Boy's Town* (1890). Looking to the present, however, many writers discovered that the union of art and realism sparked literary controversies that opened up broader opportunities than their predecessors had known.

Realism, Naturalism, and Idealism

The Civil War had ended in the spring of 1865, but the consequences of that brutal struggle continued to send shocks throughout the nation's cultural life. As the year 1900 drew nearer, a civil war of sorts continued between the literary camps of the Realists and the Romanticists. Leading writers and arbiters of taste like William Dean Howells were convinced that Realism was the only honest way to record what it was actually like to live the everyday American life. Howells and his friends (Mark Twain and Henry James) and protégés (Stephen Crane and Sarah Orne Jewett) viewed Romanticism as an adversary of truth and common humanity, with its soft-focused views that preferred sentimental, pretty, happy emotions and denied the less pleasant facts cast up by late-nineteenth-century existence. Of course, there were writers—such as Ambrose "Bitter" Bierce—who disagreed with Howells. Realism, Bierce wrote in *The Devil's Dictionary,* is "the art of depicting nature as it is seen by toads, the charm suffusing a landscape painted by a mole, or a story written by a measuring-worm."

The honor roll of the Realists includes Mark Twain, Henry James, and Edith Wharton, together with Howells, but even these champions of the cause of honesty allowed certain kinds of romanticism to infiltrate and energize their works. In his later years especially, Howells realized that the Realism versus Romanticism standoff was not quite as simple as he, or Bierce, sometimes pictured it, and he began to explore the darker reaches of the psyche, which had been the favorite stalking ground for the great American Romantics in the years prior to the war.

Just as "idealism" (the belief that the universe is run according to the principles of absolute and eternal goodness) could mean either a profound examination of important human concerns or become the slovenly basis for whatever people desired to think life ought to be like, "romanticism" also cut two ways—either toward an escapism that twisted facts past recognition (what the Realists detested) or toward a responsible reexploration of areas dismissed by the literal-minded (areas the Realists dared not ignore).

Becoming a Realist, then, could mean being expansive and exploratory or being merely a self-limiting advocate of small home truths; a Romanticist might be a student of complex reality or just one of those who glossed over unpleasantness. But American writers had more to choose between than these schools: A writer could decide to follow the lead of the literary school of Naturalism that spilled over from the Continent in the 1890s. Stephen Crane, Jack London, and Theodore Dreiser each responded differently to the precepts of objective, scientific reporting set down in France by Émile Zola in *Le Roman*

Expérimental in 1880. There was no single "Naturalism," just as there was no one "Realism" or "Romanticism," but one distinctive trait separates these several ways of seeing the world and the role taken by the individual. This difference is not a matter of setting or theme; ugly, sordid events were as much the property of the writers of Romance and of Realism as of the Naturalists. Nor is the crucial distinction based on who lays claim to being true to life; the best writers in any one of these literary groupings were confident they were doing just that. The differences among them depend, rather, on the relative amount of individual choice allowed the characters whose lives are portrayed by Naturalists, Romanticists, and Realists.

Generally speaking (for even here there must be notable exceptions), the writers in the Romantic tradition emphasized the possible triumph of the human will; the Realists qualified freedom of choice with large provisos concerning the power of outside forces; the Naturalists tended to reduce to nil all human chances of winning on their own terms. The Romanticists liked to view man as a god; the Realists said man is just that—a man; the Naturalists admitted that in the end man is not much more than a physical object, subject to forces of biology and environment well beyond his control.

This, then, was the situation American writers had to confront. From the start, they all had careers to make, and all had private needs to answer: to feel accepted, earn a living, express what had to be told, and satisfy the demands of their imaginations. During the 1890s and after, many writers also began to assume a definite sense of social obligation to their readers, even those who paid great mind to matters of style and form and went with "the art for art's sake" crowd. To write clearly and effectively about important personal and public issues might help save American society from the enemies who lay within and without. Their stories could not directly bring about changes in the social attitudes of their readers, but still these writers wanted *to have an effect*.

Some shook up their readers by writing humor (Mark Twain). Some acted as chroniclers of regional "local color" (Sarah Orne Jewett, Kate Chopin). Others took old formalities of poetic versification and introduced surprises with new words, topics, and realignments of sounds (Emily Dickinson, Walt Whitman). Still others put the strengths of the native tongue and an interest in native themes to extensive use in their novels (William Dean Howells).

The country's writers had also to contend with the many Americans who preferred to be entertained, instructed, and (sometimes) saved by what they read. On occasion, the public seemed stupidly reluctant to face the realities the writers singled out for its attention. There were times when the public was more interested in being indulged than in being startled into emotional and intellectual life. But a marvelous thing happened. The writers whom we now think of as having contributed the best and most interesting literature of the fifty years between 1865 and 1915 got themselves published, read, and to some extent or another recognized.

The careers of some (Dreiser, Chopin, Whitman) were often troubled and filled with disappointments. The writing life of Kate Chopin, for example, came to an abrupt halt when her novel *The Awakening* took liberties concerning a woman's capacity for sensuality that the general public was not willing to allow. But an exceptional number of American writers found appreciative readers, both early and late—not as many, perhaps, as the writers might have liked; not as many as Twain and Howells could regularly count on; but enough. The American literary innovators were heard then and continue to be heard now. They expressed what it meant to them and to their contemporaries to be buffeted by the changes all Americans experienced as they moved rapidly into a future that had largely discarded the past in the process of somewhat crudely creating the present. The writers were creatures of their time, but they were also capable, at their best, of transcending those times. They reflected the boundlessness and the limits of the age. Sometimes they tried to make that age better; they seldom left it worse.

What is entailed by social and technological progress and whether wars are necessary were but two of the questions to which Americans had to respond during the late 1800s and the early 1900s. They also had to ask what it meant *to do good* and *to be good* in a world where *making good* seemed to have replaced the old moral notion of "goodness." The necessity to assess society and to reexamine the literary means for expressing what it meant to live in the decades after the close of the Civil War fell with particular weight upon American writers. Sometimes they wrote from deep within the silence of their hearts, as did Emily Dickinson. Sometimes they wrote directly from the public square because of their awareness of grave social issues, as did William Dean Howells and Mark Twain. Writers and readers alike were part of a period that pushed inquiries about whether the United States was—or could become—any better as a nation than the world at large. Everyone was living through many changes taking place very fast over an immense area of American life. The one thing the writers *could* do was to express, in imaginative terms, their responses to the thickness of the surrounding facts. They realized that those facts would have no human meaning unless they as writers had the skill to reveal those facts through the stories they told about America.

The Diary of a Shirtwaist Striker

I've come to believe that this strike business is something like a catching sickness—measles or chicken-pox. Once you get it it sticks to you until it's all over.

And then again, one can't really help standing up for the girls. I went down to see Minnie; she's down in bed; some hoodlum hit her last night. God! how these people do live! I don't see how she can afford to stop for a single day.

Her brother Mack is out of work, her father never works, Minnie and her sister, Sarah, are out on strike. Talk about nerve, I really think them Jew girls have it all. I'd like a share of it myself, but somehow I aint of the brave kind. Ray said she'd rather starve to death than be a scab and take some one else's bread out of their mouths. I'm sure I couldn't have that much courage, but I'd hate to go back on the girls.

Theresa Serber Malkiel (1910)

Fictional narrative reflected in various ways the often squalid yet humanly inspiring facts of lives as actually experienced in the shock of the times. A record kept by a young woman worker in the New York City sweatshops preserves in diary form just one of the tales that American writers had to tell.

Redefinitions and New Vocabularies

With changes marking almost every corner of American existence, it was inevitable that old words had new meanings forced upon them and that new phrases spun into being. The forty years between 1888 and 1928 witnessed the introduction of one new word out of every ten. As Mark Sullivan pointed out in his six-volume study *Our Times,* three thousand new words received official recognition between 1909 and 1927 alone. Most of these words reflected the discoveries taking place continually in physics, chemistry, and medicine and in the widening use of technology. But along with *X-ray, dynamo, telephone,* and *aeroplane* were words like *flivver, Kodak, movies, skyscraper,* and *el*—slangier references to the new entities filling everyday lives.

Going west in the 1860s as a greenhorn, Samuel Clemens dragged along a massive dictionary in the stagecoach he took out of St. Joseph, Missouri. But Clemens found out that many of the words acceptable back east were of little use beyond the Mississippi. Words like *coyote* and *blind lead* were more to the point in his new life. The 1884 edition of *The Adventures of Huckleberry Finn* was drummed off the shelf of the public library in Concord, Massachusetts, because it contained the ungrammatical sentences and lower-class language of a vagabond boy without genteel schooling. Yet Mark Twain's use of the vernacular proved one of the strongest elements of the thrust toward literary independence that was well under way by the 1890s.

Mark Twain, William Dean Howells, and Henry James introduced the flavor of colloquial speech into their fiction. Stephen Crane's infantryman Henry Fleming talked like a real infantryman might talk, and Sarah Orne Jewett accurately noted the linguistic mannerisms of rural characters from New England. Kate Chopin emphasized the southern phrasings characteristic of the Creoles and Cajuns of Louisiana. As one result, the reading public was exposed to *American* speech distinctively unlike that of a "proper" literature derived from Boston or Great Britain.

The Devil's Dictionary

Conservative: A statesman who is enamored of existing evils, as distinguished from the Liberal, who wishes to replace them with others.
Vote: The instrument and symbol of a freeman's power to make a fool of himself and a wreck of his country.
Presidency: The greased pig in the field game of American politics.

Ambrose Bierce (1906)

So many new words! *Teddy bear* (inspired by the popular image of President Theodore Roosevelt), *she's a daisy,* and *ragtime* represented the simple pleasures of the nursery, the holiday outing, and the music hall. Still other words were less innocent records of current social upheavals and maladies: *Jim Crow, carpetbagger, skid row, the Four Hundred, nabobs, the Pinkertons, sweatshop,* and *the Molly Maguires.* The influx of immigrants meant the incorporation of words from Yiddish, Polish, Gaelic, and Italian into the basic pool of Yankee speech. They also kicked up new terms of insult: *Yid, Polack, Mick, Dago.* American life was turning inside out, and the good and the bad found the vocabularies needed to express their cruder emotions and deepest needs.

Older words were also redefined. On the battlefield in *The Red Badge of Courage,* Crane's Henry Fleming is forced to test accepted meanings for *heroism, glory,* and *patriotism.* Blacks in the South and the North and the slum dwellers in the cities had to reassess what it meant to live with the way words such as *values, equality,* and *freedom* were actually being used. Businessmen had to relearn what *individualism* and *business* signified in an economy where corporate organizations and new marketing techniques made the small, family-run company an anachronism. Faithful believers in American democracy had one set of definitions for *conservative, vote,* and *presidency;* Ambrose Bierce, dipping into his cynicism for *The Devil's Dictionary,* had others.

Home and the words that traditionally cluster around its values *(mother, wife, family, breadwinner)* were placed under the stress of still newer terms: *apartment, the working woman,* and *divorce. West, East, North,* and *South* were reassessed in light of what such labels meant to politicians dickering for votes, to bankers packaging far-flung mergers, to arbiters of culture attempting to create a national taste, to agronomists and economists trying to bring supply and demand into line, and to all those people piling onto the trains and wagons that moved them from one place to another in their search for a better life and true-blue American values.

Everywhere Strangers

Even the word *America* underwent severe testing. Questions arose over what constituted a *real* citizen of the United States. The religious preferences, cultural habits, racial and national antecedents of "the others" were probed to determine whether Catholics, Jews, Indians, Slavs, Slovenes, Asians, blacks, and Mexicans could ever be considered "one of us." The melting pot theory promised a massive process of national assimilation. The nativists insisted that such types would remain forever "aliens."

The debate over who would be permitted to claim the proud name "American" (native Anglo-Saxon stock only, or latecomers as well?) was complicated by the sense of national mission that reached its peak during the Spanish-American War and the takeover of the Philippines in 1898 and 1899. After all, so the argument went, it was precisely *as* Americans that the people of the United States had the duty to see to it that others became Americanized, whatever the contradictions involved in this transformation.

"Th' White Civilization"

"Ye see, Hinnissy, th' Indyun is bound f'r to give way to th' onward march iv white civilization. You an' me, Hinnissy, is th' white civilization."

"Mr. Dooley" (Finley Peter Dunne)

The strong stomach of American civilization may, and doubtless will, digest and assimilate ultimately this unsavory and repellent throng. . . . In time they catch the spirit of the country and form an element of decided worth.

The Philadelphia Press (1888)

Just as cross-fertilization is beneficial to plant life, the intermingling of peoples in this country must produce the most beautiful, most intellectual, and most powerful race of the world. . . . *[The] American, even to-day, presents the highest type of beauty which ever adorned the earth.*

Professor W. J. McGee (1906)

The members of the newly formed Anti-Imperialist League stepped in to say nay to this mood of expansionism. They stated the objections that found confirmation in Mark Twain's satiric essay "To a Person Sitting in Darkness" and in William James's "The Moral Equivalent of War." But it became increasingly difficult to interpret the words used to define America's proper role at home and abroad, just as it had been puzzling from the first to know exactly how to "read" the features of the colossal Statue of Liberty that stood at the nation's gates.

"Civilize and Christianize Them"

I walked the floor of the White House night after night until midnight; and I am not ashamed to tell you, gentlemen, that I went down on my knees and prayed Almighty God for light and guidance more than one night. And one night it came to me late this way—I don't know how it was, but it came . . . that there was nothing left for us to do but to take them all, and to educate the Filipinos, and uplift and civilize and Christianize them, and by God's grace do the very best we could for them, as our fellow-men for whom Christ also died.

President William McKinley (1899)

"Whin we plant what Hogan calls th' starry banner iv Freedom in th' Ph'lippeens," said Mr. Dooley, "an' give th' sacred blessin' iv liberty to th' poor, down-trodden people iv thim unfortunate isles—dam thim!—we'll larn thim a lesson."

"Mr. Dooley" (Finley Peter Dunne)

The New Colossus

Not like the brazen giant of Greek fame,
With conquering limbs astride from land to land;
Here at our sea-washed, sunset gates shall stand
A mighty woman with a torch, whose flame
Is the imprisoned lightning, and her name
Mother of Exiles. From her beacon-hand
Glows world-wide welcome; her mild eyes command
The air-bridged harbor that twice cities frame.
"Keep, ancient lands, your storied pomp!" cries she
With silent lips. "Give me your tired, your poor,
Your huddled masses yearning to breathe free,
The wretched refuse of your teeming shore.
Send these, the homeless, tempest-tossed to me:
I lift my lamp beside the golden door!"

Emma Lazarus (1886)

More than racial and ethnic labels were readjusted; class structures were also shifted. A sizable middle-class bloc emerged. At the high end of the spectrum lay what the newspapers liked to call "the plutocrats," while at the bottom of the heap huddled "the other half." (Reliable statistics gathered by 1915 indicate that the poor totaled sixty-five percent of the population, the lower and middle classes together made up thirty-three percent, and the wealthy constituted only two percent of the whole.)

How was one to know who was who in a society in which the signs of recognition were changing overnight? Could one distinguish friends from strangers—in class terms, at least—by the houses they lived in? Andrew Carnegie thought so. As he expounded in his 1889 essay "Wealth": "It is well, nay, essential, for the progress of the race that the houses of some should be homes for all that is highest and best in literature and the arts, and for all the refinements of civilization, rather than that none should be so. Much better this great irregularity than universal squalor."

Edith Wharton and Henry James certainly knew how to make clear the distinctions between "new" and "old" money—the differences between those who make a great show of their wealth and those who carefully keep their possessions under wraps. These were the same distinctions Thorstein Veblen made famous in his study of 1899, *The Theory of the Leisure Class.* He analyzed the look of affluence that places a successful man's possessions (wife and house) on public display. "The more reputable, 'presentable' portion of middle-class household paraphernalia are, on the one hand, items of conspicuous consumption, and on the other hand, apparatus for putting in the vicarious leisure rendered by the housewife."

In 1890 Jacob Riis attempted to do for the poor of the New York City slums what Wharton, James, and Veblen did for the well-to-do. In Riis's book of words and photographs, *How the Other Half Lives,* he analyzed the tonal differences between the families herded into Jewtown and the free-lance hoodlums who made the neighborhood of "the Bend" a synonym for crime. Willa Cather's memories of farm and village life in Nebraska also caught the distinctions between ethnic and class structures; she vividly portrayed the special vitality each immigrant servant girl (whether Bohemian, Swede, or German) brought to the Saturday night dances that threw the pallid, native-born town girls into the shade.

Transformations

If there were problems in knowing whether other people were friends or potential enemies in a world full of change, there was also the possible terror of inner transformations. William James lets it be known that the green-faced idiot he once saw sitting on a bench in an insane asylum is essentially what he, and we all, might yet become. Horatio Alger's Ragged Dick is transformed into a respectable wage-earning citizen. Dreiser's George Hurstwood, on the other hand, is plucked from the midst of health and well-being and cast down into degradation and death. Frank Norris's novels furnish many unsettling examples of characters who go through reversions to the most primitive stages. Perhaps one of the saddest, and most hilarious, of all lines from American literature comes in Norris's novel *Vandover and the Brute.* The main protagonist, Vandover, after dropping to all fours to howl at the moon, contrasts the wolfish brute he is turning into with what he had formerly been. "My God! to think I was a Harvard man once!"

Not all the transformations were as sensational as those insisted upon by Norris, Dreiser, and Jack London—writers who endorsed the current scientific and philosophical theories concerning the determining forces of heredity and environment. But even the metamorphoses taking place within the species "young American woman" proved disturbing to many who witnessed new types of the female rushing into existence. Henry James (with Daisy Miller and Isabel Archer) and William Dean Howells (with Kitty Ellison, Florida Vervain, and Lydia Blood) initiated the type of the American girl in the 1870s and 1880s. By the 1890s two of the most talked-about versions (favorites of the popular magazines and the Sunday newspaper supplements) were "the American heiress" and "the new woman."

Women as a sexual and social subclass were, by tradition, supposedly the most stable of all elements of American nineteenth-century life, fixed firmly within their sphere of home and hearth. In 1880 one of the many popular books of etiquette that taught Americans the proper "code of manners" stated flatly, "The power of a woman is in her refinement, gentleness and elegance; it is she who makes etiquette, and it is she who preserves the order and decency of society. Without women, men soon resume the savage state, and the comfort and the graces of the home are exchanged for the misery of the mining camp." But should a woman slip loose from the restraining influences of the home, she was transformed into that ancient aspect of Eve feared by "good society" and beloved of the tabloids.

The American heiress and the new woman. Left: Howard Chandler Christy, in
Our Girls, Poems in Praise of the American Girl (1907). Right: The cover of *The
Evolution of Woman* by Harry Whitney McVickar (1896).

There was no finer instance of the type of the femme fatale at the turn of the
century than Evelyn Nesbit, over whose tarnished innocence one man (her
husband, Harry Thaw) shot to death another man (her lover, the well-known
architect Stanford White). The reporter for the *New York Evening World*
covering the sensational murder trial of 1907 was agog over Nesbit's beauty—
dangerous because it seemed so innocent. Hers was "the slim, quick grace of a
fawn, a head that sat on the faultless throat as a lily on its stem, eyes that were
the color of blue-brown pansies and the size of half-dollars, a mouth made of
rumpled rose petals."

"Why Don't All These Ladies Do Something?"

And in the midst of the mild little tumult a certain Rose Lipschowsky got
upon a soap-box in Union Square to say violently: "Why don't all these ladies
do something to help the Garment Workers' Union instead of saying how good
and refined they are?" She was much applauded, got down from her soap-box
and vanished altogether, an unconscious symbol of what suffrage in the '90's
omitted from its speeches and programs.

Thomas Beer, *The Mauve Decade* (1926)

It was a shock (of delight for some, of dismay for many) to realize that there were still other forms of female behavior coming into play by the 1870s and after than those of "the Eternal Evelyn." New occupations brought women (before and after marriage) into the work place. Enhanced college programs for women led them toward an education in new ideas, as well as in professional skills hitherto relegated to men alone. The *New York Journal* of March 22, 1896, headlined its alarm: "Are We Destroying Woman's Beauty? The Startling Warning of a Great English Physician Against Higher Education of Women. How Intellectual Work Destroys Beauty."

Women also pushed their way into politics. The suffrage movement made a widely publicized comeback in the 1880s after a relatively quiescent period in the years following the Civil War. The suffragists had no clear sailing, however. The right-to-vote advocates were criticized from without and within the movement. From outside their ranks, women as well as men feared the damage that social radicalism might do to the sanctity of the home. From inside the world of political activism, working-class women charged the middle-class members of the movement with elitism and ineffectual action, as in the confrontation in 1893, reported by Thomas Beer.

To the dizzying effect of the political and economic transformations taking place in the woman's world in America, add the burst of international marriages that allied the new wealth of young American girls with the old titles held by European noblemen who were not always noble in character. "The American heiress" as a type especially piqued the interest of readers of the Hearst and Pulitzer papers and such newly flourishing women's magazines as the *Ladies' Home Journal, Cosmopolitan,* and *Good Housekeeping.* Headed for a sumptuous life abroad, the heiress was a particular pet of the public when her romantic adventures were supplemented by the illustrations of Charles Dana Gibson, Howard Chandler Christy, Albert Beck Wenzell, and others. Some, like Christy, saw the heiress going from triumph to triumph. In *The American Girl as Seen and Portrayed by Howard Chandler Christy,* Christy extolled the type as proof of Darwinistic theories of evolution, sanctified as an icon enfolded in Old Glory. "She is the culmination of mankind's long struggle upward from his barbarism into civilization. To make her all that she is countless millions have lived and died." Others, however, expressed apprehension over the buying and selling of the American girl. James and Wharton did this in their novels and stories, as did Charles Dana Gibson in satiric exposés. Commentators on the American scene decided that "one is inclined to believe that a 'palatial' residence is sometimes the rich American girl's compensation for the absence of a 'palatial' husband."

Many of the fears and aspirations released during this period of change and transformation, affecting males and females alike, focused on the image of the American girl. What happened to her represented what was going on in every area of American society. In 1895 the *New York World* featured "a Scathing Rebuke of the Unfettered Female, Her Mannish Ways, Hatred of Children, Chewing Gum, and Erotic Novels." As the *New York Journal* warned in 1896, the show of energy embodied by the girl might bring to her and to society at large a massive "disorganization of the nervous system," leading to "loss of graceful outlines, loss of appetite, lines in the face, bad teeth, bad complexion,

The ambitious mother and the obliging clergyman. Charles Dana Gibson, from The Gibson Book in Two Volumes *(1906).*

short sight and possibly hysteria, epilepsy and insanity!" No wonder that Henry Adams (at a higher intellectual level than the Hearst or Pulitzer papers offered) was studying with fascination the kinds of force represented by "the dynamo" and "the virgin." The male machine (symbolized by the Corliss engine, which dominated the American imagination after its presentation at the 1876 Philadelphia Centennial Exposition) was in power at the moment, but Adams had the premonition that female energy, hitherto frustrated and wasted, was about to force its way upon the American scene. As pupil and historian of modern times, Adams was eager to see what the outcome of such an explosion might be.

Making Contact

New people, new places, new objects, new ideas, new types—all located in new patterns of interchange and communication. There were no guarantees, however, that the newest inventions would not result in shocks and confusions rather than in clarity of meaning and the enhancement of personal and social life.

The Pullman car, the transcontinental railway, the electric trolley car, the transoceanic steamship, the bicycle, and the automobile were made possible by major advances in the technology of transportation. The telegraph, the Atlantic cable, and the telephone speeded the transport of messages. But it was in the world of the printed page that many of the most startling innovations took place. Dozens of new magazines and newspapers appeared so quickly that it was hard to keep up with the blur of words and images. Advances in printing techniques increased the amount, the kind, and the quality of illustrations that could be included in books, journals, and newspapers. Photographs were in common use for public purposes by the late 1890s. More words and pictures could be printed faster, for the viewing of more people, than ever before.

Certain Dangerous Tendencies in American Life

The young people of the mills generally read the story papers, published (most of them) in New York city, and devoted to interminably "continued" narratives, of which there are always three or four in process of publication in each paper. . . . They have usually no very distinct educational quality of tendency, good or bad. They are simply stories,—vapid, silly, turgid, and incoherent. As the robber-heroes are mostly grand-looking fellows, and all the ladies have white hands and splendid attire, it may be that some of the readers find hard work more distasteful because of their acquaintance with the gorgeous idlers and thieves, who, in these fictions are always so much more fortunate than the people who are honest and industrious. But usually . . . the only effect of this kind of reading is that it serves "to pass away the time," by supplying a kind of entertainment, a stimulus or opiate for the mind, and that these people resort to it and feel a necessity for it in much the same way that others feel they must have a whisky or opium. The reading is a narcotic, but it is less pernicious than those just named.

Jonathan Baxter Harrison (1880)

Improved print and picture meant spreading contact through all layers of society. Farmers, factory workers, city dwellers (whether in the tenements, the big houses, or the new apartment complexes), ethnic groups, and people from every geographic region now had a newspaper or a magazine addressed expressly to them. At the same time special audiences were being singled out, methods for the standardization of production and consumption were also under way. A great deal of what went into print was couched in broadly nationalistic terms. The jarring headlines or the newest best-sellers that intrigued readers on one coast aroused the interest of audiences on the opposite coast and just about everyone in between.

Together with the widening of the general readership (aided by an increased access to public schools, land-grant colleges, and special-training courses) came a vertical thrust down through the layers of class. The so-called genteel readership that had once centered in Boston and radiated out from other established eastern communities had always possessed a selection of magazines that suited its particular tastes in the arts and in politics. Now brash new publications were supplying things to read all the way down the cultural slope to the shop girls and foreign-born mechanics.

Upper- and middle-class magazines prided themselves on being responsible to the intellectual and spiritual values of their readers. Sometimes this sense of social obligation defined itself as smug support of traditional views and as fear of change. In 1889 Thomas DeWitt Talmage wrote *Social Dynamite; or, The Wickedness of Modern Society*. Talmage was certain that "poison" would replace "truth" if the unwary allowed popular romances into their homes. On other occasions, Clarence S. Darrow criticized the literature of moral evasion and urged reforms in the direction of reality. Darrow, no less than Talmage, sought the truth, but each found what he praised in the writings the other man condemned.

Social Dynamite

Look through your library, and then, having looked through your library, look on the stand where you keep your pictorials and newspapers, and apply the Christian principles I have laid down. If there is anything in your home that can not stand the test, do not give it away, for it might spoil an immortal soul; do not sell it, for the money you get would be the price of blood; but rather kindle a fire on your kitchen hearth, or in your back yard, and then drop the poison in it, and keep stirring the blaze until from preface to appendix there shall not be a single paragraph left, and the bonfire in your city shall be as consuming as that one in the streets of Ephesus.

Thomas DeWitt Talmage, *Social Dynamite; or, The Wickedness of Modern Society* (1889)

The popular press was somewhat more cheerfully cynical about its role as critic of social ills and upholder of sacred truths. Editors of the large-circulation papers and magazines directed toward the working classes were diligent enough in exposing national corruptions and local connivings since just such stories (done up in bold headlines) both did society some good and sold like hotcakes. By the 1890s Hearst and Pulitzer refined the formulas that brought their readers news that went to the extremes of sensationalism. Available facts were keyed up to make the stories splashier, or facts were invented to bring stories—even wars—into existence.

Entertainment, instruction, and reform made the interconnecting worlds of journalism, magazine publication, and book sales go; but there continued to be a deep split in tastes between one segment of the American population and another. Van Wyck Brooks, the man who helped popularize the terms *highbrow* and *lowbrow,* drove home the point that America was in the midst of a cultural civil war. Brooks saw the nation as divided: "on the one hand a quite unclouded, quite unhypocritical assumption of transcendent theory ('high ideals'); on the other a simultaneous acceptance of catchpenny realities. Between university ethic and business ethics, between American culture and American humor, between Good Government and Tammany, between academic pedantry and pavement slang, there is no community, no genial middle ground."

Along with all the other "strangers" (by virtue of race, heritage, economic status, region, and gender) American society had to contend with, those who lived by ideals were estranged from those who abided by the way things were. This cultural division made itself felt in the way American writers and artists viewed their chances at success and effectiveness in a nation where the business of being an American seemed mainly to be just that: *business.*

The Intellectual and Aesthetic Life

By the 1890s and 1900s the new professionals of the advertising and promotion world were using the picture and print industry to the utmost. New products were featured in entirely new areas of merchandising: big department stores, mail-order catalogs, national and international fairs and expositions. New approaches to the marketing of sports, theaters, and museums disclosed different ways to place entertainment on display and to "sell" the pleasures of culture. There was a riot of new things in America to desire. It was up to everyone to take advantage of the chances to make, to sell, and to buy.

Not all the new in American life came in the form of material objects or tangible events. Ideas were important too, even the more abstract, unsellable kind. The final decades of the nineteenth century were marked by a distinguished group of thinkers who tried out new intellectual methods for resolving both age-old philosophical questions and the brand-new difficulties that rushed into existence. A great deal of hard thinking went on, especially from the 1880s onwards, over matters of social justice and humanistic concerns.

The back cover of Puck *(April 1, 1885).*

"The World Asks for Facts"

The world has grown tired of preachers and sermons; to-day it asks for facts. It has grown tired of fairies and angels, and asks for flesh and blood. It looks on life as it exists to-day—both in its beauty and its horror, its joy and its sorrow. It wishes to see all; not only the prince and the millionaire, but the laborer and the beggar, the master and the slave. We see the beautiful and the ugly, and know what the world is and what it ought to be, and the true picture which the author saw and painted stirs the heart to holier feelings and to grander thoughts.

Clarence S. Darrow, "Realism in Literature and Art" (1892)

Josiah Royce, George Santayana, William James, Charles Sanders Peirce, and John Dewey as philosophers; Justice Oliver Wendell Holmes as an authority on the law; Thorstein Veblen, Herbert Croly, Lester Frank Ward, and Henry George as economists and political scientists—all countered the slipshod notions and vicious ideologies, the *bad* thinking, that crowded the mental spaces of American life. The men named here, as well as many others (women, too), argued vigorously about such sharp-edged issues as how best to educate the young, to put equitable laws into practice, to assure racial and economic fairness, to encourage ethical behavior, to initiate tax reforms, and to reshape democratic principles to fit the times. These overtly social questions battled for public attention alongside equally vital questions concerning freedom of choice, the existence of God or goodness, the ways by which complex minds work and the bodily instincts function, and—above all—the nature of truths in an ambiguous universe and the means by which to signify them in language and in deeds.

The new school of American philosophers and psychologists saw to it that seemingly abstruse queries about materialism (emphasis on things), idealism (concentration on ideas and principles), determinism (what you cannot control), and free will (the choices you can make) received recognition among thoughtful Americans as matters that concretely affected everyone's life. They wanted to prevent what many feared might take place: the loss of one's sense of humanity in a torrent of sensual impressions or the chance of that humanity being locked into grids by massive mechanistic forces.

In 1890 William James graphically imaged the mind's environment. It was precisely *that* environment out of which turn-of-the-century Americans had to make something good for themselves and their fellow citizens or go down in defeat. Somehow the life of the mind, as well as that of the body, had to be conducted under imperfect conditions. The soul was also important, at least to idealists like Josiah Royce who still held a toehold in a world of contingencies and materiality. Mind, body, or soul, the sense of *being human* had to make itself felt as an experienced fact; otherwise, it would all signify nothing. In *The Principles of Psychology*, William James hit it right on the mark: "Millions of items of the outward order are present to my senses which never properly enter into my experience. Why? Because they have no *interest for me. My experience is what I agree to attend to.*"

The Stream of Thought

Out of what is in itself an undistinguishable, swarming *continuum,* devoid of distinction or emphasis, our senses make for us, by attending to this motion and ignoring that, a world full of contrasts, of sharp accents, of abrupt changes of picturesque light and shade.

William James, *The Principles of Psychology* (1890)

Science received the kind of rapt attention of which William James spoke. In his sixties, Henry Adams, for example, tried to make up for the botched education he received as a Harvard undergraduate in the 1850s by teaching himself the essentials of the new mathematics and physics. Speculation about thermodynamics, X-rays, and "the supersensual chaos" of the universe occupied Adams's busy mind until his death in 1918, just after Albert Einstein's momentous discoveries about cosmic time, space, and energy.

From the 1860s onward Darwinism and its permutations affected the way Americans came to view their economic system (competitiveness versus regulation in the marketplace), their religious beliefs (God versus chance as the master of the universe), their bodies (theirs to direct versus control by inherited "tendencies"), and their physical surroundings (a thing of spirit versus a conglomeration of geologic earth-masses). Herbert Spencer (champion of Social Darwinism) and Pierre and Marie Curie (discoverers of radium) were names that caught the interest of the public as much as those of Thomas Edison, George Pullman, and the builders of Chicago's skyscrapers and Brooklyn's bridge. The age became known as the Age of Energy. The forces set loose by the new science heartened some and dismayed others, but no one escaped its impact.

For many Americans, *being human* meant paying attention to the aesthetic side of life in order to offset the jars of science, technology, and the business of buying and selling. The worth of literature, painting, music, architecture, the theater, and the decorative arts was reexamined (along with everything else) by the rising generation of young writers and artists, who often felt they had to fight for attention in a society that seemed more interested in the Corliss engine, the Bessemer steel-processing method, and Standard Oil takeovers than in what artists had to express or how they expressed it.

The problems that nagged the more radical among the writers and artists of the late nineteenth century were not as much caused by lack of interest in the arts on the part of the general American public as they were affected by the questionable kind and quality of art that found quickest acceptance around the country. There is an ingrained contradiction here, since admirable, often outstanding advances were made in the fine and applied arts and architecture of the period, fully commensurate with the striking triumphs achieved in literature. The paintings of Thomas Eakins, John Singer Sargent, Winslow Homer, James Abbott McNeill Whistler, and Mary Cassatt, the sculpture of Augustus Saint-Gaudens and Daniel Chester French, the architectural plans of Henry

Hobson Richardson, Stanford White, and Louis Sullivan, and the decorative designs of Louis Tiffany and John La Farge can hardly be dismissed. Photography as a skilled art form had its champions in Frances Benjamin Johnston, Gertrude Käsebier, F. Holland Day, and Clarence White, and the display poster achieved an enviable peak with the work of Will Bradley, Louis Rhead, and Edward Penfield.

Nor could anyone suggest that the American public was not avidly interested in the artistic side of life. The arts exhibits at the Centennial Exposition held in Philadelphia in 1876 and (together with a number of writers' congresses) at the Columbian Exposition in Chicago in 1893 drew large audiences. So did the expositions in St. Louis and San Francisco in subsequent years. *The Book of the Fair,* compiled by Hubert Howe Bancroft after the Columbian Exposition, proudly declared that "the Fair has been to the world a revelation, to Americans an inspiration. It has shown, as no written or spoken words could show, the power and progress of a nation where all are free to strive for the highest rewards that energy and talent can win." The museums that first opened their neo-Renaissance portals to the public during the 1890s and 1900s also stirred wide interest. The many salon showings of contemporary paintings (both American and European), the ample inclusion of fine arts reproductions in the magazines, the commissions given to muralists and sculptors to decorate the stately new municipal buildings, and the widespread practice of placing copies of famous works of art in the classrooms of the public schools indicate that there was much interest in art (and the moral values it was meant to represent) at one level of American taste or another.

What irritated the artists was that the views on "taste" sponsored by the academies and the official showplaces of aesthetic wares encouraged the public to respond negatively to themes that were demonstrably American and to techniques that were experimentally modern. And the artists' problem was shared with the writers of the period. No one could accuse the American public of not wanting to read stories, poetry, and novels; there was an insatiable appetite for almost everything in print. But what most people said they liked did not often coincide with what those who opposed traditional literary values upheld as true art.

"Sentimental Romance to Bitter Realism"

Owen Wister and Alfred Henry Lewis were busy with [the] past. . . . Kirk Munro told tales for boys. Mary Hallock Foote varied from sentimental romance to a sudden passage or two of bitter realism. . . . Stephen Crane flashed his short string of Western sketches through *McClure's* and the *Century,* refutations of melodrama in melodrama's terms. . . . The stencilled characters of Bret Harte returned thinly masked in the *Argonaut,* the *Wave* and the *Overland Monthly.* So in 1898 Harry Thurston Peck mourned: "I would have given ten Mrs. Humphrey Wards for one good realistic novel about Denver and Seattle."

Thomas Beer, *The Mauve Decade* (1926)

Artists and writers in America of an independent turn of the imagination had enemies aplenty. H. H. Boyesen named one of the worst as "the Iron Madonna," the female reader "who strangles in her fond embrace the American novelist; the Moloch upon whose altar he sacrifices, willingly or unwillingly, his chances of greatness." Thomas Beer went even further when he blamed the namby-pamby conservatism of the general imagination.

Americans who wanted to say something real, strong, and earnest usually received small encouragement from the people at the top. President Grover Cleveland put it nicely: "When I come [to the theater] I want to see something to make me laugh." But even the most shallow or timid consumers of the written word sooner or later learned that there was something more that had to be said. When Mary Roberts Coolidge examined "why women are so," she described the shock that occurs when fantasies of evasion—such as those concerning love's young dream about getting married—are jolted by the realities.

The best of the writers who rode out the storms of late-nineteenth-century American life took on the task of dealing with just these "puzzling and inevitable facts of nature." They did it in many different ways. Henry James's *Daisy Miller* does not read like Theodore Dreiser's *Sister Carrie* or Edith Wharton's *Summer*. Walt Whitman's *Leaves of Grass* makes use of other poetic means than those of Emily Dickinson's "A Narrow Fellow in the Grass." William Dean Howells and Henry Adams shake up the imagination of their readers by means of indirection. Stephen Crane pounces on the emotions straight on. Mark Twain is a realist through slam-bang humor.

Such pluralism of literary approaches was all to the good at the turn of the century since the reality of American life the writers tried to record was "the buzzing booming chaos" described by William James. Faced by a world like this, American writers needed complex minds and hearts to do it justice. Fortunately, among the best "products" coming out of late-nineteenth-century America were precisely the minds and hearts Henry James said "the complex fate" of being an American required.

Further Reading:

P. Buck, *The Road to Reunion*, 1937.
V. Brooks, *New England: Indian Summer*, 1940.
L. Mumford, *The Brown Decades*, 1941.
D. Wecter, *The Hero in America*, 1941.
R. E. Spiller et al., *Literary History of the United States*, 1948 (and supplements).
E. Wilson, *Patriotic Gore*, 1962.
T. Tanner, *The Reign of Wonder*, 1965.
L. Ziff, *The American 1890s*, 1966.
J. Martin, *Harvests of Change*, 1967.
Popular Culture and Industrialism, ed. H. Smith, 1967.

Democratic Vistas: 1860–1880, ed. A. Trachtenberg, 1970.
H. M. Jones, *The Age of Energy*, 1971.
D. McCullough, *The Great Bridge*, 1972.
D. Aaron, *The Unwritten War*, 1973.
N. Harris, *Humbug: The Art of P. T. Barnum*, 1973.
D. Boorstin, *The Americans: The Democratic Experience*, 1974.
W. S. McFeely, *Grant*, 1981.
A. Kazin, *An American Procession*, 1984.

Emily Dickinson
1830–1886

Walt Whitman and Emily Dickinson are America's nineteenth-century poetic geniuses; separately, they resisted the Anglophilia that had hobbled American verse in genteel forms. Whitman invented American free verse unrhymed and unmeasured; Dickinson invented a free form of England's most common poem, the hymn. Except for a very few early experiments, Dickinson wrote in hymn meters all her life, shaping her single form till it responded effortlessly to her intensity of perception and expression.

Dickinson, brought up in conventional Protestantism, never abandoned the metaphysical questions of her upbringing—questions of mortality, renunciation, perfection, existential meaning. But she emptied them of specifically Christian import, though she continued to employ Christian symbols, especially those of damnation, salvation, crucifixion, and heaven. "Some keep the Sabbath going to Church— / I keep it, staying at Home—" she wrote. Her poetry is frequently blasphemous, as when she indicts God as the torturer who "scalps your naked Soul." She does not evade her Puritan and Emersonian inheritance of personal ethical responsibility, but she wrenches it powerfully to her own uses.

A second Dickinson, as powerful as the metaphysical one, is the observer of nature, watching a bird eat a worm raw or coming upon a snake and feeling "Zero at the Bone—" This Dickinson hears the "unobtrusive Mass" of the crickets and perceives "a Druidic Difference" on the face of the world. She notices "a certain Slant of light, / Winter Afternoons"—a light that makes "Shadows—hold their breath." The New England seasons ("I see—New Englandly—," she said) are memorialized in her work in all their variety.

The third, and greatest, Dickinson is the psychological analyst. Herself subject to extremes of anxiety and depression, she never flinched from interrogating her own mental states, taming them (at least to some degree) by her fine-drawn descriptions of the horrors she experienced. When "a Plank in Reason, broke," or when "the Nerves sit ceremonious, like Tombs—," or when "Chaos—Stopless— cool" besets the soul, Dickinson watches, then reports. Though she concealed herself, in life, from others, she was nakedly exposed to herself.

There are other Dickinsons—the love poet, the social satirist, the observer of people, the poet of aesthetic reflection—each of them a considerable talent. The almost two thousand poems in the Dickinson canon can scarcely be fully present even to Dickinson critics, let alone to the common reader. A search through Dickinson's *Complete Poems* never fails to turn up new poems of great value.

And yet this great poet published only a dozen poems in her lifetime. It was not until 1955 that all her known poetry was published, and this was the first collection to reproduce Dickinson's texts as she wrote them, without many editorial changes; it was not until 1982 that her own arrangement of many of her poems in little books, or "fascicles," was made known in facsimile publication. Dickinson was perhaps discouraged by the criticism her poems received from

Thomas Wentworth Higginson, an editor of the *Atlantic Monthly,* to whom she sent poems in 1862; but her friend Helen Hunt Jackson, a well-known author, could have helped to ensure that more poems were published had Dickinson been willing. Dickinson's personal reclusiveness forbade self-promotion, however, and she allowed her poems to accumulate instead in her bureau drawers.

Dickinson grew up in a well-to-do household and had the run of her father's library. Her father was the treasurer of Amherst College, and her grandfather had been one of its founders. She spent a single year at the South Hadley Female Seminary (later to become Mount Holyoke College) but did not remain; she experienced there the inability to believe in institutional religion that caused her to abandon attendance at the Congregational Church. After leaving school, Dickinson became increasingly unwilling to engage in social interchange outside her own house. Though she made brief visits to Boston, Philadelphia, and Washington, D.C., she spent her entire life in her father's house, eventually seeing no visitors. Her brother Austin, after his marriage, lived next door with his wife, the difficult "Sister Sue" to whom many of Dickinson's poems were addressed. Dickinson wrote hundreds of letters and poems yearly (366 poems in the single year 1862). Her neighbors, noting her elusiveness and her constant wearing of white, considered her eccentric. They had no idea of the practical purpose served by her withdrawal, which permitted her to escape the enormous labors usually required of single women, who were freely called on to attend the young, the sick, and the dying. Dickinson reserved her energies for her genius.

Dickinson's early poetry, when it is weak, displays hysteria, self-absorption, and a coy whimsicality. To watch her develop as a poet is to see the whimsicality relax, the hysteria become disciplined by intellectual analysis, and the self-absorption strengthen itself into meditation on the human lot. Her irony turns on herself as well as on the universe; her love of paradox deepens to an examination of the laws of necessity, creative and destructive at once. In manuscript, the smallest Dickinson poem spreads, in her enlarged handwriting, to fill the whole page on which it is written, as though each blank piece of paper were the brain, or the world, filled to the margins with a single mood or insight. Dickinson's bold calligraphy and her composition by phrase—each marked off by a dash with space before and after—puts emphasis on each stamp or impress of the mind in its analysis of experience. Slant rhymes and an oblique form of expression ensure the oddness of surface in Dickinson's poems; the resonant forms of her language stand for her conviction of the baffling eccentricity of life and thought. Though her poetry reflects her reading of many English poets (Shakespeare, Keats, Mrs. Browning) and of Emerson, she is the least imitative of American poets, turning the discursive certainties of writers and philosophers alike into her own preferred thematic form, the riddle. Enigma is her genre, and pain her topic; her anatomy of psychic skepticism remains one of the great documents of American nineteenth-century attitudes. The best measure of her success in verse is the way in which her poems make themselves remembered. Without any effort on our part to memorize them, we find we cannot forget her lines. Her fame has continued to grow. Her poems, once rewritten by others for public acceptability, are now known in their full power and self-assertion.

Further Reading:
G. F. Whicher, *This Was a Poet: A Critical Biography of Emily Dickinson*, 1939.
R. Chase, *Emily Dickinson*, 1951.
C. R. Anderson, *Emily Dickinson's Poetry*, 1960.
A. J. Gelpi, *Emily Dickinson: The Mind of the Poet*, 1965.
B. Lindberg-Seyersted, *The Voice of the Poet: Aspects of Style in the Poetry of Emily Dickinson*, 1968.
R. B. Sewall, *The Life of Emily Dickinson*, 1974.

S. Cameron, *Lyric Time: Dickinson & the Limits of Genre*, 1979.
K. Keller, *The Only Kangaroo Among the Beauty: Emily Dickinson and America*, 1979.
J. F. Diehl, *Dickinson and the Romantic Imagination*, 1981.
R. W. Franklin, *The Manuscript Books of Emily Dickinson*, 1981.
R. Porter, *Dickinson, the Modern Idiom*, 1981.
S. Juhasz, *The Undiscovered Continent: Emily Dickinson and the Space of the Mind*, 1983.

Text:
The Poems of Emily Dickinson, ed. T. H. Johnson, 3 vols., 1953.

See also *The Letters of Emily Dickinson*, ed. T. H. Johnson and T. Ward, 1958.

185

"Faith" is a fine invention
When Gentlemen can *see*—
But *Microscopes* are prudent
In an Emergency.
1951

213

Did the Harebell loose her girdle
To the lover Bee
Would the Bee the Harebell *hallow*
Much as formerly?

Did the "Paradise"—persuaded—   5
Yield her moat of pearl—
Would the Eden *be* an Eden,
Or the Earl—an *Earl?*
1951

216

[Draft 1]

Safe in their Alabaster Chambers—
Untouched by Morning
And untouched by Noon—
Sleep the meek members of the Resurrection—
Rafter of satin,   5
And Roof of stone.

Light laughs the breeze
In her Castle above them—
Babbles the Bee in a stolid Ear,
Pipe the Sweet Birds in ignorant cadence—   10
Ah, what sagacity perished here!

1859/1951

[Draft 2]

Safe in their Alabaster Chambers—
Untouched by Morning—
And untouched by Noon—
Lie the meek members of the Resurrection—
Rafter of Satin—and Roof of Stone!   5

Grand go the Years—in the Crescent—above
    them—
Worlds scoop their Arcs—
And Firmaments—row—
Diadems—drop—and Doges'—surrender—
Soundless as dots—on a Disc of Snow—   10

1861/1951

241

I like a look of Agony,
Because I know it's true—
Men do not sham Convulsion,
Nor simulate, a Throe—

¹ Early chief magistrates of the Italian republics
of Venice and Genoa; in this context, rulers.

The Eyes glaze once—and that is Death—
Impossible to feign
The Beads upon the Forehead
By homely Anguish strung.
1951

254

"Hope" is the thing with feathers—
That perches in the soul—
And sings the tune without the words—
And never stops—at all—

And sweetest—in the Gale—is heard—   5
And sore must be the storm—
That could abash the little Bird
That kept so many warm—

I've heard it in the chillest land—
And on the strangest Sea—   10
Yet, never, in Extremity,
It asked a crumb—of Me.
1951

258

There's a certain Slant of light,
Winter Afternoons—
That oppresses, like the Heft
Of Cathedral Tunes—

Heavenly Hurt, it gives us—   5
We can find no scar,

But internal difference,
Where the Meanings, are—

None may teach it—Any—
'Tis the Seal Despair—   10
An imperial affliction
Sent us of the Air—

When it comes, the Landscape listens—
Shadows—hold their breath—
When it goes, 'tis like the Distance   15
On the look of Death—
1951

280

I felt a Funeral, in my Brain,
And Mourners to and fro
Kept treading—treading—till it seemed
That Sense was breaking through—

And when they all were seated,   5
A Service, like a Drum—
Kept beating—beating—till I thought
My Mind was going numb—

And then I heard them lift a Box
And creak across my Soul   10
With those same Boots of Lead, again,
Then Space—began to toll,

As all the Heavens were a Bell,
And Being, but an Ear,
And I, and Silence, some strange Race   15
Wrecked, solitary, here—

And then a Plank in Reason, broke,
And I dropped down, and down—
And hit a World, at every plunge,
And Finished knowing—then—   20
1951

290

Of Bronze—and Blaze—
The North—Tonight—
So adequate—it forms—
So preconcerted with itself
So distant—to alarms—   5
An Unconcern so sovreign
To Universe, or me—
Infects my simple spirit
With Taints of Majesty—
Till I take vaster attitudes—   10
And strut upon my stem—
Disdaining Men, and Oxygen,
For Arrogance of them—

My Splendors, are Menagerie—
But their Competeless Show   15
Will entertain the Centuries
When I, am long ago,
An Island in dishonored Grass—
Whom none but Daisies, know.
                                              1951

303

The Soul selects her own Society—
Then—shuts the Door—
To her divine Majority—
Present no more—

Unmoved—she notes the Chariots—pausing—   5
At her low Gate—
Unmoved—an Emperor be kneeling
Upon her Mat—

I've known her—from an ample nation—
Choose One—   10
Then—close the Valves of her attention—
Like Stone—
                                              1951

324

Some keep the Sabbath going to Church—
I keep it, staying at Home—
With a Bobolink for a Chorister—
And an Orchard, for a Dome—

Some keep the Sabbath in Surplice—   5
I just wear my Wings—
And instead of tolling the Bell, for Church,
Our little Sexton—sings.

God preaches, a noted Clergyman—
And the sermon is never long,   10
So instead of getting to Heaven at last—
I'm going, all along.

1951

327

Before I got my eye put out
I liked as well to see—
As other Creatures, that have Eyes
And know no other way—

But were it told to me—Today—   5
That I might have the sky
For mine—I tell you that my Heart
Would split, for size of me—

The Meadows—mine—
The Mountains—mine—   10
All Forests—Stintless Stars—
As much of Noon as I could take
Between my finite eyes—

The Motions of the Dipping Birds—
The Morning's Amber Road—   15
For mine—to look at when I liked—
The News would strike me dead—

So safer—guess—with just my soul
Upon the Window pane—
Where other Creatures put their eyes—   20
Incautious—of the Sun—

1951

332

There are two Ripenings—one—of sight—
Whose forces Spheric wind
Until the Velvet product
Drop spicy to the ground—
A homelier maturing—   5
A process in the Bur—
That teeth of Frosts alone disclose
In far October Air.

1951

338

I know that He exists.
Somewhere—in Silence—
He has hid his rare life
From our gross eyes.

'Tis an instant's play.   5
'Tis a fond Ambush—
Just to make Bliss
Earn her own surprise!

But—should the play
Prove piercing earnest—   10
Should the glee—glaze—
In Death's—stiff—stare—

Would not the fun
Look too expensive!
Would not the jest—   15
Have crawled too far!

1951

341

After great pain, a formal feeling comes—
The Nerves sit ceremonious, like Tombs—
The stiff Heart questions was it He, that bore,
And Yesterday, or Centuries before?

The Feet, mechanical, go round—   5
Of Ground, or Air, or Ought—
A Wooden way
Regardless grown,
A Quartz contentment, like a stone—

This is the Hour of Lead—   10
Remembered, if outlived,
As Freezing persons, recollect the Snow—
First—Chill—then Stupor—then the letting go—

1951

379

Rehearsal to Ourselves
Of a Withdrawn Delight—
Affords a Bliss like Murder—
Omnipotent—Acute—

We will not drop the Dirk'—   5
Because We love the Wound
The Dirk Commemorate—Itself
Remind Us that we died.

1951

---

¹ Dagger.

401

What Soft—Cherubic Creatures—
These Gentlewomen are—
One would as soon assault a Plush—
Or violate a Star—

Such Dimity Convictions—   5
A Horror so refined
Of freckled Human Nature—
Of Deity—ashamed—

It's such a common—Glory—
A Fisherman's—Degree—   10
Redemption—Brittle Lady—
Be so—ashamed of Thee—
1951

414

'Twas like a Maelstrom, with a notch,
That nearer, every Day,
Kept narrowing its boiling Wheel
Until the Agony

Toyed coolly with the final inch   5
Of your delirious Hem—
And you dropt, lost,
When something broke—
And let you from a Dream—

As if a Goblin with a Gauge—   10
Kept measuring the Hours—
Until you felt your Second
Weigh, helpless, in his Paws—

And not a Sinew—stirred—could help,
And sense was setting numb—   15
When God—remembered—and the Fiend
Let go, then, Overcome—

As if your Sentence stood—pronounced—
And you were frozen led
From Dungeon's luxury of Doubt   20
To Gibbets, and the Dead—

And when the Film had stitched your eyes
A Creature gasped "Reprieve"!
Which Anguish was the utterest—then—
To perish, or to live?
1951   25

435

Much Madness is divinest Sense—
To a discerning Eye—
Much Sense—the starkest Madness—
'Tis the Majority
In this, as All, prevail—   5
Assent—and you are sane—
Demur—you're straightway dangerous—
And handled with a Chain—
1951

441

This is my letter to the World
That never wrote to Me—
The simple News that Nature told—
With tender Majesty

Her Message is committed   5
To Hands I cannot see—
For love of Her—Sweet—countrymen—
Judge tenderly—of Me
1951

448

This was a Poet—It is That
Distills amazing sense
From ordinary Meanings—
And Attar[1] so immense

From the familiar species   5
That perished by the Door—
We wonder it was not Ourselves
Arrested it—before—

Of Pictures, the Discloser—
The Poet—it is He—   10
Entitles Us—by Contrast—
To ceaseless Poverty—

Of Portion—so unconscious—
The Robbing—could not harm—
Himself—to Him—a Fortune—   15
Exterior—to Time—

1951

449

I died for Beauty—but was scarce
Adjusted in the Tomb
When One who died for Truth, was lain
In an adjoining Room—

He questioned softly "Why I failed"?   5
"For Beauty", I replied—
"And I—for Truth—Themself are One—
We Brethren, are", He said—

[1] Distilled fragrance, usually concentrated and intense.

And so, as Kinsmen, met a Night—
We talked between the Rooms—   10
Until the Moss had reached our lips—
And covered up—our names—

1951

465

I heard a Fly buzz—when I died—
The Stillness in the Room
Was like the Stillness in the Air—
Between the Heaves of Storm—

The Eyes around—had wrung them dry—   5
And Breaths were gathering firm
For that last Onset—when the King
Be witnessed—in the Room—

I willed my Keepsakes—Signed away
What portion of me be   10
Assignable—and then it was
There interposed a Fly—

With Blue—uncertain stumbling Buzz—
Between the light—and me—
And then the Windows failed—and then   15
I could not see to see—

1951

510

It was not Death, for I stood up,
And all the Dead, lie down—
It was not Night, for all the Bells
Put out their Tongues, for Noon.

It was not Frost, for on my Flesh 5
I felt Siroccos'—crawl—
Nor Fire—for just my Marble feet
Could keep a Chancel, cool—

And yet, it tasted, like them all,
The Figures I have seen 10
Set orderly, for Burial,
Reminded me, of mine—

As if my life were shaven,
And fitted to a frame,
And could not breathe without a key, 15
And 'twas like Midnight, some—

When everything that ticked—has stopped—
And Space stares all around—
Or Grisly frosts—first Autumn morns,
Repeal the Beating Ground— 20

But, most, like Chaos—Stopless—cool—
Without a Chance, or Spar—
Or even a Report of Land—
To justify—Despair.
1951

536

The Heart asks Pleasure—first—
And then—Excuse from Pain—
And then—those little Anodynes
That deaden suffering—

And then—to go to sleep— 5
And then—if it should be
The will of its Inquisitor
The privilege to die—
1951

¹ Sirocco (Italian origin): hot, dry wind.

561

I measure every Grief I meet
With narrow, probing, Eyes—
I wonder if It weighs like Mine—
Or has an Easier size.

I wonder if They bore it long—   5
Or did it just begin—
I could not tell the Date of Mine—
It feels so old a pain—

I wonder if it hurts to live—
And if They have to try—   10
And whether—could They choose between—
It would not be—to die—

I note that Some—gone patient long—
At length, renew their smile—
An imitation of a Light   15
That has so little Oil—

I wonder if when Years have piled—
Some Thousands—on the Harm—
That hurt them early—such a lapse
Could give them any Balm—   20

Or would they go on aching still
Through Centuries of Nerve—
Enlightened to a larger Pain—
In Contrast with the Love—

The Grieved—are many—I am told—   25
There is the various Cause—
Death—is but one—and comes but once—
And only nails the eyes—

There's Grief of Want—and Grief of Cold—
A sort they call "Despair"—   30
There's Banishment from native Eyes—
In sight of Native Air—

And though I may not guess the kind—
Correctly—yet to me
A piercing Comfort it affords   3:
In passing Calvary[1]—

To note the fashions—of the Cross—
And how they're mostly worn—
Still fascinated to presume
That Some—are like My Own—   40
1951

569

I reckon—when I count at all—
First—Poets—Then the Sun—
Then Summer—Then the Heaven of God—
And then—the List is done—

But, looking back—the First so seems   5
To Comprehend the Whole—
The Others look a needless Show—
So I write—Poets—All—

Their Summer—lasts a Solid Year—
They can afford a Sun   10
The East—would deem extravagant—
And if the Further Heaven—

Be Beautiful as they prepare
For Those who worship Them—
It is too difficult a Grace—   15
To justify the Dream—
1951

[1] The hill on which Jesus was crucified.

632

The Brain—is wider than the Sky—
For—put them side by side—
The one the other will contain
With ease—and You—beside—

The Brain is deeper than the sea—   5
For—hold them—Blue to Blue—
The one the other will absorb—
As Sponges—Buckets—do—

The Brain is just the weight of God—
For—Heft them—Pound for Pound—   10
And they will differ—if they do—
As Syllable from Sound—

1951

640

I cannot live with You—
It would be Life—
And Life is over there—
Behind the Shelf

The Sexton keeps the Key to—   5
Putting up
Our Life—His Porcelain—
Like a Cup—

Discarded of the Housewife—
Quaint—or Broke—   10
A newer Sevres[1] pleases—
Old Ones crack—

I could not die—with You—
For One must wait

---

[1] Porcelain made in the town of Sèvres, France.

To shut the Other's Gaze down—   15
You—could not—

And I—Could I stand by
And see You—freeze—
Without my Right of Frost—
Death's privilege?   20

Nor could I rise—with You—
Because Your Face
Would put out Jesus'—
That New Grace

Glow plain—and foreign   25
On my homesick Eye—
Except that You than He
Shone closer by—

They'd judge Us—How—
For You—served Heaven—You know,   30
Or sought to—
I could not—

Because You saturated Sight—
And I had no more Eyes
For sordid excellence   35
As Paradise

And were You lost, I would be—
Though My Name
Rang loudest
On the Heavenly fame—   40

And were You—saved—
And I—condemned to be
Where You were not—
That self—were Hell to Me—

So We must meet apart—   45
You there—I—here—
With just the Door ajar
That Oceans are—and Prayer—
And that White Sustenance—
Despair—   50

1951

650

Pain—has an Element of Blank—
It cannot recollect
When it begun—or if there were
A time when it was not—

It has no Future—but itself—   5
Its Infinite contain
Its Past—enlightened to perceive
New Periods—of Pain.
1951

657

I dwell in Possibility—
A fairer House than Prose—
More numerous of Windows—
Superior—for Doors—

Of Chambers as the Cedars—   5
Impregnable of Eye—
And for an Everlasting Roof
The Gambrels of the Sky—

Of Visitors—the fairest—
For Occupation—This—   10
The spreading wide my narrow Hands
To gather Paradise—
1951

664

Of all the Souls that stand create—
I have elected—One—
When Sense from Spirit—files away—
And Subterfuge—is done—
When that which is—and that which was— 5
Apart—instrinsic—stand—
And this brief Drama in the flesh—
Is shifted—like a Sand—
When Figures show their royal Front—
And Mists—are carved away, 10
Behold the Atom—I preferred—
To all the lists of Clay!

1951

670

One need not be a Chamber—to be Haunted—
One need not be a House—
The Brain has Corridors—surpassing
Material Place—

Far safer, of a Midnight Meeting 5
External Ghost
Than its interior Confronting—
That Cooler Host.

Far safer, through an Abbey gallop,
The Stones a'chase— 10
Than Unarmed, one's a'self encounter—
In lonesome Place—

Ourself behind ourself, concealed—
Should startle most—
Assassin hid in our Apartment 15
Be Horror's least.

The Body—borrows a Revolver—
He bolts the Door—
O'erlooking a superior spectre—
Or More—   20

1951

675

Essential Oils—are wrung—
The Attar¹ from the Rose
Be not expressed by Suns—alone—
It is the gift of Screws—

The General Rose—decay—   5
But this—in Lady's Drawer
Make Summer—When the Lady lie
In Ceaseless Rosemary—

1951

712

Because I could not stop for Death—
He kindly stopped for me—
The Carriage held but just Ourselves—
And Immortality.

We slowly drove—He knew no haste   5
And I had put away
My labor and my leisure too,
For His Civility—

We passed the School, where Children strove
At Recess—in the Ring—   10
We passed the Fields of Gazing Grain—
We passed the Setting Sun—

¹ Distilled fragrance, usually concentrated and
intense; perfume.

Or rather—He passed Us—
The Dews drew quivering and chill—
For only Gossamer, my Gown—   15
My Tippet¹—only Tulle—

We paused before a House that seemed
A Swelling of the Ground—
The Roof was scarcely visible—
The Cornice—in the Ground—   20

Since then—'tis Centuries—and yet
Feels shorter than the Day
I first surmised the Horses' Heads
Were toward Eternity—
1951

721

Behind Me—dips Eternity—
Before Me—Immortality—
Myself—the Term between—
Death but the Drift of Eastern Gray,
Dissolving into Dawn away,   5
Before the West begin—

'Tis Kingdoms—afterward—they say—
In perfect—pauseless Monarchy—
Whose Prince—is Son of None—
Himself—His Dateless Dynasty—   10
Himself—Himself diversify—
In Duplicate divine¹—

'Tis Miracle before Me—then—
'Tis Miracle behind—between—
A Crescent in the Sea—   15
With Midnight to the North of Her—
And Midnight to the South of Her—
And Maelstrom—in the Sky—
1951

¹ Short shoulder cape or scarf.
¹ Reference to the Christian doctrine of the
Trinity, which states that the Son issues from
the Father, and the Holy Spirit from the union
of Father and Son.

745

Renunciation—is a piercing Virtue—
The letting go
A Presence—for an Expectation—
Not now—
The putting out of Eyes—   5
Just Sunrise—
Lest Day—
Day's Great Progenitor—
Outvie—
Renunciation—is the Choosing   10
Against itself—
Itself to justify
Unto itself—
When larger function—
Make that appear—   15
Smaller—that Covered Vision—Here—

1951

754

My Life had stood—a Loaded Gun—
In Corners—till a Day
The Owner passed—identified—
And carried Me away—

And now We roam in Sovereign Woods—   5
And now We hunt the Doe—
And every time I speak for Him—
The Mountains straight reply—

And do I smile, such cordial light
Upon the Valley glow—   10
It is as a Vesuvian[1] face
Had let its pleasure through—

[1] Reference to Mount Vesuvius, the famous
volcano on the Bay of Naples.

And when at Night—Our good Day done—
I guard My Master's Head—
'Tis better than the Eider-Duck's
Deep Pillow[2]—to have shared—

To foe of His—I'm deadly foe—
None stir the second time—
On whom I lay a Yellow Eye—
Or an emphatic Thumb—

Though I than He—may longer live
He longer must—than I—
For I have but the power to kill,
Without—the power to die—

1951

764

Presentiment—is that long Shadow—on the Lawn—
Indicative that Suns go down—

The Notice to the startled Grass
That Darkness—is about to pass—

1951

812

A Light exists in Spring
Not present on the Year
At any other period—
When March is scarcely here

A Color stands abroad
On Solitary Fields

[2] I.e., filled with soft feathers.

That Science cannot overtake
But Human Nature feels.

It waits upon the Lawn,
It shows the furthest Tree   10
Upon the furthest Slope you know
It almost speaks to you.

Then as Horizons step
Or Noons report away
Without the Formula of sound   15
It passes and we stay—

A quality of loss
Affecting our Content
As Trade had suddenly encroached
Upon a Sacrament.   20
1951

910

Experience is the Angled Road
Preferred against the Mind
By—Paradox—the Mind itself—
Presuming it to lead

Quite Opposite—How Complicate   5
The Discipline of Man—
Compelling Him to Choose Himself
His Preappointed Pain—
1951

986

A narrow Fellow in the Grass
Occasionally rides—
You may have met Him—did you not
His notice sudden is—

The Grass divides as with a Comb— 5
A spotted shaft is seen—
And then it closes at your feet
And opens further on—

He likes a Boggy Acre
A Floor too cool for Corn— 10
Yet when a Boy, and Barefoot—
I more than once at Noon
Have passed, I thought, a Whip lash
Unbraiding in the Sun
When stooping to secure it 15
It wrinkled, and was gone—

Several of Nature's People
I know, and they know me—
I feel for them a transport
Of cordiality— 20

But never met this Fellow
Attended, or alone
Without a tighter breathing
And Zero at the Bone—
1951

997

Crumbling is not an instant's Act
A fundamental pause
Dilapidation's processes
Are organized Decays.

'Tis first a Cobweb on the Soul 5
A Cuticle of Dust
A Borer in the Axis
An Elemental Rust—

Ruin is formal—Devil's work
Consecutive and slow— 10
Fail in an instant, no man did
Slipping—is Crash's law.
1951

1052

I never saw a Moor—
I never saw the Sea—
Yet know I how the Heather looks
And what a Billow be.

I never spoke with God   5
Nor visited in Heaven—
Yet certain am I of the spot
As if the Checks¹ were given—

1951

1062

He scanned it—staggered—
Dropped the Loop
To Past or Period—
Caught helpless at a sense as if
His Mind were going blind—   5

Groped up, to see if God was there—
Groped backward at Himself
Caressed a Trigger absently
And wandered out of Life.

1951

1068

Further in Summer than the Birds
Pathetic from the Grass
A minor Nation celebrates
Its unobtrusive Mass.

---

¹ Railway tickets.

No Ordinance be seen 5
So gradual the Grace
A pensive Custom it becomes
Enlarging Loneliness.

Antiquest felt at Noon
When August burning low 10
Arise this spectral Canticle
Repose to typify

Remit as yet no Grace
No Furrow on the Glow
Yet a Druidic Difference 15
Enhances Nature now
1951

1071

Perception of an object costs
Precise the Object's loss—
Perception in itself a Gain
Replying to its Price—

The Object Absolute—is nought— 5
Perception sets it fair
And then upbraids a Perfectness
That situates so far—
1951

1100

The last Night that She lived
It was a Common Night
Except the Dying—this to Us
Made Nature different

We noticed smallest things—   5
Things overlooked before
By this great light upon our Minds
Italicized—as 'twere.

As We went out and in
Between Her final Room   10
And Rooms where Those to be alive
Tomorrow were, a Blame

That Others could exist
While She must finish quite
A Jealousy for Her arose   15
So nearly infinite—

We waited while She passed—
It was a narrow time—
Too jostled were Our Souls to speak
At length the notice came.   20

She mentioned, and forgot—
Then lightly as a Reed
Bent to the Water, struggled scarce—
Consented, and was dead—

And We—We placed the Hair—   25
And drew the Head erect—
And then an awful leisure was
Belief to regulate—

1951

1126

Shall I take thee, the Poet said
To the propounded word?
Be stationed with the Candidates
Till I have finer tried—

The Poet searched Philology   5
And when about to ring
For the suspended Candidate
There came unsummoned in—

That portion of the Vision
The Word applied to fill
Not unto nomination
The Cherubim[1] reveal—

1951

1129

Tell all the Truth but tell it slant—
Success in Circuit lies
Too bright for our infirm Delight
The Truth's superb surprise

As Lightning to the Children eased
With explanation kind
The Truth must dazzle gradually
Or every man be blind—

1951

1177

A prompt—executive Bird is the Jay—
Bold as a Bailiff's Hymn—
Brittle and Brief in quality—
Warrant in every line—

Sitting a Bough like a Brigadier
Confident and straight—
Much is the mien of him in March
As a Magistrate—

1951

[1] The angels who guard the throne of God.

1212

A word is dead
When it is said,
Some say.
I say it just
Begins to live   5
That day.
1951

1282

[Draft 1]

Art thou the thing I wanted?
Begone—my Tooth has grown—
Supply the minor Palate
That has not starved so long—
I tell thee while I waited   5
The mystery of Food
Increased till I abjured it
And dine without Like God—
1873?/1951

[Draft 2]

Art thou the thing I wanted?
Begone—my Tooth has grown—
Affront a minor palate
Thou could'st not goad so long—

I tell thee while I waited—   5
The mystery of Food
Increased till I abjured it
Subsisting now like God—
1873?/1951

1393

Lay this Laurel[1] on the One
Too intrinsic for Renown—
Laurel—veil your deathless tree—
Him you chasten, that is He!
1951

1540

As imperceptibly as Grief
The Summer lapsed away—
Too imperceptible at last
To seem like Perfidy—
A Quietness distilled   5
As Twilight long begun,
Or Nature spending with herself
Sequestered Afternoon—
The Dusk drew earlier in—
The Morning foreign shone—   10
A courteous, yet harrowing Grace,
As Guest, that would be gone—
And thus, without a Wing
Or service of a Keel
Our Summer made her light escape   15
Into the Beautiful.
1951

[1] Traditionally, a laurel wreath signified honor
and immortality.

1545

The Bible is an antique Volume—
Written by faded Men
At the suggestion of Holy Spectres[1]—
Subjects—Bethlehem—
Eden—the ancient Homestead—   5
Satan—the Brigadier—
Judas—the Great Defaulter—
David—the Troubadour[2]—
Sin—a distinguished Precipice
Others must resist—   10
Boys that "believe" are very lonesome—
Other Boys are "lost"—
Had but the Tale a warbling Teller—
All the Boys would come—
Orpheus' Sermon captivated[3]—   15
It did not condemn—

1951

1593

There came a Wind like a Bugle—
It quivered through the Grass
And a Green Chill upon the Heat
So ominous did pass
We barred the Windows and the Doors   5
As from an Emerald Ghost—
The Doom's electric Moccasin[1]
That very instant passed—
On a strange Mob of panting Trees
And Fences fled away   10
And Rivers where the Houses ran

---

[1] The Holy Spirit is said to be the inspirer of the authors of the Bible.
[2] Beginning in line 4 Dickinson enumerates, out of order, the fall of Satan and his rebel angels, the creation of Man in Eden, Original Sin and the Fall, the composition of the Psalms by King David, the birth of Jesus in Bethlehem, and the betrayal of Jesus by Judas.
[3] In mythology, when Orpheus played his lyre and sang, trees and rocks danced, and all the animals came to listen.
[1] Soft leather shoe worn by American Indians.

Those looked that lived—that Day—
The Bell within the steeple wild
The flying tidings told—
How much can come
And much can go,   15
And yet abide the World!

1951

1624

Apparently with no surprise
To any happy Flower
The Frost beheads it at its play—
In accidental power—
The blonde Assassin passes on—   5
The Sun proceeds unmoved
To measure off another Day
For an Approving God.

1951

1651

A Word made Flesh[1] is seldom
And tremblingly partook[2]
Nor then perhaps reported
But have I not mistook
Each one of us has tasted   5
With ecstasies of stealth
The very food debated[3]
To our specific strength—

---

[1] "And the Word was made flesh and dwelt among us," are St. John's words for the Incarnation of Christ. (See John 1:14.)
[2] In the Christian rite of Holy Communion, believers "partake" of the bread and wine, symbols of Jesus' body and blood, respectively.
[3] Determined by discussion to be accurate.

A Word that breathes distinctly
Has not the power to die   10
Cohesive as the Spirit
It may expire if He—
"Made Flesh and dwelt among us"
Could condescension[4] be
Like this consent of Language   15
This loved Philology.

1951

1670

In Winter in my Room
I came upon a Worm—
Pink, lank and warm—
But as he was a worm
And worms presume   5
Not quite with him at home—
Secured him by a string
To something neighboring
And went along.

A Trifle afterward   10
A thing occurred
I'd not believe it if I heard
But state with creeping blood—
A snake with mottles rare
Surveyed my chamber floor   15
In feature as the worm before
But ringed with power—
The very string with which
I tied him—too
When he was mean and new   20
That string was there—

I shrank—"How fair you are"!
Propitiation's claw—
"Afraid," he hissed
"Of me"?   25

---

[4] Used theologically to signify Christ's descent
from the Godhead into flesh.

"No cordiality"—
He fathomed me—
Then to a Rhythm *Slim*
Secreted in his Form
As Patterns swim   30
Projected him.

That time I flew
Both eyes his way
Lest he pursue
Nor ever ceased to run   35
Till in a distant Town
Towns on from mine
I set me down
This was a dream.
1951

1732

My life closed twice before its close—
It yet remains to see
If Immortality unveil
A third event to me

So huge, so hopeless to conceive   5
As these that twice befell.
Parting is all we know of heaven,
And all we need of hell.
1951

1755

To make a prairie it takes a clover and one bee,
One clover, and a bee,
And revery.
The revery alone will do,
If bees are few.   5
1951

1760

Elysium[1] is as far as to
The very nearest Room
If in that Room a Friend await
Felicity or Doom—

What fortitude the Soul contains,   5
That it can so endure
The accent of a coming Foot—
The opening of a Door—

1951

Mark Twain
1835–1910

Mark Twain (born Samuel Longhorne Clemens) looked back with longing to
what he recalled as the innocence, simplicity, and rectitude of pre–Gold Rush
America. Yet no other writer partook so hungrily of the wealth, status, fame,
and other rewards that the Gilded Age offered. A divided sensibility who
alternately craved attention and solitude, he lived on the scale of a prince of
industry or banking in New York, Hartford, and the great cities of Europe while
his imagination remained tied to the drowsing villages of the Mississippi River
valley. The words "when I was a boy" were his mantra, with magical power to
unlock memory and emotion. "The part of him that was Western in his
Southwestern origin Clemens kept to the end," recalled William Dean Howells,
his friend for over forty years, "but he was the most desouthernized Southerner I
ever knew." Out of such oppositions came one of the dominating prose styles of
American literature, half a dozen of its classics, and an incomparably attractive
public voice and personality.

Caught up in the westward tide of expansion, Samuel Clemens's parents, poor
but blood-proud Virginia gentry, settled along what was then the southwestern
frontier, first in the crossroads hamlet of Florida, Missouri, where he was born in
1835, and four years later in Hannibal. His father, a justice of the peace, failed in
the law, shopkeeping, land speculation, and ventures in slave trading. The boy
left school at *twelve to earn* his living; he worked in a printing office and wrote
occasional newspaper items, burlesques, and humorous sketches. "One isn't a
printer ten years," he was to recall, "without setting up acres of good and bad

[1] Mythological equivalent to the Christian
heaven.

literature, and learning—unconsciously at first, consciously later—to discriminate between the two, within his mental limitations; and meanwhile he is consciously acquiring what is called a 'style.' " But he also realized the boyhood ambition he was to write about in *Old Times on the Mississippi:* In 1859, after two years of "cubbing," he earned a pilot's license and stood in princely grandeur in the wheelhouse of a river steamboat.

The coming of the Civil War put an end to this occupation and to commercial traffic on the river. Young Clemens spent a few grim weeks in the field as a Confederate irregular (an experience considerably embroidered in "The Private History of a Campaign That Failed") before going West to try his hand at prospecting in the Nevada Territory and California. While working as reporter on the *Virginia City Territorial Enterprise,* he settled finally on his vocation: "seriously scribbling to excite the *laughter* of God's creatures." He was to learn that the punishing thing about laughter is that people refuse to take it seriously, even though, as he argued time and again, laughter was a supreme moral weapon. All his life he felt compelled to defend his profession, to segregate the noun *humorist* from the adjective *mere* and the synonym *clown.* Reciprocally, Americans of his time tended to cherish him as entertainer alone and, as soon as the smiles faded from their faces, trivialize his genius and irony, his moral passion and assaults on conventional wisdom.

In 1865, two years after Samuel Clemens's pseudonym "Mark Twain" appeared in print for the first time, he published "The Notorious Jumping Frog of Calaveras County." Although he once dismissed it as "a villainous backwoods sketch," the "Jumping Frog" is a brilliant experiment in narrative technique, point of view, and language. It points the way to the tales that make up much of *Roughing It* (1872), Mark Twain's account of his life in the West, and to *Adventures of Huckleberry Finn* (1885).

With *The Innocents Abroad* (1869), a humorous travel narrative that held Europe and the Holy Land up to American standards but was equally unsparing about America, Mark Twain first established himself as a popular author. His books, sold by door-to-door salesmen taking orders in advance of publication, reached a broad, nonliterary audience, typically the families of tradesmen, farmers, and small-town professionals. His royalties (he figured that *The Innocents Abroad* sold some 100,000 copies in two years) were supplemented by his earnings as one of the rising stars of the lecture circuit, successor to Artemus Ward. He owned and edited a daily newspaper in Buffalo, New York, and married Olivia Langdon, heiress to a coal fortune, after a courtship that he made part of the folklore of love in America: "I saw her first in the form of an ivory miniature. . . ."

In 1871 they moved to Hartford, midway in values as well as distance between two literary capitals in transition, New York and Boston. They rented, and soon built, a house at Nook Farm, a tightly knit, high-minded enclave of writers and intellectuals that included Harriet Beecher Stowe and Charles Dudley Warner. *The Gilded Age* (1873), a novel Mark Twain wrote in collaboration with Warner, fed rather than exorcised his growing anger at American society and institutions. In time he would be regarded as a spokesman for American democracy, for what he called "the mighty mass of the uncultivated" instead of "the thin top crust of humanity." But during the 1870s, believing that the

American system had broken down, he raged against universal suffrage, the jury system, and what he saw as an "era of incredible rottenness." He crossed the Atlantic to "breathe the free air of Europe," indulge his worship of all things English (the English, in turn, lionized him), and write another travel book, *A Tramp Abroad* (1880). *The Gilded Age,* subtitled "A Tale of Today," helped turn his mind toward the more malleable yesterdays of *Old Times on the Mississippi* (1875), *The Adventures of Tom Sawyer* (1876), and *The Prince and the Pauper* (1882), the last a concession to genteel taste.

In 1884, after eight years of intermittent struggles with plot problems, Mark Twain completed his masterpiece, *Adventures of Huckleberry Finn.* He wrote this realistic, satiric, yet lyrical novel in the southwestern vernacular from the first-person point of view of an unlettered boy at the bottom of the white social order. "It's the best book we've had," Ernest Hemingway wrote in 1935. T. S. Eliot said Mark Twain discovered "a new way of writing" that brought literary language "up to date." But though it has now been read in millions of copies and become a fixture in world literature, *Huckleberry Finn,* like *Leaves of Grass,* entered the world under a cloud of disapproval. Demanding refined language, exemplary heroes, and elevating morals, guardians of the genteel tradition inevitably found Mark Twain's book coarse, vulgar, and immoral. In 1885 the trustees of the Concord (Massachusetts) Public Library expelled the book from their shelves as "trash and suitable only for the slums." Today, *Huckleberry Finn,* a passionately humanitarian and antiracist book, often comes under fire because readers misunderstand Mark Twain's language, his portrayal of the fugitive slave Jim, and the irony framing and shaping the entire narrative.

At fifty it seemed that Mark Twain was blessed with everything: overflowing creative energies, as *Huckleberry Finn* demonstrated; domestic happiness; world fame and social eminence; friendships with Howells and other writers; wealth; and an eye-catching brick-and-brownstone mansion—part steamboat, part medieval stronghold, part cuckoo clock—that was one of Hartford's curiosities. The house at 351 Farmington Avenue, now maintained as a memorial to its owner, served as a reminder of how far he had traveled from a clapboard dwelling "the size of a birdhouse" in Hannibal. He invested heavily in speculative business ventures. One was a New York subscription publishing house, Charles L. Webster & Company, which, in addition to Mark Twain's own books, issued *Personal Memoirs of U. S. Grant* (1885), a huge commercial success. It earned the general's widow about half a million dollars in royalties but misled Mark Twain into expecting even bigger bonanzas. Over the course of about fifteen years he also poured steadily increasing amounts of money and faith into James W. Paige's automatic typesetting machine, a device timely in concept but committed to impossibly expensive standards of perfection and hopeless competition with Ottmar Mergenthaler's superior Linotype.

The anarchic impulses unleashed in *A Connecticut Yankee in King Arthur's Court* (1889)—the book ends with a massacre and a rejection of new and old values alike—reflect Mark Twain's anguish and frustration during this period. After the final collapse of both typesetter and publishing house in 1894, he filed for bankruptcy. He copyrighted his new novel, *Pudd'nhead Wilson,* in his wife's name to keep it out of the hands of creditors. To pay off his debts he traveled to

Australia, New Zealand, India, and South Africa on a yearlong lecture tour. He was the most famous American author in the world. People in India knew only three things about the United States, he noted—"George Washington, Mark Twain, and the Chicago Fair." He had settled in England to write a book about his journey around the world, *Following the Equator* (1897), when he learned by cable from Hartford that his favorite daughter had died of meningitis.

"It is one of the mysteries of our nature," Mark Twain was to reflect, "that a man, all unprepared, can receive a thunder-stroke like that and live." For a while he walked the edge of madness in a self-induced dream state that he hoped would reveal to him where and why he had gone wrong. He worked on a series of unfinished and perhaps unfinishable symbolic stories, voyage and dream narratives characterized by dislocations of time, place, and scale. These stories of the "Great Dark" (collected and published in 1967 as *Which Was the Dream?*) deal with guilt, responsibility, and identity. They are reminders that this humorist and realist, so anchored in the particularities and textures of day-to-day existence, also sailed the spectral seas of Poe, Hawthorne, and Melville. ("Everyone is a moon," he said, "and has a dark side which he never shows to anybody.") He survived the crisis narrowly enough to give unintended irony to the statement he released to the press from London in 1897, "The report of my death was an exaggeration."

To the end of his days Mark Twain argued that personality was merely a machine driven by self-interest and the craving for approval, a doctrine he elaborated in his "bible," *What Is Man?* (first published, anonymously, in 1906). Like "The Man That Corrupted Hadleyburg" (1899), much of his late work is marked by moral and logical clarity instead of a rich sprawl of incident and anecdote. To get his juices flowing he relied on progressively larger jolts of indignation directed at God, orthodox Christianity, Mary Baker Eddy (founder of Christian Science), imperialism, racism, lynching, the martial spirit, and "corn-pone opinions" in general. His preferred forms were polemics, satire, and, above all, personal reminiscence. Mark Twain's free-form autobiography, in manuscript a million words or more of written and dictated prose, is the major work of his last years. Its chief unifying principle is the accent and rhythm and attack of his voice. (Ostensibly an integral work of Twain's last years, *The Mysterious Stranger,* published after his death, has proved to be a textual pastiche put together by his editor and his literary executor.)

Restored to financial health, Mark Twain moved back to the United States in 1900. (He had lived abroad for approximately half of the previous twenty-two years.) The ovation that welcomed him continued until his death in 1910. "The Hero as Man of Letters," newspaper editorials said, had emerged from bankruptcy with "unsullied honor." "The most conspicuous person on the planet," he was the idol of New York society and of plutocrats like the steelmaster Andrew Carnegie and Henry H. Rogers of the Standard Oil Trust; a spellbinding after-dinner speaker; a leading voice in the anti-imperialist movement; the most quotable public personality of his time; a master showman who wore white suits winter and summer, flaunted his shock of white hair, and made it a rule "never to smoke when asleep, and never to refrain when awake." In 1902 he revisited Missouri, "a great and beautiful country," for the last time and imagined Tom and Huck coming home to Hannibal old and withered. Five years later he journeyed to England to receive the degree of Doctor of Letters from Oxford University. For this honor, to himself and to the profession of humor, he said he would have been willing to "journey to Mars." He died in 1910 at Stormfield, his Italianate villa perched on a hilltop in Redding, Connecticut. He had built this last home with the proceeds from his serialized autobiography.

"Emerson, Longfellow, Lowell, Holmes—" Howells wrote in his memoir, *My Mark Twain,* "I knew them all and all the rest of our sages, poets, seers, critics, humorists; they were like one another and like other literary men; but Clemens was sole, incomparable, the Lincoln of our literature."

Further Reading:
W. D. Howells, *My Mark Twain,* 1910.
A. B. Paine, *Mark Twain: A Biography,* 3 vols., 1912.
V. Brooks, *The Ordeal of Mark Twain,* 1920.
B. DeVoto, *Mark Twain's America,* 1932.
K. Andrews, *Nook Farm: Mark Twain's Hartford Circle,* 1950.
E. Branch, *The Literary Apprenticeship of Mark Twain,* 1950.
D. Wecter, *Sam Clemens of Hannibal,* 1952.
E. H. Long, *Mark Twain Handbook,* 1957.
P. Fatout, *Mark Twain on the Lecture Circuit,* 1960.
W. Blair, *Mark Twain and Huck Finn,* 1960.
H. N. Smith, *Mark Twain: The Development of a Writer,* 1962.
J. M. Cox, *Mark Twain: The Fate of Humor,* 1966.
J. Kaplan, *Mr. Clemens and Mark Twain,* 1966.
H. Hill, *Mark Twain, God's Fool,* 1973.
L. J. Budd, *Our Mark Twain: The Making of His Public Personality,* 1983.

Texts:
"The Notorious Jumping Frog of Calaveras County," *Mark Twain's Sketches,* 1875.
Roughing It, 1872.
Old Times on the Mississippi, in the *Atlantic Monthly,* 1875.
"The Story of a Speech," "The Private History of a Campaign That Failed," "Fenimore Cooper's Literary Offenses," and "Corn-Pone Opinions" from *The Writings of Mark Twain,* 37 vols., ed. A. B. Paine, 1922–1925.
See also *The Mark Twain Papers,* ed. F. Anderson et al., 1967–.
The Works of Mark Twain, ed. J. Gerber et al., 1972–.

The Notorious Jumping Frog
of Calaveras County

In compliance with the request of a friend of mine, who wrote me from the East, I called on good-natured, garrulous old Simon Wheeler, and inquired after my friend's friend, Leonidas W. Smiley, as requested to do, and I hereunto append the result. I have a lurking suspicion that *Leonidas W.* Smiley is a myth; that my friend never knew such a personage; and that he only conjectured that if I asked old Wheeler about him. it would remind him of his infamous *Jim* Smiley, and he would go to work and bore me to death with some exasperating reminiscence of him as long and as tedious as it should be useless to me. If that was the design, it succeeded.

I found Simon Wheeler dozing comfortably by the bar-room stove of the dilapidated tavern in the decayed mining camp of Angel's, and I noticed that he was fat and bald-headed, and had an expression of winning gentleness and simplicity upon his tranquil countenance. He roused up, and gave me good-day. I told him a friend of mine had commissioned me to make some inquiries about a cherished companion of his boyhood named *Leondias W.* Smiley—*Rev. Leondias W.* Smiley, a young minister of the Gospel, who he had heard was at one time a resident of Angel's Camp. I added that if Mr. Wheeler could tell me anything about this Rev. Leonidas W. Smiley, I would feel under many obligations to him.

Simon Wheeler backed me into a corner and blockaded me there with his chair, and then sat down and reeled off the monotonous narrative which follows this paragraph. He never smiled, he never frowned, he never changed his voice from the gentle-flowing key to which he tuned his initial sentence, he never betrayed the slightest suspicion of enthusiasm; but all through the interminable narrative there ran a vein of impressive earnestness and sincerity, which showed me plainly that, so far from his imagining that there was anything ridiculous or funny about his story, he regarded it as a really important matter, and admired its two heroes as men of transcendent genius in *finesse.* I let him go on in his own way, and never interrupted him once.

"Rev. Leonidas W. H'm, Reverend Le—well, there was a feller here once by the name of *Jim* Smiley, in the winter of '49—or may be it was the spring of '50—I don't recollect exactly, somehow, though what makes me think it was one or the other is because I remember the big flume warn't finished when he first come to the camp; but any way, he was the curiosest man about always betting on anything that turned up you ever see, if he could get anybody to bet on the other side; and if he couldn't he'd change sides. Any way that suited the other man would suit *him*—any way just so's he got a bet, *he* was satisfied. But still he was lucky, uncommon lucky; he most always come out winner. He was always ready and laying for a chance; there couldn't be no solit'ry thing mentioned but that feller'd offer to bet on it, and take ary side you please, as I was just telling you. If there was a horse-race, you'd find him flush or you'd find him busted at the end of it; if there was a dog-fight, he'd bet on it; if there was a cat-fight, he'd bet on it; if there was a chicken-fight, he'd bet on it; why, if there was two birds setting on a fence, he would bet you which one would fly first; or if there was a camp-meeting, he would be there reg'lar to bet on Parson Walker, which he judged to be the best exhorter about here, and so he was too, and a good man. If he even see a straddle-bug start to go anywheres, he would bet you how long it would take him to get to—to wherever he was going to, and if you took him up, he would foller that straddle-bug to Mexico but what he would find out where he was bound for and how long he was on the road. Lots of the boys here has seen that Smiley, and can tell you about him. Why, it never made no difference to *him*—he'd bet on *any* thing—the dangdest feller. Parson Walker's wife laid very sick once, for a good while, and it seemed as if they warn't going to save her; but one morning he come in, and Smiley up and asked him how she was, and he said she was considable better—thank the Lord for his inf'nit mercy—and coming on so smart that with the blessing of Prov'dence she'd get well yet; and Smiley, before he thought says, "Well, I'll resk two-and-a-half she don't anyway."

Thish-yer Smiley had a mare—the boys called her the fifteen-minute nag, but that was only in fun, you know, because of course she was faster than that—and he used to win money on that horse, for all she was so slow and always had the asthma, or the distemper, or the consumption, or something of that kind. They used to give her two or three hundred yards' start, and then pass her under way; but always at the fag-end of the race she'd get excited and desperate-like, and come cavorting and straddling up, and scattering her legs around limber, sometimes in the air, and sometimes out to one side amongst the fences, and kicking up m-o-r-e dust and raising m-o-r-e racket with her coughing and sneezing and blowing her nose— and *always* fetch up at the stand just about a neck ahead, as near as you could cipher it down.

And he had a little small bull-pup, that to look at him you'd think he warn't worth a cent but to set around and look ornery and lay for a chance to steal something. But as soon as money was up on him he was a different dog; his under-jaw'd begin to stick out like the fo'castle of a steamboat, and his teeth would uncover and shine like the furnaces. And a dog might tackle him and bully-rag him, and bite him, and throw him over his shoulder two or three times, and Andrew Jackson—which was the name of the pup—Andrew Jackson would never let on but what *he* was satisfied, and hadn't expected nothing else—and the bets being doubled and doubled on the other side all the time, till the money was all up; and then all of a sudden he would grab that other dog jest by the j'int of his hind leg and freeze to it—not chaw, you understand, but only just grip and hang on till they throwed up the sponge, if it was a year. Smiley always come out winner on that pup, till he harnessed a dog once that didn't have no hind legs, because they'd been sawed off in a circular saw, and when the thing had gone along far enough, and the money was all up, and he come to make a snatch for his pet holt, he see in a minute how he'd been imposed on, and how the other dog had him in the door, so to speak, and he 'peared surprised, and then he looked sorter discouraged-like, and didn't try no more to win the fight, and so he got shucked out bad. He give Smiley a look, as much as to say his heart was broke, and it was *his* fault, for putting up a dog that hadn't no hind legs for him to take holt of, which was his main dependence in a fight, and then he limped off a piece and laid down and died. It was a good pup, was that Andrew Jackson, and would have made a name for hisself if he'd lived, for the stuff was in him and he had genius—I know it, because he hadn't no opportunities to speak of, and it don't stand to reason that a dog could make such a fight as he could under them circumstances if he hadn't no talent. It always makes me feel sorry when I think of that last fight of his'n, and the way it turned out.

Well, thish-yer Smiley had rat-terriers, and chicken cocks, and tom-cats and all them kind of things, till you couldn't rest, and you couldn't fetch nothing for him to bet on but he'd match you. He ketched a frog one day, and took him home, and said he cal'lated to educate him; and so he never done nothing for three months but set in his back-yard and learn that frog to jump. And you bet you he *did* learn him, too. He'd give him a little punch behind, and the next minute you'd see that frog whirling in the air like a doughnut—see him turn one summerset, or may be a couple, if he got a good start, and come down flat-footed and all right, like a cat. He got him up so in the ma'ter of ketching flies, and kep' him in practice so constant, that he'd nail a fly every time as fur as he could see him. Smiley said all a frog wanted was education, and he could do 'most anything—and I believe him. Why, I've seen him set Dan'l Webster down here on this floor—Dan'l Webster was the name of the frog—and sing out, "Flies, Dan'l, flies!" and quicker'n you could wink he'd spring straight up and snake a fly off'n the counter there, and flop down on the floor ag'in as solid as a gob of mud, and fall to scratching the side of his head with his hind foot as indifferent as if he hadn't no idea he'd been doin' any more'n any frog might do. You never see a frog so modest and straightfor'ard as he was, for all he was so gifted. And when it come to fair and square jumping on a dead level, he could get over more ground at one straddle than any animal of his breed you ever see. Jumping on a dead level was his strong suit, you understand; and when it come to that, Smiley would ante up money on him as long as he had a red. Smiley was monstrous proud of his frog, and well he might be, for fellers that had traveled and been everywheres, all said he laid over any frog that ever *they* see.

Well, Smiley kep' the beast in a little lattice box, and he used to fetch him down town sometimes and lay for a bet. One day a feller—a stranger in the camp, he was—come acrost him with his box, and says:

"What might it be that you've got in the box?"

And Smiley says, sorter indifferent-like, "It might be a parrot, or it might be a canary, maybe, but it ain't—it's only just a frog."

And the feller took it, and looked at it careful, and turned it round this way and that, and says, "H'm—so 'tis. Well, what's *he* good for?"

"Well," Smiley, says, easy and careless, "he's good enough for *one* thing, I should judge—he can outjump any frog in Calaveras county."

The feller took the box again, and took another long, particular look, and give it back to Smiley, and says, very deliberate, "Well," he says, "I don't see no p'ints about that frog that's any better'n any other frog."

"Maybe you don't," Smiley says. "Maybe you understand frogs and maybe you don't understand 'em; maybe you've had experience, and maybe you ain't only a amature, as it were. Anyways, I've got *my* opinion and I'll resk forty dollars that he can outjump any frog in Calaveras county."

And the feller studied a minute, and then says, kinder sad like, "Well, I'm only a stranger here, and I ain't got no frog; but if I had a frog, I'd bet you."

And then Smiley says, "That's all right—that's all right—if you'll hold my box a minute, I'll go and get you a frog." And so the feller took the box, and put up his forty dollars along with Smiley's, and set down to wait.

So he set there a good while thinking and thinking to hisself, and then he got the frog out and prized his mouth open and took a teaspoon and filled him full of quail shot—filled him pretty near up to his chin—and set him on the floor. Smiley he went to the swamp and slopped around in the mud for a long time, and finally he ketched a frog, and fetched him in, and give him to this feller, and says:

"Now, if you're ready, set him alongside of Dan'l, with his fore-paws just even with Dan'l's, and I'll give the word." Then he says, "One—two—three—*git!*" and him and the feller touched up the frogs from behind, and the new frog hopped off lively, but Dan'l give a heave, and hysted up his shoulders—so—like a Frenchman, but it warn't no use—he couldn't budge; he was planted as solid as a church, and he couldn't no more stir than if he was anchored out. Smiley was a good deal surprised, and he was disgusted too, but he didn't have no idea what the matter was, of course.

The feller took the money and started away; and when he was going out at the door, he sorter jerked his thumb over his shoulder—so—at Dan'l, and says again, very deliberate, "Well," he says "*I* don't see no p'ints about that frog that's any better'n any other frog."

Smiley he stood scratching his head and looking down at Dan'l a long time, and at last he says, "I do wonder what in the nation that frog throw'd off for—I wonder if there ain't something the matter with him—he 'pears to look mighty baggy, somehow." And he ketched Dan'l by the nap of the neck, and hefted him, and says, "Why blame my cats if he don't weigh five pound!" and turned him upside down and he belched out a double handful of shot. And then he see how it was, and he was the maddest man—he set the frog down and took out after that feller, but he never ketched him. And—"

(Here Simon Wheeler heard his name called from the front yard, and got up to see what was wanted.) And turning to me as he moved away, he said: "Just set where you are, stranger, and rest easy—I ain't going to be gone a second."

But, by your leave, I did not think that a continuation of the history of the enterprising vagabond *Jim* Smiley would be likely to afford me much information concerning the Rev. *Leonidas W.* Smiley, and so I started away.

At the door I met the sociable Wheeler returning, and he button-holed me and re-commenced:

"Well, thish-yer Smiley had a yaller one-eyed cow that didn't have no tail, only jest a short stump like a bannanner, and—"

However, lacking both time and inclination, I did not wait to hear about the afflicted cow, but took my leave.

1865

---

from Roughing It

Chapter 53: [Grandfather's Old Ram]

Every now and then, in these days, the boys used to tell me I ought to get one Jim Blaine to tell me the stirring story of his grandfather's old ram—but they always added that I must not mention the matter unless Jim was drunk at the time—just comfortably and sociably drunk. They kept this up until my curiosity was on the rack to hear the story. I got to haunting Blaine; but it was of no use, the boys always found fault with his condition; he was often moderately but never satisfactorily drunk. I never watched a man's condition with such absorbing interest, such anxious solicitude; I never so pined to see a man uncompromisingly drunk before. At last, one evening I hurried to his cabin, for I learned that this time his situation was such that even the most fastidious could find no fault with it—he was tranquilly, serenely, symmetrically drunk—not a hiccup to mar his voice, not a cloud upon his brain thick enough to obscure his memory. As I entered, he was sitting upon an empty powder-keg, with a clay pipe in one hand and the other raised to command silence. His face was round, red, and very serious; his throat was bare and his hair tumbled; in general appearance and costume he was a stalwart miner of the period. On the pine table stood a candle, and its dim light revealed "the boys" sitting here and there on bunks, candle-boxes, powder-kegs, etc. They said:

"Sh——! Don't speak—he's going to commence."

The Story of the Old Ram

I found a seat at once, and Blaine said:

"I don't reckon them times will ever come again. There never was a more bullier old ram than what he was. Grandfather fetched him from Illinois—got him of a man by the name of Yates—Bill Yates—maybe you might have heard of him; his father was a deacon—Baptist—and he was a rustler, too; a man had to get up ruther early to get the start of old Thankful Yates; it was him that put the Greens up to jining teams with my grandfather when he moved west. Seth Green was prob'ly the pick of the flock; he married a Wilkerson—Sarah Wilkerson—a good cretur, she was— one of the likeliest heifers that was ever raised in old Stoddard, everybody said that knowed her. She could heft a bar'l of flour as easy as I can flirt a flapjack. And spin? Don't mention it! Independent? Humph! When Sile Hawkins come a browsing around her, she let him know that for all his tin he couldn't trot in harness alongside of *her*. You see, Sile Hawkins was—no, it warn't Sile Hawkins, after all—it was a galoot by the name of Filkins—I disremember his first name; but he *was* a stump— come into pra'r meeting drunk, one night, hooraying for Nixon, becuz he thought it was a primary; and old deacon Ferguson up and scooted him through the window and he lit on old Miss Jefferson's head, poor old filly. She was a good soul—had a glass eye and used to lend it to old Miss Wagner, that hadn't any, to receive company in; it warn't big enough, and when Miss Wagner warn't noticing, it would get twisted around in the socket, and look up, maybe, or out to one side, and every which way, while t' other one was looking as straight ahead as a spy-glass. Grown people didn't mind it, but it most always made the children cry, it was so sort of scary. She tried packing it in raw cotton, but it wouldn't work, somehow—the cotton would get loose and stick out and look so kind of awful that the children couldn't stand it no way. She was always dropping it out, and turning up her old dead-light on the company empty, and making them oncomfortable, becuz she never could tell when it hopped out, being blind on that side, you see. So somebody would have to hunch her and say, "Your game eye has fetched loose, Miss Wagner dear"—and then all of them would have to sit and wait till she jammed it in again—wrong side before, as a general thing, and green as a bird's egg, being a bashful cretur and easy sot back before company. But being wrong side before warn't much difference, anyway, becuz her own eye was sky-blue and the glass one was yaller on the front side, so whichever way she turned it it didn't match nohow. Old Miss Wagner was considerable on the borrow, she was. When she had a quilting, or Dorcas S'iety' at her house she gen'ally borrowed Miss Higgins's wooden leg to stump around on; it was considerable shorter than her other pin, but much *she* minded that. She said she couldn't abide crutches when she had company, becuz they were so slow; said when she had company and things had to be done, she wanted to get up and hump herself. She was as bald as

---

' I.e., Dorcas Society, a church sewing circle.

a jug, and so she used to borrow Miss Jacops's wig—Miss Jacops was the coffin-peddler's wife—a ratty old buzzard, he was, that used to go roosting around where people was sick, waiting for 'em; and there that old rip would sit all day, in the shade, on a coffin that he judged would fit the can'idate; and if it was a slow customer and kind of uncertain, he'd fetch his rations and a blanket along and sleep in the coffin nights. He was anchored out that way, in frosty weather, for about three weeks, once, before old Robbins's place, waiting for him; and after that, for as much as two years, Jacops was not on speaking terms with the old man, on account of his disapp'inting him. He got one of his feet froze, and lost money, too, becuz old Robbins took a favorable turn and got well. The next time Robbins got sick, Jacops tried to make up with him, and varnished up the same old coffin and fetched it along; but old Robbins was too many for him; he had him in, and 'peared to be powerful weak; he bought the coffin for ten dollars and Jacops was to pay it back and twenty-five more besides if Robbins didn't like the coffin after he'd tried it. And then Robbins died, and at the funeral he bursted off the lid and riz up in his shroud and told the parson to let up on the performances, becuz he could *not* stand such a coffin as that. You see he had been in a trance once before, when he was young, and he took the chances on another, cal'lating that if he made the trip it was money in his pocket, and if he missed fire he couldn't lose a cent. And by George he sued Jacops for the rhino and got jedgment; and he set up the coffin in his back parlor and said he 'lowed to take his time, now. It was always an aggravation to Jacops, the way that miserable old thing acted. He moved back to Indiany pretty soon—went to Wellsville— Wellsville was the place the Hogadorns was from. Mighty fine family. Old Maryland stock. Old Squire Hogadorn could carry around more mixed licker, and cuss better than most any man I ever see. His second wife was the widder Billings—she that was Becky Martin; her dam was deacon Dunlap's first wife. Her oldest child, Maria, married a missionary and died in grace—et up by the savages. They et *him,* too, poor feller—biled him. It warn't the custom, so they say, but they explained to friends of his'n that went down there to bring away his things, that they'd tried missionaries every other way and never could get any good out of 'em—and so it annoyed all his relations to find out that that man's life was fooled away just out of a dern'd experiment, so to speak. But mind you, there ain't anything ever reely lost; everything that people can't understand and don't see the reason of does good if you only hold on and give it a fair shake; Prov'dence don't fire no blank ca'tridges, boys. That there missionary's substance, unbeknowns to himself, actu'ly converted every last one of them heathens that took a chance at the barbacue. Nothing ever fetched them but that. Don't tell *me* it was an accident that he was biled. There ain't no such a thing as an accident. When my uncle Lem was leaning up agin a scaffolding once, sick, or drunk, or suthin, an Irishman with a hod full of bricks fell on him out of the third story and broke the old man's back in two places. People said it was an accident. Much accident there was about that. He didn't know what he was there for, but he was there for a good object. If he hadn't been there the Irishman would have been killed. Nobody can ever make me believe anything different from that. Uncle Lem's dog was there. Why didn't the Irishman fall on the dog? Becuz the dog would a seen him a coming and stood from under. That's the reason the dog warn't appinted. A dog can't be depended on to carry out a special providence. Mark my words it was a put-up thing. Accidents don't happen, boys. Uncle Lem's dog—I wish you could a seen that dog. He was a reglar shepherd—or ruther he was part bull and part shepherd—splendid animal; belonged to parson Hagar before Uncle Lem got him. Parson Hagar belonged to the Western Reserve Hagars; prime family; his mother was a Watson; one of his sisters married a Wheeler; they settled in Morgan county, and he got nipped by the machinery in a carpet factory and went through in less than a quarter of a minute; his widder bought the piece of carpet that had his remains wove in, and people come a hundred mile to 'tend the funeral. There was fourteen yards in the piece. She wouldn't let them roll him up, but planted him just so—full length. The church was middling small where they preached the funeral, and they had to let one end of the coffin stick out of the window. They didn't bury him—they planted one end, and let him stand up, same as a monument. And they nailed a sign on it and put—put on—put on it—sacred to—the m-e-m-o-r-y—of fourteen y-a-r-d-s—of three-ply—car—pet—containing all that was—m-o-r-t-a-l—of—of—W-i-l-l-i-a-m—W-h-e—"

Jim Blaine had been growing gradually drowsy and drowsier—his head nodded, once, twice, three times—dropped peacefully upon his breast, and he fell tranquilly asleep. The tears were running down the boys' cheeks—they were suffocating with suppressed laughter—and had been from the start, though I had never noticed it. I perceived that I was "sold." I learned then that Jim Blaine's peculiarity was that whenever he reached a certain stage of intoxication, no human power could keep him from setting out, with impressive unction, to tell about a wonderful adventure which he had once had with his grandfather's old ram—and the mention of the ram in the first sentence was as far as any man had ever heard him get, concerning it. He always maundered off, interminably, from one thing to another, till his whisky got the best of him and he fell asleep. What the thing was that happened to him and his grandfather's old ram is a dark mystery to this day, for nobody had ever yet found out.

1872

from Old Times on the Mississippi

I: ["Cub" Wants to Be a Pilot]

When I was a boy, there was but one permanent ambition among my comrades in our village¹ on the west bank of the Mississippi River. That was, to be a steamboatman. We had transient ambitions of other sorts, but they were only transient. When a circus came and went, it left us all burning to become clowns; the first negro minstrel show that came to our section left us all suffering to try that kind of life; now and then we had a hope that if we lived and were good, God would permit us to be pirates. These ambitions faded out, each in its turn; but the ambition to be a steamboatman always remained.

Once a day a cheap, gaudy packet arrived upward from St. Louis, and another downward from Keokuk. Before these events had transpired, the day was glorious

---

¹ Hannibal, Missouri.

with expectancy; after they had transpired, the day was a dead and empty thing. Not only the boys, but the whole village, felt this. After all these years I can picture that old time to myself now, just as it was then: the white town drowsing in the sunshine of a summer's morning; the streets empty, or pretty nearly so; one or two clerks sitting in front of the Water Street stores, with their splint-bottomed chairs tilted back against the wall, chins on breasts, hats slouched over their faces, asleep—with shingle-shavings enough around to show what broke them down; a sow and a litter of pigs loafing along the sidewalk, doing a good business in water-melon rinds and seeds; two or three lonely little freight piles scattered about the "levee;" a pile of "skids" on the slope of the stone-paved wharf, and the fragrant town drunkard asleep in the shadow of them; two or three wood flats at the head of the wharf, but nobody to listen to the peaceful lapping of the wavelets against them; the great Mississippi, the majestic, the magnificent Mississippi, rolling its mile-wide tide along, shining in the sun; the dense forest away on the other side; the "point" above the town, and the "point" below, bounding the river-glimpse and turning it into a sort of sea, and withal a very still and brilliant and lonely one. Presently a film of dark smoke appears above one of those remote "points;" instantly a negro drayman, famous for his quick eye and prodigious voice, lifts up the cry, "S-t-e-a-m-boat a-comin'!'" and the scene changes! The town drunkard stirs, the clerks wake up, a furious clatter of drays follows, every house and store pours out a human contribution, and all in a twinkling the dead town is alive and moving. Drays, carts, men, boys, all go hurrying from many quarters to a common centre, the wharf. Assembled there, the people fasten their eyes upon the coming boat as upon a wonder they are seeing for the first time. And the boat *is* rather a handsome sight, too. She is long and sharp and trim and pretty; she has two tall, fancy-topped chimneys, with a gilded device of some kind swung between them; a fanciful pilot-house, all glass and "gingerbread," perched on top of the "texas" deck behind them; the paddle-boxes are gorgeous with a picture or with gilded rays above the boat's name; the boiler deck, the hurricane deck, and the texas deck are fenced and orna-mented with clean white railings; there is a flag gallantly flying from the jack-staff; the furnace doors are open and the fires glaring bravely; the upper decks are black with passengers; the captain stands by the big bell, calm, imposing, the envy of all; great volumes of the blackest smoke are rolling and tumbling out of the chimneys —a husbanded grandeur created with a bit of pitch pine just before arriving at a town; the crew are grouped on the forecastle; the broad stage is run far out over the port bow, and an envied deck-hand stands picturesquely on the end of it with a coil of rope in his hand; the pent steam is screaming through the gauge-cocks; the captain lifts his hand, a bell rings, the wheels stop; then they turn back, churning the water to foam, and the steamer is at rest. Then such a scramble as there is to get aboard, and to get ashore, and to take in freight and to discharge freight, all at once and the same time; and such a yelling and cursing as the mates facilitate it all with! Ten minutes later the steamer is under way again, with no flag on the jack-staff and no black smoke issuing from the chimneys. After ten more minutes the town is dead again, and the town drunkard asleep by the skids once more.

My father was a justice of the peace, and I supposed he possessed the power of life and death over all men and could hang anybody that offended him. This was distinction enough for me as a general thing; but the desire to be a steamboatman kept intruding, nevertheless. I first wanted to be a cabin-boy, so that I could come out with a white apron on and shake a table-cloth over the side, where all my old comrades could see me; later I thought I would rather be the deck-hand who stood on the end of the stageplank with the coil of rope in his hand, because he was particularly conspicuous. But these were only daydreams—they were too heavenly to be contemplated as real possibilities. By and by one of our boys went away. He was not heard of for a long time. At last he turned up as apprentice engineer or "striker" on a steamboat. This thing shook the bottom out of all my Sunday-school teachings. That boy had been notoriously worldly, and I just the reverse; yet he was exalted to this eminence, and I left in obscurity and misery. There was nothing generous about this fellow in his greatness. He would always manage to have a rusty bolt to scrub while his boat tarried at our town, and he would sit on the inside guard and scrub it, where we could all see him and envy him and loathe him. And whenever his boat was laid up he would come home and swell around the town in his blackest and greasiest clothes, so that nobody could help remembering that he was a steamboatman; and he used all sorts of steamboat technicalities in his talk, as if he were so used to them that he forgot common people could not understand them. He would speak of the "labboard" side of a horse in an easy, natural way that would make one wish he was dead. And he was always talking about "St. Looy" like an old citizen; he would refer casually to occasions when he "was coming down Fourth Street," or when he was "passing by the Planter's House," or when there was a fire and he took a turn on the brakes of "the old Big Missouri;" and then he would go on and lie about how many towns the size of ours were burned down there that day. Two or three of the boys had long been persons of consideration among us because they had been to St. Louis once and had a vague general knowledge of its wonders, but the day of their glory was over now. They lapsed into a humble silence, and learned to disappear when the ruthless "cub"-engineer approached. This fellow had money, too, and hair oil. Also an ignorant silver watch and a showy brass watch chain. He wore a leather belt and used no suspenders. If ever a youth was cordially admired and hated by his comrades, this one was. No girl could withstand his charms. He "cut out" every boy in the village. When his boat blew up at last, it diffused a tranquil contentment among us such as we had not known for months. But when he came home the next week, alive, renowned, and appeared in church all battered up and bandaged, a shining hero, stared at and wondered over by everybody, it seemed to us that the partiality of Providence for an undeserving reptile had reached a point where it was open to criticism.

This creature's career could produce but one result, and it speedily followed. Boy after boy managed to get on the river. The minister's son became an engineer. The doctor's and the postmaster's sons became "mud clerks;" the wholesale liquor dealer's son became a bar-keeper on a boat; four sons of the chief merchant, and two sons of the county judge, became pilots. Pilot was the grandest position of all. The pilot, even in those days of trivial wages, had a princely salary—from a hundred and fifty to two hundred and fifty dollars a month, and no board to pay. Two months of his wages would pay a preacher's salary for a year. Now some of us were left disconsolate. We could not get on the river—at least four parents would not let us.

So by and by I ran away. I said I never would come home again till I was a pilot and could come in glory. But somehow I could not manage it. I went meekly aboard a few of the boats that lay packed together like sardines at the long St. Louis wharf, and very humbly inquired for the pilots, but got only a cold shoulder and short words from mates and clerks. I had to make the best of this sort of treatment for the time being, but I had comforting daydreams of a future when I should be a great and honored pilot, with plenty of money, and could kill some of these mates and clerks and pay for them.

Months afterward the hope within me struggled to a reluctant death, and I found myself without an ambition. But I was ashamed to go home. I was in Cincinnati, and I set to work to map out a new career. I had been reading about the recent exploration of the river Amazon by an expedition sent out by our government. It was said that the expedition, owing to difficulties, had not thoroughly explored a part of the country lying about the head-waters, some four thousand miles from the mouth of the river. It was only about fifteen hundred miles from Cincinnati to New Orleans, where I could doubtless get a ship. I had thirty dollars left; I would go and complete the exploration of the Amazon. This was all the thought I gave to the subject. I never was great in matters of detail. I packed my valise, and took passage on an ancient tub called the Paul Jones, for New Orleans. For the sum of sixteen dollars I had the scarred and tarnished splendors of "her" main saloon principally to myself, for she was not a creature to attract the eye of wiser travelers.

When we presently got under way and went poking down the broad Ohio, I became a new being, and the subject of my own admiration. I was a traveler! A word never had tasted so good in my mouth before. I had an exultant sense of being bound for mysterious lands and distant climes which I never have felt in so uplifting a degree since. I was in such a glorified condition that all ignoble feelings departed out of me, and I was able to look down and pity the untraveled with a compassion that had hardly a trace of contempt in it. Still, when we stopped at villages and wood-yards, I could not help lolling carelessly upon the railings of the boiler deck to enjoy the envy of the country boys on the bank. If they did not seem to discover me, I presently sneezed to attract their attention, or moved to a position where they could not help seeing me. And as soon as I knew they saw me I gaped and stretched, and gave other signs of being mightily bored with traveling.

I kept my hat off all the time, and stayed where the wind and the sun could strike me, because I wanted to get the bronzed and weather-beaten look of an old traveler. Before the second day was half gone, I experienced a joy which filled me with the purest gratitude; for I saw that the skin had begun to blister and peel off my face and neck. I wished that the boys and girls at home could see me now.

We reached Louisville in time—at least the neighborhood of it. We stuck hard and fast on the rocks in the middle of the river and lay there four days. I was now beginning to feel a strong sense of being a part of the boat's family, a sort of infant son to the captain and younger brother to the officers. There is no estimating the pride I took in this grandeur, or the affection that began to swell and grow in me for those people. I could not know how the lordly steamboatman scorns that sort of presumption in a mere landsman. I particularly longed to acquire the least trifle of notice from the big stormy mate, and I was on the alert for an opportunity to do him a service to that end. It came at last. The riotous powwow of setting a spar was going on down on the forecastle, and I went down there and stood around in the way—or mostly skipping out of it—till the mate suddenly roared a general order for somebody to bring him a capstan bar. I sprang to his side and said: "Tell me where it is—I'll fetch it!"

If a rag-picker had offered to do a diplomatic service for the Emperor of Russia, the monarch could not have been more astounded than the mate was. He even stopped swearing. He stood and stared down at me. It took him ten seconds to scrape his disjointed remains together again. Then he said impressively: "Well, if this don't beat hell!" and turned to his work with the air of a man who had been confronted with a problem too abstruse for solution.

I crept away, and courted solitude for the rest of the day. I did not go to dinner; I stayed away from supper until everybody else had finished. I did not feel so much like a member of the boat's family now as before. However, my spirits returned, in installments, as we pursued our way down the river. I was sorry I hated the mate so, because it was not in (young) human nature not to admire him. He was huge and muscular, his face was bearded and whiskered all over; he had a red woman and a blue woman tattooed on his right arm,—one on each side of a blue anchor with a red rope to it; and in the matter of profanity he was perfect. When he was getting out cargo at a landing, I was always where I could see and hear. He felt all the sublimity of his great position, and made the world feel it, too. When he gave even the simplest order, he discharged it like a blast of lightning, and sent a long, reverberating peal of profanity thundering after it. I could not help contrasting the way in which the average landsman would give an order, with the mate's way of doing it. If the landsman should wish the gangplank moved a foot farther forward, he would probably say: "James, or William, one of you push that plank forward, please;" but put the mate in his place, and he would roar out: "Here, now, start that gang-plank for'ard! Lively, now! *What*'re you about! Snatch it! *snatch* it! There! there! Aft again! aft again! Don't you hear me? Dash it to dash! are you going to *sleep* over it! 'Vast heaving. 'Vast heaving, I tell you! Going to heave it clear astern? WHERE're you going with that barrel! *for'ard* with it 'fore I make you swallow it, you dash-dash-dash-*dashed* split between a tired mud-turtle and a crippled hearse-horse!"

I wished I could talk like that.

When the soreness of my adventure with the mate had somewhat worn off, I began timidly to make up to the humblest official connected with the boat—the night watchman. He snubbed my advances at first, but I presently ventured to offer him a new chalk pipe, and that softened him. So he allowed me to sit with him by the big bell on the hurricane deck, and in time he melted into conversation. He could not well have helped it, I hung with such homage on his words and so plainly showed that I felt honored by his notice. He told me the names of dim capes and shadowy islands as we glided by them in the solemnity of the night, under the winking stars, and by and by got to talking about himself. He seemed oversentimental for a man whose salary was six dollars a week—or rather he might have seemed so to an older person than I. But I drank in his words hungrily, and with a faith that might have moved mountains if it had been applied judiciously. What was it to me that he was soiled and seedy and fragrant with gin? What was it to me that his grammar was bad, his construction worse, and his profanity so void of art that it was an element of weakness rather than strength in his conversation? He was a wronged man, a man who had seen trouble, and that was enough for me. As he mellowed into his plaintive history his tears dripped upon the lantern in his lap, and I cried, too, from sympathy. He said he was the son of an English nobleman—either an earl or an alderman, he could not remember which, but believed he was both; his father, the nobleman, loved him, but his mother hated him from the cradle; and so while he was still a little boy he was sent to "one of them old, ancient colleges"—he couldn't remember which; and by and by his father died and his mother seized the property and "shook" him, as he phrased it. After his mother shook him, members of the nobility with whom he was acquainted used their influence to get him the position of "loblolly-boy in a ship;" and from that point my watchman threw off all trammels of date and locality and branched out into a narrative that bristled all along with incredible adventures; a narrative that was so reeking with bloodshed and so crammed with hair-breadth escapes and the most engaging and unconscious personal villainies, that I sat speechless, enjoying, shuddering, wondering, worshiping.

It was a sore blight to find out afterwards that he was a low, vulgar, ignorant, sentimental, half-witted humbug, an untraveled native of the wilds of Illinois, who had absorbed wildcat literature and appropriated its marvels, until in time he had woven odds and ends of the mess into this yarn, and then gone on telling it to fledgelings like me, until he had come to believe it himself.

II: [A "Cub" Pilot's Experience; or, Learning the River]

What with lying on the rocks four days at Louisville, and some other delays, the poor old Paul Jones fooled away about two weeks in making the voyage from Cincinnati to New Orleans. This gave me a chance to get acquainted with one of the pilots, and he taught me how to steer the boat, and thus made the fascination of river life more potent than ever for me.

It also gave me a chance to get acquainted with a youth who had taken deck passage —more's the pity; for he easily borrowed six dollars of me on a promise to return to the boat and pay it back to me the day after we should arrive. But he probably died or forgot, for he never came. It was doubtless the former, since he had said his parents were wealthy, and he only traveled deck passage[2] because it was cooler.

I soon discovered two things. One was that a vessel would not be likely to sail for the mouth of the Amazon under ten or twelve years; and the other was that the nine or ten dollars still left in my pocket would not suffice for so imposing an exploration as I had planned, even if I could afford to wait for a ship. Therefore it followed that I must contrive a new career. The Paul Jones was now bound for St. Louis. I planned a siege against my pilot, and at the end of three hard days he surrendered. He agreed to teach me the Mississippi River from New Orleans to St. Louis for five hundred dollars, payable out of the first wages I should receive after graduating. I entered upon the small enterprise of "learning" twelve or thirteen hundred miles of the great Mississippi River with the easy confidence of my time of life. If I had really known what I was about to require of my faculties, I should not have had the courage to begin. I supposed that all a pilot had to do was to keep his boat in the river, and I did not consider that that could be much of a trick, since it was so wide.

The boat backed out from New Orleans at four in the afternoon, and it was "our watch" until eight. Mr. B——, my chief, "straightened her up," plowed her along

[2] Steerage, the cheapest passage.

past the sterns of the other boats that lay at the Levee, and then said, "Here, take her; shave those steamships as close as you'd peel an apple." I took the wheel, and my heart went down into my boots; for it seemed to me that we were about to scrape the side off every ship in the line, we were so close. I held my breath and began to claw the boat away from the danger; and I had my own opinion of the pilot who had known no better than to get us into such peril, but I was too wise to express it. In half a minute I had a wide margin of safety intervening between the Paul Jones and the ships; and within ten seconds more I was set aside in disgrace, and Mr. B—— was going into danger again and flaying me alive with abuse of my cowardice. I was stung, but I was obliged to admire the easy confidence with which my chief loafed from side to side of his wheel, and trimmed the ships so closely that disaster seemed ceaselessly imminent. When he had cooled a little he told me that the easy water was close ashore and the current outside, and therefore we must hug the bank, up-stream, to get the benefit of the former, and stay well out, downstream, to take advantage of the latter. In my own mind I resolved to be a down-stream pilot and leave the up-streaming to people dead to prudence.

Now and then Mr. B—— called my attention to certain things. Said he, "This is Six-Mile Point." I assented. It was pleasant enough information, but I could not see the bearing of it. I was not conscious that it was a matter of any interest to me. Another time he said, "This is Nine-Mile Point." Later he said, "This is Twelve-Mile Point." They were all about level with the water's edge; they all looked about alike to me; they were monotonously unpicturesque. I hoped Mr. B—— would change the subject. But no; he would crowd up around a point, hugging the shore with affection, and then say: "The slack water ends here, abreast this bunch of China-trees; now we cross over." So he crossed over. He gave me the wheel once or twice, but I had no luck. I either came near chipping off the edge of a sugar plantation, or else I yawed too far from shore, and so I dropped back into disgrace again and got abused.

The watch was ended at last, and we took supper and went to bed. At midnight the glare of a lantern shone in my eyes, and the night watchman said:—

"Come! turn out!"

And then he left. I could not understand this extraordinary procedure; so I presently gave up trying to, and dozed off to sleep. Pretty soon the watchman was back again, and this time he was gruff. I was annoyed. I said:—

"What do you want to come bothering around here in the middle of the night for? Now as like as not I'll not get to sleep again to-night."

The watchman said:—

"Well, if this an't good, I'm blest."

The "off-watch" was just turning in, and I heard some brutal laughter from them, and such remarks as "Hello, watchman! an't the new cub turned out yet? He's delicate, likely. Give him some sugar in a rag and send for the chambermaid to sing rock-a-by-baby to him."

About this time Mr. B—— appeared on the scene. Something like a minute later I was climbing the pilot-house steps with some of my clothes on and the rest in my arms. Mr. B—— was close behind, commenting. Here was something fresh—this thing of getting up in the middle of the night to go to work. It was a detail in piloting that had never occurred to me at all. I knew that boats ran all night, but somehow I had never happened to reflect that somebody had to get up out of a warm bed to run them. I began to fear that piloting was not quite so romantic as I had imagined it was; there was something very real and work-like about this new phase of it.

It was a rather dingy night, although a fair number of stars were out. The big mate was at the wheel, and he had the old tub pointed at a star and was holding her straight up the middle of the river. The shores on either hand were not much more than a mile apart, but they seemed wonderfully far away and ever so vague and indistinct. The mate said:—

"We've got to land at Jones's plantation, sir."

The vengeful spirit in me exulted. I said to myself, I wish you joy of your job, Mr. B——; you'll have a good time finding Mr. Jones's plantation such a night as this; and I hope you never *will* find it as long as you live.

Mr. B—— said to the mate:—

"Upper end of the plantation, or the lower?"

"Upper."

"I can't do it. The stumps there are out of water at this stage. It's no great distance to the lower, and you'll have to get along with that."

"All right, sir. If Jones don't like it he'll have to lump it, I reckon."

And then the mate left. My exultation began to cool and my wonder to come up. Here was a man who not only proposed to find this plantation on such a night, but to find either end of it you preferred. I dreadfully wanted to ask a question, but I was carrying about as many short answers as my cargo-room would admit of, so I held my peace. All I desired to ask Mr. B—— was the simple question whether he was ass enough to really imagine he was going to find that plantation on a night when all plantations were exactly alike and all the same color. But I held in. I used to have fine inspirations of prudence in those days.

Mr. B—— made for the shore and soon was scraping it, just the same as if it had been daylight. And not only that, but singing—

"Father in heaven the day is declining," etc.

It seemed to me that I had put my life in the keeping of a peculiarly reckless outcast. Presently he turned on me and said:—

"What's the name of the first point above New Orleans?"

I was gratified to be able to answer promptly, and I did. I said I didn't know.

"Don't *know?*"

This manner jolted me. I was down at the foot again, in a moment. But I had to say just what I had said before.

"Well, you're a smart one," said Mr. B——. "What's the name of the *next* point?"

Once more I didn't know.

"Well this beats anything. Tell me the name of *any* point or place I told you."

I studied a while and decided that I couldn't.

"Look-a-here! What do you start out from, above Twelve-Mile Point, to cross over?"

"I—I—don't know."

"You—you—don't know?" mimicking my drawling manner of speech. "What *do* you know?"

"I—I—nothing, for certain."

"By the great Cæsar's ghost I believe you! You're the stupidest dunderhead I ever saw or ever heard of, so help me Moses! The idea of *you* being a pilot—*you!* Why, you don't know enough to pilot a cow down a lane."

Oh, but his wrath was up! He was a nervous man, and he shuffled from one side of his wheel to the other as if the floor was hot. He would boil a while to himself, and then overflow and scald me again.

"Look-a-here! What do you suppose I told you the names of those points for?"

I tremblingly considered a moment, and then the devil of temptation provoked me to say:—

"Well—to—to—be entertaining, I thought."

This was a red rag to the bull. He raged and stormed so (he was crossing the river at the time) that I judge it made him blind, because he ran over the steering-oar of a trading-scow. Of course the traders sent up a volley of red-hot profanity. Never was a man so grateful as Mr. B—— was: because he was brim full, and here were subjects who would *talk back*. He threw open a window, thrust his head out, and such an irruption followed as I never had heard before. The fainter and farther away the scowmen's curses drifted, the higher Mr. B—— lifted his voice and the weightier his adjectives grew. When he closed the window he was empty. You could have drawn a seine through his system and not caught curses enough to disturb your mother with. Presently he said to me in the gentlest way:—

"My boy, you must get a little memorandum-book, and every time I tell you a thing, put it down right away. There's only one way to be a pilot, and that is to get this entire river by heart. You have to know it just like A B C."

That was a dismal revelation to me; for my memory was never loaded with anything but blank cartridges. However, I did not feel discouraged long. I judged that it was best to make some allowances, for doubtless Mr. B—— was "stretching." Presently, he pulled a rope and struck a few strokes on the big bell. The stars were all gone, now, and the night was as black as ink. I could hear the wheels churn along the bank, but I was not entirely certain that I could see the shore. The voice of the invisible watchman called up from the hurricane deck:—

"What's this, sir?"

"Jones's plantation."

I said to myself, I wish I might venture to offer a small bet that it isn't. But I did not chirp. I only waited to see. Mr. B—— handled the engine bells, and in due time the boat's nose came to the land, a torch glowed from the forecastle, a man skipped ashore, a darky's voice on the bank said, "Gimme de carpet-bag, Mars' Jones," and the next moment we were standing up the river again, all serene. I reflected deeply a while, and then said,—but not aloud,—Well, the finding of that plantation was the luckiest accident that ever happened; but it couldn't happen again in a hundred years. And I fully believed it *was* an accident, too.

By the time we had gone seven or eight hundred miles up the river, I had learned to be a tolerably plucky upstream steersman, in daylight, and before we reached St. Louis I had made a trifle of progress in night-work, but only a trifle. I had a note-book that fairly bristled with the names of towns, "points," bars, islands, bends, reaches, etc.; but the information was to be found only in the note-book—none of it was in my head. It made my heart ache to think I had only got half of the river set down; for as our watch was four hours off and four hours on, day and night, there was a long four-hour gap in my book for every time I had slept since the voyage began.

My chief was presently hired to go on a big New Orleans boat, and I packed my satchel and went with him. She was a grand affair. When I stood in her pilot-house I was so far above the water that I seemed perched on a mountain; and her decks stretched so far away, fore and aft, below me, that I wondered how I could ever have considered the little Paul Jones a large craft. There were other differences, too. The Paul Jones's pilot-house was a cheap, dingy, battered rattle-trap, cramped for room: but here was a sumptuous glass temple; room enough to have a dance in; showy red and gold window-curtains; an imposing sofa; leather cushions and a back to the high bench where visiting pilots sit, to spin yarns and "look at the river;" bright, fanciful "cuspadores" instead of a broad wooden box filled with sawdust; nice new oil-cloth on the floor; a hospitable big stove for winter; a wheel as high as my head, costly with inlaid work; a wire tiller-rope; bright brass knobs for the bells; and a tidy, white-aproned, black "texas-tender," to bring up tarts and ices and coffee during mid-watch, day and night. Now this was "something like;" and so I began to take heart once more to believe that piloting was a romantic sort of occupation after all. The moment we were under way I began to prowl about the great steamer and fill myself with joy. She was as clean and as dainty as a drawing-room; when I looked down her long, gilded saloon, it was like gazing through a splendid tunnel; she had an oil-picture, by some gifted sign-painter, on every state-room door; she glittered with no end of prism-fringed chandeliers; the clerk's office was elegant, the bar was marvelous, and the bar-keeper had been barbered and upholstered at incredible cost. The boiler deck (*i.e.,* the second story of the boat, so to speak) was as spacious as a church, it seemed to me; so with the forecastle; and there was no pitiful handful of deckhands, firemen, and roust-abouts down there, but a whole battalion of men. The fires were fiercely glaring from a long row of furnaces, and over them were eight huge boilers! This was unutterable pomp. The mighty engines—but enough of this. I had never felt so fine before. And when I found that the regiment of natty servants respectfully "sir'd" me, my satisfaction was complete.

When I returned to the pilot-house St. Louis was gone and I was lost. Here was a piece of river which was all down in my book, but I could make neither head nor tail of it: you understand, it was turned around. I had seen it, when coming up-stream, but I had never faced about to see how it looked when it was behind me. My heart broke again, for it was plain that I had got to learn this troublesome river *both ways*.

The pilot-house was full of pilots, going down to "look at the river." What is called the "upper river" (the two hundred miles between St. Louis and Cairo, where the Ohio comes in) was low; and the Mississippi changes its channel so constantly that the pilots used to always find it necessary to run down to Cairo to take a fresh look, when their boats were to lie in port a week, that is, when the water was at a low stage. A deal of this "looking at the river" was done by poor fellows who seldom had a berth, and whose only hope of getting one lay in their being always freshly posted and therefore ready to drop into the shoes of some reputable pilot, for a single trip, on account of such pilot's sudden illness, or some other necessity. And a good many of them constantly ran up and down inspecting the river, not because they ever really hoped to get a berth, but because (they being guests of the boat) it was cheaper to "look at the river" than stay ashore and pay board. In time these fellows grew dainty in their tastes, and only infested boats that had an established reputation for setting good tables. All visiting pilots were useful, for they were always ready and willing, winter or summer, night or day, to go out in the yawl and help buoy the channel or assist the boat's pilots in any way they could. They were likewise welcome because all pilots are tireless talkers, when gathered together, and as they talk only about the river they are always understood and are always interesting. Your true pilot cares nothing about anything on earth but the river, and his pride in his occupation surpasses the pride of kings.

We had a fine company of these river-inspectors along, this trip. There were eight or ten; and there was abundance of room for them in our great pilot-house. Two or three of them wore polished silk hats, elaborate shirtfronts, diamond breastpins, kid gloves, and patent-leather boots. They were choice in their English, and bore themselves with a dignity proper to men of solid means and prodigious reputation as pilots. The others were more or less loosely clad, and wore upon their heads tall felt cones that were suggestive of the days of the Commonwealth.

I was a cipher in this august company, and felt subdued, not to say torpid. I was not even of sufficient consequence to assist at the wheel when it was necessary to put the tiller hard down in a hurry; the guest that stood nearest did that when occasion required—and this was pretty much all the time, because of the crookedness of the channel and the scant water. I stood in a corner; and the talk I listened to took the hope all out of me. One visitor said to another:—

"Jim, how did you run Plum Point, coming up?"

"It was in the night, there, and I ran it the way one of the boys on the Diana told me; started out about fifty yards above the wood pile on the false point, and held on the cabin under Plum Point till I raised the reef—quarter less twain—then straightened up for the middle bar till I got well abreast the old one-limbed cotton-wood in the bend, then got my stern on the cotton-wood and head on the low place above the point, and came through a-booming—nine and a half."

"Pretty square crossing, an't it?"

"Yes, but the upper bar's working down fast."

Another pilot spoke up and said:—

"I had better water than that, and ran it lower down; started out from the false point—mark twain—raised the second reef abreast the big snag in the bend, and had quarter less twain."

There was no more trouble after that. Mr. B—— was a hero that night; and it was some little time, too, before his exploit ceased to be talked about by river men.

Fully to realize the marvelous precision required in laying the great steamer in her marks in that murky waste of water, one should know that not only must she pick her intricate way through snags and blind reefs, and then shave the head of the island so closely as to brush the overhanging foliage with her stern, but at one place she must pass almost within arm's reach of a sunken and invisible wreck that would snatch the hull timbers from under her if she should strike it, and destroy a quarter of a million dollars' worth of steamboat and cargo in five minutes, and maybe a hundred and fifty human lives into the bargain.

The last remark I heard that night was a compliment to Mr. B——, uttered in soliloquy and with unction by one of our guests. He said:—

"By the Shadow of Death, but he's a lightning pilot!"

1875

The Story of a Speech[*]

The Speech

This is an occasion peculiarly meet for the digging up of pleasant reminiscences concerning literary folk; therefore I will drop lightly into history myself. Standing here on the shore of the Atlantic and contemplating certain of its largest literary billows, I am reminded of a thing which happened to me thirteen years ago, when I had just succeeded in stirring up a little Nevadian literary puddle myself, whose spume-flakes were beginning to blow thinly Californiaward. I started an inspection tramp through the southern mines of California. I was callow and conceited, and I resolved to try the virtue of my *nom de guerre*.

I very soon had an opportunity. I knocked at a miner's lonely log cabin in the foot-hills of the Sierras just at nightfall. It was snowing at the time. A jaded, melancholy man of fifty, barefooted, opened the door to me. When he heard my *nom de guerre* he looked more dejected than before. He let me in—pretty reluctantly, I thought—and after the customary bacon and beans, black coffee, and hot whiskey, I took a pipe. This sorrowful man had not said three words up to this time. Now he spoke up and said, in the voice of one who is secretly suffering, "You're the fourth —I'm going to move." "The fourth what?" said I. "The fourth literary man that has been here in twenty-four hours—I'm going to move." "You don't tell me!" said I; "who were the others?" "Mr. Longfellow, Mr. Emerson, and Mr. Oliver Wendell Holmes—confound the lot!"

You can easily believe I was interested. I supplicated—three hot whiskies did the rest—and finally the melancholy miner began. Said he:

"They came here just at dark yesterday evening, and I let them in, of course. Said they were going to the Yosemite. They were a rough lot, but that's nothing; everybody looks rough that travels afoot. Mr. Emerson was a seedy little bit of a chap, redheaded. Mr. Holmes was as fat as a balloon; he weighed as much as three hundred, and had double chins all the way down to his stomach. Mr. Longfellow was built like a prize-fighter. His head was cropped and bristly, like as if he had a wig made of hair-brushes. His nose lay straight down his face, like a finger with the end joint tilted up. They had been drinking, I could see that. And what queer talk they used! Mr. Holmes inspected this cabin, then he took me by the buttonhole, and says he:

" 'Through the deep caves of thought
I hear a voice that sings,
Build thee more stately mansions,
O my soul!'

"Says I, 'I can't afford it, Mr. Holmes, and moreover I don't want to.' Blamed if I liked it pretty well, either, coming from a stranger, that way. However, I started

---

[*] An address delivered in 1877, at a dinner given by the publishers of the *Atlantic Monthly*, followed by Twain's written assessment of it 29 years later.

to get out my bacon and beans, when Mr. Emerson came and looked on awhile, and then *he* takes me aside by the buttonhole and says:

> " 'Gives me agates for my meat;
> Gives me cantharids to eat;
> From air and ocean bring me foods,
> From all zones and altitudes.'

"Says I, 'Mr. Emerson, if you'll excuse me, this ain't no hotel.' You see it sort of riled me—I warn't used to the ways of littery swells. But I went on a-sweating over my work and next comes Mr. Longfellow and buttonholes me, and interrupts me. Says he:

> " 'Honor be to Mudjekeewis!
> You shall hear how Pau-Puk-Keewis—'

"But I broke in, and says I, 'Beg your pardon, Mr. Longfellow, if you'll be so kind as to hold your yawp for about five minutes and let me get this grub ready, you'll do me proud.' Well, sir, after they'd filled up I set out the jug. Mr. Holmes looks at it, and then he fires up all of sudden and yells:

> " 'Flash out a stream of blood-red wine!
> For I would drink to other days.'

"By George, I was getting kind of worked up. I don't deny it, I was getting kind of worked up. I turns to Mr. Holmes, and says I, 'Looky here, my fat friend, I'm a-running this shanty, and if the court knows herself, you'll take whisky straight or you'll go dry.' Them's the very words I said to him. Now I don't want to sass such famous littery people, but you see they kind of forced me. There ain't nothing onreasonable 'bout me; I don't mind a passel of guests a-treadin' on my tail three or four times, but when it comes to *standing* on it it's different, 'and if the court knows herself,' I says, 'you'll take whisky straight or you'll go dry.' Well, between drinks they'd swell around the cabin and strike attitudes and spout; and pretty soon they got out a greasy old deck and went to playing euchre at ten cents a corner—on trust. I began to notice some pretty suspicious things. Mr. Emerson dealt, looked at his hand, shook his head, says:

> " 'I am the doubter and the doubt—'

and ca'mly bunched the hands and went to shuffling for a new layout. Says he:

> " 'They reckon ill who leave me out;
> They know not well the subtle ways I keep
> I pass and deal again!'

Hang'd if he didn't go ahead and do it, too! Oh, he was a cool one! Well, in about a minute things were running pretty tight, but all of a sudden I see by Mr. Emerson's eye he judged he had 'em. He had already corralled two tricks, and each of the others one. So now he kind of lifts a little in his chair and says:

" 'I tire of globes and aces!—
Too long the game is played!'

—and down he fetched a right bower. Mr. Longfellow smiles as sweet as pie and says:

" 'Thanks thanks to thee, my worthy friend,
For the lesson thou hast taught,'

—and blamed if he didn't down with *another* right bower! Emerson claps his hand on his bowie, Longfellow claps his on his revolver, and I went under a bunk. There was going to be trouble; but that monstrous Holmes rose up, wobbling his double chins, and says he, 'Order, gentlemen; the first man that draws, I'll lay down on him and smother him!' All quiet on the Potomac, you bet!

"They were pretty how-come-you-so by now, and they begun to blow. Emerson says, 'The nobbiest thing I ever wrote was "Barbara Frietchie." ' Says Longfellow, 'It don't begin with my "Biglow Papers." ' Says Holmes, 'My "Thanatopsis" lays over 'em both.' They mighty near ended in a fight. Then they wished they had some more company—and Mr. Emerson pointed to me and says:

" 'Is yonder squalid peasant all
That this proud nursery could breed?'

He was a-whetting his bowie on his boot—so I let it pass. Well, sir, next they took it into their heads that they would like some music; so they made me stand up and sing "When Johnny Comes Marching Home" till I dropped—at thirteen minutes past four this morning. That's what I've been through, my friend. When I woke at seven, they were leaving, thank goodness, and Mr. Longfellow had my only boots on, and his'n under his arm. Says I, 'Hold on, there, Evangeline, what are you going to do with *them?*' He says, 'Going to make tracks with 'em; because:

" 'Lives of great men all remind us
We can make our lives sublime;
And, departing, leave behind us
Footprints on the sands of time.'

As I said, Mr. Twain, you are the fourth in twenty-four hours—and I'm going to move; I ain't suited to a littery atmosphere."

I said to the miner, "Why, my dear sir, *these* were not the gracious singers to whom we and the world pay loving reverence and homage; these were impostors."

The miner investigated me with a calm eye for awhile; then said he, "Ah! impostors, were they? Are *you?*"

I did not pursue the subject, and since then I have not traveled on my *nom de guerre* enough to hurt. Such was the reminiscence I was moved to contribute, Mr. Chairman. In my enthusiasm I may have exaggerated the details a little, but you will easily forgive me that fault, since I believe it is the first time I have ever deflected from perpendicular fact on an occasion like this.

The Story

January 11, 1906.

Answer to a letter received this morning:

> DEAR MRS. H.,—I am forever your debtor for reminding me of that curious passage in my life. During the first year or two after it happened, I could not bear to think of it. My pain and shame were so intense, and my sense of having been an imbecile so settled, established and confirmed, that I drove the episode entirely from my mind—and so all these twenty-eight or twenty-nine years I have lived in the conviction that my performance of that time was coarse, vulgar, and destitute of humor. But your suggestion that you and your family found humor in it twenty-eight years ago moved me to look into the matter. So I commissioned a Boston typewriter[1] to delve among the Boston papers of that bygone time and send me a copy of it.
>
> It came this morning, and if there is any vulgarity about it I am not to discover it. If it isn't innocently and ridiculously funny, I am no judge. I will see to it that you get a copy.

What I have said to Mrs. H. is true. I did suffer during a year or two from the deep humiliations of the episode. But at last, in 1888, in Venice, my wife and I came across Mr. and Mrs. A. P. C., of Concord, Massachusetts, and a friendship began then of the sort which nothing but death terminates. The C.'s were very bright people and in every way charming and companionable. We were together a month or two in Venice and several months in Rome, afterward, and one day that lamented break of mine was mentioned. And when I was on the point of lathering those people for bringing it to my mind when I had gotten the memory of it almost squelched, I perceived with joy that the C.'s were indignant about the way that my performance had been received in Boston. They poured out their opinions most freely and frankly about the frosty attitude of the people who were present at that performance, and about the Boston newspapers for the position they had taken in regard to the matter. That position was that I had been irreverent beyond belief, beyond imagination. Very well; I had accepted that as a fact for a year or two, and had been thoroughly miserable about it whenever I thought of it—which was not frequently, if I could help it. Whenever I thought of it I wondered how I ever could have been inspired to do so unholy a thing. Well, the C.'s comforted me, but they did not persuade me to continue to think about the unhappy episode. I resisted that. I tried to get it out of my mind, and let it die, and I succeeded. Until Mrs. H.'s letter came, it had been a good twenty-five years since I had thought of that matter; and when she said that the thing was funny I wondered if possibly she might be right. At any rate, my curiosity was aroused, and I wrote to Boston and got the whole thing copied, as above set forth.

I vaguely remembered some of the details of that gathering—dimly I can see a

---

[1] Typist.

hundred people—no, perhaps fifty—shadowy figures sitting at tables feeding, ghosts now to me, and nameless forevermore. I don't know who they were, but I can very distinctly see, seated at the grand table and facing the rest of us, Mr. Emerson, supernaturally grave, unsmiling; Mr. Whittier, grave, lovely, his beautiful spirit shining out of his face; Mr. Longfellow, with his silken white hair and his benignant face; Dr. Oliver Wendell Holmes, flashing smiles and affection and all good-fellow-ship everywhere like a rose-diamond whose facets are being turned toward the light first one way and then another—a charming man, and always fascinating, whether he was talking or whether he was sitting still (what *he* would call still, but what would be more or less motion to other people). I can see those figures with entire distinctness across this abyss of time.

One other feature is clear—Willie Winter (for these past thousand years dramatic editor of the *New York Tribune,* and still occupying that high post in his old age) was there. He was much younger then than he is now, and he showed it. It was always a pleasure to me to see Willie Winter at a banquet. During a matter of twenty years I was seldom at a banquet where Willie Winter was not also present, and where he did not read a charming poem written for the occasion. He did it this time, and it was up to standard: dainty, happy, choicely phrased, and as good to listen to as music, and sounding exactly as if it was pouring unprepared out of heart and brain.

Now at that point ends all that was pleasurable about that notable celebration of Mr. Whittier's seventieth birthday—because *I* got up at that point and followed Winter, with what I have no doubt I supposed would be the gem of the evening—the gay oration above quoted from the Boston paper. I had written it all out the day before and had perfectly memorized it, and I stood up there at my genial and happy and self-satisfied ease, and began to deliver it. Those majestic guests, that row of venerable and still active volcanoes, listened, as did everybody else in the house, with attentive interest. Well, I delivered myself of—we'll say the first two hundred words of my speech. I was expecting no returns from that part of the speech, but this was not the case as regarded the rest of it. I arrived now at the dialogue: "The old miner said, 'You are the fourth, I'm going to move.' 'The fourth what?' said I. He answered, 'The fourth littery man that has been here in twenty-four hours. I am going to move.' 'Why, you don't tell me,' said I. 'Who were the others?' 'Mr. Longfellow, Mr. Emerson, Mr. Oliver Wendell Holmes, confound the lot—' "

Now, then, the house's *attention* continued, but the expression of interest in the faces turned to a sort of black frost. I wondered what the trouble was. I didn't know. I went on, but with difficulty—I struggled along, and entered upon that miner's fearful description of the bogus Emerson, the bogus Holmes, the bogus Longfellow, always hoping—but with a gradually perishing hope—that somebody would laugh, or that somebody would at least smile, but nobody did. I didn't know enough to give it up and sit down, I was too new to public speaking, and so I went on with this awful performance, and carried it clear through to the end, in front of a body of people who seemed turned to stone with horror. It was the sort of expression their faces would have worn if I had been making these remarks about the Deity and the rest of the Trinity; there is no milder way in which to describe the petrified condition and the ghastly expression of those people.

When I sat down it was with a heart which had long ceased to beat. I shall never be as dead again as I was then. I shall never be as miserable again as I was then. I speak now as one who doesn't know what the conditions of things may be in the next world, but in this one I shall never be as wretched again as I was then. Howells, who was near me, tried to say a comforting word, but couldn't get beyond a gasp. There was no use—he understood the whole size of the disaster. He had good intentions, but the words froze before they could get out. It was an atmosphere that would freeze anything. If Benvenuto Cellini's[2] salamander had been in that place he would not have survived to be put into Cellini's autobiography. There was a frightful pause. There was an awful silence, a desolating silence. Then the next man on the list had to get up—there was no help for it. That was Bishop[3]—Bishop had just burst handsomely upon the world with a most acceptable novel, which had appeared in *The Atlantic Monthly,* a place which would make any novel respectable and any author noteworthy. In this case the novel itself was recognized as being, without extraneous help, respectable. Bishop was away up in the public favor, and he was an object of high interest, consequently there was a sort of national expectancy in the air; we may say our American millions were standing, from Maine to Texas and from Alaska to Florida, holding their breath, their lips parted, their hands ready to applaud, when Bishop should get up on that occasion, and for the first time in his life speak in public. It was under these damaging conditions that he got up to "make good," as the vulgar say. I had spoken several times before, and that is the reason why I was able to go on without dying in my tracks, as I ought to have done—but Bishop had had no experience. He was up facing those awful deities—facing those other people, those strangers—facing human beings for the first time in his life, with a speech to utter. No doubt it was well packed away in his memory, no doubt it was fresh and usable, until I had been heard from. I suppose that after that, and under the smothering pall of that dreary silence, it began to waste away and disappear out of his head like the rags breaking from the edge of a fog, and presently there wasn't any fog left. He didn't go on—he didn't last long. It was not many sentences after his first before he began to hesitate, and break, and lost his grip, and totter, and wobble, and at last he slumped down in a limp and mushy pile.

Well, the programme for the occasion was probably not more than one-third finished, but it ended there. Nobody rose. The next man hadn't strength enough to get up, and everybody looked so dazed, so stupefied, paralyzed, it was impossible for anybody to do anything, or even try. Nothing could go on in that strange atmosphere. Howells mournfully, and without words, hitched himself to Bishop and me and supported us out of the room. It was very kind—he was most generous. He towed us tottering away into some room in that building, and we sat down there. I don't know what my remark was now, but I know the nature of it. It was the kind of remark you make when you know that nothing in the world can help your case. But Howells was honest—he had to say the heart-breaking things he did say: that there was no help for this calamity, this shipwreck, this cataclysm; that this was the most disastrous thing that had ever happened in anybody's history—and then he added, "That is, for *you*—and consider what you have done for Bishop. It is bad enough in your case, you deserve to suffer. You have committed this crime, and you deserve to have all

---

[2] Benvenuto Cellini: Italian sculptor (1500–1571). The significance of the reference is obscure.
[3] William Henry Bishop (1847–1928), author of *Detmold*, a romance published in book form in 1879.

you are going to get. But here is an innocent man. Bishop had never done you any harm, and see what you have done to him. He can never hold his head up again. The world can never look upon Bishop as being a live person. He is a corpse."

That is the history of that episode of twenty-eight years ago, which pretty nearly killed me with shame during that first year or two whenever it forced its way into my mind.

Now then, I take that speech up and examine it. As I said, it arrived this morning, from Boston. I have read it twice, and unless I am an idiot, it hasn't a single defect in it from the first word to the last. It is just as good as good can be. It is smart; it is saturated with humor. There isn't a suggestion of coarseness or vulgarity in it anywhere. What could have been the matter with that house? It is amazing, it is incredible, that they didn't shout with laughter, and those deities the loudest of them all. Could the fault have been with me? Did I lose courage when I saw those great men up there whom I was going to describe in such a strange fashion? If that happened, if I showed doubt, that can account for it, for you can't be successfully funny if you show that you are afraid of it. Well, I can't account for it, but if I had those beloved and revered old literary immortals back here now on the platform at Carnegie Hall I would take that same old speech, deliver it, word for word, and melt them till they'd run all over that stage. Oh, the fault must have been with *me,* it is not in the speech at all.

1923

The Private History of a Campaign That Failed

You have heard from a great many people who did something in the war; is it not fair and right that you listen a little moment to one who started out to do something in it, but didn't? Thousands entered the war, got just a taste of it, and then stepped out again permanently. These, by their very numbers, are respectable, and are therefore entitled to a sort of voice—not a loud one, but a modest one; not a boastful one, but an apologetic one. They ought not to be allowed much space among better people —people who did something. I grant that; but they ought at least to be allowed to state why they didn't do anything, and also to explain the process by which they didn't do anything. Surely this kind of light must have a sort of value.

Out West there was a good deal of confusion in men's minds during the first months of the great trouble—a good deal of unsettledness, of leaning first this way, then that, then the other way. It was hard for us to get our bearings. I call to mind an instance of this. I was piloting on the Mississippi when the news came that South Carolina had gone out of the Union on the 20th of December, 1860. My pilot mate was a New-Yorker. He was strong for the Union; so was I. But he would not listen to me with any patience; my loyalty was smirched, to his eye, because my father had owned slaves. I said, in palliation of this dark fact, that I had heard my father say, some years before he died, that slavery was a great wrong, and that he would free the solitary negro he then owned if he could think it right to give away the property of the family when he was so straitened in means. My mate retorted that a mere impulse was nothing—anybody could pretend to a good impulse; and went on decrying my Unionism and libeling my ancestry. A month later the secession atmosphere had considerably thickened on the Lower Mississippi, and I became a rebel; so did he. We were together in New Orleans the 26th of January, when Louisiana went out of the Union. He did his full share of the rebel shouting, but was bitterly opposed to letting me do mine. He said that I came of bad stock—of a father who had been willing to set slaves free. In the following summer he was piloting a Federal gunboat and shouting for the Union again, and I was in the Confederate army. I held his note for some borrowed money. He was one of the most upright men I ever knew, but he repudiated that note without hesitation because I was a rebel and the son of a man who owned slaves.

In that summer—of 1861—the first wash of the wave of war broke upon the shores of Missouri. Our state was invaded by the Union forces. They took possession of St. Louis, Jefferson Barracks, and some other points. The Governor, Claib Jackson, issued his proclamation calling out fifty thousand militia to repel the invader.

I was visiting in the small town where my boyhood had been spent—Hannibal, Marion County. Several of us got together in a secret place by night and formed ourselves into a military company. One Tom Lyman, a young fellow of a good deal of spirit but of no military experience, was made captain; I was made second lieutenant. We had no first lieutenant; I do not know why; it was long ago. There were fifteen of us. By the advice of an innocent connected with the organization we called ourselves the Marion Rangers. I do not remember that any one found fault with the name. I did not; I thought it sounded quite well. The young fellow who proposed this title was perhaps a fair sample of the kind of stuff we were made of. He was young, ignorant, good-natured, well-meaning, trivial, full of romance, and given to reading chivalric novels and singing forlorn love-ditties. He had some pathetic little nickel-plated aristocratic instincts, and detested his name, which was Dunlap; detested it, partly because it was nearly as common in that region as Smith, but mainly because it had a plebeian sound to his ear. So he tried to ennoble it by writing it in this way: *d'Unlap.* That contented his eye, but left his ear unsatisfied, for people gave the new name the same old pronunciation—emphasis on the front end of it. He then did the bravest thing that can be imagined—a thing to make one shiver when one remembers how the world is given to resenting shams and affectations; he began to write his name so: *d'Un Lap.* And he waited patiently through the long storm of mud that was flung at this work of art, and he had his reward at last; for he lived to see that name accepted, and the emphasis put where he wanted it by people who had known him all his life, and to whom the tribe of Dunlaps had been as familiar as the rain and the sunshine for forty years. So sure of victory at last is the courage that can wait. He said he had found, by consulting some ancient French chronicles, that the name was rightly and originally written d'Un Lap; and said that if it were translated into English it would mean Peterson: *Lap,* Latin or Greek, he said, for stone or rock, same as the French *pierre,* that is to say, Peter: *d',* of or from; *un,* a or one; hence, d'Un Lap, of or from a stone or a Peter; that is to say, one who is the son of a stone, the son of a Peter

—Peterson. Our militia company were not learned, and the explanation confused them; so they called him Peterson Dunlap. He proved useful to us in his way; he named our camps for us, and he generally struck a name that was "no slouch," as the boys said.

That is one sample of us. Another was Ed Stevens, son of the town jeweler—trim-built, handsome, graceful, neat as a cat; bright, educated, but given over entirely to fun. There was nothing serious in life to him. As far as he was concerned, this military expedition of ours was simply a holiday. I should say that about half of us looked upon it in the same way; not consciously, perhaps, but unconsciously. We did not think; we were not capable of it. As for myself, I was full of unreasoning joy to be done with turning out of bed at midnight and four in the morning for a while; grateful to have a change, new scenes, new occupations, a new interest. In my thoughts that was as far as I went; I did not go into the details; as a rule, one doesn't at twenty-four.

Another sample was Smith, the blacksmith's apprentice. This vast donkey had some pluck, of a slow and sluggish nature, but a soft heart; at one time he would knock a horse down for some impropriety, and at another he would get homesick and cry. However, he had one ultimate credit to his account which some of us hadn't; he stuck to the war, and was killed in battle at last.

Jo Bowers, another sample, was a huge, good-natured, flax-headed lubber; lazy, sentimental, full of harmless brag, a grumbler by nature; an experienced, industrious, ambitious, and often quite picturesque liar, and yet not a successful one, for he had had no intelligent training, but was allowed to come up just any way. This life was serious enough to him, and seldom satisfactory. But he was a good fellow, anyway, and the boys all liked him. He was made orderly sergeant; Stevens was made corporal.

These samples will answer—and they are quite fair ones. Well, this herd of cattle started for the war. What could you expect of them? They did as well as they knew how; but, really, what was justly to be expected of them? Nothing, I should say. That is what they did.

We waited for a dark night, for caution and secrecy were necessary; then, toward midnight, we stole in couples and from various directions to the Griffith place, beyond the town; from that point we set out together on foot. Hannibal lies at the extreme southeastern corner of Marion County, on the Mississippi River; our objective point was the hamlet of New London, ten miles away, in Ralls County.

The first hour was all fun, all idle nonsense and laughter. But that could not be kept up. The steady trudging came to be like work; the play had somehow oozed out of it; the stillness of the woods and the somberness of the night began to throw a depressing influence over the spirits of the boys, and presently the talking died out and each person shut himself up in his own thoughts. During the last half of the second hour nobody said a word.

Now we approached a log farm-house where, according to report, there was a guard of five Union soldiers. Lyman called a halt; and there, in the deep gloom of the overhanging branches, he began to whisper a plan of assault upon that house, which made the gloom more depressing than it was before. It was a crucial moment; we realized, with a cold suddenness, that here was no jest—we were standing face to face with actual war. We were equal to the occasion. In our response there was no hesitation, no indecision: we said that if Lyman wanted to meddle with those soldiers, he could go ahead and do it; but if he waited for us to follow him, he would wait a long time.

Lyman urged, pleaded, tried to shame us, but it had no effect. Our course was plain, our minds were made up: we would flank the farm-house—go out around. And that was what we did.

We struck into the woods and entered upon a rough time, stumbling over roots, getting tangled in vines, and torn by briers. At last we reached an open place in a safe region, and sat down, blown and hot, to cool off and nurse our scratches and bruises. Lyman was annoyed, but the rest of us were cheerful; we had flanked the farm-house, we had made our first military movement, and it was a success; we had nothing to fret about, we were feeling just the other way. Horse-play and laughing began again; the expedition was become a holiday frolic once more.

Then we had two more hours of dull trudging and ultimate silence and depression; then, about dawn, we straggled into New London, soiled, heel-blistered, fagged with our little march, and all of us except Stevens in a sour and raspy humor and privately down on the war. We stacked our shabby old shotguns in Colonel Ralls's barn, and then went in a body and breakfasted with that veteran of the Mexican War. Afterward he took us to a distant meadow, and there in the shade of a tree we listened to an old-fashioned speech from him, full of gun-powder and glory, full of that adjective-piling, mixed metaphor and windy declamation which were regarded as eloquence in that ancient time and that remote region; and then he swore us on the Bible to be faithful to the State of Missouri and drive all invaders from her soil, no matter whence they might come or under what flag they might march. This mixed us considerably, and we could not make out just what service we were embarked in; but Colonel Ralls, the practised politician and phrase-juggler, was not similarly in doubt; he knew quite clearly that he had invested us in the cause of the Southern Confederacy. He closed the solemnities by belting around me the sword which his neighbor, Colonel Brown, had worn at Buena Vista and Molino del Rey;[1] and he accompanied this act with another impressive blast.

Then we formed in line of battle and marched four miles to a shady and pleasant piece of woods on the border of the far-reaching expanses of a flowery prairie. It was an enchanting region for war—our kind of war.

We pierced the forest about half a mile, and took up a strong position, with some low, rocky, and wooded hills behind us, and a purling, limpid creek in front. Straightway half the command were in swimming and the other half fishing. The ass with the French name gave this position a romantic title, but it was too long, so the boys shortened and simplified it to Camp Ralls.

We occupied an old maple-sugar camp, whose half-rotted troughs were still propped against the trees. A long corn-crib served for sleeping-quarters for the battalion. On our left, half a mile away, were Mason's farm and house; and he was a friend to the cause. Shortly after noon the farmers began to arrive from several directions, with mules and horses for our use, and these they lent us for as long as the war might last, which they judged would be about three months. The animals were of all sizes, all colors, and all breeds. They were mainly young and frisky, and

---

[1] American victories (February and September 1847) in the Mexican War.

nobody in the command could stay on them long at a time; for we were town boys, and ignorant of horsemanship. The creature that fell to my share was a very small mule, and yet so quick and active that it could throw me without difficulty; and it did this whenever I got on it. Then it would bray—stretching its neck out, laying its ears back, and spreading its jaws till you could see down to its works. It was a disagreeable animal in every way. If I took it by the bridle and tried to lead it off the grounds, it would sit down and brace back, and no one could budge it. However, I was not entirely destitute of military resources, and I did presently manage to spoil this game; for I had seen many a steamboat aground in my time, and knew a trick or two which even a grounded mule would be obliged to respect. There was a well by the corn-crib; so I substituted thirty fathom of rope for the bridle, and fetched him home with the windlass.

I will anticipate here sufficiently to say that we did learn to ride, after some days' practice, but never well. We could not learn to like our animals; they were not choice ones, and most of them had annoying peculiarities of one kind or another. Stevens's horse would carry him, when he was not noticing, under the huge excrescences which form on the trunks of oak-trees, and wipe him out of the saddle; in this way Stevens got several bad hurts. Sergeant Bowers's horse was very large and tall, with slim, long legs, and looked like a railroad bridge. His size enabled him to reach all about, and as far as he wanted to, with his head; so he was always biting Bowers's legs. On the march, in the sun, Bowers slept a good deal; and as soon as the horse recognized that he was asleep he would reach around and bite him on the leg. His legs were black and blue with bites. This was the only thing that could ever make him swear, but this always did; whenever his horse bit him he always swore, and of course Stevens, who laughed at everything, laughed at this, and would even get into such convulsions over it as to lose his balance and fall off his horse; and then Bowers, already irritated by the pain of the horse-bite, would resent the laughter with hard language, and there would be a quarrel; so that horse made no end of trouble and bad blood in the command.

However, I will get back to where I was—our first afternoon in the sugar-camp. The sugar-troughs came very handy as horse-troughs, and we had plenty of corn to fill them with. I ordered Sergeant Bowers to feed my mule; but he said that if I reckoned he went to war to be a dry-nurse to a mule it wouldn't take me very long to find out my mistake. I believed that this was insubordination, but I was full of uncertainties about everything military, and so I let the thing pass, and went and ordered Smith, the blacksmith's apprentice, to feed the mule; but he merely gave me a large, cold, sarcastic grin, such as an ostensibly seven-year-old horse gives you when you lift his lip and find he is fourteen, and turned his back on me. I then went to the captain, and asked if it were not right and proper and military for me to have an orderly. He said it was, but as there was only one orderly in the corps, it was but right that he himself should have Bowers on his staff. Bowers said he wouldn't serve on anybody's staff; and if anybody thought he could make him, let him try it. So, of course, the thing had to be dropped; there was no other way.

Next, nobody would cook; it was considered a degradation; so we had no dinner. We lazied the rest of the pleasant afternoon away, some dozing under the trees, some smoking cob-pipes and talking sweethearts and war, some playing games. By late supper-time all hands were famished; and to meet the difficulty all hands turned to, on an equal footing, and gathered wood, built fires, and cooked the meal. Afterward everything was smooth for a while; then trouble broke out between the corporal and the sergeant, each claiming to rank the other. Nobody knew which was the higher office; so Lyman had to settle the matter by making the rank of both officers equal. The commander of an ignorant crew like that has many troubles and vexations which probably do not occur in the regular army at all. However, with the song-singing and yarn-spinning around the camp-fire, everything presently became serene again; and by and by we raked the corn down level in one end of the crib, and all went to bed on it, tying a horse to the door, so that he would neigh if any one tried to get in.[2]

We had some horsemanship drill every forenoon; then, afternoons, we rode off here and there in squads a few miles, and visited the farmers' girls, and had a youthful good time, and got an honest good dinner or supper, and then home again to camp, happy and content.

For a time life was idly delicious, it was perfect; there was nothing to mar it. Then came some farmers with an alarm one day. They said it was rumored that the enemy were advancing in our direction from over Hyde's prairie. The result was a sharp stir among us, and general consternation. It was a rude awakening from our pleasant trance. The rumor was but a rumor—nothing definite about it; so, in the confusion, we did not know which way to retreat. Lyman was for not retreating at all in these uncertain circumstances; but he found that if he tried to maintain that attitude he would fare badly, for the command were in no humor to put up with insubordination. So he yielded the point and called a council of war—to consist of himself and the three other officers; but the privates made such a fuss about being left out that we had to allow them to remain, for they were already present, and doing the most of the talking too. The question was, which way to retreat; but all were so flurried that nobody seemed to have even a guess to offer. Except Lyman. He explained in a few calm words that, inasmuch as the enemy were approaching from over Hyde's prairie, our course was simple: all we had to do was not to retreat *toward* him; any other direction would answer our needs perfectly. Everybody saw in a moment how true this was, and how wise; so Lyman got a great many compliments. It was now decided that we should fall back on Mason's farm.

It was after dark by this time, and as we could not know how soon the enemy might arrive, it did not seem best to try to take the horses and things with us; so we only took the guns and ammunition, and started at once. The route was very rough and hilly and rocky, and presently the night grew very black and rain began to fall; so we had a troublesome time of it, struggling and stumbling along in the dark; and soon some person slipped and fell, and then the next person behind stumbled over him and fell, and so did the rest, one after the other; and then Bowers came, with

[2] Twain's note: "It was always my impression that that was what the horse was there for, and I know that it was also the impression of at least one other of the command, for we talked about it at the time, and admired the military ingenuity of the device; but when I was out West, three years ago, I was told by Mr. A. G. Fuqua, a member of our company, that the horse was his; that the leaving him tied at the door was a matter of mere forgetfulness, and that to attribute it to intelligent invention was to give him quite too much credit. In support of his position he called my attention to the suggestive fact that the artifice was not employed again. I had not thought of that before."

the keg of powder in his arms, while the command were all mixed together, arms and legs, on the muddy slope; and so he fell, of course, with the keg, and this started the whole detachment down the hill in a body, and they landed in the brook at the bottom in a pile, and each that was undermost pulling the hair and scratching and biting those that were on top of him; and those that were being scratched and bitten scratching and biting the rest in their turn, and all saying they would die before they would ever go to war again if they ever got out of this brook this time, and the invader might rot for all they cared, and the country along with him—and all such talk as that, which was dismal to hear and take part in, in such smothered, low voices, and such a grisly dark place and so wet, and the enemy, maybe, coming any moment.

The keg of powder was lost, and the guns, too; so the growling and complaining continued straight along while the brigade pawed around the pasty hillside and slopped around in the brook hunting for these things; consequently we lost considerable time at this; and then we heard a sound, and held our breath and listened, and it seemed to be the enemy coming, though it could have been a cow, for it had a cough like a cow; but we did not wait, but left a couple of guns behind and struck out for Mason's again as briskly as we could scramble along in the dark. But we got lost presently among the rugged little ravines, and wasted a deal of time finding the way again, so it was after nine when we reached Mason's stile at last; and then before we could open our mouths to give the countersign several dogs came bounding over the fence, with great riot and noise, and each of them took a soldier by the slack of his trousers and began to back away with him. We could not shoot the dogs without endangering the persons they were attached to; so we had to look on helpless at what was perhaps the most mortifying spectacle of the Civil War. There was light enough, and to spare, for the Masons had now run out on the porch with candles in their hands. The old man and his son came and undid the dogs without difficulty, all but Bowers's; but they couldn't undo his dog, they didn't know his combination; he was of the bull kind, and seemed to be set with a Yale time-lock; but they got him loose at last with some scalding water, of which Bowers got his share and returned thanks. Peterson Dunlap afterward made up a fine name for this engagement, and also for the night march which preceded it, but both have long ago faded out of my memory.

We now went into the house, and they began to ask us a world of questions, whereby it presently came out that we did not know anything concerning who or what we were running from; so the old gentleman made himself very frank, and said we were a curious breed of soldiers, and guessed we could be depended on to end up the war in time, because no government could stand the expense of the shoe-leather we should cost it trying to follow us around. "Marion *Rangers!* good name, b'gosh!" said he. And wanted to know why we hadn't had a picket-guard at the place where the road entered the prairie, and why we hadn't sent out a scouting party to spy out the enemy and bring us an account of his strength, and so on, before jumping up and stampeding out of a strong position upon a mere vague rumor—and so on, and so forth, till he made us all feel shabbier than the dogs had done, not half so enthusiastically welcome. So we went to bed shamed and low-spirited; except Stevens. Soon Stevens began to devise a garment for Bowers which could be made to automatically display his battle-scars to the grateful, or conceal them from the envious, according to his occasions; but Bowers was in no humor for this, so there was a fight, and when it was over Stevens had some battle-scars of his own to think about.

Then we got a little sleep. But after all we had gone through, our activities were not over for the night; for about two o'clock in the morning we heard a shout of warning from down the lane, accompanied by a chorus from all the dogs, and in a moment everybody was up and flying around to find out what the alarm was about. The alarmist was a horseman who gave notice that a detachment of Union soldiers was on its way from Hannibal with orders to capture and hang any bands like ours which it could find, and said we had no time to lose. Farmer Mason was in a flurry this time himself. He hurried us out of the house with all haste, and sent one of his negroes with us to show us where to hide ourselves and our telltale guns among the ravines half a mile away. It was raining heavily.

We struck down the lane, then across some rocky pasture-land which offered good advantages for stumbling; consequently we were down in the mud most of the time, and every time a man went down he blackguarded the war, and the people that started it, and everybody connected with it, and gave himself the master dose of all for being so foolish as to go into it. At last we reached the wooded mouth of a ravine, and there we huddled ourselves under the streaming trees, and sent the negro back home. It was a dismal and heart-breaking time. We were like to be drowned with the rain, deafened with the howling wind and the booming thunder, and blinded by the lightning. It was, indeed, a wild night. The drenching we were getting was misery enough, but a deeper misery still was the reflection that the halter might end us before we were a day older. A death of this shameful sort had not occurred to us as being among the possibilities of war. It took the romance all out of the campaign, and turned our dreams of glory into a repulsive nightmare. As for doubting that so barbarous an order had been given, not one of us did that.

The long night wore itself out at last, and then the negro came to us with the news that the alarm had manifestly been a false one, and that breakfast would soon be ready. Straightway we were light-hearted again, and the world was bright, and life as full of hope and promise as ever—for we were young then. How long ago that was! Twenty-four years.

The mongrel child of philology named the night's refuge Camp Devastation, and no soul objected. The Masons gave us a Missouri country breakfast, in Missourian abundance, and we needed it: hot biscuits; hot "wheat bread," prettily criss-crossed in a lattice pattern on top; hot corn-pone; fried chicken; bacon, coffee, eggs, milk, buttermilk, etc.; and the world may be confidently challenged to furnish the equal of such a breakfast, as it is cooked in the South.

We stayed several days at Mason's; and after all these years the memory of the dullness, and stillness, and lifelessness of that slumberous farm-house still oppresses my spirit as with a sense of the presence of death and mourning. There was nothing to do, nothing to think about; there was no interest in life. The male part of the household were away in the fields all day, the women were busy and out of our sight; there was no sound but the plaintive wailing of a spinning-wheel, forever moaning out from some distant room—the most lonesome sound in nature, a sound steeped and sodden with homesickness and the emptiness of life. The family went to bed about dark every night, and as we were not invited to intrude any new customs we naturally followed theirs. Those nights were a hundred years long to youths accustomed to being up till twelve. We lay awake and miserable till that hour every time, and grew old and decrepit waiting through the still eternities for the clock-strikes. This was no place for town boys. So at last it was with something very like joy that we received news that the enemy were on our track again. With a new birth of the old warrior spirit we sprang to our places in line of battle and fell back on Camp Ralls.

Captain Lyman had taken a hint from Mason's talk, and he now gave orders that our camp should be guarded against surprise by the posting of pickets. I was ordered to place a picket at the forks of the road in Hyde's prairie. Night shut down black and threatening. I told Sergeant Bowers to go out to that place and stay till midnight; and, just as I was expecting, he said he wouldn't do it. I tried to get others to go, but all refused. Some excused themselves on account of the weather; but the rest were frank enough to say they wouldn't go in any kind of weather. This kind of thing sounds odd now, and impossible, but there was no surprise in it at the time. On the contrary, it seemed a perfectly natural thing to do. There were scores of little camps scattered over Missouri where the same thing was happening. These camps were composed of young men who had been born and reared to a sturdy independence, and who did not know what it meant to be ordered around by Tom, Dick, and Harry, whom they had known familiarly all their lives, in the village or on the farm. It is quite within the probabilities that this same thing was happening all over the South. James Redpath recognized the justice of this assumption, and furnished the following instance in support of it. During a short stay in East Tennessee he was in a citizen colonel's tent one day talking, when a big private appeared at the door, and, without salute or other circumlocution, said to the colonel:

"Say, Jim, I'm a-goin' home for a few days."

"What for?"

"Well, I hain't b'en there for a right smart while, and I'd like to see how things is comin' on."

"How long are you going to be gone?"

"'Bout two weeks."

"Well, don't be gone longer than that; and get back sooner if you can."

That was all, and the citizen officer resumed his conversation where the private had broken it off. This was in the first months of the war, of course. The camps in our part of Missouri were under Brigadier-General Thomas H. Harris. He was a townsman of ours, a first-rate fellow, and well liked; but we had all familiarly known him as the sole and modest-salaried operator in our telegraph-office, where he had to send about one despatch a week in ordinary times, and two when there was a rush of business; consequently, when he appeared in our midst one day, on the wing, and delivered a military command of some sort, in a large military fashion, nobody was surprised at the response which he got from the assembled soldiery:

"Oh, now, what'll you take to *don't,* Tom Harris?"

It was quite the natural thing. One might justly imagine that we were hopeless material for war. And so we seemed, in our ignorant state; but there were those among us who afterward learned the grim trade; learned to obey like machines; became valuable soldiers; fought all through the war, and came out at the end with excellent records. One of the very boys who refused to go out on picket duty that night, and called me an ass for thinking he would expose himself to danger in such a foolhardy way, had become distinguished for intrepidity before he was a year older.

I did secure my picket that night—not by authority, but by diplomacy. I got Bowers to go by agreeing to exchange ranks with him for the time being, and go along and stand the watch with him as his subordinate. We stayed out there a couple of dreary hours in the pitchy darkness and the rain, with nothing to modify the dreariness but Bowers's monotonous growlings at the war and the weather; then we began to nod, and presently found it next to impossible to stay in the saddle; so we gave up the tedious job, and went back to the camp without waiting for the relief guard. We rode into camp without interruption or objection from anybody, and the enemy could have done the same, for there were no sentries. Everybody was asleep; at midnight there was nobody to send out another picket, so none was sent. We never tried to establish a watch at night again, as far as I remember, but we generally kept a picket out in the daytime.

In that camp the whole command slept on the corn in the big corn-crib; and there was usually a general row before morning, for the place was full of rats, and they would scramble over the boys' bodies and faces, annoying and irritating everybody; and now and then they would bite some one's toe, and the person who owned the toe would start up and magnify his English and begin to throw corn in the dark. The ears were half as heavy as bricks, and when they struck they hurt. The persons struck would respond, and inside of five minutes every man would be locked in a death-grip with his neighbor. There was a grievous deal of blood shed in the corncrib, but this was all that was spilt while I was in the war. No, that is not quite true. But for one circumstance it would have been all. I will come to that now.

Our scares were frequent. Every few days rumors would come that the enemy were approaching. In these cases we always fell back on some other camp of ours; we never stayed where we were. But the rumors always turned out to be false; so at last even we began to grow indifferent to them. One night a negro was sent to our corn-crib with the same old warning: the enemy was hovering in our neighborhood. We all said let him hover. We resolved to stay still and be comfortable. It was a fine warlike resolution, and no doubt we all felt the stir of it in our veins—for a moment. We had been having a very jolly time, that was full of horse-play and schoolboy hilarity; but that cooled down now, and presently the fast-waning fire of forced jokes and forced laughs died out altogether, and the company became silent. Silent and nervous. And soon uneasy—worried—apprehensive. We had said we would stay, and we were committed. We could have been persuaded to go, but there was nobody brave enough to suggest it. An almost noiseless movement presently began in the dark by a general but unvoiced impulse. When the movement was completed each man knew that he was not the only person who had crept to the front wall and had his eye at a crack between the logs. No, we were all there; all there with our hearts in our throats, and staring out toward the sugar-troughs where the forest footpath came through. It was late, and there was a deep woodsy stillness everywhere. There was a veiled moonlight, which was only just strong enough to enable us to mark the general shape of objects. Presently a muffled sound caught our ears, and we recognized it as the hoof-beats of a horse or horses. And right away a figure appeared in the forest path; it could have been made of smoke, its mass had so little sharpness of outline. It was a man on horse-back, and it seemed to me that there were others behind him. I got hold of a gun in the dark, and pushed it through a crack between the logs, hardly knowing what I was doing, I was so dazed with fright. Somebody said "Fire!" I pulled the trigger. I seemed to see a hundred flashes and hear a hundred reports; then I saw the man fall down out of the saddle. My first feeling was of surprised gratification; my first impulse was an apprentice-sportsman's impulse to run and pick up his game. Somebody said, hardly audibly, "Good—we've got him!—wait for the rest." But the rest did not come. We waited—listened—still no more came. There was not a sound, not the whisper of a leaf; just perfect stillness; an uncanny kind of stillness, which was all the more uncanny on account of the damp, earthy, late-night smells now rising and pervading it. Then, wondering, we crept stealthily out, and approached the man. When we got to him the moon revealed him distinctly. He was lying on his back, with his arms abroad; his mouth was open and his chest heaving with long gasps, and his white shirt-front was all splashed with blood. The thought shot through me that I was a murderer; that I had killed a man—a man who had never done me any harm. That was the coldest sensation that ever went through my marrow. I was down by him in a moment, helplessly stroking his forehead; and I would have given anything then—my own life freely—to make him again what he had been five minutes before. And all the boys seemed to be feeling in the same way; they hung over him, full of pitying interest, and tried all they could to help him, and said all sorts of regretful things. They had forgotten all about the enemy; they thought only of this one forlorn unit of the foe. Once my imagination persuaded me that the dying man gave me a reproachful look out of his shadowy eyes, and it seemed to me that I could rather he had stabbed me than done that. He muttered and mumbled like a dreamer in his sleep about his wife and his child; and I thought with a new despair, "This thing that I have done does not end with him; it falls upon *them* too, and they never did me any harm, any more than he."

In a little while the man was dead. He was killed in war; killed in fair and legitimate war; killed in battle, as you may say; and yet he was as sincerely mourned by the opposing force as if he had been their brother. The boys stood there a half-hour sorrowing over him, and recalling the details of the tragedy, and wondering who he might be, and if he were a spy, and saying that if it were to do over again they would not hurt him unless he attacked them first. It soon came out that mine was not the only shot fired; there were five others—a division of the guilt which was a great relief to me, since it in some degree lightened and diminished the burden I was carrying. There were six shots fired at once; but I was not in my right mind at the time, and my heated imagination had magnified my one shot into a volley.

The man was not in uniform, and was not armed. He was a stranger in the country; that was all we ever found out about him. The thought of him got to preying upon me every night; I could not get rid of it. I could not drive it away, the taking of that unoffending life seemed such a wanton thing. And it seemed an epitome of war; that all war must be just that—the killing of strangers against whom you feel no personal animosity; strangers whom, in other circumstances, you would help if you found them in trouble, and who would help you if you needed it. My campaign was spoiled. It seemed to me that I was not rightly equipped for this awful business; that war was intended for men, and I for a child's nurse. I resolved to retire from this avocation of sham soldiership while I could save some remnant of my self-respect. These morbid thoughts clung to me against reason; for at bottom I did not believe I had touched that man. The law of probabilities decreed me guiltless of his blood; for in all my small experience with guns I had never hit anything I had tried to hit, and I knew I had done my best to hit him. Yet there was no solace in the thought. Against a diseased imagination demonstration goes for nothing.

The rest of my war experience was of a piece with what I have already told of it. We kept monotonously falling back upon one camp or another, and eating up the farmers and their families. They ought to have shot us; on the contrary, they were as hospitably kind and courteous to us as if we had deserved it. In one of these camps we found Ab Grimes, an Upper Mississippi pilot, who afterward became famous as a dare-devil rebel spy, whose career bristled with desperate adventures. The look and style of his comrades suggested that they had not come into the war to play, and their deeds made good the conjecture later. They were fine horsemen and good revolver shots; but their favorite arm was the lasso. Each had one at his pommel, and could snatch a man out of the saddle with it every time, on a full gallop, at any reasonable distance.

In another camp the chief was a fierce and profane old blacksmith of sixty, and he had furnished his twenty recruits with gigantic home-made bowie-knives, to be swung with two hands, like the *machetes* of the Isthmus. It was a grisly spectacle to see that earnest band practising their murderous cuts and slashes under the eye of that remorseless old fanatic.

The last camp which we fell back upon was in a hollow near the village of Florida, where I was born—in Monroe County. Here we were warned one day that a Union colonel was sweeping down on us with a whole regiment at his heel. This looked decidedly serious. Our boys went apart and consulted; then we went back and told the other companies present that the war was a disappointment to us, and we were going to disband. They were getting ready themselves to fall back on some place or other, and we were only waiting for General Tom Harris, who was expected to arrive at any moment; so they tried to persuade us to wait a little while, but the majority of us said no, we were accustomed to falling back, and didn't need any of Tom Harris's help; we could get along perfectly well without him—and save time, too. So about half of our fifteen, including myself, mounted and left on the instant; the others yielded to persuasion and stayed—stayed through the war.

An hour later we met General Harris on the road, with two or three people in his company—his staff, probably, but we could not tell; none of them were in uniform; uniforms had not come into vogue among us yet. Harris ordered us back; but we told him there was a Union colonel coming with a whole regiment in his wake, and it looked as if there was going to be a disturbance; so we had concluded to go home. He raged a little, but it was of no use; our minds were made up. We had done our share; had killed one man, exterminated one army, such as it was; let him go and kill the rest, and that would end the war. I did not see that brisk young general again until last year; then he was wearing white hair and whiskers.

In time I came to know that Union colonel whose coming frightened me out of the war and crippled the Southern cause to that extent—General Grant. I came within a few hours of seeing him when he was as unknown as I was myself; at a time when anybody could have said, "Grant?—Ulysses S. Grant? I do not remember hearing the name before." It seems difficult to realize that there was once a time when such a remark could be rationally made; but there was, and I was within a few miles of the place and the occasion, too, though proceeding in the other direction.

The thoughtful will not throw this war paper of mine lightly aside as being valueless. It has this value: it is a not unfair picture of what went on in many and many a militia camp in the first months of the rebellion, when the green recruits were without discipline, without the steadying and heartening influence of trained leaders;

when all their circumstances were new and strange, and charged with exaggerated terrors, and before the invaluable experience of actual collision in the field had turned them from rabbits into soldiers. If this side of the picture of that early day has not before been put into history, then history has been to that degree incomplete, for it had and has its rightful place there. There was more Bull Run material scattered through the early camps of this country than exhibited itself at Bull Run. And yet it learned its trade presently, and helped to fight the great battles later. I could have become a soldier myself if I had waited. I had got part of it learned; I knew more about retreating than the man that invented retreating.

1885

Fenimore Cooper's Literary Offenses

The Pathfinder *and* The Deerslayer *stand at the head of Cooper's novels as artistic creations. There are others of his works which contain parts as perfect as are to be found in these, and scenes even more thrilling. Not one can be compared with either of them as a finished whole.*
   The defects in both of these tales are comparatively slight. They were pure works of art.
   Prof. Lounsbury

   The five tales reveal an extraordinary fullness of invention. . . . One of the very greatest characters in fiction, Natty Bumppo. . . .
   The craft of the woodsman, the tricks of the trapper, all the delicate art of the forest, were familiar to Cooper from his youth up.
   Prof. Brander Matthews

      Cooper is the greatest artist in the domain of romantic fiction yet produced by America.
      Wilkie Collins

It seems to me that it was far from right for the Professor of English Literature in Yale, the Professor of English Literature in Columbia, and Wilkie Collins to deliver opinions on Cooper's literature without having read some of it. It would have been much more decorous to keep silent and let persons talk who have read Cooper.

Cooper's art has some defects. In one place in *Deerslayer,* and in the restricted space of two-thirds of a page, Cooper has scored 114 offenses against literary art out of a possible 115. It breaks the record.

There are nineteen rules governing literary art in the domain of romantic fiction —some say twenty-two. In *Deerslayer* Cooper violated eighteen of them. These eighteen require:

1. That a tale shall accomplish something and arrive somewhere. But the *Deer-slayer* tale accomplishes nothing and arrives in the air.
2. They require that the episodes of a tale shall be necessary parts of the tale, and

shall help to develop it. But as the *Deerslayer* tale is not a tale, and accomplishes nothing and arrives nowhere, the episodes have no rightful place in the work, since there was nothing for them to develop.

3. They require that the personages in a tale shall be alive, except in the case of corpses, and that always the reader shall be able to tell the corpses from the others. But this detail has often been overlooked in the *Deerslayer* tale.

4. They require that the personages in a tale, both dead and alive, shall exhibit a sufficient excuse for being there. But this detail also has been overlooked in the *Deerslayer* tale.

5. They require that when the personages of a tale deal in conversation, the talk shall sound like human talk, and be talk such as human beings would be likely to talk in the given circumstances, and have a discoverable meaning, also a discoverable purpose, and a show of relevancy, and remain in the neighborhood of the subject in hand, and be interesting to the reader, and help out the tale, and stop when the people cannot think of anything more to say. But this requirement has been ignored from the beginning of the *Deerslayer* tale to the end of it.

6. They require that when the author describes the character of a personage in his tale, the conduct and conversation of that personage shall justify said description. But this law gets little or no attention in the *Deerslayer* tale, as Natty Bumppo's case will amply prove.

7. They require that when a personage talks like an illustrated, gilt-edged, tree-calf, hand-tooled, seven-dollar Friendship's Offering in the beginning of a paragraph, he shall not talk like a negro minstrel in the end of it. But this rule is flung down and danced upon in the *Deerslayer* tale.

8. They require that crass stupidities shall not be played upon the reader as "the craft of the woodsman, the delicate art of the forest," by either the author or the people in the tale. But this rule is persistently violated in the *Deerslayer* tale.

9. They require that the personages of a tale shall confine themselves to possibilities and let miracles alone; or, if they venture a miracle, the author must so plausibly set it forth as to make it look possible and reasonable. But these rules are not respected in the *Deerslayer* tale.

10. They require that the author shall make the reader feel a deep interest in the personages of his tale and in their fate; and that he shall make the reader love the good people in the tale and hate the bad ones. But the reader of the *Deerslayer* tale dislikes the good people in it, is indifferent to the others, and wishes they would all get drowned together.

11. They require that the characters in a tale shall be so clearly defined that the reader can tell beforehand what each will do in a given emergency. But in the *Deerslayer* tale this rule is vacated.

In addition to these large rules there are some little ones. These require that the author shall

12. *Say* what he is proposing to say, not merely come near it.

13. Use the right word, not its second cousin.

14. Eschew surplusage.

15. Not omit necessary details.
16. Avoid slovenliness of form.
17. Use good grammar.
18. Employ a simple and straightforward style.

Even these seven are coldly and persistently violated in the *Deerslayer* tale.

Cooper's gift in the way of invention was not a rich endowment; but such as it was he liked to work it, he was pleased with the effects, and indeed he did some quite sweet things with it. In his little box of stage-properties he kept six or eight cunning devices, tricks, artifices for his savages and woodsmen to deceive and circumvent each other with, and he was never so happy as when he was working these innocent things and seeing them go. A favorite one was to make a moccasined person tread in the tracks of the moccasined enemy, and thus hide his own trail. Cooper wore out barrels and barrels of moccasins in working that trick. Another stage-property that he pulled out of his box pretty frequently was his broken twig. He prized his broken twig above all the rest of his effects, and worked it the hardest. It is a restful chapter in any book of his when somebody doesn't step on a dry twig and alarm all the reds and whites for two hundred yards around. Every time a Cooper person is in peril, and absolute silence is worth four dollars a minute, he is sure to step on a dry twig. There may be a hundred handier things to step on, but that wouldn't satisfy Cooper. Cooper requires him to turn out and find a dry twig; and if he can't do it, go and borrow one. In fact, the Leatherstocking Series ought to have been called the Broken Twig Series.

I am sorry there is not room to put in a few dozen instances of the delicate art of the forest, as practised by Natty Bumppo and some of the other Cooperian experts. Perhaps we may venture two or three samples. Cooper was a sailor—a naval officer; yet he gravely tells us how a vessel, driving toward a lee shore in a gale, is steered for a particular spot by her skipper because he knows of an *undertow* there which will hold her back against the gale and save her. For just pure woodcraft, or sailorcraft, or whatever it is, isn't that neat? For several years Cooper was daily in the society of artillery, and he ought to have noticed that when a cannon-ball strikes the ground it either buries itself or skips a hundred feet or so; skips again a hundred feet or so —and so on, till finally it gets tired and rolls. Now in one place he loses some "females"—as he always calls women—in the edge of a wood near a plain at night in a fog, on purpose to give Bumppo a chance to show off the delicate art of the forest before the reader. These mislaid people are hunting for a fort. They hear a cannon-blast, and a cannon-ball presently comes rolling into the wood and stops at their feet. To the females this suggests nothing. The case is very different with the admirable Bumppo. I wish I may never know peace again if he doesn't strike out promptly and *follow the track* of that cannon-ball across the plain through the dense fog and find the fort. Isn't it a daisy? If Cooper had any real knowledge of Nature's ways of doing things, he had a most delicate art in concealing the fact. For instance: one of his acute Indian experts, Chingachgook (pronounced Chicago, I think), has lost the trail of a person he is tracking through the forest. Apparently that trail is hopelessly lost. Neither you nor I could ever have guessed out the way to find it. It was very different with Chicago. Chicago was not stumped for long. He turned a running stream out of its course, and there, in the slush in its old bed, were that person's moccasin tracks.

The current did not wash them away, as it would have done in all other like cases—no, even the eternal laws of Nature have to vacate when Cooper wants to put up a delicate job of woodcraft on the reader.

We must be a little wary when Brander Matthews tells us that Cooper's books "reveal an extraordinary fullness of invention." As a rule, I am quite willing to accept Brander Matthews's literary judgments and applaud his lucid and graceful phrasing of them; but that particular statement needs to be taken with a few tons of salt. Bless your heart, Cooper hadn't any more invention than a horse; and I don't mean a high-class horse, either; I mean a clothes-horse. It would be very difficult to find a really clever "situation" in Cooper's books, and still more difficult to find one of any kind which he has failed to render absurd by his handling of it. Look at the episodes of "the caves"; and at the celebrated scuffle between Maqua and those others on the table-land a few days later; and at Hurry Harry's queer water-transit from the castle to the ark; and at Deerslayer's half-hour with his first corpse; and at the quarrel between Hurry Harry and Deerslayer later; and at—but choose for yourself; you can't go amiss.

If Cooper had been an observer his inventive faculty would have worked better; not more interestingly, but more rationally, more plausibly. Cooper's proudest creations in the way of "situations" suffer noticeably from the absence of the observer's protecting gift. Cooper's eye was splendidly inaccurate. Cooper seldom saw anything correctly. He saw nearly all things as through a glass eye, darkly. Of course a man who cannot see the commonest little every-day matters accurately is working at a disadvantage when he is constructing a "situation." In the *Deerslayer* tale Cooper has a stream which is fifty feet wide where it flows out of a lake; it presently narrows to twenty as it meanders along for no given reason, and yet when a stream acts like that it ought to be required to explain itself. Fourteen pages later the width of the brook's outlet from the lake has suddenly shrunk thirty feet, and become "the narrowest part of the stream." This shrinkage is not accounted for. The stream has bends in it, a sure indication that it has alluvial banks and cuts them; yet these bends are only thirty and fifty feet long. If Cooper had been a nice and punctilious observer he would have noticed that the bends were oftener nine hundred feet long than short of it.

Cooper made the exit of that stream fifty feet wide, in the first place, for no particular reason; in the second place, he narrowed it to less than twenty to accommodate some Indians. He bends a "sapling" to the form of an arch over this narrow passage, and conceals six Indians in its foliage. They are "laying" for a settler's scow or ark which is coming up the stream on its way to the lake; it is being hauled against the stiff current by a rope whose stationary end is anchored in the lake; its rate of progress cannot be more than a mile an hour. Cooper describes the ark, but pretty obscurely. In the matter of dimensions "it was little more than a modern canal-boat." Let us guess, then, that it was about one hundred and forty feet long. It was of "greater breadth than common." Let us guess, then, that it was about sixteen feet wide. This leviathan had been prowling down bends which were but a third as long as itself, and scraping between banks where it had only two feet of space to spare on each side. We cannot too much admire this miracle. A low-roofed log dwelling occupies "two-thirds of the ark's length"—a dwelling ninety feet long and sixteen feet wide, let us say—a kind of vestibule train. The dwelling has two rooms—each forty-five feet long and sixteen feet wide, let us guess. One of them is the bedroom of the Hutter girls, Judith and Hetty; the other is the parlor in the daytime, at night it is papa's bedchamber. The ark is arriving at the stream's exit now, whose width has been reduced to less than twenty feet to accommodate the Indians—say to eighteen. There is a foot to spare on each side of the boat. Did the Indians notice that there was going to be a tight squeeze there? Did they notice that they could make money by climbing down out of that arched sapling and just stepping aboard when the ark scraped by? No, other Indians would have noticed these things, but Cooper's Indians never notice anything. Cooper thinks they are marvelous creatures for noticing, but he was almost always in error about his Indians. There was seldom a sane one among them.

The ark is one hundred and forty-feet long; the dwelling is ninety feet long. The idea of the Indians is to drop softly and secretly from the arched sapling to the dwelling as the ark creeps along under it at the rate of a mile an hour, and butcher the family. It will take the ark a minute and a half to pass under. It will take the ninety-foot dwelling a minute to pass under. Now, then, what did the six Indians do? It would take you thirty years to guess, and even then you would have to give it up, I believe. Therefore, I will tell you what the Indians did. Their chief, a person of quite extraordinary intellect for a Cooper Indian, warily watched the canal-boat as it squeezed along under him, and when he had got his calculations fined down to exactly the right shade, as he judged, he let go and dropped. And *missed the house!* That is actually what he did. He missed the house, and landed in the stern of the scow. It was not much of a fall, yet it knocked him silly. He lay there unconscious. If the house had been ninety-seven feet long he would have made the trip. The fault was Cooper's, not his. The error lay in the construction of the house. Cooper was no architect.

There still remained in the roost five Indians. The boat has passed under and is now out of their reach. Let me explain what the five did—you would not be able to reason it out for yourself. No. 1 jumped for the boat, but fell in the water astern of it. Then No. 2 jumped for the boat, but fell in the water still farther astern of it. Then No. 3 jumped for the boat, and fell a good way astern of it. Then No. 4 jumped for the boat, and fell in the water *away* astern. Then even No. 5 made a jump for the boat —for he was a Cooper Indian. In the matter of intellect, the difference between a Cooper Indian and the Indian that stands in front of the cigar-shop is not spacious. The scow episode is really a sublime burst of invention; but it does not thrill, because the inaccuracy of the details throws a sort of air of fictitiousness and general improbability over it. This comes of Cooper's inadequacy as an observer.

The reader will find some examples of Cooper's high talent for inaccurate observation in the account of the shooting-match in *The Pathfinder*.

A common wrought nail was driven lightly into the target, its head having been first touched with paint.

The color of the paint is not stated—an important omission, but Cooper deals freely in important omissions. No, after all, it was not an important omission; for this nail-head is *a hundred yards from* the marksmen, and could not be seen by them at that distance, no matter what its color might be. How far can the best eyes see a common house-fly? A hundred yards? It is quite impossible. Very well; eyes that cannot see a house-fly that is a hundred yards away cannot see an ordinary nail-head at that distance, for the size of the two objects is the same. It takes a keen eye to see a fly or a nail-head at fifty yards—one hundred and fifty feet. Can the reader do it?

The nail was lightly driven, its head painted, and game called. Then the Cooper miracles began. The bullet of the first marksman chipped an edge of the nail-head; the next man's bullet drove the nail a little way into the target—and removed all the paint. Haven't the miracles gone far enough now? Not to suit Cooper; for the purpose of this whole scheme is to show off his prodigy, Deerslayer-Hawkeye-Long-Rifle-Leatherstocking-Pathfinder-Bumppo before the ladies.

"Be all ready to clench it, boys!" cried out Pathfinder, stepping into his friend's tracks the instant they were vacant. "Never mind a new nail; I can see that, though the paint is gone, and what I can see I can hit at a hundred yards, though it were only a mosquito's eye. Be ready to clench!"

The rifle cracked, the bullet sped its way, and the head of the nail was buried in the wood, covered by the piece of flattened lead.

There, you see, is a man who could hunt flies with a rifle, and command a ducal salary in a Wild West show to-day if we had him back with us.

The recorded feat is certainly surprising just as it stands; but it is not surprising enough for Cooper. Cooper adds a touch. He has made Pathfinder do this miracle with another man's rifle; and not only that, but Pathfinder did not have even the advantage of loading it himself. He had everything against him, and yet he made that impossible shot; and not only made it, but did it with absolute confidence, saying, "Be ready to clench." Now a person like that would have undertaken that same feat with a brickbat, and with Cooper to help he would have achieved it, too.

Pathfinder showed off handsomely that day before the ladies. His very first feat was a thing which no Wild West show can touch. He was standing with the group of marksmen, observing—a hundred yards from the target, mind; one Jasper raised his rifle and drove the center of the bull's-eye. Then the Quartermaster fired. The target exhibited no result this time. There was a laugh. "It's a dead miss," said Major Lundie. Pathfinder waited an impressive moment or two; then said, in that calm, indifferent, know-it-all way of his, "No, Major, he has covered Jasper's bullet, as will be seen if any one will take the trouble to examine the target."

Wasn't it remarkable! How *could* he see that little pellet fly through the air and enter that distant bullet-hole? Yet that is what he did; for nothing is impossible to a Cooper person. Did any of those people have any deep-seated doubts about this thing? No; for that would imply sanity, and these were all Cooper people.

The respect for Pathfinder's skill and for his quickness and accuracy of sight [the italics are mine] was so profound and general, that the instant he made this declaration the spectators began to distrust their own opinions, and a dozen rushed to the target in order to ascertain the fact. There, sure enough, it was found that the Quartermaster's bullet had gone through the hole made by Jasper's, and that, too, so accurately as to require a minute examination to be certain of the circumstance, which, however, was soon clearly established by discovering one bullet over the other in the stump against which the target was placed.

They made a "minute" examination; but never mind, how could they know that there were two bullets in that hole without digging the latest one out? For neither probe nor eyesight could prove the presence of any more than one bullet. Did they dig? No; as we shall see. It is the Pathfinder's turn now; he steps out before the ladies, takes aim, and fires.

But, alas! here is a disappointment; an incredible, an unimaginable disappointment —for the target's aspect is unchanged; there is nothing there but that same old bullet-hole!

"If one dared to hint at such a thing," cried Major Duncan, "I should say that the Pathfinder has also missed the target!"

As nobody had missed it yet, the "also" was not necessary; but never mind about that, for the Pathfinder is going to speak.

"No, no, Major," said he, confidently, "that *would* be a risky declaration. I didn't load the piece, and can't say what was in it; but if it was lead, you will find the bullet driving down those of the Quartermaster and Jasper, else is not my name Pathfinder."

A shout from the target announced the truth of this assertion.

Is the miracle sufficient as it stands? Not for Cooper. The Pathfinder speaks again, as he "now slowly advances toward the stage occupied by the females":

"That's not all, boys, that's not all; if you find the target touched at all, I'll own to a miss. The Quartermaster cut the wood, but you'll find no wood cut by that last messenger."

The miracle is at last complete. He knew—doubtless *saw*—at the distance of a hundred yards—that his bullet had passed into the hole *without fraying the edges*. There were now three bullets in that one hole—three bullets embedded processionally in the body of the stump back of the target. Everybody knew this—somehow or other —and yet nobody had dug any of them out to make sure. Cooper is not a close observer, but he is interesting. He is certainly always that, no matter what happens. And he is more interesting when he is not noticing what he is about than when he is. This is a considerable merit.

The conversations in the Cooper books have a curious sound in our modern ears. To believe that such talk really ever came out of people's mouths would be to believe that there was a time when time was of no value to a person who thought he had something to say; when it was the custom to spread a two-minute remark out to ten; when a man's mouth was a rolling-mill, and busied itself all day long in turning four-foot pigs of thought into thirty-foot bars of conversational railroad iron by attenuation; when subjects were seldom faithfully stuck to, but the talk wandered all around and arrived nowhere; when conversations consisted mainly of irrelevancies, with here and there a relevancy, a relevancy with an embarrassed look, as not being able to explain how it got there.

Cooper was certainly not a master in the construction of dialogue. Inaccurate observation defeated him here as it defeated him in so many other enterprises of his. He even failed to notice that the man who talks corrupt English six days in the week must and will talk it on the seventh, and can't help himself. In the *Deerslayer* story he lets Deerslayer talk the showiest kind of book-talk sometimes, and at other times the basest of base dialects. For instance, when some one asks him if he has a sweetheart, and if so, where she abides, this is his majestic answer:

"She's in the forest—hanging from the boughs of the trees, in a soft rain—in the dew on the open grass—the clouds that float about in the blue heavens— the birds that sing in the woods—the sweet springs where I slake my thirst— and in all the other glorious gifts that come from God's Providence!"

And he preceded that, a little before, with this:

"It consarns me as all things that touches a fri'nd consarns a fri'nd."

And this is another of his remarks:

"If I was Injin born, now, I might tell of this, or carry in the scalp and boast of the expl'ite afore the whole tribe; or if my inimy had only been a bear"— [and so on].

We cannot imagine such a thing as a veteran Scotch Commander-in-Chief comporting himself in the field like a windy melodramatic actor, but Cooper could. On one occasion Alice and Cora were being chased by the French through a fog in the neighborhood of their father's fort:

"Point de quartier aux coquins!" cried an eager pursuer, who seemed to direct the operations of the enemy.

"Stand firm and be ready, my gallant 6oths!" suddenly exclaimed a voice above them; "wait to see the enemy; fire low, and sweep the glacis."

"Father! father" exclaimed a piercing cry from out the mist; "it is I! Alice! thy own Elsie! spare, O! save your daughters!"

"Hold!" shouted the former speaker, in the awful tones of parental agony, the sound reaching even to the woods, and rolling back in solemn echo. "'Tis she! God has restored me my children! Throw open the sally-port; to the field, 6oths, to the field! pull not a trigger, lest ye kill my lambs! Drive off these dogs of France with your steel!"

Cooper's word-sense was singularly dull. When a person has a poor ear for music he will flat and sharp right along without knowing it. He keeps near the tune, but it is *not* the tune. When a person has a poor ear for words, the result is a literary flatting and sharping; you perceive what he is intending to say, but you also perceive that he doesn't say it. This is Cooper. He was not a word-musician. His ear was satisfied with the *approximate* word. I will furnish some circumstantial evidence in support of this charge. My instances are gathered from half a dozen pages of the tale called *Deerslayer.* He uses "verbal" for "oral"; "precision" for "facility"; "phenomena" for "marvels"; "necessary" for "predetermined"; "unsophisticated" for "primitive"; "preparation" for "expectancy"; "rebuked" for "subdued"; "dependent on" for "resulting from"; "fact" for "condition"; "fact" for "conjecture"; "precaution" for "caution"; "explain" for "determine"; "mortified" for "disappointed"; "meretricious" for "factitious"; "materially" for "considerably"; "decreasing" for "deepening"; "increasing" for "disappearing"; "embedded" for "inclosed"; "treacherous" for "hostile"; "stood" for "stooped"; "softened" for "replaced"; "rejoined" for "remarked"; "situation" for "condition"; "different" for "differing"; "insensible" for "unsentient"; "brevity" for "celerity"; "distrusted" for "suspicious"; "mental imbecility" for "imbecility"; "eyes" for "sight"; "counteracting" for "opposing"; "funeral obsequies" for "obsequies."

There have been daring people in the world who claimed that Cooper could write English, but they are all dead now—all dead but Lounsbury. I don't remember that Lounsbury makes the claim in so many words, still he makes it, for he says that *Deerslayer* is a "pure work of art." Pure, in that connection, means faultless—faultless in all details—and language is a detail. If Mr. Lounsbury had only compared Cooper's English with the English which he writes himself—but it is plain that he didn't; and so it is likely that he imagines until this day that Cooper's is as clean and compact as his own. Now I feel sure, deep down in my heart, that Cooper wrote about the poorest English that exists in our language, and that the English of *Deerslayer* is the very worst that even Cooper ever wrote.

I may be mistaken, but it does seem to me that *Deerslayer* is not a work of art in any sense; it does seem to me that it is destitute of every detail that goes to the making of a work of art; in truth, it seems to me that *Deerslayer* is just simply a literary *delirium tremens.*

A work of art? It has no invention; it has no order, system, sequence, or result; it has no life-likeness, no thrill, no stir, no seeming of reality; its characters are confusedly drawn, and by their acts and words they prove that they are not the sort of people the author claims that they are; its humor is pathetic; its pathos is funny; its conversations are—oh! indescribable; its love-scenes odious; its English a crime against the language.

Counting these out, what is left is Art. I think we must all admit that.

1895

Corn-Pone Opinions

Fifty years ago, when I was a boy of fifteen and helping to inhabit a Missourian village on the banks of the Mississippi, I had a friend whose society was very dear to me because I was forbidden by my mother to partake of it. He was a gay and impudent and satirical and delightful young black man—a slave—who daily preached sermons from the top of his master's woodpile, with me for sole audience. He imitated the pulpit style of the several clergymen of the village, and did it well, and with fine passion and energy. To me he was a wonder. I believed he was the greatest orator in the United States and would some day be heard from. But it did not happen; in the distribution of rewards he was overlooked. It is the way, in this world.

He interrupted his preaching, now and then, to saw a stick of wood; but the sawing was a pretense—he did it with his mouth; exactly imitating the sound the bucksaw makes in shrieking its way through the wood. But it served its purpose; it kept his master from coming out to see how the work was getting along. I listened to the sermons from the open window of a lumber room at the back of the house. One of his texts was this:

"You tell me whar a man gits his corn pone, en I'll tell you what his 'pinions is."

I can never forget it. It was deeply impressed upon me. By my mother. Not upon my memory, but elsewhere. She had slipped in upon me while I was absorbed and not watching. The black philosopher's idea was that a man is not independent, and cannot afford views which might interfere with his bread and butter. If he would prosper, he must train with the majority; in matters of large moment, like politics and religion, he must think and feel with the bulk of his neighbors, or suffer damage in his social standing and in his business prosperities. He must restrict himself to corn-pone opinions—at least on the surface. He must get his opinions from other people; he must reason out none for himself; he must have no first-hand views.

I think Jerry was right, in the main, but I think he did not go far enough.

1. It was his idea that a man conforms to the majority view of his locality by calculation and intention.

This happens, but I think it is not the rule.

2. It was his idea that there is such a thing as a first-hand opinion; an original opinion; an opinion which is coldly reasoned out in a man's head, by a searching analysis of the facts involved, with the heart unconsulted, and the jury room closed against outside influences. It may be that such an opinion has been born somewhere, at some time or other, but I suppose it got away before they could catch it and stuff it and put it in the museum.

I am persuaded that a coldly-thought-out and independent verdict upon a fashion in clothes, or manners, or literature, or politics, or religion, or any other matter that is projected into the field of our notice and interest, is a most rare thing—if it has indeed ever existed.

A new thing in costume appears—the flaring hoopskirt, for example—and the passers-by are shocked, and the irreverent laugh. Six months later everybody is reconciled; the fashion has established itself; it is admired, now, and no one laughs. Public opinion resented it before, public opinion accepts it now, and is happy in it. Why? Was the resentment reasoned out? Was the acceptance reasoned out? No. The instinct that moves to conformity did the work. It is our nature to conform; it is a force which not many can successfully resist. What is its seat? The inborn requirement of self-approval. We all have to bow to that; there are no exceptions. Even the woman who refuses from first to last to wear the hoopskirt comes under that law and is its slave; she could not wear the skirt and have her own approval; and that she *must* have, she cannot help herself. But as a rule our self-approval has its source in but one place and not elsewhere—the approval of other people. A person of vast consequences can introduce any kind of novelty in dress and the general world will presently adopt it —moved to do it, in the first place, by the natural instinct to passively yield to that vague something recognized as authority, and in the second place by the human instinct to train with the multitude and have its approval. An empress introduced the hoopskirt, and we know the result. A nobody introduced the bloomer, and we know the result. If Eve should come again, in her ripe renown, and reintroduce her quaint styles—well, we know what would happen. And we should be cruelly embarrassed, along at first.

The hoopskirt runs its course and disappears. Nobody reasons about it. One woman abandons the fashion; her neighbor notices this and follows her lead; this influences the next woman; and so on and so on, and presently the skirt has vanished out of the world, no one knows how nor why; nor cares, for that matter. It will come again, by and by; and in due course will go again.

Twenty-five years ago, in England, six or eight wine glasses stood grouped by each person's plate at a dinner party, and they were used, not left idle and empty; to-day there are but three or four in the group, and the average guest sparingly uses about two of them. We have not adopted this new fashion yet, but we shall do it presently. We shall not think it out; we shall merely conform, and let it go at that. We get our notions and habits and opinions from outside influences; we do not have to study them out.

Our table manners, and company manners, and street manners change from time to time, but the changes are not reasoned out; we merely notice and conform. We are creatures of outside influences; as a rule we do not think, we only imitate. We cannot invent standards that will stick; what we mistake for standards are only fashions, and perishable. We may continue to admire them, but we drop the use of them. We notice this in literature. Shakespeare is a standard, and fifty years ago we used to write tragedies which we couldn't tell from—from somebody else's; but we don't do it any more, now. Our prose standard, three quarters of a century ago, was ornate and diffuse; some authority or other changed it in the direction of compactness and simplicity, and conformity followed, without argument. The historical novel starts up suddenly, and sweeps the land. Everybody writes one, and the nation is glad. We had historical novels before; but nobody read them, and the rest of us conformed—without reasoning it out. We are conforming in the other way, now, because it is another case of everybody.

The outside influences are always pouring in upon us, and we are always obeying their orders and accepting their verdicts. The Smiths like the new play; the Joneses go to see it, and they copy the Smith verdict. Morals, religions, politics, get their following from surrounding influences and atmospheres, almost entirely; not from study, not from thinking. A man must and will have his own approval first of all, in each and every moment and circumstance of his life—even if he must repent of a self-approved act the moment after its commission, in order to get his self-approval *again:* but, speaking in general terms, a man's self-approval in the large concerns of life has its source in the approval of the peoples about him, and not in a searching personal examination of the matter. Mohammedans are Mohammedans because they are born and reared among that sect, not because they have thought it out and can furnish sound reasons for being Mohammedans; we know why Catholics are Catholics; why Presbyterians are Presbyterians; why Baptists are Baptists; why Mormons are Mormons; why thieves are thieves; why monarchists are monarchists; why Republicans are Republicans and Democrats, Democrats. We know it is a matter of association and sympathy, not reasoning and examination; that hardly a man in the world has an opinion upon morals, politics, or religion which he got otherwise than through his associations and sympathies. Broadly speaking, there are none but corn-pone opinions. And broadly speaking, corn-pone stands for self-approval. Self-approval is acquired mainly from the approval of other people. The result is conformity. Sometimes conformity has a sordid business interest—the bread-and-butter interest—but not in most cases, I think. I think that in the majority of cases it is unconscious and not calculated; that it is born of the human being's natural yearning to stand well with his fellows and have their inspiring approval and praise—a yearning which is commonly so strong and so insistent that it cannot be effectually resisted, and must have its way.

A political emergency brings out the corn-pone opinion in fine force in its two chief varieties—the pocketbook variety, which has its origin in self-interest, and the bigger variety, the sentimental variety—the one which can't bear to be outside the pale; can't bear to be in disfavor; can't endure the averted face and the cold shoulder; wants to stand well with his friends, wants to be smiled upon, wants to be welcome, wants to hear the precious words, *"He's* on the right track!" Uttered, perhaps by an ass, but still an ass of high degree, an ass whose approval is gold and diamonds to a smaller ass, and confers glory and honor and happiness, and membership in the herd. For these gauds many a man will dump his life-long principles into the street, and his conscience along with them. We have seen it happen. In some millions of instances.

Men think they think upon great political questions, and they do; but they think with their party, not independently; they read its literature, but not that of the other side; they arrive at convictions, but they are drawn from a partial view of the matter in hand and are of no particular value. They swarm with their party, they feel with their party, they are happy in their party's approval; and where the party leads they will follow, whether for right and honor, or through blood and dirt and a mush of mutilated morals.

In our late canvass half of the nation passionately believed that in silver lay salvation, the other half as passionately believed that that way lay destruction. Do you believe that a tenth part of the people, on either side, had any rational excuse for having an opinion about the matter at all? I studied that mighty question to the bottom —came out empty. Half of our people passionately believe in high tariff, the other half believe otherwise. Does this mean study and examination, or only feeling? The latter, I think. I have deeply studied that question, too—and didn't arrive. We all do no end of feeling, and we mistake it for thinking. And out of it we get an aggregation which we consider a boon. Its name is Public Opinion. It is held in reverence. It settles everything. Some think it the Voice of God.

1923

William Dean Howells
1837–1920

William Dean Howells is best remembered for his ability to recognize how good
other writers were, not for his own merits. Rather than stressing the implications
of his first name ("he who asserts his own will"), we tend to focus on *Dean*,
picturing Howells as the person high up in the administrative order who oversees
and evaluates others. From his place in "The Editor's Study" and "The Easy
Chair," titles given the influential monthly essays he wrote for *Harper's* magazine,
Howells served as America's foremost critic and editor from 1886 into the early
years of the twentieth century. But his reputation as the acknowledged spokesman
for middle-class literary values, the cautiousness of his approach to matters of
sexuality, and the canniness with which he orchestrated his own career are
misleading. They make Howells seem older and grayer than in fact he was.

Howells started out as a brash young man with a background in a printer's
shop and local newspapers. He came out of Ohio to storm the genteel Eastern
literary redoubts in much the manner of heroes of the nineteenth-century
Bildungsromen (a novel in which climbers from the provinces make their
energetic way upward to social and professional acclaim in the major centers of
power). Another example of the same type is Mark Twain, a man Howells
helped to attain the level of success he himself already enjoyed.

Oddly enough, we think of Mark Twain as the eternal boy, even after his
hair went snowy white. But Twain and Howells were almost exact
contemporaries and shared several of the same early experiences: printing-shop
apprenticeship, jobs with regional newspapers, and moves to the East in 1866
after sitting out the Civil War in other places (for Twain, the Nevada Territory,
as secretary to the governor's secretary; for Howells, a consulship in Venice). But
Howells's early days were, probably even more than Twain's, given over to the
pugnacious attempt to get ahead. Twain seems the more energetic because he let
his wildness show, while Howells carefully kept his under cover. Howells's main
chance came through his role as critic and editor, positions that called for him to
reject the personal flamboyance Twain found useful to his role as humorist and
iconoclast. But Howells's temperament put his psychic energies to work in
controlling, not releasing, the extremes of emotion that lay concealed beneath the
smooth surface of the polite young man from Ohio.

One of eight children, Howells was born to a humble family in Martin's
Ferry, Ohio, somewhat shakily supported by the father's work as an itinerant
printer and newspaper editor. Though poor and peripatetic in their shifts around
Ohio during the early years of Howells's childhood, the family was close.
Howells was strongly affected by his father's championing of various reform
movements and by his own avid reading in the literary classics. He set to work
at once to turn himself into a capable journalist and writer of occasional poems
and sketches. By the time he was twenty-one, he had begun to make his mark in
Ohio as a writer and editor for important newspapers in and around Cincinnati
and Columbus—the *Gazette* and the *Ohio State Journal*.

Howells's ambitions exceeded what Ohio had to offer, however. In 1860 he made two crucial moves: He wrote a campaign biography for Abraham Lincoln's presidential candidacy, and he made a trip to New England to meet such literary celebrities as Emerson, Holmes, Hawthorne, Lowell, and Thoreau. The Lincoln biography led to his appointment as American consul to Venice, and his visits with famous American writers gave him a glimpse into the nation's most prominent literary circle. The introductions he received to the Boston-Concord literary powers earned him early recognition for his talents and prepared the way, upon his return from Italy in 1865, for an assistant editorship at the country's most important journal, the *Atlantic Monthly,* where he was to become editor in chief in 1871. The *Atlantic* appointment was the start of what would be Howells's special fate: to be the arbiter of American letters and the judge of the careers of the next generation of writers.

From the time Howells settled in Boston, he began to pursue a second career as a novelist. The six novels he wrote while with the *Atlantic* not only helped him perfect his craft but also determined the kind of fiction he would urge on the American reading public, which heeded his judgments. Fiction had to be realistic, he maintained. It must give its attention to the details of the everyday lives of ordinary people. It must reject romanticized plots of passion and adventure to concentrate on stories of character and close observations of contemporary American life.

In 1881 Howells resigned his post with the *Atlantic* to free-lance. His first notable novel, *A Modern Instance,* appeared in 1882. *The Rise of Silas Lapham,* published in 1885, confirmed Howells's worth as a novelist. By 1886 he was back in an editor's chair, associated with *Harper's,* which had overtaken the *Atlantic* as the country's major literary arbiter. In 1889 he moved to New York, which had replaced Boston as the place where literary reputations were made or broken. Howells could work with the assurance that what he said for Realism and against the shoddily romantic would receive serious attention from a large, receptive, and international audience. Marked by the earnestness and commitment (as well as the humor and ironic touch) Howells brought to all his professional tasks, the essays and reviews he printed in the pages of *Harper's* helped make American literature what it became by 1900. The novels in the bookshops and lending libraries and in serial form in the popular magazines were no longer limited to the sentimental "weeper" or the historical costume romance.

This is not to suggest that the sentimental romance went out of style during Howells's day as the dean of American Realism; it flourished, but it did so in the face of the strong, new force in American writing that Howells made not only acceptable but respectable. White, middle-class readers could hardly think themselves *au courant* on the newest books if they were not familiar with the writings of such Americans as Hamlin Garland, Stephen Crane, and Frank Norris and with the names of such leading Continental writers as Tolstoy, Turgenev, Galdós, and Ibsen, as well as the Briton Thomas Hardy. Howells gave his editorial attention to American women writers—Sarah Orne Jewett, Emily Dickinson, and Edith Wharton. He also encouraged new black writers like Paul

Dunbar and Charles Chesnutt. Howells took it on himself, early and late, to declare the central importance of Mark Twain and Henry James on the American cultural scene Capable of appreciating their differing qualities as writers, Howells celebrated both the rowdiness of Twain's humor and the refined specialness of James's style. Part of Howells's talent was the ability to admire in others what he himself was unable to do. Certain literary leanings, differences in temperament, and deep-seated fears carried over from his childhood prevented Howells from speaking directly in his own fiction about the sex and violence that Stephen Crane and Frank Norris, for example, placed dead center in their works.

At the same time Howells helped several generations of Realists to get the notice they deserved, he continued to build up the bulk of his own writing. His most important essays and literary reminiscences trace the growth of the imaginative movement he himself helped to create: *Criticism and Fiction* (1891), *My Literary Passions* (1895), *Literary Friends and Acquaintances* (1900), and *My Mark Twain* (1910). Also noteworthy are his accounts of his youthful Ohio days, *A Boy's Town* (1890) and *My Year in a Log Cabin* (1893). In addition to *A Modern Instance* and *The Rise of Silas Lapham,* the foremost titles among his many novels are *Their Wedding Journey* (his first, 1878), *The Undiscovered Country* (1880), *Indian Summer* (1886), *A Hazard of New Fortunes* and *The Shadow of a Dream* (1890), *An Imperative Duty* (1892), *A Traveler from Altruria* (1894), *The Landlord at Lion's Head* (1897), *The Son of Royal Langbrith* (1904), and *The Leatherwood God* (1916). If all these titles were not enough, travel books, plays, and poems extended Howells's reach into other areas of writing.

Somehow there was time for other activities as well, both public and personal. On the political side, Howells took a number of courageous, well-publicized stands in the 1880s and 1890s: a forthright defense of the so-called Haymarket Anarchists in 1886, support of the founding of the NAACP, advocacy of socialism as the solution to the problem caused by the widening margin between the rich and the poor, encouragement of the suffragist movement, and criticism of the nation's imperialistic policies. On the private side, Howells, whose own psychological makeup had been vulnerable to jolts ever since young manhood, had to stave off further assaults to his mental stability, including breakdowns that came while he was at work on *A Modern Instance* in 1881 and 1882 and again in 1885 while completing *The Rise of Silas Lapham.*

The emotional history of Howells's wife and daughter Winifred was similar to that experienced by the Clemens household, as well as by the James and Adams families. It is a sad history—all too familiar to this period—of invalidism, nervous disorders, and early death. But Howells himself persevered, while trying to hold together the pieces of his family during Winny's illness in the 1880s, her death in 1889, and his wife's subsequent invalidism.

More and more honors were heaped upon his stocky body and graying head. Honorary degrees from Oxford, Princeton, Yale, and Columbia were bestowed on a man who had never had the chance back in Ohio to earn a regular grade-school education. By 1900 Howells commanded the literary scene. Over the next decade he was still deeply revered, but attention started to drift away from him toward the energetic young writers he had often been instrumental in getting started. By the 1920s Sinclar Lewis, H. L. Mencken, and other obstreperous young critics ridiculed Howells in a manner that was just as vigorous but less polite than the tone he had used as a young man to attack literary deadwood. By the 1930s the popularity of Melville and Poe was on the rise, while this honest Realist was shunted aside. Yet Howells's literary reputation began to regain attention in the 1940s as the concerns of the critics and historians turned once more toward the solid achievements of the post–Civil War generation.

Why is the praise that Howells gets sometimes begrudging? Certainly he introduced his readers to important "new" themes, something a literature requires if it is to keep pace with the events it tries to reflect. Among Howells's major themes are many that are still topical: the young American woman as a special type who sallies forth with somewhat reckless abandon to take on the world; the effects of divorce on couples in a society where admitting one's failures in marriage may be legally permissible but can be the cause of emotional devastation; the amorality of the business and professional classes, tenuously bound to the shaky morality of older values; the loss of religious certainties, with little of worth to replace them; the weakening position of "old families"; and the faltering relationships between parents and children. Howells portrays the shabby boredom of country life set against the more glamorous squalor and frenetic pace of city living; classes set against classes, both socially, in the drawing room, and economically, when strikers take to the street in protest; the shining veneer of manners that barely cover the fundamental crudity of people on the make. He is adept at the analysis of the female character and the discussion of the dream life that resists explanation by the most severe scientific scrutiny. Howells's main theme is the most modern theme of all: people at loose ends, displaced ethnically (with the "natives" drawing in their elbows in the presence of Irish, blacks, and other "aliens") and psychically (men and women going it alone in their professions or their marriages).

In addition to the new areas Howells opened up to the novelists of Realism, he took a clear position on several ethical issues. For Howells the acts of the artist are moral acts. To see realistically is to meet the world honestly, even though it means giving up faith in abstract absolutes. To see romantically is to deceive and to be deceived, thereby to live without moral validation. He wished to reject fatalism because he believed choice is necessary so that people can be responsible for what they do. He also scorned self-isolation, excessive subjectivism, and the sentimentality of people—especially women—given over to self-sacrifice and lives ground down by excessive attention to "duty."

Howells knew his American scene, and he was careful to single out what was most characteristically "American" about it. Howells believed that ordinariness was fine; optimism and small appetites were the national traits. Without self-contradiction, he wrote stories about the way common people react when placed at the extremes possible in ordinary lives—drug addiction, madness, alcoholism, suicide, emotional incest, repressed sexuality, violent death. Without denying his statement that American literature does best with the "smiling aspects" of life, he lived and worked on the edge of his own pessimism and doubts, as when, in the brief sketch "A Scene," he describes the holiday atmosphere surrounding the discovery of a young woman, pregnant but unmarried, who drowned herself. Howells did all these things, and handled these themes, because he was an ironist as well as a realist.

Irony is both Howells's greatest strength as an honest man and the source of the weakness that sapped his verve as a writer. We blame him most for not being exciting. But he would doubtless reply that he chose to keep himself and excitement apart. The love of novelty and the desire to set crazy things happening all at once, which attracts us to Mark Twain (because novelty and craziness pulled powerfully at Twain's imagination), were exactly what Howells tried to keep out of his life, his literature, and his pronouncements on the nature of Realism. Irony let him do this. It kept his fires banked, but it also held him to the truths of his life's intention: to re-create the American imagination in the image of his own self-limiting commitment to things exactly as they are.

Further Reading:

J. Woodress, *Howells and Italy*, 1952.
E. Carter, *Howells and the Age of Realism*, 1954.
E. Cady, *The Road to Realism: The Early Years, 1837–1885*, 1956.
E. Cady, *The Realist at War: The Mature Years, 1885–1920*, 1958.
O. Fryckstedt, *In Quest of America: A Study of Howells' Early Development as a Novelist*, 1958, 1971.
G. Bennett, *William Dean Howells: The Development of a Novelist*, 1959.
V. Brooks, *Howells: His Life and World*, 1959.
R. Hough, *The Quiet Rebel: William Dean Howells as Social Commentator*, 1959.
The War of the Critics over William Dean Howells, ed. E. Cady and D. Frazier, 1962.
R. Kirk and C. Kirk, *William Dean Howells*, 1962.
C. Kirk, *William Dean Howells and Art in His Time*, 1965.
G. Carrington, *The Immense Complex Drama: The World and Art of the Howells Novels*, 1966.

K. Vanderbilt, *The Achievement of William Dean Howells*, 1968.
E. Wagenknecht, *William Dean Howells: The Friendly Eye*, 1969.
K. Lynn, *William Dean Howells: An American Life*, 1971.
G. Bennett, *The Realism of William Dean Howells*, 1973.
William Dean Howells as Critic, ed. E. Cady, 1973.
E. Carter, *On the Trail of the Truth*, 1975.
Critics on William Dean Howells, ed. P. Eschholz, 1975.
G. C. Carrington, *Plots and Characters in the Fiction of William Dean Howells*, 1976.
W. Alexander, *William Dean Howells: The Realist as Humanist*, 1981.
K. E. Eble, *William Dean Howells*, 1982.
G. R. Uba, *Native Grains: Marriage and Family in the Fiction of William Dean Howells*, 1982.
E. S. Prioleau, *The Circle of Eros: Sexuality in the Work of William Dean Howells*, 1983.

Texts:

Criticism and Fiction, 1891.
"Editha" from *Between the Dark and the Daylight*, 1907.
See also M. Howells, *Life in Letters of William Dean Howells*, 2 vols., 1928, 1968.

William Dean Howells: Representative Selections, ed. C. Kirk and R. Kirk, 1950.
Mark Twain–Howells Letters: The Correspondence of Samuel L. Clemens and William Dean Howells, 1872–1910, ed. H. Smith and W. Gibson, 1960.

---

from Criticism and Fiction

II: [Realism and the Common Man]

"As for those called critics," the author[1] says, "they have generally sought the rule of the arts in the wrong place; they have sought among poems, pictures, engravings, statues, and buildings; but art can never give the rules that make an art. This is, I believe, the reason why artists in general, and poets principally, have been confined in so narrow a circle; they have been rather imitators of one another than of nature. Critics follow them, and therefore can do little as guides. I can judge but poorly of anything while I measure it by no other standard than itself. The true standard of the arts is in every man's power; and an easy observation of the most common, sometimes of the meanest things, in nature will give the truest lights, where the greatest sagacity and industry that slights such observation must leave us in the dark, or, what is worse, amuse and mislead us by false lights."

If this should happen to be true—and it certainly commends itself to acceptance —it might portend an immediate danger to the vested interests of criticism, only that it was written a hundred years ago; and we shall probably have the "sagacity and industry that slights the observation" of nature long enough yet to allow most critics the time to learn some more useful trade than criticism as they pursue it. Nevertheless, I am in hopes that the communistic era in taste foreshadowed by Burke is approaching, and that it will occur within the lives of men now overawed by the foolish old superstition that literature and art are anything but the expression of life, and are to be judged by any other test than that of their fidelity to it. The time is coming, I hope, when each new author, each new artist, will be considered, not in his proportion to any other author or artist, but in his relation to the human nature, known to us all, which it is his privilege, his high duty, to interpret. "The true standard of the artist is in every man's power" already, as Burke says; Michelangelo's "light of the piazza," the glance of the common eye, is and always was the best light on a statue;[2] Goethe's[3] "boys and blackbirds" have in all ages been the real connoisseurs of berries; but hitherto the mass of common men have been afraid to apply their own simplicity, naturalness, and honesty to the appreciation of the beautiful. They have always cast about for the instruction of some one who professed to know better, and who browbeat wholesome common-sense into the self-distrust that ends in sophistication. They have fallen generally to the worst of this bad species, and have been "amused[4] and misled" (how pretty that quaint old use of amuse is!) "by the false lights" of critical vanity and self-righteousness. They have been taught to compare what they see and what they read, not with the things that they have observed and known, but with the things that some other artist or writer has done. Especially if they have themselves the artistic impulse in any direction they are taught to form themselves,

---

[1] Edmund Burke (1729–1797), English statesman, in *Philosophical Inquiry into the Origins of Our Ideas on the Sublime and the Beautiful* (1756).

[2] Michelangelo's *David* (1504) may be meant as an example of a statue originally on public display in a Florentine *piazza,* or open square.

[3] Goethe: Johann Wolfgang von Goethe (1749–1832), German poet and dramatist.

[4] Beguiled, deceived.

not upon life, out upon the masters who became masters only by forming themselves upon life. The seeds of death are planted in them, and they can produce only the still-born, the academic. They are not told to take their work into the public square and see if it seems true to the chance passer, but to test it by the work of the very men who refused and decried any other test of their own work. The young writer who attempts to report the phrase and carriage of every-day life, who tries to tell just how he has heard men talk and seen them look, is made to feel guilty of something low and unworthy by the stupid people who would like to have him show how Shakespeare's men talked and looked, or Scott's, or Thackeray's, or Balzac's, or Hawthorne's, or Dickens's;[5] he is instructed to idealize his personages, that is, to take the life-likeness out of them, and put the book-likeness into them. He is approached in the spirit of the wretched pedantry into which learning, much or little, always decays when it withdraws itself and stands apart from experience in an attitude of imagined superiority, and which would say with the same confidence to the scientist: "I see that you are looking at a grasshopper there which you have found in the grass, and I suppose you intend to describe it. Now don't waste your time and sin against culture in that way. I've got a grasshopper here, which has been evolved at considerable pains and expense out of the grasshopper in general; in fact, it's a type. It's made up of wire and cardboard, very prettily painted in a conventional tint, and it's perfectly indestructible. It isn't very much like a real grasshopper, but it's a great deal nicer, and it's served to represent the notion of a grasshopper ever since man emerged from barbarism. You may say that it's artificial. Well, it is artificial; but then it's ideal too; and what you want to do is cultivate the ideal. You'll find the books full of my kind of grasshopper, and scarcely a trace of yours in any of them. The thing that you are proposing to do is commonplace; but if you say that it isn't commonplace, for the very reason that it hasn't been done before, you'll have to admit that it's photographic."

As I said, I hope the time is coming when not only the artist, but the common, average man, who always "has the standard of the arts in his power," will have also the courage to apply it, and will reject the ideal grasshopper wherever he finds it, in science, in literature, in art, because it is not "simple, natural, and honest," because it is not like a real grasshopper. But I will own that I think the time is yet far off, and that the people who have been brought up on the ideal grasshopper, the heroic grasshopper, the impassioned grasshopper, the self-devoted, adventureful, good old romantic cardboard grasshopper, must die out before the simple, honest, and natural grasshopper can have a fair field. I am in no haste to compass the end of these good people, whom I find in the mean time very amusing. It is delightful to meet one of them, either in print or out of it—some sweet elderly lady or excellent gentleman whose youth was pastured on the literature of thirty or forty years ago—and to witness the confidence with which they preach their favorite authors as all the law and the prophets. They have commonly read little or nothing since, or, if they have, they have judged it by a standard taken from these authors, and never dreamed of judging it by nature; they are destitute of the documents in the case of the later writers;

---

[5] The novelists cited are Sir Walter Scott (1771–1832), William Makepeace Thackeray (1811–1863), Honoré de Balzac (1799–1850), Nathaniel Hawthorne (1804–1864), and Charles Dickens (1812–1870).

they suppose that Balzac was the beginning of realism, and that Zola[6] is its wicked end; they are quite ignorant, but they are ready to talk you down, if you differ from them, with an assumption of knowledge sufficient for any occasion. The horror, the resentment, with which they receive any question of their literary saints is genuine; you descend at once very far in the moral and social scale, and anything short of offensive personality is too good for you; it is expressed to you that you are one to be avoided, and put down even a little lower than you have naturally fallen.

These worthy persons are not to blame; it is part of their intellectual mission to represent the petrifaction of taste, and to preserve an image of a smaller and cruder and emptier world than we now live in, a world which was feeling its way towards the simple, the natural, the honest, but was a good deal "amused and misled" by lights now no longer mistakable for heavenly luminaries. They belong to a time, just passing away, when certain authors were considered authorities in certain kinds, when they must be accepted entire and not questioned in any particular. Now we are beginning to see and to say that no author is an authority except in those moments when he held his ear close to Nature's lips and caught her very accent. These moments are not continuous with any authors in the past, and they are rare with all. Therefore I am not afraid to say now that the greatest classics are sometimes not at all great, and that we can profit by them only when we hold them, like our meanest contemporaries, to a strict accounting, and verify their work by the standard of the arts which we all have in our power, the simple, the natural, and the honest.

Those good people, those curious and interesting if somewhat musty back-numbers, must always have a hero, an idol of some sort, and it is droll to find Balzac, who suffered from their sort such bitter scorn and hate for his realism while he was alive, now become a fetich in his turn, to be shaken in the faces of those who will not blindly worship him. But it is no new thing in the history of literature: whatever is established is sacred with those who do not think. At the beginning of the century, when romance was making the same fight against effete classicism which realism is making to-day against effete romanticism, the Italian poet Monti[7] declared that "the romantic was the cold grave of the Beautiful," just as the realistic is now supposed to be. The romantic of that day and the real of this are in certain degree the same. Romanticism then sought, as realism seeks now, to widen the bounds of sympathy, to level every barrier against æsthetic freedom, to escape from the paralysis of tradition. It exhausted itself in this impulse; and it remained for realism to assert that fidelity to experience and probability of motive are essential conditions of a great imaginative literature. It is not a new theory, but it has never before universally characterized literary endeavor. When realism becomes false to itself, when it heaps up facts merely, and maps life instead of picturing it, realism will perish too. Every true realist instinctively knows this, and it is perhaps the reason why he is careful of every fact, and feels himself bound to express or to indicate its meaning at the risk of overmoralizing. In life he finds nothing insignificant; all tells for destiny and character; nothing that God has made is contemptible. He cannot look upon human life and declare this thing or that

[6] Émile Zola (1840–1902), the French novelist and critic, who championed the school of literary Naturalism.

[7] Vincenzo Monti (1754–1828).

thing unworthy of notice, any more than the scientist can declare a fact of the material world beneath the dignity of his inquiry. He feels in every nerve the equality of things and the unity of men; his soul is exalted, not by vain shows and shadows and ideals, but by realities, in which alone the truth lives. In criticism it is his business to break the images of false gods and misshapen heroes, to take away the poor silly toys that many grown people would still like to play with. He cannot keep terms with Jack the Giant-killer or Puss in Boots, under any name or in any place, even when they appear as the convict Vautrec, or the Marquis de Montrivaut, or the Sworn Thirteen Noblemen.[8] He must say to himself that Balzac, when he imagined these monsters, was not Balzac, he was Dumas;[9] he was not realistic, he was romantic.

XXI: [The Nature of American Fiction]

It is no doubt such work as Mr. James's that an English essayist (Mr. E. Hughes)[10] has chiefly in mind, in a study of the differences of the English and American novel. He defines the English novel as working from within outwardly, and the American novel as working from without inwardly. The definition is very surprisingly accurate; and the critic's discovery of this fundamental difference is carried into particulars with a distinctness which is as unfailing as the courtesy he has in recognizing the present superiority of American work. He seems to think, however, that the English principle is the better though why he should think so he does not make so clear. It appears a belated and rather voluntary effect of patriotism, disappointing in a philosopher of his degree; but it does not keep him from very explicit justice to the best characteristics of our fiction. "The American novelist is distinguished for the intellectual grip which he has of his characters. . . . He penetrates below the crust, and he recognizes no necessity of the crust to anticipate what is beneath. . . . He utterly discards heroics; he often even discards anything like a plot. . . . His story proper is often no more than a natural predicament. . . . It is no stage view we have of his characters, but one behind the scenes. . . . We are brought into contact with no strained virtues, illumined by strained light upon strained heights of situation. . . . Whenever he appeals to the emotions it would seem to be with an appeal to the intellect too. . . . because he weaves his story of the finer, less self-evident though common threads of human nature, seldom calling into play the grosser and more powerful strain. . . . Everywhere in his pages we come across acquaintances undisguised. . . . The characters in an American novel are never unapproachable to the reader. . . . The naturalness, with the every-day atmosphere which surrounds it, is one great charm of the American novel. . . . It is throughout examinative, discursory, even more—quizzical. Its characters are undergoing, at the hands of the author, calm, interested observation. . . . He is never caught identifying himself with them; he must preserve impartiality at all costs . . . but . . . the touch of nature is always felt, the feeling of kinship always follows. . . . The strength of the American novel is its optimistic faith. . . . If out of this persistent

---

[8] Fictional characters depicted by Honoré de Balzac in *La Comédie Humaine,* the general title of the series of novels he wrote throughout his career.

[9] Alexandre Dumas the elder (1803–1870), French

author of romantic novels, such as *The Three Musketeers* and *The Count of Monte Cristo.*

[10] The English critic Eilian Hughes, who wrote *Some Aspects of Humanity* in 1889.

hopefulness it can evolve for men a new order of trustfulness, a tenet that between man and man there should be less suspicion, more confidence, since human nature sanctions it, its mission will have been more than an æsthetic, it will have been a moral one."

Not all of this will be found true of Mr. James, but all that relates to artistic methods and characteristics will, and the rest is true of American novels generally. For the most part in their range and tendency they are admirable. I will not say they are all good, or that any of them is wholly good; but I find in nearly every one of them a disposition to regard our life without the literary glasses so long thought desirable, and to see character, not as it is in other fiction, but as it abounds outside of all fiction. This disposition sometimes goes with poor enough performance, but in some of our novels it goes with performance that is excellent; and at any rate it is for the present more valuable than evenness of performance. It is what relates American fiction to the only living movement in imaginative literature, and distinguishes by a superior freshness and authenticity any group of American novels from a similarly accidental group of English novels, giving them the same good right to be as the like number of recent Russian novels, French novels, Spanish novels, Italian novels, Norwegian novels.

It is the difference of the American novelist's ideals from those of the English novelist that gives him his advantage, and seems to promise him the future. The love of the passionate and the heroic, as the Englishman has it, is such a crude and unwholesome thing, so deaf and blind to all the most delicate and important facts of art and life, so insensible to the subtle values in either that its presence or absence makes the whole difference, and enables one who is not obsessed by it to thank Heaven that he is not as that other man is.

There can be little question that many refinements of thought and spirit which every American is sensible of in the fiction of this continent, are necessarily lost upon our good kin beyond seas, whose thumb-fingered apprehension requires something gross and palpable for its assurance of reality. This is not their fault, and I am not sure that it is wholly their misfortune: they are made so as not to miss what they do not find, and they are simply content without those subtleties of life and character which it gives us so keen a pleasure to have noted in literature. If they perceive them at all it is as something vague and diaphanous, something that filmily wavers before their sense and teases them, much as the beings of an invisible world might mock one of our material frame by intimations of their presence. It is with reason, therefore, on the part of an Englishman, that Mr. Henley[11] complains of our fiction as a shadow-land, though we find more and more in it the faithful report of our life, its motives and emotions, and all the comparatively etherealized passions and ideals that influence it.

In fact, the American who chooses to enjoy his birthright to the full, lives in a world wholly different from the Englishman's, and speaks (too often through his nose) another language: he breathes a rarefied and nimble air full of shining possibilities and radiant promises which the fog-and-soot-clogged lungs of those less-favored islanders struggle in vain to fill themselves with. But he ought to be modest in his advantage,

[11] William Ernest Henley (1849–1903), English critic and poet.

and patient with the coughing and sputtering of his cousin who complains of finding himself in an exhausted receiver[12] on plunging into one of our novels. To be quite just to the poor fellow, I have had some such experience as that myself in the atmosphere of some of our more attenuated romances.

Yet every now and then I read a book with perfect comfort and much exhilaration, whose scenes the average Englishman would gasp in. Nothing happens; that is, nobody murders or debauches anybody else; there is no arson or pillage of any sort; there is not a ghost, or a ravening beast, or a hair-breadth escape, or a shipwreck, or a monster of self-sacrifice, or a lady five thousand years old in the whole course of the story; "no promenade, no band of music, nossing!" as Mr. Du Maurier's Frenchman said of the meet for a fox-hunt.[13] Yet it is all alive with the keenest interest for those who enjoy the study of individual traits and general conditions as they make themselves known to American experience.

These conditions have been so favorable hitherto (though they are becoming always less so) that they easily account for the optimistic faith of our novel which Mr. Hughes notices. It used to be one of the disadvantages of the practice of romance in America, which Hawthorne more or less whimsically lamented, that there were so few shadows and inequalities in our broad level of prosperity; and it is one of the reflections suggested by Dostoïevsky's novel, The Crime and the Punishment,[14] that whoever struck a note so profoundly tragic in American fiction would do a false and mistaken thing—as false and as mistaken in its way as dealing in American fiction with certain nudities which the Latin peoples seem to find edifying. Whatever their deserts, very few American novelists have been led out to be shot, or finally exiled to the rigors of a winter at Duluth; and in a land where journeymen carpenters and plumbers strike for four dollars a day the sum of hunger and cold is comparatively small, and the wrong from class to class has been almost inappreciable, though all this is changing for the worse. Our novelists, therefore, concern themselves with the more smiling aspects of life, which are the more American, and seek the universal in the individual rather than the social interests. It is worth while, even at the risk of being called commonplace, to be true to our well-to-do actualities; the very passions themselves seem to be softened and modified by conditions which formerly at least could not be said to wrong any one, to cramp endeavor, or to cross lawful desire. Sin and suffering and shame there must always be in the world, I suppose, but I believe that in this new world of ours it is still mainly from one to another one, and oftener still from one to one's self. We have death too in America, and a great deal of disagreeable and painful disease, which the multiplicity of our patent medicines does not seem to cure; but this is tragedy that comes in the very nature of things, and is not peculiarly American as the large, cheerful average of health and success and happy life is. It will not do to boast, but it is well to be true to the facts, and to see that, apart from these purely mortal troubles, the race here has enjoyed conditions in which most of the ills that have darkened its annals might be averted by honest work and unselfish behavior.

Fine artists we have among us, and right-minded as far as they go; and we must

[12] A vacuum jar used in chemical experiments.
[13] From a sketch by the English writer and illustrator George Du Maurier (1834–1896), included in his Pictures of English Society of 1884.

[14] Fédor Dostoyevski's novel Crime and Punishment was published in 1866.

not forget this at evil moments when it seems as if all the women had taken to writing hysterical improprieties, and some of the men were trying to be at least as hysterical in despair of being as improper. If we kept to the complexion of a certain school—which sadly needs a school-master—we might very well be despondent; but, after all, that school is not representative of our conditions or our intentions. Other traits are much more characteristic of our life and our fiction. In most American novels, vivid and graphic as the best of them are, the people are segregated if not sequestered, and the scene is sparsely populated. The effect may be in instinctive response to the vacancy of our social life, and I shall not make haste to blame it. There are few places, few occasions among us, in which a novelist can get a large number of polite people together, or at least keep them together. Unless he carries a snap-camera his picture of them has no probability; they affect one like the figures perfunctorily associated in such deadly old engravings as that of "Washington Irving and his Friends." Perhaps it is for this reason that we excel in small pieces with three or four figures, or in studies of rustic communities, where there is propinquity if not society. Our grasp of more urbane life is feeble; most attempts to assemble it in our pictures are failures, possibly because it is too transitory, too intangible in its nature with us, to be truthfully represented as really existent.

I am not sure that the Americans have not brought the short story nearer perfection in the all-round sense than almost any other people, and for reasons very simple and near at hand. It might be argued from the national hurry and impatience that it was a literary form peculiarly adapted to the American temperament, but I suspect that its extraordinary development among us is owing much more to more tangible facts. The success of American magazines, which is nothing less than prodigious, is only commensurate with their excellence. Their sort of success is not only from the courage to decide what ought to please, but from the knowledge of what does please; and it is probable that, aside from the pictures, it is the short stories which please the readers of our best magazines. The serial novels they must have, of course; but rather more of course they must have short stories, and by operation of the law of supply and demand, the short stories, abundant in quantity and excellent in quality, are forthcoming because they are wanted. By another operation of the same law, which political economists have more recently taken account of, the demand follows the supply, and short stories are sought for because there is a proven ability to furnish them, and people read them willingly because they are usually very good. The art of writing them is now so disciplined and diffused with us that there is no lack either for the magazines or for the newspaper "syndicates" which deal in them almost to the exclusion of the serials. In other countries the feuilleton[15] of the journals is a novel continued from day to day, but with us the papers, whether daily or weekly, now more rarely print novels, whether they get them at first hand from the writers, as a great many do, or through the syndicates, which purvey a vast variety of literary wares, chiefly for the Sunday editions of the city journals. In the country papers the short story takes place of the chapters of a serial which used to be given.

1891

---

[15] The literary section of French newspapers.

Editha

The air was thick with the war[1] feeling, like the electricity of a storm which has not yet burst. Editha sat looking out into the hot spring afternoon, with her lips parted, and panting with the intensity of the question whether she could let him go. She had decided that she could not let him stay, when she saw him at the end of the still leafless avenue, making slowly up towards the house, with his head down and his figure relaxed. She ran impatiently out on the veranda, to the edge of the steps, and imperatively demanded greater haste of him with her will before she called aloud to him: "George!"

He had quickened his pace in mystical response to her mystical urgence, before he could have heard her; now he looked up and answered, "Well?"

"Oh, how united we are!" she exulted, and then she swooped down the steps to him. "What is it?" she cried.

"It's war," he said, and he pulled her up to him and kissed her.

She kissed him back intensely, but irrelevantly, as to their passion, and uttered from deep in her throat. "How glorious!"

"It's war," he repeated, without consenting to her sense of it; and she did not know just what to think at first. She never knew what to think of him; that made his mystery, his charm. All through their courtship, which was contemporaneous with the growth of the war feeling, she had been puzzled by his want of seriousness about it. He seemed to despise it even more than he abhorred it. She could have understood his abhorring any sort of bloodshed; that would have been a survival of his old life when he thought he would be a minister, and before he changed and took up the law. But making light of a cause so high and noble seemed to show a want of earnestness at the core of his being. Not but that she felt herself able to cope with a congenital defect of that sort, and make his love for her save him from himself. Now perhaps the miracle was already wrought in him. In the presence of the tremendous fact that he announced, all triviality seemed to have gone out of him; she began to feel that. He sank down on the top step, and wiped his forehead with his handkerchief, while she poured out upon him her question of the origin and authenticity of his news.

All the while, in her duplex emotioning, she was aware that now at the very beginning she must put a guard upon herself against urging him, by any word or act, to take the part that her whole soul willed him to take, for the completion of her ideal of him. He was very nearly perfect as he was, and he must be allowed to perfect himself. But he was peculiar, and he might very well be reasoned out of his peculiarity. Before her reasoning went her emotioning: her nature pulling upon his nature, her womanhood upon his manhood, without her knowing the means she was using to the end she was willing. She had always supposed that the man who won her would

[1] The Spanish-American War of 1898.

have done something to win her: she did not know what, but something. George Gearson had simply asked her for her love, on the way home from a concert, and she gave her love to him without, as it were, thinking. But now, it flashed upon her, if he could do something worthy to *have* won her—be a hero, *her* hero—it would be even better than if he had done it before asking her; it would be grander. Besides, she had believed in the war from the beginning.

"But don't you see, dearest," she said, "that it wouldn't have come to this if it hadn't been in the order of Providence? And I call any war glorious that is for the liberation of people who have been struggling for years against the cruelest oppression. Don't you think so, too?"

"I suppose so," he returned languidly. "But war! Is it glorious to break the peace of the world?"

"That ignoble peace! It was no peace at all, with that crime and shame at our very gates." She was conscious of parroting the current phrases of the newspapers, but it was no time to pick and choose her words. She must sacrifice anything to the high ideal she had for him, and after a good deal of rapid argument she ended with the climax: "But now it doesn't matter about the how or why. Since the war has come, all that is gone. There are no two sides any more. There is nothing now but our country."

He sat with his eyes closed and his head leant back against the veranda, and he remarked, with a vague smile, as if musing aloud, "Our country—right or wrong."[2]

"Yes, right or wrong!" she returned, fervidly. "I'll go and get you some lemonade." She rose rustling, and whisked away; when she came back with two tall glasses of clouded liquid on a tray, and the ice clucking in them, he still sat as she had left him, and she said, as if there had been no interruption: "But there is no question of wrong in this case. I call it a sacred war. A war for liberty and humanity, if ever there was one. And I know you will see it just as I do, yet."

He took half the lemonade at a gulp, and he answered as he set the glass down: "I know you always have the highest ideal. When I differ from you I ought to doubt myself."

A generous sob rose in Editha's throat for the humility of a man, so very nearly perfect, who was willing to put himself below her.

Besides, she felt, more subliminally, that he was never so near slipping through her fingers as when he took that meek way.

"You shall not say that! Only, for once I happen to be right." She seized his hand in her two hands, and poured her soul from her eyes into his. "Don't you think so?" she entreated him.

He released his hand and drank the rest of his lemonade, and she added, "Have mine too," but he shook his head in answering, "I've no business to think so, unless I act so, too."

Her heart stopped a beat before it pulsed on with leaps that she felt in her neck. She had noticed that strange thing in men: they seemed to feel bound to do what they believed, and not think a thing was finished when they said it, as girls did. She knew

---

[2] During an engagement with the British fleet in 1816, this phrase was coined by Stephen Decatur, the American naval hero.

what was in his mind, but she pretended not, as she said, "Oh, I am not sure," and then faltered.

He went on as if to himself, without apparently heeding her: "There's only one way of proving one's faith in a thing like this."

She could not say that she understood, but she did understand.

He went on again. "If I believed—if I felt as you do about this war—Do you wish me to feel as you do?"

Now she was really not sure; so she said: "George, I don't know what you mean."

He seemed to muse away from her as before. "There is a sort of fascination in it. I suppose that at the bottom of his heart every man would like at times to have his courage tested, to see how he would act."

"How can you talk in that ghastly way?"

"It *is* rather morbid. Still, that's what it comes to, unless you're swept away by ambition or driven by conviction. I haven't the conviction or the ambition, and the other thing is what it comes to with me. I ought to have been a preacher, after all; then I couldn't have asked it of myself, as I must, now I'm a lawyer. And you believe it's a holy war, Editha?" he suddenly addressed her. "Oh, I know you do! But you wish me to believe so, too?"

She hardly knew whether he was mocking or not, in the ironical way he always had with her plainer mind. But the only thing was to be outspoken with him.

"George, I wish you to believe whatever you think is true, at any and every cost. If I've tried to talk you into anything, I take it all back."

"Oh, I know that, Editha. I know how sincere you are, and how—I wish I had your undoubting spirit! I'll think it over; I'd like to believe as you do. But I don't, now; I don't, indeed. It isn't this war alone; though this seems peculiarly wanton and needless; but it's every war—so stupid; it makes me sick. Why shouldn't this thing have been settled reasonably?"

"Because," she said, very throatily again, "God meant it to be war."

"You think it was God? Yes, I suppose that is what people will say."

"Do you suppose it would have been war if God hadn't meant it?"

"I don't know. Sometimes it seems as if God had put this world into men's keeping to work it as they pleased."

"Now, George, that is blasphemy."

"Well, I won't blaspheme. I'll try to believe in your pocket Providence," he said, and then he rose to go.

"Why don't you stay to dinner?" Dinner at Balcom's Works was at one o'clock.

"I'll come back to supper, if you'll let me. Perhaps I shall bring you a convert."

"Well, you may come back, on that condition."

"All right. If I don't come, you'll understand."

He went away without kissing her, and she felt it a suspension of their engagement. It all interested her intensely; she was undergoing a tremendous experience, and she was being equal to it. While she stood looking after him, her mother came out through one of the long windows onto the veranda, with a catlike softness and vagueness.

"Why didn't he stay to dinner?"

"Because—because—war has been declared," Editha pronounced, without turning. Her mother said, "Oh, my!" and then said nothing more until she had sat down in one of the large Shaker chairs[3] and rocked herself for some time. Then she closed whatever tacit passage of thought there had been in her mind with the spoken words: "Well, I hope *he* won't go."

"And *I* hope he *will*," the girl said, and confronted her mother with a stormy exaltation that would have frightened any creature less unimpressionable than a cat.

Her mother rocked herself again for an interval of cogitation. What she arrived at in speech was: "Well, I guess you've done a wicked thing, Editha Balcom."

The girl said, as she passed indoors through the same window her mother had come out by: "I haven't done anything—yet."

In her room, she put together all her letters and gifts from Gearson, down to the withered petals of the first flower he had offered, with that timidity of his veiled in that irony of his. In the heart of the packet she enshrined her engagement ring which she had restored to the pretty box he had brought it her in. Then she sat down, if not calmly yet strongly, and wrote:

"GEORGE:—I understood when you left me. But I think we had better emphasize your meaning that if we cannot be one in everything we had better be one in nothing. So I am sending these things for your keeping till you have made up your mind.

"I shall always love you, and therefore I shall never marry any one else. But the man I marry must love his country first of all, and be able to say to me,

" 'I could not love thee, dear, so much,
Loved I not honor more.'[4]

"There is no honor above America with me. In this great hour there is no other honor.

"Your heart will make my words clear to you. I had never expected to say so much, but it has come upon me that I must say the utmost. EDITHA."

She thought she had worded her letter well, worded it in a way that could not be bettered; all had been implied and nothing expressed.

She had it ready to send with the packet she had tied with red, white, and blue ribbon, when it occurred to her that she was not just to him, that she was not giving him a fair chance. He had said he would go and think it over, and she was not waiting. She was pushing, threatening, compelling. That was not a woman's part. She must leave him free, free, free. She could not accept for her country or herself a forced sacrifice.

In writing her letter she had satisfied the impulse from which it sprang; she could well afford to wait till he had thought it over. She put the packet and the letter by, and rested serene in the consciousness of having done what was laid upon her by her love itself to do, and yet used patience, mercy, justice.

She had her reward. Gearson did not come to tea, but she had given him till morning, when, late at night there came up from the village the sound of a fife and

---

[3] Designed and manufactured by the Shakers, members of a religious community noted for the fine simplicity of their artifacts.

[4] From the poem "To Lucasta, Going to the Wars," by Richard Lovelace (1618–1658).

drum, with a tumult of voices, in shouting, singing, and laughing. The noise drew nearer and nearer; it reached the street end of the avenue; there it silenced itself, and one voice, the voice she knew best, rose over the silence. It fell; the air was filled with cheers; the fife and drum struck up, with the shouting, singing, and laughing again, but now retreating; and a single figure came hurrying up the avenue.

She ran down to meet her lover and clung to him. He was very gay, and he put his arm round her with a boisterous laugh. "Well, you must call me Captain now; or Cap, if you prefer; that's what the boys call me. Yes, we've had a meeting at the town-hall, and everybody has volunteered; and they selected me for captain, and I'm going to the war, the big war, the glorious war, the holy war ordained by the pocket Providence that blesses butchery. Come along; let's tell the whole family about it. Call them from their downy beds, father, mother, Aunt Hitty, and all the folks!"

But when they mounted the veranda steps he did not wait for a larger audience; he poured the story out upon Editha alone.

"There was a lot of speaking, and then some of the fools set up a shout for me. It was all going one way, and I thought it would be a good joke to sprinkle a little cold water on them. But you can't do that with a crowd that adores you. The first thing I knew I was sprinkling hell-fire on them. 'Cry havoc, and let slip the dogs of war.'[5] That was the style. Now that it had come to the fight, there were no two parties; there was one country, and the thing was to fight to a finish as quick as possible. I suggested volunteering then and there, and I wrote my name first of all on the roster. Then they elected me—that's all. I wish I had some ice-water."

She left him walking up and down the veranda, while she ran for the ice-pitcher and a goblet, and when she came back he was still walking up and down, shouting the story he had told her to her father and mother, who had come out more sketchily dressed than they commonly were by day. He drank goblet after goblet of the ice-water without noticing who was giving it, and kept on talking, and laughing through his talk wildly. "It's astonishing," he said, "how well the worse reason looks when you try to make it appear the better. Why, I believe I was the first convert to the war in that crowd to-night! I never thought I should like to kill a man; but now I shouldn't care; and the smokeless powder lets you see the man drop that you kill. It's all for the country! What a thing it is to have a country that *can't* be wrong, but if it is, is right, anyway!"

Editha had a great, vital thought, an inspiration. She set down the ice-pitcher on the veranda floor, and ran up-stairs and got the letter she had written him. When at last he noisily bade her father and mother, "Well, good-night. I forgot I woke you up; I sha'n't want any sleep myself," she followed him down the avenue to the gate. There, after the whirling words that seemed to fly away from her thoughts and refuse to serve them, she made a last effort to solemnize the moment that seemed so crazy, and pressed the letter she had written upon him.

"What's this?" he said. "Want me to mail it?"

"No, no. It's for you. I wrote it after you went this morning. Keep it—keep it —and read it sometime—" She thought, and then her inspiration came: "Read it if ever you doubt what you've done, or fear that I regret your having done it. Read it after you've started."

They strained each other in embraces that seemed as ineffective as their words, and

---

[5] Shakespeare's *Julius Caesar*, Act III, Sc. i, l. 273.

he kissed her face with quick, hot breaths that were so unlike him, that made her feel as if she had lost her old lover and found a stranger in his place. The stranger said: "What a gorgeous flower you are, with your red hair, and your blue eyes that look black now, and your face with the color painted out by the white moonshine! Let me hold you under the chin, to see whether I love blood, you tiger-lily!" Then he laughed Gearson's laugh, and released her, scared and giddy. Within her wilfulness she had been frightened by a sense of subtler force in him, and mystically mastered as she had never been before.

She ran all the way back to the house, and mounted the steps panting. Her mother and father were talking of the great affair. Her mother said: "Wa'n't Mr. Gearson in rather of an excited state of mind? Didn't you think he acted curious?"

"Well, not for a man who'd just been elected captain and had set'em up for the whole of Company A," her father chuckled back.

"What in the world do you mean, Mr. Balcom? Oh! There's Editha!" She offered to follow the girl indoors.

"Don't come, mother!" Editha called, vanishing.

Mrs. Balcom remained to reproach her husband. "I don't see much of anything to laugh at."

"Well, it's catching. Caught it from Gearson. I guess it won't be much of a war, and I guess Gearson don't think so either. The other fellows will back down as soon as they see we mean it. I wouldn't lose any sleep over it. I'm going back to bed, myself."

Gearson came again next afternoon, looking pale and rather sick, but quite himself, even to his languid irony. "I guess I'd better tell you, Editha, that I consecrated myself to your god of battles last night by pouring too many libations to him down my own throat. But I'm all right now. One has to carry off the excitement, somehow."

"Promise me," she commanded, "that you'll never touch it again!"

"What! Not let the cannikin[6] clink? Not let the soldier drink? Well, I promise."

"You don't belong to yourself now; you don't even belong to *me*. You belong to your country, and you have a sacred charge to keep yourself strong and well for your country's sake. I have been thinking, thinking all night and all day long."

"You look as if you had been crying a little, too," he said, with his queer smile.

"That's all past. I've been thinking, and worshipping *you*. Don't you suppose I know all that you've been through, to come to this? I've followed you every step from your old theories and opinions."

"Well, you've had a long row to hoe."

"And I know you've done this from the highest motives—"

"Oh, there won't be much pettifogging to do till this cruel war is—"

"And you haven't simply done it for my sake. I couldn't respect you if you had."

"Well, then we'll say I haven't. A man that hasn't got his own respect intact wants the respect of all the other people he can corner. But we won't go into that. I'm in for the thing now, and we've got to face our future. My idea is that this isn't going to be a very protracted struggle; we shall just scare the enemy to death before it comes

[6] Cup. The reference is to the tradition of a soldier's right to drink before battle, as described in Shakespeare's *Othello,* Act II, Sc. iii, ll. 71–75.

to a fight at all. But we must provide for contingencies, Editha. If anything happens to me—"

"Oh, George!" She clung to him, sobbing.

"I don't want you to feel foolishly bound to my memory. I should hate that, wherever I happened to be."

"I am yours, for time and eternity—time and eternity." She liked the words; they satisfied her famine for phrases.

"Well, say eternity; that's all right; but time's another thing; and I'm talking about time. But there is something! My mother! If anything happens—"

She winced, and he laughed, "You're not the bold soldier-girl of yesterday!" Then he sobered. "If anything happens, I want you to help my mother out. She won't like my doing this thing. She brought me up to think war a fool thing as well as a bad thing. My father was in the Civil War; all through it; lost his arm in it." She thrilled with the sense of the arm round her; what if that should be lost? He laughed as if divining her: "Oh, it doesn't run in the family, as far as I know!" Then he added, gravely: "He came home with misgivings about war, and they grew on him. I guess he and mother agreed between them that I was to be brought up in his final mind about it; but that was before my time. I only knew him from my mother's report of him and his opinions; I don't know whether they were hers first; but they were hers last. This will be a blow to her. I shall have to write and tell her—"

He stopped, and she asked: "Would you like me to write, too, George?"

"I don't believe that would do. No, I'll do the writing. She'll understand a little if I say that I thought the way to minimize it was to make war on the largest possible scale at once—that I felt I must have been helping on the war somehow if I hadn't helped keep it from coming, and I knew I hadn't; when it came, I had no right to stay out of it."

Whether his sophistries satisfied him or not, they satisfied her. She clung to his breast, and whispered, with closed eyes and quivering lips: "Yes, yes, yes!"

"But if anything should happen, you might go to her and see what you could do for her. You know? It's rather far off; she can't leave her chair—"

"Oh, I'll go, if it's the ends of the earth! But nothing will happen! Nothing *can!* I—"

She felt herself lifted with his rising, and Gearson was saying, with his arm still round her, to her father: "Well, we're off at once, Mr. Balcom. We're to be formally accepted at the capital, and then bunched up with the rest somehow, and sent into camp somewhere, and got to the front as soon as possible. We all want to be in the van, of course; we're the first company to report to the Governor. I came to tell Editha, but I hadn't got round to it."

She saw him again for a moment at the capital, in the station, just before the train started southward with his regiment. He looked well, in his uniform, and very soldierly, but somehow girlish, too, with his clean-shaven face and slim figure. The manly eyes and the strong voice satisfied her, and his preoccupation with some unexpected details of duty flattered her. Other girls were weeping and bemoaning themselves, but she felt a sort of noble distinction in the abstraction, the almost unconsciousness, with which they parted. Only at the last moment he said: "Don't forget my mother. It mayn't be such a walk-over as I supposed," and he laughed at the notion.

He waved his hand to her as the train moved off—she knew it among a score of hands that were waved to other girls from the platform of the car, for it held a letter which she knew was hers. Then he went inside the car to read it, doubtless, and she did not see him again. But she felt safe for him through the strength of what she called her love. What she called her God, always speaking the name in a deep voice and with the implication of a mutual understanding, would watch over him and keep him and bring him back to her. If with an empty sleeve, then he should have three arms instead of two, for both of hers should be his for life. She did not see, though, why she should always be thinking of the arm his father had lost.

There were not many letters from him, but they were such as she could have wished, and she put her whole strength into making hers such as she imagined he could have wished, glorifying and supporting him. She wrote to his mother glorifying him as their hero, but the brief answer she got was merely to the effect that Mrs. Gearson was not well enough to write herself, and thanking her for her letter by the hand of some one who called herself "Yrs truly, Mrs. W. J. Andrews."

Editha determined not to be hurt, but to write again quite as if the answer had been all she expected. Before it seemed as if she could have written, there came news of the first skirmish, and in the list of the killed, which was telegraphed as a trifling loss on our side, was Gearson's name. There was a frantic time of trying to make out that it might be, must be, some other Gearson; but the name and the company and the regiment and the State were too definitely given.

Then there was a lapse into depths out of which it seemed as if she never could rise again; then a lift into clouds far above all grief, black clouds, that blotted out the sun, but where she soared with him, with George—George! She had the fever that she expected of herself, but she did not die in it; she was not even delirious, and it did not last long. When she was well enough to leave her bed, her one thought was of George's mother, of his strangely worded wish that she should go to her and see what she could do for her. In the exaltation of the duty laid upon her—it buoyed her up instead of burdening her—she rapidly recovered.

Her father went with her on the long railroad journey from northern New York to western Iowa; he had business out at Davenport, and he said he could just as well go then as any other time; and he went with her to the little country town where George's mother lived in a little house on the edge of the illimitable cornfields, under trees pushed to a top of the rolling prairie. George's father had settled there after the Civil War, as so many other old soldiers had done; but they were Eastern people, and Editha fancied touches of the East in the June rose overhanging the front door, and the garden with early summer flowers stretching from the gate of the paling fence.

It was very low inside the house, and so dim, with the closed blinds, that they could scarcely see one another: Editha tall and black in her crapes which filled the air with smell of their dyes; her father standing decorously apart with his hat on his forearm, as at funerals; a woman rested in a deep arm-chair, and the woman who had let the strangers in stood behind the chair.

The seated woman turned her head round and up, and asked the woman behind her chair: "*Who* did you say?"

Editha, if she had done what she expected of herself, would have gone down on her knees at the feet of the seated figure and said, "I am George's Editha," for answer.

But instead of her own voice she heard that other woman's voice saying: "Well,

I don't know as I *did* get the name just right. I guess I'll have to make a little more light in here," and she went and pushed two of the shutters ajar.

Then Editha's father said, in his public will-now-address-a-few-remarks tone: "My name is Balcom, ma'am—Junius H. Balcom, of Balcom's Works, New York; my daughter—"

"Oh!" the seated woman broke in, with a powerful voice, the voice that always surprised Editha from Gearson's slender frame. "Let me see you. Stand round where the light can strike on your face," and Editha dumbly obeyed. "So, you're Editha Balcom," she sighed.

"Yes," Editha said, more like a culprit than a comforter.

"What did you come for?" Mrs. Gearson asked.

Editha's face quivered and her knees shook. "I came—because—because George—" She could go no further.

"Yes," the mother said, "he told me he had asked you to come if he got killed. You didn't expect that, I suppose, when you sent him."

"I would rather have died myself than done it!" Editha said, with more truth in her deep voice than she ordinarily found in it. "I tried to leave him free—"

"Yes, that letter of yours, that came back with his other things, left him free." Editha saw now where George's irony came from.

"It was not to be read before—unless—until—I told him so," she faltered.

"Of course, he wouldn't read a letter of yours, under the circumstances, till he thought you wanted him to. Been sick?" the woman abruptly demanded.

"Very sick," Editha said, with self-pity.

"Daughter's life," her father interposed, "was almost despaired of, at one time."

Mrs. Gearson gave him no heed. "I suppose you would have been glad to die, such a brave person as you! I don't believe *he* was glad to die. He was always a timid boy, that way; he was afraid of a good many things; but if he was afraid he did what he made up his mind to. I suppose he made up his mind to go, but I knew what it cost him by what it cost me when I heard of it. I had been through *one* war before. When you sent him you didn't expect he would get killed."

The voice seemed to compassionate Editha, and it was time. "No," she huskily murmured.

"No, girls don't; women don't when they give their men up to their country. They think they'll come marching back, somehow, just as gay as they went, or if it's an empty sleeve, or even an empty pantaloon, it's all the more glory, and they're so much the prouder of them, poor things!"

The tears began to run down Editha's face; she had not wept till then; but it was now such a relief to be understood that the tears came.

"No, you didn't expect him to get killed," Mrs. Gearson repeated, in a voice which was startlingly like George's again. "You just expected him to kill some one else, some of those foreigners, that weren't there because they had any say about it, but because they had to be there, poor wretches—conscripts, or whatever they call 'em. You thought it would be all right for my George, *your* George, to kill the sons of those miserable mothers and the husbands of those girls that you would never see the faces of." The woman lifted her powerful voice in a psalmlike note. "I thank my God he didn't live to do it! I thank my God they killed him first, and that he ain't livin' with their blood on his hands!" She dropped her eyes, which she had raised with her voice, and glared at Editha. "What you got that black on for?" She lifted herself by her powerful arms so high that her helpless body seemed to hang limp its full length. "Take it off, take it off, before I tear it from your back!"

The lady who was passing the summer near Balcom's Works was sketching Editha's beauty, which lent itself wonderfully to the effects of a colorist. It had come to that confidence which is rather apt to grow between artist and sitter, and Editha had told her everything.

"To think of your having such tragedy in your life!" the lady said. She added: "I suppose there are people who feel that way about war. But when you consider the good this war has done—how much it has done for the country! I can't understand such people, for my part. And when you had come all the way out there to console her—got up out of a sick-bed! Well!"

"I think," Editha said, magnanimously, "she wasn't quite in her right mind; and so did papa."

"Yes," the lady said, looking at Editha's lips in nature and then at her lips in art, and giving an empirical touch to them in the picture. "But how dreadful of her! How perfectly—excuse me—how *vulgar!*"

A light broke upon Editha in the darkness which she felt had been without a gleam of brightness for weeks and months. The mystery that had bewildered her was solved by the word; and from that moment she rose from grovelling in shame and self-pity, and began to live again in the ideal.

1905

Henry Adams
1838–1918

To be born a member of the Adams family, one of the few dynastic powers to descend from the days of the American Revolution, portends a special fate. It was an honor and a burden keenly felt by Henry Brooks Adams, great-grandson of John Adams and grandson of John Quincy Adams, second and sixth presidents of the United States, and member of the family whose existence had helped make the United States into a nation with its own separate fate to fulfill. When the family gardener observed to the child Henry, "You'll be thinkin' you'll be President too!" the "causality of the remark made so strong an impression on [Adams's] mind that he never forgot it." But Henry Adams learned that such steady patterns of cause and effect were no guarantees in the helter-skelter society in which he grew up.

Henry Adams did not become president, or anything near. The centers of public power had been closed after the 1828 election, when Andrew Jackson blocked John Quincy Adams's attempt to gain a second term in office. The brash new values of Jacksonian democracy did not favor the eighteenth-century Federalist principles of America's premier family. Henry Adams had to create a career out of *not* being president, out of not being one of *those* Adamses. But since he could hardly escape the consequences of the evolutionary process he studied so closely, he spent a lifetime testing what it meant to be the descendent of the Adamses and of the mythic Adam (the progenitor of all human history). He also had to work out the personal significance of having been flung into one century at a time when it was speeding headlong toward the next. Henry Adams would not, therefore, make his way into the nation's history as a statesman or politician or an industrial leader. Writing served as the shaping power of his career as he became simultaneously the historian and the autobiographer of himself, of the Adams family, and of all the children of Adam.

Henry Adams was born and raised in Boston, summered at the Adamses' country residence in nearby Quincy, graduated from Harvard, studied some law in Germany, traveled around Europe, and acted as secretary to his father when Lincoln named Charles Francis Adams foreign minister to London during the Civil War years. After the war Adams, in his late twenties, knocked about for several years as a journalist writing on politics, economic matters, and historical events for the influential *Nation* and the *North American Review*. In 1870 Adams was cajoled into accepting a teaching post at Harvard. At the university he offered courses in medieval history to young men who would be unable to earn five dollars a day in the emerging commercial and industrial society with the information they got from his classes, however finely he honed their intellectual skills. He remained at Harvard until 1877 and developed an area of historical study where none had previously existed. (In the same way, his friend William James was just then teaching subjects at Harvard he had never taken as a student.)

The 1870s was a busy decade for Adams in other ways as well. He took on the editorship of the *North American Review* and used it as a forum to attack the political corruptions of the Gilded Age. In 1872 he married wealthy and clever Marion "Clover" Hooper of Boston. Adams had talent and energy to spare, together with enough of an independent income to assure him freedom to move from career to career or, as he would put it, from one kind of failed education to another.

Although Adams knew that he could never obtain political authority in the nation's capital, he decided he wanted to be where the power was. In 1877 he and Clover left New England and settled into the midst of "good" Washington, D.C., society. Here he could at least observe the nation's flaws and perhaps exert the influence of a sharp-eyed, caustic-tongued critic of the American scene.

Never an idler or quiescent observer, Adams launched himself into a full-time career as the historian of the Republic, especially of the period when the earlier Adamses had held center stage. His histories were actually extended biographies of the men who had, in addition to John Adams and John Quincy Adams, created a new country out of an old colony. Studies of Albert Gallatin (1879) and John Randolph (1882) joined with Adams's nine-volume *History of the United States of America During the Administrations of Thomas Jefferson and James Madison* (1889–1891) to give an overview of the period, one that is still considered essential to historical scholarship. He also published two anonymously written novels: *Democracy* (1880) and *Esther* (1884). Both novels make use of sensitive heroines to register the grievous flaws in American life that Adams and his wife found undermining confidence in the established beliefs—whether in government or in religion—that once gave Americans their sense of stability.

The growing loss of equilibrium on the public scene became almost unbearable for Adams when his wife committed suicide in 1885. Over and over he told his friends that he had died too, that what they saw in their midst was a dead man. The void caused by his wife's sudden death gave Adams a glimpse of "the supersensual chaos" that lay just below the surface of the elegant social world this husband and wife had shared. (Her suicide was an even greater shock than the one he had experienced as a young man when he stood at the bedside of his sister, dying terribly of lockjaw while the sun shone down upon the beauty of the world outside her window.) Marion's death also created a gap in the chronology Adams would give to his autobiography, *The Education of Henry Adams* (1918). When writing this, his most famous book, Adams deleted all mention of Marion or their marriage, omitting a twenty-year period in the chronology. But in actual life, the self-described "dead man" persevered.

Frenetic travel occupied Adams for several years after 1885. He and his friends zigzagged through Japan, Australia, the South Seas, Russia, the Middle East, as well as Europe, where he made almost annual trips. The habits of the student led him to continue his research into customs and artifacts of whatever cultures he came in contact with. *Historical Essays* about America was published in 1891, the same year as the final volume of *The History of the United States*. *Memoirs of Marau Taaroa*, about the Tahitian royal family, appeared in 1893.

As Adams's interests turned toward French history and culture, Paris and its environs became increasingly his home. The medievalist in him began to focus on the effects the Middle Ages had had on French civilization. Adams began to free himself from the weariness that had beset him since 1885 and to contemplate ways in which he might interpret his own era in terms of the past glories of Western culture. He hoped to be able to predict the future toward which he and his contemporaries were hurtling. He knew he could do nothing to control the social forces set loose by the new century. Perhaps he could learn how to interpret the laws that made it work. The cathedrals and religious monuments of northern France dedicated to the saints and the Virgin Mary attracted his imagination; so did the international expositions held in honor of the occult power of the dynamo, the most potent force of the new age of technology. *Mont-Saint-Michel and Chartres* (a "study of thirteenth-century unity") was completed and printed privately in 1904 and published in 1913. *The Education of Henry Adams* (a "study of twentieth-century multiplicity") was distributed to friends in 1907 but did not reach the hands of the general public until after Adams's death in 1918.

As Adams crisscrossed the ocean between the United States and the Continent during the final decade of his life, other writings concerned him. In 1901 Adams developed a theory of the future of human existence in "The Rule of Phase Applied to History." (With the increase in the quality of human consciousness, he noted, there was an alarming decline in the capacity of the mind to control the random forces of the universe.) While serving as the head of the American Historical Association, he gave an address that he later expanded into an essay, "A Letter to American Teachers of History" (1910), in which he argued that historical study must become more scientific and less impressionistic in its methods of research and interpretation. During an age increasingly scientific in temper and achievement, Adams thought history might become an anachronism through the acceleration of events marking the turn of the century. These two essays show Adams's continuing attempt to discover the kind of education that would permit him and his contemporaries to survive in a world of bewildering change.

In his sixties Adams turned to the study of X-rays, radiation, and thermodynamics. The new sciences were the essential education of the new age, an age neither his years at Harvard in the 1850s nor his subsequent experiences as a student of legal history, medieval philosophers, political skullduggery in London and Washington, nineteenth-century aesthetics, Darwinism, and the vagaries of the gold market had prepared him for.

Adams died the year the First World War came to its close. *The Education of Henry Adams* was published that year. It became an immediate best-seller and continues to hold its own as a masterpiece, though it has been more often praised than read. Among its fascinations are its power to foretell the course of future history: shaped by the ancient inertial weight of Russia in contention with China, by the nervous energy let loose by the New Woman, and by the explosive impersonality of the forces released by the new physics. The boy who had been born into the fourth decade of the nineteenth century with the assurance of meaning promised by his eighteenth-century mentality had lived long enough to face the fact that the twentieth century could not be mastered by any one of the forms of education available in the year 1900. The legacy Adams received from his distinguished Adams forebears had been insufficient. The value of the legacy that this childless man handed on to the sons of Adam could come only from the records he had kept of trying, failing, and trying once again—those unending processes by which the new Adam might yet make sense out of a welter of experiences.

The reasons for the somewhat begrudging attention paid to Adams's writing are not hard to find. His works are perceived to be arduous to read as literary texts. Their author is often difficult to stomach as a man because of his egotism and petty snobberies. Poe and Thoreau also wrote hard texts; as for liking their personalities, if one were making out a list of America's most lovable writers, the names of Poe and Thoreau would probably not appear either. But Adams suffers from special kinds of distaste that are brought to the reading of his big book. He wrote stories of failure that strike readers as not only depressing but arrogant. Adams has also been attacked for being too rich and privileged, somehow protected from life's trials. Even his ironic responses to social and cosmic ills make him seem more narrowly conservative than the interesting mix he claimed for himself—"Christian conservative anarchist." And there is no clear way around the often nasty bigotry by which he expressed his fear that the United States would be overrun by alien cultures and the unformed masses.

Still, Adams's merits continue to make a place for him as one of the most important writers of the late nineteenth century—perhaps even, as a steadily increasing number of readers insist, one of the major figures in American letters. Adams helped to redefine *education,* a word that Americans, from the Puritans through Franklin, Emerson, Melville, and Mark Twain, have thought crucial for the nation's survival. Adams also made himself into a masterly commentator on the nature of autobiography. His predecessors are not only Augustine, Rousseau, and Franklin (figures he specifically mentions) but also John Woolman, Frederick Douglass, and Henry David Thoreau—Americans all. In a secular age, he asked important questions about what it is we are to celebrate: the Lord, technology, or the self. He emphasized the importance of the mind at work creating facts as well as interpreting them. As a prose stylist he took earthbound words out into cosmic spaces; he grounded pure abstractions in the concrete world of political, social, and personal events. Reluctant as he was to leave the comforting tidiness of his old-fashioned boyhood in Quincy, he let himself be hurtled into the anxieties of the dynamo age.

Adams stood between Thoreau, who knew the questions and the answers—though he was unable to live according to them in the fullest sense—and the legion of twentieth-century worriers with uncertain questions and no answers. Adams shared with Gertrude Stein the brave ability to admit that he was not even certain which questions to ask or whether there were any. Snobbish, self-deprecating, a bit neurotic, and partially insulated by wealth, Adams took advantage of his privileged view to give us, in stunning literary style and with the discipline of historical scholarship, the state of affairs of the world as he found it. Subsequent generations of readers have undergone the shock of discovering that his world and the future he speculated about with such energy are essentially their world and their future. The "modern" perspective Adams brought to the writing of history reveals what a personal and universal story it is. History, as Adams writes it, is the same thing as autobiography: an unending education in what it means to experience the twentieth century and beyond.

Further Reading:

E. Samuels, *The Young Henry Adams*, 1948.

H. Jordy, *Henry Adams: Scientific Historian*, 1952, 1963.

J. C. Brunner, *Henry Adams: His Decline and Fall*, 1956.

H. H. Wasser, *The Scientific Thought of Henry Adams*, 1956.

J. Levenson, *The Mind and Art of Henry Adams*, 1957, 1968.

E. Samuels, *Henry Adams: The Middle Years*, 1958.

G. Hochfield, *Henry Adams: An Introduction and Interpretation*, 1962.

E. Samuels, *Henry Adams: The Major Phase*, 1964.

M. Lyon, *Symbol and Idea in Henry Adams*, 1969, 1970.

V. Wagner, *The Suspension of Henry Adams*, 1969.

J. Conder, *A Formula of His Own: Henry Adams' Literary Experiment*, 1970.

E. Scheyer, *The Circle of Henry Adams: Art and Artists*, 1970.

L. Auchincloss, *Henry Adams*, 1971.

J. Rowe, *Henry Adams and Henry James, The Emergence of the Modern Consciousness*, 1976.

E. Harbert, *The Force So Much Closer Home: Henry Adams and the Adams Family*, 1977.

D. R. Contosta, *Henry Adams and the American Experiment*, 1980.

W. Dusinberre, *Henry Adams: The Myth of Failure*, 1980.

Henry Adams/R. P. Blackmur, ed. V. Makowsky, 1980.

J. F. Byrnes, *The Virgin of Chartres*, 1981.

Critical Essays on Henry Adams, ed. E. N. Harbert, 1981.

Text:

The Education of Henry Adams, 1974.

See also *The Degradation of Democratic Dogma*, 1919, 1949.

Letters of Henry Adams, 2 vols., ed. W. Ford, 1930–1938.

Henry Adams and His Friends: A Collection of His Unpublished Letters, ed. H. Cater, 1947.

The Letters of Henry Adams, 3 vols., ed. J. Levenson, 1982.

from The Education of Henry Adams[*]

Chapter XXV: The Dynamo and the Virgin (1900)

Until the Great Exposition of 1900[1] closed its doors in November, Adams haunted it, aching to absorb knowledge, and helpless to find it. He would have liked to know how much of it could have been grasped by the best-informed man in the world. While he was thus meditating chaos, Langley[2] came by, and showed it to him. At Langley's behest, the Exhibition dropped its superfluous rags and stripped itself to the skin, for Langley knew what to study, and why, and how; while Adams might as well have stood outside in the night, staring at the Milky Way. Yet Langley said nothing new, and taught nothing that one might not have learned from Lord Bacon,[3] three hundred years before; but though one should have known the "Advancement of Science" as well as one knew the "Comedy of Errors,"[4] the literary knowledge counted for nothing until some teacher should show how to apply it. Bacon took a vast deal of trouble in teaching King James I and his subjects, American or other, towards the year 1620, that true science was the development or economy of forces; yet an elderly American in 1900 knew neither the formula nor the forces; or even so much as to say to himself that his historical business in the Exposition concerned only the economies or developments of force since 1893, when he began the study at Chicago.

Nothing in education is so astonishing as the amount of ignorance it accumulates in the form of inert facts. Adams had looked at most of the accumulations of art in the storehouses called Art Museums; yet he did not know how to look at the art exhibits of 1900. He had studied Karl Marx and his doctrines of history[5] with profound attention, yet he could not apply them at Paris. Langley, with the ease of a great master of experiment, threw out of the field every exhibit that did not reveal a new application of force, and naturally threw out, to begin with, almost the whole art exhibit. Equally, he ignored almost the whole industrial exhibit. He led his pupil directly to the forces. His chief interest was in new motors to make his airship feasible, and he taught Adams the astonishing complexities of the new Daimler motor,[6] and of the automobile, which, since 1893, had become a nightmare at a hundred kilometres an hour, almost as destructive as the electric tram which was only ten years older; and threatening to become as terrible as the locomotive steam-engine itself, which was almost exactly Adams's own age.

[*] Adams began work on *The Education* in 1903, completed it by 1905, and sent out the first copy of a private printing early in 1907; the Preface is dated February 16, 1907. The Massachusetts Historical Society brought out the first public edition in September 1918, after Adams's death in March of that year.
[1] On display at the Paris Exposition of 1900 was an array of the most recent advances in the technology of electric motors, transformers, and dynamos.
[2] Samuel Langley (1834–1906), American scientist.
[3] Francis Bacon (1561–1628), English scientist.
[4] Play by William Shakespeare.
[5] Marx's *Das Kapital* was published in 1867.
[6] Invented by the German Gottlieb Daimler (1834–1900), one of the primary developers of the internal combustion engine.

Then he showed his scholar the great hall of dynamos,[7] and explained how little he knew about electricity or force of any kind, even of his own special sun, which spouted heat in inconceivable volume, but which, as far as he knew, might spout less or more, at any time, for all the certainty he felt in it. To him, the dynamo itself was but an ingenious channel for conveying somewhere the heat latent in a few tons of poor coal hidden in a dirty engine-house carefully kept out of sight; but to Adams the dynamo became a symbol of infinity. As he grew accustomed to the great gallery of machines, he began to feel the forty-foot dynamos as a moral force, much as the early Christians felt the Cross. The planet itself seemed less impressive, in its old-fashioned, deliberate, annual or daily revolution, than this huge wheel, revolving within arm's-length at some vertiginous speed, and barely murmuring—scarcely humming an audible warning to stand a hair's-breadth further for respect of power —while it would not wake the baby lying close against its frame. Before the end, one began to pray to it; inherited instinct taught the natural expression of man before silent and infinite force. Among the thousand symbols of ultimate energy, the dynamo was not so human as some, but it was the most expressive.

Yet the dynamo, next to the steam-engine, was the most familiar of exhibits. For Adams's objects its value lay chiefly in its occult mechanism. Between the dynamo in the gallery of machines and the engine-house outside, the break of continuity amounted to abysmal fracture for a historian's objects. No more relation could he discover between the steam and the electric current than between the Cross and the cathedral. The forces were interchangeable if not reversible, but he could see only an absolute *fiat* in electricity as in faith. Langley could not help him. Indeed, Langley seemed to be worried by the same trouble, for he constantly repeated that the new forces were anarchical, and especially that he was not responsible for the new rays, that were little short of parricidal in their wicked spirit towards science. His own rays, with which he had doubled the solar spectrum, were altogether harmless and beneficent; but Radium denied its God[8]— or, what was to Langley the same thing, denied the truths of his Science. The force was wholly new.

A historian who asked only to learn enough to be as futile as Langley or Kelvin,[9] made rapid progress under this teaching, and mixed himself up in the tangle of ideas until he achieved a sort of Paradise of ignorance vastly consoling to his fatigued senses. He wrapped himself in vibrations and rays which were new, and he would have hugged Marconi and Branly[10] had he met them, as he hugged the dynamo; while he lost his arithmetic in trying to figure out the equation between the discoveries and the economies of force. The economies, like the discoveries, were absolute, supersensual, occult; incapable of expression in horse-power. What mathematical equivalent could he suggest as the value of a Branly coherer? Frozen air, or the electric furnace, had some scale of measurement, no doubt, if somebody could invent a thermometer

---

[7] The first electrical generator had been developed in 1831 by the British inventor Michael Faraday (1791–1867). By Adams's time the dynamo had come to stand for the forces of industrial society that lacked the personal humanity Adams associated with the Virgin Mary as worshipped during the Middle Ages.

[8] Radium's radiation, caused by atomic disintegration, went beyond any conception of cosmic force previously known, even that disclosed by Langley in 1881 in his measurements of solar radiation.

[9] William Thomson, Lord Kelvin (1824–1907), British scientist.

[10] Guglielmo Marconi (1874–1937) and Edouard Branly (1846–1940), Italian inventor of the radio telegraph and French inventor of the method for detecting radio waves, respectively.

adequate to the purpose; but X-rays had played no part whatever in man's consciousness, and the atom itself had figured only as a fiction of thought. In these seven years man had translated himself into a new universe which had no common scale of measurement with the old. He had entered a supersensual world, in which he could measure nothing except by chance collisions of movements imperceptible to his senses, perhaps even imperceptible to his instruments, but perceptible to each other, and so to some known ray at the end of the scale. Langley seemed prepared for anything, even for an indeterminable number of universes interfused—physics stark mad in metaphysics.

Historians undertake to arrange sequences,—called stories, or histories—assuming in silence a relation of cause and effect. These assumptions, hidden in the depths of dusty libraries, have been astounding, but commonly unconscious and childlike; so much so, that if any captious critic were to drag them to light, historians would probably reply, with one voice, that they had never supposed themselves required to know what they were talking about. Adams, for one, had toiled in vain to find out what he meant. He had even published a dozen volumes of American history for no other purpose than to satisfy himself whether, by the severest process of stating, with the least possible comment, such facts as seemed sure, in such order as seemed rigorously consequent, he could fix for a familiar moment a necessary sequence of human movement. The result had satisfied him as little as at Harvard College. Where he saw sequence, other men saw something quite different, and no one saw the same unit of measure. He cared little about his experiments and less about his statesmen, who seemed to him quite as ignorant as himself and, as a rule, no more honest; but he insisted on a relation of sequence, and if he could not reach it by one method, he would try as many methods as science knew. Satisfied that the sequence of men led to nothing and that the sequence of their society could lead no further, while the mere sequence of time was artificial, and the sequence of thought was chaos, he turned at last to the sequence of force; and thus it happened that, after ten years' pursuit, he found himself lying in the Gallery of Machines at the Great Exposition of 1900, with his historical neck broken by the sudden irruption of forces totally new.

Since no one else showed much concern, an elderly person without other cares had no need to betray alarm. The year 1900 was not the first to upset schoolmasters. Copernicus and Galileo[11] had broken many professional necks about 1600; Columbus had stood the world on its head towards 1500; but the nearest approach to the revolution of 1900 was that of 310, when Constantine[12] set up the Cross. The rays that Langley disowned, as well as those which he fathered, were occult, supersensual, irrational; they were a revelation of mysterious energy like that of the Cross; they were what, in terms of medieval science, were called immediate modes of the divine substance.

The historian was thus reduced to his last resources. Clearly if he was bound to reduce all these forces to a common value, this common value could have no measure but that of their attraction on his own mind. He must treat them as they had been

---

[11] Copernicus (1473–1543) and Galileo (1564–1642) reformed existing conceptions concerning the motion of the earth around the sun.

[12] Christianity was made the official religion of the Roman Empire in A.D. 313 upon the proclamation of Emperor Constantine I.

felt; as convertible, reversible, interchangeable attractions on thought. He made up his mind to venture it; he would risk translating rays into faith. Such a reversible process would vastly amuse a chemist,[13] but the chemist could not deny that he, or some of his fellow physicists, could feel the force of both. When Adams was a boy in Boston, the best chemist in the place had probably never heard of Venus except by way of scandal,[14] or of the Virgin except as idolatry; neither had he heard of dynamos or automobiles or radium; yet his mind was ready to feel the force of all, though the rays were unborn and the women were dead.

Here opened another totally new education, which promised to be by far the most hazardous of all. The knife-edge along which he must crawl, like Sir Lancelot[15] in the twelfth century, divided two kingdoms of force which had nothing in common but attraction. They were as different as a magnet is from gravitation, supposing one knew what a magnet was, or gravitation, or love. The force of the Virgin was still felt at Lourdes,[16] and seemed to be as potent as X-rays; but in America neither Venus nor Virgin ever had value as force—at most as sentiment. No American had ever been truly afraid of either.

This problem in dynamics gravely perplexed an American historian. The Woman had once been supreme; in France she still seemed potent, not merely as a sentiment, but as a force. Why was she unknown in America? For evidently America was ashamed of her, and she was ashamed of herself, otherwise they would not have strewn fig-leaves so profusely all over her. When she was a true force, she was ignorant of fig-leaves,[17] but the monthly-magazine-made American female had not a feature that would have been recognized by Adam. The trait was notorious, and often humorous, but anyone brought up among Puritans knew that sex was sin. In any previous age, sex was strength. Neither art nor beauty was needed. Everyone, even among Puritans, knew that neither Diana[18] of the Ephesians nor any of the Oriental goddesses was worshipped for her beauty. She was goddess because of her force; she was the animated dynamo; she was reproduction—the greatest and most mysterious of all energies; all she needed was to be fecund. Singularly enough, not one of Adams's many schools of education had ever drawn his attention to the opening lines of Lucretius, though they were perhaps the finest in all Latin literature, where the poet invoked Venus exactly as Dante invoked the Virgin:—

"Quae quoniam rerum naturam *sola* gubernas."[19]

The Venus of Epicurean philosophy survived in the Virgin of the Schools:[20]—

---

[13] Druggist.
[14] By way of the treatment of venereal disease, associated with Venus, the love goddess.
[15] Reference to one of the chivalric tales concerning Sir Lancelot's heroic deeds.
[16] Shrine in France dedicated to the healing powers of the Virgin Mary.
[17] According to Genesis, Eve went naked in Eden until the Fall. She then covered her body with leaves from the fig tree because of her sense of shame. Adams refers to the prudery about the unclothed female form common to American magazines of the period.
[18] Fertility goddess.
[19] From *De Rerum Natura* ("On the Nature of Things") by the Roman poet Lucretius (99?–55? B.C.): "Since thou alone dost govern the nature of things."
[20] That is, as described by the medieval scholastic philosophers.

> "Donna, sei tanto grande, e tanto vali,
> Che qual vuol grazia, e a te non ricorre,
> Sua disianza vuol volar senz' ali."[21]

All this was to American thought as though it had never existed. The true American knew something of the facts, but nothing of the feelings; he read the letter, but he never felt the law. Before this historical chasm, a mind like that of Adams felt itself helpless; he turned from the Virgin to the Dynamo as though he were a Branly coherer. On one side, at the Louvre and at Chartres, as he knew by the record of work actually done and still before his eyes, was the highest energy ever known to man, the creator of four-fifths of his noblest art, exercising vastly more attraction over the human mind than all the steam-engines and dynamos ever dreamed of; and yet this energy was unknown to the American mind. An American Virgin would never dare command; an American Venus would never dare exist.

The question, which to any plain American of the nineteenth century seemed as remote as it did to Adams, drew him almost violently to study, once it was posed; and on this point Langleys were as useless as though they were Herbert Spencers[22] or dynamos. The idea survived only as art. There one turned as naturally as though the artist were himself a woman. Adams began to ponder, asking himself whether he knew of any American artist who had ever insisted on the power of sex, as every classic had always done; but he could think only of Walt Whitman; Bret Harte, as far as the magazine would let him venture; and one or two painters, for the flesh-tones. All the rest had used sex for sentiment, never for force; to them, Eve was a tender flower, and Herodias[23] an unfeminine horror. American art, like the American language and American education, was as far as possible sexless. Society regarded this victory over sex as its greatest triumph, and the historian readily admitted it, since the moral issue, for the moment, did not concern one who was studying the relations of unmoral force. He cared nothing for the sex of the dynamo until he could measure its energy.

Vaguely seeking a clue, he wandered through the art exhibit, and, in his stroll, stopped almost every day before St. Gaudens's General Sherman,[24] which had been given the central post of honor. St. Gaudens himself was in Paris, putting on the work his usual interminable last touches, and listening to the usual contradictory suggestions of brother sculptors. Of all the American artists who gave to American art whatever life it breathed in the seventies, St. Gaudens was perhaps the most sympathetic, but certainly the most inarticulate. General Grant or Don Cameron[25] had scarcely less instinct of rhetoric than he. All the others—the Hunts, Richardson, John La Farge,

---

[21] From Dante's *Divine Comedy* (*Paradiso* xxxiii, 13–15): "Lady [the Virgin], Thou art so great and so worthy, / That one who desires grace and does not seek after thee, / Would have his wish to soar without wings."

[22] Herbert Spencer (1820–1903): English advocate of social Darwinism.

[23] The wife of King Herod, who had John the Baptist slain.

[24] The statue of General William T. Sherman, Union general, was then on display in Paris; sculpted by Augustus Saint-Gaudens (1848–1907), it now stands at the edge of New York City's Central Park.

[25] James Donald Cameron (1833–1918), Pennsylvania senator and a man considered as inarticulate as President Grant, under whom he served as secretary of war.

Stanford White[26]—were exuberant; only St. Gaudens could never discuss or dilate on an emotion or suggest artistic arguments for giving to his work the forms that he felt. He never laid down the law or affected the despot, or became brutalized like Whistler[27] by the brutalities of his world. He required no incense; he was no egoist; his simplicity of thought was excessive; he could not imitate, or give any form but his own to the creations of his hand. No one felt more strongly than he the strength of other men, but the idea that they could affect him never stirred an image in his mind.

This summer his health was poor and his spirits were low. For such a temper, Adams was not the best companion, since his own gaiety was not *folle*;[28] but he risked going now and then to the studio on Mont Parnasse to draw him out for a stroll in the Bois de Boulogne,[29] or dinner as pleased his moods, and in return St. Gaudens sometimes let Adams go about in his company.

Once St. Gaudens took him down to Amiens, with a party of Frenchmen, to see the cathedral.[30] Not until they found themselves actually studying the sculpture of the western portal, did it dawn on Adams's mind that, for his purposes, St. Gaudens on that spot had more interest to him than the cathedral itself. Great men before great monuments express great truths, provided they are not taken too solemnly. Adams never tired of quoting the supreme phrase of his idol Gibbon, before the Gothic cathedrals: "I darted a contemptuous look on the stately monuments of superstition."[31] Even in the footnotes of his history, Gibbon had never inserted a bit of humor more human than this, and one would have paid largely for a photograph of the fat little historian, on the background of Notre Dame of Amiens, trying to persuade his readers—perhaps himself—that he was darting a contemptuous look on the stately monument, for which he felt in fact the respect which every man of his vast study and active mind always feels before objects worthy of it; but besides the humor, one felt also the relation. Gibbon ignored the Virgin, because in 1789 religious monuments were out of fashion. In 1900 his remark sounded fresh and simple as the green fields to ears that had heard a hundred years of other remarks, mostly no more fresh and certainly less simple. Without malice, one might find it more instructive than a whole lecture of Ruskin. One sees what one brings, and at that moment Gibbon brought the French Revolution. Ruskin[32] brought reaction against the Revolution. St. Gaudens had passed beyond all. He liked the stately monuments much more than he liked Gibbon or Ruskin; he loved their dignity; their unity; their scale; their lines; their lights and shadows; their decorative sculpture; but he was even less conscious than they of the force that created it all—the Virgin, the Woman—by whose genius "the stately monuments of superstition" were built, through which

---

[26] Well-known artists and architects of the period: William Morris Hunt (1824–1879); Richard Morris Hunt (1828–1895); Henry Richardson (1838–1886); John La Farge (1835–1910); Stanford White (1853–1906).

[27] James Abbott McNeil Whistler (1834–1903), who was apt to unloose vitriolic attacks against the artistic conventions of his day.

[28] French: "excessive" or "mad."

[29] Montparnasse was the Parisian artists' quarter; the Bois is a large park.

[30] The largest cathedral in France, dedicated to the Virgin Mary.

[31] English historian Edward Gibbon (1737–1794), author of *The Decline and Fall of the Roman Empire* (1776–1788), wrote this entry in his *French Journal* (February 21, 1763). Adams paraphrases here.

[32] John Ruskin (1819–1900), English writer on art and architecture.

she was expressed. He would have seen more meaning in Isis with the cow's horns, at Edfoo,[33] who expressed the same thought. The art remained, but the energy was lost even upon the artist.

Yet in mind and person St. Gaudens was a survival of the 1500's; he bore the stamp of the Renaissance, and should have carried an image of the Virgin round his neck, or stuck in his hat, like Louis XI.[34] In mere time he was a lost soul that had strayed by chance into the twentieth century, and forgotten where it came from. He writhed and cursed at his ignorance, much as Adams did at his own, but in the opposite sense. St. Gaudens was a child of Benvenuto Cellini,[35] smothered in an American cradle. Adams was a quintessence of Boston, devoured by curiosity to think like Benvenuto. St. Gaudens's art was starved from birth, and Adams's instinct was blighted from babyhood. Each had but half of a nature, and when they came together before the Virgin of Amiens they ought both to have felt in her the force that made them one; but it was not so. To Adams she became more than ever a channel of force; to St. Gaudens she remained as before a channel of taste.

For a symbol of power, St. Gaudens instinctively preferred the horse, as was plain in his horse and Victory of the Sherman monument. Doubtless Sherman also felt it so. The attitude was so American that, for at least forty years, Adams had never realized that any other could be in sound taste. How many years had he taken to admit a notion of what Michael Angelo and Rubens[36] were driving at? He could not say; but he knew that only since 1895 had he begun to feel the Virgin or Venus as force, and not everywhere even so. At Chartres—perhaps at Lourdes—possibly at Cnidos if one could still find there the divinely naked Aphrodite of Praxiteles[37]—but otherwise one must look for force to the goddesses of Indian mythology. The idea died out long ago in the German and English stock. St. Gaudens at Amiens was hardly less sensitive to the force of the female energy than Matthew Arnold at the Grande Chartreuse.[38] Neither of them felt goddesses as power—only as reflected emotion, human expression, beauty, purity, taste, scarcely even as sympathy. They felt a railway train as power; yet they, and all other artists, constantly complained that the power embodied in a railway train could never be embodied in art. All the steam in the world could not, like the Virgin, build Chartres.

Yet in mechanics, whatever the mechanicians might think, both energies acted as interchangeable forces on man, and by action on man all known force may be measured. Indeed, few men of science measured force in any other way. After once admitting that a straight line was the shortest distance between two points, no serious mathematician cared to deny anything that suited his convenience, and rejected no symbol, unproved or unproveable, that helped him to accomplish work. The symbol was force, as a compass-needle or a triangle was force, as the mechanist might prove

---

[33] At Edfu on the Nile, Adams had seen such a statue of the fertility goddess Isis.

[34] King of France from 1423 to 1483.

[35] I.e., of the Italian Renaissance. The sculptor and writer Benvenuto Cellini lived from 1500 to 1571.

[36] Both the Italian artist and the Flemish painter emphasized the human form in their depiction of religious themes.

[37] Famous statue of Venus of the fourth century B.C. by the renowned Greek sculptor Praxiteles.

[38] The English poet (1822–1888) wrote "Stanzas from the Grande Chartreuse" (1855) in expression of his sense of the loss of the faith once held by the members of this medieval monastic community.

by losing it, and nothing could be gained by ignoring their value. Symbol or energy, the Virgin had acted as the greatest force the Western world ever felt, and had drawn man's activities to herself more strongly than any other power, natural or supernatural, had ever done; the historian's business was to follow the track of the energy; to find where it came from and where it went to; its complex source and shifting channels; its values, equivalents, conversions. It could scarcely be more complex than radium; it could hardly be deflected, diverted, polarized, absorbed more perplexingly than other radiant matter. Adams knew nothing about any of them, but as a mathematical problem of influence on human progress, though all were occult, all reacted on his mind, and he rather inclined to think the Virgin easiest to handle.

The pursuit turned out to be long and tortuous, leading at last into the vast forests of scholastic science. From Zeno to Descartes, hand in hand with Thomas Aquinas, Montaigne, and Pascal,[39] one stumbled as stupidly as though one were still a German student of 1860.[40] Only with the instinct of despair could one force one's self into this old thicket of ignorance after having been repulsed at a score of entrances more promising and more popular. Thus far, no path had led anywhere, unless perhaps to an exceedingly modest living. Forty-five years of study had proved to be quite futile for the pursuit of power; one controlled no more force in 1900 than in 1850, although the amount of force controlled by society had enormously increased. The secret of education still hid itself somewhere behind ignorance, and one fumbled over it as feebly as ever. In such labyrinths, the staff is a force almost more necessary than the legs; the pen becomes a sort of blind-man's dog, to keep him from falling into the gutters. The pen works for itself, and acts like a hand, modelling the plastic material over and over again to the form that suits it best. The form is never arbitrary, but is a sort of growth like crystallization, as any artist knows too well; for often the pencil or pen runs into side-paths and shapelessness, loses its relations, stops or is bogged. Then it has to return on its trail, and recover, if it can, its line of force. The result of a year's work depends more on what is struck out than on what is left in; on the sequence of the main lines of thought, than on their play or variety. Compelled once more to lean heavily on this support, Adams covered more thousands of pages with figures as formal as though they were algebra, laboriously striking out, altering, burning, experimenting, until the year had expired, the Exposition had long been closed, and winter drawing to its end, before he sailed from Cherbourg, on January 19, 1901, for home.

1905/1918

---

[39] Influential philosophers and mathematicians from the time of ancient Greece to the seventeenth century: Zeno of Elea (fifth century B.C.); René Descartes (1596–1650); St. Thomas Aquinas (1225?–1274); Michel de Montaigne (1533–1592); Blaise Pascal (1623–1662).
[40] Between 1858 and 1860 Adams studied in Germany.

Henry James
1843–1916

Literary historians of the United States and Great Britain both claim Henry James as their own. Modernist critics say he is of no country at all because he possessed an imagination that is "international" in scope. A few, like Mark Twain (who would not read one of James's novels on a bet), are indifferent as to who claims him.

It is natural that a man who has attracted so many different views of his worth has been given so many identifying labels. James is "the expatriate," the man who lived, observed, and wrote *between* cultures. Still, although he resided abroad for the bulk of his mature years and became a British citizen in the last year of his life, James is also recognized for his intensely "American" consciousness and for the slant that American quality gave to his international themes. James is also "the critic" or, in his own words, "the restless analyst." One of the first major American critical theorists, he possessed a penetrating social intelligence of the kind needed to aid Americans in better understanding their collective strengths and weaknesses. In the words of recent criticism, James is "the androgyne of the imagination." Neither exclusively male nor female in his sensibilities, he preferred to sort people out in terms of their behavior, not their gender. James is "the celibate priest," the writer who willingly sacrifices everything on what he called the altar of art. Finally, and most important, James is known as "the Master"—the influential force who helped bring an end to the nineteenth-century novel based on external plots and public events and initiated twentieth-century views of fiction as inner dramas of consciousness.

James denied himself the elements of personality that come to a man through marriage and through making his permanent home in his native country. Yet it is striking to realize that James began his life as one of the most American of children. Gertrude Stein once teasingly observed that Henry James had to suffer the ignominy of having no last name, only two first names—that is, having no real family identity. But James was born in 1843 into a securely upper-middle-class home in New York City's fashionable Washington Square neighborhood. He was very much the member of a pronounced family group, headed by the benign domination of the senior Henry James—philosopher, visionary, lecturer, and writer. The second son in a family of five precociously alert children (including William, the psychologist and philosopher, and Alice, the youngest of the lot), the younger Henry James remained somewhat to the side until his father's death in 1882. At that time, he shook himself loose from the first label he had had to wear—"Henry James, Junior," the name he used to sign the literary pieces he had presented to the public since his emergence as a professional writer in 1864.

Until his twenty-first year, Henry James was usually in tow as his father moved the family from New York to Newport, Rhode Island, and Cambridge, Massachusetts, and on to England, France, Germany, and Switzerland—always in quest of the perfect spiritual and intellectual education. In his late teens, James studied painting and then the law during a brief stint at Harvard. But it was "the life of the imagination" to which he would apply himself. Without the aid or liability of advanced schooling, James's intelligence was shaped into an acutely sensuous responsiveness by the theaters, art galleries, landscape vistas, and city scenes through which the senior James marched his troop of children. The young James responded most of all to the intricate give-and-take he saw played out in the midst of the intensely social nucleus of the James family.

James sensed very early in his career that the choreographed shifts of relationship between his fictional men and women that would form the basis of his mature literary art required settings steeped in generations of cultural and historical expressiveness. To his mind, the right people for his fictional needs were available anywhere he turned his watchful eye, but the proper background for his characters' activities was generally missing in his native country. For this reason, James left America in 1876 to take up residence abroad. Finally settling in England, he dedicated his life to the only thing that mattered: studying people having "scenes" and learning how to "make scenes" in his fiction.

James never broke loose altogether from his ties to the United States, nor did he dismiss his family or his American friends. His decision to become a British citizen in 1915 was the result of the shock caused by the First World War, when he came to view England as standing alone against the enemies of Western culture. But James remained an American of the kind that Henry Adams, Gertrude Stein, Henry David Thoreau, and even Edgar Allan Poe also represented: observers and critics who stood somewhat to the side of the American scene.

James had one of the longest and most sustained careers of any American writer, and he came to be considered one of the masters of fiction in Great Britain and the United States. In 1907 Scribner's publishing house began to put out the famous New York edition of his selected works in twenty-six volumes. James had not, however, leapt to fame overnight with the writing of a smashingly successful big book. With the exception of the relatively small popular success of *Daisy Miller* in 1879, that kind of fame always escaped him. Particularly at the very start of his career in the mid-1860s, James went through a long and often discouraging apprenticeship as a reviewer and writer of romantic tales, travel sketches, and what he later considered his "hideous" early attempts to write novels.

James's first notable appearance in print came in 1865 with a review of Walt Whitman's "Drum Taps," a collection of poems about the Civil War. (He did not care for it, but this early assessment of Whitman's poetry was revised sharply upward during his mature years.) His work as reviewer and writer of tales continued to appear in many of the more important journals of that period: the *North American Review,* the *Galaxy,* the *Nation,* and the newly formed *Atlantic Monthly.* James's first collection of stories was published in 1875, the same year that *Roderick Hudson* came out as an *Atlantic Monthly* serial; this was the novel he identified as the first serious expression of his powers as a writer of fiction. During that same decade, while on one of his frequent trips to the Continent, he met and conversed with Flaubert, Zola, Turgenev, and De Maupassant about literary matters. He also studied the works of his early favorites, Honoré de

Balzac, the French chronicler of "the human comedy," and George Eliot, the English novelist. The late 1870s found James, settled in England and well into his chosen vocation, feeling increased confidence in his powers as a technician and storyteller. *The American* was published in 1877, quickly followed in 1878 by *The Europeans* and in 1879 by *Daisy Miller*. With *The Portrait of a Lady* in 1881, James completed his literary apprenticeship; he had fully arrived on the literary scene and was ready for the next stage of his developing career.

For the sake of convenience, students of James's career usually divide it into three periods. Analogous to the histories of the British monarchy, there is James I, James II, and James III (in the opinion of some of his detractors, James the Old Pretender). If *The Portrait of a Lady* stands out as the finest of James's early full-length novels (characteristic of the reign of James I), the middle period is highlighted by *The Bostonians, The Princess Casamassima* (both 1886), and *The Tragic Muse* (1889). None of these novels achieved the notoriety of *Daisy Miller*. James always longed for fame; at the same time, he trained his eye on the creation of a pure art. He wished to be free from compromises with the moral prudery of the public as well as the cheap sensationalism and easy sentimentality that brought big sales and wide publicity to lesser talents.

During the 1890s James turned to writing for the theater. There, he hoped, he would find the approval of the large theater-going public. But he encountered the same difficulties overcoming the theater audience's bent for superficiality as he had in capturing the attention of the readers of slickly presented fictions. This phase of his career was not the demoralizing failure it has sometimes been made to be. Yet clearly it was not a time of success. By 1895 James had returned to writing fiction, taking with him the skills of scenic presentation he had learned while trying his hand at drama. The loss in one area became a gain when he returned to writing novels and stories. Ten years of notable success followed as James wrote one after another intensely felt short tales, novellas, and long novels. Among his best known are "The Real Thing," "The Turn of the Screw," "The Beast in the Jungle," "The Aspern Papers," and "The Jolly Corner," as well as *The Spoils of Poynton* and *What Maisie Knew* in 1897 and *The Awkward Age* in 1899.

James's final period—the one that has made him one of the supreme masters of fiction in the minds of many and an overrated writer in the opinion of others—includes the three novels that were published in the years between 1902 and 1904: *The Wings of the Dove, The Ambassadors,* and *The Golden Bowl*. They were preceded and followed by the stylistic oddities of *The Sacred Fount* (1901), *The Sense of the Past,* and *The Ivory Tower,* the last two narratives remaining unfinished at the time of his death in 1916.

Any listing of James's major novels and novellas tends to overshadow two other areas of his productivity: the dozens of short stories he published throughout his fifty years as a writer and the great variety of nonfiction he wrote. In the latter grouping there are travel pieces, literary reviews, biographical descriptions, personal memoirs, and analyses of the social scene in the United States and abroad, including such memorable works as *The American Scene* (1907), *A Small Boy and Others* (1913), and *Notes of a Son and Brother* (1914). His reputation as a major influence on the art of the novel extends even further. The quantity and quality of his writings as a literary theorist must still be taken into account.

It was not that other American writers before Henry James paid no attention to the theory by which effective literary expression is formulated. Poe applied himself to this task. In varying degrees, Hawthorne and Whitman laid down principles of composition. And in James's own day, William Dean Howells was a constant commentator on the nature of literary composition. But it was Henry James who over the years amassed a body of critical essays on both form and content that made him a major force in the definition of what prose fiction can do to create a sense of life on the page.

"The Art of Fiction" (1884), his notebooks, and the prefaces he supplied for each volume of the New York edition are but a few of the occasions he took to address, in public and in private, the long list of issues out of which modern literature has unfolded. James considered the essentially self-effacing role of the author who disappears inside the consciousnesses of his fictional characters or the generalized voice of the unseen narrator. He encouraged readers to give themselves willingly to a pleasureful encounter with complicated language and to delight in difficult syntax and ambiguities of verbal meaning. He experimented with the devices by which narrative time is compressed and expanded. He analyzed why emotion becomes intensified when the narrative is given over to one particularly alert fictional character whose singular point of view forms the story's drama. He refined the means for creating significant "scenes" out of barely perceptible incidents. Above all, James reiterated the importance of the literary techniques by which psychological complexities are revealed through the characters' responses to the environment that enfold them. Before James, writing good prose fiction had often been a happy accident; with James, writers and readers of literature alike became aware of fiction's conscious craft.

The same acute self-consciousness that Henry James lavished on his own and other writers' fiction provides the terms by which James himself can be assessed. Admired during his lifetime by a relatively small group of readers and fellow writers, James's loyal followers are matched by an equally intense group who find him infuriatingly or boringly difficult to read. The detail he gave to the nuances of individual consciousnesses within his stories seems liberating to many, stifling to some. Some see James responding to his characters with tender compassion for their frailties. To others he is a snob, a prude, an effete aesthete, and a social reactionary. The fact that many of the characters in his narratives are highly refined members of the leisured class, living and traveling far from American everyday doings, with all the Jamesian time in the world to linger with their exquisite consciousness, indicates for some that James was out of touch with his native land, his era, and real human life. Still others find in James's choice of subject and setting an inspired strategy for getting close to essential social and psychological concerns. These readers find their feelings mirrored by James's wide spectrum of human types—characters who discover they must (in the words of Lambert Strether, the hero of *The Ambassadors*) come to terms with what it means to live as though they were completely free, all the while remaining aware that they are gripped by binding limitations.

The value of James's influence on the art of fiction remains controversial. But all agree that, whether pernicious or inspiring, his influence has been immense and lasting. James remained convinced of his own greatness as a literary genius throughout his long devotion to his art. He would be pleased to know that his stamp is fixed on the face of fiction, altering the way we read about ourselves and others.

Further Reading:

F. Matthiessen, *Henry James: The Major Phase*, 1944.

The Question of Henry James, ed. F. Dupee, 1945.

J. Beach, *The Method of Henry James*, 1954.

Q. Anderson, *The American Henry James*, 1957.

L. Edel and D. Laurence, *A Bibliography of Henry James*, 1957.

F. Crews, *The Tragedy of Manners: Moral Drama in the Later Novels of Henry James*, 1957.

L. Levy, *Versions of Melodrama: A Study of the Fiction and Drama of Henry James, 1865–1897*, 1957.

C. Wegelin, *The Image of Europe in Henry James*, 1958.

R. Poirier, *The Comic Sense of Henry James: A Study of the Early Novels*, 1960.

O. Cargill, *The Novels of Henry James*, 1961, 1975.

J. Ward, *The Imagination of Disaster: Evil in the Fiction of Henry James*, 1961.

D. Krook, *The Ordeal of Consciousness in Henry James*, 1962.

W. Wright, *The Madness of Art: A Study of Henry James*, 1962.

Discussions of Henry James, ed. N. Lebowitz, 1962.

M. Geismar, *Henry James and the Jacobites*, 1963.

L. Holland, *The Expense of Vision: Essays on the Craft of Henry James*, 1964, 1982.

N. Lebowitz, *The Imagination of Loving*, 1965.

T. Tanner, *Henry James: Modern Comments*, 1968, 1970.

S. Sears, *The Negative Imagination: Form and Perspective in the Novels of Henry James*, 1969.

P. Buitenhuis, *The Grasping Imagination: The American Writing of Henry James*, 1970.

C. Samuel, *The Ambiguity of Henry James*, 1971.

M. Banta, *Henry James and the Occult*, 1972.

S. B. Chatman, *The Later Style of Henry James*, 1972.

Henry James's Major Novels: Essays in Criticism, ed. L. Powers, 1973.

R. A. Hocks, *Henry James and Pragmatistic Thought*, 1974.

L. Auchincloss, *Reading Henry James*, 1975.

G. H. Jones *Henry James's Psychology of Experience*, 1975.

J. G. Moseley, *A Complex Inheritance: The Idea of Self-Transcendence in the Theology of Henry James, Sr., and the Novels of Henry James*, 1975.

T. Laitiner, *Aspects of Henry James's Style*, 1975.

W. R. Veeder, *Henry James: The Lesson of the Master: Popular Fiction and Personal Style in the Nineteenth Century*, 1975.

P. Brooks, *The Melodramatic Imagination: Balzac, Henry James, Melodrama, and the Mode of Excess*, 1976.

K. Graham, *Henry James: The Drama of Fulfillment*, 1976.

G. Leeming, *Who's Who in Henry James*, 1976.

M. MacKenzie, *Communities of Honor and Love in Henry James*, 1976.

J. Rowe, *Henry Adams and Henry James, The Emergence of a Modern Consciousness*, 1976.

R. Yeazell, *Language and Knowledge in the Late Novels of Henry James*, 1976.

C. Anderson, *Person, Place, and Thing in Henry James's Novels*, 1977.

S. Rimmon, *The Concept of Ambiguity: The Example of Henry James*, 1977.

S. Donadio, *Nietzsche, Henry James, and the Artist's Will*, 1978.

S. Perosa, *Henry James and the Experimental Novel*, 1978.

M. D. Springer, *A Rhetoric of Literary Character: Some Women of Henry James*, 1978.

E. Wagenknecht, *Eve and Henry James*, 1978.

N. Bradbury, *Henry James: The Later Novels*, 1979.

T. Tanner, *Henry James*, 1968.

T. Tanner, *Henry James*, 3 vols., 1979–1981.

P. Sicker, *Love and the Quest for Identity in the Fiction of Henry James*, 1980.

D. M. Fogel, *Henry James and the Structure of the Romantic Imagination*, 1981.

A. Habegger, *Gender, Fantasy, and Realism in American Literature*, 1982.

M. E. Jacobson, *Henry James and the Mass Market*, 1983.

E. Wagenknecht, *The Novels of Henry James*, 1983.

C. Kaston, *Imagination and Desire in the Novels of Henry James*, 1984.

M. Seltzer, *Henry James and the Art of Power*, 1984.

L. Edel, *Henry James: A Life*, 1985.

Texts:

Daisy Miller, "The Beast in the Jungle," "The Jolly Corner," and preface to *The American* from *The Novels and Tales of Henry James* (New York edition), 26 vols., 1907–1917.
See also *The Art of the Novel: Critical Prefaces,* ed. R. Blackmur, 1943.
The Notebooks of Henry James, ed.
F. Matthiessen and K. Murdock, 1947.
Plays of Henry James, ed. L. Edel, 1949.
Autobiography, ed. F. Dupee, 1956, 1983.
L. Edel and D. Laurence, *A Bibliography of Henry James,* 1957.

Henry James and H. G. Wells, ed. L. Edel and G. Ray, 1958.
Discovery of a Genius: William Dean Howells and Henry James, ed. A. Mordell, 1961.
Stories of the Supernatural, ed. L. Edel, 1949.
The Complete Tales of Henry James, 12 vols., ed. L. Edel, 1962–1965.
Letters of Henry James, 2 vols., ed. P. Lubbock, 1920.
The Letters of Henry James, 4 vols., ed. L. Edel, 1974–1984.

Daisy Miller

from Preface

It was in Rome during the autumn of 1877; a friend then living there but settled now in a South less weighted with appeals and memories happened to mention—which she might perfectly not have done—some simple and uninformed American lady of the previous winter, whose young daughter, a child of nature and of freedom, accompanying her from hotel to hotel, had "picked up" by the wayside, with the best conscience in the world, a good-looking Roman, of vague identity, astonished at his luck, yet (so far as might be, by the pair) all innocently, all serenely exhibited and introduced: this at least till the occurrence of some small social check, some interrupting incident, of no great gravity or dignity, and which I forget. I had never heard, save on this showing, of the amiable but not otherwise eminent ladies, who were n't in fact named, I think, and whose case had merely served to point a familiar moral; and it must have been just their want of salience that left a margin for the small pencil-mark inveterately signifying, in such connexions, "Dramatise, dramatise!" The result of my recognising a few months later the sense of my pencil-mark was the short chronicle of "Daisy Miller," which I indited in London the following spring and then addressed, with no conditions attached, as I remember, to the editor of a magazine that had its seat of publication at Philadelphia and had lately appeared to appreciate my contributions. That gentleman however (an historian of some repute) promptly returned me my missive, and with an absence of comment that struck me at the time as rather grim—as, given the circumstances, requiring indeed some explanation: till a friend to whom I appealed for light, giving him the thing to read, declared it could only have passed with the Philadelphian critic for "an outrage on American girlhood." This was verily a light, and of bewildering intensity; though I was presently to read into the matter a further helpful inference. To the fault of being outrageous this little composition added that of being essentially and pre-eminently a *nouvelle;*[1] a signal example in fact of that type, foredoomed at the best, in more cases than not, to

---

[1] Short prose narrative, one of James's favorite literary forms.

editorial disfavour. If accordingly I was afterwards to be cradled, almost blissfully, in the conception that "Daisy" at least, among my productions, might approach "success," such success for example, on her eventual appearance, as the state of being promptly pirated in Boston—a sweet tribute I had n't yet received and was never again to know—the irony of things yet claimed its rights, I could n't but long continue to feel, in the circumstance that quite a special reprobation had waited on the first appearance in the world of the ultimately most prosperous child of my invention. So doubly discredited, at all events, this bantling met indulgence, with no great delay, in the eyes of my admirable friend the late Leslie Stephen and was published in two numbers of *The Cornhill Magazine* (1878).[2]

It qualified itself in that publication and afterwards as "a Study"; for reasons which I confess I fail to recapture unless they may have taken account simply of a certain flatness in my poor little heroine's literal denomination. Flatness indeed, one must have felt, was the very sum of her story; so that perhaps after all the attached epithet was meant but as a deprecation, addressed to the reader, of any great critical hope of stirring scenes. It provided for mere concentration, and on an object scant and superficially vulgar—from which, however, a sufficiently brooding tenderness might eventually extract a shy incongruous charm. I suppress at all events here the appended qualification—in view of the simple truth, which ought from the first to have been apparent to me, that my little exhibition is made to no degree whatever in critical but, quite inordinately and extravagantly, in poetical terms. It comes back to me that I was at a certain hour long afterwards to have reflected, in this connexion, on the characteristic free play of the whirligig of time. It was in Italy again—in Venice and in the prized society of an interesting friend, now dead, with whom I happened to wait, on the Grand Canal, at the animated water-steps of one of the hotels. The considerable little terrace there was so disposed as to make a salient stage for certain demonstrations on the part of two young girls, children *they,* if ever, of nature and of freedom, whose use of those resources, in the general public eye, and under our own as we sat in the gondola, drew from the lips of a second companion, sociably afloat with us, the remark that there before us, with no sign absent, were a couple of attesting Daisy Millers. Then it was that, in my charming hostess's prompt protest, the whirligig, as I have called it, at once betrayed itself. "How can you liken *those* creatures to a figure of which the only fault is touchingly to have transmuted so sorry a type and to have, by a poetic artifice, not only led our judgement of it astray, but made *any* judgement quite impossible?" With which this gentle lady and admirable critic turned on the author himself. "You *know* you quite falsified, by the turn you gave it, the thing you had begun with having in mind, the thing you had had, to satiety, the chance of 'observing': your pretty perversion of it, or your unprincipled mystification of our sense of it, does it really too much honour—in spite of which, none the less, as anything charming or touching always to that extent justifies itself, we after a fashion forgive and understand you. But why *waste* your romance? There are cases, too many, in which you 've done it again; in which, provoked by a spirit of observation at first no doubt sufficiently sincere, and with the measured and felt truth fairly twitching your sleeve, you have yielded to your incurable prejudice in

[2] British journal edited by Stephen, well-known writer and father of the writer Virginia Woolf.

favour of grace—to whatever it is in you that makes so inordinately for form and prettiness and pathos; not to say sometimes for misplaced drolling. Is it that you 've after all too much imagination? Those awful young women capering at the hotel-door, *they* are the real little Daisy Millers that were; whereas yours in the tale is such a one, more 's the pity, as—for pitch of the ingenuous, for quality of the artless—could n't possibly have been at all." My answer to all which bristled of course with more professions than I can or need report here; the chief of them inevitably to the effect that my supposedly typical little figure was of course pure poetry, and had never been anything else; since this is what helpful imagination, in however slight a dose, ever directly makes for. As for the original grossness of readers, I dare say I added, that was another matter—but one which at any rate had then quite ceased to signify. . . .

Daisy Miller

I

At the little town of Vevey, in Switzerland, there is a particularly comfortable hotel; there are indeed many hotels, since the entertainment of tourists is the business of the place, which, as many travellers will remember, is seated upon the edge of a remark-ably blue lake[3]—a lake that it behoves every tourist to visit. The shore of the lake presents an unbroken array of establishments of this order, of every category, from the "grand hotel" of the newest fashion, with a chalk-white front, a hundred balconies, and a dozen flags flying from its roof, to the small Swiss pension of an elder day, with its name inscribed in German-looking lettering upon a pink or yellow wall and an awkward summer-house in the angle of the garden. One of the hotels at Vevey, however, is famous, even classical, being distinguished from many of its upstart neighbours by an air both of luxury and of maturity. In this region, through the month of June, American travellers are extremely numerous; it may be said indeed that Vevey assumes at that time some of the characteristics of an American watering-place. There are sights and sounds that evoke a vision, an echo, of Newport and Saratoga.[4] There is a flitting hither and thither of "stylish" young girls, a rustling of muslin flounces, a rattle of dance-music in the morning hours, a sound of high-pitched voices at all times. You receive an impression of these things at the excellent inn of the "Trois Couronnes,"[5] and are transported in fancy to the Ocean House or to Congress Hall.[6] But at the "Trois Couronnes," it must be added, there are other features much at variance with these suggestions: neat German waiters who look like secretaries of legation: Russian princesses sitting in the garden; little Polish boys walking about, held by the hand, with their governors; a view of the snowy crest of the Dent du Midi[7] and the picturesque towers of the Castle of Chillon.[8]

I hardly know whether it was the analogies or the differences that were uppermost

[3] Lake Geneva.
[4] Fashionable resorts in Rhode Island and New York State, respectively.
[5] French: "Three Crowns."
[6] Hotels at Newport and Saratoga, respectively.

[7] Peak of Mont Blanc in the Swiss Alps.
[8] Medieval castle situated on the lake and the setting for "The Prisoner of Chillon" (1816) by Lord Byron.

in the mind of a young American, who, two or three years ago, sat in the garden of the "Trois Couronnes," looking about him rather idly at some of the graceful objects I have mentioned. It was a beautiful summer morning, and in whatever fashion the young American looked at things they must have seemed to him charming. He had come from Geneva the day before, by the little steamer, to see his aunt, who was staying at the hotel—Geneva having been for a long time his place of residence. But his aunt had a headache—his aunt had almost always a headache—and she was now shut up in her room smelling camphor, so that he was at liberty to wander about. He was some seven-and-twenty years of age; when his friends spoke of him they usually said that he was at Geneva "studying." When his enemies spoke of him they said—but after all he had no enemies: he was extremely amiable and generally liked. What I should say is simply that when certain persons spoke of him they conveyed that the reason of his spending so much time at Geneva was that he was extremely devoted to a lady who lived there—a foreign lady, a person older than himself. Very few Americans—truly I think none—had ever seen this lady, about whom there were some singular stories. But Winterbourne had an old attachment for the little capital of Calvinism:[9] he had been put to school there as a boy and had afterwards even gone, on trial—trial of the grey old "Academy"[10] on the steep and stony hillside—to college there; circumstances which had led to his forming a great many youthful friendships. Many of these he had kept, and they were a source of great satisfaction to him.

After knocking at his aunt's door and learning that she was indisposed he had taken a walk about the town and then he had come in to his breakfast. He had now finished that repast, but was enjoying a small cup of coffee which had been served him on a little table in the garden by one of the waiters who looked like *attachés*. At last he finished his coffee and lit a cigarette. Presently a small boy came walking along the path—an urchin of nine or ten. The child, who was diminutive for his years, had an aged expression of countenance, a pale complexion and sharp little features. He was dressed in knickerbockers and had red stockings that displayed his poor little spindle-shanks; he also wore a brilliant red cravat. He carried in his hand a long alpenstock, the sharp point of which he thrust into everything he approached—the flower-beds, the garden-benches, the trains of the ladies' dresses. In front of Winterbourne he paused, looking at him with a pair of bright and penetrating little eyes.

"Will you give me a lump of sugar?" he asked in a small sharp hard voice—a voice immature and yet somehow not young.

Winterbourne glanced at the light table near him, on which his coffee-service rested, and saw that several morsels of sugar remained. "Yes, you may take one," he answered; "but I don't think too much sugar good for little boys."

This little boy stepped forward and carefully selected three of the coveted fragments, two of which he buried in the pocket of his knickerbockers, depositing the other as promptly in another place. He poked his alpenstock, lance-fashion, into Winterbourne's bench and tried to crack the lump of sugar with his teeth.

"Oh blazes; it's har-r-d!" he exclaimed, divesting vowel and consonants, pertinently enough, of any taint of softness.

Winterbourne had immediately gathered that he might have the honour of claim-

[9] Bastion of John Calvin's Protestant reform activities between 1541 and 1564.

[10] University of Geneva.

ing him as a countryman. "Take care you don't hurt your teeth," he said paternally.

"I have n't got any teeth to hurt. They've all come out. I've only got seven teeth. Mother counted them last night, and one came out right afterwards. She said she'd slap me if any more came out. I can't help it. It's this old Europe. It's the climate that makes them come out. In America they did n't come out. It's these hotels."

Winterbourne was much amused. "If you eat three lumps of sugar your mother will certainly slap you," he ventured.

"She's got to give me some candy then," rejoined his young interlocutor. "I can't get any candy here—any American candy. American candy's the best candy."

"And are American little boys the best little boys?" Winterbourne asked.

"I don't know. *I'm* an American boy," said the child.

"I see you're one of the best!" the young man laughed.

"Are you an American man?" pursued this vivacious infant. And then on his friend's affirmative reply, "American men are the best," he declared with assurance.

His companion thanked him for the compliment, and the child, who had now got astride of his alpenstock, stood looking about him while he attacked another lump of sugar. Winterbourne wondered if he himself had been like this in his infancy, for he had been brought to Europe at about the same age.

"Here comes my sister!" cried his young compatriot. "She's an American girl, you bet!"

Winterbourne looked along the path and saw a beautiful young lady advancing. "American girls are the best girls," he thereupon cheerfully remarked to his visitor.

"My sister ain't the best!" the child promptly returned. "She's always blowing at me."[11]

"I imagine that's your fault, not hers," said Winterbourne. The young lady meanwhile had drawn near. She was dressed in white muslin, with a hundred frills and flounces and knots of pale-coloured ribbon. Bareheaded, she balanced in her hand a large parasol with a deep border of embroidery; and she was strikingly, admirably pretty. "How pretty they are!" thought our friend, who straightened himself in his seat as if he were ready to rise.

The young lady paused in front of his bench, near the parapet of the garden, which overlooked the lake. The small boy had now converted his alpenstock into a vaulting-pole, by the aid of which he was springing about in the gravel and kicking it up not a little. "Why Randolph," she freely began, "What *are* you doing?"

"I'm going up the Alps!" cried Randolph. "This is the way!" And he gave another extravagant jump, scattering the pebbles about Winterbourne's ears.

"That's the way they come down," said Winterbourne.

"He's an American man!" proclaimed Randolph in his harsh little voice.

The young lady gave no heed to this circumstance, but looked straight at her brother. "Well, I guess you'd better be quiet," she simply observed.

It seemed to Winterbourne that he had been in a manner presented. He got up and stepped slowly toward the charming creature, throwing away his cigarette. "This little boy and I have made acquaintance," he said with great civility. In Geneva, as he had been perfectly aware, a young man was n't at liberty to speak to a young unmarried lady save under certain rarely-occurring conditions; but here at Vevey what conditions

---

[11] Slang for "criticizing me."

could be better than these?—a pretty American girl coming to stand in front of you in a garden with all the confidence in life. This pretty American girl, whatever that might prove, on hearing Winterbourne's observation simply glanced at him; she then turned her head and looked over the parapet, at the lake and the opposite mountains. He wondered whether he had gone too far, but decided that he must gallantly advance rather than retreat. While he was thinking of something else to say the young lady turned again to the little boy, whom she addressed quite as if they were alone together. "I should like to know where you got that pole."

"I bought it!" Randolph shouted.

"You don't mean to say you're going to take it to Italy!"

"Yes, I'm going to take it t' Italy!" the child rang out.

She glanced over the front of her dress and smoothed out a knot or two of ribbon. Then she gave her sweet eyes to the prospect again. "Well, I guess you'd better leave it somewhere." she dropped after a moment.

"Are you going to Italy?" Winterbourne now decided very respectfully to enquire.

She glanced at him with lovely remoteness. "Yes, sir," she then replied. And she said nothing more.

"And are you—a—thinking of the Simplon?"[12] he pursued with a slight drop of assurance.

"I don't know," she said. "I suppose it's some mountain. Randolph, what mountain are we thinking of?"

"Thinking of?"—the boy stared.

"Why going right over."

"Going to where?" he demanded.

"Why right down to Italy"—Winterbourne felt vague emulations.

"I don't know," said Randolph. "I don't want to go t' Italy. I want to go to America."

"Oh Italy's a beautiful place!" the young man laughed.

"Can you get candy there?" Randolph asked of all the echoes.

"I hope not," said his sister. "I guess you've had enough candy, and mother thinks so too."

"I have n't had any for ever so long—for a hundred weeks!" cried the boy, still jumping about.

The young lady inspected her flounces and smoothed her ribbons again; and Winterbourne presently risked an observation on the beauty of the view. He was ceasing to be in doubt, for he had begun to perceive that she was really not in the least embarrassed. She might be cold, she might be austere, she might even be prim; for that was apparently—he had already so generalised—what the most "distant" American girls did: they came and planted themselves straight in front of you to show how rigidly unapproachable they were. There had n't been the slightest flush in her fresh fairness however; so that she was clearly neither offended nor fluttered. Only she was composed—he had seen that before too—of charming little parts that didn't match and that made no *ensemble;*[13] and if she looked another way when he spoke to her, and seemed not particularly to hear him, this was simply her habit, her manner, the result of her having no idea whatever of "form" (with such a tell-tale appendage

---

[12] Alpine pass between Switzerland and Italy.   [13] French: "harmonious whole."

as Randolph where in the world would she have got it?) in any such connexion. As he talked a little more and pointed out some of the objects of interest in the view, with which she appeared wholly unacquainted, she gradually, none the less, gave him more of the benefit of her attention; and then he saw that act unqualified by the faintest shadow of reserve. It was n't however what would have been called a "bold" front that she presented, for her expression was as decently limpid as the very cleanest water. Her eyes were the very prettiest conceivable, and indeed Winterbourne had n't for a long time seen anything prettier than his fair countrywoman's various features— her complexion, her nose, her ears, her teeth. He took a great interest generally in that range of effects and was addicted to noting and, as it were, recording them; so that in regard to this young lady's face he made several observations. It was n't at all insipid, yet at the same time was n't pointedly—what point, on earth, could she ever make?—expressive; and though it offered such a collection of small finenesses and neatnesses he mentally accused it—very forgivingly—of a want of finish. He thought nothing more likely than that its wearer would have had her own experience of the action of her charms, as she would certainly have acquired a resulting confidence; but even should she depend on this for her main amusement her bright sweet superficial little visage gave out neither mockery nor irony. Before long it became clear that, however these things might be, she was much disposed to conversation. She remarked to Winterbourne that they were going to Rome for the winter—she and her mother and Randolph. She asked him if he was a "real American"; she would n't have taken him for one; he seemed more like a German—this flower was gathered as from a large field of comparison—especially when he spoke. Winterbourne, laughing, answered that he had met Germans who spoke like Americans, but not, so far as he remembered, any American with the resemblance she noted. Then he asked her if she might n't be more at ease should she occupy the bench he had just quitted. She answered that she liked hanging round, but she none the less resignedly, after a little, dropped to the bench. She told him she was from New York State—"if you know where that is"; but our friend really quickened this current by catching hold of her small slippery brother and making him stand a few minutes by his side.

"Tell me your honest name, my boy." So he artfully proceeded.

In response to which the child was indeed unvarnished truth. "Randolph C. Miller. And I'll tell you hers." With which he levelled his alpenstock at his sister.

"You had better wait till you're asked!" said this young lady quite at her leisure.

"I should like very much to know *your* name," Winterbourne made free to reply.

"Her name's Daisy Miller!" cried the urchin. "But that ain't her real name; that ain't her name on her cards."

"It's a pity you have n't got one of my cards!" Miss Miller quite as naturally remarked.

"Her real name's Annie P. Miller," the boy went on.

It seemed, all amazingly, to do her good. "Ask him *his* now"—and she indicated their friend.

But to this point Randolph seemed perfectly indifferent; he continued to supply information with regard to his own family. "My father's name is Ezra B. Miller. My father ain't in Europe—he's in a better place than Europe." Winterbourne for a moment supposed this the manner in which the child had been taught to intimate that Mr. Miller had been removed to the sphere of celestial rewards. But Randolph immediately added: "My father's in Schenectady. He's got a big business. My father's rich, you bet."

"Well!" ejaculated Miss Miller, lowering her parasol and looking at the embroidered border. Winterbourne presently released the child, who departed, dragging his alpenstock along the path. "He don't like Europe," said the girl as with an artless instinct for historic truth. "He wants to go back."

"To Schenectady, you mean?"

"Yes, he wants to go right home. He has n't got any boys here. There's one boy here, but he always goes round with a teacher. They won't let him play."

"And your brother has n't any teacher?" Winterbourne enquired.

It tapped, at a touch, the spring of confidence. "Mother thought of getting him one—to travel round with us. There was a lady told her of a very good teacher; an American lady—perhaps you know her—Mrs. Sanders. I think she came from Boston. She told her of this teacher, and we thought of getting him to travel round with us. But Randolph said he did n't want a teacher travelling round with us. He said he would n't have lessons when he was in the cars.[14] And we *are* in the cars about half the time. There was an English lady we met in the cars—I think her name was Miss Featherstone; perhaps you know her. She wanted to know why I did n't give Randolph lessons—give him 'instruction,' she called it. I guess he could give me more instruction than I could give him. He's very smart."

"Yes," said Winterbourne; "he seems very smart."

"Mother's going to get a teacher for him as soon as we get t' Italy. Can you get good teachers in Italy?"

"Very good, I should think," Winterbourne hastened to reply.

"Or else she's going to find some school. He ought to learn some more. He's only nine. He's going to college." And in this way Miss Miller continued to converse upon the affairs of her family and upon other topics. She sat there with her extremely pretty hands, ornamented with very brilliant rings, folded in her lap, and with her pretty eyes now resting upon those of Winterbourne, now wandering over the garden, the people who passed before her and the beautiful view. She addressed her new acquaintance as if she had known him a long time. He found it very pleasant. It was many years since he had heard a young girl talk so much. It might have been said of this wandering maiden who had come and sat down beside him upon a bench that she chattered. She was very quiet, she sat in a charming tranquil attitude; but her lips and her eyes were constantly moving. She had a soft slender agreeable voice, and her tone was distinctly sociable. She gave Winterbourne a report of her movements and intentions, and those of her mother and brother, in Europe, and enumerated in particular the various hotels at which they had stopped. "That English lady in the cars," she said—"Miss Featherstone—asked me if we did n't all live in hotels in America. I told her I had never been in so many hotels in my life as since I came to Europe. I've never seen so many—it's nothing but hotels." But Miss Miller made this remark with no querulous accent; she appeared to be in the best humour with everything. She declared that the hotels were very good when once you got used to their ways and that Europe was perfectly entrancing. She was n't disappointed—not a bit. Perhaps it was because she had heard so much about it before. She had ever so

---

[14] Railway cars.

many intimate friends who had been there ever so many times, and that way she had got thoroughly posted. And then she had had ever so many dresses and things from Paris. Whenever she put on a Paris dress she felt as if she were in Europe.

"It was a kind of a wishing-cap," Winterbourne smiled.

"Yes," said Miss Miller at once and without examining this analogy; "it always made me wish I was here. But I need n't have done that for dresses. I'm sure they send all the pretty ones to America; you see the most frightful things here. The only thing I don't like," she proceeded, "is the society. There ain't any society—or if there is I don't know where it keeps itself. Do you? I suppose there's some society some-where, but I have n't seen anything of it. I'm very fond of society and I've always had plenty of it. I don't mean only in Schenectady, but in New York. I used to go to New York every winter. In New York I had lots of society. Last winter I had seventeen dinners given me, and three of them were by gentlemen," added Daisy Miller. "I've more friends in New York than in Schenectady—more gentlemen friends; and more young lady friends too," she resumed in a moment. She paused again for an instant; she was looking at Winterbourne with all her prettiness in her frank gay eyes and in her clear rather uniform smile. "I've always had," she said, "a great deal of gentlemen's society."

Poor Winterbourne was amused and perplexed—above all he was charmed. He had never yet heard a young girl express herself in just this fashion; never at least save in cases where to say such things was to have at the same time some rather complicated consciousness about them. And yet was he to accuse Miss Daisy Miller of an actual or a potential *arrière-pensée*,[15] as they said at Geneva? He felt he had lived at Geneva so long as to have got morally muddled; he had lost the right sense for the young American tone. Never indeed since he had grown old enough to appreciate things had he encountered a young compatriot of so "strong" a type as this. Certainly she was very charming, but how extraordinarily communicative and how tremendously easy! Was she simply a pretty girl from New York State—were they all like that, the pretty girls who had had a good deal of gentlemen's society? Or was she also a designing, an audacious, in short an expert young person? Yes, his instinct for such a question had ceased to serve him, and his reason could but mislead. Miss Daisy Miller looked extremely innocent. Some people had told him that after all American girls were exceedingly innocent, and others had told him that after all they were n't. He must on the whole take Miss Daisy Miller for a flirt—a pretty American flirt. He had never as yet had relations with representatives of that class. He had known here in Europe two or three women—persons older than Miss Daisy Miller and provided, for respectability's sake, with husbands—who were great coquettes; dangerous terrible women with whom one's light commerce might indeed take a serious turn. But this charming apparition was n't a coquette in that sense; she was very unsophisticated; she was only a pretty American flirt. Winterbourne was almost grateful for having found the formula that applied to Miss Daisy Miller. He leaned back in his seat; he remarked to himself that she had the finest little nose he had ever seen; he wondered what were the regular conditions and limitations of one's intercourse with a pretty American flirt. It presently became apparent that he was on the way to learn.

[15] French: "ulterior motive."

"Have you been to that old castle?" the girl soon asked, pointing with her parasol to the far-shining walls of the Château de Chillon.

"Yes, formerly, more than once," said Winterbourne. "You too, I suppose, have seen it?"

"No, we have n't been there. I want to go there dreadfully. Of course I mean to go there. I would n't go away from here without having seen that old castle."

"It's a very pretty excursion," the young man returned, "and very easy to make. You can drive, you know, or you can go by the little steamer."

"You can go in the cars," said Miss Miller.

"Yes, you can go in the cars," Winterbourne assented.

"Our courier[16] says they take you right up to the castle," she continued. "We were going last week, but mother gave out. She suffers dreadfully from dyspepsia. She said she could n't any more go—!" But this sketch of Mrs. Miller's plea remained unfinished. "Randolph would n't go either; he says he don't think much of old castles. But I guess we'll go this week if we can get Randolph."

"Your brother is n't interested in ancient monuments?" Winterbourne indulgently asked.

He now drew her, as he guessed she would herself have said, every time. "Why no, he says he don't care much about old castles. He's only nine. He wants to stay at the hotel. Mother's afraid to leave him alone, and the courier won't stay with him; so we have n't been to many places. But it will be too bad if we don't go up there." And Miss Miller pointed again at the Château de Chillon.

"I should think it might be arranged," Winterbourne was thus emboldened to reply. "Could n't you get some one to stay—for the afternoon—with Randolph?"

Miss Miller looked at him a moment, and then with all serenity, "I wish *you'd* stay with him!" she said.

He pretended to consider it. "I'd much rather go to Chillon with you."

"With me?" she asked without a shadow of emotion.

She did n't rise blushing, as a young person at Geneva would have done; and yet, conscious that he had gone very far, he thought it possible she had drawn back. "And with your mother," he answered very respectfully.

But it seemed that both his audacity and his respect were lost on Miss Daisy Miller. "I guess mother would n't go—for *you*," she smiled. "And she ain't much *bent* on going, anyway. She don't like to ride round in the afternoon." After which she familiarly proceeded: "But did you really mean what you said just now—that you'd like to go up there?"

"Most earnestly I meant it," Winterbourne declared.

"Then we may arrange it. If mother will stay with Randolph I guess Eugenio will."

"Eugenio?" the young man echoed.

"Eugenio's our courier. He does n't like to stay with Randolph—he's the most fastidious man I ever saw. But he's a splendid courier. I guess he'll stay at home with Randolph if mother does, and then we can go to the castle."

[16] Person hired to aid travelers with hotel reservations and luggage.

Winterbourne reflected for an instant as lucidly as possible: "we" could only mean Miss Miller and himself. This prospect seemed almost too good to believe; he felt as if he ought to kiss the young lady's hand. Possibly he would have done so,—and quite spoiled his chance; but at this moment another person—presumably Eugenio— appeared. A tall handsome man, with superb whiskers and wearing a velvet morning-coat and a voluminous watch-guard, approached the young lady, looking sharply at her companion. "Oh Eugenio!" she said with the friendliest accent.

Eugenio had eyed Winterbourne from head to foot; he now bowed gravely to Miss Miller. "I have the honour to inform Mademoiselle that luncheon's on table."

Mademoiselle slowly rose. "See here, Eugenio, I'm going to that old castle any-way."

"To the Château de Chillon, Mademoiselle?" the courier enquired. "Mademoiselle has made arrangements?" he added in a tone that struck Winterbourne as impertinent.

Eugenio's tone apparently threw, even to Miss Miller's own apprehension, a slightly ironical light on her position. She turned to Winterbourne with the slightest blush. "You won't back out?"

"I shall not be happy till we go!" he protested.

"And you're staying in this hotel?" she went on. "And you're really American?"

The courier still stood there with an effect of offence for the young man so far as the latter saw in it a tacit reflexion on Miss Miller's behaviour and an insinuation that she "picked up" acquaintances. "I shall have the honour of presenting to you a person who'll tell you all about me," he said, smiling, and referring to his aunt.

"Oh well, we'll go some day," she beautifully answered; with which she gave him a smile and turned away. She put up her parasol and walked back to the inn beside Eugenio. Winterbourne stood watching her, and as she moved away, drawing her muslin furbelows over the walk, he spoke to himself of her natural elegance.

II

He had, however, engaged to do more than proved feasible in promising to present his aunt, Mrs. Costello, to Miss Daisy Miller. As soon as that lady had got better of her headache he waited on her in her apartment and, after a show of the proper solicitude about her health, asked if she had noticed in the hotel an American family —a mamma, a daughter and an obstreperous little boy.

"An obstreperous little boy and a preposterous big courier?" said Mrs. Costello. "Oh yes, I've noticed them. Seen them, heard them and kept out of their way." Mrs. Costello was a widow of fortune, a person of much distinction and who frequently intimated that if she had n't been so dreadfully liable to sick-headaches she would probably have left a deeper impress on her time. She had a long pale face, a high nose and a great deal of very striking white hair, which she wore in large puffs and over the top of her head. She had two sons married in New York and another who was now in Europe. This young man was amusing himself at Homburg[17] and, though guided by his taste, was rarely observed to visit any particular city at the moment selected by his mother for her appearance there. Her nephew, who had come to Vevey

[17] German resort.

expressly to see her, was therefore more attentive than, as she said, her very own. He had imbibed at Geneva the idea that one must be irreproachable in all such forms. Mrs. Costello had n't seen him for many years and was now greatly pleased with him, manifesting her approbation by initiating him into many of the secrets of that social sway which, as he could see she would like him to think, she exerted from her stronghold in Forty-Second Street. She admitted that she was very exclusive, but if he had been better acquainted with New York he would see that one had to be. And her picture of the minutely hierarchical constitution of the society of that city, which she presented to him in many different lights, was, to Winterbourne's imagination, almost oppressively striking.

He at once recognized from her tone that Miss Daisy Miller's place in the social scale was low. "I'm afraid you don't approve of them," he pursued in reference to his new friends.

"They're horribly common"—it was perfectly simple. "They're the sort of Americans that one does one's duty by just ignoring."

"Ah you just ignore them?"—the young man took it in.

"I can't *not,* my dear Frederick. I would n't if I had n't to, but I have to."

"The little girl's very pretty," he went on in a moment.

"Of course she's very pretty. But she's of the last crudity."

"I see what you mean of course," he allowed after another pause.

"She has that charming look they all have," his aunt resumed. "I can't think where they pick it up; and she dresses in perfection—no, you don't know how well she dresses. I can't think where they get their taste."

"But, my dear aunt, she's not, after all, a Comanche savage."

"She is a young lady," said Mrs. Costello, "who has an intimacy with her mamma's courier?"

"An 'intimacy' with him?" Ah there it was!

"There's no other name for such a relation. But the skinny little mother's just as bad! They treat the courier as a familiar friend—as a gentleman and a scholar. I should n't wonder if he dines with them. Very likely they've never seen a man with such good manners, such fine clothes, so *like* a gentleman—or a scholar. He probably corresponds to the young lady's idea of a count. He sits with them in the garden of an evening. I think he smokes in their faces."

Winterbourne listened with interest to these disclosures; they helped him to make up his mind about Miss Daisy. Evidently she was rather wild. "Well," he said, "I'm not a courier and I did n't smoke in her face, and yet she was very charming to me."

"You had better have mentioned at first," Mrs. Costello returned with dignity, "that you had made her valuable acquaintance."

"We simply met in the garden and talked a bit."

"By appointment—no? Ah that's still to come! Pray what did you say?"

"I said I should take the liberty of introducing her to my admirable aunt."

"Your admirable aunt's a thousand times obliged to you."

"It was to guarantee my respectability."

"And pray who's to guarantee hers?"

"Ah you're cruel!" said the young man. "She's a very innocent girl."

"You don't say that as if you believed it," Mrs. Costello returned.

"She's completely uneducated," Winterbourne acknowledged, "but she's wonder-fully pretty, and in short she's very nice. To prove I believe it I'm going to take her to the Château de Chillon."

Mrs. Costello made a wondrous face. "You two are going off there together? I should say it proved just the contrary. How long had you known her, may I ask, when this interesting project was formed? You have n't been twenty-four hours in the house."

"I had known her half an hour!" Winterbourne smiled.

"Then she's just what I supposed."

"And what do you suppose?"

"Why that she's a horror."

Our youth was silent for some moments. "You really think then," he presently began, and with a desire for trustworthy information, "you really think that—" But he paused again while his aunt waited.

"Think what, sir?"

"That she's the sort of young lady who expects a man sooner or later to—well, we'll call it carry her off?"

"I have n't the least idea what such young ladies expect a man to do. But I really consider you had better not meddle with little American girls who are uneducated, as you mildly put it. You've lived too long out of the country. You'll be sure to make some great mistake. You're too innocent."

"My dear aunt, not so much as that comes to!" he protested with a laugh and a curl of his moustache.

"You're too guilty then!"

He continued all thoughtfully to finger the ornament in question. "You won't let the poor girl know you then?" he asked at last.

"Is it literally true that she's going to the Château de Chillon with you?"

"I've no doubt she fully intends it."

"Then, my dear Frederick," said Mrs. Costello, "I must decline the honour of her acquaintance. I'm an old woman, but I'm not too old—thank heaven—to be honestly shocked!"

"But don't they all do these things—the little American girls at home?" Winter-bourne enquired.

Mrs. Costello stared a moment. "I should like to see my granddaughters do them!" she then grimly returned.

This seemed to throw some light on the matter, for Winterbourne remembered to have heard his pretty cousins in New York, the daughters of this lady's two daughters, called "tremendous flirts." If therefore Miss Daisy Miller exceeded the liberal licence allowed to these young women it was probable she did go even by the American allowance rather far. Winterbourne was impatient to see her again, and it vexed, it even a little humiliated him, that he should n't by instinct appreciate her justly.

Though so impatient to see her again he hardly knew what ground he should give for his aunt's refusal to become acquainted with her; but he discovered promptly enough that with Miss Daisy Miller there was no great need of walking on tiptoe. He found her that evening in the garden, wandering about in the warm starlight after the manner of an indolent sylph and swinging to and fro the largest fan he had ever beheld. It was ten o'clock. He had dined with his aunt, had been sitting with her since dinner, and had just taken leave of her till the morrow. His young friend frankly rejoiced to renew their intercourse; she pronounced it the stupidest evening she had ever passed.

"Have you been all alone?" he asked with no intention of an epigram and no effect of her perceiving one.

"I've been walking round with mother. But mother gets tired walking round," Miss Miller explained.

"Has she gone to bed?"

"No, she does n't like to go to bed. She does n't sleep scarcely any—not three hours. She says she does n't know how she lives. She's dreadfully nervous. I guess she sleeps more than she thinks. She's gone somewhere after Randolph; she wants to try to get him to go to bed. He does n't like to go to bed."

The soft impartiality of her *constatations*,[18] as Winterbourne would have termed them, was a thing by itself—exquisite little fatalist as they seemed to make her. "Let us hope she'll persuade him," he encouragingly said.

"Well, she'll talk to him all she can—but he does n't like her to talk to him": with which Miss Daisy opened and closed her fan. "She's going to try to get Eugenio to talk to him. But Randolph ain't afraid of Eugenio. Eugenio's a splendid courier, but he can't make much impression on Randolph! I don't believe he'll go to bed before eleven." Her detachment from any invidious judgement of this was, to her companion's sense, inimitable; and it appeared that Randolph's vigil was in fact triumphantly prolonged, for Winterbourne attended her in her stroll for some time without meeting her mother. "I've been looking round for that lady you want to introduce me to," she resumed—"I guess she's your aunt." Then on his admitting the fact and expressing some curiosity as to how she had learned it, she said she had heard all about Mrs. Costello from the chambermaid. She was very quiet and very *comme il faut*;[19] she wore white puffs; she spoke to no one and she never dined at the common table. Every two days she had a headache. "I think that's a lovely description, headache and all!" said Miss Daisy, chattering along in her thin gay voice. "I want to know her ever so much. I know just what *your* aunt would be; I know I'd like her. She'd be very exclusive. I like a lady to be exclusive; I'm dying to be exclusive myself. Well, I guess we *are* exclusive, mother and I. We don't speak to any one—or they don't speak to us. I suppose it's about the same thing. Anyway, I shall be ever so glad to meet your aunt."

Winterbourne was embarrassed—he could but trump up some evasion. "She'd be most happy, but I'm afraid those tiresome headaches are always to be reckoned with."

The girl looked at him through the fine dusk. "Well, I suppose she does n't have a headache every day."

He had to make the best of it. "She tells me she wonderfully does." He did n't know what else to say.

Miss Miller stopped and stood looking at him. Her prettiness was still visible in the darkness; she kept flapping to and fro her enormous fan. "She does n't want to know me!" she then lightly broke out. "Why don't you say so? You need n't be afraid. *I'm* not afraid!" And she quite crowed for the fun of it.

[18] French: "matter-of-fact conclusions."   [19] Attentive to the proprieties.

Winterbourne distinguished however a wee false note in this: he was touched, shocked, mortified by it. "My dear young lady, she knows no one. She goes through life immured. It's her wretched health."

The young girl walked on a few steps in the glee of the thing. "You need n't be afraid," she repeated. "Why should she want to know me?" Then she paused again; she was close to the parapet of the garden, and in front of her was the starlit lake. There was a vague sheen on its surface, and in the distance were dimly-seen mountain forms. Daisy Miller looked out at these great lights and shades and again proclaimed a gay indifference—"Gracious! she *is* exclusive!" Winterbourne wondered if she were seriously wounded and for a moment almost wished her sense of injury might be such as to make it becoming in him to reassure and comfort her. He had a pleasant sense that she would be all accessible to a respectful tenderness at that moment. He felt quite ready to sacrifice his aunt—conversationally; to acknowledge she was a proud rude woman and to make the point that they need n't mind her. But before he had time to commit himself to this questionable mixture of gallantry and impiety, the young lady, resuming her walk, gave an exclamation in quite another tone. "Well, here's mother! I guess she *has n't* got Randolph to go to bed." The figure of a lady appeared, at a distance, very indistinct in the darkness; it advanced with a slow and wavering step and then suddenly seemed to pause.

"Are you sure it's your mother? Can you make her out in this thick dusk?" Winterbourne asked.

"Well," the girl laughed, "I guess I know my own mother! And when she has got on my shawl too. She's always wearing my things."

The lady in question, ceasing now to approach, hovered vaguely about the spot at which she had checked her steps.

"I'm afraid your mother does n't see you," said Winterbourne. "Or perhaps," he added—thinking, with Miss Miller, the joke permissible—"perhaps she feels guilty about your shawl."

"Oh it's a fearful old thing!" his companion placidly answered. "I told her she could wear it if she did n't mind looking like a fright. She won't come here because she sees you."

"Ah then," said Winterbourne, "I had better leave you."

"Oh no—come on!" the girl insisted.

"I'm afraid your mother does n't approve of my walking with you."

She gave him, he thought, the oddest glance. "It is n't for me; it's for you—that is it's for *her.* Well, I don't know who it's for! But mother does n't like any of my gentlemen friends. She's right down timid. She always makes a fuss if I introduce a gentleman. But I *do* introduce them—almost always. If I did n't introduce my gentlemen friends to mother," Miss Miller added, in her small flat monotone, "I should n't think I was natural."

"Well, to introduce me," Winterbourne remarked, "you must know my name." And he proceeded to pronounce it.

"Oh my—I can't say all that!" cried his companion, much amused. But by this time they had come up to Mrs. Miller, who, as they drew near, walked to the parapet of the garden and leaned on it, looking intently at the lake and presenting her back to them. "Mother!" said the girl in a tone of decision—upon which the elder lady turned round. "Mr. Frederick Forsyth Winterbourne," said the latter's young friend, repeating his lesson of a moment before and introducing him very frankly and prettily. "Common" she might be, as Mrs. Costello had pronounced her; yet what provision was made by that epithet for her queer little native grace?

Her mother was a small spare light person, with a wandering eye, a scarce perceptible nose, and, as to make up for it, an unmistakeable forehead, decorated—but too far back, as Winterbourne mentally described it—with thin much-frizzled hair. Like her daughter Mrs. Miller was dressed with extreme elegance; she had enormous diamonds in her ears. So far as the young man could observe, she gave him no greeting —she certainly was n't looking at him. Daisy was near her, pulling her shawl straight. "What are you doing, poking round here?" this young lady enquired—yet by no means with the harshness of accent her choice of words might have implied.

"Well, I don't know"—and the new-comer turned to the lake again.

"I should n't think you'd want that shawl!" Daisy familiarly proceeded.

"Well—I do!" her mother answered with a sound that partook for Winterbourne of an odd strain between mirth and woe.

"Did you get Randolph to go to bed?" Daisy asked.

"No, I could n't induce him"—and Mrs. Miller seemed to confess to the same mild fatalism as her daughter. "He wants to talk to the waiter. He *likes* to talk to that waiter."

"I was just telling Mr. Winterbourne," the girl went on; and to the young man's ear her tone might have indicated that she had been uttering his name all her life.

"Oh yes!" he concurred—"I've the pleasure of knowing your son."

Randolph's mamma was silent; she kept her attention on the lake. But at last a sigh broke from her. "Well, I don't see how he lives!"

"Anyhow, it is n't so bad as it was at Dover,"[20] Daisy at least opined.

"And what occurred at Dover?" Winterbourne desired to know.

"He would n't go to bed at all. I guess he sat up all night—in the public parlour. He was n't in bed at twelve o'clock: it seemed as if he could n't budge."

"It was half-past twelve when *I* gave up," Mrs. Miller recorded with passionless accuracy.

It was of great interest to Winterbourne. "Does he sleep much during the day?"

"I guess he does n't sleep *very* much," Daisy rejoined.

"I wish he just *would!*" said her mother. "It seems as if he *must* make it up somehow."

"Well, I guess it's we that make it up. I think he's real tiresome," Daisy pursued.

After which, for some moments, there was silence. "Well, Daisy Miller," the elder lady then unexpectedly broke out, "I should n't think you'd want to talk against your own brother!"

"Well, he *is* tiresome, mother," said the girl, but with no sharpness of insistence.

"Well, he's only nine," Mrs. Miller lucidly urged.

"Well, he would n't go up to that castle, anyway," her daughter replied as for accommodation. "I'm going up there with Mr. Winterbourne."

To this announcement, very placidly made, Daisy's parent offered no response. Winterbourne took for granted on this that she opposed such a course; but he said to himself at the same time that she was a simple easily-managed person and that a

---

[20] Town on the English side of the Channel.

few deferential protestations would modify her attitude. "Yes," he therefore interposed, "your daughter has kindly allowed me the honour of being her guide."

Mrs. Miller's wandering eyes attached themselves with an appealing air to her other companion, who, however, strolled a few steps further, gently humming to herself. "I presume you'll go in the cars," she then quite colourlessly remarked.

"Yes, or in the boat," said Winterbourne.

"Well, of course I don't know," Mrs. Miller returned. "I've never been up to that castle."

"It is a pity you should n't go," he observed, beginning to feel reassured as to her opposition. And yet he was quite prepared to find that as a matter of course she meant to accompany her daughter.

It was on this view accordingly that light was projected for him. "We've been thinking ever so much about going, but it seems as if we could n't. Of course Daisy —she wants to go round everywhere. But there's a lady here—I don't know her name —she says she should n't think we'd want to go to see castles *here;* she should think we'd want to wait till we got t' Italy. It seems as if there would be so many there," continued Mrs. Miller with an air of increasing confidence. "Of course we only want to see the principal ones. We visited several in England," she presently added.

"Ah yes, in England there are beautiful castles," said Winterbourne. "But Chillon here is very well worth seeing."

"Well, if Daisy feels up to it—" said Mrs. Miller in a tone that seemed to break under the burden of such conceptions. "It seems as if there's nothing she won't undertake."

"Oh I'm pretty sure she'll enjoy it!" Winterbourne declared. And he desired more and more to make it a certainty that he was to have the privilege of a *tête-à-tête* [21] with the young lady who was still strolling along in front of them and softly vocalising. "You're not disposed, madam," he enquired, "to make the so interesting excursion yourself?"

So addressed Daisy's mother looked at him an instant with a certain scared obliquity and then walked forward in silence. Then, "I guess she had better go alone," she said simply.

It gave him occasion to note that this was a very different type of maternity from that of the vigilant matrons who massed themselves in the forefront of social intercourse in the dark old city at the other end of the lake. But his meditations were interrupted by hearing his name very distinctly pronounced by Mrs. Miller's unprotected daughter. "Mr. Winterbourne!" she piped from a considerable distance.

"Mademoiselle!" said the young man.

"Don't you want to take me out in a boat?"

"At present?" he asked.

"Why of course!" she gaily returned.

"Well, Annie Miller!" exclaimed her mother.

"I beg you, madam, to let her go," he hereupon eagerly pleaded; so instantly had he been struck with the romantic side of this chance to guide through the summer starlight a skiff freighted with a fresh and beautiful young girl.

[21] Intimate conversation.

"I should n't think she'd want to," said her mother. "I should think she'd rather go indoors."

"I'm sure Mr. Winterbourne wants to *take* me," Daisy declared. "He's so awfully devoted!"

"I'll row you over to Chillon under the stars."

"I don't believe it!" Daisy laughed.

"Well!" the elder lady again gasped, as in rebuke of this freedom.

"You haven't spoken to me for half an hour," her daughter went on.

"I've been having some very pleasant conversation with your mother," Winterbourne replied.

"Oh pshaw! I want you to take me out in a boat!" Daisy went on as if nothing else had been said. They had all stopped and she had turned round and was looking at her friend. Her face wore a charming smile, her pretty eyes gleamed in the darkness, she swung her great fan about. No, he felt, it was impossible to be prettier than that.

"There are half a dozen boats moored at that landing-place," and he pointed to a range of steps that descended from the garden to the lake. "If you'll do me the honour to accept my arm we'll go and select one of them."

She stood there smiling; she threw back her head; she laughed as for the drollery of this. "I like a gentleman to be formal!"

"I assure you it's a formal offer."

"I was bound I'd make you say something," Daisy agreeably mocked.

"You see it's not very difficult," said Winterbourne. "But I'm afraid you're chaffing me."

"I think not, sir," Mrs. Miller shyly pleaded.

"Do then let me give you a row," he persisted to Daisy.

"It's quite lovely, the way you say that!" she cried in reward.

"It will be still more lovely to do it."

"Yes, it would be lovely!" But she made no movement to accompany him; she only remained an elegant image of free light irony.

"I guess you'd better find out what time it is," her mother impartially contributed.

"It's eleven o'clock, Madam," said a voice with a foreign accent out of the neighbouring darkness; and Winterbourne, turning, recognised the florid personage he had already seen in attendance. He had apparently just approached.

"Oh Eugenio," said Daisy, "I'm going out with Mr. Winterbourne in a boat!"

Eugenio bowed. "At this hour of the night, Mademoiselle?"

"I'm going with Mr. Winterbourne," she repeated with her shining smile. "I'm going this very minute."

"Do tell her she can't, Eugenio," Mrs. Miller said to the courier.

"I think you had better not go out in a boat, Mademoiselle," the man declared.

Winterbourne wished to goodness this pretty girl were not on such familiar terms with her courier; but he said nothing, and she meanwhile added to his ground. "I suppose you don't think it's proper! My!" she wailed; "Eugenio does n't think anything's proper."

"I'm nevertheless quite at your service," Winterbourne hastened to remark.

"Does Mademoiselle propose to go alone?" Eugenio asked of Mrs. Miller.

"Oh no, with this gentleman!" cried Daisy's mamma for reassurance.

"I *meant* alone with the gentleman." The courier looked for a moment at Winterbourne—the latter seemed to make out in his face a vague presumptuous intelligence as at the expense of their companions—and then solemnly and with a bow, "As Mademoiselle pleases!" he said.

But Daisy broke off at this. "Oh I hoped you'd make a fuss! I don't care to go now."

"Ah but I myself shall make a fuss if you don't go," Winterbourne declared with spirit.

"That's all I want—a little fuss!" With which she began to laugh again.

"Mr. Randolph has retired for the night!" the courier hereupon importantly announced.

"Oh Daisy, now we can go then!" cried Mrs. Miller.

Her daughter turned away from their friend, all lighted with her odd perversity. "Good-night—I hope you're disappointed or disgusted or something!"

He looked at her gravely, taking her by the hand she offered. "I'm puzzled, if you want to know!" he answered.

"Well, I hope it won't keep you awake!" she said very smartly; and, under the escort of the privileged Eugenio, the two ladies passed toward the house.

Winterbourne's eyes followed them; he was indeed quite mystified. He lingered beside the lake a quarter of an hour, baffled by the question of the girl's sudden familiarities and caprices. But the only very definite conclusion he came to was that he should enjoy deucedly "going off" with her somewhere.

Two days later he went off with her to the Castle of Chillon. He waited for her in the large hall of the hotel, where the couriers, the servants, the foreign tourists were lounging about and staring. It was n't the place he would have chosen for a tryst, but she had placidly appointed it. She came tripping downstairs, buttoning her long gloves, squeezing her folded parasol against her pretty figure, dressed exactly in the way that consorted best, to his fancy, with their adventure. He was a man of imagination and, as our ancestors used to say, of sensibility;[22] as he took in her charming air and caught from the great staircase her impatient confiding step the note of some small sweet strain of romance, not intense but clear and sweet, seemed to sound for their start. He could have believed he was *really* going "off" with her. He led her out through all the idle people assembled—they all looked at her straight and hard: she had begun to chatter as soon as she joined him. His preference had been that they should be conveyed to Chillon in a carriage, but she expressed a lively wish to go in the little steamer—there would be such a lovely breeze upon the water and they should see such lots of people. The sail was n't long, but Winterbourne's companion found time for many characteristic remarks and other demonstrations, not a few of which were, from the extremity of their candour, slightly disconcerting. To the young man himself their small excursion showed so for delightfully irregular and incongruously intimate that, even allowing for her habitual sense of freedom, he had some expectation of seeing her appear to find in it the same savour. But it must be confessed that he was in this particular rather disappointed. Miss Miller was highly animated, she was in the brightest spirits; but she was clearly not at all in a nervous flutter—as she should have been to match *his* tension; she avoided neither his eyes nor those

[22] Sensitive responses.

of any one else; she neither coloured from an awkward consciousness when she looked at him nor when she saw that people were looking at herself. People continued to look at her a great deal, and Winterbourne could at least take pleasure in his pretty companion's distinguished air. He had been privately afraid she would talk loud, laugh overmuch, and even perhaps desire to move extravagantly about the boat. But he quite forgot his fears; he sat smiling with his eyes on her face while, without stirring from her place, she delivered herself of a great number of original reflexions. It was the most charming innocent prattle he had ever heard, for, by his own experience hitherto, when young persons were so ingenuous they were less articulate and when they were so confident were more sophisticated. If he had assented to the idea that she was "common," at any rate, *was* she proving so, after all, or was he simply getting used to her commonness? Her discourse was for the most part of what immediately and superficially surrounded them, but there were moments when it threw out a longer look or took a sudden straight plunge.

"What on *earth* are you solemn about?" she suddenly demanded, fixing her agreeable eyes on her friend's.

"*Am* I solemn?" he asked. "I had an idea I was grinning from ear to ear."

"You look as if you were taking me to a prayer-meeting or a funeral. If that's a grin your ears are very near together."

"Should you like me to dance a hornpipe on the deck?"

"Pray do, and I'll carry round your hat. It will pay the expenses of our journey."

"I never was better pleased in my life," Winterbourne returned.

She looked at him a moment, then let it renew her amusement. "I like to make you say these things. You're a queer mixture!"

In the castle, after they had landed, nothing could exceed the light independence of her humour. She tripped about the vaulted chambers, rustled her skirts in the corkscrew staircases, flirted back with a pretty little cry and a shudder from the edge of the oubliettes[23] and turned a singularly well-shaped ear to everything Winterbourne told her about the place. But he saw she cared little for mediæval history and that the grim ghosts of Chillon loomed but faintly before her. They had the good fortune to have been able to wander without other society than that of their guide; and Winterbourne arranged with this companion that they should n't be hurried—that they should linger and pause wherever they chose. He interpreted the bargain generously—Winterbourne on his side had been generous—and ended by leaving them quite to themselves. Miss Miller's observations were marked by no logical consistency; for anything she wanted to say she was sure to find a pretext. She found a great many, in the tortuous passages and rugged embrasures of the place, for asking her young man sudden questions about himself, his family, his previous history, his tastes, his habits, his designs, and for supplying information on corresponding points in her own situation. Of her own tastes, habits and designs the charming creature was prepared to give the most definite and indeed the most favourable account.

"Well, I hope you know enough!" she exclaimed after Winterbourne had sketched for her something of the story of the unhappy Bonnivard.[24] "I never saw a man that

---

[23] Dungeon cells set below ground level with barred openings across the top.

[24] François de Bonnivard (1465?–1570), Swiss

patriot held prisoner in a castle for seven years; hero of Byron's poem.

knew so much!" The history of Bonnivard had evidently, as they say, gone into one ear and out of the other. But this easy erudition struck her none the less as wonderful, and she was soon quite sure she wished Winterbourne would travel with them and "go round" with them: they too in that case might learn something about something. "Don't you want to come and teach Randolph?" she asked; "I guess he'd improve with a gentleman teacher." Winterbourne was certain that nothing could possibly please him so much, but that he had unfortunately other occupations. "Other occupations? I don't believe a speck of it!" she protested. "What do you mean now? You're not in business." The young man allowed that he was not in business, but he had engagements which even within a day or two would necessitate his return to Geneva. "Oh bother!" she panted, "I don't believe it!" and she began to talk about something else. But a few moments later, when he was pointing out to her the interesting design of an antique fireplace, she broke our irrelevantly: "You don't mean to say you're going back to Geneva?"

"It is a melancholy fact that I shall have to report myself there to-morrow."

She met it with a vivacity that could only flatter him. "Well, Mr. Winterbourne, I think you're horrid!"

"Oh don't say such dreadful things!" he quite sincerely pleaded—"just at the last."

"The last?" the girl cried; "I call it the very first! I've half a mind to leave you here and go straight back to the hotel alone." And for the next ten minutes she did nothing but call him horrid. Poor Winterbourne was fairly bewildered; no young lady had as yet done him the honour to be so agitated by the mention of his personal plans. His companion, after this, ceased to pay any attention to the curiosities of Chillon or the beauties of the lake; she opened fire on the special charmer in Geneva whom she appeared to have instantly taken it for granted that he was hurrying back to see. How did Miss Daisy Miller know of that agent of his fate in Geneva? Winterbourne, who denied the existence of such a person, was quite unable to discover; and he was divided between amazement of the rapidity of her induction and amusement at the directness of her criticism. She struck him afresh, in all this, as an extraordinary mixture of innocence and crudity. "Does she never allow you more than three days at a time?" Miss Miller wished ironically to know. "Does n't she give you a vacation in summer? there's no one so hard-worked but they can get leave to go off somewhere at this season. I suppose if you stay another day she'll come right after you in the boat. Do wait over till Friday and I'll go down to the landing to see her arrive!" He began at last even to feel he had been wrong to be disappointed in the temper in which his young lady had embarked. If he missed the personal accent, the personal accent was now making its appearance. It sounded very distinctly, toward the end, in her telling him she'd stop "teasing" him if he'd promise her solemnly to come down to Rome that winter.

"That's not a difficult promise to make," he hastened to acknowledge. "My aunt has taken an apartment in Rome from January and has already asked me to come and see her."

"I don't want you to come for your aunt," said Daisy; "I want you just to come for me." And this was the only allusion he was ever to hear her make again to his invidious kinswoman. He promised her that at any rate he would certainly come, and after this she forbore from teasing. Winterbourne took a carriage and they drove back to Vevey in the dusk; the girl at his side, her animation a little spent, was now quite distractingly passive.

In the evening he mentioned to Mrs. Costello that he had spent the afternoon at Chillon with Miss Daisy Miller.

"The Americans—of the courier?" asked this lady.

"Ah happily the courier stayed at home."

"She went with you all alone?"

"All alone."

Mrs. Costello sniffed a little at her smelling-bottle. "And that," she exclaimed, "is the little abomination you wanted me to know!"

III

Winterbourne, who had returned to Geneva the day after his excursion to Chillon, went to Rome toward the end of January. His aunt had been established there a considerable time and he had received from her a couple of characteristic letters. "Those people you were so devoted to last summer at Vevey have turned up here, courier and all," she wrote. "They seem to have made several acquaintances, but the courier continues to be the most *intime.*[25] The young lady, however, is also very intimate with various third-rate Italians, with whom she rackets about in a way that makes much talk. Bring me that pretty novel of Cherbuliez's—'Paule Méré'[26]—and don't come later than the 23d."

Our friend would in the natural course of events, on arriving in Rome, have presently ascertained Mrs. Miller's address at the American banker's and gone to pay his compliments to Miss Daisy. "After what happened at Vevey I certainly think I may call upon them," he said to Mrs. Costello.

"If after what happens—at Vevey and everywhere—you desire to keep up the acquaintance, you're very welcome. Of course you're not squeamish—a man may know every one. Men are welcome to the privilege!"

"Pray what is it then that 'happens'—here for instance?" Winterbourne asked.

"Well, the girl tears about alone with her unmistakeably low foreigners. As to what happens further you must apply elsewhere for information. She has picked up half a dozen of the regular Roman fortune-hunters of the inferior sort and she takes them about to such houses as she may put *her* nose into. When she comes to a party—such a party as she can come to—she brings with her a gentleman with a good deal of manner and a wonderful moustache."

"And where's the mother?"

"I have n't the least idea. They're very dreadful people."

Winterbourne thought them over in these new lights. "They're very ignorant—very innocent only, and utterly uncivilised. Depend on it they're not 'bad.' "

"They're hopelessly vulgar," said Mrs. Costello. "Whether or no being hopelessly vulgar is being 'bad' is a question for the metaphysicians. They're bad enough to blush for, at any rate; and for this short life that's quite enough."

The news that his little friend the child of nature of the Swiss lakeside was now surrounded by half a dozen wonderful moustaches checked Winterbourne's impulse to go straightway to see her. He had perhaps not definitely flattered himself that he

[25] French: "intimate."
[26] Novel by Victor Cherbuliez (1829–1899), published in 1864.

had made an ineffaceable impression upon her heart, but he was annoyed at hearing of a state of affairs so little in harmony with an image that had lately flitted in and out of his own meditations; the image of a very pretty girl looking out of an old Roman window and asking herself urgently when Mr. Winterbourne would arrive. If, however, he determined to wait a little before reminding this young lady of his claim to her faithful remembrance, he called with more promptitude on two or three other friends. One of these friends was an American lady who had spent several winters at Geneva, where she had placed her children at school. She was a very accomplished woman and she lived in Via Gregoriana.[27] Winterbourne found her in a little crimson drawing-room on a third floor; the room was filled with southern sunshine. He had n't been there ten minutes when the servant, appearing in the doorway, announced complacently "Madame Mila!" This announcement was presently followed by the entrance of little Randolph Miller, who stopped in the middle of the room and stood staring at Winterbourne. An instant later his pretty sister crossed the threshold; and then, after a considerable interval, the parent of the pair slowly advanced.

"I guess I know you!" Randolph broke ground without delay.

"I'm sure you know a great many things"—and his old friend clutched him all interestedly by the arm. "How's your education coming on?"

Daisy was engaged in some pretty babble with her hostess, but when she heard Winterbourne's voice she quickly turned her head with a "Well, I declare!" which he met smiling. "I told you I should come, you know."

"Well, I did n't believe it," she answered.

"I'm much obliged to you for that," laughed the young man.

"You might have come to see me then," Daisy went on as if they had parted the week before.

"I arrived only yesterday."

"I don't believe any such thing!" the girl declared afresh.

Winterbourne turned with a protesting smile to her mother, but this lady evaded his glance and, seating herself, fixed her eyes on her son. "We've got a bigger place than this," Randolph hereupon broke out. "It's all gold on the walls."

Mrs. Miller, more of a fatalist apparently than ever, turned uneasily in her chair. "I told you if I was to bring you you'd say something!" she stated as for the benefit of such of the company as might hear it.

"I told *you!*" Randolph retorted. "I tell *you,* sir!" he added jocosely, giving Winterbourne a thump on the knee. "It *is* bigger too!"

As Daisy's conversation with her hostess still occupied her Winterbourne judged it becoming to address a few words to her mother—such as "I hope you've been well since we parted at Vevey."

Mrs. Miller now certainly looked at him—at his chin. "Not very well, sir," she answered.

"She's got the dyspepsia," said Randolph. "I've got it too. Father's got it bad. But I've got it worst!"

This proclamation, instead of embarrassing Mrs. Miller, seemed to soothe her by reconstituting the environment to which she was most accustomed. "I suffer from the liver," she amiably whined to Winterbourne. "I think it's this climate; it's less bracing than Schenectady, especially in the winter season. I don't know whether you know we reside at Schenectady. I was saying to Daisy that I certainly had n't found any one like Dr. Davis and I did n't believe I *would*. Oh up in Schenectady, he stands first; they think everything of Dr. Davis. He has so much to do, and yet there was nothing he would n't do for *me*. He said he never saw anything like my dyspepsia, but he was bound to get at it. I'm sure there was nothing he would n't try, and I did n't care what he did to me if he only brought me relief. He was just going to try something new, and I just longed for it, when we came right off. Mr. Miller felt as if he wanted Daisy to see Europe for herself. But I could n't help writing the other day that I supposed it was all right for Daisy, but that I did n't know as I *could* get on much longer without Dr. Davis. At Schenectady he stands at the very top; and there's a great deal of sickness there too. It affects my sleep."

Winterbourne had a good deal of pathological gossip with Dr. Davis's patient, during which Daisy chattered unremittingly to her own companion. The young man asked Mrs. Miller how she was pleased with Rome. "Well, I say I'm disappointed," she confessed. "We had heard so much about it—I suppose we had heard too much. But we could n't help that. We had been led to expect something different."

Winterbourne, however, abounded in reassurance. "Ah wait a little, and you'll grow very fond of it."

"I hate it worse and worse every day!" cried Randolph.

"You're like the infant Hannibal,"[28] his friend laughed.

"No I ain't—like any infant!" Randolph declared at a venture.

"Well, that's so—and you never *were*!" his mother concurred. "But we've seen places," she resumed, "that I'd put a long way ahead of Rome." And in reply to Winterbourne's interrogation, "There's Zürich—up there in the mountains," she instanced; "I think Zürich's real lovely, and we had n't heard half so much about it."

"The best place we've seen's the *City of Richmond*!" said Randolph.

"He means the ship," Mrs. Miller explained. "We crossed in that ship. Randolph had a good time on the *City of Richmond*."

"It's the best place *I've* struck," the child repeated. "Only it was turned the wrong way."

"Well, we've got to turn the right way sometime," said Mrs. Miller with strained but weak optimism. Winterbourne expressed the hope that her daughter at least appreciated the so various interest of Rome, and she declared with some spirit that Daisy was quite carried away. "It's on account of the society—the society's splendid. She goes round everywhere; she has made a great number of acquaintances. Of course she goes round more than I do. I must say they've all been very sweet—they've taken her right in. And then she knows a great many gentlemen. Oh she thinks there's nothing like Rome. Of course it's a great deal pleasanter for a young lady if she knows plenty of gentlemen."

By this time Daisy had turned her attention again to Winterbourne, but in quite the same free form. "I've been telling Mrs. Walker how mean you were!"

"And what's the evidence you've offered?" he asked, a trifle disconcerted, for all his superior gallantry, by her inadequate measure of the zeal of an admirer who on his way down to Rome had stopped neither at Bologna nor at Florence, simply

---

[28] Carthaginian general (243–183? B.C.), who bore a hatred of Rome from childhood on.

because of a certain sweet appeal to his fond fancy, not to say to his finest curiosity. He remembered how a cynical compatriot had once told him that American women —the pretty ones, and this gave a largeness to the axiom—were at once the most exacting in the world and the least endowed with a sense of indebtedness.

"Why you were awfully mean up at Vevey," Daisy said. "You would n't do most anything. You would n't stay there when I asked you."

"Dearest young lady," cried Winterbourne, with generous passion, "have I come all the way to Rome only to be riddled by your silver shafts?"

"Just hear him say that!"—and she gave an affectionate twist to a bow on her hostess's dress. "Did you ever hear anything so quaint?"

"So 'quaint,' my dear?" echoed Mrs. Walker more critically—quite in the tone of a partisan of Winterbourne.

"Well, I don't know."—and the girl continued to finger her ribbons. "Mrs. Walker, I want to tell you something."

"Say, mother-r," broke in Randolph with his rough ends to his words, "I tell you you've got to go. Eugenio'll raise something!"

"I'm not afraid of Eugenio," said Daisy with a toss of her head. "Look here, Mrs. Walker," she went on, "you know I'm coming to your party."

"I'm delighted to hear it."

"I've got a lovely dress."

"I'm very sure of that."

"But I want to ask a favour—permission to bring a friend."

"I shall be happy to see any of your friends," said Mrs. Walker, who turned with a smile to Mrs. Miller.

"Oh they're not my friends," cried that lady, squirming in shy repudiation. "It seems as if they did n't take to *me*—I never spoke to one of them!"

"It's an intimate friend of mine, Mr. Giovanelli," Daisy pursued without a tremor in her young clearness or a shadow on her shining bloom.

Mrs. Walker had a pause and gave a rapid glance at Winterbourne. "I shall be glad to see Mr. Giovanelli," she then returned.

"He's just the finest kind of Italian," Daisy pursued with the prettiest serenity. "He's a great friend of mine and the handsomest man in the world—except Mr. Winterbourne! He knows plenty of Italians, but he wants to know some Americans. It seems as if he was crazy about Americans. He's tremendously bright. He's perfectly lovely!"

It was settled that this paragon should be brought to Mrs. Walker's party, and then Mrs. Miller prepared to take her leave. "I guess we'll go right back to the hotel," she remarked with a confessed failure of the larger imagination.

"You may go back to the hotel, mother," Daisy replied, "but I'm just going to walk round."

"She's going to go it with Mr. Giovanelli," Randolph unscrupulously commented.

"I'm going to go it on the Pincio,"[29] Daisy peaceably smiled, while the way that she "condoned" these things almost melted Winterbourne's heart.

"Alone, my dear—at this hour?" Mrs. Walker asked. The afternoon was drawing to a close—it was the hour for the throng of carriages and of contemplative pedestrians. "I don't consider it's safe, Daisy," her hostess firmly asserted.

[29] Roman hill with a panoramic vista.

"Neither do I then," Mrs. Miller thus borrowed confidence to add. "You'll catch the fever as sure as you live. Remember what Dr. Davis told you!"

"Give her some of that medicine before she starts in," Randolph suggested.

The company had risen to its feet; Daisy, still showing her pretty teeth, bent over and kissed her hostess. "Mrs. Walker, you're too perfect," she simply said. "I'm not going alone; I'm going to meet a friend."

"Your friend won't keep you from catching the fever even if it *is* his own second nature," Mrs. Miller observed.

"Is it Mr. Giovanelli that's the dangerous attraction?" Mrs. Walker asked without mercy.

Winterbourne was watching the challenged girl; at this question his attention quickened. She stood there smiling and smoothing her bonnet-ribbons; she glanced at Winterbourne. Then, while she glanced and smiled, she brought out all affirmatively and without a shade of hesitation: "Mr. Giovanelli—the beautiful Giovanelli."

"My dear young friend"—and, taking her hand, Mrs. Walker turned to pleading —"don't prowl off to the Pincio at this hour to meet a beautiful Italian."

"Well, he speaks first-rate English," Mrs. Miller incoherently mentioned.

"Gracious me," Daisy piped up, "I don't want to do anything that's going to affect my health—or my character either! There's an easy way to settle it." Her eyes continued to play over Winterbourne. "The Pincio's only a hundred yards off, and if Mr. Winterbourne were as polite as he pretends he'd offer to walk right in with me!"

Winterbourne's politeness hastened to proclaim itself, and the girl gave him gracious leave to accompany her. They passed downstairs before her mother, and at the door he saw Mrs. Miller's carriage drawn up, with the ornamental courier whose acquaintance he had made at Vevey seated within. "Goodbye, Eugenio," cried Daisy; "I'm going to take a walk!" The distance from Via Gregoriana to the beautiful garden at the other end of the Pincian Hill is in fact rapidly traversed. As the day was splendid, however, and the concourse of vehicles, walkers and loungers numerous, the young Americans found their progress much delayed. This fact was highly agreeable to Winterbourne, in spite of his consciousness of his singular situation. The slow-moving, idly-gazing Roman crowd bestowed much attention on the extremely pretty young woman of English race who passed through it, with some difficulty, on his arm; and he wondered what on earth had been in Daisy's mind when she proposed to exhibit herself unattended to its appreciation. His own mission, to her sense, was apparently to consign her to the hands of Mr. Giovanelli; but, at once annoyed and gratified, he resolved that he would do no such thing.

"Why have n't you been to see me?" she meanwhile asked. "You can't get out of that."

"I've had the honour of telling you that I've only just stepped out of the train."

"You must have stayed in the train a good while after it stopped!" she derisively cried. "I suppose you were asleep. You've had time to go to see Mrs. Walker."

"I knew Mrs. Walker—" Winterbourne began to explain.

"I know where you knew her. You knew her at Geneva. She told me so. Well, you knew me at Vevey. That's just as good. So you ought to have come." She asked him no other question than this; she began to prattle about her own affairs. "We've got splendid rooms at the hotel; Eugenio says they're the best rooms in Rome. We're going to stay all winter—if we don't die of the fever; and I guess we'll stay then! It's a great deal nicer than I thought; I thought it would be fearfully quiet—in fact I was sure it would be deadly pokey. I foresaw we should be going round all the time with one of those dreadful old men who explain about the pictures and things. But we only had about a week of that, and now I'm enjoying myself. I know ever so many people, and they're all so charming. The society's extremely select. There are all kinds—English and Germans and Italians. I think I like the English best. I like their style of conversation. But there are some lovely Americans. I never saw anything so hospitable. There's something or other every day. There's not much dancing—but I must say I never thought dancing was everything. I was always fond of conversation. I guess I'll have plenty at Mrs. Walker's—her rooms are so small." When they had passed the gate of the Pincian Gardens Miss Miller began to wonder where Mr. Giovanelli might be. "We had better go straight to that place in front, where you look at the view."

Winterbourne at this took a stand. "I certainly shan't help you to find him."

"Then I shall find him without you," Daisy said with spirit.

"You certainly won't leave me!" he protested.

She burst into her familiar little laugh. "Are you afraid you'll get lost—or run over? But there's Giovanelli leaning against that tree. He's staring at the women in the carriages: did you ever see anything so cool?"

Winterbourne descried hereupon at some distance a little figure that stood with folded arms and nursing its cane. It had a handsome face, a hat artfully poised, a glass in one eye and a nosegay in its buttonhole. Daisy's friend looked at it a moment and then said: "Do you mean to speak to that thing?"

"Do I mean to speak to him? Why you don't suppose I mean to communicate by signs!"

"Pray understand then," the young man returned, "that I intend to remain with you."

Daisy stopped and looked at him without a sign of troubled consciousness, with nothing in her face but her charming eyes, her charming teeth and her happy dimples. "Well, she's a cool one!" he thought.

"I don't like the way you say that," she declared. "It's too imperious."

"I beg your pardon if I say it wrong. The main point's to give you an idea of my meaning."

The girl looked at him more gravely, but with eyes that were prettier than ever. "I've never allowed a gentleman to dictate to me or to interfere with anything I do."

"I think that's just where your mistake has come in," he retorted. "You should sometimes listen to a gentleman—the right one."

At this she began to laugh again. "I do nothing but listen to gentlemen! Tell me if Mr. Giovanelli is the right one."

The gentleman with the nosegay in his bosom had now made out our two friends and was approaching Miss Miller with obsequious rapidity. He bowed to Winterbourne as well as to the latter's compatriot; he seemed to shine, in his coxcombical way, with the desire to please and the fact of his own intelligent joy, though Winterbourne thought him not a bad-looking fellow. But he nevertheless said to Daisy: "No, he's not the right one."

She had clearly a natural turn for free introductions: she mentioned with the easiest grace the name of each of her companions to the other. She strolled forward with one of them on either hand; Mr. Giovanelli, who spoke English very cleverly—Winterbourne afterwards learned that he had practised the idiom upon a great many American heiresses—addressed her a great deal of very polite nonsense. He had the best possible manners, and the young American, who said nothing, reflected on that depth of Italian subtlety, so strangely opposed to Anglo-Saxon simplicity, which enables people to show a smoother surface in proportion as they're more acutely displeased. Giovanelli of course had counted upon something more intimate—he had not bargained for a party of three; but he kept his temper in a manner that suggested far-stretching intentions. Winterbourne flattered himself he had taken his measure. "He's anything but a gentleman," said the young American; "he isn't even a very plausible imitation of one. He's a music-master or a penny-a-liner[30] or a third-rate artist. He's awfully on his good behaviour, but damn his fine eyes!" Mr. Giovanelli had indeed great advantages; but it was deeply disgusting to Daisy's other friend that something in her should n't have instinctively discriminated against such a type. Giovanelli chattered and jested and made himself agreeable according to his honest Roman lights. It was true that if he was an imitation the imitation was studied. "Nevertheless," Winterbourne said to himself, "a nice girl ought to know!" And then he came back to the dreadful question of whether this *was* in fact a nice girl. Would a nice girl—even allowing for her being a little American flirt—make a rendezvous with a presumably low-lived foreigner? The rendezvous in this case indeed had been in broad daylight and in the most crowded corner of Rome; but was n't it possible to regard the choice of these very circumstances as a proof more of vulgarity than of anything else? Singular though it may seem, Winterbourne was vexed that the girl, in joining her *amoroso,*[31] should n't appear more impatient of his own company, and he was vexed precisely because of his inclination. It was impossible to regard her as a wholly unspotted flower—she lacked a certain indispensable fineness; and it would therefore much simplify the situation to be able to treat her as the subject of one of the visitations known to romancers as "lawless passions." That she should seem to wish to get rid of him would have helped him to think more lightly of her, just as to be able to think more lightly of her would have made her less perplexing. Daisy at any rate continued on this occasion to present herself as an inscrutable combination of audacity and innocence.

She had been walking some quarter of an hour, attended by her two cavaliers and responding in a tone of very childish gaiety, as it after all struck one of them, to the pretty speeches of the other, when a carriage that had detached itself from the revolving train drew up beside the path. At the same moment Winterbourne noticed that his friend Mrs. Walker—the lady whose house he had lately left—was seated in the vehicle and was beckoning to him. Leaving Miss Miller's side, he hastened to obey her summons—and all to find her flushed, excited, scandalised. "It's really too dreadful"—she earnestly appealed to him. "That crazy girl must n't do this sort of thing. She must n't walk here with you two men. Fifty people have remarked her."

Winterbourne—suddenly and rather oddly rubbed the wrong way by this—raised his grave eyebrows. "I think it's a pity to make too much fuss about it."

"It's a pity to let the girl ruin herself!"

---

[30] Low-paid hack writer.   [31] Italian: "lover"; "admirer."

"She's very innocent," he reasoned in his own troubled interest.

"She's very reckless," cried Mrs. Walker, "and goodness knows how far—left to itself—it may go. Did you ever," she proceeded to enquire, "see anything so blatantly imbecile as the mother? After you had all left me just now I could n't sit still for thinking of it. It seemed too pitiful not even to attempt to save them. I ordered the carriage and put on my bonnet and came here as quickly as possible. Thank heaven I've found you!"

"What do you propose to do with us?" Winterbourne uncomfortably smiled.

"To ask her to get in, to drive her about here for half an hour—so that the world may see she's not running absolutely wild—and then take her safely home."

"I don't think it's a very happy thought," he said after reflexion, "but you're at liberty to try."

Mrs. Walker accordingly tried. The young man went in pursuit of their young lady who had simply nodded and smiled, from her distance, at her recent patroness in the carriage and then had gone her way with her own companion. On learning, in the event, that Mrs. Walker had followed her, she retraced her steps, however, with a perfect good grace and with Mr. Giovanelli at her side. She professed herself "enchanted" to have a chance to present this gentleman to her good friend, and immediately achieved the introduction; declaring with it, and as if it were of as little importance, that she had never in her life seen anything so lovely as that lady's carriage-rug.

"I'm glad you admire it," said her poor pursuer, smiling sweetly. "Will you get in and let me put it over you?"

"Oh no, thank you!"—Daisy knew her mind. "I'll admire it ever so much more as I see you driving round with it."

"Do get in and drive round *with* me," Mrs. Walker pleaded.

"That would be charming, but it's so fascinating just as I am!"—with which the girl radiantly took in the gentlemen on either side of her.

"It may be fascinating, dear child, but it's not the custom here," urged the lady of the victoria,[32] leaning forward in this vehicle with her hands devoutly clasped.

"Well, it ought to be then!" Daisy imperturbably laughed. "If I did n't walk I'd expire."

"You should walk with your mother, dear," cried Mrs. Walker with a loss of patience.

"With my mother dear?" the girl amusedly echoed. Winterbourne saw she scented interference. "My mother never walked ten steps in her life. And then, you know," she blandly added, "I'm more than five years old."

"You're old enough to be more reasonable. You're old enough, dear Miss Miller, to be talked about."

Daisy wondered to extravagance. "Talked about? What do you mean?"

"Come into my carriage and I'll tell you."

Daisy turned shining eyes again from one of the gentlemen beside her to the other. Mr. Giovanelli was bowing to and fro, rubbing down his gloves and laughing irresponsibly; Winterbourne thought the scene the most unpleasant possible. "I don't

[32] Horse-drawn carriage.

think I want to know what you mean," the girl presently said. "I don't think I should like it."

Winterbourne only wished Mrs. Walker would tuck up her carriage-rug and drive away; but this lady, as she afterwards told him, did n't feel she could "rest there." "Should you prefer being thought a very reckless girl?" she accordingly asked.

"Gracious me!" exclaimed Daisy. She looked again at Mr. Giovanelli, then she turned to her other companion. There was a small pink flush in her cheek; she was tremendously pretty. "Does Mr. Winterbourne think," she put to him with a wonderful bright intensity of appeal, "that—to save my reputation—I ought to get into the carriage?"

It really embarrassed him; for an instant he cast about—so strange was it to hear her speak that way of her "reputation." But he himself in fact had to speak in accordance with gallantry. The finest gallantry here was surely just to tell her the truth; and the truth, for our young man, as the few indications I have been able to give have made him known to the reader, was that his charming friend should listen to the voice of civilised society. He took in again her exquisite prettiness and then said the more distinctly: "I think you should get into the carriage."

Daisy gave the rein to her amusement. "I never heard anything so stiff! If this is improper, Mrs. Walker," she pursued, "then I'm *all* improper, and you had better give me right up. Good-bye; I hope you'll have a lovely ride!"—and with Mr. Giovanelli, who made a triumphantly obsequious salute, she turned away.

Mrs. Walker sat looking after her, and there were tears in Mrs. Walker's eyes. "Get in here, sir," she said to Winterbourne, indicating the place beside her. The young man answered that he felt bound to accompany Miss Miller; whereupon the lady of the victoria declared that if he refused her this favour she would never speak to him again. She was evidently wound up. He accordingly hastened to overtake Daisy and her more faithful ally, and, offering her his hand, told her that Mrs. Walker had made a stringent claim on his presence. He had expected her to answer with something rather free, something still more significant of the perversity from which the voice of society, through the lips of their distressed friend, had so earnestly endeavoured to dissuade her. But she only let her hand slip, as she scarce looked at him, through his slightly awkward grasp; while Mr. Giovanelli, to make it worse, bade him farewell with too emphatic a flourish of the hat.

Winterbourne was not in the best possible humour as he took his seat beside the author of his sacrifice. "That was not clever of you," he said candidly, as the vehicle mingled again with the throng of carriages.

"In such a case," his companion answered, "I don't want to be clever—I only want to be *true!*"

"Well, your truth has only offended the strange little creature—it has only put her off."

"It has happened very well"—Mrs. Walker accepted her work. "If she's so perfectly determined to compromise herself the sooner one knows it the better—one can act accordingly."

"I suspect she meant no great harm, you know," Winterbourne maturely opined.

"So I thought a month ago. But she has been going too far."

"What has she been doing?"

"Everything that's not done here. Flirting with any man she can pick up; sitting in corners with mysterious Italians; dancing all the evening with the same partners; receiving visits at eleven o'clock at night. Her mother melts away when the visitors come."

"But her brother," laughed Winterbourne, "sits up till two in the morning."

"He must be edified by what he sees. I'm told that at their hotel every one's talking about her and that a smile goes round among the servants when a gentleman comes and asks for Miss Miller."

"Ah we need n't mind the servants!" Winterbourne compassionately signified. "The poor girl's only fault," he presently added, "is her complete lack of education."

"She's naturally indelicate," Mrs. Walker, on her side, reasoned. "Take that example this morning. How long had you known her at Vevey?"

"A couple of days."

"Imagine then the taste of her making it a personal matter that you should have left the place!"

He agreed that taste was n't the strong point of the Millers—after which he was silent for some moments; but only at last to add: "I suspect, Mrs. Walker, that you and I have lived too long at Geneva!" And he further noted that he should be glad to learn with what particular design she had made him enter her carriage.

"I wanted to enjoin on you the importance of your ceasing your relations with Miss Miller; that of your not appearing to flirt with her; that of your giving her no further opportunity to expose herself; that of your in short letting her alone."

"I'm afraid I can't do anything quite so enlightened as *that*," he returned. "I like her awfully, you know."

"All the more reason you should n't help her to make a scandal."

"Well, there shall be nothing scandalous in my attentions to her," he was willing to promise.

"There certainly will be in the way she takes them. But I've said what I had on my conscience," Mrs. Walker pursued. "If you wish to rejoin the young lady I'll put you down. Here, by the way, you have a chance."

The carriage was engaged in that part of the Pincian drive which overhangs the wall of Rome and overlooks the beautiful Villa Borghese.[33] It is bordered by a large parapet, near which are several seats. One of these, at a distance, was occupied by a gentleman and a lady, toward whom Mrs. Walker gave a toss of her head. At the same moment these persons rose and walked to the parapet. Winterbourne had asked the coachman to stop; he now descended from the carriage. His companion looked at him a moment in silence and then, while he raised his hat, drove majestically away. He stood where he had alighted; he had turned his eyes toward Daisy and her cavalier. They evidently saw no one; they were too deeply occupied with each other. When they reached the low garden-wall they remained a little looking off at the great flat-topped pine-clusters of Villa Borghese; then the girl's attendant admirer seated himself familiarly on the broad ledge of the wall. The western sun in the opposite sky sent out a brilliant shaft through a couple of cloud-bars; whereupon the gallant Giovanelli took her parasol out of her hands and opened it. She came a little nearer

---

[33] Former summer palace of the Borghese family and now a museum, located in a public park.

and he held the parasol over her; then, still holding it, he let it so rest on her shoulder that both of their heads were hidden from Winterbourne. This young man stayed but a moment longer; then he began to walk. But he walked—not toward the couple united beneath the parasol, rather toward the residence of his aunt Mrs. Costello.

IV

He flattered himself on the following day that there was no smiling among the servants when he at least asked for Mrs. Miller at her hotel. This lady and her daughter, however, were not at home; and on the next day after, repeating his visit, Winterbourne again was met by a denial. Mrs. Walker's party took place on the evening of the third day, and in spite of the final reserves that had marked his last interview with that social critic our young man was among the guests. Mrs. Walker was one of those pilgrims from the younger world who, while in contact with the elder, make a point, in their own phrase, of studying European society; and she had on this occasion collected several specimens of diversely-born humanity to serve, as might be, for text-books. When Winterbourne arrived the little person he desired most to find was n't there; but in a few moments he saw Mrs. Miller come in alone, very shyly and ruefully. This lady's hair, above the dead waste of her temples, was more frizzled than ever. As she approached their hostess Winterbourne also drew near.

"You see I've come all alone," said Daisy's unsupported parent. "I'm so frightened I don't know what to do; it's the first time I've ever been to a party alone—especially in this country. I wanted to bring Randolph or Eugenio or some one, but Daisy just pushed me off by myself. I ain't used to going round alone."

"And does n't your daughter intend to favour us with her society?" Mrs. Walker impressively enquired.

"Well, Daisy's all dressed," Mrs. Miller testified with that accent of the dispassionate, if not of the philosophic, historian with which she always recorded the current incidents of her daughter's career. "She got dressed on purpose before dinner. But she has a friend of hers there; that gentleman—the handsomest of the Italians—that she wanted to bring. They've got going at the piano—it seems as if they could n't leave off. Mr. Giovanelli does sing splendidly. But I guess they'll come before very long," Mrs. Miller hopefully concluded.

"I'm sorry she should come—in that particular way," Mrs. Walker permitted herself to observe.

"Well, I told her there was no use in her getting dressed before dinner if she was going to wait three hours," returned Daisy's mamma. "I did n't see the use of her putting on such a dress as that to sit round with Mr. Giovanelli."

"This is most horrible!" said Mrs. Walker, turning away and addressing herself to Winterbourne. *"Elle s'affiche, la malheureuse."* [34] It's her revenge for my having ventured to remonstrate with her. When she comes I shan't speak to her."

Daisy came after eleven o'clock, but she was n't, on such an occasion, a young lady to wait to be spoken to. She rustled forward in radiant loveliness, smiling and

[34] French: "She's making a spectacle of herself, poor girl."

chattering, carrying a large bouquet and attended by Mr. Giovanelli. Every one stopped talking and turned and looked at her while she floated up to Mrs. Walker. "I'm afraid you thought I never was coming, so I sent mother off to tell you. I wanted to make Mr. Giovanelli practise some things before he came; you know he sings beautifully, and I want you to ask him to sing. This is Mr. Giovanelli; you know I introduced him to you; he's got the most lovely voice and he knows the most charming set of songs. I made him go over them this evening on purpose; we had the greatest time at the hotel." Of all this Daisy delivered herself with the sweetest brightest loudest confidence, looking now at her hostess and now at all the room, while she gave a series of little pats, round her very white shoulders, to the edges of her dress. "Is there any one I know?" she as undiscourageably asked.

"I think every one knows you!" said Mrs. Walker as with a grand intention; and she gave a very cursory greeting to Mr. Giovanelli. This gentleman bore himself gallantly; he smiled and bowed and showed his white teeth, he curled his moustaches and rolled his eyes and performed all the proper functions of a handsome Italian at an evening party. He sang, very prettily, half a dozen songs, though Mrs. Walker afterwards declared that she had been quite unable to find out who asked him. It was apparently not Daisy who had set him in motion—this young lady being seated a distance from the piano and though she had publicly, as it were, professed herself his musical patroness or guarantor, giving herself to gay and audible discourse while he warbled.

"It's a pity these rooms are so small; we can't dance," she remarked to Winterbourne as if she had seen him five minutes before.

"I'm not sorry we can't dance," he candidly returned. "I'm incapable of a step."

"Of course you're incapable of a step," the girl assented. "I should think your legs *would* be stiff cooped in there so much of the time in that victoria."

"Well, they were very restless three days ago," he amicably laughed; "all they really wanted was to dance attendance on you."

"Oh my other friend—my friend in need—stuck to me; he seems more at one with his limbs than you are—I'll say that for him. But did you ever hear anything so cool," Daisy demanded, "as Mrs. Walker's wanting me to get into her carriage and drop poor Mr. Giovanelli, and under the pretext that it was proper? People have different ideas! It would have been most unkind; he had been talking about that walk for ten days."

"He should n't have talked about it at all," Winterbourne decided to make answer on this: "he would never have proposed to a young lady of this country to walk about the streets of Rome with him."

"About the streets?" she cried with her pretty stare. "Where then would he have proposed to her to walk? The Pincio ain't the streets either, I guess; and I besides, thank goodness, am not a young lady of this country. The young ladies of this country have a dreadfully pokey time of it, by what I can discover; I don't see why I should change my habits for *such* stupids."

"I'm afraid your habits are those of a ruthless flirt," said Winterbourne with studied severity.

"Of course they are!"—and she hoped, evidently, by the manner of it, to take his breath away. "I'm a fearful frightful flirt! Did you ever hear of a nice girl that was n't? But I suppose you'll tell me now I'm not a nice girl."

He remained grave indeed under the shock of her cynical profession. "You're a very nice girl, but I wish you'd flirt with me, and me only."

"Ah thank you, thank you very much: you're the last man I should think of flirting with. As I've had the pleasure of informing you, you're too stiff."

"You say that too often," he resentfully remarked.

Daisy gave a delighted laugh. "If I could have the sweet hope of making you angry I'd say it again."

"Don't do that—when I'm angry I'm stiffer than ever. But if you won't flirt with me do cease at least to flirt with your friend at the piano. They don't," he declared as in full sympathy with "them," "understand that sort of thing here."

"I thought they understood nothing else!" Daisy cried with startling world-knowledge.

"Not in young unmarried women."

"It seems to me much more proper in young unmarried than in old married ones," she retorted.

"Well," said Winterbourne, "when you deal with natives you must go by the custom of the country. American flirting is a purely American silliness; it has—in its ineptitude of innocence—no place in *this* system. So when you show yourself in public with Mr. Giovanelli and without your mother—"

"Gracious, poor mother!"—and she made it beautifully unspeakable.

Winterbourne had a touched sense for this, but it did n't alter his attitude. "Though *you* may be flirting Mr. Giovanelli is n't—he means something else."

"He is n't preaching at any rate," she returned. "And if you want very much to know, we're neither of us flirting—not a little speck. We're too good friends for that. We're real intimate friends."

He was to continue to find her thus at moments inimitable. "Ah," he then judged, "if you're in love with each other it's another affair altogether!"

She had allowed him up to this point to speak so frankly that he had no thought of shocking her by the force of his logic; yet she now none the less immediately rose, blushing visibly and leaving him mentally to exclaim that the name of little American flirts was incoherence. "Mr. Giovanelli at least," she answered, sparing but a single small queer glance for it, a queerer small glance, he felt, than he had ever yet had from her—"Mr. Giovanelli never says to me such very disagreeable things."

It had an effect on him—he stood staring. The subject of their contention had finished singing; he left the piano, and his recognition of what—a little awkwardly—did n't take place in celebration of this might nevertheless have been an acclaimed operatic tenor's series of repeated ducks before the curtain. So he bowed himself over to Daisy. "Won't you come to the other room and have some tea?" he asked—offering Mrs. Walker's slightly thin refreshment as he might have done all the kingdoms of the earth.

Daisy at last turned on Winterbourne a more natural and calculable light. He was but the more muddled by it, however, since so inconsequent a smile made nothing clear—it seemed at the most to prove in her a sweetness and softness that reverted instinctively to the pardon of offences. "It has never occurred to Mr. Winterbourne to offer me any tea," she said with her finest little intention of torment and triumph.

"I've offered you excellent advice," the young man permitted himself to growl.

"I prefer weak tea!" cried Daisy, and she went off with the brilliant Giovanelli. She sat with him in the adjoining room, in the embrasure of the window, for the rest of the evening. There was an interesting performance at the piano, but neither of these conversers gave heed to it. When Daisy came to take leave of Mrs. Walker this lady conscientiously repaired the weakness of which she had been guilty at the moment of the girl's arrival—she turned her back straight on Miss Miller and left her to depart with what grace she might. Winterbourne happened to be near the door; he saw it all. Daisy turned very pale and looked at her mother, but Mrs. Miller was humbly unconscious of any rupture of any law or of any deviation from any custom. She appeared indeed to have felt an incongruous impulse to draw attention to her own striking conformity. "Good-night, Mrs. Walker," she said; "we've had a beautiful evening. You see if I let Daisy come to parties without me I don't want her to go away without me." Daisy turned away, looking with a small white prettiness, a blighted grace, at the circle near the door: Winterbourne saw that for the first moment she was too much shocked and puzzled even for indignation. He on his side was greatly touched.

"That was very cruel," he promptly remarked to Mrs. Walker.

But this lady's face was also as a stone. "She never enters my drawing-room again."

Since Winterbourne then, hereupon, was not to meet her in Mrs. Walker's drawing-room he went as often as possible to Mrs. Miller's hotel. The ladies were rarely at home, but when he found them the devoted Giovanelli was always present. Very often the glossy little Roman, serene in success, but not unduly presumptuous, occupied with Daisy alone the florid salon enjoyed by Eugenio's care, Mrs. Miller being apparently ever of the opinion that discretion is the better part of solicitude. Winterbourne noted, at first with surprise, that Daisy on these occasions was neither embarrassed nor annoyed by his own entrance; but he presently began to feel that she had no more surprises for him and that he really liked, after all, not making out what she was "up to." She showed no displeasure for the interruption of her *tête-à-tête* with Giovanelli; she could chatter as freshly and freely with two gentlemen as with one, and this easy flow had ever the same anomaly for her earlier friend that it was so free without availing itself of its freedom. Winterbourne reflected that if she was seriously interested in the Italian it was odd she should n't take more trouble to preserve the sanctity of their interviews, and he liked her the better for her innocent-looking indifference and her inexhaustible gaiety. He could hardly have said why, but she struck him as a young person not formed for a troublesome jealousy. Smile at such a betrayal though the reader may, it was a fact with regard to the women who had hitherto interested him that, given certain contingencies, Winterbourne could see himself afraid—literally afraid—of these ladies. It pleased him to believe that even were twenty other things different and Daisy should love him and he should know it and like it, he would still never be afraid of Daisy. It must be added that this conviction was not altogether flattering to her: it represented that she was nothing every way if not light.

But she was evidently very much interested in Giovanelli. She looked at him whenever he spoke; she was perpetually telling him to do this and to do that; she was constantly chaffing and abusing him. She appeared completely to have forgotten that her other friend had said anything to displease her at Mrs. Walker's entertainment. One Sunday afternoon, having gone to Saint Peter's with his aunt, Winterbourne became aware that the young woman held in horror by that lady was strolling about the great church under escort of her coxcomb of the Corso.[35] It amused him, after a debate, to point out the exemplary pair—even at the cost, as it proved, of Mrs. Costello's saying when she had taken them in through her eye-glass: "That's what makes you so pensive in these days, eh?"

"I had n't the least idea I was pensive," he pleaded.

"You're very much preoccupied; you're always thinking of something."

"And what is it," he asked, "that you accuse me of thinking of?"

"Of that young lady's, Miss Baker's, Miss Chandler's—what's her name?—Miss Miller's intrigue with that little barber's block."

"Do you call it an intrigue," he asked—"an affair that goes on with such peculiar publicity?"

"That's their folly," said Mrs. Costello, "it's not their merit."

"No," he insisted with a hint perhaps of the preoccupation to which his aunt had alluded—"I don't believe there's anything to be called an intrigue."

"Well"—and Mrs. Costello dropped her glass—"I've heard a dozen people speak of it: they say she's quite carried away by him."

"They're certainly as thick as thieves," our embarrassed young man allowed.

Mrs. Costello came back to them, however, after a little; and Winterbourne recognized in this a further illustration—than that supplied by his own condition—of the spell projected by the case. "He's certainly very handsome. One easily sees how it is. She thinks him the most elegant man in the world, the finest gentleman possible. She has never seen anything like him—he's better even than the courier. It was the courier probably who introduced him, and if he succeeds in marrying the young lady the courier will come in for a magnificent commission."

"I don't believe she thinks of marrying him," Winterbourne reasoned, "and I don't believe he hopes to marry her."

"You may be very sure she thinks of nothing at all. She romps on from day to day, from hour to hour, as they did in the Golden Age. I can imagine nothing more vulgar," said Mrs. Costello, whose figure of speech scarcely went on all fours. "And at the same time," she added, "depend upon it she may tell you any moment that she is 'engaged.'"

"I think that's more than Giovanelli really expects," said Winterbourne.

"And who is Giovanelli?"

"The shiny— but, to do him justice, not greasy—little Roman. I've asked questions about him and learned something. He's apparently a perfectly respectable little man. I believe he's in a small way a *cavaliere avvocato*.[36] But he does n't move in what are called the first circles. I think it really not absolutely impossible the courier introduced him. He's evidently immensely charmed with Miss Miller. If she thinks him the finest gentleman in the world, he, on his side, has never found himself in personal contact with such splendour, such opulence, such personal daintiness, as this young lady's. And then she must seem to him wonderfully pretty and interesting. Yes, he can't really hope to pull it off. That must appear to him too impossible a piece of luck. He has nothing but his handsome face to offer, and there's a substantial, a possibly explosive Mr. Miller in that mysterious land of dollars and six-shooters. Giovanelli's but too

---

[35] Roman street.

[36] Italian: "lawyer from the upper classes."

conscious that he has n't a title to offer. If he were only a count or a *marchese!* [37] What on earth can he make of the way they've taken him up?"

"He accounts for it by his handsome face and thinks Miss Miller a young lady *qui se passe ses fantaisies!*"[38]

"It's very true," Winterbourne pursued, "that Daisy and her mamma have n't yet risen to that stage of—what shall I call it—of culture, at which the idea of catching a count or a *marchese* begins. I believe them intellectually incapable of that conception."

"Ah but the *cavaliere avvocato* does n't believe them!" cried Mrs. Costello.

Of the observation excited by Daisy's "intrigue" Winterbourne gathered that day at Saint Peter's sufficient evidence. A dozen of the American colonists in Rome came to talk with his relative, who sat on a small portable stool at the base of one of the great pilasters. The vesper-service was going forward in splendid chants and organ-tones in the adjacent choir, and meanwhile, between Mrs. Costello and her friends, much was said about poor little Miss Miller's going really "too far." Winterbourne was not pleased with what he heard; but when, coming out upon the great steps of the church, he saw Daisy, who had emerged before him, get into an open cab with her accomplice and roll away through the cynical streets of Rome, the measure of her course struck him as simply there to take. He felt very sorry for her—not exactly that he believed she had completely lost her wits, but because it was painful to see so much that was pretty and undefended and natural sink so low in human estimation. He made an attempt after this to give a hint to Mrs. Miller. He met one day in the Corso a friend—a tourist like himself—who had just come out of the Doria Palace, where he had been walking through the beautiful gallery. His friend "went on" for some moments about the great portrait of Innocent X, by Velasquez,[39] suspended in one of the cabinets of the palace; and then said: "And in the same cabinet, by the way, I enjoyed sight of an image of a different kind; that little American who's so much more a work of nature than of art and whom you pointed out to me last week." In answer to Winterbourne's enquiries his friend narrated that the little American—prettier now than ever—was seated with a companion in the secluded nook in which the papal presence is enshrined.

"All alone?" the young man heard himself disingenuously ask.

"Alone with a little Italian who sports in his button-hole a stack of flowers. The girl's a charming beauty, but I thought I understood from you the other day that she's a young lady *du meilleur monde.*"[40]

"So she is!" said Winterbourne; and having assured himself that his informant had seen the interesting pair but ten minutes before, he jumped into a cab and went to call on Mrs. Miller. She was at home, but she apologised for receiving him in Daisy's absence.

"She's gone out somewhere with Mr. Giovanelli. She's always going round with Mr. Giovanelli."

"I've noticed they're intimate indeed," Winterbourne concurred.

---

[37] Marquis; one of noble rank.
[38] French: "who submits to her caprices."
[39] Diego Rodriguez de Silva y Velàsquez

(1599–1660), Spanish painter of the portrait of Pope Innocent X.
[40] French: "of the best society."

"Oh it seems as if they could n't live without each other!" said Mrs. Miller. "Well, he's a real gentleman anyhow. I guess I have the joke on Daisy—that she *must* be engaged!"

"And how does your daughter *take* the joke?"

"Oh she just says she ain't. But she might as *well* be!" this philosophic parent resumed. "She goes on as if she was. But I've made Mr. Giovanelli promise to tell me if Daisy don't. I'd want to write to Mr. Miller about it—would n't you?"

Winterbourne replied that he certainly should; and the state of mind of Daisy's mamma struck him as so unprecedented in the annals of parental vigilance that he recoiled before the attempt to educate at a single interview either her conscience or her wit.

After this Daisy was never at home and he ceased to meet her at the houses of their common acquaintance, because, as he perceived, these shrewd people had quite made up their minds as to the length she must have gone. They ceased to invite her, intimating that they wished to make, and make strongly, for the benefit of observant Europeans, the point that though Miss Daisy Miller was a pretty American girl all right, her behaviour was n't pretty at all—was in fact regarded by her compatriots as quite monstrous. Winterbourne wondered how she felt about all the cold shoulders that were turned upon her, and sometimes found himself suspecting with impatience that she simply did n't feel and did n't know. He set her down as hopelessly childish and shallow, as such mere giddiness and ignorance incarnate as was powerless either to heed or to suffer. Then at other moments he could n't doubt that she carried about in her elegant and irresponsible little organism a defiant, passionate, perfectly observant consciousness of the impression she produced. He asked himself whether the defiance would come from the consciousness of innocence or from her being essentially a young person of the reckless class. Then it had to be admitted, he felt, that holding fast to a belief in her "innocence" was more and more but a matter of gallantry too fine-spun for use. As I have already had occasion to relate, he was reduced without pleasure to this chopping of logic and vexed at his poor fallibility, his want of instinctive certitude as to how far her extravagance was generic and national and how far it was crudely personal. Whatever it was he had helplessly missed her, and now it was too late. She was "carried away" by Mr. Giovanelli.

A few days after his brief interview with her mother he came across her at that supreme seat of flowering desolation known as the Palace of the Cæsars.[41] The early Roman spring had filled the air with bloom and perfume, and the rugged surface of the Palatine was muffled with tender verdure. Daisy moved at her ease over the great mounds of ruin that are embanked with mossy marble and paved with monumental inscriptions. It seemed to him he had never known Rome so lovely as just then. He looked off at the enchanting harmony of line and colour that remotely encircles the city—he inhaled the softly humid odours and felt the freshness of the year and the antiquity of the place reaffirm themselves in deep interfusion. It struck him also that Daisy had never showed to the eye for so utterly charming; but this had been his conviction on every occasion of their meeting. Giovanelli was of course at her side,

---

[41] Roman palace, now in ruins, on the Palatine Hill.

and Giovanelli too glowed as never before with something of the glory of his race.

"Well," she broke out upon the friend it would have been such mockery to designate as the latter's rival, "I should think you'd be quite lonesome!"

"Lonesome?" Winterbourne resignedly echoed.

"You're always going round by yourself. Can't you get any one to walk with you?"

"I'm not so fortunate," he answered, "as your gallant companion."

Giovanelli had from the first treated him with distinguished politeness; he listened with a deferential air to his remarks; he laughed punctiliously at his pleasantries; he attached such importance as he could find terms for to Miss Miller's cold compatriot. He carried himself in no degree like a jealous wooer; he had obviously a great deal of tact; he had no objection to any one's expecting a little humility of him. It even struck Winterbourne that he almost yearned at times for some private communication in the interest of his character for common sense; a chance to remark to him as another intelligent man that, bless him, *he* knew how extraordinary was their young lady and did n't flatter himself with confident—at least *too* confident and too delusive—hopes of matrimony and dollars. On this occasion he strolled away from his charming charge to pluck a sprig of almond-blossom which he carefully arranged in his button-hole.

"I know why you say that," Daisy meanwhile observed. "Because you think I go round too much with *him!*" And she nodded at her discreet attendant.

"Every one thinks so—if you care to know," was all Winterbourne found to reply.

"Of course I care to know!"—she made this point with much expression. "But I don't believe a word of it. They're only pretending to be shocked. They don't really care a straw what I do. Besides, I don't go round so much."

"I think you'll find they do care. They'll show it—disagreeably," he took on himself to state.

Daisy weighed the importance of that idea. "How—disagreeably?"

"Have n't you noticed anything?" he compassionately asked.

"I've noticed *you*. But I noticed you've no more 'give' than a ramrod the first time ever I saw you."

"You'll find at least that I've more 'give' than several others," he patiently smiled.

"How shall I find it?"

"By going to see the others."

"What will they do to me?"

"They'll show you the cold shoulder. Do you know what that means?"

Daisy was looking at him intently; she began to colour. "Do you mean as Mrs. Walker did the other night?"

"Exactly as Mrs. Walker did the other night."

She looked away at Giovanelli, still titivating with his almond-blossom. Then with her attention again on the important subject: "I should n't think you'd let people be so unkind!"

"How can I help it?"

"I should think you'd want to say something."

"I do want to say something"—and Winterbourne paused a moment. "I want to say that your mother tells me she believes you engaged."

"Well, I guess she does," said Daisy very simply.

The young man began to laugh. "And does Randolph believe it?"

"I guess Randolph does n't believe anything." This testimony to Randolph's scepticism excited Winterbourne to further mirth, and he noticed that Giovanelli was coming back to them. Daisy, observing it as well, addressed herself again to her countryman. "Since you've mentioned it," she said, "I *am* engaged." He looked at her hard—he had stopped laughing. "You don't believe it!" she added.

He asked himself, and it was for a moment like testing a heart-beat; after which, "Yes, I believe it!" he said.

"Oh no, you don't," she answered. "But *if* you possibly do," she still more perversely pursued—"well, I ain't!"

Miss Miller and her constant guide were on their way to the gate of the enclosure, so that Winterbourne, who had but lately entered, presently took leave of them. A week later on he went to dine at a beautiful villa on the Cælian Hill, and, on arriving, dismissed his hired vehicle. The evening was perfect, and he promised himself the satisfaction of walking home beneath the Arch of Constantine and past the vaguely-lighted monuments of the Forum.[42] Above was a moon half-developed, whose radiance was not brilliant but veiled in a thin cloud-curtain that seemed to diffuse and equalise it. When on his return from the villa at eleven o'clock he approached the dusky circle of the Colosseum the sense of the romantic in him easily suggested that the interior, in such an atmosphere, would well repay a glance. He turned aside and walked to one of the empty arches, near which, as he observed, an open carriage—one of the little Roman street-cabs—was stationed. Then he passed in among the cavernous shadows of the great structure and emerged upon the clear and silent arena. The place had never seemed to him more impressive. One half of the gigantic circus was in deep shade while the other slept in the luminous dusk. As he stood there he began to murmur Byron's famous lines out of "Manfred";[43] but before he had finished his quotation he remembered that if nocturnal meditation thereabouts was the fruit of a rich literary culture it was none the less deprecated by medical science. The air of other ages surrounded one; but the air of other ages, coldly analysed, was no better than a villainous miasma. Winterbourne sought, however, toward the middle of the arena, a further reach of vision, intending the next moment a hasty retreat. The great cross in the centre was almost obscured; only as he drew near did he make it out distinctly. He thus also distinguished two persons stationed on the low steps that formed its base. One of these was a woman seated; her companion hovered before her.

Presently the sound of the woman's voice came to him distinctly in the warm night-air. "Well, he looks at us as one of the old lions or tigers may have looked at the Christian martyrs!" These words were winged with their accent, so that they fluttered and settled about him in the darkness like vague white doves. It was Miss Daisy Miller who had released them for flight.

"Let us hope he's not very hungry"—the bland Giovanelli fell in with her humour. "He'll have to take *me* first; you'll serve for dessert."

Winterbourne felt himself pulled up with final horror now—and, it must be added, with final relief. It was as if a sudden clearance had taken place in the ambiguity of the poor girl's appearances and the whole riddle of her contradictions had grown easy

---

[42] Remnants of ancient constructions from the time of imperial Rome.

[43] Lord Byron's verse drama of 1817.

to read. She was a young lady about the *shades* of whose perversity a foolish puzzled gentleman need no longer trouble his head or his heart. That once questionable quantity *had* no shades—it was a mere black little blot. He stood there looking at her, looking at her companion too, and not reflecting that though he saw them vaguely he himself must have been more brightly presented. He felt angry at all his shiftings of view—he felt ashamed of all his tender little scruples and all his witless little mercies. He was about to advance again, and then again checked himself; not from the fear of doing her injustice, but from a sense of the danger of showing undue exhilaration for this disburdenment of cautious criticism. He turned away toward the entrance of the place; but as he did so he heard Daisy speak again.

"Why it was Mr. Winterbourne! He saw me and he cuts me dead!"

What a clever little reprobate she was, he was amply able to reflect at this, and how smartly she feigned, how promptly she sought to play off on him, a surprised and injured innocence! But nothing would induce him to cut her either "dead" or to within any measurable distance even of the famous "inch" of her life. He came forward again and went toward the great cross. Daisy had got up and Giovanelli lifted his hat. Winterbourne had now begun to think simply of the madness, on the ground of exposure and infection, of a frail young creature's lounging away such hours in a nest of malaria. What if she *were* the most plausible of little reprobates? That was no reason for her dying of the *perniciosa.* [44] "How long have you been 'fooling round' here?" he asked with conscious roughness.

Daisy, lovely in the sinister silver radiance, appraised him a moment, roughness and all. "Well, I guess all the evening." She answered with spirit and, he could see even then, with exaggeration. "I never saw anything so quaint."

"I'm afraid," he returned, "you'll not think a bad attack of Roman fever very quaint. This is the way people catch it. I wonder," he added to Giovanelli, "that you, a native Roman, should countenance such extraordinary rashness."

"Ah," said this seasoned subject, "for myself I have no fear."

"Neither have I—for you!" Winterbourne retorted in French. "I'm speaking for this young lady."

Giovanelli raised his well-shaped eyebrows and showed his shining teeth, but took his critic's rebuke with docility. "I assured Mademoiselle it was a grave indiscretion, but when was Mademoiselle ever prudent?"

"I never was sick, and I don't mean to be!" Mademoiselle declared. "I don't look like much, but I'm healthy! I was bound to see the Colosseum by moonlight—I would n't have wanted to go home without *that;* and we've had the most beautiful time, have n't we, Mr. Giovanelli? If there has been any danger Eugenio can give me some pills. Eugenio has got some splendid pills."

"*I* should advise you then," said Winterbourne, "to drive home as fast as possible and take one!"

Giovanelli smiled as for the striking happy thought. "What you say is very wise. I'll go and make sure the carriage is at hand." And he went forward rapidly.

Daisy followed with Winterbourne. He tried to deny himself the small fine anguish of looking at her, but his eyes themselves refused to spare him, and she seemed moreover not in the least embarrassed. He spoke no word; Daisy chattered over the

[44] Malaria, known locally as "the Roman fever."

beauty of the place: "Well, I *have* seen the Colosseum by moonlight—that's one thing I can rave about!" Then noticing her companion's silence she asked him why he was so stiff—it had always been her great word. He made no answer, but he felt his laugh an immense negation of stiffness. They passed under one of the dark archways; Giovanelli was in front with the carriage. Here Daisy stopped a moment, looking at her compatriot. *"Did* you believe I was engaged the other day?"

"It does n't matter now what I believed the other day!" he replied with infinite point.

It was a wonder how she did n't wince for it. "Well, what do you believe now?"

"I believe it makes very little difference whether you're engaged or not!"

He felt her lighted eyes fairly penetrate the thick gloom of the vaulted passage—as if to seek some access to him she had n't yet compassed. But Giovanelli, with a graceful inconsequence, was at present all for retreat. "Quick, quick; if we get in by midnight we're quite safe!"

Daisy took her seat in the carriage and the fortunate Italian placed himself beside her. "Don't forget Eugenio's pills!" said Winterbourne as he lifted his hat.

"I don't care," she unexpectedly cried out for this, "whether I have Roman fever or not!" On which the cab-driver cracked his whip and they rolled across the desultory patches of antique pavement.

Winterbourne—to do him justice, as it were—mentioned to no one that he had encountered Miss Miller at midnight in the Colosseum with a gentleman; in spite of which deep discretion, however, the fact of the scandalous adventure was known a couple of days later, with a dozen vivid details, to every member of the little American circle, and was commented accordingly. Winterbourne judged thus that the people about the hotel had been thoroughly empowered to testify, and that after Daisy's return there would have been an exchange of jokes between the porter and the cab-driver. But the young man became aware at the same moment of how thoroughly it had ceased to ruffle him that the little American flirt should be "talked about" by low-minded menials. These sources of current criticism a day or two later abounded still further: the little American flirt was alarmingly ill and the doctors now in possession of the scene. Winterbourne, when the rumour came to him, immediately went to the hotel for more news. He found that two or three charitable friends had preceded him and that they were being entertained in Mrs. Miller's salon by the all-efficient Randolph.

"It's going round at night that way, you bet—that's what has made her so sick. She's always going round at night. I should n't think she'd want to—it's so plaguey dark over here. You can't see anything over here without the moon's right up. In America they don't go round by the moon!" Mrs. Miller meanwhile wholly surrendered to her genius for unapparent uses; her salon knew her less than ever, and she was presumably now at least giving her daughter the advantage of her society. It was clear that Daisy was dangerously ill.

Winterbourne constantly attended for news from the sick-room, which reached him, however, but with worrying indirectness, though he once had speech, for a moment, of the poor girl's physician and once saw Mrs. Miller, who, sharply alarmed, struck him as thereby more happily inspired than he could have conceived and indeed as the most noiseless and light-handed of nurses. She invoked a good deal the remote shade of Dr. Davis, but Winterbourne paid her the compliment of taking her after all for less monstrous a goose. To this indulgence indeed something she further said perhaps even more insidiously disposed him. "Daisy spoke of you the other day quite pleasantly. Half the time she does n't know what she's saying, but that time I think she did. She gave me a message—she told me to tell you. She wanted you to know she never was engaged to that handsome Italian who was always round. I'm sure I'm very glad; Mr. Giovanelli has n't been near us since she was taken ill. I thought he was so much of a gentleman, but I don't call that very polite! A lady told me he was afraid I had n't approved of his being round with her so much evenings. Of course it ain't as if their evenings were as pleasant as ours—since *we* don't seem to feel that way about the poison. I guess I *don't* see the point now; but I suppose he knows I'm a lady and I'd scorn to raise a fuss. Anyway, she wants you to realise she ain't engaged. I don't know why she makes so much of it, but she said to me three times 'Mind you tell Mr. Winterbourne.' And then she told me to ask if you remembered the time you went up to that castle in Switzerland. But I said I would n't give any messages as *that*. Only if she ain't engaged I guess I'm glad to realise it too."

But, as Winterbourne had originally judged, the truth on this question had small actual relevance. A week after this the poor girl died; it had been indeed a terrible case of the *perniciosa*. A grave was found for her in the little Protestant cemetery, by an angle of the wall of imperial Rome, beneath the cypresses and the thick spring-flowers. Winterbourne stood there beside it with a number of other mourners; a number larger than the scandal excited by the young lady's career might have made probable. Near him stood Giovanelli, who came nearer still before Winterbourne turned away. Giovanelli, in decorous mourning, showed but a whiter face; his button-hole lacked its nosegay and he had visibly something urgent—and even to distress—to say, which he scarce knew how to "place." He decided at last to confide it with a pale convulsion to Winterbourne. "She was the most beautiful young lady I ever saw, and the most amiable." To which he added in a moment: "Also—naturally! —the most innocent."

Winterbourne sounded him with hard dry eyes, but presently repeated his words, "The most innocent?"

"The most innocent!"

It came somehow so much too late that our friend could only glare at its having come at all. "Why the devil," he asked, "did you take her to that fatal place?"

Giovanelli raised his neat shoulders and eyebrows to within suspicion of a shrug. "For myself I had no fear; and *she*—she did what she liked."

Winterbourne's eyes attached themselves to the ground. "She did what she liked!"

It determined on the part of poor Giovanelli a further pious, a further candid, confidence. "If she had lived I should have got nothing. She never would have married me."

It had been spoken as if to attest, in all sincerity, his disinterestedness, but Winterbourne scarce knew what welcome to give it. He said, however, with a grace inferior to his friend's: "I dare say not."

The latter was even by this not discouraged. "For a moment I hoped so. But no. I'm convinced."

Winterbourne took it in; he stood staring at the raw protuberance among the April daisies. When he turned round again his fellow mourner had stepped back.

He almost immediately left Rome, but the following summer he again met his aunt

Mrs. Costello at Vevey. Mrs. Costello extracted from the charming old hotel there a value that the Miller family had n't mastered the secret of. In the interval Winterbourne had often thought of the most interesting member of that trio—of her mystifying manners and her queer adventure. One day he spoke of her to his aunt —said it was on his conscience he had done her injustice.

"I'm sure I don't know"—that lady showed caution. "How did your injustice affect her?"

"She sent me a message before her death which I did n't understand at the time. But I've understood it since. She would have appreciated one's esteem."

"She took an odd way to gain it! But do you mean by what you say," Mrs. Costello asked, "that she would have reciprocated one's affection?"

As he made no answer to this he after a little looked round at him—he had n't been directly within sight; but the effect of that was n't to make her repeat her question. He spoke, however, after a while. "You were right in that remark that you made last summer. I was booked to make a mistake. I've lived too long in foreign parts." And this time she herself said nothing.

Nevertheless he soon went back to live at Geneva, whence there continue to come the most contradictory accounts of his motives of sojourn: a report that he's "studying" hard—an intimation that he's much interested in a very clever foreign lady.

1909

The Beast in the Jungle

I

What determined the speech that startled him in the course of their encounter scarcely matters, being probably but some words spoken by himself quite without intention —spoken as they lingered and slowly moved together after their renewal of acquaintance. He had been conveyed by friends an hour or two before to the house at which she was staying; the party of visitors at the other house, of whom he was one, and thanks to whom it was his theory, as always, that he was lost in the crowd, had been invited over to luncheon. There had been after luncheon much dispersal, all in the interest of the original motive, a view of Weatherend itself and the fine things, intrinsic features, pictures, heirlooms, treasures of all the arts, that made the place almost famous; and the great rooms were so numerous that guests could wander at their will, hang back from the principal group and in cases where they took such matters with the last seriousness give themselves up to mysterious appreciations and measurements. There were persons to be observed, singly or in couples, bending toward objects in out-of-the-way corners with their hands on their knees and their heads nodding quite as with the emphasis of an excited sense of smell. When they were two they either mingled their sounds of ecstasy or melted into silences of even deeper import, so that there were aspects of the occasion that gave it for Marcher much the air of the "look round," previous to a sale highly advertised, that excites or quenches, as may be, the dream of acquisition. The dream of acquisition at Weatherend would have had to be wild indeed, and John Marcher found himself, among such suggestions, disconcerted almost equally by the presence of those who knew too much and by that of those who knew nothing. The great rooms caused so much poetry and history to press upon him that he needed some straying apart to feel in a proper relation with them, though this impulse was not, as happened, like the gloating of some of his companions, to be compared to the movements of a dog sniffing a cupboard. It had an issue promptly enough in a direction that was not to have been calculated.

It led, briefly, in the course of the October afternoon, to his closer meeting with May Bartram, whose face, a reminder, yet not quite a remembrance, as they sat much separated at a very long table, had begun merely by troubling him rather pleasantly. It affected him as the sequel of something of which he had lost the beginning. He knew it, and for the time quite welcomed it, as a continuation, but did n't know what it continued, which was an interest or an amusement the greater as he was also somehow aware—yet without a direct sign from her—that the young woman herself had n't lost the thread. She had n't lost it, but she would n't give it back to him, he saw, without some putting forth of his hand for it; and he not only saw that, but saw several things more, things odd enough in the light of the fact that at the moment some accident of grouping brought them face to face he was still merely fumbling with the idea that any contact between them in the past would have had no importance. If it had had no importance he scarcely knew why his actual impression of her should so seem to have so much; the answer to which, however, was that in such a life as they all appeared to be leading for the moment one could but take things as they came. He was satisfied, without in the least being able to say why, that this young lady might roughly have ranked in the house as a poor relation; satisfied also that she was not there on a brief visit, but was more or less a part of the establishment—almost a working, a remunerated part. Did n't she enjoy at periods a protection that she paid for by helping, among other services, to show the place and explain it, deal with the tiresome people, answer questions about the dates of the building, the styles of the furniture, the authorship of the pictures, the favourite haunts of the ghost? It was n't that she looked as if you could have given her shillings—it was impossible to look less so. Yet when she finally drifted toward him, distinctly handsome, though ever so much older—older than when he had seen her before—it might have been as an effect of her guessing that he had, within the couple of hours, devoted more imagination to her than to all the others put together, and had thereby penetrated to a kind of truth that the others were too stupid for. She *was* there on harder terms than any one; she was there as a consequence of things suffered, one way and another, in the interval of years; and she remembered him very much as she was remembered—only a good deal better.

By the time they at last thus came to speech they were alone in one of the rooms —remarkable for a fine portrait over the chimney-place—out of which their friends had passed, and the charm of it was that even before they had spoken they had practically arranged with each other to stay behind for talk. The charm, happily, was in other things too—partly in there being scarce a spot at Weatherend without something to stay behind for. It was in the way the autumn day looked into the high windows as it waned; the way the red light, breaking at the close from under a low sombre sky, reached out in a long shaft and played over old wainscots, old tapestry, old gold, old colour. It was most of all perhaps in the way she came to him as if, since she had been turned on to deal with the simpler sort, he might, should he choose to keep the whole thing down, just take her mild attention for a part of her general business. As soon as he heard her voice, however, the gap was filled up and the missing link supplied; the slight irony he divined in her attitude lost its advantage. He almost jumped at it to get there before her. "I met you years and years ago in Rome. I remember all about it." She confessed to disappointment—she had been so sure he did n't; and to prove how well he did he began to pour forth the particular recollections that popped up as he called for them. Her face and her voice, all at his service now, worked the miracle—the impression operating like the torch of a lamplighter who touches into flame, one by one, a long row of gas-jets. Marcher flattered himself the illumination was brilliant, yet he was really still more pleased on her showing him, with amusement, that in his haste to make everything right he had got most things rather wrong. It had n't been at Rome—it had been at Naples; and it had n't been eight years before—it had been more nearly ten. She had n't been, either, with her uncle and aunt, but with her mother and her brother; in addition to which it was not with the Pembles *he* had been, but with the Boyers, coming down in their company from Rome—a point on which she insisted, a little to his confusion, and as to which she had her evidence in hand. The Boyers she had known, but did n't know the Pembles, though she had heard of them, and it was the people he was with who had made them acquainted. The incident of the thunderstorm that had raged round them with such violence as to drive them for refuge into an excavation—this incident had not occurred at the Palace of the Cæsars, but at Pompeii,[1] on an occasion when they had been present there at an important find.

He accepted her amendments, he enjoyed her corrections, though the moral of them was, she pointed out, that he *really* did n't remember the least thing about her; and he only felt it as a drawback that when all was made strictly historic there did n't appear much of anything left. They lingered together still, she neglecting her office —for from the moment he was so clever she had no proper right to him—and both neglecting the house, just waiting as to see if a memory or two more would n't again breathe on them. It had n't taken them many minutes, after all, to put down on the table, like the cards of a pack, those that constituted their respective hands; only what came out was that the pack was unfortunately not perfect—that the past, invoked, invited, encouraged, could give them, naturally, no more than it had. It had made them anciently meet—her at twenty, him at twenty-five; but nothing was so strange, they seemed to say to each other, as that, while so occupied, it had n't done a little more for them. They looked at each other as with the feeling of an occasion missed; the present would have been so much better if the other, in the far distance, in the foreign land, had n't been so stupidly meagre. There were n't apparently, all counted, more than a dozen little old things that had succeeded in coming to pass between them; trivialities of youth, simplicities of freshness, stupidities of ignorance, small possible germs, but too deeply buried—too deeply (did n't it seem?) to sprout after so many years. Marcher could only feel he ought to have rendered her some service—saved her from a capsized boat in the Bay or at least recovered her dressing-bag, filched from

---

[1] I.e., not in Rome but at the ancient city near Naples.

her cab in the streets of Naples by a lazzarone[2] with a stiletto. Or it would have been nice if he could have been taken with fever all alone at his hotel, and she could have come to look after him, to write to his people, to drive him out in convalescence. *Then* they would be in possession of the something or other that their actual show seemed to lack. It yet somehow presented itself, this show, as too good to be spoiled; so that they were reduced for a few minutes more to wondering a little helplessly why—since they seemed to know a certain number of the same people—their reunion had been so long averted. They did n't use that name for it but their delay from minute to minute to join the others was a kind of confession that they did n't quite want it to be a failure. Their attempted supposition of reasons for their not having met but showed how little they knew of each other. There came in fact a moment when Marcher felt a positive pang. It was vain to pretend she was an old friend, for all the communities were wanting, in spite of which it was as an old friend that he saw she would have suited him. He had new ones enough—was surrounded with them for instance on the stage of the other house; as a new one he probably would n't have so much as noticed her. He would have liked to invent something, get her to make-believe with him that some passage of a romantic or critical kind *had* originally occurred. He was really almost reaching out in imagination—as against time—for something that would do, and saying to himself that if it did n't come this sketch of a fresh start would show for quite awkwardly bungled. They would separate, and now for no second or no third chance. They would have tried and not succeeded. Then it was, just at the turn, as he afterwards made it out to himself, that, everything else failing, she herself decided to take up the case and, as it were, save the situation. He felt as soon as she spoke that she had been consciously keeping back what she said and hoping to get on without it; a scruple in her that immensely touched him when, by the end of three or four minutes more, he was able to measure it. What she brought out, at any rate, quite cleared the air and supplied the link—the link it was so odd he should frivolously have managed to lose.

"You know you told me something I've never forgotten and that again and again has made me think of you since; it was that tremendously hot day when we went to Sorrento,[3] across the bay, for the breeze. What I allude to was what you said to me, on the way back, as we sat under the awning of the boat enjoying the cool. Have you forgotten?"

He had forgotten and was even more surprised than ashamed. But the great thing was that he saw in this no vulgar reminder of any "sweet" speech. The vanity of women had long memories, but she was making no claim on him of a compliment or a mistake. With another woman, a totally different one, he might have feared the recall possibly even some imbecile "offer." So, in having to say that he had indeed forgotten, he was conscious rather of a loss than of a gain; he already saw an interest in the matter of her mention. "I try to think—but I give it up. Yet I remember the Sorrento day."

"I'm not very sure you do," May Bartram after a moment said; "and I'm not very sure I ought to want you to. It's dreadful to bring a person back at any time to what he was ten years before. If you've lived away from it," she smiled, "so much the better."

---

[2] Neapolitan beggar.　　　　　　　　　　　[3] On the Bay of Naples.

"Ah if *you* have n't why should I?" he asked.

"Lived away, you mean, from what I myself was?"

"From what *I* was. I was of course an ass," Marcher went on; "but I would rather know from you just the sort of ass I was than—from the moment you have something in your mind—not know anything."

Still, however, she hesitated. "But if you've completely ceased to be that sort—?"

"Why I can then all the more bear to know. Besides, perhaps I have n't."

"Perhaps. Yet if you have n't," she added, "I should suppose you'd remember. Not indeed that *I* in the least connect with my impression the invidious name you use. If I had only thought you foolish," she explained, "the thing I speak of wouldn't so have remained with me. It was about yourself." She waited as if it might come to him; but as, only meeting her eyes in wonder, he gave no sign, she burnt her ships. "Has it ever happened?"

Then it was that, while he continued to stare, a light broke for him and the blood slowly came to his face, which began to burn with recognition. "Do you mean I told you—?" But he faltered, lest what came to him shouldn't be right, lest he should only give himself away.

"It was something about yourself that it was natural one should n't forget—that is if one remembered you at all. That's why I ask you," she smiled, "if the thing you then spoke of has ever come to pass?"

Oh then he saw, but he was lost in wonder and found himself embarrassed. This, he also saw, made her sorry for him, as if her allusion had been a mistake. It took him but a moment, however, to feel it had n't been, much as it had been a surprise. After the first little shock of it her knowledge on the contrary began, even if rather strangely, to taste sweet to him. She was the only other person in the world then who would have it, and she had had it all these years, while the fact of his having so breathed his secret had unaccountably faded from him. No wonder they could n't have met as if nothing had happened. "I judge," he finally said, "that I know what you mean. Only I had strangely enough lost any sense of having taken you so far into my confidence."

"Is it because you've taken so many others as well?"

"I've taken nobody. Not a creature since then."

"So that I'm the only person who knows?"

"The only person in the world."

"Well," she quickly replied, "I myself have never spoken. I've never, never repeated of you what you told me." She looked at him so that he perfectly believed her. Their eyes met over it in such a way that he was without a doubt. "And I never will."

She spoke with an earnestness that, as if almost excessive, put him at ease about her possible derision. Somehow the whole question was a new luxury to him—that is from the moment she was in possession. If she did n't take the sarcastic view she clearly took the sympathetic, and that was what he had had, in all the long time, from no one whomsoever. What he felt was that he could n't at present have begun to tell her, and yet could profit perhaps exquisitely by the accident of having done so of old. "Please don't then. We're just right as it is."

"Oh I am," she laughed, "if you are!" To which she added: "Then you do still feel in the same way?"

It was impossible he should n't take to himself that she was really interested, though it all kept coming as perfect surprise. He had thought of himself so long as abominably alone, and lo he was n't alone a bit. He had n't been, it appeared, for an hour—since those moments on the Sorrento boat. It was *she* who had been, he seemed to see as he looked at her—she who had been made so by the graceless fact of his lapse of fidelity. To tell her what he had told her—what had it been but to ask something of her? something that she had given, in her charity, without his having, by a remembrance, by a return of the spirit, failing another encounter, so much as thanked her. What he had asked of her had been simply at first not to laugh at him. She had beautifully not done so for ten years, and she was not doing so now. So he had endless gratitude to make up. Only for that he must see just how he had figured to her. "What, exactly, was the account I gave—?"

"Of the way you did feel? Well, it was very simple. You said you had had from your earliest time, as the deepest thing within you, the sense of being kept for something rare and strange, possibly prodigious and terrible, that was sooner or later to happen to you, that you had in your bones the foreboding and the conviction of, and that would perhaps overwhelm you."

"Do you call that very simple?" John Marcher asked.

She thought a moment. "It was perhaps because I seemed, as you spoke, to understand it."

"You do understand it?" he eagerly asked.

Again she kept her kind eyes on him. "You still have the belief?"

"Oh!" he exclaimed helplessly. There was too much to say.

"Whatever it's to be," she clearly made out, "it has n't yet come."

He shook his head in complete surrender now. "It has n't yet come. Only, you know, it is n't anything I'm to *do*, to achieve in the world, to be distinguished or admired for. I'm not such an ass as *that*. It would be much better, no doubt, if I were."

"It's to be something you're merely to suffer?"

"Well, say to wait for—to have to meet, to face, to see suddenly break out in my life; possibly destroying all further consciousness, possibly annihilating me; possibly, on the other hand, only altering everything, striking at the root of all my world and leaving me to the consequences, however they shape themselves."

She took this in, but the light in her eyes continued for him not to be that of mockery. "Is n't what you describe perhaps but the expectation—or at any rate the sense of danger, familiar to so many people—of falling in love?"

John Marcher wondered. "Did you ask me that before?"

"No—I was n't so free-and-easy then. But it's what strikes me now."

"Of course," he said after a moment, "it strikes you. Of course it strikes *me*. Of course what's in store for me may be no more than that. The only thing is," he went on, "that I think if it had been that I should by this time know."

"Do you mean because you've *been* in love?" And then as he but looked at her in silence: "You've been in love, and it has n't meant such a cataclysm, has n't proved the great affair?"

"Here I am, you see. It has n't been overwhelming."

"Then it has n't been love," said May Bartram.

"Well, I at least thought it was. I took it for that—I've taken it till now. It was agreeable, it was delightful, it was miserable," he explained. "But it was n't strange. It was n't what *my* affair 's to be."

"You want something all to yourself—something that nobody else knows or *has* known?"

"It is n't a question of what I 'want'—God knows I don't want anything. It's only a question of the apprehension that haunts me—that I live with day by day."

He said this so lucidly and consistently that he could see it further impose itself. If she had n't been interested before she'd have been interested now. "Is it a sense of coming violence?"

Evidently now too again he liked to talk of it. "I don't think of it as—when it does come—necessarily violent. I only think of it as natural and as of course above all unmistakeable. I think of it simply as *the* thing. *The* thing will of itself appear natural."

"Then how will it appear strange?"

Marcher bethought himself. "It won't—to *me*."

"To whom then?"

"Well," he replied, smiling at last, "say to you."

"Oh then I'm to be present?"

"Why you *are* present—since you know."

"I see." She turned it over. "But I mean at the catastrophe."

At this, for a minute, their lightness gave way to their gravity; it was as if the long look they exchanged held them together. "It will only depend on yourself—if you'll watch with me."

"Are you afraid?" she asked.

"Don't leave me *now*," he went on.

"Are you afraid?" she repeated.

"Do you think me simply out of my mind?" he pursued instead of answering. "Do I merely strike you as a harmless lunatic?"

"No," said May Bartram. "I understand you. I believe you."

"You mean you feel how my obsession—poor old thing!—may correspond to some possible reality?"

"To some possible reality."

"Then you *will* watch with me?"

She hesitated, then for the third time put her question. "Are you afraid?"

"Did I tell you I was—at Naples?"

"No, you said nothing about it."

"Then I don't know. And I should *like* to know," said John Marcher. "You'll tell me yourself whether you think so. If you'll watch with me you'll see."

"Very good then." They had been moving by this time across the room, and at the door, before passing out, they paused as for the full wind-up of their understanding. "I'll watch with you," said May Bartram.

II

The fact that she "knew"—knew and yet neither chaffed him nor betrayed him— had in a short time begun to constitute between them a goodly bond, which became more marked when, within the year that followed their afternoon at Weatherend, the opportunities for meeting multiplied. The event that thus promoted these occasions was the death of the ancient lady her great-aunt, under whose wing, since losing her mother, she had to such an extent found shelter, and who, though but the widowed mother of the new successor to the property, had succeeded—thanks to a high tone and a high temper—in not forfeiting the supreme position at the great house. The deposition of this personage arrived but with her death, which, followed by many changes, made in particular a difference for the young woman in whom Marcher's expert attention had recognised from the first a dependent with a pride that might ache though it did n't bristle. Nothing for a long time had made him easier than the thought that the aching must have been much soothed by Miss Bartram's now finding herself able to set up a small home in London. She had acquired property, to an amount that made that luxury just possible, under her aunt's extremely complicated will, and when the whole matter began to be straightened out, which indeed took time, she let him know that the happy issue was at last in view. He had seen her again before that day, both because she had more than once accompanied the ancient lady to town and because he had paid another visit to the friends who so conveniently made of Weatherend one of the charms of their own hospitality. These friends had taken him back there; he had achieved there again with Miss Bartram some quiet detachment; and he had in London succeeded in persuading her to more than one brief absence from her aunt. They went together, on these latter occasions, to the National Gallery and the South Kensington Museum, where, among vivid reminders, they talked of Italy at large—not now attempting to recover, as at first, the taste of their youth and their ignorance. That recovery, the first day at Weatherend, had served its purpose well, had given them quite enough; so that they were, to Marcher's sense, no longer hovering about the headwaters of their stream, but had felt their boat pushed sharply off and down the current.

They were literally afloat together; for our gentleman this was marked, quite as marked as that the fortunate cause of it was just the buried treasure of her knowledge. He had with his own hands dug up this little hoard, brought to light—that is to within reach of the dim day constituted by their discretions and privacies—the object of value the hiding-place of which he had, after putting it into the ground himself, so strangely, so long forgotten. The rare luck of his having again just stumbled on the spot made him indifferent to any other question; he would doubtless have devoted more time to the odd accident of his lapse of memory if he had n't been moved to devote so much to the sweetness, the comfort, as he felt, for the future, that this accident itself had helped to keep fresh. It had never entered into his plan that any one should "know," and mainly for the reason that it was n't in him to tell any one. That would have been impossible, for nothing but the amusement of a cold world would have waited on it. Since, however, a mysterious fate had opened his mouth betimes, in spite of him, he would count that a compensation and profit by it to the utmost. That the right person *should* know tempered the asperity of his secret more even than his shyness had permitted him to imagine; and May Bartram was clearly right, because—well, because there she was. Her knowledge simply settled it; he would have been sure enough by this time had she been wrong. There was that in his situation, no doubt, that disposed him too much to see her as a mere confidant, taking all her light for him from the fact—the fact only—of her interest in his predicament; from her mercy, sympathy, seriousness, her consent not to regard him as the funniest of the funny. Aware, in fine, that her price for him was just in her giving him this constant sense of his being admirably spared, he was careful to remember that she had also a life of her own, with things that might happen to *her,* things that in friendship one should likewise take account of. Something fairly remarkable came to pass with him, for that matter, in this connexion—something represented by a certain passage of his consciousness, in the suddenest way, from one extreme to the other.

He had thought himself, so long as nobody knew, the most disinterested person in the world, carrying his concentrated burden, his perpetual suspense, ever so quietly, holding his tongue about it, giving others no glimpse of it nor of its effect upon his life, asking of them no allowance and only making on his side all those that were asked. He had n't disturbed people with the queerness of their having to know a haunted man, though he had had moments of rather special temptation on hearing them say they were forsooth "unsettled." If they were as unsettled as he was—he who had never been settled for an hour in his life—they would know what it meant. Yet it was n't, all the same, for him to make them, and he listened to them civilly enough. This was why he had such good—though possibly such rather colourless—manners; this was why, above all, he could regard himself, in a greedy world, as decently— as in fact perhaps even a little sublimely—unselfish. Our point is accordingly that he valued this character quite sufficiently to measure his present danger of letting it lapse, against which he promised himself to be much on his guard. He was quite ready, none the less, to be selfish just a little, since surely no more charming occasion for it had come to him. "Just a little," in a word, was just as much as Miss Bartram, taking one day with another, would let him. He never would be in the least coercive, and would keep well before him the lines on which consideration for her—the very highest— ought to proceed. He would thoroughly establish the heads under which her affairs, her requirements, her peculiarities—he went so far as to give them the latitude of that name—would come into their intercourse. All this naturally was a sign of how much he took the intercourse itself for granted. There was nothing more to be done about *that.* It simply existed; had sprung into being with her first penetrating question to him in the autumn light there at Weatherend. The real form it should have taken on the basis that stood out large was the form of their marrying. But the devil in this was that the very basis itself put marrying out of the question. His conviction, his apprehension, his obsession, in short, was n't a privilege he could invite a woman to share; and that consequence of it was precisely what was the matter with him. Something or other lay in wait for him, amid the twists and the turns of the months and the years, like a crouching beast in the jungle. It signified little whether the crouching beast were destined to slay him or to be slain. The definite point was the inevitable spring of the creature; and the definite lesson from that was that a man of feeling did n't cause himself to be accompanied by a lady on a tiger-hunt. Such was the image under which he had ended by figuring his life.

They had at first, none the less, in the scattered hours spent together, made no allusion to that view of it; which was a sign he was handsomely alert to give that he did n't expect, that he in fact did n't care, always to be talking about it. Such a feature in one's outlook was really like a hump on one's back. The difference it made every minute of the day existed quite independently of discussion. One discussed of course *like* a hunchback, for there was always, if nothing else, the hunchback face.

That remained, and she was watching him; but people watched best, as a general thing, in silence, so that such would be predominantly the manner of their vigil. Yet he did n't want, at the same time, to be tense and solemn; tense and solemn was what he imagined he too much showed for with other people. The thing to be, with the one person who knew, was easy and natural—to make the reference rather than be seeming to avoid it, to avoid it rather than be seeming to make it, and to keep it, in any case, familiar, facetious even, rather than pedantic and portentous. Some such consideration as the latter was doubtless in his mind for instance when he wrote pleasantly to Miss Bartram that perhaps the great thing he had so long felt as in the lap of the gods was no more than this circumstance, which touched him so nearly, of her acquiring a house in London. It was the first allusion they had yet again made, needing any other hitherto so little; but when she replied, after having given him the news, that she was by no means satisfied with such a trifle as the climax to so special a suspense, she almost set him wondering if she had n't even a larger conception of singularity for him than he had for himself. He was at all events destined to become aware little by little, as time went by, that she was all the while looking at his life, judging it, measuring it, in the light of the thing she knew, which grew to be at last, with the consecration of the years, never mentioned between them save as "the real truth" about him. That had always been his own form of reference to it, but she adopted the form so quietly that, looking back at the end of a period, he knew there was no moment at which it was traceable that she had, as he might say, got inside his idea, or exchanged the attitude of beautifully indulging for that of still more beautifully believing him.

It was always open to him to accuse her of seeing him but as the most harmless of maniacs, and this, in the long run—since it covered so much ground—was his easiest description of their friendship. He had a screw loose for her, but she liked him in spite of it and was practically, against the rest of the world, his kind wise keeper, unremunerated but fairly amused and, in the absence of other near ties, not disreputably occupied. The rest of the world of course thought him queer, but she, she only, knew how, and above all why, queer; which was precisely what enabled her to dispose the concealing veil in the right folds. She took his gaiety from him—since it had to pass with them for gaiety—as she took everything else; but she certainly so far justified by her unerring touch his finer sense of the degree to which he had ended by convincing her. *She* at least never spoke of the secret of his life except as "the real truth about you," and she had in fact a wonderful way of making it seem, as such, the secret of her own life too. That was in fine how he so constantly felt her as allowing for him; he could n't on the whole call it anything else. He allowed for himself, but she, exactly, allowed still more; partly because, better placed for a sight of the matter, she traced his unhappy perversion through reaches of its course into which he could scarce follow it. He knew how he felt, but, besides knowing that, she knew how he *looked* as well; he knew each of the things of importance he was insidiously kept from doing, but she could add up the amount they made, understand how much, with a lighter weight on his spirit, he might have done, and thereby establish how, clever as he was, he fell short. Above all she was in the secret of the difference between the forms he went through—those of his little office under Government, those of caring for his modest patrimony, for his library, for his garden in the country, for the people in London whose invitations he accepted and repaid —and the detachment that reigned beneath them and that made of all behaviour, all that could in the least be called behaviour, a long act of dissimulation. What it had come to was that he wore a mask painted with the social simper, out of the eye-holes of which there looked eyes of an expression not in the least matching the other features. This the stupid world, even after years, had never more than half-discovered. It was only May Bartram who had, and she achieved, by an art indescribable, the feat of at once—or perhaps it was only alternately—meeting the eyes from in front and mingling her own vision, as from over his shoulder, with their peep through the apertures.

So while they grew older together she did watch with him, and so she let this association give shape and colour to her own existence. Beneath *her* forms as well detachment had learned to sit, and behaviour had become for her, in the social sense, a false account of herself. There was but one account of her that would have been true all the while and that she could give straight to nobody, least of all to John Marcher. Her whole attitude was a virtual statement, but the perception of that only seemed called to take its place for him as one of the many things necessarily crowded out of his consciousness. If she had moreover, like himself, to make sacrifices to their real truth, it was to be granted that her compensation might have affected her as more prompt and more natural. They had long periods, in this London time, during which, when they were together, a stranger might have listened to them without in the least pricking up his ears; on the other hand the real truth was equally liable at any moment to rise to the surface, and the auditor would then have wondered indeed what they were talking about. They had from an early hour made up their mind that society was, luckily, unintelligent, and the margin allowed them by this had fairly become one of their commonplaces. Yet there were still moments when the situation turned almost fresh—usually under the effect of some expression drawn from herself. Her expressions doubtless repeated themselves, but her intervals were generous. "What saves us, you know, is that we answer so completely to so usual an appearance: that of the man and woman whose friendship has become such a daily habit—or almost —as to be at last indispensable." That for instance was a remark she had frequently enough had occasion to make, though she had given it at different times different developments. What we are especially concerned with is the turn it happened to take from her one afternoon when he had come to see her in honour of her birthday. This anniversary had fallen on a Sunday, at a season of thick fog and general outward gloom; but he had brought her his customary offering, having known her now long enough to have established a hundred small traditions. It was one of his proofs to himself, the present he made her on her birthday, that he had n't sunk into real selfishness. It was mostly nothing more than a small trinket, but it was always fine of its kind, and he was regularly careful to pay for it more than he thought he could afford. "Our habit saves you at least, don't you see? because it makes you, after all, for the vulgar, indistinguishable from other men. What's the most inveterate mark of men in general? Why the capacity to spend endless time with dull women—to spend it I won't say without being bored, but without minding that they are, without being driven off at a tangent by it; which comes to the same thing. I'm your dull woman, a part of the daily bread for which you pray at church. That covers your tracks more than anything."

"And what covers yours?" asked Marcher, whom his dull woman could mostly to this extent amuse. "I see of course what you mean by your saving me, in this way and that, so far as other people are concerned—I've seen it all along. Only what is it that saves *you?* I often think, you know, of that."

She looked as if she sometimes thought of that too, but rather in a different way. "Where other people, you mean, are concerned?"

"Well, you're really so in with me, you know—as a sort of result of my being so in with yourself. I mean of my having such an immense regard for you, being so tremendously mindful of all you've done for me. I sometimes ask myself if it's quite fair. Fair I mean to have so involved and—since one may say it—interested you. I almost feel as if you had n't really had time to do anything else."

"Anything else but be interested?" she asked. "Ah what else does one ever want to be? If I've been 'watching' with you, as we long ago agreed I was to do, watching's always in itself an absorption."

"Oh certainly," John Marcher said, "if you had n't had your curiosity—! Only does n't it sometimes come to you as time goes on that your curiosity is n't being particularly repaid?"

May Bartram had a pause. "Do you ask that, by any chance, because you feel at all that yours is n't? I mean because you have to wait so long."

Oh he understood what she meant! "For the thing to happen that never does happen? For the beast to jump out? No, I'm just where I was about it. It is n't a matter as to which I can *choose,* I can decide for a change. It is n't one as to which there *can* be a change. It's in the lap of the gods. One's in the hands of one's law—there one is. As to the form the law will take, the way it will operate, that's its own affair."

"Yes," Miss Bartram replied; "of course one's fate's coming, of course it *has* come in its own form and its own way, all the while. Only, you know, the form and the way in your case were to have been—well, something so exceptional and, as one may say, so particularly *your* own."

Something in this made him look at her with suspicion. "You say 'were to *have* been,' as if in your heart you had begun to doubt."

"Oh!" she vaguely protested.

"As if you believed," he went on, "that nothing will now take place."

She shook her head slowly but rather inscrutably. "You're far from my thought."

He continued to look at her. "What then is the matter with you?"

"Well," she said after another wait, "the matter with me is simply that I'm more sure than ever my curiosity, as you call it, will be but too well repaid."

They were frankly grave now; he had got up from his seat, had turned once more about the little drawing-room to which, year after year, he brought his inevitable topic; in which he had, as he might have said, tasted their intimate community with every sauce, where every object was as familiar to him as the things of his own house and the very carpets were worn with his fitful walk very much as the desks in old counting-houses are worn by the elbows of generations of clerks. The generations of his nervous moods had been at work there, and the place was the written history of his whole middle life. Under the impression of what his friend had just said he knew himself, for some reason, more aware of these things; which made him, after a moment, stop again before her. "Is it possibly that you've grown afraid?"

"Afraid?" He thought, as she repeated the word, that his question had made her, a little, change colour; so that, lest he should have touched on a truth, he explained very kindly: "You remember that that was what you asked *me* long ago—that first day at Weatherend."

"Oh yes, and you told me you did n't know—that I was to see for myself. We've said little about it since, even in so long a time."

"Precisely." Marcher interposed—"quite as if it were too delicate a matter for us to make free with. Quite as if we might find, on pressure, that I *am* afraid. For then," he said "we should n't, should we? quite know what to do."

She had for the time no answer to this question. "There have been days when I thought you were. Only, of course," she added, "there have been days when we have thought almost anything."

"Everything. Oh!" Marcher softly groaned as with a gasp, half-spent, at the face, more uncovered just then than it had been for a long while, of the imagination always with them. It had always had its incalculable moments of glaring out, quite as with the very eyes of the very Beast, and, used as he was to them, they could still draw from him the tribute of a sigh that rose from the depths of his being. All they had thought, first and last, rolled over him; the past seemed to have been reduced to mere barren speculation. This in fact was what the place had just struck him as so full of —the simplification of everything but the state of suspense. That remained only by seeming to hang in the void surrounding it. Even his original fear, if fear it had been, had lost itself in the desert. "I judge, however," he continued, "that you see I'm not afraid now."

"What I see, as I make it out, is that you've achieved something almost unprecedented in the way of getting used to danger. Living with it so long and so closely you've lost your sense of it; you know it's there, but you're indifferent, and you cease even, as of old, to have to whistle in the dark. Considering what the danger is," May Bartram wound up, "I'm bound to say I don't think your attitude could well be surpassed."

John Marcher faintly smiled. "It's heroic?"

"Certainly—call it that."

It was what he would have liked indeed to call it. "I *am* then a man of courage?"

"That's what you were to show me."

He still, however, wondered. "But does n't the man of courage know what he's afraid of—or *not* afraid of? I don't know *that,* you see. I don't focus it. I can't name it. I only know I'm exposed."

"Yes, but exposed—how shall I say?—so directly. So intimately. That's surely enough."

"Enough to make you feel then—as what we may call the end and the upshot of our watch—that I'm not afraid?"

"You're not afraid. But it is n't," she said, "the end of our watch. That is it is n't the end of yours. You've everything still to see."

"Then why have n't *you?*" he asked. He had had, all along, to-day, the sense of her keeping something back, and he still had it. As this was his first impression of that it quite made a date. The case was the more marked as she did n't at first answer; which in turn made him go on. "You know something I don't." Then his voice, for that of a man of courage, trembled a little. "You know what's to happen." Her silence, with the face she showed, was almost a confession—it made him sure. "You know, and you're afraid to tell me. It's so bad that you're afraid I'll find out."

All this might be true, for she did look as if, unexpectedly to her, he had crossed some mystic line that she had secretly drawn round her. Yet she might, after all, not have worried; and the real climax was that he himself, at all events, need n't. "You'll never find out."

III

It was all to have made, none the less, as I have said, a date; which came out in the fact that again and again, even after long intervals, other things that passed between them wore in relation to this hour but the character of recalls and results. Its immediate effect had been indeed rather to lighten insistence—almost to provoke a reaction; as if their topic had dropped by its own weight and as if moreover, for that matter, Marcher had been visited by one of his occasional warnings against egotism. He had kept up, he felt, and very decently on the whole, his consciousness of the importance of not being selfish, and it was true that he had never sinned in that direction without promptly enough trying to press the scales the other way. He often repaired his fault, the season permitting, by inviting his friend to accompany him to the opera; and it not infrequently thus happened that, to show he did n't wish her to have but one sort of food for her mind, he was the cause of her appearing there with him a dozen nights in the month. It even happened that, seeing her home at such times, he occasionally went in with her to finish, as he called it, the evening, and, the better to make his point, sat down to the frugal but always careful little supper that awaited his pleasure. His point was made, he thought, by his not eternally insisting with her on himself; made for instance, at such hours, when it befell that, her piano at hand and each of them familiar with it, they went over passages of the opera together. It chanced to be on one of these occasions, however, that he reminded her of her not having answered a certain question he had put to her during the talk that had taken place between them on her last birthday. "What is it that saves *you?*"—saved her, he meant, from that appearance of variation from the usual human type. If he had practically escaped remark, as she pretended, by doing, in the most important particular, what most men do—find the answer to life in patching up an alliance of a sort with a woman no better than himself—how had she escaped it, and how could the alliance, such as it was, since they must suppose it had been more or less noticed, have failed to make her rather positively talked about?

"I never said," May Bartram replied, "that it had n't made me a good deal talked about."

"Ah well then you're not 'saved.' "

"It has n't been a question for me. If you've had your woman I've had," she said, "my man."

"And you mean that makes you all right?"

Oh it was always as if there were so much to say! "I don't know why it should n't make me—humanly, which is what we're speaking of—as right as it makes you."

"I see," Marcher returned. " 'Humanly,' no doubt, as showing that you're living for something. Not, that is, just for me and my secret."

May Bartram smiled. "I don't pretend it exactly shows that I'm not living for you. It's my intimacy with you that's in question."

He laughed as he saw what she meant. "Yes, but since, as you say, I'm only, so far as people make out, ordinary, you're—are n't you?—no more than ordinary either. You help me to pass for a man like another. So if I *am,* as I understand you, you're not compromised. Is that it?"

She had another of her waits, but she spoke clearly enough. "That's it. It's all that concerns me—to help you to pass for a man like another."

He was careful to acknowledge the remark handsomely. "How kind, how beautiful, you are to me! How shall I ever repay you?"

She had her last grave pause, as if there might be a choice of ways. But she chose. "By going on as you are."

It was into this going on as he was that they relapsed, and really for so long a time that the day inevitably came for a further sounding of their depths. These depths, constantly bridged over by a structure firm enough in spite of its lightness and of its occasional oscillation in the somewhat vertiginous air, invited on occasion, in the interest of their nerves, a dropping of the plummet and a measurement of the abyss. A difference had been made moreover, once for all, by the fact that she had all the while not appeared to feel the need of rebutting his charge of an idea within her that she did n't dare to express—a charge uttered just before one of the fullest of their later discussions ended. It had come up for him then that she "knew" something and that what she knew was bad—too bad to tell him. When he had spoken of it as visibly so bad that she was afraid he might find it out, her reply had left the matter too equivocal to be let alone and yet, for Marcher's special sensibility, almost too formidable again to touch. He circled about it at a distance that alternately narrowed and widened and that still was n't much affected by the consciousness in him that there was nothing she could "know," after all, any better than he did. She had no source of knowledge he had n't equally—except of course that she might have finer nerves. That was what women had where they were interested; they made out things, where people were concerned, that the people often could n't have made out for themselves. Their nerves, their sensibility, their imagination, were conductors and revealers, and the beauty of May Bartram was in particular that she had given herself so to his case. He felt in these days what, oddly enough, he had never felt before, the growth of a dread of losing her by some catastrophe—some catastrophe that yet would n't at all be *the* catastrophe: partly because she had almost of a sudden begun to strike him as more useful to him than ever yet, and partly by reason of an appearance of uncertainty in her health, coincident and equally new. It was characteristic of the inner detachment he had hitherto so successfully cultivated and to which our whole account of him is a reference, it was characteristic that his complications, such as they were, had never yet seemed so as at this crisis to thicken about him, even to the point of making him ask himself if he were, by any chance, of a truth, within sight or sound, within touch or reach, within the immediate jurisdiction, of the thing that waited.

When the day came, as come it had to, that his friend confessed to him her fear of a deep disorder in her blood, he felt somehow the shadow of a change and the chill of a shock. He immediately began to imagine aggravations and disasters, and above all to think of her peril as the direct menace for himself of personal privation. This indeed gave him one of those partial recoveries of equanimity that were agreeable to him—it showed him that what was still first in his mind was the loss she herself might suffer. "What if she should have to die before knowing, before seeing—?" It would have been brutal, in the early stages of her trouble, to put that question to her; but it had immediately sounded for him to his own concern, and the possibility was what most made him sorry for her. If she did "know," moreover, in the sense of her having had some—what should he think?—mystical irresistible light, this would make the matter not better, but worse, inasmuch as her original adoption of his own curiosity had quite become the basis of her life. She had been living to see what would *be* to be seen, and it would quite lacerate her to have to give up before the accomplishment of the vision. These reflexions, as I say, quickened his generosity; yet, make them as he might, he saw himself, with the lapse of the period, more and more disconcerted. It lapsed for him with a strange steady sweep, and the oddest oddity was that it gave him, independently of the threat of much inconvenience, almost the only positive surprise his career, if career it could be called, had yet offered him. She kept the house as she had never done; he had to go to her to see her—she could meet him nowhere now, though there was scarce a corner of their loved old London in which she had n't in the past, at one time or another, done so; and he found her always seated by her fire in the deep old-fashioned chair she was less and less able to leave. He had been struck one day, after an absence exceeding his usual measure, with her suddenly looking much older to him than he had ever thought of her being; then he recognised that the suddenness was all on his side—he had just simply and suddenly noticed. She looked older because inevitably, after so many years, she *was* old, or almost; which was of course true in still greater measure of her companion. If she was old, or almost, John Marcher assuredly was, and yet it was her showing of the lesson, not his own, that brought the truth home to him. His surprises began here; when once they had begun they multiplied; they came rather with a rush: it was as if, in the oddest way in the world, they had all been kept back, sown in a thick cluster, for the late afternoon of life, the time at which for people in general the unexpected has died out.

One of them was that he should have caught himself—for he *had* so done—*really* wondering if the great accident would take form now as nothing more than his being condemned to see this charming woman, this admirable friend, pass away from him. He had never so unreservedly qualified her as while confronted in thought with such a possibility; in spite of which there was small doubt for him that as an answer to his long riddle the mere effacement of even so fine a feature of his situation would be an abject anticlimax. It would represent, as connected with his past attitude, a drop of dignity under the shadow of which his existence could only become the most grotesque of failures. He had been far from holding it a failure—long as he had waited for the appearance that was to make it a success. He had waited for quite another thing, not for such a thing as that. The breath of his good faith came short, however, as he recognised how long he had waited, or how long at least his companion had. That she, at all events, might be recorded as having waited in vain—this affected him sharply, and all the more because of his at first having done little more than amuse himself with the idea. It grew more grave as the gravity of her condition grew, and the state of mind it produced in him, which he himself ended by watching as if it had been some definite disfigurement of his outer person, may pass for another of his surprises. This conjoined itself still with another, the really stupefying consciousness of a question that he would have allowed to shape itself had he dared. What did everything mean—what, that is, did *she* mean, she and her vain waiting and her probable death and the soundless admonition of it all—unless that, at this time of day, it was simply, it was overwhelmingly too late? He had never at any stage of his queer consciousness admitted the whisper of such a correction; he had never till within these last few months been so false to his conviction as not to hold that what was to come to him had time, whether *he* struck himself as having it or not. That at last, at last, he certainly had n't it, to speak of, or had it but in the scantiest measure—such, soon enough, as things went with him, became the inference with which his old obsession had to reckon: and this it was not helped to do by the more and more confirmed appearance that the great vagueness casting the long shadow in which he had lived had, to attest itself, almost no margin left. Since it was in Time that he was to have met his fate, so it was in Time that his fate was to have acted; and as he waked up to the sense of no longer being young, which was exactly the sense of being stale, just as that, in turn, was the sense of being weak, he waked up to another matter beside. It all hung together; they were subject, he and the great vagueness, to an equal and indivisible law. When the possibilities themselves had accordingly turned stale, when the secret of the gods had grown faint, had perhaps even quite evaporated, that, and that only, was failure. It would n't have been failure to be bankrupt, dishonoured, pilloried, hanged; it was failure not to be anything. And so, in the dark valley into which his path had taken its unlooked-for twist, he wondered not a little as he groped. He did n't care what awful crash might overtake him, with what ignominy or what monstrosity he might yet be associated—since he was n't after all too utterly old to suffer—if it would only be decently proportionate to the posture he had kept, all his life, in the threatened presence of it. He had but one desire left—that he should n't have been "sold."

IV

Then it was that, one afternoon, while the spring of the year was young and new she met all in her own way his frankest betrayal of these alarms. He had gone in late to see her, but evening had n't settled and she was presented to him in that long fresh light of waning April days which affects us often with a sadness sharper than the greyest hours of autumn. The week had been warm, the spring was supposed to have begun early, and May Bartram sat, for the first time in the year, without a fire; a fact that, to Marcher's sense, gave the scene of which she formed part a smooth and ultimate look, an air of knowing, in its immaculate order and cold meaningless cheer, that it would never see a fire again. Her own aspect—he could scarce have said why —intensified this note. Almost as white as wax, with the marks and signs in her face as numerous and as fine as if they had been etched by a needle, with soft white draperies relieved by a faded green scarf on the delicate tone of which the years had further refined, she was the picture of a serene and exquisite but impenetrable sphinx, whose head, or indeed all whose person, might have been powdered with silver. She was a sphinx, yet with her white petals and green fronds she might have been a lily too— only an artificial lily, wonderfully imitated and constantly kept, without dust or stain, though not exempt from a slight droop and a complexity of faint creases, under some clear glass bell. The perfection of household care, of high polish and finish, always reigned in her rooms, but they now looked most as if everything had been wound up, tucked in, put away, so that she might sit with folded hands and with nothing more to do. She was "out of it," to Marcher's vision; her work was over; she communicated with him as across some gulf or from some island of rest that she had already reached, and it made him feel strangely abandoned. Was it—or rather was n't it—that if for so long she had been watching with him the answer to their question must have swum into her ken and taken on its name, so that her occupation was verily gone? He had as much as charged her with this in saying to her, many months before, that she even then knew something she was keeping from him. It was a point he had never since ventured to press, vaguely fearing as he did that it might become a difference, perhaps a disagreement, between them. He had in this later time turned nervous, which was what he in all the other years had never been; and the oddity was that his nervousness should have waited till he had begun to doubt, should have held off so long as he was sure. There was something, it seemed to him, that the wrong word would bring down on his head, something that would so at least ease off his tension. But he wanted not to speak the wrong word; that would make everything ugly. He wanted the knowledge he lacked to drop on him, if drop it could, by its own august weight. If she was to forsake him it was surely for her to take leave. This was why he did n't directly ask her again what she knew; but it was also why, approaching the matter from another side, he said to her in the course of his visit: "What do you regard as the very worst that at this time of day *can* happen to me?"

He had asked her that in the past often enough; they had, with the odd irregular rhythm of their intensities and avoidances, exchanged ideas about it and then had seen the ideas washed away by cool intervals, washed like figures traced in sea-sand. It had ever been the mark of their talk that the oldest allusions in it required but a little dismissal and reaction to come out again, sounding for the hour as new. She could thus at present meet his enquiry quite freshly and patiently. "Oh yes, I've repeatedly thought, only it always seemed to me of old that I could n't quite make up my mind. I thought of dreadful things, between which it was difficult to choose; and so must you have done."

"Rather! I feel now as if I had scarce done anything else. I appear to myself to have spent my life in thinking of nothing *but* dreadful things. A great many of them I've at different times named to you, but there were others I could n't name."

"They were too, too dreadful?"

"Too, too dreadful—some of them."

She looked at him a minute, and there came to him as he met it an inconsequent sense that her eyes, when one got their full clearness, were still as beautiful as they had been in youth, only beautiful with a strange cold light—a light that somehow was a part of the effect, if it was n't rather a part of the cause, of the pale hard sweetness of the season and the hour. "And yet," she said at last, "there are horrors we've mentioned."

It deepened the strangeness to see her, as such a figure in such a picture, talk of "horrors," but she was to do in a few minutes something stranger yet—though even of this he was to take the full measure but afterwards—and the note of it already trembled. It was, for the matter of that, one of the signs that her eyes were having again the high flicker of their prime. He had to admit, however, what she said. "Oh yes, there were times when we did go far." He caught himself in the act of speaking as if it all were over. Well, he wished it were; and the consummation depended for him clearly more and more on his friend.

But she had now a soft smile. "Oh far—!"

It was oddly ironic. "Do you mean you're prepared to go further?"

She was frail and ancient and charming as she continued to look at him, yet it was rather as if she had lost the thread. "Do you consider that we went far?"

"Why I thought it the point you were just making—that we *had* looked most things in the face."

"Including each other?" She still smiled. "But you're quite right. We've had together great imaginations, often great fears; but some of them have been unspoken."

"Then the worst—we have n't faced that. I *could* face it, I believe, if I knew what you think it. I feel," he explained, "as if I had lost my power to conceive such things." And he wondered if he looked as blank as he sounded. "It's spent."

"Then why do you assume," she asked, "that mine is n't?"

"Because you've given me signs to the contrary. It is n't a question for you of conceiving, imagining, comparing. It is n't a question now of choosing." At last he came out with it. "You know something I don't. You've shown me that before."

These last words had affected her, he made out in a moment, exceedingly, and she spoke with firmness. "I've shown you, my dear, nothing."

He shook his head. "You can't hide it."

"Oh, oh!" May Bartram sounded over what she could n't hide. It was almost a smothered groan.

"You admitted it months ago, when I spoke of it to you as of something you were afraid I should find out. Your answer was that I could n't, that I would n't, and I don't pretend I have. But you had something therefore in mind, and I now see how it must have been, how it still is, the possibility that, of all possibilities, has settled itself for you as the worst. This," he went on, "is why I appeal to you. I'm only afraid of ignorance to-day—I'm not afraid of knowledge." And then as for a while she said nothing: "What makes me sure is that I see in your face and feel here, in this air and amid these appearances, that you're out of it. You've done. You've had your experience. You leave me to my fate."

Well, she listened, motionless and white in her chair, as on a decision to be made, so that her manner was fairly an avowal, though still, with a small fine inner stiffness, an imperfect surrender. "It *would* be the worst," she finally let herself say. "I mean the thing I've never said."

It hushed him a moment. "More monstrous than all the monstrosities we've named?"

"More monstrous. Is n't that what you sufficiently express," she asked, "in calling it the worst?"

Marcher thought. "Assuredly—if you mean, as I do, something that includes all the loss and all the shame that are thinkable."

"It would if it *should* happen," said May Bartram. "What we're speaking of, remember, is only my idea."

"It's your belief," Marcher returned. "That's enough for me. I feel your beliefs are right. Therefore if, having this one, you give me no more light on it, you abandon me."

"No, no!" she repeated. "I'm with you—don't you see?—still." And as to make it more vivid to him she rose from her chair—a movement she seldom risked in these days—and showed herself, all draped and all soft, in her fairness and slimness. "I have n't forsaken you."

It was really, in its effort against weakness, a generous assurance, and had the success of the impulse not, happily, been great, it would have touched him to pain more than to pleasure. But the cold charm in her eyes had spread, as she hovered before him, to all the rest of her person, so that it was for the minute almost a recovery of youth. He could n't pity her for that; he could only take her as she showed—as capable even yet of helping him. It was as if, at the same time, her light might at any instant go out; wherefore he must make the most of it. There passed before him with intensity the three or four things he wanted most to know; but the question that came of itself to his lips really covered the others. "Then tell me if I shall consciously suffer."

She promptly shook her head. "Never!"

It confirmed the authority he imputed to her, and it produced on him an extraordinary effect. "Well, what's better than that? Do you call that the worst?"

"You think nothing is better?" she asked.

She seemed to mean something so special that he again sharply wondered, though still with the dawn of a prospect of relief. "Why not, if one does n't *know?*" After which, as their eyes, over his question, met in a silence, the dawn deepened and something to his purpose came prodigiously out of her very face. His own, as he took it in, suddenly flushed to the forehead, and he gasped with the force of a perception to which, on the instant, everything fitted. The sound of his gasp filled the air; then he became articulate. "I see—if I don't suffer!"

In her own look, however, was doubt. "You see what?"

"Why what you mean—what you've always meant."

She again shook her head. "What I mean is n't what I've always meant. It's different."

"It's something new?"

She hung back from it a little. "Something new. It's not what you think. I see what you think."

His divination drew breath then; only her correction might be wrong. "It is n't that I *am* a blockhead?" he asked between faintness and grimness. "It is n't that it's all a mistake?"

"A mistake?" she pityingly echoed. *That* possibility, for her, he saw, would be monstrous; and if she guaranteed him the immunity from pain it would accordingly not be what she had in mind. "Oh no," she declared; "it's nothing of that sort. You've been right."

Yet he could n't help asking himself if she were n't, thus pressed, speaking but to save him. It seemed to him he should be most in a hole if his history should prove all a platitude. "Are you telling me the truth, so that I shan't have been a bigger idiot than I can bear to know? I *have n't* lived with a vain imagination, in the most besotted illusion? I have n't waited but to see the door shut in my face?"

She shook her head again. "However the case stands *that* is n't the truth. Whatever the reality, it *is* a reality. The door is n't shut. The door's open," said May Bartram.

"Then something's to come?"

She waited once again, always with her cold sweet eyes on him. "It's never too late." She had, with her gliding step, diminished the distance between them, and she stood nearer to him, close to him, a minute, as if still charged with the unspoken. Her movement might have been for some finer emphasis of what she was at once hesitating and deciding to say. He had been standing by the chimney-piece, fireless and sparely adorned, a small perfect old French clock and two morsels of rosy Dresden constituting all its furniture; and her hand grasped the shelf while she kept him waiting, grasped it a little as for support and encouragement. She only kept him waiting, however; that is he only waited. It had become suddenly, from her movement and attitude, beautiful and vivid to him that she had something more to give him; her wasted face delicately shone with it—it glittered almost as with the white lustre of silver in her expression. She was right, incontestably, for what he saw in her face was the truth, and strangely, without consequence, while their talk of it as dreadful was still in the air, she appeared to present it as inordinately soft. This, prompting bewilderment, made him but gape the more gratefully for her revelation, so that they continued for some minutes silent, her face shining at him, her contact imponderably pressing, and his stare all kind but all expectant. The end, none the less, was that what he had expected failed to come to him. Something else took place instead, which seemed to consist at first in the mere closing of her eyes. She gave way at the same instant to a slow fine shudder, and though he remained staring—though he stared in fact but the harder—turned off and regained her chair. It was the end of what she had been intending, but it left him thinking only of that.

"Well, you don't say—?"

She had touched in her passage a bell near the chimney and had sunk back strangely pale. "I'm afraid I'm too ill."

"Too ill to tell me?" It sprang up sharp to him, and almost to his lips, the fear she might die without giving him light. He checked himself in time from so expressing his question, but she answered as if she had heard the words.

"Don't you know—now?"

" 'Now'—?" She had spoken as if some difference had been made within the moment. But her maid, quickly obedient to her bell, was already with them. "I know nothing." And he was afterwards to say to himself that he must have spoken with odious impatience, such an impatience as to show that, supremely disconcerted, he washed his hands of the whole question.

"Oh!" said May Bartram.

"Are you in pain?" he asked as the woman went to her.

"No," said May Bartram.

Her maid, who had put an arm round her as if to take her to her room, fixed on him eyes that appealingly contradicted her; in spite of which, however, he showed once more his mystification. "What then has happened?"

She was once more, with her companion's help, on her feet, and, feeling withdrawal imposed on him, he had blankly found his hat and gloves and had reached the door. Yet he waited for her answer. "What *was* to," she said.

V

He came back the next day, but she was then unable to see him, and as it was literally the first time this had occurred in the long stretch of their acquaintance he turned away, defeated and sore, almost angry—or feeling at least that such a break in their custom was really the beginning of the end—and wandered alone with his thoughts, especially with the one he was least able to keep down. She was dying and he would lose her; she was dying and his life would end. He stopped in the Park, into which he had passed, and stared before him at his recurrent doubt. Away from her the doubt pressed again; in her presence he had believed her, but as he felt his forlornness he threw himself into the explanation that, nearest at hand, had most of a miserable warmth for him and least of a cold torment. She had deceived him to save him—to put him off with something in which he should be able to rest. What could the thing that was to happen to him be, after all, but just this thing that had begun to happen? Her dying, her death, his consequent solitude—*that* was what he had figured as the Beast in the Jungle, that was what had been in the lap of the gods. He had had her word for it as he left her—what else on earth could she have meant? It was n't a thing of a monstrous order; not a fate rare and distinguished; not a stroke of fortune that overwhelmed and immortalised; it had only the stamp of the common doom. But poor Marcher at this hour judged the common doom sufficient. It would serve his turn, and even as the consummation of infinite waiting he would bend his pride to accept it. He sat down on a bench in the twilight. He had n't been a fool. Something had *been,* as she had said, to come. Before he rose indeed it had quite struck him that the final fact really matched with the long avenue through which he had had to reach it. As sharing his suspense and as giving herself all, giving her life, to bring it to an end, she had come with him every step of the way. He had lived by her aid, and to leave her behind would be cruelly, damnably to miss her. What could be more overwhelming than that?

Well, he was to know within the week, for though she kept him a while at bay, left him restless and wretched during a series of days on each of which he asked about her only again to have to turn away, she ended his trial by receiving him where she had always received him. Yet she had been brought out at some hazard into the presence of so many of the things that were, consciously, vainly, half their past, and there was scant service left in the gentleness of her mere desire, all too visible, to check his obsession and wind up his long trouble. That was clearly what she wanted, the one thing more for her own peace while she could still put out her hand. He was so affected by her state that, once seated by her chair, he was moved to let everything go; it was she herself therefore who brought him back, took up again, before she dismissed him, her last word of the other time. She showed how she wished to leave their business in order. "I'm not sure you understood. You've nothing to wait for more. It *has* come."

Oh how he looked at her! "Really?"

"Really."

"The thing that, as you said, *was* to?"

"The thing that we began in our youth to watch for."

Face to face with her once more he believed her; it was a claim to which he had so abjectly little to oppose. "You mean that it has come as a positive definite occurrence, with a name and a date?"

"Positive. Definite. I don't know about the 'name,' but oh with a date!"

He found himself again too helplessly at sea. "But come in the night—come and passed me by?"

May Bartram had her strange faint smile. "Oh no, it has n't passed you by!"

"But if I have n't been aware of it and it has n't touched me—?"

"Ah your not being aware of it"—and she seemed to hesitate an instant to deal with this—"your not being aware of it is the strangeness *in* the strangeness. It's the wonder *of* the wonder." She spoke as with the softness almost of a sick child, yet now at last, at the end of all, with the perfect straightness of a sibyl. She visibly knew that she knew, and the effect on him was of something co-ordinate, in its high character, with the law that had ruled him. It was the true voice of the law; so on her lips would the law itself have sounded. "It *has* touched you," she went on. "It has done its office. It has made you all its own."

"So utterly without my knowing it?"

"So utterly without your knowing it." His hand, as he leaned to her, was on the arm of her chair, and, dimly smiling always now, she placed her own on it. "It's enough if *I* know it."

"Oh!" he confusedly breathed, as she herself of late so often had done.

"What I long ago said is true. You'll never know now, and I think you ought to be content. You've *had* it," said May Bartram.

"But had what?"

"Why what was to have marked you out. The proof of your law. It has acted. I'm too glad," she then bravely added, "to have been able to see what it's *not.*"

He continued to attach his eyes to her, and with the sense that it was all beyond him, and that *she* was too, he would still have sharply challenged her had n't he so felt it an abuse of her weakness to do more than take devoutly what she gave him, take it hushed as to a revelation. If he did speak, it was out of the foreknowledge of his loneliness to come. "If you're glad of what it's 'not' it might then have been worse?"

She turned her eyes away, she looked straight before her; with which after a moment: "Well, you know our fears."

He wondered. "It's something then we never feared?"

On this slowly she turned to him. "Did we ever dream, with all our dreams, that we should sit and talk of it thus?"

He tried for a little to make out that they had; but it was as if their dreams, numberless enough, were in solution in some thick cold mist through which thought lost itself. "It might have been that we could n't talk?"

"Well"—she did her best for him—"not from this side. This, you see," she said, "is the *other* side."

"I think," poor Marcher returned, "that all sides are the same to me." Then, however, as she gently shook her head in correction: "We might n't, as it were, have got across—?"

"To where we are—no. We're *here*"—she made her weak emphasis.

"And much good does it do us!" was her friend's frank comment.

"It does us the good it can. It does us the good that *it* is n't here. It's past. It's behind," said May Bartram. "Before—" but her voice dropped.

He had got up, not to tire her, but it was hard to combat his yearning. She after all told him nothing but that his light had failed—which he knew well enough without her. "Before—?" he blankly echoed.

"Before, you see, it was always to *come*. That kept it present."

"Oh I don't care what comes now! Besides," Marcher added, "it seems to me I liked it better present, as you say, than I can like it absent with *your* absence."

"Oh mine!"—and her pale hands made light of it.

"With the absence of everything." He had a dreadful sense of standing there before her for—so far as anything but this proved, this bottomless drop was concerned—the last time of their life. It rested on him with a weight he felt he could scarce bear, and this weight it apparently was that still pressed out what remained in him of speakable protest. "I believe you; but I can't begin to pretend I understand. *Nothing,* for me, is past; nothing *will* pass till I pass myself, which I pray my stars may be as soon as possible. Say, however," he added, "that I've eaten my cake, as you contend, to the last crumb—how can the thing I've never felt at all be the thing I was marked out to feel?"

She met him perhaps less directly, but she met him unperturbed. "You take your 'feelings' for granted. You were to suffer your fate. That was not necessarily to know it."

"How in the world—when what is such knowledge but suffering?"

She looked up at him a while in silence. "No—you don't understand."

"I suffer," said John Marcher.

"Don't, don't!"

"How can I help at least *that?*"

"Don't!" May Bartram repeated.

She spoke it in a tone so special, in spite of her weakness, that he stared an instant —stared as if some light, hitherto hidden, had shimmered across his vision. Darkness again closed over it, but the gleam had already become for him an idea. "Because I have n't the right—?"

"Don't *know*—when you need n't," she mercifully urged. "You need n't—for we should n't."

"Should n't?" If he could but know what she meant!

"No—it's too much."

"Too much?" he still asked but, with a mystification that was the next moment of a sudden to give way. Her words, if they meant something, affected him in this light—the light also of her wasted face—as meaning *all,* and the sense of what knowledge had been for herself came over him with a rush which broke through into a question. "Is it of that then you're dying?"

She but watched him, gravely at first, as to see, with this, where he was, and she might have seen something or feared something that moved her sympathy. "I would live for you still—if I could." Her eyes closed for a little, as if, withdrawn into herself, she were for a last time trying. "But I can't!" she said as she raised them again to take leave of him.

She could n't indeed, as but too promptly and sharply appeared, and he had no vision of her after this that was anything but darkness and doom. They had parted for ever in that strange talk; access to her chamber of pain, rigidly guarded, was almost wholly forbidden him; he was feeling now moreover, in the face of doctors, nurses, the two or three relatives attracted doubtless by the presumption of what she had to "leave," how few were the rights, as they were called in such cases, that he had to put forward, and how odd it might even seem that their intimacy should n't have given him more of them. The stupidest fourth cousin had more, even though she had been nothing in such a person's life. She had been a feature of features in *his,* for what else was it to have been so indispensable? Strange beyond saying were the ways of existence, baffling for him the anomaly of his lack, as he felt it to be, of producible claim. A woman might have been, as it were, everything to him, and it might yet present him in no connexion that any one seemed held to recognise. If this was the case in these closing weeks it was the case more sharply on the occasion of the last offices rendered, in the great grey London cemetery, to what had been mortal, to what had been precious, in his friend. The concourse at her grave was not numerous, but he saw himself treated as scarce more nearly concerned with it than if there had been a thousand others. He was in short from this moment face to face with the fact that he was to profit extraordinarily little by the interest May Bartram had taken in him. He could n't quite have said what he expected, but he had n't surely expected this approach to a double privation. Not only had her interest failed him, but he seemed to feel himself unattended—and for a reason he could n't seize—by the distinction, the dignity, the propriety, if nothing else, of the man markedly bereaved. It was as if in the view of society he had not *been* markedly bereaved, as if there still failed some sign or proof of it, and as if none the less his character could never be affirmed nor the deficiency ever made up. There were moments as the weeks went by when he would have liked, by some almost aggressive act, to take his stand on the intimacy of his loss, in order that it *might* be questioned and his retort, to the relief of his spirit, so recorded; but the moments of an irritation more helpless followed fast on these, the moments during which, turning things over with a good conscience but with a bare horizon, he found himself wondering if he ought n't to have begun, so to speak, further back.

He found himself wondering indeed at many things, and this last speculation had others to keep it company. What could he have done, after all, in her lifetime, without giving them both, as it were, away? He could n't have made known she was watching him, for that would have published the superstition of the Beast. This was what closed his mouth now—now that the Jungle had been threshed to vacancy and that the Beast had stolen away. It sounded too foolish and too flat; the difference for him in this particular, the extinction in his life of the element of suspense, was such as in fact to surprise him. He could scarce have said what the effect resembled; the abrupt cessation, the positive prohibition, of music perhaps, more than anything else, in some place all adjusted and all accustomed to sonority and to attention. If he could at any rate have conceived lifting the veil from his image at some moment of the past (what had he done, after all, if not lift it to *her?*) so to do this to-day, to talk to people at large of the Jungle cleared and confide to them that he now felt it as safe, would have been not only to see them listen as to a goodwife's tale, but really to hear himself tell one. What it presently came to in truth was that poor Marcher waded through his beaten grass, where no life stirred, where no breath sounded, where no evil eye seemed to gleam from a possible lair, very much as if vaguely looking for the Beast, and still *more as if* acutely missing it. He walked about in an existence that had grown strangely more spacious, and, stopping fitfully in places where the undergrowth of life struck him as closer, asked himself yearningly, wondered secretly and sorely, if it would have lurked here or there. It would have at all events *sprung;* what was at least complete was his belief in the truth itself of the assurance given him. The change from his old sense to his new was absolute and final: what was to happen *had* so absolutely and finally happened that he was as little able to know a fear for his future as to know a hope; so absent in short was any question of anything still to come. He was to live entirely with the other question, that of his unidentified past, that of his having to see his fortune impenetrably muffled and masked.

The torment of this vision became then his occupation; he could n't perhaps have consented to live but for the possibility of guessing. She had told him, his friend, not to guess; she had forbidden him, so far as he might, to know, and she had even in a sort denied the power in him to learn: which were so many things, precisely, to deprive him of rest. It was n't that he wanted, he argued for fairness, that anything past and done should repeat itself; it was only that he should n't, as an anticlimax, have been taken sleeping so sound as not to be able to win back by an effort of thought the lost stuff of consciousness. He declared to himself at moments that he would either win it back or have done with consciousness for ever; he made this idea his one motive in fine, made it so much his passion that none other, to compare with it, seemed ever to have touched him. The lost stuff of consciousness became thus for him as a strayed or stolen child to an unappeasable father; he hunted it up and down very much as if he were knocking at doors and enquiring of the police. This was the spirit in which, inevitably, he set himself to travel; he started on a journey that was to be as long as he could make it; it danced before him that, as the other side of the globe could n't possibly have less to say to him, it might, by a possibility of suggestion, have more. Before he quitted London, however, he made a pilgrimage to May Bartram's grave, took his way to it through the endless avenues of the grim suburban metropolis, sought it out in the wilderness of tombs, and, though he had come but for the renewal of the act of farewell, found himself, when he had at last stood by it, beguiled into long intensities. He stood for an hour, powerless to turn away and yet powerless to penetrate the darkness of death; fixing with his eyes her inscribed name and date, beating his forehead against the fact of the secret they kept, drawing his breath, while he waited, as if some sense would in pity of him rise from the stones. He kneeled on the stones, however, in vain; they kept what they concealed; and if the face of the tomb did become a face for him it was because her two names became a pair of eyes that did n't know him. He gave them a last long look, but no palest light broke.

VI

He stayed away, after this, for a year; he visited the depths of Asia, spending himself on scenes of romantic interest, of superlative sanctity; but what was present to him everywhere was that for a man who had known what *he* had known the world was vulgar and vain. The state of mind in which he had lived for so many years shone out to him, in reflexion, as a light that coloured and refined, a light beside which the glow of the East was garish cheap and thin. The terrible truth was that he had lost —with everything else—a distinction as well; the things he saw could n't help being common when he had become common to look at them. He was simply now one of them himself—he was in the dust, without a peg for the sense of difference; and there were hours when, before the temples of gods and the sepulchres of kings, his spirit turned for nobleness of association to the barely discriminated slab in the London suburb. That had become for him, and more intensely with time and distance, his one witness of a past glory. It was all that was left to him for proof or pride, yet the past glories of Pharaohs were nothing to him as he thought of it. Small wonder then that he came back to it on the morrow of his return. He was drawn there this time as irresistibly as the other, yet with a confidence, almost, that was doubtless the effect of the many months that had elapsed. He had lived, in spite of himself, into his change of feeling, and in wandering over the earth had wandered, as might be said, from the circumference to the centre of his desert. He had settled to his safety and accepted perforce his extinction; figuring to himself, with some colour, in the likeness of certain little old men he remembered to have seen, of whom, all meagre and wizened as they might look, it was related that they had in their time fought twenty duels or been loved by ten princesses. They indeed had been wondrous for others while he was but wondrous for himself; which, however, was exactly the cause of his haste to renew the wonder by getting back, as he might put it, into his own presence. That had quickened his steps and checked his delay. If his visit was prompt it was because he had been separated so long from the part of himself that alone he now valued.

It's accordingly not false to say that he reached his goal with a certain elation and stood there again with a certain assurance. The creature beneath the sod *knew* of his rare experience, so that, strangely now, the place had lost for him its mere blankness of expression. It met him in mildness—not, as before, in mockery; it wore for him the air of conscious greeting that we find, after absence, in things that have closely belonged to us and which seem to confess of themselves to the connexion. The plot of ground, the graven tablet, the tended flowers affected him so as belonging to him that he resembled for the hour a contented landlord reviewing a piece of property. Whatever had happened—well, had happened. He had not come back this time with the vanity of that question, his former worrying "What, *what?*" now practically so spent. Yet he would none the less never again so cut himself off from the spot; he would come back to it every month, for if he did nothing else by its aid he at least held up his head. It thus grew for him, in the oddest way, a positive resource; he carried out his idea of periodical returns, which took their place at last among the most inveterate of his habits. What it all amounted to, oddly enough, was that in his finally so simplified world this garden of death gave him the few square feet of earth on which he could still most live. It was as if, being nothing anywhere else for any one, nothing even for himself, he were just everything here, and if not for a crowd of witnesses or indeed for any witness but John Marcher, then by clear right of the register that he could scan like an open page. The open page was the tomb of his friend, and *there* were the facts of the past, there the truth of his life, there the backward reaches in which he could lose himself. He did this from time to time with such effect that he seemed to wander through the old years with his hand in the arm of a companion who was, in the most extraordinary manner, his other, his younger self; and to wander, which was more extraordinary yet, round and round a third presence—not wandering she, but stationary, still, whose eyes, turning with his revolution, *never ceased* to follow him, and whose seat was his point, so to speak, of orientation. Thus in short he settled to live—feeding all on the sense that he once *had* lived, and dependent on it not alone for a support but for an identity.

It sufficed him in its way for months and the year elapsed; it would doubtless even have carried him further but for an accident, superficially slight, which moved him, quite in another direction, with a force beyond any of his impressions of Egypt or of India. It was a thing of the merest chance—the turn, as he afterwards felt, of a hair, though he was indeed to live to believe that if light had n't come to him in this particular fashion it would still have come in another. He was to live to believe this, I say, though he was not to live, I may not less definitely mention, to do much else. We allow him at any rate the benefit of the conviction, struggling up for him at the end, that, whatever might have happened or not happened, he would have come round of himself to the light. The incident of an autumn day had put the match to the train laid from of old by his misery. With the light before him he knew that even of late his ache had only been smothered. It was strangely drugged, but it throbbed; at the touch it began to bleed. And the touch, in the event, was the face of a fellow mortal. This face, one grey afternoon when the leaves were thick in the alleys, looked into Marcher's own, at the cemetery, with an expression like the cut of a blade. He felt it, that is, so deep down that he winced at the steady thrust. The person who so mutely assaulted him was a figure he had noticed, on reaching his own goal, absorbed by a grave a short distance away, a grave apparently fresh, so that the emotion of the visitor would probably match it for frankness. This fact alone forbade further attention, though during the time he stayed he remained vaguely conscious of his neighbour, a middle-aged man apparently, in mourning, whose bowed back, among the clustered monuments and mortuary yews, was constantly presented. Marcher's theory that these were elements in contact with which he himself revived, had suffered, on this occasion, it may be granted, a marked, an excessive check. The autumn day was dire for him as none had recently been, and he rested with a heaviness he had not yet known on the low stone table that bore May Bartram's name. He rested without power to move, as if some spring in him, some spell vouchsafed, had suddenly been broken for ever. If he could have done that moment as he wanted he would simply have stretched himself on the slab that was ready to take him, treating it as a place prepared to receive his last sleep. What in all the wide world had he now to keep awake for? He stared before him with the question, and it was then that, as one of the cemetery walks passed near him, he caught the shock of the face.

His neighbour at the other grave had withdrawn, as he himself, with force enough in him, would have done by now, and was advancing along the path on his way to one of the gates. This brought him close, and his pace was slow, so that—and all the more as there was a kind of hunger in his look—the two men were for a minute directly confronted. Marcher knew him at once for one of the deeply stricken—a perception so sharp that nothing else in the picture comparatively lived, neither his dress, his age, nor his presumable character and class; nothing lived but the deep ravage of the features he showed. He *showed* them—that was the point; he was moved, as he passed, by some impulse that was either a signal for sympathy or, more possibly, a challenge to an opposed sorrow. He might already have been aware of our friend, might at some previous hour have noticed in him the smooth habit of the scene, with which the state of his own senses so scantly consorted, and might thereby have been stirred as by an overt discord. What Marcher was at all events conscious of was in the first place that the image of scarred passion presented to him was conscious too— of something that profaned the air; and in the second that, roused, startled, shocked, he was yet the next moment looking after it, as it went, with envy. The most extraordinary thing that had happened to him—though he had given that name to other matters as well—took place, after his immediate vague stare, as a consequence of this impression. The stranger passed, but the raw glare of his grief remained, making our friend wonder in pity what wrong, what wound it expressed, what injury not to be healed. What had the man *had,* to make him by the loss of it so bleed and yet live?

Something—and this reached him with a pang—that he, John Marcher, had n't; the proof of which was precisely John Marcher's arid end. No passion had ever touched him, for this was what passion meant; he had survived and maundered and pined, but where had been *his* deep ravage? The extraordinary thing we speak of was the sudden rush of the result of this question. The sight that had just met his eyes named to him, as in letters of quick flame, something he had utterly, insanely missed, and what he had missed made these things a train of fire, made them mark themselves in an anguish of inward throbs. He had seen *outside* of his life, not learned it within, the way a woman was mourned when she had been loved for herself: such was the force of his conviction of the meaning of the stranger's face, which still flared for him as a smoky torch. It had n't come to him, the knowledge, on the wings of experience; it had brushed him, jostled him, upset him, with the disrespect of chance, the insolence of accident. Now that the illumination had begun, however, it blazed to the zenith, and what he presently stood there gazing at was the sounded void of his life. He gazed, he drew breath, in pain; he turned in his dismay, and, turning, he had before him in sharper incision than ever the open page of his story. The name on the table smote him as the passage of his neighbour had done, and what it said to him, full in the face, was that *she* was what he had missed. This was the awful thought, the answer to all the past, the vision at the dread clearness of which he grew as cold as the stone beneath him. Everything fell together, confessed, explained, overwhelmed; leaving him most of all stupefied at the blindness he had cherished. The fate he had been marked for he had met with a vengeance—he had emptied the cup to the lees; he had been the man of his time, *the* man, to whom nothing on earth was to have happened. That was the rare stroke—that was his visitation. So he saw it, as we say, in pale horror, while the pieces fitted and fitted. So *she* had seen it while he did n't, and so she served at this hour to drive the truth home. It was the truth, vivid and monstrous, that all the while he had waited the wait was itself his portion. This the companion of his vigil had at a given moment made out, and she had then offered him the chance to baffle his doom. One's doom, however, was never baffled, and on the day she told him his own had come down she had seen him but stupidly stare at the escape she offered him.

The escape would have been to love her; then, *then* he would have lived. She had lived—who could say now with what passion?—since she had loved him for himself; whereas he had never thought of her (ah how it hugely glared at him!) but in the chill of his egotism and the light of her use. Her spoken words came back to him —the chain stretched and stretched. The Beast had lurked indeed, and the Beast, at its hour, had sprung; it had sprung in that twilight of the cold April when, pale, ill, wasted, but all beautiful, and perhaps even then recoverable, she had risen from her chair to stand before him and let him imaginably guess. It had sprung as he did n't guess; it had sprung as she hopelessly turned from him, and the mark, by the time he left her, had fallen where it *was* to fall. He had justified his fear and achieved his fate; he had failed, with the last exactitude, of all he was to fail of; and a moan now rose to his lips as he remembered she had prayed he might n't know. This horror of waking—*this* was knowledge, knowledge under the breath of which the very tears in his eyes seemed to freeze. Through them, none the less, he tried to fix it and hold it; he kept it there before him so that he might feel the pain. That at least, belated and bitter, had something of the taste of life. But the bitterness suddenly sickened him, and it was as if, horribly, he saw, in the truth, in the cruelty of his image, what had been appointed and done. He saw the Jungle of his life and saw the lurking Beast; then, while he looked, perceived it, as by a stir of the air, rise, huge and hideous, for the leap that was to settle him. His eyes darkened—it was close; and, instinctively turning, in his hallucination, to avoid it, he flung himself, face down, on the tomb.

1903

from Preface to *The American*

. . . If in "The American" I invoked the romantic association without malice prepense, yet with a production of the romantic effect that is for myself unmistakeable, the occasion is of the best perhaps for penetrating a little the obscurity of that principle. By what art or mystery, what craft of selection, omission or commission, does a given picture of life appear to us to surround its theme, its figures and images, with the air of romance while another picture close beside it may affect us as steeping the whole matter in the element of reality? . . .

(. . . The real represents to my perception the things we cannot possibly *not* know, sooner or later, in one way or another; it being but one of the accidents of our hampered state, and one of the incidents of their quantity and number, that particular instances have not yet come our way. The romantic stands, on the other hand, for the things that, with all the facilities in the world, all the wealth and all the courage and all the wit and all the adventure, we never *can* directly know; the things that can reach us only through the beautiful circuit and subterfuge of our thought and our desire.) There have been, I gather, many definitions of romance, as a matter indispensably of boats, or of caravans, or of tigers, or of "historical characters," or of ghosts, or of forgers, or of detectives, or of beautiful wicked women, or of pistols and knives, but they appear for the most part reducible to the idea of the facing of danger, the acceptance of great risks for the fascination, the very love, of their uncertainty, the joy of success if possible and of battle in any case. This would be a fine formula if it bore examination; but it strikes me as weak and inadequate, as by no means covering the true ground and yet as landing us in strange confusions.

The panting pursuit of danger is the pursuit of life itself, in which danger awaits us possibly at every step and faces us at every turn; so that the dream of an intenser experience easily becomes rather some vision of a sublime security like that enjoyed on the flowery plains of heaven, where we may conceive ourselves proceeding in ecstasy from one prodigious phase and form of it to another. And if it be insisted that the measure of the type is then in the *appreciation* of danger—the sign of our projection of the real being the smallness of its dangers, and that of our projection of the romantic the hugeness, the mark of the distinction being in short, as they say of collars and gloves and shoes, the size and "number" of the danger—this discrimination again surely fails, since it makes our difference not a difference of kind, which is what we want, but a difference only of degree, and subject by that condition to the indignity of a sliding scale and a shifting measure. There are immense and flagrant dangers that are but sordid and squalid ones, as we feel, tainting with their quality the very defiances they provoke; while there are common and covert ones, that "look like nothing" and that can be but inwardly and occultly dealt with, which involve the sharpest hazards to life and honour and the highest instant decisions and intrepidities of action. It is an arbitrary stamp that keeps these latter prosaic and makes the former heroic; and yet I should still less subscribe to a mere "subjective" division— I mean one that would place the difference wholly in the temper of the imperilled agent. It would be impossible to have a more romantic temper than Flaubert's Madame Bovary,[1] and yet nothing less resembles a romance than the record of her adventures. To classify it by that aspect—the definition of the spirit that happens to animate her —is like settling the question (as I have seen it witlessly settled) by the presence or absence of "costume." Where again then does costume begin or end?—save with the "run" of one or another sort of play? We must reserve vague labels for artless mixtures.

The only *general* attribute of projected romance that I can see, the only one that fits all its cases, is the fact of the kind of experience with which it deals—experience liberated, so to speak; experience disengaged, disembroiled, disencumbered, exempt from the conditions that we usually know to attach to it and, if we wish so to put the matter, drag upon it, and operating in a medium which relieves it, in a particular interest, of the inconvenience of a *related,* a measurable state, a state subject to all our vulgar communities. The greatest intensity may so be arrived at evidently—when the sacrifice of community, of the "related" sides of situations, has not been too rash. It must to this end not flagrantly betray itself; we must even be kept if possible, for our illusion, from suspecting any sacrifice at all. The balloon of experience is in fact of course tied to the earth, and under that necessity we swing, thanks to a rope of remarkable length, in the more or less commodious car of the imagination; but it is by the rope we know where we are, and from the moment that cable is cut we are at large and unrelated: we only swing apart from the globe—though remaining as exhilarated, naturally, as we like, especially when all goes well. The art of the romancer is, "for the fun of it," insidiously to cut the cable, to cut it without our detecting him. What I have recognised then in "The American," much to my surprise and after long years, is that the experience here represented is the disconnected and uncontrolled experience—uncontrolled by our general sense of "the way things happen"—which romance alone more or less successfully palms off on us. It is a case of Newman's[2] own intimate experience all, that being my subject, the thread of which, from beginning to end, is not once exchanged, however momentarily, for any other thread; and the experience of others concerning us, and concerning him, only so far as it touches him and as he recognises, feels or divines it. There is our general sense

---

[1] The heroine of the novel by the same name (1856), created by Gustave Flaubert (1821–1880), French novelist and literary acquaintance of James. Emma Bovary's temperament is as romantic as the narrative in which she figures is severely realistic.

[2] Newman: hero of *The American.*

of the way things happen—it abides with us indefeasibly, as readers of fiction, from the moment we demand that our fiction shall be intelligible; and there is our particular sense of the way they don't happen, which is liable to wake up unless reflexion and criticism, in us, have been skilfully and successfully drugged. There are drugs enough, clearly—it is all a question of applying them with tact; in which case the way things don't happen may be artfully made to pass for the way things do. . . .

1907

The Jolly Corner

I

"Every one asks me what I 'think' of everything," said Spencer Brydon; "and I make answer as I can—begging or dodging the question, putting them off with any nonsense. It would n't matter to any of them really," he went on, "for, even were it possible to meet in that stand-and-deliver way so silly a demand on so big a subject, my 'thoughts' would still be almost altogether about something that concerns only myself." He was talking to Miss Staverton, with whom for a couple of months now he had availed himself of every possible occasion to talk; this disposition and this resource, this comfort and support, as the situation in fact presented itself, having promptly enough taken the first place in the considerable array of rather unattenuated surprises attending his so strangely belated return to America. Everything was somehow a surprise; and that might be natural when one had so long and so consistently neglected everything, taken pains to give surprises so much margin for play. He had given them more than thirty years—thirty-three, to be exact; and they now seemed to him to have organised their performance quite on the scale of that licence. He had been twenty-three on leaving New York—he was fifty-six to-day: unless indeed he were to reckon as he had sometimes, since his repatriation, found himself feeling; in which case he would have lived longer than is often allotted to man. It would have taken a century, he repeatedly said to himself, and said also to Alice Staverton, it would have taken a longer absence and a more averted mind than those even of which he had been guilty, to pile up the differences, the newnesses, the queernesses, above all the bignesses, for the better or the worse, that at present assaulted his vision wherever he looked.

The great fact all the while however had been the incalculability; since he *had* supposed himself, from decade to decade, to be allowing, and in the most liberal and intelligent manner, for brilliancy of change. He actually saw that he had allowed for nothing; he missed what he would have been sure of finding, he found what he would never have imagined. Proportions and values were upside-down; the ugly things he had expected, the ugly things of his far-away youth, when he had too promptly waked up to a sense of the ugly—these uncanny phenomena placed him rather, as it happened, under the charm; whereas the "swagger" things, the modern, the monstrous, the famous things, those he had more particularly, like thousands of ingenuous enquirers every year, come over to see, were exactly his sources of dismay. They were as so many set traps for displeasure, above all for reaction, of which his restless tread was constantly pressing the spring. It was interesting, doubtless, the whole show, but it would have been too disconcerting had n't a certain finer truth saved the situation. He had distinctly not, in this steadier light, come over *all* for the monstrosities; he had come, not only in the last analysis but quite on the face of the act, under an impulse with which they had nothing to do. He had come—putting the thing pompously— to look at his "property," which he had thus for a third of a century not been within four thousand miles of; or, expressing it less sordidly, he had yielded to the humour of seeing again his house on the jolly corner, as he usually, and quite fondly, described it—the one in which he had first seen the light, in which various members of his family had lived and had died, in which the holidays of his overschooled boyhood had been passed and the few social flowers of his chilled adolescence gathered, and which, alienated then for so long a period, had, through the successive deaths of his two brothers and the termination of old arrangements, come wholly into his hands. He was the owner of another, not quite so "good"—the jolly corner having been, from far back, superlatively extended and consecrated; and the value of the pair represented his main capital, with an income consisting, in these later years, of their respective rents which (thanks precisely to their original excellent type) had never been depressingly low. He could live in "Europe," as he had been in the habit of living, on the product of these flourishing New York leases, and all the better since, that of the second structure, the mere number in its long row, having within a twelvemonth fallen in, renovation at a high advance had proved beautifully possible.

These were items of property indeed, but he had found himself since his arrival distinguishing more than ever between them. The house within the street, two bristling blocks westward, was already in course of reconstruction as a tall mass of flats; he had acceded, some time before, to overtures for this conversion—in which, now that it was going forward, it had been not the least of his astonishments to find himself able, on the spot, and though without a previous ounce of such experience, to participate with a certain intelligence, almost with a certain authority. He had lived his life with his back so turned to such concerns and his face addressed to those of so different an order that he scarce knew what to make of this lively stir, in a compartment of his mind never yet penetrated, of a capacity for business and a sense for construction. These virtues, so common all round him now, had been dormant in his own organism—where it might be said of them perhaps that they had slept the sleep of the just. At present, in the splendid autumn weather—the autumn at least was a pure boon in the terrible place—he loafed about his "work" undeterred, secretly agitated; not in the least "minding" that the whole proposition, as they said, was vulgar and sordid, and ready to climb ladders, to walk the plank, to handle materials and look wise about them, to ask questions, in fine, and challenge explanations and really "go into" figures.

It amused, it verily quite charmed him; and, by the same stroke, it amused, and even more, Alice Staverton, though perhaps charming her perceptibly less. She was n't however going to be better-off for it, as *he* was—and so astonishingly much: nothing was now likely, he knew, ever to make her better-off than she found herself, in the afternoon of life, as the delicately frugal possessor and tenant of the small house in Irving Place to which she had subtly managed to cling through her almost unbroken New York career. If he knew the way to it now better than to any other address among the dreadful multiplied numberings which seemed to him to reduce the whole place to some vast ledger-page, overgrown, fantastic, of ruled and criss-crossed lines and figures—if he had formed, for his consolation, that habit, it was really not a little because of the charm of his having encountered and recognised, in the vast wilderness of the wholesale, breaking through the mere gross generalisation of wealth and force and success, a small still scene where items and shades, all delicate things, kept the sharpness of the notes of a high voice perfectly trained, and where economy hung about like the scent of a garden. His old friend lived with one maid and herself dusted her relics and trimmed her lamps and polished her silver; she stood off, in the awful modern crush, when she could, but she sallied forth and did battle when the challenge was really to "spirit," the spirit she after all confessed to, proudly and a little shyly, as to that of the better time, that of *their* common, their quite far-away and antediluvian social period and order. She made use of the street-cars when need be, the terrible things that people scrambled for as the panic-stricken at sea scramble for the boats; she affronted, inscrutably, under stress, all the public concussions and ordeals; and yet, with that slim mystifying grace of her appearance, which defied you to say if she were a fair young woman who looked older through trouble, or a fine smooth older one who looked young through successful indifference; with her precious reference, above all, to memories and histories into which he could enter, she was as exquisite for him as some pale pressed flower (a rarity to begin with), and, failing other sweetnesses, she was a sufficient reward of his effort. They had communities of knowledge, "their" knowledge (this discriminating possessive was always on her lips) of presences of the other age, presences all overlaid, in his case, by the experience of a man and the freedom of a wanderer, overlaid by pleasure, by infidelity, by passages of life that were strange and dim to her, just by "Europe" in short, but still unobscured, still exposed and cherished, under that pious visitation of the spirit from which she had never been diverted.

She had come with him one day to see how his "apartment-house" was rising; he had helped her over gaps and explained to her plans, and while they were there had happened to have, before her, a brief but lively discussion with the man in charge, the representative of the building-firm that had undertaken his work. He had found himself quite "standing-up" to this personage over a failure on the latter's part to observe some detail of one of their noted conditions, and had so lucidly argued his case that, besides ever so prettily flushing, at the time, for sympathy in his triumph, she had afterwards said to him (though to a slightly greater effect of irony) that he had clearly for too many years neglected a real gift. If he had but stayed at home he would have anticipated the inventor of the sky-scraper. If he had but stayed at home he would have discovered his genius in time really to start some new variety of awful architectural hare and run it till it burrowed in a goldmine. He was to remember these words, while the weeks elapsed, for the small silver ring they had sounded over the queerest and deepest of his own lately most disguised and most muffled vibrations.

It had begun to be present to him after the first fortnight, it had broken out with the oddest abruptness, this particular wanton wonderment: it met him there—and this was the image under which he himself judged the matter, or at least, not a little, thrilled and flushed with it—very much as he might have been met by some strange figure, some unexpected occupant, at a turn of one of the dim passages of an empty house. The quaint analogy quite hauntingly remained with him, when he didn't indeed rather improve it by a still intenser form: that of his opening a door behind which he would have made sure of finding nothing, a door into a room shuttered and void, and yet so coming, with a great suppressed start, on some quite erect confronting presence, something planted in the middle of the place and facing him through the dusk. After that visit to the house in construction he walked with his companion to see the other and always so much the better one, which in the eastward direction formed one of the corners, the "jolly" one precisely, of the street now so generally dishonoured and disfigured in its westward reaches, and of the comparatively conservative Avenue.[1] The Avenue still had pretensions, as Miss Staverton said, to decency; the old people had mostly gone, the old names were unknown, and here and there an old association seemed to stray, all vaguely, like some very aged person, out too late, whom you might meet and feel the impulse to watch or follow, in kindness, for safe restoration to shelter.

They went in together, our friends; he admitted himself with his key, as he kept no one there, he explained, preferring, for his reasons, to leave the place empty, under a simple arrangement with a good woman living in the neighbourhood and who came for a daily hour to open windows and dust and sweep. Spencer Brydon had his reasons and was growingly aware of them; they seemed to him better each time he was there, though he didn't name them all to his companion, any more than he told her as yet how often, how quite absurdly often, he himself came. He only let her see for the present, while they walked through the great blank rooms, that absolute vacancy reigned and that, from top to bottom, there was nothing but Mrs. Muldoon's broomstick, in a corner, to tempt the burglar. Mrs. Muldoon was then on the premises, and she loquaciously attended the visitors, preceding them from room to room and pushing back shutters and throwing up sashes—all to show them, as she remarked, how little there was to see. There was little indeed to see in the great gaunt shell where the main dispositions and the general apportionment of space, the style of an age of ampler allowances, had nevertheless for its master their honest pleading message, affecting him as some good old servant's, some lifelong retainer's appeal for a character, or even for a retiring-pension; yet it was also a remark of Mrs. Muldoon's that, glad as she was to oblige him by her noonday round, there was a request she greatly hoped he would never make of her. If he should wish her for any reason to come in after dark she would just tell him, if he "plased," that he must ask it of somebody else.

The fact that there was nothing to see didn't militate for the worthy woman against what one *might* see, and she put it frankly to Miss Staverton that no lady could be expected to like, could she? "craping up to thim top storeys in the ayvil hours." The gas and the electric light were off the house, and she fairly evoked a gruesome vision of her march through the great grey rooms—so many of them as there were too!—with her glimmering taper. Miss Staverton met her honest glare with a smile and the profession that she herself certainly would recoil from such an adventure. Spencer Brydon meanwhile held his peace—for the moment; the question of the "evil" hours in his old home had already become too grave for him. He had begun some time since to "crape," and he knew just why a packet of candles addressed to

[1] Lower Fifth Avenue near Fourteenth Street, the New York City area where James grew up.

that pursuit had been stowed by his own hand, three weeks before, at the back of a drawer of the fine old sideboard that occupied, as a "fixture," the deep recess in the dining-room. Just now he laughed at his companions—quickly however changing the subject; for the reason that, in the first place, his laugh struck him even at that moment as starting the odd echo, the conscious human resonance (he scarce knew how to qualify it) that sounds made while he was there alone sent back to his ear or his fancy; and that, in the second, he imagined Alice Staverton for the instant on the point of asking him, with a divination, if he ever so prowled. There were divinations he was unprepared for, and he had at all events averted enquiry by the time Mrs. Muldoon had left them, passing on to other parts.

There was happily enough to say, on so consecrated a spot, that could be said freely and fairly; so that a whole train of declarations was precipitated by his friend's having herself broken out, after a yearning look round: "But I hope you don't mean they want you to pull *this* to pieces!" His answer came, promptly, with his re-awakened wrath: it was of course exactly what they wanted, and what they were "at" him for, daily, with the iteration of people who could n't for their life understand a man's liability to decent feelings. He had found the place, just as it stood and beyond what he could express, an interest and a joy. There were values other than the beastly rent-values, and in short, in short—! But it was thus Miss Staverton took him up. "In short you're to make so good a thing of your sky-scraper that, living in luxury on *those* ill-gotten gains, you can afford for a while to be sentimental here!" Her smile had for him, with the words, the particular mild irony with which he found half her talk suffused; an irony without bitterness and that came, exactly, from her having so much imagination—not, like the cheap sarcasms with which one heard most people, about the world of "society," bid for the reputation of cleverness, from nobody's really having any. It was agreeable to him at this very moment to be sure that when he had answered, after a brief demur, "Well yes: so, precisely, you may put it!" her imagination would still do him justice. He explained that even if never a dollar were to come to him from the other house he would nevertheless cherish this one; and he dwelt, further, while they lingered and wandered, on the fact of the stupefaction he was already exciting, the positive mystification he felt himself create.

He spoke of the value of all he read into it, into the mere sight of the walls, mere shapes of the rooms, mere sound of the floors, mere feel, in his hand, of the old silver-plated knobs of the several mahogany doors, which suggested the pressure of the palms of the dead; the seventy years of the past in fine that these things represented, the annals of nearly three generations, counting his grandfather's, the one that had ended there, and the impalpable ashes of his long-extinct youth, afloat in the very air like microscopic motes. She listened to everything; she was a woman who answered intimately but who utterly did n't chatter. She scattered abroad therefore no cloud of words; she could assent, she could agree, above all she could encourage, without doing that. Only at the last she went a little further than he had done himself. "And then how do you know? You may still, after all, want to live here." It rather indeed pulled him up, for it was n't what he had been thinking, at least in her sense of the words. "You mean I may decide to stay on for the sake of it?"

"Well, *with* such a home—!" But, quite beautifully, she had too much tact to dot so monstrous an *i,* and it was precisely an illustration of the way she did n't rattle.

How could any one—of any wit—insist on any one else's "wanting" to live in New York?

"Oh," he said, "I *might* have lived here (since I had my opportunity early in life); I might have put in here all these years. Then everything would have been different enough—and, I dare say, 'funny' enough. But that's another matter. And then the beauty of it—I mean of my perversity, of my refusal to agree to a 'deal'—is just in the total absence of a reason. Don't you see that if I had a reason about the matter at all it would *have* to be the other way, and would then be inevitably a reason of dollars? There are no reasons here *but* of dollars. Let us therefore have none whatever—not the ghost of one."

They were back in the hall then for departure, but from where they stood the vista was large, through an open door, into the great square main saloon, with its almost antique felicity of brave spaces between windows. Her eyes came back from that reach and met his own a moment. "Are you very sure the 'ghost' of one doesn't, much rather, serve—?"

He had a positive sense of turning pale. But it was as near as they were then to come. For he made answer, he believed, between a glare and a grin: "Oh ghosts—of course the place must swarm with them! I should be ashamed of it if it didn't. Poor Mrs. Muldoon's right, and it's why I haven't asked her to do more than look in."

Miss Staverton's gaze again lost itself, and things she didn't utter, it was clear, came and went in her mind. She might even for the minute, off there in the fine room, have imagined some element dimly gathering. Simplified like the death-mask of a handsome face, it perhaps produced for her just then an effect akin to the stir of an expression in the "set" commemorative plaster. Yet whatever her impression may have been she produced instead a vague platitude. "Well, if it were only furnished and lived in—!"

She appeared to imply that in case of its being still furnished he might have been a little less opposed to the idea of a return. But she passed straight into the vestibule, as if to leave her words behind her, and the next moment he had opened the house-door and was standing with her on the steps. He closed the door and, while he re-pocketed his key, looking up and down, they took in the comparatively harsh actuality of the Avenue, which reminded him of the assault of the outer light of the Desert on the traveller emerging from an Egyptian tomb. But he risked before they stepped into the street his gathered answer to her speech. "For me it *is* lived in. For me it *is* furnished." At which it was easy for her to sigh "Ah yes—!" all vaguely and discreetly; since his parents and his favourite sister, to say nothing of other kin, in numbers, had run their course and met their end there. That represented, within the walls, ineffaceable life.

It was a few days after this that, during an hour passed with her again, he had expressed his impatience of the too flattering curiosity—among the people he met—about his appreciation of New York. He had arrived at none at all that was socially producible, and as for that matter of his "thinking" (thinking the better or the worse of anything there) he was wholly taken up with one subject of thought. It was mere vain egoism, and it was moreover, if she liked, a morbid obsession. He found all things come back to the question of what he personally might have been, how he might have led his life and "turned out," if he had not so, at the outset, given it up. And confessing for the first time to the intensity within him of this absurd speculation—which but proved also, no doubt, the habit of too selfishly thinking—he affirmed the impotence there of any other source of interest, any other native appeal. "What would it have made of me, what would it have made of me? I keep for ever wondering, all idiotically; as if I could possibly know! I see what it has made of dozens of others, those I meet, and it positively aches within me, to the point of exasperation, that it would have made something of me as well. Only I can't make out *what,* and the worry of it, the small rage of curiosity never to be satisfied, brings back what I remember to have felt, once or twice, after judging best, for reasons, to burn some important letter unopened. I've been sorry, I've hated it—I've never known what was in the letter. You may of course say it's a trifle—!"

"I don't say it's a trifle," Miss Staverton gravely interrupted.

She was seated by her fire, and before her, on his feet and restless, he turned to and fro between this intensity of his idea and a fitful and unseeing inspection, through his single eye-glass, of the dear little old objects on her chimney-piece. Her interruption made him for an instant look at her harder. "I should n't care if you did!" he laughed, however; "and it's only a figure, at any rate, for the way I now feel. *Not* to have followed my perverse young course—and almost in the teeth of my father's curse, as I may say; not to have kept it up, so, 'over there,' from that day to this, without a doubt or a pang; not, above all, to have liked it, to have loved it, so much, loved it, no doubt, with such an abysmal conceit of my own preference: some variation from *that,* I say, must have produced some different effect for my life and for my 'form.' I should have stuck here—if it had been possible; and I was too young, at twenty-three, to judge, *pour deux sous,*[2] whether it *were* possible. If I had waited I might have seen it was, and then I might have been, by staying here, something nearer to one of these types who have been hammered so hard and made so keen by their conditions. It is n't that I admire them so much—the question of any charm in them, or of any charm, beyond that of the rank money-passion, exerted by their conditions *for* them, has nothing to do with the matter: it's only a question of what fantastic, yet perfectly possible, development of my own nature I may n't have missed. It comes over me that I had then a strange *alter ego* deep down somewhere within me, as the full-blown flower is in the small tight bud, and that I just took the course, I just transferred him to the climate, that blighted him for once and for ever."

"And you wonder about the flower," Miss Staverton said. "So do I, if you want to know; and so I've been wondering these several weeks. I believe in the flower," she continued, "I feel it would have been quite splendid, quite huge and monstrous."

"Monstrous above all!" her visitor echoed; "and I imagine, by the same stroke, quite hideous and offensive."

"You don't believe that," she returned; "if you did you would n't wonder. You'd know, and that would be enough for you. What you feel—and what I feel *for* you —is that you'd have had power."

"You'd have liked me that way?" he asked.

She barely hung fire. "How should I not have liked you?"

"I see. You'd have liked me, have preferred me, a billionaire!"

"How should I not have liked you?" she simply again asked.

He stood before her still—her question kept him motionless. He took it in, so much there was of it; and indeed his not otherwise meeting it testified to that. "I know at least what I am," he simply went on; "the other side of the medal's clear enough. I've not been edifying—I believe I'm thought in a hundred quarters to have been barely decent. I've followed strange paths and worshipped strange gods; it must have come to you again and again—in fact you've admitted to me as much—that I was leading, at any time these thirty years, a selfish frivolous scandalous life. And you see what it has made of me."

She just waited, smiling at him. "You see what it has made of *me.*"

"Oh you're a person whom nothing can have altered. You were born to be what you are, anywhere, anyway: you've the perfection nothing else could have blighted. And don't you see how, without my exile, I should n't have been waiting till now—?" But he pulled up for the strange pang.

"The great thing to see," she presently said, "seems to me to be that it has spoiled nothing. It has n't spoiled your being here at last. It has n't spoiled this. It has n't spoiled your speaking—" She also however faltered.

He wondered at everything her controlled emotion might mean. "Do you believe then—too dreadfully!—that I *am* as good as I might ever have been?"

"Oh no! Far from it!" With which she got up from her chair and was nearer to him. "But I don't care," she smiled.

"You mean I'm good enough?"

She considered a little. "Will you believe it if I say so? I mean will you let that settle your question for you?" And then as if making out in his face that he drew back from this, that he had some idea which, however absurd, he could n't yet bargain away: "Oh you don't care either—but very differently: you don't care for anything but yourself."

Spencer Brydon recognised it—it was in fact what he had absolutely professed. Yet he importantly qualified. "*He* is n't myself. He's the just so totally other person. But I do want to see him," he added. "And I can. And I shall."

Their eyes met for a minute while he guessed from something in hers that she divined his strange sense. But neither of them otherwise expressed it, and her apparent understanding, with no protesting shock, no easy derision, touched him more deeply than anything yet, constituting for his stifled perversity, on the spot, an element that was like breatheable air. What she said however was unexpected. "Well, *I've* seen him."

"You—?"

"I've seen him in a dream."

"Oh a 'dream'—!" It let him down.

"But twice over," she continued. "I saw him as I see you now."

"You've dreamed the same dream—?"

"Twice over," she repeated. "The very same."

This did somehow a little speak to him, as it also gratified him. "You dream about me at that rate?"

"Ah about *him!*" she smiled.

His eyes again sounded her. "Then you know all about him." And as she said nothing more: "What's the wretch like?"

She hesitated, and it was as if he were pressing her so hard that, resisting for reasons of her own, she had to turn away. "I'll tell you some other time!"

II

It was after this that there was most of a virtue for him, most of a cultivated charm, most of a preposterous secret thrill, in the particular form of surrender to his obsession and of address to what he more and more believed to be his privilege. It was what in these weeks he was living for—since he really felt life to begin but after Mrs. Muldoon had retired from the scene and, visiting the ample house from attic to cellar, making sure he was alone, he knew himself in safe possession and, as he tacitly expressed it, let himself go. He sometimes came twice in the twenty-four hours; the moments he liked best were those of gathering dusk, of the short autumn twilight; this was the time of which, again and again, he found himself hoping most. Then he could, as seemed to him, most intimately wander and wait, linger and listen, feel his fine attention, never in his life before so fine, on the pulse of the great vague place: he preferred the lampless hour and only wished he might have prolonged each day the deep crepuscular spell. Later—rarely much before midnight, but then for a considerable vigil—he watched with his glimmering light; moving slowly, holding it high, playing it far, rejoicing above all, as much as he might, in open vistas, reaches of communication between rooms and by passages; the long straight chance or show, as he would have called it, for the revelation he pretended to invite. It was a practice he found he could perfectly "work" without exciting remark; no one was in the least the wiser for it; even Alice Staverton, who was moreover a well of discretion, did n't quite fully imagine.

He let himself in and let himself out with the assurance of calm proprietorship; and accident so far favoured him that, if a fat Avenue "officer" had happened on occasion to see him entering at eleven-thirty, he had never yet, to the best of his belief, been noticed as emerging at two. He walked there on the crisp November nights, arrived regularly at the evening's end; it was as easy to do this after dining out as to take his way to a club or to his hotel. When he left his club, if he had n't been dining out, it was ostensibly to go to his hotel; and when he left his hotel, if he had spent a part of the evening there, it was ostensibly to go to his club. Everything was easy in fine; everything conspired and promoted: there was truly even in the strain of his experience something that glossed over, something that salved and simplified, all the rest of consciousness. He circulated, talked, renewed, loosely and pleasantly, old relations—met indeed, so far as he could, new expectations and seemed to make out on the whole that in spite of the career, of such different contacts, which he had spoken of to Miss Staverton as ministering so little, for those who might have watched it, to edification, he was positively rather liked than not. He was a dim secondary social success—and all with people who had truly not an idea of him. It was all mere surface sound, this murmur of their welcome, this popping of their corks—just as his gestures of response were the extravagant shadows, emphatic in proportion as they meant little, of some game of *ombres chinoises*.[3] He projected himself all day, in thought, straight

---

[3] French: "Chinese shadows," a show in which actors' shadows are projected upon a screen.

over the bristling line of hard unconscious heads and into the other, the real, the waiting life; the life that, as soon as he had heard behind him the click of his great house-door, began for him, on the jolly corner, as beguilingly as the slow opening bars of some rich music follows the tap of the conductor's wand.

He always caught the first effect of the steel point of his stick on the old marble of the hall pavement, large black-and-white squares that he remembered as the admiration of his childhood and that had then made in him, as he now saw, for the growth of an early conception of style. This effect was the dim reverberating tinkle as of some far-off bell hung who should say where?—in the depths of the house, of the past, of that mystical other world that might have flourished for him had he not, for weal or woe, abandoned it. On this impression he did ever the same thing; he put his stick noiselessly away in a corner—feeling the place once more in the likeness of some great glass bowl, all precious concave crystal, set delicately humming by the play of a moist finger round its edge. The concave crystal held, as it were, this mystical other world, and the indescribably fine murmur of its rim was the sigh there, the scarce audible pathetic wail to his strained ear, of all the old baffled forsworn possibilities. What he did therefore by this appeal of his hushed presence was to wake them into such measure of ghostly life as they might still enjoy. They were shy, all but unappeasably shy, but they were n't really sinister; at least they weren't as he had hitherto felt them—before they had taken the Form he so yearned to make them take, the Form he at moments saw himself in the light of fairly hunting on tiptoe, the points of his evening-shoes, from room to room and from storey to storey.

That was the essence of his vision—which was all rank folly, if one would, while he was out of the house and otherwise occupied, but which took on the last verisimilitude as soon as he was placed and posted. He knew what he meant and what he wanted; it was as clear as the figure on a cheque presented in demand for cash. His *alter ego* "walked"—that was the note of his image of him, while his image of his motive for his own odd pastime was the desire to waylay him and meet him. He roamed, slowly, warily, but all restlessly, he himself did—Mrs. Muldoon had been right, absolutely, with her figure of their "craping"; and the presence he watched for would roam restlessly too. But it would be as cautious and as shifty; the conviction of its probable, in fact its already quite sensible, quite audible evasion of pursuit grew for him from night to night, laying on him finally a rigour to which nothing in his life had been comparable. It had been the theory of many superficially-judging persons, he knew, that he was wasting that life in a surrender to sensations, but he had tasted of no pleasure so fine as his actual tension, had been introduced to no sport that demanded at once the patience and the nerve of this stalking of a creature more subtle, yet at bay perhaps more formidable, than any beast of the forest. The terms, the comparisons, the very practices of the chase positively came again into play; there were even moments when passages of his occasional experience as a sportsman, stirred memories, from his younger time, of moor and mountain and desert, revived for him—and to the increase of his keenness—by the tremendous force of analogy. He found himself at moments—once he had placed his single light on some mantel-shelf or in some recess—stepping back into shelter or shade, effacing himself behind a door or in an embrasure, as he had sought of old the vantage of rock and tree; he found himself holding his breath and living in the joy of the instant, the supreme suspense created by big game alone.

He was n't afraid (though putting himself the question as he believed gentlemen on Bengal tiger-shoots or in close quarters with the great bear of the Rockies had been known to confess to having put it); and this indeed—since here at least he might be frank!—because of the impression, so intimate and so strange, that he himself produced as yet a dread, produced certainly a strain, beyond the liveliest he was likely to feel. They fell for him into categories, they fairly became familiar, the signs, for his own perception, of the alarm his presence and his vigilance created; though leaving him always to remark, portentously, on his probably having formed a relation, his probably enjoying a consciousness, unique in the experience of man. People enough, first and last, had been in terror of apparitions, but who had ever before so turned the tables and become himself, in the apparitional world, an incalculable terror? He might have found this sublime had he quite dared to think of it; but he didn't too much insist, truly, on that side of his privilege. With habit and repetition he gained to an extraordinary degree the power to penetrate the dusk of distances and the darkness of corners, to resolve back into their innocence the treacheries of uncertain light, the evil-looking forms taken in the gloom by mere shadows, by accidents of the air, by shifting effects of perspective; putting down his dim luminary he could still wander on without it, pass into other rooms and, only knowing it was there behind him in case of need, see his way about, visually project for his purpose a comparative clearness. It made him feel, this acquired faculty, like some monstrous stealthy cat; he wondered if he would have glared at these moments with large shining yellow eyes, and what it might n't verily be, for the poor hard-pressed *alter ego,* to be confronted with such a type.

He liked however the open shutters; he opened everywhere those Mrs. Muldoon had closed, closing them as carefully afterwards, so that she should n't notice: he liked —oh this he did like, and above all in the upper rooms!—the sense of the hard silver of the autumn stars through the window-panes, and scarcely less the flare of the street-lamps below, the white electric lustre which it would have taken curtains to keep out. This was human actual social; this was of the world he had lived in, and he was more at his ease certainly for the countenance, coldly general and impersonal, that all the while and in spite of his detachment it seemed to give him. He had support of course mostly in the rooms at the wide front and the prolonged side; it failed him considerably in the central shades and the parts at the back. But if he sometimes, on his rounds, was glad of his optical reach, so none the less often the rear of the house affected him as the very jungle of his prey. The place was there more subdivided; a large "extension" in particular, where small rooms for servants had been multiplied, abounded in nooks and corners, in closets and passages, in the ramifications especially of an ample back staircase over which he leaned, many a time, to look far down— not deterred from his gravity even while aware that he might, for a spectator, have figured some solemn simpleton playing at hide-and-seek. Outside in fact he might himself make that ironic *rapprochement;* [4] but within the walls, and in spite of the clear windows, his consistency was proof against the cynical light of New York.

It had belonged to that idea of the exasperated consciousness of his victim to become a real test for him; since he had quite put it to himself from the first that, oh distinctly! he could "cultivate" his whole perception. He had felt it as above all

---

[4] French: "restoration of harmonious relations."

open to cultivation—which indeed was but another name for his manner of spending his time. He was bringing it on, bringing it to perfection, by practice; in consequence of which it had grown so fine that he was now aware of impressions, attestations of his general postulate, that could n't have broken upon him at once. This was the case more specifically with a phenomenon at last quite frequent for him in the upper rooms, the recognition—absolutely unmistakeable, and by a turn dating from a particular hour, his resumption of his campaign after a diplomatic drop, a calculated absence of three nights—of his being definitely followed, tracked at a distance carefully taken and to the express end that he should the less confidently, less arrogantly, appear to himself merely to pursue. It worried, it finally quite broke him up, for it proved, of all the conceivable impressions, the one least suited to his book. He was kept in sight while remaining himself—as regards the essence of his position—sightless, and his only recourse then was in abrupt turns, rapid recoveries of ground. He wheeled about, retracing his steps, as if he might so catch in his face at least the stirred air of some other quick revolution. It was indeed true that his fully dislocalised thought of these manœuvres recalled to him Pantaloon, at the Christmas farce, buffeted and tricked from behind by ubiquitous Harlequin;[5] but it left intact the influence of the conditions themselves each time he was re-exposed to them, so that in fact this association, had he suffered it to become constant, would on a certain side have but ministered to his intenser gravity. He had made, as I have said, to create on the premises the baseless sense of a reprieve, his three absences; and the result of the third was to confirm the after-effect of the second.

On his return, that night—the night succeeding his last intermission—he stood in the hall and looked up the staircase with a certainty more intimate than any he had yet known. "He's *there,* at the top, and waiting—not, as in general, falling back for disappearance. He's holding his ground, and it's the first time—which is a proof, is n't it? that something has happened for him." So Brydon argued with his hand on the banister and his foot on the lowest stair; in which position he felt as never before the air chilled by his logic. He himself turned cold in it, for he seemed of a sudden to know what now was involved. "Harder pressed?—yes, he takes it in, with its thus making clear to him that I've come, as they say, 'to stay.' He finally does n't like and can't bear it, in the sense, I mean, that his wrath, his menaced interest, now balances with his dread. I've hunted him till he has 'turned': that, up there, is what has happened —he's the fanged or the antlered animal brought at last to bay." There came to him, as I say—but determined by an influence beyond my notation!—the acuteness of this certainty; under which however the next moment he had broken into a sweat that he would as little have consented to attribute to fear as he would have dared immediately to act upon it for enterprise. It marked none the less a prodigious thrill, a thrill that represented sudden dismay, no doubt, but also represented, and with the selfsame throb, the strangest, the most joyous, possibly the next minute almost the proudest, duplication of consciousness.

"He has been dodging, retreating, hiding, but now, worked up to anger, he'll fight!"—this intense impression made a single mouthful, as it were, of terror and

[5] Pantaloon and Harlequin were characters in traditional pantomime comedies in which tricks are played upon aging fools.

applause. But what was wondrous was that the applause, for the felt fact, was so eager, since, if it was his other self he was running to earth, this ineffable identity was thus in the last resort not unworthy of him. It bristled there—somewhere near at hand, however unseen still—as the hunted thing, even as the trodden worm of the adage *must* at last bristle; and Brydon at this instant tasted probably of a sensation more complex than had ever before found itself consistent with sanity. It was as if it would have shamed him that a character so associated with his own should triumphantly succeed in just skulking, should to the end not risk the open; so that the drop of this danger was, on the spot, a great lift of the whole situation. Yet with another rare shift of the same subtlety he was already trying to measure by how much more he himself might now be in peril of fear; so rejoicing that he could, in another form, actively inspire that fear, and simultaneously quaking for the form in which he might passively know it.

The apprehension of knowing it must after a little have grown in him, and the strangest moment of his adventure perhaps, the most memorable or really most interesting, afterwards, of his crisis, was the lapse of certain instants of concentrated conscious *combat*, the sense of a need to hold on to something, even after the manner of a man slipping and slipping on some awful incline; the vivid impulse, above all, to move, to act, to charge, somehow and upon something—to show himself, in a word, that he was n't afraid. The state of "holding-on" was thus the state to which he was momentarily reduced; if there had been anything, in the great vacancy, to seize, he would presently have been aware of having clutched it as he might under a shock at home have clutched the nearest chair-back. He had been surprised at any rate— of this he *was* aware—into something unprecedented since his original appropriation of the place; he had closed his eyes, held them tight, for a long minute, as with that instinct of dismay and that terror of vision. When he opened them the room, the other contiguous rooms, extraordinarily, seemed lighter—so light, almost, that at first he took the change for day. He stood firm, however that might be, just where he had paused; his resistance had helped him—it was as if there were something he had tided over. He knew after a little what this was—it had been in the imminent danger of flight. He had stiffened his will against going; without this he would have made for the stairs, and it seemed to him that, still with his eyes closed, he would have descended them, would have known how, straight and swiftly, to the bottom.

Well, as he had held out, here he was—still at the top, among the more intricate upper rooms and with the gauntlet of the others, of all the rest of the house, still to run when it should be his time to go. He would go at his time—only at his time: did n't he go every night very much at the same hour? He took out his watch—there was light for that: it was scarcely a quarter past one, and he had never withdrawn so soon. He reached his lodgings for the most part at two—with his walk of a quarter of an hour. He would wait for the last quarter—he would n't stir till then; and he kept his watch there with his eyes on it, reflecting while he held it that this deliberate wait, a wait with an effort, which he recognised, would serve perfectly for the attestation he desired to make. It would prove his courage—unless indeed the latter might most be proved by his budging at last from his place. What he mainly felt now was that, since he had n't originally scuttled, he had his dignities—which had never in his life seemed so many—all to preserve and to carry aloft. This was before him in truth as a physical image, an image almost worthy of an age of greater romance.

That remark indeed glimmered for him only to glow the next instant with a finer light; since what age of romance, after all, could have matched either the state of his mind or, "objectively," as they said, the wonder of his situation? The only difference would have been that, brandishing his dignities over his head as in a parchment scroll, he might then—that is in the heroic time—have proceeded downstairs with a drawn sword in his other grasp.

At present, really, the light he had set down on the mantel of the next room would have to figure his sword; which utensil, in the course of a minute, he had taken the requisite number of steps to possess himself of. The door between the rooms was open, and from the second another door opened to a third. These rooms, as he remembered, gave all three upon a common corridor as well, but there was a fourth, beyond them, without issue save through the preceding. To have moved, to have heard his step again, was appreciably a help; though even in recognising this he lingered once more a little by the chimney-piece on which his light had rested. When he next moved, just hesitating where to turn, he found himself considering a circumstance that, after his first and comparatively vague apprehension of it, produced in him the start that often attends some pang of recollection, the violent shock of having ceased happily to forget. He had come into sight of the door in which the brief chain of communication ended and which he now surveyed from the nearer threshold, the one not directly facing it. Placed at some distance to the left of this point, it would have admitted him to the last room of the four, the room without other approach or egress, had it not, to his intimate conviction, been closed *since* his former visitation, the matter probably of a quarter of an hour before. He stared with all his eyes at the wonder of the fact, arrested again where he stood and again holding his breath while he sounded its sense. Surely it had been *subsequently* closed—that is it had been on his previous passage indubitably open!

He took it full in the face that something had happened between—that he could n't not have noticed before (by which he meant on his original tour of all the rooms that evening) that such a barrier had exceptionally presented itself. He had indeed since that moment undergone an agitation so extraordinary that it might have muddled for him any earlier view; and he tried to convince himself that he might perhaps then have gone into the room and, inadvertently, automatically, on coming out, have drawn the door after him. The difficulty was that this exactly was what he never did; it was against his whole policy, as he might have said, the essence of which was to keep vistas clear. He had them from the first, as he was well aware, quite on the brain: the strange apparition, at the far end of one of them, of his baffled "prey" (which had become by so sharp an irony so little the term now to apply!) was the form of success his imagination had most cherished, projecting into it always a refinement of beauty. He had known fifty times the start of perception that had afterwards dropped; had fifty times gasped to himself "There!" under some fond brief hallucination. The house, as the case stood, admirably lent itself; he might wonder at the taste, the native architecture of the particular time, which could rejoice so in the multiplication of doors—the opposite extreme to the modern, the actual almost complete proscription of them; but it had fairly contributed to provoke this obsession of the presence encountered telescopically, as he might say, focussed and studied in diminishing perspective and as by a rest for the elbow.

It was with these considerations that his present attention was charged—they perfectly availed to make what he saw portentous. He *could n't,* by any lapse, have blocked that aperture; and if he had n't, if it was unthinkable, why what else was clear but that there had been another agent? Another agent?—he had been catching, as he felt, a moment back, the very breath of him; but when had he been so close as in this simple, this logical, this completely personal act? It was so logical, that is, that one might have *taken* it for personal; yet for what did Brydon take it, he asked himself, while, softly panting, he felt his eyes almost leave their sockets. Ah this time at last they *were,* the two, the opposed projections of him, in presence; and this time, as much as one would, the question of danger loomed. With it rose, as not before, the question of courage—for what he knew the blank face of the door to say to him was "Show us how much you have!" It stared, it glared back at him with that challenge; it put to him the two alternatives: should he just push it open or not? Oh to have this consciousness was to *think*—and to think, Brydon knew, as he stood there, was, with the lapsing moments, not to have acted! Not to have acted—that was the misery and the pang—was even still not to act; was in fact *all* to feel the thing in another, in a new and terrible way. How long did he pause and how long did he debate? There was presently nothing to measure it; for his vibration had already changed—as just by the effect of its intensity. Shut up there, at bay, defiant, and with the prodigy of the thing palpably proveably *done,* thus giving notice like some stark signboard—under that accession of accent the situation itself had turned; and Brydon at last remarkably made up his mind on what it had turned to.

It had turned altogether to a different admonition; to a supreme hint, for him, of the value of Discretion! This slowly dawned, no doubt—for it could take its time; so perfectly, on his threshold, had he been stayed, so little as yet had he either advanced or retreated. It was the strangest of all things that now when, by his taking ten steps and applying his hand to a latch, or even his shoulder and his knee, if necessary, to a panel, all the hunger of his prime need might have been met, his high curiosity crowned, his unrest assuaged—it was amazing, but it was also exquisite and rare, that insistence should have, at a touch, quite dropped from him. Discretion—he jumped at that; and yet not, verily, at such a pitch, because it saved his nerves or his skin, but because, much more valuably, it saved the situation. When I say he "jumped" at it I feel the consonance of this term with the fact that—at the end indeed of I know not how long—he did move again, he crossed straight to the door. He would n't touch it—it seemed now that he might *if* he would: he would only just wait there a little, to show, to prove, that he would n't. He had thus another station, close to the thin partition by which revelation was denied him; but with his eyes bent and his hands held off in a mere intensity of stillness. He listened as if there had been something to hear, but this attitude, while it lasted, was his own communication. "If you won't then—good: I spare you and I give up. You affect me as by the appeal positively for pity: you convince me that for reasons rigid and sublime—what do I know?—we both of us should have suffered. I respect them then, and, though moved and privileged as, I believe, it has never been given to man, I retire, I renounce—never, on my honour, to try again. So rest for ever—and let *me!*"

That, for Brydon was the deep sense of this last demonstration—solemn, measured, directed, as he felt it to be. He brought it to a close, he turned away; and now verily he knew how deeply he had been stirred. He retraced his steps, taking up his candle, burnt, he observed, well-nigh to the socket, and marking again, lighten it as he would, the distinctness of his footfall; after which, in a moment, he knew himself at the other side of the house. He did here what he had not yet done at these hours—he opened half a casement, one of those in the front, and let in the air of the night; a thing he would have taken at any time previous for a sharp rupture of his spell. His spell was broken now, and it did n't matter—broken by his concession and his surrender, which made it idle henceforth that he should ever come back. The empty street—its other life so marked even by the great lamplit vacancy—was within call, within touch; he stayed there as to be in it again, high above it though he was still perched; he watched as for some comforting common fact, some vulgar human note, the passage of a scavenger or a thief, some night-bird however base. He would have blessed that sign of life; he would have welcomed positively the slow approach of his friend the policeman, whom he had hitherto only sought to avoid, and was not sure that if the patrol had come into sight he might n't have felt the impulse to get into relation with it, to hail it, on some pretext, from his fourth floor.

The pretext that would n't have been too silly or too compromising, the explanation that would have saved his dignity and kept his name, in such a case, out of the papers, was not definite to him: he was so occupied with the thought of recording his Discretion—as an effect of the vow he had just uttered to his intimate adversary —that the importance of this loomed large and something had overtaken all ironically his sense of proportion. If there had been a ladder applied to the front of the house, even one of the vertiginous perpendiculars employed by painters and roofers and sometimes left standing overnight, he would have managed somehow, astride of the window-sill, to compass by outstretched leg and arm that mode of descent. If there had been some such uncanny thing as he had found in his room at hotels, a workable fire-escape in the form of notched cable or a canvas shoot, he would have availed himself of it as a proof—well, of his present delicacy. He nursed that sentiment, as the question stood, a little in vain, and even—at the end of he scarce knew, once more, how long—found it, as by the action on his mind of the failure of response of the outer world, sinking back to vague anguish. It seemed to him he had waited an age for some stir of the great grim hush; the life of the town was itself under a spell— so unnaturally, up and down the whole prospect of known and rather ugly objects, the blankness and the silence lasted. Had they ever, he asked himself, the hard-faced houses, which had begun to look livid in the dim dawn, had they ever spoken so little to any need of his spirit? Great builded voids, great crowded stillnesses put on, often, in the heart of cities, for the small hours, a sort of sinister mask, and it was of this large collective negation that Brydon presently became conscious—all the more that the break of day was, almost incredibly, now at hand, proving to him what a night he had made of it.

He looked again at his watch, saw what had become of his time-values (he had taken hours for minutes—not, as in other tense situations, minutes for hours) and the strange air of the streets was but the weak, the sullen flush of a dawn in which everything was still locked up. His choked appeal from his own open window had been the sole note of life, and he could but break off at last as for a worse despair. Yet while so deeply demoralised he was capable again of an impulse denoting—at least by his present measure—extraordinary resolution; of retracing his steps to the spot where he had turned cold with the extinction of his last pulse of doubt as to there being in the place another presence than his own. This required an effort strong enough to sicken him; but he had his reason, which overmastered for the moment everything else. There was the whole of the rest of the house to traverse, and how should he screw himself to that if the door he had seen closed were at present open? He could hold to the idea that the closing had practically been for him an act of mercy, a chance offered him to descend, depart, get off the ground and never again profane it. This conception held together, it worked; but what it meant for him depended now clearly on the amount of forbearance his recent action, or rather his recent inaction, had engendered. The image of the "presence," whatever it was, waiting there for him to go—this image had not yet been so concrete for his nerves as when he stopped short of the point at which certainty would have come to him. For, with all his resolution, or more exactly with all his dread, he did stop short—he hung back from really seeing. The risk was too great and his fear too definite: it took at this moment an awful specific form.

He knew—yes, as he had never known anything—that, *should* he see the door open, it would all too abjectly be the end of him. It would mean that the agent of his shame—for his shame was the deep abjection—was once more at large and in general possession; and what glared him thus in the face was the act that this would determine for him. It would send him straight about to the window he had left open, and by that window, be long ladder and dangling rope as absent as they would, he saw himself uncontrollably insanely fatally take his way to the street. The hideous chance of this he at least could avert; but he could only avert it by recoiling in time from assurance. He had the whole house to deal with, this fact was still there; only he now knew that uncertainty alone could start him. He stole back from where he had checked himself—merely to do so was suddenly like safety—and, making blindly for the greater staircase, left gaping rooms and sounding passages behind. Here was the top of the stairs, with a fine large dim descent and three spacious landings to mark off. His instinct was all for mildness, but his feet were harsh on the floors, and, strangely, when he had in a couple of minutes become aware of this, it counted somehow for help. He could n't have spoken, the tone of his voice would have scared him, and the common conceit or resource of "whistling in the dark" (whether literally or figuratively) have appeared basely vulgar; yet he liked none the less to hear himself go, and when he had reached his first landing—taking it all with no rush, but quite steadily—that stage of success drew from him a gasp of relief.

The house, withal, seemed immense, the scale of space again inordinate; the open rooms, to no one of which his eyes deflected, gloomed in their shuttered state like mouths of caverns; only the high skylight that formed the crown of the deep well created for him a medium in which he could advance, but which might have been, for queerness of colour, some watery under-world. He tried to think of something noble, as that his property was really grand, a splendid possession; but this nobleness took the form too of the clear delight with which he was finally to sacrifice it. They might come in now, the builders, the destroyers—they might come as soon as they would. At the end of two flights he had dropped to another zone, and from the middle of the third, with only one more left, he recognised the influence of the lower windows, of half-drawn blinds, of the occasional gleam of street-lamps, of the glazed spaces of the vestibule. This was the bottom of the sea, which showed an illumination of its own and which he even saw paved—when at a given moment he drew up to sink a long look over the banisters—with the marble squares of his childhood. By that time indubitably he felt, as he might have said in a commoner cause, better; it had allowed him to stop and draw breath, and the ease increased with the sight of the old black-and-white slabs. But what he most felt was that now surely, with the element of impunity pulling him as by hard firm hands, the case was settled for what he might have seen above had he dared that last look. The closed door, blessedly remote now, was still closed—and he had only in short to reach that of the house.

He came down further, he crossed the passage forming the access to the last flight; and if here again he stopped an instant it was almost for the sharpness of the thrill of assured escape. It made him shut his eyes—which opened again to the straight slope of the remainder of the stairs. Here was impunity still, but impunity almost excessive; inasmuch as the side-lights and the high fan-tracery of the entrance were glimmering straight into the hall; an appearance produced, he the next instant saw, by the fact that the vestibule gaped wide, that the hinged halves of the inner door had been thrown far back. Out of that again the *question* sprang at him, making his eyes, as he felt, half-start from his head, as they had done, at the top of the house, before the sign of the other door. If he had left that one open, had n't he left this one closed, and was n't he now in *most* immediate presence of some inconceivable occult activity? It was as sharp, the question, as a knife in his side, but the answer hung fire still and seemed to lose itself in the vague darkness to which the thin admitted dawn, glimmering archwise over the whole outer door, made a semicircular margin, a cold silvery nimbus that seemed to play a little as he looked—to shift and expand and contract.

It was as if there had been something within it, protected by indistinctness and corresponding in extent with the opaque surface behind, the painted panels of the last barrier to his escape, of which the key was in his pocket. The indistinctness mocked him even while he stared, affected him as somehow shrouding or challenging certitude, so that after faltering an instant on his step he let himself go with the sense that here *was* at last something to meet, to touch, to take, to know—something all unnatural and dreadful, but to advance upon which was the condition for him either of liberation or of supreme defeat. The penumbra, dense and dark, was the virtual screen of a figure which stood in it as still as some image erect in a niche or as some black-vizored sentinel guarding a treasure. Brydon was to know afterwards, was to recall and make out, the particular thing he had believed during the rest of his descent. He saw, in its great grey glimmering margin, the central vagueness diminish, and he felt it to be taking the very form toward which, for so many days, the passion of his curiosity had yearned. It gloomed, it loomed, it was something, it was somebody, the prodigy of a personal presence.

Rigid and conscious, spectral yet human, a man of his own substance and stature waited there to measure himself with his power to dismay. This only could it be— this only till he recognised, with his advance, that what made the face dim was the pair of raised hands that covered it and in which, so far from being offered in defiance, it was buried as for dark deprecation. So Brydon, before him, took him in; with every fact of him now, in the higher light, hard and acute—his planted stillness, his vivid truth, his grizzled bent head and white masking hands, his queer actuality of evening-dress, of dangling double eye-glass, of gleaming silk lappet and white linen, of pearl button and gold watch-guard and polished shoe. No portrait by a great modern master could have presented him with more intensity, thrust him out of his frame with more art, as if there had been "treatment," of the consummate sort, in his every shade and salience. The revulsion, for our friend, had become, before he knew it, immense—this drop, in the act of apprehension, to the sense of his adversary's inscrutable manœuvre. That meaning at least, while he gaped, it offered him; for he could but gape at his other self in this other anguish, gape as a proof that *he,* standing there for the achieved, the enjoyed, the triumphant life, could n't be faced in his triumph. Was n't the proof in the splendid covering hands, strong and completely spread?—so spread and so intentional that, in spite of a special verity that surpassed every other, the fact that one of these hands had lost two fingers, which were reduced to stumps, as if accidentally shot away, the face was effectually guarded and saved.

"Saved," though, *would* it be?—Brydon breathed his wonder till the very impunity of his attitude and the very insistence of his eyes produced, as he felt, a sudden stir which showed the next instant as a deeper portent, while the head raised itself, the betrayal of a braver purpose. The hands, as he looked, began to move, to open; then, as if deciding in a flash, dropped from the face and left it uncovered and presented. Horror, with the sight, had leaped into Brydon's throat, gasping there in a sound he could n't utter; for the bared identity was too hideous as *his,* and his glare was the passion of his protest. The face, *that* face, Spencer Brydon's?—he searched it still, but looking away from it in dismay and denial, falling straight from his height of sublimity. It was unknown, inconceivable, awful, disconnected from any possibility—! He had been "sold," he inwardly moaned, stalking such game as this: the presence before him was a presence, the horror within him a horror, but the waste of his nights had been only grotesque and the success of his adventure an irony. Such an identity fitted his at *no* point, made its alternative monstrous. A thousand times yes, as it came upon him nearer now—the face was the face of a stranger. It came upon him nearer now, quite as one of those expanding fantastic images projected by the magic lantern of childhood; for the stranger, whoever he might be, evil, odious, blatant, vulgar, had advanced as for aggression, and he knew himself give ground. Then harder pressed still, sick with the force of his shock, and falling back as under the hot breath and the roused passion of a life larger than his own, a rage of personality before which his own collapsed, he felt the whole vision turn to darkness and his very feet give way. His head went round; he was going; he had gone.

III

What had next brought him back, clearly—though after how long?—was Mrs. Muldoon's voice, coming to him from quite near, from so near that he seemed presently to see her as kneeling on the ground before him while he lay looking up at her; himself not wholly on the ground, but half-raised and upheld—conscious, yes, of tenderness of support and, more particularly, of a head pillowed in extraordinary softness and faintly refreshing fragrance. He considered, he wondered, his wit but half at his service; then another face intervened, bending more directly over him, and he finally knew that Alice Staverton had made her lap an ample and perfect cushion to him, and that she had to this end seated herself on the lowest degree of the staircase, the rest of his long person remaining stretched on his old black-and-white slabs. They were cold, these marble squares of his youth; but *he* somehow was not, in this rich return of consciousness—the most wonderful hour, little by little, that he had ever known, leaving him, as it did, so gratefully, so abysmally passive, and yet as with a treasure of intelligence waiting all round him for quiet appropriation; dissolved, he might call it, in the air of the place and producing the golden glow of a late autumn afternoon. He had come back, yes—come back from further away than any man but himself had ever travelled; but it was strange how with this sense what he had come back *to* seemed really the great thing, and as if his prodigious journey had been all for the sake of it. Slowly but surely his consciousness grew, his vision of his state thus completing itself: he had been miraculously *carried* back—lifted and carefully borne as from where he had been picked up, the uttermost end of an interminable grey passage. Even with this he was suffered to rest, and what had now brought him to knowledge was the break in the long mild motion.

It had brought him to knowledge, to knowledge—yes, this was the beauty of his state; which came to resemble more and more that of a man who has gone to sleep on some news of a great inheritance, and then, after dreaming it away, after profaning it with matters strange to it, has waked up again to serenity of certitude and has only to lie and watch it grow. This was the drift of his patience—that he had only to let it shine on him. He must moreover, with intermissions, still have been lifted and borne; since why and how else should he have known himself, later on, with the afternoon glow intenser, no longer at the foot of his stairs—situated as these now seemed at that dark other end of his tunnel—but on a deep window-bench of his high saloon, over which had been spread, couch-fashion, a mantle of soft stuff lined with grey fur that was familiar to his eyes and that one of his hands kept fondly feeling as for its pledge of truth. Mrs. Muldoon's face had gone, but the other, the second he had recognised, hung over him in a way that showed how he was still propped and pillowed. He took it all in, and the more he took it the more it seemed to suffice: he was as much at peace as if he had had food and drink. It was the two women who had found him, on Mrs. Muldoon's having plied, at her usual hour, her latch-key—and on her having above all arrived while Miss Staverton still lingered near the house. She had been turning away, all anxiety, from worrying the vain bell-handle—her calculation having been of the hour of the good woman's visit; but the latter, blessedly, had come up while she was still there, and they had entered together. He had then lain, beyond the vestibule, very much as he was lying now—quite, that is, as he appeared to have fallen, but all so wondrously without bruise or gash; only in a depth of stupor. What he most took in, however, at present, with the steadier clearance, was that Alice Staverton had for a long unspeakable moment not doubted he was dead.

"It must have been that I *was*." He made it out as she held him. "Yes—I can only have died. You brought me literally to life. Only," he wondered, his eyes rising to her, "only, in the name of all the benedictions, how?"

It took her but an instant to bend her face and kiss him, and something in the manner of it, and in the way her hands clasped and locked his head while he felt the cool charity and virtue of her lips, something in all this beatitude somehow answered everything. "And now I keep you," she said.

"Oh keep me, keep me!" he pleaded while her face still hung over him: in response to which it dropped again and stayed close, clingingly close. It was the seal of their situation—of which he tasted the impress for a long blissful moment in silence. But he came back. "Yet how did you know—?"

"I was uneasy. You were to have come, you remember—and you had sent no word."

"Yes, I remember—I was to have gone to you at one to-day." It caught on to their "old" life and relation—which were so near and so far. "I was still out there in my strange darkness—where was it, what was it? I must have stayed there so long." He could but wonder at the depth and the duration of his swoon.

"Since last night?" she asked with a shade of fear for her possible indiscretion.

"Since this morning—it must have been: the cold dim dawn of to-day. Where have I been," he vaguely wailed, "where have I been?" He felt her hold him close, and it was as if this helped him now to make in all security his mild moan. "What a long dark day!"

All in her tenderness she had waited a moment. "In the cold dim dawn?" she quavered.

But he had already gone on piecing together the parts of the whole prodigy. "As I did n't turn up you came straight—?"

She barely cast about. "I went first to your hotel—where they told me of your absence. You had dined out last evening and had n't been back since. But they appeared to know you had been at your club."

"So you had the idea of *this*—?"

"Of what?" she asked in a moment.

"Well—of what has happened."

"I believed at least you'd have been here. I've known, all along," she said, "that you've been coming."

" 'Known' it—?"

"Well, I've believed it. I said nothing to you after that talk we had a month ago —but I felt sure. I knew you *would,*" she declared.

"That I'd persist, you mean?"

"That you'd see him."

"Ah but I did n't!" cried Brydon with his long wail. "There's somebody—an awful beast; whom I brought, too horribly, to bay. But it's not me."

At this she bent over him again, and her eyes were in his eyes. "No—it's not you." And it was as if, while her face hovered, he might have made out in it, had n't it been so near, some particular meaning blurred by a smile. "No, thank heaven," she repeated—"it's not you! Of course it was n't to have been."

"Ah but it *was,*" he gently insisted. And he stared before him now as he had been staring for so many weeks. "I was to have known myself."

"You could n't!" she returned consolingly. And then reverting, and as if to account further for what she had herself done, "But it was n't only *that,* that you had n't been at home," she went on. "I waited till the hour at which we had found Mrs. Muldoon that day of my going with you; and she arrived, as I've told you, while, failing to bring any one to the door, I lingered in my despair on the steps. After a little, if she had n't come, by such a mercy, I should have found means to hunt her up. But it was n't," said Alice Staverton, as if once more with her fine intention—"it was n't only that."

His eyes, as he lay, turned back to her. "What more then?"

She met it, the wonder she had stirred. "In the cold dim dawn, you say? Well, in the cold dim dawn of this morning I too saw you."

"Saw *me*——?"

"Saw *him*," said Alice Staverton. "It must have been at the same moment."

He lay an instant taking it in——as if he wished to be quite reasonable. "At the same moment?"

"Yes——in my dream again, the same one I've named to you. He came back to me. Then I knew it for a sign. He had come to you."

At this Brydon raised himself; he had to see her better. She helped him when she understood his movement, and he sat up, steadying himself beside her there on the window-bench and with his right hand grasping her left. "*He* did n't come to me."

"You came to yourself," she beautifully smiled.

"Ah I've come to myself now——thanks to you, dearest. But this brute, with his awful face——this brute's a black stranger. He's none of *me,* even as I *might* have been," Brydon sturdily declared.

But she kept the clearness that was like the breath of infallibility. "Is n't the whole point that you'd have been different?"

He almost scowled for it. "As different as *that*——?"

Her look again was more beautiful to him than the things of this world. "Have n't you exactly wanted to know *how* different? So this morning," she said, "you appeared to me."

"Like *him?*"

"A black stranger!"

"Then how did you know it was I?"

"Because, as I told you weeks ago, my mind, my imagination, had worked so over what you might, what you might n't have been——to show you, you see, how I've thought of you. In the midst of that you came to me——that my wonder might be answered. So I knew," she went on; "and believed that, since the question held you too so fast, as you told me that day, you too would see for yourself. And when this morning I again saw I knew it would be because you had——and also then, from the first moment, because you somehow wanted me. *He* seemed to tell me of that. So why," she strangely smiled, "should n't I like him?"

It brought Spencer Brydon to his feet. "You 'like' that horror——?"

"I *could* have liked him. And to me," she said, "he was no horror. I had accepted him."

" 'Accepted'——?" Brydon oddly sounded.

"Before for the interest of his difference——yes. And as *I* did n't disown him, as *I* knew him——which you at last, confronted with him in his difference, so cruelly did n't, my dear——well, he must have been, you see, less dreadful to me. And it may have pleased him that I pitied him."

She was beside him on her feet, but still holding his hand——still with her arm supporting him. But though it all brought for him thus a dim light, "You 'pitied' him?" he grudgingly, resentfully asked.

"He has been unhappy, he has been ravaged," she said.

"And have n't I been unhappy? Am not I——you've only to look at me!——ravaged?"

"Ah I don't say I like him *better,*" she granted after a thought. "But he's grim, he's worn——and things have happened to him. He does n't make shift, for sight, with your charming monocle."

"No"—it struck Brydon: "I could n't have sported mine 'downtown.' They'd have guyed me there."

"His great convex pince-nez—I saw it, I recognised the kind—is for his poor ruined sight. And his poor right hand—!"

"Ah!" Brydon winced—whether for his proved identity or for his lost fingers. Then, "He has a million a year," he lucidly added. "But he has n't you."

"And he is n't—no, he is n't—*you!*" she murmured as he drew her to his breast.

1908

Sarah Orne Jewett
1849–1909

There is a direct line of influence from the inspiration taken by Sarah Orne Jewett from the regional stories of Harriet Beecher Stowe down to the impetus given by Jewett's writings to the young Mary Eleanor Wilkins Freeman and later to Willa Cather, who became one of Jewett's editors. With the exception of Cather, all these women were reared in New England. They gained almost immediate recognition for their talent to create literary annotations of a tight-knit way of life and a tradition of moral rigor that changed rapidly during their lifetimes. Of this group, Jewett's field of vision stands out for its attention to New England customs and local settings, made universal through its accounting of a people bound to family and community.

One of three daughters of a local practitioner and professor of medicine at Bowdoin College, Sarah Orne Jewett was born in South Berwick, Maine, a coastal town where her grandfather had been the leading sea captain and shipowner. In "The Custom House," preface to *The Scarlet Letter,* written in 1849–1850, Nathaniel Hawthorne could look back on the declining fortunes of once bustling Massachusetts port towns such as Salem. By the time of Jewett's adolescence in the 1860s, the shift from a maritime and entrepreneurial economic system to industrial America had already taken place. Spurred by her reading of Harriet Beecher Stowe's account of Maine coast life, *The Pearl of Orr's Island* (1862), and by the trips she made with her doctor-father on his buggy rounds to rural patients, Jewett decided in her teens to act as a literary amanuensis for the lives of the people of that region.

Jewett's earliest pieces, published under various pseudonyms, were written at the age of fourteen. These stories were often luridly overplotted in the manner of the popular fiction of the time, but she soon included local legends and observations of speech patterns and social mannerisms. Too sickly to receive a regular education, she read a great deal in the books of her father's library, with his constant encouragement. Most of all, she "read" the lives of people who were shaped both by the natural conditions of the villages, farms, and seaports of Maine and by the social complications introduced into a world that no longer seemed small enough to be manageable and pleasing.

By the age of twenty, Sarah Orne Jewett had had her story "Mr. Bruce" accepted by William Dean Howells for publication in the *Atlantic Monthly*. Her first collection of stories appeared as *Deephaven* (1877). In response to the praise she received for work that appeared in the country's best magazines (the *Atlantic, Harper's,* and *Scribner's*), she published more than twenty volumes of stories over the years, culminating in 1896 with *The Country of the Pointed Firs,* her single best collection.

Jewett became a recorder of times in the process of being lost forever—the "was" of her remembered childhood. She did not write rustic idylls about a perfect time and place, but in celebrating the modest pleasures and virtues of rural lives she proved how capable an unmarried woman from a sheltered background could be as the keeper of the literary annals of small-town New England. There was a large audience for such writing in her day. Later generations were reminded of a world they had never experienced personally; through Jewett, Americans came to believe they still possessed it as part of their national heritage.

Further Reading:
F. Matthiessen, *Sarah Orne Jewett,* 1960.
R. Cary, *Sarah Orne Jewett,* 1962.
M. Thorp, *Sarah Orne Jewett,* 1966.
Appreciation of Sarah Orne Jewett: 29 Interpretive Essays, ed. R. Cary, 1973.
J. Donovan, *Sarah Orne Jewett,* 1980.
P. Westbrook, *Acres of Flint: Sarah Orne Jewett and Her Contemporaries,* 1981.

Text:
Tales of New England, 1894.
See also *Deephaven and Other Stories,* ed. R. Cary, 1966.
The Uncollected Short Stories of Sarah Orne Jewett, ed. R. Cary, 1971.
Letters of Sarah Orne Jewett, ed. A. Fields, 1911.
Sarah Orne Jewett Letters, ed. R. Cary, 1956, 1967.

Miss Tempy's Watchers

The time of year was April; the place was a small farming town in New Hampshire, remote from any railroad. One by one the lights had been blown out in the scattered houses near Miss Tempy Dent's; but as her neighbors took a last look out-of-doors, their eyes turned with instinctive curiosity toward the old house, where a lamp burned steadily. They gave a little sigh. "Poor Miss Tempy!" said more than one bereft acquaintance; for the good woman lay dead in her north chamber, and the light was a watcher's light. The funeral was set for the next day, at one o'clock.

The watchers were two of the oldest friends, Mrs. Crowe and Sarah Ann Binson. They were sitting in the kitchen, because it seemed less awesome than the unused best room, and they beguiled the long hours by steady conversation. One would think that neither topics nor opinions would hold out, at that rate, all through the long spring night; but there was a certain degree of excitement just then, and the two women had risen to an unusual level of expressiveness and confidence. Each had already told the other more than one fact that she had determined to keep secret; they were again and again tempted into statements that either would have found impossible by daylight. Mrs. Crowe was knitting a blue yarn stocking for her husband; the foot was already so long that it seemed as if she must have forgotten to narrow it at the proper time. Mrs. Crowe knew exactly what she was about, however; she was of a much cooler disposition than Sister Binson, who made futile attempts at some sewing, only to drop her work into her lap whenever the talk was most engaging.

Their faces were interesting,—of the dry, shrewd, quick-witted New England type, with thin hair twisted neatly back out of the way. Mrs. Crowe could look vague and benignant, and Miss Binson was, to quote her neighbors, a little too sharp-set; but the world knew that she had need to be, with the load she must carry of supporting an inefficient widowed sister and six unpromising and unwilling nieces and nephews. The eldest boy was at last placed with a good man to learn the mason's trade. Sarah Ann Binson, for all her sharp, anxious aspect, never defended herself, when her sister whined and fretted. She was told every week of her life that the poor children never would have had to lift a finger if their father had lived, and yet she had kept her steadfast way with the little farm, and patiently taught the young people many useful things, for which, as everybody said, they would live to thank her. However pleasure-less her life appeared to outward view, it was brimful of pleasure to herself.

Mrs. Crowe, on the contrary, was well to do, her husband being a rich farmer and an easy-going man. She was a stingy woman, but for all that she looked kindly; and when she gave away anything, or lifted a finger to help anybody, it was thought a great piece of beneficence, and a compliment, indeed, which the recipient accepted with twice as much gratitude as double the gift that came from a poorer and more generous acquaintance. Everybody liked to be on good terms with Mrs. Crowe. Socially she stood much higher than Sarah Ann Binson. They were both old school-mates and friends of Temperance Dent, who had asked them, one day, not long before she died, if they would not come together and look after the house, and manage everything, when she was gone. She may have had some hope that they might become closer friends in this period of intimate partnership, and that the richer woman might better understand the burdens of the poorer. They had not kept the house the night before; they were too weary with the care of their old friend, whom they had not left until all was over.

There was a brook which ran down the hillside very near the house, and the sound of it was much louder than usual. When there was silence in the kitchen, the busy stream had a strange insistence in its wild voice, as if it tried to make the watchers understand something that related to the past.

"I declare, I can't begin to sorrow for Tempy yet. I am so glad to have her at rest," whispered Mrs. Crowe. "It is strange to set here without her, but I can't make it clear that she has gone. I feel as if she had got easy and dropped off to sleep, and I'm more scared about waking her up than knowing any other feeling."

"Yes," said Sarah Ann, "it's just like that, ain't it? But I tell you we are goin' to miss her worse than we expect. She's helped me through with many a trial, has Temperance. I ain't the only one who says the same, neither."

These words were spoken as if there were a third person listening; somebody beside Mrs. Crowe. The watchers could not rid their minds of the feeling that they were being watched themselves. The spring wind whistled in the window crack, now and then, and buffeted the little house in a gusty way that had a sort of companionable effect. Yet, on the whole, it was a very still night, and the watchers spoke in a half-whisper.

"She was the freest-handed woman that ever I knew," said Mrs. Crowe, decidedly. "According to her means, she gave away more than anybody. I used to tell her 't wa'n't right. I used really to be afraid that she went without too much, for we have a duty to ourselves."

Sister Binson looked up in a half-amused, unconscious way, and then recollected herself.

Mrs. Crowe met her look with a serious face. "It ain't so easy for me to give as it is for some," she said simply, but with an effort which was made possible only by the occasion. "I should like to say, while Tempy is laying here yet in her own house, that she has been a constant lesson to me. Folks are too kind, and shame me with thanks for what I do. I ain't such a generous woman as poor Tempy was, for all she had nothin' to do with, as one may say."

Sarah Binson was much moved at this confession, and was even pained and touched by the unexpected humility. "You have a good many calls on you"—she began, and then left her kind little compliment half finished.

"Yes, yes, but I've got means enough. My disposition's more of a cross to me as I grow older, and I made up my mind this morning that Tempy's example should be my pattern henceforth." She began to knit faster than ever.

" 'T ain't no use to get morbid: that's what Tempy used to say herself," said Sarah Ann, after a minute's silence. "Ain't it strange to say 'used to say'?" and her own voice choked a little. "She never did like to hear folks git goin' about themselves."

" 'T was only because they're apt to do it so as other folks will say 't was n't so, an' praise 'em up," humbly replied Mrs. Crowe, "and that ain't my object. There wa'n't a child but what Tempy set herself to work to see what she could do to please it. One time my brother's folks had been stopping here in the summer, from Massachusetts. The children was all little, and they broke up a sight of toys, and left 'em when they were going away. Tempy come right up after they rode by, to see if she could n't help me set the house to rights, and she caught me just as I was going to fling some of the clutter into the stove. I was kind of tired out, starting 'em off in season. 'Oh, give me them!' says she, real pleading; and she wropped 'em up and took 'em home with her when she went, and she mended 'em up and stuck 'em together, and made some young one or other happy with every blessed one. You'd thought I'd done her the biggest favor. 'No thanks to me. I should ha' burnt 'em, Tempy,' says I."

"Some of 'em came to our house, I know," said Miss Binson. "She'd take a lot o' trouble to please a child, 'stead o' shoving of it out o' the way, like the rest of us when we're drove."

"I can tell you the biggest thing she ever done, and I don't know's there's anybody left but me to tell it. I don't want it forgot," Sarah Binson went on, looking up at the clock to see how the night was going. "It was that pretty-looking Trevor girl, who taught the Corners school, and married so well afterwards, out in New York State. You remember her, I dare say?"

"Certain," said Mrs. Crowe, with an air of interest.

"She was a splendid scholar, folks said, and give the school a great start; but she'd overdone herself getting her education, and working to pay for it, and she all broke down one spring, and Tempy made her come and stop with her a while,—you remember that? Well, she had an uncle, her mother's brother, out in Chicago, who was well off and friendly, and used to write to Lizzie Trevor, and I dare say make her some presents; but he was a lively, driving man, and did n't take time to stop and think about his folks. He had n't seen her since she was a little girl. Poor Lizzie was so pale and weakly that she just got through the term o' school. She looked as if she was just going straight off in a decline. Tempy, she cosseted her up a while, and then, next thing folks knew, she was tellin' round how Miss Trevor had gone to see her uncle, and meant to visit Niagary Falls on the way, and stop over night. Now I happened to know, in ways I won't dwell on to explain, that the poor girl was in debt for her schoolin' when she come here, and her last quarter's pay had just squared it off at last, and left her without a cent ahead, hardly; but it had fretted her thinking of it, so she paid it all; those might have dunned her that she owed it to. An' I taxed Tempy about the girl's goin' off on such a journey till she owned up, rather 'n have Lizzie blamed, that she'd given her sixty dollars, same's if she was rolling in riches, and sent her off to have a good rest and vacation."

"Sixty dollars!" exclaimed Mrs. Crowe. "Tempy only had ninety dollars a year that came in to her; rest of her livin' she got by helpin' about, with what she raised off this little piece o' ground, sand one side an' clay the other. An' how often I've heard her tell, years ago, that she'd rather see Niagary than any other sight in the world!"

The women looked at each other in silence; the magnitude of the generous sacrifice was almost too great for their comprehension.

"She was just poor enough to do that!" declared Mrs. Crowe at last, in an abandonment of feeling. "Say what you may, I feel humbled to the dust," and her companion ventured to say nothing. She never had given away sixty dollars at once, but it was simply because she never had it to give. It came to her very lips to say in explanation, "Tempy was so situated;" but she checked herself in time, for she would not betray her own loyal guarding of a dependent household.

"Folks say a great deal of generosity, and this one's being public-sperited, and that one free-handed about giving," said Mrs. Crowe, who was a little nervous in the silence. "I suppose we can't tell the sorrow it would be to some folks not to give, same's 't would be to me not to save. I seem kind of made for that, as if 't was what I'd got to do. I should feel sights better about it if I could make it evident what I was savin' for. If I had a child, now, Sarah Ann," and her voice was a little husky, —"if I had a child, I should think I was heapin' of it up because he was the one trained by the Lord to scatter it again for good. But here's Mr. Crowe and me, we can't do anything with money, and both of us like to keep things same's they've always been. Now Priscilla Dance was talking away like a mill-clapper, week before last. She'd think I would go right off and get one o' them new-fashioned gilt-and-white papers for the best room, and some new furniture, an' a marble-top table. And I looked at her, all struck up. 'Why,' says I, 'Priscilla, that nice old velvet paper ain't hurt a mite. I should n't feel 't was my best room without it. Dan'el says 't is the first thing he can remember rubbin' his little baby fingers on to it, and how splendid he thought them red roses was.' I maintain," continued Mrs. Crowe stoutly, "that folks wastes sights o' good money doin' just such foolish things. Tearin' out the insides o' meetin'-houses, and fixin' the pews different; 't was good enough as 't was with mendin'; then times come, an' they want to put it all back same's 't was before."

This touched upon an exciting subject to active members of that parish. Miss Binson and Mrs. Crowe belonged to opposite parties, and had at one time come as near hard feelings as they could, and yet escape them. Each hastened to speak of other things and to show her untouched friendliness.

"I do agree with you," said Sister Binson, "that few of us know what use to make of money, beyond every-day necessities. You've seen more o' the world than I have, and know what's expected. When it comes to taste and judgment about such things, I ought to defer to others;" and with this modest avowal the critical moment passed when there might have been an improper discussion.

In the silence that followed, the fact of their presence in a house of death grew more clear than before. There was something disturbing in the noise of a mouse gnawing at the dry boards of a closet wall near by. Both the watchers looked up anxiously at the clock; it was almost the middle of the night and the whole world seemed to have left them alone with their solemn duty. Only the brook was awake.

"Perhaps we might give a look up-stairs now," whispered Mrs. Crowe, as if she hoped to hear some reason against their going just then to the chamber of death; but Sister Binson rose, with a serious and yet satisfied countenance, and lifted the small lamp from the table. She was much more used to watching than Mrs. Crowe, and much less affected by it. They opened the door into a small entry with a steep stairway; they climbed the creaking stairs, and entered the cold upper room on tiptoe. Mrs. Crowe's heart began to beat very fast as the lamp was put on a high bureau, and made long, fixed shadows about the walls. She went hesitatingly toward the solemn shape under its white drapery, and felt a sense of remonstrance as Sarah Ann gently, but in a business-like way, turned back the thin sheet.

"Seems to me she looks pleasanter and pleasanter," whispered Sarah Ann Binson impulsively, as they gazed at the white face with its wonderful smile. "To-morrow 't will all have faded out. I do believe they kind of wake up a day or two after they die, and it's then they go." She replaced the light covering, and they both turned quickly away; there was a chill in this upper room.

" 'T is a great thing for anybody to have got through, ain't it?" said Mrs. Crowe softly, as she began to go down the stairs on tiptoe. The warm air from the kitchen beneath met them with a sense of welcome and shelter.

"I don' know why it is, but I feel as near again to Tempy down here as I do up there," replied Sister Binson. "I feel as if the air was full of her, kind of. I can sense things, now and then, that she seems to say. Now I never was one to take up with no nonsense of sperits and such, but I declare I felt as if she told me just now to put some more wood into the stove."

Mrs. Crowe preserved a gloomy silence. She had suspected before this that her companion was of a weaker and more credulous disposition than herself. " 'T is a great thing to have got through," she repeated, ignoring definitely all that had last been said. "I suppose you know as well as I that Tempy was one that always feared death. Well, it's all put behind her now; she knows what 't is." Mrs. Crowe gave a little sigh, and Sister Binson's quick sympathies were stirred toward this other old friend, who also dreaded the great change.

"I'd never like to forget almost those last words Tempy spoke plain to me," she said gently, like the comforter she truly was. "She looked up at me once or twice, that last afternoon after I come to set by her, and let Mis' Owen go home; and I says, 'Can I do anything to ease you, Tempy?' and the tears come into my eyes so I could n't see what kind of a nod she give me. 'No, Sarah Ann, you can't, dear,' says she;

and then she got her breath again, and says she, looking at me real meanin', 'I'm only a-gettin' sleepier and sleepier; that's all there is,' says she, and smiled up at me kind of wishful, and shut her eyes. I knew well enough all she meant. She'd been lookin' out for a chance to tell me, and I don' know's she ever said much afterwards."

Mrs. Crowe was not knitting; she had been listening too eagerly. "Yes, 't will be a comfort to think of that sometimes," she said, in acknowledgment.

"I know that old Dr. Prince said once, in evenin' meetin', that he'd watched by many a dyin' bed, as we well knew, and enough o' his sick folks had been scared o' dyin' their whole lives through; but when they come to the last, he'd never seen one but was willin', and most were glad, to go. ' 'T is as natural as bein' born or livin' on,' he said. I don't know what had moved him to speak that night. You know he wa'n't in the habit of it, and 't was the monthly concert of prayer for foreign missions anyways," said Sarah Ann; "but 't was a great stay to the mind to listen to his words of experience."

"There never was a better man," responded Mrs. Crowe, in a really cheerful tone. She had recovered from her feeling of nervous dread, the kitchen was so comfortable with lamplight and firelight; and just then the old clock began to tell the hour of twelve with leisurely whirring strokes.

Sister Binson laid aside her work, and rose quickly and went to the cupboard. "We'd better take a little to eat," she explained. "The night will go fast after this. I want to know if you went and made some o' your nice cupcake, while you was home to-day?" she asked, in a pleased tone; and Mrs. Crowe acknowledged such a gratifying piece of thoughtfulness for this humble friend who denied herself all luxuries. Sarah Ann brewed a generous cup of tea, and the watchers drew their chairs up to the table presently, and quelled their hunger with good country appetites. Sister Binson put a spoon into a small, old-fashioned glass of preserved quince, and passed it to her friend. She was most familiar with the house, and played the part of hostess. "Spread some o' this on your bread and butter," she said to Mrs. Crowe. "Tempy wanted me to use some three or four times, but I never felt to. I know she'd like to have us comfortable now, and would urge us to make a good supper, poor dear."

"What excellent preserves she did make!" mourned Mrs. Crowe. "None of us has got her light hand at doin' things tasty. She made the most o' everything, too. Now, she only had that one old quince-tree down in the far corner of the piece, but she'd go out in the spring and tend to it, and look at it so pleasant, and kind of expect the old thorny thing into bloomin'."

"She was just the same with folks," said Sarah Ann. "And she'd never git more 'n a little apernful o' quinces, but she'd have every mite o' goodness out o' those, and set the glasses up onto her best-room closet shelf, *so* pleased. 'T wa'n't but a week ago to-morrow mornin' I fetched her a little taste o' jelly in a teaspoon; and she says 'Thank ye,' and took it, an' the minute she tasted it she looked up at me as worried as could be. 'Oh, I don't want to eat that,' says she. 'I always keep that in case o' sickness.' 'You're goin' to have the good o' one tumbler yourself,' says I. 'I'd just like to know who's sick now, if you ain't!' An' she couldn't help laughin', I spoke up so smart. Oh, dear me, how I shall miss talkin' over things with her! She always sensed things, and got just the p'int you meant."

"She did n't begin to age until two or three years ago, did she?" asked Mrs. Crowe. "I never saw anybody keep her looks as Tempy did. She looked young long after

I begun to feel like an old woman. The doctor used to say 't was her young heart, and I don't know but what he was right. How she did do for other folks! There was one spell she was n't at home a day to a fortnight. She got most of her livin' so, and that made her own potatoes and things last her through. None o' the young folks could get married without her, and all the old ones was disappointed if she wa'n't round when they was down with sickness and had to go. An' cleanin', or tailorin' for boys, or rug-hookin',—there was nothin' but what she could do as handy as most. 'I do love to work,'—ain't you heard her say that twenty times a week?"

Sarah Ann Binson nodded, and began to clear away the empty plates. "We may want a taste o' somethin' more towards mornin'," she said. "There's plenty in the closet here; and in case some comes from a distance to the funeral, we'll have a little table spread after we get back to the house."

"Yes, I was busy all the mornin'. I've cooked up a sight o' things to bring over," said Mrs. Crowe. "I felt 't was the last I could do for her."

They drew their chairs near the stove again, and took up their work. Sister Binson's rocking-chair creaked as she rocked; the brook sounded louder than ever. It was more lonely when nobody spoke, and presently Mrs. Crowe returned to her thoughts of growing old.

"Yes, Tempy aged all of a sudden. I remember I asked her if she felt as well as common, one day, and she laughed at me good. There, when Mr. Crowe begun to look old, I couldn't help feeling as if somethin' ailed him, and like as not 't was somethin' he was goin' to git right over, and I dosed him for it stiddy, half of one summer."

"How many things we shall be wanting to ask Tempy!" exclaimed Sarah Ann Binson, after a long pause. "I can't make up my mind to doin' without her. I wish folks could come back just once, and tell us how 't is where they've gone. Seems then we could do without 'em better."

The brook hurried on, the wind blew about the house now and then; the house itself was a silent place, and the supper, the warm fire, and an absence of any new topics for conversation made the watchers drowsy. Sister Binson closed her eyes first, to rest them for a minute; and Mrs. Crowe glanced at her compassionately, with a new sympathy for the hard-worked little woman. She made up her mind to let Sarah Ann have a good rest, while she kept watch alone; but in a few minutes her own knitting was dropped, and she, too, fell asleep. Overhead, the pale shape of Tempy Dent, the outworn body of that generous, loving-hearted, simple soul, slept on also in its white raiment. Perhaps Tempy herself stood near, and saw her own life and its surroundings with new understanding. Perhaps she herself was the only watcher.

Later, by some hours, Sarah Ann Binson woke with a start. There was a pale light of dawn outside the small windows. Inside the kitchen, the lamp burned dim. Mrs. Crowe awoke, too.

"I think Tempy'd be the first to say 't was just as well we both had some rest," she said, not without a guilty feeling.

Her companion went to the outer door, and opened it wide. The fresh air was none too cold, and the brook's voice was not nearly so loud as it had been in the midnight darkness. She could see the shapes of the hills, and the great shadows that lay across the lower country. The east was fast growing bright.

" 'T will be a beautiful day for the funeral," she said, and turned again, with a sigh, to follow Mrs. Crowe up the stairs.

1888

Kate Chopin
1851–1904

To the age of nineteen, Katherine O'Flaherty experienced both the pleasures and the boring aimlessness that came to her as a belle caught up in the social swirl of St. Louis, a city flourishing in the aftermath of Civil War prosperity. Her father, an immigrant from Ireland, was a successful businessman; her mother was from an old Creole family that had settled in St. Louis. Her upbringing was Catholic, affluent, and "French" in its adherence to pious convent education, society balls, and French language and culture. Kate Chopin's later remarks about that period of giddy girlhood make clear that both nuns and debutantes lived lives of fantasy that excluded "real life." Real life is what Katherine O'Flaherty confronted in 1870 when she became Mrs. Oscar Chopin (pronounced in the French way, as in the name of the pianist Frédéric Chopin). She went to live in New Orleans, then, after business reversals, to a rural community near the cotton plantation owned by her husband's family. By 1884 she was back again in St. Louis, a widow with six children. Although she was not in financial want, Kate Chopin took up the literary career she had contemplated years earlier—the one she had been too busy raising her family to enter upon.

Kate Chopin set to work to learn how to write acceptable works of fiction. For her models of stories, sketches, and poetry she drew upon French writers— her contemporaries Émile Zola and Guy de Maupassant as well as the eighteenth-century literary and intellectual figure Madame de Staël. But what influenced her most was her experiences among the diverse cultures of Louisiana. Her fiction took as its home ground the lives of Creoles (descendants of the first French and Spanish settlers in the territory), Cajuns (progeny of the French immigrants who had been ignominiously expelled from Canada by the British conquerors in the eighteenth century), and the blacks and Indians of mixed blood who lived throughout Louisiana.

The history of Kate Chopin's reception by the reading public is a revealing one. The publication in 1894 of *Bayou Folk,* a collection of tales of rural life, earned her critical acceptance. *A Night in Acadie* (1897) confirmed her popularity as a teller of stories. Her readers were pleased by her attention to local customs and dialects. (They had taken in the same way to the tales of New England written by Sarah Orne Jewett, which exerted a similar appeal with different material.) Newspapers and important national magazines, such as the newly formed *Vogue* and the well-established *Century,* featured her work. She had already written two novels of slight merit when *The Awakening* appeared in 1899. Almost immediately, her previously appreciative audience rose against her, not surprising when one realizes that the same middle-class readership had been unable to accept Stephen Crane's *Maggie, A Girl of the Streets* in 1893 and would reject Theodore Dreiser's *Sister Carrie* when it appeared in 1900.

Chopin had long been a loyal reader of Walt Whitman's *Leaves of Grass*, and the portrayal in *The Awakening* of Edna Pontellier's aroused sensuousness is indeed Whitmanesque. The young woman's increasing resentment of the constrictions imposed by married life and her flirtations with an attractive roué brought condemnation to the novel and its author; both were dropped from libraries and genteel society. Naturally upset by her fall from favor, Kate Chopin attempted little more writing before her death five years later.

The Awakening was rediscovered in the 1950s. What was once called bad behavior for a woman is now seen as good writing about a woman's turbulent feelings. During Chopin's lifetime, readers may have been drawn to her piquant tales of the exotic yet recognizably human types found in Creole and Cajun culture, but there was hardly approbation for her novel. Today appreciation comes easily to *The Awakening*, while her brief, almost anecdotal stories continue to surprise readers with their arresting portraits of passionate lives. In her accomplishments, Chopin demonstrated the characteristic American talent for writing fine short fiction heralded by Washington Irving, Edgar Allan Poe, and Nathaniel Hawthorne.

Further Reading:
D. Rankin, *Kate Chopin and Her Creole Stories*, 1932.
P. Seyersted, *Kate Chopin: A Critical Biography*, 1969, 1980.

Text:
The Complete Works of Kate Chopin, 2 vols., ed. P. Seyersted, 1969.

Désirée's Baby

As the day was pleasant, Madame Valmondé drove over to L'Abri to see Désirée and the baby.

It made her laugh to think of Désirée with a baby. Why, it seemed but yesterday that Désirée was little more than a baby herself; when Monsieur in riding through the gateway of Valmondé had found her lying asleep in the shadow of the big stone pillar.

The little one awoke in his arms and began to cry for "Dada." That was as much as she could do or say. Some people thought she might have strayed there of her own accord, for she was of the toddling age. The prevailing belief was that she had been purposely left by a party of Texans, whose canvas-covered wagon, late in the day, had crossed the ferry that Coton Maïs kept, just below the plantation. In time Madame Valmondé abandoned every speculation but the one that Désirée had been sent to her by a beneficent Providence to be the child of her affection, seeing that she was without child of the flesh. For the girl grew to be beautiful and gentle, affectionate and sincere, —the idol of Valmondé.

It was no wonder, when she stood one day against the stone pillar in whose shadow she had lain asleep, eighteen years before, that Armand Aubigny riding by and seeing her there, had fallen in love with her. That was the way all the Aubignys fell in love, as if struck by a pistol shot. The wonder was that he had not loved her before; for he had known her since his father brought him home from Paris, a boy of eight, after his mother died there. The passion that awoke in him that day, when he saw her at the gate, swept along like an avalanche, or like a prairie fire, or like anything that drives headlong over all obstacles.

Monsieur Valmondé grew practical and wanted things well considered: that is, the girl's obscure origin. Armand looked into her eyes and did not care. He was reminded that she was nameless. What did it matter about a name when he could give her one of the oldest and proudest in Louisiana? He ordered the *corbeille*[1] from Paris, and contained himself with what patience he could until it arrived; then they were married.

Madame Valmondé had not seen Désirée and the baby for four weeks. When she reached L'Abri she shuddered at the first sight of it, as she always did. It was a sad looking place, which for many years had not known the gentle presence of a mistress, old Monsieur Aubigny having married and buried his wife in France, and she having loved her own land too well ever to leave it. The roof came down steep and black like a cowl, reaching out beyond the wide galleries that encircled the yellow stuccoed house. Big, solemn oaks grew close to it, and their thick-leaved, far-reaching branches shadowed it like a pall. Young Aubigny's rule was a strict one, too, and under it his negroes had forgotten how to be gay, as they had been during the old master's easy-going and indulgent lifetime.

The young mother was recovering slowly, and lay full length, in her soft white muslins and laces, upon a couch. The baby was beside her, upon her arm, where he had fallen asleep, at her breast. The yellow nurse woman sat beside a window fanning herself.

Madame Valmondé bent her portly figure over Désirée and kissed her, holding her an instant tenderly in her arms. Then she turned to the child.

"This is not the baby!" she exclaimed, in startled tones. French was the language spoken at Valmondé in those days.

"I knew you would be astonished," laughed Désirée, "at the way he has grown. The little *cochon de lait!*[2] Look at his legs, mamma, and his hands and fingernails,— real fingernails. Zandrine had to cut them this morning. Is n't it true, Zandrine?"

The woman bowed her turbaned head majestically, "Mais si,[3] Madame."

"And the way he cries," went on Désirée, "is deafening. Armand heard him the other day as far away as La Blanche's cabin."

Madame Valmondé had never removed her eyes from the child. She lifted it and walked with it over to the window that was lightest. She scanned the baby narrowly, then looked as searchingly at Zandrine, whose face was turned to gaze across the fields.

"Yes, the child has grown, has changed," said Madame Valmondé, slowly, as she replaced it beside its mother. "What does Armand say?"

Désirée's face became suffused with a glow that was happiness itself.

---

[1] Wedding gifts from the groom to the bride.   [3] French: "But certainly."
[2] French: "Suckling pig."

"Oh, Armand is the proudest father in the parish, I believe, chiefly because it is a boy, to bear his name; though he says not,—that he would have loved a girl as well. But I know it is n't true. I know he says that to please me. And mamma," she added, drawing Madame Valmondé's head down to her, and speaking in a whisper, "he has n't punished one of them—not one of them—since baby is born. Even Négrillon, who pretended to have burnt his leg that he might rest from work—he only laughed, and said Négrillon was a great scamp. Oh, mamma, I'm so happy; it frightens me."

What Désirée said was true. Marriage, and later the birth of his son had softened Armand Aubigny's imperious and exacting nature greatly. This was what made the gentle Désirée so happy, for she loved him desperately. When he frowned she trembled, but loved him. When he smiled, she asked no greater blessing of God. But Armand's dark, handsome face had not often been disfigured by frowns since the day he fell in love with her.

When the baby was about three months old, Désirée awoke one day to the conviction that there was something in the air menacing her peace. It was at first too subtle to grasp. It had only been a disquieting suggestion; an air of mystery among the blacks; unexpected visits from far-off neighbors who could hardly account for their coming. Then a strange, an awful change in her husband's manner, which she dared not ask him to explain. When he spoke to her, it was with averted eyes, from which the old love-light seemed to have gone out. He absented himself from home; and when there, avoided her presence and that of her child, without excuse. And the very spirit of Satan seemed suddenly to take hold of him in his dealings with the slaves. Désirée was miserable enough to die.

She sat in her room, one hot afternoon, in her *peignoir,* listlessly drawing through her fingers the strands of her long, silky brown hair that hung about her shoulders. The baby, half naked, lay asleep upon her own great mahogany bed, that was like a sumptuous throne, with its satin-lined half-canopy. One of La Blanche's little quadroon boys—half naked too—stood fanning the child slowly with a fan of peacock feathers. Désirée's eyes had been fixed absently and sadly upon the baby, while she was striving to penetrate the threatening mist that she felt closing about her. She looked from her child to the boy who stood beside him, and back again; over and over. "Ah!" It was a cry that she could not help; which she was not conscious of having uttered. The blood turned like ice in her veins, and a clammy moisture gathered upon her face.

She tried to speak to the little quadroon boy; but no sound would come, at first. When he heard his name uttered, he looked up, and his mistress was pointing to the door. He laid aside the great, soft fan, and obediently stole away, over the polished floor, on his bare tiptoes.

She stayed motionless, with gaze riveted upon her child, and her face the picture of fright.

Presently her husband entered the room, and without noticing her, went to a table and began to search among some papers which covered it.

"Armand," she called to him, in a voice which must have stabbed him, if he was human. But he did not notice. "Armand," she said again. Then she rose and tottered towards him. "Armand," she panted once more, clutching his arm, "look at our child. What does it mean? tell me."

He coldly but gently loosened her fingers from about his arm and thrust the hand away from him. "Tell me what it means!" she cried despairingly.

"It means," he answered lightly, "that the child is not white; it means that you are not white."

A quick conception of all that this accusation meant for her nerved her with unwonted courage to deny it. "It is a lie; it is not true, I am white! Look at my hair, it is brown; and my eyes are gray, Armand, you know they are gray. And my skin is fair," seizing his wrist. "Look at my hand; whiter than yours, Armand," she laughed hysterically.

"As white as La Blanche's," he returned cruelly; and went away leaving her alone with their child.

When she could hold a pen in her hand, she sent a despairing letter to Madame Valmondé.

"My mother, they tell me I am not white. Armand has told me I am not white. For God's sake tell them it is not true. You must know it is not true. I shall die. I must die. I cannot be so unhappy, and live."

The answer that came was as brief:

"My own Désirée: Come home to Valmondé; back to your mother who loves you. Come with your child."

When the letter reached Désirée she went with it to her husband's study, and laid it open upon the desk before which he sat. She was like a stone image: silent, white, motionless after she placed it there.

In silence he ran his cold eyes over the written words. He said nothing. "Shall I go, Armand?" she asked in tones sharp with agonized suspense.

"Yes, go."

"Do you want me to go?"

"Yes, I want you to go."

He thought Almighty God had dealt cruelly and unjustly with him; and felt, somehow, that he was paying Him back in kind when he stabbed thus into his wife's soul. Moreover he no longer loved her, because of the unconscious injury she had brought upon his home and his name.

She turned away like one stunned by a blow, and walked slowly towards the door, hoping he would call her back.

"Good-by, Armand," she moaned.

He did not answer her. That was his last blow at fate.

Désirée went in search of her child. Zandrine was pacing the sombre gallery with it. She took the little one from the nurse's arms with no word of explanation, and descending the steps, walked away, under the live-oak branches.

It was an October afternoon; the sun was just sinking. Out in the still fields the negroes were picking cotton.

Désirée had not changed the thin white garment nor the slippers which she wore. Her hair was uncovered and the sun's rays brought a golden gleam from its brown meshes. She did not take the broad, beaten road which led to the far-off plantation of Valmondé. She walked across a deserted field, where the stubble bruised her tender feet, so delicately shod, and tore her thin gown to shreds.

She disappeared among the reeds and willows that grew thick along the banks of the deep, sluggish bayou; and she did not come back again.

Some weeks later there was a curious scene enacted at L'Abri. In the centre of the smoothly swept back yard was a great bonfire. Armand Aubigny sat in the wide hallway that commanded a view of the spectacle; and it was he who dealt out to a half dozen negroes the material which kept this fire ablaze.

A graceful cradle of willow, with all its dainty furbishings, was laid upon the pyre, which had already been fed with the richness of a priceless *layette*. Then there were silk gowns, and velvet and satin ones added to these; laces, too, and embroideries; bonnets and gloves; for the *corbeille* had been of rare quality.

The last thing to go was a tiny bundle of letters; innocent little scribblings that Désirée had sent to him during the days of their espousal. There was the remnant of one back in the drawer from which he took them. But it was not Désirée's; it was part of an old letter from his mother to his father. He read it. She was thanking God for the blessing of her husband's love:—

"But, above all," she wrote, "night and day, I thank the good God for having so arranged our lives that our dear Armand will never know that his mother, who adores him, belongs to the race that is cursed with the brand of slavery."

1892

Edith Wharton
1862–1937

There are many reasons why Mrs. Teddy Wharton (born Edith Newbold Jones) might not have become what she did, an important figure in American literature, a formidably acute recorder of social mores both here and abroad, and a sharp-minded organizer of both her own complex professional career and of relief agencies to aid refugees during the First World War. Edith Wharton was born into "old money"—that stratum of New York society that could take education, cultural refinement, and deference to class for granted. She never experienced the economic deprivations that drove, for example, Theodore Dreiser and Hamlin Garland on an upward scramble, nor did she know the uncertainties of the literary world that prompted William Dean Howells and Stephen Crane to run fast and far. As a woman of wealth and position, she could have remained throughout her lifetime essentially like many of the fictional characters in her stories and novels, characters who exist trivially in terms of glittering social events that mask their discontent and unsatisfied lives. This is not what happened, however. Slowly at first, but then with increasing momentum, Edith Wharton began to write about her life, not merely to acquiesce to its deadlier rhythms.

Edith Jones grew up in New York City, with interludes spent traveling abroad. Educated by a succession of governesses, she attained an early fluency in both foreign languages and the European outlook. This training was considered appropriate to a young woman in a patrician social circle that defined itself in terms of England and the Continent—not with any Whitmanesque democracy that lay somewhere vaguely west and north of Manhattan's chic avenues. She "came out" into society at eighteen according to the rigid rituals of her class— the class she later analyzed as rigorously as an anthropologist might the courtship habits of Fiji islanders. In the same year she also brought out some poems in the *Atlantic Monthly.* Printed anonymously, her poems signified little more than the fact that yet another young lady of good breeding believed she had something to say.

At twenty-three Edith Jones became the wife of Edward Wharton, a man of impeccable Boston ancestors. They settled into a childless, busy life. Edith Wharton threw her energies into being a society matron in New York, Newport, and Paris, and later at a large house she had built in the Massachusetts Berkshires. Marriage with Teddy (as this amiable but increasingly unstable man was known to his friends) lasted for twenty-eight generally unhappy years; it ended at last with a divorce in 1913 after his mental condition deteriorated into insanity. The decision to leave her husband pained Edith Wharton greatly. Their divorce was concluded in the courts after she proved him guilty of adultery. Everything in her nature that clung to tradition recoiled at this morally objectionable step, which she regarded as an act against "family."

She had made other, even more momentous choices than divorce prior to 1913. If the outward shows of Wharton's life continued to present her as a woman of leisure with the public style of a perennial hostess, she had long since begun to turn her private hours over to writing. Her first collection of short stories appeared in 1899 under the apt title *The Great Inclination;* it was a success that both amazed her and freed her to throw herself with even greater resolve into learning her craft. The novel *The Valley of Decision* followed in 1902, and another collection, *The Descent of Man,* in 1904. Her reputation was assured with *The House of Mirth* in 1905. From then on, Mrs. Teddy Wharton the society lady had a formidable competitor—Edith Wharton the acclaimed writer.

Wharton took up permanent residence in France in 1907. Personal and professional needs made her crave a more cosmopolitan setting than the United States could give her. Her writings poured forth, including three more collections of short stories, the last of which showed her skill at tales of the supernatural: *The Hermit and the Wild Woman and Other Stories* (1908), *Xingu and Other Stories* (1916), and *Tales of Men and Ghosts* (1910). The content of her work was by no means made up of the details of cosmopolitan society. The harshly bitter lives endured in the villages and farm areas of New England caught her attention and resulted in two powerful novels, *Ethan Frome* (1911) and *Summer* (1917). *The Custom of the Country* (1913) and *The Age of Innocence* (1920) returned Wharton to the city and to scenes of elegant society, her skill for satire still intact. Her targets continued to be both the "old society" and the "new society." The former was in the grip of outmoded values that gave idealistic young men and women little chance to survive under the new conditions. The latter was controlled by parvenues whose combative, often morally shabby actions undercut family, continuity, professional probity, and personal loyalties.

When World War I began, Wharton assumed the causes of France and Belgium as her own. She emerged from the war invigorated by the successes she had had organizing war relief programs for refugees as well as compiling several books of propaganda for the Allies.

By her midfifties Wharton had returned to her career as a literary figure. *The Age of Innocence* won her the Pulitzer Prize in 1920. *The Writing of Fiction* (1925) presented her views of her craft, and the autobiographical *A Backward Glance* (1934) revealed as much of her self as she chose. Kept out of her memoirs were mention of the difficult times she had spent as her mother's slighted child, the unhappiness of her marriage, and the brief but passionate affair she had had with an old friend, Morton Fullerton. Admitted were anecdotes of her friendships with Henry James, Sinclair Lewis, and Jean Cocteau.

Edith Wharton died in France, a member of a distinguished expatriate generation. The generation that came after—peopled by Hemingway, Stein, Dos Passos, and Fitzgerald—was also, in its own way, rebellious against convention and analytical about the mores of a newly evolving society. The life and writings of Edith Wharton might seem too special and too protected to this new throng in Paris, but she first explored some of the same literary territory settled by these later writers.

There are a number of points at which Edith Wharton's novels and stories align with those of her contemporaries. Living socially above the rank and file of Americans did not mean that Wharton existed beyond the absorptions and anxieties expressed by others. The extent to which human behavior is shaped by forces of environment and breeding is a major motif in Wharton's narratives, just as it was in those of Mark Twain and Theodore Dreiser. The manners that distinguish one group from another in a supposedly classless America called upon her powers as a social analyst, just as attention to manners absorbed Henry James and William Dean Howells in their fiction. Wharton paid the cost for sitting in judgment of her own country, just as did Henry James and Henry Adams. The annals of small-town life and the tragedies that come from the narrowing of individual aspirations are recorded in Wharton's *Ethan Frome* and *Summer,* as they were in the fiction of Sarah Orne Jewett and Mary Wilkins Freeman. A woman's experience of personal displacement and her longings to break free are presented as clearly in Wharton's stories as in those by Kate Chopin. The sharp-tongued critique of people who act like asses and rascals is as apparent in Wharton's satires as in Mark Twain's. In addition, both Wharton and Twain wrote, on occasion, reminiscences of the past that reveal their wistfulness over the loss of old values and simpler times.

Whatever the similarities between the well-bred lady from New York, Newport, and Paris and her literary contemporaries, Edith Wharton was her own woman. She frequently expressed her annoyance over being described as the too slavish pupil of Henry James. James was a friend and confidant, but she made it plain that she was not dependent on his example as a writer. Wharton's lucidity of style, her treatment of the inner life, and her eye and ear for cultural nuances

are identifiably her own. She had served an arduous apprenticeship to her craft
and to her life, and her strengths and weaknesses as a writer are to be credited to
her alone. Now, with ever increasing interest, recent criticism is establishing
Edith Wharton's place in American literary history. She is winning attention not
only as a writer but also as a woman who wrote effectively about the toll taken
on women in turn-of-the-century society and on the men who shared in their
common fate.

Further Reading:

P. Lubbock, *Portrait of Edith Wharton,* 1947.
B. Nevius, *Edith Wharton: A Study of Her
Fiction,* 1953.
M. Lyde, *Edith Wharton: Convention and
Morality in the Work of a Novelist,* 1959.
Edith Wharton: A Collection of Critical Essays,
ed. I. Home, 1962.
O. Coolidge, *Edith Wharton, 1862–1937,* 1964.
M. Bell, *Edith Wharton and Henry James: The
Story of Their Friendship,* 1965.
G. Kellogg, *The Two Lives of Edith Wharton:
The Woman and Her Work,* 1965.
L. Auchincloss, *Edith Wharton: A Woman in Her*

Time, 1971.
R. W. B. Lewis, *Edith Wharton,* 1975.
G. Lindberg, *Edith Wharton and the Novel of
Manners,* 1975.
M. McDowell, *Edith Wharton,* 1975.
M. B. McDowell, *Edith Wharton,* 1976.
R. H. Lawson, *Edith Wharton,* 1977.
C. Wolff, *A Feast of Words: The Triumph of
Edith Wharton,* 1977.
E. Ammons, *Edith Wharton's Argument with
America,* 1980.
C. Wershoven, *The Female Intruder in the Novels
of Edith Wharton,* 1982.

Text:

"The Other Two" from *The Collected Stories of
Edith Wharton,* 2 vols., ed. R. W. B. Lewis,
1968.
See also *An Edith Wharton Treasury,* ed. A.
Quinn, 1950.

Best Short Stories of Edith Wharton, ed. W.
Andrews, 1958.
The Edith Wharton Reader, ed. L. Auchincloss,
1965.

The Other Two

I

Waythorn, on the drawing-room hearth, waited for his wife to come down to dinner.

It was their first night under his own roof, and he was surprised at his thrill of
boyish agitation. He was not so old, to be sure—his glass gave him little more than
the five-and-thirty years to which his wife confessed—but he had fancied himself
already in the temperate zone; yet here he was listening for her step with a tender
sense of all it symbolised, with some old trail of verse about the garlanded nuptial
door-posts floating through his enjoyment of the pleasant room and the good dinner
just beyond it.

They had been hastily recalled from their honeymoon by the illness of Lily Haskett,
the child of Mrs. Waythorn's first marriage. The little girl, at Waythorn's desire, had
been transferred to his house on the day of her mother's wedding, and the doctor,
on their arrival, broke the news that she was ill with typhoid, but declared that all
the symptoms were favourable. Lily could show twelve years of unblemished health,
and the case promised to be a light one. The nurse spoke as reassuringly, and after

a moment of alarm Mrs. Waythorn had adjusted herself to the situation. She was very fond of Lily—her affection for the child had perhaps been her decisive charm in Waythorn's eyes—but she had the perfectly balanced nerves which her little girl had inherited, and no woman ever wasted less tissue in unproductive worry. Waythorn was therefore quite prepared to see her come in presently, a little late because of a last look at Lily, but as serene and well-appointed as if her good-night kiss had been laid on the brow of health. Her composure was restful to him; it acted as ballast to his somewhat unstable sensibilities. As he pictured her bending over the child's bed he thought how soothing her presence must be in illness: her very step would prognosticate recovery.

His own life had been a gray one, from temperament rather than circumstance, and he had been drawn to her by the unperturbed gaiety which kept her fresh and elastic at an age when most women's activities are growing either slack or febril. He knew what was said about her; for, popular as she was, there had always been a faint undercurrent of detraction. When she had appeared in New York, nine or ten years earlier, as the pretty Mrs. Haskett whom Gus Varick had unearthed somewhere—was it in Pittsburg or Utica?—society, while promptly accepting her, had reserved the right to cast a doubt on its own indiscrimination. Enquiry, however, established her undoubted connection with a socially reigning family, and explained her recent divorce as the natural result of a runaway match at seventeen; and as nothing was known of Mr. Haskett it was easy to believe the worst of him.

Alice Haskett's remarriage with Gus Varick was a passport to the set whose recognition she coveted, and for a few years the Varicks were the most popular couple in town. Unfortunately the alliance was brief and stormy, and this time the husband had his champions. Still, even Varick's stanchest supporters admitted that he was not meant for matrimony, and Mrs. Varick's grievances were of a nature to bear the inspection of the New York courts. A New York divorce is in itself a diploma of virtue, and in the semiwidowhood of this second separation Mrs. Varick took on an air of sanctity, and was allowed to confide her wrongs to some of the most scrupulous ears in town. But when it was known that she was to marry Waythorn there was a momentary reaction. Her best friends would have preferred to see her remain in the rôle of the injured wife, which was as becoming to her as crape to a rosy complexion. True, a decent time had elapsed, and it was not even suggested that Waythorn had supplanted his predecessor. People shook their heads over him, however, and one grudging friend, to whom he affirmed that he took the step with his eyes open, replied oracularly: "Yes—and with your ears shut."

Waythorn could afford to smile at these innuendoes. In the Wall Street phrase, he had "discounted" them. He knew that society has not yet adapted itself to the consequences of divorce, and that till the adaptation takes place every woman who uses the freedom the law accords her must be her own social justification. Waythorn had an amused confidence in his wife's ability to justify herself. His expectations were fulfilled, and before the wedding took place Alice Varick's group had rallied openly to her support. She took it all imperturbably: she had a way of surmounting obstacles without seeming to be aware of them, and Waythorn looked back with wonder at the trivialities over which he had worn his nerves thin. He had the sense of having found refuge in a richer, warmer nature than his own, and his satisfaction, at the moment, was humourously summed up in the thought that his wife, when she had done all she could for Lily, would not be ashamed to come down and enjoy a good dinner.

The anticipation of such enjoyment was not, however, the sentiment expressed by Mrs. Waythorn's charming face when she presently joined him. Though she had put on her most engaging teagown she had neglected to assume the smile that went with it, and Waythorn thought he had never seen her look so nearly worried.

"What is it?" he asked. "Is anything wrong with Lily?"

"No; I've just been in and she's still sleeping." Mrs. Waythorn hesitated. "But something tiresome has happened."

He had taken her two hands, and now perceived that he was crushing a paper between them.

"This letter?"

"Yes—Mr. Haskett has written—I mean his lawyer has written."

Waythorn felt himself flush uncomfortably. He dropped his wife's hands.

"What about?"

"About seeing Lily. You know the courts—"

"Yes, yes," he interrupted nervously.

Nothing was known about Haskett in New York. He was vaguely supposed to have remained in the outer darkness from which his wife had been rescued, and Waythorn was one of the few who were aware that he had given up his business in Utica and followed her to New York in order to be near his little girl. In the days of his wooing, Waythorn had often met Lily on the doorstep, rosy and smiling, on her way "to see papa."

"I am so sorry," Mrs. Waythorn murmured.

He roused himself. "What does he want?"

"He wants to see her. You know she goes to him once a week."

"Well—he doesn't expect her to go to him now, does he?"

"No—he has heard of her illness; but he expects to come here."

"Here?"

Mrs. Waythorn reddened under his gaze. They looked away from each other.

"I'm afraid he has the right. . . . You'll see. . . ." She made a proffer of the letter.

Waythorn moved away with a gesture of refusal. He stood staring about the softly lighted room, which a moment before had seemed so full of bridal intimacy.

"I'm so sorry," she repeated. "If Lily could have been moved—"

"That's out of the question," he returned impatiently.

"I suppose so."

Her lip was beginning to tremble, and he felt himself a brute.

"He must come, of course," he said. "What is—his day?"

"I'm afraid—to-morrow."

"Very well. Send a note in the morning."

The butler entered to announce dinner.

Waythorn turned to his wife. "Come—you must be tired. It's beastly, but try to forget about it," he said, drawing her hand through his arm.

"You're so good, dear. I'll try," she whispered back.

Her face cleared at once, and as she looked at him across the flowers, between the rosy candle-shades, he saw her lips waver back into a smile.

"How pretty everything is!" she sighed luxuriously.

He turned to the butler. "The champagne at once, please. Mrs. Waythorn is tired."

In a moment or two their eyes met above the sparkling glasses. Her own were quite clear and untroubled: he saw that she had obeyed his injunction and forgotten.

II

Waythorn, the next morning, went down town earlier than usual. Haskett was not likely to come till the afternoon, but the instinct of flight drove him forth. He meant to stay away all day—he had thoughts of dining at his club. As his door closed behind him he reflected that before he opened it again it would have admitted another man who had as much right to enter it as himself, and the thought filled him with a physical repugnance.

He caught the "elevated"[1] at the employés' hour, and found himself crushed between two layers of pendulous humanity. At Eighth Street the man facing him wriggled out, and another took his place. Waythorn glanced up and saw that it was Gus Varick. The men were so close together that it was impossible to ignore the smile of recognition on Varick's handsome overblown face. And after all—why not? They had always been on good terms, and Varick had been divorced before Waythorn's attentions to his wife began. The two exchanged a word on the perennial grievance of the trains, and when a seat at their side was miraculously left empty the instinct of self-preservation made Waythorn slip into it after Varick.

The latter drew the stout man's breath of relief. "Lord—I was beginning to feel like a pressed flower." He leaned back, looking unconcernedly at Waythorn. "Sorry to hear that Sellers is knocked out again."

"Sellers?" echoed Waythorn, starting at his partner's name.

Varick looked surprised. "You didn't know he was laid up with the gout?"

"No. I've been away—I only got back last night," Waythorn felt himself reddening in anticipation of the other's smile.

"Ah—yes; to be sure. And Sellers's attack came on two days ago. I'm afraid he's pretty bad. Very awkward for me, as it happens, because he was just putting through a rather important thing for me."

"Ah?" Waythorn wondered vaguely since when Varick had been dealing in "important things." Hitherto he had dabbled only in the shallow pools of speculation, with which Waythorn's office did not usually concern itself.

It occurred to him that Varick might be talking at random, to relieve the strain of their propinquity. That strain was becoming momentarily more apparent to Waythorn, and when, at Cortlandt Street, he caught sight of an acquaintance and had a sudden vision of the picture he and Varick must present to an initiated eye, he jumped up with a muttered excuse.

"I hope you'll find Sellers better," said Varick civilly, and he stammered back: "If I can be of any use to you—" and let the departing crowd sweep him to the platform.

At his office he heard that Sellers was in fact ill with the gout, and would probably not be able to leave the house for some weeks.

[1] Elevated railway.

"I'm sorry it should have happened so, Mr. Waythorn," the senior clerk said with affable significance. "Mr. Sellers was very much upset at the idea of giving you such a lot of extra work just now."

"Oh, that's no matter," said Waythorn hastily. He secretly welcomed the pressure of additional business, and was glad to think that, when the day's work was over, he would have to call at his partner's on the way home.

He was late for luncheon, and turned in at the nearest restaurant instead of going to his club. The place was full, and the waiter hurried him to the back of the room to capture the only vacant table. In the cloud of cigar-smoke Waythorn did not at once distinguish his neighbours: but presently, looking about him, he saw Varick seated a few feet off. This time, luckily, they were too far apart for conversation, and Varick, who faced another way, had probably not even seen him; but there was an irony in their renewed nearness.

Varick was said to be fond of good living, and as Waythorn sat despatching his hurried luncheon he looked across half enviously at the other's leisurely degustation of his meal. When Waythorn first saw him he had been helping himself with critical deliberation to a bit of Camembert at the ideal point of liquefaction, and now, the cheese removed, he was just pouring his *café double*[2] from its little two-storied earthen pot. He poured slowly, his ruddy profile bent above the task, and one beringed white hand steadying the lid of the coffee-pot; then he stretched his other hand to the decanter of cognac at his elbow, filled a liqueur-glass, took a tentative sip, and poured the brandy into his coffee-cup.

Waythorn watched him in a kind of fascination. What was he thinking of—only of the flavour of the coffee and the liqueur? Had the morning's meeting left no more trace in his thoughts than on his face? Had his wife so completely passed out of his life that even this odd encounter with her present husband, within a week after her remarriage, was no more than an incident in his day? And as Waythorn mused, another idea struck him: had Haskett ever met Varick as Varick and he had just met? The recollection of Haskett perturbed him, and he rose and left the restaurant, taking a circuitous way out to escape the placid irony of Varick's nod.

It was after seven when Waythorn reached home. He thought the footman who opened the door looked at him oddly.

"How is Miss Lily?" he asked in haste.

"Doing very well, sir. A gentleman—"

"Tell Barlow to put off dinner for half an hour," Waythorn cut him off, hurrying upstairs.

He went straight to his room and dressed without seeing his wife. When he reached the drawing-room she was there, fresh and radiant. Lily's day had been good; the doctor was not coming back that evening.

At dinner Waythorn told her of Sellers's illness and of the resulting complications. She listened sympathetically, adjuring him not to let himself be overworked, and asking vague feminine questions about the routine of the office. Then she gave him the chronicle of Lily's day; quoted the nurse and doctor, and told him who had called

---

[2] Strong coffee.

to inquire. He had never seen her more serene and unruffled. It struck him, with a curious pang, that she was very happy in being with him, so happy that she found a childish pleasure in rehearsing the trivial incidents of her day.

After dinner they went to the library, and the servant put the coffee and liqueurs on a low table before her and left the room. She looked singularly soft and girlish in her rosy pale dress, against the dark leather of one of his bachelor armchairs. A day earlier the contrast would have charmed him.

He turned away now, choosing a cigar with affected deliberation.

"Did Haskett come?" he asked, with his back to her.

"Oh, yes—he came."

"You didn't see him, of course?"

She hesitated a moment. "I let the nurse see him."

That was all. There was nothing more to ask. He swung round toward her, applying a match to his cigar. Well, the thing was over for a week, at any rate. He would try not to think of it. She looked up at him, a trifle rosier than usual, with a smile in her eyes.

"Ready for your coffee, dear?"

He leaned against the mantelpiece, watching her as she lifted the coffee-pot. The lamplight struck a gleam from her bracelets and tipped her soft hair with brightness. How light and slender she was, and how each gesture flowed into the next! She seemed a creature all compact of harmonies. As the thought of Haskett receded, Waythorn felt himself yielding again to the joy of possessorship. They were his, those white hands with their flitting motions, his the light haze of hair, the lips and eyes. . . .

She set down the coffee-pot, and reached for the decanter of cognac, measured off a liqueur-glass and poured it into his cup.

Waythorn uttered a sudden exclamation.

"What is the matter?" she said, startled.

"Nothing; only—I don't take cognac in my coffee."

"Oh, how stupid of me," she cried.

Their eyes met, and she blushed a sudden agonised red.

III

Ten days later, Mr. Sellers, still house-bound, asked Waythorn to call on his way down town.

The senior partner, with his swaddled foot propped up by the fire, greeted his associate with an air of embarrassment.

"I'm sorry, my dear fellow; I've got to ask you to do an awkward thing for me."

Waythorn waited, and the other went on, after a pause apparently given to the arrangement of his phrases: "The fact is, when I was knocked out I had just gone into a rather complicated piece of business for—Gus Varick."

"Well?" said Waythorn, with an attempt to put him at his ease.

"Well—it's this way: Varick came to me the day before my attack. He had evidently had an inside tip from somebody, and had made about a hundred thousand. He came to me for advice, and I suggested his going in with Vanderlyn."

"Oh, the deuce!" Waythorn exclaimed. He saw in a flash what had happened. The investment was an alluring one, but required negotiation. He listened quietly while Sellers put the case before him, and, the statement ended, he said: "You think I ought to see Varick?"

"I'm afraid I can't as yet. The doctor is obdurate. And this thing can't wait. I hate to ask you, but no one else in the office knows the ins and outs of it."

Waythorn stood silent. He did not care a farthing for the success of Varick's venture, but the honour of the office was to be considered, and he could hardly refuse to oblige his partner.

"Very well," he said, "I'll do it."

That afternoon, apprised by telephone, Varick called at the office. Waythorn, waiting in his private room, wondered what the others thought of it. The newspapers, at the time of Mrs. Waythorn's marriage, had acquainted their readers with every detail of her previous matrimonial ventures, and Waythorn could fancy the clerks smiling behind Varick's back as he was ushered in.

Varick bore himself admirably. He was easy without being undignified, and Waythorn was conscious of cutting a much less impressive figure. Varick had no experience of business, and the talk prolonged itself for nearly an hour while Waythorn set forth with scrupulous precision the details of the proposed transaction.

"I'm awfully obliged to you," Varick said as he rose. "The fact is I'm not used to having much money to look after, and I don't want to make an ass of myself—" He smiled, and Waythorn could not help noticing that there was something pleasant about his smile. "It feels uncommonly queer to have enough cash to pay one's bills. I'd have sold my soul for it a few years ago!"

Waythorn winced at the illusion. He had heard it rumoured that a lack of funds had been one of the determining causes of the Varick separation, but it did not occur to him that Varick's words were intentional. It seemed more likely that the desire to keep clear of embarrassing topics had fatally drawn him into one. Waythorn did not wish to be outdone in civility.

"We'll do the best we can for you," he said. "I think this is a good thing you're in."

"Oh, I'm sure it's immense. It's awfully good of you—" Varick broke off, embarrassed. "I suppose the thing's settled now—but if—"

"If anything happens before Sellers is about, I'll see you again," said Waythorn quietly. He was glad, in the end, to appear the more self-possessed of the two.

The course of Lily's illness ran smooth, and as the days passed Waythorn grew used to the idea of Haskett's weekly visit. The first time the day came round, he stayed out late, and questioned his wife as to the visit on his return. She replied at once that Haskett had merely seen the nurse downstairs, as the doctor did not wish any one in the child's sick-room till after the crisis.

The following week Waythorn was again conscious of the recurrence of the day, but had forgotten it by the time he came home to dinner. The crisis of the disease came a few days later, with a rapid decline of fever, and the little girl was pronounced out of danger. In the rejoicing which ensued the thought of Haskett passed out of Waythorn's mind, and one afternoon, letting himself into the house with a latch-key, he went straight to his library without noticing a shabby hat and umbrella in the hall.

In the library he found a small effaced-looking man with a thinnish gray beard sitting on the edge of a chair. The stranger might have been a piano-tuner, or one of those mysteriously efficient persons who are summoned in emergencies to adjust some detail of the domestic machinery. He blinked at Waythorn through a pair of gold-rimmed spectacles and said mildly: "Mr. Waythorn, I presume? I am Lily's father."

Waythorn flushed. "Oh—" he stammered uncomfortably. He broke off, disliking to appear rude. Inwardly he was trying to adjust the actual Haskett to the image of him projected by his wife's reminiscences. Waythorn had been allowed to infer that Alice's first husband was a brute.

"I am sorry to intrude," said Haskett, with his over-the-counter politeness.

"Don't mention it," returned Waythorn, collecting himself. "I suppose the nurse has been told?"

"I presume so. I can wait," said Haskett. He had a resigned way of speaking, as though life had worn down his natural powers of resistance.

Waythorn stood on the threshold, nervously pulling off his gloves.

"I'm sorry you've been detained. I will send for the nurse," he said; and as he opened the door he added with an effort: "I'm glad we can give you a good report of Lily." He winced as the *we* slipped out, but Haskett seemed not to notice it.

"Thank you, Mr. Waythorn. It's been an anxious time for me."

"Ah, well, that's past. Soon she'll be able to go to you." Waythorn nodded and passed out. In his own room he flung himself down with a groan. He hated the womanish sensibility which made him suffer so acutely from the grotesque chances of life. He had known when he married that his wife's former husbands were both living, and that amid the multiplied contacts of modern existence there were a thousand chances to one that he would run against one or the other, yet he found himself as much disturbed by his brief encounter with Haskett as though the law had not obligingly removed all difficulties in the way of their meeting.

Waythorn sprang up and began to pace the room nervously. He had not suffered half as much from his two meetings with Varick. It was Haskett's presence in his own house that made the situation so intolerable. He stood still, hearing steps in the passage.

"This way, please," he heard the nurse say. Haskett was being taken upstairs, then: not a corner of the house but was open to him. Waythorn dropped into another chair, staring vaguely ahead of him. On his dressing-table stood a photograph of Alice, taken when he had first known her. She was Alice Varick then—how fine and exquisite he had thought her! Those were Varick's pearls about her neck. At Waythorn's insistence they had been returned before her marriage. Had Haskett ever given her any trinkets—and what had become of them, Waythorn wondered? He realised suddenly that he knew very little of Haskett's past or present situation; but from the man's appearance and manner of speech he could reconstruct with curious precision the surroundings of Alice's first marriage. And it startled him to think that she had, in the background of her life, a phase of existence so different from anything with which he had connected her. Varick, whatever his faults, was a gentleman, in the conventional, traditional sense of the term: the sense which at that moment seemed, oddly enough, to have most meaning to Waythorn. He and Varick had the same social habits, spoke the same language, understood the same allusions. But this other man . . . it was grotesquely uppermost in Waythorn's mind that Haskett had worn a made-up tie attached with an elastic. Why should that ridiculous detail symbolise the whole man? Waythorn was exasperated by his own paltriness, but the fact of the tie expanded, forced itself on him, became as it were the key to Alice's past. He could see her, as Mrs. Haskett, sitting in a "front parlour" furnished in plush, with a pianola,[3] and a copy of "Ben Hur"[4] on the centre-table. He could see her going to the theatre with Haskett—or perhaps even to a "Church Sociable"—she in a "picture hat" and Haskett in a black frock-coat, a little creased, with the made-up tie on an elastic. On the way home they would stop and look at the illuminated shop-windows, lingering over the photographs of New York actresses. On Sunday afternoons Haskett would take her for a walk, pushing Lily ahead of them in a white enamelled perambulator, and Waythorn had a vision of the people they would stop and talk to. He could fancy how pretty Alice must have looked, in a dress adroitly constructed from the hints of a New York fashion-paper, and how she must have looked down on the other women, chafing at her life, and secretly feeling that she belonged in a bigger place.

For the moment his foremost thought was one of wonder at the way in which she had shed the phase of existence which her marriage with Haskett implied. It was as if her whole aspect, every gesture, every inflection, every allusion, were a studied negation of that period of her life. If she had denied being married to Haskett she could hardly have stood more convicted of duplicity than in this obliteration of the self which had been his wife.

Waythorn started up, checking himself in the analysis of her motives. What right had he to create a fantastic effigy of her and then pass judgment on it? She had spoken vaguely of her first marriage as unhappy, had hinted, with becoming reticence, that Haskett had wrought havoc among her young illusions. . . . It was a pity for Waythorn's peace of mind that Haskett's very inoffensiveness shed a new light on the nature of those illusions. A man would rather think that his wife has been brutalised by her first husband than that the process has been reversed.

IV

"Mr. Waythorn, I don't like that French governess of Lily's."

Haskett, subdued and apologetic, stood before Waythorn in the library, revolving his shabby hat in his hand.

Waythorn, surprised in his armchair over the evening paper, stared back perplexedly at his visitor.

"You'll excuse my asking to see you," Haskett continued. "But this is my last visit, and I thought if I could have a word with you it would be a better way than writing to Mrs. Waythorn's lawyer."

[3] An automatic piano player.
[4] Best-selling novel (1880) by General Lew

Wallace (1827–1905). Like the pianola, suggestive of lower-middle-class tastes.

Waythorn rose uneasily. He did not like the French governess either; but that was irrelevant.

"I am not so sure of that," he returned stiffly; "but since you wish it I will give your message to—my wife." He always hesitated over the possessive pronoun in addressing Haskett.

The latter sighed. "I don't know as that will help much. She didn't like it when I spoke to her."

Waythorn turned red. "When did you see her?" he asked.

"Not since the first day I came to see Lily—right after she was taken sick. I remarked to her then that I didn't like the governess."

Waythorn made no answer. He remembered distinctly that, after that first visit, he had asked his wife if she had seen Haskett. She had lied to him then, but she had respected his wishes since; and the incident cast a curious light on her character. He was sure she would not have seen Haskett that first day if she had divined that Waythorn would object, and the fact that she did not divine it was almost as disagreeable to the latter as the discovery that she had lied to him.

"I don't like the woman," Haskett was repeating with mild persistency. "She ain't straight, Mr Waythorn—she'll teach the child to be underhand. I've noticed a change in Lily—she's too anxious to please—and she don't always tell the truth. She used to be the straightest child, Mr. Waythorn—" He broke off, his voice a little thick. "Not but what I want her to have a stylish education," he ended.

Waythorn was touched. "I'm sorry, Mr. Haskett; but frankly, I don't quite see what I can do."

Haskett hesitated. Then he laid his hat on the table, and advanced to the hearth-rug, on which Waythorn was standing. There was nothing aggressive in his manner, but he had the solemnity of a timid man resolved on a decisive measure.

"There's just one thing you can do, Mr. Waythorn," he said. "You can remind Mrs. Waythorn that, by the decree of the courts, I am entitled to have a voice in Lily's bringing up." He paused, and went on more deprecatingly: "I'm not the kind to talk about enforcing my rights, Mr. Waythorn. I don't know as I think a man is entitled to rights he hasn't known how to hold on to; but this business of the child is different. I've never let go there—and I never mean to."

The scene left Waythorn deeply shaken. Shamefacedly, in indirect ways, he had been finding out about Haskett; and all that he had learned was favourable. The little man, in order to be near his daughter, had sold out his share in a profitable business in Utica, and accepted a modest clerkship in a New York manufacturing house. He boarded in a shabby street and had few acquaintances. His passion for Lily filled his life. Waythorn felt that this exploration of Haskett was like groping about with a dark-lantern in his wife's past; but he saw now that there were recesses his lantern had not explored. He had never enquired into the exact circumstances of his wife's first matrimonial rupture. On the surface all had been fair. It was she who had obtained the divorce, and the court had given her the child. But Waythorn knew how many ambiguities such a verdict might cover. The mere fact that Haskett retained a right over his daughter implied an unsuspected compromise. Waythorn was an idealist. He always refused to recognise unpleasant contingencies till he found himself confronted with them, and then he saw them followed by a special train of consequences. His next days were thus haunted, and he determined to try to lay the ghosts by conjuring them up in his wife's presence.

When he repeated Haskett's request a flame of anger passed over her face; but she subdued it instantly and spoke with a slight quiver of outraged motherhood.

"It is very ungentlemanly of him," she said.

The word grated on Waythorn. "That is neither here nor there. It's a bare question of rights."

She murmured: "It is not as if he could ever be a help to Lily—"

Waythorn flushed. This was even less to his taste. "The question is," he repeated, "what authority has he over her?"

She looked downward, twisting herself a little in her seat. "I am willing to see him —I thought you objected," she faltered.

In a flash he understood that she knew the extent of Haskett's claims. Perhaps it was not the first time she had resisted them.

"My objecting has nothing to do with it," he said coldly; "if Haskett has a right to be consulted you must consult him."

She burst into tears, and he saw that she expected him to regard her as a victim.

Haskett did not abuse his rights. Waythorn had felt miserably sure that he would not. But the governess was dismissed, and from time to time the little man demanded an interview with Alice. After the first outburst she accepted the situation with her usual adaptability. Haskett had once reminded Waythorn of the piano-tuner, and Mrs. Waythorn, after a month or two, appeared to class him with that domestic familiar. Waythorn could not but respect the father's tenacity. At first he had tried to cultivate the suspicion that Haskett might be "up to" something, that he had an object in securing a foothold in the house. But in his heart Waythorn was sure of Haskett's single-mindedness; he even guessed in the latter a mild contempt for such advantages as his relation with the Waythorns might offer. Haskett's sincerity of purpose made him invulnerable, and his successor had to accept him as a lien on the property.

Mr. Sellers was sent to Europe to recover from his gout, and Varick's affairs hung on Waythorn's hands. The negotiations were prolonged and complicated; they necessitated frequent conferences between the two men, and the interests of the firm forbade Waythorn's suggesting that his client should transfer his business to another office.

Varick appeared well in the transaction. In moments of relaxation his coarse streak appeared, and Waythorn dreaded his geniality; but in the office he was concise and clear-headed, with a flattering deference to Waythorn's judgment. Their business relations being so affably established, it would have been absurd for the two men to ignore each other in society. The first time they met in a drawing-room, Varick took up their intercourse in the same easy key, and his hostess's grateful glance obliged Waythorn to respond to it. After that they ran across each other frequently, and one evening at a ball Waythorn, wandering through the remoter rooms, came upon Varick seated beside his wife. She coloured a little, and faltered in what she was saying; but Varick nodded to Waythorn without rising, and the latter strolled on.

In the carriage, on the way home, he broke out nervously: "I didn't know you spoke to Varick."

Her voice trembled a little. "It's the first time—he happened to be standing near me; I didn't know what to do. It's so awkward, meeting everywhere—and he said you had been very kind about some business."

"That's different," said Waythorn.

She paused a moment. "I'll do just as you wish," she returned pliantly. "I thought it would be less awkward to speak to him when we meet."

Her pliancy was beginning to sicken him. Had she really no will of her own—no theory about her relation to these men? She had accepted Haskett—did she mean to accept Varick? It was "less awkward," as she had said, and her instinct was to evade difficulties or to circumvent them. With sudden vividness Waythorn saw how the instinct had developed. She was "as easy as an old shoe"—a shoe that too many feet had worn. Her elasticity was the result of tension in too many different directions. Alice Haskett—Alice Varick—Alice Waythorn—she had been each in turn, and had left hanging to each name a little of her privacy, a little of her personality, a little of the inmost self where the unknown god abides.

"Yes—it's better to speak to Varick," said Waythorn wearily.

V

The winter wore on, and society took advantage of the Waythorns' acceptance of Varick. Harassed hostesses were grateful to them for bridging over a social difficulty, and Mrs. Waythorn was held up as a miracle of good taste. Some experimental spirits could not resist the diversion of throwing Varick and his former wife together, and there were those who thought he found a zest in the propinquity. But Mrs. Waythorn's conduct remained irreproachable. She neither avoided Varick nor sought him out. Even Waythorn could not but admit that she had discovered the solution of the newest social problem.

He had married her without giving much thought to that problem. He had fancied that a woman can shed her past like a man. But now he saw that Alice was bound to hers both by the circumstances which forced her into continued relation with it, and by the traces it had left on her nature. With grim irony Waythorn compared himself to a member of a syndicate. He held so many shares in his wife's personality and his predecessors were his partners in the business. If there had been any element of passion in the transaction he would have felt less deteriorated by it. The fact that Alice took her change of husbands like a change of weather reduced the situation to mediocrity. He could have forgiven her for blunders, for excesses; for resisting Haskett, for yielding to Varick; for anything but her acquiescence and her tact. She reminded him of a juggler tossing knives; but the knives were blunt and he knew they would never cut her.

And then, gradually, habit formed a protecting surface for his sensibilities. If he paid for each day's comfort with the small change of his illusions, he grew daily to value the comfort more and set less store upon the coin. He had drifted into a dulling propinquity with Haskett and Varick and he took refuge in the cheap revenge of satirising the situation. He even began to reckon up the advantages which accrued from it, to ask himself if it were not better to own a third of a wife who knew how to make a man happy than a whole one who had lacked opportunity to acquire the art. For it *was* an art, and made up, like all others, of concessions, eliminations and embellishments; of lights judiciously thrown and shadows skilfully softened. His wife knew exactly how to manage the lights, and he knew exactly to what training she owed her skill. He even tried to trace the source of his obligations, to discriminate between the influences which had combined to produce his domestic happiness: he perceived that Haskett's commonness had made Alice worship good breeding, while Varick's liberal construction of the marriage bond had taught her to value the conjugal virtues; so that he was directly indebted to his predecessors for the devotion which made his life easy if not inspiring.

From this phase he passed into that of complete acceptance. He ceased to satirise himself because time dulled the irony of the situation and the joke lost its humour with its sting. Even the sight of Haskett's hat on the hall table had ceased to touch the springs of epigram. The hat was often seen there now, for it had been decided that it was better for Lily's father to visit her than for the little girl to go to his boarding-house. Waythorn, having acquiesced in this arrangement, had been surprised to find how little difference it made. Haskett was never obtrusive, and the few visitors who met him on the stairs were unaware of his identity. Waythorn did not know how often he saw Alice, but with himself Haskett was seldom in contact.

One afternoon, however, he learned on entering that Lily's father was waiting to see him. In the library he found Haskett occupying a chair in his usual provisional way. Waythorn always felt grateful to him for not leaning back.

"I hope you'll excuse me, Mr. Waythorn," he said rising. "I wanted to see Mrs. Waythorn about Lily, and your man asked me to wait here till she came in."

"Of course," said Waythorn, remembering that a sudden leak had that morning given over the drawing-room to the plumbers.

He opened his cigar-case and held it out to his visitor, and Haskett's acceptance seemed to mark a fresh stage in their intercourse. The spring evening was chilly, and Waythorn invited his guest to draw up his chair to the fire. He meant to find an excuse to leave Haskett in a moment; but he was tired and cold, and after all the little man no longer jarred on him.

The two were enclosed in the intimacy of their blended cigar-smoke when the door opened and Varick walked into the room. Waythorn rose abruptly. It was the first time that Varick had come to the house, and the surprise of seeing him, combined with the singular inopportuneness of his arrival, gave a new edge to Waythorn's blunted sensibilities. He stared at his visitor without speaking.

Varick seemed too preoccupied to notice his host's embarrassment.

"My dear fellow," he exclaimed in his most expansive tone, "I must apologise for tumbling in on you in this way, but I was too late to catch you down town, and so I thought—"

He stopped short, catching sight of Haskett, and his sanguine colour deepened to a flush which spread vividly under his scant blond hair. But in a moment he recovered himself and nodded slightly. Haskett returned the bow in silence, and Waythorn was still groping for speech when the footman came in carrying a tea-table.

The intrusion offered a welcome vent to Waythorn's nerves. "What the deuce are you bringing this here for?" he said sharply.

"I beg your pardon, sir, but the plumbers are still in the drawing-room, and Mrs. Waythorn said she would have tea in the library." The footman's perfectly respectful tone implied a reflection on Waythorn's reasonableness.

"Oh, very well," said the latter resignedly, and the footman proceeded to open the folding tea-table and set out its complicated appointments. While this interminable process continued the three men stood motionless, watching it with a fascinated stare, till Waythorn, to break the silence, said to Varick: "Won't you have a cigar?"

He held out the case he had just tendered to Haskett, and Varick helped himself with a smile. Waythorn looked about for a match, and finding none, proffered a light from his own cigar. Haskett, in the background, held his ground mildly, examining his cigar-tip now and then, and stepping forward at the right moment to knock its ashes into the fire.

The footman at last withdrew, and Varick immediately began: "If I could just say half a word to you about this business—"

"Certainly," stammered Waythorn; "in the dining-room—"

But as he placed his hand on the door it opened from without, and his wife appeared on the threshold.

She came in fresh and smiling, in her street dress and hat, shedding a fragrance from the boa[5] which she loosened in advancing.

"Shall we have tea in here, dear?" she began; and then she caught sight of Varick. Her smile deepened, veiling a slight tremor of surprise.

"Why, how do you do?" she said with a distinct note of pleasure.

As she shook hands with Varick she saw Haskett standing behind him. Her smile faded for a moment, but she recalled it quickly, with a scarcely perceptible side-glance at Waythorn.

"How do you do, Mr. Haskett?" she said, and shook hands with him a shade less cordially.

The three men stood awkwardly before her, till Varick, always the most self-possessed, dashed into an explanatory phrase.

"We—I had to see Waythorn a moment on business," he stammered, brick-red from chin to nape.

Haskett stepped forward with his air of mild obstinacy. "I am sorry to intrude; but you appointed five o'clock—" he directed his resigned glance to the timepiece on the mantel.

She swept aside their embarrassment with a charming gesture of hospitality.

"I'm so sorry—I'm always late; but the afternoon was so lovely." She stood drawing off her gloves, propitiatory and graceful, diffusing about her a sense of ease and familiarity in which the situation lost its grotesqueness. "But before talking business," she added brightly, "I'm sure every one wants a cup of tea."

She dropped into her low chair by the tea-table, and the two visitors, as if drawn by her smile, advanced to receive the cups she held out.

She glanced about for Waythorn, and he took the third cup with a laugh.

1904

---

[5] Long scarf of fur or feathers worn around a woman's neck or shoulders.

Edwin Arlington Robinson
1869–1935

The poets who preceded Edwin Arlington Robinson—Bryant, Whittier, Longfellow, and James Russell Lowell—have been grouped as "the fireside poets," and the name conveys their acceptability to the genteel tradition. Unlike these poets, Robinson had the lonely courage not to write conventionally pleasing verse. Instead he wrote lyrics stemming directly from his doomed sense of life. He was, in the existential bleakness of his vision, a forerunner of the disillusioned generation that created the modernist movement in art.

One of Robinson's brothers was an alcoholic, one a doctor addicted to drugs, and Robinson himself became an alcoholic. His father's business had failed, and it was only through local benefactors that Robinson managed to spend two years (like Robert Frost later) as a special student at Harvard. When he left Harvard, he returned home to Gardiner, Maine, where, trapped, unemployed, and in the force of his twenties, he wrote his most memorable poems. Robinson first anatomized his village (under the name "Tilbury Town") and its cast of local failures and eccentrics in the 1897 collection of poems *Children of the Night*. The most famous of his characters—the hopeless, backward-looking Miniver Cheevy and the immaculately dressed but suicidal Richard Cory—are perhaps self-caricatures and bear a special lyric force in their cruel self-satire. Nearing thirty, Robinson moved to New York, where he lived the rest of his life, although after 1911 he spent the summers in New Hampshire at the MacDowell Colony for artists. He never married.

In 1922 Robinson's *Collected Poems* was awarded the Pulitzer Prize. In his maturity, he was known chiefly for his long, Tennysonian poems on Arthurian themes, *Merlin* (1917), *Lancelot* (1920), and *Tristram* (1927), which have not aged well. He also wrote long psychological studies of character, among them *Cavender's House* (1929) and *Matthis at the Door* (1931). George Crabbe rather than Tennyson was Robinson's true English precursor. Crabbe's "hard, human pulse," his "plain excellence and stubborn skill," as Robinson called them, were Robinson's own aesthetic strengths. His brisk quatrains, the stern blank verse of his satires, his death-knell rhymes in "Eros Turannos"—"confusion, illusion, seclusion" or "striven, given, driven"—are marks of his care in composing.

Robinson's achievement in verse is now perceived, paradoxically, through the work of Robert Frost, who learned everything Robinson had to teach and brought it to rhythmic and lyric perfection. Without Robinson, we can scarcely imagine Frost's existence. Robinson's dark, sardonic nature appealed to Frost's grim side, and he also taught Frost how to be a regional poet. Robinson's revelation of the spoiled erotic life allowed Frost to draw aside curtains of privacy, and his insight into the tragic dramas enacted in rural life gave Frost one of his chief topics. When we look at Robinson now, we feel he must have been reading Frost; but the debt goes the other way.

Further Reading:

M. Van Doren, *Edwin Arlington Robinson,* 1927.
H. Hagedorn, *Edwin Arlington Robinson: A Biography,* 1938.
E. Kaplan, *Philosophy in the Poetry of Edwin Arlington Robinson,* 1940.
Y. Winters, *Edwin Arlington Robinson,* 1946.
E. Neff, *Edwin Arlington Robinson,* 1948.
E. Barnard, *Edwin Arlington Robinson: A Critical Study,* 1952.
E. S. Fussell, *Edwin Arlington Robinson: The Literary Background of a Traditional Poet,* 1954.
W. L. Anderson, *Edwin Arlington Robinson,*

1967.
W. R. Robinson, *Edwin Arlington Robinson: A Poetry of the Act,* 1967.
L. O. Coxe, *Edwin Arlington Robinson: The Life of Poetry,* 1968.
H. C. Franchere, *Edwin Arlington Robinson,* 1968.
Edwin Arlington Robinson: Centenary Essays, ed. E. Barnard, 1973.
R. Cary, *Early Reception of Edwin Arlington Robinson,* 1974.
N. C. Joyner, *Edwin Arlington Robinson,* 1978.

Text:

Collected Poems, 1940.
See also *Selected Poems of Edwin Arlington Robinson,* ed. M. D. Zabel, 1965, 1966.
Uncollected Poems and Prose of Edwin Arlington

Robinson, ed. R. Cary, 1975.
Selected Letters of Edwin Arlington Robinson, ed. R. Torrence, 1940.

Richard Cory

Whenever Richard Cory went down town,
We people on the pavement looked at him:
He was a gentleman from sole to crown,
Clean favored, and imperially slim.

And he was always quietly arrayed,   5
And he was always human when he talked;
But still he fluttered pulses when he said,
"Good-morning," and he glittered when he walked.

And he was rich—yes, richer than a king—
And admirably schooled in every grace: 10
In fine, we thought that he was everything
To make us wish that we were in his place.

So on we worked, and waited for the light,
And went without the meat, and cursed the bread;
And Richard Cory, one calm summer night,   15
Went home and put a bullet through his head.

1896

George Crabbe[1]

Give him the darkest inch your shelf allows,
Hide him in lonely garrets, if you will,—
But his hard, human pulse is throbbing still
With the sure strength that fearless truth endows.
In spite of all fine science disavows,   5
Of his plain excellence and stubborn skill
There yet remains what fashion cannot kill,
Though years have thinned the laurel from his brows.

Whether or not we read him, we can feel
From time to time the vigor of his name   10
Against us like a finger for the shame
And emptiness of what our souls reveal
In books that are as altars where we kneel
To consecrate the flicker, not the flame.

1896

The Corridor

It may have been the pride in me for aught
I know, or just a patronizing whim;
But call it freak or fancy, or what not,
I cannot hide that hungry face of him.

I keep a scant half-dozen words he said,   5
And every now and then I lose his name;
He may be living or he may be dead,
But I must have him with me all the same.

I knew it, and I knew it all along,—
And felt it once or twice, or thought I did;   10
But only as a glad man feels a song
That sounds around a stranger's coffin lid.

[1] English poet (1754–1832) and author of *The
Village* (1783), a bleak picture of rustic life.

I knew it, and he knew it, I believe,
But silence held us alien to the end;
And I have now no magic to retrieve   15
That year, to stop that hunger for a friend.
1902

But for the Grace of God

"There, but for the grace of God, goes . . ."

There is a question that I ask,
    And ask again:
What hunger was half-hidden by the mask
    That he wore then?

There was a word for me to say   5
    That I said not;
And in the past there was another day
    That I forgot:

A dreary, cold, unwholesome day,
    Racked overhead,—   10
As if the world were turning the wrong way,
    And the sun dead:

A day that comes back well enough
    Now he is gone.
What then? Has memory no other stuff   15
    To seize upon?

Wherever he may wander now
    In his despair,
Would he be more contented in the slough
    If all were there?   20

And yet he brought a kind of light
    Into the room;
And when he left, a tinge of something bright
    Survived the gloom.

Why will he not be where he is,   25
    And not with me?
The hours that are my life are mine, not his,—
    Or used to be.

What numerous imps invisible
   Has he at hand,
Far-flying and forlorn as what they tell
   At his command?   30

What hold of weirdness or of worth
   Can he possess,
That he may speak from anywhere on earth   35
   His loneliness?

Shall I be caught and held again
   In the old net?—
He brought a sorry sunbeam with him then,
   But it beams yet.   40

1910

Miniver Cheevy

Miniver Cheevy, child of scorn,
   Grew lean while he assailed the seasons;
He wept that he was ever born,
   And he had reasons.

Miniver loved the days of old   5
   When swords were bright and steeds were prancing;
The vision of a warrior bold
   Would set him dancing.

Miniver sighed for what was not,
   And dreamed, and rested from his labors;   10
He dreamed of Thebes[1] and Camelot,[2]
   And Priam's[3] neighbors.

Miniver mourned the ripe renown
   That made so many a name so fragrant;
He mourned Romance, now on the town,   15
   And Art, a vagrant.

[1] City in Greece made famous by Homer and the Greek tragedians.
[2] Site of King Arthur's court.
[3] Priam was king of Troy. (The Trojan War is described in Homer's *Iliad*.)

Miniver loved the Medici,[4]
  Albeit he had never seen one;
He would have sinned incessantly
  Could he have been one.   20

Miniver cursed the commonplace
  And eyed a khaki suit with loathing;
He missed the mediæval grace
  Of iron clothing.

Miniver scorned the gold he sought,   25
  But sore annoyed was he without it;
Miniver thought, and thought, and thought,
  And thought about it.

Miniver Cheevy, born too late,
  Scratched his head and kept on thinking;   30
Miniver coughed, and called it fate,
  And kept on drinking.

1910

For a Dead Lady

No more with overflowing light
Shall fill the eyes that now are faded,
Nor shall another's fringe with night
Their woman-hidden world as they did.
No more shall quiver down the days   5
The flowing wonder of her ways,
Whereof no language may requite
The shifting and the many-shaded.

The grace, divine, definitive,
Clings only as a faint forestalling;   10
The laugh that love could not forgive
Is hushed, and answers to no calling;
The forehead and the little ears
Have gone where Saturn keeps the years;
The breast where roses could not live   15
Has done with rising and with falling.

[4] One of the ruling families of the Italian
Renaissance.

The beauty, shattered by the laws
That have creation in their keeping,
No longer trembles at applause,
Or over children that are sleeping;
And we who delve in beauty's lore
Know all that we have known before
Of what inexorable cause
Makes Time so vicious in his reaping.

1910

Eros Turannos[1]

She fears him, and will always ask
   What fated her to choose him;
She meets in his engaging mask
   All reasons to refuse him;
But what she meets and what she fears
Are less than are the downward years,
Drawn slowly to the foamless weirs
   Of age, were she to lose him.

Between a blurred sagacity
   That once had power to sound him,
And Love, that will not let him be
   The Judas that she found him,
Her pride assuages her almost,
As if it were alone the cost.—
He sees that he will not be lost,
   And waits and looks around him.

A sense of ocean and old trees
   Envelops and allures him;
Tradition, touching all he sees,
   Beguiles and reassures him;
And all her doubts of what he says
Are dimmed with what she knows of days—
Till even prejudice delays
   And fades, and she secures him.

[1] Greek: "Love, the Ruler."

The falling leaf inaugurates   25
   The reign of her confusion;
The pounding wave reverberates
   The dirge of her illusion;
And home, where passion lived and died,
Becomes a place where she can hide,   30
While all the town and harbor side
   Vibrate with her seclusion.

We tell you, tapping on our brows,
   The story as it should be,—
As if the story of a house   35
   Were told, or ever could be;
We'll have no kindly veil between
Her visions and those we have seen,—
As if we guessed what hers have been,
   Or what they are or would be.   40

Meanwhile we do no harm; for they
   That with a god have striven,
Not hearing much of what we say,
   Take what the god has given;
Though like waves breaking it may be,   45
Or like a changed familiar tree,
Or like a stairway to the sea
   Where down the blind are driven.
1916

The Unforgiven

When he, who is the unforgiven,
Beheld her first, he found her fair:
No promise ever dreamt in heaven
Could then have lured him anywhere
That would have been away from there;   5
And all his wits had lightly striven,
Foiled with her voice, and eyes, and hair.

There's nothing in the saints and sages
To meet the shafts her glances had,
Or such as hers have had for ages   10
To blind a man till he be glad,

And humble him till he be mad.
The story would have many pages,
And would be neither good nor bad.

And, having followed, you would find him   1
Where properly the play begins;
But look for no red light behind him—
No fumes of many-colored sins,
Fanned high by screaming violins.
God knows what good it was to blind him,   2
Or whether man or woman wins.

And by the same eternal token,
Who knows just how it will all end?—
This drama of hard words unspoken,
This fireside farce, without a friend   25
Or enemy to comprehend
What augurs when two lives are broken,
And fear finds nothing left to mend.

He stares in vain for what awaits him,
And sees in Love a coin to toss;
He smiles, and her cold hush berates him   30
Beneath his hard half of the cross;
They wonder why it ever was;
And she, the unforgiving, hates him
More for her lack than for her loss.   35

He feeds with pride his indecision,
And shrinks from what will not occur,
Bequeathing with infirm derision
His ashes to the days that were,
Before she made him prisoner;   40
And labors to retrieve the vision
That he must once have had of her.

He waits, and there awaits an ending,
And he knows neither what nor when;
But no magicians are attending   45
To make him see as he saw then,
And he will never find again
The face that once had been the rending
Of all his purpose among men.

He blames her not, nor does he chide her,   50
And she has nothing new to say;
If he were Bluebeard he could hide her,

But that's not written in the play,
And there will be no change to-day;
Although, to the serene outsider,   55
There still would seem to be a way.
1916

The Mill

The miller's wife had waited long,
    The tea was cold, the fire was dead;
And there might yet be nothing wrong
    In how he went and what he said:
"There are no millers any more,"   5
    Was all that she had heard him say:
And he had lingered at the door
    So long that it seemed yesterday.

Sick with a fear that had no form
    She knew that she was there at last;   10
And in the mill there was a warm
    And mealy fragrance of the past.
What else there was would only seem
    To say again what he had meant;
And what was hanging from a beam   15
    Would not have heeded where she went.

And if she thought it followed her,
    She may have reasoned in the dark
That one way of the few there were
    Would hide her and would leave no mark: 20
Black water, smooth above the weir
    Like starry velvet in the night,
Though ruffled once, would soon appear
    The same as ever to the sight.
1920

The New Tenants

The day was here when it was his to know
How fared the barriers he had built between
His triumph and his enemies unseen,
For them to undermine and overthrow;
And it was his no longer to forego   5
The sight of them, insidious and serene,
Where they were delving always and had been
Left always to be vicious and to grow.

And there were the new tenants who had come,
By doors that were left open unawares,   10
Into his house, and were so much at home
There now that he would hardly have to guess,
By the slow guile of their vindictiveness,
What ultimate insolence would soon be theirs.
1920

from Not Always

II

There were long days when there was nothing said,
And there were longer nights where there was nought
But silence and recriminating thought
Between them like a field unharvested.
Antipathy was now their daily bread,   5
And pride the bitter drink they daily fought
To throw away. Release was all they sought
Of hope, colder than moonlight on the dead.

Wishing the other might at once be sure
And strong enough to shake the prison down,   10
Neither believed, although they strove together,
How long the stolid fabric would endure
That was a wall for them, and was to frown
And shine for them through many sorts of weather.
1925

New England

Here where the wind is always north-north-east
And children learn to walk on frozen toes,
Wonder begets an envy of all those
Who boil elsewhere with such a lyric yeast
Of love that you will hear them at a feast   5
Where demons would appeal for some repose,
Still clamoring where the chalice overflows
And crying wildest who have drunk the least.

Passion is here a soilure of the wits,
We're told, and Love a cross for them to bear;   10
Joy shivers in the corner where she knits
And Conscience always has the rocking-chair,
Cheerful as when she tortured into fits
The first cat that was ever killed by Care.

1925

Stephen Crane
1871–1900

At nineteen Stephen Crane was best known for his skill as a baseball player. Any
other distinctions while briefly a college student were negligible. Within ten
years Crane was dead of tuberculosis, acclaimed as a journalist and as the author
of *The Red Badge of Courage* (1894), the novel that alone assures his place in
American fiction.

Between 1890 and 1900 Crane worked as a free-lance newspaper reporter
observing life in New York's slums and as a correspondent reporting on often
violent events taking place in Mexico, the American West, Cuba, and Greece.
Because the role of the journalist and correspondent was made increasingly
glamorous by the "romantic wars" of the 1890s, Crane became a celebrity. He
lived in England in manorial splendor he could not afford with his common-law
wife, the former madam of the Hotel de Dream in Jacksonville, Florida. He was
the friend of writers of great importance, including Joseph Conrad, H. G. Wells,
and Henry James. Throughout all this commotion—public and personal—Stephen
Crane feverishly wrote the ten volumes of material that make up his collected
literary works.

The youngest of fourteen children, Crane was born in Newark, New Jersey,
the son of a Methodist minister. The peripatetic nature of the father's ministry

moved the Crane family from one small town to another in New Jersey and New York State. After Crane's abortive visits to the classrooms of Lafayette College in Pennsylvania and Syracuse University in New York, he turned full-time to the newspaper life. Crane had had some experience in the business, first as a boy working for his older brother's press bureau, then as the local correspondent of the *New York Tribune* while still a student at Syracuse University. Once he left college at the age of twenty, he had a living to earn and a good idea of how he was to do it.

Crane went to New York in 1891, held a post on the *New York Herald,* lost it, and turned to free-lance writing. He only infrequently sold filler stories to city papers that saw little merit in pieces reporting on what it feels like to live in the slums; exposés in the manner of the muckrakers were preferred. Crane lived hand to mouth, hanging about in the company of medical students and art students, with occasional stints back home in New Jersey. He knew from experience what being poor is like, and he brought to his studies of Bowery life a keenness of observation beyond that possible to the casually curious.

Maggie, a Girl of the Streets was completed in 1893 when Crane was twenty-one. Established publishers had no use for this portrayal of Irish immigrants hanging on to a Bowery existence. In contrast, Jacob Riis's *How the Other Half Lives* (1890) had quickly acquired a receptive readership for its straightforward account of the fetid places where the city's discards lived, perhaps because Riis's approach was patently that of the social reformer. Crane's fictional narrative of the short, dreary, dream-deluded life of Maggie, a young girl who goes "on the toif" as a streetwalker and ends drowned in the East River, was not so obviously uplifting. But respectable readers in 1893 preferred the didacticism of the actual photographs Riis had used to dramatize his appeals for aid and reform of the poor to Crane's seemingly impersonal, amoral, sensational effects. *Maggie* came out under the pseudonym Johnston Smith and received little attention. But what attention it got mattered. Hamlin Garland and William Dean Howells recognized Crane's talent and became his mentors—Garland through his praise in *Crumbling Idols* (1894) and Howells in reviews placed in the *Philadelphia Press* (1893) and *Harper's Weekly* (1895).

Late in 1894 Crane's novel *The Red Badge of Courage* appeared as a syndicated feature in some 750 small newspapers across the country. Early the next year the *Philadelphia Press,* part of the chain that had printed *The Red Badge of Courage,* posted their hot young property on writing assignments out West. (From these experiences Crane would write "The Bride Comes to Yellow Sky" in 1897.) In May 1895 his first collection of poems, *The Black Riders,* was published to unfavorable reviews. His experimentations in poetic form and the dark mood of his vision were too unconventional for popular acceptance. But in October 1895 *The Red Badge of Courage* was brought out by Appleton's, an important press, and Crane knew what it was like to be famous. Readers immediately took to the vivid tale of Civil War combat written by a young man born ten years after that war had been fought. Unlike *Maggie,* it created a stir among readers who were eager to read realistic accounts of Civil War battles but were uneasy with accounts of daily slum warfare. The serial publication of "Battles and Leaders of the Civil War" (published in four volumes in 1887 and 1888 by *Century* magazine) had roused public interest in the events of the war. Crane could count on excited attention from this moment on for anything he wrote or did.

For Crane, 1896 and 1897 were exceedingly productive years. *Maggie* was republished in 1896 by Appleton's under the eye of the writer-critic Frank Norris. The language of the original edition was cleaned up to meet current tastes in the printed word, and the novel received the approval it had failed to win in 1893. Also published in 1896 were *The Little Regiment*, a collection of Civil War stories, and *George's Mother*, the psychological account of the death-grip solicitude of a mother for her son. During the winter of 1896–1897 Crane was assigned to Cuba to cover the insurrection that led to the military confrontation in 1898 between Spain and the United States. He met and formed a permanent liaison with Cora Taylor of the Hotel de Dream. Early in 1897 he experienced the surprise of having the ship he was aboard sunk from under him as it headed for Cuba—an incident he immediately wrote up as a newspaper report and then developed into the short story "The Open Boat." In the midst of this activity, he published *The Third Violet*, a partly autobiographical novel about a young painter. By the summer of 1897, Crane was off to the Greco-Turkish war front, from whence he sent dispatches to American and British papers. By year's end he and Cora had gone to England to live.

Crane was once again in the Caribbean in 1898, reporting on the battles of the Spanish-American War for the famous Pulitzer paper, the *New York World*. By 1899 he had returned to England, already ill with tuberculosis and deep in debt. Over the next twelve months, Crane worked hard to earn the money he and Cora needed. He published *The Whilomville Stories* and *Wounds in the Rain;* prepared a second collection of poems, *War Is Kind;* completed the novel *Active Service;* wrote articles on major war battles published posthumously as *Great Battles of the World;* and pushed through the writing of twenty-five chapters of yet another novel, *The O'Ruddy*. Taken by Cora to a German sanatorium in the desperate hope that his illness could be arrested, Crane died on June 5, 1900.

That Crane was a literary prodigy is obvious. That he furnished American literature with a group of memorable tales and one novel-length masterwork is not at issue. The *kind* of writing Crane produced is what sparks controversy. Crane examined the inevitable conflict between self-made images that comfort and external facts that undercut romantic visions. But in his literary methods, was he primarily a realist, a naturalist, or an impressionist? Crane was a rebel against everything considered correct by the society he had left behind at twenty. The bohemian life he followed, the woman he lived with, and the material he wrote about all tell us this. But was he attempting to judge conventional society as a realist does, did he prefer to analyze its elements coolly in the manner of the naturalist, or was he most interested in imprinting impressionistic images for their own sake on his readers' minds?

The ironic tone that pervades Crane's narratives makes it difficult to determine his motives. Sometimes he appears hardly more than a very clever young man, and a rather cold one, who closes out the chance of getting at profound human feelings. At times Crane's compassion for those who yield to the stress of constant threats to their lives seems offset by a certain glibness. Those are the moments when he seems to be displaying what he knows (and his readers do not). At other times Crane appears to be trapped in unquestioned dreams of heroic male action. Consider for example, the problematic conclusion of *The Red Badge of Courage*. The young soldier Henry Fleming is now certain he knows the value of heroic action, but do the narrator's remarks in the closing sentences put the boy's certainty in doubt? Many of the endings Crane gives his stories are troublesome. They strike us as sophomoric exercises in facile cleverness—as with Mary Johnson's lament for her injured "goodness" in *Maggie*, the cash-register sign that flips up at the conclusion of "The Blue Hotel," Scratchy Wilson's double-take response to the news that the town marshal had gone and "got hisself married," and the final parade of small-town hypocrisies in "The Monster."

But Crane's imaginative force cannot be denied; nor can the way he finds apt images to encode human behavior. We detect in his writings the same discoveries made by William James's new psychology and by the theories of Charles Darwin and Herbert Spencer, which emphasize how susceptible we are to forces of inherited habits and environmental pressures. In one sense, *The Red Badge of Courage* is a determinist's primer about fears and falsehoods, but Crane manages to avoid trapping this story of a young soldier facing combat and his inner self in the doctrinaire. The novel is a very human tale, not a scientific treatise.

Crane lived quickly and wrote fast. His writing may have outrun his mind's ability or his heart's capacity to cut past the upper layers of that emotional cuticle where people under stress display their desires and terrors. But without question, Crane's reporter's eye is unfailingly accurate in its notations, just as his artist's touch is apparent in the images he has left permanently in his readers' memory.

Further Reading:
T. Beer, *Stephen Crane: A Study in American Letters*, 1923.
T. L. Raymond, *Stephen Crane*, 1923.
J. Berryman, *Stephen Crane*, 1950, 1962.
D. Hoffman, *The Poetry of Stephen Crane*, 1956, 1957.
C. Linson, *My Stephen Crane*, ed. E. Cady, 1958.
E. Cady, *Stephen Crane*, 1962, 1980.
E. Solomon, *Stephen Crane in England: A Portrait of the Artist*, 1964, 1965.
E. Solomon, *Stephen Crane: From Parody to Realism*, 1966.
Stephen Crane: A Collection of Critical Essays, ed. M. Bassan, 1967.
D. Gibson, *The Fiction of Stephen Crane*, 1968.

R. Stallman, *Stephen Crane: A Biography*, 1968.
Stephen Crane in the West and Mexico, ed. J. Katz, 1970.
R. M. Weatherford, *The Growth of Stephen Crane's Literary Reputation*, 1970.
M. La France, *A Reading of Stephen Crane*, 1971.
Stephen Crane in Transition: Centenary Essays, ed. J. Katz, 1972.
M. Holton, *Cylinder of Vision: The Fiction and Journalistic Writing of Stephen Crane*, 1972.
Stephen Crane's Career, ed. T. Gullason, 1973.
F. Bergon, *Stephen Crane's Artistry*, 1975.
J. Nagel, *Stephen Crane and Literary Impressionism*, 1980.
C. Wolford, *The Anger of Stephen Crane*, 1983.

Text:
The Works of Stephen Crane, 10 vols., ed. F. Bowers, 1969–1976.
See also R. Stallman, *Stephen Crane: An Omnibus*, 1952.
Stephen Crane: Letters, ed. R. Stallman and L. Gilkes, 1960.
Stephen Crane: Uncollected Writings, ed. O. Fryckstedt, 1963.

Completed Short Stories and Sketches, ed. T. Gullason, 1963.
The Poems of Stephen Crane: A Critical Edition, ed. J. Katz, 1966.
The Complete Novels, ed. T. Gullason, 1967.
Stephen Crane: Sullivan County Tales and Sketches, ed. R. Stallman, 1968.

The Open Boat

A Tale Intended to Be After the Fact.
Being the Experience of Four Men
*from the Sunk Steamer Commodore**

I

None of them knew the color of the sky. Their eyes glanced level, and were fastened upon the waves that swept toward them. These waves were of the hue of slate, save for the tops which were of foaming white, and all of the men knew the colors of the sea. The horizon narrowed and widened, and dipped and rose, and at all times its edge was jagged with waves that seemed thrust up in points like rocks.

Many a man ought to have a bath-tub larger than the boat which here rode upon the sea. These waves were most wrongfully and barbarously abrupt and tall, and each froth-top was a problem in small boat navigation.

The cook squatted in the bottom and looked with both eyes at the six inches of gunwale which separated him from the ocean. His sleeves were rolled over his fat forearms, and the two flaps of his unbuttoned vest dangled as he bent to bail out the boat. Often he said: "Gawd! That was a narrow clip." As he remarked it he invariably gazed eastward over the broken sea.

The oiler, steering with one of the two oars in the boat, sometimes raised himself suddenly to keep clear of water that swirled in over the stern. It was a thin little oar and it seemed often ready to snap.

The correspondent, pulling at the other oar, watched the waves and wondered why he was there.

The injured captain, lying in the bow, was at this time buried in that profound dejection and indifference which comes, temporarily at least, to even the bravest and most enduring when, willy nilly, the firm fails, the army loses, the ship goes down. The mind of the master of a vessel is rooted deep in the timbers of her, though he command for a day or a decade, and this captain had on him the stern impression of a scene in the grays of dawn of seven turned faces, and later a stump of a top-mast with a white ball on it that slashed to and fro at the waves, went low and lower, and down. Thereafter there was something strange in his voice. Although steady, it was deep with mourning, and of a quality beyond oration or tears.

"Keep' er a little more south, Billie," said he.

" 'A little more south,' sir," said the oiler in the stern.

A seat in this boat was not unlike a seat upon a bucking broncho, and, by the same token, a broncho is not much smaller. The craft pranced and reared, and plunged like

---

* Crane was on board the *Commodore* bound for Cuba to cover the revolution as a correspondent when the ship (carrying arms for the combatants) was sunk January 2, 1897, off the Florida coast. Together with four other men, Crane spent almost thirty hours in a dinghy before making a safe landing at Daytona. The New York *Press* ran Crane's account of his experiences on January 7. By June he had published his fictional version in *Scribner's Magazine* as "The Open Boat."

an animal. As each wave came, and she rose for it, she seemed like a horse making at a fence outrageously high. The manner of her scramble over these walls of water is a mystic thing, and, moreover, at the top of them were ordinarily these problems in white water, the foam racing down from the summit of each wave, requiring a new leap, and a leap from the air. Then, after scornfully bumping a crest, she would slide, and race, and splash down a long incline and arrive bobbing and nodding in front of the next menace.

A singular disadvantage of the sea lies in the fact that after successfully surmounting one wave you discover that there is another behind it just as important and just as nervously anxious to do something effective in the way of swamping boats. In a ten-foot dingey one can get an idea of the resources of the sea in the line of waves that is not probable to the average experience, which is never at sea in a dingey. As each salty wall of water approached, it shut all else from the view of the men in the boat, and it was the final outburst of the ocean, the last effort of the grim water. There was a terrible grace in the move of the waves, and they came in silence, save for the snarling of the crests.

In the wan light, the faces of the men must have been gray. Their eyes must have glinted in strange ways as they gazed steadily astern. Viewed from a balcony, the whole thing would doubtlessly have been weirdly picturesque. But the men in the boat had no time to see it, and if they had had leisure there were other things to occupy their minds. The sun swung steadily up the sky, and they knew it was broad day because the color of the sea changed from slate to emerald-green, streaked with amber lights, and the foam was like tumbling snow. The process of the breaking day was unknown to them. They were aware only of this effect upon the color of the waves that rolled toward them.

In disjointed sentences the cook and the correspondent argued as to the difference between a life-saving station and a house of refuge. The cook had said: "There's a house of refuge just north of the Mosquito Inlet Light, and as soon as they see us, they'll come off in their boat and pick us up."

"As soon as who see us?" said the correspondent.

"The crew," said the cook.

"Houses of refuge don't have crews," said the correspondent. "As I understand them, they are only places where clothes and grub are stored for the benefit of shipwrecked people. They don't carry crews."

"Oh, yes, they do," said the cook.

"No, they don't," said the correspondent.

"Well, we're not there yet, anyhow," said the oiler, in the stern.

"Well," said the cook, "perhaps it's not a house of refuge that I'm thinking of as being near Mosquito Inlet Light. Perhaps it's a life-saving station."

"We're not there yet," said the oiler, in the stern.

II

As the boat bounced from the top of each wave, the wind tore through the hair of the hatless men, and as the craft plopped her stern down again the spray slashed past them. The crest of each of these waves was a hill, from the top of which the men surveyed, for a moment, a broad tumultuous expanse, shining and wind-riven. It was probably splendid. It was probably glorious, this play of the free sea, wild with lights of emerald and white and amber.

"Bully good thing it's an on-shore wind," said the cook. "If not, where would we be? Wouldn't have a show."

"That's right," said the correspondent.

The busy oiler nodded his assent.

Then the captain, in the bow, chuckled in a way that expressed humor, contempt, tragedy, all in one. "Do you think we've got much of a show, now, boys?" said he.

Whereupon the three were silent, save for a trifle of hemming and hawing. To express any particular optimism at this time they felt to be childish and stupid, but they all doubtless possessed this sense of the situation in their mind. A young man thinks doggedly at such times. On the other hand, the ethics of their condition was decidedly against any open suggestion of hopelessness. So they were silent.

"Oh, well," said the captain, soothing his children, "we'll get ashore all right."

But there was that in his tone which made them think, so the oiler quoth: "Yes! If this wind holds!"

The cook was bailing. "Yes! If we don't catch hell in the surf."

Canton flannel gulls flew near and far. Sometimes they sat down on the sea, near patches of brown sea-weed that rolled over the waves with a movement like carpets on a line in a gale. The birds sat comfortably in groups, and they were envied by some in the dingey, for the wrath of the sea was no more to them than it was to a covey of prairie chickens a thousand miles inland. Often they came very close and stared at the men with black bead-like eyes. At these times they were uncanny and sinister in their unblinking scrutiny, and the men hooted angrily at them, telling them to be gone. One came, and evidently decided to alight on the top of the captain's head. The bird flew parallel to the boat and did not circle, but made short sidelong jumps in the air in chicken-fashion. His black eyes were wistfully fixed upon the captain's head. "Ugly brute," said the oiler to the bird. "You look as if you were made with a jack-knife." The cook and the correspondent swore darkly at the creature. The captain naturally wished to knock it away with the end of the heavy painter, but he did not dare do it, because anything resembling an emphatic gesture would have capsized this freighted boat, and so with his open hand, the captain gently and carefully waved the gull away. After it had been discouraged from the pursuit the captain breathed easier on account of his hair, and others breathed easier because the bird struck their minds at this time as being somehow grewsome and ominous.

In the meantime the oiler and the correspondent rowed. And also they rowed.

They sat together in the same seat, and each rowed an oar, then the oiler took both oars; then the correspondent took both oars; then the oiler; then the correspondent. They rowed and they rowed. The very ticklish part of the business was when the time came for the reclining one in the stern to take his turn at the oars. By the very last star of truth, it is easier to steal eggs from under a hen than it was to change seats in the dingey. First the man in the stern slid his hand along the thwart and moved with care, as if he were of Sèvres. Then the man in the rowing seat slid his hand along the other thwart. It was all done with the most extraordinary care. As the two sidled past each other, the whole party kept watchful eyes on the coming wave, and the captain cried: "Look out now! Steady there!"

The brown mats of sea-weed that appeared from time to time were like islands, bits of earth. They were travelling, apparently, neither one way nor the other. They were, to all intents, stationary. They informed the men in the boat that it was making progress slowly toward the land.

The captain, rearing cautiously in the bow, after the dingey soared on a great swell, said that he had seen the light-house at Mosquito Inlet. Presently the cook remarked that he had seen it. The correspondent was at the oars, then, and for some reason he too wished to look at the light-house, but his back was toward the far shore and the waves were important, and for some time he could not seize an opportunity to turn his head. But at last there came a wave more gentle than the others, and when at the crest of it he swiftly scoured the western horizon.

"See it?" said the captain.

"No," said the correspondent, slowly. "I didn't see anything."

"Look again," said the captain. He pointed. "It's exactly in that direction."

At the top of another wave, the correspondent did as he was bid, and this time his eyes chanced on a small still thing on the edge of the swaying horizon. It was precisely like the point of a pin. It took an anxious eye to find a light-house so tiny.

"Think we'll make it, Captain?"

"If this wind holds and the boat don't swamp, we can't do much else," said the captain.

The little boat, lifted by each towering sea, and splashed viciously by the crests, made progress that in the absence of sea-weed was not apparent to those in her. She seemed just a wee thing wallowing, miraculously, top-up, at the mercy of five oceans. Occasionally, a great spread of water, like white flame, swarmed into her.

"Bail her, cook," said the captain, serenely.

"All right, Captain," said the cheerful cook.

III

It would be difficult to describe the subtle brotherhood of men that was here established on the seas. No one said that it was so. No one mentioned it, but it dwelt in the boat, and each man felt it warm him. They were a captain, an oiler, a cook, and a correspondent, and they were friends, friends in a more curiously ironbound degree than may be common. The hurt captain, lying against the water-jar in the bow, spoke always in a low voice and calmly but he could never command a more ready and swiftly obedient crew than the motley three of the dingey. It was more than a mere recognition of what was best for the common safety. There was surely in it a quality that was personal and heartfelt. And after this devotion to the commander of the boat there was this comradeship that the correspondent, for instance, who had been taught to be cynical of men, knew even at the time was the best experience of his life. But no one said that it was so. No one mentioned it.

"I wish we had a sail," remarked the captain. "We might try my overcoat on the end of an oar and give you two boys a chance to rest." So the cook and the correspondent held the mast and spread wide the overcoat, the oiler steered, and the little boat made good way with her new rig. Sometimes the oiler had to scull sharply to keep a sea from breaking into the boat, but otherwise sailing was a success.

Meanwhile the light-house had been growing slowly larger. It had now almost assumed color, and appeared like a little gray shadow in the sky. The man at the oars could not be prevented from turning his head rather often to try for a glimpse of this little gray shadow.

At last, from the top of each wave the men in the tossing boat could see land. Even as the light-house was an upright shadow on the sky, this land seemed but a long black shadow on the sea. It certainly was thinner than paper. "We must be about opposite New Smyrna," said the cook, who had coasted this shore often in schooners. "Captain, by the way, I believe they abandoned that life-saving station there about a year ago."

"Did they?" said the captain.

The wind slowly died away. The cook and the correspondent were not now obliged to slave in order to hold high the oar. But the waves continued their old impetuous swooping at the dingey, and the little craft, no longer under way, struggled woundily over them. The oiler or the correspondent took the oars again.

Shipwrecks are *apropos* of nothing. If men could only train for them and have them occur when the men had reached pink condition, there would be less drowning at sea. Of the four in the dingey none had slept any time worth mentioning for two days and two nights previous to embarking in the dingey, and in the excitement of clambering about the deck of a foundering ship they had also forgotten to eat heartily.

For these reasons, and for others, neither the oiler nor the correspondent was fond of rowing at this time. The correspondent wondered ingenuously how in the name of all that was sane could there be people who thought it amusing to row a boat. It was not an amusement; it was a diabolical punishment, and even a genius of mental aberrations could never conclude that it was anything but a horror to the muscles and a crime against the back. He mentioned to the boat in general how the amusement of rowing struck him, and the weary-faced oiler smiled in full sympathy. Previously to the foundering, by the way, the oiler had worked double-watch in the engine-room of the ship.

"Take her easy, now, boys," said the captain. "Don't spend yourselves. If we have to run a surf you'll need all your strength, because we'll sure have to swim for it. Take your time."

Slowly the land arose from the sea. From a black line it became a line of black and a line of white—trees and sand. Finally, the captain said that he could make out a house on the shore. "That's the house of refuge, sure," said the cook. "They'll see us before long, and come out after us."

The distant light-house reared high. "The keeper ought to be able to make us out now, if he's looking through a glass," said the captain. "He'll notify the life-saving people."

"None of those other boats could have got ashore to give word of the wreck," said the oiler, in a low voice. "Else the life-boat would be out hunting us."

Slowly and beautifully the land loomed out of the sea. The wind came again. It had veered from the northeast to the southeast. Finally, a new sound struck the ears of the men in the boat. It was the low thunder of the surf on the shore. "We'll never be able to make the light-house now," said the captain. "Swing her head a little more north, Billie."

" 'A little more north,' sir," said the oiler.

Whereupon the little boat turned her nose once more down the wind, and all but the oarsmen watched the shore grow. Under the influence of this expansion doubt and direful apprehension was leaving the minds of the men. The management of the boat was still most absorbing, but it could not prevent a quiet cheerfulness. In an hour, perhaps, they would be ashore.

Their back-bones had become thoroughly used to balancing in the boat and they now rode this wild colt of a dingey like circus men. The correspondent thought that he had been drenched to the skin, but happening to feel in the top pocket of his coat, he found therein eight cigars. Four of them were soaked with seawater; four were perfectly scatheless. After a search, somebody produced three dry matches, and thereupon the four waifs rode impudently in their little boat, and with an assurance of an impending rescue shining in their eyes, puffed at the big cigars and judged well and ill of all men. Everybody took a drink of water.

IV

"Cook," remarked the captain, "there don't seem to be any signs of life about your house of refuge."

"No," replied the cook. "Funny they don't see us!"

A broad stretch of lowly coast lay before the eyes of the men. It was dunes topped with dark vegetation. The roar of the surf was plain, and sometimes they could see the white lip of a wave as it spun up the beach. A tiny house was blocked out black upon the sky. Southward, the slim light-house lifted its little gray length.

Tide, wind, and waves were swinging the dingey northward. "Funny they don't see us," said the men.

The surf's roar was here dulled, but its tone was, nevertheless, thunderous and mighty. As the boat swam over the great rollers, the men sat listening to this roar. "We'll swamp sure," said everybody.

It is fair to say here that there was not a life-saving station within twenty miles in either direction, but the men did not know this fact and in consequence they made dark and opprobrious remarks concerning the eyesight of the nation's life-savers. Four scowling men sat in the dingey and surpassed records in the invention of epithets.

"Funny they don't see us."

The light-heartedness of a former time had completely faded. To their sharpened minds it was easy to conjure pictures of all kinds of incompetency and blindness and indeed, cowardice. There was the shore of the populous land, and it was bitter and bitter to them that from it came no sign.

"Well," said the captain, ultimately, "I suppose we'll have to make a try for ourselves. If we stay out here too long, we'll none of us have strength left to swim after the boat swamps."

And so the oiler, who was at the oars, turned the boat straight for the shore. There was a sudden tightening of muscles. There was some thinking.

"If we don't all get ashore—" said the captain. "If we don't all get ashore, I suppose you fellows know where to send news of my finish?"

They then briefly exchanged some addresses and admonitions. As for the reflections of the men, there was a great deal of rage in them. Perchance they might be formulated thus: "If I am going to be drowned—if I am going to be drowned—if I am going to be drowned, why, in the name of the seven mad gods who rule the sea, was I allowed to come thus far and contemplate sand and trees? Was I brought here merely to have my nose dragged away as I was about to nibble the sacred cheese of life? It is preposterous. If this old ninny-woman, Fate, cannot do better than this, she should be deprived of the management of men's fortunes. She is an old hen who knows not her intention. If she has decided to drown me, why did she not do it in the beginning and save me all this trouble. The whole affair is absurd. . . . But, no, she cannot mean to drown me. She dare not drown me. She cannot drown me. Not after all this work." Afterward the man might have had an impulse to shake his fist at the clouds. "Just you drown me, now, and then hear what I call you!"

The billows that came at this time were more formidable. They seemed always just about to break and roll over the little boat in a turmoil of foam. There was a preparatory and long growl in the speech of them. No mind unused to the sea would have concluded that the dingey could ascend these sheer heights in time, the shore was still afar, the oiler was a wily surfman. "Boys," he said, swiftly, "she won't live three minutes more and we're too far out to swim. Shall I take her to sea again, Captain?"

"Yes! Go ahead!" said the captain.

This oiler, by a series of quick miracles, and fast and steady oarsmanship, turned the boat in the middle of the surf and took her safely to sea again.

There was a considerable silence as the boat bumped over the furrowed sea to deeper water. Then somebody in gloom spoke. "Well, anyhow, they must have seen us from the shore by now."

The gulls went in slanting flight up the wind toward the gray desolate east. A squall, marked by dingy clouds, and clouds brick-red, like smoke from a burning building, appeared from the southeast.

"What do you think of those life-saving people? Ain't they peaches?"

"Funny they haven't seen us."

"Maybe they think we're out here for sport! Maybe they think we're fishin'. Maybe they think we're damned fools."

It was a long afternoon. A changed tide tried to force them southward, but wind and wave said northward. Far ahead, where coastline, sea, and sky formed their mighty angle, there were little dots which seemed to indicate a city on the shore.

"St. Augustine?"

The captain shook his head. "Too near Mosquito Inlet."

And the oiler rowed, and then the correspondent rowed. Then the oiler rowed. It was a weary business. The human back can become the seat of more aches and pains than are registered in books for the composite anatomy of a regiment. It is a limited area, but it can become the theatre of innumerable muscular conflicts, tangles, wrenches, knots, and other comforts.

"Did you ever like to row, Billie?" asked the correspondent.

"No," said the oiler. "Hang it."

When one exchanged the rowing-seat for a place in the bottom of the boat, he suffered a bodily depression that caused him to be careless of everything save an obligation to wiggle one finger. There was cold sea-water swashing to and fro in the boat, and he lay in it. His head, pillowed on a thwart, was within an inch of the swirl of a wave crest, and sometimes a particularly obstreperous sea came in-board and drenched him once more. But these matters did not annoy him. It is almost certain that if the boat had capsized he would have tumbled comfortably out upon the ocean as if he felt sure that it was a great soft mattress.

"Look! There's a man on the shore!"

"Where?"

"There! See 'im? See 'im?"

"Yes, sure! He's walking along."

"Now he's stopped. Look! He's facing us!"

"He's waving at us!"

"So he is! By thunder!"

"Ah, now, we're all right! Now we're all right! There'll be a boat out here for us in half an hour."

"He's going on. He's running. He's going up to that house there."

The remote beach seemed lower than the sea, and it required a searching glance to discern the little black figure. The captain saw a floating stick and they rowed to it. A bath-towel was by some weird chance in the boat, and, tying this on the stick, the captain waved it. The oarsman did not dare turn his head, so he was obliged to ask questions.

"What's he doing now?"

"He's standing still again. He's looking, I think. . . . There he goes again. Toward the house. . . . Now he's stopped again."

"Is he waving at us?"

"No, not now! he was, though."

"Look! There comes another man!"

"He's running."

"Look at him go, would you."

"Why, he's on a bicycle. Now he's met the other man. They're both waving at us. Look!"

"There comes something up the beach."

"What the devil is that thing?"

"Why, it looks like a boat."

"Why, certainly it's a boat."

"No, it's on wheels."

"Yes, so it is. Well, that must be the life-boat. They drag them along shore on a wagon."

"That's the life-boat, sure."

"No, by ———, it's—it's an omnibus."

"I tell you it's a life-boat."

"It is not! It's an omnibus. I can see it plain. See? One of those big hotel omnibuses."

"By thunder, you're right. It's an omnibus, sure as fate. What do you suppose they are doing with an omnibus? Maybe they are going around collecting the life-crew, hey?"

"That's it, likely. Look! There's a fellow waving a little black flag. He's standing on the steps of the omnibus. There come those other two fellows. Now they're all talking together. Look at the fellow with the flag. Maybe he ain't waving it!"

"That ain't a flag, is it? That's his coat. Why, certainly, that's his coat."

"So it is. It's his coat. He's taken it off and is waving it around his head. But would you look at him swing it!"

"Oh, say, there isn't any life-saving station there. That's just a winter resort hotel omnibus that has brought over some of the boarders to see us drown."

"What's that idiot with the coat mean? What's he signaling, anyhow?"

"It looks as if he were trying to tell us to go north. There must be a life-saving station up there."

"No! He thinks we're fishing. Just giving us a merry hand. See? Ah, there, Willie."

"Well, I wish I could make something out of those signals. What do you suppose he means?"

"He don't mean anything. He's just playing."

"Well, if he'd just signal us to try the surf again, or to go to sea and wait, or go north, or go south, or go to hell—there would be some reason in it. But look at him. He just stands there and keeps his coat revolving like a wheel. The ass!"

"There come more people."

"Now there's quite a mob. Look! Isn't that a boat?"

"Where? Oh, I see where you mean. No, that's no boat."

"That fellow is still waving his coat."

"He must think we like to see him do that, why don't he quit it. It don't mean anything."

"I don't know. I think he is trying to make us go north. It must be that there's a life-saving station there somewhere."

"Say, he ain't tired yet. Look at 'im wave."

"Wonder how long he can keep that up. He's been revolving his coat ever since he caught sight of us. He's an idiot. Why aren't they getting men to bring a boat out. A fishing boat—one of those big yawls—could come out here all right. Why don't he do something?"

"Oh, it's all right, now."

"They'll have a boat out here for us in less than no time, now that they've seen us."

A faint yellow tone came into the sky over the low land. The shadows on the sea slowly deepened. The wind bore coldness with it, and the men began to shiver.

"Holy smoke!" said one, allowing his voice to express his impious mood, "if we keep on monkeying out here! If we've got to flounder out here all night!"

"Oh, we'll never have to stay here all night! don't you worry. They've seen us now, and it won't be long before they'll come chasing out after us."

The shore grew dusky. The man waving a coat blended gradually into the gloom, and it swallowed in the same manner the omnibus and the group of people. The spray, when it dashed uproariously over the side, made the voyagers shrink and swear like men who were being branded.

"I'd like to catch the chump who waved the coat. I feel like soaking him one, just for luck."

"Why? What did he do?"

"Oh, nothing, but then he seemed so damned cheerful."

In the meantime the oiler rowed, and then the correspondent rowed, and then the oiler rowed. Gray-faced and bowed forward, they mechanically, turn by turn, plied the leaden oars. The form of the light-house had vanished from the southern horizon, but finally a pale star appeared, just lifting from the sea. The streaked saffron in the west passed before the all-merging darkness, and the sea to the east was black. The land had vanished, and was expressed only by the low and drear thunder of the surf.

"If I am going to be drowned—if I am going to be drowned—if I am going to be drowned, why, in the name of the seven mad gods who rule the sea, was I allowed to come thus far and contemplate sand and trees? Was I brought here merely to have my nose dragged away as I was about to nibble the sacred cheese of life?"

The patient captain, drooped over the water-jar, was sometimes obliged to speak to the oarsman.

"Keep her head up! Keep her head up!"

" 'Keep her head up,' sir." The voices were weary and low.

This was surely a quiet evening. All save the oarsman lay heavily and listlessly in the boat's bottom. As for him, his eyes were just capable of noting the tall black waves that swept forward in a most sinister silence, save for an occasional subdued growl of a crest.

The cook's head was on a thwart, and he looked without interest at the water under his nose. He was deep in other scenes. Finally he spoke. "Billie," he murmured, dreamfully, "what kind of pie do you like best?"

V

"Pie," said the oiler and the correspondent, agitatedly. "Don't talk about those things, blast you!"

"Well," said the cook, "I was just thinking about ham sandwiches, and—"

A night on the sea in an open boat is a long night. As darkness settled finally, the shine of the light, lifting from the sea in the south, changed to full gold. On the northern horizon a new light appeared, a small bluish gleam on the edge of the waters. These two lights were the furniture of the world. Otherwise there was nothing but waves.

Two men huddled in the stern, and distances were so magnificent in the dingey that the rower was enabled to keep his feet partly warmed by thrusting them under his companions. Their legs indeed extended far under the rowing-seat until they touched the feet of the captain forward. Sometimes, despite the efforts of the tired oarsman, a wave came piling into the boat, an icy wave of the night, and the chilling water soaked them anew. They would twist their bodies for a moment and groan, and sleep the dead sleep once more, while the water in the boat gurgled about them as the craft rocked.

The plan of the oiler and the correspondent was for one to row until he lost the ability, and then arouse the other from his sea-water couch in the bottom of the boat.

The oiler plied the oars until his head drooped forward, and the overpowering sleep blinded him. And he rowed yet afterward. Then he touched a man in the bottom of the boat, and called his name. "Will you spell me for a little while?" he said, meekly.

"Sure, Billie," said the correspondent, awakening and dragging himself to a sitting position. They exchanged places carefully, and the oiler, cuddling down in the sea-water at the cook's side, seemed to go to sleep instantly.

The particular violence of the sea had ceased. The waves came without snarling. The obligation of the man at the oars was to keep the boat headed so that the tilt of the rollers would not capsize her, and to preserve her from filling when the crests rushed past. The black waves were silent and hard to be seen in the darkness. Often one was almost upon the boat before the oarsman was aware.

In a low voice the correspondent addressed the captain. He was not sure that the captain was awake, although this iron man seemed to be always awake. "Captain, shall I keep her making for that light north, sir?"

The same steady voice answered him. "Yes. Keep it about two points off the port bow."

The cook had tied a life-belt around himself in order to get even the warmth which this clumsy cork contrivance could donate, and he seemed almost stove-like when a rower, whose teeth invariably chattered wildly as soon as he ceased his labor, dropped down to sleep.

The correspondent, as he rowed, looked down at the two men sleeping under foot. The cook's arm was around the oiler's shoulders, and, with their fragmentary clothing and haggard faces, they were the babes of the sea, a grotesque rendering of the old babes in the wood.

Later he must have grown stupid at his work, for suddenly there was a growling of water, and a crest came with a roar and a swash into the boat, and it was a wonder that it did not set the cook afloat in his life-belt. The cook continued to sleep, but the oiler sat up, blinking his eyes and shaking with the new cold.

"Oh, I'm awful sorry, Billie," said the correspondent, contritely.

"That's all right, old boy," said the oiler, and lay down again and was asleep.

Presently it seemed that even the captain dozed, and the correspondent thought that he was the one man afloat on all the oceans. The wind had a voice as it came over the waves, and it was sadder than the end.

There was a long, loud swishing astern of the boat, and a gleaming trail of phosphorescence, like blue flame, was furrowed on the black waters. It might have been made by a monstrous knife.

Then there came a stillness, while the correspondent breathed with the open mouth and looked at the sea.

Suddenly there was another swish and another long flash of bluish light, and this time it was alongside the boat, and might almost have been reached with an oar. The correspondent saw an enormous fin speed like a shadow through the water, hurling the crystalline spray and leaving the long glowing trail.

The correspondent looked over his shoulder at the captain. His face was hidden, and he seemed to be asleep. He looked at the babes of the sea. They certainly were asleep. So, being bereft of sympathy, he leaned a little way to one side and swore softly into the sea.

But the thing did not then leave the vicinity of the boat. Ahead or astern, on one side or the other, at intervals long or short, fled the long sparkling streak, and there was to be heard the whiroo of the dark fin. The speed and power of the thing was greatly to be admired. It cut the water like a gigantic and keen projectile.

The presence of this biding thing did not affect the man with the same horror that it would if he had been a picknicker. He simply looked at the sea dully and swore in an undertone.

Nevertheless, it is true that he did not wish to be alone with the thing. He wished one of his companions to awaken by chance and keep him company with it. But the captain hung motionless over the water-jar and the oiler and the cook in the bottom of the boat were plunged in slumber.

VI

"If I am going to be drowned—if I am going to be drowned—if I am going to be drowned, why, in the name of the seven mad gods who rule the sea, was I allowed to come thus far and contemplate sand and trees?"

During this dismal night, it may be remarked that a man would conclude that it was really the intention of the seven mad gods to drown him, despite the abominable injustice of it. For it was certainly an abominable injustice to drown a man who had worked so hard, so hard. The man felt it would be a crime most unnatural. Other people had drowned at sea since galleys swarmed with painted sails, but still—

When it occurs to a man that nature does not regard him as important, and that she feels she would not maim the universe by disposing of him, he at first wishes to throw bricks at the temple, and he hates deeply the fact that there are no bricks and no temples. Any visible expression of nature would surely be pelleted with his jeers.

Then, if there be no tangible thing to hoot he feels, perhaps, the desire to confront a personification and indulge in pleas, bowed to one knee, and with hands supplicant, saying: "Yes, but I love myself."

A high cold star on a winter's night is the word he feels that she says to him. Thereafter he knows the pathos of his situation.

The men in the dingey had not discussed these matters, but each had, no doubt, reflected upon them in silence and according to his mind. There was seldom any expression upon their faces save the general one of complete weariness. Speech was devoted to the business of the boat.

To chime the notes of his emotion, a verse mysteriously entered the correspondent's head. He had even forgotten that he had forgotten this verse, but it suddenly was in his mind.

A soldier of the Legion lay dying in Algiers,
There was lack of woman's nursing, there was dearth of woman's tears;
But a comrade stood beside him, and he took that comrade's hand,
And he said: "I never more shall see my own, my native land."[1]

In his childhood, the correspondent had been made acquainted with the fact that a soldier of the legion lay dying in Algiers, but he had never regarded it as important. Myriads of his school-fellows had informed him of the soldier's plight, but the dinning had naturally ended by making him perfectly indifferent. He had never considered it his affair that a soldier of the Legion lay dying in Algiers, nor had it appeared to him as a matter for sorrow. It was less to him than the breaking of a pencil's point.

Now, however, it quaintly came to him as a human, living thing. It was no longer merely a picture of a few throes in the breast of a poet, meanwhile drinking tea and warming his feet at the grate; it was an actuality—stern, mournful, and fine.

The correspondent plainly saw the soldier. He lay on the sand with his feet out straight and still. While his pale left hand was upon his chest in an attempt to thwart the going of his life, the blood came between his fingers. In the far Algerian distance,

[1] Crane's rendition of lines from a poem by
Caroline E. S. Norton, "Bingen on the Rhine"
(1883).

a city of low square forms was set against a sky that was faint with the last sunset hues. The correspondent, plying the oars and dreaming of the slow and slower movements of the lips of the soldier, was moved by a profound and perfectly impersonal comprehension. He was sorry for the soldier of the Legion who lay dying in Algiers.

The thing which had followed the boat and waited had evidently grown bored at the delay. There was no longer to be heard the slash of the cut-water, and there was no longer the flame of the long trail. The light in the north still glimmered, but it was apparently no nearer to the boat. Sometimes the boom of the surf rang in the correspondent's ears, and he turned the craft seaward then and rowed harder. Southward, some one had evidently built a watch-fire on the beach. It was too low and too far to be seen, but it made a shimmering, roseate reflection upon the bluff back of it, and this could be discerned from the boat. The wind came stronger, and sometimes a wave suddenly raged out like a mountain-cat and there was to be seen the sheen and sparkle of a broken crest.

The captain, in the bow, moved on his water-jar and sat erect. "Pretty long night," he observed to the correspondent. He looked at the shore. "Those life-saving people take their time."

"Did you see that shark playing around?"

"Yes, I saw him. He was a big fellow, all right."

"Wish I had known you were awake."

Later the correspondent spoke into the bottom of the boat.

"Billie!" There was a slow and gradual disentanglement. "Billie, will you spell me?"

"Sure," said the oiler.

As soon as the correspondent touched the cold comfortable seawater in the bottom of the boat, and had huddled close to the cook's life-belt he was deep in sleep, despite the fact that his teeth played all the popular airs. This sleep was so good to him that it was but a moment before he heard a voice call his name in a tone that demonstrated the last stages of exhaustion. "Will you spell me?"

"Sure, Billie."

The light in the north had mysteriously vanished, but the correspondent took his course from the wide-awake captain.

Later in the night they took the boat farther out to sea, and the captain directed the cook to take one oar at the stern and keep the boat facing the seas. He was to call out if he should hear the thunder of the surf. This plan enabled the oiler and the correspondent to get respite together. "We'll give those boys a chance to get into shape again," said the captain. They curled down and, after a few preliminary chatterings and trembles, slept once more the dead sleep. Neither knew they had bequeathed to the cook the company of another shark, or perhaps the same shark.

As the boat caroused on the waves, spray occasionally bumped over the side and gave them a fresh soaking, but this had no power to break their repose. The ominous slash of the wind and the water affected them as it would have affected mummies.

"Boys," said the cook, with the notes of every reluctance in his voice, "she's drifted in pretty close. I guess one of you had better take her to sea again." The correspondent, aroused, heard the crash of the toppled crests.

As he was rowing, the captain gave him some whiskey and water, and this steadied the chills out of him. "If I ever get ashore and anybody shows me even a photograph of an oar—"

At last there was a short conversation.

"Billie. . . . Billie, will you spell me?"

"Sure," said the oiler.

VII

When the correspondent again opened his eyes, the sea and the sky were each of the gray hue of the dawning. Later, carmine and gold was painted upon the waters. The morning appeared finally, in its splendor, with a sky of pure blue, and the sunlight flamed on the tips of the waves.

On the distant dunes were set many little black cottages, and a tall white wind-mill reared above them. No man, nor dog, nor bicycle appeared on the beach. The cottages might have formed a deserted village.

The voyagers scanned the shore. A conference was held in the boat. "Well," said the captain, "if no help is coming, we might better try a run through the surf right away. If we stay out here much longer we will be too weak to do anything for ourselves at all." The others silently acquiesced in this reasoning. The boat was headed for the beach. The correspondent wondered if none ever ascended the tall wind-tower, and if then they never looked seaward. This tower was a giant, standing with its back to the plight of the ants. It represented in a degree, to the correspondent, the serenity of nature amid the struggles of the individual—nature in the wind, and nature in the vision of men. She did not seem cruel to him then, nor beneficent, nor treacherous, nor wise. But she was indifferent, flatly indifferent. It is, perhaps, plausible that a man in this situation, impressed with the unconcern of the universe, should see the innumerable flaws of his life and have them taste wickedly in his mind and wish for another chance. A distinction between right and wrong seems absurdly clear to him, then, in this new ignorance of the grave-edge, and he understands that if he were given another opportunity he would mend his conduct and his words, and be better and brighter during an introduction, or at a tea.

"Now, boys," said the captain, "she is going to swamp sure. All we can do is to work her in as far as possible, and then when she swamps, pile out and scramble for the beach. Keep cool now, and don't jump until she swamps sure."

The oiler took the oars. Over his shoulders he scanned the surf. "Captain," he said, "I think I'd better bring her about, and keep her head-on to the seas and back her in."

"All right, Billie," said the captain. "Back her in." The oiler swung the boat then and, seated in the stern, the cook and the correspondent were obliged to look over their shoulders to contemplate the lonely and indifferent shore.

The monstrous inshore rollers heaved the boat high until the men were again enabled to see the white sheets of water scudding up the slanted beach. "We won't get in very close," said the captain. Each time a man could wrest his attention from the rollers, he turned his glance toward the shore, and in the expression of the eyes during this contemplation there was a singular quality. The correspondent, observing the others, knew that they were not afraid, but the full meaning of their glances was shrouded.

As for himself, he was too tired to grapple fundamentally with the fact. He tried to coerce his mind into thinking of it, but the mind was dominated at this time by the muscles, and the muscles said they did not care. It merely occurred to him that if he should drown it would be a shame.

There were no hurried words, no pallor, no plain agitation. The men simply looked at the shore. "Now, remember to get well clear of the boat when you jump," said the captain.

Seaward the crest of a roller suddenly fell with a thunderous crash, and the long white comber came roaring down upon the boat.

"Steady now," said the captain. The men were silent. They turned their eyes from the shore to the comber and waited. The boat slid up the incline, leaped at the furious top, bounced over it, and swung down the long back of the wave. Some water had been shipped and the cook bailed it out.

But the next crest crashed also. The tumbling boiling flood of white water caught the boat and whirled it almost perpendicular. Water swarmed in from all sides. The correspondent had his hands on the gunwale at this time, and when the water entered at that place he swiftly withdrew his fingers, as if he objected to wetting them.

The little boat, drunken with this weight of water, reeled and snuggled deeper into the sea.

"Bail her out, cook! Bail her out," said the captain.

"All right, Captain," said the cook.

"Now, boys, the next one will do for us, sure," said the oiler. "Mind to jump clear of the boat."

The third wave moved forward, huge, furious, implacable. It fairly swallowed the dingey, and almost simultaneously the men tumbled into the sea. A piece of life-belt had lain in the bottom of the boat, and as the correspondent went overboard he held this to his chest with his left hand.

The January water was icy, and he reflected immediately that it was colder than he had expected to find it off the coast of Florida. This appeared to his dazed mind as a fact important enough to be noted at the time. The coldness of the water was sad; it was tragic. This fact was somehow so mixed and confused with his opinion of his own situation that it seemed almost a proper reason for tears. The water was cold.

When he came to the surface he was conscious of little but the noisy water. Afterward he saw his companions in the sea. The oiler was ahead in the race. He was swimming strongly and rapidly. Off to the correspondent's left, the cook's great white and corked back bulged out of the water, and in the rear the captain was hanging with his one good hand to the keel of the overturned dingey.

There is a certain immovable quality to a shore, and the correspondent wondered at it amid the confusion of the sea.

It seemed also very attractive, but the correspondent knew that it was a long journey, and he paddled leisurely. The piece of life-preserver lay under him, and sometimes he whirled down the incline of a wave as if he were on a hand-sled.

But finally he arrived at a place in the sea where travel was beset with difficulty. He did not pause swimming to inquire what manner of current had caught him, but there his progress ceased. The shore was set before him like a bit of scenery on a stage, and he looked at it and understood with his eyes each detail of it.

As the cook passed, much farther to the left, the captain was calling to him, "Turn over on your back, cook! Turn over on your back and use the oar."

"All right, sir." The cook turned on his back, and paddling with an oar, went ahead as if he were a canoe.

Presently the boat also passed to the left of the correspondent with the captain clinging with one hand to the keel. He would have appeared like a man raising himself to look over a board fence, if it were not for the extraordinary gymnastics of the boat. The correspondent marvelled that the captain could still hold it.

They passed on, nearer to shore—the oiler, the cook, the captain—and following them went the water-jar, bouncing gayly over the seas.

The correspondent remained in the grip of this strange new enemy—a current. The shore, with its white slope of sand and its green bluff, topped with little silent cottages, was spread like a picture before him. It was very near to him then, but he was impressed as one who in a gallery looks at a scene from Brittany or Holland.

He thought: "I am going to drown? Can it be possible? Can it be possible? Can it be possible?" Perhaps an individual must consider his own death to be the final phenomenon of nature.

But later a wave perhaps whirled him out of this small deadly current, for he found suddenly that he could again make progress toward the shore. Later still, he was aware that the captain, clinging with one hand to the keel of the dingey, had his face turned away from the shore and toward him, and was calling his name. "Come to the boat! Come to the boat!"

In his struggle to reach the captain and the boat, he reflected that when one gets properly wearied, drowning must really be a comfortable arrangement, a cessation of hostilities accompanied by a large degree of relief, and he was glad of it, for the main thing in his mind for some moments had been horror of the temporary agony. He did not wish to be hurt.

Presently he saw a man running along the shore. He was undressing with most remarkable speed. Coat, trousers, shirt, everything flew magically off him.

"Come to the boat," called the captain.

"All right, Captain." As the correspondent paddled, he saw the captain let himself down to bottom and leave the boat. Then the correspondent performed his one little marvel of the voyage. A large wave caught him and flung him with ease and supreme speed completely over the boat and far beyond it. It struck him even then as an event in gymnastics, and a true miracle of the sea. An overturned boat in the surf is not a plaything to a swimming man.

The correspondent arrived in water that reached only to his waist, but his condition did not enable him to stand for more than a moment. Each wave knocked him into a heap, and the under-tow pulled at him.

Then he saw the man who had been running and undressing, and undressing and running, come bounding into the water. He dragged ashore the cook, and then waded toward the captain, but the captain waved him away, and sent him to the correspondent. He was naked, naked as a tree in winter, but a halo was about his head, and he shone like a saint. He gave a strong pull, and a long drag, and a bully heave at the correspondent's hand. The correspondent, schooled in the minor formulae, said: "Thanks, old man." But suddenly the man cried: "What's that?" He pointed a swift finger. The correspondent said: "Go."

In the shallows, face downward, lay the oiler. His forehead touched sand that was periodically, between each wave, clear of the sea.

The correspondent did not know all that transpired afterward.

When he achieved safe ground he fell, striking the sand with each particular part of his body. It was as if he had dropped from a roof, but the thud was grateful to him.

It seems that instantly the beach was populated with men with blankets, clothes, and flasks, and women with coffee-pots and all the remedies sacred to their minds. The welcome of the land to the men from the sea was warm and generous, but a still and dripping shape was carried slowly up the beach, and the land's welcome for it could only be the different and sinister hospitality of the grave.

When it came night, the white waves paced to and fro in the moonlight, and the wind brought the sound of the great sea's voice to the men on shore, and they felt that they could then be interpreters.

1897

The Bride Comes to Yellow Sky

I

The great Pullman was whirling onward with such dignity of motion that a glance from the window seemed simply to prove that the plains of Texas were pouring eastward. Vast flats of green grass, dull-hued spaces of mesquite and cactus, little groups of frame houses, woods of light and tender trees, all were sweeping into the east, sweeping over the horizon, a precipice.

A newly married pair had boarded this coach at San Antonio. The man's face was reddened from many days in the wind and sun, and a direct result of his new black clothes was that his brick-colored hands were constantly performing in a most conscious fashion. From time to time he looked down respectfully at his attire. He sat with a hand on each knee, like a man waiting in a barber's shop. The glances he devoted to other passengers were furtive and shy.

The bride was not pretty, nor was she very young. She wore a dress of blue cashmere, with small reservations of velvet here and there and with steel buttons abounding. She continually twisted her head to regard her puff sleeves, very stiff, straight, and high. They embarrassed her. It was quite apparent that she had cooked, and that she expected to cook, dutifully. The blushes caused by the careless scrutiny of some passengers as she had entered the car were strange to see upon this plain, under-class countenance, which was drawn in placid, almost emotionless lines.

They were evidently very happy. "Ever been in a parlor-car before?" he asked, smiling with delight.

"No," she answered. "I never was. It's fine, ain't it?"

"Great! And then after a while we'll go forward to the diner and get a big lay-out. Finest meal in the world. Charge a dollar."

"Oh, do they?" cried the bride. "Charge a dollar? Why, that's too much—for us —ain't it, Jack?"

"Not this trip, anyhow," he answered bravely. "We're going to go the whole thing."

Later, he explained to her about the trains. "You see, it's a thousand miles from one end of Texas to the other, and this train runs right across it and never stops but four times." He had the pride of an owner. He pointed out to her the dazzling fittings of the coach, and in truth her eyes opened wider as she contemplated the sea-green figured velvet, the shining brass, silver, and glass, the wood that gleamed as darkly brilliant as the surface of a pool of oil. At one end a bronze figure sturdily held a support for a separated chamber, and at convenient places on the ceiling were frescoes in olive and silver.

To the minds of the pair, their surroundings reflected the glory of their marriage that morning in San Antonio. This was the environment of their new estate, and the man's face in particular beamed with an elation that made him appear ridiculous to the negro porter. This individual at times surveyed them from afar with an amused and superior grin. On other occasions he bullied them with skill in ways that did not make it exactly plain to them that they were being bullied. He subtly used all the manners of the most unconquerable kind of snobbery. He oppressed them, but of this oppression they had small knowledge, and they speedily forgot that infrequently a number of travelers covered them with stares of derisive enjoyment. Historically there was supposed to be something infinitely humorous in their situation.

"We are due in Yellow Sky at 3.42," he said, looking tenderly into her eyes.

"Oh, are we?" she said, as if she had not been aware of it. To evince surprise at her husband's statement was part of her wifely amiability. She took from a pocket a little silver watch, and as she held it before her and stared at it with a frown of attention, the new husband's face shone.

"I bought it in San Anton' from a friend of mine," he told her gleefully.

"It's seventeen minutes past twelve," she said, looking up at him with a kind of shy and clumsy coquetry. A passenger, noting this play, grew excessively sardonic, and winked at himself in one of the numerous mirrors.

At last they went to the dining-car. Two rows of negro waiters in glowing white suits surveyed their entrance with the interest and also the equanimity of men who had been forewarned. The pair fell to the lot of a waiter who happened to feel pleasure in steering them through their meal. He viewed them with the manner of a fatherly pilot, his countenance radiant with benevolence. The patronage entwined with the ordinary deference was not plain to them. And yet as they returned to their coach they showed in their faces a sense of escape.

To the left, miles down a long purple slope, was a little ribbon of mist where moved the keening Rio Grande. The train was approaching it at an angle, and the apex was Yellow Sky. Presently it was apparent that as the distance from Yellow Sky grew shorter, the husband became commensurately restless. His brick-red hands were more insistent in their prominence. Occasionally he was even rather absent-minded and far-away when the bride leaned forward and addressed him.

As a matter of truth, Jack Potter was beginning to find the shadow of a deed weigh upon him like a leaden slab. He, the town marshal of Yellow Sky, a man known, liked, and feared in his corner, a prominent person, had gone to San Antonio to meet a girl he believed he loved, and there, after the usual prayers, had actually induced her to marry him, without consulting Yellow Sky for any part of the transaction. He was now bringing his bride before an innocent and unsuspecting community.

Of course, people in Yellow Sky married as it pleased them in accordance with a general custom; but such was Potter's thought of his duty to his friends, or of their idea of his duty, or of an unspoken form which does not control men in these matters, that he felt he was heinous. He had committed an extraordinary crime. Face to face with this girl in San Antonio, and spurred by his sharp impulse, he had gone headlong over all the social hedges. At San Antonio he was like a man hidden in the dark. A knife to sever any friendly duty, any form, was easy to his hand in that remote city. But the hour of Yellow Sky, the hour of daylight, was approaching.

He knew full well that his marriage was an important thing to his town. It could only be exceeded by the burning of the new hotel. His friends would not forgive him. Frequently he had reflected on the advisability of telling them by telegraph, but a new cowardice had been upon him. He feared to do it. And now the train was hurrying him toward a scene of amazement, glee, reproach. He glanced out of the window at the line of haze swinging slowly in toward the train.

Yellow Sky had a kind of brass band which played painfully to the delight of the populace. He laughed without heart as he thought of it. If the citizens could dream of his prospective arrival with his bride, they would parade the band at the station and escort them, amid cheers and laughing congratulations, to his adobe home.

He resolved that he would use all the devices of speed and plains-craft in making the journey from the station to his house. Once within that safe citadel, he could issue some sort of a vocal bulletin, and then not go among the citizens until they had time to wear off a little of their enthusiasm.

The bride looked anxiously at him. "What's worrying you, Jack?"

He laughed again. "I'm not worrying, girl. I'm only thinking of Yellow Sky."

She flushed in comprehension.

A sense of mutual guilt invaded their minds and developed a finer tenderness. They looked at each other with eyes softly aglow. But Potter often laughed the same nervous laugh. The flush upon the bride's face seemed quite permanent.

The traitor to the feelings of Yellow Sky narrowly watched the speeding landscape. "We're nearly there," he said.

Presently the porter came and announced the proximity of Potter's home. He held a brush in his hand and, with all his airy superiority gone, he brushed Potter's new clothes as the latter slowly turned this way and that way. Potter fumbled out a coin and gave it to the porter as he had seen others do. It was a heavy and muscle-bound business, as that of a man shoeing his first horse.

The porter took their bag, and as the train began to slow they moved forward to the hooded platform of the car. Presently the two engines and their long string of coaches rushed into the station of Yellow Sky.

"They have to take water here," said Potter, from a constricted throat and in mournful cadence as one announcing death. Before the train stopped his eye had swept the length of the platform, and he was glad and astonished to see there was none upon it but the station-agent, who, with a slightly hurried and anxious air, was walking toward the water-tanks. When the train had halted, the porter alighted first and placed in position a little temporary step.

"Come on, girl," said Potter hoarsely. As he helped her down they each laughed on a false note. He took the bag from the negro, and bade his wife cling to his arm. As they slunk rapidly away, his hang-dog glance perceived that they were unloading the two trunks, and also that the station-agent far ahead near the baggage-car had turned and was running toward him, making gestures. He laughed, and groaned as he laughed, when he noted the first effect of his marital bliss upon Yellow Sky. He gripped his wife's arm firmly to his side, and they fled. Behind them the porter stood chuckling fatuously.

II

The California Express on the Southern Railway was due at Yellow Sky in twenty-one minutes. There were six men at the bar of the Weary Gentleman saloon. One was a drummer[1] who talked a great deal and rapidly; three were Texans who did not care to talk at that time; and two were Mexican sheep-herders who did not talk as a general practice in the Weary Gentleman saloon. The bar-keeper's dog lay on the board-walk that crossed in front of the door. His head was on his paws, and he glanced drowsily here and there with the constant vigilance of a dog that is kicked on occasion. Across the sandy street were some vivid green grass plots, so wonderful in appearance amid the sands that burned near them in a blazing sun that they caused a doubt in the mind. They exactly resembled the grass mats used to represent lawns on the stage. At the cooler end of the railway station a man without a coat sat in a tilted chair and smoked his pipe. The fresh-cut bank of the Rio Grande circled near the town, and there could be seen beyond it a great plum-colored plain of mesquite.

Save for the busy drummer and his companions in the saloon, Yellow Sky was dozing. The new-comer leaned gracefully upon the bar, and recited many tales with the confidence of a bard who has come upon a new field.

"—and at the moment that the old man fell down stairs with the bureau in his arms, the old woman was coming up with two scuttles of coal, and, of course—"

The drummer's tale was interrupted by a young man who suddenly appeared in the open door. He cried: "Scratchy Wilson's drunk, and has turned loose with both hands." The two Mexicans at once set down their glasses and faded out of the rear entrance of the saloon.

The drummer, innocent and jocular, answered: "All right, old man. S'pose he has. Come in and have a drink, anyhow."

But the information had made such an obvious cleft in every skull in the room that the drummer was obliged to see its importance. All had become instantly morose. "Say," said he, mystified, "what is this?" His three companions made the introductory gesture of eloquent speech, but the young man at the door forestalled them.

"It means, my friend," he answered, as he came into the saloon, "that for the next two hours this town won't be a health resort."

The bar-keeper went to the door and locked and barred it. Reaching out of the

[1] Traveling salesman.

window, he pulled in heavy wooden shutters and barred them. Immediately a solemn, chapel-like gloom was upon the place. The drummer was looking from one to another.

"But say," he cried, "what is this, anyhow? You don't mean there is going to be a gun-fight?"

"Don't know whether there'll be a fight or not," answered one man grimly. "But there'll be some shootin'—some good shootin'."

The young man who had warned them waved his hand. "Oh, there'll be a fight fast enough, if anyone wants it. Anybody can get a fight out there in the street. There's a fight just waiting."

The drummer seemed to be swayed between the interest of a foreigner and a perception of personal danger.

"What did you say his name was?" he asked.

"Scratchy Wilson," they answered in chorus.

"And will he kill anybody? What are you going to do? Does this happen often? Does he rampage around like this once a week or so? Can he break in that door?"

"No, he can't break down that door," replied the bar-keeper. "He's tried it three times. But when he comes you'd better lay down on the floor, stranger. He's dead sure to shoot at it, and a bullet may come through."

Thereafter the drummer kept a strict eye upon the door. The time had not yet been called for him to hug the floor, but as a minor precaution he sidled near to the wall. "Will he kill anybody?" he said again.

The men laughed low and scornfully at the question.

"He's out to shoot, and he's out for trouble. Don't see any good in experimentin' with him."

"But what do you do in a case like this? What do you do?"

A man responded: "Why, he and Jack Potter—"

But, in chorus, the other men interrupted: "Jack Potter's in San Anton'."

"Well, who is he? What's he got to do with it?"

"Oh, he's the town marshal. He goes out and fights Scratchy when he gets on one of these tears."

"Wow," said the drummer, mopping his brow. "Nice job he's got."

The voices had toned away to mere whisperings. The drummer wished to ask further questions which were born of an increasing anxiety and bewilderment; but when he attempted them, the men merely looked at him in irritation and motioned him to remain silent. A tense waiting hush was upon them. In the deep shadows of the room their eyes shone as they listened for sounds from the street. One man made three gestures at the bar-keeper, and the latter, moving like a ghost, handed him a glass and a bottle. The man poured a full glass of whisky, and set down the bottle noiselessly. He gulped the whisky in a swallow, and turned again toward the door in immovable silence. The drummer saw that the bar-keeper, without a sound, had taken a Winchester from beneath the bar. Later he saw this individual beckoning to him, so he tiptoed across the room.

"You better come with me back of the bar."

"No, thanks," said the drummer, perspiring. "I'd rather be where I can make a break for the back door."

Whereupon the man of bottles made a kindly but peremptory gesture. The drummer obeyed it, and finding himself seated on a box with his head below the level of the bar, balm was laid upon his soul at sight of various zinc and copper fittings that bore a resemblance to armor-plate. The bar-keeper took a seat comfortably upon an adjacent box.

"You see," he whispered, "this here Scratchy Wilson is a wonder with a gun—a perfect wonder—and when he goes on the war trail, we hunt our holes—naturally. He's about the last one of the old gang that used to hang out along the river here. He's a terror when he's drunk. When he's sober he's all right—kind of simple—wouldn't hurt a fly—nicest fellow in town. But when he's drunk—whoo!"

There were periods of stillness. "I wish Jack Potter was back from San Anton'," said the bar-keeper. "He shot Wilson up once—in the leg—and he would sail in and pull out the kinks in this thing."

Presently they heard from a distance the sound of a shot, followed by three wild yowls. It instantly removed a bond from the men in the darkened saloon. There was a shuffling of feet. They looked at each other. "Here he comes," they said.

III

A man in a maroon-colored flannel shirt, which had been purchased for purposes of decoration and made, principally, by some Jewish women on the east side of New York, rounded a corner and walked into the middle of the main street of Yellow Sky. In either hand the man held a long, heavy blue-black revolver. Often he yelled, and these cries rang through a semblance of a deserted village, shrilly flying over the roofs in a volume that seemed to have no relation to the ordinary vocal strength of a man. It was as if the surrounding stillness formed the arch of a tomb over him. These cries of ferocious challenge rang against walls of silence. And his boots had red tops with gilded imprints, of the kind beloved in winter by little sledding boys on the hillsides of New England.

The man's face flamed in a rage begot of whisky. His eyes, rolling and yet keen for ambush, hunted the still door-ways and windows. He walked with the creeping movement of the midnight cat. As it occurred to him, he roared menacing information. The long revolvers in his hands were as easy as straws; they were moved with an electric swiftness. The little fingers of each hand played sometimes in a musician's way. Plain from the low collar of the shirt, the cords of his neck straightened and sank, straightened and sank, as passion moved him. The only sounds were his terrible invitations. The calm adobes preserved their demeanor at the passing of this small thing in the middle of the street.

There was no offer of fight; no offer of fight. The man called to the sky. There were no attractions. He bellowed and fumed and swayed his revolvers here and everywhere.

The dog of the bar-keeper of the Weary Gentleman saloon had not appreciated the advance of events. He yet lay dozing in front of his master's door. At sight of the dog, the man paused and raised his revolver humorously. At sight of the man, the dog sprang up and walked diagonally away, with a sullen head and growling. The man yelled, and the dog broke into a gallop. As it was about to enter an alley, there was a loud noise, a whistling, and something spat the ground directly before it. The dog screamed, and, wheeling in terror, galloped headlong in a new direction. Again there was a noise, a whistling, and sand was kicked viciously before it. Fear-stricken, the dog turned and flurried like an animal in a pen. The man stood laughing, his weapons at his hips.

Ultimately the man was attracted by the closed door of the Weary Gentleman saloon. He went to it, and hammering with a revolver, demanded drink.

The door remaining imperturbable, he picked a bit of paper from the walk and nailed it to the framework with a knife. He then turned his back contemptuously upon this popular resort, and walking to the opposite side of the street, and spinning there on his heel quickly and lithely, fired at the bit of paper. He missed it by a half inch. He swore at himself, and went away. Later, he comfortably fusilladed the windows of his most intimate friend. The man was playing with this town. It was a toy for him.

But still there was no offer of fight. The name of Jack Potter, his ancient antagonist, entered his mind, and he concluded that it would be a glad thing if he should go to Potter's house and by bombardment induce him to come out and fight. He moved in the direction of his desire, chanting Apache scalp-music.

When he arrived at it, Potter's house presented the same still, calm front as had the other adobes. Taking up a strategic position, the man howled a challenge. But this house regarded him as might a great stone god. It gave no sign. After a decent wait, the man howled further challenges, mingling with them wonderful epithets.

Presently there came the spectacle of a man churning himself into deepest rage over the immobility of a house. He fumed at it as the winter wind attacks a prairie cabin in the North. To the distance there should have gone the sound of a tumult like the fighting of two hundred Mexicans. As necessity bade him, he paused for breath or to reload his revolvers.

IV

Potter and his bride walked sheepishly and with speed. Sometimes they laughed together shamefacedly and low.

"Next corner, dear," he said finally.

They put forth the efforts of a pair walking bowed against a strong wind. Potter was about to raise a finger to point the first appearance of the new home when, as they circled the corner, they came face to face with a man in a maroon-colored shirt who was feverishly pushing cartridges into a large revolver. Upon the instant the man dropped this revolver to the ground, and, like lightning, whipped another from its holster. The second weapon was aimed at the bridegroom's chest.

There was a silence. Potter's mouth seemed to be merely a grave for his tongue. He exhibited an instinct to at once loosen his arm from the woman's grip, and he dropped the bag to the sand. As for the bride, her face had gone as yellow as old cloth. She was a slave to hideous rites gazing at the apparitional snake.

The two men faced each other at a distance of three paces. He of the revolver smiled with a new and quiet ferocity. "Tried to sneak up on me," he said. "Tried to sneak up on me!" His eyes grew more baleful. As Potter made a slight movement, the man thrust his revolver venomously forward. "No, don't you do it, Jack Potter. Don't you move a finger toward a gun just yet. Don't you move an eyelash. The time has come for me to settle with you, and I'm goin' to do it my own way and loaf along with no interferin'. So if you don't want a gun bent on you, just mind what I tell you."

Potter looked at his enemy. "I ain't got a gun on me, Scratchy," he said. "Honest, I ain't." He was stiffening and steadying, but yet somewhere at the back of his mind a vision of the Pullman floated, the sea-green figured velvet, the shining brass, silver, and glass, the wood that gleamed as darkly brilliant as the surface of a pool of oil —all the glory of the marriage, the environment of the new estate. "You know I fight when it comes to fighting, Scratchy Wilson, but I ain't got a gun on me. You'll have to do all the shootin' yourself."

His enemy's face went livid. He stepped forward and lashed his weapon to and fro before Potter's chest. "Don't you tell me you ain't got no gun on you, you whelp. Don't tell me no lie like that. There ain't a man in Texas ever seen you without no gun. Don't take me for no kid." He eyes blazed with light, and his throat worked like a pump.

"I ain't takin' you for no kid," answered Potter. His heels had not moved an inch backward. "I'm takin' you for a ——— fool. I tell you I ain't got a gun, and I ain't. If you're goin' to shoot me up, you better begin now. You'll never get a chance like this again."

So much enforced reasoning had told on Wilson's rage. He was calmer. "If you ain't got a gun, why ain't you got a gun?" he sneered. "Been to Sunday-school?"

"I ain't got a gun because I've just come from San Anton' with my wife. I'm married," said Potter. "And if I'd thought there was going to be any galoots like you prowling around when I brought my wife home, I'd had a gun, and don't you forget it."

"Married!" said Scratchy, not at all comprehending.

"Yes, married. I'm married," said Potter distinctly.

"Married?" said Scratchy. Seemingly for the first time he saw the drooping drowning woman at the other man's side. "No!" he said. He was like a creature allowed a glimpse of another world. He moved a pace backward, and his arm with the revolver dropped to his side. "Is this—is this the lady?" he asked.

"Yes, this is the lady," answered Potter.

There was another period of silence.

"Well," said Wilson at last, slowly, "I s'pose it's all off now."

"It's all off if you say so, Scratchy. You know I didn't make the trouble." Potter lifted his valise.

"Well, I 'low it's off, Jack," said Wilson. He was looking at the ground. "Married!" He was not a student of chivalry; it was merely that in the presence of this foreign condition he was a simple child of the earlier plains. He picked up his starboard revolver, and placing both weapons in their holsters, he went away. His feet made funnel-shaped tracks in the heavy sand.

1898

An Episode of War

The lieutenant's rubber blanket lay on the ground, and upon it he had poured the company's supply of coffee. Corporals and other representatives of the grimy and hot-throated men who lined the breastwork had come for each squad's portion.

The lieutenant was frowning and serious at this task of division. His lips pursed as he drew with his sword various crevices in the heap until brown squares of coffee, astoundingly equal in size, appeared on the blanket. He was on the verge of a great triumph in mathematics and the corporals were thronging forward, each to reap a little square, when suddenly the lieutenant cried out and looked quickly at a man near him as if he suspected it was a case of personal assault. The others cried out also when they saw blood upon the lieutenant's sleeve.

He had winced like a man stung, swayed dangerously, and then straightened. The sound of his hoarse breathing was plainly audible. He looked sadly, mystically, over the breastwork at the green face of a wood where now were many little puffs of white smoke. During this moment, the men about him gazed statue-like and silent, astonished and awed by this catastrophe which had happened when catastrophes were not expected—when they had leisure to observe it.

As the lieutenant stared at the wood, they too swung their heads so that for another moment all hands, still silent, contemplated the distant forest as if their minds were fixed upon the mystery of a bullet's journey.

The officer had, of course, been compelled to take his sword at once into his left hand. He did not hold it by the hilt. He gripped it at the middle of the blade, awkwardly. Turning his eyes from the hostile wood, he looked at the sword as he held it there, and seemed puzzled as to what to do with it, where to put it. In short this weapon had of a sudden become a strange thing to him. He looked at it in a kind of stupefaction, as if he had been miraculously endowed with a trident, a sceptre, or a spade.

Finally, he tried to sheath it. To sheath a sword held by the left hand, at the middle of the blade, in a scabbard hung at the left hip, is a feat worthy of a sawdust ring. This wounded officer engaged in a desperate struggle with the sword and the wobbling scabbard, and during the time of it, he breathed like a wrestler.

But at this instant the men, the spectators, awoke from their stone-like poses and crowded forward sympathetically. The orderly-sergeant took the sword and tenderly placed it in the scabbard. At the time, he leaned nervously backward, and did not allow even his finger to brush the body of the lieutenant. A wound gives strange dignity to him who bears it. Well men shy from this new and terrible majesty. It is as if the wounded man's hand is upon the curtain which hangs before the revelations of all existence, the meaning of ants, potentates, wars, cities, sunshine, snow, a feather dropped from a bird's wing, and the power of it sheds radiance upon a bloody form, and makes the other men understand sometimes that they are little. His comrades look at him with large eyes thoughtfully. Moreover, they fear vaguely that the weight of a finger upon him might send him headlong, precipitate the tragedy, hurl him at once into the dim grey unknown. And so the orderly-sergeant while sheathing the sword leaned nervously backward.

There were others who proffered assistance. One timidly presented his shoulder and asked the lieutenant if he cared to lean upon it, but the latter waved them away mournfully. He wore the look of one who knows he is the victim of a terrible disease and understands his helplessness. He again stared over the breast-work at the forest, and then turning went slowly rearward. He held his right wrist tenderly in his left hand, as if the wounded arm was made of very brittle glass.

And the men in silence stared at the wood, then at the departing lieutenant—then at the wood, then at the lieutenant.

As the wounded officer passed from the line of battle, he was enabled to see many things which as a participant in the fight were unknown to him. He saw a general on a black horse gazing over the lines of blue infantry at the green woods which veiled his problems. An aide galloped furiously, dragged his horse suddenly to a halt, saluted, and presented a paper. It was, for a wonder, precisely like an historical painting.

To the rear of the general and his staff, a group, composed of a bugler, two or three orderlies, and the bearer of the corps standard, all upon maniacal horses, were working like slaves to hold their ground, preserve their respectful interval, while the shells bloomed in the air about them, and caused their chargers to make furious quivering leaps.

A battery, a tumultuous and shining mass, was swirling toward the right. The wild thud of hoofs, the cries of the riders shouting blame and praise, menace and encouragement, and, last, the roar of the wheels, the slant of the glistening guns, brought the lieutenant to an intent pause. The battery swept in curves that stirred the heart; it made halts as dramatic as the crash of a wave on the rocks and when it fled onward, this aggregation of wheels, levers, motors, had a beautiful unity, as if it were a missile. The sound of it was a war-chorus that reached into the depths of man's emotion.

The lieutenant, still holding his arm as if it were of glass, stood watching this battery until all detail of it was lost, save the figures of the riders, which rose and fell and waved lashes over the black mass.

Later he turned his eyes toward the battle where the shooting sometimes crackled like bush-fires, sometimes sputtered with exasperating irregularity, and sometimes reverberated like the thunder. He saw the smoke rolling upward and saw crowds of men who ran and cheered, or stood and blazed away at the inscrutable distance.

He came upon some stragglers and they told him how to find the field hospital. They described its exact location. In fact these men, no longer having part in the battle, knew more of it than others. They told the performance of every corps, every division, the opinion of every general. The lieutenant, carrying his wounded arm rearward, looked upon them with wonder.

At the roadside a brigade was making coffee and buzzing with talk like a girls' boarding-school. Several officers came out to him and inquired concerning things of which he knew nothing. One, seeing his arm, began to scold. "Why, man, that's no way to do. You want to fix that thing." He appropriated the lieutenant and the lieutenant's wound. He cut the sleeve and laid bare the arm, every nerve of which softly fluttered under his touch. He bound his handkerchief over the wound, scolding away in the meantime. He tone allowed one to think that he was in the habit of being wounded every day. The lieutenant hung his head, feeling, in this presence, that he did not know how to be correctly wounded.

The low white tents of the hospital were grouped around an old school-house. There was here a singular commotion. In the foreground two ambulances interlocked wheels in the deep mud. The drivers were tossing the blame of it back and forth, gesticulating and berating, while from the ambulances, both crammed with wounded, there came an occasional groan. An interminable crowd of bandaged men were coming and going. Great numbers sat under the trees nursing heads or arms or legs. There was a dispute of some kind raging on the steps of the school-house. Sitting with his back against a tree a man with a face as grey as a new army blanket was serenely smoking a corn-cob pipe. The lieutenant wished to rush forward and inform him that he was dying.

A busy surgeon was passing near the lieutenant. "Good morning," he said with a friendly smile. Then he caught sight of the lieutenant's arm and his face at once changed. "Well, let's have a look at it." He seemed possessed suddenly of a great contempt for the lieutenant. This would evidently placed the latter on a very low social plane. The doctor cried out impatiently. What mutton-head had tied it up that way anyhow. The lieutenant answered: "Oh, a man."

When the wound was disclosed the doctor fingered it disdainfully. "Humph," he said. "You come along with me and I'll 'tend to you." His voice contained the same scorn as if he were saying: "You will have to go to jail."

The lieutenant had been very meek but now his face flushed, and he looked into the doctor's eyes. "I guess I won't have it amputated," he said.

"Nonsense, man! nonsense! nonsense!" cried the doctor. "Come along, now. I won't amputate it. Come along. Don't be a baby."

"Let go of me," said the lieutenant, holding back wrathfully. His glance fixed upon the door of the old school-house, as sinister to him as the portals of death.

And this is the story of how the lieutenant lost his arm. When he reached home his sisters, his mother, his wife, sobbed for a long time at the sight of the flat sleeve. "Oh, well," he said, standing shamefaced amid these tears, "I don't suppose it matters so much as all that."

1899

Theodore Dreiser
1871–1945

By the end of the nineteenth century, Indiana had become a major center of literary production, able to satisfy the needs of a large body of readers across the country. There had been General Lew Wallace's best-selling novel *Ben Hur*, about early Christians in Rome and Palestine, to provide the uplift of religious inspiration mixed with the romance of exotic times and places. There were the down-home humor and sentiment of James Whitcomb Riley's verses and the popular satires of George Ade and, later, Chic Sale. Best of all, there was Booth Tarkington, "the gentleman from Indiana," who provided middle-class parlors with the novels (such as *Seventeen*) and magazine pieces (the Penrod stories) that extolled the pleasures and pain of growing up as a boy in Indianapolis. Tarkington's Indiana (closely observed, with wit and good nature) was a nice place to be a boy and a dandy place to be a rich and famous author (especially one who could, as Tarkington did, also turn out such popular historical romances as *Monsieur Beaucaire* and astute comedies of manners like *The Magnificent Ambersons*). This Indiana, however, was not the one that Theodore Herman Albert Dreiser knew. He grew up poor and unhappy, the son of German immigrant parents, in Terre Haute, a rough river town down by the Ohio River.

Dreiser's imagination was midwestern through and through. It was not the Tarkington imagination, however. Dreiser was closer to the Hoosier author of an earlier generation, Edward Eggleston, who had portrayed the seamier, more violent sides of life when Indiana had been little more than a scattering of frontier settlements. Yet Dreiser's novels are most correctly associated with the Chicago school of Realism. Just as New York began to replace Boston as the primary center for work and culture by the 1880s, Indianapolis (locale for easygoing realism and genteel romancing) was displaced by Chicago in the 1890s and early 1900s. That boom city was both the literal place and the symbolic setting for lives and literature that dramatized the naturalistic principles that Dreiser's writings commandingly represent; for Dreiser, to live in Chicago was to experience the forces of environment and physical urges emphasized by his fiction.

Chicago was not the only place to stimulate Dreiser's imagination or to offer an arena for his struggles. Dreiser was a wanderer by nature; he characterized himself as a "cosmic waif." Like others of his generation, he felt buffeted by a willful and indifferent universe. He was always sympathetic toward his unhappy fictional characters because he felt himself to be as bereft as they. He took up lodgings in St. Louis, Pittsburgh, Cleveland, Chicago, and New York. He visited the Soviet Union for eleven weeks in 1927–1928. He acted as journalist, editor, and novelist—whatever his temporary stops called upon him to do. His brother Paul became a popular songwriter with the hit "On the Banks of the Wabash"— a nostalgic bit of "down-home" melody—but home was a place neither Theodore Dreiser nor his fictional characters ever had.

Dreiser had experienced almost too much family life when he was growing up. His family, especially his sisters with their wayward lives and illegitimate children, furnished him with ideas for the stories he would write. But it was not the life Booth Tarkington gave to his boys, Penrod or Sam. The bare, though hardly barren, facts of Dreiser's life are easy to review. He was the twelfth of thirteen children. His father (severe, a religious fanatic, and often out of work) and his mother (absorbed in her family, sympathetic, and illiterate) were unable to stave off the ruin and squalor that beset them. By the age of fifteen, Dreiser was on his own, living off small jobs he scared up around Terre Haute. A year at Indiana University followed in 1889 after a high school teacher who believed in him gave him money for further schooling. But Dreiser was eager to put as much distance between himself and his childhood as possible. As it had for other young men of the period, journalism offered a way out. From 1892 on, Dreiser gained experience on newspapers around the Midwest before heading for New York. He supplemented his street knowledge as best he could with the contemporary literature that most appealed to him—the evolutionary theories of scientific and social determinism grounded on the work of Charles Darwin, Thomas Huxley, and Herbert Spencer.

The year 1900 saw the publication—and quick demise—of Dreiser's first novel, *Sister Carrie,* based in part on the elopement of one of his sisters and a story of the embezzlement of company funds that filled the newspapers at that time. *Sister Carrie* dropped from sight almost as soon as the publishers released it; they decided not to promote it because the publisher's wife found it shocking. Only recently has the full story of the tampering with Dreiser's novel come to light with the scholarly publication of the original manuscript. Dreiser had not only to suffer the evisceration of his original ideas but also to witness the disappearance from public view of the resulting bowdlerization.

Deeply disappointed by the failure of *Sister Carrie,* for which his royalties came to $68.40, Dreiser moved on to write a group of short stories. A nervous breakdown followed, debilitating him until 1904, the year he started to work for several magazines, including the Butterick publication *The Delineator.* In 1907 *Sister Carrie* was reissued and began both to receive the attention it deserved and to exert an influence on American literature's turn toward naturalism. *Jennie Gerhardt* was published in 1911; once again the plot came to Dreiser by way of a sister's experience as a rich man's mistress. In 1912 Dreiser brought out the first of three novels known as the Cowperwood trilogy: *The Financier,* followed by *The Titan* (1914) and *The Stoic* (posthumously published in 1947). A journalist by nature, Dreiser continued to base his fiction on contemporary figures whose stories were played out in the newspapers. (In the case of the Cowperwood novels, he modeled his hero on a well-known financial swashbuckler, Charles T. Yerkes.) By these means he dramatized the methods by which clever, ruthless entrepreneurs were taking control of the American system.

Autobiographical books followed: *The "Genius"* (1915) was a fictionalized version of Dreiser's early efforts as a writer; *A Book About Myself,* also known as *Newspaper Days* (1922), and *Dawn* (1931) were straightforward autobiographies. But it was the 1925 publication of *An American Tragedy,* based on an actual murder trial, that earned him the recognition he had been lumbering toward ever since his early days in Terre Haute.

Politics received most of Dreiser's attention in the last decades of his life. It is revealing that he simultaneously became a member of the Communist Party and a Quaker. He was a naive thinker and a somewhat confused social reformer, but to the end he tried to find a way out for individuals and social groups who wanted to escape the deadening grip of a mechanistic determinism that he both believed in and yearned to modify. Dreiser's example helps explain why American naturalism took a different approach to the universe from that upheld by Continental writers who worked from principles, based on their appraisal of human behavior, that attempted to be as clinically objective as any derived by laboratory observation of rats in a test cage.

Dreiser did his "homework" in the nineteenth-century evolutionary theory that had replaced Divine Providence with biology. He was a practicing journalist trained to report empirical facts. He was also a full-fledged participant in a literary movement that attempted to replace the self-delusions of romanticized fictions with honest, sobering accounts of how people react to real events. But Dreiser had to add hope to what he saw, however tragic the scene. This was how he expressed his own desires for happiness, material success, and sexual triumphs.

As Dreiser traveled around the United States—a country in the process of changing before his eyes—he wanted to be able to define the changes he witnessed as progress toward something better. He needed to associate the longings that frustrated his fictional characters and himself with the necessary birth pangs of a soul on its upward ascent. Dreiser once stopped in the middle of an outburst about the quiet farmlands of the Midwest, with their promise of stability and calm, and exclaimed, "But I have seen Pittsburgh!" That is, he had seen firsthand the hectic lives of people who worked silhouetted against the fires of the blast furnaces of the Pennsylvanian steel mills that gave the lie to an agricultural America. But if he contrasted the picture of Pittsburgh with the Ohio farmlands, he kept American ideals and rural idylls in his memory.

Carrie Meeber and George Hurstwood in *Sister Carrie* pass one another along the lines of ascent and descent that take the one to a celebrity's suite at the new Waldorf-Astoria and the other to suicide in a flophouse and a pauper's grave. In *An American Tragedy* Clyde Griffiths goes to his death for the murder of one young woman because of his longing for another, richer, more glamorous girl. His foolish dream of wealth is matched by the folly of his romantic desire for perfect love. Frank Cowperwood's life expresses his faith that he can take command of the machine that brings him financial success and sexual prowess. He rejects the notion that he can be broken by the mechanisms of a "hot" society and a "cold" universe. Money, sex, and power as the way (however abortive) to go "home" became major themes in twentieth-century literature, precisely because Dreiser made them important. His books and his life frequently demonstrate how freedom of choice and fulfillment of one's yearnings are often denied. But this did not stop him. He kept on writing as much about the power of desire as about the inevitability of defeat.

Further Reading:
D. Dudley, *Dreiser and the Land of the Free*, 1932, 1946.
R. Elias, *Theodore Dreiser, Apostle of Nature*, 1949, 1970.
H. Dreiser, *My Life with Dreiser*, 1951.
F. Matthiessen, *Theodore Dreiser*, 1951.
The Stature of Theodore Dreiser: A Critical Survey of the Man and His Work, ed. A. Kazin and C. Shapiro, 1955.
C. Shapiro, *Theodore Dreiser, Our Bitter Patriot*, 1962.
P. L. Gerber, *Theodore Dreiser*, 1964.
W. Swanberg, *Dreiser*, 1965.
M. Tjader, *Theodore Dreiser: A New Dimension*, 1965.
J. McAleer, *Theodore Dreiser: An Introduction and*

Interpretation, 1968.
R. Lehan, *Theodore Dreiser: His World and His Novels*, 1969.
E. Moers, *Two Dreisers*, 1969.
R. Warren, *Homage to Theodore Dreiser*, 1971.
Folcroft Library Editions, *Theodore Dreiser, America's Foremost Novelist*, 1973.
D. Pizer, *The Novels of Theodore Dreiser*, 1976.
P. L. Gerber, *Plots and Characters in the Fiction of Theodore Dreiser*, 1977.
Y. Hakutani, *Young Dreiser: A Critical Study*, 1980.
Critical Essays on Theodore Dreiser, ed. D. Pizer, 1981.
L. Hussman, *Dreiser and His Fiction*, 1983.

Text:
Sister Carrie, 1981.
See also *The Letters of Theodore Dreiser*, 3 vols., ed. R. Elias, 1959.

American Diaries, 1902–1926, ed. T. Riggio, 1982.

---

from Sister Carrie

Chapter III: [Looking for a Job]

Once across the river and into the wholesale district, she glanced about her for some likely door at which to apply.[1] As she contemplated the wide windows and imposing signs, she became conscious of being gazed upon and understood for what she was —a wage-seeker. She had never done this thing before and lacked courage. To avoid conspicuity and a certain indefinable shame she felt at being caught spying about for some place where she might apply for a position, she quickened her steps and assumed an air of indifference supposedly common to one upon an errand. In this way she passed many manufacturing and wholesale houses without once glancing in. At last, after several blocks of walking, she felt that this would not do, and began to look about again, though without relaxing her pace. A little way on she saw a great door which for some reason attracted her attention. It was ornamented by a small brass sign, and seemed to be the entrance to a vast hive of six or seven floors. "Perhaps," she thought, "they may want some one" and crossed over to enter, screwing up her courage to the sticking point as she went. When she came within a score of feet of the desired goal, she observed a young gentleman in a grey check suit, fumbling his watch-charm and looking out. That he had anything to do with the concern she could not tell, but because he happened to be looking in her direction, her weakening heart misgave her and she hurried by, too overcome with shame to enter in. After several blocks of walking, in which the uproar of the streets and the novelty of the situation had time to wear away the effect of this, her first defeat, she again looked about. Over the way stood a great six-story structure labeled "Storm and King," which she viewed with rising hope. It was a wholesale dry goods concern and employed women. She could see them moving about now and then upon the upper floors. This place she decided to enter, no matter what. She crossed over and walked directly toward the entrance. As she did so two men came out and paused in the door. A telegraph messenger in blue dashed past her and up the few steps which graced the entrance and disappeared. Several pedestrians out of the hurrying throng which filled the sidewalks passed about her as she paused, hesitating. She looked helplessly around and then, seeing herself observed, retreated. It was too difficult a task. She could not go past them.

So severe a defeat told sadly upon her nerves. She could scarcely understand her weakness and yet she could not think of gazing inquiringly about upon the surrounding scene. Her feet carried her mechanically forward, every foot of her progress being a satisfactory portion of a flight which she gladly made. Block after block passed by. Upon street lamps at the various corners she read names such as Madison, Monroe, La Salle, Clark, Dearborn, State; and still she went, her feet beginning to tire upon the broad stone flagging. She was pleased in part that the streets were bright and clean. The morning sun shining down with steadily increasing warmth made the shady side of the streets pleasantly cool. She looked at the blue sky overhead with more realization of its charm than had ever come to her before.

---

[1] Carrie Meeber, at 18, has arrived in Chicago from a small midwestern town in 1889 in the hope of finding a job and entering upon the exciting life of the big city.

Her cowardice began to trouble her in a way. She turned back along the street she had come, resolving to hunt up Storm and King and enter in. On the way she encountered a great wholesale shoe company, through the broad plate windows of which she saw an enclosed executive department, hidden by frosted glass. Without this enclosure, but just within the street entrance, sat a grey-haired gentleman at a small table, with a large open ledger of some kind before him. She walked by this institution several times hesitating, but finding herself unobserved she eventually gathered sufficient courage to falter past the screen door and stand humbly waiting.

"Well, young lady," observed the old gentleman looking at her somewhat kindly —"what is it you wish?"

"I am, that is, do you—I mean, do you need any help?" she stammered.

"Not just at present," he answered smiling. "Not just at present. Come in sometime next week. Occasionally we need some one."

She received the answer in silence and backed awkwardly out. The pleasant nature of her reception rather astonished her. She had expected that it would be more difficult, that something cold and harsh would be said—she knew not what. That she had not been put to shame and made to feel her unfortunate position seemed remarkable. She did not realize that it was just this which made her experience easy, but the result was the same. She felt greatly relieved.

Somewhat encouraged, she ventured into another large structure. It was a clothing company, and more people were in evidence—well-dressed men of forty and more, surrounded by brass railings and employed variously.

An office boy approached her.

"Who is it you wish to see?" he asked.

"I want to see the manager," she returned.

He ran away and spoke to one of a group of three men who were conferring together. One broke off and came towards her.

"Well?" he said, coldly. The greeting drove all courage from her at once.

"Do you need any help?" she stammered.

"No," he replied abruptly and turned upon his heel.

She went foolishly out, the office boy deferentially swinging the door for her, and gladly sank into the obscuring crowd. It was a severe set-back to her recently pleased mental state.

Now she walked quite aimlessly for a time, turning here and there, seeing one great company after another but finding no courage to prosecute her single inquiry. High noon came and with it hunger. She hunted out an unassuming restaurant and entered but was disturbed to find that the prices were exorbitant for the size of her purse. A bowl of soup was all that she could feel herself able to afford, and with this quickly eaten she went out again. It restored her strength somewhat and made her moderately bold to pursue the search.

In walking a few blocks to fix upon some probable place she again encountered the firm of Storm and King and this time managed to enter. Some gentlemen were conferring close at hand but took no notice of her. She was left standing, gazing nervously upon the floor, her confusion and mental distress momentarily increasing until at last she was ready to turn and hurry eagerly away. When the limit of her distress had been nearly reached she was beckoned to by a man at one of the many desks within the nearby railing.

"Who is it you wish to see?" he inquired.

"Why any one, if you please," she answered. "I am looking for something to do."

"Oh, you want to see Mr. McManus," he returned. "Sit down!" and he pointed to a chair against the neighboring wall. He went on leisurely writing until after a time a short stout gentleman came in from the street.

"Mr. McManus," called the man at the desk, "this young woman wants to see you."

The short gentleman turned about towards Carrie, and she arose and came forward.

"What can I do for you, Miss," he inquired surveying her curiously.

"I want to know if I can get a position," she inquired.

"As what?" he asked.

"Not as anything in particular," she faltered. "I—"

"Have you ever had any experience in the wholesale dry goods business?" he questioned.

"No sir," she replied.

"Are you a stenographer or typewriter?"[2]

"No sir."

"Well we haven't anything here," he said. "We employ only experienced help."

She began to step backward toward the door, when something about her plaintive face attracted him.

"Have you ever worked at anything before?" he inquired.

"No sir," she said.

"Well now, it's hardly possible that you would get anything to do in a wholesale house of this kind. Have you tried the department stores?"

She acknowledged that she had not.

"Well, if I were you," he said, looking at her rather genially, "I would try the department stores. They often need young women as clerks."

"Thank you," she said, her whole nature relieved by this spark of friendly interest.

"Yes," he said, as she moved toward the door, "you try the department stores," and off he went.

At that time the department store was in its earliest form of successful operation and there were not many. The first three in the United States, established about 1884, were in Chicago.[3] Carrie was familiar with the names of several through the advertisements in the "Daily News," and now proceeded to seek them. The words of Mr. McManus had somehow managed to restore her courage, which had fallen low, and she dared to hope that this new line would offer her something in the way of employment. Some time she spent in wandering up and down thinking to encounter the buildings by chance, so readily is the mind, bent upon prosecuting a hard but needful errand, eased by that self-deception which the semblance of search without the reality gives. At last she inquired of a police officer and was directed to proceed "two blocks up" where she would find The Fair. Following his advice she reached that institution and entered.

The nature of these vast retail combinations, should they ever permanently disappear, will form an interesting chapter in the commercial history of our nation. Such a flowering out of a modest trade principle the world had never witnessed up to that time. They were along the line of the most effective retail organization, with hundreds

[2] Typist.

[3] Reference to Marshall Field's, the Fair, and the Boston, stores that (although not literally the first in the country) brought commercial fame to Chicago during its time of growth after the 1871 fire.

of stores coordinated into one, and laid out upon the most imposing and economic basis. They were handsome, bustling, successful affairs, with a host of clerks and a swarm of patrons. Carrie passed along the busy aisles, much affected by the remarkable displays of trinkets, dress goods, shoes, stationery, jewelry. Each separate counter was a show place of dazzling interest and attraction. She could not help feeling the claim of each trinket and valuable upon her personally and yet she did not stop. There was nothing there which she could not have used—nothing which she did not long to own. The dainty slippers and stockings, the delicately frilled skirts and petticoats, the laces, ribbons, hair-combs, purses, all touched her with individual desire, and she felt keenly the fact that not any of these things were in the range of her purchase. She was a work-seeker, an outcast without employment, one whom the average employé could tell at a glance was poor and in need of a situation.

It must not be thought that anyone could have mistaken her for a nervous, sensitive, high-strung nature, cast unduly upon a cold, calculating and unpoetic world. Such certainly she was not. But women are peculiarly sensitive to the personal adornment or equipment of their person, even the dullest, and particularly is this true of the young. Your bright-eyed, rosy-cheeked maiden, over whom a poet might well rave for the flowerlike expression of her countenance and the lissome and dainty grace of her body, may reasonably be dead to every evidence of the artistic and poetic in the unrelated evidences of life, and yet not lack in material appreciation. Never, it might be said, does she fail in this. With her the bloom of a rose may pass unappreciated, but the bloom of a fold of silk, never. If nothing in the heavens, or the earth, or the waters, could elicit her fancy or delight her from its spiritual or artistic side, think not that the material would be lost. The glint of a buckle, the hue of a precious stone, the faintest tints of the watered silk, these she would devine and qualify as readily as your poet if not more so. The creak, the rustle, the glow—the least and best of the graven or spun—, these she would perceive and appreciate—if not because of some fashionable or hearsay quality, then on account of their true beauty, their innate fitness in any order of harmony, their place in the magical order and sequence of dress.

Not only did Carrie feel the drag of desire for all of this which was new and pleasing in apparel for women, but she noticed, too, with a touch at the heart, the fine ladies who elbowed and ignored her, brushing past in utter disregard of her presence, themselves eagerly enlisted in the materials which the store contained. Carrie was not familiar with the appearance of her more fortunate sisters of the city. Neither had she before known the nature and appearance of the shop girls, with whom she now compared poorly. They were pretty in the main, some even handsome, with a certain independence and toss of indifference which added, in the case of the more favored, a certain piquancy. Their clothes were neat, in many instances fine, and wherever she encountered the eye of one, it was only to recognize in it a keen analysis of her own position—her individual shortcomings of dress and that shadow of *manner* which she thought must hang about her and make clear to all who and what she was. A flame of envy lighted in her heart. She realized in a dim way how much the city held—wealth, fashion, ease—every adornment for women, and she longed for dress and beauty with a whole and fulsome heart.

On the second floor were the managerial offices, to which after some inquiry she was now directed. There she found other girls ahead of her, applicants like herself, but with more of that self-satisfied and independent air which experience of the city lends—girls who scrutinized her in a painful manner. After a wait of perhaps three-quarters of an hour she was called in turn.

"Now," said a sharp, quick-mannered Jew who was sitting at a roll-top desk near the window—"have you ever worked in any other store?"

"No sir," said Carrie.

"Oh, you haven't," he said, eyeing her keenly.

"No sir," she replied.

"Well, we prefer young women just now with some experience. I guess we can't use you."

Carrie stood waiting a moment, hardly certain whether the interview had terminated.

"Don't wait!" he exclaimed. "Remember we are very busy here."

Carrie began to move quickly to the door.

"Hold on," he said, calling her back. "Give me your name and address. We want girls occasionally."

When she had gotten safely out again into the street she could scarcely restrain tears. It was not so much the particular rebuff which she had just experienced, but the whole abashing trend of the day. She was tired and rather over-played upon in the nerves. She abandoned the thought of appealing to the other department stores and now wandered on, feeling a certain safety and relief in mingling with the crowd.

In her indifferent wandering she turned into Jackson Street, not far from the river, and was keeping her way along the south side of that imposing thoroughfare, when a piece of wrapping paper written on with marking ink and tacked upon a door attracted her attention. It read "Girls wanted—wrappers and stitchers." She hesitated for the moment, thinking surely to go in, but upon further consideration the added qualifications of "wrappers and stitchers" deterred her. She had no idea of what that meant. Most probably she would need to be experienced in it. She walked on a little way, mentally balancing as to whether or not to apply. Necessity triumphed however and she returned.

The entrance, which opened into a small hall, led to an elevator shaft, the elevator of which was up. It was a dingy affair, being used both as a freight and passenger entrance, and the woodwork was marked and splintered by the heavy boxes which were tumbled in and out, at intervals. A frowzy-headed German-American, about fourteen years of age, operated the elevator in his shirt sleeves and bare feet. His face was considerably marked with grease and dirt.

When the elevator stopped, the boy leisurely raised a protecting arm of wood and by grace of his superior privilege admitted her.

"Wear do you want to go?" he inquired.

"I want to see the manager," she replied.

"Wot manager?" he returned, surveying her caustically.

"Is there more than one?' she asked. "I thought it was all one firm."

"Naw," said the youth. "Der's six different people. Want to see Speigelheim?"

"I don't know," answered Carrie. She colored a little as she began to feel the necessity of explaining. "I want to see whoever put up that sign."

"Dot's Speigelheim," said the boy. "Fort floor." Therewith he proudly turned to his task of pulling the rope, and the elevator ascended.

The firm of Speigelheim and Co., makers of boys' caps, occupied one floor of fifty feet in width and some eighty feet in depth. It was a place rather dingily lighted, the darkest portions having incandescent lights, filled in part with machines and part with workbenches. At the latter labored quite a company of girls and some men. The former were drabby looking creatures, stained in face with oil and dust, clad in thin shapeless cotton dresses, and shod with more or less worn shoes. Many of them had their sleeves rolled up, revealing bare arms, and in some cases, owing to heat, their dresses were open at the neck. They were a fair type of nearly the lowest order of shop girls,—careless, rather slouchy, and more or less pale from confinement. They were not timid however, were rich in curiosity and strong in daring and slang.

Carrie looked about her, very much disturbed and quite sure that she did not want to work here. Aside from making her uncomfortable by sidelong glances, no one paid her the least attention. She waited until the whole department was aware of her presence. Then some word was sent round and a foreman in an apron and shirt sleeves, the latter rolled up to his shoulders, approached.

"Do you want to see me?" he asked.

"Do you need any help?" said Carrie, already learning directness of address.

"Do you know how to stitch caps?" he returned.

"No sir," she replied.

"Have you ever had any experience at this kind of work?" he inquired.

She owned that she hadn't.

"Well," said the foreman, scratching his ear meditatively, "we do need a stitcher. We like experienced help though. We've hardly got time to break people in." He paused and looked away out of the window. "We might, though, put you at finishing," he concluded reflectively.

"How much do you pay a week?" ventured Carrie, emboldened by a certain softness in the man's manner and his simplicity of address.

"Three and a half," he answered.

"Oh," she was about to exclaim, but checked herself, and allowed her thoughts to die without expression.

"We're not exactly in need of anybody," he went on vaguely, looking her over as one would a package. "You can come Monday morning though," he added, "and I'll put you to work."

"Thank you," said Carrie weakly.

"If you come, bring an apron," he added.

He walked away and left her standing by the elevator, never so much as inquiring her name.

While the appearance of the shop and the announcement of the price paid per week operated very much as a blow to Carrie's fancy, the fact that work of any kind, after so rude a round of experience, was offered her, was gratifying. She could not begin to believe that she would take the place, modest as her aspirations were. She had been used to better than that. Her mere experience and the free out-of-doors life of the country caused her nature to revolt at such confinement. Dirt had never been her share. Her sister's flat was clean. This place was grimy and low; the girls were careless and hardened. They must be bad-minded and -hearted, she imagined. Still a place had been offered her. Surely Chicago was not so bad if she could find one place in one day. She might find another and better later.

Her subsequent experiences were not of a reassuring nature, however. From all the more pleasing or imposing places she was turned away abruptly with the most chilling formality. In others where she applied, only the experienced were required. She met with painful rebuffs, the most trying of which had been in a cloak manufacturing house, where she had gone to the fourth floor to inquire.

"No, no," said the foreman, a rough, heavy-built individual who looked after a miserably lighted work shop, "we don't want anyone. Don't come here."

In another factory she was leered upon by a most sensual-faced individual who endeavored to turn the natural questions of the inquiry into a personal interview, asking all sorts of embarrassing questions and endeavoring to satisfy himself evidently that she was of loose enough morals to suit his purpose. In that case she had been relieved enough to get away and found the busy, indifferent streets to be again a soothing refuge.

With the wane of the afternoon went her hopes, her courage and her strength. She had been astonishingly persistent. So earnest an effort was well deserving of a better reward. On every hand, to her fatigued senses, the great business portion grew larger, harder, more stolid in its indifference. It seemed as if it was all closed to her, that the struggle was too fierce for her to hope to do anything at all. Men and women hurried by in long, shifting lines. She felt the flow of the tide of effort and interest, felt her own helplessness without quite realizing the wisp on the tide that she was. She cast about vainly for some possible place to apply but found no door which she had the courage to enter. It would be the same thing all over. The old humiliation of her pleas rewarded by curt denial. Sick at heart and in body, she turned to the west, the direction of Minnie's flat, which she had now fixed in mind, and began that wearisome, baffled retreat which the seeker for employment at nightfall too often makes. In passing through Fifth Avenue, south towards Van Buren Street, where she intended to take a car, she passed the door of a large wholesale shoe house, through the plate glass window of which she could see a middle-aged gentleman sitting at a small desk. One of those forlorn impulses which often grow out of a fixed sense of defeat, the last sprouting of a baffled and uprooted growth of ideas, seized upon her. She walked deliberately through the door and up to the gentleman who looked at her weary face with partially awakened interest.

"What is it?" he said.

"Can you give me something to do?" asked Carrie.

"Now I really don't know," he said kindly. "What kind of work is it you want —you're not a typewriter, are you?"

"Oh, no," answered Carrie.

"Well, we only employ book keepers and typewriters here. You might go round to the side and inquire upstairs. They did want some help upstairs a few days ago. Ask for Mr. Brown."

She hastened around to the side entrance and was taken up by the elevator to the fourth floor.

"Call Mr. Brown, Willie," said the elevator man to a boy near by.

Willie went off and presently returned with the information that Mr. Brown said she should sit down and that he would be around in a little while.

It was a portion of a stock room which gave no idea of the general character of the floor, and Carrie could form no opinion of the nature of the work.

"So you want something to do," said Mr. Brown, after he inquired concerning the nature of her errand. "Have you ever been employed in a shoe factory before?"

"No sir," said Carrie.

"What is your name?" he inquired, and being informed, "Well, I don't know as I have anything for you. Would you work for four and a half a week?"

Carrie was too worn by defeat not to feel that it was considerable. She had not expected that he would offer her less than six. She acquiesced, however, and he took her name and address.

"Well," he said finally—"you report here at eight o'clock Monday morning. I think I can find something for you to do."

He left her revived by the possibilities, sure that she had found something to do at last. Instantly the blood crept warmly over her body. Her nervous tension relaxed. She walked out into the busy street and discovered a new atmosphere. Behold, the throng was moving with a lightsome step. She noticed that men and women were smiling. Scraps of conversation and notes of laughter floated to her. The air was light. People were already pouring out of the buildings, their labor ended for the day. She noticed that they were pleased, and thoughts of her sister's home, and the meal that would be awaiting her, quickened her steps. She hurried on, tired perhaps, but no longer weary of foot. What would not Minnie say! Ah, the long winter in Chicago —the lights, the crowd, the amusement. This was a great, pleasing metropolis after all. Her new firm was a goodly institution. Its windows were of huge plate glass. She could probably do well there. Thoughts of Drouet[4] returned, of the things he had told her. She now felt that life was better. That it was livelier, sprightlier. She boarded a car in the best of spirits, feeling her blood still flowing pleasantly. She would live in Chicago, her mind kept saying to itself. She would have a better time than she ever had before—she would be happy.

1900

Willa Cather
1873–1947

The old settlements of Virginia and the new lands of Nebraska formed the bedding ground for Willa Cather's talents; so did the layers of memory she found elsewhere across the North American continent, from New Mexico to Canada. Cather was born on the family farm in the hills of Virginia; she lived there until she was nine, when she moved with her parents to Nebraska. After several farming ventures there proved unsuccessful, the Cathers decided to live in the small town of Red Cloud. A young community, Red Cloud nevertheless offered the usual mix of frontier activities. It was flavored by the customs of newcomers from Scandinavia, Germany, and Central Europe as well as by "eastern cultivation" based on classical languages, music, and literature.

---

[4] Charlie Drouet figures early in the novel as the traveling salesman who is Carrie's first seducer; he will be the one who introduces her to George Hurstwood, the manager of a fashionable Chicago saloon.

Willa Cather was graduated from the University of Nebraska in 1895, then returned East to Pittsburgh. She supported herself first as a journalist and later as a high school teacher. By 1900 she was placing stories and poems in such well-known, large-circulation magazines as *McClure's* and *Cosmopolitan*. *April Twilight,* a collection of poems, appeared in 1903; it was followed in 1905 by *The Troll Garden,* a grouping of short stories. On the move again, she arrived in New York in 1906 and worked as managing editor of *McClure's* until 1912, the publication date of her first novel, *Alexander's Bridge*. She decided to support herself solely by writing fiction. The appreciation commanded by her earliest work continued and grew, and her decision to be a full-time professional writer proved to be a wise one.

Until 1912 Willa Cather had only hovered around her childhood experiences in Nebraska as possible material for her writings. The next five years saw a burst of literary activity stimulated by those memories, three novels that make clear her affinity for recording dreams of an ordered life whose every moment had significance. They show her mind stimulated by the ahistorical, semimythic landscapes of Nebraska and Arizona. *O Pioneers!* (1913), *Song of the Lark* (1915), and *My Ántcnia* (1918) reveal the aspirations of young men and women on the frontier who try to trick defeat and betrayal with their hopes and unflinching will.

Youth and the Bright Medusa, a collection of stories, emerged in 1920. In 1922, the year her war novel, *One of Ours,* was published, Cather's writing career and personal life faltered when the woman she loved got married. She regained her psychic strength, however, and over the next five years wrote three more novels: *A Lost Lady* (1923), *The Professor's House* (1925), and *Death Comes for the Archbishop* (1927). *Shadows on the Rock* followed in 1931, as did other books of less note. Throughout the 1920s and early 1930s she received a number of awards, confirming her place as an important literary voice.

The twin roles of religious faith and memory are strong forces in Willa Cather's fiction. The human need for illusion, dreams, and a vision of a world that lies beyond the material frame permeates her accounts of characters whose lives are made greater, though not necessarily happier, by their insistence on linking their present desires with the aspirations experienced by previous generations Repeatedly, she portrays the psychological patterns of those who make pilgrimages of the spirit into virginal territories, either geographical or spiritual. Her confirmation as a Protestant Episcopalian in 1922 made her especially responsive to the traditions of Roman Catholicism that had led priests into the frontier areas of New Mexico and French Canada. Priests and pioneers shared the same tradition of heart's longings that are central to much of her fiction.

Cather specifically rejected the realism she associated with a journalist's itemization of facts. She worked more closely with the modernist writers of her generation who approached their subjects by means of suggestion and the power of descriptive language. But however oblique her treatment, Cather's analysis of why we dream of something better and of how those dreams result in courage and not in defeat makes her narratives of hopeful immigrants and sensitive carriers of culture seem accurate deep down at the bone of truth.

Further Reading:

A. Porterfield, *Willa Cather*, 1928.

R. Rapin, *Willa Cather*, 1930.

M. Bennett, *The World of Willa Cather*, 1951, 1961.

D. Daiches, *Willa Cather: A Critical Introduction*, 1951, 1962.

E. Brown and L. Edel, *Willa Cather: A Critical Biography*, 1953.

E. Lewis, *Willa Cather Living*, 1953.

E. Sergeant, *Willa Cather: A Memoir*, 1953, 1963.

N. W. Smith, *Willa Cather's Art of Fiction*, 1954.

J. Randall, *The Landscape and the Looking Glass: Willa Cather's Search for Value*, 1960, 1973.

E. A. Bloom, *Willa Cather's Gift of Sympathy*, 1962, 1965.

Dorothy Van Ghent, *Willa Cather*, 1964.

Willa Cather and Her Critics, ed. J. Schroeter, 1967.

R. Giannone, *Music in Willa Cather's Fiction*, 1968.

B. Bonham, *Willa Cather*, 1970.

J. Woodress, *Willa Cather: Her Life and Art*, 1970.

D. T. McFarland, *Willa Cather*, 1972.

P. L. Yongue, *The Immense Design*, 1972.

P. Gerber, *Willa Cather*, 1975.

D. McFarland, *Willa Cather's Imagination*, 1975.

M. Pers, *Willa Cather's Children*, 1975.

D. Stouck, *Willa Cather's Imagination*, 1975.

M. Brown, *Only One Point of the Compass: Willa Cather in the Northeast*, 1980.

K. Bryne, *Chrysalis: Willa Cather in Pittsburgh, 1896–1906*, 1980.

Texts:

"The Sculptor's Funeral" from *Willa Cather's Collected Short Fiction*, ed. V. Faulkner, 1970.

See also *The Novels and Stories of Willa Cather*, 13 vols., 1934–1941.

The Kingdom of Art: Willa Cather's First Principles and Critical Statements, 1893–1896, ed. B. Slote, 1966.

The World and the Parish: Willa Cather's Articles and Reviews, 1893–1902, ed. W. Curtin, 1970.

The Sculptor's Funeral

A group of the townspeople stood on the station siding of a little Kansas town, awaiting the coming of the night train, which was already twenty minutes overdue. The snow had fallen thick over everything; in the pale starlight the line of bluffs across the wide, white meadows south of the town made soft, smoke-coloured curves against the clear sky. The men on the siding stood first on one foot and then on the other, their hands thrust deep into their trousers pockets, their overcoats open, their shoulders screwed up with the cold; and they glanced from time to time toward the southeast, where the railroad track wound along the river shore. They conversed in low tones and moved about restlessly, seeming uncertain as to what was expected of them. There was but one of the company who looked as though he knew exactly why he was there; and he kept conspicuously apart; walking to the far end of the platform, returning to the station door, then pacing up the track again, his chin sunk in the high collar of his overcoat, his burly shoulders drooping forward, his gait heavy and dogged. Presently he was approached by a tall, spare, grizzled man clad in a faded Grand Army suit,[1] who shuffled out from the group and advanced with a certain deference, craning

---

[1] Uniform of members of the Grand Army of the Republic, an association of veterans of the Civil War who had fought on the Union side.

his neck forward until his back made the angle of a jack-knife three-quarters open. "I reckon she's a-goin' to be pretty late agin to-night, Jim," he remarked in a squeaky falsetto. "S'pose it's the snow?"

"I don't know," responded the other man with a shade of annoyance, speaking from out an astonishing cataract of red beard that grew fiercely and thickly in all directions.

The spare man shifted the quill toothpick he was chewing to the other side of his mouth. "It ain't likely that anybody from the East will come with the corpse, I s'pose," he went on reflectively.

"I don't know," responded the other, more curtly than before.

"It's too bad he didn't belong to some lodge or other. I like an order funeral myself. They seem more appropriate for people of some repytation," the spare man continued, with an ingratiating concession in his shrill voice, as he carefully placed his toothpick in his vest pocket. He always carried the flag at the G.A.R. funerals in the town.

The heavy man turned on his heel, without replying, and walked up the siding. The spare man shuffled back to the uneasy group. "Jim's ez full ez a tick, ez ushel," he commented commiseratingly.

Just then a distant whistle sounded, and there was a shuffling of feet on the platform. A number of lanky boys of all ages appeared as suddenly and slimily as eels wakened by the crack of thunder; some came from the waiting-room, where they had been warming themselves by the red stove, or half asleep on the slat benches; others uncoiled themselves from baggage trucks or slid out of express wagons. Two clambered down from the driver's seat of a hearse that stood backed up against the siding. They straightened their stooping shoulders and lifted their heads, and a flash of momentary animation kindled their dull eyes at that cold, vibrant scream, the world-wide call for men. It stirred them like the note of a trumpet; just as it had often stirred the man who was coming home to-night, in his boyhood.

The night express shot, red as a rocket, from out the eastward marsh lands and wound along the river shore under the long lines of shivering poplars that sentinelled the meadows, the escaping steam hanging in grey masses against the pale sky and blotting out the Milky Way. In a moment the red glare from the headlight streamed up the snow-covered track before the siding and glittered on the wet, black rails. The burly man with the dishevelled red beard walked swiftly up the platform toward the approaching train, uncovering his head as he went. The group of men behind him hesitated, glanced questioningly at one another, and awkwardly followed his example. The train stopped, and the crowd shuffled up to the express car just as the door was thrown open, the spare man in the G.A.R. suit thrusting his head forward with curiosity. The express messenger appeared in the doorway, accompanied by a young man in a long ulster and travelling cap.

"Are Mr. Merrick's friends here?" inquired the young man.

The group on the platform swayed and shuffled uneasily. Philip Phelps, the banker, responded with dignity: "We have come to take charge of the body. Mr. Merrick's father is very feeble and can't be about."

"Send the agent out here," growled the express messenger, "and tell the operator to lend a hand."

The coffin was got out of its rough box and down on the snowy platform. The townspeople drew back enough to make room for it and then formed a close semicircle about it, looking curiously at the palm leaf which lay across the black cover.

No one said anything. The baggage man stood by his truck, waiting to get at the trunks. The engine panted heavily, and the fireman dodged in and out among the wheels with his yellow torch and long oil-can, snapping the spindle boxes. The young Bostonian, one of the dead sculptor's pupils who had come with the body, looked about him helplessly. He turned to the banker, the only one of that black, uneasy, stoop-shouldered group who seemed enough of an individual to be addressed.

"None of Mr. Merrick's brothers are here?" he asked uncertainly.

The man with the red beard for the first time stepped up and joined the group. "No, they have not come yet; the family is scattered. The body will be taken directly to the house." He stooped and took hold of one of the handles of the coffin.

"Take the long hill road up, Thompson, it will be easier on the horses," called the liveryman as the undertaker snapped the door of the hearse and prepared to mount to the driver's seat.

Laird, the red-bearded lawyer, turned again to the stranger: "We didn't know whether there would be any one with him or not," he explained. "It's a long walk, so you'd better go up in the hack." He pointed to a single battered conveyance, but the young man replied stiffly: "Thank you, but I think I will go up with the hearse. If you don't object," turning to the undertaker, "I'll ride with you."

They clambered up over the wheels and drove off in the starlight up the long, white hill toward the town. The lamps in the still village were shining from under the low, snow-burdened roofs; and beyond, on every side, the plains reached out into emptiness, peaceful and wide as the soft sky itself, and wrapped in a tangible, white silence.

When the hearse backed up to a wooden sidewalk before a naked, weather-beaten frame house, the same composite, ill-defined group that had stood upon the station siding was huddled about the gate. The front yard was an icy swamp, and a couple of warped planks, extending from the sidewalk to the door, made a sort of rickety footbridge. The gate hung on one hinge, and was opened wide with difficulty. Steavens, the young stranger, noticed that something black was tied to the knob of the front door.

The grating sound made by the casket, as it was drawn from the hearse, was answered by a scream from the house; the front door was wrenched open, and a tall, corpulent woman rushed out bareheaded into the snow and flung herself upon the coffin, shrieking: "My boy, my boy! And this is how you've come home to me!"

As Steavens turned away and closed his eyes with a shudder of unutterable repulsion, another woman, also tall, but flat and angular, dressed entirely in black, darted out of the house and caught Mrs. Merrick by the shoulders, crying sharply: "Come, come, mother; you musn't go on like this!" Her tone changed to one of obsequious solemnity as she turned to the banker: "The parlour is ready, Mr. Phelps."

The bearers carried the coffin along the narrow boards, while the undertaker ran ahead with the coffin-rests. They bore it into a large, unheated room that smelled of dampness and disuse and furniture polish, and set it down under a hanging lamp ornamented with jingling glass prisms and before a "Rogers group" of John Alden and Priscilla,[2] wreathed with smilax. Henry Steavens stared about him with the

---

[2] Small plaster statuary group depicting the hero and heroine of Longfellow's poem "The Courtship of Miles Standish," manufactured by John Rogers (1829–1904). "Rogers groups" were a popular, sentimental form of art that the sculptor Merrick would have disdained.

sickening conviction that there had been some horrible mistake, and that he had somehow arrived at the wrong destination. He looked painfully about over the clover-green Brussels,[3] the fat plush upholstery; among the handpainted china plaques and panels, and vases, for some mark of identification, for something that might once conceivably have belonged to Harvey Merrick. It was not until he recognized his friend in the crayon portrait of a little boy in kilts and curls hanging above the piano, that he felt willing to let any of these people approach the coffin.

"Take the lid off, Mr. Thompson; let me see my boy's face," wailed the elder woman between her sobs. This time Steavens looked fearfully, almost beseechingly into her face, red and swollen under its masses of strong, black, shiny hair. He flushed, dropped his eyes, and then, almost incredulously, looked again. There was a kind of power about her face—a kind of brutal handsomeness, even, but it was scarred and furrowed by violence, and so coloured and coarsened by fiercer passions that grief seemed never to have laid a gentle finger there. The long nose was distended and knobbed at the end, and there were deep lines on either side of it; her heavy, black brows almost met across her forehead, her teeth were large and square, and set far apart —teeth that could tear. She filled the room; the men were obliterated, seemed tossed about like twigs in an angry water, and even Steavens felt himself being drawn into the whirlpool.

The daughter—the tall, raw-boned woman in crêpe, with a mourning comb in her hair which curiously lengthened her long face—sat stiffly upon the sofa, her hands, conspicuous for their large knuckles, folded in her lap, her mouth and eyes drawn down, solemnly awaiting the opening of the coffin. Near the door stood a mulatto woman, evidently a servant in the house, with a timid bearing and an emaciated face pitifully sad and gentle. She was weeping silently, the corner of her calico apron lifted to her eyes, occasionally suppressing a long, quivering sob. Steavens walked over and stood beside her.

Feeble steps were heard on the stairs, and an old man, tall and frail, odorous of pipe smoke, with shaggy, unkept grey hair and a dingy beard, tobacco stained about the mouth, entered uncertainly. He went slowly up to the coffin and stood rolling a blue cotton handkerchief between his hands, seeming so pained and embarrassed by his wife's orgy of grief that he had no consciousness of anything else.

"There, there, Annie, dear, don't take on so," he quavered timidly, putting out a shaking hand and awkwardly patting her elbow. She turned with a cry, and sank upon his shoulder with such violence that he tottered a little. He did not even glance toward the coffin, but continued to look at her with a dull, frightened, appealing expression, as a spaniel looks at the whip. His sunken cheeks slowly reddened and burned with miserable shame. When his wife rushed from the room, her daughter strode after her with set lips. The servant stole up to the coffin, bent over it for a moment, and then slipped away to the kitchen, leaving Steavens, the lawyer and the father to themselves. The old man stood trembling and looking down at his dead son's face. The sculptor's splendid head seemed even more noble in its rigid stillness than in life. The dark hair had crept down upon the wide forehead; the face seemed strangely long, but in it there was not that beautiful and chaste repose which we expect to find in the faces of the

---

[3] Cheap carpeting of the type made in Brussels, Belgium.

dead. The brows were so drawn that there were two deep lines above the beaked nose, and the chin was thrust forward defiantly. It was as though the strain of life had been so sharp and bitter that death could not at once wholly relax the tension and smooth the countenance into perfect peace—as though he were still guarding something precious and holy, which might even yet be wrested from him.

The old man's lips were working under his stained beard. He turned to the lawyer with timid deference: "Phelps and the rest are comin' back to set up with Harve, ain't they?" he asked. "Thank 'ee, Jim, thank 'ee." He brushed the hair back gently from his son's forehead. "He was a good boy, Jim; always a good boy. He was ez gentle ez a child and the kindest of 'em all—only we didn't none of us ever onderstand him." The tears trickled slowly down his beard and dropped upon the sculptor's coat.

"Martin, Martin. Oh, Martin! come here," his wife wailed from the top of the stairs. The old man started timorously: "Yes, Annie, I'm coming." He turned away, hesitated, stood for a moment in miserable indecision; then reached back and patted the dead man's hair softly, and stumbled from the room.

"Poor old man, I didn't think he had any tears left. Seems as if his eyes would have gone dry long ago. At his age nothing cuts very deep," remarked the lawyer.

Something in his tone made Steavens glance up. While the mother had been in the room, the young man had scarcely seen anyone else; but now, from the moment he first glanced into Jim Laird's florid face and blood-shot eyes, he knew that he had found what he had been heartsick at not finding before—the feeling, the understanding, that must exist in some one, even here.

The man was red as his beard, with features swollen and blurred by dissipation, and a hot, blazing blue eye. His face was strained—that of a man who is controlling himself with difficulty—and he kept plucking at his beard with a sort of fierce resentment. Steavens, sitting by the window, watched him turn down the glaring lamp, still its jangling pendants with an angry gesture, and then stand with his hands locked behind him, staring down into the master's face. He could not help wondering what link there could have been between the porcelain vessel and so sooty a lump of potter's clay.

From the kitchen an uproar was sounding; when the dining-room door opened, the import of it was clear. The mother was abusing the maid for having forgotten to make the dressing for the chicken salad which had been prepared for the watchers. Steavens had never heard anything in the least like it; it was injured, emotional, dramatic abuse, unique and masterly in its excruciating cruelty, as violent and unrestrained as had been her grief of twenty minutes before. With a shudder of disgust the lawyer went into the dining-room and closed the door into the kitchen.

"Poor Roxy's getting it now," he remarked when he came back. "The Merricks took her out of the poor-house years ago; and if her loyalty would let her, I guess the poor old thing could tell tales that would curdle your blood. She's the mulatto woman who was standing in here a while ago, with her apron to her eyes. The old woman is a fury; there never was anybody like her for demonstrative piety and ingenious cruelty. She made Harvey's life a hell for him when he lived at home; he was so sick ashamed of it. I never could see how he kept himself so sweet."

"He was wonderful," said Steavens slowly, "wonderful; but until to-night I have never known how wonderful."

"That is the true and eternal wonder of it, anyway; that it can come even from such a dung heap as this," the lawyer cried, with a sweeping gesture which seemed to indicate much more than the four walls within which they stood.

"I think I'll see whether I can get a little air. The room is so close I am beginning to feel rather faint," murmured Steavens, struggling with one of the windows. The sash was stuck, however, and would not yield, so he sat down dejectedly and began pulling at his collar. The lawyer came over, loosened the sash with one blow of his red fist and sent the window up a few inches. Steavens thanked him, but the nausea which had been gradually climbing into his throat for the last half hour left him with but one desire—a desperate feeling that he must get away from this place with what was left of Harvey Merrick. Oh, he comprehended well enough now the quiet bitterness of the smile that he had seen so often on his master's lips!

He remembered that once, when Merrick returned from a visit home, he brought with him a singularly feeling and suggestive bas-relief of a thin, faded old woman, sitting and sewing something pinned to her knee; while a full-lipped, full-blooded little urchin, his trousers held up by a single gallus, stood beside her, impatiently twitching her gown to call her attention to a butterfly he had caught. Steavens, impressed by the tender and delicate modelling of the thin, tired face, had asked him if it were his mother. He remembered the dull flush that had burned up in the sculptor's face.

The lawyer was sitting in a rocking-chair beside the coffin, his head thrown back and his eyes closed. Steavens looked at him earnestly, puzzled at the line of the chin, and wondering why a man should conceal a feature of such distinction under that disfiguring shock of beard. Suddenly, as though he felt the young sculptor's keen glance, he opened his eyes.

"Was he always a good deal of an oyster?" he asked abruptly. "He was terribly shy as a boy."

"Yes, he was an oyster, since you put it so," rejoined Steavens. "Although he could be very fond of people, he always gave one the impression of being detached. He disliked violent emotion; he was reflective, and rather distrustful of himself—except, of course, as regarded his work. He was sure-footed enough there. He distrusted men pretty thoroughly and women even more, yet somehow without believing ill of them. He was determined, indeed, to believe the best, but he seemed afraid to investigate."

"A burnt dog dreads the fire," said the lawyer grimly, and closed his eyes.

Steavens went on and on, reconstructing that whole miserable boyhood. All this raw, biting ugliness had been the portion of the man whose tastes were refined beyond the limits of the reasonable—whose mind was an exhaustless gallery of beautiful impressions, and so sensitive that the mere shadow of a poplar leaf flickering against a sunny wall would be etched and held there forever. Surely, if ever a man had the magic word in his finger tips, it was Merrick. Whatever he touched, he revealed its holiest secret; liberated it from enchantment and restored it to its pristine loveliness, like the Arabian prince who fought the enchantress spell for spell. Upon whatever he had come in contact with, he had left a beautiful record of the experience—a sort of ethereal signature; a scent, a sound, a colour that was his own.

Steavens understood now the real tragedy of his master's life; neither love nor wine, as many had conjectured; but a blow which had fallen earlier and cut deeper than these could have done—a shame not his, and yet so unescapably his, to hide in his heart from his very boyhood. And without—the frontier warfare; the yearning of a boy, cast ashore upon a desert of newness and ugliness and sordidness, for all that is chastened and old, and noble with traditions.

At eleven o'clock the tall, flat woman in black crêpe entered and announced that the watchers were arriving, and asked them "to step into the dining-room." As Steavens rose, the lawyer said dryly: "You go on—it'll be a good experience for you, doubtless; as for me, I'm not equal to that crowd to-night; I've had twenty years of them."

As Steavens closed the door after him he glanced back at the lawyer, sitting by the coffin in the dim light, with his chin resting on his hand.

The same misty group that had stood before the door of the express car shuffled into the dining-room. In the light of the kerosene lamp they separated and became individuals. The minister, a pale, feeble-looking man with white hair and blond chin-whiskers, took his seat beside a small side table and placed his Bible upon it. The Grand Army man sat down behind the stove and tilted his chair back comfortably against the wall, fishing his quill toothpick from his waistcoat pocket. The two bankers, Phelps and Elder, sat off in a corner behind the dinner-table where they could finish their discussion of the new usury law and its effect on chattel security loans. The real estate agent, an old man with a smiling, hypocritical face, soon joined them. The coal and lumber dealer and the cattle shipper sat on opposite sides of the hard coal-burner, their feet on the nickel-work. Steavens took a book from his pocket and began to read. The talk around him ranged through various topics of local interest while the house was quieting down. When it was clear that the members of the family were in bed, the Grand Army man hitched his shoulders and, untangling his long legs, caught his heels on the rounds of his chair.

"S'pose there'll be a will, Phelps?" he queried in his weak falsetto.

The banker laughed disagreeably and began trimming his nails with a pearl-handled pocket-knife.

"There'll scarcely be any need for one, will there?" he queried in his turn.

The restless Grand Army man shifted his position again, getting his knees still nearer his chin. "Why, the ole man says Harve's done right well lately," he chirped.

The other banker spoke up. "I reckon he means by that Harve ain't asked him to mortgage any more farms lately, so as he could go on with his education."

"Seems like my mind don't reach back to a time when Harve wasn't bein' edycated," tittered the Grand Army man.

There was a general chuckle. The minister took out his handkerchief and blew his nose sonorously. Banker Phelps closed his knife with a snap. "It's too bad the old man's sons didn't turn out better," he remarked with reflective authority. "They never hung together. He spent money enough on Harve to stock a dozen cattle-farms and he might as well have poured it into Sand Creek. If Harve had stayed at home and helped nurse what little they had, and gone into stock on the old man's bottom farm, they might all have been well fixed. But the old man had to trust everything to tenants and was cheated right and left."

"Harve never could have handled stock none," interposed the cattleman. "He hadn't it in him to be sharp. Do you remember when he bought Sander's mules for eight-year-olds, when everybody in town knew that Sander's father-in-law give 'em to his wife for a wedding present eighteen years before, an' they was full-grown mules then."

Everyone chuckled, and the Grand Army man rubbed his knees with a spasm of childish delight.

"Harve never was much account for anything practical, and he shore was never fond of work," began the coal and lumber dealer. "I mind the last time he was home; the day he left, when the old man was out to the barn helpin' his hand hitch up to take Harve to the train, and Cal Moots was patchin' up the fence, Harve, he come out on the step and sings out, in his lady-like voice: 'Cal Moots, Cal Moots! please come cord my trunk.'"

"That's Harve for you," approved the Grand Army man gleefully. "I kin hear him howlin' yet when he was a big feller in long pants and his mother used to whale him with a rawhide in the barn for lettin' the cows git foundered in the cornfield when he was drivin' 'em home from pasture. He killed a cow of mine that-a-way onct— a pure Jersey and the best milker I had, an' the ole man had to put up for her. Harve, he was watchin' the sun set acrost the marshes when the anamile got away; he argued that sunset was oncommon fine."

"Where the old man made his mistake was in sending the boy East to school," said Phelps, stroking his goatee and speaking in a deliberate, judicial tone. "There was where he got his head full of trapesing to Paris and all such folly. What Harve needed, of all people, was a course in some first-class Kansas City business college."

The letters were swimming before Steavens's eyes. Was it possible that these men did not understand, that the palm on the coffin meant nothing to them? The very name of their town would have remained forever buried in the postal guide had it not been now and again mentioned in the world in connection with Harvey Merrick's. He remembered what his master had said to him on the day of his death, after the congestion of both lungs had shut off any probability of recovery, and the sculptor had asked his pupil to send his body home. "It's not a pleasant place to be lying while the world is moving and doing and bettering," he had said with a feeble smile, "but it rather seems as though we ought to go back to the place we came from in the end. The townspeople will come in for a look at me; and after they have had their say I shan't have much to fear from the judgment of God. The wings of the Victory, in there"—with a weak gesture toward his studio—"will not shelter me."

The cattleman took up the comment. "Forty's young for a Merrick to cash in; they usually hang on pretty well. Probably he helped it along with whisky."

"His mother's people were not long lived, and Harvey never had a robust constitution," said the minister mildly. He would have liked to say more. He had been the boy's Sunday-school teacher, and had been fond of him; but he felt that he was not in a position to speak. His own sons had turned out badly, and it was not a year since one of them had made his last trip home in the express car, shot in a gambling-house in the Black Hills.

"Nevertheless, there is no disputin' that Harve frequently looked upon the wine when it was red, also variegated, and it shore made an oncommon fool of him," moralized the cattleman.

Just then the door leading into the parlour rattled loudly, and everyone started involuntarily, looking relieved when only Jim Laird came out. His red face was convulsed with anger, and the Grand Army man ducked his head when he saw the spark in his blue, blood-shot eye. They were all afraid of Jim; he was a drunkard, but he could twist the law to suit his client's needs as no other man in all western

Kansas could do; and there were many who tried. The lawyer closed the door gently behind him, leaned back against it and folded his arms, cocking his head a little to one side. When he assumed this attitude in the court-room, ears were always pricked up, as it usually foretold a flood of withering sarcasm.

"I've been with you gentlemen before," he began in a dry, even tone, "when you've sat by the coffins of boys born and raised in this town; and, if I remember rightly, you were never any too well satisfied when you checked them up. What's the matter, anyhow? Why is it that reputable young men are as scarce as millionaires in Sand City? It might almost seem to a stranger that there was some way something the matter with your progressive town. Why did Ruben Sayer, the brightest young lawyer you ever turned out, after he had come home from the university as straight as a die, take to drinking and forge a check and shoot himself? Why did Bill Merrit's son die of the shakes in a saloon in Omaha? Why was Mr. Thomas's son, here, shot in a gambling-house? Why did young Adams burn his mill to beat the insurance companies and go to the pen?"

The lawyer paused and unfolded his arms, laying one clenched fist quietly on the table. "I'll tell you why. Because you drummed nothing but money and knavery into their ears from the time they wore knickerbockers; because you carped away at them as you've been carping here to-night, holding our friends Phelps and Elder up to them for their models, as our grandfathers held up George Washington and John Adams. But the boys, worse luck, were young, and raw at the business you put them to; and how could they match coppers with such artists as Phelps and Elder? You wanted them to be successful rascals; they were only unsuccessful ones—that's all the difference. There was only one boy ever raised in this borderland between ruffianism and civilization, who didn't come to grief, and you hated Harvey Merrick more for winning out than you hated all the other boys who got under the wheels. Lord, Lord, how you did hate him! Phelps, here, is fond of saying that he could buy and sell us all out any time he's a mind to; but he knew Harve wouldn't have given a tinker's damn for his bank and all his cattle-farms put together; and a lack of appreciation, that way, goes hard with Phelps.

"Old Nimrod, here, thinks Harve drank too much; and this from such as Nimrod and me!

"Brother Elder says Harve was too free with the old man's money—fell short in filial consideration, maybe. Well, we can all remember the very tone in which brother Elder swore his own father was a liar, in the county court; and we all know that the old man came out of that partnership with his son as bare as a sheared lamb. But maybe I'm getting personal, and I'd better be driving ahead at what I want to say."

The lawyer paused a moment, squared his heavy shoulders, and went on: "Harvey Merrick and I went to school together, back East. We were dead in earnest, and we wanted you all to be proud of us some day. We meant to be great men. Even I, and I haven't lost my sense of humour, gentlemen, I meant to be a great man. I came back here to practise, and I found you didn't in the least want me to be a great man. You wanted me to be a shrewd lawyer—oh, yes! Our veteran here wanted me to get him an increase of pension, because he had dyspepsia; Phelps wanted a new county survey that would put the widow Wilson's little bottom farm inside his south line; Elder wanted to lend money at 5 per cent a month, and get it collected; old Stark here wanted to wheedle old women up in Vermont into investing their annuities in real estate mortgages that are not worth the paper they are written on. Oh, you needed me hard enough, and you'll go on needing me; and that's why I'm not afraid to plug the truth home to you this once.

"Well, I came back here and became the damned shyster you wanted me to be. You pretend to have some sort of respect for me; and yet you'll stand up and throw mud at Harvey Merrick, whose soul you couldn't dirty and whose hands you couldn't tie. Oh, you're a discriminating lot of Christians! There have been times when the sight of Harvey's name in some Eastern paper has made me hang my head like a whipped dog; and, again, times when I liked to think of him off there in the world, away from all this hog-wallow, doing his great work and climbing the big, clean up-grade he'c set for himself.

"And we? Now that we've fought and lied and sweated and stolen, and hated as only the disappointed strugglers in a bitter, dead little Western town know how to do, what have we got to show for it? Harvey Merrick wouldn't have given one sunset over your marshes for all you've got put together, and you know it. It's not for me to say why, in the inscrutable wisdom of God, a genius should ever have been called from this place of hatred and bitter waters; but I want this Boston man to know that the drivel he's been hearing here to-night is the only tribute any truly great man could ever have from such a lot of sick, side-tracked, burnt-dog, land-poor sharks as the here-present financiers of Sand City—upon which town may God have mercy!"

The lawyer thrust out his hand to Steavens as he passed him, caught up his overcoat in the hall, and had left the house before the Grand Army man had had time to lift his ducked head and crane his long neck about at his fellows.

Next day Jim Laird was drunk and unable to attend the funeral services. Steavens called twice at his office, but was compelled to start East without seeing him. He had a presentiment that he would hear from him again, and left his address on the lawyer's table; but if Laird found it, he never acknowledged it. The thing in him that Harvey Merrick had loved must have gone underground with Harvey Merrick's coffin; for it never spoke again, and Jim got the cold he died of driving across the Colorado mountains to defend one of Phelps's sons who had got into trouble out there by cutting government timber.

1905

Jack London
1876–1916

One of the most popular and most highly paid writers of his time, Jack London was born in San Francisco on January 12, 1876, the illegitimate son of William Henry Chaney, an itinerant astrologer, and Flora Wellman, a spiritualist. He took the name of his stepfather, John London, an unsuccessful rancher who moved the family to Oakland in 1886. As London records in his autobiography, *John Barleycorn* (1913), he quit Oakland High School at fourteen and began a life of odd jobs, heavy drinking, and daring adventures: He earned money as an oyster pirate in San Francisco Bay, worked long hours in a cannery, frequented the

Oakland libraries and saloons, and sailed as an able-bodied seaman to Japan. In 1894 he tramped halfway across the country with Kelley's Industrial Army, a California group of unemployed who staged a protest march on Washington. This experience not only led to his long embrace of socialism but also impelled him, especially after being arrested for vagrancy in Buffalo, New York, to begin what he called his "frantic pursuit of knowledge." In 1896 he enrolled as a special student at the University of California at Berkeley, but after a semester he decided he would rather spend the winter prospecting for gold in the Klondike. He found no gold; instead he returned with experiences and material he would mine for a lifetime as a writer. His first collection of short stories, *The Son of the Wolf,* appeared in 1900.

Three years later he published a best-selling novel, *The Call of the Wild,* in which he attempted to enter into the consciousness of an animal: "There is an ecstasy that marks the summit of life and beyond which life cannot rise. . . . This ecstasy comes when one is most alive, and it comes as a complete forgetfulness that one is alive." London believed that such elemental and ecstatic forms of consciousness could also be attained by people, though mainly in moments of violent struggle with forces larger than themselves.

Though the drama of extremely reduced states of consciousness, as depicted in such famous London stories as "To Build a Fire," informs much of his writing, there is another side to London's work, one more dependent on Marxist economics than Darwinian biology. A year before *Call of the Wild* appeared, London spent six weeks disguised as an out-of-work American sailor roaming the slums of London's East End while he gathered material for the one book he claimed to love the most, *People of the Abyss* (1903). An indictment of capitalism and the class system, the book revealed an intellectual conflict in the writer that would become increasingly strained in his later work. London never satisfactorily reconciled his intense desire for social justice with his equally intense belief in the survival of the powerful. If his Marxism was tainted by an almost ferocious faith in individualism and racial superiority ("I am first of all a white man and only then a socialist"), his Darwinism was diluted by his affection for the underdog and his collectivist sympathies. Throughout his career, he alternated between the rugged individualism of Theodore Roosevelt and the quest for solidarity of Eugene Debs.

The main difficulty with London's personal philosophy, however, was not his inability to reconcile Darwin and Marx but his inability to extend his thoughts past their crudest formulations. He once wrote in a letter:

I assert, with Hobbes, that it is impossible to separate thought from matter that thinks.

I assert, with Bacon, that all human understanding arises from the world of sensations.

I assert, with Locke, that all human ideas are due to the functions of the senses.

I assert, with Kant, the mechanical origin of the universe, and that creation is a natural and historical process.

I assert, with Laplace, that there is no need of the hypothesis of a Creator.

This manifesto typifies the blunt style of London's thinking. He tended to see ideas in much the same way that he saw nature—as elemental forces to be reckoned with. Yet, like Rudyard Kipling, whom he greatly admired, London was a natural storyteller. In its narrative energy and mythic power, London's best writing transcends whatever philosophical slogans he set out to portray.

During the height of his popularity as a novelist, London continued to lead a strenuous and adventurous life. After completing one of his most successful novels, *The Sea Wolf,* in 1904, he went to Japan and Korea to cover the Russo-Japanese War for the Hearst papers. In 1905 he ran unsuccessfully for the second time as the Socialist candidate for mayor of Oakland. He published another successful novel, *White Fang,* in 1906 and wrote one of his most highly respected books, the semiautobiographical novel *Martin Eden,* in 1908 and 1909 while sailing his homemade yacht to the South Pacific. When the Mexican Revolution broke out in 1914, he rushed to Veracruz as a correspondent for *Collier's.* In 1915, exhausted and in failing health, he traveled to Hawaii, where during the day he produced hack work to keep up his dwindling fortune (he had made over a million dollars from his writing) and at night read Freud and Jung. Back in California, suffering from acute uremia, he injected a larger dose of painkilling morphine than he had been accustomed to and died early in the morning of November 22, 1916.

Further Reading:
P. Foner, *Jack London, American Rebel,* 1947.
E. Labor, *Jack London,* 1974.
J. McClintock, *White Logic: Jack London's Short Stories,* 1975.
A. Sinclair, *Jack: A Biography of Jack London,* 1977.
C. Watson, *The Novels of Jack London: A Reappraisal,* 1982.

Text:
Lost Face, 1910.

To Build a Fire[*]

Day had broken cold and gray, exceedingly cold and gray, when the man turned aside from the main Yukon trail and climbed the high earth-bank, where a dim and little-travelled trail led eastward through the fat spruce timberland. It was a steep bank, and he paused for breath at the top, excusing the act to himself by looking at his watch. It was nine o'clock. There was no sun nor hint of sun, though there was not a cloud in the sky. It was a clear day, and yet there seemed an intangible pall over the face of things, a subtle gloom that made the day dark, and that was due to the absence of sun. This fact did not worry the man. He was used to the lack of sun. It had been

[*] An earlier version of this story first appeared in *Youth's Companion* in May 1902.

days since he had seen the sun, and he knew that a few more days must pass before that cheerful orb, due south, would just peep above the sky line and dip immediately from view.

The man flung a look back along the way he had come. The Yukon lay a mile wide and hidden under three feet of ice. On top of this ice were as many feet of snow. It was all pure white, rolling in gentle undulations where the ice jams of the freeze-up had formed. North and south, as far as his eye could see, it was unbroken white, save for a dark hairline that curved and twisted from around the spruce-covered island to the south, and that curved and twisted away into the north, where it disappeared behind another spruce-covered island. This dark hairline was the trail—the main trail —that led south five hundred miles to the Chilcoot Pass, Dyea, and salt water; and that led north seventy miles to Dawson, and still on to the north a thousand miles to Nulato, and finally to St. Michael, on Bering Sea, a thousand miles and half a thousand more.

But all this—the mysterious, far-reaching hairline trail, the absence of sun from the sky, the tremendous cold, and the strangeness and weirdness of it all—made no impression on the man. It was not because he was long used to it. He was a newcomer in the land, a *chechaquo,* and this was his first winter. The trouble with him was that he was without imagination. He was quick and alert in the things of life, but only in the things, and not in the significances. Fifty degrees below zero meant eighty-odd degrees of frost. Such fact impressed him as being cold and uncomfortable, and that was all. It did not lead him to meditate upon his frailty as a creature of temperature, and upon man's frailty in general, able only to live within certain narrow limits of heat and cold; and from there on it did not lead him to the conjectural field of immortality and man's place in the universe. Fifty degrees below zero stood for a bite of frost that hurt and that must be guarded against by the use of mittens, ear flaps, warm moccasins, and thick socks. Fifty degrees below zero was to him just precisely fifty degrees below zero. That there should be anything more to it than that was a thought that never entered his head.

As he turned to go on, he spat speculatively. There was a sharp, explosive crackle that startled him. He spat again. And again, in the air, before it could fall to the snow, the spittle crackled. He knew that at fifty below spittle crackled on the snow, but this spittle had crackled in the air. Undoubtedly it was colder than fifty below—how much colder he did not know. But the temperature did not matter. He was bound for the old claim on the left fork of Henderson Creek, where the boys were already. They had come over across the divide from the Indian Creek country, while he had come the roundabout way to take a look at the possibilities of getting out logs in the spring from the islands in the Yukon. He would be in to camp by six o'clock; a bit after dark, it was true, but the boys would be there, a fire would be going, and a hot supper would be ready. As for lunch, he pressed his hand against the protruding bundle under his jacket. It was also under his shirt, wrapped up in a handkerchief and lying against the naked skin. It was the only way to keep the biscuits from freezing. He smiled agreeably to himself as he thought of those biscuits, each cut open and sopped in bacon grease, and each enclosing a generous slice of fried bacon.

He plunged in among the big spruce trees. The trail was faint. A foot of snow had fallen since the last sled had passed over, and he was glad he was without a sled, travelling light. In fact, he carried nothing but the lunch wrapped in the handkerchief.

He was surprised, however, at the cold. It certainly was cold, he concluded, as he rubbed his numb nose and cheekbones with his mittened hand. He was a warm-whiskered man, but the hair on his face did not protect the high cheekbones and the eager nose that thrust itself aggressively into the frosty air.

At the man's heels trotted a dog, a big native husky, the proper wolf dog, gray-coated and without any visible or temperamental difference from its brother, the wild wolf. The animal was depressed by the tremendous cold. It knew that it was no time for travelling. Its instinct told it a truer tale than was told to the man by the man's judgment. In reality, it was not merely colder than fifty below zero; it was colder than sixty below, than seventy below. It was seventy-five below zero. Since the freezing point is thirty-two above zero, it meant that one hundred and seven degrees of frost obtained. The dog did not know anything about thermometers. Possibly in its brain there was no sharp consciousness of a condition of very cold such as was in the man's brain. But the brute had its instinct. It experienced a vague but menacing apprehension that subdued it and made it slink along at the man's heels, and that made it question eagerly every unwonted movement of the man as if expecting him to go into camp or to seek shelter somewhere and build a fire. The dog had learned fire, and it wanted fire, or else to burrow under the snow and cuddle its warmth away from the air.

The frozen moisture of its breathing had settled on its fur in a fine powder of frost, and especially were its jowls, muzzle, and eyelashes whitened by its crystalled breath. The man's red beard and mustache were likewise frosted, but more solidly, the deposit taking the form of ice and increasing with every warm, moist breath he exhaled. Also, the man was chewing tobacco, and the muzzle of ice held his lips so rigidly that he was unable to clear his chin when he expelled the juice. The result was that a crystal beard of the color and solidity of amber was increasing its length on his chin. If he fell down it would shatter itself, like glass, into brittle fragments. But he did not mind the appendage. It was the penalty all tobacco chewers paid in that country, and he had been out before in two cold snaps. They had not been so cold as this, he knew, but by the spirit thermometer at Sixty Mile he knew they had been registered at fifty below and at fifty-five.

He held on through the level stretch of woods for several miles, crossed a wide flat of nigger heads, and dropped down a bank to the frozen bed of a small stream. This was Henderson Creek, and he knew he was ten miles from the forks. He looked at his watch. It was ten o'clock. He was making four miles an hour, and he calculated that he would arrive at the forks at half-past twelve. He decided to celebrate that event by eating his lunch there.

The dog dropped in again at his heels, with a tail drooping discouragement, as the man swung along the creek bed. The furrow of the old sled trail was plainly visible, but a dozen inches of snow covered the marks of the last runners. In a month no man had come up or down that silent creek. The man held steadily on. He was not much given to thinking, and just then particularly he had nothing to think about save that he would eat lunch at the forks and that at six o'clock he would be in camp with the boys. There was nobody to talk to; and, had there been, speech would have been impossible because of the ice muzzle on his mouth. So he continued monotonously to chew tobacco and to increase the length of his amber beard.

Once in a while the thought reiterated itself that it was very cold and that he had never experienced such cold. As he walked along he rubbed his cheekbones and nose with the back of his mittened hand. He did this automatically, now and again changing hands. But, rub as he would, the instant he stopped his cheekbones went numb, and the following instant the end of his nose went numb. He was sure to frost his cheeks; he knew that, and experienced a pang of regret that he had not devised a nose strap of the sort Bud wore in cold snaps. Such a strap passed across the cheeks, as well, and saved them. But it didn't matter much, after all. What were frosted cheeks? A bit painful, that was all; they were never serious.

Empty as the man's mind was of thoughts, he was keenly observant, and he noticed the changes in the creek, the curves and bends and timber jams, and always he sharply noted where he placed his feet. Once, coming around a bend, he shied abruptly, like a startled horse, curved away from the place where he had been walking, and retreated several paces back along the trail. The creek he knew was frozen clear to the bottom —no creek could contain water in that arctic winter—but he knew also that there were springs that bubbled out from the hillsides and ran along under the snow and on top the ice of the creek. He knew that the coldest snaps never froze these springs, and he knew likewise their danger. They were traps. They hid pools of water under the snow that might be three inches deep, or three feet. Sometimes a skin of ice half an inch thick covered them, and in turn was covered by the snow. Sometimes there were alternate layers of water and ice skin, so that when one broke through he kept on breaking through for a while, sometimes wetting himself to the waist.

That was why he had shied in such panic. He had felt the give under his feet and heard the crackle of a snow-hidden ice skin. And to get his feet wet in such a temperature meant trouble and danger. At the very least it meant delay, for he would be forced to stop and build a fire, and under its protection to bare his feet while he dried his socks and moccasins. He stood and studied the creek bed and its banks, and decided that the flow of water came from the right. He reflected awhile, rubbing his nose and cheeks, then skirted to the left, stepping gingerly and testing the footing for each step. Once clear of the danger, he took a fresh chew of tobacco and swung along at his four-mile gait.

In the course of the next two hours he came upon several similar traps. Usually the snow above the hidden pools had a sunken, candied appearance that advertised the danger. Once again, however, he had a close call; and once, suspecting danger, he compelled the dog to go on in front. The dog did not want to go. It hung back until the man shoved it forward, and then it went quickly across the white, unbroken surface. Suddenly it broke through, floundered to one side, and got away to firmer footing. It had wet its forefeet and legs, and almost immediately the water that clung to it turned to ice. It made quick efforts to lick the ice off its legs, then dropped down in the snow and began to bite out the ice that had formed between the toes. This was matter of instinct. To permit the ice to remain would mean sore feet. It did not know this. It merely obeyed the mysterious prompting that arose from the deep crypts of its being. But the man knew, having achieved a judgment on the subject, and he removed the mitten from his right hand and helped tear out the ice particles. He did not expose his fingers more than a minute, and was astonished at the swift numbness that smote them. It certainly was cold. He pulled on the mitten hastily, and beat the hand savagely across his chest.

At twelve o'clock the day was at its brightest. Yet the sun was too far south on its winter journey to clear the horizon. The bulge of the earth intervened between it and Henderson Creek, where the man walked under a clear sky at noon and cast no shadow. At half-past twelve, to the minute, he arrived at the forks of the creek. He was pleased at the speed he had made. If he kept it up, he would certainly be with the boys by six. He unbuttoned his jacket and shirt and drew forth his lunch. The action consumed no more than a quarter of a minute, yet in that brief moment the numbness laid hold of the exposed fingers. He did not put the mitten on, but, instead, struck the fingers a dozen sharp smashes against his leg. Then he sat down on a snow-covered log to eat. The sting that followed upon the striking of his fingers against his leg ceased so quickly that he was startled. He had had no chance to take a bit of biscuit. He struck the fingers repeatedly and returned them to the mitten, baring the other hand for the purpose of eating. He tried to take a mouthful, but the ice muzzle prevented. He had forgotten to build a fire and thaw out. He chuckled at his foolishness, and as he chuckled he noted the numbness creeping into the exposed fingers. Also, he noted that the stinging which had first come to his toes when he sat down was already passing away. He wondered whether the toes were warm or numb. He moved them inside the moccasins and decided that they were numb.

He pulled the mitten on hurriedly and stood up. He was a bit frightened. He stamped up and down until the stinging returned into the feet. It certainly was cold, was his thought. That man from Sulphur Creek had spoken the truth when telling how cold it sometimes got in the country. And he had laughed at him at the time! That showed one must not be too sure of things. There was no mistake about it, it was cold. He strode up and down, stamping his feet and threshing his arms, until reassured by the returning warmth. Then he got out matches and proceeded to make a fire. From the undergrowth, where high water of the previous spring had lodged a supply of seasoned twigs, he got his firewood. Working carefully from a small beginning, he soon had a roaring fire, over which he thawed the ice from his face and in the protection of which he ate his biscuits. For the moment the cold of space was outwitted. The dog took satisfaction in the fire, stretching out close enough for warmth and far enough away to escape being singed.

When the man had finished, he filled his pipe and took his comfortable time over a smoke. Then he pulled on his mittens, settled the ear flaps of his cap firmly about his ears, and took the creek trail up the left fork. The dog was disappointed and yearned back toward the fire. This man did not know cold. Possibly all the generations of his ancestry had been ignorant of cold, of real cold, of cold one hundred and seven degrees below freezing point. But the dog knew; all its ancestry knew, and it had inherited the knowledge. And it knew that it was not good to walk abroad in such fearful cold. It was the time to lie snug in a hole in the snow and wait for a curtain of cloud to be drawn across the face of outer space whence this cold came. On the other hand, there was no keen intimacy between the dog and the man. The one was the toil slave of the other, and the only caresses it had ever received were the caresses of the whip lash and of harsh and menacing throat sounds that threatened the whip lash. So the dog made no effort to communicate its apprehension to the man. It was not concerned in the welfare of the man; it was for its own sake that it yearned back toward the fire. But the man whistled, and spoke to it with the sound of whip lashes, and the dog swung in at the man's heels and followed after.

The man took a chew of tobacco and proceeded to start a new amber beard. Also, his moist breath quickly powdered with white his mustache, eyebrows, and lashes. There did not seem to be so many springs on the left fork of the Henderson, and for half an hour the man saw no signs of any. And then it happened. At a place where there were no signs, where the soft, unbroken snow seemed to advertise solidity beneath, the man broke through. It was not deep. He wet himself halfway to the knees before he floundered out to the firm crust.

He was angry, and cursed his luck aloud. He had hoped to get into camp with the boys at six o'clock, and this would delay him an hour, for he would have to build a fire and dry out his footgear. This was imperative at that low temperature—he knew that much; and he turned aside to the bank, which he climbed. On top, tangled in the underbrush about the trunks of several small spruce trees, was a highwater deposit of dry firewood—sticks and twigs, principally, but also larger portions of seasoned branches and fine, dry, last year's grasses. He threw down several large pieces on top of the snow. This served for a foundation and prevented the young flame from drowning itself in the snow it otherwise would melt. The flame he got by touching a match to a small shred of birch bark that he took from his pocket. This burned even more readily than paper. Placing it on the foundation, he fed the young flame with wisps of dry grass and with the tiniest dry twigs.

He worked slowly and carefully, keenly aware of his danger. Gradually, as the flame grew stronger, he increased the size of the twigs with which he fed it. He squatted in the snow, pulling the twigs out from their entanglement in the brush and feeding directly to the flame. He knew there must be no failure. When it is seventy-five below zero, a man must not fail in his first attempt to build a fire—that is, if his feet are wet. If his feet are dry, and he fails, he can run along the trail for half a mile and restore his circulation. But the circulation of wet and freezing feet cannot be restored by running when it is seventy-five below. No matter how fast he runs, the wet feet will freeze the harder. All this the man knew. The old-timer on Sulphur Creek had told him about it the previous fall, and now he was appreciating the advice. Already all sensation had gone out of his feet. To build the fire he had been forced to remove his mittens, and the fingers had quickly gone numb. His pace of four miles an hour had kept his heart pumping blood to the surface of his body and to all the extremities. But the instant he stopped, the action of the pump eased down. The cold of space smote the unprotected tip of the planet, and he, being on that unprotected tip, received the full force of the blow. The blood of his body recoiled before it. The blood was alive, like the dog, and like the dog it wanted to hide away and cover itself up from the fearful cold. So long as he walked four miles an hour, he pumped that blood, willy-nilly, to the surface; but now it ebbed away and sank down into the recesses of his body. The extremities were the first to feel its absence. His wet feet froze the faster, and his exposed fingers numbed the faster, though they had not yet begun to freeze. Nose and cheeks were already freezing, while the skin of all his body chilled as it lost its blood.

But he was safe. Toes and nose and cheeks would be only touched by the frost, for the fire was beginning to burn with strength. He was feeding it with twigs the size of his finger. In another minute he would be able to feed it with branches the size of his wrist, and then he could remove his wet footgear, and, while it dried, he could keep his naked feet warm by the fire, rubbing them at first, of course, with snow. The fire was a success. He was safe. He remembered the advice of the old-timer on

Sulphur Creek, and smiled. The old-timer had been very serious in laying down the law that no man must travel alone in the Klondike after fifty below. Well, here he was; he had had the accident; he was alone; and he had saved himself. Those old-timers were rather womanish, some of them, he thought. All a man had to do was to keep his head, and he was all right. Any man who was a man could travel alone. But it was surprising, the rapidity with which his cheeks and nose were freezing. And he had not thought his fingers could go lifeless in so short a time. Lifeless they were, for he could scarcely make them move together to grip a twig, and they seemed remote from his body and from him. When he touched a twig, he had to look and see whether or not he had hold of it. The wires were pretty well down between him and his finger ends.

All of which counted for little. There was the fire, snapping and crackling and promising life with every dancing flame. He started to untie his moccasins. They were coated with ice; the thick German socks were like sheaths of iron halfway to the knees; and the moccasin strings were like rods of steel all twisted and knotted as by some conflagration. For a moment he tugged with his numb fingers, then, realizing the folly of it, he drew his sheath knife.

But before he could cut the strings, it happened. It was his own fault or, rather, his mistake. He should not have built the fire under the spruce tree. He should have built it in the open. But it had been easier to pull the twigs from the brush and drop them directly on the fire. Now the tree under which he had done this carried a weight of snow on its boughs. No wind had blown for weeks, and each bough was fully freighted. Each time he had pulled a twig he had communicated a slight agitation to the tree—an imperceptible agitation, so far as he was concerned, but an agitation sufficient to bring about the disaster. High up in the tree one bough capsized its load of snow. This fell on the boughs beneath, capsizing them. This process continued, spreading out and involving the whole tree. It grew like an avalanche, and it descended without warning upon the man and the fire, and the fire was blotted out! Where it had burned was a mantle of fresh and disordered snow.

The man was shocked. It was as though he had just heard his own sentence of death. For a moment he sat and stared at the spot where the fire had been. Then he grew very calm. Perhaps the old-timer on Sulphur Creek was right. If he had only had a trail mate he would have been in no danger now. The trail mate could have built the fire. Well, it was up to him to build the fire over again, and this second time there must be no failure. Even if he succeeded, he would most likely lose some toes. His feet must be badly frozen by now, and there would be some time before the second fire was ready.

Such were his thoughts, but he did not sit and think them. He was busy all the time they were passing through his mind. He made a new foundation for a fire, this time in the open, where no treacherous tree could blot it out. Next he gathered dry grasses and tiny twigs from the highwater flotsam. He could not bring his fingers together to pull them out, but he was able to gather them by the handful. In this way he got many rotten twigs and bits of green moss that were undesirable, but it was the best he could do. He worked methodically, even collecting an armful of the larger branches to be used later when the fire gathered strength. And all the while the dog sat and watched him, a certain yearning wistfulness in its eyes, for it looked upon him as the fire provider, and the fire was slow in coming.

When all was ready, the man reached in his pocket for a second piece of birch bark. He knew the bark was there, and, though he could not feel it with his fingers, he could hear its crisp rustling as he fumbled for it. Try as he would, he could not clutch hold of it. And all the time, in his consciousness, was the knowledge that each instant his feet were freezing. This thought tended to put him in a panic, but he fought against it and kept calm. He pulled on his mittens with his teeth, and threshed his arms back and forth, beating his hands with all his might against his sides. He did this sitting down, and he stood up to do it; and all the while the dog sat in the snow, its wolf brush of a tail curled around warmly over its forefeet, its sharp wolf ears pricked forward intently as it watched the man. And the man, as he beat and threshed with his arms and hands, felt a great surge of envy as he regarded the creature that was warm and secure in its natural covering.

After a time he was aware of the first faraway signals of sensation in his beaten fingers. The faint tingling grew stronger till it evolved into a stinging ache that was excruciating, but which the man hailed with satisfaction. He stripped the mitten from his right hand and fetched forth the birch bark. The exposed fingers were quickly going numb again. Next he brought out his bunch of sulphur matches. But the tremendous cold had already driven the life out of his fingers. In his effort to separate one match from the others, the whole bunch fell in the snow. He tried to pick it out of the snow, but failed. The dead fingers could neither touch nor clutch. He was very careful. He drove the thought of his freezing feet, and nose, and cheeks, out of his mind, devoting his whole soul to the matches. He watched, using the sense of vision in place of that of touch, and when he saw his fingers on each side the bunch, he closed them—that is, he willed to close them, for the wires were down, and the fingers did not obey. He pulled the mitten on the right hand, and beat it fiercely against his knee. Then, with both mittened hands, he scooped the bunch of matches, along with much snow, into his lap. Yet he was no better off.

After some manipulation he managed to get the bunch between the heels of his mittened hands. In this fashion he carried it to his mouth. The ice crackled and snapped when by a violent effort he opened his mouth. He drew the lower jaw in, curled the upper lip out of the way, and scraped the bunch with his upper teeth in order to separate a match. He succeeded in getting one, which he dropped on his lap. He was no better off. He could not pick it up. Then he devised a way. He picked it up in his teeth and scratched it on his leg. Twenty times he scratched before he succeeded in lighting it. As it flamed he held it with his teeth to the birch bark. But the burning brimstone went up his nostrils and into his lungs, causing him to cough spasmodically. The match fell into the snow and went out.

The old-timer on Sulphur Creek was right, he thought in the moment of controlled despair that ensued: after fifty below, a man should travel with a partner. He beat his hands, but failed in exciting any sensation. Suddenly he bared both hands, removing the mittens with his teeth. He caught the whole bunch between the heels of his hands. His arm muscles not being frozen enabled him to press the hand heels tightly against the matches. Then he scratched the bunch along his leg. It flared into flame, seventy sulphur matches at once! There was no wind to blow them out. He kept his head to one side to escape the strangling fumes, and held the blazing bunch to the birch bark. As he so held it, he became aware of sensation in his hand. His flesh was burning. He could smell it. Deep down below the surface he could feel it. The sensation developed into pain that grew acute. And still he endured it, holding the flame of the matches clumsily to the bark that would not light readily because his own burning hands were in the way, absorbing most of the flame.

At last, when he could endure no more, he jerked his hands apart. The blazing matches fell sizzling into the snow, but the birch bark was alight. He began laying dry grasses and the tiniest twigs on the flame. He could not pick and choose, for he had to lift the fuel between the heels of his hands. Small pieces of rotten wood and green moss clung to the twigs, and he bit them off as well as he could with his teeth. He cherished the flame carefully and awkwardly. It meant life, and it must not perish. The withdrawal of blood from the surface of his body now made him begin to shiver, and he grew more awkward. A large piece of green moss fell squarely on the little fire. He tried to poke it out with his fingers, but his shivering frame made him poke too far, and he disrupted the nucleus of the little fire, the burning grasses and tiny twigs separating and scattering. He tried to poke them together again, but in spite of the tenseness of the effort, his shivering got away with him, and the twigs were hopelessly scattered. Each twig gushed a puff of smoke and went out. The fire provider had failed. As he looked apathetically about him, his eyes chanced on the dog, sitting across the ruins of the fire from him, in the snow, making restless, hunching movements, slightly lifting one forefoot and then the other, shifting its weight back and forth on them with wistful eagerness.

The sight of the dog put a wild idea into his head. He remembered the tale of the man, caught in a blizzard, who killed a steer and crawled inside the carcass, and so was saved. He would kill the dog and bury his hands in the warm body until the numbness went out of them. Then he could build another fire. He spoke to the dog, calling it to him; but in his voice was a strange note of fear that frightened the animal, who had never known the man to speak in such way before. Something was the matter, and its suspicious nature sensed danger—it knew not what danger, but somewhere, somehow, in its brain arose an apprehension of the man. It flattened its ears down at the sound of the man's voice, and its restless, hunching movements and the liftings and shiftings of its forefeet became more pronounced; but it would not come to the man. He got on his hands and knees and crawled toward the dog. This unusual posture again excited suspicion, and the animal sidled mincingly away.

The man sat up in the snow for a moment and struggled for calmness. Then he pulled on his mittens, by means of his teeth, and got upon his feet. He glanced down at first in order to assure himself that he was really standing up, for the absence of sensation in his feet left him unrelated to the earth. His erect position in itself started to drive the webs of suspicion from the dog's mind; and when he spoke peremptorily, with the sound of whip lashes in his voice, the dog rendered its customary allegiance and came to him. As it came within reaching distance, the man lost his control. His arms flashed out to the dog, and he experienced genuine surprise when he discovered that his hands could not clutch, that there was neither bend nor feeling in the fingers. He had forgotten for the moment that they were frozen and that they were freezing more and more. All this happened quickly, and before the animal could get away, he encircled its body with his arms. He sat down in the snow, and in this fashion held the dog, while it snarled and whined and struggled.

But it was all he could do, hold its body encircled in his arms and sit there. He realized that he could not kill the dog. There was no way to do it. With his helpless hands he could neither draw nor hold his sheath knife nor throttle the animal. He released it, and it plunged wildly away, with tail between its legs, and still snarling. It halted forty feet away and surveyed him curiously, with ears sharply pricked forward.

The man looked down at his hands in order to locate them, and found them hanging on the ends of his arms. It struck him as curious that one should have to use his eyes in order to find out where his hands were. He began threshing his arms back and forth, beating the mittened hands against his sides. He did this for five minutes, violently, and his heart pumped enough blood up to the surface to put a stop to his shivering. But no sensation was aroused in the hands. He had an impression that they hung like weights on the ends of his arms, but when he tried to run the impression down, he could not find it.

A certain fear of death, dull and oppressive, came to him. This fear quickly became poignant as he realized that it was no longer a mere matter of freezing his fingers and toes, or of losing his hands and feet, but that it was a matter of life and death with the chances against him. This threw him into a panic, and he turned and ran up the creek bed along the old, dim trail. The dog joined in behind and kept up with him. He ran blindly, without intention, in fear such as he had never known in his life. Slowly, as he plowed and floundered through the snow, he began to see things again —the banks of the creek, the old timber jams, the leafless aspens, and the sky. The running made him feel better. He did not shiver. Maybe, if he ran on, his feet would thaw out; and, anyway, if he ran far enough, he would reach camp and the boys. Without doubt he would lose some fingers and toes and some of his face; but the boys would take care of him, and save the rest of him when he got there. And at the same time there was another thought in his mind that said he would never get to the camp and the boys; that it was too many miles away, that the freezing had too great a start on him, and that he would soon be stiff and dead. This thought he kept in the background and refused to consider. Sometimes it pushed itself forward and demanded to be heard, but he thrust it back and strove to think of other things.

It struck him as curious that he could run at all on feet so frozen that he could not feel them when they struck the earth and took the weight of his body. He seemed to himself to skim along above the surface, and to have no connection with the earth. Somewhere he had once seen a winged Mercury, and he wondered if Mercury felt as he felt when skimming over the earth.

His theory of running until he reached camp and the boys had one flaw in it: he lacked the endurance. Several times he stumbled, and finally he tottered, crumpled up, and fell. When he tried to rise, he failed. He must sit and rest, he decided, and next time he would merely walk and keep on going. As he sat and regained his breath, he noted that he was feeling quite warm and comfortable. He was not shivering, and it even seemed that a warm glow had come to his chest and trunk. And yet, when he touched his nose or cheeks, there was no sensation. Running would not thaw them out. Nor would it thaw out his hands and feet. Then the thought came to him that the frozen portions of his body must be extending. He tried to keep this thought down, to forget it, to think of something else; he was aware of the panicky feeling that it caused, and he was afraid of the panic. But the thought asserted itself, and persisted, until it produced a vision of his body totally frozen. This was too much, and he made another wild run along the trail. Once he slowed down to a walk, but the thought of the freezing extending itself made him run again.

And all the time the dog ran with him, at his heels. When he fell down a second time, it curled its tail over its forefeet and sat in front of him, facing him, curiously eager and intent. The warmth and security of the animal angered him, and he cursed it till it flattened down its ears appeasingly. This time the shivering came more quickly upon the man. He was losing in his battle with the frost. It was creeping into his body from all sides. The thought of it drove him on, but he ran no more than a hundred feet, when he staggered and pitched headlong. It was his last panic. When he had recovered his breath and control, he sat up and entertained in his mind the conception of meeting death with dignity. However, the conception did not come to him in such terms. His idea of it was that he had been making a fool of himself, running around like a chicken with its head cut off—such was the simile that occurred to him. Well, he was bound to freeze anyway, and he might as well take it decently. With this new-found peace of mind came the first glimmerings of drowsiness. A good idea, he thought, to sleep off to death. It was like taking an anesthetic. Freezing was not so bad as people thought. There were lots worse ways to die.

He pictured the boys finding his body next day. Suddenly he found himself with them, coming along the trail and looking for himself. And, still with them, he came around a turn in the trail and found himself lying in the snow. He did not belong with himself any more, for even then he was out of himself, standing with the boys and looking at himself in the snow. It certainly was cold, was his thought. When he got back to the States he could tell the folks what real cold was. He drifted on from this to a vision of the old-timer on Sulphur Creek. He could see him quite clearly, warm and comfortable, and smoking a pipe.

"You were right, old hoss; you were right," the man mumbled to the old-timer of Sulphur Creek.

Then the man drowsed off into what seemed to him the most comfortable and satisfying sleep he had ever known. The dog sat facing him and waiting. The brief day drew to a close in a long, slow twilight. There were no signs of a fire to be made, and, besides, never in the dog's experience had it known a man to sit like that in the snow and make no fire. As the twilight drew on, its eager yearning for the fire mastered it, and with a great lifting and shifting of forefeet, it whined softly, then flattened its ears down in anticipation of being chidden by the man. But the man remained silent. Later the dog whined loudly. And still later it crept close to the man and caught the scent of death. This made the animal bristle and back away. A little longer it delayed, howling under the stars that leaped and danced and shone brightly in the cold sky. Then it turned and trotted up the trail in the direction of the camp it knew, where were the other food providers and fire providers.

1908

The Literature of Modernism: Prose 1912–1940

 American writers of the early twentieth century were born into a society that was still young and a culture that was still raw. In 1890, the year in which Gertrude Stein turned sixteen and Sherwood Anderson turned fourteen, the great Sioux chief Sitting Bull died. Throughout the 1890s, the decade in which William Faulkner, F. Scott Fitzgerald, and Ernest Hemingway were born, the United States remained on the circumference of civilization. It had no palaces or castles, Henry James once noted, no cathedrals or abbeys or ivied ruins. Even its thriving cities were less elegant than those of Europe. Americans took pride in the achievement of their painters (from Benjamin West in the late eighteenth century to James McNeill Whistler in the late nineteenth) and their writers (from Edgar Allan Poe through Nathaniel Hawthorne to Mark Twain and Henry James), but they knew that their life remained comparatively crude, their art and literature comparatively thin.

To balance their sense of cultural inferiority, Americans held tightly to a sense of social and moral superiority. Many Americans respected—and some envied—Europe for its rich culture. But they scorned Europe's accumulated strata of gentility—piled, Henry James wrote, "upwards into vague regions of privilege"—and they condemned its wickedness and weariness. Even parents who sent their children to tour Europe or study there sought first to inoculate

Grant Wood,
Stone City, Iowa,
oil on canvas, 1930.
Joslyn Art Museum,
Omaha, Nebraska.

Archibald J. Motley, Jr.,
Chicken Shack,
oil on canvas, 1936.
National Archives,
Washington, D.C.

"This Vast Shaggy Continent"

The church-going classes . . . form the backbone of philanthropic social interest, of social reform through political action, of pacifism, of popular education. They embody and express the spirit of kindly goodwill towards classes which are at an economic disadvantage and towards other nations, especially when the latter show any disposition towards a republican form of government. The Middle West, the prairie country, has been the centre of active social philanthropy and political progressivism because it is the chief home of this folk.

John Dewey, "The American Intellectual Frontier" (1922)

Into this vast shaggy continent of ours poured the first feeble tide of European settlement. European men, institutions, and ideas were lodged in the American wilderness, and this great American West took them to her bosom, taught them a new way of looking upon the destiny of the common man, trained them in adaptation to the conditions of the New World, to the creation of new institutions to meet new needs; and ever as society on her eastern border grew to resemble the Old World in its social forms and its industry, ever, as it began to lose faith in the ideal of democracy, she opened new provinces, and dowered new democracies in her most distant domains with her material treasures and with the ennobling influence that the fierce love of freedom, the strength that came from hewing out a home, making a school and a church, and creating a higher future for his family, furnished to the pioneer.

Frederick Jackson Turner, The Frontier in American History (1920)

them against Europe's decadence. However crude and raw American culture might be, its "triumphant democracy" (to borrow the title of Andrew Carnegie's celebration of America) was a model of some things and proof of others: a model of political freedom, economic opportunity, and moral rectitude and proof that to remain young and vigorous a society must remain open and democratic. In a famous address delivered in Chicago at the American Historical Association in 1893, Frederick Jackson Turner announced that American democracy drew its force not from its European heritage but from its frontier experience. Twenty years later, on June 17, 1914, Turner reiterated his celebrated announcement: "American democracy was born of no theorist's dream; it was not carried in the *Susan Constant* to Virginia, nor in the *Mayflower* to Plymouth. It came stark and strong and full of life out of the American forest, and it gained new strength each time it touched a new frontier."

To live on the edge of civilization was, then, from an American point of view, to be blessed as well as deprived. Writing in the mid-nineteenth century, Henry David Thoreau captured America's characteristic ambivalence in an epigraph: "I love the wild not less than the good." Americans sometimes attributed their energy and good hope—twin tokens of superiority—to their close ties to nature, their proximity to the frontier, or their love of the wild, sometimes to what Henry James called the overriding "importance of the individual in the American world," and sometimes to the continuing presence of divine favor. But since they regarded these things as interrelated and interdependent, they also saw youth and simplicity rather than age and sophistication as the bedrock of America's strength. American culture might be raw, but American society was vital, its future assured: "The old nations of the earth creep at a snail's pace," Andrew Carnegie wrote in 1886; "the Republic thunders past with the rush of the express." As they spread across the continent, furthermore, and then later began the long trek from the soil of their farms to the sidewalks of their cities, they carried their convictions with them. The ambivalence that New Englanders learned early to feel toward Europe, mixing a sense of cultural inferiority with a sense of social and moral superiority, westerners came to feel toward easterners and rural folk toward city dwellers.

"The East Was Haunted for Me"

When I came back from the East last autumn I felt that I wanted the world to be in uniform and at a sort of moral attention forever. . . .

Even when the East excited me most, even when I was most keenly aware of its superiority to the bored, sprawling, swollen towns beyond the Ohio, with their interminable inquisitions which spared only the children and the very old —even then it had always for me a quality of distortion. West Egg, especially, still figures in my more fantastic dreams. I see it as a night scene by El Greco: a hundred houses, at once conventional and grotesque, crouching under a sullen, overhanging sky and a lustreless moon. In the foreground four solemn men in dress suits are walking along the sidewalk with a stretcher on which lies a drunken woman in a white evening dress. Her hand, which dangles over the side, sparkles cold with jewels. Gravely the men turn in at a house—the wrong house. But no one knows the woman's name, and no one cares.

After Gatsby's death the East was haunted for me like that, distorted beyond my eyes' power of correction. So when the blue smoke of brittle leaves was in the air and the wind blew the wet laundry stiff on the line I decided to come back home.

F. Scott Fitzgerald, *The Great Gatsby* (1925)

The Transformation of American Culture

By the early twentieth century, the waves of immigration that had diversified American society were also diversifying its literature. In 1908, Israel Zangwill's play *The Melting-Pot* became a major hit in New York. Although some writers of the early twentieth century came from established communities along the eastern seaboard, many came from out-of-the-way places and diverse backgrounds. Abraham Cahan (1860–1951), Gertrude Stein (1874–1946), Nathanael West (1903–1940), and Henry Roth (b. 1906) became the first major Jewish writers of American literature. Writers were more likely to be poor, more likely to be female, and more likely to be black. They came from the South: William Faulkner and Richard Wright from Mississippi, Thomas Wolfe from North Carolina, Zora Neale Hurston from Florida. They came from California, like John Steinbeck, or even from remote frontier communities like Indian Creek, Texas, the birthplace of Katherine Anne Porter. Above all they came from the Midwest: a few from its cities, John Dos Passos from Chicago and F. Scott Fitzgerald from St. Paul, and scores from its smaller

---

I Pray Thee Ask No Questions. This Is That Golden Land.

The small white steamer, *Peter Stuyvesant,* that delivered the immigrants from the stench and throb of the steerage to the stench and the throb of New York tenements, rolled slightly on the water beside the stone quay in the lee of the weathered barracks and new brick buildings of Ellis Island. Her skipper was waiting for the last of the officials, laborers and guards to embark upon her before he cast off and started for Manhattan. . . .

It was May of the year 1907, the year that was destined to bring the greatest number of immigrants to the shores of the United States. All that day, as on all the days since spring began, her decks had been thronged by hundreds upon hundreds of foreigners, natives from almost every land in the world, the jowled close-cropped Teuton, the full-bearded Russian, the scraggly-whiskered Jew, and among them Slovack peasants with docile faces, smooth-cheeked and swarthy Armenians, pimply Greeks, Danes with wrinkled eyelids. All day her decks had been colorful, a matrix of the vivid costumes of other lands, the speckled green-and-yellow aprons, the flowered kerchief, embroidered homespun, the silver-braided sheepskin vest, the gaudy scarfs, yellow boots, fur caps, caftans, dull gabardines. All day the guttural, the high-pitched voices, the astonished cries, the gasps of wonder, reiterations of gladness had risen from her decks in a motley billow of sound. But now her decks were empty, quiet, spreading out under the sunlight almost as if the warm boards were relaxing from the strain and the pressure of the myriads of feet.

Henry Roth, prologue to *Call It Sleep* (1934)

communities. Sherwood Anderson was born in Camden, Ohio; Sinclair Lewis, in Sauk Center, Minnesota; Ernest Hemingway, in Oak Park, Illinois; and Langston Hughes, in Joplin, Missouri. "The Middle West," Ford Madox Ford wrote from Paris, "was seething with literary impulse."

Together these writers transformed the cultural landscape of America and enlarged its cultural role. In the same years in which the United States was emerging as a world power, its writers were becoming a major force in the development of literary modernism. In addition to producing remarkable literature, writers like T. S. Eliot, Gertrude Stein, and Ernest Hemingway began playing prominent roles in the cultural affairs of London and Paris. At the same time, however, they reclaimed native literary traditions and transformed colloquial American English into a medium for serious fiction. "All modern American literature," Ernest Hemingway asserted, evoking America's colloquial tradition, "comes from one book by Mark Twain called *Huckleberry Finn.*"

The reassessment of American literature that began with W. C. Brownell's *American Prose Masters* (1909) and John Macy's *The Spirit of American Literature* (1913) continued through Van Wyck Brooks's *America's Coming of Age* (1915) and Waldo Frank's *Our America* (1919) to produce two works of lasting value— D. H. Lawrence's *Studies in Classic American Literature* (1922) and Lewis Mumford's *The Golden Day* (1926). Through this broad reassessment, Emily Dickinson was discovered, Herman Melville was rediscovered, and writers from James Fenimore Cooper to Mark Twain and Henry James were reinterpreted. Simultaneously, Stein and Anderson inaugurated a remarkable flowering of American fiction that culminated in the work of Faulkner, Fitzgerald, Hemingway and scores of other writers. Theirs was, as the distinguished French critic Claude-Edmonde Magny called it, *L'Age du roman américain* ("The Age of the American Novel").

The Age of the American Novel

These youngsters are attempting a first-hand examination of the national scene, and making an effort to represent it in terms that are wholly American. They are the pioneers of a literature that, whatever its defects in the abstract, will at least be a faithful reflection of the national life. . . . In England the novel subsides into formulae, the drama is submerged in artificialities, and even poetry, despite occasional revolts, moves toward scholarliness and emptiness. But in America, since the war, all three show the artless and superabundant energy of little children. They lack, only too often, manner and urbanity; it is no wonder they are often shocking to pedants. But there is the breath of life in them, and that life is nearer its beginning than its end.

H. L. Mencken, *Prejudices: Fourth Series* (1924)

The Great War and a Literature of Disenchantment

"In its essence literature is concerned with the self," Lionel Trilling has written, "and the particular concern of the literature of the last two centuries has been with the self in its standing quarrel with culture." For writers born in the 1890s, the grounds of that quarrel were shifting. Like Walt Whitman and William Dean Howells, Faulkner, Fitzgerald, and Hemingway saw life in America as a test case of life in the modern world; America remained for them, to borrow one of Howells's titles, *A Modern Instance* (1882). But for them even more than for their predecessors, the world they had inherited seemed, as James T. Farrell put it in one of his titles, *A World I Never Made* (1936). In their most characteristic moments, American writers appear both fascinated with the details of American life and ambivalent toward the values that inform it. Some of their protagonists bear the scars of old injuries and wounds; others suffer from a profound sense of disappointment that culture does so little to nourish their lives or enlarge their happiness. Virtually all of them appear ill equipped to cope both with the alluring, threatening worlds that they inhabit and with the sharp, contradictory needs that they harbor. Some are conscious of themselves primarily as people to whom things happen, as creatures shaped by social forces. Their sense of themselves is one we associate with literary Realism; they feel the force of history impinging upon them from moment to moment. Others are conscious of themselves primarily as creatures acting out of control, as creatures driven by overwhelming needs and desires. Their sense of themselves is one we associate with literary Naturalism; they feel the irresistible force of nature welling up within them from moment to moment. In both cases, however, the notion of the individual as a special force capable of fashioning or making its self and remaking its world—a notion that arose in the Renaissance and later acquired an American flavor in Benjamin Franklin's *Autobiography*—becomes deeply imperiled. Protagonists of modern fiction characteristically move back and forth between moments in which their lives are a series of set tasks and mundane repetitions and moments in which their lives become dramas of momentous decisions to which no prior experience speaks. If on one side culture fails them because it imposes rigid schedules or tedious tasks, on the other it fails them because it provides neither rules nor principles nor even useful analogies by which they can hope to give direction and purpose to their lives. When human existence consists "merely in the unique and the present," Thomas Mann once noted, people do "not know how to conduct" themselves. In modern literature, protagonists sometimes flee, sometimes withdraw, and sometimes improvise, but they rarely act with confidence in themselves or in their worlds.

The ambivalence that defines modern American literature stemmed in part from disillusionment triggered by the First World War. "That's what you all are. . . . You are a lost generation," Gertrude Stein said to Ernest Hemingway, describing those who had survived the war. To present-day readers, the literary outcry that followed World War I may well seem excessive. People had died, Ezra Pound wrote, "For an old bitch gone in the teeth, / For a botched civilization." But such words reflect more than a sense of disappointment with the untidiness of history. The Great War exacted a terrible toll. America's own substantial losses (48,000 killed, 2,900 missing, 56,000 dead from disease) pale beside those of Germany (1.8 million killed), Russia (1.7 million), France (1.4 million), Austria-Hungary (1.2 million), and Britain (947,000). Virtually the whole of Europe emerged from the war not only decimated but depleted, exhausted, and debt-ridden, still racked with inflation and political unrest. But as heinous deeds led to reprisals yet more heinous, the war had also taken on the aspect of a terrible betrayal. "All the horrors of all the ages were brought together," Winston Churchill declared, "and not only armies but whole populations were thrust into the midst of them. . . . Neither peoples nor rulers drew the line at any deed which they thought could help them to win. . . ."

A century earlier, a series of great intellectual explorers and rebels—Sir Charles Lyell, Charles Darwin, Karl Marx, Friedrich Nietzsche, and Sigmund Freud—had mounted an assault against orthodox religious faith that continued from the nineteenth century into the twentieth. Biblical criticism, historical scholarship, science, and social thought had weakened many apparently secure truths and beliefs, and with them several familiar sources of consolation and restraint. "The stupendous failure of Christianity tortured history," Henry Adams asserts in his *Education.* In exchange for religious faith, the nineteenth century offered faith in progress as assuring both continued scientific development and continued extension of rational control over the affairs of humankind—and thus promoting both prosperity and peace. Against such a backdrop, the staggering

---

"All the Horrors of All the Ages Were Brought Together"

Germany, having let Hell loose, kept well in the van of terror; but she was followed step by step by the desperate and ultimately avenging nations she had assailed. Every outrage against humanity or international law was repaid by reprisals—often of a greater scale and of longer duration. No truce or parley mitigated the strife of the armies. The wounded died between the lines: the dead mouldered into the soil. Merchant ships and neutral ships and hospital ships were sunk on the seas and all on board left to their fate, or killed as they swam. Every effort was made to starve whole nations into submission without regard to age or sex. Cities and monuments were smashed by artillery. Bombs from the air were cast down indiscriminately. Poison gas in many forms stifled or seared the soldiers. Liquid fire was projected upon their bodies. Men fell from the air in flames, or were smothered often slowly in the dark recesses of the sea. The fighting strength of armies was limited only by the manhood of their countries. Europe and large parts of Asia and Africa became one vast battlefield on which after years of struggle not armies but nations broke and ran. When all was over, Torture and Cannibalism were the only two expedients that the civilized, scientific, Christian States had been able to deny themselves: and they were of doubtful utility.

Winston Churchill (ca. 1920)

casualties and the unspeakable atrocities of the Great War made the promise of the nineteenth century seem nothing so much as a fool's paradise. "The plunge of civilization into this abyss of blood and horror," Henry James wrote, "so gives away the whole long age during which we have supposed the world to be, with whatever abatement, gradually bettering, that to have to take it all now for what the treacherous years were really making for and *meaning* is too tragic for any words."

The United States entered the war reluctantly, it entered late, and it remained uncertain of its own motives. "The world must be made safe for democracy," proclaimed Woodrow Wilson. "We are going into war upon the command of gold," countered Senator George Norris of Nebraska. Still, on April 4, 1917, the Senate voted 82 to 6 for war, and two days later, on a bleak Good Friday morning, the House followed suit, 373 to 50. Given the severe losses already suffered from England across Europe to Russia, the United States shifted the balance of power substantially. Despite its late entry, it played a major role in determining both the outcome of the war and the terms of peace. By the war's end, the United States had become a world power. Many of its citizens, including several of its writers—some as soldiers, others as ambulance drivers— had seen the war's slaughter firsthand. In the years following the war, Hemingway, who had been seriously wounded, created several almost wholly disillusioned characters: "I was always embarrassed," Frederic Henry remarks in *A Farewell to Arms* (1929), "by the words sacred, glorious, and sacrifice and the expression in vain. We had heard them . . . and had read them . . . , and I had seen nothing sacred, and the things that were glorious had no glory and the sacrifices were like the stockyards at Chicago if nothing was done with the meat except to bury it. There were many words that you could not stand to hear and finally only the names of places had dignity."

People wholly emptied of beliefs have, of course, always been rare, and they remained rare even when "the great century" became "the treacherous years." But with the war behind them, people began to see more clearly that the same intellectual explorers and rebels who had undermined traditional beliefs had also unmasked hidden realities that challenged some of the nineteenth century's most cherished assumptions—such as faith in progress, faith in human uniqueness, and faith in rationality as the shaping force of the human psyche and human society. Henry Adams's nightmare vision, of the human mind struggling "like a frightened bird to escape the chaos which caged it" and of human life terribly diminished, spoke with special force to writers of the early twentieth century as they searched for ground on which they could stand.

Politics in general and reform in particular, allied as they were with the faith that had crumbled, became almost as unfashionable among writers and intellectuals as orthodox religious belief. The populism of the 1890s, which had culminated in William Jennings Bryan's presidential campaign of 1896, was followed in the early twentieth century by the even stronger progressive movement. Yet, despite the presence of politically engaged writers like John Dos Passos, Jean Toomer, and Sinclair Lewis, the progressives' surge of reform

> ## "Looking Blankly into the Void of Death"
>
> Every fabulist has told how the human mind has always struggled like a frightened bird to escape the chaos which caged it; how—appearing suddenly and inexplicably out of some unknown and unimaginable void; passing half its known life in the mental chaos of sleep; victim even when awake, to its own ill-adjustment, to disease, to age, to external suggestion, to nature's compulsion; doubting its sensations, and, in the last resort, trusting only to instruments and averages—after sixty or seventy years of growing astonishment, the mind wakes to find itself looking blankly into the void of death. That it should profess itself pleased by this performance was all that the highest rules of good breeding could ask; but that it should actually be satisfied would prove that it existed only as idiocy.
>
> Henry Adams, *The Education of Henry Adams* (1918)

suffered major reversals after 1914. By the mid-1920s, it was in near eclipse: The Jazz Age, Fitzgerald announced, "had no interest in politics at all." Like religious belief, the appeal of social reform would not mount much of a comeback among "highbrows" until the 1930s and the heyday of New Deal politics.

In the meantime, writers turned hither and yon. The Jazz Age, Fitzgerald also asserted, "was an age of miracles, it was an age of art, it was an age of excess, and it was an age of satire." The noted drama critic George Jean Nathan adopted a deliberately cynical and hedonistic posture. "The great problems of the world—social, political, economic, and theological—do not concern me in the slightest . . . ," he proclaimed. "What concerns me alone is myself, and the interests of a few close friends. For all I care the rest of the world may go to hell at today's sunset." Others, like James G. Huneker, turned to aestheticism, as though to make a religion of art by balancing its form and beauty against the clumsy force and mess of life. "Highbrows," the journalist and novelist Ben Hecht complained, talked about art as if it were their dead grandmother. John Keats's "Ode on a Grecian Urn," William Faulkner said, with deliberate irreverence, is worth any number of old ladies. But the era's aestheticism represented more than flight. In its concern for craftsmanship and in its stress on conscious experimentation in style and form, even in its desire to isolate literature from the social and moral problems of the time, aestheticism represented a need to find in art a way of saying no to a world that seemed at once fragmented and diminished. "In an age of disbelief, or, what is the same thing, in a time that is largely humanistic, in one sense or another, it is for the poet to supply the satisfactions of belief," Wallace Stevens wrote, "in his measure and in his style."

"The Firm Foundation of Unyielding Despair"

Such, in outline, but even more purposeless, more void of meaning, is the world which Science presents for our belief. Amid such a world, if anywhere, our ideals henceforth must find a home. That Man is the product of causes which had no prevision of the end they were achieving; that his origin, his growth, his hopes and fears, his loves and his beliefs, are but the outcome of accidental collocations of atoms; that no fire, no heroism, no intensity of thought and feeling, can preserve an individual life beyond the grave; that all the labors of the ages, all the devotion, all the inspiration, all the noonday brightness of human genius, are destined to extinction in the vast death of the solar system, and that the whole temple of Man's achievement must inevitably be buried beneath the debris of a universe in ruins—all these things, if not quite beyond dispute, are yet so nearly certain, that no philosophy which rejects them can hope to stand. Only within the scaffolding of these truths, only on the firm foundation of unyielding despair, can the soul's habitation henceforth be safely built.

Bertrand Russell, "A Free Man's Worship" (1918)

Big Business and the Transformation of American Society

Another source of disillusionment, more varied than the Great War and more immediate to writers who had not seen the war firsthand, was the rapid transformation of American society that had commenced in America in the mid-nineteenth century, accelerated with the Civil War, and then accelerated again with World War I. Americans were accustomed, almost by birthright, to encounters with historical change and cultural dislocation. Their story was, at least in part, the story of a shifting frontier that had first drawn people from England and Europe to America and then across the continent to the Pacific. Many Americans were still on the road, moving on, seemingly confident of their ability to cope with motion and change. To writers born in the 1890s, however, the world's disarray seemed almost total. "We are unsettled to the very roots of our being," Walter Lippmann wrote in 1914. "There isn't a human relation, whether of parent and child, husband and wife, worker and employer, that doesn't move in a strange situation." "The civilized world has disposed of supernaturalism," H. L. Mencken reported, "and is engaged in a destructive criticism of the old faith's residuum—morality."

As early as the seventeenth century, Americans had begun to associate respectability with success and success with money—and both with what Hawthorne, in a sketch titled "The Sister Years," calls the "moral influence of wealth." But after the Civil War, America's general belief in progress became a specific belief in the beneficence of material progress—a belief shared by businessmen, politicians, social thinkers, and ministers alike. Even dissenters like Thorstein Veblen (1857–1929) found it easier to attack the distribution of wealth than to question the adequacy of material progress as an end or the feasibility of continuous economic growth as a means. By the turn of the century, changes were coming from every side. A new form of capitalism, organized and corporate, had replaced the dispersed, entrepreneurial capitalism of the early nineteenth century. A more centralized democracy that gave a greater role to people of wealth had replaced the loose confederation of the nation's beginning. Soon the nation's industry, like its government, was moving concertedly to serve the interests of business, assuming that business could satisfy as well as serve the needs of the people. The trust-busting and social reform of the late nineteenth and early twentieth centuries notwithstanding, the primary commitment of the nation—as articulated in its ideology and supported by its economy, its government, and its technology—was to making itself a model of economic growth.

Although major portions of the United States remained rural and agricultural well into the twentieth century, and though the South remained poor as well, a new pattern—urban, industrial, commercial, affluent, and secular—had been established for American life. Powerful first in the East, it spread rapidly across the upper Midwest and eventually prevailed even in the South. In the brief span between the close of the Civil War in 1865 and the outbreak of World War I in 1914, the nation saw the traditional authority of both the church and the family seriously erode; it saw its cities commence a period of rapid, unabated growth; and it saw its most successful businesses begin to produce and market on a national scale—first in cities, the easier targets, and then, as railroads, canals, and telegraphs extended their networks, in villages. Stimulated by a wartime economy, growth in productivity exploded after World War I. With national income soaring from $59.4 billion in 1920 to $87.2 billion in 1928, the United States achieved the highest standard of living the world had ever known. By 1929 it accounted for 34.4 percent of total world production, compared with 39.6 by Great Britain, France, Germany, Russia, and Japan combined.

The nation's new affluence ushered in a new mode of conspicuous consumption. Cosmetics and cigarettes, refrigerators and porcelain bathtubs, along with scores of new gadgets, fascinated the nation as they fascinated Sinclair Lewis's George Babbitt. The number of telephones installed in the nation rose from under 1.4 million in 1900 to over 20.2 million in 1930; the number of automobiles produced soared from 4,000 in 1900 to 4.8 million in 1929. In the autumn of 1920, Americans heard their first public radio broadcast; in 1929, they spent $852 million purchasing radios. Movies, boxing, and baseball became big businesses, making idols of Rudolph Valentino and Greta Garbo, heroes of Jack Dempsey and Babe Ruth. Clothing styles changed with each new season. Where the boundaries of what was permissible in language, manners, and behavior were not abolished, they were extended, and a "revolution in morals" was under way.

The Role of Artists in an Era of Wild Oscillations

Writers and artists participated in much of the remaking of America and dominated some of it. The ships that carried them to Europe almost invariably featured black jazz bands, as did many of the Parisian clubs they frequented. In

1919 and again in 1921, the "Original Dixieland Jazz Band" played in England; by 1925, black jazz performers had played in major cities from London and Paris to Berlin and Moscow. Soon the music of jazz and swing bands was altering not only the play of writers like Fitzgerald but the rhythm of their prose. In their campaign against priggishness and censorship, Randolph Bourne, Van Wyck Brooks, and H. L. Mencken made *Puritan* an epithet for people who fear pleasure and love power and *Puritanism* a scapegoat for most known forms of blindness, greed, and repression. Although the era created competing diversions—the radio, big-time sports, and the movies, for example—its technology, its expanding

---

The Writer and the Movie

Around quitting time, Tod Hackett heard a great din on the road outside his office. The groan of leather mingled with the jangle of iron and over all beat the tatoo of a thousand hooves. He hurried to the window.

An army of cavalry and foot was passing. It moved like a mob; its lines broken, as though fleeing from some terrible defeat. The dolmans of the hussars, the heavy shakos of the guards, Hanoverian light horse, with their flat leather caps and flowing red plumes, were all jumbled together in bobbing disorder. Behind the cavalry came the infantry, a wild sea of waving sabretaches, sloped muskets, crossed shoulder belts and swinging cartridge boxes. Tod recognized the scarlet infantry of England with their white shoulder pads, the black infantry of the Duke of Brunswick, the French grenadiers with their enormous white gaiters, the Scotch with bare knees under plaid skirts.

While he watched, a little fat man, wearing a cork sun-helmet, polo shirt and knickers, darted around the corner of the building in pursuit of the army.

"Stage Nine—you bastards—Stage Nine!" he screamed through a small megaphone.

The cavalry put spur to their horses and the infantry broke into a dogtrot. The little man in the cork hat ran after them, shaking his fist and cursing.

Tod watched until they had disappeared behind half a Mississippi steamboat, then put away his pencils and drawing board, and left the office. On the sidewalk outside the studio he stood for a moment trying to decide whether to walk home or take a streetcar. He had been in Hollywood less than three months and still found it a very exciting place, but he was lazy and didn't like to walk. He decided to take the streetcar as far as Vine Street and walk the rest of the way.

A talent scout for National Films had brought Tod to the Coast after seeing some of his drawings in an exhibit of undergraduate work at the Yale School of Fine Arts. He had been hired by telegram.

Nathanael West, *The Day of the Locust* (1939)

communications network, and its growing advertising industry encouraged the development of new magazines and new publishing firms (Alfred A. Knopf in 1915; Boni & Liveright in 1917; Harcourt, Brace in 1919; Viking in 1925). With publishers courting writers and magazines competing for stories, writers were able to make more money and reach a larger audience than ever before. The 1920s were the age of the Book of the Month Club and the Literary Guild. Although book prices were low, royalties were high, and magazines paid large fees for stories. Many writers shared in the nation's new affluence. Near the end of his career, Jack London made more than $75,000 per year. F. Scott Fitzgerald's first novel, *This Side of Paradise* (1920), sold more than 40,000 copies in its first year, launching Fitzgerald on a career in which he made unheard-of sums of money. After 1927, when *The Jazz Singer* transformed the use of sound in motion pictures, Hollywood began using lucrative contracts to draw hundreds of writers, including Fitzgerald and Faulkner, Dashiell Hammett and Nathanael West, to California.

Still, writers found much to offend and little to sustain them in the sharp contrasts and wild oscillations triggered by the nation's headlong rush to make money. Women had emerged from the Great War hoping for a new beginning. In 1920, after nearly a century of agitation, they won suffrage with adoption of the Nineteenth Amendment. But what followed was neither the reconstitution of American society that they had prophesied nor the disintegration of it that their enemies had predicted. The right of women to vote had little discernible impact on the nation's politics and almost none on its economy. In Dorothy Canfield Fisher's *The Home-Maker* (1924), a wife who has failed as a mother trades places with her husband, who has failed as a businessman, and both find happiness. But in fact the force of the women's movement began to dissipate rapidly after the war, leaving women who had believed in its promise disillusioned. Several older writers—Edith Wharton (1862–1937), Ellen Glasgow (1874–1945), Gertrude Stein (1874–1946), and Willa Cather (1876–1947)—survived the 1920s, and several younger ones—Katherine Anne Porter (1890–1980), Josephine Herbst (1897–1969), and Zora Neale Hurston (ca. 1901–1960)—emerged during them. But for the most part they encountered what the heroines of Fitzgerald and Hemingway novels and stories encounter—more suspicion and fear than affirmation and support. Both the literature and the life of the era reflect familiar anxieties with renewed intensity: among women, fear of being isolated or punished; among men, fear of being displaced or devoured.

At the same time, racism not only survived but flourished. On one side, it manifested itself in appeals to racial pride, particularly among so-called Aryans; on the other, it manifested itself in appeals to racial fear, particularly of "the darker types," including immigrants from southern and eastern Europe as well as black Americans. In books like *The Passing of the Great Race* (1916) and *The Rising Tide of Color* (1920), men bearing resonant names—Madison Grant and Lothrop Stoddard—not only celebrated Aryans as stalwart builders and champions of culture but also condemned people of color as fertile, dark, devious, and dangerous.

" 'The Rise of the Colored Empires' "

"Civilization's going to pieces," broke out Tom violently. "I've gotten to be a terrible pessimist about things. Have you read 'The Rise of the Colored Empires' by this man Goddard?"

"Why, no," I answered, rather surprised by his tone.

"Well, it's a fine book, and everybody ought to read it. The idea is if we don't look out the white race will be—will be utterly submerged. It's all scientific stuff; it's been proved."

"Tom's getting very profound," said Daisy, with an expression of unthoughtful sadness. "He reads deep books with long words in them. What was that word we—"

"Well, these books are all scientific," insisted Tom, glancing at her impatiently. "This fellow has worked out the whole thing. It's up to us, who are the dominant race, to watch out or these other races will have control of things."

"We've got to beat them down," whispered Daisy, winking ferociously toward the fervent sun.

"You ought to live in California—" began Miss Baker, but Tom interrupted her by shifting heavily in his chair.

"This idea is that we're Nordics. I am, and you are, and you are, and—" After an infinitesimal hesitation he included Daisy with a slight nod, and she winked at me again. "—And we've produced all the things that go to make civilization—oh, science and art, and all that. Do you see?"

F. Scott Fitzgerald, *The Great Gatsby* (1925)

On a markedly different front, Aimee Semple McPherson and Billy Sunday sought to counter the assault on religious faith by directing large evangelical enterprises designed to recruit new converts. Other citizens opposed "the revolution in morals" by attempting to legislate morality, particularly where alcohol was concerned. In 1919, when the Eighteenth Amendment established Prohibition, the tension between "highbrows" and evangelical Protestants began to intensify. Ironically, however, Prohibition tended not only to encourage lawlessness and to finance organized crime but also to associate drinking with sophistication—with consequences that are still being felt. Washington, D.C., had three hundred licensed saloons before Prohibition and seven hundred speakeasies, supplied by four thousand bootleggers, during it. Boston had more than four thousand speakeasies; Detroit, more than twenty thousand.

The era also witnessed wholesale violations of civil liberties. Both the Red Scare in 1919 and the Palmer Raids in 1920 fanned hostility toward "aliens" and "anarchists" and "Communists." The long, divisive trial of Nicola Sacco and Bartolomeo Vanzetti (1920–1927) and their execution served further to polarize the nation, as did the National Origins Act of 1924, which halted immigration from the Orient and restricted immigration from southern and eastern Europe. Encouraged by such actions, private citizens began organizing their own vigilante persecutions of political, religious, and racial minorities. In 1920, concerned citizens countered such actions by creating the American Civil Liberties Union. But the dominant mood of the nation was more clearly expressed by the Ku Klux Klan—bands of white-hooded men who rode through the night to terrorize people for not being born white and Protestant. Between 1920 and 1925, membership in the Klan rose from roughly five thousand to five million.

Given such stark contrasts, the juxtaposition of the cronyism and corruption of Warren Harding's administration (1920–1923) with the stern asceticism of Calvin Coolidge's (1923–1929) did nothing so much as reinforce the fear that America's only shared commitment was to establishing "a businessman's government." Above all, it was the materialism of the era that writers repudiated. "Feeling like aliens in the commercial world," Malcolm Cowley wrote, scores of writers, from Gertrude Stein to Ernest Hemingway to Richard Wright, sailed for Europe "as soon as they had money enough to pay for their steamer tickets." Even those like F. Scott Fitzgerald, who participated in the nation's high jinks and shared in its prosperity, felt uncomfortable in a land so totally preoccupied with business. Suddenly America seemed not merely gross and vulgar but so single-minded and so heedless in its pursuit of material progress as to doom each "new generation . . . more than the last," Fitzgerald wrote, "to the fear of poverty and the worship of success." A favorite story among writers of the period recalled the day a thirty-six-year-old man named Sherwood Anderson walked out of the office of his paint factory in Elyria, Ohio, to search for meaning in art. "I hardly know what I can teach," Anderson wrote his brother Karl, "except anti-success."

Both the inadequacy of mere success and the hostility of American society to art, or more generally to mind and spirit, coalesce in the story told of Anderson. In fact, however, Anderson's dramatic turn from business to art was triggered more by a nervous breakdown than by a startling conversion, his being one of the fortunate crises of his time. Years later, looking back, remembering especially Fitzgerald's crack-up, Edmund Wilson remarked that his own generation's journey had not been so gay "as we expected when we first started out. . . . We, too, have had our casualties." At times, a sense of hollowness seemed to touch almost everything, from the nation's dream of colossal wealth and meretricious beauty to the revolt of its highbrows and the rebellion of its youth.

Big Ideas for Big Business

What is the finest game? Business. The soundest science? Business. The truest art? Business. The fullest education? Business. The fairest opportunity? Business. The cleanest philanthropy? Business. The sanest religion? Business.

Edward Earl Purington (1921)

The Great Crash and a Revival of Reform

When the Great Crash came, bringing what Fitzgerald later termed "history's most expensive orgy" to a halt, it struck with an abruptness that remains difficult to comprehend. On December 4, 1928, in his last address to Congress, President Coolidge assured the nation that it had never "met with a more pleasing prospect." "The country can regard the present with satisfaction," he concluded, "and anticipate the future with optimism." Over the next several months, the speculative binges of the 1920s culminated in what came to be called the Great Bull Market. In 1923, the volume of sales on the New York Stock Exchange had topped 236 million shares; in 1928, the volume reached over 1.1 billion shares. As thousands rushed to borrow money and buy stock, millions rushed to read newspapers and listen to radios, making the market a spectator sport as well as business at its biggest. Between 1925 and 1928, General Motors stock climbed from 99 to 212. During three weeks in March 1929, Radio Corporation of America stock shot from 94 1/2 to 178. In the summer of 1929, industrials gained 110 points, or nearly 25 percent. Suddenly the nation's dream of overwhelming prosperity actually seemed to lie within reach. Then, in the fall of 1929, less than a year after President Coolidge's speech, the market broke: Radio Corporation of America lost 32 points in a matter of days; industrials lost 228 points between early September and early November, a decline of 50 percent. Having reached 452 in September 1929, industrials sank to 58 in 1932, at the bottom of the Great Depression. During the same period, Montgomery Ward fell from a high of 138 to a low of 4, General Motors from 212 to 8. With confidence collapsing and

---

"The *Debacle* of Idealism"

For . . . many men and women the new day so sonorously heralded by the optimists and propagandists of war-time had turned into night before it ever arrived, and in the uncertain blackness they did not know which way to turn. They could revolt against stupidity and mediocrity, they could derive a meager pleasure from regarding themselves with pity as members of a lost generation, but they could not find peace.

Frederick Lewis Allen, *Only Yesterday* (1931)

What most distinguishes the generation who have approached maturity since the *debacle* of idealism at the end of the war is not their rebellion against the religion and the moral code of their parents, but their disillusionment with their own rebellion. It is common for young men and women to rebel, but that they should rebel sadly and without faith in their rebellion, and that they should distrust the new freedom no less than the old certainties—that is something of a novelty.

Walter Lippmann, *A Preface to Morals* (1929)

---

reserves disappearing, income began to fall, banks to fail, and unemployment to rise. Soon it seemed that almost everyone was poor and that no one knew what to do—President Herbert Hoover even less than the governors and the mayors.

Bread lines and soup kitchens; "Hoovervilles," as the shantytowns that dotted the country were called; families leaving foreclosed homes in search of some place to make a new start; millions of men and hundreds of thousands of young boys riding the rails, seeking in motion a sense of release even more final than the one other people found watching movies, listening to radio programs, or dancing to the sound of the big bands—these became the trademarks of the 1930s. To those already skeptical, as many writers were, the magnitude of the Great Depression did nothing so much as confirm that something had gone drastically wrong with the nation's way of life.

"The Literary Delirium"

There has come a sort of break in the literary movement that was beginning to feel its first strength in the years 1912–1916. . . . For us [then], a variety of elements seemed to contribute to produce an atmosphere that was liberating and stimulating. The American writer . . . seemed at last to be getting all the breaks. . . . The young man or young woman was scarcely out of college when his first novel was seized on by a publisher who exploited instead of censoring whatever in it was improper or disturbing, and he soon found himself a figure of glamour in the world between the Algonquin and Greenwich Village, at a kind of fancy-dress party of frantic self-advertisement. . . .

In any case, at the end of the twenties, a kind of demoralization set in. . . . There was suddenly very little money around, and the literary delirium seemed clearing. The sexual taboos of the age before had been dismissed both from books and from life, and there was no need to be feverish about them; liquor was legal again, and the stock market lay gasping its last. The new "classes" of intellectuals—it was a feature of the post-boom period that they tended to think of themselves as "intellectuals" rather than as "writers"—were in general sober and poor, and they applied the analysis of Marxism to the scene of wreckage they faced. This at least offered a discipline for the mind, gave a coherent picture of history and promised not only employment but the triumph of the constructive intellect. But then, within the decade that followed, the young journalists and novelists and poets who had tried to base their dreams on bedrock, had the spectacle, not of the advent of "the first truly human culture," the ideal of Lenin and Trotsky, but of the rapid domination of Europe by the state socialism of Hitler and Stalin, with its strangling of political discussion and its contemptuous extermination of art; and they no longer knew what to think.

Edmund Wilson, "Thoughts on Being Bibliographed" (1943)

Given the haunting quality of the 1920s, the suddenness of the Crash inevitably provoked feelings of nostalgia and bafflement. Yet there was also, as Malcolm Cowley remarked, "a sense of relief" on coming out of the 1920s, "as on coming out of a room too full of talk and people into the sunlight of the winter streets." Soon writers began looking back on the 1920s, as Josephine Herbst later noted, less as a unified period of miracles and art than as "crumbs and pieces" that contradicted each other—as an era of "flux and change" in which "artistic movements" interacted with "political crises," and even as an era in which such seemingly abandoned ideas as "social service, justice, and religious reaction" had found "special spokesmen."

By appealing to America's idealism rather than to its established preoccupation with big business, Franklin Delano Roosevelt became the first president since Woodrow Wilson to capture the attention of writers. With the New Deal, reform politics became once again respectable. The Federal Writers' Project alone provided support for hundreds of writers. Concern for stylistic and formal experimentation in literature continued, but the 1930s also inspired a sense of urgency that literature make contact with the critical social and cultural problems of the time. Young writers wanted to prove, Alfred Kazin asserted, that they could move "the streets, the stockyards, the hiring halls into literature" and so make their "radical strength . . . carry on the experimental impulse of modern literature."

The 1930s became the heyday of documentary literature in America. In books like Ruth McKenny's *Industrial Valley,* George Leighton's *Five Cities,* Erskine Caldwell and Margaret Bourke-White's *You Have Seen Their Faces,* and the WPA's record of case histories, *These Are Our Lives,* writers sought to record the deprivation, poverty, and suffering of the poor. At the same time, an intensified fascination with the idea of culture began giving phrases like the "American dream" and the "American way of life" fresh authority in the nation's search for values. During the 1920s Sigmund Freud had taught writers, including some who had never read his writings, a new vocabulary. Beyond that, he had taught writers to regard all experience, even telltale slips of tongue and pen, as symptomatic, thus inaugurating an age of suspicion and skepticism as well as

---

"Something Has Got to Change in America"

There's a song that says, "the time ain't long." That song is right. Something has got to change in America—and change soon. We must help that change to come. . . .

We want a new and better America, where there won't be any poor, where there won't be any more Jim Crow, where there won't be any lynchings, where there won't be any munition makers, where we won't need philanthropy, nor charity, nor the New Deal, nor Home Relief.

We want an America that will be ours, a world that will be ours—we Negro workers and white workers! Black writers and white! We'll make that world.

Langston Hughes, "To Negro Writers" (1935)

critical analysis. During the 1930s, as the Depression deepened and crisis followed crisis, the influence of Karl Marx spread rapidly—particularly his critique of capitalism as interpreted by Max Eastman, Waldo Frank, and John Reed. What Freud did to human utterances—namely, insist that they should never be taken simply on their own terms but must instead be viewed skeptically—Marx did for human institutions. Soon a new form of suspicion and skepticism, as well as a new form of critical analysis, was gaining currency. Americans began wondering whether their economic system ("free enterprise capitalism") might not be at odds with their political system ("egalitarian democracy"). "Thousands were convinced and hundreds of thousands were half-persuaded that no simple operation would save us," Cowley wrote; "there had to be the complete renovation of society that Karl Marx had prophesied in 1848. Unemployment would be ended, war and fascism would vanish from the earth, but only after the revolution."

Although some writers influenced by Marx permitted their work to become propagandistic and ephemeral, others, as different as John Dos Passos, Nathanael West, and Richard Wright, did not. They wrote of the poor, often of the very poor, from the farms of the South and the ghettos of the North. Whereas writers like Theodore Dreiser had written of poor people who actually hope to escape poverty and share in power and prosperity, writers of the 1930s frequently wrote of people whose hardship, privation, and misery are intensified by hopelessness. A sense of violent protest accordingly runs through the fiction of the 1930s. If the stronger writers of the period avoided slogans—"the toiling masses," for example —it was, as Josephine Herbst asserted, in part because slogans seemed to provide no answers to "terrible questions," in part because slogans seemed to throttle struggling impulses, and in part because fiction's proper subject still seemed to them to be the individual human spirit "with its own peculiar past." But in the 1930s, more than in any other period in our history, those individual spirits tend to be marginal human beings. They are rootless poets and fierce, defiant gangsters; they are vagabonds and sharecroppers; they are people of mixed or uncertain racial identity or ambiguous sexuality; they are those Edward Dahlberg called *Bottom Dogs* (1930), Jack Conroy, *The Disinherited* (1933), Tess Slesinger, *The Unpossessed* (1934).

Despair and Compliance

One policeman sat in the rear with me while the other one drove. We were traveling very fast and the siren was blowing. It was the same kind of a siren they had used at the marathon dance when they wanted to wake us up.

"Why did you kill her?" the policeman in the rear seat asked.

"She asked me to," I said.

"You hear that, Ben?"

"Ain't he an obliging bastard?" Ben said, over his shoulder.

"Is that the only reason you got?" the policeman in the rear seat asked.

"They shoot horses, don't they?" I said.

Horace McCoy, *They Shoot Horses, Don't They?* (1935)

Shortly after the elevation of Hitler to power in 1933, the threat of war began to spread across Europe. With Hitler's staggering persecution of Jews, thousands of writers, scholars, painters, musicians, scientists, and philosophers—people like Thomas Mann, Hannah Arendt, Vladimir Nabokov, and Albert Einstein—sought refuge in the United States. Yet despite this dramatic new immigration, the United States remained throughout the 1930s preoccupied with its own internal problems and committed to neutrality. Reforms designed to offset the consequences of the Great Depression and stimulate recovery from it dominated the nation's domestic policy, just as isolationism dominated its foreign policy. Despite Roosevelt's reforms, however, recovery from the rapid economic decline and soaring unemployment of the Great Depression was painfully slow. Full economic recovery would not come until after the nation shifted its attention and abandoned its policy of neutrality by entering World War II—an event that would accelerate the United States' rise as a world power and change its literature once again.

Alienation and Experimentation

American writers of the early twentieth century began in alienation and repudiation, moods that were intensified by the Great War and transformed by the Great Depression. The sense that the world had somehow broken in two haunted them. Feeling cut off from the past, they turned to it, in search of some usable heritage. Allusions and echoes of earlier writers fill their stories. "In a city," Ezra Pound once remarked, "visual impressions succeed each other, overlap, overcross, they are 'cinematographic.'" In villages, he continued, people possess a sense of sequence and a sense of shared knowledge; because they know who did what before, during, and after the cataclysmic changes in their history, their life "is narrative." Convinced that individual experience had become disjointed and communal experience chaotic, writers of the early twentieth century struggled with the wild shifts and swings of their era, as with bits and pieces, trying to make art of them. Dos Passos shaped his fiction out of fragments taken from movies, newsreels, newspapers, and popular songs; Faulkner shaped his out of "the rag-tag and bob-ends of old tales and talking." In different ways, both sought to confront the radically discontinuous and fragmentary aspects of their world. As though to remind us that discontinuity threatens narrative as well as history, art as well as life, writers made the story sequence, a form of discontinuous narrative, one of the representative fictional forms of their era—a form highlighted in Stein's *Three Lives,* Anderson's *Winesburg, Ohio,* Hemingway's *In Our Time,* and Faulkner's *Go Down, Moses.*

At the same time, writers struggled to combine the variety and resilience of idiomatic American English with the resonance and allusional density of more traditional literary language. In some moments, they reflect a deep fascination with American life; in others, they disclose a disenchantment so profound as to approximate what the great French poet Baudelaire called the "sublime literature" of despair, in which degradation and hopelessness persuade the reader to "long for

---

"The Noises of America"

The tall, impossibly tall, incomparably tall, city shoulderingly upward into hard
sunlight leaned a little through the octaves of its parallel edges, leaningly strode
upward into firm hard snowy sunlight; the noises of America nearingly
throbbed with smokes and hurrying dots which are men and which are women
and which are things new and curious and hard and strange and vibrant and
immense, lifting with a great undulous stride firmly into immortal sunlight.

E. E. Cummings, *The Enormous Room* (1922)

Three gulls wheel above the broken boxes, orangerinds, spoiled cabbage heads
that heave between the splintered plank walls, the green waves spume under the
round bow as the ferry, skidding on the tide, crashes, gulps the broken water,
slides, settles slowly into the slip. Handwinches whirl with jingle of chains.
Gates fold upwards, feet step out across the crack, men and women press
through the manuresmelling wooden tunnel of the ferryhouse, crushed and
jostling like apples fed down a chute into a press.

John Dos Passos, *Manhattan Transfer* (1925)

---

goodness as a remedy." Some of the voices Dos Passos created are so public as to
seem familiar, while some of those Faulkner created are so private as to seem
strange, bizarre, even deranged. If, however, one part of the achievement of
Faulkner, Stein, Hemingway, Dos Passos, and Wright was to reform and extend
the language of American literature, another part was to reshape the tastes and
skills of the readers of that literature. Implicit in their works is the task of
teaching us the skills required to read them. By extending the range of our
literature, they hoped also to expand its audience.

One manifestation of the alienation that writers of the early twentieth century
felt was their need to create places more their own. "I would say," Faulkner once
remarked, "that in our culture there is really no place for the artist." In New
Orleans, Memphis, Chicago, New York, London, and Paris, writers gravitated
toward enclaves where money mattered less, literature and art more. In addition,
however, several of these enclaves were identified with specific regions (Chicago
with the Midwest; Memphis and New Orleans with the South) or with racial
minorities (Harlem) and so provided a counterbalance not only to materialism
and its consequences but also to the strong centralizing forces that had begun to
dominate American society. Although the Northeast had declined as a source of
literary art, it retained its power as literary arbiter of the nation, primarily
through the great publishing houses of New York. As a result, the writing of the
Northeast continued to be regarded as "American" literature, the writing of the
Midwest and especially the writing of the South as "regional" literature, and the
writing of black Americans as "minority" literature.

"Paris Was Always Worth It"

There is never any ending to Paris and the memory of each person who has lived in it differs from that of any other. We always returned to it no matter who we were or how it was changed or with what difficulties, or ease, it could be reached. Paris was always worth it and you received return for whatever you brought to it. But this is how Paris was in the early days when we were very poor and very happy.

Ernest Hemingway, *A Moveable Feast* (1964)

On a different front, the rise of national magazines and even more of the movies and radio was rapidly nationalizing American popular culture. In the year 1922, a total of 40 million people attended the movies; in 1930, an average of 100 million bought tickets each week. By 1928, when radio sales soared to $852 million, radio programs were reaching millions of homes each day. Writers needed places in which they could enter the world of art and find support for what they were doing; but they also needed some means of holding fast to the particular subcultures they knew, whether those subcultures were to be defined regionally, racially, or sexually. Many of the nation's stronger writers moved from regional centers to New York, London, or Paris—as was the case with Wright. A few moved back home, as was the case with Faulkner, but many found in regional enclaves precisely what they needed—a second country, slightly more romantic and considerably more supportive than any place they had known, where they could still maintain contact with the folkways and voices that fed their art, a way station poised between the worlds they actually knew and those they were trying to create.

In and outside their enclaves, they established "little magazines"—*Poetry* and *The Little Review* in Chicago; *The Criterion* and *Blast* in London; *Transition* and *Transatlantic Review* in Paris; *Broom* in Rome; *The Seven Arts* and *The Dial* in New York; *The Fugitive* in Nashville; *The Double Dealer* in New Orleans. Writers published stories in popular magazines, of course, as well as in little magazines—in *The Saturday Evening Post* as well as *The Double Dealer*—and they published many works that are now ignored as well as some that are still read. But the little magazines served an important double purpose. First, by publishing works of minor writers, they added depth and resonance to the literary life of early twentieth-century America. Second, by publishing some of the more experimental works of writers who later became famous, they provided a market for works that played a major role in revolutionizing the taste and reading skills of the nation's most avid readers, including emerging writers.

Like Whitman, writers of the twentieth century have celebrated the magic of the commonplace. And like Whitman's, their disaffection with American life has coexisted with fascination. The disaffection and alienation that mark American fiction of the early twentieth century run deep, in part because our writers have felt so acutely the failure of American life to meet the needs of mind and spirit that no material possession can ever satisfy. Like T. S. Eliot, our writers have tended to be suspicious of the dream of creating social systems so perfect that no one would need to be good, and like Herman Melville, they have tended to feel greater solidarity with the poor, the forgotten, and the defeated than with the rich and the victorious. They have confronted more honestly and courageously than most of us the incongruities and anxieties that shape our lives. One thing they had inherited from the nineteenth century, besides a suspect faith in the sufficiency of material progress itself, was the promise of more freedom: a willingness to blur or even dissolve all limitations, all restrictions, all taboos, in art as well as in life. Yet even as they enjoyed the rewards of material progress and advocated freedom, our writers have remained convinced that freedom suffices only when people truly know what they want, and then only when what they want corresponds to their deepest needs and so matches their capacity for wonder.

Recently, in another connection, I spoke of the modern self as characterized by its intense and adverse imagination of the culture in which it had its being, and by certain powers of indignant perception which, turned upon the subconscious portions of culture, have made it accessible to conscious thought. Freud's view of culture is marked by this *adverse* awareness, by this indignant perception. He does indeed see the self as formed by its culture. But he also sees the self as set against the culture, struggling against it, having been from the first reluctant to enter it. . . .

In its essence literature is concerned with the self; and the particular concern of the literature of the last two centuries has been with the self in its standing quarrel with culture. We cannot mention the name of any great writer of the modern period whose work has not in some way, and usually in a passionate and explicit way, insisted on this quarrel, who has not expressed the bitterness of his discontent with civilization, who has not said that the self made greater legitimate demands than any culture could hope to satisfy. This intense conviction of the existence of the self apart from culture is, as culture well knows, its noblest and most generous achievement. At the present moment it must be thought of as a liberating idea without which our developing ideal of community is bound to defeat itself. We can speak no greater praise of Freud than to say that he placed this idea at the very center of his thought.

Lionel Trilling, *Freud and the Crisis of Our Culture* (1955)

American writers of the early twentieth century were heirs, then, less of the dominant culture of the nineteenth century than of its great intellectual rebels. Much of the daring, even the headiness, of the assaults that Darwin, Marx, Nietzsche, and Freud had led against apparently secure truths and beliefs found new expression in the extraordinary boldness and the sheer presumption of writers as different as Stein, Dos Passos, and Faulkner as they set out to invent literature anew. When these writers looked to the past, seeking ancestors and a heritage, they often turned to forgotten, out-of-the-way figures. In fact, however, their cavalier dismissal of their most immediate heritage, that of Victorian thinking and writing, was often overstated: Many of them remained closet loyalists where the nineteenth century was concerned. In a similar vein, one may say that their brashness outstripped their assurance; even Stein, Faulkner, and Wright, as brash as any, lived on close terms with most known forms of doubt, including self-doubt. Yet their gifts survived. An almost fierce determination to deal with the past on no terms except their own not only marked them as rebels but also shaped their art. Modern American fiction is often pessimistic and violent, even brutal and despairing. But it is also infused with great boldness of spirit, as we see especially in the remarkable formal experiments that give it a special place in one of the great outpourings of innovative expression in the history of Western literature.

Further Reading:
F. L. Allen, *Only Yesterday*, 1931.
M. Cowley, *After the Genteel Tradition: American Writing, 1910–1930*, 1937.
A. Kazin, *On Native Grounds: An Interpretation of Modern American Prose Literature*, 1942.
L. Trilling, *The Liberal Imagination*, 1950.
M. Cowley, *Exile's Return: A Narrative of Ideas*, 1934, 1951.
E. Goldman, *Rendezvous with Destiny*, 1952.
E. Wilson, *The Shores of Light: A Literary Chronicle of the Twenties and Thirties*, 1952.
F. J. Hoffman, *The Twenties: American Writing in the Postwar Decade*, 1955.
R. Hofstadter, *The Age of Reform: From Bryan to FDR*, 1955.
L. Trilling, *The Opposing Self*, 1955.
L. Trilling, *Freud and the Crisis of Our Culture*, 1956.
S. P. Hays, *The Response to Industrialism: 1885–1914*, 1957,
W. Leuchtenburg, *The Perils of Prosperity: 1914–1932*, 1958.
W. Morris, *The Territory Ahead*, 1958.

D. Aaron, *Writers on the Left*, 1961
W. Berthoff, *The Ferment of Realism: American Literature 1884–1919*, 1965.
R. Bridgman, *The Colloquial Style in America*, 1966.
N. L. Huggins, *Harlem Renaissance*, 1971.
H. Kenner, *The Pound Era*, 1971.
R. Miller, *Black American Literature: 1760 to the Present*, 1971.
H. Kenner, *A Homemade World*, 1975.
M. Cowley, *And I Worked at the Writer's Trade: American Writing, Chapters of Literary History, 1918–1978*, 1978.
W. Morris, *Earthly Delights, Unearthly Adornments: American Writers as Image Makers*, 1978.
R. Stepto, *From Behind the Veil: A Study of Afro-American Narrative*, 1979.
J. Lears, *No Place of Grace: Antimodernism and the Transformation of American Culture, 1880–1920*, 1981.
P. Johnson, *Modern Times: The World from the Twenties to the Eighties*, 1983.

Gertrude Stein
1874–1946

Gertrude Stein was one of the most resolute champions in American letters for the worth of ordinary things. Live in the middle, she admonished. Yet Stein is generally thought of in terms of the experimental in writing and the unconventional in living. The first Jewish writer to have a large impact on American literature, she became the friend and patron of leaders of the avant-garde in the halcyon days before World War I. She collected juicy anecdotes as well as paintings; she entertained famous people, and she sponsored and even tutored young writers. She dispersed clever aphorisms ("You are all a lost generation"), unforgettable lines ("A rose is a rose is a rose is a rose"), and sharp admonitions ("Look facts in the face look facts in the face look facts in the face"). Having instructed others to live in the middle, she lived nearer the edge —by living as she chose and saying what she thought. She was the longtime lover of Alice B. Toklas, who became famous in her own right for her hashish fudge. Stein was frequently sharp-tongued. She studied with the experimental psychologist and philosopher William James (who praised her) and tutored Ernest Hemingway (who reluctantly gave credit where it was due).

Such items as these make good gossip. In some discussions of Paris and the surge of modernism, the mere mention of Gertrude Stein's name has been used to counteract excessive seriousness. As witty as Stein was in conversation, however, and as much amusement as she provides readers in her delightful, games-playing *Tender Buttons* or *The Autobiography of Alice B. Toklas,* her enduring importance to modern literature lies elsewhere. It lies, aptly enough, exactly where she said it should: with the middle way of familiar values and concerns. Her writings constitute a celebration and a critique of the importance of work, of the uses of self-deception, and of the importance of paying constant attention to both material things and the weight of words. Throughout her work, she resolutely places both abstract thought and complex reasoning at the service of forcefulness rather than of mere clarity.

In her own times, and in her own way, Gertrude Stein, the daughter of a talented, well-situated family one generation removed from Germany, was the intellectual child of Ralph Waldo Emerson. Both Emerson and Stein endeavored to match up linguistic signs, natural sounds, and psychic meanings. Stein also carried forward the interests of her Harvard psychology professor, William James; like him, she was fascinated with the effects of habit, memory, and the unfoldings of consciousness. In addition, she was the imaginative compatriot of William Carlos Williams, Ezra Pound, T. S. Eliot, and Sherwood Anderson. Determined to make things new, Stein broke most rules governing punctuation and syntax and many governing diction. The playfulness of her mind manifested itself in many ways, particularly in its ability to make us pay close attention to even the simplest words. Using familiar words, many of them monosyllabic, she confronted us with fundamental distinctions, such as that between being and remembering and between consciousness and self-consciousness. "At any moment when you are you you are you without the memory of yourself," she wrote in *What Are Masterpieces* (1940), "because if you remember yourself while you are you you are not for the purposes of creating you."

Gertrude Stein was born in Allegheny, Pennsylvania, a town now part of Pittsburgh, the youngest of seven children. Despite the security and privilege in which she lived, Stein never took her existence for granted. Both she and her brother Leo knew that their parents had "allowed" them to be born only because two older siblings had died. "Gertrude doesn't like to be frightened," she wrote, and she didn't; yet she persisted in testing herself at almost every turn from early in her life to its end.

The year after her birth in 1874, the Stein family went abroad, remaining there until 1879. Gertrude Stein thus had the advantage of an early exposure to European languages, but she stubbornly insisted that her only true language was English. In 1880 the Steins moved to Oakland, California, where Stein spent her youth. (Of Oakland she would later say, "There is no there there.") She was close neither to her parents nor to any of her siblings other than Leo. By 1892, both her parents were dead. Financially independent, she was free to move out into the world. In 1893 she entered Radcliffe College, which a year later affiliated with Harvard University, where she encountered the new philosophy of Josiah Royce and George Santayana and the new psychology of William James, under whose direction she worked on laboratory experiments in 1894. She graduated magna cum laude, then spent two years at Johns Hopkins University as a medical student before abandoning her plans for a career as a physiological psychologist. In 1902 she moved to London, where she immersed herself in studying the English language at the British Museum, preparing to be a writer.

Precisely why Stein decided to give up her medical studies remains unclear. She may have decided to put distance between herself and an unmanageable love affair with two women, a situation she describes in a novel *OED, or Things as They Are* (written 1903, published 1950). Or perhaps she wished to remain near Leo. She had already followed him from California to Harvard and from Harvard to Johns Hopkins. Now Leo had decided to explore the possibilities of French culture. In 1903, after one year in London, Stein moved into an apartment with Leo on the Left Bank in Paris, at 27 rue de Fleurus, near the center of Europe's literary and artistic circles, where she would live for many years.

In Paris, both Gertrude and Leo Stein found a perfect "second country." They soon turned their attention to modern painters. They promoted the art of Cézanne, Renoir, Gauguin, Manet, and Toulouse-Lautrec, as well as two even newer painters, Matisse and Picasso—all of whose works they began collecting before the artists became so famous as to be prohibitively expensive. Soon the Steins' apartment became a famous meeting place for painters and writers, making Gertrude a celebrated international hostess who ruled, as Katherine Anne Porter once reported disparagingly, "in such masterly freedom as only a few early medieval queens had equalled." But Gertrude Stein did more than collect art and entertain. She also wrote, experimenting with words as the painters she knew experimented with forms, shapes, and colors.

In 1905 Gertrude Stein completed her first book, *Three Lives*. It consists of three stories—"The Good Anna," "Melanctha," and "The Gentle Lena." These stories have been praised both for their stylistic innovations and for the poignant ways in which they explore the lives of three very different Baltimore women. In 1908 Stein completed *The Making of Americans*. In this unconventional "novel," she sets out to tell "everybody's history" by drawing heavily on the history of her family, at the same time minimizing the importance of action and avoiding dialogue. Neither *Three Lives* nor *The Making of Americans* was published commercially at the time it was written. Stein's first book was published in 1909 at her own expense; the second appeared in print in 1925, after Stein had established a name for herself with other writings.

Alice B. Toklas moved into the Steins' rue de Fleurus apartment in 1909, and she became Gertrude Stein's lifelong companion, amanuensis, lover, and joint hostess in charge of looking after the spouses of the geniuses who came to call. Later, when Leo decided to move, the Steins' valuable collection of paintings was divided; and Gertrude and Alice were left to get on with Gertrude's career.

Gertrude Stein's writing expanded in the years before World War I, and her fame seemed assured with *Tender Buttons* (1914), a series of paragraphs, some playful and witty, others brief prose poems, that focus on different subjects. Her experiments with language and literary forms coincided with and mirrored the increasing attention being given by painters to abstractions, collages, visual puns, and "in" jokes. Stein's juggling of words rejected conventional expectations of syntax, chronology, and definable meanings. As Hemingway commented in a 1948 letter, "She could never fail; nor strike out; nor be knocked out of the box because she made the rules and played under her own rules." Her portraits of people and objects were often whimsical in the extreme—seemingly thrown together at random.

But Gertrude Stein was also a theorist whose pronouncements about time, punctuation, and narration were taken seriously by other writers. In recognition of the crucial role she had come to play in the emergence of a distinctively modern literature, she was invited to present her theories as a series of lectures at Oxford and Cambridge in 1926. In 1934 and 1935 she made a triumphant tour of the United States. Both her British and American lectures, dealing with visual space as well as language and literature, were published under the titles *Composition as Explanation* (1926), *Narration* (1935), and *Geographical History of America* (1936). In them we follow Stein's pursuit of "the excitingness of pure being" and of the desire to put intensity back in language. Despite her travels, however, she continued to think of Paris as her adopted home, the vantage point from which she could best describe and interpret her native land as well as theorize about language and literature.

Stein's most famous works are autobiographical—*Everybody's Autobiography* (1937) and especially *The Autobiography of Alice B. Toklas* (1933). Both are filled with her barbed opinions about people, food, parties, writing, and the arts; both bear witness to her wide influence; and both provoked sharp rejoinders from her acquaintances and rivals. Never again would her strong-willed peers sit in silent awe of the woman Hemingway described as looking like a Roman emperor, adding that one might not prefer women to look like that. Literary critics and cultural historians joined Stein's "students" (Hemingway, Anderson, and others) in openly expressing their ambivalent feelings toward her. In 1935 a group of Parisian writers and artists published *Testimony Against Gertrude Stein,* primarily in response to *The Autobiography of Alice B. Toklas.* Yet Stein's reputation has continued to grow, especially among those who had nothing personally at stake in the issue of just how important she was.

Stein collaborated with Virgil Thompson on two operas, *Four Saints in Three Acts* (1934) and *The Mother of Us All* (1945–1946), a celebration of Susan B. Anthony. *Wars I Have Seen* (1945) provides a witty yet poignant assessment of the wars that had punctuated Stein's life. *Brewsie and Willie* (1946) offers a lively account of the popularity she enjoyed with the American soldiers who sought her out as a bona fide tourist attraction once France (where she continued to live during World War II) was liberated from German occupation in 1945. To the end of her life, however, even as she cultivated her reputation as a woman who lived an unconventional life amid people and events that stood traditional culture on its head, she remained a hardworking woman devoted to living in the middle. In 1946, following a sharp decline in her health, she entered the American hospital in Paris, where she underwent surgery that failed. On July 27, shortly before she died, she summoned the energy to say, "What is the answer?" and, hearing no reply, to murmur, "In that case, what is the question?"

Gertrude Stein sometimes acted like a comfortable anarchist. She was in fact an uneasy searcher after order who resolutely insisted on being honest about the kinds of stability the modern world could provide. She made use of all the continuities she could find—even those in "the language of dishes and daylight." But her world is a world of gerunds (her favorite verbal form, since gerunds insist on a life of continuous action), a world of consciousness where nothing stands still and where the most solid of realities is one's essential "bottom nature" caught in a flash of words and depicted verbally in "the continuous present." "Let no one think that anything has come to stay," she wrote. She held strong opinions about everything, yet she knew them for what they were—temporarily improvised certainties. After conducting a seminar at the University of Chicago in 1934, she attributed her popularity not to her sharp opinions but to this: "You see why they talk to me is that I am like them I do not know the answer. . . . I do not even know whether there is a question let alone having answers for a question."

Convinced that the twentieth century differed radically from the nineteenth, Stein sought to foster a radical shift in sensibility. Her end was immediacy of presentation in a continuous present. She wanted to give each moment its own successive emphasis, its difference, its place; her art celebrates the "thing seen at the moment it is seen." Time and again her art forces us to examine or reexamine not only relations between words and things but also relations between the composition of language and the process of consciousness: "I had in hundreds of ways related words, then sentences then paragraphs to the thing at which I was looking."

Further Reading:

W. Rogers, *When This You See, Remember Me: Gertrude Stein in Person*, 1948, 1971, 1973.
D. Sutherland, *Gertrude Stein: A Biography of Her Work*, 1951, 1971.
E. Sprigge, *Gertrude Stein: Her Life and Work*, 1957.
R. Reid, *Art by Subtraction: A Dissenting Opinion of Gertrude Stein*, 1958.
J. M. Brinnin, *The Third Rose: Gertrude Stein and Her World*, 1959.
F. Hoffman, *Gertrude Stein*, 1961.
A. Stewart, *Gertrude Stein and the Present*, 1967.
N. Weinstein, *Gertrude Stein and the Literature of the Modern Consciousness*, 1970.
R. Bridgman, *Gertrude Stein in Pieces*, 1971.
A. Burnett, *Gertrude Stein*, 1972.

H. Greenfield, *Gertrude Stein: A Biography*, 1973.
Staying Alone: Letters of Alice B. Toklas, ed. E. Burns, 1974.
J. Mellows, *Charmed Circles: Gertrude Stein and Company*, 1974.
Gertrude Stein: A Companion Portrait, ed. L. Simon, 1974.
C. Copeland, *Language & Time & Gertrude Stein*, 1975.
M. Hoffman, *Gertrude Stein*, 1976.
W. Steiner, *Exact Resemblance to Exact Resemblance: The Literary Portraiture of Gertrude Stein*, 1978.
S. Neuman, *Gertrude Stein: Autobiography and the Problem of Narration*, 1979.

Texts:

The Autobiography of Alice B. Toklas, 1960.
Three Lives, 1945.
See also *Selected Writings of Gertrude Stein*, ed. C. Van Vechten, 1946, 1962.
Two: Gertrude Stein and Her Brother, and Other Early Portraits, 1908–1912, ed. J. Flannery, 1951, 1969.
Stanzas in Meditation, and Other Poems,

1929–1933, ed. D. Sutherland, 1956.
Writings and Lectures, 1911–1945, ed. P. Meyerowitz, 1967.
Selected Operas and Plays of Gertrude Stein, ed. J. M. Brinnin, 1970.
The Yale Gertrude Stein: Selections, ed. R. Kostelanetz, 1980.

---

from The Autobiography of Alice B. Toklas

from 6: The War

Americans living in Europe before the war never really believed that there was going to be war. Gertrude Stein always tells about the little janitor's boy who, playing in the court, would regularly every couple of years assure her that papa was going to the war. Once some cousins of hers were living in Paris, they had a country girl as a servant. It was the time of the russian-japanese war and they were all talking about the latest news. Terrified she dropped the platter and cried, and are the germans at the gates.

William Cook's father was an Iowan who at seventy years of age was making his first trip in Europe in the summer of nineteen fourteen. When the war was upon them he refused to believe it and explained that he could understand a family fighting among themselves, in short a civil war, but not a serious war with one's neighbours.

Gertrude Stein in 1913 and 1914 had been very interested reading the newspapers. She rarely read french newspapers, she never read anything in french, and she always read the Herald. That winter she added the Daily Mail. She liked to read about the suffragettes and she liked to read about Lord Roberts' campaign for compulsory military service in England. Lord Roberts had been a favourite hero of hers early in her life. His Forty-One Years In India was a book she often read and she had seen Lord Roberts when she and her brother, then taking a college vacation, had seen Edward the Seventh's coronation procession. She read the Daily Mail, although, as she said, she was not interested in Ireland.

We went to England July fifth and went according to programme to see John Lane at his house Sunday afternoon.

There were a number of people there and they were talking of many things but some of them were talking about war. One of them, some one told me he was an editorial writer on one of the big London dailies, was bemoaning the fact that he would not be able to eat figs in August in Provence as was his habit. Why not, asked some one. Because of the war, he answered. Some one else, Walpole or his brother I think it was, said that there was no hope of beating Germany as she had such an excellent system, all her railroad trucks were numbered in connection with locomotives and switches. But, said the eater of figs, that is all very well as long as the trucks remain in Germany on their own lines and switches, but in an aggressive war they will leave the frontiers of Germany and then, well I promise you then there will be a great deal of numbered confusion.

This is all I remember definitely of that Sunday afternoon in July.

As we were leaving, John Lane said to Gertrude Stein that he was going out of town for a week and he made a rendezvous with her in his office for the end of July, to sign the contract for Three Lives. I think, he said, in the present state of affairs I would rather begin with that than with something more entirely new. I have confidence in that book. Mrs. Lane is very enthusiastic and so are the readers.

Having now ten days on our hands we decided to accept the invitation of Mrs. Mirlees, Hope's mother, and spend a few days in Cambridge. We went there and thoroughly enjoyed ourselves.

It was a most comfortable house to visit. Gertrude Stein liked it, she could stay in her room or in the garden as much as she liked without hearing too much conversation. The food was excellent, scotch food, delicious and fresh, and it was very amusing meeting all the University of Cambridge dignitaries. We were taken into all the gardens and invited into many of the homes. It was lovely weather, quantities of roses, morris-dancing by all the students and girls and generally delightful. We were invited to lunch at Newnham, Miss Jane Harrison, who had been Hope Mirlees' pet enthusiasm, was much interested in meeting Gertrude Stein. We sat up on the dais with the faculty and it was very awe inspiring. The conversation was not however particularly amusing. Miss Harrison and Gertrude Stein did not particularly interest each other.

We had been hearing a good deal about Doctor and Mrs. Whitehead.[1] They no longer lived in Cambridge. The year before Doctor Whitehead had left Cambridge

---

[1] Alfred North Whitehead (1861–1947), English philosopher and mathematician, was co-author, with Bertrand Russell, of *Principia Mathematica,* author of *Science in the Modern World* (1925), and proponent of the technique of "extensive abstraction" (the derivation of concepts from conscious perception).

to go to London University. They were to be in Cambridge shortly and they were to dine at the Mirlees'. They did and I met my third genius.

It was a pleasant dinner. I sat next to Housman, the Cambridge poet, and we talked about fishes and David Starr Jordan but all the time I was more interested in watching Doctor Whitehead. Later we went into the garden and he came and sat next to me and we talked about the sky in Cambridge.

Gertrude Stein and Doctor Whitehead and Mrs. Whitehead all became interested in each other. Mrs. Whitehead asked us to dine at her house in London and then to spend a week end, the last week end in July with them in their country home in Lockridge, near Salisbury Plain. We accepted with pleasure.

We went back to London and had a lovely time. We were ordering some comfortable chairs and a comfortable couch covered with chintz to replace some of the italian furniture that Gertrude Stein's brother had taken with him. This took a great deal of time. We had to measure ourselves into the chairs and into the couch and to choose chintz that would go with the pictures, all of which we successfully achieved. These chairs and this couch, and they are comfortable, in spite of war came to the door one day in January, nineteen fifteen at the rue de Fleurus and were greeted by us with the greatest delight. One needed such comforting and such comfort in those days. We dined with the Whiteheads and liked them more than ever and they liked us more than ever and were kind enough to say so.

Gertrude Stein kept her appointment with John Lane at the Bodley Head. They had a very long conversation, this time so long that I quite exhausted all the shop windows of that region for quite a distance, but finally Gertrude Stein came out with a contract. It was a gratifying climax.

Then we took the train to Lockridge to spend the week end with the Whiteheads. We had a week-end trunk, we were very proud of our week-end trunk, we had used it on our first visit and now we were actively using it again. As one of my friends said to me later, they asked you to spend the week end and you stayed six weeks. We did.

There was quite a house party when we arrived, some Cambridge people, some young men, the younger son of the Whiteheads, Eric, then fifteen years old but very tall and flower-like and the daughter Jessie just back from Newnham. There could not have been much serious thought of war because they were all talking of Jessie Whitehead's coming trip to Finland. Jessie always made friends with foreigners from strange places, she had a passion for geography and a passion for the glory of the British Empire. She had a friend, a finn, who had asked her to spend the summer with her people in Finland and had promised Jessie a possible uprising against Russia. Mrs. Whitehead was hesitating but had practically consented. There was an older son North who was away at the time.

Then suddenly, as I remember, there were the conferences to prevent the war, Lord Grey and the russian minister of foreign affairs. And then before anything further could happen the ultimatum to France. Gertrude Stein and I were completely miserable as was Evelyn Whitehead, who had french blood and who had been raised in France and had strong french sympathies. Then came the days of the invasion of Belgium and I can still hear Doctor Whitehead's gentle voice reading the papers out loud and then all of them talking about the destruction of Louvain and how they must help the brave little belgians. Gertrude Stein desperately unhappy said to me, where is Louvain. Don't you know, I said. No, she said, nor do I care, but where is it.

Our week end was over and we told Mrs. Whitehead that we must leave. But you cannot get back to Paris now, she said. No, we answered, but we can stay in London. Oh no, she said, you must stay with us until you can get back to Paris. She was very sweet and we were very unhappy and we liked them and they liked us and we agreed to stay. And then to our infinite relief England came into the war. . . .

Evelyn Whitehead was very busy planning war work and helping every one and I as far as possible helped her. Gertrude Stein and Doctor Whitehead walked endlessly around the country. They talked of philosophy and history, it was during these days that Gertrude Stein realised how completely it was Doctor Whitehead and not Russell who had had the ideas for their great book.[2] Doctor Whitehead, the gentlest and most simply generous of human beings never claimed anything for himself and enormously admired anyone who was brilliant, and Russell undoubtedly was brilliant.

Gertrude Stein used to come back and tell me about these walks and the country still the same as in the days of Chaucer, with the green paths of the early britons that could still be seen in long stretches, and the triple rainbows of that strange summer. They used, Doctor Whitehead and Gertrude Stein, to have long conversations with game-keepers and mole-catchers. The mole-catcher had said, but sir, England has never been in a war but that she has been victorious. Doctor Whitehead turned to Gertrude Stein with a gentle smile. I think we may say so, he said. The game-keeper, when Doctor Whitehead seemed discouraged said to him, but Doctor Whitehead, England is the predominant nation, is she not. I hope she is, yes I hope she is, replied Doctor Whitehead gently.

The germans were getting nearer and nearer Paris. One day Doctor Whitehead said to Gertrude Stein, they were just going through a rough little wood and he was helping her, have you any copies of your writings or are they all in Paris. They are all in Paris, she said. I did not like to ask, said Doctor Whitehead, but I have been worrying.

The germans were getting nearer and nearer Paris and the last day Gertrude Stein could not leave her room, she sat and mourned. She loved Paris, she thought neither of manuscripts nor of pictures, she thought only of Paris and she was desolate. I came up to her room, I called out, it is alright Paris is saved, the germans are in retreat. She turned away and said, don't tell me these things. But it's true, I said, it is true. And then we wept together. . . .

I remember the leaving London very little, I cannot even remember whether it was day-light or not but it must have been because when we were on the channel boat it was day-light. The boat was crowded. There were quantities of belgian soldiers and officers escaped from Antwerp, all with tired eyes. It was our first experience of the tired but watchful eyes of soldiers. We finally were able to arrange a seat for Mrs. Whitehead who had been ill and soon we were in France. Mrs. Whitehead's papers were so overpowering that there were no delays and soon we were in the train and about ten o'clock at night we were in Paris. We took a taxi and drove

---

[2] *Principia Mathematica* (1910–1913), a rigorous development of pure mathematics through formal logic.

through Paris, beautiful and unviolated, to the rue de Fleurus. We were once more at home. . . .

from 7: **After the War**

1919–1932

We were, in these days as I look back at them, constantly seeing people.

It is a confused memory those first years after the war and very difficult to think back and remember what happened before or after something else. Picasso once said, I have already told, when Gertrude Stein and he were discussing dates, you forget that when we were young an awful lot happened in a year. During the years just after the war as I look in order to refresh my memory over the bibliography of Gertrude Stein's work, I am astonished when I realise how many things happened in a year. Perhaps we were not so young then but there were a great many young in the world and perhaps that comes to the same thing.

The old crowd had disappeared. Matisse was now permanently in Nice and in any case although Gertrude Stein and he were perfectly good friends when they met, they practically never met. This was the time when Gertrude Stein and Picasso were not seeing each other. They always talked with the tenderest friendship about each other to any one who had known them both but they did not see each other. Guillaume Apollinaire was dead. Braque and his wife we saw from time to time, he and Picasso by this time were fairly bitterly on the outs. I remember one evening Man Ray brought a photograph that he had made of Picasso to the house and Braque happened to be there. The photograph was being passed around and when it came to Braque he looked at it and said, I ought to know who that gentleman is, je dois connaître ce monsieur. It was a period this and a very considerable time afterward that Gertrude Stein celebrated under the title, Of Having for a Long Time Not Continued to be Friends. . . .

We began to meet new people all the time.

Some one told us, I have forgotten who, that an american woman had started a lending library of english books in our quarter. We had in those days of economy given up Mudie's, but there was the American Library which supplied us a little, but Gertrude Stein wanted more. We investigated and we found Sylvia Beach.[3] Sylvia Beach was very enthusiastic about Gertrude Stein and they became friends. She was Sylvia Beach's first annual subscriber and Sylvia Beach was proportionately proud and grateful. Her little place was in a little street near the Ecole de Médecine. It was not then much frequented by americans. There was the author of Beebie the Beebeist and there was the niece of Marcel Schwob and there were a few stray irish poets. We saw a good deal of Sylvia those days, she used to come to the house and also go out into the country with us in the old car. We met Adrienne Monnier and she brought Valéry

---

[3] American bookseller and publisher (1887–1962). An expatriate in Paris, she ran the famous Shakespeare & Co. bookstore, located at 12 rue de l'Odéon, and encouraged new, young writers of all nationalities. Beach was the first publisher of James Joyce's Ulysses (1922), which was banned in the United States for over ten years. Her autobiography Shakespeare and Company, was published in 1959.

Larbaud to the house and they were all very interested in Three Lives and Valéry Larbaud, so we understood, meditated translating it. It was at this time that Tristan Tzara first appeared in Paris. Adrienne Monnier was much excited by his advent. Picabia had found him in Switzerland during the war and they had together created dadaism, and out of dadaism, with a great deal of struggle and quarrelling came surréalisme.

Tzara came to the house, I imagine Picabia brought him but I am not quite certain. I have always found it very difficult to understand the stories of his violence and his wickedness, at least I found it difficult then because Tzara when he came to the house sat beside me at the tea table and talked to me like a pleasant and not very exciting cousin.

Adrienne Monnier wanted Sylvia to move to the rue de l'Odéon and Sylvia hesitated but finally she did so and as a matter of fact we did not see her very often afterward. They gave a party just after Sylvia moved in and we went and there Gertrude Stein first discovered that she had a young Oxford following. There were several young Oxford men there and they were awfully pleased to meet her and they asked her to give them some manuscripts and they published them that year nineteen twenty, in the Oxford Magazine.

Sylvia Beach from time to time brought groups of people to the house, groups of young writers and some older women with them. It was at that time that Ezra Pound came, no that was brought about in another way. She later ceased coming to the house but she sent word that Sherwood Anderson had come to Paris and wanted to see Gertrude Stein and might he come. Gertrude Stein sent back word that she would be very pleased and he came with his wife and Rosenfeld, the musical critic.

For some reason or other I was not present on this occasion, some domestic complication in all probability, at any rate when I did come home Gertrude Stein was moved and pleased as she has very rarely been. Gertrude Stein was in those days a little bitter, all her unpublished manuscripts, and no hope of publication or serious recognition. Sherwood Anderson came and quite simply and directly as is his way told her what he thought of her work and what it had meant to him in his development. He told it to her then and what was even rarer he told it in print immediately after. Gertrude Stein and Sherwood Anderson have always been the best of friends but I do not believe even he realises how much his visit meant to her. It was he who thereupon wrote the introduction to Geography and Plays. . . .

As I have said there was Broom.[4]

Before the war we had known a young fellow, not known him much but a little; Elmer Harden, who was in Paris studying music. During the war we heard that Elmer Harden had joined the french army and had been badly wounded. It was rather an amazing story. Elmer Harden had been nursing french wounded in the american hospital and one of his patients, a captain with an arm fairly disabled, was going back to the front. Elmer Harden could not content himself any longer nursing. He said

---

[4] *Broom* was published from November 1921 to January 1924 and was originally edited by Harold A. Loeb and Alfred Kreymborg. The latter has been called the patron saint of the little-magazine movement, of which *Broom* is one of the best-known and more lavish examples. The term "little magazine" is usually applied specifically to small, short-lived, avant-garde publications that encourage innovation and experimentation as opposed to orthodoxy and tradition. *Broom* takes its name from the proverb "A new broom sweeps clean."

to Captain Peter, I am going with you. But it is impossible, said Captain Peter. But I am, said Elmer stubbornly. So they took a taxi and they went to the war office and to a dentist and I don't know where else, but by the end of the week Captain Peter had rejoined and Elmer Harden was in his regiment as a soldier. He fought well and was wounded. After the war we met him again and then we met often. He and the lovely flowers he used to send us were a great comfort in those days just after the peace. He and I always say that he and I will be the last people of our generation to remember the war. I am afraid we both of us have already forgotten it a little. Only the other day though Elmer announced that he had had a great triumph, he had made Captain Peter and Captain Peter is a breton admit that it was a nice war. Up to this time when he had said to Captain Peter, it was a nice war, Captain Peter had not answered, but this time when Elmer said, it was a nice war, Captain Peter said, yes Elmer, it was a nice war.

Kate Buss came from the same town as Elmer, from Medford, Mass. She was in Paris and she came to see us. I do not think Elmer introduced her but she did come to see us. She was much interested in the writings of Gertrude Stein and owned everything that up to that time could be bought. She brought Kreymborg to see us. Kreymborg had come to Paris with Harold Loeb to start Broom. Kreymborg and his wife came to the house frequently. He wanted very much to run The Long Gay Book, the thing Gertrude Stein had written just after The Making of Americans, as a serial. Of course Harold Loeb would not consent to that. Kreymborg used to read out the sentences from this book with great gusto. He and Gertrude Stein had a bond of union beside their mutual liking because the Grafton Press that had printed Three Lives had printed his first book and about the same time.

Kate Buss brought lots of people to the house. She brought Djuna Barnes and Mina Loy and they had wanted to bring James Joyce but they didn't. We were glad to see Mina whom we had known in Florence as Mina Haweis. Mina brought Glenway Wescott on his first trip to Europe. Glenway impressed us greatly by his english accent. Hemingway explained. He said, when you matriculate at the University of Chicago you write down just what accent you will have and they give it to you when you graduate. You can have a sixteenth century or modern, whatever you like. Glenway left behind him a silk cigarette case with his initials, we kept it until he came back again and then gave it to him.

Mina also brought Robert McAlmon. McAlmon was very nice in those days, very mature and very good-looking. It was much later that he published The Making of Americans in the Contact press and that everybody quarrelled. But that is Paris, except that as a matter of fact Gertrude Stein and he never became friends again.

Kate Buss brought Ernest Walsh, he was very young then and very feverish and she was very worried about him. We met him later with Hemingway and then in Belley, but we never knew him very well.

We met Ezra Pound at Grace Lounsbery's house, he came home to dinner with us and he stayed and he talked about japanese prints among other things. Gertrude Stein liked him but did not find him amusing. She said he was a village explainer, excellent if you were a village, but if you were not, not. Ezra also talked about T. S. Eliot. It was the first time any one had talked about T.S. at the house. Pretty soon everybody talked about T.S. Kitty Buss talked about him and much later Hemingway talked about him as the Major. Considerably later Lady Rothermere talked about him and invited Gertrude Stein to come and meet him. They were founding the Criterion.[5] We had met Lady Rothermere through Muriel Draper whom we had seen again for the first time after many years. Gertrude Stein was not particularly anxious to go to Lady Rothermere's and meet T. S. Eliot, but we all insisted she should, and she gave a doubtful yes. I had no evening dress to wear for this occasion and started to make one. The bell rang and in walked Lady Rothermere and T.S.

Eliot and Gertrude Stein had a solemn conversation, mostly about split infinitives and other grammatical solecisms and why Gertrude Stein used them. Finally Lady Rothermere and Eliot rose to go and Eliot said that if he printed anything of Gertrude Stein's in the Criterion it would have to be her very latest thing. They left and Gertrude Stein said, don't bother to finish your dress, now we don't have to go, and she began to write a portrait of T. S. Eliot and called it the fifteenth of November, that being this day and so there could be no doubt but that it was her latest thing. It was all about wool is wool and silk is silk or wool is woollen and silk is silken. She sent it to T. S. Eliot and he accepted it but naturally he did not print it.

Then began a long correspondence, not between Gertrude Stein and T. S. Eliot, but between T. S. Eliot's secretary and myself. We each addressed the other as Sir, I signing myself A. B. Toklas and she signing initials. It was only considerably afterwards that I found out that his secretary was not a young man. I don't know whether she ever found out that I was not.

In spite of all this correspondence nothing happened and Gertrude Stein mischievously told the story to all the english people coming to the house and at that moment there were a great many english coming in and out. At any rate finally there was a note, it was now early spring, from the Criterion asking would Miss Stein mind if her contribution appeared in the October number. She replied that nothing could be more suitable than the fifteenth of November on the fifteenth of October.

Once more a long silence and then this time came proof of the article. We were surprised but returned the proof promptly. Apparently a young man had sent it without authority because very shortly came an apologetic letter saying that there had been a mistake, the article was not to be printed just yet. This was also told to the passing english with the result that after all it was printed. Thereafter it was reprinted in the Georgian Stories. Gertrude Stein was delighted when later she was told that Eliot had said in Cambridge that the work of Gertrude Stein was very fine but not for us.

But to come back to Ezra. Ezra did come back and he came back with the editor of The Dial.[6] This time it was worse than japanese prints, it was much more violent. In his surprise at the violence Ezra fell out of Gertrude Stein's favourite little armchair, the one I have since tapestried with Picasso designs, and Gertrude Stein was furious. Finally Ezra and the editor of The Dial left, nobody too well pleased. Gertrude Stein

---

[5] Another of the so-called little magazines, published in London in 1922 and edited for a time by the poet T. S. Eliot.

[6] Published, with numerous changes in editorial policy, from 1880 to 1929. In 1916 The Dial was moved from Chicago to New York and began publishing the work of new writers. In 1919 it began to publish the works of internationally known authors. This, the most famous of the so-called little magazines, is the third of four with this name to have appeared in America since 1840.

did not want to see Ezra again. Ezra did not quite see why. He met Gertrude Stein one day near the Luxembourg gardens and said, but I do want to come to see you. I am so sorry, answered Gertrude Stein, but Miss Toklas has a bad tooth and beside we are busy picking wild flowers. All of which was literally true, like all of Gertrude Stein's literature, but it upset Ezra, and we never saw him again. . . .

The first thing that happened when we were back in Paris was Hemingway with a letter of introduction from Sherwood Anderson.

I remember very well the impression I had of Hemingway that first afternoon. He was an extraordinarily good-looking young man, twenty-three years old. It was not long after that that everybody was twenty-six. It became the period of being twenty-six. During the next two or three years all the young men were twenty-six years old. It was the right age apparently for that time and place. There were one or two under twenty, for example George Lynes but they did not count as Gertrude Stein carefully explained to them. If they were young men they were twenty-six. Later on, much later on they were twenty-one and twenty-two.

So Hemingway was twenty-three, rather foreign looking, with passionately interested, rather than interesting eyes. He sat in front of Gertrude Stein and listened and looked.

They talked then, and more and more, a great deal together. He asked her to come and spend an evening in their apartment and look at his work. Hemingway had then and has always a very good instinct for finding apartments in strange but pleasing localities and good femmes de ménage and good food. This his first apartment was just off the place du Tertre. We spent the evening there and he and Gertrude Stein went over all the writing he had done up to that time. He had begun the novel that it was inevitable he would begin and there were the little poems afterwards printed by McAlmon in the Contract Edition. Gertrude Stein rather liked the poems, they were direct Kiplingesque, but the novel she found wanting. There is a great deal of description in this, she said, and not particularly good description. Begin over again and concentrate, she said.

Hemingway was at this time Paris correspondent for a canadian newspaper. He was obliged there to express what he called the canadian viewpoint.

He and Gertrude Stein used to walk together and talk together a great deal. One day she said to him, look here, you say you and your wife have a little money between you. Is it enough to live on if you live quietly. Yes, he said. Well, she said, then do it. If you keep on doing newspaper work you will never see things, you will only see words and that will not do, that is of course if you intend to be a writer. Hemingway said he undoubtedly intended to be a writer. . . .

In those early days Hemingway liked all his contemporaries except Cummings. He accused Cummings of having copied everything, not from anybody but from somebody. Gertrude Stein who had been much impressed by The Enormous Room said that Cummings did not copy, he was the natural heir of the New England tradition with its aridity and its sterility, but also with its individuality. They disagreed about this. They also disagreed about Sherwood Anderson. Gertrude Stein contended that Sherwood Anderson had a genius for using a sentence to convey a direct emotion, this was in the great american tradition, and that really except Sherwood there was no one in America who could write a clear and passionate sentence. Hemingway did not believe this, he did not like Sherwood's taste. Taste has nothing to do with sentences, contended Gertrude Stein. She also added that Fitzgerald was the only one of the younger writers who wrote naturally in sentences.

Gertrude Stein and Fitzgerald are very peculiar in their relation to each other. Gertrude Stein had been very much impressed by This Side of Paradise. She read it when it came out and before she knew any of the young american writers. She said of it that it was this book that really created for the public the new generation. She has never changed her opinion about this. She thinks this equally true of The Great Gatsby. She thinks Fitzgerald will be read when many of his well known contemporaries are forgotten. Fitzgerald always says that he thinks Gertrude Stein says these things just to annoy him by making him think that she means them, and he adds in his favourite way, and her doing it is the cruellest thing I ever heard. They always however have a very good time when they meet. And the last time they met they had a good time with themselves and Hemingway.

Then there was McAlmon. McAlmon had one quality that appealed to Gertrude Stein, abundance, he could go on writing, but she complained that it was dull.

There was also Glenway Wescott but Glenway Wescott at no time interested Gertrude Stein. He has a certain syrup but it does not pour.

So then Hemingway's career was begun. For a little while we saw less of him and then he began to come again. He used to recount to Gertrude Stein the conversations that he afterwards used in The Sun Also Rises and they talked endlessly about the character of Harold Loeb. At this time Hemingway was preparing his volume of short stories to submit to publishers in America. One evening after we had not seen him for a while he turned up with Shipman. Shipman was an amusing boy who was to inherit a few thousand dollars when he came of age. He was not of age. He was to buy the Transatlantic Review[7] when he came of age, so Hemingway said. He was to support a surrealist review when he came of age, André Masson said. He was to buy a house in the country when he came of age, Josette Gris said. As a matter of fact when he came of age nobody who had known him then seemed to know what he did do with his inheritance. Hemingway brought him with him to the house to talk about buying the Transatlantic and incidentally he brought the manuscript he intended sending to America. He handed it to Gertrude Stein. He had added to his stories a little story of meditations and in these he said that The Enormous Room was the greatest book he had ever read. It was then that Gertrude Stein said, Hemingway, remarks are not literature. . . .

For some time now many people, and publishers, have been asking Gertrude Stein to write her autobiography and she had always replied, not possibly.

She began to tease me and say that I should write my autobiography. Just think, she would say, what a lot of money you would make. She then began to invent titles for my autobiography. My Life With The Great, Wives of Geniuses I Have Sat With, My Twenty-five Years With Gertrude Stein.

Then she began to get serious and say, but really seriously you ought to write your autobiography. Finally I promised that if during the summer I could find time I would write my autobiography.

When Ford Madox Ford was editing the Transatlantic Review he once said to

---

[7] Another of the well-known little magazines, published in Paris from 1924 to 1925 and edited by the novelist Ford Madox Ford. Its assistant editor was Ernest Hemingway, whose work it often published.

Gertrude Stein, I am a pretty good writer and a pretty good editor and a pretty good business man but I find it very difficult to be all three at once.

I am a pretty good housekeeper and a pretty good gardener and a pretty good needlewoman and a pretty good secretary and a pretty good editor and a pretty good vet for dogs and I have to do them all at once and I found it difficult to add being a pretty good author.

About six weeks ago Gertrude Stein said, it does not look to me as if you were ever going to write that autobiography. You know what I am going to do. I am going to write it for you. I am going to write it as simply as Defoe did the autobiography of Robinson Crusoe. And she has and this is it.

1933

---

from Three Lives

The Gentle Lena

Lena was patient, gentle, sweet and German. She had been a servant for four years and had liked it very well.

Lena had been brought from Germany to Bridgepoint by a cousin and had been in the same place there for four years.

This place Lena had found very good. There was a pleasant, unexacting mistress and her children, and they all liked Lena very well.

There was a cook there who scolded Lena a great deal but Lena's German patience held no suffering and the good incessant woman really only scolded so for Lena's good.

Lena's German voice when she knocked and called the family in the morning was as awakening, as soothing, and as appealing, as a delicate soft breeze in midday, summer. She stood in the hallway every morning a long time in her unexpectant and unsuffering German patience calling to the young ones to get up. She would call and wait a long time and then call again, always even, gentle, patient, while the young ones fell back often into that precious, tense, last bit of sleeping that gives a strength of joyous vigour in the young, over them that have come to the readiness of middle age, in their awakening.

Lena had good hard work all morning and on the pleasant sunny afternoons she was sent out into the park to sit and watch the little two year old girl baby of the family.

The other girls, all them that make the pleasant lazy crowd, that watch the children in the sunny afternoons out in the park, all liked the simple, gentle, German Lena very well. They all, too, liked very well to tease her, for it was so easy to make her mixed and troubled, and all helpless, for she could never learn to know just what the other quicker girls meant by the queer things they said.

The two or three of these girls, the ones that Lena always sat with, always worked together to confuse her. Still it was pleasant, all this life for Lena.

The little girl fell down sometimes and cried, and then Lena had to soothe her. When the little girl would drop her hat, Lena had to pick it up and hold it. When the little girl was bad and threw away her playthings, Lena told her she could not have them and took them from her to hold until the little girl should need them.

It was all a peaceful life for Lena, almost as peaceful as a pleasant leisure. The other girls, of course, did tease her, but then that only made a gentle stir within her.

Lena was a brown and pleasant creature, brown as blonde races often have them brown, brown, not with the yellow or the red or the chocolate brown of sun burned countries, but brown with the clear colour laid flat on the light toned skin beneath, the plain, spare brown that makes it right to have been made with hazel eyes, and not too abundant straight, brown hair, hair that only later deepens itself into brown from the straw yellow of a German childhood.

Lena had the flat chest, straight back and forward falling shoulders of the patient and enduring working woman, though her body was now still in its milder girlhood and work had not yet made these lines too clear.

The rarer feeling that there was with Lena, showed in all the even quiet of her body movements, but in all it was the strongest in the patient, old-world ignorance, and earth made pureness of her brown, flat, soft featured face. Lena had eyebrows that were a wondrous thickness. They were black, and spread, and very cool, with their dark colour and their beauty, and beneath them were her hazel eyes, simple and human, with the earth patience of the working gentle, German woman.

Yes it was all a peaceful life for Lena. The other girls, of course, did tease her, but then that only made a gentle stir within her.

"What you got on your finger Lena," Mary, one of the girls she always sat with, one day asked her. Mary was good natured, quick, intelligent and Irish.

Lena had just picked up the fancy paper made accordion that the little girl had dropped beside her, and was making it squeak sadly as she pulled it with her brown, strong, awkward finger.

"Why, what is it, Mary, paint?" said Lena, putting her finger to her mouth to taste the dirt spot.

"That's awful poison Lena, don't you know?" said Mary, "that green paint that you just tasted."

Lena had sucked a good deal of the green paint from her finger. She stopped and looked hard at the finger. She did not know just how much Mary meant by what she said.

"Ain't it poison, Nellie, that green paint, that Lena sucked just now," said Mary. "Sure it is Lena, it's real poison, I ain't foolin' this time anyhow."

Lena was a little troubled. She looked hard at her finger where the paint was, and she wondered if she had really sucked it.

It was still a little wet on the edges and she rubbed it off a long time on the inside of her dress, and in between she wondered and looked at the finger and thought, was it really poison that she had just tasted.

"Ain't it too bad, Nellie, Lena should have sucked that," Mary said.

Nellie smiled and did not answer. Nellie was dark and thin, and looked Italian. She had a big mass of black hair that she wore high up on her head, and that made her face look very fine.

Nellie always smiled and did not say much, and then she would look at Lena to perplex her.

And so they all three sat with their little charges in the pleasant sunshine a long time. And Lena would often look at her finger and wonder if it was really poison that she had just tasted and then she would rub her finger on her dress a little harder.

Mary laughed at her and teased her and Nellie smiled a little and looked queerly at her.

Then it came time, for it was growing cooler, for them to drag together the little ones, who had begun to wander, and to take each one back to its own mother. And Lena never knew for certain whether it was really poison, that green stuff that she had tasted.

During these four years of service, Lena always spent her Sundays out at the house of her aunt, who had brought her four years before to Bridgepoint.

This aunt, who had brought Lena, four years before, to Bridgepoint, was a hard, ambitious, well meaning, German woman. Her husband was a grocer in the town, and they were very well to do. Mrs. Haydon, Lena's aunt, had two daughters who were just beginning as young ladies, and she had a little boy who was not honest and who was very hard to manage.

Mrs. Haydon was a short, stout, hard built, German woman. She always hit the ground very firmly and compactly as she walked. Mrs. Haydon was all a compact and well hardened mass, even to her face, reddish and darkened from its early blonde, with its hearty, shiny, cheeks, and doubled chin well covered over with the uproll from her short, square neck.

The two daughters, who were fourteen and fifteen, looked like unkneaded, unformed mounds of flesh beside her.

The elder girl, Mathilda, was blonde, and slow, and simple, and quite fat. The younger, Bertha, who was almost as tall as her sister, was dark, and quicker, and she was heavy, too, but not really fat.

These two girls the mother had brought up very firmly. They were well taught for their position. They were always both well dressed, in the same kinds of hats and dresses, as is becoming in two German sisters. The mother liked to have them dressed in red. Their best clothes were red dresses made of good heavy cloth, and strongly trimmed with braid of a glistening black. They had stiff, red felt hats, trimmed with black velvet ribbon, and a bird. The mother dressed matronly, in a bonnet and in black, always sat between her two big daughters, firm, directing, and repressed.

The only weak spot in this good German woman's conduct was the way she spoiled her boy, who was not honest and who was very hard to manage.

The father of this family was a decent, quiet, heavy, and uninterfering German man. He tried to cure the boy of his bad ways, and make him honest, but the mother could not make herself let the father manage, and so the boy was brought up very badly.

Mrs. Haydon's girls were now only just beginning as young ladies, and so to get her niece, Lena, married, was just then the most important thing that Mrs. Haydon had to do.

Mrs. Haydon had four years before gone to Germany to see her parents, and had taken the girls with her. This visit had been for Mrs. Haydon most successful, though her children had not liked it very well.

Mrs. Haydon was a good and generous woman, and she patronized her parents grandly, and all the cousins who came from all about to see her. Mrs. Haydon's people were of the middling class of farmers. They were not peasants, and they lived in a town of some pretension, but it all seemed very poor and smelly to Mrs. Haydon's American born daughters.

Mrs. Haydon liked it all. It was familiar, and then here she was so wealthy and important. She listened and decided, and advised all of her relations how to do things better. She arranged their present and their future for them, and showed them how in the past they had been wrong in all their methods.

Mrs. Haydon's only trouble was with her two daughters, whom she could not make behave well to her parents. The two girls were very nasty to all their numerous relations. Their mother could hardly make them kiss their grandparents, and every day the girls would get a scolding. But then Mrs. Haydon was so very busy that she did not have time to really manage her stubborn daughters.

These hard working, earth-rough German cousins were to these American born children, ugly and dirty, and as far below them as were Italian or negro workmen, and they could not see how their mother could ever bear to touch them, and then all the women dressed so funny, and were worked all rough and different.

The two girls stuck up their noses at them all, and always talked in English to each other about how they hated all these people and how they wished their mother would not do so. The girls could talk some German, but they never chose to use it.

It was her eldest brother's family that most interested Mrs. Haydon. Here there were eight children, and out of the eight, five of them were girls.

Mrs. Haydon thought it would be a fine thing to take one of these girls back with her to Bridgepoint and get her well started. Everybody liked that she should do so, and they were all willing that it should be Lena.

Lena was the second girl in her large family. She was at this time just seventeen years old. Lena was not an important daughter in the family. She was always sort of dreamy and not there. She worked hard and went very regularly at it, but even good work never seemed to bring her near.

Lena's age just suited Mrs. Haydon's purpose. Lena could first go out to service, and learn how to do things, and then, when she was a little older, Mrs. Haydon could get her a good husband. And then Lena was so still and docile, she would never want to do things her own way. And then, too, Mrs. Haydon, with all her hardness had wisdom, and she could feel the rarer strain there was in Lena.

Lena was willing to go with Mrs. Haydon. Lena did not like her German life very well. It was not the hard work but the roughness that disturbed her. The people were not gentle, and the men when they were glad were very boisterous, and would lay hold of her and roughly tease her. They were good people enough around her, but it was all harsh and dreary for her.

Lena did not really know that she did not like it. She did not know that she was always dreamy and not there. She did not think whether it would be different for her away off there in Bridgepoint. Mrs. Haydon took her and got her different kinds of dresses, and then took her with them to the steamer. Lena did not really know what it was that had happened to her.

Mrs. Haydon, and her daughters, and Lena travelled second class on the steamer. Mrs. Haydon's daughters hated that their mother should take Lena. They hated to have a cousin, who was to them, little better than a nigger, and then everybody on the steamer there would see her. Mrs. Haydon's daughters said things like this to their mother, but she never stopped to hear them, and the girls did not dare to make their meaning very clear. And so they could only go on hating Lena hard, together. They could not stop her from going back with them to Bridgepoint.

Lena was very sick on the voyage. She thought, surely before it was over that she would die. She was so sick she could not even wish that she had not started. She could not eat, she could not moan, she was just blank and scared, and sure that every minute she would die. She could not hold herself in, nor help herself in her trouble. She just stayed where she had been put, pale, and scared, and weak, and sick, and sure that she was going to die.

Mathilda and Bertha Haydon had no trouble from having Lena for a cousin on the voyage, until the last day that they were on the ship, and by that time they had made their friends and could explain.

Mrs. Haydon went down every day to Lena, gave her things to make her better, held her head when it was needful, and generally was good and did her duty by her.

Poor Lena had no power to be strong in such trouble. She did not know how to yield to her sickness nor endure. She lost all her little sense of being in her suffering. She was so scared, and then at her best, Lena, who was patient, sweet and quiet, had not self-control, nor any active courage.

Poor Lena was so scared and weak, and every minute she was sure that she would die.

After Lena was on land again a little while, she forgot all her bad suffering. Mrs. Haydon got her the good place, with the pleasant unexacting mistress, and her children, and Lena began to learn some English and soon was very happy and content.

All her Sundays out Lena spent at Mrs. Haydon's house. Lena would have liked much better to spend her Sundays with the girls she always sat with, and who often asked her, and who teased her and made a gentle stir within her, but it never came to Lena's unexpectant and unsuffering German nature to do something different from what was expected of her, just because she would like it that way better. Mrs. Haydon had said that Lena was to come to her house every other Sunday, and so Lena always went there.

Mrs. Haydon was the only one of her family who took any interest in Lena. Mr. Haydon did not think much of her. She was his wife's cousin and he was good to her, but she was for him stupid, and a little simple, and very dull, and sure some day to need help and to be in trouble. All young poor relations, who were brought from Germany to Bridgepoint were sure, before long, to need help and to be in trouble.

The little Haydon boy was always very nasty to her. He was a hard child for anyone to manage, and his mother spoiled him very badly. Mrs. Haydon's daughters as they grew older did not learn to like Lena any better. Lena never knew that she did not like them either. She did not know that she was only happy with the other quicker girls, she always sat with in the park, and who laughed at her and always teased her.

Mathilda Haydon, the simple, fat, blonde, older daughter felt very badly that she had to say that this was her cousin Lena, this Lena who was little better for her than a nigger. Mathilda was an overgrown, slow, flabby, blonde, stupid, fat girl, just beginning as a woman; thick in her speech and dull and simple in her mind, and very jealous of all her family and of other girls, and proud that she could have good dresses and new hats and learn music, and hating very badly to have a cousin who was a common servant. And then Mathilda remembered very strongly that dirty nasty place that Lena came from and that Mathilda had so turned up her nose at, and where she had been made so angry because her mother scolded her and liked all those rough cow-smelly people.

Then, too, Mathilda would get very mad when her mother had Lena at their parties, and when she talked about how good Lena was, to certain German mothers in whose sons, perhaps, Mrs. Haydon might find Lena a good husband. All this would make the dull, blonde, fat Mathilda very angry. Sometimes she would get so angry that she would, in her thick, slow way, and with jealous anger blazing in her light blue eyes, tell her mother that she did not see how she could like that nasty Lena; and then her mother would scold Mathilda, and tell her that she knew her cousin Lena was poor and Mathilda must be good to poor people.

Mathilda Haydon did not like relations to be poor. She told all her girl friends what she thought of Lena, and so the girls would never talk to Lena at Mrs. Haydon's parties. But Lena in her unsuffering and unexpectant patience never really knew that she was slighted. When Mathilda was with her girls in the street or in the park and would see Lena, she always turned up her nose and barely nodded to her, and then she would tell her friends how funny her mother was to take care of people like that Lena, and how, back in Germany, all Lena's people lived just like pigs.

The younger daughter, the dark, large, but not fat, Bertha Haydon, who was very quick in her mind, and in her ways, and who was the favourite with her father, did not like Lena, either. She did not like her because for her Lena was a fool and so stupid, and she would let those Irish and Italian girls laugh at her and tease her, and everybody always made fun of Lena, and Lena never got mad, or even had sense enough to know that they were all making an awful fool of her.

Bertha Haydon hated people to be fools. Her father, too, thought Lena was a fool, and so neither the father nor the daughter ever paid any attention to Lena, although she came to their house every other Sunday.

Lena did not know how all the Haydons felt. She came to her aunt's house all her Sunday afternoons that she had out, because Mrs. Haydon had told her she must do so. In the same way Lena always saved all of her wages. She never thought of any way to spend it. The German cook, the good woman who always scolded Lena, helped her to put it in the bank each month, as soon as she got it. Sometimes before it got into the bank to be taken care of, somebody would ask Lena for it. The little Haydon boy sometimes asked and would get it, and sometimes some of the girls, the ones Lena always sat with, needed some more money; but the German cook, who always scolded Lena, saw to it that this did not happen very often. When it did happen she would scold Lena very sharply, and for the next few months she would not let Lena touch her wages, but put it in the bank for her on the same day that Lena got it.

So Lena always saved her wages, for she never thought to spend them, and she always went to her aunt's house for her Sundays because she did not know that she could do anything different.

Mrs. Haydon felt more and more every year that she had done right to bring Lena back with her, for it was all coming out just as she had expected. Lena was good and never wanted her own way, she was learning English, and saving all her wages, and soon Mrs. Haydon would get her a good husband.

All these four years Mrs. Haydon was busy looking around among all the German people that she knew for the right man to be Lena's husband, and now at last she was quite decided.

The man Mrs. Haydon wanted for Lena was a young German-American tailor, who worked with his father. He was good and all the family were very saving, and Mrs. Haydon was sure that this would be just right for Lena, and then too, this young tailor always did whatever his father and his mother wanted.

This old German tailor and his wife, the father and the mother of Herman Kreder, who was to marry Lena Mainz, were very thrifty, careful people. Herman was the only child they had left with them, and he always did everything they wanted. Herman was now twenty-eight years old, but he had never stopped being scolded and directed by his father and his mother. And now they wanted to see him married.

Herman Kreder did not care much to get married. He was a gentle soul and a little fearful. He had a sullen temper, too. He was obedient to his father and his mother. He always did his work well. He often went out on Saturday nights and on Sundays, with other men. He liked it with them but he never became really joyous. He liked to be with men and he hated to have women with them. He was obedient to his mother, but he did not care much to get married.

Mrs. Haydon and the elder Kreders had often talked the marriage over. They all three liked it very well. Lena would do anything that Mrs. Haydon wanted, and Herman was always obedient in everything to his father and his mother. Both Lena and Herman were saving and good workers and neither of them ever wanted their own way.

The elder Kreders, everybody knew, had saved up all their money, and they were hard, good German people, and Mrs. Haydon was sure that with these people Lena would never be in any trouble. Mr. Haydon would not say anything about it. He knew old Kreder had a lot of money and owned some good houses, and he did not care what his wife did with that simple, stupid Lena, so long as she would be sure never to need help or to be in trouble.

Lena did not care much to get married. She liked her life very well where she was working. She did not think much about Herman Kreder. She thought he was a good man and she always found him very quiet. Neither of them ever spoke much to the other. Lena did not care much just then about getting married.

Mrs. Haydon spoke to Lena about it very often. Lena never answered anything at all. Mrs. Haydon thought, perhaps Lena did not like Herman Kreder. Mrs. Haydon could not believe that any girl not even Lena, really had no feeling about getting married.

Mrs. Haydon spoke to Lena very often about Herman. Mrs. Haydon sometimes got very angry with Lena. She was afraid that Lena, for once, was going to be stubborn, now when it was all fixed right for her to be married.

"Why you stand there so stupid, why don't you answer, Lena," said Mrs. Haydon one Sunday, at the end of a long talking that she was giving Lena about Herman Kreder, and about Lena's getting married to him.

"Yes ma'am," said Lena, and then Mrs. Haydon was furious with this stupid Lena. "Why don't you answer with some sense, Lena, when I ask you if you don't like Herman Kreder. You stand there so stupid and don't answer just like you ain't heard a word what I been saying to you. I never see anybody like you, Lena. If you going to burst out at all, why don't you burst out sudden instead of standing there so silly and don't answer. And here I am so good to you, and find you a good husband so you can have a place to live in all your own. Answer me, Lena, don't you like Herman

Kreder? He is a fine young fellow, almost too good for you, Lena, when you stand there so stupid and don't make no answer. There ain't many poor girls that get the chance you got now to get married."

"Why, I do anything you say, Aunt Mathilda. Yes, I like him. He don't say much to me, but I guess he is a good man, and I do anything you say for me to do."

"Well then Lena, why you stand there so silly all the time and not answer when I asked you."

"I didn't hear you say you wanted I should say anything to you. I didn't know you wanted me to say nothing. I do whatever you tell me it's right for me to do. I marry Herman Kreder, if you want me."

And so for Lena Mainz the match was made.

Old Mrs. Kreder did not discuss the matter with her Herman. She never thought that she needed to talk such things over with him. She just told him about getting married to Lena Mainz who was a good worker and very saving and never wanted her own way, and Herman made his usual little grunt in answer to her.

Mrs. Kreder and Mrs. Haydon fixed the day and made all the arrangements for the wedding and invited everybody who ought to be there to see them married.

In three months Lena Mainz and Herman Kreder were to be married.

Mrs. Haydon attended to Lena's getting all the things that she needed. Lena had to help a good deal with the sewing. Lena did not sew very well. Mrs. Haydon scolded because Lena did not do it better, but then she was very good to Lena, and she hired a girl to come and help her. Lena still stayed on with her pleasant mistress, but she spent all her evenings and her Sundays with her aunt and all the sewing.

Mrs. Haydon got Lena some nice dresses. Lena liked that very well. Lena liked having new hats even better, and Mrs. Haydon had some made for her by a real milliner who made them very pretty.

Lena was nervous these days, but she did not think much about getting married. She did not know really what it was, that, which was always coming nearer.

Lena liked the place where she was with the pleasant mistress and the good cook, who always scolded, and she liked the girls she always sat with. She did not ask if she would like being married any better. She always did whatever her aunt said and expected, but she was always nervous when she saw the Kreders with their Herman. She was excited and she liked her new hats, and everybody teased her and every day her marrying was coming nearer, and yet she did not really know what it was, this that was about to happen to her.

Herman Kreder knew more what it meant to be married and he did not like it very well. He did not like to see girls and he did not want to have to have one always near him. Herman always did everything that his father and his mother wanted and now they wanted that he should be married.

Herman had a sullen temper; he was gentle and he never said much. He liked to go out with other men, but he never wanted that there should be any women with them. The men all teased him about getting married. Herman did not mind the teasing but he did not like very well the getting married and having a girl always with him.

Three days before the wedding day, Herman went away to the country to be gone over Sunday. He and Lena were to be married Tuesday afternoon. When the day came Herman had not been seen or heard from.

The older Kreder couple had not worried much about it. Herman always did everything they wanted and he would surely come back in time to get married. But when Monday night came, and there was no Herman, they went to Mrs. Haydon to tell her what had happened.

Mrs. Haydon got very much excited. It was hard enough to work so as to get everything all ready, and then to have that silly Herman go off that way, so no one could tell what was going to happen. Here was Lena and everything all ready, and now they would have to make the wedding later so that they would know that Herman would be sure to be there.

Mrs. Haydon was very much excited, and then she could not say much to the old Kreder couple. She did not want to make them angry, for she wanted very badly now that Lena should be married to their Herman.

At last it was decided that the wedding should be put off a week longer. Old Mr. Kreder would go to New York to find Herman, for it was very likely that Herman had gone there to his married sister.

Mrs. Haydon sent word around, about waiting until a week from that Tuesday, to everybody that had been invited, and then Tuesday morning she sent for Lena to come down to see her.

Mrs. Haydon was very angry with poor Lena when she saw her. She scolded her hard because she was so foolish, and now Herman had gone off and nobody could tell where he had gone to, and all because Lena always was so dumb and silly. And Mrs. Haydon was just like a mother to her, and Lena always stood there so stupid and did not answer what anybody asked her, and Herman was so silly too, and now his father had to go and find him. Mrs. Haydon did not think that any old people should be good to their children. Their children always were so thankless, and never paid any attention, and older people were always doing things for their good. Did Lena think it gave Mrs. Haydon any pleasure, to work so hard to make Lena happy, and get her a good husband, and then Lena was so thankless and never did anything that anybody wanted. It was a lesson to poor Mrs. Haydon not to do things any more for anybody. Let everybody take care of themselves and never come to her with any troubles; she knew better now than to meddle to make other people happy. It just made trouble for her and her husband did not like it. He always said she was too good, and nobody ever thanked her for it, and there Lena was always standing stupid and not answering anything anybody wanted. Lena could always talk enough to those silly girls she liked so much, and always sat with, but who never did anything for her except to take away her money, and here was her aunt who tried so hard and was so good to her and treated her just like one of her own children and Lena stood there, and never made any answer and never tried to please her aunt, or to do anything that her aunt wanted. "No, it ain't no use your standin' there and cryin', now, Lena. It's too late now to care about that Herman. You should have cared some before, and then you wouldn't have to stand and cry now, and be a disappointment to me, and then I get scolded by my husband for taking care of everybody, and nobody ever thankful. I am glad you got the sense to feel sorry now, Lena, anyway, and I try to do what I can to help you out in your trouble, only you don't deserve to have anybody take any trouble for you. But perhaps you know better next time. You go home now and take care you don't spoil your clothes and that new hat, you had no business to be wearin' that this morning, but you ain't got no sense at all, Lena. I never in my life see anybody be so stupid."

Mrs. Haydon stopped and poor Lena stood there in her hat, all trimmed with pretty flowers, and the tears coming out of her eyes, and Lena did not know what it was that she had done, only she was not going to be married and it was a disgrace for a girl to be left by a man on the very day she was to be married.

Lena went home all alone, and cried in the street car.

Poor Lena cried very hard all alone in the street car. She almost spoiled her new hat with her hitting it against the window in her crying. Then she remembered that she must not do so.

The conductor was a kind man and he was very sorry when he saw her crying. "Don't feel so bad, you get another feller, you are such a nice girl," he said to make her cheerful. "But Aunt Mathilda said now, I never get married," poor Lena sobbed out for her answer. "Why you really got trouble like that," said the conductor, "I just said that now to josh you. I didn't ever think you really was left by a feller. He must be a stupid feller. But don't you worry, he wasn't much good if he could go away and leave you, lookin' to be such a nice girl. You just tell all your trouble to me, and I help you." The car was empty and the conductor sat down beside her to put his arm around her, and to be comfort to her. Lena suddenly remembered where she was, and if she did things like that her aunt would scold her. She moved away from the man into the corner. He laughed, "Don't be scared," he said, "I wasn't going to hurt you. But you just keep up your spirit. You are a real nice girl, and you'll be sure to get a real good husband. Don't you let nobody fool you. You're all right and I don't want to scare you."

The conductor went back to his platform to help a passenger get on the car. All the time Lena stayed in the street car, he would come in every little while and reassure her, about her not to feel so bad about a man who hadn't no more sense than to go away and leave her. She'd be sure yet to get a good man, she needn't be so worried he frequently assured her.

He chatted with the other passenger who had just come in, a very well dressed old man, and then with another who came in later, a good sort of a working man, and then another who came in, a nice lady, and he told them all about Lena's having trouble, and it was too bad there were men who treated a poor girl so badly. And everybody in the car was sorry for poor Lena and the workman tried to cheer her, and the old man looked sharply at her, and said she looked like a good girl, but she ought to be more careful and not to be so careless, and things like that would not happen to her, and the nice lady went and sat beside her and Lena liked it, though she shrank away from being near her.

So Lena was feeling a little better when she got off the car, and the conductor helped her, and he called out to her, "You be sure you keep up a good heart now. He wasn't no good that feller and you were lucky for to lose him. You'll get a real man yet, one that will be better for you. Don't you be worried, you're a real nice girl as I ever see in such trouble," and the conductor shook his head and went back into his car to talk it over with the other passengers he had there.

The German cook, who always scolded Lena, was very angry when she heard the story. She never did think Mrs. Haydon would do so much for Lena, though she was always talking so grand about what she could do for everybody. The good German cook always had been a little distrustful of her. People who always thought they were so much never did really do things right for anybody. Not that Mrs. Haydon wasn't a good woman. Mrs. Haydon was a real, good, German woman, and she did really mean to do well by her niece Lena. The cook knew that very well, and she had always said so, and she always had liked and respected Mrs. Haydon, who always acted very proper to her, and Lena was so backward, when there was a man to talk to, Mrs. Haydon did have hard work when she tried to marry Lena. Mrs. Haydon was a good woman, only she did talk sometimes too grand. Perhaps this trouble would make her see it wasn't always so easy to do, to make everybody do everything just like she wanted. The cook was very sorry now for Mrs. Haydon. All this must be such a disappointment, and such a worry to her, and she really had always been very good to Lena. But Lena had better go and put on her other clothes and stop with all that crying. That wouldn't do nothing now to help her, and if Lena would be a good girl, and just be real patient, her aunt would make it all come out right yet for her. "I just tell Mrs. Aldrich, Lena, you stay here yet a little longer. You know she is always so good to you, Lena, and I know she let you and I tell her all about that stupid Herman Kreder. I got no patience, Lena, with anybody who can be so stupid. You just stop now with your crying, Lena, and take off them good clothes and put them away so you don't spoil them when you need them, and you can help me with the dishes and everything will come off better for you. You see if I ain't right by what I tell you. You just stop crying now Lena quick, or else I scold you."

Lena still choked a little and was very miserable inside her but she did everything just as the cook told her.

The girls Lena always sat with were very sorry to see her look so sad with her trouble. Mary the Irish girl sometimes got very angry with her. Mary was always very hot when she talked of Lena's aunt Mathilda, who thought she was so grand, and had such stupid, stuck up daughters. Mary wouldn't be a fat fool like that ugly tempered Mathilda Haydon, not for anything anybody could ever give her. How Lena could keep on going there so much when they all always acted as if she was just dirt to them, Mary never could see. But Lena never had any sense of how she should make people stand round for her, and that was always all the trouble with her. And poor Lena, she was so stupid to be sorry for losing that gawky fool who didn't ever know what he wanted and just said "ja" to his mamma and his papa, like a baby, and was scared to look at a girl straight, and then sneaked away the last day like as if somebody was going to do something to him. Disgrace, Lena talking about disgrace! It was a disgrace for a girl to be seen with the likes of him, let alone to be married to him. But that poor Lena, she never did know how to show herself off for what she was really. Disgrace to have him go away and leave her. Mary would just like to get a chance to show him. If Lena wasn't worth fifteen like Herman Kreder, Mary would just eat her own head all up. It was a good riddance Lena had of that Herman Kreder and his stingy, dirty parents, and if Lena didn't stop crying about it,—Mary would just naturally despise her.

Poor Lena, she knew very well how Mary meant it all, this she was always saying to her. But Lena was very miserable inside her. She felt the disgrace it was for a decent German girl that a man should go away and leave her. Lena knew very well that her aunt was right when she said the way Herman had acted to her was a disgrace to everyone that knew her. Mary and Nellie and the other girls she always sat with were always very good to Lena but that did not make her trouble any better. It was a disgrace the way Lena had been left, to any decent family, and that could never be made any different to her.

And so the slow days wore on, and Lena never saw her Aunt Mathilda. At last on Sunday she got word by a boy to go and see her Aunt Mathilda. Lena's heart beat quick for she was very nervous now with all this that had happened to her. She went just as quickly as she could to see her Aunt Mathilda.

Mrs. Haydon quick, as soon as she saw Lena, began to scold her for keeping her aunt waiting so long for her, and for not coming in all the week to see her, to see if her aunt should need her, and so her aunt had to send a boy to tell her. But it was easy, even for Lena, to see that her aunt was not really angry with her. It wasn't Lena's fault, went on Mrs. Haydon, that everything was going to happen all right for her. Mrs. Haydon was very tired taking all this trouble for her, and when Lena couldn't even take trouble to come and see her aunt, to see if she needed anything to tell her. But Mrs. Haydon really never minded things like that when she could do things for anybody. She was tired now, all the trouble she had been taking to make things right for Lena, but perhaps now Lena heard it she would learn a little to be thankful to her. "You get all ready to be married Tuesday, Lena, you hear me," said Mrs. Haydon to her. "You come here Tuesday morning and I have everything all ready for you. You wear your new dress I got you, and your hat with all them flowers on it, and you be very careful coming you don't get your things all dirty, you so careless all the time, Lena, and not thinking, and you act sometimes you never got no head at all on you. You go home now, and you tell your Mrs. Aldrich that you leave her Tuesday. Don't you go forgetting now, Lena, anything I ever told you what you should do to be careful. You be a good girl, now Lena. You get married Tuesday to Herman Kreder." And that was all Lena ever knew of what had happened all this week to Herman Kreder. Lena forgot there was anything to know about it. She was really to be married Tuesday, and her Aunt Mathilda said she was a good girl, and now there was no disgrace left upon her.

Lena now fell back into the way she always had of being always dreamy and not there, the way she always had been, except for the few days she was so excited, because she had been left by a man the very day she was to have been married. Lena was a little nervous all these last days, but she did not think much about what it meant for her to be married.

Herman Kreder was not so content about it. He was quiet and was sullen and he knew he could not help it. He knew now he just had to let himself get married. It was not that Herman did not like Lena Mainz. She was as good as any other girl could be for him. She was a little better perhaps than other girls he saw, she was so very quiet, but Herman did not like to always have to have a girl around him. Herman had always done everything that his mother and his father wanted. His father had found him in New York, where Herman had gone to be with his married sister.

Herman's father when he had found him coaxed Herman a long time and went on whole days with his complaining to him, always troubled but gentle and quite patient with him, and always he was worrying to Herman about what was the right way his boy Herman should always do, always whatever it was his mother ever wanted from him, and always Herman never made him any answer.

Old Mr. Kreder kept on saying to him, he did not see how Herman could think now, it could be any different. When you make a bargain you just got to stick right to it, that was the only way old Mr. Kreder could ever see it, and saying you would get married to a girl and she got everything all ready, that was a bargain just like one you make in business and Herman he had made it, and now Herman he would just have to do it, old Mr. Kreder didn't see there was any other way a good boy like his Herman had, to do it. And then too that Lena Mainz was such a nice girl and Herman hadn't ought to really give his father so much trouble and make him pay out all that money, to come all the way to New York just to find him, and they both lose all that time from their working, when all Herman had to do was just to stand up, for an hour, and then he would be all right married, and it would be all over for him, and then everything at home would never be any different to him.

And his father went on; there was his poor mother saying always how her Herman always did everything before she ever wanted, and now just because he got notions in him, and wanted to show people how he could be stubborn, he was making all this trouble for her, and making them pay all that money just to run around and find him. "You got no idea Herman, how bad mama is feeling about the way you been acting Herman," said old Mr. Kreder to him. "She says she never can understand how you can be so thankless Herman. It hurts her very much you been so stubborn, and she find you such a nice girl for you, like Lena Mainz who is always just so quiet and always saves up all her wages, and she never wanting her own way at all like some girls are always all the time to have it, and your mama trying so hard, just so you could be comfortable Herman to be married, and then you act so stubborn Herman. You like all young people Herman, you think only about yourself, and what you are just wanting, and your mama she is thinking only what is good for you to have, for you in the future. Do you think your mama wants to have a girl around to be a bother, for herself, Herman. It's just for you Herman she is always thinking, and she talks always about how happy she will be, when she sees her Herman married to a nice girl, and then when she fixed it all up so good for you, so it never would be any bother to you, just the way she wanted you should like it, and you say yes all right, I do it, and then you go away like this and act stubborn, and make all this trouble everybody to take for you, and we spend money, and I got to travel all round to find you. You come home now with me Herman and get married, and I tell your mama she better not say anything to you about how much it cost me to come all the way to look for you—Hey Herman," said his father coaxing, "hey, you come home now and get married. All you got to do Herman is just to stand up for an hour Herman and then you don't never to have any more bother to it—Hey Herman!— you come home with me to-morrow and get married. Hey Herman."

Herman's married sister liked her brother Herman, and she had always tried to help him, when there was anything she knew he wanted. She liked it that he was so good and always did everything that their father and their mother wanted, but still she wished it could be that he could have more his own way, if there was anything he ever wanted.

But now she thought Herman with his girl was very funny. She wanted that Herman should be married. She thought it would do him lots of good to get married. She laughed at Herman when she heard the story. Until his father came to find him, she did not know why it was Herman had come just then to New York to see her. When she heard the story she laughed a good deal at her brother Herman and teased him a good deal about his running away, because he didn't want to have a girl to be all the time around him.

Herman's married sister liked her brother Herman, and she did not want him not to like to be with women. He was good, her brother Herman, and it would surely do him good to get married. It would make him stand up for himself stronger. Herman's sister always laughed at him and always she would try to reassure him. "Such a nice man as my brother Herman acting like as if he was afraid of women. Why the girls all like a man like you Herman, if you didn't always run away when you saw them. It do you good really Herman to get married, and then you got somebody you can boss around when you want to. It do you good Herman to get married, you see if you don't like it, when you really done it. You go along home now with papa, Herman and get married to that Lena. You don't know how nice you like it Herman when you try once how you can do it. You just don't be afraid of nothing, Herman. You good enough for any girl to marry, Herman. Any girl be glad to have a man like you to be always with them Herman. You just go along home with papa and try it what I say, Herman. Oh you so funny Herman, when you sit there, and then run away and leave your girl behind you. I know she is crying like anything Herman for to lose you. Don't be bad to her Herman. You go along home with papa now and get married Herman. I'd be awful ashamed Herman, to really have a brother didn't have spirit enough to get married, when a girl is just dying for to have him. You always like me to be with you Herman. I don't see why you say you don't want a girl to be all the time around you. You always been good to me Herman, and I know you always be good to that Lena, and you soon feel just like as if she had always been there with you. Don't act like as if you wasn't a nice strong man, Herman. Really I laugh at you Herman, but you know I like awful well to see you real happy. You go home and get married to that Lena, Herman. She is a real pretty girl and real nice and good and quiet and she make my brother Herman very happy. You just stop your fussing now with Herman, papa. He go with you to-morrow papa, and you see he like it so much to be married, he make everybody laugh just to see him be so happy. Really truly, that's the way it will be with you Herman. You just listen to me what I tell you Herman." And so his sister laughed at him and reassured him, and his father kept on telling what the mother always said about her Herman, and he coaxed him and Herman never said anything in answer, and his sister packed his things up and was very cheerful with him, and she kissed him, and then she laughed and then she kissed him, and his father went and bought the tickets for the train, and at last late on Sunday he brought Herman back to Bridgepoint with him.

It was always very hard to keep Mrs. Kreder from saying what she thought, to her Herman, but her daughter had written her a letter, so as to warn her not to say anything about what he had been doing, to him, and her husband came in with Herman and said, "Here we are come home mama, Herman and me, and we are very tired it was so crowded coming," and then he whispered to her. "You be good to Herman, mama, he didn't mean to make us so much trouble," and so old Mrs. Kreder, held in what she felt was so strong in her to say to her Herman. She just said very stiffly to him, "I'm glad to see you come home to-day, Herman." Then she went to arrange it all with Mrs. Haydon.

Herman was now again just like he always had been, sullen and very good, and very quiet, and always ready to do whatever his mother and his father wanted. Tuesday morning came, Herman got his new clothes on and went with his father and his mother to stand up for an hour and get married. Lena was there in her new dress, and her hat with all the pretty flowers, and she was very nervous for now she knew she was really very soon to be married. Mrs. Haydon had everything all ready.

Everybody was there just as they should be and very soon Herman Kreder and Lena Mainz were married.

When everything was really over, they went back to the Kreder house together. They were all now to live together, Lena and Herman and the old father and the old mother, in the house where Mr. Kreder had worked so many years as a tailor, with his son Herman always there to help him.

Irish Mary had often said to Lena she never did see how Lena could ever want to have anything to do with Herman Kreder and his dirty stingy parents. The old Kreders were to an Irish nature, a stingy, dirty couple. They had not the free-hearted, thoughtless, fighting, mud bespattered, ragged, peat-smoked cabin dirt that Irish Mary knew and could forgive and love. Theirs was the German dirt of saving, of being dowdy and loose and foul in your clothes so as to save them and yourself in washing, having your hair greasy to save it in the soap and drying, having your clothes dirty, not in freedom, but because so it was cheaper, keeping the house close and smelly, because so it cost less to get it heated, living so poorly not only so as to save money but so they should never even know themselves that they had it, working all the time not only because from their nature they just had to and because it made them money but also that they never could be put in any way to make them spend their money.

This was the place Lena now had for her home and to her it was very different than it could be for an Irish Mary. She too was German and was thrifty, though she was always so dreamy and not there. Lena was always careful with things and she always saved her money, for that was the only way she knew how to do it. She never had taken care of her own money and she never had thought how to use it.

Lena Mainz had been, before she was Mrs. Herman Kreder, always clean and decent in her clothes and in her person, but it was not because she ever thought about it or really needed so to have it, it was the way her people did in the German country where she came from, and her Aunt Mathilda and the good German cook who always scolded, had kept her on and made her, with their scoldings, always more careful to keep clean and to wash real often. But there was no deep need in all this for Lena and so, though Lena did not like the old Kreders, though she really did not know that, she did not think about their being stingy dirty people.

Herman Kreder was cleaner than the old people, just because it was his nature to keep cleaner, but he was used to his mother and his father, and he never thought that they should keep things cleaner. And Herman too always saved all his money, except for that little beer he drank when he went out with other men of an evening the way he always liked to do it, and he never thought of any other way to spend it. His father had always kept all the money for them and he always was doing business with it. And then too Herman really had no money, for he always had worked for his father, and his father had never thought to pay him.

And so they began all four to live in the Kreder house together, and Lena began soon with it to look careless and a little dirty, and to be more lifeless with it, and nobody ever noticed much what Lena wanted, and she never really knew herself what she needed.

The only real trouble that came to Lena with their living all four there together, was the way old Mrs. Kreder scolded. Lena had always been used to being scolded, but this scolding of old Mrs. Kreder was very different from the way she ever before had had to endure it.

Herman, now he was married to her, really liked Lena very well. He did not care very much about her but she never was a bother to him being there around him, only when his mother worried and was nasty to them because Lena was so careless, and did not know how to save things right for them with their eating, and all the other ways with money, that the old woman had to save it.

Herman Kreder had always done everything his mother and his father wanted but he did not really love his parents very deeply. With Herman it was always only that he hated to have any struggle. It was all always all right with him when he could just go along and do the same thing over every day with his working, and not to hear things, and not to have people make him listen to their anger. And now his marriage, and he just knew it would, was making trouble for him. It made him hear more what his mother was always saying, with her scolding. He had to really hear it now because Lena was there, and she was so scared and dull always when she heard it. Herman knew very well with his mother, it was all right if one ate very little and worked hard all day and did not hear her when she scolded, the way Herman always had done before they were so foolish about his getting married and having a girl there to be all the time around him, and now he had to help her so the girl could learn too, not to hear it when his mother scolded and not to look so scared, and not to eat much, and always to be sure to save it.

Herman really did not know very well what he could do to help Lena to understand it. He could never answer his mother back to help Lena, that never would make things any better for her, and he never could feel in himself any way to comfort Lena, to make her strong not to hear his mother, in all the awful ways she always scolded. It just worried Herman to have it like that all the time around him. Herman did not know much about how a man could make a struggle with a mother, to do much to keep her quiet, and indeed Herman never knew much how to make a struggle against anyone who really wanted to have anything very badly. Herman all his life never wanted anything so badly, that he would really make a struggle against any one to get it. Herman all his life only wanted to live regular and quiet, and not talk much and to do the same way every day like every other with his working. And now his mother had made him get married to this Lena and now with his mother making all that scolding, he had all this trouble and this worry always on him.

Mrs. Haydon did not see Lena now very often. She had not lost her interest in her niece Lena, but Lena could not come much to her house to see her, it would not be right, now Lena was a married woman. And then too Mrs. Haydon had her hands full just then with her two daughters, for she was getting them ready to find them good husbands, and then too her own husband now worried her very often about her always spoiling that boy of hers, so he would be sure to turn out no good and be a disgrace to a German family, and all because his mother always spoiled him. All these things were very worrying now to Mrs. Haydon, but still she wanted to be good to Lena, though she could not see her very often. She only saw her when Mrs. Haydon went to call on Mrs. Kreder or when Mrs. Kreder came to see Mrs. Haydon, and that never could be very often. Then too these days Mrs. Haydon could not scold Lena, Mrs. Kreder was always there with her, and it would not be right to scold Lena when Mrs. Kreder was there, who had now the real right to do it. And so her aunt always said nice things now to Lena, and though Mrs. Haydon sometimes was a little worried when she saw Lena looking sad and not careful, she did not have time just then to really worry much about it.

Lena now never any more saw the girls she always used to sit with. She had no way now to see them and it was not in Lena's nature to search out ways to see them, nor did she now ever think much of the days when she had been used to see them. They never any of them had come to the Kreder house to see her. Not even Irish Mary had ever thought to come to see her. Lena had been soon forgotten by them. They had soon passed away from Lena and now Lena never thought any more that she had ever known them.

The only one of her old friends who tried to know what Lena liked and what she needed, and who always made Lena come to see her, was the good German cook who had always scolded. She now scolded Lena hard for letting herself go so, and going out when she was looking so untidy. "I know you going to have a baby Lena, but that's no way for you to be looking. I am ashamed most to see you come and sit here in my kitchen, looking so sloppy and like you never used to Lena. I never see anybody like you Lena. Herman is very good to you, you always say so, and he don't treat you bad ever though you don't deserve to have anybody good to you, you so careless all the time, Lena, letting yourself go like you never had anybody tell you what was the right way you should know how to be looking. No, Lena, I don't see no reason you should let yourself go so and look so untidy Lena, so I am ashamed to see you sit there looking so ugly, Lena. No Lena that ain't no way ever I see a woman make things come out better, letting herself go so every way and crying all the time like as if you had real trouble. I never wanted to see you marry Herman Kreder, Lena, I knew what you got to stand with that old woman always, and that old man, he is so stingy too and he don't say things out but he ain't any better in his heart than his wife with her bad ways, I know that Lena, I know they don't hardly give you enough to eat, Lena, I am real sorry for you Lena, you know that Lena, but that ain't anyway to be going round so untidy Lena, even if you have got all that trouble. You never see me do like that Lena, though sometimes I got a headache so I can't see to stand to be working hardly, and nothing comes right with all my cooking, but I always see Lena, I look decent. That's the only way a German girl can make things come out right Lena. You hear me what I am saying to you, Lena. Now you eat something rice Lena, I got it all ready for you, and you wash up and be careful Lena and the baby will come all right to you, and then I make your Aunt Mathilda see that you live in a house soon all alone with Herman and your baby, and then everything go better for you. You hear me what I say to you Lena. Now don't let me ever see you come looking like this any more Lena, and you just stop with that always crying. You ain't got no reason to be sitting there now with all that crying, I never see anybody have trouble it did them any good to do the way you are doing, Lena. You hear me Lena. You go home now and you be good the way I tell you Lena, and I see what I can do. I make your Aunt Mathilda make old Mrs. Kreder let you be till you get your baby all right. Now don't you be scared and so silly Lena. I don't like to see you act so Lena when really you got a nice man and so many things really any girl should be grateful to be having. Now you go home Lena to-day and you do the way I say, to you, and I see what I can do to help you."

"Yes Mrs. Aldrich" said the good German woman to her mistress later, "Yes Mrs. Aldrich that's the way it is with them girls when they want so to get married. They don't know when they got it good Mrs. Aldrich. They never know what it is they're really wanting when they got it, Mrs. Aldrich. There's that poor Lena, she just been here crying and looking so careless so I scold her, but that was no good that marrying for that poor Lena, Mrs. Aldrich. She do look so pale and sad now Mrs. Aldrich, it just break my heart to see her. She was a good girl was Lena, Mrs. Aldrich, and I never had no trouble with her like I got with so many young girls nowadays Mrs. Aldrich, and I never see any girl any better to work right than our Lena, and now she got to stand it all the time with that old woman Mrs. Kreder. My! Mrs. Aldrich, she is a bad old woman to her. I never see Mrs. Aldrich how old people can be so bad to young girls and not have no kind of patience with them. If Lena could only live with her Herman, he ain't so bad the way men are, Mrs. Aldrich, but he is just the way always his mother wants him, he ain't got no spirit in him, and so I don't really see no help for that poor Lena. I know her aunt, Mrs. Haydon, meant it all right for her Mrs. Aldrich, but poor Lena, it would be better for her if her Herman had stayed there in New York that time he went away to leave her. I don't like it the way Lena is looking now, Mrs. Aldrich. She looks like as if she don't have no life left in her hardly, Mrs. Aldrich, she just drags around and looks so dirty and after all the pains I always took to teach her and to keep her nice in her ways and looking. It don't do no good to them, for them girls to get married Mrs. Aldrich, they are much better when they only know it, to stay in a good place when they got it, and keep on regular with their working. I don't like it the way Lena looks now Mrs. Aldrich. I wish I knew some way to help that poor Lena, Mrs. Aldrich, but she is a bad old woman, that old Mrs. Kreder, Herman's mother. I speak to Mrs. Haydon real soon, Mrs. Aldrich, I see what we can do now to help that poor Lena."

These were really bad days for poor Lena. Herman always was real good to her and now he even sometimes tried to stop his mother from scolding Lena. "She ain't well now mama, you let her be now you hear me. You tell me what it is you want she should be doing, I tell her. I see she does it right just the way you want it mama. You let be, I say now mama, with that always scolding Lena. You let be, I say now, you wait till she is feeling better." Herman was getting really strong to struggle, for he could see that Lena with that baby working hard inside her, really could not stand it any longer with his mother and the awful ways she always scolded.

It was a new feeling Herman now had inside him that made him feel he was strong to make a struggle. It was new for Herman Kreder really to be wanting something, but Herman wanted strongly now to be a father, and he wanted badly that his baby should be a boy and healthy. Herman never had cared really very much about his father and his mother, though always, all his life, he had done everything just as they wanted, and he had never really cared much about his wife, Lena, though he always had been very good to her, and had always tried to keep his mother off her, with the awful way she always scolded, but to be really a father of a little baby, that feeling took hold of Herman very deeply. He was almost ready, so as to save his baby from all trouble, to really make a strong struggle with his mother and with his father, too, if he would not help him to control his mother.

Sometimes Herman even went to Mrs. Haydon to talk all this trouble over. They decided then together, it was better to wait there all four together for the baby, and Herman could make Mrs. Kreder stop a little with her scolding, and then when Lena was a little stronger, Herman should have his own house for her, next door to his father, so he could always be there to help him in his working, but so they could eat and sleep in a house where the old woman could not control them and they could not hear her awful scolding.

And so things went on, the same way, a little longer. Poor Lena was not feeling any joy to have a baby. She was scared the way she had been when she was so sick on the water. She was scared now every time when anything would hurt her. She was scared and still and lifeless, and sure that every minute she would die. Lena had no power to be strong in this kind of trouble, she could only sit still and be scared, and dull, and lifeless, and sure that every minute she would die.

Before very long, Lena had her baby. He was a good, healthy little boy, the baby. Herman cared very much to have the baby. When Lena was a little stronger he took a house next door to the old couple, so he and his own family could eat and sleep and do the way they wanted. This did not seem to make much change now for Lena. She was just the same as when she was waiting with her baby. She just dragged around and was careless with her clothes and all lifeless, and she acted always and lived on just as if she had no feeling. She always did everything regular with the work, the way she always had had to do it, but she never got back any spirit in her. Herman was always good and kind, and always helped her with her working. He did everything he knew to help her. He always did all the active new things in the house and for the baby. Lena did what she had to do the way she always had been taught it. She always just kept going now with her working, and she was always careless, and dirty, and a little dazed, and lifeless. Lena never got any better in herself of this way of being that she had had ever since she had been married.

Mrs. Haydon never saw any more of her niece, Lena. Mrs. Haydon had now so much trouble with her own house, and her daughters getting married, and her boy, who was growing up, and who always was getting so much worse to manage. She knew she had done right by Lena. Herman Kreder was a good man, she would be glad to get one so good, sometimes, for her own daughters, and now they had a home to live in together, separate from the old people, who had made their trouble for them. Mrs. Haydon felt she had done very well by her niece Lena, and she never thought now she needed any more to go and see her. Lena would do very well now without her aunt to trouble herself any more about her.

The good German cook who had always scolded, still tried to do her duty like a mother to poor Lena. It was very hard now to do right by Lena. Lena never seemed to hear now what anyone was saying to her. Herman was always doing everything he could to help her. Herman always, when he was home, took good care of the baby. Herman loved to take care of his baby. Lena never thought to take him out or to do anything she didn't have to.

The good cook sometimes made Lena come to see her. Lena would come with her baby and sit there in the kitchen, and watch the good woman cooking, and listen to her sometimes a little, the way she used to, while the good German woman scolded her for going around looking so careless when now she had no trouble, and sitting there so dull, and always being just so thankless. Sometimes Lena would wake up a little and get back into her face her old, gentle, patient, and unsuffering sweetness, but mostly Lena did not seem to hear much when the good German woman scolded. Lena always liked it when Mrs. Aldrich her good mistress spoke to her kindly, and then Lena would seem to go back and feel herself to be like she was when she had been in service. But mostly Lena just lived along and was careless in her clothes, and dull, and lifeless.

By and by Lena had two more little babies. Lena was not so much scared now when she had the babies. She did not seem to notice very much when they hurt her, and she never seemed to feel very much now about anything that happened to her.

They were very nice babies, all these three that Lena had, and Herman took good care of them always. Herman never really cared much about his wife, Lena. The only things Herman ever really cared for were his babies. Herman always was very good to his children. He always had a gentle, tender way when he held them. He learned to be very handy with them. He spent all the time he was not working, with them. By and by he began to work all day in his own home so that he could have his children always in the same room with him.

Lena always was more and more lifeless and Herman now mostly never thought about her. He more and more took all the care of their three children. He saw to their eating right and their washing, and he dressed them every morning, and he taught them the right way to do things, and he put them to their sleeping, and he was now always every minute with them. Then there was to come to them, a fourth baby. Lena went to the hospital near by to have the baby. Lena seemed to be going to have much trouble with it. When the baby was come out at last, it was like its mother lifeless. While it was coming, Lena had grown very pale and sicker. When it was all over Lena had died, too, and nobody knew just how it had happened to her.

The good German cook who had always scolded Lena, and had always to the last day tried to help her, was the only one who ever missed her. She remembered how nice Lena had looked all the time she was in service with her, and how her voice had been so gentle and sweet-sounding, and how she always was a good girl, and how she never had to have any trouble with her, the way she always had with all the other girls who had been taken into the house to help her. The good cook sometimes spoke so of Lena when she had time to have a talk with Mrs. Aldrich, and this was all the remembering there now ever was of Lena.

Herman Kreder now always lived very happy, very gentle, very quiet, very well content alone with his three children. He never had a woman any more to be all the time around him. He always did all his own work in his house, when he was through every day with the work he was always doing for his father. Herman always was alone, and he always worked alone, until his little ones were big enough to help him. Herman Kreder was very well content now and he always lived very regular and peaceful, and with every day just like the next one, always alone now with his three good, gentle children.

1909

Sherwood Anderson
1876–1941

Sherwood Anderson was born on September 13, 1876, in Camden, Ohio, a small town near the Kentucky border. During the first eighteen years of his life, his family moved from one Ohio town to the next, as his father, a harness maker and inveterate storyteller whom Anderson described as a "colorful no account," shifted from job to job. Anderson's formal education was brief and spotty. As a boy he worked at many jobs—as a newsboy, a housepainter, a stableboy, a farmhand, and a laborer in a bicycle factory. At fourteen, when his mother died, he dropped out of school altogether. When he was eighteen, his family settled in Clyde, Ohio, the town that he would later imaginatively transform into Winesburg, Ohio, the fictional setting that ensured his literary reputation. In 1896, however, after only two years in Clyde, Anderson moved to Chicago, where he worked as a warehouse laborer. In 1898 he enlisted in the army during the Spanish-American War and served briefly in Cuba. Back from the army, he drifted into business, first as an advertising copywriter in Chicago and later as the manager of two paint firms in Ohio. By 1904, when he married the first of his four wives, he was living the life of a successful businessman.

At the same time, Anderson was secretly writing fiction and building toward a crisis. Everything came to a head on November 27, 1912, when suddenly, in the middle of dictating a letter, he walked out of his office in Elyria, Ohio, and disappeared for several days. He turned up in Cleveland disturbed, disheveled, and disoriented. He later dramatized this apparently confused gesture as an artistic repudiation of the business world. It also became an integral part of his literary achievement. The critic Clifton Fadiman remarked of Anderson that "the dramatization of this moment is his major contribution to the interpretation of American life. . . . He is obsessed with the experience of sudden self-discovery."

Having recovered from his nervous collapse, Anderson moved again to Chicago, hoping this time to combine a career writing advertising copy with a career writing fiction. But he was now moving steadily toward art. He was reading receptively the work of Sigmund Freud, D. H. Lawrence, and Gertrude Stein. He was also receiving encouragement from some of the leading figures of the Chicago "Renaissance," including Theodore Dreiser, Ben Hecht, Floyd Dell, and Carl Sandburg. Soon he began publishing verse and short fiction in *The Little Review, Poetry, The Masses,* and *The Seven Arts.* In 1916 he published his first novel, *Windy McPherson's Son,* an autobiographical story based on memories of his father and his own recent disillusionment with the world of business. A second novel, *Marching Men* (1917), dealt with a militant brotherhood of industrial workers. In 1918 Anderson published a volume of poems in the Carl Sandburg manner, *Mid-American Chants.*

In the late fall of 1915 Anderson began writing the 23 tales that would compose the only one of his books still regarded as a major achievement, *Winesburg, Ohio* (1919). By the middle of the next year he had finished most of "The Tales and the Persons" that make up his "Book of the Grotesque." Thematically, Anderson's Winesburg tales (the name of the fictional town suggests a combination of the dreamy and the mundane) anticipate the wasteland image explored by T. S. Eliot, Ernest Hemingway, F. Scott Fitzgerald, and Nathanael West. The truncation of life that his characters experience becomes a kind of living death. Their senses seem anesthetized, their sensibilities numbed, their spirits shrunken. Though the feeling of small-town paralysis derived directly from Anderson's experiences, *Winesburg, Ohio* was structurally indebted to such collections as Ivan Turgenev's *A Sportsman's Sketches* (1852), James Joyce's *Dubliners* (1914), and particularly Edgar Lee Masters's *Spoon River Anthology* (1915). Anderson acknowledged the influence of Gertrude Stein's *Three Lives*

(1909)—"She is making new, strange and to my ears sweet combinations of words"—in the development of his repetitive, colloquial prose style. So deliberately did Anderson resist fancy writing ("I have had a great fear of phrase-making") that his prose might be said to approach a poetry of inarticulation. Nearly all of his characters struggle at self-expression and, as stories like "Hands" and "Mother" clearly reveal, live in a conversational world of unfocused feelings and awkward silences.

Winesburg, Ohio has had an enormous influence on the development of the American short story. Its sequential pattern anticipates such collections as Jean Toomer's *Cane,* Ernest Hemingway's *In Our Time,* William Faulkner's *Go Down, Moses,* and more recently, John Barth's *Lost in the Funhouse.* Its preoccupation with American eccentrics and "grotesques" foreshadowed the characterizations of such later short-story writers as Flannery O'Connor and Carson McCullers. And its spare poetry of ordinary American speech anticipates the recent working-class tales of Raymond Carver and Bobbie Ann Mason. Anderson also demonstrated in his stories and critical essays an aesthetic resistance to the literary slickness of contrived plots: No Americans, he wrote, "lived, felt, or talked as the average American novel makes them live, feel, or talk and as for the plot short stories of the magazines—those bastard children of de Maupassant, Poe, and O. Henry—it was certain that there were no plot stories ever lived in any life."

As much as any writer of his time, Anderson combined the fate of being a flawed writer ("For all my egotism," he remarked late in his life, "I know I am but a minor figure") and a major force ("He was the father of my generation of American writers and the tradition of American writing which our successors will carry on," remarked William Faulkner). None of Anderson's subsequent books had the literary impact of *Winesburg, Ohio,* though collections of short stories such as *The Triumph of the Egg* (1921), *Horses and Men* (1923), and *Death in the Woods and Other Stories* (1933) contain a number of excellent tales. Anderson continued to write novels, the most successful of which is *Poor White* (1920), the story of an aspiring midwestern inventor who realizes that his industrial genius is destroying the environment. His later novels include *Many Marriages* (1923), *Dark Laughter* (1925), *Beyond Desire* (1932), and *Kit Brandon* (1936). Anderson also published several collections of essays on American industrial and rural conditions, *Perhaps Women* (1931), *Puzzled America* (1935), and *Home Town* (1940), and a collection of literary profiles, *No Swank* (1934).

In the summer of 1922, a year after he had traveled to Europe and met Gertrude Stein, Anderson was finally able to give up copywriting. In 1924 he moved with his third wife to Marion, Virginia, where he edited two local newspapers, one Democratic and the other Republican. He collected his editorials in *Hello, Towns* (1929). In 1941, while on a State Department goodwill tour of South America, he died of peritonitis caused by his accidentally having swallowed a fragment of a toothpick at a cocktail party.

One explanation of the discrepancy between Anderson's achievement and his influence has to do with his origins. Many critics and readers were easterners who nevertheless believed, as Van Wyck Brooks put it, "that the heart of America lay in the West" and that "Sherwood was the essence of his West." A second explanation lies in the overriding importance of the theme and scene that

Anderson sought to explore: the loneliness of the modern world as manifested in the social, cultural, and spiritual impoverishment of small-town America. The isolation that haunts Anderson's characters is religious as well as social; felt as a form of orphanhood, a kind of ultimate separation, it leads them almost inevitably to flight that is undertaken as a kind of return. The struggle his characters wage, they wage in the name of reestablishing ties with a community, a family, or a self that they have somehow lost. A third explanation lies in Anderson's capacity for deliberate self-dramatization. Like Walt Whitman, Anderson viewed himself as a composite of us all; he was the American as writer. In the tales he told about himself, in his three volumes of autobiographical writing, *A Story-Teller's Story* (1924), *Tar: A Midwest Childhood* (1926), and the posthumous *Sherwood Anderson's Memoirs* (1942), and in his letters, he insisted on mixing his life and art, on making himself into a fictional character for his time as well as for himself. In this, too, his motives were mixed: They were social and even didactic as well as personal and artistic. Anderson wanted to teach us, among other things, the value of dropping out and breaking away. "I hardly know what I can teach except anti-success," he wrote his brother Karl in 1931. Most of all, Anderson wanted to teach us that the purpose of art, like the purpose of love, is self-transcendence. "I think the whole glory of writing lies in the fact that it forces us out of ourselves and into the lives of others," he said later in his life. "In the end the real writer becomes a lover."

Further Reading:
I. Howe, *Sherwood Anderson*, 1951.
R. Burbank, *Sherwood Anderson*, 1964.
B. Weber, *Sherwood Anderson*, 1964.
The Achievement of Sherwood Anderson: Essays in Criticism, ed. R. L. White, 1966.

Texts:
"The Book of the Grotesque" and "Hands" from *Winesburg, Ohio*, 1919.
"Mother" and "Departure" from the edition of 1958.

from Winesburg, Ohio

The Book of the Grotesque

The writer, an old man with a white mustache, had some difficulty in getting into bed. The windows of the house in which he lived were high and he wanted to look at the trees when he awoke in the morning. A carpenter came to fix the bed so that it would be on a level with the window.

Quite a fuss was made about the matter. The carpenter, who had been a soldier in the Civil War, came into the writer's room and sat down to talk of building a platform for the purpose of raising the bed. The writer had cigars lying about and the carpenter smoked.

For a time the two men talked of the raising of the bed and then they talked of other things. The soldier got on the subject of the war. The writer, in fact, led him to that subject. The carpenter had once been a prisoner in Andersonville prison and had lost a brother. The brother had died of starvation, and whenever the carpenter got upon that subject he cried. He, like the old writer, had a white mustache, and when he cried he puckered up his lips and the mustache bobbed up and down. The weeping old man with the cigar in his mouth was ludicrous. The plan the writer had for the raising of his bed was forgotten and later the carpenter did it in his own way and the writer, who was past sixty, had to help himself with a chair when he went to bed at night.

In his bed the writer rolled over on his side and lay quite still. For years he had been beset with notions concerning his heart. He was a hard smoker and his heart fluttered. The idea had got into his mind that he would some time die unexpectedly and always when he got into bed he thought of that. It did not alarm him. The effect in fact was quite a special thing and not easily explained. It made him more alive, there in bed, than at any other time. Perfectly still he lay and his body was old and not of much use any more, but something inside him was altogether young. He was like a pregnant woman, only that the thing inside him was not a baby but a youth. No, it wasn't a youth, it was a woman, young, and wearing a coat of mail like a knight. It is absurd, you see, to try to tell what was inside the old writer as he lay on his high bed and listened to the fluttering of his heart. The thing to get at is what the writer, or the young thing within the writer, was thinking about.

The old writer, like all of the people in the world, had got, during his long life, a great many notions in his head. He had once been quite handsome and a number of women had been in love with him. And then, of course, he had known people, many people, known them in a peculiarly intimate way that was different from the way in which you and I know people. At least that is what the writer thought and the thought pleased him. Why quarrel with an old man concerning his thoughts?

In the bed the writer had a dream that was not a dream. As he grew somewhat sleepy but was still conscious, figures began to appear before his eyes. He imagined the young indescribable thing within himself was driving a long procession of figures before his eyes.

You see the interest in all this lies in the figures that went before the eyes of the writer. They were all grotesques. All of the men and women the writer had ever known had become grotesques.

The grotesques were not all horrible. Some were amusing, some almost beautiful, and one, a woman all drawn out of shape, hurt the old man by her grotesqueness. When she passed he made a noise like a small dog whimpering. Had you come into the room you might have supposed the old man had unpleasant dreams or perhaps indigestion.

For an hour the procession of grotesques passed before the eyes of the old man, and then, although it was a painful thing to do, he crept out of bed and began to write. Some one of the grotesques had made a deep impression on his mind and he wanted to describe it.

At his desk the writer worked for an hour. In the end he wrote a book which he called "The Book of the Grotesque." It was never published, but I saw it once and it made an indelible impression on my mind. The book had one central thought that is very strange and has always remained with me. By remembering it I have been able to understand many people and things that I was never able to understand before. The thought was involved but a simple statement of it would be something like this:

That in the beginning when the world was young there were a great many thoughts but no such thing as a truth. Man made the truths himself and each truth was a composite of a great many vague thoughts. All about in the world were the truths and they were all beautiful.

The old man had listed hundreds of the truths in his book. I will not try to tell you of all of them. There was the truth of virginity and the truth of passion, the truth of wealth and of poverty, of thrift and of profligacy, of carelessness and abandon. Hundreds and hundreds were the truths and they were all beautiful.

And then the people came along. Each as he appeared snatched up one of the truths and some who were quite strong snatched up a dozen of them.

It was the truths that made the people grotesques. The old man had quite an elaborate theory concerning the matter. It was his notion that the moment one of the people took one of the truths to himself, called it his truth, and tried to live his life by it, he became a grotesque and the truth he embraced became a falsehood.

You can see for yourself how the old man, who had spent all of his life writing and was filled with words, would write hundreds of pages concerning this matter. The subject would become so big in his mind that he himself would be in danger of becoming a grotesque. He didn't, I suppose, for the same reason that he never published the book. It was the young thing inside him that saved the old man.

Concerning the old carpenter who fixed the bed for the writer, I only mentioned him because he, like many of what are called very common people, became the nearest thing to what is understandable and lovable of all the grotesques in the writer's book.

Hands

Upon the half decayed veranda of a small frame house that stood near the edge of a ravine near the town of Winesburg, Ohio, a fat little old man walked nervously up and down. Across a long field that had been seeded for clover but that had produced only a dense crop of yellow mustard weeds, he could see the public highway along which went a wagon filled with berry pickers returning from the fields. The berry pickers, youths and maidens, laughed and shouted boisterously. A boy clad in a blue shirt leaped from the wagon and attempted to drag after him one of the maidens, who screamed and protested shrilly. The feet of the boy in the road kicked up a cloud of dust that floated across the face of the departing sun. Over the long field came a thin girlish voice. "Oh, you Wing Biddlebaum, comb your hair, it's falling into your eyes," commanded the voice to the man, who was bald and whose nervous little hands fiddled about the bare white forehead as though arranging a mass of tangled locks.

Wing Biddlebaum, forever frightened and beset by a ghostly band of doubts, did not think of himself as in any way a part of the life of the town where he had lived for twenty years. Among all the people of Winesburg but one had come close to him. With George Willard, son of Tom Willard, the proprietor of the New Willard House, he had formed something like a friendship. George Willard was the reporter on the *Winesburg Eagle* and sometimes in the evenings he walked out along the highway to Wing Biddlebaum's house. Now as the old man walked up and down on the veranda, his hands moving nervously about, he was hoping that George Willard would come and spend the evening with him. After the wagon containing the berry pickers had passed, he went across the field through the tall mustard weeds and climbing a rail fence peered anxiously along the road to the town. For a moment he stood thus, rubbing his hands together and looking up and down the road, and then, fear overcoming him, ran back to walk again upon the porch on his own house.

In the presence of George Willard, Wing Biddlebaum, who for twenty years had been the town mystery, lost something of his timidity, and his shadowy personality, submerged in a sea of doubts, came forth to look at the world. With the young reporter at his side, he ventured in the light of day into Main Street or strode up and down on the rickety front porch of his own house, talking excitedly. The voice that had been low and trembling became shrill and loud. The bent figure straightened. With a kind of wriggle, like a fish returned to the brook by the fisherman, Biddlebaum the silent began to talk, striving to put into words the ideas that had been accumulated by his mind during long years of silence.

Wing Biddlebaum talked much with his hands. The slender expressive fingers, forever active, forever striving to conceal themselves in his pockets or behind his back, came forth and became the piston rods of his machinery of expression.

The story of Wing Biddlebaum is a story of hands. Their restless activity, like unto the beating of the wings of an imprisoned bird, had given him his name. Some obscure poet of the town had thought of it. The hands alarmed their owner. He wanted to keep them hidden away and looked with amazement at the quiet inexpressive hands of other men who worked beside him in the fields, or passed, driving sleepy teams on country roads.

When he talked to George Willard, Wing Biddlebaum closed his fists and beat with them upon a table or on the walls of his house. The action made him more comfortable. If the desire to talk came to him when the two were walking in the fields, he sought out a stump or the top board of a fence and with his hands pounding busily talked with renewed ease.

The story of Wing Biddlebaum's hands is worth a book in itself. Sympathetically set forth it would tap many strange, beautiful qualities in obscure men. It is a job for a poet. In Winesburg the hands had attracted attention merely because of their activity. With them Wing Biddlebaum had picked as high as a hundred and forty quarts of strawberries in a day. They became his distinguishing feature, the source of his fame. Also they made more grotesque an already grotesque and elusive individuality. Winesburg was proud of the hands of Wing Biddlebaum in the same spirit in which it was proud of Banker White's new stone house and Wesley Moyer's bay stallion, Tony Tip, that had won the two-fifteen trot at the fall races in Cleveland.

As for George Willard, he had many times wanted to ask about the hands. At times an almost overwhelming curiosity had taken hold of him. He felt that there must be a reason for their strange activity and their inclination to keep hidden away and only a growing respect for Wing Biddlebaum kept him from blurting out the questions that were often in his mind.

Once he had been on the point of asking. The two were walking in the fields on a summer afternoon and had stopped to sit upon a grassy bank. All afternoon Wing Biddlebaum had talked as one inspired. By a fence he had stopped and beating like a giant woodpecker upon the top board had shouted at George Willard, condemning his tendency to be too much influenced by the people about him. "You are destroying yourself," he cried. "You have the inclination to be alone and to dream and you are afraid of dreams. You want to be like others in town here. You hear them talk and you try to imitate them."

On the grassy bank Wing Biddlebaum had tried again to drive his point home. His voice became soft and reminiscent, and with a sigh of contentment he launched into a long rambling talk, speaking as one lost in a dream.

Out of the dream Wing Biddlebaum made a picture for George Willard. In the picture men lived again in a kind of pastoral golden age. Across a green open country came clean-limbed young men, some afoot, some mounted upon horses. In crowds the young men came to gather about the feet of an old man who sat beneath a tree in a tiny garden and who talked to them.

Wing Biddlebaum became wholly inspired. For once he forgot the hands. Slowly they stole forth and lay upon George Willard's shoulders. Something new and bold came into the voice that talked. "You must try to forget all you have learned," said the old man. "You must begin to dream. From this time on you must shut your ears to the roaring of the voices."

Pausing in his speech, Wing Biddlebaum looked long and earnestly at George Willard. His eyes glowed. Again he raised the hands to caress the boy and then a look of horror swept over his face.

With a convulsive movement of his body, Wing Biddlebaum sprang to his feet and thrust his hands deep into his trousers pockets. Tears came to his eyes. "I must be getting along home. I can talk no more with you," he said nervously.

Without looking back, the old man had hurried down the hillside and across a meadow, leaving George Willard perplexed and frightened upon the grassy slope. With a shiver of dread the boy arose and went along the road toward town. "I'll not ask him about his hands," he thought, touched by the memory of the terror he had seen in the man's eyes. "There's something wrong, but I don't want to know what it is. His hands have something to do with his fear of me and of everyone."

And George Willard was right. Let us look briefly into the story of the hands. Perhaps our talking of them will arouse the poet who will tell the hidden wonder story of the influence for which the hands were but fluttering pennants of promise.

In his youth Wing Biddlebaum had been a school teacher in a town in Pennsylvania. He was not then known as Wing Biddlebaum, but went by the less euphonic name of Adolph Myers. As Adolph Myers he was much loved by the boys of his school.

Adolph Myers was meant by nature to be a teacher of youth. He was one of those rare, little-understood men who rule by a power so gentle that it passes as a lovable weakness. In their feeling for the boys under their charge such men are not unlike the finer sort of women in their love of men.

And yet that is but crudely stated. It needs the poet there. With the boys of his school, Adolph Myers had walked in the evening or had sat talking until dusk upon the schoolhouse steps lost in a kind of dream. Here and there went his hands, caressing the shoulders of the boys, playing about the tousled heads. As he talked his voice became soft and musical. There was a caress in that also. In a way the voice and the hands, the stroking of the shoulders and the touching of the hair were a part of the schoolmaster's effort to carry a dream into the young minds. By the caress that was in his fingers he expressed himself. He was one of those men in whom the force that creates life is diffused, not centralized. Under the caress of his hands doubt and disbelief went out of the minds of the boys and they began also to dream.

And then the tragedy. A half-witted boy of the school became enamored of the young master. In his bed at night he imagined unspeakable things and in the morning went forth to tell his dreams as facts. Strange, hideous accusations fell from his loose-hung lips. Through the Pennsylvania town went a shiver. Hidden, shadowy doubts that had been in men's minds concerning Adolph Myers were galvanized into beliefs.

The tragedy did not linger. Trembling lads were jerked out of bed and questioned. "He put his arms about me," said one. "His fingers were always playing in my hair," said another.

One afternoon a man of the town, Henry Bradford, who kept a saloon, came to the schoolhouse door. Calling Adolph Myers into the school yard he began to beat him with his fists. As his hard knuckles beat down into the frightened face of the schoolmaster, his wrath became more and more terrible. Screaming with dismay, the children ran here and there like disturbed insects. "I'll teach you to put your hands on my boy, you beast," roared the saloon keeper, who, tired of beating the master, had begun to kick him about the yard.

Adolph Myers was driven from the Pennsylvania town in the night. With lanterns in their hands a dozen men came to the door of the house where he lived alone and commanded that he dress and come forth. It was raining and one of the men had a rope in his hands. They had intended to hang the schoolmaster, but something in his figure, so small, white, and pitiful, touched their hearts and they let him escape. As he ran away into the darkness they repented of their weakness and ran after him, swearing and throwing sticks and great balls of soft mud at the figure that screamed and ran faster and faster into the darkness.

For twenty years Adolph Myers had lived alone in Winesburg. He was but forty but looked sixty-five. The name of Biddlebaum he got from a box of goods seen at a freight station as he hurried through an eastern Ohio town. He had an aunt in Winesburg, a black-toothed old woman who raised chickens, and with her he lived until she died. He had been ill for a year after the experience in Pennsylvania, and after his recovery worked as a day laborer in the fields, going timidly about and striving to conceal his hands. Although he did not understand what had happened he felt that the hands must be to blame. Again and again the fathers of the boys had talked of the hands. "Keep your hands to yourself," the saloon keeper had roared, dancing with fury in the schoolhouse yard.

Upon the veranda of his house by the ravine, Wing Biddlebaum continued to walk up and down until the sun had disappeared and the road beyond the field was lost in the grey shadows. Going into his house he cut slices of bread and spread honey upon them. When the rumble of the evening train that took away the express cars loaded with the day's harvest of berries had passed and restored the silence of the summer night, he went again to walk upon the veranda. In the darkness he could not see the hands and they became quiet. Although he still hungered for the presence of the boy, who was the medium through which he expressed his love of man, the hunger became again a part of his loneliness and his waiting. Lighting a lamp, Wing Biddlebaum washed the few dishes soiled by his simple meal and, setting up a folding cot by the screen door that led to the porch, prepared to undress for the night. A few stray white bread crumbs lay on the cleanly washed floor by the table; putting the lamp upon a low stool he began to pick up the crumbs, carrying them to his mouth one by one with unbelievable rapidity. In the dense blotch of light beneath the table, the kneeling figure looked like a priest engaged in some service of his church. The nervous expressive fingers, flashing in and out of the light, might well have been mistaken for the fingers of the devotee going swiftly through decade after decade of his rosary.

Mother

Elizabeth Willard, the mother of George Willard, was tall and gaunt and her face was marked with smallpox scars. Although she was but forty-five, some obscure disease had taken the fire out of her figure. Listlessly she went about the disorderly old hotel looking at the faded wall-paper and the ragged carpets and, when she was able to be about, doing the work of a chambermaid among beds soiled by the slumbers of fat traveling men. Her husband, Tom Willard, a slender, graceful man with square shoulders, a quick military step, and a black mustache trained to turn sharply up at the ends, tried to put the wife out of his mind. The presence of the tall ghostly figure, moving slowly through the halls, he took as a reproach to himself. When he thought of her he grew angry and swore. The hotel was unprofitable and forever on the edge of failure and he wished himself out of it. He thought of the old house and the woman who lived there with him as things defeated and done for. The hotel in which he had begun life so hopefully was now a mere ghost of what a hotel should be. As he went spruce and business-like through the streets of Winesburg, he sometimes stopped and turned quickly about as though fearing that the spirit of the hotel and of the woman would follow him even into the streets. "Damn such a life, damn it!" he sputtered aimlessly.

Tom Willard had a passion for village politics and for years had been the leading Democrat in a strongly Republican community. Some day, he told himself, the tide of things political will turn in my favor and the years of ineffectual service count big in the bestowal of rewards. He dreamed of going to Congress and even of becoming governor. Once when a younger member of the party arose at a political conference and began to boast of his faithful service, Tom Willard grew white with fury. "Shut up, you," he roared, glaring about. "What do you know of service? What are you but a boy? Look at what I've done here! I was a Democrat here in Winesburg when it was a crime to be a Democrat. In the old days they fairly hunted us with guns."

Between Elizabeth and her one son George there was a deep unexpressed bond of sympathy, based on a girlhood dream that had long ago died. In the son's presence she was timid and reserved, but sometimes while he hurried about town intent upon his duties as a reporter, she went into his room and closing the door knelt by a little desk, made of a kitchen table, that sat near a window. In the room by the desk she went through a ceremony that was half a prayer, half a demand, addressed to the skies. In the boyish figure she yearned to see something half forgotten that had once been a part of herself re-created. The prayer concerned that. "Even though I die, I will in some way keep defeat from you," she cried, and so deep was her determination that her whole body shook. Her eyes glowed and she clenched her fists. "If I am dead and see him becoming a meaningless drab figure like myself, I will come back," she declared. "I ask God now to give me that privilege. I demand it. I will pay for it. God may beat me with his fists. I will take any blow that may befall if but this my boy be allowed to express something for us both." Pausing uncertainly, the woman stared about the boy's room. "And do not let him become smart and successful either," she added vaguely.

The communion between George Willard and his mother was outwardly a formal thing without meaning. When she was ill and sat by the window in her room he sometimes went in the evening to make her a visit. They sat by a window that looked over the roof of a small frame building into Main Street. By turning their heads they could see through another window, along an alleyway that ran behind the Main Street stores and into the back door of Abner Groff's bakery. Sometimes as they sat thus a picture of village life presented itself to them. At the back door of his shop appeared Abner Groff with a stick or an empty milk bottle in his hand. For a long time there was a feud between the baker and a grey cat that belonged to Sylvester West, the druggist. The boy and his mother saw the cat creep into the door of the bakery and presently emerge followed by the baker, who swore and waved his arms about. The baker's eyes were small and red and his black hair and beard were filled with flour dust. Sometimes he was so angry that, although the cat had disappeared, he hurled sticks, bits of broken glass, and even some of the tools of his trade about. Once he broke a window at the back of Sinning's Hardware Store. In the alley the grey cat crouched behind barrels filled with torn paper and broken bottles above which flew a black swarm of flies. Once when she was alone, and after watching a prolonged and ineffectual outburst on the part of the baker, Elizabeth Willard put her head down on her long white hands and wept. After that she did not look along the alleyway any more, but tried to forget the contest between the bearded man and the cat. It seemed like a rehearsal of her own life, terrible in its vividness.

In the evening when the son sat in the room with his mother, the silence made them both feel awkward. Darkness came on and the evening train came in at the station. In the street below feet tramped up and down upon a board sidewalk. In the station yard, after the evening train had gone, there was a heavy silence. Perhaps Skinner Leason, the express agent, moved a truck the length of the station platform. Over on Main Street sounded a man's voice, laughing. The door of the express office banged. George Willard arose and crossing the room fumbled for the doorknob. Sometimes he knocked against a chair, making it scrape along the floor. By the window sat the sick woman, perfectly still, listless. Her long hands, white and bloodless, could be seen drooping over the ends of the arms of the chair. "I think you had better be out among the boys. You are too much indoors," she said, striving to relieve the embarrassment of the departure. "I thought I would take a walk," replied George Willard, who felt awkward and confused.

One evening in July, when the transient guests who made the New Willard House their temporary home had become scarce, and the hallways, lighted only by kerosene lamps turned low, were plunged in gloom, Elizabeth Willard had an adventure. She had been ill in bed for several days and her son had not come to visit her. She was alarmed. The feeble blaze of life that remained in her body was blown into a flame by her anxiety and she crept out of bed, dressed and hurried along the hallway toward her son's room, shaking with exaggerated fears. As she went along she steadied herself with her hand, slipped along the papered walls of the hall and breathed with difficulty. The air whistled through her teeth. As she hurried forward she thought how foolish she was. "He is concerned with boyish affairs," she told herself. "Perhaps he has now begun to walk about in the evening with girls."

Elizabeth Willard had a dread of being seen by guests in the hotel that had once belonged to her father and the ownership of which still stood recorded in her name in the county courthouse. The hotel was continually losing patronage because of its shabbiness and she thought of herself as also shabby. Her own room was in an obscure corner and when she felt able to work she voluntarily worked among the beds, preferring the labor that could be done when the guests were abroad seeking trade among the merchants of Winesburg.

By the door of her son's room the mother knelt upon the floor and listened for some sound from within. When she heard the boy moving about and talking in low tones a smile came to her lips. George Willard had a habit of talking aloud to himself and to hear him doing so had always given his mother a peculiar pleasure. The habit in him, she felt, strengthened the secret bond that existed between them. A thousand times she had whispered to herself of the matter. "He is groping about, trying to find himself," she thought. "He is not a dull clod, all words and smartness. Within him there is a secret something that is striving to grow. It is the thing I let be killed in myself."

In the darkness in the hallway by the door the sick woman arose and started again toward her own room. She was afraid that the door would open and the boy come upon her. When she had reached a safe distance and was about to turn a corner into a second hallway she stopped and bracing herself with her hands waited, thinking to shake off a trembling fit of weakness that had come upon her. The presence of the boy in the room had made her happy. In her bed, during the long hours alone, the little fears that had visited her had become giants. Now they were all gone. "When I get back to my room I shall sleep," she murmured gratefully.

But Elizabeth Willard was not to return to her bed and to sleep. As she stood trembling in the darkness the door of her son's room opened and the boy's father, Tom Willard, stepped out. In the light that streamed out at the door he stood with the knob in his hand and talked. What he said infuriated the woman.

Tom Willard was ambitious for his son. He had always thought of himself as a successful man, although nothing he had ever done had turned out successfully. However, when he was out of sight of the New Willard House and had no fear of coming upon his wife, he swaggered and began to dramatize himself as one of the chief men of the town. He wanted his son to succeed. He it was who had secured for the boy the position on the *Winesburg Eagle*. Now, with a ring of earnestness in his voice, he was advising concerning some course of conduct. "I tell you what, George, you've got to wake up," he said sharply. "Will Henderson has spoken to me three times concerning the matter. He says you go along for hours not hearing when you are spoken to and acting like a gawky girl. What ails you?" Tom Willard laughed good-naturedly. "Well, I guess you'll get over it," he said. "I told Will that. You're not a fool and you're not a woman. You're Tom Willard's son and you'll wake up. I'm not afraid. What you say clears things up. If being a newspaper man had put the notion of becoming a writer into your mind that's all right. Only I guess you'll have to wake up to do that too, eh?"

Tom Willard went briskly along the hallway and down a flight of stairs to the office. The woman in the darkness could hear him laughing and talking with a guest who was striving to wear away a dull evening by dozing in a chair by the office door. She returned to the door of her son's room. The weakness had passed from her body as by a miracle and she stepped boldly along. A thousand ideas raced through her head. When she heard the scraping of a chair and the sound of a pen scratching upon paper, she again turned and went back along the hallway to her own room.

A definite determination had come into the mind of the defeated wife of the Winesburg hotel keeper. The determination was the result of long years of quiet and rather ineffectual thinking. "Now," she told herself, "I will act. There is something threatening my boy and I will ward it off." The fact that the conversation between Tom Willard and his son had been rather quiet and natural, as though an understanding existed between them, maddened her. Although for years she had hated her husband, her hatred had always before been a quite impersonal thing. He had been merely a part of something else that she hated. Now, and by the few words at the door, he had become the thing personified. In the darkness of her own room she clenched her fists and glared about. Going to a cloth bag that hung on a nail by the wall she took out a long pair of sewing scissors and held them in her hand like a dagger. "I will stab him," she said aloud. "He has chosen to be the voice of evil and I will kill him. When I have killed him something will snap within myself and I will die also. It will be a release for all of us."

In her girlhood and before her marriage with Tom Willard, Elizabeth had borne a somewhat shaky reputation in Winesburg. For years she had been what is called "stage-struck" and had paraded through the streets with traveling men guests at her father's hotel, wearing loud clothes and urging them to tell her of life in the cities out of which they had come. Once she startled the town by putting on men's clothes and riding a bicycle down Main Street.

In her own mind the tall dark girl had been in those days much confused. A great restlessness was in her and it expressed itself in two ways. First there was an uneasy desire for change, for some big definite movement to her life. It was this feeling that had turned her mind to the stage. She dreamed of joining some company and wandering over the world, seeing always new faces and giving something out of herself to all people. Sometimes at night she was quite beside herself with the thought, but when she tried to talk of the matter to the members of the theatrical companies that came to Winesburg and stopped at her father's hotel, she got nowhere. They did not seem to know what she meant, or if she did get something of her passion expressed, they only laughed. "It's not like that," they said. "It's as dull and uninteresting as this here. Nothing comes of it."

With the traveling men when she walked about with them, and later with Tom Willard, it was quite different. Always they seemed to understand and sympathize with her. On the side streets of the village, in the darkness under the trees, they took hold of her hand and she thought that something unexpressed in herself came forth and became a part of an unexpressed something in them.

And then there was the second expression of her restlessness. When that came she felt for a time released and happy. She did not blame the men who walked with her and later she did not blame Tom Willard. It was always the same, beginning with kisses and ending, after strange wild emotions, with peace and then sobbing repentance. When she sobbed she put her hand upon the face of the man and had always the same thought. Even though he were large and bearded she thought he had become suddenly a little boy. She wondered why he did not sob also.

In her room, tucked away in a corner of the old Willard House, Elizabeth Willard lighted a lamp and put it on a dressing table that stood by the door. A thought had come into her mind and she went to a closet and brought out a small square box and set it on the table. The box contained material for make-up and had been left with other things by a theatrical company that had once been stranded in Winesburg. Elizabeth Willard had decided that she would be beautiful. Her hair was still black and there was a great mass of it braided and coiled about her head. The scene that was to take place in the office below began to grow in her mind. No ghostly worn-out figure should confront Tom Willard, but something quite unexpected and startling. Tall and with dusky cheeks and hair that fell in a mass from her shoulders, a figure should come striding down the stairway before the startled loungers in the hotel office. The figure would be silent—it would be swift and terrible. As a tigress whose cub had been threatened would she appear, coming out of the shadows, stealing noiselessly along and holding the long wicked scissors in her hand.

With a little broken sob in her throat, Elizabeth Willard blew out the light that stood upon the table and stood weak and trembling in the darkness. The strength that had been as a miracle in her body left and she half reeled across the floor, clutching at the back of the chair in which she had spent so many long days staring out over the tin roofs into the main street of Winesburg. In the hallway there was the sound of footsteps and George Willard came in at the door. Sitting in a chair beside his mother he began to talk. "I'm going to get out of here," he said. "I don't know where I shall go or what I shall do but I am going away."

The woman in the chair waited and trembled. An impulse came to her. "I suppose you had better wake up," she said. "You think that? You will go to the city and make money, eh? It will be better for you, you think, to be a business man, to be brisk and smart and alive?" She waited and trembled.

The son shook his head. "I suppose I can't make you understand, but oh, I wish I could," he said earnestly. "I can't even talk to father about it. I don't try. There isn't any use. I don't know what I shall do. I just want to go away and look at people and think."

Silence fell upon the room where the boy and woman sat together. Again, as on the other evenings, they were embarrassed. After a time the boy tried again to talk. "I suppose it won't be for a year or two but I've been thinking about it," he said, rising and going toward the door. "Something father said makes it sure that I shall have to go away." He fumbled with the door knob. In the room the silence became unbearable to the woman. She wanted to cry out with joy because of the words that had come from the lips of her son, but the expression of joy had become impossible to her. "I think you had better go out among the boys. You are too much indoors," she said. "I thought I would go for a little walk," replied the son stepping awkwardly out of the room and closing the door.

Departure

Young George Willard got out of bed at four in the morning. It was April and the young tree leaves were just coming out of their buds. The trees along the residence streets in Winesburg are maple and the seeds are winged. When the wind blows they whirl crazily about, filling the air and making a carpet underfoot.

George came downstairs into the hotel office carrying a brown leather bag. His trunk was packed for departure. Since two o'clock he had been awake thinking of the journey he was about to take and wondering what he would find at the end of his journey. The boy who slept in the hotel office lay on a cot by the door. His mouth was open and he snored lustily. George crept past the cot and went out into the silent deserted main street. The east was pink with the dawn and long streaks of light climbed into the sky where a few stars still shone.

Beyond the last house on Trunion Pike in Winesburg there is a great stretch of open fields. The fields are owned by farmers who live in town and drive homeward at evening along Trunion Pike in light creaking wagons. In the fields are planted berries and small fruits. In the late afternoon in the hot summers when the road and the fields are covered with dust, a smoky haze lies over the great flat basin of land. To look across it is like looking out across the sea. In the spring when the land is green the effect is somewhat different. The land becomes a wide green billiard table on which tiny human insects toil up and down.

All through his boyhood and young manhood George Willard had been in the habit of walking on Trunion Pike. He had been in the midst of the great open place on winter nights when it was covered with snow and only the moon looked down at him; he had been there in the fall when bleak winds blew and on summer evenings when the air vibrated with the song of insects. On the April morning he wanted to go there again, to walk again in the silence. He did walk to where the road dipped down by a little stream two miles from town and then turned and walked silently back again. When he got to Main Street clerks were sweeping the sidewalks before the stores. "Hey, you George. How does it feel to be going away?" they asked.

The westbound train leaves Winesburg at seven forty-five in the morning. Tom Little is conductor. His train runs from Cleveland to where it connects with a great trunk line railroad with terminals in Chicago and New York. Tom has what in railroad circles is called an "easy run." Every evening he returns to his family. In the fall and spring he spends his Sundays fishing in Lake Erie. He has a round red face and small blue eyes. He knows the people in the towns along his railroad better than a city man knows the people who live in his apartment building.

George came down the little incline from the New Willard House at seven o'clock. Tom Willard carried his bag. The son had become taller than the father.

On the station platform everyone shook the young man's hand. More than a dozen people waited about. Then they talked of their own affairs. Even Will Henderson, who was lazy and often slept until nine, had got out of bed. George was embarrassed. Gertrude Wilmot, a tall thin woman of fifty who worked in the Winesburg post office, came along the station platform. She had never before paid any attention to George. Now she stopped and put out her hand. In two words she voiced what everyone felt. "Good luck," she said sharply and then turning went on her way.

When the train came into the station George felt relieved. He scampered hurriedly aboard. Helen White came running along Main Street hoping to have a parting word with him, but he had found a seat and did not see her. When the train started Tom Little punched his ticket, grinned and, although he knew George well and knew on what adventure he was just setting out, made no comment. Tom had seen a thousand George Willards go out of their towns to the city. It was a commonplace enough incident with him. In the smoking car there was a man who had just invited Tom to go on a fishing trip to Sandusky Bay. He wanted to accept the invitation and talk over details.

George glanced up and down the car to be sure no one was looking, then took out his pocketbook and counted his money. His mind was occupied with a desire not to appear green. Almost the last words his father had said to him concerned the matter of his behavior when he got to the city. "Be a sharp one," Tom Willard had said. "Keep your eyes on your money. Be awake. That's the ticket. Don't let anyone think you're a greenhorn."

After George counted his money he looked out of the window and was surprised to see that the train was still in Winesburg.

The young man, going out of his town to meet the adventure of life, began to think but he did not think of anything very big or dramatic. Things like his mother's death, his departure from Winesburg, the uncertainty of his future life in the city, the serious and larger aspects of his life did not come into his mind.

He thought of little things—Turk Smollet wheeling boards through the main street of his town in the morning, a tall woman, beautifully gowned, who had once stayed overnight at his father's hotel, Butch Wheeler the lamp lighter of Winesburg hurrying through the streets on a summer evening and holding a torch in his hand, Helen White standing by a window in the Winesburg post office and putting a stamp on an envelope.

The young man's mind was carried away by his growing passion for dreams. One looking at him would not have thought him particularly sharp. With the recollection of little things occupying his mind he closed his eyes and leaned back in the car seat. He stayed that way for a long time and when he aroused himself and again looked out of the car window the town of Winesburg had disappeared and his life there had become but a background on which to paint the dreams of his manhood.

1919

Sinclair Lewis
1885–1951

Satirists give us new vocabularies for showing how ideals degenerate into follies. Sinclair Lewis performed that service for the 1920s. The titles of his two major novels, *Main Street* and *Babbitt*, came quickly to summarize for his generation the mediocrity and narrowness of small-town life—its corruption of the American dream through an infatuation with boosterism and a worship of material wealth, as well as its betrayal of individualism through an intolerant fear of behavior that departed from accepted norms. As much as any writer of his time, Lewis extended into direct encounter with the culture of the 1920s the view of stultifying small-town life that we associate with Sarah Orne Jewett and Sherwood Anderson.

Sinclair Lewis was born in 1885 in Sauk Centre, Minnesota, into a prominent, prosperous family. A tall, ungainly, lonely boy, he became a tall, ungainly, lonely man. In both playground games and social gatherings, around children and adults, he felt awkward and ill at ease. Nearly friendless, variously pitied and teased, he soon discovered that hiking and reading could provide means of getting away from the people and scenes that oppressed him. He took long, solitary rambles through the countryside, and he began reading about other worlds. He was particularly drawn to nineteenth-century poets, especially Alfred

Lord Tennyson and Charles Swinburne, and to medieval culture. Yet Lewis was also fortunate to be born in a small town in the heartland of the United States near the turn of the century, just when the nation's literary center had begun to shift from the East to the Midwest and South and just before it began to shift from small towns to cities. By the time Lewis came to write *Main Street,* he had his fictional community of Gopher Prairie already at hand.

At age seventeen Lewis left the Midwest to attend Yale. Again friendless and alone, he continued to feel the need to get away. He read widely, particularly about medieval culture, and he began writing, signing his name "H. Sinclayre Lewys." He also began planning long excursions—two that took him to Europe by cattle boat and one that took him across Mexico in a series of long hikes. Near the beginning of his senior year, he left Yale to join Upton Sinclair's experimental commune, Helicon Hall, located outside Englewood Cliffs, New Jersey. From there he went to New York and then to Panama before returning to Yale, from which he graduated in 1908.

After graduation, Lewis lived in Iowa, California, Washington, and New York, working as a reporter for various newspapers and selling story plots for $5 each. For a short time he lived in a bohemian colony in Carmel, California, where he met Jack London. But it was not until he turned back to the Midwest, to the scenes he had encountered earliest and knew best, that fiction began to work for him. To augment his own memories and observations, he conducted research almost as an amateur sociologist might. His notebooks consist of long lists of names, turns of speech, descriptions of people and places, maps, statistics, and the like. During the next decade Lewis wrote five novels and many stories. In *Main Street* (1920) and *Babbitt* (1922), later in *Arrowsmith* (1925), *Elmer Gantry* (1927), "The Man Who Knew Coolidge" (1928), and *Dodsworth* (1929), he launched a decade-long attack against both the greediness of American business and the stifling effect of American provincialism. In 1930, having emerged from obscurity to acclaim, he became the first American writer to win the Nobel Prize for literature.

Lewis's major literary themes reach back through Edgar Lee Masters's *Spoon River Anthology* to the "Whilomville" stories of Stephen Crane and the novels of William Dean Howells. In Mark Twain's "The Man That Corrupted Hadleyburg," the Dawson's Landing setting of *Puddn'head Wilson,* and the river town described in *Huckleberry Finn,* we can locate the literary origins of similarly satiric views of village life. But it was Lewis's novels that lifted these themes to prominence immediately after World War I. In *Main Street,* Lewis presents a character who embodies some of the best and combats some of the worst qualities of "middletown" America. In *Babbitt,* he presents a character who embodies some of the worst forms of boosterism, materialism, and intolerance yet retains deeper needs and desires that he struggles to express.

If Sinclair Lewis set out to deflate myths—by satirizing evangelical preachers on the make, shrewd yet limited businessmen, hypocritical doctors and teachers, and racial bigots—he also tried to create myths of his own. This tendency is most evident in *Arrowsmith,* in which an idealistic young doctor devoted to research is pitted against people who want to exploit his contributions for profit. Satire lends itself to good/bad, either/or conflicts, and Lewis liked to pit knights of idealism against dragons of cynical materialism.

As a result, the fiction that won Lewis acclaim and helped change American literature also brought him vilification. To some readers, his works offered revelations of the unfulfilled dreams and the rising discontent of people who find little sense of shared happiness in the organizations they join, fleeting pleasure in the gadgets they buy, and limited fulfillment in the values they boost; to others, his works represented unfair depictions or even bitter denunciations of the American way of life. Both *Main Street* and *Babbitt* draw heavily on the qualities that most clearly marked Lewis's dominant frame of mind during his youth and apprenticeship: his uneasy estrangement and his restless longings. In addition, however, these novels depend heavily on his capacity for close attention to the local and the immediate. The clothes and manners, the mores and gadgets, the foibles and hypocrisies, the emptiness and aspirations of "middletown" America form the center of his best fiction. Inseparable from his capacity for close observation is the characteristic ambivalence he acquired early and cultivated throughout his life—of estrangement and kinship, judgment and affection. In his crude yet telling art, close familiarity and a detached, even bitter perspective mingle with youthful yearning. As a result, his fiction combines satire, realism, and romance in shifting and sometimes strained combinations.

Lewis continued to write until his death in 1951. But the Nobel Prize in 1930 came near the end of his short life as a writer of significant work. In some respects, he was as much a journalist of the muckraking tradition of the generation that immediately preceded him (producing, for example, Upton Sinclair's *The Jungle*) as he was a novelist. Like the muckrakers, he was skilled at satirizing his victims. His portrayals of Babbitt and Dodsworth, however, allowed Lewis to show compassion for his small-town go-getters; he recognized the basic pathos of their mistaken devotion to the idols of the marketplace—which William James called "the bitch-goddess success." When Lewis set out directly to celebrate idealistic young devotees of freedom or simply to debunk village philistines and corporate crooks, his work lost its edge. It possessed staying power only when his need to flail his misguided fools was balanced by his sense of compassion for them. In *Arrowsmith* and *Elmer Gantry,* and above all in *Main Street* and *Babbitt,* he exposes the sometimes pathetic and sometimes terrible inadequacies of the commonplace. In the process, he finds words for America's hidden fears and hopes.

Further Reading:

C. Van Doren, *Sinclair Lewis,* 1933.
P. Miller, "The Incorruptible Sinclair Lewis," *Atlantic,* April 1951.
From Main Street to Stockholm, 1919–1930, ed. H. Smith, 1952.
M. Schorer, *Sinclair Lewis: An American Life,* 1961.
S. Grebstein, *Sinclair Lewis,* 1962.
Sinclair Lewis: A Collection of Critical Essays, ed.

M. Schorer, 1962.
D. Dooley, *The Art of Sinclair Lewis,* 1967.
R. O'Connor, *Sinclair Lewis,* 1971.
S. Sherman, *The Significance of Sinclair Lewis,* 1922, 1971.
J. Lundquist, *Sinclair Lewis,* 1973.
M. Light, *The Quixotic Vision of Sinclair Lewis,* 1975.

Text:

Babbitt, 1922, 1950.
See also *Selected Short Stories of Sinclair Lewis,* 1935.

The Man from Main Street: A Sinclair Lewis Reader, ed. H. Maule and M. Cane, 1953.

from Babbitt

Chapter III: [George F. Babbitt and the Fairy Girl]

I

To George F. Babbitt, as to most prosperous citizens of Zenith, his motor car was poetry and tragedy, love and heroism. The office was his pirate ship but the car his perilous excursion ashore.

Among the tremendous crises of each day none was more dramatic than starting the engine. It was slow on cold mornings; there was the long, anxious whirr of the starter; and sometimes he had to drip ether into the cocks of the cylinders, which was so very interesting that at lunch he would chronicle it drop by drop, and orally calculate how much each drop had cost him.

This morning he was darkly prepared to find something wrong, and he felt belittled when the mixture exploded sweet and strong, and the car didn't even brush the door-jamb, gouged and splintery with many bruisings by fenders, as he backed out of the garage. He was confused. He shouted "Morning!" to Sam Doppelbrau with more cordiality than he had intended.

Babbitt's green and white Dutch Colonial house was one of three in that block on Chatham Road. To the left of it was the residence of Mr. Samuel Doppelbrau, secretary of an excellent firm of bathroom-fixture jobbers. His was a comfortable house with no architectural manners whatever; a large wooden box with a squat tower, a broad porch, and glossy paint yellow as a yolk. Babbitt disapproved of Mr. and Mrs. Doppelbrau as "Bohemian." From their house came midnight music and obscene laughter; there were neighborhood rumors of bootlegged whisky and fast motor rides. They furnished Babbitt with many happy evenings of discussion, during which he announced firmly, "I'm not strait-laced, and I don't mind seeing a fellow throw in a drink once in a while, but when it comes to deliberately trying to get away with a lot of hell-raising all the while like the Doppelbraus do, it's too rich for my blood!"

On the other side of Babbitt lived Howard Littlefield, Ph.D., in a strictly modern house whereof the lower part was dark red tapestry brick, with a leaded oriel, the upper part of pale stucco like spattered clay, and the roof red-tiled. Littlefield was the Great Scholar of the neighborhood; the authority on everything in the world except babies, cooking, and motors. He was a Bachelor of Arts of Blodgett College, and a Doctor of Philosophy in economics of Yale. He was the employment-manager and publicity-counsel of the Zenith Street Traction Company. He could, on ten hours' notice, appear before the board of aldermen or the state legislature and prove, absolutely, with figures all in rows and with precedents from Poland and New Zealand, that the street-car company loved the Public and yearned over its employees; that all its stock was owned by Widows and Orphans; and that whatever it desired to do would benefit property-owners by increasing rental values, and help the poor by lowering rents. All his acquaintances turned to Littlefield when they desired to know the date of the battle of Saragossa, the definition of the word "sabotage," the future of the German mark, the translation of *"hinc illæ lachrimæ,"*[1] or the number of products of coal tar. He awed Babbitt by confessing that he often sat up till midnight reading the figures and footnotes in Government reports, or skimming (with amusement at the author's mistakes) the latest volumes of chemistry, archeology, and ichthyology.

But Littlefield's great value was as a spiritual example. Despite his strange learnings he was as strict a Presbyterian and as firm a Republican as George F. Babbitt. He confirmed the business men in the faith. Where they knew only by passionate instinct that their system of industry and manners was perfect, Dr. Howard Littlefield proved it to them, out of history, economics, and the confessions of reformed radicals.

Babbitt had a good deal of honest pride in being the neighbor of such a savant, and in Ted's intimacy with Eunice Littlefield. At sixteen Eunice was interested in no statistics save those regarding the ages and salaries of motion-picture stars, but—as Babbitt definitively put it—"she was her father's daughter."

The difference between a light man like Sam Doppelbrau and a really fine character like Littlefield was revealed in their appearances. Doppelbrau was disturbingly young for a man of forty-eight. He wore his derby on the back of his head, and his red face was wrinkled with meaningless laughter. But Littlefield was old for a man of forty-two. He was tall, broad, thick; his gold-rimmed spectacles were engulfed in the folds of his long face; his hair was a tossed mass of greasy blackness; he puffed and rumbled as he talked; his Phi Beta Kappa key shone against a spotty black vest; he smelled of old pipes; he was altogether funereal and archidiaconal; and to real-estate brokerage and the jobbing of bathroom-fixtures he added an aroma of sanctity.

This morning he was in front of his house, inspecting the grass parking between the curb and the broad cement sidewalk. Babbitt stopped his car and leaned out to shout "Mornin'!" Littlefield lumbered over and stood with one foot up on the running-board.

"Fine morning," said Babbitt, lighting—illegally early—his second cigar of the day.

"Yes, it's a mighty fine morning," said Littlefield.

"Spring coming along fast now."

"Yes, it's real spring now, all right," said Littlefield.

"Still cold nights, though. Had to have a couple blankets, on the sleeping-porch last night."

"Yes, it wasn't any too warm last night," said Littlefield.

"But I don't anticipate we'll have any more real cold weather now."

"No, but still, there was snow at Tiflis, Montana, yesterday," said the Scholar, "and you remember the blizzard they had out West three days ago—thirty inches of snow at Greeley, Colorado—and two years ago we had a snow-squall right here in Zenith on the twenty-fifth of April."

"Is that a fact! Say, old man, what do you think about the Republican candidate? Who'll they nominate for president? Don't you think it's about time we had a real business administration?"

---

[1] Latin: "hence these tears"; from *Andria* by Terence (ca. 195–159 B.C.).

"In my opinion, what the country needs, first and foremost, is a good, sound, business-like conduct of its affairs. What we need is—a business administration!" said Littlefield.

"I'm glad to hear you say that! I certainly am glad to hear you say that! I didn't know how you'd feel about it, with all your associations with colleges and so on, and I'm glad you feel that way. What the country needs—just at this present juncture —is neither a college president nor a lot of monkeying with foreign affairs, but a good —sound—economical—business—administration, that will give us a chance to have something like a decent turnover."

"Yes. It isn't generally realized that even in China the schoolmen are giving way to more practical men, and of course you can see what that implies."

"Is that a fact! Well, well!" breathed Babbitt, feeling much calmer, and much happier about the way things were going in the world. "Well, it's been nice to stop and parleyvoo a second. Guess I'll have to get down to the office now and sting a few clients. Well, so long, old man. See you tonight. So long."

II

They had labored, these solid citizens. Twenty years before, the hill on which Floral Heights was spread, with its bright roofs and immaculate turf and amazing comfort, had been a wilderness of rank second-growth elms and oaks and maples. Along the precise streets were still a few wooded vacant lots, and the fragment of an old orchard. It was brilliant to-day; the apple boughs were lit with fresh leaves like torches of green fire. The first white of cherry blossoms flickered down a gully, and robins clamored.

Babbitt sniffed the earth, chuckled at the hysteric robins as he would have chuckled at kittens or at a comic movie. He was, to the eye, the perfect office-going executive —a well-fed man in a correct brown soft hat and frameless spectacles, smoking a large cigar, driving a good motor along a semi-suburban parkway. But in him was some genius of authentic love for his neighborhood, his city, his clan. The winter was over; the time was come for the building, the visible growth, which to him was glory. He lost his dawn depression; he was ruddily cheerful when he stopped on Smith Street to leave the brown trousers, and to have the gasoline-tank filled.

The familiarity of the rite fortified him: the sight of the tall red iron gasoline-pump, the hollow-tile and terra-cotta garage, the window full of the most agreeable accessories—shiny casings, spark-plugs with immaculate porcelain jackets, tire-chains of gold and silver. He was flattered by the friendliness with which Sylvester Moon, dirtiest and most skilled of motor mechanics, came out to serve him. "Mornin', Mr. Babbitt!" said Moon, and Babbitt felt himself a person of importance, one whose name even busy garagemen remembered—not one of these cheap-sports flying around in flivvers. He admired the ingenuity of the automatic dial, clicking off gallon by gallon; admired the smartness of the sign: "A fill in time saves getting stuck—gas to-day 31 cents"; admired the rhythmic gurgle of the gasoline as it flowed into the tank, and the mechanical regularity with which Moon turned the handle.

"How much we takin' to-day?" asked Moon, in a manner which combined the independence of the great specialist, the friendliness of a familiar gossip, and respect for a man of weight in the community, like George F. Babbitt.

"Fill 'er up."

"Who you rootin' for for Republican candidate, Mr. Babbitt?"

"It's too early to make any predictions yet. After all, there's still a good month and two weeks—no, three weeks—must be almost three weeks—well, there's more than six weeks in all before the Republican convention, and I feel a fellow ought to keep an open mind and give all the candidates a show—look 'em all over and size 'em up, and then decide carefully."

"That's a fact, Mr. Babbitt."

"But I'll tell you—and my stand on this is just the same as it was four years ago, and eight years ago, and it'll be my stand four years from now—yes, and eight years from now! What I tell everybody, and it can't be too generally understood, is that what we need first, last, and all the time is a good, sound business administration!"

"By golly, that's right!"

"How do those front tires look to you?"

"Fine! Fine! Wouldn't be much work for garages if everybody looked after their car the way you do."

"Well, I do try and have some sense about it." Babbitt paid his bill, said adequately, "Oh, keep the change," and drove off in an ecstasy of honest self-appreciation. It was with the manner of a Good Samaritan that he shouted at a respectable-looking man who was waiting for a trolley car, "Have a lift?" As the man climbed in Babbitt condescended, "Going clear down-town? Whenever I see a fellow waiting for a trolley, I always make it a practice to give him a lift—unless, of course, he looks like a bum."

"Wish there were more folks that were so generous with their machines," dutifully said the victim of benevolence.

"Oh, no, 'tain't a question of generosity, hardly. Fact, I always feel—I was saying to my son just the other night—it's a fellow's duty to share the good things of this world with his neighbors, and it gets my goat when a fellow gets stuck on himself and goes around tooting his horn merely because he's charitable."

The victim seemed unable to find the right answer. Babbitt boomed on:

"Pretty punk service the Company giving us on these car-lines. Nonsense to only run the Portland Road cars once every seven minutes. Fellow gets mighty cold on a winter morning, waiting on a street corner with the wind nipping at his ankles."

"That's right. The Street Car Company don't care a damn what kind of a deal they give us. Something ought to happen to 'em."

Babbitt was alarmed. "But still, of course it won't do to just keep knocking the Traction Company and not realize the difficulties they're operating under, like these cranks that want municipal ownership. The way these workmen hold up the Company for high wages is simply a crime, and of course the burden falls on you and me that have to pay a seven-cent fare! Fact, there's remarkable service on all their lines—considering."

"Well—" uneasily.

"Darn fine morning," Babbitt explained. "Spring coming along fast."

"Yes, it's real spring now."

The victim had no originality, no wit, and Babbitt fell into a great silence and devoted himself to the game of beating trolley cars to the corner: a spurt, a tail-chase, nervous speeding between the huge yellow side of the trolley and the jagged row of parked motors, shooting past just as the trolley stopped—a rare game and valiant.

And all the while he was conscious of the loveliness of Zenith. For weeks together he noticed nothing but clients and the vexing To Rent signs of rival brokers. To-day, in mysterious malaise, he raged or rejoiced with equal nervous swiftness, and to-day the light of spring was so winsome that he lifted his head and saw.

He admired each district along his familiar route to the office: The bungalows and shrubs and winding irregular drive-ways of Floral Heights. The one-story shops on Smith Street, a glare of plate-glass and new yellow brick; groceries and laundries and drug-stores to supply the more immediate needs of East Side housewives. The market gardens in Dutch Hollow, their shanties patched with corrugated iron and stolen doors. Billboards with crimson goddesses nine feet tall advertising cinema films, pipe tobacco, and talcum powder. The old "mansions" along Ninth Street, S.E., like aged dandies in filthy linen; wooden castles turned into boarding-houses, with muddy walks and rusty hedges, jostled by fast-intruding garages, cheap apartment-houses, and fruit-stands conducted by bland, sleek Athenians. Across the belt of railroad-tracks, factories with high-perched water-tanks and tall stacks—factories producing condensed milk, paper boxes, lighting-fixtures, motor cars. Then the business center, the thickening darting traffic, the crammed trolleys unloading, and high doorways of marble and polished granite.

It was big—and Babbitt respected bigness in anything; in mountains, jewels, muscles, wealth, or words. He was, for a spring-enchanted moment, the lyric and almost unselfish lover of Zenith. He thought of the outlying factory suburbs; of the Chaloosa River with its strangely eroded banks; of the orchard-dappled Tonawanda Hills to the North, and all the fat dairy land and big barns and comfortable herds. As he dropped his passenger he cried, "Gosh, I feel pretty good this morning!"

III

Epochal as starting the car was the drama of parking it before he entered his office. As he turned from Oberlin Avenue round the corner into Third Street, N.E., he peered ahead for a space in the line of parked cars. He angrily just missed a space as a rival driver slid into it. Ahead, another car was leaving the curb, and Babbitt slowed up, holding out his hand to the cars pressing on him from behind, agitatedly motioning an old woman to go ahead, avoiding a truck which bore down on him from one side. With front wheels nicking the wrought-steel bumper of the car in front, he stopped, feverishly cramped his steering-wheel, slid back into the vacant space and, with eighteen inches of room, manœuvered to bring the car level with the curb. It was a virile adventure masterfully executed. With satisfaction he locked a thief-proof steel wedge on the front wheel, and crossed the street to his real-estate office on the ground floor of the Reeves Building.

The Reeves Building was as fireproof as a rock and as efficient as a typewriter; fourteen stories of yellow pressed brick, with clean, upright, unornamented lines. It was filled with the offices of lawyers, doctors, agents for machinery, for emery wheels, for wire fencing, for mining-stock. Their gold signs shone on the windows. The entrance was too modern to be flamboyant with pillars; it was quiet, shrewd, neat. Along the Third Street side were a Western Union Telegraph Office, the Blue Delft Candy Shop, Shotwell's Stationery Shop, and the Babbitt-Thompson Realty Company.

Babbitt could have entered his office from the street, as customers did, but it made him feel an insider to go through the corridor of the building and enter by the back door. Thus he was greeted by the villagers.

The little unknown people who inhabited the Reeves Building corridors—elevator-runners, starter, engineers, superintendent, and the doubtful-looking lame man who conducted the news and cigar stand—were in no way city-dwellers. They were rustics, living in a constricted valley, interested only in one another and in The Building. Their Main Street was the entrance hall, with its stone floor, severe marble ceiling, and the inner windows of the shops. The liveliest place on the street was the Reeves Building Barber Shop, but this was also Babbitt's one embarrassment. Himself, he patronized the glittering Pompeian Barber Shop in the Hotel Thornleigh, and every time he passed the Reeves shop—ten times a day, a hundred times—he felt untrue to his own village.

Now, as one of the squirearchy, greeted with honorable salutations by the villagers, he marched into his office, and peace and dignity were upon him, and the morning's dissonances all unheard.

They were heard again, immediately.

Stanley Graff, the outside salesman, was talking on the telephone with tragic lack of that firm manner which disciplines clients: "Say, uh, I think I got just the house that would suit you—the Percival House, in Linton. . . . Oh, you've seen it. Well, how'd it strike you? . . . Huh? . . . Oh," irresolutely, "oh, I see."

As Babbitt marched into his private room, a coop with semi-partition of oak and frosted glass, at the back of the office, he reflected how hard it was to find employees who had his own faith that he was going to make sales.

There were nine members of the staff, besides Babbitt and his partner and father-in-law, Henry Thompson, who rarely came to the office. The nine were Stanley Graff, the outside salesman—a youngish man given to cigarettes and the playing of pool; old Mat Penniman, general utility man, collector of rents and salesman of insurance —broken, silent, gray; a mystery, reputed to have been a "crack" real-estate man with a firm of his own in haughty Brooklyn; Chester Kirby Laylock, resident salesman out at the Glen Oriole acreage development—an enthusiastic person with a silky mustache and much family; Miss Theresa McGoun, the swift and rather pretty stenographer; Miss Wilberta Bannigan, the thick, slow, laborious accountant and file-clerk; and four freelance part-time commission salesmen.

As he looked from his own cage into the main room Babbitt mourned, "McGoun's a good stenog., smart's a whip, but Stan Graff and all those bums—" The zest of the spring morning was smothered in the stale office air.

Normally he admired the office, with a pleased surprise that he should have created this sure lovely thing; normally he was stimulated by the clean newness of it and the air of bustle; but to-day it seemed flat—the tiled floor, like a bathroom, the ocher-colored metal ceiling, the faded maps on the hard plaster walls, the chairs of varnished pale oak, the desks and filing-cabinets of steel painted in olive drab. It was a vault, a steel chapel where loafing and laughter were raw sin.

He hadn't even any satisfaction in the new water-cooler! And it was the very best of water-coolers, up-to-date, scientific, and right-thinking. It had cost a great deal of money (in itself a virtue). It possessed a non-conducting fiber ice-container, a porcelain water-jar (guaranteed hygienic), a dripless non-clogging sanitary faucet, and machine-painted decorations in two tones of gold. He looked down the relentless stretch of tiled floor at the water-cooler, and assured himself that no tenant of the Reeves Building had a more expensive one, but he could not recapture the feeling of social superiority it had given him. He astoundingly grunted, "I'd like to beat it off to the woods right now. And loaf all day. And go to Gunch's again to-night, and play poker, and cuss as much as I feel like, and drink a hundred and nine-thousand bottles of beer."

He sighed; he read through his mail; he shouted "Msgoun," which meant "Miss McGoun"; and began to dictate.

This was his own version of his first letter:

"Omar Gribble, send it to his office, Miss McGoun, yours of twentieth to hand and in reply would say look here, Gribble, I'm awfully afraid if we go on shilly-shallying like this we'll just naturally lose the Allen sale, I had Allen up on carpet day before yesterday and got right down to cases and think I can assure you—uh, uh, no, change that: all my experience indicates he is all right, means to do business, looked into his financial record which is fine—that sentence seems to be a little balled up, Miss McGoun; make a couple sentences out of it if you have to, period, new paragraph.

"He is perfectly willing to pro rate the special assessment and strikes me, am dead sure there will be no difficulty in getting him to pay for title insurance, so now for heaven's sake let's get busy—no, make that: so now let's go to it and get down—no, that's enough—you can tie those sentences up a little better when you type 'em, Miss McGoun—your sincerely, etcetera."

This is the version of his letter which he received, typed, from Miss McGoun that afternoon:

BABBITT-THOMPSON REALTY CO.
Homes for Folks
Reeves Bldg., Oberlin Avenue & 3rd St., N.E.
Zenith

Omar Gribble, Esq.,
576 North American Building,
Zenith.

Dear Mr. Gribble:

Your letter of the twentieth to hand. I must say I'm awfully afraid that if we go on shilly-shallying like this we'll just naturally lose the Allen sale. I had Allen up on the carpet day before yesterday, and got right down to cases. All my experience indicates that he means to do business. I have also looked into his financial record, which is fine.

He is perfectly willing to pro rate the special assessment and there will be no difficulty in getting him to pay for title insurance.

So let's go!

Yours sincerely,

As he read and signed it, in his correct flowing business-college hand, Babbitt reflected, "Now that's a good, strong letter, and clear's a bell. Now what the— I never told McGoun to make a third paragraph there! Wish she'd quit trying to improve on my dictation! But what I can't understand is: why can't Stan Graff or Chet Laylock write a letter like that? With punch! With a kick!"

The most important thing he dictated that morning was the fortnightly form-letter, to be mimeographed and sent out to a thousand "prospects." It was diligently imitative of the best literary models of the day; of heart-to-heart-talk advertisements, "sales-pulling" letters, discourses on the "development of Will-power," and hand-shaking house-organs, as richly poured forth by the new school of Poets of Business. He had painfully written out a first draft, and he intoned it now like a poet delicate and distrait:

SAY, OLD MAN!

I just want to know can I do you a whaleuva favor? Honest! No kidding! I know you're interested in getting a house, not merely a place where you hang up the old bonnet but a love-nest for the wife and kiddies—and maybe for the flivver out beyant (be sure and spell that b-e-y-a-n-t, Miss McGoun) the spud garden. Say, did you ever stop to think that we're here to save you trouble? That's how we make a living—folks don't pay us for our lovely beauty! Now take a look:

Sit right down at the handsome carved mahogany escritoire and shoot us in a line telling us just what you want, and if we can find it we'll come hopping down your lane with the good tidings, and if we can't, we won't bother you. To save your time, just fill out the blank enclosed. On request will also send blank regarding store properties in Floral Heights, Silver Grove, Linton, Bellevue, and all East Side residential districts.

Yours for service,

P.S.—Just a hint of some plums we can pick for you—some genuine bargains that came in to-day:

SILVER GROVE.—Cute four-room California bungalow, a.m.i., garage, dandy shade tree, swell neighborhood, handy car line. $3700, $780 down and balance liberal, Babbitt-Thompson terms, cheaper than rent.

DORCHESTER.—A corker! Artistic two-family house, all oak trim, parquet floors, lovely gas log, big porches, colonial, HEATED ALL-WEATHER GARAGE, a bargain at $11,250.

Dictation over, with its need of sitting and thinking instead of bustling around and making a noise and really doing something, Babbitt sat creakily back in his revolving desk-chair and beamed on Miss McGoun. He was conscious of her as a girl, of black bobbed hair against demure cheeks. A longing which was indistinguishable from loneliness enfeebled him. While she waited, tapping a long, precise pencil-point on the desk-tablet, he half identified her with the fairy girl of his dreams. He imagined their eyes meeting with terrifying recognition; imagined touching her lips with frightened reverence and— She was chirping, "Any more, Mist' Babbitt?" He grunted, "That winds it up, I guess," and turned heavily away.

For all his wandering thoughts, they had never been more intimate than this. He often reflected, "Nev' forget how old Jake Offutt said a wise bird never goes love-making in his own office or his own home. Start trouble. Sure. But—"

In twenty-three years of married life he had peered uneasily at every graceful ankle, every soft shoulder; in thought he had treasured them; but not once had he hazarded respectability by adventuring. Now, as he calculated the cost of repapering the Styles house, he was restless again, discontented about nothing and everything, ashamed of his discontentment, and lonely for the fairy girl.

1922

Eugene O'Neill
1888–1953

Nobel Prize–winning playwright Eugene Gladstone O'Neill was born in a Broadway hotel room, in the center of New York's theater district, and grew up in the world of the American theater. "You might say I started as a trouper," he once reported. "I knew only actors and the stage. My mother nursed me in the wings and in dressing rooms." His father, James O'Neill, was an extremely successful, Irish-born actor who played the lead in over 6,000 performances of *The Count of Monte Cristo,* a melodrama based on Alexandre Dumas's famous novel. By his late teens O'Neill had begun to despise the popular Victorian theater that his father represented. Later he would set out to create a new dramatic style and idiom—to completely transform the American stage.

O'Neill was educated in Catholic boarding schools and private academies. His only regular home in childhood was in New London, Connecticut, where his family lived during the summer, and where he grew to love both the sea and the gritty waterfront life of sailors and saloons. He entered Princeton in 1906, but collegiate life soon clashed with his hard-drinking, rebellious behavior, and he was suspended in his first year. He spent several years "just drifting" and in 1909 was secretly married against the wishes of both his and his wife's parents. A few months later he embarked on the experiences as a seaman that would provide him with much of the material for his later plays. He sailed to Honduras to prospect for gold and spent two years before the mast, sailing to Buenos Aires, England, and South Africa.

On his return, divorced and the father of a two-year-old son, O'Neill hung around disreputable New York waterfront backrooms, several of which became settings for later plays; passed a few months on tour with his father's company; and found a position as a reporter for a New London newspaper, where he contributed local news items and light verse. Toward the end of 1912, however, he was hospitalized for six months with tuberculosis. The event proved to be a turning point in his life. While recovering in a Connecticut sanitorium, he started to read drama seriously—especially Strindberg, Ibsen, and the Greek tragic poets—and decided to become a playwright. In the summer of 1914 he applied to George Pierce Baker's famous drama workshop at Harvard ("because I want to be an artist or nothing") to study for one year as a special student, and that same year he published his first book, *Thirst, and Other One-Act Plays.*

After a semester at Harvard, O'Neill moved to Greenwich Village, where he became a leading member of two avant-garde groups, the Provincetown Players and the Greenwich Village Theatre, both of which helped to lay the foundation for the modern "little theater" movement. On July 28, 1916, O'Neill's first play, *Bound East for Cardiff,* was produced at the Wharf Theatre in Provincetown, Massachusetts. Written in 1914 and included as a writing sample with his Harvard application, this one-act play showed O'Neill's gift for evoking a powerful atmosphere and his keen ear for the vernacular. These two elements, voice and atmosphere, became prominent features of every O'Neill stage production.

In 1918 O'Neill remarried and, despite severe bouts of alcoholism, began working on longer plays. His first full-length play, *Beyond the Horizon,* was produced in New York in 1920 and won a Pulitzer Prize. In the same year the Provincetown Playhouse staged *The Emperor Jones.* An experimental drama that blends fantasy and reality against an incessant beat of drums, it established O'Neill as America's most promising playwright. A year later that promise seemed fulfilled when he won his second Pulitzer Prize for *Anna Christie.* To O'Neill, however, *Anna Christie* seemed a backward-looking work, full of "Broadway tricks," rather than a new theatrical form designed to get beneath conventional dramatic surfaces—"behind life," as he put it.

Following *Anna Christie,* O'Neill began a period of restless experimentation and colossal productivity. The early 1920s brought the deaths in close succession of his father, mother, and brother and were marred by his own continued drinking problems and a deteriorating marriage. Yet twenty of his plays were produced on New York stages. These included a series of experimental plays: *The Hairy Ape* (1922), *All God's Chillun Got Wings* (1924), *Desire Under the Elms* (1924), *The Great God Brown* (1926), and the nine-act *Strange Interlude* (1928), which won him a third Pulitzer Prize. With *Strange Interlude* O'Neill achieved a new dramatic language, one that stressed breakdowns in communication, with private voices submerged beneath social voices. A stage direction from the play offers an indication of the "interior dialogue" that O'Neill was striving for: "They stare straight ahead and remain motionless. They speak, ostensibly one to the other, but showing by their tone it is a thinking aloud to oneself, and neither appears to hear what the other has said." In 1929 O'Neill, recovered from his alcoholism, divorced his second wife and married the actress Carlotta Monterey in France, where they were to live for several years. Two years later, The Theatre Guild produced one of O'Neill's most ambitious plays, *Mourning Becomes Electra,* a trilogy that focuses on the passions of an old New England family at the conclusion of the Civil War.

O'Neill's later drama turned increasingly to personal memories. *Ah, Wilderness!* (1933), which featured George M. Cohan, is a domestic comedy—O'Neill called it a "comedy of recollection"—about a rebellious adolescent growing up, like O'Neill himself, in a turn-of-the-century Connecticut family. In *The Iceman Cometh* (1946), O'Neill delved back into his New York waterfront days. Set in a backroom world of drunk and hopeless individuals, the four and one-half hour drama climaxes in an astonishing soliloquy, perhaps the longest in American drama. The last of O'Neill's plays to be produced on Broadway during his lifetime, *The Iceman Cometh* achieved greater success during its revival in the 1950s than in its first production, and it is now among his most widely acclaimed works.

In 1932 O'Neill and his wife moved to Sea Island, Georgia. Four years later he was awarded the Nobel Prize. As his health continued to decline, he moved, first to California, where he lived in relative seclusion, and then to New York. During this period he wrote several plays, all of which were produced in Sweden after his death in 1953. Of these, the most impressive is another four and one-half hour play, *Long Day's Journey into Night,* for which O'Neill received posthumously his fourth Pulitzer Prize. An intense, autobiographical drama concerning a writer's miserly father, drug-addicted mother, and alcoholic brother, *Long Day's Journey into Night* is probably O'Neill's finest work. After seeing a London production of the play, T. S. Eliot called it "one of the most moving plays I have ever seen." The critic Brendan Gill considered it "the finest play written in English in my lifetime." The play opened in New York in 1956 and has been successfully revived twice on Broadway, most recently in 1986.

Three other plays received posthumous premieres: *A Touch of the Poet, Hughie,* and *More Stately Mansions.* Of these, the most successful is *Hughie,* written in 1940 but not performed in America until 1964. Echoing many of O'Neill's themes, this fifty-minute play returns to the spare, almost claustrophobic settings of his first sea plays. A drama of voice and atmosphere rather than of plot, it shows O'Neill's remarkable sensitivity to sound and to the poetry of urban slang. O'Neill once wrote that critics had generally missed the best part of his work: "But where I feel myself most neglected is just where I set most store by myself —as a bit of a poet, who has labored with the spoken word to evolve original rhythms of beauty where beauty apparently isn't." A one-act masterpiece, *Hughie* captures the essence of O'Neill's dramatic lyricism.

Further Reading:
B. H. Clark, *Eugene O'Neill: The Man and His Plays,* 1947.
E. Engel, *The Haunted Heroes of Eugene O'Neill,* 1953.
D. Alexander, *The Tempering of Eugene O'Neill,* 1962.
A. and B. Gelb, *O'Neill,* 1962, 1973.
J. Raleigh, *The Plays of Eugene O'Neill,* 1965.

L. Schaeffer, *O'Neill, Son and Playwright,* 1968.
T. Bogard, *Contour in Time: The Plays of Eugene O'Neill,* 1972.
L. Chabrowe, *Ritual and Pathos: The Theater of O'Neill,* 1976.
Eugene O'Neill: A Collection of Criticism, ed. E. Griffin, 1976.

Text:
Hughie, 1959.

Hughie

Characters

"Erie" Smith, a teller of tales

A Night Clerk

Scene: The desk and a section of lobby of a small hotel on a West Side street in midtown New York. It is between 3 and 4 A.M. of a day in the summer of 1928.

It is one of those hotels, built in the decade 1900–10 on the side streets of the Great White Way[1] sector, which began as respectable second class but soon were forced to deteriorate in order to survive. Following the First World War and Prohibition, it had given up all pretense of respectability, and now is anything a paying guest wants it to be, a third class dump, catering to the catch-as-catch-can trade. But still it does not prosper. It has not shared in the Great Hollow Boom of the twenties. The Everlasting Opulence of the New Economic Law has overlooked it. It manages to keep running by cutting the overhead for service, repairs, and cleanliness to a minimum.

The desk faces left along a section of seedy lobby with shabby chairs. The street entrance is off-stage, left. Behind the desk are a telephone switchboard and the operator's stool. At right, the usual numbered tiers of mailboxes, and above them a clock.

The NIGHT CLERK sits on the stool, facing front, his back to the switchboard. There is nothing to do. He is not thinking. He is not sleepy. He simply droops and stares acquiescently at nothing. It would be discouraging to glance at the clock. He knows there are several hours to go before his shift is over. Anyway, he does not need to look at clocks. He has been a night clerk in New York hotels so long he can tell time by sounds in the street.

He is in his early forties. Tall, thin, with a scrawny neck and jutting Adam's apple. His face is long and narrow, greasy with perspiration, sallow, studded with pimples from ingrowing hairs. His nose is

---

[1] The theatrical section of Broadway.

large and without character. So is his mouth. So are his ears. So is his thinning brown hair, powdered with dandruff. Behind horn-rimmed spectacles, his blank brown eyes contain no discernible expression. One would say they had even forgotten how it feels to be bored. He wears an ill-fitting blue serge suit, white shirt and collar, a blue tie. The suit is old and shines at the elbows as if it had been waxed and polished.

Footsteps echo in the deserted lobby as someone comes in from the street. The Night Clerk rises wearily. His eyes remain empty but his gummy lips part automatically in a welcoming The-Patron-Is-Always-Right grimace, intended as a smile. His big uneven teeth are in bad condition.

ERIE SMITH enters and approaches the desk. He is about the same age as the Clerk and has the same pasty, perspiry, night-life complexion. There the resemblance ends. Erie is around medium height but appears shorter because he is stout and his fat legs are too short for his body. So are his fat arms. His big head squats on a neck which seems part of his beefy shoulders. His face is round, his snub nose flattened at the tip. His blue eyes have drooping lids and puffy pouches under them. His sandy hair is falling out and the top of his head is bald. He walks to the desk with a breezy, familiar air, his gait a bit waddling because of his short legs. He carries a Panama hat and mops his face with a red and blue silk handkerchief. He wears a light grey suit cut in the extreme, tight-waisted, Broadway mode, the coat open to reveal an old and faded but expensive silk shirt in a shade of blue that sets teeth on edge, and a gay red and blue foulard tie, its knot stained by perspiration. His trousers are held up by a braided brown leather belt with a brass buckle. His shoes are tan and white, his socks white silk.

In manner, he is consciously a Broadway sport and a Wise Guy—the type of small fry gambler and horse player, living hand to mouth on the fringe of the rackets. Infesting corners, doorways, cheap restaurants, the bars of minor speakeasies, he and his kind imagine they are in the Real Know, cynical oracles of the One True Grapevine.

Erie usually speaks in a low, guarded tone, his droop-lidded eyes suspiciously wary of nonexistent eavesdroppers. His face is set in the prescribed pattern of gambler's dead pan. His small, pursy mouth is

> always crooked in the cynical leer of one who possesses
> superior, inside information, and his shifty once-over
> glances never miss the price tags he detects on
> everything and everybody. Yet there is something
> phoney about his characterization of himself, some
> sentimental softness behind it which doesn't belong in
> the hard-boiled picture.
>
> > *Erie avoids looking at the Night Clerk, as if he
> > resented him.*

Erie: *Peremptorily.* Key.

> > *Then as the Night Clerk gropes with his memory—
> > grudgingly.*

Forgot you ain't seen me before. Erie Smith's the name. I'm an old timer in this
fleabag. 492.

Night Clerk: *In a tone of one who is wearily relieved when he does not have to
remember anything—he plucks out the key.* 492. Yes, sir.

Erie: *Taking the key, gives the Clerk the once-over. He appears not unfavorably
impressed but his tone still holds resentment.* How long you been on the job?
Four, five days, huh? I been off on a drunk. Come to now, though. Tapering
off. Well, I'm glad they fired that young squirt they took on when Hughie
got sick. One of them fresh wise punks. Couldn't tell him nothing. Pleased to
meet you, Pal. Hope you stick around.

> > *He shoves out his hand. The Night Clerk takes it
> > obediently.*

Night Clerk. *With a compliant, uninterested smile.* Glad to know you, Mr. Smith.

Erie: What's your name?

Night Clerk: *As if he had half forgotten because what did it matter, anyway?* Hughes.
Charlie Hughes.

Erie: *Starts.* Huh? Hughes? Say, is that on the level?

Night Clerk: Charlie Hughes.

Erie: Well, I be damned! What the hell d'you know about that!

> > *Warming toward the Clerk.*

Say, now I notice, you don't look like Hughie, but you remind me of him
somehow. You ain't by any chance related?

Night Clerk: You mean to the Hughes who had this job so long and died
recently? No, sir. No relation.

Erie: *Gloomily.* No, that's right. Hughie told me he didn't have no relations left
—except his wife and kids, of course.

He pauses—more gloomily.

Yeah. The poor guy croaked last week. His funeral was what started me off on a bat.

Then boastfully, as if defending himself against gloom.

Some drunk! I don't go on one often. It's bum dope in my book. A guy gets careless and gabs about things he knows and when he comes to he's liable to find there's guys who'd feel easier if he wasn't around no more. That's the trouble with knowing things. Take my tip, Pal. Don't never know nothin'. Be a sap and stay healthy.

> *His manner has become secretive, with sinister
> undertones. But the Night Clerk doesn't notice this.
> Long experience with guests who stop at his desk in
> the small hours to talk about themselves has given him
> a foolproof technique of self-defense. He appears to
> listen with agreeable submissiveness and be impressed,
> but his mind is blank and he doesn't hear unless a
> direct question is put to him, and sometimes not even
> then. Erie thinks he is impressed.*

But hell, I always keep my noggin working, booze or no booze. I'm no sucker. What was I sayin'? Oh, some drunk. I sure hit the high spots. You shoulda seen the doll I made night before last. And did she take me to the cleaners! I'm a sucker for blondes.

> *He pauses—giving the Night Clerk a cynical,
> contemptuous glance.*

You're married, ain't you?

Night Clerk: Long ago he gave up caring whether questions were personal or not. Yes, sir.

Erie: Yeah, I'd'a laid ten to one on it. You got that old look. Like Hughie had. Maybe that's the resemblance.

> *He chuckles contemptuously.*

Kids, too, I bet?

Night Clerk: Yes, sir. Three.

Erie: You're worse off than Hughie was. He only had two. Three, huh? Well, that's what comes of being careless!

> *He laughs. The Night Clerk smiles at a guest. He had
> been a little offended when a guest first made that crack
> —must have been ten years ago—yes, Eddie, the*

*oldest, is eleven now—or is it twelve? Erie goes on
with good-natured tolerance.*

Well, I suppose marriage ain't such a bum racket, if you're made for it. Hughie
didn't seem to mind it much, although if you want my low-down, his wife is a
bum—in spades! Oh, I don't mean cheatin'. With her puss and figure, she'd
never make no one except she raided a blind asylum.

*The Night Clerk feels that he has been standing a
long time and his feet are beginning to ache and he
wishes 492 would stop talking and go to bed so he can
sit down again and listen to the noises in the street and
think about nothing. Erie gives him an amused,
condescending glance.*

How old are you? Wait! Let me guess. You look fifty or over but I'll lay ten to
one you're forty-three or maybe forty-four.
Night Clerk I'm forty-three.

He adds vaguely.

Or maybe it is forty-four.
Erie: Elated. I win, huh? I sure can call the turn on ages, Buddy. You ought to
see the dolls get sored up when I work it on them! You're like Hughie. He
looked like he'd never see fifty again and he was only forty-three. Me, I'm
forty-five. Never think it, would you? Most of the dames don't think I've hit
forty yet.

*The Night Clerk shifts his position so he can lean
more on the desk. Maybe those shoes he sees advertised
for fallen arches— But they cost eight dollars, so that's
out— Get a pair when he goes to heaven. Erie is
sizing him up with another cynical, friendly glance.*

I make another bet about you. Born and raised in the sticks, wasn't you?
Night Clerk: Faintly aroused and defensive. I come originally from Saginaw,
Michigan, but I've lived here in the Big Town so long I consider myself a
New Yorker now.

*This is a long speech for him and he wonders sadly
why he took the trouble to make it.*

Erie: I don't deserve no medal for picking that one. Nearly every guy I know
on the Big Stem[2]—and I know most of 'em—hails from the sticks. Take me.
You'd never guess it but I was dragged up in Erie, P-a. Ain't that a

[2] I.e., the larger of the two peninsulas forming
Michigan.

knockout! Erie, P-a! That's how I got my moniker. No one calls me nothing but Erie. You better call me Erie, too, Pal, or I won't know when you're talkin' to me.

Night Clerk: All right, Erie.

Erie: Atta Boy.

He chuckles.

Here's another knockout. Smith is my real name. A Broadway guy like me named Smith and it's my real name! Ain't that a knockout!

He explains carefully so there will be no misunderstanding.

I don't remember nothing much about Erie, P-a, you understand—or want to. Some punk burg! After grammar school, my Old Man put me to work in his store, dealing out groceries. Some punk job! I stuck it till I was eighteen before I took a run-out powder.

The Night Clerk seems turned into a drooping waxwork, draped along the desk. This is what he used to dread before he perfected his technique of not listening: The Guest's Story of His Life. He fixes his mind on his aching feet. Erie chuckles.

Speaking of marriage, that was the big reason I ducked. A doll nearly had me hooked for the old shotgun ceremony. Closest I ever come to being played for a sucker. This doll in Erie—Daisy's her name—was one of them dumb wide-open dolls. All the guys give her a play. Then one day she wakes up and finds she's going to have a kid. I never figured she meant to frame me in particular. Way I always figured, she didn't have no idea who, so she holds a lottery all by herself. Put about a thousand guys' names in a hat—all she could remember—and drew one out and I was it. Then she told her Ma, and her Ma told her Pa, and her Pa come round looking for me. But I was no fall guy even in them days. I took it on the lam. For Saratoga, to look the bangtails[3] over. I'd started to be a horse player in Erie, though I'd never seen a track. I been one ever since.

With a touch of bravado.

And I ain't done so bad, Pal. I've made some killings in my time the gang still gab about. I've been in the big bucks. More'n once, and I will be again. I've had tough breaks too, but what the hell, I always get by. When the horses won't run for me, there's draw or stud. When they're bad, there's a crap game. And when they're all bad, there's always bucks to pick up for little errands I ain't talkin'

---

[3] Racehorses.

about, which they give a guy who can keep his clam shut. Oh, I get along, Buddy. I get along fine.

> *He waits for approving assent from the Night Clerk, but the latter is not hearing so intently he misses his cue until the expectant silence crashes his ears.*

Night Clerk: *Hastily, gambling on "yes."* Yes, Sir.
Erie: *Bitingly.* Sorry if I'm keeping you up, Sport.

> *With an aggrieved air.*

Hughie was a wide-awake guy. He was always waiting for me to roll in. He'd say, "Hello, Erie, how'd the bangtails treat you?" Or, "How's luck?" Or, "Did you make the old bones behave?" Then I'd tell him how I'd done. He'd ask, "What's new along the Big Stem?" and I'd tell him the latest off the grapevine.

> *He grins with affectionate condescension.*

It used to hand me a laugh to hear old Hughie crackin' like a sport. In all the years I knew him, he never bet a buck on nothin'.

> *Excusingly.*

But it ain't his fault. He'd have took a chance, but how could he with his wife keepin' cases on every nickel of his salary? I showed him lots of ways he could cross her up, but he was too scared.

> *He chuckles.*

The biggest knockout was when he'd kid me about dames. He'd crack, "What? No blonde to-night, Erie? You must be slippin'." Jeez, you never see a guy more bashful with a doll around than Hughie was. I used to introduce him to the tramps I'd drag home with me. I'd wise them up to kid him along and pretend they'd fell for him. In two minutes, they'd have him hanging on the ropes. His face'd be red and he'd look like he wanted to crawl under the desk and hide. Some of them dolls was raw babies. They'd make him pretty raw propositions. He'd stutter like he was paralyzed. But he ate it up, just the same. He was tickled pink. I used to hope maybe I could nerve him up to do a little cheatin'. I'd offer to fix it for him with one of my dolls. Hell, I got plenty, I wouldn't have minded. I'd tell him, "Just let that wife of yours know you're cheatin', and she'll have some respect for you." But he was too scared.

> *He pauses—boastfully.*

Some queens I've brought here in my time, Brother—frails from the Follies, or the Scandals, or the Frolics,[4] that'd knock your eye out! And I still can make 'em. You watch. I ain't slippin'.

He looks at the Night Clerk expecting reassurance, but the Clerk's mind has slipped away to the clanging bounce of garbage cans in the outer night. He is thinking: "A job I'd like. I'd bang those cans louder than they do! I'd wake up the whole damned city!" Erie mutters disgustedly to himself.

Jesus, what a dummy!

He makes a move in the direction of the elevator, off right front—gloomily.

Might as well hit the hay, I guess.
Night Clerk: *Comes to—with the nearest approach to feeling he has shown in many a long night—approvingly.* Good night, Mr. Smith. I hope you have a good rest.

But Erie stops, glancing around the deserted lobby with forlorn distaste, jiggling the room key in his hand.

Erie: What a crummy dump! What did I come back for? I shoulda stayed on a drunk. You'd never guess it, Buddy, but when I first come here this was a classy hotel—and clean, can you believe it?

He scowls.

I've been campin' here, off and on, fifteen years, but I've got a good notion to move out. It ain't the same place since Hughie was took to the hospital.

Gloomily.

Hell with going to bed! I'll just lie there worrying—

He turns back to the desk. The Clerk's face would express despair, but the last time he was able to feel despair was back around World War days when the cost of living got so high and he was out of a job for three months. Erie leans on the desk—in a dejected, confidential tone.

Believe me, Brother, I never been a guy to worry, but this time I'm on a spot where I got to, if I ain't a sap.

---

[4] Follies; Scandals; Frolics: stage revues.

Night Clerk· In the vague tone of a corpse which admits it once overheard a favorable rumor about life. That's too bad, Mr. Smith. But they say most of the things we worry about never happen.

> *His mind escapes to the street again to play bouncing cans with the garbage men.*

Erie: Grimly. This thing happens, Pal. I ain't won a bet at nothin' since Hughie was took to the hospital. I'm jinxed. And that ain't all— But to hell with it! You're right, at that. Something always turns up for me. I was born lucky. I ain't worried. Just moaning low. Hell, who don't when they're getting over a drunk? You know how it is. The Brooklyn Boys march over the bridge with bloodhounds to hunt you down. And I'm still carrying the torch for Hughie. His checking out was a real K.O. for me. Damn if I know why. Lots of guys I've been pals with, in a way, croaked from booze or something, or got rubbed out, but I always took it as part of the game. Hell, we all gotta croak. Here today, gone tomorrow, so what's the good of beefin'? When a guy's dead, he's dead. He don't give a damn, so why should anybody else?

> *But this fatalistic philosophy is no comfort and Erie sighs.*

I miss Hughie, I guess. I guess I'd got to like him a lot.

> *Again he explains carefully so there will be no misunderstanding.*

Not that I was ever real pals with him, you understand. He didn't run in my class. He didn't know none of the answers. He was just a sucker.

> *He sighs again.*

But I sure am sorry he's gone. You missed a lot not knowing Hughie, Pal. He sure was one grand little guy.

> *He stares at the lobby floor. The Night Clerk regards him with vacant, bulging eyes full of a vague envy for the blind. The garbage men have gone their predestined way. Time is that much older. The Clerk's mind remains in the street to greet the noise of a far-off El train. Its approach is pleasantly like a memory of hope; then it roars and rocks and rattles past the nearby corner, and the noise pleasantly deafens memory; then it recedes and dies, and there is something melancholy about that. But there is hope. Only so many El trains pass in one night, and each one passing leaves one less*

> to pass, so the night recedes, too, until at last it must
> die and join all the other long nights in Nirvana,[5] the
> Big Night of Nights. And that's life. "What I always
> tell Jess when she nags me to worry about something:
> 'That's life, isn't it? What can you do about it?'"
> Erie sighs again—then turns to the Clerk, his foolishly
> wary, wise-guy eyes defenseless, his poker face as
> self-betraying as a hurt dog's—appealingly.

Say, you do remind me of Hughie somehow, Pal. You got the same look on
your map.

> But the Clerk's mind is far away attending the
> obsequies of night, and it takes it some time to get
> back. Erie is hurt—contemptuously.

But I guess it's only that old night clerk look! There's one of 'em born every
minute!
Night Clerk: His mind arrives just in time to catch this last—with a bright grimace.
Yes, Mr. Smith. That's what Barnum[6] said, and it's certainly true, isn't it?
Erie: Grateful even for this sign of companionship, growls. Nix on the Mr. Smith
stuff, Charlie. There's ten of them born every minute. Call me Erie, like I told
you.
Night Clerk: Automatically, as his mind tiptoes into the night again. All right, Erie.
Erie: Encouraged, leans on the desk, clacking his room key like a castanet. Yeah.
Hughie was one grand little guy. All the same, like I said, he wasn't the kind
of guy you'd ever figger a guy like me would take to. Because he was a
sucker, see—the kind of sap you'd take to the cleaners a million times and
he'd never wise up he was took. Why, night after night, just for a gag, I'd
get him to shoot crap with me here on the desk. With my dice. And he'd
never ask to give 'em the once-over. Can you beat that!

> He chuckles—then earnestly.

Not that I'd ever ring in no phoneys on a pal. I'm no heel.

> He chuckles again.

And anyway, I didn't need none to take Hughie because he never even made me
knock 'em against nothing. Just a roll on the desk here. Boy, if they'd ever let
me throw 'em that way in a real game, I'd be worth ten million dollars.

> He laughs.

---

[5] Paradise.
[6] P. T. Barnum (1810–1891), the American showman, was supposed to have coined the phrase "There's a sucker born every minute."

You'da thought Hughie woulda got wise something was out of order when, no matter how much he'd win on a run of luck like suckers have sometimes, I'd always take him to the cleaners in the end. But he never suspicioned nothing. All he'd say was "Gosh, Erie, no wonder you took up gambling. You sure were born lucky."

He chuckles.

Can you beat that?

He hastens to explain earnestly.

Of course, like I said, it was only a gag. We'd play with real jack,[7] just to make it look real, but it was all my jack. He never had no jack. His wife dealt him four bits a day for spending money. So I'd stake him at the start to half of what I got—in chicken feed, I mean. We'd pretend a cent was a buck, and a nickel was a fin and so on. Some big game! He got a big kick out of it. He'd get all het up.[8] It give me a kick, too—especially when he'd say, "Gosh, Erie, I don't wonder you never worry about money, with your luck."

He laughs.

That guy would believe anything! Of course, I'd stall him off when he'd want to shoot nights when I didn't have a goddamned nickel.

He chuckles.

What laughs he used to hand me! He'd always call horses "the bangtails," like he'd known 'em all his life—and he'd never seen a race horse, not till I kidnaped him one day and took him down to Belmont. What a kick he got out of that! I got scared he'd pass out with excitement. And he wasn't doing no betting either. All he had was four bits. It was just the track, and the crowd, and the horses got him. Mostly the horses.

With a surprised, reflective air.

Y'know, it's funny how a dumb, simple guy like Hughie will all of a sudden get something right. He says, "They're the most beautiful things in the world, I think." And he wins! I tell you, Pal, I'd rather sleep in the same stall with old Man o' War[9] than make the whole damn Follies. What do you think?
Night Clerk: His mind darts back from a cruising taxi and blinks bewilderedly in the light: "Say yes." Yes, I agree with you, Mr.—I mean, Erie.

---

[7] Money.
[8] Excited ("heated up").

[9] The champion racehorse that won the Belmont Stakes in 1920.

Erie: With good-natured contempt. Yeah? I bet you never seen one, except back at the old Fair Grounds in the sticks. I don't mean them kind of turtles. I mean a real horse.

> *The Clerk wonders what horses have to do with anything—or for that matter, what anything has to do with anything—then gives it up. Erie takes up his tale.*

And what d'you think happened the next night? Damned if Hughie didn't dig two bucks out of his pants and try to slip 'em to me. "Let this ride on the nose of whatever horse you're betting on tomorrow," he told me. I got sore. "Nix," I told him, "if you're going to start playin' sucker and bettin' on horse races, you don't get no assist from me."

> *He grins wryly.*

Was that a laugh! Me advising a sucker not to bet when I've spent a lot of my life tellin' saps a story to make 'em bet! I said, "Where'd you grab this dough? Outa the Little Woman's purse, huh? What tale you going to give her when you lose it? She'll start breaking up the furniture with you!" "No," he says, "she'll just cry." "That's worse," I said, "no guy can beat that racket. I had a doll cry on me once in a restaurant full of people till I had to promise her a diamond engagement ring to sober her up." Well, anyway, Hughie sneaked the two bucks back in the Little Woman's purse when he went home that morning, and that was the end of that.

> *Cynically.*

Boy Scouts got nothin' on me, Pal, when it comes to good deeds. That was one I done. It's too bad I can't remember no others.

> *He is well wound up now and goes on without noticing that the Night Clerk's mind has left the premises in his sole custody.*

Y'know I had Hughie sized up for a sap the first time I see him. I'd just rolled in from Tia Juana. I'd made a big killing down there and I was lousy with jack. Came all the way in a drawing room, and I wasn't lonely in it neither. There was a blonde movie doll on the train—and I was lucky in them days. Used to follow the horses South every winter. I don't no more. Sick of traveling. And I ain't as lucky as I was—

> *Hastily.*

Anyway, this time I'm talkin' about, soon as I hit this lobby I see there's a new night clerk, and while I'm signing up for the bridal suite I make a bet with myself he's never been nothin' but a night clerk. And I win. At first, he wouldn't open up. Not that he was cagey about gabbin' too much. But like he couldn't think of nothin' about himself worth saying. But after he'd seen me roll in here the last one every night, and I'd stop to kid him along and tell him the tale of what I'd win that day, he got friendly and talked. He'd come from a hick burg upstate. Graduated from high school, and had a shot at different jobs in the old home town but couldn't make the grade until he was took on as night clerk in the hotel there. Then he made good. But he wasn't satisfied. Didn't like being only a night clerk where everybody knew him. He'd read somewhere—in the Suckers' Almanac, I guess—that all a guy had to do was come to the Big Town and Old Man Success would be waitin' at the Grand Central[10] to give him the key to the city. What a gag that is! Even I believed that once, and no one could ever call me a sap. Well, anyway, he made the break and come here and the only job he could get was night clerk. Then he fell in love—or kidded himself he was—and got married. Met her on a subway train. It stopped sudden and she was jerked into him, and he put his arms around her, and they started talking, and the poor boob never stood a chance. She was a sales girl in some punk department store, and she was sick of standing on her dogs all day, and all the way home to Brooklyn, too. So, the way I figger it, knowing Hughie and dames, she proposed and said "yes" for him, and married him, and after that, of course, he never dared stop being a night clerk, even if he could.

He pauses.

Maybe you think I ain't giving her a square shake. Well, maybe I ain't. She never give me one. She put me down as a bad influence, and let her chips ride. And maybe Hughie couldn't have done no better. Dolls didn't call him no riot. Hughie and her seemed happy enough the time he had me out to dinner in their flat. Well, not happy. Maybe contented. No, that's boosting it, too. Resigned comes nearer, as if each was givin' the other a break by thinking, "Well, what more could I expect?"

Abruptly he addresses the Night Clerk with contemptuous good nature.

How d'you and your Little Woman hit it off, Brother?
Night Clerk: His mind has been counting the footfalls of the cop on the beat as they recede, sauntering longingly toward the dawn's release. "If he'd only shoot it out with a gunman some night! Nothing exciting has happened in any night I've ever lived through!" He stammers gropingly among the echoes of Erie's last words. Oh—you mean *my* wife? Why, we get along all right, I guess.
Erie: Disgustedly. Better lay off them headache pills, Pal. First thing you know, some guy is going to call you a dope.

---

[10] Grand Central Station, in midtown New York.

> *But the Night Clerk cannot take this seriously. It is*
> *years since he cared what anyone called him. So many*
> *guests have called him so many things. The Little*
> *Woman has, too. And, of course, he has, himself. But*
> *that's all past. Is daybreak coming now? No, too early*
> *yet. He can tell by the sound of that surface car. It is*
> *still lost in the night. Flat wheeled and tired. Distant*
> *the carbarn,*[11] *and far away the sleep. Erie, having*
> *soothed resentment with his wisecrack, goes on with a*
> *friendly grin.*

Well, keep hoping, Pal. Hughie was as big a dope as you until I give him some interest in life.

Slipping back into narrative.

That time he took me home to dinner. Was that a knockout! It took him a hell of a while to get up nerve to ask me. "Sure, Hughie," I told him, "I'll be tickled to death." I was thinking, I'd rather be shot. For one thing, he lived in Brooklyn, and I'd sooner take a trip to China. Another thing, I'm a guy that likes to eat what I order and not what somebody deals me. And he had kids and a wife, and the family racket is out of my line. But Hughie looked so tickled I couldn't welsh on him. And it didn't work out so bad. Of course, what he called home was only a dump of a cheap flat. Still, it wasn't so bad for a change. His wife had done a lot of stuff to doll it up. Nothin' with no class, you understand. Just cheap stuff to make it comfortable. And his kids wasn't the gorillas I'd expected, neither. No throwin' spitballs in my soup or them kind of gags. They was quiet like Hughie. I kinda liked 'em. After dinner I started tellin' 'em a story about a race horse a guy I know owned once. I thought it was up to me to put out something, and kids like animal stories, and this one was true, at that. This old turtle never wins a race, but he was as foxy as ten guys, a natural born crook, the goddamnedest thief, he'd steal anything in reach that wasn't nailed down— Well, I didn't get far. Hughie's wife butt in and stopped me cold. Told the kids it was bedtime and hustled 'em off like I was giving 'em measles. It got my goat, kinda. I coulda liked her—a little—if she'd give me a chance. Not that she was nothin' Ziegfeld[12] would want to glorify. When you call her plain, you give her all the breaks.

Resentfully.

Well, to hell with it. She had me tagged for a bum, and seein' me made her sure she was right. You can bet she told Hughie never invite me again, and he never did. He tried to apologize, but I shut him up quick. He says, "Irma was brought

---

[11] Bus or railway terminal.
[12] Florenz Ziegfeld (1869–1932), producer of the Follies.

up strict. She can't help being narrow-minded about gamblers." I said, "What's it to me? I don't want to hear your dame troubles. I got plenty of my own. Remember that doll I brung home night before last? She gives me an argument I promised her ten bucks. I told her, 'Listen, Baby, I got an impediment in my speech. Maybe it sounded like ten, but it was two, and that's all you get. Hell, I don't want to buy your soul! What would I do with it?' Now she's peddling the news along Broadway I'm a rat and a chiseler, and of course all the rats and chiselers believe her. Before she's through, I won't have a friend left."

He pauses—confidentially.

I switched the subject on Hughie, see, on purpose. He never did beef to me about his wife again.

He gives a forced chuckle.

Believe me, Pal, I can stop guys that start telling me their family troubles!

Night Clerk: His mind has hopped an ambulance clanging down Sixth, and is asking without curiosity: "Will he die, Doctor, or isn't he lucky?" "I'm afraid not, but he'll have to be absolutely quiet for months and months." "With a pretty nurse taking care of him?" "Probably not pretty." "Well, anyway, I claim he's lucky. And now I must get back to the hotel. 492 won't go to bed and insists on telling me jokes. It must have been a joke because he's chuckling." He laughs with a heartiness which has forgotten that heart is more than a word used in "Have a heart," an old slang expression. Ha— Ha! That's a good one, Erie. That's the best I've heard in a long time!

Erie: For a moment is so hurt and depressed he hasn't the spirit to make a sarcastic crack. He stares at the floor, twirling his room key—to himself. Jesus, this sure is a dead dump. About as homey as the Morgue.

He glances up at the clock.

Gettin' late. Better beat it up to my cell and grab some shut eye.

> *He makes a move to detach himself from the desk but fails and remains wearily glued to it. His eyes prowl the lobby and finally come to rest on the Clerk's glistening, sallow face. He summons up strength for a withering crack.*

Why didn't you tell me you was deaf, Buddy? I know guys is sensitive about them little afflictions, but I'll keep it confidential.

> *But the Clerk's mind has rushed out to follow the siren wail of a fire engine. "A fireman's life must be exciting." His mind rides the engine, and asks a*

*fireman with disinterested eagerness: "Where's the fire?
Is it a real good one this time? Has it a good start?
Will it be big enough, do you think?" Erie examines
his face—bitingly.*

Take my tip, Pal, and don't never try to buy from a dope peddler. He'll tell you
you had enough already.

*The Clerk's mind continues its dialogue with the
fireman: "I mean, big enough to burn down the whole
damn city?" "Sorry, Brother, but there's no chance.
There's too much stone and steel. There'd always be
something left." "Yes, I guess you're right. There's too
much stone and steel. I wasn't really hoping, anyway.
It really doesn't matter to me." Erie gives him up and
again attempts to pry himself from the desk, twirling
his key frantically as if it were a fetish which might
set him free.*

Well, me for the hay.

But he can't dislodge himself—dully.

Christ, it's lonely. I wish Hughie was here. By God, if he was, I'd tell him a tale
that'd make his eyes pop! The bigger the story the harder he'd fall. He was that
kind of sap. He thought gambling was romantic. I guess he saw me like a sort of
dream guy, the sort of guy he'd like to be if he could take a chance. I guess he
lived a sort of double life listening to me gabbin' about hittin' the high spots.
Come to figger it, I'll bet he even cheated on his wife that way, using me and
my dolls.

He chuckles.

No wonder he liked me, huh? And the bigger I made myself the more he lapped
it up. I went easy on him at first. I didn't lie—not any more'n a guy naturally
does when he gabs about the bets he wins and the dolls he's made. But I soon see
he was cryin' for more, and when a sucker cries for more, you're a dope if you
don't let him have it. Every tramp I made got to be a Follies' doll. Hughie liked
'em to be Follies' dolls. Or in the Scandals or Frolics. He wanted me to be the
Sheik of Araby, or something that any blonde 'd go round-heeled about. Well, I
give him plenty of that. And I give him plenty of gambling tales. I explained
my campin' in this dump was because I don't want to waste jack on nothin' but
gambling. It was like dope to me, I told him. I couldn't quit. He lapped that up.
He liked to kid himself I'm mixed up in the racket. He thought gangsters was
romantic. So I fed him some baloney about highjacking I'd done once. I told
him I knew all the Big Shots. Well, so I do, most of 'em, to say hello, and
sometimes they hello back. Who wouldn't know 'em that hangs around

Broadway and the joints? I run errands for 'em sometimes, because there's dough
in it, but I'm cagey about gettin' in where it ain't healthy. Hughie wanted to
think me and Legs Diamond[13] was old pals. So I give him that too. I give him
anything he cried for.

> *Earnestly.*

Don't get the wrong idea, Pal. What I fed Hughie wasn't all lies. The tales about
gambling wasn't. They was stories of big games and killings that really happened
since I've been hangin' round. Only I wasn't in on 'em like I made out—except
one or two from way back when I had a run of big luck and was in the bucks
for a while until I was took to the cleaners.

> *He stops to pay tribute of a sigh to the memory of
> brave days that were and that never were—then
> meditatively.*

Yeah, Hughie lapped up my stories like they was duck soup,[14] or a beakful of
heroin. I sure took him around with me in tales and showed him one hell of a
time.

> *He chuckles—then seriously.*

And, d'you know, it done me good, too, in a way. Sure. I'd get to seein' myself
like he seen me. Some nights I'd come back here without a buck, feeling lower
than a snake's belly, and first thing you know I'd be lousy with jack, bettin' a
grand a race. Oh, I was wise I was kiddin' myself. I ain't a sap. But what the
hell, Hughie loved it, and it didn't cost nobody nothin', and if every guy along
Broadway who kids himself was to drop dead there wouldn't be nobody left.
Ain't it the truth, Charlie?

> *He again stares at the Night Clerk appealingly,
> forgetting past rebuffs. The Clerk's face is taut with
> vacancy. His mind has been trying to fasten itself to
> some noise in the night, but a rare and threatening
> pause of silence has fallen on the city, and here he is,
> chained behind a hotel desk forever, awake when
> everyone else in the world is asleep, except Room 492,
> and he won't go to bed, he's still talking, and there is
> no escape.*

Night Clerk: His glassy eyes stare through Erie's face. He stammers deferentially.
      Truth? I'm afraid I didn't get— What's the truth?
Erie: Hopelessly. Nothing, Pal. Not a thing.

---

[13] John Henry Diamond (1896–1931), gangster of   [14] Something easy to take.
the prohibition era.

His eyes fall to the floor. For a while he is too defeated even to twirl his room key. The Clerk's mind still cannot make a getaway because the city remains silent, and the night vaguely reminds him of death, and he is vaguely frightened, and now that he remembers, his feet are giving him hell, but that's no excuse not to act as if the Guest is always right: "I should have paid 492 more attention. After all, he is company. He is awake and alive. I should use him to help me live through the night. What's he been talking about? I must have caught some of it without meaning to." The Night Clerk's forehead puckers perspiringly as he tries to remember. Erie begins talking again but this time it is obviously aloud to himself, without hope of a listener.

I could tell by Hughie's face before he went to the hospital, he was through. I've seen the same look on guys' faces when they knew they was on the spot, just before guys caught up with them. I went to see him twice in the hospital. The first time, his wife was there and give me a dirty look, but he cooked up a smile and said, "Hello, Erie, how're the bangtails treating you?" I see he wants a big story to cheer him, but his wife butts in and says he's weak and he mustn't get excited. I felt like crackin', "Well, the Docs in this dump got the right dope. Just leave you with him and he'll never get excited." The second time I went, they wouldn't let me see him. That was near the end. I went to his funeral, too. There wasn't nobody but a coupla his wife's relations. I had to feel sorry for her. She looked like she ought to be parked in a coffin, too. The kids was bawlin'. There wasn't no flowers but a coupla lousy wreaths. It woulda been a punk showing for poor old Hughie, if it hadn't been for my flower piece.

He swells with pride.

That was some display, Pal. It'd knock your eye out! Set me back a hundred bucks, and no kiddin'! A big horseshoe of red roses! I knew Hughie'd want a horseshoe because that made it look like he'd been a horse player. And around the top printed in forget-me-nots was "Good-by, Old Pal." Hughie liked to kid himself he was my pal.

He adds sadly.

And so he was, at that—even if he was a sucker.

He pauses, his false poker face as nakedly forlorn as an organ grinder's monkey's. Outside, the spell of abnormal quiet presses suffocatingly upon the street, enters the deserted, dirty lobby. The Night Clerk's mind cowers away from it. He cringes behind the desk, his feet aching like hell. There is only one possible escape. If his mind could only fasten onto something 492 has said. "What's he been talking about? A clerk should always be attentive. You even are duty bound to laugh at a guest's smutty jokes, no matter how often you've heard them. That's the policy of the hotel. 492 has been gassing[15] for hours. What's he been telling me? I must be slipping. Always before this I've been able to hear without bothering to listen, but now when I need company— Ah! I've got it! Gambling! He said a lot about gambling. That's something I've always wanted to know more about, too. Maybe he's a professional gambler. Like Arnold Rothstein."[16]

Night Clerk: *Blurts out with an uncanny, almost lifelike eagerness.* I beg your pardon, Mr.—Erie—but did I understand you to say you are a gambler by profession? Do you, by any chance, know the Big Shot, Arnold Rothstein?

But this time it is Erie who doesn't hear him. And the Clerk's mind is now suddenly impervious to the threat of Night and Silence as it pursues an ideal of fame and glory within itself called Arnold Rothstein.

Erie: *With mournful longing.* Christ, I wish Hughie was alive and kickin'. I'd tell him I win ten grand from the bookies, and ten grand at stud, and ten grand in a crap game! I'd tell him I bought one of those Mercedes sport roadsters with nickel pipes sticking out of the hood! I'd tell him I lay three babes from the Follies—two blondes and one brunette!

The Night Clerk dreams, a rapt hero worship transfiguring his pimply face: "Arnold Rothstein! He must be some guy! I read a story about him. He'll gamble for any limit on anything, and always wins. The story said he wouldn't bother playing in a poker game unless the smallest bet you could make—one white chip!—was a hundred dollars. Christ, that's going some! I'd like to have the dough to get in a game with him once! The last pot everyone would drop out but him and me. I'd say, 'Okay, Arnold, the sky's the limit,' and I'd raise him five grand, and he'd call, and I'd have a royal flush to his four aces. Then I'd say, 'Okay, Arnold, I'm a good sport, I'll give you a break. I'll cut you double or nothing. Just one cut. I

---

[15] Talking emptily.
[16] Rothstein (1882–1928), New York area gambler

known for high stakes, was murdered in his hotel room, supposedly for reneging on a bet.

want quick action for my dough.' And I'd cut the ace of spades and win again." Beatific vision swoons on the empty pools of the Night Clerk's eyes. He resembles a holy saint, recently elected to Paradise. Erie breaks the silence—bitterly resigned.

But Hughie's better off, at that, being dead. He's got all the luck. He needn't do no worryin' now. He's out of the racket. I mean, the whole goddamned racket. I mean life.

Night Clerk: Kicked out of his dream—with detached, pleasant acquiescence. Yes, it is a goddamned racket when you stop to think, isn't it, 492? But we might as well make the best of it, because— Well, you can't burn it all down, can you? There's too much steel and stone. There'd always be something left to start it going again.

Erie: Scowls bewilderedly. Say, what is this? What the hell you talkin' about?

Night Clerk: At a loss—in much confusion. Why, to be frank, I really don't— Just something that came into my head.

Erie: Bitingly, but showing he is comforted at having made some sort of contact. Get it out of your head quick, Charlie, or some guys in uniform will walk in here with a butterfly net and catch you.

He changes the subject—earnestly.

Listen, Pal, maybe you guess I was kiddin' about that flower piece for Hughie costing a hundred bucks? Well, I ain't! I didn't give a damn what it cost. It was up to me to give Hughie a big-time send-off, because I knew nobody else would.

Night Clerk: Oh, I'm not doubting your word, Erie. You won the money gambling, I suppose— I mean, I beg your pardon if I'm mistaken, but you are a gambler, aren't you?

Erie: Preoccupied. Yeah, sure, when I got scratch[17] to put up. What of it? But I don't win that hundred bucks. I don't win a bet since Hughie was took to the hospital. I had to get down on my knees and beg every guy I know for a sawbuck here and a sawbuck there until I raised it.

Night Clerk: His mind concentrated on the Big Ideal—insistently. Do you by any chance know—Arnold Rothstein?

Erie: His train of thought interrupted—irritably. Arnold? What's he got to do with it? He wouldn't loan a guy like me a nickel to save my grandmother from streetwalking.

Night Clerk: With humble awe. Then you do know him!

Erie: Sure I know the bastard. Who don't on Broadway? And he knows me— when he wants to. He uses me to run errands when there ain't no one else handy. But he ain't my trouble, Pal. My trouble is, some of these guys I put the bite on is dead wrong G's,[18] and they expect to be paid back next Tuesday,

---

[17] Betting money. A sawbuck (below) is a ten-dollar bill.

[18] I.e., some are owed several thousand dollars.

or else I'm outa luck and have to take it on the lam, or I'll get beat up and maybe sent to a hospital.

> *He suddenly rouses himself and there is something pathetically but genuinely gallant about him.*

But what the hell. I was wise I was takin' a chance. I've always took a chance, and if I lose I pay, and no welshing! It sure was worth it to give Hughie the big send-off.

> *He pauses. The Night Clerk hasn't paid any attention except to his own dream. A question is trembling on his parted lips, but before he can get it out Erie goes on gloomily.*

But even that ain't my big worry, Charlie. My big worry is the run of bad luck I've had since Hughie got took to the hospital. Not a win. That ain't natural. I've always been a lucky guy—lucky enough to get by and pay up, I mean. I wouldn't never worry about owing guys, like I owe them guys. I'd always know I'd make a win that'd fix it. But now I got a lousy hunch when I lost Hughie I lost my luck—I mean, I've lost the old confidence. He used to give me confidence.

> *He turns away from the desk.*

No use gabbin' here all night. You can't do me no good.

> *He starts toward the elevator.*

Night Clerk: Pleadingly. Just a minute, Erie, if you don't mind.

> *With awe.*

So you're an old friend of Arnold Rothstein! Would you mind telling me if it's really true when Arnold Rothstein plays poker, one white chip is—a hundred dollars?
Erie: Dully exasperated. Say, for Christ's sake, what's it to you—?

> *He stops abruptly, staring probingly at the Clerk. There is a pause. Suddenly his face lights up with a saving revelation. He grins warmly and saunters confidently back to the desk.*

Say, Charlie, why didn't you put me wise before, you was interested in gambling? Hell, I got you all wrong, Pal. I been tellin' myself, this guy ain't like old Hughie. He ain't got no sportin' blood. He's just a dope.

> *Generously.*

Now I see you're a right guy. Shake.

> *He shoves out his hand which the Clerk clasps with a limp pleasure. Erie goes on with gathering warmth and self-assurance.*

That's the stuff. You and me'll get along. I'll give you all the breaks, like I give Hughie.

Night Clerk: Gratefully. Thank you, Erie.

> *Then insistently.*

Is it true when Arnold Rothstein plays poker, one white chip—

Erie: With magnificent carelessness. Sets you back a hundred bucks? Sure. Why not? Arnold's in the bucks, ain't he? And when you're in the bucks, a C note[19] is chicken feed. I ought to know, Pal. I was in the bucks when Arnold was a piker.[20] Why, one time down in New Orleans I lit a cigar with a C note, just for a gag, y'understand. I was with a bunch of high class dolls and I wanted to see their eyes pop out—and believe me, they sure popped! After that, I coulda made 'em one at a time or all together! Hell, I once win twenty grand on a single race. That's action! A good crap game is action, too. Hell, I've been in games where there was a hundred grand in real folding money lying around the floor. That's travelin'!

> *He darts a quick glance at the Clerk's face and begins to hedge warily. But he needn't. The Clerk sees him now as the Gambler in 492, the Friend of Arnold Rothstein—and nothing is incredible. Erie goes on.*

Of course, I wouldn't kid you. I'm not in the bucks now—not right this moment. You know how it is, Charlie. Down today and up tomorrow. I got some dough ridin' on the nose of a turtle in the 4th at Saratoga. I hear a story he'll be so full of hop, if the joc can keep him from jumpin' over the grandstand, he'll win by a mile. So if I roll in here with a blonde that'll knock your eyes out, don't be surprised.

> *He winks and chuckles.*

Night Clerk: Ingratiatingly pally, smiling. Oh, you can't surprise me that way. I've been a night clerk in New York all my life, almost.

> *He tries out a wink himself.*

---

[19] One-hundred-dollar bill.　　　　[20] Small-time gambler.

I'll forget the house rules, Erie.
Erie: Dryly. Yeah. The manager wouldn't like you to remember something he
   ain't heard of yet.

Then slyly feeling his way.

How about shootin' a little crap, Charlie? I mean just in fun, like I used to with
Hughie. I know you can't afford takin' no chances. I'll stake you, see? I got a
coupla bucks. We gotta use real jack or it don't look real. It's all my jack, get it?
You can't lose. I just want to show you how I'll take you to the cleaners. It'll
give me confidence.

> *He has taken two one-dollar bills and some change
> from his pocket. He pushes most of it across to the
> Clerk.*

Here y'are.

> *He produces a pair of dice—carelessly.*

Want to give these dice the once-over before we start?
Night Clerk. Earnestly. What do you think I am? I know I can trust you.
Erie: Smiles. You remind me a lot of Hughie, Pal. He always trusted me. Well,
   don't blame me if I'm lucky.

> *He clicks the dice in his hand—thoughtfully.*

Y'know, it's time I quit carryin' the torch for Hughie. Hell, what's the use? It
don't do him no good. He's gone. Like we all gotta go. Him yesterday, me or
you tomorrow, and who cares, and what's the difference? It's all in the racket,
huh?

> *His soul is purged of grief, his confidence restored.*

I shoot two bits.
*Night Clerk: Manfully, with an excited dead-pan expression he hopes resembles Arnold
   Rothstein's.* I fade you.[21]
Erie: Throws the dice. Four's my point.

> *Gathers them up swiftly and throws them again.*

Four it is.

---

[21] Accept your bet. (The first roll of the dice here
becomes the point, or goal, of successive rolls.)

He takes the money.

Easy when you got my luck—and know how. Huh, Charlie?

*He chuckles, giving the Night Clerk the slyly amused,
contemptuous, affectionate wink with which a Wise
Guy regales a Sucker.*

CURTAIN

1941/1958;1959

Katherine Anne Porter
1890–1980

Katherine Anne Porter was born Callie Porter on May 15, 1890, in a simple L-shaped log cabin in Indian Creek, Texas, a small frontier community. She received, as she put it, a "fragmentary, but strangely useless and ornamental education" in various convent schools. Looking back, she saw herself as having been taught not at "schools at all but by five writers: Henry James, James Joyce, W. B. Yeats, T. S. Eliot, and Ezra Pound." Throughout her life, she spread misrepresentations, concoctions, and fabrications about her family and childhood, evoking a grand family plantation and distinguished ancestry that bore little resemblance to the actualities of the hard, uprooted life she experienced but considerable resemblance to elements of the stories she wrote.

During her long life, Porter lived in towns all over Texas and in cities throughout the United States—Denver, Chicago, New Orleans, New York, and Washington, to name a few—where she worked on newspapers and later held teaching positions. She also lived in Mexico, where she was politically active, as well as Belgium, Switzerland, France, and Germany. Approaching forty, she reported "that she had had four husbands and thirty-seven lovers." Over the last half of her life, there were two more husbands and many more lovers, including several after she reached the age of seventy. "Love," she said, is "purely a creation of the human imagination": it is the "most important example of how the imagination continually outruns the creature it inhabits." In addition to men, Porter collected furs, jewels, fine silver and china, antique furniture, gossip, and fables.

Porter's need to glamorize and enhance the facts of her life emerged early and lasted as long as she lived. Her finest fiction, however, which clearly sprang in part from needs like those expressed in her fabrications, was largely concentrated in the middle years of her life, especially the decade of the 1930s. "I went to Europe in 1931 an unknown," she later remarked, "and returned to find myself a celebrity." This success was based on two collections of stories and short novels, *Flowering Judas* (published in 1930 and augmented in 1935) and *Noon Wine*

(1937). Her critical reputation was enhanced by *Pale Horse, Pale Rider: Three Short Novels* (1938) and *The Leaning Tower and Other Stories* (1944). In his review of *The Leaning Tower,* Edmund Wilson admitted that Porter was "baffling" to him and struggled to formulate the "elusive" quality that made her "absolutely a first-rate artist":

> These stories are not illustrations of anything that is reducible to a moral law or a political or social analysis or even a principle of human behavior. What they show us are human relations in their constantly shifting phases and in the moments of which their existence is made. There is no place for general reflections; you are to live through the experience as the characters do.

Like Sherwood Anderson, Porter believed that the short story did not require a "plot." The writer, she said, "needed *first* a *theme,* and then a point of view, a certain knowledge of human nature and strong feeling about it, and style—that is to say, his own special way of telling a thing that makes it precisely his own and no one else's." As Eudora Welty pointed out in a review of *The Collected Stories of Katherine Anne Porter* (1965), she cared nothing for conventionally dramatic construction: "The suspense—so acute and so real—in Katherine Anne Porter's work never did depend for its life on disclosure of the happenings of the narrative . . . but in the writing of the story, which becomes one single long sustained moment for the reader."

Even in Porter's finest work we observe a tension between a desire to confront and disclose the significance of her experience and a countervailing desire to disguise and conceal that significance. The conflict between these impulses sometimes results in a rarefied, ethereal prose, as though Porter were reaching for the timeless and the universal before making sufficient contact with the local and the immediate. Both her aestheticism and her evasiveness, her reluctance to confront fully the significances lurking in her own experience of the world she knew best, occasionally limit her achievement. In her best works, however, she masters the tension between her sense of herself as a stylist seeking timelessness and universality and her sense of herself as a storyteller drawing upon perceptions and memories of local scenes and human actions.

Porter's only novel, *Ship of Fools,* which she wrote laboriously over a thirty-year period, appeared in 1962 and attracted considerable attention, in part because it had been so long awaited. The novel, an account of a voyage from Veracruz, Mexico, to Bremerhaven, Germany, in 1931, during the Nazi regime, explores the wreckage of modern civilization by focusing on the often vicious private histories and behavior of the ship's passengers. The vision of the book is a bleak one and apparently derives from Porter's longstanding belief that art offered the only hope, however small and fragile, in a darkening world. In 1940 she wrote in an introduction to a new edition of *Flowering Judas:* "All the conscious and recollected years of my life have been lived to this day under the heavy threat of world catastrophe, and most of the energies of my mind and spirit have been spent in the effort to grasp the meaning of those threats, to trace them to their sources and to understand the logic of this majestic and terrible failure of the life of man in the Western world." In 1952 Porter published *The Days Before:*

Collected Essays and Occasional Writings, a volume that was expanded in 1970; the essays range from an interpretation of nuclear fear to a profile of Jacqueline Kennedy. Katherine Anne Porter died on September 18, 1980, in the Carriage Hill Nursing Center in Silver Spring, Maryland.

Further Reading:
H. J. Mooney, *The Fiction and Criticism of Katherine Anne Porter,* 1962.
R. B. West, Jr., *Katherine Anne Porter,* 1963.
E. Welty, "The Eye of the Story," *Yale Review,* December 1965.
J. Givner, *Katherine Anne Porter: A Life,* 1982.

Text:
The Collected Stories of Katherine Anne Porter, 1965.

Flowering Judas

Braggioni sits heaped upon the edge of a straight-backed chair much too small for him, and sings to Laura in a furry, mournful voice. Laura has begun to find reasons for avoiding her own house until the latest possible moment, for Braggioni is there almost every night. No matter how late she is, he will be sitting there with a surly, waiting expression, pulling at his kinky yellow hair, thumbing the strings of his guitar, snarling a tune under his breath. Lupe the Indian maid meets Laura at the door, and says with a flicker of a glance towards the upper room, "He waits."

Laura wishes to lie down, she is tired of her hairpins and the feel of her long tight sleeves, but she says to him, "Have you a new song for me this evening?" If he says yes, she asks him to sing it. If he says no, she remembers his favorite one, and asks him to sing it again. Lupe brings her a cup of chocolate and a plate of rice, and Laura eats at the small table under the lamp, first inviting Braggioni, whose answer is always the same: "I have eaten, and besides, chocolate thickens the voice."

Laura says, "Sing, then," and Braggioni heaves himself into song. He scratches the guitar familiarly as though it were a pet animal, and sings passionately off key, taking the high notes in a prolonged painful squeal. Laura, who haunts the markets listening to the ballad singers, and stops every day to hear the blind boy playing his reed-flute in Sixteenth of September Street,[1] listens to Braggioni with pitiless courtesy, because she dares not smile at his miserable performance. Nobody dares to smile at him. Braggioni is cruel to everyone, with a kind of specialized insolence, but he is so vain of his talents, and so sensitive to slights, it would require a cruelty and vanity greater than his own to lay a finger on the vast cureless wound of his self-esteem. It would require courage, too, for it is dangerous to offend him, and nobody has this courage.

Braggioni loves himself with such tenderness and amplitude and eternal charity that his followers—for he is a leader of men, a skilled revolutionist, and his skin has been

[1] In Mexico City; like several other streets mentioned, it takes its name from the events of the revolution for Mexican independence (which began September 16, 1810). Many of the towns mentioned are also near Mexico City.

punctured in honorable warfare—warm themselves in the reflected glow, and say to each other: "He has a real nobility, a love of humanity raised above mere personal affections." The excess of this self-love has flowed out, inconveniently for her, over Laura, who, with so many others, owes her comfortable situation and her salary to him. When he is in a a very good humor, he tells her, "I am tempted to forgive you for being a *gringa. Gringita!*"[2] and Laura, burning, imagines herself leaning forward suddenly, and with a sound back-handed slap wiping the suety smile from his face. If he notices her eyes at these moments he gives no sign.

She knows what Braggioni would offer her, and she must resist tenaciously without appearing to resist, and if she could avoid it she would not admit even to herself the slow drift of his intention. During these long evenings which have spoiled a long month for her, she sits in her deep chair with an open book on her knees, resting her eyes on the consoling rigidity of the printed page when the sight and sound of Braggioni singing threaten to identify themselves with all her remembered afflictions and to add their weight to her uneasy premonitions of the future. The gluttonous bulk of Braggioni has become a symbol of her many disillusions, for a revolutionist should be lean, animated by heroic faith, a vessel of abstract virtues. This is nonsense, she knows it now and is ashamed of it. Revolution must have leaders, and leadership is a career for energetic men. She is, her comrades tell her, full of romantic error, for what she defines as cynicism in them is merely "a developed sense of reality." She is almost too willing to say, "I am wrong, I suppose I don't really understand the principles," and afterward she makes a secret truce with herself, determined not to surrender her will to such expedient logic. But she cannot help feeling that she has been betrayed irreparably by the disunion between her way of living and her feeling of what life should be, and at times she is almost contented to rest in this sense of grievance as a private store of consolation. Sometimes she wishes to run away, but she stays. Now she longs to fly out of this room, down the narrow stairs, and into the street where the houses lean together like conspirators under a single mottled lamp, and leave Braggioni singing to himself.

Instead she looks at Braggioni, frankly and clearly, like a good child who understands the rules of behavior. Her knees cling together under sound blue serge, and her round white collar is not purposely nun-like. She wears the uniform of an idea, and has renounced vanities. She was born Roman Catholic, and in spite of her fear of being seen by someone who might make a scandal of it, she slips now and again into some crumbling little church, kneels on the chilly stone, and says a Hail Mary on the gold rosary she bought in Tehuantepec. It is no good and she ends by examining the altar with its tinsel flowers and ragged brocades, and feels tender about the battered doll-shape of some male saint whose white, lace-trimmed drawers hang limply around his ankles below the hieratic dignity of his velvet robe. She has encased herself in a set of principles derived from her early training, leaving no detail of gesture or of personal taste untouched, and for this reason she will not wear lace made on machines. This is her private heresy, for in her special group the machine is sacred, and will be the salvation of the workers. She loves fine lace, and there is a tiny edge of fluted

[2] Spanish: "foreign woman. Foreign girl!"
(Contemptuous nicknames generally reserved for Americans.)

cobweb on this collar, which is one of twenty precisely alike, folded in blue tissue paper in the upper drawer of her clothes chest.

Braggioni catches her glance solidly as if he had been waiting for it, leans forward, balancing his paunch between his spread knees, and sings with tremendous emphasis, weighing his words. He has, the song relates, no father and no mother, nor even a friend to console him; lonely as a wave of the sea he comes and goes, lonely as a wave. His mouth opens round and yearns sideways, his balloon cheeks grow oily with the labor of song. He bulges marvelously in his expensive garments. Over his lavender collar, crushed upon a purple necktie, held by a diamond hoop: over his ammunition belt of tooled leather worked in silver, buckled cruelly around his gasping middle: over the tops of his glossy yellow shoes Braggioni swells with ominous ripeness, his mauve silk hose stretched taut, his ankles bound with the stout leather thongs of his shoes.

When he stretches his eyelids at Laura she notes again that his eyes are the true tawny yellow cat's eyes. He is rich, not in money, he tells her, but in power, and this power brings with it the blameless ownership of things, and the right to indulge his love of small luxuries. "I have a taste for the elegant refinements," he said once, flourishing a yellow silk handkerchief before her nose. "Smell that? It is Jockey Club, imported from New York." Nonetheless he is wounded by life. He will say so presently. "It is true everything turns to dust in the hand, to gall on the tongue." He sighs and his leather belt creaks like a saddle girth. "I am disappointed in everything as it comes. Everything." He shakes his head. "You, poor thing, you will be disappointed too. You are born for it. We are more alike than you realize in some things. Wait and see. Some day you will remember what I have told you, you will know that Braggioni was your friend."

Laura feels a slow chill, a purely physical sense of danger, a warning in her blood that violence, mutilation, a shocking death, wait for her with lessening patience. She has translated this fear into something homely, immediate, and sometimes hesitates before crossing the street. "My personal fate is nothing, except as the testimony of a mental attitude," she reminds herself, quoting from some forgotten philosophic primer, and is sensible enough to add, "Anyhow, I shall not be killed by an automobile if I can help it."

"It may be true I am as corrupt, in another way, as Braggioni," she thinks in spite of herself, "as callous, as incomplete," and if this is so, any kind of death seems preferable. Still she sits quietly, she does not run. Where could she go? Uninvited she has promised herself to this place; she can no longer imagine herself as living in another country, and there is no pleasure in remembering her life before she came here.

Precisely what is the nature of this devotion, its true motives, and what are its obligations? Laura cannot say. She spends part of her days in Xochimilco, near by, teaching Indian children to say in English, "The cat is on the mat." When she appears in the classroom they crowd about her with smiles on their wise, innocent, clay-colored faces, crying, "Good morning, my titcher!" in immaculate voices, and they make of her desk a fresh garden of flowers every day.

During her leisure she goes to union meetings and listens to busy important voices quarreling over tactics, methods, internal politics. She visits the prisoners of her own political faith in their cells, where they entertain themselves with counting cockroaches, repenting of their indiscretions, composing their memoirs, writing out manifestoes and plans for their comrades who are still walking about free, hands in pockets, sniffing fresh air. Laura brings them food and cigarettes and a little money, and she brings messages disguised in equivocal phrases from the men outside who dare not set foot in the prison for fear of disappearing into the cells kept empty for them. If the prisoners confuse night and day, and complain, "Dear little Laura, time doesn't pass in this infernal hole, and I won't know when it is time to sleep unless I have a reminder," she brings them their favorite narcotics, and says in a tone that does not wound them with pity, "Tonight will really be night for you," and though her Spanish amuses them, they find her comforting, useful. If they lose patience and all faith, and curse the slowness of their friends in coming to their rescue with money and influence, they trust her not to repeat everything, and if she inquires, "Where do you think we can find money, or influence?" they are certain to answer, "Well, there is Braggioni, why doesn't he do something?"

She smuggles letters from headquarters to men hiding from firing squads in back streets in mildewed houses, where they sit in tumbled beds and talk bitterly as if all Mexico were at their heels, when Laura knows positively they might appear at the band concert in the Alameda[3] on Sunday morning, and no one would notice them. But Braggioni says, "Let them sweat a little. The next time they may be careful. It is very restful to have them out of the way for a while." She is not afraid to knock on any door in any street after midnight, and enter in the darkness, and say to one of these men who is really in danger: "They will be looking for you—seriously—tomorrow morning after six. Here is some money from Vicente. Go to Vera Cruz and wait."

She borrows money from the Roumanian agitator to give to his bitter enemy the Polish agitator. The favor of Braggioni is their disputed territory, and Braggioni holds the balance nicely, for he can use them both. The Polish agitator talks love to her over café tables, hoping to exploit what he believes is her secret sentimental preference for him, and he gives her misinformation which he begs her to repeat as the solemn truth to certain persons. The Roumanian is more adroit. He is generous with his money in all good causes, and lies to her with an air of ingenuous candor, as if he were her good friend and confidant. She never repeats anything they may say. Braggioni never asks questions. He has other ways to discover all that he wishes to know about them.

Nobody touches her, but all praise her gray eyes, and the soft, round under lip which promises gayety, yet is always grave, nearly always firmly closed: and they cannot understand why she is in Mexico. She walks back and forth on her errands, with puzzled eyebrows, carrying her little folder of drawings and music and school papers. No dancer dances more beautifully than Laura walks, and she inspires some amusing, unexpected ardors, which cause little gossip, because nothing comes of them. A young captain who had been a soldier in Zapata's[4] army attempted, during a horseback ride near Cuernavaca, to express his desire for her with the noble simplicity befitting a rude folk-hero: but gently, because he was gentle. This gentleness was his defeat, for when he alighted, and removed her foot from the stirrup, and essayed to

---

[3] Park in Mexico City.
[4] Zapata: Emiliano Zapata (1877?–1919), Mexican revolutionary.

draw her down into his arms, her horse, ordinarily a tame one, shied fiercely, reared and plunged away. The young hero's horse careered blindly after his stable-mate, and the hero did not return to the hotel until rather late that evening. At breakfast he came to her table in full charro[5] dress, gray buckskin jacket and trousers with strings of silver buttons down the leg, and he was in a humorous, careless mood. "May I sit with you?" and "You are a wonderful rider. I was terrified that you might be thrown and dragged. I should never have forgiven myself. But I cannot admire you enough for your riding!"

"I learned to ride in Arizona," said Laura.

"If you will ride with me again this morning, I promise you a horse that will not shy with you," he said. But Laura remembered that she must return to Mexico City at noon.

Next morning the children made a celebration and spent their playtime writing on the blackboard, "We lov ar ticher," and with tinted chalks they drew wreaths of flowers around the words. The young hero wrote her a letter: "I am a very foolish, wasteful, impulsive man. I should have first said I love you, and then you would not have run away. But you shall see me again." Laura thought, "I must send him a box of colored crayons," but she was trying to forgive herself for having spurred her horse at the wrong moment.

A brown, shock-haired youth came and stood in her patio one night and sang like a lost soul for two hours, but Laura could think of nothing to do about it. The moonlight spread a wash of gauzy silver over the clear spaces of the garden, and the shadows were cobalt blue. The scarlet blossoms of the Judas tree were dull purple, and the names of the colors repeated themselves automatically in her mind, while she watched not the boy, but his shadow, fallen like a dark garment across the fountain rim, trailing in the water. Lupe came silently and whispered expert counsel in her ear: "If you will throw him one little flower, he will sing another song or two and go away." Laura threw the flower, and he sang a last song and went away with the flower tucked in the band of his hat. Lupe said, "He is one of the organizers of the Typographers Union, and before that he sold corridos[6] in the Merced market, and before that, he came from Guanajuato, where I was born. I would not trust any man, but I trust least those from Guanajuato."

She did not tell Laura that he would be back again the next night, and the next, nor that he would follow her at a certain fixed distance around the Merced market, through the Zócolo, up Francisco I. Madero Avenue, and so along the Paseo de la Reforma to Chapultepec Park, and into the Philosopher's Footpath, still with that flower withering in his hat, and an indivisible attention in his eyes.

Now Laura is accustomed to him, it means nothing except that he is nineteen years old and is observing a convention with all propriety, as though it were founded on a law of nature, which in the end it might well prove to be. He is beginning to write poems which he prints on a wooden press, and he leaves them stuck like handbills in her door. She is pleasantly disturbed by the abstract, unhurried watchfulness of his black eyes which will in time turn easily towards another object. She tells herself that throwing the flower was a mistake, for she is twenty-two years old and knows better; but she refuses to regret it, and persuades herself that her negation of all external events

[5] Elaborately dressed Mexican horseman.   [6] Ballads.

as they occur is a sign that she is gradually perfecting herself in the stoicism she strives to cultivate against that disaster she fears, though she cannot name it.

She is not at home in the world. Every day she teaches children who remain strangers to her, though she loves their tender round hands and their charming opportunist savagery. She knocks at unfamiliar doors not knowing whether a friend or a stranger shall answer, and even if a known face emerges from the sour gloom of that unknown interior, still it is the face of a stranger. No matter what this stranger says to her, nor what her message to him, the very cells of her flesh reject knowledge and kinship in one monotonous word. No. No. No. She draws her strength from this one holy talismanic word which does not suffer her to be led into evil. Denying everything, she may walk anywhere in safety, she looks at everything without amazement.

No, repeats this firm unchanging voice of her blood; and she looks at Braggioni without amazement. He is a great man, he wishes to impress this simple girl who covers her great round breasts with thick dark cloth, and who hides long, invaluably beautiful legs under a heavy skirt. She is almost thin except for the incomprehensible fullness of her breasts, like a nursing mother's, and Braggioni, who considers himself a judge of women, speculates again on the puzzle of her notorious virginity, and takes the liberty of speech which she permits without a sign of modesty, indeed, without any sort of sign, which is disconcerting.

"You think you are so cold, *gringita!* Wait and see. You will surprise yourself some day! May I be there to advise you!" He stretches his eyelids at her, and his ill-humored cat's eyes waver in a separate glance for the two points of light marking the opposite ends of a smoothly drawn path between the swollen curve of her breasts. He is not put off by that blue serge, nor by her resolutely fixed gaze. There is all the time in the world. His cheeks are bellying with the wind of song. "O girl with the dark eyes," he sings, and reconsiders. "But yours are not dark. I can change all that. O girl with the green eyes, you have stolen my heart away!" then his mind wanders to the song, and Laura feels the weight of his attention being shifted elsewhere. Singing thus, he seems harmless, he is quite harmless, there is nothing to do but sit patiently and say "No," when the moment comes. She draws a full breath, and her mind wanders also, but not far. She dares not wander too far.

Not for nothing has Braggioni taken pains to be a good revolutionist and a professional lover of humanity. He will never die of it. He has the malice, the cleverness, the wickedness, the sharpness of wit, the hardness of heart, stipulated for loving the world profitably. *He will never die of it.* He will live to see himself kicked out from his feeding trough by other hungry world-saviors. Traditionally he must sing in spite of his life which drives him to bloodshed, he tells Laura, for his father was a Tuscany peasant who drifted to Yucatan and married a Maya woman: a woman of race, an aristocrat. They gave him the love and knowledge of music, thus: and under the rip of his thumbnail, the strings of the instrument complain like exposed nerves.

Once he was called Delgadito[7] by all the girls and married women who ran after him; he was so scrawny all his bones showed under his thin cotton clothing, and he could squeeze his emptiness to the very backbone with his two hands. He was a poet and the revolution was only a dream then; too many women loved him and sapped

[7] Spanish: "thin."

away his youth, and he could never find enough to eat anywhere, anywhere! Now he is a leader of men, crafty men who whisper in his ear, hungry men who wait for hours outside his office for a word with him, emaciated men with wild faces who waylay him at the street gate with a timid, "Comrade, let me tell you . . ." and they blow the foul breath from their empty stomachs in his face.

He is always sympathetic. He gives them handfuls of small coins from his own pocket, he promises them work, there will be demonstrations, they must join the unions and attend the meetings, above all they must be on the watch for spies. They are closer to him than his own brothers, without them he can do nothing—until tomorrow, comrade!

Until tomorrow. "They are stupid, they are lazy, they are treacherous, they would cut my throat for nothing," he says to Laura. He has good food and abundant drink, he hires an automobile and drives in the Paseo on Sunday morning, and enjoys plenty of sleep in a soft bed beside a wife who dares not disturb him; and he sits pampering his bones in easy billows of fat, singing to Laura, who knows and thinks these things about him. When he was fifteen, he tried to drown himself because he loved a girl, his first love, and she laughed at him. "A thousand women have paid for that," and his tight little mouth turns down at the corners. Now he perfumes his hair with Jockey Club, and confides to Laura: "One woman is really as good as another for me, in the dark. I prefer them all."

His wife organizes unions among the girls in the cigarette factories, and walks in picket lines, and even speaks at meetings in the evening. But she cannot be brought to acknowledge the benefits of true liberty. "I tell her I must have my freedom, net. She does not understand my point of view." Laura has heard this many times. Braggioni scratches the guitar and meditates. "She is an instinctively virtuous woman, pure gold, no doubt of that. If she were not, I should lock her up, and she knows it."

His wife, who works so hard for the good of the factory girls, employs part of her leisure lying on the floor weeping because there are so many women in the world, and only one husband for her, and she never knows where nor when to look for him. He told her: "Unless you can learn to cry when I am not here, I must go away for good." That day he went away and took a room at the Hotel Madrid.

It is this month of separation for the sake of higher principles that has been spoiled not only for Mrs. Braggioni, whose sense of reality is beyond criticism, but for Laura, who feels herself bogged in a nightmare. Tonight Laura envies Mrs. Braggioni, who is alone, and free to weep as much as she pleases about a concrete wrong. Laura has just come from a visit to the prison, and she is waiting for tomorrow with a bitter anxiety as if tomorrow may not come, but time may be caught immovably in this hour, with herself transfixed, Braggioni singing on forever, and Eugenio's body not yet discovered by the guard.

Braggioni says: "Are you going to sleep?" Almost before she can shake her head, he begins telling her about the May-day disturbances coming on in Morelia, for the Catholics hold a festival in honor of the Blessed Virgin, and the Socialists celebrate their martyrs on that day. "There will be two independent processions, starting from either end of town, and they will march until they meet, and the rest depends . . ." He asks her to oil and load his pistols. Standing up, he unbuckles his ammunition belt, and spreads it laden across her knees. Laura sits with the shells slipping through the cleaning cloth dipped in oil, and he says again he cannot understand why she works so hard for the revolutionary idea unless she loves some man who is in it. "Are you not in love with someone?" "No," says Laura. "And no one is in love with you?" "No." "Then it is your own fault. No woman need go begging. Why, what is the matter with you? The legless beggar woman in the Alameda has a perfectly faithful lover. Did you know that?"

Laura peers down the pistol barrel and says nothing, but a long, slow faintness rises and subsides in her; Braggioni curves his swollen fingers around the throat of the guitar and softly smothers the music out of it, and when she hears him again he seems to have forgotten her, and is speaking in the hypnotic voice he uses when talking in small rooms to a listening, close-gathered crowd. Some day this world, now seemingly so composed and eternal, to the edges of every sea shall be merely a tangle of gaping trenches, of crashing walls and broken bodies. Everything must be torn from its accustomed place where it has rotted for centuries, hurled skyward and distributed, cast down again clean as rain, without separate identity. Nothing shall survive that the stiffened hands of poverty have created for the rich and no one shall be left alive except the elect spirits destined to procreate a new world cleansed of cruelty and injustice, ruled by benevolent anarchy: "Pistols are good, I love them, cannon are even better, but in the end I pin my faith to good dynamite," he concludes, and strokes the pistol lying in her hands. "Once I dreamed of destroying this city, in case it offered resistance to General Ortíz,[8] but it fell into his hands like an overripe pear."

He is made restless by his own words, rises and stands waiting. Laura holds up the belt to him: "Put that on, and go kill somebody in Morelia, and you will be happier," she says softly. The presence of death in the room makes her bold. "Today, I found Eugenio going into a stupor. He refused to allow me to call the prison doctor. He had taken all the tablets I brought him yesterday. He said he took them because he was bored."

"He is a fool, and his death is his own business," says Braggioni, fastening his belt carefully.

"I told him if he had waited only a little while longer, you would have got him set free," says Laura. "He said he did not want to wait."

"He is a fool and we are well rid of him," says Braggioni, reaching for his hat.

He goes away. Laura knows his mood has changed, she will not see him any more for a while. He will send word when he needs her to go on errands into strange streets, to speak to the strange faces that will appear, like clay masks with the power of human speech, to mutter their thanks to Braggioni for his help. Now she is free, and she thinks, I must run while there is time. But she does not go.

Braggioni enters his own house where for a month his wife has spent many hours every night weeping and tangling her hair upon her pillow. She is weeping now, and she weeps more at the sight of him, the cause of all her sorrows. He looks about the room. Nothing is changed, the smells are good and familiar, he is well acquainted with the woman who comes toward him with no reproach except grief on her face. He says to her tenderly: "You are so good, please don't cry any more, you dear good creature." She says, "Are you tired, my angel? Sit here and I will wash your feet."

[8] Pascual Ortíz Rubio (1877–1963), Mexican political leader and president (1930–1932).

She brings a bowl of water, and kneeling, unlaces his shoes, and when from her knees she raises her sad eyes under her blackened lids, he is sorry for everything, and bursts into tears. "Ah, yes, I am hungry, I am tired, let us eat something together," he says, between sobs. His wife leans her head on his arm and says, "Forgive me!" and this time he is refreshed by the solemn, endless rain of her tears.

Laura takes off her serge dress and puts on a white linen nightgown and goes to bed. She turns her head a little to one side, and lying still, reminds herself that it is time to sleep. Numbers tick in her brain like little clocks, soundless doors close of themselves around her. If you would sleep, you must not remember anything, the children will say tomorrow, good morning, my teacher, the poor prisoners who come every day bringing flowers to their jailor. 1-2-3-4-5—it is monstrous to confuse love with revolution, night with day, life with death—ah, Eugenio!

The tolling of the midnight bell is a signal, but what does it mean? Get up, Laura, and follow me: come out of your sleep, out of your bed, out of this strange house. What are you doing in this house? Without a word, without fear she rose and reached for Eugenio's hand, but he eluded her with a sharp, sly smile and drifted away. This is not all, you shall see—Murderer, he said, follow me, I will show you a new country, but it is far away and we must hurry. No, said Laura, not unless you take my hand, no; and she clung first to the stair rail, and then to the topmost branch of the Judas tree that bent down slowly and set her upon the earth, and then to the rocky ledge of a cliff, and then to the jagged wave of a sea that was not water but a desert of crumbling stone. Where are you taking me, she asked in wonder but without fear. To death, and it is a long way off, and we must hurry, said Eugenio. No, said Laura, not unless you take my hand. Then eat these flowers, poor prisoner, said Eugenio in a voice of pity, take and eat: and from the Judas tree he stripped the warm bleeding flowers, and held them to her lips. She saw that his hand was fleshless, a cluster of small white petrified branches, and his eye sockets were without light, but she ate the flowers greedily for they satisfied both hunger and thirst. Murderer! said Eugenio, and Cannibal! This is my body and my blood. Laura cried No! and at the sound of her own voice, she awoke trembling, and was afraid to sleep again.

1929

Jean Toomer
1894–1967

For a time, the poet and novelist Jean Toomer was regarded as the most talented writer of the "Harlem Renaissance," a literary movement of black writers who had congregated in New York City in the early 1920s and had transformed Harlem into the intellectual and cultural center of black America. The group included an impressive number of painters, photographers, and musicians, as well as such writers as Langston Hughes, Countee Cullen, Zora Neale Hurston, and Claude McKay. In its magazines and anthologies, the movement promoted the creative work of the "New Negro," of whom Jean Toomer was thought to be one of the outstanding examples in literature. He was so highly regarded not only because he wrote truthfully and sensitively about black life but because he did so, as one member of the movement put it, "without the surrender or compromise of the artist's vision."

Jean Toomer was born in Washington, D.C., in 1894. His father was Nathan Toomer, a black planter, and his mother was the daughter of P. B. S. Pinchback, a Reconstruction governor of Louisiana whose own racial background was apparently mixed. Toomer's early years were severely complicated by his father's desertion in 1895, when Toomer was only one year old; they were perhaps even more severely complicated by what Toomer later termed his "racial composition and position." From early on, his life took him back and forth between what he later described as the "white" world and the "black" in a land where life itself was viewed "as if it were divided into white and black." "In my body were many bloods, some dark blood, all blended . . . ," he wrote. "I was . . . either a new type of man or the very oldest." He once claimed seven blood strains ("French, Dutch, Welsh, Negro, German, Jewish, and Indian"). Yet at other times Toomer doubted "whether there is any colored blood in me or not." Both of his marriages were to white women—the first to a promising writer who was a descendant of the Puritan poet Anne Bradstreet.

Toomer lived for several years in New Rochelle, New York, then moved back to Washington, where he finished high school. He then enrolled at the University of Wisconsin but abandoned his studies there after a year and wandered about—all the while working at odd jobs, studying, and writing—to Chicago, New York, Massachusetts, Wisconsin again, and New Jersey. Returning to Washington, he began to write more concertedly. In 1921 he moved to Sparta, Georgia, near his father's original home, and took a job briefly as a teacher at the Georgia Normal and Industrial Institute. It was there that he conceived and began *Cane* (1923), the book that established him as an important literary figure.

During the early 1920s Toomer contributed regularly to such leading black journals as *The Crisis* and *Opportunity* and to such experimental magazines as *Broom, The Little Review,* and *The Double Dealer.* The experimental nature of his work, and particularly his interest in combining dramatic and narrative sketches, drew praise from a wide range of writers, including Sherwood Anderson, Allen Tate, and Hart Crane. Shortly after publishing *Cane,* Toomer became intrigued by the Russian spiritual teacher George Gurdjieff, who believed that through proper discipline and meditation an individual could achieve cosmic consciousness. Toomer traveled to France in the summer of 1926 to study at the Gurdjieff Institute and returned to Harlem prepared to set up classes in the philosophy of "Unitism." Looking back, Langston Hughes described this period in Toomer's life with a blend of humor and sorrow. People in Harlem, Hughes wrote in *The Big Sea* (1940), "had to work all day to make a living" and so turned out to be *reluctant converts:*

> Their advance toward cosmic consciousness was slow and their hope of achiev-
> ing awareness distant indeed. . . . So Jean Toomer shortly left his Harlem group
> and went downtown to drop the seeds of Gurdjieff in less dark and poverty-
> stricken fields. . . . From downtown New York, Toomer carried Gurdjieff to

Chicago's Gold Coast—and the Negroes lost one of the most talented of all their writers—the author of the beautiful book of prose and verse, *Cane.*

Though Toomer disappeared from the literary scene, he continued to write poetry, plays, essays, and fiction, much of it going unpublished. Works such as *Essentials* (1931) and *Portage Potential* (1932) reflect his mounting interests in different forms of mystical philosophy (he became deeply involved in Quaker pietism) and poetry, while the long poem *Blue Meridian* (1936) reflects his continuing effort artistically to resolve the problems generated by racial tensions in America. But Toomer's literary reputation still rests primarily on the book conceived during the four months he lived near his father's home in Georgia.

In *Cane,* Toomer draws heavily on the folk songs, the folktales, and the syncopated rhythms of the language of the black people he encountered in Georgia. By mixing poems with both dramatic and prose sketches, he not only created one of the distinctive literary experiments of the 1920s but also fashioned a work of lasting historical and artistic significance. Historically, *Cane* played a major role in the efforts of black writers to enlarge the cultural life of black people in America. Artistically, it celebrates the power of exotic and primitive impulses to triumph over the tyranny of culture. What holds these two different aspects of Toomer's achievement together is his celebration of a freedom that is physical and psychic as well as aesthetic.

Further Reading:
H. M. Gloster, *Negro Voices in American Fiction,* 1948.
A. Bontemps, "The Negro Renaissance: Jean Toomer and the Harlem Writers of the 1920's" in *Anger and Beyond: The Negro Writer in the*

United States, ed. H. Hill, 1966.
D. T. Turner, *In a Minor Chord: Three Afro-American Writers and Their Search for Identity,* 1971.
N. Y. McKay, *Jean Toomer, Artist,* 1984.

Text:
Cane, 1923.

---

from Cane

Blood-Burning Moon

1

Up from the skeleton stone walls, up from the rotting floor boards and the solid hand-hewn beams of oak of the pre-war cotton factory, dusk came. Up from the dusk the full moon came. Glowing like a fired pine-knot, it illumined the great door and soft showered the Negro shanties aligned along the single street of factory town. The full moon in the great door was an omen. Negro women improvised songs against its spell.

Louisa sang as she came over the crest of the hill from the white folks' kitchen.

Her skin was the color of oak leaves on young trees in fall. Her breasts, firm and up-pointed like ripe acorns. And her singing had the low murmur of winds in fig trees. Bob Stone, younger son of the people she worked for, loved her. By the way the world reckons things, he had won her. By measure of that warm glow which came into her mind at thought of him, he had won her. Tom Burwell, whom the whole town called Big Boy, also loved her. But working in the fields all day, and far away from her, gave him no chance to show it. Though often enough of evenings he had tried to. Somehow, he never got along. Strong as he was with hands upon the ax or plow, he found it difficult to hold her. Or so he thought. But the fact was that he held her to factory town more firmly than he thought for. His black balanced, and pulled against, the white of Stone, when she thought of them. And her mind was vaguely upon them as she came over the crest of the hill, coming from the white folks' kitchen. As she sang softly at the evil face of the full moon.

A strange stir was in her. Indolently, she tried to fix upon Bob or Tom as the cause of it. To meet Bob in the canebrake, as she was going to do an hour or so later, was nothing new. And Tom's proposal which she felt on its way to her could be indefinitely put off. Separately, there was no unusual significance to either one. But for some reason, they jumbled when her eyes gazed vacantly at the rising moon. And from the jumble came the stir that was strangely within her. Her lips trembled. The slow rhythm of her song grew agitant and restless. Rusty black and tan spotted hounds, lying in the dark corners of porches or prowling around back yards, put their noses in the air and caught its tremor. They began plaintively to yelp and howl. Chickens woke up and cackled. Intermittently, all over the countryside dogs barked and roosters crowed as if heralding a weird dawn or some ungodly awakening. The women sang lustily. Their songs were cotton-wads to stop their ears. Louisa came down into factory town and sank wearily upon the step before her home. The moon was rising towards a thick cloud-bank which soon would hide it.

> Red nigger moon. Sinner!
> Blood-burning moon. Sinner!
> Come out that fact'ry door.

2

Up from the deep dusk of a cleared spot on the edge of the forest a mellow glow arose and spread fan-wise into the low-hanging heavens. And all around the air was heavy with the scent of boiling cane. A large pile of cane-stalks lay like ribboned shadows upon the ground. A mule, harnessed to a pole, trudged lazily round and round the pivot of the grinder. Beneath a swaying oil lamp, a Negro alternately whipped out at the mule, and fed cane-stalks to the grinder. A fat boy waddled pails of fresh ground juice between the grinder and the boiling stove. Steam came from the copper boiling pan. The scent of cane came from the copper pan and drenched the forest and the hill that sloped to factory town, beneath its fragrance. It drenched the men in circle seated around the stove. Some of them chewed at the white pulp of stalks, but there was no need for them to, if all they wanted was to taste the cane. One tasted it in factory town. And from factory town one could see the soft haze thrown by the glowing stove upon the low-hanging heavens.

Old David Georgia stirred the thickening syrup with a long ladle, and ever so often drew it off. Old David Georgia tended his stove and told tales about the white folks, about moonshining and cotton picking, and about sweet nigger gals, to the men who sat there about his stove to listen to him. Tom Burwell chewed cane-stalk and laughed with the others till someone mentioned Louisa. Till some one said something about Louisa and Bob Stone, about the silk stockings she must have gotten from him. Blood ran up Tom's neck hotter than the glow that flooded from the stove. He sprang up. Glared at the men and said, "She's my gal." Will Manning laughed. Tom strode over to him. Yanked him up and knocked him to the ground. Several of Manning's friends got up to fight for him. Tom whipped out a long knife and would have cut them to shreds if they hadnt ducked into the woods. Tom had had enough. He nodded to Old David Georgia and swung down the path to factory town. Just then, the dogs started barking and the roosters began to crow. Tom felt funny. Away from the fight, away from the stove, chill got to him. He shivered. He shuddered when he saw the full moon rising towards the cloud-bank. He who didnt give a godam for the fears of old women. He forced his mind to fasten on Louisa. Bob Stone. Better not be. He turned into the street and saw Louisa sitting before her home. He went towards her, ambling, touched the brim of a marvelously shaped, spotted, felt hat, said he wanted to say something to her, and then found that he didnt know what he had to say, or if he did, that he couldnt say it. He shoved his big fists in his overalls, grinned, and started to move off.

"Youall want me, Tom?"

"Thats what us wants, sho, Louisa."

"Well, here I am——"

"An here I is, but that aint ahelpin none, all th same."

"You wanted to say something? . . ."

"I did that, sho. But words is like th spots on dice: no matter how y fumbles em, there's times when they jes wont come. I dunno why. Seems like th love I feels fo yo done stole m tongue. I got it now. Whee! Louisa, honey, I oughtnt tell y, I feel I oughtnt cause yo is young an goes t church an I has had other gals, but Louisa I sho do love y. Lil gal, Ise watched y from them first days when youall sat right here befo yo door befo th well an sang sometimes in a way that like t broke m heart. Ise carried y with me into th fields, day after day, an after that, an I sho can plow when yo is there, an I can pick cotton. Yassur! Come near beatin Barlo yesterday. I sho did. Yassur! An next year if ole Stone'll trust me, I'll have a farm. My own. My bales will buy yo what y gets from white folks now. Silk stockings an purple dresses— course I dont believe what some folks been whisperin as t how y gets them things now. White folks always did do for niggers what they likes. An they jes cant help alikin yo, Louisa. Bob Stone likes y. Course he does. But not th way folks is awhisperin. Does he, hon?"

"I dont know what you mean, Tom."

"Course y dont. Ise already cut two niggers. Had t hon, t tell em so. Niggers always tryin t make somethin out a nothin. An then besides, white folks aint up t them tricks so much nowadays. Godam better not be. Leastawise not with yo. Cause I wouldnt stand f it. Nassur."

"What would you do, Tom?"

"Cut him jes like I cut a nigger."

"No, Tom—"

"I said I would an there aint no mo to it. But that aint th talk f now. Sing, honey Louisa, an while I'm listenin t y I'll be makin love."

Tom took her hand in his. Against the tough thickness of his own, hers felt soft and small. His huge body slipped down to the step beside her. The full moon sank upward into the deep purple of the cloud-bank. An old woman brought a lighted lamp and hung it on the common well whose bulky shadow squatted in the middle of the road, opposite Tom and Louisa. The old woman lifted the well-lid, took hold the chain, and began drawing up the heavy bucket. As she did so, she sang. Figures shifted, restlesslike, between lamp and window in the front rooms of the shanties. Shadows of the figures fought each other on the gray dust of the road. Figures raised the windows and joined the old woman in song. Louisa and Tom, the whole street, singing:

> Red nigger moon. Sinner!
> Blood-burning moon. Sinner!
> Come out that fact'ry door.

3

Bob Stone sauntered from his veranda out into the gloom of fir trees and magnolias. The clear white of his skin paled, and the flush of his cheeks turned purple. As if to balance this outer change, his mind became consciously a white man's. He passed the house with its huge open hearth which, in the days of slavery, was the plantation cookery. He saw Louisa bent over that hearth. He went in as a master should and took her. Direct, honest, bold. None of this sneaking that he had to go through now. The contrast was repulsive to him. His family had lost ground. Hell no, his family still owned the niggers, practically. Damned if they did, or he wouldnt have to duck around so. What would they think if they knew? His mother? His sister? He shouldnt mention them, shouldnt think of them in this connection. There in the dusk he blushed at doing so. Fellows about town were all right, but how about his friends up North? He could see them incredible, repulsed. They didnt know. The thought first made him laugh. Then with their eyes still upon him, he began to feel embarrassed. He felt the need of explaining things to them. Explain hell. They wouldnt understand, and moreover, who ever heard of a Southerner getting on his knees to any Yankee, or anyone. No sir. He was going to see Louisa to-night, and love her. She was lovely —in her way. Nigger way. What way was that? Damned if he knew. Must know. He'd known her long enough to know. Was there something about niggers that you couldnt know? Listening to them at church didnt tell you anything. Looking at them didnt tell you anything. Talking to them didnt tell you anything—unless it was gossip, unless they wanted to talk. Of course, about farming, and licker, and craps —but those werent nigger. Nigger was something more. How much more? Something to be afraid of, more? Hell no. Who ever heard of being afraid of a nigger? Tom Burwell. Cartwell had told him that Tom went with Louisa after she reached home. No sir. No nigger had ever been with his girl. He'd like to see one try. Some position for him to be in. Him, Bob Stone, of the old Stone family, in a scrap with a nigger over a nigger girl. In the good old days . . . Ha! Those were the days. His family had lost ground. Not so much, though. Enough for him to have to cut through old Lemon's canefield by way of the woods, that he might meet her. She was worth it. Beautiful nigger gal. Why nigger? Why not, just gal? No, it was because she was nigger that he went to her. Sweet . . . The scent of boiling cane came to him. Then he saw the rich glow of the stove. He heard the voices of the men circled around it. He was about to skirt the clearing when he heard his own name mentioned. He stopped. Quivering. Leaning against a tree, he listened.

"Bad nigger. Yassur, he sho is one bad nigger when he gets started."

"Tom Burwell's been on th gang three times fo cuttin men."

"What y think he's agwine t do t Bob Stone?"

"Dunno yet. He aint found out. When he does—Baby!"

"Aint no tellin."

"Young Stone aint no quitter an I ken tell y that. Blood of th old uns in his veins."

"Thats right. He'll scrap, sho."

"Be gettin too hot f niggers round this away."

"Shut up, nigger. Y dont know what y talkin bout."

Bob Stone's ears burned as though he had been holding them over the stove. Sizzling heat welled up within him. His feet felt as if they rested on red-hot coals. They stung him to quick movement. He circled the fringe of the glowing. Not a twig cracked beneath his feet. He reached the path that led to factory town. Plunged furiously down it. Halfway along, a blindness within him veered him aside. He crashed into the bordering canebrake. Cane leaves cut his face and lips. He tasted blood. He threw himself down and dug his fingers in the ground. The earth was cool. Cane-roots took the fever from his hands. After a long while, or so it seemed to him, the thought came to him that it must be time to see Louisa. He got to his feet and walked calmly to their meeting place. No Louisa. Tom Burwell had her. Veins in his forehead bulged and distended. Saliva moistened the dried blood on his lips. He bit down on his lips. He tasted blood. Not his own blood; Tom Burwell's blood. Bob drove through the cane and out again upon the road. A hound swung down the path before him towards factory town. Bob couldnt see it. The dog loped aside to let him pass. Bob's blind rushing made him stumble over it. He fell with a thud that dazed him. The hound yelped. Answering yelps came from all over the countryside. Chickens cackled. Roosters crowed, heralding the bloodshot eyes of southern awakening. Singers in the town were silenced. They shut their windows down. Palpitant between the rooster crows, a chill hush settled upon the huddled forms of Tom and Louisa. A figure rushed from the shadow and stood before them. Tom popped to his feet.

"Whats y want?"

"I'm Bob Stone."

"Yassur—an I'm Tom Burwell. Whats y want?"

Bob lunged at him. Tom side-stepped, caught him by the shoulder, and flung him to the ground. Straddled him.

"Let me up."

"Yassur—but watch yo doins, Bob Stone."

A few dark figures, drawn by the sound of scuffle, stood about them. Bob sprang to his feet.

"Fight like a man, Tom Burwell, an I'll lick y."

Again he lunged. Tom side-stepped and flung him to the ground. Straddled him.

"Get off me, you godam nigger you."

"Yo sho has started somethin now. Get up."

Tom yanked him up and began hammering at him. Each blow sounded as if it smashed into a precious, irreplaceable soft something. Beneath them, Bob staggered back. He reached in his pocket and whipped out a knife.

"Thats my game, sho."

Blue flash, a steel blade slashed across Bob Stone's throat. He had a sweetish sick feeling. Blood began to flow. Then he felt a sharp twitch of pain. He let his knife drop. He slapped one hand against his neck. He pressed the other on top of his head as if to hold it down. He groaned. He turned, and staggered towards the crest of the hill in the direction of white town. Negroes who had seen the fight slunk into their homes and blew the lamps out. Louisa, dazed, hysterical, refused to go indoors. She slipped, crumbled, her body loosely propped against the woodwork of the well. Tom Burwell leaned against it. He seemed rooted there.

Bob reached Broad Street. White men rushed up to him. He collapsed in their arms.

"Tom Burwell. . . ."

White men like ants upon a forage rushed about. Except for the taut hum of their moving, all was silent. Shotguns, revolvers, rope, kerosene, torches. Two high-powered cars with glaring search-lights. They came together. The taut hum rose to a low roar. Then nothing could be heard but the flop of their feet in the thick dust of the road. The moving body of their silence preceded them over the crest of the hill into factory town. It flattened the Negroes beneath it. It rolled to the wall of the factory, where it stopped. Tom knew that they were coming. He couldnt move. And then he saw the search-lights of the two cars glaring down on him. A quick shock went through him. He stiffened. He started to run. A yell went up from the mob. Tom wheeled about and faced them. They poured down on him. They swarmed. A large man with dead-white face and flabby cheeks came to him and almost jabbed a gun-barrel through his guts.

"Hands behind y, nigger."

Tom's wrists were bound. The big man shoved him to the well. Burn him over it, and when the woodwork caved in, his body would drop to the bottom. Two deaths for a godam nigger. Louisa was driven back. The mob pushed in. Its pressure, its momentum was too great. Drag him to the factory. Wood and stakes already there. Tom moved in the direction indicated. But they had to drag him. They reached the great door. Too many to get in there. The mob divided and flowed around the walls to either side. The big man shoved him through the door. The mob pressed in from the sides. Taut humming. No words. A stake was sunk into the ground. Rotting floor boards piled around it. Kerosene poured on the rotting floor boards. Tom bound to the stake. His breast was bare. Nails scratches let little lines of blood trickle down and mat into the hair. His face, his eyes were set and stony. Except for irregular breathing, one would have thought him already dead. Torches were flung onto the pile. A great flare muffled in black smoke shot upward. The mob yelled. The mob was silent. Now Tom could be seen within the flames. Only his head, erect, lean, like a blackened stone. Stench of burning flesh soaked the air. Tom's eyes popped. His head settled downward. The mob yelled. Its yell echoed against the skeleton stone walls and sounded like a hundred yells. Like a hundred mobs yelling. Its yell thudded against the thick front wall and fell back. Ghost of a yell slipped through the flames and out the great door of the factory. It fluttered like a dying thing down the single street of factory town. Louisa, upon the step before her home, did not hear it, but her eyes opened slowly. They saw the full moon glowing in the great door. The full moon, an evil thing, an omen, soft showering the homes of folks she knew. Where were they, these people? She'd sing, and perhaps they'd come out and join her. Perhaps Tom Burwell would come. At any rate, the full moon in the great door was an omen which she must sing to:

Red nigger moon. Sinner!
Blood-burning moon. Sinner!
Come out that fact'ry door.

1923

John Dos Passos
1896–1970

John Roderigo Dos Passos was born on January 14, 1896, in a hotel in Chicago, Illinois, the illegitimate son of Lucy Addison Sprigg Madison, who was forty-eight when her son was born, and John Randolph Dos Passos, a wealthy attorney of Portuguese descent, who had written a book on the superiority of Anglo-Saxon political traditions. After years of living discreetly apart, Dos Passos's parents were finally married in 1910, though it was not until Dos Passos finished his college education that he was formally acknowledged by his father. Raised by his mother with his father's generous financial support, Dos Passos lived a comfortable early life. He later referred to these years as a "hotel childhood." He toured Europe extensively, and he experienced early, steady exposure to good music, art, and books as well as to fine clothes, fine food, and fine schools. Having first attended private schools in England and Connecticut, he went on to Harvard College, where he graduated with honors in 1916.

By the time he entered Harvard, Dos Passos had already substantially defined the two interests that would shape his life—literary aestheticism and reform politics. "It was characteristic of the Jazz Age," F. Scott Fitzgerald remarked, "that it had no interest in politics at all." In contrast to many of his contemporaries, however, Dos Passos was directly influenced by the leaders of the reform movements of the prewar years. At Harvard he studied Thorstein Veblen's penetrating analyses of capitalistic society as well as Walter Pater's aesthetic theories, and he read Theodore Dreiser as well as Gustave Flaubert. It was characteristic of him that his contributions to the *Harvard Advocate* included a review of the radical John Reed's *Insurgent Mexico* as well as reviews of the experimental poetry of Ezra Pound and T. S. Eliot.

After graduation, Dos Passos followed his father's advice and left for Spain to study architecture, but in 1917, upon his father's death and America's entry into the First World War, he followed his own inclinations and joined the

Norton-Harjes volunteer ambulance service in France. He later served with the
Red Cross ambulance service in Italy, then with the United States Army Medical
Corps. He also spent some time in Paris, where during one offensive he
volunteered to help with the wounded: "It was my job," he recalled, "to carry
off buckets full of amputated arms and hands and legs from an operating room."
These war experiences led to his first two novels, *One Man's Initiation, 1917*
(1920) and the critically well-received *Three Soldiers* (1921), both of which focus
on the disillusioning impact of the Great War on sensitive young American
soldiers.

With the war behind him, Dos Passos resumed the mixed career he had
envisaged earlier, as a free-lance journalist, an aspiring artist, and a political
activist. By 1920 he was publishing widely in *The Liberator, The Freeman, Dial,*
and *The Nation*. He also published a volume of poems, *A Pushcart at the Curb*
(1922), and two modernist plays, *The Garbage Man* (1926) and *Airways, Inc.*
(1928). In 1926 he joined the executive board of *New Masses,* an avowedly
Communist journal that he helped found. In 1927 he was jailed in Boston for
picketing the statehouse in support of Sacco and Vanzetti. And in 1928,
following a tour of the USSR, he agreed to serve as "contributing editor" to the
Daily Worker. Though he never joined the Communist party—in 1930 he called
himself only "a middle-class liberal"—he found himself, as the Great Depression
deepened, increasingly entangled in labor disputes and related controversies, yet
also more and more disenchanted by the strong-arm tactics of communism. In
1931 Dos Passos, along with Theodore Dreiser, was indicted for criminal
syndicalism for aiding the striking miners in Harlan County, Kentucky. He
served as treasurer of the National Committee for Defense of Political Prisoners
in 1932, and in 1940 as treasurer of the Joint Campaign for Political Refugees.

Throughout this period—in fact, throughout his life—Dos Passos traveled
extensively. Travel played a large part in his creative imagination, both as a
direct stimulus for several travel books and as a metaphor for the rootlessness of
modern technological society. Like his friend Ernest Hemingway, Dos Passos was
for a time enamored of Spain, and he immersed himself in Spanish culture and
politics. In 1922 he published a collection of essays on Spain, *Rosinante to the
Road Again*, in which he examined Spanish civilization and at the same time
explored his own Iberian background. Later his passionate disagreement with
Hemingway over the Spanish civil war—Dos Passos was disgusted by the way
the Communists used the war to their own advantage—led to an irreparable
breach in what had been a close, mutually supportive friendship. Toward the end
of his life, Dos Passos continued to use his ethnic roots as a motive for travel and
writing: He published *Brazil on the Move* in 1963 and *The Portugal Story* in 1969.

Dos Passos's fiction, like his politics, reflects his desire to confront
imaginatively the large-scale transformation of American society from a
predominantly rural, agricultural, traditional society into an increasingly urban,
industrial, commercial, secular, and disoriented one. In *Manhattan Transfer* (1925),
the impact of the First World War is placed against the larger backdrop of an
emerging urban, technological civilization. In this, his first major novel, Dos
Passos began to develop the tone that became characteristic of his work, a tone in
which protest and despair mingle with some residual, irrepressible hope. But he

also began experimenting with style and structure in ways that continued to mark his art. Sinclair Lewis said of *Manhattan Transfer* that its composition was based on the "technique of the movie, in its flashes, its cut-backs, its speed." In narrative shifts and jumps (with an absence of transitions reminiscent of Ezra Pound's *Cantos,* T. S. Eliot's *The Waste Land,* and Hart Crane's *The Bridge*), Dos Passos also began finding techniques that would convey the stark contrasts and abrupt changes of urban life. In subways and skyscrapers he began finding images of a society whose great energies and skills, lacking purpose, are surrendered to mere motion and empty innovation.

In his masterpiece, *U.S.A.* (1937), a trilogy comprising three separately published novels—*The 42nd Parallel* (1930), *1919* (1932), and *The Big Money* (1936)—Dos Passos created a story that extends chronologically from the prewar years to 1936 and reaches geographically from New York to California, from Chicago to Mexico, and beyond America to Europe. His panoramic canvas includes isolated farms and airplane factories, picket lines and ghetto streets, union offices and corporate headquarters. Matching his canvas, his cast of characters includes farmhands and factory laborers, hoboes and vagabonds, advertising executives and Hollywood actresses, entrepreneurs and financiers. Yet despite the vast sweep of his story and the shifts that characterize it, Dos Passos establishes the central conflict of his story as a conflict between "two nations"—a small group of rich and powerful people who successfully manipulate the social and economic forces that shape history and a large group of poor and sometimes hopeless people who are used by those forces only to be abandoned or destroyed.

In addition to telling the individual stories of eleven major characters in *U.S.A.,* Dos Passos employs three supplemental devices that broaden the scope of his work. In the first of these, called "Newsreel," he presents materials that create a public framework for the incidents and themes of his narrative. "Newsreel" includes headlines and snippets of articles from newspapers ("Wall Street Stunned"); lines from slogans, mottoes, and popular songs (from a ballad about Casey Jones or a union protest song); and bits and pieces from public reports and political oratory. In the second supplemental device, called "Camera Eye," he presents bits and pieces expressive of private and subjective feelings that are sometimes lyrical, sometimes elegiac, sometimes satiric, sometimes angry, and sometimes threatening (" 'all right we are two nations' "). In the third supplemental device, Dos Passos brings twenty-seven carefully crafted biographical sketches of prominent public figures (movie stars like Rudolph Valentino, politicians like Woodrow Wilson, inventors like Thomas Edison, financiers like J. P. Morgan, social critics like Thorstein Veblen, labor leaders like Eugene Debs) into his narrative. Like the stories of his own fictional characters, the stories of these actual personages focus on different modes of failure and success and on the social and economic forces that shape success and failure alike. They thus serve to extend Dos Passos's chronicle of the transformation of the United States in the first third of this century.

In *U.S.A.,* more than in any other of his novels, Dos Passos blends literary aestheticism and reformist politics by combining innovative language and technique with a detailed survey of contemporary history and politics. A less stylistically conscious reformer, Upton Sinclair, found the books deplorably difficult to read. A less politically conscious stylist, Ernest Hemingway, thought

Dos Passos might be sacrificing his fictional characters to propaganda: "Keep them people, people, people, and don't let them get to be symbols. Remember the race is older than the economic system." The French philosopher and writer Jean Paul Sartre, however, regarded *U.S.A.* as a supreme literary and political achievement and called Dos Passos the greatest novelist of the twentieth century.

The idea of calling his trilogy *U.S.A.* came to Dos Passos at about the same time that he broke with Hemingway and returned to the United States planning to write the "truth" about the Communist activities in Spain. In 1937 Dos Passos wrote an article, "Farewell to Europe," and began an intensive program of reading in American history that not only culminated in such books as *The Living Thoughts of Tom Paine* (1940), *The Ground We Stand On* (1941), *The Head and Heart of Thomas Jefferson* (1954), and a narrative history, *The Men Who Made the Nation* (1957), but also reinforced an increasingly patriotic and conservative stance. Although he remained aware of the many imperfections of the United States, Dos Passos also became convinced that in a corrupt world the United States remained the best hope for individual liberty and human progress. As early as 1937 he had described "the one hope for the future of the type of western civilization which furnishes the frame of our lives" as "the system of popular government based on individual liberty." In 1939 his disillusionment with the Spanish civil war found fictional form in *The Adventures of a Young Man,* which became the first volume in a second trilogy, *District of Columbia* (1952). The second volume of the trilogy, *Number One* (1943), is a novelistic exposé of political corruption loosely based on the career of Huey Long; the third, *The Grand Design* (1949), is a satire on New Deal bureaucracy. In *Mid-Century* (1961), Dos Passos attempted to revive the style and methods of *U.S.A.* in a fictional attack on the power of financiers and labor unions.

Largely because of the success of *U.S.A.,* Dos Passos tends to be identified as a writer of the 1930s. Yet he wrote passionately and productively from the 1920s through the Cold War era of the 1950s and the counterculture of the 1960s. In *Mid-Century* he laments what he considers the loss of heroic ideals among "kids who'd been soaked in wartime prosperity . . . raised on the gibblegabble of the radio between the family car and the corner drugstore and the Five and Ten." Staunchly anti-Communist, he supported President Nixon's 1970 invasion of Cambodia ("the first rational military step taken in the whole war"). In June 1970 he wrote his daughter cantankerously about the impact that the documentary movie *Woodstock* had on his conception of the young: "To me it was endlessly depressing. . . . If Nixon fails [in Cambodia] it is just this generation that is raising such cain that will have to bear the brunt of the results. I'll be in my grave re-entering the carbon cycle." Three months later, on September 27, 1970, he died of a heart attack in Baltimore, Maryland.

Further Reading:
J. H. Wrenn, *John Dos Passos,* 1961.
R. G. Davis, *John Dos Passos,* 1962.
Studies in U.S.A., ed. D. Sanders, 1972.
M. Landesberg, *Dos Passos' Path to U.S.A.: A Political Biography, 1912–1936,* 1972.
Ludington, T. *John Dos Passos: Twentieth Century Odyssey,* 1980.

Text:
U.S.A., 1974.
See also *The Fourteenth Chronicle: Letters and Diaries of John Dos Passos,* ed. T. Ludington, 1973.

from U.S.A.*

from The Big Money

Newsreel LXVI

HOLMES DENIES STAY

A better world's in birth

Tiny wasps imported from Korea in battle to death with Asiatic beetle

BOY CARRIED MILE DOWN SEWER; SHOT OUT
ALIVE

CHICAGO BARS MEETINGS

For justice thunders condemnation

WASHINGTON KEEPS EYE ON RADICALS

Arise rejected of the earth

PARIS BRUSSELS MOSCOW GENEVA ADD THEIR
VOICES

It is the final conflict
Let each stand in his place

GEOLOGIST LOST IN CAVE SIX DAYS

The International Party

SACCO AND VANZETTI MUST DIE

Shall be the human race.

Much I thought of you when I was lying in the death house—the singing, the kind tender voices of the children from the playground where there was all the life and the joy of liberty —just one step from the wall that contains the buried agony of three buried souls. It would remind me so often of you and your sister and I wish I could see you every moment, but I feel better that you will not come to the death house so that you could not see the horrible picture of three living in agony waiting to be electrocuted.

---

* The trilogy *U.S.A.*, containing the three novels *The 42nd Parallel, 1919,* and *The Big Money,* was first published in 1938. These novels had been published separately in 1930, 1932, and 1936, respectively.

The Camera Eye (50)

they have clubbed us off the streets   they are stronger   they are rich   they hire and fire the politicians the newspapereditors the old judges the small men with reputations the collegepresidents the wardheelers (listen businessmen collegepresidents judges America will not forget her betrayers) they hire the men with guns the uniforms the policecars the patrolwagons

all right you have won   you will kill the brave men our friends tonight

there is nothing left to do   we are beaten   we the beaten crowd together in these old dingy schoolrooms on Salem Street   shuffle up and down the gritty creaking stairs sit hunched with bowed heads on benches and hear the old words of the haters of oppression   made new in sweat and agony tonight

our work is over   the scribbled phrases   the nights typing releases the smell of the printshop the sharp reek of newprinted leaflets the rush for Western Union stringing words into wires the search for stinging words to make you feel who are your oppressors America

America our nation has been beaten by strangers who have turned our language inside out who have taken the clean words our fathers spoke and made them slimy and foul

their hired men sit on the judge's bench they sit back with their feet on the tables under the dome of the State House they are ignorant of our beliefs they have the dollars the guns the armed forces the powerplants

they have built the electricchair and hired the executioner to throw the switch

all right we are two nations

America our nation has been beaten by strangers who have bought the laws and fenced off the meadows and cut down the woods for pulp and turned our pleasant cities into slums and sweated the wealth out of our people and when they want to they hire the executioner to throw the switch

but do they know that the old words of the immigrants are being renewed in blood and agony tonight do they know that the old American speech of the haters of oppression is new tonight in the mouth of an old woman from Pittsburgh of a husky boilermaker from Frisco who hopped freights clear from the Coast to come here in the mouth of a Back Bay socialworker in the mouth of an Italian printer of a hobo from Arkansas   the language of the beaten nation is not forgotten in our ears tonight

the men in the deathhouse made the old words new before they died

If it had not been for these things, I might have lived out my life talking at streetcorners to scorning men. I might have died unknown, unmarked, a failure. This is our career and our triumph. Never in our full life can we hope to do such work for tolerance, for justice, for man's understanding of man as now we do by an accident.

now their work is over   the immigrants haters of oppression lie quiet in black suits in the little undertaking parlor in the North End   the city is quiet   the men of the conquering nation are not to be seen on the streets

they have won why are they scared to be seen on the streets?   on the streets you see only the downcast faces of the beaten   the streets belong to the beaten nation all the way to the cemetery where the bodies of the immigrants are to be burned   we line the curbs in the drizzling rain we crowd the wet sidewalks elbow to elbow silent pale looking with scared eyes at the coffins

we stand defeated America

Newsreel LXVIII

WALL STREET STUNNED

This is not Thirtyeight but it's old Ninetyseven
You must put her in Center on time

MARKET SURE TO RECOVER FROM SLUMP

DECLINE IN CONTRACTS

POLICE TURN MACHINE GUNS ON COLORADO
MINE STRIKERS KILL 5 WOUND 40

sympathizers appeared on the scene just as thousands of office workers were pouring out of the buildings at the lunch hour. As they raised their placard high and started an indefinite march from one side to the other, they were jeered and hooted not only by the office workers but also by workmen on a building under construction

NEW METHODS OF SELLING SEEN

RESCUE CREWS TRY TO UPEND ILL-FATED CRAFT
WHILE WAITING FOR PONTOONS

He looked 'round an' said to his black greasy fireman
Jus' shovel in a little more coal
And when we cross that White Oak Mountain
You can watch your Ninety-seven roll

I find your column interesting and need advice. I have saved four thousand dollars which I want to invest for a better income. Do you think I might buy stocks?

POLICE KILLER FLICKS CIGARETTE AS HE GOES
TREMBLING TO DOOM

PLAY AGENCIES IN RING OF SLAVE GIRL MARTS

MAKER OF LOVE DISBARRED AS LAWYER

Oh the right wing clothesmakers
And the Socialist fakers
They make by the workers . . . .
Double cross

They preach Social-ism
But practice Fasc-ism
To keep capitalism
By the boss

MOSCOW CONGRESS OUSTS OPPOSITION

It's a mighty rough road from Lynchburg to Danville
An' a line on a three mile grade
It was on that grade he lost his average
An' you see what a jump he made

MILL THUGS IN MURDER RAID

here is the most dangerous example of how at the decisive moment the bourgeois ideology liquidates class solidarity and turns a friend of the workingclass of yesterday into a most miserable propagandist for imperialism today

RED PICKETS FINED FOR PROTESTS HERE

We leave our home in the morning
We kiss our children goodbye

OFFICIALS STILL HOPE FOR RESCUE OF MEN

He was goin' downgrade makin' ninety miles an hour
When his whistle broke into a scream
He was found in the wreck with his hand on the throttle
An' was scalded to death with the steam

RADICALS FIGHT WITH CHAIRS AT UNITY MEETING

PATROLMEN PROTECT REDS

U.S. CHAMBER OF COMMERCE URGES CONFIDENCE

REAL VALUES UNHARMED

While we slave for the bosses
Our children scream an' cry
But when we draw our money
Our grocery bills to pay

PRESIDENT SEES PROSPERITY NEAR

Not a cent to spend for clothing
Not a cent to lay away

STEAMROLLER IN ACTION AGAINST MILITANTS

MINERS BATTLE SCABS

But we cannot buy for our children
Our wages are too low
Now listen to me you workers
Both you women and men
Let us win for them the victory
I'm sure it ain't no sin

CARILLON PEALS IN SINGING TOWER

the President declared it was impossible to view the increased advantages for the many without smiling at those who a short time ago expressed so much fear lest our country might come under the control of a few individuals of great wealth.

HAPPY CROWDS THRONG CEREMONY

on a tiny island nestling like a green jewel in the lake that mirrors the singing tower, the President today participated in the dedication of a bird sanctuary and its pealing carillon, fulfilling the dream of an immigrant boy

The Camera Eye (51)

at the head of the valley in the dark of the hills on the broken floor of a lurchedover cabin a man halfsits halflies propped up by an old woman two wrinkled girls that might be young   chunks of coal flare in the hearth flicker in his face white and sagging as dough   blacken the cavedin mouth the taut throat the belly swelled enormous with the wound he got working on the minetipple

the barefoot girl brings him a tincup of water   the woman wipes sweat off his streaming face with a dirty denim sleeve   the firelight flares in his eyes stretched big with fever in the women's scared eyes and in the blanched faces of the foreigners

without help in the valley hemmed by dark strikesilent hills the man will die (my father died we know what it is like to see a man die) the women will lay him out on the rickety cot the miners will bury him

in the jail it's light too hot the steamheat hisses we talk through the greenpainted iron bars to a tall white mustachioed old man some smiling miners in shirtsleeves a boy   faces white from mining have already the tallowy look of jailfaces

foreigners what can we say to the dead?   foreigners what can we say to the jailed?

the representative of the political party talks fast through the bars join up with us and no other union we'll send you tobacco candy solidarity our lawyers will write briefs speakers will shout your names at meetings they'll carry your names on cardboards on picketlines   the men in jail shrug their shoulders smile thinly our eyes look in their eyes through the bars   what can I say?

(in another continent I have seen the faces looking out through the barred basement windows behind the ragged sentry's boots I have seen before day the straggling footsore prisoners herded through the streets limping between bayonets   heard the volley

I have seen the dead lying out in those distant deeper valleys) what can we say to the jailed?

in the law's office we stand against the wall the law is a big man with eyes angry in a big pumpkinface   who sits and stares at us meddling foreigners through the door the deputies crane with their guns   they stand guard at the mines   they blockade the miners' soupkitchens   they've cut off the road up the valley   the hiredmen with guns stand ready to shoot (they have made us foreigners in the land where we were born they are the conquering army that has filtered into the country unnoticed they have taken the hilltops by stealth they levy toll they stand at the minehead   they stand at the polls   they stand by when the bailiffs carry the furniture of the family evicted from the city tenement out on the sidewalk they are there when the bankers foreclose on a farm they are ambushed and ready to shoot down the strikers marching behind the flag up the switchback road to the mine   those that the guns spare they jail)

the law stares across the desk out of angry eyes his face reddens in splotches like a gobbler's neck with the strut of the power of submachineguns sawedoffshotguns teargas and vomitinggas the power that can feed you or leave you to starve

sits easy at his desk his back is covered he feels strong behind him he feels the prosecutingattorney the judge an owner himself the political boss the minesuperintendent the board of directors   the president of the utility the manipulator of the holdingcompany

he lifts his hand towards the telephone
the deputies crowd in the door
we have only words against

Power Superpower

In eighteen-eighty when Thomas Edison's agent was hooking up the first telephone in London, he put an ad in the paper for a secretary and stenographer. The eager young cockney with sprouting muttonchop whiskers who answered it

had recently lost his job as officeboy. In his spare time he had been learning shorthand and bookkeeping and taking dictation from the editor of the English *Vanity Fair* at night and jotting down the speeches in Parliament for the papers. He came of temperance smallshopkeeper stock; already he was butting his bullethead against the harsh structure of caste that doomed boys of his class to a life of alpaca jackets, penmanship, subordination. To get a job with an American firm was to put a foot on the rung of a ladder that led up into the blue.

He did his best to make himself indispensable; they let him operate the switchboard for the first halfhour when the telephone service was opened. Edison noticed his weekly reports on the electrical situation in England

and sent for him to be his personal secretary.

Samuel Insull landed in America on a raw March day in eightyone. Immediately he was taken out to Menlo Park, shown about the little group of laboratories, saw the strings of electriclightbulbs shining at intervals across the snowy lots, all lit from the world's first central electric station. Edison put him right to work and he wasn't through till midnight. Next morning at six he was on the job; Edison had no use for any nonsense about hours or vacations. Insull worked from that time on until he was seventy without a break; no nonsense about hours or vacations. Electric power turned the ladder into an elevator.

Young Insull made himself indispensable to Edison and took more and more charge of Edison's business deals. He was tireless, ruthless, reliable as the tides, Edison used to say, and fiercely determined to rise.

In ninetytwo he induced Edison to send him to Chicago and put him in as president of the Chicago Edison Company. Now he was on his own. *My engineering,* he said once in a speech, when he was sufficiently czar of Chicago to allow himself the luxury of plain speaking, *has been largely concerned with engineering all I could out of the dollar.*

He was a stiffly arrogant redfaced man with a closecropped mustache; he lived on Lake Shore Drive and was at the office at 7:10 every morning. It took him fifteen years to merge the five electrical companies into the Commonwealth Edison Company. *Very early I discovered that the first essential, as in other public utility business, was that it should be operated as a monopoly.*

When his power was firm in electricity he captured gas, spread out into the surrounding townships in northern Illinois. When politicians got in his way, he bought them, when laborleaders got in his way he bought them. Incredibly his power grew. He was scornful of bankers, lawyers were his hired men. He put his own lawyer in as corporation counsel and through him ran Chicago. When he found to his amazement that there were men (even a couple of young lawyers, Richberg and Ickes) in Chicago that he couldn't buy, he decided he'd better put on a show for the public;

Big Bill Thompson, the Builder:
punch King George in the nose,
the hunt for the treeclimbing fish,
the Chicago Opera.

It was too easy; the public had money, there was one of them born every minute, with the founding of Middlewest Utilities in nineteen twelve Insull began to use the public's money to spread his empire. His companies began to have open stockholders' meetings, to ballyhoo service, the small investor could sit there all day hearing the bigwigs talk. It's fun to be fooled. Companyunions hypnotized his employees; everybody had to buy stock in his companies, employees had to go out and sell stock, officeboys, linemen, trolleyconductors. Even Owen D. Young was afraid of him. *My experience is that the greatest aid in the efficiency of labor is a long line of men waiting at the gate.*

War shut up the progressives (no more nonsense about trustbusting, controlling monopoly, the public good) and raised Samuel Insull to the peak.

He was head of the Illinois State Council of Defense. *Now,* he said delightedly, *I can do anything I like.* With it came the perpetual spotlight, the purple taste of empire. If anybody didn't like what Samuel Insull did he was a traitor. Chicago damn well kept its mouth shut.

The Insull companies spread and merged put competitors out of business until Samuel Insull and his stooge brother Martin controlled through the leverage of holdingcompanies and directorates and blocks of minority stock

light and power, coalmines and tractioncompanies

in Illinois, Michigan, the Dakotas, Nebraska, Arkansas, Oklahoma, Missouri, Maine, Kansas, Wisconsin, Virginia, Ohio, North Carolina, Indiana, New York, New Jersey, Texas, in Canada, in Louisiana, in Georgia, in Florida and Alabama.

(It has been figured out that one dollar in Middle West Utilities controlled seventeen hundred and fifty dollars invested by the public in the subsidiary companies that actually did the work of producing electricity. With the delicate lever of a voting trust controlling the stock of the two top holdingcompanies he controlled a twelfth of the power output of America.)

Samuel Insull began to think he owned all that the way a man owns the roll of bills in his back pocket.

Always he'd been scornful of bankers. He owned quite a few in Chicago. But the New York bankers were laying for him; they felt he was a bounder, whispered that this financial structure was unsound. Fingers itched to grasp the lever that so delicately moved this enormous power over lives,

superpower, Insull liked to call it.

A certain Cyrus S. Eaton of Cleveland, an exBaptistminister, was the David that brought down this Goliath. Whether it was so or not he made Insull believe that Wall Street was behind him.

He started buying stock in the three Chicago utilities. Insull in a panic for fear he'd lose his control went into the market to buy against him. Finally the Reverend Eaton let himself be bought out, shaking down the old man for a profit of twenty million dollars.

The stockmarket crash.

Paper values were slipping. Insull's companies were intertwined in a tangle that no bookkeeper has ever been able to unravel.

The gas hissed out of the torn balloon. Insull threw away his imperial pride and went on his knees to the bankers.

The bankers had him where they wanted him. To save the face of the tottering czar he was made a receiver of his own concerns. But the old man couldn't get out of his head the illusion that the money was all his. When it was discovered that he was using the stockholders' funds to pay off his brothers' brokerage accounts it was too thick even for a federal judge. Insull was forced to resign.

He held directorates in eightyfive companies, he was chairman of sixtyfive, president of eleven: it took him three hours to sign his resignations.

As a reward for his services to monopoly his companies chipped in on a pension of eighteen thousand a year. But the public was shouting for criminal prosecution. When the handouts stopped newspapers and politicians turned on him. Revolt against the moneymanipulators was in the air. Samuel Insull got the wind up and ran off to Canada with his wife.

Extradition proceedings. He fled to Paris. When the authorities began to close in on him there he slipped away to Italy, took a plane to Tirana, another to Saloniki and then the train to Athens. There the old fox went to earth. Money talked as sweetly in Athens as it had in Chicago in the old days.

The American ambassador tried to extradite him. Insull hired a chorus of Hellenic lawyers and politicos and sat drinking coffee in the lobby of the Grande Bretagne, while they proceeded to tie up the ambassador in a snarl of chicanery as complicated as the bookkeeping of his holdingcompanies. The successors of Demosthenes were delighted. The ancestral itch in many a Hellenic palm was temporarily assuaged. Samuel Insull settled down cozily in Athens, was stirred by the sight of the Parthenon, watched the goats feeding on the Pentelic slopes, visited the Areopagus, admired marble fragments ascribed to Phidias, talked with the local bankers about reorganizing the public utilities of Greece, was said to be promoting Macedonian lignite. He was the toast of the Athenians; Madame Kouryoumdjouglou, the vivacious wife of a Bagdad datemerchant, devoted herself to his comfort. When the first effort at extradition failed, the old gentleman declared in the courtroom, as he struggled out from the embraces of his four lawyers: *Greece is a small but great country.*

The idyll was interrupted when the Roosevelt Administration began to put the heat on the Greek Foreign Office. Government lawyers in Chicago were accumulating truckloads of evidence and chalking up more and more drastic indictments.

Finally after many a postponement (he had hired physicians as well as lawyers, they cried to high heaven that it would kill him to leave the genial climate of the Attic plain),

he was ordered to leave Greece as an undesirable alien, to the great indignation of Balkan society and of Madame Kouryoumdjouglou.

He hired the *Maiotis* a small and grubby Greek freighter and panicked the foreign-news services by slipping off for an unknown destination.

It was rumored that the new Odysseus was bound for Aden, for the islands of the South Seas, that he'd been invited to Persia. After a few days he turned up rather seasick in the Bosporus on his way, it was said, to Rumania where Madame Kouryoumdjouglou had advised him to put himself under the protection of her friend la Lupescu.

At the request of the American ambassador the Turks were delighted to drag him off the Greek freighter and place him in a not at all comfortable jail. Again money had been mysteriously wafted from England, the healing balm began to flow, lawyers were hired, interpreters expostulated, doctors made diagnoses;

but Angora was boss

and Insull was shipped off to Smyrna to be turned over to the assistant federal districtattorney who had come all that way to arrest him.

The Turks wouldn't even let Madame Kouryoumdjouglou, on her way back from making arrangements in Bucharest, go ashore to speak to him. In a scuffle with the officials on the steamboat the poor lady was pushed overboard

and with difficulty fished out of the Bosporus.

Once he was cornered the old man let himself tamely be taken home on the *Exilona,* started writing his memoirs, made himself agreeable to his fellow passengers, was taken off at Sandy Hook and rushed to Chicago to be arraigned.

In Chicago the government spitefully kept him a couple of nights in jail; men he'd never known, so the newspapers said, stepped forward to go on his twohundredand-fiftythousanddollar bail. He was moved to a hospital that he himself had endowed. Solidarity. The leading businessmen in Chicago were photographed visiting him there. Henry Ford paid a call.

The trial was very beautiful. The prosecution got bogged in finance technicalities. The judge was not unfriendly. The Insulls stole the show.

They were folks, they smiled at reporters, they posed for photographers, they went down to the courtroom by bus. Investors might have been ruined but so, they allowed it to be known, were the Insulls; the captain had gone down with the ship.

Old Samuel Insull rambled amiably on the stand, told his lifestory: from officeboy to powermagnate, his struggle to make good, his love for his home and the kiddies. He didn't deny he'd made mistakes; who hadn't, but they were honest errors. Samuel Insull wept. Brother Martin wept. The lawyers wept. With voices choked with emotion headliners of Chicago business told from the witnessstand how much Insull had done for business in Chicago. There wasn't a dry eye in the jury.

Finally driven to the wall by the prosecutingattorney Samuel Insull blurted out that yes, he had made an error of some ten million dollars in accounting but that it had been an honest error.

Verdict: Not Guilty.

Smiling through their tears the happy Insulls went to their towncar amid the cheers of the crowd. Thousands of ruined investors, at least so the newspapers said, who had lost their life savings sat crying over the home editions at the thought of how Mr. Insull had suffered. The bankers were happy, the bankers had moved in on the properties.

In an odor of sanctity the deposed monarch of superpower, the officeboy who made good, enjoys his declining years spending the pension of twentyone thousand a year that the directors of his old companies dutifully restored to him. *After fifty years of work,* he said, *my job is gone.*

1936

F. Scott Fitzgerald
1896–1940

Francis Scott Key Fitzgerald belonged, as Edmund Wilson once noted, as much to "the middle west of large cities and country clubs" as Sinclair Lewis belonged to "the middle west of the prairies and little towns." Born in St. Paul, Minnesota, on September 24, 1896, Fitzgerald was descended on his father's side from a socially prominent family of once-prosperous landowners and legislators, including the author of "The Star-Spangled Banner," and on his mother's from a family of newly prosperous and still thriving Irish immigrants. The former, he later noted, possessed "that series of reticences and obligations that go under the poor old shattered word 'breeding,'" while the latter "had the money." From this divided heritage, Fitzgerald acquired not only a deep ambivalence toward both status and money but also a sense of entanglement in America's history. "I look out at it," he once said of that history, "and I think it is the most beautiful history in the world. It is the history of me and my people. . . . It is the history of all aspiration—not just the American dream but the human dream." Yet Fitzgerald's hold on his heritage, as on almost everything, remained precarious.

"That was always my experience," he observed near the end of his life, "a poor boy in a rich town; a poor boy in a rich boy's school; a poor boy in a rich man's club."

From St. Paul, Fitzgerald went on to Princeton and New York and Paris and Hollywood. No major writer of his time lived so extravagant a version of success, and none experienced a more devastating version of failure. He was at once a striking embodiment and a scathing critic of his age, primarily because he possessed, as his friend John Peale Bishop remarked, "the rare faculty of being able to experience romantic and ingenuous emotions and a half hour later regard them with satiric detachment." Many of Fitzgerald's emotions, like those of his age, derived from the almost religious awe that he felt toward the idealization of great wealth and the romanticization of sexual love, by both of which he felt simultaneously attracted and repulsed, enchanted and offended. At the same time, however, his fiction discloses a preoccupation with and a sensitivity to social class that is unusual in American fiction. In both his writing and his life, Fitzgerald continually demonstrated the tensions of a divided consciousness. Toward the end of his life, in a series of remarkably personal and vulnerable essays about his "crack-up," he said that "the test of a first-rate intelligence is the ability to hold two opposed ideas in the mind at the same time, and still retain the ability to function."

At a Catholic prep school in New Jersey and then at Princeton, where poor examination scores barely qualified him in 1913 for admission "with conditions," Fitzgerald sacrificed academic achievement to social success. He very early equated literature with celebrity and success, claiming in "The Crack-up" (1936) that "it seemed a romantic business to be a successful literary man—you were not ever going to be famous as a movie star but what note you had was probably longer-lived—you were never going to have the power of a man of strong political or religious convictions but you were certainly more independent." At Princeton, Fitzgerald compiled a dismal scholastic record—he was in academic trouble every semester—yet managed to distinguish himself socially and intellectually through his writing. He wrote clever plots and lyrics for Triangle Club shows (in one he played a glamorous show girl, and a photograph of him in costume appeared in the *New York Times*), along with short stories, poems, and plays for literary and humor magazines.

In 1917 Fitzgerald conveniently eased himself out of Princeton, where he had fallen a year behind because of poor grades, by accepting a commission in the U.S. Infantry. That winter, at Fort Leavenworth, Kansas (where his platoon captain was Dwight David Eisenhower), Fitzgerald began a novel, *The Romantic Egoist*, which, after several drafts and rejections, was eventually salvaged as *This Side of Paradise* (1920). Fitzgerald worked desperately at the novel—keeping at it while in the army, including a tour in Montgomery, Alabama (he never got overseas), and then after the army while working briefly in New York and while living at his parents' house in St. Paul—because he optimistically equated its publication with both literary and romantic success. While stationed in Montgomery, Fitzgerald had fallen in love with a recent high school graduate, a beautiful, high-spirited, talented, precariously balanced debutante named Zelda Sayre. "If I stopped working to finish the novel," Fitzgerald later wrote, "I lost the girl." With the publication of *This Side of Paradise,* an autobiographical novel set in Princeton, Fitzgerald not only won Zelda's hand but also made himself a cultural hero to the "flappers and philosophers" of the era he named "the Jazz Age." A whole generation of college students listened to Fitzgerald as one might listen to an oracle.

The novel proved to be an immediate sensation; it sold over 40,000 copies in its first year and made Fitzgerald an overnight celebrity. It also immensely improved his income: "Counting the bag, I found that in 1919 I had made $800 by writing, that in 1920 I had made $18,000 [from] stories, picture rights, and book. My story price had gone from $30 to $1,000." Fitzgerald had been publishing his short stories since the spring of 1919, first in H. L. Mencken's *The Smart Set* and later in the mass-circulation *Saturday Evening Post,* where he published story after story for the next seventeen years. Though Fitzgerald remains one of the finest American short-story writers, he often expressed contempt for the form—"I don't enjoy it & just do it for the money"—and considered the novel as the best expression of his art. Nevertheless, Fitzgerald would publish in his lifetime four significant collections of stories: *Flappers and Philosophers* (1920), *Tales of the Jazz Age* (1922), *All the Sad Young Men* (1926) (which featured "The Rich Boy" as the lead story), and *Taps at Reveille* (1935). Several collections of stories were also published posthumously. Edmund Wilson, who met Fitzgerald at Princeton and who became one his closest friends, had warned Fitzgerald after reading *This Side of Paradise* that he was in danger of becoming a "very popular trashy novelist." In selling scores of stories to popular magazines over the years, Fitzgerald, it is apparent, did not always heed Wilson's warning.

After their marriage in April 1920, Fitzgerald and Zelda set out on a life together that was glamorous, extravagant, emotionally stormy, and usually good publicity. Through the 1920s and into the 1930s they dressed fashionably, stayed in expensive hotels, swam in public fountains, and danced on restaurant tables. They partied for nights at a time, drank excessively, and enjoyed being evicted from public places, all the while spending money even more rapidly than Fitzgerald could earn it. A second novel, *The Beautiful and Damned,* a story of moral and sexual dissolution partly stimulated by the fast style of the Fitzgeralds' marriage, appeared in 1922 and received many disappointing reviews. Between 1922 and 1924 Fitzgerald lived in Great Neck, Long Island, where he became friends with Ring Lardner and where he tried his hand at an unsuccessful play, *The Vegetable* (1923). In 1924 the Fitzgeralds sailed for an extended European trip, during which Fitzgerald met Gertrude Stein and Ezra Pound and began a tense, competitive friendship with Ernest Hemingway. In 1925 Fitzgerald published his finest novel, *The Great Gatsby,* which has continued to exercise a remarkable hold on both the popular and the academic imagination. Three movies have been based on it, and scores of critical articles have been written about it. The novel is about the mysterious, fabulously wealthy Jay Gatsby, who throws lavish parties at his Long Island estate and who tries to relive a previous idyllic romance. For all his vulgarity, Gatsby possesses "some heightened sensitivity to the promises of life . . . an extraordinary gift for hope, a romantic readiness." The enormous popularity of the book derives in part from its focus on two of Fitzgerald's favorite themes, love and money, while its enormous critical success derives from Fitzgerald's ability to imbue a popular subject with cultural myth and literary seriousness.

Fitzgerald returned to the United States in December 1926 and spent a few months scriptwriting in Hollywood. The Fitzgeralds then settled outside of Wilmington, Delaware, where they tried to piece their lives together. Zelda felt unproductive and frustrated; Fitzgerald's drinking had reached dangerous proportions. In the summer of 1928 they returned to Paris, where Zelda, always a talented dancer and desperately searching for an independent identity, tried too late to find a creative outlet in ballet. Two years later, while on another trip to Europe, Zelda suffered the first of a series of mental breakdowns that forced her to spend most of the last seventeen years of her life in sanatoriums. By 1931, when the Fitzgeralds returned to America, the Great Depression was deepening and Fitzgerald was experiencing an abrupt reversal of fortune. Guilt-ridden and depressed by Zelda's collapse, humbled by his own rising self-doubts, he began drinking more and writing less.

In 1932 Zelda Fitzgerald published a novel, *Save Me the Waltz,* which she had written while she was receiving treatment at the Johns Hopkins clinic. Two years later Fitzgerald published *Tender Is the Night,* the story of an alcoholic American psychiatrist who falls in love with and disastrously marries one of his wealthy patients. (The book's title comes from "Ode to a Nightingale," one of several Keats poems that had long exerted a powerful influence on Fitzgerald's fiction.) But nothing could revitalize Fitzgerald's financial situation. The royalties on works that had earned hundreds of thousands of dollars in the 1920s brought him a total of $50 in 1932 and 1933. Sorely in debt, Fitzgerald returned to Hollywood in 1937 on a lucrative contract as a scriptwriter. But his effort to translate his genius for narrative fiction into screenplays also failed. Although he worked on numerous scripts, he managed to receive only one screen credit over the next two years. His drinking binges continued to get him in trouble with the studios, and he gradually drifted into free-lance jobs. In 1940, at the age of forty-four, he died in Hollywood of a heart attack at the home of the journalist Sheilah Graham. His new novel—Fitzgerald liked to think of it as "a Western" —about a self-made Hollywood producer, *The Last Tycoon,* remained unfinished. Over the next eight years, Zelda continued to struggle with bouts of severe depression. In 1947, she was burned to death in a North Carolina hospital fire.

"I am not a great man," Fitzgerald said to his daughter, near the end of his life, "but sometimes I think the impersonal and objective quality of my talent and the sacrifices of it, in pieces, to preserve its essential value has some sort of epic grandeur." At the time of his death, Fitzgerald's reputation, like his income, had fallen very low. In the years since, however, readers have discovered, in *The Great Gatsby, Tender Is the Night,* and a handful of stories, including "The Rich Boy," works of permanent value. At its best, the lyricism of his prose arises from and is interlaced with dramatic situations that disclose something of the emptiness and something of the hope of our world. The critic Lionel Trilling regarded Fitzgerald as "perhaps the last notable writer to affirm the Romantic fantasy, descended from the Renaissance, of personal ambition or heroism, of life committed to, or thrown away for, some ideal of self."

Further Reading:
K. Eble, *F. Scott Fitzgerald*, 1963.
W. Goldhurst, *F. Scott Fitzgerald and His Contemporaries*, 1963.
A. Mizener, *The Far Side of Paradise*, rev. ed., 1965.
J. F. Callahan, *The Illusions of a Nation: Myth and History in the Novels of F. Scott Fitzgerald*, 1972.
M. J. Bruccoli, *Some Sort of Epic Grandeur: The Life of F. Scott Fitzgerald*, 1981.

Text:
"The Rich Boy" from *Babylon Revisited and Other Stories*, 1950.

The Rich Boy

[I]

Begin with an individual, and before you know it you find that you have created a type; begin with a type, and you find that you have created—nothing. That is because we are all queer fish, queerer behind our faces and voices than we want any one to know or than we know ourselves. When I hear a man proclaiming himself an "average, honest, open fellow," I feel pretty sure that he has some definite and perhaps terrible abnormality which he has agreed to conceal—and his protestation of being average and honest and open is his way of reminding himself of his misprision.

There are no types, no plurals. There is a rich boy, and this is his and not his brothers' story. All my life I have lived among his brothers but this one has been my friend. Besides, if I wrote about his brothers I should have to begin by attacking all the lies that the poor have told about the rich and the rich have told about themselves —such a wild structure they have erected that when we pick up a book about the rich, some instinct prepares us for unreality. Even the intelligent and impassioned reporters of life have made the country of the rich as unreal as fairy-land.

Let me tell you about the very rich. They are different from you and me. They possess and enjoy early, and it does something to them, makes them soft where we are hard, and cynical where we are trustful, in a way that, unless you were born rich, it is very difficult to understand. They think, deep in their hearts, that they are better than we are because we had to discover the compensations and refuges of life for ourselves. Even when they enter deep into our world or sink below us, they still think that they are better than we are. They are different. The only way I can describe young Anson Hunter is to approach him as if he were a foreigner and cling stubbornly to my point of view. If I accept his for a moment I am lost—I have nothing to show but a preposterous movie.

II

Anson was the eldest of six children who would some day divide a fortune of fifteen million dollars, and he reached the age of reason—is it seven?—at the beginning of the century when daring young women were already gliding along Fifth Avenue in electric "mobiles." In those days he and his brother had an English governess who spoke the language very clearly and crisply and well, so that the two boys grew to speak as she did—their words and sentences were all crisp and clear and not run together as ours are. They didn't talk exactly like English children but acquired an accent that is peculiar to fashionable people in the city of New York.

In the summer the six children were moved from the house on 71st Street to a big estate in northern Connecticut. It was not a fashionable locality—Anson's father wanted to delay as long as possible his children's knowledge of that side of life. He was a man somewhat superior to his class, which composed New York society, and to his period, which was the snobbish and formalized vulgarity of the Gilded Age, and he wanted his sons to learn habits of concentration and have sound constitutions and grow up into right-living and successful men. He and his wife kept an eye on them as well as they were able until the two older boys went away to school, but in huge establishments this is difficult—it was much simpler in the series of small and medium-sized houses in which my own youth was spent—I was never far out of the reach of my mother's voice, of the sense of her presence, her approval or disapproval.

Anson's first sense of his superiority came to him when he realized the half-grudging American deference that was paid to him in the Connecticut village. The parents of the boys he played with always inquired after his father and mother, and were vaguely excited when their own children were asked to the Hunters' house. He accepted this as the natural state of things, and a sort of impatience with all groups of which he was not the centre—in money, in position, in authority—remained with him for the rest of his life. He disdained to struggle with other boys for precedence —he expected it to be given him freely, and when it wasn't he withdrew into his family. His family was sufficient, for in the East money is still a somewhat feudal thing, a clan-forming thing. In the snobbish West, money separates families to form "sets."

At eighteen, when he went to New Haven, Anson was tall and thick-set, with a clear complexion and a healthy color from the ordered life he had led in school. His hair was yellow and grew in a funny way on his head, his nose was beaked—these two things kept him from being handsome—but he had a confident charm and a certain brusque style, and the upper-class men who passed him on the street knew without being told that he was a rich boy and had gone to one of the best schools. Nevertheless, his very superiority kept him from being a success in college—the independence was mistaken for egotism, and the refusal to accept Yale standards with the proper awe seemed to belittle all those who had. So, long before he graduated, he began to shift the centre of his life to New York.

He was at home in New York—there was his own house with "the kind of servants you can't get any more"—and his own family, of which, because of his good humor and a certain ability to make things go, he was rapidly becoming the centre, and the débutante parties, and the correct manly world of the men's clubs, and the occasional wild spree with the gallant girls' whom New Haven only knew from the fifth row. His aspirations were conventional enough—they included even the irreproachable

---

' I.e., chorus girls or performers in burlesque theaters.

shadow he would some day marry, but they differed from the aspirations of the majority of young men in that there was no mist over them, none of that quality which is variously known as "idealism" or "illusion." Anson accepted without reservation the world of high finance and high extravagance, of divorce and dissipation, of snobbery and of privilege. Most of our lives end as a compromise—it was as a compromise that his life began.

He and I first met in the late summer of 1917 when he was just out of Yale, and, like the rest of us, was swept up into the systematized hysteria of the war. In the blue-green uniform of the naval aviation he came down to Pensacola, where the hotel orchestras played "I'm sorry, dear," and we young officers danced with the girls. Every one liked him, and though he ran with the drinkers and wasn't an especially good pilot, even the instructors treated him with a certain respect. He was always having long talks with them in his confident, logical voice—talks which ended by his getting himself, or, more frequently, another officer, out of some impending trouble. He was convivial, bawdy, robustly avid for pleasure, and we were all surprised when he fell in love with a conservative and rather proper girl.

Her name was Paula Legendre, a dark, serious beauty from somewhere in California. Her family kept a winter residence just outside of town, and in spite of her primness she was enormously popular; there is a large class of men whose egotism can't endure humor in a woman. But Anson wasn't that sort, and I couldn't understand the attraction of her "sincerity"—that was the thing to say about her—for his keen and somewhat sardonic mind.

Nevertheless, they fell in love—and on her terms. He no longer joined the twilight gathering at the De Soto bar, and whenever they were seen together they were engaged in a long, serious dialogue, which must have gone on several weeks. Long afterward he told me that it was not about anything in particular but was composed on both sides of immature and even meaningless statements—the emotional content that gradually came to fill it grew up not out of the words but out of its enormous seriousness. It was a sort of hypnosis. Often it was interrupted, giving way to that emasculated humor we call fun; when they were alone it was resumed again, solemn, low-keyed, and pitched so as to give each other a sense of unity in feeling and thought. They came to resent any interruptions of it, to be unresponsive to facetiousness about life, even to the mild cynicism of their contemporaries. They were only happy when the dialogue was going on, and its seriousness bathed them like the amber glow of an open fire. Toward the end there came an interruption they did not resent—it began to be interrupted by passion.

Oddly enough, Anson was as engrossed in the dialogue as she was and as profoundly affected by it, yet at the same time aware that on his side much was insincere, and on hers much was merely simple. At first, too, he despised her emotional simplicity as well, but with his love her nature deepened and blossomed, and he could despise it no longer. He felt that if he could enter into Paula's warm safe life he would be happy. The long preparation of the dialogue removed any constraint—he taught her some of what he had learned from more adventurous women, and she responded with a rapt holy intensity. One evening after a dance they agreed to marry, and he wrote a long letter about her to his mother. The next day Paula told him that she was rich, that she had a personal fortune of nearly a million dollars.

III

It was exactly as if they could say "Neither of us has anything: we shall be poor together"—just as delightful that they should be rich instead. It gave them the same communion of adventure. Yet when Anson got leave in April, and Paula and her mother accompanied him North, she was impressed with the standing of his family in New York and with the scale on which they lived. Alone with Anson for the first time in the rooms where he had played as a boy, she was filled with a comfortable emotion, as though she were pre-eminently safe and taken care of. The pictures of Anson in a skull cap at his first school, of Anson on horseback with the sweetheart of a mysterious forgotten summer, of Anson in a gay group of ushers and bridesmaids at a wedding, made her jealous of his life apart from her in the past, and so completely did his authoritative person seem to sum up and typify these possessions of his that she was inspired with the idea of being married immediately and returning to Pensacola as his wife.

But an immediate marriage wasn't discussed—even the engagement was to be secret until after the war. When she realized that only two days of his leave remained, her dissatisfaction crystallized in the intention of making him as unwilling to wait as she was. They were driving to the country for dinner, and she determined to force the issue that night.

Now a cousin of Paula's was staying with them at the Ritz, a severe, bitter girl who loved Paula but was somewhat jealous of her impressive engagement, and as Paula was late in dressing, the cousin, who wasn't going to the party, received Anson in the parlor of the suite.

Anson had met friends at five o'clock and drunk freely and indiscreetly with them for an hour. He left the Yale Club at a proper time, and his mother's chauffeur drove him to the Ritz, but his usual capacity was not in evidence, and the impact of the steam-heated sitting-room made him suddenly dizzy. He knew it, and he was both amused and sorry.

Paula's cousin was twenty-five, but she was exceptionally naïve, and at first failed to realize what was up. She had never met Anson before, and she was surprised when he mumbled strange information and nearly fell off his chair, but until Paula appeared it didn't occur to her that what she had taken for the odor of a dry-cleaned uniform was really whiskey. But Paula understood as soon as she appeared; her only thought was to get Anson away before her mother saw him, and at the look in her eyes the cousin understood too.

When Paula and Anson descended to the limousine they found two men inside, both asleep; they were the men with whom he had been drinking at the Yale Club, and they were also going to the party. He had entirely forgotten their presence in the car. On the way to Hempstead they awoke and sang. Some of the songs were rough, and though Paula tried to reconcile herself to the fact that Anson had few verbal inhibitions, her lips tightened with shame and distaste.

Back at the hotel the cousin, confused and agitated, considered the incident, and then walked into Mrs. Legendre's bedroom, saying: "Isn't he funny?"

"Who is funny?"

"Why—Mr. Hunter. He seemed so funny."

Mrs. Legendre looked at her sharply.

"How is he funny?"

"Why, he said he was French. I didn't know he was French."

"That's absurd. You must have misunderstood." She smiled: "It was a joke."

The cousin shook her head stubbornly.

"No. He said he was brought up in France. He said he couldn't speak any English, and that's why he couldn't talk to me. And he couldn't!"

Mrs. Legendre looked away with impatience just as the cousin added thoughtfully, "Perhaps it was because he was so drunk," and walked out of the room.

This curious report was true. Anson, finding his voice thick and uncontrollable, had taken the unusual refuge of announcing that he spoke no English. Years afterwards he used to tell that part of the story, and he invariably communicated the uproarious laughter which the memory aroused in him.

Five times in the next hour Mrs. Legendre tried to get Hempstead on the phone. When she succeeded, there was a ten-minute delay before she heard Paula's voice on the wire.

"Cousin Jo told me Anson was intoxicated."

"Oh, no. . . ."

"Oh, yes. Cousin Jo says he was intoxicated. He told her he was French, and fell off his chair and behaved as if he was very intoxicated. I don't want you to come home with him."

"Mother, he's all right! Please don't worry about—"

"But I do worry. I think it's dreadful. I want you to promise me not to come home with him."

"I'll take care of it, mother. . . ."

"I don't want you to come home with him."

"All right, mother. Good-by."

"Be sure now, Paula. Ask some one to bring you."

Deliberately Paula took the receiver from her ear and hung it up. Her face was flushed with helpless annoyance. Anson was stretched out asleep in a bedroom up-stairs, while the dinner-party below was proceeding lamely toward conclusion.

The hour's drive had sobered him somewhat—his arrival was merely hilarious—and Paula hoped that the evening was not spoiled, after all, but two imprudent cocktails before dinner completed the disaster. He talked boisterously and somewhat offensively to the party at large for fifteen minutes, and then slid silently under the table; like a man in an old print—but, unlike an old print, it was rather horrible without being at all quaint. None of the young girls present remarked upon the incident—it seemed to merit only silence. His uncle and two other men carried him up-stairs, and it was just after this that Paula was called to the phone.

An hour later Anson awoke in a fog of nervous agony, through which he perceived after a moment the figure of his uncle Robert standing by the door.

". . . I said are you better?"

"What?"

"Do you feel better, old man?"

"Terrible," said Anson.

"I'm going to try you on another bromo-seltzer. If you can hold it down, it'll do you good to sleep."

With an effort Anson slid his legs from the bed and stood up.

"I'm all right," he said dully.

"Take it easy."

"I thin' if you gave me a glassbrandy I could go down-stairs."

"Oh, no—"

"Yes, that's the only thin'. I'm all right now. . . . I suppose I'm in Dutch dow' there."

"They know you're a little under the weather," said his uncle deprecatingly. "But don't worry about it. Schuyler didn't even get here. He passed away in the locker-room over at the Links."

Indifferent to any opinion, except Paula's, Anson was nevertheless determined to save the débris of the evening, but when after a cold bath he made his appearance most of the party had already left. Paula got up immediately to go home.

In the limousine the old serious dialogue began. She had known that he drank, she admitted, but she had never expected anything like this—it seemed to her that perhaps they were not suited to each other, after all. Their ideas about life were too different, and so forth. When she finished speaking, Anson spoke in turn, very soberly. Then Paula said she'd have to think it over; she wouldn't decide to-night; she was not angry but she was terribly sorry. Nor would she let him come into the hotel with her, but just before she got out of the car she leaned and kissed him unhappily on the cheek.

The next afternoon Anson had a long talk with Mrs. Legendre while Paula sat listening in silence. It was agreed that Paula was to brood over the incident for a proper period and then, if mother and daughter thought it best, they would follow Anson to Pensacola. On his part he apologized with sincerity and dignity—that was all; with every card in her hand Mrs. Legendre was unable to establish any advantage over him. He made no promises, showed no humility, only delivered a few serious comments on life which brought him off with rather a moral superiority at the end. When they came South three weeks later, neither Anson in his satisfaction nor Paula in her relief at the reunion realized that the psychological moment had passed forever.

IV

He dominated and attracted her, and at the same time filled her with anxiety. Confused by his mixture of solidity and self-indulgence, of sentiment and cynicism—incongruities which her gentle mind was unable to resolve—Paula grew to think of him as two alternating personalities. When she saw him alone, or at a formal party, or with his casual inferiors, she felt a tremendous pride in his strong, attractive presence, the paternal, understanding stature of his mind. In other company she became uneasy when what had been a fine imperviousness to mere gentility showed its other face. The other face was gross, humorous, reckless of everything but pleasure. It startled her mind temporarily away from him, even led her into a short covert experiment with an old beau, but it was no use—after four months of Anson's enveloping vitality there was an anæmic pallor in all other men.

In July he was ordered abroad, and their tenderness and desire reached a crescendo. Paula considered a last-minute marriage—decided against it only because there were always cocktails on his breath now, but the parting itself made her physically ill with grief. After his departure she wrote him long letters of regret for the days of love they had missed by waiting. In August Anson's plane slipped down into the North Sea. He was pulled onto a destroyer after a night in the water and sent to hospital with pneumonia; the armistice was signed before he was finally sent home.

Then, with every opportunity given back to them, with no material obstacle to overcome, the secret weavings of their temperaments came between them, drying up their kisses and their tears, making their voices less loud to one another, muffling the intimate chatter of their hearts until the old communication was only possible by letters, from far away. One afternoon a society reporter waited for two hours in the Hunters' house for a confirmation of their engagement. Anson denied it; nevertheless an early issue carried the report as a leading paragraph—they were "constantly seen together at Southhampton, Hot Springs, and Tuxedo Park." But the serious dialogue had turned a corner into a long-sustained quarrel, and the affair was almost played out. Anson got drunk flagrantly and missed an engagement with her, whereupon Paula made certain behavioristic demands. His despair was helpless before his pride and his knowledge of himself: the engagement was definitely broken.

"Dearest," said their letters now, "Dearest, Dearest, when I wake up in the middle of the night and realize that after all it was not to be, I feel that I want to die. I can't go on living any more. Perhaps when we meet this summer we may talk things over and decide differently—we were so excited and sad that day, and I don't feel that I can live all my life without you. You speak of other people. Don't you know there are no other people for me, but only you. . . ."

But as Paula drifted here and there around the East she would sometimes mention her gaieties to make him wonder. Anson was too acute to wonder. When he saw a man's name in her letters he felt more sure of her and a little disdainful—he was always superior to such things. But he still hoped that they would some day marry.

Meanwhile he plunged vigorously into all the movement and glitter of post-bellum New York, entering a brokerage house, joining half a dozen clubs, dancing late, and moving in three worlds—his own world, the world of young Yale graduates, and that section of the half-world which rests one end on Broadway. But there was always a thorough and infractible eight hours devoted to his work in Wall Street, where the combination of his influential family connection, his sharp intelligence, and his abundance of sheer physical energy brought him almost immediately forward. He had one of those invaluable minds with partitions in it; sometimes he appeared at his office refreshed by less than an hour's sleep, but such occurrences were rare. So early as 1920 his income in salary and commissions exceeded twelve thousand dollars.

As the Yale tradition slipped into the past he became more and more of a popular figure among his classmates in New York, more popular than he had ever been in college. He lived in a great house, and had the means of introducing young men into other great houses. Moreover, his life already seemed secure, while theirs, for the most part, had arrived again at precarious beginnings. They commenced to turn to him for amusement and escape, and Anson responded readily, taking pleasure in helping people and arranging their affairs.

There were no men in Paula's letters now, but a note of tenderness ran through them that had not been there before. From several sources he heard that she had "a heavy beau," Lowell Thayer, a Bostonian of wealth and position, and though he was sure she still loved him, it made him uneasy to think that he might lose her, after all. Save for one unsatisfactory day she had not been in New York for almost five months, and as the rumors multiplied he became increasingly anxious to see her. In February he took his vacation and went down to Florida.

Palm Beach sprawled plump and opulent between the sparkling sapphire of Lake Worth, flawed here and there by house-boats at anchor, and the great turquoise bar of the Atlantic Ocean. The huge bulks of the Breakers and the Royal Poinciana rose as twin paunches from the bright level of the sand, and around them clustered the Dancing Glade, Bradley's House of Chance, and a dozen modistes and milliners with goods at triple prices from New York. Upon the trellised veranda of the Breakers two hundred women stepped right, stepped left, wheeled, and slid in that then celebrated calisthenic known as the double-shuffle, while in half-time to the music two thousand bracelets clicked up and down on two hundred arms.

At the Everglades Club after dark Paula and Lowell Thayer and Anson and a casual fourth played bridge with hot cards. It seemed to Anson that her kind, serious face was wan and tired—she had been around now for four, five, years. He had known her for three.

"Two spades."

"Cigarette? . . . Oh, I beg your pardon. By me."

"By."

"I'll double three spades."

There were a dozen tables of bridge in the room, which was filling up with smoke. Anson's eyes met Paula's, held them persistently even when Thayer's glance fell between them. . . .

"What was bid?" he asked abstractedly.

"Rose of Washington Square"

sang the young people in the corners:

"I'm withering there
    In basement air—"

The smoke banked like fog, and the opening of a door filled the room with blown swirls of ectoplasm. Little Bright Eyes streaked past the tables seeking Mr. Conan Doyle among the Englishmen who were posing as Englishmen about the lobby.

"You could cut it with a knife."

". . . cut it with a knife."

". . . a knife."

At the end of the rubber Paula suddenly got up and spoke to Anson in a tense, low voice. With scarcely a glance at Lowell Thayer, they walked out the door and descended a long flight of stone steps—in a moment they were walking hand in hand along the moonlit beach.

"Darling, darling. . . ." They embraced recklessly, passionately, in a shadow. . . . Then Paula drew back her face to let his lips say what she wanted to hear—she could feel the words forming as they kissed again. . . . Again she broke away, listening, but as he pulled her close once more she realized that he had said nothing—

only *"Darling! Darling!"* in that deep, sad whisper that always made her cry. Humbly, obediently, her emotions yielded to him and the tears streamed down her face, but her heart kept on crying: "Ask me—oh, Anson, dearest, ask me!"

"Paula. . . . *Paula!"*

The words wrung her heart like hands, and Anson, feeling her tremble, knew that emotion was enough. He need say no more, commit their destinies to no practical enigma. Why should he, when he might hold her so, biding his own time, for another year—forever? He was considering them both, her more than himself. For a moment, when she said suddenly that she must go back to her hotel, he hesitated, thinking, first, "This is the moment, after all," and then: "No, let it wait—she is mine. . . ."

He had forgotten that Paula too was worn away inside with the strain of three years. Her mood passed forever in the night.

He went back to New York next morning filled with a certain restless dissatisfaction. Late in April, without warning, he received a telegram from Bar Harbor in which Paula told him that she was engaged to Lowell Thayer, and that they would be married immediately in Boston. What he never really believed could happen had happened at last.

Anson filled himself with whiskey that morning, and going to the office, carried on his work without a break—rather with a fear of what would happen if he stopped. In the evening he went out as usual, saying nothing of what had occurred; he was cordial, humorous, unabstracted. But one thing he could not help—for three days, in any place, in any company, he would suddenly bend his head into his hands and cry like a child.

V

In 1922 when Anson went abroad with the junior partner to investigate some London loans, the journey intimated that he was to be taken into the firm. He was twenty-seven now, a little heavy without being definitely stout, and with a manner older than his years. Old people and young people liked him and trusted him, and mothers felt safe when their daughters were in his charge, for he had a way, when he came into a room, of putting himself on a footing with the oldest and most conservative people there. "You and I," he seemed to say, "we're solid. We understand."

He had an instinctive and rather charitable knowledge of the weaknesses of men and women, and, like a priest, it made him the more concerned for the maintenance of outward forms. It was typical of him that every Sunday morning he taught in a fashionable Episcopal Sunday-school—even though a cold shower and a quick change into a cutaway coat were all that separated him from the wild night before.

After his father's death he was the practical head of his family, and, in effect, guided the destinies of the younger children. Through a complication his authority did not extend to his father's estate, which was administrated by his Uncle Robert, who was the horsey member of the family, a good-natured, hard-drinking member of that set which centres about Wheatley Hills.

Uncle Robert and his wife, Edna, had been great friends of Anson's youth, and the former was disappointed when his nephew's superiority failed to take a horsey form. He backed him for a city club which was the most difficult in America to enter —one could only join if one's family had "helped to build up New York" (or, in other words, were rich before 1880)—and when Anson, after his election, neglected it for the Yale Club, Uncle Robert gave him a little talk on the subject. But when on top of that Anson declined to enter Robert Hunter's own conservative and somewhat neglected brokerage house, his manner grew cooler. Like a primary teacher who has taught all he knew, he slipped out of Anson's life.

There were so many friends in Anson's life—scarcely one for whom he had not done some unusual kindness and scarcely one whom he did not occasionally embarrass by his bursts of rough conversation or his habit of getting drunk whenever and however he liked. It annoyed him when any one else blundered in that regard—about his own lapses he was always humorous. Odd things happened to him and he told them with infectious laughter.

I was working in New York that spring, and I used to lunch with him at the Yale Club, which my university was sharing until the completion of our own. I had read of Paula's marriage, and one afternoon, when I asked him about her, something moved him to tell me the story. After that he frequently invited me to family dinners at his house and behaved as though there was a special relation between us, as though with his confidence a little of that consuming memory had passed into me.

I found that despite the trusting mothers, his attitude toward girls was not indiscriminately protective. It was up to the girl—if she showed an inclination toward looseness, she must take care of herself, even with him.

"Life," he would explain sometimes, "has made a cynic of me."

By life he meant Paula. Sometimes, especially when he was drinking, it became a little twisted in his mind, and he thought that she had callously thrown him over.

This "cynicism," or rather his realization that naturally fast girls were not worth sparing, led to his affair with Dolly Karger. It wasn't his only affair in those years, but it came nearest to touching him deeply, and it had a profound effect upon his attitude toward life.

Dolly was the daughter of a notorious "publicist" who had married into society. She herself grew up into the Junior League, came out at the Plaza, and went to the Assembly; and only a few old families like the Hunters could question whether or not she "belonged," for her picture was often in the papers, and she had more enviable attention than many girls who undoubtedly did. She was dark-haired, with carmine lips and a high, lovely color, which she concealed under pinkish-gray powder all through the first year out, because high color was unfashionable—Victorian-pale was the thing to be. She wore black, severe suits and stood with her hands in her pockets leaning a little forward, with a humorous restraint on her face. She danced exquisitely —better than anything she liked to dance—better than anything except making love. Since she was ten she had always been in love, and, usually, with some boy who didn't respond to her. Those who did—and there were many—bored her after a brief encounter, but for her failures she reserved the warmest spot in her heart. When she met them she would always try once more—sometimes she succeeded, more often she failed.

It never occurred to this gypsy of the unattainable that there was a certain resemblance in those who refused to love her—they shared a hard intuition that saw through to her weakness, not a weakness of emotion but a weakness of rudder. Anson perceived this when he first met her, less than a month after Paula's marriage. He was drinking rather heavily, and he pretended for a week that he was falling in love with her. Then he dropped abruptly and forgot—immediately he took up the commanding position in her heart.

Like so many girls of that day Dolly was slackly and indiscreetly wild. The unconventionality of a slightly older generation had been simply one facet of a post-war movement to discredit obsolete manners—Dolly's was both older and shabbier, and she saw in Anson the two extremes which the emotionally shiftless woman seeks, an abandon to indulgence alternating with a protective strength. In his character she felt both the sybarite and the solid rock, and these two satisfied every need of her nature.

She felt that it was going to be difficult, but she mistook the reason—she thought that Anson and his family expected a more spectacular marriage, but she guessed immediately that her advantage lay in his tendency to drink.

They met at the large débutante dances, but as her infatuation increased they managed to be more and more together. Like most mothers, Mrs. Karger believed that Anson was exceptionally reliable, so she allowed Dolly to go with him to distant country clubs and suburban houses without inquiring closely into their activities or questioning her explanations when they came in late. At first these explanations might have been accurate, but Dolly's worldly ideas of capturing Anson were soon engulfed in the rising sweep of her emotion. Kisses in the back of taxis and motor-cars were no longer enough; they did a curious thing:

They dropped out of their world for a while and made another world just beneath it where Anson's tippling and Dolly's irregular hours would be less noticed and commented on. It was composed, this world, of varying elements—several of Anson's Yale friends and their wives, two or three young brokers and bond salesmen and a handful of unattached men, fresh from college, with money and a propensity to dissipation. What this world lacked in spaciousness and scale it made up for by allowing them a liberty that it scarcely permitted itself. Moreover, it centred around them and permitted Dolly the pleasure of a faint condescension—a pleasure which Anson, whose whole life was a condescension from the certitudes of his childhood, was unable to share.

He was not in love with her, and in the long feverish winter of their affair he frequently told her so. In the spring he was weary—he wanted to renew his life at some other source—moreover, he saw that either he must break with her now or accept the responsibility of a definite seduction. Her family's encouraging attitude precipitated his decision—one evening when Mr. Karger knocked discreetly at the library door to announce that he had left a bottle of old brandy in the dining-room, Anson felt that life was hemming him in. That night he wrote her a short letter in which he told her that he was going on his vacation, and that in view of all the circumstances they had better meet no more.

It was June. His family had closed up the house and gone to the country, so he was living temporarily at the Yale Club. I had heard about his affair with Dolly as it developed—accounts salted with humor, for he despised unstable women, and granted them no place in the social edifice in which he believed—and when he told me that night that he was definitely breaking with her I was glad. I had seen Dolly here and there, and each time with a feeling of pity at the hopelessness of her struggle, and of shame at knowing so much about her that I had no right to know. She was what is known as "a pretty little thing," but there was a certain recklessness which rather fascinated me. Her dedication to the goddess of waste would have been less obvious had she been less spirited—she would most certainly throw herself away, but I was glad when I heard that the sacrifice would not be consummated in my sight.

Anson was going to leave the letter of farewell at her house next morning. It was one of the few houses left open in the Fifth Avenue district, and he knew that the Kargers, acting upon erroneous information from Dolly, had foregone a trip abroad to give their daughter her chance. As he stepped out the door of the Yale Club into Madison Avenue the postman passed him, and he followed back inside. The first letter that caught his eye was in Dolly's hand.

He knew what it would be—a lonely and tragic monologue, full of the reproaches he knew, the invoked memories, the "I wonder if's"—all the immemorial intimacies that he had communicated to Paula Legendre in what seemed another age. Thumbing over some bills, he brought it on top again and opened it. To his surprise it was a short, somewhat formal note, which said that Dolly would be unable to go to the country with him for the week-end, because Perry Hull from Chicago had unexpectedly come to town. It added that Anson had brought this on himself: "—if I felt that you loved me as I love you I would go with you at any time, any place, but Perry is *so* nice, and he so much wants me to marry him—"

Anson smiled contemptuously—he had had experience with such decoy epistles. Moreover, he knew how Dolly had labored over this plan, probably sent for the faithful Perry and calculated the time of his arrival—even labored over the note so that it would make him jealous without driving him away. Like most compromises, it had neither force nor vitality but only a timorous despair.

Suddenly he was angry. He sat down in the lobby and read it again. Then he went to the phone, called Dolly and told her in his clear, compelling voice that he had received her note and would call for her at five o'clock as they had previously planned. Scarcely waiting for the pretended uncertainty of her "Perhaps I can see you for an hour," he hung up the receiver and went down to his office. On the way he tore his own letter into bits and dropped it in the street.

He was not jealous—she meant nothing to him—but at her pathetic ruse everything stubborn and self-indulgent in him came to the surface. It was a presumption from a mental inferior and it could not be overlooked. If she wanted to know to whom she belonged she would see.

He was on the door-step at quarter past five. Dolly was dressed for the street, and he listened in silence to the paragraph of "I can only see you for an hour," which she had begun on the phone.

"Put on your hat, Dolly," he said, "we'll take a walk."

They strolled up Madison Avenue and over to Fifth while Anson's shirt dampened upon his portly body in the deep heat. He talked little, scolding her, making no love to her, but before they had walked six blocks she was his again, apologizing for the note, offering not to see Perry at all as an atonement, offering anything. She thought that he had come because he was beginning to love her.

"I'm hot," he said when they reached 71st Street. "This is a winter suit. If I stop by the house and change, would you mind waiting for me down-stairs? I'll only be a minute."

She was happy; the intimacy of his being hot, of any physical fact about him, thrilled her. When they came to the iron-grated door and Anson took out his key she experienced a sort of delight.

Down-stairs it was dark, and after he ascended in the lift Dolly raised a curtain and looked out through opaque lace at the houses over the way. She heard the lift machinery stop, and with the notion of teasing him pressed the button that brought it down. Then on what was more than an impulse she got into it and sent it up to what she guessed was his floor.

"Anson," she called, laughing a little.

"Just a minute," he answered from his bedroom . . . then after a brief delay: "Now you can come in."

He had changed and was buttoning his vest.

"This is my room," he said lightly. "How do you like it?"

She caught sight of Paula's picture on the wall and stared at it in fascination, just as Paula had stared at the pictures of Anson's childish sweethearts five years before. She knew something about Paula—sometimes she tortured herself with fragments of the story.

Suddenly she came close to Anson, raising her arms. They embraced. Outside the area window a soft artificial twilight already hovered, though the sun was still bright on a back roof across the way. In half an hour the room would be quite dark. The uncalculated opportunity overwhelmed them, made them both breathless, and they clung more closely. It was imminent, inevitable. Still holding one another, they raised their heads—their eyes fell together upon Paula's picture, staring down at them from the wall.

Suddenly Anson dropped his arms, and sitting down at his desk tried the drawer with a bunch of keys.

"Like a drink?" he asked in a gruff voice.

"No, Anson."

He poured himself half a tumbler of whiskey, swallowed it, and then opened the door into the hall.

"Come on," he said.

Dolly hesitated.

"Anson—I'm going to the country with you tonight, after all. You understand that, don't you?"

"Of course," he answered brusquely.

In Dolly's car they rode on to Long Island, closer in their emotions than they had ever been before. They knew what would happen—not with Paula's face to remind them that something was lacking, but when they were alone in the still, hot Long Island night they did not care.

The estate in Port Washington where they were to spend the weekend belonged to a cousin of Anson's who had married a Montana copper operator. An interminable drive began at the lodge and twisted under imported poplar saplings toward a huge, pink Spanish house. Anson had often visited there before.

After dinner they danced at the Linx Club. About midnight Anson assured himself that his cousins would not leave before two—then he explained that Dolly was tired; he would take her home and return to the dance later. Trembling a little with excitement, they got into a borrowed car together and drove to Port Washington. As they reached the lodge he stopped and spoke to the night-watchman.

"When are you making a round, Carl?"

"Right away."

"Then you'll be here till everybody's in?"

"Yes, sir."

"All right. Listen: if any automobile, no matter whose it is, turns in at this gate, I want you to phone the house immediately." He put a five-dollar bill into Carl's hand. "Is that clear?"

"Yes, Mr. Anson." Being of the Old World, he neither winked nor smiled. Yet Dolly sat with her face turned slightly away.

Anson had a key. Once inside he poured a drink for both of them—Dolly left hers untouched—then he ascertained definitely the location of the phone, and found that it was within easy hearing distance of their rooms, both of which were on the first floor.

Five minutes later he knocked at the door of Dolly's room.

"Anson?" He went in, closing the door behind him. She was in bed, leaning up anxiously with elbows on the pillow; sitting beside her he took her in his arms.

"Anson, darling."

He didn't answer.

"Anson. . . . Anson! I love you. . . . Say you love me. Say it now—can't you say it now? Even if you don't mean it?"

He did not listen. Over her head he perceived that the picture of Paula was hanging here upon this wall.

He got up and went close to it. The frame gleamed faintly with thrice-reflected moonlight—within was a blurred shadow of a face that he saw he did not know. Almost sobbing, he turned around and stared with abomination at the little figure on the bed.

"This is all foolishness," he said thickly. "I don't know what I was thinking about. I don't love you and you'd better wait for somebody that loves you. I don't love you a bit, can't you understand?"

His voice broke, and he went hurriedly out. Back in the salon he was pouring himself a drink with uneasy fingers, when the front door opened suddenly, and his cousin came in.

"Why, Anson, I hear Dolly's sick," she began solicitously. "I hear she's sick. . . ."

"It was nothing," he interrupted, raising his voice so that it would carry into Dolly's room. "She was a little tired. She went to bed."

For a long time afterward Anson believed that a protective God sometimes interfered in human affairs. But Dolly Karger, lying awake and staring at the ceiling, never again believed in anything at all.

VI

When Dolly married during the following autumn, Anson was in London on business. Like Paula's marriage, it was sudden, but it affected him in a different way. At first he felt that it was funny, and had an inclination to laugh when he thought of it. Later it depressed him—it made him feel old.

There was something repetitive about it—why, Paula and Dolly had belonged to different generations. He had a foretaste of the sensation of a man of forty who hears that the daughter of an old flame has married. He wired congratulations and, as was not the case with Paula, they were sincere—he had never really hoped that Paula would be happy.

When he returned to New York, he was made a partner in the firm, and, as his responsibilities increased, he had less time on his hands. The refusal of a life-insurance company to issue him a policy made such an impression on him that he stopped drinking for a year, and claimed that he felt better physically, though I think he missed the convivial recounting of those Celliniesque adventures[2] which, in his early twenties, had played such a part in his life. But he never abandoned the Yale Club. He was a figure there, a personality, and the tendency of his class, who were now seven years out of college, to drift away to more sober haunts was checked by his presence.

His day was never too full nor his mind too weary to give any sort of aid to any one who asked it. What had been done at first through pride and superiority had become a habit and a passion. And there was always something—a younger brother in trouble at New Haven, a quarrel to be patched up between a friend and his wife, a position to be found for this man, an investment for that. But his specialty was the solving of problems for young married people. Young married people fascinated him and their apartments were almost sacred to him—he knew the story of their love-affair, advised them where to live and how, and remembered their babies' names. Toward young wives his attitude was circumspect: he never abused the trust which their husbands—strangely enough in view of his unconcealed irregularities—invariably reposed in him.

He came to take a vicarious pleasure in happy marriages, and to be inspired to an almost equally pleasant melancholy by those that went astray. Not a season passed that he did not witness the collapse of an affair that perhaps he himself had fathered. When Paula was divorced and almost immediately remarried to another Bostonian, he talked about her to me all one afternoon. He would never love any one as he had loved Paula, but he insisted that he no longer cared.

"I'll never marry," he came to say; "I've seen too much of it, and I know a happy marriage is a very rare thing. Besides, I'm too old."

But he did believe in marriage. Like all men who spring from a happy and successful marriage, he believed in it passionately—nothing he had seen would change his belief, his cynicism dissolved upon it like air. But he did really believe he was too old. At twenty-eight he began to accept with equanimity the prospect of marrying without romantic love; he resolutely chose a New York girl of his own class, pretty, intelligent, congenial, above reproach—and set about falling in love with her. The things he had said to Paula with sincerity, to other girls with grace, he could no longer say at all without smiling, or with the force necessary to convince.

"When I'm forty," he told his friends, "I'll be ripe. I'll fall for some chorus girl like the rest."

Nevertheless, he persisted in his attempt. His mother wanted to see him married, and he could now well afford it—he had a seat on the Stock Exchange, and his earned income came to twenty-five thousand a year. The idea was agreeable: when his friends

---

[2] I.e., love affairs like those of Benvenuto Cellini (1500–1571), Italian sculptor and legendary lover.

—he spent most of his time with the set he and Dolly had evolved—closed themselves in behind domestic doors at night, he no longer rejoiced in his freedom. He even wondered if he should have married Dolly. Not even Paula had loved him more, and he was learning the rarity, in a single life, of encountering true emotion.

Just as this mood began to creep over him a disquieting story reached his ear. His Aunt Edna, a woman just this side of forty, was carrying on an open intrigue with a dissolute, hard-drinking young man named Cary Sloane. Every one knew of it except Anson's Uncle Robert, who for fifteen years had talked long in clubs and taken his wife for granted.

Anson heard the story again and again with increasing annoyance. Something of his old feeling for his uncle came back to him, a feeling that was more than personal, a reversion toward that family solidarity on which he had based his pride. His intuition singled out the essential point of the affair, which was that his uncle shouldn't be hurt. It was his first experiment in unsolicited meddling, but with his knowledge of Edna's character he felt that he could handle the matter better than a district judge or his uncle.

His uncle was in Hot Springs. Anson traced down the sources of the scandal so that there should be no possibility of mistake and then he called Edna and asked her to lunch with him at the Plaza next day. Something in his tone must have frightened her, for she was reluctant, but he insisted, putting off the date until she had no excuse for refusing.

She met him at the appointed time in the Plaza lobby, a lovely, faded, gray-eyed blonde in a coat of Russian sable. Five great rings, cold with diamonds and emeralds, sparkled on her slender hands. It occurred to Anson that it was his father's intelligence and not his uncle's that had earned the fur and the stones, the rich brilliance that buoyed up her passing beauty.

Though Edna scented his hostility, she was unprepared for the directness of his approach.

"Edna, I'm astonished at the way you've been acting," he said in a strong, frank voice. "At first I couldn't believe it."

"Believe what?" she demanded sharply.

"You needn't pretend with me, Edna. I'm talking about Cary Sloane. Aside from any other consideration, I didn't think you could treat Uncle Robert—"

"Now look here, Anson—" she began angrily, but his peremptory voice broke through hers:

"—and your children in such a way. You've been married eighteen years, and you're old enough to know better."

"You can't talk to me like that! You—"

"Yes, I can. Uncle Robert has always been my best friend." He was tremendously moved. He felt a real distress about his uncle, about his three young cousins.

Edna stood up, leaving her crab-flake cocktail untasted.

"This is the silliest thing—"

"Very well, if you won't listen to me I'll go to Uncle Robert and tell him the whole story—he's bound to hear it sooner or later. And afterward I'll go to old Moses Sloane."

Edna faltered back into her chair.

"Don't talk so loud," she begged him. Her eyes blurred with tears. "You have no idea how your voice carries. You might have chosen a less public place to make all these crazy accusations."

He didn't answer.

"Oh, you never liked me, I know," she went on. "You're just taking advantage of some silly gossip to try and break up the only interesting friendship I've ever had. What did I ever do to make you hate me so?"

Still Anson waited. There would be the appeal to his chivalry, then to his pity, finally to his superior sophistication—when he had shouldered his way through all these there would be the admissions, and he could come to grips with her. By being silent, by being impervious, by returning constantly to his main weapon, which was his own true emotion, he bullied her into frantic despair as the luncheon hour slipped away. At two o'clock she took out a mirror and a handkerchief, shined away the marks of her tears and powdered the slight hollows where they had lain. She had agreed to meet him at her own house at five.

When he arrived she was stretched on a *chaise-longue* which was covered with cretonne for the summer, and the tears he had called up at luncheon seemed still to be standing in her eyes. Then he was aware of Cary Sloane's dark anxious presence upon the cold hearth.

"What's this idea of yours?" broke out Sloane immediately. "I understand you invited Edna to lunch and then threatened her on the basis of some cheap scandal."

Anson sat down.

"I have no reason to think it's only scandal."

"I hear you're going to take it to Robert Hunter, and to my father."

Anson nodded.

"Either you break it off—or I will," he said.

"What God damned business is it of yours, Hunter?"

"Don't lose your temper, Cary," said Edna nervously. "It's only a question of showing him how absurd—"

"For one thing, it's my name that's being handed around," interrupted Anson. "That's all that concerns you, Cary."

"Edna isn't a member of your family."

"She most certainly is!" His anger mounted. "Why—she owes this house and the rings on her fingers to my father's brains. When Uncle Robert married her she didn't have a penny."

They all looked at the rings as if they had a significant bearing on the situation. Edna made a gesture to take them from her hand.

"I guess they're not the only rings in the world," said Sloane.

"Oh, this is absurd," cried Edna. "Anson, will you listen to me? I've found out how the silly story started. It was a maid I discharged who went right to the Chilicheffs—all these Russians pump things out of their servants and then put a false meaning on them." She brought down her fist angrily on the table: "And after Robert lent them the limousine for a whole month when we were South last winter—"

"Do you see?" demanded Sloane eagerly. "This maid got hold of the wrong end of the thing. She knew that Edna and I were friends, and she carried it to the Chilicheffs. In Russia they assume that if a man and a woman—"

He enlarged the theme to a disquisition upon social relations in the Caucasus.

"If that's the case it better be explained to Uncle Robert," said Anson dryly, "so that when the rumors do reach him he'll know they're not true."

Adopting the method he had followed with Edna at luncheon he let them explain it all away. He knew that they were guilty and that presently they would cross the line from explanation into justification and convict themselves more definitely than he could ever do. By seven they had taken the desperate step of telling him the truth —Robert Hunter's neglect, Edna's empty life, the casual dalliance that had flamed up into passion—but like so many true stories it had the misfortune of being old, and its enfeebled body beat helplessly against the armor of Anson's will. The threat to go to Sloane's father sealed their helplessness, for the latter, a retired cotton broker out of Alabama, was a notorious fundamentalist who controlled his son by a rigid allowance and the promise that at his next vagary the allowance would stop forever.

They dined at a small French restaurant, and the discussion continued—at one time Sloane resorted to physical threats, a little later they were both imploring him to give them time. But Anson was obdurate. He saw that Edna was breaking up, and that her spirit must not be refreshed by any renewal of their passion.

At two o'clock in a small night-club on 53d Street, Edna's nerves suddenly collapsed, and she cried to go home. Sloane had been drinking heavily all evening, and he was faintly maudlin, leaning on the table and weeping a little with his face in his hands. Quickly Anson gave them his terms. Sloane was to leave town for six months, and he must be gone within forty-eight hours. When he returned there was to be no resumption of the affair, but at the end of a year Edna might, if she wished, tell Robert Hunter that she wanted a divorce and go about it in the usual way.

He paused, gaining confidence from their faces for his final word.

"Or there's another thing you can do," he said slowly, "if Edna wants to leave her children, there's nothing I can do to prevent your running off together."

"I want to go home!" cried Edna again. "Oh, haven't you done enough to us for one day?"

Outside it was dark, save for a blurred glow from Sixth Avenue down the street. In that light those two who had been lovers looked for the last time into each other's tragic faces, realizing that between them there was not enough youth and strength to avert their eternal parting. Sloane walked suddenly off down the street and Anson tapped a dozing taxi-driver on the arm.

It was almost four; there was a patient flow of cleaning water along the ghostly pavement of Fifth Avenue, and the shadows of two night women flitted over the dark façade of St. Thomas's church. Then the desolate shrubbery of Central Park where Anson had often played as a child, and the mounting numbers, significant as names, of the marching streets. This was his city, he thought, where his name had flourished through five generations. No change could alter the permanence of its place here, for change itself was the essential substratum by which he and those of his name identified themselves with the spirit of New York. Resourcefulness and a powerful will—for his threats in weaker hands would have been less than nothing—had beaten the gathering dust from his uncle's name, from the name of his family, from even this shivering figure that sat beside him in the car.

Cary Sloane's body was found next morning on the lower shelf of a pillar of Queensboro Bridge. In the darkness and in his excitement he had thought that it was the water flowing black beneath him, but in less than a second it made no possible difference—unless he had planned to think one last thought of Edna, and call out her name as he struggled feebly in the water.

VII

Anson never blamed himself for his part in this affair—the situation which brought it about had not been of his making. But the just suffer with the unjust, and he found that his oldest and somehow his most precious friendship was over. He never knew what distorted story Edna told, but he was welcome in his uncle's house no longer.

Just before Christmas Mrs. Hunter retired to a select Episcopal heaven, and Anson became the responsible head of his family. An unmarried aunt who had lived with them for years ran the house, and attempted with helpless inefficiency to chaperone the younger girls. All the children were less self-reliant than Anson, more conventional both in their virtues and in their shortcomings. Mrs. Hunter's death had postponed the début of one daughter and the wedding of another. Also it had taken something deeply material from all of them, for with her passing the quiet, expensive superiority of the Hunters came to an end.

For one thing, the estate, considerably diminished by two inheritance taxes and soon to be divided among six children, was not a notable fortune any more. Anson saw a tendency in his youngest sisters to speak rather respectfully of families that hadn't "existed" twenty years ago. His own feeling of precedence was not echoed in them—sometimes they were conventionally snobbish, that was all. For another thing, this was the last summer they would spend on the Connecticut estate; the clamor against it was too loud: "Who wants to waste the best months of the year shut up in that dead old town?" Reluctantly he yielded—the house would go into the market in the fall, and next summer they would rent a smaller place in Westchester County. It was a step down from the expensive simplicity of his father's idea, and, while he sympathized with the revolt, it also annoyed him; during his mother's lifetime he had gone up there at least every other week-end—even in the gayest summers.

Yet he himself was part of this change, and his strong instinct for life had turned him in his twenties from the hollow obsequies of that abortive leisure class. He did not see this clearly—he still felt that there was a norm, a standard of society. But there was no norm, it was doubtful if there ever had been a true norm in New York. The few who still paid and fought to enter a particular set succeeded only to find that as a society it scarcely functioned—or, what was more alarming, that the Bohemia from which they fled sat above them at table.

At twenty-nine Anson's chief concern was his own growing loneliness. He was sure now that he would never marry. The number of weddings at which he had officiated as best man or usher was past all counting—there was a drawer at home that bulged with the official neckties of this or that wedding-party, neckties standing for romances that had not endured a year, for couples who had passed completely from his life. Scarf-pins, gold pencils, cuff-buttons, presents from a generation of grooms had passed through his jewel-box and been lost—and with every ceremony he was less and less able to imagine himself in the groom's place. Under his hearty good-will toward all those marriages there was despair about his own.

And as he neared thirty he became not a little depressed at the inroads that marriage, especially lately, had made upon his friendships. Groups of people had a disconcerting tendency to dissolve and disappear. The men from his own college—and it was upon them he had expended the most time and affection—were the most elusive of all. Most of them were drawn deep into domesticity, two were dead, one lived abroad, one was in Hollywood writing continuities for pictures that Anson went faithfully to see.

Most of them, however, were permanent commuters with an intricate family life centring around some suburban country club, and it was from these that he felt his estrangement most keenly.

In the early days of their married life they had all needed him; he gave them advice about their slim finances, he exorcised their doubts about the advisability of bringing a baby into two rooms and a bath, especially he stood for the great world outside. But now their financial troubles were in the past and the fearfully expected child had evolved into an absorbing family. They were always glad to see old Anson, but they dressed up for him and tried to impress him with their present importance, and kept their troubles to themselves. They needed him no longer.

A few weeks before his thirtieth birthday the last of his early and intimate friends was married. Anson acted in his usual rôle of best man, gave his usual silver tea-service, and went down to the usual *Homeric* [3] to say good-by. It was a hot Friday afternoon in May, and as he walked from the pier he realized that Saturday closing had begun and he was free until Monday morning.

"Go where?" he asked himself.

The Yale Club, of course; bridge until dinner, then four or five raw cocktails in somebody's room and a pleasant confused evening. He regretted that this afternoon's groom wouldn't be along—they had always been able to cram so much into such nights: they knew how to attach women and how to get rid of them, how much consideration any girl deserved from their intelligent hedonism. A party was an adjusted thing—you took certain girls to certain places and spent just so much on their amusement; you drank a little, not much more than you ought to drink, and at a certain time in the morning you stood up and said you were going home. You avoided college boys, sponges, future engagements, fights, sentiment, and indiscretions. That was the way it was done. All the rest was dissipation.

In the morning you were never violently sorry—you made no resolutions, but if you had overdone it and your heart was slightly out of order, you went on the wagon for a few days without saying anything about it, and waited until an accumulation of nervous boredom projected you into another party.

The lobby of the Yale Club was unpopulated. In the bar three very young alumni looked up at him, momentarily and without curiosity.

"Hello, there, Oscar," he said to the bartender. "Mr. Cahill been around this afternoon?"

"Mr. Cahill's gone to New Haven."

"Oh . . . that so?"

"Gone to the ball game. Lot of men gone up."

Anson looked once again into the lobby, considered for a moment, and then walked out and over to Fifth Avenue. From the broad window of one of his clubs—one that

[3] An ocean liner; a cruise was a popular honeymoon trip.

he had scarcely visited in five years—a gray man with watery eyes stared down at him. Anson looked quickly away—that figure sitting in vacant resignation, in supercilious solitude, depressed him. He stopped and, retracing his steps, started over 47th Street toward Teak Warden's apartment. Teak and his wife had once been his most familiar friends—it was a household where he and Dolly Karger had been used to go in the days of their affair. But Teak had taken to drink, and his wife had remarked publicly that Anson was a bad influence on him. The remark reached Anson in an exaggerated form—when it was finally cleared up, the delicate spell of intimacy was broken, never to be renewed.

"Is Mr. Warden at home?" he inquired.

"They've gone to the country."

The fact unexpectedly cut at him. They were gone to the country and he hadn't known. Two years before he would have known the date, the hour, come up at the last moment for a final drink, and planned his first visit to them. Now they had gone without a word.

Anson looked at his watch and considered a week-end with his family, but the only train was a local that would jolt through the aggressive heat for three hours. And to-morrow in the country, and Sunday—he was in no mood for porch-bridge with polite undergraduates, and dancing after dinner at a rural roadhouse, a diminutive of gaiety which his father had estimated too well.

"Oh, no," he said to himself. . . . "No."

He was a dignified, impressive young man, rather stout now, but otherwise unmarked by dissipation. He could have been cast for a pillar of something—at times you were sure it was not society, at others nothing else—for the law, for the church. He stood for a few minutes motionless on the sidewalk in front of a 47th Street apartment-house; for almost the first time in his life he had nothing whatever to do.

Then he began to walk briskly up Fifth Avenue, as if he had just been reminded of an important engagement there. The necessity of dissimulation is one of the few characteristics that we share with dogs, and I think of Anson on that day as some well-bred specimen who had been disappointed at a familiar back door. He was going to see Nick, once a fashionable bartender in demand at all private dances, and now employed in cooling non-alcoholic champagne among the labyrinthine cellars of the Plaza Hotel.

"Nick," he said, "what's happened to everything?"

"Dead," Nick said.

"Make me a whiskey sour." Anson handed a pint bottle over the counter. "Nick, the girls are different; I had a little girl in Brooklyn and she got married last week without letting me know."

"That a fact? Ha-ha-ha," responded Nick diplomatically. "Slipped it over on you."

"Absolutely," said Anson. "And I was out with her the night before."

"Ha-ha-ha," said Nick, "ha-ha-ha!"

"Do you remember the wedding, Nick, in Hot Springs where I had the waiters and the musicians singing 'God save the King'?"

"Now where was that, Mr. Hunter?" Nick concentrated doubtfully. "Seems to me that was—"

"Next time they were back for more, and I began to wonder how much I'd paid them," continued Anson.

"—seems to me that was at Mr. Trenholm's wedding."

"Don't know him," said Anson decisively. He was offended that a strange name should intrude upon his reminiscences; Nick perceived this.

"Na—aw—" he admitted, "I ought to know that. It was one of *your* crowd—Brakins . . . Baker—"

"Bicker Baker," said Anson responsively. "They put me in a hearse after it was over and covered me up with flowers and drove me away."

"Ha-ha-ha," said Nick. "Ha-ha-ha."

Nick's simulation of the old family servant paled presently and Anson went up-stairs to the lobby. He looked around—his eyes met the glance of an unfamiliar clerk at the desk, then fell upon a flower from the morning's marriage hesitating in the mouth of a brass cuspidor. He went out and walked slowly toward the blood-red sun over Columbus Circle. Suddenly he turned around and, retracing his steps to the Plaza, immured himself in a telephone-booth.

Later he said that he tried to get me three times that afternoon, that he tried every one who might be in New York—men and girls he had not seen for years, an artist's model of his college days whose faded number was still in his address book—Central told him that even the exchange existed no longer. At length his quest roved into the country, and he held brief disappointing conversations with emphatic butlers and maids. So-and-so was out, riding, swimming, playing golf, sailed to Europe last week. Who shall I say phoned?

It was intolerable that he should pass the evening alone—the private reckonings which one plans for a moment of leisure lose every charm when the solitude is enforced. There were always women of a sort, but the ones he knew had temporarily vanished, and to pass a New York evening in the hired company of a stranger never occurred to him—he would have considered that that was something shameful and secret, the diversion of a travelling salesman in a strange town.

Anson paid the telephone bill—the girl tried unsuccessfully to joke with him about its size—and for the second time that afternoon started to leave the Plaza and go he knew not where. Near the revolving door the figure of a woman, obviously with child, stood sideways to the light—a sheer beige cape fluttered at her shoulders when the door turned and, each time, she looked impatiently toward it as if she were weary of waiting. At the first sight of her a strong nervous thrill of familiarity went over him, but not until he was within five feet of her did he realize that it was Paula.

"Why, Anson Hunter!"

His heart turned over.

"Why, Paula—"

"Why, this is wonderful. I can't believe it, *Anson!*"

She took both his hands, and he saw in the freedom of the gesture that the memory of him had lost poignancy to her. But not to him—he felt that old mood that she evoked in him stealing over his brain, that gentleness with which he had always met her optimism as if afraid to mar its surface.

"We're at Rye for the summer. Pete had to come East on business—you know of course I'm Mrs. Peter Hagerty now—so we brought the children and took a house. You've got to come out and see us."

"Can I?" he asked directly. "When?"

"When you like. Here's Pete." The revolving door functioned, giving up a fine tall man of thirty with a tanned face and a trim mustache. His immaculate fitness made a sharp contrast with Anson's increasing bulk, which was obvious under the faintly tight cut-away coat.

"You oughtn't to be standing," said Hagerty to his wife. "Let's sit down here." He indicated lobby chairs, but Paula hesitated.

"I've got to go right home," she said. "Anson, why don't you—why don't you come out and have dinner with us to-night? We're just getting settled, but if you can stand that—"

Hagerty confirmed the invitation cordially.

"Come out for the night."

Their car waited in front of the hotel, and Paula with a tired gesture sank back against silk cushions in the corner.

"There's so much I want to talk to you about," she said, "it seems hopeless."

"I want to hear about you."

"Well"—she smiled at Hagerty—"that would take a long time too. I have three children—by my first marriage. The oldest is five, then four, then three." She smiled again. "I didn't waste much time having them, did I?"

"Boys?"

"A boy and two girls. Then—oh, a lot of things happened, and I got a divorce in Paris a year ago and married Pete. That's all—except that I'm awfully happy."

In Rye they drove up to a large house near the Beach Club, from which there issued presently three dark, slim children who broke from an English governess and approached them with an esoteric cry. Abstractedly and with difficulty Paula took each one into her arms, a caress which they accepted stiffly, as they had evidently been told not to bump into Mummy. Even against their fresh faces Paula's skin showed scarcely any weariness—for all her physical languor she seemed younger than when he had last seen her at Palm Beach seven years ago.

At dinner she was preoccupied, and afterward, during the homage to the radio, she lay with closed eyes on the sofa, until Anson wondered if his presence at this time were not an intrusion. But at nine o'clock, when Hagerty rose and said pleasantly that he was going to leave them by themselves for a while, she began to talk slowly about herself and the past.

"My first baby," she said—"the one we call Darling, the biggest little girl—I wanted to die when I knew I was going to have her, because Lowell was like a stranger to me. It didn't seem as though she could be my own. I wrote you a letter and tore it up. Oh, you were *so* bad to me, Anson."

It was the dialogue again, rising and falling. Anson felt a sudden quickening of memory.

"Weren't you engaged once?" she asked—"a girl named Dolly something?"

"I wasn't ever engaged. I tried to be engaged, but I never loved anybody but you, Paula."

"Oh," she said. Then after a moment: "This baby is the first one I ever really wanted. You see, I'm in love now—at last."

He didn't answer, shocked at the treachery of her remembrance. She must have seen that the "at last" bruised him, for she continued:

"I was infatuated with you, Anson—you could make me do anything you liked. But we wouldn't have been happy. I'm not smart enough for you. I don't like things to be complicated like you do." She paused. "You'll never settle down," she said.

The phrase struck at him from behind—it was an accusation that of all accusations he had never merited.

"I could settle down if women were different," he said. "If I didn't understand so much about them, if women didn't spoil you for other women, if they had only a little pride. If I could go to sleep for a while and wake up into a home that was really mine—why, that's what I'm made for, Paula, that's what women have seen in me and liked in me. It's only that I can't get through the preliminaries any more."

Hagerty came in a little before eleven; after a whiskey Paula stood up and announced that she was going to bed. She went over and stood by her husband.

"Where did you go, dearest?" she demanded.

"I had a drink with Ed Saunders."

"I was worried. I thought maybe you'd run away."

She rested her head against his coat.

"He's sweet, isn't he, Anson?" she demanded.

"Absolutely," said Anson, laughing.

She raised her face to her husband.

"Well, I'm ready," she said. She turned to Anson: "Do you want to see our family gymnastic stunt?"

"Yes," he said in an interested voice.

"All right. Here we go!"

Hagerty picked her up easily in his arms.

"This is called the family acrobatic stunt," said Paula. "He carries me up-stairs. Isn't it sweet of him?"

"Yes," said Anson.

Hagerty bent his head slightly until his face touched Paula's.

"And I love him," she said. "I've just been telling you, haven't I, Anson?"

"Yes," he said.

"He's the dearest thing that ever lived in this world; aren't you, darling? . . . Well, good night. Here we go. Isn't he strong?"

"Yes," Anson said.

"You'll find a pair of Pete's pajamas laid out for you. Sweet dreams—see you at breakfast."

"Yes," Anson said.

VIII

The older members of the firm insisted that Anson should go abroad for the summer. He had scarcely had a vacation in seven years, they said. He was stale and needed a change. Anson resisted.

"If I go," he declared, "I won't come back any more."

"That's absurd, old man. You'll be back in three months with all this depression gone. Fit as ever."

"No." He shook his head stubbornly. "If I stop, I won't go back to work. If I stop, that means I've given up—I'm through."

"We'll take a chance on that. Stay six months if you like—we're not afraid you'll leave us. Why, you'd be miserable if you didn't work."

They arranged his passage for him. They liked Anson—every one liked Anson—and the change that had been coming over him cast a sort of pall over the office. The enthusiasm that had invariably signalled up business, the consideration toward his equals and his inferiors, the lift of his vital presence—within the past four months his intense nervousness had melted down these qualities into the fussy pessimism of a man of forty. On every transaction in which he was involved he acted as a drag and a strain.

"If I go I'll never come back," he said.

Three days before he sailed Paula Legendre Hagerty died in childbirth. I was with him a great deal then, for we were crossing together, but for the first time in our friendship he told me not a word of how he felt, nor did I see the slightest sign of emotion. His chief preoccupation was with the fact that he was thirty years old—he would turn the conversation to the point where he could remind you of it and then fall silent, as if he assumed that the statement would start a chain of thought sufficient to itself. Like his partners, I was amazed at the change in him, and I was glad when the *Paris* moved off into the wet space between the worlds, leaving his principality behind.

"How about a drink?" he suggested.

We walked into the bar with that defiant feeling that characterizes the day of departure and ordered four Martinis. After one cocktail a change came over him—he suddenly reached across and slapped my knee with the first joviality I had seen him exhibit for months.

"Did you see that girl in the red tam?" he demanded, "the one with the high color who had the two police dogs down to bid her good-by."

"She's pretty," I agreed.

"I looked her up in the purser's office and found out that she's alone. I'm going down to see the steward in a few minutes. We'll have dinner with her to-night."

After a while he left me, and within an hour he was walking up and down the deck with her, talking to her in his strong, clear voice. Her red tam was a bright spot of color against the steel-green sea, and from time to time she looked up with a flashing bob of her head, and smiled with amusement and interest, and anticipation. At dinner we had champagne, and were very joyous—afterward Anson ran the pool with infectious gusto, and several people who had seen me with him asked me his name. He and the girl were talking and laughing together on a lounge in the bar when I went to bed.

I saw less of him on the trip than I had hoped. He wanted to arrange a foursome, but there was no one available, so I saw him only at meals. Sometimes, though, he would have a cocktail in the bar, and he told me about the girl in the red tam, and his adventures with her, making them all bizarre and amusing, as he had a way of doing, and I was glad that he was himself again, or at least the self that I knew, and with which I felt at home. I don't think he was ever happy unless some one was in love with him, responding to him like filings to a magnet, helping him to explain himself, promising him something. What it was I do not know. Perhaps they promised that there would always be women in the world who would spend their brightest, freshest, rarest hours to nurse and protect that superiority he cherished in his heart.

1926

William Faulkner
1897–1962

Eudora Welty said that to be a writer in Mississippi after Faulkner was like living next door to a mountain. Brilliant and erratic (even after he won the Nobel Prize in 1949, he was still capable of producing work his editors hesitated to publish), Faulkner is today generally regarded as the greatest twentieth-century American writer of fiction, and his work is routinely ranked with the literary achievements of Hawthorne, Melville, Twain, and James. Although Faulkner's novels and tales have been frequently described as difficult and obscure, his explanation of them was simple: He wrote, he said in his Nobel Prize acceptance speech, of "the problems of the human heart in conflict with itself which alone can make good writing because only that is worth writing about, worth the agony and the sweat."

Born on September 25, 1897, in New Albany, Mississippi, Faulkner soon moved with his family to Oxford, Mississippi, where he lived most of his life. He grew up with legends about his ancestors, most notably his great-grandfather, William Clark Falkner, a lawyer and a Civil War colonel prominent in the region for his colorful exploits, his political influence and wealth, his keen sense of honor, and his popular romantic novel, *The White Rose of Memphis* (1881). "When I was a little boy," Faulkner said, "there'd be sometimes twenty or thirty people in the house, mostly relatives, . . . some maybe coming for overnight and staying on for months, swapping stories about the family and about the past, while I sat in a corner and listened. That's where I got my books." The Falkner family had made its money in railroad and banking enterprises during the post–Civil War era, but after the family railroad was sold in 1902, Faulkner's father ran a livery stable, then a hardware store, and eventually became business manager of the University of Mississippi.

A good student in his early years, Faulkner soon became restive in school and was often truant. Though he liked to read, draw, and write poetry, he attended classes during his last two years of high school mainly to play football. In 1915 he dropped out of school for good, planning to work in his grandfather's bank. For two years he frequented the University of Mississippi campus, writing poems and submitting his drawings to student publications. Distressed when his childhood sweetheart decided to marry another man, Faulkner tried to enlist in the U.S. Army, only to be told that he was too small (he was five feet five and a half inches tall). In the spring of 1918 he moved to New Haven, Connecticut, to be close to an Oxford friend, Phil Stone, who was attending Yale Law School and who had already begun to encourage and promote Faulkner's literary talents. Later that year Faulkner changed the spelling of his name from Falkner to Faulkner and enlisted with the Royal Air Force in Canada. After spending several months in Toronto, he returned to Oxford dressed in an officer's uniform and armed with dramatic tales of his adventures in the skies over France.

As a veteran, Faulkner was allowed in the fall of 1919 to enroll as a special student at the University of Mississippi, where he studied French and wrote for

University periodicals. He had a poem accepted by *The New Republic,* and his first published short story, an aviation tale, appeared in the college newspaper. But Faulkner soon found college little more to his liking than high school had been, and after a year and a half he again dropped out. He continued to read, write, and sketch while working for brief intervals as a salesman in a New York City bookstore and as a carpenter, a house painter, and a university postmaster in Oxford, earning for himself a reputation as a ne'er-do-well. "Count No Count," the people of Oxford called him.

During his early years as a writer, Faulkner thought of himself as a poet (he would later describe himself as a "failed poet"). His reading continued to range widely, from French and English poetry of the nineteenth and early twentieth centuries to Cervantes and Shakespeare, Fielding and Dickens, Hawthorne and Melville, Balzac, Conrad, and Joyce. But most of his early writing is poetry, much of it written in the pastoral mode and all of it full not only of echoes but of borrowed words and borrowed sentiments, taken especially from the Romantics, particularly John Keats; from the Victorians, particularly Alfred Lord Tennyson; from the aesthetes and decadents of the late nineteenth and early twentieth centuries, particularly Algernon Charles Swinburne and A. E. Housman; and from his own contemporaries, particularly T. S. Eliot. In 1924, with the energetic help of his friend Phil Stone, who acted from time to time as critic, editor, agent, and publicist, Faulkner published his first book, a slim volume of poetry called—in echo of Hawthorne—*The Marble Faun.* Stone also wrote the book's preface, promoting Faulkner as a promising local celebrity, "a man steeped in the soil of his native land, a Southerner by every instinct, and, more than that, a Mississippian."

The first major turning point in Faulkner's career came in the fall of 1924, when he visited New Orleans and met Sherwood Anderson, whose writing he admired; at the time, Faulkner thought Conrad's *Heart of Darkness* and Anderson's "I'm a Fool" the two best stories he had ever read. The following year, he spent several months with Anderson, discussing books, spinning yarns, and drinking, while he contributed to the new literary magazine, *The Double Dealer,* and wrote sketches of New Orleans for the *Times-Picayune* (these were collected in 1968 as *New Orleans Sketches*). With Anderson's encouragement, Faulkner was turning increasingly to prose. While in New Orleans he finished *Soldiers' Pay* (1926), a novel about the homecoming of a badly scarred and dying air force veteran. In the summer of 1925 Faulkner traveled to Europe, visiting Italy, Switzerland, France, and England. Upon his return, he alternated between Oxford and New Orleans.

In 1937 Faulkner brought out his second novel, *Mosquitoes,* a story about a sophisticated New Orleans literary crowd on a yachting expedition that is written in the "conversational" mode Aldous Huxley had made fashionable in the 1920s. It is, however, in the work that followed *Mosquitoes,* the work set in his mythical Mississippi county, Yoknapatawpha, that Faulkner established the special themes—having to do with the complexities of sexual, familial, social, and racial identities and the force and burden of the past—that would eventually make him famous. In writing a book originally called *Flags in the Dust* but published as *Sartoris* (1929), Faulkner made the discovery that marked the second turning point in his career: "I discovered that my own little postage stamp of native soil was worth writing about and that I would never live long enough to exhaust it, and that by sublimating the actual into the apocryphal I might have complete liberty to use whatever talent I might have to its absolute top. I opened up a gold mine of other people, so I created a cosmos of my own." In *Sartoris,* a novel about the history of several generations of a distinguished Mississippi family, modeled in part on his own family, Faulkner introduced many of the characters and themes he would work with in his fiction throughout his career.

In the best of the Yoknapatawpha fiction, Faulkner created works unequaled in America in this century. Of his twenty novels, fifteen are set in Yoknapatawpha County, a location based on Lafayette County in northern Mississippi. *The Sound and the Fury* (1929), one of the great twentieth-century novels, treats the economic and emotional deterioration of the Compson family in four magnificent chapters, each one dramatizing a different consciousness with a different conception of time and language. The famous opening chapter, for example, is narrated by Benjy Compson, a thirty-three-year-old idiot, as his mind alternates between sense impressions and memories. No less innovative in its narrative method is Faulkner's next novel, *As I Lay Dying* (1930), which he wrote while working the night shift in a University of Mississippi boiler room. The novel, told from the multiple perspectives of fifteen "interior monologues," moves between horror and comedy as it recounts the adventures of a poor white family's efforts to fulfill the mother's wish to have her body decently buried in her hometown. Plot summary can give no sense of Faulkner's stylistic achievement in these books and those that were to follow. Trying to capture the effect on the reader of Faulkner's narrative technique, Jean-Paul Sartre wrote:

> Faulkner's vision of the world can be compared to that of a man sitting in a convertible looking backward. At every moment shadows emerge on his right, and on his left flickering and quavering points of light, which become trees, men, and cars only when they are seen in perspective. The past here gains a surrealistic quality; its outline is hard, clear, and immutable. The indefinable and elusive present is helpless before it; it is full of holes through which past things, fixed, motionless, and silent, invade it.

In 1929 Faulkner finally succeeded in marrying his childhood sweetheart, not long after she had divorced her first husband and moved back to Oxford with her two children. The following year he bought and restored an antebellum mansion; he was also beginning to sell his fiction to national magazines. In 1931 he published *Sanctuary,* the tale of a collegiate "flapper," Temple Drake, who gets involved with criminals, drugs, and prostitution. Following *Sanctuary,* the first of his novels to enjoy any commercial success, Faulkner immediately wrote several of his finest novels. In 1932 he published *Light in August,* a story of sexual passion, racism, and religious fanaticism that traces the parallel destinies of two wandering orphans—a pregnant country girl, Lena Grove, who is searching for her fleeing lover, and a presumed murderer, Joe Christmas, who is eventually shot and castrated. In *Absalom, Absalom!* (1936), Faulkner explored the intricate family history of a poor white man, Thomas Sutpen, whose dream of founding a dynasty in Mississippi ends in the tragic ruin of almost everyone involved. In 1938 Faulkner collected seven stories concerning the Sartoris family in *The Unvanquished*. He also published two non-Yoknapatawpha books during this period: *Pylon* (1935), a novel that grew out of Faulkner's flying lessons in 1933 and that traces the adventures of barnstorming airplane pilots, and *Wild Palms* (1939), a novel with two stories arranged in alternating chapters—one the tale of two doomed lovers and the other the story of a convict caught in a flood.

In 1940 Faulkner completed *The Hamlet*, the story of a grasping and rising family of poor whites, the Snopeses, who are described as "just Snopes, like colonies of rats or termites." Faulkner later added two more episodic novels about the Snopes family, *The Town* (1957) and *The Mansion* (1959), the three books usually being referred to as the Snopes trilogy. In 1942 Faulkner completed *Go Down, Moses*, which explores the history of the racially mixed McCaslin family. Faulkner frequently incorporated stories into his novels. "Spotted Horses," for example, evolved into a section of *The Hamlet*. Many stories, furthermore, deal with characters who also appear in the novels. The Compsons of "That Evening Sun," for example, are the central characters in *The Sound and the Fury*.

Because of his complex narrative methods and his morally oriented subject matter, Faulkner did not greatly interest sociologically minded critics during the Depression years; by the mid-1940s, of all his books, only *Sanctuary* remained in print. During the late 1940s and the early 1950s, however, a reappraisal of Faulkner's achievement began, spurred in part by the publication in 1948 of *Intruder in the Dust*, a "detective" story about an elderly black man who refuses to "act like a nigger" and whose surprising innocence in a murder case leaves him a "tyrant over the whole county's white conscience." In 1950, shortly after the appearance of his *Collected Stories*, Faulkner learned that he had won the Nobel Prize for literature. In the early 1950s he made several trips to Europe and lectured frequently on college campuses. In 1954 he published *The Fable*, a dense allegory that takes place during the false armistice of 1918. The novel won both the National Book Award and the Pulitzer Prize. A month before his death from a heart attack in 1962, Faulkner published his last novel, *The Reivers*, a nostalgic and comic story based on events remembered from his childhood.

Although Faulkner's finest fiction deals with one imaginary county in Mississippi, it explores the whole of human experience, a fact recognized when Faulkner received the Nobel Prize. No American writer of his time has exerted wider influence. His fiction has been translated into many languages, and it has exercised a deep, varied influence on writers not only in Europe, especially France, but throughout South America and even Japan, where he traveled on a State Department trip in 1955. In his work readers have discovered a feeling for the American South—and for the South's history—that bespeaks a concern for human beings both in the modern world and in some larger, more inclusive realm as well. In addition, readers have recognized that Faulkner's work is strikingly innovative in structure, form, and style. In its rhetorical extravagance and its dry understatement, in its rich allusions and intricate design, readers have found themselves amply challenged and amply rewarded. "The study of Faulkner," said Robert Penn Warren, "is the most challenging single task in contemporary American literature for criticism to undertake. Here is a novelist who, in mass of work, in scope of material, in range of effect, in reportorial accuracy and symbolic subtlety, in philosophical weight can be put beside the masters of our own past literature."

Shortly before Faulkner died on July 6, 1962, he wrote in a letter to a friend that he had finally gotten "some perspective on all that I have done. I mean, the work apart from me, the work which I did, apart from what I am. . . . And now I realise for the first time what an amazing gift I had. . . . I don't know where it came from." Though Faulkner sometimes feared that words bore too little relation to life, his fiction demonstrates the power of words—their power to serve, as one of his characters puts it, as a "meager and fragile thread . . . by which the little surface corners and edges of men's secret and solitary lives may be joined for an instant now and then," and their power, as another of his characters puts it, when brought "into a happy conjunction" to "produce something that lives."

Further Reading:
C. Brooks, *William Faulkner: The Yoknapatawpha Country*, 1963.
J. Blotner, *Faulkner: A Biography*, 1974.
C. Brooks, *William Faulkner: Toward Yoknapatawpha and Beyond*, 1978.
D. Kartiganer, *The Fragile Thread: The Meaning of Form in Faulkner's Novels*, 1979.
D. Minter, *William Faulkner: His Life and Work*, 1980.
Faulkner: New Perspectives, ed. R. H. Brodhead, 1983.

Texts:
"Spotted Horses" from *Uncollected Stories of William Faulkner*, 1979.
"That Evening Sun" from *Collected Stories of William Faulkner*, 1950.

Spotted Horses

I

Yes, sir. Flem Snopes has filled that whole country full of spotted horses. You can hear folks running them all day and all night, whooping and hollering, and the horses running back and forth across them little wooden bridges ever now and then kind of like thunder. Here I was this morning pretty near half way to town, with the team ambling along and me setting in the buckboard about half asleep, when all of a sudden something come swurging up outen the bushes and jumped the road clean, without touching hoof to it. It flew right over my team, big as a billboard and flying through the air like a hawk. It taken me thirty minutes to stop my team and untangle the harness and the buckboard and hitch them up again.

That Flem Snopes. I be dog if he ain't a case, now. One morning about ten years ago, the boys was just getting settled down on Varner's porch for a little talk and tobacco, when here come Flem out from behind the counter, with his coat off and his hair all parted, like he might have been clerking for Varner for ten years already. Folks all knowed him; it was a big family of them about five miles down the bottom. That year, at least. Share-cropping. They never stayed on any place over a year. Then they would move on to another place, with the chap or maybe the twins of that year's litter. It was a regular nest of them. But Flem. The rest of them stayed tenant farmers, moving ever year, but here come Flem one day, walking out from behind Jody Varner's counter like he owned it. And he wasn't there but a year or two before folks knowed that, if him and Jody was both still in that store in ten years more, it would be Jody clerking for Flem Snopes. Why, that fellow could make a nickel where it wasn't but four cents to begin with. He skun me in two trades, myself, and the fellow that can do that, I just hope he'll get rich before I do; that's all.

All right. So here Flem was, clerking at Varner's, making a nickel here and there and not telling nobody about it. No, sir. Folks never knowed when Flem got the better of somebody lessen the fellow he beat told it. He'd just set there in the store-chair, chewing his tobacco and keeping his own business to hisself, until about a week later we'd find out it was somebody else's business he was keeping to hisself—provided the fellow he trimmed was mad enough to tell it. That's Flem.

We give him ten years to own ever thing Jody Varner had. But he never waited no ten years. I reckon you-all know that gal of Uncle Billy Varner's, the youngest one; Eula. Jody's sister. Ever Sunday ever yellow-wheeled buggy and curried riding horse in that country would be hitched to Bill Varner's fence, and the young bucks setting on the porch, swarming around Eula like bees around a honey pot. One of these here kind of big, soft-looking gals that could giggle richer than plowed new-ground. Wouldn't none of them leave before the others, and so they would set there on the porch until time to go home, with some of them with nine and ten miles to ride and then get up tomorrow and go back to the field. So they would all leave together and they would ride in a clump down to the creek ford and hitch them curried horses and yellow-wheeled buggies and get out and fight one another. Then they would get in the buggies again and go on home.

Well, one day about a year ago, one of them yellow-wheeled buggies and one of them curried saddle-horses quit this country. We heard they was heading for Texas. The next day Uncle Billy and Eula and Flem come in to town in Uncle Bill's surrey, and when they come back, Flem and Eula was married. And on the next day we heard that two more of them yellow-wheeled buggies had left the country. They mought have gone to Texas, too. It's a big place.

Anyway, about a month after the wedding, Flem and Eula went to Texas, too. They was gone pretty near a year. Then one day last month, Eula come back, with a baby. We figgured up, and we decided that it was as well-growed a three-months-old baby as we ever see. It can already pull up on a chair. I reckon Texas makes big men quick, being a big place. Anyway, if it keeps on like it started, it'll be chewing tobacco and voting time it's eight years old.

And so last Friday here come Flem himself. He was on a wagon with another fellow. The other fellow had one of these two-gallon hats and a ivory-handled pistol and a box of gingersnaps sticking out of his hind pocket, and tied to the tail-gate of the wagon was about two dozen of them Texas ponies, hitched to one another with barbed wire. They was colored like parrots and they was quiet as doves, and ere a one of them would kill you quick as a rattlesnake. Nere a one of them had two eyes the same color, and nere a one of them had ever see a bridle, I reckon; and when that Texas man got down offen the wagon and walked up to them to show how gentle they was, one of them cut his vest clean offen him, same as with a razor.

Flem had done already disappeared; he had went on to see his wife, I reckon, and to see if that ere baby had done gone on to the field to help Uncle Billy plow maybe. It was the Texas man that taken the horses on to Mrs. Littlejohn's lot. He had a little trouble at first, when they come to the gate, because they hadn't never see a fence before, and when he finally got them in and taken a pair of wire cutters and unhitched them and got them into the barn and poured some shell corn into the trough, they durn nigh tore down the barn. I reckon they thought that shell corn was bugs, maybe. So he left them in the lot and he announced that the auction would begin at sunup to-morrow.

That night we was setting on Mrs. Littlejohn's porch. You-all mind the moon was nigh full that night, and we could watch them spotted varmints swirling along the fence and back and forth across the lot same as minnows in a pond. And then now and then they would all kind of huddle up against the barn and rest themselves by biting and kicking one another. We would hear a squeal, and then a set of hoofs would go Bam! against the barn, like a pistol. It sounded just like a fellow with a pistol, in a nest of cattymounts, taking his time.

II

It wasn't ere a man knowed yet if Flem owned them things or not. They just knowed one thing: that they wasn't never going to know for sho if Flem did or not, or if maybe he didn't just get on that wagon at the edge of town, for the ride or not. Even Eck Snopes didn't know, Flem's own cousin. But wasn't nobody surprised at that. We knowed that Flem would skin Eck quick as he would ere a one of us.

They was there by sunup next morning, some of them come twelve and sixteen miles, with seed-money tied up in tobacco sacks in their overalls, standing along the fence, when the Texas man come out of Mrs. Littlejohn's after breakfast and clumb onto the gate post with that ere white pistol butt sticking outen his hind pocket. He taken a new box of gingersnaps outen his pocket and bit the end offen it like a cigar and spit out the paper, and said the auction was open. And still they was coming up in wagons and a horse- and mule-back and hitching the teams across the road and coming to the fence. Flem wasn't nowhere in sight.

But he couldn't get them started. He begun to work on Eck, because Eck holp him last night to get them into the barn and feed them that shell corn. Eck got out just in time. He come outen that barn like a chip on the crest of a busted dam of water, and clumb into the wagon just in time.

He was working on Eck when Henry Armstid come up in his wagon. Eck was saying he was skeered to bid on one of them, because he might get it, and the Texas man says, "Them ponies? Them little horses?" He clumb down offen the gate post and went toward the horses. They broke and run, and him following them, kind of chirping to them, with his hand out like he was fixing to catch a fly, until he got three or four of them cornered. Then he jumped into them, and then we couldn't see nothing for a while because of the dust. It was a big cloud of it, and them blare-eyed, spotted things swoaring outen it twenty foot to a jump, in forty directions without counting up. Then the dust settled and there they was, that Texas man and the horse. He had its head twisted clean around like a owl's head. Its legs was braced and it was trembling like a new bride and groaning like a saw mill, and him holding its head wrung clean around on its neck so it was snuffing sky. "Look it over," he says, with his heels dug too and that white pistol sticking outen his pocket and his neck swole up like a spreading adder's until you could just tell what he was saying, cussing the horse and talking to us all at once: "Look him over, the fiddleheaded son of fourteen fathers. Try him, buy him; you will get the best—" Then it was all dust again, and we couldn't see nothing but spotted hide and mane, and that ere Texas man's boot-heels like a couple of walnuts on two strings, and after a while that two-gallon hat come sailing out like a fat old hen crossing a fence.

When the dust settled again, he was just getting outen the far fence corner, brushing himself off. He come and got his hat and brushed it off and come and clumb onto the gate post again. He was breathing hard. He taken the gingersnap box outen his pocket and et one, breathing hard. The hammer-head horse was still running round and round the lot like a merry-go-round at a fair. That was when Henry Armstid come shoving up to the gate in them patched overalls and one of them dangle-armed shirts of hisn. Hadn't nobody noticed him until then. We was all watching the Texas man and the horses. Even Mrs. Littlejohn; she had done come out and built a fire under the wash-pot in her back yard, and she would stand at the fence a while and then go back into the house and come out again with a arm full of wash and stand at the fence again. Well, here come Henry shoving up, and then we see Mrs. Armstid right behind him, in that ere faded wrapper and sunbonnet and them tennis shoes. "Git on back to that wagon," Henry says.

"Henry," she says.

"Here, boys," the Texas man says; "make room for missus to git up and see. Come on, Henry," he says; "here's your chance to buy that saddle-horse missus has been wanting. What about ten dollars, Henry?"

"Henry," Mrs. Armstid says. She put her hand on Henry's arm. Henry knocked her hand down.

"Git on back to that wagon, like I told you," he says.

Mrs. Armstid never moved. She stood behind Henry, with her hands rolled into her dress, not looking at nothing. "He hain't no more despair than to buy one of them things," she says. "And us not five dollars ahead of the pore house, he hain't no more despair." It was the truth, too. They ain't never made more than a bare living offen that place of theirs, and them with four chaps and the very clothes they wears she earns by weaving by the firelight at night while Henry's asleep.

"Shut your mouth and git on back to that wagon," Henry says. "Do you want I taken a wagon stake to you here in the big road?"

Well, that Texas man taken one look at her. Then he begun on Eck again, like Henry wasn't even there. But Eck was skeered. "I can git me a snapping turtle or a water moccasin for nothing. I ain't going to buy none."

So the Texas man said he would give Eck a horse. "To start the auction, and because you holp me last night. If you'll start the bidding on the next horse," he says, "I'll give you that fiddle-head horse."

I wish you could have seen them, standing there with their seed-money in their pockets, watching that Texas man give Eck Snopes a live horse, all fixed to call him a fool if he taken it or not. Finally Eck says he'll take it. "Only I just starts the bidding," he says. "I don't have to buy the next one lessen I ain't overtopped." The Texas man said all right, and Eck bid a dollar on the next one, with Henry Armstid standing there with his mouth already open, watching Eck and the Texas man like a mad-dog or something. "A dollar," Eck says.

The Texas man looked at Eck. His mouth was already open too, like he had started to say something and what he was going to say had up and died on him. "A dollar?" he says. "One dollar? You mean, *one* dollar, Eck?"

"Durn it," Eck says; "two dollars, then."

Well, sir, I wish you could a seen that Texas man. He taken out that gingersnap box and held it up and looked into it, careful, like it might have been a diamond ring in it, or a spider. Then he throwed it away and wiped his face with a bandanna. "Well," he says. "Well. Two dollars. Two dollars. Is your pulse all right, Eck?" he says. "Do you have ager-sweats at night, maybe?" he says. "Well," he says, "I got to take it. But are you boys going to stand there and see Eck get two horses at a dollar a head?"

That done it. I be dog if he wasn't nigh as smart as Flem Snopes. He hadn't no more than got the words outen his mouth before here was Henry Armstid, waving his hand. "Three dollars," Henry says. Mrs. Armstid tried to hold him again. He knocked her hand off, shoving up to the gate post.

"Mister," Mrs. Armstid says, "we got chaps in the house and not corn to feed the stock. We got five dollars I earned my chaps a-weaving after dark, and him snoring in the bed. And he hain't no more despair."

"Henry bids three dollars," the Texas man says. "Raise him a dollar, Eck, and the horse is yours."

"Henry," Mrs. Armstid says.

"Raise him, Eck," the Texas man says.

"Four dollars," Eck says.

"Five dollars," Henry says, shaking his fist. He shoved up right under the gate post. Mrs. Armstid was looking at the Texas man too.

"Mister," she says, "if you take that five dollars I earned my chaps a-weaving for one of them things, it'll be a curse onto you and yourn during all the time of man."

But it wasn't no stopping Henry. He had shoved up, waving his fist at the Texas man. He opened it; the money was in nickels and quarters, and one dollar bill that looked like a cow's cud. "Five dollars," he says. "And the man that raises it'll have to beat my head off, or I'll beat hisn."

"All right," the Texas man says. "Five dollars is bid. But don't you shake your hand at me."

III

It taken till nigh sundown before the last one was sold. He got them hotted up once and the bidding got up to seven dollars and a quarter, but most of them went around three or four dollars, him setting on the gate post and picking the horses out one at a time by mouth-word, and Mrs. Littlejohn pumping up and down at the tub and stopping and coming to the fence for a while and going back to the tub again. She had done got done too, and the wash was hung on the line in the back yard, and we could smell supper cooking. Finally they was all sold; he swapped the last two and the wagon for a buckboard.

We was all kind of tired, but Henry Armstid looked more like a mad-dog than ever. When he bought, Mrs. Armstid had went back to the wagon, setting in it behind them two rabbit-sized, bone-pore mules, and the wagon itself looking like it would fall all to pieces soon as the mules moved. Henry hadn't even waited to pull it outen the road; it was still in the middle of the road and her setting in it, not looking at nothing, ever since this morning.

Henry was right up against the gate. He went up to the Texas man. "I bought a horse and I paid cash," Henry says. "And yet you expect me to stand around here until they are all sold before I can get my horse. I'm going to take my horse outen that lot."

The Texas man looked at Henry. He talked like he might have been asking for a cup of coffee at the table. "Take your horse," he says.

Then Henry quit looking at the Texas man. He begun to swallow, holding onto the gate. "Ain't you going to help me?" he says.

"It ain't my horse," the Texas man says.

Henry never looked at the Texas man again, he never looked at nobody. "Who'll help me catch my horse?" he says. Never nobody said nothing. "Bring the plowline," Henry says. Mrs. Armstid got outen the wagon and brought the plowline. The Texas man got down offen the post. The woman made to pass him, carrying the rope.

"Don't you go in there, missus," the Texas man says.

Henry opened the gate. He didn't look back. "Come on here," he says.

"Don't you go in there, missus," the Texas man says.

Mrs. Armstid wasn't looking at nobody, neither, with her hands across her middle, holding the rope. "I reckon I better," she says. Her and Henry went into the lot. The horses broke and run. Henry and Mrs. Armstid followed.

"Get him into the corner," Henry says. They got Henry's horse cornered finally, and Henry taken the rope, but Mrs. Armstid let the horse get out. They hemmed it up again, but Mrs. Armstid let it get out again, and Henry turned and hit her with the rope. "Why didn't you head him back?" Henry says. He hit her again. "Why didn't you?" It was about that time I looked around and see Flem Snopes standing there.

It was the Texas man that done something. He moved fast for a big man. He caught the rope before Henry could hit the third time, and Henry whirled and made like he would jump at the Texas man. But he never jumped. The Texas man went and taken Henry's arm and led him outen the lot. Mrs. Armstid come behind them and the Texas man taken some money outen his pocket and he give it into Mrs. Armstid's hand. "Get him into the wagon and take him on home," the Texas man says, like he might have been telling them he enjoyed his supper.

Then here come Flem. "What's that for, Buck?" Flem says.

"Thinks he bought one of them ponies," the Texas man says. "Get him on away, missus."

But Henry wouldn't go. "Give him back that money," he says. "I bought that horse and I aim to have him if I have to shoot him."

And there was Flem, standing there with his hands in his pockets, chewing, like he had just happened to be passing.

"You take your money and I take my horse," Henry says. "Give it back to him," he says to Mrs. Armstid.

"You don't own no horse of mine," the Texas man says. "Get him on home, missus."

Then Henry seen Flem. "You got something to do with these horses," he says. "I bought one. Here's the money for it." He taken the bill outen Mrs. Armstid's hand. He offered it to Flem. "I bought one. Ask him. Here. Here's the money," he says, giving the bill to Flem.

When Flem taken the money, the Texas man dropped the rope he had snatched outen Henry's hand. He had done sent Eck Snopes's boy up to the store for another box of gingersnaps, and he taken the box outen his pocket and looked into it. It was empty and he dropped it on the ground. "Mr. Snopes will have your money for you to-morrow," he says to Mrs. Armstid. "You can get it from him to-morrow. He don't own no horse. You get him into the wagon and get him on home." Mrs. Armstid went back to the wagon and got in. "Where's that ere buckboard I bought?" the Texas man says. It was after sundown then. And then Mrs. Littlejohn come out on the porch and rung the supper bell.

IV

I come on in and et supper. Mrs. Littlejohn would bring in a pan of bread or something, then she would go out to the porch a minute and come back and tell us. The Texas man had hitched his team to the buckboard he had swapped them last two horses for, and him and Flem had gone, and then she told that the rest of them that never had ropes had went back to the store with I. O. Snopes to get some ropes, and wasn't nobody at the gate but Henry Armstid, and Mrs. Armstid setting in the wagon in the road, and Eck Snopes and that boy of hisn. "I don't care how many of them fool men gets killed by them things," Mrs. Littlejohn says, "but I ain't going to let Eck Snopes take that boy into that lot again." So she went down to the gate, but she come back without the boy or Eck neither.

"It ain't no need to worry about that boy," I says. "He's charmed." He was right behind Eck last night when Eck went to help feed them. The whole drove of them jumped clean over that boy's head and never touched him. It was Eck that touched him. Eck snatched him into the wagon and taken a rope and frailed the tar outen him.

So I had done et and went to my room and was undressing, long as I had a long trip to make next day; I was trying to sell a machine to Mrs. Bundren up past Whiteleaf; when Henry Armstid opened that gate and went in by hisself. They couldn't make him wait for the balance of them to get back with their ropes. Eck Snopes said he tried to make Henry wait, but Henry wouldn't do it. Eck said Henry walked right up to them and that when they broke, they run clean over Henry like a hay-mow breaking down. Eck said he snatched that boy of hisn out of the way just in time and that them things went through that gate like a creek flood and into the wagons and teams hitched side the road, busting wagon tongues and snapping harness like it was fishing-line, with Mrs. Armstid still setting in their wagon in the middle of it like something carved outen wood. Then they scattered, wild horses and tame mules with pieces of harness and single trees dangling offen them, both ways up and down the road.

"There goes ourn, paw!" Eck says his boy said. "There it goes, into Mrs. Little-john's house." Eck says it run right up the steps and into the house like a boarder late for supper. I reckon so. Anyway, I was in my room, in my underclothes, with one sock on and one sock in my hand, leaning out the window when the commotion busted out, when I heard something run into the melodeon in the hall; it sounded like a railroad engine. Then the door to my room come sailing in like when you throw a tin bucket top into the wind and I looked over my shoulder and see something that looked like a fourteen-foot pinwheel a-blaring its eyes at me. It had to blare them fast, because I was already done jumped out the window.

I reckon it was anxious, too. I reckon it hadn't never seen barbed wire or shell corn before, but I know it hadn't never seen underclothes before, or maybe it was a sewing-machine agent it hadn't never seen. Anyway, it swirled and turned to run back up the hall and outen the house, when it met Eck Snopes and that boy just coming in, carrying a rope. It swirled again and run down the hall and out the back door just in time to meet Mrs. Littlejohn. She had just gathered up the clothes she had washed, and she was coming onto the back porch with a armful of washing in one hand and a scrubbing-board in the other, when the horse skidded up to her, trying to stop and swirl again. It never taken Mrs. Littlejohn no time a-tall.

"Git outen here, you son," she says. She hit it across the face with the scrubbing-board; that ere scrubbing-board split as neat as ere a axe could have done it, and when the horse swirled to run back up the hall, she hit it again with what was left of the scrubbing-board, not on the head this time. "And stay out," she says.

Eck and that boy was half-way down the hall by this time. I reckon that horse looked like a pinwheel to Eck too. "Git to hell outen here, Ad!" Eck says. Only there wasn't time. Eck dropped flat on his face, but the boy never moved. The boy was about a yard tall maybe, in overhalls just like Eck's; that horse swoared over his head without touching a hair. I saw that, because I was just coming back up the front steps, still carrying that ere sock and still in my underclothes, when the horse come onto the porch again. It taken one look at me and swirled again and run to the end of the porch and jumped the banisters and the lot fence like a hen-hawk and lit in the lot running and went out the gate again and jumped eight or ten upside-down wagons and went on down the road. It was a full moon then. Mrs. Armstid was still setting in the wagon like she had done been carved outen wood and left there and forgot.

That horse. It ain't never missed a lick. It was going about forty miles a hour when it come to the bridge over the creek. It would have had a clear road, but it so happened that Vernon Tull was already using the bridge when it got there. He was coming back from town; he hadn't heard about the auction; him and his wife and three daughters and Mrs. Tull's aunt, all setting in chairs in the wagon bed, and all asleep, including the mules. They waked up when the horse hit the bridge one time, but Tull said the first he knew was when the mules tried to turn the wagon around in the middle of the bridge and he seen that spotted varmint run right twixt the mules and run up the wagon tongue like a squirrel. He said he just had time to hit it across the face with his whip-stock, because about that time the mules turned the wagon around on that ere one-way bridge and that horse clumb across one of the mules and jumped down onto the bridge again and went on, with Vernon standing up in the wagon and kicking at it.

Tull said the mules turned in the harness and clumb back into the wagon too, with Tull trying to beat them out again, with the reins wrapped around his wrist. After that he says all he seen was overturned chairs and womenfolks' legs and white drawers shining in the moonlight, and his mules and that spotted horse going on up the road like a ghost.

The mules jerked Tull outen the wagon and drug him a spell on the bridge before the reins broke. They thought at first that he was dead, and while they was kneeling around him, picking the bridge splinters outen him, here come Eck and that boy, still carrying the rope. They was running and breathing a little hard. "Where'd he go?" Eck says.

V

I went back and got my pants and shirt and shoes on just in time to go and help get Henry Armstid outen the trash in the lot. I be dog if he didn't look like he was dead, with his head hanging back and his teeth showing in the moonlight, and a little rim of white under his eyelids. We could still hear them horses, here and there; hadn't none of them got more than four-five miles away yet, not knowing the country, I reckon. So we could hear them and folks yelling now and then: "Whooey. Head him!"

We toted Henry into Mrs. Littlejohn's. She was in the hall; she hadn't put down the armful of clothes. She taken one look at us, and she laid down the busted scrubbing-board and taken up the lamp and opened a empty door. "Bring him in here," she says.

We toted him in and laid him on the bed. Mrs. Littlejohn set the lamp on the dresser, still carrying the clothes. "I'll declare, you men," she says. Our shadows was way up the wall, tiptoeing too; we could hear ourselves breathing. "Better get his wife," Mrs. Littlejohn says. She went out, carrying the clothes.

"I reckon we had," Quick says. "Go get her, somebody."

"Whyn't you go?" Winterbottom says.

"Let Ernest git her," Durley says. "He lives neighbors with them."

Ernest went to fetch her. I be dog if Henry didn't look like he was dead. Mrs. Littlejohn come back, with a kettle and some towels. She went to work on Henry, and then Mrs. Armstid and Ernest come in. Mrs. Armstid come to the foot of the bed and stood there, with her hands rolled into her apron, watching what Mrs. Littlejohn was doing, I reckon.

"You men git outen the way," Mrs. Littlejohn says. "Git outside," she says. "See if you can't find something else to play with that will kill some more of you."

"Is he dead?" Winterbottom says.

"It ain't your fault if he ain't," Mrs. Littlejohn says. "Go tell Will Varner to come up here. I reckon a man ain't so different from a mule, come long come short. Except maybe a mule's got more sense."

We went to get Uncle Billy. It was a full moon. We could hear them, now and then, four mile away: "Whooey. Head him." The country was full of them, one on ever wooden bridge in the land, running across it like thunder: "Whooey. There he goes. Head him."

We hadn't got far before Henry begun to scream. I reckon Mrs. Littlejohn's water had brung him to; anyway, he wasn't dead. We went on to Uncle Billy's. The house was dark. We called to him, and after a while the window opened and Uncle Billy put his head out, peart as a peckerwood, listening. "Are they still trying to catch them durn rabbits?" he says.

He come down, with his britches on over his night-shirt and his suspenders dangling, carrying his horse-doctoring grip. "Yes, sir," he says, cocking his head like a woodpecker; "they're still a-trying."

We could hear Henry before we reached Mrs. Littlejohn's. He was going Ah-Ah-Ah. We stopped in the yard. Uncle Billy went on in. We could hear Henry. We stood in the yard, hearing them on the bridges, this-a-way and that: "Whooey. Whooey."

"Eck Snopes ought to caught hisn," Ernest says.

"Looks like he ought," Winterbottom said.

Henry was going Ah-Ah-Ah steady in the house; then he begun to scream. "Uncle Billy's started," Quick says. We looked into the hall. We could see the light where the door was. Then Mrs. Littlejohn come out.

"Will needs some help," she says. "You, Ernest. You'll do." Ernest went into the house.

"Hear them?" Quick said. "That one was on Four Mile bridge." We could hear them; it sounded like thunder a long way off; it didn't last long:

"Whooey."

We could hear Henry: "Ah-Ah-Ah-Ah-Ah."

"They are both started now," Winterbottom says. "Ernest too."

That was early in the night. Which was a good thing, because it taken a long night for folks to chase them things right and for Henry to lay there and holler, being as Uncle Billy never had none of this here chloryfoam to set Henry's leg with. So it was considerate in Flem to get them started early. And what do you reckon Flem's com-ment was?

That's right. Nothing. Because he wasn't there. Hadn't nobody see him since that Texas man left.

VI

That was Saturday night. I reckon Mrs. Armstid got home about daylight, to see about the chaps. I don't know where they thought her and Henry was. But lucky the oldest one was a gal, about twelve, big enough to take care of the little ones. Which she did for the next two days. Mrs. Armstid would nurse Henry all night and work in the kitchen for hern and Henry's keep, and in the afternoon she would drive home (it was about four miles) to see to the chaps. She would cook up a pot of victuals and leave it on the stove, and the gal would bar the house and keep the little ones quiet. I would hear Mrs. Littlejohn and Mrs. Armstid talking in the kitchen. "How are the chaps making out?" Mrs. Littlejohn says.

"All right," Mrs. Armstid says.

"Don't they git skeered at night?" Mrs. Littlejohn says.

"Ina May bars the door when I leave," Mrs. Armstid says. "She's got the axe in bed with her. I reckon she can make out."

I reckon they did. And I reckon Mrs. Armstid was waiting for Flem to come back to town; hadn't nobody seen him until this morning; to get her money the Texas man said Flem was keeping for her. Sho. I reckon she was.

Anyway, I heard Mrs. Armstid and Mrs. Littlejohn talking in the kitchen this morning while I was eating breakfast. Mrs. Littlejohn had just told Mrs. Armstid that Flem was in town. "You can ask him for that five dollars," Mrs. Littlejohn says.

"You reckon he'll give it to me?" Mrs. Armstid says.

Mrs. Littlejohn was washing dishes, washing them like a man, like they was made out of iron. "No," she says. "But asking him won't do no hurt. It might shame him. I don't reckon it will, but it might."

"If he wouldn't give it back, it ain't no use to ask," Mrs. Armstid says.

"Suit yourself," Mrs. Littlejohn says. "It's your money."

I could hear the dishes.

"Do you reckon he might give it back to me?" Mrs. Armstid says. "That Texas man said he would. He said I could get it from Mr. Snopes later."

"Then go and ask him for it," Mrs. Littlejohn says.

I could hear the dishes.

"He won't give it back to me," Mrs. Armstid says.

"All right," Mrs. Littlejohn says. "Don't ask him for it, then."

I could hear the dishes; Mrs. Armstid was helping. "You don't reckon he would, do you?" she says. Mrs. Littlejohn never said nothing. It sounded like she was throwing the dishes at one another. "Maybe I better go and talk to Henry about it," Mrs. Armstid says.

"I would," Mrs. Littlejohn says. I be dog if it didn't sound like she had two plates in her hands, beating them together. "Then Henry can buy another five-dollar horse with it. Maybe he'll buy one next time that will out and out kill him. If I thought that, I'd give you back the money, myself."

"I reckon I better talk to him first," Mrs. Armstid said. Then it sounded like Mrs. Littlejohn taken up all the dishes and throwed them at the cook-stove, and I come away.

That was this morning. I had been up to Bundren's and back, and I thought that things would have kind of settled down. So after breakfast, I went up to the store. And there was Flem, setting in the store-chair and whittling, like he might not have ever moved since he come to clerk for Jody Varner. I. O. was leaning in the door, in his shirt sleeves and with his hair parted too, same as Flem was before he turned the clerking job over to I. O. It's a funny thing about them Snopes: they all looks alike, yet there ain't ere a two of them that claims brothers. They're always just cousins, like Flem and Eck and Flem and I. O. Eck was there too, squatting against the wall, him and that boy, eating cheese and crackers outen a sack; they told me that Eck hadn't been home a-tall. And that Lon Quick hadn't got back to town, even. He followed his horse clean down to Samson's Bridge, with a wagon and a camp outfit. Eck finally caught one of hisn. It run into a blind lane at Freeman's and Eck and the boy taken and tied their rope across the end of the lane, about three foot high. The horse come to the end of the lane and whirled and run back without ever stopping. Eck says it never seen the rope a-tall. He says it looked just like one of these here Christmas pinwheels. "Didn't it try to run again?" I says.

"No," Eck says, eating a bite of cheese offen his knife blade. "Just kicked some."

"Kicked some?" I says.

"It broke its neck," Eck says.

Well, they was squatting there, about six of them, talking, talking at Flem; never nobody knowed yet if Flem had ere a interest in them horses or not. So finally I come right out and asked him. "Flem's done skun all of us so much," I says, "that we're proud of him. Come on, Flem," I says, "how much did you and that Texas man make offen them horses? You can tell us. Ain't nobody here but Eck that bought one of them; the others ain't got back to town yet, and Eck's your own cousin; he'll be proud to hear, too. How much did you-all make?"

They was all whittling, not looking at Flem, making like they was studying. But you could a heard a pin drop. And I. O. He had been rubbing his back up and down on the door, but he stopped now, watching Flem like a pointing dog. Flem finished cutting the sliver offen his stick. He spit across the porch, into the road. " 'Twarn't none of my horses," he says.

I. O. cackled, like a hen, slapping his legs with both hands. "You boys might just as well quit trying to get ahead of Flem," he said.

Well, about that time I see Mrs. Armstid come outen Mrs. Littlejohn's gate, coming up the road. I never said nothing. I says, "Well, if a man can't take care of himself in a trade, he can't blame the man that trims him."

Flem never said nothing, trimming at the stick. He hadn't seen Mrs. Armstid. "Yes, sir," I says. "A fellow like Henry Armstid ain't got nobody but hisself to blame."

"Course he ain't," I. O. says. He ain't seen her, neither. "Henry Armstid's a born fool. Always is been. If Flem hadn't a got his money, somebody else would."

We looked at Flem. He never moved. Mrs. Armstid come on up the road.

"That's right," I says. "But, come to think of it, Henry never bought no horse." We looked at Flem; you could a heard a match drop. "That Texas man told her to get that five dollars back from Flem next day. I reckon Flem's done already taken that money to Mrs. Littlejohn's and give it to Mrs. Armstid."

We watched Flem. I. O. quit rubbing his back against the door again. After a while Flem raised his head and spit across the porch, into the dust. I. O. cackled, just like a hen. "Ain't he a beating fellow, now?" I. O. says.

Mrs. Armstid was getting closer, so I kept on talking, watching to see if Flem would look up and see her. But he never looked up. I went on talking about Tull, about how he was going to sue Flem, and Flem setting there, whittling his stick, not saying nothing else after he said they wasn't none of his horses.

Then I. O. happened to look around. He seen Mrs. Armstid. "Pssst!" he says. Flem looked up. "Here she comes!" I. O. says. "Go out the back. I'll tell her you done went in to town to-day."

But Flem never moved. He just set there, whittling, and we watched Mrs. Armstid come up onto the porch, in that ere faded sunbonnet and wrapper and them tennis shoes that made a kind of hissing noise on the porch. She come onto the porch and stopped, her hands rolled into her dress in front, not looking at nothing.

"He said Saturday," she says, "that he wouldn't sell Henry no horse. He said I could get the money from you."

Flem looked up. The knife never stopped. It went on trimming off a sliver same as if he was watching it. "He taken that money off with him when he left," Flem says.

Mrs. Armstid never looked at nothing. We never looked at her, neither, except that boy of Eck's. He had a half-et cracker in his hand, watching her, chewing.

"He said Henry hadn't bought no horse," Mrs. Armstid says. "He said for me to get the money from you today."

"I reckon he forgot about it," Flem said. "He taken that money off with him Saturday." He whittled again. I. O. kept on rubbing his back, slow. He licked his lips. After a while the woman looked up the road, where it went on up the hill, toward the graveyard. She looked up that way for a while, with that boy of Eck's watching her and I. O. rubbing his back slow against the door. Then she turned back toward the steps.

"I reckon it's time to get dinner started," she says.

"How's Henry this morning, Mrs. Armstid?" Winterbottom says.

She looked at Winterbottom; she almost stopped. "He's resting, I thank you kindly," she says.

Flem got up, outen the chair, putting his knife away. He spit across the porch. "Wait a minute, Mrs. Armstid," he says. She stopped again. She didn't look at him. Flem went on into the store, with I. O. done quit rubbing his back now, with his head craned after Flem, and Mrs. Armstid standing there with her hands rolled into her dress, not looking at nothing. A wagon come up the road and passed; it was Freeman, on the way to town. Then Flem come out again, with I. O. still watching him. Flem had one of these little striped sacks of Jody Varner's candy; I bet he still owes Jody that nickel, too. He put the sack into Mrs. Armstid's hand, like he would have put it into a hollow stump. He spit again across the porch. "A little sweetening for the chaps," he says.

"You're right kind," Mrs. Armstid says. She held the sack of candy in her hand, not looking at nothing. Eck's boy was watching the sack, the half-et cracker in his hand; he wasn't chewing now. He watched Mrs. Armstid roll the sack into her apron. "I reckon I better get on back and help with dinner," she says. She turned and went back across the porch. Flem set down in the chair again and opened his knife. He spit across the porch again, past Mrs. Armstid where she hadn't went down the steps yet. Then she went on, in that ere sunbonnet and wrapper all the same color, back down the road toward Mrs. Littlejohn's. You couldn't see her dress move, like a natural woman walking. She looked like a old snag still standing up and moving along on a high water. We watched her turn in at Mrs. Littlejohn's and go outen sight. Flem was whittling. I. O. begun to rub his back on the door. Then he begun to cackle, just like a durn hen.

"You boys might just as well quit trying," I. O. says. "You can't git ahead of Flem. You can't touch him. Ain't he a sight, now?"

I be dog if he ain't. If I had brung a herd of wild cattymounts into town and sold them to my neighbors and kinfolks, they would have lynched me. Yes, sir.

1931

That Evening Sun[1]

I

Monday is no different from any other weekday in Jefferson now. The streets are paved now, and the telephone and electric companies are cutting down more and more of the shade trees—the water oaks, the maples and locusts and elms—to make room for iron poles bearing clusters of bloated and ghostly and bloodless grapes, and we

[1] Probably an echo of "I hate to see that evening
sun go down," from the 1914 song "St. Louis
Blues," by W. C. Handy.

have a city laundry which makes the rounds on Monday morning, gathering the bundles of clothes into bright-colored, specially-made motor cars: the soiled wearing of a whole week now flees apparitionlike behind alert and irritable electric horns, with a long diminishing noise of rubber and asphalt like tearing silk, and even the Negro women who still take in white people's washing after the old custom, fetch and deliver it in automobiles.

But fifteen years ago, on Monday morning the quiet, dusty, shady streets would be full of Negro women with, balanced on their steady, turbaned heads, bundles of clothes tied up in sheets, almost as large as cotton bales, carried so without touch of hand between the kitchen door of the white house and the blackened washpot beside a cabin door in Negro Hollow.

Nancy would set her bundle on the top of her head, then upon the bundle in turn she would set the black straw sailor hat which she wore winter and summer. She was tall, with a high, sad face sunken a little where her teeth were missing. Sometimes we would go a part of the way down the lane and across the pasture with her, to watch the balanced bundle and the hat that never bobbed nor wavered, even when she walked down into the ditch and up the other side and stooped through the fence. She would go down on her hands and knees and crawl through the gap, her head rigid, uptilted, the bundle steady as a rock or a balloon, and rise to her feet again and go on.

Sometimes the husbands of the washing women would fetch and deliver the clothes, but Jesus never did that for Nancy, even before father told him to stay away from our house, even when Dilsey was sick and Nancy would come to cook for us.

And then about half the time we'd have to go down the lane to Nancy's cabin and tell her to come on and cook breakfast. We would stop at the ditch, because father told us to not have anything to do with Jesus—he was a short black man, with a razor scar down his face—and we would throw rocks at Nancy's house until she came to the door, leaning her head around it without any clothes on.

"What yawl mean, chunking my house?" Nancy said. "What you little devils mean?"

"Father says for you to come on and get breakfast," Caddy said. "Father says it's over a half an hour now, and you've got to come this minute."

"I aint studying no breakfast," Nancy said. "I going to get my sleep out."

"I bet you're drunk," Jason said. "Father says you're drunk. Are you drunk, Nancy?"

"Who says I is?" Nancy said. "I got to get my sleep out. I aint studying no breakfast."

So after a while we quit chunking the cabin and went back home. When she finally came, it was too late for me to go to school. So we thought it was whisky until that day they arrested her again and they were taking her to jail and they passed Mr Stovall. He was the cashier in the bank and a deacon in the Baptist church, and Nancy began to say:

"When you going to pay me, white man? When you going to pay me, white man? It's been three times now since you paid me a cent—" Mr Stovall knocked her down, but she kept on saying, "When you going to pay me, white man? It's been three times now since—" until Mr Stovall kicked her in the mouth with his heel and the marshal caught Mr Stovall back, and Nancy lying in the street, laughing. She turned her head and spat out some blood and teeth and said, "It's been three times now since he paid me a cent."

That was how she lost her teeth, and all that day they told about Nancy and Mr Stovall, and all that night the ones that passed the jail could hear Nancy singing and yelling. They could see her hands holding to the window bars, and a lot of them stopped along the fence, listening to her and to the jailer trying to make her stop. She didn't shut up until almost daylight, when the jailer began to hear a bumping and scraping upstairs and he went up there and found Nancy hanging from the window bar. He said that it was cocaine and not whisky, because no nigger would try to commit suicide unless he was full of cocaine, because a nigger full of cocaine wasn't a nigger any longer.

The jailer cut her down and revived her; then he beat her, whipped her. She had hung herself with her dress. She had fixed it all right, but when they arrested her she didn't have on anything except a dress and so she didn't have anything to tie her hands with and she couldn't make her hands let go of the window ledge. So the jailer heard the noise and ran up there and found Nancy hanging from the window, stark naked, her belly already swelling out a little, like a little balloon.

When Dilsey was sick in her cabin and Nancy was cooking for us, we could see her apron swelling out; that was before father told Jesus to stay away from the house. Jesus was in the kitchen, sitting behind the stove, with his razor scar on his black face like a piece of dirty string. He said it was a watermelon that Nancy had under her dress.

"It never come off of your vine, though," Nancy said.

"Off of what vine?" Caddy said.

"I can cut down the vine it did come off of," Jesus said.

"What makes you want to talk like that before these chillen?" Nancy said. "Whyn't you go on to work? You done et. You want Mr Jason to catch you hanging around his kitchen, talking that way before these chillen?"

"Talking what way?" Caddy said. "What vine?"

"I cant hang around white man's kitchen," Jesus said. "But white man can hang around mine. White man can come in my house, but I cant stop him. When white man want to come in my house, I aint got no house. I cant stop him, but he cant kick me outen it. He cant do that."

Dilsey was still sick in her cabin. Father told Jesus to stay off our place. Dilsey was still sick. It was a long time. We were in the library after supper.

"Isn't Nancy through in the kitchen yet?" mother said. "It seems to me that she has had plenty of time to have finished the dishes."

"Let Quentin go and see," father said. "Go and see if Nancy is through, Quentin. Tell her she can go on home."

I went to the kitchen. Nancy was through. The dishes were put away and the fire was out. Nancy was sitting in a chair, close to the cold stove. She looked at me.

"Mother wants to know if you are through," I said.

"Yes," Nancy said. She looked at me. "I done finished." She looked at me.

"What is it?" I said. "What is it?"

"I aint nothing but a nigger," Nancy said. "It aint none of my fault."

She looked at me, sitting in the chair before the cold stove, the sailor hat on her head. I went back to the library. It was the cold stove and all, when you think of a kitchen being warm and busy and cheerful. And with a cold stove and the dishes all put away, and nobody wanting to eat at that hour.

"Is she through?" mother said.

"Yessum," I said.

"What is she doing?" mother said.

"She's not doing anything. She's through."

"I'll go and see," father said.

"Maybe she's waiting for Jesus to come and take her home," Caddy said.

"Jesus is gone," I said. Nancy told us how one morning she woke up and Jesus was gone.

"He quit me," Nancy said. "Done gone to Memphis, I reckon. Dodging them city *po*-lice for a while, I reckon."

"And a good riddance," father said. "I hope he stays there."

"Nancy's scaired of the dark," Jason said.

"So are you," Caddy said.

"I'm not," Jason said.

"Scairy cat," Caddy said.

"I'm not," Jason said.

"You, Candace!" mother said. Father came back.

"I am going to walk down the lane with Nancy," he said. "She says that Jesus is back."

"Has she seen him?" mother said.

"No. Some Negro sent her word that he was back in town. I wont be long."

"You'll leave me alone, to take Nancy home?" mother said. "Is her safety more precious to you than mine?"

"I wont be long," father said.

"You'll leave these children unprotected, with that Negro about?"

"I'm going too," Caddy said. "Let me go, Father."

"What would he do with them, if he were unfortunate enough to have them?" father said.

"I want to go, too," Jason said.

"Jason!" mother said. She was speaking to father. You could tell that by the way she said the name. Like she believed that all day father had been trying to think of doing the thing she wouldn't like the most, and that she knew all the time that after a while he would think of it. I stayed quiet, because father and I both knew that mother would want him to make me stay with her if she just thought of it in time. So father didn't look at me. I was the oldest. I was nine and Caddy was seven and Jason was five.

"Nonsense," father said. "We wont be long."

Nancy had her hat on. We came to the lane. "Jesus always been good to me," Nancy said. "Whenever he had two dollars, one of them was mine." We walked in the lane. "If I can just get through the lane," Nancy said, "I be all right then."

The lane was always dark. "This is where Jason got scared on Hallowe'en," Caddy said.

"I didn't," Jason said.

"Cant Aunt Rachel do anything with him?" father said. Aunt Rachel was old. She lived in a cabin beyond Nancy's, by herself. She had white hair and she smoked a pipe in the door, all day long; she didn't work any more. They said she was Jesus' mother. Sometimes she said she was and sometimes she said she wasn't any kin to Jesus.

"Yes, you did," Caddy said. "You were scairder than Frony. You were scairder than T.P. even. Scairder than niggers."

"Cant nobody do nothing with him," Nancy said. "He say I done woke up the devil in him and aint but one thing going to lay it down again."

"Well, he's gone now," father said. "There's nothing for you to be afraid of now. And if you'd just let white men alone."

"Let what white men alone?" Caddy said. "How let them alone?"

"He aint gone nowhere," Nancy said. "I can feel him. I can feel him now, in this lane. He hearing us talk, every word, hid somewhere, waiting. I aint seen him, and I aint going to see him again but once more, with that razor in his mouth. That razor on that string down his back, inside his shirt. And then I aint going to be even surprised."

"I wasn't scaired," Jason said.

"If you'd behave yourself, you'd have kept out of this," father said. "But it's all right now. He's probably in St. Louis now. Probably got another wife by now and forgot all about you."

"If he has, I better not find out about it," Nancy said. "I'd stand there right over them, and every time he wropped her, I'd cut that arm off. I'd cut his head off and I'd slit her belly and I'd shove—"

"Hush," father said.

"Slit whose belly, Nancy?" Caddy said.

"I wasn't scaired," Jason said. "I'd walk right down this lane by myself."

"Yah," Caddy said. "You wouldn't dare to put your foot down in it if we were not here too."

II

Dilsey was still sick, so we took Nancy home every night until mother said, "How much longer is this going on? I to be left alone in this big house while you take home a frightened Negro?"

We fixed a pallet in the kitchen for Nancy. One night we waked up, hearing the sound. It was not singing and it was not crying, coming up the dark stairs. There was a light in mother's room and we heard father going down the hall, down the back stairs, and Caddy and I went into the hall. The floor was cold. Our toes curled away from it while we listened to the sound. It was like singing and it wasn't like singing, like the sounds that Negroes make.

Then it stopped and we heard father going down the back stairs, and we went to the head of the stairs. Then the sound began again, in the stairway, not loud, and we could see Nancy's eyes halfway up the stairs, against the wall. They looked like cat's eyes do, like a big cat against the wall, watching us. When we came down the steps to where she was, she quit making the sound again, and we stood there until father came back up from the kitchen, with his pistol in his hand. He went back down with Nancy and they came back with Nancy's pallet.

We spread the pallet in our room. After the light in mother's room went off, we could see Nancy's eyes again. "Nancy," Caddy whispered, "are you asleep, Nancy?"

Nancy whispered something. It was oh or no, I dont know which. Like nobody had made it, like it came from nowhere and went nowhere, until it was like Nancy was not there at all; that I had looked so hard at her eyes on the stairs that they had got printed on my eyeballs, like the sun does when you have closed your eyes and there is no sun. "Jesus," Nancy whispered. "Jesus."

"Was it Jesus?" Caddy said. "Did he try to come into the kitchen?"

"Jesus," Nancy said. Like this: Jeeeeeeeeeeeeeeeesus, until the sound went out, like a match or a candle does.

"It's the other Jesus she means," I said.

"Can you see us, Nancy?" Caddy whispered. "Can you see our eyes too?"

"I aint nothing but a nigger," Nancy said. "God knows. God knows."

"What did you see down there in the kitchen?" Caddy whispered. "What tried to get in?"

"God knows," Nancy said. We could see her eyes. "God knows."

Dilsey got well. She cooked dinner. "You'd better stay in bed a day or two longer," father said.

"What for?" Dilsey said. "If I had been a day later, this place would be to rack and ruin. Get on out of here now, and let me get my kitchen straight again."

Dilsey cooked supper too. And that night, just before dark, Nancy came into the kitchen.

"How do you know he's back?" Dilsey said. "You aint seen him."

"Jesus is a nigger," Jason said.

"I can feel him," Nancy said. "I can feel him laying yonder in the ditch."

"Tonight?" Dilsey said. "Is he there tonight?"

"Dilsey's a nigger too," Jason said.

"You try to eat something," Dilsey said.

"I dont want nothing," Nancy said.

"I aint a nigger," Jason said.

"Drink some coffee," Dilsey said. She poured a cup of coffee for Nancy. "Do you know he's out there tonight? How come you know it's tonight?"

"I know," Nancy said. "He's there, waiting. I know. I done lived with him too long. I know what he is fixing to do fore he know it himself."

"Drink some coffee," Dilsey said. Nancy held the cup to her mouth and blew into the cup. Her mouth pursed out like a spreading adder's, like a rubber mouth, like she had blown all the color out of her lips with blowing the coffee.

"I aint a nigger," Jason said. "Are you a nigger, Nancy?"

"I hellborn, child," Nancy said. "I wont be nothing soon. I going back where I come from soon."

III

She began to drink the coffee. While she was drinking, holding the cup in both hands, she began to make the sound again. She made the sound into the cup and the coffee sploshed out onto her hands and her dress. Her eyes looked at us and she sat there, her elbows on her knees, holding the cup in both hands, looking at us across the wet cup, making the sound. "Look at Nancy," Jason said. "Nancy cant cook for us now. Dilsey's got well now."

"You hush up," Dilsey said. Nancy held the cup in both hands, looking at us, making the sound, like there were two of them: one looking at us and the other making the sound. "Whyn't you let Mr Jason telefoam the marshal?" Dilsey said. Nancy stopped then, holding the cup in her long brown hands. She tried to drink some coffee again, but it sploshed out of the cup, onto her hands and her dress, and she put the cup down. Jason watched her.

"I cant swallow it," Nancy said. "I swallows but it wont go down me."

"You go down to the cabin," Dilsey said. "Frony will fix you a pallet and I'll be there soon."

"Wont no nigger stop him," Nancy said.

"I aint a nigger," Jason said. "Am I, Dilsey?"

"I reckon not," Dilsey said. She looked at Nancy. "I dont reckon so. What you going to do, then?"

Nancy looked at us. Her eyes went fast, like she was afraid there wasn't time to look, without hardly moving at all. She looked at us, at all three of us at one time. "You member that night I stayed in yawls' room?" she said. She told about how we waked up early the next morning, and played. We had to play quiet, on her pallet, until father woke up and it was time to get breakfast. "Go and ask your maw to let me stay here tonight," Nancy said. "I wont need no pallet. We can play some more."

Caddy asked mother. Jason went too. "I cant have Negroes sleeping in the bedrooms," mother said. Jason cried. He cried until mother said he couldn't have any dessert for three days if he didn't stop. Then Jason said he would stop if Dilsey would make a chocolate cake. Father was there.

"Why dont you do something about it?" mother said. "What do we have officers for?"

"Why is Nancy afraid of Jesus?" Caddy said. "Are you afraid of father, mother?"

"What could the officers do?" father said. "If Nancy hasn't seen him, how could the officers find him?"

"Then why is she afraid?" mother said.

"She says he is there. She says she knows he is there tonight."

"Yet we pay taxes," mother said. "I must wait here alone in this big house while you take a Negro woman home."

"You know that I am not lying outside with a razor," father said.

"I'll stop if Dilsey will make a chocolate cake," Jason said. Mother told us to go out and father said he didn't know if Jason would get a chocolate cake or not, but he knew what Jason was going to get in about a minute. We went back to the kitchen and told Nancy.

"Father said for you to go home and lock the door, and you'll be all right," Caddy said. "All right from what, Nancy? Is Jesus mad at you?" Nancy was holding the coffee cup in her hands again, her elbows on her knees and her hands holding the cup between her knees. She was looking into the cup. "What have you done that made Jesus mad?" Caddy said. Nancy let the cup go. It didn't break on the floor, but the coffee spilled out, and Nancy sat there with her hands still making the shape of the cup. She began to make the sound again, not loud. Not singing and not unsinging. We watched her.

"Here," Dilsey said. "You quit that, now. You get aholt of yourself. You wait here. I going to get Versh to walk home with you." Dilsey went out.

We looked at Nancy. Her shoulders kept shaking, but she quit making the sound. We watched her. "What's Jesus going to do to you?" Caddy said. "He went away."

Nancy looked at us. "We had fun that night I stayed in yawls' room, didn't we?"

"I didn't," Jason said. "I didn't have any fun."

"You were asleep in mother's room," Caddy said. "You were not there."

"Let's go down to my house and have some more fun," Nancy said.

"Mother wont let us," I said. "It's too late now."

"Dont bother her," Nancy said. "We can tell her in the morning. She wont mind."

"She wouldn't let us," I said.

"Dont ask her now," Nancy said. "Dont bother her now."

"She didn't say we couldn't go," Caddy said.

"We didn't ask," I said.

"If you go, I'll tell," Jason said.

"We'll have fun," Nancy said. "They won't mind, just to my house. I been working for yawl a long time. They won't mind."

"I'm not afraid to go," Caddy said. "Jason is the one that's afraid. He'll tell."

"I'm not," Jason said.

"Yes, you are," Caddy said. "You'll tell."

"I won't tell," Jason said. "I'm not afraid."

"Jason ain't afraid to go with me," Nancy said. "Is you, Jason?"

"Jason is going to tell," Caddy said. The lane was dark. We passed the pasture gate. "I bet if something was to jump out from behind that gate, Jason would holler."

"I wouldn't," Jason said. We walked down the lane. Nancy was talking loud.

"What are you talking so loud for, Nancy?" Caddy said.

"Who; me?" Nancy said. "Listen at Quentin and Caddy and Jason saying I'm talking loud."

"You talk like there was five of us here," Caddy said. "You talk like father was here too."

"Who; me talking loud, Mr Jason?" Nancy said.

"Nancy called Jason 'Mister,'" Caddy said.

"Listen how Caddy and Quentin and Jason talk," Nancy said.

"We're not talking loud," Caddy said. "You're the one that's talking like father—"

"Hush," Nancy said; "hush, Mr Jason."

"Nancy called Jason 'Mister' aguh—"

"Hush," Nancy said. She was talking loud when we crossed the ditch and stooped through the fence where she used to stoop through with the clothes on her head. Then we came to her house. We were going fast then. She opened the door. The smell of the house was like the lamp and the smell of Nancy was like the wick, like they were waiting for one another to begin to smell. She lit the lamp and closed the door and put the bar up. Then she quit talking loud, looking at us.

"What're we going to do?" Caddy said.

"What do yawl want to do?" Nancy said.

"You said we would have some fun," Caddy said.

There was something about Nancy's house; something you could smell besides Nancy and the house. Jason smelled it, even. "I don't want to stay here," he said. "I want to go home."

"Go home, then," Caddy said.

"I don't want to go by myself," Jason said.

"We're going to have some fun," Nancy said.

"How?" Caddy said.

Nancy stood by the door. She was looking at us, only it was like she had emptied her eyes, like she had quit using them. "What do you want to do?" she said.

"Tell us a story," Caddy said. "Can you tell a story?"

"Yes," Nancy said.

"Tell it," Caddy said. We looked at Nancy. "You don't know any stories."

"Yes," Nancy said. "Yes, I do."

She came and sat in a chair before the hearth. There was a little fire there. Nancy built it up, when it was already hot inside. She built a good blaze. She told a story. She talked like her eyes looked, like her eyes watching us and her voice talking to us did not belong to her. Like she was living somewhere else, waiting somewhere else. She was outside the cabin. Her voice was inside and the shape of her, the Nancy that could stoop under a barbed wire fence with a bundle of clothes balanced on her head as though without weight, like a balloon, was there. But that was all. "And so this here queen come walking up to the ditch, where that bad man was hiding. She was walking up to the ditch, and she say, 'If I can just get past this here ditch,' was what she say . . ."

"What ditch?" Caddy said. "A ditch like that one out there? Why did a queen want to go into a ditch?"

"To get to her house," Nancy said. She looked at us. "She had to cross the ditch to get into her house quick and bar the door."

"Why did she want to go home and bar the door?" Caddy said.

IV

Nancy looked at us. She quit talking. She looked at us. Jason's legs stuck straight out of his pants where he sat on Nancy's lap. "I don't think that's a good story," he said. "I want to go home."

"Maybe we had better," Caddy said. She got up from the floor. "I bet they are looking for us right now." She went toward the door.

"No," Nancy said. "Don't open it." She got up quick and passed Caddy. She didn't touch the door, the wooden bar.

"Why not?" Caddy said.

"Come back to the lamp," Nancy said. "We'll have fun. You don't have to go."

"We ought to go," Caddy said. "Unless we have a lot of fun." She and Nancy came back to the fire, the lamp.

"I want to go home," Jason said. "I'm going to tell."

"I know another story," Nancy said. She stood close to the lamp. She looked at Caddy, like when your eyes look up at a stick balanced on your nose. She had to look down to see Caddy, but her eyes looked like that, like when you are balancing a stick.

"I won't listen to it," Jason said. "I'll bang on the floor."

"It's a good one," Nancy said. "It's better than the other one."

"What's it about?" Caddy said. Nancy was standing by the lamp. Her hand was on the lamp, against the light, long and brown.

"Your hand is on that hot globe," Caddy said. "Don't it feel hot to your hand?"

Nancy looked at her hand on the lamp chimney. She took her hand away, slow. She stood there, looking at Caddy, wringing her long hand as though it were tied to her wrist with a string.

"Let's do something else," Caddy said.

"I want to go home," Jason said.

"I got some popcorn," Nancy said. She looked at Caddy and then at Jason and then at me and then at Caddy again. "I got some popcorn."

"I don't like popcorn," Jason said. "I'd rather have candy."

Nancy looked at Jason. "You can hold the popper." She was still wringing her hand; it was long and limp and brown.

"All right," Jason said. "I'll stay a while if I can do that. Caddy can't hold it. I'll want to go home again if Caddy holds the popper."

Nancy built up the fire. "Look at Nancy putting her hands in the fire," Caddy said. "What's the matter with you, Nancy?"

"I got popcorn," Nancy said. "I got some." She took the popper from under the bed. It was broken. Jason began to cry.

"Now we can't have any popcorn," he said.

"We ought to go home, anyway," Caddy said. "Come on, Quentin."

"Wait," Nancy said; "wait. I can fix it. Don't you want to help me fix it?"

"I don't think I want any," Caddy said. "It's too late now."

"You help me, Jason," Nancy said. "Don't you want to help me?"

"No," Jason said. "I want to go home."

"Hush," Nancy said; "hush. Watch. Watch me. I can fix it so Jason can hold it and pop the corn." She got a piece of wire and fixed the popper.

"It won't hold good," Caddy said.

"Yes, it will," Nancy said. "Yawl watch. Yawl help me shell some corn."

The popcorn was under the bed too. We shelled it into the popper and Nancy helped Jason hold the popper over the fire.

"It's not popping," Jason said. "I want to go home."

"You wait," Nancy said. "It'll begin to pop. We'll have fun then." She was sitting close to the fire. The lamp was turned up so high it was beginning to smoke.

"Why don't you turn it down some?" I said.

"It's all right," Nancy said. "I'll clean it. Yawl wait. The popcorn will start in a minute."

"I don't believe it's going to start," Caddy said. "We ought to start home, anyway. They'll be worried."

"No," Nancy said. "It's going to pop. Dilsey will tell um yawl with me. I been working for yawl long time. They won't mind if yawl at my house. You wait, now. It'll start popping any minute now."

Then Jason got some smoke in his eyes and he began to cry. He dropped the popper into the fire. Nancy got a wet rag and wiped Jason's face, but he didn't stop crying.

"Hush," she said. "Hush." But he didn't hush. Caddy took the popper out of the fire.

"It's burned up," she said. "You'll have to get some more popcorn, Nancy."

"Did you put all of it in?" Nancy said.

"Yes," Caddy said. Nancy looked at Caddy. Then she took the popper and opened it and poured the cinders into her apron and began to sort the grains, her hands long and brown, and we watching her.

"Haven't you got any more?" Caddy said.

"Yes," Nancy said; "yes. Look. This here ain't burnt. All we need to do is—"

"I want to go home," Jason said. "I'm going to tell."

"Hush," Caddy said. We all listened. Nancy's head was already turned toward the barred door, her eyes filled with red lamplight. "Somebody is coming," Caddy said.

Then Nancy began to make that sound again, not loud, sitting there above the fire, her long hands dangling between her knees; all of a sudden water began to come out on her face in big drops, running down her face, carrying in each one a little turning ball of firelight like a spark until it dropped off her chin. "She's not crying," I said.

"I ain't crying," Nancy said. Her eyes were closed. "I ain't crying. Who is it?"

"I don't know," Caddy said. She went to the door and looked out. "We've got to go now," she said. "Here comes father."

"I'm going to tell," Jason said. "Yawl made me come."

The water still ran down Nancy's face. She turned in her chair. "Listen. Tell him. Tell him we going to have fun. Tell him I take good care of yawl until in the morning. Tell him to let me come home with yawl and sleep on the floor. Tell him I won't need no pallet. We'll have fun. You member last time how we had so much fun?"

"I didn't have fun," Jason said. "You hurt me. You put smoke in my eyes. I'm going to tell."

V

Father came in. He looked at us. Nancy did not get up.

"Tell him," she said.

"Caddy made us come down here," Jason said. "I didn't want to."

Father came to the fire. Nancy looked up at him. "Can't you go to Aunt Rachel's and stay?" he said. Nancy looked up at father, her hands between her knees. "He's not here," father said. "I would have seen him. There's not a soul in sight."

"He in the ditch," Nancy said. "He waiting in the ditch yonder."

"Nonsense," father said. He looked at Nancy. "Do you know he's there?"

"I got the sign," Nancy said.

"What sign?"

"I got it. It was on the table when I come in. It was a hog-bone, with blood meat still on it, laying by the lamp. He's out there. When yawl walk out that door, I gone."

"Gone where, Nancy?" Caddy said.

"I'm not a tattletale," Jason said.

"Nonsense," father said.

"He out there," Nancy said. "He looking through that window this minute, waiting for yawl to go. Then I gone."

"Nonsense," father said. "Lock up your house and we'll take you on to Aunt Rachel's."

" 'Twont do no good," Nancy said. She didn't look at father now, but he looked down at her, at her long, limp, moving hands. "Putting it off wont do no good."

"Then what do you want to do?" father said.

"I don't know," Nancy said. "I can't do nothing. Just put it off. And that don't do no good. I reckon it belong to me. I reckon what I going to get ain't no more than mine."

"Get what?" Caddy said. "What's yours?"

"Nothing," father said. "You all must get to bed."

"Caddy made me come," Jason said.

"Go on to Aunt Rachel's," father said.

"It won't do no good," Nancy said. She sat before the fire, her elbows on her knees, her long hands between her knees. "When even your own kitchen wouldn't do no good. When even if I was sleeping on the floor in the room with your chillen, and the next morning there I am, and blood—"

"Hush," father said. "Lock the door and put out the lamp and go to bed."

"I scared of the dark," Nancy said. "I scared for it to happen in the dark."

"You mean you're going to sit right here with the lamp lighted?" father said. Then Nancy began to make the sound again, sitting before the fire, her long hands between her knees. "Ah, damnation," father said. "Come along, chillen. It's past bedtime."

"When yawl go home, I gone," Nancy said. She talked quieter now, and her face looked quiet, like her hands. "Anyway, I got my coffin money saved up with Mr. Lovelady." Mr. Lovelady was a short, dirty man who collected the Negro insurance, coming around to the cabins or the kitchens every Saturday morning, to collect fifteen cents. He and his wife lived at the hotel. One morning his wife committed suicide. They had a child, a little girl. He and the child went away. After a week or two he came back alone. We would see him going along the lanes and the back streets on Saturday mornings.

"Nonsense," father said. "You'll be the first thing I'll see in the kitchen tomorrow morning."

"You'll see what you'll see, I reckon," Nancy said. "But it will take the Lord to say what that will be."

VI

We left her sitting before the fire.

"Come and put the bar up," father said. But she didn't move. She didn't look at us again, sitting quietly there between the lamp and the fire. From some distance down the lane we could look back and see her through the open door.

"What, Father?" Caddy said. "What's going to happen?"

"Nothing," father said. Jason was on father's back, so Jason was the tallest of all of us. We went down into the ditch. I looked at it, quiet. I couldn't see much where the moonlight and the shadows tangled.

"If Jesus is hid here, he can see us, can't he?" Caddy said.

"He's not there," father said. "He went away a long time ago."

"You made me come," Jason said, high; against the sky it looked like father had two heads, a little one and a big one. "I didn't want to."

We went up out of the ditch. We could still see Nancy's house and the open door, but we couldn't see Nancy now, sitting before the fire with the door open, because she was tired. "I just done got tired," she said. "I just a nigger. It ain't no fault of mine."

But we could hear her, because she began just after we came up out of the ditch, the sound that was not singing and not unsinging. "Who will do our washing now, Father?" I said.

"I'm not a nigger," Jason said, high and close above father's head.

"You're worse," Caddy said, "you are a tattletale. If something was to jump out, you'd be scairder than a nigger."

"I wouldn't," Jason said.

"You'd cry," Caddy said.

"Caddy," father said.

"I wouldn't!" Jason said.

"Scairy cat," Caddy said.

"Candace!" father said.

1931

Ernest Hemingway
1899–1961

No other major American writer has ever equaled the popular success and worldwide reputation of Ernest Hemingway. During his lifetime he attained the status of an international celebrity; his activities were reported by gossip columnists along with the disport of the movie stars and the athletes he became friends with. His prose style became one of the most recognizable literary "trademarks" of all time and is still widely imitated and parodied.

Hemingway was born on July 21, 1899, in Oak Park, Illinois, a suburb just west of Chicago. His father was a prosperous physician; his mother, a devoted member of the Congregational church who, having tried to pursue a career as an opera singer, taught music. In high school Hemingway participated in several organized sports, including football and boxing. He played the cello in the school orchestra (his mother hoped he would become a cellist) and wrote for the school's newspaper and literary magazine. But the most intense of his early experiences, if we may judge by the memories he carried with him, centered on the hunting and fishing he did with his father near the family cottage on the upper peninsula of northern Michigan. There, under his father's tutelage, he learned things he never forgot—the ritual of the hunt and the code of the hunter, lessons that stressed the primacy of elemental physical confrontations and the importance of physical prowess, physical endurance, and physical courage. His father, who committed suicide in 1928, gave Hemingway his first fishing rod at age two and his first gun at age ten: "I am so pleased and proud you have grown to be such a fine big manly fellow," he wrote his son in 1915.

In 1917, having finished high school, Hemingway decided to forgo college. Setting out on his own, he found work as a cub reporter on the Kansas City *Star,* where he began cultivating the restrained yet vigorous prose style that later, when he shaped it into literature under the influence of Sherwood Anderson, Ezra Pound, and Gertrude Stein, would make him famous. Though he enjoyed newspaper work, he soon left it for Europe, drawn by the first of several wars in which he would serve. Rejected by the army because of an eye defect, he volunteered for the Red Cross ambulance corps. In 1918, after a brief stay in France, he entered active duty in Italy, where he was severely wounded by the explosion of a mortar shell. Throughout his life he wore a platinum kneecap and bore numerous shrapnel scars. Yet the experience proved exhilarating as well as traumatic. "Wounds don't matter," he wrote his family jauntily in a letter from a Milan hospital that was published in the Oak Park newspaper; "I wouldn't mind being wounded again so much because I know just what it is like . . . and it does give you an awfully satisfactory feeling to be wounded." Wounds— physical and psychic—would play a significant role not only in Hemingway's writing but also in his life. Remarkably accident-prone, he was repeatedly injured —in car crashes, plane crashes, shooting mishaps, freak accidents, and fires. Nearly everywhere he went—Italy, Spain, France, England, Africa, Montana, Idaho, the Florida Keys, Cuba—something happened, making his scarred body a personal geography of wounds.

After the war Hemingway returned home, decorated by the Italians for conspicuous valor. For the next two years he tried to resume the life he had left behind. He hunted and fished with friends in northern Michigan and began writing for the Toronto *Star.* But he could not adjust to the United States and Canada and itched to return to Europe. He would always be attacked by critics for not concentrating on the "American scene" ("Difference with us guys," he wrote Faulkner, "is I always lived out of country"), and most of his writing is set in other countries. In 1921 he married the first of his four wives and left the United States to join the growing band of self-exiled artists and writers who were gathering in Paris.

Paris attracted Americans such as Hemingway not only because it was the exciting center of a modernist revolution in art and literature but also because of its more liberal moral climate, the availability of liquor (Prohibition had gone into effect in the United States in 1919), and the highly favorable exchange rate. Back in the spring of 1921 Hemingway had met Sherwood Anderson, and it was through Anderson's courteous letters of introduction that the younger midwestern writer met Gertrude Stein and Ezra Pound. Later, Hemingway would get to know John Dos Passos, James Joyce (whose *Ulysses* he considered a "most goddamn wonderful book"), and F. Scott Fitzgerald. Though all of these writers in one way or another helped Hemingway launch his literary career, he ended up quarreling—at times nastily—with nearly everyone who had helped him.

"That's what you are, that's what you all are," Gertrude Stein said to Hemingway, speaking of those who had survived the war. "You are a lost generation." And it was in part a sense of loss, disillusionment, and disenchantment that Hemingway shared with the other expatriates in Paris. The Great War, like the grand words used to justify it, seemed to him a terrible betrayal. He was beginning to discover in violence and the consequences of violence one of his major themes and in war and its aftermath one of his favorite settings. The violence of the modern world, ritualized in hunting, fishing, and bullfighting (in which he saw a combination of "valor and art"), began to preoccupy his imagination. At the same time, he continued to write articles as the European correspondent of the Toronto *Star:* He interviewed Mussolini, covered the Greco-Turkish War, and wrote about crime. In 1923 he published his first book, *Three Stories and Ten Poems,* and returned to Toronto, where he resumed newspaper work and where his first child was born.

A year later Hemingway was back in Paris, trying to support a family on his meager income from journalism and publishing short stories in small literary journals. One of his early stories, "My Old Man," was selected for an anthology of the best stories of 1923, though the editor of the volume consistently misspelled Hemingway's name. Gradually, however, Hemingway was building a reputation as a meticulous craftsman. His stories, he warned a publisher, "are written so tight and so hard that the alteration of a word can throw an entire story out of key." In 1925 he published *In Our Time,* a story sequence that included several stories set in the Michigan of his boyhood. A year earlier he had published a slightly different collection in Paris under the lowercase title *in our time.* The main sequence of stories, which concludes with "Big Two-Hearted River, Parts I and II," is introduced and interspersed with a series of brief and elliptically related interchapters that begins with the violence of the Turkish War and concludes with the violence of bullfighting and political execution.

Although, as its title indicates, Hemingway clearly intended *In Our Time* to have the immediacy and impact of journalism, its style is far from the representational realism of modern reporting. In a 1958 interview, Hemingway expressed his literary concern in a way that shows how his art both depends on and radically departs from conventional "realism": "From things that have happened and from things as they exist and from all the things that you know and all those that you cannot know, you make something through your invention that is not a representation but a whole new thing truer than any thing true and alive." The two parts of "Big Two-Hearted River" are firmly grounded in Hemingway's firsthand knowledge of fishing the Fox River north of Seney, Michigan, yet, as he said to Gertrude Stein, in writing the story he was "trying to do the country like Cézanne," a reference to Cézanne's now famous landscape paintings of the Provence countryside, which became the creative force behind cubism.

By 1926 Hemingway had grown increasingly annoyed at critical references to his artistic indebtedness to Sherwood Anderson. As a response, he published an insensitive and even vicious parody of Anderson called *The Torrents of Spring,* a book that is widely regarded as one of his weakest efforts. Yet in the same year he published *The Sun Also Rises,* which brought him international fame and is still widely regarded as the best of his novels. *The Sun Also Rises* centers on a group of heavy-drinking, tough-talking, and hard-living expatriates and is narrated by an American reporter in Paris. For many readers, *The Sun Also Rises* perfectly captured the postwar mood of the "lost generation"; to emphasize the point, Hemingway used Gertrude Stein's phrase as an epigraph to the book. A second collection of stories, *Men Without Women,* followed in 1927, and two years later his second serious novel, *A Farewell to Arms,* the story of an American ambulance officer in Italy who is seriously wounded and falls in love with a British nurse. After discovering that she is pregnant, he deserts the service and escapes with her to Switzerland, where for a few idyllic months in the mountains they find a "separate peace" that is disastrously shattered when both mother and infant die in childbirth.

In 1930, at the suggestion of John Dos Passos, Hemingway bought a house in Key West, Florida. By this time he was married for a second time, was sporting a full beard, weighed a burly 208 pounds, and was already referring to himself as "Papa." It was a persona he would use for the rest of his life. In Key West,

Hemingway developed a lifelong passion for sailing and deep-sea fishing. "A sportsman," James Joyce had called him, "and ready to live the life he writes about. He would never have written it if his body had not allowed him to live it." In his writing and behavior, Hemingway consistently promoted a conventionally "masculine" way of life; for a biographical sketch, he once listed his hobbies as "ski-ing, fishing, shooting, and drinking." Yet even during his life, his insistently male performances, though good for publicity, were the subject of critical ridicule. Edmund Wilson had been among the first to praise Hemingway's early stories. In the Key West Hemingway, however, "the Hemingway of the handsome photographs with the sportsman's tan and the outdoor grin, with the ominous resemblance to Clark Gable, who poses with giant marlin which he has just hauled in," Wilson saw an "arrogant, belligerent and boastful" man who was "certainly the worst-invented character to be found in the author's work."

For all his public posturing, however, Hemingway continued to write. In 1932 he published a now classic book about bullfighting, *Death in the Afternoon,* which contains much of what can be called the author's "philosophy of life"—his fascination with danger and death and his unswerving commitment to honor, valor, and a quality of style he called "grace under pressure." Another excellent collection of short stories, *Winner Take Nothing,* appeared in 1933, and in 1935 Hemingway used the experiences gathered on African safaris to write *The Green Hills of Africa,* a book that blends literary commentary and travel description with a metaphysics of big-game hunting. Out of his African experience also came two of his finest stories, "The Snows of Kilimanjaro" and "The Short Happy Life of Francis Macomber."

Throughout the 1930s Hemingway was criticized by leftist critics for ignoring progressive causes and retreating into a hedonistic sporting life. Hemingway was always suspicious of politically motivated fiction: "There is no left and right in writing," he claimed; "there is only good and bad writing." Yet in his next book, *To Have and Have Not* (1937), his only novel that uses an American setting, Hemingway created the hard-bitten, pragmatic hero Harry Morgan, a Florida fishing boat captain who fights a separate war against the Depression by smuggling rum from Cuba to Key West. Morgan's often-quoted dying words— "One man alone ain't got no bloody f——ing chance"—appealed to "socially aware" readers who were perhaps too eager to see in the book a statement of Hemingway's social conscience. In 1936 Hemingway went to Spain with Dos Passos to work on an anti-Fascist documentary film, *The Spanish Earth.* His journalistic coverage of the civil war in Spain provided him with the material for a play called *The Fifth Column* (1938) and a novel called *For Whom the Bell Tolls* (1940), an enormously popular story about an American academic, Robert Jordan, who teams up with a small group of peasant guerrillas and heroically sacrifices his life in what proves to be a losing cause.

In 1940, married for the third time, Hemingway moved to an estate in Cuba, where he fished for marlin, drank excessively, raised fighting cocks, and played lavish host to actors and actresses, matadors, fighters, politicos, and an assortment of international celebrities. When the United States entered the Second World War, Hemingway volunteered his prized fishing vessel for antisubmarine duty. In 1944, as a war correspondent, he participated in the Normandy invasion and eventually took such an "active" role with the U.S. Army's 4th Infantry Division in France and Germany that he was awarded the Bronze Star. After the war, he married again and spent time in Venice, the city that served as the setting for one of his most poorly received novels, the idyllic romance, *Across the River and into the Trees* (1950). He returned to Cuba and started working on a long "sea novel" that he had much difficulty with and that eventually was published posthumously as *Islands in the Stream* (1970). In 1952, however, Hemingway selected one long self-contained section of that novel and published it as *The Old Man and the Sea* —a parable-like tale of an old Cuban fisherman who catches a giant marlin but is unable to keep the sharks from mutilating it before he can get it safely to shore. This novella became Hemingway's biggest-selling book, won him the Pulitzer Prize, and led directly to his being awarded the Nobel Prize in 1954.

During the final years of his life, Hemingway made several trips to Spain and engaged in another African safari, during which he barely survived back-to-back plane crashes. But his health was giving out. As political tension mounted in Cuba, he left his estate and moved to Ketchum, Idaho, where he underwent both medical and psychiatric treatment. In 1960 he used some notes and reportage that had survived from the 1920s as the basis for a collection of reminiscences, *A Moveable Feast,* which appeared posthumously in 1964. In 1961 he found himself unable to write one sentence for a volume to be presented to President John F. Kennedy: "It just won't come any more," he said. "How simple the writing of literature would be," he had written in his Nobel Prize acceptance speech, "if it were only necessary to write in another way what has been well written."

A sense of loss and the threat of violence had informed almost everything Hemingway wrote. In a deceptively simple, spare, disciplined prose (he said of *In Our Time,* "There is no writing in it that anybody with a high-school education cannot read"), he labored to find ways of restoring the force of words that had lost their edge. His heroes bear scars that are psychological as well as physical, and they carry with them memories of violence as well as premonitions of death. Facing a disordered, hypocritical world, they seek to discover some code by which to live, some style for comporting themselves in reality. Their cause, that of finding some way gracefully to endure the pain and accept the futility of life without cant or illusion, is based on the assumption that learning how to live life can sometimes help us to understand it. On July 2, 1961, in Ketchum, Idaho, Hemingway chose, as his father had before him, to end his own life violently. He pressed a double-barreled shotgun to his forehead and pulled both triggers.

Further Reading:
Ernest Hemingway: The Man and His Work, ed.
J. K. M. McCaffrey, 1950.
P. Young, *Ernest Hemingway,* rev. ed., 1966.
C. Baker, *Ernest Hemingway: A Life Story,* 1969.
G. H. Hemingway, *Papa,* 1976.
A. Burgess, *Ernest Hemingway and His World,* 1978.

Text:
"Big Two-Hearted River" from *In Our Time,* 1925.

Big Two-Hearted River

Part I

The train went on up the track out of sight, around one of the hills of burnt timber. Nick sat down on the bundle of canvas and bedding the baggage man had pitched out of the door of the baggage car. There was no town, nothing but the rails and the burned-over country. The thirteen saloons that had lined the one street of Seney had not left a trace. The foundations of the Mansion House hotel stuck up above the ground. The stone was chipped and split by the fire. It was all that was left of the town of Seney. Even the surface had been burned off the ground.

Nick looked at the burned-over stretch of hillside, where he had expected to find the scattered houses of the town and then walked down the railroad track to the bridge over the river. The river was there. It swirled against the log spiles of the bridge. Nick looked down into the clear, brown water, colored from the pebbly bottom, and watched the trout keeping themselves steady in the current with wavering fins. As he watched them they changed their positions by quick angles, only to hold steady in the fast water again. Nick watched them a long time.

He watched them holding themselves with their noses into the current, many trout in deep, fast moving water, slightly distorted as he watched far down through the glassy convex surface of the pool, its surface pushing and swelling smooth against the resistance of the log-driven piles of the bridge. At the bottom of the pool were the big trout. Nick did not see them at first. Then he saw them at the bottom of the pool, big trout looking to hold themselves on the gravel bottom in a varying mist of gravel and sand, raised in spurts by the current.

Nick looked down into the pool from the bridge. It was a hot day. A kingfisher flew up the stream. It was a long time since Nick had looked into a stream and seen trout. They were very satisfactory. As the shadow of the kingfisher moved up the stream, a big trout shot upstream in a long angle, only his shadow marking the angle, then lost his shadow as he came through the surface of the water, caught the sun, and then, as he went back into the stream under the surface, his shadow seemed to float down the stream with the current, unresisting, to his post under the bridge where he tightened facing up into the current.

Nick's heart tightened as the trout moved. He felt all the old feeling.

He turned and looked down the stream. It stretched away, pebbly-bottomed with shallows and big boulders and a deep pool as it curved away around the foot of a bluff.

Nick walked back up the ties to where his pack lay in the cinders beside the railway track. He was happy. He adjusted the pack harness around the bundle, pulling straps tight, slung the pack on his back, got his arms through the shoulder straps and took some of the pull off his shoulders by leaning his forehead against the wide band of the tump-line. Still, it was too heavy. It was much too heavy. He had his leather rod-case in his hand and leaning forward to keep the weight of the pack high on his shoulders he walked along the road that paralleled the railway track, leaving the burned town behind in the heat, and then turned off around a hill with a high, fire-scarred hill on either side onto a road that went back into the country. He walked along the road feeling the ache from the pull of the heavy pack. The road climbed steadily. It was hard work walking up-hill. His muscles ached and the day was hot, but Nick felt happy. He felt he had left everything behind, the need for thinking, the need to write, other needs. It was all back of him.

From the time he had gotten down off the train and the baggage man had thrown his pack out of the open car door things had been different. Seney was burned, the country was burned over and changed, but it did not matter. It could not all be burned. He knew that. He hiked along the road, sweating in the sun, climbing to cross the range of hills that separated the railway from the pine plains.

The road ran on, dipping occasionally, but always climbing. Nick went on up. Finally the road after going parallel to the burnt hillside reached the top. Nick leaned back against a stump and slipped out of the pack harness. Ahead of him, as far as he could see, was the pine plain. The burned country stopped off at the left with the range of hills. On ahead islands of dark pine trees rose out of the plain. Far off to the left was the line of the river. Nick followed it with his eye and caught glints of the water in the sun.

There was nothing but the pine plain ahead of him, until the far blue hills that marked the Lake Superior height of land. He could hardly see them, faint and far away in the heat-light over the plain. If he looked too steadily they were gone. But if he only half-looked they were there, the far off hills of the height of land.

Nick sat down against the charred stump and smoked a cigarette. His pack balanced on the top of the stump, harness holding ready, a hollow molded in it from his back. Nick sat smoking, looking out over the country. He did not need to get his map out. He knew where he was from the position of the river.

As he smoked, his legs stretched out in front of him, he noticed a grasshopper walk along the ground and up onto his woolen sock. The grasshopper was black. As he had walked along the road, climbing, he had started many grasshoppers from the dust. They were all black. They were not the big grasshoppers with yellow and black or red and black wings whirring out from their black wing sheathing as they fly up. These were just ordinary hoppers, but all a sooty black in color. Nick had wondered about them as he walked, without really thinking about them. Now, as he watched the black hopper that was nibbling at the wool of his sock with its fourway lip, he realized that they had all turned black from living in the burned-over land. He realized that the fire must have come the year before, but the grasshoppers were all black now. He wondered how long they would stay that way.

Carefully he reached his hand down and took hold of the hopper by the wings. He turned him up, all his legs walking in the air, and looked at his jointed belly. Yes, it was black too, iridescent where the back and head were dusty.

"Go on, hopper," Nick said, speaking out loud for the first time, "Fly away somewhere."

He tossed the grasshopper up into the air and watched him sail away to a charcoal stump across the road.

Nick stood up. He leaned his back against the weight of his pack where it rested upright on the stump and got his arms through the shoulder straps. He stood with the pack on his back on the brow of the hill looking out across the country, toward the distant river and then struck down the hillside away from the road. Underfoot the ground was good walking. Two hundred yards down the hillside the fire line stopped. Then it was sweet fern, growing ankle high, to walk through, and clumps of jack pines; a long undulating country with frequent rises and descents, sandy underfoot and the country alive again.

Nick kept his direction by the sun. He knew where he wanted to strike the river and he kept on through the pine plain, mounting small rises to see other rises ahead of him and sometimes from the top of a rise a great solid island of pines off to his right or his left. He broke off some sprigs of the heathery sweet fern, and put them under his pack straps. The chafing crushed it and he smelled it as he walked.

He was tired and very hot, walking across the uneven, shadeless pine plain. At any time he knew he could strike the river by turning off to his left. It could not be more than a mile away. But he kept on toward the north to hit the river as far upstream as he could go in one day's walking.

For some time as he walked Nick had been in sight of one of the big islands of pine standing out above the rolling high ground he was crossing. He dipped down and then as he came slowly up to the crest of the ridge he turned and made toward the pine trees.

There was no underbrush in the island of pine trees. The trunks of the trees went straight up or slanted toward each other. The trunks were straight and brown without branches. The branches were high above. Some interlocked to make a solid shadow on the brown forest floor. Around the grove of trees was a bare space. It was brown and soft underfoot as Nick walked on it. This was the over-lapping of the pine needle floor, extending out beyond the width of the high branches. The trees had grown tall and the branches moved high, leaving in the sun this bare space they had once covered with shadow. Sharp at the edge of this extension of the forest floor commenced the sweet fern.

Nick slipped off his pack and lay down in the shade. He lay on his back and looked up into the pine trees. His neck and back and the small of his back rested as he stretched. The earth felt good against his back. He looked up at the sky, through the branches, and then shut his eyes. He opened them and looked up again. There was a wind high up in the branches. He shut his eyes again and went to sleep.

Nick woke stiff and cramped. The sun was nearly down. His pack was heavy and the straps painful as he lifted it on. He leaned over with the pack on and picked up the leather rod-case and started out from the pine trees across the sweet fern swale, toward the river. He knew it could not be more than a mile.

He came down a hillside covered with stumps into a meadow. At the edge of the meadow flowed the river. Nick was glad to get to the river. He walked upstream through the meadow. His trousers were soaked with the dew as he walked. After the hot day, the dew had come quickly and heavily. The river made no sound. It was too fast and smooth. At the edge of the meadow, before he mounted to a piece of high ground to make camp, Nick looked down the river at the trout rising. They were rising to insects come from the swamp on the other side of the stream when the sun went down. The trout jumped out of water to take them. While Nick walked through the little stretch of meadow alongside the stream, trout had jumped high out of water. Now as he looked down the river, the insects must be settling on the surface, for the trout were feeding steadily all down the stream. As far down the long stretch as he could see, the trout were rising, making circles all down the surface of the water, as though it were starting to rain.

The ground rose, wooded and sandy, to overlook the meadow, the stretch of river and the swamp. Nick dropped his pack and rod-case and looked for a level piece of ground. He was very hungry and he wanted to make his camp before he cooked. Between two jack pines, the ground was quite level. He took the ax out of the pack and chopped out two projecting roots. That leveled a piece of ground large enough to sleep on. He smoothed out the sandy soil with his hand and pulled all the sweet fern bushes by their roots. His hands smelled good from the sweet fern. He smoothed the uprooted earth. He did not want anything making lumps under the blankets. When he had the ground smooth, he spread his three blankets. One he folded double, next to the ground. The other two he spread on top.

With the ax he slit off a bright slab of pine from one of the stumps and split it into pegs for the tent. He wanted them long and solid to hold in the ground. With the tent unpacked and spread on the ground, the pack, leaning against a jackpine, looked much smaller. Nick tied the rope that served the tent for a ridge-pole to the trunk of one of the pine trees and pulled the tent up off the ground with the other end of the rope and tied it to the other pine. The tent hung on the rope like a canvas blanket on a clothes line. Nick poked a pole he had cut up under the back peak of the canvas and then made it a tent by pegging out the sides. He pegged the sides out taut and drove the pegs deep, hitting them down into the ground with the flat of the ax until the rope loops were buried and the canvas was drum tight.

Across the open mouth of the tent Nick fixed cheese cloth to keep out mosquitoes. He crawled inside under the mosquito bar with various things from the pack to put at the head of the bed under the slant of the canvas. Inside the tent the light came through the brown canvas. It smelled pleasantly of canvas. Already there was something mysterious and homelike. Nick was happy as he crawled inside the tent. He had not been unhappy all day. This was different though. Now things were done. There had been this to do. Now it was done. It had been a hard trip. He was very tired. That was done. He had made his camp. He was settled. Nothing could touch him. It was a good place to camp. He was there, in the good place. He was in his home where he had made it. Now he was hungry.

He came out, crawling under the cheese cloth. It was quite dark outside. It was lighter in the tent.

Nick went over to the pack and found, with his fingers, a long nail in a paper sack of nails, in the bottom of the pack. He drove it into the pine tree, holding it close and hitting it gently with the flat of the ax. He hung the pack up on the nail. All his supplies were in the pack. They were off the ground and sheltered now.

Nick was hungry. He did not believe he had ever been hungrier. He opened and emptied a can of pork and beans and a can of spaghetti into the frying pan.

"I've got a right to eat this kind of stuff, if I'm willing to carry it," Nick said. His voice sounded strange in the darkening woods. He did not speak again.

He started a fire with some chunks of pine he got with the ax from a stump. Over the fire he stuck a wire grill, pushing the four legs down into the ground with his boot. Nick put the frying pan on the grill over the flames. He was hungrier. The beans and spaghetti warmed. Nick stirred them and mixed them together. They began to bubble, making little bubbles that rose with difficulty to the surface. There was a good smell. Nick got out a bottle of tomato catchup and cut four slices of bread. The little bubbles were coming faster now. Nick sat down beside the fire and lifted the frying pan off. He poured about half the contents out into the tin plate. It spread slowly on the plate. Nick knew it was too hot. He poured on some tomato catchup. He knew the beans and spaghetti were still too hot. He looked at the fire, then at the tent, he was not going to spoil it all by burning his tongue. For years he had never enjoyed fried bananas because he had never been able to wait for them to cool. His tongue was very sensitive. He was very hungry. Across the river in the swamp, in the almost dark, he saw a mist rising. He looked at the tent once more. All right. He took a full spoonful from the plate.

"Chrise," Nick said, "Geezus Chrise," he said happily.

He ate the whole plateful before he remembered the bread. Nick finished the second plateful with the bread, mopping the plate shiny. He had not eaten since a cup of coffee and a ham sandwich in the station restaurant at St. Ignace. It had been a very fine experience. He had been that hungry before, but had not been able to satisfy it. He could have made camp hours before if he had wanted to. There were plenty of good places to camp on the river. But this was good.

Nick tucked two big chips of pine under the grill. The fire flared up. He had forgotten to get water for the coffee. Out of the pack he got a folding canvas bucket and walked down the hill, across the edge of the meadow, to the stream. The other bank was in the white mist. The grass was wet and cold as he knelt on the bank and dipped the canvas bucket into the stream. It bellied and pulled hard in the current. The water was ice cold. Nick rinsed the bucket and carried it full up to the camp. Up away from the stream it was not so cold.

Nick drove another big nail and hung up the bucket full of water. He dipped the coffee pot half full, put some more chips under the grill onto the fire and put the pot on. He could not remember which way he made coffee. He could remember an argument about it with Hopkins, but not which side he had taken. He decided to bring it to a boil. He remembered now that was Hopkins's way. He had once argued about everything with Hopkins. While he waited for the coffee to boil, he opened a small can of apricots. He liked to open cans. He emptied the can of apricots out into a tin cup. While he watched the coffee on the fire, he drank the juice syrup of the apricots, carefully at first to keep from spilling, then meditatively, sucking the apricots down. They were better than fresh apricots.

The coffee boiled as he watched. The lid came up and coffee and grounds ran down the side of the pot. Nick took it off the grill. It was a triumph for Hopkins. He put sugar in the empty apricot cup and poured some of the coffee out to cool. It was too hot to pour and he used his hat to hold the handle of the coffee pot. He would not let it steep in the pot at all. Not the first cup. It should be straight Hopkins all the way. Hop deserved that. He was a very serious coffee maker. He was the most serious man Nick had ever known. Not heavy, serious. That was a long time ago. Hopkins spoke without moving his lips. He had played polo. He made millions of dollars in Texas. He had borrowed carfare to go to Chicago, when the wire came that his first big well had come in. He could have wired for money. That would have been too slow. They called Hop's girl the Blonde Venus. Hop did not mind because she was not his real girl. Hopkins said very confidently that none of them would make fun of his real girl. He was right. Hopkins went away when the telegram came. That was on the Black River. It took eight days for the telegram to reach him. Hopkins gave away his .22 caliber Colt automatic pistol to Nick. He gave his camera to Bill. It was to remember him always by. They were all going fishing again next summer. The Hop Head was rich. He would get a yacht and they would all cruise along the north shore of Lake Superior. He was excited but serious. They said good-bye and all felt bad. It broke up the trip. They never saw Hopkins again. That was a long time ago on the Black River.

Nick drank the coffee, the coffee, according to Hopkins. The coffee was bitter. Nick laughed. It made a good ending to the story. His mind was starting to work. He knew he could choke it because he was tired enough. He spilled the coffee out of the pot and shook the grounds loose into the fire. He lit a cigarette and went inside the tent. He took off his shoes and trousers, sitting on the blankets, rolled the shoes up inside the trousers for a pillow and got in between the blankets.

Out through the front of the tent he watched the glow of the fire, when the night wind blew on it. It was a quiet night. The swamp was perfectly quiet. Nick stretched under the blanket comfortably. A mosquito hummed close to his ear. Nick sat up and lit a match. The mosquito was on the canvas, over his head. Nick moved the match quickly up to it. The mosquito made a satisfactory hiss in the flame. The match went out. Nick lay down again under the blankets. He turned on his side and shut his eyes. He was sleepy. He felt sleep coming. He curled up under the blanket and went to sleep.

Part II

In the morning the sun was up and the tent was starting to get hot. Nick crawled out under the mosquito netting stretched across the mouth of the tent, to look at the morning. The grass was wet on his hands as he came out. He held his trousers and his shoes in his hands. The sun was just up over the hill. There was the meadow, the river and the swamp. There were birch trees in the green of the swamp on the other side of the river.

The river was clear and smoothly fast in the early morning. Down about two hundred yards were three logs all the way across the stream. They made the water smooth and deep above them. As Nick watched, a mink crossed the river on the logs and went into the swamp. Nick was excited. He was excited by the early morning and the river. He was really too hurried to eat breakfast, but he knew he must. He built a little fire and put on the coffee pot. While the water was heating in the pot he took an empty bottle and went down over the edge of the high ground to the meadow. The meadow was wet with dew and Nick wanted to catch grasshoppers for bait before the sun dried the grass. He found plenty of good grasshoppers. They were at the base of the grass stems. Sometimes they clung to a grass stem. They were cold and wet with the dew, and could not jump until the sun warmed them. Nick picked them up, taking only the medium sized brown ones, and put them into the bottle. He turned over a log and just under the shelter of the edge were several hundred hoppers. It was a grasshopper lodging house. Nick put about fifty of the medium browns into the bottle. While he was picking up the hoppers the others warmed in the sun and commenced to hop away. They flew when they hopped. At first they made one flight and stayed stiff when they landed, as though they were dead.

Nick knew that by the time he was through with breakfast they would be as lively as ever. Without dew in the grass it would take him all day to catch a bottle full of good grasshoppers and he would have to crush many of them, slamming at them with his hat. He washed his hands at the stream. He was excited to be near it. Then he walked up to the tent. The hoppers were already jumping stiffly in the grass. In the bottle, warmed by the sun, they were jumping in a mass. Nick put in a pine stick as a cork. It plugged the mouth of the bottle enough, so the hoppers could not get out and left plenty of air passage.

He had rolled the log back and knew he could get grasshoppers there every morning.

Nick laid the bottle full of jumping grasshoppers against a pine trunk. Rapidly he mixed some buckwheat flour with water and stirred it smooth, one cup of flour, one cup of water. He put a handful of coffee in the pot and dipped a lump of grease out of a can and slid it sputtering across the hot skillet. On the smoking skillet he poured smoothly the buckwheat batter. It spread like lava, the grease spitting sharply. Around the edges the buckwheat cake began to firm, then brown, then crisp. The surface was bubbling slowly to porousness. Nick pushed under the browned under surface with a fresh pine chip. He shook the skillet sideways and the cake was loose on the surface. I won't try and flop it, he thought. He slid the chip of clean wood all the way under the cake, and flopped it over onto its face. It sputtered in the pan.

When it was cooked Nick regreased the skillet. He used all the batter. It made another big flapjack and one smaller one.

Nick ate a big flapjack and a smaller one, covered with apple butter. He put apple butter on the third cake, folded it over twice, wrapped it in oiled paper and put it in his shirt pocket. He put the apple butter jar back in the pack and cut bread for two sandwiches.

In the pack he found a big onion. He sliced it in two and peeled the silky outer skin. Then he cut one half into slices and made onion sandwiches. He wrapped them in oiled paper and buttoned them in the other pocket of his khaki shirt. He turned the skillet upside down on the grill, drank the coffee, sweetened and yellow brown with the condensed milk in it, and tidied up the camp. It was a nice little camp.

Nick took his fly rod out of the leather rod-case, jointed it, and shoved the rod-case back into the tent. He put on the reel and threaded the line through the guides. He had to hold it from hand to hand, as he threaded it, or it would slip back through its own weight. It was a heavy, double tapered fly line. Nick had paid eight dollars for it a long time ago. It was made heavy to lift back in the air and come forward flat and heavy and straight to make it possible to cast a fly which has no weight. Nick opened the aluminum leader box. The leaders were coiled between the damp flannel pads. Nick had wet the pads at the water cooler on the train up to St. Ignace. In the damp pads the gut leaders had softened and Nick unrolled one and tied it by a loop at the end to the heavy fly line. He fastened a hook on the end of the leader. It was a small hook; very thin and springy.

Nick took it from his hook book, sitting with the rod across his lap. He tested the knot and the spring of the rod by pulling the line taut. It was a good feeling. He was careful not to let the hook bite into his finger.

He started down to the stream, holding his rod, the bottle of grasshoppers hung from his neck by a thong tied in half hitches around the neck of the bottle. His landing net hung by a hook from his belt. Over his shoulder was a long flour sack tied at each corner into an ear. The cord went over his shoulder. The sack flapped against his legs.

Nick felt awkward and professionally happy with all his equipment hanging from him. The grasshopper bottle swung against his chest. In his shirt the breast pockets bulged against him with the lunch and his fly book.

He stepped into the stream. It was a shock. His trousers clung tight to his legs. His shoes felt the gravel. The water was a rising cold shock.

Rushing, the current sucked against his legs. Where he stepped in, the water was over his knees. He waded with the current. The gravel slid under his shoes. He looked down at the swirl of water below each leg and tipped up the bottle to get a grasshopper.

The first grasshopper gave a jump in the neck of the bottle and went out into the water. He was sucked under in the whirl by Nick's right leg and came to the surface a little way down stream. He floated rapidly, kicking. In a quick circle, breaking the smooth surface of the water, he disappeared. A trout had taken him.

Another hopper poked his head out of the bottle. His antennæ wavered. He was getting his front legs out of the bottle to jump, Nick took him by the head and held him while he threaded the slim hook under his chin, down through his thorax and into the last segments of his abdomen. The grasshopper took hold of the hook with his front feet, spitting tobacco juice on it. Nick dropped him into the water.

Holding the rod in his right hand he let out line against the pull of the grasshopper in the current. He stripped off line from the reel with his left hand and let it run free. He could see the hopper in the little waves of the current. It went out of sight.

There was a tug on the line. Nick pulled against the taut line. It was his first strike. Holding the now living rod across the current he brought in the line with his left hand. The rod bent in jerks, the trout pumping against the current. Nick knew it was a small one. He lifted the rod straight up in the air. It bowed with the pull.

He saw the trout in the water jerking with his head and body against the shifting tangent of the line in the stream.

Nick took the line in his left hand and pulled the trout, thumping tiredly against the current, to the surface. His back was mottled the clear, water-over-gravel color, his side flashing in the sun. The rod under his right arm, Nick stooped, dipping his right hand into the current. He held the trout, never still, with his moist right hand, while he unhooked the barb from his mouth, then dropped him back into the stream.

He hung unsteadily in the current, then settled to the bottom beside a stone. Nick reached down his hand to touch him, his arm to the elbow under water. The trout was steady in the moving stream, resting on the gravel, beside a stone. As Nick's fingers touched him, touched his smooth, cool, underwater feeling he was gone, gone in a shadow across the bottom of the stream.

He's all right, Nick thought. He was only tired.

He had wet his hand before he touched the trout, so he would not disturb the delicate mucus that covered him. If a trout was touched with a dry hand, a white fungus attacked the unprotected spot. Years before when he had fished crowded streams, with fly fishermen ahead of him and behind him, Nick had again and again come on dead trout, furry with white fungus, drifted against a rock, or floating belly up in some pool. Nick did not like to fish with other men on the river. Unless they were of your party, they spoiled it.

He wallowed down the stream, above his knees in the current, through the fifty yards of shallow water above the pile of logs that crossed the stream. He did not rebait his hook and held it in his hand as he waded. He was certain he could catch small trout in the shallows, but he did not want them. There would be no big trout in the shallows this time of day.

Now the water deepened up his thighs sharply and coldly. Ahead was the smooth dammed-back flood of water above the logs. The water was smooth and dark; on the left, the lower edge of the meadow; on the right the swamp.

Nick leaned back against the current and took a hopper from the bottle. He threaded the hopper on the hook and spat on him for good luck. Then he pulled several yards of line from the reel and tossed the hopper out ahead onto the fast, dark water. It floated down towards the logs, then the weight of the line pulled the bait under the surface. Nick held the rod in his right hand, letting the line run out through his fingers.

There was a long tug. Nick struck and the rod came alive and dangerous, bent double, the line tightening, coming out of water, tightening, all in a heavy, dangerous, steady pull. Nick felt the moment when the leader would break if the strain increased and let the line go.

The reel ratcheted into a mechanical shriek as the line went out in a rush. Too fast. Nick could not check it, the line rushing out, the reel note rising as the line ran out.

With the core of the reel showing, his heart feeling stopped with the excitement, leaning back against the current that mounted icily his thighs, Nick thumbed the reel hard with his left hand. It was awkward getting his thumb inside the fly reel frame.

As he put on pressure the line tightened into sudden hardness and beyond the logs a huge trout went high out of water. As he jumped, Nick lowered the tip of the rod. But he felt, as he dropped the tip to ease the strain, the moment when the strain was too great; the hardness too tight. Of course, the leader had broken. There was no mistaking the feeling when all spring left the line and it became dry and hard. Then it went slack.

His mouth dry, his heart down, Nick reeled in. He had never seen so big a trout. There was a heaviness, a power not to be held, and then the bulk of him, as he jumped. He looked as broad as a salmon.

Nick's hand was shaky. He reeled in slowly. The thrill had been too much. He felt vaguely, a little sick, as though it would be better to sit down.

The leader had broken where the hook was tied to it. Nick took it in his hand. He thought of the trout somewhere on the bottom, holding himself steady over the gravel, far down below the light, under the logs, with the hook in his jaw. Nick knew the trout's teeth would cut through the snell of the hook. The hook would imbed itself in his jaw. He'd bet the trout was angry. Anything that size would be angry. That was a trout. He had been solidly hooked. Solid as a rock. He felt like a rock, too, before he started off. By God, he was a big one. By God, he was the biggest one I ever heard of.

Nick climbed out onto the meadow and stood, water running down his trousers and out of his shoes, his shoes squlchy. He went over and sat on the logs. He did not want to rush his sensations any.

He wriggled his toes in the water, in his shoes, and got out a cigarette from his breast pocket. He lit it and tossed the match into the fast water below the logs. A tiny trout rose at the match, as it swung around in the fast current. Nick laughed. He would finish the cigarette.

He sat on the logs, smoking, drying in the sun, the sun warm on his back, the river shallow ahead entering the woods, curving into the woods, shallows, light glittering, big water-smooth rocks, cedars along the bank and white birches, the logs warm in the sun smooth to sit on, without bark, gray to the touch; slowly the feeling of disappointment left him. It went away slowly, the feeling of disappointment that came sharply after the thrill that made his shoulders ache. It was all right now. His rod lying out on the logs, Nick tied a new hook on the leader, pulling the gut tight until it grimped into itself in a hard knot.

He baited up, then picked up the rod and walked to the far end of the logs to get into the water, where it was not too deep. Under and beyond the logs was a deep pool. Nick walked around the shallow shelf near the swamp shore until he came out on the shallow bed of the stream.

On the left, where the meadow ended and the woods began, a great elm tree was uprooted. Gone over in a storm, it lay back into the woods, its roots clotted with dirt, grass growing in them, rising a solid bank beside the stream. The river cut to the edge of the uprooted tree. From where Nick stood he could see deep channels, like ruts, cut in the shallow bed of the stream by the flow of the current. Pebbly where he stood and pebbly and full of boulders beyond; where it curved near the tree roots, the bed of the stream was marly and between the ruts of deep water green weed fronds swung in the current.

Nick swung the rod back over his shoulder and forward, and the line, curving forward, laid the grasshopper down on one of the deep channels in the weeds. A trout struck and Nick hooked him.

Holding the rod far out toward the uprooted tree and sloshing backward in the current, Nick worked the trout, plunging, the rod bending alive, out of the danger of the weeds into the open river. Holding the rod, pumping alive against the current, Nick brought the trout in. He rushed, but always came, the spring of the rod yielding to the rushes, sometimes jerking under water, but always bringing him in. Nick eased downstream with the rushes. The rod above his head he led the trout over the net, then lifted.

The trout hung heavy in the net, mottled trout back and silver sides in the meshes. Nick unhooked him; heavy sides, good to hold, big undershot jaw, and slipped him, heaving and big sliding, into the long sack that hung from his shoulders in the water.

Nick spread the mouth of the sack against the current and it filled, heavy with water. He held it up, the bottom in the stream, and the water poured out through the sides. Inside at the bottom was the big trout, alive in the water.

Nick moved downstream. The sack out ahead of him, sunk, heavy in the water, pulling from his shoulders.

It was getting hot, the sun hot on the back of his neck.

Nick had one good trout. He did not care about getting many trout. Now the stream was shallow and wide. There were trees along both banks. The trees of the left bank made short shadows on the current in the forenoon sun. Nick knew there were trout in each shadow. In the afternoon, after the sun had crossed toward the hills, the trout would be in the cool shadows on the other side of the stream.

The very biggest ones would lie up close to the bank. You could always pick them up there on the Black. When the sun was down they all moved out into the current. Just when the sun made the water blinding in the glare before it went down, you were liable to strike a big trout anywhere in the current. It was almost impossible to fish then, the surface of the water was blinding as a mirror in the sun. Of course, you could fish upstream, but in a stream like the Black, or this, you had to wallow against the current and in a deep place, the water piled up on you. It was no fun to fish upstream with this much current.

Nick moved along through the shallow stretch watching the banks for deep holes. A beech tree grew close beside the river, so that the branches hung down into the water. The stream went back in under the leaves. There were always trout in a place like that.

Nick did not care about fishing that hole. He was sure he would get hooked in the branches.

It looked deep though. He dropped the grasshopper so the current took it under water, back in under the overhanging branch. The line pulled hard and Nick struck. The trout threshed heavily, half out of water in the leaves and branches. The line was caught. Nick pulled hard and the trout was off. He reeled in and holding the hook in his hand, walked down the stream.

Ahead, close to the left bank, was a big log. Nick saw it was hollow; pointing up river the current entered it smoothly, only a little ripple spread each side of the log. The water was deepening. The top of the hollow log was gray and dry. It was partly in the shadow.

Nick took the cork out of the grasshopper bottle and a hopper clung to it. He picked him off, hooked him and tossed him out. He held the rod far out so that the hopper on the water moved into the current flowing into the hollow log. Nick lowered the rod and the hopper floated in. There was a heavy strike. Nick swung the rod against the pull. It felt as though he were hooked into the log itself, except for the live feeling.

He tried to force the fish out into the current. It came, heavily.

The line went slack and Nick thought the trout was gone. Then he saw him, very near, in the current, shaking his head, trying to get the hook out. His mouth was clamped shut. He was fighting the hook in the clear flowing current.

Looping in the line with his left hand, Nick swung the rod to make the line taut and tried to lead the trout toward the net but he was gone, out of sight, the line pumping. Nick fought him against the current, letting him thump in the water against the spring of the rod. He shifted the rod to his left hand, worked the trout upstream, holding his weight, fighting on the rod, and then let him down into the net. He lifted him clear of the water, a heavy half circle in the net, the net dripping, unhooked him and slid him into the sack.

He spread the mouth of the sack and looked down in at the two big trout alive in the water.

Through the deepening water, Nick waded over to the hollow log. He took the sack off, over his head, the trout flopping as it came out of water, and hung it so the trout were deep in the water. Then he pulled himself up on the log and sat, the water from his trousers and boots running down into the stream. He laid his rod down, moved along to the shady end of the log and took the sandwiches out of his pocket. He dipped the sandwiches in the cold water. The current carried away the crumbs. He ate the sandwiches and dipped his hat full of water to drink, the water running out through his hat just ahead of his drinking.

It was cool in the shade, sitting on the log. He took a cigarette out and struck a match to light it. The match sunk into the gray wood, making a tiny furrow. Nick leaned over the side of the log, found a hard place and lit the match. He sat smoking and watching the river.

Ahead the river narrowed and went into a swamp. The river became smooth and deep and the swamp looked solid with cedar trees, their trunks close together, their branches solid. It would not be possible to walk through a swamp like that. The branches grew so low. You would have to keep almost level with the ground to move at all. You could not crash through the branches. That must be why the animals that lived in swamps were built the way they were, Nick thought.

He wished he had brought something to read. He felt like reading. He did not feel like going on into the swamp. He looked down the river. A big cedar slanted all the way across the stream. Beyond that the river went into the swamp.

Nick did not want to go in there now. He felt a reaction against deep wading with the water deepening up under his armpits, to hook big trout in places impossible to land them. In the swamp the banks were bare, the big cedars came together overhead, the sun did not come through, except in patches; in the fast deep water, in the half light, the fishing would be tragic. In the swamp fishing was a tragic adventure. Nick did not want it. He did not want to go down the stream any further today.

He took out his knife, opened it and stuck it in the log. Then he pulled up the sack, reached into it and brought out one of the trout. Holding him near the tail, hard to hold, alive, in his hand, he whacked him against the log. The trout quivered, rigid. Nick laid him on the log in the shade and broke the neck of the other fish the same way. He laid them side by side on the log. They were fine trout.

Nick cleaned them, slitting them from the vent to the tip of the jaw. All the insides and the gills and tongue came out in one piece. They were both males; long gray-white strips of milt, smooth and clean. All the insides clean and compact, coming out all together. Nick tossed the offal ashore for the minks to find.

He washed the trout in the stream. When he held them back up in the water they looked like live fish. Their color was not gone yet. He washed his hands and dried them on the log. Then he laid the trout on the sack spread out on the log, rolled them up in it, tied the bundle and put it in the landing net. His knife was still standing, blade stuck in the log. He cleaned it on the wood and put it in his pocket.

Nick stood up on the log, holding his rod, the landing net hanging heavy, then stepped into the water and splashed ashore. He climbed the bank and cut up into the woods, toward the high ground. He was going back to camp. He looked back. The river just showed through the trees. There were plenty of days coming when he could fish the swamp.

1925

Zora Neale Hurston
ca. 1901–1960

Zora Neale Hurston was born—the date is uncertain—in Eatonville, Florida, a town she described as "the first [incorporated] Negro community" and "the first attempt at organized self-government on the part of Negroes in America." After her mother's death in 1904, her father, a tenant farmer and preacher, placed her in a school in Jacksonville. At fourteen, when want of money forced her father to remove her from school, she joined a traveling Gilbert and Sullivan troupe as a maid, hoping to save money so that she could return to school. Near the end of her life, Hurston entered another period of wandering: She worked again as a maid, then as a librarian, as a part-time teacher, and as a reporter. On January 28, 1960, she died in the County Welfare Home in Fort Pierce, Florida. Between her troubled beginnings and her lonely end, however, during the 1920s, the 1930s, and into the 1940s, Hurston lived a remarkably full and varied life, one she autobiographically recorded in what may be her finest book, *Dust Tracks on the Road* (1942).

In 1923 Hurston entered Howard University, where she began to write. In 1926 she won a scholarship to Barnard College, where she was the first black woman to be admitted and where she continued to write. She also began to cultivate an interest in anthropology. By the time she graduated in 1928, she had attracted the attention of Columbia University's distinguished anthropologist Franz Boas, with whom she worked off and on for more than ten years. From 1928 to 1931 she collected folklore throughout the South and in 1935 published *Mules & Men,* anthropological stories of voodoo among southern blacks. In 1937 and 1938, sponsored by two successive Guggenheim fellowships, she did field research in Jamaica, Haiti, and Bermuda, investigations that led to another book of anthropology, *Tell My Horse* (1938). Later still, she collected folklore in Florida for the Works Progress Administration. "Voodooism" and "black magic" became abiding interests, as did the oral folk literature of the black South and the Caribbean. "She was always getting scholarships and things from wealthy white people," Langston Hughes recalled, "some of whom simply paid her just to sit around and represent the Negro race for them. . . . She was full of side-splitting anecdotes, humorous tales, and tragicomic stories, remembered out of her life in the South as a daughter of a travelling minister of God."

In part because she was a flamboyant, charismatic woman, and especially because she was a remarkably gifted writer, Hurston played a major role in the Harlem Renaissance during the late 1920s and the early 1930s. No writer of the period did more than she to show the glamour, the excitement, and the promise that enabled American cities to draw hundreds of thousands of black people to them. And none did more than she to expose the loneliness, emptiness, and brutality that people often found once they had reached their destinations. Her deeper subject, however, one embedded in the move of people from the farms and villages to the cities, lay in the strength and wisdom that people found in the folkways, the music, and the stories they carried with them. Many of these themes were explored in a series of novels: *Jonah's Gourd Vine* (1934), a narrative based on the lives of Hurston's parents; *Their Eyes Were Watching God* (1937), a love story set in Eatonville and the surrounding farm community; *Moses, Man of the Mountain* (1939), a re-creation and reinterpretation of the Old Testament Hebrews in the form of Negro folktales; and *Seraph on the Suwanee* (1948), the tale of a love affair between a white man and a black woman.

Hurston's point of view was so distinctly and powerfully her own that she seldom pleased anyone entirely and sometimes pleased no one at all. Since her writing often went counter to the more recent literature of black protest, making her seem politically unrealistic, Hurston's reputation suffered in the 1950s a severe decline that continued in the years following her lonely death. During the last several years, however, her achievement has received new recognition, based, as Alice Walker has noted, on the sense that she was "before her time" in presenting "black people as complete, complex, *undiminished* human beings, a sense that is lacking in so much black writing and literature."

Further Reading:
L. Hughes, *The Big Sea*, 1940.
A. Rayson, "The Novels of Zora Neale Hurston," *Studies in Black Literature*, Winter 1974.
A. Walker, "In Search of Zora Neale Hurston," *Ms. Magazine*, March 1975.
R. E. Hemenway, *Zora Neale Hurston: A Literary Biography*, 1977.

Text:
"The Gilded Six-bits" from *The Best Short Stories by Negro Writers*, ed. Langston Hughes, 1967.

The Gilded Six-bits[1]

It was a Negro yard around a Negro house in a Negro settlement that looked to the payroll of the G. and G. Fertilizer works for its support.

But there was something happy about the place. The front yard was parted in the middle by a sidewalk from gate to doorstep, a sidewalk edged on either side by quart bottles driven neck down into the ground on a slant. A mess of homey flowers planted without a plan but blooming cheerily from their helter-skelter places. The fence and house were whitewashed. The porch and steps scrubbed white.

The front door stood open to the sunshine so that the floor of the front room could finish drying after its weekly scouring. It was Saturday. Everything clean from the front gate to the privy house. Yard raked so that the strokes of the rake would make a pattern. Fresh newspaper cut in fancy edge on the kitchen shelves.

Missie May was bathing herself in the galvanized washtub in the bedroom. Her dark-brown skin glistened under the soapsuds that skittered down from her washrag. Her stiff young breasts thrust forward aggressively, like broad-based cones with the tips lacquered in black.

She heard men's voices in the distance and glanced at the dollar clock on the dresser.

"Humph! Ah'm way behind time t'day! Joe gointer be heah 'fore Ah git mah clothes on if Ah don't make haste."

She grabbed the clean meal sack at hand and dried herself hurriedly and began to dress. But before she could tie her slippers, there came the ring of singing metal on wood. Nine times.

Missie May grinned with delight. She had not seen the big tall man come stealing

[1] Seventy-five cents.

in the gate and creep up the walk grinning happily at the joyful mischief he was about to commit. But she knew that it was her husband throwing silver dollars in the door for her to pick up and pile beside her plate at dinner. It was this way every Saturday afternoon. The nine dollars hurled into the open door, he scurried to a hiding place behind the Cape jasmine bush and waited.

Missie May promptly appeared at the door in mock alarm.

"Who dat chunkin' money in mah do'way?" she demanded. No answer from the yard. She leaped off the porch and began to search the shrubbery. She peeped under the porch and hung over the gate to look up and down the road. While she did this, the man behind the jasmine darted to the chinaberry tree. She spied him and gave chase.

"Nobody ain't gointer be chunkin' money at me and Ah not do 'em nothin'," she shouted in mock anger. He ran around the house with Missie May at his heels. She overtook him at the kitchen door. He ran inside but could not close it after him before she crowded in and locked with him in a rough-and-tumble. For several minutes the two were a furious mass of male and female energy. Shouting, laughing, twisting, turning, tussling, tickling each other in the ribs; Missie May clutching onto Joe and Joe trying, but not too hard, to get away.

"Missie May, take yo' hand out mah pocket!" Joe shouted out between laughs.

"Ah ain't, Joe, not lessen you gwine gimme whateve' it is good you got in yo' pocket. Turn it go, Joe, do Ah'll tear yo' clothes."

"Go on tear 'em. You de one dat pushes de needles round heah. Move yo' hand, Missie May."

"Lemme git dat paper sack out yo' pocket. Ah bet it's candy kisses."

"Tain't. Move yo' hand. Woman ain't got no business in a man's clothes nohow. Go way."

Missie May gouged way down and gave an upward jerk and triumphed.

"Unhhunh! Ah got it! It 'tis so candy kisses. Ah knowed you had somethin' for me in yo' clothes. Now Ah got to see whut's in every pocket you got."

Joe smiled indulgently and let his wife go through all of his pockets and take out the things that he had hidden there for her to find. She bore off the chewing gum, the cake of sweet soap, the pocket handkerchief as if she had wrested them from him, as if they had not been bought for the sake of this friendly battle.

"Whew! dat play-fight done got me all warmed up!" Joe exclaimed. "Got me some water in de kittle?"

"Yo' water is on de fire and yo' clean things is cross de bed. Hurry up and wash yo'self and git changed so we kin eat. Ah'm hongry." As Missie said this, she bore the steaming kettle into the bedroom.

"You ain't hongry, sugar," Joe contradicted her. "Youse jes' a little empty. Ah'm de one whut's hongry. Ah could eat up camp meetin', back off 'ssociation, and drink Jurdan dry. Have it on de table when Ah git out de tub."

"Don't you mess wid mah business, man. You git in yo' clothes. Ah'm a real wife, not no dress and breath. Ah might not look lak one, but if you burn me, you won't git a thing but wife ashes."

Joe splashed in the bedroom and Missie May fanned around in the kitchen. A fresh red-and-white checked cloth on the table. Big pitcher of buttermilk beaded with pale drops of butter from the churn. Hot fried mullet, crackling bread, ham hock atop a mound of string beans and new potatoes, and perched on the windowsill a pone of spicy potato pudding.

Very little talk during the meal but that little consisted of banter that pretended to deny affection but in reality flaunted it. Like when Missie May reached for a second helping of the tater pone. Joe snatched it out of her reach.

After Missie May had made two or three unsuccessful grabs at the pan, she begged, "Aw, Joe, gimme some mo' dat tater pone."

"Nope, sweetenin' is for us menfolks. Y'all pritty lil frail eels don't need nothin' lak dis. You too sweet already."

"Please, Joe."

"Naw, naw. Ah don't want you to git no sweeter than whut you is already. We goin' down de road a lil piece t'night so you go put on yo' Sunday-go-to-meetin' things."

Missie May looked at her husband to see if he was playing some prank. "Sho nuff, Joe?"

"Yeah. We goin' to de ice cream parlor."

"Where de ice cream parlor at, Joe?"

"A new man done come heah from Chicago and he done got a place and took and opened it up for a ice cream parlor, and bein' as it's real swell, Ah wants you to be one de first ladies to walk in dere and have some set down."

"Do Jesus, Ah ain't knowed nothin' bout it. Who de man done it?"

"Mister Otis D. Slemmons, of spots and places—Memphis, Chicago, Jacksonville, Philadelphia and so on."

"Dat heavyset man wid his mouth full of gold teeths?"

"Yeah. Where did you see 'im at?"

"Ah went down to de sto' tuh git a box of lye and Ah seen 'im standin' on de corner talkin' to some of de mens, and Ah come on back and went to scrubbin' de floor, and he passed and tipped his hat whilst Ah was scourin' de steps. Ah thought Ah never seen *him* befo'."

Joe smiled pleasantly. "Yeah, he's up-to-date. He got de finest clothes Ah ever seen on a colored man's back."

"Aw, he don't look no better in his clothes than you do in yourn. He got a puzzlegut[2] on 'im and he so chuckleheaded[3] he got a pone behind his neck."

Joe looked down at his own abdomen and said wistfully: "Wisht Ah had a build on me lak he got. He ain't puzzlegutted, honey. He jes' got a corperation. Dat make 'm look lak a rich white man. All rich mens is got some belly on 'em."

"Ah seen de pitchers of Henry Ford and he's a spare-built man and Rockefeller look lak he ain't got but one gut. But Ford and Rockefeller and dis Slemmons and all de rest kin be as many-gutted as dey please, Ah's satisfied wid you jes' lak you is, baby. God took pattern after a pine tree and built you noble. Youse a pritty man, and if Ah knowed any way to make you mo' pritty still Ah'd take and do it."

Joe reached over gently and toyed with Missie May's ear. "You jes' say dat cause you love me, but Ah know Ah can't hold no light to Otis D. Slemmons. Ah ain't never been nowhere and Ah ain't got nothin' but you."

---

[2] Potbelly.   [3] Stupid.

Missie May got on his lap and kissed him and he kissed back in kind. Then he went on. "All de womens is crazy 'bout 'im everywhere he go."

"How you know dat, Joe?"

"He tole us so hisself."

"Dat don': make it so. His mouf is cut crossways, ain't it? Well, he kin lie jes' lak anybody else."

"Good Lawd, Missie! You womens sho is hard to sense into things. He's got a five-dollar gold piece for a stickpin and he got a ten-dollar gold piece on his watch chain and his mouf is jes' crammed full of gold teeths. Sho wisht it wuz mine. And whut make it so cool, he got money 'cumulated. And womens give it all to 'im."

"Ah don': see whut de womens see on 'im. Ah wouldn't give 'im a wink if de sheriff wuz after 'im."

"Well, he tole us how de white womens in Chicago give 'im all dat gold money. So he don't 'low nobody to touch it at all. Not even put day finger on it. Dey tole 'im not to. You kin make 'miration at it, but don't tetch it."

"Whyn't he stay up dere where dey so crazy 'bout 'im?"

"Ah reckon dey done made 'im vast-rich and he wants to travel some. He says dey wouldn't leave 'im hit a lick of work. He got mo' lady people crazy 'bout him than he kin shake a stick at."

"Joe, Ah hates to see you so dumb. Dat stray nigger jes' tell y'all anything and y'all b'lieve it."

"Go 'head on now, honey, and put on yo' clothes. He talkin' 'bout his pritty womens—Ah want 'im to see *mine.*"

Missie May went off to dress and Joe spent the time trying to make his stomach punch out like Slemmons's middle. He tried the rolling swagger of the stranger, but found that his tall bone-and-muscle stride fitted ill with it. He just had time to drop back into his seat before Missie May came in dressed to go.

On the way home that night Joe was exultant. "Didn't Ah say ole Otis was swell? Can't he talk Chicago talk? Wuzn't dat funny whut he said when great big fat ole Ida Armstrong come in? He asted me, 'Who is dat broad wid de forte shake?' Dat's a new word. Us always thought forty was a set of figgers but he showed us where it means a whole heap of things. Sometimes he don't say forty, he jes' say thirty-eight and two and dat mean de same thing. Know whut he tole me when Ah wuz payin' for our ice cream? He say, Ah have to hand it to you, Joe. Dat wife of yours is jes' thirty-eight and two. Yessuh, she's forte!' Ain't he killin'?"

"He'll do in case of a rush. But he sho is got uh heap uh gold on 'im. Dat's de first time Ah ever seed gold money. It lookted good on him sho nuff, but it'd look a whole heap better on you."

"Who, me? Missie May, youse crazy! Where would a po' man lak me git gold money from?"

Missie May was silent for a minute, then she said, "Us might find some goin' long de road some time. Us could."

"Who would be losin' gold money round heah? We ain't even seen none dese white folks wearin' no gold money on dey watch chain. You must be figgerin' Mister Packard or Mister Cadillac goin' pass through heah."

"You don't know whut been lost 'round heah. Maybe somebody way back in memorial times lost they gold money and went on off and it ain't never been found. And then if we wuz to find it, you could wear some 'thout havin' no gang of womens lak dat Slemmons say he got."

Joe laughed and hugged her. "Don't be so wishful 'bout me. Ah'm satisfied de way Ah is. So long as Ah be yo' husband. Ah don't keer 'bout nothin' else. Ah'd ruther all de other womens in de world to be dead than for you to have de toothache. Less we go to bed and git our night rest."

It was Saturday night once more before Joe could parade his wife in Slemmons's ice cream parlor again. He worked the night shift and Saturday was his only night off. Every other evening around six o'clock he left home, and dying dawn saw him hustling home around the lake, where the challenging sun flung a flaming sword from east to west across the trembling water.

That was the best part of life—going home to Missie May. Their whitewashed house, the mock battle on Saturday, the dinner and ice cream parlor afterwards, church on Sunday nights when Missie outdressed any woman in town—all, everything, was right.

One night around eleven the acid ran out at the G. and G. The foreman knocked off the crew and let the steam die down. As Joe rounded the lake on his way home, a lean moon rode the lake in a silver boat. If anybody had asked Joe about the moon on the lake, he would have said he hadn't paid it any attention. But he saw it with his feelings. It made him yearn painfully for Missie. Creation obsessed him. He thought about children. They had been married more than a year now. They had money put away. They ought to be making little feet for shoes. A little boy child would be about right.

He saw a dim light in the bedroom and decided to come in through the kitchen door. He could wash the fertilizer dust off himself before presenting himself to Missie May. It would be nice for her not to know that he was there until he slipped into his place in bed and hugged her back. She always liked that.

He eased the kitchen door open slowly and silently, but when he went to set his dinner bucket on the table he bumped it into a pile of dishes, and something crashed to the floor. He heard his wife gasp in fright and hurried to reassure her.

"Iss me, honey. Don't git skeered."

There was a quick, large movement in the bedroom. A rustle, a thud, and a stealthy silence. The light went out.

What? Robbers? Murderers? Some varmint attacking his helpless wife, perhaps. He struck a match, threw himself on guard and stepped over the doorsill into the bedroom.

The great belt on the wheel of Time slipped and eternity stood still. By the match light he could see the man's legs fighting with his breeches in his frantic desire to get them on. He had both chance and time to kill the intruder in his helpless condition —half in and half out of his pants—but he was too weak to take action. The shapeless enemies of humanity that live in the hours of Time had waylaid Joe. He was assaulted in his weakness. Like Samson awakening after his haircut. So he just opened his mouth and laughed.

The match went out and he struck another and lit the lamp. A howling wind raced across his heart, but underneath its fury he heard his wife sobbing and Slemmons pleading for his life. Offering to buy it with all that he had. "Please, suh, don't kill me. Sixty-two dollars at de sto'. Gold money."

Joe just stood. Slemmons looked at the window, but it was screened. Joe stood out like a rough-backed mountain between him and the door. Barring him from escape, from sunrise, from life.

He considered a surprise attack upon the big clown that stood there laughing like a chessy cat. But before his fist could travel an inch, Joe's own rushed out to crush him like a battering ram. Then Joe stood over him.

"Git into yo' damn rags, Slemmons, and dat quick."

Slemmons scrambled to his feet and into his vest and coat. As he grabbed his hat, Joe's fury overrode his intentions and he grabbed at Slemmons with his left hand and struck at him with his right. The right landed. The left grazed the front of his vest. Slemmons was knocked a somersault into the kitchen and fled through the open door. Joe found himself alone with Missie May, with the golden watch charm clutched in his left fist. A short bit of broken chain dangled between his fingers.

Missie May was sobbing. Wails of weeping without words. Joe stood, and after a while he found out that he had something in his hand. And then he stood and felt without thinking and without seeing with his natural eyes. Missie May kept on crying and Joe kept on feeling so much, and not knowing what to do with all his feelings, he put Slemmons's watch charm in his pants pocket and took a good laugh and went to bed.

"Missie May, whut you cryin' for?"

"Cause Ah love you so hard and Ah know you don't love *me* no mo'."

Joe sank his face into the pillow for a spell, then he said huskily, "You don't know de feelings of dat yet, Missie May."

"Oh Joe, honey, he said he wuz gointer give me dat gold money and he jes' kept on after me—"

Joe was very still and silent for a long time. Then he said, "Well, don't cry no mo', Missie May. Ah got yo' gold piece for you."

The hours went past on their rusty ankles. Joe still and quiet on one bed rail and Missie May wrung dry of sobs on the other. Finally the sun's tide crept upon the shore of night and drowned all its hours. Missie May with her face stiff and streaked towards the window saw the dawn come into her yard. It was day. Nothing more. Joe wouldn't be coming home as usual. No need to fling open the front door and sweep off the porch, making it nice for Joe. Never no more breakfast to cook; no more washing and starching of Joe's jumper-jackets and pants. No more nothing. So why get up?

With this strange man in her bed, she felt embarrassed to get up and dress. She decided to wait till he had dressed and gone. Then she would get up, dress quickly and be gone forever beyond reach of Joe's looks and laughs. But he never moved. Red light turned to yellow, then white.

From beyond the no-man's land between them came a voice. A strange voice that yesterday had been Joe's.

"Missie May, ain't you gonna fix me no breakfus'?"

She sprang out of bed. "Yeah, Joe. Ah didn't reckon you wuz hongry."

No need to die today. Joe needed her for a few more minutes anyhow.

Soon there was a roaring fire in the cookstove. Water bucket full and two chickens killed. Joe loved fried chicken and rice. She didn't deserve a thing and good Joe was letting her cook him some breakfast. She rushed hot biscuits to the table as Joe took his seat.

He ate with his eyes in his plate. No laughter, no banter.

"Missie May, you ain't eatin' yo' breakfus'."

"Ah don't choose none, Ah thank yuh."

His coffee cup was empty. She sprang to refill it. When she turned from the stove and bent to set the cup beside Joe's plate, she saw the yellow coin on the table between them.

She slumped into her seat and wept into her arms.

Presently Joe said calmly, "Missie May, you cry too much. Don't look back lak Lot's wife and turn to salt."

The sun, the hero of every day, the impersonal old man that beams as brightly on death as on birth, came up every morning and raced across the blue dome and dipped into the sea of fire every morning. Water ran downhill and birds nested.

Missie knew why she didn't leave Joe. She couldn't. She loved him too much, but she could not understand why Joe didn't leave her. He was polite, even kind at times, but aloof.

There were no more Saturday romps. No ringing silver dollars to stack beside her plate. No pockets to rifle. In fact, the yellow coin in his trousers was like a monster hiding in the cave of his pockets to destroy her.

She often wondered if he still had it, but nothing could have induced her to ask nor yet to explore his pockets to see for herself. Its shadow was in the house whether or no.

One night Joe came home around midnight and complained of pains in the back. He asked Missie to rub him down with liniment. It had been three months since Missie had touched his body and it all seemed strange. But she rubbed him. Grateful for the chance. Before morning youth triumphed and Missie exulted. But the next day, as she joyfully made up their bed, beneath her pillow she found the piece of money with the bit of chain attached.

Alone to herself, she looked at the thing with loathing, but look she must. She took it into her hands with trembling and saw first thing that it was no gold piece. It was a gilded half dollar. Then she knew why Slemmons had forbidden anyone to touch his gold. He trusted village eyes at a distance not to recognize his stickpin as a gilded quarter, and his watch charm as a four-bit piece.

She was glad at first that Joe had left it there. Perhaps he was through with her punishment. They were man and wife again. Then another thought came clawing at her. He had come home to buy from her as if she were any woman in the longhouse. Fifty cents for her love. As if to say that he could pay as well as Slemmons. She slid the coin into his Sunday pants pocket and dressed herself and left his house.

Halfway between her house and the quarters she met her husband's mother, and after a short talk she turned and went back home. Never would she admit defeat to that woman who prayed for it nightly. If she had not the substance of marriage she had the outside show. Joe must leave *her.* She let him see she didn't want his old gold four-bits, too.

She saw no more of the coin for some time though she knew that Joe could not help finding it in his pocket. But his health kept poor, and he came home at least every ten days to be rubbed.

The sun swept around the horizon, trailing its robes of weeks and days. One morning as Joe came in from work, he found Missie May chopping wood. Without a word he took the ax and chopped a huge pile before he stopped.

"You ain't got no business choppin' wood, and you know it."

"How come? Ah been choppin' it for de last longest."

"Ah ain't blind. You makin' feet for shoes."

"Won't you be glad to have a lil baby chile, Joe?"

"You know dat 'thout astin' me."

"Iss gointer be a boy chile and de very spit of you."

"You reckon, Missie May?"

"Who else could it look lak?"

Joe said nothing, but he thrust his hand deep into his pocket and fingered something there.

It was almost six months later Missie May took to bed and Joe went and got his mother to come wait on the house.

Missie May was delivered of a fine boy. Her travail was over when Joe came in from work one morning. His mother and the old women were drinking great bowls of coffee around the fire in the kitchen.

The minute Joe came into the room his mother called him aside.

"How did Missie May make out?" he asked quickly.

"Who, dat gal? She strong as a ox. She gointer have plenty mo'. We done fixed her wid de sugar and lard to sweeten her for de nex' one."

Joe stood silent awhile.

"You ain't ask 'bout de baby, Joe. You oughter be mighty proud cause he sho is de spittin' image of yuh, son. Dat's yourn all right, if you never git another one, dat un is yourn. And you know Ah'm mighty proud too, son, cause Ah never thought well of you marryin' Missie May cause her ma used tuh fan her foot round right smart and Ah been mighty skeered dat Missie May wuz gointer git misput on her road."

Joe said nothing. He fooled around the house till late in the day, then, just before he went to work, he went and stood at the foot of the bed and asked his wife how she felt. He did this every day during the week.

On Saturday he went to Orlando to make his market. It had been a long time since he had done that.

Meat and lard, meal and flour, soap and starch. Cans of corn and tomatoes. All the staples. He fooled around town for a while and bought bananas and apples. Way after while he went around to the candy store.

"Hello, Joe," the clerk greeted him. "Ain't seen you in a long time."

"Nope, Ah ain't been heah. Been round in spots and places."

"Want some of them molasses kisses you always buy?"

"Yessuh." He threw the gilded half dollar on the counter. "Will dat spend?"

"What is it, Joe? Well, I'll be doggone! A gold-plated four-bit piece. Where'd you git it, Joe?"

"Offen a stray nigger dat come through Eatonville. He had it on his watch chain for a charm—goin' round making out iss gold money. Ha ha! He had a quarter on his tiepin and it wuz all golded up too. Tryin' to fool people. Makin' out he so rich and everything. Ha! Ha! Tryin' to tole off folkses wives from home."

"How did you git it, Joe? Did he fool you, too?"

"Who, me? Naw suh! He ain't fooled me none. Know whut Ah done? He come round me wid his smart talk. Ah hauled off and knocked 'im down and took his old four-bits away from 'im. Gointer buy my wife some good ole lasses kisses wid it. Gimme fifty cents worth of dem candy kisses."

"Fifty cents buys a mighty lot of candy kisses, Joe. Why don't you split it up and take some chocolate bars, too? They eat good, too."

"Yessuh, dey do, but Ah wants all dat in kisses. Ah got a lil boy chile home now. Tain't a week old yet, but he kin suck a sugar tit and maybe eat one them kisses hisself."

Joe got his candy and left the store. The clerk turned to the next customer. "Wisht I could be like these darkies. Laughin' all the time. Nothin' worries 'em."

Back in Eatonville, Joe reached his own front door. There was the ring of singing metal on wood. Fifteen times. Missie May couldn't run to the door, but she crept there as quickly as she could.

"Joe Banks, Ah hear you chunkin' money in mah do'way. You wait till Ah got mah strength back and Ah'm gointer fix you for dat."

1933

Langston Hughes
1902–1967

The most influential black writer in the history of American literature, Langston Hughes was at the center of the Harlem Renaissance of the 1920s and was one of its most productive figures. Besides editing numerous anthologies of black writing, Hughes published ten volumes of poetry, nine books of fiction, nine plays, two autobiographies, several biographies and histories, and an impressive amount of humor and journalism. Practically a cultural institution in himself, by the mid-1930s he had become the first black American writer to establish a truly international reputation. Hughes was also the first American black to carve out for himself a wholly independent literary career.

James Langston Hughes was born in Joplin, Missouri, on February 1, 1902. His racial ancestry was complex: black, Jewish, Scottish, English, and Cherokee. His grandmother had been married to one of the men killed in John Brown's attack on Harpers Ferry. Hughes's parents separated when he was still quite young (Hughes's father, a lawyer and engineer, moved to Mexico to escape American racism), and Hughes was brought up by his mother and grandmother in Kansas and later in Cleveland, Ohio, where he graduated from high school. Hughes then spent a year in Mexico with his father, who offered to finance his education at Columbia, provided he study engineering. Quarrels with his father drove Hughes nearly to the brink of suicide, but he nevertheless entered Columbia in 1921. Dissatisfied with his studies, restless, and determined to be a writer, Hughes left college the following year and in 1923 joined the merchant marines. He worked as a cook's helper, traveling to Africa, Italy, and France, where he spent a year working as a dishwasher in a Paris nightclub. Hughes returned to the United States in 1925; while working as a busboy in a Washington, D.C., hotel, he met the then prominent poet Vachel Lindsay, who immediately publicized the "bus-boy poet" in local papers and thus helped launch Hughes's literary career.

A precocious writer, Hughes began composing poetry in early adolescence. In high school he read Carl Sandburg and Edgar Lee Masters and wrote for the literary magazine. One of his best-known poems, "The Negro Speaks of Rivers," was written while he was still in high school and was published (as were several other of his poems) in *The Crisis,* the magazine of the National Association for the Advancement of Colored People (NAACP). Eleven of Hughes's poems were selected for *The New Negro* (1925), Alain Locke's influential anthology representing the best work of the Harlem Renaissance. In 1926 Hughes returned to college, enrolling at Lincoln University in Pennsylvania, from which he graduated in 1929. During this period he published two books of poetry, *The Weary Blues* (1926) and *Fine Clothes to the Jew* (1927), and wrote a novel about everyday black life, *Not Without Laughter* (1930), which won an award and convinced him that he could make a living—however precarious—by writing.

After graduation Hughes received a monthly sum from an affluent white woman and so was able to live in suburban New Jersey and write. Soon, however, sensing that he was disappointing his patroness (who wanted him "to be more African than Harlem—primitive in the simple, intuitive and noble sense of the word"), he set out on his own. After a tour of Cuba and Haiti, he began supporting himself by conducting an extensive reading tour that took him throughout the South, the Southwest, and California. In 1932 he was invited to participate in a movie about American race relations to be filmed in the Soviet Union; the film was never made, but it permitted Hughes to travel throughout Russia, China, and Japan. Hughes's childhood years and the account of his many travels are the subjects of his two autobiographical books, *The Big Sea* (1940) and *I Wonder as I Wander* (1956).

While in Russia, Hughes discovered the stories of D. H. Lawrence and began writing short fiction: "If D. H. Lawrence," he thought, "can write such psychologically powerful accounts of folks in England, that send shivers up and down my spine, maybe I could write stories like his about folks in America." The results of Hughes's efforts were contained in two collections of stories, *The Ways of White Folks* (1934) and *Laughing to Keep from Crying* (1952), stories mostly written while Hughes lived at the artists' colony in Carmel, California. In 1935 his play *Mulatto* (written in 1930), which he called "a problem play on race relations," was successfully produced on Broadway, and in 1937 Hughes traveled to Spain, where he covered the civil war for the Baltimore *Afro-American* and met many writers, including Ernest Hemingway. Throughout his career, Hughes continued to write plays, the most famous of which is *Tambourines to Glory* (1963), based on his 1959 novel of that name. A remarkably versatile writer, Hughes also tried his hand at librettos, film scripts, songs, children's books, and translations. He never, however, lost touch with poetry: In 1951 he published one of his most famous books, *Montage of a Dream Deferred*, which he followed with *Ask Your Mama: Twelve Moods for Jazz* (1961) and *The Panther and the Lash: Poems of Our Times* (1967).

Aside from his own considerable body of published work, Hughes left several indelible marks on American cultural life. He collaborated on projects with Zora Neale Hurston and Arna Bontemps; he organized and led poetry-reading tours for black writers; he fostered the reading of poetry to musical accompaniment; he promoted the work of a host of other writers as well as several musicians; and he founded the Harlem Suitcase Theater in New York (1938), the New Negro Theater in Los Angeles (1939), and the Skyloft Players in Chicago (1942). In his own work he used elements taken from black songs and folktales as well as the rhythms of blues and jazz. In many of his poems he employs the metrical forms of the blues and the improvisational techniques of the jam session. His was an effort to capture the cunning and the richness of the idiomatic black English he had heard both in the rural South and in the urban North. Through it he sought to convey the resilience and strength of the dispossessed as they struggled to develop popular art forms that would combat the debilitating monotony, weariness, fear, and pain of their lives.

In 1943 Hughes began a long series of character vignettes for the *Chicago Defender* that now ranks among his most important work. At the center of the series is a humorous, street-wise Harlem workingman, Jesse B. Simple, whose musings and opinions on contemporary affairs—war, racism, feminism, cities, poverty, sports, and so on—are communicated to an educated black narrator. Hughes claimed that the origins of Simple were probably to be found in his reading of *Don Quixote*, though he also claimed that he modeled Simple after a factory worker he had interviewed in 1942 in a Harlem café. Hughes asked the man what he made at the plant:

"Cranks," he answered.

"What kind of cranks?"

"Oh, man, I don't know what kind of cranks."

"Well," asked Hughes, "do they crank cars, trucks, buses, planes, or what?"

"I don't know what them cranks cranks," he said.

At which his girl friend, a little annoyed, put in, "You've been working there long enough. By now you ought to know what them cranks crank."

"Aw woman," he said, "you know white folks don't tell colored folks what cranks cranks."

The first collection of sketches, *Simple Speaks His Mind*, appeared in 1950; it was followed by *Simple Takes a Wife* (1952), *Simple Stakes a Claim* (1957), *The Best* of *Simple* (1961), and *Simple's Uncle Sam* (1965). Langston Hughes died on May 22, 1967.

Further Reading:
J. Emmanuel, *Langston Hughes*, 1967.
M. Meltzer, *Langston Hughes: A Biography*, 1968.
T. B. O'Daniel *Langston Hughes, Black Genius: A Critical Evaluation*, 1972.
F. Berry, *Langston Hughes: Before and Beyond Harlem*, 1983.

Texts:
"Feet Live Their Own Life" from *The Best of Simple*, 1961.
"Thank You M'am" from *Something in Common*, 1963.
See also *The Big Sea*, 1940.

Feet Live Their Own Life

"If you want to know about my life," said Simple as he blew the foam from the top of the newly filled glass the bartender put before him, "don't look at my face, don't look at my hands. Look at my feet and see if you can tell how long I been standing on them."

"I cannot see your feet through your shoes," I said.

"You do not need to see through my shoes," said Simple. "Can't you tell by the shoes I wear—not pointed, not rockingchair, not French-toed, not nothing but big, long, broad and flat—that I been standing on these feet a long time and carrying some heavy burdens? They ain't flat from standing at no bar, neither, because I always sets at a bar. Can't you tell that? You know I do not hang out in a bar unless it has stools, don't you?"

"That I have observed," I said, "but I did not connect it with your past life."

"Everything I do is connected up with my past life," said Simple. "From Virginia to Joyce, from my wife to Zarita, from my mother's milk to this glass of beer, everything is connected up."

"I trust you will connect up with that dollar I just loaned you when you get paid," I said. "And who is Virginia? You never told me about her."

"Virginia is where I was borned," said Simple. "I *would* be borned in a state named after a woman. From that day on, women never give me no peace."

"You, I fear, are boasting. If the women were running after you as much as you run after them, you would not be able to sit here on this bar stool in peace. I don't see any women coming to call you out to go home, as some of these fellows' wives do around here."

"Joyce better not come in no bar looking for me," said Simple. "That is why me and my wife busted up—one reason. I do not like to be called out of no bar by a female. It's a man's perogative to just set and drink sometimes."

"How do you connect that prerogative with your past?" I asked.

"When I was a wee small child," said Simple, "I had no place to set and think in, being as how I was raised up with three brothers, two sisters, seven cousins, one married aunt, a common-law uncle, and the minister's grandchild—and the house only had four rooms. I never had no place just to set and think. Neither to set and drink—not even much my milk before some hongry child snatched it out of my hand. I were not the youngest, neither a girl, nor the cutest. I don't know why, but I don't think nobody liked me much. Which is why I was afraid to like anybody for a long time myself. When I did like somebody, I was full-grown and then I picked out the wrong woman because I had no practice in liking anybody before that. We did not get along."

"Is that when you took to drink?"

"Drink took to me," said Simple. "Whiskey just naturally likes me but beer likes me better. By the time I got married I had got to the point where a cold bottle was almost as good as a warm bed, especially when the bottle could not talk and the bed-warmer could. I do not like a woman to talk to me too much—I mean about me. Which is why I like Joyce. Joyce most in generally talks about herself."

"I am still looking at your feet," I said, "and I swear they do not reveal your life to me. Your feet are no open book."

"You have eyes but you see not," said Simple. "These feet have stood on every rock from the Rock of Ages to 135th and Lenox. These feet have supported everything from a cotton bale to a hongry woman. These feet have walked ten thousand miles working for white folks and another ten thousand keeping up with colored. These feet have stood at altars, crap tables, free lunches, bars, graves, kitchen doors, betting windows, hospital clinics, WPA desks, social security railings, and in all kinds of lines from soup lines to the draft. If I just had four feet, I could have stood in more places longer. As it is, I done wore out seven hundred pairs of shoes, eighty-nine tennis shoes, twelve summer sandals, also six loafers. The socks that these feet have bought could build a knitting mill. The corns I've cut away would dull a German razor. The bunions I forgot would make you ache from now till Judgment Day. If anybody was to write the history of my life, they should start with my feet."

"Your feet are not all that extraordinary," I said. "Besides, everything you are saying is general. Tell me specifically some one thing your feet have done that makes them different from any other feet in the world, just one."

"Do you see that window in that white man's store across the street?" asked Simple. "Well, this right foot of mine broke out that window in the Harlem riots right smack in the middle. Didn't no other foot in the world break that window but mine. And this left foot carried me off running as soon as my right foot came down. Nobody else's feet saved me from the cops that night but these *two* feet right here. Don't tell me these feet ain't had a life of their own."

"For shame," I said, "going around kicking out windows. Why?"

"Why?" said Simple. "You have to ask my great-great-grandpa why. He must of been simple—else why did he let them capture him in Africa and sell him for a slave to breed my great-grandpa in slavery to breed my grandpa in slavery to breed my pa to breed me to look at that window and say, 'It ain't mine! Bam-mmm-mm-m!' and kick it out?"

"This bar glass is not yours either," I said. "Why don't you smash it?"

"It's got my beer in it," said Simple.

Just then Zarita came in wearing her Thursday-night rabbit-skin coat. She didn't

stop at the bar, being dressed up, but went straight back to a booth. Simple's hand
went up, his beer went down, and the glass back to its wet spot on the bar.

"Excuse me a minute," he said, sliding off the stool.

Just to give him pause, the dozens, that old verbal game of maligning a friend's
female relatives, came to mind. "Wait," I said. "You have told me about what to ask
your great-great-grandpa. But I want to know what to ask your great-great-grand-
ma."

"I don't play the dozens that far back," said Simple, following Zarita into the
smoky juke-box blue of the back room.

1950

Thank You, M'am

She was a large woman with a large purse that had everything in it but a hammer
and nails. It had a long strap, and she carried it slung across her shoulder. It was
about eleven o'clock at night, dark, and she was walking alone, when a boy ran up
behind her and tried to snatch her purse. The strap broke with the sudden single tug
the boy gave it from behind. But the boy's weight and the weight of the purse
combined caused him to loose his balance. Instead of taking off full blast as he had
hoped, the boy fell on his back on the sidewalk and his legs flew up. The large
woman simply turned around and kicked him right square in his blue-jeaned sitter.
Then she reached down, picked the boy up by his shirt front, and shook him until
his teeth rattled.

After that the woman said, "Pick up my pocketbook, boy, and give it here."

She still held him tightly. But she bent down enough to permit him to stoop and
pick up her purse. Then she said, "Now ain't you ashamed of yourself?"

Firmly gripped by his shirt front, the boy said, "Yes'm."

The woman said, "What did you want to do it for?"

The boy said, "I didn't aim to."

She said, "You a lie!"

By that time two or three people passed, stopped, turned to look, and some stood
watching.

"If I turn you loose, will you run?" asked the woman.

"Yes'm," said the boy.

"Then I won't turn you loose," said the woman. She did not release him.

"Lady, I'm sorry," whispered the boy.

"Um-hum! Your face is dirty. I got a great mind to wash your face for you. Ain't
you got nobody home to tell you to wash your face?"

"No'm," said the boy.

"Then it will get washed this evening," said the large woman, starting up the street,
dragging the frightened boy behind her.

He looked as if he were fourteen or fifteen, frail and willow-wild, in tennis shoes and blue jeans.

The woman said, "You ought to be my son. I would teach you right from wrong. Least I can do right now is to wash your face. Are you hungry?"

"No'm," said the being-dragged boy. "I just want you to turn me loose."

"Was I bothering *you* when I turned that corner?" asked the woman.

"No'm."

"But you put yourself in contact with *me,*" said the woman. "If you think that that contact is not going to last awhile, you got another thought coming. When I get through with you, sir, you are going to remember Mrs. Luella Bates Washington Jones."

Sweat popped out on the boy's face and he began to struggle. Mrs. Jones stopped, jerked him around in front of her, put a half nelson about his neck, and continued to drag him up the street. When she got to her door, she dragged the boy inside, down a hall, and into a large kitchenette-furnished room at the rear of the house. She switched on the light and left the door open. The boy could hear other roomers laughing and talking in the large house. Some of their doors were open, too, so he knew he and the woman were not alone. The woman still had him by the neck in the middle of her room.

She said, "What is your name?"

"Roger," answered the boy.

"Then, Roger, you go to that sink and wash your face," said the woman, whereupon she turned him loose—at last. Roger looked at the door—looked at the woman—looked at the door—*and went to the sink.*

"Let the water run until it gets warm," she said. "Here's a clean towel."

"You gonna take me to jail?" asked the boy, bending over the sink.

"Not with that face, I would not take you nowhere," said the woman. "Here I am trying to get home to cook me a bite to eat, and you snatch my pocketbook! Maybe you ain't been to your supper either, late as it be. Have you?"

"There's nobody home at my house," said the boy.

"Then we'll eat," said the woman. "I believe you're hungry—or been hungry—to try to snatch my pocketbook!"

"I want a pair of blue suede shoes," said the boy.

"Well, you didn't have to snatch *my* pocketbook to get some suede shoes," said Mrs. Luella Bates Washington Jones. "You could of asked me."

"M'am?"

The water dripping from his face, the boy looked at her. There was a long pause. A very long pause. After he had dried his face and not knowing what else to do, dried it again, the boy turned around, wondering what next. The door was open. He could make a dash for it down the hall. He could run, run, run, *run!*

The woman was sitting on the day bed. After a while she said, "I were young once and I wanted things I could not get."

There was another long pause. The boy's mouth opened. Then he frowned, not knowing he frowned.

The woman said, "Um-hum! You thought I was going to say *but,* didn't you? You thought I was going to say, *but I didn't snatch people's pocketbooks.* Well, I wasn't going to say that." Pause. Silence. "I have done things, too, which I would not tell you, son—neither tell God, if He didn't already know. Everybody's got something in common. So you set down while I fix us something to eat. You might run that comb through your hair so you will look presentable."

In another corner of the room behind a screen was a gas plate and an icebox. Mrs. Jones got up and went behind the screen. The woman did not watch the boy to see if he was going to run now, nor did she watch her purse, which she left behind her on the day bed. But the boy took care to sit on the far side of the room, away from the purse, where he thought she could easily see him out of the corner of her eye if she wanted to. He did not trust the woman *not* to trust him. And he did not want to be mistrusted now.

"Do you need somebody to go to the store," asked the boy, "maybe to get some milk or something?"

"Don't believe I do," said the woman, "unless you just want sweet milk yourself. I was going to make cocoa out of this canned milk I got here."

"That will be fine," said the boy.

She heated some lima beans and ham she had in the icebox, made the cocoa, and set the table. The woman did not ask the boy anything about where he lived, or his folks, or anything else that would embarrass him. Instead, as they ate, she told him about her job in a hotel beauty shop that stayed open late, what the work was like, and how all kinds of women came in and out, blondes, redheads, and Spanish. Then she cut him a half of her ten-cent cake.

"Eat some more, son," she said.

When they were finished eating, she got up and said, "Now here, take this ten dollars and buy yourself some blue suede shoes. And next time, do not make the mistake of latching onto *my* pocketbook *nor nobody else's*—because shoes got by devilish ways will burn your feet. I got to get my rest now. But from here on in, son, I hope you will behave yourself."

She led him down the hall to the front door and opened it. "Good night! Behave yourself, boy!" she said, looking out into the street as he went down the steps.

The boy wanted to say something other than, "Thank you, m'am," to Mrs. Luella Bates Washington Jones, but although his lips moved, he couldn't even say that as he turned at the foot of the barren stoop and looked up at the large woman in the door. Then she shut the door.

1958

John Steinbeck
1902–1968

John Steinbeck was born on February 27, 1902, in Salinas, California, in the heart of Monterey County and the Salinas Valley, whose scenery and people left indelible marks on much of his finest fiction. His father was county treasurer and his mother a schoolteacher. In high school, Steinbeck participated in basketball and track, wrote for the school paper, and was elected president of the senior class. In 1919 he entered Stanford University, where he attended classes off and on for several years without taking a degree. During this period he also worked sporadically at odd jobs—as a hand on farms and ranches, a laborer on a road gang, a seaman on a cattle boat, a bricklayer, a surveyor, and a reporter. His single-minded ambition, however, from the age of seventeen, was to become a writer. For ten years he consistently wrote stories and novels—which publishers consistently rejected. But Steinbeck managed to stick through this period, even though he had very little money, apparently because his need to write was deeper than his need to be published. "If my characters are sad or happy," he said in 1931, "I reflect their emotions. I have no personal nor definitive emotions of my own. Indeed, when there is no writing in progress, I feel like an uninhabited body. I think I am only truly miserable at such times."

In 1926 Steinbeck left California, determined to establish himself as a writer and convinced that New York was the place to do it. Soon he was back in California, working again at odd jobs and writing persistently. His first novel, *Cup of Gold,* a fictionalized account of the pirate Henry Morgan, was published in 1929. But neither it nor Steinbeck's next two books—*The Pastures of Heaven* (1932), a collection of short stories about a California farming community, and *To a God Unknown* (1933), a novel about a California farmer's pagan fertility cult—attracted much attention.

In 1930, however, Steinbeck met a marine biologist and naturalist, Edward F. Ricketts, who exerted an enormous influence over his thinking and writing. Ricketts introduced Steinbeck to theories of organisms that today would probably be regarded as sociobiology. Steinbeck responded with an intellectual enthusiasm that was at once deep and decisive; he realized not only that he had found his "theme" but that he had been heading toward similar notions in his writing for some time ("I have written this theme over and over and did not know what I was writing"). The main idea was that the essential biological difference between individuals and groups was *qualitative* rather than quantitative. As Steinbeck put it, "When acting as a group, men do not partake of their ordinary natures at all. The group can change its nature. . . . The greatest group unit, that is the whole race, has qualities which the individual lacks entirely." Armed with such biological ideas as well as with his innate storytelling power, Steinbeck became, for a brief time, one of the most prominent writers in America.

Between 1935 and 1941 Steinbeck published his finest work: *Tortilla Flat* (1935), a novel that deals with the *paisanos* of the Salinas Valley in a manner deliberately reminiscent of Malory's tales of King Arthur and the Knights of the Round Table; *In Dubious Battle* (1936), the story of a strike by migrant fruit pickers; *Of Mice and Men* (1937), a folk parable of itinerent farmhands who dream of a piece of land they can call their own; *The Long Valley* (1938), a collection of short fiction that contains many of Steinbeck's most famous tales, such as "The Red Pony," "The Snake," "The Chrysanthemums," and "The Leader of the People"; *The Grapes of Wrath* (1939), the Pulitzer Prize–winning odyssey of a family of dispossessed sharecroppers who migrate from the Oklahoma dust bowl to the "promised land" of California; and *The Sea of Cortez*

(1941), the record of a biological expedition to collect specimens along the California peninsula that Steinbeck wrote in collaboration with Edward Ricketts.

All of Steinbeck's major works, and especially the stories of *The Long Valley,* are populated by characters who—like those of his fellow-Californian predecessor Jack London—display severely reduced states of consciousness. Steinbeck is fond of portraying simpletons, idiots, illiterates, and animals. In fact, animal imagery and animal behavior, as Edmund Wilson pointed out, pervade Steinbeck's books, from the Pirate in *Tortilla Flat,* who lives with his dogs in a kennel, to the famous description of a turtle crossing a highway in *The Grapes of Wrath,* a progress that prefigures the human journey. Even Steinbeck's "group" consciousness finds its equivalent in animal behavior. The westward migration in "The Leader of the People" is described as "a whole bunch of people made into one big crawling beast. . . . Every man wanted something for himself, but the big beast that was all of them wanted only westering."

During the Second World War, Steinbeck worked as a war correspondent and in 1942 wrote a popular tale about Norway's resistance to the Nazis, *The Moon Is Down* (1942), which like many of his later books seemed to be originally conceived as a play and was quickly turned into a highly successful Broadway production. Steinbeck's ability to write stories that were almost scenarios was perhaps first apparent in *Of Mice and Men,* and it led not only to numerous film adaptations of his works but to many screenwriting assignments. In 1944 Steinbeck published *Cannery Row,* a "down-and-out" tale of the Monterey docks based on the work of Edward Ricketts; it was followed by the story of a microcosmic group of stranded travelers, *The Wayward Bus* (1947), then by another symbolic examination of society, *The Pearl* (1948), a parable of a poor Mexican fisherman whose sudden wealth brings only misery to his community. In 1952 Steinbeck brought out a family saga patterned after the biblical tale of Cain and Abel, *East of Eden.* (While he wrote it, he simultaneously kept a journal documenting his writing process; this was published posthumously in 1969 as *Journal of a Novel: The East of Eden Letters.*) His two last novels were *The Short Reign of Pippin IV* (1957), a slight comedy about a contemporary French king, and *The Winter of Our Discontent* (1961), a story of moral and political corruption that he described as "part Kafka and part Booth Tarkington." In 1962, the year he was awarded the Nobel Prize for literature, Steinbeck published *Travels with Charlie in Search of America,* the record of an automobile tour of forty states.

Steinbeck's greatest subject, the story of lowly, dispossessed people, of their indignant fear and their inherent dignity, had a poignancy during the Great Depression that it has since lost for some readers. Yet it is not a subject we can afford to lose. In *The Pastures of Heaven,* Steinbeck pictures an old man, looking down into a valley, wishing that he "could go down there and . . . think over all" the events of his life; "maybe," he concludes, "I could make something out of them, something all in one piece that had a meaning, instead of all these trailing ends." Some such motive, the desire to become a cohesive imagination and an articulate voice for the broken dreams and lives of common people, lies at the heart of the work for which Steinbeck is now best remembered.

Further Reading:
P. Lisca, *The Wide World of John Steinbeck*, 1958.
W. French, *John Steinbeck*, 1961.
J. Fontenrose, *John Steinbeck: An Introduction and Interpretation*, 1963.
T. Kiernan, *The Intricate Music: A Biography of John Steinbeck*, 1979.
J. J. Benson, *The True Adventures of John Steinbeck, Writer: A Biography*, 1984.

Text:
The Long Valley, 1938.

The Leader of the People*

On Saturday afternoon Billy Buck, the ranch-hand, raked together the last of the old year's haystack and pitched small forkfuls over the wire fence to a few mildly interested cattle. High in the air small clouds like puffs of cannon smoke were driven eastward by the March wind. The wind could be heard whishing in the brush on the ridge crests, but no breath of it penetrated down into the ranch-cup.

The little boy, Jody, emerged from the house eating a thick piece of buttered bread. He saw Billy working on the last of the haystack. Jody tramped down scuffing his shoes in a way he had been told was destructive to good shoe-leather. A flock of white pigeons flew out of the black cypress tree as Jody passed, and circled the tree and landed again. A half-grown tortoise-shell cat leaped from the bunkhouse porch, galloped on stiff legs across the road, whirled and galloped back again. Jody picked up a stone to help the game along, but he was too late, for the cat was under the porch before the stone could be discharged. He threw the stone into the cypress tree and started the white pigeons on another whirling flight.

Arriving at the used-up haystack, the boy leaned against the barbed wire fence. "Will that be all of it, do you think?" he asked.

The middle-aged ranch-hand stopped his careful raking and stuck his fork into the ground. He took off his black hat and smoothed down his hair. "Nothing left of it that isn't soggy from ground moisture," he said. He replaced his hat and rubbed his dry leathery hands together.

"Ought to be plenty mice," Jody suggested.

"Lousy with them," said Billy. "Just crawling with mice."

"Well, maybe, when you get all through, I could call the dogs and hunt the mice."

"Sure, I guess you could," said Billy Buck. He lifted a forkful of the damp ground-hay and threw it into the air. Instantly three mice leaped out and burrowed frantically under the hay again.

---

* Originally Part IV of *The Red Pony*, published in 1937, "The Leader of the People" was published for the first time as a separate collected work in *The Long Valley* (1938).

Jody sighed with satisfaction. Those plump, sleek, arrogant mice were doomed. For eight months they had lived and multiplied in the haystack. They had been immune from cats, from traps, from poison and from Jody. They had grown smug in their security, overbearing and fat. Now the time of disaster had come; they would not survive another day.

Billy looked up at the top of the hills that surrounded the ranch. "Maybe you better ask your father before you do it," he suggested.

"Well, where is he? I'll ask him now."

"He rode up to the ridge ranch after dinner. He'll be back pretty soon."

Jody slumped against the fence post. "I don't think he'd care."

As Billy went back to his work he said ominously, "You'd better ask him anyway. You know how he is."

Jody did know. His father, Carl Tiflin, insisted upon giving permission for anything that was done on the ranch, whether it was important or not. Jody sagged farther against the post until he was sitting on the ground. He looked up at the little puffs of wind-driven cloud. "Is it like to rain, Billy?"

"It might. The wind's good for it, but not strong enough."

"Well, I hope it don't rain until after I kill those damn mice." He looked over his shoulder to see whether Billy had noticed the mature profanity. Billy worked on without comment.

Jody turned back and looked at the side-hill where the road from the outside world came down. The hill was washed with lean March sunshine. Silver thistles, blue lupins and a few poppies bloomed among the sage bushes. Halfway up the hill Jody could see Doubletree Mutt, the black dog, digging in a squirrel hole. He paddled for a while and then paused to kick bursts of dirt out between his hind legs, and he dug with an earnestness which belied the knowledge he must have had that no dog had ever caught a squirrel by digging in a hole.

Suddenly, while Jody watched, the black dog stiffened, and backed out of the hole and looked up the hill toward the cleft in the ridge where the road came through. Jody looked up too. For a moment Carl Tiflin on horseback stood out against the pale sky and then he moved down the road toward the house. He carried something white in his hand.

The boy started to his feet. "He's got a letter," Jody cried. He trotted away toward the ranch house, for the letter would probably be read aloud and he wanted to be there. He reached the house before his father did, and ran in. He heard Carl dismount from his creaking saddle and slap the horse on the side to send it to the barn where Billy would unsaddle it and turn it out.

Jody ran into the kitchen. "We got a letter!" he cried.

His mother looked up from a pan of beans. "Who has?"

"Father has. I saw it in his hand."

Carl strode into the kitchen then, and Jody's mother asked, "Who's the letter from, Carl?"

He frowned quickly. "How did you know there was a letter?"

She nodded her head in the boy's direction. "Big-Britches Jody told me."

Jody was embarrassed.

His father looked down at him contemptuously. "He *is* getting to be a Big-

Britches," Carl said. "He's minding everybody's business but his own. Got his big nose into everything."

Mrs. Tiflin relented a little. "Well, he hasn't enough to keep him busy. Who's the letter from?"

Carl still frowned on Jody. "I'll keep him busy if he isn't careful." He held out a sealed letter. "I guess it's from your father."

Mrs. Tiflin took a hairpin from her head and slit open the flap. Her lips pursed judiciously. Jody saw her eyes snap back and forth over the lines. "He says," she translated, "he says he's going to drive out Saturday to stay for a little while. Why, this is Saturday. The letter must have been delayed." She looked at the postmark. "This was mailed day before yesterday. It should have been here yesterday." She looked up questioningly at her husband, and then her face darkened angrily. "Now what have you got that look on you for? He doesn't come often."

Carl turned his eyes away from her anger. He could be stern with her most of the time, but when occasionally her temper arose, he could not combat it.

"What's the matter with you?" she demanded again.

In his explanation there was a tone of apology Jody himself might have used. "It's just that he talks," Carl said lamely. "Just talks."

"Well, what of it? You talk yourself."

"Sure I do. But your father only talks about one thing."

"Indians!" Jody broke in excitedly. "Indians and crossing the plains!"

Carl turned fiercely on him. "You get out, Mr. Big-Britches! Go on, now! Get out!"

Jody went miserably out the back door and closed the screen with elaborate quietness. Under the kitchen window his shamed, downcast eyes fell upon a curiously shaped stone, a stone of such fascination that he squatted down and picked it up and turned it over in his hands.

The voices came clearly to him through the open kitchen window. "Jody's damn well right," he heard his father say. "Just Indians and crossing the plains. I've heard that story about how the horses got driven off about a thousand times. He just goes on and on, and he never changes a word in the things he tells."

When Mrs. Tiflin answered her tone was so changed that Jody, outside the window, looked up from his study of the stone. Her voice had become soft and explanatory. Jody knew how her face would have changed to match the tone. She said quietly, "Look at it this way, Carl. That was the big thing in my father's life. He led a wagon train clear across the plains to the coast, and when it was finished, his life was done. It was a big thing to do, but it didn't last long enough. Look!" she continued, "it's as though he was born to do that, and after he finished it, there wasn't anything more for him to do but think about it and talk about it. If there'd been any farther west to go, he'd have gone. He's told me so himself. But at last there was the ocean. He lives right by the ocean where he had to stop."

She had caught Carl, caught him and entangled him in her soft tone.

"I've seen him," he agreed quietly. "He goes down and stares off west over the ocean." His voice sharpened a little. "And then he goes up to the Horseshoe Club in Pacific Grove, and he tells people how the Indians drove off the horses."

She tried to catch him again. "Well, it's everything to him. You might be patient with him and pretend to listen."

Carl turned impatiently away. "Well, if it gets too bad, I can always go down to the bunkhouse and sit with Billy," he said irritably. He walked through the house and slammed the front door after him.

Jody ran to his chores. He dumped the grain to the chickens without chasing any of them. He gathered the eggs from the nests. He trotted into the house with the wood and interlaced it so carefully in the wood-box that two armloads seemed to fill it to overflowing.

His mother had finished the beans by now. She stirred up the fire and brushed off the stove-top with a turkey wing. Jody peered cautiously at her to see whether any rancor toward him remained. "Is he coming today?" Jody asked.

"That's what his letter said."

"Maybe I better walk up the road to meet him."

Mrs. Tiflin clanged the stove-lid shut. "That would be nice," she said. "He'd probably like to be met."

"I guess I'll just do it then."

Outside, Jody whistled shrilly to the dogs. "Come on up the hill," he commanded. The two dogs waved their tails and ran ahead. Along the roadside the sage had tender new tips. Jody tore off some pieces and rubbed them on his hands until the air was filled with the sharp wild smell. With a rush the dogs leaped from the road and yapped into the brush after a rabbit. That was the last Jody saw of them, for when they failed to catch the rabbit, they went back home.

Jody plodded on up the hill toward the ridge top. When he reached the little cleft where the road came through, the afternoon wind struck him and blew up his hair and ruffled his shirt. He looked down on the little hills and ridges below and then out at the huge green Salinas Valley. He could see the white town of Salinas far out in the flat and the flash of its windows under the waning sun. Directly below him, in an oak tree, a crow congress had convened. The tree was black with crows all cawing at once.

Then Jody's eyes followed the wagon road down from the ridge where he stood, and lost it behind a hill, and picked it up again on the other side. On that distant stretch he saw a cart slowly pulled by a bay horse. It disappeared behind the hill. Jody sat down on the ground and watched the place where the cart would reappear again. The wind sang on the hilltops and the puff-ball clouds hurried eastward.

Then the cart came into sight and stopped. A man dressed in black dismounted from the seat and walked to the horse's head. Although it was so far away, Jody knew he had unhooked the check-rein, for the horse's head dropped forward. The horse moved on, and the man walked slowly up the hill beside it. Jody gave a glad cry and ran down the road toward them. The squirrels bumped along off the road, and a road-runner flirted its tail and raced over the edge of the hill and sailed out like a glider.

Jody tried to leap into the middle of his shadow at every step. A stone rolled under his foot and he went down. Around a little bend he raced, and there, a short distance ahead, were his grandfather and the cart. The boy dropped from his unseemly running and approached at a dignified walk.

The horse plodded stumble-footedly up the hill and the old man walked beside it. In the lowering sun their giant shadows flickered darkly behind them. The grandfather was dressed in a black broadcloth suit and he wore kid congress gaiters[1] and a black tie on a short, hard collar. He carried his black slouch hat in his hand. His white beard was cropped close and his white eyebrows overhung his eyes like moustaches. The blue eyes were sternly merry. About the whole face and figure there was a granite dignity, so that every motion seemed an impossible thing. Once at rest, it seemed the old man would be stone, would never move again. His steps were slow and certain. Once made, no step could ever be retraced; once headed in a direction, the path would never bend nor the pace increase nor slow.

When Jody appeared around the bend, Grandfather waved his hat slowly in welcome, and he called, "Why, Jody! Come down to meet me, have you?"

Jody sidled near and turned and matched his step to the old man's step and stiffened his body and dragged his heels a little. "Yes, sir," he said. "We got your letter only today."

"Should have been here yesterday," said Grandfather. "It certainly should. How are all the folks?"

"They're fine, sir." He hesitated and then suggested shyly, "Would you like to come on a mouse hunt tomorrow, sir?"

"Mouse hunt, Jody?" Grandfather chuckled. "Have the people of this generation come down to hunting mice? They aren't very strong, the new people, but I hardly thought mice would be game for them."

"No, sir. It's just play. The haystack's gone. I'm going to drive out the mice to the dogs. And you can watch, or even beat the hay a little."

The stern, merry eyes turned down on him. "I see. You don't eat them, then. You haven't come to that yet."

Jody explained, "The dogs eat them, sir. It wouldn't be much like hunting Indians, I guess."

"No, not much—but then later, when the troops were hunting Indians and shooting children and burning teepees, it wasn't much different from your mouse hunt."

They topped the rise and started down into the ranch cup, and they lost the sun from their shoulders. "You've grown," Grandfather said. "Nearly an inch, I should say."

"More," Jody boasted. "Where they mark me on the door, I'm up more than an inch since Thanksgiving even."

Grandfather's rich throaty voice said, "Maybe you're getting too much water and turning to pith and stalk. Wait until you head out, and then we'll see."

Jody looked quickly into the old man's face to see whether his feelings should be hurt, but there was no will to injure, no punishing nor putting-in-your-place light in the keen blue eyes. "We might kill a pig," Jody suggested.

"Oh, no! I couldn't let you do that. You're just humoring me. It isn't the time and you know it."

"You know Riley, the big boar, sir?"

"Yes. I remember Riley well."

"Well, Riley ate a hole into that same haystack, and it fell down on him and smothered him."

---

[1] Ankle-high shoes with elastic in the sides (also called "congress boots").

"Pigs do that when they can," said Grandfather.

"Riley was a nice pig, for a boar, sir. I rode him sometimes, and he didn't mind."

A door slammed at the house below them, and they saw Jody's mother standing on the porch waving her apron in welcome. And they saw Carl Tiflin walking up from the barn to be at the house for the arrival.

The sun had disappeared from the hills by now. The blue smoke from the house chimney hung in flat layers in the purpling ranch-cup. The puff-ball clouds, dropped by the falling wind, hung listlessly in the sky.

Billy Buck came out of the bunkhouse and flung a wash basin of soapy water on the ground. He had been shaving in mid-week, for Billy held Grandfather in reverence, and Grandfather said that Billy was one of the few men of the new generation who had not gone soft. Although Billy was in middle age, Grandfather considered him a boy. Now Billy was hurrying toward the house too.

When Jody and Grandfather arrived, the three were waiting for them in front of the yard gate.

Carl said, "Hello, sir. We've been looking for you."

Mrs. Tiflin kissed Grandfather on the side of his beard, and stood still while his big hand patted her shoulder. Billy shook hands solemnly, grinning under his straw moustache. "I'll put up your horse," said Billy, and he led the rig away.

Grandfather watched him go, and then, turning back to the group, he said as he had said a hundred times before, "There's a good boy. I knew his father, old Mule-tail Buck. I never knew why they called him Mule-tail except he packed mules."

Mrs. Tiflin turned and led the way into the house. "How long are you going to stay, Father? Your letter didn't say."

"Well, I don't know. I thought I'd stay about two weeks. But I never stay as long as I think I'm going to."

In a short while they were sitting at the white oilcloth table eating their supper. The lamp with the tin reflector hung over the table. Outside the dining-room windows the big moths battered softly against the glass.

Grandfather cut his steak into tiny pieces and chewed slowly. "I'm hungry," he said. "Driving out here got my appetite up. It's like when we were crossing. We all got so hungry every night we could hardly wait to let the meat get done. I could eat about five pounds of buffalo meat every night."

"It's moving around does it," said Billy. "My father was a government packer. I helped him when I was a kid. Just the two of us could about clean up a deer's ham."

"I knew your father, Billy," said Grandfather. "A fine man he was. They called him Mule-tail Buck. I don't know why except he packed mules."

"That was it," Billy agreed. "He packed mules."

Grandfather put down his knife and fork and looked around the table. "I remember one time we ran out of meat—" His voice dropped to a curious low sing-song, dropped into a tonal groove the story had worn for itself. "There was no buffalo, no antelope; not even rabbits. The hunters couldn't even shoot a coyote. That was the time for the leader to be on the watch. I was the leader, and I kept my eyes open. Know why? Well, just the minute the people began to get hungry they'd start slaughtering the team oxen. Do you believe that? I've heard of parties that just ate up their draft cattle. Started from the middle and worked toward the ends. Finally they'd eat the lead pair, and then the wheelers. The leader of a party had to keep them from doing that."

In some manner a big moth got into the room and circled the hanging kerosene lamp. Billy got up and tried to clap it between his hands. Carl struck with a cupped palm and caught the moth and broke it. He walked to the window and dropped it out.

"As I was saying," Grandfather began again, but Carl interrupted him. "You'd better eat some more meat. All the rest of us are ready for our pudding."

Jody saw a flash of anger in his mother's eyes. Grandfather picked up his knife and fork. "I'm pretty hungry, all right," he said. "I'll tell you about that later."

When supper was over, when the family and Billy Buck sat in front of the fireplace in the other room, Jody anxiously watched Grandfather. He saw the signs he knew. The bearded head leaned forward; the eyes lost their sternness and looked wonderingly into the fire; the big lean fingers laced themselves on the black knees. "I wonder," he began, "I just wonder whether I ever told you how those thieving Piutes drove off thirty-five of our horses."

"I think you did," Carl interrupted. "Wasn't it just before you went up into the Tahoe country?"

Grandfather turned quickly toward his son-in-law. "That's right. I guess I must have told you that story."

"Lots of times," Carl said cruelly, and he avoided his wife's eyes. But he felt the angry eyes on him, and he said, "'Course I'd like to hear it again."

Grandfather looked back at the fire. His fingers unlaced and laced again. Jody knew how he felt, how his insides were collapsed and empty. Hadn't Jody been called a Big-Britches that very afternoon? He arose to heroism and opened himself to the term Big-Britches again. "Tell about Indians," he said softly.

Grandfather's eyes grew stern again. "Boys always want to hear about Indians. It was a job for men, but boys want to hear about it. Well, let's see. Did I ever tell you how I wanted each wagon to carry a long iron plate?"

Everyone but Jody remained silent. Jody said, "No. You didn't."

"Well, when the Indians attacked, we always put the wagons in a circle and fought from between the wheels. I thought that if every wagon carried a long plate with rifle holes, the men could stand the plates on the outside of the wheels when the wagons were in the circle and they would be protected. It would save lives and that would make up for the extra weight of the iron. But of course the party wouldn't do it. No party had done it before and they couldn't see why they should go to the expense. They lived to regret it, too."

Jody looked at his mother, and knew from her expression that she was not listening at all. Carl picked at a callus on his thumb and Billy Buck watched a spider crawling up the wall.

Grandfather's tone dropped into its narrative groove again. Jody knew in advance exactly what words would fall. The story droned on, speeded up for the attack, grew sad over the wounds, struck a dirge at the burials on the great plains. Jody sat quietly watching Grandfather. The stern blue eyes were detached. He looked as though he were not very interested in the story himself.

When it was finished, when the pause had been politely respected as the frontier of the story, Billy Buck stood up and stretched and hitched his trousers. "I guess I'll turn in," he said. Then he faced Grandfather. "I've got an old powder horn and a cap and ball pistol down to the bunkhouse. Did I ever show them to you?"

Grandfather nodded slowly. "Yes, I think you did, Billy. Reminds me of a pistol I had when I was leading the people across." Billy stood politely until the little story was done, and then he said, "Good night," and went out of the house.

Carl Tiflin tried to turn the conversation then. "How's the country between here and Monterey? I've heard it's pretty dry."

"It is dry," said Grandfather. "There's not a drop of water in the Laguna Seca. But it's a long pull from '87. The whole country was powder then, and in '61 I believe all the coyotes starved to death. We had fifteen inches of rain this year."

"Yes, but it all came too early. We could do with some now." Carl's eye fell on Jody. "Hadn't you better be getting to bed?"

Jody stood up obediently. "Can I kill the mice in the old haystack, sir?"

"Mice? Oh! Sure, kill them all off. Billy said there isn't any good hay left."

Jody exchanged a secret and satisfying look with Grandfather. "I'll kill every one tomorrow," he promised.

Jody lay in his bed and thought of the impossible world of Indians and buffaloes, a world that had ceased to be forever. He wished he could have been living in the heroic time, but he knew he was not of heroic timber. No one living now, save possibly Billy Buck, was worthy to do the things that had been done. A race of giants had lived then, fearless men, men of a staunchness unknown in this day. Jody thought of the wide plains and of the wagons moving across like centipedes. He thought of Grandfather on a huge white horse, marshaling the people. Across his mind marched the great phantoms, and they marched off the earth and they were gone.

He came back to the ranch for a moment, then. He heard the dull rushing sound that space and silence make. He heard one of the dogs, out in the doghouse, scratching a flea and bumping his elbow against the floor with every stroke. Then the wind arose again and the black cypress groaned and Jody went to sleep.

He was up half an hour before the triangle sounded for breakfast. His mother was rattling the stove to make the flames roar when Jody went through the kitchen. "You're up early," she said. "Where are you going?"

"Out to get a good stick. We're going to kill the mice today."

"Who is 'we'?"

"Why, Grandfather and I."

"So you've got him in it. You always like to have someone in with you in case there's blame to share."

"I'll be right back," said Jody. "I just want to have a good stick ready for after breakfast."

He closed the screen door after him and went out into the cool blue morning. The birds were noisy in the dawn and the ranch cats came down from the hill like blunt snakes. They had been hunting gophers in the dark, and although the four cats were full of gopher meat, they sat in a semi-circle at the back door and mewed piteously for milk. Doubletree Mutt and Smasher moved sniffing along the edge of the brush, performing the duty with rigid ceremony, but when Jody whistled, their heads jerked up and their tails waved. They plunged down to him, wriggling their skins and yawning. Jody patted their heads seriously, and moved on to the weathered scrap pile. He selected an old broom handle and a short piece of inch-square scrap wood. From his pocket he took a shoelace and tied the ends of the sticks loosely together to make a flail. He whistled his new weapon through the air and struck the ground experimentally, while the dogs leaped aside and whined with apprehension.

Jody turned and started down past the house toward the old haystack ground to look over the field of slaughter, but Billy Buck, sitting patiently on the back steps, called to him, "You better come back. It's only a couple of minutes till breakfast."

Jody changed his course and moved toward the house. He leaned his flail against the steps. "That's to drive the mice out," he said. "I'll bet they're fat. I'll bet they don't know what's going to happen to them today."

"No, nor you either," Billy remarked philosophically, "nor me, nor anyone."

Jody was staggered by this thought. He knew it was true. His imagination twitched away from the mouse hunt. Then his mother came out on the back porch and struck the triangle, and all thoughts fell in a heap.

Grandfather hadn't appeared at the table when they sat down. Billy nodded at his empty chair. "He's all right? He isn't sick?"

"He takes a long time to dress," said Mrs. Tiflin. "He combs his whiskers and rubs up his shoes and brushes his clothes."

Carl scattered sugar on his mush. "A man that's led a wagon train across the plains has got to be pretty careful how he dresses."

Mrs. Tiflin turned on him. "Don't do that, Carl! Please don't!" There was more of threat than of request in her tone. And the threat irritated Carl.

"Well, how many times do I have to listen to the story of the iron plates, and the thirty-five horses? That time's done. Why can't he forget it, now it's done?" He grew angrier while he talked, and his voice rose. "Why does he have to tell them over and over? He came across the plains. All right! Now it's finished. Nobody wants to hear about it over and over."

The door into the kitchen closed softly. The four at the table sat frozen. Carl laid his mush spoon on the table and touched his chin with his fingers.

Then the kitchen door opened and Grandfather walked in. His mouth smiled tightly and his eyes were squinted. "Good morning," he said, and he sat down and looked at his mush dish.

Carl could not leave it there. "Did—did you hear what I said?"

Grandfather jerked a little nod.

"I don't know what got into me, sir. I didn't mean it. I was just being funny."

Jody glanced in shame at his mother, and he saw that she was looking at Carl, and that she wasn't breathing. It was an awful thing that he was doing. He was tearing himself to pieces to talk like that. It was a terrible thing to him to retract a word, but to retract it in shame was infinitely worse.

Grandfather looked sidewise. "I'm trying to get right side up," he said gently. "I'm not being mad. I don't mind what you said, but it might be true, and I would mind that."

"It isn't true," said Carl. "I'm not feeling well this morning. I'm sorry I said it."

"Don't be sorry, Carl. An old man doesn't see things sometimes. Maybe you're right. The crossing is finished. Maybe it should be forgotten, now it's done."

Carl got up from the table. "I've had enough to eat. I'm going to work. Take your time, Billy!" He walked quickly out of the dining-room. Billy gulped the rest of his food and followed soon after. But Jody could not leave his chair.

"Won't you tell any more stories?" Jody asked.

"Why, sure I'll tell them, but only when—I'm sure people want to hear them."

"I like to hear them, sir."

"Oh! Of course you do, but you're a little boy. It was a job for men, but only little boys like to hear about it."

Jody got up from his place. "I'll wait outside for you, sir. I've got a good stick for those mice."

He waited by the gate until the old man came out on the porch. "Let's go down and kill the mice now," Jody called.

"I think I'll just sit in the sun, Jody. You go kill the mice."

"You can use my stick if you like."

"No, I'll just sit here a while."

Jody turned disconsolately away, and walked down toward the old haystack. He tried to whip up his enthusiasm with thoughts of the fat juicy mice. He beat the ground with his flail. The dogs coaxed and whined about him, but he could not go. Back at the house he could see Grandfather sitting on the porch, looking small and thin and black.

Jody gave up and went to sit on the steps at the old man's feet.

"Back already? Did you kill the mice?"

"No, sir. I'll kill them some other day."

The morning flies buzzed close to the ground and the ants dashed about in front of the steps. The heavy smell of sage slipped down the hill. The porch boards grew warm in the sunshine.

Jody hardly knew when Grandfather started to talk. "I shouldn't stay here, feeling the way I do." He examined his strong old hands. "I feel as though the crossing wasn't worth doing." His eyes moved up the side-hill and stopped on a motionless hawk perched on a dead limb. "I tell those old stories, but they're not what I want to tell. I only know how I want people to feel when I tell them.

"It wasn't Indians that were important, nor adventures, nor even getting out here. It was a whole bunch of people made into one big crawling beast. And I was the head. It was westering and westering. Every man wanted something for himself, but the big beast that was all of them wanted only westering. I was the leader, but if I hadn't been there, someone else would have been the head. The thing had to have a head.

"Under the little bushes the shadows were black at white noonday. When we saw the mountains at last, we cried—all of us. But it wasn't getting here that mattered, it was movement and westering.

"We carried life out here and set it down the way those ants carry eggs. And I was the leader. The westering was as big as God, and the slow steps that made the movement piled up and piled up until the continent was crossed.

"Then we came down to the sea, and it was done." He stopped and wiped his eyes until the rims were red. "That's what I should be telling instead of stories."

When Jody spoke, Grandfather started and looked down at him. "Maybe I could lead the people some day," Jody said.

The old man smiled. "There's no place to go. There's the ocean to stop you. There's a line of old men along the shore hating the ocean because it stopped them."

"In boats I might, sir."

"No place to go, Jody. Every place is taken. But that's not the worst—no, not the worst. Westering has died out of the people. Westering isn't a hunger any more.

It's all done. Your father is right. It is finished." He laced his fingers on his knee and looked at them.

Jody felt very sad. "If you'd like a glass of lemonade I could make it for you."

Grandfather was about to refuse, and then he saw Jody's face. "That would be nice," he said. "Yes, it would be nice to drink a lemonade."

Jody ran into the kitchen where his mother was wiping the last of the breakfast dishes. "Can I have a lemon to make a lemonade for Grandfather?"

His mother mimicked—"And another lemon to make a lemonade for you."

"No, ma'am. I don't want one."

"Jody! You're sick!" Then she stopped suddenly. "Take a lemon out of the cooler," she said softly. "Here, I'll reach the squeezer down to you."

1938

Nathanael West
1903–1940

As a teenager, Nathan Weinstein went to a summer camp in the Adirondack Mountains called Camp Paradox—an appropriate start to the strange, brief life of the writer who changed his name to Nathanael West, wrote four vividly grotesque short novels in eight years, and died with his bride of six months in a car crash at the age of thirty-seven. West was born in New York City, the first child of prosperous Lithuanian Jewish immigrants. But his parents' hope that he would prove to be a success in school and then in business soon was dashed. An indifferent student, West spent most of his boyhood and youth playing baseball and reading unassigned books. Tolstoy, Dostoevski, Flaubert, and Henry James were far more important to him than school assignments. In 1921, having left high school without a diploma, he forged the documents he needed to gain admittance to Tufts University, only to withdraw within two months because of poor grades. Still restless, he gained admission to Brown University by passing himself off as another student, also named Nathan Weinstein, who possessed the proper credentials for admission and had already matriculated.

While at Brown, West appropriated the clothes of a dandy and the manner of a gentile in a somewhat frantic attempt to disown his own Jewishness. Intellectually and imaginatively, he experimented with different strains of the aesthete, the decadent, and the mystic. He reveled in readings from medieval Catholicism, the French Symbolists, Friedrich Nietzsche, and James Joyce and in the bizarre stories of J. K. Huysmans and Arthur Machen, as well as in the latest experiments in literary form. Discovering that his double had already conveniently passed the subjects he most disliked, such as science and mathematics, he began to concentrate on English and other more congenial subjects. Two and one-half years later, in 1924, he graduated.

Degree in hand, West persuaded his father to postpone the time when he, as the only son, would be expected to join the family's business as a building contractor. He spent the next two years in Paris, reading and trying to write, then returned to New York, where he again begged off working for his father, this time to clerk first in one small hotel and then another. Over the next several years he continued to write and began to cadge free rooms for such indigent writer-friends as Dashiell Hammett, Erskine Caldwell, and James T. Farrell.

By ruining his family's business, the stock market crash of 1929 saved West from ever having to return to the fold. In 1931 he published his first novel, *The Dream Life of Balso Snell,* under his new name, Nathanael West. Although *Balso Snell* went virtually unnoticed, West's second novel, *Miss Lonelyhearts* (written at the slow speed of a hundred words a day), attracted considerable attention when it first appeared in 1933. Then, just as the demand for copies was increasing, West's publisher went bankrupt, with only eight hundred copies sold.

Between 1932 and 1934 West did a stint editing little magazines, including work with the poet William Carlos Williams on *Contact.* In 1934 he published a novel, *A Cool Million,* which vanished from sight almost as soon as it had appeared. Disheartened, West moved to Hollywood to try his luck at screenwriting, which he took to with surprising ease. Disillusioned by California, West returned to New York, only to decide that the East was a dead end. In 1935 he went back to Hollywood, trying once again to follow the advice of Horace Greeley's nineteenth-century motto—"Go west, young man"—which West insisted had been both the inspiration for the name he had created for himself in 1931 and the catalyst for his first trip to California in 1934.

Back in Hollywood, West soon began making a great deal of money. He had time not only for writing but also for hunting, which he loved, and radical politics, which he needed. A speedy scriptwriter, he spent his spare time hunting, joining in Communist rallies, and completing *The Day of the Locust.* Published in 1939, *The Day of the Locust* received good reviews but had poor sales because, according to his publisher, women did not take to the story. Happiness came to him in 1940 with marriage in April to Eileen McKenney, the subject of Ruth McKenney's *My Sister Eileen* (1938), as well as with a better job at Columbia Pictures and the sale of the movie rights to *A Cool Million.* In December he and his wife were killed in an automobile accident near El Centro, California, on their return from a hunting trip in Mexico. His body was returned to the East at his family's request and laid to rest in a Jewish cemetery.

During the years following his death, Nathanael West gradually acquired a large underground reputation. It was not until 1957, however, with the publication of his collected novels, that he began to receive public acclaim. His talent for parody, brilliant nastiness, grotesquerie, and unsympathetically rendered characters is immense. At the time of his death, West was planning to move on to serious political novels as well as "simple, warm, and kindly books." But his enormous conscience did not lend itself to earnest expression, which in his hands too easily became maudlin. He cared about the people he portrayed, but preaching about their failings was not his way of showing his concern. His satires are fast and funny rather than somber and uplifting. His vision of horror and betrayal, apocalypse and self-delusion sometimes combines the brevity of Poe and the mordancy of Melville, but it always retains the disillusionment of the bright and strangely earnest young man who had read a great deal of Dostoevski and Nietzsche while conning his way through college.

In West's strange art, bizarre fantasies, sexual confusion, social alienation, and tortured sensibilities mingle and collide. The masks his characters don and the roles they play, like the role of Miss Lonelyhearts, come somehow to dominate and even tyrannize them. In his art, society tends rather to manipulate and use human beings, even to mock and taunt them, than to support, serve, and sustain them. At times the world of Miss Lonelyhearts seems almost like a cartoon. It is a stark world, a world of grotesque, misshapen characters, of strange, contorted images, of apocalyptic signs. Yet despite the stark contrasts that define it, it is not a simple world. Miss Lonelyhearts, West's fool of pity, is only in part a victim of his world and its confusions; he is also a victim of himself.

Further Reading:
J. Light, *Nathanael West: An Interpretive Study*, 1961.
S. Hyman, *Nathanael West*, 1962.
R. Reid, *Nathanael West*, 1962.
V. Comerchero, *Nathanael West, The Ironic Prophet*, 1964.
R. Reid, *The Fiction of Nathanael West: No Redeemer, No Promised Land*, 1967.
J. Martin, *Nathanael West: The Art of His Life*, 1970.
Nathanel West: A Collection of Critical Essays, ed. J. Martin, 1971.
N. Scott, *Nathanael West: A Critical Essay*, 1971.
I. Malin, *Nathanael West's Novels*, 1972.
Nathanael West: The Cheaters and the Cheated: A Collection of Critical Essays, ed. D. Madden, 1973.
K. Widmer, *Nathanael West*, 1982.

Text:
The Complete Works of Nathanael West, 1957, 1960, 1970.
See also *The Collected Works of Nathanael West*, 1975.

from Miss Lonelyhearts

Miss Lonelyhearts, Help Me, Help Me

The Miss Lonelyhearts of The New York *Post-Dispatch* (Are-you-in-trouble?—Do-you-need-advice?—Write-to-Miss-Lonelyhearts-and-she-will-help-you) sat at his desk and stared at a piece of white cardboard. On it a prayer had been printed by Shrike, the feature editor.

> "Soul of Miss L, glorify me.
> Body of Miss L, nourish me
> Blood of Miss L, intoxicate me.
> Tears of Miss L, wash me.
> Oh good Miss L, excuse my plea,
> And hide me in your heart,
> And defend me from mine enemies.
> Help me, Miss L, help me, help me.
> In sæcula sæculorum.[1] Amen."

Although the deadline was less than a quarter of an hour away, he was still working on his leader. He had gone as far as: "Life *is* worth while, for it is full of dreams and peace, gentleness and ecstasy, and faith that burns like a clear white flame on a

[1] Latin: "world without end."

grim dark altar." But he found it impossible to continue. The letters were no longer funny. He could not go on finding the same joke funny thirty times a day for months on end. And on most days he received more than thirty letters, all of them alike, stamped from the dough of suffering with a heart-shaped cookie knife.

On his desk were piled those he had received this morning. He started through them again, searching for some clue to a sincere answer.

Dear Miss Lonelyhearts—

I am in such pain I don't know what to do sometimes I think I will kill myself my kidneys hurt so much. My husband thinks no woman can be a good catholic and not have children irregardless of the pain. I was married honorable from our church but I never knew what married life meant as I never was told about man and wife. My grandmother never told me and she was the only mother I had but made a big mistake by not telling me as it dont pay to be inocent and is only a big disapointment. I have 7 children in 12 yrs and ever since the last 2 I have been so sick. I was operatored on twice and my husband promised no more children on the doctors advice as he said I might die but when I got back from the hospital he broke his promise and now I am going to have a baby and I dont think I can stand it my kidneys hurt so much. I am so sick and scared because I cant have an abortion on account of being a catholic and my husband so religious. I cry all the time it hurts so much and I dont know what to do.

> *Yours respectfully,*
> *Sick-of-it-all*

Miss Lonelyhearts threw the letter into an open drawer and lit a cigarette.

Dear Miss Lonelyhearts—

I am sixteen years old now and I dont know what to do and would appreciate it if you could tell me what to do. When I was a little girl it was not so bad because I got used to the kids on the block makeing fun of me, but now I would like to have boy friends like the other girls and go out on Saturday nites, but no boy will take me because I was born without a nose—although I am a good dancer and have a nice shape and my father buys me pretty clothes.

I sit and look at myself all day and cry. I have a big hole in the middle of my face that scares people even myself so I cant blame the boys for not wanting to take me out. My mother loves me, but she crys terrible when she looks at me.

What did I do to deserve such a terrible bad fate? Even if I did do some bad things I didnt do any before I was a year old and I was born this way. I asked Papa and he says he doesnt know, but that maybe I did something in the other world before I was born or that maybe I was being punished for his sins. I dont believe that because he is a very nice man. Ought I commit suicide?

> *Sincerely yours,*
> *Desperate*

The cigarette was imperfect and refused to draw. Miss Lonelyhearts took it out of his mouth and stared at it furiously. He fought himself quiet, then lit another one.

Dear Miss Lonelyhearts—

I am writing to you for my little sister Gracie because something awfull hapened to her and I am afraid to tell mother about it. I am 15 years old and Gracie is 13 and we live in Brooklyn. Gracie is deaf and dumb and biger than me but not very smart on account of being deaf and dumb. She plays on the roof of our house and dont go to school except to deaf and dumb school twice a week on tuesdays and thursdays. Mother makes her play on the roof because we dont want her to get run over as she aint very smart. Last week a man came on the roof and did something dirty to her. She told me about it and I dont know what to do as I am afraid to tell mother on account of her being liable to beat Gracie up. I am afraid that Gracie is going to have a baby and I listened to her stomack last night for a long time to see if I could hear the baby but I couldn't. If I tell mother she will beat Gracie up awfull because I am the only one who loves her and last time when she tore her dress they loked her in the closet for 2 days and if the boys on the blok hear about it they will say dirty things like they did on Peewee Conors sister the time she got caught in the lots. So please what would you do if the same hapened in your family.

Yours truly,
Harold S.

He stopped reading. Christ was the answer, but, if he did not want to get sick, he had to stay away from the Christ business. Besides, Christ was Shrike's particular joke. "Soul of Miss L, glorify me. Body of Miss L, save me. Blood of . . ." He turned to his typewriter.

Although his cheap clothes had too much style, he still looked like the son of a Baptist minister. A beard would become him, would accent his Old-Testament look. But even without a beard no one could fail to recognize the New England puritan. His forehead was high and narrow. His nose was long and fleshless. His bony chin was shaped and cleft like a hoof. On seeing him for the first time, Shrike had smiled and said, "The Susan Chesters, the Beatrice Fairfaxes and the Miss Lonelyhearts are the priests of twentieth-century America."

A copy boy came up to tell him that Shrike wanted to know if the stuff was ready. He bent over the typewriter and began pounding its keys.

But before he had written a dozen words, Shrike leaned over his shoulder. "The same old stuff," Shrike said. "Why don't you give them something new and hopeful? Tell them about art. Here, I'll dictate:

"Art Is a Way Out.

"Do not let life overwhelm you. When the old paths are choked with the débris of failure, look for newer and fresher paths. Art is just such a path. Art is distilled from suffering. As Mr. Polnikoff exclaimed through his fine Russian beard, when, at the age of eighty-six, he gave up his business to learn Chinese, 'We are, as yet, only at the beginning. . . .'

"Art Is One of Life's Richest Offerings.

"For those who have not the talent to create, there is appreciation. For those . . .

"Go on from there."

Miss Lonelyhearts and the Cripple

Miss Lonelyhearts dodged Betty because she made him feel ridiculous. He was still trying to cling to his humility, and the farther he got below self-laughter, the easier it was for him to practice it. When Betty telephoned, he refused to answer and after he had twice failed to call her back, she left him alone.

One day, about a week after he had returned from the country, Goldsmith asked him out for a drink. When he accepted, he made himself so humble that Goldsmith was frightened and almost suggested a doctor.

They found Shrike in Delehanty's and joined him at the bar. Goldsmith tried to whisper something to him about Miss Lonelyhearts' condition, but he was drunk and refused to listen. He caught only part of what Goldsmith was trying to say.

"I must differ with you, my good Goldsmith," Shrike said. "Don't call sick those who have faith. They are the well. It is you who are sick."

Goldsmith did not reply and Shrike turned to Miss Lonelyhearts. "Come, tell us, brother, how it was that you first came to believe. Was it music in a church, or the death of a loved one, or mayhap, some wise old priest?"

The familiar jokes no longer had any effect on Miss Lonelyhearts. He smiled at Shrike as the saints are supposed to have smiled at those about to martyr them.

"Ah, but how stupid of me," Shrike continued. "It was the letters, of course. Did I myself not say that the Miss Lonelyhearts are the priests of twentieth-century America?"

Goldsmith laughed, and Shrike, in order to keep him laughing, used an old trick; he appeared to be offended. "Goldsmith, you are the nasty product of this unbelieving age. You cannot believe, you can only laugh. You take everything with a bag of salt and forget that salt is the enemy of fire as well as of ice. Be warned, the salt you use is not Attic salt, it is coarse butcher's salt. It doesn't preserve; it kills."

The bartender who was standing close by, broke in to address Miss Lonelyhearts. "Pardon me, sir, but there's a gent here named Doyle who wants to meet you. He says you know his wife."

Before Miss Lonelyhearts could reply, he beckoned to someone standing at the other end of the bar. The signal was answered by a little cripple, who immediately started in their direction. He used a cane and dragged one of his feet behind him in a box-shaped shoe with a four-inch sole. As he hobbled along, he made many waste motions, like those of a partially destroyed insect.

The bartender introduced the cripple as Mr. Peter Doyle. Doyle was very excited and shook hands twice all around, then with a wave that was meant to be sporting, called for a round of drinks.

Before lifting his glass, Shrike carefully inspected the cripple. When he had finished, he winked at Miss Lonelyhearts and said, "Here's to humanity." He patted Doyle on the back. "Mankind, mankind . . ." he sighed, wagging his head sadly. "What is man that . . ."

The bartender broke in again on behalf of his friend and tried to change the conversation to familiar ground. "Mr. Doyle inspects meters for the gas company."

"And an excellent job it must be," Shrike said. "He should be able to give us the benefit of a different viewpoint. We newspapermen are limited in many ways and I like to hear both sides of a case."

Doyle had been staring at Miss Lonelyhearts as though searching for something, but he now turned to Shrike and tried to be agreeable. "You know what people say, Mr. Shrike?"

"No, my good man, what is it that people say?"

"Everybody's got a frigidaire nowadays, and they say that we meter inspectors take the place of the iceman in the stories." He tried, rather diffidently, to leer.

"What!" Shrike roared at him. "I can see, sir, that you are not the man for us. You can know nothing about humanity; you are humanity. I leave you to Miss Lonelyhearts." He called to Goldsmith and stalked away.

The cripple was confused and angry. "Your friend is a nut," he said. Miss Lonelyhearts was still smiling, but the character of his smile had changed. It had become full of sympathy and a little sad.

The new smile was for Doyle and he knew it. He smiled back gratefully.

"Oh, I forgot," Doyle said, "the wife asked me, if I bumped into you, to ask you to our house to eat. That's why I made Jake introduce us."

Miss Lonelyhearts was busy with his smile and accepted without thinking of the evening he had spent with Mrs. Doyle. The cripple felt honored and shook hands for a third time. It was evidently his only social gesture.

After a few more drinks, when Doyle said that he was tired, Miss Lonelyhearts suggested that they go into the back room. They found a table and sat opposite each other.

The cripple had a very strange face. His eyes failed to balance; his mouth was not under his nose; his forehead was square and bony; and his round chin was like a forehead in miniature. He looked like one of those composite photographs used by screen magazines in guessing contests.

They sat staring at each other until the strain of wordless communication began to excite them both. Doyle made vague, needless adjustments to his clothing. Miss Lonelyhearts found it very difficult to keep his smile steady.

When the cripple finally labored into speech, Miss Lonelyhearts was unable to understand him. He listened hard for a few minutes and realized that Doyle was making no attempt to be understood. He was giving birth to groups of words that lived inside of him as things, a jumble of the retorts he had meant to make when insulted and the private curses against fate that experience had taught him to swallow.

Like a priest, Miss Lonelyhearts turned his face slightly away. He watched the play of the cripple's hands. At first they conveyed nothing but excitement, then gradually they became pictorial. They lagged behind to illustrate a matter with which he was already finished, or ran ahead to illustrate something he had not yet begun to talk about. As he grew more articulate, his hands stopped trying to aid his speech and began to dart in and out of his clothing. One of them suddenly emerged from a pocket of his coat, dragging some sheets of letter paper. He forced these on Miss Lonelyhearts.

Dear Miss Lonelyhearts—

I am kind of ashamed to write you because a man like me dont take stock in things like that but my wife told me you were a man and not some dopey woman so I thought I would write to you after reading your answer to Disillusioned. I am a cripple 41 yrs of age which I have been all my life and I have never let myself get blue until lately when I have been feeling lousy all the time on account of not getting anywhere and asking myself what is it all for. You have a education so I figured may be you no. What I want to no is why I go around pulling my leg up and down stairs reading meters for the gas company for a stinking $22.50 per while the bosses ride around in swell cars living off the fat of the land. Dont think

I am a greasy red. I read where they shoot cripples in Russia because they cant work but I can work better than any park bum and support a wife and child to. But thats not what I am writing you about. What I want to no is what is it all for my pulling my god damed leg along the streets and down in stinking cellars with it all the time hurting fit to burst so that near quitting time I am crazy with pain and when I get home all I hear is money money which aint no home for a man like me. What I want to no is what in hell is the use day after day with a foot like mine when you have to go around pulling and scrambling for a lousy three squares with a toothache in it that comes from useing the foot so much. The doctor told me I ought to rest it for six months but who will pay me when I am resting it. But that aint what I mean either because you might tell me to change my job and where could I get another one I am lucky to have one at all. It aint the job that I am complaining about but what I want to no is what is the whole stinking business for.

Please write me an answer not in the paper because my wife reads your stuff and I dont want her to no I wrote to you because I always said the papers is crap but I figured maybe you no something about it because you have read a lot of books and I never even finished high.

Yours truly,
Peter Doyle

While Miss Lonelyhearts was puzzling out the crabbed writing, Doyle's damp hand accidentally touched his under the table. He jerked away, but then drove his hand back and forced it to clasp the cripple's. After finishing the letter, he did not let go, but pressed it firmly with all the love he could manage. At first the cripple covered his embarrassment by disguising the meaning of the clasp with a handshake, but he soon gave in to it and they sat silently, hand in hand.

Miss Lonelyhearts Has a Religious Experience

After a long night and morning, towards noon, Miss Lonelyhearts welcomed the arrival of fever. It promised heat and mentally unmotivated violence. The promise was soon fulfilled; the rock became a furnace.

He fastened his eyes on the Christ that hung on the wall opposite his bed. As he stared at it, it became a bright fly, spinning with quick grace on a background of blood velvet sprinkled with tiny nerve stars.

Everything else in the room was dead—chairs, table, pencils, clothes, books. He thought of this black world of things as a fish. And he was right, for it suddenly rose to the bright bait on the wall. It rose with a splash of music and he saw its shining silver belly.

Christ is life and light.

"Christ! Christ!" This shout echoed through the innermost cells of his body.

He moved his head to a cooler spot on the pillow and the vein in his forehead became less swollen. He felt clean and fresh. His heart was a rose and in his skull another rose bloomed.

The room was full of grace. A sweet, clean grace, not washed clean, but clean as the innersides of the inner petals of a newly forced rosebud.

Delight was also in the room. It was like a gentle wind, and his nerves rippled under it like small blue flowers in a pasture.

He was conscious of two rhythms that were slowly becoming one. When they became one, his identification with God was complete. His heart was the one heart, the heart of God. And his brain was likewise God's.

God said, "Will you accept it, now?"

And he replied, "I accept, I accept."

He immediately began to plan a new life and his future conduct as Miss Lonelyhearts. He submitted drafts of his column to God and God approved them. God approved his every thought.

Suddenly the door bell rang. He climbed out of bed and went into the hall to see who was coming. It was Doyle, the cripple, and he was slowly working his way up the stairs.

God had sent him so that Miss Lonelyhearts could perform a miracle and be certain of his conversion. It was a sign. He would embrace the cripple and the cripple would be made whole again, even as he, a spiritual cripple, had been made whole.

He rushed down the stairs to meet Doyle with his arms spread for the miracle.

Doyle was carrying something wrapped in a newspaper. When he saw Miss Lonelyhearts, he put his hand inside the package and stopped. He shouted some kind of a warning, but Miss Lonelyhearts continued his charge. He did not understand the cripple's shout and heard it as a cry for help from Desperate, Harold S., Catholic-mother, Broken-hearted, Broad-shoulders, Sick-of-it-all, Disillusioned-with-tubercular-husband. He was running to succor them with love.

The cripple turned to escape, but he was too slow and Miss Lonelyhearts caught him.

While they were struggling, Betty came in through the street door. She called to them to stop and started up the stairs. The cripple saw her cutting off his escape and tried to get rid of the package. He pulled his hand out. The gun inside the package exploded and Miss Lonelyhearts fell, dragging the cripple with him. They both rolled part of the way down the stairs.

1933

Richard Wright
1908–1960

Richard Wright was born into an impoverished black sharecropper family on a cotton plantation near Natchez, Mississippi, on September 4, 1908. His father deserted the family when Wright was five years old, and when he was ten his mother suffered the first of a series of strokes that left her partially paralyzed. As a child Wright was shuttled about among various relatives and spent some time in an orphanage. A good student, he graduated from Smith-Robinson High School in Jackson, Mississippi, in 1925 and moved to Memphis, where he took menial jobs and began writing. Two years later he moved to Chicago, then in 1937 to New York City. In 1947 he moved to Paris, where he lived as an expatriate until his fatal heart attack on November 28, 1960.

Although each of the places Wright lived marked his life, none marked it more deeply than Mississippi, which inspired the characteristic tone of anguish and anger that we find in all his best work. The deprivation that Wright felt in the Deep South was partly physical—he was often hungry, and he was always poor. But it was also psychological, intellectual, and spiritual. Both his mother and his maternal grandmother, who helped raise him, were rigidly moralistic and believed in harsh corporal punishment. In the society around him, the threat of far worse forms of violence was constant. In the schools he attended, education was not only limited but restrictive. In Memphis he once tried to get books from the library by forging a note from a white borrower: *"Dear Madam:"* he later wrote in "The Library Card," *"Will you please let this nigger boy . . . have some books by H. L Mencken?"* The deception reflects not only the iconoclastic role Mencken later came to play for Wright but also the sense Wright had of having been deliberately denied access to the books he most needed. An avid reader, Wright often turned to books for the emotional fulfillment he could not find in life: "It had been only through books," he wrote, ". . . that I had managed to keep myself alive."

After his move to Chicago, Wright worked as a porter, a dishwasher, a salesman for a disreputable burial insurance agency, and as a postal worker. With the onset of the Depression, he was forced to go on relief and work as a street sweeper before gravitating toward the Federal Negro Theater and the Federal Writer's Project, both of which were sponsored by the WPA. Wright also became active in radical politics; he began writing poetry for leftist journals, and in 1933 he joined the Chicago John Reed Club shortly before officially becoming a member of the Communist party. In 1935 Wright began to contribute articles and reviews to the intellectual and politically radical journal, *The New Masses.*

With his move to New York City in 1937, Wright became Harlem editor of the Communist newspaper *The Daily Worker* and soon began writing the books that made him famous. That year he finished his first novel, *Lawd Today,* an experimental work (not published until 1963) about twenty-four hours in the life of a middle-class Chicago black that Wright self-consciously modeled after James Joyce's *Ulysses* and John Dos Passos's *U.S.A.* A year later Wright published his first book, *Uncle Tom's Children: Four Novellas,* a collection of stories that viscerally concern racial prejudice, black resistance, and violence in the Deep South. Wright said of one of the stories that he was influenced by both Gertrude Stein and Ernest Hemingway as he tried to find a way to handle serious social issues in a simple, naturalistic style. In 1940, while on a Guggenheim fellowship, Wright published *Native Son,* the grim, nightmarish tale of a young black man who accidentally murders the liberal daughter of his white employer. As Theodore Dreiser had done with *An American Tragedy* (1925), Wright based his story on an actual murder case; like Dreiser's, Wright's intentions were more literary than documentary. He wanted, he wrote, to put the case of the Negro squarely into American literary tradition:

We do have in the Negro the embodiment of a past, tragic enough to appease the spiritual hunger of even a [Henry] James and we have in the oppression of the Negro a shadow athwart our national life dense and heavy enough to satisfy even the gloomy broodings of a Hawthorne. And if Poe were alive, he would not have to invent horror; horror would invent him.

An enormous publishing success, *Native Son* was the first book written by an American black to be selected for the Book of the Month Club.

In 1941 Wright wrote the text for *Twelve Million Black Voices,* a book that combined words and pictures to express the "folk history of the Negro in the United States." The following year, while giving a talk at Fisk University on growing up black in America, Wright decided to compose his autobiography:

It was not half-way through my speech that it crashed upon me that I was saying things that whites had forbidden Negroes to say. . . . Later, I learned that I had accidentally blundered into the secret, black, hidden core of race relations in the United States. That core is this: nobody is ever expected to speak honestly about this problem.

The result of his autobiographical efforts was another best-selling book, *Black Boy* (1945), which contained the story of his life up until his move to Chicago. Deleted at the time were several chapters dealing with his life in Chicago and his increasing disenchantment with the Communist party; this material was eventually published posthumously as *American Hunger* (1977). Wright had left the Communist party in 1944, following a bitter struggle in which the party accused him of harboring anti-Stalinist sentiments and resisting party discipline.

In the spring of 1946 Wright and his family visited France for several months on the invitation of Gertrude Stein. The Wrights returned to Paris in 1947, where they settled permanently and where Wright, by now a vehement anti-Communist, met Jean-Paul Sartre and immersed himself in existentialist philosophy. Wright's work had long concerned itself with such issues as freedom, alienation, dread, and identity through violence ("When a man kills, it's for something. . . . I didn't know I was really alive in this world until I felt things hard enough to kill for 'em," says the hero of *Native Son*), but in his later work, such as *The Outsider* (1953), *Savage Holiday* (1954), and *The Long Dream* (1958), philosophy became a more explicit and less effective part of his fiction. These novels focus on heroes who, finding themselves cut off from the world around them as well as from the past, determine to make virtues of isolation and rootlessness. Throughout the 1950s Wright also traveled extensively in an attempt to understand the origins and legacy of black slavery: *Black Power: A Report of Reactions in a Land of Pathos* (1954) is an account of a trip to the Gold Coast (Ghana); *The Color Curtain* (1956) reports on his coverage of a conference in Indonesia; and *Pagan Spain* (1957) is an attempt to find answers to the history of slavery in the paradoxes of Spanish culture. In 1957 Wright also brought out a collection of his European lectures on politics, racism, and black literature. A collection of short stories, *Eight Men,* was published posthumously in 1961.

Wright's early work, which is also his most powerful, focuses on the large demographic shift of black people from the rural South toward the urban North. In these works his heroes struggle against accepting both the "place" of powerlessness and the "role" of subservience and silence that their society has assigned them. Since this struggle often leads Wright's heroes into defiance that society regards as criminal—and sometimes leads them directly into criminality—they characteristically find themselves threatened by social rejection as well as terrible punishment. Both of these threats, one psychological, the other physical, haunt Wright's characters as they attempt to force people who occupy positions of power and prestige to see, hear, and acknowledge them. It was a struggle Wright, too, continually endured: "I had elected," he wrote in *American Hunger,* "in my fevered search for honorable adjustment to the American scene, not to submit and in doing so I had embraced the daily horror of anxiety, of tension, of eternal disquiet."

Further Reading:
J. Baldwin, "Everybody's Protest Novel" in *Notes of a Native Son,* 1955.
I. Howe, "Black Boys and Native Sons" in *A World More Attractive,* 1963.
R. Ellison, "Richard Wright's Blues" in *Shadow and Act,* 1964.
C. Webb, *Richard Wright: A Biography,* 1968.
D. McCall, *The Example of Richard Wright,* 1969.

Text:
Black Boy, 1945.

---

from Black Boy

Chapter Thirteen: [The Library Card]

One morning I arrived early at work and went into the bank lobby where the Negro porter was mopping. I stood at a counter and picked up the Memphis *Commercial Appeal* and began my free reading of the press. I came finally to the editorial page and saw an article dealing with one H. L. Mencken. I knew by hearsay that he was the editor of the *American Mercury,* but aside from that I knew nothing about him. The article was a furious denunciation of Mencken, concluding with one, hot, short sentence: Mencken is a fool.

I wondered what on earth this Mencken had done to call down upon him the scorn of the South. The only people I had ever heard denounced in the South were Negroes, and this man was not a Negro. Then what ideas did Mencken hold that made a newspaper like the *Commercial Appeal* castigate him publicly? Undoubtedly he must be advocating ideas that the South did not like. Were there, then, people other than Negroes who criticized the South? I knew that during the Civil War the South had hated northern whites, but I had not encountered such hate during my life. Knowing no more of Mencken than I did at that moment, I felt a vague sympathy for him. Had not the South, which had assigned me the role of a non-man, cast at him its hardest words?

Now, how could I find out about this Mencken? There was a huge library near the riverfront, but I knew that Negroes were not allowed to patronize its shelves any more than they were the parks and playgrounds of the city. I had gone into the library several times to get books for the white men on the job. Which of them would now help me to get books? And how could I read them without causing concern to the white men with whom I worked? I had so far been successful in hiding my thoughts and feelings from them, but I knew that I would create hostility if I went about this business of reading in a clumsy way.

I weighed the personalities of the men on the job. There was Don, a Jew; but I distrusted him. His position was not much better than mine and I knew that he was uneasy and insecure; he had always treated me in an offhand, bantering way that barely concealed his contempt. I was afraid to ask him to help me to get books; his frantic desire to demonstrate a racial solidarity with the whites against Negroes might make him betray me.

Then how about the boss? No, he was a Baptist and I had the suspicion that he would not be quite able to comprehend why a black boy would want to read Mencken. There were other white men on the job whose attitudes showed clearly that they were Kluxers or sympathizers, and they were out of the question.

There remained only one man whose attitude did not fit into an anti-Negro category, for I had heard the white men refer to him as a "Pope lover." He was an Irish Catholic and was hated by the white Southerners. I knew that he read books, because I had got him volumes from the library several times. Since he, too, was an object of hatred, I felt that he might refuse me but would hardly betray me. I hesitated, weighing and balancing the imponderable realities.

One morning I paused before the Catholic fellow's desk.

"I want to ask you a favor," I whispered to him.

"What is it?"

"I want to read. I can't get books from the library. I wonder if you'd let me use your card?"

He looked at me suspiciously.

"My card is full most of the time," he said.

"I see," I said and waited, posing my question silently.

"You're not trying to get me into trouble, are you, boy?" he asked, staring at me.

"Oh, no, sir."

"What book do you want?"

"A book by H. L. Mencken."

"Which one?"

"I don't know. Has he written more than one?"

"He has written several."

"I didn't know that."

"What makes you want to read Mencken?"

"Oh, I just saw his name in the newspaper," I said.

"It's good of you to want to read," he said. "But you ought to read the right things."

I said nothing. Would he want to supervise my reading?

"Let me think," he said. "I'll figure out something."

I turned from him and he called me back. He stared at me quizzically.

"Richard, don't mention this to the other white men," he said.

"I understand," I said. "I won't say a word."

A few days later he called me to him.

"I've got a card in my wife's name," he said. "Here's mine."

"Thank you, sir."

"Do you think you can manage it?"

"I'll manage fine," I said.

"If they suspect you, you'll get in trouble," he said.

"I'll write the same kind of notes to the library that you wrote when you sent me for books," I told him. "I'll sign your name."

He laughed.

"Go ahead. Let me see what you get," he said.

That afternoon I addressed myself to forging a note. Now, what were the names of books written by H. L. Mencken? I did not know any of them. I finally wrote what I thought would be a foolproof note: *Dear Madam: Will you please let this nigger boy*—I used the word "nigger" to make the librarian feel that I could not possibly be the author of the note—*have some books by H. L. Mencken?* I forged the white man's name.

I entered the library as I had always done when on errands for whites, but I felt that I would somehow slip up and betray myself. I doffed my hat, stood a respectful distance from the desk, looked as unbookish as possible, and waited for the white patrons to be taken care of. When the desk was clear of people, I still waited. The white librarian looked at me.

"What do you want, boy?"

As though I did not possess the power of speech, I stepped forward and simply handed her the forged note, not parting my lips.

"What books by Mencken does he want?" she asked.

"I don't know, ma'am," I said, avoiding her eyes.

"Who gave you this card?"

"Mr. Falk," I said.

"Where is he?"

"He's at work, at the M—— Optical Company," I said. "I've been in here for him before."

"I remember," the woman said. "But he never wrote notes like this."

Oh, God, she's suspicious. Perhaps she would not let me have the books? If she had turned her back at that moment, I would have ducked out the door and never gone back. Then I thought of a bold idea.

"You can call him up, ma'am," I said, my heart pounding.

"You're not using these books, are you?" she asked pointedly.

"Oh, no, ma'am. I can't read."

"I don't know what he wants by Mencken," she said under her breath.

I knew now that I had won; she was thinking of other things and the race question had gone out of her mind. She went to the shelves. Once or twice she looked over her shoulder at me, as though she was still doubtful. Finally she came forward with two books in her hand.

"I'm sending him two books," she said. "But tell Mr. Falk to come in next time, or send me the names of the books he wants. I don't know what he wants to read."

I said nothing. She stamped the card and handed me the books. Not daring to glance at them, I went out of the library, fearing that the woman would call me back for further questioning. A block away from the library I opened one of the books and read a title: *A Book of Prefaces.* I was nearing my nineteenth birthday and I did not know how to pronounce the word "preface." I thumbed the pages and saw strange words and strange names. I shook my head, disappointed. I looked at the other book; it was called *Prejudices.* I knew what that word meant; I had heard it all my life. And right off I was on guard against Mencken's books. Why would a man want to call a book *Prejudices?* The word was so stained with all my memories of racial hate that I could not conceive of anybody using it for a title. Perhaps I had made a mistake about Mencken? A man who had prejudices must be wrong.

When I showed the books to Mr. Falk, he looked at me and frowned.

"That librarian might telephone you," I warned him.

"That's all right," he said. "But when you're through reading those books, I want you to tell me what you get out of them."

That night in my rented room, while letting the hot water run over my can of pork and beans in the sink, I opened *A Book of Prefaces* and began to read. I was jarred and shocked by the style, the clear, clean, sweeping sentences. Why did he write like that? And how did one write like that? I pictured the man as a raging demon, slashing with his pen, consumed with hate, denouncing everything American, extolling everything European or German, laughing at the weaknesses of people, mocking God, authority. What was this? I stood up, trying to realize what reality lay behind the meaning of the words . . . Yes, this man was fighting, fighting with words. He was using words as a weapon, using them as one would use a club. Could words be weapons? Well, yes, for here they were. Then, maybe, perhaps, I could use them as a weapon? No. It frightened me. I read on and what amazed me was not what he said, but how on earth anybody had the courage to say it.

Occasionally I glanced up to reassure myself that I was alone in the room. Who were these men about whom Mencken was talking so passionately? Who was Anatole France? Joseph Conrad? Sinclair Lewis, Sherwood Anderson, Dostoevski, George Moore, Gustave Flaubert, Maupassant, Tolstoy, Frank Harris, Mark Twain, Thomas Hardy, Arnold Bennett, Stephen Crane, Zola, Norris, Gorky, Bergson, Ibsen, Balzac, Bernard Shaw, Dumas, Poe, Thomas Mann, O. Henry, Dreiser, H. G. Wells, Gogol, T. S. Eliot, Gide, Baudelaire, Edgar Lee Masters, Stendhal, Turgenev, Huneker, Nietzsche, and scores of others? Were these men real? Did they exist or had they existed? And how did one pronounce their names?

I ran across many words whose meanings I did not know, and I either looked them up in a dictionary or, before I had a chance to do that, encountered the word in a context that made its meaning clear. But what strange world was this? I concluded the book with the conviction that I had somehow overlooked something terribly important in life. I had once tried to write, had once reveled in feeling, had let my crude imagination roam, but the impulse to dream had been slowly beaten out of me by experience. Now it surged up again and I hungered for books, new ways of looking and seeing. It was not a matter of believing or disbelieving what I read, but of feeling something new, of being affected by something that made the look of the world different.

As dawn broke I ate my pork and beans, feeling dopey, sleepy. I went to work, but the mood of the book would not die; it lingered, coloring everything I saw, heard, did. I now felt that I knew what the white men were feeling. Merely because I had

read a book that had spoken of how they lived and thought, I identified myself with
that book. I felt vaguely guilty. Would I, filled with bookish notions, act in a manner
that would make the whites dislike me?

I forged more notes and my trips to the library became frequent. Reading grew
into a passion. My first serious novel was Sinclair Lewis's *Main Street*. It made me
see my boss, Mr. Gerald, and identify him as an American type. I would smile when
I saw him lugging his golf bags into the office. I had always felt a vast distance
separating me from the boss, and now I felt closer to him, though still distant. I felt
now that I knew him, that I could feel the very limits of his narrow life. And this
had happened because I had read a novel about a mythical man called George F.
Babbitt.

The plots and stories in the novels did not interest me so much as the point of view
revealed. I gave myself over to each novel without reserve, without trying to criticize
it; it was enough for me to see and feel something different. And for me, everything
was something different. Reading was like a drug, a dope. The novels created moods
in which I lived for days. But I could not conquer my sense of guilt, my feeling that
the white men around me knew that I was changing, that I had begun to regard them
differently.

Whenever I brought a book to the job, I wrapped it in newspaper—a habit that
was to persist for years in other cities and under other circumstances. But some of
the white men pried into my packages when I was absent and they questioned me.

"Boy, what are you reading those books for?"

"Oh, I don't know, sir."

"That's deep stuff you're reading, boy."

"I'm just killing time, sir."

"You'll addle your brains if you don't watch out."

I read Dreiser's *Jennie Gerhardt* and *Sister Carrie* and they revived in me a vivid
sense of my mother's suffering; I was overwhelmed. I grew silent, wondering about
the life around me. It would have been impossible for me to have told anyone what
I derived from these novels, for it was nothing less than a sense of life itself. All my
life had shaped me for the realism, the naturalism of the modern novel, and I could
not read enough of them.

Steeped in new moods and ideas, I bought a ream of paper and tried to write; but
nothing would come, or what did come was flat beyond telling. I discovered that more
than desire and feeling were necessary to write and I dropped the idea. Yet I still
wondered how it was possible to know people sufficiently to write about them? Could
I ever learn about life and people? To me, with my vast ignorance, my Jim Crow
station in life, it seemed a task impossible of achievement. I now knew what being
a Negro meant. I could endure the hunger. I had learned to live with hate. But to
feel that there were feelings denied me, that the very breath of life itself was beyond
my reach, that more than anything else hurt, wounded me. I had a new hunger.

In buoying me up, reading also cast me down, made me see what was possible,
what I had missed. My tension returned, new, terrible, bitter, surging, almost too great
to be contained. I no longer *felt* that the world about me was hostile, killing; I *knew*
it. A million times I asked myself what I could do to save myself, and there were
no answers. I seemed forever condemned, ringed by walls.

I did not discuss my reading with Mr. Falk, who had lent me his library card; it would have meant talking about myself and that would have been too painful. I smiled each day, fighting desperately to maintain my old behavior, to keep my disposition seemingly sunny. But some of the white men discerned that I had begun to brood.

"Wake up there, boy!" Mr. Olin said one day.

"Sir!" I answered for the lack of a better word.

"You act like you've stolen something," he said.

I laughed in the way I knew he expected me to laugh, but I resolved to be more conscious of myself, to watch my every act, to guard and hide the new knowledge that was dawning within me.

If I went north, would it be possible for me to build a new life then? But how could a man build a life upon vague, unformed yearnings? I wanted to write and I did not even know the English language. I bought English grammars and found them dull. I felt that I was getting a better sense of the language from novels than from grammars. I read hard, discarding a writer as soon as I felt that I had grasped his point of view. At night the printed page stood before my eyes in sleep.

Mrs. Moss, my landlady, asked me one Sunday morning:

"Son, what is this you keep on reading?"

"Oh, nothing. Just novels."

"What you get out of 'em?"

"I'm just killing time," I said.

"I hope you know your own mind," she said in a tone which implied that she doubted if I had a mind.

I knew of no Negroes who read the books I liked and I wondered if any Negroes ever thought of them. I knew that there were Negro doctors, lawyers, newspapermen, but I never saw any of them. When I read a Negro newspaper I never caught the faintest echo of my preoccupation in its pages. I felt trapped and occasionally, for a few days, I would stop reading. But a vague hunger would come over me for books, books that opened up new avenues of feeling and seeing, and again I would forge another note to the white librarian. Again I would read and wonder as only the naïve and unlettered can read and wonder, feeling that I carried a secret, criminal burden about with me each day.

That winter my mother and brother came and we set up housekeeping, buying furniture on the installment plan, being cheated and yet knowing no way to avoid it. I began to eat warm food and to my surprise found that regular meals enabled me to read faster. I may have lived through many illnesses and survived them, never suspecting that I was ill. My brother obtained a job and we began to save toward the trip north, plotting our time, setting tentative dates for departure. I told none of the white men on the job that I was planning to go north; I knew that the moment they felt I was thinking of the North they would change toward me. It would have made them feel that I did not like the life I was living, and because my life was completely conditioned by what they said or did, it would have been tantamount to challenging them.

I could calculate my chances for life in the South as a Negro fairly clearly now.

I could fight the southern whites by organizing with other Negroes, as my grandfather had done. But I knew that I could never win that way; there were many whites and there were but few blacks. They were strong and we were weak. Outright black rebellion could never win. If I fought openly I would die and I did not want to die. News of lynchings were frequent.

I could submit and live the life of a genial slave, but that was impossible. All of my life had shaped me to live by my own feelings and thoughts. I could make up to Bess and marry her and inherit the house. But that, too, would be the life of a slave; if I did that, I would crush to death something within me, and I would hate myself as much as I knew the whites already hated those who had submitted. Neither could I ever willingly present myself to be kicked, as Shorty had done. I would rather have died than do that.

I could drain off my restlessness by fighting with Shorty and Harrison. I had seen many Negroes solve the problem of being black by transferring their hatred of themselves to others with a black skin and fighting them. I would have to be cold to do that, and I was not cold and I could never be.

I could, of course, forget what I had read, thrust the whites out of my mind, forget them; and find release from anxiety and longing in sex and alcohol. But the memory of how my father had conducted himself made that course repugnant. If I did not want others to violate my life, how could I voluntarily violate it myself?

I had no hope whatever of being a professional man. Not only had I been so conditioned that I did not desire it, but the fulfillment of such an ambition was beyond my capabilities. Well-to-do Negroes lived in a world that was almost as alien to me as the world inhabited by whites.

What, then, was there? I held my life in my mind, in my consciousness each day, feeling at times that I would stumble and drop it, spill it forever. My reading had created a vast sense of distance between me and the world in which I lived and tried to make a living, and that sense of distance was increasing each day. My days and nights were one long, quiet, continuously contained dream of terror, tension, and anxiety. I wondered how long I could bear it.

1937

Walker Evans,
Brooklyn Bridge,
photograph, ca. 1928.
The J. Paul Getty Museum.

Georgia O'Keeffe,
Brooklyn Bridge,
oil on masonite, 1948.
The Brooklyn Museum.
Bequest of Mary Childs Draper.

The Literature
of Modernism:
Poetry
1912–1940

 The generation of poets that came to adulthood in
the early years of the twentieth century had been
brought up to believe that American culture was far
inferior to European culture. Black poets, like
Langston Hughes bore the double burden of having
been told that their race had no culture and that the
only way to be literary was to imitate a white
tradition. The great accomplishment of American
poetry of the modernist period was to equal English
poetry—not by the work of a single genius like
Whitman or Dickinson but rather by the productions
of a long line of poets changing the face of the art.
The new American poets defiantly claimed equal
status with the parent literature and explored to the
full the native resources of the American language. A
number of black poets, for instance, encouraged by
the example of Langston Hughes, began to write in
the black vernacular, taking as their rhythmic base
not the English pentameter but the syncopation of
jazz, the first black art form to be incorporated into
American life.

Hughes's vignettes of Harlem life participated in
the large democratization of poetry sponsored by
his contemporaries. Dissatisfied with the historically
aristocratic role of poetry in Europe, some modern
American poets—Robert Frost, E. E. Cummings,
William Carlos Williams—began writing poetry for
a mass audience, a poetry in which that audience
could find reflected its own environment and
concerns. "My nonliterary listeners," said Langston
Hughes in *I Wonder as I Wander* (1956), "would

be ready [at this point in the reading] to think in terms of their own problems":

> Then I read poems about women domestics, workers on the Florida roads, poor black students wanting to shatter the darkness of ignorance and prejudice, and one about the sharecroppers of Mississippi. . . . Many of my verses were documentary, journalistic, and topical.

While Hughes was documenting Harlem and Mississippi, Cummings was sketching, in slang, the flappers of the jazz age, Williams was writing proletarian portraits, and Frost was describing, in terms the common reader could understand, the bleak isolation, hostility, and seclusion of rural New England. But American readers, on the whole, were not prepared for the new poets, even these most accessible ones; all of the American modernists found themselves writing in a raw culture not yet ready for them.

American Culture and the International Style

In the early part of the century, when the poets were exploring Europe and European avant-garde writing, America was firmly isolationist. Even America's late participation in World War I only confirmed in most Americans a sense that the country's strength lay in its turning its back on European quarrels. After all, most Americans had repudiated Europe (for political, religious, or economic reasons) in deciding to emigrate to America, and many immigrant families Americanized themselves, linguistically and culturally, as fast as possible.

World War I, decimating Europe, had left America relatively untouched. After Woodrow Wilson's death, America returned to its isolationist mood during the "normalcy" of the twenties under Warren Harding, Calvin Coolidge, and Herbert Hoover. The business boom of the twenties collapsed in the crash of the stock market in October 1929, an event that plunged America into a depression that turned American attention even more drastically toward its own concerns. Despite the efforts of Franklin Delano Roosevelt after 1932, the depression was finally ended only by the increase in manufacturing caused by America's entrance into World War II in 1941. Until the end of that war, America remained a provincial nation, wary of all things European.

The writers of this era responded variously to American isolationism and provinciality. Many writers left America for London or Paris—among them T. S. Eliot, Ezra Pound, Cummings, and Frost (though of these only Eliot and Pound became permanent expatriates). The first books of poetry by Pound, Frost, and Marianne Moore were all published abroad, where public taste was more accustomed to avant-garde art. Pound wrote, in disgust, that "the age demanded an image / Of its accelerated grimace, / . . . a mould in plaster, / Made with no loss of time, / . . . [not] alabaster / Or the 'sculpture' of rhyme" ("Hugh Selwyn Mauberley"). American taste preferred genteel Anglophilia or robust American good sense to the sort of experimentation being carried on by its new poets.

Credo

If a certain thing was said once for all in Atlantis or Arcadia, in 450 before Christ or in 1290 after, it is not for us moderns to go saying it over, or to go obscuring the memory of the dead by saying the same thing with less skill and less conviction.

My pawing over the ancients and semi-ancients has been one struggle to find out what has been done, once for all, better than it can ever be done again, and to find out what remains for us to do, and plenty does remain, for if we still feel the same emotions as those which launched the thousand ships, it is quite certain that we come on these feelings differently, through different nuances, by different intellectual gradations. Each age has its own abounding gifts yet only some ages transmute them into matter of duration. No good poetry is ever written in a manner twenty years old, for to write in such a manner shows conclusively that the writer thinks from books, convention and *cliché*, and not from life.

Ezra Pound (1911)

That experimentation, as observed with the advantage of hindsight, directed itself chiefly against the prescribed English models. The "international style" that American modernist work exhibits (in common with modern French and Italian poetry) distinguishes it sharply from nineteenth-century American poetry. Though some nineteenth-century poets, notably Longfellow, had borrowed from European literature, their borrowings were domesticated into a "fireside" style and on the whole did not exhibit linguistic experimentation. But now Eliot, who had studied comparative literature at Harvard, began to imitate topics and tones that he had found in French poets—the urban *ennui* of Charles Baudelaire, the satire of the bourgeoisie of Jules Laforgue. Pound, who had studied comparative literature at the University of Pennsylvania, looked for his inspiration to a European period before the English Renaissance, imitating the *dolce stil nuovo* ("sweet new style") of fourteenth-century Italian poets such as Guido Cavalcanti. This hybridizing of the English poetic heritage with French and Italian models produced the poems that appeared in Pound's *A Lume Spento* (1908) and Eliot's *Prufrock and Other Observations* (1917). Eliot's European poems adopted a weary irony foreign to American literature, and Pound's poems took on archaic language and medieval postures. Later, Eliot, who had studied Sanskrit and Buddhism, would turn to the religious poetry of the Indian Upanishads as a lyric source, and Pound would incorporate Chinese, Anglo-Saxon, and Latin models into his *Cantos*. It must quickly be added that, for all this display of foreign influence, both Pound and Eliot wrote solidly in the British tradition. Pound's masters were Robert Browning, for the dramatic monologue, and Dante Gabriel Rossetti, who wrote poems derived from medieval Italian models, especially Dante, Petrarch, and Cavalcanti. Eliot's masters were Matthew Arnold, Browning, Tennyson (whose musicality he imitated), and the post-Shakespearean Jacobean dramatists (whom Eliot admired for their macabre theatricality of style).

Tradition and the Individual Talent

No poet, no artist of any art, has his complete meaning alone. His significance, his appreciation is the appreciation of his relation to the dead poets and artists. You cannot value him alone; you must set him, for contrast and comparison, among the dead. I mean this as a principle of æsthetic, not merely historical, criticism. The necessity that he shall conform, that he shall cohere, is not one-sided; what happens when a new work of art is created is something that happens simultaneously to all the works of art which preceded it. The existing monuments form an ideal order among themselves, which is modified by the introduction of the new (the really new) work of art among them. The existing order is complete before the new work arrives; for order to persist after the supervention of novelty, the *whole* existing order must be, if ever so slightly, altered; and so the relations, proportions, values of each work of art toward the whole are readjusted; and this is conformity between the old and the new. Whoever has approved this idea of order, of the form of European, of English literature, will not find it preposterous that the past should be altered by the present as much as the present is directed by the past. And the poet who is aware of this will be aware of great difficulties and responsibilities.

T. S. Eliot (1919)

Eliot and Pound were not the only poets to borrow from foreign sources. E. E. Cummings learned his typographical play from the French modernist poets Guillaume Apollinaire and Stéphane Mallarmé, and he adopted an aesthetic based on the manifestos issued by the French Surrealists and Dadaists, poets who detached literature from referential meaning and linked it to experimental play. (The Surrealist manifestos were imitated by Pound, who, in his short-lived journal *Blast* in 1914 and 1915 issued irascible proclamations of his own, influenced by the Italian Futurist writers, who wanted a poetry geared to a technological world.)

In quieter ways, Frost, Wallace Stevens, and Moore were also influenced by international models. Frost wrote a rural poetry influenced not only by the English tradition from Wordsworth to Hardy but also by Latin eclogues and georgic poetry. He rightly suspected that he might find a more cordial reception in England for such poetry than in America, and his friendship with the English poet Edward Thomas (who reviewed Frost's work enthusiastically) gave him the support he sought. Although Frost returned to America after three years in England, it is symptomatic of the condition of American culture that it was in London that he and Pound should meet. Pound, finding in Frost an indigenous American voice of the sort he had been calling for, sponsored Frost's first American publication.

Stevens, though he never in his long life traveled abroad, was a devoted reader of French poetry and collector of French painting. "French and English," he wrote, "constitute a single language," and he composed his inventive lines as though they did: "The gaiety of language is our seigneur." For all the depth of his roots in Wordsworth and Keats, Stevens, like Eliot, found his way as a young poet at Harvard only by imitating the new harmonies—abrupt, nonchalant, oblique—of the French symbolists. And Marianne Moore, though she went abroad only once, served for four years (1925–1929) as the editor of *The Dial,* the New York magazine that, more than any other, brought the news of avant-garde art (including painting, sculpture, and music) to the American audience. Her expert knowledge of French was probably instrumental in her form of rebellion against English prosody when she decided to count syllables in her verse, as the French do, in lieu of feet.

Almost all the modernist American poets lived their creative years in cities. The American hinterland offered no base for poetry. Eliot left St. Louis for Cambridge and, eventually, London; Pound's family went from Idaho to Philadelphia, and Pound left the United States for Venice, Paris, London, and eventually various cities in Italy; Frost's family moved back east from San Francisco, and Frost remained always within easy reach of Boston. In the United States, only New York (and to a lesser extent Boston and Cambridge) contained enough artists for company, support, and journal publishing.

New York became the center toward which most poets converged. Moore's family made their way from St. Louis to Carlisle, Pennsylvania, to New York; E. E. Cummings left Cambridge for New York; William Carlos Williams, though he practiced medicine in New Jersey, joined, as did Stevens, the New York group clustered around *The Dial* and *Others* (a journal of experimental writing); Hart Crane left Ohio for Manhattan; and the writers of the Harlem Renaissance, though they may have been born in the South, found in New York the personal and intellectual stimulus necessary for a black literary movement.

But New York was not the only city to produce poetry. There was a "Chicago school" of poets that included Edgar Lee Masters and Carl Sandburg; and the magazine *Poetry,* founded and edited by Harriet Monroe, was published in Chicago. There was also a "southern school" of poetry clustered around John Crowe Ransom, a school that would produce Allen Tate, Robert Penn Warren, and even Robert Lowell. Still, New York was where the modernist movement in poetry, supported from abroad by its expatriate wing, was created and sustained. The poets were sustained, too, by artistic events in New York, notably the famous Armory show of 1913, which introduced modernist French painting to the American audience and radically changed American conceptions of art. Even though American poetry in the first part of the century was, for the most part, confined to one city on one coast, it was no longer narrowly parochial in content or in form.

American Themes in the New Poetry

Though the international aesthetic of modernism is the one that gave American poetry a wider perspective on the world, there were American poets who embraced a different, and no less powerful, aesthetic. William Carlos Williams

---

American Scenes

Mr. Frost is an honest writer, writing from himself, from his own knowledge and emotion; not simply picking up the manner which magazines are accepting at the moment, and applying it to topics in vogue. He is quite consciously and definitely putting New England rural life into verse. He is not using themes that anybody could have cribbed out of Ovid.

There are only two passions in art; there are only love and hate—with endless modifications. Frost has been honestly fond of the New England people, I dare say with spells of irritation. He has given their life honestly and seriously. He has never turned aside to make fun of it. He has taken their tragedy as tragedy, their stubbornness as stubbornness. I know more of farm life than I did before I had read his poems. That means I know more of 'Life.'

Ezra Pound, reviewing *North of Boston* (1914)

---

and Hart Crane opposed Eliot's and Pound's search for foreign materials for poetry. Williams, whose father was English and mother Puerto Rican, experienced the shakiness of being a first-generation child in America. His early Anglophile poetry imitated Keats, but he soon became defiantly American. Though Williams was powerfully influenced by the concepts of modernist art (he knew the French painters Francis Picabia and Marcel Duchamp), he embodied those concepts in poems treating American scenes, poems expressed in a resolutely colloquial language. Crane, believing that Eliot had taken a fatally wrong turn in using continental materials in *The Waste Land,* set himself, as had Williams in *Paterson,* the task of writing an American epic, which he called *The Bridge.* As *Paterson* uses documentary materials concerning the history and ongoing life of an ordinary American city, so *The Bridge* confronts modern American technology (the Brooklyn Bridge), the American past (Pocahontas and Rip Van Winkle), and the American present (hoboes riding the rails during the Depression).

Both Crane and Williams, though themselves from the middle class, felt social and political sympathy for the poor. This sympathy may have arisen in Williams through his practice of medicine among New Jersey's immigrants and in Crane through his sexual companionship with working-class men. The "Europeanizing" modernists, on the other hand, were conservative in their social and political alignments: Eliot declared himself an Anglo–Catholic royalist, Pound eventually came to sympathize with Fascism, and Frost and Stevens became increasingly Republican. The southern writers, though Democrats, preached an agrarianism that was profoundly conservative in its preference for the southern agricultural past over the northern technological present.

The division in American literary life between left and right wings has been the cause of bitter quarrels and literary scandals, the most famous centering on Ezra Pound, who in 1948 was awarded the Library of Congress Bollingen Prize for poetry while under indictment for treason for his World War II Italian radio broadcasts supporting Mussolini. Pound's literary supporters—of all political persuasions—argued that the poetry could be separated from the politics, since Pound had been declared of unsound mind and was incarcerated in St. Elizabeth's mental hospital; political antagonists replied that Pound's alliance with Fascism and his declared anti-Semitism should have precluded any award for his poetry. The controversy revealed the persistent American tendency to judge a poet's work by his life and to demand an ethical standard for literature to the exclusion of an aesthetic one.

American poets of the twentieth century did not, in short, enter a sympathetic culture. American suspicion of poetry originated long before the modernist period, however. In a frontier society, it has been argued, the fine arts have no practical value. It is also true that the dissenting founders of the northeastern colonies adopted a moral and instrumental, rather than aesthetic, view of literature. But the deepening of the estrangement between the common reader and the poet came about partly because of the gap in learning between the modernist poets and a reading public that knew no foreign cultures, ancient or modern, and partly because of the obliquity and nondiscursive form of the new poetry.

Longfellow, for instance, had been careful to explain his sources and allusions and to present his foreign material to his audience in an accommodated form. But *The Waste Land* and Pound's *Cantos* scattered bits of the literary and historical past over the page and expected the reader to perform as archaeologist, piecing together the fragments of a ruined culture. Even in *Paterson* and *The Bridge,* development was neither linear nor logical. These works, American in theme, were nonetheless radically modernist in form. *Paterson* mixed prose with poetry, history with lyricism, personal letters with dramatic vignettes; *The Bridge* mixed myth with history, narrative with rhapsody, stanzaic forms with free verse. Moore's patchwork of quotations, united by a quirky intellectual associationism, was no easier for the common reader to appreciate. The public embraced Frost and Cummings because they seemed accessible, brief, and explicit. Yet the public simplified both poets, seeking the sage more than the skeptic in Frost and preferring the sentimental to the satiric Cummings, reducing the one to a benign pastoral poet and the other to a poet of easy eroticism.

Yet the modernist poets, whatever their early estranged relation with the immediate public, were not indifferent to the common life of their generation. Like everyone else of the period, they were affected by World War I and the Depression and reacted variously to these events. Because Eliot and Pound saw the war from the European side, they felt a shock similar to that experienced by European poets, and the total work of each can be seen as a long meditation on the dissolution of the cultural past. Both used anthropological and archaeological methods to explore the myths that have sustained the West. Pound's reaction to

"What Is the Poet's Function?"

Certainly it is not to lead people out of the confusion in which they find themselves. Nor is it, I think, to comfort them while they follow their leaders to and fro. I think that his function is to make his imagination theirs and that he fulfills himself only as he sees his imagination become the light in the minds of others. His role, in short, is to help people live their lives.

> Wallace Stevens, from *The Necessary Angel* (1951)

Ethics are no more a part of poetry than they are of painting.

The aesthetic order includes all other orders but is not limited to them.

Poetry is a purging of the world's poverty and change and evil and death. It is a present perfecting, a satisfaction in the irremediable poverty of life.

We never arrive intellectually. But emotionally we arrive constantly (as in poetry, happiness, high mountains, vistas).

> Wallace Stevens, from *Adagia*

World War I was to attack capitalism itself and to urge a return to an economic system that did not permit "usury," the making of money by lending money. Williams, Crane, and Hughes, on the other hand, dealt more immediately with domestic events. Williams wrote about the 1920 trial of Sacco and Vanzetti (two Italian anarchist immigrants who were executed, perhaps wrongly, for murder), but he also treated the urban poverty and squalor that he saw among his patients. Crane wrote about the gains and losses of a technological society, criticizing the quantification of life but admiring the mastery of technological power; Hughes commemorated the wrongful trial, in 1931, of the Scottsboro "boys," nine blacks accused of the rape of two white women. The skepticism about the American dream generated by the Depression reached even such a politically inactive poet as Stevens. He was stung by the criticism (voiced in the Marxist journal *The Masses* by the critic Stanley Burnshaw) that his poetry averted its gaze from those suffering in the Depression. As a result, Stevens embarked on *Owl's Clover,* a long poem treating the social function of art and raising questions of the permanence and relevance of European art to the future.

All of the modernist poets, by their interest in the social fabric and its intellectual base, enlarged the range of topics considered appropriate to poetry. In the Pre-Raphaelite and Georgian poets of turn-of-the-century England, poetry had become almost purely "lyric," attenuated, inward-looking. Eliot made the revolutionary move of including, in *The Waste Land,* a sordid lower-class pub discussion of abortion and also a meaningless copulation between a bored typist and her "young man carbuncular." In another surprising move, Frost retold, in an American locale and with American characters, what the English poet Thomas Gray had called "the short and simple annals of the poor," including those who were backward, criminal, or mad. Pound, although he never abandoned entirely his Pre-Raphaelite lyric beginnings, thrust up against lyric passages inconsequential and trivial details of ordinary experience. Williams sketched the urban underclass, while Crane brought into his poetry all sorts of diverse social realities—Charlie Chaplin, advertising, Indian dances, black oppression, urban suicide. Cummings introduced comic obscenity and political satire; Hughes and Toomer began to make visible in poetry the life of blacks, northern and southern. And Wallace Stevens, though he was rarely a poet of historical events, introduced into modern poetry topics of philosophical and cognitive subtlety.

A New American Literary Language

But modernist poetry did not stake its claim chiefly by being innovative in thematic ways. Rather, like all interesting poetry, it distinguished itself, in W. H. Auden's words, by "new styles of architecture, a change of heart." The new style manifested itself in many ways. Some poetry could be distinctively American in language, as in Frost's "sentence sounds" and Hughes's black vernacular, or it could rewrite in American idiom (as in Frost and Robinson) traditional genres like the Wordsworthian pastoral narrative. Frost learned from Longfellow and Whittier and Bryant that rural New England was worthy poetic territory, but he learned even more, stylistically, from the Latin poets, especially Horace and Lucretius. His domestication, in American poetry, of the language of Roman stoicism is a brilliant native achievement. Prosody too is a distinguishing feature of modernist poetry: Both Eliot and Pound, but in different ways, brought free verse into prominence. Eliot's extreme musicality, visible throughout all his work, culminated in his calling his last poems "quartets" after the example of Beethoven; Pound, on the other hand, amassed Imagist phrases into a fragmentary line that broke off after each breath.

Modernist poetry is distinguished by structure, too, from the traditional poetry of earlier centuries; it is a poetry of fragments. Many of the modernist poets wrote long poems, but they constructed them on a principle different from the apparent unity that governs the sustained epics of Milton and Wordsworth. *The Waste Land,* the *Cantos, Paterson,* and *The Bridge* are all discontinuous epics, coming at their topics from a variety of perspectives. They borrow from art the metonymic technique of collage, in which one thing after another is glued onto a surface, and they borrow from film the technique of montage, in which one frame is contrasted with the next. They also change disconcertingly from "high" to "low" language instead of keeping a constant level of diction. The *ars poetica* of Wallace Stevens, a long poem called *Notes Toward a Supreme Fiction,* is similarly unpredictable in diction and form; it is sometimes serious, sometimes farcical, sometimes philosophical, sometimes anecdotal.

"A Machine Made of Words"

A poem is a small (or large) machine made of words. When I say there's nothing sentimental about a poem I mean that there can be no part, as in any other machine, that is redundant.

Prose may carry a load of ill-defined matter like a ship. But poetry is the machine which drives it, pruned to a perfect economy. As in all machines its movement is intrinsic, undulant, a physical more than a literary character. In a poem this movement is distinguished in each case by the character of the speech from which it arises. . . .

There is no poetry of distinction without formal invention, for it is in the intimate form that works of art achieve their exact meaning, in which they most resemble the machine, to give language its highest dignity, its illumination in the environment to which it is native.

William Carlos Williams (1944)

All poetry is experimental poetry.

Wallace Stevens, from *Adagia*

By the end of the modernist period, there was no longer a single American literary language—elevated, discursive, logical, genteel, expository. Instead, literary language had been shattered into a thousand bright reflecting parts, and the literary artists turned the kaleidoscope of poetry to make successive new patterns of the shining fragments. Not only language, but topics and conventions had been reworked. All the poetic genres—elegy, epic, love poetry, the sonnet— had been given new American embodiments. The Muse, as Whitman had predicted in "Song of the Exposition," had come as an "illustrious émigré" to these shores.

The view of America that we can gather from modernist testimony is full of contradictory elements. Except for Frost and Crane, the modernist poets are sharply critical of their country, either explicitly or implicitly—and even Frost and Crane see much that they deplore, such as the deprivation and misery present among both the rural and the urban poor. Pound, in a fervor driven by mounting eccentricity rising to madness, attempted to persuade America away from its entanglements with munition makers and back to what he believed to be its political first principles. Eliot satirized Boston provinciality, and Cummings mocked "the Cambridge ladies that live in furnished souls." Hughes uttered bitter indictments of the oppressive racism of the American majority. Stevens wondered how a country with more wilderness than settled land, and only a brief history of cultural production, could ever generate a native aesthetic.

"I Am Concerned with the Future of America"

I am concerned with the Future of America, but not because I think that America has any so-called par value as a state or as a group of people. . . . It is only because I feel persuaded that here are destined to be discovered certain as yet undefined spiritual quantities, perhaps a new hierarchy of faith not to be developed so completely elsewhere. And in this process I like to feel myself as a potential factor; certainly I must speak in its terms and what discoveries I may make are situated in its experience.

Hart Crane, "General Aims and Theories" (1937)

And yet, for all this criticism, a certain piety toward America distills itself from this poetry. Eliot displays piety toward Gloucester and the New England past; Frost takes pride in the stubbornness of the New England conscience; Crane makes a radiant claim for a single American tradition reaching from Indian dances to the suspension bridge; Williams expresses a humorous and tolerant love of life in a small American city; Moore asserts that superiority, which "has never been confined to one locality," can exist in America as well as in the older cultures of Europe or China; Cummings finds ebullient amusement in watching the American character, appealing in spite of its foolishness; and Hughes makes appreciative notations of the resilience of his Harlem neighbors even in hard times. It is the ambivalence of American poetry about American social reality that renders it believable.

If we look to the philosophical base of modernity, we can see that the modernist poets—except for the later Eliot—create either a world without a God or a world in which a corrosive skepticism attaches itself to belief. Their secular sense of the world revises the subject matter, attitude, and style of poetry. Wallace Stevens wrote:

To see the gods dispelled in mid-air and dissolve like clouds is one of the great human experiences. . . . It was their annihilation, not ours, and yet it left us feeling that in a measure, we, too, had been annihilated.

In varying degrees, this is the story of one whole generation of poets. They look to an Emersonian natural transcendence but find that it fails to sustain them. They can settle on no doctrinal or communal form of belief. Each of them— again, the later Eliot excepted—constructs a world of which the individual is, necessarily, the center and in which human mortality defines a final horizon of expectation. Even when these poets are believers—as Moore was—the aesthetic of the poetry is founded on social, not supernatural, meaning.

"The Figure a Poem Makes"

The figure a poem makes. It begins in delight and ends in wisdom. The figure is the same as for love. No one can really hold that the ecstasy should be static and stand still in one place. It begins in delight, it inclines to the impulse, it assumes direction with the first line laid down, it runs a course of lucky events, and ends in a clarification of life—not necessarily a great clarification, such as sects and cults are founded on, but in a momentary stay against confusion. It has denouement. It has an outcome that though unforeseen was predestined from the first image of the original mood—and indeed from the very mood. It is but a trick poem and no poem at all if the best of it was thought of first and saved for the last. It finds its own name as it goes and discovers the best waiting for it in some final phrase at once wise and sad—the happy-sad blend of the drinking song.

Robert Frost (1939)

Faced with the absence of a prescriptive religious or social order, many of these poets eventually find an exhilarating sense of personal freedom. An exploration of this freedom, coupled with a parallel exploration of linguistic possibility, becomes for these poets the chief avenue to creative work. They become historians of modernist culture, examining the possible representations—both individual and communal—of our century. As they cleanse language and culture of old and worn-out meanings and introduce to poetry what is American in thought, sensibility, perception, observation, and diction, they become exemplary of the modern endeavors of consciousness itself.

Further Reading:

S. Brown, *Negro Poetry and Drama,* 1937.

H. Gregory and M. Zaturenska, *A History of American Poetry, 1900–1940,* 1946.

L. Bogan, *Achievement in American Poetry 1900–1950,* 1951.

R. H. Pearce, *The Continuity of American Poetry,* 1961.

M. Cowley, *After the Genteel Tradition: American Writers 1910–1930,* rev. ed. 1964.

J. H. Miller, *Poets of Reality,* 1965.

R. Bridgman, *The Colloquial Style in America,* 1966.

E. Margolies, *Native Sons: A Critical Study of Twentieth-Century Negro Authors,* 1968.

H. H. Waggoner, *American Poets: From the Puritans to the Present Day,* 1968.

J. Mazzaro, *Modern American Poetry,* 1970.

N. I. Huggins, *Harlem Renaissance,* 1971.

H. Kenner, *The Pound Era,* 1971.

A. Gelpi, *The Tenth Muse: The Psyche of the American Poet,* 1975.

D. Perkins, *History of Modern Poetry,* 1976.

E. S. Watts, *The Poetry of American Women from 1632 to 1945,* 1977.

M. L. Rosenthal, *Sailing into the Unknown: Yeats, Pound, and Eliot,* 1978.

M. Borroff, *Language and the Poet: Verbal Artistry in Frost, Stevens, and Moore,* 1979.

H. Vendler, *Part of Nature, Part of Us: Modern American Poets,* 1980.

M. Perloff, *The Poetics of Indeterminacy: Rimbaud to Cage,* 1981.

D. E. Stanford, *Revolution and Convention in Modern Poetry,* 1983.

Robert Frost
1875–1963

Robert Frost is the best known of our modern American poets: His poems find their way into high school textbooks and into popular memory far more quickly than do the poems of his contemporaries. In part, Frost's popularity may be due to the apparent simplicity of his subject matter, but it is surely more profoundly due to his uncanny feeling for what he called "sentence sounds," the sounds and syntactic patterns into which the American language naturally falls. Frost's lines are remembered without effort: "The land was ours before we were the land's"; "But I have promises to keep"; "Nothing gold can stay"; "Earth's the right place for love"; "Good fences make good neighbors." Frost's immense talent as a reader of his own work made him something of a national institution; the gravel-voiced old man with a shock of white hair who was seen on television reading "The Gift Outright" at John F. Kennedy's inauguration in 1961 was already a figure known to most viewers. But they also knew his work; he was probably the one living poet whose poetry had touched them in school.

Frost's gift for an intimate lyricism was learned in part from Whitman; "You come too" (from "The Pasture") was an invitation that Whitman had often extended to his readers. Whitman's patriotism, too, finds a kindred echo in Frost's faith in the continuity of American principle, evident in a poem like "Immigrants," where every immigrant ship is said to have the *Mayflower* as its convoy. And Emerson, the ancestor of both Whitman and Frost, stands behind Frost's resolute transcendental confidence that we can stay—anchor—our minds on something like a star.

And yet these American ancestors do not fully account for Frost. Since Lionel Trilling first emphasized the darker side of Frost's imagination, critics have increasingly seen how many-sided Frost is. Biographers have drawn links between the events of Frost's own life—a Gothic chronicle of disasters—and the poetry. Frost's father, a transplanted easterner, died in San Francisco when Frost was eleven. (Frost's mother returned to New Hampshire, and Frost took the region for his own.) But it was not only the early death of his father that convinced Frost of the evil in existence. His own first child died in infancy; his only son committed suicide; one daughter died after childbirth, and another was mentally ill; his embittered wife refused on her deathbed to admit him to her room. The "rage" that Frost saw in the natural order ("Once by the Pacific") had for him its counterpart in the social order, where any "flower" could be subverted; the poem "The Subverted Flower" suggests a fundamental incompatibility between male sexual desire and female fear and disgust. In many of his grimmer poems (like "Design") Frost comes close to Thomas Hardy in suspecting that the universe may be governed by a malevolent God or, worse, not governed at all— by anyone.

Like many American writers, Frost had to expatriate himself to find his first success. Before he went to England in 1912 at the age of thirty-eight, he had been writing poetry for a long time. He had been class poet at his graduation in

1892 from high school in Lawrence, Massachusetts, where his future wife, Elinor White, was co-valedictorian with him. Frost went on to Dartmouth but dropped out after only one term. He continued to write while working at odd jobs— bobbin boy at a cotton mill, cobbler, schoolteacher, journalist. In 1897 he came to Harvard for two years as a special student, where he carried on the study of Latin that he had begun in high school. At Harvard he attended the philosophy lectures of George Santayana and read William James; their skepticism and pragmatism influenced the philosophical temper of his poetry. In 1899 his grandfather bought a farm for him in Derry, New Hampshire; but though Frost lived there and worked the farm for ten years, he was no nearer to publishing a book. After three more years of teaching at Pinkerton Academy in Derry, Frost left for England, where he published his first volume, *A Boy's Will* (1913). The title comes from Longfellow: "A boy's will is the wind's will, / And the thoughts of youth are long, long thoughts." In choosing this title, Frost made explicit his own derivation from and competition with Longfellow, New England's regional poet, and in fact Longfellow's "Schooner Hesperus" and "Hiawatha" have now been displaced in our literary history by Frost's regional poetry of New Hampshire.

In England, Frost met Ezra Pound, who helped publish Frost's second book, *North of Boston* (1914), a volume containing several of Frost's most stunning poems, including "Mending Wall," "Home Burial," and "After Apple-Picking." His reputation made, Frost returned to the United States to take a teaching position at Amherst College in 1917, through he taught there only intermittently. His many other teaching stints and his poetry readings, together with his royalties, supported Frost for the rest of his life. He was far more popular, and more successful financially, than the majority of his contemporaries.

Frost's poems tend to fall, formally speaking, into two groups: the long blank-verse poems like "Home Burial," often embodying some form of New England rural suffering, and the short, exquisite, rhymed lyrics, including philosophical sonnets like "Design." The narratives, which reopen a vein already worked by Edwin Arlington Robinson, represent the strains of life lived under pinched, emotionally thwarting conditions. They are a powerful corrective to the European pastoral tradition that represents nature as bountiful and gracious and man's life in nature as healing and joyful. They are also a corrective to the optimistic Emersonian view of nature as an authentic teacher. After reading the harsh accusations in "Home Burial," no reader can continue to think nature or domesticity merciful. The troglodytic farmer in "Mending Wall" is more a savage than a noble savage.

Frost's songlike lyrics ("Reluctance" or "Stopping by Woods on a Snowy Evening") stem directly from the most musical of English poems (Shakespeare's songs, Keats's odes, Shelley's choruses); his more philosophical lyrics are given their sternness by Horace and Lucretius. Frost's long reading in the Latin poets is visible not merely in his use of hendecasyllabics (eleven-syllable lines) in "For Once, Then, Something," but more powerfully in his pre-Christian view of nature. In repudiating the Christian tradition of a sacramental nature in favor of a nature enigmatic ("The Most of It"), elusive ("For Once, Then, Something"), or unreadable ("Time Out"), Frost adds to his nature poetry a metaphysical element of philosophic commentary. But his deftness of touch ("If design govern in a thing so small") retains his poetry within a colloquial tradition, just as his reliance on rhyme (he objected to free verse, saying it was like playing tennis without a net) retains his poetry within the tradition of the European lyric.

Frost represents a powerful antithesis to the modernist poetic represented by Pound and Eliot. As they face Europe, he faces America; as they assume and display learning, he is only obliquely allusive; as they write free verse, he writes in meter; as they lament a fragmented culture, he records a culture that can still muster a living, if forgotten, tradition. No one has better incorporated American speed into verse; Frost was delighted when he wrote, as a final line to "The Pauper Witch of Grafton," "I might have, but it doesn't seem as if"—a line that, in its vernacular lilt, could never have closed a British poem. In his grimly comic, sometimes even mischievous poetry, Frost preserved a vein of American humor that we are more likely to associate with prose like Twain's. And in his essays on poetry—aphoristic, pithy, and profound—Frost is one of the best theorists of a skeptical, questioning modern poetry that settles for no easy answers.

Further Reading:
L. R. Thompson, *Fire and Ice: The Art and Thought of Robert Frost*, 1942.
S. Cox, *A Swinger of Birches*, 1957.
R. L. Cook, *The Dimensions of Robert Frost*, 1959.
J. F. Lynan, *The Pastoral Art of Robert Frost*, 1960.
R. Squires, *The Major Themes of Robert Frost*, 1963.
R. Brower, *The Poetry of Robert Frost*, 1963.
P. L. Gerber, *Robert Frost*, 1966.
L. R. Thompson, *Robert Frost: The Early Years*, 1966.
L. R. Thompson, *Robert Frost: The Years of Triumph*, 1970.
F. Lentricchia, *Robert Frost: Modern Poetics and the Landscape of Self*, 1975.
L. R. Thompson and R. H. Winnick, *Robert Frost: The Later Years*, 1976.
F. Lentricchia and M. C. Lentricchia, *Robert Frost: A Bibliography*, 1976.
R. Poirier, *Robert Frost: The Work of Knowing*, 1977.
L. Wagner, *Robert Frost: The Critical Reception*, 1977.
J. C. Kemp, *Robert Frost and New England*, 1979.
L. R. Thompson, *Robert Frost*, 1981.
Critical Essays on Robert Frost, ed. P. L. Gerber, 1982.

Text:
The Poetry of Robert Frost, ed. E. C. Lathem, 1969 (punctuation corrected from *The Selected Poems of Robert Frost*, 1963).
See also *Selected Letters of Robert Frost*, ed. L. R. Thompson, 1964.
Selected Prose of Robert Frost, ed. H. Cox and E. C. Lathem, 1966.

Mowing

There was never a sound beside the wood but one,
And that was my long scythe whispering to the ground.
What was it it whispered? I knew not well myself;
Perhaps it was something about the heat of the sun,

Something, perhaps, about the lack of sound— 5
And that was why it whispered and did not speak.
It was no dream of the gift of idle hours,
Or easy gold at the hand of fay or elf:
Anything more than the truth would have seemed too weak
To the earnest love that laid the swale[1] in rows, 10
Not without feeble-pointed spikes of flowers
(Pale orchises), and scared a bright green snake.
The fact is the sweetest dream that labor knows.
My long scythe whispered and left the hay to make.
1913

October

O hushed October morning mild,
Thy leaves have ripened to the fall;
Tomorrow's wind, if it be wild,
Should waste them all.
The crows above the forest call; 5
Tomorrow they may form and go.
O hushed October morning mild,
Begin the hours of this day slow.
Make the day seem to us less brief.
Hearts not averse to being beguiled, 10
Beguile us in the way you know.
Release one leaf at break of day;
At noon release another leaf;
One from our trees, one far away.
Retard the sun with gentle mist; 15
Enchant the land with amethyst.
Slow, slow!
For the grapes' sake, if they were all,
Whose leaves already are burnt with frost,
Whose clustered fruit must else be lost— 20
For the grapes' sake along the wall.
1913

---

[1] Low-lying meadow.

Reluctance

Out through the fields and the woods
And over the walls I have wended;
I have climbed the hills of view
And looked at the world, and descended;
I have come by the highway home,   5
And lo, it is ended.

The leaves are all dead on the ground,
Save those that the oak is keeping
To ravel them one by one
And let them go scraping and creeping   10
Out over the crusted snow,
When others are sleeping.

And the dead leaves lie huddled and still,
No longer blown hither and thither;
The last lone aster is gone;   15
The flowers of the witch hazel wither;
The heart is still aching to seek,
But the feet question "Whither?"

Ah, when to the heart of man
Was it ever less than a treason   20
To go with the drift of things,
To yield with a grace to reason,
And bow and accept the end
Of a love or a season?
1913

Mending Wall

Something there is that doesn't love a wall,[1]
That sends the frozen-ground-swell under it
And spills the upper boulders in the sun,
And makes gaps even two can pass abreast.

[1] It is frost (a pun on Frost himself) that is
inimical to walls.

The work of hunters is another thing: 5
I have come after them and made repair
Where they have left not one stone on a stone,
But they would have the rabbit out of hiding,
To please the yelping dogs. The gaps I mean,
No one has seen them made or heard them made, 10
But at spring mending-time we find them there.
I let my neighbor know beyond the hill;
And on a day we meet to walk the line
And set the wall between us once again.
We keep the wall between us as we go. 15
To each the boulders that have fallen to each.
And some are loaves and some so nearly balls
We have to use a spell to make them balance:
"Stay where you are until our backs are turned!"
We wear our fingers rough with handling them. 20
Oh, just another kind of outdoor game,
One on a side. It comes to little more:
There where it is we do not need the wall:
He is all pine and I am apple orchard.
My apple trees will never get across 25
And eat the cones under his pines, I tell him.
He only says, "Good fences make good neighbors."
Spring is the mischief in me, and I wonder
If I could put a notion in his head:
"*Why* do they make good neighbors? Isn't it 30
Where there are cows? But here there are no cows.
Before I built a wall I'd ask to know
What I was walling in or walling out,
And to whom I was like to give offense.
Something there is that doesn't love a wall, 35
That wants it down." I could say "Elves" to him,
But it's not elves exactly, and I'd rather
He said it for himself. I see him there,
Bringing a stone grasped firmly by the top
In each hand, like an old-stone savage armed. 40
He moves in darkness as it seems to me,
Not of woods only and the shade of trees.
He will not go behind his father's saying,
And he likes having thought of it so well
He says again, "Good fences make good neighbors." 45

1914

Home Burial

He saw her from the bottom of the stairs
Before she saw him. She was starting down,
Looking back over her shoulder at some fear.
She took a doubtful step and then undid it
To raise herself and look again. He spoke   5
Advancing toward her: "What is it you see
From up there always—for I want to know."
She turned and sank upon her skirts at that,
And her face changed from terrified to dull.
He said to gain time: "What is it you see,"   10
Mounting until she cowered under him.
"I will find out now—you must tell me, dear."
She, in her place, refused him any help,
With the least stiffening of her neck and silence.
She let him look, sure that he wouldn't see,   15
Blind creature; and awhile he didn't see.
But at last he murmured, "Oh," and again, "Oh."

"What is it—what?" she said.

                       "Just that I see."

"You don't," she challenged. "Tell me what it is."

"The wonder is I didn't see at once.   20
I never noticed it from here before.
I must be wonted to it—that's the reason.
The little graveyard where my people are!
So small the window frames the whole of it.
Not so much larger than a bedroom, is it?   25
There are three stones of slate and one of marble,
Broad-shouldered little slabs there in the sunlight
On the sidehill. We haven't to mind *those*.
But I understand: it is not the stones,
But the child's mound——"

                   "Don't, don't, don't, don't," she cried.   30

She withdrew, shrinking from beneath his arm
That rested on the banister, and slid downstairs;
And turned on him with such a daunting look,
He said twice over before he knew himself:
"Can't a man speak of his own child he's lost?"   35

"Not you! Oh, where's my hat? Oh, I don't need it!
I must get out of here. I must get air.
I don't know rightly whether any man can."

"Amy! Don't go to someone else this time.
Listen to me. I won't come down the stairs."   40
He sat and fixed his chin between his fists.
"There's something I should like to ask you, dear."

"You don't know how to ask it."

                                   "Help me, then."

Her fingers moved the latch for all reply.

"My words are nearly always an offense.   45
I don't know how to speak of anything
So as to please you. But I might be taught
I should suppose. I can't say I see how.
A man must partly give up being a man
With womenfolk. We could have some arrangement   50
By which I'd bind myself to keep hands off
Anything special you're a-mind to name.
Though I don't like such things 'twixt those that love.
Two that don't love can't live together without them.
But two that do can't live together with them."   55
She moved the latch a little. "Don't—don't go.
Don't carry it to someone else this time.
Tell me about it if it's something human.
Let me into your grief. I'm not so much
Unlike other folks as your standing there   60
Apart would make me out. Give me my chance.
I do think, though, you overdo it a little.
What was it brought you up to think it the thing
To take your mother-loss of a first child
So inconsolably—in the face of love.   65
You'd think his memory might be satisfied——"

"There you go sneering now!"

                                   "I'm not, I'm not!
You make me angry. I'll come down to you.
God, what a woman! And it's come to this,
A man can't speak of his own child that's dead."   70

"You can't because you don't know how to speak.
If you had any feelings, you that dug

With your own hand—how could you?—his little grave;
I saw you from that very window there,
Making the gravel leap and leap in air,   75
Leap up, like that, like that, and land so lightly
And roll back down the mound beside the hole.
I thought, Who is that man? I didn't know you.
And I crept down the stairs and up the stairs
To look again, and still your spade kept lifting.   80
Then you came in. I heard your rumbling voice
Out in the kitchen, and I don't know why,
But I went near to see with my own eyes.
You could sit there with the stains on your shoes
Of the fresh earth from your own baby's grave   85
And talk about your everyday concerns.
You had stood the spade up against the wall
Outside there in the entry, for I saw it."

"I shall laugh the worst laugh I ever laughed.
I'm cursed. God, if I don't believe I'm cursed."   90

"I can repeat the very words you were saying.
'Three foggy mornings and one rainy day
Will rot the best birch fence a man can build.'
Think of it, talk like that at such a time!
What had how long it takes a birch to rot   95
To do with what was in the darkened parlor.
You *couldn't* care! The nearest friends can go
With anyone to death, comes so far short
They might as well not try to go at all.
No, from the time when one is sick to death,   100
One is alone, and he dies more alone.
Friends make pretense of following to the grave,
But before one is in it, their minds are turned
And making the best of their way back to life
And living people, and things they understand.   105
But the world's evil. I won't have grief so
If I can change it. Oh, I won't, I won't!"

"There, you have said it all and you feel better.
You won't go now. You're crying. Close the door.
The heart's gone out of it: why keep it up.   110
Amy! There's someone coming down the road!"

"*You*—oh, you think the talk is all. I must go—
Somewhere out of this house. How can I make you——"

"If—you—do!" She was opening the door wider.
"Where do you mean to go? First tell me that.
I'll follow and bring you back by force. I *will!*—"
1914

After Apple-Picking

My long two-pointed ladder's sticking through a
    tree
Toward heaven still,
And there's a barrel that I didn't fill
Beside it, and there may be two or three
Apples I didn't pick upon some bough.   5
But I am done with apple-picking now.
Essence of winter sleep is on the night,
The scent of apples: I am drowsing off.
I cannot rub the strangeness from my sight
I got from looking through a pane of glass   10
I skimmed this morning from the drinking trough
And held against the world of hoary grass.
It melted, and I let it fall and break.
But I was well
Upon my way to sleep before it fell,   15
And I could tell
What form my dreaming was about to take.
Magnified apples appear and disappear,
Stem end and blossom end,
And every fleck of russet showing clear.   20
My instep arch not only keeps the ache,
It keeps the pressure of a ladder-round.
I feel the ladder sway as the boughs bend.
And I keep hearing from the cellar bin
The rumbling sound   25
Of load on load of apples coming in.
For I have had too much
Of apple-picking: I am overtired
Of the great harvest I myself desired.
There were ten thousand thousand fruit to touch,   30
Cherish in hand, lift down, and not let fall.
For all
That struck the earth,
No matter if not bruised or spiked with stubble,

Went surely to the cider-apple heap   35
As of no worth.
One can see what will trouble
This sleep of mine, whatever sleep it is.
Were he not gone,
The woodchuck could say whether it's like his   40
Long sleep, as I describe its coming on,
Or just some human sleep.

1914

The Road Not Taken

Two roads diverged in a yellow wood,
And sorry I could not travel both
And be one traveler, long I stood
And looked down one as far as I could
To where it bent in the undergrowth;   5

Then took the other, as just as fair,
And having perhaps the better claim,
Because it was grassy and wanted wear;
Though as for that the passing there
Had worn them really about the same,   10

And both that morning equally lay
In leaves no step had trodden black.
Oh, I kept the first for another day!
Yet knowing how way leads on to way,
I doubted if I should ever come back.   15

I shall be telling this with a sigh
Somewhere ages and ages hence:
Two roads diverged in a wood, and I—
I took the one less traveled by,
And that has made all the difference.   20

1916

The Oven Bird

There is a singer everyone has heard,
Loud, a mid-summer and a mid-wood bird,
Who makes the solid tree trunks sound again.
He says that leaves are old and that for flowers
Mid-summer is to spring as one to ten.   5
He says the early petal-fall is past
When pear and cherry bloom went down in
   showers
On sunny days a moment overcast;
And comes that other fall we name the fall.[1]
He says the highway dust is over all.   10
The bird would cease and be as other birds
But that he knows in singing not to sing.
The question that he frames in all but words
Is what to make of a diminished thing.
1916

Birches

When I see birches bend to left and right
Across the lines of straighter darker trees,
I like to think some boy's been swinging them.
But swinging doesn't bend them down to stay
As ice storms do. Often you must have seen them   5
Loaded with ice a sunny winter morning
After a rain. They click upon themselves
As the breeze rises, and turn many-colored
As the stir cracks and crazes their enamel.
Soon the sun's warmth makes them shed crystal shells   10
Shattering and avalanching on the snow crust—
Such heaps of broken glass to sweep away
You'd think the inner dome of heaven had fallen.
They are dragged to the withered bracken[1] by the load,
And they seem not to break; though once they are bowed   15
So low for long, they never right themselves:

[1] The English call the season "autumn."   [1] Fern.

You may see their trunks arching in the woods
Years afterwards, trailing their leaves on the ground
Like girls on hands and knees that throw their hair
Before them over their heads to dry in the sun.   20
But I was going to say when Truth broke in
With all her matter of fact about the ice storm
I should prefer to have some boy bend them
As he went out and in to fetch the cows—
Some boy too far from town to learn baseball,   25
Whose only play was what he found himself,
Summer or winter, and could play alone.
One by one he subdued his father's trees
By riding them down over and over again
Until he took the stiffness out of them,   30
And not one but hung limp, not one was left
For him to conquer. He learned all there was
To learn about not launching out too soon
And so not carrying the tree away
Clear to the ground. He always kept his poise   35
To the top branches, climbing carefully
With the same pains you use to fill a cup
Up to the brim, and even above the brim.
Then he flung outward, feet first, with a swish,
Kicking his way down through the air to the ground.   40
So was I once myself a swinger of birches.
And so I dream of going back to be.
It's when I'm weary of considerations,
And life is too much like a pathless wood
Where your face burns and tickles with the cobwebs   45
Broken across it, and one eye is weeping
From a twig's having lashed across it open.
I'd like to get away from earth awhile
And then come back to it and begin over.
May no fate willfully misunderstand me   50
And half grant what I wish and snatch me away
Not to return. Earth's the right place for love:
I don't know where it's likely to go better.
I'd like to go by climbing a birch tree,
And climb black branches up a snow-white trunk   55
Toward heaven, till the tree could bear no more,
But dipped its top and set me down again.
That would be good both going and coming back.
One could do worse than be a swinger of birches.
1916

Fire and Ice

Some say the world will end in fire,
Some say in ice.
From what I've tasted of desire
I hold with those who favor fire.
But if it had to perish twice,   5
I think I know enough of hate
To say that for destruction ice
Is also great
And would suffice.

1923

Nothing Gold Can Stay

Nature's first green is gold,
Her hardest hue to hold.
Her early leaf's a flower;
But only so an hour.
Then leaf subsides to leaf.   5
So Eden sank to grief,
So dawn goes down to day.
Nothing gold can stay.

1923

Stopping by Woods on a Snowy Evening

Whose woods these are I think I know.
His house is in the village, though;
He will not see me stopping here
To watch his woods fill up with snow.

My little horse must think it queer   5
To stop without a farmhouse near
Between the woods and frozen lake
The darkest evening of the year.

He gives his harness bells a shake
To ask if there is some mistake.   10
The only other sound's the sweep
Of easy wind and downy flake.

The woods are lovely, dark and deep,
But I have promises to keep,
And miles to go before I sleep,   15
And miles to go before I sleep.
1923

For Once, Then, Something*

Others taunt me with having knelt at well-curbs
Always wrong to the light, so never seeing
Deeper down in the well than where the water
Gives me back in a shining surface picture
Me myself in the summer heaven godlike   5
Looking out of a wreath of fern and cloud puffs.
Once, when trying with chin against a well-curb,
I discerned, as I thought, beyond the picture,
Through the picture, a something white, uncertain,
Something more of the depths—and then I lost it.   10
Water came to rebuke the too clear water.
One drop fell from a fern, and lo, a ripple
Shook whatever it was lay there at bottom,
Blurred it, blotted it out. What was that whiteness?
Truth? A pebble of quartz? For once, then, something.[1] 15
1923

* The poem is written in hendecasyllabics, a Latin form of 11 syllables per line.
[1] Cf. Diogenes (412?–323 B.C.), Greek Cynic philosopher: "Truth lies at the bottom of a well."

To Earthward

Love at the lips was touch
As sweet as I could bear;
And once that seemed too much;
I lived on air

That crossed me from sweet things,   5
The flow of—was it musk
From hidden grapevine springs
Down hill at dusk?

I had the swirl and ache
From sprays of honeysuckle   10
That when they're gathered shake
Dew on the knuckle.

I craved strong sweets, but those
Seemed strong when I was young;
The petal of the rose   15
It was that stung.

Now no joy but lacks salt
That is not dashed with pain
And weariness and fault;
I crave the stain   20

Of tears, the aftermark
Of almost too much love,
The sweet of bitter bark
And burning clove.

When stiff and sore and scarred   25
I take away my hand
From leaning on it hard
In grass and sand,

The hurt is not enough:
I long for weight and strength   30
To feel the earth as rough
To all my length.

1923

The Need of Being Versed in Country Things

The house had gone to bring again
To the midnight sky a sunset glow.
Now the chimney was all of the house that stood,
Like a pistil after the petals go.

The barn opposed across the way,   5
That would have joined the house in flame
Had it been the will of the wind, was left
To bear forsaken the place's name.

No more it opened with all one end
For teams that came by the stony road   10
To drum on the floor with scurrying hoofs
And brush the mow with the summer load.

The birds that came to it through the air
At broken windows flew out and in,
Their murmur more like the sigh we sigh   15
From too much dwelling on what has been.

Yet for them the lilac renewed its leaf,
And the aged elm, though touched with fire;
And the dry pump flung up an awkward arm;
And the fence post carried a strand of wire.   20

For them there was really nothing sad.
But though they rejoiced in the nest they kept,
One had to be versed in country things
Not to believe the phoebes wept.

1923

Once by the Pacific

The shattered water made a misty din.
Great waves looked over others coming in,
And thought of doing something to the shore
That water never did to land before.
The clouds were low and hairy in the skies,   5
Like locks blown forward in the gleam of eyes.
You could not tell, and yet it looked as if
The shore was lucky in being backed by cliff,
The cliff in being backed by continent;
It looked as if a night of dark intent   10
Was coming, and not only a night, an age.
Someone had better be prepared for rage.
There would be more than ocean-water broken
Before God's last *Put out the Light* was spoken.[1]

1928

Immigrants

No ship of all that under sail or steam
Have gathered people to us more and more
But Pilgrim-manned the *Mayflower* in a dream
Has been her anxious convoy in to shore.

1928

Desert Places

Snow falling and night falling fast, oh, fast
In a field I looked into going past,
And the ground almost covered smooth in snow,
But a few weeds and stubble showing last.

---

[1] God's first words in Genesis are, "Let there be
Light."

The woods around it have it—it is theirs.   5
All animals are smothered in their lairs.
I am too absent-spirited to count;
The loneliness includes me unawares.

And lonely as it is, that loneliness
Will be more lonely ere it will be less—   10
A blanker whiteness of benighted[1] snow
With no expression, nothing to express.

They cannot scare me with their empty spaces
Between stars—on stars where no human race is.
I have it in me so much nearer home   15
To scare myself with my own desert places.
1936

Design[1]

I found a dimpled spider, fat and white,
On a white heal-all,[2] holding up a moth
Like a white piece of rigid satin cloth—
Assorted characters of death and blight
Mixed ready to begin the morning right,   5
Like the ingredients of a witches' broth—
A snow-drop spider, a flower like a froth,[3]
And dead wings carried like a paper kite.

What had that flower to do with being white,
The wayside blue and innocent heal-all?   10
What brought the kindred spider to that height,
Then steered the white moth thither in the night?
What but design of darkness to appall?—
If design govern in a thing so small.
1936

---

[1] Ignorant; overtaken by spiritual and physical darkness.
[1] The argument from design (order in nature) was often urged as a proof for the existence of God.
[2] A flower, normally blue.

[3] In the octave (first eight lines), Frost complicates his task by using the only four common words ending with the sound *ŏth;* he also continues the octave rhyme sound *īte* in the sestet (last six lines).

Provide, Provide

The witch that came (the withered hag)
To wash the steps with pail and rag
Was once the beauty Abishag,[1]

The picture pride of Hollywood.
Too many fall from great and good   5
For you to doubt the likelihood.

Die early and avoid the fate.
Or if predestined to die late,
Make up your mind to die in state.

Make the whole stock exchange your own!   10
If need be occupy a throne,
Where nobody can call *you* crone.

Some have relied on what they knew,
Others on being simply true.
What worked for them might work for you.   15

No memory of having starred
Atones for later disregard,
Or keeps the end from being hard.

Better to go down dignified
With boughten friendship at your side   20
Than none at all. Provide, provide!
1936

The Most of It

He thought he kept the universe alone;
For all the voice in answer he could wake
Was but the mocking echo of his own
From some tree-hidden cliff across the lake.

[1] Young girl brought in as a sexual partner for
King David in his old age (see 1 Kings 1:2–4).

Some morning from the boulder-broken beach   5
He would cry out on life, that what it wants
Is not its own love back in copy speech,
But counter-love, original response.
And nothing ever came of what he cried
Unless it was the embodiment that crashed   10
In the cliff's talus'[1] on the other side,
And then in the far-distant water splashed,
But after a time allowed for it to swim,
Instead of proving human when it neared
And someone else additional to him,   15
As a great buck it powerfully appeared,
Pushing the crumpled water up ahead,
And landed pouring like a waterfall,
And stumbled through the rocks with horny tread,
And forced the underbrush—and that was all.   20

1942

The Gift Outright

The land was ours before we were the land's.
She was our land more than a hundred years
Before we were her people. She was ours
In Massachusetts, in Virginia,
But we were England's, still colonials,   5
Possessing what we still were unpossessed by,
Possessed by what we now no more possessed.
Something we were withholding made us weak
Until we found out that it was ourselves
We were withholding from our land of living,   10
And forthwith found salvation in surrender.
Such as we were we gave ourselves outright
(The deed of gift was many deeds of war)
To the land vaguely realizing westward,
But still unstoried, artless, unenhanced,   15
Such as she was, such as she would become.

1942

---

[1] Slope.

Time Out

It took that pause to make him realize
The mountain he was climbing had the slant
As of a book held up before his eyes
(And was a text albeit done in plant).
Dwarf cornel, gold-thread, and maianthemum,   5
He followingly fingered as he read,
The flowers fading on the seed to come;
But the thing was the slope it gave his head:
The same for reading as it was for thought,
So different from the hard and level stare   10
Of enemies defied and battles fought.
It was the obstinately gentle air
That may be clamored at by cause and sect,
But it will have its moment to reflect.

1942

Carl Sandburg
1878–1967

With his fellow Chicago poet Edgar Lee Masters, Carl Sandburg was one of the
early rebels of the modern period, reacting against the genteel tradition in the
name of Walt Whitman and America. Writing in free verse and about such
unpoetic subjects as the vigorous, even violent poor of Chicago, the "Hog
Butcher for the World," he sought to be a poet of the people in the Whitman
tradition. Sandburg was strongly populist in his political sympathies; he celebrated
grass-roots American characters and circumstances, often in poems that drew
clearly on Whitman for their verse technique. "Chicago," for example, teems
with people and attempts to recreate, in a modern and stridently vitalist way, the
energy of Whitman's chants. His main concern as a poet was the vivid
presentation of unrefined reality, and poems like "Fog" resemble the work of the
Imagists in their brevity, their juxtaposition of images to catch objective reality,
and their clean, simple language. Sandburg characteristically wrote other kinds of
poems as well—most notably poems of social protest, such as "Graceland," and
emotional, reflective poems, such as "Cool Tombs" and "Grass."

Carl Sandburg was born in 1878 to a family of Swedish immigrants in Illinois,
where his father was employed in the railroad yards. Raised in poverty, Sandburg
was forced to quit school at the age of thirteen to earn money at a variety of
odd jobs—milkman, porter, dishwasher. After the Spanish-American war, in
which he volunteered for the army and was sent to Puerto Rico, he enrolled in

Lombard College, supporting himself while there by working for the local fire department; he left abruptly in 1902 without graduating. He again found work of various sorts, including a stint as salesman of stereoscopic photographs. He even spent some time riding the rails with hoboes and served a short jail term in Pittsburgh. His experiences helped reinforce his strong populist convictions, and in 1907 and 1908 he worked for the Social Democratic party as journalist and organizer. Meanwhile he was trying to settle down, and in 1908 he married the sister of the photographer Edward Steichen.

In 1914 Harriet Monroe published a group of his poems, entitled "Chicago Poems," in *Poetry;* two years later a book with the same title appeared. It marked the start of Sandburg's fame, which by the end of his life was considerable. *Cornhuskers* appeared in 1918, followed by *Smoke and Steel* (1920), *Slabs of the Sunburnt West* (1922), and *The People, Yes* (1936). His six-volume biography of Abraham Lincoln (1940) earned him the Pulitzer Prize for history. Other prose writings include children's stories (beginning with *Rootabaga Stories,* 1922), historical commentary (*Storm over the Land,* 1942, and *Home Front Memos,* 1943), and a novel (*Remembrance Rock,* 1950). The poet who toured the country, reading and singing folksongs while accompanying himself on guitar, interspersing his performances with homespun philosophizing, became a celebrated public figure. He was asked to be a candidate for the presidency in 1940, and his birthplace was made a museum that same year; his 75th birthday was declared Carl Sandburg Day by the governor of Illinois. Sandburg received the Presidential Medal of Freedom in 1964.

He was not admired, on the whole, by his fellow poets. Ezra Pound once suggested that the University of Pennsylvania set up a fellowship for creative ability; he had Sandburg in mind as a possible recipient, for he feared Sandburg would remain imperfect for lack of culture. William Carlos Williams also criticized Sandburg's artlessness, but Frost's observation, after their first meeting, was the most acid:

> We've been having a dose of Carl Sandburg. He's another person I find it hard to do justice to. He was possibly [three] hours in town and he spent one of those washing his white hair and toughening his expression for his public performance. His mandolin pleased some people, his poetry a very few, and his infantile talk none. His affectations have almost buried him out of sight. He is probably the most artificial and studied ruffian the world has had.

Often as artless in life as he appeared to be in his writing, Sandburg had walked away from that meeting feeling that a friendship had begun. "Met Frost," he wrote, "about the strongest, loneliest, friendliest personality among the poets today; I'm going to write him once a year; and feel the love of him every day."

In a tradition in which the poet as primitive occupies a central, if complicated, place, Sandburg might have become an important figure. But, from Whitman on, to be "one of the roughs," to be artless in American literature, has been a creation of highly self-conscious art. By those standards Sandburg was lacking. Where others sought to create the illusion of unsophisticated spontaneity, Sandburg *was* artistically unsophisticated; almost paradoxically, he therefore seemed, at least to an observer like Frost, affected. Behind Pound's and Williams's apparently casual Imagist poems lay an almost obsessive concern with craft and, in Pound's case in particular, considerable acquaintance with the literary past that he sought to make new. Behind Whitman's chants of America lay far more than the desire to present American figures in all their vitality. The Americans Whitman wrote of, including himself in his own complicated self-portrayal, were part of a comprehensive vision of divine, natural, social, and psychological reality, and Whitman's language ranged from the demotic to the sublime in his attempt to give flesh to this vision. Against that achievement, Sandburg's work as a whole seems notable primarily for its part in the modernist revolution in literature. It is best appreciated for the real power of some of the individual poems, where Sandburg achieved a memorable freshness and vigor of expression.

Further Reading:

B. Weirick, *From Whitman to Sandburg*, 1924.

K. Detzer, *Carl Sandburg*, 1941.

H. Durnell, *The America of Carl Sandburg*, 1945.

R. Crowder, *Carl Sandburg*, 1964.

J. Haas, *Carl Sandburg*, 1967.

N. Callahan, *Carl Sandburg, Lincoln of Our Literature*, 1969.

G. W. Allen, *Carl Sandburg*, 1972.

Text:

Complete Poems, 1950.

Chicago

> Hog Butcher for the World,
> Tool Maker, Stacker of Wheat,
> Player with Railroads and the Nation's Freight Handler;
> Stormy, husky, brawling,
> City of the Big Shoulders: 5

They tell me you are wicked and I believe them, for I have seen your painted
  women under the gas lamps luring the farm boys.
And they tell me you are crooked and I answer: Yes, it is true I have seen the
  gunman kill and go free to kill again.
And they tell me you are brutal and my reply is: On the faces of women and
  children I have seen the marks of wanton hunger.
And having answered so I turn once more to those who sneer at this my city,
  and I give them back the sneer and say to them:
Come and show me another city with lifted head singing so proud to be alive
  and coarse and strong and cunning.   10
Flinging magnetic curses amid the toil of piling job on job, here is a tall bold
  slugger set vivid against the little soft cities;
Fierce as a dog with tongue lapping for action, cunning as a savage pitted
  against the wilderness,

Bareheaded,
Shoveling,
Wrecking,   15
Planning,
Building, breaking, rebuilding,
Under the smoke, dust all over his mouth, laughing with white teeth,
Under the terrible burden of destiny laughing as a young man laughs,
Laughing even as an ignorant fighter laughs who has never lost a battle,   20
Bragging and laughing that under his wrist is the pulse, and under his ribs the
    heart of the people,
               Laughing!
Laughing the stormy, husky, brawling laughter of Youth, half-naked, sweating,
    proud to be Hog Butcher, Tool Maker, Stacker of Wheat, Player with
    Railroads and Freight Handler to the Nation.

1914

Graceland

Tomb of a millionaire,
A multi-millionaire, ladies and gentlemen,
Place of the dead where they spend every year
The usury of twenty-five thousand dollars
    For upkeep and flowers   5
To keep fresh the memory of the dead.
The merchant prince gone to dust
Commanded in his written will
Over the signed name of his last testament
Twenty-five thousand dollars be set aside   10
For roses, lilacs, hydrangeas, tulips,
For perfume and color, sweetness of remembrance
Around his last long home.

(A hundred cash girls want nickels to go to the movies tonight.
In the back stalls of a hundred saloons, women are at tables   15
Drinking with men or waiting for men jingling loose silver dollars in their
    pockets.
In a hundred furnished rooms is a girl who sells silk or dress goods or leather
    stuff for six dollars a week wages
And when she pulls on her stockings in the morning she is reckless about God
    and the newspapers and the police, the talk of her home town or the name
    people call her.)

1916

Fog

The fog comes
on little cat feet.

It sits looking
over harbor and city
on silent haunches
and then moves on.   5
1916

Portrait of a Motorcar

It's a lean car . . . a long-legged dog of a car . . . a gray-ghost eagle car.
The feet of it eat the dirt of a road . . . the wings of it eat the hills.
Danny the driver dreams of it when he sees women in red skirts and red sox in
    his sleep.
It is in Danny's life and runs in the blood of him . . . a lean gray-ghost car.
1918

Cool Tombs

When Abraham Lincoln was shoveled into the tombs, he forgot the copperheads[1]
    and the assassin . . . in the dust, in the cool tombs.

And Ulysses Grant lost all thought of con men and Wall Street, cash and
    collateral turned ashes . . . in the dust, in the cool tombs.

Pocahontas' body, lovely as a poplar, sweet as a red haw[2] in November or a
    pawpaw[3] in May, did she wonder? does she remember? . . . in the dust, in
    the cool tombs?

[1] Copperhead: species of poisonous snake, but here a derogatory epithet for Northerners who sided with the Confederacy during the Civil War.

[2] Hawthorn berry.

[3] Fruit of the pawpaw tree, much like papaya.

Take any streetful of people buying clothes and groceries, cheering a hero or
   throwing confetti and blowing tin horns . . . tell me if the lovers are losers
   . . . tell me if any get more than the lovers . . . in the dust . . . in the cool
   tombs.

1918

Grass

Pile the bodies high at Austerlitz¹ and Waterloo.
Shovel them under and let me work—
                    I am the grass; I cover all.

And pile them high at Gettysburg
And pile them high at Ypres and Verdun.   5
Shovel them under and let me work.
Two years, ten years, and passengers ask the conductor:
                    What place is this?
                    Where are we now?

                    I am the grass.   10
                    Let me work.

1918

Wallace Stevens
1879–1955

Wallace Stevens's extraordinary first book, *Harmonium* (1923), is one of those
books, like T. S. Eliot's *Prufrock and Other Observations* and Marianne Moore's
Observations, by which we have come to define American modernism. Each of
these collections struck a clear new note in formal terms; each was in some way
self-displaying. Stevens's book was not a success; even in 1931, when it was
reprinted in an expanded form, it had only a *succès d'estime.* It was full of odd
poems with odd names, like "Thirteen Ways of Looking at a Blackbird" and
"Metaphors of a Magnifico." These strange-looking poems did not at all resemble
the other poems in the volume, which were recognizably in a traditional vein,

---

¹ The places named in the poem were the scenes
of major battles during the Napoleonic Wars,
the Civil War, and World War I, respectively.

with reminiscences of Wordsworth, Keats, Browning, and Tennyson. Even the seemingly conventional poems, however, had strange titles like "Le Monocle de Mon Oncle" and "The Comedian as the Letter C." The book did contain one conventionally named poem in a conventional style—"Sunday Morning." But this poem, soon to become very famous, was unconventional in theme; it was a bold declaration of the death of God. In the poem a sensuous aestheticism and agnosticism became substitutes for religious observance.

At least one of those who read the second edition of *Harmonium* when it appeared in the depths of the Great Depression found it shocking that the poet was not addressing the social ills of the day. Stanley Burnshaw's criticism of *Harmonium* in *The New Masses* stung Stevens into his attempts, in *Owl's Clover* (1936) and *Parts of a World* (1942), to treat social issues, including the war in Ethiopia and World War II. But these poems achieved no real stylistic success, and Stevens remained, for the rest of his career, preeminently a poet of the inner life. Nonetheless, Stevens never lost his concern with the social function of poetry, that "postcard from a volcano" addressed to future generations.

Stevens's nature was both religious and romantic; yet the two beliefs he had wholeheartedly entered into, religion and romantic love, both turned out, in his eyes, to be delusory. By these striking evidences of the mind's capacity to delude itself he was led to meditate on the ways that the mind contructs objects and worlds responsive to desire, then sees them shatter and dissolve. The inadequacy of the world to our desire, coupled with our apparently incorrigible pursuit of belief and desire, gave Stevens the great paradox on which he was to brood all his life, the incommensurability of desire and its object. For him, the imagination was what desired; "reality" was what the imagination constructed as a response to desire. "Reality" therefore changes always, as desire is frustrated and a new fictive construct must be shaped yet once again. In this way, new political states are constructed after the collapse of old ones, new art forms are invented when the old become withered, and a new religion replaces the stale religion of the past. Stevens's skepticism about these successive reconstructions of reality comes from his taking the long historical view of the psyche's inner life.

At the same time, though Stevens held seriously to the absolute power of the imagination in the construction of the self and culture, he could treat his theme with gaiety, mockery, and brio. Many of the short poems in *Harmonium* are what we would now call "conceptual art"—the originality of the idea behind them, rather than the linguistic execution, gives them their poetic energy. "Anecdote of the Jar" is such a poem, in its witty reversal of Keats's "Ode on a Grecian Urn." The British poet may have an illustrated marble urn in the British Museum, but the American poet has only a bare gray stoneware jar in the Tennessee wilderness. And whereas the British poet can write in opulent stanzas derived from Shakespeare and the sonnet, the American poet cannot find any diction or stanza form that he is comfortable in. In this respect, Stevens's laconic wit is often turned against himself as the clumsy American trying to utter "heavenly labials in a world of gutturals." In the many volumes following *Harmonium*, Stevens's seriousness of subject and gaiety of treatment continue to create a style peculiar to him, in which he deepens his exploration of the inner life of desire.

During his life as a poet, Stevens carried on a parallel life as a lawyer and insurance executive. He was the son of a Reading, Pennsylvania, lawyer who sent all three of his sons to law school. After three years at Harvard, where he wrote poetry and was president of the literary magazine, Stevens left without taking a degree; his father would not pay for a final year, as only three years of college were required for admission at some law schools. Since the Harvard Law School required four years of college, Stevens could not be admitted there; instead, he entered New York Law School, but after graduation he was relatively unsuccessful in his first professional jobs. At this time in New York, Stevens associated with other young poets, especially his Harvard classmate Alfred Kreymborg, who edited a journal called *Others*. In the *Others* group Stevens met William Carlos Williams and Marianne Moore, a lifelong friend. But as Stevens's professional duties increased, he drifted away from literary society; his move to Hartford, Connecticut in 1916 removed him from the New York scene. He eventually became a very successful insurance lawyer; at his death he was a vice-president of the Hartford Accident and Indemnity Company.

From 1916 to his death in 1955, Stevens lived in Hartford, and although he made many business trips in America, he never went to Europe. His chief literary life, aside from poetry, took place through correspondence with friends and students of his poetry. His marriage to Elsie Kachel seems to have been unhappy. They had one child, born in 1924, named by Stevens, because her birth came near Christmas, Holly Bright.

By the end of his life, Stevens was recognized as a major poet. His *Collected Poems* (1955) won the National Book Award and a Pulitzer Prize. Although Stevens's daughter has published, in *The Palm at the End of the Mind* (1971), a group of his poems arranged in chronological order, the *Collected Poems* remains the way to know Stevens, to read the poems as he himself arranged them in successive volumes. To Stevens, his *Collected Poems*, when he saw them bound, seemed like the whole world in reduced form, like the terrestrial globe used in geography classes. The volume was "the planet on the table," and he, as poet, was like Shakespeare's airy spirit Ariel: "Ariel was glad he had written his poems."

In 1951 Stevens published a remarkable collection of essays, *The Necessary Angel*. Here, and in essays published after his death in *Opus Posthumous* (1957), he displays the outlines of his theory of poetry. Stevens saw poetry as an "accuracy with respect to the structure of reality"; it was formed by the pressure of the mind against the outside pressure of reality. Imagination was for him a "third planet," comparable in power to the sun and moon, allowing us to see the world in a personal way, different with each mood. Poetry is "the gaiety of language," "a holiday in reality"; but it is also a voice, speaking in "ghostlier demarcations, keener sounds," "of ourselves and of our origins." Stevens's most concise view of the poet's role in society appears in the poem "Academic Discourse at Havana," where he says of the poet:

As part of nature he is part of us.
His rarities are ours: may they be fit
And reconcile us to our selves in those
True reconcilings, dark, pacific words,
And the adroiter harmonies of their fall.

Stevens showed American poetry a new way of being American—not by regionalism (though he wrote memorable poems about Connecticut), not by patriotism, not through use of the common vernacular, but by an adaptation of English literature to the American language. In his long poems he invented a new pentameter, freer in its metric than the English model, returning to Whitman's largeness of motion. And in his skeptical, ironic, and whimsical humor he lightens into modern American speculativeness the seriousness of English discursive verse.

Further Reading:

F. Kermode, *Wallace Stevens*, 1961.
J. G. Benziger, *Images of Eternity*, 1962.
The Achievement of Wallace Stevens, ed.
A. Brown and R. Haller, 1962.
D. Fuchs, *The Comic Spirit of Wallace Stevens*, 1962.
G. Cambon, *The Inclusive Flame*, 1963.
J. J. Enck, *Wallace Stevens: Images and Judgments*, 1964.
H. Wells, *Introduction to Wallace Stevens*, 1964.
J. N. Riddell, *The Clairvoyant Eye*, 1965.
E. P. Nasser, *Wallace Stevens: An Anatomy of Figuration*, 1965.
F. Doggett, *Stevens' Poetry of Thought*, 1966.
H. J. Stern, *Wallace Stevens: Art of Uncertainty*, 1966.
R. Buttel, *Wallace Stevens: The Making of "Harmonium,"* 1967.
R. Sukenick, *Wallace Stevens: Musing the Obscure*, 1967.
J. Baird, *The Dome and the Rock: Structure in the Poetry of Wallace Stevens*, 1968.
W. Burney, *Wallace Stevens*, 1968.

H. Vendler, *On Extended Wings: Wallace Stevens' Longer Poems*, 1969.
R. Blessing, *Wallace Stevens's "Whole Harmonium,"* 1970.
S. F. Morse, *Wallace Stevens: Poetry as Life*, 1970.
M. Benamou, *Wallace Stevens and the Symbolist Imagination*, 1972.
W. A. Litz, *Introspective Voyage: The Poetic Development of Wallace Stevens*, 1972.
L. Beckett, *Wallace Stevens*, 1977.
H. Bloom, *Wallace Stevens: The Poems of Our Climate*, 1977.
H. Stevens, *Souvenirs and Prophecies: The Young Wallace Stevens*, 1977.
S. B. Weston, *Wallace Stevens: An Introduction*, 1977.
F. Doggett, *Wallace Stevens: The Making of a Poem*, 1980.
Wallace Stevens: A Celebration, ed. F. Doggett and R. Buttel, 1980.
H. Vendler, *Wallace Stevens: Words Chosen out of Desire*, 1985.

Text:
The Palm at the End of the Mind, ed.
H. Stevens, 1971.

Sunday Morning

I

Complacencies of the peignoir, and late
Coffee and oranges in a sunny chair,[1]
And the green freedom of a cockatoo
Upon a rug mingle to dissipate
The holy hush of ancient sacrifice.[2]   5
She dreams a little, and she feels the dark
Encroachment of that old catastrophe,
As a calm darkens among water-lights.
The pungent oranges and bright, green wings
Seem things in some procession of the dead,   10
Winding across wide water, without sound.
The day is like wide water, without sound,
Stilled for the passing of her dreaming feet
Over the seas, to silent Palestine,
Dominion of the blood and sepulchre.[3]   15

II

Why should she give her bounty to the dead?
What is divinity if it can come
Only in silent shadows and in dreams?
Shall she not find in comforts of the sun,
In pungent fruit and bright, green wings, or else   20
In any balm or beauty of the earth,
Things to be cherished like the thought of heaven?
Divinity must live within herself:
Passions of rain, or moods in falling snow;
Grievings in loneliness, or unsubdued   25
Elations when the forest blooms; gusty
Emotions on wet roads on autumn nights;
All pleasures and all pains, remembering
The bough of summer and the winter branch.
These are the measures destined for her soul.   30

III

Jove[4] in the clouds had his inhuman birth.
No mother suckled him, no sweet land gave

---

[1] The agnostic lady does not attend a Sunday
church service; instead, she remains in her
peignoir and breakfasts.

[2] The death of Jesus.
[3] The passion and entombment of Jesus.
[4] In mythology, the king of the gods.

Large-mannered motions to his mythy mind.
He moved among us, as a muttering king,
Magnificent, would move among his hinds,   35
Until our blood, commingling, virginal,[5]
With heaven, brought such requital to desire
The very hinds[6] discerned it, in a star.
Shall our blood fail? Or shall it come to be
The blood of paradise? And shall the earth   40
Seem all of paradise that we shall know?
The sky will be much friendlier then than now,
A part of labor and a part of pain,
And next in glory to enduring love,
Not this dividing and indifferent blue.   45

IV

She says, "I am content when wakened birds,
Before they fly, test the reality
Of misty fields, by their sweet questionings;
But when the birds are gone, and their warm fields
Return no more, where, then, is paradise?"   50
There is not any haunt of prophecy,
Nor any old chimera[7] of the grave,
Neither the golden underground,[8] nor isle
Melodious,[9] where spirits gat them home,
Nor visionary south, nor cloudy palm[10]   55
Remote on heaven's hill, that has endured
As April's green endures; or will endure
Like her remembrance of awakened birds,
Or her desire for June and evening, tipped
By the consummation of the swallow's wings.   60

V

She says, "But in contentment I still feel
The need of some imperishable bliss."
Death is the mother of beauty; hence from her,
Alone, shall come fulfilment to our dreams
And our desires. Although she strews the leaves   65
Of sure obliteration on our paths,
The path sick sorrow took, the many paths

---

[5] Like the Virgin Mary, impregnated by the Holy Spirit.
[6] The shepherds who saw the Christmas star.
[7] Ghost, illusion.
[8] The Elysian fields, in mythology the heaven of heroes.
[9] Avalon, where King Arthur was taken after death.
[10] The palm was the reward given to Christian martyrs in heaven.

Where triumph rang its brassy phrase, or love
Whispered a little out of tenderness,
She makes the willow shiver in the sun   70
For maidens who were wont to sit and gaze
Upon the grass, relinquished to their feet.
She causes boys to pile new plums and pears
On disregarded plate." The maidens taste
And stray impassioned in the littering leaves.   75

VI

Is there no change of death in paradise?
Does ripe fruit never fall? Or do the boughs
Hang always heavy in that perfect sky,
Unchanging, yet so like our perishing earth,
With rivers like our own that seek for seas   80
They never find, the same receding shores
That never touch with inarticulate pang?
Why set the pear upon those river-banks
Or spice the shores with odors of the plum?
Alas, that they should wear our colors there,   85
The silken weavings of our afternoons,
And pick the strings of our insipid lutes!
Death is the mother of beauty, mystical,
Within whose burning bosom we devise
Our earthly mothers waiting, sleeplessly.   90

VII

Supple and turbulent, a ring of men
Shall chant in orgy on a summer morn
Their boisterous devotion to the sun,
Not as a god, but as a god might be,
Naked among them, like a savage source.   95
Their chant shall be a chant of paradise,
Out of their blood, returning to the sky;
And in their chant shall enter, voice by voice,
The windy lake wherein their lord delights,
The trees, like serafin," and echoing hills,   100
That choir among themselves long afterward.
They shall know well the heavenly fellowship
Of men that perish and of summer morn.
And whence they came and whither they shall go
The dew upon their feet shall manifest.   105

" Silver dishes.   " Seraphim; angels.

VIII

She hears, upon that water without sound,
A voice that cries, "The tomb in Palestine
Is not the porch of spirits lingering.[13]
It is the grave of Jesus, where he lay."
We live in an old chaos of the sun,   11
Or old dependency of day and night,
Or island solitude, unsponsored, free,
Of that wide water, inescapable.
Deer walk upon our mountains, and the quail
Whistle about us their spontaneous cries;   11
Sweet berries ripen in the wilderness;
And, in the isolation of the sky,
At evening, casual flocks of pigeons make
Ambiguous undulations as they sink,
Downward to darkness, on extended wings.   12

1923

Thirteen Ways of Looking at a Blackbird

I

Among twenty snowy mountains,
The only moving thing
Was the eye of the blackbird.

II

I was of three minds,
Like a tree   5
In which there are three blackbirds.

III

The blackbird whirled in the autumn winds.
It was a small part of the pantomime.

---

[13] When Jesus' friends went to the sepulcher, they found that the door-stone had been rolled away and the tomb was empty. An angel sat on the stone and said, "He is not here, for he is risen" (Matthew 28:2–6; Mark 16:4–6). (In Luke 24:1–6 and in John 20:11–12, there are two angels at the tomb.)

IV

A man and a woman
Are one.   10
A man and a woman and a blackbird
Are one.

V

I do not know which to prefer,
The beauty of inflections
Or the beauty of innuendoes,   15
The blackbird whistling
Or just after.

VI

Icicles filled the long window
With barbaric glass.
The shadow of the blackbird   20
Crossed it, to and fro.
The mood
Traced in the shadow
An indecipherable cause.

VII

O thin men of Haddam,[1]   25
Why do you imagine golden birds?
Do you not see how the blackbird
Walks around the feet
Of the women about you?

VIII

I know noble accents   30
And lucid, inescapable rhythms;
But I know, too,
That the blackbird is involved
In what I know.

IX

When the blackbird flew out of sight,   35
It marked the edge
Of one of many circles.

[1] Town in Connecticut.

X

At the sight of blackbirds
Flying in a green light,
Even the bawds of euphony[2]
Would cry out sharply.

XI

He rode over Connecticut
In a glass coach.
Once a fear pierced him,
In that he mistook
The shadow of his equipage
For blackbirds.

XII

The river is moving.
The blackbird must be flying.

XIII

It was evening all afternoon.
It was snowing
And it was going to snow.
The blackbird sat
In the cedar-limbs.

1923

Anecdote of the Jar

I placed a jar in Tennessee,
And round it was, upon a hill.
It made the slovenly wilderness
Surround that hill.

The wilderness rose up to it,
And sprawled around, no longer wild.
The jar was round upon the ground
And tall and of a port in air.

---

[2] Those touting harmony as the highest aesthetic
virtue.

It took dominion everywhere.
The jar was gray and bare. 10
It did not give of bird or bush,
Like nothing else in Tennessee.

1923

The Paltry Nude Starts on a Spring Voyage

But not on a shell,[1] she starts,
Archaic, for the sea.
But on the first-found weed
She scuds[2] the glitters,
Noiselessly, like one more wave. 5

She too is discontent
And would have purple stuff upon her arms,
Tired of the salty harbors,
Eager for the brine and bellowing
Of the high interiors of the sea. 10

The wind speeds her,
Blowing upon her hands
And watery back.
She touches the clouds, where she goes
In the circle of her traverse of the sea. 15

Yet this is meagre play
In the scurry[3] and water-shine,
As her heels foam—
Not as when the goldener nude
Of a later day 20

Will go, like the centre of sea-green pomp,
In an intenser calm,
Scullion[4] of fate,
Across the spick torrent, ceaselessly,
Upon her irretrievable way. 25

1923

---

[1] In classical myth the spring goddess, Venus, was born of sea-foam and appears in paintings (as in Botticelli's *Birth of Venus*) nude, borne on a seashell, and with drapery of royal purple.
[2] Runs swiftly, as if driven forward.
[3] An invented word.
[4] Here, the "new broom" that "sweeps clean"; literally, a kitchen servant whose chief task is cleaning dishes.

The Snow Man

One must have a mind of winter
To regard the frost and the boughs
Of the pine-trees crusted with snow;

And have been cold a long time
To behold the junipers shagged with ice,   5
The spruces rough in the distant glitter

Of the January sun; and not to think
Of any misery in the sound of the wind,
In the sound of a few leaves,

Which is the sound of the land   10
Full of the same wind
That is blowing in the same bare place

For the listener, who listens in the snow,
And, nothing himself, beholds
Nothing that is not there and the nothing that is.   15
1923

The Emperor of Ice-Cream

Call the roller of big cigars,
The muscular one,[1] and bid him whip
In kitchen cups concupiscent curds.
Let the wenches dawdle in such dress
As they are used to wear, and let the boys   5
Bring flowers in last month's newspapers.
Let be be finale of seem.
The only emperor is the emperor of ice-cream.

[1] It required muscles to operate the large machines that rolled tobacco leaves flat in cigar factories. The poem may be a Key West poem; at Cuban wakes in Key West, Florida, ice cream was often served.

Take from the dresser of deal,[2]
Lacking the three glass knobs, that sheet   10
On which she embroidered fantails[3] once
And spread it so as to cover her face.
If her horny feet protrude, they come
To show how cold she is, and dumb.
Let the lamp affix its beam.   15
The only emperor is the emperor of ice-cream.

1923

The Idea of Order at Key West

She sang beyond the genius of the sea.
The water never formed to mind or voice,
Like a body wholly body, fluttering
Its empty sleeves; and yet its mimic motion
Made constant cry, caused constantly a cry,   5
That was not ours although we understood,
Inhuman, of the veritable ocean.

The sea was not a mask. No more was she.
The song and water were not medleyed sound
Even if what she sang was what she heard,   10
Since what she sang was uttered word by word.
It may be that in all her phrases stirred
The grinding water and the gasping wind;
But it was she and not the sea we heard.

For she was the maker of the song she sang.   15
The ever-hooded, tragic-gestured sea
Was merely a place by which she walked to sing.
Whose spirit is this? we said, because we knew
It was the spirit that we sought and knew
That we should ask this often as she sang.   20

If it was only the dark voice of the sea
That rose, or even colored by many waves;
If it was only the outer voice of sky

---

[2] Pine (the cheapest wood).
[3] Embroidery pattern resembling the tails of
fantail pigeons.

And cloud, of the sunken coral water-walled,
However clear, it would have been deep air,
The heaving speech of air, a summer sound
Repeated in a summer without end
And sound alone. But it was more than that,
More even than her voice, and ours, among
The meaningless plungings of water and the wind,
Theatrical distances, bronze shadows heaped
On high horizons, mountainous atmospheres
Of sky and sea.

        It was her voice that made
The sky acutest at its vanishing.
She measured to the hour its solitude.
She was the single artificer of the world
In which she sang. And when she sang, the sea,
Whatever self it had, became the self
That was her song, for she was the maker. Then we,
As we beheld her striding there alone,
Knew that there never was a world for her
Except the one she sang and, singing, made.

Ramon Fernandez,[1] tell me, if you know,
Why, when the singing ended and we turned
Toward the town, tell why the glassy lights,
The lights in the fishing boats at anchor there,
As the night descended, tilting in the air,
Mastered the night and portioned out the sea,
Fixing emblazoned zones and fiery poles,[2]
Arranging, deepening, enchanting night.

Oh! Blessed rage for order, pale Ramon,
The maker's rage to order words of the sea,
Words of the fragrant portals, dimly-starred,
And of ourselves and of our origins,
In ghostlier demarcations, keener sounds.

1936

---

[1] Stevens said that he invented this name.
[2] The zones and poles are like those geographers
invent to demarcate the terrestrial globe.

A Postcard from the Volcano[*]

Children picking up our bones
Will never know that these were once
As quick as foxes on the hill;

And that in autumn, when the grapes
Made sharp air sharper by their smell   5
These had a being, breathing frost;

And least will guess that with our bones
We left much more, left what still is
The look of things, left what we felt

At what we saw. The spring clouds blow   10
Above the shuttered mansion-house,
Beyond our gate and the windy sky

Cries out a literate despair.
We knew for long the mansion's look
And what we said of it became   15

A part of what it is . . . Children,
Still weaving budded aureoles,
Will speak our speech and never know,

Will say of the mansion that it seems
As if he that lived there left behind   20
A spirit storming in blank walls,

A dirty house in a gutted world,
A tatter of shadows peaked to white,
Smeared with the gold of the opulent sun.

1936

---

[*] The poem is written as a message from an inhabitant of a town covered over by lava after a volcanic eruption long ago. The dead man lived in a "mansion-house" still visible.

Arrival at the Waldorf [1]

Home from Guatemala, back at the Waldorf.
This arrival in the wild country of the soul,
All approaches gone, being completely there,

Where the wild poem is a substitute
For the woman one loves or ought to love,   5
One wild rhapsody a fake for another.

You touch the hotel the way you touch moonlight
Or sunlight and you hum and the orchestra
Hums and you say "The world in a verse,

A generation sealed, men remoter than mountains,   10
Women invisible in music and motion and color,"
After that alien, point-blank, green and actual Guatemala.

1942

No Possum, No Sop, No Taters [1]

He is not here, the old sun,
As absent as if we were asleep.

The field is frozen. The leaves are dry.
Bad is final in this light.

In this bleak air the broken stalks   5
Have arms without hands. They have trunks

Without legs or, for that, without heads.
They have heads in which a captive cry

Is merely the moving of a tongue.
Snow sparkles like eyesight falling to earth,   10

[1] Famous and expensive hotel in New York City.
[1] Rustic American for "No meat (opossum), no
bread to dip in gravy, no potatoes."

Like seeing fallen brightly away.
The leaves hop, scraping on the ground.

It is deep January. The sky is hard.
The stalks are firmly rooted in ice.

It is in this solitude, a syllable,   15
Out of these gawky flitterings,

Intones its single emptiness,
The savagest hollow of winter-sound.

It is here, in this bad, that we reach
The last purity of the knowledge of good.   20

The crow looks rusty as he rises up.
Bright is the malice in his eye . . .

One joins him there for company.
But at a distance, in another tree.

1947

Angel Surrounded by Paysans*

One of the countrymen:

                                                        There is
A welcome at the door to which no one comes?
The angel:
I am the angel of reality,   5
Seen for a moment standing in the door.

I have neither ashen wing nor wear of ore[1]
And live without a tepid aureole,

---

* In his *Letters* (New York: Knopf, 1966), Stevens says that the poem was written about a still life representing a Venetian glass bowl (the "angel") standing on a table amid other glass and pottery vessels (the "peasants"). "The point of the poem," Stevens writes, "is that there must be in the world about us things that solace us quite as fully as any heavenly visitation could."
[1] Gold.

Or stars that follow me, not to attend,
But, of my being and its knowing, part.

I am one of you and being one of you
Is being and knowing what I am and know.

Yet I am the necessary angel of earth,
Since, in my sight, you see the earth again,

Cleared of its stiff and stubborn, man-locked set,
And, in my hearing, you hear its tragic drone

Rise liquidly in liquid lingerings,
Like watery words awash; like meanings said

By repetitions of half-meanings. Am I not,
Myself, only half of a figure of a sort,

A figure half seen, or seen for a moment, a man
Of the mind, an apparition apparelled in

Apparels of such lightest look that a turn
Of my shoulder and quickly, too quickly, I am gone?

1950

Final Soliloquy of the Interior Paramour[*]

Light the first light of evening, as in a room
In which we rest and, for small reason, think
The world imagined is the ultimate good.

This is, therefore, the intensest rendezvous.
It is in that thought that we collect ourselves,
Out of all the indifferences, into one thing:

Within a single thing, a single shawl
Wrapped tightly round us, since we are poor, a warmth,
A light, a power, the miraculous influence.

[*] The poem is spoken by the "interior
paramour," or muse, to the poet.

Here, now, we forget each other and ourselves.   10
We feel the obscurity of an order, a whole,
A knowledge, that which arranged the rendezvous,

Within its vital boundary, in the mind.
We say God and the imagination are one . . .
How high that highest candle lights the dark.   15

Out of this same light, out of the central mind,
We make a dwelling in the evening air,
In which being there together is enough.
1953

The Plain Sense of Things

After the leaves have fallen, we return
To a plain sense of things. It is as if
We had come to an end of the imagination,
Inanimate in an inert savoir.[1]

It is difficult even to choose the adjective   5
For this blank cold, this sadness without cause.
The great structure has become a minor house.
No turban walks across the lessened floors.

The greenhouse never so badly needed paint.
The chimney is fifty years old and slants to one side.   10
A fantastic effort has failed, a repetition
In a repetitiousness of men and flies.

Yet the absence of the imagination had
Itself to be imagined. The great pond,
The plain sense of it, without reflections, leaves,   15
Mud, water like dirty glass, expressing silence

Of a sort, silence of a rat come out to see,
The great pond and its waste of the lilies, all this
Had to be imagined as an inevitable knowledge,
Required, as a necessity requires.   20
1954

[1] French: "knowledge."

The Planet on the Table[1]

Ariel[2] was glad he had written his poems.
They were of a remembered time
Or of something seen that he liked.

Other makings of the sun
Were waste and welter   5
And the ripe shrub writhed.

His self and the sun were one
And his poems, although makings of his self,
Were no less makings of the sun.

It was not important that they survive.   10
What mattered was that they should bear
Some lineament or character,

Some affluence, if only half-perceived,
In the poverty of their words,
Of the planet of which they were part.   15

1954

The River of Rivers in Connecticut[1]

There is a great river this side of Stygia,[2]
Before one comes to the first black cataracts
And trees that lack the intelligence of trees.

In that river, far this side of Stygia,
The mere flowing of the water is a gayety,   5
Flashing and flashing in the sun. On its banks,

---

[1] The "planet" is a terrestrial globe, representing
the world in miniature. Stevens uses this as an
image for his *Collected Poems* (1954).
[2] The tree spirit in Shakespeare's play *The
Tempest*. The character Ariel sings several songs
in the course of the play. Here, Ariel
symbolizes the poet.
[1] *Connecticut* is an Indian word meaning "land of

many rivers." The Connecticut River is the
largest in the state, where Stevens lived. The
phrase "River of Rivers" is formed in imitation
of such Biblical phrases as "King of Kings" and
"Holy of Holies."
[2] The land of the dead, named from the River
Styx, which the shades of the dead must cross
in the boatman Charon's ferry.

No shadow walks. The river is fateful,
Like the last one. But there is no ferryman.
He could not bend against its propelling force.

It is not to be seen beneath the appearances   10
That tell of it. The steeple at Farmington
Stands glistening and Haddam[3] shines and sways.

It is the third commonness with light and air,
A curriculum,[4] a vigor, a local abstraction . . .
Call it, once more, a river, an unnamed flowing,   15

Space-filled, reflecting the seasons, the folk-lore
Of each of the senses; call it, again and again,
The river that flows nowhere, like a sea.
1954

Not Ideas About the Thing
but the Thing Itself[1]

At the earliest ending of winter,
In March, a scrawny cry from outside
Seemed like a sound in his mind.

He knew that he heard it,
A bird's cry, at daylight or before,   5
In the early March wind.

The sun was rising at six,
No longer a battered panache[2] above snow . . .
It would have been outside.

It was not from the vast ventriloquism   10
Of sleep's faded papier-mâché . . .[3]
The sun was coming from outside.

---

[3] Farmington and Haddam are towns in Connecticut.
[4] Body of knowledge; the word has the same root as *current*.
[1] The *Ding-an-sich* (German) or "thing as it is in itself," was thought by Kantian philosophers to be beyond the reach of our perceptions, which could attain only to phenomena. Stevens put this poem last in his *Collected Poems* (1954).
[2] Tuft of feathers on a helmet.
[3] Material of paper and paste used to make ephemeral masks, statues, etc.

That scrawny cry—It was
A chorister whose c preceded the choir.[4]
It was part of the colossal sun,

Surrounded by its choral rings,
Still far away. It was like
A new knowledge of reality.

1954

The Course of a Particular

Today the leaves cry, hanging on branches swept by wind,
Yet the nothingness of winter becomes a little less.
It is still full of icy shades and shapen snow.

The leaves cry . . . One holds off and merely hears the cry.
It is a busy cry, concerning someone else.   5
And though one says that one is part of everything,

There is a conflict, there is a resistance involved;
And being part is an exertion that declines:
One feels the life of that which gives life as it is.

The leaves cry. It is not a cry of divine attention,   10
Nor the smoke-drift of puffed-out heroes, nor human cry.
It is the cry of leaves that do not transcend themselves,

In the absence of fantasia, without meaning more
Than they are in the final finding of the ear, in the thing
Itself, until, at last, the cry concerns no one at all.   15

1957

---

[4] The chorister sounds the note C on a pitch pipe
to give the choir its starting key.

Of Mere Being

The palm at the end of the mind,
Beyond the last thought, rises
In the bronze decor,

A gold-feathered bird
Sings in the palm, without human meaning,   5
Without human feeling, a foreign song.

You know then that it is not the reason
That makes us happy or unhappy.
The bird sings. Its feathers shine.

The palm stands on the edge of space.   10
The wind moves slowly in the branches.
The bird's fire-fangled feathers dangle down.

1957

William Carlos Williams
1883–1963

William Carlos Williams was long viewed as the homespun poet for the
technological age. A New Jersey physician, he was mistaken for a hobbyist-poet
jotting verses at odd moments between patients. Only with the 1946 publication
of Book One of his modern industrial-age American epic, *Paterson,* did readers
begin to appreciate Williams's achievement as a major twentieth-century
American writer. Thereafter, students, young poets, and critics looked closely and
with increasing admiration at his formally innovative books of poetry, fiction,
drama, and criticism. Dr. Williams had been writing in relative obscurity since
before 1920. At last, at midcentury, his readers caught up with the poet and
began to realize that Williams deserved the recognition and honor already
accorded to the select group of twentieth-century American poets that included
T. S. Eliot, Robert Frost, and Wallace Stevens.

His *Autobiography* (1951) presents young Billy Williams as an all-American
boy playing baseball and pranks, but in several ways his youth was not typically
American. Williams was born in 1883 in Rutherford, a northern New Jersey
town across the Meadowlands from New York City. He was the elder son of
William George and Raquel Helene Hoheb Williams. His father, an Englishman
earning his living as a traveling salesman in the Caribbean and in Latin America,
had met Helene, of Basque and Jewish origins, in Puerto Rico. After their

marriage he settled with her in Rutherford, where neither had friends or family. "Imagine," Williams later wrote of the town in the 1880s, "no sewers, no water supply, no gas even, not even a trolley car. The sidewalks were of wood." Williams's father was periodically away on business, while his mother, knowing little English, was somewhat reclusive in the town. More difficult still, there was mental disorder in the family. His father's brother, Uncle Godwin, who lived with them, terrified young Billy with his erratic behavior. Helene herself was subject periodically to seizures combined with changes of voice, which embarrassed and doubtless frightened the child.

Yet Williams's parents were a cultured couple. As a young woman, his mother had studied art in the *beaux arts* tradition in Paris, and throughout her life she conveyed her love of all things European, especially art, which Williams later considered studying. His father passed along his literary interests to the boy by reading aloud from the Afro-American poet Paul Lawrence Dunbar, from Gilbert and Sullivan, and from a collection of English Romantic and Victorian poets, including Keats. The household was bilingual in English and Spanish, and in boyhood the Williams sons, including Billy's younger brother Edgar, took music lessons and tasted life abroad, including a year of school in Switzerland and several months in Paris. This family background has proved significant to Williams's readers, who continue to discover important strains of European artistic influence in writing that is self-professedly American.

Ambitious for his sons' education, George Williams sent them, at considerable financial sacrifice, to Horace Mann High School in New York City, a two-hour daily commute each way. With the family's blessing, Edgar, evidently the academically superior student, prepared to study architecture, while William was readied for a career in dentistry. At the turn of the century, college work was not required for admission to some American medical schools, and Williams entered the School of Medicine at the University of Pennsylvania in Philadelphia following his graduation from high school. In retrospect, it was a happy choice. Within the year he had transferred from dentistry into medicine. Meanwhile, in a moment crucial for his life as a writer, he met the aspiring artist Charles Demuth, the young poet H. D. (Hilda Doolittle), and a graduate student, Ezra Pound, who became his lifelong friend and critic.

Through medical school and his interning years in New York (1902–1909), Williams, an earnest and dutiful young man, remained a Sunday painter and sustained his literary ambitions. Unknown to him then, his medical education, emphasizing rapid diagnosis and note-taking on cases, would later become an integral part of his poetic practice. In those early years, however, Williams still wrote well-meant clichés ("the only way to be truly happy is to make others happy") that echoed the Christian liberalism of his Rutherford culture. His first book, *Poems* (1909), self-published, was ambitious but sentimental and derivative —"bad Keats" he later called it. At that point poetry was his haven, a respite from the daily experience of blood and childbirth, roach-infested laboratories and disease.

At twenty-six, while a medical intern, Williams began the courtship of Charlotte Herman, the daughter of a prosperous German-American printer in Rutherford whose family became the subject of Williams's Stecher trilogy of novels (*White Mule*, 1937; *In the Money*, 1940; *The Build-Up*, 1952). When she refused him, Williams immediately proposed to her quieter, plainer, younger sister Florence. Williams and "Flossie" became informally engaged in 1909, just before he left for a year of postgraduate medical study in Leipzig, Germany. He also visited Pound in London and saw his brother Ed, who was studying architecture at the American Academy in Rome. After touring in Spain, Williams returned to America to begin medical practice in his hometown. He married Flossie in December 1912, and within two years had a mortgage, the first of two infant sons, and a practice that included evening office hours and house calls. Nonetheless, he determined to continue his literary life.

Manhattan, Rutherford, and their surroundings thereafter became Williams's main compass points. The Rutherford area provided abundant material for his writing, while an hour's drive away in a Model-T Ford, a wide circle of cosmopolitan artists and writers in New York kept him abreast of the contemporary movement in the arts known as modernism. In 1913, the year in which Pound arranged for the publication of Williams's second book of poems, *The Tempers,* Williams probably learned of the latest European work of artists like Matisse, Cézanne, and Braque, whose works were displayed at the New York Armory. By the midteens, Williams had affiliated with the Others group of artists and writers and had met Marianne Moore, Wallace Stevens, and Marcel Duchamp, who were revolutionizing the arts through their efforts to break down and restructure space and time.

But the cultural influences on Williams were broad-based. One was the efficiency movement of the 1910s, which was meant to encourage more productive labor and which taught Americans to think in ever finer, more precise subdivisions of time and motion. Even as Williams criticized this glorification of speed, he was writing prodigiously and sustaining a busy, multifaceted life.

Williams's break with traditional forms and subject matter came with *Al Que Quiere!* ("To Him Who Wants It!"), a book of iconoclastic lyrics, and with *Kora in Hell: Improvisations* (1920). *Kora* was an experimental montage of passages written "automatically" to tap subconscious funds of poetic energy; portions of unpremeditated writing were coupled with Williams's commentary on them. *Kora* appeared in the same issues of *The Little Review* that carried James Joyce's *Ulysses,* a work that was to influence Williams profoundly, as it did numerous other American writers. (Williams met Joyce in 1924, while on sabbatical in Europe with Flossie.)

The 1920s were an especially prolific period for Williams. Continuously experimenting in form, he spoke in the voice that is unmistakably his. Often angry and irreverent in tone, it was defiant of all conventions—formal, political, and religious. A self-consciously American poet, he was angered by—and jealous of—T. S. Eliot, whose insistence on the British tradition Williams thought retrograde. During those years, various small presses published many of Williams's most lasting works, including *Spring and All* (1923), which combined prose and poetry, *The Great American Novel* (1923), and *In the American Grain* (1925), a personal revision of American history and culture. Williams always remained innovative. He believed the repetition of familiar forms to be a kind of living death for a poet.

During the Great Depression, Williams published a collection of short stories aptly entitled *The Knife of the Times* (1932) and saw two major collections of poems through the press. From the wartime 1940s, as successive books of his long poem *Paterson* appeared and his reputation grew, Williams began to suffer health problems. Through heart attacks and strokes he continued, with the tireless help of Flossie, to read, write, travel, and lecture. Two major works, *The Desert Music* (1954) and *Pictures from Brueghel* (1962) came from the efforts of those years, as he struggled toward a flexible verse form he called the variable foot.

By now Williams was earning prestigious prizes for his poetry. Still he resolutely encouraged the younger poets who wrote him letters and appeared on his Rutherford doorstep. He never forgot how hard it was to make his way or how difficult his isolation had often been. He remarked in 1950, "I think the artist, generally speaking, feels lonely. Perhaps his recourse to art, in any form, comes from his essential loneliness. He is usually in rebellion against the world."

Further Reading:

J. H. Miller, *Poets of Reality*, 1965.
J. Guimond, *The Art of William Carlos Williams*, 1968.
S. Paul, *The Music of Survival*, 1968.
B. Dijkstra, *The Hieroglyphics of a New Speech*, 1969.
J. Breslin, *William Carlos Williams*, 1970.
J. Conarroe, *William Carlos Williams'*

"Paterson," 1970.
B. Sankey, *A Companion to William Carlos Williams' "Paterson,"* 1971.
D. Tashjian, *William Carlos Williams and the American Scene, 1920–1940*, 1978.
P. Mariani, *William Carlos Williams*, 1981.
William Carlos Williams: Man and Poet, ed. C. Terrell, 1983.

Texts:

The Collected Earlier Poems of William Carlos Williams, 1966.

The Collected Later Poems of William Carlos Williams, 1967.

The Young Housewife

At ten A.M. the young housewife
moves about in negligee behind
the wooden walls of her husband's house.
I pass solitary in my car.

Then again she comes to the curb   5
to call the ice-man, fish-man, and stands
shy, uncorseted, tucking in
stray ends of hair, and I compare her
to a fallen leaf.

The noiseless wheels of my car   10
rush with a crackling sound over
dried leaves as I bow and pass smiling.
        1917

El Hombre[1]

It's a strange courage
you give me ancient star:

Shine alone in the sunrise
toward which you lend no part!
1917

Danse Russe[1]

If when my wife is sleeping
and the baby and Kathleen
are sleeping
and the sun is a flame-white disc
in silken mists   5
above shining trees,—
if I in my north room
dance naked, grotesquely
before my mirror
waving my shirt round my head   10
and singing softly to myself:
"I am lonely, lonely.
I was born to be lonely,
I am best so!"
If I admire my arms, my face,   15
my shoulders, flanks, buttocks
against the yellow drawn shades,—
Who shall say I am not
the happy genius of my household?[2]
1917

[1] Spanish: "the man" or "the brave man."   [2] The *genius loci* (Latin) is the tutelary deity of a
[1] French: "Russian dance."   place.

Love Song

I lie here thinking of you:—

the stain of love
is upon the world!
Yellow, yellow, yellow
it eats into the leaves,   5
smears with saffron
the horned branches that lean
heavily
against a smooth purple sky!
There is no light   10
only a honey-thick stain
that drips from leaf to leaf
and limb to limb
spoiling the colors
of the whole world—   15

you far off there under
the wine-red selvage[1] of the west!
1917

Queen Anne's Lace[1]

Her body is not so white as
anemone petals nor so smooth—nor
so remote a thing. It is a field
of the wild carrot taking
the field by force; the grass   5
does not raise above it.
Here is no question of whiteness,
white as can be, with a purple mole
at the center of each flower.
Each flower is a hand's span   10
of her whiteness. Wherever

[1] Finished edge of fabric.
[1] The wild carrot; its flower is composed of multiple white blossoms, giving a lacelike appearance.

his hand has lain there is
a tiny purple blemish. Each part
is a blossom under his touch
to which the fibres of her being   15
stem one by one, each to its end,
until the whole field is a
white desire, empty, a single stem,
a cluster, flower by flower,
a pious wish to whiteness gone over—   20
or nothing.

1921

Paterson[1]

Before the grass is out the people are out
and bare twigs still whip the wind—
when there is nothing, in the pause between
snow and grass in the parks and at the street ends
—Say it, no ideas but in things—   5
nothing but the blank faces of the houses
and cylindrical trees
bent, forked by preconception and accident
split, furrowed, creased, mottled, stained
secret—into the body of the light—   10
These are the ideas, savage and tender
somewhat of the music, et cetera
of Paterson, that great philosopher—

From above, higher than the spires, higher
even than the office towers, from oozy fields   15
abandoned to grey beds of dead grass
black sumac, withered weed stalks
mud and thickets cluttered with dead leaves—
the river comes pouring in above the city
and crashes from the edge of the gorge   20
in a recoil of spray and rainbow mists—
—Say it, no ideas but in things—
and factories crystallized from its force,
like ice from spray upon the chimney rocks

[1] The New Jersey city is anthropomorphized here
and in Williams's epic narrative.

Say it! No ideas but in things. Mr.
Paterson has gone away
to rest and write. Inside the bus one sees
his thoughts sitting and standing. His thoughts
alight and scatter—

Who are these people (how complex
this mathematic) among whom I see myself
in the regularly ordered plateglass of
his thoughts, glimmering before shoes and bicycles—?
They walk incommunicado, the
equation is beyond solution, yet
its sense is clear—that they may live
his thought is listed in the Telephone
Directory—
       and there's young Alex Shorn
whose dad the boot-black bought a house
and painted it inside
with seascapes of a pale green monochrome[2]—
the infant Dionysus springing from
Apollo's arm—the floors oakgrained in
Balkan fashion—Hermes' nose, the body
of a gourmand, the lips of Cupid, the eyes
the black eyes of Venus' sister—

But who! who are these people? It is
his flesh making the traffic, cranking the car
buying the meat—
Defeated in achieving the solution they
fall back among cheap pictures, furniture
filled silk, cardboard shoes, bad dentistry
windows that will not open, poisonous gin
scurvy, toothache—

But never, in despair and anxiety
forget to drive wit in, in till it
discover that his thoughts are decorous and simple
and never forget that though his thoughts are decorous
and simple, the despair and anxiety
the grace and detail of
a dynamo—

Divine thought! Jacob fell backwards off the press
and broke his spine. What pathos, what mercy

---

[2] The bootblack's paintings are of mythological subjects; his house borrows its floor pattern from Europe. In the incongruity of these transplanted fashions Williams questions the suitability of European themes for American art and architecture.

of nurses (who keep birthday books)   65
and doctors who can't speak proper english—
is here correctly on a spotless bed
painless to the Nth power—the two legs
perfect without movement or sensation

Twice a month Paterson receives letters   70
from the Pope, his works are translated
into French, the clerks in the post office
ungum the rare stamps from his packages
and steal them for their children's albums
So in his high decorum he is wise   75

What wind and sun of children stamping the snow
stamping the snow and screaming drunkenly
The actual, florid detail of cheap carpet
amazingly upon the floor and paid for
as no portrait ever was—Canary singing   80
and geraniums in tin cans spreading their leaves
reflecting red upon the frost—
They are the divisions and imbalances
of his whole concept, made small by pity
and desire, they are—no ideas beside the facts—   85
1921

Spring and All

By the road to the contagious hospital
under the surge of the blue
mottled clouds driven from the
northeast—a cold wind. Beyond, the
waste of broad, muddy fields   5
brown with dried weeds, standing and fallen

patches of standing water
the scattering of tall trees

All along the road the reddish
purplish, forked, upstanding, twiggy   10
stuff of bushes and small trees
with dead, brown leaves under them
leafless vines—

Lifeless in appearance, sluggish
dazed spring approaches—   15

They enter the new world naked,
cold, uncertain of all
save that they enter. All about them
the cold, familiar wind—

Now the grass, tomorrow   20
the stiff curl of wildcarrot leaf
One by one objects are defined—
It quickens: clarity, outline of leaf

But now the stark dignity of
entrance—Still, the profound change   25
has come upon them: rooted they
grip down and begin to awaken

1923

The Red Wheelbarrow

so much depends
upon

a red wheel
barrow

glazed with rain   5
water

beside the white
chickens

1923

This Is Just to Say

I have eaten
the plums
that were in
the icebox

and which
you were probably
saving
for breakfast

Forgive me
they were delicious   10
so sweet
and so cold
1934

To a Poor Old Woman

munching a plum on
the street a paper bag
of them in her hand

They taste good to her
They taste good   5
to her. They taste
good to her

You can see it by
the way she gives herself
to the one half   10
sucked out in her hand

Comforted
a solace of ripe plums
seeming to fill the air
They taste good to her   15
1935

The Yachts

contend in a sea which the land partly encloses
shielding them from the too-heavy blows
of an ungoverned ocean which when it chooses

tortures the biggest hulls, the best man knows
to pit against its beatings, and sinks them pitilessly.   5
Mothlike in mists, scintillant in the minute

brilliance of cloudless days, with broad bellying sails
they glide to the wind tossing green water
from their sharp prows while over them the crew crawls

ant-like, solicitously grooming them, releasing,   10
making fast as they turn, lean far over and having
caught the wind again, side by side, head for the mark.

In a well guarded arena of open water surrounded by
lesser and greater craft which, sycophant, lumbering
and flittering follow them, they appear youthful, rare   15

as the light of a happy eye, live with the grace
of all that in the mind is fleckless, free and
naturally to be desired. Now the sea which holds them

is moody, lapping their glossy sides, as if feeling
for some slightest flaw but fails completely.   20
Today no race. Then the wind comes again. The yachts

move, jockeying for a start, the signal is set and they
are off. Now the waves strike at them but they are too
well made, they slip through, though they take in canvas.

Arms with hands grasping seek to clutch at the prows.   25
Bodies thrown recklessly in the way are cut aside.
It is a sea of faces about them in agony, in despair

until the horror of the race dawns staggering the mind,
the whole sea become an entanglement of watery bodies
lost to the world bearing what they cannot hold. Broken,   30

beaten, desolate, reaching from the dead to be taken up
they cry out, failing, failing! their cries rising
in waves still as the skillful yachts pass over.

1935

The Poor

It's the anarchy of poverty
delights me, the old
yellow wooden house indented
among the new brick tenements

Or a cast-iron balcony   5
with panels showing oak branches
in full leaf. It fits
the dress of the children

reflecting every stage and
custom of necessity—   10
Chimneys, roofs, fences of
wood and metal in an unfenced

age and enclosing next to
nothing at all: the old man
in a sweater and soft black   15
hat who sweeps the sidewalk—

his own ten feet of it
in a wind that fitfully
turning his corner has
overwhelmed the entire city   20

1938

These

are the desolate, dark weeks
when nature in its barrenness
equals the stupidity of man.

The year plunges into night
and the heart plunges   5
lower than night

to an empty, windswept place
without sun, stars or moon
but a peculiar light as of thought

that spins a dark fire—
whirling upon itself until,
in the cold, it kindles

to make a man aware of nothing
that he knows, not loneliness
itself—Not a ghost but

would be embraced—emptiness,
despair—(They
whine and whistle) among

the flashes and booms of war;
houses of whose rooms
the cold is greater than can be thought,   20

the people gone that we loved,
the beds lying empty, the couches
damp, the chairs unused—

Hide it away somewhere   25
out of the mind, let it get roots
and grow, unrelated to jealous

ears and eyes—for itself.
In this mine they come to dig—all.
Is this the counterfoil to sweetest   30

music? The source of poetry that
seeing the clock stopped, says,
The clock has stopped

that ticked yesterday so well?
and hears the sound of lakewater   35
splashing—that is now stone.
1938

Paterson: The Falls

What common language to unravel?
The falls, combed into straight lines
from that rafter of a rock's
lip. Strike in! the middle of

some trenchant phrase, some   5
well packed clause. Then . . .
This is my plan. 4 sections: First,
the archaic persons of the drama.

An eternity of bird and bush,
resolved. An unraveling: 10
the confused streams aligned, side
by side, speaking! Sound

married to strength, a strength
of falling—from a height! The wild
voice of the shirt-sleeved   15
Evangelist[1] rivaling, Hear

me! I am the Resurrection
and the Life! echoing
among the bass and pickerel, slim
eels from Barbados, Sargasso   20

Sea,[2] working up the coast to that
bounty, ponds and wild streams—
Third, the old town: Alexander Hamilton
working up from St. Croix,[3]

from that sea! and a deeper, whence   25
he came! stopped cold
by that unmoving roar, fastened
there: the rocks silent

but the water, married to the stone,
voluble, though frozen; the water   30
even when and though frozen
still whispers and moans—

And in the brittle air
a factory bell clangs, at dawn, and
snow whines under their feet. Fourth,   35
the modern town, a

disembodied roar! the cataract and
its clamor broken apart—and from
all learning, the empty
ear struck from within, roaring . . .   40

1944

---

[1] I.e., preaching in the park.
[2] Eels migrate to New Jersey from foreign seas.
[3] Hamilton was born in St. Croix, in the West Indies.

The Last Words of My English Grandmother

1920

There were some dirty plates
and a glass of milk
beside her on a small table
near the rank, disheveled bed—

Wrinkled and nearly blind   5
she lay and snored
rousing with anger in her tones
to cry for food,

Gimme something to eat—
They're starving me—   10
I'm all right I won't go
to the hospital. No, no, no

Give me something to eat
Let me take you
to the hospital, I said   15
and after you are well

you can do as you please.
She smiled, Yes
you do what you please first
then I can do what I please—   20

Oh, oh, oh! she cried
as the ambulance men lifted
her to the stretcher—
Is this what you call

making me comfortable?   25
By now her mind was clear—
Oh you think you're smart
you young people,

she said, but I'll tell you
you don't know anything.   30
Then we started.
On the way

we passed a long row
of elms. She looked at them
awhile out of   35
the ambulance window and said,

What are all those
fuzzy-looking things out there?
Trees? Well, I'm tired
of them and rolled her head away.   40

1949

Ezra Pound
1885–1972

Ezra Pound set himself the goal of knowing by the age of thirty "more about poetry than any man living." Accomplished and influential as a poet and—perhaps more notably—as critic, translator, and literary entrepreneur, he pursued his many-sided literary career with ambition and intensity. There can be "no doubt," a reviewer remarked, "as to his vitality and his determination to burst his way into Parnassus." He remains one of the writers most responsible for the modernist revolution in English poetry and prose.

Pound was born in Hailey, Idaho, and raised in Philadelphia in middle-class circumstances. At Hamilton College and the University of Pennsylvania, he specialized in medieval and Renaissance literature in Spanish, Italian, French, and Latin, including a "special study" of Martial, Catullus, and Tacitus. By the time he received his M.A. in 1906, he had "spatted with nearly everybody" and decided against continuing toward the Ph.D. A short period teaching at Wabash College ("the last or at least sixth circle of desolation") only confirmed him in his often heated contempt of American college professors. Dismissed abruptly after a scandal about keeping a woman overnight in his room, Pound traveled to Venice. There he began his lifelong struggle to live for and, wherever possible, on his writing.

In Venice, he had his first book, *A Lume Spento* (1908), published, but at his own expense. He tried working as a gondolier (he was not strong enough) and, briefly, as a publicist for a friend ("the greatest livin' she pianist") before moving in 1908 to London, "the place for poetry." He immediately began to transform English literature—without, however, sacrificing his pleasure in ostentatiously playing the raw and vital American. He frequently cultivated, in speech and writing, a parodic version of the American language; he also was an occasional self-appointed expert on native manners, as when, at lunch with the novelists D. H. Lawrence and Ford Madox Ford, he demonstrated, in a suitably barbaric fashion, how an American ate an apple.

In London, Pound entered a milieu of poets dedicated to writing what, he determined, had already been written in language that was already worn. He responded with poetry that was at once conservative and revolutionary. His famous rallying cry—"make it new!"—meant not a break with the past, but remaining faithful to the spirit of the past while attempting to modernize it, to rediscover its vigor through the creation of new forms. This was something that, Pound vehemently believed, most did not do, because of the sterile academism of most scholarship and the formulaic rhetoric of conventional literary styles. Pound was thus a maverick iconoclast who denounced both the academic scholarship and conventional verse of his day; he was, at the same time, however eccentrically, a passionately learned, even bookish writer. These apparently contradictory tendencies account for much of the energy in an early poem like "Sestina: Altaforte," which is in the difficult sestina form, on a historical subject, and in the tradition of the dramatic monologue associated with Robert Browning. Despite all this indebtedness to literary tradition and history, Pound sought to project himself into the speaker so completely that he became him, and to make thereby a poem that was not archaizing but vitally alive—so alive that when Pound read the poem at a poets' dinner at the Tour Eiffel restaurant, the management put a screen around his table.

Pound's success in infusing the books he touched and the history he recounted with immediacy and passion was so great that some have seen in his intense immersion in experience a sort of mysticism. The English writer and artist Wyndham Lewis observed that Pound "has really walked with Sophocles beside the Aegean; he has *seen* the Florence of Cavalcanti." When Pound continually exhorted himself and others that "every literaryism, every book word, fritters away a scrap of the reader's patience, a scrap of his sense of your sincerity," he did so with an evangelist's intensity. Literature was for him an intensification of life, and he treated his own lapses into "literaryisms"—his poems that echoed the dead letter of an old language rather than the living spirit of the past—with as much severity as he did those of others. After Ford Madox Ford looked through the copy of Pound's third book of poetry, *Canzoni* (1911), he rolled on the floor of his room in mock horror at the book's artificial language. That roll, Pound wrote, "saved me at least two years, perhaps more."

Pound's engagement with the past throughout his career encompassed a wide variety of literary traditions and historical eras, from classical Greece and Rome to medieval Europe, ancient China, and eighteenth-century America. The result was frequently poetry studded with covert references, difficult to the point of inaccessibility. Yet part of the reason for this difficulty was Pound's increasing exploration of an essentially simple poetic technique. At the beginning of his career he called it the technique of the "luminous detail"; later it became the "ideogrammatic method." In his early work it meant to evoke by means of a few, spare words, used without narrative context, moments of transcendent beauty. Later, employed with greater compression and allusiveness, the same technique could evoke the "intelligence of a period."

The first uses of the technique were purely literary. The luminous detail was essential to the Imagist movement in poetry, of which Pound was the originator and, for a little while, the leader. Under the banner of Imagism, he advocated poetry that eschewed all rhetoric and "emotional slither," that would be, objectively and concretely, an image—which Pound defined as "that which presents an intellectual and emotional 'complex' in an instant of time." The Imagist poem showed with as much immediacy as possible a luminous moment; it sought to owe little or nothing, therefore, to narrative or expository structures. When, shortly after defining the Imagist poem, Pound discovered Ernest Fenellosa's essay on the Chinese written character, he was able to extend the implications of the Imagist aesthetic considerably. In that essay, Fenellosa argued that Chinese characters were pictographs and that Chinese poetry was a succession of these "concrete pictures." Poetry of this sort could, Pound felt, in its presentation of a succession of luminous moments, approach the grammarless immediacy of perception, an ontological ideal that remained crucial to his poetry throughout his career. In 1914 Pound joined Wyndham Lewis in founding the Vorticism movement, which stood in essence for an aggressive version of these ideas.

The short Imagist poem "In a Station of the Metro" is representative, in compressed form, of Pound's technique. Pound presents concretely a moment of perception. The language is economical, free of "emotional slither." And, thanks to the unexplained juxtaposition of the two lines—a juxtaposition that avoids the use of logical and narrative connectives—the poem approaches, Pound would maintain, the grammarless immediacy of nature. Reality, the poem implies, is a construction of such relationships, and poetic perception is a succession of moments in which those relationships become luminously manifest.

By the end of the decade, Pound was the author of a number of books of poetry, of which *Personae* (1909), *Ripostes* (1912), and *Lustra* (1915) are the most important. The best poems from the latter two were later added to an expanded version of *Personae*. Pound also distinguished himself during this time as one of the century's outstanding, though sometimes controversial, translators of poetry. The most famous of his translations are those from the Chinese, done from the notes of Fenellosa and collected under the title *Cathay* (1915), and from the Latin poet Propertius, published as *Homage to Sextus Propertius* (1917).

With the appearance in 1920 of *Hugh Selwyn Mauberley: Life and Contacts* and the first sections of the poem that was to occupy him for the rest of his life, *The Cantos,* it was clear that Pound had decisively expanded on and complicated his poetic technique. With his friends T. S. Eliot and James Joyce, he shared the ambition to exploit and to overcome the often depressing, often comic disparity between ancient and modern cultures by writing an epic for the modern world. Increasingly concerned with the relationships of art and society, Pound began working in longer, more complex forms. *Hugh Selwyn Mauberley* was a sequence of short, crisp cameos; it was, Pound wrote, "a study in form, an attempt to condense the James novel." *The Cantos,* by contrast, were not condensations but a finally unending, encyclopedic long poem in open form, one that could include, however chaotically, all that was on Pound's mind, from personal anecdotes to literary allusions of an enormous variety and range. Both these works extended the technique of the luminous detail. It became, in the *Mauberley* poems, more decisively a historiographical technique, as details, allusions, and fragments of quotations were inserted in the separate sections of the poem as means of evoking the whole flavor of the society and era from which they came. Once again, narrative structure, though hard to avoid, was suppressed wherever possible. In

The Cantos this technique of often cryptic, fragmented, and highly allusive references was vastly extended, and narrative and expository structure was more daringly put aside. The result is a poem of greater flexibility and difficulty, if one that finally lacks the coherence of an overall design.

While Pound was attempting to establish his own career as a poet, he was passionately interested in the careers of other writers. Indeed, his own work was often overshadowed by that of the writers he admired and worked on behalf of. Pound was as passionately generous as he was egoistic. He attempted to aid, practically and artistically, an astonishing number of the century's most important writers. A short list would include Lawrence, Joyce, Eliot, Lewis, William Butler Yeats, William Carlos Williams, Robert Frost, and Ernest Hemingway. He served as corresponding editor in Europe for Harriet Monroe's Chicago-based *Poetry,* the literary magazine most responsible for exporting the modernist revolution to America, and as editor or contributing editor for numerous other magazines. He once made unauthorized changes in some poems that Yeats had entrusted to him for submission to *Poetry;* once Yeats got over his shock, he sought Pound's help in modernizing his style. Pound acted as an editor for Eliot's *Waste Land,* cutting a number of lines and passages from it. Pound also tried to help Eliot at one point by setting up a fund to enable his friend to stop working in a bank and to devote himself to writing poetry full-time. On numerous occasions, Pound helped writers financially from his own pocket. He encouraged other writers even when their achievements made him jealous (*The Waste Land* evoked from Pound the response "Complimenti, you bitch. I am wracked by the seven jealousies") or when he detested them, as he did Lawrence.

Between 1915 and 1920, as Pound worked on the *Mauberley* poems and the beginning of *The Cantos,* he became a committed social critic and theorist. The *Mauberley* poems show vividly how Pound's bitter reaction to World War I, which convinced him of the bankruptcy of Western history, helped launch him on his ultimately disastrous career as social analyst and critic. "There died a myriad, / And of the best, among them, / For an old bitch gone in the teeth / For a botched civilization," he wrote in Section V; among the best who were killed, he was doubtless thinking of his friend the sculptor Henri Gaudier-Brzeska, who died at the front in 1915. But the crucial point in Pound's transformation into a passionately engaged social critic came with his discovery of the economic theories of Major C. H. Douglas. Pound felt he had discovered in them the answer to many of the evils of the current system. In particular, he saw in Douglas's theories of social credit the basis for a monetary system that would change the disenfranchised position of the artist in the modern commercial world. Governments would grant citizens social credit for work done. They would consider, in doing so, the inherent and social value of the work that went into making something; the laws of the marketplace, the laws of cost, supply, and demand would be set aside. Pound threw himself as passionately into the fray as social critic as he had as literary critic. "Usurers"—a category which for Pound consisted of capitalists, Jews, and bankers—acted against the common good. As a prose work like *Jefferson and Mussolini* (1935) illustrates, he made them the targets of repeated virulent attacks.

Pound left England for France in 1921. Dissatisfied there, he moved in 1924 to Rapallo, Italy, where he stayed until the end of World War II. He became more and more obsessed with his missionary role as social critic, turning his enormous vigor in that direction in letters, essays, and poems. He met Mussolini in 1933 and was greatly impressed; Mussolini had found Pound's *A Draft of XXX Cantos* "entertaining," and Pound saw in Mussolini someone who had outdone the aesthetes in their own field. Feeling that Fascist Italy was a nation that was likely to adopt his economic theories, Pound supported it more and more vigorously. The most notorious form of that support was his broadcasting a regular program on Rome Radio in which he discussed both aesthetic and political matters and propagandized for Fascism even after America had entered the war. In 1939 he wrote, "Usury is the cancer of the world, and only the surgeon's knife of Fascism can cut it out of the life of the nations." His support of Fascism included an equally strenuous anti-Semitism.

At the end of the war Pound was imprisoned in an American camp for prisoners of war at Pisa. He was first put in a cage that had been reinforced with heavy steel, where he was exposed to the weather. After three weeks, he became so thin and weak that he was transferred to a tent in the medical compound. There, on the dispensary typewriter, he wrote (along with letters for other prisoners) what many regard as his best poems, *The Pisan Cantos*. At the end of six months he was taken to America to stand trial for treason. Declared legally insane, he was transferred to St. Elizabeth's mental hospital in Washington, D.C., where he was incarcerated for thirteen years. At last, after receiving the Bollingen Prize for poetry and after work on his behalf by a number of writers, including Frost, Hemingway, Archibald MacLeish, and the ever-faithful Eliot, he was released to return to Italy. He died in 1972, last of the great leaders of the modernist movement.

Though he spent his formative years as an artist in England and lived abroad most of his life, and though he uttered, on more than one occasion, the sentiment that "residence in America is most revolting to think of," Pound remains a distinctively American author. Like Walt Whitman, the poet he likened to a "pig-headed father" in "Pact," Pound was pig-headed, exhibitionistic, and egoistic, yet equally generous in both his attachments and his commitment to the renewal of poetry in his age. He wrote poetry that was as indecorous as it was sublime, in the way that Whitman's verse had echoed for Emerson both the Bhagavad-Gita and the *New York Herald*. And Pound spent the bulk of his poetic career working on a long poem in the Whitmanesque tradition. *The Cantos* has been variously assessed, by Pound and others, as a success or a failure in its accomplishment; it is, at least in ambition, based on an epic model and frequently messianic in impulse. Confused and confusing, it is often capricious in its use of juxtaposition without structural connection, the technique that Pound came to label in later years the ideogrammatic method. In its confusion, however, *The Cantos* too, like Walt Whitman's "Song of Myself," contains multitudes—of ideas, insights, characters, and events—from the wide-ranging play of Pound's sometimes nobly impassioned, sometimes violently satiric personality. Though the theater of the poems is not the American scene and circumstance but world history, it was here that Pound came closest to living up to the egotism of his early comment about Whitman: "I honor him for he prophesized me." Pound's place as critic, aesthetician, and central figure in the tradition of American poetry is still disputed. But though his work is variously assessed, none would deny

Pound's importance to the modernist movement: as literary entrepreneur, generous publicist for the work of others, and literary journalist.

Further Reading:

C. Norman, *Ezra Pound*, 1960.
L. Dembo, *The Confucian Odes of Ezra Pound*, 1963.
G. Dekker, *The Cantos of Ezra Pound*, 1963.
N. de Nagy, *Ezra Pound's Poetics and Literary Tradition*, 1966.
K. L. Goodwin, *The Influence of Ezra Pound*, 1966.
J. Cornell, *The Trial of Ezra Pound*, 1966.
N. Stock, *Reading the Cantos*, 1967.
T. H. Jackson, *The Early Poetry of Ezra Pound*, 1968.
W. Yip, *Ezra Pound's Cathay*, 1969.
New Approaches to Ezra Pound, ed. E. Hesse, 1969.
N. Stock, *The Life of Ezra Pound*, 1970.
M. de Rachewiltz, *Discretions*. 1971.
C. Brooke-Rose, *A ZBC of Ezra Pound*, 1971.
H. Kenner, *The Pound Era*, 1972.
D. Davie, *Ezra Pound*, 1976.

R. Bush, *The Genesis of Pound's Cantos*, 1976.
J. Wilhelm, *The Later Cantos of Ezra Pound*, 1977.
M. Alexander, *The Poetic Achievement of Ezra Pound*, 1979.
M. S. Bernstein, *The Tale of the Tribe: Ezra Pound and Modern Verse Epic*, 1980.
W. Flory, *Ezra Pound and the Cantos*, 1980.
G. Kearn, *Guide to Ezra Pound's Selected Cantos*, 1980.
C. Terrell, *A Companion to the Cantos of Ezra Pound*, 1980.
P. Ackroyd, *Ezra Pound and His World*, 1981.
I. F. A. Bell, *Critic as Scientist: The Modernist Poetics of Ezra Pound*, 1981.
C. Froula, *A Guide to Ezra Pound's Selected Poems*, 1982.
E. Fuller Torrey, *The Roots of Treason: Ezra Pound and the Secret of St. Elizabeth's*, 1983.

Texts:

Personae, 1949.
The Cantos of Ezra Pound, 1970.
See also *The Letters of Ezra Pound, 1907–1941*, ed. D. D. Paige, 1950.
Pound/Joyce: Letters and Essays, ed. F. Read, 1967.

Sestina: Altaforte

LOQUITUR: En Bertrans de Born.[1]
    Dante Alighieri put this man in hell for that he was a stirrer up of strife.
    Eccovi![2]
    Judge ye!
    Have I dug him up again?
    The scene is at his castle, Altaforte. "Papiols" is his jongleur.[3]
    "The Leopard," the device[4] *of Richard Cœur de Lion.*

I

Damn it all! all this our South stinks peace.
You whoreson dog, Papiols, come! Let's to music!
I have no life save when the swords clash.

[1] "Lord Bertrans de Born speaks." Bertrans de Born, Provençal poet (1140–1209), appears in Dante's *Inferno*, 28, as the promoter of strife between two brothers, Henry Plantagenet and King Richard I of England (1157–1199), called Richard Cœur de Lion (the Lionhearted).

[2] "Behold!"
[3] *Altaforte*, in Italian, means "high and strong"; jongleur: minstrel.
[4] Heraldic emblem.

But ah! when I see the standards gold, vair,[5] purple,
    opposing
And the broad fields beneath them turn crimson,   5
Then howl I my heart nigh mad with rejoicing.

II

In hot summer have I great rejoicing
When the tempests kill the earth's foul peace,
And the lightnings from black heav'n flash crimson,
And the fierce thunders roar me their music   10
And the winds shriek through the clouds mad,
    opposing,
And through all the riven skies God's swords clash.

III

Hell grant soon we hear again the swords clash!
And the shrill neighs of destriers[6] in battle rejoicing,
Spiked breast to spiked breast opposing!   15
Better one hour's stour[7] than a year's peace
With fat boards, bawds, wine and frail music!
Bah! there's no wine like the blood's crimson!

IV

And I love to see the sun rise blood-crimson.
And I watch his spears through the dark clash   20
And it fills all my heart with rejoicing
And pries wide my mouth with fast music
When I see him so scorn and defy peace,
His lone might 'gainst all darkness opposing.

V

The man who fears war and squats opposing   25
My words for stour, hath no blood of crimson
But is fit only to rot in womanish peace
Far from where worth's won and the swords clash
For the death of such sluts I go rejoicing;
Yea, I fill all the air with my music.   30

VI

Papiols, Papiols, to the music!
There's no sound like to swords swords opposing,

---

[5] Alternating argent (silver) and azure bell-shapes
on a standard, resembling those on a heraldic
emblem.

[6] Battle horses.
[7] Combat.

No cry like the battle's rejoicing
When our elbows and swords drip the crimson
And our charges 'gainst "The Leopard's" rush clash.   35
May God damn for ever all who cry "Peace!"

VII

And let the music of the swords make them
    crimson!
Hell grant soon we hear again the swords clash!
Hell blot black for alway the thought "Peace"!
1909

The River-Merchant's Wife: A Letter*

While my hair was still cut straight across my forehead
I played about the front gate, pulling flowers.
You came by on bamboo stilts, playing horse,
You walked about my seat, playing with blue plums.
And we went on living in the village of Chokan: 5
Two small people, without dislike or suspicion.

At fourteen I married My Lord you.
I never laughed, being bashful.
Lowering my head, I looked at the wall.
Called to, a thousand times, I never looked back.   10

At fifteen I stopped scowling,
I desired my dust to be mingled with yours
Forever and forever and forever.
Why should I climb the look out?

At sixteen you departed,   15
You went into far Ku-to-yen, by the river of swirling eddies,
And you have been gone five months.
The monkeys make sorrowful noise overhead.

* Adapted from the Chinese of Li Po (700?–762).   orientalist and collector, made the translation
Ernest Fenollosa (1853–1908), an American   from which Pound worked.

You dragged your feet when you went out.
By the gate now, the moss is grown, the different mosses,   20
Too deep to clear them away!
The leaves fall early this autumn, in wind.
The paired butterflies are already yellow with August
Over the grass in the West garden;
They hurt me. I grow older.   25
If you are coming down through the narrows of the river Kiang,
Please let me know beforehand,
And I will come out to meet you
                    As far as Cho-fu-Sa.

1915

The Garden

En robe de parade.[1]
        Samain

Like a skein of loose silk blown against a wall
She walks by the railing of a path in Kensington Gardens,
And she is dying piece-meal
        of a sort of emotional anæmia.

And round about there is a rabble   5
Of the filthy, sturdy, unkillable infants of the very poor.
They shall inherit the earth.

In her is the end of breeding.
Her boredom is exquisite and excessive.
She would like some one to speak to her,   10
And is almost afraid that I
        will commit that indiscretion.

1916

---

[1] French: "dressed for going out."

Salutation

O generation of the thoroughly smug
      and thoroughly uncomfortable,
I have seen fishermen picknicking in the sun,
I have seen them with untidy families,
I have seen their smiles full of teeth 5
      and heard ungainly laughter.
And I am happier than you are,
And they were happier than I am;
And the fish swim in the lake
      and do not even own clothing. 10

1916

A Pact

I make a pact with you, Walt Whitman—
I have detested you long enough.
I come to you as a grown child
Who has had a pig-headed father;
I am old enough now to make friends. 5
It was you that broke the new wood,
Now is a time for carving.
We have one sap and one root—
Let there be commerce between us.

1916

In a Station of the Metro[1]

The apparition of these faces in the crowd;
Petals on a wet, black bough.

1916

---

[1] The Paris subway.

from Hugh Selwyn Mauberley
(Life and Contacts)

"Vocat æstus in umbram"[1]
NEMESIANUS, *Ec. IV*

I: E. P. Ode pour l'Election de Son Sepulchre[2]

For three years, out of key with his time,
He strove to resuscitate the dead art
Of poetry; to maintain "the sublime"
In the old sense. Wrong from the start—

No, hardly, but seeing he had been born   5
In a half savage country, out of date;
Bent resolutely on wringing lilies from the acorn;
Capaneus;[3] trout for factitious bait;

'Ἴδμεν γάρ τοι πάνθ', ὅσ' ἐνὶ Τροίη[4]
Caught in the unstopped ear;   10
Giving the rocks small lee-way
The chopped seas held him, therefore, that year.

His true Penelope was Flaubert,[5]
He fished by obstinate isles;
Observed the elegance of Circe's[6] hair   15
Rather than the mottoes on sun-dials.

Unaffected by "the march of events,"
He passed from men's memory in *l'an trentiesme*
De son eage;[7] the case presents
No adjunct to the Muses' diadem.   20

II

The age demanded an image
Of its accelerated grimace,

---

[1] Latin: "Heat summons us into the shade." From the fourth *Eclogue* of Nemesianus, Roman poet (fl. A.D. 283).
[2] Adaptation of the title of an ode by the French Renaissance poet Pierre de Ronsard (1524–1585), *On the Selection of His Tomb.*
[3] One of the Seven against Thebes, struck by lightning for his rebellion.
[4] From the song the Sirens sang (*Odyssey* 12.189): "For we know all the toils [endured] in wide Troy." Odysseus stopped his comrades' ears

with wax so they would not be seduced by the song.
[5] Penelope: Odysseus' faithful wife; Flaubert: Gustave Flaubert (1821–1880), French novelist who cultivated "the right word," *le mot juste.*
[6] Circe: Enchantress with whom Odysseus remained for a year.
[7] "His thirtieth year." Adapted from *The Testament* of François Villon, French Renaissance poet.

Something for the modern stage,
Not, at any rate, an Attic grace;

Not, not certainly, the obscure reveries
Of the inward gaze;
Better mendacities
Than the classics in paraphrase!

The "age demanded" chiefly a mould in plaster,
Made with no loss of time,
A prose kinema,[8] not, not assuredly, alabaster
Or the "sculpture" of rhyme.

III

The tea-rose tea-grown, etc.
Supplants the mousseline of Cos,[9]
The pianola "replaces"
Sappho's barbitos.[10]

Christ follows Dionysus,[11]   5
Phallic and ambrosial
Made way for macerations;[12]
Caliban casts out Ariel.[13]

All things are a flowing,
Sage Heracleitus[14] says;   10
But a tawdry cheapness
Shall outlast our days.

Even the Christian beauty
Defects—after Samothrace;[15]
We see τὸ καλόν[16]   15
Decreed in the market place.

Faun's flesh is not to us,
Nor the saint's vision.
We have the press for wafer;
Franchise for circumcision.   20

[8] Greek for "motion"; also the root of *cinema*, motion pictures.
[9] Mousseline of Cos: light fabric woven in the Aegean island of Cos.
[10] Lyrelike instrument used by Sappho, Greek woman poet who lived during the sixth century B.C.
[11] Greek god of wine and sexual frenzy.
[12] Mortification of the flesh.
[13] Caliban; Ariel: in Shakespeare's *Tempest*, the earth-bound and airy figures, respectively.
[14] Greek philosopher who taught that all things are in flux.
[15] Aegean island where the statute *The Winged Victory* was found.
[16] Greek: "the beautiful."

All men, in law, are equals.
Free of Pisistratus,[17]
We choose a knave or an eunuch
To rule over us.

O bright Apollo,   25
τίν᾽ ἄνδρα, τίν᾽ ἥρωα, τίνα θεόν,[18]
What god, man, or hero
Shall I place a tin wreath upon!

IV

These fought in any case,
and some believing,
                          pro domo,[19] in any case . . .

Some quick to arm,
some for adventure,   5
some from fear of weakness,
some from fear of censure,
some for love of slaughter, in imagination,
learning later . . .
some in fear, learning love of slaughter;   10

Died some, pro patria,
                          non "dulce" non
                          "et decor" . . .[20]
walked eye-deep in hell
believing in old men's lies, then unbelieving
came home, home to a lie,   15
home to many deceits,
home to old lies and new infamy;
usury age-old and age-thick
and liars in public places.

Daring as never before, wastage as never before.   20
Young blood and high blood,
fair cheeks, and fine bodies;

fortitude as never before

frankness as never before,
disillusions as never told in the old days,   25

---

[17] Athenian tyrant.
[18] "What god, what hero, what man shall we loudly praise?" From Pindar's *Olympian Odes,* II, 2.

[19] Latin: "for the home."
[20] "For the homeland, not sweetly, not gloriously." Adapted from Horace: "Dulce et decorum est pro patria mori" (*Odes,* III, ii, 13).

hysterias, trench confessions,
laughter out of dead bellies.

V

There died a myriad,
And of the best, among them,
For an old bitch gone in the teeth,
For a botched civilization,

Charm, smiling at the good mouth,   5
Quick eyes gone under earth's lid,

For two gross of broken statues,
For a few thousand battered books.

1920

---

from **The Cantos**

I

And then went down to the ship,[1]
Set keel to breakers, forth on the godly sea, and
We set up mast and sail on that swart ship,
Bore sheep aboard her, and our bodies also
Heavy with weeping, and winds from sternward   5
Bore us out onward with bellying canvas,
Circe's[2] this craft, the trim-coifed goddess.
Then sat we amidships, wind jamming the tiller,
Thus with stretched sail, we went over sea till day's end.
Sun to his slumber, shadows o'er all the ocean,   10
Came we then to the bounds of deepest water,
To the Kimmerian lands,[3] and peopled cities
Covered with close-webbed mist, unpierced ever
With glitter of sun-rays
Nor with stars stretched, nor looking back from heaven   15
Swartest night stretched over wretched men there.
The ocean flowing backward, came we then to the place
Aforesaid by Circe.
Here did they rites, Perimedes and Eurylochus,[4]

---

[1] Adapted from Book XI of Homer's *Odyssey,* retelling Odysseus' sacrifice, summoning up the spirits of the dead in Hades.
[2] In myth, Circe was the enchantress who turned men to beasts; she sent Odysseus into the underworld to seek Tiresias, who would give him directions for returning home to Ithaca.
[3] Lands of darkness at the edge of the earth; the entrance to Hades.
[4] Two of Odysseus' companions.

And drawing sword from my hip   20
I dug the ell-square pitkin;[5]
Poured we libations unto each the dead,
First mead and then sweet wine, water mixed with white flour.
Then prayed I many a prayer to the sickly death's-heads;
As set in Ithaca, sterile bulls of the best   25
For sacrifice, heaping the pyre with goods,
A sheep to Tiresias only, black and a bell-sheep.
Dark blood flowed in the fosse,
Souls out of Erebus,[6] cadaverous dead, of brides
Of youths and of the old who had borne much;   30
Souls stained with recent tears, girls tender,
Men many, mauled with bronze lance heads,
Battle spoil, bearing yet dreory[7] arms,
These many crowded about me; with shouting,
Pallor upon me, cried to my men for more beasts;   35
Slaughtered the herds, sheep slain of bronze;
Poured ointment, cried to the gods,
To Pluto the strong, and praised Proserpine;[8]
Unsheathed the narrow sword,
I sat to keep off the impetuous impotent dead,   40
Till I should hear Tiresias.
But first Elpenor[9] came, our friend Elpenor,
Unburied, cast on the wide earth,
Limbs that we left in the house of Circe,
Unwept, unwrapped in sepulchre, since toils urged other.   45
Pitiful spirit. And I cried in hurried speech:
"Elpenor, how art thou come to this dark coast?
"Cam'st thou afoot, outstripping seamen?"
                And he in heavy speech:
"Ill fate and abundant wine. I slept in Circe's ingle.[10]   50
"Going down the long ladder unguarded,
"I fell against the buttress,
"Shattered the nape-nerve, the soul sought Avernus.[11]
"But thou, O King, I bid remember me, unwept, unburied,
"Heap up mine arms, be tomb by sea-bord, and inscribed: 55
"*A man of no fortune, and with a name to come.*
"And set my oar up, that I swung mid fellows."

And Anticlea[12] came, whom I beat off, and then Tiresias Theban,
Holding his golden wand, knew me, and spoke first:
"A second time?[13] why? man of ill star,   60

---

[5] Small pit.
[6] Hades.
[7] Old English: "bloody."
[8] Pluto; Proserpine: king and queen of Hades.
[9] Companion of Ulysses who died in a fall from Circe's roof and was left unburied.

[10] Corner (i.e., house).
[11] Lake thought to be the entrance of Hades.
[12] Odysseus' mother; he may not speak to her until Tiresias speaks, having drunk the blood of the libation.
[13] They had met once in life.

"Facing the sunless dead and this joyless region?
"Stand from the fosse, leave me my bloody bever[14]
"For soothsay."
        And I stepped back,
And he strong with the blood, said then: "Odysseus   65
"Shalt return through spiteful Neptune,[15] over dark seas,
"Lose all companions." And then Anticlea came.
Lie quiet Divus. I mean, that is Andreas Divus,
In officina Wecheli, 1538, out of Homer.[16]
And he sailed, by Sirens and thence outward and away   70
And unto Circe.
        Venerandam,[17]
In the Cretan's phrase, with the golden crown, Aphrodite,[18]
Cypri munimenta sortita est,[19] mirthful, orichalchi,[20] with golden
Girdles and breast bands, thou with dark eyelids   75
Bearing the golden bough of Argicida.[21] So that:

1925

from **XLV**

With *Usura*[22]

With usura hath no man a house of good stone
each block cut smooth and well fitting
that design might cover their face,
with usura
hath no man a painted paradise on his church wall   5
harpes et luz[23]
or where virgin receiveth message
and halo projects from incision,
with usura
seeth no man Gonzaga[24] his heirs and his concubines   10
no picture is made to endure nor to live with
but it is made to sell and sell quickly

[14] Libation (from French *boire*: "to drink").
[15] Neptune, god of the sea, would delay by a storm Odysseus' return to Ithaca.
[16] Pound used the Latin translation of the *Odyssey* produced in the workshop ("officina") of Wechel in Paris by Andreas Divus.
[17] "Worthy of veneration." Phrase used of Aphrodite in the second Homeric Hymn, translated into Latin verse in the fifteenth century by the Cretan Georgius Dartona.
[18] Goddess of sexual love and beauty.
[19] Latin: "She won by lot from the fortresses of Cyprus."

[20] "Of copper," a phrase referring to the gifts given to Aphrodite, recounted in the second Homeric Hymn.
[21] *Argicida* means "killer of Argus." This is a refernce to the god Hermes, whose caduceus, or magic wand, is here associated with the golden bough offered by Odysseus to Proserpina.
[22] Latin: "usury," exorbitant interest paid for money borrowed; more generally, avarice of all sorts.
[23] French: "harps and lutes," from Jacques Villon's prayer for his mother.
[24] Luigi Gonzaga (1267–1360), ruler of Mantua.

with usura, sin against nature,
is thy bread ever more of stale rags   15
is thy bread dry as paper,
with no mountain wheat, no strong flour
with usura the line grows thick
with usura is no clear demarcation
and no man can find site for his dwelling.   20
Stonecutter is kept from his stone
weaver is kept from his loom
WITH USURA
wool comes not to market
sheep bringeth no gain with usura   25
Usura is a murrain,[25] usura
blunteth the needle in the maid's hand
and stoppeth the spinner's cunning. Pietro Lombardo[26]
came not by usura
Duccio[27] came not by usura   30
nor Pier della Francesca;[28] Zuan Bellin'[29] not by usura
nor was 'La Calunnia'[30] painted.
Came not by usura Angelico;[31] came not Ambrogio Praedis,[32]
Came no church of cut stone signed: Adamo me fecit.[33]
Not by usura St Trophime[34]   35
Not by usura Saint Hilaire,[35]
Usura rusteth the chisel
It rusteth the craft and the craftsman
It gnaweth the thread in the loom
None learneth to weave gold in her pattern;   40
Azure hath a canker by usura; cramoisi[36] is unbroidered
Emerald findeth no Memling[37]
Usura slayeth the child in the womb
It stayeth the young man's courting
It hath brought palsey to bed, lyeth   45
between the young bride and her bridegroom
                    CONTRA NATURAM[38]
They have brought whores for Eleusis[39]
Corpses are set to banquet
at behest of usura.   50
1937

---

[25] Disease.
[26] Italian sculptor (1435–1515).
[27] Sienese painter (1260?–1318?).
[28] Florentine painter (1420?–1492).
[29] Giovanni Bellini (1430?–1516), Venetian painter.
[30] Italian: "Calumny," painting by Sandro Botticelli (1445?–1510).
[31] Fra Angelico (1387?–1455), Florentine painter.
[32] Ambrogio de Predis (1455?–1506), Italian painter.

[33] Latin: "Adam made me," the inscription by the architect on the Church of San Zeno Maggiore in Verona.
[34] Church in Arles, France.
[35] Church in Poitiers, France.
[36] Crimson cloth.
[37] Hans Memling (1430?–1495), Flemish painter.
[38] Latin: "against nature."
[39] Shrine of Demeter, the mother goddess.

Robinson Jeffers
1887–1962

Robinson Jeffers was a poet of long forms who remained a poetic conservative, choosing traditional narrative over the innovative open form of Walt Whitman's "Song of Myself." Yet, as much as Whitman, Jeffers worked to articulate with evangelical intensity a vision of America and the cosmos, a vision that was at once religious, historical, psychological, and scientific in its points of reference. He differed from Whitman in depicting his primitive American characters against the background of classical tragedy rather than the epic tradition; he once professed to be pleased by a description of himself as "striding morosely over the hills with a copy of Aeschylus in one hand and a shilling shocker in the other."

Jeffers was born in 1887 to a prosperous family in Pittsburgh, Pennsylvania. His father, a Presbyterian preacher and theologian who taught at Western Theological Seminary, could afford to send his son to study in Switzerland and Germany. After graduation in 1905 from Occidental College (his family having moved west to Long Beach, California, in 1903), the young Jeffers began work on an M.A. at the University of Southern California, studied in Zurich in 1906, and returned to U.S.C. as a medical student in 1907.

At U.S.C. Jeffers met Una Call Kuster, who was then married to a prominent Los Angeles lawyer. It was the first of what he later called the two "accidents that changed and directed my life." As their relationship deepened and grew to trouble them both, Jeffers broke away to study forestry in Washington State; but within an hour of his return to California in 1911, he saw Una in the street, and their relationship recommenced. In a last attempt to save the marriage, her husband persuaded her to spend a year abroad; it did not succeed. In 1913 Una divorced Kuster and married Jeffers. Years later, Jeffers touchingly acknowledged his personal debt to Una with a characteristically self-deprecating tribute: "My nature is cold and undiscriminating; she excited and focused it, gave it eyes and nerves and sympathies. She never saw any of my poems until they were typed, yet by her presence and conversation she has coauthored every one of them." Una also served, as Jeffers wrote in 1953, in many practical ways as a mediator between him and the world, something that his extreme shyness made necessary.

In 1914, aided by a modest inheritance, Jeffers settled in Carmel, California. Happening upon that region was the second of the two accidents that directed his life. There, Jeffers wrote, he "could see people living—amid magnificent unspoiled scenery—essentially as they did in the Idylls, or the Sagas, or in Homer's Ithaca." The region was to furnish much of both the settings and the spirit of his major poetry. In 1919 he started work on Tor House and Hawk Tower, the stone buildings that became his lifelong home. As Jeffers "helped the mason shift and place the wave and wind-worn granite," Una wrote, he became "aware of strengths in himself unknown before." In a poem published in 1951, "The Old Stonemason," Jeffers linked working with stone with some of the major preoccupations of his poetry, the strength that allows one to struggle out of the "tidewash" of human passions and illusions, and the ability to face the "enormous inhuman beauty of things." In 1924 Jeffers's first major work, *Tamar and Other Poems*, was privately published; it was reissued with the narrative "Roan Stallion" in 1925. The success of these poems marked the beginning of his public career as a poet and his emerging identity as a sort of cult figure. From the nature of his poetry, which was often sensational, tragic, and philosophical (he also, though less frequently, philosophized in prose), it was not difficult to picture him as a solitary, brooding, prophetic figure who, from his rugged house overlooking the Pacific, wrote of the suicidal passions of a self-deluded mankind.

By now the pattern of the rest of his reclusive, outwardly uneventful life was set. With Una to manage his limited contact with the public world, he could stay in the seclusion he so required, a seclusion that had less to do with the misanthropy many readers have found in his works than it did with Jeffers's shyness and extreme self-protectiveness. When he did have contact with others, he showed himself consistently to be a conscientious and considerate man. Though a stoical detachment from the passions of mankind was an important theme and a heroic posture in much of his poetry, Jeffers's personal need for solitude had humbler and tenderer roots. As Una remarked, "Many people work best, I think, when they are stimulated by outside influences and clashing with other minds, but not my husband, who gets quite *numb* when he cannot pursue his own quiet and solitary way." So shy of contact was he that once, when Una was away, he hid in the bedroom with their dog to avoid two strangers who had knocked at the door. The great tragedy of his life was Una's death in 1950. The "passage of time does not make it more endurable," he wrote a year later, in refusing an invitation to give a reading in Chicago. He died after years of illness in 1962.

Jeffers's work consists primarily of two kinds of poems. Long tragic narratives like *Tamar* and "Roan Stallion" and, later, *The Women at Point Sur, Cawdor, Thurso's Landing,* and *Give Your Heart to the Hawks* are complemented by short meditative lyrics, typically set on the dramatic Pacific coastline. In all his poems, Jeffers saw himself as an exponent of what he called "inhumanism," a philosophy so austere and forbidding that it has, along with the sensationalistic plots of his longer works, limited Jeffers's appeal. His view of the world, molded as it was by the disillusionment that followed World War I, was as prophetically stern as his domestic life was quiet and devoted. He believed that "man is a part of nature, but a nearly infinitesimal part; the human race will cease after a while and leave no trace, but the great splendors of nature will go on." Most fear to face this truth, Jeffers believed; as a result, the life of the bulk of humankind is characterized by "immoderate racial introversion," with "ninety-odd percent of people's activities turned in on other people instead of outward on the world." Human social and historical concerns, he believed, are blind and vain. They isolate humankind as a species from awareness of the far greater, inhuman beauty of the cosmos it inhabits. Jeffers occasionally took comfort in the thought of the *extinction* of the human race, when nature will have purified itself of man. More frequently, he condemned his fellows for their many forms of self-degradation. Jeffers interpreted such differing phenomena as urbanization and world war as signs of the self-destructive self-preoccupation of the species, and he could sound quite strident, even foolish in his condemnations. He once described the life of the masses with disgust as "this horrible entwining of people libidinously listening to *crooners,* etc." His work frequently uses the theme of incest to express symbolically how the species causes its own suffering by turning away from the grandeur of nonhuman nature to focus its energies and passions on itself.

Against this collective degradation, lonely individuals of a higher sort could stand out in bold relief insofar as they sought the triumph of an extreme and painful self-transcendence. In such moments, moments that usually came in the midst of a great tragedy that burned away the all-too-human in them, a few of Jeffers's heroes were capable of looking directly on inhuman reality in all its terrible beauty. For Jeffers, this was the equivalent of looking directly at God. In these moments his characters found in themselves an austere, stony stoicism. Jeffers once wrote a characteristically stern version of the biblical commandments: One must love God with all one's heart and soul and one's neighbor as oneself—"as much as that, but as *little* as that."

Further Reading:

L. Powell, *Robinson Jeffers, The Man and His Work,* 1934, 1940.
R. Gilbert, *Shine, Perishing Republic: Robinson Jeffers and the Tragic Sense in Modern Poetry,* 1936.
R. Squires, *The Loyalties of Robinson Jeffers,* 1956, 1963.
M. C. Monjian, *Robinson Jeffers, a Study in Inhumanism,* 1958.
M. Bennett, *The Stone Mason of Tor House: The Life and Work of Robinson Jeffers,* 1966.

Brother Antonius (W. Everson), *Robinson Jeffers: Fragments of an Older Fury,* 1968.
A. B. Coffin, *Robinson Jeffers: Poet of Inhumanism,* 1970.
R. Brophy, *Robinson Jeffers: Myth, Ritual, and Symbol in the Narrative Poems,* 1973.
J. Shebl, *In This Wild Water,* 1976.
W. Nolte, *Rock and Hawk: Robinson Jeffers and the Romantic Agony,* 1978.
R. Zaller, *The Cliffs of Solitude: A Reading of Robinson Jeffers,* 1983.

Texts:
The Selected Poetry of Robinson Jeffers, 1959.
See also *The Selected Letters of Robinson Jeffers, 1897–1962,* ed. A. Ridgeway, 1968.

Boats in a Fog

Sports and gallantries, the stage, the arts, the antics of dancers,
The exuberant voices of music,
Have charm for children but lack nobility; it is bitter earnestness
That makes beauty; the mind
Knows, grown adult.
            A sudden fog-drift muffled the ocean,   5
A throbbing of engines moved in it,
At length, a stone's throw out, between the rocks and the vapor,
One by one moved shadows
Out of the mystery, shadows, fishing-boats, trailing each other
Following the cliff for guidance,   10

Holding a difficult path between the peril of the sea-fog
And the foam on the shore granite.
One by one, trailing their leader, six crept by me,
Out of the vapor and into it,
The throb of their engines subdued by the fog, patient and cautious,   15
Coasting all round the peninsula
Back to the buoys in Monterey[1] harbor. A flight of pelicans
Is nothing lovelier to look at;
The flight of the planets is nothing nobler; all the arts lose virtue
Against the essential reality   20
Of creatures going about their business among the equally
Earnest elements of nature.

1925

Apology for Bad Dreams

I

In the purple light, heavy with redwood, the slopes drop seaward,
Headlong convexities of forest, drawn in together to the steep ravine. Below,
    on the sea-cliff,
A lonely clearing; a little field of corn by the streamside, a roof under spared
    trees. Then the ocean
Like a great stone someone has cut to a sharp edge and polished to shining.
    Beyond it, the fountain
And furnace of incredible light flowing up from the sunk sun. In the little
    clearing a woman   5
Is punishing a horse; she had tied the halter to a sapling at the edge of the
    wood, but when the great whip
Clung to the flanks, the creature kicked so hard she feared he would snap the
    halter; she called from the house
The young man her son; who fetched a chain tie-rope, they working together
Noosed the small rusty links round the horse's tongue
And tied him by the swollen tongue to the tree.   10
Seen from this height they are shrunk to insect size.
Out of all human relation. You cannot distinguish
The blood dripping from where the chain is fastened,
The beast shuddering; but the thrust neck and the legs
Far apart. You can see the whip fall on the flanks . . .   15

---

[1] California coastal town just to the north of
Carmel, the site of Jeffers's Tor House.

The gesture of the arm. You cannot see the face of the woman.[1]

The enormous light beats up out of the west across the cloud-bars of the trade-wind. The ocean

Darkens, the high clouds brighten, the hills darken together. Unbridled and unbelievable beauty

Covers the evening world . . . not covers, grows apparent out of it, as Venus down there grows out

From the lit sky. What said the prophet? "I create good: and I create evil: I am the Lord."[2]   2

II

This coast crying out for tragedy like all beautiful places,

(The quiet ones ask for quieter suffering: but here the granite cliff the gaunt cypresses crown

Demands what victim? The dykes of red lava and black what Titan? The hills like pointed flames

Beyond Soberanes,[3] the terrible peaks of the bare hills under the sun, what immolation?)

This coast crying out for tragedy like all beautiful places: and like the passionate spirit of humanity   25

Pain for its bread: God's, many victims', the painful deaths, the horrible transfigurations: I said in my heart,

"Better invent than suffer: imagine victims

Lest your own flesh be chosen the agonist, or you

Martyr some creature in the beauty of the place." And I said,

"Burn sacrifices once a year to magic   30

Horror away from the house, this little house here

You have built over the ocean with your own hands

Beside the standing boulders: for what are we,

The beast that walks upright, with speaking lips

And little hair, to think we should always be fed,   35

Sheltered, intact, and self-controlled? We sooner more liable

Than the other animals. Pain and terror, the insanities of desire; not accidents but essential,

And crowd up from the core:" I imagined victims for those wolves, I made them phantoms to follow,

They have hunted the phantoms and missed the house. It is not good to forget over what gulfs the spirit

Of the beauty of humanity, the petal of a lost flower blown seaward by the night-wind, floats to its quietness.   40

[1] In a letter, Jeffers provides a source for this scene: "The woman who tied up the horse to the tree to lash, with the chain around its tongue—*she* was real and she did just that. *And* this isnt *[sic]* in the poem[:] we heard later she was killed by one of her horses falling on her as they were crossing a stream. Pinioned her in the water!"

[2] For Jeffers, God is not bound by the human categories of good and evil; God includes all phenomena.

[3] Point on the California coast.

III

Boulders blunted like an old bear's teeth break up from the headland; below
    them
All the soil is thick with shells, the tide-rock feasts of a dead people.
Here the granite flanks are scarred with ancient fire, the ghosts of the tribe
Crouch in the nights beside the ghost of a fire, they try to remember the
    sunlight,
Light has died out of their skies. These have paid something for the future   45
Luck of the country, while we living keep old griefs in memory: though God's
Envy is not a likely fountain of ruin, to forget evils calls down
Sudden reminders from the cloud: remembered deaths be our redeemers;
Imagined victims our salvation: white as the half moon at midnight
Someone flamelike passed me, saying, "I am Tamar Cauldwell,[4] I have my
    desire,"   50
Then the voice of the sea returned, when she had gone by, the stars to their
    towers.
. . . Beautiful country burn again. Point Pinos down to the Sur Rivers
Burn as before with bitter wonders, land and ocean and the Carmel water.

IV

He brays[5] humanity in a mortar[6] to bring the savor
From the bruised root: a man having bad dreams, who invents victims, is only
    the ape of that God.   55
He washes it out with tears and many waters, calcines it with fire in the red
    crucible,
Deforms it, makes it horrible to itself: the spirit flies out and stands naked, he
    sees the spirit,
He takes it in the naked ecstasy; it breaks in his hand, the atom is broken, the
    power that massed it
Cries to the power that moves the stars, "I have come home to myself, behold
    me.
I bruised myself in the flint mortar and burnt me   60
In the red shell, I tortured myself, I flew forth,
Stood naked of myself and broke me in fragments,
And here am I moving the stars that are me."
I have seen these ways of God:[7] I know of no reason

---

[4] Heroine of Jeffers's early narrative poem *Tamar*.
Her "desire" ultimately leads to a
sensationalistic *liebestod* (love-death), in which
she and her "three lovers" (a group that
includes her brother and father) are burned to
death.
[5] Crushes or grinds.
[6] Vessel for pulverizing and pounding.
[7] Jeffers's comment about his poem "At the Birth
of an Age" is relevant here: "All the prevalent
religions think of God as blessed or happy, or
at least at peace; even the pantheist mystic finds

peace in God. Therefore this conception of
God as pain is hardly admitted by the reader's
mind. . . . It is a conception that runs through
my verses. . . . If God is all, he must be
suffering, since an unreckoned part of the
universe is always suffering. But his suffering
must be self-inflicted, for he is all; there is no
one outside himself to inflict it.—I suppose the
idea carries psychological as well as cosmic or
religious implications. Man as well as God must
suffer in order to discover; and it is often
voluntary—self-inflicted suffering."

For fire and change and torture and the old returnings.

He being sufficient might be still. I think they admit no reason; they are the
  ways of my love.

Unmeasured power, incredible passion, enormous craft: no thought apparent but
  burns darkly

Smothered with its own smoke in the human brain-vault: no thought outside: a
  certain measure in phenomena:

The fountains of the boiling stars, the flowers on the foreland, the
  ever-returning roses of dawn.

1925

Marianne Moore
1887–1972

Marianne Moore, by the end of her long life, was treated somewhat as a lovable
mascot to be patronized by those who thought her eccentricities (the black
tricorn hat or her love of the Brooklyn Dodgers) charming. This latter image
obscured the real person, the clever and scornful writer who came on the literary
scene praised by T. S. Eliot, in 1921. Moore's clear and avant-garde intelligence
made *The Dial,* under her editorship (1925–1929), the magazine anyone interested
in new art and writing in the 1920s had to read. In her poetry, she was a precise
artist for whom a few words sketched an ethical problem, an exotic animal, or a
landscape.

Moore was born within a year of Emily Dickinson's death; it was not, in fact,
until Moore was in her twenties that Dickinson's art was understood and her
rank as a major poet established. Moore looked to Dickinson as a model, but
looked even more to various English sources, especially George Herbert, John
Bunyan, and other religious writers. She had been brought up in strict
Presbyterianism, and the strong ethical bent that this training produced in her
remained in lifelong tension (at first productive, later destructive) with her
appreciation of the multiplicity and aesthetic diversity of life's natural and human
products. She gazed at lizards and medieval tapestries with equal interest; she
relished the lore of bestiaries and newspaper quotations, advertising copy and
guidebooks, fashion reporting and the Bible. But her moral side urged the
strictness of principles, the plainness of axioms, and the geometry of the righteous
life. Her relish she called "gusto," her love of the plain style she called
"sincerity," and in the antiphony between "gusto" and "sincerity" her poetry
takes form.

The form it takes is both strict and free. Moore would write out a stanza
until the phrases all fell right and the lines were satisfactory. Then she would
create other stanzas on the model of the first, counting the syllables in each line
of the original stanza and replicating that number in subsequent stanzas. She
insisted that she wrote by stanzas, not in syllabic lines. By fixing a relatively
inflexible number of syllables in each line, she established the rule of control that

a poet needs for ingenious invention to be pressed into service. Though many of her poems are written in free verse, the elegant and quirky motion of her syllabic poems (including "The Fish" and "Poetry") made her famous.

Moore's father went insane before she was born; she never knew him. For the first seven years of her life she lived with her mother and her elder brother in the house of her maternal grandparents in St. Louis. Her mother took a teaching job and moved the family to Carlisle, Pennsylvania; there they continued the intense closeness reflected in their subsequent lives. Moore lived with her mother all her life and remained closely attached to her brother. Moore graduated from Bryn Mawr College; her grades were not good enough for her to major in English—an ironic fate—so she majored in biology, beginning that training of the eye that, together with the act of the commenting mind, gave her second book its punning title, *Observations* (1924).

In fact, that book contained mostly poems reprinted from her first book, *Poems* (1921), published (without her knowledge or permission) by two of her friends, American writers living in London, Winifred Bryher and Hilda Dolittle. Moore's poems had already appeared in such American avant-garde journals as *Poetry* and *Others*. She was moving in a circle that included Alfred Kreymborg (the editor of *Others*), Wallace Stevens, William Carlos Williams, and various painters and sculptors. She was thought beautiful by many who knew her, but marriage (which it takes "all one's criminal ingenuity to avoid") was something she turned away from, though her long poem "Marriage" shows she had considered both its seductions and its rewards. Her mother's bitter experience may have deterred her, or, like Emily Dickinson, she may have reserved her attention for her work.

"One detects creative power," wrote Moore, "by its capacity to conquer one's detachment." To read Moore's best pages is to find one's detachment conquered as one is drawn into an odd, unpredictable, satiric, learned mind, offering "neatness of finish! neatness of finish!" side by side with the sprawling grandeur of "an octopus of ice"—as Moore called the many-armed glacier covering Mt. Rainier. A great deal of Moore's creative power was spent thinking about America, both critically and approvingly. Her symbol for America is Mt. Rainier itself—enormous, half threat, half invitation, hospitable to all sorts of enterprising and hardy mountain fauna but at the same time the site of terrible geographic, climatic, and aesthetic extremes. Moore was tart when she looked at American failings: Against the American disposition to listen to "snake-charming controversialists" she argued that "it is one thing to change one's mind, / another to eradicate it." Against those who saw in New York only a commercial center she argued "it is not the plunder, / but 'accessibility to experience.'" Against Anglophiles she argued that excellence "has never been confined to one locality." She hated the "half limping and half-ladyfied" rhetoric of diplomats; she scoffed at those who complacently announced that woman was "circumscribed by a / heritage of blindness and native / incompetence." Generally, the prejudiced, in Moore's poetry, condemn themselves; their words, quoted back at them and embedded in Moore's surgical cleanness of style, resound in foolishness. Moore's habit of quoting, however, extended far beyond the satirical quoting of the words of fools; she collected with the temperament of a magpie all sorts of things to quote. The Rosenbach Foundation Museum in Philadelphia preserves her living room; its drawers are full of the accumulation of a lifetime— conversation notebooks in which she recorded sayings (especially of her mother and brother) and files of clippings. Her poems are mosaics, or collages; many pieces are arranged until they fit together. The impossible ideal hovering under the surface is that of an assemblage so perfect that it would need no authorially supplied connective tissue.

The aesthetic pleasures to be found in Moore are those of exquisite appositeness, lightness of touch combined with depth of feeling, ingenuity and surprise, and conversational urbanity and wit. In her later years her morality ("this is mortality, / this is eternity") and her whimsy ("O to be a dragon") disturbed the delicate balance maintained in the best of her poetry, but *Observations* remains, like T. S. Eliot's *Prufrock and Other Observations* and Wallace Stevens's *Harmonium,* one of the treasures of American modernist writing.

Further Reading:
F. Engel, *Marianne Moore,* 1964.
J. Garrigue, *Marianne Moore,* 1965.
A. K. Weatherhead, *The Edge of the Image: Marianne Moore, William Carlos Williams, and Some Other Poets,* 1967.
G. W. Nitchie, *Marianne Moore: An Introduction to the Poetry,* 1969.
Marianne Moore: A Collection of Critical Essays, ed. C. Tomlinson, 1969.
D. Hall, *Marianne Moore: The Cage and the Animal,* 1970.
C. S. Abbot, *Marianne Moore: A Reference Guide,* 1980.
B. Costello, *Marianne Moore: Imaginary Possessions,* 1981.

Texts:
"Poetry" from *Collected Poems,* 1951.
All other selections from *The Complete Poems of Marianne Moore,* 1981.
See also *A Marianne Moore Reader,* 1961.

Poetry*

I, too, dislike it: there are things that are important beyond all this fiddle.
  Reading it, however, with a perfect contempt for it, one discovers in
  it after all, a place for the genuine.
     Hands that can grasp, eyes
      that can dilate, hair that can rise
        if it must, these things are important not because a   5

---

* This poem was revised several times and in the end (1967) reduced to its first two sentences. The version here is from *Collected Poems* (1951).

high-sounding interpretation can be put upon them but because they are
   useful. When they become so derivative as to become unintelligible,
     the same thing may be said for all of us, that we
       do not admire what   10
        we cannot understand: the bat
          holding on upside down or in quest of something to

eat, elephants pushing, a wild horse taking a roll, a tireless wolf under
   a tree, the immovable critic twitching his skin like a horse that feels a flea,
     the base-   15
     ball fan, the statistician—
       nor is it valid
         to discriminate against 'business documents and

school-books';' all these phenomena are important. One must make a
   distinction
   however: when dragged into prominence by half poets, the result is not
     poetry,   20
   nor till the poets among us can be
     'literalists of
       the imagination'²—above
         insolence and triviality and can present

for inspection, 'imaginary gardens with real toads in them', shall we have   25
   it. In the meantime, if you demand on the one hand,
     the raw material of poetry in
       all its rawness³ and
       that which is on the other hand
         genuine, you are interested in poetry.   30

1921

---

¹ Moore's note: "*Diary of Tolstoy* (Dutton), p. 84. 'Where the boundary between prose and poetry lies, I shall never be able to understand. The question is raised in manuals of style, yet the answer to it lies beyond me. Poetry is verse; prose is not verse. Or else poetry is everything with the exception of business documents and school books.'"

² Moore's note: "*Yeats: Ideas of Good and Evil* (A. H. Bullen), p. 182. 'The limitation of his view was from the very intensity of his vision; he was a too literal realist of imagination, as others are of nature; and because he believed that the figures seen by the mind's eye, when exalted by inspiration, were "eternal existences," symbols of divine essences, he hated every grace of style that might obscure their lineaments.'"

³ Moore saved a clipping from *The Spectator* (London) for May 10, 1913, in which a contributor, called "C," asked why the Greek Anthology still charms us, says: "All [of its poems] appeal to emotions which endure for all time, and which, it has been aptly said, are the true raw material of poetry."

The Fish

wade
through black jade.[1]
    Of the crow-blue mussel-shells, one keeps
    adjusting the ash-heaps;[2]
        opening and shutting itself like   5

an
injured fan.
    The barnacles which encrust the side
    of the wave, cannot hide
        there for the submerged shafts of the   10

sun,
split like spun
    glass, move themselves with spotlight swiftness
    into the crevices—
        in and out, illuminating   15

the
turquoise sea
    of bodies. The water drives a wedge
    of iron through the iron edge
        of the cliff; whereupon the stars,[3]   20

pink
rice-grains, ink-
    bespattered jelly-fish, crabs like green
    lilies, and submarine
        toadstools, slide each on the other.   25

All
external
    marks of abuse are present on this
    defiant edifice—
        all the physical features of   30

ac-
cident—lack
    of cornice, dynamite grooves, burns, and

---

[1] The ocean waters.
[2] I.e., the heaps of mussels look like lumps of
burnt coal.

[3] Starfish.

$$\begin{array}{l}
\text{hatchet strokes, these things stand} \\
\quad\text{out on it; the chasm-side is} \qquad\qquad 35
\end{array}$$

dead.
Repeated
    evidence has proved that it can live
      on what can not revive
        its youth. The sea grows old in it.   40

    1924

When I Buy Pictures

or what is closer to the truth,
when I look at that of which I may regard myself as the imaginary possessor,
I fix upon what would give me pleasure in my average moments:
the satire upon curiosity in which no more is discernible
than the intensity of the mood;   5
or quite the opposite—the old thing, the medieval decorated hat-box,
in which there are hounds with waists diminishing like the waist of the
    hour-glass,
and deer and birds and seated people;
it may be no more than a square of parquetry; the literal biography perhaps,
in letters standing well apart upon a parchment-like expanse;   10
an artichoke in six varieties of blue; the snipe-legged hieroglyphic in three parts;[1]
the silver fence protecting Adam's grave,[2] or Michael taking Adam by the wrist.
Too stern an intellectual emphasis upon this quality or that detracts from one's
    enjoyment.
It must not wish to disarm anything; nor may the approved triumph easily be
    honored—
that which is great because something else is small.   15
It comes to this: of whatever sort it is,
it must be "lit with piercing glances into the life of things";[3]
it must acknowledge the spiritual forces which have made it.

1921

---

[1] These are instances of various forms of illustration and calligraphy.

[2] Moore's note: " 'A silver fence was erected by Constantine to enclose the grave of Adam.'

Literary Digest, January 5, 1918; descriptive paragraph with photograph."

[3] Moore's note: "A. R. Gordon, *The Poets of the Old Testament* (Hodder and Stoughton, 1919)."

A Grave

Man looking into the sea,
taking the view from those who have as much right to it as you have to it
   yourself,
it is human nature to stand in the middle of a thing,
but you cannot stand in the middle of this;
the sea has nothing to give but a well excavated grave.   5
The firs stand in a procession, each with an emerald turkey-foot at the top,
reserved as their contours, saying nothing;
repression, however, is not the most obvious characteristic of the sea;
the sea is a collector, quick to return a rapacious look.
There are others besides you who have worn that look—   10
whose expression is no longer a protest; the fish no longer investigate them
for their bones have not lasted:
men lower nets, unconscious of the fact that they are desecrating a grave,
and row quickly away—the blades of the oars
moving together like the feet of water-spiders as if there were no such thing as
   death.   15
The wrinkles progress among themselves in a phalanx—beautiful under
   networks of foam,
and fade breathlessly while the sea rustles in and out of the seaweed;
the birds swim through the air at top speed, emitting cat-calls as heretofore—
the tortoise-shell scourges about the feet of the cliffs, in motion beneath them;
and the ocean, under the pulsation of lighthouses and noise of bell-buoys,   20
advances as usual, looking as if it were not that ocean in which dropped things
   are bound to sink—
in which if they turn and twist, it is neither with volition nor consciousness.
1924

No Swan So Fine[*]

"No water so still as the
     dead fountains of Versailles."[1] No swan,
with swart blind look askance

---

[*] According to Moore, the poem concerns a pair of Louis XV (1723–1774) candelabra ornamented with Dresden china flowers and swans, a piece of art still "alive" though the king in whose reign it was made is long dead.

[1] The king's palace at Versailles, near Paris, has elaborate fountains. Moore's note: " 'There is no water so still as the dead fountains of Versailles.' Percy Phillip, *New York Times Magazine,* May 10, 1931."

and gondoliering legs, so fine
    as the chintz china one with fawn-
brown eyes and toothed gold
collar on to show whose bird it was.   5

Lodged in the Louis Fifteenth
    candelabrum-tree of cockscomb-
tinted buttons, dahlias,
sea-urchins, and everlastings,   10
    it perches on the branching foam
of polished sculptured
flowers—at ease and tall. The king is dead.

1935

The Monkey Puzzle[1]

A kind of monkey or pine-lemur
not of interest to the monkey,
in a kind of Flaubert's Carthage,[2] it defies one—
this "Paduan cat with lizard," this "tiger in a bamboo thicket."
"An interwoven somewhat," it will not come out.   5
Ignore the Foo dog and it is forthwith more than a dog,
its tail superimposed upon itself in a complacent half spiral,
this pine-tree—this pine-tiger, is a tiger, not a dog.
It knows that if a nomad may have dignity,
Gibraltar has had more—   10
that "it is better to be lonely than unhappy."
A conifer contrived in imitation of the glyptic work of jade and hard-stone
    cutters,
a true curio in this bypath of curio-collecting,
it is worth its weight in gold, but no one takes it
from these woods in which society's not knowing is colossal,   15
the lion's ferocious chrysanthemum head seeming kind by comparison.
This porcupine-quilled, complicated starkness—

[1] The tree, popularly called the monkey-puzzle tree, belongs to the species *Araucaria imbricata* and is also known as the Chile pine. Its large branches curl in on themselves.

[2] Moore quoted in an interview the injunction of the French novelist Gustave Flaubert (1821–1880): "Describe a tree so no other tree could be mistaken for it," an act she accomplishes in this poem. Flaubert, in his novel *Salammbô* (1863), describes in exact detail the ancient city of Carthage; thus "Flaubert's Carthage" refers to a meticulously descriptive system.

this is beauty—"a certain proportion in the skeleton which gives the best results."[3]

One is at a loss, however, to know why it should be here,
in this morose part of the earth—
to account for its origin at all;
but we prove, we do not explain our birth.

1935

T. S. Eliot
1888–1965

T. S. Eliot's *The Waste Land,* like Walt Whitman's "Song of Myself," changed the course of American literary history. Eliot's long poem, published in 1922, consolidated the despair felt throughtout Europe after World War I and thus spoke for the collapse of a whole culture. Its fragments of civilization seemed like the rubbish heap of history. But it was the exquisite musicality of the poem, its instantly memorable lines, that made it haunt the literary imagination.

The poet of *The Waste Land* was an expatriate American living in London. At the time he wrote the poem he had been driven, by fears of a permanent breakdown, to psychiatric treatment in Lausanne. There, in the midst of polyglot Switzerland, in the center of Europe, he looked inward to his own nervous collapse and outward to the fragmentation of Europe. But behind the European voices and landscapes of this famous poem lay an American story. In fact, Eliot had originally begun his poem with a scene in Boston's Scollay Square (the home of brothels and burlesque shows). In deleting his original opening scene and affixing instead an opening unmistakably European, Eliot turned his back on the New World and placed himself resolutely in the Old.

Eliot's family had come to the United States from England, and the pull back to family origins in East Coker, Somersetshire, is given its due in the second poem of his later sequence, *Four Quartets.* Eliot's own branch of the family had moved from Gloucester, Massachusetts, to St. Louis, where Eliot's grandfather founded Washington University in 1853. Eliot's father made money manufacturing bricks from Mississippi clay; it was Eliot's mother (author of a long verse-drama on Savonarola, which her son paid to have published) who sponsored the literary education of the poet. Eliot was a brilliantly successful student at Harvard (1906–1910 as an undergraduate studying literature, 1911–1914 as a graduate student in Sanskrit and philosophy). Though he completed a Ph.D. dissertation on the work of the skeptical idealist philosopher F. H. Bradley, Eliot

---

[3] Moore's note for this quotation, the only one in the poem for which she cites a source, is: "Lafcadio Hearn, *Talks to Writers* (Dodd, Mead)." Moore often put into quotation marks remarks by others, which she had noted in her "conversation notebooks." The quoted

fragments in this poem may be remarks of this kind made perhaps by her mother, with whom she lived. Lafcadio Hearn (1850–1904) was a naturalized American citizen, born in Greece, famous for his travel books.

never took the degree. He was studying at Oxford when World War I broke out; by the time it ended, when he could have returned to America to defend the dissertation, he had married and had chosen poetry over the academic life.

The marriage was unhappy from the beginning. Eliot's wife, Vivien Haigh-Wood, was constantly ill with an assortment of maladies, in part psychosomatic but nonetheless agonizing. Eliot's father, disapproving of the marriage, changed his will and died leaving Eliot only the income, not the capital, from his share of the estate. It was after his father's death, the punishment of the will, and a London visit by his mother and sister that Eliot experienced the breakdown preceding the composition of *The Waste Land*.

With the recovery of his health, a change of job from banking to publishing (at Faber & Faber), and the publication of *The Waste Land* in *The Criterion* (a journal that he edited), Eliot's life found renewed stability. In 1932 he obtained a legal separation from his wife, whose condition had considerably worsened and who eventually died in a mental hospital in 1947. After World War II, Eliot lived for over ten years in London with John Hayward, a bibliophile, editor, and reviewer who was confined to a wheelchair by muscular dystrophy. In 1957, at age sixty-eight, Eliot married Valerie Fletcher, for many years his secretary at Faber.

Eliot's sensibility sometimes seems, to use Ezra Pound's term, a "vortex" into which the whole of modern culture was absorbed. Even as an undergraduate, Eliot adopted the irony and *ennui* of the French poets Charles Baudelaire and Jules Laforgue, whom he had discovered through Arthur Symons's influential book, *The Symbolist Movement in Literature*. In "The Love Song of J. Alfred Prufrock" the French influence is brilliantly crossed with a Tennysonian music and a Browningesque dramatic monologue. Eliot's surrealism, combining the etherized patient, the catlike fog, the butt-ends of days, and the impaled Prufrock wriggling on the wall, was something altogether new in American poetry, far from the inert Imagism of Amy Lowell and equally far from the pieties of the nineteenth-century "fireside poets."

Prufrock and Other Observations (1917) is, like Wallace Stevens's *Harmonium* (1923) and Marianne Moore's *Observations* (1924), one of the landmarks of American modernism. It was followed rapidly by *Gerontion* (1919), *Poems* (1920), and *Poems 1909–1925*, which contained *The Waste Land*. These books remain Eliot's chief poetic achievement. In them we see Eliot's most striking lyric invention, a play of voices deployed almost as instruments in an orchestra, as he drew into lyric the vocal theatricality he had found in Elizabethan and Jacobean drama. Eliot's original title for *The Waste Land* had been "He do the police in different voices," a quotation from Dickens's *Our Mutual Friend*, describing a character who would read aloud newspaper accounts of police-blotter business, giving all the characters different dramatic voicings. Escaping from "personality" (the lyric self of the conventional lyric speaker), Eliot found freedom in multiplying his poetic voices, both in *The Waste Land* and in his later plays.

At the same time, Eliot was becoming the most brilliant literary critic in English since Coleridge. As assistant editor of *The Egoist* from 1917 to 1919 and editor of *The Criterion* for seventeen years (1922–1939), he wrote the essays collected in *The Sacred Wood* (1920), *Homage to Dryden* (1924), and *For Lancelot*

Andrewes (1928). Eliot's essays took up polemical positions in the service of his own theory of poetry, projecting his own "dissociation of sensibility" back into the post-metaphysical poets, defending the macabre extremes of tension in the Jacobeans, and (after his conversion to Anglicanism in 1927) arguing for the glories of Anglican literature (Lancelot Andrewes, George Herbert). Eliot's most influential essay, "Tradition and the Individual Talent," published in *The Sacred Wood,* repudiates both the avant-garde conviction that modern poetry should break utterly from the past and the Wordsworthian definition of poetry as "emotion recollected in tranquillity." It argues that the modern poet cannot succeed without a profound incorporation of the literature of the past. It argues as well that the poet is a medium, serving as a catalyst for new combinations of language, and that the poet must therefore escape from individual personality and emotion in composing poetry. In turning away from biographical and historical information and toward language and style in his essays on individual poets (Milton, Herbert), Eliot gave a new direction to the practice of literary criticism. The so-called New Criticism, advocated in England by I. A. Richards and in the United States by such followers of Eliot as Allen Tate and John Crowe Ransom, brought a new sophistication, after the manner of Eliot, to the analysis of poetry.

Eliot's valuing of complexity, irony, and paradox, his powerful sense of the unity of a literary work, and his conviction that the work provided an "objective correlative" for the state of mind of its creator pervaded his critical writing in the 1920s. In later essays Eliot's political views became increasingly conservative until, in 1934, in a book he later retracted, *After Strange Gods* (based on lectures given at the University of Virginia), he argued against the desirability of "any large number of free-thinking Jews" in any Christian society. Eliot, who remained in many ways a Victorian intellectual preoccupied with the dissolution of social consensus and Christian belief, was pained by the increasing democratization of society and the increasing secularism of education. Both of these, he thought, entailed the loss of the fabric of common culture he believed indispensable to literature and government alike.

Though Eliot was acquainted with the avant-garde English writers of Bloomsbury, he could not greet with any joy their enthusiasm for change, reflected in Virginia Woolf's statement that in 1910 the world had changed, had become modern. His own balance was too precarious to welcome any external disruptions. Eliot may have displayed a failure of nerve in being unable to embrace social change, but that change found no more sensitive seismographer than its horrified poet-witness.

Eliot's major work after *The Waste Land* was the sequence now known as *Four Quartets* ("Burnt Norton," "East Coker," "The Dry Salvages," and "Little Gidding"). The first was written in 1935, the others during World War II; they were published together in the United States in 1943. They should be read, in part, as war poems, as well as poems having a relation, as Eliot said, to "the four seasons and the four elements." In wartime, Eliot's confidence in the value of writing was momentarily shaken: "It is hard . . . to feel confident that morning after morning spent fiddling with words and rhythms is justified activity— especially as there is never any certainty that the whole thing won't have to be scrapped."

Yet Eliot's career as a writer continued, not only in the autobiographical and historical accounts of temporal mutability in the *Quartets* but also in a series of plays. He had earlier composed *Sweeney Agonistes* (1926–1927), a brilliant adaptation of vaudeville rhythms; *Murder in the Cathedral* (1935), a dramatization of the temptation of Thomas à Becket; and *The Family Reunion* (1939), a play about marital guilt. After the *Quartets*, Eliot wrote more plays—*The Cocktail Party* (1949), which introduced a psychiatrist into a drama of Christian expiation of guilt; *The Confidential Clerk* (1953); and *The Elder Statesman* (1959). Only the first of these succeeded on the stage.

In 1948 Eliot was awarded the Nobel Prize for literature. His reputation fluctuated even during his lifetime, and it will require the publication of manuscripts, letters, and other such documents before a full history of his significance and influence can be written. He is indubitably the greatest writer of modern free verse in America and the greatest of our literary critics, a man whose taste set the taste of his era. Eliot's conviction that he was witnessing the death of culture, conveyed most powerfully in his myths of historical decline, gripped his first auditors. More skeptical readers may believe his later ironic statement that *The Waste Land* represented merely "a personal grudge," a catastrophe of the inner life rather than of the life of civilization. Those readers will see it as one of the great lyrics of a crisis in consciousness, an American long poem to be ranked with Milton's "Lycidas" and Wordsworth's "Ode: On the Intimations of Immortality" as a comprehensive account of the human predicament.

Further Reading:
F. R. Leavis, *New Bearings in English Poetry*, 1932.
F. O. Matthiessen, *The Achievement of T. S. Eliot*, 1935, 1947.
T. S. Eliot: A Selected Critique, ed. L. Unger, 1948.
E. Drew, *T. S. Eliot: The Design of His Poetry*, 1949.
H. Gardner, *The Art of T. S. Eliot*, 1949.
D. E. S. Maxwell, *The Poetry of T. S. Eliot*, 1952.
G. Williamson, *A Reader's Guide to T. S. Eliot*, 1953.
G. Smith, *T. S. Eliot's Poetry and Plays*, 1956.
H. Kenner, *The Invisible Poet: T. S. Eliot*, 1959.
D. E. Jones, *The Plays of T. S. Eliot*, 1960.
K. Smidt, *Poetry and Belief in the Work of T. S. Eliot*, 1961.
A. G. George, *T. S. Eliot: His Mind and Art*, 1962.
P. R. Headings, *T. S. Eliot*, 1964.
H. Howarth, *Notes of Some Figures Behind T. S. Eliot*, 1964.
L. Unger, *T. S. Eliot: Monuments and Patterns*, 1966.
H. Blamires, *Word Unheard: A Guide Through Eliot's Four Quartets*, 1969.
A. Austin, *T. S. Eliot: The Literary and Social Criticism*, 1971.
B. Bergonzi, *T. S. Eliot*, 1971.
G. Patterson, *T. S. Eliot: Poems in the Making*, 1971.
R. Sencourt, *T. S. Eliot: A Memoir*, 1971.
R. Kirk, *Eliot and His Age*, 1972.
R. Kojecky, *T. S. Eliot's Social Criticism*, 1972.
J. D. Margolis, *T. S. Eliot's Intellectual Development*, 1972.
B. Rajan, *The Overwhelming Question: A Study of the Poetry of T. S. Eliot*, 1976.
S. Spender, *T. S. Eliot*, 1976.
D. Traversi, *T. S. Eliot: The Longer Poems*, 1976.
H. Gardner, *The Composition of the "Four Quartets,"* 1977.
L. Gordon, *Eliot's Early Years*, 1977.
J. E. Miller, *T. S. Eliot's Personal Waste Land*, 1977.
The Literary Criticism of T. S. Eliot: New Essays, ed. D. Newton-DeMolina, 1977.
N. Frye, *T. S. Eliot*, 1981.
C. Behr, *T. S. Eliot: A Chronology of His Life and Works*, 1982.
E. K. Hay, *T. S. Eliot's Negative Way*, 1982.
R. Bush, *T. S. Eliot: A Study in Character and Style*, 1983.

Texts:
"Death of St. Narcissus" from *Poems Written in Early Youth*, 1967.

Remaining selections from *Complete Poems and Plays*, 1962.

The Death of Saint Narcissus[1]

Come under the shadow of this gray rock—
Come in under the shadow of this gray rock,
And I will show you something different from either
Your shadow sprawling over the sand at daybreak, or
Your shadow leaping behind the fire against the red rock: 5
I will show you his bloody cloth and limbs
And the gray shadow on his lips.

He walked once between the sea and the high cliffs
When the wind made him aware of his limbs smoothly passing each other
And of his arms crossed over his breast.   10
When he walked over the meadows
He was stifled and soothed by his own rhythm.
By the river
His eyes were aware of the pointed corners of his eyes
And his hands aware of the pointed tips of his fingers.   15

Struck down by such knowledge
He could not live men's ways, but became a dancer before God.
If he walked in city streets
He seemed to tread on faces, convulsive thighs and knees.
So he came out under the rock.   20

First he was sure that he had been a tree,[2]
Twisting its branches among each other.
And tangling its roots among each other.

Then he knew that he had been a fish
With slippery white belly held tight in his own fingers,   25
Writhing in his own clutch, his ancient beauty
Caught fast in the pink tips of his new beauty.

Then he had been a young girl
Caught in the woods by a drunken old man
Knowing at the end the taste of his own whiteness,   30
The horror of his own smoothness,
And he felt drunken and old.

---

[1] The title represents a conflation of the mythological Narcissus—who fell in love with his own image in a pool and is consequently the symbol of autoeroticism—and Saint Sebastian, a Christian who was martyred by being shot through with arrows. The death of Saint Sebastian was a favorite subject in the Renaissance for painters wishing to depict the male nude.

[2] The doctrine of the transmigration of the soul here shows the soul rising in the evolutionary scale as it passes from one body to another.

So he became a dancer to God.
Because his flesh was in love with the burning arrows
He danced on the hot sand
Until the arrows came.   35
As he embraced them his white skin surrendered itself to the redness of
    blood, and satisfied him.
Now he is green, dry and stained
With the shadow in his mouth.

1967

The Love Song of J. Alfred Prufrock

S'io credesse che mia risposta fosse
A persona che mai tornasse al mondo,
Questa fiamma staria senza piu scosse.
Ma perciocche giammai di questo fondo
Non torno vivo alcun, s'i'odo il vero,
Senza tema d'infamia it rispondo.[1]

Let us go then, you and I,
When the evening is spread out against the sky
Like a patient etherised upon a table;
Let us go, through certain half-deserted streets,
The muttering retreats   5
Of restless nights in one-night cheap hotels
And sawdust restaurants with oyster-shells:
Streets that follow like a tedious argument
Of insidious intent
To lead you to an overwhelming question. . .   10
Oh, do not ask, "What is it?"
Let us go and make our visit.

In the room the women come and go
Talking of Michelangelo.

The yellow fog that rubs its back upon the window-panes,   15
The yellow smoke that rubs its muzzle on the window-panes,
Licked its tongue into the corners of the evening,

[1] From Dante's *Inferno*, XXVII, 61–66. Guido da Montefeltro speaks, after Dante questions him: "If I thought that my reply were to be to someone who would ever return to the world, this flame would be still, without further motion. But since no one has ever returned alive from this depth, if what I hear is true, I answer you without fear of shame." In the poem, Prufrock speaks, similarly, an inner truth to an unnamed "you."

Lingered upon the pools that stand in drains,
Let fall upon its back the soot that falls from chimneys,
Slipped by the terrace, made a sudden leap,
And seeing that it was a soft October night,
Curled once about the house, and fell asleep.

    And indeed there will be time
For the yellow smoke that slides along the street,
Rubbing its back upon the window-panes;
There will be time, there will be time
To prepare a face to meet the faces that you meet;
There will be time to murder and create,
And time for all the works and days² of hands
That lift and drop a question on your plate;
Time for you and time for me,
And time yet for a hundred indecisions,
And for a hundred visions and revisions,
Before the taking of a toast and tea.

    In the room the women come and go
Talking of Michelangelo.

    And indeed there will be time
To wonder, "Do I dare?" and, "Do I dare?"
Time to turn back and descend the stair,
With a bald spot in the middle of my hair—
(They will say: "How his hair is growing thin!")
My morning coat, my collar mounting firmly to the chin,
My necktie rich and modest, but asserted by a simple pin—
(They will say: "But how his arms and legs are thin!")
Do I dare
Disturb the universe?
In a minute there is time
For decisions and revisions which a minute will reverse.

    For I have known them all already, known them all—
Have known the evenings, mornings, afternoons,
I have measured out my life with coffee spoons;
I know the voices dying with a dying fall
Beneath the music from a farther room.
    So how should I presume?

    And I have known the eyes already, known them all—
The eyes that fix you in a formulated phrase,
And when I am formulated, sprawling on a pin,

---

² The Greek poet Hesiod (eighth century B.C.)
wrote *Works and Days,* a georgic poem.

When I am pinned and wriggling on the wall,
Then how should I begin
To spit out all the butt-ends of my days and ways?   60
    And how should I presume?

    And I have known the arms already, known them all—
Arms that are braceleted and white and bare
(But in the lamplight, downed with light brown hair!)
Is it perfume from a dress   65
That makes me so digress?
Arms that lie along a table, or wrap about a shawl.
    And should I then presume?
    And how should I begin?
        . . . . .
    Shall I say, I have gone at dusk through narrow streets   70
And watched the smoke that rises from the pipes
Of lonely men in shirt-sleeves, leaning out of windows? . . .

    I should have been a pair of ragged claws
Scuttling across the floors of silent seas.
        . . . . .

    And the afternoon, the evening, sleeps so peacefully!   75
Smoothed by long fingers,
Asleep . . . tired . . . or it malingers,
Stretched on the floor, here beside you and me.
Should I, after tea and cakes and ices,
Have the strength to force the moment to its crisis?   80
But though I have wept and fasted, wept and prayed,
Though I have seen my head (grown slightly bald) brought in upon a platter,[3]
I am no prophet—and here's no great matter;
I have seen the moment of my greatness flicker,
And I have seen the eternal Footman hold my coat, and snicker,   85
And in short, I was afraid.

    And would it have been worth it, after all,
After the cups, the marmalade, the tea,
Among the porcelain, among some talk of you and me,
Would it have been worth while,   90
To have bitten off the matter with a smile,
To have squeezed the universe into a ball
To roll it toward some overwhelming question,
To say: "I am Lazarus, come from the dead,[4]
Come back to tell you all, I shall tell you all"—   95

---

[3] The head of John the Baptist was delivered on a platter to Salome (Matthew 14:1–11).

[4] Lazarus was raised from the dead by Jesus (John 11:1–44).

If one, settling a pillow by her head,
   Should say: "That is not what I meant at all.
   That is not it, at all."

   And would it have been worth it, after all,
Would it have been worth while,
After the sunsets and the dooryards and the sprinkled streets,
After the novels, after the teacups, after the skirts that trail along the floor—
And this, and so much more?—
It is impossible to say just what I mean!
But as if a magic lantern threw the nerves in patterns on a screen:
Would it have been worth while
If one, settling a pillow or throwing off a shawl,
And turning toward the window, should say:
   "That is not it at all,
   That is not what I meant, at all."
      . . . . .

No! I am not Prince Hamlet,[5] nor was meant to be;
Am an attendant lord, one that will do
To swell a progress,[6] start a scene or two,
Advise the prince; no doubt, an easy tool,
Deferential, glad to be of use,
Politic, cautious, and meticulous;
Full of high sentence,[7] but a bit obtuse;
At times, indeed, almost ridiculous—
Almost, at times, the Fool.

   I grow old . . . I grow old . . .
I shall wear the bottoms of my trousers rolled.

   Shall I part my hair behind? Do I dare to eat a peach?
I shall wear white flannel trousers, and walk upon the beach.
I have heard the mermaids singing, each to each.

I do not think that they will sing to me.

I have seen them riding seaward on the waves
Combing the white hair of the waves blown back
When the wind blows the water white and black.

We have lingered in the chambers of the sea
By sea-girls wreathed with seaweed red and brown
Till human voices wake us, and we drown.
1917

---

[5] I.e., Prufrock will be, not like Hamlet the hero, but rather like Polonius, a fussy court advisor.   [6] Royal procession.   [7] Sententiousness.

La Figlia Che Piange[1]

O quam te memorem virgo . . .[2]

Stand on the highest pavement of the stair—
Lean on a garden urn—
Weave, weave the sunlight in your hair—
Clasp your flowers to you with a pained surprise—
Fling them to the ground and turn   5
With a fugitive resentment in your eyes:
But weave, weave the sunlight in your hair.

So I would have had him leave,
So I would have had her stand and grieve,
So he would have left   10
As the soul leaves the body torn and bruised,
As the mind deserts the body it has used.
I should find
Some way incomparably light and deft,
Some way we both should understand,   15
Simple and faithless as a smile and shake of the hand.

She turned away, but with the autumn weather
Compelled my imagination many days,
Many days and many hours:
Her hair over her arms and her arms full of flowers.   20
And I wonder how they should have been together!
I should have lost a gesture and a pose.
Sometimes these cogitations still amaze
The troubled midnight and the noon's repose.

1917

Whispers of Immortality

Webster[1] was much possessed by death
And saw the skull beneath the skin;
And breastless creatures under ground
Leaned backward with a lipless grin.

---

[1] Italian: "The Weeping Girl."
[2] From Virgil's *Aeneid*, I, 327: "By what name
shall I call thee, O maiden?" This is Aeneas'
salutation to the huntress who is in fact his
mother, Venus.

[1] John Webster, English dramatist (1580?–1634)
and author of the play *The Duchess of Malfi* (ca.
1614).

Daffodil bulbs instead of balls   5
Stared from the sockets of the eyes!
He knew that thought clings round dead limbs
Tightening its lusts and luxuries.

Donne, I suppose, was such another
Who found no substitute for sense,   10
To seize and clutch and penetrate;
Expert beyond experience,

He knew the anguish of the marrow
The ague of the skeleton;
No contact possible to flesh   15
Allayed the fever of the bone.

. . . . .

Grishkin is nice: her Russian eye
Is underlined for emphasis;
Uncorseted, her friendly bust
Gives promise of pneumatic bliss.   20

The couched Brazilian jaguar
Compels the scampering marmoset
With subtle effluence of cat;
Grishkin has a maisonette;[2]

The sleek Brazilian jaguar   25
Does not in its arboreal gloom
Distil so rank a feline smell
As Grishkin in a drawing-room.

And even the Abstract Entities
Circumambulate her charm;   30
But our lot crawls between dry ribs
To keep our metaphysics warm.

1920

---

[2] Apartment with two stories.

Sweeney Among the Nightingales

ὤμοι, πέπληγμαι καιρίαν πληγὴν ἔσω.[1]

Apeneck Sweeney[2] spreads his knees
Letting his arms hang down to laugh,
The zebra stripes along his jaw
Swelling to maculate[3] giraffe.

The circles of the stormy moon   5
Slide westward toward the River Plate,[4]
Death and the Raven drift above
And Sweeney guards the hornèd gate.[5]

Gloomy Orion and the Dog[6]
Are veiled; and hushed the shrunken seas;   10
The person in the Spanish cape
Tries to sit on Sweeney's knees

Slips and pulls the table cloth
Overturns a coffee-cup,
Reorganized upon the floor   15
She yawns and draws a stocking up;

The silent man in mocha brown
Sprawls at the window-sill and gapes;
The waiter brings in oranges
Bananas figs and hothouse grapes;   20

The silent vertebrate in brown
Contracts and concentrates, withdraws;
Rachel *née* Rabinovitch
Tears at the grapes with murderous paws;

She and the lady in the cape   25
Are suspect, thought to be in league;
Therefore the man with heavy eyes
Declines the gambit, shows fatigue,

[1] "Alas, I am struck a mortal blow within,"
Agamemnon's cry as he is murdered by his wife
and her lover (Aeschylus, *Agamemnon*, l. 1343).
[2] Sweeney, with his apelike neck and gorillalike
arms, is Eliot's figure for brutish man.
[3] Spotted.

[4] In Argentina.
[5] In Hades, the gate through which true dreams
pass.
[6] The constellation Orion and the Dog Star,
Sirius.

Leaves the room and reappears
Outside the window, leaning in,   3
Branches of wistaria
Circumscribe a golden grin;

The host with someone indistinct
Converses at the door apart,
The nightingales are singing near   35
The Convent of the Sacred Heart,

And sang within the bloody wood
When Agamemnon cried aloud,
And let their liquid siftings fall
To stain the stiff dishonoured shroud.   40

1920

The Waste Land

The Waste Land was printed first in 1922 in *The Criterion* and *The Dial;* when it was expanded to book form later that year, Eliot added notes. "In the early poems," said Eliot at seventy-six in a *Paris Review* interview, "it was a question of . . . having more to say than one knew how to say. . . . In *The Waste Land,* I wasn't even bothering whether I understood what I was saying." In his thirties Eliot was perhaps writing under the compulsions of extreme marital unhappiness and self-disgust, yet his agile and retentive mind was not quite so unconscious as he later suggested.

The Waste Land is based on a few well-known literary and aesthetic sources, most of them myths manipulated so that they yield unhappy endings (the death of the vegetation god; the death of the father; shipwreck; the devastation of the land when its king, symbolically wounded in the thigh, is impotent). Eliot also found for his poem myths that already had unhappy endings: the destruction of Valhalla through human greed, dramatized by Wagner in *The Ring of the Nibelung;* the death of the cities that symbolize civilization (Jerusalem, Athens, Alexandria, Rome, London); and the death of cultures, like that of Renaissance England personified in Queen Elizabeth. These myths are for Eliot macrocosmic cultural versions of the death of personal love between man and wife and the death of generosity and freedom in the heart. *The Waste Land* sees history—both universal history and personal history—as unredeemable on its own terms.

Sexual malaise lies at the heart of *The Waste Land*. The neurasthenic upper-class couple driven mad by each other's presence are paired, in "A Game of Chess," with a squalid lower-class couple whose marriage is foundering because of bad teeth, abortion, and sexual infidelity. Girls at Margate are seduced and abandoned, just as Philomela was raped and tortured long ago; Tristan sees only a blank sea instead of Isolde; Ophelia goes mad after Hamlet's desertion. Sexual squalor appears in the joyless affair of the typist and the "young man carbuncular," in Sweeney's vulgar conjunction with Mrs. Porter, and in the unsavory offer of a homosexual weekend by Mr. Eugenides. Women become surreal seducers surrounded by bats with baby faces. Salome, enraged by John the Baptist's persistence in speaking of Jesus from the cistern in which he is imprisoned, takes revenge for his rejection of her by ordering his execution.

The central figure in the poem, one who has "foresuffered all," is Tiresias, the prophet who had experienced sexuality as both man and woman. The androgynous voice of this "old man with wrinkled female breasts" mediates this poem, so full of loathing for the sexual principle.

The poem is also an elegy. It begins with the ritual of the burial of the dead, and at its nerve center we see the immemorial topic of elegy, the death of the beautiful young man, "Phlebas, who was once handsome and tall as you." (Eliot had dedicated *Prufrock and Other Observations* to the memory of Jean Verdenal, a young doctor he had known in Paris, who had drowned during World War I.) The elegiac subject is also multiple—the "so many" undone by death, the drowned Phoenician Sailor, the Hanged Man, the corpse planted in the garden, "the king my brother's wreck," and "the king my father's death before him."

Against the twin horrors of sexuality and death, Eliot sets certain luminous fragments of value—the young steersman's love song to his Irish love, Spenser's refrain in his betrothal song, Ophelia's poignant "goodnight" spoken in madness, the Rhinemaidens' ecstatic water song, the repentance of St. Augustine, the Buddha's fire sermon. He asserts also the consolatory powers of literature; he has shored fragments of literature as his only bulwark against his ruins. Seen in this way, the poem is an assemblage of what Matthew Arnold called "touchstones," those lines of literature that move us deeply and against which we test other lines for greatness. In these closing "touchstones," the poem reminds itself of the chant of salvation (sung by boy sopranos in Wagner's *Parsifal*), when the grail knight cures the impotent king and restores the land to fertility. It invokes a Dantesque purgation in the refining fire and recalls a sonnet in which the disinherited speaker ("El Desdichado") says that he is the inconsolable widower whose beloved has died, whose tower is ruined. It invokes ideas of madness and vengeance in its allusion to *The Spanish Tragedy*. In finding lines of poetry appropriate to his own disinherited and mad state, to his dead father's cruelty and his own sexual failure, Eliot condensed his wide and polyglot reading to "touchstones," ending with one line of sexual longing ("The swallow has its mate; when shall I be as the swallow?") and one line of ethical and religious Buddhist resignation ("Give. Sympathize. Control. Peace. Peace. Peace.").

This collage of literary fragments, this archaeological heap of literary ruins, is the mirror of Eliot's acute inspection of his own spiritual and literary predicament. How could he forge a new literature out of the ruins of European culture? The refusal here to end with a Christian solution marks only one resting place of Eliot's long mental and aesthetic journey. It is, however, deservedly, the most famous pause in his career. In spite of its initial difficulty, *The Waste Land* has rapidly become domesticated in our literature, its combination of the ferociously colloquial and a stylized exaltation of diction setting a new level of literary daring.

The manuscript of *The Waste Land* was edited by Ezra Pound into its present form, gaining him Eliot's grateful dedication as "the better craftsman." But it should not be forgotten that Eliot could have edited it himself—as he did previous and subsequent poems—and that its glories are his invention. Its music is so pervasive that long stretches resound in the mind long after the pages are closed. At a time of suicidal grief—the epigraph, after all, says "I want to die"— Eliot raised himself, in this one poem, to a fury of self-analysis and cultural polemic that remains unsurpassed in modern literature.

The Waste Land*

"Nam Sibyllam quidem Cumis ego ipse oculis meis vidi in ampulla pendere, et cum illi pueri dicerent: Σίβυλλα τί θέλεις; respondebat illa: ἀποθανεῖν θέλω."

For Ezra Pound
il miglior fabbro. [2]

I. The Burial of the Dead [3]

April is the cruellest month, breeding
Lilacs out of the dead land, mixing
Memory and desire, stirring
Dull roots with spring rain.
Winter kept us warm, covering   5
Earth in forgetful snow, feeding
A little life with dried tubers.
Summer surprised us, coming over the Starnbergersee[4]
With a shower of rain; we stopped in the colonnade,
And went on in sunlight, into the Hofgarten,[5]   10
And drank coffee, and talked for an hour.
Bin gar keine Russin, stamm' aus Litauen, echt deutsch.[6]
And when we were children, staying at the archduke's,
My cousin's, he took me out on a sled,

* Eliot's notes are printed after the text of the poem. His notes are referred to in parentheses in the footnotes that follow by an *E* followed by the section number of the poem in Roman numerals and the line number in Arabic, e.g., (E.,II,32).

[1] "For I myself saw with my own eyes the Cumaean Sibyl hanging in a bottle, and when the boys said to her, 'Sibyl, what do you want?,' she would reply, 'I want to die'" (Petronius, *Satyricon,* XLVIII). The Sibyl, in requesting longevity from Apollo, had forgotten to ask for perpetual youth and had therefore shriveled with age.

[2] "The better craftsman" (Dante, *Purgatorio,* XXVI, 117). Eliot's tribute to Pound, whose editorial help can be seen in the facsimile *Waste Land* (1971), which transcribes the original manuscript of the poem.
[3] Title of the funeral service in the Anglican *Book of Common Prayer.*
[4] Lake near Munich.
[5] Park in Munich.
[6] German: "I'm not Russian at all, I come from Lithuania, pure German."

And I was frightened. He said, Marie,   15
Marie, hold on tight. And down we went.
In the mountains, there you feel free.
I read, much of the night, and go south in the winter.

What are the roots that clutch, what branches grow
Out of this stony rubbish? Son of man,[7]   20
You cannot say, or guess, for you know only
A heap of broken images, where the sun beats,
And the dead tree gives no shelter, the cricket no relief,[8]
And the dry stone no sound of water. Only
There is shadow under this red rock,   25
(Come in under the shadow of this red rock),[9]
And I will show you something different from either
Your shadow at morning striding behind you
Or your shadow at evening rising to meet you;
I will show you fear in a handful of dust.[10]   30
  Frisch weht der Wind
  Der Heimat zu
  Mein Irisch Kind,
  Wo weilest du?[11]
"You gave me hyacinths first a year ago;   35
"They called me the hyacinth girl."
—Yet when we came back, late, from the Hyacinth garden,
Your arms full, and your hair wet, I could not
Speak, and my eyes failed, I was neither
Living nor dead, and I knew nothing,   40
Looking into the heart of light, the silence.
Oed' und leer das Meer.[12]

Madame Sosostris, famous clairvoyante,
Had a bad cold, nevertheless
Is known to be the wisest woman in Europe,   45
With a wicked pack of cards.[13] Here, said she,
Is your card, the drowned Phoenician Sailor,
(Those are pearls that were his eyes.[14] Look!)
Here is Belladonna, the Lady of the Rocks,
The lady of situations.   50

---

[7] God's address to the prophet Ezekiel (E.,I,20).
[8] "The grasshopper shall be a burden" in old age, when "desire shall fail," says the Preacher in Ecclesiastes (E.,I,23).
[9] Cf. Isaiah 32:1–2, where the coming of the Messiah will be "as the shadow of a great rock in a weary land."
[10] "Dust thou art, and unto dust thou shalt return," as in the funeral service.
[11] From Richard Wagner's opera *Tristan und Isolde*

(E.,I,34), the young steersman's lyric song: "The wind blows fresh / To the homeland / My Irish girl, / Where are you waiting?"
[12] "Empty and barren the sea" (E.,I, 42), Tristan's lament as he lies dying, thinking that he will die before Isolde arrives.
[13] Tarot cards, used to tell fortunes (E.,I,46).
[14] From Shakespeare's *The Tempest* (Act I, Sc. ii, l. 398); said of a drowned father.

Here is the man with three staves, and here the Wheel,
And here is the one-eyed merchant, and this card,
Which is blank, is something he carries on his back,
Which I am forbidden to see. I do not find
The Hanged Man. Fear death by water. 55
I see crowds of people, walking round in a ring.
Thank you. If you see dear Mrs. Equitone,
Tell her I bring the horoscope myself:
One must be so careful these days.

Unreal City, 60
Under the brown fog of a winter dawn,
A crowd flowed over London Bridge, so many,
I had not thought death had undone so many.[15]
Sighs, short and infrequent, were exhaled,
And each man fixed his eyes before his feet. 65
Flowed up the hill and down King William Street,
To where Saint Mary Woolnoth[16] kept the hours
With a dead sound on the final stroke of nine.
There I saw one I knew, and stopped him, crying: "Stetson!
"You who were with me in the ships at Mylae![17] 70
"That corpse you planted last year in your garden,
"Has it begun to sprout? Will it bloom this year?
"Or has the sudden frost disturbed its bed?
"Oh keep the Dog far hence, that's friend to men,
"Or with his nails he'll dig it up again![18] 75
"You! hypocrite lecteur!—mon semblable,—mon frère!"[19]

II. A Game of Chess[20]

The Chair she sat in, like a burnished throne,
Glowed on the marble,[21] where the glass
Held up by standards wrought with fruited vines
From which a golden Cupidon[22] peeped out 80
(Another hid his eyes behind his wing)
Doubled the flames of sevenbranched candelabra
Reflecting light upon the table as
The glitter of her jewels rose to meet it,

[15] Quoted from Dante's *Inferno* (E.,I,63).
[16] London church.
[17] Naval battle (260 B.C.) in which the Romans defeated the Carthaginians.
[18] An echo from the play *The White Devil* (1612) by John Webster. The original reads: "But keep the wolf far thence, that's foe to men, / For with his nails he'll dig them up again" (Act V, Sc. iv, ll. 97–98).
[19] Quote from Baudelaire's poem "Au Lecteur"("To the Reader"): "Hypocrite reader! —my double,—my brother!" (E.,I,76).
[20] Title of a play by Thomas Middleton (1627) about a marriage of convenience.
[21] Echo of a passage in Shakespeare's *Antony and Cleopatra* (Act II, Sc. ii, ll. 196–197), referring to Cleopatra's barge: "The barge she sat in, like a burnish'd throne, / Burn'd on the water."
[22] Statue of Cupid, god of love in Roman mythology.

From satin cases poured in rich profusion;
In vials of ivory and coloured glass
Unstoppered, lurked her strange synthetic perfumes,
Unguent, powdered, or liquid—troubled, confused
And drowned the sense in odours; stirred by the air
That freshened from the window, these ascended   90
In fattening the prolonged candle-flames,
Flung their smoke into the laquearia,[23]
Stirring the pattern on the coffered ceiling.
Huge sea-wood fed with copper
Burned green and orange, framed by the coloured stone,   95
In which sad light a carvèd dolphin swam.
Above the antique mantel was displayed
As though a window gave upon the sylvan scene[24]
The change of Philomel,[25] by the barbarous king
So rudely forced; yet there the nightingale   100
Filled all the desert with inviolable voice
And still she cried, and still the world pursues,
"Jug Jug"[26] to dirty ears.
And other withered stumps of time
Were told upon the walls; staring forms   105
Leaned out, leaning, hushing the room enclosed.
Footsteps shuffled on the stair.
Under the firelight, under the brush, her hair
Spread out in fiery points
Glowed into words, then would be savagely still.   110

    "My nerves are bad to-night. Yes, bad. Stay with me.
"Speak to me. Why do you never speak. Speak.
    "What are you thinking of? What thinking? What?
"I never know what you are thinking. Think."

    I think we are in rats' alley   115
Where the dead men lost their bones.

    "What is that noise?"
                        The wind under the door.
"What is that noise now? What is the wind doing?"
                        Nothing again nothing.   120
                                            "Do
"You know nothing? Do you see nothing? Do you remember
"Nothing?"

[23] Paneled ceiling as described in a passage in
Virgil's *Aeneid* telling of Dido's welcome of
Aeneas to Carthage. When Aeneas left her,
Dido committed suicide (E.,II,92).
[24] Allusion to the Garden of Eden in John
Milton's *Paradise Lost* (IV, 140).

[25] Ovid, in the *Metamorphoses,* retells the story of
the rape of Philomel by her brother-in-law
Tereus; he cut out her tongue, but the gods, in
compensation, turned her into a nightingale.
[26] Conventional Elizabethan rendering of the
nightingale's song.

I remember
Those are pearls that were his eyes.
"Are you alive, or not? Is there nothing in your head?"

But

O O O O that Shakespeherian Rag—
It's so elegant
So intelligent[27]   13
"What shall I do now? What shall I do?"
"I shall rush out as I am, and walk the street
"With my hair down, so. What shall we do to-morrow?
"What shall we ever do?"
                                    The hot water at ten.   13:
And if it rains, a closed car at four.
And we shall play a game of chess,
Pressing lidless eyes and waiting for a knock upon the door.

When Lil's husband got demobbed,[28] I said—
I didn't mince my words, I said to her myself,   140
HURRY UP PLEASE ITS TIME[29]
Now Albert's coming back, make yourself a bit smart.
He'll want to know what you done with that money he gave you
To get yourself some teeth. He did, I was there.
You have them all out, Lil, and get a nice set,   145
He said, I swear, I can't bear to look at you.
And no more can't I, I said, and think of poor Albert,
He's been in the army four years, he wants a good time,
And if you don't give it him, there's others will, I said.
Oh is there, she said. Something o' that, I said.   150
Then I'll know who to thank, she said, and give me a straight look.
HURRY UP PLEASE ITS TIME
If you don't like it you can get on with it, I said.
Others can pick and choose if you can't.
But if Albert makes off, it won't be for lack of telling.   155
You ought to be ashamed, I said, to look so antique.
(And her only thirty-one.)
I can't help it, she said, pulling a long face,
It's them pills I took, to bring it off,[30] she said.
(She's had five already, and nearly died of young George.)   160
The chemist[31] said it would be all right, but I've never been the same.
You are a proper fool, I said.
Well, if Albert won't leave you alone, there it is, I said,
What you get married for if you don't want children?
HURRY UP PLEASE ITS TIME   165

[27] Lines adapted from a popular song, "That Shakesperian Rag."
[28] Demobilized from the army (slang).
[29] English pubkeeper's announcement of closing time.
[30] I.e., to cause an abortion.
[31] In England: "pharmacist."

Well, that Sunday Albert was home, they had a hot gammon,[32]
And they asked me in to dinner, to get the beauty of it hot—
HURRY UP PLEASE ITS TIME
HURRY UP PLEASE ITS TIME
Goonight Bill. Goodnight Lou. Goonight May. Goonight.   170
Ta ta. Goonight. Goonight.
Good night, ladies, good night, sweet ladies, good night, good night.[33]

III. The Fire Sermon[34]

The river's tent is broken: the last fingers of leaf
Clutch and sink into the wet bank. The wind
Crosses the brown land, unheard. The nymphs are departed.   175
Sweet Thames, run softly, till I end my song.[35]
The river bears no empty bottles, sandwich papers,
Silk handkerchiefs, cardboard boxes, cigarette ends
Or other testimony of summer nights. The nymphs are departed.
And their friends, the loitering heirs of city directors;[36]   180
Departed, have left no addresses.
By the waters of Leman I sat down and wept . . .[37]
Sweet Thames, run softly till I end my song,
Sweet Thames, run softly, for I speak not loud or long.
But at my back in a cold blast I hear[38]   185
The rattle of the bones, and chuckle spread from ear to ear.
A rat crept softly through the vegetation
Dragging its slimy belly on the bank
While I was fishing in the dull canal
On a winter evening round behind the gashouse   190
Musing upon the king my brother's wreck
And on the king my father's death before him.[39]
White bodies naked on the low damp ground
And bones cast in a little low dry garret,
Rattled by the rat's foot only, year to year.   195
But at my back from time to time I hear
The sound of horns and motors, which shall bring

---

[32] Bacon.

[33] From Ophelia's mad speech, after Hamlet has repudiated her (Shakespeare's *Hamlet*, Act IV, Sc. ii, ll. 72–74).

[34] Title of a sermon by the Buddha, denouncing the fires of passion, hatred, and infatuation with which the senses burn (E.,III,308).

[35] From Edmund Spenser's "Prothalamion," a nuptial eulogy describing a wedding party on the river Thames, including nymphs and swans.

[36] The "city" is London's financial district.

[37] Echo of Psalm 137, lamenting the Jews' exile from Jerusalem: "By the rivers of Babylon, there we sat down, yea, we wept, when we remembered Zion." Eliot substitutes "Leman," the French name for Lake Geneva. (Eliot was hospitalized in Lausanne, Switzerland, while writing *The Waste Land*.)

[38] Adapted from "To His Coy Mistress" by Andrew Marvell (1621–1678): "But at my back I always hear / Time's wingèd chariot hurrying near."

[39] Adapted from Shakespeare's *Tempest* (Act I, Sc. ii, ll. 389–391), as Ferdinand laments his father's presumed death: "Sitting on a bank, / Weeping against the king my father's wreck, / This music crept by me upon the waters."

Sweeney to Mrs. Porter in the spring.[40]
O the moon shone bright on Mrs. Porter
And on her daughter
They wash their feet in soda water
Et O ces voix d'enfants, chantant dans la coupole![41]

   Twit twit twit
Jug jug jug jug jug jug
So rudely forc'd.
Tereu[42]

   Unreal City
Under the brown fog of a winter noon
Mr. Eugenides, the Smyrna[43] merchant
Unshaven, with a pocket full of currants
C.i.f. London:[44] documents at sight,
Asked me in demotic[45] French
To luncheon at the Cannon Street Hotel[46]
Followed by a weekend at the Metropole.

   At the violet hour, when the eyes and back   215
Turn upward from the desk, when the human engine waits
Like a taxi throbbing waiting,
I Tiresias, though blind, throbbing between two lives,[47]
Old man with wrinkled female breasts, can see
At the violet hour, the evening hour that strives   220
Homeward, and brings the sailor home from sea,[48]
The typist home at teatime, clears her breakfast, lights
Her stove, and lays out food in tins.
Out of the window perilously spread
Her drying combinations[49] touched by the sun's last rays,   225
On the divan are piled (at night her bed)
Stockings, slippers, camisoles, and stays.[50]

---

[40] Sweeney, as in Eliot's other poems, represents vulgar humanity. Mrs. Porter and her daughter appear in a bawdy song from World War I. The allusion (E.,III,197) is to a poem by John Day (1574–1640?) that mentions Actaeon's violation of the goddess Diana's privacy as he spied on her as she was bathing, an offense that was punished by death.

[41] French: "And O those treble voices, singing in the dome!" This is the closing line of the sonnet "Parsifal" by Paul Verlaine (1844–1896). In Wagner's opera *Parsifal,* the voices of boy sopranos are heard up high, from the wings, in the final affirmation of Parsifal's salvation once he has defeated the seductress Kundry, thereby preserving his sexual purity.

[42] A reprise of the nightingale's song and the story of Philomel and Tereus.

[43] Turkish port.

[44] "Carriage and insurance free" to London.

[45] Vulgar.

[46] Presumably, a homosexual assignation in a luxury hotel in Brighton.

[47] Tiresias, a blind prophet, had been transformed into a woman for seven years; when asked by the gods who had greater pleasure in sex, men or women, he answered that it was women (E.,III,218).

[48] The allusion is to Sappho's poem (CXLIX) on the evening star, which brings all things home that the morning had dispersed.

[49] Underwear.

[50] Corsets.

I Tiresias, old man with wrinkled dugs[51]
Perceived the scene, and foretold the rest—
I too awaited the expected guest.
He, the young man carbuncular,[52] arrives,　　　　　　　　　　230
A small house agent's clerk, with one bold stare,
One of the low on whom assurance sits
As a silk hat on a Bradford millionaire.[53]
The time is now propitious, as he guesses,
The meal is ended, she is bored and tired,　　　　　　　　　235
Endeavours to engage her in caresses
Which still are unreproved, if undesired.
Flushed and decided, he assaults at once;
Exploring hands encounter no defence;　　　　　　　　　　240
His vanity requires no response,
And makes a welcome of indifference.
(And I Tiresias have foresuffered all
Enacted on this same divan or bed;
I who have sat by Thebes below the wall　　　　　　　　　245
And walked among the lowest of the dead.)[54]
Bestows one final patronising kiss,
And gropes his way, finding the stairs unlit . . .

　　She turns and looks a moment in the glass,
Hardly aware of her departed lover;　　　　　　　　　　　250
Her brain allows one half-formed thought to pass:
"Well now that's done: and I'm glad it's over."
When lovely woman stoops to folly and
Paces about her room again, alone,
She smoothes her hair with automatic hand,　　　　　　　255
And puts a record on the gramophone.[55]

　　"This music crept by me upon the waters"
And along the Strand,[56] up Queen Victoria Street.
O City city, I can sometimes hear
Beside a public bar in Lower Thames Street,　　　　　　　260
The pleasant whining of a mandoline
And a clatter and a chatter from within
Where fishmen lounge at noon: where the walls
Of Magnus Martyr[57] hold
Inexplicable splendour of Ionian white and gold.　　　　265

---

[51] Breasts.
[52] I.e., suffering from acne.
[53] A *nouveau riche* industrialist from Bradford, Yorkshire.
[54] Tiresias lived in Thebes, and in the afterlife in Hades.
[55] Echo of *The Vicar of Wakefield* by Oliver Goldsmith (1728–1774), in which Olivia recalls

her seduction: "When lovely woman stoops to folly, / And finds too late that men betray, / What charm can soothe her melancholy? / What art can wash her guilt away?"
[56] London street.
[57] London church built by the famous architect Sir Christopher Wren (1632–1723) (E.,III,264).

The river sweats
Oil and tar
The barges drift
With the turning tide
Red sails
Wide
To leeward, swing on the heavy spar.
The barges wash
Drifting logs
Down Greenwich reach[58]
Past the Isle of Dogs.[59]
        Weialala leia
        Wallala leialala[60]

Elizabeth and Leicester[61]
Beating oars
The stern was formed
A gilded shell
Red and gold
The brisk swell
Rippled both shores
Southwest wind
Carried down stream
The peal of bells
White towers
        Weialala leia
        Wallala leialala

"Trams[62] and dusty trees.
Highbury bore me. Richmond and Kew
Undid me.[63] By Richmond I raised my knees
Supine on the floor of a narrow canoe."

"My feet are at Moorgate,[64] and my heart
Under my feet. After the event
He wept. He promised 'a new start.'
I made no comment. What should I resent?"

---

[58] Along the Thames River at Greenwich.
[59] Peninsula in the Thames opposite Greenwich where Queen Elizabeth I was born.
[60] From the song of the Rhinemaidens in Wagner's *Ring* cycle. These are the river nymphs who open the tetralogy and who repossess their Rhinegold at the end.
[61] Queen Elizabeth I and Robert Dudley, earl of Leicester. The account of their boat ride on the Thames (E.,III,279) is drawn from an incident, retold by the Spanish ambassador, in which Elizabeth and Leicester joked about their marrying. Of course no marriage took place.
[62] Streetcars.
[63] Highbury, Richmond, and Kew are areas near London. The passage rephrases Dante's "Siena bore me; Maremma undid me" (E.,III,64).
[64] Slum in East London.

"On Margate Sands.⁶⁵

I can connect

Nothing with nothing.

The broken fingernails of dirty hands.

My people humble people who expect

Nothing." 305

        la la

To Carthage then I came⁶⁶

    Burning burning burning burning⁶⁷

O Lord Thou pluckest me out⁶⁸

O Lord Thou pluckest 310

burning

IV. Death by Water⁶⁹

Phlebas the Phoenician, a fortnight dead,

Forgot the cry of gulls, and the deep sea swell

And the profit and loss.

                A current under sea 315

Picked his bones in whispers. As he rose and fell

He passed the stages of his age and youth

Entering the whirlpool.

              Gentile or Jew

O you who turn the wheel and look to windward, 320

Consider Phlebas, who was once handsome and tall as you.

V. What the Thunder Said⁷⁰

After the torchlight red on sweaty faces

After the frosty silence in the gardens

After the agony in stony places

The shouting and the crying 325

Prison and palace and reverberation

Of thunder of spring over distant mountains

He who was living is now dead⁷¹

We who were living are now dying

With a little patience 330

⁶⁵ Resort on the Thames estuary.
⁶⁶ From the *Confessions* of St. Augustine; in Carthage, Augustine continued his life of sexual sin (E.,III,309).
⁶⁷ From the Buddha's Fire Sermon.
⁶⁸ St. Augustine (*Confessions*) thanks God for having plucked him out of the life of sin.
⁶⁹ Eliot had dedicated his first volume of verse to the memory of his French friend Jean Verdenal,
who had drowned. (See Madame Sosostris's warning [I, 55].)
⁷⁰ The thunder is the voice of God in the Indian *Upanishads* (E.,V,402).
⁷¹ The opening of this section recalls Jesus' agony in the Garden of Gethsemane, his betrayal by Judas, his judging by Pontius Pilate in the palace, and his death.

Here is no water but only rock
Rock and no water and the sandy road
The road winding above among the mountains
Which are mountains of rock without water
If there were water we should stop and drink
Amongst the rock one cannot stop or think
Sweat is dry and feet are in the sand
If there were only water amongst the rock
Dead mountain mouth of carious[72] teeth that cannot spit
Here one can neither stand nor lie nor sit
There is not even silence in the mountains
But dry sterile thunder without rain
There is not even solitude in the mountains
But red sullen faces sneer and snarl
From doors of mudcracked houses
                 If there were water

   And no rock
   If there were rock
   And also water
   And water
   A spring
   A pool among the rock
   If there were the sound of water only
   Not the cicada
   And dry grass singing
   But sound of water over a rock
   Where the hermit-thrush sings in the pine trees
   Drip drop drip drop drop drop drop
   But there is no water

Who is the third who walks always beside you?[73]
When I count, there are only you and I together
But when I look ahead up the white road
There is always another one walking beside you
Gliding wrapt in a brown mantle, hooded
I do not know whether a man or a woman
—But who is that on the other side of you?

   What is that sound high in the air
Murmur of maternal lamentation
Who are those hooded hordes swarming
Over endless plains, stumbling in cracked earth
Ringed by the flat horizon only
What is the city over the mountains

300

305

340

345

350

355

360

365

370

---

[72] Decayed.
[73] Eliot suggests here the hallucinations of Antarctic explorers; he also recalls (E.,V, introductory note) Christ's accompanying, unrecognized, two disciples to Emmaus after his resurrection.

Cracks and reforms and bursts in the violet air
Falling towers
Jerusalem Athens Alexandria
Vienna London   375
Unreal

    A woman drew her long black hair out tight
And fiddled whisper music on those strings
And bats with baby faces in the violet light   380
Whistled, and beat their wings
And crawled head downward down a blackened wall
And upside down in air were towers
Tolling reminiscent bells, that kept the hours
And voices singing out of empty cisterns and exhausted wells.   385

    In this decayed hole among the mountains
In the faint moonlight, the grass is singing
Over the tumbled graves, about the chapel
There is the empty chapel,[74] only the wind's home.
It has no windows, and the door swings,   390
Dry bones can harm no one.
Only a cock stood on the rooftree
Co co rico co co rico
In a flash of lightning. Then a damp gust
Bringing rain   395

    Ganga[75] was sunken, and the limp leaves
Waited for rain, while the black clouds
Gathered far distant, over Himavant.[76]
The jungle crouched, humped in silence.
Then spoke the thunder   400
DA
Datta:[77] what have we given?
My friend, blood shaking my heart
The awful daring of a moment's surrender
Which an age of prudence can never retract   405
By this, and this only, we have existed
Which is not to be found in our obituaries
Or in memories draped by the beneficent spider
Or under seals broken by the lean solicitor
In our empty rooms   410
DA
Dayadhvam:[78] I have heard the key

---

[74] In Arthurian legend, the Chapel Perilous, where the Grail knights prayed before they set out to find the Holy Grail.
[75] The Ganges, India's sacred river.

[76] The Himalayas.
[77] Sanskrit for "give," the first word of the thunder in the Upanishads.
[78] Sanskrit: "sympathize."

Turn in the door once and turn once only
We think of the key, each in his prison
Thinking of the key, each confirms a prison
Only at nightfall, aethereal rumours
Revive for a moment a broken Coriolanus[79]
DA
Damyata:[80] The boat responded
Gaily, to the hand expert with sail and oar
The sea was calm, your heart would have responded
Gaily, when invited, beating obedient
To controlling hands

                                  I sat upon the shore
Fishing,[81] with the arid plain behind me
Shall I at least set my lands in order?[82]
London Bridge is falling down falling down falling down
Poi s'ascose nel foco che gli affina[83]
Quando fiam uti chelidon[84]—O swallow swallow
Le Prince d'Aquitaine à la tour abolie[85]
These fragments I have shored against my ruins
Why then Ile fit you. Hieronymo's mad againe.[86]
Datta. Dayadhvam. Damyata.
            Shantih shantih shantih[87]

1922

Notes on "The Waste Land"[88]

Not only the title, but the plan and a good deal of the incidental symbolism of the poem were suggested by Miss Jessie L. Weston's book on the Grail legend: *From Ritual to Romance* (Cambridge). Indeed, so deeply am I indebted, Miss Weston's book will elucidate the difficulties of the poem much better than my notes can do; and I

[79] Shakespeare's tragic hero who betrayed his own country and then betrayed the opposite camp.
[80] Sanskrit: "Control yourselves."
[81] Eliot's note refers to the Fisher King of the Grail legend (E.,V,425).
[82] Allusion to God's command in Isaiah 38:1: "Set thine house in order: for thou shalt die, and not live."
[83] In the *Purgatorio* (*Purgatory*) of Dante's *Divine Comedy,* the Provençal poet Arnaut Daniel implores Dante's regard: "Then he hid himself in the fire that refines them."
[84] "When will I be like the swallow" (and have a mate and be able to sing again)? From the late Latin poem *Pervigilium Veneris* (*The Vigil of Venus*), a love complaint (E.,V,429).
[85] French: "The prince of Aquitaine of the ruined tower." From the sonnet "El Desdichado" ("The Disinherited Son") by Gérard de Nerval (1808–1855). The passage reads: "I am the man

of shadows, the widower, unconsoled, / The prince of Aquitaine of the ruined tower, / My only star is dead, and my starry lute / Bears the black sun of melancholia."
[86] Lines from Elizabethan playwright Thomas Kyd's revenge play *The Spanish Tragedy.* "I'll suit your wish," says the bereaved father Hieronymo, agreeing to write a play by means of which, even though mad, he revenges himself for the murder of his son and then kills himself.
[87] Sanskrit: the formal ending of an Upanishad; equivalent, says Eliot, to "the peace which passeth understanding" (E.,v.,434).
[88] In its original appearance in journals in both England and America, The Waste Land had no notes. When it appeared as a separate publication, Eliot was asked to fill out the pages and added the notes.

recommend it (apart from the great interest of the book itself) to any who think such elucidation of the poem worth the trouble. To another work of anthropology I am indebted in general, one which has influenced our generation profoundly; I mean *The Golden Bough*;[89] I have used especially the two volumes *Adonis, Attis, Osiris*.[90] Anyone who is acquainted with these works will immediately recognise in the poem certain references to vegetation ceremonies.

I. The Burial of the Dead

Line 20. Cf. Ezekiel II, i.

    23. Cf. Ecclesiastes XII, v.

    31. V. Tristan und Isolde, I, verses 5–8.

    42. Id. III, verse 24.

    46. I am not familiar with the exact constitution of the Tarot pack of cards, from which I have obviously departed to suit my own convenience. The Hanged Man, a member of the traditional pack, fits my purpose in two ways: because he is associated in my mind with the Hanged God of Frazer, and because I associate him with the hooded figure in the passage of the disciples to Emmaus in Part V. The Phoenician Sailor and the Merchant appear later; also the "crowds of people," and Death by Water is executed in Part IV. The Man with Three Staves (an authentic member of the Tarot pack) I associate, quite arbitrarily, with the Fisher King himself.

    60. Cf. Baudelaire:

    "Fourmillante cité, cité pleine de rêves,

    "Où le spectre en plein jour raccroche le passant."[91]

    63. Cf. Inferno III, 55–57:

                                "si lunga tratta

    di gente, ch'io non avrei mai creduto

    che morte tanta n'avesse disfatta."[92]

    64. Cf. Inferno IV, 25–27:

    "Quivi, secondo che per ascoltare,

    "non avea pianto, ma' che di sospiri,

    "che l'aura eterna facevan tremare."[93]

    68. A phenomenon which I have often noticed.

    74. Cf. the Dirge in Webster's *White Devil*.

    76. V. Baudelaire, Preface to *Fleurs du Mal*.

II. A Game of Chess

    77. Cf. *Antony and Cleopatra*, II, ii, l. 190.

    92. Laquearia. V. *Aeneid*, I, 726:

---

[89] Sir James Frazer's compendium of myths and religions (1890).

[90] Vegetation gods who die and are reborn.

[91] From "Les Sept Vieillards" ("The Seven Old Men") of Charles Baudelaire (1821–1867): "Swarming city, city of dreams, / Where in broad daylight a ghost accosts the passerby."

[92] Dante: "such a long train / of people, that I would never have believed / that death had undone so many."

[93] Dante: "Here, as far as hearing could ascertain, / was no complaint, except for sighs, / that made the eternal air tremble."

dependent lychni laquearibus aureis incensi / et noctem flammis funalia vincunt.[94]

98. Sylvan scene. V. Milton, *Paradise Lost,* IV, 140.

99. V. Ovid, *Metamorphoses,* VI, Philomela.

100. Cf. Part III, l. 204.

115. Cf. Part III, l. 195.

118. Cf. Webster: "Is the wind in that door still?"[95]

126. Cf. Part I, l. 37, 48.

138. Cf. the game of chess in Middleton's *Women beware Women.*[96]

III. The Fire Sermon

176. V. Spenser, *Prothalamion.*

192. Cf. *The Tempest,* I, ii.

196. Cf. Marvell, *To His Coy Mistress.*

197. Cf. Day, *Parliament of Bees:*

"When of the sudden, listening, you shall hear,

"A noise of horns and hunting, which shall bring

"Actaeon to Diana in the spring,

"Where all shall see her naked skin . . ."

199. I do not know the origin of the ballad from which these lines are taken: it was reported to me from Sydney, Australia.

202. V. Verlaine, *Parsifal.*

210. The currants were quoted at a price "carriage and insurance free to London"; and the Bill of Lading etc. were to be handed to the buyer upon payment of the sight draft.

218. Tiresias, although a mere spectator and not indeed a "character," is yet the most important personage in the poem, uniting all the rest. Just as the one-eyed merchant, seller of currants, melts into the Phoenician Sailor, and the latter is not wholly distinct from Ferdinand Prince of Naples,[97] so all the women are one woman, and the two sexes meet in Tiresias. What Tiresias *sees,* in fact, is the substance of the poem. The whole passage from Ovid is of great anthropological interest:

. . . Cum Iunone iocos et 'maior vestra profecto est

Quam, quae contingit maribus,' dixisse, 'voluptas.'

Illa negat; placuit quae sit sententia docti

Quaerere Tiresiae: venus huic erat utraque nota.

Nam duo magnorum viridi coeuntia silva

Corpora serpentum baculi violaverat ictu

Deque viro factus, mirabile, femina septem

Egerat autumnos; octavo rursus eosdem

Vidit et 'est vestrae si tanta potentia plagae,'

Dixit 'ut auctoris sortem in contraria mutet,

[94] "Lighted lamps hang from the gold-paneled ceiling, and flaming torches vanquish the night."

[95] In John Webster's play *The Devil's Law-Case* (1623) this is said of a dying man, meaning "Is there still breath coming from his mouth?"

[96] In this play by Thomas Middleton (1657), a guardian plays a game of chess while her ward is seduced.

[97] In Shakespeare's *The Tempest.*

Nunc quoque vos feriam!' percussis anguibus isdem
Forma prior rediit genetivaque venit imago.
Arbiter hic igitur sumptus de lite iocosa
Dicta Iovis firmat; gravius Saturnia iusto
Nec pro materia fertur doluisse suique
Iudicis aeterna damnavit lumina nocte,
At pater omnipotens (neque enim licet inrita cuiquam
Facta dei fecisse deo) pro lumine adempto
Scire futura dedit poenamque levavit honore.[98]

221. This may not appear as exact as Sappho's lines, but I had in mind the "longshore" or "dory" fisherman, who returns at nightfall.

253. V. Goldsmith, the song in *The Vicar of Wakefield*.

257. V. *The Tempest*, as above.

264. The interior of St. Magnus Martyr is to my mind one of the finest among Wren's interiors. See *The Proposed Demolition of Nineteen City Churches*: (P. S. King & Son, Ltd.).

266. The Song of the (three) Thames-daughters begins here. From line 292 to 306 inclusive they speak in turn. V. *Götterdämmerung*, III, i: the Rhine-daughters.

279. V. Froude, *Elizabeth*, Vol. I, ch. iv, letter of De Quadra to Philip of Spain:

"In the afternoon we were in a barge, watching the games on the river. (The queen) was alone with Lord Robert and myself on the poop, when they began to talk nonsense, and went so far that Lord Robert at last said, as I was on the spot there was no reason why they should not be married if the queen pleased."

293. Cf. *Purgatorio*, V, 133:

"Ricorditi di me, che son la Pia;
"Siena mi fe', disfecemi Maremma."[99]

307. V. St. Augustine's *Confessions*: "to Carthage then I came, where a cauldron of unholy loves sang all about mine ears."

308. The complete text of the Buddha's Fire Sermon (which corresponds in importance to the Sermon on the Mount) from which these words are taken, will be found translated in the late Henry Clarke Warren's *Buddhism in Translation* (Harvard Oriental Series). Mr. Warren was one of the great pioneers of Buddhist studies in the Occident.

---

[98] The passage Eliot quotes is from Ovid's *Metamorphoses* II, 421–43: "Jove said jestingly to Juno: 'You wives have greater pleasure in love than husbands.' She denied it. It pleased them to ask the opinion of the learned Tiresias, who knew both sorts of love. For once, with a blow of his staff, he had separated two copulating snakes in the forest, and was miraculously changed instantly from a man into a woman, remaining so for seven years. In the eighth year he saw the same snakes again and said, 'If striking you is so powerful that it changes the sex of the one dealing the blow, then I will now strike you again.' As soon as he struck them, his former shape and masculine form were restored. As arbiter of the jesting quarrel, he supported Jove's opinion. Juno, disturbed by the decision, decreed that he should be condemned to eternal blindness. But the omnipotent god (since no god can undo what has been done by another god) gave him the power to know the future, with this honor redeeming his loss of sight."

[99] La Pia, born in Siena, was murdered by her husband in his castle at Maremma: "Remember me, who am La Pia; / Siena made me, Maremma undid me."

309. From St. Augustine's *Confessions* again. The collocation of these two representatives of eastern and western asceticism, as the culmination of this part of the poem,
is not an accident.

V. What the Thunder Said

In the first part of Part V three themes are employed: the journey to Emmaus, the
approach to the Chapel Perilous (see Miss Weston's book) and the present decay of
Eastern Europe.

357. This is *Turdus aonalaschkae pallasii*, the hermit-thrush which I have heard in
Quebec Province. Chapman says (*Handbook of Birds of Eastern North America*) "it is
most at home in secluded woodland and thickety retreats. . . . Its notes are not
remarkable for variety or volume, but in purity and sweetness of tone and exquisite
modulation they are unequalled." Its "water-dripping song" is justly celebrated.

360. The following lines were stimulated by the account of one of the Antarctic
expeditions (I forget which, but I think one of Shackleton's): it was related that the
party of explorers, at the extremity of their strength, had the constant delusion that
there was *one more member* than could actually be counted.

367–77. Cf. Hermann Hesse, *Blick ins Chaos:* "Schon ist halb Europa, schon ist
zumindest der halbe Osten Europas auf dem Wege zum Chaos, fährt betrunken im
heiligem Wahn am Abgrund entlang und singt dazu, singt betrunken und hymnisch
wie Dmitri Karamasoff sang. Ueber diese Lieder lacht der Bürger beleidigt, der
Heilige und Seher hört sie mit Tränen."[100]

402. "Datta, dayadhvam, damyata" (Give, sympathise, control). The fable of the
meaning of the Thunder is found in the *Brihadaranyaka—Upanishad*, 5, 1. A translation
is found in Deussen's *Sechzig Upanishads des Veda*, p. 489.

408. Cf. Webster, *The White Devil*, V, vi:

> ". . . they'll remarry
> Ere the worm pierce your winding-sheet, ere the spider
> Make a thin curtain for your epitaphs."

412. Cf. *Inferno*, XXXIII, 46:

> "ed io senti chiavar l'uscio di sotto
> all'orribile torre."[101]

Also F. H. Bradley, *Appearance and Reality*, p. 346.

"My external sensations are no less private to myself than are my thoughts or my
feelings. In either case my experience falls within my own circle, a circle closed on
the outside; and, with all its elements alike, every sphere is opaque to the others which
surround it. . . . In brief, regarded as an existence which appears in a soul, the whole
world for each is peculiar and private to that soul."

425. V. Weston: *From Ritual to Romance;* chapter on the Fisher King.

428. V. *Purgatorio*, XXVI, 148.

[100] "Already half of Europe, already at least half of
Eastern Europe, is on the way to chaos,
traveling drunken in a sort of holy ecstasy,
headlong toward the abyss, singing the while,
singing drunken hymns, as Dmitri Karamazov
sang. The offended bourgeois laughs at these
songs; the saint and the seer hear them with
tears."

[101] Ugolino was imprisoned with his children, and
they starved to death: "And I heard the key
turn below in the door / of the horrible
tower."

" 'Ara vos prec per aquella valor
  'que vos guida al som de l'escalina,
  'sovegna vos a temps de ma dolor.'
  Poi s'ascose nel foco che gli affina."[102]

429. V. *Pervigilium Veneris.* Cf. Philomela in Parts II and III.

430. V. Gérard de Nerval, Sonnet *El Desdichado.*

432. V. Kyd's *Spanish Tragedy.*

434. Shantih. Repeated as here, a formal ending to an Upanishad. "The peace which passeth understanding" is our equivalent to this word.

1922

---

from Four Quartets

Burnt Norton[*]

τοῦ λόγου δ'ἐόντος ξυνοῦ ζώουσιν οἱ πολλοί
ὡς ἰδίαν ἔχοντες φρόνησιν.
                            I. p. 77. Fr. 2.
ὁδὸς ἄνω κάτω μία καὶ ωὐτή.
                            I. p. 89. Fr. 60.
Diels: Die Fragmente der Vorsokratiker [*Herakleitos*].[1]

I

Time present and time past
Are both perhaps present in time future,
And time future contained in time past.
If all time is eternally present
All time is unredeemable.   5
What might have been is an abstraction
Remaining a perpetual possibility
Only in a world of speculation.
What might have been and what has been
Point to one end, which is always present.   10
Footfalls echo in the memory
Down the passage which we did not take
Towards the door we never opened

[102] The speaker is the troubadour poet Arnaut Daniel: " 'I pray you now, by the goodness / that guides you to the top of the staircase, / remember my suffering in due time.' / Then he hid himself in the fire that refines them."

[*] The poem is the first of Eliot's "Four Quartets," the other three being "East Coker," "The Dry Salvages," and "Little Gidding." Burnt Norton was a country house in Gloucestershire, visited by Eliot in 1934.

[1] Both epigraphs, quoted from Diels's *Fragments of the Presocratics,* are from the Greek philosopher Heraclitus (sixth century B.C.), who believed the whole world to be constantly in flux: "Although the Word, the Logos, is universal, most people live as though they had their own special rules." "The way up and the way down are one and the same."

Into the rose-garden. My words echo
Thus, in your mind.
                    But to what purpose   15
Disturbing the dust on a bowl of rose-leaves
I do not know.
                    Other echoes
Inhabit the garden. Shall we follow?
Quick, said the bird, find them, find them,
Round the corner. Through the first gate,   20
Into our first world, shall we follow
The deception of the thrush? Into our first world.
There they were, dignified, invisible,
Moving without pressure, over the dead leaves,
In the autumn heat, through the vibrant air,   25
And the bird called, in response to
The unheard music hidden in the shrubbery,
And the unseen eyebeam crossed, for the roses
Had the look of flowers that are looked at.
There they were as our guests, accepted and accepting.   30
So we moved, and they, in a formal pattern,
Along the empty alley, into the box circle,
To look down into the drained pool.
Dry the pool, dry concrete, brown edged,
And the pool was filled with water out of sunlight,   35
And the lotos rose, quietly, quietly,
The surface glittered out of heart of light,
And they were behind us, reflected in the pool.
Then a cloud passed, and the pool was empty.
Go, said the bird, for the leaves were full of children,   40
Hidden excitedly, containing laughter.
Go, go, go, said the bird: human kind
Cannot bear very much reality.
Time past and time future
What might have been and what has been   45
Point to one end, which is always present.

II

Garlic and sapphires in the mud
Clot the bedded axle-tree.[2]
The trilling wire in the blood
Sings below inveterate scars   50
And reconciles forgotten wars.
The dance along the artery
The circulation of the lymph

---

[2] The axle on which the world turns.

Are figured in the drift of stars
Ascend to summer in the tree
We move above the moving tree
In light upon the figured leaf
And hear upon the sodden floor
Below, the boarhound and the boar
Pursue their pattern as before   60
But reconciled among the stars.

    At the still point of the turning world. Neither flesh nor fleshless;
Neither from nor towards; at the still point, there the dance is,
But neither arrest nor movement. And do not call it fixity,
Where past and future are gathered. Neither movement from nor towards,   65
Neither ascent nor decline. Except for the point, the still point,
There would be no dance, and there is only the dance.
I can only say, *there* we have been: but I cannot say where.
And I cannot say, how long, for that is to place it in time.

    The inner freedom from the practical desire,   70
The release from action and suffering, release from the inner
And the outer compulsion, yet surrounded
By a grace of sense, a white light still and moving,
Erhebung,[3] without motion, concentration
Without elimination, both a new world   75
And the old made explicit, understood
In the completion of its partial ecstasy,
The resolution of its partial horror.
Yet the enchainment of past and future
Woven in the weakness of the changing body,   80
Protects mankind from heaven and damnation
Which flesh cannot endure.
                        Time past and time future
Allow but a little consciousness.
To be conscious is not to be in time
But only in time can the moment in the rose-garden,   85
The moment in the arbour where the rain beat,
The moment in the draughty church at smokefall
Be remembered; involved with past and future.
Only through time time is conquered.

III

Here is a place of disaffection   90
Time before and time after
In a dim light: neither daylight

---

[3] German: "exaltation."

Investing form with lucid stillness
Turning shadow into transient beauty
With slow rotation suggesting permanence   95
Nor darkness to purify the soul
Emptying the sensual with deprivation
Cleansing affection from the temporal.
Neither plenitude nor vacancy. Only a flicker
Over the strained time-ridden faces   10
Distracted from distraction by distraction
Filled with fancies and empty of meaning
Tumid apathy with no concentration
Men and bits of paper, whirled by the cold wind
That blows before and after time,   105
Wind in and out of unwholesome lungs
Time before and time after.
Eructation[4] of unhealthy souls
Into the faded air, the torpid
Driven on the wind that sweeps the gloomy hills of London, 110
Hampstead and Clerkenwell, Campden and Putney,
Highgate, Primrose and Ludgate. Not here
Not here the darkness, in this twittering world.

    Descend lower, descend only
Into the world of perpetual solitude,   115
World not world, but that which is not world,
Internal darkness, deprivation
And destitution of all property,
Desiccation of the world of sense,
Evacuation of the world of fancy,   120
Inoperancy of the world of spirit;
This is the one way, and the other
Is the same, not in movement
But abstention from movement; while the world moves
In appetency, on its metalled ways   125
Of time past and time future.

IV

Time and the bell have buried the day,
The black cloud carries the sun away.
Will the sunflower turn to us, will the clematis
Stray down, bend to us; tendril and spray   130
Clutch and cling?
Chill
Fingers of yew be curled

[4] Belching.

Down on us? After the kingfisher's wing
Has answered light to light, and is silent, the light is still   135
At the still point of the turning world.

V

Words move, music moves
Only in time; but that which is only living
Can only die. Words, after speech, reach
Into the silence. Only by the form, the pattern,   140
Can words or music reach
The stillness, as a Chinese jar still
Moves perpetually in its stillness.
Not the stillness of the violin, while the note lasts,
Not that only, but the co-existence,   145
Or say that the end precedes the beginning,
And the end and the beginning were always there
Before the beginning and after the end.
And all is always now. Words strain,
Crack and sometimes break, under the burden,   150
Under the tension, slip, slide, perish,
Decay with imprecision, will not stay in place,
Will not stay still. Shrieking voices
Scolding, mocking, or merely chattering,
Always assail them. The Word in the desert   155
Is most attacked by voices of temptation,⁵
The crying shadow in the funeral dance,
The loud lament of the disconsolate chimera.

The detail of the pattern is movement,
As in the figure of the ten stairs.⁶   160
Desire itself is movement
Not in itself desirable;
Love is itself unmoving,
Only the cause and end of movement,
Timeless, and undesiring   165
Except in the aspect of time
Caught in the form of limitation
Between un-being and being.
Sudden in a shaft of sunlight
Even while the dust moves   170
There rises the hidden laughter

---

⁵ Reference to Satan's temptation of Jesus in the desert (Luke 4:1–12).
⁶ The stairway to perfection, a Christian concept derived from the ladder on which Jacob saw angels ascending to and descending from heaven. St. John of the Cross said that the soul ascends to God by way of "the Ten Degrees of the Mystical Ladder of Divine Love."

Of children in the foliage
Quick now, here, now, always—
Ridiculous the waste sad time
Stretching before and after.
1936

John Crowe Ransom
1888–1974

John Crowe Ransom, the best southern poet of his generation, combined faultless irony with a faultless civility and tenderness, achieving a tone quite unlike that of any other poet, a tone as far as possible from the dryly angular metaphysical poetry of another southern poet and critic, Allen Tate. Ransom was a poet of line rather than of color. Though he, like Tate, was influenced as an adult reader by the English seventeenth-century poets, he also received the literary past indirectly through the southern culture into which he was born.

The son of a Methodist minister in Tennessee, Ransom studied Latin and Greek at Vanderbilt before going on to Oxford as a Rhodes scholar. After military service between 1917 and 1919, he returned to teach at Vanderbilt for almost twenty years. In 1937 he left Vanderbilt for Kenyon College in Ohio, where he founded *The Kenyon Review* in 1939. Ransom wrote most of his poetry between 1914 and 1927, roughly between the ages of twenty-five and forty. *Poems About God* (1919), *Chills and Fever* (1924), and *Two Gentlemen in Bonds* (1926) made his reputation as a poet, though in his *Selected Poems* (1945) he did not include any work from his first volume. Revised editions of the *Selected Poems* (1963, 1969) were awarded the Bollingen Prize and the National Book Award. In his later life, Ransom was known chiefly as the writer of the book *The New Criticism* (1941), which gave its name to a literary school. In that book, Ransom discussed the critical work of four eminent contemporary writers— I. A. Richards, T. S. Eliot, Yvor Winters, and William Empson—and suggested, in closing, that what was wanted for the modern age was "an ontological critic," one who would see the literary work as a part of "the world's body," a being rich in its own right, not one to be appropriated to abstract ideological ends. In his own writing about poetry, Ransom emphasized the "texture" of the literary artifact, its highly wrought fabric of language.

While Ransom was at Vanderbilt, he and a group that included Allen Tate and Robert Penn Warren became known as the Fugitives, after the name of their journal, a little magazine that ran for only nineteen issues over three years. The conservative political philosophy of the Fugitives, based on a wish to preserve the religious and economic status quo of the old South, consorted oddly with their avant-garde taste in poetry and critical theory.

Ransom, their chief theorist, knew from his own experience the work of making a poem, the delicate interrelations of its parts, the weaving of its motivations, its figures, and its rhetorical drama. As a poet, he objected to teachers' filling up time in class by discussing, for example, the Puritan revolution or Puritan theology in preference to, or to the exclusion of, any discussion of Milton's aesthetic work in making his epic poem. In arguing for pedagogical attention to the complexity of poetic texture and to the aesthetic achievement of the poem, Ransom wished to correct the philological, philosophical, and historical emphasis in American literary study. It was logical that such a corrective should come from the South, always the region in which belles lettres were best understood, while the Northeast had been formed in the theologically serious mode of Puritan reading.

Ransom's own poetry has all the delight in texture, all the irony and subtlety that one would expect from the mind that argued that attention should be paid to such matters. Though Ransom wrote in formal rhyming stanzas, his metric was accentual, based on the number of beats per line rather than on isometric feet. His tone is always at once light and grave, classical in its reserve but gracious in its tenderness. Ransom writes often about the conflict between body and spirit, about death, and about aspirations that end in defeat. He reflected on the nature of poetry in the New World: In a poem about Philomela, the grieving nightingale who stands symbolically for poetry, he asks despairingly about her status in America:

How could her delicate dirge run democratic,
Delivered in a cloudless boundless public place
To an inordinate race?

Ransom brought to American literature qualities we associate with classical poetry—urbanity, shapeliness, and equilibrium. In perceiving the distinct separateness of the civilization and literature of the South, Ransom helped preserve and continue our oldest American belletristic tradition. And by turning American academic minds to the ontological uniqueness of art, Ransom profoundly influenced the aesthetic development of a generation.

Further Reading:

J. L. Stewart, *John Crowe Ransom*, 1962.
K. F. Knight, *The Poetry of John Crowe Ransom*, 1964.
R. Buffington, *The Equilibrist: A Study of John Crowe Ransom's Poems 1916–1963*, 1967.
John Crowe Ransom: Critical Essays and a Bibliography, ed. N. H. Young, 1968.
T. H. Parsons, *John Crowe Ransom*, 1969.

J. E. Magner, Jr., *John Crowe Ransom: Critical Principles and Preoccupations*, 1971.
T. D. Young, ed., *John Crowe Ransom*, 1971.
J. L. Stewart, *John Crowe Ransom*, 1972.
M. Williams, *The Poetry of John Crowe Ransom*, 1972.
T. H. Young, *Gentleman in a Dustcoat: A Biography of John Crowe Ransom*, 1977.

Text:

Selected Poems, 1978.
See also The New Criticism, 1941.

Piazza Piece

—I am a gentleman in a dustcoat trying
To make you hear. Your ears are soft and small
And listen to an old man not at all,
They want the young men's whispering and sighing.
But see the roses on your trellis dying   5
And hear the spectral singing of the moon;
For I must have my lovely lady soon,
I am a gentleman in a dustcoat trying.

—I am a lady young in beauty waiting
Until my truelove comes, and then we kiss.   10
But what grey man among the vines is this
Whose words are dry and faint as in a dream?
Back from my trellis, Sir, before I scream!
I am a lady young in beauty waiting.

1927

Dead Boy

The little cousin is dead, by foul subtraction,
A green bough from Virginia's aged tree,
And none of the county kin like the transaction,
Nor some of the world of outer dark, like me.

A boy not beautiful, nor good, nor clever,   5
A black cloud full of storms too hot for keeping,
A sword beneath his mother's heart—yet never
Woman bewept her babe as this is weeping.

A pig with a pasty face, so I had said,
Squealing for cookies, kinned by poor pretense   10
With a noble house. But the little man quite dead,
I see the forbears' antique lineaments.

The elder men have strode by the box of death
To the wide flag porch, and muttering low send round

The bruit[1] of the day. O friendly waste of breath! 15
Their hearts are hurt with a deep dynastic wound.

He was pale and little, the foolish neighbors say;
The first-fruits, saith the Preacher, the Lord hath taken;
But this was the old tree's late branch wrenched away,
Grieving the sapless limbs, the shorn and shaken. 20
1927

The Equilibrists

Full of her long white arms and milky skin
He had a thousand times remembered sin.
Alone in the press of people traveled he,
Minding her jacinth, and myrrh, and ivory.

Mouth he remembered: the quaint orifice 5
From which came heat that flamed upon the kiss,
Till cold words came down spiral from the head,
Grey doves from the officious tower illsped.

Body: it was a white field ready for love,
On her body's field, with the gaunt tower above, 10
The lilies grew, beseeching him to take,
If he would pluck and wear them, bruise and break.

Eyes talking: Never mind the cruel words,
Embrace my flowers, but not embrace the swords.
But what they said, the doves came straightway flying 15
And unsaid: Honor, Honor, they came crying.

Importunate her doves. Too pure, too wise,
Clambering on his shoulder, saying, Arise,
Leave me now, and never let us meet,
Eternal distance now command thy feet. 20

Predicament indeed, which thus discovers
Honor among thieves, Honor between lovers.

[1] Rumor.

O such a little word is Honor, they feel!
But the grey word is between them cold as steel.

At length I saw these lovers fully were come   25
Into their torture of equilibrium;
Dreadfully had forsworn each other, and yet
They were bound each to each, and they did not forget.

And rigid as two painful stars, and twirled
About the clustered night their prison world,   30
They burned with fierce love always to come near,
But Honor beat them back and kept them clear.

Ah, the strict lovers, they are ruined now!
I cried in anger. But with puddled brow
Devising for those gibbeted and brave   35
Came I descanting: Man, what would you have?

For spin your period out, and draw your breath,
A kinder sæculum¹ begins with Death.
Would you ascend to Heaven and bodiless dwell?
Or take your bodies honorless to Hell?   40

In Heaven you have heard no marriage is,
No white flesh tinder to your lecheries,
Your male and female tissue sweetly shaped
Sublimed away, and furious blood escaped.

Great lovers lie in Hell, the stubborn ones   45
Infatuate of the flesh upon the bones;
Stuprate,² they rend each other when they kiss,
The pieces kiss again, no end to this.

But still I watched them spinning, orbited nice.
Their flames were not more radiant than their ice.   50
I dug in the quiet earth and wrought the tomb
And made these lines to memorize their doom:—

EPITAPH

Equilibrists lie here; stranger, tread light;
Close, but untouching in each other's sight;   55
Mouldered the lips and ashy the tall skull.
Let them lie perilous and beautiful.
1927

---

¹ World.   ² Violated.

E. E. Cummings
1894–1962

Cummings belongs to the part of the modernist movement that wanted to experiment with the visual appearance of the printed page. Both Guillaume Apollinaire and Stéphane Mallarmé in France had scattered typography over the page, and Cummings adopted their inventions (which would later engender "concrete poetry") to his own purposes. Numbers and letters fall like confetti down his pages, giving his *Collected Poems* the look of a volume printed by a tipsy typesetter. Cummings's typographical experiments arose in part from his visual gifts. He was a painter all his life, and his sophisticated and humorous paintings and drawings are still regularly shown in museums. But his experiments arose perhaps even more from his wish to upset the predictability of the printed page and the expectations of conventional readers.

Cummings was born in Cambridge, Massachusetts, the child of cultured parents. His father was a Congregational minister and professor at Harvard, but it was chiefly his mother, to whom Cummings was devoted all his life, who encouraged her son's writing. It seems likely that a good deal of Cummings's wish to shock stemmed originally from his repudiation of his father's way of life. For all Cummings's protestations of filial piety in "my father moved through dooms of love," he was irritated by his father's unremitting seriousness, so alien to his own volatile temperament; the role of *enfant terrible* was one Cummings never tired of playing.

Cummings's father taught English and social ethics at Harvard, and Cummings himself graduated from Harvard in 1915 and took an M.A. in literature there the following year. At Harvard, through knowledgeable friends like Scofield Thayer and Witter Bynner, Cummings discovered new art and music. At his Harvard graduation, having won the privilege of delivering one of the commencement "parts" (or speeches), Cummings praised cubist painting and Stravinsky's music. He knew such tastes were opposed by the majority of his teachers and fellow students. In his writing he continually pitted the values of what he scornfully called "mostpeople" against the bohemian tastes of the artist.

Cummings went off to France in 1917 as a volunteer ambulance driver for the Red Cross. Through his own unconventional behavior, he was suspected of being a spy and was detained, with his friend Slater Brown, for three months in a French internment camp. His father wrote letters to friends in Washington pleading for intervention on his son's behalf; through the influence of President Woodrow Wilson, Cummings was freed. He described his imprisonment in *The Enormous Room* (1922), the book that first brought him fame.

Cummings lived in France from 1921 to 1923, where he was exposed to a bohemian culture that he imitated when he finally settled, in 1924, in New York's Greenwich Village, where he spent the rest of his life writing and painting. His mother helped to support him until she died. Cummings married three times and had a daughter by his first wife, who concealed Cummings's paternity from the child because she had remarried and wished the child to believe that her second husband was the father. Cummings acknowledged his daughter when she was in her twenties, and they became affectionately attached to each other.

Cummings's first poems were published in *The Dial* in 1920. In his lifetime, his most frequently anthologized poems were those in which he was most sentimental. But his greatest gift was as a satirist. He could take the measure of literary falsity, patriotic cant, or intellectual humbug with a scathing phrase; he scorned conventional verbal and political pieties and conventional standards of behavior. He preached a neo-paganism of untroubled sexual pleasure, childlike egotism, and irrepressible impudence; a myth of spontaneity animated his aesthetic. Of course, the ingenuity visible in his poems about the grasshopper and the falling leaf demonstrates how unspontaneous such compositions actually are. An acrobat of words, Cummings scorned discursive logic and political strategy. If this world did not suit, "there's a hell / of a good universe next door; let's go." He establishes only two poles of thought, ignorance and belief; there is, to him, something suspect about the middle ground of learning, on the one hand, and skepticism, on the other.

In American literary history, Cummings ranks as a memorable documentary writer because of *The Enormous Room* and *Eimi* (1933), his account of travels in Russia after the rise of Stalin (whom he hated). Both books are vivid in rapidly noted sensory detail and irrepressibly energetic in style. Cummings's early poetry remains a body of inventive and ebullient work, raising provocative aesthetic questions. Is something that cannot be read aloud a poem? If so, what do we mean by the word *poem?* Can a poem incorporate slang, obscenity, advertising jargon, dialect? Is all language material for poetry? Must the line be the unit of the poem? Does the eye have as much right to the poem as the ear? Is the sonnet dead or can it be resuscitated? Can satiric lyrics be written in puritanical America? These questions are still relevant.

Cummings's wish to believe that all people are at heart alike in love and that all desires are simple ones led him into a conventional sentimentalizing of the erotic life. But his capacity for play in language and for vivid satire of America and its institutions ensures him a permanent place in American literature.

Further Reading:
C. Norman, *The Magic Maker, E. E. Cummings,* 1958.
N. Friedman, *E. E. Cummings: The Art of His Poetry,* 1960.
N. Friedman, *E. E. Cummings: The Growth of a Writer,* 1964.
B. A. Marks, *E. E. Cummings,* 1964.
R. E. Wegner, *The Poetry and Prose of E. E. Cummings,* 1965.
E. Triem, *E. E. Cummings,* 1969.
B. K. Dumas, *A Remembrance of Miracles,* 1974.
G. Lane, *I Am: A Study of E. E. Cummings' Poems,* 1976.
P. Lauter, *E. E. Cummings,* 1976.
R. Kidder, *E. E. Cummings: An Introduction to the Poetry,* 1979.
R. S. Kennedy, *Dreams in the Mirror: A Biography of E. E. Cummings,* 1980.
A Concordance to the Poems of E. E. Cummings, ed. K. McBride, 1982.

Text:
Complete Poems, 1972.
See also *Selected Letters of E. E. Cummings,* ed. F. W. Dupee and G. Stade, 1969.

[in Just-]

in Just-
spring   when the world is mud-
luscious the little
lame balloonman

whistles   far   and wee   5

and eddieandbill come
running from marbles and
piracies and it's
spring

when the world is puddle-wonderful   10

the queer
old balloonman whistles
far   and   wee
and bettyandisbel come dancing

from hop-scotch and jump-rope and   15
it's
spring
and
    the

            goat-footed[1]   20

balloonMan   whistles
far
and
wee

1923

[1] Characteristic of Pan, ancient Greek god of
woods and shepherds.

[the Cambridge ladies who live in furnished souls]

the Cambridge ladies who live in furnished souls
are unbeautiful and have comfortable minds
(also, with the church's protestant blessings
daughters, unscented shapeless spirited)
they believe in Christ and Longfellow,[1] both dead,   5
are invariably interested in so many things—
at the present writing one still finds
delighted fingers knitting for the is it Poles?
perhaps. While permanent faces coyly bandy
scandal of Mrs. N and Professor D   10
. . . . the Cambridge ladies do not care, above
Cambridge if sometimes in its box of
sky lavender and cornerless, the
moon rattles like a fragment of angry candy

1923

[mr youse needn't be so spry]

mr youse needn't be so spry
concernin questions arty

each has his tastes but as for i
i likes a certain party

gimme the he-man's solid bliss   5
for youse ideas i'll match youse

a pretty girl who naked is
is worth a million statues

1926

---

[1] Henry Wadsworth Longfellow (1807–1882),
Cambridge poet and Harvard professor.

[she being Brand]

she being Brand

-new; and you
know consequently a
little stiff i was
careful of her and(having   5

thoroughly oiled the universal
joint tested my gas felt of
her radiator made sure her springs were O.

K.)i went right to it flooded-the-carburetor cranked her

up,slipped the   10
clutch(and then somehow got into reverse she
kicked what
the hell)next
minute i was back in neutral tried and

again slo-wly; bare,ly nudg.   ing(my   15

lev-er Right-
oh and her gears being in
A 1 shape passed
from low through
second-in-to-high like   20
greasedlightning)just as we turned the corner of Divinity

avenue¹ i touched the accelerator and give

her the juice,good

            (it
was the first ride and believe i we was   25
happy to see how nice she acted right up to
the last minute coming back down by the Public
Gardens² i slammed on
the

¹ Street in Cambridge, Massachusetts, where the   ² Properly, the Public Garden, a park in Boston.
Harvard Divinity School is located.

internalexpanding
&
externalcontracting
brakes Bothatonce and
brought allofher tremB
-ling
to a: dead.

stand-
;Still)
1926

["next to of course god america i]

"next to of course god america i
love you land of the pilgrims' and so forth oh
say can you see by the dawn's early my
country 'tis of centuries come and go
and are no more what of it we should worry   5
in every language even deafanddumb
thy sons acclaim your glorious name by gorry
by jingo by gee by gosh by gum
why talk of beauty what could be more beautiful than these heroic happy dead   10
who rushed like lions to the roaring slaughter
they did not stop to think they died instead
then shall the voice of liberty be mute?"

He spoke. And drank rapidly a glass of water
1926

[my sweet old etcetera]

my sweet old etcetera
aunt lucy during the recent

war could and what
is more did tell you just
what everybody was fighting   5

for,
my sister

isabel created hundreds
(and
hundreds) of socks not to   10
mention shirts fleaproof earwarmers

etcetera wristers etcetera, my
mother hoped that

i would die etcetera
bravely of course my father used   15
to become hoarse talking about how it was
a privilege and if only he
could meanwhile my

self etcetera lay quietly
in the deep mud et   20

cetera
(dreaming,
et
    cetera, of
Your smile   25
eyes knees and of your Etcetera)
1926

[i sing of Olaf glad and big]

i sing of Olaf glad and big
whose warmest heart recoiled at war:
a conscientious object-or

his wellbelovéd colonel(trig
westpointer most succinctly bred)   5
took erring Olaf soon in hand;
but—though an host of overjoyed
noncoms(first knocking on the head
him)do through icy waters roll

that helplessness which others stroke   I
with brushes recently employed
anent this muddy toiletbowl,
while kindred intellects evoke
allegiance per blunt instruments—
Olaf(being to all intents   I
a corpse and wanting any rag
upon what God unto him gave)
responds, without getting annoyed
"I will not kiss your fucking flag"

straightway the silver bird looked grave   2
(departing hurriedly to shave)

but—though all kinds of officers
(a yearning nation's blueeyed pride)
their passive prey did kick and curse
until for wear their clarion   25
voices and boots were much the worse,
and egged the firstclassprivates on
his rectum wickedly to tease
by means of skilfully applied
bayonets roasted hot with heat—   30
Olaf(upon what were once knees)
does almost ceaselessly repeat
"there is some shit I will not eat"

our president, being of which
assertions duly notified   35
threw the yellowsonofabitch
into a dungeon, where he died

Christ(of His mercy infinite)
i pray to see; and Olaf, too

preponderatingly because   40
unless statistics lie he was
more brave than me:more blond than you.
1931

[r-p-o-p-h-e-s-s-a-g-r]

                              r-p-o-p-h-e-s-s-a-g-r
                        who
          a)s w(e loo)k
          upnowgath
                    PPEGORHRASS   5
                                      eringint(o-
          aThe):l
               eA
                  !p:
          S   a   10
                        (r
          rIvInG   gRrEaPsPhOs)
                                          to
          rea(be)rran(com)gi(e)ngly
          ,grasshopper;   15
          1935

[may i feel said he]

          may i feel said he
          (i'll squeal said she
          just once said he)
          it's fun said she

          (may i touch said he   5
          how much said she
          a lot said he)
          why not said she

          (let's go said he
          not too far said she   10
          what's too far said he
          where you are said she)

          may i stay said he
          (which way said she
          like this said he   15
          if you kiss said she

may i move said he
is it love said she)
if you're willing said he
(but you're killing said she   20

but it's life said he
but your wife said she
now said he)
ow said she

(tiptop said he   25
don't stop said she
oh no said he)
go slow said she

(cccome?said he   30
ummm said she)
you're divine!said he
(you are Mine said she)
1935

[this little bride & groom are]

this little bride & groom are
standing)in a kind
of crown he dressed
in black candy she

veiled with candy white   5
carrying a bouquet of
pretend flowers this
candy crown with this candy

little bride & little
groom in it kind of stands on   10
a thin ring which stands on a much
less thin very much more

big & kinder of ring & which
kinder of stands on a
much more than very much   15
biggest & thickest & kindest

of ring & all one two three rings
are cake & everything is protected by-
cellophane against anything(because
nothing really exists   20
1938

[anyone lived in a pretty how town]

anyone lived in a pretty how town
(with up so floating many bells down)
spring summer autumn winter
he sang his didn't he danced his did.

Women and men(both little and small)   5
cared for anyone not at all
they sowed their isn't they reaped their same
sun moon stars rain

children guessed(but only a few
and down they forgot as up they grew   10
autumn winter spring summer)
that noone loved him more by more

when by now and tree by leaf
she laughed his joy she cried his grief
bird by snow and stir by still   15
anyone's any was all to her

someones married their everyones
laughed their cryings and did their dance
(sleep wake hope and then)they
said their nevers they slept their dream   20

stars rain sun moon
(and only the snow can begin to explain
how children are apt to forget to remember
with up so floating many bells down)

one day anyone died i guess   25
(and noone stooped to kiss his face)

busy folk buried them side by side
little by little and was by was

all by all and deep by deep   30
and more by more they dream their sleep
noone and anyone earth by april
wish by spirit and if by yes.

Women and men(both dong and ding)
summer autumn winter spring   35
reaped their sowing and went their came
sun moon stars rain
1940

[1(a]

l(a

le

af

fa

ll

s)

one
l

iness
1958

Hart Crane
1899–1932

In his short life, Hart Crane left a small legacy of highly worked and powerfully thought-through poems in which the legacy of the modernist French poets Rimbaud and Mallarmé first entered our literature. Like Rimbaud in his "Bateau Ivre," Crane wrote a poetry of headlong momentum, his precipitous current flowing, like the Mississippi, toward a revelatory ocean. Like Mallarmé, Crane pressed syntax to its utmost compression, and by transferred epithets and periphrases he made up a heady texture rich with music and light. Crane's poems name Emily Dickinson, Herman Melville, and Walt Whitman as his predecessors, but Robert Lowell was right in calling Crane "the Shelley of our age"; Crane had learned from Shelley the ecstatic hope and incandescent love that opposed themselves to skepticism and irony, which they both nonetheless knew well.

Nothing in Crane's life or background explains his meteoric poetic genius. He was born in Cleveland, Ohio, of unhappily married parents, who were divorced when he was seventeen. Crane's businessman father, a candy manufacturer, hoped that his son would enter his business. Crane's predatory mother, from whom he had eventually to cut himself off, bound her son ever more tightly to her. Crane's schooling was interrupted by his mother's insisting he accompany her on trips; lacking enough credits at the end of high school to enter college, Crane took jobs in advertising, first in Cleveland and then New York. The jobs bored him, but as he moved, he found friends. In New York these included Sherwood Anderson, Allen Tate, and Gorham Munson, editor of *The Pagan*, where in 1916 Crane had published a poem. In Cleveland again, from 1919 to 1921, while working for his father, Crane made the acquaintance of other artists, who recognized him as one of their own.

Crane returned to New York, where he published his first collection, *White Buildings*, in 1926 and began work on *The Bridge* (he had already completed *Voyages*, his love sequence for Emil Opffer, a sailor with whom he shared an apartment with a view of the Brooklyn Bridge). Grants from the philanthropist Otto Kahn, as well as money from his family and friends, enabled Crane to live without steady work. But already Crane's drinking and his search for homosexual liaisons in dock bars were proving dangerous.

Crane's uncontrollable alcoholism proved so destructive that it led him to his early suicide. Toward the end of his life there was a chaotic period in Mexico, where he attempted to forsake his lifelong homosexuality by beginning an affair with Peggy Cowley (previously married to the critic Malcolm Cowley). In Mexico, Crane was imprisoned for disturbing the peace. In 1932 he set sail for New York but jumped into the Gulf of Mexico, the last impulsive act of an impulsive life.

Although the surface of Crane's poetry is difficult, behind his opaque texture lie careful reasons for his choice of words, as his patient letters to his friends show and as close reading will confirm. He had epic ambitions (fulfilled only partly by his sequence *The Bridge*), and many of his poems attempt epic scope within a lyric compass as they retell a decisive journey or voyage. They do this with a profound commitment to modernity.

The modern poet must, Crane thought, "absorb the machine." In opposing himself to Eliot's more conservative Europeanizing of American poetry, Crane looked resolutely not eastward to Europe but westward to America's frontiers. In *The Bridge*, Crane connects the bridge, the technological symbol of the machine age, to the dance of Pocahontas, to Whitman's mapping of the American continent, to the hoboes riding the freight trains, and to New Yorkers in the subway. Each portion of the sequence has its own form, ranging from first-person monologue to third-person description to second-person colloquy; the sequence employs both rhyme and free verse. In recognizing the Indian dance as the primal American aesthetic and religious form, and, later, in wanting to write an epic called *The Conquistadors*, Crane demonstrated his conviction that the present is constructed upon the past. America, he thought, must retain historical memory, not the memory of Europe so much as the memory of what has occurred on American soil. And unlike Pound and Frost, he turned not only to the New England past but to Spanish sources. *The Bridge* included not only political events (Columbus's voyage) but also aesthetic ones, from *Rip Van Winkle* to the works of Poe.

In 1930, after the publication of *The Bridge* (to mixed reviews), Crane received a Guggenheim fellowship and traveled to Mexico, but it became increasingly difficult for him to write. In the brief peaceful period with Peggy Cowley, he completed his last lyric, "The Broken Tower." In it what Crane called "the logic of metaphor" appears fully coherent, and the poem becomes an example of the sort of verse that would assemble itself into one great organized "single new word, never before spoken." At their best, Crane's assimilative powers produce a poetry that is at once rapidly cumulative and disintegrating, in which atmospheres dissolve as fast as they are created. This instability of essence in Crane affronted conservative critics, among them Yvor Winters, who argued that Crane's suicide was the logical result of his Emersonian and Whitmanesque individualism.

Crane's ambition was halted by his rapidly worsening alcoholism. But he left, besides the uneven *Bridge,* many exquisite smaller pieces (from the tender "Chaplinesque" to the symphonic *Voyages*) by which he will be remembered, and in his essays and letters he bequeathed a strict body of working aesthetic theory. Its chief tenet is the forsaking of a discursive or expository appearance to the poem. The logic of the poem must be impeccable, but it is not the explanatory or instructional logic of versified prose. Instead, the logic of the poem is associational, governed by the succession of feelings acted out by the words of the poem. Crane often uses transferred epithets—for example, "adagios of islands" —to combine two ideas—here, moving slowly (as in a musical adagio) and an ocean voyage through islands. Such writing conveys much information in a small compass, and subsequent poets (especially Robert Lowell in his sonnets and Allen Ginsberg in his telegraphic descriptions) have learned to write in Crane's rapid notation. In turning poetry away from the instructional and toward the associational, Crane taught other poets how to render brilliant impressions, in language duplicating the dazzling multiplicity of human sensations and thoughts.

Further Reading:

B. Weber, *Hart Crane: A Biographical and Critical Study,* 1948, 1970.
V. Quinn, *Hart Crane,* 1963.
R. W. B. Lewis, *The Poetry of Hart Crane,* 1969.
J. E. Unterecker, *Voyager: A Life of Hart Crane,* 1969.
S. Paul, *Hart's Bridge,* 1972.
M. D. Uroff, *Hart Crane: The Patterns of His Poetry,* 1974.

P. Horton, *Hart Crane,* 1976.
R. Sugg, *Hart Crane's* The Bridge, 1976.
H. Nilsen, *Hart Crane's Divided Vision: An Analysis of* The Bridge, 1980.
D. R. Clark, *Critical Essays on Hart Crane,* 1982.
A. Trachtenberg, *Hart Crane: A Collection of Critical Essays,* 1982.
J. Schwartz, *Hart Crane: A Reference Guide,* 1983.

Text:
The Complete Poems and Selected Letters and Prose of Hart Crane, ed. B. Weber, 1966.

See also *The Letters of Hart Crane, 1916–1932,* ed. B. Weber, 1952, 1965.

Chaplinesque[1]

We make our meek adjustments,
Contented with such random consolations
As the wind deposits
In slithered and too ample pockets.

For we can still love the world, who find   5
A famished kitten on the step, and know
Recesses for it from the fury of the street,
Or warm torn elbow coverts.

We will sidestep, and to the final smirk
Dally the doom of that inevitable thumb   10
That slowly chafes its puckered index toward us,
Facing the dull squint with what innocence
And what surprise!

And yet these fine collapses are not lies
More than the pirouettes of any pliant cane;   15
Our obsequies are, in a way, no enterprise.
We can evade you, and all else but the heart:
What blame to us if the heart live on.

The game enforces smirks; but we have seen
The moon in lonely alleys make   20
A grail of laughter of an empty ash can,
And through all sound of gaiety and quest
Have heard a kitten in the wilderness.
1926

Repose of Rivers

The willows carried a slow sound,
A sarabande the wind mowed on the mead.
I could never remember
That seething, steady leveling of the marshes
Till age had brought me to the sea.   5

[1] In the manner of Charles Chaplin.

Flags, weeds. And remembrance of steep alcoves
Where cypresses shared the noon's
Tyranny; they drew me into hades almost.
And mammoth turtles climbing sulphur dreams
Yielded, while sun-silt rippled them   10
Asunder . . .

How much I would have bartered! the black gorge
And all the singular nestings in the hills
Where beavers learn stitch and tooth.
The pond I entered once and quickly fled—   15
I remember now its singing willow rim.

And finally, in that memory all things nurse;
After the city that I finally passed
With scalding unguents spread and smoking darts
The monsoon cut across the delta   20
At gulf gates . . . There, beyond the dykes

I heard wind flaking sapphire, like this summer,
And willows could not hold more steady sound.
1926

Passage

Where the cedar leaf divides the sky
I heard the sea.
In sapphire arenas of the hills
I was promised an improved infancy.

Sulking, sanctioning the sun,   5
My memory I left in a ravine,—
Casual louse that tissues the buckwheat,
Aprons rocks, congregates pears
In moonlit bushels
And wakens alleys with a hidden cough.   10

Dangerously the summer burned
(I had joined the entrainments of the wind).
The shadows of boulders lengthened my back:
In the bronze gongs of my cheeks
The rain dried without odour.   15

"It is not long, it is not long;
See where the red and black
Vine-stanchioned valleys—": but the wind
Died speaking through the ages that you know
And hug, chimney-sooted heart of man!   20

So was I turned about and back, much as your smoke
Compiles a too well-known biography.

The evening was a spear in the ravine
That throve through very oak. And had I walked
The dozen particular decimals of time?   25
Touching an opening laurel, I found
A thief beneath, my stolen book in hand.

"Why are you back here—smiling an iron coffin?"
"To argue with the laurel," I replied:
"Am justified in transience, fleeing   30
Under the constant wonder of your eyes—."

He closed the book. And from the Ptolemies
Sand troughed us in a glittering abyss.
A serpent swam a vertex to the sun
—On unpaced beaches leaned its tongue and drummed.   35
What fountains did I hear? what icy speeches?
Memory, committed to the page, had broke.
1926

At Melville's Tomb[*]

Often beneath the wave, wide from this ledge
The dice of drowned men's bones he saw bequeath
An embassy. Their numbers as he watched,
Beat on the dusty shore and were obscured.

And wrecks passed without sound of bells,   5
The calyx[1] of death's bounty giving back
A scattered chapter, livid hieroglyph,
The portent wound in corridors of shells.

[*] Written in memory of Herman Melville
(1819–1891), author of *Moby-Dick* (1851). The
poem imitates the French convention of the
poem at the tomb of the artist-predecessor.

[1] Used metaphorically of the vortex made in the
ocean by a sinking ship.

> Then in the circuit calm of one vast coil,
> Its lashings charmed and malice reconciled,   10
> Frosted eyes there were that lifted altars;
> And silent answers crept across the stars.
>
> Compass, quadrant and sextant[2] contrive
> No farther tides . . . High in the azure steeps
> Monody[3] shall not wake the mariner.   15
> This fabulous shadow only the sea keeps.
>
> 1926

---

from The Bridge

To Brooklyn Bridge

How many dawns, chill from his rippling rest
The seagull's wings shall dip and pivot him,
Shedding white rings of tumult, building high
Over the chained bay waters Liberty—

Then, with inviolate curve, forsake our eyes   5
As apparitional as sails that cross
Some page of figures to be filed away;
—Till elevators drop us from our day . . .

I think of cinemas, panoramic sleights
With multitudes bent toward some flashing scene   10
Never disclosed, but hastened to again,
Foretold to other eyes on the same screen;

And Thee, across the harbor, silver-paced
As though the sun took step of thee, yet left
Some motion ever unspent in thy stride,—   15
Implicitly thy freedom staying thee!

Out of some subway scuttle, cell or loft
A bedlamite[1] speeds to thy parapets,
Tilting there momently, shrill shirt ballooning,
A jest falls from the speechless caravan.   20

Down Wall,[2] from girder into street noon leaks,
A rip-tooth of the sky's acetylene;

---

[2] Instruments used in navigation.   [1] Madman.
[3] Ode sung by one voice.   [2] Wall Street in New York City.

All afternoon the cloud-flown derricks turn . . .
Thy cables breathe the North Atlantic still.

And obscure as that heaven of the Jews,   25
Thy guerdon[3] . . . Accolade[4] thou dost bestow
Of anonymity time cannot raise:
Vibrant reprieve and pardon thou dost show.

O harp and altar, of the fury fused,
(How could mere toil align thy choiring strings!)   30
Terrific threshold of the prophet's pledge,
Prayer of pariah,[5] and the lover's cry,—

Again the traffic lights that skim thy swift
Unfractioned idiom, immaculate sigh of stars,
Beading thy path—condense eternity: 35
And we have seen night lifted in thine arms.

Under thy shadow by the piers I waited;
Only in darkness is thy shadow clear.
The City's fiery parcels all undone,
Already snow submerges an iron year . . .   40

O Sleepless as the river under thee,
Vaulting the sea, the prairies' dreaming sod,
Unto us lowliest sometime sweep, descend
And of the curveship lend a myth to God.
1930

The Dance

The swift red flesh, a winter king—
Who squired the glacier woman down the sky?
She ran the neighing canyons all the spring;
She spouted arms; she rose with maize—to die.

And in the autumn drouth, whose burnished hands   5
With mineral wariness found out the stone
Where prayers, forgotten, streamed the mesa sands?
He holds the twilight's dim, perpetual throne.

Mythical brows we saw retiring—loth,
Disturbed and destined, into denser green.   10
Greeting they sped us, on the arrow's oath:
Now lie incorrigibly what years between . . .

---

[3] Reward.   [5] Outcast.
[4] Award of special merit.

There was a bed of leaves, and broken play;
There was a veil upon you, Pocahontas, bride—
O Princess whose brown lap was virgin May;
And bridal flanks and eyes hid tawny pride.

I left the village for dogwood. By the canoe
Tugging below the mill-race, I could see
Your hair's keen crescent running, and the blue
First moth of evening take wing stealthily.

What laughing chains the water wove and threw!
I learned to catch the trout's moon whisper; I
Drifted how many hours I never knew,
But, watching, saw that fleet young crescent die,—

And one star, swinging, take its place, alone,
Cupped in the larches of the mountain pass—
Until, immortally, it bled into the dawn.
I left my sleek boat nibbling margin grass . . .

I took the portage climb, then chose
A further valley-shed; I could not stop.
Feet nozzled wat'ry webs of upper flows;
One white veil gusted from the very top.

O Appalachian Spring! I gained the ledge;
Steep, inaccessible smile that eastward bends
And northward reaches in that violet wedge
Of Adirondacks!—wisped of azure wands,

Over how many bluffs, tarns, streams I sped!
—And knew myself within some boding shade:—
Grey tepees tufting the blue knolls ahead,
Smoke swirling through the yellow chestnut glade . . .

A distant cloud, a thunder-bud—it grew,
That blanket of the skies: the padded foot
Within,—I heard it; 'til its rhythm drew,
—Siphoned the black pool from the heart's hot root!

A cyclone threshes in the turbine crest,
Swooping in eagle feathers down your back;
Know, Maquokeeta,[6] greeting; know death's best;
—Fall, Sachem,[7] strictly as the tamarack!

---

[6] Indian god of the thunderstorm.   [7] Chief.

10

20

25

30

35

40

45

A birch kneels. All her whistling fingers fly.
The oak grove circles in a crash of leaves;   50
The long moan of a dance is in the sky.
Dance, Maquokeeta: Pocahontas grieves . . .

And every tendon scurries toward the twangs
Of lightning deltaed down your saber hair.
Now snaps the flint in every tooth; red fangs   55
And splay tongues thinly busy the blue air . . .

Dance, Maquokeeta! snake[8] that lives before,
That casts his pelt, and lives beyond! Sprout, horn!
Spark, tooth! Medicine-man, relent, restore—
Lie to us,—dance us back the tribal morn!   60

Spears and assemblies: black drums thrusting on—
O yelling battlements,—I, too, was liege
To rainbows currying each pulsant bone:
Surpassed the circumstance, danced out the siege!

And buzzard-circleted, screamed from the stake;   65
I could not pick the arrows from my side.
Wrapped in that fire, I saw more escorts wake—
Flickering, sprint up the hill groins like a tide.

I heard the hush of lava wrestling your arms,
And stag teeth foam about the raven throat;   70
Flame cataracts of heaven in seething swarms,
Fed down your anklets to the sunset's moat.

O, like the lizard in the furious noon,
That drops his legs and colors in the sun,
—And laughs, pure serpent, Time itself, and moon   75
Of his own fate, I saw thy change begun!

And saw thee dive to kiss that destiny
Like one white meteor, sacrosanct and blent
At last with all that's consummate and free
There, where the first and last gods keep thy tent.   80

                    *   *   *

Thewed of the levin, thunder-shod and lean,
Lo, through what infinite seasons dost thou gaze—
Across what bivouacs of thine angered slain,
And see'st thy bride immortal in the maize!

[8] The snake that sheds its skin symbolizes
self-renewing time.

Totem and fire-gall, slumbering pyramid—
Though other calendars now stack the sky,
Thy freedom is her largesse, Prince, and hid
On paths thou knewest best to claim her by.

High unto Labrador the sun strikes free
Her speechless dream of snow, and stirred again,
She is the torrent and the singing tree;
And she is virgin to the last of men . . .

West, west and south! winds over Cumberland
And winds across the llano[9] grass resume
Her hair's warm sibilance. Her breasts are fanned
O stream by slope and vineyard—into bloom!

And when the caribou slant down for salt
Do arrows thirst and leap? Do antlers shine
Alert, star-triggered in the listening vault
Of dusk?—And are her perfect brows to thine?

We danced, O Brave, we danced beyond their farms,
In cobalt desert closures made our vows . . .
Now is the strong prayer folded in thine arms,
The serpent with the eagle in the boughs.

1930

Atlantis[10]

*Music is then the knowledge of that which
relates to love in harmony and system.*[11]
                                          Plato

Through the bound cable strands, the arching path
Upward, veering with light, the flight of strings,—
Taut miles of shuttling moonlight syncopate
The whispered rush, telepathy of wires.
Up the index of night, granite and steel—
Transparent meshes—fleckless the gleaming staves—
Sibylline[12] voices flicker, waveringly stream
As though a god were issue of the strings. . . .

And through that cordage, threading with its call
One arc synoptic of all tides below—
Their labyrinthine mouths of history
Pouring reply as though all ships at sea

---

[9] Plain without trees.
[10] The legendary sunken continent.

[11] Plato's *Republic*, III, 403.
[12] Prophetic.

Complighted in one vibrant breath made cry,—
"Make thy love sure—to weave whose song we ply!"
—From black embankments, moveless soundings hailed,   15
So seven oceans answer from their dream.

And on, obliquely up bright carrier bars
New octaves trestle the twin monoliths
Beyond whose frosted capes the moon bequeaths
Two worlds of sleep (O arching strands of song!)—   20
Onward and up the crystal-flooded aisle
White tempest nets file upward, upward ring
With silver terraces the humming spars,
The loft of vision, palladium[13] helm of stars.

Sheerly the eyes, like seagulls stung with rime[14]—   25
Slit and propelled by glistening fins of light—
Pick biting way up towering looms that press
Sidelong with flight of blade on tendon blade
—Tomorrows into yesteryear—and link
What cipher-script of time no traveller reads   30
But who, through smoking pyres of love and death,
Searches the timeless laugh of mythic spears.

Like hails, farewells—up planet-sequined heights
Some trillion whispering hammers glimmer Tyre:[15]
Serenely, sharply up the long anvil cry   35
Of inchling æons silence rivets Troy.[16]
And you, aloft there—Jason![17] hesting Shout!
Still wrapping harness to the swarming air!
Silvery the rushing wake, surpassing call,
Beams yelling Æolus![18] splintered in the straits!   40

From gulfs unfolding, terrible of drums,
Tall Vision-of-the-Voyage, tensely spare—
Bridge, lifting night to cycloramic crest
Of deepest day—O Choir, translating time
Into what multitudinous Verb the suns   45
And synergy of waters ever fuse, recast
In myriad syllables,—Psalm of Cathay![19]
O Love, thy white, pervasive Paradigm . . . !

We left the haven hanging in the night—
Sheened harbor lanterns backward fled the keel.   50

[13] A statue of Pallas Athena; also, an element of
the platinum group.
[14] Frost.
[15] Ancient Phoenician port.
[16] City destroyed in the Trojan War.

[17] Captain of the Greek Argonauts in the quest
for the fabled Golden Fleece.
[18] God of the winds.
[19] Ancient name for China.

Pacific here at time's end, bearing corn,—
Eyes stammer through the pangs of dust and steel.
And still the circular, indubitable frieze
Of heaven's meditation, yoking wave
To kneeling wave, one song devoutly binds—   5
The vernal strophe chimes from deathless strings!

O Thou steeled Cognizance whose leap commits
The agile precincts of the lark's return;
Within whose lariat sweep encinctured sing
In single chrysalis the many twain,—   60
Of stars Thou art the stitch and stallion glow
And like an organ, Thou, with sound of doom—
Sight, sound and flesh Thou leadest from time's realm
As love strikes clear direction for the helm.

Swift peal of secular light, intrinsic Myth   65
Whose fell unshadow is death's utter wound,—
O River-throated—iridescently upborne
Through the bright drench and fabric of our veins;
With white escarpments[20] swinging into light,
Sustained in tears the cities are endowed   70
And justified conclamant with ripe fields
Revolving through their harvests in sweet torment.

Forever Deity's glittering Pledge, O Thou
Whose canticle fresh chemistry assigns
To wrapt inception and beatitude,—   75
Always through blinding cables, to our joy,
Of thy white seizure springs the prophecy:
Always through spiring cordage,[21] pyramids
Of silver sequel, Deity's young name
Kinetic of white choiring wings . . . ascends.   80

Migrations that must needs void memory,
Inventions that cobblestone the heart,—
Unspeakable Thou Bridge to Thee, O Love.
Thy pardon for this history, whitest Flower,
O Answerer of all,—Anemone,—   85
Now while thy petals spend the suns about us, hold—
(O Thou whose radiance doth inherit me)
Atlantis,—hold thy floating singer late!

So to thine Everpresence, beyond time,
Like spears ensanguined of one tolling star   90

---

[20] Steep slopes.   [21] Ropes in the rigging of a ship.

That bleeds infinity—the orphic strings,[22]
Sidereal[23] phalanxes, leap and converge:
—One Song, one Bridge of Fire! Is it Cathay,
Now pity steeps the grass and rainbows ring
The serpent with the eagle in the leaves . . . ?   95
Whispers antiphonal in azure swing.

1930

O Carib Isle!

The tarantula rattling at the lily's foot
Across the feet of the dead, laid in white sand
Near the coral beach—nor zigzag fiddle crabs
Side-stilting from the path (that shift, subvert
And anagrammatize your name)—No, nothing here   5
Below the palsy that one eucalyptus lifts
In wrinkled shadows—mourns.

               And yet suppose
I count these nacreous frames of tropic death,
Brutal necklaces of shells around each grave
Squared off so carefully. Then   10

To the white sand I may speak a name, fertile
Albeit in a stranger tongue. Tree names, flower names
Deliberate, gainsay death's brittle crypt. Meanwhile
The wind that knots itself in one great death—
Coils and withdraws. So syllables want breath.   15

But where is the Captain of this doubloon isle
Without a turnstile? Who but catchword crabs
Patrols the dry groins of the underbrush?
What man, or What
Is Commissioner of mildew throughout the ambushed senses?   20
His Carib mathematics web the eyes' baked lenses!

Under the poinciana, of a noon or afternoon
Let fiery blossoms clot the light, render my ghost
Sieved upward, white and black along the air
Until it meets the blue's comedian host.   25

[22] Suggesting the lyre of Orpheus.   [23] Starry.

Let not the pilgrim see himself again
For slow evisceration bound like those huge terrapin
Each daybreak on the wharf, their brine-caked eyes;
—Spiked, overturned; such thunder in their strain!
And clenched beaks coughing for the surge again!

Slagged of the hurricane—I, cast within its flow,
Congeal by afternoons here, satin and vacant.
You have given me the shell, Satan,—carbonic amulet
Sere of the sun exploded in the sea.

1933

The Idiot

Sheer over to the other side,—for see—
The boy straggling under those mimosas, daft
With squint lanterns in his head, and it's likely
Fumbling his sex. That's why those children laughed

In such infernal circles round his door   5
Once when he shouted, stretched in ghastly shape.
I hurried by. But back from the hot shore
Passed him again . . . He was alone, agape;

One hand dealt out a kite string, a tin can
The other tilted, peeled end clapped to eye.   10
That kite aloft—you should have watched him scan
Its course, though he'd clamped midnight to noon sky!

And since, through these hot barricades of green,
A Dios gracias, graç¹—I've heard his song
Above all reason lifting, halt serene—   15
My trespass vision shrinks to face his wrong.

1933

¹ Spanish: "Thanks be to God, thanks."

The Broken Tower

The bell-rope that gathers God at dawn
Dispatches me as though I dropped down the knell
Of a spent day—to wander the cathedral lawn
From pit to crucifix, feet chill on steps from hell.

Have you not heard, have you not seen that corps   5
Of shadows in the tower, whose shoulders sway
Antiphonal carillons launched before
The stars are caught and hived in the sun's ray?

The bells, I say, the bells break down their tower;
And swing I know not where. Their tongues engrave   10
Membrane through marrow, my long-scattered score
Of broken intervals . . . And I, their sexton slave!

Oval encyclicals in canyons heaping
The impasse high with choir. Banked voices slain!
Pagodas, campaniles with reveilles outleaping—   15
O terraced echoes prostrate on the plain! . . .

And so it was I entered the broken world
To trace the visionary company of love, its voice
An instant in the wind (I know not whither hurled)
But not for long to hold each desperate choice.   20

My word I poured. But was it cognate, scored
Of that tribunal monarch of the air
Whose thigh embronzes earth, strikes crystal Word
In wounds pledged once to hope—cleft to despair?

The steep encroachments of my blood left me   25
No answer (could blood hold such a lofty tower
As flings the question true?)—or is it she
Whose sweet mortality stirs latent power?—

And through whose pulse I hear, counting the strokes
My veins recall and add, revived and sure   30
The angelus[1] of wars my chest evokes:
What I hold healed, original now, and pure . . .

[1] Prayer recounting the Incarnation of Christ.

And builds, within, a tower that is not stone
(Not stone can jacket heaven)—but slip
Of pebbles,—visible wings of silence sown
In azure circles, widening as they dip

The matrix[2] of the heart, lift down the eye
That shrines the quiet lake and swells a tower . . .
The commodious, tall decorum of that sky
Unseals her earth, and lifts love in its shower.

1933

Allen Tate
1899–1979

Allen Tate, poet, biographer, and essayist, was an influential man of letters from his twenties at Vanderbilt University to his death in Sewanee, Tennessee. He was born in Kentucky to a wealthy family who maintained a conventional interest in books and general culture. His father's business failures, however, made for a disrupted childhood. Tate entered Vanderbilt in 1919 and roomed with Robert Penn Warren; they both came under the influence of the poet John Crowe Ransom and the group known as the Fugitives; their journal, *The Fugitive,* printed Tate's first poems, and Tate himself edited the journal from 1923 to 1925. Tate and other southern writers, including Ransom and Warren, published a collection of essays, *I'll Take My Stand: The South and Agrarian Tradition* (1930), defending the antebellum values of an agrarian South against the industrial values of the North. Tate's biographies of Stonewall Jackson (1928) and Jefferson Davis (1929) were also implicit arguments for the preservation of southern culture.

It has always been true that the aristocratic South has been more hospitable to belles lettres than the Puritan North, where intellectuals preferred theological or philosophical prose to novels and poetry. The leisured class of the South (made possible, of course, by slavery) sponsored an aristocratic culture, centered rather in law and letters than in religious disputation, and allying itself more with the aristocratic literature produced in England than with the polemic literature of dissent. Tate's poetry is in this sense aristocratic: Its models come from the Latin literature he studied at Vanderbilt. His poetry is often latinate in diction, measured in rhythm, intellectual in content, and historical in emphasis. Though he turns to local color in some southern poems like "The Swimmers," even there the fundamental emphasis of the poem is intellectual and moral rather than sensuous.

Tate's long life was spent chiefly as an essayist (he wrote for *The New Republic, The Nation, Hound and Horn,* and the *Sewanee Review*) and professor (he taught from 1951 to 1968 at the University of Minnesota). He was friend and

[2] Womb.

mentor to both Hart Crane and Robert Lowell, and his influence can be seen in Lowell's early poetry. Tate preferred a literature of ideas in which propositions were stated, explored, defended, and summarized in a lofty diction. He believed, with Aristotle, that poetry is more philosophical than history; he thought it should express large moral truths, drawn from history, perhaps, but broadened into universality. At the same time, he wanted a complexity in poetry, a constant tension and historical irony, that would save the ideas from platitudinousness. He found a poetic ideal in Eliot and imitated him as a poet and as a critic. Like Eliot, Tate adopted in his criticism a tone of dry instructiveness, but his criticism lacks the passion that animates Eliot's views. Together with Ransom, Tate founded the New Criticism (Ransom's term), which aimed to change the way in which literature was taught; instead of spending time on historical and biographical data, the critic should direct readers or students to look at the qualities of the work itself—its tensions and ambiguities, its complex of positions, its structural completeness. As a movement that turned attention back to the art object, the New Criticism was immensely valuable. But Tate could not envisage a poetry other than the metaphysical poetry he admired, imitated in his own work, and fostered in his pupils. He disliked Robert Lowell's abandonment of strict forms and classical reticence when *Life Studies* (1959) appeared.

Strict in conscience, intellectual in temperament, severe in criticism, Tate lacked the freedom and play of imagination that mark the great poet. As one of the exponents of the New Criticism, with its emphasis on the artistry of the poet visible in the text, he helped turn American criticism away from its former uncritical reliance on biography and the history of ideas. He remains, with John Crowe Ransom (a more talented poet), one of the founders of contemporary southern poetry.

Further Reading:
W. B. Arnold, *The Social Ideas of Allen Tate,* 1955.
R. K. Meiners, *The Last Alternatives,* 1963.
G. Hemphill, *Allen Tate,* 1964.
F. Bishop, *Allen Tate,* 1967.
R. Squires, *Allen Tate: A Literary Biography,* 1971.
Allen Tate and His Work: Critical Evaluations, ed. R. Squires, 1972.
R. S. Dupree, *Allen Tate and the Augustinian Imagination: A Study of the Poetry,* 1983.

Text:
Collected Poems, 1919–1976, 1977.
See also *The Poetry Reviews of Allen Tate, 1924–1944,* ed. A. Brown and F. N. Cheney, 1983.

Ode to the Confederate Dead

Row after row with strict impunity
The headstones yield their names to the element,
The wind whirrs without recollection;

In the riven troughs the splayed leaves
Pile up, of nature the casual sacrament
To the seasonal eternity of death;
Then driven by the fierce scrutiny
Of heaven to their election in the vast breath,
They sough[1] the rumour of mortality.

Autumn is desolation in the plot
Of a thousand acres where these memories grow
From the inexhaustible bodies that are not
Dead, but feed the grass row after rich row.
Think of the autumns that have come and gone!—
Ambitious November with the humors of the year,   10
With a particular zeal for every slab,
Staining the uncomfortable angels that rot
On the slabs, a wing chipped here, an arm there:
The brute curiosity of an angel's stare
Turns you, like them, to stone,   20
Transforms the heaving air
Till plunged to a heavier world below
You shift your sea-space blindly
Heaving, turning like the blind crab.

    Dazed by the wind, only the wind   25
    The leaves flying, plunge

You know who have waited by the wall
The twilight certainty of an animal,
Those midnight restitutions of the blood
You know—the immitigable pines, the smoky frieze   30
Of the sky, the sudden call: you know the rage,
The cold pool left by the mounting flood,
Of muted Zeno and Parmenides.[2]
You who have waited for the angry resolution
Of those desires that should be yours tomorrow,   35
You know the unimportant shrift of death
And praise the vision
And praise the arrogant circumstance
Of those who fall
Rank upon rank, hurried beyond decision—   40
Here by the sagging gate, stopped by the wall.

    Seeing, seeing only the leaves
    Flying, plunge and expire

---

[1] Sigh.
[2] Greek philosophers of the fifth century B.C. who denied the reality of change and believed in the permanence of "being."

Turn your eyes to the immoderate past,
Turn to the inscrutable infantry rising   45
Demons out of the earth—they will not last.
Stonewall, Stonewall,[3] and the sunken fields of hemp,
Shiloh, Antietam, Malvern Hill, Bull Run.[4]
Lost in that orient of the thick-and-fast
You will curse the setting sun.   50

    Cursing only the leaves crying
    Like an old man in a storm

You hear the shout, the crazy hemlocks point
With troubled fingers to the silence which
Smothers you, a mummy, in time.   55

               The hound bitch
Toothless and dying, in a musty cellar
Hears the wind only.

         Now that the salt of their blood
Stiffens the saltier oblivion of the sea,   60
Seals the malignant purity of the flood,
What shall we who count our days and bow
Our heads with a commemorial woe
In the ribboned coats of grim felicity,
What shall we say of the bones, unclean,   65
Whose verdurous anonymity will grow?
The ragged arms, the ragged heads and eyes
Lost in these acres of the insane green?
The gray lean spiders come, they come and go;
In a tangle of willows without light   70
The singular screech-owl's tight
Invisible lyric seeds the mind
With the furious murmur of their chivalry.

    We shall say only the leaves
    Flying, plunge and expire   75

We shall say only the leaves whispering
In the improbable mist of nightfall
That flies on multiple wing;
Night is the beginning and the end
And in between the ends of distraction   80
Waits mute speculation, the patient curse

[3] Confederate general Stonewall Jackson (1824–1863).

[4] Shiloh; Antietam; Malvern Hill; Bull Run: battles of the Civil War.

That stones the eyes, or like the jaguar leaps
For his own image in a jungle pool, his victim.
What shall we say who have knowledge
Carried to the heart? Shall we take the act
To the grave? Shall we, more hopeful, set up the grave
In the house? The ravenous grave?

Leave now
The shut gate and the decomposing wall:
The gentle serpent, green in the mulberry bush,
Riots with his tongue through the hush—
Sentinel of the grave who counts us all!

1930

Langston Hughes
1902–1967

Langston Hughes's short stories won him an enormous audience among the black
population. The stories, like the poems, showed the average struggle of ordinary
blacks in their everyday lives. The edge of bitter humor animating Hughes's
work does not take away from its essential comedy; his satire of both white and
black, while establishing with perfect clarity the extent of social injustice in
America, creates a cast of characters who are resourceful and hapless, courageous
and foolish, altruistic and self-serving.

Hughes's realistic descriptions in verse and prose of the life of poor blacks
earned him hatred and condemnation from black intellectuals who wished black
writing to be improving, to show black life only at its best. When his second
book of poetry, *Fine Clothes to the Jew* (1929), appeared, the headline in the
widely circulated black newspaper *The Amsterdam News* was "Langston Hughes—
The Sewer Dweller."

Hughes's father, who had left his wife shortly after his son's birth, disavowed
all connection with American blacks and went to live in Mexico, where Hughes
lived with him in his adolescent years. Hughes grew to hate his father and,
reversing his father's attitude, decided to immerse himself in the life of black
Americans, to write about the entire community:

Workers, roustabouts, and singers, and job hunters on Lenox Avenue in New
York, or Seventh Street in Washington or South State in Chicago—people up
today and down tomorrow, working this week and fired the next, beaten and
baffled, but determined not to be wholly beaten, buying furniture on the
installment plan, filling the house with roomers to help pay the rent, hoping
to get a new suit for Easter—and pawning that suit before the Fourth of July.

James Langston Hughes dropped his first name, which he shared with his father, and adopted his middle name, his mother's maiden name, for his writing career.

After an unsuccessful year at Columbia University, Hughes dropped out of school, but he later received the A.B. from Lincoln University in Pennsylvania, an all-black college. In his long writing life he was able to support himself by his writing and his public readings. Besides poems and short stories, he wrote novels, children's books, plays, nonfiction, opera libretti, and lyrics for musicals, notably for Kurt Weill's *Street Scene* (1948). He was in the center of the group making up the Harlem Renaissance in the 1920s. At that time, Negro intellectuals took on as a self-conscious task the construction of an aesthetic and intellectual culture for black Americans. Hughes was drawn into the group by Dr. Alain Locke, who had included some of Hughes's poems in his 1925 anthology *The New Negro.* Hughes was also sponsored by the poet Vachel Lindsay and the novelist Carl Van Vechten. Eventually Hughes set out on his own, reading widely to southern audiences, traveling to Russia, reporting the Spanish Civil War for the *Baltimore Afro-American,* and translating García Lorca and Gabriela Mistral. He was a force for the establishing of black theaters; he anthologized his fellow black writers.

The fullness of Hughes's literary achievement will only be seen when his collected works have been compiled; he left his mark on every phase of literary activity in America. His writing created a new audience for poetry—the black community, who, in spite of the criticism of black intellectuals and moralists, saw in Hughes's direct, frank, open verse a reflection of their music and their language, their social debasement and their persistent hope and despair. In drawing on the poems of Carl Sandburg to make his own verse, Hughes continued a populist tradition in American poetry, one that depends as much on the spoken word as on the written page. In his "documentary, journalistic, and topical" poems (as he described them), Hughes reached the hearts of his listeners and validated a poetry with a strong oral base. The "Beat" poets—especially Allen Ginsberg in his blues chants—continued Hughes's emphasis on the spoken or sung poem, and subsequent black poets (Gwendolyn Brooks, Don Lee) have emphasized the colloquial vigor of black speech as Hughes himself did, transforming it into poetry.

Further Reading:
D. C. Dickinson, *A Bio-Bibliography of Langston Hughes, 1902–1967,* 1967.
J. Emanuel, *Langston Hughes,* 1967.
C. H. Rollins, *Black Troubadour,* 1970.
Langston Hughes, Black Genius, ed. T. B. O'Daniel, 1971.
O. Jemie, *Langston Hughes: An Introduction to the Poetry,* 1976.
R. K. Barksdale, *Langston Hughes: The Poet and His Critics,* 1977.
E. P. Myers, *Langston Hughes,* 1981.
F. Berry, *Langston Hughes: Before and After Harlem,* 1983.

Texts:
"The Negro Speaks of Rivers" from *Selected Poems,* 1959.
Remaining selections from *Montage of a Dream Deferred,* 1951.
See also *I Wonder as I Wander: An Autobiographical Journey,* 1956.
The Langston Hughes Reader, 1958.

The Negro Speaks of Rivers

I've known rivers:
I've known rivers ancient as the world and older than the flow of human blood
   in human veins.

My soul has grown deep like the rivers.

I bathed in the Euphrates when dawns were young.
I built my hut near the Congo and it lulled me to sleep.
I looked upon the Nile and raised the pyramids above it.   5
I heard the singing of the Mississippi when Abe Lincoln went down to New
   Orleans, and I've seen its muddy bosom turn all golden in the sunset.

I've known rivers:
Ancient, dusky rivers.

My soul has grown deep like the rivers.   10
1926

Dream Boogie

Good morning, daddy!
Ain't you heard
The boogie-woogie rumble
Of a dream deferred?

Listen closely: 5
You'll hear their feet
Beating out and beating out a——

    You think
    It's a happy beat?

Listen to it closely:
Ain't you heard   10
something underneath
like a——

What did I say?

Sure,   15
I'm happy!
Take it away!

> *Hey, pop!*
> *Re–bop!*
> *Mop!*   20
>
> *Y–e–a–h!*
> *What don't bug*
> *them white kids*
> *sure bugs me:*
> *We knows everybody*   25
> *ain't free!*

Some of these young ones is cert'ly bad——
One batted a hard ball right through my window
and my gold fish et the glass.

> *What's written down*   30
> *for white folks*
> *ain't for us a-tall:*
> *"Liberty And Justice——*
> *Huh—For All."*
>
> *Oop-pop-a-da!*   35
> *Skee! Daddle-de-do!*
> *Be-bop!*
>
> *Salt'peanuts!*
>
> *De-dop!*

1951

Movies

The Roosevelt, Renaissance, Gem, Alhambra:
Harlem laughing in all the wrong places
    at the crocodile tears
    of crocodile art

that you know
in your heart
is crocodile: 5

(Hollywood
laughs at me,
black——   10
so I laugh
back.)

1951

Harlem

What happens to a dream deferred?

Does it dry up
like a raisin in the sun?
Or fester like a sore——
And then run?
Does it stink like rotten meat?   5
Or crust and sugar over——
like a syrupy sweet?

Maybe it just sags
like a heavy load.   10

Or does it explode?
1951

Same in Blues

I said to my baby,
Baby, take it slow.
I can't, she said, I can't!
I got to go!

There's a certain   5
amount of traveling
in a dream deferred.

Lulu said to Leonard,
I want a diamond ring.
Leonard said to Lulu,   10
You won't get a goddamn thing!

    A certain
    amount of nothing
    in a dream deferred.

Daddy, daddy, daddy,   15
All I want is you.
You can have me, baby———
but my lovin' days is through.

    A certain
    amount of impotence   20
    in a dream deferred.

Three parties
On my party line———
But that third party,
Lord, ain't mine!   25

    There's liable
    to be confusion
    in a dream deferred.

From river to river,
Uptown and down,   30
There's liable to be confusion
when a dream gets kicked around.

1951

Robert Rauschenberg,
Estate,
oil and printer's ink, 1963.
Philadelphia Museum of Art.
Given by the Friends of the
Philadelphia Museum of Art.

The Literature of Postwar America: Prose 1940–1973

By 1940 American literature was being taught in universities not only in the United States but also in England and Europe, and it was being taught by professors of American literature. The Nobel Prize that Sinclair Lewis received in 1930 was in part a tribute to Lewis's achievement, but it was also a tribute to American literature. "Yes," the secretary of the Swedish Academy said, "Sinclair Lewis is an American. He writes the new language—American—as one of the representatives of a hundred and twenty million souls" who have created the "new great American literature." In creating this new great literature, American writers transformed writing into a profession, sometimes a lucrative one. During the 1920s and the 1930s their books were marketed and read widely in England and Europe as well as America. By the 1950s they were available in translations in scores of languages, including Arabic and Hebrew, Japanese and Estonian. Today, no literature reaches a wider international audience. American writers have been assisted by their government, particularly through the WPA (Works Progress Administration), by a growing advertising industry, by magazines, publishers, foundations, and universities; and they have benefited enormously from the relative affluence of their society, from the growing attraction of English as a second language, and from the prodigious prominence and power of their nation.

Yet, despite the rising fame and affluence that surrounds them, recent American writers describe their position as somehow diminished. In 1967 John Barth described the fiction he and his colleagues were writing as "the literature of exhaustion," or more precisely, "the literature of exhausted possibility"—as though to suggest that earlier writers had left more recent ones the task of working depleted ground. Nine years later John Updike announced that "the profession of writer in the United States has been sharply devalued in the last thirty years, and has suffered loss both in the dignity assigned to it by non-writers, and in the sense of purpose that shapes a profession from within."

Just before and after World War I, a new generation of writers set out to reinvent literature, confident that they could deal with the past on their own terms. By midcentury, young writers had begun to feel that they were surrounded by giants. Being a writer in Mississippi after William Faulkner, Eudora Welty remarked, "was like living near a big mountain." Finally, however, the concerns that Barth and Updike locate have more to do with the pace of change and the force of history than with the prodigious achievement of their forebears. Continuities exist, of course, even surprising ones. We have still our hermits and our celebrants, though it is strange as well as useful to think of the reclusive Thomas Pynchon as an heir of Emily Dickinson and to regard the self-advertising Norman Mailer as an heir of Walt Whitman. But it is change that abounds—change so rapid as to make America appear almost formless. The shift of large segments of our population from farms and villages to large cities; the continued unraveling of our national ethos, of the manners, mores, and beliefs that shape our thought and action; and the dramatic unfolding of new technologies, especially in weaponry, in medicine, and in telecommunications, have altered every aspect of American life and art.

Like our century, our writers have become more diverse—racially, sexually, and politically—and our fiction has become more urban. During the 1920s the literary center of the United States shifted from the East to the Midwest and the South; by mid-century it was shifting from towns and villages to cities and suburbs. Despite the emergence of exceptions like Scott Momaday (Anadarko, Oklahoma), writers are less likely to come from small towns than from cities— Chicago (Saul Bellow), New York (Bernard Malamud, Norman Mailer, James Baldwin), Tulsa, Oklahoma (Ralph Ellison), Houston, Texas (Donald Barthelme) —or from suburbs (John Cheever from Quincy, Massachusetts, Thomas Pynchon from Glen Cove, Long Island).

Amid the urbanization and diversification of America, writers have encountered a welter of staggering events, some of them almost cataclysmic: three wars (World War II, Korea, and Vietnam) and many conflicts and skirmishes; the explosion of the first atomic bomb (1945); the production of the first electronic computer (1946); the beginning of full-time television broadcasting (1948); the development of the transistor (1948); the explosion of the first hydrogen bomb (1952); the deciphering of the double-helix configuration of the molecule of deoxyribonucleic acid (DNA) in 1953; the civil rights revolution of the 1950s and 1960s, and with it the rise of blacks and of women; the rapid exploration of space; the first successful heart transplant (1968); and the dramatic development of computer technology, including speculation about artificial intelligence.

Thus bombarded, American writers seem at times to have lost their sense of place and purpose. "I grew up, and formulated my ambition to be a 'creative artist' of some sort," John Updike asserts, "in a world where the radio and the cinema were the mass media. Both bathed the American consciousness in emanations from worlds distinctly artificial. . . . These films and radio shows were made things, fictions," he adds, noting that fictions were also "the chief staple of the book industry." Now, he laments, "so-called nonfiction dominates" the publishing world, "and the dominant mass medium is television," featuring events rather than plays, happenings rather than fictions—"the sports event, the panel discussion, the talk show, the quiz show."

At once interlaced with the media and scrutinized by them, our society has become more interconnected and self-conscious, and our culture has become more diverse and less coherent. Simultaneously, our literature has undergone a transformation, as seen especially in the rising authority of nonfiction and in the blurring of lines between fiction and nonfiction. To comprehend these changes is, of course, no easy task. But the place to begin is with the force of history and the impact of our new means of reporting it.

A Second Great War

The United States entered World War II as it had entered World War I—reluctantly. In 1935 Italy conquered Ethiopia; in 1936 the Spanish civil war broke out; in 1937 Japan increased hostilities against China; in 1938 Germany invaded Austria. Soon the flow of refugees from Asia and Europe quickened, and the flow of warnings and appeals as well. The Spanish civil war, with Russia intervening on one side, Germany and Italy on the other, was a sign of things to come, and it galvanized the attention of many writers, including André Malraux from France; George Orwell, W. H. Auden, and Stephen Spender from England; and John Dos Passos and Ernest Hemingway from America. In the title of his novel *For Whom the Bell Tolls* (1940), which was based on his experiences as a war correspondent in Spain, Hemingway suggested that the bells tolling in Europe were tolling for the world as well. In January 1936, however, ten million American workers remained unemployed, and America's face still turned inward, waiting for full recovery to arrive. America First was the name of one isolationist organization, and it was the slogan of many Americans. It stood for neutrality and against all unnecessary entanglements—whether alliances, aid, or intervention.

As the decade of the 1930s drew to a close, the pace of aggression accelerated. In March 1939 Germany declared the state of Czechoslovakia dissolved; in April Italy invaded Albania; in September Germany invaded Poland. In 1938 and again in 1939 Hitler both intensified and broadened his persecution of Europe's Jews. Still America's reluctance persisted. A remarkable phrase, characterizing the whole European debacle as "the phony war," gained rather than lost currency during the dark fall and winter of 1939–1940. The message America sent abroad was blunt: Germany, Italy, and Japan would have to be stopped without American involvement.

A World Grown Suddenly Small

There comes a time in the affairs of men when they must prepare to defend not their homes alone, but the tenets of faith and humanity on which their churches, their government and their very civilization are founded. . . . The world has grown so small and weapons of attack so swift that no nation can be safe in its will to pursue peace so long as any other single nation refuses to settle its grievances at the council table. . . . In our foreign relations we have learned from the past what not to do. From new wars we have learned . . . that effective timing of defense and the distant points from which attacks may be launched are completely different from what they were twenty years ago.

Franklin Delano Roosevelt (1939)

Throughout the bleak spring of 1940, lights continued going out all over Europe. In April Germany invaded Denmark and Norway; in May, Belgium; in June, France. Within a matter of months, Allied resistance had crumbled, the last British troops had been forced off the Continent, and England stood virtually alone, isolated and under siege. Almost immediately, both public opinion and government policy in America began to shift. Citizens moved to organize—the Committee to Defend America by Aiding the Allies sprang up in the Midwest in May, soon to be followed by a like-minded organization, the Century Group, based in New York. In June President Roosevelt pledged to send aid "to the opponents of force"—a pledge he honored, first, in the fall of 1940, by sending Britain fifty destroyers, and second, in the spring of 1941, by initiating the "lend-lease" agreement that would eventually send Britain approximately $7 billion in aid. Although neutrality remained the official policy of the United States, it had ceased strictly to control action, and events were running hard against its revival. In June 1941 Germany invaded Russia; in July Japan occupied southern Indochina. Then, on the morning of December 7, 1941, a day President Roosevelt said would "live in infamy," Japan bombed Pearl Harbor.

Japan's attack on Pearl Harbor was one of the most successful surprise attacks in military history, and it left the United States reeling. It would be months before good news came from either the Atlantic or the Pacific. But the attack also put an end to effective dissent, if not to isolationist murmurings. The unity of purpose that the president had first articulated in June 1940—"In our unity, our American unity," he had said, we shall support "the opponents of force" and shall prove "equal to the task of every emergency and every defense"—quickly took shape. Families began and ended their days gathered around radios, listening to news reports on the war or "fireside chats" by the president.

In going to war, the nation also went back to work. Volunteers, female and male, black and white, poured in record numbers into factories as well as the armed services. Soon people who had been unemployed were saving money to buy "Victory Bonds" through payroll deductions, and Hollywood was making movies about factory workers (*Blondie for Victory*) as well as pilots, soldiers, and sailors *(Salute to Courage* and *To the Shores of Tripoli).* Stage and screen stars traveled around the world to entertain the troops, while directors like Frank Capra, John Huston, and John Ford began making documentary films—some pieced together from stock war footage, others shot on location. Leaders of the American Federation of Labor and the Congress of Industrial Organizations adopted a no-strike policy, and the manufacture of war supplies soared. In 1940 the aviation industry produced 12,000 planes; in 1943 it produced more than 100,000. In addition to arming its own troops, the United States sent thousands of planes, tanks, and trucks to Russia and England. The result was the most successful war effort the world has ever seen.

"A Tremendous Flash of Light"

At exactly fifteen minutes past eight in the morning, on August 6, 1945, Japanese time, . . . the atomic bomb flashed above Hiroshima. . . . There was no sound of planes. The morning was still; the place was cool and pleasant.

Then a tremendous flash of light cut across the sky. . . .

Early . . . [on] August 7th, the Japanese radio broadcast for the first time a succinct announcement that very few, if any, of the people most concerned with its content, the survivors in Hiroshima, happened to hear: "Hiroshima suffered considerable damage as the result of an attack by a few B-29s. It is believed that a new type of bomb was used. The details are being investigated." Nor is it probable that any of the survivors happened to be tuned in on a short-wave rebroadcast of an extraordinary announcement by the President of the United States, which identified the new bomb as atomic: "That bomb had more power than twenty thousand tons of TNT. It had more than two thousand times the blast power of the British Grand Slam, which is the largest bomb ever yet used in the history of warfare." Those victims who were able to worry at all about what had happened thought of it and discussed it in more primitive, childish terms—gasoline sprinkled from an airplane, maybe, or some combustible gas, or a big cluster of incendiaries, or the work of parachutists; but, even if they had known the truth, most of them were too busy or too weary or too badly hurt to care that they were the objects of the first great experiment in the use of atomic power, which (as the voices on the short wave shouted) no country except the United States, with its industrial know-how, its willingness to throw two billion gold dollars into an important wartime gamble, could possibly have developed. . . .

At two minutes after eleven o'clock on the morning of August 9th, the second atomic bomb was dropped, on Nagasaki. It was several days before the survivors of Hiroshima knew they had company, because the Japanese radio and newspapers were being extremely cautious on the subject of the strange weapon.

John Hersey, *Hiroshima* (1946)

In June 1942, seven months after Pearl Harbor, Allied forces halted Japan's advance across the Pacific at the Battle of Midway; in August they launched a successful counteroffensive at Guadalcanal, turning the tide of battle in the Pacific. On November 8, 1942, Allied forces invaded North Africa to start on the long road toward liberating Europe. Less than two years later, they staged major new offensives in both the Atlantic and the Pacific: On June 6, 1944, they invaded Normandy, piercing Germany's hold on northern Europe; two weeks later they won a decisive victory over the Japanese fleet in the Battle of Leyte Gulf. Less than one year later, when the war in Europe ended, on May 7, 1945, with Germany's "unconditional surrender," Allied forces had taken Iwo Jima and Okinawa and were poised to invade the mainland of Japan.

Given the unparalleled magnitude of World War II and the unparalleled horror of the Holocaust—including the systematic annihilation of six million Jews—the twentieth century's second "Great War" was certain to mark the consciousness of the world for decades to come. As it turned out, however, one cataclysmic event remained to reinforce one of the haunting lessons of the twentieth century—that nations have done whatever their weapons made possible. More than any war in history, World War II was a war of technology—of new developments in synthetic rubber, radar, microwaves, and rockets as well as ships, planes, and weaponry. In the summer of 1939, after a group of physicists that included Albert Einstein and Enrico Fermi met in Washington, D.C., President Roosevelt established the Advisory Committee on Uranium and thus initiated development of the atomic bomb. On July 16, 1945, in Alamogordo, New Mexico, the United States successfully tested the world's first atomic bomb. Less than one month later, on August 6 and August 9, the United States dropped atomic bombs on Hiroshima and Nagasaki, ushering in a new era even as it brought World War II to an end.

Literature and Reform in an Age of Conformity

World War II was in many ways "bad for writing," William Faulkner wrote his agent in 1944. For several younger writers and a few older ones, the war's interruption was direct. Saul Bellow served in the merchant marine, John Cheever and Norman Mailer in the U.S. Army, Ernest Hemingway once again as a war correspondent. Having failed to get a commission, Faulkner spent considerable time in Hollywood, working on screenplays about Nazi spies (*Northern Pursuit*) or great heroes (*The De Gaulle Story*). But the larger problem was the preemptive force of the war itself, which seemed to put almost everything that was not directly related to the war effort, including most literature, on hold for the duration.

Americans emerged from World War II convinced that they had participated in the great adventure of their time. Literary appropriation of the war commenced immediately and continued long. It reaches from the 1940s, with John Hersey's *Hiroshima* (1946), James Gould Cozzens's *Guard of Honor* (1948), and Norman Mailer's *The Naked and the Dead* (1948); through the 1950s, with James Jones's *From Here to Eternity* (1951), Herman Wouk's *The Caine Mutiny*

(1951), and Thomas Berger's *Crazy in Berlin* (1958), and the 1960s, with Joseph Heller's *Catch-22* (1961); to the 1970s, with Thomas Pynchon's *Gravity's Rainbow* (1973). Other works, such as Harriette Arnow's *The Dollmaker* (1954), reflected the impact of the war on "the home front," as it came to be called.

Many of these works emanate from troubled sensibilities and constitute counterrealities. They are imaginative violences from within that seek to match physical violences from without. As such, they offer minority reports—each what Wallace Stevens once called an "unofficial view of being." But they do not disclose disillusionment comparable to that seen in the literature of World War I. Despite the sacrifices and losses that it inflicted, World War II fostered a sense of unity that ran deep and proved durable.

Confident that the war had tested their nation many times and hopeful that most of the tests lay behind them, Americans emerged from World War II impatient to get on with life. The troops were ready to come home, and their families and friends were ready to welcome them. Demobilization was rapid. Yet, contrary to expectations, problems surfaced almost immediately. In 1946 the nation lost a colossal 107,475,000 workdays to strikes, slowing production and increasing prices. Disputes between labor and management remained a problem for years to come. Some servicemen returned home only to find themselves feeling lost without the sense of high purpose that the war had given them. Many women emerged from the war hoping that their large contributions to the war effort would provide a basis for a new start, only to find that they were expected to step aside as returning servicemen moved back into the work force.

In 1946 Mary Beard published *Woman as a Force in History,* hoping to push the beginnings of the women's movement back beyond the nineteenth century through the Renaissance to the Middle Ages. *Life* magazine described Beard's work as "simply ridiculous," then went on to suggest that the nation might cure such madness by drafting women into the army so that men could teach them the meaning of discipline and responsibility. As it turned out, however, apathy proved more damaging than hostility: Beard's book remained widely unread, her cause largely unfulfilled. In 1912 the distinguished anthropologist Ruth Benedict had written, "My real me was a creature I dared not look upon. . . . No one had ever heard that me. If they had, they would have thought it an interesting pose. The mask was tightly adjusted." Despite scattered changes and many promises, Benedict's words were almost as pertinent in the 1940s and the 1950s as they had been in 1912.

For black Americans, on the other hand, World War II marked a significant, if modest, turning point. "A change will come out of this war," Faulkner wrote in a letter of July 4, 1943, referring to the heroic actions of black servicemen in the war, that will force "the politicians and the people who run this country . . . to make good the shibboleth they glibly talk about freedom, liberty, human rights." In 1945 Richard Wright published *Black Boy.* Two years later Jackie Robinson, Branch Rickey, and the Brooklyn Dodgers defied baseball's rigid racial line, and so began the long struggle to integrate professional sports. A decade later, in 1957, while Congress was passing its first piece of civil rights legislation since Reconstruction, Althea Gibson, a young black woman born in South

Carolina and reared in Harlem, murmured "at last, at last" as she curtsied before the Queen of England to receive tennis's most coveted award, the Wimbledon trophy. Between Robinson's achievement in the summer of 1947 and Gibson's in the summer of 1957, President Truman integrated the U.S. armed services (1948), the Supreme Court struck down segregation in the public schools (1954), and Martin Luther King organized a successful bus boycott in Montgomery, Alabama (1956), launching a campaign that would eventually win the support of thousands of people working in hundreds of towns and cities.

More striking, however, than either the disappointments or the reforms of American life in the late 1940s and the 1950s was the strong sense of unity that rolled across the land. Despite ups and downs, the nation's economy remained strong; despite frustrations, its expectations remained high. In 1947 some four million men and women were attending colleges and universities on the G.I. Bill. When details of the wreckage that Germany had wrought in Europe and that Japan had wrought in Asia began to emerge, and especially when details of the atrocities inflicted on the Jews of Europe began to circulate, World War II became even more clearly a great crusade. The sheer magnitude of the Holocaust was staggering: six million Jews—men, women, and children—annihilated. But as seared memories and ghastly reports began to disclose details of what had happened in the gas chambers, in the medical and military "experimental" stations, in the crematoriums, and in the torture chambers of the Nazi concentration camps, the United States was forced to confront what its soldiers had confronted as they liberated those camps: "There," wrote Colonel William W. Quinn, who led U.S. 7th Army troops in rescuing the survivors of Dachau, "our troops found sights, sounds, and stenches horrible beyond belief, cruelties so enormous as to be incomprehensible to the normal mind."

"Ashes in the Stream of the Sola"

Then they would feel the gas and crowd together away from the menacing columns and finally stampede towards the huge metal door with its little window, where they piled up in one blue clammy blood-spattered pyramid, clawing and mauling at each other even in death. Twenty-five minutes later the "exhauster" electric pumps removed the gas-laden air, the great metal door slid open, and the men of the Jewish *Sonderkommando* entered, wearing gas-masks and gumboots and carrying hoses, for their first task was to remove the blood and defecations before dragging the clawing dead apart with nooses and hooks, the prelude to the ghastly search for gold and the removal of the teeth and hair which were regarded by the Germans as strategic materials. Then the journey by lift or rail-wagon to the furnaces, the mill that ground the clinker to fine ash, and the lorry that scattered the ashes in the stream of the Sola.

quoted in Gerald Reitlinger, *The Final Solution* (1953)

"But I Had No More Tears"

There was silence all round now, broken only by groans. In front of the block, the SS were giving orders. An officer passed by the beds. My father begged me:

"My son, some water. . . . I'm burning. . . . My stomach. . . ."

"Quiet, over there!" yelled the officer.

"Eliezer," went on my father, "some water. . . ."

The officer came up to him and shouted at him to be quiet. But my father did not hear him. He went on calling me. The officer dealt him a violent blow on the head with his truncheon.

I did not move. I was afraid. My body was afraid of also receiving a blow.

Then my father made a rattling noise and it was my name: "Eliezer."

I could see that he was still breathing—spasmodically.

I did not move.

When I got down after roll call, I could see his lips trembling as he murmured something. Bending over him, I stayed gazing at him for over an hour, engraving into myself the picture of his blood-stained face, his shattered skull.

Then I had to go to bed. I climbed into my bunk, above my father, who was still alive. It was January 28, 1945.

I awoke on January 29 at dawn. In my father's place lay another invalid. They must have taken him away before dawn and carried him to the crematory. He may still have been breathing.

There were no prayers at his grave. No candles were lit to his memory. His last word was my name. A summons, to which I did not respond.

I did not weep, and it pained me that I could not weep. But I had no more tears.

Elie Wiesel, Night (1958)

Soon Russia began to bolster the strong sense of American unity that came out of the war through a series of aggressive acts in Europe. "We have got to understand," Dean Acheson announced early in 1946, "that all our lives the danger, the uncertainty, the need for alertness, for effort, for discipline will be upon us. It will be hard for us." On March 5, 1946, Winston Churchill journeyed from England to Missouri to warn that an "iron curtain" had descended across Europe, separating the East from the West. One year later, on March 12, 1947, President Truman outlined the Truman Doctrine: "I believe that it must be the policy of the United States to support free peoples who are resisting attempted subjugation by armed minorities or by outside pressures." But Russia's response to such declarations was clear: Having already occupied Poland, Russia overran Hungary in April, and a year later, in February 1948, Czechoslovakia. On June 5, 1947, General George Marshall, secretary of state, moved to counter Russia's expansion into Europe by setting in motion the Marshall Plan—a plan designed to combat the "hunger, poverty, desperation, and chaos" that threatened western Europe by restoring the region's economy and permitting "the emergence of political and social conditions in which free institutions can exist." A year later, on June 19, 1948, Russia blockaded Berlin, forcing the United States to organize an airlift that would last until the blockade was lifted on May 12, 1949. Eventually, however, Russia's aggressive acts worked to alienate all but the most determined of its friends, perhaps in part because they bore too close a resemblance to Germany's expansion in the 1930s.

Despite domestic tensions, therefore, the dominant forces at work in the United States between 1945 and 1960 were centripetal. Never before had there been so little resistance to the integration of intellectuals, including writers and artists, into the government, the media, and the universities. One result was the rush of novels set in universities, including Mary McCarthy's *The Groves of Academe* (1952), Randall Jarrell's *Pictures from an Institution* (1954), and John Barth's *The End of the Road* (1958). Soon artists and intellectuals were less concerned with the crippling impact of alienation than with the debilitating impact of assimilation. In 1952 *Partisan Review* organized a symposium called "Our Country and Our Culture" and invited twenty-five of the nation's leading literary critics, writers, sociologists, political theorists, anthropologists, and philosophers to respond to the proposition that "American intellectuals now regard America and its institutions in a new way." The clear consensus was not only that intellectuals did in fact regard America in a new way, but also that *new* meant "less critical." Having once appeared skeptical and even jaundiced toward their country, writers now seemed sympathetic and even protective—in part because they regarded America as less hostile to art, and in part because they regarded America as offering the only viable alternative to "Russian totalitarianism."

Such thinking troubled a few participants in the *Partisan Review* symposium. Norman Mailer described the symposium's assumptions as "shocking." Two years later, in an essay called "This Age of Conformity" (1954), Irving Howe declared dangerous the tendency to endorse America's "claim to a unique and immaculate destiny." But unity and its corollary, conformity, remained the dominant forces of the age, particularly during the Eisenhower years (1953–1961) and especially in the business world. David Riesman's sociological study *The Lonely Crowd* (1950) —which traced the rise of "other-directed people," people whose actions are based less on internal convictions than on responses "to the signals" provided by their contemporary peers—became one of the classics of the age, anticipating Sloan Wilson's novel, *The Man in the Gray Flannel Suit* (1955), as well as William S. Whyte's work of social analysis, *The Organization Man* (1956).

With the rise of unity and conformity came clear political dangers, as Senator Joe McCarthy (Republican, Wisconsin) promptly proved. Between February 1950, when he made his first dramatic accusations, and December 1954, when he became the fourth senator in 167 years to be censured by the Senate, McCarthy headed an inquisition that dominated the American political scene as few events ever had before. On one side, McCarthy exploited the nation's legitimate concerns for issues of national security; on the other, he exploited the nation's uneasiness with everything strange or foreign. In the process, he accused hundreds

"Other-Directed People"

What is common to all the other-directed people is that their contemporaries are the source of direction for the individual—either those known to [them] or those with whom [they are] indirectly acquainted, through friends and through the mass media. . . .

Of course, it matters very much who these "others" are: whether they are the individual's immediate circle or a "higher" circle or the anonymous voices of the mass media; whether the individual fears the hostility of chance acquaintances or only of those who "count." But his need for approval and direction from others—and contemporary others rather than ancestors—goes beyond the reasons that lead most people in any era to care very much what others think of them. While all people want and need to be liked by some of the people some of the time, it is only the modern other-directed types who make this their chief source of direction and chief area of sensitivity.

David Riesman, *The Lonely Crowd: A Study of the Changing American Character* (1950)

of people—composers like Aaron Copland, writers like Howard Fast and Lillian Hellman, professors like Owen Lattimore and Philip Jessup—of being either Communists, Communist sympathizers, or Communist dupes. Before he was done, he had impugned the loyalty of Secretary of State George Marshall, the Department of State, the U.S. Information Service, the U.S. Army, and even President Eisenhower.

The McCarthy debacle tested the nation's commitment to civil liberties—its tolerance of dissent and its respect for freedom of conscience—many times. Among direct literary responses to the ordeal, the most notable was Arthur Miller's *The Crucible* (1953). Still, the sense of unity that remained dominant also proved useful, enabling the nation to confront a series of international crises, including the blockade of Berlin (1948–1949); the emergence of Communist China (1949); Russia's development of the atomic bomb (1949); the development of the hydrogen bomb, first in the United States (1952) and then in Russia (1953); the Suez Canal crisis (1956–1958); the launchings of *Sputnik I* and *Sputnik II* (1957); Castro's victory in Cuba (1959); and especially a hard, ambiguous war in Korea in which more than 50,000 men died and nearly 100,000 were wounded. Furthermore, although unity clearly carried cultural as well as political implications, including some that were alarming, it proved to be stimulating rather than stultifying. If only by provoking what Robert Frost once called "counter-love, original response," the 1950s produced both an impressive culture and a lively counterculture.

The Literature of the 1950s

The counterculture of the 1950s—the hippies and the "beat generation"— appealed, as one young writer put it, to those unable to find gray flannel suits to fit their souls. Centered around such poets as Allen Ginsberg and Lawrence Ferlinghetti and such prose writers as Jack Kerouac, the hippies made the City Lights Book Store in the North Beach area of San Francisco famous. College students across the country listened to recordings of Ginsberg reading "Howl." One of the striking features of the counterculture of the 1950s, however, is the extent to which its very considerable political potential remained quiescent, in both poetry and music.

The rock and roll music of Elvis Presley came in part out of the rhythm and blues tradition—music played by blacks for blacks—and it came in part out of the country and western tradition—music played largely by whites for whites. Presley's music thus drew on two different traditions of protest, much of it bitter. Yet the protest in Presley's music dealt more with natural desires, sad fates, and repressive mores than with the oppressive power of American culture and thus remained largely innocent of politics. It was later—with Bob Dylan in the 1960s more than with Elvis Presley in the 1950s, and with the Rolling Stones more than with the Beatles—that America's counterculture became a political force.

At the same time, literature flourished. Scores of writers—Eudora Welty from Mississippi; Saul Bellow from the West Side of Chicago; Norman Mailer, Arthur Miller, and Bernard Malamud from Brooklyn, New York; Ralph Ellison from Oklahoma, by way of Alabama and Harlem; James Baldwin from Harlem; and Flannery O'Connor from Milledgeville, Georgia—emerged to confront us with protagonists whose indignation bespeaks an involvement in their worlds and whose dissent signals a love for it. Some of the protagonists of the 1950s are hampered and preshrunk by fear of being different; others are too dangling or lonely ever to be complete; still others are so dominated by intolerance, poorly repressed hostilities, hidden doubts, or secret fears that their violence finally turns either against themselves or against others. Like Mailer's Sam Slovoda in "The Man Who Studied Yoga," they frequently find themselves torn between "the loss of a country" they love yet have "never seen" and "repudiation" of the only country in which they have ever lived. Blacks, Jews, and southerners alike find it difficult to be what they are—and just as difficult not to be what they are. As a result, they are tested many times. In their affirmations and celebrations, as in their denials and renunciations, they are at least as apt to fail as to succeed. Most of them feel alienated, and some of them, particularly those created by Flannery O'Connor, are so estranged that their emotions seem borrowed, their actions accidental. Yet at mid-century art remained a way of reaching for the timeless— or, as Eudora Welty put it, a way of making "time give back all it has taken, through turning life by way of the memory into art."

Writing in "The Territory Ahead," Wright Morris states that "an element of despair, a destructive element, is one of the signs" by which we must recognize "the modern temper" and that another "is the constructive use to which this element is put." Like the writers of the 1920s and 1930s, writers of the 1950s force their disillusionment to serve the purposes of experimentation and reinvention. Their indignation, their dissent, and even their despair, they direct toward discovery. In their fiction, the inherited is transformed into the new, and the bleak is merged with the experimental.

The End of Unity

Compared with the drastic dislocations of the 1960s, the crises that punctuated the 1950s have come almost inevitably to seem much tamer than they were. For the 1960s, as the phrase goes, were "something else." To one recent historian, they represent "the unraveling of America"; to another, they constitute "America's suicide attempt." Given the countermoves of the 1970s, both phrases may seem extreme, but the 1960s, dominated by extreme actions, now lend themselves to extreme statements.

In May 1960 the Russians shot down an American spy plane over their territory, then proceeded to watch as one American official after another, including President Eisenhower, embarrassed themselves by issuing false denials and misleading reports. Five months later a judge in Georgia invoked a technicality in order to put Martin Luther King in jail. But neither the deceit of May nor the hypocrisy of October could foreshadow what was to come. In January 1961 John Fitzgerald Kennedy became the first Roman Catholic to be sworn in as president of the United States. A few months later, with summer on its way, Bob Dylan left Minnesota for Greenwich Village, where he launched a spectacular career writing and singing songs whose titles—"Blowin' in the Wind," "A Hard Rain's Gonna Fall," "The Times They Are A-Changing"— anticipated the sharp turns and twists that lay ahead. That same summer, violence broke out across the South, as "freedom riders" sought to integrate public transportation.

Rock and Roll

Starting simply as a vehicle for solo performers, rock and roll didn't differ radically from some of the popular music that had preceded it. Out of Negro rhythm and blues and country and western came Elvis Presley . . . with his long sideburns, tight pants and suggestive gyrations. . . . The Beatles, bursting onto the scene in the early '60s with Edwardian clothes and English schoolboy haircuts, transformed the original primitive Negro sound, making it acceptable to the mass of young white people all over the world. They brought to prominence Group Rock, one of the most attractive symbols of our non-private, corporate, thoroughly electronic age. Now literally "armies of minstrels"—the Beach Boys, the Jefferson Airplane, the Grateful Dead, the Who, the Bee Gees, the Doors, the Mothers of Invention, the Buffalo Springfield, and so on—indicate the awesome potential of electronic sound.

Joan Peyser, "The Music of Sound, or, The Beatles and the Beatless" (1967)

The civil rights movement of the late 1950s and the 1960s is often associated with the violent confrontations that it triggered and with the way it touched every region of the country, spawning clashes in the North, the Midwest, and the West as well as the South. But race riots had occurred in Atlanta around the turn of the century, in Detroit in 1943, and in Harlem in 1935 and 1943. What distinguished the movement of the 1950s and the 1960s was its success in arousing the moral conscience of people everywhere and its success in marshaling the power of the federal government, as seen in the historic Civil Rights Act of 1964 and the Voting Rights Act of 1965.

In September 1962 it took both a federal court order and federal marshals to integrate the University of Mississippi. On April 3, 1963, King launched his campaign to demolish segregation in Birmingham. "Downtown Birmingham," he wrote later, "echoed to the strains of the freedom songs." Four months later, on August 28, in what was perhaps the greatest day in the history of the civil rights movement, King led 200,000 Americans in a march on Washington. Gathered at the Lincoln Memorial, the crowd listened first to such performers as Dick Gregory, Joan Baez, and Bob Dylan, then to Martin Luther King:

> When the architects of our great republic wrote the magnificent words of the Constitution and the Declaration of Independence, they were signing a promissory note to which every American was to fall heir. This note was a promise that all men, yes, black men as well as white men, would be guaranteed the inalienable rights of life, liberty, and the pursuit of happiness.

"The Racist Cancer in the Body of America"

You watch. I will be labeled as, at best, an "irresponsible" black man. I have always felt about this accusation that the black "leader" whom white men consider to be "responsible" is invariably the black "leader" who never gets any results. You only get action as a black man if you are regarded by the white man as "irresponsible." In fact, this much I had learned when I was just a little boy. And since I have been some kind of a "leader" of black people here in the racist society of America, I have been more reassured each time the white man resisted me, or attacked me harder—because each time made me more certain that I was on the right track in the American black man's best interests. The racist white man's opposition automatically made me know that I did offer the black man something worthwhile.

Yes, I have cherished my "demagogue" role. I know that societies often have killed the people who have helped to change those societies. And if I can die having brought any light, having exposed any meaningful truth that will help to destroy the racist cancer that is malignant in the body of America—then, all of the credit is due to Allah. Only the mistakes have been mine.

The Autobiography of Malcolm X (1964)

Compared with the voices of leaders like Malcolm X, John Lewis, H. Rap Brown, and Stokely Carmichael, King's was a moderate voice. But nerves were raw and suspicions ran high in the 1960s. Before the end of 1963, Robert Kennedy, attorney general of the United States, had agreed with J. Edgar Hoover, director of the Federal Bureau of Investigation, that King was a dangerous man. In October the FBI set up wiretaps on King's telephone; in December FBI officials gathered in Washington to explore ways of "neutralizing King as an effective Negro leader." They would expose him, one official promised, as the "clerical fraud and Marxist he is."

"These Disillusioned Colored Pioneers"

I want to talk about the first Northern urban generation of Negroes. . . . This is a story of their searching, their dreams, their sorrows, their small and futile rebellions, and their endless battle to establish their own place in America's greatest metropolis—and in America itself.

The characters are sons and daughters of former Southern sharecroppers. These were the poorest people of the South, who poured into New York City during the decade following the Great Depression. These migrants were told that unlimited opportunities for prosperity existed in New York and that there was no "color problem" there. They were told that Negroes lived in houses with bathrooms, electricity, running water, and indoor toilets. To them, this was the "promised land" that Mammy had been singing about in the cotton fields for many years.

Going to New York was good-bye to the cotton fields, good-bye to "Massa Charlie," good-bye to the chain gang, and, most of all, good-bye to those sunup-to-sundown working hours. One no longer had to wait to get to heaven to lay his burden down; burdens could be laid down in New York.

So, they came, from all parts of the South, like all the black chillun o' God following the sound of Gabriel's horn on that long-overdue Judgment Day. . . . Even while planning the trip, they sang spirituals as "Jesus Take My Hand" and "I'm On My Way" and chanted, "Hallelujah, I'm on my way to the promised land!"

It seems that Cousin Willie, in his lying haste, had neglected to tell the folks down home about one of the most important aspects of the promised land: it was a slum ghetto. There was a tremendous difference in the way life was lived up North. There were too many people full of hate and bitterness crowded into a dirty, stinky, uncared-for closet-size section of a great city. . . .

The children of these disillusioned colored pioneers inherited the total lot of their parents—the disappointments, the anger. To add to their misery, they had little hope of deliverance. For where does one run to when he's already in the promised land?

Claude Brown, *Manchild in the Promised Land* (1965)

Throughout 1963, protesters marched in the South, from Raleigh, North Carolina, to Jackson, Mississippi, and in the North, the Midwest and the West, from New York to St. Louis to Los Angeles. In the fall school boycotts broke out in Boston, Chicago, and New York. The next July race riots erupted in Harlem and then upstate in Rochester; by August they had spread to Paterson and Elizabeth in New Jersey; by September they had reached Philadelphia, Pennsylvania. A year later, on August 11, 1965, the spirit of violent confrontation reached a new peak when the worst of the decade's riots broke out in Watts, a ghetto in southeast Los Angeles, to the chant of "Burn, baby, burn"—a story recounted in Robert Conot's *Rivers of Blood, Years of Darkness* (1967).

Between the freedom riders of 1961 and the burning of Watts in 1965, the United States wandered from involvement in the ill-considered and inept invasion of Cuba at the Bay of Pigs, to a dangerous confrontation with Russia in the Cuban missile crisis, to a fateful intensification of hostilities in Vietnam, first under President Kennedy and then under President Johnson. Soon the spirit of protest generated by the civil rights movement began discovering, in the women's movement and especially in Vietnam, new causes and new voices.

Having been largely stymied for a decade or more, the women's movement entered a new era. From Betty Friedan's *Feminine Mystique* (1963) through Kate Millett's *Sexual Politics* (1970) to the writings of Elizabeth Janeway and Gloria Steinem, a new generation of women writers not only surpassed the sophistication of such precedessors as Mary Beard but also set new standards for influencing public consciousness and public policy, particularly in the 1970s.

In the mid-1960s, however, it was Vietnam more than either civil rights or women's rights that dominated American life. Efforts to close down military induction centers or to impede the flow of military personnel and supplies spread across the land. "We're now in the business of wholesale disruption and widespread resistance and dislocation of the American society," Jerry Rubin announced, adding that for the sake of their cause they were willing "to risk injuries, even deaths." Writers and intellectuals who had remained largely supportive of the government during the 1950s (taken in, Irving Howe had suggested, by an "age of conformity") suddenly found themselves at odds with

---

Of Blood and Darkness

We'll give this country a chance. We'll give 'em a chance to make up for what they've done in the past, we'll give 'em a chance to say "We know we've done you wrong, and we're gonna do our best to change it!" But I'm not gonna have nobody tell me what to do. . . . I'm gonna be the master of my life, and if they try to run over me, I'm gonna demolish them! And next time, baby, let me tell you, it's not gonna be a gentle war like it was, it's not gonna be the soul people doing all the bleeding. . . . If we get pushed again, it's gonna be goodbye, baby.

Robert Conot, *Rivers of Blood, Years of Darkness* (1967)

their government. Soon the era of unity and support seemed little more than a faded memory, to some a shameful one. Writers like Norman Mailer, Bernard Malamud, and Susan Sontag, poets like Robert Lowell and Robert Penn Warren, linguists like Noam Chomsky, and philosophers like Hannah Arendt joined in protesting the nation's deepening involvement in Vietnam. "We are in danger of imperceptibly becoming an explosive and suddenly chauvinistic nation, and we may even be drifting on our way to the last nuclear ruin," Robert Lowell wrote President Johnson in 1965, in what he described as an "anguished, delicate and perhaps determining moment."

The sense of crisis that marked the 1960s had, of course, several sources. But much of its particular intensity derived from a changed assessment of where responsibility for international crises lay. At the *Partisan Review* symposium in 1952, "Russian totalitarianism" was perceived to "threaten world domination." In 1965 "an explosive and suddenly chauvinistic" United States was seen to threaten world peace. In October 1967 protesters organized a march on the Pentagon as part of a nationwide "Stop the Draft Week." From this remarkable event came Mailer's *Armies of the Night* (1968). Shortly before the march, a dissenter named Paul Goodman informed a group of business executives gathered at the State Department that they, as shapers of America's military-industrial might, were "the most dangerous body of men at the present in the world." Goodman then joined Lowell and Mailer and fifty thousand other Americans in a march that took them from the steps of the Lincoln Memorial to the steps of the Pentagon.

By the mid-1960s, strong centrifugal forces were pulling the country apart. Some protesters believed that all forms of central economic planning, from welfare programs to corporate capitalism, inevitably undermined freedom, carrying people, as Friedrich A. von Hayek had put it, along *The Road to Serfdom* (1944). Others saw repression, above all sexual repression, as the enemy. "Dionysus, the mad god, breaks down the boundaries; releases the prisoners; abolishes repression," Norman O. Brown wrote in *Love's Body* (1966), in order to restore "the unity of man and the unity of man with nature." Still others, committed to those after whom Frantz Fanon titled his book *The Wretched of the Earth* (published in French in 1961, in English in 1965), believed that only violence could cleanse the land. "It is a struggle of total revolution," Stokely Carmichael said, "in which we propose to change the imperialist, capitalist and racialist structure" that oppresses people within the United States and threatens people beyond it.

Assassinations tell a part of the story: John Kennedy, November 22, 1963; Malcolm X, February 21, 1965; Martin Luther King, April 4, 1968; Robert Kennedy, June 4, 1968. But violence erupted in many places and took many forms. In August 1968, at the Democratic national convention, an army of 10,000 protesters clashed with an army of 22,000 law enforcers, and blood ran in the streets in what Mailer called "the siege of Chicago." "We Want Revolution," Mark Rudd wrote a month later, in a piece published in the *Saturday Evening Post*.

As the decade drew to a close, no one saw an end to the turmoil. Earlier President Kennedy had spoken of a "New Frontier" and President Johnson of a

"The Center Was Not Holding"

The center was not holding. It was a country of . . . commonplace reports of casual killings and misplaced children and abandoned homes and vandals who misspelled even the four-letter words they scrawled. . . . Adolescents drifted from city to torn city, sloughing off both the past and the future as snakes shed their skins, children who were never taught and would never now learn the games that had held the society together. . . .

It was not a country in open revolution. It was not a country under enemy siege. It was the United States of America in the cold late spring of 1967, and the market was steady and the G.N.P. high and a great many articulate people seemed to have a sense of high social purpose and it might have been a spring of brave hopes and national promise, but it was not, and more and more people had the uneasy apprehension that it was not. All that seemed clear was that at some point we had aborted ourselves and butchered the job, and because nothing else seemed so relevant I decided to go to San Francisco. San Francisco was where the social hemorrhaging was showing up. San Francisco was where the missing children were gathering and calling themselves "hippies."

Joan Didion, *Slouching Towards Bethlehem* (1968)

"Great Society"; both had dreamed of extending the blessings of American life to the poor and the black, hoping to renew the nation's sense of purpose and reinforce its sense of unity. But their plans had gone badly awry, undone by frustrations that ran too deep, anxieties that touched too much. In the early 1950s the nation had endured the Korean "conflict" under the leadership of President Truman, who could never quite decide whether the nation was or was not at war. Gradually, the American people had learned to live with phrases like "limited engagement" and "Cold War" and without phrases like "decisive victory" and "unconditional surrender." Later still, the nation had overcome the self-doubt that followed its failed efforts to match the success of *Sputnik I* and *Sputnik II*— "Flopnik," "Stay-putnik," and "Kaputnik," the British press called America's first ventures in space. "General annihilation beckons," Albert Einstein said when he learned that President Truman had ordered the Atomic Energy Commission to continue development of the hydrogen bomb. But the war in Vietnam, which had no clear beginning and would come to no clear end, seemed suddenly to have exhausted the nation's capacity for tolerating failure, uncertainty, and ambiguity. As a result, Vietnam bathed the nation not only in blood but also in the language of blood. "Minutemen" and "Black Panthers" sprang up to preach as well as practice violence; people talked of armies clashing by night, of sieges and marches, of fires in the earth. In May 1970, in the wake of President Nixon's decision to invade Cambodia, angry confrontations swept across the country, closing down everything from subways and buses to universities, including Kent State University, where a detachment of young National Guardsmen killed four students.

Still, the war that Secretary of Defense Robert McNamara had once budgeted to end by June 30, 1967, dragged on. By April 1975, when the United States finally withdrew from Vietnam, more Americans had died there than had died in Korea. The Vietnam Memorial that stands in Washington, D.C., commemorating American victims of the war, bears more than 55,000 names. Yet when the war finally ended, it ended not with victory nor even with a genuine truce but rather, as Arnold Isaacs has written, with "the collapse of the U.S.-backed armies in South Vietnam and Cambodia and the Communist conquest of all of Indochina, amid scenes of terror and suffering that will forever sear the memories of those who were there."

"So Many Casualties"

Out on the street I couldn't tell the Vietnam veterans from the rock and roll veterans. The Sixties had made so many casualties, its war and its music had run power off the same circuit for so long they didn't even have to fuse. The war rimed you for lame years while rock and roll turned more lurid and dangerous than bullfighting, rock stars started falling like second lieutenants; ecstasy and death and (of course and for sure) life, but it didn't seem so then. What I'd thought of as two obsessions were really only one, I don't know how to tell you how complicated that made my life. Freezing and burning and going down again into the sucking mud of the culture, hold on tight and move real slow.

That December I got a Christmas card from a Marine I'd known in Hue. It showed a psychotic-art Snoopy in battered jungle fatigues, a cigarette clenched in his teeth, blasting away with an M-16. "Peace on Earth, Good Will Toward Men," it read, "and Best Wishes for a Happy One-Niner-Six-Niner."

Maybe it was classic, maybe it was my twenties I was missing and not the Sixties, but I began missing them both before either had really been played out. The year had been so hot that I think it shorted out the whole decade, what followed was mutation, some kind of awful 1969-X. It wasn't just that I was growing older, I was leaking time, like I'd taken a frag from one of those anti-personnel weapons we had that were so small they could kill a man and never show up on X-rays. Hemingway once described the glimpse he'd had of his soul after being wounded, it looked like a fine white handkerchief drawing out of his body, floating away and then returning. What floated out of me was more like a huge gray 'chute, I hung there for a long time waiting for it to open. Or not. My life and my death got mixed up with their lives and deaths, doing the Survivor Shuffle between the two, testing the pull of each and not wanting either very much. I was once in such a bad head about it that I thought the dead had only been spared a great deal of pain.

Michael Herr, *Dispatches* (1978)

The Counterculture of the 1960s and a Changed Literature

In the dominant counterculture of the period, the cult of violence merged with the cult of escape. In some respects, the hippie culture of the 1960s derived from the hip culture of Harlem in the 1920s. More immediately, it was linked to the "beat generation" of the 1950s, particularly Allen Ginsberg's bitter lament ("I saw the best minds of my generation destroyed by madness, starving hysterical naked, / dragging themselves through the negro streets at dawn looking for an angry fix") in "Howl" (1956) and Jack Kerouac's dirge for the lost promise of the New World in *On the Road* (1957). But the new music of the 1960s was the music of the Rolling Stones and the Grateful Dead, and the new drug was the synthetic hallucinogen diethylamide of lysergic acid, which was called LSD or acid by its self-appointed high priest, Timothy Leary. Having first dedicated himself to converting the elite of the country—"the ancient underground society of alchemists, artists, mystics, alienated visionaries, dropouts and the disenchanted young"—Leary later set his sights on an entire generation. By 1966 LSD was big news: *Newsweek* and *Life* had done cover stories on it, Congress had outlawed it, and the Food and Drug Administration had mailed letters to thousands of colleges and universities warning of its danger. In 1968 Tom Wolfe published *The Electric Kool-Aid Acid Test,* depicting Ken Kesey and his "Merry Pranksters" as the epitome of hippie culture.

"A Farewell to All the Promises of America"

The last pages [of Kerouac's *Visions of Cody*] say, "All America marching to this last land." The book was a dirge for America, for its heroes' deaths too, but then who could know except in the unconscious—A dirge for the American Hope that Jack (& his hero Neal) carried so valiantly through the land after Whitman—an America of pioneers and generosity—and selfish glooms & exploitations implicit in the pioneers' entry into Foreign Indian & Moose lands —but the great betrayal of that manly America was made by the pseudo-heroic pseudo-responsible masculines of Army and Industry and Advertising and Construction and Transport and toilets and Wars.

Last pages . . . a farewell to all the promises of America, an explanation & prayer for innocence, a tearful renunciation of victory & accomplishment, a humility in the face of "the necessary blankness of men" in hopeless America, hopeless World, in hopeless wheel of Heaven, a compassionate farewell to Love.

Allen Ginsberg, Introduction to Jack Kerouac's
Visions of Cody (1972)

"Amid the Peaceful Houston Elms"

And they went with the flow, the whole goddamn flow of America. The bus barrels into the superhighway toll stations and the microphones on top of the bus pick up all the clacking and ringing and the mumbling by the toll-station attendant and the brakes squeaking and the gears shifting, all the sounds of the true America that are screened out everywhere else, it all came amplified back inside the bus, while Hagen's camera picked up the faces, the faces in Phoenix, the cops, the service-station owners, the stragglers and the strugglers of America . . . hitting the American asphalt, the open road at 70 miles an hour . . . and they *had* it on tape—and played it back in variable lag skakkkkkk-akkk-akkkk-akkkooooooooooooo.

ooooooooooooooooooooooooooo—Stark Naked, waxing weirder and weirder, huddled in the black blanket shivering, then out, bobbing wraith, her little deep red aureolae bobbing in the crazed vibrations—finally they pull into Houston and head for Larry McMurtry's house. They pull up to McMurtry's house, . . . and the door of the house opens and out comes McMurtry, a slight, slightly wan, kingly-looking shy-looking guy, ambling out, with his little boy, his son, and Cassady opens the door of the bus so everybody can get off, and suddenly Stark Naked shrieks out: "Frankie! Frankie! Frankie! Frankie!"—this being the name of her own divorced-off little boy—and she whips off the blanket and leaps off the bus . . . stark naked, and rushes up to McMurtry's little boy and scoops him up and presses him to her skinny breast, crying and shrieking, "Frankie! oh Frankie! my little Frankie! oh! oh! oh!"—while McMurtry doesn't know what in the name of hell to do, reaching tentatively toward her stark-naked shoulder and saying, "Ma'am! Ma'am! Just a minute, ma'am!"—

—while the Pranksters, spilling out of the bus—stop. The bus is stopped. No roar, no crazed bounce or vibrations, no crazed car beams, no tapes, no microphones. Only Stark Naked, with somebody else's little boy in her arms, is bouncing and vibrating.

And there, amid the peaceful Houston elms on Quenby Road, it dawned on them all that this woman—which one of us even knows her?—had completed her trip. She had gone with the flow. She had gone stark raving mad.

Tom Wolfe, The Electric Kool-Aid Acid Test (1968)

Like the nation surrounding it, the hippie culture of the 1960s was almost violently at odds with itself—torn between its avowed love of American Indians and its obvious fascination with all manner of electronic gadgets; torn, too, between its desire for the beautiful magic of blissful at-onement and its demonstrated fascination with violence. Besides being torn, the hippies were caught. They were heavily dependent on their dread enemy, modern mass technological society—for developing and manufacturing their drugs; for amplifying and recording their music; and for organizing, publicizing, and marketing their "happenings" and their "be-ins." Seeking freedom, they planned a symposium on obscenity. When that failed, they planned one on spontaneity. Once, in the spring of 1967, Allen Ginsberg joined other sponsors in planning a be-in to be staged in the Grand Canyon. Needing the cooperation of the Hopi Indians, they went out to the reservation to talk. "No," the tribe's spokesman said after listening for a time; "you mean well but you are foolish. . . . You are a tribe of strangers to yourselves."

Although folk and rock concerts provided the central cultural "happenings" of the 1960s, the era's larger fascination was with history, or more precisely with the making of history. Soon people who had never dreamt of being movers and shakers participated in marches, sieges, sit-ins, and lock-ins expecting to see themselves on the evening news. By the late 1960s violence seemed to dominate almost everything, particularly television reporting and movies. The movie *Medium Cool* (1969) confronts not only the violence of a nation divided by war but also the consternation of a veteran cameraman who realizes how deeply his cool, detached instrument is implicated in intensifying or distorting the events he "reports."

As it turned out, writers were not only embroiled in the great rumblings of the era but also were changed by them. To John Updike, the turning point was 1959, when Norman Mailer published *Advertisements for Myself.* The date is as good as any, and Mailer is the almost inevitable choice as the representative figure of the 1960s. No writer lived its ups and downs, its turns and twists with more openness or as much energy. Having begun as a novelist, Mailer began during the 1960s both to play prominent roles in events of the time and to publish vast quantities of prose, most of it nonfiction, about those events—about conventions, elections, marches, moon shots, and public executions in books he

---

Legacies of the Beat Generation

Chester Anderson is a legacy of the Beat Generation, a man in his middle thirties whose peculiar hold on the District derives from his possession of a mimeograph machine, on which he prints communiqués signed "the communication company." It is another tenet of the official District mythology that the communication company will print anything anybody has to say, but in fact Chester Anderson prints only what he writes himself, agrees with, or considers harmless or dead matter. . . . An Anderson communiqué might be doing something as specific as fingering someone who is said to have set up a marijuana bust, or it might be working in a more general vein: "Pretty little 16-year-old middle-class chick comes to the Haight to see what it's all about & gets picked up by a 17-year-old street dealer who spends all day shooting her full of speed again & again, then feeds her 3,000 mikes and raffles off her temporarily unemployed body for the biggest Haight Street gangbang since the night before last. The politics and ethics of ecstasy. . . . Kids are starving on the Street. Minds and bodies are being maimed as we watch, a scale model of Vietnam."

Joan Didion, *Slouching Towards Bethlehem* (1968)

called *The Presidential Papers* (1963), *Cannibals and Christians* (1966), *The Armies of the Night* (1968), *Miami and the Siege of Chicago* (1968), *Of a Fire on the Moon* (1970), *The Prisoner of Sex* (1971), and *The Executioner's Song* (1979). In the second of these books, *Cannibals and Christians,* Mailer announced that both of the two dominant "impulses in American letters had failed"—the "realistic impulse," which manifested itself in efforts to represent or mirror life, and the "aristocratic impulse," which manifested itself in efforts to subordinate life to art by transforming life's muddle into art's order and beauty.

What Mailer seeks in nonfiction is a way of redefining these impulses—an undertaking shared by several of his contemporaries. James Baldwin, for example, and Walker Percy and William Gass, have combined the writing of fiction and nonfiction, while several younger contemporaries, including Susan Sontag and Joan Didion, have tended to move from fiction to nonfiction, finding it more congenial. Still others—Tom Wolfe, John McPhee, and Edward Hoagland— simply began with nonfiction. Together writers such as these have brought the "new journalism" to a point where it vies with fiction on equal footing. By 1976 nonfiction appeared to John Updike almost to have supplanted fiction.

From one perspective, of course, the rising authority of nonfiction clearly possesses a history of its own. In 1922 Tristran Tzara, in his "Lecture on Dada," had denied that art is "the most precious manifestation of life," insisting that "Life is far more interesting." But the sheer force of recent events—rapid, dramatic, almost apocalyptic—has clearly promoted nonfiction by reinforcing the notion that life is at least as strange and compelling as fiction can ever be. And from this perspective, John Hersey's *Hiroshima* (1946), one of the first books of the postwar period, becomes a harbinger of the kind of combative journalism that Mailer practices in *The Armies of the Night,* when for the first time we explicitly see "History as a Novel" and then see "The Novel as History."

The rise of nonfiction also has been fostered by the interconnectedness and self-consciousness of American society, which has become more and more avid in its desire to look at itself. Although "Watergate" began as a clumsy spy operation, it led to several elaborate media re-creations—in newspapers, on television, in a best-selling book, and in a popular movie. Together these media events extended the original event by leading not only to clumsy "stonewalling" and "cover-ups" but also to heroic counterspying and investigations, to dramatic exposés, confessions, and conversions. Together these developments forced several government officials, including the president, from office; it made villains of some people, heroes of others. If in Mailer's *Armies of the Night* we may be said to see history as a novel and the novel as history, in Watergate we may be said to see history as the media and the media as history. In a similar vein, one of the crucial scenes in the film *Gimme Shelter* provides an example of what it means to see history as a film and the film as history. For what appears at first as simply another scene in another movie (of a white man knifing a black man within a few feet of a stage where the Rolling Stones are playing music) turns out to have been an actual event. Opportunistically caught on camera, this event (of one of the Hell's Angels knifing a man named Meredith Hunter while the Rolling Stones played at the Altamont Raceway near San Francisco in December 1969) became a scene, first when it was reported in the news and again when it was incorporated into a movie.

The Much-Changed Situation of the Writer

"The Americans of the 1850's wrote with a confidence impossible" to Americans of today. Behind so seemingly simple a statement as this by John Updike lies more than mere nostalgia. "Not now could Melville write, 'The world is as young today as when it was created; and this Vermont morning dew is as wet to my feet, as Eden's dew to Adam's,' " Updike continues, reminding us that sophistication and power and recognition and prestige and affluence and comfort are not all that art, or for that matter life, requires. The authority our culture bestows on events, the authority of fascination, it bestows on events that are

---

The Age of the Combine

The Big Nurse tends to get real put out if something keeps her outfit from running like a smooth, accurate, precision-made machine. The slightest thing messy or out of kilter or in the way ties her into a little white knot of tight-smiled fury. She walks around with that same doll smile crimped between her chin and her nose and that same calm whir coming from her eyes, but down inside of her she's tense as steel. I know, I can feel it. And she don't relax a hair till she gets the nuisance attended to—what she calls "adjusted to surroundings."

Under her rule the ward Inside is almost completely adjusted to surroundings. But the thing is she can't be on the ward all the time. She's got to spend some time Outside. So she works with an eye to adjusting the Outside world too. Working alongside others like her who I call the "Combine," which is a huge organization that aims to adjust the Outside as well as she has the Inside, has made her a real veteran at adjusting things. She was already the Big Nurse in the old place when I came in from the Outside so long back, and she'd been dedicating herself to adjustment for God knows how long.

And I've watched her get more and more skillful over the years. Practice has steadied and strengthened her until now she wields a sure power that extends in all directions on hairlike wires too small for anybody's eye but mine; I see her sit in the center of this web of wires like a watchful robot, tend her network with mechanical insect skill, know every second which wire runs where and just what current to send up to get the results she wants. I was an electrician's assistant in training camp before the Army shipped me to Germany and I had some electronics in my year in college is how I learned about the way these things can be rigged.

What she dreams of there in the center of those wires is a world of precision efficiency and tidiness like a pocket watch with a glass back, a place where the schedule is unbreakable . . .

Ken Kesey, *One Flew Over the Cuckoo's Nest* (1962)

---

recorded and reported as no events have ever been before. It bestows its deepest fascination, furthermore, on certain kinds of events—on invasions, spy missions, and covert operations; on sports extravaganzas, "human be-ins," rock concerts, and psychedelic multimedia happenings; on nuclear tests, space launches, organ transplants, test-tube babies, and genetic engineering; on assassinations, hijackings, kidnappings, sit-ins, and marches, whether in Poland, Iran, France, or Alabama— that exist under carefully planned conditions yet reflect a limited degree of human control. Such events mirror a world that is more organized, more regulated, more scrutinized, more bureaucratized, and more interconnected than people have ever known, or for that matter cared to know. But the planning, the control, the precision that such events epitomize—governed as they are by rules and regulations and codes, by set procedures, checklists, agreements, and schedules, by programs and agendas, by fallback positions and backup equipment—coexist with the random, the unpredictable, the accidental, the indeterminate, as though to mirror a world that, for all its organization, regulation, and planning, is also more precarious, more explosive, more dangerous than people have ever known.

Drawn into a world preoccupied with its own rigidity, fragility, and violence, writers have tried, as did their predecessors, to extend the language of fiction and its range. As one result of their efforts, no words remain forbidden, particularly after publication of William Burroughs's *Naked Lunch* (1959). As another, most boundaries have become blurred—particularly those between life and art, history and fiction, fiction and nonfiction—in the far-reaching literary experiments of our time. Among writers like John Barth, the fabulation of myth, not simply as a refuge to which one can flee, but as a counterreality, has become a dominant mode. Irony lies at the heart of most of the era's comic experiments, in part because irony allows writers to confront even a terribly torn world on something like equal footing. Donald Barthelme's advice—"only trust the fragments"—has become for writers so much a byword that the notion of the synthesizing imagination is in danger of being discredited. Forced to conduct their literary experiments among seemingly endless possibilities and uncertainties, writers sometimes seem scarcely to know where to turn. "What happens to a man to whom all things seem possible and every course of action open?" Walker Percy asks in *The Last Gentleman* (1966). "Nothing of course. Except war. If a man lives in the sphere of the possible and waits for something to happen, what he is waiting for is war—or the end of the world." At least one kind of uncertainty now haunting writers lies close to home: "The nature of existence cannot be felt any more," Mailer said in 1976. "As novelists, we cannot locate our center of values."

Yet despite uncertainty and confusion that seem at times to touch everything, Mailer and his contemporaries, in the immortal words of O. C. Smith, "keep on keepin' on." No doubt they have been aided in part by what Updike calls a "native optimism" that matches their "native pessimism." To be sustained, however, a writer's effort must be founded on the conviction that under proper pressure, language possesses the power to command attention. Among recent writers this conviction has been shaken by the force of history and the power of the media, but it has also been reinforced by the sense that language has always come to us under the aspect of the unpredictable, the accidental, and the indeterminate as well as the deliberate, the planned, and the controlled.

Further Reading:

E. Wilson, *Classics and Commercials: A Literary Chronicle of the Forties,* 1950.
E. Goldman, *The Crucial Decade and After: America, 1945–1960,* 1956, 1960.
H. Agar, *The Price of Power: America Since 1945,* 1957.
D. Perkins, *The New Age of Franklin Roosevelt: 1932–45,* 1957.
W. Morris, *The Territory Ahead,* 1958.
D. Aaron, *Writers on the Left,* 1961.
A. Mizener, *The Sense of Life in the Modern Novel,* 1964.
T. Wolfe, *The Electric Kool-Aid Acid Test,* 1968.
W. Berthoff, *Fictions and Events,* 1971.
L. Fiedler, *Collected Essays,* 1971.
R. Poirier, *The Performing Self,* 1971.
T. Tanner, *City of Words: American Fiction 1935–1970,* 1971.
A. Kazin, *Bright Book of Life,* 1973.

M. Dickstein, *Gates of Eden: American Culture in the Sixties,* 1977.
F. McConnell, *Four Postwar American Novelists,* 1977.
W. Morris, *Earthly Delights, Unearthly Adornments: American Writers as Image Makers,* 1978.
W. Berthoff, *A Literature Without Qualities: American Writing Since 1945,* 1979.
R. Sale, *On Not Being Good Enough,* 1979.
R. H. King, *A Southern Renaissance: The Cultural Awakening of the American South, 1930–1955,* 1980.
A. R. Isaacs, *Without Honor: Defeat in Vietnam and Cambodia,* 1983.
P. Johnson, *Modern Times: The World from the Twenties to the Eighties,* 1983.
A. J. Matusow, *The Unraveling of America: A History of Liberalism in the 1960s,* 1984.

Vladimir Nabokov
1899–1977

"I am an American writer, born in Russia and educated in England, where I studied French literature, before spending fifteen years in Germany. I came to America in 1940 and decided to become an American citizen and made America my home." Such was Vladimir Nabokov's reply when asked in a 1963 interview if he felt any strong sense of national identity. John Updike responded to Nabokov's mixed identities by calling him "the best writer of English prose at present holding American citizenship."

Nabokov was born in St. Petersburg, Russia, on April 23, 1899. His father, a wealthy professor of criminal law and a prominent liberal statesman, made certain that his precocious son received a solid education in English and French: "I learned to read English," Nabokov recalled, "before I could read Russian." In 1919, following the Revolution, the family escaped to Berlin, and Nabokov won a scholarship to Trinity College, Cambridge, where he studied French and Russian literature and proved to be an accomplished soccer and tennis player. After receiving his B.A. in 1922, he returned to Berlin, took a job with a bank —which lasted three hours—and then managed to support himself by teaching English, French, boxing, tennis, and poetry. But, as he later said, his "main occupation was writing." In 1923 he published a Russian translation of *Alice in Wonderland,* and he soon became a leading contributor of fiction, poetry, criticism, and chess columns (he was an excellent composer of chess problems) to Russian émigré journals. In 1926 he published his first novel, *Mary,* under the pseudonym V. Sirin, the name he used for a succession of books: *King, Queen, Knave* (1928), *The Defence* (1930), *The Eye* (1930), *Glory* (1932), *Laughter in the Dark* (1933), *Despair* (1936), and *Invitation to a Beheading* (1938). By the time he

wrote *The Gift* (1937–1938), Nabokov had established himself as a major
European novelist.

Nabokov fled Nazi Germany in 1937 and, after spending a few years in Paris,
sailed for the United States with his wife and son in 1940. He taught literature at
Stanford, Wellesley, and Cornell between 1941 and 1959. While actively pursuing
his lifelong passion for butterfly collecting (he published a number of scientific
papers on lepidopterology), he continued to write fiction, now entirely in
English. He wrote his first novel in English, *The Real Life of Sebastian Knight*
(1941), while in Paris; it was followed by *Bend Sinister* (1947), *Lolita* (1955),
Pnin (1957), *Pale Fire* (1962), *Ada* (1969), *Transparent Things* (1972), and *Look at
the Harlequins!* (1974). During this period Nabokov, with the help of his son,
Dmitri, translated his earlier Russian novels into English. His other works include
six collections of short stories; a critical study of Nicolai Gogol (1944); a
memoir, *Speak, Memory* (1966); and a monumental translation of Aleksandr
Pushkin's *Eugene Onegin* (4 vols., 1964). In 1959, following the enormous success
of *Lolita,* Nabokov and his wife, Vera, moved to Montreux, Switzerland, where
he died in 1977.

Lolita is not only Nabokov's best-known novel, it is also his most American
book. The twelve-year-old Lolita ("the loveliest nymphet")—whom the
European narrator, Humbert Humbert, passionately adores—represents in her
adolescent demands and dreams the "philistine vulgarity" that Nabokov found to
be such an artistically exhilarating aspect of contemporary life: "She it was to
whom ads were dedicated: the ideal consumer, the subject and object of every
foul poster." Writers often write most dazzlingly about the things they despise,
and some of Nabokov's most brilliant passages occur when Humbert Humbert's
aristocratic sensibility confronts some singularly pretentious vulgarity or cultural
absurdity of American taste and education. In his study of Nicolai Gogol,
Nabokov used a Russian word, *poshlust,* to express what "is not only the
obviously trashy but also the falsely important, the falsely beautiful, the falsely
clever, the falsely aristocratic." A scrutinizing attention to the countless
manifestations of *poshlust* in everyday life can be found in nearly all of
Nabokov's writing, but in *Lolita* it reaches the giddy summits of comic poetry.

Despite such achievements as the hilariously and realistically itemized
Americana of *Lolita,* Nabokov's work continually reminds us that fiction is an
illusion—an illusion not so much of reality but of what we call reality. "It is
childish," he wrote in an "afterword" to *Lolita,* "to study a work of fiction in
order to gain information about a country or about a social class or about the
author." Fiction is a country of its own, a "terra incognita" that lies somewhere
at the intersection of art and life. Nabokov scorned any fiction that purported to
give readers a "realistic," documentary version of life; he did so not only because
such endeavors invariably simplify art but also because in doing so they grossly
distort life.

For Nabokov it would be a kind of imaginative *poshlust* to read a novel as
though it were "about" characters one "identified" with and who inhabited a
world one considered to be socially, politically, or economically "realistic." But
though Nabokov's works and worlds are intricately woven with images, patterns,
word games, parodies, and an incredible variety of self-referential devices—all

designed to nudge the reader's attention, saying, "Don't forget, this is a *novel!*"— Nabokov surprisingly never loses contact with the rich texture of life. He is often criticized for writing literature that seems to be only about itself, to exist for merely aesthetic purposes, yet few modern novelists have so consistently evoked such lavishly detailed locations, have created so many memorable characters, and have suffused their work with such a convincing range of human feelings and passions.

Further Reading:
A. Field, *Nabokov: His Life in Art,* 1967.
"For Vladimir Nabokov on His Seventieth
Birthday," *TriQuarterly,* Winter 1970.
W. W. Rowe, *Nabokov's Deceptive World,*
1971.
J. Bader, *Crystal Land: Patterns of Artifice in
Vladimir Nabokov's English Novels,* 1973.
A. Appel, Jr., *Nabokov's Dark Cinema,* 1974.
A. Field, *Nabokov: His Life in Part,* 1977.
J. Karges, *Nabokov's Lepidoptera: Genres and
Genera,* 1985.

Text:
Lolita, 1957.

---

from Lolita[*]

from Part II

1

It was then that began our extensive travels all over the States. To any other type of tourist accommodation I soon grew to prefer the Functional Motel—clean, neat, safe nooks, ideal places for sleep, argument, reconciliation, insatiable illicit love. At first, in my dread of arousing suspicion, I would eagerly pay for both sections of one double unit, each containing a double bed. I wondered what type of foursome this arrangement was ever intended for, since only a pharisaic[1] parody of privacy could be attained by means of the incomplete partition dividing the cabin or room into two communicating love nests. By and by, the very possibilities that such honest promiscuity suggested (two young couples merrily swapping mates or a child shamming sleep to earwitness[2] primal sonorities) made me bolder, and every now and then I would take a bed-and-cot or twin-bed cabin, a prison cell of paradise, with yellow window shades pulled down to create a morning illusion of Venice and sunshine when actually it was Pennsylvania and rain.

---

[*] Rejected by American publishers afraid of censorship, *Lolita* was originally published by Olympia Press in Paris in 1955. The text printed here is from the *Anchor Review* edition (1957), an excerpted edition prepared by the editor, Jason Epstein, with Vladimir Nabokov's approval. Several typographical errors have been silently corrected.
[1] Broadly, self-righteous and critical of manners and behavior. The Pharisees were an ancient sect of elite Jews known for their strict orthodoxy.
[2] Nabokov's own coinage.

We came to know—*nous connûmes,*[3] to use a Flaubertian[4] intonation—the stone cottages under enormous Chateaubriandesque trees,[5] the brick unit, the adobe unit, the stucco court, on what the Tour Book of the Automobile Association describes as "shaded" or "spacious" or "landscaped" grounds. The log kind finished in knotty pine, reminded Lo, by its golden-brown glaze, of fried-chicken bones. We held in contempt the plain whitewashed clapboard Kabins, with their faint sewerish smell or some other gloomy self-conscious stench and nothing to boast of (except "good beds"), and an unsmiling landlady always prepared to have her gift (". . . well, I could give you . . .") turned down.

Nous connûmes (this is royal fun) the would-be enticements of their repetitious names—all those Sunset Motels, U-Beam Cottages, Hillcrest Courts, Pine View Courts, Mountain View Courts, Skyline Courts, Park Plaza Courts, Green Acres, Mac's Courts. There was sometimes a special line in the write-up, such as "Children welcome, pets allowed" (*You* are welcome, *you* are allowed). The baths were mostly tiled showers, with an endless variety of spouting mechanisms, but with one definitely non-Laodicean[6] characteristic in common, a propensity, while in use, to turn instantly beastly hot or blindingly cold upon you, depending on whether your neighbor turned on his cold or his hot to deprive you of its complement in the shower you had so carefully blended. Some motels had instructions pasted above the toilet (on whose tank the towels were unhygienically heaped) asking guests not to throw into its bowl garbage, beer cans, cartons, stillborn babes; others had special notices under glass, such as Things to Do (Riding: "You will often see riders coming down Main Street on their way back from a romantic moonlight ride." "Often at 3 a.m.," sneered unromantic Lo).

Nous connûmes the various types of motor court operators, the reformed criminal, the retired teacher and the business flop, among the males; and the motherly, pseudo-ladylike and madamic variants among the females. And sometimes trains would cry in the monstrously hot and humid night with heart-rending and ominous plangency, mingling power and hysteria in one desperate scream.

We avoided Tourist Homes, country cousins of Funeral ones, old-fashioned, genteel and showerless, with elaborate dressing tables in depressingly white-and-pink little bedrooms, and photographs of the landlady's children in all their instars.[7] But I did surrender, n   and then, to Lo's predilection for "real" hotels. She would pick out in the book, while I petted her in the parked car in the silence of a dusk-mellowed, mysterious side-road, some highly recommended lake lodge which offered all sorts of things magnified by the flashlight she moved over them, such as congenial company, between-meals snacks, outdoor barbecues—but which in my mind conjured up odious visions of stinking highschool boys in sweatshirts and an ember-red cheek pressing against hers, while poor Dr. Humbert, embracing

---

[3] French for the preceding phrase ("We came to know").

[4] In the style of the French novelist Gustave Flaubert (1821–1880), author of the novel *Madame Bovary.*

[5] Nabokov invokes the descriptions of America by François-René de Chateaubriand (1768–1848). Like many of the early European artists and writers who toured the new

continent, Chateaubriand marveled at the lushness and size of American trees.

[6] An early Christian community; the Laodiceans were considered "lukewarm, and neither cold nor hot" on points of religious doctrine. (See Revelation 3:14–16.)

[7] Any one of several forms assumed by insects during their various stages of growth.

nothing but two masculine knees, would cold-humor[8] his piles on the damp turf. Most tempting to her, too, were those "Colonial" Inns, which apart from "gracious atmosphere" and picture-windows, promised "unlimited quantities of M-m-m food." Treasured recollections of my father's palatial hotel sometimes led me to seek for its like in the strange country we traveled through. I was soon discouraged; but Lo kept following the scent of rich food ads, while I derived a not exclusively economic kick from such roadside signs as "Timber Hotel, Children under 14 Free." On the other hand, I shudder when recalling that *soi-disant*[9] "highclass" resort in a Midwestern State, which advertised "raid-the-icebox" midnight snacks and, intrigued by my accent, wanted to know my dead wife's and dead mother's maiden names. A two-days' stay there cost me a hundred and twenty-four dollars! And do you remember, Miranda,[10] that other "ultrasmart" robbers' den with complimentary morning coffee and circulating ice water, and no children under sixteen (no Lolitas, of course)?

Immediately upon arrival at one of the plainer motor courts which became our habitual haunts, she would set the electric fan a-whirr, or induce me to drop a quarter into the radio, or she would read all the signs and inquire with a whine why she could not go riding up some advertised trail or swimming in that local pool of warm mineral water. . . .

A combination of naïveté and deception, of charm and vulgarity, of blue sulks and rosy mirth, Lolita, when she chose, could be a most exasperating brat. I was not really quite prepared for her fits of disorganized boredom, intense and vehement griping, her sprawling, droopy, dopey-eyed style, and what is called goofing off—a kind of diffused clowning which she thought was tough in a boyish hoodlum way. Mentally, I found her to be a disgustingly conventional little girl. Sweet hot jazz, square dancing, gooey fudge sundaes, musicals, movie magazines and so forth—these were the obvious items in her list of beloved things. The Lord knows how many nickels I fed to the gorgeous music boxes that came with every meal we had! I still hear the nasal voices of those invisibles serenading her, people with names like Sammy and Jo and Eddy and Tony and Peggy and Guy and Patty and Rex,[11] and sentimental song hits, all of them as similar to my ear as her various candies were to my palate. She believed, with a kind of celestial trust, any advertisement or advice that appeared in *Movie Love* or *Screen Land*—Starasil[12] Starves Pimples, or "You better watch out if you're wearing your shirttails outside your jeans, gals, because Jill says you shouldn't." If a roadside sign said: Visit Our Gift Shop—we *had* to visit it, *had* to buy its Indian curios, dolls, copper jewelry, cactus candy. The words "novelties and souvenirs" simply entranced her by their trochaic lilt.[13] If some café sign proclaimed Icecold Drinks, she was automatically stirred, although all drinks everywhere were ice-cold. She it was to whom ads were dedicated: the ideal consumer, the subject and object of every foul poster.

---

[8] Nabokov's coinage: take a treatment for hemorrhoids.

[9] French: "so-called" or "self-styled."

[10] From the opening lines of "Tarantella" by the poet Hilaire Belloc (1870–1953): "Do you remember an Inn, / Miranda? / Do you remember an Inn?"

[11] Popular singers of the 1950s.

[12] An acne medication.

[13] A *trochee* is a prosodic foot of two syllables, of which the first is accented and the second is unaccented.

And she attempted—unsuccessfully—to patronize only those restaurants where the holy spirit of Huncan Dines[14] had descended upon the cute paper napkins and cottage cheese-crested salads. . . .

My lawyer has suggested I give a clear, frank account of the itinerary we followed, and I suppose I have reached here a point where I cannot avoid that chore. Roughly, during that mad year (August 1947 to August 1948), our route began with a series of wiggles and whorls in New England, then meandered south, up and down, east and west; dipped deep into *ce qu'on appelle*[15] Dixieland, avoided Florida because the Farlows[16] were there, veered west, zig-zagged through corn belts and cotton belts (this is not too clear I am afraid, Clarence,[17] but I did not keep any notes, and have at my disposal only an atrociously crippled Tour Book in three volumes, almost a symbol of my torn and tattered past, in which to check these recollections); crossed and recrossed the Rockies, straggled through southern deserts where we wintered; reached the Pacific, turned north through the pale lilac fluff of flowering shrubs along forest roads; almost reached the Canadian border; and proceeded east, across good lands and bad lands, back to agriculture on a grand scale, avoiding, despite little Lo's strident remonstrations, little Lo's birthplace, in a corn, coal and hog producing area; and finally returned to the fold of the East, petering out in the college town of Beardsley.

2

Now, in perusing what follows, the reader should bear in mind not only the general circuit as adumbrated above, with its many sidetrips and tourist traps, secondary circles and skittish deviations, but also the fact that far from being an indolent *partie de plaisir*,[18] our tour was a hard, twisted, teleological growth, whose sole *raison d'être*[19] (these French clichés are symptomatic) was to keep my companion in passable humor from kiss to kiss.

Thumbing through that battered tour book, I dimly evoke that Magnolia Garden in a southern State which cost me four bucks and which, according to the ad in the book you must visit for three reasons: because John Galsworthy[20] (a stonedead writer of sorts) acclaimed it as the world's fairest garden; because in 1900 Baedeker's Guide had marked it with a star; and finally, because . . . O, Reader, My Reader, guess! . . . because children (and by Jingo was not my Lolita a child!) will "walk starry-eyed and reverently through this foretaste of Heaven, drinking in beauty that can influence a life." "Not mine," said grim Lo, and settled down on a bench with the fillings of two Sunday papers in her lovely lap.

We passed and re-passed through the whole gamut of American roadside restaurants, from the lowly Eat with its deer-head (dark trace of long tear at inner can-

---

[14] Play on the name of the American recipe king, Duncan Hines (1880–1959).

[15] French: "what one calls."

[16] Former neighbors of Lolita's from her hometown.

[17] Humbert's attorney, Clarence Choate Clark, in

whose care Humbert left the manuscript of *Lolita.*

[18] Day trip or picnic.

[19] French: "reason for existing."

[20] Prolific and popular British novelist (1867–1933), author of *The Forsyte Saga.*

thus[21]), "humorous" picture postcards of the posterior "Kurort"[22] type, impaled guest checks, life savers, sunglasses, adman visions of celestial sundaes, one half of a chocolate cake under glass, and several horribly experienced flies zigzagging over the sticky sugar-pour on the ignoble counter; and all the way to the expensive place with the subdued lights, preposterously poor table linen, inept waiters (ex-convicts or college boys), the roan[23] back of a screen actress, the sable eyebrows of her male of the moment, and an orchestra of zootsuiters with trumpets. . . .

We had rows, minor and major. The biggest ones we had took place: at Lacework Cabins, Virginia; on Park Avenue, Little Rock, near a school; on Milner Pass, 10,759 feet high, in Colorado; at the corner of Seventh Street and Central Avenue in Phoenix, Arizona; on Third Street, Los Angeles, because the tickets to some studio or other were sold out; at a motel called Poplar Shade in Utah, where six pubescent trees were scarcely taller than my Lolita, and where she asked, *à propos de rien,*[24] how long did I think we were going to live in stuffy cabins, doing filthy things together and never behaving like ordinary people? On N. Broadway, Burns, Oregon, corner of W. Washington, facing Safeway, a grocery. In some little town in the Sun Valley of Idaho, before a brick hotel, pale and flushed bricks, nicely mixed, with, opposite, a poplar playing its liquid shadows all over the local Honor Roll. In a sage brush wilderness, between Pinedale and Farson. Somewhere in Nebraska, on Main Street, near the First National Bank, established 1889, with a view of a railway crossing in the vista of the street, and beyond that the white organ pipes of a multiple silo. And on McEwen St., corner of Wheaton Ave., in a Michigan town bearing his first name.[25]

We came to know the curious roadside species, Hitchhiking Man, *Homo pollex*[26] of science, with all its many subspecies and forms: the modest soldier, spic and span, quietly waiting, quietly conscious of khaki's viatic[27] appeal; the schoolboy wishing to go two blocks; the killer wishing to go two thousand miles; the mysterious, nervous, elderly gent, with brandnew suitcase and clipped mustache; a trio of optimistic Mexicans; the college student displaying the grime of vacational outdoor work as proudly as the name of the famous college arching across the front of his sweatshirt; the desperate lady whose battery has just died on her; the cleancut, glossy-haired, shifty-eyed, white-faced young beasts in loud shirts and coats, vigorously, almost priapically[28] thrusting out tense thumbs to tempt lone women or sad-sack salesmen with fancy cravings.

"Let's take him," Lo would often plead, rubbing her knees together in a way she had, as some particularly disgusting *pollex,* some man of my age and shoulder breadth, with the *face à claques*[29] of an unemployed actor, walked backwards, practically in the path of our car.

Oh, I had to keep a very sharp eye on Lo, little limp Lo! . . . . She radiated, despite

---

[21] Location of the tear duct at the inner corner of the eye.

[22] German term for a health spa, or resort with therapeutic waters.

[23] Chestnut color mottled with spots of white or gray.

[24] French: "out of the blue"; literally, "relevant to nothing."

[25] I.e., Clare, Michigan. Clare Quilty is a playwright who has been following Humbert and Lolita.

[26] Combination of the Latin words *Homo* (the genus of humans) and *pollex* ("thumb").

[27] Pertaining to road travel.

[28] Like a phallus (from Priapus, god of fertility).

[29] French: roughly, "with a face aching to be slapped."

her very childish appearance, some special languorous glow which threw garage fellows, hotel pages, vacationists, goons in luxurious cars, maroon morons near blued pools, into fits of concupiscence which might have tickled my pride, had it not incensed my jealousy. For little Lo was aware of that glow of hers, and I would often catch her *coulant un regard*[30] in the direction of some amiable male, some grease monkey, with a sinewy golden-brown forearm and watch-braceleted wrist, and hardly had I turned my back to go and buy this very Lo a lollipop, than I would hear her and the fair mechanic burst into a perfect love song of wisecracks.

When, during our longer stops, I would relax, and out of the goodness of my lulled heart allow her—indulgent Hum!—to visit the rose garden or children's library across the street with a motor court neighbor's plain little Mary and Mary's eight-year old brother, Lo would come back an hour late, with barefoot Mary lagging far behind, and the little boy metamorphosed into two gangling, golden-haired highschool uglies, all muscles and gonorrhea. The reader may well imagine what I answered my pet when—rather uncertainly, I admit—she would ask me if she could go with Carl and Al here to the roller skating rink.

I remember the first time, a dusty windy afternoon, I did let her go to one such rink. Cruelly she said it would be no fun if I accompanied her, since that time of day was reserved for teenagers. We wrangled out a compromise: I remained in the car, among other (empty) cars, with their noses to the canvas-topped open-air rink, where some fifty young people, many in pairs, were endlessly rolling round and round to mechanical music, and the wind silvered the trees. Dolly wore blue jeans and white high shoes, as most of the other girls did. I kept counting the revolutions of the rolling crowd—and suddenly she was missing. When she rolled past again, she was together with three hoodlums whom I had heard analyze a moment before the girl skaters from the outside—and jeer at a lovely leggy young thing who had arrived clad in red shorts instead of those jeans or slacks.

At inspection stations on highways entering Arizona or California, a policeman's cousin would peer with such intensity at us that my poor heart wobbled. "Any honey?" he would inquire, and every time my sweet fool giggled. I still have, vibrating all along my optic nerve, visions of Lo on horseback, a link in the chain of a guided trip along a bridle trail: Lo bobbing at a walking pace, with an old woman rider in front and a lecherous red-necked dude-rancher behind; and I behind him, hating his fat flowery-shirted back even more fervently than a motorist does a slow truck on a mountain road. Or else, at a ski lodge, I would see her floating away from me, celestial and solitary, in an ethereal chairlift, up and up, to a glittering summit where laughing athletes stripped to the waist were waiting for her, for her. . . .

I tried to teach her to play tennis so we might have more amusements in common; but although I had been a good player in my prime, I proved to be hopeless as a teacher; and so, in California, I got her to take a number of very expensive lessons with a famous coach,[31] a husky, wrinkled oldtimer, with a harem of ball boys; he looked an awful wreck off the court, but now and then, when, in the course of a lesson, to keep up the exchange, he would put out as it were an exquisite spring blossom

---

[30] French: "glancing slyly."
[31] The "famous coach" is based on William Tilden (1893–1953), a brilliant American tennis player who had his heyday in the 1920s and 1930s.

of a stroke and twang the ball back to his pupil, that divine delicacy of absolute power made me recall that, thirty years before, I had seen *him* in Cannes demolish the great Gobbert![32] Until she began taking those lessons, I thought she would never learn the game. On this or that hotel court I would drill Lo, and try to relive the days when in a hot gale, a daze of dust, and queer lassitude, I fed ball after ball to gay, innocent, elegant Annabel (gleam of bracelet, pleated white skirt, black velvet hair band). With every word of persistent advice I would only augment Lo's sullen fury. To our games, oddly enough, she preferred—at least, before we reached California—formless pat ball approximations—more ball hunting than actual play—with a wispy, weak, wonderfully pretty in an *ange gauche*[33] way coeval. A helpful spectator, I would go up to that other child, and, inhale her faint musky fragrance as I touched her forearm and held her knobby wrist, and push this way or that her cool thigh to show her the backhand stance. In the meantime, Lo, bending forward, would let her sunny-brown curls hang forward as she stuck her racket, like a cripple's stick, into the ground and emitted a tremendous ugh of disgust at my intrusion. I would leave them to their game and look on, comparing their bodies in motion, a silk scarf round my throat; this was in south Arizona I think—and the days had a lazy lining of warmth, and awkward Lo would slash at the ball and miss it, and curse, and send a simulacrum of a serve into the net, and show the wet glistening young down of her armpit as she brandished her racket in despair, and her even more insipid partner would dutifully rush out after every ball, and retrieve none; but both were enjoying themselves beautifully, and in clear ringing tones kept the exact score of their ineptitudes all the time.

One day, I remember, I offered to bring them cold drinks from the hotel, and went up the gravel path, and came back with two tall glasses of pineapple juice, soda and ice; and then a sudden void within my chest made me stop as I saw that the tennis court was deserted. I stooped to set down the glasses on a bench and for some reason, with a kind of icy vividness, saw Charlotte's face[34] in death, and I glanced around, and noticed Lo in white shorts receding through the speckled shadow of a garden path in the company of a tall man who carried two tennis rackets. I sprang after them, but as I was crashing through the shrubbery, I saw, in an alternate vision, as if life's course constantly branched, Lo, in slacks, and her companion, in shorts, trudging up and down a small weedy area, and beating bushes with their rackets in listless search for their last lost ball.

I itemize these sunny nothings mainly to prove to my judges that I did everything in my power to give my Lolita a really good time. How charming it was to see her, a child herself, showing another child, some of her few accomplishments, such as for example a special way of jumping rope. With her right hand holding her left arm behind her untanned back, the lesser nymphet, a diaphanous darling, would be all eyes, as the pavonian sun was all eyes on the gravel under the flowering trees, while in the midst of that oculate paradise, my freckled and raffish lass, skipped, repeating the movements of so many others I had gloated over on the sun-shot, watered, damp-smelling sidewalks and ramparts of ancient Europe. . . .

1955

[32] Andre H. Gobbert, a French tennis pro.
[33] Clumsily angelic.
[34] Charlotte Haze, Lolita's mother and Humbert's ex-wife. Shortly after arriving in America and meeting Lolita, Humbert married Charlotte. She was run over by a car while hysterical after reading Humbert's private diary, in which he candidly expresses his obsession for Lolita.

Eudora Welty
b. 1909

Admirers of Eudora Welty's fiction have always been in good company: Ford
Madox Ford, Katherine Anne Porter, and Robert Penn Warren were among her
earliest supporters. Like those who have followed them, they praised Welty's
fiction for its evocative sense of place and even more for its compelling and
honest presentation of human experience on all levels. Welty's most recent novel,
The Optimist's Daughter (1972), focuses primarily on the social elite of a modern
southern town, while her early, famous short story, "A Worn Path," is a realistic
and uncondescending account of an old black woman's strength and dignity.
Convinced that "to write honestly and with all our powers is the least we can
do, and the most," Welty persists in confronting the flaws she sees in her
characters and her region, but she does so without bitterness. She brings to life
"the turn of mind, the nature of temperament, of a privileged observer," but
"owing to the way I became so," she has remarked, "it turned out that I became
the loving kind."

A native of Jackson, Mississippi, where she has lived most of her life, Eudora
Welty was born on April 13, 1909. She attended the Mississippi State College for
Women for two years before transferring to the University of Wisconsin, from
which she was graduated in 1929. She then enrolled at the Columbia University
Graduate School of Business to study advertising. "As certain as I was of wanting
to be a writer," she says, "I was certain of *not* wanting to be a teacher." After
two years in New York, she returned to Jackson, where she worked in
advertising with a local radio station and a state commission on tourism and as a
society correspondent for a Memphis newspaper. As a publicist for the Works
Progress Administration in the early 1930s, she took a series of photographs on
southern rural poverty, some of which were exhibited in a one-woman show at
the Museum of Modern Art in 1973. In 1936 she published her first short story,
"Death of a Travelling Salesman," and followed it in rapid succession with two
collections of stories, *A Curtain of Green and Other Stories* (1941) and *The Wide
Net* (1943). Her first novel, *The Robber Bridegroom,* a fairy-tale-like story,
appeared in 1942. Other novels, all dealing with various aspects of Mississippi
life, include the story of a modern plantation family in *Delta Wedding* (1946), the
comic first-person narrative of small-town life in *The Ponder Heart* (1954), and
the complex tale of a large rural family in *Losing Battles* (1970), her most
ambitious book. Her most recent work, *One Writer's Beginnings,* a collection of
three autobiographical pieces, appeared in 1984. She has published additional
collections of short stories—some realistic and others more fantastic—as well as
several collections of essays on criticism and fictional theory, including *Place in
Fiction* (1957) and *The Eye of the Story* (1977). Although *The Optimist's Daughter*
has received widespread popular and critical acclaim, Welty remains best known
for her finely crafted and often extremely funny short stories, which were
published in 1980 as *The Collected Stories of Eudora Welty.*

Welty's fiction draws heavily on her deep knowledge of her region and her keen powers of observation. She has said that her imagination is predominantly visual, yet her ear for dialect matches her mastery of descriptive detail. Welty's major achievement, however, lies in her ability to reach through detailed surfaces to less tangible dimensions of reality. In "Why I Live at the P.O.," for example, Sister's obsessive monologue reveals not only the comic interaction of her extended family, nor merely her own deep-rooted feelings of alienation and lost opportunity, but also a sense of the mystery of human relationships. Like many southern writers, Welty is known for the creation of "grotesque" characters. Her characters, including Sister, are often physically, mentally, or emotionally handicapped and are thus at odds with their community. Yet even as they show the pain that isolation inflicts, they also show a freedom that a small, tightly-knit community does not permit.

In an early story, Welty describes a young girl who often looks at the world through a frame that she makes with her fingers. A frame, as Welty has since observed, not only involves focus and distance and selection; it also involves a viewer's values and commitments, her preferences, even her beliefs. The "frame through which I viewed the world changed too, with time," she has written recently, in *One Writer's Beginnings*. "Greater than scene, I came to see, is situation. Greater than situation is implication. Greater than all of these is a single, entire human being, who will never be confined in any frame." Over the years, Welty has concentrated on refining her frame, believing that the integrity of a work largely determines its quality. She makes her stories, she says, not directly out of her own life nor directly out of the lives of other people but out of "the *whole* fund of my feelings, my responses to the real experiences of my own life, to the relationships that formed and changed it, that I have given most of myself to." She writes of familiar themes—the power of the community and the power of the past in shaping the lives of individuals, the power of love and the power of memory, and the pain of loneliness and the pain of loss. Yet the character she feels closest to is the spinster piano teacher Miss Eckhart in "June Recital": "What I have put into her is my passion for my own life work, my own art. Exposing yourself to risk is a truth Miss Eckhart and I had in common. What animates and possesses me is what drives Miss Eckhart, the love of her art and the love of giving it, the desire to give it until there is no more left."

Further Reading:
R. P. Warren, "The Love and Separateness in Miss Welty" in *Selected Essays,* 1958.
R. M. Vande Kieft, *Eudora Welty,* 1962.
L. D. Rubin, Jr., "The Golden Apples of the Sun" in *The Faraway Country: Writers of the Modern South,* 1963.
J. A. Bryant, Jr., *Eudora Welty,* 1968.
M. Kreyling, *Eudora Welty's Achievement of Order,* 1980.

Text:
Collected Stories, 1980.

Why I Live at the P.O.

I was getting along fine with Mama, Papa-Daddy and Uncle Rondo until my sister Stella-Rondo just separated from her husband and came back home again. Mr. Whitaker! Of course I went with Mr. Whitaker first, when he first appeared here in China Grove, taking "Pose Yourself" photos, and Stella-Rondo broke us up. Told him I was one-sided. Bigger on one side than the other, which is a deliberate, calculated falsehood: I'm the same. Stella-Rondo is exactly twelve months to the day younger than I am and for that reason she's spoiled.

She's always had anything in the world she wanted and then she'd throw it away. Papa-Daddy gave her this gorgeous Add-a-Pearl necklace when she was eight years old and she threw it away playing baseball when she was nine, with only two pearls.

So as soon as she got married and moved away from home the first thing she did was separate! From Mr. Whitaker! This photographer with the popeyes she said she trusted. Came home from one of those towns up in Illinois and to our complete surprise brought this child of two.

Mama said she like to made her drop dead for a second. "Here you had this marvelous blonde child and never so much as wrote your mother a word about it," says Mama. "I'm thoroughly ashamed of you." But of course she wasn't.

Stella-Rondo just calmly takes off this *hat,* I wish you could see it. She says, "Why, Mama, Shirley-T.'s adopted. I can prove it."

"How?" says Mama, but all I says was, "H'm!" There I was over the hot stove, trying to stretch two chickens over five people and a completely unexpected child into the bargain, without one moment's notice.

"What do you mean—'H'm!'?" says Stella-Rondo, and Mama says, "I heard that, Sister."

I said that oh, I didn't mean a thing, only that whoever Shirley-T. was, she was the spit-image of Papa-Daddy if he'd cut off his beard, which of course he'd never do in the world. Papa-Daddy's Mama's papa and sulks.

Stella-Rondo got furious! She said, "Sister, I don't need to tell you you got a lot of nerve and always did have and I'll thank you to make no future reference to my adopted child whatsoever."

"Very well," I said. "Very well, very well. Of course I noticed at once she looks like Mr. Whitaker's side too. That frown. She looks like a cross between Mr. Whitaker and Papa-Daddy."

"Well, all I can say is she isn't."

"She looks exactly like Shirley Temple to me," says Mama, but Shirley-T. just ran away from her.

So the first thing Stella-Rondo did at the table was turn Papa-Daddy against me.

"Papa-Daddy," she says. He was trying to cut up his meat. "Papa-Daddy!" I was taken completely by surprise. Papa-Daddy is about a million years old and's got this long-long beard. "Papa-Daddy, Sister says she fails to understand why you don't cut off your beard."

So Papa-Daddy l-a-y-s down his knife and fork! He's real rich. Mama says he is, he says he isn't. So he says, "Have I heard correctly? You don't understand why I don't cut off my beard?"

"Why," I says, "Papa-Daddy, of course I understand, I did not say any such of a thing, the idea!"

He says, "Hussy!"

I says, "Papa-Daddy, you know I wouldn't any more want you to cut off your beard than the man in the moon. It was the farthest thing from my mind! Stella-Rondo sat there and made that up while she was eating breast of chicken."

But he says, "So the postmistress fails to understand why I don't cut off my beard. Which job I got you through my influence with the government. 'Bird's nest'—is that what you call it?"

Not that it isn't the next to smallest P.O. in the entire state of Mississippi.

I says, "Oh, Papa-Daddy," I says, "I didn't say any such of a thing, I never dreamed it was a bird's nest, I have always been grateful though this is the next to smallest P.O. in the state of Mississippi, and I do not enjoy being referred to as a hussy by my own grandfather."

But Stella-Rondo says, "Yes, you did say it too. Anybody in the world could of heard you, that had ears."

"Stop right there," says Mama, looking at *me*.

So I pulled my napkin straight back through the napkin ring and left the table.

As soon as I was out of the room Mama says, "Call her back, or she'll starve to death," but Papa-Daddy says, "This is the beard I started growing on the Coast when I was fifteen years old." He would of gone on till nightfall if Shirley-T. hadn't lost the Milky Way she ate in Cairo.

So Papa-Daddy says, "I am going out and lie in the hammock, and you can all sit here and remember my words: I'll never cut off my beard as long as I live, even one inch, and I don't appreciate it in you at all." Passed right by me in the hall and went straight out and got in the hammock.

It would be a holiday. It wasn't five minutes before Uncle Rondo suddenly appeared in the hall in one of Stella-Rondo's flesh-colored kimonos, all cut on the bias, like something Mr. Whitaker probably thought was gorgeous.

"Uncle Rondo!" I says. "I didn't know who that was! Where are you going?"

"Sister," he says, "get out of my way, I'm poisoned."

"If you're poisoned stay away from Papa-Daddy," I says. "Keep out of the hammock. Papa-Daddy will certainly beat you on the head if you come within forty miles of him. He thinks I deliberately said he ought to cut off his beard after he got me the P.O., and I've told him and told him and told him, and he acts like he just don't hear me. Papa-Daddy must of gone stone deaf."

"He picked a fine day to do it then," says Uncle Rondo, and before you could say "Jack Robinson" flew out in the yard.

What he'd really done, he'd drunk another bottle of that prescription. He does it every single Fourth of July as sure as shooting, and it's horribly expensive. Then he falls over in the hammock and snores. So he insisted on zigzagging right on out to the hammock, looking like a half-wit.

Papa-Daddy woke up with this horrible yell and right there without moving an inch he tried to turn Uncle Rondo against me. I heard every word he said. Oh, he told Uncle Rondo I didn't learn to read till I was eight years old and he didn't see how in the world I ever got the mail put up at the P.O., much less read it all, and he said if Uncle Rondo could only fathom the lengths he had gone to get me that job! And he said on the other hand he thought Stella-Rondo had a brilliant mind and deserved credit for getting out of town. All the time he was just lying there swinging as pretty as you please and looping out his beard, and poor Uncle Rondo was *pleading* with him to slow down the hammock, it was making him as dizzy as a witch to watch it. But that's what Papa-Daddy likes about a hammock. So Uncle Rondo was too dizzy to get turned against me for the time being. He's Mama's only brother and is a good case of a one-track mind. Ask anybody. A certified pharmacist.

Just then I heard Stella-Rondo raising the upstairs window. While she was married she got this peculiar idea that it's cooler with the windows shut and locked. So she has to raise the window before she can make a soul hear her outdoors.

So she raises the window and says, *"Oh!"* You would have thought she was mortally wounded.

Uncle Rondo and Papa-Daddy didn't even look up, but kept right on with what they were doing. I had to laugh.

I flew up the stairs and threw the door open! I says, "What in the wide world's the matter, Stella-Rondo? You mortally wounded?"

"No," she says, "I am not mortally wounded but I wish you would do me the favor of looking out that window there and telling me what you see."

So I shade my eyes and look out the window.

"I see the front yard," I says.

"Don't you see any human beings?" she says.

"I see Uncle Rondo trying to run Papa-Daddy out of the hammock," I says. "Nothing more. Naturally, it's so suffocating-hot in the house, with all the windows shut and locked, everybody who cares to stay in their right mind will have to go out and get in the hammock before the Fourth of July is over."

"Don't you notice anything different about Uncle Rondo?" asks Stella-Rondo.

"Why, no, except he's got on some terrible-looking flesh-colored contraption I wouldn't be found dead in, is all I can see," I says.

"Never mind, you won't be found dead in it, because it happens to be part of my trousseau, and Mr. Whitaker took several dozen photographs of me in it," says Stella-Rondo. "What on earth could Uncle Rondo *mean* by wearing part of my trousseau out in the broad open daylight without saying so much as 'Kiss my foot,' *knowing* I only got home this morning after my separation and hung my negligee up on the bathroom door, just as nervous as I could be?"

"I'm sure I don't know, and what do you expect me to do about it?" I says. "Jump out the window?"

"No, I expect nothing of the kind. I simply declare that Uncle Rondo looks like a fool in it, that's all," she says. "It makes me sick to my stomach."

"Well, he looks as good as he can," I says. "As good as anybody in reason could." I stood up for Uncle Rondo, please remember. And I said to Stella-Rondo, "I think I would do well not to criticize so freely if I were you and came home with a two-year-old child I had never said a word about, and no explanation whatever about my separation."

"I asked you the instant I entered this house not to refer one more time to my adopted child, and you gave me your word of honor you would not," was all Stella-Rondo would say, and started pulling out every one of her eyebrows with some cheap Kress tweezers.

So I merely slammed the door behind me and went down and made some green-tomato pickle. Somebody had to do it. Of course Mama had turned both the Negroes loose; she always said no earthly power could hold one anyway on the Fourth of July, so she wouldn't even try. It turned out that Jaypan fell in the lake and came within a very narrow limit of drowning.

So Mama trots in. Lifts up the lid and says, "H'm! Not very good for your Uncle Rondo in his precarious condition, I must say. Or poor little adopted Shirley-T. Shame on you!"

That made me tired. I says, "Well, Stella-Rondo had better thank her lucky stars it was her instead of me came trotting in with that very peculiar-looking child. Now if it had been me that trotted in from Illinois and brought a peculiar-looking child of two, I shudder to think of the reception I'd of got, much less controlled the diet of an entire family."

"But you must remember, Sister, that you were never married to Mr. Whitaker in the first place and didn't go up to Illinois to live," says Mama, shaking a spoon in my face. "If you had I would of been just as overjoyed to see you and your little adopted girl as I was to see Stella-Rondo, when you wound up with your separation and came on back home."

"You would not," I says.

"Don't contradict me, I would," says Mama.

But I said she couldn't convince me though she talked till she was blue in the face. Then I said, "Besides, you know as well as I do that that child is not adopted."

"She most certainly is adopted," says Mama, stiff as a poker.

I says, "Why, Mama, Stella-Rondo had her just as sure as anything in this world, and just too stuck up to admit it."

"Why, Sister," said Mama. "Here I thought we were going to have a pleasant Fourth of July, and you start right out not believing a word your own baby sister tells you!"

"Just like Cousin Annie Flo. Went to her grave denying the facts of life," I remind Mama.

"I told you if you ever mentioned Annie Flo's name I'd slap your face," says Mama, and slaps my face.

"All right, you wait and see," I says.

"I," says Mama, "*I* prefer to take my children's word for anything when it's humanly possible." You ought to see Mama, she weighs two hundred pounds and has real tiny feet.

Just then something perfectly horrible occurred to me.

"Mama," I says, "can that child talk?" I simply had to whisper! "Mama, I wonder if that child can be—you know—in any way? Do you realize," I says, "that she hasn't spoken one single, solitary word to a human being up to this minute? This is the way she looks," I says, and I looked like this.

Well, Mama and I just stood there and stared at each other. It was horrible!

"I remember well that Joe Whitaker frequently drank like a fish," says Mama. "I believed to my soul he drank *chemicals.*" And without another word she marches to the foot of the stairs and calls Stella-Rondo.

"Stella-Rondo? O-o-o-o-o! Stella-Rondo!"

"What?" says Stella-Rondo from upstairs. Not even the grace to get up off the bed.

"Can that child of yours talk?" asks Mama.

Stella-Rondo says, "Can she what?"

"Talk! Talk!" says Mama. "Burdyburdyburdyburdy!"

So Stella-Rondo yells back, "Who says she can't talk?"

"Sister says so," says Mama.

"You didn't have to tell me, I know whose word of honor don't mean a thing in this house," says Stella-Rondo.

And in a minute the loudest Yankee voice I ever heard in my life yells out, "OE'm Pop-OE the Sailor-r-r Ma-a-an!" and then somebody jumps up and down in the upstairs hall. In another second the house would of fallen down.

"Not only talks, she can tap-dance!" calls Stella-Rondo. "Which is more than some people I won't name can do."

"Why, the little precious darling thing!" Mama says, so surprised. "Just as smart as she can be!" Starts talking baby talk right there. Then she turns on me. "Sister, you ought to be thoroughly ashamed! Run upstairs this instant and apologize to Stella-Rondo and Shirley-T."

"Apologize for what?" I says. "I merely wondered if the child was normal, that's all. Now that she's proved she is, why, I have nothing further to say."

But Mama just turned on her heel and flew out, furious. She ran right upstairs and hugged the baby. She believed it was adopted. Stella-Rondo hadn't done a thing but turn her against me from upstairs while I stood there helpless over the hot stove. So that made Mama, Papa-Daddy and the baby all on Stella-Rondo's side.

Next, Uncle Rondo.

I must say that Uncle Rondo has been marvelous to me at various times in the past and I was completely unprepared to be made to jump out of my skin, the way it turned out. Once Stella-Rondo did something perfectly horrible to him—broke a chain letter from Flanders Field—and he took the radio back he had given her and gave it to me. Stella-Rondo was furious! For six months we all had to call her Stella instead of Stella-Rondo, or she wouldn't answer. I always thought Uncle Rondo had all the brains of the entire family. Another time he sent me to Mammoth Cave, with all expenses paid.

But this would be the day he was drinking that prescription, the Fourth of July.

So at supper Stella-Rondo speaks up and says she thinks Uncle Rondo ought to try to eat a little something. So finally Uncle Rondo said he would try a little cold biscuits and ketchup, but that was all. So *she* brought it to him.

"Do you think it wise to disport with ketchup in Stella-Rondo's flesh-colored kimono?" I says. Trying to be considerate! If Stella-Rondo couldn't watch out for her trousseau, somebody had to.

"Any objections?" asks Uncle Rondo, just about to pour out all the ketchup.

"Don't mind what she says, Uncle Rondo," says Stella-Rondo. "Sister has been devoting this solid afternoon to sneering out my bedroom window at the way you look."

"What's that?" says Uncle Rondo. Uncle Rondo has got the most terrible temper in the world. Anything is liable to make him tear the house down if it comes at the wrong time.

So Stella-Rondo says, "Sister says, 'Uncle Rondo certainly does look like a fool in that pink kimono!' "

Do you remember who it was really said that?

Uncle Rondo spills out all the ketchup and jumps out of his chair and tears off the kimono and throws it down on the dirty floor and puts his foot on it. It had to be sent all the way to Jackson to the cleaners and re-pleated.

"So that's your opinion of your Uncle Rondo, is it?" he says. "I look like a fool, do I? Well, that's the last straw. A whole day in this house with nothing to do, and then to hear you come out with a remark like that behind my back!"

"I didn't say any such of a thing, Uncle Rondo," I says, "and I'm not saying who did, either. Why, I think you look all right. Just try to take care of yourself and not talk and eat at the same time," I says. "I think you better go lie down."

"Lie down my foot," says Uncle Rondo. I ought to of known by that he was fixing to do something perfectly horrible.

So he didn't do anything that night in the precarious state he was in—just played Casino with Mama and Stella-Rondo and Shirley-T. and gave Shirley-T. a nickel with a head on both sides. It tickled her nearly to death, and she called him "Papa." But at 6:30 A.M. the next morning, he threw a whole five-cent package of some unsold one-inch firecrackers from the store as hard as he could into my bedroom and they every one went off. Not one bad one in the string. Anybody else, there'd be one that wouldn't go off.

Well, I'm just terribly susceptible to noise of any kind, the doctor has always told me I was the most sensitive person he had ever seen in his whole life, and I was simply prostrated. I couldn't eat! People tell me they heard it as far as the cemetery, and old Aunt Jep Patterson, that had been holding her own so good, thought it was Judgment Day and she was going to meet her whole family. It's usually so quiet here.

And I'll tell you it didn't take me any longer than a minute to make up my mind what to do. There I was with the whole entire house on Stella-Rondo's side and turned against me. If I have anything at all I have pride.

So I just decided I'd go straight down to the P.O. There's plenty of room there in the back, I says to myself.

Well! I made no bones about letting the family catch on to what I was up to. I didn't try to conceal it.

The first thing they knew, I marched in where they were all playing Old Maid and pulled the electric oscillating fan out by the plug, and everything got real hot. Next I snatched the pillow I'd done the needlepoint on right off the davenport from behind Papa-Daddy. He went "Ugh!" I beat Stella-Rondo up the stairs and finally found my charm bracelet in her bureau drawer under a picture of Nelson Eddy.

"So that's the way the land lies," says Uncle Rondo. There he was, piecing on the ham. "Well, Sister, I'll be glad to donate my army cot if you got any place to set it up, providing you'll leave right this minute and let me get some peace." Uncle Rondo was in France.

"Thank you kindly for the cot and 'peace' is hardly the word I would select if I had to resort to firecrackers at 6:30 A.M. in a young girl's bedroom," I says back to him. "And as to where I intend to go, you seem to forget my position as postmistress of China Grove, Mississippi," I says. "I've always got the P.O."

Well, that made them all sit up and take notice.

I went out front and started digging up some four-o'clocks to plant around the P.O.

"Ah-ah-ah!" says Mama, raising the window. "Those happen to be my four-o'clocks. Everything planted in that star is mine. I've never known you to make anything grow in your life."

"Very well," I says. "But I take the fern. Even you, Mama, can't stand there and deny that I'm the one watered that fern. And I happen to know where I can send in a box top and get a packet of one thousand mixed seeds, no two the same kind, free."

"Oh, where?" Mama wants to know.

But I says, "Too late. You 'tend to your house, and I'll 'tend to mine. You hear things like that all the time if you know how to listen to the radio. Perfectly marvelous offers. Get anything you want free."

So I hope to tell you I marched in and got that radio, and they could of all bit a nail in two, especially Stella-Rondo, that it used to belong to, and she well knew she couldn't get it back, I'd sue for it like a shot. And I very politely took the sewing-machine motor I helped pay the most on to give Mama for Christmas back in 1929, and a good big calendar, with the first-aid remedies on it. The thermometer and the Hawaiian ukulele certainly were rightfully mine, and I stood on the step-ladder and got all my watermelon-rind preserves and every fruit and vegetable I'd put up, every jar. Then I began to pull the tacks out of the bluebird wall vases on the archway to the dining room.

"Who told you you could have those, Miss Priss?" says Mama, fanning as hard as she could.

"I bought 'em and I'll keep track of 'em," I says. "I'll tack 'em up one on each side the post-office window, and you can see 'em when you come to ask me for your mail, if you're so dead to see 'em."

"Not I! I'll never darken the door to that post office again if I live to be a hundred," Mama says. "Ungrateful child! After all the money we spent on you at the Normal.[1]"

"Me either," says Stella-Rondo. "You can just let my mail lie there and *rot*, for all I care. I'll never come and relieve you of a single, solitary piece."

"I should worry," I says. "And who you think's going to sit down and write you all those big fat letters and postcards, by the way? Mr. Whitaker? Just because he was the only man ever dropped down in China Grove and you got him—unfairly—is he going to sit down and write you a lengthy correspondence after you come home giving no rhyme nor reason whatsoever for your separation and no explanation for the presence of that child? I may not have your brilliant mind, but I fail to see it."

So Mama says, "Sister, I've told you a thousand times that Stella-Rondo simply got homesick, and this child is far too big to be hers," and she says, "Now, why don't you all just sit down and play Casino?"

Then Shirley-T. sticks out her tongue at me in this perfectly horrible way. She has no more manners than the man in the moon. I told her she was going to cross her eyes like that some day and they'd stick.

"It's too late to stop me now," I says. "You should have tried that yesterday. I'm going to the P.O. and the only way you can possibly see me is to visit me there."

So Papa-Daddy says, "You'll never catch me setting foot in that post office, even

---

[1] I.e., normal school, which trained teachers, chiefly for the elementary grades.

if I should take a notion into my head to write a letter some place." He says, "I won't have you reachin' out of that little old window with a pair of shears and cuttin' off any beard of mine. I'm too smart for you!"

"We all are," says Stella-Rondo.

But I said, "If you're so smart, where's Mr. Whitaker?"

So then Uncle Rondo says, "I'll thank you from now on to stop reading all the orders I get on postcards and telling everybody in China Grove what you think is the matter with them," but I says, "I draw my own conclusions and will continue in the future to draw them." I says, "If people want to write their inmost secrets on penny postcards, there's nothing in the wide world you can do about it, Uncle Rondo."

"And if you think we'll ever *write* another postcard you're sadly mistaken," says Mama.

"Cutting off your nose to spite your face then," I says. "But if you're all determined to have no more to do with the U.S. mail, think of this: What will Stella-Rondo do now, if she wants to tell Mr. Whitaker to come after her?"

"Wah!" says Stella-Rondo. I knew she'd cry. She had a conniption fit right there in the kitchen.

"It will be interesting to see how long she holds out," I says. "And now—I am leaving."

"Good-bye," says Uncle Rondo.

"Oh, I declare," says Mama, "to think that a family of mine should quarrel on the Fourth of July, or the day after, over Stella-Rondo leaving old Mr. Whitaker and having the sweetest little adopted child! It looks like we'd all be glad!"

"Wah!" says Stella-Rondo, and has a fresh conniption fit.

"*He* left *her*—you mark my words," I says. "That's Mr. Whitaker. I know Mr. Whitaker. After all, I knew him first. I said from the beginning he'd up and leave her. I foretold every single thing that's happened."

"Where did he go?" asks Mama.

"Probably to the North Pole, if he knows what's good for him," I says.

But Stella-Rondo just bawled and wouldn't say another word. She flew to her room and slammed the door.

"Now look what you've gone and done, Sister," says Mama. "You go apologize."

"I haven't got time, I'm leaving," I says.

"Well, what are you waiting around for?" asks Uncle Rondo.

So I just picked up the kitchen clock and marched off, without saying "Kiss my foot" or anything, and never did tell Stella-Rondo good-bye.

There was a girl going along on a little wagon right in front.

"Girl," I says, "come help me haul these things down the hill, I'm going to live in the post office."

Took her nine trips in her express wagon. Uncle Rondo came out on the porch and threw her a nickel.

And that's the last I've laid eyes on any of my family or my family laid eyes on me for five solid days and nights. Stella-Rondo may be telling the most horrible tales in the world about Mr. Whitaker, but I haven't heard them. As I tell everybody, I draw my own conclusions.

But oh, I like it here. It's ideal, as I've been saying. You see, I've got everything cater-cornered, the way I like it. Hear the radio? All the war news. Radio, sewing machine, book ends, ironing board and that great big piano lamp—peace, that's what I like. Butter-bean vines planted all along the front where the strings are.

Of course, there's not much mail. My family are naturally the main people in China Grove, and if they prefer to vanish from the face of the earth, for all the mail they get or the mail they write, why, I'm not going to open my mouth. Some of the folks here in town are taking up for me and some turned against me. I know which is which. There are always people who will quit buying stamps just to get on the right side of Papa-Daddy.

But here I am, and here I'll stay. I want the world to know I'm happy.

And if Stella-Rondo should come to me this minute, on bended knees, and *attempt* to explain the incidents of her life with Mr. Whitaker, I'd simply put my fingers in both my ears and refuse to listen.

1941

Tennessee Williams
1911–1983

Tennessee Williams's one-act play *Portrait of a Madonna* made its debut in 1946 at the Actors' Laboratory Theater in Los Angeles, where reviewers hailed it as an outstanding example of Williams's mastery of the one-act form. Hume Cronyn directed the first production, which featured the celebrated actress Jessica Tandy as Miss Lucretia Collins, a tattered remnant of the genteel Old South who resolutely clings to her youthful delusions despite the squalor that engulfs her. Before the aging spinster is led from her dingy rented room to an asylum, she manages to evoke virtually all of the dramatic themes that have earned Williams his reputation as one of America's most important playwrights. In Lucretia Collins's world we recognize Williams's characteristic lyric rendition of a decaying physical and psychological environment populated with semigrotesques. Since that first acclaimed production, *Portrait of a Madonna* has enjoyed several revivals, most recently in 1986 as part of a highly successful off-Broadway production entitled *Ten by Tennessee.*

Williams's critical reputation has wavered over the years. His first recognized work, *Battle of Angels,* was assailed at its 1940 opening in Boston. One critic charged it with giving "the audience the sensation of having been dunked in mire." However, with his second work, *The Glass Menagerie,* which opened in Chicago on December 26, 1944, and moved to New York the following March, Williams immediately created an indelible presence for himself in American drama. Soon he was also providing gossip columnists with extravagant incidents from his troubled and unconventional personal life.

Born in Columbus, Mississippi, in 1911, Thomas Lanier Williams was descended on his father's side from "pioneer Tennessee stock" and on his mother's from early Quaker "settlers of Nantucket Island in New England," a mix of

"Cavalier" and "Puritan" he later saw as a possible source "for the conflicting impulses I often represent in the people I write about." During his early years Williams lived in several Mississippi towns and in Nashville, Tennessee, with his mother, his older sister Rose, and his grandfather, an Episcopalian minister. In his early adolescence, his family made what he later described as "a tragic move" to St. Louis, where his father, a traveling salesman, had accepted an appointment as the manager of a shoe company.

> Neither my sister nor I could adjust ourselves to life in a midwestern city. The schoolchildren made fun of our southern speech and manners. I remember gangs of kids following me home yelling "Sissy!" and home was not a very pleasant refuge. It was a perpetually dim little apartment in a wilderness of identical brick and concrete structures with no grass and no trees nearer than the park.

It was also a place where his parents seemed constantly to quarrel and where his father, disappointed at not having a more athletic son, began calling his son "Miss Nancy." Soon Williams's frail physical and psychological condition weakened into partial paralysis in his legs. His sister Rose, suffering comparable pressures, experienced a mental breakdown that culminated when a suitor died— circumstances similar to those that form the narrative basis for *Portrait of a Madonna*.

Early in his troubled life, writing became Williams's sanctuary.

> At the age of fourteen I discovered writing as an escape from a world of reality in which I felt acutely uncomfortable. It immediately became my place of retreat, my cave, my refuge.

At age eleven Williams had his own typewriter; at fourteen he garnered recognition with a first-place award (and $25.00) in a nationwide writing contest sponsored by the prestigious *Smart Set* magazine. After high school, he studied briefly at the University of Missouri, then worked in "a clerical job in the shoe company that employed my father." It was two years of "indescribable torment to me as an individual but of immense value to me as a writer for they gave me first-hand knowledge of what it meant to be a small wage earner in a hopelessly routine job." Williams continued to write—often late into the night—without regard for his poor health. After recuperating from another nervous collapse, he lived briefly with his grandparents in Memphis and then returned to college, first at Washington University in St. Louis, where he wrote and produced several plays, and then at the University of Iowa, where he took a B.A. in 1938, with a major in playwriting.

In the years following graduation, Williams traveled and lived briefly in Chicago, St. Louis, Mexico, Los Angeles, New Orleans, and New York, experiencing the kind of life he was so often to present on stage: lonely and uncertain, trapped in a painful past, and struggling to survive in a world essentially indifferent to personal illusions. During this period he also changed his name. Thomas Lanier Williams was, he observed, a nice enough name, perhaps a little too nice. . . . It sounds like it might belong to the son of a writer who turns out sonnet sequences to Spring. . . . Under that name I published a good deal of lyric poetry which was a bad imitation of Edna Millay. When I grew up I realized this poetry wasn't much good and I felt the name had been compromised so I changed it to Tennessee Williams, the justification being mainly that the Williamses had fought the Indians for Tennessee and I had already discovered that the life of a young writer was going to be something similar to the dilemma of a stockade against a band of savages.

Williams supported himself mainly through odd jobs, including working as a scriptwriter at MGM studios, running the night elevator in a large hotel, and ushering at the Strand Theater on Broadway. "All the while I kept on writing, writing, not with any hope of making a living at it but because I found no other means of expressing things that seemed to demand expression."

By 1945, however, with *The Glass Menagerie* written and produced, Williams began to enjoy both critical praise, including a New York Drama Critics Circle Award, and financial rewards. In its first appearance on Broadway, *The Glass Menagerie* ran for 561 performances. In 1947 Williams won a Pulitzer Prize as well as a second Drama Critics Circle Award for *A Streetcar Named Desire,* which ran for 855 performances. *The Rose Tatoo,* with 300 performances, followed in 1951, and four years later *Cat on a Hot Tin Roof* earned Williams a third Drama Critics Circle Award and a second Pulitzer Prize. In 1953 the play *Camino Real* provoked controversy that was rekindled in 1956 when the film *Baby Doll* was released. These in turn were followed by well-received stage and film versions of *Suddenly Last Summer* (1958), *Sweet Bird of Youth* (1959), and *The Night of the Iguana* (1961), which is widely recognized as Williams's last important play. Although he continued to write until quite close to his death in 1983, none of his later plays received the acclaim of his earlier works.

During his last twenty years, Williams's depression became, in his own words, "almost clinical," and alcohol and drugs began to dominate his life. In the 1970s Williams published a string of theatrical failures, two works of fiction (*Eight Mortal Ladies Possessed* and *Noise and the World of Reason*), and a collection of poems (*Androgyne, Mon Amour*), along with his collected essays (*Where I Live,* 1978) and his *Memoirs* (1975). By the time of his death, only the extravagances of his personal life succeeded in bringing his name to public attention.

Williams wrote about such subjects as murder, rape, homosexuality, nymphomania and drug and alcohol addiction at a time when many of these were still regarded as too controversial for the American stage. But his characters transcend their exaggerated roles—neurotics, victims, would-be artists, and outsiders. In *Portrait of a Madonna,* for example, Lucretia Collins conveys the stubborn dignity as well as the debilitating paranoia of the southern gentlewoman, primarily because Williams renders her personal dilemma in intensely lyric terms. Her mother's death fifteen years earlier has turned her into a sexually obsessed, frustrated recluse, adrift in the world of her own fantasies. Convinced that she at last has won back her married former love and is now expecting his child, Lucretia Collins becomes increasingly dependent on the kindness of strangers. The play's artful blend of repression and guilt anticipates many of Williams's later, longer works, and Lucretia is often seen as a forerunner of both Blanche du Bois in *Streetcar* and Alma Winemiller in *Summer and Smoke.* Yet the play has its own remarkable dramatic intensity. As its first star, Jessica Tandy, has remarked, *Portrait of a Madonna* has "got everything in it. It's a perfect little jewel of a play. A lot of Tennessee's one-act ones are. He really mastered the one-act play."

Further Reading:

N. Tischler, *Tennessee Williams: Rebellious Puritan,* 1961.

Tennessee Williams: A Tribute, ed. J. Tharpe, 1977.

S. L. Falk, *Tennessee Williams,* 2nd ed., 1978.

F. Hirsch, *A Portrait of the Artist: The Plays of Tennessee Williams,* 1979.

F. H. Londre, *Tennessee Williams,* 1979.

J. S. McCann, *The Critical Reputation of Tennessee Williams: A Reference Guide,* 1983.

D. Rader, *Tennessee, Cry of the Heart,* 1983.

D. Williams and S. Mead, *Tennessee Williams: An Intimate Biography,* 1983.

D. Spoto, *The Kindness of Strangers: The Life of Tennessee Williams,* 1985.

Text:
27 Wagons Full of Cotton and Other Plays, 1945.

Portrait of a Madonna

Characters

Miss Lucretia Collins

The Porter

The Elevator Boy

The Doctor

The Nurse

Mr. Abrams

> *Scene: The living room of a moderate-priced city apartment. The furnishings are old-fashioned and everything is in a state of neglect and disorder. There is a door in the back wall to a bedroom, and on the right to the outside hall.*

Miss Collins: Richard! *(The door bursts open and Miss Collins rushes out, distractedly. She is a middle-aged spinster, very slight and hunched of figure with a desiccated face that is flushed with excitement. Her hair is arranged in curls that would become a* *young girl and she wears a frilly negligee which might have come from an old hope chest of a period considerably earlier.)* No, no, no, no! I don't care if the whole church hears about it! *(She frenziedly snatches up the phone.)* Manager, I've got to speak to the manager! Hurry, oh, please hurry, there's a *man*—! *(wildly aside as if to an invisible figure)* Lost all respect, absolutely no respect! . . . Mr. Abrams? *(in a tense hushed voice)* I don't want any reporters to hear about this but something awful has been going on upstairs. Yes, this is Miss Collins' apartment on the top floor. I've refrained from making any complaint because of my connections with the church. I used to be assistant to the Sunday School superintendent and I once had the primary class. I helped them put on the Christmas pageant. I made the dress for the Virgin and Mother, made robes for the Wise Men. Yes, and now this has happened, I'm not responsible for it, but night after night after night this man has been coming into my apartment and—indulging his senses! Do you understand? Not once but repeatedly, Mr. Abrams! I don't know whether he comes in the door or the window or up the fire-escape or whether there's some secret entrance they know about at the church, but he's here now, in my bedroom, and I can't force him to leave, I'll have to have some assistance! No, he isn't a thief, Mr. Abrams, he comes of a very fine family in Webb, Mississippi, but this woman has ruined his character, she's destroyed his respect for ladies! Mr. Abrams? Mr. Abrams! Oh, goodness! *(She slams up the receiver and looks distractedly about for a moment; then rushes back into the bedroom.)* Richard! *(The door slams shut. After a few moments an old porter enters in drab gray cover-alls. He looks about with a sorrowfully humorous curiosity, then timidly calls.)*

Porter: Miss Collins? *(The elevator door slams open in hall and the Elevator Boy, wearing a uniform, comes in.)*

Elevator Boy: Where is she?

Porter: Gone in 'er bedroom.

Elevator Boy: *(grinning)* She got him in there with her?

Porter: Sounds like it. *(Miss Collins' voice can be heard faintly protesting with the mysterious intruder.)*

Elevator Boy: What'd Abrams tell yuh to do?

Porter: Stay here an' keep a watch on 'er till they git here.

Elevator Boy: Jesus.

Porter: Close 'at door.

Elevator Boy: I gotta leave it open a little so I can hear the buzzer. Ain't this place a holy sight though?

Porter: Don't look like it's had a good cleaning in fifteen or twenty years. I bet it ain't either. Abrams'll bust a blood-vessel when he takes a lookit them walls.

Elevator Boy: How comes it's in this condition?

Porter: She wouldn't let no one in.

Elevator Boy: Not even the paper-hangers?

Porter: Naw. Not even the plumbers. The plaster washed down in the bathroom underneath hers an' she admitted her plumbin' had been stopped up. Mr. Abrams had to let the plumber in with this here pass-key when she went out for a while.

Elevator Boy: Holy Jeez. I wunner if she's got money stashed around here. A lotta freaks do stick away big sums of money in ole mattresses an' things.

Porter: She ain't. She got a monthly pension check or something she always turned over to Mr. Abrams to dole it out to 'er. She tole him that Southern ladies was never brought up to manage finanshul affairs. Lately the checks quit comin'.

Elevator Boy: Yeah?

Porter: The pension give out or somethin'. Abrams says he got a contribution from the church to keep 'er on here without 'er knowin' about it. She's proud as a peacock's tail in spite of 'er awful appearance.

Elevator Boy: Lissen to 'er in there!

Porter: What's she sayin'?

Elevator Boy: Apologizin' to him! For callin' the *police!*

Porter: She thinks police 're comin'?

Miss Collins: (from bedroom) Stop it, it's got to stop!

Elevator Boy: Fightin' to protect her honor again! What a commotion, no wunner folks are complainin'!

Porter: (lighting his pipe) This here'll be the last time.

Elevator Boy: She's goin' out, huh?

Porter: (blowing out the match) Tonight.

Elevator Boy: Where'll she go?

Porter: (slowly moving to the old gramophone) She'll go to the state asylum.

Elevator Boy: Holy G!

Porter: Remember this ole number? *(He puts on a record of "I'm Forever Blowing Bubbles.")*

Elevator Boy: Naw. When did that come out?

Porter: Before your time, sonny boy. Machine needs oilin'. *(He takes out small oil-can and applies oil about the crank and other parts of gramophone.)*

Elevator Boy: How long is the old girl been here?

Porter: Abrams says she's been livin' here twenty-five, thirty years, since before he got to be manager even.

Elevator Boy: Livin' alone all that time?

Porter: She had an old mother died of an operation about fifteen years ago. Since then she ain't gone out of the place excep' on Sundays to church or Friday nights to some kind of religious meeting.

Elevator Boy: Got an awful lot of ol' magazines piled aroun' here.

Porter: She used to collect 'em. She'd go out in back and fish 'em out of the incinerator.

Elevator Boy: What'n hell for?

Porter: Mr. Abrams says she used to cut out the Campbell soup kids. Them red-tomato-headed kewpie dolls that got with the soup advertisements. You seen 'em, ain'tcha?

Elevator Boy: Uh-huh.

Porter: She made a collection of 'em. Filled a big lot of scrapbooks with them paper kiddies an' took 'em down to the Children's Hospitals on Xmas Eve an' Easter Sunday, exactly twicet a year. Sounds better, don't it? *(referring to gramophone, which resumes its faint, wheedling music)* Eliminated some a that crankin' noise . . .

Elevator Boy: I didn't know that she'd been nuts *that* long.

Porter: Who's nuts an' who ain't? If you ask me the world is populated with people that's just as peculiar as she is.

Elevator Boy: Hell. She don't have brain *one.*

Porter: There's important people in Europe got less'n she's got. Tonight they're takin' her off 'n' lockin' her up. They'd do a lot better to leave 'er go an' lock up some a them maniacs over there. She's harmless; they ain't. They kill millions of people an' go scot free!

Elevator Boy: An ole woman like her is disgusting, though, imaginin' somebody's raped her.

Porter: Pitiful, not disgusting. Watch out for them cigarette ashes.

Elevator Boy: What's uh diff'rence? So much dust you can't see it. All a this here goes out in the morning, don't it?

Porter: Uh-huh.

Elevator Boy: I think I'll take a couple a those ole records as curiosities for my girl friend. She's got a portable in 'er bedroom, she says it's better with music!

Porter: Leave 'em alone. She's still got 'er property rights.

Elevator Boy: Aw, she's got all she wants with them dream-lovers of hers!

Porter: Hush up! *(He makes a warning gesture as Miss Collins enters from bedroom. Her appearance is that of a ravaged woman. She leans exhaustedly in the doorway, hands clasped over her flat, virginal bosom.)*

Miss Collins: *(breathlessly)* Oh, Richard—Richard . . . .

Porter: *(coughing)* Miss—Collins.

Elevator Boy: Hello, Miss Collins.

Miss Collins: *(just noticing the men)* Goodness! You've arrived already! Mother didn't tell me you were here! *(Self-consciously she touches her ridiculous corkscrew curls with the faded pink ribbon tied through them. Her manner becomes that of a slightly coquettish but prim little Southern belle.)* I must ask you gentlemen to excuse the terrible disorder.

Porter: That's all right, Miss Collins.

Miss Collins: It's the maid's day off. Your No'thern girls receive such excellent domestic training, but in the South it was never considered essential for a girl to have anything but prettiness and charm! *(She laughs girlishly.)* Please do sit down. Is it too close? Would you like a window open?

Porter: No, Miss Collins.

Miss Collins: *(advancing with delicate grace to the sofa)* Mother will bring in something cool after while. . . . Oh, my! *(She touches her forehead.)*

Porter: *(kindly)* Is anything wrong, Miss Collins?

Miss Collins: Oh, no, no, thank you, nothing! My head is a little bit heavy. I'm always a little bit—malarial—this time of year! *(She sways dizzily as she starts to sink down on the sofa.)*

Porter: *(helping her)* Careful there, Miss Collins.

Miss Collins: *(vaguely)* Yes, it is, I hadn't noticed before. *(She peers at them near-sightedly with a hesitant smile.)* You gentlemen have come from the church?

Porter: No, ma'am. I'm Nick, the porter, Miss Collins, and this boy here is Frank that runs the elevator.

Miss Collins: (stiffening a little) Oh? . . . I don't understand.

Porter: (gently) Mr. Abrams just asked me to drop in here an' see if you was getting along all right.

Miss Collins: Oh! Then he must have informed you of what's been going on in here!

Porter: He mentioned some kind of—disturbance.

Miss Collins: Yes! Isn't it outrageous? But it mustn't go any further, you understand. I mean you mustn't repeat it to other people.

Porter: No, I wouldn't say nothing.

Miss Collins: Not a word of it, please!

Elevator Boy: Is the man still here, Miss Collins?

Miss Collins: Oh, no. No, he's gone now.

Elevator Boy: How did he go, out the bedroom window, Miss Collins?

Miss Collins: (vaguely) Yes. . . .

Elevator Boy: I seen a guy that could do that once. He crawled straight up the side of the building. They called him The Human Fly! Gosh, that's a wonderful publicity angle, Miss Collins—"Beautiful Young Society Lady Raped by The Human Fly!"

Porter: (nudging him sharply) Git back in your cracker box!

Miss Collins: Publicity? No! It would be so humiliating! Mr. Abrams surely hasn't reported it to the papers!

Porter: No, ma'am. Don't listen to this smarty pants.

Miss Collins: (touching her curls) Will pictures be taken, you think? There's one of him on the mantel.

Elevator Boy: (going to the mantel) This one here, Miss Collins?

Miss Collins: Yes. Of the Sunday School faculty picnic. I had the little kindergardeners that year and he had the older boys. We rode in the cab of a railroad locomotive from Webb to Crystal Springs. *(She covers her ears with a girlish grimace and toss of her curls.)* Oh, how the steam-whistle blew! Blew! *(giggling) Blewwwww!* It frightened me so, he put his arm round my shoulders! But she was there, too, though she had no business being. She grabbed his hat and stuck it on the back of her head and they—they *rassled* for it, they actually *rassled* together! Everyone said it was *shameless!* Don't you think that it was?

Porter: Yes, Miss Collins.

Miss Collins: That's the picture, the one in the silver frame up there on the mantel. We cooled the watermelon in the springs and afterwards played games. She hid somewhere and he took ages to find her. It got to be dark and he hadn't found her yet and everyone whispered and giggled about it and finally they came back together—her hangin' on to his arm like a common little strumpet—and Daisy Belle Huston shrieked out, "Look, everybody, the seat of Evelyn's skirt!" It was—covered with—grass-stains! Did you ever hear of anything as outrageous? It didn't faze her, though, she laughed like it was something very, very amusing! Rather *triumphant* she was!

Elevator Boy: Which one is him, Miss Collins?

Miss Collins: The tall one in the blue shirt holding onto one of my curls. He
loved to play with them.

Elevator Boy: Quite a Romeo—1910 model, huh?

Miss Collins: (vaguely) Do you? It's nothing, really, but I like the lace on the
collar. I said to Mother, "Even if I don't wear it, Mother, it will be *so* nice
for my hope-chest!"

Elevator Boy: How was he dressed tonight when he climbed into your balcony,
Miss Collins?

Miss Collins: Pardon?

Elevator Boy: Did he still wear that nifty little stick-candy-striped blue shirt with
the celluloid collar?

Miss Collins: He hasn't changed.

Elevator Boy: Oughta be easy to pick him up in that. What color pants did he
wear?

Miss Collins: (vaguely) I don't remember.

Elevator Boy: Maybe he didn't wear any. Shimmied out of 'em on the way up
the wall! You could get him on grounds of indecent exposure, Miss Collins!

Porter: (grasping his arm) Cut that or git back in your cage! Understand?

Elevator Boy: (snickering) Take it easy. She don't hear a thing.

Porter: Well, you keep a decent tongue or get to hell out. Miss Collins here is a
lady. You understand that?

Elevator Boy: Okay. She's Shoiley Temple.

Porter: She's a *lady!*

Elevator Boy: Yeah! *(He returns to the gramophone and looks through the records.)*

Miss Collins: I really shouldn't have created this disturbance. When the officers
come I'll have to explain that to them. But you can understand my feelings,
can't you?

Porter: Sure, Miss Collins.

Miss Collins: When men take advantage of common white-trash women who
smoke in public there is probably some excuse for it, but when it occurs to a
lady who is single and always com-*pletely* above reproach in her moral
behavior, there's really nothing to do but call for police protection! Unless of
course the girl is fortunate enough to have a father and brothers who can take
care of the matter privately without any scandal.

Porter: Sure. That's right, Miss Collins.

Miss Collins: Of course it's bound to cause a great deal of very disagreeable talk.
Especially 'round the *church!* Are you gentlemen Episcopalian?

Porter: No, ma'am. Catholic, Miss Collins.

Miss Collins: Oh. Well, I suppose you know in England we're known as the
English Catholic church. We have direct Apostolic succession through St. Paul
who christened the Early Angles—which is what the original English people
were called—and established the English branch of the Catholic church over
there. So when you hear ignorant people claim that our church was founded
by—by Henry the *Eighth*—that horrible, *lech*erous old man who had so many
wives—as many as *Blue*-beard they say!—you can see how ridiculous it *is* and
how thoroughly ob*nox*-ious to anybody who really *knows* and under*stands*
Church *His*tory!

Porter: (comfortingly) Sure, Miss Collins. Everybody knows that.

Miss Collins: I wish they *did*, but they need to be in*struc*ted! Before he died, my father was Rector at the Church of St. Michael and St. George at Glorious Hill, Mississippi. . . . I've literally grown up right in the very *shad*ow of the Episcopal church. At Pass Christian and Natchez, Biloxi, Gulfport, Port Gibson, Columbus and Glorious Hill! *(with gentle, bewildered sadness)* But you know I sometimes suspect that there has been some kind of spiritual schism in the modern church. These northern dioceses have completely departed from the good old church traditions. For instance our Rector at the Church of the Holy Communion has never darkened my door. It's a fashionable church and he's terribly busy, but even so you'd think he might have time to make a stranger in the congregation feel at home. But he doesn't though! Nobody seems to have the time any more. . . . *(She grows more excited as her mind sinks back into illusion.)* I ought not to mention this, but do you know they actually take a malicious de-*light* over there at the Holy Communion—where I've recently transferred my letter—in what's been going on here at night in this apartment? *Yes!! (She laughs wildly and throws up her hands.)* They take a malicious de*LIGHT* in it!! *(She catches her breath and gropes vaguely about her wrapper.)*

Porter: You lookin' for somethin', Miss Collins?

Miss Collins: My—handkerchief . . . *(She is blinking her eyes against tears.)*

Porter: (removing a rag from his pocket) Here. Use this, Miss Collins. It's just a rag but it's clean, except along that edge where I wiped off the phonograph handle.

Miss Collins: Thanks. You gentlemen are very kind. Mother will bring in something cool after while. . . .

Elevator Boy: (placing a record on machine) This one is got some kind of foreign title. *(The record begins to play Tschaikowsky's "None But the Lonely Heart.")*[1]

Miss Collins: (stuffing the rag daintily in her bosom) Excuse me, please. Is the weather nice outside?

Porter: (huskily) Yes, it's nice, Miss Collins.

Miss Collins: (dreamily) So wa'm for this time of year. I wore my little astrakhan cape to service but had to *carry* it *home*, as the weight of it actually seemed *oppres*sive to me. *(Her eyes fall shut.)* The sidewalks seem so dreadfully long in summer. . . .

Elevator Boy: This ain't summer, Miss Collins.

Miss Collins: (dreamily) I used to think I'd never get to the end of that last block. And that's the block where all the trees went down in the big tornado. The walk is simple *glit*-tering with sunlight. *(pressing her eyelids)* Impossible to shade your face and I *do* perspire so freely! *(She touches her forehead daintily with the rag.)* Not a branch, not a leaf to give you a little protection! You simply *have* to en-*dure* it. Turn your hideous red face away from all the front-porches and walk as fast as you decently *can* till you get *by* them! Oh,

[1] Song by Peter Ilyich Tchaikovsky (1840–1893), Russian composer.

dear, dear Savior, sometimes you're not so lucky and you *meet* people and have to *smile!* You can't *avoid* them unless you cut *across* and that's so *obvious*, you know. . . . People would say you're pe*cu*liar. . . . His house is right in the middle of that awful leafless block, *their* house, his and *hers,* and they have an automobile and always get home early and sit on the porch and *watch* me walking by—Oh, Father in Heaven—with a malicious de*light! (She averts her face in remembered torture.)* She has such *penetrating* eyes, they look straight through me. She sees that terrible choking thing in my throat and the pain I have in *here—(touching her chest)*—and she points it out and laughs and whispers to him, "There she goes with her shiny big red nose, the poor old maid—that *loves* you!" *(She chokes and hides her face in the rag.)*

Porter: Maybe you better forget all that, Miss Collins.

Miss Collins: Never, never forget it! Never, never! I left my parasol once—the one with long white fringe that belonged to Mother—I left it behind in the cloak-room at the church so I didn't have anything to cover my face with when I walked by, and I couldn't turn back either, with all those people behind me—giggling back of me, poking fun at my clothes! Oh, dear, dear! I had to walk straight forward—past the last elm tree and into that *merciless* sunlight. Oh! It beat down on me, *scorching* me! *Whips! . . .* Oh, Jesus! . . . Over my face and my body! . . . I tried to walk on fast but was dizzy and they kept closer behind me—! I stumbled, I nearly fell, and all of them burst out laughing! My face turned so *horribly* red, it got so red and wet, I knew how ugly it was in all that merciless glare—not a single shadow to hide in! And then—*(Her face contorts with fear.)*—their automobile drove up in front of their house, right where I had to pass by it, and *she* stepped out, in white, so fresh and easy, her stomach round with a baby, the first of the *six.* Oh, God! . . . And he stood smiling behind her, white and easy and cool, and they stood there waiting for me. *Waiting!* I had to keep on. What else could I do? I couldn't turn *back,* could I? *No!* I said dear *God,* strike me *dead!* He didn't, though. I put my head way down like I couldn't see them! You know what she did? She stretched out her hand to *stop* me! And *he*—he stepped up straight in front of me, *smiling,* blocking the walk with his terrible big white body! *"Lucretia,"* he said, *"Lucretia Collins!"* I—I tried to speak but I couldn't, the breath went out of my body! I covered my face and—ran! . . . Ran! . . . *Ran! (beating the arm of the sofa)* Till I reached the end of the block —and the elm trees—*started* again. . . . Oh, Merciful Christ in Heaven, how *kind* they were! *(She leans back exhaustedly, her hand relaxed on sofa. She pauses and the music ends.)* I said to Mother, "Mother, we've got to leave town!" We *did* after that. And now after all these years he's finally remembered and come *back!* Moved away from that house and the woman and come *here*—I saw him in the back of the church one day. I wasn't sure—but it *was.* The night after that was the night that he first broke in—and indulged his senses with me. . . . He doesn't realize that I've changed, that I can't feel again the way that I used to feel, now that he's got six children by that Cincinnati girl— three in high-school already! Six! Think of that? Six children! I don't know what he'll say when he knows another one's coming! He'll probably blame *me* for it because a man always *does!* In spite of the fact that he *forced* me!

Elevator Boy: (grinning) Did you say—a *baby,* Miss Collins?

Miss Collins: (lowering her eyes but speaking with tenderness and pride) Yes—I'm expecting a *child.*

Elevator Boy: Jeez! *(He claps his hand over his mouth and turns away quickly.)*

Miss Collins: Even if it's not legitimate, I think it has a perfect right to its father's name—don't you?

Porter: Yes. Sure, Miss Collins.

Miss Collins: A child is innocent and pure. No matter how it's conceived. And it must *not* be made to suffer! So I intend to dispose of the little property cousin Ethel left me and give the child a private education where it won't come under the evil influence of the Christian church! I want to make sure that it doesn't grow up in the shadow of the cross and then have to walk along blocks that scorch you with terrible sunlight! *(The elevator buzzer sounds from the hall.)*

Porter: Frank! Somebody wants to come up. *(The Elevator Boy goes out. The elevator door bangs shut. The Porter clears his throat.)* Yes, it'd be better—to go off some place else.

Miss Collins: If only I had the courage—but I don't. I've grown so used to it here, and people outside—it's always so *hard* to *face* them!

Porter: Maybe you won't—have to face nobody, Miss Collins. *(The elevator door clangs open.)*

Miss Collins: (rising fearfully) Is someone coming—here?

Porter: You just take it easy, Miss Collins.

Miss Collins: If that's the officers coming for Richard, tell them to go away. I've decided not to prosecute Mr. Martin. *(Mr. Abrams enters with the Doctor and the Nurse. The Elevator Boy gawks from the doorway. The Doctor is the weary, professional type, the Nurse hard and efficient. Mr. Abrams is a small, kindly person, sincerely troubled by the situation.)*

Miss Collins: (shrinking back, her voice faltering) I've decided not to—prosecute Mr. Martin . . .

Doctor: Miss Collins?

Mr. Abrams: (with attempted heartiness) Yes, this is the lady you wanted to meet, Dr. White.

Doctor: Hmmm. *(briskly to the Nurse)* Go in her bedroom and get a few things together.

Nurse: Yes, sir. *(She goes quickly across to the bedroom.)*

Miss Collins: (fearfully shrinking) Things?

Doctor: Yes, Miss Tyler will help you pack up an overnight bag. *(smiling mechanically)* A strange place always seems more homelike the first few days when we have a few of our little personal articles around us.

Miss Collins: A strange—place?

Doctor: (carelessly, making a memorandum) Don't be disturbed, Miss Collins.

Miss Collins: I know! *(excitedly)* You've come from the Holy Communion to place me under arrest! On moral charges!

Mr. Abrams: Oh, no, Miss Collins, you got the wrong idea. This is a doctor who—

Doctor: (impatiently) Now, now, you're just going away for a while till things get straightened out. *(He glances at his watch.)* Two-twenty-five! Miss Tyler?

Nurse: Coming!

Miss Collins: (with slow and sad comprehension) Oh. . . . I'm going away. . . .

Mr. Abrams: She was always a lady, Doctor, such a perfect lady.

Doctor: Yes. No doubt.

Mr. Abrams: It seems too bad!

Miss Collins: Let me—write him a note. A pencil? Please?

Mr. Abrams: Here, Miss Collins. *(She takes the pencil and crouches over the table. The Nurse comes out with a hard, forced smile, carrying a suitcase.)*

Doctor: Ready, Miss Tyler?

Nurse: All ready, Dr. White. *(She goes up to Miss Collins.)* Come along, dear, we can tend to that later!

Mr. Abrams: (sharply) Let her finish the note!

Miss Collins: (straightening with a frightened smile) It's—finished.

Nurse: All right, dear, come along. *(She propels her firmly toward the door.)*

Miss Collins: (turning suddenly back) Oh, Mr. Abrams!

Mr. Abrams: Yes, Miss Collins?

Miss Collins: If he should come again—and find me gone—I'd rather you didn't tell him—about the baby. . . . I think its better for *me* to tell him *that. (gently smiling)* You know how men *are,* don't you?

Mr. Abrams: Yes, Miss Collins.

Porter: Goodbye, Miss Collins. *(The Nurse pulls firmly at her arm. She smiles over her shoulder with a slight apologetic gesture.)*

Miss Collins: Mother will bring in—something cool—after while . . . *(She disappears down the hall with the Nurse. The elevator door clangs shut with the metallic sound of a locked cage. The wires hum.)*

Mr. Abrams: She wrote him a note.

Porter: What did she write, Mr. Abrams?

Mr. Abrams: "Dear—Richard. I'm going away for a while. But don't worry, I'll be back. I have a secret to tell you. Love—Lucretia." *(He coughs.)* We got to clear out this stuff an' pile it down in the basement till I find out where it goes.

Porter: (dully) Tonight, Mr. Abrams?

Mr. Abrams: (roughly to hide his feeling) No, no, not tonight, you old fool. Enough has happened tonight! *(then gently)* We can do it tomorrow. Turn out that bedroom light—and close the window. *(Music playing softly becomes audible as the men go out slowly, closing the door, and the light fades out.)*

CURTAIN

1941–1944/1946

John Cheever
1912–1982

A book reviewer once referred to John Cheever as the "Chekhov of the suburbs" —a double-edged comment that acknowledged his great talent as a short story writer but limited his fictional scope. Cheever's stories, however, though they frequently chronicle the manners and mores of upper-middle-class suburban life, offer more than social documentation. His overriding theme has less to do with the social customs of a particular class than with his profound disappointment that civilization can do so little for human happiness. In one of his tales, a character gazes out the window of a commuter train "looking with some delicacy, not into a formidable and challenging wilderness but into a half-finished civilization embracing glass towers, oil derricks, suburban continents and abandoned movie houses and wondering why, in this most prosperous, equitable, and accomplished world—where even the cleaning women practice Chopin preludes in their spare time—everyone should seem to be so disappointed."

John Cheever was born on May 27, 1912, in Quincy, Massachusetts. He went through a deeply troubled adolescence as a result of his father's business failure in the stock market crash of 1929 and his parent's separation. He attended Thayer Academy in South Braintree, Massachusetts, but his refusal to memorize the names of the Greek playwrights, along with other breaches of discipline, led to his dismissal in his junior year. Determined to be a writer, Cheever sent sketches of his expulsion to literary critic Malcolm Cowley, then editor of the *New Republic*. Cowley, who became Cheever's lifelong friend, published the sketches and thus launched the seventeen-year-old Cheever's literary career. Cheever promptly moved to New York City, where he contributed stories to numerous magazines and lived in such squalor that Walker Evans, the famous photographer of rural poverty, couldn't resist taking a picture of his room. Cheever married in 1941 and afterward spent four years with the U.S. Army during World War II. In the early 1950s Cheever worked for the Columbia Broadcasting System, writing scripts for such radio shows as "Life with Father." He died of cancer in 1982.

Cheever's first volume of short stories, *The Way Some People Live,* appeared in 1942, while he was serving in the army. His next volume, *The Enormous Radio and Other Stories* (1953), consisted of fourteen tales that had originally been published in *The New Yorker,* to which Cheever had been contributing regularly since 1940. In subsequent collections, *The Housebreaker of Shady Hill* (1958), *Some People, Places, and Things That Will Not Appear in My Next Novel* (1961), *The Brigadier and the Golf Widow* (1964), and *The World of Apples* (1972), Cheever's tone remained predominantly elegaic, though it was increasingly counterbalanced, as in "The Fourth Alarm," by a grittier, more absurd view of human nature. Taking a retrospective look at his career in a foreword to the Pulitzer Prize–winning *Stories of John Cheever* (1978), he noted that "Calvin played no part at all in my religious education, but his presence seemed to abide in the barns of my childhood and to have left me with some undue bitterness."

Cheever's literary reputation seems to rest more on his short stories than on his longer works, though his first novel, *The Wapshot Chronicle* (1957), won the National Book Award. Cheever continued the story of the urbane, eccentric New England family in *The Wapshot Scandal* (1964), then produced two novels that recast some of the grimmer themes of his short fiction: *Bullet Park* (1969), the tale of an insane attempt at ritual murder in an affluent suburb, and *Falconer* (1977), a story of fratricide, homosexuality, and imprisonment that grew out of his experiences teaching creative writing at Ossining State Prison in New York. In his last book, *Oh What a Paradise It Seems* (1982), Cheever managed to compress into a very short novel the concerns of a lifetime: the search for love, the restoration of the world's physical beauty, the quest, however illusory, to regain a paradise lost.

Further Reading:
S. Coale, *John Cheever*, 1977.
L. Waldeland, *John Cheever*, 1979.
G. Hunt, *John Cheever: The Company of Love*, 1983.
S. Cheever, *Home Before Dark*, 1984.

Text:
The Stories of John Cheever, 1978.

The Fourth Alarm

I sit in the sun drinking gin. It is ten in the morning. Sunday. Mrs. Uxbridge is off somewhere with the children. Mrs. Uxbridge is the housekeeper. She does the cooking and takes care of Peter and Louise.

It is autumn. The leaves have turned. The morning is windless, but the leaves fall by the hundreds. In order to see anything—a leaf or a blade of grass—you have, I think, to know the keenness of love. Mrs. Uxbridge is sixty-three, my wife is away, and Mrs. Smithsonian (who lives on the other side of town) is seldom in the mood these days, so I seem to miss some part of the morning as if the hour had a threshold or a series of thresholds that I cannot cross. Passing a football might do it but Peter is too young and my only football-playing neighbor goes to church.

My wife, Bertha, is expected on Monday. She comes out from the city on Monday and returns on Tuesday. Bertha is a good-looking young woman with a splendid figure. Her eyes, I think, are a little close together and she is sometimes peevish. When the children were young she had a peevish way of disciplining them. "If you don't eat the nice breakfast Mummy has cooked for you before I count three," she would say, "I will send you back to bed. One. Two. *Three*. . . ." I heard it again at dinner. "If you don't eat the nice dinner Mummy has cooked for you before I count three I will send you to bed without any supper. One. Two. Three. . . ." I heard it again. "If you don't pick up your toys before Mummy counts three Mummy will throw them all away. One. Two. Three. . . ." So it went on through the bath and bedtime and one two three was their lullaby. I sometimes thought she must have learned to count when she was an infant and that when the end came she would call a countdown for the Angel of Death. If you'll excuse me I'll get another glass of gin.

When the children were old enough to go to school, Bertha got a job teaching social studies in the sixth grade. This kept her occupied and happy and she said she had always wanted to be a teacher. She had a reputation for strictness. She wore dark clothes, dressed her hair simply, and expected contrition and obedience from her pupils. To vary her life she joined an amateur theatrical group. She played the maid in *Angel Street* and the old crone in *Desmonds Acres*. The friends she made in the theatre were all pleasant people and I enjoyed taking her to their parties. It is important to know that Bertha does not drink. She will take a Dubonnet politely but she does not enjoy drinking.

Through her theatrical friends, she learned that a nude show called *Ozamanides II* was being cast. She told me this and everything that followed. Her teaching contract gave her ten days' sick leave, and claiming to be sick one day she went into New York. *Ozamanides* was being cast at a producer's office in midtown, where she found a line of a hundred or more men and women waiting to be interviewed. She took an unpaid bill out of her pocketbook, and waving this as if it were a letter she bucked the line saying, "Excuse me please, excuse me, I have an appointment. . . ." No one protested and she got quickly to the head of the line, where a secretary took her name, Social Security number, etc. She was told to go into a cubicle and undress. She was then shown into an office where there were four men. The interview, considering the circumstances, was very circumspect. She was told that she would be nude throughout the performance. She would be expected to simulate or perform copulation twice during the performance and participate in a love pile that involved the audience.

I remember the night when she told me all of this. It was in our living room. The children had been put to bed. She was very happy. There was no question about that. "There I was naked," she said, "but I wasn't in the least embarrassed. The only thing that worried me was that my feet might get dirty. It was an old-fashioned kind of place with framed theatre programs on the wall and a big photograph of Ethel Barrymore. There I sat naked in front of these strangers and I felt for the first time in my life that I'd found myself. I found myself in nakedness. I felt like a new woman, a better woman. To be naked and unashamed in front of strangers was one of the most exciting experiences I've ever had. . . ."

I didn't know what to do. I still don't know, on this Sunday morning, what I should have done. I guess I should have hit her. I said she couldn't do it. She said I couldn't stop her. I mentioned the children and she said this experience would make her a better mother. "When I took off my clothes," she said, "I felt as if I had rid myself of everything mean and small." Then I said she'd never get the job because of her appendicitis scar. A few minutes later the phone rang. It was the producer offering her a part. "Oh, I'm so happy," she said. "Oh, how wonderful and rich and strange life can be when you stop playing out the roles that your parents and their friends wrote out for you. I feel like an explorer."

The fitness of what I did then or rather left undone still confuses me. She broke her teaching contract, joined Equity, and began rehearsals. As soon as *Ozamanides* opened she hired Mrs. Uxbridge and took a hotel apartment near the theatre. I asked for a divorce. She said she saw no reason for a divorce. Adultery and cruelty have well marked courses of action but what can a man do when his wife wants to appear naked on the stage? When I was younger I had known some burlesque girls and some of them were married and had children. However, they did what Bertha was going to do only on the midnight Saturday show, and as I remember their husbands were third-string comedians and the kids always looked hungry.

A day or so later I went to a divorce lawyer. He said a consent decree was my only hope. There are no precedents for simulated carnality in public as grounds for divorce in New York State and no lawyer will take a divorce case without a precedent. Most of my friends were tactful about Bertha's new life. I suppose most of them went to see her, but I put it off for a month or more. Tickets were expensive and hard to get. It was snowing the night I went to the theatre, or what had been a theatre. The proscenium arch had been demolished, the set was a collection of used tires, and the only familiar features were the seats and the aisles. Theatre audiences have always confused me. I suppose this is because you find an incomprehensible variety of types thrust into what was an essentially domestic and terribly ornate interior. There were all kinds there that night. Rock music was playing when I came in. It was that deafening old fashioned kind of rock they used to play in places like Arthur. At eight-thirty the houselights dimmed, and the cast—there were fourteen —came down the aisles. Sure enough, they were all naked excepting Ozamanides, who wore a crown.

I can't describe the performance. Ozamanides had two sons, and I think he murdered them, but I'm not sure. The sex was general. Men and women embraced one another and Ozamanides embraced several men. At one point a stranger, sitting in the seat on my right, put his hand on my knee. I didn't want to reproach him for a human condition, nor did I want to encourage him. I removed his hand and experienced a deep nostalgia for the innocent movie theatres of my youth. In the little town where I was raised there was one—the Alhambra. My favorite movie was called *The Fourth Alarm*. I saw it first one Tuesday after school and stayed on for the evening show. My parents worried when I didn't come home for supper and I was scolded. On Wednesday I played hooky and was able to see the show twice and get home in time for supper. I went to school on Thursday but I went to the theatre as soon as school closed and sat partway through the evening show. My parents must have called the police, because a patrolman came into the theatre and made me go home. I was forbidden to go to the theatre on Friday, but I spent all Saturday there, and on Saturday the picture ended its run. The picture was about the substitution of automobiles for horse-drawn fire engines. Four fire companies were involved. Three of the teams had been replaced by engines and the miserable horses had been sold to brutes. One team remained, but its days were numbered. The men and the horses were sad. Then suddenly there was a great fire. One saw the first engine, the second, and the third race off to the conflagration. Back at the horse-drawn company, things were very gloomy. Then the fourth alarm rang—it was their summons—and they sprang into action, harnassed the team, and galloped across the city. They put out the fire, saved the city, and were given an amnesty by the Mayor. Now on the stage Ozamanides was writing something obscene on my wife's buttocks.

Had nakedness—its thrill—annihilated her sense of nostalgia? Nostalgia—in spite of her close-set eyes—was one of her principal charms. It was her gift gracefully to carry the memory of some experience into another tense. Did she, mounted in public by a naked stranger, remember any of the places where we had made love—the rented houses close to the sea, where one heard in the sounds of a summer rain the prehistoric promises of love, peacefulness, and beauty? Should I stand up in the theatre and shout for her to return, return, return in the name of love, humor, and serenity? It was nice driving home after parties in the snow. I thought. The snow flew into the headlights and made it seem as if we were going a hundred miles an hour. It was nice driving home in the snow after parties. Then the cast lined up and urged us—commanded us in fact—to undress and join them.

This seemed to be my duty. How else could I approach understanding Bertha? I've always been very quick to get out of my clothes. I did. However, there was a problem. What should I do with my wallet, wrist watch, and car keys? I couldn't safely leave them in my clothes. So, naked, I started down the aisle with my valuables in my right hand. As I came up to the action a naked young man stopped me and shouted—sang —"Put down your lendings. Lendings are impure."

"But it's my wallet and my watch and the car keys," I said.

"Put down your lendings," he sang.

"But I have to drive home from the station," I said, "and I have sixty or seventy dollars in cash."

"Put down your lendings."

"I can't, I really can't. I have to eat and drink and get home."

"Put down your lendings."

Then one by one they all, including Bertha, picked up the incantation. The whole cast began to chant: "Put down your lendings, put down your lendings."

The sense of being unwanted has always been for me acutely painful. I suppose some clinician would have an explanation. The sensation is reverberative and seems to attach itself as the last link in a chain made up of all similar experience. The voices of the cast were loud and scornful, and there I was, buck naked, somewhere in the middle of the city and unwanted, remembering missed football tackles, lost fights, the contempt of strangers, the sound of laughter from behind shut doors. I held my valuables in my right hand, my literal identification. None of it was irreplaceable, but to cast it off would seem to threaten my essence, the shadow of myself that I could see on the floor, my name.

I went back to my seat and got dressed. This was difficult in such a cramped space. The cast was still shouting. Walking up the sloping aisle of the ruined theatre was powerfully reminiscent. I had made the same gentle ascent after *King Lear* and *The Cherry Orchard*. I went outside.

It was still snowing. It looked like a blizzard. A cab was stuck in front of the theatre and I remembered then that I had snow tires. This gave me a sense of security and accomplishment that would have disgusted Ozamanides and his naked court; but I seemed not to have exposed my inhibitions but to have hit on some marvelously practical and obdurate part of myself. The wind flung the snow into my face and so, singing and jingling the car keys, I walked to the train.

1970

Tillie Olsen
b. 1913

Tillie Olsen was fifteen years old when she paid ten cents for a water-soaked copy of the April 1861 issue of the *Atlantic Monthly* in an Omaha used-book store. In this sixty-seven-year-old magazine, she read an excerpt from Rebecca Harding Davis's anonymously published *Life in the Iron Mills* and learned, as she reports in *Silences,* that "literature can be made out of the lives of despised people." Although some readers have praised Olsen as a great prose stylist, most are convinced that the power of her work turns on its eloquent rendering of the pain and the possibility of the lives of the "despised"—the white working-class women and men who together with their black brothers and sisters populate the world of her fiction.

Born Tillie Lerner to Russian immigrant parents in Omaha, Nebraska, Olsen received more formal education than most women during the Depression. She completed the eleventh grade and, as she has reported, used the local public library as her college classroom. At the age of nineteen she began working on what to date has been her only novel. Within a short time, however, she put the manuscript aside and lost it. Years later, having accidentally recovered it, she decided to reconstruct and finish it. Published in 1974 as *Yonnonido: From the Thirties,* the book recounts the impoverished odyssey, anguished relations, and eventual survival of an unflinchingly hopeful mother and daughter. Above all, as one reviewer puts it, *Yonnonido* demonstrates Olsen's profound understanding of "what a great weight poor women carry" as well as a "deep sympathy for the restlessness and degraded pride" of working-class men.

Olsen's first publications—a few poems and a short story ("The Iron Throat," later the opening chapter of *Yonnonido*)—appeared in the initial volume of the *Partisan Review* in 1934. That same year *The New Republic* printed her autobiographical essay "Thousand-Dollar Vagrant." After this promising beginning, however, Olsen dropped from sight. For the next twenty-two years she published nothing. Having married Jack Olsen, a printer, in 1936, she spent the next two decades trying to write while also rearing four children and working—not only as a typist-transcriber for a dairy-equipment company but also, as she notes in *Silences,* "full time on temporary jobs, a Kelly, a Western Agency girl, (girl!), wandering from office to office, always hoping to manage two, three writing months ahead." Time in which to write came as "stolen moments" on a bus or on the job, she reports, or more often in "the deep night hours for as long as I could stay awake, after the kids were in bed, after the household tasks were done, sometimes during. It is no accident," she adds, "that the first work I considered publishable began: 'I stand here ironing, and what you asked me moves tormented back and forth with the iron.'"

"Eventually," however, Olsen reports, "there was time." The story that begins "I stand here ironing," reprinted here, was written in 1953 and 1954 and first published under the title "Help Her to Believe" in a small magazine, *The Pacific Spectator.* Its theme (how women contend with familial trauma) and its style (lyric rhythms cast in achingly beautiful terms) mark all of Olsen's best work. Retitled "I Stand Here Ironing," the story was included in what is to date Olsen's only collection of fiction, *Tell Me a Riddle* (1961). In that same year, the title story of the collection won the O. Henry Award for best American short story. Since then, Olsen's stories have been reprinted in numerous anthologies, and her contributions—as a writer, critic, teacher, and feminist—have received wide recognition. When *Tell Me a Riddle* was reissued in 1971, it earned even greater praise, as work comparable to Faulkner's "The Bear" and Melville's "Benito Cereno" in the way in which it "carries us through despair to a renewal of hope."

In recent years Tillie Olsen has received numerous honors and awards, including Guggenheim and Radcliffe fellowships, a National Endowment for the Arts grant, and several honorary degrees. She has also been writer-in-residence or visiting professor at several colleges and universities, including Amherst, Stanford, Massachusetts Institute of Technology, and the University of Massachusetts at Boston.

In 1972 Olsen revived Rebecca Harding Davis's *Life in the Iron Mills,* to which she had been so indebted in her youth. Reissued by the Feminist Press, *Life in the Iron Mills* now carries with it an incisive "biographical interpretation" written by Olsen. Olsen's most important recent book is *Silences* (1978), a collection of finely woven pieces concerned, as Olsen has noted, "with the relationship of circumstances—including class, color, sex; the times, climate into which one is born—to the creation of literature." The poet Adrienne Rich has hailed *Silences* as a "prose poem" that is enriched not only by "Olsen's unique connection and resonance with other writers" but also by its explorations of the "losses, the empty spaces, she, above all, has been equipped to recognize."

Although Olsen's body of work is relatively small, her influence on other writers has been large. Margaret Atwood has written of the "reverence" with which other women writers regard Olsen's work. And Alice Walker has observed that there have been few other writers "who manage in their work and in their sharing of their understanding to actually help us to live, to work, to create, day by day." Compelling on many counts, Olsen's work is especially unforgettable for its poor, forgotten female characters—archetypal in their ordinariness—who struggle to claim a dignified place for themselves in circumstances that nurture but also restrain the creative self.

Further Reading:
F. Howe, "Literacy and Literature," *PMLA,* May 1974.
C. Stimpson, "Tillie Olsen: Witness as Servant," *Polit,* Fall 1977.
M. Atwood, "Obstacle Course," *The New York Times Book Review,* July 30, 1978.
S. Cunneen, "Tillie Olsen: Storyteller of Working America," *Christian Century,* May 21, 1980.

Text:
Tell Me a Riddle, 1961.

I Stand Here Ironing

I stand here ironing, and what you asked me moves tormented back and forth with the iron.

"I wish you would manage the time to come in and talk with me about your daughter. I'm sure you can help me understand her. She's a youngster who needs help and whom I'm deeply interested in helping."

"Who needs help." Even if I came, what good would it do? You think because I am her mother I have a key, or that in some way you could use me as a key? She has lived for nineteen years. There is all that life that has happened outside of me, beyond me.

And when is there time to remember, to sift, to weigh, to estimate, to total? I will start and there will be an interruption and I will have to gather it all together again. Or I will become engulfed with all I did or did not do, with what should have been and what cannot be helped.

She was a beautiful baby. The first and only one of our five that was beautiful at birth. You do not guess how new and uneasy her tenancy in her now-loveliness. You did not know her all those years she was thought homely, or see her poring over her baby pictures, making me tell her over and over how beautiful she had been—and would be, I would tell her—and was now, to the seeing eye. But the seeing eyes were few or nonexistent. Including mine.

I nursed her. They feel that's important nowadays. I nursed all the children, but with her, with all the fierce rigidity of first motherhood, I did like the books then said. Though her cries battered me to trembling and my breasts ached with swollenness, I waited till the clock decreed.

Why do I put that first? I do not even know if it matters, or if it explains anything.

She was a beautiful baby. She blew shining bubbles of sound. She loved motion, loved light, loved color and music and textures. She would lie on the floor in her blue overalls patting the surface so hard in ecstasy her hands and feet would blur. She was a miracle to me, but when she was eight months old I had to leave her daytimes with the woman downstairs to whom she was no miracle at all, for I worked or looked for work and for Emily's father, who "could no longer endure" (he wrote in his good-bye note) "sharing want with us."

I was nineteen. It was the pre-relief, pre-WPA world of the depression. I would start running as soon as I got off the streetcar, running up the stairs, the place smelling sour, and awake or asleep to startle awake, when she saw me she would break into a clogged weeping that could not be comforted, a weeping I can hear yet.

After a while I found a job hashing at night so I could be with her days, and it was better. But it came to where I had to bring her to his family and leave her.

It took a long time to raise the money for her fare back. Then she got chicken pox and I had to wait longer. When she finally came, I hardly knew her, walking quick and nervous like her father, looking like her father, thin, and dressed in a shoddy red that yellowed her skin and glared at the pockmarks. All the baby loveliness gone.

She was two. Old enough for nursery school they said, and I did not know then what I know now—the fatigue of the long day, and the lacerations of group life in nurseries that are only parking places for children.

Except that it would have made no difference if I had known. It was the only place there was. It was the only way we could be together, the only way I could hold a job.

And even without knowing, I knew. I knew the teacher that was evil because all these years it has curdled into my memory, the little boy hunched in the corner, her rasp, "why aren't you outside, because Alvin hits you? that's no reason, go out, scaredy." I knew Emily hated it even if she did not clutch and implore "don't go Mommy" like the other children, mornings.

She always had a reason why we should stay home. Momma, you look sick, Momma. I feel sick. Momma, the teachers aren't there today, they're sick. Momma, we can't go, there was a fire there last night. Momma, it's a holiday today, no school, they told me.

But never a direct protest, never rebellion. I think of our others in their three-, four-year-oldness—the explosions, the tempers, the denunciations, the demands—and I feel suddenly ill. I put the iron down. What in me demanded that goodness in her? And what was the cost, the cost to her of such goodness?

The old man living in the back once said in his gentle way: "You should smile at Emily more when you look at her." What *was* in my face when I looked at her? I loved her. There were all the acts of love.

It was only with the others I remembered what he said, and it was the face of joy, and not of care or tightness or worry I turned to them—too late for Emily. She does not smile easily, let alone almost always as her brothers and sisters do. Her face is closed and sombre, but when she wants, how fluid. You must have seen it in her pantomimes, you spoke of her rare gift for comedy on the stage that rouses a laughter out of the audience so dear they applaud and applaud and do not want to let her go.

Where does it come from, that comedy? There was none of it in her when she came back to me that second time, after I had had to send her away again. She had a new daddy now to learn to love, and I think perhaps it was a better time.

Except when we left her alone nights, telling ourselves she was old enough.

"Can't you go some other time, Mommy, like tomorrow?" she would ask. "Will it be just a little while you'll be gone? Do you promise?"

The time we came back, the front door open, the clock on the floor in the hall. She rigid awake. "It wasn't just a little while. I didn't cry. Three times I called you, just three times, and then I ran downstairs to open the door so you could come faster. The clock talked loud. I threw it away, it scared me what it talked."

She said the clock talked loud again that night I went to the hospital to have Susan. She was delirious with the fever that comes before red measles, but she was fully conscious all the week I was gone and the week after we were home when she could not come near the new baby or me.

She did not get well. She stayed skeleton thin, not wanting to eat, and night after night she had nightmares. She would call for me, and I would rouse from exhaustion to sleepily call back: "You're all right, darling, go to sleep, it's just a dream," and if she still called, in a sterner voice, "now go to sleep, Emily, there's nothing to hurt you." Twice, only twice, when I had to get up for Susan anyhow, I went in to sit with her.

Now when it is too late (as if she would let me hold and comfort her like I do the others) I get up and go to her at once at her moan or restless stirring. "Are you awake, Emily? Can I get you something?" And the answer is always the same: "No, I'm all right, go back to sleep, Mother."

They persuaded me at the clinic to send her away to a convalescent home in the country where "she can have the kind of food and care you can't manage for her, and you'll be free to concentrate on the new baby." They still send children to that place. I see pictures on the society page of sleek young women planning affairs to raise money for it, or dancing at the affairs, or decorating Easter eggs or filling Christmas stockings for the children.

They never have a picture of the children so I do not know if the girls still wear those gigantic red bows and the ravaged looks on the every other Sunday when parents can come to visit "unless otherwise notified"—as we were notified the first six weeks.

Oh it is a handsome place, green lawns and tall trees and fluted flower beds. High up on the balconies of each cottage the children stand, the girls in their red bows and white dresses, the boys in white suits and giant red ties. The parents stand below shrieking up to be heard and the children shriek down to be heard, and between them the invisible wall "Not To Be Contaminated by Parental Germs or Physical Affection."

There was a tiny girl who always stood hand in hand with Emily. Her parents never came. One visit she was gone. "They moved her to Rose College," Emily shouted in explanation. "They don't like you to love anybody here."

She wrote once a week, the labored writing of a seven-year-old. "I am fine. How is the baby. If I write my letter nicly I will have a star. Love." There never was a star. We wrote every other day, letters she could never hold or keep but only hear read—once. "We simply do not have room for children to keep any personal possessions," they patiently explained when we pieced one Sunday's shrieking together to plead how much it would mean to Emily, who loved so to keep things, to be allowed to keep her letters and cards.

Each visit she looked frailer. "She isn't eating," they told us.

(They had runny eggs for breakfast or mush with lumps, Emily said later, I'd hold it in my mouth and not swallow. Nothing ever tasted good, just when they had chicken.)

It took us eight months to get her released home, and only the fact that she gained back so little of her seven lost pounds convinced the social worker.

I used to try to hold and love her after she came back, but her body would stay stiff, and after a while she'd push away. She ate little. Food sickened her, and I think much of life too. Oh she had physical lightness and brightness, twinkling by on skates, bouncing like a ball up and down up and down over the jump rope, skimming over the hill; but these were momentary.

She fretted about her appearance, thin and dark and foreign-looking at a time when every little girl was supposed to look or thought she should look a chubby blonde replica of Shirley Temple. The doorbell sometimes rang for her, but no one seemed to come and play in the house or be a best friend. Maybe because we moved so much.

There was a boy she loved painfully through two school semesters. Months later she told me how she had taken pennies from my purse to buy him candy. "Licorice was his favorite and I brought him some every day, but he still liked Jennifer better'n me. Why, Mommy?" The kind of question for which there is no answer.

School was a worry to her. She was not glib or quick in a world where glibness and quickness were easily confused with ability to learn. To her overworked and exasperated teachers she was an overconscientious "slow learner" who kept trying to catch up and was absent entirely too often.

I let her be absent, though sometimes the illness was imaginary. How different from my now-strictness about attendance with the others. I wasn't working. We had a new baby, I was home anyhow. Sometimes, after Susan grew old enough, I would keep her home from school, too, to have them all together.

Mostly Emily had asthma, and her breathing, harsh and labored, would fill the house with a curiously tranquil sound. I would bring the two old dresser mirrors and her boxes of collections to her bed. She would select beads and single earrings, bottle tops and shells, dried flowers and pebbles, old postcards and scraps, all sorts of oddments; then she and Susan would play Kingdom, setting up landscapes and furniture, peopling them with action.

Those were the only times of peaceful companionship between her and Susan. I have edged away from it, that poisonous feeling between them, that terrible balancing of hurts and needs I had to do between the two, and did so badly, those earlier years.

Oh there are conflicts between the others too, each one human, needing, demanding, hurting, taking—but only between Emily and Susan, no, Emily toward Susan that corroding resentment. It seems so obvious on the surface, yet it is not obvious. Susan, the second child, Susan, golden- and curly-haired and chubby, quick and articulate and assured, everything in appearance and manner Emily was not; Susan, not able to resist Emily's precious things, losing or sometimes clumsily breaking them; Susan telling jokes and riddles to company for applause while Emily sat silent (to say to me later: that was *my* riddle, Mother, I told it to Susan); Susan, who for all the five years' difference in age was just a year behind Emily in developing physically.

I am glad for that slow physical development that widened the difference between her and her contemporaries, though she suffered over it. She was too vulnerable for that terrible world of youthful competition, of preening and parading, of constant measuring of yourself against every other, of envy, "If I had that copper hair," "If I had that skin. . . ." She tormented herself enough about not looking like the others, there was enough of the unsureness, the having to be conscious of words before you speak, the constant caring—what are they thinking of me? without having it all magnified by the merciless physical drives.

Ronnie is calling. He is wet and I change him. It is rare there is such a cry now. That time of motherhood is almost behind me when the ear is not one's own but must always be racked and listening for the child cry, the child call. We sit for a while and I hold him, looking out over the city spread in charcoal with its soft aisles of light. *"Shoogily,"* he breathes and curls closer. I carry him back to bed, asleep. *Shoogily.* A funny word, a family word, inherited from Emily, invented by her to say: *comfort.*

In this and other ways she leaves her seal, I say aloud. And startle at my saying it. What do I mean? What did I start to gather together, to try and make coherent? I was at the terrible, growing years. War years. I do not remember them well. I was working, there were four smaller ones now, there was not time for her. She had to help be a mother, and housekeeper, and shopper. She had to set her seal. Mornings of crisis and near hysteria trying to get lunches packed, hair combed, coats and shoes found, everyone to school or Child Care on time, the baby ready for transportation. And always the paper scribbled on by a smaller one, the book looked at by Susan then mislaid, the homework not done. Running out to that huge school where she was one, she was lost, she was a drop; suffering over the unpreparedness, stammering and unsure in her classes.

There was so little time left at night after the kids were bedded down. She would struggle over books, always eating (it was in those years she developed her enormous appetite that is legendary in our family) and I would be ironing, or preparing food for the next day, or writing V-mail to Bill, or tending the baby. Sometimes, to make me laugh, or out of her despair, she would imitate happenings or types at school.

I think I said once: "Why don't you do something like this in the school amateur show?" One morning she phoned me at work, hardly understandable through the weeping: "Mother, I did it. I won, I won; they gave me first prize; they clapped and clapped and wouldn't let me go."

Now suddenly she was Somebody, and as imprisoned in her difference as she had been in anonymity.

She began to be asked to perform at other high schools, even in colleges, then at city and statewide affairs. The first one we went to, I only recognized her that first moment when thin, shy, she almost drowned herself into the curtains. Then: Was this Emily? The control, the command, the convulsing and deadly clowning, the spell, then the roaring, stamping audience, unwilling to let this rare and precious laughter out of their lives.

Afterwards: You ought to do something about her with a gift like that—but without money or knowing how, what does one do? We have left it all to her, and the gift has as often eddied inside, clogged and clotted, as been used and growing.

She is coming. She runs up the stairs two at a time with her light graceful step, and I know she is happy tonight. Whatever it was that occasioned your call did not happen today.

"Aren't you ever going to finish the ironing, Mother? Whistler painted his mother in a rocker. I'd have to paint mine standing over an ironing board." This is one of her communicative nights and she tells me everything and nothing as she fixes herself a plate of food out of the icebox.

She is so lovely. Why did you want me to come in at all? Why were you concerned? She will find her way.

She starts up the stairs to bed. "Don't get me up with the rest in the morning." "But I thought you were having midterms." "Oh, those," she comes back in, kisses me, and says quite lightly, "in a couple of years when we'll all be atom-dead they won't matter a bit."

She has said it before. She *believes* it. But because I have been dredging the past, and all that compounds a human being is so heavy and meaningful in me, I cannot endure it tonight.

I will never total it all. I will never come in to say: She was a child seldom smiled at. Her father left me before she was a year old. I had to work her first six years when *there* was work, or I sent her home and to his relatives. There were years she had care she hated. She was dark and thin and foreign-looking in a world where the prestige went to blondeness and curly hair and dimples, she was slow where glibness was prized. She was a child of anxious, not proud, love. We were poor and could not afford for her the soil of easy growth. I was a young mother, I was a distracted mother. There were the other children pushing up, demanding. Her younger sister seemed all that she was not. There were years she did not want me to touch her. She kept too much in herself, her life was such she had to keep too much in herself. My wisdom came too late. She has much to her and probably nothing will come of it. She is a child of her age, of depression, of war, of fear.

Let her be. So all that is in her will not bloom—but in how many does it? There is still enough left to live by. Only help her to know—help make it so there is cause for her to know—that she is more than this dress on the ironing board, helpless before the iron.

1953–1954/1956

Ralph Ellison
b. 1914

When Ralph Ellison published *Invisible Man* in 1952, he was thirty-eight years old. At that time he had published a number of reviews primarily in "little magazines" and radical periodicals, most notably *The New Masses.* He had also published several stories, including "Slick Gonna Learn," "That I had the Wings," "In a Strange Country," "Flying Home," and "King of the Bingo Game." Twelve years after *Invisible Man,* he published *Shadow and Act* (1964), a work that includes several distinguished essays. Since the mid 1950s he has been at work on a second novel, several parts of which have been published. To date, however, Ellison's reputation as one of the major writers of the mid-twentieth century clearly rests on *Invisible Man.* The winner of several prizes when it was published, including the National Book Award for 1953, *Invisible Man* has been widely praised. In a poll of two hundred authors, critics, and editors conducted by *Book Week,* it was selected as the "most distinguished work" published in the United States between 1945 and 1965.

Ralph Waldo Ellison was born in Oklahoma City on March 1, 1914. His father, Lewis Ellison, a native of South Carolina, worked both as a construction foreman and as an independent businessman selling ice and coal. His mother, Ida Milsap Ellison, a native of Mississippi, worked as a maid. Three years after Ellison's birth, his father died, but despite the ensuing poverty, Ellison's family managed to keep him in school, where he was drawn particularly to the study of music, sacred and secular, classical and jazz. By 1933, when he left home to enter Tuskegee Institute, Ellison had had twelve years' instruction in playing the soprano saxophone and several brass instruments. At Tuskegee he studied literature, painting, and photography but still concentrated on music, hoping to become a composer. Forced by lack of funds to quit school after three years, he left for New York, where he worked as a receptionist, file clerk, and factory hand while also playing music and trying to compose it. He also experimented briefly with photography and sculpture. As he came under the influence of Richard Wright and Langston Hughes, however, he began reading more widely, especially the works of the great modernists. In André Malraux he found an interesting merging of literature and politics. In T. S. Eliot's *The Waste Land* he found something that reminded him of the rhythms and allusional density he heard in black music but often missed in black writing. Soon Ellison was also writing. Hoping to combine a commitment to art with a commitment to politics, he found himself working for the WPA Federal Writer's Project and at the same time writing reviews and stories for radical magazines. For a brief period in 1942 and 1943 he was managing editor of *The Negro Quarterly,* a "Review of Negro Life and Culture" that regularly published leftist artists and scholars.

Ellison's political concerns derived in part from the example of his mother, who had been an ardent supporter of Eugene Debs's Socialist party, and they were intensified by his mother's death in 1937. By the time he began writing *Invisible Man* in 1945, however, most organized forms of radical politics had begun to seem to him too restrictive. More and more he was convinced that literature, like music, could capture the revolutionary implications of black life only by discovering techniques commensurate with the complexities of that life. With this emerging conviction came a new mode of fiction that combined elements of "social realism" with elements of "surrealism." In addition to music, which continued strongly to influence his writing, Ellison began to infuse his fiction with black folklore out of a conviction that black folklore captured and conveyed the sense of black experience "with a complexity of vision that seldom gets into our writing." As he labored to write his way through these interrelated shifts, Ellison also began to move away from short fiction toward the novel as his appropriate form. The novel, he says, "is a form which attempts to deal with the contradictions of life and ambivalence and ambiguities of values." On a personal level, the novel seemed to him to provide a means of discovering some deeper, "more universal meaning" in his own experience—in "remembered conversations" and "local customs." Beyond that, on broader social and political levels, the novel seemed to him to provide a way of discovering "the heroic component" of the experience of black people in America. "Let's not forget," he states in *Shadow and Act,* "that the great tragedies not only treat of negative matters, of violence, brutalities, defeats, but they treat them within a context of man's will to act, to challenge reality and to snatch triumph from the teeth of destruction."

Further Reading:
A. Chester and V. Howard, "The Art of Fiction: An Interview," *Paris Review,* Spring 1955.
Ralph Ellison: A Collection of Critical Essays, ed. J. Hersey, 1970.
Twentieth Century Interpretations of Invisible Man, ed. J. M. Reilly, 1970.

Text:
Invisible Man, 1952.

---

from Invisible Man

Chapter 1: [The Battle Royal]

It goes a long way back, some twenty years. All my life I had been looking for something, and everywhere I turned someone tried to tell me what it was. I accepted their answers too, though they were often in contradiction and even self-contradictory. I was naïve. I was looking for myself and asking everyone except myself questions which I, and only I, could answer. It took me a long time and much painful boomeranging of my expectations to achieve a realization everyone else appears to have been born with: That I am nobody but myself. But first I had to discover that I am an invisible man!

And yet I am no freak of nature, nor of history. I was in the cards, other things having been equal (or unequal) eighty-five years ago. I am not ashamed of my grandparents for having been slaves. I am only ashamed of myself for having at one time been ashamed. About eighty-five years ago they were told that they were free, united with others of our country in everything pertaining to the common good, and, in everything social, separate like the fingers of the hand. And they believed it. They exulted in it. They stayed in their place, worked hard, and brought up my father to do the same. But my grandfather is the one. He was an odd old guy, my grandfather, and I am told I take after him. It was he who caused the trouble. On his deathbed he called my father to him and said, "Son, after I'm gone I want you to keep up the good fight. I never told you, but our life is a war and I have been a traitor all my born days, a spy in the enemy's country ever since I give up my gun back in the Reconstruction. Live with your head in the lion's mouth. I want you to overcome 'em with yeses, undermine 'em with grins, agree 'em to death and destruction, let 'em swoller you till they vomit or bust wide open." They thought the old man had gone out of his mind. He had been the meekest of men. The younger children were rushed from the room, the shades drawn and the flame of the lamp turned so low that it sputtered on the wick like the old man's breathing. "Learn it to the younguns," he whispered fiercely; then he died.

But my folks were more alarmed over his last words than over his dying. It was as though he had not died at all, his words caused so much anxiety. I was warned emphatically to forget what he had said and, indeed, this is the first time it has been mentioned outside the family circle. It had a tremendous effect upon me, however. I could never be sure of what he meant. Grandfather had been a quiet old man who never made any trouble, yet on his deathbed he had called himself a traitor and a spy, and he had spoken of his meekness as a dangerous activity. It became a constant puzzle which lay unanswered in the back of my mind. And whenever things went well for me I remembered my grandfather and felt guilty and uncomfortable. It was as though I was carrying out his advice in spite of myself. And to make it worse, everyone loved me for it. I was praised by the most lily-white men of the town. I was considered an example of desirable conduct—just as my grandfather had been. And what puzzled me was that the old man had defined it as *treachery*. When I was praised for my conduct I felt a guilt that in some way I was doing something that was really against the wishes of the white folks, that if they had understood they would have desired me to act just the opposite, that I should have been sulky and mean, and that that really would have been what they wanted, even though they were fooled and thought they wanted me to act as I did. It made me afraid that some day they would look upon me as a traitor and I would be lost. Still I was more afraid to act any other way because they didn't like that at all. The old man's words were like a curse. On my graduation day I delivered an oration in which I showed that humility was the secret, indeed, the very essence of progress. (Not that I believed this—how could I, remembering my grandfather?—I only believed that it worked.) It was a great success. Everyone praised me and I was invited to give the speech at a gathering of the town's leading white citizens. It was a triumph for our whole community.

It was in the main ballroom of the leading hotel. When I got there I discovered that it was on the occasion of a smoker, and I was told that since I was to be there anyway I might as well take part in the battle royal to be fought by some of my schoolmates as part of the entertainment. The battle royal came first.

All of the town's big shots were there in their tuxedoes, wolfing down the buffet foods, drinking beer and whiskey and smoking black cigars. It was a large room with a high ceiling. Chairs were arranged in neat rows around three sides of a portable boxing ring. The fourth side was clear, revealing a gleaming space of polished floor. I had some misgivings over the battle royal, by the way. Not from a distaste for fighting, but because I didn't care too much for the other fellows who were to take part. They were tough guys who seemed to have no grandfather's curse worrying their minds. No one could mistake their toughness. And besides, I suspected that fighting a battle royal might detract from the dignity of my speech. In those pre-invisible days I visualized myself as a potential Booker T. Washington. But the other fellows didn't care too much for me either, and there were nine of them. I felt superior to them in my way, and I didn't like the manner in which we were all crowded together into the servants' elevator. Nor did they like my being there. In fact, as the warmly lighted floors flashed past the elevator we had words over the fact that I, by taking part in the fight, had knocked one of their friends out of a night's work.

We were led out of the elevator through a rococo hall into an anteroom and told to get into our fighting togs. Each of us was issued a pair of boxing gloves and ushered out into the big mirrored hall, which we entered looking cautiously about us and whispering, lest we might accidentally be heard above the noise of the room. It was foggy with cigar smoke. And already the whiskey was taking effect. I was shocked to see some of the most important men of the town quite tipsy. They were all there —bankers, lawyers, judges, doctors, fire chiefs, teachers, merchants. Even one of the more fashionable pastors. Something we could not see was going on up front. A clarinet was vibrating sensuously and the men were standing up and moving eagerly forward. We were a small tight group, clustered together, our bare upper bodies touching and shining with anticipatory sweat; while up front the big shots were becoming increasingly excited over something we still could not see. Suddenly I heard the school superintendent, who had told me to come, yell, "Bring up the shines, gentlemen! Bring up the little shines!"

We were rushed up to the front of the ballroom, where it smelled even more strongly of tobacco and whiskey. Then we were pushed into place. I almost wet my pants. A sea of faces, some hostile, some amused, ringed around us, and in the center, facing us, stood a magnificent blonde—stark naked. There was dead silence. I felt a blast of cold air chill me. I tried to back away, but they were behind me and around me. Some of the boys stood with lowered heads, trembling. I felt a wave of irrational guilt and fear. My teeth chattered, my skin turned to goose flesh, my knees knocked. Yet I was strongly attracted and looked in spite of myself. Had the price of looking been blindness, I would have looked. The hair was yellow like that of a circus kewpie doll, the face heavily powdered and rouged, as though to form an abstract mask, the eyes hollow and smeared a cool blue, the color of a baboon's butt. I felt a desire to spit upon her as my eyes brushed slowly over her body. Her breasts were firm and round as the domes of East Indian temples, and I stood so close as to see the fine skin texture and beads of pearly perspiration glistening like dew around the pink and erected buds of her nipples. I wanted at one and the same time to run from the room, to sink through the floor, or go to her and cover her from my eyes and the eyes of the others with my body; to feel the soft thighs, to caress her and destroy her, to love her and murder her, to hide from her, and yet to stroke where below the small American flag tattooed upon her belly her thighs formed a capital V. I had a notion that of all in the room she saw only me with her impersonal eyes.

And then she began to dance, a slow sensuous movement; the smoke of a hundred cigars clinging to her like the thinnest of veils. She seemed like a fair bird-girl girdled in veils calling to me from the angry surface of some gray and threatening sea. I was transported. Then I became aware of the clarinet playing and the big shots yelling at us. Some threatened us if we looked and others if we did not. On my right I saw one boy faint. And now a man grabbed a silver pitcher from a table and stepped close as he dashed ice water upon him and stood him up and forced two of us to support him as his head hung and moans issued from his thick bluish lips. Another boy began to plead to go home. He was the largest of the group, wearing dark red fighting trunks much too small to conceal the erection which projected from him as though in answer to the insinuating low-registered moaning of the clarinet. He tried to hide himself with his boxing gloves.

And all the while the blonde continued dancing, smiling faintly at the big shots who watched her with fascination, and faintly smiling at our fear. I noticed a certain merchant who followed her hungrily, his lips loose and drooling. He was a large man who wore diamond studs in a shirtfront which swelled with the ample paunch underneath, and each time the blonde swayed her undulating hips he ran his hand through the thin hair of his bald head and, with his arms upheld, his posture clumsy like that of an intoxicated panda, wound his belly in a slow and obscene grind. This creature was completely hypnotized. The music had quickened. As the dancer flung herself about with a detached expression on her face, the men began reaching out to touch her. I could see their beefy fingers sink into the soft flesh. Some of the others tried to stop them and she began to move around the floor in graceful circles, as they gave chase, slipping and sliding over the polished floor. It was mad. Chairs went crashing, drinks were spilt, as they ran laughing and howling after her. They caught her just as she reached a door, raised her from the floor, and tossed her as college boys are tossed at a hazing, and above her red, fixed-smiling lips I saw the terror and disgust in her eyes, almost like my own terror and that which I saw in some of the other boys. As I watched, they tossed her twice and her soft breasts seemed to flatten against the air and her legs flung wildly as she spun. Some of the more sober ones helped her to escape. And I started off the floor, heading for the anteroom with the rest of the boys.

Some were still crying and in hysteria. But as we tried to leave we were stopped and ordered to get into the ring. There was nothing to do but what we were told. All ten of us climbed under the ropes and allowed ourselves to be blindfolded with broad bands of white cloth. One of the men seemed to feel a bit sympathetic and tried to cheer us up as we stood with our backs against the ropes. Some of us tried to grin. "See that boy over there?" one of the men said. "I want you to run across at the bell and give it to him right in the belly. If you don't get him, I'm going to get you. I don't like his looks." Each of us was told the same. The blindfolds were put on. Yet even then I had been going over my speech. In my mind each word was as bright as flame. I felt the cloth pressed into place, and frowned so that it would be loosened when I relaxed.

But now I felt a sudden fit of blind terror. I was unused to darkness. It was as though I had suddenly found myself in a dark room filled with poisonous cotton-mouths. I could hear the bleary voices yelling insistently for the battle royal to begin.

"Get going in there!"

"Let me at that big nigger!"

I strained to pick up the school superintendent's voice, as though to squeeze some security out of that slightly more familiar sound.

"Let me at those black sonsabitches!" someone yelled.

"No, Jackson, no!" another voice yelled. "Here, somebody, help me hold Jack."

"I want to get at that ginger-colored nigger. Tear him limb from limb," the first voice yelled.

I stood against the ropes trembling. For in those days I was what they called ginger-colored, and he sounded as though he might crunch me between his teeth like a crisp ginger cookie.

Quite a struggle was going on. Chairs were being kicked about and I could hear voices grunting as with a terrific effort. I wanted to see, to see more desperately than ever before. But the blindfold was tight as a thick skin-puckering scab and when I raised my gloved hands to push the layers of white aside a voice yelled, "Oh, no you don't, black bastard! Leave that alone!"

"Ring the bell before Jackson kills him a coon!" someone boomed in the sudden silence. And I heard the bell clang and the sound of the feet scuffling forward.

A glove smacked against my head. I pivoted, striking out stiffly as someone went past, and felt the jar ripple along the length of my arm to my shoulder. Then it seemed as though all nine of the boys had turned upon me at once. Blows pounded me from all sides while I struck out as best I could. So many blows landed upon me that I wondered if I were not the only blindfolded fighter in the ring, or if the man called Jackson hadn't succeeded in getting me after all.

Blindfolded, I could no longer control my motions. I had no dignity. I stumbled about like a baby or a drunken man. The smoke had become thicker and with each new blow it seemed to sear and further restrict my lungs. My saliva became like hot bitter glue. A glove connected with my head, filling my mouth with warm blood. It was everywhere. I could not tell if the moisture I felt upon my body was sweat or blood. A blow landed hard against the nape of my neck. I felt myself going over, my head hitting the floor. Streaks of blue light filled the black world behind the blindfold. I lay prone, pretending that I was knocked out, but felt myself seized by hands and yanked to my feet. "Get going, black boy! Mix it up!" My arms were like lead, my head smarting from blows. I managed to feel my way to the ropes and held on, trying to catch my breath. A glove landed in my mid-section and I went over again, feeling as though the smoke had become a knife jabbed into my guts. Pushed this way and that by the legs milling around me, I finally pulled erect and discovered that I could see the black, sweat-washed forms weaving in the smoky-blue atmosphere like drunken dancers weaving to the rapid drum-like thuds of blows.

Everyone fought hysterically. It was complete anarchy. Everybody fought everybody else. No group fought together for long. Two, three, four, fought one, then turned to fight each other, were themselves attacked. Blows landed below the belt and in the kidney, with the gloves open as well as closed, and with my eye partly opened now there was not so much terror. I moved carefully, avoiding blows, although not too many to attract attention, fighting from group to group. The boys groped about like blind, cautious crabs crouching to protect their mid-sections, their heads pulled in short against their shoulders, their arms stretched nervously before them, with their fists testing the smoke-filled air like the knobbed feelers of hypersensitive snails. In one corner I glimpsed a boy violently punching the air and heard him scream in pain as he smashed his hand against a ring post. For a second I saw him bent over holding his hand, then going down as a blow caught his unprotected head. I played one group against the other, slipping in and throwing a punch then stepping out of range while pushing the others into the melee to take the blows blindly aimed at me. The smoke was agonizing and there were no rounds, no bells at three minute intervals to relieve our exhaustion. The room spun round me, a swirl of lights, smoke, sweating bodies surrounded by tense white faces. I bled from both nose and mouth, the blood spattering upon my chest.

The men kept yelling, "Slug him, black boy! Knock his guts out!"

"Uppercut him! Kill him! Kill that big boy!"

Taking a fake fall, I saw a boy going down heavily beside me as though we were felled by a single blow, saw a sneaker-clad foot shoot into his groin as the two who had knocked him down stumbled upon him. I rolled out of range, feeling a twinge of nausea.

The harder we fought the more threatening the men became. And yet, I had begun to worry about my speech again. How would it go? Would they recognize my ability? What would they give me?

I was fighting automatically when suddenly I noticed that one after another of the boys was leaving the ring. I was surprised, filled with panic, as though I had been left alone with an unknown danger. Then I understood. The boys had arranged it among themselves. It was the custom for the two men left in the ring to slug it out for the winner's prize. I discovered this too late. When the bell sounded two men in tuxedoes leaped into the ring and removed the blindfold. I found myself facing Tatlock, the biggest of the gang. I felt sick at my stomach. Hardly had the bell stopped ringing in my ears than it clanged again and I saw him moving swiftly toward me. Thinking of nothing else to do I hit him smash on the nose. He kept coming, bringing the rank sharp violence of stale sweat. His face was a black blank of a face, only his eyes alive—with hate of me and aglow with a feverish terror from what had happened to us all. I became anxious. I wanted to deliver my speech and he came at me as though he meant to beat it out of me. I smashed him again and again, taking his blows as they came. Then on a sudden impulse I struck him lightly and as we clinched, I whispered, "Fake like I knocked you out, you can have the prize."

"I'll break your behind," he whispered hoarsely.

"For *them?*"

"For *me,* sonofabitch!"

They were yelling for us to break it up and Tatlock spun me half around with a blow, and as a joggled camera sweeps in a reeling scene, I saw the howling red faces crouching tense beneath the cloud of blue-gray smoke. For a moment the world wavered, unraveled, flowed, then my head cleared and Tatlock bounced before me. That fluttering shadow before my eyes was his jabbing left hand. Then falling forward, my head against his damp shoulder, I whispered,

"I'll make it five dollars more."

"Go to hell!"

But his muscles relaxed a trifle beneath my pressure and I breathed, "Seven?"

"Give it to your ma," he said, ripping me beneath the heart.

And while I still held him I butted him and moved away. I felt myself bombarded with punches. I fought back with hopeless desperation. I wanted to deliver my speech more than anything else in the world, because I felt that only these men could judge truly my ability, and now this stupid clown was ruining my chances. I began fighting carefully now, moving in to punch him and out again with my greater speed. A lucky blow to his chin and I had him going too—until I heard a loud voice yell, "I got my money on the big boy."

Hearing this, I almost dropped my guard. I was confused: Should I try to win against the voice out there? Would not this go against my speech, and was not this a moment for humility, for nonresistance? A blow to my head as I danced about sent my right eye popping like a jack-in-the-box and settled my dilemma. The room went red as I fell. It was a dream fall, my body languid and fastidious as to where to land, until the floor became impatient and smashed up to meet me. A moment later I came to. An hypnotic voice said FIVE emphatically. And I lay there, hazily watching a dark red spot of my own blood shaping itself into a butterfly, glistening and soaking into the soiled gray world of the canvas.

When the voice drawled TEN I was lifted up and dragged to a chair. I sat dazed. My eye pained and swelled with each throb of my pounding heart and I wondered if now I would be allowed to speak. I was wringing wet, my mouth still bleeding. We were grouped along the wall now. The other boys ignored me as they congratulated Tatlock and speculated as to how much they would be paid. One boy whimpered over his smashed hand. Looking up front, I saw attendants in white jackets rolling the portable ring away and placing a small square rug in the vacant space surrounded by chairs. Perhaps, I thought, I will stand on the rug to deliver my speech.

Then *the* M.C. called to us, "Come on up here boys and get your money."

We ran forward to where the men laughed and talked in their chairs, waiting. Everyone seemed friendly now.

"There it is on the rug," the man said. I saw the rug covered with coins of all dimensions and a few crumpled bills. But what excited me, scattered here and there, were the gold pieces.

"Boys, it's all yours," the man said. "You get all you grab."

"That's right, Sambo," a blond man said, winking at me confidentially.

I trembled with excitement, forgetting my pain. I would get the gold and the bills, I thought. I would use both hands. I would throw my body against the boys nearest me to block them from the gold.

"Get down around the rug now," the man commanded, "and don't anyone touch it until I give the signal."

"This ought to be good," I heard.

As told, we got around the square rug on our knees. Slowly the man raised his freckled hand as we followed it upward with our eyes.

I heard, "These niggers look like they're about to pray!"

Then, "Ready," the man said. "Go!"

I lunged for a yellow coin lying on the blue design of the carpet, touching it and sending a surprised shriek to join those rising around me. I tried frantically to remove my hand but could not let go. A hot, violent force tore through my body, shaking me like a wet rat. The rug was electrified. The hair bristled up on my head as I shook myself free. My muscles jumped, my nerves jangled, writhed. But I saw that this was not stopping the other boys. Laughing in fear and embarrassment, some were holding back and scooping up the coins knocked off by the painful contortions of the others. The men roared above us as we struggled.

"Pick it up, goddamnit, pick it up!" someone called like a bass-voiced parrot. "Go on, get it!"

I crawled rapidly around the floor, picking up the coins, trying to avoid the coppers and to get greenbacks and the gold. Ignoring the shock by laughing, as I brushed the coins off quickly, I discovered that I could contain the electricity—a contradiction, but it works. Then the men began to push us onto the rug. Laughing embarrassedly, we struggled out of their hands and kept after the coins. We were all wet and slippery and hard to hold. Suddenly I saw a boy lifted into the air, glistening with sweat like a circus seal, and dropped, his wet back landing flush upon the charged rug, heard him yell and saw him literally dance upon his back, his elbows beating a frenzied tattoo upon the floor, his muscles twitching like the flesh of a horse stung by many flies. When he finally rolled off, his face was gray and no one stopped him when he ran from the floor amid booming laughter.

"Get the money," the M.C. called. "That's good hard American cash!"

And we snatched and grabbed, snatched and grabbed. I was careful not to come too close to the rug now, and when I felt the hot whiskey breath descend upon me like a cloud of foul air I reached out and grabbed the leg of a chair. It was occupied and I held on desperately.

"Leggo, nigger! Leggo!"

The huge face wavered down to mine as he tried to push me free. But my body was slippery and he was too drunk. It was Mr. Colcord, who owned a chain of movie houses and "entertainment palaces." Each time he grabbed me I slipped out of his hands. It became a real struggle. I feared the rug more than I did the drunk, so I held on, surprising myself for a moment by trying to topple *him* upon the rug. It was such an enormous idea that I found myself actually carrying it out. I tried not to be obvious, yet when I grabbed his leg, trying to tumble him out of the chair, he raised up roaring with laughter, and, looking at me with soberness dead in the eye, kicked me viciously in the chest. The chair leg flew out of my hand and I felt myself going and rolled.

It was as though I had rolled through a bed of hot coals. It seemed a whole century would pass before I would roll free, a century in which I was seared through the deepest levels of my body to the fearful breath within me and the breath seared and heated to the point of explosion. It'll all be over in a flash, I thought as I rolled clear. It'll all be over in a flash.

But not yet, the men on the other side were waiting, red faces swollen as though from apoplexy as they bent forward in their chairs. Seeing their fingers coming toward me I rolled away as a fumbled football rolls off the receiver's fingertips, back into the coals. That time I luckily sent the rug sliding out of place and heard the coins ringing against the floor and the boys scuffling to pick them up and the M.C. calling, "All right, boys, that's all. Go get dressed and get your money."

I was limp as a dish rag. My back felt as though it had been beaten with wires.

When we had dressed the M.C. came in and gave us each five dollars, except Tatlock, who got ten for being last in the ring. Then he told us to leave. I was not to get a chance to deliver my speech, I thought. I was going out into the dim alley in despair when I was stopped and told to go back. I returned to the ballroom, where the men were pushing back their chairs and gathering in groups to talk.

The M.C. knocked on a table for quiet. "Gentlemen," he said, "we almost forgot an important part of the program. A most serious part, gentlemen. This boy was brought here to deliver a speech which he made at his graduation yesterday . . ."

"Bravo!"

"I'm told that he is the smartest boy we've got out there in Greenwood. I'm told that he knows more big words than a pocket-sized dictionary."

Much applause and laughter.

"So now, gentlemen, I want you to give him your attention."

There was still laughter as I faced them, my mouth dry, my eye throbbing. I began slowly, but evidently my throat was tense, because they began shouting, "Louder! Louder!"

"We of the younger generation extol the wisdom of that great leader and educator," I shouted, "who first spoke these flaming words of wisdom: 'A ship lost at sea for many days suddenly sighted a friendly vessel. From the mast of the unfortunate vessel was seen a signal: "Water, water; we die of thirst!" The answer from the friendly vessel came back: "Cast down your bucket where you are." The captain of the distressed vessel, at last heeding the injunction, cast down his bucket, and it came up full of fresh sparkling water from the mouth of the Amazon River.' And like him I say, and in his words, 'To those of my race who depend upon bettering their condition in a foreign land, or who underestimate the importance of cultivating friendly relations with the Southern white man, who is his next-door neighbor, I would say: "Cast down your bucket where you are"—cast it down in making friends in every manly way of the people of all races by whom we are surrounded . . .'"

I spoke automatically and with such fervor that I did not realize that the men were still talking and laughing until my dry mouth, filling up with blood from the cut, almost strangled me. I coughed, wanting to stop and go to one of the tall brass, sand-filled spittoons to relieve myself, but a few of the men, especially the superintendent, were listening and I was afraid. So I gulped it down, blood, saliva and all, and continued. (What powers of endurance I had during those days! What enthusiasm!

What a belief in the rightness of things!) I spoke even louder in spite of the pain. But still they talked and still they laughed, as though deaf with cotton in dirty ears. So I spoke with greater emotional emphasis. I closed my ears and swallowed blood until I was nauseated. The speech seemed a hundred times as long as before, but I could not leave out a single word. All had to be said, each memorized nuance considered, rendered. Nor was that all. Whenever I uttered a word of three or more syllables a group of voices would yell for me to repeat it. I used the phrase "social responsibility" and they yelled:

"What's that word you say, boy?"

"Social responsibility," I said.

"What?"

"Social . . ."

"Louder."

". . . responsibility."

"More!"

"Respon——"

"Repeat!"

"——sibility."

The room filled with the uproar of laughter until, no doubt, distracted by having to gulp down my blood, I made a mistake and yelled a phrase I had often seen denounced in newspaper editorials, heard debated in private.

"Social . . ."

"What?" they yelled.

". . . equality—"

The laughter hung smokelike in the sudden stillness. I opened my eyes, puzzled. Sounds of displeasure filled the room. The M.C. rushed forward. They shouted hostile phrases at me. But I did not understand.

A small dry mustached man in the front row blared out, "Say that slowly, son!"

"What, sir?"

"What you just said!"

"Social responsibility, sir," I said.

"You weren't being smart, were you, boy?" he said, not unkindly.

"No, sir!"

"You sure that about 'equality' was a mistake?"

"Oh, yes, sir," I said. "I was swallowing blood."

"Well, you had better speak more slowly so we can understand. We mean to do right by you, but you've got to know your place at all times. All right, now, go on with your speech."

I was afraid. I wanted to leave but I wanted also to speak and I was afraid they'd snatch me down.

"Thank you, sir," I said, beginning where I had left off, and having them ignore me as before.

Yet when I finished there was a thunderous applause. I was surprised to see the superintendent come forth with a package wrapped in white tissue paper, and, gesturing for quiet, address the men.

"Gentlemen, you see that I did not overpraise this boy. He makes a good speech and some day he'll lead his people in the proper paths. And I don't have to tell you that that is important in these days and times. This is a good, smart boy, and so to encourage him in the right direction, in the name of the Board of Education I wish to present him a prize in the form of this . . ."

He paused, removing the tissue paper and revealing a gleaming calfskin brief case. ". . . in the form of this first-class article from Shad Whitmore's shop."

"Boy," he said, addressing me, "take this prize and keep it well. Consider it a badge of office. Prize it. Keep developing as you are and some day it will be filled with important papers that will help shape the destiny of your people."

I was so moved that I could hardly express my thanks. A rope of bloody saliva forming a shape like an undiscovered continent drooled upon the leather and I wiped it quickly away. I felt an importance that I had never dreamed.

"Open it and see what's inside," I was told.

My fingers a-tremble, I complied, smelling the fresh leather and finding an official-looking document inside. It was a scholarship to the state college for Negroes. My eyes filled with tears and I ran awkwardly off the floor.

I was overjoyed; I did not even mind when I discovered that the gold pieces I had scrambled for were brass pocket tokens advertising a certain make of automobile.

When I reached home everyone was excited. Next day the neighbors came to congratulate me. I even felt safe from grandfather, whose deathbed curse usually spoiled my triumphs. I stood beneath his photograph with my brief case in hand and smiled triumphantly into his stolid black peasant's face. It was a face that fascinated me. The eyes seemed to follow everywhere I went.

That night I dreamed I was at a circus with him and that he refused to laugh at the clowns no matter what they did. Then later he told me to open my brief case and read what was inside and I did, finding an official envelope stamped with the state seal; and inside the envelope I found another and another, endlessly, and I thought I would fall of weariness. "Them's years," he said. "Now open that one." And I did and in it I found an engraved document containing a short message in letters of gold. "Read it," my grandfather said. "Out loud!"

"To Whom It May Concern," I intoned. "Keep This Nigger-Boy Running."

I awoke with the old man's laughter ringing in my ears.

(It was a dream I was to remember and dream again for many years after. But at that time I had no insight into its meaning. First I had to attend college.)

1952

Bernard Malamud
1914–1986

Bernard Malamud's most memorable characters, like Leo Finkle, the young rabbinical student in "The Magic Barrel," are usually impoverished Jews who lead socially meager lives—losers and loners, the unloved and the loveless. But they are people who also live on the threshold of miracle. Magical intervention operates in Malamud's stories largely for the redemption of lost souls: Leo Finkle's passionless life is transformed by the manipulations of a destitute, shadowy marriage broker, who during the course of the story assumes the mythic proportions of Pan, a trickster, a magician. Yet, unlike most fairy tales, Malamud's stories of the miraculous proceed against a strong undertow of hardheaded skepticism. Miracles do occur, Malamud seems to be saying, but they may only be—in the words of Robert Frost—"a momentary stay against confusion."

Bernard Malamud was born in Brooklyn, New York, on April 26, 1914. The son of comparatively poor Russian-Jewish immigrants, he attended Erasmus Hall High School and received his B.A. in 1936 from New York's City College and his M.A. in 1942 from Columbia University. He taught evening classes in high school English from 1940 to 1949, then took a position as an instructor at Oregon State. Malamud was a member of the American Academy of Arts and Sciences and the National Institute of Arts and Letters, and from 1961 until his death in 1986 he taught "imaginative writing" at Bennington College in Vermont.

Malamud's first novel, *The Natural* (1952), uses a semirealistic and semifantastic re-creation of the world of major league baseball as the background for a predominantly comic exploration of the mythic hero. In his next novel, *The Assistant* (1957), Malamud creates a far more mundane environment—a small Jewish grocery store—as the setting for a tale of oppression and the regenerative power of suffering. Renewal also figures as the theme of the largely satirical novel *A New Life* (1961), in which a young English instructor tries unsuccessfully to break out of the psychological confines of an academic wasteland. Malamud won the National Book Award for his first collection of short stories, *The Magic Barrel* (1958), and both the National Book Award and the Pulitzer Prize for *The Fixer* (1966), a grim parable of human courage set in anti-Semitic Czarist Russia. Malamud's other novels include *Pictures of Fidelman* (1969), a comic story about an art student "ever a sucker for strange beauty and all sorts of experiences"; *The Tenants* (1971), a tense tale of acute loneliness and the uneasy racial relationship between two writers, one white, the other black; *Dubin's Lives* (1979), a story of infidelity and insight; and *God's Grace* (1982), a visionary account of the end of the world and two shipwrecked survivors—a Jewish paleologist and a talking (and talkative) chimpanzee. Among Malamud's collections of short stories are *Idiots First* (1963) and *Rembrandt's Hat* (1973). *The Stories of Bernard Malamud* appeared in 1983.

At the heart of Malamud's fiction is a characteristically Yiddish interplay between inscrutable suffering and deadpan humor, one that finds expression in such old Yiddish proverbs as "God will provide—but if only He would till He does!" Malamud's writing is pervaded with references to the Old Testament, but if he were to re-create the Book of Job, it would most likely feature Charlie Chaplin. Malamud, in fact, claimed that as a writer he learned a great deal from Chaplin's films: "The rhythm, the snap of comedy; the reserved comic presence— that beautiful distancing; the funny with the sad; the surprise of surprise." And like Chaplin's comedy, Malamud's fiction holds us in a suspended state of disequilibrium, where the emotional tempo alternates between hurting and joking. In *God's Grace,* Calvin Cohn, the last man on earth, faces the Divine wrath: "He danced in a shower of rocks; but that may have been his imagining. Yet those that hit the head hurt."

Further Reading:
S. Cohen, *Bernard Malamud and the Trial by Love,* 1974.
R. Ducharme, *Art and Idea in the Novels of Bernard Malamud,* 1974.
R. Astro and J. Benson, eds., *The Fiction of Bernard Malamud,* 1977.

Text:
The Magic Barrel, 1958.

The Magic Barrel

Not long ago there lived in uptown New York, in a small, almost meager room, though crowded with books, Leo Finkle, a rabbinical student in the Yeshiva University. Finkle, after six years of study, was to be ordained in June and had been advised by an acquaintance that he might find it easier to win himself a congregation if he were married. Since he had no present prospects of marriage, after two tormented days of turning it over in his mind, he called in Pinye Salzman, a marriage broker whose two-line advertisement he had read in the *Forward.*

The matchmaker appeared one night out of the dark fourth-floor hallway of the graystone rooming house where Finkle lived, grasping a black, strapped portfolio that had been worn thin with use. Salzman, who had been long in the business, was of slight but dignified build, wearing an old hat, and an overcoat too short and tight for him. He smelled frankly of fish, which he loved to eat, and although he was missing a few teeth, his presence was not displeasing, because of an amiable manner curiously contrasted with mournful eyes. His voice, his lips, his wisp of beard, his bony fingers were animated, but give him a moment of repose and his mild blue eyes revealed a depth of sadness, a characteristic that put Leo a little at ease although the situation, for him, was inherently tense.

He at once informed Salzman why he had asked him to come, explaining that his home was in Cleveland, and that but for his parents, who had married comparatively late in life, he was alone in the world. He had for six years devoted himself almost entirely to his studies, as a result of which, understandably, he had found himself without time for a social life and the company of young women. Therefore he thought it the better part of trial and error—of embarrassing fumbling—to call in an experienced person to advise him on these matters. He remarked in passing that the function of the marriage broker was ancient and honorable, highly approved in the Jewish community, because it made practical the necessary without hindering joy. Moreover, his own parents had been brought together by a matchmaker. They had made, if not a financially profitable marriage—since neither had possessed any worldly goods to speak of—at least a successful one in the sense of their everlasting devotion to each other. Salzman listened in embarrassed surprise, sensing a sort of apology. Later, however, he experienced a glow of pride in his work, an emotion that had left him years ago, and he heartily approved of Finkle.

The two went to their business. Leo had led Salzman to the only clear place in the room, a table near a window that overlooked the lamp-lit city. He seated himself at the matchmaker's side but facing him, attempting by an act of will to suppress the unpleasant tickle in his throat. Salzman eagerly unstrapped his portfolio and removed a loose rubber band from a thin packet of much-handled cards. As he flipped through them, a gesture and sound that physically hurt Leo, the student pretended not to see and gazed steadfastly out the window. Although it was still February, winter was on its last legs, signs of which he had for the first time in years begun to notice. He now observed the round white moon, moving high in the sky through a cloud menagerie, and watched with half-open mouth as it penetrated a huge hen, and dropped out of her like an egg laying itself. Salzman, though pretending through eyeglasses he had just slipped on to be engaged in scanning the writing on the cards, stole occasional glances at the young man's distinguished face, noting with pleasure the long, severe scholar's nose, brown eyes heavy with learning, sensitive yet ascetic lips, and a certain, almost hollow quality of the dark cheeks. He gazed around at shelves upon shelves of books and let out a soft, contented sigh.

When Leo's eyes fell upon the cards, he counted six spread out in Salzman's hand.

"So few?" he asked in disappointment.

"You wouldn't believe me how much cards I got in my office," Salzman replied. "The drawers are already filled to the top, so I keep them now in a barrel, but is every girl good for a new rabbi?"

Leo blushed at this, regretting all he had revealed of himself in a curriculum vitae he had sent to Salzman. He had thought it best to acquaint him with his strict standards and specifications, but in having done so, felt he had told the marriage broker more than was absolutely necessary.

He hesitantly inquired, "Do you keep photographs of your clients on file?"

"First comes family, amount of dowry, also what kind promises," Salzman replied, unbuttoning his tight coat and settling himself in the chair. "After comes pictures, rabbi."

"Call me Mr. Finkle. I'm not yet a rabbi."

Salzman said he would, but instead called him doctor, which he changed to rabbi when Leo was not listening too attentively.

Salzman adjusted his horn-rimmed spectacles, gently cleared his throat and read in an eager voice the contents of the top card:

"Sophie P. Twenty four years. Widow one year. No children. Educated high school and two years college. Father promises eight thousand dollars. Has wonderful wholesale business. Also real estate. On the mother's side comes teachers, also one actor. Well known on Second Avenue."

Leo gazed up in surprise. "Did you say a widow?"

"A widow don't mean spoiled, rabbi. She lived with her husband maybe four months. He was a sick boy she made a mistake to marry him."

"Marrying a widow has never entered my mind."

"This is because you have no experience. A widow, especially if she is young and healthy like this girl, is a wonderful person to marry. She will be thankful to you the rest of her life. Believe me, if I was looking now for a bride, I would marry a widow."

Leo reflected, then shook his head.

Salzman hunched his shoulders in an almost imperceptible gesture of disappointment. He placed the card down on the wooden table and began to read another:

"Lily H. High school teacher. Regular. Not a substitute. Has savings and new Dodge car. Lived in Paris one year. Father is successful dentist thirty-five years. Interested in professional man. Well-Americanized family. Wonderful opportunity."

"I knew her personally," said Salzman. "I wish you could see this girl. She is a doll. Also very intelligent. All day you could talk to her about books and theyater and what not. She also knows current events."

"I don't believe you mentioned her age?"

"Her age?" Salzman said, raising his brows. "Her age is thirty-two years."

Leo said after a while, "I'm afraid that seems a little too old."

Salzman let out a laugh. "So how old are you, rabbi?"

"Twenty-seven."

"So what is the difference, tell me, between twenty-seven and thirty-two? My own wife is seven years older than me. So what did I suffer?—Nothing. If Rothschild's a daughter wants to marry you, would you say on account her age, no?"

"Yes," Leo said dryly.

Salzman shook off the no in the yes. "Five years don't mean a thing. I give you my word that when you will live with her for one week you will forget her age. What does it mean five years—that she lived more and knows more than somebody who is younger? On this girl, God bless her, years are not wasted. Each one that it comes makes better the bargain."

"What subject does she teach in high school?"

"Languages. If you heard the way she speaks French, you will think it is music. I am in the business twenty-five years, and I recommend her with my whole heart. Believe me, I know what I'm talking, rabbi."

"What's on the next card?" Leo said abruptly.

Salzman reluctantly turned up the third card:

"Ruth K. Nineteen years. Honor student. Father offers thirteen thousand cash to the right bridegroom. He is a medical doctor. Stomach specialist with marvelous practice. Brother in law owns own garment business. Particular people."

Salzman looked as if he had read his trump card.

"Did you say nineteen?" Leo asked with interest.

"On the dot."

"Is she attractive?" He blushed. "Pretty?"

Salzman kissed his finger tips. "A little doll. On this I give you my word. Let me call the father tonight and you will see what means pretty."

But Leo was troubled. "You're sure she's that young?"

"This I am positive. The father will show you the birth certificate."

"Are you positive there isn't something wrong with her?" Leo insisted.

"Who says there is wrong?"

"I don't understand why an American girl her age should go to a marriage broker."

A smile spread over Salzman's face.

"So for the same reason you went, she comes."

Leo flushed. "I am pressed for time."

Salzman, realizing he had been tactless, quickly explained. "The father came, not her. He wants she should have the best, so he looks around himself. When we will locate the right boy he will introduce him and encourage. This makes a better marriage than if a young girl without experience takes for herself. I don't have to tell you this."

"But don't you think this young girl believes in love?" Leo spoke uneasily.

Salzman was about to guffaw but caught himself and said soberly, "Love comes with the right person, not before."

Leo parted dry lips but did not speak. Noticing that Salzman had snatched a glance at the next card, he cleverly asked, "How is her health?"

"Perfect," Salzman said, breathing with difficulty. "Of course, she is a little lame on her right foot from an auto accident that it happened to her when she was twelve years, but nobody notices on account she is so brilliant and also beautiful."

Leo got up heavily and went to the window. He felt curiously bitter and upbraided himself for having called in the marriage broker. Finally, he shook his head.

"Why not?" Salzman persisted, the pitch of his voice rising.

"Because I detest stomach specialists."

"So what do you care what is his business? After you marry her do you need him? Who says he must come every Friday night in your house?"

Ashamed of the way the talk was going, Leo dismissed Salzman, who went home with heavy, melancholy eyes.

Though he had felt only relief at the marraige broker's departure, Leo was in low spirits the next day. He explained it as arising from Salzman's failure to produce a suitable bride for him. He did not care for his type of clientele. But when Leo found himself hesitating whether to seek out another matchmaker, one more polished than Pinye, he wondered if it could be—his protestations to the contrary, and although he honored his father and mother—that he did not, in essence, care for the matchmaking institution? This thought he quickly put out of mind yet found himself still upset. All day he ran around in the woods—missed an important appointment, forgot to give out his laundry, walked out of a Broadway cafeteria without paying and had to run back with the ticket in his hand; had even not recognized his landlady in the street when she passed with a friend and courteously called out, "A good evening to you, Doctor Finkle." By nightfall, however, he had regained sufficient calm to sink his nose into a book and there found peace from his thoughts.

Almost at once there came a knock on the door. Before Leo could say enter, Salzman, commercial cupid, was standing in the room. His face was gray and meager, his expression hungry, and he looked as if he would expire on his feet. Yet the marriage broker managed, by some trick of the muscles, to display a broad smile.

"So good evening. I am invited?"

Leo nodded, disturbed to see him again, yet unwilling to ask the man to leave.

Beaming still, Salzman laid his portfolio on the table. "Rabbi, I got for you tonight good news."

"I've asked you not to call me rabbi. I'm still a student."

"Your worries are finished. I have for you a first-class bride."

"Leave me in peace concerning this subject." Leo pretended lack of interest.

"The world will dance at your wedding."

"Please, Mr. Salzman, no more."

"But first must come back my strength," Salzman said weakly. He fumbled with the portfolio straps and took out of the leather case an oily paper bag, from which he extracted a hard, seeded roll and a small, smoked white fish. With a quick motion of his hand he stripped the fish out of its skin and began ravenously to chew. "All day in a rush," he muttered.

Leo watched him eat.

"A sliced tomato you have maybe?" Salzman hesitantly inquired.

"No."

The marriage broker shut his eyes and ate. When he had finished he carefully cleaned up the crumbs and rolled up the remains of the fish, in the paper bag. His spectacled eyes roamed the room until he discovered, amid some piles of books, a one-burner gas stove. Lifting his hat he humbly asked, "A glass tea you got, rabbi?"

Conscience-stricken, Leo rose and brewed the tea. He served it with a chunk of lemon and two cubes of lump sugar, delighting Salzman.

After he had drunk his tea, Salzman's strength and good spirits were restored.

"So tell me, rabbi," he said amiably, "you considered some more the three clients I mentioned yesterday?"

"There was no need to consider."

"Why not?"

"None of them suits me."

"What then suits you?"

Leo let it pass because he could give only a confused answer.

Without waiting for a reply, Salzman asked, "You remember this girl I talked to you—the high school teacher?"

"Age thirty-two?"

But, surprisingly, Salzman's face lit in a smile. "Age twenty-nine."

Leo shot him a look. "Reduced from thirty-two?"

"A mistake," Salzman avowed. "I talked today with the dentist. He took me to his safety deposit box and showed me the birth certificate. She was twenty-nine years last August. They made her a party in the mountains where she went for her vacation. When her father spoke to me the first time I forgot to write the age and I told you thirty-two, but now I remember this was a different client, a widow."

"The same one you told me about? I thought she was twenty-four?"

"A different. Am I responsible that the world is filled with widows?"

"No, but I'm not interested in them, nor for that matter, in school teachers."

Salzman pulled his clasped hands to his breast. Looking at the ceiling he devoutly exclaimed, "Yiddishe kinder,[1] what can I say to somebody that he is not interested in high school teachers? So what then you are interested?"

Leo flushed but controlled himself.

"In what else will you be interested," Salzman went on, "If you not interested in this fine girl that she speaks four languages and has personally in the bank ten thousand dollars? Also her father guarantees further twelve thousand. Also she has a new car, wonderful clothes, talks on all subjects, and she will give you a first-class home and children. How near do we come in our life to paradise?"

"*If she's so wonderful, why wasn't she married ten years ago?*"

"Why?" said Salzman with a heavy laugh. "—Why? Because she is *partikiler*. This is why. She wants the *best.*"

Leo was silent, amused at how he had entangled himself. But Salzman had aroused

[1] Yiddish children.

his interest in Lily H., and he began seriously to consider calling on her. When the marriage broker observed how intently Leo's mind was at work on the facts he had supplied, he felt certain they would soon come to an agreement.

Late Saturday afternoon, conscious of Salzman, Leo Finkle walked with Lily Hirschorn along Riverside Drive. He walked briskly and erectly, wearing with distinction the black fedora he had that morning taken with trepidation out of the dusty hat box on his closet shelf, and the heavy black Saturday coat he had thoroughly whisked clean. Leo also owned a walking stick, a present from a distant relative, but quickly put temptation aside and did not use it. Lily, petite and not unpretty, had on something signifying the approach of spring. She was au courant, animatedly, with all sorts of subjects, and he weighed her words and found her surprisingly sound— score another for Salzman, whom he uneasily sensed to be somewhere around, hiding perhaps high in a tree along the street, flashing the lady signals with a pocket mirror; or perhaps a cloven-hoofed Pan, piping nuptial ditties as he danced his invisible way before them, strewing wild buds on the walk and purple grapes in their path, symbolizing fruit of a union, though there was of course still none.

Lily startled Leo by remarking, "I was thinking of Mr. Salzman, a curious figure, wouldn't you say?"

Not certain what to answer, he nodded.

She bravely went on, blushing, "I for one am grateful for his introducing us. Aren't you?"

He courteously replied, "I am."

"I mean," she said with a little laugh—and it was all in good taste, or at least gave the effect of being not in bad—"do you mind that we came together so?"

He was not displeased with her honesty, recognizing that she meant to set the relationship aright, and understanding that it took a certain amount of experience in life, and courage, to want to do it quite that way. One had to have some sort of past to make that kind of beginning.

He said that he did not mind. Salzman's function was traditional and honorable —valuable for what it might achieve, which, he pointed out, was frequently nothing.

Lily agreed with a sigh. They walked on for a while and she said after a long silence, again with a nervous laugh, "Would you mind if I asked you something a little bit personal? Frankly, I find the subject fascinating." Although Leo shrugged, she went on half embarrassedly, "How was it that you came to your calling? I mean was it a sudden passionate inspiration?"

Leo, after a time, slowly replied, "I was always interested in the Law."

"You saw revealed in it the presence of the Highest?"

He nodded and changed the subject. "I understand that you spent a little time in Paris, Miss Hirschorn?"

"Oh, did Mr. Salzman tell you, Rabbi Finkle?" Leo winced but she went on, "It was ages ago and almost forgotten. I remember I had to return for my sister's wedding."

And Lily would not be put off. "When," she asked in a trembly voice, "did you become enamored of God?"

He stared at her. Then it came to him that she was talking not about Leo Finkle, but of a total stranger, some mystical figure, perhaps even passionate prophet that

Salzman had dreamed up for her—no relation to the living or dead. Leo trembled with rage and weakness. The trickster had obviously sold her a bill of goods, just as he had him, who'd expected to become acquainted with a young lady of twenty-nine, only to behold, the moment he laid eyes upon her strained and anxious face, a woman past thirty-five and aging rapidly. Only his self control had kept him this long in her presence.

"I am not," he said gravely, "a talented religious person," and in seeking words to go on, found himself possessed by shame and fear. "I think," he said in a strained manner, "that I came to God not because I loved Him, but because I did not."

This confession he spoke harshly because its unexpectedness shook him.

Lily wilted. Leo saw a profusion of loaves of bread go flying like ducks high over his head, not unlike the winged loaves by which he had counted himself to sleep last night. Mercifully, then, it snowed, which he would not put past Salzman's machinations.

He was infuriated with the marriage broker and swore he would throw him out of the room the minute he reappeared. But Salzman did not come that night, and when Leo's anger had subsided, an unaccountable despair grew in its place. At first he thought this was caused by his disappointment in Lily, but before long it became evident that he had involved himself with Salzman without a true knowledge of his own intent. He gradually realized—with an emptiness that seized him with six hands —that he had called in the broker to find him a bride because he was incapable of doing it himself. This terrifying insight he had derived as a result of his meeting and conversation with Lily Hirschorn. Her probing questions had somehow irritated him into revealing—to himself more than her—the true nature of his relationship to God, and from that it had come upon him, with shocking force, that apart from his parents, he had never loved anyone. Or perhaps it went the other way, that he did not love God so well as he might, because he had not loved man. It seemed to Leo that his whole life stood starkly revealed and he saw himself for the first time as he truly was —unloved and loveless. This bitter but somehow not fully unexpected revelation brought him to a point of panic, controlled only by extraordinary effort. He covered his face with his hands and cried.

The week that followed was the worst of his life. He did not eat and lost weight. His beard darkened and grew ragged. He stopped attending seminars and almost never opened a book. He seriously considered leaving the Yeshiva, although he was deeply troubled at the thought of the loss of all his years of study—saw them like pages torn from a book, strewn over the city—and at the devastating effect of this decision upon his parents. But he had lived without knowledge of himself and never in the Five Books[2] and all the Commentaries—mea culpa[3]—had the truth been revealed to him. He did not know where to turn, and in all this desolating loneliness there was no *to whom,* although he often thought of Lily but not once could bring himself to go downstairs and make the call. He became touchy and irritable, especially with his landlady, who asked him all manner of personal questions; on the other hand, sensing his own disagreeableness, he waylaid her on the stairs and apologized abjectly, until

---

[2] The first five books of the Old Testament, known collectively as the Pentateuch. [3] Latin: "my fault."

mortified, she ran from him. Out of this, however, he drew the consolation that he was a Jew and that a Jew suffered. But gradually, as the long and terrible week drew to a close, he regained his composure and some idea of purpose in life: to go on as planned. Although he was imperfect, the ideal was not. As for his quest of a bride, the thought of continuing afflicted him with anxiety and heartburn, yet perhaps with this new knowledge of himself he would be more successful than in the past. Perhaps love would now come to him and a bride to that love. And for this sanctified seeking who needed a Salzman?

The marriage broker, a skeleton with haunted eyes, returned that very night. He looked, withal, the picture of frustrated expectancy—as if he had steadfastly waited the week at Miss Lily Hirschorn's side for a telephone call that never came.

Casually coughing, Salzman came immediately to the point: "So how did you like her?"

Leo's anger rose and he could not refrain from chiding the matchmaker: "Why did you lie to me, Salzman?"

Salzman's pale face went dead white, the world had snowed on him.

"Did you not state that she was twenty-nine?" Leo insisted.

"I give you my word—"

"She was thirty-five, if a day. *At least* thirty-five."

"Of this don't be too sure. Her father told me—"

"Never mind. The worst of it was that you lied to her."

"How did I lie to her, tell me?"

"You told her things about me that weren't true. You made me out to be more, consequently less than I am. She had in mind a totally different person, a sort of semimystical Wonder Rabbi."

"All I said, you was a religious man."

"I can imagine."

Salzman sighed. "This is my weakness that I have," he confessed. "My wife says to me I shouldn't be a salesman, but when I have two fine people that they would be wonderful to be married, I am so happy that I talk too much." He smiled wanly. "This is why Salzman is a poor man."

Leo's anger left him. "Well, Salzman, I'm afraid that's all."

The marriage broker fastened hungry eyes on him.

"You don't want any more a bride?"

"I do," said Leo, "but I have decided to seek her in a different way. I am no longer interested in an arranged marriage. To be frank, I now admit the necessity of premarital love. That is, I want to be in love with the one I marry."

"Love?" said Salzman, astounded. After a moment he remarked, "For us, our love is our life, not for the ladies. In the ghetto they—"

"I know, I know," said Leo. "I've thought of it often. Love, I have said to myself, should be a by-product of living and worship rather than its own end. Yet for myself I find it necessary to establish the level of my need and fulfill it."

Salzman shrugged but answered, "Listen, rabbi, if you want love, this I can find for you also. I have such beautiful clients that you will love them the minute your eyes will see them."

Leo smiled unhappily. "I'm afraid you don't understand."

But Salzman hastily unstrapped his portfolio and withdrew a manila packet from it.

"Pictures," he said, quickly laying the envelope on the table.

Leo called after him to take the pictures away, but as if on the wings of the wind, Salzman had disappeared.

March came. Leo had returned to his regular routine. Although he felt not quite himself yet—lacked energy—he was making plans for a more active social life. Of course it would cost something, but he was an expert in cutting corners; and when there were no corners left he would make circles rounder. All the while Salzman's pictures had lain on the table, gathering dust. Occasionally as Leo sat studying, or enjoying a cup of tea, his eyes fell on the manila envelope, but he never opened it.

The days went by and no social life to speak of developed with a member of the opposite sex—it was difficult, given the circumstances of his situation. One morning Leo toiled up the stairs to his room and stared out the window at the city. Although the day was bright his view of it was dark. For some time he watched the people in the street below hurrying along and then turned with a heavy heart to his little room. On the table was the packet. With a sudden relentless gesture he tore it open. For a half-hour he stood by the table in a state of excitement, examining the photographs of the ladies Salzman had included. Finally, with a deep sigh he put them down. There were six, of varying degrees of attractiveness, but look at them long enough and they all became Lily Hirschorn: all past their prime, all starved behind bright smiles, not a true personality in the lot. Life, despite their frantic yoohooings, had passed them by; they were pictures in a briefcase that stank of fish. After a while, however, as Leo attempted to return the photographs into the envelope, he found in it another, a snapshot of the type taken by a machine for a quarter. He gazed at it a moment and let out a cry.

Her face deeply moved him. Why, he could at first not say. It gave him the impression of youth—spring flowers, yet age—a sense of having been used to the bone, wasted; this came from the eyes, which were hauntingly familiar, yet absolutely strange. He had a vivid impression that he had met her before, but try as he might he could not place her although he could almost recall her name, as if he had read it in her own handwriting. No, this couldn't be; he would have remembered her. It was not, he affirmed, that she had an extraordinary beauty—no, though her face was attractive enough; it was that *something* about her moved him. Feature for feature, even some of the ladies of the photographs could do better; but she leaped forth to his heart—had *lived,* or wanted to—more than just wanted, perhaps regretted how she had lived—had somehow deeply suffered: it could be seen in the depths of those reluctant eyes, and from the way the light enclosed and shone from her, and within her, opening realms of possibility: this was her own. Her he desired. His head ached and eyes narrowed with the intensity of his gazing, then as if an obscure fog had blown up in the mind, he experienced fear of her and was aware that he had received an impression, somehow, of evil. He shuddered, saying softly, it is thus with us all. Leo brewed some tea in a small pot and sat sipping it without sugar, to calm himself. But before he had finished drinking, again with excitement he examined the face and found it good: good for Leo Finkle. Only such a one could understand him and help him seek whatever he was seeking. She might, perhaps, love him. How she had happened to be among the discards in Salzman's barrel he could never guess, but he knew he must urgently go find her.

Leo rushed downstairs, grabbed up the Bronx telephone book, and searched for Salzman's home address. He was not listed, nor was his office. Neither was he in the Manhattan book. But Leo remembered having written down the address on a slip of paper after he had read Salzman's advertisement in the "personals" column of the *Forward*. He ran up to his room and tore through his papers, without luck. It was exasperating. Just when he needed the matchmaker he was nowhere to be found. Fortunately Leo remembered to look in his wallet. There on a card he found his name written and a Bronx address. No phone number was listed, the reason—Leo now recalled—he had originally communicated with Salzman by letter. He got on his coat, put a hat on over his skull cap and hurried to the subway station. All the way to the far end of the Bronx he sat on the edge of his seat. He was more than once tempted to take out the picture and see if the girl's face was as he remembered it, but he refrained, allowing the snapshot to remain in his inside coat pocket, content to have her so close. When the train pulled into the station he was waiting at the door and bolted out. He quickly located the street Salzman had advertised.

The building he sought was less than a block from the subway, but it was not an office building, nor even a loft, nor a store in which one could rent office space. It was a very old tenement house. Leo found Salzman's name in pencil on a soiled tag under the bell and climbed three dark flights to his apartment. When he knocked, the door was opened by a thin, asthmatic, gray-haired woman, in felt slippers.

"Yes?" she said, expecting nothing. She listened without listening. He could have sworn he had seen her, too, before but knew it was an illusion.

"Salzman—does he live here? Pinye Salzman," he said, "the matchmaker?"

She stared at him a long minute. "Of course."

He felt embarrassed. "Is he in?"

"No." Her mouth, though left open, offered nothing more.

"The matter is urgent. Can you tell me where his office is?"

"In the air." She pointed upward.

"You mean he has no office?" Leo asked.

"In his socks."

He peered into the apartment. It was sunless and dingy, one large room divided by a half-open curtain, beyond which he could see a sagging metal bed. The near side of a room was crowded with rickety chairs, old bureaus, a three-legged table, racks of cooking utensils, and all the apparatus of a kitchen. But there was no sign of Salzman or his magic barrel, probably also a figment of the imagination. An odor of frying fish made Leo weak to the knees.

"Where is he?" he insisted. "I've got to see your husband."

At length she answered, "So who knows where he is? Every time he thinks a new thought he runs to a different place. Go home, he will find you."

"Tell him Leo Finkle."

She gave no sign she had heard.

He walked downstairs, depressed.

But Salzman, breathless, stood waiting at his door.

Leo was astounded and overjoyed. "How did you get here before me?"

"I rushed."

"Come inside."

They entered. Leo fixed tea, and a sardine sandwich for Salzman. As they were drinking he reached behind him for the packet of pictures and handed them to the marriage broker.

Salzman put down his glass and said expectantly, "You found somebody you like?"

"Not among these."

The marriage broker turned away.

"Here is the one I want." Leo held forth the snapshot.

Salzman slipped on his glasses and took the picture into his trembling hand. He turned ghastly and let out a groan.

"What's the matter?" cried Leo.

"Excuse me. Was an accident this picture. She isn't for you."

Salzman frantically shoved the manila packet into his portfolio. He thrust the snapshot into his pocket and fled down the stairs.

Leo, after momentary paralysis, gave chase and cornered the marriage broker in the vestibule. The landlady made hysterical outcries but neither of them listened.

"Give me back the picture, Salzman."

"No." The pain in his eyes was terrible.

"Tell me who she is then."

"This I can't tell you. Excuse me."

He made to depart, but Leo, forgetting himself, seized the matchmaker by his tight coat and shook him frenziedly.

"Please," sighed Salzman. *"Please."*

Leo ashamedly let him go. "Tell me who she is," he begged. "It's very important for me to know."

"She is not for you. She is a wild one—wild, without shame. This is not a bride for a rabbi."

"What do you mean wild?"

"Like an animal. Like a dog. For her to be poor was a sin. This is why to me she is dead now."

"In God's name, what do you mean?"

"Her I can't introduce to you," Salzman cried.

"Why are you so excited?"

"Why, he asks," Salzman said, bursting into tears. "This is my baby, my Stella, she should burn in hell."

Leo hurried up to bed and hid under the covers. Under the covers he thought his life through. Although he soon fell asleep he could not sleep her out of his mind. He woke, beating his breast. Though he prayed to be rid of her, his prayers went unanswered. Through days of torment he endlessly struggled not to love her; fearing success, he escaped it. He then concluded to convert her to goodness, himself to God. The idea alternately nauseated and exalted him.

He perhaps did not know that he had come to a final decision until he encountered Salzman in a Broadway cafeteria. He was sitting alone at a rear table, sucking the bony remains of a fish. The marriage broker appeared haggard, and transparent to the point of vanishing.

Salzman looked up at first without recognizing him. Leo had grown a pointed beard and his eyes were weighted with wisdom.

"Salzman," he said, "love has at last come to my heart."

"Who can love from a picture?" mocked the marriage broker.

"It is not impossible."

"If you can love her, then you can love anybody. Let me show you some new clients that they just sent me their photographs. One is a little doll."

"Just her I want," Leo murmured.

"Don't be a fool, doctor. Don't bother with her."

"Put me in touch with her, Salzman," Leo said humbly. "Perhaps I can be of service."

Salzman had stopped eating and Leo understood with emotion that it was now arranged.

Leaving the cafeteria, he was, however, afflicted by a tormenting suspicion that Salzman had planned it all to happen this way.

Leo was informed by letter that she would meet him on a certain corner, and she was there one spring night, waiting under a street lamp. He appeared, carrying a small bouquet of violets and rosebuds. Stella stood by the lamp post, smoking. She wore white with red shoes, which fitted his expectations, although in a troubled moment he had imagined the dress red, and only the shoes white. She waited uneasily and shyly. From afar he saw that her eyes—clearly her father's—were filled with desperate innocence. He pictured, in her, his own redemption. Violins and lit candles revolved in the sky. Leo ran forward with flowers outthrust.

Around the corner, Salzman, leaning against a wall, chanted prayers for the dead.

1954

Saul Bellow
b. 1915

Saul Bellow was born on June 10, 1915, in the small town of Lachine in Quebec, Canada. Nine years later his family—deeply religious Jewish immigrants from St. Petersburg, Russia—moved to Chicago, where Bellow grew up in a multilingual neighborhood. He attended the University of Chicago and in 1935 transferred to Northwestern to study sociology and anthropology. After graduation in 1937, Bellow began working for an advanced degree in anthropology at the University of Wisconsin in Madison, but in 1938 he withdrew and returned to Chicago, hoping to write fiction. Over the next several years he taught school, served briefly in the merchant marine, and worked on the editorial staff of the *Encyclopaedia Britannica,* assembling the index to the Great Books series.

In 1941 Bellow's first story was published. Since that time he has devoted himself to writing, though he has also held a series of university appointments. Bellow taught at the University of Minnesota (1946–1948, 1957–1959); New York University (1950–1951); Princeton University (1952–1953), where he met the poet John Berryman; and Bard College (1953–1954). Between 1948 and 1950 Bellow lived in Paris and traveled in Europe, and afterward he spent over ten years in New York City and Dutchess County, New York. He returned to the University of Chicago in 1963 as a professor on the Committee on Social Thought. Bellow has had perhaps the most distinguished literary career of any contemporary novelist in the United States; his numerous honors and awards have included the National Book Award in 1954, 1965, and 1971. In 1976 he became the seventh American writer to win the Nobel Prize.

In the course of reaching a wider American audience than any other major writer of his time, Bellow has clearly marked several modern themes— particularly the theme of the displaced person—as his own. Bellow introduced this theme in his first novel, *Dangling Man* (1944), the story of a man waiting anxiously to be inducted into the army. In that book, narrated, like Sartre's *Nausea* (1938), in the form of a journal, the hero fears the presence of "the unhuman in the all too human city," a fear that is elaborated in Bellow's next two novels, *The Victim* (1947), a story about the personal conflicts between a Jew and a Gentile that tough-mindedly explores the meaning of "human," and *The Adventures of Augie March* (1953), in which Bellow's philosophic sense of what it means to be human is dramatized by the picaresque experiences of a persistently optimistic young Chicago man from an impoverished Jewish family who finds that "you do all you can to humanize and familiarize the world, and suddenly it becomes more strange than ever." At the core of Bellow's next book, *Seize the Day* (1956), a short novel many critics regard as a modern masterpiece, is the unrelievable need for human contact in a world where people feel so displaced that they find it almost impossible to communicate their need even for a simple glass of water. "Nobody truly occupies a station in life any more," we read in Bellow's fifth novel, *Henderson the Rain King* (1958), the story of a Connecticut millionaire who searches for self-understanding in the African jungles. "There are mostly people who feel that they occupy the place that belongs to another by rights. There are displaced persons everywhere."

Bellow's protagonists tend to be social creatures, and urban ones as well. To them, nature remains a largely alien world. Yet the cities where they live are likely to leave them feeling dulled, exhausted, and spent rather than sustained, nourished, or excited. They move amid incessant change, feeling themselves entangled by worlds to which they never quite belong. Like the protagonist of Bellow's next novel, *Herzog* (1964)—an intellectual who lives on the edge of suicide yet refuses to yield to despair—Bellow's main characters retain both a strong sense of family and a strong sense of religion without finding support or consolation in either. Their personalities are often dominated in part by feelings of shame or guilt that they carry as a burden, and in part by a longing for deliverance that they carry as an unfulfilled need. They are characteristically introspective people who, like the elderly hero of *Mr. Sammler's Planet* (1970), have come bitterly to hate modern ideals of self-fulfillment, and they often possess both a disordered sense of history and a fear of social disorder. Like their sense of family and their religious impulses, however, their talent for self-analysis and their sense of history are more often burdens to be borne than blessings to be cherished. "The spirit, the peculiar burden of his existence," we read of Tommy

Wilhelm in *Seize the Day*, "lay upon him like an accretion, a load, a hump . . . of nameless things which it was the business of his life to carry about. That must be what a man was for."

Bellow's tone is sometimes self-mocking and sometimes grandiose—as it can be in *Humboldt's Gift* (1975), the story of a man trying to balance a fast-paced, ambitious life with a "listening soul that can hear the essence of things and comes to understand the marvelous." In most of his fiction Bellow seems determined to discover moral, creative, even noble possibilities among the unpromising displacements that characterize the urban, secular world he so vividly depicts. In his latest novel, *The Dean's December* (1982), he examines the human dislocations of three worlds—the university, the urban streets, and a Communist regime. Bellow has long been fascinated with the ancient myth of the displaced wanderer. In his hands it becomes a story that is at once intensely Jewish, intensely American, and intensely modern.

Further Reading:
R. Dutton, *Saul Bellow*, 1961.
G. L. Harper, "Saul Bellow: An Interview,"
Paris Review, Winter 1965.
J. Clayton, *Saul Bellow, In Defense of Man*,
1967.
I. Malin, *Saul Bellow and the Critics*, 1967.

Text:
Mosby's Memoirs & Other Stories, 1968.

Looking for Mr. Green

Whatsoever thy hand findeth to do, do it with thy might. . . .[1]

Hard work? No, it wasn't really so hard. He wasn't used to walking and stair-climbing, but the physical difficulty of his new job was not what George Grebe felt most. He was delivering relief checks in the Negro district, and although he was a native Chicagoan this was not a part of the city he knew much about—it needed a depression to introduce him to it. No, it wasn't literally hard work, not as reckoned in foot-pounds, but yet he was beginning to feel the strain of it, to grow aware of its peculiar difficulty. He could find the streets and numbers, but the clients were not where they were supposed to be, and he felt like a hunter inexperienced in the camouflage of his game. It was an unfavorable day, too—fall, and cold, dark weather, windy. But, anyway, instead of shells in his deep trenchcoat pocket he had the cardboard of checks, punctured for the spindles of the file, the holes reminding him of the holes in player-piano paper. And he didn't look much like a hunter, either; his was a city figure entirely, belted up in this Irish conspirator's coat. He was slender without being tall, stiff in the back, his legs looking shabby in a pair of old tweed pants gone through and fringy at the cuffs. With this stiffness, he kept his head forward, so that his face was red from the sharpness of the weather; and it was an

[1] See Ecclesiastes 9:10.

indoors sort of face with gray eyes that persisted in some kind of thought and yet seemed to avoid definiteness of conclusion. He wore sideburns that surprised you somewhat by the tough curl of the blond hair and the effect of assertion in their length. He was not so mild as he looked, nor so youthful; and nevertheless there was no effort on his part to seem what he was not. He was an educated man; he was a bachelor; he was in some ways simple; without lushing, he liked a drink; his luck had not been good. Nothing was deliberately hidden.

He felt that his luck was better than usual today. When he had reported for work that morning he had expected to be shut up in the relief office at a clerk's job, for he had been hired downtown as a clerk, and he was glad to have, instead, the freedom of the streets and welcomed, at least at first, the vigor of the cold and even the blowing of the hard wind. But on the other hand he was not getting on with the distribution of the checks. It was true that it was a city job; nobody expected you to push too hard at a city job. His supervisor, that young Mr. Raynor, had practically told him that. Still, he wanted to do well at it. For one thing, when he knew how quickly he could deliver a batch of checks, he would know also how much time he could expect to clip for himself. And then, too, the clients would be waiting for their money. That was not the most important consideration, though it certainly mattered to him. No, but he wanted to do well, simply for doing-well's sake, to acquit himself decently of a job because he so rarely had a job to do that required just this sort of energy. Of this peculiar energy he now had a superabundance; once it had started to flow, it flowed all too heavily. And, for the time being anyway, he was balked. He could not find Mr. Green.

So he stood in his big-skirted trenchcoat with a large envelope in his hand and papers showing from his pocket, wondering why people should be so hard to locate who were too feeble or sick to come to the station to collect their own checks. But Raynor had told him that tracking them down was not easy at first and had offered him some advice on how to proceed. "If you can see the postman, he's your first man to ask, and your best bet. If you can't connect with him, try the stores and tradespeople around. Then the janitor and the neighbors. But you'll find the closer you come to your man the less people will tell you. They don't want to tell you anything."

"Because I'm a stranger."

"Because you're white. We ought to have a Negro doing this, but we don't at the moment, and of course you've got to eat, too, and this is public employment. Jobs have to be made. Oh, that holds for me too. Mind you, I'm not letting myself out. I've got three years of seniority on you, that's all. And a law degree. Otherwise, you might be back of the desk and I might be going out into the field this cold day. The same dough pays us both and for the same, exact, identical reason. What's my law degree got to do with it? But you have to pass out these checks, Mr. Grebe, and it'll help if you're stubborn, so I hope you are."

"Yes, I'm fairly stubborn."

Raynor sketched hard with an eraser in the old dirt of his desk, left-handed, and said, "Sure, what else can you answer to such a question. Anyhow, the trouble you're going to have is that they don't like to give information about anybody. They think you're a plain-clothes dick or an installment collector, or summons-server or something like that. Till you've been seen around the neighborhood for a few months and people know you're only from the relief."

It was dark, ground-freezing, pre-Thanksgiving weather; the wind played hob with the smoke, rushing it down, and Grebe missed his gloves, which he had left in Raynor's office. And no one would admit knowing Green. It was past three o'clock and the postman had made his last delivery. The nearest grocer, himself a Negro, had never heard the name Tulliver Green, or said he hadn't. Grebe was inclined to think that it was true, that he had in the end convinced the man that he wanted only to deliver a check. But he wasn't sure. He needed experience in interpreting looks and signs and, even more, the will not to be put off or denied and even the force to bully if need be. If the grocer did know, he had got rid of him easily. But since most of his trade was with reliefers, why should he prevent the delivery of a check? Maybe Green, or Mrs. Green, if there was a Mrs. Green, patronized another grocer. And was there a Mrs. Green? It was one of Grebe's great handicaps that he hadn't looked at any of the case records. Raynor should have let him read files for a few hours. But he apparently saw no need for that, probably considering the job unimportant. Why prepare systematically to deliver a few checks?

But now it was time to look for the janitor. Grebe took in the building in the wind and gloom of the late November day—trampled, frost-hardened lots on one side; on the other, an automobile junk yard and then the infinite work of Elevated frames, weak-looking, gaping with rubbish fires; two sets of leaning brick porches three stories high and a flight of cement stairs to the cellar. Descending, he entered the underground passage, where he tried the doors until one opened and he found himself in the furnace room. There someone rose toward him and approached, scraping on the coal grit and bending under the canvas-jacketed pipes.

"Are you the janitor?"

"What do you want?"

"I'm looking for a man who's supposed to be living here. Green."

"What Green?"

"Oh, you maybe have more than one Green?" said Grebe with new, pleasant hope. "This is Tulliver Green."

"I don't think I c'n help you, mister. I don't know any."

"A crippled man."

The janitor stood bent before him. Could it be that he was crippled? Oh, God! what if he was. Grebe's gray eyes sought with excited difficulty to see. But no, he was only very short and stooped. A head awakened from meditation, a strong-haired beard, low, wide shoulders. A staleness of sweat and coal rose from his black shirt and the burlap sack he wore as an apron.

"Crippled how?"

Grebe thought and then answered with the light voice of unmixed candor, "I don't know. I've never seen him." This was damaging, but his only other choice was to make a lying guess, and he was not up to it. "I'm delivering checks for the relief to shut-in cases. If he weren't crippled he'd come to collect himself. That's why I said crippled. Bedridden, chair-ridden—is there anybody like that?"

This sort of frankness was one of Grebe's oldest talents, going back to childhood. But it gained him nothing here.

"No suh. I've got four buildin's same as this that I take care of. I don't know all the tenants, leave alone the tenants' tenants. The rooms turn over so fast, people movin' in and out every day. I can't tell you."

The janitor opened his grimy lips but Grebe did not hear him in the piping of the valves and the consuming pull of air to flame in the body of the furnace. He knew, however, what he had said.

"Well, all the same, thanks. Sorry I bothered you. I'll prowl around upstairs again and see if I can turn up someone who knows him."

Once more in the cold air and early darkness he made the short circle from the cellarway to the entrance crowded between the brickwork pillars and began to climb to the third floor. Pieces of plaster ground under his feet; strips of brass tape from which the carpeting had been torn away marked old boundaries at the sides. In the passage, the cold reached him worse than in the street; it touched him to the bone. The hall toilets ran like springs. He thought grimly as he heard the wind burning around the building with a sound like that of the furnace, that this was a great piece of constructed shelter. Then he struck a match in the gloom and searched for names and numbers among the writings and scribbles on the walls. He saw WHOODY-DOODY GO TO JESUS, and zigzags, caricatures, sexual scrawls, and curses. So the sealed rooms of pyramids were also decorated, and the caves of human dawn.

The information on his card was, TULLIVER GREEN—APT 3D. There were no names, however, and no numbers. His shoulders drawn up, tears of cold in his eyes, breathing vapor, he went the length of the corridor and told himself that if he had been lucky enough to have the temperament for it he would bang on one of the doors and bawl out "Tulliver Green!" until he got results. But it wasn't in him to make an uproar and he continued to burn matches, passing the light over the walls. At the rear, in a corner off the hall, he discovered a door he had not seen before and he thought it best to investigate. It sounded empty when he knocked, but a young Negress answered, hardly more than a girl. She opened only a bit, to guard the warmth of the room.

"Yes suh?"

"I'm from the district relief station on Prairie Avenue. I'm looking for a man named Tulliver Green to give him his check. Do you know him?"

No, she didn't; but he thought she had not understood anything of what he had said. She had a dream-bound, dream-blind face, very soft and black, shut off. She wore a man's jacket and pulled the ends together at her throat. Her hair was parted in three directions, at the sides and transversely, standing up at the front in a dull puff.

"Is there somebody around here who might know?"

"I jus' taken this room las' week."

He observed that she shivered, but even her shiver was somnambulistic and there was no sharp consciousness of cold in the big smooth eyes of her handsome face.

"All right, miss, thank you. Thanks," he said, and went to try another place.

Here he was admitted. He was grateful, for the room was warm. It was full of people, and they were silent as he entered—ten people, or a dozen, perhaps more, sitting on benches like a parliament. There was no light, properly speaking, but a tempered darkness that the window gave, and everyone seemed to him enormous, the men padded out in heavy work clothes and winter coats, and the women huge, too, in their sweaters, hats, and old furs. And, besides, bed and bedding, a black cooking range, a piano piled towering to the ceiling with papers, a dining-room table of the old style of prosperous Chicago. Among these people Grebe, with his cold-heightened fresh color and his smaller stature, entered like a schoolboy. Even though he was met with smiles and good will, he knew, before a single word was spoken, that all the currents ran against him and that he would make no headway. Nevertheless he began. "Does anybody here know how I can deliver a check to Mr. Tulliver Green?"

"Green?" It was the man that had let him in who answered. He was in short sleeves, in a checkered shirt, and had a queer, high head, profusely overgrown and long as a shako;[2] the veins entered it strongly from his forehead. "I never heard mention of him. Is this where he live?"

"This is the address they gave me at the station. He's a sick man, and he'll need his check. Can't anybody tell me where to find him?"

He stood his ground and waited for a reply, his crimson wool scarf wound about his neck and drooping outside his trenchcoat, pockets weighted with the block of checks and official forms. They must have realized that he was not a college boy employed afternoons by a bill collector, trying foxily to pass for a relief clerk, recognized that he was an older man who knew himself what need was, who had had more than an average seasoning in hardship. It was evident enough if you looked at the marks under his eyes and at the sides of his mouth.

"Anybody know this sick man?"

"No suh." On all sides he saw heads shaken and smiles of denial. No one knew. And maybe it was true, he considered, standing silent in the earthen, musky human gloom of the place as the rumble continued. But he could never really be sure.

"What's the matter with this man?" said shako-head.

"I've never seen him. All I can tell you is that he can't come in person for his money. It's my first day in this district."

"Maybe they given you the wrong number?"

"I don't believe so. But where else can I ask about him?" He felt that this persistence amused them deeply, and in a way he shared their amusement that he should stand up so tenaciously to them. Though smaller, though slight, he was his own man, he retracted nothing about himself, and he looked back at them, gray-eyed, with amusement and also with a sort of courage. On the bench some man spoke in his throat, the words impossible to catch, and a woman answered with a wild, shrieking laugh, which was quickly cut off.

"Well, so nobody will tell me?"

"Ain't nobody who knows."

"At least, if he lives here, he pays rent to someone. Who manages the building?"

"Greatham Company. That's on Thirty-ninth Street."

Grebe wrote it in his pad. But, in the street again, a sheet of wind-driven paper clinging to his leg while he deliberated what direction to take next, it seemed a feeble lead to follow. Probably this Green didn't rent a flat, but a room. Sometimes there were as many as twenty people in an apartment; the real-estate agent would know only the lessee. And not even the agent could tell you who the renters were. In some places the beds were even used in shifts, watchmen or jitney drivers or short-order cooks in night joints turning out after a day's sleep and surrendering their beds to a sister, a nephew, or perhaps a stranger, just off the bus. There were large numbers of newcomers in this terrific, blight-bitten portion of the city between Cottage Grove and Ashland, wandering from house to house and room to room. When you saw them, how could you know them? They didn't carry bundles on their backs or look

---

[2] Tall, stiff military cap.

picturesque. You only saw a man, a Negro, walking in the street or riding in the car, like everyone else, with his thumb closed on a transfer. And therefore how were you supposed to tell? Grebe thought the Greatham agent would only laugh at his question.

But how much it would have simplified the job to be able to say that Green was old, or blind, or consumptive. An hour in the files, taking a few notes, and he needn't have been at such a disadvantage. When Raynor gave him the block of checks he asked, "How much should I know about these people?" Then Raynor had looked as though he were preparing to accuse him of trying to make the job more important than it was. He smiled, because by then they were on fine terms, but nevertheless he had been getting ready to say something like that when the confusion began in the station over Staika and her children.

Grebe had waited a long time for this job. It came to him through the pull of an old schoolmate in the Corporation Counsel's office, never a close friend, but suddenly sympathetic and interested—pleased to show, moreover, how well he had done, how strongly he was coming on even in these miserable times. Well, he was coming through strongly, along with the Democratic administration itself. Grebe had gone to see him in City Hall, and they had had a counter lunch or beers at least once a month for a year, and finally it had been possible to swing the job. He didn't mind being assigned the lowest clerical grade, nor even being a messenger, though Raynor thought he did.

This Raynor was an original sort of guy and Grebe had taken to him immediately. As was proper on the first day, Grebe had come early, but he waited long, for Raynor was late. At last he darted into his cubicle of an office as though he had just jumped from one of those hurtling huge red Indian Avenue cars. His thin, rough face was wind-stung and he was grinning and saying something breathlessly to himself. In his hat, a small fedora, and his coat, the velvet collar a neat fit about his neck, and his silk muffler that set off the nervous twist of his chin, he swayed and turned himself in his swivel chair, feet leaving the ground; so that he pranced a little as he sat. Meanwhile he took Grebe's measure out of his eyes, eyes of an unusual vertical length and slightly sardonic. So the two men sat for a while, saying nothing, while the supervisor raised his hat from his miscombed hair and put it in his lap. His cold-darkened hands were not clean. A steel beam passed through the little makeshift room, from which machine belts once had hung. The building was an old factory.

"I'm younger than you; I hope you won't find it hard taking orders from me," said Raynor. "But I don't make them up, either. You're how old, about?"

"Thirty-five."

"And you thought you'd be inside doing paper work. But it so happens I have to send you out."

"I don't mind."

"And it's mostly a Negro load we have in this district."

"So I thought it would be."

"Fine. You'll get along. *C'est un bon boulot.*[3] Do you know French?"

"Some."

"I thought you'd be a university man."

"Have you been in France?" said Grebe.

[3] French: "It's a good job."

"No, that's the French of the Berlitz School. I've been at it for more than a year, just as I'm sure people have been, all over the world, office boys in China and braves in Tanganyika. In fact, I damn well know it. Such is the attractive power of civilization. It's overrated, but what do you want? *Que voulez-vous?*[4] I get *Le Rire*[5] and all the spicy papers, just like in Tanganyika. It must be mystifying, out there. But my reason is that I'm aiming at the diplomatic service. I have a cousin who's a courier, and the way he describes it is awfully attractive. He rides in the *wagon-lits*[6] and reads books. While we— What did you do before?"

"I sold."

"Where?"

"Canned meat at Stop and Shop. In the basement."

"And before that?"

"Window shades, at Goldblatt's."

"Steady work?"

"No, Thursdays and Saturdays. I also sold shoes."

"You've been a shoe-dog too. Well. And prior to that? Here it is in your folder." He opened the record. "Saint Olaf's College, instructor in classical languages. Fellow, University of Chicago, 1926–27. I've had Latin, too. Let's trade quotations—'*Dum spiro spero.*'"

"'*Da dextram misero.*'"

"'*Alea jacta est.*'"

"'*Excelsior.*'"[7]

Raynor shouted with laughter, and other workers came to look at him over the partition. Grebe also laughed, feeling pleased and easy. The luxury of fun on a nervous morning.

When they were done and no one was watching or listening, Raynor said rather seriously, "What made you study Latin in the first place? Was it for the priesthood?"

"No."

"Just for the hell of it? For the culture? Oh, the things people think they can pull!" He made his cry hilarious and tragic. "I ran my pants off so I could study for the bar, and I've passed the bar, so I get twelve dollars a week more than you as a bonus for having seen life straight and whole.[8] I'll tell you, as a man of culture, that even though nothing looks to be real, and everything stands for something else, and that thing for another thing, and that thing for a still further one—there ain't any comparison between twenty-five and thirty-seven dollars a week, regardless of the last reality. Don't you think that was clear to your Greeks? They were a thoughtful people, but they didn't part with their slaves."

This was a great deal more than Grebe had looked for in his first interview with his supervisor. He was too shy to show all the astonishment he felt. He laughed a little, aroused, and brushed at the sunbeam that covered his head with its dust. "Do you think my mistake was so terrible?"

---

4. French: "What do you want?"
5. French periodical; its title means "laughter."
6. Railway sleeping cars.
7. Latin: "Where there's life, there's hope." "Give your right hand to the wretched." "The die is cast." "Ever upward."

8. An echo of "to see life steadily and see it whole," from the novel *Howard's End* by E. M. Forster (1879–1970).

"Damn right it was terrible, and you know it now that you've had the whip of hard times laid on your back. You should have been preparing yourself for trouble. Your people must have been well off to send you to the university. Stop me, if I'm stepping on your toes. Did your mother pamper you? Did your father give in to you? Were you brought up tenderly, with permission to go and find out what were the last things that everything else stands for while everybody else labored in the fallen world of appearances?"

"Well, no, it wasn't exactly like that." Grebe smiled. *The fallen world of appearances!* no less. But now it was his turn to deliver a surprise. "We weren't rich. My father was the last genuine English butler in Chicago—"

"Are you kidding?"

"Why should I be?"

"In a livery?"

"In livery. Up on the Gold Coast."[9]

"And he wanted you to be educated like a gentleman?"

"He did not. He sent me to the Armour Institute to study chemical engineering. But when he died I changed schools."

He stopped himself, and considered how quickly Raynor had reached him. In no time he had your valise on the table and all your stuff unpacked. And afterward, in the streets, he was still reviewing how far he might have gone, and how much he might have been led to tell if they had not been interrupted by Mrs. Staika's great noise.

But just then a young woman, one of Raynor's workers, ran into the cubicle exclaiming, "Haven't you heard all the fuss?"

"We haven't heard anything."

"It's Staika, giving out with all her might. The reporters are coming. She said she phoned the papers, and you know she did."

"But what is she up to?" said Raynor.

"She brought her wash and she's ironing it here, with our current, because the relief won't pay her electric bill. She has her ironing board set up by the admitting desk, and her kids are with her, all six. They never are in school more than once a week. She's always dragging them around with her because of her reputation."

"I don't want to miss any of this," said Raynor, jumping up. Grebe, as he followed with the secretary, said, "Who is this Staika?"

"They call her the 'Blood Mother of Federal Street.' She's a professional donor at the hospitals. I think they pay ten dollars a pint. Of course it's no joke, but she makes a very big thing out of it and she and the kids are in the papers all the time."

A small crowd, staff and clients divided by a plywood barrier, stood in the narrow space of the entrance, and Staika was shouting in a gruff, mannish voice, plunging the iron on the board and slamming it on the metal rest.

"My father and mother came in a steerage, and I was born in our house, Robey by Huron. I'm no dirty immigrant. I'm a U.S. citizen. My husband is a gassed veteran from France with lungs weaker'n paper, that hardly can he go to the toilet by himself. These six children of mine, I have to buy the shoes for their feet with my own blood. Even a lousy little white Communion necktie, that's a couple of drops of blood; a

---

[9] Fashionable neighborhood in northern Chicago.

little piece of mosquito veil for my Vadja so she won't be ashamed in church for the other girls, they take my blood for it by Goldblatt. That's how I keep goin'. A fine thing if I had to depend on the relief. And there's plenty of people on the rolls—fakes! There's nothin' *they* can't get, that can go and wrap bacon at Swift and Armour any time. They're lookin' for them by the Yards. They never have to be out of work. Only they rather lay in their lousy beds and eat the public's money." She was not afraid, in a predominantly Negro station, to shout this way about Negroes.

Grebe and Raynor worked themselves forward to get a closer view of the woman. She was flaming with anger and with pleasure at herself, broad and huge, a golden-headed woman who wore a cotton cap laced with pink ribbon. She was barelegged and had on black gym shoes, her Hoover apron[10] was open and her great breasts, not much restrained by a man's undershirt, hampered her arms as she worked at the kid's dress on the ironing board. And the children, silent and white, with a kind of locked obstinacy, in sheepskins and lumberjackets, stood behind her. She had captured the station, and the pleasure this gave her was enormous. Yet her grievances were true grievances. She was telling the truth. But she behaved like a liar. The look of her small eyes was hidden, and while she raged she also seemed to be spinning and planning.

"They send me out college case workers in silk pants to talk me out of what I got comin'. Are they better'n me? Who told them? Fire them. Let 'em go and get married, and then you won't have to cut electric from people's budget."

The chief supervisor, Mr. Ewing, couldn't silence her and he stood with folded arms at the head of his staff, bald, bald-headed, saying to his subordinates like the ex-school principal he was, "Pretty soon she'll be tired and go."

"No she won't," said Raynor to Grebe. "She'll get what she wants. She knows more about the relief even than Ewing. She's been on the rolls for years, and she always gets what she wants because she puts on a noisy show. Ewing knows it. He'll give in soon. He's only saving face. If he gets bad publicity, the Commissioner'll have him on the carpet, downtown. She's got him submerged; she'll submerge everybody in time, and that includes nations and governments."

Grebe replied with his characteristic smile, disagreeing completely. Who would take Staika's orders, and what changes could her yelling ever bring about?

No, what Grebe saw in her, the power that made people listen, was that her cry expressed the war of flesh and blood, perhaps turned a little crazy and certainly ugly, on this place and this condition. And at first, when he went out, the spirit of Staika somehow presided over the whole district for him, and it took color from her; he saw her color, in the spotty curb fires, and the fires under the El, the straight alley of flamy gloom. Later, too, when he went into a tavern for a shot of rye, the sweat of beer, association with West Side Polish streets, made him think of her again.

He wiped the corners of his mouth with his muffler, his handkerchief being inconvenient to reach for, and went out again to get on with the delivery of his checks. The air bit cold and hard and a few flakes of snow formed near him. A train struck by and left a quiver in the frames and a bristling icy hiss over the rails.

Crossing the street, he descended a flight of board steps into a basement grocery, setting off a little bell. It was a dark, long store and it caught you with its stinks of smoked meat, soap, dried peaches, and fish. There was a fire wrinkling and flapping

[10] Kind of woman's coverall.

in the little stove, and the proprietor was waiting, an Italian with a long, hollow face and stubborn bristles. He kept his hands warm under his apron.

No, he didn't know Green. You knew people but not names. The same man might not have the same name twice. The police didn't know, either, and mostly didn't care. When somebody was shot or knifed they took the body away and didn't look for the murderer. In the first place, nobody would tell them anything. So they made up a name for the coroner and called it quits. And in the second place, they didn't give a goddamn anyhow. But they couldn't get to the bottom of a thing even if they wanted to. Nobody would get to know even a tenth of what went on among these people. They stabbed and stole, they did every crime and abomination you ever heard of, men and men, women and women, parents and children, worse than the animals. They carried on their own way, and the horrors passed off like a smoke. There was never anything like it in the history of the whole world.

It was a long speech, deepening with every word in its fantasy and passion and becoming increasingly senseless and terrible: a swarm amassed by suggestion and invention, a huge, hugging, despairing knot, a human wheel of heads, legs, bellies, arms, rolling through his shop.

Grebe felt that he must interrupt him. He said sharply, "What are you talking about! All I asked was whether you knew this man."

"That isn't even the half of it. I been here six years. You probably don't want to believe this. But suppose it's true?"

"All the same," said Grebe, "there must be a way to find a person."

The Italian's close-spaced eyes had been queerly concentrated, as were his muscles, while he leaned across the counter trying to convince Grebe. Now he gave up the effort and sat down on his stool. "Oh—I suppose. Once in a while. But I been telling you, even the cops don't get anywhere."

"They're always after somebody. It's not the same thing."

"Well, keep trying if you want. I can't help you."

But he didn't keep trying. He had no more time to spend on Green. He slipped Green's check to the back of the block. The next name on the list was FIELD, WINSTON.

He found the back-yard bungalow without the least trouble; it shared a lot with another house, a few feet of yard between. Grebe knew these two-shack arrangements. They had been built in vast numbers in the days before the swamps were filled and the streets raised, and they were all the same—a boardwalk along the fence, well under street level, three or four ball-headed posts for clotheslines, greening wood, dead shingles, and a long, long flight of stairs to the rear door.

A twelve-year-old boy let him into the kitchen, and there the old man was, sitting by the table in a wheel chair.

"Oh, it's d' Government man," he said to the boy when Grebe drew out his checks. "Go bring me my box of papers." He cleared a space on the table.

"Oh, you don't have to go to all that trouble," said Grebe. But Field laid out his papers: Social Security card, relief certification, letters from the state hospital in Manteno, and a naval discharge dated San Diego, 1920.

"That's plenty," Grebe said. "Just sign."

"You got to know who I am," the old man said. "You're from the Government. It's not your check, it's a Government check and you got no business to hand it over till everything is proved."

He loved the ceremony of it, and Grebe made no more objections. Field emptied his box and finished out the circle of cards and letters.

"There's everything I done and been. Just the death certificate and they can close book on me." He said this with a certain happy pride and magnificence. Still he did not sign; he merely held the little pen upright on the golden-green corduroy of his thigh. Grebe did not hurry him. He felt the old man's hunger for conversation.

"I got to get better coal," he said. "I send my little gran'son to the yard with my order and they fill his wagon with screening. The stove ain't made for it. It fall through the grate. The order says Franklin County egg-size coal."

"I'll report it and see what can be done."

"Nothing can be done, I expect. You know and I know. There ain't no little ways to make things better, and the only big thing is money. That's the only sunbeams, money. Nothing is black where it shines, and the only place you see black is where it ain't shining. What we colored have to have is our own rich. There ain't no other way."

Grebe sat, his reddened forehead bridged levelly by his close-cut hair and his cheeks lowered in the wings of his collar—the caked fire shone hard within the isinglass-and-iron frames but the room was not comfortable—sat and listened while the old man unfolded his scheme. This was to create one Negro millionaire a month by subscription. One clever, good-hearted young fellow elected every month would sign a contract to use the money to start a business employing Negroes. This would be advertised by chain letters and word of mouth, and every Negro wage earner would contribute a dollar a month. Within five years there would be sixty millionaires.

"That'll fetch respect," he said with a throat-stopped sound that came out like a foreign syllable. "You got to take and organize all the money that gets thrown away on the policy wheel and horse race. As long as they can take it away from you, they got no respect for you. Money, that's d' sun of human kind!" Field was a Negro of mixed blood, perhaps Cherokee, or Natchez; his skin was reddish. And he sounded, speaking about a golden sun in this dark room, and looked, shaggy and slab-headed, with the mingled blood of his face and broad lips, the little pen still upright in his hand, like one of the underground kings of mythology, old judge Minos himself.

And now he accepted the check and signed. Not to soil the slip, he held it down with his knuckles. The table budged and creaked, the center of the gloomy, heathen midden of the kitchen covered with bread, meat, and cans, and the scramble of papers.

"Don't you think my scheme'd work?"

"It's worth thinking about. Something ought to be done, I agree."

"It'll work if people will do it. That's all. That's the only thing, any time. When they understand it in the same way, all of them."

"That's true," said Grebe, rising. His glance met the old man's.

"I know you got to go," he said. "Well, God bless you, boy, you ain't been sly with me. I can tell it in a minute."

He went back through the buried yard. Someone nursed a candle in a shed, where a man unloaded kindling wood from a sprawl-wheeled baby buggy and two voices carried on a high conversation. As he came up the sheltered passage he heard the hard boost of the wind in the branches and against the house fronts, and then, reaching the sidewalk, he saw the needle-eye red of cable towers in the open icy height hundreds of feet above the river and the factories—those keen points. From here, his view was obstructed all the way to the South Branch and its timber banks, and the cranes beside the water. Rebuilt after the Great Fire, this part of the city was, not fifty years later, in ruins again, factories boarded up, buildings deserted or fallen, gaps of prairie between. But it wasn't desolation that this made you feel, but rather a faltering of organization that set free a huge energy, an escaped, unattached, un-regulated power from the giant raw place. Not only must people feel it but, it seemed to Grebe, they were compelled to match it. In their very bodies. He no less than others, he realized. Say that his parents had been servants in their time, whereas he was not supposed to be one. He thought that they had never done any service like this, which no one visible asked for, and probably flesh and blood could not even perform. Nor could anyone show why it should be performed; or see where the performance would lead. That did not mean that he wanted to be released from it, he realized with a grimly pensive face. On the contrary. He had something to do. To be compelled to feel this energy and yet have no task to do—that was horrible; that was suffering; he knew what that was. It was now quitting time. Six o'clock. He could go home if he liked, to his room, that is, to wash in hot water, to pour a drink, lie down on his quilt, read the paper, eat some liver paste on crackers before going out to dinner. But to think of this actually made him feel a little sick, as though he had swallowed hard air. He had six checks left, and he was determined to deliver at least one of these: Mr. Green's check.

So he started again. He had four or five dark blocks to go, past open lots, condemned houses, old foundations, closed schools, black churches, mounds, and he reflected that there must be many people alive who had once seen the neighborhood rebuilt and new. Now there was a second layer of ruins; centuries of history accom-plished through human massing. Numbers had given the place forced growth; enor-mous numbers had also broken it down. Objects once so new, so concrete that it could never have occurred to anyone they stood for other things, had crumbled. Therefore, reflected Grebe, the secret of them was out. It was that they stood for themselves by agreement, and were natural and not unnatural by agreement, and when the things themselves collapsed the agreement became visible. What was it, otherwise, that kept cities from looking peculiar? Rome, that was almost permanent, did not give rise to thoughts like these. And was it abidingly real? But in Chicago, where the cycles were so fast and the familiar died out, and again rose changed, and died again in thirty years, you saw the common agreement or covenant, and you were forced to think about appearances and realities. (He remembered Raynor and he smiled. Raynor was a clever boy.) Once you had grasped this, a great many things became intelligible. For instance, why Mr. Field should conceive such a scheme. Of course, if people were to agree to create a millionaire, a real millionaire would come into existence. And if you wanted to know how Mr. Field was inspired to think of this, why, he had within sight of his kitchen window the chart, the very bones of a successful scheme—the El with its blue and green confetti of signals. People consented to pay dimes and ride the crash-box cars, and so it was a success. Yet how absurd it looked; how little reality there was to start with. And yet Yerkes,[11] the great financier who built it, had known

---

[11] Charles Tyson Yerkes (1837–1905), who gained
control of and developed the Chicago elevated
rails.

that he could get people to agree to do it. Viewed as itself, what a scheme of a scheme it seemed, how close to an appearance. Then why wonder at Mr. Field's idea? He had grasped a principle. And then Grebe remembered, too, that Mr. Yerkes had established the Yerkes Observatory and endowed it with millions. Now how did the notion come to him in his New York museum of a palace or his Aegean-bound yacht to give money to astronomers? Was he awed by the success of his bizarre enterprise and therefore ready to spend money to find out where in the universe being and seeming were identical? Yes, he wanted to know what abides; and whether flesh is Bible grass; and he offered money to be burned in the fire of suns.[12] Okay, then, Grebe thought further, these things exist because people consent to exist with them—we have got so far— and also there is a reality which doesn't depend on consent but within which consent is a game. But what about need, the need that keeps so many vast thousands in position? You tell me that, you *private* little gentleman and *decent* soul—he used these words against himself scornfully. Why is the consent given to misery? And why so painfully ugly? Because there is *something* that is dismal and permanently ugly? Here he sighed and gave it up, and thought it was enough for the present moment that he had a real check in his pocket for a Mr. Green who must be real beyond question. If only his neighbors didn't think they had to conceal him.

This time he stopped at the second floor. He struck a match and found a door. Presently a man answered his knock and Grebe had the check ready and showed it even before he began. "Does Tulliver Green live here? I'm from the relief."

The man narrowed the opening and spoke to someone at his back.

"Does he live here?"

"Uh-uh. No."

"Or anywhere in this building? He's a sick man and he can't come for his dough." He exhibited the check in the light, which was smoky—the air smelled of charred lard—and the man held off the brim of his cap to study it.

"Uh-uh. Never seen the name."

"There's nobody around here that uses crutches?"

He seemed to think, but it was Grebe's impression that he was simply waiting for a decent interval to pass.

"No, suh. Nobody I ever see."

"I've been looking for this man all afternoon"—Grebe spoke out with sudden force —"and I'm going to have to carry this check back to the station. It seems strange not to be able to find a person to *give* him something when you're looking for him for a good reason. I suppose if I had bad news for him I'd find him quick enough."

There was a responsive motion in the other man's face. "That's right, I reckon."

"It almost doesn't do any good to have a name if you can't be found by it. It doesn't stand for anything. He might as well not have any," he went on, smiling. It was as much of a concession as he could make to his desire to laugh.

"Well, now, there's a little old knot-back man I see once in a while. He might be the one you lookin' for. Downstairs."

"Where? Right side or left? Which door?"

"I don't know which. Thin-face little knot-back with a stick."

But no one answered at any of the doors on the first floor. He went to the end

---

[12] Echoes of biblical prophets (see, e.g., Isaiah 40:6).

of the corridor, searching by matchlight, and found only a stairless exit to the yard, a drop of about six feet. But there was a bungalow near the alley, an old house like Mr. Field's. To jump was unsafe. He ran from the front door, through the underground passage and into the yard. The place was occupied. There was a light through the curtains, upstairs. The name on the ticket under the broken, scoop-shaped mailbox was Green! He exultantly rang the bell and pressed against the locked door. Then the lock clicked faintly and a long staircase opened before him. Someone was slowly coming down—a woman. He had the impression in the weak light that she was shaping her hair as she came, making herself presentable, for he saw her arms raised. But it was for support that they were raised; she was feeling her way downward, down the wall, stumbling. Next he wondered about the pressure of her feet on the treads; she did not seem to be wearing shoes. And it was a freezing stairway. His ring had got her out of bed, perhaps, and she had forgotten to put them on. And then he saw that she was not only shoeless but naked; she was entirely naked, climbing down while she talked to herself, a heavy woman, naked and drunk. She blundered into him. The contact of her breasts, though they touched only his coat, made him go back against the door with a blind shock. See what he had tracked down, in his hunting game!

The woman was saying to herself, furious with insult, "So I cain't fuck, huh? I'll show that son of a bitch kin I, cain't I."

What should he do now? Grebe asked himself. Why, he should go. He should turn away and go. He couldn't talk to this woman. He couldn't keep her standing naked in the cold. But when he tried he found himself unable to turn away.

He said, "Is this where Mr. Green lives?"

But she was still talking to herself and did not hear him.

"Is this Mr. Green's house?"

At last she turned her furious drunken glance on him. "What do you want?"

Again her eyes wandered from him; there was a dot of blood in their enraged brilliance. He wondered why she didn't feel the cold.

"I'm from the relief."

"Awright, what?"

"I've got a check for Tulliver Green."

This time she heard him and put out her hand.

"No, no, for *Mr.* Green. He's got to sign," he said. How was he going to get Green's signature tonight!

"I'll take it. He cain't."

He desperately shook his head, thinking of Mr. Field's precautions about identification. "I can't let you have it. It's for him. Are you Mrs. Green?"

"Maybe I is, and maybe I ain't. Who want to know?"

"Is he upstairs?"

"Awright. Take it up yourself, you goddamn fool."

Sure, he was a goddamn fool. Of course he could not go up because Green would probably be drunk and naked, too. And perhaps he would appear on the landing soon. He looked eagerly upward. Under the light was a high narrow brown wall. Empty! It remained empty!

"Hell with you, then!" he heard her cry. To deliver a check for coal and clothes, he was keeping her in the cold. She did not feel it, but his face was burning with frost and self-ridicule. He backed away from her.

"I'll come tomorrow, tell him."

"Ah, hell with you. Don' never come. What you doin' here in the nighttime? Don' come back." She yelled so that he saw the breadth of her tongue. She stood astride in the long cold box of the hall and held on to the banister and the wall. The bungalow itself was shaped something like a box, a clumsy, high box pointing into the freezing air with its sharp, wintry lights.

"If you are Mrs. Green, I'll give you the check," he said, changing his mind.

"Give here, then." She took it, took the pen offered with it in her left hand, and tried to sign the receipt on the wall. He looked around, almost as though to see whether his madness was being observed, and came near believing that someone was standing on a mountain of used tires in the auto–junking shop next door.

"But are you Mrs. Green?" he now thought to ask. But she was already climbing the stairs with the check, and it was too late, if he had made an error, if he was now in trouble, to undo the thing. But he wasn't going to worry about it. Though she might not be Mrs. Green, he was convinced that Mr. Green was upstairs. Whoever she was, the woman stood for Green, whom he was not to see this time. Well, you silly bastard, he said to himself, so you think you found him. So what? Maybe you really did find him—what of it? But it was important that there was a real Mr. Green whom they could not keep him from reaching because he seemed to come as an emissary from hostile appearances. And though the self-ridicule was slow to diminish, and his face still blazed with it, he had, nevertheless, a feeling of elation, too. "For after all," he said, "he *could* be found!"

1951

Arthur Miller
b. 1915

Arthur Miller was born in Brooklyn, New York, on October 17, 1915. Thwarted in his desire to attend college because "nobody in the house was in possession of the fare," he worked for two and a half years in an automobile-parts warehouse before saving enough money to attend the University of Michigan. His first plays, written in his sophomore and junior years and produced at the university theater in Ann Arbor, won the Hopwood Award for both 1936 and 1937. After graduation in 1938 (in that year he also won the Theater Guild National Award), Miller returned to New York, where he wrote numerous scripts for network radio and also worked as a laborer in the Brooklyn Navy Yard and in a cardboard factory. In 1944 he published *Situation Normal,* a report on military life at army bases, and wrote his first Broadway play, *The Man Who Had All the Luck.* Although it represented Miller's first engagement with America's myth of success, which he would later explore in his most famous work, *The Man Who Had All the Luck* was not itself a success. The following year Miller published *Focus,* an ironic novel dealing with anti–Semitism.

"Drama," Miller asserts, "is one of the things that makes possible a solution to the problem of socializing people." For Miller, significant dramatic conflict must deal with the way people live together. The meaning of a life cannot be evaluated in a vacuum; it depends on its relationship to others and to social decisions. So important is our social existence to Miller that in his plays the interrelations of family and society become almost as tangible as the characters themselves. Miller reinforces this sense of interrelatedness by creating dialogue in which characters habitually and emphatically punctuate their conversation with each other's names, as though they needed continually to reaffirm each other's presence. (*Death of a Salesman,* for example, opens with the calling out of the protagonist's name.) In Miller, too, as in few other prominent American writers, jobs play a central role in the dramatic conflict. Miller remains keenly aware that one of the primary features of modern society is the often painfully close connection between an individual's work and that person's sense of worth, between occupation and self-identity. His awareness of the real social pressures faced by real people ("A play," he said, "ought to make sense to common-sense people") has perhaps more than any other aspect of his work made him one of the most successful playwrights in the history of American theater.

Miller's first Broadway success was *All My Sons* (1947), a three-act play about a wealthy manufacturer who is accused of murder by one of his sons because he sold defective aircraft parts during wartime. Miller followed *All My Sons* with another drama of a man's difficult and guilt-ridden relation to his family and society, *Death of a Salesman,* which in 1949 began one of the longest runs for serious drama in Broadway history. The play not only won the Drama Critics' Circle Award and the Pulitzer Prize but has also sold well over three million copies in book form, making it possibly America's best-known play. In 1951 Miller adapted for the stage one of the world's masterpieces of social drama, Ibsen's *An Enemy of the People,* and in 1953 he wrote *The Crucible,* a four-act drama about the Salem witchcraft trials that is also an attack on Senator McCarthy's anti-Communist "witch hunts" of the 1950s. The film version of *The Crucible* was eventually made in France because Miller, as a result of the play and his refusal to name names during his appearance before the House Un-American Activities Committee in 1956, had been blacklisted by Hollywood. In 1955 Miller won the Pulitzer Prize for *A View from the Bridge,* a play about the charged family relations of an Italian longshoreman. A year later he married the movie star Marilyn Monroe—an event that was especially dramatic because of his having been blacklisted by Hollywood. In 1961, the year in which Miller and Monroe were divorced, Hollywood released a movie, *The Misfits,* based on a screenplay written by Miller for Monroe that also starred Clark Gable and Montgomery Clift.

In his next play, *After the Fall* (1964), Miller created a semiautobiographical drama about a man trying to make sense of his past. It was soon followed by *Incident at Vichy* (1965), a play set during the Nazi occupation of France. Miller's most recent plays are *The Price* (1968), *The Creation of the World and Other Business* (1972), and *The Archbishop's Ceiling* (1976). He has also published a volume of short stories, *I Don't Need You Anymore* (1967), and several travel books with photographs taken by his wife. *The Theatre Essays of Arthur Miller* appeared in 1978.

Throughout his career, but particularly in *Death of a Salesman,* Miller has sought to blend the larger force of tragic drama with the immediate pertinence of social drama. As social drama, *Death of a Salesman* focuses on Willy Loman as a victim of society, and particularly as a victim of a harsh economic system that first uses and then discards him. As a moden tragedy, on the other hand, *Death of a Salesman* focuses on Willy Loman as a victim of his own inadequate values and ideals. There is, as a result, terror as well as pity in Loman's story, as he struggles and fails to find values that can give his life purpose and dignity and so deliver him from the sense of hollowness that runs even deeper than the sense of betrayal and failure that haunts him.

Further Reading:
D. Welland, *Arthur Miller*, 1961.
S. Huftel, *Arthur Miller: The Burning Glass*, 1965.
Arthur Miller: A Collection of Critical Essays, ed. R. W. Corrigan, 1969.

Text:
Death of a Salesman, 1976.

Death of a Salesman

ACT ONE

A melody is heard, played upon a flute. It is small and fine, telling of grass and trees and the horizon. The curtain rises.

Before us is the Salesman's house. We are aware of towering, angular shapes behind it, surrounding it on all sides. Only the blue light of the sky falls upon the house and forestage; the surrounding area shows an angry glow of orange. As more light appears, we see a solid vault of apartment houses around the small, fragile-seeming home. An air of the dream clings to the place, a dream rising out of reality. The kitchen at center seems actual enough, for there is a kitchen table with three chairs, and a refrigerator. But no other fixtures are seen. At the back of the kitchen there is a draped entrance, which leads to the living-room. To the right of the kitchen, on a level raised two feet, is a bedroom furnished only with a brass bedstead and a straight chair. On a shelf over the bed a silver athletic trophy stands. A window opens onto the apartment house at the side.

Behind the kitchen, on a level raised six and a half feet, is the boys' bedroom, at present barely visible. Two beds are dimly seen, and at the back of the room a dormer window. (This bedroom is above the unseen living-room.) At the left a stairway curves up to it from the kitchen.

The entire setting is wholly, or, in some places, partially transparent. The roof-line of the house is one-dimensional; under and over it we see the apartment buildings. Before the house lies an apron, curving beyond the forestage into the orchestra. This forward area serves as the back yard as well as the locale of all Willy's imaginings and of his city scenes. Whenever the action is in the present the actors observe the imaginary wall-lines, entering the house only through its door at the left. But in the scenes of the past these boundaries are broken, and characters enter or leave a room by stepping "through" a wall onto the forestage.

From the right, Willy Loman, the Salesman, enters, carrying two large sample cases. The flute plays on. He hears but is not aware of it. He is past sixty years of age, dressed quietly. Even as he crosses the stage to the doorway of the house, his exhaustion is apparent. He unlocks the door, comes into the kitchen, and thankfully lets his burden down, feeling the soreness of his palms. A word-sigh escapes his lips—it might be "Oh, boy, oh, boy." He closes the door, then carries his cases out into the living-room, through the draped kitchen doorway.

Linda, his wife, has stirred in her bed at the right. She gets out and puts on a robe, listening. Most often jovial, she has developed an iron repression of her exceptions to Willy's behavior —she more than loves him, she admires him, as though his mercurial nature, his temper, his massive dreams and little cruelties, served her only as sharp reminders of the turbulent longings within him, longings which she shares but lacks the temperament to utter and follow to their end.

Linda: hearing Willy outside the bedroom, calls with some trepidation: Willy!

Willy: It's all right. I came back.

Linda: Why? What happened? *Slight pause.* Did something happen, Willy?

Willy: No, nothing happened.

Linda: You didn't smash the car, did you?

Willy: with casual irritation: I said nothing happened. Didn't you hear me?

Linda: Don't you feel well?

Willy: I'm tired to the death. *The flute has faded away. He sits on the bed beside her, a little numb.* I couldn't make it. I just couldn't make it, Linda.

Linda: very carefully, delicately: Where were you all day? You look terrible.

Willy: I got as far as a little above Yonkers. I stopped for a cup of coffee. Maybe it was the coffee.

Linda: What?

Willy: after a pause: I suddenly couldn't drive any more. The car kept going off onto the shoulder, y'know?

Linda: helpfully: Oh. Maybe it was the steering again. I don't think Angelo knows the Studebaker.

Willy: No, it's me, it's me. Suddenly I realize I'm goin' sixty miles an hour and I don't remember the last five minutes. I'm—I can't seem to—keep my mind to it.

Linda: Maybe it's your glasses. You never went for your new glasses.

Willy: No, I see everything. I came back ten miles an hour. It took me nearly four hours from Yonkers.

Linda: resigned: Well, you'll just have to take a rest, Willy, you can't continue this way.

Willy: I just got back from Florida.

Linda: But you didn't rest your mind. Your mind is overactive, and the mind is what counts, dear.

Willy: I'll start out in the morning. Maybe I'll feel better in the morning. *She is taking off his shoes.* These goddam arch supports are killing me.

Linda: Take an aspirin. Should I get you an aspirin? It'll soothe you.

Willy: with wonder: I was driving along, you understand? And I was fine. I was even observing the scenery. You can imagine, me looking at scenery, on the road every week of my life. But it's so beautiful up there, Linda, the trees are so thick, and the sun is warm. I opened the windshield and just let the warm air bathe over me. And then all of a sudden I'm goin' off the road! I'm tellin' ya, I absolutely forgot I was driving. If I'd've gone the other way over the white line I might've killed somebody. So I went on again—and five minutes later I'm dreamin' again, and I nearly—*He presses two fingers against his eyes.* I have such thoughts, I have such strange thoughts.

Linda: Willy, dear. Talk to them again. There's no reason why you can't work in New York.

Willy: They don't need me in New York. I'm the New England man. I'm vital in New England.

Linda: But you're sixty years old. They can't expect you to keep traveling every week.

Willy: I'll have to send a wire to Portland. I'm supposed to see Brown and Morrison tomorrow morning at ten o'clock to show the line. Goddammit, I could sell them! *He starts putting on his jacket.*

Linda: taking the jacket from him: Why don't you go down to the place tomorrow and tell Howard you've simply got to work in New York? You're too accommodating, dear.

Willy: If old man Wagner was alive I'd a been in charge of New York now! That man was a prince, he was a masterful man. But that boy of his, that Howard, he don't appreciate. When I went north the first time, the Wagner Company didn't know where New England was!

Linda: Why don't you tell those things to Howard, dear?

Willy: encouraged: I will, I definitely will. Is there any cheese?

Linda: I'll make you a sandwich.

Willy: No, go to sleep. I'll take some milk. I'll be up right away. The boys in?

Linda: They're sleeping. Happy took Biff on a date tonight.

Willy: interested: That so?

Linda: It was so nice to see them shaving together, one behind the other, in the bathroom. And going out together. You notice? The whole house smells of shaving lotion.

Willy: Figure it out. Work a lifetime to pay off a house. You finally own it, and there's nobody to live in it.

Linda: Well, dear, life is a casting off. It's always that way.

Willy: No, no, some people—some people accomplish something. Did Biff say anything after I went this morning?

Linda: You shouldn't have criticized him, Willy, especially after he just got off the train. You mustn't lose your temper with him.

Willy: When the hell did I lose my temper? I simply asked him if he was making any money. Is that a criticism?

Linda: But, dear, how could he make any money?

Willy: worried and angered: There's such an undercurrent in him. He became a moody man. Did he apologize when I left this morning?

Linda: He was crestfallen. Willy. You know how he admires you. I think if he finds himself, then you'll both be happier and not fight any more.

Willy: How can he find himself on a farm? Is that a life? A farmhand? In the beginning, when he was young. I thought, well, a young man, it's good for him to tramp around, take a lot of different jobs. But it's more than ten years now and he has yet to make thirty-five dollars a week!

Linda: He's finding himself, Willy.

2063 Miller · Death of a Salesman

Willy: Not finding yourself at the age of thirty-four is a disgrace!

Linda: Shh!

Willy: The trouble is he's lazy, goddammit!

Linda: Willy, please!

Willy: Biff is a lazy bum!

Linda: They're sleeping. Get something to eat. Go on down.

Willy: Why did he come home? I would like to know what brought him home.

Linda: I don't know. I think he's still lost, Willy. I think he's very lost.

Willy: Biff Loman is lost. In the greatest country in the world a young man with such—personal attractiveness, gets lost. And such a hard worker. There's one thing about Biff—he's not lazy.

Linda: Never.

Willy: with pity and resolve: I'll see him in the morning; I'll have a nice talk with him. I'll get him a job selling. He could be big in no time. My God! Remember how they used to follow him around in high school? When he smiled at one of them their faces lit up. When he walked down the street . . . *He loses himself in reminiscences.*

Linda: trying to bring him out of it: Willy, dear, I got a new kind of American-type cheese today. It's whipped.

Willy: Why do you get American when I like Swiss?

Linda: I just thought you'd like a change—

Willy: I don't want a change! I want Swiss cheese. Why am I always being contradicted?

Linda: with a covering laugh: I thought it would be a surprise.

Willy: Why don't you open a window in here, for God's sake?

Linda: with infinite patience: They're all open, dear.

Willy: The way they boxed us in here. Bricks and windows, windows and bricks.

Linda: We should've bought the land next door.

Willy: The street is lined with cars. There's not a breath of fresh air in the neighborhood. The grass don't grow any more, you can't raise a carrot in the back yard. They should've had a law against apartment houses. Remember those two beautiful elm trees out there? When I and Biff hung the swing between them?

Linda: Yeah, like being a million miles from the city.

Willy: They should've arrested the builder for cutting those down. They massacred the neighborhood. *Lost:* More and more I think of those days, Linda. This time of year it was lilac and wisteria. And then the peonies would come out, and the daffodils. What fragrance in this room!

Linda: Well, after all, people had to move somewhere.

Willy: No, there's more people now.

Linda: I don't think there's more people. I think—

Willy: There's more people! That's what's ruining this country! Population is getting out of control. The competition is maddening! Smell the stink from that apartment house! And another one on the other side . . . How can they whip cheese?

On Willy's last line, Biff and Happy raise themselves up in their beds, listening.

Linda: Go down, try it. And be quiet.

Willy: turning to Linda, guiltily: You're not worried about me, are you, sweetheart?

Biff: What's the matter?

Happy: Listen!

Linda: You've got too much on the ball to worry about.

Willy: You're my foundation and my support, Linda.

Linda: Just try to relax, dear. You make mountains out of molehills.

Willy: I won't fight with him any more. If he wants to go back to Texas, let him go.

Linda: He'll find his way.

Willy: Sure. Certain men just don't get started till later in life. Like Thomas Edison, I think. Or B. F. Goodrich. One of them was deaf. *He starts for the bedroom doorway.* I'll put my money on Biff.

Linda: And Willy—if it's warm Sunday we'll drive in the country. And we'll open the windshield, and take lunch.

Willy: No, the windshields don't open on the new cars.

Linda: But you opened it today.

Willy: Me? I didn't. *He stops.* Now isn't that peculiar! Isn't that a remarkable— *He breaks off in amazement and fright as the flute is heard distantly.*

Linda: What, darling?

Willy: That is the most remarkable thing.

Linda: What, dear?

Willy: I was thinking of the Chevvy. *Slight pause.* Nineteen twenty-eight . . . when I had that red Chevvy—*Breaks off.* That funny? I coulda sworn I was driving that Chevvy today.

Linda: Well, that's nothing. Something must've reminded you.

Willy: Remarkable. Ts. Remember those days? The way Biff used to simonize that car? The dealer refused to believe there was eighty thousand miles on it. *He shakes his head.* Heh! *To Linda:* Close your eyes, I'll be right up. *He walks out of the bedroom.*

Happy: to Biff: Jesus, maybe he smashed up the car again!

Linda: calling after Willy: Be careful on the stairs, dear! The cheese is on the middle shelf! *She turns, goes over to the bed, takes his jacket, and goes out of the bedroom.*

Light has risen on the boys' room. Unseen, Willy is heard talking to himself. "Eighty thousand miles," and a little laugh. Biff gets out of bed, comes downstage a bit, and stands attentively. Biff is two years older than his brother, Happy, well built, but in these days bears a worn air and seems less self-assured. He has succeeded less, and his dreams are stronger and less acceptable than Happy's. Happy is tall, powerfully made. Sexuality is like a visible color on him, or a scent that many women have discovered. He, like his brother, is lost, but in a different way, for he has never allowed himself to turn his face toward defeat and is thus more confused and hard-skinned, although seemingly more content.

Happy: getting out of bed: He's going to get his license taken away if he keeps that up. I'm getting nervous about him, y'know, Biff?

Biff: His eyes are going.

Happy: No, I've driven with him. He sees all right. He just doesn't keep his mind on it. I drove into the city with him last week. He stops at a green light and then it turns red and he goes. *He laughs.*

Biff: Maybe he's color-blind.

Happy: Pop? Why he's got the finest eye for color in the business. You know that.

Biff: sitting down on his bed: I'm going to sleep.

Happy: You're not still sour on Dad, are you, Biff?

Biff: He's all right, I guess.

Willy: underneath them, in the living-room: Yes, sir, eighty thousand miles— eighty-two thousand!

Biff: You smoking?

Happy: holding out a pack of cigarettes: Want one?

Biff: taking a cigarette: I can never sleep when I smell it.

Willy: What a simonizing job, heh!

Happy: with deep sentiment: Funny, Biff, y'know? Us sleeping in here again? The old beds. *He pats his bed affectionately.* All the talk that went across those two beds, huh? Our whole lives.

Biff: Yeah. Lotta dreams and plans.

Happy: with a deep and masculine laugh: About five hundred women would like to know what was said in this room.

They share a soft laugh.

Biff: Remember that big Betsy something—what the hell was her name—over on Bushwick Avenue?

Happy: combing his hair: With the collie dog!

Biff: That's the one. I got you in there, remember?

Happy: Yeah, that was my first time—I think. Boy, there was a pig! *They laugh, almost crudely.* You taught me everything I know about women. Don't forget that.

Biff: I bet you forgot how bashful you used to be. Especially with girls.

Happy: Oh, I still am, Biff.

Biff: Oh, go on.

Happy: I just control it, that's all. I think I got less bashful and you got more so. What happened, Biff? Where's the old humor, the old confidence? *He shakes Biff's knee. Biff gets up and moves restlessly about the room.* What's the matter?

Biff: Why does Dad mock me all the time?

Happy: He's not mocking you, he—

Biff: Everything I say there's a twist of mockery on his face. I can't get near him.

Happy: He just wants you to make good, that's all. I wanted to talk to you about Dad for a long time, Biff. Something's—happening to him. He—talks to himself.

Biff: I noticed that this morning. But he always mumbled.

Happy: But not so noticeable. It got so embarrassing I sent him to Florida. And you know something? Most of the time he's talking to you.

Biff: What's he say about me?

Happy: I can't make it out.

Biff: What's he say about me?

Happy: I think the fact that you're not settled, that you're still kind of up in the air . . .

Biff: There's one or two other things depressing him, Happy.

Happy: What do you mean?

Biff: Never mind. Just don't lay it all to me.

Happy: But I think if you just got started—I mean—is there any future for you out there?

Biff: I tell ya, Hap, I don't know what the future is. I don't know—what I'm supposed to want.

Happy: What do you mean?

Biff: Well, I spent six or seven years after high school trying to work myself up. Shipping clerk, salesman, business of one kind or another. And it's a measly manner of existence. To get on that subway on the hot mornings in summer. To devote your whole life to keeping stock, or making phone calls, or selling or buying. To suffer fifty weeks of the year for the sake of a two-week vacation, when all you really desire is to be outdoors, with your shirt off. And always to have to get ahead of the next fella. And still—that's how you build a future.

Happy: Well, you really enjoy it on a farm? Are you content out there?

Biff: with rising agitation: Hap, I've had twenty or thirty different kinds of jobs since I left home before the war, and it always turns out the same. I just realized it lately. In Nebraska when I herded cattle, and the Dakotas, and Arizona, and now in Texas. It's why I came home now. I guess, because I realized it. This farm I work on, it's spring there now, see? And they've got about fifteen new colts. There's nothing more inspiring or—beautiful than the sight of a mare and a new colt. And it's cool there now, see? Texas is cool now, and it's spring. And whenever spring comes to where I am, I suddenly get the feeling, my God, I'm not gettin' anywhere! What the hell am I doing, playing around with horses, twenty-eight dollars a week! I'm thirty-four years old, I oughta be makin' my future. That's when I come running home. And now, I get here, and I don't know what to do with myself. *After a pause:* I've always made a point of not wasting my life, and everytime I come back here I know that all I've done is to waste my life.

Happy: You're a poet, you know that, Biff? You're a—you're an idealist!

Biff: No, I'm mixed up very bad. Maybe I oughta get married. Maybe I oughta get stuck into something. Maybe that's my trouble. I'm like a boy. I'm not married, I'm not in business, I just—I'm like a boy. Are you content, Hap? You're a success, aren't you? Are you content?

Happy: Hell, no!

Biff: Why? You're making money, aren't you?

Happy: moving about with energy, expressiveness: All I can do now is wait for the merchandise manager to die. And suppose I get to be merchandise manager? He's a good friend of mine, and he just built a terrific estate on Long Island. And he lived there about two months and sold it, and now he's building another one. He can't enjoy it once it's finished. And I know that's just what I would do. I don't know what the hell I'm workin' for. Sometimes I sit in my apartment—all alone. And I think of the rent I'm paying. And it's crazy. But then, it's what I always wanted. My own apartment, a car, and plenty of women. And still, goddammit, I'm lonely.

Biff: with enthusiasm: Listen, why don't you come out West with me?

Happy: You and I, heh?

Biff: Sure, maybe we could buy a ranch. Raise cattle, use our muscles. Men built like we are should be working out in the open.

Happy: avidly: The Loman Brothers, heh?

Biff: with vast affection: Sure, we'd be known all over the counties!

Happy: enthralled: That's what I dream about, Biff. Sometimes I want to just rip my clothes off in the middle of the store and outbox that goddam merchandise manager. I mean I can outbox, outrun, and outlift anybody in that store, and I have to take orders from those common, petty sons-of-bitches till I can't stand it any more.

Biff: I'm tellin' you, kid, if you were with me I'd be happy out there.

Happy: enthused: See, Biff, everybody around me is so false that I'm constantly lowering my ideals . . .

Biff: Baby, together we'd stand up for one another, we'd have someone to trust.

Happy: If I were around you—

Biff: Hap, the trouble is we weren't brought up to grub for money. I don't know how to do it.

Happy: Neither can I!

Biff: Then let's go!

Happy: The only thing is—what can you make out there?

Biff: But look at your friend. Builds an estate and then hasn't the peace of mind to live in it.

Happy: Yeah, but when he walks into the store the waves part in front of him. That's fifty-two thousand dollars a year coming through the revolving door, and I got more in my pinky finger than he's got in his head.

Biff: Yeah, but you just said—

Happy: I gotta show some of those pompous, self-important executives over there that Hap Loman can make the grade. I want to walk into the store the way he walks in. Then I'll go with you. Biff. We'll be together yet, I swear. But take those two we had tonight. Now weren't they gorgeous creatures?

Biff: Yeah, yeah, most gorgeous I've had in years.

Happy: I get that any time I want, Biff. Whenever I feel disgusted. The only trouble is, it gets like bowling or something. I just keep knockin' them over and it doesn't mean anything. You still run around a lot?

Biff: Naa. I'd like to find a girl—steady, somebody with substance.

Happy: That's what I long for.

Biff: Go on! You'd never come home.

Happy: I would! Somebody with character, with resistance! Like Mom, y'know?

You're gonna call me a bastard when I tell you this, That girl Charlotte I was with tonight is engaged to be married in five weeks. *He tries on his new hat.*

Biff: No kiddin'!

Happy: Sure, the guy's in line for the vice-presidency of the store. I don't know what gets into me, maybe I just have an overdeveloped sense of competition or something, but I went and ruined her, and furthermore I can't get rid of her. And he's the third executive I've done that to. Isn't that a crummy characteristic? And to top it all, I go to their weddings! *Indignantly, but laughing:* Like I'm not supposed to take bribes. Manufacturers offer me a hundred-dollar bill now and then to throw an order their way. You know how honest I am, but it's like this girl, see. I hate myself for it. Because I don't want the girl, and, still, I take it and—I love it!

Biff: Let's go to sleep.

Happy: I guess we didn't settle anything, heh?

Biff: I just got one idea that I think I'm going to try.

Happy: What's that?

Biff: Remember Bill Oliver?

Happy: Sure, Oliver is very big now. You want to work for him again?

Biff: No, but when I quit he said something to me. He put his arm on my shoulder, and he said, "Biff, if you ever need anything, come to me."

Happy: I remember that. That sounds good.

Biff: I think I'll go to see him. If I could get ten thousand or even seven or eight thousand dollars I could buy a beautiful ranch.

Happy: I bet he'd back you. 'Cause he thought highly of you, Biff. I mean, they all do. You're well liked, Biff. That's why I say to come back here, and we both have the apartment. And I'm tellin' you, Biff, any babe you want . . .

Biff: No, with a ranch I could do the work I like and still be something. I just wonder though. I wonder if Oliver still thinks I stole that carton of basketballs.

Happy: Oh, he probably forgot that long ago. It's almost ten years. You're too sensitive. Anyway, he didn't really fire you.

Biff: Well, I think he was going to. I think that's why I quit. I was never sure whether he knew or not. I know he thought the world of me, though. I was the only one he'd let lock up the place.

Willy: below: You gonna wash the engine, Biff?

Happy: Shh!

Biff looks at Happy, who is gazing down, listening. Willy is mumbling in the parlor.

Happy: You hear that?

They listen. Willy laughs warmly.

Biff: growing angry: Doesn't he know Mom can hear that?

Willy: Don't get your sweater dirty, Biff!

A look of pain crosses Biff's face.

Happy: Isn't that terrible? Don't leave again, will you? You'll find a job here. You gotta stick around. I don't know what to do about him, it's getting embarrassing.

Willy: What a simonizing job!

Biff: Mom's hearing that!

Willy: No kiddin', Biff, you got a date? Wonderful!

Happy: Go on to sleep. But talk to him in the morning, will you?

Biff: reluctantly getting into bed: With her in the house. Brother!

Happy: getting into bed: I wish you'd have a good talk with him.

The light on their room begins to fade.

Biff: to himself in bed: That selfish, stupid . . .

Happy: Sh . . . Sleep, Biff.

Their light is out. Well before they have finished speaking, Willy's form is dimly seen below in the darkened kitchen. He opens the refrigerator, searches in there, and takes out a bottle of milk. The apartment houses are fading out, and the entire house and surroundings become covered with leaves. Music insinuates itself as the leaves appear.

Willy: Just wanna be careful with those girls. Biff, that's all. Don't make any promises. No promises of any kind. Because a girl, y'know, they always believe what you tell 'em, and you're very young, Biff, you're too young to be talking seriously to girls.

Light rises on the kitchen. Willy, talking, shuts the refrigerator door and comes downstage to the kitchen table. He pours milk into a glass. He is totally immersed in himself, smiling faintly.

Willy: Too young entirely, Biff. You want to watch your schooling first. Then when you're all set, there'll be plenty of girls for a boy like you. *He smiles broadly at a kitchen chair.* That so? The girls pay for you? *He laughs.* Boy, you must really be makin' a hit.

Willy is gradually addressing—physically—a point offstage, speaking through the wall of the kitchen, and his voice has been rising in volume to that of a normal conversation.

Willy: I been wondering why you polish the car so careful. Ha! Don't leave the hubcaps, boys. Get the chamois to the hubcaps. Happy, use newspaper on the windows, it's the easiest thing. Show him how to do it, Biff! You see, Happy? Pad it up, use it like a pad. That's it, that's it, good work. You're doin' all right, Hap. *He pauses, then nods in approbation for a few seconds, then looks upward.* Biff, first thing we gotta do when we get time is clip that big branch over the house. Afraid it's gonna fall in a storm and hit the roof. Tell you what. We get a rope and sling her around, and then we climb up there with a couple of saws and take her down. Soon as you finish the car, boys, I wanna see ya. I got a surprise for you, boys.

Biff: offstage: Whatta ya got, Dad?

Willy: No, you finish first. Never leave a job till you're finished—remember that.

Looking toward the "big trees": Biff, up in Albany I saw a beautiful hammock. I think I'll buy it next trip, and we'll hang it right between those two elms. Wouldn't that be something? Just swinging' there under those branches. Boy, that would be . . .

Young Biff and Young Happy appear from the direction Willy was addressing. Happy carries rags and a pail of water. Biff, wearing a sweater with a block "S," carries a football.

Biff: pointing in the direction of the car offstage: How's that, Pop, professional?
Willy: Terrific. Terrific job, boys. Good work, Biff.
Happy: Where's the surprise, Pop?
Willy: In the back seat of the car.
Happy: Boy! *He runs off.*
Biff: What is it, Dad? Tell me, what'd you buy?
Willy: laughing, cuffs him: Never mind, something I want you to have.
Biff: turns and starts off: What is it, Hap?
Happy: offstage: It's a punching bag!
Biff: Oh, Pop!
Willy: It's got Gene Tunney's signature on it!

Happy runs onstage with a punching bag.

Biff: Gee, how'd you know we wanted a punching bag?
Willy: Well, it's the finest thing for the timing.
Happy: lies down on his back and pedals with his feet: I'm losing weight, you notice, Pop?
Willy: to Happy: Jumping rope is good too.
Biff: Did you see the new football I got?
Willy: examining the ball: Where'd you get a new ball?
Biff: The coach told me to practice my passing.
Willy: That so? And he gave you the ball, heh?
Biff: Well, I borrowed it from the locker room. *He laughs confidentially.*
Willy: laughing with him at the theft: I want you to return that.
Happy: I told you he wouldn't like it!
Biff: angrily: Well, I'm bringing it back!
Willy: stopping the incipient argument, to Happy: Sure, he's gotta practice with a regulation ball, doesn't he? *To Biff:* Coach'll probably congratulate you on your initiative!
Biff: Oh, he keeps congratulating my initiative all the time, Pop.
Willy: That's because he likes you. If somebody else took that ball there'd be an uproar. So what's the report, boys, what's the report?
Biff: Where'd you go this time, Dad? Gee we were lonesome for you.
Willy: pleased, puts an arm around each boy an they come down to the apron: Lonesome, heh?
Biff: Missed you every minute.
Willy: Don't say? Tell you a secret, boys. Don't breathe it to a soul. Someday I'll have my own business, and I'll never have to leave home any more.

Happy: Like Uncle Charley, heh?

Willy: Bigger than Uncle Charley! Because Charley is not—liked. He's liked, but he's not—well liked.

Biff: Where'd you go this time, Dad?

Willy: Well, I got on the road, and I went north to Providence. Met the Mayor.

Biff: The Mayor of Providence!

Willy: He was sitting in the hotel lobby.

Biff: What'd he say?

Willy: He said, "Morning!" And I said, "You got a fine city here, Mayor." And then he had coffee with me. And then I went to Waterbury. Waterbury is a fine city. Big clock city, the famous Waterbury clock. Sold a nice bill there. And then Boston—Boston is the cradle of the Revolution. A fine city. And a couple of other towns in Mass., and on to Portland and Bangor and straight home!

Biff: Gee, I'd love to go with you sometime, Dad.

Willy: Soon as summer comes.

Happy: Promise?

Willy: You and Hap and I, and I'll show you all the towns. America is full of beautiful towns and fine, upstanding people. And they know me, boys, they know me up and down New England. The finest people. And when I bring you fellas up, there'll be open sesame for all of us, 'cause one thing, boys: I have friends. I can park my car in any street in New England, and the cops protect it like their own. This summer, heh?

Biff and Happy, together: Yeah! You bet!

Willy: We'll take our bathing suits.

Happy: We'll carry your bags. Pop!

Willy: Oh, won't that be something! Me comin' into the Boston stores with you boys carryin' my bag. What a sensation!

Biff is prancing around, practicing passing the ball.

Willy: You nervous, Biff, about the game?

Biff: Not if you're gonna be there.

Willy: What do they say about you in school, now that they made you captain?

Happy: There's a crowd of girls behind him everytime the classes change.

Biff: taking Willy's hand: This Saturday, Pop, this Saturday—just for you, I'm going to break through for a touchdown.

Happy: You're supposed to pass.

Biff: I'm takin' one play for Pop. You watch me, Pop, and when I take off my helmet, that means I'm breakin' out. Then you watch me crash through that line!

Willy: kisses Biff: Oh, wait'll I tell this in Boston!

Bernard enters in knickers. He is younger than Biff, earnest and loyal, a worried boy.

Bernard: Biff, where are you? You're supposed to study with me today.

Willy: Hey, looka Bernard. What're you lookin' so anemic about, Bernard?

Bernard: He's gotta study, Uncle Willy. He's got Regents' next week.

Happy: tauntingly, spinning Bernard around: Let's box, Bernard!

Bernard: Biff! *He gets away from Happy.* Listen, Biff, I heard Mr. Birnbaum say that if you don't start studyin' math he's gonna flunk you, and you won't graduate. I heard him!

Willy: You better study with him, Biff. Go ahead now.

Bernard: I heard him!

Biff: Oh, Pop, you didn't see my sneakers! *He holds up a foot for Willy to look at.*

Willy: Hey, that's a beautiful job of printing!

Bernard: wiping his glasses: Just because he printed University of Virginia on his sneakers doesn't mean they've got to graduate him, Uncle Willy!

Willy: angrily: What're you talking about? With scholarships to three universities they're gonna flunk him?

Bernard: But I heard Mr. Birnbaum say—

Willy: Don't be a pest, Bernard! *To his boys:* What an anemic!

Bernard: Okay, I'm waiting for you in my house, Biff.

Bernard goes off. The Lomans laugh.

Willy: Bernard is not well liked, is he?

Biff: He's liked, but he's not well liked.

Happy: That's right, Pop.

Willy: That's just what I mean. Bernard can get the best marks in school, y'understand, but when he gets out in the business world, y'understand, you are going to be five times ahead of him. That's why I thank Almighty God you're both built like Adonises. Because the man who makes an appearance in the business world, the man who creates personal interest, is the man who gets ahead. Be liked and you will never want. You take me, for instance. I never have to wait in line to see a buyer. "Willy Loman is here!" That's all they have to know, and I go right through.

Biff: Did you knock them dead, Pop?

Willy: Knocked 'em cold in Providence, slaughtered 'em in Boston.

Happy: on his back, pedaling again: I'm losing weight, you notice, Pop?

Linda enters, as of old, a ribbon in her hair, carrying a basket of washing.

Linda: with youthful energy: Hello, dear!

Willy: Sweetheart!

Linda: How'd the Chevvy run?

Willy: Chevrolet, Linda, is the greatest car ever built. *To the boys:* Since when do you let your mother carry wash up the stairs?

Biff: Grab hold there, boy!

Happy: Where to, Mom?

Linda: Hang them up on the line. And you better go down to your friends, Biff. The cellar is full of boys. They don't know what to do with themselves.

---

[1] Competitive examinations required for graduation from high schools in New York State.

Biff: Ah, when Pop comes home they can wait!

Willy: laughs appreciatively: You better go down and tell them what to do, Biff.

Biff: I think I'll have them sweep out the furnace room.

Willy: Good work, Biff.

Biff: goes through wall-line of kitchen to doorway at back and calls down: Fellas! Everybody sweep out the furnace room! I'll be right down!

Voices: All right! Okay, Biff.

Biff: George and Sam and Frank, come out back! We're hangin' up the wash! Come on, Hap, on the double! *He and Happy carry out the basket.*

Linda: The way they obey him!

Willy: Well, that's training, the training. I'm tellin' you, I was sellin' thousands and thousands, but I had to come home.

Linda: Oh, the whole block'll be at that game. Did you sell anything?

Willy: I did five hundred gross in Providence and seven hundred gross in Boston.

Linda: No! Wait a minute, I've got a pencil. *She pulls pencil and paper out of her apron pocket.* That makes your commission . . . Two hundred—my God! Two hundred and twelve dollars!

Willy: Well, I didn't figure it yet, but . . .

Linda: How much did you do?

Willy: Well, I—I did—about a hundred and eighty gross in Providence. Well, no—it came to—roughly two hundred gross on the whole trip.

Linda: without hesitation: Two hundred gross. That's . . . *She figures.*

Willy: The trouble was that three of the stores were half closed for inventory in Boston. Otherwise I woulda broke records.

Linda: Well, it makes seventy dollars and some pennies. That's very good.

Willy: What do we owe?

Linda: Well, on the first there's sixteen dollars on the refrigerator—

Willy: Why sixteen?

Linda: Well, the fan belt broke, so it was a dollar eighty.

Willy: But it's brand new.

Linda: Well, the man said that's the way it is. Till they work themselves in, y'know.

They move through the wall-line into the kitchen.

Willy: I hope we didn't get stuck on that machine.

Linda: They got the biggest ads of any of them!

Willy: I know, it's a fine machine. What else?

Linda: Well, there's nine-sixty for the washing machine. And for the vacuum cleaner there's three and a half due on the fifteenth. Then, the roof, you got twenty-one dollars remaining.

Willy: It don't leak, does it?

Linda: No, they did a wonderful job. Then you owe Frank for the carburetor.

Willy: I'm not going to pay that man! That goddam Chevrolet, they ought to prohibit the manufacture of that car!

Linda: Well, you owe him three and a half. And odds and ends, comes to around a hundred and twenty dollars by the fifteenth.

Willy: A hundred and twenty dollars! My God, if business don't pick up I don't know what I'm gonna do!

Linda: Well, next week you'll do better.

Willy: Oh, I'll knock 'em dead next week. I'll go to Hartford. I'm very well liked in Hartford. You know, the trouble is, Linda, people don't seem to take to me.

They move onto the forestage.

Linda: Oh, don't be foolish.

Willy: I know it when I walk in. They seem to laugh at me.

Linda: Why? Why would they laugh at you? Don't talk that way, Willy.

Willy moves to the edge of the stage. Linda goes into the kitchen and starts to darn stockings.

Willy: I don't know the reason for it, but they just pass me by. I'm not noticed.

Linda: But you're doing wonderful, dear. You're making seventy to a hundred dollars a week.

Willy: But I gotta be at it ten, twelve hours a day. Other men—I don't know— they do it easier. I don't know why—I can't stop myself—I talk too much. A man oughta come in with a few words. One thing about Charley. He's a man of few words, and they respect him.

Linda: You don't talk too much, you're just lively.

Willy: smiling: Well, I figure, what the hell, life is short, a couple of jokes. *To himself:* I joke too much! *The smile goes.*

Linda: Why? You're—

Willy: I'm fat. I'm very—foolish to look at, Linda. I didn't tell you, but Christmas time I happened to be calling on F. H. Stewarts, and a salesman I know, as I was going in to see the buyer I heard him say something about— walrus. And I—I cracked him right across the face. I won't take that. I simply will not take that. But they do laugh at me. I know that.

Linda: Darling . . .

Willy: I gotta overcome it. I know I gotta overcome it. I'm not dressing to advantage, maybe.

Linda: Willy, darling, you're the handsomest man in the world—

Willy: Oh, no, Linda.

Linda: To me you are. *Slight pause.* The handsomest.

From the darkness is heard the laughter of a woman. Willy doesn't turn to it, but it continues through Linda's lines.

Linda: And the boys, Willy. Few men are idolized by their children the way you are.

Music is heard as behind a scrim, to the left of the house, The Woman, dimly seen, is dressing.

Willy: with great feeling: You're the best there is. Linda, you're a pal, you know that? On the road—on the road I want to grab you sometimes and just kiss the life outa you.

The laughter is loud now, and he moves into a brightening area at the left, where The Woman has come from behind the scrim and is standing, putting on her hat, looking into a "mirror" and laughing.

Willy: 'Cause I get so lonely—especially when business is bad and there's nobody to talk to. I get the feeling that I'll never sell anything again, that I won't making a living for you, or a business, a business for the boys. *He talks through The Woman's subsiding laughter; The Woman primps at the "mirror."* There's so much I want to make for—
The Woman: Me? You didn't make me, Willy. I picked you.
Willy: pleased: You picked me?
The Woman: who is quite proper-looking, Willy's age: I did. I've been sitting at that desk watching all the salesmen go by, day in, day out. But you've got such a sense of humor, and we do have such a good time together, don't we?
Willy: Sure, sure. *He takes her in his arms.* Why do you have to go now?
The Woman: It's two o'clock . . .
Willy: No, come on in! *He pulls her.*
The Woman: . . . my sisters'll be scandalized. When'll you be back?
Willy: Oh, two weeks about. Will you come up again?
The Woman: Sure thing. You do make me laugh. It's good for me. *She squeezes his arm, kisses him.* And I think you're a wonderful man.
Willy: You picked me, heh?
The Woman: Sure. Because you're so sweet. And such a kidder.
Willy: Well, I'll see you next time I'm in Boston.
The Woman: I'll put you right through to the buyers.
Willy: slapping her bottom: Right. Well, bottoms up!
The Woman: slaps him gently and laughs: You just kill me, Willy. *He suddenly grabs her and kisses her roughly.* You kill me. And thanks for the stockings. I love a lot of stockings. Well, good night.
Willy: Good night. And keep your pores open!
The Woman: Oh, Willy!

The Woman bursts out laughing, and Linda's laughter blends in. The Woman disappears into the dark. Now the area at the kitchen table brightens. Linda is sitting where she was at the kitchen table, but now is mending a pair of her silk stockings.

Linda: You are, Willy. The handsomest man. You've got no reason to feel that—
Willy: coming out of The Woman's dimming area and going over to Linda: I'll make it all up to you, Linda, I'll—
Linda: There's nothing to make up, dear. You're doing fine, better than—
Willy: noticing her mending: What's that?
Linda: Just mending my stockings. They're so expensive—
Willy: angrily, taking them from her: I won't have you mending stockings in this house! Now throw them out!

Linda puts the stockings in her pocket.

Bernard: entering on the run: Where is he? If he doesn't study!

Willy: moving to the forestage, with great agitation: You'll give him the answers!

Bernard: I do, but I can't on a Regents! That's a state exam! They're liable to arrest me!

Willy: Where is he? I'll whip him, I'll whip him!

Linda: And he'd better give back that football, Willy, it's not nice.

Willy: Biff! Where is he? Why is he taking everything?

Linda: He's too rough with the girls, Willy. All the mothers are afraid of him!

Willy: I'll whip him!

Bernard: He's driving the car without a license!

The Woman's laugh is heard.

Willy: Shut up!

Linda: All the mothers—

Willy: Shut up!

Bernard: backing quietly away and out: Mr. Birnbaum says he's stuck up.

Willy: Get outa here!

Bernard: If he doesn't buckle down he'll flunk math! *He goes off.*

Linda: He's right. Willy, you've gotta—

Willy: exploding at her: There's nothing the matter with him! You want him to be a worm like Bernard? He's got spirit, personality . . .

As he speaks, Linda, almost in tears, exits into the living-room. Willy is alone in the kitchen, wilting and staring. The leaves are gone. It is night again, and the apartment houses look down from behind.

Willy: Loaded with it. Loaded! What is he stealing? He's giving it back, isn't he? Why is he stealing? What did I tell him? I never in my life told him anything but decent things.

Happy in pajamas has come down the stairs; Willy suddenly becomes aware of Happy's presence.

Happy: Let's go now, come on.

Willy: sitting down at the kitchen table: Huh! Why did she have to wax the floors herself? Everytime she waxes the floors she keels over. She knows that!

Happy: Shh! Take it easy. What brought you back tonight?

Willy: I got an awful scare. Nearly hit a kid in Yonkers.[2] God! Why didn't I go to Alaska with my brother Ben that time! Ben! That man was a genius, that man was success incarnate! What a mistake! He begged me to go.

Happy: Well, there's no use in—

Willy: You guys! There was a man started with the clothes on his back and ended up with diamond mines!

---

[2] Suburb north of New York City.

Happy: Boy, someday I'd like to know how he did it.

Willy: What's the mystery? The man knew what he wanted and went out and got it! Walked into a jungle, and comes out, the age of twenty-one, and he's rich! The world is an oyster, but you don't crack it open on a mattress!

Happy: Pop, I told you I'm gonna retire you for life.

Willy: You'll retire me for life on seventy goddam dollars a week? And your women and your car and your apartment, and you'll retire me for life! Christ's sake, I couldn't get past Yonkers today! Where are you guys, where are you? The woods are burning! I can't drive a car!

Charley has appeared in the doorway. He is a large man, slow of speech, laconic, immovable. In all he says, despite what he says, there is pity, and, now, trepidation. He has a robe over pajamas, slippers on his feet. He enters the kitchen.

Charley: Everything all right?

Happy: Yeah, Charley, everything's . . .

Willy: What's the matter?

Charley: I heard some noise. I thought something happened. Can't we do something about the walls? You sneeze in here, and in my house hats blow off.

Happy: Let's go to bed, Dad. Come on.

Charley signals to Happy to go.

Willy: You go ahead, I'm not tired at the moment.

Happy: to Willy: Take it easy, huh? *He exits.*

Willy: What're you doin' up?

Charley: sitting down at the kitchen table opposite Willy: Couldn't sleep good. I had a heartburn.

Willy: Well, you don't know how to eat.

Charley: I eat with my mouth.

Willy: No, you're ignorant. You gotta know about vitamins and things like that.

Charley: Come on, let's shoot. Tire you out a little.

Willy: hesitantly: All right. You got cards?

Charley: taking a deck from his pocket: Yeah, I got them. Someplace. What is it with those vitamins?

Willy: dealing: They build up your bones. Chemistry.

Charley: Yeah, but there's no bones in a heartburn.

Willy: What are you talkin' about? Do you know the first thing about it?

Charley: Don't get insulted.

Willy: Don't talk about something you don't know anything about.

They are playing. Pause.

Charley: What're you doin' home?

Willy: A little trouble with the car.

Charley: Oh. *Pause.* I'd like to take a trip to California.

Willy: Don't say.

Charley: You want a job?

Willy: I got a job, I told you that. *After a slight pause:* What the hell are you offering me a job for?

Charley: Don't get insulted.

Willy: Don't insult me.

Charley: I don't see no sense in it. You don't have to go on this way.

Willy: I got a good job. *Slight pause.* What do you keep comin' in here for?

Charley: You want me to go?

Willy: after a pause, withering: I can't understand it. He's going back to Texas again. What the hell is that?

Charley: Let him go.

Willy: I got nothin' to give him, Charley, I'm clean, I'm clean.

Charley: He won't starve. None a them starve. Forget about him.

Willy: Then what have I got to remember?

Charley: You take it too hard. To hell with it. When a deposit bottle is broken you don't get your nickel back.

Willy: That's easy enough for you to say.

Charley: That ain't easy for me to say.

Willy: Did you see the ceiling I put up in the living-room?

Charley: Yeah, that's a piece of work. To put up a ceiling is a mystery to me. How do you do it?

Willy: What's the difference?

Charley: Well, talk about it.

Willy: You gonna put up a ceiling?

Charley: How could I put up a ceiling?

Willy: Then what the hell are you bothering me for?

Charley: You're insulted again.

Willy: A man who can't handle tools is not a man. You're disgusting.

Charley: Don't call me disgusting, Willy.

Uncle Ben, carrying a valise and an umbrella, enters the forestage from around the right corner of the house. He is a stolid man, in his sixties, with a mustache and an authoritative air. He is utterly certain of his destiny, and there is an aura of far places about him. He enters exactly as Willy speaks.

Willy: I'm getting awfully tired, Ben.

Ben's music is heard. Ben looks around at everything.

Charley: Good, keep playing; you'll sleep better. Did you call me Ben?

Ben looks at his watch.

Willy: That's funny. For a second there you reminded me of my brother Ben.

Ben: I only have a few minutes. *He strolls, inspecting the place. Willy and Charley continue playing.*

Charley: You never heard from him again, heh? Since that time?

Willy: Didn't Linda tell you? Couple of weeks ago we got a letter from his wife
in Africa. He died.

Charley: That so.

Ben: chuckling: So this is Brooklyn, eh?

Charley: Maybe you're in for some of his money.

Willy: Naa, he had seven sons. There's just one opportunity I had with that
man . . .

Ben: I must make a train, William. There are several properties I'm looking at in
Alaska.

Willy: Sure, sure! If I'd gone with him to Alaska that time, everything would've
been totally different.

Charley: Go on, you'd froze to death up there.

Willy: What're you talking about?

Ben: Opportunity is tremendous in Alaska, William. Surprised you're not up
there.

Willy: Sure, tremendous.

Charley: Heh?

Willy: There was the only man I ever met who knew the answers.

Charley: Who?

Ben: How are you all?

Willy: taking a pot, smiling: Fine, fine.

Charley: Pretty sharp tonight.

Ben: Is Mother living with you?

Willy: No, she died a long time ago.

Charley: Who?

Ben: That's too bad. Fine specimen of a lady, Mother.

Willy: to Charley: Heh?

Ben: I'd hoped to see the old girl.

Charley: Who died?

Ben: Heard anything from Father, have you?

Willy: unnerved: What do you mean, who died?

Charley: taking a pot: What're you talkin' about?

Ben: looking at his watch: William, it's half-past eight!

Willy: as though to dispel his confusion he angrily stops Charley's hand: That's my
build!

Charley: I put the ace—

Willy: If you don't know how to play the game I'm not gonna throw my
money away on you!

Charley: rising: It was my ace, for God's sake!

Willy: I'm through, I'm through!

Ben: When did Mother die?

Willy: Long ago. Since the beginning you never knew how to play cards.

Charley: picks up the cards and goes to the door: All right! Next time I'll bring a
deck with five aces.

Willy: I don't play that kind of game!

Charley: turning to him: You ought to be ashamed of yourself!

Willy: Yeah?

Charley: Yeah! *He goes out.*

Willy: slamming the door after him: Ignoramus!

Ben: as Willy comes toward him through the wall-line of the kitchen: So you're William.

Willy: shaking Ben's hand: Ben! I've been waiting for you so long! What's the answer? How did you do it?

Ben: Oh, there's a story in that.

Linda enters the forestage, as of old, carrying the wash basket.

Linda: Is this Ben?

Ben: gallantly: How do you do, my dear.

Linda: Where've you been all these years? Willy's always wondered why you—

Willy: pulling Ben away from her impatiently: Where is Dad? Didn't you follow him? How did you get started?

Ben: Well, I don't know how much you remember.

Willy: Well, I was just a baby, of course, only three or four years old—

Ben: Three years and eleven months.

Willy: What a memory, Ben!

Ben: I have many enterprises, William, and I have never kept books.

Willy: I remember I was sitting under the wagon in—was it Nebraska?

Ben: It was South Dakota, and I gave you a bunch of wild flowers.

Willy: I remember you walking away down some open road.

Ben: laughing: I was going to find Father in Alaska.

Willy: Where is he?

Ben: At that age I had a very faulty view of geography, William. I discovered after a few days that I was heading due south, so instead of Alaska, I ended up in Africa.

Linda: Africa!

Willy: The Gold Coast!

Ben: Principally diamond mines.

Linda: Diamond mines!

Ben: Yes, my dear. But I've only a few minutes—

Willy: No! Boys! Boys! *Young Biff and Happy appear.* Listen to this. This is your Uncle Ben, a great man! Tell my boys, Ben!

Ben: Why, boys, when I was seventeen I walked into the jungle, and when I was twenty-one I walked out. *He laughs.* And by God I was rich.

Willy: to the boys: You see what I been talking about? The greatest things can happen!

Ben: glancing at his watch: I have an appointment in Ketchikan Tuesday week.

Willy: No, Ben! Please tell about Dad. I want my boys to hear. I want them to know the kind of stock they spring from. All I remember is a man with a big beard, and I was in Mamma's lap, sitting around a fire, and some kind of high music.

Ben: His flute. He played the flute.

Willy: Sure, the flute, that's right!

New music is heard, a high, rollicking tune.

Ben: Father was a very great and a very wild-hearted man. We would start in Boston, and he'd toss the whole family into the wagon, and then he'd drive the team right across the country; through Ohio, and Indiana, Michigan, Illinois, and all the Western states. And we'd stop in the towns and sell the flutes that he'd made on the way. Great inventor, Father. With one gadget he made more in a week than a man like you could make in a lifetime.

Willy: That's just the way I'm bringing them up, Ben—rugged, well liked, all-around.

Ben: Yeah? *To Biff:* Hit that, boy—hard as you can. *He pounds his stomach.*

Biff: Oh, no, sir!

Ben: taking boxing stance: Come on, get to me! *He laughs.*

Willy: Go to it, Biff! Go ahead, show him!

Biff: Okay! *He cocks his fists and starts in.*

Linda: to Willy: Why must he fight, dear?

Ben: sparring with Biff: Good boy! Good boy!

Willy: How's that, Ben, heh?

Happy: Give him the left, Biff!

Linda: Why are you fighting?

Ben: Good boy! *Suddenly comes in, trips Biff, and stands over him, the point of his umbrella poised over Biff's eye.*

Linda: Look out, Biff!

Biff: Gee!

Ben: patting Biff's knee: Never fight fair with a stranger, boy. You'll never get out of the jungle that way. *Taking Linda's hand and bowing:* It was an honor and a pleasure to meet you, Linda.

Linda: withdrawing her hand coldly, frightened: Have a nice—trip.

Ben: to Willy: And good luck with your—what do you do?

Willy: Selling.

Ben: Yes. Well . . . *He raises his hand in farewell to all.*

Willy: No, Ben, I don't want you to think . . . *He takes Ben's arm to show him.* It's Brooklyn, I know, but we hunt too.

Ben: Really, now.

Willy: Oh, sure, there's snakes and rabbits and—that's why I moved out here. Why, Biff can fell any one of these trees in no time! Boys! Go right over to where they're building the apartment house and get some sand. We're gonna rebuild the entire front stoop right now! Watch this, Ben!

Biff: Yes, sir! On the double, Hap!

Happy: as he and Biff run off: I lost weight, Pop, you notice?

Charley enters in knickers, even before the boys are gone.

Charley: Listen, if they steal any more from that building the watchman'll put the cops on them!

Linda: to Willy: Don't let Biff . . .

Ben laughs lustily.

Willy: You shoulda seen the lumber they brought home last week. At least a dozen six-by-tens worth all kinds a money.

Charley: Listen, if that watchman——

Willy: I gave them hell, understand. But I got a couple of fearless characters there.

Charley: Willy, the jails are full of fearless characters.

Ben: clapping Willy on the back, with a laugh at Charley: And the stock exchange, friend!

Willy: joining in Ben's laughter: Where are the rest of your pants?

Charley: My wife bought them.

Willy: Now all you need is a golf club and you can go upstairs and go to sleep. *To Ben:* Great athlete! Between him and his son Bernard they can't hammer a nail!

Bernard: rushing in: The watchman's chasing Biff!

Willy: angrily: Shut up! He's not stealing anything!

Linda: alarmed, hurrying off left: Where is he? Biff, dear! *She exits.*

Willy: moving toward the left, away from Ben: There's nothing wrong. What's the matter with you?

Ben: Nervy boy. Good!

Willy: laughing: Oh, nerves of iron, that Biff!

Charley: Don't know what it is. My New England man comes back and he's bleedin', they murdered him up there.

Willy: It's contacts, Charley, I got important contacts!

Charley: sarcastically: Glad to hear it, Willy. Come in later, we'll shoot a little casino. I'll take some of your Portland money. *He laughs at Willy and exits.*

Willy: turning to Ben: Business is bad, it's murderous. But not for me, of course.

Ben: I'll stop by on my way back to Africa.

Willy: longingly: Can't you stay a few days? You're just what I need, Ben, because I—I have a fine position here, but I—well, Dad left when I was such a baby and I never had a chance to talk to him and I still feel—kind of temporary about myself.

Ben: I'll be late for my train.

They are at opposite ends of the stage.

Willy: Ben, my boys—can't we talk? They'd go into the jaws of hell for me, see, but I—

Ben: William, you're being first-rate with your boys. Outstanding, manly chaps!

Willy: hanging on to his words: Oh, Ben, that's good to hear! Because sometimes I'm afraid that I'm not teaching them the right kind of—Ben, how should I teach them?

Ben: giving great weight to each word, and with a certain vicious audacity: William, when I walked into the jungle, I was seventeen. When I walked out I was twenty-one. And, by God, I was rich! *He goes off into the darkness around the right corner of the house.*

Willy: . . . was rich! That's just the spirit I want to imbue them with! To walk into a jungle! I was right! I was right! I was right!

*Ben is gone, but Willy is still speaking to him as Linda, in nightgown and robe, enters
the kitchen, glances around for Willy, then goes to the door of the house, looks out and
sees him. Comes down to his left. He looks at her.*

Linda: Willy, dear? Willy?

Willy: I was right!

Linda: Did you have some cheese? *He can't answer.* It's very late, darling. Come
to bed, heh?

Willy: looking straight up: Gotta break your neck to see a star in this yard.

Linda: You coming in?

Willy: Whatever happened to that diamond watch fob? Remember? When Ben
came from Africa that time? Didn't he give me a watch fob with a diamond
in it?

Linda: You pawned it, dear. Twelve, thirteen years ago. For Biff's radio
correspondence course.

Willy: Gee, that was a beautiful thing. I'll take a walk.

Linda: But you're in your slippers.

Willy: starting to go around the house at the left: I was right! I was! *Half to Linda,
as he goes, shaking his head:* What a man! There was a man worth talking to. I
was right!

Linda: calling after Willy: But in your slippers, Willy!

*Willy is almost gone when Biff, in his pajamas, comes down the stairs and enters the
kitchen.*

Biff: What is he doing out there?

Linda: Sh!

Biff: God Almighty, Mom, how long has he been doing this?

Linda: Don't, he'll hear you.

Biff: What the hell is the matter with him?

Linda: It'll pass by morning.

Biff: Shouldn't we do anything?

Linda: Oh, my dear, you should do a lot of things, but there's nothing to do, so
go to sleep.

Happy comes down the stairs and sits on the steps.

Happy: I never heard him so loud, Mom.

Linda: Well, come around more often; you'll hear him. *She sits down at the table
and mends the lining of Willy's jacket.*

Biff: Why didn't you ever write me about this, Mom?

Linda: How would I write to you? For over three months you had no address.

Biff: I was on the move. But you know I thought of you all the time. You
know that, don't you, pal?

Linda: I know, dear, I know. But he likes to have a letter. Just to know that
there's still a possibility for better things.

Biff: He's not like this all the time, is he?

Linda: It's when you come home he's always the worst.

Biff: When I come home?

Linda: When you write you're coming, he's all smiles, and talks about the future, and—he's just wonderful. And then the closer you seem to come, the more shaky he gets, and then, by the time you get here, he's arguing, and he seems angry at you. I think it's just that maybe he can't bring himself to—to open up to you. Why are you so hateful to each other? Why is that?

Biff: evasively: I'm not hateful, Mom.

Linda: But you no sooner come in the door than you're fighting!

Biff: I don't know why. I mean to change. I'm tryin', Mom, you understand?

Linda: Are you home to stay now?

Biff: I don't know. I want to look around, see what's doin'.

Linda: Biff, you can't look around all your life, can you?

Biff: I just can't take hold, Mom. I can't take hold of some kind of a life.

Linda: Biff, a man is not a bird, to come and go with the springtime.

Biff: Your hair . . . *He touches her hair.* Your hair got so gray.

Linda: Oh, it's been gray since you were in high school. I just stopped dyeing it, that's all.

Biff: Dye it again, will ya? I don't want my pal looking old. *He smiles.*

Linda: You're such a boy! You think you can go away for a year and . . . You've got to get it into your head now that one day you'll knock on this door and there'll be strange people here—

Biff: What are you talking about? You're not even sixty, Mom.

Linda: But what about your father?

Biff: lamely: Well, I meant him too.

Happy: He admires Pop.

Linda: Biff, dear, if you don't have any feeling for him, then you can't have any feeling for me.

Biff: Sure I can, Mom.

Linda: No. You can't just come to see me, because I love him. *With a threat, but only a threat, of tears:* He's the dearest man in the world to me, and I won't have anyone making him feel unwanted and low and blue. You've got to make up your mind now, darling, there's no leeway any more. Either he's your father and you pay him that respect, or else you're not to come here. I know he's not easy to get along with—nobody knows that better than me— but . . .

Willy: from the left, with a laugh: Hey, hey, Biffo!

Biff: starting to go out after Willy: What the hell is the matter with him? *Happy stops him.*

Linda: Don't—don't go near him!

Biff: Stop making excuses for him! He always, always wiped the floor with you. Never had an ounce of respect for you.

Happy: He's always had respect for—

Biff: What the hell do you know about it?

Happy: surlily: Just don't call him crazy!

Biff: He's got no character—Charley wouldn't do this. Not in his own house— spewing out that vomit from his mind.

Happy: Charley never had to cope with what he's got to.

Biff: People are worse off than Willy Loman. Believe me, I've seen them!

Linda: Then make Charley your father, Biff. You can't do that, can you? I don't say he's a great man. Willy Loman never made a lot of money. His name was never in the paper. He's not the finest character that ever lived. But he's a human being, and a terrible thing is happening to him. So attention must be paid. He's not to be allowed to fall into his grave like an old dog. Attention, attention must be finally paid to such a person. You called him crazy—

Biff: I didn't mean—

Linda: No, a lot of people think he's lost his—balance. But you don't have to be very smart to know what his trouble is. The man is exhausted.

Happy: Sure!

Linda: A small man can be just as exhausted as a great man. He works for a company thirty-six years this March, opens up unheard-of territories to their trademark, and now in his old age they take his salary away.

Happy: indignantly: I didn't know that, Mom.

Linda: You never asked, my dear! Now that you get your spending money someplace else you don't trouble your mind with him.

Happy: But I gave you money last—

Linda: Christmas time, fifty dollars! To fix the hot water it cost ninety-seven fifty! For five weeks he's been on straight commission, like a beginner, an unknown!

Biff: Those ungrateful bastards!

Linda: Are they any worse than his sons? When he brought them business, when he was young, they were glad to see him. But now his old friends, the old buyers that loved him so and always found some order to hand him in a pinch—they're all dead, retired. He used to be able to make six, seven calls a day in Boston. Now he takes his valises out of the car and puts them back and takes them out again and he's exhausted. Instead of walking he talks now. He drives seven hundred miles, and when he gets there no one knows him any more, no one welcomes him. And what goes through a man's mind, driving seven hundred miles home without having earned a cent? Why shouldn't he talk to himself? Why? When he has to go to Charley and borrow fifty dollars a week and pretend to me that it's his pay? How long can that go on? How long? You see what I'm sitting here and waiting for? And you tell me he has no character? The man who never worked a day but for your benefit? When does he get the medal for that? Is this his reward—to turn around at the age of sixty-three and find his sons, who he loved better than his life, one a philandering bum—

Happy: Mom!

Linda: That's all you are, my baby! *To Biff:* And you! What happened to the love you had for him? You were such pals! How you used to talk to him on the phone every night! How lonely he was till he could come home to you!

Biff: All right, Mom. I'll live here in my room, and I'll get a job. I'll keep away from him, that's all.

Linda: No, Biff. You can't stay here and fight all the time.

Biff: He threw me out of this house, remember that.

Linda: Why did he do that? I never knew why.

Biff: Because I know he's a fake and he doesn't like anybody around who knows!

Linda: Why a fake? In what way? What do you mean?

Biff: Just don't lay it all at my feet. It's between me and him—that's all I have to say. I'll chip in from now on. He'll settle for half my pay check. He'll be all right. I'm going to bed. *He starts for the stairs.*

Linda: He won't be all right.

Biff: turning on the stairs, furiously: I hate this city and I'll stay here. Now what do you want?

Linda: He's dying, Biff.

Happy turns quickly to her, shocked.

Biff: after a pause: Why is he dying?

Linda: He's been trying to kill himself.

Biff: with great horror: How?

Linda: I live from day to day.

Biff: What're you talking about?

Linda: Remember I wrote you that he smashed up the car again? In February?

Biff: Well?

Linda: The insurance inspector came. He said that they have evidence. That all these accidents in the last year—weren't—weren't—accidents.

Happy: How can they tell that? That's a lie.

Linda: It seems there's a woman . . . *She takes a breath as*

Biff: sharply but contained: What woman?

Linda: simultaneously: . . . and this woman . . .

Linda: What?

Biff: Nothing. Go ahead.

Linda: What did you say?

Biff: Nothing. I just said what woman?

Happy: What about her?

Linda: Well, it seems she was walking down the road and saw his car. She says that he wasn't driving fast at all, and that he didn't skid. She says he came to that little bridge, and then deliberately smashed into the railing, and it was only the shallowness of the water that saved him.

Biff: Oh, no, he probably just fell asleep again.

Linda: I don't think he fell asleep.

Biff: Why not?

Linda: Last month . . . *With great difficulty:* Oh, boys, it's so hard to say a thing like this! He's just a big stupid man to you, but I tell you there's more good in him than in many other people. *She chokes, wipes her eyes.* I was looking for a fuse. The lights blew out, and I went down the cellar. And behind the fuse box—it happened to fall out—was a length of rubber pipe—just short.

Happy: No kidding?

Linda: There's a little attachment on the end of it. I knew right away. And sure enough, on the bottom of the water heater there's a new little nipple on the gas pipe.

Happy: angrily: That—jerk.

Biff: Did you have it taken off?

Linda: I'm—I'm ashamed to. How can I mention it to him? Every day I go down and take away that little rubber pipe. But, when he comes home, I put it back where it was. How can I insult him that way? I don't know what to do. I live from day to day, boys. I tell you, I know every thought in his mind. It sounds so old-fashioned and silly, but I tell you he put his whole life into you and you've turned your backs on him. *She is bent over in the chair, weeping, her face in her hands.* Biff, I swear to God! Biff, his life is in your hands!

Happy: to Biff: How do you like that damned fool!

Biff: kissing her: All right, pal, all right. It's all settled now. I've been remiss. I know that, Mom. But now I'll stay, and I swear to you, I'll apply myself. *Kneeling in front of her, in a fever of self-reproach:* It's just—you see, Mom, I don't fit in business. Not that I won't try. I'll try, and I'll make good.

Happy: Sure you will. The trouble with you in business was you never tried to please people.

Biff: I know, I—

Happy: Like when you worked for Harrison's. Bob Harrison said you were tops, and then you go and do some damn fool thing like whistling whole songs in the elevator like a comedian.

Biff: against Happy: So what? I like to whistle sometimes.

Happy: You don't raise a guy to a responsible job who whistles in the elevator!

Linda: Well, don't argue about it now.

Happy: Like when you'd go off and swim in the middle of the day instead of taking the line around.

Biff: his resentment rising: Well, don't you run off? You take off sometimes, don't you? On a nice summer day?

Happy: Yeah, but I cover myself!

Linda: Boys!

Happy: If I'm going to take a fade the boss can call any number where I'm supposed to be and they'll swear to him that I just left. I'll tell you something that I hate to say, Biff, but in the business world some of them think you're crazy.

Biff: angered: Screw the business world!

Happy: All right, screw it! Great, but cover yourself!

Linda: Hap, Hap!

Biff: I don't care what they think! They've laughed at Dad for years, and you know why? Because we don't belong in this nuthouse of a city! We should be mixing cement on some open plain, or—or carpenters. A carpenter is allowed to whistle!

Willy walks in from the entrance of the house, at left.

Willy: Even your grandfather was better than a carpenter. *Pause. They watch him.* You never grew up. Bernard does not whistle in the elevator, I assure you.

Biff: as though to laugh Willy out of it: Yeah, but you do, Pop.

Willy: I never in my life whistled in an elevator! And who in the business world thinks I'm crazy?

Biff: I didn't mean it like that, Pop. Now don't make a whole thing out of it, will ya?

Willy: Go back to the West! Be a carpenter, a cowboy, enjoy yourself!

Linda: Willy, he was just saying—

Willy: I heard what he said!

Happy: trying to quiet Willy: Hey, Pop, come on now . . .

Willy: continuing over Happy's line: They laugh at me, heh? Go to Filene's, go to the Hub, go to Slattery's, Boston. Call out the name Willy Loman and see what happens! Big shot!

Biff: All right, Pop.

Willy: Big!

Biff: All right!

Willy: Why do you always insult me?

Biff: I didn't say a word. *To Linda:* Did I say a word?

Linda: He didn't say anything, Willy.

Willy: going to the doorway of the living-room: All right, good night, good night.

Linda: Willy, dear, he just decided . . .

Willy: to Biff: If you get tired hanging around tomorrow, paint the ceiling I put up in the living-room.

Biff: I'm leaving early tomorrow.

Happy: He's going to see Bill Oliver, Pop.

Willy: interestedly: Oliver? For what?

Biff: with reserve, but trying, trying: He always said he'd stake me. I'd like to go into business, so maybe I can take him up on it.

Linda: Isn't that wonderful?

Willy: Don't interrupt. What's wonderful about it? There's fifty men in the City of New York who'd stake him. *To Biff:* Sporting goods?

Biff: I guess so. I know something about it and—

Willy: He knows something about it! You know sporting goods better than Spalding, for God's sake! How much is he giving you?

Biff: I don't know, I didn't even see him yet, but—

Willy: Then what're you talkin' about?

Biff: getting angry: Well, all I said was I'm gonna see him, that's all!

Willy: turning away: Ah, you're counting your chickens again.

Biff: starting left for the stairs: Oh, Jesus, I'm going to sleep!

Willy: calling after him: Don't curse in this house!

Biff: turning: Since when did you get so clean?

Happy: trying to stop them: Wait a . . .

Willy: Don't use that language to me! I won't have it!

Happy: grabbing Biff, shouts: Wait a minute! I got an idea. I got a feasible idea. Come here, Biff, let's talk this over now, let's talk some sense here. When I was down in Florida last time, I thought of a great idea to sell sporting goods. It just came back to me. You and I, Biff—we have a line, the Loman Line. We train a couple of weeks, and put on a couple of exhibitions, see?

Willy: That's an idea!

Happy: Wait! We form two basketball teams, see? Two water-polo teams. We play each other. It's a million dollars' worth of publicity. Two brothers, see? The Loman Brothers. Displays in the Royal Palms—all the hotels. And banners over the ring and the basketball court: "Loman Brothers." Baby, we could sell sporting goods!

Willy: That is a one-million-dollar idea!

Linda: Marvelous!

Biff: I'm in great shape as far as that's concerned.

Happy: And the beauty of it is, Biff, it wouldn't be like a business. We'd be out playin' ball again . . .

Biff: enthused: Yeah, that's . . .

Willy: Million-dollar . . .

Happy: And you wouldn't get fed up with it, Biff. It'd be the family again. There'd be the old honor, and comradeship, and if you wanted to go off for a swim or somethin'—well, you'd do it! Without some smart cooky gettin' up ahead of you!

Willy: Lick the world! You guys together could absolutely lick the civilized world.

Biff: I'll see Oliver tomorrow. Hap, if we could work that out . . .

Linda: Maybe things are beginning to—

Willy: wildly enthused, to Linda: Stop interrupting! *To Biff:* But don't wear sport jacket and slacks when you see Oliver.

Biff: No, I'll—

Willy: A business suit, and talk as little as possible, and don't crack any jokes.

Biff: He did like me. Always liked me.

Linda: He loved you!

Willy: to Linda: Will you stop! *To Biff:* Walk in very serious. You are not applying for a boy's job. Money is to pass. Be quiet, fine, and serious. Everybody likes a kidder, but nobody lends him money.

Happy: I'll try to get some myself, Biff. I'm sure I can.

Willy: I see great things for you kids, I think your troubles are over. But remember, start big and you'll end big. Ask for fifteen. How much you gonna ask for?

Biff: Gee, I don't know—

Willy: And don't say "Gee." "Gee" is a boy's word. A man walking in for fifteen thousand dollars does not say "Gee!"

Biff: Ten, I think, would be top though.

Willy: Don't be so modest. You always started too low. Walk in with a big laugh. Don't look worried. Start off with a couple of your good stories to lighten things up. It's not what you say, it's how you say it—because personality always wins the day.

Linda: Oliver always thought the highest of him—

Willy: Will you let me talk?

Biff: Don't yell at her, Pop, will ya?

Willy: angrily: I was talking, wasn't I?

Biff: I don't like you yelling at her all the time, and I'm tellin' you, that's all.

Willy: What're you, takin' over this house?

Linda: Willy—

Willy: turning on her: Don't take his side all the time, goddammit!

Biff: furiously: Stop yelling at her!

Willy: suddenly pulling on his cheek, beaten down, guilt ridden: Give my best to Bill Oliver—he may remember me. *He exits through the living-room doorway.*

Linda: her voice subdued: What'd you have to start that for? *Biff turns away.* You see how sweet he was as soon as you talked hopefully? *She goes over to Biff.* Come up and say good night to him. Don't let him go to bed that way.

Happy: Come on, Biff, let's buck him up.

Linda: Please, dear. Just say good night. It takes so little to make him happy. Come. *She goes through the living-room doorway, calling upstairs from within the living-room:* Your pajamas are hanging in the bathroom, Willy!

Happy: looking toward where Linda went out: What a woman! They broke the mold when they made her. You know that, Biff?

Biff: He's off salary. My God, working on commission!

Happy: Well, let's face it: he's no hot-shot selling man. Except that sometimes, you have to admit, he's a sweet personality.

Biff: deciding: Lend me ten bucks, will ya? I want to buy some new ties.

Happy: I'll take you to a place I know. Beautiful stuff. Wear one of my striped shirts tomorrow.

Biff: She got gray. Mom got awful old. Gee, I'm gonna go in to Oliver tomorrow and knock him for a—

Happy: Come on up. Tell that to Dad. Let's give him a whirl. Come on.

Biff: steamed up: You know, with ten thousand bucks, boy!

Happy: as they go into the living-room: That's the talk, Biff, that's the first time I've heard the old confidence out of you! *From within the living-room, fading off:* You're gonna live with me, kid, and any babe you want just say the word . . . *The last lines are hardly heard. They are mounting the stairs to their parents' bedroom.*

Linda: entering her bedroom and addressing Willy, who is in the bathroom. She is straightening the bed for him: Can you do anything about the shower? It drips.

Willy: from the bathroom: All of a sudden everything falls to pieces! Goddam plumbing, oughta be sued, those people. I hardly finished putting it in and the thing . . . *His words rumble off.*

Linda: I'm just wondering if Oliver will remember him. You think he might?

Willy: coming out of the bathroom in his pajamas: Remember him? What's the matter with you, you crazy? If he'd've stayed with Oliver he'd be on top by now! Wait'll Oliver gets a look at him. You don't know the average caliber any more. The average young man today—*he is getting into bed*—is got a caliber of zero. Greatest thing in the world for him was to bum around.

Biff and Happy enter the bedroom. Slight pause.

Willy: stops short, looking at Biff: Glad to hear it, boy.

Happy: He wanted to say good night to you, sport.

Willy: to Biff: Yeah. Knock him dead, boy. What'd you want to tell me?

Biff: Just take it easy, Pop. Good night. *He turns to go.*

Willy: unable to resist: And if anything falls off the desk while you're talking to him—like a package or something—don't you pick it up. They have office boys for that.

Linda: I'll make a big breakfast—

Willy: Will you let me finish? *To Biff:* Tell him you were in the business in the West. Not farm work.

Biff: All right, Dad.

Linda: I think everything—

Willy: going right through her speech: And don't undersell yourself. No less than fifteen thousand dollars.

Biff: unable to bear him: Okay. Good night, Mom. *He starts moving.*

Willy: Because you got a greatness in you, Biff, remember that. You got all kinds a greatness . . . *He lies back, exhausted. Biff walks out.*

Linda: calling after Biff: Sleep well, darling!

Happy: I'm gonna get married, Mom. I wanted to tell you.

Linda: Go to sleep, dear.

Happy: going: I just wanted to tell you.

Willy: Keep up the good work. *Happy exits.* God . . . remember that Ebbets Field[3] game? The championship of the city?

Linda: Just rest. Should I sing to you?

Willy: Yeah. Sing to me. *Linda hums a soft lullaby.* When that team came out— he was the tallest, remember?

Linda: Oh, yes. And in gold.

Biff enters the darkened kitchen, takes a cigarette, and leaves the house. He comes downstage into a golden pool of light. He smokes, staring at the night.

Willy: Like a young god. Hercules—something like that. And the sun, the sun all around him. Remember how he waved to me? Right up from the field, with the representatives of three colleges standing by? And the buyers I brought, and the cheers when he came out—Loman, Loman, Loman! God Almighty, he'll be great yet. A star like that, magnificent, can never really fade away!

The light on Willy is fading. The gas heater begins to glow through the kitchen wall, near the stairs, a blue flame beneath red coils.

Linda: timidly: Willy dear, what has he got against you?

Willy: I'm so tired. Don't talk any more.

Biff slowly returns to the kitchen. He stops, stares toward the heater.

Linda: Will you ask Howard to let you work in New York?

Willy: First thing in the morning. Everything'll be all right.

---

[3] Home of the Brooklyn Dodgers at the time *Death of a Salesman* was written.

Biff reaches behind the heater and draws out a length of rubber tubing. He is horrified and turns his head toward Willy's room, still dimly lit, from which the strains of Linda's desperate but monotonous humming rise.

Willy: staring through the window into the moonlight: Gee, look at the moon moving between the buildings!

Biff wraps the tubing around his hand and quickly goes up the stairs.
  Curtain

ACT TWO

Music is heard, gay and bright. The curtain rises as the music fades away. Willy, in shirt sleeves, is sitting at the kitchen table, sipping coffee, his hat in his lap. Linda is filling his cup when she can.

Willy: Wonderful coffee. Meal in itself.
Linda: Can I make you some eggs?
Willy: No. Take a breath.
Linda: You look so rested, dear.
Willy: I slept like a dead one. First time in months. Imagine, sleeping till ten on a Tuesday morning. Boys left nice and early, heh?
Linda: They were out of here by eight o'clock.
Willy: Good work!
Linda: It was so thrilling to see them leaving together. I can't get over the shaving lotion in this house!
Willy: smiling: Mmm—
Linda: Biff was very changed this morning. His whole attitude seemed to be hopeful. He couldn't wait to get downtown to see Oliver.
Willy: He's heading for a change. There's no question, there simply are certain men that take longer to get—solidified. How did he dress?
Linda: His blue suit. He's so handsome in that suit. He could be a—anything in that suit!

Willy gets up from the table. Linda holds his jacket for him.

Willy: There's no question, no question at all. Gee, on the way home tonight I'd like to buy some seeds.
Linda: laughing: That'd be wonderful. But not enough sun gets back there. Nothing'll grow any more.
Willy: You wait, kid, before it's all over we're gonna get a little place out in the country, and I'll raise some vegetables, a couple of chickens . . .
Linda: You'll do it yet, dear.

Willy walks out of his jacket. Linda follows him.

Willy: And they'll get married, and come for a weekend. I'd build a little guest
  house. 'Cause I got so many fine tools, all I'd need would be a little lumber
  and some peace of mind.

Linda: joyfully: I sewed the lining . . .

Willy: I could build two guest houses, so they'd both come. Did he decide how
  much he's going to ask Oliver for?

Linda: getting him into the jacket: He didn't mention it, but I imagine ten or
  fifteen thousand. You going to talk to Howard today?

Willy: Yeah. I'll put it to him straight and simple. He'll just have to take me off
  the road.

Linda: And Willy, don't forget to ask for a little advance, because we've got the
  insurance premium. It's the grace period now.

Willy: That's a hundred . . .?

Linda: A hundred and eight, sixty-eight. Because we're a little short again.

Willy: Why are we short?

Linda: Well, you had the motor job on the car . . .

Willy: That goddam Studebaker!

Linda: And you got one more payment on the refrigerator . . .

Willy: But it just broke again!

Linda: Well, it's old, dear.

Willy: I told you we should've bought a well-advertised machine. Charley
  bought a General Electric and it's twenty years old and it's still good, that
  son-of-a-bitch.

Linda: But, Willy—

Willy: Whoever heard of a Hastings refrigerator? Once in my life I would like
  to own something outright before it's broken! I'm always in a race with the
  junkyard! I just finished paying for the car and it's on its last legs. The
  refrigerator consumes belts like a goddam maniac. They time those things.
  They time them so when you finally paid for them, they're used up.

Linda: buttoning up his jacket as he unbuttons it: All told, about two hundred
  dollars would carry us, dear. But that includes the last payment on the
  mortgage. After this payment, Willy, the house belongs to us.

Willy: It's twenty-five years!

Linda: Biff was nine years old when we bought it.

Willy: Well, that's a great thing. To weather a twenty-five year mortgage is—

Linda: It's an accomplishment.

Willy: All the cement, the lumber, the reconstruction I put in this house! There
  ain't a crack to be found in it any more.

Linda: Well, it served its purpose.

Willy: What purpose? Some stranger'll come along, move in, and that's that. If
  only Biff would take this house, and raise a family . . . *He starts to go.*
  Good-by, I'm late.

Linda: suddenly remembering: Oh, I forgot! You're supposed to meet them for dinner.

Willy: Me?

Linda: At Frank's Chop House on Forty-eighth near Sixth Avenue.

Willy: Is that so! How about you?

Linda: No, just the three of you. They're gonna blow you to a big meal!

Willy: Don't say! Who thought of that?

Linda: Biff came to me this morning, Willy, and he said, "Tell Dad, we want to blow him to a big meal." Be there six o'clock. You and your two boys are going to have dinner.

Willy: Gee whiz! That's really somethin'. I'm gonna knock Howard for a loop, kid. I'll get an advance, and I'll come home with a New York job. Goddammit, now I'm gonna do it!

Linda: Oh, that's the spirit, Willy!

Willy: I will never get behind a wheel the rest of my life!

Linda: It's changing, Willy, I can feel it changing!

Willy: Beyond a question. G'by, I'm late. *He starts to go again.*

Linda: calling after him as she runs to the kitchen table for a handkerchief: You got your glasses?

Willy: feels for them, then comes back in: Yeah, yeah, got my glasses.

Linda: giving him the handkerchief: And a handkerchief.

Willy: Yeah, handkerchief.

Linda: And your saccharine?

Willy: Yeah, my saccharine.

Linda: Be careful on the subway stairs.

She kisses him, and a silk stocking is seen hanging from her hand. Willy notices it.

Willy: Will you stop mending stockings? At least while I'm in the house. It gets me nervous. I can't tell you. Please.

Linda hides the stocking in her hand as she follows Willy across the forestage in front of the house.

Linda: Remember, Frank's Chop House.

Willy: passing the apron: Maybe beets would grow out there.

Linda: laughing: But you tried so many times.

Willy: Yeah. Well, don't work hard today. *He disappears around the right corner of the house.*

Linda: Be careful!

As Willy vanishes, Linda waves to him. Suddenly the phone rings. She runs across the stage and into the kitchen and lifts it.

Linda: Hello? Oh, Biff! I'm so glad you called, I just . . . Yes, sure, I just told him. Yes, he'll be there for dinner at six o'clock, I didn't forget. Listen, I was just dying to tell you. You know that little rubber pipe I told you about? That he connected to the gas heater? I finally decided to go down the cellar this morning and take it away and destroy it. But it's gone! Imagine? He took it away himself, it isn't there! *She listens.* When? Oh, then you took it. Oh— nothing, it's just that I'd hoped he'd taken it away himself. Oh, I'm not worried, darling, because this morning he left in such high spirits, it was like the old days! I'm not afraid any more. Did Mr. Oliver see you? . . . Well, you wait there then. And make a nice impression on him, darling. Just don't perspire too much before you see him. And have a nice time with Dad. He may have big news too! . . . That's right, a New York job. And be sweet to him tonight, dear. Be loving to him. Because he's only a little boat looking for a harbor. *She is trembling with sorrow and joy.* Oh, that's wonderful, Biff, you'll save his life. Thanks, darling. Just put your arm around him when he comes into the restaurant. Give him a smile. That's the boy . . . Good-by, dear. . . . You got your comb? . . . That's fine. Good-by, Biff dear.

In the middle of her speech, Howard Wagner, thirty-six, wheels in a small typewriter table on which is a wire-recording machine[4] and proceeds to plug it in. This is on the left forestage. Light slowly fades on Linda as it rises on Howard. Howard is intent on threading the machine and only glances over his shoulder as Willy appears.

Willy: Pst! Pst!
Howard: Hello, Willy, come in.
Willy: Like to have a little talk with you, Howard.
Howard: Sorry to keep you waiting. I'll be with you in a minute.
Willy: What's that, Howard?
Howard: Didn't you ever see one of these? Wire recorder.
Willy: Oh. Can we talk a minute?
Howard: Records things. Just got delivery yesterday. Been driving me crazy, the most terrific machine I ever saw in my life. I was up all night with it.
Willy: What do you do with it?
Howard: I bought it for dictation, but you can do anything with it. Listen to this. I had it home last night. Listen to what I picked up. The first one is my daughter. Get this. *He flicks the switch and "Roll out the Barrel!" is heard being whistled.* Listen to that kid whistle.
Willy: That is lifelike, isn't it?
Howard: Seven years old. Get that tone.
Willy: Ts, ts. Like to ask a little favor if you . . .

The whistling breaks off, and the voice of Howard's daughter is heard.

His Daughter: "Now you, Daddy."
Howard: She's crazy for me! *Again the same song is whistled.* That's me! Ha! *He winks.*
Willy: You're very good!

The whistling breaks off again. The machine runs silent for a moment.

Howard: Sh! Get this now, this is my son.
His Son: "The capital of Alabama is Montgomery; the capital of Arizona is Phoenix; the capital of Arkansas is Little Rock; the capital of California is Sacramento . . ." *and on, and on.*
Howard: holding up five fingers: Five years old, Willy!
Willy: He'll make an announcer some day!

[4] Precursor of the modern tape recorder.

His Son: continuing: "The capital . . ."

Howard: Get that—alphabetical order! *The machine breaks off suddenly.* Wait a minute. The maid kicked the plug out.

Willy: It certainly is a—

Howard: Sh, for God's sake!

His Son: "It's nine o'clock, Bulova watch time. So I have to go to sleep."

Willy: That really is—

Howard: Wait a minute! The next is my wife.

They wait.

Howard's Voice: "Go on, say something." *Pause.* "Well, you gonna talk?"

His Wife: "I can't think of anything."

Howard's Voice: "Well, talk—it's turning."

His Wife: shyly, beaten: "Hello." *Silence.* "Oh, Howard, I can't talk into this . . ."

Howard: snapping the machine off: That was my wife.

Willy: That is a wonderful machine. Can we—

Howard: I tell you, Willy, I'm gonna take my camera, and my bandsaw, and all my hobbies, and out they go. This is the most fascinating relaxation I ever found.

Willy: I think I'll get one myself.

Howard: Sure, they're only a hundred and a half. You can't do without it. Supposing you wanna hear Jack Benny, see? But you can't be at home at that hour. So you tell the maid to turn the radio on when Jack Benny comes on, and this automatically goes on with the radio . . .

Willy: And when you come home you . . .

Howard: You can come home twelve o'clock, one o'clock, any time you like, and you get yourself a Coke and sit yourself down, throw the switch, and there's Jack Benny's program in the middle of the night!

Willy: I'm definitely going to get one. Because lots of time I'm on the road, and I think to myself, what I must be missing on the radio!

Howard: Don't you have a radio in the car?

Willy: Well, yeah, but who ever thinks of turning it on?

Howard: Say, aren't you supposed to be in Boston?

Willy: That's what I want to talk to you about, Howard. You got a minute? *He draws a chair in from the wing.*

Howard: What happened? What're you doing here?

Willy: Well . . .

Howard: You didn't crack up again, did you?

Willy: Oh, no. No . . .

Howard: Geez, you had me worried there for a minute. What's the trouble?

Willy: Well, tell you the truth, Howard, I've come to the decision that I'd rather not travel any more.

Howard: Not travel! Well, what'll you do?

Willy: Remember, Christmas time, when you had the party here? You said you'd try to think of some spot for me here in town.

Howard: With us?

Willy: Well, sure.

Howard: Oh, yeah, yeah. I remember. Well, I couldn't think of anything for you, Willy.

Willy: I tell ya, Howard. The kids are all grown up, y'know. I don't need much any more. If I could take home—well, sixty-five dollars a week, I could swing it.

Howard: Yeah, but Willy, see I—

Willy: I tell ya why, Howard. Speaking frankly and between the two of us, y'know—I'm just a little tired.

Howard: Oh, I could understand that, Willy. But you're a road man, Willy, and we do a road business. We've only got a half-dozen salesmen on the floor here.

Willy: God knows, Howard, I never asked a favor of any man. But I was with the firm when your father used to carry you in here in his arms.

Howard: I know that, Willy, but—

Willy: Your father came to me the day you were born and asked me what I thought of the name of Howard, may he rest in peace.

Howard: I appreciate that, Willy, but there just is no spot here for you. If I had a spot I'd slam you right in, but I just don't have a single solitary spot.

He looks for his lighter. Willy has picked it up and gives it to him. Pause.

Willy: with increasing anger: Howard, all I need to set my table is fifty dollars a week.

Howard: But where am I going to put you, kid?

Willy: Look, it isn't a question of whether I can sell merchandise, is it?

Howard: No, but it's a business, kid, and everybody's gotta pull his own weight.

Willy: desperately: Just let me tell you a story, Howard—

Howard: 'Cause you gotta admit, business is business.

Willy: angrily: Business is definitely business, but just listen for a minute. You don't understand this. When I was a boy—eighteen, nineteen—I was already on the road. And there was a question in my mind as to whether selling had a future for me. Because in those days I had a yearning to go to Alaska. See, there were three gold strikes in one month in Alaska, and I felt like going out. Just for the ride, you might say.

Howard: barely interested: Don't say.

Willy: Oh, yeah, my father lived many years in Alaska. He was an adventurous man. We've got quite a little streak of self-reliance in our family. I thought I'd go out with my older brother and try to locate him, and maybe settle in the North with the old man. And I was almost decided to go, when I met a salesman in the Parker House. His name was Dave Singleman. And he was eighty-four years old, and he'd drummed merchandise in thirty-one states. And old Dave, he'd go up to his room, y'understand, put on his green velvet slippers—I'll never forget—and pick up his phone and call the buyers, and without ever leaving his room, at the age of eighty-four, he made his living. And when I saw that, I realized that selling was the greatest career a man could want. 'Cause what could be more satisfying than to be able to go, at the age of eighty-four, into twenty or thirty different cities, and pick up a phone, and be remembered and loved and helped by so many different people? Do you know? when he died—and by the way he died the death of a salesman, in his green velvet slippers in the smoker of the New York, New Haven and Hartford, going into Boston—when he died, hundreds of salesmen and buyers were at his funeral. Things were sad on a lotta trains for months after that. *He stands up. Howard has not looked at him.* In those days there was personality in it, Howard. There was respect, and comradeship, and gratitude in it. Today, it's all cut and dried, and there's no chance for bringing friendship to bear—or personality. You see what I mean? They don't know me any more.

Howard: moving away, to the right: That's just the thing, Willy.

Willy: If I had forty dollars a week—that's all I'd need. Forty dollars, Howard.

Howard: Kid, I can't take blood from a stone. I—

Willy: desperation is on him now: Howard, the year Al Smith[5] was nominated, your father came to me and—

Howard: starting to go off: I've got to see some people, kid.

Willy: stopping him: I'm talking about your father! There were promises made across this desk! You mustn't tell me you've got people to see—I put thirty-four years into this firm, Howard, and now I can't pay my insurance! You can't eat the orange and throw the peel away—a man is not a piece of fruit! *After a pause:* Now pay attention. Your father—in 1928 I had a big year. I averaged a hundred and seventy dollars a week in commissions.

Howard: impatiently: Now, Willy, you never averaged—

Willy: banging his hand on the desk: I averaged a hundred and seventy dollars a week in the year of 1928! And your father came to me—or rather, I was in the office here—it was right over this desk—and he put his hand on my shoulder—

Howard: getting up: You'll have to excuse me, Willy, I gotta see some people. Pull yourself together. *Going out:* I'll be back in a little while.

On Howard's exit, the light on his chair grows very bright and strange.

Willy: Pull myself together! What the hell did I say to him? My God, I was yelling at him! How could I! *Willy breaks off, staring at the light, which occupies the chair, animating it. He approaches this chair, standing across the desk from it.* Frank, Frank, don't you remember what you told me that time? How you put your hand on my shoulder, and Frank . . . *He leans on the desk and as he speaks the dead man's name he accidentally switches on the recorder, and instantly*

Howard's Son: " . . . of New York is Albany. The capital of Ohio is Cincinnati, the capital of Rhode Island is . . ." *The recitation continues.*

Willy: leaping away with fright, shouting: Ha! Howard! Howard! Howard!

Howard: rushing in: What happened?

---

[5] Alfred Emanuel Smith (1873–1944), American politician, governor of New York, and presidential candidate in 1928.

Willy: pointing at the machine, which continues nasally, childishly, with the capital cities: Shut it off! Shut it off!

Howard: pulling the plug out: Look, Willy . . .

Willy: pressing his hands to his eyes: I gotta get myself some coffee. I'll get some coffee . . .

Willy starts to walk out. Howard stops him.

Howard: rolling up the cord: Willy, look . . .

Willy: I'll go to Boston.

Howard: Willy, you can't go to Boston for us.

Willy: Why can't I go?

Howard: I don't want you to represent us. I've been meaning to tell you for a long time now.

Willy: Howard, are you firing me?

Howard: I think you need a good long rest, Willy.

Willy: Howard—

Howard: And when you feel better, come back, and we'll see if we can work something out.

Willy: But I gotta earn money, Howard. I'm in no position to—

Howard: Where are your sons? Why don't your sons give you a hand?

Willy: They're working on a very big deal.

Howard: This is no time for false pride, Willy. You go to your sons and you tell them that you're tired. You've got two great boys, haven't you?

Willy: Oh, no question, no question, but in the meantime . . .

Howard: Then that's that, heh?

Willy: All right, I'll go to Boston tomorrow.

Howard: No, no.

Willy: I can't throw myself on my sons. I'm not a cripple!

Howard: Look, kid, I'm busy this morning.

Willy: grasping Howard's arm: Howard, you've got to let me go to Boston!

Howard: hard, keeping himself under control: I've got a line of people to see this morning. Sit down, take five minutes, and pull yourself together, and then go home, will ya? I need the office, Willy. *He starts to go, turns, remembering the recorder, starts to push off the table holding the recorder.* Oh, yeah. Whenever you can this week, stop by and drop off the samples. You'll feel better, Willy, and then come back and we'll talk. Pull yourself together, kid, there's people outside.

Howard exits, pushing the table off left. Willy stares into space, exhausted. Now the music is heard—Ben's music—first distantly, then closer, closer. As Willy speaks, Ben enters from the right. He carries valise and umbrella.

Willy: Oh, Ben, how did you do it? What is the answer? Did you wind up the Alaska deal already?

Ben: Doesn't take much time if you know what you're doing. Just a short business trip. Boarding ship in an hour. Wanted to say good-by.

Willy: Ben, I've got to talk to you.

Ben: glancing at his watch: Haven't the time, William.

Willy: crossing the apron to Ben: Ben, nothing's working out. I don't know what to do.

Ben: Now, look here, William. I've bought timberland in Alaska and I need a man to look after things for me.

Willy: God, timberland! Me and my boys in those grand outdoors!

Ben: You've a new continent at your doorstep, William. Get out of these cities, they're full of talk and time payments and courts of law. Screw on your fists and you can fight for a fortune up there.

Willy: Yes, yes! Linda, Linda!

Linda enters as of old, with the wash.

Linda: Oh, you're back?

Ben: I haven't much time.

Willy: No, wait! Linda, he's got a proposition for me in Alaska.

Linda: But you've got—*To Ben:* He's got a beautiful job here.

Willy: But in Alaska, kid, I could—

Linda: You're doing well enough, Willy!

Ben: to Linda: Enough for what, my dear?

Linda: frightened of Ben and angry at him: Don't say those things to him! Enough to be happy right here, right now. *To Willy, while Ben laughs:* Why must everybody conquer the world? You're well liked, and the boys love you, and someday—*to Ben*—why, old man Wagner told him just the other day that if he keeps it up he'll be a member of the firm, didn't he, Willy?

Willy: Sure, sure. I am building something with this firm. Ben, and if a man is building something he must be on the right track, mustn't he?

Ben: What are you building? Lay your hand on it. Where is it?

Willy: hesitantly: That's true, Linda, there's nothing.

Linda: Why? *To Ben:* There's a man eighty-four years old—

Willy: That's right, Ben, that's right. When I look at that man I say, what is there to worry about?

Ben: Bah!

Willy: It's true, Ben. All he has to do is go into any city, pick up the phone, and he's making his living and you know why?

Ben: picking up his valise: I've got to go.

Willy: holding Ben back: Look at this boy!

Biff, in his high school sweater, enters carrying suitcase. Happy carries Biff's shoulder guards, gold helmet, and football pants.

Willy: Without a penny to his name, three great universities are begging for him, and from there the sky's the limit, because it's not what you do, Ben. It's who you know and the smile on your face! It's contacts, Ben, contacts! The whole wealth of Alaska passes over the lunch table at the Commodore Hotel, and that's the wonder, the wonder of this country, that a man can end with diamonds here on the basis of being liked! *He turns to Biff.* And that's why when you get out on that field today it's important. Because thousands of people will be rooting for you and loving you. *To Ben, who has again begun to leave:* And Ben! when he walks into a business office his name will sound out like a bell and all the doors will open to him! I've seen it, Ben, I've seen it a thousand times! You can't feel it with your hand like timber, but it's there!

Ben: Good-by, William.

Willy: Ben, am I right? Don't you think I'm right? I value your advice.

Ben: There's a new continent at your doorstep, William. You could walk out rich. Rich! *He is gone.*

Willy: We'll do it here, Ben! You hear me? We're gonna do it here!

Young Bernard rushes in. The gay music of the Boys is heard.

Bernard: Oh, gee, I was afraid you left already!

Willy: Why? What time is it?

Bernard: It's half-past one!

Willy: Well, come on, everybody! Ebbets Field next stop! Where's the pennants? *He rushes through the wall-line of the kitchen and out into the living-room.*

Linda: to Biff: Did you pack fresh underwear?

Biff: who has been limbering up: I want to go!

Bernard: Biff, I'm carrying your helmet, ain't I?

Happy: No, I'm carrying the helmet.

Bernard: Oh, Biff, you promised me.

Happy: I'm carrying the helmet.

Bernard: How am I going to get in the locker room?

Linda: Let him carry the shoulder guards. *She puts her coat and hat on in the kitchen.*

Bernard: Can I, Biff? 'Cause I told everybody I'm going to be in the locker room.

Happy: In Ebbets Field it's the clubhouse.

Bernard: I meant the clubhouse. Biff!

Happy: Biff!

Biff: grandly, after a slight pause: Let him carry the shoulder guards.

Happy: as he gives Bernard the shoulder guards: Stay close to us now.

Willy rushes in with the pennants.

Willy: handing them out: Everybody wave when Biff comes out on the field. *Happy and Bernard run off.* You set now, boy?

The music has died away.

Biff: Ready to go, Pop. Every muscle is ready.

Willy: at the edge of the apron: You realize what this means?

Biff: That's right, Pop.

Willy: feeling Biff's muscles: You're comin' home this afternoon captain of the All-Scholastic Championship Team of the City of New York.

Biff: I got it, Pop. And remember, pal, when I take off my helmet, that
touchdown is for you.

Willy: Let's go! *He is starting out, with his arm around Biff, when Charley enters, as
of old, in knickers.* I got no room for you, Charley.

Charley: Room? For what?

Willy: In the car.

Charley: You goin' for a ride? I wanted to shoot some casino.

Willy: furiously: Casino! *Incredulously:* Don't you realize what today is?

Linda: Oh, he knows, Willy. He's just kidding you.

Willy: That's nothing to kid about!

Charley: No, Linda, what's goin' on?

Linda: He's playing in Ebbets Field.

Charley: Baseball in this weather?

Willy: Don't talk to him. Come on, come on! *He is pushing them out.*

Charley: Wait a minute, didn't you hear the news?

Willy: What?

Charley: Don't you listen to the radio? Ebbets Field just blew up.

Willy: You go to hell! *Charley laughs. Pushing them out.* Come on, come on!
We're late.

Charley: as they go: Knock a homer, Biff, knock a homer!

Willy: the last to leave, turning to Charley: I don't think that was funny, Charley.
This is the greatest day of his life.

Charley: Willy, when are you going to grow up?

Willy: Yeah, heh? When this game is over, Charley, you'll be laughing out of
the other side of your face. They'll be calling him another Red Grange.[6]
Twenty-five thousand a year.

Charley: kidding: Is that so?

Willy: Yeah, that's so.

Charley: Well, then, I'm sorry, Willy. But tell me something.

Willy: What?

Charley: Who is Red Grange?

Willy: Put up your hands. Goddam you, put up your hands!

*Charley, chuckling, shakes his head and walks away, around the left corner of the stage.
Willy follows him. The music rises to a mocking frenzy.*

Willy: Who the hell do you think you are, better than everybody else? You
don't know everything, you big, ignorant, stupid . . . Put up your hands!

*Light rises, on the right side of the forestage, on a small table in the reception room of
Charley's office. Traffic sounds are heard. Bernard, now mature, sits whistling to himself.
A pair of tennis rackets and an overnight bag are on the floor beside him.*

---

[6] Harold Edward Grange (b. 1903), legendary
American football player at the University of
Illinois and with the Chicago Bears.

Willy: offstage: What are you walking away for? Don't walk away! If you're going to say something say it to my face! I know you laugh at me behind my back. You'll laugh out of the other side of your goddam face after this game. Touchdown! Touchdown! Eighty thousand people! Touchdown! Right between the goal posts.

Bernard is a quiet, earnest, but self-assured young man. Willy's voice is coming from right upstage now. Bernard lowers his feet off the table and listens. Jenny, his father's secretary, enters.

Jenny: distressed: Say, Bernard, will you go out in the hall?
Bernard: What is that noise? Who is it?
Jenny: Mr. Loman. He just got off the elevator.
Bernard: getting up: Who's he arguing with?
Jenny: Nobody. There's nobody with him. I can't deal with him any more, and your father gets all upset everytime he comes. I've got a lot of typing to do, and your father's waiting to sign it. Will you see him?
Willy: entering: Touchdown! Touch—*He sees Jenny.* Jenny, Jenny, good to see you. How're ya? Workin'? Or still honest?
Jenny: Fine. How've you been feeling?
Willy: Not much any more, Jenny. Ha, ha! *He is surprised to see the rackets.*
Bernard: Hello, Uncle Willy.
Willy: almost shocked: Bernard! Well, look who's here! *He comes quickly, guiltily, to Bernard and warmly shakes his hand.*
Bernard: How are you? Good to see you.
Willy: What are you doing here?
Bernard: Oh, just stopped by to see Pop. Get off my feet till my train leaves. I'm going to Washington in a few minutes.
Willy: Is he in?
Bernard: Yes, he's in his office with the accountant. Sit down.
Willy: sitting down: What're you going to do in Washington?
Bernard: Oh, just a case I've got there, Willy.
Willy: That so? *Indicating the rackets:* You going to play tennis there?
Bernard: I'm staying with a friend who's got a court.
Willy: Don't say. His own tennis court. Must be fine people, I bet.
Bernard: They are, very nice. Dad tells me Biff's in town.
Willy: with a big smile: Yeah, Biff's in. Working on a very big deal, Bernard.
Bernard: What's Biff doing?
Willy: Well, he's been doing very big things in the West. But he decided to establish himself here. Very big. We're having dinner. Did I hear your wife had a boy?
Bernard: That's right. Our second.
Willy: Two boys! What do you know!
Bernard: What kind of a deal has Biff got?
Willy: Well, Bill Oliver—very big sporting-goods man—he wants Biff very badly. Called him in from the West. Long distance, carte blanche, special deliveries. Your friends have their own private tennis court?

Bernard: You still with the old firm, Willy?

Willy: after a pause: I'm—I'm overjoyed to see how you made the grade, Bernard, overjoyed. It's an encouraging thing to see a young man really— really—Looks very good for Biff—very—*He breaks off, then:* Bernard—*He is so full of emotion, he breaks off again.*

Bernard: What is it, Willy?

Willy: small and alone: What—what's the secret?

Bernard: What secret?

Willy: How—how did you? Why didn't he ever catch on?

Bernard: I wouldn't know that, Willy.

Willy: confidentially, desperately: You were his friend, his boyhood friend. There's something I don't understand about it. His life ended after that Ebbets Field game. From the age of seventeen nothing good ever happened to him.

Bernard: He never trained himself for anything.

Willy: But he did, he did. After high school he took so many correspondence courses. Radio mechanics; television; God knows what, and never made the slightest mark.

Bernard: taking off his glasses: Willy, do you want to talk candidly?

Willy: rising, faces Bernard: I regard you as a very brilliant man, Bernard. I value your advice.

Bernard: Oh, the hell with the advice, Willy. I couldn't advise you. There's just one thing I've always wanted to ask you. When he was supposed to graduate, and the math teacher flunked him—

Willy: Oh, that son-of-a-bitch ruined his life.

Bernard: Yeah, but, Willy, all he had to do was go to summer school and make up that subject.

Willy: That's right, that's right.

Bernard: Did you tell him not to go to summer school?

Willy: Me? I begged him to go. I ordered him to go!

Bernard: Then why wouldn't he go?

Willy: Why? Why! Bernard, that question has been trailing me like a ghost for the last fifteen years. He flunked the subject, and laid down and died like a hammer hit him!

Bernard: Take it easy, kid.

Willy: Let me talk to you—I got nobody to talk to. Bernard, Bernard, was it my fault? Y'see? It keeps going around in my mind, maybe I did something to him. I got nothing to give him.

Bernard: Don't take it so hard.

Willy: Why did he lay down? What is the story there? You were his friend!

Bernard: Willy, I remember, it was June, and our grades came out. And he'd flunked math.

Willy: That son-of-a-bitch!

Bernard: No, it wasn't right then. Biff just got very angry, I remember, and he was ready to enroll in summer school.

Willy: surprised: He was?

Bernard: He wasn't beaten by it at all. But then, Willy, he disappeared from the block for almost a month. And I got the idea that he'd gone up to New England to see you. Did he have a talk with you then?

Willy stares in silence.

Bernard: Willy?

Willy: *with a strong edge of resentment in his voice:* Yeah, he came to Boston. What about it?

Bernard: Well, just that when he came back—I'll never forget this, it always mystifies me. Because I'd thought so well of Biff, even though he'd always taken advantage of me. I loved him, Willy, y'know? And he came back after that month and took his sneakers—remember those sneakers with "University of Virginia" printed on them? He was so proud of those, wore them every day. And he took them down in the cellar, and burned them up in the furnace. We had a fist fight. It lasted at least half an hour. Just the two of us, punching each other down the cellar, and crying right through it. I've often thought of how strange it was that I knew he'd given up his life. What happened in Boston, Willy?

Willy looks at him as at an intruder.

Bernard: I just bring it up because you asked me.

Willy: *angrily:* Nothing. What do you mean, "What happened?" What's that got to do with anything?

Bernard: Well, don't get sore.

Willy: What are you trying to do, blame it on me? If a boy lays down is that my fault?

Bernard: Now, Willy, don't get—

Willy: Well, don't—don't talk to me that way! What does that mean, "What happened?"

Charley enters. He is in his vest, and he carries a bottle of bourbon.

Charley: Hey, you're going to miss that train. *He waves the bottle.*

Bernard: Yeah, I'm going. *He takes the bottle.* Thanks, Pop. *He picks up his rackets and bag.* Good-by, Willy, and don't worry about it. You know, "If at first you don't succeed . . ."

Willy: Yes, I believe in that.

Bernard: But sometimes, Willy, it's better for a man just to walk away.

Willy: Walk away?

Bernard: That's right.

Willy: But if you can't walk away?

Bernard: *after a slight pause:* I guess that's when it's tough. *Extending his hand:* Good-by, Willy.

Willy: *shaking Bernard's hand:* Good-by, boy.

Charley: *an arm on Bernard's shoulder:* How do you like this kid? Gonna argue a case in front of the Supreme Court.

Bernard: *protesting:* Pop!

Willy: genuinely shocked, pained, and happy: No! The Supreme Court!
Bernard: I gotta run. 'By, Dad!
Charley: Knock 'em dead, Bernard!

Bernard goes off.

Willy: as Charley takes out his wallet: The Supreme Court! And he didn't even
   mention it!
Charley: counting out money on the desk: He don't have to—he's gonna do it.
Willy: And you never told him what to do, did you? You never took any
   interest in him.
Charley: My salvation is that I never took any interest in anything. There's some
   money—fifty dollars. I got an accountant inside.
Willy: Charley, look . . . *With difficulty:* I got my insurance to pay. If you can
   manage it—I need a hundred and ten dollars.

Charley doesn't reply for a moment; merely stops moving.

Willy: I'd draw it from my bank but Linda would know, and I . . .
Charley: Sit down, Willy.
Willy: moving toward the chair: I'm keeping an account of everything, remember.
   I'll pay every penny back. *He sits.*
Charley: Now listen to me, Willy.
Willy: I want you to know I appreciate . . .
Charley: sitting down on the table: Willy, what're you doin'? What the hell is
   goin' on in your head?
Willy: Why? I'm simply . . .
Charley: I offered you a job. You can make fifty dollars a week. And I won't
   send you on the road.
Willy: I've got a job.
Charley: Without pay? What kind of a job is a job without pay? *He rises.* Now,
   look, kid, enough is enough. I'm no genius but I know when I'm being
   insulted.
Willy: Insulted!
Charley: Why don't you want to work for me?
Willy: What's the matter with you? I've got a job.
Charley: Then what're you walkin' in here every week for?
Willy: getting up: Well, if you don't want me to walk in here—
Charley: I am offering you a job.
Willy: I don't want your goddam job!
Charley: When the hell are you going to grow up?
Willy: furiously: You big ignoramus, if you say that to me again I'll rap you
   one! I don't care how big you are! *He's ready to fight.*

Pause.

Charley: kindly, going to him: How much do you need, Willy?

Willy: Charley, I'm strapped, I'm strapped. I don't know what to do. I was just fired.

Charley: Howard fired you?

Willy: That snotnose. Imagine that? I named him. I named him Howard.

Charley: Willy, when're you gonna realize that them things don't mean anything? You named him Howard, but you can't sell that. The only thing you got in this world is what you can sell. And the funny thing is that you're a salesman, and you don't know that.

Willy: I've always tried to think otherwise, I guess. I always felt that if a man was impressive, and well liked, that nothing—

Charley: Why must everybody like you? Who liked J. P. Morgan? Was he impressive? In a Turkish bath he'd look like a butcher. But with his pockets on he was very well liked. Now listen, Willy, I know you don't like me, and nobody can say I'm in love with you, but I'll give you a job because—just for the hell of it, put it that way. Now what do you say?

Willy: I—I just can't work for you, Charley.

Charley: What're you, jealous of me?

Willy: I can't work for you, that's all, don't ask me why.

Charley: angered, takes out more bills: You been jealous of me all your life, you damned fool! Here, pay your insurance. *He puts the money in Willy's hand.*

Willy: I'm keeping strict accounts.

Charley: I've got some work to do. Take care of yourself. And pay your insurance.

Willy: moving to the right: Funny, y'know? After all the highways, and the trains, and the appointments, and the years, you end up worth more dead than alive.

Charley: Willy, nobody's worth nothin' dead. *After a slight pause:* Did you hear what I said?

Willy stands still, dreaming.

Charley: Willy!

Willy: Apologize to Bernard for me when you see him. I didn't mean to argue with him. He's a fine boy. They're all fine boys, and they'll end up big—all of them. Someday they'll all play tennis together. Wish me luck, Charley. He saw Bill Oliver today.

Charley: Good luck.

Willy: on the verge of tears: Charley, you're the only friend I got. Isn't that a remarkable thing? *He goes out.*

Charley: Jesus!

Charley stares after him a moment and follows. All light blacks out. Suddenly raucous music is heard, and a red glow rises behind the screen at right. Stanley, a young waiter, appears, carrying a table, followed by Happy, who is carrying two chairs.

Stanley: putting the table down: That's all right, Mr. Loman, I can handle it myself. *He turns and takes the chairs from Happy and places them at the table.*

Happy: glancing around: Oh, this is better.

Stanley: Sure, in the front there you're in the middle of all kinds a noise. Whenever you got a party, Mr. Loman, you just tell me and I'll put you back here. Y'know, there's a lotta people they don't like it private, because when they go out they like to see a lotta action around them because they're sick and tired to stay in the house by theirself. But I know you, you ain't from Hackensack.[7] You know what I mean?

Happy: sitting down: So how's it coming, Stanley?

Stanley: Ah, it's a dog's life. I only wish during the war they'd a took me in the Army. I coulda been dead by now.

Happy: My brother's back, Stanley.

Stanley: Oh, he come back, heh? From the Far West.

Happy: Yeah, big cattle man, my brother, so treat him right. And my father's coming too.

Stanley: Oh, your father too!

Happy: You got a couple of nice lobsters?

Stanley: Hundred per cent, big.

Happy: I want them with the claws.

Stanley: Don't worry, I don't give you no mice. *Happy laughs.* How about some wine? It'll put a head on the meal.

Happy: No. You remember, Stanley, that recipe I brought you from overseas? With the champagne in it?

Stanley: Oh, yeah, sure. I still got it tacked up yet in the kitchen. But that'll have to cost a buck apiece anyways.

Happy: That's all right.

Stanley: What'd you, hit a number or somethin'?

Happy: No, it's a little celebration. My brother is—I think he pulled off a big deal today. I think we're going into business together.

Stanley: Great! That's the best for you. Because a family business, you know what I mean?—that's the best.

Happy: That's what I think.

Stanley: 'Cause what's the difference? Somebody steals? It's in the family. Know what I mean? *Sotto voce:*[8] Like this bartender here. The boss is goin' crazy what kinda leak he's got in the cash register. You put it in but it don't come out.

Happy: raising his head: Sh!

Stanley: What?

Happy: You notice I wasn't lookin' right or left, was I?

Stanley: No.

Happy: And my eyes are closed.

Stanley: So what's the—?

Happy: Strudel's comin'.

Stanley: catching on, looks around: Ah, no, there's no—

---

[7] City in New Jersey; here meant as an example of a small, industrialized, middle-class town.

[8] Italian: "in a low voice."

He breaks off as a furred, lavishly dressed girl enters and sits at the next table. Both follow her with their eyes.

Stanley: Geez, how'd ya know?

Happy: I got radar or something. *Staring directly at her profile:* Ooooooooo . . . Stanley.

Stanley: I think that's for you, Mr. Loman.

Happy: Look at that mouth. Oh, God. And the binoculars.

Stanley: Geez, you got a life, Mr. Loman.

Happy: Wait on her.

Stanley: going to the girl's table: Would you like a menu, ma'am?

Girl: I'm expecting someone, but I'd like a—

Happy: Why don't you bring her—excuse me, miss, do you mind? I sell champagne, and I'd like you to try my brand. Bring her a champagne, Stanley.

Girl: That's awfully nice of you.

Happy: Don't mention it. It's all company money. *He laughs.*

Girl: That's a charming product to be selling, isn't it?

Happy: Oh, gets to be like everything else. Selling is selling, y'know.

Girl: I suppose.

Happy: You don't happen to sell, do you?

Girl: No, I don't sell.

Happy: Would you object to a compliment from a stranger? You ought to be on a magazine cover.

Girl: looking at him a little archly: I have been.

Stanley comes in with a glass of champagne.

Happy: What'd I say before, Stanley? You see? She's a cover girl.

Stanley: Oh, I could see, I could see.

Happy: to the Girl: What magazine?

Girl: Oh, a lot of them. *She takes the drink.* Thank you.

Happy: You know what they say in France, don't you? "Champagne is the drink of the complexion"—Hya, Biff!

Biff has entered and sits with Happy.

Biff: Hello, kid. Sorry I'm late.

Happy: I just got here. Uh, Miss—?

Girl: Forsythe.

Happy: Miss Forsythe, this is my brother.

Biff: Is Dad here?

Happy: His name is Biff. You might've heard of him. Great football player.

Girl: Really? What team?

Happy: Are you familiar with football?

Girl: No, I'm afraid I'm not.

Happy: Biff is quarterback with the New York Giants.

Girl: Well, that is nice, isn't it? *She drinks.*

Happy: Good health.

Girl: I'm happy to meet you.

Happy: That's my name. Hap. It's really Harold, but at West Point they called me Happy.

Girl: now really impressed: Oh, I see. How do you do? *She turns her profile.*

Biff: Isn't Dad coming?

Happy: You want her?

Biff: Oh, I could never make that.

Happy: I remember the time that idea would never come into your head. Where's the old confidence, Biff?

Biff: I just saw Oliver—

Happy: Wait a minute. I've got to see that old confidence again. Do you want her? She's on call.

Biff: Oh, no. *He turns to look at the Girl.*

Happy: I'm telling you. Watch this. *Turning to the Girl:* Honey? *She turns to him.* Are you busy?

Girl: Well, I am . . . but I could make a phone call.

Happy: Do that, will you, honey? And see if you can get a friend. We'll be here for a while. Biff is one of the greatest football players in the country.

Girl: standing up: Well, I'm certainly happy to meet you.

Happy: Come back soon.

Girl: I'll try.

Happy: Don't try, honey, try hard.

The Girl exits. Stanley follows, shaking his head in bewildered admiration.

Happy: Isn't that a shame now? A beautiful girl like that? That's why I can't get married. There's not a good woman in a thousand. New York is loaded with them, kid!

Biff: Hap, look—

Happy: I told you she was on call!

Biff: strangely unnerved: Cut it out, will ya? I want to say something to you.

Happy: Did you see Oliver?

Biff: I saw him all right. Now look, I want to tell Dad a couple of things and I want you to help me.

Happy: What? Is he going to back you?

Biff: Are you crazy? You're out of your goddam head, you know that?

Happy: Why? What happened?

Biff: breathlessly: I did a terrible thing today, Hap. It's been the strangest day I ever went through. I'm all numb, I swear.

Happy: You mean he wouldn't see you?

Biff: Well, I waited six hours for him, see? All day. Kept sending my name in. Even tried to date his secretary so she'd get me to him, but no soap.

Happy: Because you're not showin' the old confidence, Biff. He remembered you, didn't he?

Biff: stopping Happy with a gesture: Finally, about five o'clock, he comes out. Didn't remember who I was or anything. I felt like such an idiot, Hap.

Happy: Did you tell him my Florida idea?

Biff: He walked away. I saw him for one minute. I got so mad I could've torn the walls down! How the hell did I ever get the idea I was a salesman there? I even believed myself that I'd been a salesman for him! And then he gave me one look and—I realized what a ridiculous lie my whole life has been! We've been talking in a dream for fifteen years. I was a shipping clerk.

Happy: What'd you do?

Biff: with great tension and wonder: Well, he left, see. And the secretary went out. I was all alone in the waiting-room. I don't know what came over me, Hap. The next thing I know I'm in his office—paneled walls, everything. I can't explain it. I—Hap, I took his fountain pen.

Happy: Geez, did he catch you?

Biff: I ran out. I ran down all eleven flights. I ran and ran and ran.

Happy: That was an awful dumb—what'd you do that for?

Biff: agonized: I don't know, I just—wanted to take something, I don't know. You gotta help me, Hap, I'm gonna tell Pop.

Happy: You crazy? What for?

Biff: Hap, he's got to understand that I'm not the man somebody lends that kind of money to. He thinks I've been spiting him all these years and it's eating him up.

Happy: That's just it. You tell him something nice.

Biff: I can't.

Happy: Say you got a lunch date with Oliver tomorrow.

Biff: So what do I do tomorrow?

Happy: You leave the house tomorrow and come back at night and say Oliver is thinking it over. And he thinks it over for a couple of weeks, and gradually it fades away and nobody's the worse.

Biff: But it'll go on forever!

Happy: Dad is never so happy as when he's looking forward to something!

Willy enters.

Happy: Hello, scout!

Willy: Gee, I haven't been here in years!

Stanley has followed Willy in and sets a chair for him. Stanley starts off but Happy stops him.

Happy: Stanley!

Stanley stands by, waiting for an order.

Biff: going to Willy with guilt, as to an invalid: Sit down, Pop. You want a drink?

Willy: Sure, I don't mind.

Biff: Let's get a load on.

Willy: You look worried.

Biff: N-no. *To Stanley:* Scotch all around. Make it doubles.

Stanley: Doubles, right. *He goes.*

Willy: You had a couple already, didn't you?

Biff: Just a couple, yeah.

Willy: Well, what happened, boy? *Nodding affirmatively, with a smile:* Everything go all right?

Biff: takes a breath, then reaches out and grasps Willy's hand: Pai . . . *He is smiling bravely, and Willy is smiling too.* I had an experience today.

Happy: Terrific, Pop.

Willy: That so? What happened?

Biff: high, slightly alcoholic, above the earth: I'm going to tell you everything from first to last. It's been a strange day. *Silence. He looks around, composes himself as best he can, but his breath keeps breaking the rhythm of his voice.* I had to wait quite a while for him, and—

Willy: Oliver?

Biff: Yeah, Oliver. All day, as a matter of cold fact. And a lot of—instances—facts, Pop, facts about my life came back to me. Who was it, Pop? Who ever said I was a salesman with Oliver?

Willy: Well, you were.

Biff: No, Dad, I was a shipping clerk.

Willy: But you were practically—

Biff: with determination: Dad, I don't know who said it first, but I was never a salesman for Bill Oliver.

Willy: What're you talking about?

Biff: Let's hold on to the facts tonight, Pop. We're not going to get anywhere bullin' around. I was a shipping clerk.

Willy: angrily: All right, now listen to me—

Biff: Why don't you let me finish?

Willy: I'm not interested in stories about the past or any crap of that kind because the woods are burning, boys, you understand? There's a big blaze going on all around. I was fired today.

Biff: shocked: How could you be?

Willy: I was fired, and I'm looking for a little good news to tell your mother, because the woman has waited and the woman has suffered. The gist of it is that I haven't got a story left in my head, Biff. So don't give me a lecture about facts and aspects. I am not interested. Now what've you got to say to me?

Stanley enters with three drinks. They wait until he leaves.

Willy: Did you see Oliver?

Biff: Jesus, Dad!

Willy: You mean you didn't go up there?

Happy: Sure he went up there.

Biff: I did. I—saw him. How could they fire you?

Willy: on the edge of his chair: What kind of a welcome did he give you?

Biff: He won't even let you work on commission?

Willy: I'm out! *Driving:* So tell me, he gave you a warm welcome?

Happy: Sure, Pop, sure!

Biff: driven: Well, it was kind of—

Willy: I was wondering if he'd remember you. *To Happy:* Imagine, man doesn't see him for ten, twelve years and gives him that kind of a welcome!

Happy: Damn right!

Biff: trying to return to the offensive: Pop, look—

Willy: You know why he remembered you, don't you? Because you impressed him in those days.

Biff: Let's talk quietly and get this down to the facts, huh?

Willy: as though Biff had been interrupting: Well, what happened? It's great news, Biff. Did he take you into his office or'd you talk in the waiting-room?

Biff: Well, he came in, see, and—

Willy: with a big smile: What'd he say? Betcha he threw his arm around you.

Biff: Well, he kinda—

Willy: He's a fine man. *To Happy:* Very hard man to see, y'know.

Happy: agreeing: Oh, I know.

Willy: to Biff: Is that where you had the drinks?

Biff: Yeah, he gave me a couple of—no, no!

Happy: cutting in: He told him my Florida idea.

Willy: Don't interrupt. *To Biff:* How'd he react to the Florida idea?

Biff: Dad, will you give me a minute to explain?

Willy: I've been waiting for you to explain since I sat down here! What happened? He took you into his office and what?

Biff: Well—I talked. And—and he listened, see.

Willy: Famous for the way he listens, y'know. What was his answer?

Biff: His answer was—*He breaks off, suddenly angry.* Dad, you're not letting me tell you what I want to tell you!

Willy: accusing, angered: You didn't see him, did you?

Biff: I did see him!

Willy: What'd you insult him or something? You insulted him, didn't you?

Biff: Listen, will you let me out of it, will you just let me out of it!

Happy: What the hell!

Willy: Tell me what happened!

Biff: to Happy: I can't talk to him!

A single trumpet note jars the ear. The light of green leaves stains the house, which holds the air of night and a dream. Young Bernard enters and knocks on the door of the house.

Young Bernard: frantically: Mrs. Loman, Mrs. Loman!

Happy: Tell him what happened!

Biff: to Happy: Shut up and leave me alone!

Willy: No, no! You had to go and flunk math!

Biff: What math? What're you talking about?

Young Bernard: Mrs. Loman, Mrs. Loman!

Linda appears in the house, as of old.

Willy: wildly: Math, math, math!
Biff: Take it easy, Pop!
Young Bernard: Mrs. Loman!
Willy: furiously: If you hadn't flunked you'd've been set by now!
Biff: Now, look, I'm gonna tell you what happened, and you're going to listen to me.
Young Bernard: Mrs. Loman!
Biff: I waited six hours—
Happy: What the hell are you saying?
Biff: I kept sending in my name but he wouldn't see me. So finally he . . . *He continues unheard as light fades low on the restaurant.*
Young Bernard: Biff flunked math!
Linda: No!
Young Bernard: Birnbaum flunked him! They won't graduate him!
Linda: But they have to. He's gotta go to the university. Where is he? Biff! Biff!
Young Bernard: No, he left. He went to Grand Central.[9]
Linda: Grand—You mean he went to Boston!
Young Bernard: Is Uncle Willy in Boston?
Linda: Oh, maybe Willy can talk to the teacher. Oh, the poor, poor boy!

Light on house area snaps out.

Biff: at the table, now audible, holding up a gold fountain pen: . . . so I'm washed up with Oliver, you understand? Are you listening to me?
Willy: at a loss: Yeah, sure. If you hadn't flunked—
Biff: Flunked what? What're you talking about?
Willy: Don't blame everything on me! I didn't flunk math—you did! What pen?
Happy: That was awful dumb, Biff, a pen like that is worth—
Willy: seeing the pen for the first time: You took Oliver's pen?
Biff: weakening: Dad, I just explained it to you.
Willy: You stole Bill Oliver's fountain pen!
Biff: I didn't exactly steal it! That's just what I've been explaining to you!
Happy: He had it in his hand and just then Oliver walked in, so he got nervous and stuck it in his pocket!
Willy: My God, Biff!
Biff: I never intended to do it, Dad!
Operator's Voice: Standish Arms, good evening!
Willy: shouting: I'm not in my room!
Biff: frightened: Dad, what's the matter? *He and Happy stand up.*
Operator: Ringing Mr. Loman for you!
Willy: I'm not there, stop it!

---

[9] Grand Central Station in New York City, a main transportation terminal.

Biff: horrified, gets down on one knee before Willy: Dad, I'll make good, I'll make good. *Willy tries to get to his feet. Biff holds him down.* Sit down now.

Willy: No, you're no good, you're no good for anything.

Biff: I am, Dad, I'll find something else, you understand? Now don't worry about anything. *He holds up Willy's face:* Talk to me, Dad.

Operator: Mr. Loman does not answer. Shall I page him?

Willy: attempting to stand, as though to rush and silence the Operator: No, no, no!

Happy: He'll strike something, Pop.

Willy: No, no . . .

Biff: desperately, standing over Willy: Pop, listen! Listen to me! I'm telling you something good. Oliver talked to his partner about the Florida idea. You listening? He—he talked to his partner, and he came to me . . . I'm going to be all right, you hear? Dad, listen to me, he said it was just a question of the amount!

Willy: Then you . . . got it?

Happy: He's gonna be terrific, Pop!

Willy: trying to stand: Then you got it, haven't you? You got it! You got it!

Biff: agonized, holds Willy down: No, no. Look, Pop. I'm supposed to have lunch with them tomorrow. I'm just telling you this so you'll know that I can still make an impression, Pop. And I'll make good somewhere, but I can't go tomorrow, see?

Willy: Why not? You simply—

Biff: But the pen, Pop!

Willy: You give it to him and tell him it was an oversight!

Happy: Sure, have lunch tomorrow!

Biff: I can't say that—

Willy: You were doing a crossword puzzle and accidentally used his pen!

Biff: Listen, kid, I took those balls years ago, now I walk in with his fountain pen? That clinches it, don't you see? I can't face him like that! I'll try elsewhere.

Page's Voice: Paging Mr. Loman!

Willy: Don't you want to be anything?

Biff: Pop, how can I go back?

Willy: You don't want to be anything, is that what's behind it?

Biff: now angry at Willy for not crediting his sympathy: Don't take it that way! You think it was easy walking into that office after what I'd done to him? A team of horses couldn't have dragged me back to Bill Oliver!

Willy: Then why'd you go?

Biff: Why did I go? Why did I go! Look at you! Look at what's become of you!

Off left, The Woman laughs.

Willy: Biff, you're going to go to that lunch tomorrow, or—

Biff: I can't go. I've got no appointment!

Happy: Biff, for . . . !

Willy: Are you spiting me?

Biff: Don't take it that way! Goddammit!

Willy: strikes Biff and falters away from the table: You rotten little louse! Are you spiting me?

The Woman: Someone's at the door, Willy!

Biff: I'm not good, can't you see what I am?

Happy: separating them: Hey, you're in a restaurant! Now cut it out, both of you! *The girls enter.* Hello, girls, sit down.

The Woman laughs, off left.

Miss Forsythe: I guess we might as well. This is Letta.

The Woman: Willy, are you going to wake up?

Biff: ignoring Willy: How're ya, miss, sit down. What do you drink?

Miss Forsythe: Letta might not be able to stay long.

Letta: I gotta get up very early tomorrow. I got jury duty. I'm so excited! Were you fellows ever on a jury?

Biff: No, but I been in front of them! *The girls laugh.* This is my father.

Letta: Isn't he cute? Sit down with us, Pop.

Happy: Sit him down, Biff!

Biff: going to him: Come on, slugger, drink us under the table. To hell with it! Come on, sit down, pal.

On Biff's last insistence, Willy is about to sit.

The Woman: now urgently: Willy, are you going to answer the door!

The Woman's call pulls Willy back. He starts right, befuddled.

Biff: Hey, where are you going?

Willy: Open the door.

Biff: The door?

Willy: The washroom . . . the door . . . where's the door?

Biff: leading Willy to the left: Just go straight down.

Willy moves left.

The Woman: Willy, Willy, are you going to get up, get up, get up, get up?

Willy exits left.

Letta: I think it's sweet you bring your daddy along.

Miss Forsythe: Oh, he isn't really your father!

Biff: at left, turning to her resentfully: Miss Forsythe, you've just seen a prince walk by. A fine, troubled prince. A hard-working, unappreciated prince. A pal, you understand? A good companion. Always for his boys.

Letta: That's so sweet.

Happy: Well, girls, what's the program? We're wasting time. Come on, Biff. Gather round. Where would you like to go?

Biff: Why don't you do something for him?

Happy: Me!

Biff: Don't you give a damn for him, Hap?

Happy: What're you talking about? I'm the one who—

Biff: I sense it, you don't give a good goddam about him. *He takes the rolled-up hose from his pocket and puts it on the table in front of Happy.* Look what I found in the cellar, for Christ's sake. How can you bear to let it go on?

Happy: Me? Who goes away? Who runs off and—

Biff: Yeah, but he doesn't mean anything to you. You could help him—I can't! Don't you understand what I'm talking about? He's going to kill himself, don't you know that?

Happy: Don't I know it! Me!

Biff: Hap, help him! Jesus . . . help him . . . Help me, help me, I can't bear to look at his face! *Ready to weep, he hurries out, up right.*

Happy: starting after him: Where are you going?

Miss Forsythe: What's he so mad about?

Happy: Come on, girls, we'll catch up with him.

Miss Forsythe: as Happy pushes her out: Say, I don't like that temper of his!

Happy: He's just a little overstrung, he'll be all right!

Willy: off left, as The Woman laughs: Don't answer! Don't answer!

Letta: Don't you want to tell your father—

Happy: No, that's not my father. He's just a guy. Come on, we'll catch Biff, and, honey, we're going to paint this town! Stanley, where's the check! Hey, Stanley!

They exit. Stanley looks toward left.

Stanley: calling to Happy indignantly: Mr. Loman! Mr. Loman!

Stanley picks up a chair and follows them off. Knocking is heard off left. The Woman enters, laughing. Willy follows her. She is in a black slip; he is buttoning his shirt. Raw, sensuous music accompanies their speech.

Willy: Will you stop laughing? Will you stop?

The Woman: Aren't you going to answer the door? He'll wake the whole hotel.

Willy: I'm not expecting anybody.

The Woman: Whyn't you have another drink, honey, and stop being so damn self-centered?

Willy: I'm so lonely.

The Woman: You know you ruined me, Willy? From now on, whenever you come to the office, I'll see that you go right through to the buyers. No waiting at my desk any more, Willy. You ruined me.

Willy: That's nice of you to say that.

The Woman: Gee, you are self-centered! Why so sad? You are the saddest, self-centeredest soul I ever did see-saw. *She laughs. He kisses her.* Come on inside, drummer boy. It's silly to be dressing in the middle of the night. *As knocking is heard:* Aren't you going to answer the door?

Willy: They're knocking on the wrong door.

The Woman: But I felt the knocking. And he heard us talking in here. Maybe the hotel's on fire!

Willy: his terror rising: It's a mistake.

The Woman: Then tell him to go away!

Willy: There's nobody there.

The Woman: It's getting on my nerves, Willy. There's somebody standing out there and it's getting on my nerves!

Willy: pushing her away from him: All right, stay in the bathroom here, and don't come out. I think there's a law in Massachusetts about it, so don't come out. It may be that new room clerk. He looked very mean. So don't come out. It's a mistake, there's no fire.

The knocking is heard again. He takes a few steps away from her, and she vanishes into the wing. The light follows him, and now he is facing Young Biff, who carries a suitcase. Biff steps toward him. The music is gone.

Biff: Why didn't you answer?

Willy: Biff! What are you doing in Boston?

Biff: Why didn't you answer? I've been knocking for five minutes, I called you on the phone—

Willy: I just heard you. I was in the bathroom and had the door shut. Did anything happen home?

Biff: Dad—I let you down.

Willy: What do you mean?

Biff: Dad . . .

Willy: Biffo, what's this about? *Putting his arm around Biff:* Come on, let's go downstairs and get you a malted.

Biff: Dad, I flunked math.

Willy: Not for the term?

Biff: The term. I haven't got enough credits to graduate.

Willy: You mean to say Bernard wouldn't give you the answers?

Biff: He did, he tried, but I only got a sixty-one.

Willy: And they wouldn't give you four points?

Biff: Birnbaum refused absolutely. I begged him, Pop, but he won't give me those points. You gotta talk to him before they close the school. Because if he saw the kind of man you are, and you just talked to him in your way, I'm sure he'd come through for me. The class came right before practice, see, and I didn't go enough. Would you talk to him? He'd like you, Pop. You know the way you could talk.

Willy: You're on. We'll drive right back.

Biff: Oh, Dad, good work! I'm sure he'll change it for you!

Willy: Go downstairs and tell the clerk I'm checkin' out. Go right down.

Biff: Yes, sir! See, the reason he hates me, Pop—one day he was late for class so I got up at the blackboard and imitated him. I crossed my eyes and talked with a lithp.

Willy: laughing: You did? The kids like it?

Biff: They nearly died laughing!

Willy: Yeah? What'd you do?

Biff: The thquare root of thixty twee is . . . *Willy bursts out laughing; Biff joins him.* And in the middle of it he walked in!

Willy laughs and The Woman joins in offstage.

Willy: without hesitation: Hurry downstairs and—

Biff: Somebody in there?

Willy: No, that was next door.

The Woman laughs offstage.

Biff: Somebody got in your bathroom!

Willy: No, it's the next room, there's a party—

The Woman: enters, laughing. She lisps this: Can I come in? There's something in the bathtub, Willy, and it's moving!

Willy looks at Biff, who is staring open-mouthed and horrified at The Woman.

Willy: Ah—you better go back to your room. They must be finished painting by now. They're painting her room so I let her take a shower here. Go back, go back . . . *He pushes her.*

The Woman: resisting: But I've got to get dressed, Willy, I can't—

Willy: Get out of here! Go back, go back . . . *Suddenly striving for the ordinary:* This is Miss Francis, Biff, she's a buyer. They're painting her room. Go back, Miss Francis, go back . . .

The Woman: But my clothes, I can't go out naked in the hall!

Willy: pushing her offstage: Get outa here! Go back, go back!

Biff slowly sits down on his suitcase as the argument continues offstage.

The Woman: Where's my stockings? You promised me stockings, Willy!

Willy: I have no stockings here!

The Woman: You had two boxes of size nine sheers for me, and I want them!

Willy: Here, for God's sake, will you get outa here!

The Woman: enters holding a box of stockings: I just hope there's nobody in the hall. That's all I hope. *To Biff:* Are you football or baseball?

Biff: Football.

The Woman: angry, humiliated: That's me too. G'night. *She snatches her clothes from Willy, and walks out.*

Willy: after a pause: Well, better get going. I want to get to the school first thing in the morning. Get my suits out of the closet. I'll get my valise. *Biff doesn't move.* What's the matter? *Biff remains motionless, tears falling.* She's a buyer. Buys for J. H. Simmons. She lives down the hall—they're painting. You don't imagine—*He breaks off. After a pause:* Now listen, pal, she's just a buyer. She sees merchandise in her room and they have to keep it looking just so . . . *Pause. Assuming command:* All right, get my suits. *Biff doesn't move.* Now stop crying and do as I say. I gave you an order. Biff, I gave you an order! Is that what you do when I give you an order? How dare you cry! *Putting his arm around Biff:* Now look, Biff, when you grow up you'll understand about these things. You mustn't—you mustn't overemphasize a thing like this. I'll see Birnbaum first thing in the morning.

Biff: Never mind.

Willy: getting down beside Biff: Never mind! He's going to give you those points. I'll see to it.

Biff: He wouldn't listen to you.

Willy: He certainly will listen to me. You need those points for the U. of Virginia.

Biff: I'm not going there.

Willy: Heh? If I can't get him to change that mark you'll make it up in summer school. You've got all summer to—

Biff: his weeping breaking from him: Dad . . .

Willy: infected by it: Oh, my boy . . .

Biff: Dad . . .

Willy: She's nothing to me, Biff. I was lonely, I was terribly lonely.

Biff: You—you gave her Mama's stockings! *His tears break through and he rises to go.*

Willy: grabbing for Biff: I gave you an order!

Biff: Don't touch me, you—liar!

Willy: Apologize for that!

Biff: You fake! You phony little fake! You fake! *Overcome, he turns quickly and weeping fully goes out with his suitcase. Willy is left on the floor on his knees.*

Willy: I gave you an order! Biff, come back here or I'll beat you! Come back here! I'll whip you!

Stanley comes quickly in from the right and stands in front of Willy.

Willy: shouts at Stanley: I gave you an order . . .

Stanley: Hey, let's pick it up, pick it up. Mr. Loman. *He helps Willy to his feet.* Your boys left with the chippies. They said they'll see you home.

A second waiter watches some distance away.

Willy: But we were supposed to have dinner together.

Music is heard, Willy's theme.

Stanley: Can you make it?

Willy: I'll—sure, I can make it. *Suddenly concerned about his clothes:* Do I—I look all right?

Stanley: Sure, you look all right. *He flicks a speck off Willy's lapel.*

Willy: Here—here's a dollar.

Stanley: Oh, your son paid me. It's all right.

Willy: putting it in Stanley's hand: No, take it. You're a good boy.

Stanley: Oh, no, you don't have to . . .

Willy: Here—here's some more, I don't need it any more. *After a slight pause:* Tell me—is there a seed store in the neighborhood?

Stanley: Seeds? You mean like to plant?

As Willy turns. Stanley slips the money back into his jacket pocket.

Willy: Yes. Carrots, peas . . .

Stanley: Well, there's hardware stores on Sixth Avenue, but it may be too late now.

Willy: anxiously: Oh, I'd better hurry. I've got to get some seeds. *He starts off to the right.* I've got to get some seeds, right away. Nothing's planted. I don't have a thing in the ground.

Willy hurries out as the light goes down. Stanley moves over to the right after him, watches him off. The other waiter has been staring at Willy.

Stanley: to the waiter: Well, whatta you looking at?

The waiter picks up the chairs and moves off right. Stanley takes the table and follows him. The light fades on this area. There is a long pause, the sound of the flute coming over. The light gradually rises on the kitchen, which is empty. Happy appears at the door of the house, followed by Biff. Happy is carrying a large bunch of long-stemmed roses. He enters the kitchen, looks around for Linda. Not seeing her, he turns to Biff, who is just outside the house door, and makes a gesture with his hands, indicating "Not here, I guess." He looks into the living-room and freezes. Inside, Linda, unseen, is seated, Willy's coat on her lap. She rises ominously and quietly and moves toward Happy, who backs up into the kitchen, afraid.

Happy: Hey, what're you doing up? *Linda says nothing but moves toward him implacably.* Where's Pop? *He keeps backing to the right, and now Linda is in full view in the doorway to the living-room.* Is he sleeping?

Linda: Where were you?

Happy: trying to laugh it off: We met two girls, Mom, very fine types. Here, we brought you some flowers. *Offering them to her:* Put them in your room, Ma.

She knocks them to the floor at Biff's feet. He has now come inside and closed the door behind him. She stares at Biff, silent.

Happy: Now what'd you do that for? Mom, I want you to have some flowers—

Linda: cutting Happy off, violently to Biff: Don't you care whether he lives or dies?

Happy: going to the stairs: Come upstairs, Biff.

Biff: with a flare of disgust, to Happy: Go away from me! *To Linda:* What do you mean, lives or dies? Nobody's dying around here, pal.

Linda: Get out of my sight! Get out of here!

Biff: I wanna see the boss.

Linda: You're not going near him!

Biff: Where is he? *He moves into the living-room and Linda follows.*

Linda: shouting after Biff: You invite him for dinner. He looks forward to it all day—*Biff appears in his parents' bedroom, looks around, and exits*—and then you desert him there. There's no stranger you'd do that to!

Happy: Why? He had a swell time with us. Listen, when I—*Linda comes back into the kitchen*—desert him I hope I don't outlive the day!

Linda: Get out of here!

Happy: Now look, Mom . . .

Linda: Did you have to go to women tonight? You and your lousy rotten whores!

Biff re-enters the kitchen.

Happy: Mom, all we did was follow Biff around trying to cheer him up! *To Biff:* Boy, what a night you gave me!

Linda: Get out of here, both of you, and don't come back! I don't want you tormenting him any more. Go on now, get your things together! *To Biff:* You can sleep in his apartment. *She starts to pick up the flowers and stops herself.* Pick up this stuff, I'm not your maid any more. Pick it up, you bum, you!

Happy turns his back to her in refusal. Biff slowly moves over and gets down on his knees, picking up the flowers.

Linda: You're a pair of animals! Not one, not another living soul would have had the cruelty to walk out on that man in a restaurant!

Biff: not looking at her: Is that what he said?

Linda: He didn't have to say anything. He was so humiliated he nearly limped when he came in.

Happy: But, Mom, he had a great time with us—

Biff: cutting him off violently: Shut up!

Without another word, Happy goes upstairs.

Linda: You! You didn't even go in to see if he was all right!

Biff: still on the floor in front of Linda, the flowers in his hand; with self-loathing: No. Didn't. Didn't do a damned thing. How do you like that, heh? Left him babbling in a toilet.

Linda: You louse, You . . .

Biff: Now you hit it on the nose! *He gets up, throws the flowers in the wastebasket.* The scum of the earth, and you're looking at him!

Linda: Get out of here!

Biff: I gotta talk to the boss, Mom. Where is he?

Linda: You're not going near him. Get out of this house!

Biff: with absolute assurance, determination: No. We're gonna have an abrupt conversation, him and me.

Linda: You're not talking to him!

Hammering is heard from outside the house, off right. Biff turns toward the noise.

Linda: suddenly pleading: Will you please leave him alone?
Biff: What's he doing out there?
Linda: He's planting the garden!
Biff: quietly: Now? Oh, my God!

Biff moves outside, Linda following. The light dies down on them and comes up on the center of the apron as Willy walks into it. He is carrying a flashlight, a hoe, and a handful of seed packets. He raps the top of the hoe sharply to fix it firmly, and then moves to the left, measuring off the distance with his foot. He holds the flashlight to look at the seed packets, reading off the instructions. He is in the blue of night.

Willy: Carrots . . . quarter-inch apart. Rows . . . one-foot rows. *He measures it off.* One foot. *He puts down a package and measures off.* Beets. *He puts down another package and measures again.* Lettuce. *He reads the package, puts it down.* One foot—*He breaks off as Ben appears at the right and moves slowly down to him.* What a proposition, ts, ts. Terrific, terrific. 'Cause she's suffered, Ben, the woman has suffered. You understand me? A man can't go out the way he came in, Ben, a man has got to add up to something. You can't, you can't—*Ben moves toward him as though to interrupt.* You gotta consider, now. Don't answer so quick. Remember, it's a guaranteed twenty-thousand–dollar proposition. Now look, Ben, I want you to go through the ins and outs of this thing with me. I've got nobody to talk to, Ben, and the woman has suffered, you hear me?
Ben: standing still, considering: What's the proposition?
Willy: It's twenty thousand dollars on the barrelhead. Guaranteed, gilt-edged, you understand?
Ben: You don't want to make a fool of yourself. They might not honor the policy.
Willy: How can they dare refuse? Didn't I work like a coolie to meet every premium on the nose? And now they don't pay off? Impossible!
Ben: It's called a cowardly thing, William.
Willy: Why? Does it take more guts to stand here the rest of my life ringing up a zero?
Ben: yielding: That's a point, William. *He moves, thinking, turns.* And twenty thousand—that *is* something one can feel with the hand, it is there.
Willy: now assured, with rising power: Oh, Ben, that's the whole beauty of it! I see it like a diamond, shining in the dark, hard and rough, that I can pick up and touch in my hand. Not like—like an appointment! This would not be another damned-fool appointment, Ben, and it changes all the aspects. Because he thinks I'm nothing, see, and so he spites me. But the funeral—*Straightening up:* Ben, that funeral will be massive! They'll come from Maine, Massachusetts, Vermont, New Hampshire! All the old-timers with the strange license plates—that boy will be thunder-struck, Ben, because he never realized—I am known! Rhode Island, New York, New Jersey—I am known, Ben, and he'll see it with his eyes once and for all. He'll see what I am, Ben! He's in for a shock, that boy!
Ben: coming down to the edge of the garden: He'll call you a coward.

Willy: suddenly fearful: No, that would be terrible.
Ben: Yes. And a damned fool.
Willy: No, no, he mustn't, I won't have that! *He is broken and desperate.*
Ben: He'll hate you, William.

The gay music of the Boys is heard.

Willy: Oh, Ben, how do we get back to all the great times? Used to be so full
of light, and comradeship, the sleigh-riding in winter, and the ruddiness on his
cheeks. And always some kind of good news coming up, always something
nice coming up ahead. And never even let me carry the valises in the house,
and simonizing, simonizing that little red car! Why, why can't I give him
something and not have him hate me?
Ben: Let me think about it. *He glances at his watch.* I still have a little time.
Remarkable proposition, but you've got to be sure you're not making a fool
of yourself.

Ben drifts off upstage and goes out of sight. Biff comes down from the left.

*Willy: suddenly conscious of Biff, turns and looks up at him, then begins picking up the
packages of seeds in confusion:* Where the hell is that seed? *Indignantly:* You
can't see nothing out here! They boxed in the whole goddam neighborhood!
Biff: There are people all around here. Don't you realize that?
Willy: I'm busy. Don't bother me.
Biff: taking the hoe from Willy: I'm saying good-by to you, Pop. *Willy looks at
him, silent, unable to move.* I'm not coming back any more.
Willy: You're not going to see Oliver tomorrow?
Biff: I've got no appointment, Dad.
Willy: He put his arm around you, and you've got no appointment?
Biff: Pop, get this now, will you? Everytime I've left it's been a fight that sent
me out of here. Today I realized something about myself and I tried to
explain it to you and I—I think I'm just not smart enough to make any sense
out of it for you. To hell with whose fault it is or anything like that. *He
takes Willy's arm.* Let's just wrap it up, heh? Come on in, we'll tell Mom. *He
gently tries to pull Willy to left.*
Willy: frozen, immobile, with guilt in his voice: No, I don't want to see her.
Biff: Come on! *He pulls again, and Willy tries to pull away.*
Willy: highly nervous: No, no, I don't want to see her.
Biff: tries to look into Willy's face, as if to find the answer there: Why don't you
want to see her?
Willy: more harshly now: Don't bother me, will you?
Biff: What do you mean, you don't want to see her? You don't want them
calling you yellow, do you? This isn't your fault; it's me, I'm a bum. Now
come inside! *Willy strains to get away.* Did you hear what I said to you?

Willy pulls away and quickly goes by himself into the house. Biff follows.

Linda: to Willy: Did you plant, dear?

Biff: at the door, to Linda: All right, we had it out. I'm going and I'm not writing any more.

Linda: going to Willy in the kitchen: I think that's the best way, dear. 'Cause there's no use drawing it out, you'll just never get along.

Willy doesn't respond.

Biff: People ask where I am and what I'm doing, you don't know, and you don't care. That way it'll be off your mind and you can start brightening up again. All right? That clears it, doesn't it? *Willy is silent, and Biff goes to him.* You gonna wish me luck, scout? *He extends his hand.* What do you say?

Linda: Shake his hand, Willy.

Willy: turning to her, seething with hurt: There's no necessity to mention the pen at all, y'know.

Biff: gently: I've got no appointment, Dad.

Willy: erupting fiercely: He put his arm around . . . ?

Biff: Dad, you're never going to see what I am, so what's the use of arguing? If I strike oil I'll send you a check. Meantime forget I'm alive.

Willy: to Linda: Spite, see?

Biff: Shake hands, Dad.

Willy: Not my hand.

Biff: I was hoping not to go this way.

Willy: Well, this is the way you're going. Good-by.

Biff looks at him a moment, then turns sharply and goes to the stairs.

Willy: stops him with: May you rot in hell if you leave this house!

Biff: turning: Exactly what is it that you want from me?

Willy: I want you to know, on the train, in the mountains, in the valleys, wherever you go, that you cut down your life for spite!

Biff: No, no.

Willy: Spite, spite, is the word of your undoing! And when you're down and out, remember what did it. When you're rotting somewhere beside the railroad tracks, remember, and don't you dare blame it on me!

Biff: I'm not blaming it on you!

Willy: I won't take the rap for this, you hear?

Happy comes down the stairs and stands on the bottom step, watching.

Biff: That's just what I'm telling you!

Willy: sinking into a chair at the table, with full accusation: You're trying to put a knife in me—don't think I don't know what you're doing!

Biff: All right, phony! Then let's lay it on the line. *He whips the rubber tube out of his pocket and puts it on the table.*

Happy: You crazy—

Linda: Biff! *She moves to grab the hose, but Biff holds it down with his hand.*

Biff: Leave it there! Don't move it!

Willy: not looking at it: What is that?

Biff: You know goddam well what that is.

Willy: caged, wanting to escape: I never saw that.

Biff: You saw it. The mice didn't bring it into the cellar! What is this supposed to do, make a hero out of you? This supposed to make me sorry for you?

Willy: Never heard of it.

Biff: There'll be no pity for you, you hear it? No pity!

Willy: to Linda: You hear the spite!

Biff: No, you're going to hear the truth—what you are and what I am!

Linda: Stop it!

Willy: Spite!

Happy: coming down toward Biff: You cut it now!

Biff: to Happy: The man don't know who we are! The man is gonna know! *To Willy:* We never told the truth for ten minutes in this house!

Happy: We always told the truth!

Biff: turning on him: You big blow, are you the assistant buyer? You're one of the two assistants to the assistant, aren't you?

Happy: Well, I'm practically—

Biff: You're practically full of it! We all are! And I'm through with it. *To Willy:* Now hear this, Willy, this is me.

Willy: I know you!

Biff: You know why I had no address for three months? I stole a suit in Kansas City and I was in jail. *To Linda, who is sobbing:* Stop crying. I'm through with it.

Linda turns away from them, her hands covering her face.

Willy: I suppose that's my fault!

Biff: I stole myself out of every good job since high school!

Willy: And whose fault is that?

Biff: And I never got anywhere because you blew me so full of hot air I could never stand taking orders from anybody! That's whose fault it is!

Willy: I hear that!

Linda: Don't, Biff!

Biff: It's goddam time you heard that! I had to be boss big shot in two weeks, and I'm through with it!

Willy: Then hang yourself! For spite, hang yourself!

Biff: No! Nobody's hanging himself, Willy! I ran down eleven flights with a pen in my hand today. And suddenly I stopped, you hear me? And in the middle of that office building, do you hear this? I stopped in the middle of that building and I saw—the sky. I saw the things that I love in this world. The work and the food and time to sit and smoke. And I looked at the pen and said to myself, what the hell am I grabbing this for? Why am I trying to become what I don't want to be? What am I doing in an office, making a contemptuous, begging fool of myself, when all I want is out there, waiting for me the minute I say I know who I am! Why can't I say that, Willy? *He tries to make Willy face him, but Willy pulls away and moves to the left.*

Willy: with hatred, threateningly: The door of your life is wide open!

Biff: Pop! I'm a dime a dozen, and so are you!

Willy: turning on him now in an uncontrolled outburst: I am not a dime a dozen! I am Willy Loman, and you are Biff Loman!

Biff starts for Willy, but is blocked by Happy. In his fury, Biff seems on the verge of attacking his father.

Biff: I am not a leader of men, Willy, and neither are you. You were never anything but a hard-working drummer[10] who landed in the ash can like all the rest of them! I'm one dollar an hour. Willy! I tried seven states and couldn't raise it. A buck an hour! Do you gather my meaning? I'm not bringing home any prizes any more, and you're going to stop waiting for me to bring them home!

Willy: directly to Biff: You vengeful, spiteful mutt!

Biff breaks from Happy. Willy, in fright, starts up the stairs. Biff grabs him.

Biff: at the peak of his fury: Pop, I'm nothing! I'm nothing, Pop. Can't you understand that? There's no spite in it any more. I'm just what I am, that's all.

Biff's fury has spent itself, and he breaks down, sobbing, holding on to Willy, who dumbly fumbles for Biff's face.

Willy: astonished: What're you doing? What're you doing? *To Linda:* Why is he crying?

Biff: crying, broken: Will you let me go, for Christ's sake? Will you take that phony dream and burn it before something happens? *Struggling to contain himself, he pulls away and moves to the stairs.* I'll go in the morning. Put him— put him to bed. *Exhausted, Biff moves up the stairs to his room.*

Willy: after a long pause, astonished, elevated: Isn't that—isn't that remarkable? Biff—he likes me!

Linda: He loves you, Willy!

Happy: deeply moved: Always did, Pop.

Willy: Oh, Biff! *Staring wildly:* He cried! Cried to me. *He is choking with his love, and now cries out his promise:* That boy—that boy is going to be magnificent!

Ben appears in the light just outside the kitchen.

Ben: Yes, outstanding, with twenty thousand behind him.

Linda: sensing the racing of his mind, fearfully, carefully: Now come to bed, Willy. It's all settled now.

Willy: finding it difficult not to rush out of the house: Yes, we'll sleep. Come on. Go to sleep, Hap.

Ben: And it does take a great kind of a man to crack the jungle.

[10] American slang: traveling salesman.

In accents of dread, Ben's idyllic music starts up.

Happy: his arm around Linda: I'm getting married, Pop, don't forget it. I'm changing everything. I'm gonna run that department before the year is up. You'll see, Mom. *He kisses her.*

Ben: The jungle is dark but full of diamonds, Willy.

Willy turns, moves, listenig to Ben.

Linda: Be good. You're both good boys, just act that way, that's all.

Happy: 'Night, Pop. *He goes upstairs.*

Linda: to Willy: Come, dear.

Ben: with greater force: One must go in to fetch a diamond out.

Willy: to Linda, as he moves slowly along the edge of the kitchen, toward the door: I just want to get settled down, Linda. Let me sit alone for a little.

Linda: almost uttering her fear: I want you upstairs.

Willy: taking her in his arms: In a few minutes, Linda. I couldn't sleep right now. Go on, you look awful tired. *He kisses her.*

Ben: Not like an appointment at all. A diamond is rough and hard to the touch.

Willy: Go on now. I'll be right up.

Linda: I think this is the only way, Willy.

Willy: Sure, it's the best thing.

Ben: Best thing!

Willy: The only way. Everything is gonna be—go on, kid, get to bed. You look so tired.

Linda: Come right up.

Willy: Two minutes.

Linda goes into the living-room, then reappears in her bedroom. Willy moves just outside the kitchen door.

Willy: Loves me. *Wonderingly:* Always loved me. Isn't that a remarkable thing? Ben, he'll worship me for it!

Ben: with promise: It's dark there, but full of diamonds.

Willy: Can you imagine that magnificence with twenty thousand dollars in his pocket?

Linda: calling from her room: Willy! Come up!

Willy: calling into the kitchen: Yes! Yes. Coming! It's very smart, you realize that, don't you, sweetheart? Even Ben sees it. I gotta go, baby, 'By! 'By! *Going over to Ben, almost dancing:* Imagine? When the mail comes he'll be ahead of Bernard again!

Ben: A perfect proposition all around.

Willy: Did you see how he cried to me? Oh, if I could kiss him, Ben!

Ben: Time, William, time!

Willy: Oh, Ben, I always knew one way or another we were gonna make it, Biff and I!

Ben: looking at his watch: The boat. We'll be late. *He moves slowly off into the darkness.*

Willy: elegiacally, turning to the house: Now when you kick off, boy, I want a seventy-yard boot, and get right down the field under the ball, and when you hit, hit low and hit hard, because it's important, boy. *He swings around and faces the audience.* There's all kinds of important people in the stands, and the first thing you know . . . *Suddenly realizing he is alone:* Ben! Ben, where do I . . . ? *He makes a sudden movement of search.* Ben, how do I . . . ?

Linda: calling: Willy, you coming up?

Willy: uttering a gasp of fear, whirling about as if to quiet her: Sh! *He turns around as if to find his way; sounds, faces, voices, seem to be swarming in upon him and he flicks at them, crying,* Sh! Sh! *Suddenly music, faint and high, stops him. It rises in intensity, almost to an unbearable scream. He goes up and down on his toes, and rushes off around the house.* Shhh!

Linda: Willy?

There is no answer. Linda waits. Biff gets up off his bed. He is still in his clothes. Happy sits up. Biff stands listening.

Linda: with real fear: Willy, answer me! Willy!

There is the sound of a car starting and moving away at full speed.

Linda: No!

Biff: rushing down the stairs: Pop!

As the car speeds off, the music crashes down in a frenzy of sound, which becomes the soft pulsation of a single cello string. Biff slowly returns to his bedroom. He and Happy gravely don their jackets. Linda slowly walks out of her room. The music has developed into a dead march. The leaves of day are appearing over everything. Charley and Bernard, somberly dressed, appear and knock on the kitchen door. Biff and Happy slowly descend the stairs to the kitchen as Charley and Bernard enter. All stop a moment when Linda, in clothes of mourning, bearing a little bunch of roses, comes through the draped doorway into the kitchen. She goes to Charley and takes his arm. Now all move toward the audience, through the wall-line of the kitchen. At the limit of the apron, Linda lays down the flowers, kneels, and sits back on her heels. All stare down at the grave.

REQUIEM

Charley: It's getting dark, Linda.

Linda doesn't react. She stares at the grave.

Biff: How about it, Mom? Better get some rest, heh? They'll be closing the gate soon.

Linda makes no move. Pause.

Happy: deeply angered: He had no right to do that. There was no necessity for it. We would've helped him.

Charley: grunting: Hmmm.

Biff: Come along, Mom.

Linda: Why didn't anybody come?

Charley: It was a very nice funeral.

Linda: But where are all the people he knew? Maybe they blame him.

Charley: Naa. It's a rough world, Linda. They wouldn't blame him.

Linda: I can't understand it. At this time especially. First time in thirty-five years we were just about free and clear. He only needed a little salary. He was even finished with the dentist.

Charley: No man only needs a little salary.

Linda: I can't understand it.

Biff: There were a lot of nice days. When he'd come home from a trip; or on Sundays, making the stoop; finishing the cellar; putting on the new porch; when he built the extra bathroom; and put up the garage. You know something, Charley, there's more of him in that front stoop than in all the sales he ever made.

Charley: Yeah. He was a happy man with a batch of cement.

Linda: He was so wonderful with his hands.

Biff: He had the wrong dreams. All, all, wrong.

Happy: almost ready to fight Biff: Don't say that!

Biff: He never knew who he was.

Charley: stopping Happy's movement and reply. To Biff: Nobody dast blame this man. You don't understand: Willy was a salesman. And for a salesman, there is no rock bottom to the life. He don't put a bolt to a nut, he don't tell you the law or give you medicine. He's a man way out there in the blue, riding on a smile and a shoeshine. And when they start not smiling back—that's an earthquake. And then you get yourself a couple of spots on your hat, and you're finished. Nobody dast blame this man. A salesman is got to dream, boy. It comes with the territory.

Biff: Charley, the man didn't know who he was.

Happy: infuriated: Don't say that!

Biff: Why don't you come with me, Happy?

Happy: I'm not licked that easily. I'm staying right in this city, and I'm gonna beat this racket! *He looks at Biff, his chin set.* The Loman Brothers!

Biff: I know who I am, kid.

Happy: All right, boy. I'm gonna show you and everybody else that Willy Loman did not die in vain. He had a good dream. It's the only dream you can have—to come out number-one man. He fought it out here, and this is where I'm gonna win it for him.

Biff: with a hopeless glance at Happy, bends toward his mother: Let's go, Mom.

Linda: I'll be with you in a minute. Go on, Charley. *He hesitates.* I want to, just for a minute. I never had a chance to say good-by.

Charley moves away, followed by Happy. Biff remains a slight distance up and left of Linda. She sits there, summoning herself. The flute begins, not far away, playing behind her speech.

Linda: Forgive me, dear. I can't cry. I don't know what it is, but I can't cry. I
don't understand it. Why did you ever do that? Help me, Willy, I can't cry.
It seems to me that you're just on another trip. I keep expecting you. Willy,
dear, I can't cry. Why did you do it? I search and search and I search, and I
can't understand it, Willy. I made the last payment on the house today.
Today, dear. And there'll be nobody home. *A sob rises in her throat.* We're
free and clear. *Sobbing more fully, released:* We're free. *Biff comes slowly toward
her.* We're free . . . We're free . . .

*Biff lifts her to her feet and moves out up right with her in his arms. Linda sobs
quietly. Bernard and Charley come together and follow them, followed by Happy. Only
the music of the flute is left on the darkening stage as over the house the hard towers of
the apartment buildings rise into sharp focus, and*
      The Curtain Falls
1949

Norman Mailer
b. 1923

Norman Mailer was born in Long Branch, New Jersey, on January 31, 1923, and
grew up in Brooklyn, New York. At Harvard College he studied aeronautical
engineering but also spent much of his time writing. In 1941 he won *Story*
magazine's annual award for college fiction. Two years later he left Harvard with
an honors degree in engineering, joined the army, and headed for the Philippines
as a rifleman in the 112th Cavalry.

Mailer's first novel, *The Naked and the Dead* (1948), the account of an
American invasion of a small Pacific island held by the Japanese, drew directly on
his military experiences and is generally considered one of the finest novels to
come out of the Second World War. An enormous success, it gave Mailer an
immediate literary reputation. In the early 1950s Mailer settled in New York
City and, as he says in his first collection of essays, *Advertisements for Myself*
(1959), resolved to make "a revolution in the consciousness of our time." He set
about doing so through fiction, essays, journalism, and publishing. His second
novel, *Barbary Shore* (1951), grew out of his reflections on the difficulties that
necessarily surround reform politics in a world where all values seem to have
gone dead. *The Deer Park* (1955), his third novel, in which he pays literary dues
to Ernest Hemingway and F. Scott Fitzgerald, is still regarded as one of the best
novels yet written about Hollywood. In 1959 Mailer attempted through a long
essay, "The White Negro," to define the existential characteristics of "hip," a
style of thought and behavior that he opposed to the "square" and that he
believed typified the most desirable mode of contemporary consciousness. In 1953
he became a coeditor of *Dissent* and a year later helped found *The Village Voice.*

During the 1960s and early 1970s Mailer's work became increasingly political as he began to explore more deeply the various sources of power in America. He published two collections of essays on politics and culture, *The Presidential Papers* (1963) and *Cannibals and Christians* (1966). He wrote *An American Dream* in 1965, a novel about a war hero, excongressman, and friend of John F. Kennedy who murders his socially prominent wife and then apparently purges himself clean—a baptism by fire—by a deliberate immersion into what he bleakly sees as his country's cultural disintegration. In 1967 he published his fifth novel, *Why Are We in Vietnam?*, a contemporary tall tale that examines American violence through the pulsating narrative voice of an eighteen-year-old Dallas disc jockey. But much of Mailer's best work of the period was in the budding genre of "New Journalism"—writing that combined a sense of the occasions and objectivity of journalism with many of the techniques and freedoms of fiction. In 1968 Mailer wrote one of his finest books (it won both the Pulitzer Prize and the National Book Award), *The Armies of the Night,* which he subtitled *History as a Novel/The Novel as History* and which deals with his experiences in the 1967 peace march on the Pentagon to protest the Vietnam War. In the same vein he wrote about the presidential conventions of 1968 and 1972 in *Miami and the Seige of Chicago: An Informal History of the Republican and Democratic Conventions of 1968* (1969) and *St. George and the Godfather* (1972). In 1968 he published a collection of earlier political essays, *The Idol and the Octopus: Political Writings on the Kennedy and Johnson Administrations,* and in the same year reinforced his political theme by running as an independent candidate for mayor of New York City.

Like Yeats's poetry, Mailer's prose grows out of a dialectic between a fascination with his own life and a matching fascination with the life of his times. Mailer is often seen trying to balance a desire to be a public figure—a performer, an oracle, and a celebrity—with the desire to be a serious man of letters. His writing, too, draws heavily on his abiding concern for the American culture—for its heroes and heroines, its gadgets and gimmicks, its aberrations and achievements, and above all its spiritual endangerment as it seeks to open up new worlds and yet find enduring values. In recent years he has written a number of books that investigate various aspects of contemporary American society and culture: the space program and first moon landing in *Of a Fire on the Moon* (1970), a personal polemic against feminism and the women's movement in *The Prisoner of Sex* (1971), a biographical essay on Marilyn Monroe in *Marilyn* (1973), an interpretation of urban graffiti in *The Faith of Graffiti* (1974), a report of a famous Muhammad Ali championship bout in *The Fight* (1975), and a searching account of a convicted murderer's Utah background in *The Executioner's Song* (1979). In keeping with his remarkable versatility, Mailer has also written a long novel set in the Egypt of the Pharaohs, *Ancient Evenings* (1983), and a murder mystery, *Tough Guys Don't Dance* (1984).

Both controversy and acclaim have greeted Mailer's efforts to make the tension between his art and his life as compellingly interesting to others as it is to himself. Even so, both his work and his career surely stand among the more remarkable achievements of our time. For more than thirty years now he has displayed an artistic restlessness—deriving from what he once described as an instinctive feeling that "the best way to grow was not to write one novel after another but to move from activity to activity"—that has carried him from one telling experiment to another. As much as any writer of his time, he has reached beyond familiar attitudes, themes, styles, and modes into new areas and so has broadened literature in our time. Furthermore, though he has sometimes simplified and reduced the realities of modern American life, he has also, at his best, brought unusual imaginative force, and unusually supple prose, to bear on them. "I suppose," he once remarked,

> that the virtue I should like most to achieve as a writer is to be genuinely disturbing . . . to see life . . . as others do not see it, or only partially see it, and therefore open for the reader that literary experience . . . of having one's experience enlarged, one's perceptions deepened, and one's illusions about one-self rendered even more untenable. For me, this is the highest function of art, precisely that it is disturbing, that it does not let man rest.

Further Reading:
"Norman Mailer: An Interview" in *Writers at Work: The Paris Review Interviews*, 3d series, 1967, intro. by A. Kazin.
R. Poirier, *Norman Mailer*, 1973.
R. Solotaroff, *Down Mailer's Way*, 1974.

Text:
The Armies of the Night: History as a Novel/The Novel as History, 1968.

from The Armies of the Night*
Book I: History As a Novel:
The Steps of the Pentagon

from Part I: Thursday Evening

5: Toward a Theater of Ideas

The guests were beginning to leave the party for the Ambassador, which was two blocks away. Mailer did not know this yet, but the audience there had been waiting almost an hour. They were being entertained by an electronic folk rock guitar group, so presumably the young were more or less happy, and the middle-aged dim. Mailer was feeling the high sense of clarity which accompanies the light show of the aurora borealis when it is projected upon the inner universe of the chest, the lungs, and the heart. He was happy. On leaving, he had appropriated a coffee mug and filled it with bourbon. The fresh air illumined the bourbon, gave it a cerebrative edge; words entered his brain with the agreeable authority of fresh minted coins. Like all good professionals, he was stimulated by the chance to try a new if related line of work. Just as professional football players love sex because it is so close to football, so he

---

* *The Armies of the Night* is based on the march to the Pentagon in October 1967 in opposition to the Vietnam War.

was fond of speaking in public because it was thus near to writing. An extravagant analogy? Consider that a good half of writing consists of being sufficiently sensitive to the moment to reach for the next promise which is usually hidden in some word or phrase just a shift to the side of one's conscious intent. (Consciousness, that blunt tool, bucks in the general direction of the truth; instinct plucks the feather. Cheers!) Where public speaking is an exercise from prepared texts to demonstrate how successfully a low order of consciousness can beat upon the back of a collective flesh, public speaking being, therefore, a sullen expression of human possibility metaphorically equal to a bugger on his victim, speaking-in-public (as Mailer liked to describe any speech which was more or less improvised, impromptu, or dangerously written) was an activity like writing; one had to trick or seize or submit to the grace of each moment, which, except for those unexpected and sometimes well-deserved moments when consciousness and grace came together (and one felt on the consequence, heroic) were usually occasions of some mystery. The pleasure of speaking in public was the sensitivity it offered: with every phrase one was better or worse, close or less close to the existential promise of truth, *it feels true,* which hovers on good occasions like a presence between speaker and audience. Sometimes one was better, and worse, at the same moment; so strategic choices on the continuation of the attack would soon have to be decided, a moment to know the blood of the gambler in oneself.

Intimations of this approaching experience, obviously one of Mailer's preferred pleasures in life, at least when he did it well, were now connected to the professional sense of intrigue at the new task: tonight he would be both speaker and master of ceremonies. The two would conflict, but interestingly. Already he was looking in his mind for kind even celebrative remarks about Paul Goodman[1] which would not violate every reservation he had about Goodman's dank glory. But he had it. It would be possible with no violation of truth to begin by saying that the first speaker looked very much like Nelson Algren,[2] because in fact the first speaker was Paul Goodman, and both Nelson Algren and Paul Goodman looked like old cons. Ladies and Gentlemen, without further ado let me introduce one of young America's favorite old cons, Paul Goodman! (It would not be necessary to add that where Nelson Algren looked like the sort of skinny old con who was in on every make in the joint, and would sign away Grandma's farm to stay in the game, Goodman looked like the sort of old con who had first gotten into trouble in the YMCA, and hadn't spoken to anyone since.)

All this while, Mailer had in clutch *Why Are We In Vietnam?* He had neglected to bring his own copy to Washington and so had borrowed the book from his hostess on the promise he would inscribe it. (Later he was actually to lose it—working apparently on the principle that if you cannot make a hostess happy, the next best charity is to be so evil that the hostess may dine out on tales of your misconduct.) But the copy of the book is now noted because Mailer, holding it in one hand and the mug of whisky in the other, was obliged to notice on entering the Ambassador Theater that he had an overwhelming urge to micturate. The impulse to pass urine, being for some reason more difficult to restrain when both hands are occupied, there

---

[1] American poet and cultural critic (1911–1972), and author of *Growing Up Absurd* (1959).
[2] Contemporary American novelist (b. 1909) and author of *The Man With the Golden Arm* (1949).

was no thought in the Master of Ceremonies' mind about the alternatives—he would have to find The Room before he went on stage.

That was not so immediately simple as one would have thought. The twenty guests from the party, looking a fair piece subdued under the fluorescent lights, had therefore the not unhaggard look of people who have arrived an hour late at the theater. No matter that the theater was by every evidence sleazy (for neighborhood movie houses built on the dream of the owner that some day Garbo or Harlow or Lombard would give a look in, aged immediately they were not used for movies anymore) no matter, the guests had the uneasiness of very late arrivals. Apologetic, they were therefore in haste for the speakers to begin.

Mailer did not know this. He was off already in search of The Room, which, it developed was up on the balcony floor. Imbued with the importance of his first gig as Master of Ceremonies, he felt such incandescence of purpose that he could not quite conceive it necessary to notify de Grazia[3] he would be gone for a minute. Incandescence is the *satori*[4] of the Romantic spirit which spirit would insist—this is the essence of the Romantic—on accelerating time. The greater the power of any subjective state, the more total is a Romantic's assumption that everyone understands exactly what he is about to do, therefore waste not a moment by stopping to tell them.

Flush with his incandescence, happy in all the anticipations of liberty which this Götterdämmerung[5] of a urination was soon to provide, Mailer did not know, but he had already and unwitting to himself metamorphosed into the Beast. Wait and see!

He was met on the stairs by a young man from *Time* magazine, a stringer presumably, for the young man lacked that I-am-damned look in the eye and rep tie of those whose work for *Time* has become a life addiction. The young man had a somewhat ill-dressed look, a map showed on his skin of an old adolescent acne, and he gave off the unhappy furtive presence of a fraternity member on probation for the wrong thing, some grievous mis-deposit of vomit, some hanky panky with frat-house tickets.

But the Beast was in a great good mood. He was soon to speak; that was food for all. So the Beast greeted the *Time* man with the geniality of a surrogate Hemingway unbending for the Luce-ites (Loo-sights was the pun) made some genial cryptic remark or two about finding Herr John, said cheerfully in answer to why he was in Washington that he had come to protest the war in Vietnam, and taking a sip of bourbon from the mug he kept to keep all fires idling right, stepped off into the darkness of the top balcony floor, went through a door into a pitch-black men's room, and was alone with his need. No chance to find the light switch for he had no matches, he did not smoke. It was therefore a matter of locating what's what with the probing of his toes. He found something finally which seemed appropriate, and pleased with the precision of these generally unused senses in his feet, took aim between them at a point twelve inches ahead, and heard in the darkness the sound of his water striking the floor. Some damn mistake had been made, an assault from the side doubtless instead

---

[3] Ed de Grazia, one of the organizers of the march.
[4] State of spiritual enlightenment sought in Zen Buddhism.

[5] German: "twilight of the gods." Hence, catastrophic and grandiose like the Wagnerian opera of that title.

of the front, the bowl was relocated now, and Master of Ceremonies breathed deep of the great reveries of this utterly non-Sisyphian release—at last!!—and thoroughly enjoyed the next forty-five seconds, being left on the aftermath not a note depressed by the condition of the premises. No, he was off on the Romantic's great military dream, which is: seize defeat, convert it to triumph. Of course, pissing on the floor was bad; very bad; the attendant would probably gossip to the police (if the *Time* man did not sniff it out first) and The Uniformed in turn would report it to The Press who were sure to write about the scandalous condition in which this meeting had left the toilets. And all of this contretemps merely because the management, bitter with their lost dream of Garbo and Harlow and Lombard, were now so pocked and stingy they doused the lights. (Out of such stuff is a novelist's brain.)

Well, he could convert this deficiency to an asset. From gap to gain is very American. He would confess straight out to all aloud that he was the one who wet the floor in the men's room, he alone! While the audience was recovering from the existential anxiety of encountering an orator who confessed to such a crime, he would be able—their attention now riveted—to bring them up to a contemplation of deeper problems, of, indeed, the deepest problems, the most chilling alternatives, and would from there seek to bring them back to a restorative view of man. Man might be a fool who peed in the wrong pot, man was also a scrupulous servant of the self-damaging admission; man was therefore a philosopher who possessed the magic stone; he could turn loss to philosophical gain, and so illumine the deeps, find the poles, and eventually learn to cultivate his most special fool's garden: *satori,* incandescence, and the hard gem-like flame of bourbon burning in the furnaces of metabolism.

Thus composed, illumined by these first stages of Emersonian transcendence, Mailer left the men's room, descended the stairs, entered the back of the orchestra, all opening remarks held close file in his mind like troops ranked in order before the parade, and then suddenly, most suddenly saw, with a cancerous swoop of albatross wings, that de Grazia was on the stage, was acting as M.C., was—no calling it back—launched into the conclusion of a gentle stammering stumbling—small orator, de Grazia!—introduction of Paul Goodman. All lost! The magnificent opening remarks about the forces gathered here to assemble on Saturday before the Pentagon, this historic occasion, let us hold it in our mind and focus on a puddle of passed water on the floor above and see if we assembled here can as leftists and proud dissenters contain within our minds the grandeur of the two—all lost!—no chance to do more than pick up later—later! after de Grazia and Goodman had finished dead-assing the crowd. Traitor de Grazia! Sicilian de Grazia!

As Mailer picked his way between people sitting on the stone floor (orchestra seats had been removed—the movie house was a dance hall now with a stage) he made a considerable stir in the orchestra. Mailer had been entering theaters for years, mounting stages—now that he had put on weight, it would probably have been fair to say that he came to the rostrum like a poor man's version of Orson Welles, some minor note of the same contemplative presence. A titter and rise of expectation followed him. He could not resist its appeal. As he passed de Grazia, he scowled, threw a look from Lower Shakespearia "Èt tu Bruté," and proceeded to slap the back of his hand against de Grazia's solar plexus. It was not a heavy blow, but then de Grazia was not a heavy man; he wilted some hint of an inch. And the audience pinched off a howl, squeaked on their squeal. It was not certain to them what had taken place.

Picture the scene two minutes later from the orchestra floor. Paul Goodman, now up at the microphone with no podium or rostrum, is reading the following lines:

> . . . these days my contempt
> for the misrulers of my country
> is icy and my indignation raucous.

It is impossible to tell what he is reading. Off at the wing of the stage where the others are collected—stout Macdonald, noble Lowell, beleaguered de Grazia, and Mailer, Prince of Bourbon, the acoustics are atrocious. One cannot hear a word the speaker is saying. Nor are there enough seats. If de Grazia and Macdonald are sitting in folding chairs, Mailer is squatting on his haunches, or kneeling on one knee like a player about to go back into the ball game. Lowell has the expression on his face of a dues payer who is just about keeping up with the interest on some enormous debt. As he sits on the floor with his long arms clasped mournfully about his long Yankee legs, "I am here," says his expression, "but I do not have to pretend I like what I see." The hollows in his cheeks give a hint of the hanging judge. Lowell is of a good weight, not too heavy, not too light, but the hollows speak of the great Puritan gloom in which the country was founded—man was simply not good enough for God.

At this moment, it is hard not to agree with Lowell. The cavern of the theater seems to resonate behind the glare of the footlights, but this is no resonance of a fine bass voice—it is rather electronics on the march. The public address system hisses, then rings in a random chorus of electronic music, sounds of cerebral mastication from some horror machine of Outer Space (where all that electricity doubtless comes from, child!) then a hum like the squeak in the hinges of the gates of Hell—we are in the penumbra of psychedelic netherworlds, ghost-odysseys from the dead brain cells of adolescent trysts with LSD, some ultrapurple spotlight from the balcony (not ultraviolet—ultrapurple, deepest purple one could conceive) there out in the dark like some neon eye of the night, the media is the message, and the message is purple, speaks of the monarchies of Heaven, madnesses of God, and clam-vaults of people on a stone floor. Mailer's senses are now tuned to absolute pitch or sheer error—he marks a ballot for absolute pitch—he is certain there is a profound pall in the audience. Yes, they sit there, stricken, inert, in terror of what Saturday will bring, and so are unable to rise to a word the speaker is offering them. It will take dynamite to bring life. The shroud of burned-out psychedelic dreams is in this audience, Cancer Gulch with open maw—and Mailer thinks of the vigor and the light (from marijuana?) in the eyes of those American soldiers in Vietnam who have been picked by the newsreel cameras to say their piece, and the happy healthy never unintelligent faces of all those professional football players he studies so assiduously on television come Sunday (he has neglected to put his bets in this week) and wonders how they would poll out on sentiment for the war.

HAWKS 95 · DOVES 6
NFL Footballers Approve Vietnam War

Doubtless. All the healthy Marines, state troopers, professional athletes, movie stars, rednecks, sensuous life-loving Mafia, cops, mill workers, city officials, nice healthy-looking easy-grafting politicians full of the light (from marijuana?) in their eye of a life they enjoy—yes, they would be for the war in Vietnam. Arrayed against them as hard-core troops: an elite! the Freud-ridden embers of Marxism, good old American anxiety strata—the urban middle-class with their proliferated monumental adenoidal resentments, their secret slavish love for the oncoming hegemony of the computer and the suburb, yes, they and their children, by the sheer ironies, the sheer ineptitude, the *kinks* of history, were now being compressed into more and more militant stands, their resistance to the war some hopeless melange, somehow firmed, of Pacifism and closet Communism. And their children—on a freak-out from the suburbs to a love-in on the Pentagon wall.

It was the children in whom Mailer had some hope, a gloomy hope. These mad middle-class children with their lobotomies from sin, their nihilistic embezzlement of all middle-class moral funds, their innocence, their lust for apocalypse, their unbelievable indifference to waste: twenty generations of buried hopes perhaps engraved in their chromosomes, and now conceivably burning like faggots in the secret inquisitional fires of LSD. It was a devil's drug—designed by the Devil to consume the love of the best, and leave them liver-wasted, weeds of the big city. If there had been a player piano, Mailer might have put in a quarter to hear "In the Heart of the City Which Has No Heart."

Yes, these were the troops: middle-class cancer-pushers and drug-gutted flower children. And Paul Goodman to lead them. Was he now reading this?

Once American faces
were beautiful to me
but now they look cruel
and as if they had narrow thoughts.

Not much poetry, but well put prose. And yet there was always Goodman's damnable tolerance for all the varieties of sex. Did he know nothing of evil or entropy? Sex was the superhighway to your own soul's entropy if it was used without a constant sharpening of the taste. And orgies? What did Goodman know of orgies, real ones, not lib-lab college orgies to carry out the higher program of the Great Society, but real ones with murder in the air, and witches on the shoulder. The collected Tory in Mailer came roaring to the surface like a cocked hat in a royal coach.

"When Goodman finishes, I'm going to take over as M.C.," he whispered to de Grazia. (The revery we have just attended took no more in fact than a second. Mailer's melancholy assessment of the forces now mounting in America took place between two consecutive lines of Goodman's poem—not because Mailer cerebrated that instantly, but because he had had the revery many a time before—he had to do no more than sense the audience, whisper Cancer Gulch to himself and the revery went by with a mental ch-ch-ch Click! reviewed again.) In truth, Mailer was now in a state. He had been prepared to open the evening with apocalyptic salvos to announce the real gravity of the situation, and the intensely peculiar American aspect of it—which is that the urban and suburban middle class were to be offered on Saturday an opportunity for glory—what other nation could boast of such option for its middle class? Instead—lost. The benignity and good humor of his planned opening remarks now subjugated to the electronic hawking and squabbling and *hum* of the P.A., the maniacal necessity to *wait* was on this hiatus transformed into a violent concentration of purpose, all intentions reversed. He glared at de Grazia. "How could you do this?" he whispered to his ear.

De Grazia looked somewhat confused at the intensity. Meetings to de Grazia were obviously just meetings, assemblages of people who coughed up for large admissions or kicked in for the pitch; at best, some meetings were less boring than others. De Grazia was much too wise and guilty-spirited to brood on apocalypse. "I couldn't find you," he whispered back.

"You didn't trust me long enough to wait one minute?"

"We were over an hour late," de Grazia whispered again. "We had to begin."

Mailer was all for having the conversation right then on stage: to hell with reciprocal rights and polite incline of the ear to the speaker. The Beast was ready to grapple with the world. "Did you think I wouldn't show up?" he asked de Grazia.

"Well, I was wondering."

In what sort of mumbo-jumbo of promise and betrayal did de Grazia live? How could de Grazia ever suppose he would not show up? He had spent his life showing up at the most boring and onerous places. He gave a blast of his eyes to de Grazia. But Macdonald gave a look at Mailer, as if to say, "You're creating disturbance."

Now Goodman was done.

Mailer walked to the stage. He did not have any idea any longer of what he would say, his mind was empty, but in a fine calm, taking for these five instants a total rest. While there was no danger of Mailer ever becoming a demagogue since if the first idea he offered could appeal to a mob, the second in compensation would be sure to enrage them, he might nonetheless have made a fair country orator, for he loved to speak, he loved in fact to holler, and liked to hear a crowd holler back. (Of how many New York intellectuals may that be said?)

"I'm here as your original M.C., temporarily displaced owing to a contretemps" —which was pronounced purposefully as contretempse—"in the men's room," he said into the microphone for opening, but the gentle high-strung beast of a device pushed into a panic by the electric presence of a real Beast, let loose a squeal which shook the welds in the old foundation of the Ambassador. Mailer immediately decided he had had enough of public address systems, electronic fields of phase, impedance, and spooks in the circuitry. A hex on collaborating with Cancer Gulch. He pushed the microphone away, squared off before the audience. "Can you hear me?" he bellowed.

"Yes."

"Can you hear me in the balcony?"

"Yes."

"Then let's do away with electronics," he called out.

Cries of laughter came back. A very small pattern of applause. (Not too many on his side for electrocuting the public address system, or so his orator's ear recorded the vote.)

"Now I missed the beginning of this occasion, or I would have been here to introduce Paul Goodman, for which we're all sorry, right?"

Confused titters. Small reaction.

"What are you, dead-heads?" he bellowed at the audience. "Or are you all"—here he put on his false Irish accent—"in the nature of becoming dead ahsses?" Small laughs. A whistle or two. "No," he said, replying to the whistles, "I invoke these dead asses as part of the gravity of the occasion. The middle class plus one hippie surrealistic symbolic absolutely insane March on the Pentagon, bless us all," beginning of a big applause which offended Mailer for it came on "bless" and that was too cheap a way to win votes, "bless us all—shit!" he shouted, "I'm trying to say the middle class plus shit, I mean plus revolution, is equal to one big collective dead ass." Some yells of approval, but much shocked curious rather stricken silence. He had broken the shank of his oratorical charge. Now he would have to sweep the audience together again. (Perhaps he felt like a surgeon delivering a difficult breech—nothing to do but plunge to the elbows again.)

"To resume our exposition," a good warm titter, then a ripple of laughter, not unsympathetic to his ear; the humor had been unwitting, but what was the life of an orator without some bonus? "To resume this orderly marshalling of concepts"— a conscious attempt at humor which worked less well; he was beginning to recognize for the first time that bellowing without a mike demanded a more forthright style —"I shall now *engage* in confession." More Irish accent. (He blessed Brendan Behan for what he had learned from him.) "A public speaker may offer you two opportunities. Instruction or confession." Laughter now. "Well, you're all college heads, so my instruction would be as pearls before—I dare not say it." Laughs. Boos. A voice from the balcony: "Come on, Norman, say something!"

"Is there a black man in the house?" asked Mailer. He strode up and down the stage pretending to peer at the audience. But in fact they were illumined just well enough to emphasize one sad discovery—if black faces there were they were certainly not in plenty. "Well ah'll just have to be the *impromptu* Black Power for tonight. Woo-eeeeee! Woo-eeeeee! HMmmmmmm." He grunted with some partial success, showing hints of Cassius Clay. "Get your white butts moving."

"The confession. The confession!" screamed some adolescents from up front.

He came to a stop, shifted his voice. Now he spoke in a relaxed tone. "The confession, yeah!" Well, at least the audience was awake. He felt as if he had driven away some sepulchral phantoms of a variety which inhabited the profound middle-class schist. Now to charge the center of vested spookery.

"Say," he called out into the semidarkness with the ultrapurple light coming off the psychedelic lamp on the rail of the balcony, and the spotlights blaring against his eyes, "say," all happiness again, "I think of Saturday, and that March and do you know, fellow carriers of the holy unendurable grail, for the first time in my life I don't know whether I have the piss or the shit scared out of me most." It was an interesting concept, thought Mailer, for there was a difference between the two kinds of fear—pursue the thought, he would, in quieter times—"we are up, face this, all of you, against an existential situation—we do not know how it is going to turn out, and what is even more inspiring of dread is that the government doesn't know either."

Beginning of a real hand, a couple of rebel yells. "We're going to try to stick it up the government's ass," he shouted, "right into the sphincter of the Pentagon." Wild yells and chills of silence from different reaches of the crowd. Yeah, he was cooking now. "Will reporters please get every word accurately," he called out dryly to warm the chill.

But humor may have been too late. *The New Yorker* did not have strictures against the use of sh*t for nothing; nor did Dwight Macdonald love *The New Yorker* for nothing, he also had strictures against sh*t's metaphorical associations. Mailer looked to his right to see Macdonald approaching, a book in his hands, arms at his side, a sorrowing look of concern in his face. "Norman," said Macdonald quietly, "I can't possibly follow you after all this. Please introduce me, and get it over with."

Mailer was near to stricken. On the one hand interrupted on a flight; on the other, he had fulfilled no duty whatsoever as M.C. He threw a look at Macdonald which said: give me this. I'll owe you one.

But de Grazia was there as well. "Norman, let me be M.C. now," he said.

They were being monstrous unfair, thought Mailer. They didn't understand what he had been doing, how good he had been, what he would do next. Fatal to walk off now—the verdict would claim he was unbalanced. Still, he could not hold the stage by force. That was unthinkably worse.

For the virtuous, however, deliverance (like buttercups) pops up everywhere. Mailer now took the microphone and turned to the audience. He was careful to speak in a relaxed voice. "We are having a disagreement about the value of the proceedings. Some think de Grazia should resume his post as Master of Ceremonies. I would like to keep the position. It is an existential moment. We do not know how it will turn out. So let us vote on it." Happy laughter from the audience at these comic effects. Actually Mailer did not believe it was an existential situation any longer. He reckoned the vote would be well in his favor. "Will those," he asked, "who are in favor of Mr. de Grazia succeeding me as Master of Ceremonies please say aye."

A good sound number said aye.

Now for the ovation. "Will those opposed to this, please say no." The no's to Mailer's lack of pleasure were no greater in volume. "It seems the ayes and no's are about equal," said Mailer. (He was thinking to himself that he had posed the issue all wrong—the ayes should have been reserved for those who would keep him in office.) "Under the circumstances," he announced, "I will keep the chair." Laughter at this easy cheek. He stepped into the middle of such laughter. "You have all just learned an invaluable political lesson." He waved the microphone at the audience. "In the absence of a definitive vote, the man who holds the power, keeps it."

"Hey, de Grazia," someone yelled from the audience, "why do you let him have it?"

Mailer extended the microphone to de Grazia who smiled sweetly into it. "Because if I don't," he said in a gentle voice, "he'll beat the shit out of me." The dread word had been used again.

"Please, Norman," said Macdonald retreating.

So Mailer gave his introduction to Macdonald. It was less than he would have attempted if the flight had not been grounded, but it was certainly respectable. Under the military circumstances, it was a decent cleanup operation. For about a minute he proceeded to introduce Macdonald as a man with whom one might seldom agree, but could never disrespect because he always told the truth as he saw the truth, a man therefore of the most incorruptible integrity. "Pray heaven, I am right," said Mailer to himself, and walked past Macdonald who was on his way to the mike. Both men nodded coolly to each other.

In the wing, visible to the audience, Paul Goodman sat on a chair clearly avoiding any contaminatory encounter with The Existentialist. De Grazia gave his "It's tough all over" smile. Lowell sat in a mournful hunch on the floor, his eyes peering over his glasses to scrutinize the metaphysical substance of his boot, now hide? now machine? now, where the joining and to what? foot to boot, boot to earth—cease all speculations as to what was in Lowell's head. "The one mind a novelist cannot enter is the mind of a novelist superior to himself," said once to Mailer by Jean Malaquais. So, by corollary, the one mind a minor poet may not enter . . .

Lowell looked most unhappy. Mailer, minor poet, had often observed that Lowell had the most disconcerting mixture of strength and weakness in his presence, a blending so dramatic in its visible sign of conflict that one had to assume he would be sensationally attractive to women. He had something untouchable, all insane in its force; one felt immediately there were any number of causes for which the man would be ready to die, and for some he would fight, with an axe in his hand and a Cromwellian light in his eye. It was even possible that physically he was very strong —one couldn't tell at all—he might be fragile, he might have the sort of farm mechanic's strength which could manhandle the rear axle and differential off a car and into the back of a pickup. But physical strength or no, his nerves were all too apparently delicate. Obviously spoiled by everyone for years, he seemed nonetheless to need the spoiling. These nerves—the nerves of a consummate poet—were not tuned to any battering. The squalls of the mike, now riding up a storm on the erratic piping breath of Macdonald's voice, seemed to tear along Lowell's back like a gale. He detested tumult—obviously. And therefore saw everything which was hopeless in a rife situation: the dank middle-class depths of the audience, the strident squalor of the mike, the absurdity of talent gathered to raise money—for what, dear God? who could finally know what this March might convey, or worse, purvey, and worst of all—to be associated now with Mailer's butcher boy attack. Lowell's eyes looked up from the shoe, and passed one withering glance by the novelist, saying much, saying, "Every single bad thing I have ever heard about you is not exaggerated."

Mailer, looking back, thought bitter words he would not say: "You, Lowell, beloved poet of many, what do you know of the dirt and the dark deliveries of the necessary? What do you know of dignity hard-achieved, and dignity lost through innocence, and dignity lost by sacrifice for a cause one cannot name. What do you know about getting fat against your will, and turning into a clown of an arriviste baron when you would rather be an eagle or a count, or rarest of all, some natural aristocrat from these damned democratic states. No, the only subject we share, you and I, is that species of perception which shows that if we are not very loyal to our unendurable and most exigent inner light, then some day we may burn. How dare you condemn me! You know the diseases which inhabit the audience in this accursed psychedelic house. How dare you scorn the explosive I employ?"

And Lowell with a look of the greatest sorrow as if all this *mess* were finally too shapeless for the hard Protestant smith of his own brain, which would indeed burst if it could not forge his experience into the iron edge of the very best words and the most unsinkable relation of words, now threw up his eyes like an epileptic as if turned out of orbit by a turn of the vision—and fell backward, his head striking the floor with no last instant hesitation to cushion the blow, but like a baby, downright sudden, savagely to himself, as if from the height of a foot he had taken a pumpkin and dropped it splat on the floor. "There, much-regarded, much-protected brain, you have finally taken a blow," Lowell might have said to himself, for he proceeded to lie there, resting quietly, while Macdonald went on reading from "The White Man's Burden," Lowell seeming as content as if he had just tested the back of his cranium against a policeman's club. What a royal head they had all to lose!

1968

James Baldwin
b. 1924

"An artist," says James Baldwin, "is here not to give you answers but to ask you questions." In his long career as a novelist, essayist, and civil rights activist, Baldwin's questions have most often taken the form of moral alternatives. In both his fiction and his essays, he deals with controversial subjects, posing questions about race, politics, sex, and love that address the sources of human suffering and human joy. Baldwin's characters succeed through knowledge that is hard won, and they are usually closest to triumph in moments of maximum risk.

James Baldwin was born on August 2, 1924, in Harlem. Three years later his mother, Emma Jones, married David Baldwin, a preacher whom Baldwin later admitted was the only person he had ever hated. Baldwin and his eight brothers and sisters grew up in abject poverty in the Harlem ghetto, and Baldwin says of himself that he "wanted to become rich and famous simply so no one could evict my family again." In 1938 he was converted and became a preacher at the Fireside Pentecostal Assembly, experiences that form the basis for his first novel, *Go Tell It on the Mountain* (1953). In 1942 he graduated from high school and left the ministry, convinced that religion provided inadequate answers to the problems of poor blacks. That same year he began a ten-year struggle to write *Go Tell It on the Mountain.* "In a sense," he said, "I wrote to redeem my father. I had to understand the forces, the experience, the life that shaped him before I could grow up myself, before I could become a writer." While working on the novel, he moved to Greenwich Village, where he met Richard Wright. With Wright's help, he received a Eugene Saxton fellowship and began writing essays and reviews for *The Nation* and *Commentary.* In 1948 he published his first short story, "Previous Condition," and received a Rosenwald fellowship, which allowed him to move to Paris where he remained for the next nine years.

The publication of *Go Tell It on the Mountain* marked Baldwin's emergence as a major writer. He followed it with a collection of essays, *Notes of a Native Son* (1955), and the controversial novel *Giovanni's Room* (1956), which deals with a young, white homosexual's attempt to accept himself as he is. Over the next several years Baldwin's work moved back and forth between efforts to deal with the racial situation in America—*Another Country* (1962) and *The Fire Next Time* (1963)—and efforts to deal with the subject of homosexuality—*Tell Me How Long the Train's Been Gone* (1965). In "Sonny's Blues," which was first published in *Going to Meet the Man* (1965), as in his novel *Just Above My Head* (1979), Baldwin presents an older brother's account of his relationship with a younger brother who is a musician. In the story as well as the novel, Baldwin uses music to explore the relationship of art to life.

Baldwin has always thought of writing—of art—as a public act. Writing, he says, "involves, after all, disturbing the peace." For him, artists are revolutionaries not simply as a result of their perspectives but also as a result of the potential their work has to effect social change. Yet the artist's role is not simply to affirm political rhetoric: "You got to be aware that a slogan is only a slogan," for "what you have to do is insist on complexity which people in the battle don't want to think about."

Baldwin's own involvement in the civil rights movement began with his return from France in 1957; by 1962 he had become a nationally recognized leader for the movement. In "Fifth Avenue, Uptown: A Letter from Harlem" (1960) he says that "it is a terrible, an inexorable, law that one cannot deny the humanity of another without diminishing one's own: in the face of one's victim, one sees himself." To "be a Negro in this country," he says, "and to be relatively conscious is to be in a rage almost all the time."

In his fiction, as well as in his essays and speeches, Baldwin consistently depicts the political, economic, and social injustice he sees in American society, but he also affirms the importance of accepting the past, both personal and collective, even when it involves pain. Accepting "one's past—one's history—is not the same thing as drowning in it, it is learning how to use it." In his work, religion tends to reinforce oppression while art serves as a bridge between people, as music does in "Sonny's Blues." Like art, love is almost always a liberating force in Baldwin's work, even though in its less socially acceptable forms, such as interracial or homosexual love, it can also cause intense pain. "You write," Baldwin says,

> in order to change the world, knowing perfectly well that you probably can't, but also knowing that literature is indispensable to the world. In some way, your aspirations and concern for a single man in fact do begin to change the world. The world changes according to the way people see it, and if you alter, even by a millimeter, the way a person looks or people look at reality, then you can change it.

Further Reading:
F. Eckman, *The Furious Passage of James Baldwin,* 1966.
W. J. Weatherby, *Squaring Off: Mailer vs. Baldwin,* 1976.
L. H. Pratt, *James Baldwin,* 1978.
C. W. Sylvander, *James Baldwin,* 1980.

Text:
Going to Meet the Man, 1965.

Sonny's Blues

I read about it in the paper, in the subway, on my way to work. I read it, and I couldn't believe it, and I read it again. Then perhaps I just stared at it, at the newsprint spelling out his name, spelling out the story. I stared at it in the swinging lights of the subway car, and in the faces and bodies of the people, and in my own face, trapped in the darkness which roared outside.

It was not to be believed and I kept telling myself that, as I walked from the subway station to the high school. And at the same time I couldn't doubt it. I was scared, scared for Sonny. He became real to me again. A great block of ice got settled in my belly and kept melting there slowly all day long, while I taught my classes algebra. It was a special kind of ice. It kept melting, sending trickles of ice water all up and down my veins, but it never got less. Sometimes it hardened and seemed to expand until I felt my guts were going to come spilling out or that I was going to choke or scream. This would always be at a moment when I was remembering some specific thing Sonny had once said or done.

When he was about as old as the boys in my classes his face had been bright and open, there was a lot of copper in it; and he'd had wonderfully direct brown eyes, and great gentleness and privacy. I wondered what he looked like now. He had been picked up, the evening before, in a raid on an apartment downtown, for peddling and using heroin.

I couldn't believe it: but what I mean by that is that I couldn't find any room for it anywhere inside me. I had kept it outside me for a long time. I hadn't wanted to know. I had had suspicions, but I didn't name them, I kept putting them away. I told myself that Sonny was wild, but he wasn't crazy. And he'd always been a good boy, he hadn't ever turned hard or evil or disrespectful, the way kids can, so quick, so quick, especially in Harlem. I didn't want to believe that I'd ever see my brother going down, coming to nothing, all that light in his face gone out, in the condition I'd already seen so many others. Yet it had happened and here I was, talking about algebra to a lot of boys who might, every one of them for all I knew, be popping off needles every time they went to the head. Maybe it did more for them than algebra could.

I was sure that the first time Sonny had ever had horse, he couldn't have been much older than these boys were now. These boys, now, were living as we'd been living then, they were growing up with a rush and their heads bumped abruptly against the low ceiling of their actual possibilities. They were filled with rage. All they really knew were two darknesses, the darkness of their lives, which was now closing in on them, and the darkness of the movies, which had blinded them to that other darkness, and in which they now, vindictively, dreamed, at once more together than they were at any other time, and more alone.

When the last bell rang, the last class ended, I let out my breath. It seemed I'd been holding it for all that time. My clothes were wet—I may have looked as though I'd been sitting in a steam bath, all dressed up, all afternoon. I sat alone in the classroom a long time. I listened to the boys outside, downstairs, shouting and cursing and laughing. Their laughter struck me for perhaps the first time. It was not the joyous laughter which—God knows why—one associates with children. It was mocking and insular, its intent was to denigrate. It was disenchanted, and in this, also, lay the authority of their curses. Perhaps I was listening to them because I was thinking about my brother and in them I heard my brother. And myself.

One boy was whistling a tune, at once very complicated and very simple, it seemed to be pouring out of him as though he were a bird, and it sounded very cool and moving through all that harsh, bright air, only just holding its own through all those other sounds.

I stood up and walked over to the window and looked down into the courtyard. It was the beginning of the spring and the sap was rising in the boys. A teacher passed through them every now and again, quickly, as though he or she couldn't wait to get out of that courtyard, to get those boys out of their sight and off their minds. I started collecting my stuff. I thought I'd better get home and talk to Isabel.

The courtyard was almost deserted by the time I got downstairs. I saw this boy standing in the shadow of a doorway, looking just like Sonny. I almost called his name. Then I saw that it wasn't Sonny, but somebody we used to know, a boy from around our block. He'd been Sonny's friend. He'd never been mine, having been too young for me, and, anyway, I'd never liked him. And now, even though he was a grown-up man, he still hung around that block, still spent hours on the street corners, was always high and raggy. I used to run into him from time to time and he'd often work around to asking me for a quarter or fifty cents. He always had some real good excuse, too, and I always gave it to him, I don't know why.

But now, abruptly, I hated him. I couldn't stand the way he looked at me, partly like a dog, partly like a cunning child. I wanted to ask him what the hell he was doing in the school courtyard.

He sort of shuffled over to me, and he said, "I see you got the papers. So you already know about it."

"You mean about Sonny? Yes, I already know about it. How come they didn't get you?"

He grinned. It made him repulsive and it also brought to mind what he'd looked like as a kid. "I wasn't there. I stay away from them people."

"Good for you." I offered him a cigarette and I watched him through the smoke. "You come all the way down here just to tell me about Sonny?"

"That's right." He was sort of shaking his head and his eyes looked strange, as though they were about to cross. The bright sun deadened his damp dark brown skin and it made his eyes look yellow and showed up the dirt in his kinked hair. He smelled funky. I moved a little away from him and I said, "Well, thanks. But I already know about it and I got to get home."

"I'll walk you a little ways," he said. We started walking. There were a couple of kids still loitering in the courtyard and one of them said goodnight to me and looked strangely at the boy beside me.

"What're you going to do?" he asked me. "I mean, about Sonny?"

"Look. I haven't seen Sonny for over a year, I'm not sure I'm going to do anything. Anyway, what the hell *can* I do?"

"That's right," he said quickly, "ain't nothing you can do. Can't much help old Sonny no more, I guess."

It was what I was thinking and so it seemed to me he had no right to say it.

"I'm surprised at Sonny, though," he went on—he had a funny way of talking, he looked straight ahead as though he were talking to himself—"I thought Sonny was a smart boy, I thought he was too smart to get hung."

"I guess he thought so too," I said sharply, "and that's how he got hung. And now about you? You're pretty goddamn smart, I bet."

Then he looked directly at me, just for a minute. "I ain't smart," he said. "If I was smart, I'd have reached for a pistol a long time ago."

"Look. Don't tell *me* your sad story, if it was up to me, I'd give you one." Then I felt guilty—guilty, probably, for never having supposed that the poor bastard *had* a story of his own, much less a sad one, and I asked, quickly, "What's going to happen to him now?"

He didn't answer this. He was off by himself some place. "Funny thing," he said, and from his tone we might have been discussing the quickest way to get to Brooklyn, "when I saw the papers this morning, the first thing I asked myself was if I had anything to do with it. I felt sort of responsible."

I began to listen more carefully. The subway station was on the corner, just before us, and I stopped. He stopped, too. We were in front of a bar and he ducked slightly, peering in, but whoever he was looking for didn't seem to be there. The juke box was blasting away with something black and bouncy and I half watched the barmaid as she danced her way from the juke box to her place behind the bar. And I watched her face as she laughingly responded to something someone said to her, still keeping time to the music. When she smiled one saw the little girl, one sensed the doomed, still-struggling woman beneath the battered face of the semi-whore.

"I never *give* Sonny nothing," the boy said finally, "but a long time ago I come to school high and Sonny asked me how it felt." He paused, I couldn't bear to watch him, I watched the barmaid, and I listened to the music which seemed to be causing the pavement to shake. "I told him it felt great." The music stopped, the barmaid paused and watched the juke box until the music began again. "It did."

All this was carrying me some place I didn't want to go. I certainly didn't want to know how it felt. It filled everything, the people, the houses, the music, the dark, quicksilver barmaid, with menace; and this menace was their reality.

"What's going to happen to him now?" I asked again.

"They'll send him away some place and they'll try to cure him." He shook his head. "Maybe he'll even think he's kicked the habit. Then they'll let him loose"—he gestured, throwing his cigarette into the gutter. "That's all."

"What do you mean, that's *all?*"

But I knew what he meant.

"I *mean,* that's *all.*" He turned his head and looked at me, pulling down the corners of his mouth. "Don't you know what I mean?" he asked, softly.

"How the hell *would* I know what you mean?" I almost whispered it, I don't know why.

"That's right," he said to the air, "how would *he* know what I mean?" He turned toward me again, patient and calm, and yet I somehow felt him shaking, shaking as though he were going to fall apart. I felt that ice in my guts again, the dread I'd felt all afternoon; and again I watched the barmaid, moving about the bar, washing glasses, and singing. "Listen. They'll let him out and then it'll just start all over again. That's what I mean."

"You mean—they'll let him out. And then he'll just start working his way back in again. You mean he'll never kick the habit. Is that what you mean?"

"That's right," he said, cheerfully. "*You* see what I mean."

"Tell me," I said it last, "why does he want to die? He must want to die, he's killing himself, why does he want to die?"

He looked at me in surprise. He licked his lips. "He don't want to die. He wants to live. Don't nobody want to die, ever."

Then I wanted to ask him—too many things. He could not have answered, or if he had, I could not have borne the answers. I started walking. "Well, I guess it's none of my business."

"It's going to be rough on old Sonny," he said. We reached the subway station. "This is your station?" he asked. I nodded. I took one step down. "Damn!" he said, suddenly. I looked up at him. He grinned again. "Damn it if I didn't leave all my money home. You ain't got a dollar on you, have you? Just for a couple of days, is all."

All at once something inside gave and threatened to come pouring out of me. I didn't hate him any more. I felt that in another moment I'd start crying like a child.

"Sure," I said. "Don't sweat." I looked in my wallet and didn't have a dollar, I only had a five. "Here," I said. "That hold you?"

He didn't look at it—he didn't want to look at it. A terrible, closed look came over his face, as though he were keeping the number on the bill a secret from him and me. "Thanks," he said, and now he was dying to see me go. "Don't worry about Sonny. Maybe I'll write him or something."

"Sure," I said. "You do that. So long."

"Be seeing you," he said. I went on down the steps.

And I didn't write Sonny or send him anything for a long time. When I finally did, it was just after my little girl died, he wrote me back a letter which made me feel like a bastard.

Here's what he said:

> Dear brother,
>
> You don't know how much I needed to hear from you. I wanted to write you many a time but I dug how much I must have hurt you and so I didn't write. But now I feel like a man who's been trying to climb up out of some deep, real deep and funky hole and just saw the sun up there, outside. I got to get outside.
>
> I can't tell you much about how I got here. I mean I don't know how to tell you. I guess I was afraid of something or I was trying to escape from something and you know I have never been very strong in the head (smile). I'm glad Mama and Daddy are dead and can't see what's happened to their son and I swear if I'd known what I was doing I would never have hurt you so, you and a lot of other fine people who were nice to me and who believed in me.
>
> I don't want you to think it had anything to do with me being a musician. It's more than that. Or maybe less than that. I can't get anything straight in my head down here and I try not to think about what's going to happen to me when

I get outside again. Sometime I think I'm going to flip and *never* get outside
and sometime I think I'll come straight back. I tell you one thing, though, I'd
rather blow my brains out than go through this again. But that's what they all
say, so they tell me. If I tell you when I'm coming to New York and if you
could meet me, I sure would appreciate it. Give my love to Isabel and the kids
and I was sure sorry to hear about little Gracie. I wish I could be like Mama
and say the Lord's will be done, but I don't know it seems to me that trouble
is the one thing that never does get stopped and I don't know what good it does
to blame it on the Lord. But maybe it does some good if you believe it.

Your brother,
Sonny

Then I kept in constant touch with him and I sent him whatever I could and I
went to meet him when he came back to New York. When I saw him many things
I thought I had forgotten came flooding back to me. This was because I had begun,
finally, to wonder about Sonny, about the life that Sonny lived inside. This life,
whatever it was, had made him older and thinner and it had deepened the distant
stillness in which he had always moved. He looked very unlike my baby brother. Yet,
when he smiled, when we shook hands, the baby brother I'd never known looked out
from the depths of his private life, like an animal waiting to be coaxed into the light.

"How you been keeping?" he asked me.

"All right. And you?"

"Just fine." He was smiling all over his face. "It's good to see you again."

"It's good to see you."

The seven years' difference in our ages lay between us like a chasm: I wondered
if these years would ever operate between us as a bridge. I was remembering, and it
made it hard to catch my breath, that I had been there when he was born; and I had
heard the first words he had ever spoken. When he started to walk, he walked from
our mother straight to me. I caught him just before he fell when he took the first
steps he ever took in this world.

"How's Isabel?"

"Just fine. She's dying to see you."

"And the boys?"

"They're fine, too. They're anxious to see their uncle."

"Oh, come on. You know they don't remember me."

"Are you kidding? Of course they remember you."

He grinned again. We got into a taxi. We had a lot to say to each other, far too
much to know how to begin.

As the taxi began to move, I asked, "You still want to go to India?"

He laughed. "You still remember that. Hell, no. This place is Indian enough for
me."

"It used to belong to them," I said.

And he laughed again. "They damn sure knew what they were doing when they
got rid of it."

Years ago, when he was around fourteen, he'd been all hipped on the idea of going
to India. He read books about people sitting on rocks, naked, in all kinds of weather,
but mostly bad, naturally, and walking barefoot through hot coals and arriving at

wisdom. I used to say that it sounded to me as though they were getting away from wisdom as fast as they could. I think he sort of looked down on me for that.

"Do you mind," he asked, "if we have the driver drive alongside the park? On the west side—I haven't seen the city in so long."

"Of course not," I said. I was afraid that I might sound as though I were humoring him, but I hoped he wouldn't take it that way.

So we drove along, between the green of the park and the stony, lifeless elegance of hotels and apartment buildings, toward the vivid, killing streets of our childhood. These streets hadn't changed, though housing projects jutted up out of them now like rocks in the middle of a boiling sea. Most of the houses in which we had grown up had vanished, as had the stores from which we had stolen, the basements in which we had first tried sex, the rooftops from which we had hurled tin cans and bricks. But houses exactly like the houses of our past yet dominated the landscape, boys exactly like the boys we once had been found themselves smothering in these houses, came down into the streets for light and air and found themselves encircled by disaster. Some escaped the trap, most didn't. Those who got out always left something of themselves behind, as some animals amputate a leg and leave it in the trap. It might be said, perhaps, that I had escaped, after all, I was a school teacher; or that Sonny had, he hadn't lived in Harlem for years. Yet, as the cab moved uptown through streets which seemed, with a rush, to darken with dark people, and as I covertly studied Sonny's face, it came to me that what we both were seeking through our separate cab windows was that part of ourselves which had been left behind. It's always at the hour of trouble and confrontation that the missing member aches.

We hit 110th Street and started rolling up Lenox Avenue. And I'd known this avenue all my life, but it seemed to me again, as it had seemed on the day I'd first heard about Sonny's trouble, filled with a hidden menace which was its very breath of life.

"We almost there," said Sonny.

"Almost." We were both too nervous to say anything more.

We live in a housing project. It hasn't been up long. A few days after it was up it seemed uninhabitably new, now, of course, it's already rundown. It looks like a parody of the good, clean, faceless life—God knows the people who live in it do their best to make it a parody. The beat-looking grass lying around isn't enough to make their lives green, the hedges will never hold out the streets, and they know it. The big windows fool no one, they aren't big enough to make space out of no space. They don't bother with the windows, they watch the TV screen instead. The playground is most popular with the children who don't play at jacks, or skip rope, or roller skate, or swing, and they can be found in it after dark. We moved in partly because it's not too far from where I teach, and partly for the kids; but it's really just like the houses in which Sonny and I grew up. The same things happen, they'll have the same things to remember. The moment Sonny and I started into the house I had the feeling that I was simply bringing him back into the danger he had almost died trying to escape.

Sonny has never been talkative. So I don't know why I was sure he'd be dying to talk to me when supper was over the first night. Everything went fine, the oldest boy remembered him, and the youngest boy liked him, and Sonny had remembered to bring something for each of them; and Isabel, who is really much nicer than I am, more open and giving, had gone to a lot of trouble about dinner and was genuinely glad to see him. And she's always been able to tease Sonny in a way that I haven't. It was nice to see her face so vivid again and to hear her laugh and watch her make Sonny laugh. She wasn't, or, anyway, she didn't seem to be, at all uneasy or embarrassed. She chatted as though there were no subject which had to be avoided and she got Sonny past his first, faint stiffness. And thank God she was there, for I was filled with that icy dread again. Everything I did seemed awkward to me, and everything I said sounded freighted with hidden meaning. I was trying to remember everything I'd heard about dope addiction and I couldn't help watching Sonny for signs. I wasn't doing it out of malice. I was trying to find out something about my brother. I was dying to hear him tell me he was safe.

"Safe!" my father grunted, whenever Mama suggested trying to move to a neighborhood which might be safer for children. "Safe, hell! Ain't no place safe for kids, nor nobody."

He always went on like this, but he wasn't, ever, really as bad as he sounded, not even on weekends, when he got drunk. As a matter of fact, he was always on the lookout for "something a little better," but he died before he found it. He died suddenly, during a drunken weekend in the middle of the war, when Sonny was fifteen. He and Sonny hadn't ever got on too well. And this was partly because Sonny was the apple of his father's eye. It was because he loved Sonny so much and was frightened for him, that he was always fighting with him. It doesn't do any good to fight with Sonny. Sonny just moves back, inside himself, where he can't be reached. But the principal reason that they never hit it off is that they were so much alike. Daddy was big and rough and loud-talking, just the opposite of Sonny, but they both had—that same privacy.

Mama tried to tell me something about this, just after Daddy died. I was home on leave from the army.

This was the last time I ever saw my mother alive. Just the same, this picture gets all mixed up in my mind with pictures I had of her when she was younger. The way I always see her is the way she used to be on a Sunday afternoon, say, when the old folks were talking after the big Sunday dinner. I always see her wearing pale blue. She'd be sitting on the sofa. And my father would be sitting in the easy chair, not far from her. And the living room would be full of church folks and relatives. There they sit, in chairs all around the living room, and the night is creeping up outside, but nobody knows it yet. You can see the darkness growing against the windowpanes and you hear the street noises every now and again, or maybe the jangling beat of a tambourine from one of the churches close by, but it's real quiet in the room. For a moment nobody's talking, but every face looks darkening, like the sky outside. And my mother rocks a little from the waist, and my father's eyes are closed. Everyone is looking at something a child can't see. For a minute they've forgotten the children. Maybe a kid is lying on the rug, half asleep. Maybe somebody's got a kid in his lap and is absent-mindedly stroking the kid's head. Maybe there's a kid, quiet and big-eyed, curled up in a big chair in the corner. The silence, the darkness coming, and the darkness in the faces frightens the child obscurely. He hopes that the hand which strokes his forehead will never stop—will never die. He hopes that there will never come a time when the old folks won't be sitting around the living room, talking about where they've come from, and what they've seen, and what's happened to them and their kinfolk.

But something deep and watchful in the child knows that this is bound to end, is already ending. In a moment someone will get up and turn on the light. Then the old folks will remember the children and they won't talk any more that day. And when light fills the room, the child is filled with darkness. He knows that every time this happens he's moved just a little closer to that darkness outside. The darkness outside is what the old folks have been talking about. It's what they've come from. It's what they endure. The child knows that they won't talk any more because if he knows too much about what's happened to *them,* he'll know too much too soon, about what's going to happen to *him.*

The last time I talked to my mother, I remember I was restless. I wanted to get out and see Isabel. We weren't married then and we had a lot to straighten out between us.

There Mama sat, in black, by the window. She was humming an old church song, *Lord, you brought me from a long ways off.* Sonny was out somewhere. Mama kept watching the streets.

"I don't know," she said, "if I'll ever see you again, after you go off from here. But I hope you'll remember the things I tried to teach you."

"Don't talk like that," I said, and smiled. "You'll be here a long time yet."

She smiled, too, but she said nothing. She was quiet for a long time. And I said, "Mama, don't you worry about nothing. I'll be writing all the time, and you be getting the checks. . . ."

"I want to talk to you about your brother," she said, suddenly. "If anything happens to me he ain't going to have nobody to look out for him."

"Mama," I said, "ain't nothing going to happen to you *or* Sonny. Sonny's all right. He's a good boy and he's got good sense."

"It ain't a question of his being a good boy," Mama said, "nor of his having good sense. It ain't only the bad ones, nor yet the dumb ones that gets sucked under." She stopped, looking at me. "Your Daddy once had a brother," she said, and she smiled in a way that made me feel she was in pain. "You didn't never know that, did you?"

"No," I said, "I never knew that," and I watched her face.

"Oh, yes," she said, "your Daddy had a brother." She looked out of the window again. "I know you never saw your Daddy cry. But *I* did—many a time, through all these years."

I asked her, "What happened to his brother? How come nobody's ever talked about him?"

This was the first time I ever saw my mother look old.

"His brother got killed," she said, "when he was just a little younger than you are now. I knew him. He was a fine boy. He was maybe a little full of the devil, but he didn't mean nobody no harm."

Then she stopped and the room was silent, exactly as it had sometimes been on those Sunday afternoons. Mama kept looking out into the streets.

"He used to have a job in the mill," she said, "and, like all young folks, he just liked to perform on Saturday nights. Saturday nights, him and your father would drift around to different place, go to dances and things like that, or just sit around with people they knew, and your father's brother would sing, he had a fine voice, and play along with himself on his guitar. Well, this particular Saturday night, him and your father was coming home from some place, and they were both a little drunk and there was a moon that night, it was bright like day. Your father's brother was feeling kind of good, and he was whistling to himself, and he had his guitar slung over his shoulder. They was coming down a hill and beneath them was a road that turned off from the highway. Well, your father's brother, being always kind of frisky, decided to run down this hill, and he did, with that guitar banging and clanging behind him, and he ran across the road, and he was making water behind a tree. And your father was sort of amused at him and he was still coming down the hill, kind of slow. Then he heard a car motor and that same minute his brother stepped from behind the tree, into the road, in the moonlight. And he started to cross the road. And your father started to run down the hill, he says he don't know why. This car was full of white men. They was all drunk, and when they seen your father's brother they let out a great whoop and holler and they aimed the car straight at him. They was having fun, they just wanted to scare him, the way they do sometimes, you know. But they was drunk. And I guess the boy, being drunk, too, and scared, kind of lost his head. By the time he jumped it was too late. Your father says he heard his brother scream when the car rolled over him, and he heard the wood of that guitar when it give, and he heard them strings go flying, and he heard them white men shouting, and the car kept on a-going and it ain't stopped till this day. And, time your father got down the hill, his brother weren't nothing but blood and pulp."

Tears were gleaming on my mother's face. There wasn't anything I could say.

"He never mentioned it," she said, "because I never let him mention it before you children. Your Daddy was like a crazy man that night and for many a night thereafter. He says he never in his life seen anything as dark as that road after the lights of that car had gone away. Weren't nothing, weren't nobody on that road, just your Daddy and his brother and that busted guitar. Oh, yes. Your Daddy never did really get right again. Till the day he died he weren't sure but that every white man he saw was the man that killed his brother."

She stopped and took out her handkerchief and dried her eyes and looked at me.

"I ain't telling you all this," she said, "to make you scared or bitter or to make you hate nobody. I'm telling you this because you got a brother. And the world ain't changed."

I guess I didn't want to believe this. I guess she saw this in my face. She turned away from me, toward the window again, searching those streets.

"But I praise my Redeemer," she said at last, "that He called your Daddy home before me. I ain't saying it to throw no flowers at myself, but, I declare, it keeps me from feeling too cast down to know I helped your father get safely through this world. Your father always acted like he was the roughest, strongest man on earth. And everybody took him to be like that. But if he hadn't had *me* there—to see his tears!"

She was crying again. Still, I couldn't move. I said, "Lord, Lord, Mama, I didn't know it was like that."

"Oh, honey," she said, "there's a lot that you don't know. But you are going to *find it out.*" She stood up from the window and came over to me. "You got to hold on to your brother," she said, "and don't let him fall, no matter what it looks like is happening to him and no matter how evil you gets with him. You going to be evil with him many a time. But don't you forget what I told you, you hear?"

"I won't forget," I said. "Don't you worry, I won't forget. I won't let nothing happen to Sonny."

My mother smiled as though she were amused at something she saw in my face. Then, "You may not be able to stop nothing from happening. But you got to let him know you's *there*."

Two days later I was married, and then I was gone. And I had a lot of things on my mind and I pretty well forgot my promise to Mama until I got shipped home on a special furlough for her funeral.

And, after the funeral, with just Sonny and me alone in the empty kitchen, I tried to find out something about him.

"What do you want to do?" I asked him.

"I'm going to be a musician," he said.

For he had graduated, in the time I had been away, from dancing to the juke box to finding out who was playing what, and what they were doing with it, and he had bought himself a set of drums.

"You mean, you want to be a drummer?" I somehow had the feeling that being a drummer might be all right for other people but not for my brother Sonny.

"I don't think," he said, looking at me very gravely, "that I'll ever be a good drummer. But I think I can play a piano."

I frowned. I'd never played the role of the older brother quite so seriously before, had scarcely ever, in fact, *asked* Sonny a damn thing. I sensed myself in the presence of something I didn't really know how to handle, didn't understand. So I made my frown a little deeper as I asked: "What kind of musician do you want to be?"

He grinned. "How many kinds do you think there are?"

"Be *serious*," I said.

He laughed, throwing his head back, and then looked at me. "I *am* serious."

"Well, then, for Christ's sake, stop kidding around and answer a serious question. I mean, do you want to be a concert pianist, you want to play classical music and all that, or—or what?" Long before I finished he was laughing again. "For Christ's sake, Sonny!"

He sobered, but with difficulty. "I'm sorry. But you sound so—*scared!*" and he was off again.

"Well, you may think it's funny now, baby, but it's not going to be so funny when you have to make your living at it, let me tell you *that*." I was furious because I knew he was laughing at me and I didn't know why.

"No," he said, very sober now, and afraid, perhaps, that he'd hurt me, "I don't want to be a classical pianist. That isn't what interests me. I mean"—he paused, looking hard at me, as though his eyes would help me to understand, and then gestured helplessly, as though perhaps his hand would help—"I mean, I'll have a lot of studying to do, and I'll have to study *everything*, but, I mean, I want to play *with*—jazz musicians." He stopped. "I want to play jazz," he said.

Well, the word had never before sounded as heavy, as real, as it sounded that afternoon in Sonny's mouth. I just looked at him and I was probably frowning a real frown by this time. I simply couldn't see why on earth he'd want to spend his time hanging around nightclubs, clowning around on bandstands, while people pushed each other around a dance floor. It seemed—beneath him, somehow. I had never thought about it before, had never been forced to, but I suppose I had always put jazz musicians in a class with what Daddy called "good-time people."

"Are you *serious?*"

"Hell, *yes,* I'm serious."

He looked more helpless than ever, and annoyed, and deeply hurt.

I suggested, helpfully: "You mean—like Louis Armstrong?"

His face closed as though I'd struck him. "No. I'm not talking about none of that old-time, down home crap."

"Well, look, Sonny, I'm sorry, don't get mad. I just don't altogether get it, that's all. Name somebody—you know, a jazz musician you admire."

"Bird."

"Who?"

"Bird! Charlie Parker! Don't they teach you nothing in the goddamn army?"

I lit a cigarette. I was surprised and then a little amused to discover that I was trembling. "I've been out of touch," I said. "You'll have to be patient with me. Now. Who's this Parker character?"

"He's just one of the greatest jazz musicians alive," said Sonny, sullenly, his hands in his pockets, his back to me. "Maybe *the* greatest," he added, bitterly, "that's probably why *you* never heard of him."

"All right," I said, "I'm ignorant. I'm sorry. I'll go out and buy all the cat's records right away, all right?"

"It don't," said Sonny, with dignity, "make any difference to me. I don't care what you listen to. Don't do me no favors."

I was beginning to realize that I'd never seen him so upset before. With another part of my mind I was thinking that this would probably turn out to be one of those things kids go through and that I shouldn't make it seem important by pushing it too hard. Still, I didn't think it would do any harm to ask: "Doesn't all this take a lot of time? Can you make a living at it?"

He turned back to me and half leaned, half sat, on the kitchen table. "Everything takes time," he said, "and—well, yes, sure, I can make a living at it. But what I don't seem to be able to make you understand is that it's the only thing I want to do."

"Well, Sonny," I said, gently, "you know people can't always do exactly what they *want* to do—"

"*No,* I don't know that," said Sonny, surprising me. "I think people *ought* to do what they want to do, what else are they alive for?"

"You getting to be a big boy," I said desperately, "it's time you started thinking about your future."

"I'm thinking about my future," said Sonny, grimly. "I think about it all the time."

I gave up. I decided, if he didn't change his mind, that we could always talk about it later. "In the meantime," I said, "you got to finish school." We had already decided that he'd have to move in with Isabel and her folks. I knew this wasn't the ideal arrangement because Isabel's folks are inclined to be dicty[1] and they hadn't especially wanted Isabel to marry me. But I didn't know what else to do. "And we have to get you fixed up at Isabel's."

There was a long silence. He moved from the kitchen table to the window. "That's a terrible idea. You know it yourself."

"Do you have a *better* idea?"

---

[1] Snobbish or bossy.

He just walked up and down the kitchen for a minute. He was as tall as I was. He had started to shave. I suddenly had the feeling that I didn't know him at all.

He stopped at the kitchen table and picked up my cigarettes. Looking at me with a kind of mocking, amused defiance, he put one between his lips. "You mind?"

"You smoking already?"

He lit the cigarette and nodded, watching me through the smoke. "I just wanted to see if I'd have the courage to smoke in front of you." He grinned and blew a great cloud of smoke to the ceiling. "It was easy." He looked at my face. "Come on, now. I bet you was smoking at my age, tell the truth."

I didn't say anything but the truth was on my face, and he laughed. But now there was something very strained in his laugh. "Sure. And I bet that ain't all you was doing."

He was frightening me a little. "Cut the crap," I said. "We already decided that you was going to go and live at Isabel's. Now what's got into you all of a sudden?"

"*You* decided it," he pointed out. "*I* didn't decide nothing." He stopped in front of me, leaning against the stove, arms loosely folded. "Look, brother. I don't want to stay in Harlem no more, I really don't." He was very earnest. He looked at me, then over toward the kitchen window. There was something in his eyes I'd never seen before, some thoughtfulness, some worry all his own. He rubbed the muscle of one arm. "It's time I was getting out of here."

"Where do you want to *go*, Sonny?"

"I want to join the army. Or the navy, I don't care. If I say I'm old enough, they'll believe me."

Then I got mad. It was because I was so scared. "You must be crazy. You goddamn fool, what the hell do you want to go and join the *army* for?"

"I just told you. To get out of Harlem."

"Sonny, you haven't even finished *school*. And if you really want to be a musician, how do you expect to study if you're in the *army?*"

He looked at me, trapped, and in anguish. "There's ways. I might be able to work out some kind of deal. Anyway, I'll have the G.I. Bill when I come out."

"*If* you come out." We stared at each other. "Sonny, please. Be reasonable. I know the setup is far from perfect. But we got to do the best we can."

"I ain't learning nothing in school," he said. "Even when I go." He turned away from me and opened the window and threw his cigarette out into the narrow alley. I watched his back. "At least, I ain't learning nothing you'd want me to learn." He slammed the window so hard I thought the glass would fly out, and turned back to me. "And I'm sick of the stink of these garbage cans!"

"Sonny," I said, "I know how you feel. But if you don't finish school now, you're going to be sorry later that you didn't." I grabbed him by the shoulders. "And you only got another year. It ain't so bad. And I'll come back and I swear I'll help you do *whatever* you want to do. Just try to put up with it till I come back. Will you please do that? For me?"

He didn't answer and he wouldn't look at me.

"Sonny. You hear me?"

He pulled away. "I hear you. But you never hear anything *I* say."

I didn't know what to say to that. He looked out of the window and then back at me. "OK," he said, and sighed. "I'll try."

Then I said, trying to cheer him up a little, "They got a piano at Isabel's. You can practice on it."

And as a matter of fact, it did cheer him up for a minute. "That's right," he said to himself. "I forgot that." His face relaxed a little. But the worry, the thoughtfulness, played on it still, the way shadows play on a face which is staring into the fire.

But I thought I'd never hear the end of that piano. At first, Isabel would write me, saying how nice it was that Sonny was so serious about his music and how, as soon as he came in from school, or wherever he had been when he was supposed to be at school, he went straight to that piano and stayed there until suppertime. And, after supper, he went back to that piano and stayed there until everybody went to bed. He was at the piano all day Saturday and all day Sunday. Then he bought a record player and started playing records. He'd play one record over and over again, all day long sometimes, and he'd improvise along with it on the piano. Or he'd play one section of the record, one chord, one change, one progression, then he'd do it on the piano. Then back to the record. Then back to the piano.

Well, I really don't know how they stood it. Isabel finally confessed that it wasn't like living with a person at all, it was like living with sound. And the sound didn't make any sense to her, didn't make any sense to any of them—naturally. They began, in a way, to be afflicted by this presence that was living in their home. It was as though Sonny were some sort of god, or monster. He moved in an atmosphere which wasn't like theirs at all. They fed him and he ate, he washed himself, he walked in and out of their door; he certainly wasn't nasty or unpleasant or rude, Sonny isn't any of those things; but it was as though he were all wrapped up in some cloud, some fire, some vision all his own; and there wasn't any way to reach him.

At the same time, he wasn't really a man yet, he was still a child, and they had to watch out for him in all kinds of ways. They certainly couldn't throw him out. Neither did they dare to make a great scene about that piano because even they dimly sensed, as I sensed, from so many thousands of miles away, that Sonny was at that piano playing for his life.

But he hadn't been going to school. One day a letter came from the school board and Isabel's mother got it—there had, apparently, been other letters but Sonny had torn them up. This day, when Sonny came in, Isabel's mother showed him the letter and asked where he'd been spending his time. And she finally got it out of him that he'd been down in Greenwich Village, with musicians and other characters, in a white girl's apartment. And this scared her and she started to scream at him and what came up, once she began—though she denies it to this day—was what sacrifices they were making to give Sonny a decent home and how little he appreciated it.

Sonny didn't play the piano that day. By evening, Isabel's mother had calmed down but then there was the old man to deal with, and Isabel herself. Isabel says she did her best to be calm but she broke down and started crying. She says she just watched Sonny's face. She could tell, by watching him, what was happening with him. And what was happening was that they penetrated his cloud, they had reached him. Even if their fingers had been a thousand times more gentle than human fingers ever are, he could hardly help feeling that they had stripped him naked and were spitting on that nakedness. For he also had to see that his presence, that music, which was life or death to him, had been torture for them and that they had endured it, not at all for his sake, but only for mine. And Sonny couldn't take that. He can take it a little better today than he could then but he's still not very good at it and, frankly, I don't know anybody who is.

The silence of the next few days must have been louder than the sound of all the music ever played since time began. One morning, before she went to work, Isabel was in his room for something and she suddenly realized that all of his records were gone. And she knew for certain that he was gone. And he was. He went as far as the navy would carry him. He finally sent me a postcard from some place in Greece and that was the first I knew that Sonny was still alive. I didn't see him any more until we were both back in New York and the war had long been over.

He was a man by then, of course, but I wasn't willing to see it. He came by the house from time to time, but we fought almost every time we met. I didn't like the way he carried himself, loose and dreamlike all the time, and I didn't like his friends, and his music seemed to be merely an excuse for the life he led. It sounded just that weird and disordered.

Then we had a fight, a pretty awful fight, and I didn't see him for months. By and by I looked him up, where he was living, in a furnished room in the Village, and I tried to make it up. But there were lots of other people in the room and Sonny just lay on his bed, and he wouldn't come downstairs with me, and he treated these other people as though they were his family and I weren't. So I got mad and then he got mad, and then I told him that he might just as well be dead as live the way he was living. Then he stood up and he told me not to worry about him any more in life, that he *was* dead as far as I was concerned. Then he pushed me to the door and the other people looked on as though nothing were happening, and he slammed the door behind me. I stood in the hallway, staring at the door. I heard somebody laugh in the room and then the tears came to my eyes. I started down the steps, whistling to keep from crying, I kept whistling to myself, *You going to need me, baby, one of these cold, rainy days.*

I read about Sonny's trouble in the spring. Little Grace died in the fall. She was a beautiful little girl. But she only lived a little over two years. She died of polio and she suffered. She had a slight fever for a couple of days, but it didn't seem like anything and we just kept her in bed. And we would certainly have called the doctor, but the fever dropped, she seemed to be all right. So we thought it had just been a cold. Then, one day, she was up, playing, Isabel was in the kitchen fixing lunch for the two boys when they'd come in from school, and she heard Grace fall down in the living room. When you have a lot of children you don't always start running when one of them falls, unless they start screaming or something. And, this time, Grace was quiet. Yet, Isabel says that when she heard that *thump* and then that silence, something happened in her to make her afraid. And she ran to the living room and there was little Grace on the floor, all twisted up, and the reason she hadn't screamed was that she couldn't get her breath. And when she did scream, it was the worst sound, Isabel says, that she'd ever heard in all her life, and she still hears it sometimes in her dreams. Isabel will sometimes wake me up with a low, moaning, strangled sound and I have to be quick to awaken her and hold her to me and where Isabel is weeping against me seems a mortal wound.

I think I may have written Sonny the very day that little Grace was buried. I was sitting in the living room in the dark, by myself, and I suddenly thought of Sonny. My trouble made his real.

One Saturday afternoon, when Sonny had been living with us, or, anyway, been in our house, for nearly two weeks, I found myself wandering aimlessly about the living room, drinking from a can of beer, and trying to work up the courage to search Sonny's room. He was out, he was usually out whenever I was home, and Isabel had taken the children to see their grandparents. Suddenly I was standing still in front of the living room window, watching Seventh Avenue. The idea of searching Sonny's room made me still. I scarcely dared to admit to myself what I'd be searching for. I didn't know what I'd do if I found it. Or if I didn't.

On the sidewalk across from me, near the entrance to a barbecue joint, some people were holding an old-fashioned revival meeting. The barbecue cook, wearing a dirty white apron, his conked hair[2] reddish and metallic in the pale sun, and a cigarette between his lips, stood in the doorway, watching them. Kids and older people paused in their errands and stood there, along with some older men and a couple of very tough-looking women who watched everything that happened on the avenue, as though they owned it, or were maybe owned by it. Well, they were watching this, too. The revival was being carried on by three sisters in black, and a brother. All they had were their voices and their Bibles and a tambourine. The brother was testifying and while he testified two of the sisters stood together, seeming to say, amen, and the third sister walked around with the tambourine outstretched and a couple of people dropped coins into it. Then the brother's testimony ended and the sister who had been taking up the collection dumped the coins into her palm and transferred them to the pocket of her long black robe. Then she raised both hands, striking the tambourine against the air, and then against one hand, and she started to sing. And the two other sisters and the brother joined in.

It was strange, suddenly, to watch, though I had been seeing these street meetings all my life. So, of course, had everybody else down there. Yet, they paused and watched and listened and I stood still at the window. *"Tis the old ship of Zion,"* they sang, and the sister with the tambourine kept a steady, jangling beat, *"it has rescued many a thousand!"* Not a soul under the sound of their voices was hearing this song for the first time, not one of them had been rescued. Nor had they seen much in the way of rescue work being done around them. Neither did they especially believe in the holiness of the three sisters and the brother, they knew too much about them, knew where they lived, and how. The woman with the tambourine, whose voice dominated the air, whose face was bright with joy, was divided by very little from the woman who stood watching her, a cigarette between her heavy, chapped lips, her hair a cuckoo's nest, her face scarred and swollen from many beatings, and her black eyes glittering like coal. Perhaps they both knew this, which was why, when, as rarely, they addressed each other, they addressed each other as Sister. As the singing filled the air the watching, listening faces underwent a change, the eyes focusing on something within; the music seemed to soothe a poison out of them; and time seemed, nearly, to fall away from the sullen, belligerent, battered faces, as though they were fleeing back to their first condition, while dreaming of their last. The barbecue cook

---

[2] Hair that has been straightened and coated heavily with grease.

half shook his head and smiled, and dropped his cigarette and disappeared into his joint. A man fumbled in his pockets for change and stood holding it in his hand impatiently, as though he had just remembered a pressing appointment further up the avenue. He looked furious. Then I saw Sonny, standing on the edge of the crowd. He was carrying a wide, flat notebook with a green cover, and it made him look, from where I was standing, almost like a schoolboy. The coppery sun brought out the copper in his skin, he was very faintly smiling, standing very still. Then the singing stopped, the tambourine turned into a collection plate again. The furious man dropped in his coins and vanished, so did a couple of the women, and Sonny dropped some change in the plate, looking directly at the woman with a little smile. He started across the avenue, toward the house. He has a slow, loping walk, something like the way Harlem hipsters walk, only he's imposed on this his own half-beat. I had never really noticed it before.

I stayed at the window, both relieved and apprehensive. As Sonny disappeared from my sight, they began singing again. And they were still singing when his key turned in the lock.

"Hey," he said.

"Hey, yourself. You want some beer?"

"No. Well, maybe." But he came up to the window and stood beside me, looking out. "What a warm voice," he said.

They were singing *If I could only hear my mother pray again!*

"Yes," I said, "and she can sure beat that tambourine."

"But what a terrible song," he said, and laughed. He dropped his notebook on the sofa and disappeared into the kitchen. "Where's Isabel and the kids?"

"I think they went to see their grandparents. You hungry?"

"No." He came back into the living room with his can of beer. "You want to come some place with me tonight?"

I sensed, I don't know how, that I couldn't possibly say no. "Sure. Where?"

He sat down on the sofa and picked up his notebook and started leafing through it. "I'm going to sit in with some fellows in a joint in the Village."

"You mean, you're going to play, tonight?"

"That's right." He took a swallow of his beer and moved back to the window. He gave me a sidelong look. "If you can stand it."

"I'll try," I said.

He smiled to himself and we both watched as the meeting across the way broke up. The three sisters and the brother, heads bowed, were singing *God be with you till we meet again.* The faces around them were very quiet. Then the song ended. The small crowd dispersed. We watched the three women and the lone man walk slowly up the avenue.

"When she was singing before," said Sonny, abruptly, "her voice reminded me for a minute of what heroin feels like sometimes—when it's in your veins. It makes you feel sort of warm and cool at the same time. And distant. And—and sure." He sipped his beer, very deliberately not looking at me. I watched his face. "It makes you feel —in control. Sometimes you've got to have that feeling."

"Do you?" I sat down slowly in the easy chair.

"Sometimes." He went to the sofa and picked up his notebook again. "Some people do."

"In order," I asked, "to play?" And my voice was very ugly, full of contempt and anger.

"Well"—he looked at me with great, troubled eyes, as though, in fact, he hoped his eyes would tell me things he could never otherwise say—"they *think* so. And *if* they think so—!"

"And what do *you* think?" I asked.

He sat on the sofa and put his can of beer on the floor. "I don't know," he said, and I couldn't be sure if he were answering my question or pursuing his thoughts. His face didn't tell me. "It's not so much to *play*. It's to *stand* it, to be able to make it at all. On any level." He frowned and smiled: "In order to keep from shaking to pieces."

"But these friends of yours," I said, "they seem to shake themselves to pieces pretty goddamn fast."

"Maybe." He played with the notebook. And something told me that I should curb my tongue, that Sonny was doing his best to talk, that I should listen. "But of course you only know the ones that've gone to pieces. Some don't—or at least they haven't *yet* and that's just about all *any* of us can say." He paused. "And then there are some who just live, really, in hell, and they know it and they see what's happening and they go right on. I don't know." He sighed, dropped the notebook, folded his arms. "Some guys, you can tell from the way they play, they on something *all* the time. And you can see that, well, it makes something real for them. But of course," he picked up his beer from the floor and sipped it and put the can down again, "they *want* to, too, you've got to see that. Even some of them that say they don't—*some, not all*."

"And what about you?" I asked—I couldn't help it. "What about you? Do *you* want to?"

He stood up and walked to the window and remained silent for a long time. Then he sighed. "Me," he said. Then: "While I was downstairs before, on my way here, listening to that woman sing, it struck me all of a sudden how much suffering she must have had to go through—to sing like that. It's *repulsive* to think you have to suffer that much."

I said: "But there's no way not to suffer—is there, Sonny?"

"I believe not," he said and smiled, "but that's never stopped anyone from trying." He looked at me. "Has it?" I realized, with this mocking look, that there stood between us, forever, beyond the power of time or forgiveness, the fact that I had held silence—so long!—when he had needed human speech to help him. He turned back to the window. "No, there's no way not to suffer. But you try all kinds of ways to keep from drowning in it, to keep on top of it, and to make it seem—well, like *you*. Like you did something, all right, and now you're suffering for it. You know?" I said nothing. "Well you know," he said, impatiently, "why *do* people suffer? Maybe it's better to do something to give it a reason, *any* reason."

"But we just agreed," I said, "that there's no way not to suffer. Isn't it better, then, just to—take it?"

"But nobody just takes it," Sonny cried, "that's what I'm telling you! *Everybody* tries not to. You're just hung up on the *way* some people try—it's not *your* way!"

The hair on my face began to itch, my face felt wet. "That's not true," I said, "that's not true. I don't give a damn what other people do, I don't even care how they suffer.

I just care how *you* suffer." And he looked at me. "Please believe me," I said, "I don't want to see you—die—trying not to suffer."

"I won't," he said, flatly, "die trying not to suffer. At least, not any faster than anybody else."

"But there's no need," I said, trying to laugh, "is there? in killing yourself."

I wanted to say more, but I couldn't. I wanted to talk about will power and how life could be—well, beautiful. I wanted to say that it was all within; but was it? or, rather, wasn't that exactly the trouble? And I wanted to promise that I would never fail him again. But it would all have sounded—empty words and lies.

So I made the promise to myself and prayed that I would keep it.

"It's terrible sometimes, inside," he said, "that's what's the trouble. You walk these streets, black and funky and cold, and there's not really a living ass to talk to, and there's nothing shaking, and there's no way of getting it out—that storm inside. You can't talk it and you can't make love with it, and when you finally try to get with it and play it, you realize *nobody's* listening. So *you've* got to listen. You got to find a way to listen."

And then he walked away from the window and sat on the sofa again, as though all the wind had suddenly been knocked out of him. "Sometimes you'll do *anything* to play, even cut your mother's throat." He laughed and looked at me. "Or your brother's." Then he sobered. "Or your own." Then: "Don't worry. I'm all right now and I think I'll *be* all right. But I can't forget—where I've been. I don't mean just the physical place I've been, I mean where I've *been*. And *what* I've been."

"What have you been, Sonny?" I asked.

He smiled—but sat sideways on the sofa, his elbow resting on the back, his fingers playing with his mouth and chin, not looking at me. "I've been something I didn't recognize, didn't know I could be. Didn't know anybody could be." He stopped, looking inward, looking helplessly young, looking old. "I'm not talking about it now because I feel *guilty* or anything like that—maybe it would be better if I did, I don't know. Anyway, I can't really talk about it. Not to you, not to anybody," and now he turned and faced me. "Sometimes, you know, and it was actually when I was most *out* of the world, I felt that I was in it, that I was *with* it, really, and I could play or I didn't really have to *play*, it just came out of me, it was there. And I don't know how I played, thinking about it now, but I know I did awful things, those times, sometimes, to people. Or it wasn't that I *did* anything to them—it was that they weren't real." He picked up the beer can; it was empty; he rolled it between his palms: "And other times—well, I needed a fix, I needed to find a place to lean, I needed to clear a space to *listen*—and I couldn't find it, and I—went crazy, I did terrible things to *me*, I was terrible *for* me." He began pressing the beer can between his hands, I watched the metal begin to give. It glittered, as he played with it, like a knife, and I was afraid he would cut himself, but I said nothing. "Oh well. I can never tell you. I was all by myself at the bottom of something, stinking and sweating and crying and shaking, and I smelled it, you know? *my* stink, and I thought I'd die if I couldn't get away from it and yet, all the same, I knew that everything I was doing was just locking me in with it. And I didn't know," he paused, still flattening the beer can, "I didn't know, I still *don't* know, something kept telling me that maybe it was good to smell your own stink, but I didn't think that *that* was what I'd been trying to do—and—

who can stand it?" and he abruptly dropped the ruined beer can, looking at me with a small, still smile, and then rose, walking to the window as though it were the lodestone rock. I watched his face, he watched the avenue, "I couldn't tell you when Mama died—but the reason I wanted to leave Harlem so bad was to get away from drugs. And then, when I ran away, that's what I was running from—really. When I came back, nothing had changed, *I* hadn't changed, I was just—older." And he stopped, drumming with his fingers on the windowpane. The sun had vanished, soon darkness would fall. I watched his face. "It can come again," he said, almost as though speaking to himself. Then he turned to me. "It can come again," he repeated. "I just want you to know that."

"All right," I said, at last. "So it can come again. All right."

He smiled, but the smile was sorrowful. "I had to try to tell you," he said.

"Yes," I said. "I understand that."

"You're my brother," he said, looking straight at me, and not smiling at all.

"Yes," I repeated, "yes. I understand that."

He turned back to the window, looking out. "All that hatred down there," he said, "all that hatred and misery and love. It's a wonder it doesn't blow the avenue apart."

We went to the only nightclub on a short, dark street, downtown. We squeezed through the narrow, chattering, jam-packed bar to the entrance of the big room, where the bandstand was. And we stood there for a moment, for the lights were very dim in this room and we couldn't see. Then, "Hello, boy," said a voice and an enormous black man, much older than Sonny or myself, erupted out of all that atmospheric lighting and put an arm around Sonny's shoulder. "I been sitting right here," he said, "waiting for you."

He had a big voice, too, and heads in the darkness turned toward us.

Sonny grinned and pulled a little away, and said, "Creole, this is my brother. I told you about him."

Creole shook my hand. "I'm glad to meet you, son," he said, and it was clear that he was glad to meet me *there,* for Sonny's sake. And he smiled, "You got a real musician in *your* family," and he took his arm from Sonny's shoulder and slapped him, lightly, affectionately, with the back of his hand.

"Well. Now I've heard it all," said a voice behind us. This was another musician, and a friend of Sonny's, a coal-black, cheerful-looking man, built close to the ground. He immediately began confiding to me, at the top of his lungs, the most terrible things about Sonny, his teeth gleaming like a lighthouse and his laugh coming up out of him like the beginning of an earthquake. And it turned out that everyone at the bar knew Sonny, or almost everyone; some were musicians, working there, or nearby, or not working, some were simply hangers-on, and some were there to hear Sonny play. I was introduced to all of them and they were all very polite to me. Yet, it was clear that, for them, I was only Sonny's brother. Here, I was in Sonny's world. Or, rather: his kingdom. Here, it was not even a question that his veins bore royal blood.

They were going to play soon and Creole installed me, by myself, at a table in a dark corner. Then I watched them, Creole, and the little black man, and Sonny, and the others, while they horsed around, standing just below the bandstand. The light from the bandstand spilled just a little short of them and, watching them laughing and gesturing and moving about, I had the feeling that they, nevertheless, were being most careful not to step into that circle of light too suddenly: that if they moved into the light too suddenly, without thinking, they would perish in flame. Then, while I watched, one of them, the small, black man, moved into the light and crossed the bandstand and started fooling around with his drums. Then—being funny and being, also, extremely ceremonious—Creole took Sonny by the arm and led him to the piano. A woman's voice called Sonny's name and a few hands started clapping. And Sonny, also being funny and being ceremonious, and so touched, I think, that he could have cried, but neither hiding it nor showing it, riding it like a man, grinned, and put both hands to his heart and bowed from the waist.

Creole then went to the bass fiddle and a lean, very bright-skinned brown man jumped up on the bandstand and picked up his horn. So there they were, and the atmosphere on the bandstand and in the room began to change and tighten. Someone stepped up to the microphone and announced them. Then there were all kinds of murmurs. Some people at the bar shushed others. The waitress ran around, frantically getting in the last orders, guys and chicks got closer to each other, and the lights on the bandstand, on the quartet, turned to a kind of indigo. Then they all looked different there. Creole looked about him for the last time, as though he were making certain that all his chickens were in the coop, and then he—jumped and struck the fiddle. And there they were.

All I know about music is that not many people ever really hear it. And even then, on the rare occasions when something opens within, and the music enters, what we mainly hear, or hear corroborated, are personal, private, vanishing evocations. But the man who creates the music is hearing something else, is dealing with the roar rising from the void and imposing order on it as it hits the air. What is evoked in him, then, is of another order, more terrible because it has no words, and triumphant, too, for that same reason. And his triumph, when he triumphs, is ours. I just watched Sonny's face. His face was troubled, he was working hard, but he wasn't with it. And I had the feeling that, in a way, everyone on the bandstand was waiting for him, both waiting for him and pushing him along. But as I began to watch Creole, I realized that it was Creole who held them all back. He had them on a short rein. Up there, keeping the beat with his whole body, wailing on the fiddle, with his eyes half closed, he was listening to everything, but he was listening to Sonny. He was having a dialogue with Sonny. He wanted Sonny to leave the shoreline and strike out for the deep water. He was Sonny's witness that deep water and drowning were not the same thing—he had been there, and he knew. And he wanted Sonny to know. He was waiting for Sonny to do the things on the keys which would let Creole know that Sonny was in the water.

And, while Creole listened, Sonny moved, deep within, exactly like someone in torment. I had never before thought of how awful the relationship must be between the musician and his instrument. He has to fill it, this instrument, with the breath of life, his own. He has to make it do what he wants it to do. And a piano is just a piano. It's made out of so much wood and wires and little hammers and big ones, and ivory. While there's only so much you can do with it, the only way to find this out is to try; to try and make it do everything.

And Sonny hadn't been near a piano for over a year. And he wasn't on much better terms with his life, not the life that stretched before him now. He and the piano stammered, started one way, got scared, stopped; started another way, panicked, marked time, started again; then seemed to have found a direction, panicked again, got stuck. And the face I saw on Sonny I'd never seen before. Everything had been burned out of it, and, at the same time, things usually hidden were being burned in, by the fire and fury of the battle which was occurring in him up there.

Yet, watching Creole's face as they neared the end of the first set, I had the feeling that something had happened, something I hadn't heard. Then they finished, there was scattered applause, and then, without an instant's warning, Creole started into something else, it was almost sardonic, it was *Am I Blue*. And, as though he commanded, Sonny began to play. Something began to happen. And Creole let out the reins. The dry, low, black man said something awful on the drums, Creole answered, and the drums talked back. Then the horn insisted, sweet and high, slightly detached perhaps, and Creole listened, commenting now and then, dry, and driving, beautiful and calm and old. Then they all came together again, and Sonny was part of the family again. I could tell this from his face. He seemed to have found, right there beneath his fingers, a damn brand-new piano. It seemed that he couldn't get over it. Then, for awhile, just being happy with Sonny, they seemed to be agreeing with him that brand-new pianos certainly were a gas.

Then Creole stepped forward to remind them that what they were playing was the blues. He hit something in all of them, he hit something in me, myself, and the music tightened and deepened, apprehension began to beat the air. Creole began to tell us what the blues were all about. They were not about anything very new. He and his boys up there were keeping it new, at the risk of ruin, destruction, madness, and death, in order to find new ways to make us listen. For, while the tale of how we suffer, and how we are delighted, and how we may triumph is never new, it always must be heard. There isn't any other tale to tell, it's the only light we've got in all this darkness.

And this tale, according to that face, that body, those strong hands on those strings, has another aspect in every country, and a new depth in every generation. Listen, Creole seemed to be saying, listen. Now these are Sonny's blues. He made the little black man on the drums know it, and the bright, brown man on the horn. Creole wasn't trying any longer to get Sonny in the water. He was wishing him Godspeed. Then he stepped back, very slowly, filling the air with the immense suggestion that Sonny speak for himself.

Then they all gathered around Sonny and Sonny played. Every now and again one of them seemed to say, amen. Sonny's fingers filled the air with life, his life. But that life contained so many others. And Sonny went all the way back, he really began with the spare, flat statement of the opening phrase of the song. Then he began to make it his. It was very beautiful because it wasn't hurried and it was no longer a lament. I seemed to hear with what burning he had made it his, with what burning we had *yet to make* it ours, how we could cease lamenting. Freedom lurked around us and I understood, at last, that he could help us to be free if we would listen, that he would never be free until we did. Yet, there was no battle in his face now. I heard what he had gone through, and would continue to go through until he came to rest in earth. He had made it his: that long line, of which we knew only Mama and Daddy. And he was giving it back, as everything must be given back, so that, passing through death, it can live forever. I saw my mother's face again, and felt, for the first time, how the stones of the road she had walked on must have bruised her feet. I saw the moonlit road where my father's brother died. And it brought something else back to me, and carried me past it, I saw my little girl again and felt Isabel's tears again, and I felt my own tears begin to rise. And I was yet aware that this was only a moment, that the world waited outside, as hungry as a tiger, and that trouble stretched above us, longer than the sky.

Then it was over. Creole and Sonny let out their breath, both soaking wet, and grinning. There was a lot of applause and some of it was real. In the dark, the girl came by and I asked her to take drinks to the bandstand. There was a long pause, while they talked up there in the indigo light and after awhile I saw the girl put a Scotch and milk on top of the piano for Sonny. He didn't seem to notice it, but just before they started playing again, he sipped from it and looked toward me, and nodded. Then he put it back on top of the piano. For me, then, as they began to play again, it glowed and shook above my brother's head like the very cup of trembling.

1957

Flannery O'Connor
1925–1964

"Fiction," Flannery O'Connor wrote, "can transcend its limitations only by staying within them." That paradox informed her entire career as well. She was a determined regionalist whose work never lapses into a comfortable provinciality, a devout Catholic who found her themes and characters in the "Christ-haunted" southern Protestant Bible belt, and, for much of her adult life, a confined invalid who could be as resistant to sentimentality and what she called "hazy compassion" as the most hard-boiled detective novelist. Like such earlier southern regionalists as George Washington Harris, she wanted nothing to do with mansions, magnolias, and mockingbirds, and like Harris, too, she shaped her stories around moments of unexpected comic violence. Yet unlike Harris, her literary commitment to comedy and violence never seems gratuitous but rather was deeply rooted in religious and aesthetic convictions. "My subject in fiction," she said, "is the action of grace in territory held largely by the devil."

Mary Flannery O'Connor was born in Savannah, Georgia, on March 25, 1925. Her family moved when she was twelve to Milledgeville, Georgia, where she graduated from the Women's College of Georgia. She studied creative writing at the State University of Iowa, earning an M.F.A. in 1947. In 1948 she was invited to join Yaddo, the prestigious writer's colony in Saratoga Springs, New York, but resigned, along with her new friends Robert Lowell and Elizabeth Hardwick, over the internal handling of a political incident. She lived for a few months in New York City and then spent a year with the writers Sally and Robert Fitzgerald at their Connecticut home.

In 1950, after she learned that she was dying of lupus, an incurable tubercular disease that had killed her father, she returned to Milledgeville to live with her mother on the family dairy farm. Her first novel, *Wise Blood,* the story of a young Tennessee religious fanatic who preaches a Church Without Christ, appeared in 1952. It was followed by a collection of ten short stories, *A Good Man Is Hard to Find* (1955), from which the story that follows has been reprinted. She published her second novel, another grotesque tale of religious aberration, *The Violent Bear It Away,* in 1960. Suffering from acute anemia, Flannery O'Connor underwent what may have been an ill-advised operation to remove a benign tumor. The operation reactivated the lupus, and she died in Milledgeville on August 3, 1964. Her second collection of stories, *Everything That Rises Must Converge* (its title derives from the Catholic theologian Teilhard de Chardin), appeared in 1965.

Flannery O'Connor hated abstraction. "The first and most obvious characteristic of fiction is that it deals with reality, through what can be seen, heard, smelt, tasted, and touched." Following the great Catholic philosopher, St. Thomas Aquinas, she believed that human knowledge begins through the senses. She disliked critical abstractions as well, feeling that a good story must resist sociological, psychological, philosophical, or religious paraphrase. She recalled that once after a reading of her short story "A Good Man Is Hard to Find," an earnest teacher began asking her questions:

"Miss O'Connor," he said, "why was the Misfit's hat *black?*" I said most countrymen in Georgia wore black hats. He looked pretty disappointed. Then he said, "Miss O'Connor, the Misfit represents Christ, does he not?" "He does not," I said. He looked crushed. "Well, Miss O'Connor," he said, "what is the significance of the Misfit's hat?" I said it was to cover his head; and after that he left me alone. Anyway, that's what's happening to the teaching of literature.

Her irritation with the questions has less to do with a dislike for symbolism than with a dislike for a symbol-hunting mentality that thinks it has "understood" a story when it has completely discarded the work's literal level and discovered, as in an algebraic equation, what every detail "stands for."

In Flannery O'Connor's own critical articles, collected posthumously in *Mystery and Manners* (1969), she is always careful to respect the essential mystery of art. She saw the preservation of mystery as fundamental to both art and religion: "Christian dogma," she claimed, "is about the only thing left in the world that surely guards and respects mystery." The novelist's sense of mystery, she believed, grows out of a recognition of the world's incompleteness; the writer's profound sense of something lacking in the world gives serious fiction its value and meaning. In one of her finest essays, "Some Aspects of the Grotesque in Southern Fiction," she expressed this belief in a way that bears directly on her own literary achievement: For a certain kind of writer, she noted, "the meaning of a story does not begin except at a depth where adequate motivation and adequate psychology and the various determinations have been exhausted. Such a writer will be interested in what we don't understand rather than in what we do."

Further Reading:
The Art and Mind of Flannery O'Connor, ed.
M. J. Freedman and L. A. Lawson, 1966.
S. E. Hyman, *Flannery O'Connor,* 1966.
J. Hendin, *The World of Flannery O'Connor,*
1970.
D. Walters, *Flannery O'Connor,* 1973.
J. R. May, *The Pruning Word: The Parables of
Flannery O'Connor,* 1976.
C. Shloss, *Flannery O'Connor's Dark Comedies,*
1980.

Text:
The Complete Stories, 1971.
See also *The Habit of Being: Letters of Flannery
O'Connor,* ed. S. Fitzgerald, 1979.

A Good Man Is Hard to Find

The grandmother didn't want to go to Florida. She wanted to visit some of her connections in east Tennessee and she was seizing every chance to change Bailey's mind. Bailey was the son she lived with, her only boy. He was sitting on the edge of his chair at the table, bent over the orange sports section of the *Journal.* "Now look here, Bailey," she said, "see here, read this," and she stood with one hand on her thin hip and the other rattling the newspaper at his bald head. "Here this fellow that calls himself The Misfit is aloose from the Federal Pen and headed toward Florida and you read here what it says he did to these people. Just you read it. I wouldn't take my children in any direction with a criminal like that aloose in it. I couldn't answer to my conscience if I did."

Bailey didn't look up from his reading so she wheeled around then and faced the children's mother; a young woman in slacks, whose face was as broad and innocent as a cabbage and was tied around with a green headkerchief that had two points on the top like rabbit's ears. She was sitting on the sofa, feeding the baby his apricots out of a jar. "The children have been to Florida before," the old lady said. "You all ought to take them somewhere else for a change so they would see different parts of the world and be broad. They never have been to east Tennessee."

The children's mother didn't seem to hear her, but the eight-year-old boy, John Wesley, a stocky child with glasses, said, "If you don't want to go to Florida, why dontcha stay at home?" He and the little girl, June Star, were reading the funny papers on the floor.

"She wouldn't stay at home to be queen for a day," June Star said without raising her yellow head.

"Yes, and what would you do if this fellow, The Misfit, caught you?" the grandmother asked.

"I'd smack his face," John Wesley said.

"She wouldn't stay at home for a million bucks," June Star said. "Afraid she'd miss something. She has to go everywhere we go."

"All right, Miss," the grandmother said. "Just remember that the next time you want me to curl your hair."

June Star said her hair was naturally curly.

The next morning the grandmother was the first one in the car, ready to go. She had her big black valise that looked like the head of a hippopotamus in one corner, and underneath it she was hiding a basket with Pitty Sing, the cat, in it. She didn't intend for the cat to be left alone in the house for three days because he would miss her too much and she was afraid he might brush against one of the gas burners and accidentally asphyxiate himself. Her son, Bailey, didn't like to arrive at a motel with a cat.

She sat in the middle of the back seat with John Wesley and June Star on either side of her. Bailey and the children's mother and the baby sat in the front and they left Atlanta at eight forty-five with the mileage on the car at 55890. The grandmother wrote this down because she thought it would be interesting to say how many miles they had been when they got back. It took them twenty minutes to reach the outskirts of the city.

The old lady settled herself comfortably, removing her white cotton gloves and putting them up with her purse on the shelf in front of the back window. The children's mother still had on slacks and still had her head tied up in a green kerchief, but the grandmother had on a navy blue straw sailor hat with a bunch of white violets on the brim and a navy blue dress with a small white dot in the print. Her collar and cuffs were white organdy trimmed with lace and at her neckline she had pinned a purple spray of cloth violets containing a sachet. In case of an accident, anyone seeing her dead on the highway would know at once that she was a lady.

She said she thought it was going to be a good day for driving, neither too hot nor too cold, and she cautioned Bailey that the speed limit was fifty-five miles an hour and that the patrolmen hid themselves behind bill-boards and small clumps of trees and sped out after you before you had a chance to slow down. She pointed out interesting details of the scenery: Stone Mountain; the blue granite that in some places came up to both sides of the highway; the brilliant red clay banks slightly streaked with purple; and the various crops that made rows of green lace-work on the ground. The trees were full of silver-white sunlights and the meanest of them sparkled. The children were reading comic magazines and their mother had gone back to sleep.

"Let's go through Georgia fast so we won't have to look at it much," John Wesley said.

"If I were a little boy," said the grandmother, "I wouldn't talk about my native state that way. Tennessee has the mountains and Georgia has the hills."

"Tennessee is just a hillbilly dumping ground," John Wesley said, "and Georgia is a lousy state too."

"You said it," June Star said.

"In my time," said the grandmother, folding her thin veined fingers, "children were more respectful of their native states and their parents and everything else. People did right then. Oh look at the cute little pickaninny!" she said and pointed to a Negro child standing in the door of a shack. "Wouldn't that make a picture, now?" she asked and they all turned and looked at the little Negro out of the back window. He waved.

"He didn't have any britches on," June Star said.

"He probably didn't have any," the grandmother explained. "Little niggers in the country don't have things like we do. If I could paint, I'd paint that picture," she said.

The children exchanged comic books.

The grandmother offered to hold the baby and the children's mother passed him over the front seat to her. She set him on her knee and bounced him and told him about the things they were passing. She rolled her eyes and screwed up her mouth and stuck her leathery thin face into his smooth bland one. Occasionally he gave her a faraway smile. They passed a large cotton field with five or six graves fenced in the middle of it, like a small island. "Look at the graveyard!" the grandmother said, pointing it out. "That was the old family burying ground. That belonged to the plantation."

"Where's the plantation?" John Wesley asked.

"Gone With the Wind," said the grandmother. "Ha. Ha."

When the children finished all the comic books they had brought, they opened the lunch and ate it. The grandmother ate a peanut butter sandwich and an olive and would not let the children throw the box and the paper napkins out the window. When there was nothing else to do they played a game by choosing a cloud and making the other two guess what shape it suggested. John Wesley took one the shape of a cow and June Star guessed a cow and John Wesley said, no, an automobile, and June Star said he didn't play fair, and they began to slap each other over the grandmother.

The grandmother said she would tell them a story if they would keep quiet. When she told a story, she rolled her eyes and waved her head and was very dramatic. She said once when she was a maiden lady she had been courted by a Mr. Edgar Atkins Teagarden from Jasper, Georgia. She said he was a very good-looking man and a gentleman and that he brought her a watermelon every Saturday afternoon with his initials cut in it, E.A.T. Well, one Saturday, she said, Mr. Teagarden brought the watermelon and there was nobody at home and he left it on the front porch and returned in his buggy to Jasper, but she never got the watermelon, she said, because a nigger boy ate it when he saw the initials, E.A.T.! This story tickled John Wesley's funny bone and he giggled and giggled but June Star didn't think it was any good. She said she wouldn't marry a man that just brought her a watermelon on Saturday. The grandmother said she would have done well to marry Mr. Teagarden because he was a gentleman and had bought Coca-Cola stock when it first came out and that he had died only a few years ago, a very wealthy man.

They stopped at The Tower for barbecued sandwiches. The Tower was a part-stucco and part-wood filling station and dance hall set in a clearing outside of Timothy. A fat man named Red Sammy Butts ran it and there were signs stuck here and there on the building and for miles up and down the highway saying, TRY RED SAMMY'S FAMOUS BARBECUE. NONE LIKE FAMOUS RED SAMMY'S! RED SAM! THE FAT BOY WITH THE HAPPY LAUGH. A VETERAN! RED SAMMY'S YOUR MAN!

Red Sammy was lying on the bare ground outside The Tower with his head under a truck while a gray monkey about a foot high, chained to a small chinaberry tree, chattered nearby. The monkey sprang back into the tree and got on the highest limb as soon as he saw the children jump out of the car and run toward him.

Inside, The Tower was a long dark room with a counter at one end and tables at the other and dancing space in the middle. They all sat down at a broad table next to the nickelodeon and Red Sam's wife, a tall burnt-brown woman with hair and eyes lighter than her skin, came and took their order. The children's mother put a dime in the machine and played "The Tennessee Waltz," and the grandmother said that tune always made her want to dance. She asked Bailey if he would like to dance but he only glared at her. He didn't have a naturally sunny disposition like she did and trips made him nervous. The grandmother's brown eyes were very bright. She swayed her head from side to side and pretended she was dancing in her chair. June Star said play something she could tap to so the children's mother put in another dime and played a fast number and June Star stepped out onto the dance floor and did her tap routine.

"Ain't she cute?" Red Sam's wife said, leaning over the counter. "Would you like to come be my little girl?"

"No, I certainly wouldn't," June Star said. "I wouldn't live in a broken-down place like this for a million bucks!" and she ran back to the table.

"Ain't she cute?" the woman repeated, stretching her mouth politely.

"Aren't you ashamed?" hissed the grandmother.

Red Sam came in and told his wife to quit lounging on the counter and hurry up with these people's order. His khaki trousers reached just to his hip bones and his stomach hung over them like a sack of meal swaying under his shirt. He came over and sat down at a table nearby and let out a combination sigh and yodel. "You can't win," he said. "You can't win," and he wiped his sweating red face off with a gray handkerchief. "These days you don't know who to trust," he said. "Ain't that the truth?"

"People are certainly not nice like they used to be," said the grandmother.

"Two fellers come in here last week," Red Sammy said, "driving a Chrysler. It was an old beat-up car but it was a good one and these boys looked all right to me. Said they worked at the mill and you know I let them fellers charge the gas they bought? Now why did I do that?"

"Because you're a good man!" the grandmother said at once.

"Yes'm, I suppose so," Red Sam said as if he were struck with this answer.

His wife brought the orders, carrying the five plates all at once without a tray, two in each hand and one balanced on her arm. "It isn't a soul in this green world of God's that you can trust," she said. "And I don't count nobody out of that, not nobody," she repeated, looking at Red Sammy.

"Did you read about that criminal, The Misfit, that's escaped?" asked the grandmother.

"I wouldn't be a bit surprised if he didn't attack this place right here," said the woman. "If he hears about it being here, I wouldn't be none surprised to see him. If he hears it's two cent in the cash register, I wouldn't be a tall surprised if he. . . ."

"That'll do," Red Sam said. "Go bring these people their Co'-Colas," and the woman went off to get the rest of the order.

"A good man is hard to find," Red Sammy said. "Everything is getting terrible. I remember the day you could go off and leave your screen door unlatched. Not no more."

He and the grandmother discussed better times. The old lady said that in her opinion Europe was entirely to blame for the way things were now. She said the way Europe acted you would think we were made of money and Red Sam said it was no use talking about it, she was exactly right. The children ran outside into the white sunlight and looked at the monkey in the lacy chinaberry tree. He was busy catching fleas on himself and biting each one carefully between his teeth as if it were a delicacy.

They drove off again into the hot afternoon. The grandmother took cat naps and woke up every few minutes with her own snoring. Outside of Toombsboro she woke up and recalled an old plantation that she had visited in this neighborhood once when she was a young lady. She said the house had six white columns across the front and that there was an avenue of oaks leading up to it and two little wooden trellis arbors on either side in front where you sat down with your suitor after a stroll in the garden. She recalled exactly which road to turn off to get to it. She knew that Bailey would not be willing to lose any time looking at an old house, but the more she talked about it, the more she wanted to see it once again and find out if the little twin arbors were still standing. "There was a secret panel in this house," she said craftily, not telling the truth but wishing that she were, "and the story went that all the family silver was hidden in it when Sherman¹ came through but it was never found. . . . "

"Hey!" John Wesley said. "Let's go see it! We'll find it! We'll poke all the wood work and find it! Who lives there? Where do you turn off at? Hey Pop, can't we turn off there?"

"We never have seen a house with a secret panel!" June Star shrieked. "Let's go to the house with the secret panel! Hey, Pop, can't we go see the house with the secret panel!"

"It's not far from here, I know," the grandmother said. "It wouldn't take over twenty minutes."

Bailey was looking straight ahead. His jaw was as rigid as a horseshoe. "No," he said.

The children began to yell and scream that they wanted to see the house with the secret panel. John Wesley kicked the back of the front seat and June Star hung over her mother's shoulder and whined desperately into her ear that they never had any fun even on their vacation, that they could never do what THEY wanted to do. The baby began to scream and John Wesley kicked the back of the seat so hard that his father could feel the blows in his kidney.

"All right!" he shouted and drew the car to a stop at the side of the road. "Will you all shut up? Will you all just shut up for one second? If you don't shut up, we won't go anywhere."

"It would be very educational for them," the grandmother murmured.

"All right," Bailey said, "but get this. This is the only time we're going to stop for anything like this. This is the one and only time."

"The dirt road that you have to turn down is about a mile back," the grandmother directed. "I marked it when we passed."

"A dirt road," Bailey groaned.

After they had turned around and were headed toward the dirt road, the grandmother recalled other points about the house, the beautiful glass over the front doorway and the candle lamp in the hall. John Wesley said that the secret panel was probably in the fireplace.

"You can't go inside this house," Bailey said. "You don't know who lives there."

¹ William Tecumseh Sherman, the Union general who marched his troops through Atlanta to the Georgia coast in the winter of 1864.

"While you all talk to the people in front, I'll run around behind and get in a window," John Wesley suggested.

"We'll all stay in the car," his mother said.

They turned onto the dirt road and the car raced roughly along in a swirl of pink dust. The grandmother recalled the times when there were no paved roads and thirty miles was a day's journey. The dirt road was hilly and there were sudden washes in it and sharp curves on dangerous embankments. All at once they would be on a hill, looking down over the blue tops of trees for miles around, then the next minute, they would be in a red depression with the dust-coated trees looking down on them.

"This place had better turn up in a minute," Bailey said, "or I'm going to turn around."

The road looked as if no one had traveled on it in months.

"It's not much farther," the grandmother said and just as she said it, a horrible thought came to her. The thought was so embarrassing that she turned red in the face and her eyes dilated and her feet jumped up, upsetting her valise in the corner. The instant the valise moved, the newspaper top she had over the basket under it rose with a snarl and Pitty Sing, the cat, sprang onto Bailey's shoulder.

The children were thrown to the floor and their mother, clutching the baby, was thrown out the door onto the ground; the old lady was thrown into the front seat. The car turned over once and landed right-side-up in a gulch on the side of the road. Bailey remained in the driver's seat with the cat—gray-striped with a broad white face and an orange nose—clinging to his neck like a caterpillar.

As soon as the children saw they could move their arms and legs, they scrambled out of the car, shouting, "We've had an ACCIDENT!" The grandmother was curled up under the dashboard, hoping she was injured so that Bailey's wrath would not come down on her all at once. The horrible thought she had had before the accident was that the house she had remembered so vividly was not in Georgia but in Tennessee.

Bailey removed the cat from his neck with both hands and flung it out the window against the side of a pine tree. Then he got out of the car and started looking for the children's mother. She was sitting against the side of the red gutted ditch, holding the screaming baby, but she only had a cut down her face and a broken shoulder. "We've had an ACCIDENT!" the children screamed in a frenzy of delight.

"But nobody's killed," June Star said with disappointment as the grandmother limped out of the car, her hat still pinned to her head but the broken front brim standing up at a jaunty angle and the violet spray hanging off the side. They all sat down in the ditch, except the children, to recover from the shock. They were all shaking.

"Maybe a car will come along," said the children's mother hoarsely.

"I believe I have injured an organ," said the grandmother, pressing her side, but no one answered her. Bailey's teeth were clattering. He had on a yellow sport shirt with bright blue parrots designed in it and his face was as yellow as the shirt. The grandmother decided that she would not mention that the house was in Tennessee.

The road was about ten feet above and they could see only the tops of the trees on the other side of it. Behind the ditch they were sitting in there were more woods, tall and dark and deep. In a few minutes they saw a car some distance away on top of a hill, coming slowly as if the occupants were watching them. The grandmother stood up and waved both arms dramatically to attract their attention. The car continued to come on slowly, disappeared around a bend and appeared again, moving even slower on top of the hill they had gone over. It was a big black battered hearselike automobile. There were three men in it.

It came to a stop just over them and for some minutes, the driver looked down with a steady expressionless gaze to where they were sitting, and didn't speak. Then he turned his head and muttered something to the other two and they got out. One was a fat boy in black trousers and a red sweat shirt with a silver stallion embossed on the front of it. He moved around on the right side of them and stood staring, his mouth partly open in a kind of loose grin. The other had on khaki pants and a blue striped coat and a gray hat pulled down very low, hiding most of his face. He came around slowly on the left side. Neither spoke.

The driver got out of the car and stood by the side of it, looking down at them. He was an older man than the other two. His hair was just beginning to gray and he wore silver-rimmed spectacles that gave him a scholarly look. He had a long creased face and didn't have on any shirt or undershirt. He had on blue jeans that were too tight for him and was holding a black hat and a gun. The two boys also had guns.

"We've had an ACCIDENT!" the children screamed.

The grandmother had the peculiar feeling that the bespectacled man was someone she knew. His face was as familiar to her as if she had known him all her life but she could not recall who he was. He moved away from the car and began to come down the embankment, placing his feet carefully so that he wouldn't slip. He had on tan and white shoes and no socks, and his ankles were red and thin. "Good afternoon," he said. "I see you all had you a little spill."

"We turned over twice!" said the grandmother.

"Oncet," he corrected. "We see it happen. Try their car and see will it run, Hiram," he said quietly to the boy with the gray hat.

"What you got that gun for?" John Wesley asked. "Whatcha gonna do with that gun?"

"Lady," the man said to the children's mother, "would you mind calling them children to sit down by you? Children make me nervous. I want all you to sit down right together there where you're at."

"What are you telling us what to do for?" June Star asked.

Behind them the line of woods gaped like a dark open mouth. "Come here," said their mother.

"Look here now," Bailey began suddenly, "we're in a predicament! We're in. . . . "

The grandmother shrieked. She scrambled to her feet and stood staring. "You're The Misfit!" she said. "I recognized you at once!"

"Yes'm," the man said, smiling slightly as if he were pleased in spite of himself to be known. "but it would have been better for all of you, lady, if you hadn't of reckernized me."

Bailey turned his head sharply and said something to his mother that shocked even the children. The old lady began to cry and The Misfit reddened.

"Lady," he said, "don't you get upset. Sometimes a man says things he don't mean. I don't reckon he meant to talk to you thataway."

"You wouldn't shoot a lady, would you?" the grandmother said and removed a clean handkerchief from her cuff and began to slap at her eyes with it.

The Misfit pointed the toe of his shoe into the ground and made a little hole and then covered it up again. "I would hate to have to," he said.

"Listen," the grandmother almost screamed, "I know you're a good man. You don't look a bit like you have common blood. I know you must come from nice people!"

"Yes mam," he said, "finest people in the world." When he smiled he showed a row of strong white teeth. "God never made a finer woman than my mother and my daddy's heart was pure gold," he said. The boy with the red sweat shirt had come around behind them and was standing with his gun at his hip. The Misfit squatted down on the ground. "Watch them children, Bobby Lee," he said. "You know they make me nervous." He looked at the six of them huddled together in front of him and he seemed to be embarrassed as if he couldn't think of anything to say. "Ain't a cloud in the sky," he remarked, looking up at it. "Don't see no sun but don't see no cloud neither."

"Yes, it's a beautiful day," said the grandmother. "Listen," she said, "you shouldn't call yourself The Misfit because I know you're a good man at heart. I can just look at you and tell."

"Hush!" Bailey yelled. "Hush! Everybody shut up and let me handle this!" He was squatting in the position of a runner about to sprint forward but he didn't move.

"I pre-chate that, lady," The Misfit said and drew a little circle in the ground with the butt of his gun.

"It'll take a half a hour to fix this here car," Hiram called, looking over the raised hood of it.

"Well, first you and Bobby Lee get him and that little boy to step over yonder with you," The Misfit said, pointing to Bailey and John Wesley. "The boys want to ask you something," he said to Bailey. "Would you mind stepping back in them woods there with them?"

"Listen," Bailey began, "we're in a terrible predicament! Nobody realizes what this is," and his voice cracked. His eyes were as blue and intense as the parrots in his shirt and he remained perfectly still.

The grandmother reached up to adjust her hat brim as if she were going to the woods with him but it came off in her hand. She stood staring at it and after a second she let it fall on the ground. Hiram pulled Bailey up by the arm as if he were assisting an old man. John Wesley caught hold of his father's hand and Bobby Lee followed. They went off toward the woods and just as they reached the dark edge, Bailey turned and supporting himself against a gray naked pine trunk, he shouted, "I'll be back in a minute, Mamma, wait on me!"

"Come back this instant!" his mother shrilled but they all disappeared into the woods.

"Bailey Boy!" the grandmother called in a tragic voice but she found she was looking at The Misfit squatting on the ground in front of her. "I just know you're a good man," she said desperately. "You're not a bit common!"

"Nome, I ain't a good man," The Misfit said after a second as if he had considered her statement carefully, "but I ain't the worst in the world neither. My daddy said I was a different breed of dog from my brothers and sisters. 'You know,' Daddy said, 'it's some that can live their whole life without asking about it and it's others has to know why it is, and this boy is one of the latters. He's going to be into everything!' " He put on his black hat and looked up suddenly and then away deep into the woods as if he were embarrassed again. "I'm sorry, I don't have on a shirt before you ladies," he said, hunching his shoulders slightly. "We buried our clothes that we had on when we escaped and we're just making do until we can get better. We borrowed these from some folks we met," he explained.

"That's perfectly all right," the grandmother said. "Maybe Bailey has an extra shirt in his suitcase."

"I'll look and see terrectly," The Misfit said.

"Where are they taking him?" the children's mother screamed.

"Daddy was a card himself," The Misfit said. "You couldn't put anything over on him. He never got in trouble with the Authorities though. Just had the knack of handling them."

"You could be honest too if you'd only try," said the grandmother. "Think how wonderful it would be to settle down and live a comfortable life and not have to think about somebody chasing you all the time."

The Misfit kept scratching in the ground with the butt of his gun as if he were thinking about it. "Yes'm, somebody is always after you," he murmured.

The grandmother noticed how thin his shoulder blades were just behind his hat because she was standing up looking down on him. "Do you ever pray?" she asked.

He shook his head. All she saw was the black hat wiggle between his shoulder blades. "Nome," he said.

There was a pistol shot from the woods, followed closely by another. Then silence. The old lady's head jerked around. She could hear the wind move through the tree tops like a long satisfied insuck of breath. "Bailey Boy!" she called.

"I was a gospel singer for a while," The Misfit said. "I been most everything. Been in the arm service, both land and sea, at home and abroad, been twict married, been an undertaker, been with the railroads, plowed Mother Earth, been in a tornado, seen a man burnt alive oncet," and he looked up at the children's mother and the little girl who were sitting close together, their faces white and their eyes glassy; "I even seen a woman flogged," he said.

"Pray, pray," the grandmother began, "pray, pray. . . . "

"I never was a bad boy that I remember of," The Misfit said in an almost dreamy voice, "but somewheres along the line I done something wrong and got sent to the penitentiary. I was buried alive," and he looked up and held her attention to him by a steady stare.

"That's when you should have started to pray," she said. "What did you do to get sent to the penitentiary that first time?"

"Turn to the right, it was a wall," The Misfit said, looking up again at the cloudless sky. "Turn to the left, it was a wall. Look up it was a ceiling, look down it was a floor. I forget what I done, lady. I set there and set there, trying to remember what it was I done and I ain't recalled it to this day. Oncet in a while, I would think it was coming to me, but it never come."

"Maybe they put you in by mistake," the old lady said vaguely.

"Nome," he said. "It wasn't no mistake. They had the papers on me."

"You must have stolen something," she said.

The Misfit sneered slightly. "Nobody had nothing I wanted," he said. "It was a head-doctor at the penitentiary said what I had done was kill my daddy but I known that for a lie. My daddy died in nineteen ought nineteen of the epidemic flu[2] and I never had a thing to do with it. He was buried in the Mount Hopewell Baptist churchyard and you can go there and see for yourself."

"If you would pray," the old lady said, "Jesus would help you."

"That's right," The Misfit said.

"Well then, why don't you pray?" she asked trembling with delight suddenly.

"I don't want no hep," he said. "I'm doing all right by myself."

Bobby Lee and Hiram came ambling back from the woods. Bobby Lee was dragging a yellow shirt with bright blue parrots in it.

"Throw me that shirt, Bobby Lee," The Misfit said. The shirt came flying at him and landed on his shoulder and he put it on. The grandmother couldn't name what the shirt reminded her of. "No, lady," The Misfit said while he was buttoning it up, "I found out the crime don't matter. You can do one thing or you can do another, kill a man or take a tire off his car, because sooner or later you're going to forget what it was you done and just be punished for it."

The children's mother had begun to make heaving noises as if she couldn't get her breath. "Lady," he asked, "would you and that little girl like to step off yonder with Bobby Lee and Hiram and join your husband?"

"Yes, thank you," the mother said faintly. Her left arm dangled helplessly and she was holding the baby, who had gone to sleep, in the other. "Hep that lady up, Hiram," The Misfit said as she struggled to climb out of the ditch, "and Bobby Lee, you hold onto that little girl's hand."

"I don't want to hold hands with him," June Star said. "He reminds me of a pig."

The fat boy blushed and laughed and caught her by the arm and pulled her off into the woods after Hiram and her mother.

Alone with The Misfit, the grandmother found that she had lost her voice. There was not a cloud in the sky nor any sun. There was nothing around her but woods. She wanted to tell him that he must pray. She opened and closed her mouth several times before anything came out. Finally she found herself saying, "Jesus. Jesus," meaning, Jesus will help you, but the way she was saying it, it sounded as if she might be cursing.

"Yes'm," The Misfit said as if he agreed. "Jesus thrown everything off balance. It was the same case with Him as with me except He hadn't committed any crime and they could prove I had committed one because they had the papers on me. Of course," he said, "they never shown me my papers. That's why I sign myself now. I said long ago, you get you a signature and sign everything you do and keep a copy of it. Then you'll know what you done and you can hold up the crime to the punishment and see do they match and in the end you'll have something to prove you ain't been treated right. I call myself The Misfit," he said, "because I can't make what all I done wrong fit what all I gone through in punishment."

There was a piercing scream from the woods, followed closely by a pistol report.

[2] I.e., the worldwide flu epidemic of 1919.

"Does it seem right to you, lady, that one is punished a heap and another ain't punished at all?"

"Jesus!" the old lady cried. "You've got good blood! I know you wouldn't shoot a lady! I know you come from nice people! Pray! Jesus, you ought not to shoot a lady. I'll give you all the money I've got!"

"Lady," The Misfit said, looking beyond her far into the woods, "there never was a body that give the undertaker a tip."

There were two more pistol reports and the grandmother raised her head like a parched old turkey hen crying for water and called, "Bailey Boy, Bailey Boy!" as if her heart would break.

"Jesus was the only One that ever raised the dead," The Misfit continued, "and He shouldn't have done it. He thrown everything off balance. If He did what He said, then it's nothing for you to do but throw away everything and follow Him, and if He didn't then it's nothing for you to do but enjoy the few minutes you got left the best way you can—by killing somebody or burning down his house or doing some other meanness to him. No pleasure but meanness," he said and his voice had become almost a snarl.

"Maybe He didn't raise the dead," the old lady mumbled, not knowing what she was saying and feeling so dizzy that she sank down in the ditch with her legs twisted under her.

"I wasn't there so I can't say He didn't," The Misfit said. "I wisht I had of been there," he said, hitting the ground with his fist. "It ain't right I wasn't there because if I had of been there I would of known. Listen lady," he said in a high voice, "if I had of been there I would of known and I wouldn't be like I am now." His voice seemed about to crack and the grandmother's head cleared for an instant. She saw the man's face twisted close to her own as if he were going to cry and she murmured, "Why, you're one of my babies. You're one of my own children!" She reached out and touched him on the shoulder. The Misfit sprang back as if a snake had bitten him and shot her three times through the chest. Then he put his gun down on the ground and took off his glasses and began to clean them.

Hiram and Bobby Lee returned from the woods and stood over the ditch, looking down at the grandmother who half sat and half lay in a puddle of blood with her legs crossed under her like a child's and her face smiling up at the cloudless sky.

Without his glasses, The Misfit's eyes were red-rimmed and pale and defenseless-looking. "Take her off and throw her where you thrown the others," he said, picking up the cat that was rubbing itself against his leg.

"She was a talker, wasn't she?" Bobby Lee said, sliding down the ditch with a yodel.

"She would of been a good woman," The Misfit said, "if it had been somebody there to shoot her every minute of her life."

"Some fun!" Bobby Lee said.

"Shut up, Bobby Lee," The Misfit said. "It's no real pleasure in life."

1953

Donald Barthelme
b. 1931

Donald Barthelme was born in Philadelphia on April 7, 1931, and grew up in Houston, Texas. He began writing stories and poems in high school and continued writing, combining journalism with poetry and fiction, at the University of Houston, where he studied for several years without taking a degree. After serving with the U.S. Army in Japan and Korea, Barthelme returned to the University of Houston. Over the next several years he founded the literary magazine, *Forum,* and worked as a reporter for the *Houston Post.* In addition, he became a sponsor and then the director of Houston's Contemporary Arts Museum.

With his long, rather mixed apprenticeship behind him, Barthelme moved to New York in 1962 and began a period of remarkable productivity. Throughout the 1950s and into the 1960s he had sought a style of his own, only to remain dissatisfied. Suddenly, however, in 1963 he found what he wanted, and after publishing his first story, "L'Lapse," in *The New Yorker,* he began contributing regularly to that magazine. In 1964 he published his first collection of stories, *Come Back, Dr. Caligari,* and three years later his first novel, *Snow White,* which had originally been published in its entirety in *The New Yorker.* A kind of surrealistic version of a classic fairy tale combined with a critique of a consumer society (fiction, too, being part of what is "consumed" in contemporary culture), *Snow White* contains a self-parodic questionnaire asking its readers for suggestions about how the novel should proceed. In his other novel, *The Dead Father* (1975), the narrative is interrupted by the inclusion of an old-fashioned "Manual for Sons" that lists types of fathers and means of dealing with them.

Since the late 1960s Barthelme has published several collections of short stories: *Unspeakable Practices, Unnatural Acts* (1968), *City Life* (1970), *Sadness* (1972), *Guilty Pleasures* (1974), *Amateurs* (1976), *Great Days* (1979), and a selection, *Sixty Stories* (1981). Together these works demonstrate an interest in mythology that dates back to Barthelme's childhood and a knowledge of modern art that derives from the influence of his father, an architect. They also reveal Barthelme's early reading of the French Symbolists and such great modernists as Pound, Eliot, and Joyce. In both *Forum* and *Location,* a literary magazine he edited during his early months in New York, Barthelme published writers ranging from Jean-Paul Sartre and Alain Robbe-Grillet to Saul Bellow and William Gass. More than any of these writers, however, and as much as any writer of his time, Barthelme's distinctive style turns on experiments with language. Painters "had to go out and reinvent painting because of the invention of photography," he once remarked, "and I think films have done something of the sort for us."

Fiction possesses, as Barthleme sees it, both "the enormous resources" of language and different ways of "investigating" those resources. His characters often seem odd and abstract partly because they are so completely creations not simply of language but of something very like linguistic investigations. As "Robert Kennedy Saved from Drowning" clearly shows, Barthelme delights in odd combinations of words—unexpected terms injected into hackneyed idioms and clichés (especially those of the mass media), pop allusions, odd statistics, and jargon picked up from science, technology, sociology, and government bureaucracies. Traditional literary allusions are often wedged together with comic-strip characters, film references, Walt Disney–like figures, and brand-name advertised products.

Barthelme investigates by combining, and he combines at a rate that is frequently disorienting. As a consequence, his stories seem sometimes to deaden as well as to prick and delight. As a writer, he takes great risks, leaving himself little margin for error. When his style works, however, his characters become creators as well as creatures of the odd, even the startlingly odd, combination, the telling juxtaposition, and they do so in the name of making such old, familiar issues as time and mortality new. Like their creator, they evince a conviction that "there is a realm of possible knowledge which can be reached by artists, which is not susceptible of mathematical verification but which is true."

Further Reading:
J. Klinkowitz, *Literary Disruptions: The Making of a Post-Contemporary American Fiction*, 1975.
M. Zavarzadeh, *The Mythopoeic Reality*, 1976.
L. Gordon, *Donald Barthelme*, 1981.

Text:
Sixty Stories, 1981.

Robert Kennedy Saved from Drowning

K. at His Desk

He is neither abrupt with nor excessively kind to associates. Or he is both abrupt and kind.

The telephone is, for him, a whip, a lash, but also a conduit for soothing words, a sink into which he can hurl gallons of syrup if it comes to that.

He reads quickly, scratching brief comments ("Yes," "No") in corners of the paper. He slouches in the leather chair, looking about him with a slightly irritated air for new visitors, new difficulties. He spends his time sending and receiving messengers.

"I spend my time sending and receiving messengers," he says, "Some of these messages are important. Others are not."

Described by Secretaries

A: "Quite frankly I think he forgets a lot of things. But the things he forgets are those which are inessential. I even think he might forget deliberately, to leave his mind free. He has the ability to get rid of unimportant details. And he does."

B: "Once when I was sick, I hadn't heard from him, and I thought he had forgotten me. You know usually your boss will send flowers or something like that. I was in the hospital, and I was mighty blue. I was in a room with another girl, and *her* boss hadn't sent her anything either. Then suddenly the door opened and there he was with the biggest bunch of yellow tulips I'd ever seen in my life. And the other girl's boss was with him, and he had tulips too. They were standing there with all those tulips, smiling."

Behind the Bar

At a crowded party, he wanders behind the bar to make himself a Scotch and water. His hand is on the bottle of Scotch, his glass is waiting. The bartender, a small man in a beige uniform with gilt buttons, politely asks K. to return to the other side, the guests' side, of the bar. "You let one behind here, they all be behind here," the bartender says.

K. Reading the Newspaper

His reactions are impossible to catalogue. Often he will find a note that amuses him endlessly, some anecdote involving, say, a fireman who has propelled his apparatus at record-breaking speed to the wrong address. These small stories are clipped, carried about in a pocket, to be produced at appropriate moments for the pleasure of friends. Other manifestations please him less. An account of an earthquake in Chile, with its thousands of dead and homeless, may depress him for weeks. He memorizes the terrible statistics, quoting them everywhere and saying, with a grave look: "We must do something." Important actions often follow, sometimes within a matter of hours. (On the other hand, these two kinds of responses may be, on a given day, inexplicably reversed.)

The more trivial aspects of the daily itemization are skipped. While reading, he maintains a rapid drumming of his fingertips on the desktop. He receives twelve newspapers, but of these, only four are regarded as serious.

Attitude Toward His Work

"Sometimes I can't seem to do anything. The work is there, piled up, it seems to me an insurmountable obstacle, really out of reach. I sit and look at it, wondering where to begin, how to take hold of it. Perhaps I pick up a piece of paper, try to read it but my mind is elsewhere, I am thinking of something else, I can't seem to get the gist of it, it seems meaningless, devoid of interest, not having to do with human affairs, drained of life. Then, in an hour, or even a moment, everything changes suddenly: I realize I only have to *do* it, hurl myself into the midst of it, proceed mechanically, the first thing and then the second thing, that it is simply a matter of moving from one step to the next, plowing through it. I become interested, I become excited, I work very fast, things fall into place, I am exhilarated, amazed that these things could ever have seemed dead to me."

Sleeping on the Stones of Unknown Towns (Rimbaud)[1]

K. is walking, with that familiar slight dip of the shoulders, through the streets of a small city in France or Germany. The shop signs are in a language which alters when

[1] Arthur Rimband (1854–1891), French poet famous for his dramatically unconventional life.

inspected closely, MÖBEL becoming MEUBLES[2] for example, and the citizens mutter to themselves with dark virtuosity a mixture of languages. K. is very interested, looks closely at everything, at the shops, the goods displayed, the clothing of the people, the tempo of street life, the citizens themselves, wondering about them. What are their water needs?

"In the West, wisdom is mostly gained at lunch. At lunch, people tell you things."
The nervous eyes of the waiters.
The tall bald cook, white apron, white T-shirt, grinning through an opening in the wall.
"Why is that cook looking at me?"

Urban Transportation

"The transportation problems of our cities and their rapidly expanding suburbs are the most urgent and neglected transportation problems confronting the country. In these heavily populated and industrialized areas, people are dependent on a system of transportation that is at once complex and inadequate. Obsolete facilities and growing demands have created seemingly insoluble difficulties and present methods of dealing with these difficulties offer little prospect of relief."

K. Penetrated with Sadness

He hears something playing on someone else's radio, in another part of the building.
The music is wretchedly sad; now he can (barely) hear it, now it fades into the wall.
He turns on his own radio. There it is, on his own radio, the same music. The sound fills the room.

Karsh of Ottawa

"We sent a man to Karsh of Ottawa[3] and told him that we admired his work very much. Especially, I don't know, the Churchill thing and, you know, the Hemingway thing, and all that. And we told him we wanted to set up a sitting for K. sometime in June, if that would be convenient for him, and he said yes, that was okay, June was okay, and where did we want to have it shot, there or in New York or where. Well, that was a problem because we didn't know exactly what K.'s schedule would be for June, it was up in the air, so we tentatively said New York around the fifteenth. And he said, that was okay, he could do that. And he wanted to know how much time he could have, and we said, well, how much time do you need? And he said he didn't know, it varied from sitter to sitter. He said some people were very restless and that made it difficult to get just the right shot. He said there was one shot in each sitting that was, you know, the key shot, the right one. He said he'd have to see, when the time came."

---

[2] German and French, respectively: "furniture."
[3] Yousef Karsh, renowned contemporary photographer noted for his portraits of powerful and famous personalities.

Dress

He is neatly dressed in a manner that does not call attention to itself. The suits are soberly cut and in dark colors. He must at all times present an aspect of freshness difficult to sustain because of frequent movements from place to place under conditions which are not always the most favorable. Thus he changes clothes frequently, especially shirts. In the course of a day he changes his shirt many times. There are always extra shirts about, in boxes.

"Which of you has the shirts?"

A Friend Comments: K.'s Aloneness

"The thing you have to realize about K. is that essentially he's absolutely alone in the world. There's this terrible loneliness which prevents people from getting too close to him. Maybe it comes from something in his childhood, I don't know. But he's very hard to get to know, and a lot of people who think they know him rather well don't really know him at all. He says something or does something that surprises you, and you realize that all along you really didn't know him at all.

"He has surprising facets. I remember once we were out in a small boat. K. of course was the captain. Some rough weather came up and we began to head back in. I began worrying about picking up a landing and I said to him that I didn't think the anchor would hold, with the wind and all. He just looked at me. Then he said: 'Of course it will hold. That's what it's for.' "

K. on Crowds

"There are exhausted crowds and vivacious crowds.

"Sometimes, standing there, I can sense whether a particular crowd is one thing or the other. Sometimes the mood of the crowd is disguised, sometimes you only find out after a quarter of an hour what sort of crowd a particular crowd is.

"And you can't speak to them in the same way. The variations have to be taken into account. You have to say something to them that is meaningful to them *in that mood*."

Gallery-going

K. enters a large gallery on Fifty-seventh Street, in the Fuller Building. His entourage includes several ladies and gentlemen. Works by a geometricist are on show. K. looks at the immense, rather theoretical paintings.

"Well, at least we know he has a ruler."

The group dissolves in laughter. People repeat the remark to one another, laughing. The artist, who has been standing behind a dealer, regards K. with hatred.

K. Puzzled by His Children

The children are crying. There are several children, one about four, a boy, then another boy, slightly older, and a little girl, very beautiful, wearing blue jeans, crying.

There are various objects on the grass, an electric train, a picture book, a red ball, a plastic bucket, a plastic shovel.

K. frowns at the children whose distress issues from no source immediately available to the eye, which seems indeed uncaused, vacant, a general anguish. K. turns to the mother of these children who is standing nearby wearing hip-huggers which appear to be made of linked marshmallows studded with diamonds but then I am a notoriously poor observer.

"Play with them," he says.

This mother of ten quietly suggests that K. himself "play with them."

K. picks up the picture book and begins to read to the children. But the book has a German text. It has been left behind, perhaps, by some foreign visitor. Nevertheless K. perseveres.

"A ist der Affe, er isst mit der Pfote." ("A is the Ape, he eats with his Paw.") The crying of the children continues.

A Dream

Orange trees.

Overhead, a steady stream of strange aircraft which resemble kitchen implements, bread boards, cookie sheets, colanders.

The shiny aluminum instruments are on their way to complete the bombings of Sidi-Madani.

A farm in the hills.

Matters (from an Adminstrative Assistant)

"A lot of matters that had been pending came to a head right about that time, moved to the front burner, things we absolutely had to take care of. And we couldn't find K. Nobody knew where he was. We had looked everywhere. He had just withdrawn, made himself unavailable. There was this one matter that was probably more pressing than all the rest put together. Really crucial. We were all standing around wondering what to do. We were getting pretty nervous because this thing was really . . . Then K. walked in and disposed of it with a quick phone call. A quick phone call!"

Childhood of K. As Recalled by a Former Teacher

"He was a very alert boy, very bright, good at his studies, very thorough, very conscientious. But that's not unusual; that describes a good number of the boys who pass through here. It's not unusual, that is, to find these qualities which are after all the qualities that we look for and encourage in them. What *was* unusual about K. was his compassion, something very rare for a boy of that age—even if they have it, they're usually very careful not to display it for fear of seeming soft, girlish. I remember, though, that in K. this particular attribute was very marked. I would almost say that it was his strongest characteristic."

Speaking to No One but Waiters He—

"The dandelion salad with bacon, I think."

"The *rysstafel*."[4]

"The poached duck."

"The black bean purée."

"The cod fritters."

K. Explains a Technique

"It's an expedient in terms of how not to destroy a situation which has been a long time gestating, or, again, how to break it up if it appears that the situation has changed, during the gestation period, into one whose implications are not quite what they were at the beginning. What I mean is that in this business things are constantly altering (usually for the worse) and usually you want to give the impression that you're not watching this particular situation particularly closely, that you're paying no special attention to it, until you're ready to make your move. That is, it's best to be sudden, if you can manage it. Of course you can't do that all the time. Sometimes you're just completely wiped out, cleaned out, totaled, and then the only thing to do is shrug and forget about it."

K. on His Own Role

"Sometimes it seems to me that it doesn't matter what I do, that it is enough to exist, to sit somewhere, in a garden for example, watching whatever is to be seen there, the small events. At other times, I'm aware that other people, possibly a great number of other people, could be affected by what I do or fail to do, that I have a responsibility, as we all have, to make the best possible use of whatever talents I've been given, for the common good. It is not enough to sit in that garden, however restful or pleasurable it might be. The world is full of unsolved problems, situations that demand careful, reasoned and intelligent action. In Latin America, for example."

As Entrepreneur

The original cost estimates for burying the North Sea pipeline have been exceeded by a considerable margin. Everyone wonders what he will say about this contretemps which does not fail to have its dangers for those responsible for the costly miscalculations, which are viewed in many minds as inexcusable.

He says only: "Exceptionally difficult rock conditions."

[4] Dutch-Indonesian: "rice-table," a meal consisting
of many different dishes, all served with rice.

With Young People

K., walking the streets of unknown towns, finds himself among young people. Young people line these streets, narrow and curving, which are theirs, dedicated to them. They are everywhere, resting on the embankments, their guitars, small radios, long hair. They sit on the sidewalks, back to back, heads turned to stare. They stand implacably on street corners, in doorways, or lean on their elbows in windows, or squat in small groups at that place where the sidewalk meets the walls of buildings. The streets are filled with these young people who say nothing, reveal only a limited interest, refuse to declare themselves. Street after street contains them, a great number, more displayed as one turns a corner, rank upon rank stretching into the distance, drawn from the arcades, the plazas, staring.

He Discusses the French Writer Poulet

"For Poulet, it is not enough to speak of *seizing the moment*. It is rather a question of, and I quote, 'recognizing in the instant which lives and dies, which surges out of nothingness and which ends in dream, an intensity and depth of significance which ordinarily attaches only to the whole of existence.'

"What Poulet is describing is neither an ethic nor a prescription but rather what he has discovered in the work of Marivaux. Poulet has taken up the Marivaudian canon and squeezed it with both hands to discover the essence of what may be called the Marivaudian being, what Poulet in fact calls the Marivaudian being.

"The Marivaudian being is, according to Poulet, a pastless futureless man, born anew at every instant. The instants are points which organize themselves into a line, but what is important is the instant, not the line. The Marivaudian being has in a sense no history. Nothing follows from what has gone before. He is constantly surprised. He cannot predict his own reaction to events. He is constantly being *overtaken* by events. A condition of breathlessness and dazzlement surrounds him. In consequence he exists in a certain freshness which seems, if I may say so, very desirable. This freshness Poulet, quoting Marivaux, describes very well."

K. Saved from Drowning

K. in the water. His flat black hat, his black cape, his sword are on the shore. He retains his mask. His hands beat the surface of the water which tears and rips about him. The white foam, the green depths. I throw a line, the coils leaping out over the surface of the water. He has missed it. No, it appears that he has it. His right hand (sword arm) grasps the line that I have thrown him. I am on the bank, the rope wound round my waist, braced against a rock. K. now has both hands on the line. I pull him out of the water. He stands now on the bank, gasping.

"Thank you."

1968

John Updike
b. 1932

John Updike was born on March 18, 1932, in the small town of Shillington, Pennsylvania, where he acquired an overwhelming sense of place that has continued to yield richly detailed memories—of buildings and pets, scenes and playmates, and above all of family. None of this would be remarkable were Updike's sense of life not inseparable from his sense of place and his sense of art from his sense of life.

Art began for Updike "as a method of riding a thin pencil line out of Shillington, out of time altogether, into an infinity of unseen and even unborn hearts." Yet, having begun as a mode of flight, writing quickly became for him a method of return—or more precisely, a method of transcribing the world he had known: "middleness with all its grits, bumps, and anonymities, in its fullness of satisfaction and mystery." Whether such a thing as transcribing is "possible" or, in view of the world's wild suffering, "worth doing" is a question Updike explicitly puts to himself. "Possibly not," he replies, only to conclude that it is nevertheless necessary since "the horse chestnut trees, the telephone poles, the porches, the green hedges recede to a calm point that in my subjective geography is still the center of the world."

Between his beginnings in Shillington and his emergence as a writer, Updike spent four years at Harvard, from which he was graduated *summa cum laude* in 1954. After studying art for a year in England, Updike returned to the United States in 1955. He worked as a staff reporter for *The New Yorker* for two years and soon began contributing stories there regularly, establishing a relationship with that magazine that has continued to the present. In 1957 he left New York to practice his "solitary trade" in Ipswich, Massachusetts.

In 1959 Updike published a collection of short stories, *The Same Door,* and his first novel—partly inspired by his early reading of Huxley and Orwell—*The Poorhouse Fair,* a futuristic story set in a county home for the elderly poor. The following year Updike published a successful second novel, *Rabbit, Run,* about a former high school basketball star who, nostalgic for a lost past, finds himself continually on the run from the demands of adult responsibility. Updike continued the story of Harry ("Rabbit") Angstrom, taking him through the cultural turmoil of the late 1960s in *Rabbit Redux* (1971) and into upper-middle-class prosperity—though not necessarily peace of mind—in *Rabbit Is Rich* (1981). Updike has frequently connected his themes to classical mythology, a technique that came fully to the surface in his third novel, *The Centaur* (1963), the story of three days in the life of a high school science teacher and his son.

By the mid-1960s it had become clear that one of Updike's dominant subjects was marriage. Many of his short stories—among them "Separating"—deal exclusively with the difficulties of married life in a world where the traditional religious values that once nourished and sanctioned marital love and sex have lost their meaning. In *Of the Farm* (1965) Updike explores the inner dynamics of a marriage during a couple's weekend visit to the husband's dying mother. The problems of marriage in our time are given ritualistic and religious significance in *Couples* (1968), a novel about sexual love and infidelity among ten couples in a small New England community. In *A Month of Sundays* (1975) Updike explores the themes of love and sex, marriage and infidelity within the framework of American Protestant morality. The theme of marriage and infidelity is also at the center of Updike's eighth novel, *Marry Me* (1976), the story of a summer love affair that is also a story of modern morality: We live in "the twilight of the old morality," the book's hero argues, "and there's just enough to torment us, and not enough to hold us in." In 1979 Updike collected his stories about a married couple, the Maples, in *Too Far to Go* and in the same year also published *Problems and Other Stories,* which contains "Separating," another of the Maples stories.

Though continually drawn to the problems of love, sex, and modern domesticity, Updike has nevertheless kept a close eye on literature, culture, and politics. In 1970 he published *Bech: A Book,* a series of linked stories about an American Jewish writer that dealt humorously with the meaning of a literary career; Updike continued the adventures of Henry Bech in another collection of tales, *Bech Is Back* (1982). In 1973 Updike toured Africa as a Fulbright lecturer, and out of his experiences he wrote *The Coup* (1978), a political novel about a violent, imaginary African regime. Updike's enormous output of essays, criticism, and literary reviews have been collected in several volumes: *Assorted Prose* (1965), *Picked-Up Pieces* (1975), and *Hugging the Shore* (1983). Updike has also written a play and several volumes of poetry. His latest novels are *The Witches of Eastwick* (1984), which uses a contemporary instance of witchcraft as a way of commenting on a modern culture habituated to television and popular media, and *Roger's Version* (1986).

Updike's stories, a large number of them set in "Olinger," the small imaginary town that evokes the Shillington of Updike's boyhood and youth, often center on adolescent protagonists. Over the stories hovers a certain nostalgia, a remorse for time. One source of that nostalgia is Updike's feeling for youth itself—for its openness, its honesty, its innocence, its brave sense of immortality. Another source is his feeling for preurban America and the life it spawned. But there is always an edge to Updike's journeys back toward the source, not simply because he is suspicious of nostalgia but also because such journeys always follow lines toward the unseen and the unknown. His larger quest is for some form of work or play or love that can approximate—or some religious experience that can satisfy—our longing for permanence.

Further Reading:
C. T. Samuels, *John Updike,* 1969.

Text:
Problems and Other Stories, 1979.

Separating

The day was fair. Brilliant. All that June the weather had mocked the Maples' internal misery with solid sunlight—golden shafts and cascades of green in which their conversations had wormed unseeing, their sad murmuring selves the only stain in Nature. Usually by this time of the year they had acquired tans; but when they met their elder daughter's plane on her return from a year in England they were almost as pale as she, though Judith was too dazzled by the sunny opulent jumble of her native land to notice. They did not spoil her homecoming by telling her immediately. Wait a few days, let her recover from jet lag, had been one of their formulations, in that string of gray dialogues—over coffee, over cocktails, over Cointreau—that had shaped the strategy of their dissolution, while the earth performed its annual stunt of renewal unnoticed beyond their closed windows. Richard had thought to leave at Easter; Joan had insisted they wait until the four children were at last assembled, with all exams passed and ceremonies attended, and the bauble of summer to console them. So he had drudged away, in love, in dread, repairing screens, getting the mowers sharpened, rolling and patching their new tennis court.

The court, clay, had come through its first winter pitted and windswept bare of redcoat. Years ago the Maples had observed how often, among their friends, divorce followed a dramatic home improvement, as if the marriage were making one last effort to live; their own worst crisis had come amid the plaster dust and exposed plumbing of a kitchen renovation. Yet, a summer ago, as canary-yellow bulldozers gaily churned a grassy, daisy-dotted knoll into a muddy plateau, and a crew of pigtailed young men raked and tamped clay into a plane, this transformation did not strike them as ominous, but festive in its impudence; their marriage could rend the earth for fun. The next spring, waking each day at dawn to a sliding sensation as if the bed were being tipped, Richard found the barren tennis court—its net and tapes still rolled in the barn—an environment congruous with his mood of purposeful desolation, and the crumbling of handfuls of clay into cracks and holes (dogs had frolicked on the court in a thaw; rivulets had eroded trenches) an activity suitably elemental and interminable. In his sealed heart he hoped the day would never come.

Now it was here. A Friday. Judith was re-acclimated; all four children were assembled, before jobs and camps and visits again scattered them. Joan thought they should be told one by one. Richard was for making an announcement at the table. She said, "I think just making an announcement is a cop-out. They'll start quarrelling and playing to each other instead of focusing. They're each individuals, you know, not just some corporate obstacle to your freedom."

"O.K., O.K. I agree." Joan's plan was exact. That evening, they were giving Judith a belated welcome-home dinner, of lobster and champagne. Then, the party over, they, the two of them, who nineteen years before would push her in a baby carriage along Fifth Avenue to Washington Square, were to walk her out of the house, to the bridge across the salt creek, and tell her, swearing her to secrecy. Then Richard Jr., who was going directly from work to a rock concert in Boston, would be told, either late when he returned on the train or early Saturday morning before he went off to his job; he was seventeen and employed as one of a golf-course maintenance crew. Then the two younger children, John and Margaret, could, as the morning wore on, be informed.

"Mopped up, as it were," Richard said.

"Do you have any better plan? That leaves you the rest of Saturday to answer any questions, pack, and make your wonderful departure."

"No," he said, meaning he had no better plan, and agreed to hers, though to him it showed an edge of false order, a hidden plea for control, like Joan's long chore lists and financial accountings and, in the days when he first knew her, her too-copious lecture notes. Her plan turned one hurdle for him into four—four knife-sharp walls, each with a sheer blind drop on the other side.

All spring he had moved through a world of insides and outsides, of barriers and partitions. He and Joan stood as a thin barrier between the children and the truth. Each moment was a partition, with the past on one side and the future on the other, a future containing this unthinkable now. Beyond four knifelike walls a new life for him waited vaguely. His skull cupped a secret, a white face, a face both frightened and soothing, both strange and known, that he wanted to shield from tears, which he felt all about him, solid as the sunlight. So haunted, he had become obsessed with battening down the house against his absence, replacing screens and sash cords, hinges and latches —a Houdini making things snug before his escape.

The lock. He had still to replace a lock on one of the doors of the screened porch. The task, like most such, proved more difficult than he had imagined. The old lock, aluminum frozen by corrosion, had been deliberately rendered obsolete by manufacturers. Three hardware stores had nothing that even approximately matched the mortised hole its removal (surprisingly easy) left. Another hole had to be gouged, with bits too small and saws too big, and the old hole fitted with a block of wood—the chisels dull, the saw rusty, his fingers thick with lack of sleep. The sun poured down, beyond the porch, on a world of neglect. The bushes already needed pruning, the windward side of the house was shedding flakes of paint, rain would get in when he was gone, insects, rot, death. His family, all those he would lose, filtered through the edges of his awareness as he struggled with screw holes, splinters, opaque instructions, minutiae of metal.

Judith sat on the porch, a princess returned from exile. She regaled them with stories of fuel shortages, of bomb scares in the Underground, of Pakistani workmen loudly lusting after her as she walked past on her way to dance school. Joan came and went, in and out of the house, calmer than she should have been, praising his struggles with the lock as if this were one more and not the last of their long succession of shared chores. The younger of his sons for a few minutes held the rickety screen door while his father clumsily hammered and chiseled, each blow a kind of sob in Richard's ears. His younger daughter, having been at a slumber party, slept on the porch hammock through all the noise—heavy and pink, trusting and forsaken. Time, like the sunlight, continued relentlessly; the sunlight slowly slanted. Today was one of the longest days. The lock clicked, worked. He was through. He had a drink; he drank it on the porch, listening to his daughter. "It was so sweet," she was saying, "during the worst of it, how all the butchers and bakery shops kept open by candlelight. They're all so plucky and cute. From the papers, things sounded so much worse here—people shooting people in gas lines, and everybody freezing."

Richard asked her, "Do you still want to live in England forever?" *Forever:* the concept, now a reality upon him, pressed and scratched at the back of his throat.

"No," Judith confessed, turning her oval face to him, its eyes still childishly far apart, but the lips set as over something succulent and satisfactory. "I was anxious to come home. I'm an American." She was a woman. They had raised her; he and Joan had endured together to raise her, alone of the four. The others had still some raising left in them. Yet it was the thought of telling Judith—the image of her, their first baby, walking between them arm in arm to the bridge—that broke him. The partition between his face and the tears broke. Richard sat down to the celebratory meal with the back of his throat aching; the champagne, the lobster seemed phases of sunshine; he saw them and tasted them through tears. He blinked, swallowed, croakily joked about hay fever. The tears would not stop leaking through; they came not through a hole that could be plugged but through a permeable spot in a membrane, steadily, purely, endlessly, fruitfully. They became, his tears, a shield for himself against these others—their faces, the fact of their assembly, a last time as innocents, at a table where he sat the last time as head. Tears dropped from his nose as he broke the lobster's back; salt flavored his champagne as he sipped it; the raw clench at the back of his throat was delicious. He could not help himself.

His children tried to ignore his tears. Judith, on his right, lit a cigarette, gazed upward in the direction of her too energetic, too sophisticated exhalation; on her other side, John earnestly bent his face to the extraction of the last morsels—legs, tail segments—from the scarlet corpse. Joan, at the opposite end of the table, glanced at him surprised, her reproach displaced by a quick grimace, of forgiveness, or of salute to his superior gift of strategy. Between them, Margaret, no longer called Bean, thirteen and large for her age, gazed from the other side of his pane of tears as if into a shopwindow at something she coveted—at her father, a crystalline heap of splinters and memories. It was not she, however, but John who, in the kitchen, as they cleared the plates and carapaces away, asked Joan the question: *"Why is Daddy crying?"*

Richard heard the question but not the murmured answer. Then he heard Bean cry, "Oh, no-oh!"—the faintly dramatized exclamation of one who had long expected it.

John returned to the table carrying a bowl of salad. He nodded tersely at his father and his lips shaped the conspiratorial words "She told."

"Told what?" Richard asked aloud, insanely.

The boy sat down as if to rebuke his father's distraction with the example of his own good manners. He said quietly, "The separation."

Joan and Margaret returned; the child, in Richard's twisted vision, seemed diminished in size, and relieved, relieved to have had the bogieman at last proved real. He called out to her—the distances at the table had grown immense—"You knew, you always knew," but the clenching at the back of his throat prevented him from making sense of it. From afar he heard Joan talking, levelly, sensibly, reciting what they had prepared: it was a separation for the summer, an experiment. She and Daddy both agreed it would be good for them; they needed space and time to think; they liked each other but did not make each other happy enough, somehow.

Judith, imitating her mother's factual tone, but in her youth off-key, too cool, said, "I think it's silly. You should either live together or get divorced."

Richard's crying, like a wave that has crested and crashed, had become tumultuous; but it was overtopped by another tumult, for John, who had been so reserved, now grew larger and larger at the table. Perhaps his younger sister's being credited with knowing set him off. "Why didn't you *tell* us?" he asked, in a large round voice quite unlike his own. "You should have *told* us you weren't getting along."

Richard was startled into attempting to force words through his tears. "We *do* get along, that's the trouble, so it doesn't show even to us—" *That we do not love each other* was the rest of the sentence; he couldn't finish it.

Joan finished for him, in her style. "And we've always, *especially,* loved our children."

John was not mollified. "What do you care about *us?*" he boomed. "We're just little things you *had.*" His sisters' laughing forced a laugh from him, which he turned hard and parodistic: "Ha ha *ha.*" Richard and Joan realized simultaneously that the child was drunk, on Judith's homecoming champagne. Feeling bound to keep the center of the stage, John took a cigarette from Judith's pack, poked it into his mouth, let it hang from his lower lip, and squinted like a gangster.

"You're not little things we had," Richard called to him. "You're the whole point. But you're grown. Or almost."

The boy was lighting matches. Instead of holding them to his cigarette (for they had never seen him smoke; being "good" had been his way of setting himself apart), he held them to his mother's face, closer and closer, for her to blow out. Then he lit the whole folder—a hiss and then a torch, held against his mother's face. Prismed by tears, the flame filled Richard's vision; he didn't know how it was extinguished. He heard Margaret say, "Oh stop showing off," and saw John, in response, break the cigarette in two and put the halves entirely into his mouth and chew, sticking out his tongue to display the shreds to his sister.

Joan talked to him, reasoning—a fountain of reason, unintelligible. "Talked about it for years . . . our children must help us . . . Daddy and I both want . . ." As the boy listened, he carefully wadded a paper napkin into the leaves of his salad, fashioned a ball of paper and lettuce, and popped it into his mouth, looking around the table for the expected laughter. None came. Judith said, "Be mature," and dismissed a plume of smoke.

Richard got up from this stifling table and led the boy outside. Though the house was in twilight, the outdoors still brimmed with light, the lovely waste light of high summer. Both laughing, he supervised John's spitting out the lettuce and paper and tobacco into the pachysandra. He took him by the hand—a square gritty hand, but for its softness a man's. Yet, it held on. They ran together up into the field, past the tennis court. The raw banking left by the bulldozers was dotted with daisies. Past the court and a flat stretch where they used to play family baseball stood a soft green rise glorious in the sun, each weed and species of grass distinct as illumination on parchment. "I'm sorry, so sorry," Richard cried. "You were the only one who ever tried to help me with all the goddam jobs around this place."

Sobbing, safe within his tears and the champagne, John explained, "It's not just the separation, it's the whole crummy year, I *hate* that school, you can't make any friends, the history teacher's a scud."

They sat on the crest of the rise, shaking and warm from their tears but easier in their voices, and Richard tried to focus on the child's sad year—the weekdays long with homework, the weekends spent in his room with model airplanes, while his parents murmured down below, nursing their separation. How selfish, how blind, Richard thought; his eyes felt scoured. He told his son, "We'll think about getting you transferred. Life's too short to be miserable."

They had said what they could, but did not want the moment to heal, and talked on, about the school, about the tennis court, whether it would ever again be as good as it had been that first summer. They walked to inspect it and pressed a few more tapes more firmly down. A little stiltedly, perhaps trying now to make too much of the moment, Richard led the boy to the spot in the field where the view was best, of the metallic blue river, the emerald marsh, the scattered islands velvety with shadow in the low light, the white bits of beach far away. "See," he said. "It goes on being beautiful. It'll be here tomorrow."

"I know," John answered, impatiently. The moment had closed.

Back in the house, the others had opened some white wine, the champagne being drunk, and still sat at the table, the three females, gossiping. Where Joan sat had become the head. She turned, showing him a tearless face, and asked, "All right?"

"We're fine," he said, resenting it, though relieved, that the party went on without him.

In bed she explained, "I couldn't cry I guess because I cried so much all spring. It really wasn't fair. It's your idea, and you made it look as though I was kicking you out."

"I'm sorry," he said. "I couldn't stop. I wanted to but couldn't."

"You *didn't* want to. You loved it. You were having your way, making a general announcement."

"I love having it over," he admitted. "God, those kids were great. So brave and funny." John, returned to the house, had settled to a model airplane in his room, and kept shouting down to them, "I'm O.K. No sweat." "And the way," Richard went on, cozy in his relief, "they never questioned the reasons we gave. No thought of a third person. Not even Judith."

"That *was* touching," Joan said.

He gave her a hug. "You were great too. Very reassuring to everybody. Thank you." Guiltily, he realized he did not feel separated.

"You still have Dickie to do," she told him. These words set before him a black mountain in the darkness; its cold breath, its near weight affected his chest. Of the four children, his elder son was most nearly his conscience. Joan did not need to add, "That's one piece of your dirty work I won't do for you."

"I know. I'll do it. You go to sleep."

Within minutes, her breathing slowed, became oblivious and deep. It was quarter to midnight. Dickie's train from the concert would come in at one-fourteen. Richard set the alarm for one. He had slept atrociously for weeks. But whenever he closed his lids some glimpse of the last hours scorched them—Judith exhaling toward the ceiling in a kind of aversion, Bean's mute staring, the sunstruck growth in the field where he and John had rested. The mountain before him moved closer, moved within him; he was huge, momentous. The ache at the back of his throat felt stale. His wife slept as if slain beside him. When, exasperated by his hot lids, his crowded heart, he rose from bed and dressed, she awoke enough to turn over. He told her then, "Joan, if I could undo it all, I would."

"Where would you begin?" she asked. There was no place. Giving him courage, she was always giving him courage. He put on shoes without socks in the dark. The children were breathing in their rooms, the downstairs was hollow. In their confusion they had left lights burning. He turned off all but one, the kitchen overhead. The car started. He had hoped it wouldn't. He met only moonlight on the road; it seemed a diaphanous companion, flickering in the leaves along the roadside, haunting his rearview mirror like a pursuer, melting under his headlights. The center of town, not quite deserted, was eerie at this hour. A young cop in uniform kept company with a gang of T-shirted kids on the steps of the bank. Across from the railroad station, several bars kept open. Customers, mostly young, passed in and out of the warm night, savoring summer's novelty. Voices shouted from cars as they passed; an immense conversation seemed in progress. Richard parked and in his weariness put his head on the passenger seat, out of the commotion and wheeling lights. It was as when, in the movies, an assassin grimly carries his mission through the jostle of a carnival—except the movies cannot show the precipitous, palpable slope you cling to within. You cannot climb back down; you can only fall. The synthetic fabric of the car seat, warmed by his cheek, confided to him an ancient, distant scent of vanilla.

A train whistle caused him to lift his head. It was on time; he had hoped it would be late. The slender drawgates descended. The bell of approach tingled happily. The great metal body, horizontally fluted, rocked to a stop, and sleepy teen-agers disembarked, his son among them. Dickie did not show surprise that his father was meeting him at this terrible hour. He sauntered to the car with two friends, both taller than he. He said "Hi" to his father and took the passenger's seat with an exhausted promptness that expressed gratitude. The friends got in the back, and Richard was grateful; a few more minutes' postponement would be won by driving them home.

He asked, "How was the concert?"

"Groovy," one boy said from the back seat.

"It bit," the other said.

"It was O.K.," Dickie said, moderate by nature, so reasonable that in his childhood the unreason of the world had given him headaches, stomach aches, nausea. When the second friend had been dropped off at his dark house, the boy blurted, "Dad, my eyes are killing me with hay fever! I'm out there cutting that mothering grass all day!"

"Do we still have those drops?"

"They didn't do any good last summer."

"They might this." Richard swung a U-turn on the empty street. The drive home took a few minutes. The mountain was here, in his throat. "Richard," he said, and felt the boy, slumped and rubbing his eyes, go tense at his tone, "I didn't come to meet you just to make your life easier. I came because your mother and I have some news for you, and you're a hard man to get ahold of these days. It's sad news."

"That's O.K." The reassurance came out soft, but quick, as if released from the tip of a spring.

Richard had feared that his tears would return and choke him, but the boy's manliness set an example, and his voice issued forth steady and dry. "It's sad news, but it needn't be tragic news, at least for you. It should have no practical effect on your life, though it's bound to have an emotional effect. You'll work at your job, and go back to school in September. Your mother and I are really proud of what you're making of your life; we don't want that to change at all."

"Yeah," the boy said lightly, on the intake of his breath, holding himself up. They turned the corner; the church they went to loomed like a gutted fort. The home of the woman Richard hoped to marry stood across the green. Her bedroom light burned.

"Your mother and I," he said, "have decided to separate. For the summer. Nothing legal, no divorce yet. We want to see how it feels. For some years now, we haven't been doing enough for each other, making each other as happy as we should be. Have you sensed that?"

"No," the boy said. It was an honest, unemotional answer: true or false in a quiz.

Glad for the factual basis, Richard pursued, even garrulously, the details. His apartment across town, his utter accessibility, the split vacation arrangements, the advantages to the children, the added mobility and variety of the summer. Dickie listened, absorbing. "Do the others know?"

"Yes."

"How did they take it?"

"The girls pretty calmly. John flipped out; he shouted and ate a cigarette and made a salad out of his napkin and told us how much he hated school."

His brother chuckled. "He did?"

"Yeah. The school issue was more upsetting for him than Mom and me. He seemed to feel better for having exploded."

"He did?" The repetition was the first sign that he was stunned.

"Yes. Dickie, I want to tell you something. This last hour, waiting for your train to get in, has been about the worst of my life. I hate this. *Hate* it. My father would have died before doing it to me." He felt immensely lighter, saying this. He had dumped the mountain on the boy. They were home. Moving swiftly as a shadow, Dickie was out of the car, through the bright kitchen. Richard called after him, "Want a glass of milk or anything?"

"No thanks."

"Want us to call the course tomorrow and say you're too sick to work?"

"No, that's all right." The answer was faint, delivered at the door to his room; Richard listened for the slam that went with a tantrum. The door closed normally, gently. The sound was sickening.

Joan had sunk into that first deep trough of sleep and was slow to awake. Richard had to repeat, "I told him."

"What did he say?"

"Nothing much. Could you go say goodnight to him? Please."

She left their room, without putting on a bathrobe. He sluggishly changed back into his pajamas and walked down the hall. Dickie was already in bed, Joan was sitting beside him, and the boy's bedside clock radio was murmuring music. When she stood, an inexplicable light—the moon?—outlined her body through the nightie. Richard sat on the warm place she had indented on the child's narrow mattress. He asked him, "Do you want the radio on like that?"

"It always is."

"Doesn't it keep you awake? It would me."

"No."

"Are you sleepy?"

"Yeah."

"Good. Sure you want to get up and go to work? You've had a big night."

"I want to."

Away at school this winter he had learned for the first time that you can go short of sleep and live. As an infant he had slept with an immobile, sweating intensity that had alarmed his babysitters. In adolescence he had often been the first of the four children to go to bed. Even now, he would go slack in the middle of a television show, his sprawled legs hairy and brown. "O.K. Good boy. Dickie, listen. I love you so much, I never knew how much until now. No matter how this works out, I'll always be with you. Really."

Richard bent to kiss an averted face but his son, sinewy, turned and with wet cheeks embraced him and gave him a kiss, on the lips, passionate as a woman's. In his father's ear he moaned one word, the crucial, intelligent word: *"Why?"*

Why. It was a whistle of wind in a crack, a knife thrust, a window thrown open on emptiness. The white face was gone, the darkness was featureless. Richard had forgotten why.

1975

N. Scott Momaday
b. 1934

N. Scott Momaday, a Kiowa Indian, is a Pulitzer Prize–winning novelist and university professor who believes that the strength of American Indian culture rests on its close identification with the land. His grandmother, Aho, typifies for him the Indian experience: "The immense landscape of the continental interior," he says, "lay like memory in her blood." Yet for as long as she lived after witnessing the outlawing of the Sun Dance, the Kiowa ritual of worship, "she bore a vision of deicide," the killing of a god. In his fiction and nonfiction Momaday celebrates the spiritual awareness that his grandmother possessed even as he laments the cultural alienation imposed on her by the United States.

Navarre Scott Momaday, whose Kiowa name is Tsoai-talee, was born on February 27, 1934, near Anadarko, the Oklahoma Kiowa Indian agency. In 1935 his family moved to northern New Mexico, where he grew up on Navajo,

Apache, and Jemez Pueblo Indian reservations. He received a B.A. in political science from the University of New Mexico in 1958, an M.A. from Stanford in 1960, and a Ph.D. from Stanford in 1963. Currently on the English and Comparative Literature faculty at Stanford, Momaday has also taught at the Berkeley and Santa Barbara campuses of the University of California and at the Las Cruces campus of New Mexico State University. His scholarly interest is in nineteenth-century American poetry, and he is editor of *The Complete Poems of Frederick Goddard Tuckerman* (1965).

Momaday lives another life, however, as a Kiowa tribal dancer and chronicler of Indian experience in this country. "None but an Indian, I think," he has said, "knows so much what it is like to have existence in two worlds and security in neither." In *House Made of Dawn* (1968), his prizewinning first novel, Momaday recounts the adventures of an Indian named Abel, a man who survives World War II only to discover, as Momaday put it, that he can neither "recover his tribal identity nor . . . escape the cultural context in which he grew up. He is torn, as they say, between two worlds, neither of which he can enter and be a whole man. The story is that of his struggle to survive. . . ." The language of *House Made of Dawn* paradoxically conjoins the lyrical and the violent. Abel and his fellow runners run, we read, "with great dignity and calm, not in hope of anything, but hopelessly; neither in fear nor hatred nor despair of evil, but simply in recognition and with respect. Evil was. Evil was abroad in the night; they must venture out to the confrontation; they must reckon dues and divide the world."

In Momaday's nonfiction the "sacred earth" becomes a redemptive agent in the human quest for knowledge and wholeness. In *The Journey of Tai-me* (1967), the story of the tribal god of the Kiowa whose death his grandmother witnessed at the last Sun Dance, and again in *The Way to Rainy Mountain* (1969), Momaday confronts a world in which experience typically seems fragmentary and inadequate and in which knowledge typically comes as "a moment of truth and exile." But Momaday also writes as one who is convinced that "man's idea of himself" finds "old and essential being in language," in the act of naming and the process of remembering, activities of the mind that are "legendary as well as historical, personal as well as cultural."

Further Reading:
C. Oleson, "The Remembered Earth: Momaday's *House Made of Dawn*," *South Dakota Review*, Spring 1973.
M. S. Trimble, *N. Scott Momaday*, 1973.

Text:
House Made of Dawn, 1956.

from House Made of Dawn

from The Priest of the Sun

from January 26

The Priest of the Sun lived with his disciple Cruz on the first floor of a two-story red-brick building in Los Angeles. The upstairs was maintained as a storage facility by the A. A. Kaul Office Supply Company. The basement was a kind of church. There was a signboard on the wall above the basement steps, encased in glass. In neat, movable white block letters on a black field it read:

LOS ANGELES
HOLINESS PAN–INDIAN RESCUE MISSION
Rev. J. B. B. Tosamah, Pastor & Priest of the Sun
Saturday 8:30 P.M.
"The Gospel According to John"
Sunday 8:30 P.M.
"The Way to Rainy Mountain"
Be kind to a white man today

The basement was cold and dreary, dimly illuminated by two 40-watt bulbs which were screwed into the side walls above the dais. This platform was made out of rough planks of various woods and dimensions, thrown together without so much as a hammer and nails; it stood seven or eight inches above the floor, and it supported the tin firebox and the crescent altar. Off to one side was a kind of lectern, decorated with red and yellow symbols of the sun and moon. In back of the dais there was a screen of purple drapery, threadbare and badly faded. On either side of the aisle which led to the altar there were chairs and crates, fashioned into pews. The walls were bare and gray and streaked with water. The only windows were small, rectangular openings near the ceiling, at ground level; the panes were covered over with a thick film of coal oil and dust, and spider webs clung to the frames or floated out like smoke across the room. The air was heavy and stale; odors of old smoke and incense lingered all around. The people had filed into the pews and were waiting silently.

Cruz, a squat, oily man with blue-black hair that stood out like spines from his head, stepped forward on the platform and raised his hands as if to ask for the quiet that already was. Everyone watched him for a moment; in the dull light his skin shone yellow with sweat. Turning slightly and extending his arm behind him, he said, "The Right Reverend John Big Bluff Tosamah."

There was a ripple in the dark screen; the drapes parted and the Priest of the Sun appeared, moving shadow-like to the lectern. He was shaggy and awful-looking in the thin, naked light: big, lithe as a cat, narrow-eyed, suggesting in the whole of his look and manner both arrogance and agony. He wore black like a cleric; he had the voice of a great dog:

" '*In principio erat Verbum.*'[1] Think of Genesis. Think of how it was before the world was made. There was nothing, the Bible says. 'And the earth was without form, and void; and darkness was upon the face of the deep.' It was dark, and there was nothing. There were no mountains, no trees, no rocks, no rivers. There was nothing. But there was darkness all around, and in the darkness something happened. *Something happened!* There was a single sound. Far away in the darkness there was a single sound. Nothing made it, but it was there; and there was no one to hear it, but it was there. It was there, and there was nothing else. It rose up in the darkness, little and still, almost nothing in itself—like a single soft breath, like the wind arising; yes, like the whisper of the wind rising slowly and going out into the early morning. But there was no wind. There was only the sound, little and soft. It was almost nothing in itself, the smallest seed of sound—but it took hold of the darkness and there was light; it took hold of the stillness and there was motion forever; it took hold of the silence and there was sound. It was almost nothing in itself, a single sound, a word—a word broken off at the darkest center of the night and let go in the awful void, forever and forever. And it was almost nothing in itself. It scarcely was; but it was, and everything began."

Just then a remarkable thing happened. The Priest of the Sun seemed stricken; he let go of his audience and withdrew into himself, into some strange potential of himself. His voice, which had been low and resonant, suddenly became harsh and flat; his shoulders sagged and his stomach protruded, as if he had held his breath to the limit of endurance; for a moment there was a look of amazement, then utter carelessness in his face. Conviction, caricature, callousness: the remainder of his sermon was a going back and forth among these.

"Thank you *so* much, Brother Cruz. Good evening, blood brothers and sisters, and welcome, welcome. Gracious me, I see lots of new faces out there tonight. *Gracious me!* May the Great Spirit—can we knock off that talking in the back there?—be with you always.

" 'In the beginning was the Word.' I have taken as my text this evening the almighty Word itself. Now get this: 'There was a man sent from God, whose name was John. The same came for a witness, to bear witness of the Light, that all men through him might believe.' Amen, brothers and sisters, *Amen.* And the riddle of the Word, 'In the beginning was the Word. . . .' Now what do you suppose old John *meant* by that? That cat was a preacher, and, well, you know how it is with preachers; he had something big on his mind. Oh my, it was big; it was the *Truth,* and it was heavy, and old John hurried to set it down. And in his hurry he said too much. 'In the beginning was the Word, and the Word was with God, and the Word was God.' It was the Truth, all right, but it was more than the Truth. The Truth was overgrown with fat, and the fat was God. The fat was *John's* God, and God stood between John and the Truth. Old John, see, he got up one morning and caught sight of the Truth. It must have been like a bolt of lightning, and the sight of it made him blind. And *for a moment* the vision burned on in back of his eyes, and he *knew* what it was. In that instant he saw something he had never seen before and would never see again. That was the instant of revelation, inspiration, Truth. And old John, he must have

[1] Latin: "In the beginning was the Word." (See John 1:1.)

fallen down on his knees. Man, he must have been shaking and laughing and crying and yelling and praying—all at the same time—and he must have been drunk and delirious with the Truth. You see, he had lived all his life waiting for that one moment, and it came, and it took him by surprise, and it was gone. And he said, 'In the beginning was the Word. . . .' And, man, right then and there he should have stopped. There was nothing more to say, but he went on. He had said all there was to say, everything, but he went on. 'In the beginning was the Word. . . .' Brothers and sisters, *that* was the Truth, the whole of it, the essential and eternal Truth, the bone and blood and muscle of the Truth. But he went on, old John, because he was a preacher. The perfect vision faded from his mind, and he went on. The instant passed, and then he had nothing but a memory. He was desperate and confused, and in his confusion he stumbled and went on. 'In the beginning was the Word, and the Word was with God, and the Word was God.' He went on to talk about Jews and Jerusalem, Levites and Pharisees, Moses and Philip and Andrew and Peter. Don't you see? Old John *had* to go on. That cat had a whole lot at stake. He couldn't let the Truth alone. He couldn't see that he had come to the end of the Truth, and he went on. He tried to make it bigger and better than it was, but instead he only demeaned and encumbered it. He made it soft and big with fat. He was a preacher, and he made a complex sentence of the Truth, two sentences, three, a paragraph. He made a sermon and theology of the Truth. He imposed his idea of God upon the everlasting Truth. 'In the beginning was the Word. . . .' And that is all there was, and it was enough.

"Now, brothers and sisters, old John was a white man, and the white man has his ways. Oh gracious me, he has his ways. He talks about the Word. He talks through it and around it. He builds upon it with syllables, with prefixes and suffixes and hyphens and accents. He adds and divides and multiplies the Word. And in all of this he subtracts the Truth. And, brothers and sisters, you have come here to live in the white man's world. Now the white man deals in words, and he deals easily, with grace and sleight of hand. And in his presence, here on his own ground, you are as children, mere babes in the woods. You must not mind, for in this you have a certain advantage. A child can listen and learn. The Word is sacred to a child.

"My grandmother was a storyteller; she knew her way around words. She never learned to read and write, but somehow she knew the good of reading and writing; she had learned how to listen and delight. She had learned that in words and in language, and there only, she could have whole and consummate being. She told me stories, and she taught me how to listen. I was a child and I listened. She could neither read nor write, you see, but she taught me how to live among her words, how to listen and delight. 'Storytelling; to utter and to hear . . .' And the simple act of listening is crucial to the concept of language, more crucial even than reading and writing, and language in turn is crucial to human society. There is proof of that, I think, in all the histories and prehistories of human experience. When that old Kiowa woman told me stories, I listened with only one ear. I was a child, and I took the words for granted. I did not know what all of them meant, but somehow I held on to them; I remembered them, and I remember them now. The stories were old and dear; they meant a great deal to my grandmother. It was not until she died that I knew how much they meant to her. I began to think about it, and then I knew. When she told me those old stories, something strange and good and powerful was going on. I was a child, and that old woman was asking me to come directly into the presence of her mind and spirit; she was taking hold of my imagination, giving me to share in the great fortune of her wonder and delight. She was asking me to go with her to the confrontation of something that was sacred and eternal. It was a timeless, *timeless* thing; nothing of her old age or of my childhood came between us.

"Children have a greater sense of the power and beauty of words than have the rest of us in general. And if that is so, it is because there occurs—or reoccurs—in the mind of every child something like a reflection of all human experience. I have heard that the human fetus corresponds in its development, stage by stage, to the scale of evolution. Surely it is no less reasonable to suppose that the waking mind of a child corresponds in the same way to the whole evolution of human thought and perception.

"In the white man's world, language, too—and the way in which the white man thinks of it—has undergone a process of change. The white man takes such things as words and literatures for granted, as indeed he must, for nothing in his world is so commonplace. On every side of him there are words by the millions, an unending succession of pamphlets and papers, letters and books, bills and bulletins, commentaries and conversations. He has diluted and multiplied the Word, and words have begun to close in upon him. He is sated and insensitive; his regard for language—for the Word itself—as an instrument of creation has diminished nearly to the point of no return. It may be that he will perish by the Word.

"But it was not always so with him, and it is not so with you. Consider for a moment that old Kiowa woman, my grandmother, whose use of language was confined to speech. And be assured that her regard for words was always keen in proportion as she depended upon them. You see, for her words were medicine; they were magic and invisible. They came from nothing into sound and meaning. They were beyond price; they could neither be bought nor sold. And she never threw words away.

"My grandmother used to tell me the story of Tai-me, of how Tai-me came to the Kiowas. The Kiowas were a sun dance culture, and Tai-me was their sun dance doll, their most sacred fetish; no medicine was ever more powerful. There is a story about the coming of Tai-me. This is what my grandmother told me:

Long ago there were bad times. The Kiowas were hungry and there was no food. There was a man who heard his children cry from hunger, and he began to search for food. He walked four days and became very weak. On the fourth day he came to a great canyon. Suddenly there was thunder and lightning. A Voice spoke to him and said, "Why are you following me? What do you want?" The man was afraid. The thing standing before him had the feet of a deer, and its body was covered with feathers. The man answered that the Kiowas were hungry. "Take me with you," the Voice said, "and I will give you whatever you want." From that day Tai-me has belonged to the Kiowas.

"Do you see? There, far off in the darkness, something happened. Do you see? Far, far away in the nothingness something happened. There was a voice, a sound, a word —and everything began. The story of the coming of Tai-me has existed for hundreds of years by word of mouth. It represents the oldest and best idea that man has of himself. It represents a very rich literature, which, because it was never written down, was always but one generation from extinction. But for the same reason it was cherished and revered. I could see that reverence in my grandmother's eyes, and I could hear it in her voice. It was that, I think, that old Saint John had in mind when he said, 'In the beginning was the Word. . . .' But he went on. He went on to lay a scheme about the Word. He could find no satisfaction in the simple fact that the Word was; he had to account for it, not in terms of that sudden and profound insight, which must have devastated him at once, but in terms of the moment afterward, which was irrelevant and remote; not in terms of his imagination, but only in terms of his prejudice.

"Say this: 'In the beginning was the Word. . . .' There was nothing. There was *nothing!* Darkness. There was darkness, and there was no end to it. You look up sometimes in the night and there are stars; you can see all the way to the stars. And you begin to know the universe, how awful and great it is. The stars lie out against the sky and do not fill it. A single star, flickering out in the universe, is enough to fill the mind, but it is nothing in the night sky. The darkness looms around it. The darkness flows among the stars, and beyond them forever. In the beginning that is how it was, but there were no stars. There was only the dark infinity in which nothing was. And something happened. At the distance of a star something happened, and everything began. The Word did not come into being, but *it was.* It did not break upon the silence, but *it was older than the silence and the silence was made of it.*

"Old John caught sight of something terrible. The thing standing before him said, 'Why are you following me? What do you want?' And from that day the Word has belonged to us, who have heard it for what it is, who have lived in fear and awe of it. In the Word was the beginning; *'In the beginning was the Word. . . .'* "

The Priest of the Sun appeared to have spent himself. He stepped back from the lectern and hung his head, smiling. In his mind the earth was spinning and the stars rattled around in the heavens. The sun shone, and the moon. Smiling in a kind of transport, the Priest of the Sun stood silent for a time while the congregation waited to be dismissed.

"Good night," he said, at last, "and get yours." . . .

from January 27

Tosamah, orator, physician, Priest of the Sun, son of Hummingbird, spoke:

"A single knoll rises out of the plain in Oklahoma, north and west of the Wichita range. For my people it is an old landmark, and they gave it the name Rainy Mountain. There, in the south of the continental trough, is the hardest weather in the world. In winter there are blizzards which come down the Williston corridor, bearing hail and sleet. Hot tornadic winds arise in the spring, and in summer the prairie is an anvil's edge. The grass turns brittle and brown, and it cracks beneath your feet. There are green belts along the rivers and creeks, linear groves of hickory and pecan, willow and witch hazel. At a distance in July or August the steaming foliage seems almost to writhe in fire. Great green and yellow grasshoppers are everywhere in the tall grass, popping up like corn to sting the flesh, and tortoises crawl about on the red earth, going nowhere in the plenty of time. Loneliness is there as an aspect of the land. All things in the plain are isolate; there is no confusion of objects in the eye, but one hill or one tree or one man. At the slightest elevation you can see to the end of the world. To look upon that landscape in the early morning, with the sun at your back, is to lose the sense of proportion. Your imagination comes to life, and this, you think, is where Creation was begun.

"I returned to Rainy Mountain in July. My grandmother had died in the spring, and I wanted to be at her grave. She had lived to be very old and at last infirm. Her only living daughter was with her when she died, and I was told that in death her face was that of a child.

"I like to think of her as a child. When she was born, the Kiowas were living the last great moment of their history. For more than a hundred years they had controlled the open range from the Smoky Hill River to the Red, from the headwaters of the Canadian to the fork of the Arkansas and Cimarron. In alliance with the Comanches, they had ruled the whole of the Southern Plains. War was their sacred business, and they were the finest horsemen the world has ever known. But warfare for the Kiowas was pre-eminently a matter of disposition rather than survival, and they never understood the grim, unrelenting advance of the U.S. Cavalry. When at last, divided and ill-provisioned, they were driven onto the Staked Plain in the cold of autumn, they fell into panic. In Palo Duro Canyon they abandoned their crucial stores to pillage and had nothing then but their lives. In order to save themselves, they surrendered to the soldiers at Fort Sill and were imprisoned in the old stone corral that now stands as a military museum. My grandmother was spared the humiliation of those high gray walls by eight or ten years, but she must have known from birth the affliction of defeat, the dark brooding of old warriors.

"Her name was Aho, and she belonged to the last culture to evolve in North America. Her forebears came down from the high north country nearly three centuries ago. The earliest evidence of their existence places them close to the source of the Yellowstone River in western Montana. They were a mountain people, a mysterious tribe of hunters whose language has never been classified in any major group. In the late seventeenth century they began a long migration to the south and east. It was a journey toward the dawn, and it led to a golden age. Along the way the Kiowas were befriended by the Crows, who gave them the culture and religion of the plains. They acquired horses, and their ancient nomadic spirit was suddenly free of the ground. They acquired Tai-me, the sacred sun dance doll, from that moment the chief object and symbol of their worship, and so shared in the divinity of the sun. Not least, they acquired the sense of destiny, therefore courage and pride. When they entered upon the Southern Plains, they had been transformed. No longer were they slaves to the simple necessity of survival; they were a lordly and dangerous society of fighters and thieves, hunters and priests of the sun. According to their origin myth, they entered the world through a hollow log. From one point of view, their migration was the fruit of an old prophecy, for indeed they emerged from a sunless world.

"I could see that. I followed their ancient way to my grandmother's grave. Though she lived out her long life in the shadow of Rainy Mountain, the immense landscape of the continental interior—all of its seasons and its sounds—lay like memory in her blood. She could tell of the Crows, whom she had never seen, and of the Black Hills, where she had never been. I wanted to see in reality what she had seen more perfectly in the mind's eye.

"I began my pilgrimage on the course of the Yellowstone. There, it seemed to me, was the top of the world, a region of deep lakes and dark timber, canyons and waterfalls. But, beautiful as it is, one might have the sense of confinement there. The skyline in all directions is close at hand, the high wall of the woods and deep cleavages of shade. There is a perfect freedom in the mountains, but it belongs to the eagle and the elk, the badger and the bear. The Kiowas reckoned their stature by the distance they could see, and they were bent and blind in the wilderness.

"Descending eastward, the highland meadows are a stairway to the plain. In July the inland slope of the Rockies is luxuriant with flax and buckwheat, stonecrop and larkspur. The earth unfolds and the limit of the land recedes. Clusters of trees, and animals grazing far in the distance, cause the vision to reach away and wonder to build upon the mind. The sun follows a longer course in the day, and the sky is immense beyond all comparison. The great billowing clouds that sail upon it are shadows that move upon the grass and grain like water, dividing light. Farther down, in the land of the Crows and the Blackfeet, the plain is yellow. Sweet clover takes hold of the hills and bends upon itself to cover and seal the soil. There the Kiowas paused on their way; they had come to the place where they must change their lives. The sun is at home on the plains. Precisely there does it have the certain character of a god. When the Kiowas came to the land of the Crows, they could see the dark lees of the hills at dawn across the Bighorn River, the profusion of light on the grain shelves, the oldest deity ranging after the solstices. Not yet would they veer south to the caldron of the land that lay below; they must wean their blood from the northern winter and hold the mountains a while longer in their view. They bore Tai-me in procession to the east.

"A dark mist lay over the Black Hills, and the land was like iron. At the top of a ridge I caught sight of Devils Tower—the uppermost extremity of it, like a file's end on the gray sky—and then it fell away behind the land. I was a long time then in coming upon it, and I did not see it again until I saw it whole, suddenly there across the valley, as if in the birth of time the core of the earth had broken through its crust and the motion of the world was begun. It stands in motion, like certain timeless trees that aspire too much into the sky, and imposes an illusion on the land. There are things in nature which engender an awful quiet in the heart of man; Devils Tower is one of them. Man must account for it. He must never fail to explain such a thing to himself, or else he is estranged forever from the universe. Two centuries ago, because they could not do otherwise, the Kiowas made a legend at the base of the rock. My grandmother said:

Eight children were there at play, seven sisters and their brother. Suddenly the boy was struck dumb; he trembled and began to run upon his hands and feet. His fingers became claws, and his body was covered with fur. There was a bear where the boy had been. The sisters were terrified; they ran, and the bear after them. They came to the stump of a great tree, and the tree spoke to them. It bade them climb upon it, and as they did so it began to rise into the air. The bear came to kill them, but they were just beyond its reach. It reared against the tree and scored the bark all around with its claws. The seven sisters were borne into the sky, and they became the stars of the Big Dipper.

"From that moment, and so long as the legend lives, the Kiowas have kinsmen in the night sky. Whatever they were in the mountains, they could be no more. However tenuous their well-being, however much they had suffered and would suffer again, they had found a way out of the wilderness.

"The first man among them to stand on the edge of the Great Plains saw farther over land than he had ever seen before. There is something about the heart of the continent that resides always in the end of vision, some essence of the sun and wind. That man knew the possible quest. There was nothing to prevent his going out; he could enter upon the land and be alive, could bear at once the great hot weight of its silence. In a sense the question of survival had never been more imminent, for no land is more the measure of human strength. But neither had wonder been more accessible to the mind nor destiny to the will.

"My grandmother had a reverence for the sun, a certain holy regard which now is all but gone out of mankind. There was a wariness in her, and an ancient awe. She was a Christian in her later years, but she had come a long way about, and she never forgot her birthright. As a child, she had been to the sun dances; she had taken part in that annual rite, and by it she had learned the restoration of her people in the presence of Tai-me. She was about seven years old when the last Kiowa sun dance was held in 1887 on the Washita River above Rainy Mountain Creek. The buffalo were gone. In order to consummate the ancient sacrifice—to impale the head of a buffalo bull upon the Tai-me tree—a delegation of old men journeyed into Texas, there to beg and barter for an animal from the Goodnight herd. She was ten when the Kiowas came together for the last time as a living sun dance culture. They could find no buffalo; they had to hang an old hide from the sacred tree. That summer was known to my grandmother as Ä'poto Etódǎ-de K'ádó, Sun Dance When the Forked Poles Were Left Standing, and it is entered in the Kiowa calendars as the figure of a tree standing outside the unfinished framework of a medicine lodge. Before the dance could begin, a company of armed soldiers rode out from Fort Sill under orders to disperse the tribe. Forbidden without cause the essential act of their faith, having seen the wild herds slaughtered and left to rot upon the ground, the Kiowas backed away forever from the tree. That was July 20, 1890, at the great bend of the Washita. My grandmother was there. Without bitterness, and for as long as she lived, she bore a vision of deicide.

"Now that I can have her only in memory, I see my grandmother in the several postures that were peculiar to her: standing at the wood stove on a winter morning and turning meat in a great iron skillet; sitting at the south window, bent above her beadwork, and afterward, when her vision failed, looking down for a long time into the fold of her hands; going out upon a cane, very slowly as she did when the weight of age came upon her; praying. I remember her most often at prayer. She made long, rambling prayers out of suffering and hope, having seen many things. I was never sure that I had the right to hear, so exclusive were they of all mere custom and company. The last time I saw her, she prayed standing by the side of her bed at night, naked to the waist, the light of a kerosene lamp moving upon her dark skin. Her long black hair, always drawn and braided in the day, lay upon her shoulders and against her breasts like a shawl. I did not always understand her prayers; I believe they were made of an older language than that of ordinary speech. There was something inherently sad in the sound, some slight hesitation upon the syllables of sorrow. She began in a high and descending pitch, exhausting her breath to silence; then again and again —and always the same intensity of effort, of something that is, and is not, like urgency in the human voice. Transported so in the dim and dancing light among the shadows of her room, she seemed beyond the reach of time, as if age could not lay hold of her. But that was illusion; I think I knew then that I should not see her again. . . .

1966

Thomas Pynchon
b. 1937

The sense of mystery that permeates Pynchon's fiction, emanating from elusive characters and plots, elusive concepts and themes, also shrouds his life. Thomas Pynchon is an intensely private person. He has never permitted his photograph to be publicly printed, and he has discouraged the circulation not only of rumors about his life but of accurate information as well. As a result, we have but few basic facts. Pynchon was born in Glen Cove, New York, on May 8, 1937. He attended Cornell University and, after serving two years in the U.S. Navy, graduated in 1958. After graduation he lived for a year in Greenwich Village, followed by a year in Seattle, Washington, where he worked for Boeing Aircraft on the corporation's in-house magazine. He then moved to Mexico to concentrate on his first novel. According to some sources, he now lives somewhere in California, though other sources place him in New York City.

Pynchon's first book, *V,* appeared in 1963. It is an intricately plotted novel that moves from alligator hunts through the sewers of New York to an elusive quest to find the enigamtic V, a woman mysteriously connected to the disastrous events of twentieth-century European history. His second book, *The Crying of Lot 49* (1966), is a short novel that features another elusive, paranoiac quest, this one to discover the significance of a secret postal system. Pynchon's third novel, *Gravity's Rainbow* (1973), won the National Book Award. Although it concerns an American officer forced into desertion toward the end of World War II, it is impossible to summarize. In its unremitting mixture of literary and popular styles, its unrelenting parody and paranoia, its technical jargon and multilayered plot structure, the novel not only portrays a labyrinthine world but becomes one itself. Though Pynchon studied English at Cornell, he also took a heavy dose of science courses, especially physics. In his collection of early short stories, *Slow Learner* (1984), Pynchon included "Entropy," a story he claims was inspired by his reading of Henry Adams and the mathematician Norbert Wiener. Connections —sometimes bizarre, sometimes terrifying—among modern history, technology, and communications consistently form the core of Pynchon's fiction.

Praised for its inventiveness and criticized for its obscurity, Pynchon's fiction continues to be controversial. Like James Joyce's and Vladimir Nabokov's, Pynchon's prose bristles with puns, cross-references, and layered meanings. Like

Edgar Allan Poe's and Nathanael West's, Pynchon's characteristic imaginative mode combines the comic, the satiric, and the apocalyptic. Like John Barth and Walker Percy, Pynchon moves with considerable confidence and authority in handling complex philosophical, psychological, and even scientific concepts. Like Herman Melville, he displays an affinity for arcane, offbeat information—an affinity so deep that one suspects him not only of reading almanacs but of being able to write them. His grasp of contemporary data and materials is especially remarkable.

What holds such rare talents together, enabling Pynchon to balance and control them, is an overriding concern with plot, a concern that begins with his own elaborate arrangements, in which he takes delight in everything from intricate entanglements to outrageous coincidences. Yet Pynchon's own plots are only a beginning. They have analogues everywhere—in the plots his characters concoct for themselves, in the divergent plots of their co-conspirators and their enemies, and in the crazy quilt of competing designs that emanate from the technologies, organizations, bureaucracies, and governments that surround them. Pynchon's characters frequently become the manipulated objects of their own plots, of the designs they initiate and the roles they choose. But they are the objects of endless machinations long before they begin foolishly to dream of possessing manipulative powers. Even their scramble merely to understand the plots and the tangles that enclose them is finally doomed. They work in the dark, and they work alone. One vestige of a shared community resides in their memory of loss, which is sometimes elegiac, sometimes ironic. Another, more telling vestige—the last, as it were—consists of wariness and suspicion that fade into paranoia as people wait apprehensively to see which encompassing plot will take control of their lives, which encompassing conspiracy will take over their world. Pynchon frequently writes as though he were standing at the end of time, examining and describing, even celebrating, the death not only of freedom but of culture. As much, perhaps, as any artist of his time, he is willing to question everything, including his own need to question everything. Finally, however, language is for him a means of resisting as well as examining and describing the end, and the celebration we sense in his style is not of the end but of our resistance to it.

Further Reading:
Mindful Pleasures: Essays on Thomas Pynchon, ed. G. Levine and D. Leverenz, 1976.
Pynchon: A Collection of Critical Essays, ed. E. Mendelson, 1978.
T. Schaub, *Listening to Pynchon: The Voice of Ambiguity*, 1981.
P. L. Cooper, *Contemporary World*, 1983.

Text:
Kenyon Review, Spring 1960.

Entropy

> *Boris has just given me a summary of his views. He is a weather prophet.*
> *The weather will continue bad, he says. There will be more calamities,*
> *more death, more despair. Not the slightest indication of a change any-*
> *where.* . . . *We must get into step, a lockstep toward the prison of death.*
> *There is no escape. The weather will not change.*
>
> Tropic of Cancer[1]

Downstairs, Meatball Mulligan's lease-breaking party was moving into its 40th hour. On the kitchen floor, amid a litter of empty champagne fifths, were Sandor Rojas and three friends, playing spit in the ocean and staying awake on Heidsieck and benzedrine pills. In the living room Duke, Vincent, Krinkles and Paco sat crouched over a 15-inch speaker which had been bolted into the top of a wastepaper basket, listening to 27 watts' worth of *The Heroes' Gate at Kiev.*[2] They all wore horn rimmed sunglasses and rapt expressions, and smoked funny-looking cigarettes which contained not, as you might expect, tobacco, but an adulterated form of *cannabis sativa.*[3] This group was the Duke di Angelis quartet. They recorded for a local label called Tambú and had to their credit one 10″ LP entitled *Songs of Outer Space.* From time to time one of them would flick the ashes from his cigarette into the speaker cone to watch them dance around. Meatball himself was sleeping over by the window, holding an empty magnum to his chest as if it were a teddy bear. Several government girls, who worked for people like the State Department and NSA,[4] had passed out on couches, chairs and in one case the bathroom sink.

This was in early February of '57 and back then there were a lot of American expatriates around Washington, D.C., who would talk, every time they met you, about how someday they were going to go over to Europe for real but right now it seemed they were working for the government. Everyone saw a fine irony in this. They would stage, for instance, polyglot parties where the newcomer was sort of ignored if he couldn't carry on simultaneous conversations in three or four languages. They would haunt Armenian delicatessens for weeks at a stretch and invite you over for bulghour and lamb in tiny kitchens whose walls were covered with bullfight posters. They would have affairs with sultry girls from Andalucía or the Midi who studied economics at Georgetown. Their Dôme was a collegiate Rathskeller out on Wisconsin Avenue called the Old Heidelberg and they had to settle for cherry blossoms instead of lime trees when spring came, but in its lethargic way their life provided, as they said, kicks.

At the moment, Meatball's party seemed to be gathering its second wind. Outside there was rain. Rain splatted against the tar paper on the roof and was fractured into a fine spray off the noses, eyebrows and lips of wooden gargoyles under the eaves, and ran like drool down the windowpanes. The day before, it had snowed and the

---

[1] Novel by Henry Miller (b. 1891), American writer.
[2] The final section of "Pictures at an Exhibition"; the suite for piano by Modest Mussorgsky (1835–1881), Russian composer, was orchestrated by the French composer Maurice Ravel (1875–1937).
[3] Botanical name of marijuana.
[4] National Security Agency.

day before that there had been winds of gale force and before that the sun had made the city glitter bright as April, though the calendar read early February. It is a curious season in Washington, this false spring. Somewhere in it are Lincoln's Birthday and the Chinese New Year, and a forlornness in the streets because cherry blossoms are weeks away still and, as Sarah Vaughan has put it, spring will be a little late this year. Generally crowds like the one which would gather in the Old Heidelberg on weekday afternoons to drink Würtzburger and to sing Lili Marlene (not to mention The Sweetheart of Sigma Chi) are inevitably and incorrigibly Romantic. And as every good Romantic knows, the soul (*spiritus, ruach, pneuma*)[5] is nothing, substantially, but air; it is only natural that warpings in the atmosphere should be recapitulated in those who breathe it. So that over and above the public components—holidays, tourist attractions—there are private meanderings, linked to the climate as if this spell were a *stretto*[6] passage in the year's fugue: haphazard weather, aimless loves, unpredicted commitments: months one can easily spend *in* fugue, because oddly enough, later on, winds, rains, passions of February and March are never remembered in that city, it is as if they had never been.

The last bass notes of *The Heroes' Gate* boomed up through the floor and woke Callisto from an uneasy sleep. The first thing he became aware of was a small bird he had been holding gently between his hands, against his body. He turned his head sidewise on the pillow to smile down at it, at its blue hunched-down head and sick, lidded eyes, wondering how many more nights he would have to give it warmth before it was well again. He had been holding the bird like that for three days: it was the only way he knew to restore its health. Next to him the girl stirred and whimpered, her arm thrown across her face. Mingled with the sounds of the rain came the first tentative, querulous morning voices of the other birds, hidden in philodendrons and small fan palms: patches of scarlet, yellow and blue laced through this Rousseau-like fantasy, this hothouse jungle it had taken him seven years to weave together. Hermetically sealed, it was a tiny enclave of regularity in the city's chaos, alien to the vagaries of the weather, of national politics, of any civil disorder. Through trial-and-error Callisto had perfected its ecological balance, with the help of the girl its artistic harmony, so that the swayings of its plant life, the stirrings of its birds and human inhabitants were all as integral as the rhythms of a perfectly-executed mobile. He and the girl could no longer, of course, be omitted from that sanctuary; they had become necessary to its unity. What they needed from outside was delivered. They did not go out.

"Is he all right," she whispered. She lay like a tawny question mark facing him, her eyes suddenly huge and dark and blinking slowly. Callisto ran a finger beneath the feathers at the base of the bird's neck; caressed it gently. "He's going to be well, I think. See: he hears his friends beginning to wake up." The girl had heard the rain and the birds even before she was fully awake. Her name was Aubade:[7] she was part French and part Annamese,[8] and she lived on her own curious and lonely planet, where

---

[5] The Latin, Hebrew, and Greek words, respectively, for "soul."

[6] The summing-up in a fugue, in which the subject and its answers overlap in rapid succession. (From the Italian for "close" or "narrow.")

[7] French: "dawn song."

[8] Resident of Annam, a region of Vietnam situated partly in the north, partly in the south.

the clouds and the odor of poincianas, the bitterness of wine and the accidental fingers at the small of her back or feathery against her breasts came to her reduced inevitably to the terms of sound: of music which emerged at intervals from a howling darkness of discordancy. "Aubade," he said, "go see." Obedient, she arose; padded to the window, pulled aside the drapes and after a moment said: "It is 37. Still 37." Callisto frowned. "Since Tuesday, then," he said. "No change." Henry Adams, three generations before his own, had stared aghast at Power; Callisto found himself now in much the same state over Thermodynamics, the inner life of that power, realizing like his predecessor that the Virgin and the dynamo stand as much for love as for power; that the two are indeed identical; and that love therefore not only makes the world go 'round but also makes the boccie ball spin, the nebula precess. It was this latter or sidereal element which disturbed him. The cosmologists had predicted an eventual heat-death for the universe (something like Limbo:[9] form and motion abolished, heat-energy identical at every point in it); the meteorologists, day-to-day, staved it off by contradicting with a reassuring array of varied temperatures.

But for three days now, despite the changeful weather, the mercury had stayed at 37 degrees Fahrenheit. Leery at omens of apocalypse, Callisto shifted beneath the covers. His fingers pressed the bird more firmly, as if needing some pulsing or suffering assurance of an early break in the temperature.

It was that last cymbal crash that did it. Meatball was hurled wincing into consciousness as the synchronized wagging of heads over the wastebasket stopped. The final hiss remained for an instant in the room, then melted into the whisper of rain outside. "Aarrgghh," announced Meatball in the silence, looking at the empty magnum. Krinkles, in slow motion, turned, smiled and held out a cigarette. "Tea time, man," he said. "No, no," said Meatball. "How many times I got to tell you guys. Not at my place. You ought to know, Washington is lousy with Feds." Krinkles looked wistful. "Jeez, Meatball," he said, "you don't want to do nothing no more." "Hair of dog," said Meatball. "Only hope. Any juice left?" He began to crawl toward the kitchen. "No champagne, I don't think," Duke said. "Case of tequila behind the icebox." They put on an Earl Bostic side.[10] Meatball paused at the kitchen door, glowering at Sandor Rojas. "Lemons," he said after some thought. He crawled to the refrigerator and got out three lemons and some cubes, found the tequila and set about restoring order to his nervous system. He drew blood once cutting the lemons and had to use two hands squeezing them and his foot to crack the ice tray but after about ten minutes he found himself, through some miracle, beaming down into a monster tequila sour. "That looks yummy," Sandor Rojas said. "How about you make me one." Meatball blinked at him. *"Kitchi lofass a shegítbe,"*[11] he replied automatically, and wandered away into the bathroom. "I say," he called out a moment later to no one in particular. "I say, there seems to be a girl or something sleeping in the sink." He took her by the shoulders and shook. "Wha," she said. "You don't look too comfortable," Meatball said. "Well," she agreed. She stumbled to the shower, turned on the cold water and sat down crosslegged in the spray. "That's better," she smiled.

[9] In Catholic theology, the border state between heaven and hell. It is reserved for the just who died before the resurrection or for children who die before being baptized—i.e., for those who are neither saved nor damned.

[10] I.e., a record by Earl Bostic, a well-known jazz saxophonist of the 1950s. (The characters are jazz fans, and many famous jazz musicians, like Gerry Mulligan, Chet Baker, John Lewis, and Charlie Mingus, are mentioned later in the story.)

[11] Phonetic Hungarian: equivalent of "Up yours."

"Meatball," Sandor Rojas yelled from the kitchen. "Somebody is trying to come in the window. A burglar, I think. A second-story man." "What are you worrying about," Meatball said. "We're on the third floor." He loped back into the kitchen. A shaggy woebegone figure stood out on the fire escape, raking his fingernails down the windowpane. Meatball opened the window. "Saul," he said.

"Sort of wet out," Saul said. He climbed in, dripping. "You heard, I guess."

"Miriam left you," Meatball said, "or something, is all I heard."

There was a sudden flurry of knocking at the front door. "Do come in," Sandor Rojas called. The door opened and there were three coeds from George Washington, all of whom were majoring in philosophy. They were each holding a gallon of Chianti. Sandor leaped up and dashed into the living room. "We heard there was a party," one blonde said. "Young blood," Sandor shouted. He was an ex-Hungarian freedom fighter who had easily the worst chronic case of what certain critics of the middle class have called Don Giovannism in the District of Columbia. *Purche porti la gonnella, voi sapete quel che fa.*[12] Like Pavlov's dog: a contralto voice or a whiff of Arpege and Sandor would begin to salivate. Meatball regarded the trio blearily as they filed into the kitchen; he shrugged. "Put the wine in the icebox," he said "and good morning."

Aubade's neck made a golden bow as she bent over the sheets of foolscap, scribbling away in the green murk of the room. "As a young man at Princeton," Callisto was dictating, nestling the bird against the gray hairs of his chest, "Callisto had learned a mnemonic device for remembering the Laws of Thermodynamics: you can't win, things are going to get worse before they get better, who says they're going to get better.[13] At the age of 54, confronted with Gibbs' notion of the universe, he suddenly realized that undergraduate cant had been oracle, after all. That spindly maze of equations became, for him, a vision of ultimate, cosmic heat-death. He had known all along, of course, that nothing but a theoretical engine or system ever runs at 100% efficiency; and about the theorem of Clausius, which states that the entropy of an isolated system always continually increases. It was not, however, until Gibbs and Boltzmann brought to this principle the methods of statistical mechanics that the horrible significance of it all dawned on him: only then did he realize that the isolated system—galaxy, engine, human being, culture, whatever—must evolve spontaneously toward the Condition of the More Probable. He was forced, therefore, in the sad dying fall of middle age, to a radical reevaluation of everything he had learned up to then; all the cities and seasons and casual passions of his days had now to be looked at in a new and elusive light. He did not know if he was equal to the task. He was aware of the dangers of the reductive fallacy and, he hoped, strong enough not to drift into the graceful decadence of an enervated fatalism. His had always been a vigorous, Italian sort of pessimism: like Machiavelli, he allowed the forces of *virtú* and *fortuna*[14] to be about 50/50; but the equations now introduced a random factor which pushed the odds to some unutterable and indeterminate ratio which he found himself afraid to calculate." Around him loomed vague hothouse shapes; the pitifully small heart fluttered against his own. Counterpointed against his words the girl heard

[12] Italian: "As long as she wears a skirt, you know what she does" (from the opera *Don Giovanni*).

[13] Roughly speaking, the three laws of thermodynamics state that energy can neither be created nor destroyed, that the entropy (randomness or disorder) of a closed system always increases, and that there is an absolute zero.

[14] Italian: "virtue" and "fortune."

the chatter of birds and fitful car honkings scattered along the wet morning and Earl Bostic's alto rising in occasional wild peaks through the floor. The architectonic purity of her world was constantly threatened by such hints of anarchy: gaps and excrescences and skew lines, and a shifting or tilting of planes to which she had continually to readjust lest the whole structure shiver into a disarray of discrete and meaningless signals. Callisto had described the process once as a kind of "feedback": she crawled into dreams each night with a sense of exhaustion, and a desperate resolve never to relax that vigilance. Even in the brief periods when Callisto made love to her, soaring above the bowing of taut nerves in haphazard double-stops would be the one singing string of her determination.

"Nevertheless," continued Callisto, "he found in entropy or the measure of disorganization for a closed system an adequate metaphor to apply to certain phenomena in his own world. He saw, for example, the younger generation responding to Madison Avenue with the same spleen his own had once reserved for Wall Street: and in American 'consumerism' discovered a similar tendency from the least to the most probable, from differentiation to sameness, from ordered individuality to a kind of chaos. He found himself, in short, restating Gibbs' prediction in social terms, and envisioned a heat-death for his culture in which ideas, like heat-energy, would no longer be transferred, since each point in it would ultimately have the same quantity of energy; and intellectual motion would, accordingly, cease." He glanced up suddenly. "Check it now," he said. Again she rose and peered out at the thermometer. "37," she said. "The rain has stopped." He bent his head quickly and held his lips against a quivering wing. "Then it will change soon," he said, trying to keep his voice firm.

Sitting on the stove Saul was like any big rag doll that a kid has been taking out some incomprehensible rage on. "What happened," Meatball said. "If you feel like talking, I mean."

"Of course I feel like talking," Saul said. "One thing I did, I slugged her."

"Discipline must be maintained."

"Ha, ha. I wish you'd been there. Oh Meatball, it was a lovely fight. She ended up throwing a *Handbook of Chemistry and Physics* at me, only it missed and went through the window, and when the glass broke I reckon something in her broke too. She stormed out of the house crying, out in the rain. No raincoat or anything."

"She'll be back."

"No."

"Well." Soon Meatball said: "It was something earth-shattering, no doubt. Like who is better, Sal Mineo or Ricky Nelson."

"What it was about," Saul said, "was communication theory. Which of course makes it very hilarious."

"I don't know anything about communication theory."

"Neither does my wife. Come right down to it, who does? That's the joke."

When Meatball saw the kind of smile Saul had on his face he said: "Maybe you would like tequila or something."

"No. I mean, I'm sorry. It's a field you can go off the deep end in, is all. You get where you're watching all the time for security cops: behind bushes, around corners. MUFFET is top secret."

"Wha."

"Multi-unit factorial field electronic tabulator."

"You were fighting about that."

"Miriam has been reading science-fiction again. That and *Scientific American*. It seems she is, as we say, bugged at this idea of computers acting like people. I made the mistake of saying you can just as well turn that around, and talk about human behavior like a program fed into an IBM machine."

"Why not," Meatball said.

"Indeed, why not. In fact it is sort of crucial to communication, not to mention information theory. Only when I said that she hit the roof. Up went the balloon. And I can't figure out *why*. If anybody should know why, I should. I refuse to believe the government is wasting taxpayers' money on me, when it has so many bigger and better things to waste it on."

Meatball made a moue. "Maybe she thought you were acting like a cold, dehumanized amoral scientist type."

"My god," Saul flung up an arm. "Dehumanized. How much more human can I get? I worry, Meatball, I do. There are Europeans wandering around North Africa these days with their tongues torn out of their heads because those tongues have spoken the wrong words. Only the Europeans thought they were the right words."

"Language barrier," Meatball suggested.

Saul jumped down off the stove. "That," he said, angry, "is a good candidate for sick joke of the year. No, ace, it is *not* a barrier. If it is anything it's a kind of leakage. Tell a girl: 'I love you.' No trouble with two-thirds of that, it's a closed circuit. Just you and she. But that nasty four-letter word in the middle, *that's* the one you have to look out for. Ambiguity. Redundance. Irrelevance, even. Leakage. All this is noise. Noise screws up your signal, makes for disorganization in the circuit."

Meatball shuffled around. "Well, now, Saul," he muttered, "you're sort of, I don't know, expecting a lot from people. I mean, you know. What it is is, most of the things we say, I guess, are mostly noise."

"Ha! Half of what you just said, for example."

"Well, you do it too."

"I know." Saul smiled grimly. "It's a bitch, ain't it."

"I bet that's what keeps divorce lawyers in business. Whoops."

"Oh I'm not sensitive. Besides," frowning, "you're right. You find I think that most 'successful' marriages—Miriam and me, up to last night—are sort of founded on compromises. You never run at top efficiency, usually all you have is a minimum basis for a workable thing. I believe the phrase is Togetherness."

"Aarrgghh."

"Exactly. You find that one a bit noisy, don't you. But the noise content is different for each of us because you're a bachelor and I'm not. Or wasn't. The hell with it."

"Well sure," Meatball said, trying to be helpful, "you were using different words. By 'human being' you meant something that you can look at like it was a computer. It helps you think better on the job or something. But Miriam meant something entirely—"

"The hell with it."

Meatball fell silent. "I'll take that drink," Saul said after a while.

The card game had been abandoned and Sandor's friends were slowly getting wasted on tequila. On the living room couch, one of the coeds and Krinkles were engaged in amorous conversation. "No," Krinkles was saying, "no, I can't put Dave *down*. In fact I give Dave a lot of credit, man. Especially considering his accident and all." The girl's smile faded. "How terrible," she said. "What accident?" "Hadn't you heard?" Krinkles said. "When Dave was in the army, just a private E-2, they sent him down to Oak Ridge[15] on special duty. Something to do with the Manhattan Project.[16] He was handling hot stuff one day and got an overdose of radiation. So now he's got to wear lead gloves all the time." She shook her head sympathetically. "What an awful break for a piano-player."

Meatball had abandoned Saul to a bottle of tequila and was about to go to sleep in a closet when the front door flew open and the place was invaded by five enlisted personnel of the U.S. Navy, all in varying stages of abomination. "This is the place," shouted a fat, pimply seaman apprentice who had lost his white hat. "This here is the hoorhouse that chief was telling us about." A stringy-looking 3rd class boatswain's mate pushed him aside and cased the living room. "You're right, Slab," he said. "But it don't look like much, even for Stateside. I seen better tail in Naples, Italy." "How much, hey," boomed a large seaman with adenoids, who was holding a Mason jar full of white lightning. "Oh, my god," said Meatball.

Outside the temperature remained constant at 37 degrees Fahrenheit. In the hot-house Aubade stood absently caressing the branches of a young mimosa, hearing a motif of sap-rising, the rough and unresolved anticipatory theme of those fragile pink blossoms which, it is said, insure fertility. That music rose in a tangled tracery: arabesques of order competing fugally with the improvised discords of the party downstairs, which peaked sometimes in cusps and ogees of noise. That precious signal-to-noise ratio, whose delicate balance required every calorie of her strength, seesawed inside the small tenuous skull as she watched Callisto, sheltering the bird. Callisto was trying to confront any idea of the heat-death now, as he nuzzled the feathery lump in his hands. He sought correspondences. Sade, of course. And Temple Drake, gaunt and hopeless in her little park in Paris, at the end of *Sanctuary*. Final equilibrium. *Nightwood*.[17] And the tango. Any tango, but more than any perhaps the sad sick dance in Stravinsky's *L'Histoire du Soldat*.[18] He thought back: what had tango music been for them after the war, what meanings had he missed in all the stately coupled automatons in the *cafés-dansants*,[19] or in the metronomes which had ticked behind the eyes of his own partners? Not even the clean constant winds of Switzerland could cure the *grippe espagnole*:[20] Stravinsky had had it, they all had had it. And now many musicians were left after Passchendaele, after the Marne?[21] It came down in this case to seven: violin, double-bass. Clarinet, bassoon. Cornet, trombone. Tympani. Almost as if any tiny troupe of saltimbanques had set about conveying the same information as a full pit-orchestra. There was hardly a full complement left in Europe. Yet with violin and tympani Stravinsky had managed to communicate in that tango

---

[15] City in Tennessee, site of production of uranium for the atomic bomb.

[16] Research project sponsored by the U.S. government that produced the first atomic bomb in 1945.

[17] *Sanctuary* (1931) by William Faulkner and *Nightwood* (1936) by Djuna Barnes are novels that deal explicitly with sexuality.

[18] French: "The Story of the Soldier," spoken text with music by the Russian-born composer Igor Stravinsky (1882–1971).

[19] French: "dance halls."

[20] French: "Spanish flu."

[21] Passchendaele, Flanders, a province of Belgium, and the Marne, a river in France, were both scenes of heavy fighting in World War I.

the same exhaustion, the same airlessness one saw in the slicked-down youths who were trying to imitate Vernon Castle, and in their mistresses, who simply did not care. *Ma maitresse.*[22] Celeste. Returning to Nice after the second war he had found that cafe replaced by a perfume shop which catered to American tourists. And no secret vestige of her in the cobblestones or in the old pension next door; no perfume to match her breath heavy with the sweet Spanish wine she always drank. And so instead he had purchased a Henry Miller novel and left for Paris, and read the book on the train so that when he arrived he had been given at least a little forewarning. And saw that Celeste and the others and even Temple Drake were not all that had changed. "Aubade," he said, "my head aches." The sound of his voice generated in the girl an answering scrap of melody. Her movement toward the kitchen, the towel, the cold water, and his eyes following her formed a weird and intricate canon; as she placed the compress on his forehead his sigh of gratitude seemed to signal a new subject, another series of modulations.

"No," Meatball was still saying, "no, I'm afraid not. This is not a house of ill repute. I'm sorry, really I am." Slab was adamant. "But the chief said," he kept repeating. The seaman offered to swap the moonshine for a good piece. Meatball looked around frantically, as if seeking assistance. In the middle of the room, the Duke di Angelis quartet were engaged in a historic moment. Vincent was seated and the others standing: they were going through the motions of a group having a session, only without instruments. "I say," Meatball said. Duke moved his head a few times, smiled faintly, lit a cigarette, and eventually caught sight of Meatball. "Quiet, man," he whispered. Vincent began to fling his arms around, his fists clenched; then, abruptly, was still, then repeated the performance. This went on for a few minutes while Meatball sipped his drink moodily. The navy had withdrawn to the kitchen. Finally at some invisible signal the group stopped tapping their feet and Duke grinned and said, "At least we ended together."

Meatball glared at him. "I say," he said. "I have this new conception, man," Duke said. "You remember your namesake. You remember Gerry."

"No," said Meatball. "I'll Remember April,[23] if that's any help."

"As a matter of fact," Duke said, "it was Love for Sale. Which shows how much you know. The point is, it was Mulligan, Chet Baker and that crew, way back then, out yonder. You dig?"

"Baritone sax," Meatball said. "Something about a baritone sax."

"But no piano, man. No guitar. Or accordion. You know what that means."

"Not exactly," Meatball said.

"Well first let me just say, that I am no Mingus, no John Lewis. Theory was never my strong point. I mean things like reading were always difficult for me and all—"

"I know," Meatball said drily. "You got your card taken away because you changed key on Happy Birthday at a Kiwanis Club picnic."

"Rotarian. But it occurred to me, in one of these flashes of insight, that if that first quartet of Mulligan's had no piano, it could only mean one thing."

[22] French: "My mistress."
[23] A popular tune that was adapted for jazz. The characters play a verbal game in which they try to incorporate titles and lyrics of jazz and popular song into their conversations. (These are generally recognizable by the capitalization, as here.)

"No chords," said Paco, the baby-faced bass.

"What is he trying to say," Duke said, "is no root chords. Nothing to listen to while you blow a horizontal line. What one does in such a case is, one *thinks* the roots."

A horrified awareness was dawning on Meatball. "And the next logical extension," he said.

"Is to think everything," Duke announced with simple dignity. "Roots, line, everything."

Meatball looked at Duke, awed. "But," he said.

"Well," Duke said modestly, "there are a few bugs to work out."

"But," Meatball said.

"Just listen," Duke said. "You'll catch on." And off they went again into orbit, presumably somewhere around the asteroid belt. After a while Krinkles made an embouchure and started moving his fingers[24] and Duke clapped his hand to his forehead. "Oaf!" he roared. "The new head[25] we're using, you remember, I wrote last night?" "Sure," Krinkles said, "the new head. I come in on the bridge. All your heads I come in then." "Right," Duke said. "So why—" "Wha," said Krinkles, "16 bars, I wait, I come in—" "16?" Duke said. "No. No, Krinkles. Eight you waited. You want me to sing it? A cigarette that bears a lipstick's traces, an airline ticket to romantic places." Krinkles scratched his head. "These Foolish Things, you mean." "Yes," Duke said, "yes, Krinkles. Bravo." "Not I'll Remember April," Krinkles said. "*Minghe morte,*"[26] said Duke. "I *figured* we were playing it a little slow," Krinkles said. Meatball chuckled. "Back to the old drawing board," he said. "No, man," Duke said, "back to the airless void." And they took off again, only it seemed Paco was playing in G sharp while the rest were in E flat, so they had to start all over.

In the kitchen two of the girls from George Washington and the sailors were singing Let's All Go Down and Piss on the Forrestal. There was a two-handed, bilingual *mura*[27] game on over by the icebox. Saul had filled several paper bags with water and was sitting on the fire escape, dropping them on passersby in the street. A fat government girl in a Bennington sweatshirt, recently engaged to an ensign attached to the Forrestal, came charging into the kitchen, head lowered, and butted Slab in the stomach. Figuring this was as good an excuse for a fight as any, Slab's buddies piled in. The *mura* players were nose-to-nose, screaming *trois, sette*[28] at the tops of their lungs. From the shower the girl Meatball had taken out of the sink announced that she was drowning. She had apparently sat on the drain and the water was now up to her neck. The noise in Meatball's apartment had reached a sustained, ungodly crescendo.

Meatball stood and watched, scratching his stomach lazily. The way he figured, there were only about two ways he could cope: (a) lock himself in the closet and maybe eventually they would all go away, or (b) try to calm everybody down, one by one. (a) was certainly the more attractive alternative. But then he started thinking about that closet. It was dark and stuffy and he would be alone. He did not feature

---

[24] I.e., began to play. (An embouchure is the position of the lips against a horn.)

[25] Lead-in to a part or song.

[26] Probably, corruption of *Minchia morte,* vulgar Italian exclamation.

[27] Probably, corruption of *morra,* Italian game; a player guesses the number of fingers held up by another player.

[28] French: "three"; and Italian: "seven."

being alone. And then this crew off the good ship Lollipop or whatever it was might take it upon themselves to kick down the closet door, for a lark. And if that happened he would be, at the very least, embarrassed. The other way was more a pain in the neck, but probably better in the long run.

So he decided to try and keep his lease-breaking party from deteriorating into total chaos: he gave wine to the sailors and separated the *mura* players; he introduced the fat government girl to Sandor Rojas, who would keep her out of trouble; he helped the girl in the shower to dry off and get into bed; he had another talk with Saul; he called a repairman for the refrigerator, which someone had discovered was on the blink. This is what he did until nightfall, when most of the revellers had passed out and the party trembled on the threshold of its third day.

Upstairs Callisto, helpless in the past, did not feel the faint rhythm inside the bird begin to slacken and fail. Aubade was by the window, wandering the ashes of her own lovely world; the temperature held steady, the sky had become a uniform darkening gray. Then something from downstairs—a girl's scream, an overturned chair, a glass dropped on the floor, he would never know what exactly—pierced that private time-warp and he became aware of the faltering, the constriction of muscles, the tiny tossings of the bird's head; and his own pulse began to pound more fiercely, as if trying to compensate. "Aubade," he called weakly, "he's dying." The girl, flowing and rapt, crossed the hothouse to gaze down at Callisto's hands. The two remained like that, poised, for one minute, and two, while the heartbeat ticked a graceful diminuendo down at last into stillness. Callisto raised his head slowly. "I held him," he protested, impotent with the wonder of it, "to give him the warmth of my body. Almost as if I were communicating life to him, or a sense of life. What has happened? Has the transfer of heat ceased to work? Is there no more . . ." He did not finish.

"I was just at the window," she said. He sank back, terrified. She stood a moment more, irresolute; she had sensed his obsession long ago, realized somehow that that constant 37 was now decisive. Suddenly then, as if seeing the single and unavoidable conclusion to all this she moved swiftly to the window before Callisto could speak; tore away the drapes and smashed out the glass with two exquisite hands which came away bleeding and glistening with splinters; and turned to face the man on the bed and wait with him until the moment of equilibrium was reached, when 37 degrees Fahrenheit should prevail both outside and inside, and forever, and the hovering, curious dominant of their separate lives should resolve into a tonic[29] of darkness and the final absence of all motion.

1960

---

[29] Typically, songs conclude by returning ("resolving") to the tonic, or principal chord.

Joyce Carol Oates
b. 1938

One of the most prolific and popular of recent American writers, Joyce Carol Oates is perhaps best known for the extremities of violence in her fiction. One critic, Marvin Mudrick, has said that "typical activities in Oates's novels are arson, rape, riot, mental breakdown, murder (plain and fancy, with excursions into patricide, matricide, uxoricide, mass filicide), and suicide." For Oates, violence is inseparable from the psychic dislocation she sees as endemic to contemporary society. Like Joan Didion, she professes a strong commitment to family and tradition as defining forces for the individual, and like Didion, she sees modern culture as hostile to the individual. Specific acts of violence thus reflect culture's basic disposition, just as physical danger reflects the psychic risks inherent in our acceptance of modern values. Asked about the preponderance of violence in her fiction, Oates said, "These things do not have to be contrived. This is America."

Joyce Carol Oates was born on June 16, 1938, in Millerport, New York, to working-class, devoutly Catholic parents. A talented student, she won a scholarship to Syracuse University in 1956, and in 1960 she received a B.A. in English, graduating Phi Beta Kappa and valedictorian of her class. The next year she married Raymond Smith, received an M.A. in English literature from the University of Wisconsin, and enrolled in the doctoral program in English at Rice University, only to withdraw soon after one of her stories was listed on the Honor Roll in *Best American Short Stories.* Since publication of her first collection of stories, *By the North Gate,* in 1963, Oates has continued to write, as she puts it, in flurries. Besides numerous collections of short stories, poetry, and critical essays, she has written sixteen novels over the past twenty years—an output that surely places her among the most productive serious writers in the history of American literature.

Her first novel, *With Shuddering Fall* (1964), the story of an intense and violent love affair between an impressionable seventeen-year-old girl and a thirty-year-old stock-car racer, introduced the themes of emotional derangement, tragic love, and compulsive behavior that have characterized much of her fiction. With her second novel, *A Garden of Earthly Delights* (1967), she began an American trilogy that took her from the Arkansas migrant camps of the 1920s to the suburbs of the 1960s and, with *Expensive People* (1968), to the story of a child murderer. The third novel in the trilogy, *Them* (1969), which won the National Book Award, moves from Depression-era Detroit to the shattering violence of the 1967 riots. In *Wonderland* (1971), Oates turned to the region of her childhood with a grisly, obsessive story about a boy who alone survives his insane father's massacre of an entire family. She turned again to childhood trauma in *Do with Me What You Will* (1973), the tale of a woman who as a child had been abducted by her father. In her next two novels, *The Assassins* (1975) and *Childwold* (1976), Oates experimented with intricate narrative techniques to portray the dissolving boundaries of dream and reality, the self and others. In

1978 she published a novel about intense religious experience, *Son of the Morning,* and in the following year turned to a university setting with *Unholy Lives.* In 1980 Oates broke new ground with *Bellefleur,* a novel that combines surrealist elements with a Gothic atmosphere as it traces the story of six generations of an American family in the Adirondack Valley. A year later she published *Angel of Light* (1981), a story of violence and political power whose title comes from Thoreau's description of John Brown. In these and in her latest novels, *A Bloodsmoor Romance* (1982), *Mysteries of Winterthurn* (1984), *Solstice* (1985), and *Marya: A Life* (1986), she seems to be simultaneously using and commenting on popular forms of American fiction.

As an artist, Oates allies herself more with D. H. Lawrence than with such experimentalists as James Joyce and Virginia Woolf, though she also insists that she is a committed Anti-Romantic. The individual's desire for autonomy is the primary source of the human moral failure that manifests itself in—and is punished by—the acts of violence that pervade her fiction. One of her recurring themes has to do with "recognizing limits" that are implicit in the conjunction that an individual's history makes with the contours of culture. When her characters attempt to ignore or deny these limits, the givens of their lives, as does the narrator of "How I Contemplated the World," violence and meaninglessness threaten both them and the people around them.

Despite her rejection of Romanticism, Oates mixes realistic settings and characters with surreal and even supernatural experiences, often to disclose some hidden tie between the authors and the victims of violence. Such unexpected connections are important to her for many reasons, the chief one being their potential as a basis for community. In one way or another, her stories center on the importance of establishing a sense of community that is grounded biologically as well as socially, morally, and culturally. To her mind, the great failing of modern literature is its "solipsistic" tendency, its self-indulgent creation of "art forms in which language is arranged and rearranged in such a manner as to give pleasure to the artist and his readers, excluding any referent to an available exterior world." By contrast, her own effort, the only one she finally deems worthy, "is to do no less than attempt the sanctification of the world!"

Further Reading:
M. K. Grant, *The Tragic Vision of Joyce Carol Oates,* 1978.
R. Phillips, "Joyce Carol Oates: The Art of Fiction," *Paris Review,* Fall–Winter 1978.
J. V. Creighton, *Joyce Carol Oates,* 1979.
E. G. Friedman, *Joyce Carol Oates,* 1980.

Text:
The Wheel of Love and Other Stories, 1970.

from How I Contemplated the World
from the Detroit House of
Correction and Began My Life
Over Again

Notes for an Essay for an English Class at Baldwin
Country Day School; Poking Around in Debris;
Disgust and Curiosity; a Revelation of the Meaning
of Life; a Happy Ending . . .

I: Events

1. The girl (myself) is walking through Branden's, that excellent store. Suburb of a large famous city that is a symbol for large famous American cities. The event sneaks up on the girl, who believes she is herding it along with a small fixed smile, a girl of fifteen, innocently experienced. She dawdles in a certain style by a counter of costume jewelry. Rings, earrings, necklaces. Prices from $5 to $50, all within reach. All ugly. She eases over to the glove counter, where everything is ugly too. In her close-fitted coat with its black fur collar she contemplates the luxury of Branden's, which she has known for many years: its many mild pale lights, easy on the eye and the soul, its elaborate tinkly decorations, its women shoppers with their excellent shoes and coats and hairdos, all dawdling gracefully, in no hurry.

Who was ever in a hurry here?

2. The girl seated at home. A small library, paneled walls of oak. Someone is talking to me. An earnest, husky, female voice drives itself against my ears, nervous, frightened, groping around my heart, saying, "If you wanted gloves, why didn't you say so? Why didn't you ask for them?" That store, Branden's is owned by Raymond Forrest who lives on Du Maurier Drive. We live on Sioux Drive. Raymond Forrest. A handsome man? An ugly man? A man of fifty or sixty, with gray hair, or a man of forty with earnest, courteous eyes, a good golf game; who is Raymond Forrest, this man who is my salvation? Father has been talking to him. Father is not his physician; Dr. Berg, is his physician. Father and Dr. Berg refer patients to each other. There is a connection. Mother plays bridge with . . . On Mondays and Wednesdays our maid Billie works at . . . The strings draw together in a cat's cradle, making a net to save you when you fall. . . .

3. *Harriet Arnold's.* A small shop, better than Branden's. Mother in her black coat, I in my close-fitted blue coat. Shopping. Now look at this, isn't this cute, do you want this, why don't you want this, try this on, take this with you to the fitting room, take this also, what's wrong with you, what can I do for you, why are you so strange . . . ? "I wanted to steal but not to buy," I don't tell her. The girl droops

along in her coat and gloves and leather boots, her eyes scan the horizon, which is pastel pink and decorated like Branden's, tasteful walls and modern ceilings with graceful glimmering lights.

4. Weeks later, the girl at a bus stop. Two o'clock in the afternoon, a Tuesday; obviously she has walked out of school.

5. The girl stepping down from a bus. Afternoon, weather changing to colder. Detroit. Pavement and closed-up stores; grill-work over the windows of a pawnshop. What is a pawnshop, exactly?

II: Characters

1. The girl stands five feet five inches tall. An ordinary height. Baldwin Country Day School draws them up to that height. She dreams along the corridors and presses her face against the Thermoplex glass. No frost or steam can ever form on that glass. A smudge of grease from her forehead . . . could she be boiled down to grease? She wears her hair loose and long and straight in suburban teen-age style, 1968. Eyes smudged with pencil, dark brown. Brown hair. Vague green eyes. A pretty girl? An ugly girl? She sings to herself under her breath, idling in the corridor, thinking of her many secrets (the thirty dollars she once took from the purse of a friend's mother, just for fun, the basement window she smashed in her own house just for fun) and thinking of her brother who is at Susquehanna Boys' Academy, an excellent preparatory school in Maine, remembering him unclearly . . . he has long manic hair and a squeaking voice and he looks like one of the popular teen-age singers of 1968, one of those in a group. *The Certain Forces, The Way Out, The Maniacs Responsible.* The girl in her turn looks like one of those fieldsful of girls who listen to the boys' singing, dreaming and mooning restlessly, breaking into high sullen laughter, innocently experienced.

2. The mother. A Midwestern woman of Detroit and suburbs. Belongs to the Detroit Athletic Club. Also the Detroit Golf Club. Also the Bloomfield Hills Country Club. The Village Women's Club at which lectures are given each winter on Genet and Sartre and James Baldwin, by the Director of the Adult Education Program at Wayne State University. . . . The Bloomfield Art Association. Also the Founders Society of the Detroit Institute of Arts. Also . . . Oh, she is in perpetual motion, this lady, hair like blown-up gold and finer than gold, hair and fingers and body of inestimable grace. Heavy weighs the gold on the back of her hairbrush and hand mirror. Heavy heavy the candlesticks in the dining room. Very heavy is the big car, a Lincoln, long and black, that on one cool autumn day split a squirrel's body in two unequal parts.

3. The father. Dr.   . He belongs to the same clubs as #2. A player of squash and golf; he has a golfer's umbrella of stripes. Candy stripes. In his mouth nothing turns

to sugar, however; saliva works no miracles here. His doctoring is of the slightly sick. The sick are sent elsewhere (to Dr. Berg?), the deathly sick are sent back for more tests and their bills are sent to their homes, the unsick are sent to Dr. Coronet (Isabel, a lady), an excellent psychiatrist for unsick people who angrily believe they are sick and want to do something about it. If they demand a male psychiatrist, the unsick are sent by Dr.   (my father) to Dr. Lowenstein, a male psychiatrist, excellent and expensive, with a limited practice.

4. Clarita. She is twenty, twenty-five, she is thirty or more? Pretty, ugly, what? She is a woman lounging by the side of a road, in jeans and a sweater, hitchhiking, or she is slouched on a stool at a counter in some roadside diner. A hard line of jaw. Curious eyes. Amused eyes. Behind her eyes processions move, funeral pageants, cartoons. She says, "I never can figure out why girls like you bum around down here. What are you looking for anyway?" An odor of tobacco about her. Unwashed underclothes, or no underclothes, unwashed skin, gritty toes, hair long and falling into strands, not recently washed.

5. Simon. In this city the weather changes abruptly, so Simon's weather changes abruptly. He sleeps through the afternoon. He sleeps through the morning. Rising, he gropes around for something to get him going, for a cigarette or a pill to drive him out to the street, where the temperature is hovering around 35°. Why doesn't it drop? Why, why doesn't the cold clean air come down from Canada; will he have to go up into Canada to get it? will he have to leave the Country of his Birth and sink into Canada's frosty fields . . . ? Will the F.B.I. (which he dreams about constantly) chase him over the Canadian border on foot, hounded out in a blizzard of broken glass and horns . . . ?

"Once I was Huckleberry Finn," Simon says, "but now I am Roderick Usher." Beset by frenzies and fears, this man who makes my spine go cold, he takes green pills, yellow pills, pills of white and capsules of dark blue and green . . . he takes other things I may not mention, for what if Simon seeks me out and climbs into my girl's bedroom here in Bloomfield Hills and strangles me, what then . . . ? (As I write this I begin to shiver. Why do I shiver? I am now sixteen and sixteen is not an age for shivering.) It comes from Simon, who is always cold.

III: World Events

Nothing.

IV: People & Circumstances Contributing to This Delinquency

Nothing.

V: Sioux Drive

George, Clyde G. 240 Sioux. A manufacturer's representative; children, a dog, a wife. Georgian with the usual columns. You think of the White House, then of Thomas Jefferson, then your mind goes blank on the white pillars and you think of nothing. Norris, Ralph W. 246 Sioux. Public relations. Colonial. Bay window, brick, stone, concrete, wood, green shutters, sidewalk, lantern, grass, trees, blacktop drive, two children, one of them my classmate Esther (Esther Norris) at Baldwin. Wife, cars. Ramsey, Michael D. 250 Sioux. Colonial. Big living room, thirty by twenty-five, fireplaces in living room, library, recreation room, paneled walls wet bar five bathrooms five bedrooms two lavatories central air conditioning automatic sprinkler automatic garage door three children one wife two cars a breakfast room a patio a large fenced lot fourteen trees a front door with a brass knocker never knocked. Next is our house. Classic contemporary. Traditional modern. Attached garage, attached Florida room, attached patio, attached pool and cabana, attached roof. A front door mail slot through which pour *Time Magazine, Fortune, Life, Business Week,* the *Wall Street Journal,* the *New York Times,* the *New Yorker,* the *Saturday Review, M.D., Modern Medicine, Disease of the Month* . . . and also. . . . And in addition to all this, a quiet sealed letter from Baldwin saying: *Your daughter is not doing work compatible with her performance on the Stanford-Binet.* . . . And your son is not doing well, not well at all, very sad. Where is your son anyway? Once he stole trick-and-treat candy from some six-year-old kids, he himself being a robust ten. The beginning. Now your daughter steals. In the Village Pharmacy she made off with, yes she did, don't deny it, she made off with a copy of *Pageant Magazine* for no reason, she swiped a roll of Life Savers in a green wrapper and was in no need of saving her life or even in need of sucking candy; when she was no more than eight years old she stole, don't blush, she stole a package of Tums only because it was out on the counter and available, and the nice lady behind the counter (now dead) said nothing. . . . Sioux Drive. Maples, oaks, elms. Diseased elms cut down. Sioux Drive runs into Roosevelt Drive. Slow, turning lanes, not streets, all drives and lanes and ways and passes. A private police force. Quiet private police, in unmarked cars. Cruising on Saturday evenings with paternal smiles for the residents who are streaming in and out of houses, going to and from parties, a thousand parties, slightly staggering, the women in their furs alighting from automobiles bought of Ford and General Motors and Chrysler, very heavy automobiles. No foreign cars. Detroit. In 275 Sioux, down the block in that magnificent French-Normandy mansion, lives   himself, who has the C   account itself, imagine that! Look at where he lives and look at the enormous trees and chimneys, imagine his many fireplaces, imagine his wife and children, imagine his wife's hair, imagine her fingernails, imagine her bathtub of smooth clean glowing pink, imagine their embraces, his trouser pockets filled with odd coins and keys and dust and peanuts, imagine their ecstasy on Sioux Drive, imagine their income tax returns, imagine their little boy's pride in his experimental car, a scaled-down C   , as he roars around the neighborhood on the sidewalks frightening dogs and Negro maids, oh imagine all these things, imagine everything, let your mind roar out all over Sioux

Drive and Du Maurier Drive and Roosevelt Drive and Ticonderoga Pass and Burning Bush Way and Lincolnshire Pass and Lois Lane.

When spring comes, its winds blow nothing to Sioux Drive, no odors of hollyhocks or forsythia, nothing Sioux Drive doesn't already possess, everything is planted and performing. The weather vanes, had they weather vanes, don't have to turn with the wind, don't have to contend with the weather. There is no weather.

VI: Detroit

There is always weather in Detroit. Detroit's temperature is always 32°. Fast-falling temperatures. Slow-rising temperatures. Wind from the north-northeast four to forty miles an hour, small craft warnings, partly cloudy today and Wednesday changing to partly sunny through Thursday . . . small warnings of frost, soot warnings, traffic warnings, hazardous lake conditions small craft and swimmers, restless Negro gangs, restless cloud formations, restless temperatures aching to fall out the very bottom of the thermometer or shoot up over the top and boil everything over in red mercury.

Detroit's temperature is 32°. Fast-falling temperatures. Slow-rising temperatures. Wind from the north-northeast four to forty miles an hour. . . .

VII: Events

1. The girl's heart is pounding. In her pocket is a pair of gloves! In a plastic bag! Airproof breathproof plastic bag, gloves selling for twenty-five dollars on Branden's counter! In her pocket! Shoplifted! . . . In her purse is a blue comb, not very clean. In her purse is a leather billfold (a birthday present from her grandmother in Philadelphia) with snapshots of the family in clean plastic windows, in the billfold are bills, she doesn't know how many bills. . . . In her purse is an ominous note from her friend Tykie *What's this about Joe H. and the kids hanging around at Louise's Sat. night? You heard anything? . . .* passed in French class. In her purse is a lot of dirty yellow Kleenex, her mother's heart would break to see such very dirty Kleenex, and at the bottom of her purse are brown hairpins and safety pins and a broken pencil and a ballpoint pen (blue) stolen from somewhere forgotten and a purse-size compact of Cover Girl Make-Up, Ivory Rose. . . . Her lipstick is Broken Heart, a corrupt pink; her fingers are trembling like crazy; her teeth are beginning to chatter; her insides are alive; her eyes glow in her head; she is saying to her mother's astonished face *I want to steal but not to buy.*

2. At Clarita's. Day or night? What room is this? A bed, a regular bed, and a mattress on the floor nearby. Wallpaper hanging in strips. Clarita says she tore it like that with her teeth. She was fighting a barbaric tribe that night, high from some pills; she was battling for her life with men wearing helmets of heavy iron and their faces no more than Christian crosses to breathe through, every one of

those bastards looking like her lover Simon, who seems to breathe with great difficulty through the slits of mouth and nostrils in his face. Clarita has never heard of Sioux Drive. Raymond Forrest cuts no ice with her, nor does the C account and its millions; Harvard Business School could be at the corner of Vernor and 12th Street for all she cares, and Vietnam might have sunk by now into the Dead Sea under its tons of debris, for all the amazement she could show . . . her face is overworked, overwrought, at the age of twenty (thirty?) it is already exhausted but fanciful and ready for a laugh. Clarita says mournfully to me *Honey somebody is going to turn you out let me give you warning.* In a movie shown on late television Clarita is not a mess like this but a nurse, with short neat hair and a dedicated look, in love with her doctor and her doctor's patients and their diseases, enamored of needles and sponges and rubbing alcohol. . . . Or no: she is a private secretary. Robert Cummings is her boss. She helps him with fantastic plots, the canned audience laughs, no, the audience doesn't laugh because nothing is funny, instead her boss is Robert Taylor and they are not boss and secretary but husband and wife, she is threatened by a young starlet, she is grim, handsome, wifely, a good companion for a good man. . . . She is Claudette Colbert. Her sister too is Claudette Colbert. They are twins, identical. Her husband Charles Boyer is a very rich handsome man and her sister, Claudette Colbert, is plotting her death in order to take her place as the rich man's wife, no one will know because they are *twins.* . . . All these marvelous lives Clarita might have lived, but she fell out the bottom at the age of thirteen. At the age when I was packing my overnight case for a slumber party at Toni Deshield's she was tearing filthy sheets off a bed and scratching up a rash on her arms. . . . Thirteen is uncommonly young for a white girl in Detroit, Miss Brock of the Detroit House of Correction said in a sad newspaper interview for the *Detroit News;* fifteen and sixteen are more likely. Eleven, twelve, thirteen are not surprising in colored . . . they are more precocious. What can we do? Taxes are rising and the tax base is falling. The temperature rises slowly but falls rapidly. Everything is falling out the bottom, Woodward Avenue is filthy, Livernois Avenue is filthy! Scraps of paper flutter in the air like pigeons, dirt flies up and hits you right in the eye, oh Detroit is breaking up into dangerous bits of newspaper and dirt, watch out. . . .

Clarita's apartment is over a restaurant. Simon her lover emerges from the cracks at dark. Mrs. Olesko, a neighbor of Clarita's, an aged white wisp of a woman, doesn't complain but sniffs with contentment at Clarita's noisy life and doesn't tell the cops, hating cops, when the cops arrive. I should give more fake names, more blanks, instead of telling all these secrets. I myself am a secret; I am a minor.

3. My father reads a paper at a medical convention in Los Angeles. There he is, on the edge of the North American continent, when the unmarked detective put his hand so gently on my arm in the aisle of Branden's and said, "Miss, would you like to step over here for a minute?"

And where was he when Clarita put her hand on my arm, that wintry dark sulphurous aching day in Detroit, in the company of closed-down barber shops, closed-down diners, closed-down movie houses, homes, windows, basements, faces . . . she put her hand on my arm and said, "Honey, are you looking for somebody down here?"

And was he home worrying about me, gone for two weeks solid, when they carried me off . . . ? It took three of them to get me in the police cruiser, so they said, and they put more than their hands on my arm.

4. I work on this lesson. My English teacher is Mr. Forest, who is from Michigan State. Not handsome, Mr. Forest, and his name is plain, unlike Raymond Forrest's, but he is sweet and rodentlike, he has conferred with the principal and my parents, and everything is fixed . . . treat her as if nothing has happened, a new start, begin again, only sixteen years old, what a shame, how did it happen?—nothing happened, nothing could have happened, a slight physiological modification known only to a gynecologist or to Dr. Coronet. I work on my lesson. I sit in my pink room. I look around the room with my sad pink eyes. I sigh, I dawdle, I pause, I eat up time, I am limp and happy to be home, I am sixteen years old suddenly, my head hangs heavy as a pumpkin on my shoulders, and my hair has just been cut by Mr. Faye at the Crystal Salon and is said to be very becoming.

(Simon too put his hand on my arm and said, "Honey, you have got to come with me," and in his six-by-six room we got to know each other. Would I go back to Simon again? Would I lie down with him in all that filth and craziness? Over and over again.

a Clarita is being betrayed as in front of a Cunningham Drug Store she is nervously eyeing a colored man who may or may not have money, or a nervous white boy of twenty with sideburns and an Appalachian look, who may or may not have a knife hidden in his jacket pocket, or a husky red-faced man of friendly countenance who may or may not be a member of the Vice Squad out for an early twilight walk.)

I work on my lesson for Mr. Forest. I have filled up eleven pages. Words pour out of me and won't stop. I want to tell everything . . . what was the song Simon was always humming, and who was Simon's friend in a very new trench coat with an old high school graduation ring on his finger . . . ? Simon's bearded friend? When I was down too low for him, Simon kicked me out and gave me to him for three days, I think, on Fourteenth Street in Detroit, an airy room of cold cruel drafts with newspapers on the floor. . . . Do I really remember that or am I piecing it together from what they told me? Did they tell the truth? Did they know much of the truth?

VIII: Characters

1. Wednesdays after school, at four; Saturday mornings at ten. Mother drives me to Dr. Coronet. Ferns in the office, plastic or real, they look the same. Dr. Coronet is queenly, an elegant nicotine-stained lady who would have studied with Freud had circumstances not prevented it, a bit of a Catholic, ready to offer you some mystery if your teeth will ache too much without it. Highly recommended by Father! Forty dollars an hour, Father's forty dollars! Progress! Looking up! Looking better! That

new haircut is so becoming, says Dr. Coronet herself, showing how normal she is for a woman with an I.Q. of 180 and many advanced degrees.

2. Mother. A lady in a brown suede coat. Boots of shiny black material, black gloves, a black fur hat. She would be humiliated could she know that of all the people in the world it is my ex-lover Simon who walks most like her . . . self-conscious and unreal, listening to distant music, a little bowlegged with craftiness. . . .

3. Father. Tying a necktie. In a hurry. On my first evening home he put his hand on my arm and said, "Honey, we're going to forget all about this."

4. Simon. Outside, a plane is crossing the sky, in here we're in a hurry. Morning. It must be morning. The girl is half out of her mind, whimpering and vague; Simon her dear friend is wretched this morning . . . he is wretched with morning itself . . . he forces her to give him an injection with that needle she knows is filthy, she has a dread of needles and surgical instruments and the odor of things that are to be sent into the blood, thinking somehow of her father. . . . This is a bad morning, Simon says that his mind is being twisted out of shape, and so he submits to the needle that he usually scorns and bites his lip with his yellowish teeth, his face going very pale. *Ah baby!* he says in his soft mocking voice, which with all women is a mockery of love, *do it like this—Slowly—*And the girl, terrified, almost drops the precious needle but manages to turn it up to the light from the window . . . is it an extension of herself then? She can give him this gift then? *I wish you wouldn't do this to me,* she says, wise in her terror, because it seems to her that Simon's danger—in a few minutes he may be dead—is a way of pressing her against him that is more powerful than any other embrace. She has to work over his arm, the knotted corded veins of his arm, her forehead wet with perspiration as she pushes and releases the needle, staring at that mixture of liquid now stained with Simon's bright blood. . . . When the drug hits him she can feel it herself, she feels that magic that is more than any woman can give him, striking the back of his head and making his face stretch as if with the impact of a terrible sun. . . . She tries to embrace him but he pushes her aside and stumbles to his feet. *Jesus Christ,* he says. . . .

5. Princess, a Negro girl of eighteen. What is her charge? She is closed-mouthed about it, shrewd and silent, you know that no one had to wrestle her to the sidewalk to get her in here; she came with dignity. In the recreation room she sits reading *Nancy Drew and the Jewel Box Mystery,* which inspires in her face tiny wrinkles of alarm and interest: what a face! Light brown skin, heavy shaded eyes, heavy eyelashes, a serious sinister dark brow, graceful fingers, graceful wristbones, graceful legs, lips, tongue, a sugar-sweet voice, a leggy stride more masculine than Simon's and my mother's, decked out in a dirty white blouse and dirty white slacks; vaguely nautical is Princess' style. . . . At breakfast she is in charge of clearing the table and leans over me, saying, *Honey you sure you ate enough?*

6. The girl lies sleepless, wondering. Why here, why not there? Why Bloomfield Hills and not jail? Why jail and not her pink room? Why downtown Detroit and not Sioux Drive? What is the difference? Is Simon all the difference? The girl's head

is a parade of wonders. She is nearly sixteen, her breath is marvelous with wonders, not long ago she was coloring with crayons and now she is smearing the landscape with paints that won't come off and won't come off her fingers either. She says to the matron *I am not talking about anything*, not because everyone has warned her not to talk but because, because she will not talk; because she won't say anything about Simon, who is her secret. And she says to the matron, *I won't go home*, up until that night in the lavatory when everything was changed. . . . "No, I won't go home I want to stay here," she says, listening to her own words with amazement, thinking that weeds might climb everywhere over that marvelous $180,000 house and dinosaurs might return to muddy the beige carpeting, but never never will she reconcile four o'clock in the morning in Detroit with eight o'clock breakfasts in Bloomfield Hills. . . . oh, she aches still for Simon's hands and his caressing breath, though he gave her little pleasure, he took everything from her (five-dollar bills, ten-dollar bills, passed into her numb hands by men and taken out of her hands by Simon) until she herself was passed into the hands of other men, police, when Simon evidently got tired of her and her hysteria. . . . *No, I won't go home, I don't want to be bailed out*. The girl thinks as a *Stubborn and Wayward Child* (one of several charges lodged against her), and the matron understands her crazy white-rimmed eyes that are seeking out some new violence that will keep her in jail, should someone threaten to let her out. Such children try to strangle the matrons, the attendants, or one another . . . they want the locks locked forever, the doors nailed shut . . . and this girl is no different up until that night her mind is changed for her. . . .

IX: That Night

Princess and Dolly, a little white girl of maybe fifteen, hardy however as a sergeant and in the House of Correction for armed robbery, corner her in the lavatory at the farthest sink and the other girls look away and file out to bed, leaving her. God, how she is beaten up! Why is she beaten up? Why do they pound her, why such hatred? Princess vents all the hatred of a thousand silent Detroit winters on her body, this girl whose body belongs to me, fiercely she rides across the Midwestern plains on this girl's tender bruised body . . . revenge on the oppressed minorities of America! revenge on the slaughtered Indians! revenge on the female sex, on the male sex, revenge on Bloomfield Hills, revenge revenge. . . .

X: Detroit

In Detroit, weather weighs heavily upon everyone. The sky looms large. The horizon shimmers in smoke. Downtown the buildings are imprecise in the haze. Perpetual haze. Perpetual motion inside the haze. Across the choppy river is the city of Windsor, in Canada. Part of the continent has bunched up here and is bulging outward, at the tip of Detroit; a cold hard rain is forever falling on the expressways. . . . Shoppers shop grimly, their cars are not parked in safe places, their windshields may be smashed and graceful ebony hands may drag them out through their shatterproof smashed windshields, crying, *Revenge for the Indians!* Ah, they all fear leaving Hudson's and being dragged to the very tip of the city and thrown off the parking roof of Cobo Hall, that expensive tomb, into the river. . . .

XI: Characters We Are Forever Entwined with

1. Simon drew me into his tender rotting arms and breathed gravity into me. Then I came to earth, weighed down. He said, *You are such a little girl,* and he weighed me down with his delight. In the palms of his hands were teeth marks from his previous life experiences. He was thirty-five, they said. Imagine Simon in this room, in my pink room: he is about six feet tall and stoops slightly, in a feline cautious way, always thinking, always on guard, with his scuffed light suede shoes and his clothes that are anyone's clothes, slightly rumpled ordinary clothes that ordinary men might wear to not-bad jobs. Simon has fair long hair, curly hair, spent languid curls that are like . . . exactly like the curls of wood shavings to the touch, I am trying to be exact . . . and he smells of unheated mornings and coffee and too many pills coating his tongue with a faint green-white scum. . . . Dear Simon, who would be panicked in this room and in this house (right now Billie is vacuuming next door in my parents' room; a vacuum cleaner's roar is a sign of all good things), Simon who is said to have come from a home not much different from this, years ago, fleeing all the carpeting and the polished banisters . . . Simon has a deathly face, only desperate people fall in love with it. His face is bony and cautious, the bones of his cheeks prominent as if with the rigidity of his ceaseless thinking, plotting, for he has to make money out of girls to whom money means nothing, they're so far gone they can hardly count it, and in a sense money means nothing to him either except as a way of keeping on with his life. *Each Day's Proud Struggle,* the title of a novel we could read at jail. . . . Each day he needs a certain amount of money. He devours it. It wasn't love he uncoiled in me with his hollowed-out eyes and his courteous smile, that remnant of a prosperous past, but a dark terror that needed to press itself flat against him, or against another man . . . but he was the first, he came over to me and took my arm, a claim. We struggled on the stairs and I said, *Let me loose, you're hurting my neck, my face,* it was such a surprise that my skin hurt where he rubbed it, and afterward we lay face to face and he breathed everything into me. In the end I think he turned me in.

2. Raymond Forrest. I just read this morning that Raymond Forrest's father, the chairman of the board at   died of a heart attack on a plane bound for London. I would like to write Raymond Forrest a note of sympathy. I would like to thank him for not pressing charges against me one hundred years ago, saving me, being so generous . . . well, men like Raymond Forrest are generous men, not like Simon. I would like to write him a letter telling of my love, or of some other emotion that *is positive* and healthy. Not like Simon and his poetry, which he scrawled down when he was high and never changed a word . . . but when I try to think of something to say, it is Simon's language that comes back to me, caught in my head like a bad song, it is always Simon's language:

There is no reality only dreams
Your neck may get snapped when you wake
My love is drawn to some violent end
She keeps wanting to get away
My love is heading downward
And I am heading upward
She is going to crash on the sidewalk
And I am going to dissolve into the clouds

XII: Events

1. Out of the hospital, bruised and saddened and converted, with Princess' grunts still tangled in my hair . . . and Father in his overcoat looking like a prince himself, come to carry me off. Up the expressway and out north to home. Jesus Christ, but the air is thinner and cleaner here. Monumental houses. Heartbreaking sidewalks, so clean.

2. Weeping in the living room. The ceiling is two stories high and two chandeliers hang from it. Weeping, weeping, though Billie the maid is *probably listening.* I will never leave home again. Never. Never leave home. Never leave this home again, never.

3. Sugar doughnuts for breakfast. The toaster is very shiny and my face is distorted in it. Is that my face?

4. The car is turning in the driveway. Father brings me home. Mother embraces me. Sunlight breaks in movieland patches on the roof of our traditional-contemporary home, which was designed for the famous automotive stylist whose identity, if I told you the name of the famous car he designed, you would all know, so I can't tell you because my teeth chatter at the thought of being sued . . . or having someone climb into my bedroom with a rope to strangle me. . . . The car turns up the blacktop drive. The house opens to me like a doll's house, so lovely in the sunlight, the big living room beckons to me with its walls falling away in a delirium of joy at my return. Billie the maid is *no doubt* listening from the kitchen as I burst into tears and the hysteria Simon got so sick of. Convulsed in Father's arms, I say I will never leave again, never, why did I leave, where did I go, what happened, my mind is gone wrong, my body is one big bruise, my backbone was sucked dry, it wasn't the men who hurt me and Simon never hurt me but only those girls . . . my God, how they hurt me . . . I will never leave home again. . . . The car is perpetually turning up the drive and I am perpetually breaking down in the living room and we are perpetually taking the right exit from the expressway (Lahser Road) and the wall of the rest room is perpetually banging against my head and perpetually are Simon's hands moving across my body and adding everything up and so too are Father's hands on my shaking bruised back, far from the surface of my skin on the surface of my good blue cashmere coat (dry-cleaned for my release). . . . I weep for all the money here, for God in gold

and beige carpeting, for the beauty of chandeliers and the miracle of a clean polished gleaming toaster and faucets that run both hot and cold water, and I tell them, *I will never leave home, this is my home, I love everything here, I am in love with everything here. . . .*

I am home.

1969

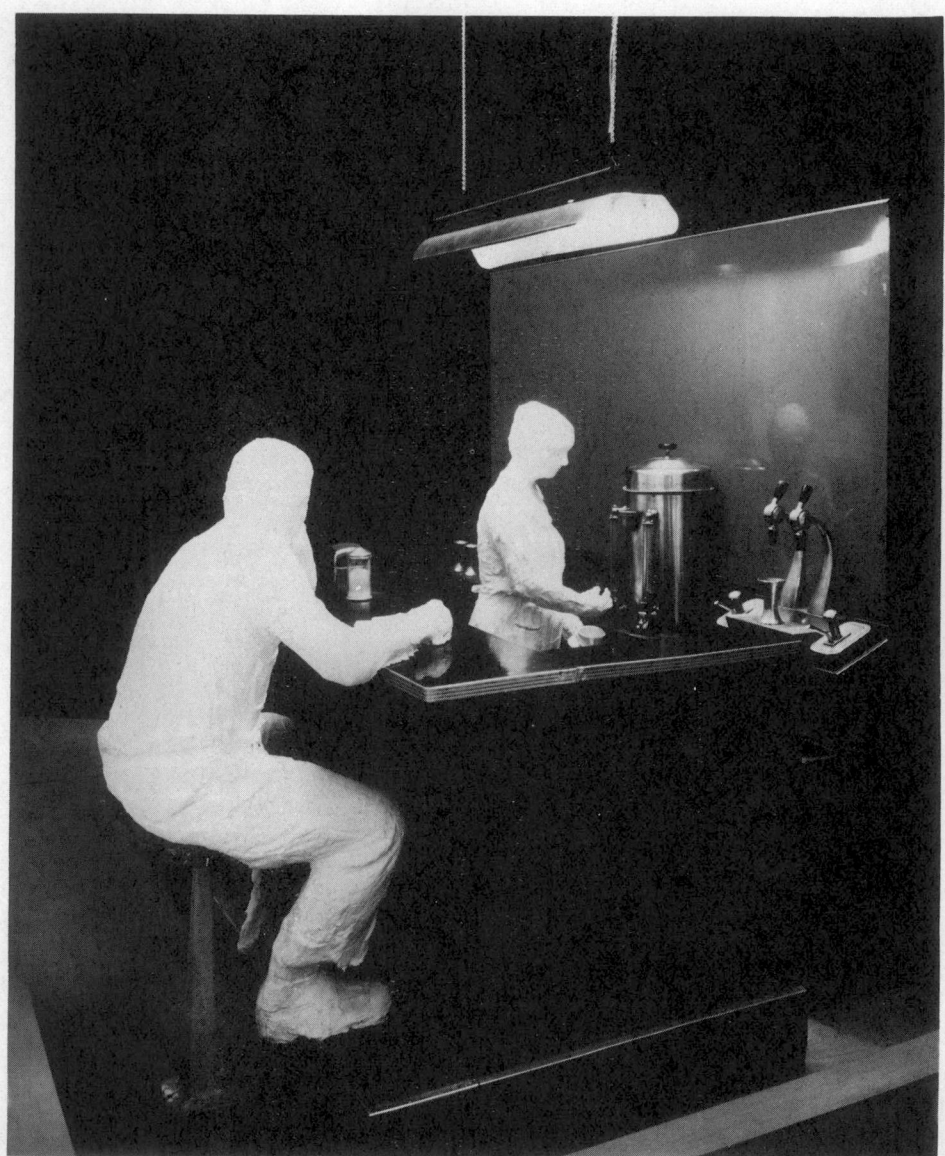

George Segal,
The Diner,
plaster and assemblage, 1964–1966.
Collection Walker Art Center, Minneapolis.
Gift of the T. B. Walker Foundation, 1966.

The Literature of Postwar America: Poetry 1940–1973

 The generation of poets who flourished after World
War II—poets as diverse as Robert Lowell and
Elizabeth Bishop, Theodore Roethke and Frank
O'Hara, John Berryman and John Ashbery, Allen
Ginsberg and A. R. Ammons, Adrienne Rich and James
Wright—had one thing in common: They had to define
themselves against the achievements of their great
modernist predecessors. American poetics and American
aesthetics had been broadly defined by the first
generation of twentieth-century American poets. T. S.
Eliot and Ezra Pound, on the one hand, had made
American poetry international and had established free
verse as the modernist mode *par excellence.* They wrote
as educated men, readers of history and foreign
languages, raiders of culture; their poems demanded a
readership that did not flinch at phrases quoted from
Sanskrit or Chinese, historical references, and cultivated
allusion. Robert Frost, on the other hand, had
established the right of American poetry to be sturdily
American in syntax and local accent, and William
Carlos Williams had founded a laconic urban poetry of
hard-edged realism. Langston Hughes and other writers
of the Harlem Renaissance had claimed poetic value for
the black vernacular and for the representation of ghetto
life. Wallace Stevens, the most elusive of the
modernists, had brought philosophic skepticism into
American poetry and had found a meditative style—
ironic and syntactically elaborate—adequate to the
complexity of his subject. The second generation,
inheriting these victories, chose in part to continue, in
part to correct or reject, the work of their predecessors.

Modernism in an American Vernacular

The poets after World War II seem, in retrospect, more American, less European, than most of their poetic forebears. The wave of international modernism had receded, and the new poets no longer exhibited the defensiveness so common to American poetry since its inception. With the rise of American world power in the wake of the war, fewer writers believe in American inferiority to Europe. There would be influxes, as we shall see, into American poetry from the poetry of other countries, but there was no longer the need for American poets to remake themselves into European or English writers.

The chief European influence on the poets of the second generation was not a poet but, strange to say, Freud, the Viennese inventor of a new psychology. The Freudian model for man's inner life (which replaced the classical and Christian model of "faculties" such as the intellect, the will, and the imagination) divided the self into three components: the superego, which urged the standards of behavior and conscience absorbed from parents and social norms; the id, which represented the instincts and drives often disapproved of by society and therefore repressed; and the ego, the integrated self that mediates the conflicting demands of the superego and the id. It was perhaps not surprising that Freud's emphasis on dark and unruly drives, driven underground only to erupt disastrously in violence or madness, appealed to a generation that had just experienced World War II.

But it was a second part of the Freudian theory—the conjecture that the behavior of one's parents contributes greatly to one's sense of self and one's later life—that appears most conspicuously as an influence in American poetry. Many of the second-generation poets had undergone psychoanalysis or psychoanalytic therapy, and the work of the therapeutic hour—a recalling of incidents of childhood and youth—soon appeared in poetry. Roethke, Jarrell, Berryman, Lowell, Anne Sexton, and Sylvia Plath all made poetry out of the family constellation described in psychoanalytic terms. Lowell's *Life Studies* (1959) was the first full anatomy of the family; Sexton's *To Bedlam and Part Way Back* (1960) was written at the suggestion of a therapist after Sexton had been hospitalized for a mental breakdown; Berryman's *77 Dream Songs* (1964) showed the id (renamed

---

Confessional Poetry

Notebook: as my title intends, the poems in this book are written as one poem, intuitive in arrangement, but not a pile or sequence of related material. It is less an almanac than the story of my life. Many events turn up, many others of equal or greater personal reality do not. This is not my private lash, or confession, or a puritan's too literal pornographic honesty, glad to share secret embarrassment and triumph. The time is a summer, an autumn, a winter, a spring, another summer. . . . My plot rolls with the seasons, but one year is confused with another. I have flashbacks to what I remember, and fables inspired by impulse. Accident threw up subjects, and the plot swallowed them— famished for human chances.

Robert Lowell, "Afterthought" in *Notebook* (1970)

Henry) in full spate; and Plath's "Daddy" (1966) became the most notorious poem exposing the underside of the family romance. The Freudian therapeutic approach, urging the exploration of one's darkest impulses, led to "confessions" being made not only on the analyst's couch but also on the printed page.

In describing such writing as confessional poetry, critics often did not distinguish between life and art, nor did they admit that such personal revelations in art have a long history in poetry in English, reaching back as far as Shakespeare's sonnets. "When Shakespeare said 'Two loves have I,' reader, he was not kidding," wrote John Berryman. The label "confessional poetry" has usually been applied pejoratively—and there was just enough truth in the phrase to make it a popular one. One "confessional poet," Robert Lowell, defended his practice in his last printed poem, "Epilogue," with the retort to his critics, "Yet why not say what happened?" The motive underlying all art, after all, is the drive toward accuracy: Without the artist's record of "what happened," we would remain only transient statistics:

> We are poor passing facts,
> warned by that to give
> each figure in the photograph
> his living name.

If Freud was the chief external influence on American poetry after 1945, there was nonetheless a continuing influence of foreign poetry as well. In part, this came about because some of our poets lived abroad; though the great period of expatriation had ended, several of the second-generation poets lived for some time in foreign countries. Bishop spent years in Brazil, Snyder in Japan, Lowell (in his fifties) in England, Ashbery in France, Plath in England (where she died). Even poets who did not live abroad often traveled widely, through Fulbright fellowships and international poetry festivals. The cross-fertilization of American literature that took place in this generation imported Arthur Rimbaud (through O'Hara and Ashbery), Rainer Maria Rilke and Herman Hesse (through Jarrell and Wright), Cesar Vallejo, Pablo Neruda, Carlos Drummond de Andrade, and other South American poets (through Robert Bly and Elizabeth Bishop), Ted Hughes (via his wife, Sylvia Plath), Buddhist poetry (through Ginsberg and Snyder), and Constantine Cavafy (through James Merrill). The special case of Auden's residence in America caused him to be the chief British influence on the young. The art of translation received new energy through Lowell's *Imitations* (1961), in which Lowell translated classical and European originals in a new way: He borrowed the subject matter and structure of the parent poem while giving the syntax and diction an unmistakably Lowellesque ring.

But though the poets after 1945 interested themselves in foreign poetry, they did not, in the manner of Eliot and Pound, adopt European modes of speech in their poetry. Pound's archaisms, Eliot's anglicisms, were purged from the new American poetry. The foreign poets read by the later poets were silently absorbed into the American vernacular. It is chiefly by new structures in the lyric and new kinds of imagery that we recognize the presence of European or South American or Asian poetry. There is very little attempt at a European or international speaking voice, and even when the perspective of the poet is a global or

The Long Line

Its natural inspiration of the moment that keeps it moving, disparate things put down together, shorthand notations of visual imagery, juxtapositions of hydrogen juke-box—abstract haikus sustain the mystery & put iron poetry back into the line: the last line of *Sunflower Sutra* is the extreme, one stream of single word associations, summing up. Mind is shapely, Art is shapely. Meaning Mind practiced in spontaneity invents forms in its own image & gets to Last Thoughts.

Allen Ginsberg, notes for *Howl* (1959)

international one—as in Lowell, Ginsberg, or Snyder—the perspective is expressed in indigenous American tones.

And the tones became increasingly varied. Whitman, in the nineteenth century, had represented himself as the channel for the "varied carols" of America; through him, the "many long dumb voices" would find utterance. He implied a hope that one day the silent voices would be able to speak for themselves, and in this century they have begun to fulfill his prophecy. Through Allen Ginsberg, the American immigrant voice first entered American poetry in a powerful way. In his long sequence "Kaddish," Ginsberg presented the life of his mother, a Jewish immigrant from Russia, as typical of the unbearable strain put on the psyche by such a violent break in experience. Ginsberg's rich social documentation marked a new era in American lyric; in his phenomenally successful *Howl* (1956) and the volumes that followed it in quick succession, Jews, beatniks, Vietnam protesters, and urban homosexuals all appeared in believable form.

Through the activity of Dudley Randall, the Broadside Press in Detroit began to publish a steady stream of black poets (Etheredge Knight, Don Lee, and others), while in New York, trade presses, over the years, published other black poets (including Gwendolyn Brooks, June Jordan, Audre Lorde, Michael Harper, Sonia Sanchez, and Nikki Giovanni). Many black poets responded to the late 1960s' black consciousness movement by consciously writing as a black for black audiences.

A New Diversity

The acknowledging of ethnicity in poetry, not only in subject matter but also in language, marked a new diversity in American poetry and a reaction against the modernist impersonality of voice. Against the conventional history of American poetry—as a descendant of English poetry—the new ethnicity insisted that a poetry belongs also to its physical location and that the proper predecessor of American poetry was the poetry of the first inhabitants of this country, the American Indians. The resurgence of Native American poetry as a source of inspiration, especially in the work of Gary Snyder, has been an impetus to Native Americans to repossess their own literature and to add to it.

An increased regional diversity also entered American poetry after World War II as, for the first time, a strong poetic school was founded on the West Coast. Though several of the "beat" writers (notably Ginsberg and Kerouac) were easterners, others (Snyder, Robert Duncan) were natives of the West Coast. Both groups celebrated the landscape and mores of the Pacific states. Strong ecological concern began to be voiced by Gary Snyder and by the Alaskan poet John Haines. Even Allen Ginsberg was later to write a rueful poem called "Ecologue" (the title is a triple pun on *echo, eclogue,* and *ecology*) about his own ill-fated attempt at living a rural life. Though Ginsberg remains an urban poet, he is imaginatively moved by the preservation of life on the land.

Other regions maintained or began poetic activity. In the South, Allen Tate, John Crowe Ransom, and Robert Penn Warren continued the southern tradition of belles lettres: Their most famous pupil, Robert Lowell, though a northerner, absorbed their principles of poetry. As creative writing programs began to proliferate across the country in American universities, the clustering of older and younger poets in workshops changed the constitution of English departments (themselves newly engaged in the close examination of texts). Universities increasingly became the base for journals and for poetry readings. The poetry reading became a popular social rite; on T. S. Eliot's occasional visits from England, huge throngs would gather to hear him read. Frost too drew enormous audiences in the 1950s and was the official poet at the 1960 presidential inauguration of John F. Kennedy. In a different mode, Ginsberg (protesting American involvement in Vietnam) and Adrienne Rich (protesting the oppression of women) also drew large audiences. As poets read in state after state, in university after university, poetry increasingly seemed a possession common to all the states, not simply a monopoly of New England.

Various "schools" of poetry seemed to form after World War II. The "New York school" (Ashbery, O'Hara, and Kenneth Koch) had particularly close relations with painters, especially with the abstract expressionists. They turned inward to a spontaneous recording of imaginative moments and wished above all to be amusing, intimate, secular, and colloquial—a contrast with both the political fierceness of Pound and the elegiac solemnity of Eliot. Their affinities were neither with philosophy nor with history but with the fine arts—painting, sculpture, theater, and ballet.

The Beats (the name, conferred by journalists, suggests the downtrodden, the jazzy, and the beatified) wrote a poetry characterized by a linguistic freedom that included words commonly considered obscene. Perhaps more disturbing to the common reader was the open admission in poetry, by Ginsberg and others, of the use of drugs, of homosexual experience, of promiscuity in sexual life, and of *disillusionment with* American government and politics. The humor of the Beats, their cheerful and unpredictable readings, their spontaneity in aesthetic matters ("First thought, best thought") was a revelation to more formal American poets; Robert Lowell changed his own early style (modeled on that of Allen Tate) after hearing a Beat reading and realizing that the Beats were closer to the American reality than he was.

Black Mountain

A poem is energy transferred from where the poet got it (he will have some several causations), by way of the poem itself to, all the way over to, the reader. Okay. Then the poem itself must, at all points, be a high energy–construct and, at all points, an energy–discharge. . . .

And I think it can be boiled down to one statement: . . . ONE PERCEPTION MUST IMMEDIATELY AND DIRECTLY LEAD TO A FURTHER PERCEPTION. It means exactly what it says, is a matter of, at *all* points (even, I should say, of our management of daily reality as of the daily work) get on with it, keep moving, keep in, speed, the nerves, their speed, the perceptions, theirs, the acts, the split second acts, the whole business, keep it moving as fast as you can, citizen. And if you also set up as a poet, USE USE USE the process at all points, in any given poem always, always one perception must must must MOVE, INSTANTER, ON ANOTHER!

Charles Olson, "Projective Verse" (1950)

A more complicated and less successful school was that of the "Black Mountain poets," so called because they had been connected with Black Mountain, an avant-garde college in North Carolina where the poet Charles Olson was rector. The best-known members of the group, besides Olson, are Robert Creeley, Robert Duncan, and Denise Levertov. At Black Mountain, the faculty included the dancer Merce Cunningham, the painters Franz Kline, Josef Albers, and Robert Rauschenberg, and the composer John Cage. Olson was an admirer of Pound—for years he visited Pound at St. Elizabeth's hospital in Washington, where Pound was confined for mental illness. All of the Black Mountain poets derive (perhaps too closely) from Pound. In Olson's epic about his native Gloucester, *The Maximus Poems,* one sees Pound's influence most

Imagism

An "Image" is that which presents an intellectual and emotional complex in an instant of time. . . .

It is the presentation of such a "complex" instantaneously which gives that sense of sudden liberation; that sense of freedom from time limits and space limits; that sense of sudden growth, which we experience in the presence of the greatest works of art.

It is better to present one Image in a lifetime than to produce voluminous works.

Ezra Pound, "A Few Don'ts" (1913)

clearly. Though without Pound's social urgency, *The Maximus Poems* adopt Pound's method of historical collage, by which one fragment of historical information is placed against another, over and over, until a jagged accumulation is achieved. The followers of Pound have tended to emphasize, as he did, a montage of phrases and a collocation of images over syntactic complexity and intellectual or logical connection; in this they are the descendants of the American Imagist poets.

The combination of interest in irrational forces within (via Freud and Jung) and disturbance by irrational forces without (especially war) aroused in one group of poets (known as "deep image poets") a wish to tap the unconscious psychic sources of poetry. Robert Bly, James Wright, and W. S. Merwin turned aside, in different ways, from the 1950s' poetry of formal intellectualization and attempted to express, chiefly by mysterious images, "deeper" animal and preconscious motives. They turned to the model of the American Indian shaman (or other such figures of inspiration) as their image of the poet; Bly has given poetry readings wearing a variety of masks resembling the totemic masks worn by witch doctors or shamans. The brooding poetry of Bly and the bleak poetry of Wright and Merwin appealed especially to the antiestablishment young, who associated the poetry of formal prosody and intellectual content with a conservative political stance.

The chief woman poets of this period—Elizabeth Bishop, Anne Sexton, Sylvia Plath, and Adrienne Rich—do not in any sense form a "school" with a common aesthetic. However, consciously feminist poetry (including lesbian poetry such as that written by Rich and Audre Lorde) sees itself as having a common political aim, the claiming of literary space for the voices of women, who, before this generation, have not had access, to the same degree as men, to a literary education. And all the women poets—like Emily Dickinson and Marianne Moore —rebel against the conventional "woman's voice" in literature—obedient, docile, religious, coy, demure, self-deprecating. One can see this rebellion even in minor poets like Edna St. Vincent Millay, Elinor Wylie, and Sara Teasdale; in more powerful voices the terrain of subject matter available to women is enlarged and amplified. In the nineteenth-century past, women wrote chiefly of nature, love,

---

The Voice of Women

Women's work and thinking has been made to seem sporadic, errant, orphaned of any tradition of its own.

In fact, we do have a long feminist tradition, both oral and written, a tradition which has built on itself over and over, recovering essential elements even when those have been strangled or wiped out. . . .

Today women are talking to each other, recovering an oral culture, telling our life-stories, reading aloud to one another the books that have moved and healed us, analyzing the language that has lied about us, reading our own words aloud to each other . . . to name and found a culture of our own.

Adrienne Rich, *On Lies, Secrets, and Silence* (1978)

God, and death; Moore, while not abandoning such subjects altogether, had staked out a precise territory of her own, strongly voiced, unapologetic, full of gusto. Bishop, encouraged by Moore, took travel as her subject—a topic thought to be more suited to men and to the narrative than to women and to the lyric. Sexton, who had from her days as a model a powerfully satiric sense of social demands on women, mocked the infantile roles assigned to them. Rich took on a voice—prophetic, denunciatory—reserved by convention to men, especially to preachers. And Plath wrote a powerful poetry of ambivalence about herself as a daughter, wife, and mother (roles scarcely treated in earlier poetry). Nonetheless, the modernist inheritance is strong in these later women. Bishop would not have been the poet she was without Stevens (whose visual sense she admired and whose limpidity of line she learned from); Rich's first masters were Frost and Auden, and she has never forsaken her allegiance to a Frostian "common language."

Poetry and Society

It has usually not been characteristic of the lyric to include a great deal of social detail; that work has been left to the novel. But both Pound and the poets of the second generation decided to reclaim history and social reality for poetry. What Pound did in the epic, the later poets did in lyric, and anyone looking at Pre-Raphaelite or Georgian lyric in England would find it hard to believe that a half century later this thin and attenuated form would be bursting with political and social information. World War II itself produced rather little in the way of lyric documentation, though the war poems of Randall Jarrell are a notable exception. The chief political events affecting later poets were the war in Vietnam and the political assassinations of the 1960s. Though some poems comment directly on the Vietnam War, it was chiefly important in the way that it polarized society, with the poets generally aligning themselves with the draft-liable young and against official government policy. The sense among poets that they had an important message to utter to the country awoke poetry from the formal and meditative stance that it had adopted during the "tranquillized fifties" (as Lowell called them) and gave a new impulse to poetry spoken or chanted aloud to a listening public.

The March on the Pentagon in 1967, in which Lowell and other writers participated (described by Norman Mailer in *The Armies of the Night*) consolidated the powerful entry of authors into American political protest. Merwin, Ginsberg, Rich, and others protested the Vietnam War: Merwin wrote about Asians dying, Ginsberg about the politics behind the war, Rich of the human waste of battle. In the same decade, the assassinations, in turn, of John F. Kennedy, Robert Kennedy, and Martin Luther King powerfully affected poets, black and white; many elegies were written about both President Kennedy and Dr. King. The bitterness with respect to America that entered the poetry of Lowell, Ginsberg, and many others at this time directly reflects the double disillusionment of the war abroad and the assassinations at home. With the ending of the war, the political force of poetry abated, and it seemed (with the exception of feminist poetry) to be entering a new meditative phase. At the same time, poets experienced a nostalgia for the time when they felt necessary to the social good, and American poets know that their poetry is not formed under the pressure that poets feel in societies where to utter a protest poem is to put oneself in danger of arrest. Since the 1930s, America has been a refuge for émigré writers from Germany, Russia, and other countries; American poets can envy the seriousness of purpose with which such poets write and the degree to which they feel their writing is necessary.

If the subject matter of American poetry in this period turned radically to the subconscious and the social, it also, though more subtly, turned to the scientific. It may be in the future that the acceptance of the scientific model for knowledge will be seen as the most profound change in poetry of this period. Not all poets by any means accept such a model, at least not consciously; the poetry of Roethke, for instance, can be seen as a violent striving against such a model. On the other hand, most of the poets of this generation have neither a religious nor a political creed. Their conception of the universe no longer contains a presiding God or a teleological purpose. They are familiar with physical and chemical descriptions of the universe unknown to poets of earlier centuries, descriptions comparable in their revolutionary force to the Copernican hypothesis. The neutrino and the double helix, invisible though they are to the naked eye, are part of our conceptual world. The poets of this generation are aware of interstellar distances and of electron microscopy. Only a few poets incorporate the vocabulary of science (A. R. Ammons, because of his scientific training, does it entirely naturally; James Merrill does it imaginatively). But even Lowell, the most unscientific of poets, could not continue to write the poetry he wrote in his young manhood, when he had become a Roman Catholic convert. "Against my will," he wrote, "I left the City of God where it belongs." In becoming an unbeliever, Lowell had to become a different poet; his poems could no longer have the neatness of closure, the linear purpose, that they had in their religious phase. The formal properties of a successful poem always mirror the formal properties of the universe it represents—and a universe displaying several "layers" of order (macrocosmic to microcosmic), a complex dynamic of physical and biological evolution, and a tendency toward entropy cannot be mirrored by a single static structure. The freedom of modern free verse is philosophical as well as experimental, and the diffuseness of closure in recent poetry is a gesture toward the multiplicity of process in the universe as we now understand it.

"The Inroads of Science"

The function of poetry in a Machine Age is identical to its function in any other age; and its capacities for presenting the most complete synthesis of human values remain essentially immune from any of the so-called inroads of science.

Hart Crane, "Modern Poetry" (1930)

The language of the poetry of an era must also reflect its understanding of the self. In this period, the distrust of the excessively "rational" appears in many poets' distrust of "adult" language. To give the unconscious a language, Berryman's Henry and Roethke's "lost son" speak in baby talk; Sexton and Plath turn to fairy tales. Poetic language is widened, in this era, in other ways as well —through Ginsberg's defiant use of obscenities, in the self-consciously ironic "camp" talk of O'Hara, Ashbery, and Merrill, in colloquialism of all sorts (from street vernacular in Don Lee to the language of political protest in Rich). The notion of the self as a composite of its own past furnishes Lowell with his rich amalgam of language, in which personal history is interwoven with on the history of the world. A reversal of the emblematic language of Emerson (in which a natural object is made to reveal spiritual reality) appears in A. R. Ammons (who makes an inner state real by attaching it to nature). The language of Chinese and Japanese poetry, introduced to American poetry by Amy Lowell in Imagism, has taken on new life in the minimalist verse of W. S. Merwin and Gary Snyder, and Buddhist chants have influenced Ginsberg. The American language, always in a process of change, was first made into notable poetry by Whitman and Dickinson. But their example was too daring, and the indigenous freedom of the American language has had to assert its rights in poetry once again in each generation. It no longer, at least, has subject status with respect to the English language.

In the poetry of the 1950s and 1960s we can see the continuation of many of the attempts begun by early modernism. The American long poem continues to be written, whether in Poundian collage (as by Olson) or by means of the poetic sequence (the way favored by Eliot and Stevens, and after them by Robert Lowell in *Life Studies* and *History,* for instance and Ammons in *The Snow Poems* and other sequences). The long discursive poem is written by Ashbery ("Self-portrait in a Convex Mirror") as well as by Ammons ("Sphere"); Merrill has done a long "conversation poem" in three books, *The Changing Light at Sandover.* Experiments in the arrangement of words on the page continue: Ammons has written on an adding-machine tape ("Tape for the Turn of the Year"); Merrill has taken dictation from a Ouija board; Ashbery has written a double-column poem ("Litany"). The prose poem (most brilliantly done in Ashbery's *Three Poems*) has been successfully attempted by Ginsberg and Rich, among others. Free verse and formal verse continue to dispute the field, with Lowell oscillating back and forth between them throughout his career. The implication of this variety of form is that all poetic forms are possible, that modes of expression and formulation are as various as the human psyche, and that America's chief contribution to poetry will be its encouraging of extreme diversity.

Of course, we see too many poets, so to speak, when we look at the production of our own century. Poets in their own time are often noticed chiefly for their topicality, as they comment on current events, delineate common problems, or voice conventionally acceptable sentiments. It is always sobering to look at journals, book reviews, and anthologies of a hundred years ago. In them

> ### "The Form of the Poem Need Not Be Foreclosed"
>
> The history of contemporary American poetry will record massive movement toward conventionally open styles. Ginsberg, Warren, Wright, Lowell, Roethke, Simpson, Dickey, and others have been accused of abandoning something like an ideal music for an inferior form. This argument is not resolvable because it masks political, economic, and cultural arguments metastasized to aesthetics. All we can really ask, must ask, of a poet is that his poem in part and in whole give pleasure, be durable, and lead us to better know what we dimly intuit as the reality of life.
>
> Dave Smith, *Local Assays* (1985)

we see poets now judged to be minor or negligible being published in great quantity, reviewed in ecstatic terms, and massively anthologized. Today their names are forgotten, since history winnows literature to the few poets of each century that subsequent poets can admire for their language and form. An observer a hundred years hence will be able to see resemblances among our poets where we see chiefly differences, and may be able to find a single descriptive rubric by which to characterize poetry after World War II. As yet, we seem to have found only the feebly linear term "postmodernist," which abandons any attempt at substantive description. Perhaps the era will finally seem to fall into a political period and a domestic period, with the more intimate verse of Merrill, Ammons, and Ashbery succeeding to the passions of the Vietnam War years. Poetic styles arise by reaction; after the quiet formality of the 1950s came the overt declarations and strenuous political rhetoric of the 1960s; this was followed by an inward-turning and more ironic stance in the 1970s. All of these forms continue to perform the task of poetry: to record and analyze in each age the inner life of mankind, and to maintain for each generation the freshness and inventiveness of imagination and language.

Further Reading:

R. Jarrell, *Poetry and the Age*, 1953.
S. Stepanchev, *American Poetry Since 1945*, 1965.
R. Howard, *Alone with America*, 1969.
The Survival of Poetry, ed. M. Dodsworth, 1970.
H. Bloom, *The Ringers in the Tower*, 1971.
Contemporary Poetry in America: Essays and Introductions, ed. R. Boyers, 1973.
K. Malkoff, *Crowell's Handbook of Contemporary American Poetry*, 1973.
E. Faas, *Towards a New American Poetics: Essays and Interviews: Olson, Duncan, Snyder, Creeley, Bly, Ginsberg*, 1976.
D. Kalstone, *Five Temperaments: Elizabeth Bishop, Robert Lowell, James Merrill, Adrienne Rich, John Ashbery*, 1977.
L. Lieberman, *Unassigned Frequencies*, 1977.
R. Pinsky, *The Situation of Poetry*, 1977.
H. Nemerov, *Figures of Thought*, 1978.
C. Altieri, *Enlarging the Temple: New Directions in American Poetry During the 1960s*, 1979.

Harvard Guide to Comtemporary American
Writing, ed. D. Hoffman, 1979.
C. Molesworth, The Fierce Embrace: A Study of
Contemporary American Poetry, 1979.
H. Vendler, Part of Nature, Part of Us: Modern
American Poets, 1980.
A. Williamson, Introspection and Contemporary

Poetry, 1984.
R. Hass, Twentieth-Century Pleasures: Prose on
Poetry, 1985.
D. Smith, Local Assays: On Contemporary
American Poetry, 1985.
R. von Hallberg, American Poetry and Culture,
1945–1980, 1985.

Theodore Roethke
1908–1963

Theodore Roethke's childhood intimacy with the world of his father's greenhouse provided a rich vein of poetic material, from which his most individual poems issued. American poets (except for Whitman) have traditionally been bookish; the soil has been relatively absent from our verse. Roethke knew swamp and soil, cuttings and roots, the dark life of plants in the earth before their time for blossoming. He knew, too, the authoritarian structure of the greenhouse, where his German grandfather and his father ruled with an iron hand; there he was helpless, small, frightened, "the lost son."

The voice of the child he was is Roethke's most notable poetic invention (imitated, since he invented it, by poets as various as Robert Lowell, Anne Sexton, and Sylvia Plath). Of course, Roethke did not entirely invent this child-voice; he learned it in part from William Blake, whose Songs of Innocence first memorably introduced the voice of the child into poetry in English. But Roethke's child has, so to speak, studied Freud and discovered his unconscious. His preconscious language is full of brilliant linguistic and poetic invention; its quick, elusive rhythms and slippery sounds convey the daring investigations of the bewildered child.

Roethke's greenhouse poems occur in the volume The Lost Son (1948). His volumes subsequent to Praise to the End! (1952) and The Waking (1953) became both more formal (with many imitations of William Butler Yeats and T. S. Eliot) and more prolix in their use of free verse, while still containing some lyrics of terse power, especially some short bitter poems about confinement for mental illness.

Roethke was born in Saginaw, Michigan, and educated at the University of Michigan; he spent most of his teaching life (1948–1963) at the University of Washington in Seattle, where he served as mentor to many younger poets and creative writing students, including James Wright. Roethke's successive breakdowns and recurrent alcoholism made his life increasingly difficult until his early death in his fifties.

His influence on the emergence of West Coast writing was a powerful one, and his advocacy of formal prosody (both in his own work and in his teaching) was one of the countermeasures against the domination by free verse of the American poetic scene. Though he was a large, powerfully built man, the truest self for which he found a voice was the small soul that trembled in childhood before the mysteries of nature.

Further Reading:
R. J. Mills, Jr., *Theodore Roethke,* 1963.
Theodore Roethke: Essays on the Poetry, ed. A. Stein, 1965.
K. Malkoff, *Theodore Roethke: An Introduction to the Poetry,* 1966.
A. Seager, *The Glass House: The Life of Theodore Roethke,* 1968.
R. A. Blessing, *Theodore Roethke's Dynamic Vision,* 1974.
R. Sullivan, *Theodore Roethke: The Garden Master,* 1975.
J. La Belle, *The Echoing Wood of Theodore Roethke,* 1976.
Keith R. Moul, *Theodore Roethke's Career: An Annotated Bibliography,* 1977.
H. Williams, *"The Edge Is What I Have": Theodore Roethke and After,* 1977.
J. Parini, *Theodore Roethke: An American Romantic,* 1979.

Text:
Collected Poems, 1966.
See also *On the Poet and His Craft: Selected Prose of Theodore Roethke,* ed. R. J. Mills, Jr., 1965.
Selected Letters of Theodore Roethke, ed. R. J. Mills, Jr., 1968.
Straw for the Fire: From the Notebooks of Theodore Roethke, 1943–1963, ed. D. Wagoner, 1972.

Cuttings

Sticks-in-a-drowse droop over sugary loam,
Their intricate stem-fur dries;
But still the delicate slips keep coaxing up water;
The small cells bulge;

One nub of growth   5
Nudges a sand-crumb loose,
Pokes through a musty sheath
Its pale tendrilous horn.

1948

Cuttings

(later)

This urge, wrestle, resurrection of dry sticks,
Cut stems struggling to put down feet,
What saint strained so much,
Rose on such lopped limbs to a new life?

I can hear, underground, that sucking and sobbing,   5
In my veins, in my bones I feel it,—

The small waters seeping upward,
The tight grains parting at last.
When sprouts break out,
Slippery as fish,
I quail, lean to beginnings, sheath-wet.   10
1948

My Papa's Waltz

The whiskey on your breath
Could make a small boy dizzy;
But I hung on like death:
Such waltzing was not easy.

We romped until the pans   5
Slid from the kitchen shelf;
My mother's countenance
Could not unfrown itself.

The hand that held my wrist
Was battered on one knuckle;   10
At every step you missed
My right ear scraped a buckle.

You beat time on my head
With a palm caked hard by dirt,
Then waltzed me off to bed   15
Still clinging to your shirt.
1948

Dolor

I have known the inexorable sadness of pencils,
Neat in their boxes, dolor of pad and paper-weight,
All the misery of manila folders and mucilage,
Desolation in immaculate public places,
Lonely reception room, lavatory, switchboard,   5

The unalterable pathos of basin and pitcher,
Ritual of multigraph, paper-clip, comma,
Endless duplication of lives and objects.
And I have seen dust from the walls of institutions,
Finer than flour, alive, more dangerous than silica,   10
Sift, almost invisible, through long afternoons of tedium,
Dropping a fine film on nails and delicate eyebrows,
Glazing the pale hair, the duplicate grey standard faces.

1948

Elegy for Jane

My student, thrown by a horse

I remember the neckcurls, limp and damp as tendrils;
And her quick look, a sidelong pickerel smile;
And how, once startled into talk, the light syllables leaped for her,
And she balanced in the delight of her thought,
A wren, happy, tail into the wind,   5
Her song trembling the twigs and small branches.
The shade sang with her;
The leaves, their whispers turned to kissing;
And the mold sang in the bleached valleys under the rose.

Oh, when she was sad, she cast herself down into such a pure depth,   10
Even a father could not find her:
Scraping her cheek against straw;
Stirring the clearest water.

My sparrow, you are not here,
Waiting like a fern, making a spiny shadow.   15
The sides of wet stones cannot console me,
Nor the moss, wound with the last light.

If only I could nudge you from this sleep,
My maimed darling, my skittery pigeon.
Over this damp grave I speak the words of my love: 20
I, with no rights in this matter,
Neither father nor *lover*.

1953

The Waking

I wake to sleep, and take my waking slow.
I feel my fate in what I cannot fear.
I learn by going where I have to go.

We think by feeling. What is there to know?
I hear my being dance from ear to ear.   5
I wake to sleep, and take my waking slow.

Of those so close beside me, which are you?
God bless the Ground! I shall walk softly there,
And learn by going where I have to go.

Light takes the Tree; but who can tell us how?   10
The lowly worm climbs up a winding stair;
I wake to sleep, and take my waking slow.

Great Nature has another thing to do
To you and me; so take the lively air,
And, lovely, learn by going where to go.   15

This shaking keeps me steady. I should know.
What falls away is always. And is near.
I wake to sleep, and take my waking slow.
I learn by going where I have to go.

1953

Heard in a Violent Ward

In heaven, too,
You'd be institutionalized.
But that's all right,—
If they let you eat and swear
With the likes of Blake,   5
And Christopher Smart,
And that sweet man, John Clare.[1]

1964

[1] William Blake (1757–1827), Christopher Smart (1722–1771), and John Clare (1793–1864) were English poets thought mad by some of their contemporaries. (Both Smart and Clare were institutionalized.)

Elizabeth Bishop
1911–1979

Elizabeth Bishop's poetry is that of a skeptic who looks on everything she sees with the eye of estrangement. Bishop was, in effect, orphaned early. Her father died before she was a year old, and her mother had a breakdown that led to insanity and permanent commitment to an asylum when Bishop was five. Bishop was raised in Massachusetts by an aunt but spent summers until she was thirteen with her grandparents in Nova Scotia. After graduating from Vassar (in the class commemorated by Mary McCarthy in *The Group*), she lived for some time in Key West; she also lived in France and Mexico. Eventually, during a trip to Brazil, she renewed acquaintance with Lota de Macedo Soares, with whom she lived for the next nineteen years. She then returned to the United States and during the last years of her life taught at Harvard. Bishop's continual geographic displacements reinforced her sense of homelessness and lack of parents. In effect, she was always piecing together a world out of unfamiliar elements.

Bishop's career unfolded slowly. In college, she wrote imitations of Hopkins and Herbert, but even in these bits of pastiche her humor and self-scrutiny are already evident. Her first book, *North and South* (1946), shows her as an accomplished poet aware already of her major metaphor, the resemblance between a map and a poem. Each represents—but in an arbitrary, schematic, and conventionalized way—a reality independent of its charting. Maps and poems both distort in the service of representation; both are miniature versions of the world. Bishop also poses, in her first book, questions of spirit and flesh, truth and nature, and establishes her polarities of North and South—polarities that also dominate her later books, *A Cold Spring* (1955), *Questions of Travel* (1965), and *Geography III* (1976), which followed the *Collected Poems* of 1969.

Bishop's first critics compared her to Marianne Moore, who was for a long time Bishop's poetic mentor; Bishop had met Moore through the librarian at Vassar. But in fact Bishop's roots go back to the religious poetry of the seventeenth-century poet George Herbert, to Protestant hymnody, and to the plain style of William Cowper and William Wordsworth. Bishop's skepticism unfolds against the backdrop of a lost religious faith. The seriality of existence without a religious meaning, ending only in the dust of the grave, appalls her: "Why couldn't we have seen this old Nativity while we were at it?" she asks, reproducing in the Christmas scene that "family with pets" that she had never had. But nostalgia is powerless against the icy truth of human solitude in the universe. Bishop's tableau of the fishhouses, in the poem named for them, is inhabited by three solitaries: the Wordsworthian fisherman, Bishop herself, and *the single* seal. Bishop's solitary "total immersion" in knowledge—"dark, salt, clear, moving, utterly free"—stands against the permanent inscrutability of the world.

In her experiments in reproducing the thought processes of a child, an animal, a tourist, or an exile, Bishop invents a language lucid in its simple diction but surreal in its bewildered disjunction of space and time. While she retained an interest in rhyme and formal patterns, she began early to introduce natural speech rhythms and slant rhymes to her stanzas. Her naturalness earned Robert Lowell's admiration; he dedicated "Skunk Hour" to her, saying that he had learned from "The Armadillo" how to loosen up his own lines. Lowell and Bishop remained close friends; "North Haven," her elegy for him, expresses not only her loss but also their aesthetic difference. Lowell, a copious writer, revised constantly, treating even his printed work as manuscript, while Bishop, a perfectionist, kept poems unpublished for years while she sought the *mot juste* to fill a gap.

In an American literature largely preoccupied with the transcendental, the emblematic, the Christian, and the chauvinistic, Bishop's skeptical, observant, and ironic tone (learned in part from Emily Dickinson) comes as a welcome note. Her gaze takes in the whole hemisphere, from Cape Breton to Rio de Janeiro. Though she sees the dangers of travel—the exploitative cruelty of the conquistadors, the superficiality of tourist experience—in the end she values those questions that are provoked only by travel; and values as well, almost against her will, the resulting lessons in skepticism and loss.

Further Reading:
A. Stevenson, *Elizabeth Bishop*, 1966.
C. McMahon, *Elizabeth Bishop: A Bibliography,*
1980.
L. Schwartz and S. Estess, *Elizabeth Bishop and Her Art,* 1982.

Text:
Complete Poems, 1982.

The Fish

I caught a tremendous fish
and held him beside the boat
half out of water, with my hook
fast in a corner of his mouth.
He didn't fight.   5
He hadn't fought at all.
He hung a grunting weight,
battered and venerable
and homely. Here and there
his brown skin hung in strips   10
like ancient wallpaper,
and its pattern of darker brown
was like wallpaper:
shapes like full-blown roses
stained and lost through age.   15
He was speckled with barnacles,
fine rosettes of lime,
and infested
with tiny white sea-lice,

and underneath two or three   20
rags of green weed hung down.
While his gills were breathing in
the terrible oxygen
—the frightening gills,
fresh and crisp with blood,   25
that can cut so badly—
I thought of the coarse white flesh
packed in like feathers,
the big bones and the little bones,
the dramatic reds and blacks   30
of his shiny entrails,
and the pink swim-bladder
like a big peony.
I looked into his eyes
which were far larger than mine   35
but shallower, and yellowed,
the irises backed and packed
with tarnished tinfoil
seen through the lenses
of old scratched isinglass.   40
They shifted a little, but not
to return my stare.
—It was more like the tipping
of an object toward the light.
I admired his sullen face,   45
the mechanism of his jaw,
and then I saw
that from his lower lip
—if you could call it a lip—
grim, wet, and weaponlike,   50
hung five old pieces of fish-line,
or four and a wire leader
with the swivel still attached,
with all their five big hooks
grown firmly in his mouth.   55
A green line, frayed at the end
where he broke it, two heavier lines,
and a fine black thread
still crimped from the strain and snap
when it broke and he got away.   60
Like medals with their ribbons
frayed and wavering,
a five-haired beard of wisdom
trailing from his aching jaw.
I stared and stared   65
and victory filled up

the little rented boat,
from the pool of bilge
where oil had spread a rainbow
around the rusted engine   7°
to the bailer rusted orange,
the sun-cracked thwarts,
the oarlocks on their strings,
the gunnels—until everything
was rainbow, rainbow, rainbow!   75
And I let the fish go.

1946

Over 2000 Illustrations
and a Complete Concordance[1]

Thus should have been our travels:
serious, engravable.
The Seven Wonders of the World are tired
and a touch familiar, but the other scenes,
innumerable, though equally sad and still,   5
are foreign. Often the squatting Arab,
or group of Arabs, plotting, probably,
against our Christian Empire,
while one apart, with outstretched arm and hand
points to the Tomb, the Pit, the Sepulcher.   10
The branches of the date-palms look like files.
The cobbled courtyard, where the Well is dry,
is like a diagram, the brickwork conduits
are vast and obvious, the human figure
far gone in history or theology,   15
gone with its camel or its faithful horse.
Always the silence, the gesture, the specks of birds
suspended on invisible threads above the Site,
or the smoke rising solemnly, pulled by threads.
Granted a page alone or a page made up   20
of several scenes arranged in cattycornered
    rectangles
or circles set on stippled gray,
granted a grim lunette,
caught in the toils of an initial letter,
when dwelt upon, they all resolve themselves.   25

---

[1] The title is a phrase describing the type of old   in the Holy Land as well as a *concordance,* or
Bible that often included illustrations of places   index of important names and words.

The eye drops, weighted, through the lines
the burin[2] made, the lines that move apart
like ripples above sand,
dispersing storms, God's spreading fingerprint,
and painfully, finally, that ignite   30
in watery prismatic white-and-blue.
Entering the Narrows at St. Johns[3]
the touching bleat of goats reached to the ship.
We glimpsed them, reddish, leaping up the cliffs
among the fog-soaked weeds and butter-and-eggs.   35
And at St. Peter's[4] the wind blew and the sun shone
    madly.
Rapidly, purposefully, the Collegians[5] marched in
    lines,
crisscrossing the great square with black, like ants.
In Mexico the dead man lay
in a blue arcade; the dead volcanoes   40
glistened like Easter lilies.
The jukebox went on playing "Ay, Jalisco!"
And at Volubilis[6] there were beautiful poppies
splitting the mosaics; the fat old guide made eyes.
In Dingle[7] harbor a golden length of evening   45
the rotting hulks held up their dripping plush.
The Englishwoman poured tea, informing us
that the Dutchess was going to have a baby.
And in the brothels of Marrakesh[8]
the little pockmarked prostitutes   50
balanced their tea-trays on their heads
and did their belly-dances; flung themselves
naked and giggling against our knees,
asking for cigarettes. It was somewhere near there
I saw what frightened me most of all: 55
A holy grave, not looking particularly holy,
one of a group under a keyhole-arched stone
    baldaquin
open to every wind from the pink desert.
An open, gritty, marble trough, carved solid
with exhortation, yellowed   60
as scattered cattle-teeth;
half-filled with dust, not even the dust
of the poor prophet paynim[9] who once lay there.
In a smart burnoose[10] Khadour looked on amused.

---

[2] Engraver's tool.
[3] Capital of Newfoundland.
[4] The church in Rome.
[5] American priests from the North American
    College in Rome.
[6] Ancient Roman city in Morocco.

[7] Town in the southwest of Ireland.
[8] City in Morocco.
[9] Archaic word for an infidel, especially a
    Muslim.
[10] Hooded cloak worn by Arabs.

Everything only connected by "and" and "and."
Open the book. (The gilt rubs off the edges
of the pages and pollinates the fingertips.)
Open the heavy book. Why couldn't we have seen
this old Nativity while we were at it?
—the dark ajar, the rocks breaking with light,
an undisturbed, unbreathing flame,
colorless, sparkless, freely fed on straw,
and, lulled within, a family with pets,
—and looked and looked our infant sight away.

1955

At the Fishhouses

Although it is a cold evening,
down by one of the fishhouses
an old man sits netting,
his net, in the gloaming almost invisible
a dark purple-brown,
and his shuttle worn and polished.
The air smells so strong of codfish
it makes one's nose run and one's eyes water.
The five fishhouses have steeply peaked roofs
and narrow, cleated gangplanks slant up
to storerooms in the gables
for the wheelbarrows to be pushed up and down on.
All is silver: the heavy surface of the sea,
swelling slowly as if considering spilling over,
is opaque, but the silver of the benches,
the lobster pots, and masts, scattered
among the wild jagged rocks,
is of an apparent translucence
like the small old buildings with an emerald moss
growing on their shoreward walls.
The big fish tubs are completely lined
with layers of beautiful herring scales
and the wheelbarrows are similarly plastered
with creamy iridescent coats of mail,
with small iridescent flies crawling on them.
Up on the little slope behind the houses,
set in the sparse bright sprinkle of grass,

is an ancient wooden capstan,[1]
cracked, with two long bleached handles
and some melancholy stains, like dried blood,   30
where the ironwork has rusted.
The old man accepts a Lucky Strike.
He was a friend of my grandfather.
We talk of the decline in the population
and of codfish and herring   35
while he waits for a herring boat to come in.
There are sequins on his vest and on his thumb.
He has scraped the scales, the principal beauty,
from unnumbered fish with that black old knife,
the blade of which is almost worn away.   40

Down at the water's edge, at the place
where they haul up the boats, up the long ramp
descending into the water, thin silver
tree trunks are laid horizontally
across the gray stones, down and down   45
at intervals of four or five feet.

Cold dark deep and absolutely clear,
element bearable to no mortal,
to fish and to seals . . . One seal particularly
I have seen here evening after evening.   50
He was curious about me. He was interested in music;
like me a believer in total immersion,[2]
so I used to sing him Baptist hymns.
I also sang "A Mighty Fortress Is Our God."[3]
He stood up in the water and regarded me   55
steadily, moving his head a little,
Then he would disappear, then suddenly emerge
almost in the same spot, with a sort of shrug
as if it were against his better judgment.
Cold dark deep and absolutely clear,   60
the clear gray icy water . . . Back, behind us,
the dignified tall firs begin.
Bluish, associating with their shadows,
a million Christmas trees stand
waiting for Christmas. The water seems suspended   65
above the rounded gray and blue-gray stones.
I have seen it over and over, the same sea, the same,

---

[1] Machine for raising weights by winding cable
around a vertical rotating drum.
[2] Form of baptism practiced by some Christian
sects.

[3] Hymn of which the original German version
was written by Martin Luther (1483–1546).

slightly, indifferently swinging above the stones,
icily free above the stones,
above the stones and then the world.   70
If you should dip your hand in,
your wrist would ache immediately,
your bones would begin to ache and your hand would burn
as if the water were a transmutation of fire
that feeds on stones and burns with a dark gray flame.   75
If you tasted it, it would first taste bitter,
then briny, then surely burn your tongue.
It is like what we imagine knowledge to be:
dark, salt, clear, moving, utterly free,
drawn from the cold hard mouth   80
of the world, derived from the rocky breasts
forever, flowing and drawn, and since
our knowledge is historical, flowing, and flown.
1955

Questions of Travel

There are too many waterfalls here; the crowded streams
hurry too rapidly down to the sea,
and the pressure of so many clouds on the mountaintops
makes them spill over the sides in soft slow-motion,
turning to waterfalls under our very eyes.   5
—For if those streaks, those mile-long, shiny, tearstains,
aren't waterfalls yet,
in a quick age or so, as ages go here,
they probably will be.
But if the streams and clouds keep travelling, travelling,   10
the mountains look like the hulls of capsized ships,
slime-hung and barnacled.

Think of the long trip home.
Should we have stayed at home and thought of here?
Where should we be today?
Is it right to be watching strangers in a play   15
in this strangest of theatres?
What childishness is it that while there's a breath of life
in our bodies, we are determined to rush
to see the sun the other way around?   20
The tiniest green hummingbird in the world?
To stare at some inexplicable old stonework,

inexplicable and impenetrable,
at any view,
instantly seen and always, always delightful? 25
Oh, must we dream our dreams
and have them, too?
And have we room
for one more folded sunset, still quite warm?

But surely it would have been a pity 30
not to have seen the trees along this road,
really exaggerated in their beauty,
not to have seen them gesturing
like noble pantomimists, robed in pink.
—Not to have had to stop for gas and heard 35
the sad, two-noted, wooden tune
of disparate wooden clogs
carelessly clacking over
a grease-stained filling-station floor.
(In another country the clogs would all be tested. 40
Each pair there would have identical pitch.)
—A pity not to have heard
the other, less primitive music of the fat brown bird
who sings above the broken gasoline pump
in a bamboo church of Jesuit baroque:[1] 45
three towers, five silver crosses.
—Yes, a pity not to have pondered,
blurr'dly and inconclusively,
on what connection can exist for centuries
between the crudest wooden footwear 50
and, careful and finicky,
the whittled fantasies of wooden cages.
—Never to have studied history in
the weak calligraphy of songbirds' cages.
—And never to have had to listen to rain 55
so much like politicians' speeches:
two hours of unrelenting oratory
and then a sudden golden silence
in which the traveller takes a notebook, writes:

"Is it lack of imagination that makes us come 60
to imagined places, not just stay at home?
Or could Pascal[2] have been not entirely right
about just sitting quietly in one's room?

[1] Style of architecture introduced into South
America in the seventeenth century by Jesuit
missionaries.

[2] Blaise Pascal, French philosopher (1623–1662).

Continent, city, country, society:
the choice is never wide and never free.
And here, or there . . . No. Should we have stayed at home,
wherever that may be?"
1965

The Armadillo

(For Robert Lowell)

This is the time of year
when almost every night
the frail, illegal fire balloons appear.
Climbing the mountain height,

rising toward a saint   5
still honored in these parts,
the paper chambers flush and fill with light
that comes and goes, like hearts.

Once up against the sky it's hard
to tell them from the stars—   10
planets, that is—the tinted ones:
Venus going down, or Mars,

or the pale green one. With a wind,
they flare and falter, wobble and toss;
but if it's still they steer between   15
the kite sticks of the Southern Cross,[1]

receding, dwindling, solemnly
and steadily forsaking us,
or, in the downdraft from a peak,
suddenly turning dangerous.   20

Last night another big one fell.
It splattered like an egg of fire
against the cliff behind the house.
The flame ran down. We saw the pair

of owls who nest there flying up   25
and up, their whirling black-and-white

---

[1] Constellation visible only in the Southern
hemisphere.

stained bright pink underneath, until
they shrieked up out of sight.

The ancient owls' nest must have burned.
Hastily, all alone,   30
a glistening armadillo left the scene,
rose-flecked, head down, tail down,

and then a baby rabbit jumped out,
short-eared, to our surprise.
So soft!—a handful of intangible ash   35
with fixed, ignited eyes.

Too pretty, dreamlike mimicry!
O falling fire and piercing cry
and panic, and a weak mailed fist
clenched ignorant against the sky!   40
1965

Sestina

September rain falls on the house.
In the failing light, the old grandmother
sits in the kitchen with the child
beside the Little Marvel Stove,
reading the jokes from the almanac,   5
laughing and talking to hide her tears.

She thinks that her equinoctial[1] tears
and the rain that beats on the roof of the house
were both foretold by the almanac,
but only known to a grandmother.   10
The iron kettle sings on the stove.
She cuts some bread and says to the child,

It's time for tea now; but the child
is watching the teakettle's small hard tears
dance like mad on the hot black stove,   15
the way the rain must dance on the house.

[1] At the time of the (autumn) equinox; an
oblique reference to September rain.

Tidying up, the old grandmother
hangs up the clever almanac

on its string. Bird-like, the almanac
hovers half open above the child,   2[0]
hovers above the old grandmother
and her teacup full of dark brown tears.
She shivers and says she thinks the house
feels chilly, and puts more wood in the stove.

It was to be, says the Marvel Stove.   25
I know what I know, says the almanac.
With crayons the child draws a rigid house
and a winding pathway. Then the child
puts in a man with buttons like tears
and shows it proudly to the grandmother.   30

But secretly, while the grandmother
busies herself about the stove,
the little moons fall down like tears
from between the pages of the almanac
into the flower bed the child   35
has carefully placed in the front of the house.

Time to plant tears, says the almanac.
The grandmother sings to the marvellous stove
and the child draws another inscrutable house.

1965

Filling Station

Oh, but it is dirty!
—this little filling station,
oil-soaked, oil-permeated
to a disturbing, over-all
black translucency.   5
Be careful with that match!

Father wears a dirty,
oil-soaked monkey suit

that cuts him under the arms,
and several quick and saucy   10
and greasy sons assist him
(it's a family filling station),
all quite thoroughly dirty.

Do they live in the station?
It has a cement porch   15
behind the pumps, and on it
a set of crushed and grease-
impregnated wickerwork;
on the wicker sofa
a dirty dog, quite comfy.   20

Some comic books provide
the only note of color—
of certain color. They lie
upon a big dim doily
draping a taboret   25
(part of the set), beside
a big hirsute begonia.

Why the extraneous plant?
Why the taboret?
Why, oh why, the doily?   30
(Embroidered in daisy stitch
with marguerites, I think,
and heavy with gray crochet.)

Somebody embroidered the doily.
Somebody waters the plant,   35
or oils it, maybe. Somebody
arranges the rows of cans
so that they softly say:
ESSO—SO—SO—SO
to high-strung automobiles.   40
Somebody loves us all.
1965

In the Waiting Room

In Worcester, Massachusetts,
I went with Aunt Consuelo
to keep her dentist's appointment
and sat and waited for her
in the dentist's waiting room.   5
It was winter. It got dark
early. The waiting room
was full of grown-up people,
arctics and overcoats,
lamps and magazines.   10
My aunt was inside
what seemed like a long time
and while I waited I read
the *National Geographic*
(I could read) and carefully   15
studied the photographs:
the inside of a volcano,
black, and full of ashes;
then it was spilling over
in rivulets of fire.   20
Osa and Martin Johnson[1]
dressed in riding breeches,
laced boots, and pith helmets.
A dead man slung on a pole
—"Long Pig,"[2] the caption said.   25
Babies with pointed heads
wound round and round with string;
black, naked women with necks
wound round and round with wire
like the necks of light bulbs.   30
Their breasts were horrifying.
I read it right straight through.
I was too shy to stop.
And then I looked at the cover:
the yellow margins, the date.   35

Suddenly, from inside,
came an *oh!* of pain

---

[1] Osa Johnson (1894–1953) and Martin Johnson
(1884–1937), tropical explorers and authors of
travel books.

[2] Name given by cannibals to a dead man to be
eaten.

—Aunt Consuelo's voice—
not very loud or long.
I wasn't at all surprised;   40
even then I knew she was
a foolish, timid woman.
I might have been embarrassed,
but wasn't. What took me
completely by surprise   45
was that it was *me:*
my voice, in my mouth.
Without thinking at all
I was my foolish aunt,
I—we—were falling, falling,   50
our eyes glued to the cover
of the National Geographic,
February, 1918.

I said to myself: three days
and you'll be seven years old.   55
I was saying it to stop
the sensation of falling off
the round, turning world
into cold, blue-black space.
But I felt: you are an *I,*   60
you are an *Elizabeth,*
you are one of *them.*
Why should you be one, too?
I scarcely dared to look
to see what it was I was.   65
I gave a sidelong glance
—I couldn't look any higher—
at shadowy gray knees,
trousers and skirts and boots
and different pairs of hands   70
lying under the lamps.
I knew that nothing stranger
had ever happened, that nothing
stranger could ever happen.
Why should I be my aunt,   75
or me, or anyone?
What similarities—
boots, hands, the family voice
I felt in my throat, or even
the National Geographic   80
and those awful hanging breasts—
held us all together
or made us all just one?

How—I didn't know any
word for it—how "unlikely" . . .   8
How had I come to be here,
like them, and overhear
a cry of pain that could have
got loud and worse but hadn't?

The waiting room was bright   9(
and too hot. It was sliding
beneath a big black wave,
another, and another.

Then I was back in it.
The War was on. Outside,   9!
in Worcester, Massachusetts,
were night and slush and cold,
and it was still the fifth
of February, 1918.
1976

Robert Hayden
1913–1980

Robert Hayden's two most ambitious poems directly confront the intolerable social evil of slavery by retelling the history of slave rebellions. "Middle Passage" recounts the seizure of the slave ship *Amistad* by Cinquez, one of the slaves being transported in the "middle passage" from Africa to America. "Runagate Runagate" retells the 1849 escape from slavery of Harriet Tubman, who subsequently led more than three hundred slaves to freedom. Hayden's form of protest poetry is solidly rooted in historical antecedents, as though to argue that one cannot write about the phenomenon of racism without understanding its historical causes. In this way he differs both from the black writers who confined themselves to the contemporary plight of blacks in American society and from those who tried to write conventional "English" poetry on conventional themes.

Hayden was a learned poet. He received a B.A. from Detroit City College (now Wayne State University) in 1942, at the age of twenty-nine, but he had already won the Hopwood Award for poetry at the University of Michigan in 1938 and in 1942, and had published his first book, *Heart-Shaped in the Dust,* in 1940. After returning to Michigan to take an M.A., he taught at Fisk University for twenty-three years, eventually leaving Fisk to become professor of English at Michigan, where he taught until his death.

Hayden's poems appeared, after 1940, in successive arrestingly named volumes: *A Ballad of Remembrance* (1962), *Words in Mourning Time* (1970), *The Night-Blooming Cereus* (1972), *Angle of Ascent* (1975), and *American Journal*

(1978). His poetry ranged through many subjects and forms; it was marked by a consistent experimentation in voices, allusiveness, patterns on the page, and choice of speaker. He wished to avoid writing agitprop verse, and his career offers an implicit rebuke to an aesthetic that would disregard the importance of form in art. Hayden once said:

> I write poetry because I prefer it to prose, for one thing. Because, for another, I'm driven, impelled to make patterns of words in the special ways that poetry demands. . . . I suppose I could say, with fear of contradicting myself later, that writing poetry is one way I have of coming to grips with both inner and external realities. I also think of my writing as a form of prayer—a prayer for illumination, perfection.

Hayden's example has been important for such subsequent black poets as Michael Harper and Rita Dove. The poetic implicit in his work, and theirs, is a reconstructive one: The contemporary black poet must speak not only for living blacks but also for all the dead blacks deprived of voice. The voice of the living, it suggests, cannot be properly vocal if it does not know its own antecedents. It will be thin if it speaks out of the present alone, depriving the present of the very past that constituted it. The past of slavery, peculiar to blacks, is preserved, Hayden's poetry suggests, in the consciousness and imagination of blacks, and a poetry that represses it is bound to falsify. Michael Harper's allusions to black history and Rita Dove's recreations of slave voices are attempts to enlarge and consolidate Hayden's model—a poetic language committed to adequate historical self-knowledge.

At the same time, Hayden was a vigorous commentator on the general American scene. In the late poem "American Journal" he adopted the voice of a visiting alien from outer space, reporting on America:

> There among them the americans this baffling
> multi people extremes and variegations their
> noise restlessness their almost frightening
> energy . . .

As he studies these "charming savages enlightened primitives brash / new comers lately sprung up in our galaxy," the alien commentator takes precisely the very tone that whites have often used historically about blacks. Hayden's ironic social mirror silently shows American society in a devastating light. In 1985, Hayden's *Complete Poems* appeared, making widely available once again the work of a neglected American poet.

Text:
Angle of Ascent, 1966.

Those Winter Sundays

Sundays too my father got up early
and put his clothes on in the blueblack cold,
then with cracked hands that ached
from labor in the weekday weather made
banked fires blaze. No one ever thanked him.   5

I'd wake and hear the cold splintering, breaking.
When the rooms were warm, he'd call,
and slowly I would rise and dress,
fearing the chronic angers of that house,

Speaking indifferently to him,   10
who had driven out the cold
and polished my good shoes as well.
What did I know, what did I know
of love's austere and lonely offices?
1966

Middle Passage[1]

I

Jesús, Estrella, Esperanza, Mercy:[2]

Sails flashing to the wind like weapons,
sharks following the moans the fever and the dying;
horror the corposant[3] and compass rose.

Middle Passage:
            voyage through death   5
                        to life upon these shores.

"10 April 1800—
Blacks rebellious. Crew uneasy. Our linguist says

---

[1] The passage of slave ships from Africa to the New World.
[2] Names of slave ships. The irony of names like *Jesus, Star, Hope,* and *Mercy* is evident.
[3] St. Elmo's fire.

their moaning is a prayer for death, 10
ours and their own. Some try to starve themselves.
Lost three this morning leaped with crazy laughter
to the waiting sharks, sang as they went under."

Desire, Adventure, Tartar, Ann:

Standing to America, bringing home 15
black gold, black ivory, black seed.

> *Deep in the festering hold thy father lies,*
> *of his bones New England pews are made,*
> *those are altar lights that were his eyes.*[4]

Jesus   Saviour   Pilot   Me 20
Over   Life's   Tempestuous   Sea

We pray that Thou wilt grant, O Lord,
safe passage to our vessels bringing
heathen souls unto Thy chastening.

Jesus Saviour 25
    "8 bells. I cannot sleep, for I am sick
    with fear, but writing eases fear a little
    since still my eyes can see these words take shape
    upon the page & so I write, as one
    would turn to exorcism. 4 days scudding, 30
    but now the sea is calm again. Misfortune
    follows in our wake like sharks (our grinning
    tutelary gods). Which one of us
    has killed an albatross?[5] A plague among
    our blacks—Ophthalmia: blindness—& we 35
    have jettisoned the blind to no avail.
    It spreads, the terrifying sickness spreads.
    Its claws have scratched sight from the Capt.'s eyes
    & there is blindness in the fo'c'sle
    & we must sail 3 weeks before we come 40
    to port."

> *What port awaits us, Davy Jones*[6]
> *or home? I've heard of slavers drifting, drifting,*
> *playthings of wind and storm and chance, their crews*

---

[4] Allusion to Ariel's song in Shakespeare's *The Tempest:* "'Full fathom five thy father lies; Of his bones are coral made; Those are pearls that were his eyes. . . .'"

[5] The killing of an albatross was thought to bring bad luck.

[6] In nautical vernacular the sea bottom is called "Davy Jones' locker."

> *gone blind, the jungle hatred*
> *crawling up on deck.*

4

Thou Who Walked On Galilee

"Deponent further sayeth *The Bella*
left the Guinea Coast
with cargo of five hundred blacks and odd
for the barracoons[7] of Florida:

50

"That there was hardly room 'tween–decks for half
the sweltering cattle stowed spoon-fashion there;
that some went mad of thirst and tore their flesh
and sucked the blood:

55

"That Crew and Captain lusted with the comeliest
of the savage girls kept naked in the cabins;
that there was one they called The Guinea Rose
and they cast lots and fought to lie with her:

"That when the Bo's'n piped all hands, the flames
spreading from starboard already were beyond
control, the negroes howling and their chains
entangled with the flames:

60

"That the burning blacks could not be reached,
that the Crew abandoned ship,
leaving their shrieking negresses behind,
that the Captain perished drunken with the wenches:

65

"Further Deponent sayeth not."

Pilot   Oh   Pilot   Me

II

Aye, lad, and I have seen those factories,
Gambia, Rio Pongo, Calabar;
have watched the artful mongos baiting traps
of war wherein the victor and the vanquished

70

Were caught as prizes for our barracoons.
Have seen the nigger kings whose vanity
and greed turned wild black hides of Fellatah,
Mandingo, Ibo, Kru[8] to gold for us.

75

---

[7] Barracks for slaves.   [8] African tribes.

And there was one—King Anthracite we named him—
fetish face beneath French parasols
of brass and orange velvet, impudent mouth   80
whose cups were carven skulls of enemies:

He'd honor us with drum and feast and conjo
and palm-oil-glistening wenches deft in love,
and for tin crowns that shone with paste,
red calico and German-silver trinkets   85

Would have the drums talk war and send
his warriors to burn the sleeping villages
and kill the sick and old and lead the young
in coffles[9] to our factories.

Twenty years a trader, twenty years,   90
for there was wealth aplenty to be harvested
from those black fields, and I'd be trading still
but for the fevers melting down my bones.

III

Shuttles in the rocking loom of history,
the dark ships move, the dark ships move,   95
their bright ironical names
like jests of kindness on a murderer's mouth;
plough through thrashing glister toward
fata morgana's[10] lucent melting shore,
weave toward New World littorals that are   100
mirage and myth and actual shore.

Voyage through death,
                    voyage whose chartings are unlove.

A charnel stench, effluvium of living death
spreads outward from the hold,   105
where the living and the dead, the horribly dying,
lie interlocked, lie foul with blood and excrement.

> *Deep in the festering hold thy father lies,*
> *the corpse of mercy rots with him,*
> *rats eat love's rotten gelid eyes.*   110
> But, oh, the living look at you
> *with human eyes whose suffering accuses you,*

---

[9] Manacled together in a group.   [10] Fata morgana: mirage.

whose hatred reaches through the swill of dark
to strike you like a leper's claw.

You cannot stare that hatred down
or chain the fear that stalks the watches
and breathes on you its fetid scorching breath;
cannot kill the deep immortal human wish,
the timeless will.

"But for the storm that flung up barriers
of wind and wave, *The Amistad,*[11] señores,
would have reached the port of Principe[12] in two,
three days at most; but for the storm we should
have been prepared for what befell.
Swift as the puma's leap it came. There was
that interval of moonless calm filled only
with the water's and the rigging's usual sounds,
then sudden movement, blows and snarling cries
and they had fallen on us with machete
and marlinspike. It was as though the very
air, the night itself were striking us.
Exhausted by the rigors of the storm,
we were no match for them. Our men went down
before the murderous Africans. Our loyal
Celestino ran from below with gun
and lantern and I saw, before the cane-
knife's wounding flash, Cinquez,
that surly brute who calls himself a prince,
directing, urging on the ghastly work.
He hacked the poor mulatto down, and then
he turned on me. The decks were slippery
when daylight finally came. It sickens me
to think of what I saw, of how these apes
threw overboard the butchered bodies of
our men, true Christians all, like so much jetsam.
Enough, enough. The rest is quickly told:
Cinquez was forced to spare the two of us
you see to steer the ship to Africa,
and we like phantoms doomed to rove the sea
voyaged east by day and west by night,
deceiving them, hoping for rescue,
prisoners on our own vessel, till
at length we drifted to the shores of this
your land, America, where we were freed
from our unspeakable misery. Now we

[11] The ship's name: *Friendship.*   [12] Portuguese island in the Atlantic Ocean.

demand, good sirs, the extradition of
Cinquez and his accomplices to La
Havana.[13] And it distresses us to know
there are so many here who seem inclined
to justify the mutiny of these blacks.   160
We find it paradoxical indeed
that you whose wealth, whose tree of liberty
are rooted in the labor of your slaves
should suffer the august John Quincy Adams
to speak with so much passion of the right   165
of chattel slaves to kill their lawful masters
and with his Roman rhetoric weave a hero's
garland for Cinquez. I tell you that
we are determined to return to Cuba
with our slaves and there see justice done. Cinquez—   170
or let us say 'the Prince'—Cinquez shall die."

The deep immortal human wish,
the timeless will:

    Cinquez its deathless primaveral image,
    life that transfigures many lives.   175

Voyage through death
                 to life upon these shores.

1966

Randall Jarrell
1914–1965

Randall Jarrell (the accent is on the second syllable) was a divided soul, half
critic, half poet. By the time of his early death (he walked either by accident or
design into the path of a car on a freeway), he was the best-known critic of
poetry in America, serving as poetry editor of *The Nation* (1946) and writing
brilliantly witty essays on American poetry from Whitman to Elizabeth Bishop.
His essay on Whitman helped restore Whitman to the American pantheon of
poets, he understood Marianne Moore better than anyone else, and he greeted
(from his privileged position as Robert Lowell's college roommate) Lowell's first
book of verse, *Lord Weary's Castle* (1946), as the achievement of a major poet. It
was his own poetic sensibility, of course, that made Jarrell's criticism so acute; he
saw into the workings of verse with a poet's eye. And his criticism was also a
reflection of his rapid, abrasive, allusive, and mercurial conversation that made

---

[13] In Cuba.

willing hearers of his gifted friends—Lowell, Peter Taylor, John Berryman. Jarrell's critical books—*Poetry and the Age* (1953), *A Sad Heart at the Supermarket* (1962), and *The Third Book of Criticism* (1971)—brought American poetry reviewing from a generally depressing exhibition of puffery to the level of a high accomplishment.

Yet Jarrell's own heart was with his poetry, where he wrote chiefly with a yearning pity for the fallibility, weakness, and sadness of human beings. He could insert himself with uncanny insight into the mind of his characters. That Keatsian degree of empathy may have been what led him to major in psychology at Vanderbilt; Freud was to become one of his major intellectual points of reference. In going to Vanderbilt, Jarrell was remaining in Nashville, where he had been born and had lived since the age of twelve. Yet the impressionable years of his early childhood had been spent in California, and a deep nostalgia for Hollywood, where he had lived for a year with his grandparents, never left him. He called it his "lost world" in the reminiscent title poem of his last book (1965), and its movie lots, with their temporary fantasy constructions, were for him symbols of the imagination.

Jarrell took an M.A. in English from Vanderbilt in 1938 and, except for his military service from 1942 to 1946, spent the rest of his life teaching in various colleges, notably Kenyon, the University of Texas, Sarah Lawrence, Princeton, and the Women's College of the University of North Carolina (1947–1965, with occasional interruptions). Jarrell first became known for his poignant war poetry. He had served in the air force in World War II, and his first volumes, *Little Friend, Little Friend* (1945) and *Losses* (1948), show soldiers as pitiful high school boys plunged, unequipped and ignorant, into war, bombing, and death. In 1965, after a long and brilliant career, Jarrell was hospitalized for a nervous breakdown; he died not long thereafter. His *Complete Poems* appeared posthumously, in 1969.

Jarrell liked the English blank verse line, adapted (via the example of Frost) to American speech rhythms; he was also capable (as in "Next Day") of beautiful inventions in stanza form and rhyme scheme. He had an eye for the poetry of the ordinary ("Moving from Cheer to Joy, from Joy to All"), and his rendering of the pathos of a young soldier, of a woman in a supermarket or at a zoo, of a girl falling asleep over her homework, is exact and touching.

Further Reading:

Randall Jarrell, 1914–1965, ed. R. Lowell, P. Taylor, and R. P. Warren, 1967.
K. Shapiro, *Randall Jarrell*, 1967.
The Achievement of Randall Jarrell, ed. F. Hoffman, 1970.
S. Ferguson, *The Poetry of Randall Jarrell*, 1971.
M. L. Rosenthal, *Randall Jarrell*, 1972.

H. Hagenbuchle, *The Black Goddess: A Study of the Archetypal Feminine in the Poetry of Randall Jarrell*, 1975.
B. Quinn, *Randall Jarrell*, 1981.
S. Ferguson, *Critical Essays on Randall Jarrell*, 1983.

Text:

Complete Poems, 1969.
See also *Poetry and the Age*, 1953.
Pictures from an Institution, 1954.

A Sad Heart at the Supermarket, 1962.
The Third Book of Criticism, 1969.

The Death of the Ball Turret[1] Gunner

From my mother's sleep I fell into the State,
And I hunched in its belly till my wet fur froze.
Six miles from earth, loosed from its dream of life,
I woke to black flak and the nightmare fighters.
When I died they washed me out of the turret with a hose.   5

1955

Losses

It was not dying: everybody died.
It was not dying: we had died before
In the routine crashes—and our fields
Called up the papers, wrote home to our folks,
And the rates rose, all because of us.   5
We died on the wrong page of the almanac,
Scattered on mountains fifty miles away;
Diving on haystacks, fighting with a friend,
We blazed up on the lines we never saw.
We died like aunts or pets or foreigners.   10
(When we left high school nothing else had died
For us to figure we had died like.)

In our new planes, with our new crews, we bombed
The ranges by the desert or the shore,
Fired at towed targets, waited for our scores—   15
And turned into replacements and woke up
One morning, over England, operational.
It wasn't different: but if we died
It was not an accident but a mistake

[1] A *ball turret* was a revolvable plexiglass sphere set into the underside of a B-17 or B-24 bomber, from which a man, in a crouched position, could fire a mounted .50 caliber machine gun at other aircraft aloft.

(But an easy one for anyone to make).
We read our mail and counted up our missions—
In bombers named for girls, we burned
The cities we had learned about in school—
Till our lives wore out; our bodies lay among
The people we had killed and never seen.
When we lasted long enough they gave us medals;
When we died they said, "Our casualties were low."
They said, "Here are the maps"; we burned the cities.

It was not dying—no, not ever dying;
But the night I died I dreamed that I was dead,
And the cities said to me: "Why are you dying?
We are satisfied, if you are; but why did I die?"
1955

A Lullaby

For wars his life and half a world away
The soldier sells his family and days.
He learns to fight for freedom and the State;
He sleeps with seven men within six feet.

He picks up matches and he cleans out plates;   5
Is lied to like a child, cursed like a beast.
They crop his head, his dog tags ring like sheep
As his stiff limbs shift wearily to sleep.

Recalled in dreams or letters, else forgot,
His life is smothered like a grave, with dirt;   10
And his dull torment mottles like a fly's
The lying amber of the histories.
1955

The Woman at the Washington Zoo

The saris¹ go by me from the embassies.

Cloth from the moon. Cloth from another planet.
They look back at the leopard like the leopard.

And I. . . .
    this print of mine, that has kept its color   5
Alive through so many cleanings; this dull null
Navy I wear to work, and wear from work, and so
To my bed, so to my grave, with no
Complaints, no comment: neither from my chief,
The Deputy Chief Assistant, nor his chief—   10
Only I complain. . . . this serviceable
Body that no sunlight dyes, no hand suffuses
But, dome-shadowed, withering among columns,
Wavy beneath fountains—small, far-off, shining
In the eyes of animals, these beings trapped   15
As I am trapped but not, themselves, the trap,
Aging, but without knowledge of their age,
Kept safe here, knowing not of death, for death—
Oh, bars of my own body, open, open!

The world goes by my cage and never sees me.   20
And there come not to me, as come to these,
The wild beasts, sparrows pecking the llamas' grain,
Pigeons settling on the bears' bread, buzzards
Tearing the meat the flies have clouded. . . .
            Vulture,   25
When you come for the white rat that the foxes left,
Take off the red helmet of your head, the black
Wings that have shadowed me, and step to me as man:
The wild brother at whose feet the white wolves fawn,
To whose hand of power the great lioness   30
Stalks, purring. . . .
      You know what I was,
You see what I am: change me, change me!

1960

¹ Long flowing garments worn by women of
India.

Next Day

Moving from Cheer to Joy, from Joy to All,
I take a box
And add it to my wild rice, my Cornish game hens.
The slacked or shorted, basketed, identical
Food-gathering flocks   5
Are selves I overlook. Wisdom, said William James,[1]

Is learning what to overlook. And I am wise
If that is wisdom.
Yet somehow, as I buy All from these shelves
And the boy takes it to my station wagon,   10
What I've become
Troubles me even if I shut my eyes.

When I was young and miserable and pretty
And poor, I'd wish
What all girls wish: to have a husband,   15
A house and children. Now that I'm old, my wish
Is womanish:
That the boy putting groceries in my car

See me. It bewilders me he doesn't see me.
For so many years   20
I was good enough to eat: the world looked at me
And its mouth watered. How often they have undressed me,
The eyes of strangers!
And, holding their flesh within my flesh, their vile

Imaginings within my imagining,   25
I too have taken
The chance of life. Now the boy pats my dog
And we start home. Now I am good.
The last mistaken,
Ecstatic, accidental bliss, the blind   30

Happiness that, bursting, leaves upon the palm
Some soap and water—
It was so long ago, back in some Gay
Twenties, Nineties, I don't know . . . Today I miss

[1] American philosopher and psychologist
(1842–1910).

My lovely daughter   35
Away at school, my sons away at school,

My husband away at work—I wish for them.
The dog, the maid,
And I go through the sure unvarying days
At home in them. As I look at my life,   40
I am afraid
Only that it will change, as I am changing:

I am afraid, this morning, of my face.
It looks at me
From the rear-view mirror, with the eyes I hate,   45
The smile I hate. Its plain, lined look
Of gray discovery
Repeats to me: "You're old." That's all, I'm old.

And yet I'm afraid, as I was at the funeral
I went to yesterday.   50
My friend's cold made-up face, granite among its flowers,
Her undressed, operated-on, dressed body
Were my face and body.
As I think of her I hear her telling me

How young I seem; I *am* exceptional;   55
I think of all I have.
But really no one is exceptional,
No one has anything, I'm anybody,
I stand beside my grave
Confused with my life, that is commonplace and solitary.   60

1965

John Berryman
1914–1972

John Berryman's fame rests chiefly on the odd personal language he invented in
77 Dream Songs (1964), a compound of baby talk, slang, minstrel-show imitation
of black English, deviant grammar and syntax, and intimate address. This
language, derived in part from the syntactic and grammatical disruptions of
Gerard Manley Hopkins and E. E. Cummings, appeared in extended form in
Berryman's long dramatic poem "Homage to Mistress Bradstreet" (1956). This
explosive poem, coming after Berryman's earlier imitations of William Butler
Yeats, W. H. Auden, and Hopkins in *The Dispossessed* (1948), represented
Berryman's discovery of his Americanness, through his identification with Ann

Bradstreet, the first American poet. It also enabled Berryman to find his true topic, the utterance of what Freud would have called the id, the irrepressible vehemence of pure untutored and uncivilized desire.

The division of Berryman's self into two voices—the one American and untamable, the other a reproachful voice, whether of an inhibited English "literary" superego or of the conscience—mirrors his own division in life. On the one hand, he was a formidable scholar, critic, and teacher, author of a Columbia Ph.D. thesis on the writer Stephen Crane (published as a book in 1950), and author as well of brilliant critical essays posthumously collected as *The Freedom of the Poet* (1976). On the other hand, he was a rebellious student, an alcoholic in adult life, and finally a suicide (he leaped from a bridge in Minneapolis) after he despaired of curing his alcoholism.

Berryman's true name was John Smith. His father, a banker, committed suicide by shooting himself when Berryman was twelve, and Berryman adopted the name of the man whom his adoring and possessive mother subsequently married. After private school in Connecticut, Berryman received his B.A. in 1936 from Columbia and, as the ranking English scholar, was awarded a Kellett fellowship to Clare College of Cambridge University in England. The ambitious, intense, and exploratory years at Cambridge are recalled in *Love and Fame* (1970).

Berryman taught at Wayne State, Harvard, and Princeton; in 1955 he joined the faculty of the University of Minnesota, where he continued to teach until his death. Among the pieces included in *The Freedom of the Poet* is an account, in fictional form, of Berryman's class on Milton's "Lycidas"; the story conveys the intensity and passion behind Berryman's teaching. At the same time, Berryman's alcoholic illness, complicated by addiction to sedatives and tranquilizers, caused more and more unpredictable and undependable behavior; his immense learning and conversational charm protected him for some time, but in his last years his self-destructive behavior affected his private and public life and his writing. These desperate later years are chronicled in Berryman's novel *Recovery* (published posthumously in 1973, with an introduction by Saul Bellow).

"Huffy Henry" is the character Berryman invented in his *Dream Songs* to speak for the id. Henry—sulky, eager, manic and depressive by turns—craves the whole world but is haunted by a nameless and all-encompassing guilt:

> But never did Henry, as he thought he did,
> end anyone and hacks her body up
> and hide the pieces, where they may be found.
> He knows: he went over everyone, & nobody's missing.

Berryman's Roman Catholic upbringing contributes to Henry's sense of a religious standard that condemns his uncontrolled desires. In one poem, the "profiled reproach" of a Sienese madonna oppresses him. In another, he wishes for the peace he sees in the art of a Zen garden. But such religious order and harmony elude him; he continues to act, gaze, and suffer, the more so as his friends die and his own life lurches to ruin.

If we ask why Berryman turned to splitting himself in two in *The Dream Songs,* we can answer, perhaps, by looking at his elegy for Stevens. Berryman's

critique of Wallace Stevens—that he was too cold, too narrow, too metaphysical
—suggests a self-critique. If the "scholarly" and "philosophical" Berryman seemed
inhibited to himself, he would release his more volcanic, heated, physical self in
the person of Henry. But how should Henry speak? Where does Henry live?
And what language does Henry use? Berryman's departure in the *Dream Songs*
from his earlier practice in "Homage to Mistress Bradstreet" is to the point here:
Bradstreet lives in history, Henry lives in the world of desire and dream;
Bradstreet speaks, Henry sings; Bradstreet uses adult language, Henry uses an
invented language of the unconscious. Henry has only one formal resource—a
three-stanza, eighteen-line song into which all content spills and in which it is
contained. Elegance, comedy, pathos, and horror meet in Henry's songs. It is the
comedy with which Berryman's tragic topics are treated that is striking. Robert
Lowell, in his elegy for Berryman, realized "how we differ: humor." The black
humor of the songs, their violent beauty, and their suicidal momentum make
them part of literature. They continue the line of song in the lyric, a line that
interested, among others, Shakespeare, Blake, Yeats, and Auden but that had been
neglected by the earlier American modernists (except for Frost and Cummings)
until revived by Berryman.

Further Reading:
W. J. Martz, *John Berryman*, 1969.
J. M. Linebarger, *John Berryman*, 1974.
J. Conarroe, *John Berryman: An Introduction to
the Poetry*, 1977.
G. Arpin, *The Poetry of John Berryman*, 1978.
J. Haffenden, *John Berryman: A Critical
Commentary*, 1980.
J. Haffenden, *The Life of John Berryman*, 1982.

Texts:
Through "77" from *77 Dream Songs*, 1964.
Remaining "Dream Songs" from *His Toy, His
Dream, His Rest*, 1968.
Other poems from *Henry's Fate*, 1977.

---

from The Dream Songs*

1

Huffy Henry hid   the day,
unappeasable Henry sulked.
I see his point,—a trying to put things over.
It was the thought that they thought
they could *do* it made Henry wicked & away.   5
But he should have come out and talked.

All the world like a woolen lover
once did seem on Henry's side.

---

* The first of Berryman's Dream Songs were
published as *77 Dream Songs* in 1964. More
Dream Songs appeared in *His Toy; His Dream;*

His Rest in 1968. *The Dream Songs* (1969)
combines the poems of these two groups in
sequence.

Then came a departure.
Thereafter nothing fell out as it might or ought.   10
I don't see how Henry, pried
open for all the world to see, survived.

What he has now to say is a long
wonder the world can bear & be.
Once in a sycamore I was glad   15
all at the top, and I sang.
Hard on the land wears the strong sea
and empty grows every bed.
     1964

4

Filling her compact & delicious body
with chicken páprika, she glanced at me
twice.
Fainting with interest, I hungered back
and only the fact of her husband & four other people   5
kept me from springing on her

or falling at her little feet and crying
'You are the hottest one for years of night
Henry's dazed eyes
have enjoyed, Brilliance.' I advanced upon   10
(despairing) my spumoni.[1] —Sir Bones: is stuffed,
de world, wif feeding girls.

—Black hair, complexion Latin, jewelled eyes
downcast . . . The slob beside her   feasts . . . What wonders is
she sitting on, over there?
The restaurant buzzes. She might as well be on Mars.   15
Where did it all go wrong? There ought to be a law against Henry.
—Mr. Bones: there is.
1964

5

Henry sats in de bar & was odd,
off in the glass from the glass,
at odds wif de world & its god,
his wife is a complete nothing,

---

[1] Italian ice cream.

St Stephen[2]   5
getting even.

Henry sats in de plane & was gay.
Careful Henry nothing said aloud
but where a Virgin[3] out of cloud
to her Mountain dropt in light,   10
his thought made pockets & the plane buckt.
'Parm me, lady.' 'Orright.'

Henry lay in de netting,[4] wild,
while the brainfever bird did scales;
Mr Heartbreak, the New Man,   15
come to farm a crazy land;
an image of the dead on the fingernail
of a newborn child.
1964

14

Life, friends, is boring. We must not say so.
After all, the sky flashes, the great sea yearns,
we ourselves flash and yearn,
and moreover my mother told me as a boy
(repeatingly) 'Ever to confess you're bored   5
means you have no

Inner Resources.' I conclude now I have no
inner resources, because I am heavy bored.
Peoples bore me,
literature bores me, especially great literature,   10
Henry bores me, with his plights & gripes
as bad as achilles,[5]

who loves people and valiant art, which bores me.
And the tranquil hills, & gin, look like a drag
and somehow a dog   15
has taken itself & its tail considerably away
into mountains or sea or sky, leaving
behind: me, wag.
1964

---

[2] First martyr of the Christian church; he was
stoned to death, without resisting his attackers.
[3] The Virgin Mary.

[4] Mosquito netting.
[5] Hero of the *Iliad*. His anger at his fellow
Greeks keeps him from joining them in battle.

26

The glories of the world struck me, made me aria,[6] once.
—What happen then, Mr Bones?
if be you cares to say.
—Henry. Henry became interested in women's bodies,
his loins were & were the   scene of stupendous achievement.   5
Stupor. Knees, dear. Pray.

All the knobs & softnesses of, my God,
the ducking & trouble it swarm on Henry,
at one time.
—What happen then, Mr Bones?   10
you seems excited-like.
—Fell Henry back into   the original crime: art, rime

besides a sense of others, my God, my God,
and a jealousy for the honour (alive) of his country,
what can get more odd?   15
and discontent with the thriving gangs & pride.
—What happen then, Mr. Bones?
—I had a most marvellous   piece of luck. I died.
1964

29

There sat down, once, a thing on Henry's heart
só heavy, if he had a hundred years
& more, & weeping, sleepless, in all them time
Henry could not make good.
Starts again always in Henry's ears   5
the little cough somewhere, an odour, a chime.

And there is another thing he has in mind
like a grave Sienese face[7] a thousand years
would fail to blur the still profiled reproach of. Ghastly,
with open eyes, he attends, blind.   10
All the bells say: too late. This is not for tears;
thinking.

But never did Henry, as he thought he did,
end anyone and hacks her body up
and hide the pieces, where they may be found.   15
He knows: he went over everyone, & nobody's missing.
Often he reckons, in the dawn, them up.
Nobody is ever missing.
1964

---

[6] I.e., sing an operatic song.
[7] The face of a saint or Virgin in a painting of   the Sienese school (thirteenth to fourteenth century).

45

He stared at ruin. Ruin stared straight back.
He thought they was old friends. He felt on the stair
where her papa found them bare
they became familiar. When the papers were lost
rich with pals' secrets, he thought he had the knack   5
of ruin. Their paths crossed

and once they crossed in jail; they crossed in bed;
and over an unsigned letter their eyes met,
and in an Asian city
directionless & lurchy at two & three,   10
or trembling to a telephone's fresh threat,
and when some wired his head

to reach a wrong opinion, 'Epileptic'.
But he noted now that: they were not old friends.
He did not know this one.   15
This one was a stranger, come to make amends
for all the imposters, and to make it stick.
Henry nodded, un-.

1964

77

Seedy Henry rose up shy in de world
& shaved & swung his barbells, duded Henry up
and p.a.'d[8] poor thousands of persons on topics of grand
moment to Henry, ah to those less & none.
Wif a book of his in either hand   5
he is stript down to move on.

—Come away, Mr Bones.

—Henry is tired of the winter,
& haircuts, & a squeamish comfy   ruin-prone proud national mind,   & Spring
      (in the city so called).   10
Henry likes Fall.
Hé would be prepared to líve in a world of Fáll
for ever, impenitent Henry.
But the snows and summers grieve & dream;

thése fierce & airy occupations, and love,   15
raved away so many of Henry's years

---

[8] Publicly addressed.

it is a wonder that, with in each hand
one of his own mad books and all,
ancient fires for eyes, his head full
& his heart full, he's making ready to move on.

1964

164

Three limbs, three seasons smashed; well, one to go.
Henry fell smiling through the air below
and through the air above,
the middle air as well did he not neglect
but carefully in all these airs was wrecked   5
which he got truly tired of.

His friends alas went all about their ways
intact. Couldn't William break at least a collar-bone?
O world so ill arranged!
Henry holds in addition pharmacies   10
for all his other ills, pills of his own
which frequently get changed

as his despairing doctors change their minds
about what must be best for wilful Henry.
There seems to firm no answer   15
save from the sexton in the place that blinds
& stones and does not hurt: Henry springs youthfully
in his six-by-two like a dancer.

1968

219: So Long? Stevens[9]

He lifted up, among the actuaries,
a grandee crow. Ah ha & he crowed good.
That funny money-man.
Mutter we all must as well as we can.
He mutter spiffy. He make wonder Henry's   5
wits, though, with a odd

. . . something . . . something . . . not there in his flourishing art.
O veteran of death, you will not mind
a counter-mutter.
What was it missing, then, at the man's heart   10

[9] Wallace Stevens (1879–1955), American poet
and vice-president of the Hartford Insurance
company.

so that he does not wound? It is our kind
to wound, as well as utter

a fact of happy world. That metaphysics
he hefted up until we could not breathe
the physics. *On our side,*   15
monotonous (or ever-fresh)—it sticks
in Henry's throat to judge—brilliant, he seethe;
better than us; less wide.

1968

384

The marker slants, flowerless, day's almost done,
I stand above my father's grave with rage,
often, often before
I've made this awful pilgrimage to one
who cannot visit me, who tore his page   5
out: I come back for more,

I spit upon this dreadful banker's grave
who shot his heart out in a Florida dawn
O ho alas alas
When will indifference come, I moan & rave   10
I'd like to scrabble till I got right down
away down under the grass

and ax the casket open ha to see
just how he's taking it, which he sought so hard
we'll tear apart   15
the mouldering grave clothes ha & then Henry
will heft the ax once more, his final card,
and fell it on the start.

1968

[With arms outflung]

With arms outflung the clock announced: Ten-twenty.
Dozens of demons sprang & preyed on Henry.
All on a heavy morning.
The baby was ill, the sky was dark, the I

was Id,[1] somebody put the sky on like a lid,
somebody who is not returning.

Oh we'll wait. After all, after all.
The Doubter[2] & the rest. They rested all,
on the night of the crucifying.
Perhaps their dreams were something truly remarkable.
Perhaps their dreams had what to do with his dying—
but that was very lonely.

Haldol & Serax, phenobarbital,
Vivactil, by day; by deep night Tuinal
& Thorazine,[3]
kept Henry going, like a natural man.
I'm waiting for them to work, as sometimes they can,
honey, in the bloodstream.

1977

[Old codger Henry]

Old codger Henry contain within hisself
Henry young, Henry almost beautiful
Henry the seducer
Henry the mad young artist, with *no* interest in pelf
whereas now he takes steps to keep both his bank accounts full
just like: you, Sir!

Henry could never put up with litter.
Litter grew on him as he grew, until
you couldn't see his tables
for the damned *litter* of papers, glasses,
visible incoherences—& so was the floor, pal;
Henry lived like something from Aesop's Fables.

Codger Henry, desperatingly tired,
nevertheless got *fed up* with this state
which alas only he could fix.

[1] Freud's word for the unconscious portion of the mind.
[2] The Apostle Thomas, who doubted the reports of the resurrection of Christ.
[3] Haldol, etc.: major tranquilizers and antipsychotic drugs.

I draw the veil over whom then he hired
but I promise they did not solve his fate.
He bared his rare watch. *It* ticks.

1977

[All projects failed]

All projects failed, in the August afternoon
he lay & cursed himself & cursed his lot
like Housman's lad[1] forsooth.
A breeze sometimes came by. His sunburn itcht.
His wife was out on errands. He sighed & scratcht.   5
The little girls were fiddling with the telephone.

They wanted candy, the which he gave them.
His entire soul contorted with the phlegm.
The sun burned down.
Photos of him in despair flooded the town   10
or city. Mourned his many friends, or so.
The little girls were fiddling with the piano.

He crusht a cigarette out. Crusht him out
surprising God, at last, in a wink of time.
His soul was forwarded.   15
Adressat unbekannt.[2] The little girls with a shout
welcomed the dazzling package. In official rime
the official verdict was: dead.

1977

Robert Lowell
1917–1977

Robert Lowell's poems are so various in theme and form that it is difficult to
believe they were all written by the same man. With *Lord Weary's Castle* (1946),
he burst on the literary scene as a "Roman Catholic poet," writing a poetry of
social protest in icily formal meters swelling with Miltonic rage; with *Day by*

---

[1] The persona of A. E. Housman's poems *A*   [2] German: "addressee unknown."
Shropshire Lad (1896).

Day (1977), he left the American literary scene as a Horatian poet of quiet stoicism, writing verse "day by day." In having the daring to break his own aesthetic several times over, Lowell helped to reshape twentieth-century poetry. His poetic powers, trained in Greek and Latin and developed further by "imitations" of many famous European poems, were formidable.

The accident of Lowell's quasi-aristocratic birth determined his poetic life; he was a Lowell first, and a husband, lover, father, teacher, or political protester second. The other determinant of his life was his recurrent manic-depressive illness, which caused a part of almost every year of his adult life to be spent in confinement in an asylum. In the last ten years of his life his condition was stabilized by lithium. But the uncertainty of his behavior made it for a long time impossible for him to be regularly employed; his family income luckily made that unnecessary. His large poetic output has yet to be fully absorbed by critics and the public.

Robert Lowell's father was a vacant and inept man who made the mistake of leaving the navy, at his wife's insistence, to take up stockbroking. The firm kept him on for his name and social connections, but he had, according to his son's memoir, *91 Revere Street,* no clients. Lowell's mother, a Winslow by birth, was intelligent, possessive, and domineering. After an unsuccessful two years at Harvard, Lowell fled his parents and, advised by Ford Madox Ford, went off to Kenyon College to study under John Crowe Ransom. There he succeeded brilliantly, majored in classics, and was valedictorian of his class.

Lowell married the novelist Jean Stafford (all three of his wives were writers) and for a brief period became a Roman Catholic (the one thing that would most enrage his Puritan-descended family). After attempting to enlist in the navy during World War II and being refused for bad eyesight, he decided on pacifist grounds to become a conscientious objector, flouting the family naval tradition. Finally, in full mania, he wrote a letter to President Roosevelt ("I made my manic statement"), explaining his choice of conscientious objector status. After spending several months in jail, Lowell was released. Lowell's first marriage ended after bouts of drinking, insanity, and infidelity. His second, more stable marriage was to the writer Elizabeth Hardwick, who enabled him to survive moves, breakdowns, and hospitalizations. He entered psychoanalytic therapy, and the reflection on his past entailed by therapy is visible in *Life Studies* (1960), a book of pitilessly naked portraits of his family.

These poems were written in a new laconic free verse (retaining some underpinnings of rhyme) that Lowell ascribed to the influence of both Elizabeth Bishop's natural cadences and the new oral poetry of the Beats. In writing *Life Studies,* Lowell was continuing the historical portraiture of his Puritan stock that had begun in his early poems about the Winslows (whom he scandalously called "Indian killers") and Jonathan Edwards (to whom, as a Puritan intellectual of crisis mentality, he was very much drawn). *Life Studies* also records Lowell's repudiation of Roman Catholicism; here, in a symbolic decision, he leaves Rome and travels "Beyond the Alps" to Paris.

Life Studies was excoriated by Lowell's old mentor Allen Tate, who said the poems were not poetry. Seeing Lowell's agnostic stance, Catholics regretted losing an apologist. Young poets, on the other hand, recognized that Lowell had crystallized a new plain style into form. But no sooner had Lowell consolidated that free-verse style in *For the Union Dead* (1964) than he confused the reading world (he was by this time a much-read poet here and abroad) by publishing the formal Marvellian poems of *Near the Ocean* (1967). He next poured out an apparently inexhaustible stream of unrhymed sonnets, first as *Notebook 1967–68*, next (augmented and revised) as *Notebook* (1970), next rearranged and split in two as *History* and *For Lizzie and Harriet* (1973). At the same time, he published a coda in *The Dolphin* (1973), a set of sonnets about his third marriage, in England, to Lady Caroline Blackwood, a journalist and novelist.

The sonnets are full of events, public and private, that took place during their composition; they are also full of allusiveness. Often they seemed unreadable to those who did not possess Lowell's learning and could not know the events of his private life. For those who liked them, the sonnets seemed yet another form of Lowellesque energy—as though the poet had determined to put into his poetry his entire complex mind, not simply some selection from it. The sonnets often resemble, in diction, the denser passages of Milton or Shakespeare. As they are clarified by time and annotation, they will be better understood. In their political dimension, they represent a gripping testimony to one intellectual's revulsion at the Vietnam War, the March on the Pentagon in 1967 (in which Lowell participated), and the state of government and society in America in the late 1960s.

It might be said that all of Lowell's writing was driven into being by some cause or belief—religious, political, or historical. The consistent linking of his own family's history with the history of the United States made Lowell see, for most of his life, every political event as one intimately addressed to himself. And he viewed the Puritan theocratic obsessions, toward which he felt both admiration and revulsion, as a form of familial legacy. But when he broke his style for the last time in *Day by Day,* he abandoned all fictions of battle and now saw his past religious and political positions chiefly as constructs of his own embattled psyche. In the brief hope that he could be, with the help of lithium, an ordinary person, he had moved to England in 1970, entered his last marriage, and had a son. The early idyll of the new marriage, the recurrence of his mental illness, and the unhappiness of the later years in England are all reflected in the new, spare free verse of *Day by Day,* a verse that is pared to the bone, dry and plangent at once in its anticipation of death. Lowell died of a heart attack in a taxicab in New York City shortly before he was due to return to Harvard, where he had been teaching literature and writing for several years.

Lowell wrote occasional prose (not yet collected) and several plays. He adapted Melville's *Benito Cereno,* three stories by Hawthorne, and Thomas Morton's 1637 *New Canaan* for the stage under the title *The Old Glory* (1965); he translated Racine's *Phèdre* (1961) and Aeschylus' *Prometheus Bound* (1969). In times of depression, when he could not write poetry, he turned to translation. Eventually, his practice in translating was to turn the foreign original into a poem that could have been written by himself. These extraordinary "translations" were collected under the title *Imitations* (1961), and, for all their willfulness, raised the level of both translation and the theory of translation in America.

However, Lowell will be judged, finally, by his revolutionizing of American poetry. He took it from the formal patterns of Tate and Ransom into a new era of boldly revolutionary free verse, then into a torrential new formality. Finally, he invented, in *Day by Day*, a new kind of lyric—wayward, structurally free, and intimate—that reflects formally his abandonment of transcendence and teleology in favor of an unforced perception of earthly transience.

Further Reading:

H. Staples, *Robert Lowell: The First Twenty Years*, 1961.
J. Mazzaro, *The Poetic Themes of Robert Lowell*, 1965.
Robert Lowell: A Collection of Critical Essays, ed. T. Parkinson, 1968.
P. Cooper, *The Autobiographical Myth of Robert Lowell*, 1970.
P. Cosgrave, *The Public Poetry of Robert Lowell*, 1970.
R. J. Fein, *Robert Lowell*, 1970.
J. Martin, *Robert Lowell*, 1970.
R. K. Meiners, *Everything to Be Endured: An Essay on Robert Lowell*, 1970.

M. Perloff, *The Poetic Art of Robert Lowell*, 1973.
A. Williamson, *Pity the Monsters: The Political Vision of Robert Lowell*, 1974.
S. Yenser, *Circle to Circle: The Poetry of Robert Lowell*, 1975.
S. G. Axelrod, *Robert Lowell: Life and Art*, 1978.
S. G. Axelrod and H. Deese, *Robert Lowell: A Reference Guide*, 1982.
V. M. Bell, *Robert Lowell: Nihilist as Hero*, 1983.
I. Hamilton, *Robert Lowell: A Biography*, 1983.
M. Rudman, *Robert Lowell: An Introduction to the Poetry*, 1983.

Texts:

"Waking in the Blue" and "Skunk Hour" from *Life Studies*, 1960.
"For the Union Dead" from *For the Union Dead*, 1964.
"Waking Early Sunday Morning" from *Near the Ocean*, 1967.

"The March I" from *Notebook*, 1970.
"Harriet" from *For Lizzie and Harriet*, 1973.
"History" and "Reading Myself" from *History*, 1973.
"Fishnet" from *Dolphin*, 1973.
Remaining poems from *Day by Day*, 1977.

Waking in the Blue

The night attendant, a B. U.[1] sophomore,
rouses from the mare's-nest of his drowsy head
propped on *The Meaning of Meaning.*[2]
He catwalks down our corridor.
Azure day
makes my agonized blue window bleaker.   5
Crows maunder on the petrified fairway.
Absence! My heart grows tense
as though a harpoon were sparring for the kill.
(This is the house for the "mentally ill.")   10

[1] Boston University.
[2] Philosophical treatise by Charles Kay Ogden and I. A. Richards.

What use is my sense of humor?
I grin at Stanley, now sunk in his sixties,
once a Harvard all-American fullback,
(if such were possible!)
still hoarding the build of a boy in his twenties,   15
as he soaks, a ramrod
with the muscle of a seal
in his long tub,
vaguely urinous from the Victorian plumbing.
A kingly granite profile in a crimson golf-cap,   20
worn all day, all night,
he thinks only of his figure,
of slimming on sherbet and ginger ale—
more cut off from words than a seal.

This is the way day breaks in Bowditch Hall at McLean's;[3]   25
the hooded night lights bring out "Bobbie,"
Porcellian '29,[4]
a replica of Louis XVI
without the wig—
redolent and roly-poly as a sperm whale,   30
as he swashbuckles about in his birthday suit
and horses at chairs.

These victorious figures of bravado ossified young.

In between the limits of day,
hours and hours go by under the crew haircuts   35
and slightly too little nonsensical bachelor twinkle
of the Roman Catholic attendants.
(There are no Mayflower
screwballs in the Catholic Church.)

After a hearty New England breakfast,   40
I weigh two hundred pounds
this morning. Cock of the walk,
I strut in my turtle-necked French sailor's jersey
before the metal shaving mirrors,
and see the shaky future grow familiar   45
in the pinched, indigenous faces
of these thoroughbred mental cases,

[3] Psychiatric hospital in Belmont, Massachusetts.
[4] I.e., elected in 1929 to the exclusive Porcellian
Club at Harvard.

twice my age and half my weight.
We are all old-timers,
each of us holds a locked razor.   50

1960

Skunk Hour

(For Elizabeth Bishop)

Nautilus Island's[1] hermit
heiress still lives through winter in her Spartan cottage;
her sheep still graze above the sea.
Her son's a bishop. Her farmer
is first selectman in our village;   5
she's in her dotage.

Thirsting for
the hierarchic privacy
of Queen Victoria's century,
she buys up all   10
the eyesores facing her shore,
and lets them fall.

The season's ill—
we've lost our summer millionaire,
who seemed to leap from an L. L. Bean[2]   15
catalogue. His nine-knot yawl
was auctioned off to lobstermen.
A red fox stain[3] covers Blue Hill.

And now our fairy
decorator brightens his shop for fall;   20
his fishnet's filled with orange cork,
orange, his cobbler's bench and awl;
there is no money in his work,
he'd rather marry.

One dark night,   25
my Tudor[4] Ford climbed the hill's skull;

---

[1] In Maine, near Castine, where Lowell often
spent summers.
[2] Store in Freeport, Maine, specializing in
outdoor clothing and camping goods.

[3] The autumn leaves.
[4] Make of two-door Ford.

I watched for love-cars. Lights turned down,
they lay together, hull to hull,
where the graveyard shelves on the town. . . .
My mind's not right.   30

A car radio bleats,
"Love, O careless Love. . . ." I hear
my ill-spirit sob in each blood cell,
as if my hand were at its throat. . . .
I myself am hell;[5]   35
nobody's here—

only skunks, that search
in the moonlight for a bite to eat.
They march on their soles up Main Street:
white stripes, moonstruck eyes' red fire   40
under the chalk-dry and spar spire
of the Trinitarian Church.

I stand on top
of our back steps and breathe the rich air—
a mother skunk with her column[6] of kittens swills the garbage pail.   45
She jabs her wedge-head in a cup
of sour cream, drops her ostrich tail,
and will not scare.

1960

For the Union Dead[1]

"Relinquunt Omnia Servare Rem Publicam."[2]

The old South Boston Aquarium stands
in a Sahara of snow now. Its broken windows are boarded.
The bronze weathervane cod[3] has lost half its scales.
The airy tanks are dry.

[5] "Myself am hell," Satan says in Milton's
Paradise Lost, IV, 75.
[6] A military formation.
[1] Soldiers who died fighting for the North in the
Civil War. The poem is written about a bronze
bas-relief opposite the Massachusetts State House
on Beacon Street, in Boston; the monument, by
Augustus St. Gaudens (1848–1897),
commemorates Colonel Robert Gould Shaw
(1837–1863), who commanded the first

all-Negro regiment in the North, and who was
killed while leading an attack on Fort Wagner
in South Carolina. The monument represents
Shaw on horseback flanked by Negro foot
soldiers.
[2] Lowell has changed the inscription on the
monument from singular to plural, so that it
reads: "They leave everything behind to serve
the Republic."
[3] Codfish, the symbol of Boston.

Once my nose crawled like a snail on the glass;   5
my hand tingled
to burst the bubbles
drifting from the noses of the cowed, compliant fish.

My hand draws back. I often sigh still
for the dark downward and vegetating kingdom   10
of the fish and reptile. One morning last March,
I pressed against the new barbed and galvanized

fence on the Boston Common.[4] Behind their cage,
yellow dinosaur steamshovels were grunting
as they cropped up tons of mush and grass   15
to gouge their underworld garage.[5]

Parking spaces luxuriate like civic
sandpiles in the heart of Boston.
A girdle of orange, Puritan-pumpkin colored girders
braces the tingling Statehouse,   20

shaking over the excavations, as it faces Colonel Shaw
and his bell-cheeked Negro infantry
on St. Gaudens' shaking Civil War relief,
propped by a plank splint against the garage's earthquake.

Two months after marching through Boston,   25
half the regiment was dead;
at the dedication,
William James[6] could almost hear the bronze Negroes breathe.

Their monument sticks like a fishbone
in the city's throat.   30
Its Colonel is as lean
as a compass-needle.

He has an angry wrenlike vigilance,
a greyhound's gentle tautness;
he seems to wince at pleasure,   35
and suffocate for privacy.

He is out of bounds now. He rejoices in man's lovely,
peculiar power to choose life and die—
when he leads his black soldiers to death,
he cannot bend his back.   40

---

[4] Park facing the State House.   [6] Philosopher and psychologist (1842–1910); the
[5] The construction of the garage beneath the   allusion is to a letter.
Common was attended by graft and corruption.

On a thousand small town New England greens,[7]
the old white churches hold their air
of sparse, sincere rebellion; frayed flags
quilt the graveyards of the Grand Army of the Republic.

The stone statues of the abstract Union Soldier   45
grow slimmer and younger each year—
wasp-waisted, they doze over muskets
and muse through their sideburns . . .

Shaw's father wanted no monument
except the ditch,   50
where his son's body was thrown
and lost with his "niggers."[8]

The ditch is nearer.
There are no statues for the last war[9] here;
on Boylston Street, a commercial photograph   55
shows Hiroshima boiling

over a Mosler Safe, the "Rock of Ages"
that survived the blast. Space is nearer.
When I crouch[10] to my television set,
the drained faces of Negro school-children[11] rise like balloons. 60

Colonel Shaw
is riding on his bubble,
he waits
for the blessèd break.

The Aquarium is gone. Everywhere,   65
giant finned cars nose forward like fish;
a savage servility
slides by on grease.

1964

---

[7] Lowell is thinking of the village green in
Castine.
[8] Shaw's father could have had his son's body
brought home (officers *had that privilege,* while
infantry were buried where they fell), but he
refused, knowing his son's affection for his men.
[9] Perhaps the Korean War (1950–1953); or, as
Lowell's mention of Hiroshima suggests, World
War II, which ended with the dropping of the
atom bomb; the exploitation of the survival of
the safe for advertising purposes is a sign of
callousness, while the use in the advertisement
of the phrase "Rock of Ages," normally a
reference to Christ, proclaims the collapse of
religion.
[10] The posture of a "savage" worshipping a
"god."
[11] Schools in the South were being forcibly
desegregated in 1960.

Waking Early Sunday Morning[*]

O to break loose, like the chinook
salmon jumping and falling back,
nosing up to the impossible
stone and bone-crushing waterfall—
raw-jawed, weak-fleshed there, stopped by ten   5
steps of the roaring ladder, and then
to clear the top on the last try,
alive enough to spawn and die.

Stop, back off. The salmon breaks
water, and now my body wakes   10
to feel the unpolluted joy
and criminal leisure of a boy—
no rainbow smashing a dry fly[1]
in the white run is free as I,
here squatting like a dragon on   15
time's hoard before the day's begun!

Vermin run for their unstopped holes;
in some dark nook a fieldmouse rolls
a marble, hours on end, then stops;
the termite in the woodwork sleeps—   20
listen, the creatures of the night
obsessive, casual, sure of foot,
go on grinding, while the sun's
daily remorseful blackout dawns.

Fierce, fireless mind, running downhill.   25
Look up and see the harbor fill:
business as usual in eclipse
goes down to the sea in ships—
wake of refuse, dacron rope,
bound for Bermuda or Good Hope,   30
all bright before the morning watch
the wine-dark hulls of yawl and ketch.

I watch a glass of water wet
with a fine fuzz of icy sweat,

---

[*] Two other poems on refusing to attend church on Sunday are Emily Dickinson's "Some keep the Sabbath going to Church" ("324") and Wallace Stevens's "Sunday Morning," both in this anthology.

[1] Rainbow trout smashing a trout lure (fly).

silvery colors touched with sky,   35
serene in their neutrality—
yet if I shift, or change my mood,
I see some object made of wood,
background behind it[2] of brown grain,
to darken it, but not to stain.   40

O that the spirit could remain
tinged but untarnished by its strain!
Better dressed and stacking birch,
or lost with the Faithful at Church—
anywhere, but somewhere else!   45
And now the new electric bells,
clearly chiming, "Faith of our fathers,"
and now the congregation gathers.

O Bible chopped and crucified
in hymns we hear but do not read,   50
none of the milder subtleties
of grace or art will sweeten these
stiff quatrains shovelled out four-square—
they sing of peace, and preach despair;
yet they gave darkness some control,   55
and left a loophole for the soul.

No, put old clothes on, and explore
the corners of the woodshed for
its dregs and dreck:[3] tools with no handle,
ten candle-ends not worth a candle,   60
old lumber banished from the Temple,[4]
damned by Paul's precept and example,
cast from the kingdom, banned in Israel,
the wordless sign, the tinkling cymbal.[5]

When will we see Him face to face?   65
Each day, He shines through darker glass.[6]
In this small town where everything
is known, I see His vanishing
emblems, His white spire and flag-
pole sticking out above the fog,   70

[2] I.e., behind the glass of water.
[3] Yiddish for "refuse" or "junk."
[4] The Hebrew temple, standing for the "old law"
replaced by the Christian dispensation, whose
apostle was St. Paul.
[5] I Corinthians 13:1: "Though I speak with the
tongues of men and of angels, and have not

charity, I am become as sounding brass, or a
tinkling cymbal."
[6] I Corinthians 13:12: "For now we see through a
glass, darkly; but then face to face." Lowell
reverses the hope of the second part of the
quotation.

like old white china doorknobs, sad,
slight, useless things to calm the mad.
Hammering military splendor,
top-heavy Goliath[7] in full armor—
little redemption in the mass   75
liquidations of their brass,
elephant and phalanx moving
with the times and still improving,
when that kingdom hit the crash:
a million foreskins stacked like trash . . .   80

Sing softer! But what if a new
diminuendo[8] brings no true
tenderness, only restlessness,
excess, the hunger for success,
sanity of self-deception   85
fixed and kicked by reckless caution,
while we listen to the bells—
anywhere, but somewhere else!

O to break loose. All life's grandeur
is something with a girl in summer . . .   90
elated as the President[9]
girdled by his establishment
this Sunday morning, free to chaff
his own thoughts with his bear-cuffed staff,
swimming nude, unbuttoned, sick   95
of his ghost-written rhetoric!

No weekends for the gods now. Wars
flicker, earth licks its open sores,
fresh breakage, fresh promotions, chance
assassinations, no advance.   100
Only man thinning out his kind
sounds through the Sabbath noon, the blind
swipe of the pruner and his knife
busy about the tree of life . . .

Pity the planet, all joy gone   105
from this sweet volcanic cone;
peace to our children when they fall

[7] Philistine giant, slain by David with a slingshot.
King Saul demanded from David a hundred
foreskins of Philistines (as proof that David had
killed them) in lieu of dowry when David
married the king's daughter; David returned
with two hundred foreskins. (See 1 Samuel 17

and 18.) Lowell may have been thinking of
Hitler's liquidation of the Jews as well.
[8] Reduction in volume of sound.
[9] Lyndon B. Johnson, who would playfully cuff
members of his staff.

in small war on the heels of small
war—until the end of time
to police the earth, a ghost
orbiting forever lost
in our monotonous sublime.   110

1967

The March I[1]

(For Dwight Macdonald)

Under the too white marmoreal Lincoln Memorial,
the too tall marmoreal Washington Obelisk,
gazing into the too long reflecting pool,
the reddish trees, the withering autumn sky,
the remorseless, amplified harangues for peace—   5
lovely to lock arms, to march absurdly locked
(unlocking to keep my wet glasses from slipping)
to see the cigarette match quaking in my fingers,
then to step off like green Union Army recruits
for the first Bull Run,[2] sped by photographers,   10
the notables, the girls . . . fear, glory, chaos, rout . . .
our green army staggered out on the miles-long green fields,
met by the other army,[3] the Martian, the ape, the hero,
his new-fangled rifle, his green new steel helmet.

1970

Harriet[1]

Spring moved to summer—the rude cold rain
hurries the ambitious, flowers and youth;
our flash-tones crackle for an hour, and then
we too follow nature, imperceptibly
change our mouse-brown to white lion's mane,   5
thin white fading to a freckled, knuckled skull,

---

[1] A peace march during the Vietnam War.
[2] Union defeat (July 21, 1861) in the Civil War.
[3] Troops of the U.S. Army.

[1] Lowell's daughter by Elizabeth Hardwick
Lowell, his second wife.

bronzed by decay, by many, many suns. . . .
Child of ten, three quarters animal,
three years from Juliet,[2] half Juliet,
already ripened for the night on stage—   10
beautiful petals, what shall we hope for,
knowing one choice not two is all you're given,
health beyond the measure, dangerous
to yourself, more dangerous to others?

1973

History

History has to live with what was here,
clutching and close to fumbling all we had—
it is so dull and gruesome how we die,
unlike writing, life never finishes.
Abel was finished; death is not remote,   5
a flash-in-the-pan electrifies the skeptic,
his cows crowding like skulls against high-voltage wire,
his baby crying all night like a new machine.
As in our Bibles, white-faced, predatory,
the beautiful, mist-drunken hunter's moon ascends—   10
a child could give it a face: two holes, two holes,
my eyes, my mouth, between them a skull's no-nose—
O there's a terrifying innocence in my face
drenched with the silver salvage of the mornfrost.

1973

Reading Myself

Like thousands, I took just pride and more than just,
struck matches that brought my blood to a boil;
I memorized the tricks to set the river on fire—
somehow never wrote something to go back to.
Can I suppose I am finished with wax flowers   5
and have earned my grass on the minor slopes of Parnassus. . . .[1]

---

[2] Shakespeare's Juliet, 14 years old.
[1] Mountain in Greece; in mythology, the home
of Apollo and the Muses.

No honeycomb is built without a bee
adding circle to circle, cell to cell,
the wax and honey of a mausoleum—
this round dome proves its maker is alive;   10
the corpse of the insect lives embalmed in honey,
prays that its perishable work live long
enough for the sweet-tooth bear to desecrate—
this open book . . . my open coffin.

1973

Fishnet

Any clear thing that blinds us with surprise,
your wandering silences and bright trouvailles,[1]
dolphin let loose to catch the flashing fish. . . .
Poets die adolescents, their beat embalms them,
the archetypal voices sing offkey;   5
the old actor cannot read his friends,
and nevertheless he reads himself aloud,
genius hums the auditorium dead.
The line must terminate.
Yet my heart rises, I know I've gladdened a lifetime   10
knotting, undoing a fishnet of tarred rope;
the net will hang on the wall when the fish are eaten,
nailed like illegible bronze[2] on the futureless future.

1973

For John Berryman

(After reading his last *Dream Song*)[1]

The last years we only met
when you were on the road,
and lit up for reading

---

[1] French: "discoveries."

[2] Lowell is remembering the Roman poet
Horace's boast (*Odes*, III, 30) that a poem is
more lasting than bronze ("*Exegi monumentum
aere perennius*"), but the artifacts of culture all
eventually become unintelligible.

[1] The poet John Berryman, Lowell's
contemporary, committed suicide in 1972 after
episodes of acute alcoholism and mental
breakdown; the sequence of lyrics called *The
Dream Songs* became Berryman's major poetic
undertaking.

your battering *Dream*—
audible, deaf . . .   5
in another world then as now.
I used to want to live
to avoid your elegy.
Yet really we had the same life,
the generic one   1
our generation offered
(*Les Maudits*[2]—the compliment
each American generation
pays itself in passing):
first students, then with our own,   1
our galaxy of grands maîtres,[3]
our fifties' fellowships
to Paris, Rome and Florence,
veterans of the Cold War[4] not the War—
all the best of life . . .   2
then daydreaming to drink at six,
waiting for the iced fire,
even the feel of the frosted glass,
like waiting for a girl . . .
if you had waited.   2
We asked to be obsessed with writing,
and we were.

Do you wake dazed like me,
and find your lost glasses in a shoe?

Something so heavy lies on my heart—   3
there, still here, the good days
when we sat by a cold lake in Maine,
talking about the *Winter's Tale,*
Leontes' jealousy[5]
in Shakespeare's broken syntax.   3
You got there first.
Just the other day,
I discovered how we differ—humor . . .
even in this last *Dream Song,*
to mock your catlike flight   4
from home and classes—
to leap from the bridge.

---

[2] The *poète maudit* (French: "accursed poet" or
"damned poet") was a cliché of the later
nineteenth century.
[3] "Great teachers" (poetic mentors).
[4] Diplomatic estrangement between the United
States and Russia during the 1950s.

[5] In Shakespeare's *The Winter's Tale,* Leontes
orders his wife killed, unreasonably suspecting
her of infidelity.

Girls will not frighten the frost from the grave.[6]

To my surprise, John,
I pray *to* not for you,   45
think of you not myself,
smile and fall asleep.

1977

For Sheridan[1]

We only live between
before we are and what we were.

In the lost negative[2]
you exist,
a smile, a cypher,   5
an old-fashioned face
in an old-fashioned hat.

Three ages in a flash:
the same child in the same picture,
he, I, you,   10
chockablock, one stamp[3]
like mother's wedding silver—

gnome, fish, brute cherubic force.

We could see clearly
and all the same things   15
before the glass was hurt.

Past fifty, we learn with surprise and a sense
of suicidal absolution
that what we intended and failed
could never have happened—   20
and must be done better.

1977

---

[6] Lowell is recalling the last two lines from a
song in *The Sad Shepherd* by Ben Jonson
(1572/3–1637): " 'Except Love's fires the virtue
have, / To fright the frost out of the grave.' "

[1] Lowell's son by Caroline Blackwood, his third
wife.
[2] Of a picture of Robert Lowell as a small boy.
[3] The family monogram, as on silver cutlery.

Epilogue*

Those blessèd structures, plot and rhyme—
why are they no help to me now
I want to make
something imagined, not recalled?
I hear the noise of my own voice: 5
The painter's vision is not a lens,
it trembles to caress the light.
But sometimes everything I write
with the threadbare art of my eye
seems a snapshot,   10
lurid, rapid, garish, grouped,
heightened from life,
yet paralyzed by fact.
All's misalliance.
Yet why not say what happened?   15
Pray for the grace of accuracy
Vermeer[1] gave to the sun's illumination
stealing like the tide across a map
to his girl solid with yearning.
We are poor passing facts,   20
warned by that to give
each figure in the photograph
his living name.

1977

Howard Nemerov
b. 1920

Howard Nemerov's sardonic observations of American life are turned with a morose wit that makes them more than light verse. Nothing escapes his sharp eye; he sees the world, in his more acerbic moments, as a caricature of itself— politicians and evangelists retailing cant, a foolish public deluding itself, bourgeois illusion reigning except where war and carnage rule. But in other poems, throughout his long career, there is a harmonious, if grim, song that Nemerov

---

* This is the closing poem in Lowell's last volume of poetry, *Day by Day* (1977).
[1] Jan Vermeer (1632–1675), Dutch painter; the painting in question, *Girl Reading a Letter,* has in the background a map hanging on the wall on which light shines from an open casement, which the girl reading the letter is facing in profile.

sings—the song of the processions of the stars and the seasons. He senses what
Emily Dickinson called "the process in the burr"; he is, like Keats's swallows,
"intelligent of seasons." Natural law is to him a guarantee at least of periodicity
and rhythm, if not of meaning, and it is no accident that his first book was
entitled *The Image and the Law* (1947). His metaphysical and moral poems have
an Old Testament sternness about them that corresponds to the law of the
physical heavens; the paradoxical creations and destructions of the universe serve
as matter for Nemerov's brooding mind.

Nemerov is a formalist, as one would expect from his love of the law of
recurrence. His serious verse moves with gravity and resonance; in the clarity and
weight of his reasoning there is something philosophic; in the satisfying closure
of many of the poems—as in *Gnomes and Occasions* (1973)—there is an iron ring
at the last words.

Nemerov grew up in New York and went to Harvard, where he won the
Bowdoin Prize in 1940. After he graduated in 1941, he joined the Royal
Canadian Air Force, and, in 1944, the U.S. Army Air Force. He taught at
Hamilton, Bennington, and Brandeis before joining the faculty of Washington
University in St. Louis, where he is now the Edward Mallinckrodt Distinguished
University Professor of English. Though he began by writing fiction as well as
poetry, more recently Nemerov has written, in addition to his poetry, remarkable
critical reflections on the art of poetry, collected in *Figures of Thought* (1978). His
Collected Poems, published in 1977, won both the Pulitzer Prize and the National
Book Award.

Nemerov continues, in our day, a didactic poetic tradition begun by Emerson.
He adds to it an Old Testament weight foreign to Emerson's airy rapidity
(Nemerov is Jewish, but philosophically rather than ethnically so). In joining
together the proverbial and prophetic Hebraic wisdom tradition, the Latin
tradition of epigram, and the Puritan strain of moral verse (from Wigglesworth
to Lowell), Nemerov creates a new compound, distinctive in its tart, grave, and
ironic resonance. In his long meditative poems on art (like "The Painter
Dreaming in the Scholar's House"), Nemerov has established a model through
which some younger poets, most recently Michael Blumenthal, have found ways
to join poetic and philosophic discourse.

Further Reading:
P. Meinke, *Howard Nemerov*, 1968.
J. A. Bartholomay, *The Shield of Perseus: The
Vision and Imagination of Howard Nemerov*, 1972.
W. Mills, *The Stillness in Moving Things: The
World of Howard Nemerov*, 1975.
R. Labrie, *Howard Nemerov*, 1980.
D. E. Wyllie, *Elizabeth Bishop and Howard
Nemerov: A Reference Guide*, 1983.

Text:
The Collected Poems, 1977.
Figures of Thought, 1979.
Sentences, 1980.
See also *Journal of the Fictive Life*, 1965.

The Daily Globe[1]

Each day another installment of the old
Romance of Order brings to the breakfast table
The paper flowers of catastrophe.
One has this recurrent dream about the world.

Headlines declare the ambiguous oracles,   5
The comfortable old prophets mutter doom.
Man's greatest intellectual pleasure is
To repeat himself, yet somehow the daily globe

Rolls on, while the characters in comic strips
Prolong their slow, interminable lives   10
Beyond the segregated photographs
Of the girls that marry and the men that die.

1962

To David,[1] About His Education

The world is full of mostly invisible things,
And there is no way but putting the mind's eye,
Or its nose, in a book, to find them out,
Things like the square root of Everest
Or how many times Byron goes into Texas,   5
Or whether the law of the excluded middle
Applies west of the Rockies. For these
And the like reasons, you have to go to school
And study books and listen to what you are told,
And sometimes try to remember. Though I don't know   10
What you will do with the mean annual rainfall
On Plato's Republic, or the calorie content
Of the Diet of Worms, such things are said to be
Good for you, and you will have to learn them
In order to become one of the grown-ups   15

---

[1] Boston daily newspaper.   [1] Nemerov's son.

Who sees invisible things neither steadily nor whole,[2]
But keeps gravely the grand confusion of the world
Under his hat, which is where it belongs,
And teaches small children to do this in their turn.

1962

Thirtieth Anniversary Report
of the Class of '41[1]

We who survived the war and took to wife
And sired the kids and made the decent living,
And piecemeal furnished forth the finished life
Not by grand theft so much as petty thieving—

Who had the routine middle-aged affair   5
And made our beds and had to lie in them
This way or that because the beds were there,
And turned our bile and choler in for phlegm—

Who saw grandparents, parents, to the vault
And wives and selves grow wrinkled, grey and fat   10
And children through their acne and revolt
And told the analyst about all that—

Are done with it. What is there to discuss?
There's nothing left for us to say of us.

1973

Richard Wilbur
b. 1921

Richard Wilbur's verse combines a Latin elegance and wit with the New
England skepticism and wisdom we associate with Robert Frost (whom Wilbur
met as an undergraduate at Amherst College). Wilbur's first book, *The Beautiful
Changes and Other Poems* (1947), published when he was in his twenties, reflected

---

[2] "He saw life steadily and saw it whole":
Matthew Arnold's remark on Sophocles in "To
a Friend."

[1] Nemerov's class at Harvard.

his war service in Italy and France (1943–1945) and his admiration for the landscape and architecture of Europe. The book drew immediate critical praise, and Wilbur's poetry has continued to attract readers who see the continuity of American poetry with the formal verse of the English past. The rougher line of American verse, from Emerson through Whitman to Ashbery, insists on discontinuity, rupture, and spontaneity, whereas the Europeanized tradition exemplified by Stevens, Frost, Merrill, and Wilbur values continuity, gradualism, and musicality.

Wilbur's alignment with Europe arises, in part, from his affiliation with Eliot as a "civilized poet" and from his superb command of French. He has translated Molière into excellent English verse for the stage; he was one of the lyricists for Leonard Bernstein's musical version of *Candide* (1956).

Unlike the *poètes maudits* ("accursed poets") of the modern tradition like Baudelaire and Rimbaud, who emphasize the role of the poet as social outcast, Wilbur, who has remained a Christian believer, considers himself "a poet–citizen rather than an alienated artist. . . . Poetry is sterile unless it arises from a sense of community, or, at least, from the hope of community." By meditating on the conflicts like those between sensual pleasure and transcendence or between the stationary and the restless, the poet, says Wilbur, is "acknowledging the contradictions that inhere in life." The chief contradiction is that between "the tangible world and the intuitions of the spirit." Though Wilbur's use of stanzaic structures and regular meters reflects his attachment to poetic tradition, his genial, understated American voice has naturalized older English forms into new indigenous ones. His intricately musical meditative writing continues, in a secular vein, the reflective verse of such seventeenth-century religious poets as George Herbert and Thomas Traherne. Wilbur, the son of a painter, writes poetry of the eye, but he wishes to find, behind the eye, the workings of the soul.

Wilbur has taught at Harvard (where he took an M.A.), at Wellesley, and at Wesleyan; he is now a professor of English at Smith. His poems were collected in 1963; since then, he has published *Walking to Sleep* (1969) and *The Mind-Reader* (1976). His essays have been collected in *Responses: Prose Pieces, 1948–1976* (1976).

Further Reading:
D. L. Hill, *Richard Wilbur*, 1967.
H. Stevens, *Richard Wilbur*, 1977.
Richard Wilbur's Creation, ed. W. Salinger, 1983.

Texts:
"The Beautiful Changes" and "Mind" from *The Poems of Richard Wilbur*, 1963.
"The Writer" and "Cottage Street, 1953" from *The Mind-Reader*, 1976.

The Beautiful Changes

One wading a Fall meadow finds on all sides
The Queen Anne's Lace¹ lying like lilies
On water; it glides
So from the walker, it turns
Dry grass to a lake, as the slightest shade of you   5
Valleys my mind in fabulous blue Lucernes.²

The beautiful changes as a forest is changed
By a chameleon's tuning his skin to it;
As a mantis, arranged
On a green leaf, grows   10
Into it, makes the leaf leafier, and proves
Any greenness is deeper than anyone knows.

Your hands hold roses always in a way that says
They are not only yours; the beautiful changes
In such kind ways,   15
Wishing ever to sunder
Things and things' selves for a second finding, to lose
For a moment all that it touches back to wonder.

1947

Mind

Mind in its purest play is like some bat
That beats about in caverns all alone,
Contriving by a kind of senseless wit
Not to conclude against a wall of stone.

It has no need to falter or explore;   5
Darkly it knows what obstacles are there,
And so may weave and flitter, dip and soar
In perfect courses through the blackest air.

¹ American wildflower with white, lacelike
blossoms.   ² Lucerne: town in mountainous Switzerland.

And has this simile a like perfection?
The mind is like a bat. Precisely. Save   10
That in the very happiest intellection
A graceful error may correct the cave.
1956

The Writer

In her room at the prow of the house
Where light breaks, and the windows are tossed with linden,
My daughter is writing a story.

I pause in the stairwell, hearing
From her shut door a commotion of typewriter-keys   5
Like a chain hauled over a gunwale.

Young as she is, the stuff
Of her life is a great cargo, and some of it heavy:
I wish her a lucky passage.

But now it is she who pauses,   10
As if to reject my thought and its easy figure.
A stillness greatens, in which

The whole house seems to be thinking,
And then she is at it again with a bunched clamor
Of strokes, and again is silent.   15

I remember the dazed starling
Which was trapped in that very room, two years ago;
How we stole in, lifted a sash

And retreated, not to affright it;
And how for a helpless hour, through the crack of the door, 20
We watched the sleek, wild, dark

And iridescent creature
Batter against the brilliance, drop like a glove
To the hard floor, or the desk-top,

And wait then, humped and bloody,   25
For the wits to try it again; and how our spirits
Rose when, suddenly sure,

It lifted off from a chair-back,
Beating a smooth course for the right window
And clearing the sill of the world.   30

It is always a matter, my darling,
Of life or death, as I had forgotten. I wish
What I wished you before, but harder.
1976

Cottage Street, 1953

Framed in her phoenix fire-screen, Edna Ward
Bends to the tray of Canton,[1] pouring tea
For frightened Mrs. Plath; then, turning toward
The pale, slumped daughter, and my wife, and me,

Asks if we would prefer it weak or strong.   5
Will we have milk or lemon, she enquires?
The visit seems already strained and long.
Each in his turn, we tell her our desires.

It is my office to exemplify
The published poet in his happiness,   10
Thus cheering Sylvia, who has wished to die;[2]
But half-ashamed, and impotent to bless,

I am a stupid life-guard who has found,
Swept to his shallows by the tide, a girl
Who, far from shore, has been immensely drowned.   15
And stares through water now with eyes of pearl.

How large is her refusal; and how slight
The genteel chat whereby we recommend
Life, of a summer afternoon, despite
The brewing dusk which hints that it may end.   20

And Edna Ward shall die in fifteen years,
After her eight-and-eighty summers of

[1] Blue-and-white patterned Chinese-export
porcelain ware; in this case, the tea service.
[2] The poet Sylvia Plath (1932–1963) attempted
suicide after her junior year at Smith College.
Later, she died by suicide.

Such grace and courage as permit no tears,
The thin hand reaching out, the last word *love*,

Outliving Sylvia who, condemned to live,   25
Shall study for a decade, as she must,
To state at last her brilliant negative
In poems free and helpless and unjust.
1976

James Dickey
b. 1923

James Dickey made his mark as a poet with his striking early poems—published in *Drowning with Others* (1962) and *Helmets* (1964)—about his experience in the Air Force during World War II. He had enlisted in 1942 after a year at Clemson College, in South Carolina; after the war he returned to college at Vanderbilt and began to write. Dickey's poetry has always celebrated the animal life of man and man's response to states of extraordinary pressure. It is a poetry of violence, often carried to extremes (as Dickey's own life tends to have been carried to extremes of danger in motorcycle driving and drinking). Dickey's poems are spread across the page in bursts of language; syntactic articulation is often sacrificed to a brutality of enunciation. His mystical or visionary side is perhaps not altogether unexpected in a southern poet (Dickey was born in Atlanta, Georgia); his moments of "second sight" belong perhaps to his tendency to mythologize experience, as he did in the novel *Deliverance* (1970), which he adapted for Hollywood. Dickey's work can spin off into regions of incoherence, but when he trims his sails and refuses the temptation to be over-rhetorical, he can write with point and tenderness. His book of literary criticism, *Babel to Byzantium* (1968), reveals a different Dickey—formal, even scholarly, in his discussion of the poetry of others. In his recent attempts to write in the voice of women, Dickey has turned aside from the almost exclusively male world that he made famous in *Buckdancer's Choice* (1965) and subsequent books; however, the sprawl of his lines has not changed, and Dickey's energy remains still uncontained by form.

Further Reading:
Babel to Byzantium, 1968.
Self-interviews, 1970.
Sorties, Journals, and New Essays, 1971.
James Dickey: The Expansive Imagination, ed.
R. J. Calhoun, 1973.
J. Elledge, *James Dickey: A Bibliography*,
1947–1974, 1979.

Text:
Poems, 1947–1967, 1967.

The Hospital Window

I have just come down from my father.
Higher and higher he lies
Above me in a blue light
Shed by a tinted window.
I drop through six white floors   5
And then step out onto pavement.

Still feeling my father ascend,
I start to cross the firm street,
My shoulder blades shining with all
The glass the huge building can raise.   10
Now I must turn round and face it,
And know his one pane from the others.

Each window possesses the sun
As though it burned there on a wick.
I wave, like a man catching fire.   15
All the deep-dyed windowpanes flash,
And, behind them, all the white rooms
They turn to the color of Heaven.

Ceremoniously, gravely, and weakly,
Dozens of pale hands are waving   20
Back, from inside their flames.
Yet one pure pane among these
Is the bright, erased blankness of nothing.
I know that my father is there,

In the shape of his death still living.   25
The traffic increases around me
Like a madness called down on my head.
The horns blast at me like shotguns,
And drivers lean out, driven crazy—
But now my propped-up father   30

Lifts his arm out of stillness at last.
The light from the window strikes me
And I turn as blue as a soul,
As the moment when I was born.
I am not afraid for my father—   35
Look! He is grinning; he is not

Afraid for my life, either,
As the wild engines stand at my knees
Shredding their gears and roaring,
And I hold each car in its place   4○
For miles, inciting its horn
To blow down the walls of the world

That the dying may float without fear
In the bold blue gaze of my father.
Slowly I move to the sidewalk   45
With my pin-tingling hand half dead
At the end of my bloodless arm.
I carry it off in amazement,

High, still higher, still waving,
My recognized face fully mortal,   50
Yet not; not at all, in the pale,
Drained, otherworldly, stricken,
Created hue of stained glass.
I have just come down from my father.

1962

Buckdancer's Choice

So I would hear out those lungs,
The air split into nine levels,
Some gift of tongues of the whistler

In the invalid's bed: my mother,
Warbling all day to herself   5
The thousand variations of one song;

It is called Buckdancer's Choice.
For years, they have all been dying
Out, the classic buck-and-wing[1] men

Of traveling minstrel shows;   10
With them also an old woman
Was dying of breathless angina,

[1] Traditional solo tap dance done by blacks in a
minstrel show.

Yet still found breath enough
To whistle up in my head
A sight like a one-man band,   15

Freed black, with cymbals at heel,
An ex-slave who thrivingly danced
To the ring of his own clashing light

Through the thousand variations of one song
All day to my mother's prone music,   20
The invalid's warbler's note,

While I crept close to the wall
Sock-footed, to hear the sounds alter,
Her tongue like a mockingbird's break

Through stratum after stratum of a tone   25
Proclaiming what choices there are
For the last dancers of their kind,

For ill women and for all slaves
Of death, and children enchanted at walls
With a brass-beating glow underfoot,   30

Not dancing but nearly risen
Through barnlike, theatrelike houses
On the wings of the buck and wing.

1965

The Sheep Child

Farm boys wild to couple
With anything   with soft-wooded trees
With mounds of earth   mounds
Of pinestraw   will keep themselves off
Animals by legends of their own: 5
In the hay-tunnel dark
And dung of barns, they will
Say   I have heard tell

That in a museum in Atlanta
Way back in a corner somewhere   10

There's this thing that's only half
Sheep   like a woolly baby
Pickled in alcohol   because
Those things can't live   his eyes
Are open   but you can't stand to look   15
I heard from somebody who . . .

But this is now almost all
Gone. The boys have taken
Their own true wives in the city,
The sheep are safe in the west hill   20
Pasture   but we who were born there
Still are not sure. Are we,
Because we remember, remembered
In the terrible dust of museums?

Merely with his eyes, the sheep-child may   25

Be saying   saying

> *I am here, in my father's house.*
> *I who am half of your world, came deeply*
> *To my mother in the long grass*
> *Of the west pasture, where she stood like moonlight*   30
> *Listening for foxes. It was something like love*
> *From another world that seized her*
> *From behind, and she gave, not lifting her head*
> *Out of dew, without ever looking, her best*
> *Self to that great need. Turned loose, she dipped her face*   35
> *Farther into the chill of the earth, and in a sound*
> *Of sobbing   of something stumbling*
> *Away, began, as she must do,*
> *To carry me. I woke, dying,*
>
> *In the summer sun of the hillside, with my eyes*   40
> *Far more than human. I saw for a blazing moment*
> *The great grassy world from both sides,*
> *Man and beast in the round of their need,*
> *And the hill wind stirred in my wool,*
> *My hoof and my hand clasped each other,*   45
> *I ate my one meal*
> *Of milk, and died*
> *Staring. From dark grass I came straight*
>
> *To my father's house, whose dust*
> *Whirls up in the halls for no reason*   50
> *When no one comes   piling deep in a hellish mild corner,*

And, through my immortal waters,
I meet the sun's grains eye
To eye, and they fail at my closet of glass.
Dead, I am most surely living   55
In the minds of farm boys: I am he who drives
Them like wolves from the hound bitch and calf
And from the chaste ewe in the wind.
They go into woods   into bean fields   they go
Deep into their known right hands. Dreaming of me,   60
They groan   they wait   they suffer
Themselves, they marry, they raise their kind.

1967

A. R. Ammons
b. 1926

Archibald Randolph Ammons is a poet whose work incorporates American life
from its agricultural beginnings to its nuclear present. He was born and raised on
a farm in North Carolina, and the habit of noticing the seasons, the stars, the
growth of trees and crops, and the destructions of storm and fire persists in his
poetry. After his wartime service in the navy, he enrolled in Wake Forest
University on the GI Bill. Although he had begun writing poetry during his
navy watches, he was, he has said, afraid of the part of himself the poems
represented, and in college he majored in chemistry. Still, he took enough
English courses to make it possible to be admitted as a candidate for an M.A. in
English at Berkeley, where the poet Josephine Miles encouraged him to continue
to write poetry. Ammons left Berkeley in 1952 without the degree, however, and
went to work for his father-in-law's glass manufacturing company in New Jersey.
Ammons remained there for ten years, continuing to write; he published his first
book, Ommateum (1955), at his own expense. Later, the poet John Logan helped
to get his second book, Expressions of Sea Level (1964), published. Cornell
University invited Ammons to join its faculty in 1964, and he has remained in
Ithaca, New York, as professor of English there. His Collected Poems (1972) won
the National Book Award. He has since published Diversifications (1976), The
Snow Poems (1977), A Coast of Trees (1981), and Worldly Hopes (1983). Recently,
he was awarded a five-year MacArthur fellowship.

Ammons's early Protestant religious training formed his mind in ways we
associate with the American Transcendentalists, especially Ralph Waldo Emerson.
Early he began to see the natural world as emblematic of spiritual or intellectual
meaning. But his use of the allegorical tradition reverses the usual religious
practice, visible in poems like Oliver Wendell Holmes's "The Chambered
Nautilus." Holmes fastens first on the natural object: He describes the successively
larger chambers of the nautilus, then draws a moral lesson from it for himself.
Ammons, on the other hand, begins with his own emotional perplexity. He goes

into the world bearing an inchoate freight of thought and feeling and then sees—as he does in "Grace Abounding"—a natural scene that exhibits an uncanny correspondence to his unarticulated emotion. In describing a hedge encased in ice, Ammons can make us feel a heart encased in misery.

The usual reach of emblematic verse in the past extended only to what could be perceived by the unaided senses, but Ammons's youthful familiarity with the microscope and the telescope extended his perceptual reach into the domain of the invisible, on the one hand, and the astronomical, on the other. Algae and galaxies are no more strange to him than roses and stars were to his English predecessors. And Ammons's years of work with chemical processes have made the complex interchanges and metamorphoses of the elements second nature to him. His view of the universe is at home with technological and scientific language, which appears in his poetry with unassuming naturalness. In Ammons, for the first time, modern American poetry has found a poet who can write with ease in the full range of scientific acquaintance.

The poets from whom Ammons derives are very diverse: They range from Emerson, Whitman, and Dickinson to Williams, Moore, and Stevens. Like Emerson and Dickinson, Ammons is emblematic; like Whitman, he is democratic and curious about the world; like Williams, he is unaffectedly colloquial; like Moore, he is observant and scientific; like Stevens, he is reflective and philosophical. Ammons is nonetheless a recognizably new voice. He is a poet of violent griefs, severe feelings of isolation and loneliness, and sudden elations. He assimilates these gusts of feeling to a perceptual grounding in the natural world and to an intellectual grounding in the impalpable; he speaks in a remarkably natural voice.

Ammons's verse is only imperfectly represented here, since he writes long poems of great variety and versatility, abandoning his terse and shapely short forms for a long stream of utterance, of clauses separated not by periods but by colons. Ammons has allowed chance a part in his long poems; one of them, *Tape for the Turn of the Year* (1965), is determined, in line width and total length, by the shape of the paper on which it is written, a roll of adding-machine tape. Another journal volume, *The Snow Poems* (1977), takes its daily cue from the Ithaca weather throughout the winter of Ammons's fiftieth year. Ammons's humor and self-deprecation, visible here in his colloquy with the mountain, are the obverse of his moments of loss and estrangement.

Ammons is a poet who has translated many English genres into indigenous American terms. Gray's "Elegy in a Country Churchyard" has been given us in native form in Ammons's exquisite "Easter Morning," a poem ending with a reminiscence, in natural rather than religious terms, of Bryant's "To a Waterfowl." His "scribbling," in a form like the water "uncapturable and vanishing," partakes of the linearity of all flow, but it leaves behind those shapes of emotion captured: "Shadows are bodiless shapes, yet they have a song." Whitman said that the poet judges not as a judge judges but as the light falling round a helpless thing. Ammons, remembering this injunction, takes as his example the radiance that "does not withhold itself." Poetry for Ammons can use and absorb all that the world contains.

Further Reading:
R. Howard, *Alone with America: Essays on the Art of Poetry in the United States Since 1950*, 1969.
A. Holder, *A. R. Ammons*, 1978.
S. T. Wright, *A. R. Ammons: A Bibliography*, 1980.

Texts:
"Easter Morning" from *A Coast of Trees*, 1981.
All other poems from *Collected Poems, 1951–1971*, 1972.

Hardweed Path Going

Every evening, down into the hardweed
going,
the slop bucket heavy, held-out, wire handle
freezing in the hand, put it down a minute, the jerky
smooth unspilling levelness of the knees,   5
    meditation of a bucket rim,
lest the wheat meal,
floating on clear greasewater, spill,
down the grown-up path:

    don't forget to slop the hogs,   10
    feed the chickens,
    water the mule,
    cut the kindling,
    build the fire,
    call up the cow: 15

    supper is over, it's starting to get
dark early,
better get the scraps together, mix a little meal in,
nothing but swill.

    The dead-purple woods hover on the west.   20
I know those woods.
Under the tall, ceiling-solid pines, beyond the edge of
field and brush, where the wild myrtle grows,
    I let my jo-reet loose.
A jo-reet is a bird. Nine weeks of summer he   25
sat on the well bench in a screened box,
a stick inside to walk on,
    "jo-reet," he said, "jo-reet."
    and I

would come up to the well and draw the bucket down
deep into the cold place where red and white marbled
clay oozed the purest water, water celebrated
throughout the county: 30

　　　　"Grits all gone?"
　　　　"jo-reet."
Throw a dipper of cold water on him. Reddish-black
flutter. 35

　　　　　　"reet, reet, reet!"

　　　　Better turn him loose before
cold weather comes on.
　　　　Doom caving in 40
　　　　inside
　　　　any pleasure, pure
　　　　attachment
　　　　of love. 45

Beyond the wild myrtle away from cats I turned him loose
and his eye asked me what to do, where to go;
he hopped around, scratched a little, but looked up at me.
Don't look at me. Winter is coming.
Disappear in the bushes. I'm tired of you and will 50
be alone hereafter. I will go dry in my well.
　　　　I will turn still.
Go south. Grits is not available in any natural form.
Look under leaves, try mushy logs, the floors of pinywoods.
South into the dominion of bugs. 55

　　　　They're good woods.
But lay me out if a mourning dove far off in the dusky pines
　　　　starts.

　　　　Down the hardweed path going,
leaning, balancing, away from the bucket, to 60
Sparkle, my favorite hog, sparse, fine black hair,
grunted while feeding if rubbed,
scratched against the hair, or if talked to gently:
got the bottom of the slop bucket:
　　　　　　"Sparkle . . . 65
　　　　　　You hungry?
　　　　　　Hungry, girly?"
blowing, bubbling in the trough.

　　　　Waiting for the first freeze:
"Think it's going to freeze tonight?" say the neighbors, 70
the neighbors, going by.

Hog-killing.

Oh, Sparkle, when the axe tomorrow morning falls
and the rush is made to open your throat,
I will sing, watching dry-eyed as a man, sing my   75
          love for you in the tender feedings.

          She's nothing but a hog, boy.

Bleed out, Sparkle, the moon-chilled bleaches
          of your body hanging upside-down
hardening through the mind and night of the first freeze.   80
1964

Cascadilla Falls[1]

I went down by Cascadilla
Falls this
evening, the
stream below the falls,
and picked up a   5
handsized stone
kidney-shaped, testicular, and

thought all its motions into it,
the 800 mph earth spin,
the 190-million-mile yearly   10
displacement around the sun,
the overriding
grand
haul

of the galaxy with the 30,000   15
mph of where
the sun's going:
thought all the interweaving
motions
into myself: dropped   20

[1] Waterfall in Ithaca, New York, near Ammons's
house.

the stone to dead rest:
the stream from other motions
broke
rushing over it:
shelterless,
I turned

to the sky and stood still:
Oh
I do
not know where I am going
that I can live my life
by this single creek.
1970

Transaction

I attended the burial of all my rosy feelings:
I performed the rites, simple and decisive:
the long box took the spilling of gray ground in
with little evidence of note: I traded slow

work for the usual grief: the services were private: 5
there was little cause for show, though no cause not
to show: it went indifferently, with an appropriate
gravity and lack of noise: the ceremonies of the self

seem always to occur at a distance from the ruins of men
where there is nothing really much to expect, no arms,   10
no embraces: the day was all right: certain occasions
outweigh the weather: the woods just to the left

were average woods: well, I turned around finally from
the process, the surface smoothed into a kind of seal,
and tried to notice what might be thought to remain: 15
everything was there, the sun, the breeze, the woods

(as I said), the little mound of troublesome tufts of
grass: but the trees were upright shadows, the breeze
was as against a shade, the woods stirred gray
as deep water: I looked around for what was left,   20

the tools, and took them up and went away, leaving
all my treasures where they might never again disturb
me, increase or craze: decision quietens:
shadows are bodiless shapes, yet they have a song.

1970

Treaties

My great wars close:
ahead, papers,
signatures, the glimmering
in shade of
leaf and raised wine: 5
orchards, orchards,
vineyards, fields:
spiralling slow time while
the medlar
smarts and glows and   10
empty nests
come out in the open:
fall rain then stirs
the black creek and
the small leaf slips in.   15

1971

The City Limits

When you consider the radiance, that it does not withhold
itself but pours its abundance without selection into every
nook and cranny not overhung or hidden; when you consider

that birds' bones make no awful noise against the light but
lie low in the light as in a high testimony; when you consider   5
the radiance, that it will look into the guiltiest

swervings of the weaving heart and bear itself upon them,
not flinching into disguise or darkening; when you consider
the abundance of such resource as illuminates the glow-blue

bodies and gold-skeined wings of flies swarming the dumped
guts of a natural slaughter or the coil of shit and in no
way winces from its storms of generosity; when you consider

that air or vacuum, snow or shale, squid or wolf, rose or lichen,
each is accepted into as much light as it will take, then
the heart moves roomier, the man stands and looks about, the   1.

leaf does not increase itself above the grass, and the dark
work of the deepest cells is of a tune with May bushes
and fear lit by the breadth of such calmly turns to praise.
1971

The Eternal City[1]

After the explosion or cataclysm, that big
display that does its work but then fails
out with destructions, one is left with the

pieces: at first, they don't look very valuable,
but nothing sizable remnant around for   5
gathering the senses on, one begins to take

an interest, to sort out, to consider closely
what will do and won't, matters having become
not only small but critical: bulbs may have been

uprooted: they should be eaten, if edible, or   10
got back in the ground: what used to be garages,
even the splinters, should be collected for

fires: some unusually deep holes or cleared
woods may be turned to water supplies or
sudden fields: ruinage is hardly ever a   15

pretty sight but it must when splendor goes
accept into itself piece by piece all the old
perfect human visions, all the old perfect loves.
1972

[1] Appellation for Rome and for the Christian
heaven.

Grace Abounding[1]

for E.C.

What is the misery in one that turns one with gladness
to the hedge strung lucid with ice: is it that one's
misery, penetrating there as sight, meets neither

welcome nor reprimand but finds nevertheless a picture
of itself sympathetic, held as the ice-blurred stems   5
increased: ah, what an abundance is in the universe

when one can go for gladness to the indifferent ghastly,
feel alliances where none may ever take: find one's
misery made clear, borne, as if also, by a hedge of ice.

1972

Easter Morning

I have a life that did not become,
that turned aside and stopped,
astonished:
I hold it in me like a pregnancy or
as on my lap a child   5
not to grow or grow old but dwell on

it is to his grave I most
frequently return and return
to ask what is wrong, what was
wrong, to see it all by   10
the light of a different necessity
but the grave will not heal
and the child,
stirring, must share my grave
with me, an old man having   15
gotten by on what was left

---

[1] The title is borrowed from John Bunyan's
(1628–1688) *Grace Abounding to the Chief of
Sinners* (1666), his spiritual autobiography,
allegorically retold in *The Pilgrim's Progress*
(1678).

when I go back to my home country in these
fresh far-away days, it's convenient to visit
everybody, aunts and uncles, those who used to say,
look how he's shooting up, and the   20
trinket aunts who always had a little
something in their pocketbooks, cinnamon bark
or a penny or nickel, and uncles who
were the rumored fathers of cousins
who whispered of them as of great, if   25
troubled, presences, and school
teachers, just about everybody older
(and some younger) collected in one place
waiting, particularly, but not for
me, mother and father there, too, and others   30
close, close as burrowing
under skin, all in the graveyard
assembled, done for, the world they
used to wield, have trouble and joy
in, gone   35

the child in me that could not become
was not ready for others to go,
to go on into change, blessings and
horrors, but stands there by the road
where the mishap occurred, crying out for   40
help, come and fix this or we
can't get by, but the great ones who
were to return, they could not or did
not hear and went on in a flurry and
now, I say in the graveyard, here   45
lies the flurry, now it can't come
back with help or helpful asides, now
we all buy the bitter
incompletions, pick up the knots of
horror, silently raving, and go on   50
crashing into empty ends not
completions, not rondures the fullness
has come into and spent itself from
I stand on the stump
of a child, whether myself   55
or my little brother who died, and
yell as far as I can, I cannot leave this place, for
for me it is the dearest and the worst,
it is life nearest to life which is
life lost: it is my place where   60
I must stand and fail,
calling attention with tears

to the branches not lofting
boughs into space, to the barren
air that holds the world that was my world   65

though the incompletions
(& completions) burn out
standing in the flash high-burn
momentary structure of ash, still it
is a picture-book, letter-perfect   70
Easter morning: I have been for a
walk: the wind is tranquil: the brook
works without flashing in an abundant
tranquility: the birds are lively with
voice: I saw something I had   75
never seen before: two great birds,
maybe eagles, blackwinged, whitenecked
and -headed, came from the south oaring
the great wings steadily; they went
directly over me, high up, and kept on   80
due north: but then one bird,
the one behind, veered a little to the
left and the other bird kept on seeming
not to notice for a minute: the first
began to circle as if looking for   85
something, coasting, resting its wings
on the down side of some of the circles:
the other bird came back and they both
circled, looking perhaps for a draft;
they turned a few more times, possibly   90
rising—at least, clearly resting—
then flew on falling into distance till
they broke across the local bush and
trees: it was a sight of bountiful
majesty and integrity: the having   95
patterns and routes, breaking
from them to explore other patterns or
better ways to routes, and then the
return: a dance sacred as the sap in
the trees, permanent in its descriptions   100
as the ripples round the brook's
ripplestone: fresh as this particular
flood of burn breaking across us now
from the sun.

1981

Allen Ginsberg
b. 1926

Allen Ginsberg brought a raw new power into American poetry with the publication of *Howl* (1956). It was a recognizable descendant of *Leaves of Grass,* but Whitman's poetry had been out of favor during the ascendancy of the difficult and "European" poetry of Eliot, Pound, and Stevens. Ginsberg had crossed Whitman's long lines with the long lines of the Hebrew psalms and Whitman's protests against gentility with the Hebrew prophets' denunciations of their society. In the relatively quiet 1950s, Ginsberg's excoriation of America rang out with explosive force: "I saw the best minds of my generation destroyed by madness, starving hysterical naked. . . ."

Yet Ginsberg's declamations, considering his early life, were not surprising. As we learn from "Kaddish" and other poems, he had grown up in a milieu of protest, among Jewish socialists and communists, in Paterson, New Jersey. The faith that rhetoric and political action can be effective was bred into him, and it might have been predicted that William Blake, the English protest-poet, would become Ginsberg's favorite writer. Blake's hatred of the forces of repression found expression in both small lyrics (the *Songs of Innocence* and *Experience*) and in giant mythic narratives like *Jerusalem*. Ginsberg, too, writes both songs and long journey poems, and he has never turned aside from his stance of protest.

Allen Ginsberg saw at close hand the enormous psychic strain endured by American immigrant populations. In his elegy for his mother, Naomi, the long poem entitled "Kaddish" (after the Hebrew prayer for the dead), Ginsberg traces Naomi's life from her first arrival in America from Russia through her brief idyllic youth in the Young People's Socialist League and on to her marriage and long decline into paranoia, confinement in an asylum, eventual lobotomy, and death. Naomi's life became for Ginsberg a paradigm of all the lives of the suffering poor, the confined, and the oppressed. Ginsberg's openly proclaimed homosexuality, which made him a criminal in the eyes of the law, reinforced his belief that the legal system is unnecessarily oppressive, directed by American fundamentalist morality rather than by a concern for public order.

Large public issues—the stockpiling of nuclear bombs, the Korean and Vietnam wars, FBI wiretappings, racism, ecology—continue to enter Ginsberg's poems, but the poetry contains as well Ginsberg's ruefully humorous account of his private life—his travels, his sexual history, his experiments with drugs, his interest in Buddhism, his mourning for his father.

Ginsberg's father was a high school teacher of English and a writer of inept conventional verse (Ginsberg gave poetry readings jointly with his father in the later years of his father's life, as if to demonstrate that family solidarity outweighs aesthetic compatibility). Ginsberg's mother ("from whose pained head I first took Vision," says Ginsberg) may have been his muse, but in his father's verse he found his introduction to English poetry. Ginsberg went to Columbia

University, was expelled as a sophomore for writing an obscene phrase in the dust on his dormitory windowpane, lived for a while with William Burroughs and Jack Kerouac, reentered Columbia, and graduated in 1948. Shortly after graduation, implicated in a friend's thefts because the stolen goods had been stored in his apartment, Ginsberg pleaded insanity to avoid imprisonment and was confined for eight months in the Columbia Psychiatric Institute. In the early 1950s, in San Francisco, he met the poets who were to be known collectively with him as the Beat generation—Kenneth Rexroth, Lawrence Ferlinghetti, and Gary Snyder. The City Lights Press, founded by Ferlinghetti, published Ginsberg's verse from *Howl* until 1985, including such volumes as *Reality Sandwiches* (1963), *Planet News* (1968), *The Fall of America* (1973) and *Mind Breaths* (1977). In 1985 Harper & Row issued Ginsberg's *Collected Poems;* the volume *White Shroud* followed in 1986.

Ginsberg's return to the oral tradition in poetry had far-reaching effects, as did his allegiance to the line of poetry stretching from Whitman through Williams. (As one New Jersey poet to another, Williams had encouraged Ginsberg's early verse, and contributed an introduction to *Howl;* he had even included letters from Ginsberg in *Paterson.*) Even such formal poets as Robert Lowell became conscious, by the example of the beat poets, of the necessity of incorporating in poetry the rhythms of American speech. The uninhibited poetry readings Ginsberg has given—which have included, over the years, occasional nakedness, references to drugs, chants with a harmonium and finger cymbals, the reading aloud of sexual diaries, Buddhist mantras, and audience participation—immensely changed the nature of the poetry reading as a communal occasion. Ginsberg's humorous and candid poetry suggested that self-revelation need not be shaming or self-abasing and that political protest need not be dour or hateful. His spiritual evolution—his repudiation of drugs, his travels in India, his adoption of Buddhism—appears in his poetry as a dramatic thread giving continuity to the whole. He remains a powerful presence in American poetry today and is probably the only American poet whose name is known throughout the world.

Further Reading:

T. F. Merrill, *Allen Ginsberg,* 1969.
J. Kramer, *Allen Ginsberg in America,* 1970.
J. Tytell, *Naked Angels: The Lives and Literature of the Beat Generation,* 1976.
M. P. Kraus, *Allen Ginsberg: An Annotated Bibliography, 1969–1977,* 1978.
P. C. Portages, *The Visionary Poetics of Allen Ginsberg,* 1978.

Texts:

"Howl," "A Supermarket in California," "Sunflower Sutra," and "America" from *Howl,* 1956.
"Mugging" from *Mind Breaths,* 1979.

from Howl

for Carl Solomon

I

I saw the best minds of my generation destroyed by madness, starving hysterical
naked,

dragging themselves through the negro streets at dawn looking for an angry fix,

angelheaded hipsters burning for the ancient heavenly connections to the starry
dynamo in the machinery of night,

who poverty and tatters and hollow-eyed and high sat up smoking in the
supernatural darkness of cold-water flats floating across the tops of cities
contemplating jazz,

who bared their brains to Heaven under the El and saw Mohammedan angels
staggering on tenement roofs illuminated,   5

who passed through universities with radiant cool eyes hallucinating Arkansas
and Blake-light tragedy among the scholars of war,

who were expelled from the academies for crazy & publishing obscene odes on
the windows of the skull,[1]

who cowered in unshaven rooms in underwear, burning their money in
wastebaskets and listening to the Terror through the wall,

who got busted in their pubic beards returning through Laredo with a belt of
marijuana for New York,

who ate fire in paint hotels or drank turpentine in Paradise Alley,[2] death, or
purgatoried their torsos night after night   10

with dreams, with drugs, with waking nightmares, alcohol and cock and endless
balls,

incomparable blind streets of shuddering cloud and lightning in the mind
leaping toward poles of Canada & Paterson, illuminating all the motionless
world of Time between,

Peyote solidities of halls, backyard green tree cemetery dawns, wine drunkenness
over the rooftops, storefront boroughs of teahead joyride neon blinking
traffic light, sun and moon and tree vibrations in the roaring winter dusks of
Brooklyn, ashcan rantings and kind king light of mind,

who chained themselves to subways for the endless ride from Battery to holy
Bronx on benzedrine until the noise of wheels and children brought them
down shuddering mouth-wracked and battered bleak of brain all drained of
brilliance in the drear light of Zoo,

who sank all night in submarine light of Bickford's floated out and sat through
the stale beer afternoon in desolate Fugazzi's, listening to the crack of doom
on the hydrogen jukebox,   15

---

[1] Ginsberg was expelled from Columbia
University for writing an obscenity in the dust
on his dormitory windowpane.

[2] Ginsberg's note: "A slum courtyard N.Y. Lower
East Side, site of [the writer Jack] Kerouac's
Subterraneans, 1958."

who talked continuously seventy hours from park to pad to bar to Bellevue to
   museum to the Brooklyn Bridge,
a lost battalion of platonic conversationalists jumping down the stoops off fire
   escapes off windowsills off Empire State out of the moon,
yacketayakking screaming vomiting whispering facts and memories and
   anecdotes and eyeball kicks and shocks of hospitals and jails and wars,
whole intellects disgorged in total recall for seven days and nights with brilliant
   eyes, meat for the Synagogue cast on the pavement,
who vanished into nowhere Zen New Jersey leaving a trail of ambiguous
   picture postcards of Atlantic City Hall,   20
suffering Eastern sweats and Tangerian bone-grindings and migraines of China
   under junk-withdrawal of Newark's bleak furnished room,
who wandered around and around at midnight in the railroad yard wondering
   where to go, and went, leaving no broken hearts,
who lit cigarettes in boxcars boxcars boxcars racketing through snow toward
   lonesome farms in grandfather night,
who studied Plotinus Poe St. John of the Cross telepathy and bop kaballa
   because the cosmos instinctively vibrated at their feet in Kansas,
who loned it through the streets of Idaho seeking visionary indian angels who
   were visionary indian angels,   25
who thought they were only mad when Baltimore gleamed in supernatural
   ecstasy,
who jumped in limousines with the Chinaman of Oklahoma on the impulse of
   winter midnight streetlight smalltown rain,
who lounged hungry and lonesome through Houston seeking jazz or sex or
   soup, and followed the brilliant Spaniard to converse about America and
   Eternity, a hopeless task, and so took ship to Africa,
who disappeared into the volcanoes of Mexico leaving behind nothing but the
   shadow of dungarees and the lava and ash of poetry scattered in fireplace
   Chicago,
who reappeared on the West Coast investigating the F.B.I. in beards and shorts
   with big pacifist eyes sexy in their dark skin passing out incomprehensible
   leaflets,   30
who burned cigarette holes in their arms protesting the narcotic tobacco haze of
   Capitalism,
who distributed Supercommunist pamphlets in Union Square weeping and
   undressing while the sirens of Los Alamos wailed them down, and wailed
   down Wall, and the Staten Island ferry also wailed,
who broke down crying in white gymnasiums naked and trembling before the
   machinery of other skeletons,
who bit detectives in the neck and shrieked with delight in policecars for
   committing no crime but their own wild cooking pederasty and
   intoxication,
who howled on their knees in the subway and were dragged off the roof
   waving genitals and manuscripts,   35
who let themselves be fucked in the ass by saintly motorcyclists, and screamed
   with joy,

who blew and were blown by those human seraphim, the sailors, caresses of
    Atlantic and Caribbean love,

who balled in the morning in the evenings in rosegardens and the grass of
    public parks and cemeteries scattering their semen freely to whomever come
    who may,

who hiccupped endlessly trying to giggle but wound up with a sob behind a
    partition in a Turkish Bath when the blonde & naked angel came to pierce
    them with a sword,

who lost their loveboys to the three old shrews of fate the one eyed shrew of
    the heterosexual dollar the one eyed shrew that winks out of the womb and
    the one eyed shrew that does nothing but sit on her ass and snip the
    intellectual golden threads of the craftsman's loom,   40

who copulated ecstatic and insatiate with a bottle of beer a sweetheart a package
    of cigarettes a candle and fell off the bed, and continued along the floor and
    down the hall and ended fainting on the wall with a vision of ultimate cunt
    and come eluding the last gyzym of consciousness,

who sweetened the snatches of a million girls trembling in the sunset, and were
    red eyed in the morning but prepared to sweeten the snatch of the sunrise,
    flashing buttocks under barns and naked in the lake,

who went out whoring through Colorado in myriad stolen night-cars, N.C.,[3]
    secret hero of these poems, cocksman and Adonis of Denver—joy to the
    memory of his innumerable lays of girls in empty lots & diner backyards,
    moviehouses' rickety rows, on mountaintops in caves or with gaunt waitresses
    in familiar roadside lonely petticoat upliftings & especially secret gas-station
    solipsisms of johns, & hometown alleys too,

who faded out in vast sordid movies, were shifted in dreams, woke on a sudden
    Manhattan, and picked themselves up out of basements hungover with
    heartless Tokay and horrors of Third Avenue iron dreams & stumbled to
    unemployment offices,

who walked all night with their shoes full of blood on the snowbank docks
    waiting for a door in the East River to open to a room full of steamheat
    and opium,   45

who created great suicidal dramas on the apartment cliff-banks of the Hudson
    under the wartime blue floodlight of the moon & their heads shall be
    crowned with laurel in oblivion,

who ate the lamb stew of the imagination or digested the crab at the muddy
    bottom of the rivers of Bowery,

who wept at the romance of the streets with their pushcarts full of onions and
    bad music,

who sat in boxes breathing in the darkness under the bridge, and rose up to
    build harpsichords in their lofts,

who coughed on the sixth floor of Harlem crowned with flame under the
    tubercular sky surrounded by orange crates of theology,   50

[3] Neal Cassady, a friend of Ginsberg and Jack
Kerouac, who appears as the character Dean
Moriarty in Kerouac's novel *On the Road*.

who scribbled all night rocking and rolling over lofty incantations which in the
   yellow morning were stanzas of gibberish,
who cooked rotten animals lung heart feet tail borsht & tortillas dreaming of
   the pure vegetable kingdom,
who plunged themselves under meat trucks looking for an egg,
who threw their watches off the roof to cast their ballot for Eternity outside of
   Time, & alarm clocks fell on their heads every day for the next decade,
who cut their wrists three times successively unsuccessfully, gave up and were
   forced to open antique stores where they thought they were growing old and
   cried,   55
who were burned alive in their innocent flannel suits on Madison Avenue amid
   blasts of leaden verse & the tanked-up clatter of the iron regiments of fashion
   & the nitroglycerine shrieks of the fairies of advertising & the mustard gas of
   sinister intelligent editors, or were run down by the drunken taxicabs of
   Absolute Reality,
who jumped off the Brooklyn Bridge this actually happened and walked away
   unknown and forgotten into the ghostly daze of Chinatown soup alleyways
   & firetrucks, not even one free beer,
who sang out of their windows in despair, fell out of the subway window,
   jumped in the filthy Passaic, leaped on negroes, cried all over the street,
   danced on broken wineglasses barefoot smashed phonograph records of
   nostalgic European 1930's German jazz finished the whiskey and threw up
   groaning into the bloody toilet, moans in their ears and the blast of colossal
   steamwhistles,
who barreled down the highways of the past journeying to each other's
   hotrod-Golgotha jail-solitude watch or Birmingham jazz incarnation,
who drove crosscountry seventytwo hours to find out if I had a vision or you
   had a vision or he had a vision to find out Eternity,   60
who journeyed to Denver, who died in Denver, who came back to Denver &
   waited in vain, who watched over Denver & brooded & loned in Denver
   and finally went away to find out the Time, & now Denver is lonesome for
   her heroes,
who fell on their knees in hopeless cathedrals praying for each other's salvation
   and light and breasts, until the soul illuminated its hair for a second,
who crashed through their minds in jail waiting for impossible criminals with
   golden heads and the charm of reality in their hearts who sang sweet blues to
   Alcatraz,
who retired to Mexico to cultivate a habit, or Rocky Mount to tender Buddha
   or Tangiers to boys or Southern Pacific to the black locomotive or Harvard
   to Narcissus to Woodlawn to the daisychain or grave,
who demanded sanity trials accusing the radio of hypnotism & were left with
   their insanity & their hands & a hung jury,   65
who threw potato salad at CCNY[4] lecturers on Dadaism and subsequently
   presented themselves on the granite steps of the madhouse with shaven heads
   and harlequin speech of suicide, demanding instantaneous lobotomy,

[4] City College of New York.

and who were given instead the concrete void of insulin metrasol[5] electricity
   hydrotherapy psychotherapy occupational therapy pingpong & amnesia,
who in humorless protest overturned only one symbolic pingpong table, resting
   briefly in catatonia,
returning years later truly bald except for a wig of blood, and tears and fingers,
   to the visible madman doom of the wards of the madtowns of the East,
Pilgrim State's Rockland's and Greystone's[6] foetid halls, bickering with the
   echoes of the soul, rocking and rolling in the midnight solitude-bench
   dolmen-realms of love, dream of life a nightmare, bodies turned to stone as
   heavy as the moon,
with mother finally ******,[7] and the last fantastic book flung out of the
   tenement window, and the last door closed at 4 AM and the last telephone
   slammed at the wall in reply and the last furnished room emptied down to
   the last piece of mental furniture, a yellow paper rose twisted on a wire
   hanger in the closet, and even that imaginary, nothing but a hopeful little bit
   of hallucination—
ah, Carl, while you are not safe I am not safe, and now you're really in the
   total animal soup of time—
and who therefore ran through the icy streets obsessed with a sudden flash of
   the alchemy of the use of the ellipse the catalog the meter & the vibrating
   plane,
who dreamt and made incarnate gaps in Time & Space through images
   juxtaposed, and trapped the archangel of the soul between 2 visual images
   and joined the elemental verbs and set the noun and dash of consciousness
   together jumping with sensation of Pater Omnipotens Aeterna Deus[8]
to recreate the syntax and measure of poor human prose and stand before you
   speechless and intelligent and shaking with shame, rejected yet confessing out
   the soul to conform to the rhythm of thought in his naked and endless head,
the madman bum and angel beat in Time, unknown, yet putting down here
   what might be left to say in time come after death,
and rose reincarnate in the ghostly clothes of jazz in the goldhorn shadow of
   the band and blew the suffering of America's naked mind for love into an eli
   eli lamma lamma sabacthani[9] saxophone cry that shivered the cities down to
   the last radio
with the absolute heart of the poem of life butchered out of their own bodies
   good to eat a thousand years.

70

75

1956

---

[5] A tranquilizing drug.
[6] Pilgrim State, Rockland, and Greystone: state
mental hospitals. Carl Solomon was confined in
Rockland.
[7] Asterisks replace *fucked*.
[8] Latin, from the Creed: "Omnipotent Father
Eternal God." Ginsberg uses the feminine of the
adjective "aeternus," as does the French painter

Paul Cézanne (1839–1906), from whose letters
Ginsberg borrowed the phrase. Cézanne meant
all of created nature (conventionally imagined
as female).
[9] Hebrew: "My God, my God, why hast thou
forsaken me?" These were Jesus' words on the
cross (Matthew 4:26).

A Supermarket in California

What thoughts I have of you tonight, Walt Whitman, for I walked down the sidestreets under the trees with a headache, self-conscious looking at the full moon.

In my hungry fatigue, and shopping for images, I went into the neon fruit supermarket, dreaming of your enumerations!

What peaches and what penumbras! Whole families shopping at night! Aisles full of husbands! Wives in the avocados, babies in the tomatoes!—and you, Garcia Lorca,[1] what were you doing down by the watermelons?

I saw you, Walt Whitman, childless, lonely old grubber, poking among the meats in the refrigerator and eyeing the grocery boys.

I heard you asking questions of each: Who killed the pork chops? What price bananas? Are you my Angel?   5

I wandered in and out of the brilliant stacks of cans following you, and followed in my imagination by the store detective.

We strode down the open corridors together in our solitary fancy tasting artichokes, possessing every frozen delicacy, and never passing the cashier.

Where are we going, Walt Whitman? The doors close in an hour. Which way does your beard point tonight?

(I touch your book and dream of our odyssey in the supermarket and feel absurd.)

Will we walk all night through solitary streets? The trees add shade to shade, lights out in the houses, we'll both be lonely.   10

Will we stroll dreaming of the lost America of love past blue automobiles in driveways, home to our silent cottage?

Ah, dear father, graybeard, lonely old courage-teacher, what America did you have when Charon[2] quit poling his ferry and you got out on a smoking bank and stood watching the boat disappear on the black waters of Lethe?

1956

---

[1] Homosexual Spanish poet (1898–1936), shot by French soldiers in the Spanish Civil War. He wrote an "Ode to Walt Whitman."
[2] In mythology Charon is the ferryman who carries souls across the river Styx to Hades, where they drink from the river Lethe, causing them to forget their life before death.

Sunflower Sutra[1]

I walked on the banks of the tincan banana dock and sat down under the huge
   shade of a Southern Pacific locomotive to look at the sunset over the box
   house hills and cry.
Jack Kerouac sat beside me on a busted rusty iron pole, companion, we thought
   the same thoughts of the soul, bleak and blue and sad-eyed, surrounded by
   the gnarled steel roots of trees of machinery.
The oily water on the river mirrored the red sky, sun sank on top of final
   Frisco peaks, no fish in that stream, no hermit in those mounts, just ourselves
   rheumy-eyed and hungover like old bums on the riverbank, tired and wily.
Look at the Sunflower, he said, there was a dead gray shadow against the sky,
   big as a man, sitting dry on top of a pile of ancient sawdust—
—I rushed up enchanted—it was my first sunflower, memories of Blake[2]—my
   visions—Harlem   5
and Hells of the Eastern rivers, bridges, clanking Joes Greasy Sandwiches, dead
   baby carriages, black treadless tires forgotten and unretreaded, the poem of
   the riverbank, condoms & pots, steel knives, nothing stainless, only the dank
   muck and the razor sharp artifacts passing into the past—
and the gray Sunflower poised against the sunset, crackly bleak and dusty with
   the smut and smog and smoke of olden locomotives in its eye—
corolla[3] of bleary spikes pushed down and broken like a battered crown, seeds
   fallen out of its face, soon-to-be-toothless mouth of sunny air, sunrays
   obliterated on its hairy head like a dried wire spiderweb,
leaves stuck out like arms out of the stem, gestures from the sawdust root,
   broke pieces of plaster fallen out of the black twigs, a dead fly in its ear,
Unholy battered old thing you were, my sunflower O my soul, I loved you
   then!   10
The grime was no man's grime but death and human locomotives,
all that dress of dust, that veil of darkened railroad skin, that smog of cheek,
   that eyelid of black mis'ry, that sooty hand or phallus or protuberance of
   artificial worse-than-dirt—industrial—modern—all that civilization spotting
   your crazy golden crown—
and those blear thoughts of death and dusty loveless eyes and ends and withered
   roots below, in the home-pile of sand and sawdust, rubber dollar bills, skin
   of machinery, the guts and innards of the weeping coughing car, the empty
   lonely tincans with their rusty tongues alack, what more could I name, the
   smoked ashes of some cock cigar, the cunts of wheelbarrows and the milky
   breasts of cars, wornout asses out of chairs & sphincters of dynamos—all
   these

---

[1] Buddhist religious text.
[2] William Blake (1757–1827), English poet and
author of "Ah! Sunflower." Ginsberg in 1948

had had a vision in which he heard Blake's
voice reciting this poem.
[3] Petals surrounding the center of a flower.

entangled in your mummied roots—and you there standing before me in the
    sunset, all your glory in your form!
A perfect beauty of a sunflower! a perfect excellent lovely sunflower existence!
    a sweet natural eye to the new hip moon, woke up alive and excited
    grasping in the sunset shadow sunrise golden monthly breeze!   15
How many flies buzzed round you innocent of your grime, while you cursed
    the heavens of the railroad and your flower soul?
Poor dead flower? when did you forget you were a flower? when did you look
    at your skin and decide you were an impotent dirty old locomotive? the
    ghost of a locomotive? the specter and shade of a once powerful mad
    American locomotive?
You were never no locomotive, Sunflower, you were a sunflower!
And you Locomotive, you are a locomotive, forget me not!
So I grabbed up the skeleton thick sunflower and stuck it at my side like a
    scepter,   20
and deliver my sermon to my soul, and Jack's soul too, and anyone who'll
    listen,
—We're not our skin of grime, we're not our dread bleak dusty imageless
    locomotive, we're all beautiful golden sunflowers inside, we're blessed by our
    own seed & golden hairy naked accomplishment-bodies growing into mad
    black formal sunflowers in the sunset, spied on by our eyes under the shadow
    of the mad locomotive riverbank sunset Frisco hilly tincan evening sitdown
    vision.

1956

America

America I've given you all and now I'm nothing.
America two dollars and twentyseven cents January 17, 1956.
I can't stand my own mind.
America when will we end the human war?
Go fuck yourself with your atom bomb.   5
I don't feel good don't bother me.
I won't write my poem till I'm in my right mind.
America when will you be angelic?
When will you take off your clothes?
When will you look at yourself through the grave?   10
When will you be worthy of your million Trotskyites?[1]
America why are your libraries full of tears?

---

[1] Communist idealists, followers of Leon Trotsky
(1879–1940), the opponent of Stalin.

America when will you send your eggs to India?[2]
I'm sick of your insane demands.
When can I go into the supermarket and buy what I need with my good
    looks?   15
America after all it is you and I who are perfect not the next world.
Your machinery is too much for me.
You made me want to be a saint.
There must be some other way to settle this argument.
Burroughs is in Tangiers[3] I don't think he'll come back it's sinister.   20
Are you being sinister or is this some form of practical joke?
I'm trying to come to the point.
I refuse to give up my obsession.
America stop pushing I know what I'm doing.
America the plum blossoms are falling.   25
I haven't read the newspapers for months, everyday somebody goes on trial for
    murder.
America I feel sentimental about the Wobblies.[4]
America I used to be a communist when I was a kid I'm not sorry.
I smoke marijuana every chance I get.
I sit in my house for days on end and stare at the roses in the closet.   30
When I go to Chinatown I get drunk and never get laid.
My mind is made up there's going to be trouble.
You should have seen me reading Marx.[5]
My psychoanalyst thinks I'm perfectly right.
I won't say the Lord's Prayer.   35
I have mystical visions and cosmic vibrations.
America I still haven't told you what you did to Uncle Max after he came over
    from Russia.

I'm addressing you.
Are you going to let your emotional life be run by Time Magazine?
I'm obsessed by Time Magazine.   40
I read it every week.
Its cover stares at me every time I slink past the corner candystore.
I read it in the basement of the Berkeley Public Library.
It's always telling me about responsibility. Businessmen are serious. Movie
    producers are serious. Everybody's serious but me.
It occurs to me that I am America.   45
I am talking to myself again.

---

[2] India was suffering a famine, while America had
an agricultural surplus.
[3] William Burroughs (b. 1914), a friend of
Ginsberg and author of the novel *Naked Lunch*
(1959), was living in Morocco.
[4] Nickname for members of the Industrial

Workers of the World, a revolutionary union
founded in Chicago in 1905.
[5] Karl Marx (1818–1883), German social
philosopher and author, with Friedrich Engels,
of *The Communist Manifesto* (1848).

Asia is rising against me.
I haven't got a chinaman's chance.
I'd better consider my national resources.
My national resources consist of two joints of marijuana millions of genitals an
    unpublishable private literature that goes 1400 miles an hour and
    twentyfive-thousand mental institutions.   50
I say nothing about my prisons nor the millions of underprivileged who live in
    my flowerpots under the light of five hundred suns.
I have abolished the whorehouses of France, Tangiers is the next to go.
My ambition is to be President despite the fact that I'm a Catholic.

America how can I write a holy litany in your silly mood?
I will continue like Henry Ford my strophes are as individual as his
    automobiles more so they're all different sexes.   55
America I will sell you strophes $2500 apiece $500 down on your old strophe
America free Tom Mooney[6]
America save the Spanish Loyalists[7]
America Sacco & Vanzetti[8] must not die
America I am the Scottsboro boys.[9]   60
America when I was seven momma took me to Communist Cell meetings they
    sold us garbanzos[10] a handful per ticket a ticket costs a nickel and the
    speeches were free everybody was angelic and sentimental about the workers
    it was all so sincere you have no idea what a good thing the party was in
    1935 Scott Nearing was a grand old man a real mensch Mother Bloor made
    me cry I once saw Israel Amter[11] plain. Everybody must have been a spy.
America you don't really want to go to war.
America it's them bad Russians.
Them Russians them Russians and them Chinamen. And them Russians.
The Russia wants to eat us alive. The Russia's power mad. She wants to take
    our cars from out our garages.   65
Her wants to grab Chicago. Her needs a Red Readers' Digest. Her wants our
    auto plants in Siberia. Him big bureaucracy running our fillingstations.
That no good. Ugh. Him make Indians learn read. Him need big black niggers.
Hah. Her make us all work sixteen hours a day. Help.
America this is quite serious.

[6] American labor agitator in California, accused of bomb killings and sentenced to death in 1916 but pardoned in 1939.
[7] Those fighting against Franco in the Spanish Civil War.
[8] Nicola Sacco and Bartolomeo Vanzetti were *executed* in Massachusetts in 1927 for a murder connected with a robbery; sentiment ran high against them because of their radical political beliefs.
[9] The "Scottsboro boys" were nine blacks who were convicted in Alabama of the rape of two white women in 1931. Liberals and radicals believed the conviction to be unproved. Four years later the sentences were reduced in four cases and the charges dropped in five.
[10] Chick peas.
[11] Scott Nearing (1883–1983), Ella ("Mother") Bloor (1862–1951), and Israel Amter (1881–1954): well-known American Socialists and Communists.

America this is the impression I get from looking in the television set.
America is this correct?   70
I'd better get right down to the job.
It's true I don't want to join the Army or turn lathes in precision parts
    factories, I'm nearsighted and psychopathic anyway.
America I'm putting my queer shoulder to the wheel.
1956

---

from Mugging

I

Tonite I walked out of my red apartment door on East tenth street's dusk—
Walked out of my home ten years, walked out in my honking neighborhood
Tonite at seven walked out past garbage cans chained to concrete anchors
Walked under black painted fire escapes, giant castiron plate covering a hole in
    ground
—Crossed the street, traffic lite red, thirteen bus roaring by liquor store,   5
past corner pharmacy iron grated, past Coca Cola & My-Lai[1] posters fading
    scraped on brick
Past Chinese Laundry wood door'd, & broken cement stoop steps For Rent hall
    painted green & purple Puerto Rican style
Along E. 10th's glass splattered pavement, kid blacks & Spanish oiled hair
    adolescents' crowded house fronts—
Ah, tonite I walked out on my block NY City under humid summer sky
    Halloween,
thinking what happened Timothy Leary[2] joining brain police for a season?   10
thinking what's all this Weathermen,[3] secrecy & selfrighteousness beyond reason
    —F.B.I. plots?
Walked past a taxicab controlling the bottle strewn curb—
past young fellows with their umbrella handles & canes leaning against ravaged
    Buick
—and as I looked at the crowd of kids on the stoop—a boy stepped up, put
    his arm around my neck
tenderly I thought for a moment, squeezed harder, his umbrella handle against
    my skull,   15
and his friends took my arm, a young brown companion tripped his foot 'gainst
    my ankle—

[1] Site of an atrocity in the Vietnam War.
[2] Professor fired from Harvard University for
espousing drug use.
[3] Revolutionary radical group.

as I went down shouting Om Ah Hūm[4] to gangs of lovers on the stoop
    watching
slowly appreciating, why this is a raid, these strangers mean strange business
with what—my pockets, bald head, broken-healed-bone leg, my softshoes, my
    heart—
Have they knives? Om Ah Hūm—Have they sharp metal wood to shove in eye
    ear ass? Om Ah Hūm   20
& slowly reclined on the pavement, struggling to keep my woolen bag of
    poetry address calendar & Leary-lawyer notes hung from my shoulder
dragged in my neat orlon shirt over the crossbar of a broken metal door
dragged slowly onto the fire-soiled floor an abandoned store, laundry candy
    counter 1929—
now a mess of papers & pillows & plastic covers cracked cockroach-corpsed
    ground—
my wallet back pocket passed over the iron foot step guard   25
and fell out, stole by God Muggers' lost fingers, Strange—
Couldn't tell—snakeskin wallet actually plastic, 70 dollars my bank money for a
    week,
old broken wallet—and dreary plastic contents—Amex card & Manf. Hanover
    Trust Credit too—business card from Mr. Spears British Home Minister
    Drug Squad—my draft card—membership ACLU[5] & Naropa Institute[6]
    Instructor's identification
Om Ah Hūm I continued chanting Om Ah Hūm
Putting my palm on the neck of an 18 year old boy fingering my back pocket
    crying "Where's the money"   30
"Om Ah Hūm there isn't any"
My card Chief Boo-Hoo Neo American Church New Jersey & Lower East
    Side
Om Ah Hūm—what not forgotten crowded wallet—Mobil Credit, Shell? old
    lovers addresses on cardboard pieces, booksellers calling cards—
—"Shut up or we'll murder you"—"Om Ah Hūm take it easy"
Lying on the floor shall I shout more loud?—the metal door closed on
    blackness   35
one boy felt my broken healed ankle, looking for hundred dollar bills behind
    my stocking weren't even there—a third boy untied my Seiko Hong Kong
    watch rough from right wrist leaving a clasp-prick skin tiny bruise
"Shut up and we'll get out of here"—and so they left,
as I rose from the cardboard mattress thinking Om Ah Hūm didn't stop em
    enough,
the tone of voice too loud—my shoulder bag with 10,000 dollars full of poetry
    left on the broken floor—

1974

---

[4] Buddhist chanted prayer (mantra).   [6] Ginsberg's Institute of Poetics.
[5] American Civil Liberties Union.

James Merrill
b. 1926

In 1983 James Merrill published two collections. One, called *From the First Nine*, is a selection of lyrics from his first nine volumes of poetry, and the second, *The Changing Light at Sandover*, collects the three "books" of his verse trilogy—*The Book of Ephraim*, *Mirabell*, and *Scripts for the Pageant*. Merrill's writing has been advancing on these two fronts—lyric and narrative—since his thirties, but his first narrative experiments, *The Seraglio* (1957) and *The [Diblos] Notebook* (1965), were in prose. Merrill's gift for social observation, for the comedy of manners, appears in both lyric and narrative forms. He is an expert observer of both ordinary surroundings and the world to which he was born (the New York world of the very rich). His father, Charles Merrill, founded the Merrill, Lynch stockbrokerage. His parents were divorced when he was young; he writes about them in "The Broken Home," and about his lonely childhood in "Lost in Translation." Merrill's life as an adult has been marked by wide reading, frequent travel, and an international perspective. He has taught from time to time and is at present the judge for the Yale Younger Poet series, the series in which his own first book appeared, chosen by W. H. Auden.

It is the natural tendency of lyric to divest itself of social detail; consequently, the lyric alone did not suffice for the working out of Merrill's talent. When Merrill, after the 1960s, abandoned the novel as a narrative medium, he began to write a conversation-narrative in mixed forms of verse, one that eventually grew to fill three volumes. The generating medium (or pretext) for the conversation is the Ouija board, and by means of it Merrill "converses" with dead friends (including W. H. Auden) as well as with various immortal beings, who gradually reveal to him a new cosmology, itself perhaps less interesting than the human interchanges surrounding it.

The trilogy represents one extreme of Merrill's writing. At the other extreme are lyrics of intense delicacy, delighted complexity, and pained apprehension. Laughter, pain, and love are the ingredients of Merrill's social comedy, and the dominant topic of his lyrics is a love tinged by finely discriminated shades of sensuality. His palette of words is luxuriously rich; he descends from both Keats and Byron, but perhaps most of all from Proust (on whom he did his senior honors thesis at Amherst). The nostalgias of love seen through the filters of memory are a perpetual subject for Merrill; he is a poet of the embarrassments as well as the rewards of desire.

Merrill's *First Poems* (1950), published a few years after his graduation from Amherst College, were already accomplished in technique but oblique in their manner, probably because of his legitimate fear (at a time when homosexuality still had criminal status) of revealing his sexual orientation. Succeeding volumes —*The Country of a Thousand Years of Peace* (1959) and *Water Street* (1962)— widened his canvas. He had left New York City, where he lived after college, for Stonington, Connecticut, and he began to spend part of each year in Greece, where his landscape poetry took on particular brilliance and his love poetry deepened and grew better acquainted with loss. The influence of the modern

Greek poet Constantine Cavafy is reflected in *Nights and Days* (1966). In *Braving the Elements* (1972) Merrill included landscape poetry of the American West, where deserts and geodes and cacti give the poems a different barbarism from that of Greece.

Merrill is as tireless as George Herbert (another of his English masters) in the reinvention of poetic forms. His many sonnet sequences (see "Matinees") have redescribed that genre, as they change rhyme-schemes, reshape proportions, and take up surprising levels of diction. Language in Merrill's hands is a gauzy and spangled fabric, a form of enchantment. Merrill is fond of metaphors of shadow play, magician's tents, illusion successfully practiced; he is the "sleight-of-hand man" that Wallace Stevens thought the poet should be.

Under the dense and shimmering glow of language, Merrill treats human experiences—the isolation of childhood, the terrors of betrayal in love, the gaiety and mystery of love rewarded, the fidelities of friendship—that concern everyone; and in his witty self-portrait of the American innocent abroad, he continues a national tradition magisterially exemplified in Henry James. "I feel exotic at home, American abroad," Merrill has said; the uneasy accommodation between the parent continent (with its worldliness and cynicism) and our American naiveté is a constant source of poetry for Merrill.

Merrill has rarely, in lyrics, written free verse; his love for pattern, though it took him at first into some gymnastic exercises perhaps too strict to be called poetry, has proved a revivifying force for the claims of formal verse in a field where free verse, based on an American phrasal rhythm, seemed to have won the day. In admitting worldliness, sophistication, and mixed emotions into his verse, Merrill, even more than Robert Lowell, acts as a civilized poet in the classical tradition, undistorted by the pragmatic American habit of seeing only one side of a question. He has preserved a tone of lightness and discretion and a texture of charm and ease while treating the most profound topics—love and death—proper to lyric.

Further Reading:
R. Labrie, *James Merrill*, 1982.
J. Moffett, *James Merrill: An Introduction to the Poetry*, 1984.

Text:
Selected Poems, 1982.

The Broken Home[1]

Crossing the street,
I saw the parents and the child
At their window, gleaming like fruit
With evening's mild gold leaf.

[1] The cliché is used with some irony here.

In a room on the floor below,   5
Sunless, cooler—a brimming
Saucer of wax, marbly and dim—
I have lit what's left of my life.

I have thrown out yesterday's milk
And opened a book of maxims.   10
The flame quickens. The word stirs.

Tell me, tongue of fire,
That you and I are as real
At least as the people upstairs.

My father,[2] who had flown in World War I,   15
Might have continued to invest his life
In cloud banks well above Wall Street and wife.
But the race was run below, and the point was to win.

Too late now, I make out in his blue gaze
(Through the smoked glass of being thirty-six)   20
The soul eclipsed by twin black pupils, sex
And business; time was money in those days.

Each thirteenth year he married. When he died
There were already several chilled wives
In sable orbit—rings, cars, permanent waves.   25
We'd felt him warming up for a green bride.

He could afford it. He was "in his prime"
At three score ten. But money was not time.

When my parents were younger this was a popular act:
A veiled woman would leap from an electric, wine-dark car   30
To the steps of no matter what—the Senate or the Ritz Bar—
And bodily, at newsreel speed, attack

No matter whom—Al Smith or José Maria Sert
Or Clemenceau[3]—veins standing out on her throat
As she yelled War mongerer! Pig! Give us the vote!,   35
And would have to be hauled away in her hobble skirt.

What had the man done? Oh, made history.
Her business (he had implied) was giving birth,
Tending the house, mending the socks.

[2] Charles Merrill, who was a financier and
founder of the brokerage firm Merrill, Lynch.
He and Merrill's mother eventually divorced.

[3] Alfred E. Smith (1873–1944) and Georges
Clemenceau (1841–1929) were politicians; José
Maria Sert (1876–1945) was a painter.

Always that same old story—
Father Time and Mother Earth,[4]
A marriage on the rocks.   40

One afternoon, red, satyr-thighed
Michael, the Irish setter, head
Passionately lowered, led
The child I was to a shut door. Inside,   45

Blinds beat sun from the bed.
The green-gold room throbbed like a bruise.
Under a sheet, clad in taboos
Lay whom we sought, her hair undone, outspread,   50

And of a blackness found, if ever now, in old
Engravings where the acid bit.
I must have needed to touch it
Or the whiteness—was she dead?
Her eyes flew open, startled strange and cold.   55

The dog slumped to the floor. She reached for me. I fled.
Tonight they have stepped out onto the gravel.
The party is over. It's the fall
Of 1931. They love each other still.

She: Charlie, I can't stand the pace.   60
He: Come on, honey—why, you'll bury us all!

A lead soldier guards my windowsill:
Khaki rifle, uniform, and face.
Something in me grows heavy, silvery, pliable.

How intensely people used to feel!   65
Like metal poured at the close of a proletarian novel,
Refined and glowing from the crucible,
I see those two hearts, I'm afraid,
Still. Cool here in the graveyard of good and evil,
They are even so to be honored and obeyed.   70

. . . Obeyed, at least, inversely. Thus
I rarely buy a newspaper, or vote.
To do so, I have learned, is to invite
The tread of a stone guest[5] within my house.

---

[4] In mythology, Cronus (Time) and Rhea
(mother of the gods) were the parents of Zeus,
who dethroned his father.

[5] In Mozart's opera *Don Giovanni* the statue of
the Commendatore, whom Don Giovanni had
murdered, enters the house to seek vengeance.

Shooting this rusted bolt, though, against him,
I trust I am no less time's child than some
Who on the heath impersonate Poor Tom[6]
Or on the barricades risk life and limb.

Nor do I try to keep a garden, only
An avocado in a glass of water—
Roots pallid, gemmed with air. And later,

When the small gilt leaves have grown
Fleshy and green, I let them die, yes, yes,
And start another. I am earth's no less.

A child, a red dog roam the corridors,
Still, of the broken home. No sound. The brilliant
Rag runners halt before wide-open doors.
My old room! Its wallpaper—cream, medallioned
With pink and brown—brings back the first nightmares,
Long summer colds, and Emma, sepia-faced,
Perspiring over broth carried upstairs
Aswim with golden fats I could not taste.

The real house became a boarding-school.
Under the ballroom ceiling's allegory
Someone at last may actually be allowed
To learn something; or, from my window, cool
With the unstiflement of the entire story,
Watch a red setter[7] stretch and sink in cloud.

1966

Syrinx[1]

Bug, flower, bird on slipware[2] fired and fluted,
The summer day breaks everywhere at once.

Worn is the green of things that have known dawns
Before this, and the darkness before them.

---

[6] The name adopted, in Shakespeare's *King Lear*, by Edgar, disinherited by his father, Gloucester.
[7] There is a pun on *setter*—i.e., the dog and the setting sun.
[1] In mythology, the nymph who, escaping from Pan, was turned into a reed. Out of the reeds, Pan made a panpipe and blew through it, creating music. Merrill turns the reed into a flute, and Pan into Pain. The poem is spoken by Syrinx.
[2] A kind of ceramic.

Among the wreckage, bent in Christian weeds,   5
Illiterate—X my mark—I tremble, still

A thinking reed.³ Who puts his mouth to me
Draws out the scale of love and dread—

O ramify, sole antidote!⁴ Foxglove
Each year, cloud, hornet, fatal growths   10

Proliferating by metastasis
Rooted their total in the gliding stream.

Some formula not relevant any more
To flower children might express it yet

Like $\sqrt{\left(\dfrac{x}{y}\right)^{n}} = 1$ 15

—Or equals zero, one forgets—

The y standing for you, dear friend, at least
Until that hour he reaches for me, then

Leaves me cold, the great god Pain,
Letting me slide back into my scarred case   20

Whose silvery breath-tarnished tones
No longer rivet bone and star in place

Or keep from shriveling, leather round a stone,
The sunbather's precocious apricot⁵

Or stop the four winds racing overhead   25

        Nought
    Waste   Eased
        Sought

1972

³ The French philosopher Blaise Pascal
(1623–1662) called man a "thinking reed."
⁴ I.e., the reed's music is the only antidote to
life's poisons.

⁵ Reference to the male genitals.

Samos[1]

And still, at sea all night, we had a sense
Of sunrise, golden oil poured upon water,
Soothing its heave, letting the sleeper sense
What inborn, amniotic homing sense
Was ferrying him—now through the dream-fire   5
In which (it has been felt) each human sense
Burns, now through ship's radar's cool sixth sense,
Or mere unerring starlight—to an island.
Here we were. The twins of Sea and Land,
Up and about for hours—hues, cries, scents—   10
Had placed at eye level a single light
Croissant:[2] the harbor glazed with warm pink light.

Fire-wisps were weaving a string bag of light
For sea stones. Their astounding color sense!
Porphyry, alabaster, chrysolite   15
Translucences that go dead in daylight
Asked only the quick dip in holy water
For the saint of cell on cell to come alight—
Illuminated crystals thinking light,
Refracting it, the gray prismatic fire   20
Or yellow-gray of sea's dilute sapphire . . .
Wavelengths daily deeply score the leit-
Motifs[3] of Loom and Wheel upon this land.
To those who listen, it's the Promised Land.

A little spin today? Dirt roads inland   25
Jounce and revolve in a nerve-jangling light,
Doing the ancient dances of the land
Where, gnarled as olive trees that shag the land
With silver, old men—their two-bladed sense
Of spendthrift poverty, the very land   30
Being, if not loaf, tomb—superbly land
Upright on the downbeat. We who water
The local wine, which "drinks itself" like water,
Clap for more, cry out to *be* this island
Licked all over by a white, salt fire,   35
Be noon's pulsing ember raked by fire,

---

[1] One of the Greek islands.
[2] French: "crescent."
[3] Leitmotifs: leading motives; i.e., musical themes often repeated.

Know nothing, now, but Earth, Air, Water, Fire!
For once out of the frying pan to land
Within their timeless, everlasting fire!
Blood's least red monocle, O magnifier   40
Of the great Eye that sees by its own light
More pictures in "the world's enchanted fire"
Than come and go in any shrewd crossfire
Upon the page, of syllable and sense,
We want unwilled excursions and ascents,   45
Crave the upward-rippling rungs of fire,
The outward-rippling rings (enough!) of water . . .
(Now some details—how else will this hold water?)

Our room's three flights above the whitewashed water-
front where Pythagoras[4] was born. A fire   50
Escape of sky-blue iron leads down to water.
Yachts creak on mirror berths, and over water
Voices from Sweden or Somaliland
Tell how this or that one crossed the water
To Ephesus,[5] came back with toilet water   55
And a two kilo box of Turkish delight[6]
—Trifles. Yet they shine with such pure light
In memory, even they, that the eyes water.
As with the setting sun, or innocence,
Do things that fade especially make sense?   60

Samos. We keep trying to make sense
Of what we can. Not souls of the first water—
Although we've put on airs, and taken fire—
We shall be dust of quite another land
Before the seeds here planted come to light.   65

1980

Frank O'Hara
1926–1966

Frank O'Hara died tragically young in a car accident at night on Fire Island,
New York. During his lifetime, his poetry was known in a rather restricted circle
because his poems had come out in small special editions. Only after his death

---

[4] Pre-Socratic Greek philosopher who first
discovered that the relation between musical
notes could be expressed mathematically.

[5] Greek city in Asia Minor.
[6] Type of nougat candy.

was his work gathered up, edited by Donald Allen, and published as the *Collected Poems* (1971). Two more volumes have since been issued: *Early Poems* (1977) and *Poems Retrieved* (1977). The first full critical study appeared only in 1979.

The sheer personal charm visible in the poems seems to have been characteristic of O'Hara in life; every party, according to legend, was better if O'Hara, with his sense of fun, was present. The people O'Hara knew best were painters and poets, and, grouped as the "New York school," O'Hara, John Ashbery, James Schuyler, and Kenneth Koch have been seen as a new movement in American poetry. This movement borrows from visual artists the sense of spontaneity that can enter drawings or graffiti, the amusement that can follow from sketching on a napkin or a memo, the liberation that follows from thinking of art as something one does freely and all the time, rather than something fully "composed" and "finished." By bringing the colloquial, the intimate, the transient, and the quickly observed into poetry, O'Hara and his friends offered an alternative to the constructed or ponderous "philosophical" verse being written by imitators of T. S. Eliot, Wallace Stevens, and Allen Tate. Against the aesthetic that sought philosophical clarification in poetry, O'Hara said:

> What is happening to me, allowing for lies and exaggerations which I try to avoid, goes into my poems. I don't think my experiences are clarified or made beautiful for myself or anyone else, they are just there in whatever form I can find them. What is clear to me in my work is probably obscure to others, and vice versa. . . . It may be that poetry makes life's nebulous events tangible to me and restores their detail; or conversely, that poetry brings forth the intangible quality of incidents which are all too concrete and circumstantial. Or each on specific occasions, or both all the time.

O'Hara wrote candid and happy homosexual love poems, freed from the various tonalities—of secrecy, shame, protestation—that had troubled such verse from Whitman on. He captured the insignificant but momentous meetings of lovers, the pleasures of "having a Coke with you," the joy of dropping in on someone loved. Other poems recorded sudden moments of grief ("The Day Lady Died") or delight ("A Step Away from Them"); others are vignettes full of relish for life in New York.

O'Hara was born in Baltimore and grew up in Worcester, Massachusetts. At Harvard, he majored in English and music, graduating late, in 1950, because of his two-year service in the navy during and after World War II. After a year at the University of Michigan, where he took an M.A. and won the Hopwood Award for poetry, he went to New York and began working for the Museum of Modern Art, where he rose to become an assistant curator in the department of painting and sculpture exhibitions. He also worked as an editor and critic for *Art News*. He was at the center of the explosion of creativity among artists— including Willem de Kooning, Robert Motherwell, Helen Frankenthaler, Jackson Pollock, and Franz Kline—that made New York the art center of the world. Abstract expressionism sought a more "expressionist" warmth, excitement, and depth than had been allowed by pure abstraction, the sort found in Mondrian. The painters' emphasis on color, free movement, and expansive gesture is reflected in O'Hara's longer surrealist poems, where process and exuberant invention tend to dominate.

O'Hara's humor appears in everything he writes, but he is well aware of the classic, serious, lyric tradition and participates in it in his elegies for friends who died, in his love songs, and in his poems about childhood and adolescence—phases with which he never lost touch. He reflects, too, on the differences between his medium and that of his painter friends, continuing in poems like "Why I Am Not a Painter" a lyric topic as old as Horace. In his exuberance, cheerful interest in the sideshow of city life, sophisticated childlikeness, and syncopated rhythms, O'Hara is the descendant of the French Surrealist poets and of E. E. Cummings, their American representative.

Further Reading:
A. Feldman, *Frank O'Hara*, 1979.
M. Perloff, *Frank O'Hara, Poet Among Painters*,
1979.
A. Smith, Jr., *Frank O'Hara: A Comprehensive Bibliography*, 1979.

Text:
Selected Poems, 1974.

To the Harbormaster

I wanted to be sure to reach you;
though my ship was on the way it got caught
in some moorings. I am always tying up
and then deciding to depart. In storms and
at sunset, with the metallic coils of the tide   5
around my fathomless arms, I am unable
to understand the forms of my vanity
or I am hard alee with my Polish rudder
in my hand and the sun sinking. To
you I offer my hull and the tattered cordage   10
of my will. The terrible channels where
the wind drives me against the brown lips
of the reeds are not all behind me. Yet
I trust the sanity of my vessel; and
if it sinks, it may well be in answer   15
to the reasoning of the eternal voices,
the waves which have kept me from reaching you.

1956

A Step Away from Them[1]

It's my lunch hour, so I go
for a walk among the hum-colored
cabs.[2] First, down the sidewalk
where laborers feed their dirty
glistening torsos sandwiches   5
and Coca-Cola, with yellow helmets
on. They protect them from falling
bricks, I guess. Then onto the
avenue where skirts are flipping
above heels and blow up over   10
grates. The sun is hot, but the
cabs stir up the air. I look
at bargains in wristwatches. There
are cats playing in sawdust.
                           On   15
to Times Square, where the sign
blows smoke over my head, and higher
the waterfall pours lightly. A
Negro stands in a doorway with a
toothpick, languorously agitating.   20
A blonde chorus girl clicks: he
smiles and rubs his chin. Everything
suddenly honks: it is 12:40 of
a Thursday.
                    Neon in daylight is a   25
great pleasure, as Edwin Denby[3] would
write, as are light bulbs in daylight.
I stop for a cheeseburger at JULIET'S
CORNER. Giulietta Masina, wife of
Federico Fellini, è bell' attrice.[4]   30
And chocolate malted. A lady in
foxes[5] on such a day puts her poodle
in a cab.
            There are several Puerto
Ricans on the avenue today, which   35
makes it beautiful and warm. First
Bunny died, then John Latouche,

---

[1] O'Hara observes the passersby from a slight
distance.
[2] Yellow Cabs, like bumblebees with their
black-on-yellow coloring.

[3] Dance critic.
[4] Italian: "is a fine actress."
[5] I.e., with a fox fur around her neck.

then Jackson Pollock.[6] But is the
earth as full as life was full, of them?
And one has eaten and one walks,   40
past the magazines with nudes
and the posters for BULLFIGHT and
the Manhattan Storage Warehouse,
which they'll soon tear down. I
used to think they had the Armory   45
Show[7] there.
                       A glass of papaya juice
and back to work. My heart is in my
pocket, it is Poems by Pierre Reverdy.[8]
1964

The Day Lady[1] Died

It is 12:20 in New York a Friday
three days after Bastille day,[2] yes
it is 1959 and I go get a shoeshine
because I will get off the 4:19 in Easthampton
at 7:15 and then go straight to dinner   5
and I don't know the people who will feed me

I walk up the muggy street beginning to sun
and have a hamburger and a malted and buy
an ugly NEW WORLD WRITING to see what the poets
in Ghana are doing these days   10
                    I go on to the bank
and Miss Stillwagon (first name Linda I once heard)
doesn't even look up my balance for once in her life
and in the GOLDEN GRIFFIN I get a little Verlaine[3]
for Patsy with drawings by Bonnard[4] although I do   15
think of Hesiod,[5] trans. Richmond Lattimore or
Brendan Behan's[6] new play or Le Balcon or Les Nègres
of Genet,[7] but I don't, I stick with Verlaine
after practically going to sleep with quandariness

---

[6] Bunny Lang, John Latouche, and the painter
Jackson Pollock were close friends of O'Hara.
[7] Show of modernist art in 1913 that
revolutionized American painting.
[8] French poet (1889–1960).
[1] Billie Holliday (1915–1959), American jazz
singer, known as Lady Day.

[2] July 14.
[3] French poet (1844–1896).
[4] French painter (1867–1941).
[5] Greek poet of the eighth century B.C.
[6] Behan: Irish playwright (1923–1964).
[7] French novelist and playwright (b. 1910).

and for Mike I just stroll into the PARK LANE 20
Liquor Store and ask for a bottle of Strega and
then I go back where I came from to 6th Avenue
and the tobacconist in the Ziegfeld Theatre and
casually ask for a carton of Gauloises and a carton
of Picayunes, and a NEW YORK POST with her face on it 25

and I am sweating a lot by now and thinking of
leaning on the john door in the 5 SPOT[8]
while she whispered a song along the keyboard
to Mal Waldron and everyone and I stopped breathing
1960

Poetry

The only way to be quiet
is to be quick, so I scare
you clumsily, or surprise
you with a stab. A praying
mantis knows time more 5
intimately than I and is
more casual. Crickets use
time for accompaniment to
innocent fidgeting. A zebra
races counterclockwise. 10
All this I desire. To
deepen you by my quickness
and delight as if you
were logical and proven,
but still be quiet as if 15
I were used to you; as if
you would never leave me
and were the inexorable
product of my own time.
1971

[8] Manhattan nightclub noted for its jazz
music.

Why I Am Not a Painter

I am not a painter, I am a poet.
Why? I think I would rather be
a painter, but I am not. Well,

for instance, Mike Goldberg
is starting a painting. I drop in.   5
"Sit down and have a drink" he
says. I drink; we drink. I look
up. "You have SARDINES in it."
"Yes, it needed something there."
"Oh." I go and the days go by   10
and I drop in again. The painting
is going on, and I go, and the days
go by. I drop in. The painting is
finished. "Where's SARDINES?"
All that's left is just   15
letters, "It was too much," Mike says.

But me? One day I am thinking of
a color: orange. I write a line
about orange. Pretty soon it is a
whole page of words, not lines.   20
Then another page. There should be
so much more, not of orange, of
words, of how terrible orange is
and life. Days go by. It is even in
prose, I am a real poet. My poem   25
is finished and I haven't mentioned
orange yet. It's twelve poems, I call
it ORANGES. And one day in a gallery
I see Mike's painting, called SARDINES.

1971

John Ashbery
b. 1927

John Ashbery's poems resemble a score for performance by the reader. Some
experience of interest, depth, and importance is being retold—a journey, a
catastrophe, a loss—but we are given the general outline rather than the specific
details. Ashbery invites us to involve ourselves in the flow of events, filling in

from our own past the appropriate incidents. The disturbances of life, its energies and hates, are transformed into the towers and "lacustrine cities" of art, "things offered," the poet says to his reader, "to your participation." Since the grid of human experience takes on repetitive patterns, Ashbery trusts to an aesthetic of algebraic outline expressed in his masterly syntax and invokes the cooperation of his reader in following his graph. A poem by Ashbery is the occasion for a dazzling unfolding of inventive language, which borrows from popular sources like slang and advertising as well as from intellectual sources like art history and theater. It is impossible to predict what color or shape or tone an Ashbery poem will take on next; the configurations in his kaleidoscope fall into new shapes as the poem turns.

Ashbery's own training centered on language, literature, theater, and the visual arts. His early years were spent on a farm in upstate New York. After preparing at Deerfield Academy, he attended Harvard (B.A., 1949) and then took an M.A. in English at Columbia. Later, a Fulbright scholarship took him to Montpellier and Paris (1955–1957). In 1958, living in Paris, he became the art critic for the *International Herald Tribune* and wrote reviews of art shows for *Art News* and *Arts International*. After his return to America in 1965, he served until 1972 as executive editor of *Art News;* he is currently the art critic for *Newsweek*. Recently he has taught creative writing at Brooklyn College.

Ashbery's lyrical first volume, *Some Trees* (1956), selected by W. H. Auden for the Yale Younger Poet series, was followed by the unsettling collection *The Tennis Court Oath* (1962), in which many of the poems, notably "Europe," were baffling in their discontinuity, allusiveness, and surreal effects. With *Rivers and Mountains* (1966), Ashbery assumed the cursive, seductive, musical style with which he is now identified. Together with Frank O'Hara (a close friend), he drew poetry away from the deliberateness of Eliot's diction and into the mainstream of urbane American conversational exchange.

Ashbery's poetry has been influenced by our century's experiments in the visual arts, notably cubism and abstraction. Cubism in sculpture suggested that the various forms of the world could be schematized into elementary geometric forms; cubism in painting (as in Picasso's paintings, where we see a profile superimposed on a full face) suggested that any number of perspectives of an object are "true" and that we should attempt to keep all views in mind at once. Ashbery's preference for an elemental outline may be seen as a recourse to a cubist simplicity, while his frequent (and often unsettling) changes of perspective may derive from the multiplicity of perspectives visible, for instance, in Picasso. Other aspects of modern art—the playfulness of Klee, the cartoon sketches of Matisse, the parodic elements of the Dada movement—have all created a revolution that has passed, in linguistic form, into Ashbery's daring loosening of the usual structures of writing. But his liberties with metaphor and pronominal reference (indebted perhaps to the experiments of Gertrude Stein) accompany a deeply traditional sense of the historic genres of poetry in English. Ashbery's use of forms like the sonnet and the sestina; his obedience to the conventions of the elegy, of love poetry, of the ode, and of the landscape poem; and his frequent allusions to his predecessors (especially Keats, Eliot, Stevens, and Auden) establish his homage to the perennial life of poetry.

Ashbery's attention turns frequently to self-reflective poetry, in which he examines the conditions of creation for the contemporary poet. "Our question of a place of origin hangs / Like smoke," he writes; the poet no longer thinks that in creating he imitates the divine freedom of God. Art is a repetitive traditional function but contains an inner freedom:

> So I cradle this average violin that knows
> Only forgotten showtunes, but argues
> The possibility of free declamation anchored
> To a dull refrain.

The function of art is to be a deposit of human physicality, sexuality, and material culture; to affect by its presence the landscape around it; and to serve as a means of self-creation:

> [We] left
> Our trash, sperm and excrement everywhere, smeared
> On the landscape, to make of us what we could.

Art is the "pyrography"—writing (or playing) with fire—undertaken by the artist while life continues its circular journey. In spite of the absence of an origin or goal, life still presents itself to us, Ashbery suggests, as precious and worthy of preservation, so we must "model all these unimportant details" and include them if art is truly to represent the ephemeral truths of culture.

In his love poetry, Ashbery creates compelling sketches of loss, betrayal, and fidelity: Other wagons may go on to the gold rush, "But we stay behind, among them, / The injured, the adored." Lovers keep trying "to get it right," to phrase, in the midst of a night's attrition, their "notes to each other, always repeated, always the same." Ashbery can be brutal as well as tender; his light exploratory tones, his jokes, his parodies often mask the harshness of his vision, as when he imagines life as a damaged carousel constantly climbed onto by blighted supplicants ("Landscapepeople"). The end is certain; but at least, like a medieval illuminator, the poet ornaments the black-letter text of life, "filling up the margins of the days / With pictures of fruit, light, colors, music, and vines, / Until it ceases to be a problem."

In recent years, Ashbery has continued his inventiveness, not only in the brilliant prose poems of *Three Poems* (1972) but also in the Pulitzer Prize–winning *Self-portrait in a Convex Mirror* (1975), the lyrics of *Houseboat Days* (1977), the double-column long poem "Litany" in *As We Know* (1979), the unrhymed "sonnets" of *Shadow Train* (1981), and the elegiac title poem of *A Wave* (1984).

Further Reading:
D. Shapiro, *John Ashbery: An Introduction to the Poetry*, 1979.
Beyond Amazement: New Essays on John Ashbery, ed. D. Lehman, 1980.

Texts:
"Some Trees" from *Some Trees*, 1956.
"These Lacustrine Cities" from *Rivers and Mountains*, 1966.
"Soonest Mended" and "Years of Indiscretion" from *The Double Dream of Spring*, 1970.
"As One Put Drunk into the Packet-Boat" from *Self-portrait in a Convex Mirror*, 1975.
"Pyrography" from *Houseboat Days*, 1977.
"A Love Poem" from *As We Know*, 1979.
"Drunken Americans" from *Shadow Train*, 1981.

Some Trees

These are amazing: each
Joining a neighbor, as though speech
Were a still performance.
Arranging by chance

To meet as far this morning   5
From the world as agreeing
With it, you and I
Are suddenly what the trees try

To tell us we are:
That their merely being there   10
Means something; that soon
We may touch, love, explain.

And glad not to have invented
Such comeliness, we are surrounded:
A silence already filled with noises,   15
A canvas on which emerges

A chorus of smiles, a winter morning.
Placed in a puzzling light, and moving,
Our days put on such reticence
These accents seem their own defense.   20

1956

These Lacustrine[1] Cities

These lacustrine cities grew out of loathing
Into something forgetful, although angry with history.
They are the product of an idea: that man is horrible, for instance,
Though this is only one example.

They emerged until a tower
Controlled the sky, and with artifice dipped back   5

---

[1] Built on stilts in lakes.

Into the past for swans and tapering branches,
Burning, until all that hate was transformed into useless love.

Then you are left with an idea of yourself
And the feeling of ascending emptiness of the afternoon   10
Which must be charged to the embarrassment of others
Who fly by you like beacons.

The night is a sentinel.
Much of your time has been occupied by creative games
Until now, but we have all-inclusive plans for you.   15
We had thought, for instance, of sending you to the middle of the desert,

To a violent sea, or of having the closeness of the others be air
To you, pressing you back into a startled dream
As sea-breezes greet a child's face.
But the past is already here, and you are nursing some private project.   20

The worst is not over, yet I know
You will be happy here. Because of the logic
Of your situation, which is something no climate can outsmart.
Tender and insouciant by turns, you see

You have built a mountain of something,   25
Thoughtfully pouring all your energy into this single monument,
Whose wind is desire starching a petal,
Whose disappointment broke into a rainbow of tears.
1966

Soonest Mended

Barely tolerated, living on the margin
In our technological society, we were always having to be rescued
On the brink of destruction, like heroines in *Orlando Furioso*[1]
Before it was time to start all over again.
There would be thunder in the bushes, a rustling of coils,   5
And Angelica, in the Ingres[2] painting, was considering
The colorful but small monster near her toe, as though wondering whether
    forgetting

-----

[1] Epic (1532) by Lodovico Ariosto (1474–1533),   [2] French painter (1780–1867).
of which the heroine is Angelica.

The whole thing might not, in the end, be the only solution.
And then there always came a time when
Happy Hooligan[3] in his rusted green automobile   1
Came plowing down the course, just to make sure everything was O.K.,
Only by that time we were in another chapter and confused
About how to receive this latest piece of information.
Was it information? Weren't we rather acting this out
For someone else's benefit, thoughts in a mind   1
With room enough and to spare for our little problems (so they began to
    seem),
Our daily quandary about food and the rent and bills to be paid?
To reduce all this to a small variant,
To step free at last, minuscule on the gigantic plateau—
This was our ambition: to be small and clear and free.   2(
Alas, the summer's energy wanes quickly,
A moment and it is gone. And no longer
May we make the necessary arrangements, simple as they are.
Our star was brighter perhaps when it had water in it.
Now there is no question even of that, but only   2'
Of holding on to the hard earth so as not to get thrown off,
With an occasional dream, a vision: a robin flies across
The upper corner of the window, you brush your hair away
And cannot quite see, or a wound will flash
Against the sweet faces of the others, something like: 3(
This is what you wanted to hear, so why
Did you think of listening to something else? We are all talkers
It is true, but underneath the talk lies
The moving and not wanting to be moved, the loose
Meaning, untidy and simple like a threshing floor.   35

These then were some hazards of the course,
Yet though we knew the course *was* hazards and nothing else
It was still a shock when, almost a quarter of a century later,
The clarity of the rules dawned on you for the first time.
They were the players, and we who had struggled at the game   40
Were merely spectators, though subject to its vicissitudes
And moving with it out of the tearful stadium, borne on shoulders, at last.
Night after night this message returns, repeated
In the flickering bulbs of the sky, raised past us, taken away from us,
Yet ours over and over until the end that is past truth,   45
The being of our sentences, in the climate that fostered them,
Not ours to own, like a book, but to be with, and sometimes
To be without, alone and desperate.
But the fantasy makes it ours, a kind of fence-sitting
Raised to the level of an esthetic ideal. These were moments, years,   50

---

[3] Comic strip character.

Solid with reality, faces, namable events, kisses, heroic acts,
But like the friendly beginning of a geometrical progression
Not too reassuring, as though meaning could be cast aside some day
When it had been outgrown. Better, you said, to stay cowering
Like this in the early lessons, since the promise of learning   55
Is a delusion, and I agreed, adding that
Tomorrow would alter the sense of what had already been learned,
That the learning process is extended in this way, so that from this standpoint
None of us ever graduates from college,
For time is an emulsion, and probably thinking not to grow up   60
Is the brightest kind of maturity for us, right now at any rate.
And you see, both of us were right, though nothing
Has somehow come to nothing; the avatars[4]
Of our conforming to the rules and living
Around the home have made—well, in a sense, "good citizens" of us,   65
Brushing the teeth and all that, and learning to accept
The charity of the hard moments as they are doled out,
For this is action, this not being sure, this careless
Preparing, sowing the seeds crooked in the furrow,
Making ready to forget, and always coming back   70
To the mooring of starting out, that day so long ago.

1970

Years of Indiscretion

Whatever your eye alights on this morning is yours:
Dotted rhythms of colors as they fade to the color,
A gray agate, translucent and firm, with nothing
Beyond its purifying reach. It's all there.
These are things offered to your participation.   5

These pebbles in a row are the seasons.
This is a house in which you may wish to live.
There are more than any of us to choose from
But each must live its own time.

And with the urging of the year each hastens onward separately   10
In strange sensations of emptiness, anguish, romantic
Outbursts, visions and wraiths. One meeting
Cancels another. "The seven-league boot

---

[4] Embodiments.

Gliding hither and thither of its own accord"
Salutes these forms for what they now are: 15

Fables that time invents
To explain its passing. They entertain
The very young and the very old, and not
One's standing up in them to shoulder
Task and vision, vision in the form of a task   20
So that the present seems like yesterday
And yesterday the place where we left off a little while ago.
1970

As One Put Drunk
into the Packet-Boat[1]

I tried each thing, only some were immortal and free.
Elsewhere we are as sitting in a place where sunlight
Filters down, a little at a time,
Waiting for someone to come. Harsh words are spoken,
As the sun yellows the green of the maple tree. . . .   5

So this was all, but obscurely
I felt the stirrings of new breath in the pages
Which all winter long had smelled like an old catalogue.
New sentences were starting up. But the summer
Was well along, not yet past the mid-point   10
But full and dark with the promise of that fullness,
That time when one can no longer wander away
And even the least attentive fall silent
To watch the thing that is prepared to happen.

A look of glass stops you   15
And you walk on shaken: was I the perceived?
Did they notice me, this time, as I am,
Or is it postponed again? The children
Still at their games, clouds that arise with a swift
Impatience in the afternoon sky, then dissipate   20
As limpid, dense twilight comes.

[1] Borrowed from the first line of the poem
"Tom May's Death" by Andrew Marvell
(1621–1678).

Only in that tooting of a horn
Down there, for a moment, I thought
The great, formal affair was beginning, orchestrated,
Its colors concentrated in a glance, a ballade[2]   25
That takes in the whole world, now, but lightly,
Still lightly, but with wide authority and tact.

The prevalence of those gray flakes falling?
They are sun motes. You have slept in the sun
Longer than the sphinx, and are none the wiser for it.   30
Come in. And I thought a shadow fell across the door
But it was only her come to ask once more
If I was coming in, and not to hurry in case I wasn't.

The night sheen takes over. A moon of cistercian[3] pallor
Has climbed to the center of heaven, installed,   35
Finally involved with the business of darkness.
And a sigh heaves from all the small things on earth,
The books, the papers, the old garters and union-suit buttons
Kept in a white cardboard box somewhere, and all the lower
Versions of cities flattened under the equalizing night.   40
The summer demands and takes away too much,
But night, the reserved, the reticent, gives more than it takes.

1975

Pyrography[1]

Out here on Cottage Grove it matters. The galloping
Wind balks at its shadow. The carriages
Are drawn forward under a sky of fumed oak.
This is America calling:
The mirroring of state to state,   5
Of voice to voice on the wires,
The force of colloquial greetings like golden
Pollen sinking on the afternoon breeze.
In service stairs the sweet corruption thrives;
The page of dusk turns like a creaking revolving stage in Warren, Ohio. 10

[2] Musical composition, usually for piano.   [1] The art of using fire to etch patterns on wood.
[3] I.e., the color of unbleached white robes worn
   by Cistercian monks.

If this is the way it is let's leave,
They agree, and soon the slow boxcar journey begins,
Gradually accelerating until the gyrating fans of suburbs
Enfolding the darkness of cities are remembered
Only as a recurring tic. And midway   15
We meet the disappointed, returning ones, without its
Being able to stop us in the headlong night
Toward the nothing of the coast. At Bolinas
The houses doze and seem to wonder why through the
Pacific haze, and the dreams alternately glow and grow dull.   20
Why be hanging on here? Like kites, circling,
Slipping on a ramp of air, but always circling?

But the variable cloudiness is pouring it on,
Flooding back to you like the meaning of a joke.
The land wasn't immediately appealing; we built it   25
Partly over with fake ruins, in the image of ourselves:
An arch that terminates in mid-keystone, a crumbling stone pier
For laundresses, an open-air theater, never completed
And only partially designed. How are we to inhabit
This space from which the fourth wall is invariably missing,   30
As in a stage-set or dollhouse, except by staying as we are,
In lost profile, facing the stars, with dozens of as yet
Unrealized projects, and a strict sense
Of time running out, of evening presenting
The tactfully folded-over bill? And we fit   35
Rather too easily into it, become transparent,
Almost ghosts. One day
The birds and animals in the pasture have absorbed
The color, the density of the surroundings,
The leaves are alive, and too heavy with life.   40

A long period of adjustment followed.
In the cities at the turn of the century they knew about it
But were careful not to let on as the iceman and the milkman
Disappeared down the block and the postman shouted
His daily rounds. The children under the trees knew it   45
But all the fathers returning home
On streetcars after a satisfying day at the office undid it:
The climate was still floral and all the wallpaper
In a million homes all over the land conspired to hide it.
One day we thought of painted furniture, of how   50
It just slightly changes everything in the room
And in the yard outside, and how, if we were going
To be able to write the history of our time, starting with today,
It would be necessary to model all these unimportant details
So as to be able to include them; otherwise the narrative   55

Would have that flat, sandpapered look the sky gets
Out in the middle west toward the end of summer,
The look of wanting to back out before the argument
Has been resolved, and at the same time to save appearances
So that tomorrow will be pure. Therefore, since we have to do our business   60
In spite of things, why not make it in spite of everything?
That way, maybe the feeble lakes and swamps
Of the back country will get plugged into the circuit
And not just the major events but the whole incredible
Mass of everything happening simultaneously and pairing off,   65
Channeling itself into history, will unroll
As carefully and as casually as a conversation in the next room,
And the purity of today will invest us like a breeze,
Only be hard, spare, ironical: something one can
Tip one's hat to and still get some use out of.   70

The parade is turning into our street.
My stars, the burnished uniforms and prismatic
Features of this instant belong here. The land
Is pulling away from the magic, glittering coastal towns
To an aforementioned rendezvous with August and December.   75
The hunch is it will always be this way,
The look, the way things first scared you
In the night light, and later turned out to be,
Yet still capable, all the same, of a narrow fidelity
To what you and they wanted to become;   80
No sighs like Russian music, only a vast unravelling
Out toward the junctions and to the darkness beyond
To these bare fields, built at today's expense.

1977

A Love Poem

And they have to get it right. We just need
A little happiness, and when the clever things
Are taken up (O has the mouth shaped that letter?
What do we have bearing down on it?) as the last thin curve
("Positively the last," they say) before the dark: 5
(The sky is pure and faint, the pavement still wet) and

The dripping is in the walls, within sleep
Itself. I mean there is no escape

From me, from it. The night is itself sleep
And what goes on in it, the naming of the wind,   10
Our notes to each other, always repeated, always the same.
1979

Drunken Americans

I saw the reflection in the mirror
And it doesn't count, or not enough
To make a difference, fabricating itself
Out of the old, average light of a college town,

And afterwards, when the bus trip   5
Had depleted my pocket of its few pennies
He was seen arguing behind steamed glass,
With an invisible proprietor. What if you can't own

This one either? For it seems that all
Moments are like this: thin, unsatisfactory   10
As gruel, worn away more each time you return to them.
Until one day you rip the canvas from its frame

And take it home with you. You think the god-given
Assertiveness in you has triumphed
Over the stingy scenario: these objects are real as meat,   15
As tears. We are all soiled with this desire, at the last moment, the last.
1981

W. S. Merwin
b. 1927

W. S. Merwin's volume *The Lice* (1967) became a central book for those
opposed to the war in Vietnam; the poem "The Asians Dying," in its brevity and
conclusiveness, focused the anguish of social protest in an apprehensible form. At
his best, Merwin says a great deal in a very few words. His mature art is the
work of a minimalist who reduces a problem to its most abstract or skeletal
form; stripped of particulars, the essence stands luminously revealed.

Merwin was born in New York City, the son of a Presbyterian minister, and grew up in Scranton, Pennsylvania. As an undergraduate at Princeton, he knew John Berryman and the critic R. P. Blackmur. In his boyhood and youth, Merwin recalls:

> I started writing hymns for my father almost as soon as I could write at all. . . . In Scranton there was an anthology of *Best Loved Poems of the American People* in the house, which seemed for a time to afford some clues. But the first real writers that held me were not poets; Conrad first, and then Tolstoy, and it was not until I had received a scholarship and gone away to the university that I began to read poetry steadily and try incessantly, and with abiding desperation, to write it. . . . While I was there, John Berryman and R. P. Blackmur helped me, by example as much as by design, to find out some things about writing.

After his graduation, Merwin moved to Europe and became private tutor to the son of the British poet Robert Graves. Between 1951 and 1954 he lived in London, translating for the BBC Third Programme. In 1956 he returned to America and was active in the Poets' Theatre in Cambridge (with which Frank O'Hara and John Ashbery were also associated). He moved to New York in the 1960s; recently he has lived in Hawaii.

Merwin was chosen by Auden as Yale Younger Poet for 1952. His early volumes—*A Masque for Janus* (1952), *The Dancing Bears* (1954), *Green with Beasts* (1956), and *The Drunk in the Furnace* (1960)—reflect the formalist influence of the 1950s. In *The Moving Target* (1963), Merwin exhibits the sparse poetry that was to become his chosen form, one that found a home in prose in *The Miner's Pale Children* (1970) as well as in poetry.

The abstract rendering of motifs in Merwin's verse has caused some readers to overlook his social concern. He has criticized America as "a society whose triumphs one after the other emerge as new symbols of death, and that frees itself by poisoning the earth." In writing about the extinction of whales or about the use of technology for genocidal purposes, Merwin became one of the most fervent spokesmen of the 1960s. His later volumes—*The Carrier of Ladders* (1970), *Writings to an Unfinished Accompaniment* (1973), *The Compass Flower* (1977), and *Opening the Hand* (1983)—display the purity of diction and brevity of statement that have characterized all his mature work.

Merwin has been a translator of many classics written in Spanish—*The Poem of the Cid* (1959) and *The Life of Lazarillo de Tormes* (1962), as well as works by Neruda and García Lorca. The considerable influence of medieval Spanish poetry on his formal, musical, unrhymed stanzas has been noticed by his commentators.

In American verse, Merwin represents a tendency—collective and impersonal—completely opposed to the autobiographical "confessional" verse of Lowell, Plath, and Sexton. In his moral emphasis and social focus, his work might be compared to that of Adrienne Rich, but its deliberate reliance on generality links it as well to that of John Ashbery. In his elegance and intensity of formulation, as well as in his secularized Protestant morality, Merwin continues a line of concise, gnomic, ethical American poetry begun by Emerson and Dickinson.

Texts:
"The Fishermen" from *The First Four Books of Poems*, 1975.
"Noah's Raven" from *The Moving Target*, 1963.
"For the Anniversary of My Death," "The Asians Dying," and "For a Coming Extinction" from *The Lice*, 1967.
"Tool" and "The Chase" from *Writings to an*

Unfinished Accompaniment, 1973.
"Line" from *The Compass Flower*, 1977.
See also *Houses and Travellers: A Book of Prose*, 1977.
Selected Translations, 1968–1978, 1979.
Unframed Originals: Recollections, 1982.

The Fishermen

When you think how big their feet are in black rubber
And it slippery underfoot always, it is clever
How they thread and manage among the sprawled nets, lines,
Hooks, spidery cages with small entrances.
But they are used to it. We do not know their names.   5
They know our needs, and live by them, lending them wiles
And beguilements we could never have fashioned for them;
They carry the ends of our hungers out to drop them
To wait swaying in a dark place we could never have chosen.
By motions we have never learned they feed us.   10
We lay wreaths on the sea when it has drowned them.
1956

Noah's Raven[1]

Why should I have returned?
My knowledge would not fit into theirs.
I found untouched the desert of the unknown,
Big enough for my feet. It is my home.
It is always beyond them. The future   5
Splits the present with the echo of my voice.
Hoarse with fulfilment, I never made promises.
1963

---

[1] After the Deluge, Noah's ark landed on Mount Ararat. Noah sent out a raven and a dove to see whether the waters had subsided. The dove returned but the raven did not (see Genesis 8:7, 8).

For the Anniversary of My Death

Every year without knowing it I have passed the day
When the last fires will wave to me
And the silence will set out
Tireless traveller
Like the beam of a lightless star   5

Then I will no longer
Find myself in life as in a strange garment
Surprised at the earth
And the love of one woman
And the shamelessness of men   10
As today writing after three days of rain
Hearing the wren sing and the falling cease
And bowing not knowing to what

1967

The Asians Dying[1]

When the forests have been destroyed their darkness remains
The ash the great walker follows the possessors
Forever
Nothing they will come to is real
Nor for long   5
Over the watercourses
Like ducks in the time of the ducks
The ghosts of the villages trail in the sky
Making a new twilight

Rain falls into the open eyes of the dead   10
Again again with its pointless sound
When the moon finds them they are the color of everything

[1] In the Vietnam War, 1964–1973.

The nights disappear like bruises but nothing is healed
The dead go away like bruises
The blood vanishes into the poisoned farmlands   1

Pain the horizon
Remains
Overhead the seasons rock
They are paper bells
Calling to nothing living   20

The possessors move everywhere under Death their star
Like columns of smoke they advance into the shadows
Like thin flames with no light
They with no past
And fire their only future   25

1967

For a Coming Extinction

Gray whale
Now that we are sending you to The End
That great god
Tell him
That we who follow you invented forgiveness
And forgive nothing   5

I write as though you could understand
And I could say it
One must always pretend something
Among the dying
When you have left the seas nodding on their stalks   10
Empty of you
Tell him that we were made
On another day

The bewilderment will diminish like an echo   15
Winding along your inner mountains
Unheard by us
And find its way out
Leaving behind it the future
Dead   20
And ours

When you will not see again
The whale calves trying the light
Consider what you will find in the black garden'
And its court   25
The sea cows the Great Auks the gorillas
The irreplaceable hosts ranged countless
And fore-ordaining as stars
Our sacrifices

Join your word to theirs   30
Tell him
That it is we who are important
1967

Tool

If it's invented it will be used

maybe not for some time

then all at once
a hammer rises from under a lid
and shakes off its cold family   5

its one truth is stirring in its head
order order saying

and a surprised nail leaps
into darkness
that a moment before had been nothing   10

waiting
for the law
1973

The Chase

On the first day of Ruin
a crack appears running

then what do they know to do
they shout Thief Thief
and run after   5

like cracks converging across a wall

they strike at it
they pick it up by tails
they throw pieces into the air
where the pieces join hands   10
join feet run on

through the first day

while the wren sings and sings
1973

Line

Those waiting in line
for a cash register at a supermarket
pushing wire baby carriages
full of food in packages
past signs about coupons   5
in the blank light
do not look at each other
frankly
pretend not to stare at each other's
soft drinks and white bread   10
do not think of themselves as
part of a line
ordinarily
and the clerk often does not
look at them   15

giving them change
and the man who puts the things
they have chosen
into bags
talks to the clerk   20
as he never talks to her
at any other time
1977

James Wright
1927–1980

When James Wright died of throat cancer at the early age of fifty-three, he was mourned as the poet who had put the Midwest into verse—its rural despair, its urban poor, its suburban frustration. He was born in Martins Ferry, Ohio, a town he recalled in many poems. Wright's deepest sense of life came to him from his earliest days, when he experienced life as a child of the Depression: "Hundreds of times I must have heard a man returning home after a long day's futile search for work, any work at all, and dispiritedly whispering to his anxious wife, or mumbling absent-mindedly to himself in his baffled loneliness: 'I ain't got a pot to piss in or a window to throw it out of.'" Wright's father worked for fifty years in Wheeling, West Virginia, for the Hazel-Atlas glass factory but was often "laid off," which meant, as Wright said, being "told by the management to just go home and stay there, often for weeks at a time, without being paid." In representing the dark underside of America, Wright follows Whitman's injunction in the preface to *Leaves of Grass* to "stand up for the stupid and crazy."

W. H. Auden chose Wright as Yale Younger Poet for 1957 for the book *The Green Wall,* a book formal in its meters and stanza forms, influenced by Wright's literary studies with John Crowe Ransom at Kenyon College, from which he received an A.B. in 1952, and with Theodore Roethke at the University of Washington, where he took a Ph.D. in 1959. Wright then began, in collaboration with Robert Bly, a series of translations from foreign poets: the Austrian Georg Trakl in 1961 (Wright had been a Fulbright student in Vienna), César Vallejo in 1962, Pablo Neruda in 1968. These translations influenced his own third and fourth books, *The Branch Will Not Break* (1963) and *Shall We Gather at the River* (1968). The stark imagism of Trakl and the uninhibited surrealism of Neruda, combined with the directness and honesty of Vallejo, broke through Wright's formalism and induced in him a new starkness and simplicity of presentation: "I have wasted my life"; "If I stepped out of my body I would break / Into blossom." In subsequent volumes, *Two Citizens* (1973) and *To a Blossoming Pear Tree* (1977), Wright's elegiac plangency threatened to dissolve into sentimentality. Alcoholism sapped his creative energy and induced poems of self-hatred and disgust, of terror at the uncontrolled disintegration of his life. Eventually he gave up alcohol and found a new sweetness in life in America as well as in travel in Europe with his wife, Annie.

Wright's poetry won him a wide following in the late 1960s when the war in Vietnam made readers long for a poetry of direct statement, pity, and elegiac sympathy. During the later years of his life, Wright taught literature at Hunter College in New York, but he remains a poet of "the heart of the heart of the country," that Midwest as yet underrepresented in American verse. Following the example set by Robinson and Frost in their scenes of crabbed rural life in New England, Wright revealed how a transplanted genre could flourish in a new geographic setting, in the flat, despairing tones of Middle America.

Further Reading:
G. S. Lensing and R. Moran, *Four Poets and Emotive Imagination*, 1976.
W. S. Saunders, *James Wright: An Introduction*, 1980.
The Pure Clear Word: Essays on the Poetry of James Wright, ed. D. Smith, 1982.

Text:
Collected Poems, 1971.
See also *Collected Prose*, ed. A. Wright, 1983.

At the Executed Murderer's Grave

(for J. L. D.)

Why should we do this? What good is it to us? Above all, how can we do such a thing? How can it possibly be done?
Freud

1

My name is James A. Wright, and I was born
Twenty-five miles from this infected grave,
In Martins Ferry, Ohio, where one slave
To Hazel-Atlas Glass became my father.
He tried to teach me kindness. I return   5
Only in memory now, aloof, unhurried,
To dead Ohio, where I might lie buried,
Had I not run away before my time.
Ohio caught George Doty. Clean as lime,
His skull rots empty here. Dying's the best   10
Of all the arts men learn in a dead place.
I walked here once. I made my loud display,
Leaning for language on a dead man's voice.
Now sick of lies, I turn to face the past.
I add my easy grievance to the rest: 15

2

Doty, if I confess I do not love you,
Will you let me alone? I burn for my own lies.
The nights electrocute my fugitive,
My mind. I run like the bewildered mad
At St. Clair Sanitarium, who lurk,   20
Arch and cunning, under the maple trees,
Pleased to be playing guilty after dark.
Staring to bed, they croon self-lullabies.
Doty, you make me sick. I am not dead.
I croon my tears at fifty cents per line.   25

3

Idiot, he demanded love from girls,
And murdered one. Also, he was a thief.
He left two women, and a ghost with child.
The hair, foul as a dog's upon his head,
Made such revolting Ohio animals   30
Fitter for vomit than a kind man's grief.
I waste no pity on the dead that stink,
And no love's lost between me and the crying
Drunks of Belaire, Ohio, where police
Kick at their kidneys till they die of drink.   35
Christ may restore them whole, for all of me.
Alive and dead, those giggling muckers who
Saddled my nightmares thirty years ago
Can do without my widely printed sighing
Over their pains with paid sincerity.   40
I do not pity the dead, I pity the dying.

4

I pity myself, because a man is dead.
If Belmont County killed him, what of me?
His victims never loved him. Why should we?
And yet, nobody had to kill him either.   45
It does no good to woo the grass, to veil
The quicklime hole of a man's defeat and shame.
Nature-lovers are gone. To hell with them.
I kick the clods away, and speak my name.

5

This grave's gash festers. Maybe it will heal,   50
When all are caught with what they had to do

In fear of love, when every man stands still
By the last sea,
And the princes of the sea come down
To lay away their robes, to judge the earth   55
And its dead, and we dead stand undefended everywhere,
And my bodies—father and child and unskilled criminal—
Ridiculously kneel to bare my scars,
My sneaking crimes, to God's unpitying stars.

6

Staring politely, they will not mark my face   60
From any murderer's, buried in this place.
Why should they? We are nothing but a man.

7

Doty, the rapist and the murderer,
Sleeps in a ditch of fire, and cannot hear;
And where, in earth or hell's unholy peace,   65
Men's suicides will stop, God knows, not I.
Angels and pebbles mock me under trees.
Earth is a door I cannot even face.
Order be damned, I do not want to die,
Even to keep Belaire, Ohio, safe.   70
The hackles on my neck are fear, not grief.
(Open, dungeon! Open, roof of the ground!)
I hear the last sea in the Ohio grass,
Heaving a tide of gray disastrousness.
Wrinkles of winter ditch the rotted face   75
Of Doty, killer, imbecile, and thief:
Dirt of my flesh, defeated, underground.

1959

Autumn Begins in Martins Ferry, Ohio

In the Shreve High football stadium,
I think of Polacks¹ nursing long beers in Tiltonsville,
And gray faces of Negroes in the blast furnace at Benwood,

¹ Derogatory epithet for Polish-Americans.

And the ruptured[2] night watchman of Wheeling Steel,
Dreaming of heroes.   5

All the proud fathers are ashamed to go home.
Their women cluck like starved pullets,
Dying for love.

Therefore,
Their sons grow suicidally beautiful   10
At the beginning of October,
And gallop terribly against each other's bodies.

1963

Lying in a Hammock
at William Duffy's Farm
in Pine Island, Minnesota

Over my head, I see the bronze butterfly,
Asleep on the black trunk,
Blowing like a leaf in green shadow.
Down the ravine behind the empty house,
The cowbells follow one another   5
Into the distances of the afternoon.
To my right,
In a field of sunlight between two pines,
The droppings of last year's horses
Blaze up into golden stones.   10
I lean back, as the evening darkens and comes on.
A chicken hawk floats over, looking for home.
I have wasted my life.

1963

Anne Sexton
1928–1975

Anne Sexton was born in Newton, Massachusetts, grew up in Wellesley, attended
Garland Junior College, and married at twenty. After suffering a mental
breakdown, she was urged to write poetry by her therapist. Like Sylvia Plath, she

---

[2] I.e., with a hernia supported by a truss.

studied with Robert Lowell at Boston University in the 1950s. Sexton's first book, *To Bedlam and Part Way Back* (1960), was published when she was thirty-two, and her third book, *Live or Die* (1967), was awarded the Pulitzer Prize, a recognition that crowned the amazing rise to fame of a woman who a few years before had been a suburban housewife without a college degree.

Sexton's poetic talents were a brisk diction, a devastating honesty, a gift for black humor, and a lethal talent for exposing the fraudulence and foolishness of the familial and social world, especially in the socialization of women. Her bold dramatic sense led her, in *Transformations* (1971), to adapt well-known fairy tales (about such heroines as Snow White and Briar Rose) in ways that expose the myths of female acceptability underlying those stories.

At the same time, Sexton's poetry dealt in pathos, often the pathos of the abandoned child. Sexton's capacity to resort to the childlike, even the infantile, in language and then to snap quickly to a disillusioned worldliness gave her poems their linguistic energy. The events of Sexton's life—her breakdown, her time in a mental hospital, her therapy, her troubled marriage (ending in divorce), her affairs, and her relationship with her two daughters—became transparently the stuff of her poetry. Her verse, far more directly than that of Lowell or Plath, can be called confessional poetry (a name first applied in 1959 by the critic M. L. Rosenthal). In her forties, after her marriage had ended in divorce, Sexton, who had been teaching at Boston University, committed suicide by carbon monoxide poisoning, leaving behind manuscripts posthumously published as *The Awful Rowing Toward God* (1975) and *45 Mercy Street* (1976), the volumes following *The Death Notebooks* (1974). Her *Complete Poems* was published posthumously in 1981.

The religious guilt evident in these books may perhaps be traced to Sexton's Roman Catholic upbringing. Her preoccupation with self-abasement, sin, sexual transgression, and bodily disgust worked against the efforts she made in years of therapy to find personal equilibrium. Her good looks and her performing spirit (she had been a fashion model as a girl and later founded her own jazz group, called Anne Sexton and Her Kind) made for gallantry of bearing and a winning insouciance in the poetry. But her last years, complicated by dependence on alcohol, made her become repetitive and self-pitying in the writing and to lose formal control of the poetry. Her surreal images became disconnected; the poems grew overlong. She will be remembered chiefly for her poems of the 1960s, those sharp, observant, satiric vignettes of American life, whether in a mental hospital, in a suburban kitchen, or at a country club dance. Her truthtelling wit and her ruthless self-examination gave her poetry a freshness and candor rarely equaled in domestic poetry.

Further Reading:
A Self-portrait in Letters, ed. L. G. Sexton and L. Ames, 1977.
Anne Sexton: The Artist and Her Critics, ed. J. D. McClatchy, 1978.

Text:
The Complete Poems, 1981.

Her Kind

I have gone out, a possessed witch,
haunting the black air, braver at night;
dreaming evil, I have done my hitch
over the plain houses, light by light:
lonely thing, twelve-fingered,[1] out of mind.   5
A woman like that is not a woman, quite.
I have been her kind.

I have found the warm caves in the woods,
filled them with skillets, carvings, shelves,
closets, silks, innumerable goods;   10
fixed the suppers for the worms and the elves:
whining, rearranging the disaligned.
A woman like that is misunderstood.
I have been her kind.

I have ridden in your cart, driver,   15
waved my nude arms at villages going by,
learning the last bright routes, survivor
where your flames still bite my thigh
and my ribs crack where your wheels wind.[2]
A woman like that is not ashamed to die.   20
I have been her kind.

1960

Ringing the Bells

And this is the way they ring
the bells in Bedlam[1]
and this is the bell-lady

[1] Witches were thought to have six fingers on
each hand.
[2] In Europe and America in the seventeenth
century, women thought to be witches were
often burned at the stake after being tortured
on the wheel, which stretched the victim's body
till the bones broke.

[1] "Bedlam" is the English name for a hospital for
the insane. The word is a contraction of
Bethlehem, after the London hospital St. Mary
of Bethlehem. The poem is based on the
nursery rhyme "This is the House That Jack
Built."

who comes each Tuesday morning
to give us a music lesson   5
and because the attendants make you go
and because we mind by instinct,
like bees caught in the wrong hive,
we are the circle of the crazy ladies
who sit in the lounge of the mental house   10
and smile at the smiling woman
who passes us each a bell,
who points at my hand
that holds my bell, E flat,
and this is the gray dress next to me   15
who grumbles as if it were special
to be old, to be old,
and this is the small hunched squirrel girl
on the other side of me
who picks at the hairs over her lip,   20
who picks at the hairs over her lip all day,
and this is how the bells really sound,
as untroubled and clean
as a workable kitchen,
and this is always my bell responding   25
to my hand that responds to the lady
who points at me, E flat;
and although we are no better for it,
they tell you to go. And you do.
1960

For My Lover, Returning to His Wife

She is all there.
She was melted carefully down for you
and cast up from your childhood,
cast up from your one hundred favorite aggies.[1]

She has always been there, my darling.   5
She is, in fact, exquisite.
Fireworks in the dull middle of February
and as real as a cast-iron pot.

---

[1] Agate marbles.

Let's face it, I have been momentary.
A luxury. A bright red sloop in the harbor.   10
My hair rising like smoke from the car window.
Littleneck clams out of season.

She is more than that. She is your have to have,
has grown you your practical your tropical growth.
This is not an experiment. She is all harmony.   15
She sees to oars and oarlocks for the dinghy,

has placed wild flowers at the window at breakfast,
sat by the potter's wheel at midday,
set forth three children under the moon,
three cherubs drawn by Michelangelo,   20

done this with her legs spread out
in the terrible months in the chapel.
If you glance up, the children are there
like delicate balloons resting on the ceiling.

She has also carried each one down the hall   25
after supper, their heads privately bent,
two legs protesting, person to person,
her face flushed with a song and their little sleep.

I give you back your heart.
I give you permission—   30

for the fuse inside her, throbbing
angrily in the dirt, for the bitch in her
and the burying of her wound—
for the burying of her small red wound alive—

for the pale flickering flare under her ribs,   35
for the drunken sailor who waits in her left pulse,
for the mother's knee, for the stockings,
for the garter belt, for the call—

the curious call
when you will burrow in arms and breasts   40

and tug at the orange ribbon in her hair
and answer the call, the curious call.

She is so naked and singular.
She is the sum of yourself and your dream.

Climb her like a monument, step after step.
She is solid.

As for me, I am a watercolor.
I wash off.
1969

January 1st

Today is favorable for joint financial affairs but do
not take any chances with speculation.

My daddy played the market.
My mother cut her coupons.
The children ran in circles.
The maid announced, the soup's on.

The guns were cleaned on Sunday.   5
The family went out to shoot.
We sat in the blind for hours.
The ducks fell down like fruit.

The big fat war was going on.
So profitable for daddy.   10
She drove a pea green Ford.
He drove a pearl gray Caddy.

In the end they used it up.
All that pale green dough.
The rest I spent on doctors   15
who took it like gigolos.[1]

My financial affairs are small.
Indeed they seem to shrink.
My heart is on a budget.
It keeps me on the brink.   20

I tell it stories now and then
and feed it images like honey.
I will not speculate today
with poems that think they're money.
1978

[1] Paid male lovers.

Adrienne Rich
b. 1929

Adrienne Rich was a precocious poet; her first book, *A Change of World* (1951), was selected by W. H. Auden for the Yale Younger Poets series when Rich was still a student at Radcliffe. The daughter of a Jewish doctor and professor of medicine at Johns Hopkins University and a non-Jewish mother, Rich grew up under the intense tutelage of her father. She became estranged from him when, against his assimilationist wishes, she married a Jewish economist, Alfred Conrad, a professor at Harvard. (The family conflicts have been repeatedly examined in Rich's verse.) Rich quickly had three sons; she writes in *Of Woman Born* (1976) of her unhappiness as a wife and mother and of the conflict she felt between those roles, as socially defined, and that of the writer. In 1963, at the age of thirty-four, Rich published *Snapshots of a Daughter-in-Law,* in which the themes of rebellion and disaffection present in masked forms in her first two books became overt. In the 1960s Rich and her husband moved to New York; the marriage dissolved, and Rich's husband committed suicide. Some years later, Rich declared herself to be a lesbian and joined lesbian political action to the other forms of social action in which she had engaged during the 1960s, when she had taught in the open admissions program at the City College of New York and had joined in protests against the Vietnam War.

Rich has lived a politically committed life and has not always escaped the dangers of politically inspired writing—a preference for bluntness over complexity of response, a certain predictability of stance. At the same time, she has been a seismograph of American protest, registering in turn the convulsions of the peace movement, the women's movement, and, later, the gay rights movement.

More recently, Rich has turned to reexamining the traditional life of women in the past, hoping to reconstruct a connection between those older female arts and skills and the inner life of contemporary women. After living for some years in western Massachusetts, Rich has now moved to California.

Though Rich's accomplished early verse in *A Change of World* (1951) and *The Diamond Cutters* (1955) imitated the formal patterns she found in Yeats, Auden, and Frost, she moved during the 1960s into free verse and has only rarely returned to formal prosody. She has experimented with the prose poem as well as with forms, such as "jump cuts," borrowed from the cinema and from photography. Her forms seem, however, subordinate to the urgency of the voice that speaks in the poems, whether in rage or in measured attack. It is typical of Rich to utter a theme first in a crude oppositional cartoon, like a political caricaturist; in a subsequent volume the same theme, often a myth or an archetype, is likely to be more subtly and deeply explored. *Leaflets* (1969), as its title implies, had the urgency of a set of bulletins from a political strategy center; *The Will to Change* (1971) explored inner personal drama, that drama that Rich has continued to trace in her metaphors of exile, toil, burning, sickness, devastation, rape, imprisonment, nakedness, and struggle. "I am trying to hold in one steady glance / all the parts of my life," she says in "Toward the Solstice," echoing Matthew Arnold's wish "to see life steadily and see it whole."

It is in fact the Victorians whom Rich most resembles in her earnestness, her direct gaze at social conditions, and her tone of public moral assertion. Her poetry lacks suppleness, play, wit, and humor; she is always serious. But she has never been content simply to be a propagandist. Her drive to make poetry of her autobiography reveals a subjectivity not entirely willing to be absorbed in the role of collective spokesperson. Her recent books—*The Dream of a Common Language* (1978), *A Wild Patience Has Taken Me This Far* (1981), and *The Fact of a Doorframe* (1985)—show an increasingly complex and searching response to the deprivations and yearning of the human condition.

Further Reading:
Adrienne Rich's Poetry: Text of the Poems; The Poet on Her Work; Reviews and Criticism, ed. B. C. Gelpi and A. Gelpi, 1975.

Texts:
"Upper Broadway" from *The Dream of a Common Language,* 1978.
All other selections from *Poems Selected and New, 1950–1974,* 1975.
See also *Of Woman Born: Motherhood as Experience and Institution,* 1976.
Women and Honor: Some Notes on Lying, 1977.
On Lies, Secrets, and Silence: Selected Prose, 1966–1978, 1979.

"I Am in Danger—Sir—"[1]

"Half-cracked" to Higginson, living,
afterward famous in garbled versions,

your hoard of dazzling scraps a battlefield,
now your old snood

mothballed at Harvard[2]   5
and you in your variorum monument
equivocal to the end—
who are you?

Gardening the day-lily,
wiping the wine-glass stems,   10
your thought pulsed on behind
a forehead battered paper-thin,

[1] From Emily Dickinson's letter of June 7, 1862, to Thomas Wentworth Higginson (1823–1911), then editor of the *Atlantic Monthly.*
[2] Memorabilia of the Dickinson homestead, as well as the packets of manuscript poems by Emily Dickinson, are kept in the Dickinson Room of the Houghton Library at Harvard University.

you, woman, masculine
in single-mindedness,
for whom the word was more   15
than a symptom—

a condition of being.
Till the air buzzing with spoiled language
sang in your ears
of Perjury   20

and in your half-cracked way you chose
silence for entertainment,
chose to have it out at last
on your own premises.
1966

Trying to Talk with a Man

Out in this desert we are testing bombs,

that's why we came here.

Sometimes I feel an underground river
forcing its way between deformed cliffs
an acute angle of understanding   5
moving itself like a locus of the sun
into this condemned scenery.

What we've had to give up to get here—
whole LP collections, films we starred in
playing in the neighborhoods, bakery windows   10
full of dry, chocolate-filled Jewish cookies,
the language of love-letters, of suicide notes,
afternoons on the riverbank
pretending to be children

Coming out to this desert   15
we meant to change the face of
driving among dull green succulents
walking at noon in the ghost town
surrounded by a silence

that sounds like the silence of the place   20
except that it came with us
and is familiar
and everything we were saying until now
was an effort to blot it out—
coming out here we are up against it   25

Out here I feel more helpless
with you than without you

You mention the danger
and list the equipment
we talk of people caring for each other   30
in emergencies—laceration, thirst—
but you look at me like an emergency

Your dry heat feels like power
your eyes are stars of a different magnitude
they reflect lights that spell out: EXIT   35
when you get up and pace the floor

talking of the danger
as if it were not ourselves
as if we were testing anything else.
1973

Diving into the Wreck

First having read the book of myths,
and loaded the camera,
and checked the edge of the knife-blade,
I put on
the body-armor of black rubber   5
the absurd flippers
the grave and awkward mask.
I am having to do this
not like Cousteau[1] with his
assiduous team   10

---

[1] Jacques Cousteau (b. 1910), French underwater
explorer, inventor of the aqualung, author, and
filmmaker.

aboard the sun-flooded schooner
but here alone.

There is a ladder.
The ladder is always there
hanging innocently   15
close to the side of the schooner.
We know what it is for,
we who have used it.
Otherwise
it's a piece of maritime floss   20
some sundry equipment.

I go down.
Rung after rung and still
the oxygen immerses me
the blue light   25
the clear atoms
of our human air.
I go down.
My flippers cripple me,
I crawl like an insect down the ladder   30
and there is no one
to tell me when the ocean
will begin.

First the air is blue and then
it is bluer and then green and then   35
black I am blacking out and yet
my mask is powerful
it pumps my blood with power
the sea is another story
the sea is not a question of power   40
I have to learn alone
to turn my body without force
in the deep element.

And now: it is easy to forget
what I came for   45
among so many who have always
lived here
swaying their crenellated fans
between the reefs
and besides   50
you breathe differently down here.

I came to explore the wreck.
The words are purposes.

The words are maps.
I came to see the damage that was done
and the treasures that prevail.
I stroke the beam of my lamp
slowly along the flank
of something more permanent
than fish or weed

the thing I came for:
the wreck and not the story of the wreck
the thing itself and not the myth
the drowned face always staring
toward the sun
the evidence of damage
worn by salt and sway into this threadbare beauty
the ribs of the disaster
curving their assertion
among the tentative haunters.

This is the place.
And I am here, the mermaid whose dark hair
streams black, the merman in his armored body
We circle silently
about the wreck
we dive into the hold.
I am she: I am he

whose drowned face sleeps with open eyes
whose breasts still bear the stress
whose silver, copper, vermeil cargo lies
obscurely inside barrels
half-wedged and left to rot
we are the half-destroyed instruments
that once held to a course
the water-eaten log
the fouled compass

We are, I am, you are
by cowardice or courage
the one who find our way
back to this scene
carrying a knife, a camera
a book of myths
in which
our names do not appear.

1973

Translations

You show me the poems of some woman
my age, or younger
translated from your language

Certain words occur: *enemy, oven, sorrow*
enough to let me know   5
she's a woman of my time

obsessed

with Love, our subject:
we've trained it like ivy to our walls
baked it like bread in our ovens   10
worn it like lead on our ankles
watched it through binoculars as if
it were a helicopter
bringing food to our famine
or the satellite   15
of a hostile power

I begin to see that woman
doing things: stirring rice
ironing a skirt
typing a manuscript till dawn   20

trying to make a call
from a phonebooth

The phone rings unanswered
in a man's bedroom
she hears him telling someone else   25
Never mind. She'll get tired—
hears him telling her story to her sister
who becomes her enemy
and will in her own time
light her own way to sorrow   30

ignorant of the fact this way of grief
is shared, unnecessary
and political

1973

From a Survivor

The pact that we made was the ordinary pact
of men & women in those days

I don't know who we thought we were
that our personalities
could resist the failures of the race   5

Lucky or unlucky, we didn't know
the race had failures of that order
and that we were going to share them

Like everybody else, we thought of ourselves as special

Your body is as vivid to me   10
as it ever was: even more

since my feeling for it is clearer:
I know what it could and could not do

it is no longer
the body of a god   15
or anything with power over my life

Next year it would have been 20 years
and you are wastefully dead
who might have made the leap
we talked, too late, of making   20

which I live now
not as a leap
but a succession of brief, amazing movements
each one making possible the next
1973

Upper Broadway

The leafbud straggles forth
toward the frigid light of the airshaft   this is faith
this pale extension of a day

when looking up   you know   something is changing
winter has turned   though the wind is colder   5
Three streets away   a roof collapses   onto people
who thought they still had time.   Time out of mind

I have written so many words
wanting to live inside you
to be of use to you   10

Now I must write for myself   for this blind
woman scratching the pavement   with her wand of thought
this slippered crone   inching on icy streets
reaching into wire trashbaskets   pulling out
what was thrown away   and infinitely precious   15

I look at my hands and see   they are still unfinished
I look at the vine and see the leafbud
inching towards life

I look at my face in the glass   and see
a halfborn woman   20
1978

Gary Snyder
b. 1930

Gary Snyder has brought both Zen Buddhism and ecological concerns into
contemporary American poetry. He is a notable landscape poet of the American
Northwest, who sees the West Coast as one border of the "Pacific basin" and
links it to the Orient and to the Alaskan Indian and Eskimo culture. In
symbolically turning away from the East Coast, the traditional "hub" of
American poetry, and in rejecting as well the Anglo-Saxon Protestant ethnic base
of American poetry, Snyder reminds his readers that many different American
orientations are possible, that the West, as well as the East, can be the center
from which allegiances are measured. He reminds us, too, that we are not the
first inhabitants of our country.

Snyder was born in San Francisco, but soon after his birth his family moved
to a small farm near Seattle, where he grew up. He went to Reed College on a
scholarship, working summers with the U.S. Forest Service and in logging camps
in the Northwest. His senior thesis at Reed, *He Who Invented Birds in His
Father's Village,* showed his early acquaintance with the culture of the American
Indians. Later he studied linguistics and American Indian culture at the University
of Indiana; he then moved to San Francisco and completed all requirements
except the thesis for a doctorate in Japanese at Berkeley. In the 1950s he was

associated in San Francisco with Allen Ginsberg, Jack Kerouac, and others who introduced the "Beat" movement in literature. (He was the hero of Kerouac's 1958 novel *The Dharma Bums.*) He worked as a wiper on an American tanker that went to the Persian Gulf and the South Pacific islands; from 1956 to 1968 he lived chiefly in Japan and spent several years in residence at Zen Buddhist monasteries. He considers himself "a Buddhist of the Mahayana-Vajrayana line" and now lives in the Sierra Nevada foothills with his third wife and children.

Snyder's first book was called *Riprap* (1959)—"a cobble of stone laid on steep slick rock / to make a trail for horses in the mountain." In the last poem of that book he defines poetry as "a riprap on the slick rock of metaphysics"—the graspable tactile surface giving us a purchase on the path of thought that we travel. The subsequently published *Myths and Texts* (1960) contains poems from the 1950s concerned with logging and hunting, activities (in which Snyder has participated) that destroy or alter the environment. In later books, Snyder continues his exploration of the West Coast and our relation to nature, most notably in the book called, after the Indian name for North America, *Turtle Island* (1974). His most recent volume is *Axe Handles* (1983).

In his prosody, Snyder derives most immediately from Pound. He has said that his lines are influenced by "five-and-seven-character-line Chinese poems . . . and the songs and dances of Great Basin Indian tribes." The longer poems are digressive and episodic, held together more by moral concern than by an inner architecture. "As a poet," says Snyder, "I hold the most archaic values on earth. They go back to the Neolithic: the fertility of the soil, the magic of animals, the power-vision in solitude, the terrifying initiation and rebirth, the love and ecstasy of the dance, the common work of the tribe." Snyder's work, embodying these values, can be considered either nostalgically regressive or prophetic of the earth's future necessities. Snyder considers poetry "a social and traditional art that is linked to its past and particularly its language. . . . Poetry is intimately linked to any culture's fundamental world view, body of lore, which is its myth base, its symbol-base, and the source of much of its values. . . . That's the ongoing work of major poets, to restate the society's whole body of world-view lore periodically." In turning to Asia and to Buddhism, Snyder, like Ginsberg, suggests to American readers the limitation of a cultural perspective that knows only Western values. But it puts in question, too, the extent to which a country can adopt values and attitudes not culturally indigenous. Since the time of Whitman, there has been a stubborn effort on the part of American poets to enlarge the frame of reference of American literature beyond the European point of view: Snyder's work is part of the history of that long-standing effort.

Further Reading:
B. Steuding, *Gary Snyder*, 1976.

Texts:
"This Poem Is for Bear" from *Myths and Texts,* 1960.
"Riprap" from *Riprap and Cold Mountain Poems,* 1965.
"Sixth-Month Song in the Foothills" and "Trail Crew Camp. . . ." from *The Back Country,* 1968.
"I Went into the Maverick Bar" from *Turtle Island,* 1974.

This Poem Is for Bear

"As for me I am a child of the god of the mountains."

A bear down under the cliff.
She is eating huckleberries.
They are ripe now
Soon it will snow, and she
Or maybe he, will crawl into a hole   5
And sleep. You can see
Huckleberries in bearshit if you
Look, this time of year
If I sneak up on the bear
It will grunt and run   10

The others had all gone down
From the blackberry brambles, but one girl
Spilled her basket, and was picking up her
Berries in the dark.
A tall man stood in the shadow, took her arm,   15
Led her to his home. He was a bear.
In a house under the mountain
She gave birth to slick dark children
With sharp teeth, and lived in the hollow
Mountain many years.   20
            snare a bear: call him out:

honey-eater
forest apple
light-foot
Old man in the fur coat, Bear! come out!   25
Die of your own choice!
Grandfather black-food!
            this girl married a bear
Who rules in the mountains, Bear!
            you have eaten many berries   30
            you have caught many fish
            you have frightened many people
Twelve species north of Mexico
Sucking their paws in the long winter
Tearing the high-strung caches down   35
Whining, crying, jacking off
(Odysseus was a bear)

Bear-cubs gnawing the soft tits
Teeth gritted, eyes screwed tight
            but she let them.   40

Til her brothers found the place
Chased her husband up the gorge
Cornered him in the rocks.
Song of the snared bear:
    "Give me my belt.
    "I am near death.
    "I came from the mountain caves
    "At the headwaters,
    "The small streams there
    "Are all dried up.

—I think I'll go hunt bears.
        "hunt bears?
Why shit Snyder,
You couldn't hit a bear in the ass
        with a handful of rice!"

1960

Riprap[1]

Lay down these words
Before your mind like rocks.
        placed solid, by hands
In choice of place, set
Before the body of the mind
        in space and time:
Solidity of bark, leaf, or wall
        riprap of things:
Cobble of milky way,
        straying planets,
These poems, people,
        lost ponies with
Dragging saddles—
        and rocky sure-foot trails.
The worlds like an endless
        four-dimensional
Game of *Go.*
        ants and pebbles

[1] Snyder's note: "Riprap: a cobble of stone laid on steep slick rock to make a trail for horses in the mountains."

In the thin loam, each rock a word
   a creek-washed stone   20
Granite: ingrained
   with torment of fire and weight
Crystal and sediment linked hot
   all change, in thoughts,
As well as things.   25
 1959

Sixth-Month Song in the Foothills

In the cold shed sharpening saws.
   a swallow's nest hangs by the door
setting rakers in sunlight
falling from meadow through doorframe
   swallows flit under the eaves.   5

Grinding the falling axe
sharp for the summer
   a swallow shooting out over.
over the river, snow on low hills
sharpening wedges for splitting.   10

Beyond the low hills, white mountains
and now snow is melting.   sharpening tools;
   pack horses grazing new grass
bright axes—and swallows
   fly in to my shed.   15
 1968

Trail Crew Camp at Bear Valley, 9000 Feet
Northern Sierra—White Bone and Threads of Snowmelt Water

Cut branches back for a day—
trail a thin line through willow
   up buckbrush meadows,

<pre>
                                      creekbed for twenty yards
                               winding in boulders
                                      zigzags the hill   5
                               into timber, white pine.

                                      gooseberry bush on the turns.
                               hooves clang on the riprap¹
                                             dust, brush, branches.   10
                                      a stone
                                cairn² at the pass—
                               strippt mountains hundreds of miles.

                               sundown went back
                                             the clean switchbacks to camp.   15
                               bell on the gelding,
                               stew in the cook tent,
                               black coffee in a big tin can.
                               1968
</pre>

I Went into the Maverick Bar

I went into the Maverick Bar
In Farmington, New Mexico.
And drank double shots of bourbon
                         backed with beer.
My long hair was tucked up under a cap   5
I'd left the earring in the car.

Two cowboys did horseplay
                      by the pool tables,
A waitress asked us
                      where are you from?   10
a country-and-western band began to play
"We don't smoke Marijuana in Muskokie"
And with the next song,
                         a couple began to dance.

¹ Stone cobbles laid on rock to make a trail for   ² Pile of stones.
horses.

They held each other like in High School dances   15
          in the fifties;
I recalled when I worked in the woods
          and the bars of Madras, Oregon.
That short-haired joy and roughness—
          America—your stupidity.   20
I could almost love you again.

We left—onto the freeway shoulders—
          under the tough old stars—
In the shadow of bluffs
          I came back to myself,   25
To the real work, to
          "What is to be done."
    1974

Sylvia Plath
1932–1963

The intensity, purity, and spareness of Sylvia Plath's last poems have given her short career a weight out of proportion to its brevity. Though they come from a tragic life and often have a tragic subject, these poems are exhilarated, sure, certain of their path. They are poems of cool mastery, of a talent unafraid of its own extremes. It is also a well-schooled talent, one that has assimilated the poetry of D. H. Lawrence, Theodore Roethke, and Robert Lowell and has added a wild, dark comedy of its own (visible in "Daddy" and "Lady Lazarus") not learned from any of those masters.

Plath worked obsessively at being a poet from childhood; her first published poem appeared in a Boston newspaper when she was eight and a half. By the time she was in college at Smith, she was publishing in *Seventeen* and *Mademoiselle.* As her journals show, she had unlimited ambition and equally unlimited anxiety; cycles of manic planning followed by depressive collapses recurred throughout her life, causing an unsuccessful suicide attempt at nineteen and a successful one at thirty-one. Manic-depressive illness was not well understood at the time, and Plath, like Lowell, underwent electroconvulsive therapy, involuntary confinement in an asylum, and psychiatric therapy. These palliative treatments did not prevent the recurrence of symptoms.

Plath's distress at her own emotional volatility caused her to channel her explosive nature at first into rigidly controlled and conventionally acceptable poems, published in *The Colossus* (1960). With her marriage to the Yorkshire poet Ted Hughes, her expatriation to England, and the birth of her two children, her emotional life deepened and, under the tutelage of Hughes, who approved of the "demonic" forces in poetry, became freer to express itself. She turned savagely against what she regarded as the German oppressiveness of her professor-father (whose academic specialty was bees) and the bourgeois gentility of her mother (who taught secretarial subjects). Her rage turned as well against her husband when she discovered his infidelity; it was after their separation, in the coldest London winter in years, that she killed herself by turning on the kitchen gas. Plath's best-selling autobiographical (and pseudonymously published) novel, *The Bell Jar* (1963), has none of the talent of her poetry, but it remains a reference point as one of the changing scenarios of explanation that Plath continuously constructed for her life.

Most of Plath's best poetry—*Ariel* (1966), *Crossing the Water* (1971), and *Winter Trees* (1972)—was published posthumously. It caught the public imagination by the topicality of its subject matter (marriage, childbearing, infidelity, the woman artist), but it also caught the literary imagination by its ardent language, its compression, its violence in metaphor, and its authoritative tone. Plath had studied at Boston University with Robert Lowell, and it was probably his example that she followed in writing her later poetry in free verse. Her free verse, however, has none of the loose and low-keyed quality of Lowell's *Life Studies;* rather, it is so firmly supported by internal rhymes, eye rhymes, parallelism, apposition, alliteration, and other binding devices that it seems as fully controlled as any formal verse could be.

Like Emily Dickinson, Plath repudiated the language of conventional female verse for a fierce and daring explicitness. At the same time, her acute and cold self-observation dominated her fiery lines, taming them to form, mediating her tormented states of mind by a high intelligence. Her reputation has grown steadily since her death; *The Collected Poems,* edited by Ted Hughes, was published in 1981 and the *Journals of Sylvia Plath* in 1982. Her short fiction is collected in *Johnny Panic and the Bible of Dreams* (1979), and a selection of her letters, edited with commentary by her mother, Aurelia Schober Plath, was published as *Letters Home* (1975).

Further Reading:
The Art of Sylvia Plath, ed. C. Newman, 1970.
N. H. Steiner, *A Closer Look at Ariel: A Memory of Sylvia Plath,* 1973.
E. Butscher, *Sylvia Plath: Method and Madness,* 1976.
D. Holbrook, *Sylvia Plath: Poetry and Existence,* 1976.
J. Kroll, *Chapters in a Mythology: The Poetry of Sylvia Plath,* 1976.

G. Lane and M. Stevens, *Sylvia Plath: A Bibliography,* 1978.
Sylvia Plath: New Views on Poetry, ed. G. Lane, 1979.
M. D. Uroff, *Sylvia Plath and Ted Hughes,* 1979.
J. Rosenblatt, *Sylvia Plath: The Poetry of Initiation,* 1979.

Text:
The Collected Poems, 1981.

Black Rook in Rainy Weather

On the stiff twig up there
Hunches a wet black rook
Arranging and rearranging its feathers in the rain.
I do not expect a miracle
Or an accident   5

To set the sight on fire
In my eye, nor seek
Any more in the desultory weather some design,
But let spotted leaves fall as they fall,
Without ceremony, or portent.   10

Although, I admit, I desire,
Occasionally, some backtalk
From the mute sky, I can't honestly complain:
A certain minor light may still
Lean incandescent   15

Out of kitchen table or chair
As if a celestial burning took
Possession of the most obtuse objects now and then—
Thus hallowing an interval
Otherwise inconsequent   20

By bestowing largesse, honor,
One might say love. At any rate, I now walk
Wary (for it could happen
Even in this dull, ruinous landscape); skeptical,
Yet politic; ignorant   25

Of whatever angel may choose to flare
Suddenly at my elbow. I only know that a rook
Ordering its black feathers can so shine
As to seize my senses, haul
My eyelids up, and grant   30

A brief respite from fear
Of total neutrality. With luck,
Trekking stubborn through this season
Of fatigue, I shall
Patch together a content   35

Of sorts. Miracles occur,
If you care to call those spasmodic
Tricks of radiance miracles. The wait's begun again,
The long wait for the angel,
For that rare, random descent.

1960

The Colossus

I shall never get you put together entirely,
Pieced, glued, and properly jointed.
Mule-bray, pig-grunt and bawdy cackles
Proceed from your great lips.
It's worse than a barnyard.

Perhaps you consider yourself an oracle,
Mouthpiece of the dead, or of some god or other.
Thirty years now I have labored
To dredge the silt from your throat.
I am none the wiser.

Scaling little ladders with gluepots and pails of Lysol
I crawl like an ant in mourning
Over the weedy acres of your brow
To mend the immense skull-plates and clear
The bald, white tumuli[1] of your eyes.

A blue sky out of the Oresteia[2]
Arches above us. O father, all by yourself
You are pithy and historical as the Roman Forum.[3]
I open my lunch on a hill of black cypress.
Your fluted bones and acanthine[4] hair are littered

In their old anarchy to the horizon-line.
It would take more than a lightning-stroke

---

[1] Grave mounds.
[2] The Greek trilogy, by Aeschylus (525–426 B.C.), recounting the tragic story of the house of Atreus.
[3] The large public market and meeting place in ancient Rome.
[4] Like an acanthus leaf, the stylized ornate leaf that was used as a motif in Greek art.

To create such a ruin.
Nights, I squat in the cornucopia
Of your left ear, out of the wind,   25

Counting the red stars and those of plum-color.
The sun rises under the pillar of your tongue.
My hours are married to shadow.
No longer do I listen for the scrape of a keel
On the blank stones of the landing.   30
1960

Morning Song

Love set you going like a fat gold watch.
The midwife slapped your footsoles, and your bald cry
Took its place among the elements.

Our voices echo, magnifying your arrival. New statue.
In a drafty museum, your nakedness   5
Shadows our safety. We stand round blankly as walls.

I'm no more your mother
Than the cloud that distills a mirror to reflect its own slow
Effacement at the wind's hand.

All night your moth-breath   10
Flickers among the flat pink roses.[1] I wake to listen:
A far sea moves in my ear.

One cry, and I stumble from bed, cow-heavy and floral
In my Victorian nightgown.
Your mouth opens clean as a cat's. The window square   15

Whitens and swallows its dull stars. And now you try
Your handful of notes;
The clear vowels rise like balloons.
1965

---

[1] I.e., of the wallpaper.

The Moon and the Yew Tree

This is the light of the mind, cold and planetary.
The trees of the mind are black. The light is blue.
The grasses unload their griefs on my feet as if I were God,
Prickling my ankles and murmuring of their humility.
Fumy, spiritous mists inhabit this place   5
Separated from my house by a row of headstones.
I simply cannot see where there is to get to.

The moon is no door. It is a face in its own right,
White as a knuckle and terribly upset.
It drags the sea after it like a dark crime; it is quiet   10
With the O-gape of complete despair. I live here.
Twice on Sunday, the bells startle the sky——
Eight great tongues affirming the Resurrection.
At the end, they soberly bong out their names.

The yew tree points up. It has a Gothic shape.   15
The eyes lift after it and find the moon.
The moon is my mother. She is not sweet like Mary.[1]
Her blue garments unloose small bats and owls.
How I would like to believe in tenderness——
The face of the effigy, gentled by candles,   20
Bending, on me in particular, its mild eyes.

I have fallen a long way. Clouds are flowering
Blue and mystical over the face of the stars.
Inside the church, the saints will be all blue,
Floating on their delicate feet over the cold pews,   25
Their hands and faces stiff with holiness.
The moon sees nothing of this. She is bald and wild.
And the message of the yew tree is blackness—blackness and silence.

1965

---

[1] The Virgin Mary, usually depicted as dressed in
blue.

Crossing the Water

Black lake, black boat, two black, cut-paper people.
Where do the black trees go that drink here?
Their shadows must cover Canada.

A little light is filtering from the water flowers.
Their leaves do not wish us to hurry: 5
They are round and flat and full of dark advice.

Cold worlds shake from the oar.
The spirit of blackness is in us, it is in the fishes.
A snag is lifting a valedictory, pale hand;

Stars open among the lilies.   10
Are you not blinded by such expressionless sirens?[1]
This is the silence of astounded souls.

1965

The Bee Meeting

Who are these people at the bridge to meet me? They are the villagers——
The rector, the midwife, the sexton, the agent for bees.
In my sleeveless summery dress I have no protection,
And they are all gloved and covered, why did nobody tell me?
They are smiling and taking out veils tacked to ancient hats.   5

I am nude as a chicken neck, does nobody love me?
Yes, here is the secretary of bees with her white shop smock,
Buttoning the cuffs at my wrists and the slit from my neck to my knees.
Now I am milkweed silk, the bees will not notice.
They will not smell my fear, my fear, my fear.   10

Which is the rector now, is it that man in black?
Which is the midwife, is that her blue coat?
Everybody is nodding a square black head, they are knights in visors,

---

[1] Mermaids who, according to classical legend,
enticed sailors to their death.

Breastplates of cheesecloth knotted under the armpits.
Their smiles and their voices are changing. I am led through a beanfield.

Strips of tinfoil winking like people,
Feather dusters fanning their hands in a sea of bean flowers,
Creamy bean flowers with black eyes and leaves like bored hearts.
Is it blood clots the tendrils are dragging up that string?
No, no, it is scarlet flowers that will one day be edible.

Now they are giving me a fashionable white straw Italian hat
And a black veil that molds to my face, they are making me one of them.
They are leading me to the shorn grove, the circle of hives.
Is it the hawthorn that smells so sick?
The barren body of hawthorn, etherizing its children.

Is it some operation that is taking place?
It is the surgeon my neighbors are waiting for,
This apparition in a green helmet,
Shining gloves and white suit.
Is it the butcher, the grocer, the postman, someone I know?

I cannot run, I am rooted, and the gorse hurts me
With its yellow purses, its spiky armory.
I could not run without having to run forever.
The white hive is snug as a virgin,
Sealing off her brood cells, her honey, and quietly humming.

Smoke rolls and scarves in the grove.
The mind of the hive thinks this is the end of everything.
Here they come, the outriders, on their hysterical elastics.[1]
If I stand very still, they will think I am cow-parsley,
A gullible head untouched by their animosity,

Not even nodding, a personage in a hedgerow.
The villagers open the chambers, they are hunting the queen.
Is she hiding, is she eating honey? She is very clever.
She is old, old, old, she must live another year, and she knows it.
While in their fingerjoint cells the new virgins[2]

Dream of a duel they will win inevitably,
A curtain of wax dividing them from the bride flight,
The upflight of the murderess[3] into a heaven that loves her.
The villagers are moving the virgins, there will be no killing.
The old queen does not show herself, is she so ungrateful?

[1] The outgoing bees, who then "snap back" to the hive.
[2] Embryonic female bees.
[3] The queen bee.

I am exhausted, I am exhausted——
Pillar of white in a blackout of knives.
I am the magician's girl who does not flinch.
The villagers are untying their disguises, they are shaking hands.
Whose is that long white box in the grove, what have they accomplished, why
    am I cold.   55

1965

Daddy

You do not do, you do not do
Any more, black shoe
In which I have lived like a foot
For thirty years, poor and white,
Barely daring to breathe or Achoo.   5

Daddy, I have had to kill you.
You died before I had time——
Marble-heavy, a bag full of God,
Ghastly statue with one gray toe[1]
Big as a Frisco seal   10

And a head in the freakish Atlantic
Where it pours bean green over blue
In the waters off beautiful Nauset.
I used to pray to recover you.
Ach, du.[2]   15

In the German tongue, in the Polish town
Scraped flat by the roller
Of wars, wars, wars.
But the name of the town is common.
My Polack[3] friend   20

Says there are a dozen or two.
So I never could tell where you
Put your foot, your root,
I never could talk to you.
The tongue stuck in my jaw.   25

---

[1] Otto Plath's diabetes caused a gangrenous toe,
which led to the septicemia that killed him.
[2] German: "Ah, you." The second-person familiar
form is used for intimates.

[3] Derogatory slang for "Polish."

It stuck in a barb wire snare.
Ich, ich, ich, ich,[4]
I could hardly speak.
I thought every German was you.
And the language obscene   30

An engine, an engine
Chuffing me off like a Jew.
A Jew to Dachau, Auschwitz, Belsen.[5]
I began to talk like a Jew.
I think I may well be a Jew.   35

The snows of the Tyrol,[6] the clear beer of Vienna[7]
Are not very pure or true.
With my gipsy ancestress and my weird luck
And my Taroc pack and my Taroc pack[8]
I may be a bit of a Jew.   40

I have always been scared of *you*,
With your Luftwaffe,[9] your gobbledygoo.
And your neat mustache
And your Aryan[10] eye, bright blue.
Panzer-man, panzer-man,[11] O You——   45

Not God but a swastika[12]
So black no sky could squeak through.
Every woman adores a Fascist,
The boot in the face, the brute
Brute heart of a brute like you.   50

You stand at the blackboard, daddy,[13]
In the picture I have of you,
A cleft in your chin instead of your foot
But no less a devil for that, no not
Any less the black man who   55

Bit my pretty red heart in two.
I was ten when they buried you.
At twenty I tried to die
And get back, back, back to you.
I thought even the bones would do.   60

[4] German: "I, I, I, I."
[5] Nazi concentration camps.
[6] Alpine region of Austria.
[7] Capital of Austria.
[8] Pack of cards used in fortune telling.
[9] The Nazi air force.

[10] Word used by Nazis to characterize those of "pure" or unadulterated German stock.
[11] Man resembling a German armored tank.
[12] Symbol of the Nazi party.
[13] Otto Plath was a professor of biology at Boston University.

But they pulled me out of the sack,
And they stuck me together with glue.
And then I knew what to do.
I made a model of you,
A man in black with a Meinkampf[14] look   65

And a love of the rack and the screw.[15]
And I said I do, I do.
So daddy, I'm finally through.
The black telephone's off at the root,
The voices just can't worm through.   70

If I've killed one man, I've killed two——
The vampire who said he was you
And drank my blood for a year,
Seven years, if you want to know.
Daddy, you can lie back now.   75

There's a stake in your fat black heart[16]
And the villagers never liked you.
They are dancing and stamping on you.
They always *knew* it was you.
Daddy, daddy, you bastard, I'm through.   80

1965

Ariel[1]

Stasis in darkness.
Then the substanceless blue
Pour of tor[2] and distances.

God's lioness,
How one we grow,
Pivot of heels and knees!—The furrow   5

Splits and passes, sister to
The brown arc
Of the neck I cannot catch,

---

[14] German: "My struggle," the title of Hitler's manifesto.
[15] Rack; screw: instruments of torture.
[16] Traditionally, a vampire was buried at a crossroads with a stake through the heart.

[1] Plath's horse.
[2] High, craggy hill.

Nigger-eye   1
Berries cast dark
Hooks——

Black sweet blood mouthfuls,
Shadows.
Something else   1.

Hauls me through air——
Thighs, hair;
Flakes from my heels.

White   20
Godiva,[3] I unpeel——
Dead hands, dead stringencies.

And now I
Foam to wheat, a glitter of seas.
The child's cry

Melts in the wall.   25
And I
Am the arrow,

The dew that flies
Suicidal, at one with the drive
Into the red   30

Eye, the cauldron of morning.
1965

Poppies in October

Even the sun-clouds this morning cannot manage such skirts.
Nor the woman in the ambulance
Whose red heart blooms through her coat so astoundingly——

A gift, a love gift
Utterly unasked for
By a sky   5

[3] Lady Godiva, in the legend, rode naked on her
horse.

Palely and flamily
Igniting its carbon monoxides, by eyes
Dulled to a halt under bowlers.

O my God, what am I   10
That these late mouths should cry open
In a forest of frost, in a dawn of cornflowers.

1965

Lady Lazarus[1]

I have done it again.
One year in every ten
I manage it——

A sort of walking miracle, my skin
Bright as a Nazi lampshade,[2]   5
My right foot

A paperweight,
My face a featureless, fine
Jew linen.

Peel off the napkin[3]   10
O my enemy.
Do I terrify?——

The nose, the eye pits, the full set of teeth?
The sour breath
Will vanish in a day.   15

Soon, soon the flesh
The grave cave ate will be
At home on me

And I a smiling woman.
I am only thirty.   20
And like the cat I have nine times to die.

[1] Lazarus was raised from the dead by Jesus.
[2] The Nazis, in concentration camps, made lampshades of human skin.
[3] According to legend, the veil or napkin with which Veronica wiped Jesus' face, as he bore the Cross, was then impressed with his visage.

This is Number Three.
What a trash
To annihilate each decade.

What a million filaments.
The peanut-crunching crowd   2
Shoves in to see

Them unwrap me hand and foot——
The big strip tease.
Gentlemen, ladies   3

These are my hands
My knees.
I may be skin and bone,

Nevertheless, I am the same, identical woman.
The first time it happened I was ten.   35
It was an accident.

The second time I meant
To last it out and not come back at all.
I rocked shut

As a seashell.   40
They had to call and call
And pick the worms off me like sticky pearls.

Dying
Is an art, like everything else.
I do it exceptionally well.   45

I do it so it feels like hell.
I do it so it feels real.
I guess you could say I've a call.

It's easy enough to do it in a cell.
It's easy enough to do it and stay put.   50
It's the theatrical

Comeback in broad day
To the same place, the same face, the same brute
Amused shout:

'A miracle!'   55
That knocks me out.
There is a charge

For the eyeing of my scars, there is a charge
For the hearing of my heart——
It really goes.   60

And there is a charge, a very large charge
For a word or a touch
Or a bit of blood

Or a piece of my hair or my clothes.
So, so, Herr Doktor.   65
So, Herr Enemy.

I am your opus,
I am your valuable,
The pure gold baby

That melts to a shriek.   70
I turn and burn.
Do not think I underestimate your great concern.

Ash, ash——
You poke and stir.
Flesh, bone, there is nothing there——   75

A cake of soap,
A wedding ring,
A gold filling.[4]

Herr God, Herr Lucifer
Beware   80
Beware.

Out of the ash
I rise with my red hair
And I eat men like air.

1965

Death & Co.

Two, of course there are two.
It seems perfectly natural now——
The one who never looks up, whose eyes are lidded

---

[4] Items left in the crematoria of the Nazi concentration camps after the bodies of prisoners had been burned. (The rendered fat of the bodies was used to make soap.)

And balled, like Blake's,[1]
Who exhibits   5

The birthmarks that are his trademark——
The scald scar of water,
The nude
Verdigris of the condor.
I am red meat. His beak   10

Claps sidewise: I am not his yet.
He tells me how badly I photograph.
He tells me how sweet
The babies look in their hospital
Icebox, a simple   15

Frill at the neck,
Then the flutings of their Ionian[2]
Death-gowns,
Then two little feet.
He does not smile or smoke.   20

The other does that,
His hair long and plausive.
Bastard
Masturbating a glitter,
He wants to be loved.   25

I do not stir.
The frost makes a flower,
The dew makes a star,
The dead bell,
The dead bell.   30

Somebody's done for.
1965

Winter Trees

The wet dawn inks are doing their blue dissolve.
On their blotter of fog the trees
Seem a botanical drawing—

---

[1] The plaster death mask of the English poet   [2] Greek.
William Blake (1757–1827) represents his eyes
"lidded and balled."

Memories growing, ring on ring,
A series of weddings.   5

Knowing neither abortions nor bitchery,
Truer than women,
They seed so effortlessly!
Tasting the winds, that are footless,
Waist-deep in history—   10

Full of wings, otherworldliness.
In this, they are Ledas.[1]
O mother of leaves and sweetness
Who are these pietàs?[2]
The shadows of ringdoves chanting, but easing nothing.   15

1971

[1] In Greek mythology, Leda, after being
impregnated by Zeus in the form of a swan,
gave birth to Helen of Troy.

[2] Pietà: traditional sculptural group depicting
Mary with the dead Jesus.

Richard Estes,
Double Self-Portrait,
oil on canvas, 1976.
Collection, The Museum of Modern Art, New York.
Mr. and Mrs. Stuart M. Speiser Fund.

The Literature of Contemporary America: Prose

The years between the assassination of John F. Kennedy (November 1963) and the final withdrawal of American troops from Vietnam (April 1975) battered everyone living in the United States, especially the thoughtful young. Allen Matusow called his history of these convulsive years *The Unraveling of America;* to another historian, Paul Johnson, they represent America's "suicide attempt." In an essay published in July 1984, the literary critic Benjamin DeMott refers to them as "the killer decade."

Such assessments of American society of the late 1960s and early 1970s—"finished, ruined, to hell in a handbasket" (as DeMott sums up the more extreme judgments)—may strike readers today as excessive, particularly in light of the resurgent hope and apparent unity of the Reagan era. But even the most critical assessments gain credibility when we realize that the dominant theme in recent years has been recovery and the dominant force, reaction against protest.

Following his narrow victory over Hubert Humphrey in 1968, Richard Nixon used his first term as president (1969–1972) to marshal what he called America's "great, silent majority" against the "excesses" of the 1960s. In 1972 that emergent majority carried Nixon to a landslide victory over George McGovern (the margin in the electoral college was 521 to 17). In less than a year, however, the Watergate scandal revived the nation's interest in reform. It not only forced Nixon from office; it set the stage for Jimmy Carter's victory over Gerald Ford in 1976. Finally, however, Watergate inflicted only temporary damage to the nation's reaction against protest and reform. Since then, in both the election (1980) and reelection (1984) of Ronald Reagan as president, three conservative groups have dominated national issues and political campaigns: first, the "neoconservatives," a group of intellectuals centered in New York City; second, the "moral majority," Nixon's "silent majority" become organized and powerful primarily through the work of evangelical Protestant groups; and third, the "New Right," a loose band of conservative individuals and organizations.

There are, of course, many reasons for the shift that has carried the United States from the heyday of the "hippies" to the heyday of Reaganomics. But at least four are worth special attention. First, with American involvement in Vietnam halted, with Nixon out of office, and with the rights of women and racial and sexual minorities (Chicanos, American Indians, Asian-Americans, and blacks as well as "gays") gradually receiving more attention, fewer issues cried out for protest. Second, as the "flower children" of the 1960s aged, their energies waned and their attention wandered. Rennie Davis, one of the folk heroes of the counterculture of the 1960s, became an insurance salesman. Eldridge Cleaver, leader of the Black Panthers and author of *Soul on Ice* (1968), became a supporter of Ronald Reagan. As ex-rebels everywhere became preoccupied with their careers, their younger sisters and brothers began to lose track of what all the protest had been about.

A third, larger reason for the shift lay in the roller-coaster events of the late 1960s and early 1970s. By 1974 the United States was emotionally exhausted. From the heroic accomplishments of the civil rights movement during the late 1950s and early 1960s ("still, for many of us," Benjamin DeMott remarks, "the best proof in our lives of the possibilities of human solidarity") the nation plunged into its longest and most confusing war. No one in the United States escaped its reach, for Vietnam was also the nation's most photographed, televised, and reported war. As the fighting and the protests dragged on, both the noblest and the basest instincts of the nation seemed more and more exposed. By the time the ordeal was finally over, no one stood on firm ground. Convinced of the war's brutality and futility, its opponents had still to question their own right to evade its dangers while leaving their poorer, less privileged contemporaries to die or be maimed. Convinced that citizens should fight when their nation's security and honor were at stake, supporters of the war had still to wonder why so much suffering and sacrifice had yielded so little—an illusory peace agreement followed by the Communist conquest of all of Indochina.

Another reason for the shift in mood, as though from a different world, lay in the narrowed focus, the increasing self-absorption, of American life. In the dominant culture of the nation, presided over by the business and professional worlds, self-absorption takes the form of an unbridled "careerism." During the Renaissance, at the dawn of the modern era, individuals began to dream of committing themselves to (or even throwing themselves away for) an ideal conception of what they should be. Some such drama is what Lionel Trilling discerned in the life of F. Scott Fitzgerald—and what Fitzgerald created in the story of Jay Gatsby. To focus exclusively on one's career, however, is to devote

> ### The War That Won't Go Away
>
> Ten years have passed since Saigon fell to the advancing North Vietnamese
> Army—an event that marked the extinction of South Vietnam as a nation and
> the humiliating finale to the American effort to hold the line in Indochina.
> Vietnam was America's longest, most debilitating war, and its memory still
> haunts the national psyche. . . .
>
> The events of the past decade—the occupation of Cambodia, the flight of the
> boat people, the dreary neo-Stalinist isolation of Vietnam today—have deflated
> the hopeful expectations of those who saw Ho Chi Minh as the liberator of his
> country. America's Vietnam veterans, once viewed with a mixture of
> indifference and outright hostility by their countrymen, are now widely
> regarded as national heroes. But America remains ambivalent about the war and
> its costs, and in some respects the ongoing national reconciliation is incomplete.
>
> *Newsweek,* "The Legacy of Vietnam: The War That Won't Go
> Away" (April 15, 1985)

oneself not to the realization of some ideal conception of self but to the
single-minded pursuit of one's own professional advancement—in the name of
money, power, and status. By contrast, the counterculture of the 1960s and 1970s
scorned such self-promotion, only to celebrate other forms of self-gratification. In
its drugs, its music, and its casual sex, it urged indulgence of individual needs and
desires.

Contrastive though these two cultures were, they remained interactive on
many levels and mutually supportive on one: strong elements of both fostered the
subordination of larger social and moral claims to private and personal ones.
Shorn of both its more violent elements and its political missions, the
counterculture of the 1960s and the 1970s became socially more acceptable. In the
"yuppies" of the 1980s, the careerism promoted by the business and professional
worlds merges with the drugs, the music, and the casual sex espoused by the
"hippies." As a result, social and moral claims have eroded further. No major
issue—from the Equal Rights Amendment and genetic engineering to artificial
intelligence and nuclear disarmament—has inspired the young people of America
as both the civil rights movement and the war in Vietnam once inspired them.
Even at the University of California, Berkeley, the birthplace of campus unrest
in the 1960s, the Republican Club "has taken off," says Jack Abramoff, chair of
the College Republican National Committee. "It's a sign that, like on campuses
all over the country, there's a strong move to the right," Abramoff adds. In fact,
however, the more telling move on college campuses is away from politics, as it
is away from concern with the claims of public realities. "Student politics at the
moment" come to "nothing," Charles Muscatine, professor of English at
Berkeley, asserted in September 1984. "What you have now is not so much
conservative thought but prepolitical behavior."

One consequence of the nation's changed cultural situation is the diminished role that contemporary writers play in the public arena. Writers continue to come from every region (Ann Beattie from Washington, D.C.; Leslie Silko from Albuquerque; Alice Walker from Eatonton, Georgia). Sexually and racially, our literary scene is more varied than ever before. For the first time in our history, women are doing a large portion of the most interesting work—itself a tribute to the force of the women's movement. Writers continue to show concern for a large, varied set of social and political issues—from the environment to the rights of minorities, from organ transplants and genetic engineering to nuclearism. But no writer of the 1970s and 1980s, not even such powerful feminists as Gloria Steinem and Alice Walker, has emerged to play the social role that H. L. Mencken played in the 1920s, that John Dos Passos played in the 1930s—to say nothing of the social roles that Norman Mailer and James Baldwin played in the 1960s.

A second consequence of our changed cultural situation is a deepening anxiety that literature is becoming still more marginal. Television reporting of such stunning events as the Vietnam War and America's space missions has reinforced fear that television is destined to finish what movies began. Nothing, including the direct challenges of Norman Mailer, the acknowledged master of the public occasion, has effectively countered the impression that the role of primary witness to the disorders and adventures of history has shifted from the writer to the reporter. The interpenetration of literature with other media, including movies, television, and music, continues to accelerate, especially in stage performances that blend not only the rehearsed and the improvised but also music, dance, poetry, prose, and drama.

Like the line between poetry and prose, the line between fiction and nonfiction continues to blur, as writers search for new ways of endowing their experience with aesthetic purpose. One sign of our times is the continued development of nonfiction, including a wide range of issues-oriented nonfiction. Another is the resurgence of short fiction. If, furthermore, the spread of nonfiction, as practiced by John McPhee and Tom Wolfe, may be said to reassert the authority of literary "realism" and thus to question the imagination's role in mastering social realities by transmuting them into art, the resurgence of short fiction, one of the most demanding of literary forms, may be said to reassert the primacy of form. Self-conscious experimentation in fiction (like that of Donald Barthelme, for example) has almost certainly lost ground in recent years. But formal experimentation and even elaborate game playing have survived as a way of making old themes new.

Still, even the strongest of recent writers has found it difficult to combat the feeling that the burgeoning telecommunications revolution of the last several decades has taken a heavy toll. At the dawn of the modern era, the development of printing made possible a new, enlarged role for literature. In the twentieth century, the radio industry (recently revitalized through what David Mamet calls "the theater of the air") and the movie and television industries have become increasingly powerful. Today no one escapes their reach, and the result is a diminished role for literature.

Interacting with the crisis about the cultural role of art is a crisis about the vocation of the artist. The direction of art in the second half of the twentieth century—in sharp contrast to its direction in the first—has been to blur the line between the artist and the artist's work. Caught in such a climate and also pushed by the need to reassert their cultural role and help market their works, through giving interviews and readings and lectures, writers have found it more and more difficult to square the private discipline and dedication that writing demands with the public performances that success requires. Henry James knew that a life dedicated to art meant going without many things. Renunciation became one of his earliest themes and remained one of his greatest. But James ended his life as he lived it, basically confident that to choose art was also to choose life—that, far from being an evasion of experience or a retreat from life, the imaginative act of exposing, revealing, and creating life in art was a way of living in the most engaged, intense, revivified manner possible.

Signs of uncertainty about both the cultural role of art and the vocation of the artist—the latest crisis of nerve in American literature—can be discerned in older as well as younger writers. Norman Mailer and Philip Roth not only remember an earlier, seemingly simpler era when the line between fiction and nonfiction remained clearer and the line between the artist and the artist's work remained stark; they also remember a shining moment in the 1960s and 1970s when they became dominant personalities as well as dominant voices in their culture and thus experienced a kind of cultural centrality that few writers have ever known. Having written a series of books—from *The Presidential Papers* (1963) through *The Armies of the Night* (1968) and *Of a Fire on the Moon* (1970) to *The Executioner's Song* (1979)—that constitute direct engagements with the major adventures and dislocations of his age, Mailer responded to the suddenly changed situation of the early 1980s by fleeing to the Egypt of the pharaohs in a long novel called *Ancient Evenings* (1983). Having seen *Portnoy's Complaint* (1969) catapult him into the middle of the sexual revolution of the 1960s and 1970s, Philip Roth proceeded to write three overlapping novels—*The Ghost Writer* (1979), *Zuckerman Unbound* (1981), and *The Anatomy Lesson* (1983)—about the guilt-ridden, self-doubting author of a novel that resembles *Portnoy's Complaint.*

Among younger writers, signs of uncertainty are less direct but more disturbing. In Roth's *The Anatomy Lesson,* Nathan Zuckerman wonders openly whether the life of a writer is not an "evasion of experience," a "retreat" from life rather than an "intensification" of it. In the stories of Ann Beattie and Raymond Carver, both the life and the work of the artist have at least one thing in common with all manner of things: that they are not so much objects of suspicion as objects of indifference. One of the dominant themes of the literature of the last several years—the theme of impassivity, of internal blankness that merges with interpersonal blankness, of selves as coexisting deserts—draws support from philosophic analysis as well as historical experience. Several philosophers now in vogue—Michel Foucault, for example, and Jacques Derrida —reinforce the wrenching experiences of the 1960s and 1970s in at least one important way: They extend the web of suspicion to include everything from art to human feeling. Charles Darwin drew the relation of human beings to nature into this web; Karl Marx drew the relation of human beings to historical institutions into it; Sigmund Freud drew the relation of selves to their psyches into it. Among more recent thinkers, however, nothing—neither art nor human responsiveness—escapes. Henry James thought of the artist as occupying "a sacred office," and he could and did speak of the terrible possibility of betraying that office. Concomitantly, James's declared preference was for characters so engaged, responsive, and vulnerable that no experience in life was lost on them. In much contemporary writing, art is not thought of as distinctively profane, let alone sacred, and the cult of responsiveness is viewed as another dubious bourgeois creation of the self-interested, sentimental, and mindlessly optimistic nineteenth century.

Thus reinforced, the wrenching ordeals of the 1960s and 1970s have fostered a literature of characters who neither feel nor express much of anything. Mark Twain's Huck Finn fled from civilization in search of the wild; F. Scott Fitzgerald's Jay Gatsby fled in search of a bride, a mansion, and a fortune from the inadequate fate of being born James Gatz. But much recent art records flight of a different sort—flight from all forms of responsiveness to life. The self of Robert Frost's poem "Desert Places" (1936) ("With no expression, nothing to express") becomes the self as impervious and blank in the 1960s song "I Am a Rock" by Paul Simon and Art Garfunkel ("I am a rock. I am an island. And a rock feels no pain, and an island never cries"). In recent fiction, such as that of Ann Beattie and Raymond Carver, we meet protagonists in whom not only feeling but even the memory of feeling and the desire for it are dead. It is as though we have moved a step beyond even the terribly wounding experiences of the Holocaust—in which, as Elie Wiesel and Susan Sontag have noted, some feelings were deepened even while others were imperiled—to the triumph of impassivity.

In Joan Didion's novel *Play It as It Lays* (1970), for example, we encounter a character so completely modern that nothing moves her. Asked what she wants, she replies, "Nothing"; asked what she feels, she again replies, "Nothing"; threatened with violence, she shrugs. Such characters feel skeptical about everything. But they feel most deeply skeptical about the notion that human beings ever believed or doubted passionately, ever felt wonder before the mysterious, or ever experienced the currents of sympathy, compassion, or love. "The most beautiful experience we can have is the mysterious," Albert Einstein wrote. "It is the fundamental emotion which stands at the cradle of true art and true science." What we confront instead in recent fiction is not merely a world in which all human values are threatened; it is a world in which the capacity, or even desire, for the human feeling of wonder is imperiled.

"Something Went Dead; Something Is Still Crying"

Nothing I have seen—in photographs or in real life—ever cut me as sharply, deeply, instantaneously. . . . When I looked at those photographs [of Bergen-Belsen and Dachau in 1945], something broke. Some limit had been reached, and not only that of horror; I felt irrevocably grieved, wounded, but a part of my feelings started to tighten; something went dead; something is still crying.

Susan Sontag, *On Photography* (1977)

Still, within the diversity of voices that constitute recent American fiction, there are clear signs that reports of the death of responsiveness and vulnerability as human virtues are exaggerated. Those signs appear not only in writers like Leslie Silko and Alice Walker, for whom heritage and race and sex have continued to bear heavily on the dynamics of individual existence, but also in the most recent works of Ann Beattie and Raymond Carver—*The Burning House* (1982) and *Cathedral* (1983).

Irony, not sentiment, dominates the tone of contemporary fiction. At times contemporary writers seem almost as bored and disaffected as their characters. They clearly remain skeptical about the possibility of bringing imaginative form to the damaged lives they see around them. Yet they continue to draw on diverse traditions and to find in those traditions different strengths. Oral history, myth, and legend are strong forces in the fiction of Leslie Silko, who also shows great sensitivity to older, more primitive states of consciousness. Although most contemporary writers seem increasingly irreverent toward grand intellectual schemes, particularly Freudian analysis and Marxist doctrine, many writers are clearly on friendlier terms with science and technology, an attitude presaged by Thomas Pynchon. Other writers—Raymond Carver and Bobbie Ann Mason, for example—have made a serious effort to bring the white working-class ethos into serious fiction. At the same time, minority writers and women writers have demonstrated great determination in exploring their own neglected traditions. "And that's why a lot of women are doing interesting work," Grace Paley notes: "Because they're really taking these lives that haven't been seen" and illuminating them. In an increasingly fragmented, decentered world, contemporary fiction has been firm in its determination to celebrate the special authority of distinctly "minority" points of view. Whereas writers like Herman Melville and William Faulkner may be said to have explored the moral authority of failure, contemporary writers may be said to have explored the moral authority of marginality.

At the same time, American literature has become not simply more international but also less predictable in its alliances. As general editor of the excellent series "Writers from the Other Europe," Philip Roth has played a major role in introducing writers of eastern Europe (Milan Kundera, for example) into the literary world of the United States. Writers like Chinua Achebe from Africa; R. K. Narayan and Salman Rashdie from India; Jorge Luis Borges, Jorge Amado, and Gabriel García Márquez from South America; and V. S. Naipaul, whose ties are with both the West Indies and India, are now as important to American literature as any writers from England or Europe.

Did the 1960s Damage Fiction?

One truth about the 60's, obscured at this moment but assuredly not forever, is that for a while the period showed us, unambiguously, amid its horrors, some growing points for democratic culture. Another truth, visible everywhere in American writing, is that the 60's did injure us all.

Benjamin De Mott, *The New York Times Book Review* (July 8, 1984)

Writers of contemporary America clearly bear witness to the pain of recent history—and to the threat that history presents not only to our literature but also to our capacity for human feeling. One of the characteristic struggles in our time as well as our literature is the struggle between impassivity and responsiveness, between apathy and concern, between staying cool and risking vulnerability. Sooner or later, in one way or another, this struggle brings almost everything that is specifically human under the aspect of a contest between the appeal and the danger of moral indifference, on one side, and the appeal and the danger of moral commitment, on the other. But present-day writers also bear witness to the promise of recent history, both in the sheer diversity of their voices, as they open American literature to new perspectives and heritages, and in the sheer persistence with which they present for our inspection new models of human possibility.

Raymond Carver
b. 1939

"It's possible," says Raymond Carver, "to write about commonplace things and objects using commonplace but precise language, and to endow these things—a chair, a window curtain, a fork, a stone, a woman's earring—with immense, even startling power. It is possible to write a line of seemingly innocuous dialogue and have it send a chill along the reader's spine." Carver's short stories and poems often turn on just such moments of unexpected revelation of beauty or terror. Like many other contemporary writers, Carver doubts the power of fiction to effect social, political, or even personal change ("perhaps it's different in poetry," he says). Instead, he believes, "it just has to be there for the fierce pleasure we take in doing it, and the different kind of pleasure that's taken in reading something that's durable and made to last, as well as beautiful in and of itself. Something that throws off these sparks—a persistent and steady glow, however dim."

Carver was born on May 25, 1939, in Clatskanie, Oregon, and grew up in the small town of Yakima, Washington, where his father worked as a laborer in a local sawmill. In 1957, at age eighteen, Carver married, but by working evenings he still managed to attend Chico State College, where he studied with the novelist John Gardner. After graduating from Chico State in 1963, he spent a year at the writers' workshop of the University of Iowa and then returned to California, first taking a job as a night janitor at a Sacramento hospital and then as an editor with a textbook publisher in Palo Alto. Carver has also lectured in creative writing at the University of California at Santa Cruz and at Berkeley, the University of Texas, the University of Iowa, and Syracuse University.

Deeply influenced, like Sherwood Anderson, by his father's storytelling ability, Carver tried writing stories as a boy. As an undergraduate, he began publishing stories and poems. In 1967 one of his stories, "Will You Please Be Quiet, Please?" was selected for the *Best American Short Stories* anthology; later, in 1976, it became the title story of his first collection of short fiction. Two collections of

stories followed—*What We Talk About When We Talk About Love* (1981) and
Cathedral (1983)—both of which received high critical acclaim. Carver is also the
author of several volumes of poetry, including *Near Klamath* (1968), *Winter
Insomnia* (1970), and *At Night the Salmon Move* (1976), and of *Fires: Essays,
Poems, Stories* (1983).

   Widely anthologized, Carver's stories have appeared in numerous literary
magazines and have won many awards. Nearly all his stories deal with people
living on the fringe of subsistence and articulation. His style is often spare to the
point of asceticism, and it characteristically retains a tense, close touch with the
diction and rhythm of ordinary speech. "One of Mr. Carver's great gifts," as the
critic Michael Wood has noted, "is to make audible the eloquence of the
apparently inarticulate. It's not that he lends speech to his characters or talks on
their behalf. He hears what they are saying when the words run out."

Text:
Cathedral, 1983.

Cathedral

This blind man, an old friend of my wife's, he was on his way to spend the night.
His wife had died. So he was visiting the dead wife's relatives in Connecticut. He
called my wife from his in-laws'. Arrangements were made. He would come by train,
a five-hour trip, and my wife would meet him at the station. She hadn't seen him
since she worked for him one summer in Seattle ten years ago. But she and the blind
man had kept in touch. They made tapes and mailed them back and forth. I wasn't
enthusiastic about his visit. He was no one I knew. And his being blind bothered me.
My idea of blindness came from the movies. In the movies, the blind moved slowly
and never laughed. Sometimes they were led by seeing-eye dogs. A blind man in my
house was not something I looked forward to.

   That summer in Seattle she had needed a job. She didn't have any money. The man
she was going to marry at the end of the summer was in officers' training school. He
didn't have any money, either. But she was in love with the guy, and he was in love
with her, etc. She'd seen something in the paper: HELP WANTED—*Reading to Blind Man*,
and a telephone number. She phoned and went over, was hired on the spot. She'd
worked with this blind man all summer. She read stuff to him, case studies, reports,
that sort of thing. She helped him organize his little office in the county social-service
department. They'd become good friends, my wife and the blind man. How do I know
these things? She told me. And she told me something else. On her last day in the
office, the blind man asked if he could touch her face. She agreed to this. She told
me he touched his fingers to every part of her face, her nose—even her neck! She
never forgot it. She even tried to write a poem about it. She was always trying to

write a poem. She wrote a poem or two every year, usually after something really important had happened to her.

When we first started going out together, she showed me the poem. In the poem, she recalled his fingers and the way they had moved around over her face. In the poem, she talked about what she had felt at the time, about what went through her mind when the blind man touched her nose and lips. I can remember I didn't think much of the poem. Of course, I didn't tell her that. Maybe I just don't understand poetry. I admit it's not the first thing I reach for when I pick up something to read.

Anyway, this man who'd first enjoyed her favors, the officer-to-be, he'd been her childhood sweetheart. So okay. I'm saying that at the end of the summer she let the blind man run his hands over her face, said goodbye to him, married her childhood etc., who was now a commissioned officer, and she moved away from Seattle. But they'd kept in touch, she and the blind man. She made the first contact after a year or so. She called him up one night from an Air Force base in Alabama. She wanted to talk. They talked. He asked her to send him a tape and tell him about her life. She did this. She sent the tape. On the tape, she told the blind man about her husband and about their life together in the military. She told the blind man she loved her husband but she didn't like it where they lived and she didn't like it that he was a part of the military-industrial thing. She told the blind man she'd written a poem and he was in it. She told him that she was writing a poem about what it was like to be an Air Force officer's wife. The poem wasn't finished yet. She was still writing it. The blind man made a tape. He sent her the tape. She made a tape. This went on for years. My wife's officer was posted to one base and then another. She sent tapes from Moody AFB,[1] McGuire, McConnell, and finally Travis, near Sacramento, where one night she got to feeling lonely and cut off from people she kept losing in that moving-around life. She got to feeling she couldn't go it another step. She went in and swallowed all the pills and capsules in the medicine chest and washed them down with a bottle of gin. Then she got into a hot bath and passed out.

But instead of dying, she got sick. She threw up. Her officer—why should he have a name? he was the childhood sweetheart, and what more does he want?—came home from somewhere, found her, and called the ambulance. In time, she put it all on a tape and sent the tape to the blind man. Over the years, she put all kinds of stuff on tapes and sent the tapes off lickety-split. Next to writing a poem every year, I think it was her chief means of recreation. On one tape, she told the blind man she'd decided to live away from her officer for a time. On another tape, she told him about her divorce. She and I began going out, and of course she told her blind man about it. She told him everything, or so it seemed to me. Once she asked me if I'd like to hear the latest tape from the blind man. This was a year ago. I was on the tape, she said. So I said okay, I'd listen to it. I got us drinks and we settled down in the living room. We made ready to listen. First she inserted the tape into the player and adjusted a couple of dials. Then she pushed a lever. The tape squeaked and someone began to talk in this loud voice. She lowered the volume. After a few minutes of harmless chitchat, I heard my own name in the mouth of this stranger, this blind man I didn't even know! And then this: "From all you've said about him, I can only conclude—" But we were interrupted, a

[1] Air Force Base.

knock at the door, something, and we didn't ever get back to the tape. Maybe it was just as well. I'd heard all I wanted to.

Now this same blind man was coming to sleep in my house.

"Maybe I could take him bowling," I said to my wife. She was at the draining board doing scalloped potatoes. She put down the knife she was using and turned around.

"If you love me," she said, "you can do this for me. If you don't love me, okay. But if you had a friend, any friend, and the friend came to visit, I'd make him feel comfortable." She wiped her hands with the dish towel.

"I don't have any blind friends," I said.

"You don't have *any* friends," she said. "Period. Besides," she said, "goddamn it, his wife's just died! Don't you understand that? The man's lost his wife!"

I didn't answer. She'd told me a little about the blind man's wife. Her name was Beulah. Beulah! That's a name for a colored woman.

"Was his wife a Negro?" I asked.

"Are you crazy?" my wife said. "Have you just flipped or something?" She picked up a potato. I saw it hit the floor, then roll under the stove. "What's wrong with you?" she said. "Are you drunk?"

"I'm just asking," I said.

Right then my wife filled me in with more detail than I cared to know. I made a drink and sat at the kitchen table to listen. Pieces of the story began to fall into place.

Beulah had gone to work for the blind man the summer after my wife had stopped working for him. Pretty soon Beulah and the blind man had themselves a church wedding. It was a little wedding—who'd want to go to such a wedding in the first place?—just the two of them, plus the minister and the minister's wife. But it was a church wedding just the same. It was what Beulah had wanted, he'd said. But even then Beulah must have been carrying the cancer in her glands. After they had been inseparable for eight years—my wife's word, *inseparable*—Beulah's health went into a rapid decline. She died in a Seattle hospital room, the blind man sitting beside the bed and holding on to her hand. They'd married, lived and worked together, slept together—had sex, sure—and then the blind man had to bury her. All this without his having ever seen what the goddamned woman looked like. It was beyond my understanding. Hearing this, I felt sorry for the blind man for a little bit. And then I found myself thinking what a pitiful life this woman must have led. Imagine a woman who could never see herself as she was seen in the eyes of her loved one. A woman who could go on day after day and never receive the smallest compliment from her beloved. A woman whose husband could never read the expression on her face, be it misery or something better. Someone who could wear makeup or not— what difference to him? She could, if she wanted, wear green eye-shadow around one eye, a straight pin in her nostril, yellow slacks and purple shoes, no matter. And then to slip off into death, the blind man's hand on her hand, his blind eyes streaming tears —I'm imagining now—her last thought maybe this: that he never even knew what she looked like, and she on an express to the grave. Robert was left with a small insurance policy and half of a twenty-peso Mexican coin. The other half of the coin went into the box with her. Pathetic.

So when the time rolled around, my wife went to the depot to pick him up. With nothing to do but wait—sure, I blamed him for that—I was having a drink and watching the TV when I heard the car pull into the drive. I got up from the sofa with my drink and went to the window to have a look.

I saw my wife laughing as she parked the car. I saw her get out of the car and shut the door. She was still wearing a smile. Just amazing. She went around to the other side of the car to where the blind man was already starting to get out. This blind man, feature this, he was wearing a full beard! A beard on a blind man! Too much, I say. The blind man reached into the back seat and dragged out a suitcase. My wife took his arm, shut the car door, and, talking all the way, moved him down the drive and then up the steps to the front porch. I turned off the TV. I finished my drink, rinsed the glass, dried my hands. Then I went to the door.

My wife said, "I want you to meet Robert. Robert, this is my husband. I've told you all about him." She was beaming. She had this blind man by his coat sleeve.

The blind man let go of his suitcase and up came his hand.

I took it. He squeezed hard, held my hand, and then he let it go.

"I feel like we've already met," he boomed.

"Likewise," I said. I didn't know what else to say. Then I said, "Welcome. I've heard a lot about you." We began to move then, a little group, from the porch into the living room, my wife guiding him by the arm. The blind man was carrying his suitcase in his other hand. My wife said things like, "To your left here, Robert. That's right. Now watch it, there's a chair. That's it. Sit down right here. This is the sofa. We just bought this sofa two weeks ago."

I started to say something about the old sofa. I'd liked that old sofa. But I didn't say anything. Then I wanted to say something else, small-talk, about the scenic ride along the Hudson. How going *to* New York, you should sit on the right-hand side of the train, and coming *from* New York, the left-hand side.

"Did you have a good train ride?" I said. "Which side of the train did you sit on, by the way?"

"What a question, which side!" my wife said. "What's it matter which side?" she said.

"I just asked," I said.

"Right side," the blind man said. "I hadn't been on a train in nearly forty years. Not since I was a kid. With my folks. That's been a long time. I'd nearly forgotten the sensation. I have winter in my beard now," he said. "So I've been told, anyway. Do I look distinguished, my dear?" the blind man said to my wife.

"You look distinguished, Robert," she said. "Robert," she said. "Robert, it's just so good to see you."

My wife finally took her eyes off the blind man and looked at me. I had the feeling she didn't like what she saw. I shrugged.

I've never met, or personally known, anyone who was blind. This blind man was late forties, a heavy-set, balding man with stooped shoulders, as if he carried a great weight there. He wore brown slacks, brown shoes, a light-brown shirt, a tie, a sports coat. Spiffy. He also had this full beard. But he didn't use a cane and he didn't wear dark glasses. I'd always thought dark glasses were a must for the blind. Fact was, I wished he had a pair. At first glance, his eyes looked like anyone else's eyes. But if you looked close, there was something different about them. Too much white in the iris, for one thing, and the pupils seemed to move around in the sockets without his knowing it or being able to stop it. Creepy. As I stared at his face, I saw the left pupil turn in toward his nose while the other made an effort to keep in one place. But it was only an effort, for that eye was on the roam without his knowing it or wanting it to be.

I said, "Let me get you a drink. What's your pleasure? We have a little of everything. It's one of our pastimes."

"Bub, I'm a Scotch man myself," he said fast enough in this big voice.

"Right," I said. Bub! "Sure you are. I knew it."

He let his fingers touch his suitcase, which was sitting alongside the sofa. He was taking his bearings. I didn't blame him for that.

"I'll move that up to your room," my wife said.

"No, that's fine," the blind man said loudly. "It can go up when I go up."

"A little water with the Scotch?" I said.

"Very little," he said.

"I knew it," I said.

He said, "Just a tad. The Irish actor, Barry Fitzgerald? I'm like that fellow. When I drink water, Fitzgerald said, I drink water. When I drink whiskey, I drink whiskey." My wife laughed. The blind man brought his hand up under his beard. He lifted his beard slowly and let it drop.

I did the drinks, three big glasses of Scotch with a splash of water in each. Then we made ourselves comfortable and talked about Robert's travels. First the long flight from the West Coast to Connecticut, we covered that. Then from Connecticut up here by train. We had another drink concerning that leg of the trip.

I remembered having read somewhere that the blind didn't smoke because, as speculation had it, they couldn't see the smoke they exhaled. I thought I knew that much and that much only about blind people. But this blind man smoked his cigarette down to the nubbin and then lit another one. This blind man filled his ashtray and my wife emptied it.

When we sat down at the table for dinner, we had another drink. My wife heaped Robert's plate with cube steak, scalloped potatoes, green beans. I buttered him up two slices of bread. I said, "Here's bread and butter for you." I swallowed some of my drink. "Now let us pray," I said, and the blind man lowered his head. My wife looked at me, her mouth agape. "Pray the phone won't ring and the food doesn't get cold," I said.

We dug in. We ate everything there was to eat on the table. We ate like there was no tomorrow. We didn't talk. We ate. We scarfed. We grazed that table. We were into serious eating. The blind man had right away located his foods, he knew just where everything was on his plate. I watched with admiration as he used his knife and fork on the meat. He'd cut two pieces of meat, fork the meat into his mouth, and then go all out for the scalloped potatoes, the beans next, and then he'd tear off a hunk of buttered bread and eat that. He'd follow this up with a big drink of milk. It didn't seem to bother him to use his fingers once in a while, either.

We finished everything, including half a strawberry pie. For a few moments, we sat as if stunned. Sweat beaded on our faces. Finally, we got up from the table and left the dirty plates. We didn't look back. We took ourselves into the living room and sank into our places again. Robert and my wife sat on the sofa. I took the big chair. We had us two or three more drinks while they talked about the major things that had come to pass for them in the past ten years. For the most part, I just listened. Now and then I joined in. I didn't want him to think I'd left the room, and I didn't want her to think I was feeling left out. They talked of things that had happened to them—to them!—these past ten years. I waited in vain to hear my name on my wife's sweet lips: "And then my dear husband came into my life"—something like that. But I heard nothing of the sort. More talk of Robert. Robert had done a little of everything, it seemed, a regular blind jack-of-all-trades. But most recently he and his wife had had an Amway distributorship, from which, I gathered, they'd earned their living, such as it was. The blind man was also a ham radio operator. He talked in his loud voice about conversations he'd had with fellow operators in Guam, in the Philippines, in Alaska, and even in Tahiti. He said he'd have a lot of friends there if he ever wanted to go visit those places. From time to time, he'd turn his blind face toward me, put his hand under his beard, ask me something. How long had I been in my present position? (Three years.) Did I like my work? (I didn't.) Was I going to stay with it? (What were the options?) Finally, when I thought he was beginning to run down, I got up and turned on the TV.

My wife looked at me with irritation. She was heading toward a boil. Then she looked at the blind man and said, "Robert, do you have a TV?"

The blind man said, "My dear, I have two TVs. I have a color set and a black-and-white thing, an old relic. It's funny, but if I turn the TV on, and I'm always turning it on, I turn on the color set. It's funny, don't you think?"

I didn't know what to say to that. I had absolutely nothing to say to that. No opinion. So I watched the news program and tried to listen to what the announcer was saying.

"This is a color TV," the blind man said. "Don't ask me how, but I can tell."

"We traded up a while ago," I said.

The blind man had another taste of his drink. He lifted his beard, sniffed it, and let it fall. He leaned forward on the sofa. He positioned his ashtray on the coffee table, then put the lighter to his cigarette. He leaned back on the sofa and crossed his legs at the ankles.

My wife covered her mouth, and then she yawned. She stretched. She said, "I think I'll go upstairs and put on my robe. I think I'll change into something else. Robert, you make yourself comfortable," she said.

"I'm comfortable," the blind man said.

"I want you to feel comfortable in this house," she said.

"I am comfortable," the blind man said.

After she'd left the room, he and I listened to the weather report and then to the sports roundup. By that time, she'd been gone so long I didn't know if she was going to come back. I thought she might have gone to bed. I wished she'd come back downstairs. I didn't want to be left alone with a blind man. I asked him if he wanted another drink, and he said sure. Then I asked if he wanted to smoke some dope with me. I said I'd just rolled a number. I hadn't, but I planned to do so in about two shakes.

"I'll try some with you," he said.

"Damn right," I said. "That's the stuff."

I got our drinks and sat down on the sofa with him. Then I rolled us two fat numbers. I lit one and passed it. I brought it to his fingers. He took it and inhaled.

"Hold it as long as you can," I said. I could tell he didn't know the first thing.

My wife came back downstairs wearing her pink robe and her pink slippers.

"What do I smell?" she said.

"We thought we'd have us some cannabis," I said.

My wife gave me a savage look. Then she looked at the blind man and said, "Robert, I didn't know you smoked."

He said, "I do now, my dear. There's a first time for everything. But I don't feel anything yet."

"This stuff is pretty mellow," I said. "This stuff is mild. It's dope you can reason with," I said. "It doesn't mess you up."

"Not much it doesn't, bub," he said, and laughed.

My wife sat on the sofa between the blind man and me. I passed her the number. She took it and toked and then passed it back to me. "Which way is this going?" she said. Then she said, "I shouldn't be smoking this. I can hardly keep my eyes open as it is. That dinner did me in. I shouldn't have eaten so much."

"It was the strawberry pie," the blind man said. "That's what did it," he said, and he laughed his big laugh. Then he shook his head.

"There's more strawberry pie," I said.

"Do you want some more, Robert?" my wife said.

"Maybe in a little while," he said.

We gave our attention to the TV. My wife yawned again. She said, "Your bed is made up when you feel like going to bed, Robert. I know you must have had a long day. When you're ready to go to bed, say so." She pulled his arm. "Robert?"

He came to and said, "I've had a real nice time. This beats tapes, doesn't it?"

I said, "Coming at you," and I put the number between his fingers. He inhaled, held the smoke, and then let it go. It was like he'd been doing it since he was nine years old.

"Thanks, bub," he said. "But I think this is all for me. I think I'm beginning to feel it," he said. He held the burning roach out for my wife.

"Same here," she said. "Ditto. Me, too." She took the roach and passed it to me. "I may just sit here for a while between you two guys with my eyes closed. But don't let me bother you, okay? Either one of you. If it bothers you, say so. Otherwise, I may just sit here with my eyes closed until you're ready to go to bed," she said. "Your bed's made up, Robert, when you're ready. It's right next to our room at the top of the stairs. We'll show you up when you're ready. You wake me up now, you guys, if I fall asleep." She said that and then she closed her eyes and went to sleep.

The news program ended. I got up and changed the channel. I sat back down on the sofa. I wished my wife hadn't pooped out. Her head lay across the back of the sofa, her mouth open. She'd turned so that her robe had slipped away from her legs, exposing a juicy thigh. I reached to draw her robe back over her, and it was then that I glanced at the blind man. What the hell! I flipped the robe open again.

"You say when you want some strawberry pie," I said.

"I will," he said.

I said, "Are you tired? Do you want me to take you up to your bed? Are you ready to hit the hay?"

"Not yet," he said. "No, I'll stay up with you, bub. If that's all right. I'll stay up until you're ready to turn in. We haven't had a chance to talk. Know what I mean?

I feel like me and her monopolized the evening." He lifted his beard and he let it fall. He picked up his cigarettes and his lighter.

"That's all right," I said. Then I said, "I'm glad for the company."

And I guess I was. Every night I smoked dope and stayed up as long as I could before I fell asleep. My wife and I hardly ever went to bed at the same time. When I did go to sleep, I had these dreams. Sometimes I'd wake up from one of them, my heart going crazy.

Something about the church and the Middle Ages was on the TV. Not your run-of-the-mill TV fare. I wanted to watch something else. I turned to the other channels. But there was nothing on them, either. So I turned back to the first channel and apologized.

"Bub, it's all right," the blind man said. "It's fine with me. Whatever you want to watch is okay. I'm always learning something. Learning never ends. It won't hurt me to learn something tonight. I got ears," he said.

We didn't say anything for a time. He was leaning forward with his head turned at me, his right ear aimed in the direction of the set. Very disconcerting. Now and then his eyelids drooped and then they snapped open again. Now and then he put his fingers into his beard and tugged, like he was thinking about something he was hearing on the television.

On the screen, a group of men wearing cowls was being set upon and tormented by men dressed in skeleton costumes and men dressed as devils. The men dressed as devils wore devil masks, horns, and long tails. This pageant was part of a procession. The Englishman who was narrating the thing said it took place in Spain once a year. I tried to explain to the blind man what was happening.

"Skeletons," he said. "I know about skeletons," he said, and he nodded.

The TV showed this one cathedral. Then there was a long, slow look at another one. Finally, the picture switched to the famous one in Paris, with its flying buttresses and its spires reaching up to the clouds. The camera pulled away to show the whole of the cathedral rising above the skyline.

There were times when the Englishman who was telling the thing would shut up, would simply let the camera move around over the cathedrals. Or else the camera would tour the countryside, men in fields walking behind oxen. I waited as long as I could. Then I felt I had to say something. I said, "They're showing the outside of this cathedral now. Gargoyles. Little statues carved to look like monsters. Now I guess they're in Italy. Yeah, they're in Italy. There's paintings on the walls of this one church."

"Are those fresco paintings, bub?" he asked, and he sipped from his drink.

I reached for my glass. But it was empty. I tried to remember what I could remember. "You're asking me are those frescoes?" I said. "That's a good question. I don't know."

The camera moved to a cathedral outside Lisbon. The differences in the Portuguese cathedral compared with the French and Italian were not that great. But they were there. Mostly the interior stuff. Then something occurred to me, and I said, "Something has occurred to me. Do you have any idea what a cathedral is? What they look like, that is? Do you follow me? If somebody says cathedral to you, do you have any notion what they're talking about? Do you know the difference between that and a Baptist church, say?"

He let the smoke dribble from his mouth. "I know they took hundreds of workers fifty or a hundred years to build," he said. "I just heard the man say that, of course. I know generations of the same families worked on a cathedral. I heard him say that, too. The men who began their life's work on them, they never lived to see the completion of their work. In that wise, bub, they're no different from the rest of us, right?" He laughed. Then his eyelids drooped again. His head nodded. He seemed to be snoozing. Maybe he was imagining himself in Portugal. The TV was showing another cathedral now. This one was in Germany. The Englishman's voice droned on. "Cathedrals," the blind man said. He sat up and rolled his head back and forth. "If you want the truth, bub, that's about all I know. What I just said. What I heard him say. But maybe you could describe one to me? I wish you'd do it. I'd like that. If you want to know, I really don't have a good idea."

I stared hard at the shot of the cathedral on the TV. How could I even begin to describe it? But say my life depended on it. Say my life was being threatened by an insane guy who said I had to do it or else.

I stared some more at the cathedral before the picture flipped off into the countryside. There was no use. I turned to the blind man and said, "To begin with, they're very tall." I was looking around the room for clues. "They reach way up. Up and up. Toward the sky. They're so big, some of them, they have to have these supports. To help hold them up, so to speak. These supports are called buttresses. They remind me of viaducts, for some reason. But maybe you don't know viaducts, either? Sometimes the cathedrals have devils and such carved into the front. Sometimes lords and ladies. Don't ask me why this is," I said.

He was nodding. The whole upper part of his body seemed to be moving back and forth.

"I'm not doing so good, am I?" I said.

He stopped nodding and leaned forward on the edge of the sofa. As he listened to me, he was running his fingers through his beard. I wasn't getting through to him, I could see that. But he waited for me to go on just the same. He nodded, like he was trying to encourage me. I tried to think what else to say. "They're really big," I said. "They're massive. They're built of stone. Marble, too, sometimes. In those olden days, when they built cathedrals, men wanted to be close to God. In those olden days, God was an important part of everyone's life. You could tell this from their cathedral-building. I'm sorry," I said, "but it looks like that's the best I can do for you. I'm just no good at it."

"That's all right, bub," the blind man said. "Hey, listen. I hope you don't mind my asking you. Can I ask you something? Let me ask you a simple question, yes or no. I'm just curious and there's no offense. You're my host. But let me ask if you are in any way religious? You don't mind my asking?"

I shook my head. He couldn't see that, though. A wink is the same as a nod to a blind man. "I guess I don't believe in it. In anything. Sometimes it's hard. You know what I'm saying?"

"Sure, I do," he said.

"Right," I said.

The Englishman was still holding forth. My wife sighed in her sleep. She drew a long breath and went on with her sleeping.

"You'll have to forgive me," I said. "But I can't tell you what a cathedral looks like. It just isn't in me to do it. I can't do any more than I've done."

The blind man sat very still, his head down, as he listened to me.

I said, "The truth is, cathedrals don't mean anything special to me. Nothing. Cathedrals. They're something to look at on late-night TV. That's all they are."

It was then that the blind man cleared his throat. He brought something up. He took a handkerchief from his back pocket. Then he said, "I get it, bub. It's okay. It happens. Don't worry about it," he said. "Hey, listen to me. Will you do me a favor? I got an idea. Why don't you find us some heavy paper? And a pen. We'll do something. We'll draw one together. Get us a pen and some heavy paper. Go on, bub, get the stuff," he said.

So I went upstairs. My legs felt like they didn't have any strength in them. They felt like they did after I'd done some running. In my wife's room, I looked around. I found some ballpoints in a little basket on her table. And then I tried to think where to look for the kind of paper he was talking about.

Downstairs, in the kitchen, I found a shopping bag with onion skins in the bottom of the bag. I emptied the bag and shook it. I brought it into the living room and sat down with it near his legs. I moved some things, smoothed the wrinkles from the bag, spread it out on the coffee table.

The blind man got down from the sofa and sat next to me on the carpet.

He ran his fingers over the paper. He went up and down the sides of the paper. The edges, even the edges. He fingered the corners.

"All right," he said. "All right, let's do her."

He found my hand, the hand with the pen. He closed his hand over my hand. "Go ahead, bub, draw," he said. "Draw. You'll see. I'll follow along with you. It'll be okay. Just begin now like I'm telling you. You'll see. Draw," the blind man said.

So I began. First I drew a box that looked like a house. It could have been the house I lived in. Then I put a roof on it. At either end of the roof, I drew spires. Crazy.

"Swell," he said. "Terrific. You're doing fine," he said. "Never thought anything like this could happen in your lifetime, did you, bub? Well, it's a strange life, we all know that. Go on now. Keep it up."

I put in windows with arches. I drew flying buttresses. I hung great doors. I couldn't stop. The TV station went off the air. I put down the pen and closed and opened my fingers. The blind man felt around over the paper. He moved the tips of his fingers over the paper, all over what I had drawn, and he nodded.

"Doing fine," the blind man said.

I took up the pen again, and he found my hand. I kept at it. I'm no artist. But I kept drawing just the same.

My wife opened up her eyes and gazed at us. She sat up on the sofa, her robe hanging open. She said, "What are you doing? Tell me, I want to know."

I didn't answer her.

The blind man said, "We're drawing a cathedral. Me and him are working on it. Press hard," he said to me. "That's right. That's good," he said. "Sure. You got it, bub. I can tell. You didn't think you could. But you can, can't you? You're cooking with gas now. You know what I'm saying? We're going to really have us something here in a minute. How's the old arm?" he said. "Put some people in there now. What's a cathedral without people?"

My wife said, "What's going on? Robert, what are you doing? What's going on?"

"It's all right," he said to her. "Close your eyes now," the blind man said to me. I did it. I closed them just like he said.

"Are they closed?" he said. "Don't fudge."

"They're closed," I said.

"Keep them that way," he said. He said, "Don't stop now. Draw."

So we kept on with it. His fingers rode my fingers as my hand went over the paper. It was like nothing else in my life up to now.

Then he said, "I think that's it. I think you got it," he said. "Take a look. What do you think?"

But I had my eyes closed. I thought I'd keep them that way for a little longer. I thought it was something I ought to do.

"Well?" he said. "Are you looking?"

My eyes were still closed. I was in my house. I knew that. But I didn't feel like I was inside anything.

"It's really something," I said.

1981

Bobbie Ann Mason
b. 1940

Of earlier southern writers, such as William Faulkner and Allen Tate, Bobbie Ann Mason says simply that they possessed "a romantic vision." Her own work she describes as "southern Gothic going to the supermarket." The landscape of her fiction, usually rural Kentucky fast being overtaken by urban culture, is dotted with supermarkets, discount stores, video arcades, and vocational training centers. Her characters watch Phil Donahue and Johnny Carson on television; they take up weight training, make zucchini bread, and buy *The Sixties Songbook*. Or they drive trucks, eat "poke salet," and listen to Hank Williams. Caught between the country and the city, they constantly feel, she says, a "tension between their rural traditional past and the modern world." Like the woman who buys *The Sixties Songbook* ten years too late, they often find themselves struggling not to get any further behind.

Mason attributes her own and other contemporary writers' use of popular culture to cultural changes that come so rapidly that "it seems necessary to get a fix on a certain moment—or it may be different by tomorrow." Through a strange blend of colloquialisms and more formal diction, she reflects in the language of her fiction the same cultural gap that she renders in its action.

Reared on a dairy farm in western Kentucky, Mason was encouraged by her parents, neither of whom had finished high school, to continue her education. Unlike most of her friends, she went to high school in the "city"—Mayfield, Kentucky, population 10,725. She is, she now feels, "haunted by the kids I went to grade school with." After high school she went to the University of

Kentucky, where she majored in journalism, and then to New York, where she experienced a culture shock so great that it temporarily turned her from a writing career to graduate school.

After receiving an M.A. from the State University of New York at Binghamton and a Ph.D. from the University of Connecticut, Mason became a professor at Mansfield State College (1972–1979). In 1974 she published a study of Vladimir Nabokov's novel *Ada* called *Nabokov's Garden: A Nature Guide to "Ada,"* and in 1975 she published an analysis of fiction especially designed for girls called *The Girl Sleuth: A Feminist Guide to the Bobbsey Twins, Nancy Drew, and Their Sisters.* But it was the writing of fiction that more and more engaged her. In 1980 she published her first story, "Offerings," in *The New Yorker.* Two years later a collection of her stories, *Shiloh and Other Stories,* in which "Detroit Skyline, 1949" appeared, won the Ernest Hemingway Award for the year's most distinguished first work of fiction and was nominated for the National Book Critics Circle Award. Having received a grant from the National Endowment for the Arts, Mason began work on a novel, *In Country* (1985).

Out of anonymity, Mason has emerged, according to the writer Anne Tyler and others, as a recognized master of the short story, a sudden transformation that Mason says has left her "absolutely *stunned.*" In "Nancy Culpepper," her own favorite among her stories, the protagonist's mother says, "I guess you think we're just ignorant. The way we talk." "No," Nancy says, "I don't." Like Nancy Culpepper, Mason clearly respects the people she remembers and writes about, perhaps in part because she shares a feeling of kinship with them. "I write," she says, "about people in trapped circumstances. . . . I identify with people who are ambivalent about their situation. And I guess, in my stories, I'm in a way imagining myself as I would have felt if I had not gotten away and gotten a different perspective on things—if, for example, I had gotten pregnant in high school and had to marry a truck driver as the woman did in my story 'Shiloh.' " In her best fiction, Mason offers us not only different perspectives but also new ways of imagining ourselves.

Text:
Atlantic Monthly, June 1981.

Detroit Skyline, 1949

When I was nine, my mother took me on a long journey up North, because she wanted me to have a chance to see the tall buildings of Detroit. We lived on a farm in western Kentucky, not far from the U.S. highway that took so many Southerners northward to work in the auto industry just after World War II. We went to visit Aunt Mozelle, Mama's sister, and Uncle Boone Cashon, who had headed north soon after Boone's discharge from the service. They lived in a suburb of Detroit, and my mother had visited them once before. She couldn't get the skyscrapers she had seen out of her mind.

The Brocks bus took all day and all night to get there. On our trip, my mother threw up and a black baby cried all the way. I couldn't sleep for thinking about Detroit. Mama had tried in vain to show me how high the buildings were, pointing at the straight horizon beyond the cornfields. I had the impression that they towered halfway to the moon.

"Don't let the Polacks get you," my father had warned when we left. He had to stay home to milk the cows. My two-year-old brother, Johnny, stayed behind with him.

My aunt and uncle met us in a taxi at the bus station, and before I got a good look at them, they had engulfed me in their arms.

"I wouldn't have knowed you, Peggy Jo," my uncle said. "You was just a little squirt the last time I saw you."

"Don't this beat all?" said Aunt Mozelle. "Boone here could have built us a car by now—and us coming in a taxi."

"We've still got that old plug, but it gets us to town," said Mama.

"How could I build a car?" said Uncle Boone. "All I know is bumpers."

"That's what he does," my aunt said to me. "He puts on bumpers."

"We'll get a car someday soon," Uncle Boone said to his wife.

My uncle was a thin, delicate man with a receding hairline. His speckled skin made me think of the fragile shells of sparrow eggs. My aunt, on the other hand, was stout and tanned, with thick, dark hair draped like wings over her ears. I gazed at my aunt and uncle, trying to match them with the photograph my mother had shown me.

"Peggy's all worked up over seeing the tall buildings," said Mama as we climbed into the taxi. "The cat's got her tongue."

"It has *not!*"

"I'm afraid we've got bad news," said Aunt Mozelle. "The city buses is on strike and there's no way to get into Detroit."

"Don't say it!" cried Mama. "After we come all this way."

"It's trouble with the unions," said Boone. "But they might start up before y'all go back." He patted my knee and said, "Don't worry, littlun."

"The unions is full of reds," Aunt Mozelle whispered to my mother.

"Would it be safe to go?" Mama asked.

"We needn't worry," said Aunt Mozelle.

From the window of the squat yellow taxi, driven by a froglike man who grunted, I scrutinized the strange and vast neighborhoods we were passing through. I had never seen so many houses, all laid out in neat rows. The houses were new, and their pastel colors seemed peaceful and alluring. The skyscrapers were still as remote to me as the castles in fairy tales, but these houses were real, and they were nestled next to each other in a thrilling intimacy. I knew at once where I wanted to live when I grew up—in a place like this, with neighbors.

My relatives' house, on a treeless new street, had venetian blinds and glossy hardwood floors. The living room carpet had giant pink roses that made me think you could play hopscotch on them. The guest room had knotty-pine paneling and a sweet-smelling cedar closet. Aunt Mozelle had put His and Her towels in our room.

They had dogs on them and were pleasurably soft. At home, all of our washrags came out of detergent boxes, and our towels were faded and thin. The house was grand. And I had never seen my mother sparkling so. When she saw the kitchen, she whirled around happily, like a young girl, forgetting her dizziness on the bus. Aunt Mozelle had a toaster, a Mixmaster, an electric stove, and a large electric clock shaped like a rooster. On the wall, copper-bottomed pans gleamed in a row like golden-eyed cats lined up on a fence.

"Ain't it the berries?" my mother said to me. "Didn't I tell you?"

"Sometimes I have to pinch myself," said my aunt.

Just then, the front door slammed and a tall girl with a ponytail bounded into the house, saying "Hey!" in an offhand manner.

"Corn!" I said timidly, which seemed to perplex her, for she stared at me as though I were some odd sort of pet allowed into the house. This was my cousin Betsy Lou, in bluejeans rolled up halfway to her knees.

"Our kinfolks is here," Aunt Mozelle announced.

"Law, you've growed into a beanpole," said Mama to Betsy Lou.

"Welcome to our fair city, and I hope you don't get polio," Betsy Lou said to me.

"Watch what you're saying!" cried her mother. "You'll scare Peggy Jo."

"I imagine it'll be worse this summer than last," said Mama, looking worried.

"If we're stuck here without a car, you won't be any place to catch polio," Aunt Mozelle said, smiling at me.

"Polio spreads at swimming pools," Betsy Lou said.

"Then I'm not going to any swimming pool," I announced flatly.

Aunt Mozelle fussed around in her splendid kitchen, making dinner. I sat at the table, listening to Mama and her sister talk, in a gentle, flowing way, exchanging news, each stopping now and then to smile at the other in disbelief, or to look at me with pride. I couldn't take my eyes off my aunt, because she looked so much like my mother. She was older and heavier, but they had the same wide smile, the same unaffected laughter. They had similar sharp tips on their upper lips, which they filled in with bright red lipstick.

Mama said, "Boone sure is lucky. He's still young and ain't crippled and has a good job."

"Knock on wood," said Aunt Mozelle, rapping the door facing.

They had arranged for me to have a playmate, a girl my age who lived in the neighborhood. At home, in the summertime, I did not play with anyone, for the girls I knew at school lived too far away. Suddenly I found myself watching a chubby girl in a lilac piqué playsuit zoom up and down the sidewalk on roller skates.

"Come on," she said. "It's not hard."

"I'm coming." Betsy Lou had let me have her old skates, but I had trouble fastening them on my Weather-Bird sandals. I had never been on skates. At home there was no sidewalk. I decided to try skating on one foot, like a kid on a scooter, but the skate came loose.

"Put both of them on," said the girl, laughing at me.

Her name was Sharon Belletieri. She had to spell it for me. She said my name over and over until it sounded absurd. "Peggy Peggy Peggy Peggy Peggy." She made my name sound like "piggy."

"Don't you have a permanent?" she asked.

"No," I said, touching my pigtails. "My hair's in plaits 'cause it's summer."

"Hai? Oh, you mean *hair?* Like air?" She waved at the air. She was standing there, perfectly balanced on her skates. She pronounced "hair" with two syllables. *Hayer.* I said something like a cross between *herr* and *harr.*

Sharon turned and whizzed down the sidewalk, then skidded to a stop at the corner, twisted around, and faced me.

"Are you going to skate or not?" she asked.

My uncle smoked Old Golds, and he seemed to have excess nervous energy. He was always jumping up from his chair to get something, or to look outside at the thermometer. He had found his name in a newspaper ad recently and had won a free pint of Cunningham's ice cream. My aunt declared that that made him somewhat famous. When I came back that day with the skates, he was sitting on the porch fanning himself with a newspaper. There was a heat wave, he said.

"What did you think of Sharon Belletieri?" he asked.

"She talks funny," I said, sitting down beside him.

"Folks up here all talk funny. I've noticed that too."

Uncle Boone had been a clerk in the war. He told me about the time he had spent in the Pacific theater, sailing around on a battleship, looking for Japs.

"Me and some buddies went to a Pacific island where there was a tribe of people with little tails," he said.

"Don't believe a word he says," said my aunt, who had been listening.

"It's true," said Uncle Boone. "Cross my heart and hope to die." He solemnly crossed his hands on his chest, then looked at his watch and said abruptly to me, "What do you think of Gorgeous George?"

"I don't know."

"How about Howdy Doody?"

"Who's Howdy Doody?"

"This child don't know nothing," he said to my aunt. "She's been raised with a bunch of country hicks."

"He's fooling," said Aunt Mozelle. "Go ahead and show her, Boone, for gosh sakes. Don't keep it a secret."

He was talking about television. I hadn't noticed the set in the living room because it had a sliding cover over the screen. It was a ten-inch table model with an upholstered sound box in a rosewood cabinet.

"We've never seen a television," my mother said.

"This will ruin her," said my aunt. "It's ruined Boone."

Uncle Boone turned on the television set. A wrestling match appeared on the screen, and I could see Gorgeous George flexing his muscles and tossing his curls. The television set resembled our radio. For a long time I was confused, thinking that I would now be able to see all my favorite radio programs.

"It's one of those sets you can look at in normal light and not go blind," my aunt said, to reassure us. "It's called Daylight TV."

"Wait till you see Howdy Doody," said Uncle Boone.

The picture on the television set was not clear. The reception required some imagination, and the pictures frequently dissolved, but I could see Gorgeous George moving across the screen, his curls bouncing. I could see him catch hold of his opponent and wrestle him to the floor, holding him so tight I thought he would choke.

That night, I lay in the cedar-perfumed room, too excited to sleep. I did not know what to expect next. The streetlamps glowed like moons through the venetian blinds, and as I lay there, my guardian angel slowly crept into my mind. In *Uncle Arthur's Bedtime Stories*, there was a picture of a child with his guardian angel hovering over him. It was a man angel, and gigantic, with immense white feathery bird's wings. Probably the boy could never see him because the angel stayed in what drivers of automobiles call a blind spot. I had a feeling that my own guardian angel had accompanied the bus to Michigan and was in the house with me. I imagined him floating above the bus. I knew that my guardian angel was supposed to keep me from harm, but I did not want anyone to know about him. I was very afraid of him. It was a long time before I fell asleep.

In the North, they drank coffee. Aunt Mozelle made a large pot of coffee in the mornings, and she kept it in a Thermos so she could drink coffee throughout the day.

Mama began drinking coffee. "Whew! I'm higher than a kite!" she would say. "I'll be up prowling half the night."

"Little girls shouldn't ought to drink coffee," Uncle Boone said to me more than once. "It turns them black."

"I don't even want any!" I protested. But I did like the enticing smell, which awoke me early in the mornings.

My aunt made waffles with oleomargarine. She kneaded a capsule of yellow dye into the pale margarine.

"It's a law," she told me one morning.

"They don't have that law down home anymore," said Mama. "People's turning to oleo and it's getting so we can't sell butter."

"I guess everybody forgot how it tasted," said Aunt Mozelle.

"I wouldn't be surprised if that business about the dye was a Communist idea," said my uncle. "A buddy of mine at the plant thinks so. He says they want to make it look like butter. The big companies, they're full of reds now."

"That makes sense to me," said Mama. "Anything to hurt the farmer."

It didn't make sense to me. When they talked about reds, all I could imagine was a bunch of little devils in red suits, carrying pitchforks. I wondered if they were what my uncle had seen in the Pacific, since devils had tails. Everything about the North was confusing. Lunetta Jones, for instance, bewildered me. She came for coffee every morning, after my uncle had left in a car pool. Lunetta, a seventh-grade teacher, was from Kentucky, and her parents were old friends of my aunt's, so Mozelle and Boone took a special interest in her welfare. Lunetta's life was tragic, my aunt said. Her sailor-boy husband had died in the war. Lunetta never spoke to me, so I often stared at her unselfconsciously. She resembled one of the Toni twins,[1] except for her horsey teeth. She wore her hair curled tight at the bottom, with a fluffy topknot, and she

---

[1] Reference to an advertisement of the time for home permanent waves: "Which twin has the Toni?"

put hard, precise *g*'s on the ends of words like "talking" and "going," the way both Sharon Belletieri and Betsy Lou did. And she wore elaborate dresses—rayon marquisette dresses with Paris pockets, dresses with tiered tucks, others of tissue chambray, with what she called "taffeta understudies." Sometimes I thought her dresses could carry her away on a frantic ride through the sky, they were so billowy and thin.

"Lunetta's man-crazy," my aunt explained to me. "She's always dressed up in one of them Sunday-go-to-meetin' outfits in case she might come across a man to marry."

Uncle Boone called her thick lipstick "man bait."

The buses remained on strike, and I spent the days in the house. I avoided Sharon Belletieri, preferring to be alone, or to sit entranced before the television set. Sometimes the facing outlines of the characters on the screen were like ghosts. I watched Milton Berle, Morey Amsterdam, *Believe It Or Not, Wax Wackies,* and even *Blind Date.* Judy Splinters, a ventriloquist's dummy with pigtails like mine, was one of my favorites, and I liked the magician Foodini on *Lucky Pup* better than Howdy Doody. Betsy Lou teased me, saying I was too old for those baby shows. She was away most of the time, out on "jelly dates." A jelly date was a Coke date. She had jelly dates with Bob and Jim and Sam all on the same day. She was fond of singing "Let's Take an Old-Fashioned Walk," although one of her boyfriends had a car and she liked to go riding in it more than anything else. Why couldn't he take us to Detroit? I wondered, but I was afraid to ask. I had a sick feeling that we were never going to get to see the buildings of the city.

In the mornings, when there was nothing but snow[2] on television, and the women were gossiping over their coffee in the kitchen, I sat on the enclosed porch and watched the people and the cars pass. During the heat wave, it was breezy there. I sat on the rattan chaise lounge and read Aunt Mozelle's scrapbooks, which I had found on a shelf above the television set. They were filled with brittle newspaper clippings mounted in overlapping rows. The clippings included household hints and cradle notes, but most of the stories were about bizarre occurrences around the world—diseases and kidnappings and disasters. One headline that fascinated me read: TIBETAN STOMACH STOVE DECLARED CANCER CAUSE. The story said that people in Tibet who carry little hot stoves against their abdomens in winter frequently develop cancer from the irritation. I was thankful that I didn't live in a cold climate. Another story was about a boa constrictor that swallowed a horse blanket. And there were a number of strange stories about blue babies. When my aunt found me reading the scrapbooks, she said to me, "Life is amazing. I keep these to remind me of just how strange everything is. And how there are always people worse off." I nodded agreement. The porch was my favorite place. I felt secure there, as I read about these faraway wonders and afflictions. I would look up now and then and imagine I could see the tall buildings of Detroit in the distance.

"This is a *two*-tone gabardine spectator dress with a low-slung belt in the back," said Lunetta one morning as she turned to model her new dress for us. Lunetta always had official descriptions for her extravagant costumes.

[2] The white spots on an empty television screen resulting either from a weak signal or, as was common in the early days of television, from an absence of programming.

My mother said in a wistful voice, "Law me, that's beautiful. But what would I look like, feeding the chickens in that getup?"

"Just look at them shoes," Aunt Mozelle said.

Lunetta's shoes had butterfly bows and sling heels and open toes. She sat down and tapped her toes as Aunt Mozelle poured coffee for her. She said then, "Is Boone worried about his job now that they caught that red?"

"Well, he is, but he don't let on," said Aunt Mozelle, frowning.

Lunetta seized yesterday's newspaper and spread it out on the table. She pointed at the headlines. I remember the way the adults had murmured over the newspaper the day before. Aunt Mozelle had said, "Don't worry, Boone. You don't work for that company." He had replied, "But the plant is full of sympathizers." Now Lunetta said, "Just think. That man they caught could have given Russia all the plans for the power plant. Nothing's safe. You never know who might turn out to be a spy."

My mother was disturbed. "Everything you all have worked so hard for—and the reds could just come in and take it." She waved her hand at the kitchen. In my mind a strange scene appeared: a band of little red devils marching in with their pitchforks and taking the entire Kelvinator[3] kitchen to hell. Later, it occurred to me that they would take the television set first.

When my uncle came home from work, I greeted him at the door and asked him bluntly, "Are you going to get fired because of the reds?"

He only laughed and twitched my plaits. "No, sugar," he said.

"That don't concern younguns," Aunt Mozelle told me. She said to her husband, "Lunetta was here, spreading ideas."

"Leave it to Lunetta," said Uncle Boone wearily.

That evening they were eager to watch the news on the television set. When the supervisor who had been fired was shown, my uncle said, "I hope they give him what-for."

"He was going to tell Russia about the power plant," I said.

"Hush, Peggy," said Mama.

That evening, I could hear their anxious voices on the porch, as I watched Arthur Godfrey, wrestling, and the barbershop quartets. It seemed odd to me that my uncle did not want to watch the wrestling. He had told me wrestling was his favorite program.

Sharon Belletieri had a birthday party. Aunt Mozelle took Mama and me to a nearby Woolworth's, where I selected a coloring book for a present. The store was twice the size of ours at home. I also bought a souvenir of my trip—a pair of china dogs, with a label that read "Made in Japan." And my mother bought me a playsuit like Sharon's.

"It's Sanforized. That's good," she said with an air of satisfaction, as she examined seams and labels.

My mother looked pale and tired. At breakfast she had suddenly thrown up, the way she had during our bus trip. "I can't keep anything down this early," she had said. My aunt urged her to drink more coffee, saying it would settle her stomach.

Sharon Belletieri lived with her parents in a famous kind of sanitary house where you couldn't get TB or rheumatic fever because it had no drafts. "You won't have

---

[3] Leading manufacturer of kitchen appliances.

to worry about polio," Betsy Lou had told me. The house had venetian blinds like my aunt's, and there was also a television set, an immense one, on legs. Howdy Doody was on, but no one was watching. I did not know what to say to the children. They all knew each other, and their screams and giggles had a natural continuity, something like the way my mother talked with her sister, and like the splendid houses of the neighborhood, all set so close together.

For her birthday, Sharon's parents gave her a Toni doll that took my breath away. It had a bolero sundress, lace-edged panties and slip, and white shoes and socks—an outfit as fine as any of Lunetta's. It came with a Play Wave, including plastic spin curlers and Toni Creme Rinse. The doll's magic nylon hair was supposed to grow softer in texture the more you gave it permanent waves. Feeling self-conscious in my new playsuit, I sat quietly at the party, longing to give that doll a permanent.

Eventually, even though I had hardly opened my mouth, someone laughed at my accent. I had said the unfortunate word "hair" again, in reference to the doll.

Sharon said, *"She's from Kentucky."*

Growing bold and inspired, I said, "Well, we don't have any reds in Kentucky."

Some of the children laughed, and Sharon took me aside and told me a secret, making me cross my heart and hope to die. "I know who's a red," she told me in a whisper. "My father knows him."

"Who?"

"One of the men your uncle rides with to work. The one who drives the car on Thursdays. He's a red and I can prove it."

Before I could find out more, it was my turn to pin the tail on the donkey. Sharon's mother blindfolded me and spun me around. The children were squealing, and I could feel them shrinking from me. When I took the blindfold off, I was dizzy. I had pinned the donkey's tail on the wallpaper, in the center of a large yellow flower.

That evening Betsy Lou went out with a boy named Sam, the one with the car, and Lunetta came to play canasta with the adults. During *Cavalcade of Stars,* I could hear them in the kitchen, accusing each other of hiding reds, when they meant hearts and diamonds. They laughed so loudly I sometimes missed some of Jack Carter's jokes. The wrestling came on afterward, but my uncle did not notice, so I turned off the television and looked at a magazine. I spent a long time trying to write the last line to a Fab jingle so that I could win a television set and five hundred dollars a month for life. I knew that life in Kentucky would be unbearable without a television.

Between hands, Uncle Boone and Lunetta got into an argument. My uncle claimed there were more reds teaching school than making cars, and Lunetta said it was just the opposite.

"They're firing schoolteachers too," he said to Lunetta.

"Don't look at *me,*" she said. "I signed the loyalty oath."

"Hush your mouth, Boone," said Aunt Mozelle.

"I know who a red is," I said suddenly, coming to the table.

They all looked at me and I explained what Sharon had told me. Too late, I remembered my promise not to tell.

"Don't let anybody hear you say that," said Lunetta. "Your uncle would lose his job. If they even *think* you know somebody that knows somebody, you can get in trouble."

"You better not say anything, hon," said Uncle Boone.

"Peggy, it's past your bedtime," my mother said.

"What did *I* do?"

"Talk gets around," said Lunetta. "There's sympathizers even in the woodwork."

The next day, after a disturbing night in which my guardian angel did nothing to protect me from my terrible secret, I was glum and cranky, and for the first time I refused Aunt Mozelle's waffles.

"Are you burnt out on them?" she asked me.

"No, I just ain't hungry."

"She played too hard at the birthday party," Mama said knowingly to my aunt.

When Lunetta arrived and Mama told her I had played too hard at the birthday party, I burst into tears.

"It's nobody's business if I played too hard," I cried. "Besides," I shrieked at Mama, "you don't feel good at breakfast either. You always say you can't keep anything down."

"Don't be ugly," my mother said sharply. To the others, she said apologetically, "I reckon sooner or later she was bound to show out."[4]

It was Sunday, and the heat wave continued. We all sat on the porch, looking at the Sunday papers. Betsy Lou was reading *Pleasant Valley* by Louis Bromfield.[5] Uncle Boone read the Sunday comics aloud to himself. Actually, he was trying to get my attention, for I sat in a corner, determined to ignore everyone. Uncle Boone read "Abbie an' Slats," "The Gumps," and "Little Orphan Annie." He pretended he was Milton Berle as he read them, but I wouldn't laugh.

Lunetta and Uncle Boone seemed to have forgotten their argument. Lunetta had dressed up for church, but the man she planned to go with had gone to visit his mother's grave instead.

"That man sure did love his mother," she said.

"Why don't you go to church anyway?" asked Betsy Lou. "You're all dressed up."

"I just don't have it in me," said Lunetta. She was wearing a shell-tucked summer shantung dress and raffia T-strap sandals.

"Ain't you hot in that outfit?" asked my aunt. "We're burning up."

"I guess so." Lunetta seemed gloomy and distracted. I almost forgave her for upsetting me about the sympathizers, but then she launched into a complicated story about a baby-sitter who got double-crossed. "This woman baby-sat for her best friend, who was divorced and had two little babies. And come to find out, the friend was going out on dates with the woman's own husband!"

"If that don't beat all," said Mama, her eyes wide. She was drinking her second cup of coffee.

"No telling how long that could have kept up," said my aunt.

"It made a big divorce case," Lunetta said.

"I never saw so many divorce cases," said Mama.

"Would you divorce somebody if you found out they were a Communist?" Lunetta asked.

"I don't know as I would," said Aunt Mozelle. "Depends."

"*I* would," said Mama.

"I probably would," said Lunetta. "How about you, Boone?"

[4] Southern colloquialism for "misbehave."
[5] Prolific novelist and journalist (1896–1956); *Pleasant Valley* (1945) was a book about scientific farming.

"If I found out Mozelle was a red?" Boone asked, grinning. "I'd probably string her up and tickle her feet till she hollered uncle."

"Oh, Boone," Lunetta said with a laugh. "I know you'd stick up for Mozelle, no matter what."

They sat around that morning talking like this, good-naturedly. In the light of day, the reds were only jokes after all, like the comics. I had decided to eat a bowl of Pep cereal, and "Some Enchanted Evening" was playing on the radio. Suddenly everything changed, as if a black storm had appeared to break the heat wave. My mother gave out a loud whoop and clutched her stomach in pain.

"Where does it hurt?" my aunt cried, grabbing at Mama.

Mama was too much in pain to speak. Her face was distorted, her sharp-pointed lips stretched out like a slingshot. My aunt helped her to the bathroom, and a short while later, my aunt and uncle flew away with her in a taxi. Mama had straightened up enough to say that the pain had subsided, but she looked scared, and the blood had drained from her face. I said nothing to her, not even good-bye.

Betsy Lou, left alone with me, said, "I hope she hasn't got polio."

"Only children get polio," I said, trembling. "She don't have polio."

The telephone rang, and Betsy Lou chattered excitedly, telling one of her boyfriends what had happened. Alone and frightened, I sat on the porch, hugging a fat pile of newspapers and gazing at the street. I could see Sharon Belletieri, skating a block away with two other girls. She was wearing a blue playsuit. She and her friends reminded me of those privileged children in the Peanut Gallery on *Howdy Doody.*

To keep from thinking, I began searching the newspaper for something to put in Aunt Mozelle's scrapbook, but at first nothing seemed so horrible as what had just happened. Some babies had turned blue from a diaper dye, but that story didn't impress me. Then I found an item about a haunted house, and my heart began to race. A priest claimed that mysterious disturbances in a house in Wisconsin were the work of an angelic spirit watching over an eight-year-old boy. Cryptic messages were found on bits of paper in the boy's room. The spirit manifestation had occurred fifteen times. I found my aunt's scissors and cut out the story.

Within two hours, my aunt and uncle returned, with broad smiles on their faces, but I knew they were pretending.

"She's just fine," said Aunt Mozelle. "We'll take you to see her afterwhile, but right now they gave her something to make her sleep and take away the pain."

"She'll get to come home in the morning," said my uncle.

He had brought ice cream, and while he went to the kitchen to dish it out, I showed my aunt the clipping I had found. I helped her put it in her scrapbook.

"Life sure is strange," I said.

"Didn't I tell you?" she said. "Now, don't you worry about your mama, hon. She's going to be all right."

Later that day, my aunt and uncle stood in the corridor of the hospital while I visited my mother. The hospital was large and gray and steaming with the heat. Mama lay against a mound of pillows, smiling weakly.

"*I'm* the one that showed out," she said, looking ashamed. She took my hand and made me sit on the bed next to her. "You *were* going to have a little brother or sister," she said. "But I was mistaken."

"What happened to it?"

"I lost it. That happens sometimes."

When I looked at her blankly, she tried to explain that there wasn't *really* a baby, as there was when she had Johnny two years before.

She said, "You know how sometimes one or two of the chicken eggs don't hatch? The baby chick just won't take hold. That's what happened."

It occurred to me to ask what the baby's name would have been.

"I don't know," she said. "I'm trying to tell you there wasn't really a baby. I didn't know about it, anyway."

"You didn't even know there was a baby?"

"No. I didn't know about it till I lost it."

She tried to laugh, but she was weak, and she seemed as confused as I was. She squeezed my hand and closed her eyes for a moment. Then she said, "Boone says the buses will start up this week. You could go with your aunt to Detroit and see the big buildings."

"Without you?"

"The doctor said I should rest up before we go back. But you go ahead. Mozelle will take you." She smiled at me sleepily. "I wanted to go so bad—just to see those big fancy store windows. And I wanted to see your face when you saw the city."

That evening, *Toast of the Town* was on television, and then Fred Waring, and *Garroway at Large*. I was lost among the screen phantoms—the magic acts, puppets, jokes, clowns, dancers, singers, wisecracking announcers. My aunt and uncle laughed uproariously. Uncle Boone was drinking beer, something I had not seen him do, and the room stank with the smoke of his Old Golds. Now and then I was aware of all of us sitting there together, laughing in the dim light from the television, while my mother was in the hospital. Even Betsy Lou was watching with us. Later, I went to the guest room and sat on the large bed, trying to concentrate on finishing the Fab jingle.

> Here's to a fabulous life with Fab
> There's no soap scum to make wash drab
> Your clothes get cleaner—whiter, too—

I heard my aunt calling to me excitedly. I was missing something on the television screen. I had left because the news was on.

"Pictures of Detroit!" she cried. "Come quick. You can see the big buildings."

I raced into the living room in time to see some faint, dark shapes, hiding behind the snow, like a forest in winter, and then the image faded into the snow.

"Mozelle can take you into Detroit in a day or two," my uncle said. "The buses is starting up again."

"I don't want to go," I said.

"You don't want to miss the chance," said my aunt.

"Yes, I do."

That night, alone in the pine-and-cedar room, I saw everything clearly, like the sharpened images that floated on the television screen. My mother had said an egg didn't hatch, but I knew better. The reds had stolen the baby. They took things. They were after my aunt's copper-bottomed pans. They stole the butter. They wanted my uncle's job. They were invisible, like the guardian angel, although they might wear disguises. You didn't know who might be a red. You never knew when you might lose a baby that you didn't know you had. I understood it all. I hadn't trusted my guardian angel, and so he had failed to protect me. During the night, I hit upon a last line to the Fab jingle, but when I awoke I saw how silly and inappropriate it was. It was going over and over in my mind: *Red soap makes the world go round.*

On the bus home a few days later, I slept with my head in my mother's lap, and she dozed with her head propped against my seat back. She was no longer sick, but we were both tired and we swayed, unresisting, with the rhythms of the bus. When the bus stopped in Fort Wayne, Indiana, at midnight, I suddenly woke up, and at the sight of an unfamiliar place, I felt—with a new surge of clarity—the mystery of travel, the vastness of the world, the strangeness of life. My own life was a curiosity, an item for a scrapbook. I wondered what my mother would tell my father about the baby she had lost. She had been holding me tightly against her stomach as though she feared she might lose me too.

I had refused to let them take me into Detroit. At the bus station, Aunt Mozelle had hugged me and said, "Maybe next time you come we can go to Detroit."

"If there *is* a next time," Mama said. "This may be her only chance, but she had to be contrary."

"I didn't want to miss *Wax Wackies* and *Judy Splinters*," I said, protesting.

"We'll have a car next time you come," said my uncle. "If they don't fire everybody," he added with a laugh.

"If that happens, y'all can always come back to Kentucky and help us get a crop out," Mama told him.

The next afternoon, we got off the bus on the highway at the intersection with our road. Our house was half a mile away. The bus driver got our suitcases out of the bus for us, and then drove on down the highway. My father was supposed to meet us, but he was not there.

"I better not carry this suitcase," said Mama. "My insides might drop."

We left our suitcases in a ditch and started walking, expecting to meet Daddy on the way.

My mother said, "You don't remember this, but when you was two years old I went to Jackson, Tennessee, for two weeks to see Mozelle and Boone—back before Boone was called overseas?—and when I come back the bus driver let me off here and I come walking down the road to the house carrying my suitcase. You was playing in the yard and you saw me walk up and you didn't recognize me. For the longest time, you didn't know who I was. I never *will* forget how funny you looked."

"They won't recognize us," I said solemnly. "Daddy and Johnny."

As we got to the top of the hill, we could see that our little white house was still there. The tin roof of the barn was barely visible through the tall oak trees.

1981

Maxine Hong Kingston
b. 1940

"When I write most deeply, fly the highest, reach the furthest, I write like a diarist," asserts Maxine Hong Kingston, as though to remind us that writing begins for her as a private act. "My audience is myself," she says. "I dare to write anything because I can burn my papers at any moment." Using her own life and the lives of her family, Kingston addresses not the experience of being Chinese in America but the experience of being a Chinese-American. Her work demands an understanding of three cultures—American, Chinese, and Chinese-American. "Some readers," she says, "will just have to do some background reading." At the same time, she continues to believe both in "the timelessness and universality of individual vision" and in the "miracle" of being understood. Of *The Woman Warrior* (1976), from which "No Name Woman" is taken, she says that it is not merely "a family book or an American book or a woman's book but a world book, and, at the same moment, my book."

Born in Stockton, California, on October 27, 1940, Maxine Hong Kingston is a first-generation American. She received a B.A. from the University of California at Berkeley in 1962 and has taught at various high schools in California and Hawaii. From 1970 to 1977 she was on the faculty of the Mid-Pacific Institute in Honolulu, and she is currently assistant professor of English and visiting writer at the University of Hawaii. Meanwhile, her writing has met with consistent critical acclaim. Her first book, *The Woman Warrior: Memoirs of a Girlhood Among Ghosts*, won the National Book Critics Circle Award for nonfiction; her second, *China Men* (1980), won the 1981 American Book Award. Her short stories, articles, and poems have appeared in such publications as *The New Yorker, New West, Ms.*, and *American Heritage*. Kingston has also received a *Mademoiselle* award (1977), an NEA writing fellowship (1980), and a Guggenheim fellowship (1981).

Given the autobiographical focus of Kingston's fiction, it is fitting that one of her major concerns revolves around the relation between fiction and nonfiction. "My characters are story tellers," she says, "and I suspect that some of them are telling me fiction. So when I write their lives down is it fiction or nonfiction?" The answer, she believes, lies in perspective. Rather than depend solely on verifiable "facts," she also explores impressions, emotions, and interpretations, both her own and those of her characters. At the same time, she carefully delineates the sources on which she has drawn so that her readers can in turn devise interpretations of their own. "When I tell . . . all these versions," she says, "I'm actually giving the culture of these people in a very accurate way. You can see where the people make up these fictions about themselves, and it's not just for fun. It's a terrible necessity." Writing of herself and the mixed world that forms a backdrop for her experiences, Kingston creates a truth that transcends literary and ethnic categories and is as beautiful as it is necessary.

Text:
*The Woman Warrior: Memoirs of a Girlhood
Among Ghosts*, 1976.

from The Woman Warrior

No Name Woman

"You must not tell anyone," my mother said, "what I am about to tell you. In China your father had a sister who killed herself. She jumped into the family well. We say that your father has all brothers because it is as if she had never been born.

"In 1924 just a few days after our village celebrated seventeen hurry-up weddings —to make sure that every young man who went 'out on the road' would responsibly come home—your father and his brothers and your grandfather and his brothers and your aunt's new husband sailed for America, the Gold Mountain. It was your grandfather's last trip. Those lucky enough to get contracts waved goodbye from the decks. They fed and guarded the stowaways and helped them off in Cuba, New York, Bali, Hawaii. 'We'll meet in California next year,' they said. All of them sent money home.

"I remember looking at your aunt one day when she and I were dressing; I had not noticed before that she had such a protruding melon of a stomach. But I did not think, 'She's pregnant,' until she began to look like other pregnant women, her shirt pulling and the white tops of her black pants showing. She could not have been pregnant, you see, because her husband had been gone for years. No one said anything. We did not discuss it. In early summer she was ready to have the child, long after the time when it could have been possible.

"The village had also been counting. On the night the baby was to be born the villagers raided our house. Some were crying. Like a great saw, teeth strung with lights, files of people walked zigzag across our land, tearing the rice. Their lanterns doubled in the disturbed black water, which drained away through the broken bunds. As the villagers closed in, we could see that some of them, probably men and women we knew well, wore white masks. The people with long hair hung it over their faces. Women with short hair made it stand up on end. Some had tied white bands around their foreheads, arms, and legs.

"At first they threw mud and rocks at the house. Then they threw eggs and began slaughtering our stock. We could hear the animals scream their deaths—the roosters, the pigs, a last great roar from the ox. Familiar wild heads flared in our night windows; the villagers encircled us. Some of the faces stopped to peer at us, their eyes rushing like searchlights. The hands flattened against the panes, framed heads, and left red prints.

"The villagers broke in the front and the back doors at the same time, even though we had not locked the doors against them. Their knives dripped with the blood of our animals. They smeared blood on the doors and walls. One woman swung a chicken, whose throat she had slit, splattering blood in red arcs about her. We stood together in the middle of our house, in the family hall with the pictures and tables of the ancestors around us, and looked straight ahead.

"At that time the house had only two wings. When the men came back, we would build two more to enclose our courtyard and a third one to begin a second courtyard. The villagers pushed through both wings, even your grandparents' rooms, to find your aunt's, which was also mine until the men returned. From this room a new wing for one of the younger families would grow. They ripped up her clothes and shoes and broke her combs, grinding them underfoot. They tore her work from the loom. They scattered the cooking fire and rolled the new weaving in it. We could hear them in the kitchen breaking our bowls and banging the pots. They overturned the great waist-high earthenware jugs; duck eggs, pickled fruits, vegetables burst out and mixed in acrid torrents. The old woman from the next field swept a broom through the air and loosed the spirits-of-the-broom over our heads. 'Pig.' 'Ghost.' 'Pig,' they sobbed and scolded while they ruined our house.

"When they left, they took sugar and oranges to bless themselves. They cut pieces from the dead animals. Some of them took bowls that were not broken and clothes that were not torn. Afterward we swept up the rice and sewed it back up into sacks. But the smells from the spilled preserves lasted. Your aunt gave birth in the pigsty that night. The next morning when I went for the water, I found her and the baby plugging up the family well.

"Don't let your father know that I told you. He denies her. Now that you have started to menstruate, what happened to her could happen to you. Don't humiliate us. You wouldn't like to be forgotten as if you had never been born. The villagers are watchful."

Whenever she had to warn us about life, my mother told stories that ran like this one, a story to grow up on. She tested our strength to establish realities. Those in the emigrant generations who could not reassert brute survival died young and far from home. Those of us in the first American generations have had to figure out how the invisible world the emigrants built around our childhoods fit in solid America.

The emigrants confused the gods by diverting their curses, misleading them with crooked streets and false names. They must try to confuse their offspring as well, who, I suppose, threaten them in similar ways—always trying to get things straight, always trying to name the unspeakable. The Chinese I know hide their names; sojourners take new names when their lives change and guard their real names with silence.

Chinese-Americans, when you try to understand what things in you are Chinese, how do you separate what is peculiar to childhood, to poverty, insanities, one family, your mother who marked your growing with stories, from what is Chinese? What is Chinese tradition and what is the movies?

If I want to learn what clothes my aunt wore, whether flashy or ordinary, I would have to begin, "Remember Father's drowned-in-the-well sister?" I cannot ask that. My mother has told me once and for all the useful parts. She will add nothing unless powered by Necessity, a riverbank that guides her life. She plants vegetable gardens rather than lawns; she carries the odd-shaped tomatoes home from the fields and eats food left for the gods.

Whenever we did frivolous things, we used up energy; we flew high kites. We children came up off the ground over the melting cones our parents brought home from work and the American movie on New Year's Day—*Oh, You Beautiful Doll* with Betty Grable one year, and *She Wore a Yellow Ribbon* with John Wayne another year. After the one carnival ride each, we paid in guilt; our tired father counted his change on the dark walk home.

Adultery is extravagance. Could people who hatch their own chicks and eat the embryos and the heads for delicacies and boil the feet in vinegar for party food, leaving only the gravel, eating even the gizzard lining—could such people engender a prodigal aunt? To be a woman, to have a daughter in starvation time was a waste enough. My aunt could not have been the lone romantic who gave up everything for sex. Women in the old China did not choose. Some man had commanded her to lie with him and be his secret evil. I wonder whether he masked himself when he joined the raid on her family.

Perhaps she encountered him in the fields or on the mountain where the daughters-in-law collected fuel. Or perhaps he first noticed her in the marketplace. He was not a stranger because the village housed no strangers. She had to have dealings with him other than sex. Perhaps he worked an adjoining field, or he sold her the cloth for the dress she sewed and wore. His demand must have surprised, then terrified her. She obeyed him; she always did as she was told.

When the family found a young man in the next village to be her husband, she stood tractably beside the best rooster, his proxy, and promised before they met that she would be his forever. She was lucky that he was her age and she would be the first wife, an advantage secure now. The night she first saw him, he had sex with her. Then he left for America. She had almost forgotten what he looked like. When she tried to envision him, she only saw the black and white face in the group photograph the men had had taken before leaving.

The other man was not, after all, much different from her husband. They both gave orders: she followed. "If you tell your family, I'll beat you. I'll kill you. Be here again next week." No one talked sex, ever. And she might have separated the rapes from the rest of living if only she did not have to buy her oil from him or gather wood in the same forest. I want her fear to have lasted just as long as rape lasted so that the fear could have been contained. No drawn-out fear. But women at sex hazarded birth and hence lifetimes. The fear did not stop but permeated everywhere. She told the man, "I think I'm pregnant." He organized the raid against her.

On nights when my mother and father talked about their life back home, sometimes they mentioned an "outcast table" whose business they still seemed to be settling, their voices tight. In a commensal tradition,[1] where food is precious, the powerful older people made wrongdoers eat alone. Instead of letting them start separate new lives like the Japanese, who could become samurais and geishas,[2] the Chinese family, faces averted but eyes glowering sideways, hung on to the offenders and fed them leftovers. My aunt must have lived in the same house as my parents and eaten at an outcast table. My mother spoke about the raid as if she had seen it, when she and my aunt, a daughter-in-law to a different household, should not have been living together at all. Daughters-in-law lived with their husbands' parents, not their own; a synonym for marriage in Chinese is "taking a daughter-in-law." Her husband's parents could have sold her, mortgaged her, stoned her. But they had sent her back to her own mother and father, a mysterious act hinting at disgraces not told me. Perhaps they had thrown her out to deflect the avengers.

She was the only daughter; her four brothers went with her father, husband, and uncles "out on the road" and for some years became western men. When the goods were divided among the family, three of the brothers took land, and the youngest, my father, chose an education. After my grandparents gave their daughter away to

[1] One in which all members eat at the same table.
[2] Samurai: member of the Japanese feudal military aristocracy; geisha: Japanese girl trained in singing, dancing, and the art of conversation so as to serve as a hired companion to men.

her husband's family, they had dispensed all the adventure and all the property. They expected her alone to keep the traditional ways, which her brothers, now among the barbarians, could fumble without detection. The heavy, deep-rooted women were to maintain the past against the flood, safe for returning. But the rare urge west had fixed upon our family, and so my aunt crossed boundaries not delineated in space.

The work of preservation demands that the feelings playing about in one's guts not be turned into action. Just watch their passing like cherry blossoms. But perhaps my aunt, my forerunner, caught in a slow life, let dreams grow and fade and after some months or years went toward what persisted. Fear at the enormities of the forbidden kept her desires delicate, wire and bone. She looked at a man because she liked the way the hair was tucked behind his ears, or she liked the question-mark line of a long torso curving at the shoulder and straight at the hip. For warm eyes or a soft voice or a slow walk—that's all—a few hairs, a line, a brightness, a sound, a pace, she gave up family. She offered us up for a charm that vanished with tiredness, a pigtail that didn't toss when the wind died. Why, the wrong lighting could erase the dearest thing about him.

It could very well have been, however, that my aunt did not take subtle enjoyment of her friend, but, a wild woman, kept rollicking company. Imagining her free with sex doesn't fit, though. I don't know any women like that, or men either. Unless I see her life branching into mine, she gives me no ancestral help.

To sustain her being in love, she often worked at herself in the mirror, guessing at the colors and shapes that would interest him, changing them frequently in order to hit on the right combination. She wanted him to look back.

On a farm near the sea, a woman who tended her appearance reaped a reputation for eccentricity. All the married women blunt-cut their hair in flaps about their ears or pulled it back in tight buns. No nonsense. Neither style blew easily into heart-catching tangles. And at their weddings they displayed themselves in their long hair for the last time. "It brushed the backs of my knees," my mother tells me. "It was braided, and even so, it brushed the backs of my knees."

At the mirror my aunt combed individuality into her bob. A bun could have been contrived to escape into black streamers blowing in the wind or in quiet wisps about her face, but only the older women in our picture album wear buns. She brushed her hair back from her forehead, tucking the flaps behind her ears. She looped a piece of thread, knotted into a circle between her index fingers and thumbs, and ran the double strand across her forehead. When she closed her fingers as if she were making a pair of shadow geese bite, the string twisted together catching the little hairs. Then she pulled the thread away from her skin, ripping the hairs out neatly, her eyes watering from the needles of pain. Opening her fingers, she cleaned the thread, then rolled it along her hairline and the tops of her eyebrows. My mother did the same to me and my sisters and herself. I used to believe that the expression "caught by the short hairs" meant a captive held with a depilatory string. It especially hurt at the temples, but my mother said we were lucky we didn't have to have our feet bound when we were seven. Sisters used to sit on their beds and cry together, she said, as their mothers or their slaves removed the bandages for a few minutes each night and let the blood gush back into their veins. I hope that the man my aunt loved appreciated a smooth brow, that he wasn't just a tits-and-ass man.

Once my aunt found a freckle on her chin, at a spot that the almanac said predestined her for unhappiness. She dug it out with a hot needle and washed the wound with peroxide.

More attention to her looks than these pullings of hairs and pickings at spots would have caused gossip among the villagers. They owned work clothes and good clothes, and they wore good clothes for feasting the new seasons. But since a woman combing her hair hexes beginnings, my aunt rarely found an occasion to look her best. Women looked like great sea snails—the corded wood, babies, and laundry they carried were the whorls on their backs. The Chinese did not admire a bent back; goddesses and warriors stood straight. Still there must have been a marvelous freeing of beauty when a worker laid down her burden and stretched and arched.

Such commonplace loveliness, however, was not enough for my aunt. She dreamed of a lover for the fifteen days of New Year's, the time for families to exchange visits, money, and food. She plied her secret comb. And sure enough she cursed the year, the family, the village, and herself.

Even as her hair lured her imminent lover, many other men looked at her. Uncles, cousins, nephews, brothers would have looked, too, had they been home between journeys. Perhaps they had already been restraining their curiosity, and they left, fearful that their glances, like a field of nesting birds, might be startled and caught. Poverty hurt, and that was their first reason for leaving. But another, final reason for leaving the crowded house was the never-said.

She may have been unusually beloved, the precious only daughter, spoiled and mirror gazing because of the affection the family lavished on her. When her husband left, they welcomed the chance to take her back from the in-laws; she could live like the little daughter for just a while longer. There are stories that my grandfather was different from other people, "crazy ever since the little Jap bayoneted him in the head." He used to put his naked penis on the dinner table, laughing. And one day he brought home a baby girl, wrapped up inside his brown western-style greatcoat. He had traded one of his sons, probably my father, the youngest, for her. My grandmother made him trade back. When he finally got a daughter of his own, he doted on her. They must have all loved her, except perhaps my father, the only brother who never went back to China, having once been traded for a girl.

Brothers and sisters, newly men and women, had to efface their sexual color and present plain miens. Disturbing hair and eyes, a smile like no other threatened the ideal of five generations living under one roof. To focus blurs, people shouted face to face and yelled from room to room. The immigrants I know have loud voices, unmodulated to American tones even after years away from the village where they called their friendships out across the fields. I have not been able to stop my mother's screams in public libraries or over telephones. Walking erect (knees straight, toes pointed forward, not pigeon-toed, which is Chinese-feminine) and speaking in an inaudible voice, I have tried to turn myself American-feminine. Chinese communication was loud, public. Only sick people had to whisper. But at the dinner table, where the family members came nearest one another, no one could talk, not the outcasts nor any eaters. Every word that falls from the mouth is a coin lost. Silently they gave and accepted food with both hands. A preoccupied child who took his bowl with one hand got a sideways glare. A complete moment of total attention is due everyone alike. Children and lovers have no singularity here, but my aunt used a secret voice, a separate attentiveness.

She kept the man's name to herself throughout her labor and dying; she did not accuse him that he be punished with her. To save her inseminator's name she gave silent birth.

He may have been somebody in her own household, but intercourse with a man outside the family would have been no less abhorrent. All the village were kinsmen, and the titles shouted in loud country voices never let kinship be forgotten. Any man within visiting distance would have been neutralized as a lover—"brother," "younger brother," "older brother"—one hundred and fifteen relationship titles. Parents researched birth charts probably not so much to assure good fortune as to circumvent incest in a population that has but one hundred surnames. Everybody has eight million relatives. How useless then sexual mannerisms, how dangerous.

As if it came from an atavism deeper than fear, I used to add "brother" silently to boys' names. It hexed the boys, who would or would not ask me to dance, and made them less scary and as familiar and deserving of benevolence as girls.

But, of course, I hexed myself also—no dates. I should have stood up, both arms waving, and shouted out across libraries, "Hey, you! Love me back." I had no idea, though, how to make attraction selective, how to control its direction and magnitude. If I made myself American-pretty so that the five or six Chinese boys in the class fell in love with me, everyone else—the Caucasian, Negro, and Japanese boys—would too. Sisterliness, dignified and honorable, made much more sense.

Attraction eludes control so stubbornly that whole societies designed to organize relationships among people cannot keep order, not even when they bind people to one another from childhood and raise them together. Among the very poor and the wealthy, brothers married their adopted sisters, like doves. Our family allowed some romance, paying adult brides' prices and providing dowries so that their sons and daughters could marry strangers. Marriage promises to turn strangers into friendly relatives—a nation of siblings.

In the village structure, spirits shimmered among the live creatures, balanced and held in equilibrium by time and land. But one human being flaring up into violence could open up a black hole, a maelstrom that pulled in the sky. The frightened villagers, who depended on one another to maintain the real, went to my aunt to show her a personal, physical representation of the break she had made in the "roundness." Misallying couples snapped off the future, which was to be embodied in true offspring. The villagers punished her for acting as if she could have a private life, secret and apart from them.

If my aunt had betrayed the family at a time of large grain yields and peace, when many boys were born, and wings were being built on many houses, perhaps she might have escaped such severe punishment. But the men—hungry, greedy, tired of planting in dry soil, cuckolded—had had to leave the village in order to send food-money home. There were ghost plagues, bandit plagues, wars with the Japanese, floods. My Chinese brother and sister had died of an unknown sickness. Adultery, perhaps only a mistake during good times, became a crime when the village needed food.

The round moon cakes and round doorways, the round tables of graduated size that fit one roundness inside another, round windows and rice bowls—these talismen had lost their power to warn this family of the law: a family must be whole, faithfully keeping the descent line by having sons to feed the old and the dead, who in turn look after the family. The villagers came to show my aunt and her lover-in-hiding a broken house. The villagers were speeding up the circling of events because she was too shortsighted to see that her infidelity had already harmed the village, that waves of consequences would return unpredictably, sometimes in disguise, as now, to hurt her. This roundness had to be made coin-sized so that she would see its circumference: punish her at the birth of her baby. Awaken her to the inexorable. People who refused fatalism because they could invent small resources insisted on culpability. Deny accidents and wrest fault from the stars.

After the villagers left, their lanterns now scattering in various directions toward home, the family broke their silence and cursed her. "Aiaa, we're going to die. Death is coming. Death is coming. Look what you've done. You've killed us. Ghost! Dead ghost! Ghost! You've never been born." She ran out into the fields, far enough from the house so that she could no longer hear their voices, and pressed herself against the earth, her own land no more. When she felt the birth coming, she thought that she had been hurt. Her body seized together. "They've hurt me too much," she thought. "This is gall, and it will kill me." Her forehead and knees against the earth, her body convulsed and then released her onto her back. The black well of sky and stars went out and out and out forever; her body and her complexity seemed to disappear. She was one of the stars, a bright dot in blackness, without home, without a companion, in eternal cold and silence. An agoraphobia rose in her, speeding higher and higher, bigger and bigger; she would not be able to contain it; there would be no end to fear.

Flayed, unprotected against space, she felt pain return, focusing her body. This pain chilled her—a cold, steady kind of surface pain. Inside, spasmodically, the other pain, the pain of the child, heated her. For hours she lay on the ground, alternately body and space. Sometimes a vision of normal comfort obliterated reality: she saw the family in the evening gambling at the dinner table, the young people massaging their elders' backs. She saw them congratulating one another, high joy on the mornings the rice shoots came up. When these pictures burst, the stars drew yet further apart. Black space opened.

She got to her feet to fight better and remembered that old-fashioned women gave birth in their pigsties to fool the jealous, pain-dealing gods, who do not snatch piglets. Before the next spasms could stop her, she ran to the pigsty, each step a rushing out into emptiness. She climbed over the fence and knelt in the dirt. It was good to have a fence enclosing her, a tribal person alone.

Laboring, this woman who had carried her child as a foreign growth that sickened her every day, expelled it at last. She reached down to touch the hot, wet, moving mass, surely smaller than anything human, and could feel that it was human after all —fingers, toes, nails, nose. She pulled it up on to her belly, and it lay curled there, butt in the air, feet precisely tucked one under the other. She opened her loose shirt and buttoned the child inside. After resting, it squirmed and thrashed and she pushed it up to her breast. It turned its head this way and that until it found her nipple. There, it made little snuffling noises. She clenched her teeth at its preciousness, lovely as a young calf, a piglet, a little dog.

She may have gone to the pigsty as a last act of responsibility: she would protect this child as she had protected its father. It would look after her soul, leaving supplies on her grave. But how would this tiny child without family find her grave when there would be no marker for her anywhere, neither in the earth nor the family hall? No one would give her a family hall name. She had taken the child with her into the wastes. At its birth the two of them had felt the same raw pain of separation, a wound that only the family pressing tight could close. A child with no descent line would not soften her life but only trail after her, ghostlike, begging her to give it purpose. At dawn the villagers on their way to the fields would stand around the fence and look.

Full of milk, the little ghost slept. When it awoke, she hardened her breasts against the milk that crying loosens. Toward morning she picked up the baby and walked to the well.

Carrying the baby to the well shows loving. Otherwise abandon it. Turn its face into the mud. Mothers who love their children take them along. It was probably a girl; there is some hope of forgiveness for boys.

"Don't tell anyone you had an aunt. Your father does not want to hear her name. She has never been born." I have believed that sex was unspeakable and words so strong and fathers so frail that "aunt" would do my father mysterious harm. I have thought that my family, having settled among immigrants who had also been their neighbors in the ancestral land, needed to clean their name, and a wrong word would incite the kinspeople even here. But there is more to this silence: they want me to participate in her punishment. And I have.

In the twenty years since I heard this story I have not asked for details nor said my aunt's name; I do not know it. People who can comfort the dead can also chase after them to hurt them further—a reverse ancestor worship. The real punishment was not the raid swiftly inflicted by the villagers, but the family's deliberately forgetting her. Her betrayal so maddened them, they saw to it that she would suffer forever, even after death. Always hungry, always needing, she would have to beg food from other ghosts, snatch and steal it from those whose living descendants give them gifts. She would have to fight the ghosts massed at crossroads for the buns a few thoughtful citizens leave to decoy her away from village and home so that the ancestral spirits could feast unharassed. At peace, they could act like gods, not ghosts, their descent lines providing them with paper suits and dresses, spirit money, paper houses, paper automobiles, chicken, meat, and rice into eternity—essences delivered up in smoke and flames, steam and incense rising from each rice bowl. In an attempt to make the Chinese care for people outside the family, Chairman Mao encourages us now to give our paper replicas to the spirits of outstanding soldiers and workers, no matter whose ancestors they may be. My aunt remains forever hungry. Goods are not distributed evenly among the dead.

My aunt haunts me—her ghost drawn to me because now, after fifty years of neglect, I alone devote pages of paper to her, though not origamied[3] into houses and clothes. I do not think she always means me well. I am telling on her, and she was a spite suicide, drowning herself in the drinking water. The Chinese are always very frightened of the drowned one, whose weeping ghost, wet hair hanging and skin bloated, waits silently by the water to pull down a substitute.

1975

[3] I.e., folded. (Origami is the Japanese art of folding paper into representational or decorative shapes.)

Alice Walker
b. 1944

Alice Walker—novelist, poet, essayist, biographer, and editor—has described herself as "preoccupied with the spiritual survival, the survival *whole* of my people." But Walker was a young black woman before she became a writer, and she also describes herself as specifically "committed to exploring the oppressions, the insanities, the loyalties, and the triumphs of black women." Too often, Walker believes, black and female experience, both in life and in literature, has been devalued by a culture that is dominated by white males. She not only sees Zora Neale Hurston as a tragic case of unappreciated—even suppressed— achievement and isolated suffering; she also sees Hurston's neglected achievement as representing a particularly terrible loss to those for whom it should have been an inspiring example. Walker's most recent book, *In Search of Our Mothers' Gardens* (1984), celebrates the many women who, like Walker's own mother, were left without any traditional outlet for artistic expression and still managed to hand down an abiding "respect for the possibilities [of life]—and the will to grasp them."

Walker learned early the need for indomitable will. Born in 1944 in Eatonton, Georgia—one of her early residences was a shack near Flannery O'Connor's Andalusia Farm—Walker was initially discouraged in her artistic ambition by critics who felt that a poor black farmer's daughter would face obstacles impossible to overcome. Walker's response was twofold. First, although she agreed that a "shack with only a dozen or so books" was "an unlikely place to discover a young Keats," she was convinced that it was narrow to think of Keats as "the only kind of poet one would want to grow up to be." Second, like the young Richard Wright, Walker began early to broaden her education. Graduating from Sarah Lawrence College in 1965, she began teaching writing and black literature in Mississippi, at Jackson State College and Tougaloo College. More recently, she has taught at Wellesley College, the University of Massachusetts, and Yale University and has served as a consulting and contributing editor of *Ms.* magazine and *Freedomways*, a quarterly journal of the Black Freedom Movement.

A mother as well as a socially engaged teacher, Walker believes that her maternal experiences as well as her political and educational experiences have enriched her writings. She has published three novels, *The Third Life of Grange Copeland* (1970), *Meridian* (1976), and *The Color Purple* (1982); four volumes of poetry, *Once* (1968), *Revolutionary Petunias* (1973), *Good Night, Willie Lee, I'll See You in the Morning* (1979), and *Horses Make a Landscape Look More Beautiful* (1984); a children's biography of Langston Hughes; and one collection of stories, *In Love and Trouble* (1974), from which "The Child Who Favored Daughter" is taken. Many of Walker's writings render moments of pain and moments of beauty in the lives of black women. Individual stories, poems, and essays have appeared in publications as diverse as *Harper's* and *Mother Jones,* and Walker's awards and grants range from a Guggenheim fellowship to a creative writing award from the National Endowment for the Arts and the Front Page Award for best magazine criticism by the Newswomen's Club of New York. Walker currently lives in San Francisco.

Walker's fiction reflects the full range of her interests and experience. From her mother, whose literary heritage derived primarily from the oral tradition of the black South, Walker inherited not only stories but also an urgent sense that her grandmother's "stories—like her life—must be recorded" if they were not to be lost. From the slave narratives of her ancestors, she gathered a sense that "family relationships are sacred" and that life is a "moral and/or physical struggle, the result of which is expected to be some kind of larger freedom." In her literary models, black and white, Walker discovered knowledge that "the strength of the artist" consists of the "courage to look at every old thing with fresh eyes." As a result, although she deals primarily with the experiences of poor black women, she addresses not only those who believe, as Henry James put it, that the house of fiction has many windows but also those who recognize that black and white writers (and, by extension, male and female writers) are "writing one immense story—the same story, for the most part—with different parts of this immense story coming from a multitude of different perspectives." By exploring the effects of racism and sexism, by giving "voice to centuries not only of silent bitterness and hate but also of neighborly kindness and sustaining love," Walker obviously hopes to enrich the lives of those who share the same race or sex as her most memorable characters. In addition, however, she clearly hopes to touch the lives of those with "different perspectives" who nevertheless can learn from hearing the pained voices she has heard and seeing the troubled gardens she has seen.

Text:
In Love and Trouble, 1974.

The Child Who Favored[1] Daughter

"That my daughter should
fancy herself in love
with any *man!*
How can this be?"
Anonymous

[1]

She knows he has read the letter. He is sitting on the front porch watching her make the long trek from the school bus down the lane into the front yard. *Father, judge, giver of life.* Shadowy clouds indicating rain hang low on either side of the four o'clock

---

[1] In southern vernacular, resembled.

sun and she holds her hand up to her eyes and looks out across the rows of cotton that stretch on one side of her from the mailbox to the house in long green hedges. After an initial shutting off of breath caused by fear, a calm numbness sets in and as she makes her way slowly down the lane she shuffles her feet in the loose red dust and tries to seem unconcerned. But she wonders how he knows about the letter. Her lover has a mother who dotes on the girl he married. It could have been her, preserving the race. Or the young bride herself, brittled to ice to find a letter from her among keepsakes her husband makes no move to destroy. Or—? But that notion does not develop in her mind. She loves him.

> Fire of earth
> Lure of flower smells
> The sun

Down the lane with slow deliberate steps she walks in the direction of the house, toward the heavy silent man on the porch. The heat from the sun is oppressively hot but she does not feel its heat so much as its warmth, for there is a cold spot underneath the hot skin of her back that encloses her heart and reaches chilled arms around the bottom cages of her ribs.

> Lure of flower smells
> The sun

She stops to gaze intently at a small wild patch of black-eyed Susans and a few stray buttercups. Her fingers caress lightly the frail petals and she stands a moment wondering.

> The lure of flower smells
> The sun
> Softly the scent of—
> Softly the scent of flowers
> And petals
> Small, bright last wishes

2

He is sitting on the porch with his shotgun leaning against the banister within reach. If he cannot frighten her into chastity with his voice he will threaten her with the gun. He settles tensely in the chair and waits. He watches her from the time she steps from the yellow bus. He sees her shade her eyes from the hot sun and look widely over the rows of cotton running up, nearly touching him where he sits. He sees her look, knows its cast through any age and silence, knows she knows he has the letter.

Above him among the rafters in a half-dozen cool spots shielded from the afternoon sun the sound of dirt daubers. And busy wasps building onto their paper houses a dozen or more cells. Late in the summer, just as the babies are getting big enough to fly he will have to light paper torches and burn the paper houses down, singeing the wings of the young wasps before they get a chance to fly or to sting him as he sits in the cool of the evening reading his Bible.

Through eyes half closed he watches her come, her feet ankle deep in the loose red dust. Slowly, to the droning of the enterprising insects overhead, he counts each step, surveys each pause. He sees her looking closely at the bright patch of flowers. She is near enough for him to see clearly the casual slope of her arm that holds the schoolbooks against her hip. The long dark hair curls in bits about her ears and runs in corded plainness down her back. Soon he will be able to see her eyes, perfect black-eyed Susans. Flashing back fragmented bits of himself. Reflecting his mind.

Memories of years
Unknowable women—
sisters
spouses
illusions of soul

When he was a boy he had a sister called "Daughter." She was like honey, tawny, wild, and sweet. She was a generous girl and pretty, and he could not remember a time when he did not love her intensely, with his whole heart. She would give him anything she had, give anybody anything she had. She could not keep money, clothes, health. Nor did she seem to care for the love that came to her too easily. When he begged her not to go out, to stay with him, she laughed at him and went her way, sleeping here, sleeping there. Wherever she was needed, she would say, and laugh. But this could not go on forever; coming back from months with another woman's husband, her own mind seemed to have struck her down. He was struck down, too, and cried many nights on his bed; for she had chosen to give her love to the very man in whose cruel, hot, and lonely fields he, her brother, worked. Not treated as a man, scarcely as well as a poor man treats his beast.

Memories of years
Unknowable women—
sisters
spouses
illusions of soul

When she came back all of her long strong hair was gone, her teeth wobbled in her gums when she ate, and she recognized no one. All day and all night long she would sing and scream and tell them she was on fire. He was still a boy when she began playing up to him in her cunning way, exploiting again his love. And he, tears never showing on his face, would let her bat her lashless eyes at him and stroke his cheeks with her frail, clawlike hands. Tied on the bed as she was she was at the mercy of everyone in the house. They threw her betrayal at her like sharp stones, until they satisfied themselves that she could no longer feel their ostracism or her own pain. Gradually, as it became apparent she was not going to die, they took to flinging her food to her as if she were an animal and at night when she howled at the shadows thrown over her bed by the moon his father rose up and lashed her into silence with his belt.

On a day when she seemed nearly her old self she begged him to let her loose from the bed. He thought that if he set her free she would run away into the woods and never return. His love for her had turned into a dull ache of constant loathing, and he dreamed vague fearful dreams of a cruel revenge on the white lover who had shamed them all. But Daughter, climbing out of bed like a wary animal, knocked him unconscious to the floor and night found her impaled on one of the steel-spike fence posts near the house.

That she had given herself to the lord of his own bondage was what galled him! And that she was cut down so! He could not forgive her the love she gave that knew nothing of master and slave. For though her own wound was a bitter one and in the end fatal, he bore a hurt throughout his life that slowly poisoned him. In a world where innocence and guilt became further complicated by questions of color and race, he felt hesitant and weary of living as though all the world were out to trick him. His only guard against the deception he believed life had in store for him was a knowledge that evil and deception *would come* to him; and a readiness to provide them with a match.

The women in his life faced a sullen barrier of distrust and hateful mockery. He could not seem to help hating even the ones who loved him, and laughed loudest at the ones who cared for him, as if they were fools. His own wife, beaten into a cripple to prevent her from returning the imaginary overtures of the white landlord, killed herself while she was still young enough and strong enough to escape him. But she left a child, a girl, a daughter; a replica of Daughter, his dead sister. A replica in every way.

Memories of once
like a mirror reflecting—
all hope, all loss

His hands are not steady and he makes a clawing motion across the air in front of his face. She is walking, a vivid shape in blue and white, across the yard, underneath the cedar trees. She pauses at the low limb of the big magnolia and seems to contemplate the luminous gloss of the cone-shaped flowers beyond her reach. In the hand away from the gun is the open letter. He holds it tightly by a corner. The palms of his hands are sweating, his throat is dry. He swallows compulsively and rapidly bats his eyes. The slight weight of her foot sends vibrations across the gray boards of the porch. Her eyes flicker over him and rest on the open letter. Automatically his hand brings the letter upward a little although he finds he cannot yet, facing her strange familiar eyes, speak.

With passive curiosity the girl's eyes turn from the letter to the gun leaning against the banister to his face, which he feels growing blacker and tighter as if it is a mask that, when it is completely hardened, will drop off. Almost casually she sways back *against the porch post*, looking at him and from time to time looking over his head at the brilliant afternoon sky. Without wanting it his eyes travel heavily down the slight, roundly curved body and rest on her offerings to her lover in the letter. He is a black man but he blushes, the red underneath his skin glowing purple, and the coils of anger around his tongue begin to loosen.

"White man's slut!" he hisses at her through nearly sealed lips and clenched teeth.

Her body reacts as if hit by a strong wind and lightly she sways on her slender legs and props herself more firmly against the post. At first she gazes directly into his eyes as if there is nowhere else to look. Soon she drops her head.

She leads the way to the shed behind the house. She is still holding her books loosely against her thigh and he makes his eyes hard as they cover the small light tracks made in the dust. The brown of her skin is full of copper tints and her arms are like long golden fruits that take in and throw back the hues of the sinking sun. Relentlessly he hurries her steps through the sagging door of boards, with hardness he shoves her down into the dirt. She is like a young willow without roots under his hands and as she does not resist he beats her for a long time with a harness from the stable and where the buckles hit there is a welling of blood which comes to be level with the tawny skin then spills over and falls curling into the dust of the floor.

Stumbling weakly toward the house through the shadows of the trees, he tries to look up beseechingly to the stars, but the sky is full of clouds and rain beats down around his ears and drenches him by the time he reaches the back steps. The dogs run excitedly and hungry around the damp reaches of the back porch and although he feeds them not one will stand unmoving beneath his quickscratching fingers. Dully he watches them eat and listens to the high winds in the trees. Shuddering with chill he walks through the house to the front porch and picks up the gun that is getting wet and sits with it across his lap, rocking it back and forth on his knees like a baby.

It is rainsoaked, but he can make out "I love you" written in a firm hand across the blue face of the letter. He hates the very paper of the letter and crumples it in his fist. A wet storm wind lifts it lightly and holds it balled up against the taut silver screen on the side of the porch. He is glad when the wind abandons it and leaves it sodden and limp against the slick wet boards under his feet. He rests his neck heavily on the back of his chair. Words of the letter—her letter to the white devil who has disowned her to marry one of his own kind—are running on a track in his mind. "Jealousy is being nervous about something that has never, and probably won't ever, belong to you." A wet waning moon fills the sky before he nods.

3

No amount of churchgoing changed her ways. Prayers offered nothing to quench her inner thirst. Silent and lovely, but barren of essential hope if not of the ability to love, hers was a world of double images, as if constantly seen through tears. It was Christianity as it invaded her natural wonderings that threw color into high and fast relief, but its hard Southern rudeness fell flat outside her house, its agony of selfishness failed completely to pervade the deep subterranean country of her mind. When asked to abandon her simple way of looking at simple flowers, she could only yearn the more to touch those glowing points of bloom that lived and died away among the foliage over there, rising and falling like certain stars of which she was told, coming and being and going on again, always beyond her reach. Staring often and intently into the ivory hearts of fallen magnolia blossoms she sought the answer to the question that had never really been defined for her, although she was expected to know it, but she only learned from this that it is the fallen flower most earnestly hated, most easily bruised.

The lure of flower smells
The sun

In the morning, finding the world newly washed but the same, he rises from stiff-jointed sleep and wanders through the house looking at old photographs. In a frame of tarnish and gilt, her face forming out of the contours of a peach, the large dead eyes of beautiful Daughter, his first love. For the first time he turns it upside down then makes his way like a still sleeping man, wonderingly, through the house. At the back door he runs his fingers over the long blade of his pocket-knife and puts it, with gentleness and resignation, into his pocket. He knows that as one whose ultimate death must conform to an aged code of madness, resignation is a kind of dying. A preparation for the final event. He makes a step in the direction of the shed. His eyes hold the panicked calm of fishes taken out of water, whose bodies but not their eyes beat a frantic maneuver over dry land.

In the shed he finds her already awake and for a long time she lies as she was, her dark eyes reflecting the sky through the open door. When she looks at him it is not with hate, but neither is it passivity he reads in her face. Gone is the silent waiting of yesterday, and except for the blood she is strong looking and the damp black hair trailing loose along the dirt floor excites him and the terror she has felt in the night is nothing to what she reads now in his widestretched eyes.

He begs her hoarsely, when it clears for him that she is his daughter, and not Daughter, his first love, if she will deny the letter. Deny the letter; the paper eaten and the ink drunk, the words never wrung from the air. Her mouth curls into Daughter's own hilarity. She says quietly no. No, with simplicity, a shrug, finality. No. Her slow tortured rising is a strong advance and scarcely bothering to look at him, she reflects him silently, pitilessly with her black-pond eyes.

"Going," she says, as if already there, and his heart buckles. He can only strike her with his fist and send her sprawling once more into the dirt. She gazes up at him over her bruises and he sees her blouse, wet and slippery from the rain, has slipped completely off her shoulders and her high young breasts are bare. He gathers their fullness in his fingers and begins a slow twisting. The barking of the dogs creates a frenzy in his ears and he is suddenly burning with unnamable desire. In his agony he draws the girl away from him as one pulling off his own arm and with quick slashes of his knife leaves two bleeding craters the size of grapefruits on her bare bronze chest and flings what he finds in his hands to the yelping dogs.

Memories of once
constant and silent
like a mirror
reflecting

Today he is slumped in the same chair facing the road. The yellow school bus sends up clouds of red dust on its way. If he stirs it may be to Daughter shuffling lightly along the red dirt road, her dark hair down her back and her eyes looking intently at buttercups and stray black-eyed Susans along the way. If he stirs it may be he will see his own child, a black-eyed Susan from the soil on which she walks. A slight, pretty flower that grows on any ground; and flowers pledge no allegiance to banners of any man. If he stirs he might see the perfection of an ancient dream, his own nightmare; the answer to the question still whispered about, undefined. If he stirs he might feel the energetic whirling of wasps about his head and think of ripe late-summer days and time when scent makes a garden of the air. If he stirs he might wipe the dust from the dirt daubers out of his jellied eyes. If he stirs he might take up the heavy empty shotgun and rock it back and forth on his knees, like a baby.

1967

Ann Beattie
b. 1947

In some respects Ann Beattie's characters hearken back to America's old dream of success. Spiritual descendants of John Cheever's New England suburbanites, they epitomize the young, upwardly mobile professional class now emerging as a dominant force in American life. Yet, as one critic has noted, Beattie's characters are, "above all, hoping not to dissolve," for they are, "in every sense, between engagements, forever commuting between one another's homes and lives, both of which they enter and leave with casual frequency." Survivors of the turbulent 1960s, they continue to experiment with drugs, to sing old protest songs, and to engage in casual sex, even as they are engulfed by the apathy and disillusionment of the 1970s and 1980s. "I'm exhausted," one of them remarks, as if to summarize his life, "from sitting all day, drinking, and doing nothing." Possessing ties to several worlds yet fully belonging to none, they are never far from the chaos that Beattie regards as the subject of her fiction.

Beattie was born in Washington, D.C., in 1947. She received a B.A. from American University in 1969 and an M.A. the following year from the University of Connecticut, where she continued graduate studies for two more years. In 1978 she received a Guggenheim fellowship, and she has since been a visiting writer and lecturer at both Harvard and the University of Virginia. A prolific writer, she has published three novels—*Chilly Scenes of Winter* (1976), *Falling in Place* (1980), and *Love Always* (1985), the first of which was made into a movie in 1979—and four collections of short stories—*Distortions* (1976), *Secrets and Surprises* (1979), *The Burning House* (1984), from which "Jacklighting" is taken, and *Where You'll Find Me* (1986).

Many of Beattie's stories first appeared in *The New Yorker*, which has been a forum for such chroniclers of upper-middle-class life as J. D. Salinger, John Cheever, and John Updike, and in fact Beattie's work has been criticized for its faithfulness to the genre. Yet no one disputes her talent. Her uninflected prose style recalls Ernest Hemingway's in its flat, declarative sentences, but the almost bewildering detail and disjointed, oblique narrative are singularly suited to her purposes. "Many of the flat statements that I bring together," she says, "are usually non sequiturs or bordering on being non sequiturs—which reinforces the chaos." But, as John Updike has noted, Beattie's "resolutely unmetaphorical style" builds around us "a maze of familiar truths that nevertheless has something airy, eerie, and in the end lovely about it." Perhaps it is this that has moved another of her contemporaries to remark that she is beginning to sound less like a disaffected hippie and more like Chekhov.

Text:
The Burning House, 1982.

Jacklighting[1]

It is Nicholas's birthday. Last year he was alive, and we took him presents: a spiral notebook he pulled the pages out of, unable to write but liking the sound of paper tearing; magazines he flipped through, paying no attention to pictures, liking the blur of color. He had a radio, so we could not take a radio. More than the radio, he seemed to like the sound the metal drawer in his bedside table made, sliding open, clicking shut. He would open the drawer and look at the radio. He rarely took it out.

Nicholas's brother Spence has made jam. For days the cat has batted grapes around the huge homemade kitchen table; dozens of bloody rags of cheesecloth have been thrown into the trash. There is grape jelly, raspberry jelly, strawberry, quince, and lemon. Last month, a neighbor's pig escaped and ate Spence's newly planted fraise des bois plants, but overlooked the strawberry plants close to the house, heavy with berries. After that, Spence captured the pig and called his friend Andy, who came for it with his truck and took the pig to his farm in Warrenton. When Andy got home and looked in the back of the truck, he found three piglets curled against the pig.

In this part of Virginia, it is a hundred degrees in August. In June and July you can smell the ground, but in August it has been baked dry; instead of smelling the earth you smell flowers, hot breeze. There is a haze over the Blue Ridge Mountains that stays in the air like cigarette smoke. It is the same color as the eye shadow Spence's girlfriend, Pammy, wears. The rest of us are sunburned, with pink mosquito bites on our bodies, small scratches from gathering raspberries. Pammy has just arrived from Washington. She is winter-pale. Since she is ten years younger than the rest of us, a few scratches wouldn't make her look as if she belonged, anyway. She is in medical school at Georgetown, and her summer-school classes have just ended. She arrived with leather sandals that squeak. She is exhausted and sleeps half the day, upstairs, with the fan blowing on her. All weekend the big fan has blown on Spence, in the kitchen, boiling and bottling his jams and jellies. The small fan blows on Pammy.

Wynn and I have come from New York. Every year we borrow his mother's car and drive from Hoboken to Virginia. We used to take the trip to spend the week of Nicholas's birthday with him. Now we come to see Spence, who lives alone in the house. He is making jam early, so we can take jars back with us. He stays in the

[1] The practice of stunning game animals, usually deer, by shining a focused light in their eyes. Hunting by this method is illegal in most states.

kitchen because he is depressed and does not really want to talk to us. He scolds the cat, curses when something goes wrong.

Wynn is in love. The girl he loves is twenty, or twenty-one. Twenty-two. When he told me (top down on the car, talking into the wind), I couldn't understand half of what he was saying. There were enough facts to daze me; she had a name, she was one of his students, she had canceled her trip to Rome this summer. The day he told me about her, he brought it up twice; first in the car, later in Spence's kitchen. "That was *not* my mother calling the other night to say she got the car tuned," Wynn said, smashing his glass on the kitchen counter. I lifted his hand off the large shard of glass, touching his fingers as gently as I'd touch a cactus. When I steadied myself on the counter, a chip of glass nicked my thumb. The pain shot through my body and pulsed in my ribs. Wynn examined my hands; I examined his. A dust of fine glass coated our hands, gently touching, late at night, as we looked out the window at the moon shining on Spence's lemon tree with its one lemon, too heavy to be growing on the slender branch. A jar of Lipton iced tea was next to the tub the lemon tree grew out of—a joke, put there by Wynn, to encourage it to bear more fruit.

Wynn is standing in the field across from the house, pacing, head down, the bored little boy grown up.

"When wasn't he foolish?" Spence says, walking through the living room. "What kind of sense does it make to turn against him now for being a fool?"

"He calls it mid-life crisis, Spence, and he's going to be thirty-two in September."

"I know when his birthday is. You hint like this every year. Last year at the end of August you dropped it into conversation that the two of you were doing something or other to celebrate *his birthday*."

"We went to one of those places where a machine shoots baseballs at you. His birthday present was ten dollars' worth of balls pitched at him. I gave him a Red Sox cap. He lost it the same day."

"How did he lose it?"

"We came out of a restaurant and a Doberman was tied by its leash to a stop sign, barking like mad—a very menacing dog. He tossed the cap, and it landed on the dog's head. It was funny until he wanted to get it back, and he couldn't go near it."

"He's one in a million. He deserves to have his birthday remembered. Call me later in the month and remind me." Spence goes to the foot of the stairs. "Pammy," he calls.

"Come up and kill something for me," she says. The bed creaks. "Come kill a wasp on the bedpost. I hate to kill them. I hate the way they crunch."

He walks back to the living room and gets a newspaper and rolls it into a tight tube, slaps it against the palm of his hand.

Wynn, in the field, is swinging a broken branch, batting hickory nuts and squinting into the sun.

Nicholas lived for almost a year, brain-damaged, before he died. Even before the accident, he liked the way things felt. He always watched shadows. He was the man looking to the side in Cartier-Bresson's[2] photograph, instead of putting his eye to the

[2] Henri Cartier-Bresson (1908–1983), renowned French photographer.

wall. He'd find pennies on the sidewalk when the rest of us walked down city streets obliviously, spot the chipped finger on a mannequin flawlessly dressed, sidestep the one piece of glass among shells scattered on the shoreline. It would really have taken something powerful to do him in. So that's what happened: a drunk in a van, speeding, head-on, Nicholas out for a midnight ride without his helmet. Earlier in the day he'd assembled a crazy nest of treasures in the helmet, when he was babysitting the neighbors' four-year-old daughter. Spence showed it to us—holding it forward as carefully as you'd hold a bomb, looking away the way you'd avoid looking at dead fish floating in a once nice aquarium, the way you'd look at an ugly scar, once the bandages had been removed, and want to lay the gauze back over it. While he was in the hospital, his fish tank overheated and all the black mollies died. The doctor unwound some of the bandages and the long brown curls had been shaved away, and there was a red scar down the side of his head that seemed as out of place as a line dividing a highway out west, a highway that nobody traveled anyway. It could have happened to any of us. We'd all ridden on the Harley, bodies pressed into his back, hair whipped across our faces. How were we going to feel ourselves again, without Nicholas? In the hospital, it was clear that the thin intravenous tube was not dripping life back into him—that was as farfetched as the idea that the too-thin branch of the lemon tree could grow one more piece of fruit. In the helmet had been dried chrysanthemums, half of a robin's blue shell, a cat's eye marble, yellow twine, a sprig of grapes, a piece of a broken ruler. I remember Wynn actually jumping back when he saw what was inside. I stared at the strangeness such ordinary things had taken on. Wynn had been against his teaching me to ride his bike, but he had. He taught me to trust myself and not to settle for seeing things the same way. The lobster claw on a necklace he made me was funny and beautiful. I never felt the same way about lobsters or jewelry after that. "Psychologists have figured out that infants start to laugh when they've learned to be skeptical of danger," Nicholas had said. Laughing on the back of his motorcycle. When he lowered the necklace over my head, rearranging it, fingers on my throat.

It is Nicholas's birthday, and so far no one has mentioned it. Spence has made all the jam he can make from the fruit and berries and has gone to the store and returned with bags of flour to make bread. He brought the *Daily Progress* to Pammy, and she is reading it, on the side porch where there is no screening, drying her hair and stiffening when bees fly away from the Rose of Sharon bushes. Her new sandals are at the side of the chair. She has red toenails. She rubs the small pimples on her chin the way men finger their beards. I sit on the porch with her, catcher's mitt on my lap, waiting for Wynn to get back from his walk so we can take turns pitching to each other.

"Did he tell you I was a drug addict? Is that why you hardly speak to me?" Pammy says. She is squinting at her toes. "I'm older than I look," she says. "He says I'm twenty-one, because I look so young. He doesn't know when to let go of a joke, though. I don't like to be introduced to people as some child prodigy."

"What were you addicted to?" I say.

"Speed," she says. "I had another life." She has brought the bottle of polish with her, and begins brushing on a new layer of red, the fingers of her other hand stuck between her toes from underneath, separating them. "I don't get the feeling you people had another life," she says. "After all these years, I still feel funny when I'm around people who've never lived the way I have. It's just snobbishness, I'm sure."

I cup the catcher's mitt over my knee. A bee has landed on the mitt. This is the most Pammy has talked. Now she interests me; I always like people who have gone through radical changes. It's snobbishness—it shows me that other people are confused, too.

"That was the summer of sixty-seven," she says. "I slept with a stockbroker for money. Sat through a lot of horror movies. That whole period's a blur. What I remember about it is being underground all the time, going places on the subway. I only had one real friend in the city. I can't remember where I was going." Pammy looks at the newspaper beside her chair. "Charlottesville, Virginia," she says. "My, my. Who would have thought twitchy little Pammy would end up here?"

Spence tosses the ball. I jump, mitt high above my head, and catch it. Spence throws again. Catch. Again. A hard pitch that lets me know the palm of my hand will be numb when I take off the catcher's mitt. Spence winds up. Pitches. As I'm leaning to get the ball, another ball sails by on my right. Spence has hidden a ball in his pocket all this time. Like his brother, he's always trying to make me smile.

"It's too hot to play ball," he says. "I can't spend the whole day trying to distract you because Wynn stalked off into the woods today."

"Come on," I say. "It was working."

"Why don't we all go to Virginia Beach next year instead of standing around down here smoldering? This isn't any tribute to my brother. How did this get started?"

"We came to be with you because we thought it would be hard. You didn't tell us about Pammy."

"Isn't that something? What that tells you is that you matter, and Wynn matters, and Nicholas mattered, but I don't even think to mention the person who's supposedly my lover."

"She said she had been an addict."

"She probably tried to tell you she wasn't twenty-one, too, didn't she?"

I sidestep a strawberry plant, notice one croquet post stuck in the field.

"It was a lie?" I say.

"No," he says. "I never know when to let my jokes die."

When Nicholas was alive, we'd celebrate his birthday with mint juleps and croquet games, stuffing ourselves with cake, going for midnight skinny-dips. Even if he were alive, I wonder if today would be anything like those birthdays of the past, or whether we'd have bogged down so hopelessly that even his childish enthusiasm would have had little effect. Wynn is sure that he's having a crisis and that it's not the real thing with his student because he also has a crush on Pammy. We are open about everything: he tells me about taking long walks and thinking about nothing but sex; Spence bakes the French bread too long, finds that he's lightly tapping a rock, sits on the kitchen counter, puts his hands over his face, and cries. Pammy says that she does not feel close to any of us—that Virginia was just a place to come to cool out. She isn't sure she wants to go on with medical school. I get depressed and think that if the birds could talk, they'd say that they didn't enjoy flying. The mountains have disappeared in the summer haze.

Late at night, alone on the porch, toasting Nicholas with a glass of wine, I remember that when I was younger, I assumed he'd be our guide: he saw us through acid trips, planned our vacations, he was always there to excite us and to give us advice. He started a game that went on for years. He had us close our eyes after we'd stared at something and made us envision it again. We had to describe it with our eyes closed. Wynn and Spence could talk about the things and make them more vivid than they were in life. They remembered well. When I closed my eyes, I squinted until the thing was lost to me. It kept going backwards into darkness.

Tonight, Nicholas's birthday, it is dark and late and I have been trying to pay him some sort of tribute by seeing something and closing my eyes and imagining it. Besides realizing that two glasses of wine can make me drunk, I have had this revelation: that you can look at something, close your eyes and see it again and still know nothing —like staring at the sky to figure out the distances between stars.

The drunk in the van that hit Nicholas thought that he had hit a deer.

Tonight, stars shine over the field with the intensity of flashlights. Every year, Spence calls the state police to report that on his property, people are jacklighting.

1980

David Mamet
b. 1947

David Mamet's view of his craft is starkly simple: "I don't have any theories about how to write plays," he asserts in an interview. "That's something you can't possibly learn from reading a book of plays. You do it by doing it. You can sort of be guided in the pursuit of this knowledge by what other people have done, and by what you see happening on the stage, but you have to teach yourself." Mamet's self-education combined studying at Goddard College in Vermont and working at the Neighborhood Playhouse in New York with taking on odd jobs for money—in a canning plant, a truck factory, and a real estate agency ("one of those offices on the way to the airport," as he describes it). He has also driven a taxi, washed windows, waited on tables at a gay bar, and written captions for *Oui* magazine ("I got paid for sitting all day looking at pictures of naked women and making up lies about them").

Born and raised in Chicago, Mamet managed to coordinate acting in community theaters and working backstage at the Hull House Theater with graduating from the prestigious Francis Parker School. After earning a degree at Goddard College in 1969, he taught at Marlboro College in Vermont and then returned to his alma mater as artist-in-residence. While at Goddard, he helped form a group of actors that became the St. Nicholas Theater Company, which moved to Chicago in 1974 with Mamet as artistic director. In 1976 and 1977 he worked at the Yale Drama School under the auspices of a CBS creative writing fellowship and produced two new plays, *Dark Pony* and *Reunion,* to favorable reviews. In 1978 he was named associate artistic director and playwright in residence at Chicago's Goodman Theater, for which he wrote several plays. In the same year he was appointed special lecturer at the University of Chicago. "I'm a pedagogue by nature," he reports. "My wife [the actress Lindsay Crouse] says I can't burp without quoting Aristotle. Teaching is what I'm best at." Most recently, students at New York University have had the benefit of his irreverent views of his craft and the state of the American theater.

David Mamet is one of contemporary America's most prolific and honored playwrights. His works include two celebrated one-act comedies, *Duck Variations* (1973) and *Sexual Perversity in Chicago* (1974), the second of which won the *Village Voice* Obie award for distinguished playwrighting. In *Sexual Perversity in Chicago* we observe two young men engaged in a search for women; in *Duck Variations* we listen to two old men commiserating over their inability to do anything but talk. In 1977 Mamet premiered *American Buffalo,* which won the New York Drama Critics' Award as best American play. In 1978 Mamet won the John Gassner Award for his distinguished contributions to the theater. Four years later he received a second Obie for a play called *Edmond,* which traces the fate of a middle-class New Yorker who abandons his family and enters the city's underworld. *Glengarry Glen Ross* (1983), Mamet's best-known play, deals with the sordidly deceptive world of real estate hustlers. Named best play of the year by the Society of West End Theatres in London, *Glengarry Glen Ross* was nominated for four TONY awards and won the Pulitzer Prize in drama. Mamet has also written the screenplay for *The Postman Always Rings Twice* (1980) and *The Verdict* (1982), for which he was nominated for an Academy Award. In 1982 he began writing a third screenplay, on the life of Malcolm X.

Mamet's plays address quintessential American concerns. Most recently, his interest has centered on the personal costs of doing business in "a nation of entrepreneurs." In *The Vermont Sketches,* four of which were performed in 1984, he presents the underbelly of that world, the debased values and vulgar lives of small-time entrepreneurs as they struggle to survive against the threat of being eliminated by or made subservient to the corporations and franchises of America. Above all, it is Mamet's ability to capture the poignant, obscene, and humorous thoughts of his characters in colloquial cadences that distinguishes his work. "What the characters say to each other," he asserts, "must contain and give birth to what they do to each other." When asked to comment on the American theater, Mamet sardonically notes that there are grown men and women trying "to bring a tradition back. . . . This stuff is not chopped liver."

Text:
The Vermont Sketches, 1986.

---

from The Vermont Sketches

Pint's a Pound the World Around

A: . . . don't have the twelve-inch. We have the ten-inch and the fourteen-inch.
B: Isn't that always the way?
A: Seems it is. A number two do?

B: No.

A: Alright. The guy should have been in *Tuesday,* I spect him *Friday,* if he don't come then . . . I'll tell you, I've been thinking of switching. 'Merican *United,* I can get twenty percent over a year, you sign on to their Ownership Subscriber Plan, you get a basis of twenty percent, you want something it's *there.* The next day. Six days.

B: Where they out of?

A: Down in Manchester. *Basis* of twenty percent, they've got a *newspaper,* what do you call it, a *flyer,* the *specials,* they can go, sometimes they beat the Marketway sixty percent.

B: No.

A: Absolutely.

B: How's the quality?

A: Same, better. Most things better, much of . . . what they *do. You* know, they've got their *brand* . . .

B: Uh-huh . . .

A: Good stuff. Heavy gauge stuff. Some of . . . *you* know their stuff . . .

B: . . . sure . . .

A: . . . same patterns eighteen ninety-eight . . .

B: When's that, when they got started?

A: When they got started. Yes. Fellow name of . . . I had the guy in here, I was looking at their stuff since I came in. You have to sign *up,* what you do, you buy stock in the *company,* the minimum buy-in thirty-two hundred dollars, you own *stock,* at the end of the year they go and pro*rate* you the amount of your sales, and you're discounted based on that.

B: And what do you do with the discount?

A: What do you do?

B: What, do you apply it to your . . .

A: Well, I guess you do. I never thought of it. I suppose that you . . . or you could take it in cash. I had the guy here just the other day.

B: They want you to sign up.

A: The closest, *Jims,* in *Brandenburgs* American . . .

B: He is . . . ?

A: Oh yeah. You see his prices in there? Beat the *Marketway* fifteen percent *easily.* On *everything.* He *has* to . . .

B: They spend their money on advertising.

A: That's what I'm *saying.* It ain't going in the *stock,* in stock improvement . . . dealer *relations* . . . it's going in the *television* ads. Schiff, started eighteen ninety-eight. American United, the whole operation's built on one thing: the relation with the *dealer.*

B: Mm.

A: Stockholders are the dealer, *customers* the dealer. Everything. Geared toward one man. I pick up the phone, I say, "Where are the . . . *whatever,* he said that they'd be here on *Thursday."* Marketway, what do *they* care . . . ? No *displays,* very few *incentives* . . . like I'm buying *retail* from them. You complain to someone, their attitude, basically, I think, I don't think they do it on *purpose,* but what you get is: if you don't want the franchise, you can turn back. They don't care. What they think, they're doing you a *favor,* all the money they've spent on the TV ads. Some stores, maybe, though I doubt it. Not in *here*. A fella comes in here he wants three of those, four of those, something he broke on a job, he wants it this afternoon: *I'm* built on *service*. He goes down the road, he can go to the *Star* supply in *Worth*, he's in the habit to come here, I want to *keep* him here. Two things they told me: Never change your hours, never cut your stock.

B: Uh-huh.

A: A fellow comes by some hour you're spose to be open and you're *closed*, next time he thinks heavily fore he drives out of his way. "Maybe he's closed . . ."

B: That's very true.

A: . . . it makes no difference it only happened one time. It's like adultery. I'm not foolin you. He thinks, "It happened once, it could happen again."

B: Uh-huh.

A: Fellow comes in here something he needs on a job, he needs it this afternoon, I'm *out* of it, what does he think? *"Shit,* I could of drove the same distance to *Star* and had it, and probably *cheaper* . . ." Something else: If I can get with the *American* I'm going to beat Marketway, I'm going to beat *Star*. I'm going to have them coming *here* from Worth . . .

B: You think?

A: There's no two ways about it. I'll have the stock, I'll have the variety, I'll have *quality*. . . . They marshall their *franchises very* careful. Forty-two miles to Brandenburgs, the closest they could have another is here. I've got no competition. I'll have them coming in from Worth, from *Peacham* . . .

B: And it's just the down payment . . .

A: What it is, yes, it's a down payment, it's an *investment*, you're actually buying stock. Whatever it is, I looked it up a week ago, a couple of weeks ago, seventeen dollars a share. What is that? Two into thirty-five, two shares for thirty-five, two hundred shares, thirty-five hundred dollars. Which you earn the dividend on, too, whatever that is . . .

B: On the stock.

A: Yes.

B: You should go with them.

A: I *would*. I *would* and I think I will. I think June and I have almost decided to *go* with them. It's a big step, but I think it's worth it. That's what I think. Many things. You have to look down the road. It's a big step now, it's a big *investment*, it's a *commitment*, in certain ways it would mean taking on more stock. . . .

B: Why is that?

A: Well, you have a basic *order*. Whatever your *size* is: the classification that they give you . . . on your *footage* . . . on your *overhead* . . . then when you order you have a minimum order that you have to file. *(Pause)* You also have a minimum order per *month* . . . they come in and they do the inventory . . .

B: *They* do.

A: Yep. They do. At the end of the year . . . I think that that's a good idea. They come in, a team, ten people, something, calculators, they're out in an afternoon, they come in Sunday afternoon . . . whenever you're closed, they work through the night, they're out Monday morning. *That's* a good idea . . . you ever do an inventory?

B: No.

A: Hell on Earth. I worked in a shoestore once. I thought I was going to go mad . . . But it's a big step. *(Pause)*

B: Mm.

A: *(Pause)* It's a big step. *(Pause)*

B: Well—

A: Yeaaah! Five of the number three. Twelve-inch. I'm almost sure I'll have them Friday.

B: I'll be back.

A: I'm going to call him again today. I would say ninety percent. Ninety-five percent. I'll have them Friday. I'll tell you: If he *doesn't* come in, I'm going to be down in Worth, Friday night, if he *doesn't* come in, I'll pick them up, you stop in Saturday morning . . .

B: That's okay . . .

A: No. I should *have* 'em. No trouble at all. You come in Friday, he hasn't stopped in, I'll have 'em Saturday first thing.

B: That's alright.

A: No trouble at all. I'm sorry I don't *have* 'em. I *should*. It doesn't help *you* to tell you that the *man* didn't come in.

B: Well, *thank* you.

A: That's alright. You take care, now.

B: You, too.

A: It's nice talking to you.

1981–1983/1986

Leslie Marmon Silko
b. 1948

On Tuesday, May 19, 1981, the *New York Times* announced that the MacArthur Foundation had selected twenty-one "exceptionally talented individuals" to receive five-year awards of support. Among these twenty-one American "geniuses" were two writers—Robert Penn Warren, born in Guthrie, Kentucky, in 1905, and Leslie Marmon Silko, born in Albuquerque, New Mexico, in 1948. Of mixed ancestry—part Pueblo Indian, part Mexican, and part white—Silko is today considered one of the best American writers of her generation.

Reared on the Laguna Pueblo, Silko says that her "earliest memories are of my grandmother telling me stories while she watered the morning-glories in her yard. Her stories were about incidents from long ago," Silko continues, "incidents which occurred before she was born but which she told as certainly as if she had been there." Like "Storyteller," included here, all of Silko's finest fiction "captures the essence of the oral tradition." On one side, it possesses an aura of certainty and authenticity: "I will not change the story," says the narrator of "Storyteller." On the other, it possesses a sense of indefiniteness and ambiguity: knowledge has been lost, the narrator's grandmother says; "otherwise I could tell you more."

Silko has written two books, a novel called *Ceremony* (1978) and a montage of stories, legends, poems, and photographs called *Storyteller* (1981). Also a screenwriter, Silko is the author of the screenplay for Marlon Brando's film *Black Elks*. In addition, her work has appeared in such anthologies as *The Man to Send Rain Clouds, Best Short Stories of 1975,* and *200 Years of Great American Short Stories* as well as in numerous magazines and journals. Besides writing, Silko teaches English at her alma mater, the University of New Mexico, and has been writer in residence at Vassar College.

Silko's numerous, powerful readings have created an enthusiastic audience for her work on many college campuses. From her Pueblo Indian heritage Silko derives many of the concerns that are apparent in *Ceremony* and *Storyteller,* especially concern for injustice, violence, and despair as forces that shape contemporary Indian life. Like Scott Momaday, who has praised her work, Silko explores both the rich heritage of Native Americans and their tragic loss of identity as they find themselves trapped between a culture that no longer exists and a culture that for them is not yet fully available. Also like Momaday, Silko possesses an affinity with "moments of considerable beauty and intensity, moments in which, according to the central tenet of storytelling, language is celebrated." As a result, her chronicle is a celebration as much as it is a lament: To tell the story "the way it must be told, year after year . . . , without lapse or silence" is a victory that Silko—like her ancestors and her characters—creates from defeat.

Text:
Storyteller, 1981.

Storyteller

Every day the sun came up a little lower on the horizon, moving more slowly until one day she got excited and started calling the jailer. She realized she had been sitting there for many hours, yet the sun had not moved from the center of the sky. The color of the sky had not been good lately; it had been pale blue, almost white, even when there were no clouds. She told herself it wasn't a good sign for the sky to be indistinguishable from the river ice, frozen solid and white against the earth. The tundra rose up behind the river but all the boundaries between the river and hills and sky were lost in the density of the pale ice.

She yelled again, this time some English words which came randomly into her mouth, probably swear words she'd heard from the oil drilling crews last winter. The jailer was an Eskimo, but he would not speak Yupik[1] to her. She had watched people in other cells, when they spoke to him in Yupik he ignored them until they spoke English.

He came and stared at her. She didn't know if he understood what she was telling him until he glanced behind her at the small high window. He looked at the sun, and turned and walked away. She could hear the buckles on his heavy snowmobile boots jingle as he walked to the front of the building.

It was like the other buildings that white people, the Gussucks,[2] brought with them: BIA[3] and school buildings, portable buildings that arrived sliced in halves, on barges coming up the river. Squares of metal panelling bulged out with the layers of insulation stuffed inside. She had asked once what it was and someone told her it was to keep out the cold. She had not laughed then, but she did now. She walked over to the small double-pane window and she laughed out loud. They thought they could keep out the cold with stringy yellow wadding. Look at the sun. It wasn't moving; it was frozen, caught in the middle of the sky. Look at the sky, solid as the river with ice which had trapped the sun. It had not moved for a long time; in a few more hours it would be weak, and heavy frost would begin to appear on the edges and spread across the face of the sun like a mask. Its light was pale yellow, worn thin by the winter.

She could see people walking down the snow-packed roads, their breath steaming out from their parka hoods, faces hidden and protected by deep ruffs of fur. There were no cars or snowmobiles that day; the cold had silenced their machines. The metal froze; it split and shattered. Oil hardened and moving parts jammed solidly. She had seen it happen to their big yellow machines and the giant drill last winter when they came to drill their test holes. The cold stopped them, and they were helpless against it.

Her village was many miles upriver from this town, but in her mind she could see it clearly. Their house was not near the village houses. It stood alone on the bank upriver from the village. Snow had drifted to the eaves of the roof on the north side, but on the west side, by the door, the path was almost clear. She had nailed scraps of red tin over the logs last summer. She had done it for the bright red color, not for added warmth the way the village people had done. This final winter had been coming even then; there had been signs of its approach for many years.

She went because she was curious about the big school where the Government sent all the other girls and boys. She had not played much with the village children while she was growing up because they were afraid of the old man, and they ran when her grandmother came. She went because she was tired of being alone with the old woman whose body had been stiffening for as long as the girl could remember. Her knees and knuckles were swollen grotesquely, and the pain had squeezed the brown skin of her face tight against the bones; it left her eyes hard like river stone. The girl asked once what it was that did this to her body, and the old woman had raised up from sewing a sealskin boot, and stared at her.

---

[1] Eskimo-Aleut language spoken across arctic America from western Alaska to Greenland.
[2] Presumably the Yupik term for "white people."
[3] Bureau of Indian Affairs.

"The joints," the old woman said in a low voice, whispering like wind across the roof, "the joints are swollen with anger."

Sometimes she did not answer and only stared at the girl. Each year she spoke less and less, but the old man talked more—all night sometimes, not to anyone but himself; in a soft deliberate voice, he told stories, moving his smooth brown hands above the blankets. He had not fished or hunted with the other men for many years, although he was not crippled or sick. He stayed in his bed, smelling like dry fish and urine, telling stories all winter; and when warm weather came, he went to his place on the river bank. He sat with a long willow stick, poking at the smoldering moss he burned against the insects while he continued with the stories.

The trouble was that she had not recognized the warnings in time. She did not see what the Gussuck school would do to her until she walked into the dormitory and realized that the old man had not been lying about the place. She thought he had been trying to scare her as he used to when she was very small and her grandmother was outside cutting up fish. She hadn't believed what he told her about the school because she knew he wanted to keep her there in the log house with him. She knew what he wanted.

The dormitory matron pulled down her underpants and whipped her with a leather belt because she refused to speak English.

"Those backwards village people," the matron said, because she was an Eskimo who had worked for the BIA a long time, "they kept this one until she was too big to learn." The other girls whispered in English. They knew how to work the showers, and they washed and curled their hair at night. They ate Gussuck food. She lay on her bed and imagined what her grandmother might be sewing, and what the old man was eating in his bed. When summer came, they sent her home.

The way her grandmother had hugged her before she left for school had been a warning too, because the old woman had not hugged or touched her for many years. Not like the old man, whose hands were always hunting, like ravens circling lazily in the sky, ready to touch her. She was not surprised when the priest and the old man met her at the landing strip, to say that the old lady was gone. The priest asked her where she would like to stay. He referred to the old man as her grandfather, but she did not bother to correct him. She had already been thinking about it; if she went with the priest, he would send her away to a school. But the old man was different. She knew he wouldn't send her back to school. She knew he wanted to keep her.

He told her one time, that she would get too old for him faster than he got too old for her; but again she had not believed him because sometimes he lied. He had lied about what he would do with her if she came into his bed. But as the years passed, she realized what he said was true. She was restless and strong. She had no patience with the old man who had never changed his slow smooth motions under the blankets.

The old man was in his bed for the winter; he did not leave it except to use the slop bucket in the corner. He was dozing with his mouth open slightly; his lips quivered and sometimes they moved like he was telling a story even while he dreamed. She pulled on the sealskin boots, the mukluks with the bright red flannel linings her grandmother had sewn for her, and she tied the braided red yarn tassels around her ankles over the gray wool pants. She zipped the wolfskin parka. Her grandmother had worn it for many years, but the old man said that before she died, she instructed him to bury her in an old black sweater, and to give the parka to the girl. The wolf pelts were creamy colored and silver, almost white in some places, and when the old lady had walked across the tundra in the winter, she was invisible in the snow.

She walked toward the village, breaking her own path through the deep snow. A team of sled dogs tied outside a house at the edge of the village leaped against their chains to bark at her. She kept walking, watching the dusky sky for the first evening stars. It was warm and the dogs were alert. When it got cold again, the dogs would lie curled and still, too drowsy from the cold to bark or pull at the chains. She laughed loudly because it made them howl and snarl. Once the old man had seen her tease the dogs and he shook his head. "So that's the kind of woman you are," he said, "in the wintertime the two of us are no different from those dogs. We wait in the cold for someone to bring us a few dry fish."

She laughed out loud again, and kept walking. She was thinking about the Gussuck oil drillers. They were strange; they watched her when she walked near their machines. She wondered what they looked like underneath their quilted goose-down trousers; she wanted to know how they moved. They would be something different from the old man.

The old man screamed at her. He shook her shoulders so violently that her head bumped against the log wall. "I smelled it!" he yelled, "as soon as I woke up! I am sure of it now. You can't fool me!" His thin legs were shaking inside the baggy wool trousers; he stumbled over her boots in his bare feet. His toenails were long and yellow like bird claws; she had seen a gray crane last summer fighting another in the shallow water on the edge of the river. She laughed out loud and pulled her shoulder out of his grip. He stood in front of her. He was breathing hard and shaking; he looked weak. He would probably die next winter.

"I'm warning you," he said, "I'm warning you." He crawled back into his bunk then, and reached under the old soiled feather pillow for a piece of dry fish. He lay back on the pillow, staring at the ceiling and chewed dry strips of salmon. "I don't know what the old woman told you," he said, "but there will be trouble." He looked over to see if she was listening. His face suddenly relaxed into a smile, his dark slanty eyes were lost in wrinkles of brown skin. "I could tell you, but you are too good for warnings now. I can smell what you did all night with the Gussucks."

She did not understand why they came there, because the village was small and so far upriver that even some Eskimos who had been away to school did not want to come back. They stayed downriver in the town. They said the village was too quiet. They were used to the town where the boarding school was located, with electric lights and running water. After all those years away at school, they had forgotten how to set nets in the river and where to hunt seals in the fall. When she asked the old man why the Gussucks bothered to come to the village, his narrow eyes got bright with excitement.

"They only come when there is something to steal. The fur animals are too difficult for them to get now, and the seals and fish are hard to find. Now they come for oil deep in the earth. But this is the last time for them." His breathing was wheezy and fast; his hands gestured at the sky. "It is approaching. As it comes, ice will push across the sky." His eyes were open wide and he stared at the low ceiling rafters for hours without blinking. She remembered all this clearly because he began the story that day, the story he told from that time on. It began with a giant bear which he described muscle by muscle, from the curve of the ivory claws to the whorls of hair at the top of the massive skull. And for eight days he did not sleep, but talked continuously of the giant bear whose color was pale blue glacier ice.

The snow was dirty and worn down in a path to the door. On either side of the path, the snow was higher than her head. In front of the door there were jagged yellow stains melted into the snow where men had urinated. She stopped in the entry way and kicked the snow off her boots. The room was dim; a kerosene lantern by the cash register was burning low. The long wooden shelves were jammed with cans of beans and potted meats. On the bottom shelf a jar of mayonnaise was broken open, leaking oily white clots on the floor. There was no one in the room except the yellowish dog sleeping in the front of the long glass display case. A reflection made it appear to be lying on the knives and ammunition inside the case. Gussucks kept dogs inside their houses with them; they did not seem to mind the odors which seeped out of the dogs. "They tell us we are dirty for the food we eat—raw fish and fermented meat. But we do not live with dogs," the old man once said. She heard voices in the back room, and the sound of bottles set down hard on tables.

They were always confident. The first year they waited for the ice to break up on the river, and then they brought their big yellow machines up river on barges. They planned to drill their test holes during the summer to avoid the freezing. But the imprints and graves of their machines were still there, on the edge of the tundra above the river, where the summer mud had swallowed them before they ever left sight of the river. The village people had gathered to watch the white men, and to laugh as they drove the giant machines, one by one, off the steel ramp into the bogs; as if sheer numbers of vehicles would somehow make the tundra solid. But the old man said they behaved like desperate people, and they would come back again. When the tundra was frozen solid, they returned.

Village women did not even look through the door to the back room. The priest had warned them. The storeman was watching her because he didn't let Eskimos or Indians sit down at the tables in the back room. But she knew he couldn't throw her out if one of his Gussuck customers invited her to sit with him. She walked across the room. They stared at her, but she had the feeling she was walking for someone else, not herself, so their eyes did not matter. The red-haired man pulled out a chair and motioned for her to sit down. She looked back at the storeman while the red-haired man poured her a glass of red sweet wine. She wanted to laugh at the storeman the way she laughed at the dogs, straining against the chains, howling at her.

The red-haired man kept talking to the other Gussucks sitting around the table, but he slid one hand off the top of the table to her thigh. She looked over at the storeman to see if he was still watching her. She laughed out loud at him and the red-haired man stopped talking and turned to her. He asked if she wanted to go. She nodded and stood up.

Someone in the village had been telling him things about her, he said as they walked down the road to his trailer. She understood that much of what he was saying, but the rest she did not hear. The whine of the big generators at the construction camp sucked away the sound of his words. But English was of no concern to her anymore, and neither was anything the Christians in the village might say about her or the old man. She smiled at the effect of the subzero air on the electric lights around the trailers; they did not shine. They left only flat yellow holes in the darkness.

It took him a long time to get ready, even after she had undressed for him. She waited in the bed with the blankets pulled close, watching him. He adjusted the thermostat and lit candles in the room, turning out the electric lights. He searched through a stack of record albums until he found the right one. She was not sure about the last thing he did: he taped something on the wall behind the bed where he could see it while he lay on top of her. He was shriveled and white from the cold; he pushed against her body for warmth. He guided her hands to his thighs; he was shivering.

She had returned a last time because she wanted to know what it was he stuck on the wall above the bed. After he finished each time, he reached up and pulled it loose, folding it carefully so that she could not see it. But this time she was ready; she waited for his fast breathing and sudden collapse on top of her. She slid out from under him and stood up beside the bed. She looked at the picture while she got dressed. He did not raise his face from the pillow, and she thought she heard teeth rattling together as she left the room.

She heard the old man move when she came in. After the Gussuck's trailer, the log house felt cool. It smelled like dry fish and cured meat. The room was dark except for the blinking yellow flame in the mica window of the oil stove. She squatted in front of the stove and watched the flames for a long time before she walked to the bed where her grandmother had slept. The bed was covered with a mound of rags and fur scraps the old woman had saved. She reached into the mound until she felt something cold and solid wrapped in a wool blanket. She pushed her fingers around it until she felt smooth stone. Long ago, before the Gussucks came, they had burned whale oil in the big stone lamp which made light and heat as well. The old woman had saved everything they would need when the time came.

In the morning, the old man pulled a piece of dry caribou meat from under the blankets and offered it to her. While she was gone, men from the village had brought a bundle of dry meat. She chewed it slowly, thinking about the way they still came from the village to take care of the old man and his stories. But she had a story now, about the red-haired Gussuck. The old man knew what she was thinking, and his smile made his face seem more round than it was.

"Well," he said, "what was it?"

"A woman with a big dog on top of her."

He laughed softly to himself and walked over to the water barrel. He dipped the tin cup into the water.

"It doesn't surprise me," he said.

"Grandma," she said, "there was something red in the grass that morning. I remember." She had not asked about her parents before. The old woman stopped splitting the fish bellies open for the willow drying racks. Her jaw muscles pulled so tightly against her skull, the girl thought the old woman would not be able to speak.

"They bought a tin can full of it from the storeman. Late at night. He told them it was alcohol safe to drink. They traded a rifle for it." The old woman's voice sounded like each word stole strength from her. "It made no difference about the rifle. That year the Gussuck boats had come, firing big guns at the walrus and seals. There was nothing left to hunt after that anyway. So," the old lady said, in a low soft voice the girl had not heard for a long time, "I didn't say anything to them when they left that night."

"Right over there," she said, pointing at the fallen poles, half buried in the river sand and tall grass, "in the summer shelter. The sun was high half the night then. Early in the morning when it was still low, the policeman came around. I told the interpreter to tell him that the storeman had poisoned them." She made outlines in the air in front of her, showing how their bodies lay twisted on the sand; telling the story was like laboring to walk through deep snow; sweat shone in the white hair around her forehead. "I told the priest too, after he came. I told him the storeman lied." She turned away from the girl. She held her mouth even tighter, set solidly, not in sorrow or anger, but against the pain, which was all that remained. "I never believed," she said, "not much anyway. I wasn't surprised when the priest did nothing."

The wind came off the river and folded the tall grass into itself like river waves. She could feel the silence the story left, and she wanted to have the old woman go on.

"I heard sounds that night, grandma. Sounds like someone was singing. It was light outside. I could see something red on the ground." The old woman did not answer her; she moved to the tub full of fish on the ground beside the workbench. She stabbed her knife into the belly of a whitefish and lifted it onto the bench. "The Gussuck storeman left the village right after that," the old woman said as she pulled the entrails from the fish, "otherwise, I could tell you more." The old woman's voice flowed with the wind blowing off the river; they never spoke of it again.

When the willows got their leaves and the grass grew tall along the river banks and around the sloughs, she walked early in the morning. While the sun was still low on the horizon, she listened to the wind off the river; its sound was like the voice that day long ago. In the distance, she could hear the engines of the machinery the oil drillers had left the winter before, but she did not go near the village or the store. The sun never left the sky and the summer became the same long day, with only the winds to fan the sun into brightness or allow it to slip into twilight.

She sat beside the old man at his place on the river bank. She poked the smoky fire for him, and felt herself growing wide and thin in the sun as if she had been split from belly to throat and strung on the willow pole in preparation for the winter to come. The old man did not speak anymore. When men from the village brought him fresh fish he hid them deep in the river grass where it was cool. After he went inside, she split the fish open and spread them to dry on the willow frame the way the old woman had done. Inside, he dozed and talked to himself. He had talked all winter, softly and incessantly, about the giant polar bear stalking a lone hunter across Bering Sea ice. After all the months the old man had been telling the story, the bear was within a hundred feet of the man; but the ice fog had closed in on them now and the man could only smell the sharp ammonia odor of the bear, and hear the edge of the snow crust crack under the giant paws.

One night she listened to the old man tell the story all night in his sleep, describing each crystal of ice and the slightly different sounds they made under each paw; first the left and then the right paw, then the hind feet. Her grandmother was there suddenly, a shadow around the stove. She spoke in her low wind voice and the girl was afraid to sit up to hear more clearly. Maybe what she said had been to the old man because he stopped telling the story and began to snore softly the way he had long ago when the old woman had scolded him for telling his stories while others in the house were trying to sleep. But the last words she heard clearly: "It will take a long time, but the story must be told. There must not be any lies." She pulled the blankets up around her chin, slowly, so that her movements would not be seen. She thought her grandmother was talking about the old man's bear story; she did not know about the other story then.

She left the old man wheezing and snoring in his bed. She walked through river grass glistening with frost; the bright green summer color was already fading. She watched the sun move across the sky, already lower on the horizon, already moving away from the village. She stopped by the fallen poles of the summer shelter where her parents had died. Frost glittered on the river sand too; in a few more weeks there would be snow. The predawn light would be the color of an old woman. An old woman sky full of snow. There had been something red lying on the ground the morning they died. She looked for it again, pushing aside the grass with her foot. She knelt in the sand and looked under the fallen structure for some trace of it. When she found it, she would know what the old woman had never told her. She squatted down close to the gray poles and leaned her back against them. The wind made her shiver.

The summer rain had washed the mud from between the logs; the sod blocks stacked as high as her belly next to the log walls had lost their square-cut shape and had grown into soft mounds of tundra moss and stiff-bladed grass bending with clusters of seed bristles. She looked at the northwest, in the direction of the Bering Sea. The cold would come down from there to find narrow slits in the mud, rainwater holes in the outer layer of sod which protected the log house. The dark green tundra stretched away flat and continuous. Somewhere the sea and the land met; she knew by their dark green colors there were no boundaries between them. That was how the cold would come: when the boundaries were gone the polar ice would range across the land into the sky. She watched the horizon for a long time. She would stand in that place on the north side of the house and she would keep watch on the northwest horizon, and eventually she would see it come. She would watch for its approach in the stars, and hear it come with the wind. These preparations were unfamiliar, but gradually she recognized them as she did her own footprints in the snow.

She emptied the slop jar beside his bed twice a day and kept the barrel full of water melted from river ice. He did not recognize her anymore, and when he spoke to her, he called her by her grandmother's name and talked about people and events from long ago, before he went back to telling the story. The giant bear was creeping across the new snow on its belly, close enough now that the man could hear the rasp of its breathing. On and on in a soft singing voice, the old man caressed the story, repeating the words again and again like gentle strokes.

The sky was gray like a river crane's egg; its density curved into the thin crust of frost already covering the land. She looked at the bright red color of the tin against the ground and the sky and she told the village men to bring the pieces for the old man and her. To drill the test holes in the tundra, the Gussucks had used hundreds of barrels of fuel. The village people split open the empty barrels that were abandoned on the river bank, and pounded the red tin into flat sheets. The village people were using the strips of tin to mend walls and roofs for winter. But she nailed it on the log walls for its color. When she finished, she walked away with the hammer in her hand, not turning around until she was far away, on the ridge above the river banks, and then she looked back. She felt a chill when she saw how the sky and the land were already losing their boundaries, already becoming lost in each other. But the red tin penetrated the thick white color of earth and sky; it defined the boundaries like a wound revealing the ribs and heart of a great caribou about to bolt and be lost to the hunter forever. That night the wind howled and when she scratched a hole through the heavy frost on the inside of the window, she could see nothing but the impenetrable white; whether it was blowing snow or snow that had drifted as high as the house, she did not know.

It had come down suddenly, and she stood with her back to the wind looking at the river, its smoky water clotted with ice. The wind had blown the snow over the frozen river, hiding thin blue streaks where fast water ran under ice translucent and fragile as memory. But she could see shadows of boundaries, outlines of paths which were slender branches of solidity reaching out from the earth. She spent days walking on the river, watching the colors of ice that would safely hold her, kicking the heel of her boot into the snow crust, listening for a solid sound. When she could feel the paths through the soles of her feet, she went to the middle of the river where the fast gray water churned under a thin pane of ice. She looked back. On the river bank in the distance she could see the red tin nailed to the log house, something not swallowed up by the heavy white belly of the sky or caught in the folds of the frozen earth. It was time.

The wolverine fur around the hood of her parka was white with the frost from her breathing. The warmth inside the store melted it, and she felt tiny drops of water on her face. The storeman came in from the back room. She unzipped the parka and stood by the oil stove. She didn't look at him, but stared instead at the yellowish dog, covered with scabs of matted hair, sleeping in front of the stove. She thought of the Gussuck's picture, taped on the wall above the bed and she laughed out loud. The sound of her laughter was piercing; the yellow dog jumped to its feet and the hair bristled down its back. The storeman was watching her. She wanted to laugh again because he didn't know about the ice. He did not know that it was prowling the earth, or that it had already pushed its way into the sky to seize the sun. She sat down in the chair by the stove and shook her long hair loose. He was like a dog tied up all winter, watching while the others got fed. He remembered how she had gone with the oil drillers, and his blue eyes moved like flies crawling over her body. He held his thin pale lips like he wanted to spit on her. He hated the people because they had something of value, the old man said, something which the Gussucks could never have. They thought they could take it, suck it out of the earth or cut it from the mountains; but they were fools.

There was a matted hunk of dog hair on the floor by her foot. She thought of the yellow insulation coming unstuffed: their defense against the freezing going to pieces as it advanced on them. The ice was crouching on the northwest horizon like the old man's bear. She laughed out loud again. The sun would be down now; it was time.

The first time he spoke to her, she did not hear what he said, so she did not answer or even look up at him. He spoke to her again but his words were only noises coming from his pale mouth, trembling now as his anger began to unravel. He jerked her up and the chair fell over behind her. His arms were shaking and she could feel his hands tense up, pulling the edges of the parka tighter. He raised his fist to hit her, his thin body quivering with rage; but the fist collapsed with the desire he had for the valuable things, which, the old man had rightly said, was the only reason they came. She could hear his heart pounding as he held her close and arched his hips against her, groaning and breathing in spasms. She twisted away from him and ducked under his arms.

She ran with a mitten over her mouth, breathing through the fur to protect her lungs from the freezing air. She could hear him running behind her, his heavy breathing, the occasional sound of metal jingling against metal. But he ran without his parka or mittens, breathing the frozen air; its fire squeezed the lungs against the ribs and it was enough that he could not catch her near his store. On the river bank he realized how far he was from his stove, and the wads of yellow stuffing that held off the cold. But the girl was not able to run very fast through the deep drifts at the edge of the river. The twilight was luminous and he could still see clearly for a long distance; he knew he could catch her so he kept running.

When she neared the middle of the river she looked over her shoulder. He was not following her tracks; he went straight across the ice, running the shortest distance to reach her. He was close then; his face was twisted and scarlet from the exertion and the cold. There was satisfaction in his eyes; he was sure he could outrun her.

She was familiar with the river, down to the instant ice flexed into hairline fractures, and the cracking bone-sliver sounds gathered momentum with the opening ice until the churning gray water was set free. She stopped and turned to the sound of the river and the rattle of swirling ice fragments where he fell through. She pulled off a mitten and zipped the parka to her throat. She was conscious then of her own rapid breathing.

She moved slowly, kicking the ice ahead with the heel of her boot, feeling for sinews of ice to hold her. She looked ahead and all around herself; in the twilight, the dense white sky had merged into the flat snow-covered tundra. In the frantic running she had lost her place on the river. She stood still. The east bank of the river was lost in the sky; the boundaries had been swallowed by the freezing white. But then, in the distance, she saw something red, and suddenly it was as she had remembered it all those years.

She sat on her bed and while she waited, she listened to the old man. The hunter had found a small jagged knoll on the ice. He pulled his beaver fur cap off his head; the fur inside it steamed with his body heat and sweat. He left it upside down on the ice for the great bear to stalk, and he waited downwind on top of the ice knoll; he was holding the jade knife.

She thought she could see the end of his story in the way he wheezed out the words; but still he reached into his cache of dry fish and dribbled water into his mouth from the tin cup. All night she listened to him describe each breath the man took, each motion of the bear's head as it tried to catch the sound of the man's breathing, and tested the wind for his scent.

The state trooper asked her questions, and the woman who cleaned house for the priest translated them into Yupik. They wanted to know what happened to the storeman, the Gussuck who had been seen running after her down the road onto the river late last evening. He had not come back, and the Gussuck boss in Anchorage was concerned about him. She did not answer for a long time because the old man suddenly sat up in his bed and began to talk excitedly, looking at all of them—the trooper in his dark glasses and the housekeeper in her corduroy parka. He kept saying, "The story! The story! Eh-ya! The great bear! The hunter!"

They asked her again, what happened to the man from the Northern Commercial store. "He lied to them. He told them it was safe to drink. But I will not lie." She stood up and put on the gray wolfskin parka. "I killed him," she said, "but I don't lie."

The attorney came back again, and the jailer slid open the steel doors and opened the cell to let him in. He motioned for the jailer to stay to translate for him. She laughed when she saw how the jailer would be forced by this Gussuck to speak Yupik to her. She liked the Gussuck attorney for that, and for the thinning hair on his head. He was very tall, and she liked to think about the exposure of his head to the freezing; she wondered if he would feel the ice descending from the sky before the others did. He wanted to know why she told the state trooper she had killed the storeman. Some village children had seen it happen, he said, and it was an accident. "That's all you have to say to the judge: it was an accident." He kept repeating it over and over again to her, slowly in a loud but gentle voice: "It was an accident. He was running after you and he fell through the ice. That's all you have to say in court. That's all. And they will let you go home. Back to your village." The jailer translated the words sullenly, staring down at the floor. She shook her head. "I will not change the story, not even to escape this place and go home. I intended that he die. The story must be told as it is." The attorney exhaled loudly; his eyes looked tired. "Tell her that she could not have killed him that way. He was a white man. He ran after her without a parka or mittens. She could not have planned that." He paused and turned toward the cell door. "Tell her I will do all I can for her. I will explain to the judge that her mind is confused." She laughed out loud when the jailer translated what the attorney said. The Gussucks did not understand the story; they could not see the way it must be told, year after year as the old man had done, without lapse or silence.

She looked out the window at the frozen white sky. The sun had finally broken loose from the ice but it moved like a wounded caribou running on strength which only dying animals find, leaping and running on bullet-shattered lungs. Its light was weak and pale; it pushed dimly through the clouds. She turned and faced the Gussuck attorney.

"It began a long time ago," she intoned steadily, "in the summertime. Early in the morning, I remember, something red in the tall river grass. . . ."

The day after the old man died, men from the village came. She was sitting on the edge of her bed, across from the woman the trooper hired to watch her. They came into the room slowly and listened to her. At the foot of her bed they left a king salmon that had been slit open wide and dried last summer. But she did not pause or hesitate; she went on with the story, and she never stopped, not even when the woman got up to close the door behind the village men.

The old man would not change the story even when he knew the end was approaching. Lies could not stop what was coming. He thrashed around on the bed, pulling the blankets loose, knocking bundles of dried fish and meat on the floor. The hunter had been on the ice for many hours. The freezing winds on the ice knoll had numbed his hands in the mittens, and the cold had exhausted him. He felt a single muscle tremor in his hand that he could not stop, and the jade knife fell; it shattered on the ice, and the blue glacier bear turned slowly to face him.

1981

Jasper Johns,
Savarin,
brush, pen, and ink, 1977.
Collection, The Museum of Modern Art,
New York.
Gift of the Lauder Foundation.

The Literature of Contemporary America: Poetry

 As the critic Hugh Kenner once wrote, "No Englishman alive in 1600 was living in the Age of Shakespeare: . . . that age was invented long afterwards." The last quarter of the twentieth century may eventually be well represented in the anthologies of the far future, but we cannot now know how many of these new voices, who have flourished since 1973, will become part of the canon of American poetry. That canon is decided on chiefly by subsequent poets, who find only some of their predecessors worthy of admiration, imitation, and homage. To a contemporary reader, the amount of poetry being written in the United States seems formidable: Publishers report thousands of submissions for any poetry prize; *The New Yorker* alone receives a thousand poems a week in submissions. The few poets represented here are diverse in theory and practice and represent no commanding "school."

Although the intensity of American political life slackened in the 1970s with the withdrawal of United States forces from Vietnam, the aftermath of the war remained in the consciousness of young writers. Many novelists commemorated the events of the war, and some poets attempted to express the horror of battle; but beyond that local literary effect, there was a large change in the public perception of America's role in international affairs. Among writers, a distrust of military policy and a new isolationism went, paradoxically, hand in hand with a new sense of responsibility for the whole planet. Ethnological and anthropological discoveries put in question the "superiority" of colonizers over colonized; it seemed as though America's empire, like those of England and France, had ended with the defeat in Vietnam and the rise of resistance in South America to American political influence. Young writers found themselves pressed into various national and global causes—opposition to nuclear arms, defense of civil rights, conservation—while earlier causes, notably the feminist movement, remained vividly present.

During the 1970s several major poets, whose work had been important to younger writers, died: Charles Olson (1970), John Berryman (1972), Anne Sexton (1975), Robert Lowell (1977), Elizabeth Bishop (1979), and James Wright (1980). Some poets belonging chronologically to this generation had already died young by accident or suicide (Frank O'Hara, Sylvia Plath, Randall Jarrell). Still other poets, nearing sixty, seemed to be declaring their canon largely complete by bringing out collected poems (A. R. Ammons, James Merrill, Allen Ginsberg).

In this comparative vacancy, new poets became more visible. They continue to perform the immemorial task of poetry—to process some portion of nature or history into a portion of culture by endowing it with aesthetic purpose. A number of younger poets are continuing, for example, the process begun by Langston Hughes and Allen Ginsberg—recording the history of illiterate or marginally literate members of society who, because they were unschooled or

---

The Responsibility of Creative Writing

Creative writing is no panacea for individual or social ills. If it were we should have long ago discovered how to prevent Vietnam and the collapse of Chrysler. Because of the horror of the Holocaust, George Steiner said, "After Auschwitz, no more poetry." And it is hard to sustain a fervent belief in art as humanly effective when we know that Nazis read Goethe, heard Mozart, and cultivated refined tastes by night after a hard day of eliminating Jews. Yet did not art always tell us about that darkness in the human spirit, and what worse would we have been without those images of ourselves in Homer, Chaucer, Dante, Shakespeare, Dickens, the Brothers Grimm, Kafka? I have mentioned critics who complain of the spread of writing instruction and argue it dilutes the quality of our writing. Have they got their facts in perspective? One of their complaints is the size, the cost of a writing program. It is worth remembering that one Air Force bomber costs more than the entire budget for the National Endowment for the Arts; that no school in this country provides the salaries, support, or attention to creative writing that it does for computers, music, engineering, biology, or ROTC; that in every state university we have the athletic budget for laundry alone exceeds the budget for creative writing. The point is that we are a tiny, tiny operation but we are entrusted with envisioning, recording, and even sustaining the best that has been and will be thought and felt about human nature. When we seek to measure what we are doing, and we must do that, let us do so in appropriate contexts.

Dave Smith, *Local Assays* (1985)

---

were enslaved or were immigrants speaking a language other than English, left
little English record of their own American lives. Michael Harper's commitment
to historical particulars, Albert Goldbarth's transcriptions of Yiddish-speaking
ancestors, and Dave Smith's anecdotes of the taciturn Chesapeake Bay oyster
fishermen reflect not only the poet's wish to rescue, in full pathos, lost portions
of experience but also the lyric poet's deep desire to speak through other voices,
to "borrow" voice from a wide historical range. These poets follow Whitman,
who promised, in "Song of Myself":

> Through me many long dumb voices,
> Voices of the interminable generations of prisoners and slaves,
> Voices of the diseas'd and despairing and of thieves and dwarfs. . . .
> Through me forbidden voices,
> Voices of sexes and lusts, voices veil'd and I remove the veil,
> Voices indecent by me clarified and transfigur'd.

At the same time these poets, concerned with the larger historical record, have
written poems of the private life. Harper mourns a dead son; Smith writes about
his rebellious youth.

There are poets represented in the pages that follow who are historical in a
different way from the more narrative poets just mentioned. In this second group,
the use of the past is not narrative but exemplary. Jorie Graham's examples of the
past are frequently paintings—from those of Piero della Francesca to those of
Gustav Klimt. Graham takes the measure of her own aesthetic life by a deep
immersion in an objectified form rendered in a moment far in the past. Frank
Bidart, too, uses the voices of past artists (the opera singer Maria Callas, the
ballet dancer Nijinsky) as a way to measure the inexorable price exacted by the
will to form.

Yet another way of being "historical" appears in the poetry of Charles
Simic, whose childhood was spent in Yugoslavia during World War II. In
Simic's work the algebra of parable replaces the mimesis of historical narrative:
The Europe of the Second World War is reduced, allegorically, to a place
where stark and horrible events take place—a shooting, a disappearance, a
famine. Voices become disembodied; men are seen archetypally rather than
individually—a father, a son, a soldier. Form is reduced to the simplest of
quatrains, the commonest words.

In various ways, then—by historical narrative, historical voices, historical
works of art, historical anecdote—the poets of the past decade continue the
twentieth-century impulse to historicize the lyric, to make it embody a social
reality greater than the reality of a single poet alone. The American impulse
to enfranchise the "en masse" (as Whitman called it), to expose the whole
social fabric of a culture rather than an individual predicament, stems from the
American ideal of poetry as a common cultural possession, a voice expressive
of all classes, a regard democratic in its vistas. This view remains in tension
with the indisputable fact that the linguistic and cultural ease with language
necessary for any accomplished writing of poetry is usually the possession of
the educated.

The poets of the past decade continue another vein of twentieth-century lyric. Like Roethke, Lowell, Plath, and Sexton, they hark back to the theme of problematic identity, expressed in terms of parents, ancestry, gender, and ethnic and regional origins. This theme—unthinkable in a similar form in centrally English writers like Shakespeare, Keats, or Hopkins, but present in many provincial writers—marks the continuing American unease felt within an unsettled and pluralistic society. Many American writers emerge from a class unaccustomed to belles lettres; many women writers emerge from a group that feels disenfranchised in the world of letters. Finding one's feet, so to speak, demands a retracing of the original unsteadiness in the community. The new poets' emphasis on childhood origins suggests the persistence of the Freudian model of identity, shaped by family relations more than by social circumstance.

If there are continuities between the new poets and their predecessors, there are also discontinuities. The single most striking disparity between recent poets and their American forebears in this century is the difference in philosophical orientation between the generations. The poets of high modernism were still working out for themselves the Victorian crisis of religious faith (Frost, Eliot, Stevens, Crane) or the crisis of technology and modernity (Pound, Moore, Williams); the poets flourishing after World War II were working out the implications of Freud and of gender difference (Lowell, Plath, Rich, Roethke). But for the most part the recent poets find these issues less urgent and take them almost for granted. The religious impulse in these younger poets is not doctrinally based but voices itself in yearnings or aspirations rather than in the crisis of belief. Technology and modernity are, for these poets, indisputably present, often to be genially used as new sources of language. The Freudian model (though it has undergone modifications) remains the basic model for introspection. The real energy, philosophically speaking, for these poets comes from the crisis in knowledge that has absorbed philosophers most acutely since Kant and most visibly since Wittgenstein—two philosophers voicing an acute critique of the nature of language.

The model of the artist as one who holds a mirror up to nature implies an adequacy of words to things and suggests that there is no gap in reality between

Recital

But as the days and years sped by it became apparent that the naming of all the new things we now possessed had become our chief occupation; that very little time for the mere tasting and having of them was left over, and that even these simple, tangible experiences were themselves subject to description and enumeration, or else they too became fleeting and transient as the song of a bird that is uttered only once and disappears into the backlog of vague memories where it becomes as a dried, pressed flower, a wistful parody of itself. . . .

John Ashbery, *Three Poems* (1972)

the things contemplated and the language "recreating" them. More recent theorists of language suggest that we cannot get "behind" language; we cannot attain things in their unmediated being. Nor can we remove language from its function of signification in order to see what language would be before it signified a "thing," before it had "meaning." The view that language, and only language, is what constitutes the world, that there can be no world prior to the world constituted by language, appears in some of Stevens's poetry, but it was not an axiom of poets until recently. The concept of *poesis,* or imagining a world, is now seen to be the action that itself constitutes culture. Cultures change because a new imagining of the world—by thinkers, inventors, scientists, writers —has slowly come about. New cultural "languages" remodel the world. With new conceptualizations and new words, we achieve what W. H. Auden called "new styles of architecture, a change of heart." In the work of reconstituting culture, the poets—the most imaginative of imaginative writers, those who touch the core of the inner life—play a central role.

　　This perception of the role of the poet is interpreted differently by different temperaments. Utopian poets imagine that they are reconceiving the world in new codes that will overturn the old conceptions (of blacks, of women, of a "good citizen" in the docile sense). Poets who want to understand the relevance of older imaginative codes (say, those of Renaissance painters) to our own day attempt to reenter a conceptual world foreign to them, not to urge the virtues of modernity but rather to see what might be perennial about the

---

"Negative Capability"

". . . that is, when a man is capable of being in uncertainties, mysteries, doubts, without any irritable reaching after fact and reason."
John Keats

Today what Keats said could be made even more specific. In place of "uncertainties," "mysteries" and "doubts," we could substitute a long list of intellectual and aesthetic events which question, revise and contradict one another on all fundamental issues. We could also bring in recent political history: all the wars, all the concentration camps and other assorted modern sufferings, and then return to Keats and ask how, in this context, are we capable of being in anything *but* uncertainties? Or, since we are thinking about poetry, ask how do we render this now overwhelming consciousness of uncertainty, mystery and doubt in our poems?

To be "capable of being in uncertainties" is to be literally in the midst. The poet is in the midst. The poem, too, is in the midst, a kind of magnet for complex historical, literary and psychological forces, as well as a way of maintaining oneself in the face of that multiplicity.

Charles Simic, "Negative Capability and Its Children" (1984)

work of the imagination. The sense of emptiness in W. S. Merwin, Charles Wright, and Mark Strand (frequently remarked by their readers) is the space left by religious nostalgia, as yet unentered by any energy other than that of speculation on the power of language to fill a void. Their poetic forms, stripped of personal or circumstantial detail, aim at a purity of diction that will let the mind float free, in pure *poesis,* removed from quotidian or historical moorings.

In the past, the lyric has been the genre most broadly available to readers. In continuing to write of human loss, philosophical problems, fluctuations of desire, or the contemplation of art, the poets of the past decade search for authentic contemporary treatments of perennial human concerns. Religious and social doctrines no longer offer our society authoritative models in which to see the human predicament. Poets like Strand, Wright, and Graham attempt to do without such preexistent authoritative models, and their work, for the most part, does without a narrative base. They are thus writing squarely in the traditional mode of the lyric, using the native radial form of poetry that issues from, and returns to, a center of inner concern. Wright has emphasized his debt to Cézanne in arriving at a form by which "patches" of substance are applied in overlapping patterns on a blank ground. Strand has adopted a mode of disembodied allegory; Graham has used in her work motions of entering and leaving, of transgression over boundaries. These tentative inner motions reflect a distrust of definitive narrative or philosophical closure. The lines of these poets give off quanta of linguistic energy and resemble waves rather than straight lines. Closure in them becomes a suspension rather than a ringing conclusion.

The physical terrain of the United States is being mapped by these poets as by earlier ones. Amy Clampitt, in a group of powerfully descriptive poems, has charted the Maine coast as well as the Iowa of her childhood; Wright has written intensely of the southern Episcopalian atmosphere in which he was reared; Smith, in addition to his Virginia poems, has written about Wyoming and Utah; Strand has recorded elements of life in Nova Scotia; Bidart gave his first book *(Golden State)* the nickname of the state where he was born; Pinsky has written about New Jersey, Harper about both coasts. By European standards, America is still, to quote Frost, "unstoried, artless, unenhanced," but the poetic map is slowly being filled in.

The map of various self-constituting "affinity groups" is being filled in as well. Gay, lesbian, feminist, Native American, and Hispanic-American poetry have all defined themselves in anthologies and in journals. In the past, creating a movement outside the presumed "center" has been a way for dissident or avant-garde poets to find a hearing among sympathizers, fellow writers, and interested readers. A critical mass of readers (almost always, in the past, found in cities—Jerusalem, Athens, Rome, Byzantium, London, Paris) is now to be found not only in movements or in cities but also in universities, where young writers gather to undergo an apprenticeship in a creative writing program. None of these ways of finding an audience—joining a movement, heading for a city, or enrolling in a program—is indispensable, but all enable the poet to find others with a common interest or a common stance.

The interpenetration of poetry and prose, and poetry with other vocal media (television, music, stage performance), continues to be explored in "performance poetry" and "language poetry," forms exhibiting powerful reliance on such strategies as improvisation, fragmentation of language, the intermittent presence of language, the dissociation of sentence parts, and the abandoning of visible form. These strategies (many of them borrowed from the composer John Cage, one of the original teachers at Black Mountain) help to destroy the "illusion" of continuous form. The dislocations of "ordinary language" present in all poetry—whether through the mere presence of the unjustified line or through condensation, rapid metaphorical change, syntactic oddity, iteration, and other forms of overdetermination—are brought strongly into view by language poets and performance poets, for whom the disruptive imagination, rather than any element of continuous form, is the constitutive quality of poetry.

Finally, it is of course to the American language and to American forms of social expression that our poets are most deeply obligated. The inner life of an epoch must find, in its own linguistic and cultural forms, the means of its own reflection. For the poets of the past decade, this obligation means that they must find imaginative constructs, sentence forms, images, and language faithful to the sensibility of a generation that looks at television as well as at paintings, possesses the concept of the fourth dimension as well as of the magnet, and knows unisex clothing, test-tube babies, nuclear force, and planetary travel. Concepts of space and time have changed; concepts of rates of change have altered; the visual field is different; the roles of the sexes are in question. It is not that such modern realities need to be mentioned (though they do) or that new words need to be incorporated in poetry (though they do). It is rather that new conceptual models, new rates of change, and new pacings of distance must find their appropriate linear, temporal, and spatial poetic forms (a search in which John Ashbery has so

---

Some Notes on Silence

If in the form is each man's uncounterfeitable relationship with the mysteries, then the degree of his fear or grace are also in some measure legible there. It is hard to name these things: but in those poets who confront the unknown, the holy, most head-on, the syntax begins to buckle and bend back and break, very much like Saint Teresa first witnessing the host and twisting back, both to look away and, strangely, to better receive it. From the labyrinthine ritual cave paintings of the Stone Age, through every period of human time, when we have sought to enter, to break the surface, one of the ways in has been crooked —the blindness that one may see. And in the poets that go that way, twisted syntax, breaks against smooth sequence or sense, line breaks of queer kinds, white spaces, interruptions, dashes, overpunctuation, delays, clotted rich diction, obscurity, disorder, ellipses, sentence fragments, digressive strategies—every modulation in certainty—are all tools for storming the walls. Whether of hell or paradise is another matter.

Jorie Graham (1984)

far been most daring). It is too early to specify the new inner structures that will be discovered in the last quarter of this century. But the remarkable variety of the United States—intellectual, ethnic, and geographic—suggests that, as Wallace Stevens said, "The vegetation still abounds in forms."

Amy Clampitt
b. 1920

Amy Clampitt writes, "I come from a late-blooming family. My grandfather wrote and published his autobiography when he was past seventy; my father received an honorary doctorate of humane letters at the age of eighty-three. They were both farmers, and of an anxious temperament. I grew up in the same rural community," New Providence, Iowa. Clampitt's father was "a Quaker activist," and the political concern in many of her poems may be thought to derive from her father's example. After college at Grinnell, Clampitt worked for Oxford University Press and the Audubon Society; later, she became a free-lance editor and writer. In 1973 she published a small, privately printed collection of poems entitled *Multitudes, Multitudes.* Later in the decade she published poetry in *The New Yorker,* and in 1983 Knopf brought out her first widely circulated book, *The Kingfisher.* It appeared as the work of a wholly mature poet, one who had had long practice in writing. (Clampitt had written three unpublished novels before returning to poetry.) In 1985 Knopf published Clampitt's second collection, *What the Light Was Like.*

Clampitt writes passionately about her adolescence in Iowa, about the fears and deprivations of living as a young girl—and aspiring writer—in desolate rural America. In her elegies for her mother and father ("Procession at Candlemas" and "Beethoven Opus 111") she considers, respectively, what the worship of the female has meant in culture, and the nature and achievement of those born with a revolutionary temperament. Clampitt has also written poems (about the Maine coast and other landscapes) that rival Gerard Manley Hopkins's poetry in intense contemplation of the visual scene. Her long sequence on the life of John Keats reveals the psychological acuteness with which she can enter the realities, both physical and mental, of another life.

Clampitt's writing is strenuous, dense, and charged with impetus and momentum. Her sentences press on, full of reflection, argument, qualification, impressions, and queries, unwilling to come to a halt until the mind has had time to think enough and the tongue to say enough. This is a poetry of intelligence, owing something to Marianne Moore, but it is also a poetry of urgent feeling, able to recall with uncanny accuracy the confusions and rages of childhood and adolescence.

Clampitt's many poems about Europe take up once again the predicament of the American writer confronting the past—finding what is usable, what is relieving, what is admirable, what is frightening, about the legacy of history. It may be that Clampitt's most extraordinary achievement, however, is to have put on paper the Midwest region in which she was born—a region still relatively uncharted in poetry—and to have done so in a style very far from the minimalist fashion, set by Merwin and Strand, that reigned so long in American midcentury verse.

Text:
The Kingfisher, 1983.

A Procession at Candlemas[1]

1

Moving on or going back to where you came
    from,
    bad news is what you mainly travel with:
    a breakup or a breakdown, someone running off

or walking out, called up or called home:
    death in the family. Nudged from their stanchions   5
    outside the terminal, anonymous of purpose

as a flock of birds, the bison of the highway
    funnel westward onto Route 80, mirroring
    an entity that cannot look into itself and know

what makes it what it is. Sooner or later   10
    every trek becomes a funeral procession.
    The mother curtained in Intensive Care—

a scene the mind leaves blank, fleeing instead
    toward scenes of transhumance,[2] the belled sheep
    moving up the Pyrenees, red-tasseled pack llamas   15

footing velvet-green precipices, the Kurdish
    women, jingling with bangles, gorgeous
    on their rug-piled mounts—already lying dead,

---

[1] Feast of the Catholic church, held February 2, in honor of the purification of the Virgin and the presentation of Christ in the Temple. Candles used in sacred services are blessed on this day.

[2] The moving of flocks from one pasturage to another.

bereavement altering the moving lights
to a processional, a feast of Candlemas.   20
Change as child-bearing, birth as a kind

of shucking off: out of what began
as a Mosaic insult³—such a loathing
of the common origin, even a virgin,

having given birth, needs purifying—   25
to carry fire as though it were a flower,
the terror and the loveliness entrusted

into naked hands, supposing God might have,
might actually need a mother: people have
at times found this a way of being happy.   30

A Candlemas of moving lights along Route 80;
lighted candles in a corridor from Arlington⁴
over the Potomac, for every carried flame

the name of a dead soldier: an element
fragile as ego, frightening as parturition,   35
necessary and intractable as dreaming.

The lapped, wheelborne integument,⁵ layer
within layer, at the core a dream of
something precious, ripped: Where are we?

The sleepers groan, stir, rewrap themselves   40
about the self's imponderable substance,
or clamber down, numb-footed, half in a drowse

of freezing dark, through a Stonehenge
of fuel pumps, the bison hulks slantwise
beside them, drinking. What is real except   45

what's fabricated? The jellies glitter
cream-capped in the cafeteria showcase;
gumball globes, Life Savers cinctured

---

³ I.e., the regarding of women in Old Testament
law as unclean and in need of ritual purification
at certain times—for example, after childbirth.
⁴ Site near Washington, D.C., of Arlington
National Cemetary, military burial place.

⁵ I.e., the traveler herself, borne westward on the
bus.

in parcel gilt, plop from their housings
perfect, like miracles. Comb, nail clipper,   50
lip rouge, mirrors and emollients embody,

niched into the washroom wall case,
the pristine seductiveness of money.
Absently, without inhabitants, this

nowhere oasis wears the place name   55
of Indian Meadows. The westward-trekking
transhumance, once only, of a people[6] who,

in losing everything they had, lost even
the names they went by, stumbling past
like caribou, perhaps camped here. Who   60

can assign a trade-in value to that sorrow?
The monk in sheepskin over tucked-up saffron
intoning to a drum becomes the metronome

of one more straggle up Pennsylvania Avenue
in falling snow, a whirl of tenderly   65
remorseless corpuscles, street gangs

amok among magnolias' pregnant wands,
a stillness at the heart of so much whirling:
beyond the torn integument of childbirth,

sometimes, wrapped like a papoose into a grief   70
not merely of the ego, you rediscover almost
the rest-in-peace of the placental coracle.

2

Of what the dead were, living, one knows
so little as barely to recognize
the fabric of the backward-ramifying   75

antecedents, half-noted presences
in darkened rooms: the old, the feared,
the hallowed. Never the same river

drowns the unalterable doorsill. An effigy
in olive wood or pear wood, dank   80
with the sweat of age, walled in the dark

---

[6] I.e., Native Americans.

at Brauron, Argos, Samos:[7] even the unwed
Athene,[8] who had no mother, born—it's declared—
of some man's brain like every other pure idea,

had her own wizened cult object, kept   85
out of sight like the incontinent whimperer
in the backstairs bedroom, where no child

ever goes—to whom, year after year,
the fair linen of the sacred peplos
was brought in ceremonial procession—   90

flutes and stringed instruments, wildflower-
hung cattle, nubile Athenian girls, young men
praised for the beauty of their bodies. Who

can unpeel the layers of that seasonal
returning to the dark where memory fails,   95
as birds re-enter the ancestral flyway?

Daylight, snow falling, knotting of gears:
Chicago. Soot, the rotting backsides
of tenements, grimed trollshapes of ice

underneath the bridges, the tunnel heaving   100
like a birth canal. Disgorged, the infant
howling in the restroom; steam-table cereal,

pale coffee; wall-eyed TV receivers, armchairs
of molded plastic: the squalor of the day
resumed, the orphaned litter taken up again   105

unloved, the spawn of botched intentions,
grief a mere hardening of the gut,
a set piece of what can't be avoided:

parents by the tens of thousands living
unthanked, unpaid but in the sour coin   110
of resentment. Midmorning gray as zinc

along Route 80, corn-stubble quilting
the underside of snowdrifts, the cadaverous
belvedere[9] of windmills, the sullen stare

---

[7] Greek islands.
[8] Virgin goddess of wisdom in Greek mythology.
The ancient olive-wood statue of Athene kept
at the Parthenon, was the cult-object of the

yearly Panathenaic procession, in which a linen
cloth, or *peplos,* was carried.
[9] Building commanding a fine prospect.

of feedlot cattle; black creeks puncturing   115
white terrain, the frozen bottomland
a mush of willow tops; dragnetted in ice,

the Mississippi. Westward toward the dark,
the undertow of scenes come back to, fright
riddling the structures of interior history: 120

Where is it? Where, in the shucked-off
bundle, the hampered obscurity that has been
for centuries the mumbling lot of women,

did the thread of fire, too frail
ever to discover what it meant, to risk   125
even the taking of a shape, relinquish

the seed of possibility, unguessed-at
as a dream of something precious? Memory,
that exquisite blunderer, stumbling

like a migrant bird that finds the flyway   130
it hardly knew it knew except by instinct,
down the long-unentered nave of childhood,

late on a midwinter afternoon, alone
among the snow-hung hollows of the windbreak
on the far side of the orchard, encounters   135

sheltering among the evergreens, a small
stilled bird, its cap of clear yellow
slit by a thread of scarlet—the untouched

nucleus of fire, the lost connection
hallowing the wizened effigy, the mother   140
curtained in Intensive Care: a Candlemas

of moving lights along Route 80, at nightfall,
in falling snow, the stillness and the sorrow
of things moving back to where they came from.
1983

The Kingfisher

In a year the nightingales were said to be so loud
they drowned out slumber, and peafowl strolled screaming
beside the ruined nunnery, through the long evening
of a dazzled pub crawl, the halcyon color, portholed
by those eye-spots' stunning tapestry, unsettled   5
the pastoral nightfall with amazements opening.

Months later, intermission in a pub on Fifty-fifth Street
found one of them still breathless, the other quizzical,
acting the philistine, puncturing Stravinsky[1]—"Tell
me, what *was* that racket in the orchestra about?"—   10
hauling down the Firebird,[2] harum-scarum, like a kite,
a burnished, breathing wreck that didn't hurt at all.

Among the Bronx Zoo's exiled jungle fowl, they heard
through headphones of a separating panic the bellbird
reiterate its single *chong,* a scream nobody answered.   15
When he mourned, "The poetry is gone," she quailed,
seeing how his hands shook, sobered into feeling old.
By midnight, yet another fifth would have been killed.

A Sunday morning, the November of their cataclysm
(Dylan Thomas[3] brought in *in extremis*[4] to St. Vincent's   20
that same week, a symptomatic datum) found them
wandering a downtown churchyard. Among its headstones,
while from unruined choirs the noise of Christendom
poured over Wall Street, a benison in vestments,

a late thrush paused, in transit from some grizzled   25
spruce bog to the humid equatorial fireside: berry-
eyed, bark-brown above, with dark hints of trauma
in the stigmata[5] of its underparts—or so, too bruised
just then to have invented anything so fancy,
later, reembroidering a retrospect, she had supposed.   30

In gray England, years of muted recrimination (then
dead silence) later, she could not have said how many
spoiled takeoffs, how many entanglements gone sodden,

---

[1] Igor Stravinsky (1882–1971), Russian composer.
He became first a French, then an American
citizen.
[2] Ballet composed by Stravinsky in 1910.

[3] British poet (1914–1953).
[4] Latin: "dying."
[5] In tradition, the wounds of Christ.

how many gaudy evenings made frantic by just one
insomniac nightingale, how many liaisons gone down   35
screaming in a stroll beside the ruined nunnery;

a kingfisher's burnished plunge, the color
of felicity afire, came glancing like an arrow
through landscapes of untended memory: ardor
illuminating with its terrifying currency   40
now no mere glimpse, no porthole vista
but, down on down, the uninhabitable sorrow.

1983

Mark Strand
b. 1934

Mark Strand has published, besides his own poetry, several distinguished books of
translations, children's books, short stories, and essays on literature, painting, and
photography. He is a Canadian by birth, born on Prince Edward Island. He took
a B.F.A. at Yale and an M.A. at the University of Iowa after graduating from
Antioch College, and spent a year (1960–1961) at the University of Florence on a
Fulbright. He later (1965–1966) went to Rio de Janeiro as Fulbright lecturer on
American literature and became translator of the great Brazilian poet Carlos
Drummond de Andrade. He has also translated Rafael Alberti and Jorge Luis
Borges. Strand has taught at several universities and is now at the University of
Utah.

Strand's most distinctive characteristic as a poet, visible even in his first book,
Sleeping with One Eye Open (1964), is the dreamlike nature of his writing. A
gulf opens between stanzas, and even between lines, of his verse. He is a poet of
inner blank, whose lines appear with difficulty, and slowly, enacting the
arduousness of rendering and formulating the contents of consciousness. Each of
Strand's lines is long-meditated and firm in its isolation from others. The inner
loneliness in Strand would be unremarkable if it had not found an aesthetic in
which to embody itself—a large canvas full of unpainted space, like a late
Cézanne. In subsequent books—*Reasons for Moving* (1968), *Darker* (1970), *The
Story of Our Lives* (1973), and *The Late Hour* (1978)—Strand has continued to
work within a spare and economic style, exhibiting affinities with abstract
painting.

Strand's minimalist poetry represents a revulsion from the confessional mode;
he writes (and in this he resembles W. S. Merwin) a poetry of parable, a spare
poetry in which the tokens representing emotional experience are widely
representative. His poetry betrays the influence of Spanish and Latin American
surrealism, in its strange inflexible logic and its willingness to assume a
hallucinatory atmosphere. Recently, he has become more openly autobiographical
in poems recalling his childhood and youth on Prince Edward Island. He and

Elizabeth Bishop (who grew up in Nova Scotia) have become the poets of the maritime provinces of Canada as well as poets of Brazil. (They met when Bishop was living in Brazil.) Like Bishop, Strand is a poet of fastidious choices; unlike her, he writes at a second remove from the world of travels north and south, preferring an inner geography of vision.

Text:
Selected Poems, 1980.

The Tunnel

A man has been standing
in front of my house
for days. I peek at him
from the living room
window and at night,   5
unable to sleep,
I shine my flashlight
down on the lawn.
He is always there.

After a while   10
I open the front door
just a crack and order
him out of my yard.
He narrows his eyes
and moans. I slam   15
the door and dash back
to the kitchen, then up
to the bedroom, then down.

I weep like a schoolgirl
and make obscene gestures   20
through the window. I
write large suicide notes
and place them so he
can read them easily.
I destroy the living   25
room furniture to prove
I own nothing of value.

When he seems unmoved
I decide to dig a tunnel
to a neighboring yard.   30
I seal the basement off
from the upstairs with
a brick wall. I dig hard
and in no time the tunnel
is done. Leaving my pick   35
and shovel below,

I come out in front of a house
and stand there too tired to
move or even speak, hoping
someone will help me.   40
I feel I'm being watched
and sometimes I hear
a man's voice,
but nothing is done
and I have been waiting for days.   45
1969

Keeping Things Whole

In a field
I am the absence
of field.
This is
always the case.   5
Wherever I am
I am what is missing.

When I walk
I part the air
and always   10
the air moves in
to fill the spaces
where my body's been.

We all have reasons
for moving.   15
I move
to keep things whole.
1969

Coming to This

We have done what we wanted.
We have discarded dreams, preferring the heavy industry
of each other, and we have welcomed grief
and called ruin the impossible habit to break.

And now we are here.   5
The dinner is ready and we cannot eat.
The meat sits in the white lake of its dish.
The wine waits.

Coming to this
has its rewards: nothing is promised, nothing is taken away.   10
We have no heart or saving grace,
no place to go, no reason to remain.
1970

Charles Wright
b. 1935

"Poems," said Charles Wright in an interview, "are both reliquary and
transubstantiational, as our lives should be." That is, the poem preserves
something of life, while leaving it behind; the poem changes the substance of
experience into the substance of art. Wright attempted (in an early sequence
called "Tattoos") to write lyrics devoid of narrative explanatory material; the
occasion for each poem was given in an endnote. Later he experimented with
other ways of transubstantiating the narratives of life into the images of poetry,
describing his work as analogous to that of a painter, who must find the image
that will be the equivalent of his impression of the world. In his use of the
"deep image," Wright has been compared to W. S. Merwin and Mark Strand,
but though he is both remote and unearthly, his verse has a songlike base
(derived, as he says, from country music) that distinguishes him from his
contemporaries.

Ultimately, Wright derives his interest in the image from Ezra Pound. It has
taken him into translating the Italian poet Montale and into reading the German
poets Trakl and Rilke, among others. For Wright, images hover around the
white spaces in a poem: "The line, of course, is what separates us from the beasts.
I think a line has specific weight and heft, that it is melodic and tactile. It is as
though the lines were each sections of the poem attached by invisible strings to
the title." One recent poem attempts, as he says, a "non-linear approach to plot. . . .

The structure of the poem is presentational, and it works accumulatively. . . . I was conscious of working in blocks of lines, stanzas and pages, much as Cézanne might have used his dabs and columns and blotches of color (in many of the Mt. St. Victoire landscapes you can't find a line at all—everything is dab and spread and knife-stroke)." It is by the massing of many parallel items that one recognizes a poem by Charles Wright.

Wright's themes often derive from his Episcopalian upbringing in the South, which issues in a persistent wish to become disembodied, to die and be resurrected at once, to disappear into the earth and the air at a single stroke. Wright was born in Tennessee and grew up there and in North Carolina. He took an M.F.A. at Iowa after graduating from Davidson College. From 1957 to 1961 he served in Verona, Italy, in U.S. Army intelligence; from 1963 to 1965 he was a Fulbright student in Rome; and in 1968 and 1969 he was a Fulbright lecturer at the University of Padua. He taught from 1966 to 1983 at the Irvine campus of the University of California; since 1983 he has been professor of English at the University of Virginia.

Many of Wright's poems occur in a southern landscape; others are set in Italy or in California. But Wright remains a poet of grave ethereal music, tethered only lightly by earthly scenes. He is probably most southern in the emotions bequeathed him by his childhood religious experience and in his wish that poetry should have a sacramental grace.

Texts:
"Northhanger Ridge" and "Reunion" from
Country Music: Selected Early Poems, 1982.
"Virginia Reel" from *The Southern Cross*, 1981.

Northhanger Ridge[1]

Half-bridge over nothingness,
White sky of the palette knife; blot orange,
Vertical blacks; blue, birdlike,
Drifting up from the next life,
The heat-waves, like consolation, wince—   5
One cloud, like a trunk, stays shut
Above the horizon; off to the left, dream-wires,
Hill-snout like a crocodile's.

Or so I remember it,
Their clenched teeth in their clenched mouths,   10

[1] A children's summer Bible camp where Wright
was a camper.

Their voices like shards of light,
Brittle, unnecessary.
Ruined shoes, roots, the cabinet of lost things:
This is the same story,
Its lips in flame, its throat a dark water,   15
The page stripped of its meaning.

Sunday, and Father Dog is turned loose:
Up the long road the children's feet
Snick in the dust like raindrops; the wind
Excuses itself and backs off; inside, heat   20
Lies like a hand on each head;
Slither and cough. Now Father Dog
Addles our misconceptions, points, preens,
His finger a white flag, run up, run down.

Bow-wow and arf, the Great Light;   25
O, and the Great Yes, and the Great No;
Redemption, the cold kiss of release,
&c.; sentences, sentences.
(Meanwhile, docile as shadows, they stare
From their four corners, looks set: 30
No glitter escapes
This evangelical masonry.)

Candleflame; vigil and waterflow:
Like dust in the night the prayers rise:
From 6 to 6, under the sick Christ,   35
The children talk to the nothingness,
Crossrack and wound; the dark room
Burns like a coal, goes
Ash to the touch, ash to the tongue's tip;
Blood turns in the wheel: 40

Something drops from the leaves; the drugged moon
Twists and turns in its sheets; sweet breath
In a dry corner, the black widow reknits her dream.
Salvation again declines,
And sleeps like a skull in the hard ground,   45
Nothing for ears, nothing for eyes;
It sleeps as it's always slept, without
Shadow, waiting for nothing.

                                           Bible Camp, 1949

1973

Reunion

Already one day has detached itself from all the rest up ahead.
It has my photograph in its soft pocket.
It wants to carry my breath into the past in its bag of wind.

I write poems to untie myself, to do penance and disappear
Through the upper right-hand corner of things, to say grace.   5

1977

Virginia Reel*[1]

In Clarke County, the story goes, the family name
Was saved by a single crop of wheat,
The houses and land kept in a clear receipt for the subsequent suicides,
The hard times and non-believers to qualify and disperse:
Woodburn and Cedar Hall, Smithfield, Auburn and North Hill: 5
Names like white moths kicked up from the tall grass,
Spreading across the countryside
From the Shenandoah to Charles Town and the Blue Ridge.

And so it happened. But none of us lives here now, in any of them,
Though Aunt Roberta is still in town,   10
Close to the place my great-great-grandfather taught Nelly Custis's children
   once
Answers to Luther.[2] And Cardinal Newman[3] too.
Who cares? Well, I do. It's worth my sighs
To walk here, on the wrong road, tracking a picture back
To its bricks and its point of view.   15
It's worth my while to be here, crumbling this dirt through my bare hands.

I've come back for the first time in 20 years,
Sand in my shoes, my pockets full of the same wind

* Wright's note: "*Virginia Reel* is for Mark
Strand."
[1] Name of an American square dance performed
by two facing lines of people.
[2] Martin Luther (1483–1546), German monk and
theologian, and founder of Protestantism.

[3] John Henry Newman (1801–1890), English
cardinal and writer. Newman, a convert from
Protestantism to Roman Catholicism, was a
Victorian apologist.

That brought me before, my flesh
Remiss in the promises it made then, the absolutes it's heir to.   20
This is the road they drove on. And this is the rise
Their blood repaired to, removing its gloves.
And this is the dirt their lives were made of, the dirt the world is,
Immeasurable emptiness of all things.

I stand on the porch of Wickliffe Church,   25
My kinfolk out back in the bee-stitched vines and weeds,
The night coming on, my flat shirt drawing the light in,
Bright bud on the branch of nothing's tree.
In the new shadows, memory starts to shake out its dark cloth.
Everyone settles down, transparent and animate,   30
Under the oak trees.
Hampton passes the wine around, Jaq toasts to our health.

And when, from the blear and glittering air,
A hand touches my shoulder,
I want to fall to my knees, and keep on falling, here,   35
Laid down by the articles that bear my names,
The limestone and marble and locust wood.
But that's for another life. Just down the road, at Smithfield, the last of the
     apple blossoms
Fishtails to earth through the shot twilight,
A little vowel for the future, a signal from us to them.   40

1981

Michael Harper
b. 1938

Born in Brooklyn, Michael Harper studied in Los Angeles, taking a B.A. and an
M.A. at what is now California State University. He then took a second M.A. at
the University of Iowa. After leaving Iowa in 1963, he traveled in Mexico and
Europe: "Those landscapes," he has said, "broadened my scope and interest in
poetry and culture of other countries while I searched my own family and racial
history for folklore, history and myth for themes that would give my writing
the tradition and context where I could find my own voice." Harper has been a
resolutely historical poet, seeking in the narratives of the past explanatory models
by which to understand the present. He has studied "the tension between stated
moral idealism and brute historical realities," not only to understand American
racism and the reality of black life in America but also to understand universal
moral questions and perennial human suffering.

Harper's underlying music grows out of jazz. "Billie Holiday played piano in
my family's house when I was 12," he has said; he has written memorable elegies

for her and for John Coltrane, the jazz musician whose name is attached to Harper's first volume, *Dear John, Dear Coltrane* (1970). In that volume, and in subsequent ones such as *Nightmare Begins Responsibility* (1975), *Images of Kin* (1977), and *Healing Song for the Inner Ear* (1985), Harper has sought in language for some equivalent to the syncopations and improvisations of jazz and has disturbed the usual prosody deriving from speech rhythms, from what Frost called "sentence sounds." By writing a deliberately "educated" poetry, Harper has distanced himself from the black poets who write in simple "folk" forms and in black dialect; by writing a deliberately historical poetry, Harper has turned away from the confessional mode that reigned in the 1950s and 1960s. Though Harper's poetry is often autobiographical (as in the poems about his boyhood in Brooklyn or in the elegies for his two sons, his brother, and such fellow poets as Robert Hayden and James Wright), the autobiographical core is never without a meditative enlargement.

Recently, Harper has edited an anthology of black art and literature, *Chant of Saints* (1973), which takes advantage of the sophistication with which the literary forms of Afro-American literature are now being explored and classified. Harper is a professor of English at Brown University, where he directs the writing program.

Text:
Images of Kin, 1977.

Dear John, Dear Coltrane[1]

a love supreme, a love supreme
a love supreme, a love supreme[2]

Sex fingers toes
in the marketplace
near your father's church
in Hamlet, North Carolina—
witness to this love   5
in this calm fallow
of these minds,
there is no substitute for pain:
genitals gone or going,
seed burned out,   10
you tuck the roots in the earth,
turn back, and move
by river through the swamps,

---

[1] John Coltrane (1926–1967), American jazz saxophonist.

[2] "A Love Supreme," one of the songs Coltrane played, contained this chant.

singing: *a love supreme, a love supreme;*
what does it all mean?   15
Loss, so great each black
woman expects your failure
in mute change, the seed gone.
You plod up into the electric city—
your song now crystal and   20
the blues. You pick up the horn
with some will and blow
into the freezing night:
a love supreme, a love supreme—

Dawn comes and you cook   25
up the thick sin 'tween
impotence and death, fuel
the tenor sax cannibal
heart, genitals and sweat
that makes you clean—   30
a love supreme, a love supreme—

Why you so black?
cause I am
why you so funky?
cause I am
why you so black?   35
cause I am
why you so sweet?
cause I am
why you so black?   40
cause I am
a love supreme, a love supreme:

So sick
you couldn't play *Naima,*[3]
so flat we ached   45
for song you'd concealed
with your own blood,
your diseased liver gave
out its purity,
the inflated heart   50
pumps out, the tenor[4] kiss,
tenor love:
a love supreme, a love supreme—
a love supreme, a love supreme—
1970

---

[3] Another song often played by Coltrane.
[4] Allusion to the tenor saxophone, Coltrane's
primary instrument.

Martin's[1] Blues

He came apart in the open,
the slow motion cameras
falling quickly
neither alive nor kicking;
stone blind dead   5
on the balcony[2]
that old melody
etched his black lips
in a pruned echo:
We shall overcome   10
some day[3]—

Yes we did!
Yes we did!
1971

Charles Simic
b. 1938

Charles Simic, who is a professor of English at the University of New
Hampshire, was born in Yugoslavia and came to the United States in 1949. He
attended the University of Chicago and received his B.A. from New York
University after serving in the U.S. Army from 1961 to 1963. In 1967 he
published his first book of poems, *What the Grass Says,* beginning a distinguished
career. In 1984 he was awarded a five-year MacArthur fellowship. Simic's poetry,
especially in such collections as *Dismantling the Silence* (1971) and *Charon's
Cosmology* (1977), retains the flavor of folktale: In it, sinister and simple events
gather into doomed assemblages. World War II was the backdrop to Simic's
Yugoslavian childhood; deaths, wounds, exiles, treacheries, and terrors mark the
nameless and placeless parables of his inner world. A farcical comedy and a grim
humor ornament the tragic plots that animate his poems. Though these are often
miniature narratives in quatrains, much is accomplished in a few lines.

Simic learned some of his bleak techniques from eastern European postwar
poets, many of whom he has translated, most notably Vasco Popa. Together with
Mark Strand, Simic edited *Another Republic* (1976), an anthology of seventeen

---

[1] Martin Luther King (1929–1968), American
clergyman and civil rights leader, was
assassinated April 4, 1968.

[2] I.e., the motel balcony where King was shot.

[3] "We Shall Overcome" was the hymn made
famous by King's followers during the 1960s
civil rights movement.

European and South American writers. The cross-fertilization of American poetry by foreign poetry, which began in the early years of this century with the assimilation of French symbolist verse and Chinese poetry and continued in the 1960s with the adoption of Spanish and Latin American sources, has now incorporated the poetry of Russia and Eastern Europe, aided by the influence of Simic and other émigré writers such as Joseph Brodsky and Czesław Miłosz.

Simic's poems are written out of unforgettable details seen with a child's clarity, recalled against the amnesia of time, and repeatedly anatomized for significance. As he forces the gates of memory, he finds broken treasures that he pores over like an archaeologist, full of nostalgia for some unknown ancient coherence. Written in peacetime, Simic's poems are nevertheless part of the poetry of the Second World War. His *Selected Poems* appeared in 1985.

Text:
Dismantling the Silence, 1971.

Hearing Steps

Someone is walking through the snow:
An ancient sound. Perhaps the Mongols are migrating again?
Perhaps, once more we'll go hanging virgins
From bare trees, plundering churches,
Raping widows in the deep snow?   5

Perhaps, the time has come again
To go back into forests and snow fields,
Live alone killing wolves with our bare hands,
Until the last word and the last sound
Of this language I am speaking is forgotten.   10

1971

My Shoes

Shoes, secret face of my inner life:
Two gaping toothless mouths,
Two partly decomposed animal skins
Smelling of mice-nests.

My brother and sister who died at birth   5
Continuing their existence in you,
Guiding my life
Toward their incomprehensible innocence.

What use are books to me
When in you it is possible to read   10
The Gospel of my life on earth
And still beyond, of things to come?

I want to proclaim the religion
I have devised for your perfect humility
And the strange church I am building   15
With you as the altar.

Ascetic and maternal, you endure:
Kin to oxen, to Saints, to condemned men,
With your mute patience, forming
The only true likeness of myself.   20

1971

Frank Bidart
b. *1939*

Frank Bidart grew up in California, "crazy about movies. In Bakersfield, I think movies were the most accessible art form. . . . We didn't have [ballet or symphony or plays]. But we did have, each week, surrounded by publicity, glamour, and controversy, these incredibly interesting movies. As early as I can remember, I wanted to be an artist; I certainly knew I didn't want to be a farmer, as my father was. Briefly, I imagined becoming an actor; but very quickly it was clear to me that the person who really made movies was the director. . . . So, in college, I was determined to be a film director." In fact, Bidart majored in English at the University of California at Riverside and went on to take an M.A. at Harvard, where he studied writing with Robert Lowell. There, Bidart says, he realized that "subject matter"—"confronting the dilemmas, issues, 'things' with which the world had confronted me—had to be at the center of the poems if they were to have force. . . . I needed a way to embody the mind moving through the elements of its world, actively contending with and organizing them, while they somehow retain the illusion of their independence and nature, are felt as 'out there' or 'other.'" Bidart moved toward "deploying the words on the page through voice; syntax; punctuation"—a prosody marking "speed and tension and emphasis" by everything from line breaks to capital letters.

Bidart quotes Frost's saying that sentences are saved for poetry only by "the speaking tone of voice somehow entangled in the words and fastened to the page for the ear of the imagination." Bidart's first poems in *Golden State* (1973) were spoken in his own voice; some later poems, in *The Book of the Body* (1977) and *The Sacrifice* (1983), have assumed the voice of historical characters—the anorexic Ellen West, the ballet dancer Nijinsky. Through the volatile voices of characters in extreme anguish (Ellen West commits suicide; Nijinsky goes mad), Bidart choreographs on the page issues such as the relation of mind to body and the persistence of guilt, issues that have, as he says, no "answer," no "solution." Bidart's dramatic monologues resemble operatic arias more than the self-betraying verse of a Browning character; they exist not so much to define character as to display the virtuosity of voice itself. And in their rapid cuts from voice to voice and scene to scene, his polyphonic poems of many voices resemble the movies that gave Bidart his first vision of what art could be. Bidart is a professor of English at Wellesley College and has taught at Brandeis and the University of California at Berkeley.

Texts:
"Self-Portrait, 1969" from *Golden State,* 1973.
"Happy Birthday" from *The Book of the Body,*
1977.

Self-Portrait, 1969

He's *still* young—; thirty, but looks younger—
or does he? . . . In the eyes and cheeks, tonight,
turning in the mirror, he saw his mother,—
puffy; angry; bewildered . . . Many nights
now, when he stares there, he gets angry:—   5
something *unfulfilled* there, something dead
to what he once thought he surely could be—
Now, just the glamour of habits . . .

                                  Once, instead,
he thought insight would remake him, he'd reach
—what? The thrill, the exhilaration   10
unravelling disaster, that seemed to teach
necessary knowledge . . . became just jargon.

Sick of being decent, he craves another
crash. What *reaches* him except disaster?
1973

Happy Birthday

Thirty-three, goodbye—
the awe I feel

is not that you won't come again, or why—

or even that after
a time, we think of those who are dead   5

with a sweetness that cannot be explained—

but that I've read the trading-cards:
RALPH TEMPLE CYCLIST CHAMPION TRICK RIDER

WILLIE HARRADON CYCLIST
THE YOUTHFUL PHENOMENON   10

F. F. IVES CYCLIST
100 MILES 6 H. 25 MIN. 30 SEC.

—as the fragile metal of their
wheels stopped turning, as they
took on wives, children, accomplishments, all those   15
predilections which also insisted on ending,

they could not tell themselves from what they had done.

Terrible to dress in the clothes
of a period that must end.

They didn't plan it that way—   20
they didn't plan it that way.
1977

Robert Pinsky
b. 1940

The work of Robert Pinsky, a pupil at Stanford of the late poet and critic Yvor Winters, has come to represent a recoil of poetry into full discursive "sense," away from surrealist techniques, mysterious symbolist visions, political rhetoric, and minimalist reduction. Winters insisted that poetry should be rational and logical and should forgo the destructive appetite for transcendence, initiated by Emerson, that led, in Winters's view, to such excesses as the suicide of his friend Hart Crane. In a critical book, *The Situation of Poetry* (1976), Pinsky has presented a Wintersian program for postmodernist poetry, a program defending the representation of an objective world within the world of art.

As teacher and, until recently, poetry editor for *The New Republic,* Pinsky has been influential in recommending poetry that is circumstantial in its faithfulness to the quotidian appearances of life. In its reaction against introspection as a sufficient motive for poetry, the work of Pinsky and other recent poets ventures into the realm of the essay, the disquisition, and the description. Pinsky's poetry in this vein aims at a Horatian moderation; in fact, Pinsky translates one of Horace's epistles in the course of writing a long poem addressed to his daughter, entitled "An Explanation of America" (1979). Temperate in its tone, ironic in its stance, didactic much of the time in its intent, Pinsky's poetry argues that almost any subject (America, psychiatrists, tennis) will serve as sufficient occasion for the meditation of an inquiring and curious mind. Pinsky's prosody is unobtrusive, his syntax clear (if complex), and the argument of his poetry at once logical and sinuous. The poetry represents a principled turning away from the discontinuities of high modernism and a return to a more Augustan civil mode.

Pinsky was born in New Jersey and educated at Rutgers (B.A., 1962) and Stanford, where he took a Ph.D. in English literature. His first published book was *Landor's Poetry* (1968), a critical commentary on the work of the Victorian classicizing poet. Pinsky has published two volumes of poetry, *Sadness and Happiness* (1975) and *The History of My Heart* (1984). After teaching for many years at Wellesley College, Pinsky is now a professor of English at the University of California at Berkeley.

Texts:
"Memorial" from *An Explanation of America,* 1979.
"Dying" from *History of My Heart,* 1984.

Memorial

(J.E. and N.M.S.)

Here lies a man. And here, a girl. They live
In the kind of artificial life we give

To birds or statues: imagining what they feel,
Or that like birds the dead each had one call,

Repeated, or a gesture that suspends   5
Their being in a forehead or the hands.

A man comes whistling from a house. The screen
Snaps shut behind him. Though there is no man

And no house, memory sends him to get tools
From a familiar shed, and so he strolls   10

Through summer shade to work on the family car.
He is my uncle, and fresh home from the war,

With little for me to remember him doing yet.
The clock of the cancer ticks in his body, or not,

Depending if it is there, or waits. The search   15
Of memory gains and fails like surf: the porch

And trim are painted cream, the shakes are stained.
The shadows could be painted (so little wind

Is blowing there) or stains on the crazy-paving
Of the front walk. . . . Or now, the shadows are moving: 20

Another house, unrelated; a woman says,
Is this your special boy, and the girl says, yes,

Moving her hand in mine. The clock in her, too—
As someone told me a month or two ago,

Months after it finally took her. A public building   25
Is where the house was: though a surf, unyielding

And sickly, seethes and eddies at the stones
Of the foundation. The dead are made of bronze,

But dying they were like birds with clocklike hearts—
Unthinkable, how much pain the tiny parts   30

Of even the smallest bird might yet contain.
We become larger than life in how much pain

Our bodies may encompass . . . all Titans in that,
Or heroic statues. Although there is no heat

Brimming in the fixed, memorial summer, the brows   35
Of lucid metal sweat a faint warm haze

As I try to think the pain I never saw.
Though there is no pain there, the small birds draw

Together in crowds above the houses—and cry
Over the surf: as if there were a day,   40

Memorial, marked on the calendar for dread
And pain and loss—although among the dead

Are no hurts, but only emblematic things;
No hospital beds, but a lifting of metal wings.
1979

Dying

Nothing to be said about it, and everything—
The change of changes, closer or further away:
The Golden Retriever next door, Gussie, is dead,

Like Sandy, the Cocker Spaniel from three doors down
Who died when I was small; and every day   5
Things that were in my memory fade and die.

Phrases die out: first, everyone forgets
What doornails are; then after certain decades
As a dead metaphor, *"dead as a doornail"* flickers

And fades away. But someone I know is dying—   10
And though one might say glibly, "everyone is,"
The different pace makes the difference absolute.

The tiny invisible spores in the air we breathe,
That settle harmlessly on our drinking water
And on our skin, happen to come together   15

With certain conditions on the forest floor,
Or even a shady corner of the lawn—
And overnight the fleshy, pale stalks gather,

The colorless growth without a leaf or flower;
And around the stalks, the summer grass keeps growing   20
With steady pressure, like the insistent whiskers

That grow between shaves on a face, the nails
Growing and dying from the toes and fingers
At their own humble pace, oblivious

As the nerveless moths, that live their night or two—   25
Though like a moth a bright soul keeps on beating,
Bored and impatient in the monster's mouth.
1984

Dave Smith
b. 1942

Dave Smith is one of the most prolific of the younger poets now writing in
America; his restless and large talent has poured itself out in several books,
including a novel, *Onliness* (1981), a collection of short stories, and a collection
of prose pieces, *Local Assays* (1985); he has also edited a collection of essays on
the poetry of James Wright. Smith was born in Portsmouth, Virginia, and
graduated from the University of Virginia. After serving for three years in the
air force, he took an M.A. at Southern Illinois University and a Ph.D. at Ohio
University (1976). He has taught at the University of Utah and is now a
professor of English at Virginia Commonwealth University in Richmond.

"My subjects," says Smith, "have been, generally, the Atlantic seacoast, the
American West, and people. I care little for poems that do not create a narrative
or contextual event in which people are involved with something that is
happening or has happened. I am concerned to write a thickly textured poem
whose speech as well as whose event will be memorable." Smith has linked his
own work with that of Robert Penn Warren and James Dickey; he sees himself
as a southern writer and has been a rich ethnographer of southern life.

Smith's early poems about the Chesapeake Bay oyster fishermen in *The
Fisherman's Whore* (1974) show his fierce sense of locale and of natural struggle.
Later, his more spacious and vast poems in *Goshawk, Antelope* (1979), written
from the Utah landscape, suggest a more allegorical measure of our place in the

universe: between the predatory hawk and the peaceful antelope. Catastrophes and disasters often appear as the backdrop to Smith's poetry: family ruin; the dissolution of mining, railroading, and fishing communities; the erosion of American rural life; the potential for erotic dismay; nameless male violence—all of these themes course through the poetry, attended by language bearing an electric charge of feeling. Smith's effects can sometimes be coarse, when his subject outruns his technique; but with each volume there has been an expansion of imagination and an investigation into new expressive regions.

Smith has said himself that his poems "appear to devolve to the theme of obligation," to *pietas* (the Roman name for that virtue). The moral insistence in Smith's earlier poetry has, in his recent work, *Dream Flights* (1981) and *Homage to Edgar Allan Poe* (1981), evolved into a more reflective and brooding consciousness of the necessary and the fated in life; the poems are less full of vaulting ambition and more aware of the grimness of human existence. His poems have become longer, freer in their verse line and in their narrative energies, as willing to float in "dream flights" as to drive forward with relentless momentum. In his insistence on a narrative base to the lyric, Smith allies himself with the remnants of the epic tradition, claiming for lyric poetry a brotherhood with the story and the novel. Smith's *New and Selected Poems* appeared in 1985.

Texts:
"Hawktree" from *Goshawk, Antelope*, 1979.
"Reading . . ." from *Homage to Edgar Allan Poe*, 1981.

"Smithfield Ham" from *In the House of the Judge*, 1983.

Hawktree

Tonight in the hills there was a light
that leaped out of the head
and yellow longing of a young boy.
It was spring and he had walked
through the toy-littered yards   5
to the edge of town, and beyond.
In the tall spare shadow of a pine
he saw her standing, she of skin
whiter than the one cloud
each day loaned to the long sky,   10
whiter even than the pure moon.
But she would not speak to one
who kept her name to himself
when boys laughed in the courtyard.
He watched her burn like a candle   15

in the cathedral of needles.
After a while he saw the other light,
the sun's leveling blister, bring
its change to her wheaten hair.
In growing dark he waited, certain   20
she would hear the pine's whisper,
counting on nature's mediation.
But she would not speak and even
as he watched she vanished.
Slowly he knew his arms furred   25
with a fragrant green darkness
and as the moon cut its swaths
on the ground, as trucks rooted
along the road of colored pleasures,
he felt his feet pushing through   30
his shoes, his hair go sharply stiff.
He could hear her laugh, could see
her long finger loop a man's ear,
but this did not matter. Already
he felt himself sway a little   35
in the desert wind, in the wordless
emptied gnarling he had become.
1979

Reading the Books Our Children Have Written

They come into this room while the quail are crying to huddle up,
the canyon winds just beginning. They pass my big brown desk,
their faces damp and glistening like the first peaches washed,
and offer themselves to be kissed. I am their father still,
I kiss them, I say *See you tomorrow!* Their light steps fade   5
down the stairs, what they are saying like the far stars
shrill, hard to understand. They are saying their father
writes a book and they are in it, for they are his children.
Then they lie in their beds waiting for sleep, sometimes singing.

Later I get up and go down in darkness and find the hour they played   10
before they were scrubbed, before they brought me those faces.
There on the floor I find the stapled pages, the strange mild
countenances of animals no one has ever seen, the tall dark man

who writes an endless story of birds homeless in the night. They have
numbered every page, they have named each colorful wing.   15
They have done all this to surprise me, surprising themselves.
On the last lined yellow page, one has written *This is a poem.*
Under this the other one has answered *See tomorrow.*
1981

Smithfield Ham

Aged, bittersweet, in salt crusted, the pink meat
lined with the sun's flare, fissured
as a working man's skin at hat level,
I see far back the flesh fall
as the honed knife goes   5
through to the plate, the lost
voice saying ". . . it cuts easy as butter. . . ."

Brown sugar and grease tries to hold itself
still beneath the sawed knee's white.
Around the table the clatter of china   10
kept in the highboy echoes,
children squeal in a near room.

The hand sawing is grandfather's, knuckled,
steadily starting each naked plate
heaped when it ends. Mine   15
waits shyly to receive
under the tall ceiling
all aunts, uncles have gathered to hold.

My shirt white as the creased linen, I shine
before the wedge of cherry pie, coffee   20
black as the sugarless future.[1]
My mother, proud in his glance,
whispers he has called for me and for ham.

Tonight I come back to eat in that house the sliced
muscle that fills me with an old thirst.
With each swallow, unslaked, I feel   25
his hand fall more upon mine,

[1] Smith is a diabetic.

that odd endless blessing
I cannot say the name of . . .
it comes again with her family   30
tale, the dead recalled, Depression,
the jobless, china sold, low sobs, sickness.

Chewing, I ask how he is. Close your mouth, she says.
This time, if he saw me, maybe he'd remember
himself, who thanklessly carved us   35
that cured meat. The Home has to
let us in, we've paid, maybe we
have to go. I gnaw a roll
left too long on the table.
When my knife screeches the plate,   40
my mother shakes her head, whining like a child.

Nothing's sharp anymore, I can't help it, she says.
Almost alone, I lift the scalded coffee
steeped black and bitter.
My mouth, as if incontinent,   45
dribbles and surprises us.
Her face is streaked with summer
dusk where katydids drill and die.

Wanting to tell her there's always tomorrow,
I say you're sunburned, beautiful as ever,   50
Gardening has put the smell of dirt on her.
Like a blade, her hand touches mine.
More? she whispers. Then, ". . . you think
you'll never get enough, so sweet,
until the swelling starts, the ache . . .   55
it's that thirst that wants
to bust a person open late at night."
I fill my cup again, drink, nod, listen.
1983

Albert Goldbarth
b. 1948

Albert Goldbarth, a vividly abundant writer, publishes both short lyrics and long
sequences; the sequences almost always incorporate and embody historical
material. The 1974 sequence called *Optics* contains, for instance, material about
glassblowers, glassmaking, stained glass windows, and so on. He has also written
sequences on a transvestite Paris entertainer and on an American painter.

Goldbarth was born and raised in Chicago, and many of his autobiographical lyrics concern Jewish family life, with its beginnings in immigration, its decimation by the Holocaust, its religious rituals, its kinship relations, its social presence. Goldbarth writes as one who has left that life but wishes to perpetuate it as it recedes.

After graduating from the University of Illinois at Chicago Circle, Goldbarth took an M.F.A. at Iowa and subsequently has taught at the University of Utah, Cornell, and the University of Texas at Austin, where he is now a professor of English. His writing takes many risks as it leaps into associative patterns heedless of formal or logical connections. The connections are there (Goldbarth is not a surrealist but rather an expressionist writer), but the poet wishes to imitate the mind's creative elation and generalized play as the imagination reconstructs the world. His historical imagination is strong; he thinks himself into another century as powerfully as he can think himself into a dead ballet dancer. He likes, as he has said, "the extended poem that includes narrative, or has scope enough to play with large bodies of time, or that finds room for dialogue or quoted source materials, that can build up litany or weave motifs in and out with the huge sweep a suite has." His *Different Fleshes* (1977) is a "novel/poem," with alternating sections of poetry and prose. In it, Goldbarth wishes "to allow moments of pure lyric visionary intensity to take place within a novel-like framework: plot, historic and invented characters, quoted conversation." In this way, the poem attempts to imitate the diversity of life and of perception.

Though Goldbarth can be sentimental in his commemorative poetry, he can also be remarkably brusque and brisk about his childhood surroundings. His play of language is as various as the play of his imagination; words from many different registers jostle each other on the page—technical words, dialect words, philosophical words, demotic words. What is most exhilarating about reading Goldbarth is the constant surprise one encounters on each page as the poem continues a protean development, unforeseen and beautiful, of its basic premises. Goldbarth's most recent collection, *Arts and Sciences,* appeared in 1986.

Texts:
"How the Sky Counts Years" from *Faith,* 1981.
"A History of Civilization" from *Original Light: New and Selected Poems, 1973–1983,* 1983.

How the Sky Counts Years

Somewhere, on a far star, my mother
was saying "This should be" then it sputters
"the worst" a long dark space "that ever
happens to you." It was something trivial

I guess, and so the irony. Such small things   5
tug attention!—/a bee at a rose's spirals
like yoga's focus on mandalas;[1] this
milkeye nipple; whose heart holds exactly the volume
of blood of the trap-snapped mouse?; fresh
lemon wedge; your stare's two pupils, caught like   10
faltered trapezists: in their red nets/—how
can anyone master a discipline? Then

one night, walking, a man understands
astronomy. It's a cinder, cold
in the sky now; though here, in my life, I   15
first see the light, and by it.

1981

A History of Civilization

In the dating bar, the potted ferns lean down
conspiratorially, little spore-studded
elopement ladders. The two top buttons
of every silk blouse have already half-undone all
introduction. Slices of smile, slices of sweet brie,[1]   5
dark and its many white wedges. In back

of the bar, the last one-family grocer's is necklaced
over and over: strings of leeks, greek olives, sardines.
The scoops stand at attention in the millet barrel,
the cordovan sheen of the coffee barrel, the kidney beans.   10
And a woman whose pride is a clean linen apron polishes
a register as intricate as a Sicilian shrine. In back

of the grocery, dozing and waking in fitful starts
by the guttering hearth, a ring of somber-gabardined grandpas
plays dominoes. Their stubble picks up the flicker like filaments   15
still waiting for the bulb or the phone to be invented. Even their
coughs, their phlegms, are in an older language. They move the simple
pieces of matching numbers. In back

[1] A meditative technique used by Eastern
practitioners of yoga is to focus on one sacred
image, or mandala.

[1] A French cheese.

of the back room, in the unlit lengths of storage, it's
that season: a cat eyes a cat. The sacks and baskets
are sprayed with the sign of a cat's having eyed a cat, and
everything to do with rut[2] and estrus[3] comes down to a few
sure moves. The dust motes drift, the continents.
In the fern bar a hand tries a knee, as if unplanned.

20

1983

Jorie Graham
b. 1951

Jorie Graham, the daughter of American parents, grew up in Italy. She was sent
to a French lycée in Rome and so became trilingual, speaking Italian with
friends, English at home, and French in school. (One of her poems retells her
bafflement as a child that the chestnut tree had three names.) She attended the
Sorbonne for a year (1968) studying philosophy, then came to the United States,
where she entered the program in cinema studies (directed by Martin Scorcese) at
New York University, and began to write poetry. After her B.A. (1972), she
worked for NBC television and attended poetry workshops and seminars at
Columbia. She took an M.F.A. at the University of Iowa in 1978, where she is
now on the permanent faculty.

Graham was exposed very early to the visual arts (her mother is a painter and
sculptor) and to the churches and museums of Italy. Many of her poems meditate
on the relation between the expressive possibilities of language and those of the
visual arts. They also reflect on the inevitable tension between the damage of life
and the beauty of art: "Contained damage makes for beauty," one of the poems
ventures to say. How the violent and the sexual are to be handled within the
fabric of art; how art can accommodate itself to the infinite shades of nuance that
experience demands; how art mends life; how the wish of the spirit to become
pure spirit is matched by the wish of the spirit to reenter the body; how time
preserves the past in death—all these metaphysical questions are present repeatedly
in Graham's work. (Her philosophy studies at the lycée included works of Pascal,
Kant, Heidegger, Sartre, and Merleau-Ponty, with weekly papers, as she writes,
"on such subjects as 'Reason and Morality,' or 'La Passion.' ")

Graham's voice tends to move in phrases, in recurrent pulses of tentative
exploration as she moves over a field of preoccupation, testing its limits,
weighing its powers, looking for a way into feeling, "fingering all the stops." In
this way the movement of the poem tends to imitate the searchings and
depth-soundings of the mind seeking to replicate the starts and questionings of
the heart.

"As a young woman," Graham writes, "I read quantities of Baudelaire,

---

[2] In this context, the periodic sexual excitement
of a male animal.

[3] The period during which a female animal is in
heat.

Rimbaud, Mallarmé, Apollinaire, and Supervielle; at school we had to bring in
huge passages from Racine and Corneille by heart—to this day I hear 'Ô rage,
ô désespoir, ô vieillesse ennemie, / Ai-je donc tant vécu que pour cette infamie,'
etc." She also read, as was inevitable for someone raised in Italy, Dante and Tasso
and Petrarch. Among the Americans, besides the modernist poets, Graham read
and was attracted to the poetry of Elizabeth Bishop: "I feel strong kinship with
her notion of boundaries—the poem as an act of confrontation between two
worlds." Graham's musicality and her feeling for etymologies put her poetry in
the long tradition of the "pure lyric," stretching from Petrarch and Ronsard to
Rilke and Stevens.

Text:
Hybrids of Plants and Ghosts, 1980.

The Geese

Today as I hang out the wash I see them again, a code
as urgent as elegant,
tapering with goals.
For days they have been crossing. We live beneath these geese

as if beneath the passage of time, or a most perfect heading.   5
Sometimes I fear their relevance.
Closest at hand,
between the lines,

the spiders imitate the paths the geese won't stray from,
imitate them endlessly to no avail: 10
things will not remain connected,
will not heal,

and the world thickens with texture instead of history,
texture instead of place.
Yet the small fear of the spiders   15
binds and binds

the pins to the lines, the lines to the eaves, to the pincushion bush,
as if, at any time, things could fall further apart
and nothing could help them
recover their meaning. And if these spiders had their way,   20

chainlink over the visible world,
would we be in or out? I turn to go back in.
There is a feeling the body gives the mind
of having missed something, a bedrock poverty, like falling

without the sense that you are passing through one world,   25
that you could reach another
anytime. Instead the real
is crossing you,

your body an arrival
you know is false but can't outrun. And somewhere in between   30
these geese forever entering and
these spiders turning back,

this astonishing delay, the everyday, takes place.
1980

Mind

The slow overture of rain,
each drop breaking
without breaking into
the next, describes
the unrelenting, syncopated   5
mind. Not unlike
the hummingbirds
imagining their wings
to be their heart, and swallows
believing the horizon   10
to be a line they lift
and drop. What is it
they cast for? The poplars,
advancing or retreating,
lose their stature   15
equally, and yet stand firm,
making arrangements
in order to become
imaginary. The city
draws the mind in streets,   20
and streets compel it
from their intersections

where a little
belongs to no one. It is
what is driven through   25
all stationary portions
of the world, gravity's
stake in things. The leaves,
pressed against the dank
window of November   30
soil, remain unwelcome
till transformed, parts
of a puzzle unsolvable
till the edges give a bit
and soften. See how   35
then the picture becomes clear,
the mind entering the ground
more easily in pieces,
and all the richer for it.

1980

Acknowledgments

Abigail Adams: Reprinted by permission of the publishers from *The Book of Abigail and John: Selected Letters of the Adams Family*, edited by L. H. Butterfield, Marc Friedlaender and Mary-Jo Kline, Cambridge, Mass: Harvard University Press, Copyright © 1975 by the Massachusetts Historical Society.

Henry Adams: From *The Education of Henry Adams*. Copyright 1918 by the Massachusetts Historical Society. Copyright 1946 by Charles F. Adams. Reprinted by permission of Houghton Mifflin Company.

Frederick Lewis Allen: Excerpt from p. 244 in *Only Yesterday*, by Frederick Lewis Allen. Copyright 1939, 1940 by Harper & Row, Publishers, Inc.

A. R. Ammons: "The City Limits," "Transaction," "The Eternal City," "Grace Abounding," "Cascadilla Falls," "Treaties," and "Hardweed Path Going," from *Collected Poems, 1941–1971*, by A. R. Ammons. Copyright © 1972 by A. R. Ammons. "Easter Morning" from *A Coast of Trees, Poems*, by A. R. Ammons. Copyright © 1981 by A. R. Ammons. All reprinted by permission of W. W. Norton & Company, Inc.

Sherwood Anderson: "Departure," "Mother," "Hands," and "The Book of the Grotesque." From *Winesburg, Ohio*, by Sherwood Anderson. Copyright 1919 by B. W. Huebsch. Copyright renewed 1947 by Eleanor Copenhaver Anderson. Reprinted by permission of Viking Penguin Inc.

John Ashbery: "Some Trees" from *Some Trees*. Copyright © 1956 by John Ashbery. "These Lacustrine Cities" from *Rivers and Mountains*. Copyright © 1962 by John Ashbery. "Soonest Mended," "Years of Indiscretion" from *The Double Dream of Spring*. Copyright © 1970 by John Ashbery. Reprinted by permission of Georges Borchardt, Inc. and the author. "Pyrography" from *Houseboat Days*, by John Ashbery. Copyright © 1975, 1976, 1977 by John Ashbery. "Drunken Americans" from *Shadow Train*, by John Ashbery. Copyright © 1980, 1981 by John Ashbery. "A Love Poem" from *As We Know*, by John Ashbery. Copyright © 1979 by John Ashbery. "As One Put Drunk into the Packet-Boat" from *Self-Portrait in a Convex Mirror*, by John Ashbery. Copyright © 1972, 1973, 1974, 1975 by John Ashbery. From "The Recital" from *Three Poems*, by John Ashbery. Copyright © 1970, 1971, 1972 by John Ashbery. Reprinted by permission of Viking Penguin Inc.

James Baldwin: "Sonny's Blues" from *Going to Meet the Man*, by James Baldwin. Copyright © 1948, 1951, 1957, 1958, 1960, 1965 by James Baldwin. Reprinted by permission of Doubleday & Company, Inc.

John Barth: Excerpt from *The Sot-Weed Factor*, by John Barth. Copyright © 1960, 1967 by John Barth. Reprinted by permission of Doubleday & Company, Inc.

Donald Barthelme: "Robert Kennedy Saved from Drowning" from *Unspeakable Practices, Unnatural Acts*, by Donald Barthelme. Copyright © 1968 by Donald Barthelme. Reprinted by permission of Farrar, Straus and Giroux, Inc.

Ann Beattie: "Jacklighting" from *The Burning House*, by Ann Beattie. Copyright © 1982 by Irony and Pity, Inc. Reprinted by permission of Random House, Inc.

Thomas Beer: From *The Mauve Decade: American Life at the End of the Nineteenth Century* (Alfred A. Knopf, Inc., 1926).

Saul Bellow: "Looking for Mr. Green" from *Mosby's Memoirs and Other Stories,* by Saul Bellow. Copyright 1951, renewed © 1979 by Saul Bellow. Reprinted by permission of Viking Penguin Inc.

William Ralganal Benson: "The Facts of the Stone and Kelsey Massacre in Lake County, California." Reprinted by permission of the California Historical Society and The Bancroft Library, University of California, Berkeley.

John Berryman: "Huffy Henry," "Filling her compact & delicious body," "Henry sats," "Life, friends," "The glories of the world," "There sat down once," "He stared at ruin," "Seedy Henry" from *77 Dream Songs,* by John Berryman. Copyright © 1959, 1962, 1963, 1964 by John Berryman. "Three Limbs," "So Long? Stevens," "The Marker slants" from *His Toy, His Dream, His Rest,* by John Berryman. Copyright © 1964, 1965, 1966, 1967, 1968 by John Berryman. "With arms outflung," "Old Codger Henry," "All projects failed" from *Henry's Fate,* by John Berryman. Copyright © 1977 by Mrs. Kate Berryman. Excerpt from *Homage to Mistress Bradstreet,* by John Berryman. Copyright © 1956 by John Berryman. Copyright renewed © 1984 by Mrs. Kate Berryman. Reprinted by permission of Farrar, Straus and Giroux, Inc.

Frank Bidart: "Self-Portrait" from *Golden State,* by Frank Bidart. Reprinted by permission of the publisher, George Braziller Inc., New York. "Happy Birthday" copyright © 1974, 1977 by Frank Bidart. From *The Book of the Body.* Reprinted by permission of the author.

Elizabeth Bishop: "The Fish," "Over 2000 Illustrations and a Complete Concordance," "At the Fishhouses," "Questions of Travel," "The Armadillo," "Sestina," "Filling Station," "In the Waiting Room," from *The Complete Poems 1927–1979,* by Elizabeth Bishop. Copyright © 1940, 1947, 1948, 1955, 1956, 1957 by Elizabeth Bishop. Copyright renewed © 1974, 1976 by Elizabeth Bishop. Copyright © 1983 by Alice Helen Methfessel. "At the Fishhouses," "Questions of Travel," "The Armadillo," "Sestina," originally appeared in *The New Yorker.* Reprinted by permission of Farrar, Straus and Giroux, Inc.

William Bradford: From *Of Plymouth Plantation,* by William Bradford, edited by Samuel Eliot Morison. Copyright 1952 by Samuel Eliot Morison and renewed 1980 by Emily M. Beck. Reprinted by permission of Alfred A. Knopf, Inc.

Anne Bradstreet: Reprinted by permission of the publishers of *The Works of Anne Bradstreet,* edited by Jeannine Hensley, Cambridge, Mass.: The Belknap Press of Harvard University Press, Copyright © 1967 by the President and Fellows of Harvard College.

Claude Brown: From *Manchild in the Promised Land,* by Claude Brown. Copyright © 1965 by Claude Brown. Reprinted with permission of the publisher.

William Byrd II: Reprinted by permission of the publishers from *The Prose Works of William Byrd of Westover,* edited by Louis B. Wright, Cambridge, Mass.: The Belknap Press of Harvard University Press, Copyright © 1966 by the President and Fellows of Harvard College.

Raymond Carver: "Cathedral" from *Cathedral,* by Raymond Carver. Copyright © 1981, 1982, 1983 by Raymond Carver. Reprinted by permission of Alfred A. Knopf, Inc.

John Cheever: "The Fourth Alarm." Copyright © 1970 by John Cheever. Reprinted from *The Stories of John Cheever,* by permission of Alfred A. Knopf, Inc.

Winston S. Churchill: From Winston S. Churchill, Volume IV, 1916–1922: *The Stricken World,* edited by Martin Gilbert. Copyright © 1975 by C&T Publications, Ltd. Published by Heinemann and Houghton Mifflin. Reprinted by permission of Houghton Mifflin Company and Curtis Brown Ltd.

Amy Clampitt: "A Procession at Candlemas," "The Kingfisher." Copyright © 1981, 1983 by Amy Clampitt. Reprinted from *The Kingfisher,* by Amy Clampitt, by permission of Alfred A. Knopf, Inc.

Columbus: From *The Columbus Journals,* ed. by Samuel Eliot Morison. Copyright © 1964 by Samuel Eliot Morison. Reprinted by permission of Curtis Brown, Ltd.

Hart Crane: "The Broken Tower," "Proem: To Brooklyn Bridge," "The Dance," "Atlantis," "Chaplinesque," "Repose of Rivers," "Passage," "At Melville's Tomb," "O Carib Isle," "The Idiot," "I am concerned with the future of America," "The function of poetry" are reprinted from *The Complete Poems and Selected Letters and Prose of Hart Crane,* Edited by Brom Weber, by permission of Liveright Publishing Corporation. Copyright 1933 © 1958, 1966 by Liveright Publishing Corporation.

Stephen Crane: "The Bride Came to Yellow Sky" and "The Open Boat" from *The University of Virginia Edition of Works of Stephen Crane* Vol. 5, *Tales of Adventure,* Edited by Fredson Bowers, Charlottesville: The University Press of Virginia, 1970. "An Episode of War" from *The University of Virginia Edition of Works of Stephen Crane* Vol. VI, *Tales of War,* Edited by Fredson Bowers, Charlottesville: The University Press of Virginia, 1970.

permission of the publishers from *The Collected Works of Ralph Waldo Emerson*, volume I: Nature, Addresses, and Lectures, edited by R. E. Spiller and A. R. Ferguson. Cambridge, Mass.: The Belknap Press of Harvard University Press, Copyright © 1971 by the President and Fellows of Harvard College. Reprinted by permission from the publishers from *The Collected Works of Ralph Waldo Emerson*, Volume II: Essays.: First Series, edited by J. Slater, A. R. Ferguson and J. F. Carr. Cambridge, Mass: The Belknap Press of Harvard University Press, Copyright © 1979 by the President and Fellows of Harvard College.

William Faulkner: "Spotted Horses." Copyright 1931 and renewed 1959 by William Faulkner. Reprinted from *Scribner's* Magazine by permission of Random House, Inc. An extended version of this story appears as part of *The Hamlet*, by William Faulkner. "That Evening Sun." Copyright © 1959 by William Faulkner. Reprinted from *Collected Stories of William Faulkner*, by permission of Random House, Inc.

F. Scott Fitzgerald: Excerpted from *The Great Gatsby*. Copyright 1925 Charles Scribner's Sons; copyright renewed 1953 Frances Scott Fitzgerald Lanahan. "The Rich Boy" from *All the Sad Young Men*. Copyright 1925, 1926 Consolidated Magazines Corporation; copyright renewed 1953, 1954 Frances Scott Fitzgerald Lanahan. Reprinted with the permission of Charles Scribner's Sons.

Benjamin Franklin: Autobiography of Benjamin Franklin as edited by Leonard W. Labaree, et al. for Yale University Press, 1964 [Parts I & II]. HMII9999. Reprinted by permission of The Huntington Library, San Marino, California. "On Literary Style" reprinted courtesy of Historical Society of Pennsylvania. "Preface" to *Poor Richard Improved* (1758), by Benjamin Franklin from *The Papers of Benjamin Franklin*, ed. by Labaree et al. Reprinted by permission by Yale University Library.

Philip Freneau: "To a Honey Bee" from *The Poems of Philip Freneau*, vol. 3, ed. by Fred L. Pattee. Reprinted by permission of Princeton University Library.

Robert Frost: "Mowing," "October," "Reluctance," "Mending Wall," "Home Burial," "After Apple-Picking," "The Road Not Taken," "The Oven Bird," "Birches," "Fire and Ice," "Nothing Gold Can Stay," "Stopping by Woods on a Snowy Evening," "For Once, Then, Something," "To Earthward," "The Need of Being Versed in Country Things," "Once by the Pacific," "Immigrants," "Desert Places," "Design," "Provide, Provide," "The Most of It," "The Gift Outright," and "Time Out" from *The Poetry of Robert Frost*, edited by Edward Connery Lathem. Copyright 1916, 1923, 1928, 1930, 1934, 1939, 1947, © 1969 by Holt, Rinehart and Winston. Copyright 1936,

1942, 1944, 1951, © 1956, 1958, 1962 by Robert Frost. Copyright © 1964, 1967, 1970, 1975 by Lesley Frost Ballantine. From "The Figure a Poem Makes" in *Selected Prose of Robert Frost*, edited by Hyde Cox and Edward Connery Lathem. Copyright 1939, © 1967 by Holt, Rinehart and Winston, Publishers. Reprinted by permission of Holt, Rinehart and Winston, Publishers.

Margaret Fuller: From *The Writings of Margaret Fuller*, edited by Mason Wade. Copyright 1941, renewed © 1968 by The Viking Press, Inc. Reprinted by permission of Viking Penguin Inc.

Ray Ginger: From *An Age of Excess: The United States from 1877 to 1914*, Second Edn., by Ray Ginger (Copyright © 1965, 1975 by Ray Ginger). Reprinted with permission of the publisher.

Allen Ginsberg: "Howl," Part I, copyright © 1955 by Allen Ginsberg. "A Supermarket in California" copyright © 1955 by Allen Ginsberg. "Sunflower Sutra" copyright © 1955 by Allen Ginsberg. "America" copyright © 1959 by Allen Ginsberg. "Mugging" copyright © 1974 by Allen Ginsberg. All from *Collected Poems 1947–1980*, by Allen Ginsberg (1984). Reprinted by permission of Harper & Row, Publishers, Inc. From notes for *Howl*. Copyright © 1959, 1985 by Allen Ginsberg. From Introduction to Jack Kerouac's *Visions of Cody*. © Allen Ginsberg. Reprinted by permission of Andrew Wylie Agency and the author.

Albert Goldbarth: "How the Sky Counts Years" from *Faith* (New Rivers Press). © 1981 by Albert Goldbarth. Reprinted by permission of the author. "A History of Civilization" copyright © 1973, 1974, 1976, 1980, 1981, 1983 by Albert Goldbarth. Reprinted from *Original Light: New & Selected Poems 1973–1983* by permission of Ontario Review Press.

Jorie Graham: "The Geese," "Mind" from *Hybrids of Plants and of Ghosts* (in The Princeton Series of Contemporary Poets), by Jorie Graham. Copyright © 1980 by Princeton University Press. ("The Geese" first appeared in *The Iowa Review*. "Mind" first appeared in *Water Table*.) Reprinted by permission of Princeton University Press. "Some Notes on Silence." Reprinted by permission of the author.

Richard Hakluyt: "The First New England" from *The Principal Navigations, Voyages, Traffiques, and Discoveries of the English Nation*, Second Edition, 1598–1600. Ed. and Abridged by Jack Beeching (Penguin Books, 1972).

Michael S. Harper: "Dear John, Dear Coltrane," and "Martin's Blues," from *Images of Kin: New and Selected Poems* © 1970, 1971, 1972, 1973, 1974, 1975, 1976, 1977 by Michael S. Harper. Reprinted by permission of the publisher University of Illinois Press.

Robert Hayden: "Those Winter Sundays," "Middle Passage" are reprinted from *Angle of Ascent, New and Selected Poems,* by Robert Hayden, by permission of Liveright Publishing Corporation. Copyright © 1975, 1972, 1970, 1966 by Robert Hayden.

Ernest Hemingway: Excerpted from *A Moveable Feast.* Copyright © 1964 Mary Hemingway. "Big Two-Hearted River" from *In Our Time.* Copyright 1925 Charles Scribner's Sons; copyright renewed 1953 Ernest Hemingway. Reprinted with the permission of Charles Scribner's Sons.

Michael Herr: From *Dispatches,* by Michael Herr. Copyright © 1977 by Michael Herr. Reprinted by permission of Alfred A. Knopf, Inc.

John Hersey: From *Hiroshima,* by John Hersey. Copyright 1946 and renewed 1974 by John Hersey. Reprinted by permission of Alfred A. Knopf, Inc.

Langston Hughes: "To Black Writers." Copyright 1935 by International Publishers Co., Inc. "Dream Boogie," "Movies," and "Same in Blues." Copyright 1951 by Langston Hughes. Copyright renewed 1979 by George Houston Bass. "Thank You, M'am." Copyright © 1958 by Langston Hughes. Copyright renewed 1986 by George Houston Bass. Reprinted by permission of Harold Ober Associates Incorporated. "Feet Live Their Own Life" from *The Best of Simple,* by Langston Hughes. Copyright © 1961 by Langston Hughes. Reprinted by permission of Hill & Wang, a division of Farrar, Straus and Giroux, Inc. "The Negro Speaks of Rivers," "Harlem." Copyright 1926 by Alfred A. Knopf, Inc. and renewed 1954 by Langston Hughes. Copyright 1951 by Langston Hughes. Reprinted from *Selected Poems of Langston Hughes,* by permission of Alfred A. Knopf, Inc.

Zora Neale Hurston: "The Gilded Six-Bits." Reprinted by permission of the Zora Neale Hurston Estate.

Randall Jarrell: "The Woman at the Washington Zoo," in *The Woman at the Washington Zoo.* Copyright © 1960 by Randall Jarrell. Reprinted with the permission of Atheneum Publishers. "Next Day." Reprinted with permission of Macmillan Publishing Company from *The Lost World,* by Randall Jarrell. Copyright © Randall Jarrell 1963, 1965. Originally appeared in *The New Yorker.* "The Death of the Ball Turret Gunner," "Losses," "A Lullaby" from *The Complete Poems,* by Randall Jarrell. Copyright 1942, 1944, 1948, copyright renewed © 1969, 1971, 1972 by Mrs. Randall Jarrell. Reprinted by permission of Farrar, Straus and Giroux, Inc.

Robinson Jeffers: "Apology for Bad Dreams," "Boats in a Fog." Copyright 1925 and renewed 1953 by Robinson Jeffers. Reprinted from *Selected Poems,* by Robinson Jeffers, by permission of Random House, Inc.

Thomas Jefferson: From *Notes on the State of Virginia,* by Thomas Jefferson. Ed. by William Peden. Copyright, 1954, the University of North Carolina Press. Published for the Institute of Early American History and Culture, Williamsburg. Used with permission of the Publisher.

Ken Kesey: From *One Flew Over the Cuckoo's Nest,* by Ken Kesey. Copyright © 1962 by Ken Kesey. Reprinted by permission of Viking Penguin Inc.

Maxine Hong Kingston: "No Name Woman" from *The Woman Warrior: Memoirs of a Girlhood Among Ghosts,* by Maxine Hong Kingston. Copyright © 1975, 1976 by Maxine Hong Kingston. Reprinted by permission of Alfred A. Knopf, Inc.

Emma Lazarus: "The New Colossus" from Morris U. Schappes, ed., *Emma Lazarus: Selections from Her Poetry and Prose,* 5th ed., 1982. Published by Emma Lazarus Federation of Jewish Women's Clubs, New York.

Sinclair Lewis: Chapter 3 from *Babbitt,* by Sinclair Lewis. Reprinted from *Babbitt,* by Sinclair Lewis by permission of Harcourt Brace Jovanovich, Inc.; copyright 1922 by Harcourt Brace Jovanovich, Inc., renewed 1950 by Sinclair Lewis. *Babbitt* is published in paperback by The New American Library, Inc.

Walter Lippmann: From *A Preface to Morals,* by Walter Lippmann (Copyright 1929, and renewed 1957, by Walter Lippmann). Reprinted with permission of the publisher.

Robert Lowell: "Mr. Edwards and the Spider" from *Lord Weary's Castle,* by Robert Lowell. Copyright 1946, 1974 by Robert Lowell. Reprinted by permission of Harcourt Brace Jovanovich, Inc. "Waking in the Blue," "Skunk Hour" from *Life Studies,* by Robert Lowell. Copyright © 1956, 1959 by Robert Lowell. "For the Union Dead" from *For the Union Dead,* by Robert Lowell. Copyright © 1960, 1964 by Robert Lowell. "Waking Early One Sunday Morning" from *Near the Ocean,* by Robert Lowell. Copyright © 1963, 1965, 1966, 1967 by Robert Lowell. "The March I," excerpt from "Afterthought" from *Notebook,* by Robert Lowell. Copyright © 1967, 1968, 1969 by Robert Lowell. "Harriet," from *For Lizzie and Harriet,* by Robert Lowell. Copyright © 1967, 1968, 1969, 1970, 1973 by Robert Lowell. "History," "Reading Myself" from *History,* by Robert Lowell. Copyright © 1967, 1968, 1969, 1970, 1973 by Robert Lowell. "Fishnet" from *Dolphin,* by Robert Lowell. Copyright © 1973 by Robert Lowell. "For John Berryman," "For Sheridan," "Epilogue" from *Day by Day,* by Robert Lowell. Copyright © 1975, 1976, 1977 by Robert Lowell.

Flannery O'Connor: "A Good Man Is Hard to Find" from *A Good Man Is Hard to Find and Other Stories,* by Flannery O'Connor, copyright 1955 by Flannery O'Connor; renewed 1983 by Regina O'-Connor. Reprinted by permission of Harcourt Brace Jovanovich, Inc.

Frank O'Hara: "The Day Lady Died." Copyright © 1964 by Frank O'Hara. Reprinted by permission of City Lights Books. "To the Harbormaster" from *Meditations in an Emergency.* Copyright © 1957 by Frank O'Hara. Reprinted by permission of Grove, Press, Inc. "A Step Away from Them," "Why I Am Not a Painter," "Poetry." From *The Selected Poems of Frank O'Hara,* edited by Donald Allen. Copyright © 1973 by Maureen Granville-Smith, Administratrix of the Estate of Frank O'-Hara. Reprinted by permission of Alfred A. Knopf, Inc.

Tillie Olsen: "I Stand Here Ironing" excerpted from the book *Tell Me a Riddle,* by Tillie Olsen. Copyright © 1956 by Tillie Olsen. Reprinted by permission of Delacorte Press/Seymour Lawrence.

Charles Olson: From "Projective Verse." Copyright © 1950, 1967 by Charles Olson. Reprinted by permission of the Estate of Charles Olson.

Eugene O'Neill: *Hughie,* by Eugene O'Neill. © 1959 by Carlotta Monterey O'Neill. © as an unpublished work 1959 by Carlotta Monterey O'-Neill. Reprinted by permission of the publishers, Yale University Press.

Thomas Paine: *The American Crisis* and *Common Sense* from *The Complete Writings of Thomas Paine.* Ed. by Philip S. Foner. Published by arrangement with Lyle Stuart.

Dexter Perkins: From *The New Age of Franklin Roosevelt, 1932–45.* © 1957 by The University of Chicago. Reprinted by permission of The University of Chicago Press.

Joan Peyser: "The Music of Sound or, The Beatles and the Beatless." Reprinted by permission from *The Columbia Forum.* Copyright © 1967 by The Trustees of Columbia University in the City of New York. All rights reserved.

Robert Pinsky: "Memorial." Copyright © 1979 by Robert Pinsky. Reprinted by permission of the author. "Dying" from *History of My Heart* copyright © 1984 by Robert Pinsky. Published by The Ecco Press in 1984. Reprinted by permission.

Sylvia Plath: From *The Collected Poems of Sylvia Plath,* edited by Ted Hughes: "The Moon and the Yew Tree," "The Bee Meeting," "Daddy," "Lady Lazarus," "Death & Co.," and "Winter Trees," Copyright © 1963 by Ted Hughes. "Black Rook in Rainy Weather." Copyright © 1960 by Ted Hughes. "Crossing the Water." Copyright © 1962 by Ted Hughes. "Morning Song." Copyright © 1961 by Ted Hughes. "Ariel," Copyright © 1965 by Ted Hughes. "Poppies in October." Copyright © 1963 by the Estate of Sylvia Plath. Reprinted by permission of Harper & Row, Publishers, Inc. "The Colussus." Copyright © 1961 by Sylvia Plath. Reprinted from *The Colossus and Other Poems,* by Sylvia Plath, by permission of Alfred A. Knopf, Inc. All poems from *Ariel, The Colossus,* and *Crossing the Water,* by Sylvia Plath. Published by Faber & Faber, London. Copyright Ted Hughes 1971, 1967, and 1965. Reprinted by permission of Olwyn Hughes.

Edgar Allan Poe: Reprinted by permission of the publishers from *The Collected Works of Edgar Allan Poe,* edited by Thomas Olive Mabbott. Cambridge, Mass.: The Belknap Press of Harvard University Press, Copyright © 1969 (vol. I, Poems) and © 1978 (vols. II and III, Tales and Sketches) by the President and Fellows of Harvard College.

Katherine Anne Porter: "Flowering Judas." Copyright 1930, 1958 by Katherine Anne Porter. Reprinted from her volume *Flowering Judas and Other Stories* by permission of Harcourt Brace Jovanovich, Inc.

Ezra Pound: "In a Station of the Metro," "Sestina: Altaforte," "The Garden," "Salutation," "A Pact," "The River Merchant's Wife: A Letter," and "From Hugh Selwyn Mauberley, I–V" from *Personae.* Copyright 1926 Ezra Pound. "Canto I" and "Canto XLV" from *The Cantos of Ezra Pound.* Copyright 1934, 1948, © 1962 by Ezra Pound. "A Few Don'ts," "American Scenes," and "Credo" from *The Literary Essays of Ezra Pound.* Copyright 1935 by Ezra Pound. Reprinted by permission of New Directions Publishing Corporation.

Thomas Pynchon: "Entropy" from *Slow Learner,* by Thomas Pynchon. Copyright © by Thomas Pynchon. First appeared in *The Kenyon Review.* By permission of Little, Brown and Company in association with Atlantic Monthly Press.

John Crowe Ransom: "Piazza Piece," "Dead Boy," "The Equilibrists." Copyright 1927 by Alfred A. Knopf, Inc. and renewed 1955 by John Crowe Ransom. Reprinted from *Selected Poems, Third Edition Revised and Enlarged,* by John Crowe Ransom, by permission of the publisher.

David Reisman: From *The Lonely Crowd: A Study of the Changing American Character.* Reprinted by permission of Yale University Press.

Gerald Reitlinger: From *The Final Solution,* by Gerald Reitlinger. Published by George Weidenfeld & Nicolson Limited.

Adrienne Rich: "I Am in Danger—Sir," "Trying to Talk with a Man," "Diving into the Wreck," "Translations," "From a Survivor," from *Poems, Selected and New, 1950–1971,* by Adrienne Rich. Copyright © 1975, 1973, 1971, 1969, 1966 by W.

Wallace Stevens: "The Course of a Particular," "Of Mere Being," from "Adagia" Copyright © 1957 by Elsie Stevens and Holly Stevens. Reprinted from *Opus Posthumous*, by Wallace Stevens, edited by Samuel French Morse. "Sunday Morning," "Thirteen Ways of Looking at a Blackbird," "Anecdote of the Jar," "The Paltry Nude Starts on a Spring Voyage," "The Snow Man," "The Emperor of Ice-Cream," "The Idea of Order at Key West," "A Postcard from the Volcano," "Arrival at the Waldorf," "No Possum, No Sop, No Taters," "Angel Surrounded by Paysans," "Final Soliloquy of the Interior Paramour," "The Plain Sense of Things," "The Planet on the Table," "The River of Rivers in Connecticut," "Not Ideas About the Thing but the Thing Itself" from *The Collected Poems of Wallace Stevens*. Copyright 1954 by Wallace Stevens. "What Is the Poet's Function?" from *The Necessary Angel*, by Wallace Stevens. All reprinted by permission of Alfred A. Knopf, Inc.

Mark Strand: "The Tunnel," "Keeping Things Whole," "Coming To This," from *SELECTED POEMS*, by Mark Strand. Copyright © 1980 by Mark Strand. All reprinted with the permission of Atheneum Publishers.

Allen Tate: "Ode to the Confederate Dead," from *Collected Poems*, by Allen Tate. Copyright © 1952, 1953, 1970, 1977 by Allen Tate. Copyright 1931, 1932, 1937, 1948 by Charles Scribner's Sons. Copyright renewed © 1959, 1960, 1965 by Allen Tate. Reprinted by permission of Farrar, Straus and Giroux, Inc.

Edward Taylor: From *The Poems of Edward Taylor*, edited by Donald E. Stanford. Copyright © 1960 by Donald E. Stanford. Reprinted by permission of Donald E. Stanford.

Henry David Thoreau: J. Lyndon Stanley, ed., *Henry D. Thoreau: Walden*. Copyright © 1971 by Princeton University Press. Reprinted by permission of Princeton University Press. Henry D. Thoreau, *Journal*, Vol. 1: *1837–1844*, ed. Elizabeth Hall Witherell. Copyright © 1981 by Princeton University Press. Selections reprinted by permission of Princeton University Press.

Jean Toomer: "Blood-Burning Moon" is reprinted from *Cane* by Jean Toomer, by permission of Liveright Publishing Corporation. Copyright 1923 by Boni & Liveright. Copyright renewed 1951 by Jean Toomer.

Mark Twain: From pp. 64–65 in *The Autobiography of Mark Twain*, edited by Charles Neider. Copyright © 1959 by Charles Neider. Copyright © 1959 by The Mark Twain Company. "The Story of a Speech" from *Mark Twain's Speeches*, by Mark Twain. Copyright 1923 by the Mark Twain Company. Renewed 1951 by Mark Twain Company. "Corn-Pone Opinions" from *Europe and Elsewhere*, by Mark Twain. Copyright 1923 by the Mark Twain Company. Renewed 1951 by the Mark Twain Company. "The Private History of a Campaign That Failed" from *The American Claimant*, by Mark Twain. "Fenimore Cooper's Literary Offences" from *How To Tell a Story*, by Mark Twain. Reprinted by permission of Harper & Row, Publishers, Inc.

John Updike: "Separating," Copyright © 1975 by John Updike. Reprinted from *Problems and Other Stories*, by John Updike, by permission of Alfred A. Knopf, Inc.

Alice Walker: "The Child Who Favored Daughter" from *In Love & Trouble*, by Alice Walker. Copyright © 1967 by Alice Walker. Reprinted by permission of Harcourt Brace Jovanovich, Inc.

Eudora Welty: "Why I Live at the P.O." from *A Curtain of Green and Other Stories*, by Eudora Welty. Copyright 1941, 1969 by Eudora Welty. Reprinted by permission of Harcourt Brace Jovanovich, Inc.

Nathanael West: From *Miss Lonelyhearts & The Day of the Locust*. Copyright 1939 by the Estate of Nathanael West. From *The Day of the Locust*. Copyright 1939 by the Estate of Nathanael West. Reprinted by permission of New Directions Publishing Corporation.

Edith Wharton: "The Other Two" from *The Descent of Man*. Copyright under the Berne Convention. Reprinted with the permission of Charles Scribner's Sons.

Phillis Wheatley: "On the Death of the Rev. Mr. George Whitefield, 1770," "On Being Brought from Africa to America," and "To S.M. A Young African Painter, on Seeing His Works," from *The Poems of Phillis Wheatley*. Edited with an Introduction by Julian D. Mason, Jr., Copyright 1966 The University of North Carolina Press. By permission of the publisher.

Elie Wiesel: Excerpt from *Night*, by Elie Wiesel. Copyright © 1960 by McGibbon and Kee. Reprinted by permission of Farrar, Straus and Giroux.

Richard Wilbur: "The Beautiful Changes" from *The Beautiful Changes and Other Poems*, copyright 1947, 1975 by Richard Wilbur. "Mind" from *Things of This World*, copyright 1956, 1984 by Richard Wilbur. "The Writer," and "Cottage Street, 1953," from *The Mind Reader* copyright © 1975, 1972, 1971 by Richard Wilbur. All reprinted by permission of Harcourt Brace Jovanovich, Inc.

Tennessee Williams: "Portrait of a Madonna" from *27 Wagons Full of Cotton*. Copyright 1945 by Tennessee Williams. Reprinted by permission of New Directions Publishing Corporation.

Index of Authors, Titles, and First Lines of Poems